THE
CHURCHILL
DOCUMENTS

Books by Martin Gilbert
The Churchill Biography
Volume I: *Youth, 1874–1900* by Randolph S. Churchill
The Churchill Documents, Volume 1, *Youth, 1874–1896*
The Churchill Documents, Volume 2, *Young Soldier, 1896–1901*
Volume II: *Young Statesman, 1900–1914* by Randolph S. Churchill
The Churchill Documents, Volume 3, *Early Years in Politics, 1901–1907*
The Churchill Documents, Volume 4, *Minister of the Crown, 1907–1911*
The Churchill Documents, Volume 5, *At the Admiralty, 1911–1914*
Volume III: *The Challenge of War, 1914–1916* by Martin Gilbert
The Churchill Documents, Volume 6, *At the Admiralty, July 1914–April 1915*
The Churchill Documents, Volume 7, *"The Escaped Scapegoat", May 1915–December 1916*
Volume IV: *World in Torment, 1917–1922* by Martin Gilbert
The Churchill Documents, Volume 8, *War and Aftermath, December 1916–June 1919*
The Churchill Documents, Volume 9, *Disruption and Chaos, July 1919–March 1921*
The Churchill Documents, Volume 10, *Conciliation and Reconstruction, April 1921–November 1922*
Volume V: *The Prophet of Truth, 1922–1939* by Martin Gilbert
The Churchill Documents, Volume 11, *The Exchequer Years, 1922–1929*
The Churchill Documents, Volume 12, *The Wilderness Years, 1929–1935*
The Churchill Documents, Volume 13, *The Coming of War, 1936–1939*
Volume VI: *Finest Hour, 1939–1941* by Martin Gilbert
The Churchill Documents, Volume 14, *At the Admiralty, September 1939–May 1940*
The Churchill Documents, Volume 15, *Never Surrender, May 1940–December 1940*
The Churchill Documents, Volume 16, *The Ever-Widening War, 1941*
Volume VII: *Road to Victory, 1941–1945* by Martin Gilbert
The Churchill Documents, Volume 17, *Testing Times, 1942*
Volume VIII: *Never Despair, 1945–1965* by Martin Gilbert

Other Books
The Appeasers (with Richard Gott)
The European Powers, 1900–1945
The Roots of Appeasement
Winston Churchill (Clarendon edition)
Sir Horace Rumbold: Portrait of a Diplomat
Churchill: A Photographic Portrait
Exile and Return: The Struggle for Jewish Statehood
Final Journey: The Fate of the Jews of Nazi Europe
Churchill: An Illustrated Biography
Auschwitz and the Allies
Churchill's Political Philosophy
Winston Churchill: The Wilderness Years
Jews of Hope: The Plight of Soviet Jewry Today
Jerusalem: Rebirth of a City
The Holocaust: The Jewish Tragedy
Shcharansky: Hero of Our Time
The Second World War
In Search of Churchill
The First World War
The Day the War Ended: VE Day 1945
Jerusalem in the Twentieth Century
The Boys: Triumph over Adversity
Holocaust Diary: Travelling in Search of the Past
Israel: A History

History of the Twentieth Century, Volume I
Empires in Conflict, 1900–1933
History of the Twentieth Century, Volume II
Descent into Barbarism, 1934–1951
History of the Twentieth Century, Volume III
Challenge to Civilization, 1952–1999
'Never Again': A History of the Holocaust
The Jewish Century: An Illustrated History
Letters to Auntie Fori: The 5,000 Year History of the Jewish People and Their Faith
The Righteous: The Unsung Heroes of the Holocaust
Churchill at War in Photographs
Churchill's War Leadership: Continue to Pester, Nag and Bite
D-Day
Churchill and America
Kristallnacht: Prelude to Destruction
The Will of the People: Churchill and Parliamentary Democracy
Somme: Heroism and Horror in the First World War
Churchill and the Jews
The Story of Israel
In Ishmael's House: A History of Jews in Muslim Lands
Churchill: The Power of Words

Historical Atlases
Atlas of American History
Atlas of the Arab–Israel Conflict
Atlas of British Charities
Atlas of British History
Atlas of the First World War
Children's Illustrated Bible Atlas
Atlas of the Holocaust
Historical Atlas of Jerusalem
Atlas of Jewish History
Atlas of Russian History
Atlas of the Second World War

Editions of Documents
Britain and Germany Between the Wars
Plough My Own Furrow: The Life of Lord Allen of Hurtwood
Servant of India: Diaries of the Viceroy's Private Secretary, 1905–1910
Churchill: Great Lives Observed
Lloyd George: Great Lives Observed
Surviving the Holocaust: The Kovno Ghetto Diary of Avraham Tory
Winston Churchill and Emery Reves: Correspondence, 1937–1964

THE CHURCHILL DOCUMENTS

EDITORS
MARTIN GILBERT
AND
LARRY P. ARNN

VOLUME 23
NEVER FLINCH, NEVER WEARY
NOVEMBER 1951 TO FEBRUARY 1965

Hillsdale College Press, Hillsdale, Michigan

Hillsdale College Press
33 East College Street
Hillsdale, Michigan 49242
www.hillsdale.edu

© 2019 Hillsdale College
portions © C & T Publications Limited
All rights reserved.

Printed in the United States of America

Printed and bound by Sheridan Books, Chelsea, Michigan

Cover design adapted from Hesseltine & DeMason

THE CHURCHILL DOCUMENTS
Volume 23: *Never Flinch, Never Weary, November 1951 to February 1965*

Library of Congress Control Number: 2006934101
ISBN: 978-0-916308-48-3
First printing 2019

To Randolph S. Churchill
and
Sir Martin Gilbert

Contents

Note	ix
Preface *by Larry P. Arnn*	xi
Acknowledgments	xxxvii
Sources and Bibliography	xli
NOVEMBER 1951	1
DECEMBER 1951	90
JANUARY 1952	159
FEBRUARY 1952	249
MARCH 1952	298
APRIL 1952	373
MAY 1952	415
JUNE 1952	478
JULY 1952	518
AUGUST 1952	586
SEPTEMBER 1952	633
OCTOBER 1952	657
NOVEMBER 1952	700
DECEMBER 1952	744
JANUARY 1953	793
FEBRUARY 1953	832
MARCH 1953	866
APRIL 1953	929
MAY 1953	982
JUNE 1953	1056
JULY 1953	1140
AUGUST 1953	1180
SEPTEMBER 1953	1200
OCTOBER 1953	1223
NOVEMBER 1953	1268
DECEMBER 1953	1316

JANUARY 1954	1381
FEBRUARY 1954	1410
MARCH 1954	1458
APRIL 1954	1510
MAY 1954	1560
JUNE 1954	1592
JULY 1954	1641
AUGUST 1954	1720
SEPTEMBER 1954	1770
OCTOBER 1954	1789
NOVEMBER 1954	1810
DECEMBER 1954	1829
JANUARY 1955	1862
FEBRUARY 1955	1887
MARCH 1955	1926
APRIL 1955	1975
MAY 1955	1992
JUNE 1955	2013
JULY 1955	2023
AUGUST 1955	2029
SEPTEMBER 1955	2041
OCTOBER 1955	2045
NOVEMBER 1955	2053
DECEMBER 1955	2064
1956	2073
1957	2151
1958	2196
1959	2229
1960	2279
1961	2299
1962	2320
1963	2340
1964	2354
1965	2364

APPENDICES

A: Ministerial Appointments, 1 November 1951 to 5 April 1955	2389
B: Abbreviations	2392
C: Churchill's Travels, December 1951 to 1963	2400
D: Two Additional Documents	2406
E: Orders, Decorations, Medals and Honours Conferred on Winston Churchill, 1951 to 1965	2408
INDEX	2413

Note

Winston Churchill's personal papers are among the most comprehensive ever assembled relating to the life and times of one man. They are so extensive that it was only possible to include in the narrative volumes of his biography a part of the relevant documents.

The Companion volumes, now titled *The Churchill Documents*, were planned to run parallel with the narrative volumes, and with them to form a whole. When an extract or quotation appears in a narrative volume, the complete document appears in an accompanying volume of *The Churchill Documents*. Where space prevented the inclusion of a contemporary letter in the narrative volume, it is included in the document volume.

This volume contains transcriptions of over 2,100 documents, each of which we have formatted to the style that has prevailed in all these document volumes. That style includes these features:

- For verbatim diary transcriptions, we use in the heading the author's name at the time of writing, e.g. John Colville, not Sir John Colville. For "recollections" (memoirs, reflections, etc.), we use the name of the author as it was at the time of publication of the document, e.g. Lord Avon, not Anthony Eden, for his writings published after he was elevated to the peerage.
- We use italicized text in diary entries to denote text not original to the diary. For example, italicized text in John Colville's diary entries was written by himself in preparing the diaries for publication.
- Reflections and memoirs occasionally include lengthy quotes from a primary document. These quotations are displayed with a further left indent within the document to keep the two types of text distinct.
- Ellipses not bracketed are original to the document reproduced. Bracketed ellipses denote our decisions to omit text.
- For documents taken from published sources, publication details are given in the 'Sources and Bibliography' below. This list also contains publication details for works cited in the footnotes.

Preface

THE OFFICIAL BIOGRAPHY

This twenty-third volume of documents in the official biography of Winston Churchill is the last step in a journey that began fifty-eight years ago, having been prepared for decades earlier. One will find in this volume a letter that Churchill wrote to his son Randolph in 1960:

> I think that your biography[1] of Derby is a remarkable work, and I should be happy that you should write my official biography when the time comes. But I must ask you to defer this until after my death.
>
> I would not like to release my papers piece-meal, and I think that you should wait for the time being and then get all your material from my own Archives and from the Trust. In any case I do not want anything to be published until at least five years after my death.[2]

Here Churchill finalizes a suggestion he had made years earlier: his son Randolph was to be his official biographer. The work would begin a year later in 1961. Randolph hired the young historian Martin Gilbert in 1962 as his research assistant. They would inherit a treasure trove of information and then proceed to add to its volume and value over the ensuing decades.

The documents from which this biography has been written come from hundreds of archives, but mostly from that of Churchill himself. Not only did he live the large life that this biography describes, but he also began at an early day to preserve the evidence of it. Churchill made a practice, even a principle, of conducting his business in writing. When he became Prime Minister he directed that no instruction from him would be binding unless it were written down.[3] In 1946 he wrote to his successor in the post, Clement Attlee:

> An unusually large proportion of my work was done in writing, i.e. by shorthand dictation, and there is therefore in existence an unbroken series

---

[1] In 1959 Randolph published *Lord Derby, 'King of Lancashire', The Official Life of Edward, Seventeenth Earl of Derby, 1865–1948*.

[2] Churchill to Randolph Churchill, reproduced below (p. 2285).

[3] Churchill to Ismay, Dill and Bridges, 19 Jul. 1940, reproduced in *The Churchill Documents*, vol. 15, *Never Surrender, May 1940–December 1940*, p. 549.

of minutes, memoranda, telegrams, etc., covering the whole period of my Administration, all of which were my own personal composition, subject to Staff or Departmental checking.[1]

Churchill was a fluent writer, from 1921 often by dictation, which enabled him to move rapidly and to discharge the public business on an immense scale. He thought that doing business in writing helped to ensure clarity of purpose and consistency in action.

In contrast to recent political practices, the vast majority of things written and said by Churchill were composed by him. Martin Gilbert once told me of a conversation he had with three prime ministers, current or former, at a reception. One of them[2] asked him who wrote Churchill's speeches. The question came naturally to a statesman in the late 1970s. One of the others knew enough about Churchill to find this amusing.

In addition to the working efficiency of his system, Churchill also recognized the historical value of this written record. In his 1946 letter to Attlee, quoted above, Churchill writes that he hopes his written work products "may some time see the light of day in their textual form." He goes on to describe their historical value:

> These pieces, written at the moment and under the impact of events, with all their imperfections and fallacies of judgment, show far better than anything composed in subsequent years could do the hopes and fears and difficulties through which we made our way. I am by no means certain that I should wish to publish these documents in my life time, but I think they would certainly win sympathy for our country, particularly in the United States, and make them understand the awful character of the trials through which we passed especially when we were fighting alone, and the moral debt owed to us by other countries.[3]

Churchill believed that the contemporaneous documents, "with all their imperfections and fallacies of judgment," conveyed the times "far better" than "anything composed in subsequent years." This includes necessarily Churchill's own works of history and everything like them, including this biography. Except, that is, for one crucial point: Churchill's two official biographers endorsed the same principle. When Randolph Churchill commenced the work in 1961 he made his theme "he shall be his own biographer." In his two volumes, long passages and even whole documents are interspersed throughout his narrative text. Randolph's successor, Sir Martin Gilbert, the

---

[1] Churchill to Attlee, 29 May 1946, reproduced in *The Churchill Documents*, vol. 22, *Leader of the Opposition, August 1945 to October 1951*, pp. 354–5.
[2] I will not say which one, for Martin would probably not have wished it.
[3] Churchill to Attlee, 29 May 1946, reproduced in *The Churchill Documents*, vol. 22, *Leader of the Opposition, August 1945 to October 1951*, p. 355.

author of the last six volumes of narrative history and editor of most of the document volumes, believed in the reality of history as it is shown in the evidence for it: the more evidence, the more real. He explained the idea behind the histories he wrote in this telling passage:

> On the tomb of the nineteenth century Church historian Bishop Mandell Creighton are inscribed the words: "He tried to write true history."
>
> Like the bishop – who was a member of my own college at Oxford – I believe that there is such a thing as "true history."
>
> What happened in the past is unalterable and definite. To uncover it – or as much of it as possible – the historian has several tools, among them chronology, documentation, memoirs, and the vast apparatus of scholarly work in which others have delved and laboured in the same vineyard.[1]

In this deconstructionist age, many view history as little more than a mirror for our own views and influences. Churchill and his biographers agreed with Agathon, quoted by Aristotle, that "Of this power alone is even a god deprived, To make undone whatever has been done."[2] In this view the task of the historian is to recover what happened and make it available for others to understand. In doing this he exhibits aspects of the nature of human life that we can grasp today.

To use old language, one might say that the material cause of this biography is the evidence, mostly documentary, from which it is written. The efficient cause is the two men who wrote it; later, my colleagues and I have done a lesser but important work in editing and completing the document volumes. Also, Hillsdale College is keeping the whole biography in print. All of these factors combine to enable the story of Churchill to be told in detail.

Churchill was also careful in keeping the written evidence of his life in an orderly fashion. For example, on 23 January 1925, as Chancellor of the Exchequer, Churchill wrote to Sir Warren Fisher, Permanent Secretary of the Treasury and Official Head of the Civil Service. Churchill had prickly relations with Fisher, and in this correspondence they have a disagreement about how to organize papers within files. The method Churchill proposed was the product of "long, and I think unequalled, experience in Public Offices," and entailed the distinction between minutes (documents intended to record brief steps toward decisions) and memoranda (documents of an informative and argumentative character). The two were to be separated: "A clear distinction is needed between the terseness and precision which are required in Minutes and the necessary more expansive forms of argument which are suitable to Memoranda."[3] Both were to be arranged within their folders in reverse

---

[1] Martin Gilbert, "On History," https://www.martingilbert.com/sir-martin-on-history/.
[2] Aristotle, *Nicomachean Ethics*, trans. Sachs (Newburyport, MA: Focus Publishing, 2002), 104.
[3] Churchill to Fisher, 23 Jan. 1925, reproduced in *The Churchill Documents*, vol. 11, *The Exchequer Years, 1922–1929*, p. 353.

chronological order. This, Churchill wrote, would be advantageous both to department heads and those who advise them.

This was the method Churchill followed to organize his own files. When I began work on the biography in 1977, most of the papers were still in Oxford, on the third floor below ground of the New Library, part of the university's Bodleian Libraries. The papers were still in the filing cabinets that Churchill preferred. In a memo entitled "The Filing Cabinet," which I remember distinctly but cannot find, he described one manufactured by Chubb & Son's Lock & Safe Co. Ltd. It was fireproof, large, and heavy – hard to damage or to steal.

Within these cabinets, the file folders were organized most always in accordance with the scheme he described above. Filing cabinets contained related items; so also file drawers; so also file folders. In the upper left of each file folder and of each page within it a hole was punched. Through these holes, all lined up, string fasteners with metal ends, known as "Treasury tags," were threaded to hold the papers in place. As public business was carried on, it would have been quick and easy to add additional pages, as the new ones would go right on top.

For the historian and researcher, this arrangement was not quite so convenient. It was difficult to remove a page from its place, for example to photocopy it, and then put it back. Martin Gilbert was careful – as was I, under his direction – to preserve the original order in removing and replacing the documents. There was a lot of this, for Martin wanted the documents arranged in chronological, not reverse chronological order, and he did not want the papers grouped by subject matter. The evidence from which Martin wrote the biography was arranged entirely according to a single timeline, from the first document when Churchill was an infant (or even before) until the last one when he died (or even after). Martin wanted to see the documents in the sequence in which they were generated, one after another, and he wanted to see them together because events are not presented to any statesman, or any of us, grouped tidily by subject matter.

Given Randolph's and Martin's devotion to documentary history, one might wonder why they wrote history at all? Why not just read the documents? Martin's answer was that not everyone can, and that would be true even now, when most of the documents are available online. Nor can everyone develop the skill to absorb the evidence and render it faithfully, but in an entirely different form. If the material and efficient causes of the biography are the documents and the biographers, the form of the biography is eight volumes of narrative history and twenty-three volumes of documents. This is a vast work, and yet it is only a fraction of the all the records that survive from the period. For all its magnitude, it is a selection.

This biography is, then, a kind of middle way between learning from the original documents alone and reading a narrative. In the official biography

Preface

of Winston Churchill, we have a long and careful narrative written by two people who believed not only in following the evidence, but also in walking side by side with it. And then we have the documents from which they wrote, and more documents still, reproduced and available, most of them in full. They are indexed, annotated, and published. The reader may then use the biography either as the great story it is, or as a tool to do historical research. The narrative volumes are a guide to the document volumes, the document volumes evidence for the narrative.

In these last six document volumes, we have followed the practices that Randolph and Martin established. I was not privileged to meet Randolph Churchill, but I knew and worked with Martin Gilbert for almost four decades. He combined a sweeping knowledge of modern history with a meticulous attention to detail and citation. Becoming famous and eventually a knight, he did not forget that his job was not the same as Churchill's. Churchill wrote that you must "nail your life to a cross of thought or action," and then he did both. Martin, a thinker, undertook to represent the thought and action of Churchill as it was. He was aware of his advantage over Churchill or anyone of the past: the historian looks back on a series of events fixed in time, and he knows their outcome. Martin's awareness of this is one of the reasons he was never given to second-guessing or smugness.

We at Hillsdale College became the publishers of the biography in 2004. Martin finished document volumes 6–16 while he lived. Volume 17 was mostly done, and we completed it. After that, we have done the rest, volumes 18–23. Since Martin's death, the work has been done by me and an able staff led by the young, but now experienced Soren Geiger. We have selected, formatted, and annotated 14,000 pages of documents and 14,800 footnotes. Now, for the first time in these fifty-eight years, the entire biography, narrative and documents, is in print and available electronically as well.

"NEVER WEARY, NEVER DESPAIR . . ."

This volume begins in November 1951, the month of Churchill's 77th birthday. It ends with his death on 24 January 1965 at the age of 90 years and 55 days. During these years Churchill traveled over 100,000 miles, gave over 130 speeches, and published eleven books.

As this book opens, the Conservative Party had clawed its way back from the beating it took in the 1945 election. Churchill is still its leader. With a gain of ninety seats in the election of February 1950, the Conservative Party achieved near parity in parliamentary representation with the Labour Party. In the October 1951 election it gained another twenty-three seats to give it 321 against Labour's 295 and the Liberals' six. Labour's margin of the popular vote over the Conservatives was just over 230,000, or 0.8 percent. Whereas the Conservative gains in the 1950 election were mostly at the expense of Labour, in 1951 it was the Liberals who suffered. Labour's popular vote was actually higher in 1951 by 2.7 percent. The Conservative vote was up 4.6 percent.

Overall, Churchill came back into power in a narrow victory, and Labour was by no means routed. These electoral facts reinforced his long-standing wish to unite with the Liberals to build a party of the center, anti-socialist to be sure, but built upon the social reforms that Churchill advocated all his life. This kind of party, he hoped, could assemble an enduring majority. Some of the Liberals, called National Liberals, operated hand in glove with the Conservative Government throughout this time. There were 19 of them, and those Liberals who remained aloof numbered six.

The new Conservative Government soon came to think it was in an emergency. In 1951, Great Britain was straining to find foreign exchange to buy food and other necessities. Housing was in short supply. Six years after the war's end, rationing was still severe; this was more than a year after it had ended, excepting sugar, in vanquished Germany.

The severely strained budget included greatly expanded expenditure for defense – undertaken by the previous Labour Government with Conservative support. With the Soviet Union looming over Europe, this increase was inadequate. It was also unaffordable. Guns and butter were both scarce in Britain, and she was running out of money.

On December 13, the Cabinet decided that Churchill should broadcast "about the gravity of the situation which had confronted the Government when they took office."[1] He did so on December 22. The Conservatives had fought the 1951 and 1952 campaigns on a platform of removing socialist restrictions. In this broadcast, Churchill explained it would be necessary to increase them.

He began with "the broad truths of our national life and policy," stating them "without regard to party propaganda and without seeking popularity at the public expense."[2]

Six years of Socialist rule, he continued, had placed the country "on the verge of insolvency." "Two years of electioneering" had divided the country and distracted it from the work necessary to recovery. This was not "the fault of one party or the other," but it had to stop. His Government would not engage in electioneering or "party brawling." However "we shall answer attacks made upon us and give back as good as we get." The government deserved a "fair try."[3] As it would prove in foreign policy, so in domestic policy Churchill adopted a strategy of armed if not aggressive defense.

There was, Churchill continued, a strong foundation of unity upon which to build. The parties were agreed on social services, foreign affairs, and national defense. "Nine-tenths of the British people agree on nine-tenths of what has

---

[1] Cabinet: conclusions, 13 Dec. 1951, reproduced below (p. 129).
[2] Churchill: broadcast, 22 Dec. 1951, reproduced below (p. 145).
[3] Ibid., pp. 145, 146.

Preface

been done and is being done and is going to go on being done." Churchill would, then, continue 90 percent of what Labour had done. Still, he said that Britain was "running on the wrong lines downhill at sixty miles an hour," but "it is no good trying to stop it by building a brick wall across the track."[1]

This was not quite "blood, toil, tears and sweat," but Churchill promised harder times. Meat stocks were lower, he said, than they had been since 1941 "during the crunch of the war and the U-boats." The new Government had begun raising prices and restricting supply, even though he called that a bad practice in principle: "the legacy we received from those who during six years of peace have tried to buy the food for this island under wartime controls and through Government planners. They aimed at restriction. They got scarcity."[2]

At the heart of these troubles was the acute foreign-exchange problem. Gold and dollar reserves were falling, Churchill said, at an annual rate of £1,400 million a year: total reserves were only £1,000 million. To cut imports and enhance exports, Churchill said, hard steps had already been taken and new ones were coming that would "be unpleasant." This meant more rationing.

Thus Churchill's second premiership began in the uncomfortable position of intensifying a policy it condemned and had been elected to reverse. This would continue, though it soon began to moderate, for most of Churchill's administration. He told John Colville in March 1952 that "'not being broke' is going to be our major difficulty and preoccupation."[3]

Despite this opening talk of emergency, Churchill sought in his second premiership to inspire an atmosphere of confidence and calm. At the Conservative Party conference in October 1953 he said that "my prime thought at this moment is to simplify." He continued:

> But the world also needs patience. It needs a period of calm rather than vehement attempts to produce clear-cut solutions. There have been many periods when prompt and violent action might have averted calamities. This is not one of them. . . . So long as the cause of freedom is sustained by strength, beware of that, never forget that, and guided by wisdom it might well be that after those five or ten years improvement would be continued on an even larger scale. Patience.[4]

One might forget that Churchill had spent his life attempting to avoid situations of "blood, toil, tears and sweat." In 1951 he hoped to end the atmosphere of emergency, and to a considerable extent he did. In this, Churchill intended his second premiership to be precisely opposite to his first.

The search for economy in government spending during this administration was persistent and farreaching. In January 1952, during a visit to Washington,

---

[1] Churchill: broadcast, 22 Dec. 1951, reproduced below (p. 146).
[2] Ibid., p. 147.
[3] Colville: diary, 22–23 Mar. 1952, reproduced below (p. 363).
[4] Churchill: speech, 10 Oct. 1953, reproduced below (pp. 1243–4).

Churchill assembled the staff at the British Embassy for a greeting. He was astonished at the number of them, for apparently the embassy was still on a wartime footing. John Colville records that he issued a "peremptory order, in his capacity as Minister of Defence, and a drastic reduction was effected."[1]

The Cabinet decided against a Coronation Naval Review on grounds of economy. James Thomas, the First Lord of the Admiralty, appealed to Churchill to overturn the decision. To conduct the review the Navy needed about £100,000 and was prepared to find this sum in its own budget. The Naval Review, Thomas wrote, was "so traditional a feature of Coronations that it is becoming increasingly difficult to stall."[2] In correspondence Churchill and Thomas whittled the expenditure down to a display of fireworks and the charter of "a liner in which distinguished visitors could steam round the Fleet."[3] The Naval Review went forward, but cheaply.

Asked at a press conference in New York how he justified such great expenditure on the Coronation when the country was in financial straits, Churchill replied: "Everybody likes to wear a flower when he goes to see his girl."[4] He still had his wit.

Churchill pressed for an end to rationing as soon as could be. He had a history with the policy. During the war, his Government had imposed rationing upon many foodstuffs and other products. He had successfully opposed bread rationing during the war, but the Labour Government had implemented it, then abolished it, during its time. Rationing of clothing was eliminated in March 1949; of petrol in May 1950.

By early 1953, as the foreign exchange crisis eased, the Conservatives moved to eliminate all rationing. In the months leading up to the Coronation in June 1953, Churchill found himself in dispute with Gwilym Lloyd George, the Minister of Food, who wished to continue with rationing of chocolate and sweets. Churchill wanted the rationing abolished before the crowds gathered in London for the Coronation. Lloyd George warned, however, that if the ration were abolished, it might lead to a "chaotic shortage" of sugar. Churchill was emphatic, and on February 5 the ration was abolished. Within six months, there was a glut of sugar. In his diary, John Colville saluted the passing of the last of the "emblems of austerity."[5]

Cheese, butter, and margarine rationing did not end until 8 May 1954. Rationing ceased for meat and all other foodstuffs on 3 July 1954. As the normal operations of supply and demand were restored, supplies increased – as Churchill had predicted.

The heart of the socialist program was the nationalization of major

---

[1] Colville: diary, 9 Jan. 1952, reproduced below (p. 194).
[2] Thomas to Churchill, 2 Sep. 1952, reproduced below (p. 635).
[3] Cabinet: conclusions, 1 Oct. 1952, reproduced below (p. 658).
[4] Colville: diary, 3 Jan. 1953, reproduced below (p. 796).
[5] Colville: diary, 12 June 1953, reproduced below (p. 1108).

Preface

industries. Of the eight industries nationalized by the Labour Government, only two, steel and transport, were denationalized by the second Churchill Government. Transport had been only partially socialized. Steel had been the last of the industries to nationalize, only nine months before the Conservatives regained power in October 1951. The other six remained nationalized until the Thatcher administrations of 1979–90.

Given the consistent intensity with which Churchill had spoken against socialism, his restraint in denationalizing industries is remarkable. He gave reasons for it, some of them principled, some practical.

The chief practical reason was the slim majority Churchill commanded. If with a small majority his administration reversed the largest things the socialists had done, Labour would have a precedent for reversing them again. He did not campaign in 1950 or 1951 on a platform of denationalization, except in the case of steel. He might not have won if he had. The country was divided. Most any policy is better than frequent revolutions of policy. Anyway, the capital markets were depressed. What price could he get for the public industries?

Moreover, Churchill admitted that he had not been an absolute opponent of nationalization. During May 1952 he reminded the House of Commons that "before almost all the Members of the House had even thought about going to Parliament,"[1] he had himself proposed nationalization of the railways.[2] He did not maintain that opinion in later life, but said it made no difference now. Now, "we have to face the facts. The railways are and will remain nationalized, and the Tory Party will do their utmost to make them a great, living, lasting success in the vital, though limited, sphere that is open to them."[3]

A larger reason was constitutional. Churchill took seriously the fact that Labour had won the 1945 election handsomely on a platform of nationalization. The industries that were nationalized from 1945–7 were taken over with the backing of a strong public vote.

The industries nationalized later, chiefly steel, seemed to Churchill a different matter. The reason is implicit in an argument that Churchill had had in 1947 with the Attlee Government. Churchill objected to a measure to reduce from two years to one year the delay that the House of Lords could impose on a Bill passed through the Commons. The measure was a proposed amendment to the Parliament Act of 1911, which Churchill had helped to fashion and lead through the Commons. This Act stripped the House of Lords of its power to veto a Bill that had passed the Commons; after that, the Lords could delay legislation for two years, but not veto it.

---

[1] Churchill: speech, 21 May 1952, reproduced below (p. 453).
[2] During October 1906 Churchill had said: "I am sorry we have not got the railways of this country in our hands." He also said that he wanted the state to assume "the position of the reserve employer of labour." This was an instance of his often repeated view that the Government should establish universally "minimum standards of life and labour, and their progressive elevation as the increased energies of production may permit." See Martin Gilbert, *Churchill: A Life*, p. 184.
[3] Churchill: speech, 21 May 1952, reproduced below (p. 453).

This seemed to Churchill the correct duration. He argued that, the life of a parliament being typically five years, governments should do only in the first two years the controversial things for which they had been elected. Fresh from the election, they had the specific approval of the people. The next three years should be spent doing things that had not been at issue in the previous election, but which were less controversial. In that way, large changes of policy would be made only with the conscious authority of the people. Churchill thought that representation was not merely a matter of elections, but also of the constant attention and abiding agreement of the people. Big changes required a vote of the people.

In 1950, Churchill opposed the Steel Nationalization Bill on this ground. He said that the Labour Government were not nationalizing steel "because [they] want more *steel* but because they want more *power*."[1] At the same time they announced the nationalization of steel, they said they were looking for other industries to nationalize. This, Churchill said, was a warning: Keep your heads down or we will take your business. It was an example, therefore, of the Government using force to trammel public debate. It being six years since Labour had won its mandate for nationalization, and with another election soon to be held, it was not clear Labour had the authority of the people for nationalizing steel. He warned that the Conservatives would reverse any nationalization when they regained power.

In the debate over the Bill to denationalize steel, Churchill said that it would "not have been right" to denationalize steel either "merely to undo the work of our opponents, or to condemn a doctrine which we deem fallacious."[2] Churchill had called socialism much more than a "fallacious" doctrine: he had called it fatal to both freedom and civilization, and he never retracted that claim. On the other hand, if the people approved socialist policies, and the Government refused to implement them, that too would be a step toward despotism.

In this debate and others affecting socialist policy, Churchill was at pains to present an argument more practical than principled. Churchill would often draw sharp lines of principle between one choice and another, as he did about Nazism and communism, and as he did in general about socialism. But he had a narrow majority, and he hoped to make it bigger. In keeping with that aim, he justified the denationalization of steel not "upon political doctrine and theory," but upon "practical needs and experience." This was the basis of "all Conservative policies."[3] In that same statement he proposed that the trade unions should be represented, along with employers and consumers, on a board to govern the newly privatized steel industry. Churchill was looking for a middle way, as often he did.

---

[1] Churchill: speech, 28 Jan. 1950, reproduced in *The Churchill Documents*, vol. 22, *Leader of the Opposition, August 1945 to October 1951*, p. 1610.
[2] Churchill: speech, 6 Sep. 1952, reproduced below (p. 644).
[3] Ibid., p. 643.

Preface

Still, Churchill continued to make clear the advantages of free enterprise. As the balance of payments troubles eased, the Conservative Government began to deregulate and privatize international trade. Churchill told the Conservative Party conference on 10 October 1953: "We stand for the restoration of buying and selling between individual importers and exporters in different countries instead of the clumsy bargainings of one state against another, biased by politics and national feelings as these must necessarily be."[1]

Churchill also moved to deregulate several industries, especially the transport industry. In seeking to nationalize transport, the Labour Government had acquired only 41,000 lorries out of a total of more than a million. Of this million, 800,000 were operating under a "C licence," which required that they carry only goods owned by the owner of the lorry. This resulted in many inefficiencies, including lorries returning empty from delivery journeys. The repeal of this restriction gave 75 percent of the transport fleet the flexibility to respond to need.[2]

Other major initiatives of the Churchill Government were concerned with housing and tax cuts. The two were linked in Churchill's mind. In a constituency speech in September 1952, Churchill said that the housing policy was of a piece with the exemption of two million wage-earners altogether from income tax. This would help them to produce more "in the hard times through which we are passing." He continued:

> Another form of incentive is the possibility of having, and still more of owning, a home of your own where a family can live and grow and have its own front door, which none may pass except by invitation or with proper warrant. Insufficient and bad housing is a hindrance to production, and this is especially true in times of rearmament and change. More than that, it is destructive of happiness and morality and a reproach to a Christian nation.[3]

Churchill had for decades worked for "a property-owning democracy."[4] Houses were the place to start. He appointed as Minister of Housing his long-time colleague Harold Macmillan, with whom he had worked when Chancellor of the Exchequer in 1924–9, when Macmillan was a young and freshly elected MP. Macmillan's views on social reform were amenable to Churchill's. Churchill had pledged at the 1950 Conservative Conference that any government he was able to form would build 300,000 houses per year, up from 200,000. Many houses had been bombed during the war and many others were dilapidated. Churchill directed Macmillan to build "homes for the people."[5]

---

[1] Churchill: speech, 10 Oct. 1953, reproduced below (p. 1243).
[2] Churchill: speech, 6 Sep. 1952, reproduced below (p. 640).
[3] Ibid., p. 641.
[4] Churchill: speech, 9 Oct. 1954, reproduced below (p. 1795).
[5] Churchill: speech, 3 Nov. 1953, reproduced below (p. 1272).

Churchill's political opponents, he said, "used to mock us because we have set before ourselves as our goal a rate of building 300,000 houses a year."[1] Macmillan achieved that goal by the end of 1953, a year early.

After the Coronation in June 1953, John Colville reflected that the celebration seemed "to usher in a period of prosperity and relaxation."[2] Things were indeed improving. On September 6, 1952 Churchill forecast "that we in this island will in the second half of this year, after taking credit for defence aid, be in general balance with the non-sterling world, and that the whole sterling area will be in balance with the rest of the world."[3] The Marshall Plan aid of £400–500 million per year had been reduced to military aid alone of £175 million.[4]

The economy under Conservative rule had crossed a divide. Britain had begun an economic expansion that lasted 15 years. Economically, it was the beginning of what is called the modern "Golden Age" of Britain.

Churchill was proud of the expanded majority that Anthony Eden won in the election of May 1955, less than two months after Churchill retired. In the election of 1959 Harold Macmillan increased the majority again, even after the British embarrassment in the 1956 Suez Crisis, which led to Eden's resignation and his succession by Macmillan. The second Churchill premiership established policies that would remain in effect until the election of Harold Wilson's Labour Government in 1964.

The great facts in the strategic situation during Churchill's second premiership were the offsetting and opposed might of the United States and the Soviet Union. Churchill and Britain were on the side of the United States, but Churchill also sought ways to moderate the conflict and prevent war. The danger of catastrophic war loomed throughout his second administration. Much went wrong, but that, at least, was avoided.

During his second premiership, Churchill developed, articulated, and pursued a new and more restrained strategy for British foreign policy. That strategy included strong elements of aggression, chiefly diplomatic, but it involved pulling back from areas more remote from Britain and concentrating on areas closer to home.

At the beginning of his administration he named his goals:

Whatever happens we shall stand up with all our strength in defence of the free world against Communist tyranny and aggression. We shall do our utmost to preserve the British Commonwealth and Empire as an independent factor in world affairs. We shall cherish the fraternal association of the

---

[1] Churchill: speech, 6 Sep. 1952, reproduced below (p. 641).
[2] Colville: diary, 12 June 1953, reproduced below (p. 1108).
[3] Churchill: speech, 6 Sep. 1952, reproduced below (p. 642).
[4] Churchill: speech, 30 July 1952, reproduced below (p. 573).

English-speaking world. We shall work in true comradeship for and with United Europe. It may be that this land will have the honour of helping civilization climb the hill amid the toils of peace as we once did in the terrors of war.[1]

These were the goals Churchill had pursued for most of his life. Now he would pursue them with a restraint made necessary by the relative weakness of Britain after the war. Nothing better signifies this than his attitude toward the Egyptian troubles that plagued his administration and would culminate after he retired in the Suez Crisis of 1956.

Churchill's attitude to Egypt recognized the "changed constitutional position of India and Pakistan."[2] This altered the British interest in the Suez Canal. Churchill commented at a conference at the White House on 8 January 1952 that communications with the remaining Commonwealth countries of Australia and New Zealand could be maintained around the Cape of Good Hope. The British, he said, had also lost their direct interest in Persia. "Palestine was now an independent state." The British remained in Egypt to perform an international duty, and only that.[3] Britain, he complained, was keeping more than 50,000 troops in Egypt, its whole strategic reserve. He wanted to wind that down.

The British position in Egypt became increasingly difficult. The change in Egyptian politics that would bring Gamal Abdul Nasser to power began to develop under his predecessor, Mohamed Naguib. Demonstrations and attacks of terror occurred frequently, and Churchill appealed again and again for American "moral support" in Egypt.[4] Churchill emphasized that it was no part of British imperial policy to be involved in Egypt: Britain had no more interest there than other powers. He said he did not need American troops, only diplomatic efforts in Egypt to support the British position.

The strategic thinking behind this position was laid out on 3 April 1952 in a note that Churchill sent to the Minister of Defence, Field Marshal Lord Alexander, his close and admired wartime colleague. He was responding to a memorandum referring to an "anticipated Russian invasion of the Middle East." Churchill could not imagine how such a thing could happen. It could only happen as part of a global war, including a Soviet attack in Europe. That attack would be successful within "a month or six weeks." It would, however, soon be met with a United States atomic attack that would "paralyse all communications between their advancing armies and the central Government." The Soviet Union would be "shattered as an organic military force." It would not be "in a position to cross the Sinai Peninsula and play about in the Western

---

[1] Churchill: broadcast, 22 Dec. 1951, reproduced below (p. 148).
[2] US–UK discussions: minutes, 8 Jan. 1952, reproduced below (p. 180).
[3] Ibid., 181.
[4] See Bermuda Conference: minutes, 7 Dec. 1953, reproduced below (p. 1338).

Desert." He concluded: "the whole proportion of events in the Middle East is petty compared to the terrible decisions which would be reached at the outbreak of the War."[1]

With British finance strained and the nation generally weaker, Churchill looked for the cheapest way to maintain British security and influence. He continued efforts begun under the previous administration to build up the British military, though on a slower timetable than the Labour Government had planned. He was not trying to match the Soviets in conventional weapons, but to build a serious deterrent force. He continued efforts to build an independent British atomic force, including later in his administration the Hydrogen bomb. He sought independence of action and to make Britain a stronger ally.

Supporting America with troops in Korea, Churchill sought to confine that conflict to Korea alone. He understood that the Far East was more important to the United States than to Britain, and he counseled his colleagues to be patient with the United States. In a speech in the House of Commons on 1 July 1952 he urged that it would be a "great mistake" for the United States to be involved in war with the Communist Government inside China. But, he continued, "do not let us blind ourselves to the terrible cost that is being paid for their patience by the people of the United States."[2] John Colville records in his diary for 5 July 1954 "the importance of not quarrelling violently with the Americans over Far Eastern questions (which affected them more than us)."[3]

Egypt and the Far East came together in a revealing way when Admiral Radford, chairman of the American Joint Chiefs of Staff, came to see Churchill at Chequers on 26 April 1954. The admiral came to ask for British help in Vietnam, where the French position in Dien Bien Phu was under siege.

The admiral described the dangers of the French collapse in Vietnam. If Dien Bien Phu fell and the French were ejected from Indochina, rebellions against the French would spread around the world. There would be a nationalist uprising in Morocco. The food supply to Japan would be lost, and that of Australia and New Zealand threatened. Communist infiltration in all these places would increase. This was so important that the United States would be willing to help Britain "in other spheres and . . . he thought that there would be no difficulty in revoking the present American policy of aloofness with regard to our difficulties in Egypt."[4]

This mention of U.S. "aloofness" toward British policy in Egypt was more candid than American communications had been. Churchill had been

---

[1] Churchill to Alexander, 3 Apr. 1952, reproduced below (p. 378).
[2] Churchill: speech, 1 July 1952, reproduced below (p. 522).
[3] Colville: diary, 5 July 1954, reproduced below (p. 1649).
[4] Record of a conversation, 26 Apr. 1954, reproduced below (p. 1550).

pleading for help with little result but no firm denials. Radford was offering a powerful inducement.

Churchill replied that the fall of Dien Bien Phu might well be a critical moment in history. It reminded him of the situation in Warsaw in 1919 when the Russian revolutionary armies were thrown back by Piłsudski. "The tide had been checked and rolled backwards." This was another such point, "but how to roll back the tide in this instance was a very different problem. The British people would not be easily influenced by what happened in the distant jungles of SE Asia; but they did know that there was a powerful American base in East Anglia and that war with China, who would invoke the Sino-Russian Pact, might mean an assault by Hydrogen bombs on these islands." The British, Churchill said, could not commit themselves – when all these matters were about to be discussed at Geneva – to "a policy which might lead by slow stages to catastrophe."[1]

Churchill warned Radford of the danger of "war on the fringes, where the Russians were strong and could mobilise the enthusiasm of nationalist and oppressed peoples." He preferred instead "conversations at the centre." These conversations must not lead either to appeasement or to an ultimatum. They would be calculated "to bring home to the Russians the full implications of Western strength and to impress upon them the folly of war." This might not work, but it would be "understood by people in this country far better than fighting in SE Asia."[2]

The proposed action in Vietnam "was almost certain to be ineffective."[3] The French did not have the force to hold all Indochina. They should retire to the places that they could hold. Churchill complained in other conversations that the French were not serious about their empire, for they would not alter their law forbidding them to send conscripts abroad. Their army in Indochina was therefore heavily staffed by officers from France, which weakened the French army in Europe, and by enlisted men from the Foreign Legion and from mercenary forces. This, Churchill thought, was not a strategy for winning.

Churchill was disappointed with the French on many grounds. Premier Reynaud pressed him to bring Britain into the proposed European Defence Community. Churchill took the same view that he took of the European Union: Britain would be an independent friend.[4] Then in June 1954 the French Assembly voted not to join the EDC, which put an end to the idea. Churchill thought that French fears of Germany had an obvious basis, but West Germany was a necessary ally, and Churchill greatly admired Chancellor Adenauer, to whom he referred in a telegram to President Eisenhower as

---

[1] Record of a conversation, 26 Apr. 1954, reproduced below (p. 1550).
[2] Ibid., p. 1551.
[3] Ibid.
[4] Churchill to Cabinet, 29 Nov. 1951, reproduced below (p. 83).

"the best German we have found for a long time."¹ France failed to understand that resistance to the most urgent threat should have priority. Never a friend of communism or its Bolshevik incarnation, Churchill had sought alliance with the Soviet Union to meet the Nazi threat. He urged this kind of thinking upon the French.

Churchill also thought, however, that it would be a "very serious decision for us to authorise the Germans to make atomic weapons." Anyway, if they were on the right side of a future war they would get "all the advantage of the vast American production."²

Churchill closed his remarks to Radford, which amounted to a refusal, with an appeal for the close alliance of the English-speaking peoples and the continued effective cooperation of Great Britain and the United States.

Radford replied that he would tell Eisenhower, and he agreed that cooperation with Great Britain was the keystone of his policy and without it "both the United States and the United Kingdom would drift to disaster."³

One thing was established: Churchill was not willing to go to Vietnam, even to please the United States, even if it would bring American help in Egypt. He was pulling back.

This difference of British and American views led to what Anthony Eden reported as "embarrassments" at the Geneva conference the following month. At the next Cabinet meeting Churchill said: "it must be recognized that the fall of Dien Bien Phu, which now seemed inevitable, would afford great encouragement to Communists throughout the world." Britain must counter this effect by pressing forward with "efforts to establish an effective system of collective defence for Southeast Asia and the Western Pacific."⁴

Churchill was seeking to build collective security arrangements in every troubled spot in the world. These would operate under the aegis of the United Nations and be based upon American power and, to the extent possible, American partnership with Great Britain. In a letter to Eisenhower on 21 June 1954 Churchill proposed NATO arrangements for South-East Asia and the Middle East: a SEATO and a MEATO. This would perfect "in a coherent structure the world front against Communist aggression."⁵

Although Churchill after his retirement made few public statements about policy and none that were controversial, he continued to have reservations about heavy commitments in Egypt. In August 1956, as the Suez Crisis was building, Churchill wrote a note that was apparently not sent to anyone. It

---

¹ Churchill to Eisenhower, 12 Apr. 1953, reproduced below (p. 945).
² Churchill to Alexander, 10 May 1952, reproduced below (p. 431).
³ Record of a conversation, 26 Apr. 1954, reproduced below (p. 1552).
⁴ Cabinet: conclusions, 3 May 1954, reproduced below (p. 1560).
⁵ Churchill to Eisenhower, 21 June 1954, reproduced below (p. 1615).

suggested that the Prime Minister should become in fact and perhaps in name also Minister of Defence, which he was in principle anyway. Alternatively, Harold Macmillan, then Chancellor of the Exchequer, could take the job. To Churchill, the military operation seemed "very serious." There would be a long delay while British intentions were known. There might be reinforcements from Russia to "take over the cream of the Egyptian aircraft and tanks.... The more one thinks about taking over the Canal, the less one likes it." The Canal could be easily mined.[1]

Some days later, Churchill wrote to his wife that he had seen Harold Macmillan the week before. Macmillan thought it futile to take the canal and have 100,000 troops to guard it; better to send the army to Cairo. John Colville records in his diary that Churchill called the Suez operation "the most ill-conceived and ill-executed imaginable." Asked if he would have done it, Churchill said: "I would never have dared; and if I had dared, I would certainly never have dared stop." Churchill "also said that if Eden resigned he thought Harold Macmillan would be a better successor than R. A. Butler."[2]

These stories are interesting because they take us as near as we can get to answering the question: what would Churchill do if he were in our circumstances? When we are tempted to answer that question, we should remember that in retirement Churchill said nothing like this out loud. Prudential decisions were made in keeping with principle, but the principle does not apply except when it is embedded in the circumstances. The one responsible must be allowed to judge the circumstances.

THE CORONATION OF A NEW QUEEN

A signal event during Churchill's second premiership was the Coronation of Elizabeth II, today the longest-serving monarch in British history. Her father George VI died on 6 February 1952. Churchill became close to the King during the war, and in his eulogy Churchill told the story of the bombing of Buckingham Palace. If the windows of the room he was in had not been open, he and the Queen would have been showered by shattered glass. Churchill did not hear of this episode until long after, and then not from the King. The King and Queen thought it of no "more significance than a soldier in their armies would of a shell bursting near him."[3]

Churchill also admired the young Queen greatly, as he had done from her youth. He described her as "a fair and youthful figure, Princess, wife and mother" and the "heir to all our traditions and glories, never greater than in her father's days." She also inherited, he says, "all our perplexities and

---
[1] Churchill: note, 6 Aug. 1956, reproduced below (pp. 2122–3).
[2] Colville: recollection, 29 Nov. 1956, reproduced below (p. 2149).
[3] Churchill: broadcast, 7 Feb. 1952, reproduced below (p. 258).

dangers, never greater in peace-time than now." She came to the throne at a time "when a tormented mankind stands uncertainly poised between world catastrophe and a golden age."[1]

TOWARDS RETIREMENT

Churchill's retirement was not the occasion of a power struggle among contending candidates. Most, including Churchill himself, expected that his successor would be his long-time colleague Anthony Eden, Foreign Secretary during both of Churchill's premierships. The controversial question was *when* Churchill would retire. That question took over two years to answer, involved many senior people in Churchill's Government, provoked a Cabinet reshuffle, and became entwined with Churchill's wish to organize and attend a summit meeting of the United States, the Soviet Union, and Britain.

Eden broached the subject of succession with Churchill in December 1952, almost two and a half years before Churchill would step down. Churchill assured him that he would "hand over his powers and authority with the utmost smoothness and surety" to him. Eden replied yes, but "when would that be?" The response was a moment of silence, then Churchill replied: "Often, I think there are things I could say, speeches I could make more easily if I were not Prime Minister."[2] Eden regarded this conversation as inconclusive, as several more would be; nor was this the last time Churchill would indicate a wish, even a longing, to step down.

Eden would speak to Churchill on the same subject on many more occasions. On 7 June 1954 he pushed for the transition to occur before the parliamentary recess that summer. Churchill replied that he could not commit himself before he saw what would happen in the talks in Washington coming at the end of the month. He said that he hoped that the delay might not extend "beyond the autumn."[3] Eden wrote again in August, as the autumn was drawing near. Churchill replied on August 24: "I have no intention of abandoning my post at the present crisis in the world. I feel sure that with my influence I can be of help to the cause of 'peace through strength.'" Churchill trusted that he could "count on [Eden's] loyalty and friendship."[4]

And so it went on. Harold Macmillan, who would succeed Eden as Prime Minister, and who was himself a long-standing colleague, even a protégé, of Churchill, spoke to Churchill several times to encourage him to step down.[5]

---

[1] Churchill: speech, 11 Feb. 1952, reproduced below (p. 264).
[2] Shuckburgh: diary, 8 Dec. 1952, reproduced below (p. 767).
[3] Churchill to Eden, 11 June 1954, reproduced below (p. 1603).
[4] Churchill to Eden, 24 Aug. 1954, reproduced below (p. 1751).
[5] See Macmillan: recollections, 2 July 1953 and 24 Aug. 1954, reproduced below (pp. 1146–8, 1753–4).

Preface

Lord Salisbury did the same. Their arguments were similar: the party needed new blood and more youth; an election had to be held soon, and the new Prime Minister should have time to get his legs under him; and – especially from Macmillan – the party needed a new theme and Churchill could not give it. It was often implied to Churchill, and more often said by and to others in the Cabinet, that he was simply too old to continue.

Churchill frequently replied to these points with the reasons why he wanted to stay. He closed his remarks to the October 1953 Conservative Party conference with this explanation:

> One word personally about myself. If I stay on for the time being bearing the burden at my age it is not because of love for power or office. I have had an ample share of both. If I stay it is because I have a feeling that I may through things that have happened have an influence on what I care about above all else, the building of a sure and lasting peace.[1]

Churchill wanted to talk face-to-face with the Soviets, preferably with the United States by his side and no one else. He had not done this since the end of the war. He feared that by poor judgment or malice world catastrophe could come. He thought he had the arguments to appeal to the Soviets: that war would be catastrophe for all; that peace could bring unimagined benefits and prosperity and well-being; that the Western allies would join the Soviet Union in protection of its security. By experience, knowledge, and reputation Churchill was uniquely qualified to impart this message. During the war, he had traveled tens of thousands of miles, much more than Roosevelt or Stalin, sometimes at risk to his life and health, to cultivate cooperation among the Allies.

The questions were: Was he too near the end of his career to command sufficient authority at home? Did Britain have the weight any longer to make such conversations fruitful? Or simply, was he too old?

In July 1954 the issue of Churchill meeting with the Soviets came to a head. At the end of June Churchill led a delegation to Washington for discussions with the United States. Everyone on the British side, including Churchill, considered them a great success. According to John Colville's diary, Churchill thought for a time during the discussions that Eisenhower was agreeing to meet with him and the Soviets.[2] If Eisenhower did ever think that, he had cooled towards the idea by the end of the conference.[3] Churchill retreated to the position that he would meet the Soviets alone. Just before leaving Washington Churchill met with Secretary of State Dulles, who discouraged Churchill from going. He said the United States might have to make clear that Churchill

---
[1] Churchill: speech, 10 Oct. 1953, reproduced below (p. 1246).
[2] Colville: diary, 25 June 1954, reproduced below (p. 1625).
[3] Colville: diary, 27 June 1954, reproduced below (pp. 1628–9).

was not speaking for it. Churchill replied he would not go as an intermediary between the United States and the Soviet Union.

Churchill left the conference under the impression that he had permission, albeit grudging, to proceed on his own. On the ship on the way home he drafted a note to Soviet Foreign Minister Molotov.[1] While still on board ship he showed it to Eden, who reluctantly approved.[2] He then cabled it to Chancellor of the Exchequer Butler, over the weekend, seeking advice, but without a definite instruction to consult the entire Cabinet. Butler responded with a few amendments and Churchill sent the cable to Molotov. Molotov responded warmly, and it seemed that Churchill was on his way.

Then Churchill arrived home. On July 7 he sent the text of his Molotov telegram to Eisenhower. Eisenhower responded immediately. He had thought that Churchill was in an "undecided mood about this matter," and that he would receive "some notice" before the program was put into action. Still, he said, that was "past history" and they must now hope the steps Churchill had taken would lead to a good result. He would need to make a statement when Churchill made the program public. He would say that the summit had not been agreed between them, though they had discussed it. He feared that the promptness with which the message had been sent after their meeting would give an impression that it had been agreed.[3]

Churchill told the Cabinet about his letter to Molotov on July 7. He read them Eisenhower's response to it on July 8. The Cabinet then discussed what Lord Salisbury called the "constitutional aspects of this matter." The Prime Minister could determine policy, but if he took a decision of policy that involved the collective responsibility of the whole Government without prior consultation with his Cabinet colleagues, any of his colleagues who dissented "might thereby be forced to the remedy of resignation." Churchill replied that this was a personal communication to explore a meeting rather than a formal proposal to hold one. Butler told the Cabinet that his message from Churchill, while Churchill was on the voyage home, had not asked him to show it to the Cabinet. Churchill admitted that in his anxiety to lose no opportunity of "furthering the cause of world peace," he might have taken "an exaggerated view of the urgency of the matter. There had seemed no reason to delay what he regarded as a personal and informal enquiry which could not commit his colleagues." Salisbury said that he was opposed in principle to a meeting between Britain and the Soviet Union, and he had made that clear to the Prime Minister in a letter.[4] A few days later Macmillan went to Clementine Churchill to say that the Cabinet was in danger of breaking up.[5]

---

[1] Churchill to Butler, 2 July 1954, reproduced below (p. 1645).
[2] Colville: diary, 2 July 1954, reproduced below (pp. 1643–4).
[3] Eisenhower to Churchill, 7 July 1954, reproduced below (pp .1651–2).
[4] Cabinet: Confidential Annex, 8 July 1954, reproduced below (pp. 1663–4).
[5] Colville: diary, 16 July 1954, reproduced below (p. 1695).

Preface

In a letter to Churchill of July 22, not on its face connected to this issue, President Eisenhower suggested a plan for Churchill to put a capstone on his career. Churchill should give a speech of international importance on the right of self-determination of all peoples. This would help to undercut the Soviet efforts to recruit oppressed peoples to their cause. The President wrote that he agreed with Churchill that some peoples were not yet able to exercise the right of self-government, and that "any attempt to make them now responsible for their own governing would be to condemn them to lowered standards of life and probably to communistic domination." But Eisenhower suggested that Churchill set a timetable of twenty-five years for the end of colonialism. "Possibly it might be said that our two nations plan to undertake every kind of applicable program to insure that within a space of twenty-five years (or by some other agreed upon, definite, date), all peoples will have achieved the necessary political, cultural and economic standards to permit the attainment of their goals."[1]

Churchill did many surprising things in his life; a favorable answer to this letter would have been one of them. He answered Eisenhower on August 8:

> One has to do one's duty as one sees it from day to day and, as you know, the mortal peril which overhangs the human race is never absent from my thoughts. I am not looking about for the means of making a dramatic exit or of finding a suitable Curtain. It is better to take things as they come. I am however convinced that the present method of establishing the relations between the two sides of the world by means of endless discussions between Foreign Offices, will not produce any decisive result.[2]

Churchill repudiated the insult implicit in Eisenhower's letter, whether Eisenhower intended it or not. Churchill habitually spoke of his personal service in humble – or sometimes in jocular – terms, as in his famous comment that the British people were the lion, and he was called upon to give the roar. Deeply interested in honor, he knew that it was dishonorable to seek it directly. Rather, one ought to seek to *deserve* honor. But what could he do in 1954 to match the deeds of 1940? Those deeds were done in the supreme emergency. In 1954, he was seeking to meet the Soviets specifically to avoid the recurrence of such an emergency.

It is worth saying that Eisenhower's correspondence with Churchill is warm and kind to a greater degree and with greater frequency than that of either Roosevelt or Truman. One will see in this volume that this continued even after Churchill retired. Eisenhower's diaries and memoirs are not always in the same tone, but one cannot doubt his respect for Churchill.

---

[1] Eisenhower to Churchill, 22 July 1954, reproduced below (pp. 1703–6).
[2] Churchill to Eisenhower, 8 Aug. 1954, reproduced below (p. 1724).

On 23 July 1954 the Cabinet had another lengthy discussion of Churchill's wish for a summit. No member who spoke favored the idea. Anthony Eden said, however, that although he did not believe good could come of the meeting, if "the Prime Minister, with all his long experience, felt so strongly that the attempt was worth making, the Foreign Secretary was ready to acquiesce – so long as the meeting was not held on Russian soil."[1] Again the Cabinet decided to think about it further.

Churchill did not at any point commit himself to giving up the idea of a summit, but he met an obstacle that would prove decisive for the rest of his premiership. On July 26 came a Russian invitation for a conference of all the European powers. Churchill could not pursue his plan for a small meeting while this big one was on the table. The Cabinet agreed that he should write to Molotov to say that in these circumstances the two men could not meet. Churchill had but eight months left in office; he was running out of time.

This final object of Churchill's career was not to be achieved. He was unable by his own efforts to substitute "conversations at the centre" for "war on the fringes." He had been aware all along that his efforts to do so might be in vain. With reason, he thought himself best qualified to get results.

In fact, there soon was a meeting among the Soviet Union, Great Britain, and the United States – in July 1955, three months after Churchill retired. On the eve of that conference, Eisenhower wrote to Churchill:

> I cannot escape a feeling of sadness that the delay brought about by the persistently hostile Soviet attitude toward NATO has operated to prevent your personal attendance at the meeting.
>
> Foster and I know – as does the world – that your courage and vision will be missed at the meeting. But your long quest for peace daily inspires much that we do. I hope that in your wisdom you will consider that we there do well; certainly we shall do the best of which we are capable in the opportunities we may encounter in Geneva.[2]

Churchill replied:

> I am very glad that the meeting "at the summit" is now taking place, and I will gladly do anything in my power from a distance and a private station to help it to a good result. I have never indulged in extravagant hopes of a vast, dramatic transformation of human affairs, but my belief is that, so long as we do not relax our unity or our vigilance, the Soviets and the Russian people will be increasingly convinced that it is in their interests to live peaceably with us.[3]

The discussions at this Four Power conference were deemed civil, and there

---

[1] Cabinet: Confidential Annex, 23 July 1954, reproduced below (p. 1709).
[2] Eisenhower to Churchill, 15 July 1955, reproduced below (p. 2024).
[3] Churchill to Eisenhower, 18 July 1955, reproduced below (p. 2025).

was talk of free international trade among all nations. The German question was not settled, nor would it be until 1989. The Cold War continued at higher and lower temperatures until the Soviet Union itself disbanded. The overriding blessing was no war with the Soviet Union.

The frustration of Churchill's wish for a meeting with the Soviets was not by any means the first time his high hopes had been dashed. He tried to prevent the world wars. He tried to prevent the rise of socialism. He tried to prevent the loss of the British Empire. He tried many times to build a party of the center around the central themes of his career: freedom, parliamentary and constitutional government, empire, and national security as cheaply as it could be had. He was a man of many failures.

There were many complaints during Churchill's last premiership that he was holding on to power beyond his capacity to use it. He was surely old and slower. These pages are replete with those complaints, but they also contain many instances of his continued fluency, nimbleness of mind, and profundity. His wit did not fail him. For example, John Colville was impressed with Churchill's answer to a journalist in New York:

> Qn: What are your views, Mr Churchill, on the present stalemate in Korea?
> Ans: Better a stalemate than a checkmate.[1]

Churchill's last major speech in the House of Commons is a more serious example. Churchill spoke on 1 March 1955, a month before he retired, on the subject of nuclear deterrence. He began by describing the age in which we live, "happily unique in human history." The whole world is divided "intellectually and to a large extent geographically between the creeds of Communist discipline and individual freedom." Both sides possess "the obliterating weapons of the nuclear age." These antagonisms are "as deep as those of the Reformation. . . . But now they are spread over the whole world." Churchill did not pretend "to have a solution for a permanent peace." Rather, he offered some general reflections, beginning with a quotation from an essay he wrote a quarter-century before.[2] The essay was "50 Years Hence," in which he predicted the invention of nuclear weapons. Yet more significantly than that, he developed his theme, common with his contemporary C. S. Lewis, that the conquest of man over nature would also result in the conquest of man over man, more specifically some men over the rest.

In this last speech, Churchill spoke of the hydrogen bomb. It had been announced on 17 February 1954, a year earlier. With that announcement, he said, "the entire foundation of human affairs was revolutionised, and mankind placed in a situation both measureless and laden with doom."[3]

---

[1] Colville: diary, 3 Jan. 1955, reproduced below (p. 796).
[2] Churchill: speech, 1 Mar. 1955, reproduced below (p. 1926).
[3] Ibid., pp. 1927–8.

What was to be done? The best defense would be "bona fide disarmament all around." This was impossible because of the "gulf between the Soviet Government and the NATO Powers." Another difficulty was that the United States had "the overwhelming mastery in nuclear weapons," whereas "the Soviets and their Communist satellites have immense superiority in what are called 'conventional' forces."[1] Churchill did not say it, but he and others in his Cabinet had worried that the United States might be quicker to make nuclear war than those allies in Europe who would suffer most from it. But much more than that, they feared the extension of Soviet despotism across Europe. Churchill's strategy throughout his second premiership was to stay close to the United States, support her, and guide her when he could. In this speech he said: "We must also never allow, above all, I hold, the growing sense of unity and brotherhood between the United Kingdom and the United States and throughout the English-speaking world to be injured or retarded."[2] Churchill believed in the association of the free countries, especially those who could speak with one another freely.

Major wars of the future would differ, he said, from all in the past and in one significant respect: "that each side, at the outset, will suffer what it dreads the most, the loss of everything that it has ever known of."[3]

Churchill offered hope: "After a certain point has been passed it may be said, 'The worse things get the better.'"[4] There could develop something like a "saturation" in which both sides might destroy one another quickly. And then "by a process of sublime irony" we shall reach "a stage in this story where safety will be the sturdy child of terror, and survival the twin brother of annihilation."[5] But Churchill also admitted that this kind of deterrence did not cover the case of "lunatics or dictators in the mood of Hitler when he found himself in his final dug-out. That is a blank."[6]

He concluded with hope and determination:

> The deterrent may well reach its acme and reap its final reward. The day may dawn when fair play, love for one's fellow men, respect for justice and freedom, will enable tormented generations to march forth serene and triumphant from the hideous epoch in which we have to dwell.[7]

Churchill closed the speech with what may be taken as his final words to his beloved House of Commons and his country: "Meanwhile, never flinch, never weary, never despair."[8]

---

[1] Churchill: speech, 1 Mar. 1955, reproduced below (p. 1928).
[2] Ibid., p. 1935.
[3] Ibid., p. 1933.
[4] Ibid., p. 1930.
[5] Ibid., p. 1931.
[6] Ibid., p. 1932.
[7] Ibid., p.1935.
[8] Ibid., p. 1935.

Young or old, very few have been born who could weave together such a strategy for freedom in such language.

Churchill announced his retirement on 5 April 1955. Frictions of politics forgotten, the minutes of Churchill's last Cabinet meeting are moving:

> The Prime Minister said that he intended to submit his resignation to Her Majesty at an audience that afternoon. His resignation would carry with it the resignation of the whole Administration. Other Ministers need not tender their resignations to The Queen, but they should regard their offices as at the disposal of his successor. Meanwhile they should carry on the necessary administration of their Departments until a new Government was formed. Ministers of Cabinet rank who were not members of the Cabinet would be so informed at a meeting which he was holding later in the day. Junior Ministers would be similarly informed by letter.
>
> The Prime Minister said that it remained for him to wish his colleagues all good fortune in the difficult, but hopeful, situation which they had to face. He trusted that they would be enabled to further the progress already made in rebuilding the domestic stability and economic strength of the United Kingdom and in weaving still more closely the threads which bound together the countries of the Commonwealth or, as he still preferred to call it, the Empire.
>
> The Foreign Secretary said that his Cabinet colleagues had asked him to speak on this occasion on behalf of them all. It therefore fell to him to express their sense of abiding affection and esteem for the Prime Minister and their pride in the privilege of having served as his colleagues. He himself had enjoyed this privilege for sixteen years, others for varying shorter periods; but all, whatever the length of their service, had the same strong feelings of affection for him. If in a succeeding Government they met with success, this would be largely due to the example which he had shown them: if they did less well, it would be because they had failed to learn from his experience and skill as a statesman. They would remember him always – for his magnanimity, for his courage at all times and for his unfailing humour, founded in his unrivalled mastery of the English language. They would always be grateful for his leadership, and for his friendship, over the years that had passed; and they would hope to enjoy in future his continuing interest and support in their endeavours.[1]

In a magnificent gesture, the Queen offered to make Churchill a duke, the highest level of the peerage. There was an understanding, not known to him, that he would refuse it, and he did. On the day before his resignation she came to dinner at 10 Downing Street – his house for the last night.

---

[1] Cabinet: conclusions, 5 Apr. 1955, reproduced below (pp. 1980–1).

Churchill would live for almost ten more years. Many of them were spent in relative happiness, painting and traveling to the sunshine, having compliments paid – or, better, consultation sought – by presidents and prime ministers and monarchs. These years passed, and at the end he was infirm.

This volume brings the official biography of Churchill to its inevitably sad conclusion in death. Great lives generate the largest sense of loss. Richard Crossman, a gifted writer and thinker, said he felt that not only the age but perhaps even the nation was coming to an end. The 300,000 who braved a biting and damp wind to stand for hours to file past Churchill's casket felt something of the same. There are videos of a few of them saying precisely that.

Churchill himself felt this sadness in his decline. Articulate always, he said that "when you let all these responsibilities drop you feel your power falls with the thing it held."[1] He spoke often of the vivid events of his life, and one could feel the energy, the determination, the joy he had brought to them, and the love he still cherished for them.

One does feel sadness for the very old Churchill, hardly mobile and, worse, bored. It is the loss of the man in his full powers, charging the Dervishes on his horse, walking amidst the bullets beside the armored train, taking on the titans of the Parliament when he had only just arrived. One thinks of his hard stand for free trade, speaking as he believed for the ordinary folk who ought not to pay dear for their bread. One thinks of the supreme energy he brought both to the prevention and to the fighting of war. One thinks of his favorite statement of his driving ideas: the people must own the government, not the government the people.

When one thinks of these things one feels loss; but also one remembers that the story is not over. It lives in memory, and through memory it provides a better way to see for all who must make hard choices, which is all of us. We have named above three of the four causes of this biography. The most important is last. The final cause of this biography is to find the truth about this remarkable man and thereby to see human nature in both its triumphs and its tragedies.

Larry P. Arnn
Hillsdale College
Hillsdale, Michigan
September 2019

---

[1] Churchill to Tudor, 25 Aug. 1955, reproduced below (p. 2037).

Acknowledgments

This being likely the longest biography ever written, it is the work of thousands. Most of them have been young, as I was when I began, and as Sir Martin was when he began. Especially the document volumes demand the energy and ingenuity of youth. The names of the almost sixty graduate and undergraduate students who have assisted with this volume read like an honor roll of superior students at Hillsdale College. They are: Bryce Asberg, Luke Barbrick, Rachael Behr, Colin Brown, Morgan Brownfield, Adrienne Carrier, Johnathon Case, Nathanael Cheng, Colleen Coleman, Peter Cross, Amber Crump, Emma Cummins, Connor Daniels, Juan Davalos, Katherine Davenport, Jessica De Gree, Madison Estell, Christopher Goffos, Stephen Goniprow, Lynette Grundvig, Luke Grzywacz, John Hancock, Ross Hatley, Andrew Heim, Guenevere Hellickson, Jessica Higa, Adelaide Holmes, Clifford Humphrey, Annalyssa Lee, Josiah Leinbach, Jennifer Matthes, Evyn Melanson, Kristiana Mork, Ryan Murphy, Taryn Murphy, Mark Naida, Stevi Nichols, Zachary Palmer, Anthony Pestritto, Lillian Quinones, Zack Reynolds, Tess Skehan, Krystina Skurk, Genevieve Suchyta, Thomas Tacoma, Joseph Toates, Tara Ung, Keith Vrotsos, Julia Wacker, Joshua Waechter, Jonathan Walker, Doyle Wang, Jacob Weaver, Dominic Whalen, Christian Yiu, and Daniel Ziegler. I am grateful to them not only for the work they have done, evident in this volume, but also for the fun they have given me from hearing and seeing them work.

In 1979 my friend of now many decades Christopher Flannery came to Oxford from America to spend a few weeks researching with me. Some of the documents we found are in this volume. I am grateful for Christopher's work as for his friendship.

Dr Anne Theobald and Dr Stephen Naumann, excellent language professors at Hillsdale College, assisted with the translation of French and German documents respectively.

Allen Packwood, Director of the Churchill Archives Centre at Churchill College Cambridge, has been a friend of this project since he joined the Centre in 1995. He has been his usual supportive self for this volume as for its predecessors. I am grateful for the wise counsel he has given and for his ability to find anything and everything in the Churchill Archive.

Acknowledgments

Hillsdale College has secured the various rights it holds to produce and publish this biography through Winston Churchill's own literary agent, Curtis Brown Ltd, which now acts for Churchill's descendants and trusts. I am grateful to the firm and to its employees, especially Anthea Morton-Saner, with whom I began working in 1984, and Gordon Wise, with whom I have been working since 2010.

I have come to know many members of the Churchill family in the years since I began work for Martin Gilbert. I met the late Lady Soames, Churchill's youngest child, in 1984, and since then I have met most of the Churchill grandchildren. I have found them unfailingly pleasant, helpful, and respectful of the achievements of their great ancestor. I give special thanks to granddaughter-in-law Minnie Churchill, to grandchildren Julian, Celia, and Edwina Sandys, and in the next generation to Duncan and the late Jonathan Sandys. Great-grandson Randolph Churchill is a delight and tireless in discharging the family responsibilities. All of them have been generous with their time and support for many years. The entire family guards Sir Winston's legacy faithfully.

My friend and colleague of decades Richard Langworth has brought to this volume the same deep knowledge, attention to detail, and tireless labors that he has to several of their predecessors. He is a treasure of Churchilliana.

In London, significant research was accomplished by Hillsdale graduate Jack Shannon and his team at the National Archives. Judson Alphin also assisted with research in England. Aaron Kilgore, first a student in and now a librarian of Hillsdale College, has continued to apply his meticulous habits to Churchill research.

This volume being about as big as it is possible to bind a book, correcting the copy requires singular persistence and care. Sheila Ryan contributed those qualities in writing the index; Jennifer Omner in setting the type; Ann Hart in proofreading the manuscript. Gillian Somerscales, who won the confidence of Martin Gilbert back in 2012, has copy-edited each of the document volumes since volume 17. She and Ann Hart are the last line of defense against errors, and any that remain are my fault and not theirs.

Douglas Jeffrey, superior editor, has made this volume better everywhere, especially in the preface.

Soren Geiger, effectively the managing editor of the volumes that we have produced at Hillsdale College, has now left us to attend law school. He is a brilliant young man, and his work has been indispensable to this and earlier volumes. I expect you will hear of him as he builds his career. His work has been assumed by graduate student Colin Brown, who is doing very well.

This biography is as financially impractical as it is academically important. Many generous people have supported the work. They include the following foundations and individuals: the Lynde and Harry Bradley Foundation, Milwaukee, Wisconsin; the Earhart Foundation, Ann Arbor, Michigan; the late George B. Ferguson, Peoria, Arizona; Mr and Mrs William L. Grewcock, Omaha, Nebraska; Mr and Mrs Thomas N. Jordan, Jr, Healdsburg, California; Mr and Mrs Robert S. Pettengill, Brighton, Michigan; the late Tim M. Roudebush and Mrs Ruth Roudebush, Lenexa, Kansas; the Saul N. Silbert Charitable Trust, Sun City, Arizona; and Mr and Mrs Emil A. Voelz, Jr, Akron, Ohio.

During the writing of this volume the great William L. Grewcock, husband of Berniece for seventy years, passed away. We remember Bill with deep respect and repeat our condolences to Berniece. They have supported the Churchill biography for close to twenty years.

The Board of Trustees of Hillsdale College have given me time and resources to carry on this work amidst the incessant and swirling business of the college. I am personally grateful to them for this and many other evidences of their support and friendship. All who wish to know about Churchill have reason to be grateful to them.

Last June Hillsdale College held a party, premature as it turns out, to celebrate the completion of this biography. Some 150 people came to the big dining room at the Liberal Club, founded in the nineteenth century by William Gladstone. It is a beautiful place, and Baron Dobbs of Wylye, Lady Esther Gilbert, and Randolph Churchill spoke beautifully in honor of all those who prosecuted for 58 years the campaign to build this biography. I am grateful to them.

Finally I am grateful to Lady Gilbert, who in her grief carried out the transfer of Sir Martin's papers to us at Hillsdale, which enabled us to complete the work. She worked for months, a labor of love and mourning. She still contributes her intelligence and affection to sustain the legacy of Sir Martin.

Larry P. Arnn
Hillsdale College
Hillsdale, Michigan
September 2019

Sources and Bibliography

The principal archival collection used in the course of compiling this volume is the Churchill papers, now permanently housed at Churchill College, Cambridge. Access has also been granted to material in the National Archives (Cabinet, Foreign Office and Premier papers). In addition, the following collections of private papers have been used: Lord Beaverbrook papers, Lord Camrose papers, Lord Chelwood papers, Randolph Churchill papers, Sir Martin Gilbert papers, Government of Israel Archives, Lady Lytton papers, Wendy and Emery Reves Collection, Baroness Spencer-Churchill papers, Chaim Weizmann papers, Westminster College papers.

The authors, editors and compilers of the following published works, from which documents, recollections and other quotations have been drawn, are gratefully acknowledged.

American Presidency Project, University of California at Santa Barbara.
American Rhetoric Online Speech Bank.
Dean Acheson, *Present at the Creation: My Years in the State Department*, New York, 1969.
BBC Sound Archives.
Peter G. Boyle (editor), *The Churchill Eisenhower Correspondence, 1953–1955*, Chapel Hill, NC, 1990.
Anthony Montague Browne, *Long Sunset: Memoirs of Winston Churchill's Last Private Secretary*, London, 1995.
Piers Brendon, *Churchill's Bestiary: His Life through Animals*, London, 2018.
R. A. Butler, *The Art of the Possible: The Memoirs of Lord Butler*, London, 1971.
Henry Channon, *Chips, The Diaries of Sir Henry Channon*, ed. Robert Rhodes James, London, 1967.
Winston S. Churchill, *The Second World War*, vol. 6, *Triumph and Tragedy*, London, 1954.
Winston S. Churchill, *Stemming the Tide, Speeches 1951 and 1952*, ed. Randolph S. Churchill, London, 1953.
Winston S. Churchill, *The Unwritten Alliance, Speeches 1953–1959*, ed. Randolph S. Churchill, London, 1961.

Winston S. Churchill, *Winston S. Churchill, His Complete Speeches, 1897–1963*, ed. Robert Rhodes James, volume 8, London and New York, 1974.
Sir John Colville, *The Fringes of Power, Downing Street Diaries 1939–1955*, London, 1985.
Richard Crossman, *The Diaries of a Cabinet Minister*, vol. 1, *Minister of Housing, 1964–1966*, London, 1975.
Finest Hour, Nos. 79, Spring 1993; 114, Spring 2002; 117, Winter 2002–2003; 135, Summer 2007
Foreign Relations of the United States, 1952–1954, vol. IX (Washington DC, 1984).
Martin Gilbert, *Winston S. Churchill*, vol. 6, *Finest Hour, 1939–1941*, London, 1983.
Martin Gilbert, *Winston S. Churchill*, vol. 8, *Never Despair, 1945–1965*, London, 1988.
Martin Gilbert (editor), *The Churchill Documents*, vol. 16, *The Ever-Widening War, 1941*, Hillsdale, MI, 2011.
Martin Gilbert (editor), *The Churchill Documents*, vol. 17, *Testing Times, 1942*, Hillsdale, MI, 2014.
Martin Gilbert and Larry P. Arnn (editors), *The Churchill Documents*, vol. 18, *One Continent Redeemed, January–August 1943*, Hillsdale, MI, 2015.
Martin Gilbert and Larry P. Arnn (editors), *The Churchill Documents*, vol. 21, *The Shadows of Victory, January–July 1945*, Hillsdale, MI, 2018.
Martin Gilbert and Larry P. Arnn (editors), *The Churchill Documents*, vol. 22, *Leader of the Opposition, August 1945 to October 1951*, Hillsdale, MI, 2019.
Kay Halle (compiler), *The Irrepressible Churchill*, London, 1985.
Hansard (House of Commons Debates), London, various years.
Richard Hough, *Mountbatten: A Biography*, London, 1981.
David Hunt, *On the Spot: An Ambassador Remembers*, London, 1975.
Robert Rhodes James, *Anthony Eden: A Biography*, London, 1986.
Harold Macmillan, *Tides of Fortune, 1945–1955*, London, 1969.
Nigel Nicolson (editor), *Harold Nicolson, Diaries and Letters 1939–1945*, New York, 1967.
Nigel Nicolson (editor), *Harold Nicolson, Diaries and Letters: The Later Years*, New York, 1968.
S. W. Roskill, *The War at Sea, 1939–1945*, vol. 1, *The Defensive*, London, 1954.
G. W. Sand (editor), *Defending the West, The Truman–Churchill Correspondence, 1945–1960*, New York, 2004.
Evelyn Shuckburgh, *Descent to Suez: Diaries 1951–56*, London, 1986.
Mary Soames, *A Churchill Family Album: A Personal Anthology*, London, 1982.
Mary Soames, *Clementine Churchill*, London, 1979.
James Stuart, *Within the Fringe: An Autobiography*, London, 1967.
Margaret Truman, 'After the Presidency', *Life Magazine*, 1 December 1972.
Harold Wilson, *The Labour Government, 1964–1970*, London, 1971.

November 1951

Cabinet: conclusions
(Cabinet papers, 128/23)

1 November 1951
Secret
11 a.m.
Cabinet Meeting No. 2 of 1951

[...]

3. The Cabinet considered a memorandum by the Chancellor of the Exchequer[1] (C(51)1) analysing the current economic position of the United Kingdom and outlining the measures necessary to remedy the situation.

The Chancellor of the Exchequer said that there had been two meetings of the Committee which the Cabinet had appointed on the 30th October to assist him in considering this situation, and his memorandum took account of suggestions which had been made by his colleagues on the Committee.

In a preliminary discussion of this memorandum the following points were made:

(a) Would the proposed reduction in the building programme make it impossible to achieve any increase in the number of houses to be completed in 1952? The Minister of Housing and Local Government[2] said that, by concentrating on completing the houses already

---

[1] Richard Austen Butler, 1902–82. Educated at Marlborough and Pembroke College, Cambridge. President, Cambridge Union, 1924. MP (Cons.) for Saffron Walden, 1929–65. Under-Secretary of State, India Office, 1932–7. Parliamentary Secretary, Ministry of Labour, 1937–8. Under-Secretary of State for Foreign Affairs, 1938–41. PC, 1939. Minister of Education, 1941–5. Minister of Labour, 1945. Chancellor of the Exchequer, 1951–5. Lord Privy Seal, 1955–61. Home Secretary, 1957–62. Deputy PM, 1962–3. Secretary of State for Foreign Affairs, 1963–4. Baron, 1965. Master of Trinity College, Cambridge, 1965–78.

[2] (Maurice) Harold Macmillan, 1894–1986. Educated at Eton and Balliol College, Oxford. On active service, Grenadier Guards, 1914–18 (wounded three times). MP (Cons.) for Stockton-on-Tees, 1924–9, 1931–45. Author of *Reconstruction: A Plea for a National Policy* (1933); *Planning for Employment* (1935); *The Next Five Years* (1935); *The Middle Way* (1938); and *Economic Aspects of Defence* (1939). Parliamentary Secretary, Ministry of Supply, 1940–2. PC, 1942. Minister Resident, Allied HQ, North-West Africa, 1942–5. Secretary for Air, 1945. Minister of Housing and Local Government, 1951–4. Minister of Defence, 1954–5. Secretary of State for Foreign Affairs, 1955. Chancellor of the Exchequer, 1955–7. PM, 1957–63. Chancellor of the University of Oxford, 1960. Earl of Stockton, 1984.

in course of construction and preventing more from being started, it should be possible to achieve some increase in the numbers planned to be completed in 1952. In subsequent years any expansion of the programme would depend on success in exploiting substitute materials and other improvisations. The main difficulty was the shortage of softwood timber.

(b) The Chancellor of the Exchequer said that there must be some increase in the rate of interest on loans raised by local authorities. Special steps must, however, be taken to ensure that this did not result in an immediate increase in the rent of local authority houses. He was prepared in principle to increase the housing subsidy by an amount sufficient to offset the increased rate of interest on the loans raised by local authorities for housing purposes. He would discuss the details of this arrangement with the Housing Ministers.

(c) The Secretary of State for the Colonies[1] said that the Colonies might be able to give some assistance in this emergency, particularly with sugar and timber. He had instructed his Department to consider urgently what contribution the Colonies could make towards relieving the situation.

(d) Reference was made to the increasing indebtedness of the United Kingdom to the Colonies. The Chancellor of the Exchequer said that this was part of the general problem of sterling balances, on which he was proposing to submit a memorandum to the Cabinet.

(e) Would the proposed suspension of strategic stockpiling have an adverse effect on the defence production programmes? The Chancellor of the Exchequer said that the materials mainly affected were food, tobacco, softwood and rubber; that even under his proposals about £180 million of these supplies would have been accumulated by the end of 1952; and that he doubted whether his proposals would have any direct adverse effect on the defence production programmes.

(f) The Secretary of State for the Co-ordination of Transport, Fuel and Power[2] said that he was satisfied that it would be necessary for us to buy some foreign coal during the coming winter. It should, however, suffice to import about 1 million tons, at a cost of £8 or

---

[1] Oliver Lyttelton, 1893–1972. Educated at Eton and Trinity College, Cambridge. Active service on the Western Front, 1915–18 (MC, DSO, despatches thrice, wounded Apr. 1918). President of the Board of Trade, and PC, July 1940. MP (Cons.) for Aldershot, 1940–54. Minister of State, Middle East (based in Cairo), and Member of the War Cabinet, June 1941 to Mar. 1942. Minister of Production, Mar. 1942 to May 1945. Chairman, Associated Electrical Industries, 1945–51, 1954–63. Secretary of State for Colonial Affairs, 1951–4. Viscount Chandos, 1954. KG, 1970.

[2] Frederick James Leathers, 1883–1965. Managing director of Steamship Owners Coal Association, 1916. Adviser to Ministry of Shipping, 1914–18, 1940–1. Minister of War Transport, 1941–5. Baron, 1941. CH, 1943. Secretary of State for Coordination of Transport, Fuel and Power, 1951–3 (when position abolished). Viscount, 1954.

NOVEMBER 1951

£9 million. The figure of 4½ million tons, which had been mentioned in earlier conversations, was unnecessarily large and could not in any event be obtained in the time now available. The United States was the only source from which this coal could now be obtained, and it would be necessary to arrange for it to be brought here in the United States ships.

(g) It was proposed in C(51)1 that there should be a reduction of £100 million in private imports of unrationed food, including wines and spirits. The Lord President[1] said that he would do his utmost to secure the total cut in food imports suggested by the Chancellor; but he asked for discretion to decide, in consultation with the Minister of Food,[2] which particular imports should be reduced or dispensed with. The detailed proposals submitted by the Treasury included a substantial reduction in the importation of canned meats from Europe. He was satisfied that, in spite of their high cost, these were being bought by workers, e.g., for packed mid-day meals; and he would prefer to dispense with other imports which were more clearly in the category of luxuries.

(h) The Chancellor of the Exchequer said that it was essential to secure a substantial reduction in Government expenditure. This would, however, involve some changes of policy, and he needed more time in which to discuss these with the Departmental Ministers concerned. He would therefore prefer to confine himself, in the initial statement to be made in the Debate on the Address, to a broad statement of the Government's firm intention to reduce Government expenditure and to refrain at that stage from going into the matter in any detail. He would circulate to his Cabinet colleagues a draft of the statement which he proposed to make on this point in the Debate.

There was general agreement with the Chancellor's suggestion. The Prime Minister said that the Treasury should call on all Departments to reduce their expenditure, and should suggest specific means of doing so. In addition, all Ministers in charge of Departments should themselves consider what proposals they could make for reducing expenditure. By a combination of both these methods, substantial savings could be secured.

[1] Frederick James Marquis, 1883–1964. Knighted, 1935. Baron Woolton, 1939. Director-General of Equipment and Stores, Ministry of Supply, 1939–40. PC, 1940. Minister of Food, 1940–3. CH, 1942. Member of the War Cabinet and Minister of Reconstruction, 1943–5. Chairman, Conservative and Unionist Central Office, 1946–55. Lord President of the Council, 1951–2. Chancellor of the Duchy of Lancaster, 1952–5. Viscount, 1953. Earl, 1956.

[2] Gwilym Lloyd George, 1894–1967. Second son of David Lloyd George. Educated at Eastbourne College and Jesus College, Cambridge. On active service in France, 1914–19 (Maj., Royal Artillery; despatches). MP (Lib.) for Pembrokeshire, 1922–4, 1929–50; for Newcastle North, 1951–7. Parliamentary Secretary, Ministry of Food, 1941–2. Minister of Fuel and Power, 1942–5. Minister of Food, 1951–4. Home Secretary and Minister for Welsh Affairs, 1954–7. Viscount Tenby, 1957.

(i) Every effort should be made to enlist the support of the Trades Union Congress for the measures outlined in the Chancellor's memorandum. No approach could, however, be made to them until after the Chancellor had made his statement to Parliament. The Prime Minister said that he intended to see representatives of the Trades Union Congress at an early date, and he would take that opportunity of discussing these matters with them.

The Prime Minister, summing up the discussion, said that the Cabinet approved in principle the general approach to this problem which was outlined in the Chancellor's memorandum (C(51)1). Some of the detailed proposals in the memorandum would need to be discussed further with the Departmental Ministers concerned; and the Cabinet itself should have an opportunity of considering the broad outline of the statement which the Chancellor would be making in the Debate on the Address. The Cabinet would meet for this purpose on 5th November: meanwhile further consultations should be held between the Ministers principally concerned.

The Cabinet –

(1) Invited the Chancellor of the Exchequer to discuss with the Lord President and the Minister of Food the detailed proposals for reducing the programme of food imports.

(2) Invited the Chancellor of the Exchequer to discuss with the Prime Minister, and to circulate to the Cabinet, a draft of the statement which he proposed to make in the Debate on the Address regarding reductions in Government expenditure.

(3) Took note that the Chancellor of the Exchequer would submit to the Prime Minister a note on the effect which his proposal to suspend strategic stockpiling was likely to have on the defence production programmes.

(4) Took note that the Chancellor of the Exchequer would in due course submit to the Cabinet a memorandum on the general problem of the sterling balances.

(5) Invited the Secretary of State for the Colonies to submit to the Cabinet a memorandum on any emergency measures which the Colonies might take to relieve the current economic difficulties of the United Kingdom.

(6) Agreed to resume their discussion of C(51)1 at a meeting on 5th November.

NOVEMBER 1951

Anthony Eden[1] to Winston S. Churchill
(*Churchill papers, 2/517*)

1 November 1951
Top secret
PM/51/113

DISARMAMENT

The United States intend in the very near future to put forward disarmament proposals for use at the United Nations Assembly. They propose to do so in a statement to be made by the President on the 5th November, and they hope, also, by yourself and the French Prime Minister. I will very shortly send you, for your approval, a draft text which we will try to clear with the other two Powers in Paris.

2. The Americans intend that the statement should be followed by the presentation by the three Powers in the United Nations General Assembly of a plan on the lines outlined in the draft statement. It is based on a reduction of the armed forces of all States with substantial military resources to a percentage of their populations, with a maximum in the case of States with very large populations; and on a phased programme of inspection by a United Nations Commission, each phase to be completed before the next phase is begun.

3. The proposals have been approved textually by Mr Acheson,[2] by Mr Lovett[3] and by the American Chiefs of Staff. The President has cleared them in principle and himself outlined the form in which they should be presented. The Americans are anxious that the French and ourselves should join with them but, if necessary, they intend to go forward alone.

4. The four 'old' Commonwealth Governments have been informed but have not so far commented. The French Government have also been informed.

---

[1] (Robert) Anthony Eden, 1897–1977. Educated at Eton and Christ Church, Oxford. Served on the Western Front, 1915–18 (MC). MP (Cons.) for Warwick and Leamington, 1923–57. Parliamentary Under-Secretary, FO, 1931–3. Lord Privy Seal, 1934–5. Minister for League of Nations Affairs, 1935. Foreign Secretary, 1935–8; Dec. 1940 to July 1945; Oct. 1951 to Apr. 1955. Secretary of State for Dominion Affairs, Sep. 1939 to May 1940. Secretary of State for War, May to Dec. 1940. Deputy Prime Minister, 1951–5. KG, 1954. PM, 1955–7. Earl of Avon, 1961. One of his brothers was killed near Ypres in Oct. 1914; another in 1916 at the Battle of Jutland. His elder son was killed in action in Burma on 23 June 1945, aged 20.

[2] Dean Gooderham Acheson, 1893–1971. Educated at Yale University and Harvard Law School. Married, 1917, Alice Stanley: three children. Law clerk to Supreme Court Justice Louis Brandeis, 1919–21. Covington and Burling law firm, 1921–33. Under-Secretary of the Treasury, 1933. Asst Secretary of State, 1941–5. Under-Secretary of State, 1945–9. Medal for Merit, 1947. Secretary of State, 1949–53. Author of *Power and Diplomacy* (1958); *Morning and Noon* (1965); *Present at the Creation* (1969); *The Korean War* (1971); *Grapes from Thorns* (1972).

[3] Robert Abercrombie Lovett, 1895–1986. Born in Huntsville, Tex. Educated at Yale University, 1918. Special Asst to Secretary of War, 1940–1. Asst Secretary of War for Air, 1941–5. Under-Secretary of State, 1947–9. Deputy Secretary of Defense, 1950–1. Secretary of Defense, 1951–3.

We do not know their final views but unofficially they are not much impressed. Nor am I.

5. A question for consideration is whether it is appropriate for any disarmament proposals at all to be put forward at the forthcoming General Assembly since they might be represented as a sign of weakness and have a depressing effect on non-Communist countries, especially in the Middle and Far East.

6. We think it likely that the Russians will, at the United Nations, revive the proposal for a cut of one third in the arms and armed forces of the five Great Powers which Vyshinsky[1] made with some éclat in 1948. This is a deceptively appealing proposal which would have perpetuated the disparity of forces in favour of the Soviet Union. But if the Russians couple it with demands for a Five Power Peace Pact and the abolition of the atomic bomb, I am afraid the American proposals will look tame by comparison.

7. All the same, I think we ought to fall in with the American proposals. Though we had urged that, for propaganda purposes, it would be better to propose some plan based on parity between the East and the West, there is now no chance of inducing the Americans to drop or modify their plan. It is evident that a most unfortunate impression would be created if it became clear that we and the Americans disagreed over a subject of such major political importance. While the United States proposals are unlikely to serve any very useful purpose, it does not seem that any British interest will be prejudiced by their being put forward in their present form.

8. I therefore recommend that we should agree to associate ourselves with the American initiative.

The Chiefs of Staff agree.

---

[1] Andrei Yanuarevich Vyshinsky, 1883–1954. Born in Odessa. Prof. of Criminal Law, Moscow, 1923. Deputy State Prosecutor, 1933; State Prosecutor, 1935. Principal public figure conducting the 'purge trials'. First Deputy Minister for Foreign Affairs, 1940. Soviet Representative to Allied Commissions for the Mediterranean and Italy during WWII. Foreign Minister, 1949–53. Principal Soviet Delegate at the UN, 1953–4.

NOVEMBER 1951

Sir Norman Brook[1] to Winston S. Churchill
(*Premier papers, 11/176*)

1 November 1951

MINISTRY OF DEFENCE

When you were Minister of Defence during the war there was no Ministry of Defence but merely an Office of the Minister of Defence. This consisted of the military wing of the War Cabinet Secretariat: it was a handful of officers – in your own words a 'handling machine'.

2. The present situation is different. The Ministry of Defence is now a full-blown Ministry with a Permanent Secretary and the normal Civil Service hierarchy. It has 30 administrative officers (including serving officers) apart from scientists and subordinate staff.

3. The Minister of Defence has been responsible, under the Cabinet, for:
   (a) the whole range of Chiefs of Staff work – notably the formulations of the strategic plan for the employment of the Armed Forces and the size and shape of the Armed Forces;
   (b) the size and content of the rearmament programme and the progress and co-ordination of defence production programmes;
   (c) defence research and development; and
   (d) administrative problems of common concern to the three Services.

(A fuller statement of the work and staff of the Ministry of Defence is attached.)

You will wish to assume direct responsibility for (a) above and it might be of assistance to you and the Chiefs of Staff if the Secretary of State for Commonwealth Relations[2] attended some of your staff conferences. In view of his experience of your methods of work, he would be of great help to the Chief Staff Officer who now fills the post that he himself held in the war and also to the Chiefs of Staff, but you would not have the time, and it is probably not your wish, to undertake all the duties falling under (b), (c) and (d).

These duties could not be undertaken by the Secretary of State for Commonwealth Relations without grave prejudice to the work of his own office.

[1] Norman Craven Brook, 1902–67. Educated at Wadham College, Oxford. Entered Civil Service, 1925. Principal Private Secretary to Sir John Anderson, 1938–42. Deputy Secretary of the Cabinet, 1942–5. Secretary of the Cabinet, 1947–56. Secretary to the Treasury, 1956–62. Baron, 1963. Chairman of the Governors, BBC, 1964–7. Suggested the title *The Hinge of Fate* for vol. 4 of Churchill's war memoirs.

[2] Hastings Lionel Ismay, 1887–1965. Known as 'Pug'. Educated at Charterhouse and Sandhurst. 2nd Lt, 1905; Capt., 1914. On active service in India, 1908, and Somaliland, 1914–20 (DSO). Staff College, Quetta, 1922. Asst Secretary, Committee of Imperial Defence, 1925–30. Military Secretary to Viceroy of India (Lord Willingdon), 1931–3. Col., 1932. Deputy Secretary, Committee of Imperial Defence, 1936–8; Secretary, 1938. Maj.-Gen., 1939. CoS to Minister of Defence (Churchill), 1940–5. Knighted, 1940. Deputy Secretary (Military) to War Cabinet, 1940–5. Lt-Gen., 1942. Gen., 1944. CoS to Viceroy of India (Lord Mountbatten), 1947. Baron, 1947. Secretary of State for Commonwealth Relations, 1951–2. Secretary-General of NATO, 1952–7. KG, 1957. Author of *The Memoirs of General the Lord Ismay* (1960).

Will it not be necessary for you to appoint a Minister to be responsible to you for the duties under (b), (c) and (d) and to assist you generally in the defence field? A Parliamentary Secretary might suffice for some purposes – especially if it is understood that the First Lord of the Admiralty,[1] as senior Service Minister, will answer some of your Questions in the Commons and preside at meetings of the Service Ministers. But there ought to be some Minister, sitting in the Ministry of Defence, from whom officials can obtain decisions on the day to day problems which are likely to arise under (b), (c) and (d) above and are not of sufficient importance to warrant submission to you. This seems to point to someone with the authority of a Minister of State, rather than a Parliamentary Secretary.

4. If some such appointment could be made the position would, in outline, be as follows:

(a) You would yourself retain responsibility for questions of major policy over the whole defence field.

(b) You would retain sole responsibility for strategic policy, presiding over the Chiefs of Staff Committee for this purpose.

(c) You would also preside over a Defence Committee, which could be of varying composition according to the nature of the business. The Secretary of State for Commonwealth Relations might be of the permanent nucleus of the Committee, as would the Foreign Secretary, the Service Ministers and the Minister of Supply. When the Service Ministers are excluded from the Cabinet it is specially important that they should be members of a Defence Committee – as otherwise their relations with their Chiefs of Staff become difficult.

(d) On questions of day to day administration the Minister of State or Parliamentary Secretary could give decisions on your behalf. Matters of importance would be referred through him to you.

(e) The Chief Staff Officer, though he would at all times keep the Minister of State or Parliamentary Secretary informed, should have a right of direct access to you as Minister of Defence.

5. I have written this minute after consultation with General Ismay and Sir Edward Bridges.[2] May the three of us wait upon you to discuss the problem?

---

[1] James Purdon Lewes Thomas, 1903–60. Educated at Oriel College, Oxford. Private Secretary to Stanley Baldwin, 1929–31. MP (Cons.) for Hereford, 1931–55. Parliamentary Private Secretary to Secretary of State for the Dominions, 1932–5; to Secretary of State for the Colonies, 1935–8. Lord Commissioner of the Treasury, 1939–43. Parliamentary Private Secretary to Secretary of State for War, 1940. Financial Secretary to the Admiralty, 1943–5. 1st Lord of the Admiralty, 1951–6. PC, 1951. Viscount Cilcennin, 1956.

[2] Edward Bridges, 1892–1969. On active service, 1914–18 (MC). Served in Treasury, 1919–39. Secretary to the Cabinet, 1938–46. Knighted, 1939. Permanent Secretary, Treasury, 1945–56. Baron, 1957. KG, 1965.

Henry Channon:[1] diary
('Chips', page 462)

1 November 1951

I took the oath for the 6th time at 5.45. By then the queue was short, so I was able to chat with 'Shakes',[2] looking very austere and dignified. At 6.14 Winston came in; the Chamber was almost empty, a few attendants, two Whips and a few desultory spectators in the Gallery. The old man, smiling, good-tempered slowly signed his name, beamed, and approached the Chair and I heard him apologise to 'Shakes' whom he correctly called 'Mr Speaker' for being late. He has a new habit of raising his voice. Then, still grinning, he passed through the door. Only four MPs witnessed Winston taking the oath, perhaps for the last time. The light and the atmosphere made it a touching little scene . . . now I go home.

Cabinet: conclusions
(Churchill papers, 128/23)

2 November 1951
Secret
11.30 a.m.
Cabinet Meeting No. 3 of 1951

1. The Foreign Secretary said that a grave situation was developing in Egypt owing to the action of the British military authorities in suspending supplies of oil which were essential to the life of the civil population. The Cabinet were informed that, according to the latest reports, the supply of oil had now been resumed. There seemed, however, to be need for closer political control over the actions of the British military authorities in the Canal Zone.

2. The Minister of Health[3] reported that his Committee on the future of

---

[1] Henry Channon, 1897–1958. Known as 'Chips'. Educated at Christ Church, Oxford. Married, 1933, Honor Guinness: one child (div. 1945). MP (Cons.) for Southend-on-Sea, 1935–50; for Southend-on-Sea (West), 1950–8. Parliamentary Private Secretary to Under-Secretary of State for Foreign Affairs, 1938–41. Knighted, 1957.

[2] William Shepherd Morrison, 1893–1961. Known as 'Shakes'. Served in Royal Field Artillery, France, 1914–18 (wounded, MC, despatches three times). Capt., 1919. President, Edinburgh University Union, 1920. Called to the Bar, 1923. Married, 1924, Catherine Allison Swan: four children. MP (Cons.) for Cirencester and Tewkesbury, 1929–59. KC, 1934. Financial Secretary, Treasury, 1935–6. PC, 1936. A member of the Other Club from 1936. Minister of Agriculture and Fisheries, 1936–9. Chancellor of the Duchy of Lancaster and Minister of Food, 1939–40. Postmaster-General, 1940–3. Minister of Town and Country Planning, 1943–5. Speaker of the House of Commons, 1951–9.

[3] Harry Frederick Comfort Crookshank, 1893–1961. On active service, 1914–18. Capt., 1919. FO, 1919–24 (Constantinople and Washington DC). MP (Cons.) for Gainsborough, 1924–56. Secretary for Mines, 1936–9. Financial Secretary, Treasury, 1939–43. Postmaster-General, 1943–5. Minister for Health, 1951–2. Leader of the House of Commons, 1951–5. Lord Privy Seal, 1952–5. Viscount (under Eden), 1956.

the iron and steel industry had now come to the conclusion that it would not be practicable to pass before Christmas legislation restoring the industry to private ownership.

3. The Prime Minister said that he understood that it would be gratifying to public opinion in Wales if the Home Secretary[1] who was to be the member of the Cabinet responsible for Welsh Affairs, could have an additional Under-Secretary to assist him in this part of his duties. He therefore proposed to recommend the appointment of an additional Under-Secretary of state for the Home Department, who would be a Welshman.

4. The Cabinet had before them a note by the Minister of Health (C(51)2) covering a draft of The King's Speech on the Opening of Parliament.

The Prime Minister said that he had discussed this draft with the Minister of Health on the previous evening and had suggested various amendments: he handed to the Cabinet copies of a revised draft incorporating these amendments.

In discussion of the draft various changes of wording were suggested and approved. The following specific points were also made:

- (a) The Cabinet were informed that the Home Guard could not be established in time of peace without legislation. They agreed, however, that the Speech should include a reference to the re-establishment of the Home Guard. If legislation was in fact required for this purpose, the Secretary of State for War[2] should submit proposals in time for legislation to be passed before Christmas.
- (b) The reference (paragraph 8 of the draft) to the Government's intention to preserve the free use of the Suez Canal should not be framed in terms which would be read in the Middle East as implying a determination to force the passage through the Canal of oil tankers bound for Haifa. After discussion it was agreed that it would suffice to refer to the Government's intention to 'safeguard the international highway'.
- (c) A reference to the Sudan should be included, in the following terms: 'Nothing can be allowed to interfere with the rights of the Sudanese to decide for themselves the future status of their country.'
- (d) It was suggested that if the University franchise were restored, as proposed, on the basis of one vote only by each voter, it was possible

---

[1] David Patrick Maxwell Fyfe, 1900–67. Educated at George Watson College, Edinburgh, and Balliol College, Oxford, Called to the Bar, 1922. Married, 1925, Sylvia Margaret Harrison: three children. KC, 1934. MP (Cons.) for Liverpool West Derby Div., 1935–54. Knighted, 1942. Solicitor-General, 1942–5. PC, 1942. Attorney-General, 1945. Deputy Prosecutor, Nuremberg Trials, 1945–6. Home Secretary, 1951–4. Viscount Kilmuir, 1954. Lord Chancellor, 1954–62.

[2] Antony Henry Head, 1906–83. Educated at Eton and Royal Military College, Sandhurst. MC, 1940. Brig. General Staff, Combined Operations HQ, 1943. MP (Cons.) for Carshalton, 1945–60. Secretary of State for War, 1951–6. PC, 1951. Minister of Defence, 1956–7. Viscount, 1960. High Commissioner to Nigeria, 1960–3; to Malaysia, 1963–6.

that very few people would choose to use their University vote and that University Members would be elected by disproportionately small constituencies. Some Ministers thought that for this reason the Government should not at this stage commit themselves finally to the view that, when the University franchise was restored, it should be on the basis of one vote only by each voter. On the other hand it was argued that, if their intentions on this point were not made clear in The King's Speech, the Government would at once be asked in the Debate on the Address whether they proposed that persons entitled to the University franchise should have a second vote in the constituencies where they lived. The preponderant view in the Cabinet was against this restoration of plural voting; and it was agreed that the paragraph on this subject in The King's Speech should be framed as follows: 'A bill will be laid before you to make provision in the next Parliament for the representation of the Universities in the House of Commons, on the basis of one vote only by each voter.'

(e) The Lord Chancellor[1] said that an earlier draft of the Speech had promised legislation improving the salaries of county court judges and comparable judicial officers. He hoped that the omission of this reference from the later draft would not be taken to imply that the Government were unwilling to proceed with this measure, which had been agreed between the political Parties before the General Election. The Prime Minister said that, in his view, this Bill was not of such importance as to warrant specific mention in the Speech; but this was no reason why the Bill should not, if the Cabinet so decided, be included in the Government's Legislative Programme for the Session and introduced at an early date.

The Cabinet –

Approved the draft for The King's Speech on the Opening of Parliament in the form annexed to C(51)2, subject to the amendments noted in the paragraphs (b)–(d) above and to the other drafting amendments which had been agreed in the course of their discussion.

[. . .]

---

[1] Gavin Turnbull Simonds, 1881–1971. Educated at Winchester College and New College, Oxford. Called to the Bar, 1906. KC, 1924. Judge, Chancery Division of High Court of Justice, 1937–44. Knighted, 1937. Lord Appeal in Ordinary, 1944, 1954–62. PC, 1944. Baron, 1944. Lord High Chancellor, 1951–4. Viscount, 1954. High Steward of Oxford, 1954–67.

NOVEMBER 1951

Winston S. Churchill to Harold Parker[1]
Prime Minister's Personal Minute M.5c/51
(Premier papers, 11/62)

2 November 1951

Your minute of November 2.

I am keeping this report with me. Kindly let me know what the stock was at the end of July 1945. We had over 5 million men under arms and there must have been at least 2 million reserve of rifles. Total perhaps 7 million. Now there are 2 and a quarter million. In addition we had all the German and Italian rifles when over 2 million men surrendered to our Armies. Therefore there are about 9 million rifles to be accounted for. What has happened to them? Pray let me have an account of the way in which they have been dispersed. Rifles keep for a generation. Witness the 250 thousand we got from America in 1940 which were actually made for us and put aside after the First World War.

Pray also send copies of your report of today and also your report on these questions of mine to Lord Cherwell,[2] whose statistical department is getting to work as fast as possible.

Winston S. Churchill to Field Marshal Lord Alanbrooke[3]
Prime Minister's Personal Minute M.6c/51
(Premier papers, 11/176)

3 November 1951

Your minute of November 1.*

Pray let me have a list of the thirty administrative officers and officials; their

---

[1] Harold Parker, 1895–1980. On active service during WWI, 1914–18. Deputy Secretary, Ministry of Pensions, 1941–5; Secretary, 1946–8. Permanent Secretary, Ministry of Defence, 1948–56. KCB, 1949.

[2] Frederick Alexander Lindemann, 1886–1957. Known as 'the Prof'. Educated in Scotland, Darmstadt and Berlin. PhD, Berlin University, 1910. Studied physical chemistry in Paris, 1912–14. Worked at the Physical Laboratory, RAF, 1915–18. Prof. of Experimental Philosophy, Oxford, 1919–56. Member, Expert Committee on Air Defence Research, Committee of Imperial Defence, 1935–9. Unsuccessful by-election candidate, Oxford University, 1937. Personal Assistant to PM, 1940–1. Baron Cherwell, 1941. Paymaster-General, 1942–5, 1951–3. PC, 1943. Viscount, 1956.

[3] Alan Francis Brooke, 1883–1963. Entered Army, 1902. On active service, 1914–18 (DSO and bar, despatches six times). GOC-in-C, Anti-Aircraft Command, 1939. Commanded II Army Corps, BEF, 1939–40. Knighted, 1940. GOC-in-C, Home Forces, 1940–1. CIGS, 1941–6. FM, 1944. Baron, 1945. Viscount Alanbrooke, 1946. OM, 1945. Master Gunner, St James's Park, 1946–56. His brother Victor, a fellow subaltern and close friend of Churchill in 1895–6, died from exhaustion on the retreat from Mons in 1914. Churchill was also a good friend of Brooke's brother Ronnie, whose Asst Adjutant he was in South Africa for some months, and with whom he galloped into Ladysmith on the night of its liberation in 1900.

salaries; also how many secretaries, typists, messengers and other personnel are paid on the Ministry of Defence vote.

Para. 11. Pray give me the amounts involved in 11 (iii).

Also give me a much fuller account of the organization of NATO infrastructure which accounts for 7 million.

* Note on organisation and functions of the Ministry of Defence.

Lady Soames[1]: recollection
('Clementine Churchill', pages 429–30)

4 November 1951

While Winston addressed himself to the formation of his first and only all-Conservative and peacetime Government, Clementine[2] prepared to move back, once more, into No 10. She must have felt – for his sake alone – some sense of satisfaction after the bitter defeat of six years before: but of elation she felt none. Nothing that had happened had changed the conviction she held in 1945, namely, that Winston should have retired at the end of the war. Nevertheless – here they were again, and she set about reorganising their life yet once more. Ronnie Tree[3] had written to her after the election, and in her reply on 4th November she wrote: 'I do hope Winston will be able to help the country. It will be up-hill work, but he has a willing eager heart.' By contrast, her spirit was one of dogged, somewhat weary determination, rather than that of enthusiasm. Physically she was only six months from a major operation, and as always when her morale was low, difficulties loomed large. One event, however, that caused her (and indeed everyone in our circle) great pleasure and reassurance, was the return of Jock Colville[4] to the Private Office as Joint

---

[1] Mary Churchill, 1922–2014. Churchill's youngest child. Served in WWII in Red Cross and WVS, 1939–41; in ATS, 1941–6. MBE (Military), 1945. Married, 1947, Christopher Soames. DBE, 1980. Chairman, Royal National Theatre Board, 1989–95. Author of *Clementine Churchill by her Daughter Mary Soames* (1979) and *A Daughter's Tale* (2011); editor of *Speaking for Themselves, the Personal Letters of Winston and Clementine Churchill* (1998).

[2] Clementine Hozier, 1885–1977. Married, 1908, Winston Churchill: five children. Active in WWI in YWCA, providing canteens for munitions workers; in WWII, presided over Red Cross Aid to Russia Fund and Fulmer Chase Maternity Home. Chairman, YWCA National Hostels Committee, 1949–51; President, YWCA War and National Fund, 1951–7. Baroness Spencer-Churchill, 1965.

[3] Arthur Ronald Lambert Field Tree, 1897–1976. Educated at Winchester College. Editor, *Forum Magazine*, 1922. Married, 1927, Nancy Keene Perkins: two children (div. 1947); 1947, Marietta Peabody Fitzgerald: one child. MP (Cons.) for Harborough, 1933–45.

[4] John Rupert Colville, 1915–87. Known as 'Jock'. Page of Honour to King George V, 1927–31. Educated at Harrow and Trinity College, Cambridge. Entered Diplomatic Service, 1937. Asst Private Secretary to Neville Chamberlain, 1939–40; to Churchill, 1940–1. RAFVR, 1941–3. Asst Private Secretary to Churchill, 1943–5; to Clement Attlee, 1945. Private Secretary to Princess Elizabeth, 1947–9. CVO, 1949. Head of Chancery, British Embassy in Lisbon, 1949–51. Joint Principal Private

Principal Private Secretary. After 1945 he had for two years been Private Secretary to Princess Elizabeth,[1] and had since 1949 been at the British Embassy in Lisbon as Head of Chancery. In 1948 he had married Lady Margaret Egerton[2] – Meg – who became as dear and trusted a friend to Winston and Clementine as was Jock himself. During these years of Winston's last Prime Ministership, when there were many private anxieties and problems, it was a wonderful support to have someone at hand who knew the public and private side of it all. He understood Clementine very well, and he was a friend and confidant whose sense, loyalty and humour never failed.

Winston S. Churchill to Josef Stalin[3]
Prime Minister's Personal Telegram T.24c/51
(Premier papers, 11/276)

5 November 1951
Immediate
Secret
No. 966

Now that I am again in charge of His Majesty's Government let me reply in one word to your farewell telegram from Berlin of August, 1945. 'Greetings'.[4]

Secretary to Churchill, 1951–5. CB, 1955. Active in the development of Churchill College, Cambridge. Knighted, 1974. Author of a number of volumes of recollections and history, as well as *The Fringes of Power, 10 Downing Street Diaries* (1985).

[1] Elizabeth Alexandra Mary Windsor, 1926–. Married, 1947, Philip Mountbatten. Succeeded her father as Queen Elizabeth II, 1952.

[2] Margaret Egerton, 1918–2004. Lady-in-Waiting to Queen Elizabeth, 1945–8. Married, 1948, John Colville.

[3] Josef Vissarionovich Djugashvili, 1879–1953. Born in Georgia. A Bolshevik revolutionary, he took the name Stalin (man of steel). In exile in the Siberian Arctic, 1913–16. Active in Petrograd during October Revolution, 1917. Commissar for Nationalities, 1917–18. General Secretary, Central Committee of Communist Party, 1922. Effective ruler of Russia from 1923. Purged his opponents with show trials, 1936–8, murdering without compunction opponents, critics and ordinary citizens who had committed no crime. Authorized Nazi–Soviet Pact, Aug. 1939. Succeeded Molotov as Head of Government, May 1941. Marshal of the Soviet Union, May 1943. Buried beside Lenin in the Lenin Mausoleum, 1953. 'Downgraded' to the Kremlin Wall, 1960. In 1989 Mikhail Gorbachev began the official process inside the Soviet Union of denouncing Stalin's crimes.

[4] Stalin responded: 'Thank you for greetings.'

Winston S. Churchill to Oliver Lyttelton[1]
Prime Minister's Personal Minute M.7c/51
(Premier papers, 11/122)

5 November 1951

Your PM(51)1.[2]

I highly approve of your wish to see the Singapore situation on the spot. We do not think the Session will end before December 4 or 5. We cannot afford to reduce our majority. Unless a special pair can be obtained for you the various functionaries you have to meet should rearrange their dates to suit you.

Cabinet: conclusions
(Cabinet papers, 128/23)

5 November 1951
Secret
3 p.m.
Cabinet Meeting No. 4 of 1951

The Prime Minister invited the Cabinet to review their decision that legislation to restore the University franchise should be introduced in the first Session of the present Parliament. If, as the Government intended, there was to be no representation of the Universities in the present Parliament, this legislation was not of such urgency that it must be passed in the current Session. And, if this Bill were now given a prominent place in the legislative programme for the first Session, it might be represented as a mere manoeuvre in Party politics.

In discussion there was general support for the view that it would be preferable to postpone this legislation until a later Session. This would give the Government more time to consider the difficulties involved in restoring the University franchise on the basis of one vote only by each voter. It would also enable them to ascertain what views were held on this question by Government supporters generally.

The Prime Minister said that in the course of his speech in the Debate on the Address he would make it clear that it was the Government's intention to legislate on this subject, though not in the current Session. He would also

---

[1] Oliver Lyttelton, 1893–1972. Educated at Eton and Trinity College, Cambridge. 2nd Lt, Grenadier Guards, 1914; active service on Western Front, 1915–18 (MC, DSO, despatches thrice, wounded Apr. 1918). Entered merchant banking, 1919. Joined British Metal Corp., 1920; later Managing Director. Controller of Non-Ferrous Metals, Sep. 1939. President of the Board of Trade, and PC, July 1940. MP (Cons.) for Aldershot, 1940–54. Minister of State, Middle East (based in Cairo), and Member of the War Cabinet, June 1941 to Mar. 1942. Minister of Production, Mar. 1942 to May 1945. Chairman, Associated Electrical Industries, 1945–51, 1954–63. Secretary of State for Colonial Affairs, 1951–4. Viscount Chandos, 1954. KG, 1970.

[2] Reproduced in *The Churchill Documents*, vol. 22, *Leader of the Opposition, August 1945 to October 1951*, p. 227.

state that the legislation would not provide for university representation in the present Parliament, and that, as at present advised, the Government considered that the University franchise should be exercisable in future on the basis of one vote only by each voter.

The Lord Privy Seal[1] said that another matter which, he hoped, would be taken up in a later Session was the reform of the House of Lords. The Government should not allow it to be inferred that, because this was not mentioned in The King's Speech on this occasion, the Government had abandoned the idea of dealing with it during the life-time of the present Parliament.

The Prime Minister said that he had one further amendment to propose in the text of The King's Speech which the Cabinet had approved on 2nd November. He suggested that the paragraph on the social services should refer, not to 'promoting economy', but to 'providing value for money spent'.

The Cabinet –
  (1) Agreed that The King's Speech on the Opening of Parliament should contain no reference to the restoration of the University franchise, and that the paragraph on this subject should be deleted from the draft which they had approved on 2nd November.
  (2) Agreed that the paragraph in The King's Speech dealing with the social services should be amended to read: 'In their policy towards the social services My Government will pursue the aim of ensuring efficiency and providing value for money spent.'

[. . .]

3. The Prime Minister said that it had been brought to his notice that there might be some doubt whether a provision in the Ministers' Salaries Act, 1946, which enabled a Minister whose salary was less than £5,000 a year to draw £500 a year as a Member of the House of Commons, might apply to Ministers who had accepted a voluntary reduction in salary. Any arrangement enabling them to draw part of their House of Commons salary would of course defeat the Cabinet's intention. He had therefore thought it right to mention the matter to the Cabinet so that all Ministers who had undertaken to draw only £4,000 of their Ministerial salary would understand that they were also expected to refrain from drawing any salary as Members of the House of Commons even if, on a strict construction of the law, they might be technically entitled to do so.

The Cabinet –
Took note of the Prime Minister's statement.

4. The Cabinet resumed their discussion of the economic situation.

---

[1] Robert Arthur James Gascoyne-Cecil, 1893–1972. Known as 'Bobbety'. Eldest son of 4th Marquess of Salisbury. MP (Cons.) for South Dorset, 1929–41. Parliamentary Secretary of State for Foreign Affairs, 1935–8. Paymaster-General, 1940. Baron Cecil of Essendon, 1941. Secretary of State for Dominion Affairs, 1940–2, 1943–5; for the Colonies, 1942. Lord Privy Seal, 1942–3, 1951–2. Leader of the House of Lords, 1942–5, 1951–7. KG, 1946. Succeeded his father as 5th Marquess, 1947. Secretary of State for Commonwealth Relations, Mar.–Nov. 1952. Lord President of the Council, 1952–7.

November 1951

They first considered a note by the Chancellor of the Exchequer (C(51)3) covering a draft of what he proposed to say about Government expenditure in his speech in the Debate on the Address. In discussion of this draft the following points were made:

(a) The draft dealt mainly with economy in administration, and it might perhaps be taken to imply that no savings were to be sought by changes in policy. It was recognised that the Chancellor would not be in a position, when he spoke in the Debate to announce any specific changes in policy; but it would be expedient that he should make it clear in his statement that changes of policy were not excluded.

(b) The draft included a promise that the Government would announce their economy measures as soon as they had been determined. It would be preferable to omit this phrase, since it might lead to repeated requests for information about the progress of the Chancellor's proposed review of Government expenditure.

(c) The Chancellor of the Exchequer said that he was anxious to emphasise the fact that in his efforts to reduce Government expenditure he could count on the full support of all his Ministerial colleagues. The Cabinet agreed that this point should be stressed in the statement.

(d) The Prime Minister said that he relied upon the Treasury to be specially vigilant on this occasion in their scrutiny of the Estimates for the coming financial year. The Chancellor of the Exchequer should not hesitate to bring to the Cabinet any questions on which he could not reach agreement with the Departmental Minister concerned.

[. . .]

5. The Cabinet had before them (i) a note by the Secretary of State for the Co-ordination of Transport, Fuel and Power (C(51)5) covering a memorandum by the Minister of Fuel and Power[1] proposing that immediate steps should be taken to import half a million tons of coal from the United States; and (ii) a memorandum by the Minister of Supply[2] (C(51)6) on the possible effects of this plan on steel production in the United Kingdom.

---

[1] Geoffrey William Geoffrey-Lloyd, 1902–84. Educated at Harrow and Trinity College, Cambridge. Private Secretary to Samuel Hoare, 1926–9; to Stanley Baldwin, 1929–31. MP (Cons.) for Birmingham Ladywood, 1931–45; for Birmingham King's Norton, 1950–5; for Sutton Coldfield, 1955–74. Under-Secretary of State for Home Dept, 1935–9. Secretary for Mines, 1939–40. Secretary for Petroleum, 1940–2. Chairman of Oil Control Board, 1939–45. Parliamentary Secretary to Ministry of Fuel and Power, 1942–5. PC, 1943. Minister of Information, 1945. A Governor of the BBC, 1946–9. Minister of Fuel and Power, 1951–5. Minister of Education, 1957–9. Baron, 1974.

[2] Duncan Edwin Sandys, 1908–87. Educated at Eton and Magdalen College, Oxford. MP (Cons.) for Norwood, 1935–45; for Streatham, 1950–74. Married, 1935, Diana Churchill (div. 1960). On active service in Norway with BEF, 1939–41. Financial Secretary, War Office, 1941–3. Chairman of War Cabinet Committee for defence against German flying bombs and rockets, 1943. Joint Parliamentary Secretary, Ministry of Supply, 1943–4. Minister of Works, 1944–5. Minister of Supply, 1951–4. Minister of Housing and Local Government, 1954–7. Minister of Defence, 1957–9. Minister of Aviation, 1959–60. Secretary of State for Commonwealth Relations, 1960–4. Secretary of State for the Colonies, 1962–4. Baron, 1974.

The Secretary of State for the Co-ordination of Transport, Fuel and Power said that, in order to avert a breakdown in coal supplies during the coming winter, he would have liked to be able to import 1 million tons of foreign coal. At this late date not more than half a million tons could be imported in time to be of service; but it was essential that all practicable steps should be taken to secure this limited amount without delay. This was bound to involve some interference with other import programmes; but he hoped to be able to mitigate this to some extent by the use of United States reserve shipping and possibly by the diversion of coal shipments already allocated to France.

In discussion the following points were raised:

(a) The Minister of Supply drew attention to the reduction in shipments of iron ore which had resulted from the importation of coal from the United States in the previous winter. If the present proposal were carried through at the expense of iron ore shipments, United Kingdom steel production in 1952 might be reduced by some 200,000 ingot tons. This deficiency, if it fell entirely on exports by the engineering industries, might reduce our export earnings by as much as £50 million.

The Prime Minister said that every effort should be made to compensate for this by obtaining increased supplies of finished steel from the United States.

(b) The cost of importing half a million tons of coal from the United States would be in the neighbourhood of £4 million, including freight charges.

(c) This emergency programme of coal imports was likely to encourage some general increase in freight rates.

(d) The United States Government would find great difficulty in increasing substantially the rate at which they were repairing and manning ships from their reserve fleet. It was not likely that the United Kingdom could help by providing crews for these ships: there was already some difficulty in manning existing British ships.

(e) This proposal to import coal might have some adverse effect on food imports, especially the import of oil seeds from West Africa.

(f) Ministers should at an early date review the coal budget for the coming year. Exports of coal and steel were an important bargaining-counter in trade negotiations, and our bargaining position had been seriously weakened by the failure to provide an adequate amount of coal for export. Special difficulties were arising from our inability to supply Sweden with the coal which she needed.

(g) The Prime Minister said that statements on the coal situation should be made in both Houses of Parliament during the Debate on the Address. These statements should make it clear that the

Government had been compelled to import foreign coal in order to avert a crisis with which they had been faced on assuming office; and that, if this crisis had been foreseen, the coal could have been imported during the summer with far less risk of dislocating other import programmes.

The Cabinet –

Approved the proposal made in C(51)5, and authorised the Secretary of State for the Co-ordination of Transport, Fuel and Power, in consultation with the Ministers of Transport and Fuel and Power, to take immediate steps to secure the early importation into this country of half a million tons of coal from the United States.

[. . .]

Winston S. Churchill: speech
(Hansard)

6 November 1951   House of Commons

Before I enter upon the task of replying to the right hon. Member for Walthamstow, West (Mr Attlee),[1] I should like to congratulate him upon the honour he has received from the Crown of the Order of Merit. The news of this was especially gratifying to those who served so many years with him in the hard days of the war.

I join with the right hon. Gentleman in the compliments he has paid to the speeches of the mover[2] and seconder[3] of the Address. We all thought they

---

[1] Clement Richard Attlee, 1883–1967. Educated at Haileybury and University College, Oxford. Called to the Bar, 1906. Tutor and Lecturer, London School of Economics, 1913–23. On active service, Gallipoli, Mesopotamia (wounded) and France, 1914–19; Maj., 1917. First Lab. Mayor of Stepney, 1919, 1920; Alderman, 1920–7. MP (Lab.) for Limehouse, 1922–50; for West Walthamstow, 1950–5. Parliamentary Private Secretary to Ramsay MacDonald, 1922–4. Under-Secretary of State for War, 1924. Chancellor of the Duchy of Lancaster, 1930–1. Postmaster-General, 1931. Deputy Leader of the Labour Party in the House of Commons, 1931–45. PC, 1935. Leader of the Opposition, 1935–40. Lord Privy Seal, 1940–2. Deputy PM, 1942–5. Secretary of State for Dominion Affairs, 1942–3. Lord President of the Council, 1943–5. CH, 1945. PM, 1945–51 (Minister of Defence, 1945–6). FRS, 1947. OM, 1951. Leader of the Opposition, 1951–5. Earl, 1955.

[2] Arthur Douglas Dodds-Parker, 1909–2006. Educated at Winchester College and Magdalen College, Oxford. Sudan Political Service, 1930–9. Served in Grenadier Guards, 1939–45. MP (Cons.) for Banbury, 1945–59; for Cheltenham, 1964–74. Married, 1946, Aileen Coster: one child. Joint Parliamentary Under-Secretary of State for Foreign Affairs, 1953–4, 1955–7. Parliamentary Under-Secretary for Commonwealth Relations, 1954–5. Led Parliamentary Delegation to China, 1972. Knighted, 1973.

[3] Anthony Perrinott Lysberg Barber, 1920–2005. Educated at Oriel College, Oxford. Served in King's Own Yorkshire Light Infantry, 1939; RAF, 1940–5. Barrister-at-law, Inner Temple, 1948. Married, 1950, Jean Patricia Asquith (d. 1983): two children; 1989, Rosemary Youens. MP (Cons.) for Doncaster, 1951–64; for Altrincham and Sale, 1965–74. Private Parliamentary Secretary to Under-Secretary of State for Air, 1952–5. Asst Whip, 1955–7. Lord Commissioner of the Treasury, 1957–8. Parliamentary Private Secretary to PM, 1958–9. Economic Secretary to Treasury, 1959–62; Financial Secretary, 1962–3. PC, 1963. Minister of Health, 1963–4. Chairman, Conservative Party

were admirable, and it is no mere repetition of a happy form of words which has led to these praises offered by the right hon. Gentleman being accepted with goodwill by the House. Both hon. Gentlemen distinguished themselves, and one overcame the double ordeal of making a maiden speech in conditions of exceptional formality and importance.

The right hon. Gentleman will excuse me if I say that he does not seem quite to have got clear of the General Election. A great deal of his speech was made up of very effective points and quips which gave a great deal of satisfaction to those behind him. We all understand his position: 'I am their leader, I must follow them.' A hard task lies before His Majesty's Government and grave responsibilities weigh upon the new Parliament. For two whole years our island has been distracted by party strife and electioneering. I do not see how this could have been avoided. Our Parliamentary institutions express themselves through party government, at any rate in times of peace. The nation is deeply and painfully divided, and the opposing forces are more or less evenly balanced. Naturally, neither side approves of what the other has done or said in the course of the conflict. We think on this side that the 'Warmonger' campaign did us great harm, and is probably answerable for the slender majority upon which His Majesty's Government must rest, with all its many Parliamentary disadvantages and uncertainties. We are, however, now in a position to answer this cruel and ungrateful charge not merely by words but by deeds. It may well be, therefore, that in due course of time it will recoil with compound interest upon the heads of those who profited by it.

We meet together here with an apparent gulf between us as great as I have known in 50 years of House of Commons life. What the nation needs is several years of quiet, steady administration, if only to allow Socialist legislation to reach its full fruition. What the House needs is a period of tolerant and constructive debating on the merits of the questions before us without nearly every speech on either side being distorted by the passions of one election or the preparations for another. Whether we shall get this or not is, to say the least, doubtful. We ask no favours in the conduct of Parliamentary business. We believe ourselves capable of coping with whatever may confront us. Still, it would not be good for our country if, for instance, events so shaped themselves that a third General Election came upon us in, say, a year or 18 months. Still worse for our country if that conflict, in its turn, led only to a continuance of an evenly matched struggle in the House and out of doors.

We must all be conscious of the realities of our position. Fifty millions of people are now crowded in our small island which produces food for only three-fifths of them, and has to earn the rest from over the seas by exporting manufactures for which we must also first import the raw material. No community of such a size, and standing at so high a level of civilisation, has ever

---

Organization, 1967–70. Chancellor of the Duchy of Lancaster, 1970. Chancellor of the Exchequer, 1970–4. Baron, 1974.

been economically so precariously poised. An ever larger and more formidable world is growing up around us. Very soon severe competition from Germany and Japan must be expected in our export markets. The problem of earning our independent livelihood stares us in the face. All our united strength will be needed to maintain our standards at home and our rank among the nations. If in these circumstances the electioneering atmosphere is to continue indefinitely, with the nation split in half in class and ideological strife, it will present a spectacle which the world will watch with wonder, and I believe, on the whole, with dismay.

My hope is that the instinct of self-preservation may grow steadily during this Parliament. Controversy there must be in some of the issues before us, but this will be but a small part of the work and interests we have in common. Although, while present conditions last, we all live in the shadow of another General Election, the Government will not fear to do unpopular things where these are found, in our opinion, to be indispensable to the general welfare. I trust, however, that British good sense may avoid an era of annual elections, narrow majorities, and fierce, bitter, exciting class and party war.

Do not let us forget, in reviewing our position as a community, that during the last six years immense financial help has been loaned or given to us by the United States and our Dominions. (*Interruption.*) Why should I say, 'Do not let us forget it?' It would be very foolish to forget it, for but for this help the true facts of our situation would have been brought brutally home to all classes and parties – and may be coming home now.

We have thought it right to make certain reductions in Ministerial salaries. They are not intended as a reproach upon the party opposite, but only as a signal which may be helpful for all. Realising the gravity of the period upon which we have entered, I consider that this period of re-armament, when all the priorities of labour and materials are necessarily distorted and diverted from the normal peacetime flow, is one in which exceptional measures must be taken. The reductions are intended to mark the emergency character of the period upon which we have entered – into which we have been led by the leader of hon. Gentlemen opposite. They are limited to the period of re-armament or three years, whichever ends the first.

Mr Percy Schurmer[1] (Birmingham, Sparkbrook): How much did the right hon. Gentleman sacrifice?

The Prime Minister: I am discussing it seriously. Hon. Members will not gain anything by interrupting me, because I have had so much experience both of being interrupted and of interrupting. They are limited to this period of three years or to the re-armament period, and, therefore, will not affect conditions in future Parliaments or under a different Government. They are not intended as a reproach, but only as a signal for an abnormal period.

---

[1] Percy Lionel Edward Schurmer, 1888–1959. MP (Lab.) for Birmingham Sparkbrook, 1945–59.

The Gracious Speech contains only one obviously controversial measure, the annulment – that is I understand, a term of art, but it may well be expressed by the more familiar word 'repeal' – the annulment of the nationalisation of the iron and steel industry. The restoration of the university representation was one definite issue at both the General Elections. On a strict interpretation of our mandate we should be entitled to make a change in university representation operative immediately, for that was the intention most clearly expressed; but, on reaching the moment of decision, I and my colleagues felt that for the Government to add to their majority in a Parliament already elected would create a questionable precedent. We should look a little like the London County Council – not that I should think of comparing University Members with so docile and trustworthy a band as those have proved to be. We therefore decided that it was better that any alteration of the franchise should follow the normal course of franchise Measures and be operative only at the Dissolution.

I do not intend to repeat today the familiar arguments about the university seats. We have always felt that their abolition was harmful to the House. (*Interruption.*) It is possible to differ from a speaker without making verbal protests; we should have to make a great many if we followed that process out continuously. We have always felt that their abolition was harmful to the House. The House has benefited greatly by the contribution which the universities made. Moreover, we thought it unfair that a Government, exulting in its enormous majority of 1945, should depart from the agreement reached by all parties at the Speaker's Conference of 1943, in which matters were balanced fairly to agreement on both sides.

Mr Herbert Morrison[1] (Lewisham South) *indicated dissent.*

The Prime Minister: The right hon Gentleman is shaking his head, but he will have to shake it a great deal to shake off his personal responsibility in this matter. This agreement was reached by all parties at the Speaker's Conference of 1943 under the Coalition Government. We have in no way departed from our intention to restore the university franchise, but the Measure is no longer urgent and it will not become operative until the end of the Parliament.

Now, the repeal of the steel nationalization Act was a much larger and equally definite issue between parties at both elections. In the first, the Government commanded a majority of six in the House but were in a considerable minority in the country. In the second, we have a substantial majority for repeal in the country and, we believe, an effective majority in the House. I do not attempt today to argue again the rights and wrongs of the nationalization of steel. There will certainly be plenty of time for that. I did not think it was

---

[1] Herbert Stanley Morrison, 1888–1965. Began work as an errand boy at the age of 14. Secretary to the London Labour Party, 1915–40. MP (Lab.) for South Hackney, 1923–4, 1929–31, 1935–59. Minister of Transport, 1929–31. Minister of Supply, May–Oct. 1940. Home Secretary and Minister of Home Security, 1940–5 (Member of the War Cabinet, 1942–5). Lord President of the Council (responsible for economic planning and co-ordination) and Leader of the House of Commons, 1945–51. Secretary of State for Foreign Affairs, 1951. Life Peer, 1959.

a wise Measure or one conceived in the national interest. When in September, 1950, the Leader of the Opposition, as Prime Minister, announced his immense rearmament programme and raised the period of National Service to two years in the Armed Forces, and when we gave him our support in these momentous decisions, I was very sorry indeed that he should have chosen that moment to retort upon us with his nakedly partisan Measure. Had he not done so the great common task to which both parties had bound themselves might have led to wider understandings which, without any formal coalition or division of offices, would have prolonged the life of the late Parliament and restored a new sense of unity to our country amid all its difficulties. As the future years roll by, and as history is written – and I do not propose myself to write this part of it – it will be possible to judge whether things would have worked out better or worse for us all if some unity had been achieved at that moment. The denationalization of steel cannot be taken before Christmas. It will occupy us very fully, no doubt, next year.

We desire to bring this Session to an end as soon as the necessary business has been disposed of, and after providing full and customary opportunities for the discussion of the general situation. We hope that the House will adjourn early in December and will meet again in February, subject of course to the usual arrangements for recall in case of emergency. This period will give Ministers the opportunity which we need of acquainting ourselves with every detail of the administration, and of shaping with knowledge and study the many necessary measures which must be taken to secure our livelihood as a community and our safety as a nation. When we re-assemble after Christmas we shall be able to speak – (*Interruption.*) I really think I might be treated with ordinary courtesy. This is quite unusual. I have not tried to go beyond the ordinary limits which are observed on these occasions. Hon. Members, many of whom sat in the last Parliament, know quite well that nothing very much is gained by interrupting a speaker; it only prolongs the proceedings. When we reassemble after Christmas we shall be able to speak with much greater precision than is possible for men who have been six years away from official information, and for others, quite a number of whom have never held office before. We shall be able to make plans for dealing with our many cares and problems, which we have not been able to do in the 10 busy days since we took office.

The King's Speech in no way limits the legislation which may be brought before Parliament if the public interest so requires. I am sure that it would not be wise for us to commit ourselves to complicated constructive proposals until we have had full and reasonable opportunity for studying the whole situation – (*Interruption.*) Well, in justice to hon. Gentlemen opposite whose work can now be seen – until we have had full and reasonable opportunity for studying the whole situation, and for using the machinery of the Departments to aid us in framing and shaping policy. Time is required for thought and decision, and we shall not hesitate to submit to Parliament additional Measures not mentioned in the Gracious Speech if we consider at any time that this is necessary.

I might mention, however, that before we rise I shall require to have a day's debate on the defence position, on which I wish to give the House the fullest information possible. For this purpose I shall ask for a Secret Session. That is not because I shall tell the House State secrets which are not known to the General Staffs of Europe and America, but because I think that Members of Parliament should be equally well informed, and that it is better that we should talk these matters over among ourselves in the first instance without what we say becoming a matter of headlines and discussion all over the world.

The Debate on the Address will occupy the remainder of the present week, and will, it is hoped, be brought to a conclusion in the early part of next week. Under your guidance, Mr Speaker, we shall endeavour to arrange the debates, whether on Amendments or otherwise, to the general contentment of the House. The House is aware that my right hon. Friend the Foreign Secretary is attending the opening in Paris of the General Assembly of the United Nations, but special arrangements will be made for a Foreign Affairs Debate on his return. That is additional to the days taken in the course of discussing the reply to the Gracious Speech. It will be necessary for the Government to take the full time of the House till the Adjournment for Christmas, and I now give notice that my right hon. Friend the Leader of the House will make the necessary Motion tomorrow. When we meet again in the New Year, the Friday sittings will be devoted to Private Members' Bills and Motions, and there will then be no restriction upon Bills under the Ten Minutes' Rule procedure.

Before I come to the most anxious and serious part of what I have to say this afternoon, I will deal with one or two criticisms that have been made about the formation of the Government. There are those which the Leader of the Opposition made when he asked me to define the exact relationship between supervising Ministers and the Ministers responsible to this House. He is very well familiar with it, because it was a process which continually operated during all the years of the Great War and was found very beneficial in many ways. But the rights and responsibilities of the Members of Parliament are in no way affected by the fact that these problems are studied in the larger bracket from a position of some detachment from the Departments which are grouped together. I believe very much in the policy of grouping Departments where it is possible, and that really is the designing principle upon which the Government was constructed.

The right hon. Gentleman asked me whether I was not burdening myself too much by taking the Ministry of Defence as well as the office of Prime Minister. I am well aware of the burden of both these offices, but I did feel that I must, at any rate at the outset, master the situation in the sphere of defence and leave the future to be decided later on. That is what I propose to do. I do not feel that I shall have difficulty in discharging these two functions, at any rate until I am fully possessed of the actual situation in which we stand at the present time.

Then there is the question of whether the Minister of Education ought not to have a seat in the Cabinet. There is great importance in keeping the Cabinet small. It is now sixteen. There is not much difference between that and the eighteen which the right hon. Gentleman had, but the fact that some Ministers holding important offices are not in the Cabinet does not deny them access. Any head of a great Department has only to ask the Prime Minister for him to be given every opportunity of presenting the case of the Department. Quite apart from this, the Minister of Education would always be summoned when anything directly or indirectly affected education and its many concomitants were under discussion. I cannot think that that will form any great difficulty.

Then the right hon. Gentleman turned to speaking about the other place. I gather he suggested that there were too many noble Lords in the Government. The right hon. Gentleman not only employed noble Lords but even created them in considerable numbers. The position now is that there are eighteen Tory Lords as against sixteen Socialist Lords in the Government. If all our differences could be reduced to such modest proportions, how much better our fortunes would be.

There was also a complaint, so far confined to the newspapers, that the new representation we have given to the Principality of Wales should have been entrusted to a Scotsman. The reason why I placed it under the Home Secretary was because that is the Senior Secretaryship of State. I wonder whether it is a wise attitude for Welshmen to take, that their affairs can only be dealt with in the United Kingdom Parliament by one of their own race and nation. It seems to me that this principle might even be carried too far. Looking back upon the past – a long past – and even perhaps forward into the future, I should have thought that Welshmen might well expect a very much larger share in our affairs than a strict numerical computation of the population would warrant. Nevertheless, when one is trying to give pleasure it is always well to do it in the best possible way. We have therefore appointed an Under-Secretary under the Home Office who is a Welshman, and whose name is, I believe, quite well known throughout the Principality.

Mr George Thomas[1] (Cardiff, West): Pronounce his name.

The Prime Minister: I will – Llewellyn[2] 'Môr o gân yw Cymru i gyd.'[3]

This additional Under-Secretaryship to the Home Office will require legislation, and we shall present a Bill to enable my hon. Friend the Member for

---

[1] Thomas George Thomas, 1909–97. MP (Lab.) for Cardiff Central, 1945–50; for Cardiff West, 1950–83. Joint Under-Secretary of State for Home Dept, 1964–7. Joint Minister of State for Commonwealth Affairs, 1967–8. Secretary of State for Wales, 1968–70. Chairman of Ways and Means, 1974–6. Speaker of House of Commons, 1976–83. Viscount, 1983.

[2] David Treharne Llewellyn, 1916–92. MP (Cons.) for Cardiff North, 1950–9. Under-Secretary of State for Home Dept, 1951–2.

[3] In Welsh: 'All Wales is a sea of song.'

Cardiff, North (Mr Llewellyn) to take up his duties formally, and for the Home Secretary to be assisted by another Under-Secretary. The case will be so presented that the issue will be for or against the new Secretary specially charged with Welsh affairs. That, I think, is more likely to bring us all together than any other presentation of the case.

Now I come to the greatest matter that I have to bring before the House today – the financial and economic situation. The right hon. Gentleman spoke in a jocular manner about making bricks without straw, but I quote that only to emphasize by contrast the seriousness of the position. We were confronted on taking over with a Treasury report setting forth the position as it stood at that date, ten days ago. I sent a copy of this to the Leader of the Opposition in order that he might know our starting point. It was certainly scratch. In overseas payments we are in a deficit crisis worse than 1949, and in many ways worse than even 1947. Confidence in sterling is impaired. In the present half-year, we are running into an external deficit at the rate of £700 million a year compared with an annual rate of surplus of about £350 million in the same period a year ago. That means a deterioration of more than £1,000 million a year.

The latest estimates show that in 1952, on present trends and policies and without making any allowance for further speculative losses, the United Kingdom would have a deficit on its general balance of overseas payments of between £500 million and £600 million, and the loss to the central gold and dollar reserves in the transactions of the sterling areas as a whole with the rest of the world might be appreciably more. These figures mean, in short, that we are buying much more than we can afford to pay for from current earnings, and this can only in time lead to national bankruptcy. The position has been made worse by the loss of confidence in sterling and by the additional strain of the loss of Persian oil supplies, to which the Leader of the Opposition has made reference in some of his speeches. Such was the statement presented to us within a few hours of our taking office, and it has taken first place in our minds and discussions since. We are convinced that it is necessary to present the facts plainly to the nation in order that they may realize where we stand. We do not believe that a full and frank statement of our position will aggravate the loss of confidence abroad which has been taking place. On the contrary, many of the facts are known in foreign and financial circles and are, in some cases, exaggerated by foreign speculation. We feel that a solemn resolve by Parliament and the British people to set their house in order without delay, and the measures necessary to give effect to that resolve, would act as a tonic to our credit all the world over. A full statement of the financial position and the remedial measures which, in the time we have had to consider these matters we consider imperative, will be made by my right hon. Friend the Chancellor of the Exchequer at the opening of tomorrow's debate. I will not now elaborate the matter further.

We also find a bad position about coal supplies. Stocks of house coal are only half of what they were last year, and they are lower than they have ever been since the war. It is a tragedy that this great coal producing country should have to import coal, and a comedy that at the same time we should be exporting coal with our limited shipping. I know that there are explanations for all this, but the resulting fact remains, and we cannot let our people suffer cold or our industries and rearmament be hampered if there is anything that we can do at this stage to prevent it. The failure to build up house coal stocks was evident during the summer, and it seems a pity that coal was not imported at that time to restore the position when import, although no doubt not easy, would have been less difficult than it is now across the winter Atlantic. In spite of this difficulty, the Government will do all they can to get more coal from abroad. It will not be possible in the time available to bring in enough for us to guarantee that there will not be hardship before the winter ends.

We have had to reduce the meat ration to 1s. 5d. worth a week. Our predecessors had already given notice that this would be necessary. (*Interruption.*) I am only reciting facts. It is a great pity to get into a state of mind when we fear facts. They hoped that it would not fall lower during the winter and spring. My right hon. Friend the Minister of Food, in consultation with Lord Woolton, felt it essential to reduce the ration to 1s. 5d. without delay. The meat supply is really worse than it was in wartime. In the period from April 1942 to 1945, the weekly ration averaged about 1s. 2d. That would be equal to about 1s. 9½d. to 1s. 10d. at our present prices. On the reverse calculation, the ration of 1s. 5d. of today's weekly ration would equal a ration of about 11d. at wartime prices.

The prospect of supplies in the first half of next year is far from ample, but we trust it will grow. The imports from the Southern Dominions and from foreign sources such as the Argentine, even if all are made good, could not relieve the anxiety. There can be no assurance that the 1s. 5d. level can be held. We hope to do so, but I cannot disguise from the House that there are many uncertainties. A serious shortage of meat cannot be overcome quickly. To regain a pre-war consumption we should need 600,000 tons more meat a year than we are getting. I cannot hold out any hope of that in the near future. We shall do our best, and my right hon. Friend the Minister of Food will, I hope, deal with this matter later in the debate. So will the Lord President of the Council[1] in another place.

I do not propose to deal at any length this afternoon with the foreign situation. When the Foreign Secretary has returned from the conferences in Paris he will make his report to the House in a special debate. We cannot accept the ill-treatment we have received about Persian oil supplies. His Majesty's Government are always ready to negotiate a settlement on the basis of a fair partnership for the actual benefit of those who live in the country which

---

[1] Lord Woolton.

provides the oil, and for those who have created the wonderful industry and have the technical experience to extract the oil and to market it. We have so far suffered a great injustice and disaster, and we shall strive patiently and resolutely to repair the position as far as that is now possible.

In Egypt and the Sudan we are pursuing the policy adopted by the late Government and by the right hon. Gentleman the Member for Lewisham, South (Mr H. Morrison), who was Foreign Secretary. We are resolved to maintain our rightful position in the Canal Zone in spite of the illegal and one-sided Egyptian action over the 1936 Treaty. We shall do our utmost to safeguard the Canal as an international highway, using, of course, no more force than is necessary. Here again I think that time, within certain limits, and restraint and forbearance – not so strictly limited – may give the best chance of the crisis being successfully surmounted.

But our great hope in foreign affairs is, of course, to bring about an abatement of what is called 'the cold war' by negotiation at the highest level from strength and not from weakness. Perhaps I may read again to the House, as I have already read to them, what I wrote to Mr Stalin and his colleagues in April 1945.

> There is not much comfort in looking into a future where you and the countries you dominate, plus the Communist parties in many other States are all drawn up on one side, and those who rally to the English-speaking nations and their associates, or Dominions are on the other. It is quite obvious that their quarrel would tear the world to pieces and that all of us leading men on either side who had anything to do with that would be shamed before history. Even embarking on a long period of suspicions, of abuse and counter-abuse and of opposing policies would be a disaster, hampering the great developments of world prosperity for the masses which are attainable only by our trinity.[1]

That was written more than six years ago, and, alas, all came to pass with horrible exactitude. I must explain that in speaking of our trinity I was, of course, referring to a period when France had not fully resumed her rightful place in the international sphere.

At Edinburgh, in February 1950, I appealed for a conference between the heads of States or Governments,[2] and I and my right hon Friend the Foreign Secretary, who have acted in the closest, spontaneous accord in all these matters, still hold to the idea of a supreme effort to bridge the gulf between the two worlds, so that each can live its life, if not in friendship at least without the fear, the hatreds, and the frightful waste of the cold war.

---

[1] T.675/5, reproduced in *The Churchill Documents*, vol. 21, *The Shadows of Victory, January–July 1945*, pp. 1197–202.
[2] Speech of 14 Feb. 1950, reproduced in *The Churchill Documents*, vol. 22, *Leader of the Opposition, August 1945 to October 1951*, pp. 1642–50.

I must, however, today utter a word of caution. The realities which confront us are numerous, adverse and stubborn. We must be careful not to swing on a wave of emotion from despondency to over-confidence; but even if the differences between West and East are, for the time being, intractable, the creation of a new atmosphere and climate of thought, and of a revived relationship and sense of human comradeship, would, I believe, be an enormous gain to all nations.

Never must we admit that a third World War is inevitable. I heard some months ago of a foreign diplomatist who was asked: 'In which year do you think the danger of war will be the greatest?' He replied: 'Last year.' If that should prove true, as we pray it may, no one will deny their salute to the memory of Ernest Bevin,[1] or their compliments to those who worked faithfully with him. Let us, in these supreme issues with party politics far beneath them, move forward together in our united fight as faithful servants of our common country, and as unwearying guardians of the peace and freedom of the world.

Randolph S. Churchill[2] to Winston S. Churchill
(Churchill papers, 1/51)

7 November 1951

My Dearest Papa,

Now that your Government is complete, I would like to congratulate you upon it. Many of the Appointments are imaginative and I am sure the public have been impressed by the marked all round superiority to the previous Government. I thought your speech yesterday was a masterpiece.

[. . .]

---

[1] Ernest Bevin, 1881–1951. National Organiser, Dockers' Union, 1910–21. General Secretary, Transport and General Workers' Union, 1921–40. Member of TUC General Council, 1925–40. MP (Lab.) for Central Wandsworth, 1940–50; for East Woolwich, 1950–1. Minister of Labour and National Service in Churchill's Coalition Government, 1940–5. Secretary of State for Foreign Affairs, 1945–51. Lord Privy Seal, 1951.

[2] Randolph Frederick Edward Spencer Churchill, 1911–68. Educated at Eton and Christ Church, Oxford. Worked briefly for Imperial Chemical Industries as Asst Editor of their house magazine. Joined the *Sunday Graphic*, 1932. Wrote for many newspapers, including *Evening Standard,*1937–9. MP (Cons.) for Preston, 1940–5. On active service, North Africa and Italy, 1941–3. Maj., British Mission to Yugoslav Army of National Liberation, 1943–4. Unsuccessful Parliamentary candidate for Plymouth Devonport, 1950, 1951. Edited several volumes of his father's speeches, and author of first two volumes of his official biography.

Cabinet: conclusions
(*Cabinet papers, 128/23*)

8 November 1951
Secret
11.30 a.m.
Cabinet Meeting No. 5 of 1951

[...]
2. The Cabinet were informed that the Legislation Committee had considered the draft of a Judicial Office (Salaries, &c.) Bill, which would increase the salaries of County Court Judges, Metropolitan Magistrates and certain other judicial officers. The proposals in this Bill had been put forward by the previous Government and welcomed by other political Parties; and the Legislation Committee recommended that the Bill should be introduced forthwith.

The Prime Minister said that as this was a non-controversial measure, it might go forward at once. He hoped, however, that the Lord Chancellor would examine the possibility of granting some form of expense allowance to Judges of the High Court. This proposal, if it were found feasible, might be put forward when Parliament met again after the Christmas Recess.

The Cabinet –
(1) Agreed that the Judicial Offices (Salaries, &c.) Bill should be introduced into Parliament forthwith, in the form approved by the Legislation Committee.
(2) Invited the Lord Chancellor to consider, in consultation with the Chancellor of the Exchequer, whether some form of allowance should not be granted to Judges of the High Court.

3. The Prime Minister said that he was disturbed at the high cost of our military commitments in Malaya. He suggested that the Secretary of State for the Colonies, before he left for Malaya on the 26th November, should submit to the Cabinet an appreciation of the present position and his proposals for remedying it.

The Cabinet –
Invited the Secretary of State for the Colonies to submit for their consideration a memorandum on Malaya.

[...]
6. The Prime Minister said that he discussed with the Chiefs of Staff their latest proposals regarding the organization of the Middle East Command, which it was desired to form following the admission of Greece and Turkey to the North Atlantic Treaty Organization. The Turks were most reluctant to join any command structure which would be confined to the Middle East and placed under a British Commander. They were anxious to be included within General Eisenhower's[1] European Command, partly because this would

---

[1] Dwight David Eisenhower, 1890–1969. Known as 'Ike'. Graduated from West Point Military Academy, 1915. Drafted the War Dept's study and plans for industrial mobilisation, 1929–33. Asst

imply recognition of their claim to be a European country and partly because it would give them a better assurance of receiving military equipment from the United States. In these circumstances the Chiefs of Staff had formulated new proposals for the establishment of a Supreme Allied Command for Eastern Mediterranean and Middle East, which would be divided into four sub-commands, namely, Greece, Turkey, the Mediterranean and Aegean, and Middle East.

The Prime Minister said that he doubted whether this plan would prove acceptable to the other Governments concerned. After consultation with the Chiefs of Staff, however, he had accepted the Foreign Secretary's suggestion that it should be put forward as a basis for further discussion by the Standing Group in Washington. The important objective, which must be kept in mind throughout all of these discussions, was to secure that the United States should commit some forces to the defence of the Middle East.

The Cabinet took note of the Prime Minister's statement.

[...]

Winston S. Churchill: speech
('Winston S. Churchill, His Complete Speeches', volume 8, pages 8297–9)

9 November 1951   Lord Mayor's Banquet
The Guildhall, London

THE PATH OF DUTY

Though I have very often in the last forty years or so been present at your famous Guildhall banquets to salute the new Lord Mayor, this is the first occasion when I have addressed this assembly here as Prime Minister. The explanation is convincing. When I should have come here as Prime Minister the Guildhall was blown up and before it was repaired I was blown out! I thought at the time they were both disasters. But now we are here together in a union which I hope will bring good luck. I am sure we all wish the Lord Mayor[1] a successful year of his arduous office. I share his regrets that we have no Member for the City of London in the House of Commons. It is an error to believe that the world began when any particular party or statesmen got

---

Military Adviser, Commonwealth of Philippine Islands, 1935–40. Asst CoS, in charge of Operations Div., War Dept, General Staff, Washington DC, 1941. OC US Forces in England (for European operations), 1942. C-in-C, Allied Forces in North Africa, Nov. 1942 to Jan. 1944. Hon. knighthood, 1943. Supreme Cdr, Allied Expeditionary Force in Western Europe, Jan. 1944 to May 1945. Hon. OM, 1945. Cdr, American Zone of Occupation, Germany, 1945. CoS, US Army, 1945–8. Supreme Cdr, NATO Forces in Europe, 1950–2. US President, 1953–61.

[1] Harold Leslie Boyce, 1895–1955. Educated at Balliol College, Oxford. On active service with Australian Infantry, Egypt, Gallipoli and France, 1915–18. Called to the Bar, Inner Temple, 1922. Legal Adviser at 3rd Assembly of League of Nations, 1922. MP (Cons.) for Gloucester, 1929–45. Alderman, City of London, 1942–54. Knighted, 1944. Lord Mayor of London, 1951–2. Bt, 1952.

into office. It has all been going on quite a long time, and many movements and parties will rise and decline, and I trust many politicians will catch the fleeting glint of popular acclaim before the continuity of our island life is cut asunder or fades away. It's only by studying the past that we can foresee, however dimly, the future. I cannot help feeling the impact of these thoughts in this war-scarred Hall. Its battered monuments remind us of other struggles against the Continental tyrants of the past, in generations before the supreme ordeal of 1940 which we all endured and won together.

I am so glad my Lord Mayor that you have decided to replace the effigies of Gog and Magog.[1] It was to me a painful blow when they were burnt to ashes by Hitler's bomb. They will look fine in the gallery up there. Indeed I think they are not only ancient but up-to-date. It seems to me that they represent none too badly the present state of world politics. World politics, like the history of Gog and Magog, are very confused and much disputed. Still I think there is room for both of them. On the one side is Gog and on the other is Magog. But be careful my Lord Mayor, when you put them back, to keep them from colliding with each other, for if that happens both Gog and Magog would be smashed to pieces and we should all have to begin all over again – and begin from the bottom of the pit.

Whatever were the differences between Gog and Magog, at any rate they were made out of the same materials. Let me tell you what the materials are: vast masses of warm-hearted, hard-working human beings wanting to do their best for their country and their neighbours, and longing to build their homes and bring up their children in peace, freedom, and the hope of better times for the young when they grow up. That is all they ask of their rulers and governors and guides. That is the dear wish in the hearts of all the peoples of mankind. How easy it ought to be with modern science standing tiptoe ready to open the doors of a Golden Age, to grant them this humble modest desire. But then there come all these tribes of nationalists, ideologues, revolutionaries, these warfare experts, and imperialists with their nasty regiment of academic doctrines, striving night and day to work them all up against one another so that the homes instead of being built are bombed and the breadwinner is killed and the broken housewife left to pick the starving children out of the ashes. There is the structure: that is the composition which Gog and Magog have in common and there is the fate which both will suffer if you, my Lord Mayor, and others concerned in our City Affairs or those who deal with world affairs do not act with ordinary common sense and keep Gog and Magog from falling upon one another.

---

[1] Gog and Magog: biblical figures mentioned in Old and New Testaments as enemies of God's people. In British folklore, effigies of Gog and Magog were built during the reign of Henry V (1413–22) to represent two giants who were taken to London to serve as porters at the gate of the royal palace after their race was destroyed by Brutus the Trojan, legendary founder of London. These two statues were destroyed in the Great Fire of London in 1666, and replaced first by a pair made of wickerwork and pasteboard, and later, in 1708, by a pair of wooden statues that were eventually destroyed by a German air raid in 1940. The current statues of Gog and Magog were erected in 1953.

Somehow or other these ideas about Gog and Magog seem to have some suggestive relationship to the discussions which are taking place in Paris at the present time. But we must not let our thoughts be complicated by our imagery. So here I leave Gog and Magog, hoping I may have the chance to see them both in their proper places one of these days.

What is the world scene as presented to us today? Mighty forces armed with fearful weapons are baying at each other across a gulf which I have the feeling tonight neither wishes, and both fear to cross, into which they may tumble or drag each other to their common ruin. On the one side stand all the armies and air forces of Soviet Russia and all their Communists satellites, agents and devotees in so many countries. On the other are what are called 'the Western Democracies' with their far superior resources, at present only partly organized, gathering themselves together around the United States with its mastery of the atomic bomb. Now there is no doubt on which side we stand. Britain and the Commonwealth and Empire still centring upon our island, are woven by ever-growing ties of strength and comprehension of common need and self-preservation to the great Republic across the Atlantic Ocean.

The sacrifices and exertions which the United States are making to deter, and if possible prevent, Communist aggression from making further inroads upon the free world are the main foundation of peace. A tithe of the efforts now being made by America would have prevented the Second World War and would have probably led to the downfall of Hitler with scarcely any blood being shed except perhaps his own. I feel a deep gratitude towards our great American Ally. They have risen to the leadership of the world without any other ambition but to serve its highest causes faithfully. I am anxious that Britain should also play her full part, and I hope to see a revival of her former influence and initiative among the Allied Powers.

It must not be forgotten that under the late Government we took peculiar risks in providing the principal atomic base for the United States in East Anglia, and that in consequence we placed ourselves in the very forefront of Soviet antagonism. We have therefore every need and every right to seek and to receive the fullest consideration from Americans for our point of view, and I feel sure this will not be denied us.

In order to regain our position we must do our utmost to re-establish as quickly as possible our economic and financial sovereignty and independence. We were shocked and surprised by the situation with which we were confronted after accepting responsibility a fortnight ago. This resulted partly from world causes, but also partly from the prolonged electioneering atmosphere in which we have dwelt for nearly two years, and especially for the past two months. We have certainly been left a tangled web of commitments and shortages, the like of which I have never seen before, and I hope and pray we may be granted the wisdom and the strength to cope with them effectively. If these conditions of furious political warfare between the two halves of our party-divided Britain are to continue indefinitely, and we are all to live under the shadow of a third General Election, it will not be at all good for the main life interests of the British nation, or for her influence in world affairs. Nevertheless, whatever way things may go, we shall not fail to do our duty however unpopular that may be. It is not cheers that we seek to win or votes we are playing to catch, but respect and confidence. This cannot come from words alone, but only from action which proves itself by results. Results cannot be achieved by the wave of a wand. Time is needed for a new administration to grasp and measure the facts which surround us in baffling and menacing array. More time is needed for the remedies we propose and will propose to produce their curative effects. Nothing would be easier than for this country, politically rent asunder as it is, to shake and chatter itself into bankruptcy and ruin. But under grave pressures in the past we have proved ourselves to be a wise and unconquerable people, and I am sure that we shall succeed. No doubt His Majesty's Government will make mistakes. We shall not hesitate to admit them. I made many in the war. It is, however, always a comfort in times of crisis to feel that you are treading the path of duty according to the lights that are granted you. Then one need not fear whatever may happen. It was in this spirit that we all came through our worst perils eleven years ago; and I have a good and buoyant hope that the great mass of the nation will give us its ungrudging aid in all matters of truly national import. If this happens they may feel in two or three years' time that they have not been led on wrong courses and that Britain stands erect again, calm, resolute and independent, the faithful servant of peace, the valiant champion of freedom, and an honoured member of a united world instrument for preserving both.

Mary Soames to Winston S. Churchill
(Churchill papers, 1/52)[1]

10 November 1951   Chartwell Farm

My darling Papa,

It is indeed kind and generous of you and Mama to make this wonderful settlement on your grandchildren.[2] It is a great security for them, and an enormous help to us both in providing for them. It is terribly difficult for Christopher[3] to tell you how deeply grateful we do feel to you and Mama, not

---

[1] This letter was handwritten.

[2] Churchill had created a special Family Trust whereby all earnings from his war memoirs would go to the benefit of his children and grandchildren without the burden of taxation. See also responses from Randolph and Diana below (pp. 154–5, 44–5).

[3] Arthur Christopher John Soames, 1920–87. Educated at Eton and Sandhurst. 2nd Lt, Coldstream Guards, 1939; Capt., 1942. Asst Military Attaché, British Embassy, Paris, 1946–7. Married, 1947, Mary Churchill: five children. MP (Cons.) for Bedford Div. of Bedfordshire, 1950–66. Parliamentary Private Secretary to PM, 1952–5. Parliamentary Under-Secretary of State, Air Ministry, 1955–7. Parliamentary and Financial Secretary, Admiralty, 1957–8. Secretary of State for War, 1958–60. Minister

only for this latest blessing, but for the continual flow of kindness and generosity, which you have poured out on us and our children.

I think you know we are happy – deeply happy with each other – happy in the dear home and haven you have given us here – Happy in our growing family – and happy in the loving bonds which bind us to you both.

We cannot in any way repay you, except by our loving gratitude, which overflows. And trying to show to our children and dependants the same largeness of heart and steadfastness of love which you have always shown to yours.

It is hardly in the nature of things that your descendants should inherit your genius – but I earnestly hope that they may share in some way the qualities of your heart.

With my dearest love and thanks.
Always your devoted daughter, Mary

Winston S. Churchill to Anthony Eden
Prime Minister's Personal Minute M.25c/51
(Premier papers, 11/545)

11 November 1951

Please see Foreign Office telegram to Khartoum No. 220 of November 8. Surely we are not called upon to hurry this process in this way?[1] I hope this may be considered maturely by the Cabinet before any such a date is fixed.

---

of Agriculture, Fisheries and Food, 1960–4. Director, Decca Ltd, 1964–8; James Hole & Co. Ltd, 1964–8. British Ambassador to France, 1968–72. European Commissioner for Trade, 1973–7. European Commissioner for External Relations, 1973–7. Lord President of the Council, 1979–81. Leader of House of Lords, 1979–81. Governor of Southern Rhodesia, 1979–80.

[1] The Constitutional Amendment Commission had presented recommendations to the Governor-General (Robert George Howe, 1893–1981) that, if successful, would result in the Sudanese holding early elections for an all-Sudanese, representative Legislative Assembly and choosing an all-Sudanese Council of Ministers in order to lay a foundation for Sudanese self-government by 1952. In fact, independence and a democratic parliament were not achieved until Jan. 1956. Nationalist and Communist unrest continued to plague Sudan until the 1969 coup, at which point Col. Gaafar Nimiery's new regime abolished parliament and outlawed all political parties.

Winston S. Churchill to Foreign Office
Prime Minister's Personal Minute M.22c/51
(Premier papers, 11/92)

11 November 1951

What does Sir R. Stevenson[1] mean by 'intervention if the worst comes to the worst'? (See telegram from Cairo No. 962 of November 9.)[2] Does he mean the forcible occupation of Cairo?

The Cabinet must be consulted before any movements are made to 'intervene' outside the Canal Zone. There is no objection to movements inside that Zone of a preparatory character.

Cabinet: conclusions
(Cabinet papers, 128/23)

12 November 1951
Secret
12 p.m.
Cabinet Meeting No. 6 of 1951

[...]
6. The Prime Minister said that it would be convenient if regular times were fixed for meetings of the Cabinet. He proposed that the Cabinet should normally meet on Tuesdays and Thursdays at 11.30 a.m. Additional meetings would be called as necessary.

---

[1] Ralph Clarmont Skrine Stevenson, 1895–1977. On active service with Rifle Bde, 1914–18. Entered Diplomatic Service, 1919. Principal Private Secretary to Foreign Secretary, 1939–41. Minister at Montevideo, 1941–3. Ambassador to Yugoslavia, 1943–6; to China, 1946–50; to Egypt, 1950–5. Knighted, 1946.

[2] The paragraph in question read:

'3. I have no desire to be an alarmist and it may well be that nothing will go wrong next week, but there is at present no firm ground on which to base so comforting a forecast. I am naturally doing what I can to impress The King and the Minister of the Interior with the dangerous possibilities of the situation but I think that you and the Commanders-in-Chief should be prepared for intervention if the worst comes to the worst. I would suggest that troops should be held in readiness to take rapid action if necessary, but there should be no (repeat no) military moves, such as forward concentrations near the "Erskine line", which could be regarded as provocative, as the Egyptians might well then lose their heads.'

Winston S. Churchill to Sir Edward Bridges and Sir Norman Brook
Prime Minister's Personal Minute M.32c/51
(Premier papers, 11/174)

12 November 1951

Please let me have a list of the Committees, Sub-Committees and Working Parties at present sitting in Whitehall, both Ministerial and official.

*Winston S. Churchill to Lieutenant-General Kenneth McLean,[1]
for the Chiefs of Staff Committee*
Prime Minister's Personal Minute M.36c/51
(Premier papers, 11/50)

12 November 1951

1. All this must await the discussions we shall have in Washington after the New Year. There is no necessity for a Supreme Commander. The integrity of the reception end and its approaches is vital to Britain and to any United Nations armies on the Continent. They can only be managed from the Admiralty, under the executive authority of the First Sea Lord. The actual moving of convoys is worked from Derby House, Liverpool. The actual meridian or line where we and the Americans exchange the outward and the inward convoys ought to be easy to agree. The nearer the Americans will carry their ocean responsibility to Europe the better, provided always that the complete integrity of the reception and launching of convoys is settled by the Admiralty, with their administrative machine at Derby House.

2. The present line of coastal waters seems to me much too restricted. The 100-fathom line would be more agreeable, at any rate up as far as North of the Shetlands where Admiral Brind's[2] Command begins to operate.

3. The idea of the French looking after the Bay of Biscay as a kind of enclave in the British approaches or coastal waters seems open to serious criticism. In the Mediterranean the French are a great naval power and should have much consideration, but I gather they are only providing about a flotilla for the Atlantic.

[1] Kenneth Graeme McLean, 1896–1987. On active service, WWI. Asst Secretary, Committee of Imperial Defence, 1938. GSO, War Office, 1940–1. Director of Selection of Personnel, 1941. Chief Operations Officer, 21st Army Group, 1943. Deputy Adjutant-General, Allied Land Forces, South-East Asia, 1945–6; Middle East Command, 1946. Vice Adjutant-General, War Office, 1947–9. CoS, Allied Control Commission, Germany, 1949; Deputy Military Governor, British Zone, Germany, 1949. Military Secretary to Secretary of State for War, 1949–51. Chief Staff Officer, Ministry of Defence, 1951–2.

[2] Eric James Patrick Brind, 1892–1963. On active service, 1914–18. Capt., 1933. CoS to C-in-C Home Fleet, 1940–2; RAdm., 1942. Asst CNS, 1942–4. VAdm., 1945. President, Royal Naval College, Greenwich, 1946–8. Adm., 1949. C-in-C, Far East Station, 1949–51. C-in-C, Allied Forces, Northern Europe, 1951–3.

4. This idea of setting up different Commanders-in-Chief on shore under the Admiralty, with far-reaching activities and (?) sometimes direct contact with the Supreme Commander, must be very sparingly indulged in. You may quite easily find that what would have worked quite smoothly in the Admiralty building under the First Sea Lord will now become a new frontier of correspondence with the local Commander-in-Chief.

I need scarcely say that Commanders-in-Chief at sea cannot possibly judge anything but the safety and victory of their fleets. Again and again the Admiralty have had to intervene in the direction even of the movement of their outlying squadrons, because the Admiralty knew and they did not know what was happening. Also they often have to observe wireless silence, so cannot even speak.

5. So far I have only considered this matter in its relation to coping with mine-laying and U-boat warfare by British surface craft. I presume however that as far as Russian U-boats are concerned the Coastal Command Air Force, or whatever it is called, now plays not only an indispensable but possibly the major part. Let me have a short paper on this.

6. What allocation of American aircraft and anti-U-boat vessels are proposed for our waters and under our command under the present scheme?

Sir William Strang[1] to Winston S. Churchill
(*Premier papers, 11/545*)

12 November 1951
PM/WS/51/122

THE SUDAN

I am sending to the Foreign Secretary your minute M 25(C)/51 of the 11th November.[2]

2. Mr Eden had already asked me to ensure that his telegrams Nos. 539, 540 and 542 from Paris are brought to your attention. I attach copies of these.

3. The Foreign Secretary proposes to make a statement on the lines of his

---

[1] William Strang, 1893–1978. Educated at Palmer's School, University College, London, and the Sorbonne. On active service with Worcestershire Rgt, 1915–18. MBE, 1918. Served at British Embassy in Belgrade, 1919–22; FO, 1922–30; Embassy in Moscow, 1930–3. CMG, 1932. Head of League of Nations Section at FO, 1933–7; Central Dept, 1937–9. CB, 1939. Asst Under-Secretary of State for Europe, 1939–43. KCMG, 1943. UK Representative, European Advisory Commission, 1943–5. Political Adviser to C-in-C British Forces in Germany, 1945–7. Permanent Under-Secretary of State for German Section of FO, 1947–9. Permanent Under-Secretary for Foreign Affairs, 1949–53. GCMG, 1950. Retired from FO, 1953. KCB, 1953. Baron, 1954. Convenor of Cross-Bench Peers, 1968–74. Author of *The Foreign Office* (1955), *Home and Abroad* (1956), *Britain in World Affairs* (1961) and *Diplomatic Career* (1962).

[2] M.22c/51, reproduced above (p. 36).

telegram No. 540 in the House of Commons on Wednesday or Thursday of this week.

4. There is at present great uneasiness and impatience in the Sudan. The immediate cause of this is the purported Egyptian abrogation of the Condominium Agreement of 1899. Even before this the growth of political consciousness in the Sudan had been rapid, under the impact of recent events in the Middle East and the imminent granting of independence to Libya.

5. In order to unite Sudanese opinion, the Governor General[1] this year set up a Sudanese Commission to recommend to him the next steps toward self-government. This Commission is expected to make its report in the near future and to recommend steps that will lead to self-government before the end of 1952. Meanwhile the Commission, very unwisely, has sent a telegram to the United Nations asking for the appointment of an international commission to reside in the Sudan.

6. It is in order to allay the uncertainty of the Sundanese, which is already finding expression in demonstrations, and to sidetrack the Commission's request to the United Nations, that it is proposed to make a statement about our own intentions.

7. We think that something on the lines of the proposed statement is the least that can be said if we are to give the necessary lead to the Sudanese. The Governor-General has been pressing us for early action.

Winston S. Churchill to General Lord Ismay, Lord Cherwell,
Sir Edward Bridges and Sir Norman Brook
Prime Minister's Personal Minute M.37c/51
(Cabinet papers, 21/3057)

12 November 1951

We must now begin to study what we want to discuss in Washington after January 3. I should be very much obliged if you would consult together and give me at any rate a first outline. The discussions will cover the economic as well as the military side, and large questions of foreign policy. It is not necessary to approach the Departments at this stage. I feel you all know a great deal about it. Presently I will add my own quota.

---

[1] Robert George Howe, 1893–1981. Educated at Cambridge University. Married, 1919, Loveday Mary Hex (d. 1970). 3rd Secretary, Copenhagen, 1920. 2nd Secretary, Belgrade, 1922; Rio de Janeiro, 1924. 1st Secretary, Bucharest, 1926. FO, 1930. Acting Counsellor, Peking, 1934; Counsellor, 1936. CMG, 1937. Minister in Riga, 1940; in Addis Ababa, 1942–5. Asst Under-Secretary of State, FO, 1945. KCMG, 1947. Governor-General, Sudan, 1947–55. GBE, 1949. JP, Cornwall, 1955–68.

Sir Norman Brook to Winston S. Churchill
(Cabinet papers, 21/3057)

13 November 1951

On behalf of the others to whom you addressed your Minute M.37(c)/51 of yesterday, I submit a first outline of the subjects which might be covered in your discussions in Washington. This list was drawn up at a meeting which we held this morning. We have not approached the Departments concerned; and we imagine that your next step will be to talk to the Foreign Secretary on his return.

When the list of subjects is settled, I will submit proposals for organising the preparation of papers and other preparatory work.

OUTLINE OF SUBJECTS FOR DISCUSSION AT WASHINGTON
1. The 'Cold War'

(a) Policy of the West towards Russia.
(b) Germany – Unification.
    Contribution to Western Defence.
(c) Trade with countries behind the Iron Curtain.

2. Policy in the Far East

(a) China (including Korea).
(b) Future relations with Japan (including the revival of Japanese competition in export markets).
(c) The Communist threat in South-East Asia.

3. Middle East

Anglo/American understanding on the three-fold importance of the Middle East –
(i) strategic
(ii) political
(iii) economic.

The underlying problem is to find a new basis on which the Anglo/Saxon countries can maintain their position of influence and authority in the Middle East now that (i) conditions no longer favour the straight commercial concession; and (ii) nationalism resents 'occupation' by foreign troops in time of peace.

The particular problems of Egypt and Persia should be considered against this general background.

4. Defence

(a) North Atlantic Command.
(b) Integration of Greece and Turkey into NATO Command structure.
(c) Commitment of US Forces to Middle East.

(d) Supreme Political Direction in peace and in war.
(e) The .280 Rifle.

5. United States support for our defence effort

(a) General economic aid (i.e. dollars).
(b) Steel.
(c) Finished military equipment.
(d) Concerted policy on stockpiling and the purchase of raw materials.
(e) Duration of United States aid.

6. Atomic Energy

(a) Co-operation between US, UK and Canada (including request for further information on results of US tests).
(b) Strategic Air Plan.

Anthony Eden to Winston S. Churchill
(Churchill papers, 2/517)

13 November 1951
Secret
PM/51/123

CONTRACTUAL NEGOTIATION WITH GERMANY
SECURITY CONTROLS

1. At their meeting in Washington in September, the Foreign Ministers of the United Kingdom, France[1] and the United States of America considered whether the Contractual Settlement with Germany (i.e. the political settlement which will be linked with a German contribution to Western Defence) should impose any restrictions upon the German armament industry. They agreed that certain items already recommended should be prohibited; and that civil aircraft should be added to these.

2. The NATO Governments have recommended that Germany should be prohibited from manufacturing:
   (a) atomic, biological and chemical weapons;
   (b) naval vessels other than minor defensive craft;
   (c) military aircraft;
   (d) guided missiles;
   (e) heavy military equipment.

[1] Jean-Baptiste Nicolas Robert Schuman, 1886–1963. Educated at Athénée de Luxembourg and Lycée Impérial in Metz, and the Universities of Berlin, Munich, Bonn and Strasbourg. French citizen, 1919. Député to French Parliament, 1919–58. PM, 1947–8. Foreign Minister, 1948–53. Minister of Justice, 1955–6. President, European Parliamentary Assembly, 1955–61.

3. Officials of the three Western Occupying Powers met in London to prepare instructions to the Allied High Commission in Germany. They have agreed upon the definitions of (a), (b), (c), and (d). They have not, however been able to agree on the definition of (e).

4. Instead, on the suggestion of the United States and French representatives, they have recommended the prohibition of the manufacture of:
- (i) gun barrels over 60 mm calibre;
- (ii) armour plate of a thickness greater than 50 mm;
- (iii) all forms of propellant;
- (iv) specialized plant for the production of these articles.

They consider that this will achieve the same object.

5. The Chiefs of Staff examined the recommendations; and consider that they meet in full – and indeed exceed – the requirements of security.

6. Contrary to expectation, however, the United States Government have rejected the recommendation regarding heavy military equipment; Mr Acheson intends to reopen the question with M Schuman and myself in the course of our consideration of German affairs in Paris on the 21st and 22nd of November. The American view is that the Germans should be able to make the maximum possible contribution to arming the forces they contribute to the European Army. Mr Acheson will probably also argue that the Germans will not be prepared to accept the restriction proposed in the field of heavy military equipment; and ask us to agree either that, given the prohibitions under (a)–(d) in paragraph 2 above:
- (a) the manufacture of heavy military equipment should not be prohibited at all; or that
- (b) only the production of the heaviest categories of tanks and artillery should be prohibited.

7. The Chiefs of Staff have considered the matter. Their view is that we could safely accept the proposal by Mr Acheson on the lines of (a) or (b) of the preceding paragraph if this were necessary to secure a German defence contribution.

8. In these circumstances I must consider whether I should not fall in with Mr Acheson's wishes if agreement between the three Allies on this point can be achieved. It is likely, however, that M Schuman will be adamant. If so, I shall urge Mr Acheson to accept as the Allied starting point in negotiation with Germans the compromise already proposed by the tripartite official conference. This is the solution I should prefer.

9. Acceptance by His Majesty's Government of the recommendation of the tripartite official conference or of a wider American proposal would involve a decision of principle in the financial field. In either event Germany would not, on security grounds, be precluded from the producing in the future of a substantial volume of conventional war material. If she does so, the proportion of her defence budget which could otherwise contribute to the build-up of the

German defence contribution and to the maintenance in Germany of Allied troops will be considerably reduced. On the other hand, potential German commercial competition in the export field would also be reduced.

10. I am sending a copy of this minute to the Chancellor of the Exchequer for his comments.

David Hunt[1] to Alan Campbell[2]
(Premier papers, 11/545)

13 November 1951

The Prime Minister has seen Sir William Strang's minute PM/WS/51/122 of the 12th November[3] and has discussed the matter with the Foreign Secretary on the telephone. He is not entirely happy about the inclusion of a date in paragraph 2 of the statement in Paris telegram No. 540.[4]

The Prime Minister is arranging for the text of the statement in that telegram to be circulated to Cabinet for consideration Thursday.

---

[1] David Wathen Stather Hunt, 1913–98. Served in British Army, 1940–7. OBE, 1943. US Bronze Star, 1945. Private Secretary to Clement Attlee, 1950–1; to Winston Churchill, 1951–2. Deputy High Commissioner in Lahore, 1954–6. Head, Central African Dept, Commonwealth Relations Office, 1956–9. CMG, 1959. Asst Under-Secretary of State, Commonwealth Relations Office, 1959–60. Deputy High Commissioner in Lagos, Nigeria, 1960–2. High Commissioner in Uganda, 1962–5; in Cyprus, 1965–7; in Nigeria, 1967–9. KCMG, 1963. Ambassador to Brazil, 1969–73. Chairman, Attlee Foundation, 1995–6.

[2] Alan Hugh Campbell, 1919–2007. Married, 1947, Margaret Jean Taylor: three children. Educated at Sherborne School and Caius College, Cambridge. On active duty in WWII. Entered Foreign Office, 1946. Private Secretary to Permanent Under-Secretary of State, 1950. FO, 1951. First Secretary at Rome and Beijing, 1952–7. Imperial Defence College, 1958. Asst Head of News Dept, 1959. Member of British Mission to the UN, 1961. CMG, 1964. Head of Western Dept, FO, 1965–7. Counsellor in Paris, 1967– 9. Ambassador to Ethiopia, 1969–72. Asst Under-Secretary of State, FCO, 1972–4. Deputy Under-Secretary of State, 1974–6. Ambassador to Italy, 1976–9. KCMG, 1976. GCMG, 1979.

[3] Reproduced above (pp. 38–9).

[4] This paragraph read: 'His Majesty's Government will give the Governor General their full support for the steps he is taking to bring the Sudanese rapidly to the stage of self-Government as a prelude to self-determination. While awaiting the recommendations of the present Amendment Commission His Majesty's Government are glad to know that a constitution providing for self-Government may be completed and in operation by the end of 1952.'

Winston S. Churchill to R. A. Butler
Prime Minister's Personal Minute M.40c/51
(Premier papers, 11/98)

14 November 1951

1. I am very glad all passed off so well. I attach the greatest importance to the erection of power stations and thus increasing generating capacity. I have been disturbed at the reports that such valuable machinery for this purpose was going to Soviet Russia and Poland. I am quite sure that we need more power and that power stations might be set up in very much lighter structures than the palaces now planned for them in many places. This should be considered.

2. I hope you will consider with Lord Leathers the plan which Cherwell showed me of reviewing the method of calculating the electricity charges. When private companies were concerned and the expansion of the business was important, and before the shortage of electricity arose owing to artificially fomented demands it was natural that the highest prices should be charged by the companies for the first slice, and that increasing consumption should be encouraged at the lower rates. Now I think it is the other way round. The basic rate should be the lowest. That could meet the smaller class of consumers' needs, and if the people like to spend their money in buying more electricity let them pay for it. This would be much better than introducing arbitrary cuts unexpectedly from moment to moment. Pray talk to Leathers and Geoffrey Lloyd about this. I have already put the matter before them.

Diana Sandys[1] to Winston S. Churchill
(Churchill papers, 1/52)[2]

15 November 1951

Darling Papa,

Duncan and I want to thank you for the wonderful settlements you have made on our children. We are overwhelmed by your generosity to us. It will be lovely for Julian,[3] Edwina,[4] and Celia[5] to have their own nest eggs from you

---

[1] Diana Churchill, 1909–63. Churchill's eldest child. Married, 1932, Sir John Milner Bailey (div. 1935); 1935, Duncan Sandys (div. 1960). Officer in WRNS, 1939–41. Air Raid Warden, 1941–5. Began working as volunteer for Samaritans, 1962. Committed suicide, 1963.

[2] This letter was handwritten.

[3] Julian Winston Sandys, 1936–97. Educated at Eton and Melbourne University (Australia). Called to the Bar, Inner Temple, 1959. Practised on Midland Circuit, 1960–76; Western Circuit, 1982–9; Gray's Inn, 1979–97. Married, 1970, Elisabeth Jane Martin: four children. QC, 1983.

[4] Edwina Sandys, 1938–. Married, 1960, Piers John Shirley Dixon: two children (div. 1973). Co-editor of *Painting as a Pastime, The Paintings of Winston S. Churchill* (1984).

[5] Celia Mary Sandys, 1943–. Married, 1965, Michael Kennedy: one child (div. 1970); 1970, Dennis Walters: one child (div. 1979); 1985, Kenneth Perkins: two children. Co-editor of *Painting as a Pastime,*

when they are grown up. And, in the meantime, the income which we shall be spending on their behalf will be a tremendous relief to us.

Thank you so much for this wonderful gift and for all the ingenuity and resourcefulness which we know went into its preparation –

With love and blessings

Harold Nicolson[1]: diary
('Harold Nicolson, Diaries and Letters', page 212)

15 November 1951

In the evening I take the chair at a BBC Forum on the theme 'Are cliques necessary?' I have Bob Boothby[2] and Kingsley Martin,[3] and we have a good discussion. I speak about Souls, Kingsley about Bloomsbury and Bob about Cliveden and Sibyl (Colefax).[4] We say that the disappearance of Society means that young men have no opportunity of meeting the great men of their age.

Bob had been to see Winston this afternoon. He says he is getting 'very, very old; tragically old'. Winston wants him to lead the British Delegation to the discussions on the United Europe. If he does well he may get a job. 'I would have you know', said Winston, 'what a deep concern I take in your career.' Bob was pleased but not convinced.

The Paintings of Winston S. Churchill (1984); author of *The Young Churchill, The Early Years of Winston Churchill* (1995), *Churchill Wanted Dead or Alive* (1999) and *Chasing Churchill, The Travels of Winston Churchill* (2004).

[1] Harold George Nicolson, 1886–1968. Educated at Wellington and Balliol College, Oxford. Entered FO, 1909. Counsellor, 1925. Served at Paris Peace Conference, 1919; Teheran, 1925–7; Berlin, 1927–9. On editorial staff of *Evening Standard*, 1930. MP (Nat. Lab.) for West Leicester, 1935–45. Parliamentary Secretary, Ministry of Information, 1940–1. A Governor of the BBC, 1941–6. Joined Labour Party, 1947. Knighted, 1953.

[2] Robert John Graham Boothby, 1900–86. Educated at Eton and Magdalen College, Oxford. MP (Cons.) for East Aberdeenshire, 1924–58. Parliamentary Private Secretary to the Chancellor of the Exchequer, 1926–9. Parliamentary Secretary, Ministry of Food, 1940–1. British Delegate to the Consultative Assembly, Council of Europe, 1949–57. Knighted, 1953. Baron, 1958. Chairman, Royal Philharmonic Orchestra, 1961–3. Author of *The New Economy* (1943), *I Fight to Live* (1947), *My Yesterday, Your Tomorrow* (1962) and *Recollections of a Rebel* (1978).

[3] Basil Kingsley Martin, 1897–1969. Educated at Magdalene College, Cambridge. Editorial staff, *Manchester Guardian*, 1927–31. Editor, *New Statesman and Nation*, 1930–60.

[4] Sibyl Halsey, 1874–1950. Married, 1901, Arthur Colefax: two children. Founder and owner, Sibyl Colefax Ltd, 1929–44.

Winston S. Churchill to Sir Norman Brook
Prime Minister's Personal Minute M.50c/51
(Premier papers, 11/174)

16 November 1951

The object of my minute of 12 November 1951[1] was to lead to the slaughter of a great number of second- and third- grade committees which now, I am assured, cumber the ground. In reply you present me with a new crop on the highest level. However there is no difference between us on this point. It is a necessary step in Cabinet organization. You should consult the Chancellor of the Exchequer and the Lord President upon the two committees to be entrusted to them, and let me know whether they are agreeable and content. The Paymaster-General should be added to the Defence Committee, pray return me your list in due course.

But now I want you to get on with the real work and give me a list of all the committees which I am assured are luxuriating. In the first place, you need not deal with any committees on which only one department is represented.

Winston S. Churchill to Antony Head
Prime Minister's Personal Minute M.51c/51
(Premier papers, 11/62)

16 November 1951
Top Secret

I send you the attached file which please return.* I think it may become necessary to have a Parliamentary Inquiry into the loss of our rifles since the war ended.

Perhaps you may have more accurate figures than those which have so far been given to me.

* File on Loss of Rifles (Defence Org).

Winston S. Churchill to Anthony Eden
Prime Minister's Personal Minute M.53c/51
(Premier papers, 11/112)

16 November 1951

No one here knows what is going on in Korea or which side is benefiting in strength from the humbug and grimaces at Panmunjom. We must try to

---

[1] M.32c/51, reproduced above (p. 37).

penetrate the American mind and purpose. We may find this out when we are at Washington. Nobody knows it now. The other side clearly do not want an agreement. It is important to think out how prolonging the deadlock can benefit them. Obviously it diverts United Nations resources. But what else do they hope for.

Meanwhile a war is being carried on, and British troops are engaged, with sharp losses.

Winston S. Churchill to Anthony Eden
Prime Minister's Personal Minute M.59c/51
(Premier papers, 11/92)

16 November 1951

The governing words in this verbose telegram appear to be in paragraph 7, 'the next month', meaning thereby that we are to go on as we are for a month before any 'show down'.[1] This may be quite right. It would presumably mean that we should put pressure on from time to time by restricting the oil supplies and in other ways retaliating for minor affronts and injuries. The crucial point is: Are we to go on as at present for another month and see what happens, meanwhile making preparations for the 'show down' if nothing happens? Is this the policy you recommend?

Secondly, what actually are we to do to carry out the 'show down', should that become necessary during the month or when the month is over? Here again we should have precise proposals before taking a decision.

---

[1] Paragraph 7 of Sir Ralph Stevenson's No. 1002 to the Foreign Office read:
'7. I conclude from the foregoing that:
(1) if the results described in the preceding paragraph do not come about from natural causes during the next month, the time will probably have come to give that "impulse to push over the Egyptian Government" mentioned in paragraph 5 of your telegram under reference;
(2) This process will need full United States support and will have to be carried out with some delicacy if it is not to defeat its own objects;
(3) It may well lead to grave internal security dangers in Cairo and Alexandria of a continuing nature, since they seem likely to be greater with the Wafd in opposition than with the Wafd in power;
(4) Our action should accordingly be timed to coincide with the highest point of our military preparedness in this theatre; and an essential part of it should be to ensure that special emergency measures are taken by the King and the Egyptian army to maintain order.'

NOVEMBER 1951

Winston S. Churchill to Lord Leathers
Prime Minister's Personal Minute M.62c/51
(Premier papers, 11/98)

16 November 1951

I mentioned to you the other day the idea Cherwell suggested to me about a reversal in the scale of payments by consumers of electricity.

When private companies operated the industry and before the great developments in electric fires, cooking appliances and other conveniences had been so widely spread, it was natural that the private companies should work on a high original basic rate and encourage people to take more of their product by cheaper prices for more consumption. Now these conditions are reversed. The State controls the industry. A vast expansion of the use of electricity has occurred. The difficulty is to supply the demand and not in the present period to expand it. It would seem reasonable to make the first rate the low one so that the smaller consumer got relief, and increase the rate by steps as individual consumption increased. This would be much better than having arbitrary cuts, with all the uncertainty and dislocation they entail. Those who could afford to pay the very highest rates have a right to spend their money that way, but the smaller the consumer and the more economical he is, the easier it should be for him. The rates can of course be modified from year to year as production increases. Now that we face a grave shortage for several years, a progressive scale of charges would be the greatest incentive to economy.

Could you let me have a brief preliminary report on this sort of plan and some figures showing how the existing revenue could be obtained by reversal in the rate of charge.

Winston S. Churchill to Patrick Buchan-Hepburn[1]
Prime Minister's Personal Minute M.64c/51
(Premier papers, 11/136)

17 November 1951

I think it of high importance that the facts of the position when we took over should be got together. The method and moment of publication can be settled later. It seems a pity that the food position could not have been more clearly disclosed, especially the meat. That was no doubt due to fear of making our bargaining power less. This situation must pass in a few weeks,

---

[1] Patrick George Thomas Buchan-Hepburn, 1901–74. Private Secretary to Churchill, 1929–30. MP (Cons.) for East Toxteth, 1931–50; for Beckenham, 1950–7. Served in Royal Artillery, 1940–3. Cons. Deputy Chief Whip, 1945–8; Chief Whip, 1948–51. PC, 1951. Government Chief Whip, 1951–5. Minister of Works, 1955–7. Baron Hailes, 1957. Governor-General of the West Indies, 1958–62. CH, 1962.

and the exact state of the Nation on this and other matters at the time of 'changing the guard' must be made public.

Winston S. Churchill to R. A. Butler
Prime Minister's Personal Minute M.66c/51
(Premier papers, 11/176)

17 November 1951

Pray let me have the Treasury view on the reductions which should be made in the Ministry of Defence Headquarters. You have called for reductions in all departments and I should like to set an example.

Winston S. Churchill to Lieutenant-General Kenneth McLean
Prime Minister's Personal Minute M.69c/51
(Premier papers, 11/50)

18 November 1951

See paragraph 5(a).[1]

I understand no agreement is possible on this at the present time and that it must be brought forward at the meeting in January. Is this so?

Paragraph 5(b).

I hope to win the assent of the President of the United States at Washington in January to an arrangement whereby there will be no Supreme Allied Commander in the Atlantic. The questions at issue between the British Admiralty and the American Navy Department will be settled in the first instance between their Service chiefs, or if need be on a higher level. Questions involving the other European Powers who have very small resources to contribute but great needs to have good arrangements at the reception end, should be dealt with as in the late war by the agreement of the British and United States Naval Chiefs, or failing that, by the Heads of the two Governments overwhelmingly concerned.

Paragraph 5(c).

I hope to reach a decision upon this in the next two or three days, namely there should be no production, other than experimental or preparation for production, of the .280 rifle pending further discussion, and that the production and repair of the .303 rifle should continue at normal rate.

We should endeavour to reach agreement on standardization with the

---

[1] Paragraph 5 read: '5. There are three items on the draft agenda for the Military Committee which it is hoped to exclude from discussion, viz: (a) Command arrangements in the Mediterranean and Middle East. (b) Terms of reference for the Supreme Allied Commander, Atlantic.' Item (c) was not included in the source document.

United States and Canada. If they will take the .280 all my objections would disappear. If not, it is necessary for them to produce at the earliest date an equally good rifle, acceptable to the vast majority of Allied Powers concerned. Uniform production would then be organized.

Anthony Eden to Winston S. Churchill
(Churchill papers, 2/517)

19 November 1951
Secret
PM/51/127

CONTRACTUAL NEGOTIATIONS WITH GERMANY
SECURITY CONTROLS

On November 13th I sent you a minute PM/51/123,[1] about the restrictions to be imposed upon the German armament industry in the proposed Contractual Settlement with Germany, in which I explained the line I proposed to take with Mr Acheson and Monsieur Schuman in Paris next week.

2. It is probable that I shall also have to discuss in Paris the connected question of the <u>machinery</u> for imposing and operating any prohibitions.

3. I favour a solution on the following lines. The Federal Government should declare that they intend to prohibit certain agreed branches of war industry unless and until they are requested by the Supreme Allied Commander, Europe to do otherwise. This could be represented to German public opinion as inspired not by motives of Allied dictation, but by general and military considerations.

4. The Chiefs of Staff, who have been consulted, consider that a solution on these lines would safeguard our security requirements. They also suggest that the Supreme Commander's readiness to undertake this responsibility could be ascertained through the Standing Group of the North Atlantic Treaty Organisation, through whom his instructions would normally come.

5. I do not propose to commit us to any such solution in Paris, but I hope you will agree that I should explore its possibilities further with Mr Acheson and Monsieur Schuman.

---

[1] Reproduced above (pp. 41–3).

NOVEMBER 1951

Winston S. Churchill to President Chaim Weizmann[1]
(Chaim Weizmann papers)

19 November 1951

My dear Weizmann,

Thank you so much for your letter and good wishes. The wonderful exertions which Israel is making in these times of difficulty are cheering to an old Zionist like me. I trust you may work in with Jordan and the rest of the Moslem world. With true comradeship there will be enough for all.

Every good wish my old friend.

Lady Moran[2] to Winston S. Churchill
(Churchill papers, 1/54)[3]

19 November 1951

Dearest Mr Churchill,

A week ago, Charles[4] came out from seeing you and told me in the car that he had lost his temper and had said some very foolish things. And then he broke down. He said he had been entirely to blame. It has been a horrible experience for both of us, for we are both, as I told you that night at Guildhall, truly devoted to you. It would distress him very much at any time to displease you, but what keeps him from sleeping and breaks his heart, is the feeling that you may no longer respect him. I asked Charles why he did not go and just say to you that he was sorry, but he says that much as he would like to, he dare not take up any more of your time over personal matters, and that it was unforgivable of him to have done this at any time, but especially when you were working under stress.

I want you please to forgive him for both our sakes.

Yours affectionately,
Dorothy

I would have brought this to you myself but I am in bed.

---

[1] Chaim Weizmann, 1874–1952. Born in Russia. Educated in Germany. Reader in Biochemistry, University of Manchester, 1906. Naturalised as a British subject, 1910. Director, Admiralty Laboratories, 1916–19. President of World Zionist Organisation, and of Jewish Agency for Palestine, 1921–31, 1935–46. Chairman, Board of Governors, Hebrew University of Jerusalem, 1932–50. Adviser to Ministry of Supply, London, 1939–45. First President of State of Israel from 1949 until his death.

[2] Dorothy Dufton, 1895–1983. MBE, 1918. Married, 1919, Charles McMoran Wilson: two children.

[3] This letter was handwritten.

[4] Charles McMoran Wilson, 1882–1977. Physician. On active service as Medical Officer, 1914–18, Maj., RAMC (MC, despatches). Dean, St Mary's Hospital Medical School, 1920–45. Knighted, 1938. Churchill's private physician, 1940–55. President, Royal College of Physicians, 1941–50. Baron, 1943. Author of *Winston Churchill, The Struggle for Survival* (1966).

November 1951

General Lord Ismay to Members of the Cabinet
(Cabinet papers, 129/48)

19 November 1951
Secret
Cabinet Paper No. 21 of 1951

BAMANGWATO AFFAIRS

Bamangwato affairs demand action by His Majesty's Government urgently. The Reserve is in a turmoil. The people are perplexed about the Government's intentions. Parliamentary questions are being asked. Tshekedi[1] is returning to London.

2. A summary of the past is attached in Annex B.

3. The question requiring immediate decision is Tshekedi's future, but my colleagues should know in broad outline the over-all solution I have in mind.

4. There is no solution which does not include factors open to justifiable criticism. We must therefore be content with finding a solution which contains the greatest number of good points and is otherwise defensible. It calls for a gradual approach and its announcement will require careful timing.

5. The comprehensive solution I have in mind is:

   (1) the effective exclusion of Tshekedi Khama from the political life of the Bamangwato allied with his return to the Reserve as a private person at the earliest moment consistent with the peace of the tribe and his own safety;

   (2) reconciliation between the tribe and Rasebolai Khama, chief lieutenant of Tshekedi and third in adult succession to the chieftainship, and his promotion as a prospective nominee by the tribe for the chieftainship; and

   (3) the announcement, after an appropriate interval, of the permanent exclusion of Seretse Khama[2] from the chieftainship of the tribe as a necessary preliminary to their nomination of Rasebolai.

(1) will quiet the tribe and make possible its effective administration under the District Commissioner, who for the present will continue as Native Authority, in which capacity he exercises some of the functions of chief. (2) will offer

---

[1] Tshekedi Khama, 1905–59. Educated at Fort Hare University, South Africa, 1923–5. Uncle of Seretse Khama. In 1926, became Regent of Bechuanaland because his nephew, the king, was only four years old.

[2] Seretse Khama, 1921–80. Son of Chief Sekgoma and Queen Tebogo Khama. Succeeded his father as King of Bechuanaland, 1925. Educated at Fort Hare University, South Africa, and Balliol College, Oxford. Called to the Bar, Inner Temple, 1946. Married, 1948, Ruth Williams. Exiled for his interracial marriage, 1951; returned on condition of abdication, 1956. Elected to Tribal Council, 1957. Founder, Bechuanaland Democratic Party, 1961. PM, Bechuanaland, 1965–6. First President, Republic of Botswana, 1966–80. Grand Comrade, Order of the Lion of Malawi, 1967. Royal Order of Sobhuza II Grand Counsellor, Swaziland, 1978.

a rallying point, alternative to Seretse, for the traditional allegiance of the tribe. (3) will remove permanently from the Union Government a potentially powerful weapon in its campaign for incorporation of the High Commission Territories and the declaration of a Republic.

6. Under an exclusion order issued in accordance with the White Paper policy, Tshekedi cannot enter the Reserve save with permission, which is granted or withheld according to the situation in the Reserve (see paragraphs 13 and 14 of Annex B). He smarts under a sense of injustice. As soon as we can we must permit him to return to look after his large personal interests. But the observers' reports confirm the existence of such strong feeling against him in the tribe that his return now could only lead to serious disorders and danger to his life. He himself, by recent provocative actions, has aggravated feeling against him. The tribe do not believe his renunciation of claim to the chieftainship and blame him for Seretse's exclusion. The immediate need is to quiet their fear of his return to power and to do this Government must make it evident that he will be effectively excluded from their political life. The frequency of his visits and the prospects of his ultimate residence in the Reserve will depend upon his own actions.

7. The Bamangwato are so firmly wedded to the hereditary chieftainship that the idea of a council system, put forward in the original White Paper, of itself offers no alternative. The only satisfactory solution is the promotion of a suitable person as chief instead of Seretse. With both Seretse and Tshekedi out of the running for the chieftainship, Rasebolai would be the obvious choice. He would be acceptable to Government, but his advancement towards office must be cautious, since his association with Tshekedi has made him suspect by the tribe.

8. Most of the tribe want Seretse back. To let him and his white wife return in any capacity would provoke an immediate demand in South Africa for the transfer of the Territories, a demand in which all white South Africans, including those of British descent, would be united. This was the view of General Smuts[1] and is confirmed by the present leader of the United Party[2] in South Africa. (South Africans are very sensitive and emotional over racial purity; mixed marriages are prohibited and sexual relations between persons of different colour are a criminal offence.) A strong indication has been given

---

[1] Jan Christian Smuts, 1870–1950. Born in Cape Colony. Gen. commanding Boer Commando Forces, Cape Colony, 1901. Colonial Secretary, Transvaal, 1907. Minister of Defence, Union of South Africa, 1910–20. Second-in-Command of the South African forces that defeated the Germans in South-West Africa, July 1915. Hon. Member of the Other Club (founded by Churchill and F. E. Smith), 1917. South African Representative at Imperial War Cabinet, 1917 and 1918. PM of South Africa, 1919–24, 1939–48. Minister of Justice, 1933–9. FM, 1941. OM, 1947. One of Churchill's last public speeches was at the unveiling of Smuts' statue in Parliament Square in 1956.

[2] Jacobus Gideon Nel Strauss, 1900–90. Born in Calvinia, South Africa. Educated at Universities of Cape Town and South Africa. Private Secretary to PM of South Africa, 1923–4. Married, 1928, Joy Carpenter: five children. MP for Germiston, 1932–4 (South African Party); 1934–57 (United Party). Minister of Agriculture and Forestry, 1944. Leader of South African United Party, 1950–6.

that the present Government of South Africa would resort to economic sanctions against Territories, which, geographically and economically, are virtually defenceless. All our relations with the Union would be seriously impaired and we would probably lose the Territories. Our interests in Southern Africa therefore demand the continued exclusion of Seretse. But if his exclusion is to be permanent it is unfair to him and to the tribe to keep alive hopes of his ultimate return. Moreover, it makes any permanent solution of the problem impossible. But to announce his permanent exclusion before the tribe has been suitably conditioned for it by the removal of their fears about Tshekedi and the promotion of a possible alternative chief, would provoke an explosion from them. Moreover, the effect on colonial opinion of substituting permanent exclusion in place of the undertaking to review the position in not less than five years would be serious and would have to be carefully considered.

9. In short, my purposes would be to restore peaceful conditions in the Reserve by determining forthwith the future of Tshekedi, doing all that is possible for him while at the same time allaying the fears of the tribe; to secure the return of Rasebolai to the Reserve and to promote his popularity with the tribe; and, at as early a date as possible, and certainly before the end of the five-year period laid down in the White Paper, to announce the permanent exclusion of Seretse and to bring about the nomination by the tribe of Rasebolai as chief.

10. At this stage, I ask only for approval of the first step which is to make clear our intentions regarding Tshekedi. In Annex A, I submit the draft of parliamentary question and reply indicating these intentions. In it we make clear that we are sympathetic over the present deprivation of his liberty of movement in the Reserve and that, provided he will co-operate in allaying the tribe's fears, we mean to work towards its restoration. I would give Tshekedi, who has asked for an interview with me, opportunity to see me before the reply is given in the House. I would accord the same courtesy to Seretse, who has also asked for an interview.

11. There is no reason why the observers' reports (Annexes C and D) should not be published. My proposals are kinder to Tshekedi than their recommendations.

Jo Sturdee[1] to John Colville
(Churchill papers, 1/66)

19 November 1951
Personal

Dear Mr Colville,

I want to thank you for your sympathy and help in seeing us and arranging our duties so that, although we are now temporary Civil Servants and under the authority and guidance of you and the other Private Secretaries, we shall also keep our personal contacts and responsibilities towards Mr Churchill. It was tiresome for you to have to add to your work like that, but I am very happy at the result, and with the work you have been good enough to entrust us. I know Miss Gilliatt[2] and Miss Portal[3] feel the same.

I am sorry I had to protest at the sordid subject of remuneration, but, as you probably noticed from what Miss Gilliatt and I said, it is a matter upon which we have our point of view and feelings which, considering our age and experience I think is understandable. However I hope we may settle that justly and amicably.

I need hardly say that, having been granted privileges and consideration by you and the Civil Service authorities, we shall always try to do our work well, and I hope happily at No. 10 and of course in the closest liaison with you and everyone else here. We shall no doubt be flying to you and everybody for advice and help, but I hope you will not mind that and that we shall not be too much of a nuisance.

Attached is a more formal note of what we have talked about.

Sir Norman Brook to Winston S. Churchill
(Premier papers, 11/174)

20 November 1951

OFFICIAL COMMITTEES

This is the second instalment of my reply to your Minute of 12th of November.[4] It covers all the official Committees controlled by the Cabinet Office and the Ministry of Defence. In addition, there are many interdepartmental

---

[1] Nina Edith Sturdee, 1922–2006. Known as 'Jo'. Secretary to Winston Churchill. Married, 1962, William Arthur Bampfylde Onslow.
[2] Elizabeth Gilliatt, Private Secretary to Winston S. Churchill, 1946–55.
[3] Jane Gillian Portal, 1929–. Married, 1955, Gavin Bramhall Welby: two children (div. 1959); 1975, Charles Cuthbert Powell Williams. Private Secretary to Winston Churchill, 1949–55.
[4] M.32c/51, reproduced above (p. 37).

Committees centred on other Departments, of which I have no record. I am calling for a return of these, and will make a further report about them as soon as possible.

The attached sheets give particulars of the 60 Committees, 47 Sub-Committees, and 17 Working Parties which formed part of the Cabinet Committee system at the date of the Election. The descriptions have been compressed, for brevity, and you may need further information about some. If so, you may wish to send for me and go through the list with me.

These 'central' Committees have been pruned annually by the Prime Minister, on my recommendation; and there may be less scope for surgery here than among the committees centred on Departments. But there are certainly some Committees in this list which could now be abolished. I have marked these with an asterisk.

Some of the Committees which ought to be maintained could suffer a reduction in membership. The deletions in red ink in the attached list are designed to show where this could be done.

This list includes (particularly in the Section on Defence) a number of standing Committees which seldom meet but which are useful because they afford a rapid means of transacting occasional business. I suggest that these be left in being. The wasteful time of Committee work arises, not only from having too many Committees, but also from the inefficient conduct of Committee business. Some of the instructions which you gave in 1941 (see attached paper WP(G)(41)34) could usefully be repeated – in particular, about those 'hunting in couples' (or worse), brisk conduct of business by Committee Chairmen, and the duty of permanent members of a Committee to refrain from attending meetings at which nothing directly affecting their Departments is to be discussed. Instructions on these points could best be considered after I have reported on the Committees run by other Departments.[1]

Anthony Eden to Winston S. Churchill
(Churchill papers, 2/517)

20 November 1951
PM/51/128

Your personal minute M.59c/51 of the 16th November.[2]

2. We cannot foresee with any confidence how events in Egypt will develop. I think it may be well to wait a while before coming to a decision to use further means of pressure. There is of course always the danger that an incident or

---

[1] Churchill replied on Nov. 23: 'You seem to have got very few birds out of this enormous covey. Pray let me have a list of the ones you say could now be dispensed with so that at least we can make a beginning' (M.84c/51, *Premier papers, 11/174*).

[2] Reproduced above (p. 47).

series of incidents may compel us to take drastic action, such as the establishment of Military Government in the Canal Zone.

3. Meanwhile I understand that a paper on possible economic sanctions, prepared by the Foreign Office, the Treasury and other Departments concerned, will shortly be ready. I would suggest that this should be sent out to Cairo and Fayid. The ambassador and the Commanders-in-Chief should be asked to take this into account and to prepare joint recommendations. These would include political, military and economic measures which we might take, and the order in which we might take them, in the event of a decision to embark on further action against Egypt. This action might be within or beyond the lines of policy already laid down in my telegram to Cairo No. 1249 of which I attach a copy.

4. If you agree, I will instruct the Ambassador accordingly, and I would suggest that you might ask the Chiefs of Staff to send similar instructions to the Commanders-in-Chief, Middle East.

Lord De L'Isle and Dudley[1] to Members of the Cabinet
(Premier papers, 11/75)

20 November 1951
Top Secret
Cabinet Paper No. 28 of 1951

PRODUCTION OF AIRCRAFT FOR THE ROYAL AIR FORCE

1. In C(51)27 the Minister of Supply refers to the aircraft supply programme.
2. I emphasise the seriousness of the present position of supplies for the Royal Air Force.
3. The Royal Air Force is small. Its front line numbers only 1,600 aircraft. (The comparable size of the RAF in 1939 was 3,250, and that of the Soviet Air Force today is thought to be in the region of 20,000.) It is therefore essential that its quality should be high.
4. We have today no fighter in service to match the MIG 15, which was introduced in 1949 and of which the Soviet Air Force now has very large quantities. On the Minister of Supply's forecasts, we shall not have a single squadron of British fighters superior to the MIG 15 until late in 1953.
5. We have today only one squadron of Canberra light bombers (the

[1] William Philip Sidney, 1909–91. Educated at Eton and Magdalene College, Cambridge. Joined Grenadier Guards, 1929. Married, 1940, Jacqueline Corrine Yvonne Vereker: five children (d. 1962); 1966, Margaret Eldrydd Shoubridge. On active service during WWII, 1939–44; wounded in Battle of Anzio, 1944. VC, 1944. MP (Cons.) for Chelsea, 1944–5. Ministry of Pensions, 1945. Succeeded as Baron De L'Isle and Dudley, 1945. PC, 1951. Secretary of State for Air, 1951–5. Viscount De L'Isle, 1956. GCMG, 1961. Governor-General, Australia, 1961–5. KG, 1968. Chancellor, Order of St Michael and St George, 1968–91.

replacement for the Mosquito). By March, 1953, we shall have only five squadrons (50 aircraft).

6. Of the Valiant medium bomber (the replacement for the Lincoln) we shall not have a single squadron till well on in 1954.

7. Production of the Venom fighter bomber, which is inferior in speed to the MIG 15, will not reach its peak until 1954. Meanwhile much of our expansion for our contribution to General Eisenhower's force and to strengthen the defence of the Middle East will have to be done with obsolescent Vampires.

8. We have no war reserve of jet fighters or jet bombers. We shall not have any war reserves of modern interceptor fighters or of Canberras before 1955.

9. We have no ammunition for our fighters, except some war-time stocks which have deteriorated and become unsafe. We are producing in one month enough ammunition for one sortie by two squadrons. When the new fighters (the F.3 and the Swift) are delivered, there is every prospect that we shall be short of the guns, ammunition and rockets they need to fight with.

10. The position about electronic equipment is also very bad. The Canberra has not got, and will not have before 1954 at the earliest, the gear for which it was designed. The navigation and bombing gear for the Valiant looks like falling behind the aircraft. Even the navigational equipment for the Lincoln is unsatisfactory and unreliable. The United Kingdom radar chain covers only part of the country and can easily be flown round, and its equipment is out of date. Adequate radar cover for the most vital areas of the United Kingdom cannot be completed before the end of 1953.

11. I cannot believe that a major improvement is impossible. There is no lack of skill in design. If in production the country is trying to do too much, then at least let us ensure, whatever else we do, that we have the air power without which we cannot defend these islands and without which we should be at an overwhelming disadvantage on land and at sea. Our whole rearmament programme is threatened by the deplorable weakness of the preparations made to supply the Royal Air Force.

12. We have no justification for hoping that American production will come to our rescue. We are already counting on a great deal – probably more than they can spare – to fill the gaps in our own programme.

Conclusion

13. I urge that the Government should examine every possibility of improving air supplies. The measures proposed by the Minister of Supply would be an immediate step forward, but a great deal more is needed if we are to make up the ground that has been lost.

Anthony Eden to Winston S. Churchill
(*Premier papers, 11/112*)

21 November 1951
PM/51/132

Your minute M.53c/51 of November 16th about the Korean armistice talks.[1]

It has been very difficult to follow the recent course of the armistice talks at Panmunjom, but the position is at last becoming clearer.

2. The United Nations Delegates proposed on November 17th that the demarcation line should be the present line of contact but that if agreement is not reached on the remaining items of the agenda within 30 days, a new demarcation line should be drawn on the line of contact as it will then be.

3. In the last ten days the United Nations negotiators have feared that the Communists, having secured agreement on the demarcation line, which must inevitably act as a check on the scale of later military operations, would delay indefinitely over the remaining items on the agenda, with the result that we would have no guarantee against a secret build-up for a later attack and no agreement on prisoners of war. The November 17th proposals are designed to guard against this.

4. The Communists are now considering these proposals, and their final reply is expected from day to day.

5. This morning brings a fresh complication in a message from the North Korean Foreign Minister to the United Nations General Assembly, proposing a settlement in four parts:
    (1) Cease-fire.
    (2) Withdrawal to a depth of 2 kilometres on each side to establish a demilitarised zone.
    (3) Withdrawal of foreign troops from Korea.
    (4) Punishment of 'War criminals'.

It is impossible to be sure what is the significance of this proposal and what is its relevance to the Panmunjom talks. We can only wait and see what reply the Communist negotiators give to the latest United Nations Command proposals.[2]

---

[1] Reproduced above (pp. 46–7).
[2] Churchill wrote on the original minute: 'But it gives no clue to motive.'

NOVEMBER 1951

Sir Norman Brook: note
(Cabinet papers, 131/12)

21 November 1951
Confidential

TERMS OF REFERENCE AND COMPOSITION

By direction of the Prime Minister a Defence Committee is being appointed with the following terms of reference:
 '(1) To handle current defence problems.
 (2) To co-ordinate Departmental plans and preparations for war.'
The Prime Minister will preside over the Committee. Its composition will be variable according to the subjects under discussion; but the following will normally be summoned:
 Foreign Secretary
 Secretary of State for Commonwealth Relations
 Paymaster-General
 First Lord of the Admiralty
 Secretary of State for War
 Secretary of State for Air
 Minister of Supply
 The Chiefs of Staff
Sir Norman Brook and Lt.-General Sir Kenneth McLean will act as Joint Secretaries of the Committee.
 Meetings of the Committee will normally be held on Wednesday, at 11.30 a.m., or 12 noon, at No. 10, Downing Street.

General Lord Ismay to Winston S. Churchill
(Premier papers, 11/227)

22 November 1951
Secret

Your minute M.21(C)51 of the 11th November.
There is some truth in the allegations which Sir Firoz Khan Noon[1] makes against India. But many of our Indian friends would put forward equally strong charges against Pakistan.

---

[1] Firoz Khan Noon, 1893–1970. Educated in Lahore and Oxford. Advocate, Lahore High Court, 1917–26. Minister for Education and Medical and Public Health, Punjab, 1931–6. Knighted, 1933. High Commissioner for India in United Kingdom, 1936–41. Member of Viceroy's Executive Council for Labour Affairs, 1941–2; for Defence, 1942–5. Indian Envoy to British War Cabinet, 1944–5. Member of All-Pakistan Legislature, 1947–50. Governor of East Pakistan, 1950–3. Chief Minister of West Punjab, 1953–5. Foreign Minister of Pakistan, 1956–7. Prime Minister (and Foreign Minister and Minister of the Interior), 1957–8.

The situation between India and Pakistan, which is admittedly very difficult, is not one where one side is all right and the other all wrong.

I am sure therefore that you should, as you suggest, send an entirely non-committal reply. If you did anything else it would certainly become public. I attach a draft for your consideration.

DRAFT REPLY TO SIR FIROZ KHAN NOON

Secret
Private and Personal

Thank you very much for your private and personal letter of the 27th October.

I greatly appreciate your good wishes. I have many memories of our collaboration during the war and of your help to our counsels in those dark days.

The difficulties which exist between your country and India are much in my mind; the development of happier relations would be assured of a welcome from your friends everywhere and especially here in this country.

Sir Alan Lascelles[1] to Winston S. Churchill
(Premier papers, 11/194)

23 November 1951 Buckingham Palace
Personal and Top Secret

My dear Prime Minister,
The King hopes to go away for six or eight weeks early in March; the Admiralty have told His Majesty that HMS *Vanguard* can be put at his disposal then.

There are various places to which His Majesty might go in search of sunshine, but the one which at present appeals to him most is South Africa.

Some time ago, Dr Malan[2] sent me a private message through Dr Geyer,[3] to the effect that if the King should feel inclined to come to South Africa,

---

[1] Alan Frederick Lascelles, 1887–1981. Known as 'Tommy'. On active service in France, 1914–18. Capt., 1916. ADC to Lord Lloyd (then Governor of Bombay), 1919–20. Asst Private Secretary to Prince of Wales, 1920–9. Secretary to Governor-General of Canada, 1931–5. Asst Private Secretary to King George V, 1935; to King Edward VIII, 1936; to King George VI, 1936–43. Knighted, 1939. PC, 1943. Private Secretary to King George VI, 1943–52; to Queen Elizabeth II, 1952–3.

[2] Daniel François Malan, 1874–1959. Born in Riebeek West, Cape Providence, South Africa. Educated at Victoria College and University of Utrecht. Dutch Reformed minister in Heidelberg, Transvaal, 1906. Provincial leader of National Party, 1915. MP (Nat.) for Calvinia, 1918–38; for Piketberg, 1938–54. Minister of Interior, Education, and Public Health, 1924–33. Married, 1926, Martha Margaretha Elizabeth van Tonder (d. 1930): two children. PM of South Africa, 1948–54.

[3] Albertus Lourens Geyer, 1894–1969. Educated at University of Stellenbosch. Married, 1921, Anna Elizabeth Joubert: one daughter. Editor of *Die Burger*, Cape Town, 1923–45. Editor-in-Chief, publications of Nasionale Pers Co., 1945–50. High Commissioner in London for South Africa, 1950–4.

he would personally undertake to find a suitable house, in a suitable climate, where absolute privacy could be guaranteed.

He has been as good as his word, and, a few days ago, Dr Geyer brought me particulars of Botha House, on the Natal coast south of Pondoland, which, as you may know, has been the South African Chequers since its original owner, Mr Reynolds,[1] handed it over to General Botha[2] for the use of himself and his successors.

Dr Malan has offered to put this house at the King's disposal. It has many attractive features – it stands in a park of 1500 acres, has a private railway station, golf-course, and bathing beach, and appears to be reasonably commodious. Altogether, I feel that The King and Queen might be very glad to accept Dr Malan's offer, and that there is nowhere else they could go which would be likely to do them so much good. Moreover, it is appropriate that The King, when in search of health, should seek it within the Commonwealth.

Although the scheme is a satisfactory one from every other point of view, The King is, however, doubtful if it is practicable for political reasons. His Majesty is well aware that, in a not very distant future, there is a prospect of a series of head-on collisions between his Government in the United Kingdom and his Government in the Union of South Africa, and that the issues at stake would involve him personally as Sovereign. In the circumstances, The King has grave doubts whether it would be wise for him to go and stay in the Union during the period in question – approximately from the middle of March to the end of April.

The King has therefore instructed me to ask you if you would consider the matter from this aspect, and, perhaps in consultation with the Secretary of State for Commonwealth Relations, advise him whether he can prudently accept Dr Malan's offer.

His Majesty would be grateful if, for the present, you would discuss this with none of your colleagues except Ismay.

---

[1] Frank Umhlali Reynolds, 1852–1930. Sugar planter in South Africa. Born Umhlali, Natal. Married, 1894, Euphemia Chamberlain: two children. Served during Anglo-Boer War in Natal Mounted Rifle Rgt, 1899–1902. Member of Union Parliament, 1915. Knighted, 1916.

[2] Louis Botha, 1862–1919. Member of Volksraad, Parliament of the Transvaal, 1897–9. Led ambush during Boer War that captured the British armoured train on which Winston Churchill was a passenger, Nov. 1899. PM of Transvaal, 1907–10; of Union of South Africa, 1910–19.

Sir William Strang to Winston S. Churchill
(Premier papers, 11/92)

23 November 1951
Top Secret
PM/WS/51/133

EGYPT – GAZA STRIP

Before leaving for Paris and Rome, the Foreign Secretary asked me to send you a minute on this subject.

2. When Nuri Pasha,[1] the Prime Minister of Iraq, called on the Foreign Secretary on the 17th November to discuss Egypt, he suggested that a settlement would be easier if we could transfer the combatant troops in the Canal Zone to the Gaza strip. He said that the Egyptians, who occupied the Gaza strip during the hostilities with Israel but have not annexed it, find that it is costing them £E50,000 a day and would be glad to get rid of it.

3. This idea was considered by the Foreign Office and the Chiefs of Staff just over a year ago. Our conclusions then were:

   (a) The Israelis would object to the stationing of British troops on their frontier. We could not proceed with the scheme unless they agreed.
   (b) Our troops would be strategically well-placed in Gaza.
   (c) Suitable accommodation would first have to be built. This would cost a lot and take a long time. Maintenance would be costly.

4. There are 200,000 Arab refugees in the Gaza strip, maintained on subsistence level by the United Nations Relief and Works Agency. Arrangements would have to be made for them. The huts which we built there during our occupation of Palestine are now derelict and inhabited by these refugees. If we went there, we should have to improve the water supply and build a couple of airfields. Training facilities would be inadequate unless we could make an arrangement with Israel. It was estimated in 1950 that the cost of providing accommodation for a Brigade Group in the Gaza area would be £11 million; it might be more now.

5. Nevertheless it may be that transfer to the Gaza area might provide the solution to the Egyptian problem for which we are looking. The objections from the Israeli side might be less strong now, especially if Israel becomes associated with the Middle East Command.

6. The Foreign Secretary left instructions that we should ask the Chiefs of

---

[1] Nuri Pasha es Said, 1888–1958. Born in Baghdad. Iraqi Minister of Defence, 1922, 1953. Minister for Foreign Affairs, 1932. Withdrew from Iraq during the pro-German revolt, 1941. PM, 1930, 1938–40, 1941–5, 1949–52, 1958. Assassinated (together with the King and the Crown Prince) during the Baghdad uprising, 14 June 1958.

Staff to reconsider the Gaza strip proposal in the light of the present situation. If you agree, I will ask them to do this.[1]

Winston S. Churchill to Sir William Strang
Prime Minister's Personal Minute M.88c/51
(Premier papers, 11/167)

24 November 1951

It would be an advantage if a short summary – one printed page – could be prepared in the Foreign Office presenting the salient points and conclusions of the discussions in Paris with Germany, contained in the many telegrams from the Secretary of State.

Sir William Strang to Winston S. Churchill
(Premier papers, 11/167)

24 November 1951

MEETING OF THE THREE FOREIGN MINISTERS WITH THE
GERMAN FEDERAL CHANCELLOR IN PARIS ON 22ND NOVEMBER

1. This meeting was the first at which the German Federal Chancellor[2] was present on equal terms.

2. The four Ministers provisionally approved the draft of an <u>Agreement on General Relations</u>. This provides for the revocation of the Occupation Statute and the replacement of the Allied High Commission by Ambassadors. The Federal Republic agrees that the three Powers shall retain rights relating to (a) the stationing of armed forces in Germany; (b) Berlin; and (c) Germany as a whole, including the unification of Germany and a peace settlement.

3. The General Agreement will not enter into force until negotiations are complete for (a) <u>further conventions</u> providing e.g. for the juridical status and security of our forces in Germany; (b) a <u>European Defence Community</u> including Germany.

4. The three Foreign Ministers stated (a) that <u>Germany's financial</u>

---

[1] Churchill wrote at the bottom of the minute: 'No objection. So proceed.'

[2] Konrad Adenauer, 1876–1967. Studied Law at Universities of Freiburg, Munich and Bonn. Practised law, Cologne, from 1900. Deputy Mayor, Cologne, 1906; Senior Deputy Mayor, 1909; Lord Mayor, 1917–33, 1945. Member, Provincial Diet of Rhine Province, 1917–18. Member, Executive Committee of Centre Party, 1917–33. Member, Prussian Herrenhaus, 1917–18. Member, Prussian State Council, 1918–33; President, 1926–33. Dismissed from all offices by Goering, 1933. Imprisoned for political reasons, 1933, 1944. Member and President, Parliamentary Council of Bonn, 1948–9. Member, German Council of European Movement, 1949. Chancellor, Federal Republic of Germany, 1949–63; President, 1950–66; Foreign Minister, 1951–5.

contribution to defence would have to include provision for the continued support of the British and American forces now in Germany and to be on a scale comparable to the burdens borne for Western defence by other Western Governments; (b) that there would have to be an agreement providing for certain limitations on Germany's freedom to manufacture arms. Both these topics will now be discussed with the Germans.

5. Provisional agreement was also reached on a security guarantee for the Federal Republic, to come into force at the same time as the other arrangements. This reaffirms that the three Powers will treat any attack against the Federal Republic or Berlin as an attack upon themselves. It states that the three Powers consider the integrity of the Federal Republic and of Berlin an essential element of the peace of the free world and that they will maintain armed forces in both areas so long as they deem necessary in view of their responsibilities in Germany and the world situation.

6. The communiqué published after the meeting made the points that the common aim was to secure a unified Germany integrated within the European community, and a peace settlement for the whole of Germany. The determination of the boundaries of Germany must await such a settlement.

Winston S. Churchill to Anthony Eden
Prime Minister's Personal Telegram T.68c/51
(Premier papers, 11/122)

25 November 1951
No. 1013

Casey[1] is of the opinion that if Oliver Lyttelton is to obtain the best possible understanding of the problems in Malaya he should also visit Saigon, Rangoon and Djakarta. I hope you will agree to my putting this suggestion to Oliver.

---

[1] Richard Gardiner Casey, 1890–1976. Born in Australia. Educated in Australia and at Trinity College, Cambridge. On active service at Gallipoli and in France (DSO, MC), 1915–18. Australian Minister for Supply and Development, 1939–40. Australian Minister to the US, 1940–2. British Minister of State Resident in Middle East (based in Cairo) and Member of the British War Cabinet, 1942–3. Governor of Bengal, 1944–6. Minister of External Affairs, Australia, 1951–60. Baron, 1960. Governor-General of Australia, 1965–9.

November 1951

Winston S. Churchill to Patrick Buchan-Hepburn
Prime Minister's Personal Minute M.92c/51
(Premier papers, 11/136)

25 November 1951

1. The question of a Factual Record should be mentioned at the Cabinet on Tuesday. I favour it strongly. All Departments concerned should be called on for an epitome of the situation on taking over. What should be published must of course be carefully considered, but much that cannot be published now may remain on record for subsequent publication.

2. I am trying to get out of the electioneering atmosphere and therefore deprecate our starting Party Political Broadcasts at this juncture. On the other hand, if Lord Woolton would undertake a fireside chat on food and other domestic matters as a Ministerial Statement, December 15 would be a convenient date. I should be very glad not to be burdened with a broadcast before Christmas. This again should be mentioned at Tuesday's Cabinet.

Winston S. Churchill to Gwilym Lloyd George
Prime Minister's Personal Minute M.93c/51
(Premier papers, 11/143)

25 November 1951

Give me please, on a single sheet of paper, the reasons why you cut down the Christmas bonuses. How much was the saving involved? The other side was making a certain amount of Party capital out of the point. 'Scrooge!'

John Colville to Winston S. Churchill
(Churchill papers, 1/66)

25 November 1951

I have discussed with Miss Sturdee and Miss Gilliatt the question of their, and Miss Portal's, status at No. 10 and of the work that they should do. Subject to your approval, I make the following proposals, with which the young ladies concerned are in agreement:

They will be described as Personal Private Secretaries to the Prime Minister.

They will be rated and paid as civil servants as from October 25th, 1951. Their pay will be at the rates they would have been earning if they had been constantly employed in the Civil Service in the case of Miss Sturdee from 1941 and that of Miss Gilliatt from 1943. Their pay will be approximately:

Miss Sturdee .... £469 per annum.
Miss Gilliatt .... £469 per annum.

Miss Portal .... £360 per annum (plus £45 after a proficiency test).

Their duties will be as follows:

1. They will deal with all gifts which are sent to you. In this, as in other matters, they will keep in close touch with the other Private Secretaries.

2. They will be responsible for all questions relating to the appointments which you hold in a private capacity (e.g. Lord Warden, the 4th Hussars, 615 Squadron, Bristol University), Freedoms of cities, etc. They would also deal with any arrangements which might arise from your connection with these.

3. They would be responsible for your travel arrangements inside the country, but not when you go abroad.

4. One or more of them would always accompany you on your journeys abroad.

5. Part of the correspondence from the general public would be allotted to them and they would deal with government departments on your behalf in connection with this correspondence.

6. They would be generally responsible for your personal requisites.

7. Questions relating to your patronage of or association with outside bodies.

8. One of the three, together with one of the young ladies from No. 10, would be on duty each weekend.

9. Each would be on duty one night a week. Assuming that you are normally four nights in London, the remaining night would be the responsibility of one of the young ladies in the office for dictation.

Sir John Colville: recollection
('The Fringes of Power', pages 635–6)

25 November 1951

On November 25th, 1951, I made the following note of a dinner-party conversation at Chequers. There was present Richard Casey, Australian Minister of Foreign Affairs, at one stage of the war a much praised Minister of State in Cairo and a future Governor General of Australia.

> The Prime Minister said that he did not believe total war was likely. If it came, it would be on one of two accounts. Either the Americans, unable or unwilling any longer to pay for the maintenance of Europe, would say to the Russians you must by certain dates withdraw from certain points and meet us on certain requirements: otherwise we shall attack you. Or, the Russians, realising that safety did not come from being strong, but only from being the strongest, might for carefully calculated and not for emotional reasons, decide that they must attack before it was too late. If they did

so their first target would be the British Isles, which is the aircraft carrier. It was for that reason that Mr Churchill was anxious to convert this country from its present status of a rabbit into that of a hedgehog.

Mr Casey said that there was an ancient Lebanese proverb to the effect that one did not cut a man's throat when one had already poisoned his soup. Mr Churchill said he agreed: it was a matter of supererogation. Mr Casey thought that until the sores in Malaya, Indo-China and the Middle East had been cured, the Russians might consider that the soup was poisoned.

Churchill wasted no time in setting forth for America. There were defence matters to discuss and the progress of the Korean War. The Americans were bearing the brunt of the fighting, but there was also a sizable British contingent, including the gallant Gloucestershire Regiment, and the representative forces from other members of the United Nations. At the Potsdam Conference Churchill thought well of Truman[1] who had assumed Roosevelt's mantle with shrewdness and determination. Since then there had been the Truman doctrine, relieving Britain of her burden in liberated Greece; and the two men had established an immediate friendship in 1946, travelling together by train to Fulton, Missouri, where Churchill roused the world with the eloquent warning he gave in his Iron Curtain Speech.

Winston S. Churchill to Lieutenant-General Kenneth McLean,
for the Chiefs of Staff Committee
Prime Minister's Personal Minute M.94c/51
(Premier papers, 11/112)

26 November 1951

I should like a brief considered opinion of the COS on the present military situation in Korea. Before the armistice discussions began on Russian suggestion, the United Nations forces appeared to be gaining a mastery. A great many weeks have now passed, during which the Chinese have been steadily increasing and improving their artillery and Air Force. Thus our previous advantage must have been markedly diminished. Have the American and other United Nations forces been equally reinforced, or to what extent? Is there any reason for suspecting that the Chinese are making plans for a renewed major offensive and that they have been prolonging the negotiations in order to gain the needed time for this? What are the key points on the Chinese communications in Manchuria which the Americans would wish to attack by air if any fighting started again?

[1] Harry S Truman, 1884–1972. Educated at Kansas City School of Law. 1st Lt, 129th Field Artillery, 1918–19. Married, 1919, Bess Wallace. Judge, Jackson County Court, Mo., 1922–4; Presiding Judge, 1926–34. US Senator, 1934–44. US Vice-President, 1945. US President, 1945–53.

The control and responsibility for the Korean War do not lie with us, who only contribute a small fraction of the United Nations' forces. At the same time it is our duty to have a clear and continuous view of what is going on.

*Winston S. Churchill to Harold Parker, James Thomas
and Admiral of the Fleet Sir Rhoderick McGrigor[1]
Prime Minister's Personal Minute M.95c/51
(Premier papers, 11/83)*

26 November 1951
Top Secret

1. It seems a pity that we must build four different classes of frigates for specialized duties in place of the all-purpose destroyer. Specialization involves so much loss of flexibility and such increased supply and replacement difficulties. But if it is true that no destroyer of acceptable size can carry all the latest equipment I suppose we must accept these penalties. Presumably the Admiralty has made certain that an all-purpose ship cannot be produced and that the equipment itself cannot be made more compact and less complex without losing efficiency.

2. There is scarcely any reference in this paper to progress in the vital apparatus and armament to deal with the U-boats and mines for which the ships are required. The new aluminium and wood designs only touch on the fringe of the problems. What advances have been made in:
    (i)   detecting U-boats;
    (ii) attacking U-boats;
    (iii) detecting mines;
    (iv) sweeping mines.

---

[1] Rhoderick Robert McGrigor, 1893–1959. Educated at Royal Navy Colleges Osborne and Dartmouth. Lt, 1914. Served at Gallipoli, 1915; on HMS *Malaya* at Jutland, 1916. Married, 1931, Louise Gwendoline Glyn. Capt., 1933. CoS to C-in-C China Station, 1938. Lord Commissioner of Admiralty, 1941–3. Naval Force Commander for capture of Pantelleria and invasion of Sicily. DSO, 1943. RAdm., 1944. VAdm., 1945. GCB, 1945. C-in-C, Home Fleet, 1945–50. Adm. of the Fleet, 1948. C-in-C, Plymouth, 1950–1. KCB, 1951.1st Sea Lord, 1951–5. Naval ADC to Queen Elizabeth II, 1952–3.

November 1951

Winston S. Churchill to Sir Norman Brook
Prime Minister's Personal Minute M.99c/51
(Premier papers, 11/75)

26 November 1951

See the circulations by the Minister of Supply and the Secretary of State for Air,[1] dated November 20. These were to have been discussed at last week's Cabinet and are now, I presume, on the agenda for discussion when the Secretary of State for Air returns.

2. What is the procedure about Service Departments circulating memoranda direct to the Cabinet? Surely papers like these should be reported on by the COS to me, as Minister of Defence, in the first instance. The Air paper, if true, is a shocking story for estimates of nearly £350 millions. I have not yet had time to compare it with other accounts I have called for from the Ministry of Defence.

3. On the other hand I have received at my request the attached statement on the air position procured by the Ministry of Defence. Have these two papers been collated and do they clash?

4. Pray report about all this. To whom has C(51)28 been circulated? I have marked it and the Minister of Supply's paper to the COS Committee for their comments.

5. The matter should be brought before the COS Committee forthwith. Pray send me your own reply separately.

Winston S. Churchill to Harold Parker
Prime Minister's Personal Minute M.100c/51
(Premier papers, 11/69)

26 November 1951

1. In the notes about the Royal Navy, does 'Volunteer Reservists' mean or comprise the RNVR?

2. Let me have as far as possible comparable figures (written in ink) before mobilization in 1939. Also see what was the figure I prescribed for the Royal Navy in my speech on Demobilization in 1946. (Mr Christ[2] could help find this.)

3. Let me have an analysis on one of these sheets of 750 naval and 9,471 civilian people at Admiralty Headquarters together with comparable figures of 1939.

4. I presume 'Civilians at Admiralty Out-stations' means principally

---

[1] Reproduced above (pp. 57–8).
[2] George Elgie Christ, 1904–72. Political Correspondent, *Daily Telegraph*, 1940–5. Parliamentary Liaison Office, Conservative Party, 1945–65.

dockyards. What actually has happened to Chatham? Is the Nore still a first-class naval command?

5. Do your figures include new construction? I cannot think they do. I gather the Controller's Department is separate now and grouped under Lord Swinton.[1] If my view is right let me have a page on new construction.

6. I am keeping the Army and Air Force notes until later.

Winston S. Churchill to Lieutenant-General Kenneth McLean,
for the Chiefs of Staff Committee
Prime Minister's Personal Minute M.101c/51
(Premier papers, 11/91)

26 November 1951

I hope we shall have reached a conclusion one way or the other in Egypt at least by April Fool's Day. What is needed now is not a long term separation of our slowly established contacts and connections with Egypt, but an abrupt suspension of new arrivals. Pray consider whether the Egyptian Government should not be informed that this will begin forthwith.

2. At the same time let me know what other things we are doing for them, e.g., giving or selling them ships, weapons, or munitions of any kind. What is being done about money payments, or payments in goods on account of sterling balances?

3. Let me have a full programme of immediate suspension rather than of deferred cessation which I can discuss with the Foreign Secretary when he returns on Thursday. Make it the best programme you can, i.e., what they would like least.

---

[1] Philip Cunliffe-Lister, 1884–1972. On active service, 1914–17 (MC). Joint Secretary, Ministry of National Service, 1917–18. MP (Cons.) for Hendon, 1918–35. President of the Board of Trade, 1922–3, 1924–9, 1931. Secretary of State for the Colonies, 1931–5. Viscount Swinton, 1935. Secretary of State for Air, 1935–8 (when he advocated a larger Air Force expansion than the Government was prepared to accept). Brought back into Government on the outbreak of war as Chairman of UK Commercial Corp., responsible for pre-empting purchases of supplies and materials overseas that were needed by the German war machine. Appointed by Churchill in May 1940 as Chairman of the Security Executive, concerned with measures against sabotage in Britain and overseas. Organized supply route to the Soviet Union through the Persian Gulf, 1941–2. Cabinet Minister Resident in West Africa, 1942–4. Minister for Civil Aviation, 1944–5. Minister of Materials, 1951–2. Chancellor of the Duchy of Lancaster, 1951–2. Deputy Leader, House of Lords, 1951–5. Secretary of State for Commonwealth Relations, 1952–5. Earl of Swinton, 1955.

Anthony Eden to Winston S. Churchill
Prime Minister's Personal Telegram T.72c/51
(Premier papers, 11/122)

26 November 1951
Immediate
Secret
No. 564

Your 1013.[1]

I am sure that this is not necessary. We have an office at Singapore which can give him all information about the three territories. They have just had a conference there at which all our missions in the Far East were represented together with the Commanders-in-Chief and at which an Under Secretary from the Foreign Office was present.

I really think it would be a waste of time for Oliver to wander round these countries. The position at Djakarta is particularly tricky at this time and he would not want to become involved in it. He can of course at any time summon any of our representatives to Singapore if he needs their help.[2]

Cabinet: conclusions
(Cabinet papers, 128/23)

27 November 1951
Secret
12 p.m.
Cabinet Meeting No. 11 of 1951

1. The Prime Minister said that he wished to have prepared a comprehensive account of the state of the nation's affairs at the date on which the Government assumed office. It had been suggested to him that this might be presented to Parliament as a White Paper. Some of its contents could not, however, be published at the present time – for example, those relating to the state of our defences. And there would be objection to the publishing in the form of a White Paper a document which might be said to serve the purposes of Party politics. The statement should therefore be prepared, not with a view to publication, but for the use of the Cabinet.

The Cabinet –

Instructed the Secretary of the Cabinet to collect from the Departments concerned factual statements which could be assembled into a comprehensive account of the state of the nation's affairs at the date when the Government assumed office.

---

[1] T.68c/51, reproduced above (p. 65).
[2] Churchill telegraphed Lyttelton on Nov. 26: 'You need not bother about Saigon, Rangoon and Djakarta' (T.73c/51, *Premier papers 11/122*).

2. The Prime Minister said that he had now formulated his proposals regarding the use of official cars by Ministers. Those Ministers for whom police protection was provided must be able to use official cars for all purposes. No other Ministers would, however, have cars allotted to them. Cabinet Ministers or Ministers in charge of Departments would draw on a central pool of cars for official purposes, including journeys to and from their official work within seven miles of the Palace of Westminster. The arrangement by which Ministers had been able to use official cars for private purposes on repayment would be discontinued. All official cars in London would be operated from a single central pool. Consequential arrangements would be made for the use of cars by serving officers and civil servants in the London area.

In discussion the following points were raised:
  (a) The Prime Minister said that he wished to consider further whether those Ministers who used official cars for all purposes because they were provided with police protection should not make some payment for their use of these cars for private purposes.
  (b) It was suggested that there might be some loss of efficiency if all official cars in London were operated from a single pool. Car pools were now being operated in London by several Departments other than the Ministry of Supply, and there might be an advantage in allowing some of these to continue.

The Cabinet –

Approved the Prime Minister's proposals regarding the use of official cars by Ministers, subject to further consideration of the two points noted above.

3. The Cabinet agreed that a debate on Defence should be held in the House of Commons, in open session, on 6th December. The Prime Minister would speak in that debate.

The Opposition were anxious that the House of Commons should have an opportunity to debate, before the Christmas Recess, the proposals for federation of the Rhodesias and the Nyasalands. If this were conceded it would be impossible to hold before Christmas the usual debate on Welsh Affairs. The Cabinet agreed that the Leader of the House of Commons, in his discussions with the Opposition, should indicate a preference for a debate on Welsh affairs, but might, if pressed, accept the alternative of a debate on federation in Central Africa.

4. The Prime Minister reported the results of the discussion which he had held with the Ministers primarily concerned, since the Cabinet's meeting on the 22nd November, on the proposals in C(51)21[1] regarding the Chieftainship of the Bamangwato Tribe.

The Cabinet –

1. Authorised the Commonwealth Secretary, in his future handling of this question, to pursue the general policy outlined in C(51)21.

---

[1] Reproduced above (pp. 52–4).

2. Agreed that a statement regarding Tshekedi Khama should be made in the House of Commons on 6th December in the following terms: 'His Majesty's Government have decided that Tshekedi Khama's private rights in the Bamangwato Reserve should not be restricted for longer than is necessary in the public interest. He has already renounced the Chieftainship; and His Majesty's Government are convinced that the interests of peace in the Reserve demand that he should be excluded from the political life of the tribe. The sooner this exclusion is shown to be effective, and it is His Majesty's Government's intention to make it so, the sooner will it be possible to allow him progressively greater freedom to look after his private interests in the Reserve and ultimately, if all goes well, to let him live there as a private person.'

3. Agreed that the answer to any supplementary Question about Seretse Khama should be: 'As regards Seretse Khama, the Government intends to adhere to the policy of their predecessors as set forth in the White Paper on the Bechuanaland Protectorate which was presented in March 1950.'

4. Agreed that the reports of the observers who visited the Bamangwato Reserve in July 1951 (reproduced in Annexes C and D of C(51)21) should be published as a White Paper on 6th December.

[. . .]

Gwilym Lloyd George to Winston S. Churchill
(Premier papers, 11/143)

27 November 1951
PM/51/1

1. You asked me in your minute of 25th November[1] why I had not given Christmas bonuses.

2. I consider that all available food supplies can best be used in keeping ordinary rations at the highest possible level and that we should so far as possible avoid any unnecessary fluctuation of the rations such as has happened over the last few years.

3. The following would have been the consequences of trying to give bonuses this year.

Sugar. A bonus at Christmas would have made it necessary to reduce the ration for some time during next year to 8 ozs. I intend to keep it up to its present level of 10 ozs.

Sweets. Owing to a heavy cut in the allocation of sugar to manufacturers (made by the previous Government) the sweets ration will have to be cut in the new year. A bonus would have meant an earlier cut.

Cooking Fat. The cuts we are now having to make in food imports will

---

[1] Reproduced above (p. 66).

mean cutting allocations to manufacturers next year. A bonus would have meant an increased cut.

Tea. The delay in supplies due to labour troubles at Tilbury meant that the ordinary ration was in some danger. We could have given a tea bonus to old people (this would have taken 700,000 lbs).

The supply position of all other rationed foods (meat, cheese, butter and margarine) is such that we must husband our supplies to keep up the present rations.

4. On balance, I decided that it was honest and realistic not to issue any meagre and fictitious bonuses. A tea bonus for the over 70s on its own would have been derisory.

5. I believe the other side are over-reaching themselves on this matter, and I hope to show this in the debate on Thursday.

Harold Parker to Winston S. Churchill
(Premier papers, 11/59)

27 November 1951

ADMIRALTY PROGRESS REPORT ON DEFENCE PROGRAMME

I return your copy of the report.[1]

Paras. 3 and 4, page 1.

The following are the tonnages of the ships referred to:

	Tonnage
Fleet Carrier	37,000
Light Fleet Carrier (*Triumph*)	13,000
Fast Minelayers	2,650 each
Destroyers:	
Daring Class	2,610
Others	about 2,460
A/S Frigates:	
Full conversion – *Rocket and Relentless*	1,841
Limited conversion – *Tenacious*	1,866
Others	about 1,650
Submarines (surface displacement)	815
Minesweepers:	
Ocean	1,000 each
Coastal	260
Inshore	120
Motor Torpedo Boats (all short boats)	45

[1] Progress Report on the Defence Programme, 14 Nov. 1951.

A/S Trawlers	600
Landing Ship Headquarters	15,000
Minesweeping Motor Launches	751 each

<u>Para. 18, page 6</u>

Retained officers and men. Since August 1950 when the war in Korea developed all three Services have retained time expired regulars with the colours. In the Navy the period is for up to 18 months. The general future policy is now under review but the Navy sees no possibility of making any change for the next two or three years.

Recalled officers and men. The Navy and Army also recalled regular reservists for the Korea emergency. The Army will have released all their recalled reservists (some 7,000) by next February. The Navy find it necessary to continue calling up reservists, whose numbers will reach a peak of 6,000 in 1952.

<u>Para. 21, page 7</u>

Naval Reserves. About 88,000 Naval Class 'Z' Reservists have been screened. It is anticipated that 63,000 such men will be required in the first 6 months of hostilities.

<u>Para. 22, page 7</u>

Royal Naval Volunteer Supplementary Reserve. This Reserve consists of officers, commissioned during the 1939/45 Emergency, who have voluntarily undertaken to be recalled to the Navy in a future emergency. Normally they have no training liability in peace and receive no pay. They are encouraged, however, to volunteer for short refresher courses of between 3 and 14 days duration, during attendance at which they receive pay and allowances.

<u>Para. 42, page 10.</u>

VT Fuses. A VT or influence fuze is in principle a minute radar set, fitted into the nose of a shell, which sends out pulses: on approaching a target the pulses are reflected and at an appropriate range the reflected pulse sets off the fuse. 'VT' means 'Variable Time'.

I will submit in a day or so, a full note about the loan of Hunt Class Destroyers.

Winston S. Churchill to Lieutenant-General Kenneth McLean
Prime Minister's Personal Minute M.105c/51
(Premier papers, 11/74A)

28 November 1951

1. See paras. 1 and 2 of your memorandum of November 22 attached.[1] I am much concerned at this information. I had gathered that the Air Force was playing an ever-greater part in the detection of U-boats, and that sonobuoys and other devices opened an increasingly hopeful sphere. You should look up what I said about this two or three years ago in the House of Commons. The information on which I spoke was supposed to be the best available at the time. Send me the extract when you have found it. Meanwhile Lord Cherwell should see the memorandum of November 22, together with my comments.

2. About the relative strengths in the Atlantic, it would seem that, on the whole, our forces are stronger than those assigned by the United States. Pray let the two Fleets be compared (a) in tonnage, and (b) in personnel.

3. Let me see also the relative strengths of the Air contribution by Coastal Command and the Americans. I thought they had a large preponderance in this assigned to the Atlantic. The fact that this method of destroying submarines is not opening out at the present time would minimize the importance of any predominance they have in this matter.

4. All the above must be considered in relation to the claim for an American Supreme Commander.

Lieutenant-General Kenneth McLean to Winston S. Churchill
(Premier papers, 11/112)

28 November 1951
KGM/361

In your minute No. M.94c/51[2] you asked for a brief opinion from the Chiefs of Staff on the present military situation in Korea.

[1] These read:
 '1. It is unfortunately no longer true that the Coastal Command can be expected to play the major part in an Anti-Submarine campaign in the near future as it did in the crucial year of the Battle of the Atlantic, 1943. It is in fact regrettably true that, unless and until some new scientific device more effective than the sonobuoy can be developed for detecting U-boats from the air, the U-boat with snort and high submerged speed has largely neutralized the Air.
 2. Aircraft are still a useful supplement to surface anti-submarine vessels, for reconnaissance and to keep submarines submerged in the vicinity of convoys. But radar has little chance of picking up a snort except in calm seas. And offensive patrols in the transit areas, which paid such high dividends in the Battle of the Bay last time, would now require far larger numbers of aircraft than we have any chance of having in another war. Even then they could not be expected to be as effective. The days when the U-boat had to surface to change batteries for 5 or 6 hours in the 24, and when they used to stay on the surface fighting back, giving us excellent opportunities for killing them, are gone.'
[2] Reproduced above (pp. 68–9).

2. Attached at Annex is a note in reply which has been approved by the Chiefs of Staff.

ANNEX
Situation in Korea

Reinforcement by Communists and United Nations

1. The Communists have increased their forces during the Cease Fire talks by 60,000 ground troops, including two armoured divisions and artillery. The firepower of their supporting arms has shown a marked increase both in quantity and quality, and it is evident that the period of the armistice talks has enabled them to build up their battle potential to a point where a major offensive could be launched. The Communist Air Force has increased by 230 fighters (150 MIG 15) and 50 light bombers. There has been no significant change in Communist Naval forces.

2. There has been no increase of UN forces during the same period, but their tactical positions have been considerably strengthened.

3. According to current British estimates the relative strengths are now:

Communist	UN Forces
570,000 ground troops (including 235,000 North Koreans)	418,000 ground troops (including 130,000 South Koreans)
720 Fighter aircraft (400 MIG 15)	988 Fighter aircraft
90 Light Bombers	100 Light Bombers
95 Medium Bombers	

Communist Intentions

4. We believe that the Communists intend ultimately to gain control over all Korea, but that they have not yet decided whether to achieve this by force of arms or by negotiation of a formal armistice from a position of strength followed by subversion and cold war pressure. We think that they are in fact building up their strength largely in the hope that they will succeed by the latter method. In the event of failure, however, they would wish to be in a position to launch an offensive and this they could now do.

[. . .]

Winston S. Churchill to Harold Parker
Prime Minister's Personal Minute M.106c/51
(Premier papers, 11/59)

28 November 1951

1. Paras. 3 and 4.[1] I note the very large size of the Daring Class. They are virtually cruisers and are becoming 'hunted' instead of 'hunters'.
2. Para. 18. Does this mean that you keep the time-expired regulars in the Navy for eighteen months additional, and let them go then?
3. Para. 21. What do you mean by 'screened?' What exactly is the process?
4. The loan of Hunt Class destroyers. Make sure no action is taken on this until I am fully informed. I should have thought we could not afford to lend any destroyers at the present time.

Winston S. Churchill to Sir Norman Brook
Prime Minister's Personal Minute M.107c/51
(Premier papers, 11/75)

28 November 1951

This Cabinet paper, C(51)28,[2] ought not to have been circulated so widely. It should be recalled as sent in error from all those I have marked on your list. I am astonished that a document of this character can be flung about so widely.

I will discuss with you later the procedure we must follow to examine the Estimates of the Rearmament Programme. I agree with your general method. We can do nothing till Parliament has risen.

Sarah Beauchamp[3] to Winston S. Churchill
(Churchill papers, 7/50)[4]

28 November 1951   New York

Darling darling Papa,

I hope that this letter will reach you, like my one did last year right on the

---

[1] Reference Parker's minute of 27 Nov. 1951, reproduced above (pp. 75–6).
[2] Reproduced above (pp. 57–8).
[3] Sarah Millicent Hermione Spencer Churchill, 1914–83. Married, 1936, Vic Oliver (div. 1945); 1949, Antony Beauchamp (d. 1957); 1962, Thomas Touchet-Jesson (d. July 1963). Appeared on stage in Birmingham, Southampton, Weston-super-Mare and London, 1937–9; on tour with Vic Oliver in the play *Idiot's Delight*, 1938; in London in *Quiet Wedding*, 1939; and in J. M. Barrie's *Mary Rose*, 1940. Appeared in the film *Spring Meeting*, 1940. Entered WAAF, 1941. Asst Section Officer, Photographic Interpretation Unit, Medmenham, 1941–5. ADC to her father at Tehran (Nov. 1943) and Yalta (Feb. 1945). In 1951, appeared on US stage in *Grammercy Ghost*. Author of *The Empty Spaces* (1966), *A Thread in the Tapestry* (1967), *Collected Poems* (1974) and *Keep on Dancing* (1981).
[4] This letter was handwritten.

day – but if for any reason it shouldn't I will of course cable – but I have been thinking so much about you, and the momentous task you have embraced.

On paper everything looks very bleak – but I feel out of a shining and glorious life – this chapter will be one of the most thrilling and deeply satisfying. The last prize you said. I think it would be more, a fitting reward to those qualities in you which are not so quickly recognised – those of philosophical and humanitarian. If I read this letter I'll probably tear it up. It sounds already in echo like the introduction of a chairman before you have to make a speech – !! I didn't mean it to – I just pray God that He will give you life and strength to achieve the last prize for the struggling world, and for me, the ever growing joy and happiness of our relation which without much words seems to seep into me even away from you.

Please take care of yourself and take some joy in knowing how beloved you are by men and women everywhere and of your daughter.

Sarah

Wow – my darling

Many many many happy returns of the day. I will think of you all at dinner.

Winston S. Churchill to Lieutenant-General Kenneth McLean
Prime Minister's Personal Minute M.108c/51
(Premier papers, 11/112)

29 November 1951

Annex to your Minute KGM/361.[1]

Paragraph 2. Is there much wire and concrete? What minefields have been laid? Have artillery been sited to bring convergent fire on approaches? What camouflage? Have we really tried to make a strong line in depth?

Paragraph 3. I did not know we were so nearly balanced in the air. Our position certainly seems to have worsened during the armistice talks.

Paragraph 4, last line. This is a serious statement.

Paragraph 7. This is comforting, but does it really pay the United Nations to keep forces tied up in such great numbers indefinitely at enormous cost in this worthless Peninsula? Are we not clearly up to date the losers by the armistice negotiations period? Surely the Americans have ideas of their own upon these points?

---

[1] Reproduced above (pp. 77–8).

Winston S. Churchill to Members of the Cabinet
(*Cabinet papers, 129/48*)

29 November 1951
Secret
Cabinet Paper No. 32 of 1951

UNITED EUROPE

It may simplify discussion if I set forth briefly my own view and the line I have followed so far.

1. At Zürich in 1946 I appealed to France to take the lead in Europe by making friends with the Germans, 'burying the thousand-year quarrel', &c. This caused a shock at the time but progress has been continual. I always recognised that, as Germany is potentially so much stronger than France, militarily and economically, Britain and if possible the United States should be associated with United Europe, to make an even balance and to promote the United Europe Movement.

2. As year by year the project advanced, the Federal Movement in many European countries who participated became prominent. It has in the last two years lost much of its original force. The American mind jumps much too lightly over its many difficulties. I am not opposed to a European Federation including (eventually) the countries behind the Iron Curtain, provided that this comes about naturally and gradually. But I never thought that Britain or the British Commonwealths should, either individually or collectively, become an integral part of a European Federation, and have never given the slightest support to the idea. We should not, however, obstruct but rather favour the movement to closer European unity and try to get the United States' support in this work.

3. There can be no effective defence of Western Europe without the Germans. As things developed my idea has always been as follows: There is the NATO Army. Inside the NATO Army there is the European Army, and inside the European Army there is the German Army. The European Army should be formed by all the European parties to NATO *plus* Germany, 'dedicating' from their own national armies their quota of divisions to the Army now under General Eisenhower's command. Originally at Strasbourg in 1950 the Germans did not press for a national army. On the contrary they declared themselves ready to join a European Army without having a national army. The opportunity was lost and there seems very little doubt that Germany will have to have a certain limited national army from which to 'dedicate'. The size and strength of this army, and its manufacture of weapons, would have to be agreed with the victorious Powers of the late war. In any case the recruiting arrangements for covering the German quota would have involved a considerable machinery.

4. In the European Army all dedicated quotas of participating nations would be treated with strict honourable military equality. The national characteristics should be preserved up to the divisional level, special arrangements being made about the 'tail', heavy weapons, &c. I should doubt very much the military spirit of a 'sludgy amalgam' of volunteers or conscripts to defend the EDC or other similar organisations. The national spirit must animate all troops up to and including the divisional level. On this basis and within these limits national pride may be made to promote and serve international strength.

5. France does not seem to be playing her proper part in these arrangements. France is not France without 'L'Armeé Française'. I warned MM Pleven[1] and Monnet[2] several times that 'a Pleven Army' would not go down in France. The French seem to be trying to get France defended by Europe. Their proposed contribution for 1952 of five, rising to ten, divisions is pitiful, even making allowances for the fact that they are still trying to hold their Oriental Empire. They have no grounds of complaint against us who have already dedicated four divisions to General Eisenhower's Command. We must not lose all consciousness of our insular position. I noticed some time ago the faulty structure of the present French arrangements, and in particular how the few combatant divisional formations they have will be deprived of all training efficiency by the vast mass of recruits annually flowing in upon them.

6. On the economic side, I welcome the Schuman Coal and Steel Plan as a step in the reconciliation of France and Germany, and as probably rendering another Franco-German war physically impossible. I never contemplated Britain joining in this plan on the same terms as Continental partners. We should, however, have joined in all discussions, and had we done so not only a better plan would probably have emerged, but our own interests would have been watched at every stage. Our attitude towards further economic developments on the Schuman lines resembles that which we adopt about the European Army. We help, we dedicate, we play a part, but we are not merged and do not forfeit our insular or Commonwealth-wide character. I should resist any American pressure to treat Britain as on the same footing as the European States, none of whom have the advantages of the Channel and who were subsequently conquered.

7. Our first object is the unity and the consolidation of the British

[1] René Pleven, 1901–93. French Minister of Colonies, 1943–4. Minister of Finance, 1944–6. PM of France, July 1950 to Mar. 1951, Aug. 1951 to Jan. 1952. Minister of Defence, 1952–4. Author of the 'Pleven Plan' for a European Army including full German participation (rejected by the French Assembly, 1954). Foreign Minister, 13–30 May 1958.

[2] Jean Monnet, 1888–1979. French representative on Allied Executive Committee for Relocation of Common Resources, 1916–8. Deputy Secretary-General, League of Nations, 1919. Chairman, Franco-British Economic Co-ordination Committee, 1939. Member, British Supply Council, Washington DC, 1940–3. Commissioner for Armament, Supplies and Reconstruction, French National Committee, Algiers, 1943–4. General Commissioner, Plan for Modernisation and Equipment of France (Monnet Plan), 1946. Hon. GBE, 1947. President, European Coal and Steel Community, 1952–5. Chairman, Action Committee for the United States of Europe, 1956–75. Hon. CH, 1972.

Commonwealths and what is left of the former British Empire. Our second, the 'fraternal association' of the English-speaking world; and third, United Europe, to which we are a separate closely- and specially-related ally and friend.

Paul Reynaud[1] to Winston S. Churchill
(Premier papers, 11/73)

29 November 1951 Strasbourg
Translation

My dear and great friend,

I owe it to my old friendship for England, without speaking of that which unites us, to tell you of the anxiety and trouble provoked by the attitude of your Government on the subject of the European Army.

Last week, at the time of the meeting of the European delegates with a delegation from the United States Congress, I was astonished at the communiqué published by the Foreign Office declaring that Great Britain would not participate in the European Army. The next day, after referring it to the Foreign Office, Mr Boothby declared that this news was incorrect, nothing having been settled on this subject by the British Government.

The day before yesterday in Rome, General Eisenhower declared that the creation of a European Army was an absolute necessity for the defence of Europe. Yesterday morning, Sir David Maxwell Fyfe made a statement on this subject from which it appeared that nothing was yet decided by his Government; this appeared to me to be most disquieting. I drew his attention to the gravity of the effect which the refusal of Great Britain to participate in a European Army would have on Europe. This would, in effect, give a strong argument to the opposers of the plan in the French Parliament. They would be able to say, more or less, that England would keep her Army which would preserve her authority in international conferences while France lost hers, having merged her Army with the European one.

After the meeting, Sir David gave a Press Conference which yesterday's *Continental Daily Mail* summarised thus:

'The storm quietened down somewhat when Sir David emphasised at a two-hour Press Conference immediately after his speech, that Britain has not yet "closed the door on the European Army".'

Unfortunately, at the same time, Mr Eden declared in Rome, in a categorical

---

[1] Paul Reynaud, 1878–1966. On active service, 1914–18 (twice decorated). Entered Chamber of Deputies, 1919. Minister of Colonies, 1931–2. Minister of Finance, 1930, 1938–40. Minister of Justice, 1938. PM, 1940. Foreign Minister, 1940. Arrested by Vichy Government, Sep. 1940. Deported to Germany, 1943–5. Released, 1945. Minister of Finance, 1948. Deputy PM, June 1953 to July 1954. President of Finance Committee of the National Assembly, 1958.

manner, that the British Government would not participate in the European Army.

This declaration contradicts the recommendation which you put to the vote at the Strasbourg Assembly on 11th August, 1950, in which you demanded 'the immediate creation of a unified European Army, under the authority of a European Minister of Defence, subject to democratic control and acting in co-operation with the United States and Canada.'

Nobody here understands the reasons for which you have abandoned a position so firm and clear. In effect, Great Britain has today less obligation towards her overseas possessions than France has for the Union Française.

General Eisenhower having declared that the utilisation of German forces is necessary for the defence of free Europe, it is clear that if the European Army is not created or if it is rejected by the French Parliament, the Americans will attempt to create a German Army. If they succeed in this, the result will be a resurrection of the Wehrmacht and of the German general staff with all the political consequences which that entails. If they fail, General Eisenhower will state that European disagreements have hindered him in the carrying out of his mission. In this case, the route to the Atlantic will be open to the Soviet armies.

Yesterday a Labour speaker, Mr Glenvil Hall,[1] rejoiced to see you following in the footsteps of your predecessor.

I believe I am expressing the opinion of all your friends and of the French when I draw your attention to the gravity of the decision which, if it were confirmed, would contradict the recommendation for which you obtained the Assembly's vote. It does not agree, I believe, with what Europe and the world expects from one of the big figures of history.

Winston S. Churchill to Sir Norman Brook
Prime Minister's Personal Minute M.114c/51
(Premier papers, 11/174)

30 November 1951

I approve the Committee,[2] but let us be careful we do not spawn too many of these Cabinet Committees. Let me see a list of what we have already appointed. They may overlap or be capable of combination. For instance, topics may be added to the work of an existing committee. All this is a fertile field.

[1] William Glenvil Hall, 1887–1962. Barrister-at-law. On active service, 1914–18 (wounded, despatches). MP (Lab.) for Portsmouth Central, 1929–31; for Colne Valley, 1939–62. Financial Secretary to the Treasury, 1945–50. British Representative, UN General Assembly, 1945, 1946, 1948; Consultative Assembly, Strasbourg, 1950, 1951, 1952. PC, 1947. Chairman, Parliamentary Labour Party, 1950, 1951.
[2] Committee on Government Information Services.

2. See last line.[1] What is this 'general education work on a considerable scale' in Germany? Is it teaching the Germans not to be naughty in the future? I do not think this is a hopeful process. Nations are acted on by the spirit in which foreigners treat them, and not by sermons and lectures. A release of German Generals now in prison would bring much more good feeling in Germany, if timed at the right moment – now perhaps too late – than many lectures. Let me know how much is being spent on lectures.

Chiefs of Staff Committee: minutes
(Premier papers, 11/112)

30 November 1951
Top Secret
3 p.m.
Chiefs of Staff Meeting No. 3 of 1951

KOREA

The Meeting considered a draft telegram prepared by the Foreign Office in reply to two telegrams which the Foreign Secretary had despatched after his meeting with Mr Acheson in Rome to discuss the Korea Armistice negotiations.

In discussion the following points arose:

Likelihood of the Armistice Terms being Honoured

(a) There was a difference of opinion over the likelihood of the Armistice being honoured. We felt that the Communists would probably keep the Armistice: the Americans, on the other hand, were pessimistic.

Warning Statement

(b) It was necessary to be realistic over the warning statement. The Americans would insist on issuing a statement whatever we might say about it, and whether or not we considered it more likely to prove provocative than to act as a deterrent.

(c) In our opinion the warning statements should be in very general terms, as in the case of Berlin: it would be unwise to be precise. As far as possible the statements made by the different participants should be in identical terms.

(d) We should tell the Americans that we would, of course, like to discuss a draft statement with them beforehand. However, it was not necessary to discuss the terms of any statement with the Dominions yet.

---

[1] Of note on work of Overseas Information Services.

A Naval Blockade

(e) It was felt that a blockade was more likely to start World War III than bombing across the Yolu. To avoid blundering into World War III, we should have to exclude from our blockade the Russian ports, in which case a blockade would be largely ineffective.

(f) In the long run bombing of the Chinese ports and centres of communication would be much more effective than blockade, and less likely to precipitate general war.

Bombing Across the River Yalu

(g) When this problem first arose, we had been worried because of the agreement between Russia and China. The Prime Minister, however, considered that Russia would start World War III when she wanted to: she certainly would not do so merely to honour her pledge to China. He was, therefore, not unduly worried about bombing targets in Manchuria. As regards a war with China, he considered that China was not a country against which one declared war; rather a country against which war was waged.

The Dominions

(h) The Secretary of State for Commonwealth Relations raised the question of consultation with the Dominions. The Dominions disliked having their minds made up for them in matters of major policy. The Canadians already knew about the American proposals, and they were alarmed.

(i) The Prime Minister considered that Canada, Australia and New Zealand should be told that HM Government had considered it necessary to send this telegram to the State Department because of the extreme urgency of the matter. This was the first time since the Korean war began that the Americans had seen fit to consult us on any matter of major policy – this might even mark the beginning of a closer relationship between us.

Conclusions

The Prime Minister directed that:
(1) The draft telegram to Mr Acheson should be amended as agreed in discussion and despatched forthwith by the Foreign Secretary.
(2) The Foreign Secretary should later dispatch a telegram to the State Department giving facts and figures regarding trade with China.
(3) The Secretary of State for Commonwealth Relations should inform the Governments of Canada, Australia and New Zealand – but not India – of this exchange of views between HM Government and the State Department, giving them the argument in (i) above.

NOVEMBER 1951

POTENTIAL AIR THREAT TO THE UNITED NATIONS FORCES IN KOREA
Air Strength

1. There are at present in Manchuria about 400 MIG 15 jet fighter aircraft and about 170 more on training duties in China. The Chinese could also make available in the North Korean area an operational force of some 80 ground attack aircraft, 60 light bombers and 160 piston engine fighters. The nationality of the jet units is unknown, although we suspect that they are partly piloted by Russians. The North Korean Air Force is now insignificant.

2. The Russians have some 4,400 aircraft suitable for use in a tactical role in their Far East command. These could intervene in Korea and alter significantly the balance of air power.

3. During recent months the Communists have made great and successful efforts, in spite of UN bombing, to increase the number of jet airfields in North Korea. One of these is now in operational use. The Communists clearly aim to extend southwards their operational use of jet airfields.

Combat Effectiveness

4. The chief threat from the enemy air force comes from the MIG 15 aircraft. From their existing bases these can operate as far south as the 38th Parallel. Should the Communists succeed in operating from their bases in the Pyongyang area, the MIG 15 could operate effectively as far south as the 36th Parallel. Although we have no evidence that Communist jet pilots have been given training in close support operations they could carry out low flying attacks. The Communists have recently been using their piston engine day-fighters in a night-fighter role, but so far without success. There is still no definite evidence of the use of airborne interception radar.

5. Up to date the Communist air force has been primarily a defensive force, and as such it has only recently shown signs of being able to impede seriously UN daylight operations over North Korea. Its effectiveness is, however, steadily increasing: recently UN aircraft have had to concentrate more on night operations for their attacks against Communist airfields and communications.

Communist Air Defences in North Korea

6. The Communists have been making increasing efforts to build up their anti-aircraft defences, in particular on air-fields, and to increase the efficiency of their radar reporting system, which already stretches over the Western half of North Korea to well south of Pyongyang. The increasing effectiveness of these defences is likely to reduce the effectiveness of UN air attacks.

Soviet Intervention

7. We still believe that, if the UN forces bomb targets in Manchuria, the Soviet Air Force will intervene in a defensive role. Beyond this, overt

intervention by the Soviet Far Eastern Air Force is thought unlikely, since this would greatly increase the risk of global war which we believe the Russians do not want. The Russians have been supplying MIG 15 aircraft, flying instructors and technical and staff assistance to the units in Manchuria: they are likely to continue doing so on an increasing scale. However, we believe that the Russians are most anxious to avoid capture of Communist jet pilots and aircraft, and this will make the Russians reluctant to use these pilots and aircraft over and south of the battle-line.

Conclusion

8. We conclude that the Communist Air Force in the area of North Korea at present represents no great threat to UN ground forces. On the other hand, it is already restricting UN daylight air operations over North Korea. As its strength increases and the AA defences improve, it is likely to restrict increasingly UN air operations over North Korea and to enable the Communists to extend southwards their operational use of jet airfields in North Korea. In that event the potential threat to the UN ground forces would be considerably increased, although it is unlikely that the United Nations would lose air superiority over and south of the battle area.

R. A. Butler to Winston S. Churchill
(*Premier papers, 11/20*)

30 November 1951

The methods now in force for the control of Civil Service numbers include an arrangement whereby the Treasury fixes a ceiling for each Department, related to a date six months ahead, which the total staff of the Department must not exceed.

I have sent an instruction to all Civil Departments that the total staff now serving in each Department must be taken as the present ceiling for that Department, i.e. no Department may increase its staff beyond the present figure. This is a holding operation while the Treasury work out lower ceilings to be imposed on Departments, to which their staff must be reduced. For the moment I do not need your help in dealing with the staff of the Civil Departments. But I do need your support about the staff of the Service and Supply Departments.

Before the last war these employed 49,000 civil servants. In 1948 the figure was 126,000. Now it is 131,600, within a ceiling of 135,000. But on present trends this total is likely to expand to about 150,000 as the rearmament programme gets under way.

I think it is essential that this process of increasing the civil staffs of the Service Departments should be brought to an end at once. The Departments concerned will resent any stop in their growth, which they say will hamper the rearmament programme. But the Treasury believe that there is ample room for improvement in the use of staffs in these Departments, and that a standstill on the basis of the present numbers, though it would cause some inconvenience, would in the end drive these Departments to make better use of their manpower.

I therefore invite you to send a minute to the Service and Supply Departments making it clear that they must not increase their staffs beyond the figures suggested in the draft minute, which I attach for your consideration. The figures in the draft represent in all cases a small excess over the figures in post on 1st October, 1951.[1]

---

[1] Churchill responded on Dec. 3: 'I really do not think that I should waste my power in calling for this petty reduction. Let us look into this further and cut far deeper' (M.126c/51, *Premier papers, 11/20*).

December 1951

Winston S. Churchill to Sir Norman Brook
Prime Minister's Personal Minute M.127c/51
(Premier papers, 11/136)

1 December 1951

The Cabinet decided last week that careful records were to be made by each department of the position at the date of our taking over, which may be considered as November 1, 1951. It is my intention that these records shall be compiled in a secret Blue book to be kept for reference.

Winston S. Churchill to James Thomas, Antony Head,
Lord De L'Isle and Dudley, and Duncan Sandys
(Premier papers, 11/20)

2 December 1951
Confidential
Draft

The very large numbers of non-industrial staff employed in the Service and Supply Departments taken together, on 1st October, 1951 totalled 131,600 as compared with 59,000 before the war. I am told that on present trends the number is likely to expand to a total of about 150,000.

This growth must stop. I ask you to arrange that the staffs of your Department do not exceed the total on October, 1951 plus a tolerance of a few hundred in each case. (See sheet annexed.)

If any Department is of opinion that staff additions must be made to some particular branch in order to help the rearmament programme, they must first make compensating reductions elsewhere.

Economy in Civil Service staffs must not be met by increasing the numbers of members of the Armed Services employed on office duties.

December 1951

Winston S. Churchill to Harold Parker and Chiefs of Staff
Prime Minister's Personal Minute M.124/51
(Premier papers, 11/66)

3 December 1951

Please have these passages in my speech considered, checked and amplified. Several more items will be coming in but I should like to have your advice so far as I have gone.

2. The first question is whether we can greatly improve the training this year by adding three or four week-days so practically doubling the time available for training without increasing the overheads of disturbance, assembly and departure.

3. The other point about keeping two Territorial Divisions permanently mobilized in this Island in rotation is most important. If this is to be done Cabinet sanction must be obtained before any announcement is made. I might have to have a special Cabinet on Wednesday afternoon as it imposes a heavy burden, perhaps £20 million upon the Chancellor of the Exchequer. I am sure it ought to be done now but it might have to be put off until after Christmas, in which case I would not mention it. I presume it would require legislation. I feel very heavily the responsibility for keeping this country without any strategic reserves. I cannot bear to let the 6th Armoured Division go unless some major formation stands in its place. This really requires hard thought and decision by Wednesday.

Mary Soames to Winston S. Churchill
(Churchill papers, 1/52)

3 December 1951   Chartwell Farm

My darling Papa,

Some little time ago you spoke to us both about the possibility of us staying on here at Chartwell Farm more or less indefinitely. Naturally we were deeply touched and grateful that you should want us to be here now, and later on. But Christopher and I have thought about this very much, and for several reasons we think that we ought not, and cannot think of Chartwell Farm as anything but a perfect and idyllic 'Honeymoon House'.

In the first place, the house is now getting rather small for the needs of a growing family.

But perhaps the most cogent reason of all is that I know we could not live here in the future without causing bitter and disappointed feelings to Randolph. I am not closely intimate with him, but I could not bear for him to feel that we were in any way living where he or little Winston[1] might in the natural course of events hope to live themselves. I am sure that our continuing here would sour our relationship with him, and further embitter an already rather overburdened nature.

Christopher and I have therefore decided that we must now begin to look around in a leisurely and 'choosy' way for a place which we can look upon as our permanent home. (For we are sure that Sheffield Park will be quite out of the question in all events.)

We have not spoken about this to you before because first there was the Election, and now you are beset with so much; and we quite expected that we should not see anything at all suitable for many months. Tomorrow however we are going to see a house near Newmarket, which if it is all it seems from the written details would appear to be our 'dream house', big enough and small enough – elegant and simple – in the country – near Bedford – and we believe a reasonable price.

Mama knows about this – we told her last week. She has even mentioned the Trust perhaps helping us – this of course would be wonderful. Because when we leave the shelter of your wing here we shall of course find it more expensive to live.

Of course all this may come to nothing – but anyway Christopher and I feel we want you to know what is in our mind. I hope and believe you will understand. For both of us it will be a sadness to leave here – and to move further away from you both. For me it will be more than a sadness – it will be an uprooting. But I know we must do it some time.

You have given us a golden start to our married life, and wherever we go and whatever happens to us our years here with you will glow and gleam in our hearts.

And I know that 53 miles will not prevent us from 'invading' you constantly and the 'Chimp'[2] will be by you so much in the House.

---

[1] Winston Spencer-Churchill, 1940–2010. Son of Randolph and Pamela Churchill. Educated at Eton and Christ Church, Oxford. Married, 1964, Mary Caroline 'Minnie' d'Erlanger (div. 1997); 1997, Luce Engelen. A newspaper correspondent from 1963. MP (Cons.) for Stretford, 1970–83; for Davyhulme, 1983–97. Parliamentary Private Secretary to Minister of Housing and Construction, 1970–2; to Minister of State, FCO, 1972–3. A Governor of the English-Speaking Union, 1975–80. Conservative Party front-bench spokesman on defence, 1976–8. Executive Member of 1922 Committee, 1979–85. Member of Select Committee on Defence, 1983–97. Among his published books are *First Journey* (1964); *The Six Day War*, written with his father (1967); *Defending the West* (1981); *Memories and Adventures* (1989); and a biography of his father, *His Father's Son* (1996).

[2] Nickname for Christopher Soames.

Anthony Eden to Winston S. Churchill
(Churchill papers, 2/517)

4 December 1951
PM/51/138

Here is the brief note on the Persian negotiations for which you asked me last week.

PERSIA

The United States Government are still considering Dr Mossadeq's[1] application for financial assistance but have assured us that no early decision is expected. Our views on the effect of United States aid to Persia at this juncture have been made clear to them.

2. The tone of the United States press has recently become much more critical of Dr Mossadeq, and favourable to the United Kingdom viewpoint, than hitherto, and the danger to the West of Persian and Egyptian nationalism seems now better recognized. We have worked hard to bring this about.

Prospects of a Settlement

3. During Dr Mossadeq's visit to Washington, the United States Government had lengthy discussions with him on the terms of a possible settlement of the oil dispute. Although he was evasive and refused to commit himself, the United States Government were sufficiently encouraged to draw up a scheme for a possible settlement and to invite HM Government's comments. After careful consideration we decided that the scheme was not only impracticable but likely to endanger HM Government's vital interests in the Middle East. In the absence of any sign of a change of heart on the part of Dr Mossadeq, the Secretary of State explained to Mr Acheson why we could not accept the American scheme as a basis of negotiation.

4. A more hopeful development has been a suggestion from the International Bank that the Bank should try to make temporary arrangements for the operation of the Persian oil industry pending a final settlement. Both HM Government and the Anglo-Iranian Oil Company see considerable possibilities in the Bank's proposals. The Secretary of State had some discussions in Rome with Mr Garner,[2] Vice President of the Bank. Since then the Cabinet Persia Committee have examined the proposals with Mr Garner and handed him a memorandum commenting on the Bank's proposals (PO(M)(51)6 attached). This memorandum had been agreed with the Anglo-Iranian Oil Company.

[1] Mohammed Mossadeq (or Mossadegh), 1882–1957. Iranian PM, 1951–3. Nationalized Iranian oil industry, 1951. Overthrown by a coup directed by the CIA at the request of MI6 known as Operation Ajax, 1953.
[2] Robert L. Garner, 1894–1975. Educated at Vanderbilt University. Served as Capt. in 305th Infantry, 77th Div., WWI. Vice-President of World Bank, 1947–56. President, International Finance Corp., 1956–61.

5. The Bank's representatives will now be given all factual information they require about the Persian oil industry. It has been made clear to them that the Bank itself will have to decide whether a suitable basis has been found for negotiations with the Persians and on the method and timing of any approach from the Bank to the Persian Government. While, however, it would be their decision, they will ask the Americans and ourselves for advice. It might in any case be advisable to wait until after the Persian elections.

Winston S. Churchill: speech
(Hansard)

6 December 1951

DEFENCE

The Prime Minister (Mr Winston Churchill): Frankly, Mr Deputy-Speaker,[1] looking around the galleries I am sorry that I cannot spy any strangers today, for I think it would have been more useful if we could have had a private talk about our common affairs. But I must also recognise that there is no lack of topics on which public statements can and should be made, and I will address myself to these aspects.

Let me, first of all, make my acknowledgements to the late Government for several most important decisions about our defence policy which they took during their six years of office and which form the foundation on which we stand today. There was the establishment of national compulsory service, now raised to two years, as a feature in our island life, and this was a measure without which our national safety could not probably have been preserved.

The Atlantic Pact and the creation of what, for short, we call NATO was a very great event in which the Leader of the Opposition and the late Mr Bevin played a distinguished part. The tremendous re-armament programme upon which they and the former Minister of Defence led us has enabled us to stand beyond question second only to the United States in our share of the measures upon which our hopes of a lasting peace are based.

The Conservative Party, when in opposition, gave full and constructive support to the Government of the day in all these dominant acts of national policy, and we hope we shall be able to compliment our opponents, or most of them, in their turn on their steadfast perseverance in the courses on which they launched us. These policies do not arise so much from the danger of war

---

[1] Charles Glen MacAndrew, 1888–1979. Educated at Uppingham School and Trinity College, Cambridge. MP (Scottish Unionist) for Kilmarnock, 1924–9; for Glasgow Partick, 1931–5; for Bute and Northern Ayrshire, 1935–59. Deputy Chairman of Ways and Means, 1945, 1950–1; Deputy Speaker of House of Commons and Chairman of Ways and Means, 1951–9. Knighted, 1935. PC, 1952. Baron, 1959.

as from the importance of the free world creating deterrents against aggression, so the theme which His Majesty's Government will pursue and which I will illustrate this afternoon is the idea of deterrents rather than the idea of danger.

Looking back over the last few years, I cannot feel that the danger of a third war is so great now as it was at the time of the Berlin Air Lift crisis in 1948, when the Labour Government, acting in harmony with the United States, and with our full support, took great risks in a firm and resolute manner. Of course, no one can predict the future, but our feeling, on assuming responsibility, is that the deterrents have increased and that, as the deterrents have increased, the danger has become more unlikely; and we should be wise, as a House of Commons, to go on treading the same path in the immediate future with constancy, with hope and, I trust, with a broad measure of unity. That is at any rate the desire and intention of His Majesty's Government.

In saying all this, I have no wish to minimise the important differences of method and execution which exist between us in the sphere of defence. They will have to be argued out by the usual Parliamentary processes, but I should not like to dwell, as I must, on these differences – and they are neither few nor small – without setting things first of all in their broad framework of national agreement.

We must examine promptly but carefully the question of whether we are getting full value in fighting power for the immense sums of money and numbers of men provided for the three fighting Services. For the current year £420 million have been voted for the Army and over 450,000 men, soldiers, stand in uniform today. I recognise the severe strain that has been put upon the War Office by the crisis in Egypt and the Middle East, by Malaya, and by our share in the war in Korea, with its consequential reactions at Hong Kong. There is also the prime need to carry out our agreements under the North Atlantic Treaty for the reinforcement of our troops in Europe.

We found, on taking office, that important increases were contemplated both in money and manpower in the coming year and in those that followed. Before presenting such proposals to the House, we must satisfy ourselves that every possible effort has been used so to organise our forces as to procure a true economy with its twin sister, efficiency. To say such a thing is to utter platitudes. To do them is to render public service. We must ask for a reasonable time to translate words into actions, and in this, as in other matters, we seek to be judged by results.

In military matters, as well as in the economic and financial sphere, we are having a full, detailed statement prepared in every Department of the situation as we found it when we assumed office. In two or three years it will be possible to compare the new position with this record, and this may be of help to the House in forming its opinion of our performances, for good or for ill.

There are many things, one knows, in which improvements can be made.

There are, for instance, no less than 30,000 British troops awaiting orders to move or moving to and fro by land and sea in what is called the pipe-line of our communications. The cost of this movement alone is about £7 million a year. All this is partly due to our being forced to send National Service men to the Far and Middle East, where their tour of duty is necessarily very short. It will be greatly to our advantage to have a higher proportion of young men volunteering for even three years in the Regular Army.

To this end, a scheme has been introduced by the War Office whereby a man may volunteer for a short Regular engagement of three years in the Regular Army, and thus by adding only one year to his National Service liability, he gains the advantage of the higher Regular rate of pay. First indications make it hopeful that this new offer, which was already far advanced when we took over, may prove popular and fruitful.

The Navy Estimates for the current year amount to £278 million, including £30 million for new construction, modernisation and conversion. This is an immense sum. It has also to be noted that nearly 10,000 civilians and 650 naval officers are employed in the Admiralty Departments compared with 4,000 in 1938, when the Navy was larger though, of course, much less complicated than it is at present. I would not pass from the Navy without saying that, as ever, it has played its full part under circumstances most difficult and trying in all the crises of what is called the cold war, whether in Korea or Malaya or the Middle East, and has always gained distinction.

The greatest source of concern in the Services is the slow progress made in developing the Royal Air Force, especially in the supply of the latest machines. To read the complaints that are made about the disappointments experienced in re-equipment, one would hardly believe that over £300 million is being spent this year. I must make it plain that what is being produced today is governed by decisions taken months, and in many cases years, ago. The whole system of supply and production is suffering from what might be described as acute indigestion. The sum of £4,700 million in three years as a plan represented an increased annual rate of expenditure on the Royal Air Force alone of nearly £100 million in the first year and much more in later years.

It is scarcely surprising that at many points, in research as well as production, the aircraft programme is disjointed. We must not forget that the Soviet Air Force is formidable not only in numbers but in quality. The Korean war has proved how good the Russian jet fighter, the MiG-15, is. We must strive to bring to our squadrons aircraft not only as good as but better than those to which they may be opposed. All this, as I have said, is a matter for active and earnest attention, and here again we must be judged by results.

Coming now to more controversial topics, I do not feel there ought to be any great difference between us about the European Army. We are, I believe, most of us agreed that there should be a European Army and that Germany must take an honourable place in it. When I proposed this at Strasbourg

18 months ago I said – perhaps I may be permitted to quote myself when I find it convenient –

> I am very glad that the Germans amid their own problems have come here to share our perils and augment our strength. They ought to have been here a year ago. A year has been wasted, but still it is not too late. There is no revival of Europe, no safety or freedom for any of us except in standing together united and unflinching. I ask this Assembly to assure our German friends that if they throw in their lot with us we shall hold their safety and freedom as sacred as our own.[1]

This assurance has now been formally given by the Allied Governments.

I went on:

> There must be created, and in the shortest possible time, a real defensive front in Europe. Great Britain and the United States must send large forces to the Continent. France must again revive her famous Army. We welcome our Italian comrades. All – Greece, Turkey, Holland, Belgium, Luxemburg, the Scandinavian States – must bear their share and do their best.

We seem to have made good progress since then. General Eisenhower is in supreme command on the Continent. All the Powers mentioned have contributed, or are contributing, or are about to contribute, contingents and many of their contingents are growing. The front is not covered yet. The potential aggressor has a vast superiority of numbers. Nevertheless, the gathering of our deterrents has been continued. As things have developed, my own ideas have always been as follows. There is the NATO Army. Inside the NATO Army there is the European Army, and inside the European Army there is the German Army. The European Army should be formed by all the European parties to NATO dedicating from their own national armies their quota of divisions to the Army or Armies now under General Eisenhower's command.

At Strasbourg in 1950 the Germans did not press for a national army. On the contrary, they declared themselves ready to join a European Army without having a national army. Dr Adenauer has renewed to us this assurance, and that is still the German position and their preference – no national army. This is a very great and helpful fact which we must all take into consideration. The size and strength of any German army, whether contingent or otherwise, and its manufacture of weapons, would in any case have to be agreed between the Allied Powers concerned. There, in short, is the policy which I have always advocated and which I am very glad to find is steadily going forward.

Difficulties have, however, arisen about the texture of the European Army. Should it be an amalgam of the European nations divested of all national characteristics and traditions, or should it be composed of elements essentially

---

[1] Speech of 11 Aug. 1950, reproduced in *The Churchill Documents*, vol. 22, *Leader of the Opposition, August 1945 to October 1951*, pp. 1827–32.

national but woven together by alliance, common organisation and unified command? On this point the discussions have at times assumed an almost metaphysical character, and the logic of continental minds has produced a scheme for what is called the European Defence Community. That is, at least, an enlightened if not an inspiring title. The European Defence Force, which is to be a vital element in the defence of Western Europe, will be closely and effectively associated with the British Forces which constitute another element in the same defence system through their common allegiance to NATO.

The European Defence Community has not yet taken its final shape. The Paris Conference has been sitting for nine months, and it is now on the point of producing its Report. I am sorry the late Government did not send a delegation to this Conference instead of only an observer. The technical discussions have proceeded smoothly and in great detail, and at last the far-reaching political issues which have been raised and which surround the military questions have been reached. We do not know how these will be settled, and we have had no voice or share in the long argument. As soon as the Conference reaches its final conclusions we shall consider the way to establish the most effective form of association with the resultant organisations. In this way a European Army, containing a German contribution of agreed size and strength, will stand alongside the British and United States Armies in a common defensive front. That, after all, is what really matters to the life or death of the free world.

As far as Britain is concerned, we do not propose to merge in the European Army but we are already joined to it. Our troops are on the spot, and we shall do our utmost to make a worthy and effective contribution to the deterrents against aggression and to the causes of freedom and democracy which we seek to serve. These matters will, of course, require to be further discussed as the weeks pass by, and we shall probably know much more about what is the decision taken on the Continent than we can attempt to anticipate and imagine at this moment.

What I have called the most formidable step taken by the late Government was the establishment in July, 1948, of the great and ever-growing American air base in East Anglia for using the atomic weapon against Soviet Russia should the Soviets become aggressors. As in the other great measures of national defence taken by the Labour Government, we supported this policy. I have on several occasions pointed out to the House the gravity of the late Government's decision and have quoted publicly the expression used in Soviet publications that our island had become an aircraft carrier. Certainly we must recognise that the step then taken by the right hon. Gentleman the Leader of the Opposition places us in the front line should there be a third World War. The measure adds to the deterrents against war, but it may throw the brunt on to us should war come.

Mr Sydney Silverman[1] (Nelson and Colne) rose.

The Prime Minister: We shall not flinch from the duty which Britain has accepted, but we should never let the facts pass from our minds, so that they govern our actions.

Mr Silverman rose.

The Prime Minister: I was not making any attack on the hon. Gentleman.

Mr C. R. Attlee (Walthamstow, West): I am not quite sure exactly what the right hon. Gentleman means. We certainly agreed to the stationing of American bombers in this country as part of Atlantic defence, but it was never put forward specifically as a base for using the atomic bomb against Russia. We never suggested it.

The Prime Minister: That is the impression which, however mistakenly, they seem to have derived.

Mr Attlee: The right hon. Gentleman must be very careful about this. We have had conversations. The Americans have no illusions whatever as regards our position in this matter.

The Prime Minister: I am very well informed about it, and I have not said anything this afternoon that I have not frequently said in public before. I think it is absolutely necessary that the House should realise the serious effects to which the course of events and the policy of the party opposite, which we have supported and shared, have brought us. It is no use going on blinking at the great underlying realities of the position.

Mr Silverman rose.

The Prime Minister: I really would like to be allowed to make my speech. The hon. Gentleman is very skilled at interruptions of all kinds –

Mr Silverman: I do not intend to do anything like that.

The Prime Minister: Usually interruptions ought to be limited to questions where a misunderstanding has been created.

Mr Silverman: I think this is one. I think this is one. I think this is one.

The Prime Minister: All right.

Mr Silverman: I only want to ask the right hon. Gentleman – and I shall quite understand it if he feels unable to answer – whether he could at this point answer the Question which stood on the Order Paper, addressed to him today, namely, whether the effect of this agreement for bombers on our shores would not have the result of removing from our control the question of whether we were to take part or not to take part in any war in which the United States happened to be involved. Does it not make us, therefore, a belligerent unless the agreement contains a provision for their removal at our request?

The Prime Minister: I thought the hon. Gentleman was going to raise a point arising from the course of the debate, but it appears that he only wants

---

[1] Samuel Sydney Silverman, 1895–1968. MP (Lab.) for Nelson and Colne, 1935–68. Member of Parliamentary delegation to Buchenwald Concentration Camp, 1945. Chairman of World Jewish Congress.

to get a Question which he put on the Paper, and which was not reached today, answered by a different method. He will see the reply to the Question when it is circulated in the ordinary course.

This brings me to the strength of the Forces we have in this country, as I found them on becoming responsible. Practically all our Regular formations have been sent to the Army in Europe or are engaged in distant theatres. The facts are, of course, already known to foreign countries, and the Communists have particular advantages in gathering information in many countries.

I have spoken before of the danger of paratroop descents on a considerable scale, and everything I have learned since assuming office convinces me of the need to accumulate deterrents against this particular form of attack, for this reason. We have taken the first steps to re-establish the network of the Home Guard units throughout the country, and we have already permitted the raising of a proportion of the Home Guard in the south-eastern part of England. The Royal Observer Corps is being strengthened, and we have decided to set up and begin the recruiting next year of a Royal Naval mine-watching organisation.

Moreover, I have given directions that the numerous Regular military establishments in this country which contain a very large number of men – nearly 250,000 – the training schools, depots and other units, should acquire an immediate combatant value. They must be armed and ready to defend themselves, and not only themselves, in an emergency. Arrangements are being made for their use away from their local centres, as far as other reasons and mobility permits. It is a mistake to keep so many thousands of our men in uniform without their playing a direct part in our safety.

These measures are not particularly costly. The cost is the men, and here again we are in the field of deterrents. Our country should suggest to the mind of a potential paratrooper the back of a hedgehog rather than the paunch of a rabbit. We shall have next year to repeat the process adopted last year by our predecessors of calling up a proportion of the 'Z' reservists in order to enable a number of Territorial divisions, antiaircraft and other specialist units to be assembled and exercised. The results were more valuable than I had expected from such a very short period of effective training. At any rate, there was the sense of assembly and incorporation in the regimental units.

Thanks to the National Service Measures of the late Government we have a reserve of trained manhood, now beginning to flow from two years' service in the Army, of a quality and character superior to anything we have ever had before in time of peace. This enables us to raise our Territorial divisions on mobilisation far more quickly and to a quality far in advance of anything that was previously possible in former periods. The reserve is only just beginning to come to us in strength, and we should indeed be failing in our duty if we did not take the necessary and consequential steps to secure full value in deterrent resources from the cost and sacrifice which two years' compulsory service involves.

Growth and efficiency of the Territorial Army and of its speedy mobilisation in an emergency is essential to repair the inroads upon our strategic resources from which we suffer today. The House will no doubt wish to know more precisely the detailed conditions of the call-up. The Government proposes that the provisions of the Reserve and Auxiliary Forces (Training) Act, 1951, should be applied again in 1952, and the necessary Affirmative Resolution will be introduced immediately after the Recess.

Mr E. Shinwell[1] (Easington): Can the right hon. Gentleman say for how long?

The Prime Minister: Just a little patience, and the right hon. Gentleman's natural interest will be satisfied.

In the case of the Army, this training will be on the same lines as it was this year, and it will involve the recall for 15 days' training of up to 250,000 men, mainly 'Z' reservists. I agree I wish it could be longer than 15 days. Another three or four working days would add greatly to the value of it, without any marked addition to the cost. Then there is the effect that might be produced upon the permanent cadres of the Territorial volunteers, to whom we already owe so much. I did not appreciate that fact fully, but I do now and I have to consider it. I wish indeed that we could have a longer period for considering the cost involved, but I think it would be imprudent at this stage to run the risk of making the voluntary service which the Territorial Army bears so heavy a burden. The majority of the men will be trained in the units which they will attend in the event of an emergency, and the remainder, including up to 3,000 officers and certain specialists, will undergo particular courses of refresher training.

The Royal Air Force will be calling up 5,500 men of their equivalent class 'G' reserve. The Royal Navy will continue the call-up of members of the Royal Fleet Reserves for service on a small scale.

Now I come to the other side. I have been dealing with the personnel aspects, and I come now to the other side of the re-armament plans, namely, the manufacture in this country of munitions and military supplies of all kinds. I found on taking over that, under the increased programme of £4,700 million, we were committed to an expenditure in the present year of up to £1,250 million, and, in 1952–53, on the basis of 1950 prices, which have since been exceeded, to a further £1,500 million.

We shall not, however, succeed in spending the £1,250 million this year,

---

[1] Emanuel Shinwell, 1884–1986. MP (Lab.) for Linlithgowshire, 1922–4, 1928–31; for Seaham, 1935–50; for Easington, 1950–70. Parliamentary Secretary, Mines Dept, 1924, 1930–1; Minister of Fuel and Power, 1945–7; Secretary of State for War, 1947–50; Minister of Defence, 1950–1. Labour Party Chairman, 1964–7. Baron, 1970.

and some of the late Government's programme must necessarily roll forward into a future year. This point was, I believe, made by the right hon. Gentleman the Member for Ebbw Vale (Mr Bevan)[1] after his resignation. I do not reproach the late Government on this score. They tried their best to carry out what they had declared was necessary for our safety. I have never yet seen a munitions programme – and I have seen several – which did not lag behind the plans. This will, of course, be helpful to my right hon. Friend the Chancellor of the Exchequer in his special problems.

We must, however, be careful to distinguish between reductions in expenditure which are due to *bona fide* economies, or to improved methods of using available forces, and those reductions which merely push payments forward to a later date. A very careful scrutiny is being made over the whole field of this immense new re-armament programme of the late Government in all its main aspects, and many of these items will be reviewed in the light of changing events. This process must be highly selective, so that we get first what we need most and in order that bottle-necks of any kind are eliminated. It is perfectly clear that, in the sphere of the material needs, the claims of the Royal Air Force must have first and special emphasis and priority. This will be made fully effective in any rearrangement of the programme upon which we may decide.

I have been trying to show –

Mr Aneurin Bevan (Ebbw Vale): Will the right hon. Gentleman give way? He has made an exceedingly important statement, the effect of which, as I understand it, is that it will not be found possible to spend the £4,700 million in the three years. (Hon. Members: 'No.') That is the effect of his statement. (Hon. Members: 'No.') It is really no use his trying to conceal this intention behind a mass of verbiage. If this first programme is not to be accomplished, then the second year's programme and the arrears of the first year's programme will not be carried out, unless the period is more than three years. Am I, therefore, to understand that the Government has abandoned the three-year period and has added some unknown period to the length of the rearmament programme?

The Prime Minister: As events develop, the right hon. Gentleman will no doubt watch them with attention, and the discussions which, from time to time, he will have with his former colleagues will no doubt be both instructive and animated on both sides. (Hon. Members: 'Answer.') I am not really wishing to embark on a debate with the right hon. Gentleman. I was giving him an honourable mention in despatches for having, by accident –

Mr Bevan rose.

---

[1] Aneurin Bevan, 1897–1960. Known as 'Nye'. Coal miner from the age of 13. Miners' Disputes Agent, 1926. MP (Lab.) for Ebbw Vale, 1929–60. Required, 1944, to give Labour Party a written assurance of loyalty or be expelled. As Minister of Health, 1945–51, introduced National Health Service. Minister of Labour and National Service, 1951; resigned in protest against defence spending and NHS charges. Treasurer of Labour Party and Deputy Leader of Opposition, 1956–60. His often acerbic manner caused Churchill to dub him a 'merchant of discourtesy'.

December 1951

Mr Deputy-Speaker (Colonel Sir Charles MacAndrew): If the Prime Minister does not give way, hon. and right hon. Gentlemen must resume their seats.

The Prime Minister: I will give way in a moment. I was giving the right hon. Gentleman an honourable mention for having, it appears by accident, perhaps not from the best of motives, happened to be right.

Mr Bevan: As the right hon. Gentleman knows, when the statement on rearmament was made in the House of Commons by myself when Minister of Labour, I said, and the Prime Minister also said, that it may not be found possible, because of the shortage of raw materials and the lack of machine tools, to carry out the £4,700 million programme. The right hon. Gentleman ought to try to be honest about this programme. Now, what period has he, in fact, substituted for the three years?

The Prime Minister: We shall get on as best we can. We shall do our best, but I should be wrong not to warn the House that there will be a lag, as there has been in all the munitions programmes which I have ever seen or with which I have been connected.

So far, I have been endeavouring to allay controversy and hasty feelings in every direction. I have, indeed, paid many compliments to the Front Bench opposite and some other quarters and so on, but now I come to two issues which are controversial in this House.

Great Britain requires a pool of three million or four million rifles – that is what I am coming to – with the proportionate ammunition and supply arrangements. At the end of the war, we had over five million rifles; we have got less than half of that now. The causes for this are being examined. The Army of a major Power must live under a large body of rifles, because exceptional needs cannot be foreseen and the wastage of rifles in war is very high. The only other large pools in the United Nations are the United States, Canada and France.

Our annual rate of rifle production is not large, nor is it easily expanded. In 1941, for instance, after two years of war and bombing, we had only managed to make about 200,000 rifles. The changeover from one pattern of rifle to another must, therefore, be a very lengthy process, which could not be even partially effective in under six or seven years. During this period, an additional burden would be placed on our resources of labour and materials, already so heavily strained, if there were two kinds of rifles in the British Forces. We cannot abandon the manufacture of one kind until we have enough to get on with of the other.

A decision to re-arm with the new rifle is one of high policy, involving the world situation and the position of our Allies. Standardisation, not only of rifles, but of other weapons, must be regarded as a cardinal principle and aim among the Atlantic Powers. It can, of course, only be attained gradually. A marked departure from this principle in, say, small arms would prolong for many years the existing inconvenient differences of weapons, bore and ammunition. Every effort should therefore be made, in changes which can take place only so very slowly, to achieve agreement and convergence of thought on new types.

Now I come to the proposed new British .280 rifle, which can only be rightly considered in the setting I have described. It may well be that we have now the best rifle and ammunition yet made. The hon. Member for Aston (Mr Wyatt[1]) urged me to go and see it for myself. I can assure him I followed his request, and I have had the opportunity of firing both the British and American weapons. I do not pose as a technical expert in these matters at all, but I will say that these are matters of technical dispute. Great credit in any case is due to the designers and all concerned with the creation of this weapon and also with the cartridge. I never argued against the quality of the rifle.

We have at present 20 of these rifles, not 20,000, and if the re-tooling, etc. of our factories is carried out on the plans proposed by the late Government we could begin production in 1953, and by the end of 1954 we should be producing at the rate of about 100,000 a year. But the pool we should like to swim in would be over 2 million. This production would, at a time when we are so short of skilled labour, be additional, as I have just pointed out, to the indispensable maintenance of the .303 as the only weapon we can have in large numbers for a long time.

Mr Shinwell: As a point of elucidation, when the right hon. Gentleman refers to the .303, does he mean the existing American rifle, or the proposed one?

The Prime Minister: I was speaking of the British .303. The American is called a .300. It is not exactly that, but it is called that. We cannot leave our pool and cease to replenish that pool until we have got something very considerable to go to. Therefore, we have to keep the two together.

The Americans are also seeking a replacement for their present Garand rifle, of which they have a large pool. They also seek for an improvement in the cartridge, which again entails great changes in the design. But none of these changes will affect the military position substantially in the next three or four years. They are long-term projects, and a further effort should be made to secure their harmonious evolution among allies and thus prevent new rifts of organisation being opened up in the common front, and especially between Britain and Canada who, I hope, will move in unity in standardisation. It is in the light of these considerations that a final decision should not be taken

---

[1] Woodrow Lyle Wyatt, 1918–97. Educated at Eastbourne College and Worcester College, Oxford. Married, 1939, Susan Cox (div. 1944); 1948, Nora Robbins (div. 1957); 1957, Moorea Hastings : one child (div. 1966); 1966, Veronica Banszky von Ambroz: one child. Dispatch officer in WWII, 1939–45. Maj., 1944. MP (Lab.) for Birmingham Aston, 1945–55; for Bosworth, Leicester, 1959–70. Contributor to *Daily Mirror*, 1965–73; to *Sunday Mirror*, 1973–83. Knighted, 1983. Baron, 1987.

hastily. Indeed, I think it is our duty on both sides of the Atlantic to make new efforts to harmonise our long-term policy, and I propose to persevere in this and I trust that we may reach a good decision.

Mr Woodrow Wyatt (Birmingham, Aston): May I ask the right hon. Gentleman whether, while this decision is being made, he is now going to stop the preparations which are being made to put the .280 rifle into production or not, because if a final decision is made that we should go ahead with it, it is very important not to stop all the preparatory work now going on?

The Prime Minister: If the hon. Gentleman had followed what I said he would have noted that I pointed out that production would not begin until the end of 1953 and that it would not reach 100,000 a year until the end of 1954. Obviously, a few months one way or another in trying to reach a general agreement would not be wasted. I do not propose at this moment to go forward with the re-tooling until we have had some further talks about it and to see more surely where we stand.

Mr Shinwell: Does not the right hon. Gentleman realise that if we do not proceed to production of the new rifle and ammunition at a fairly early stage, we have either to rely on the existing British rifle and go on increasing production of it – a rifle which is now regarded as out of date – or accept the existing American pattern which is regarded by them as being out of date?

The Prime Minister: I was not thinking of accepting the existing American pattern at all, but we have to go on with our existing rifle until we reach a conclusion about a new rifle, which I hope may be reached with common agreement between all the Powers concerned. At any rate, I would not give that up for the sake of beginning two or three months earlier. I am not at all sure it is in our interest to embark single-handed on a lonely venture, even if that rifle is better than others put before us. At any rate, this is not a matter which can be said to be urgent as it will not affect our position for a good many years to come.

I now come to another controversial matter. I am not at present, as the House knows, convinced of the need for a Supreme Commander in the Atlantic. The question of the nationality of the commander is secondary once the need is proved. I should have thought that the method which was successful during our six years of struggle with the U-boats in the last war, with any improvements which experience may suggest, would have sufficed.

The essence is that the British Admiralty should have complete control of direction of the reception end of trans-Atlantic convoys and shipping. This ought to be managed by the First Sea Lord through his handling machine at Liverpool. The integrity of the management from hour to hour at the reception end is the key to the whole process by which any trans-Atlantic or British Armies can be landed or maintained in Western Europe. It is also the foundation of the process by which 50 million people in the British Isles have been kept alive in the teeth of the U-boat and the mining menace.

It is not a question of national pride, but a question of a good working arrangement on which victory and also life would in certain circumstances depend. As long as complete control of the approaches and reception end is exercised by the Admiralty from this small island all the rest of the problems can be solved. But conflict or duality of control on the command level or between a Supreme Commander and the Admiralty might very well be injurious. The British Admiralty and the United States and Canadian naval chiefs should work together as they always did, and any question of transference of Forces which could not be settled between the respective Admiralties could be adjusted, as they always were, at a higher level.

I am very glad that the United States should come as far east as they propose provided that the management of the reception end is unimpaired. It does not seem also – but this is a technical point – that the definition of coastal waters around Great Britain which has been agreed upon is satisfactory. The 100-fathom limit should be examined as an alternative. There should, moreover, of course, be no question of treating the Bay of Biscay differently from any other part of the approaches to this island or Western Europe.

The problem must be solved as a whole, and I have no doubt it can be by further friendly discussions. It is certainly not solved now. I hope that we may reach some conclusions which will, without offending national pride on either side of the Atlantic, have the effect of enabling us to do the work, for which we have unequalled experience and expert knowledge, of bringing safely in to the Western shores the aid and supplies that come from across the Atlantic Ocean.

There are only one or two points to which I must refer. Statements have appeared in the Press suggesting that we contemplate widespread departures in the policy of manufacturing atomic bombs. Two years ago I commented unfavourably on the fact that the Socialist Government had not been able to make a specimen atomic bomb although they had been trying to do so for four years. When we came into office, we found that a great deal of work had been done, not only on making the crucial materials required for making atomic bombs, but in preparing to manufacture these weapons. I think the House ought to know about that. Considerable if slow progress has been made.

The House will realise that this is not the moment to discuss the British research and manufacture of atomic bombs in detail. All that I will say is that we have taken over the very costly production of the Socialist Government. We have not decided on any important change in policy or principle. We hope, however, in this as in other matters, by different methods of organisation and administration to effect some improvements, and there are certain aspects of this delicate subject which I hope we may clarify by discussions with the United States authorities.

Dull tragedy rolls forward in Malaya. The first thought of the Secretary of State for the Colonies on being appointed was to go to Malaya, the black spot in his Department. No decision can be taken until after his return. It is becoming painfully evident that there must be one mind with effective power over the administration in all its branches, including particularly the military and the police.

Some brutal statistics may in the meanwhile be presented to the House. We have in Malaya over 25,000 British troops, over 10,000 Gurkhas, and over 7,000 other soldiers. Added to this there are 60,000 local police in different stages of armament and many part-time auxiliaries. Thus the whole amounts to over 100,000 men employed in a most costly manner. The total expense of the Fighting Forces is nearly £50 million a year, quite apart from any other emergency expenses falling upon the Malayan Government.

We are also suffering heavy loss in the restriction through terrorism of our tin mines and rubber plantations. It is said that the bandits, or whatever they should be called, number 3,000 to 5,000, and I do not suppose that their maintenance cost is comparably at all heavy. Certainly it seems some improvement should be made in this theatre of tragedy and waste, but we had better wait before debating the subject until the Secretary of State comes home when we can weigh and measure the report which he will make.

I have nothing to add to the statements which have been made to the House about the position in Egypt and Korea. In Korea we all hope that the armistice negotiations will reach agreement and that this agreement will lead to a wider settlement in the country. In Egypt and the Suez Canal we stand by the Four Power proposals for the organisation of the defence of the Middle East and the safeguarding of the international waterway, and we hope eventually to associate the other countries in the area with the Four Powers in their joint task.

In the meanwhile we shall do our duty in accordance with our Treaty rights in the Canal Zone, and we hope for an increasing measure of aid from the Egyptian Government in preventing mob violence and other forms of lawless and murderous attack. We believe our Forces in the Canal Zone, or within reach of it, are strong enough for any work they may have to do. We welcome the fact that good relations prevail between them and the Egyptian Army. Everyone would like to see a speedy and friendly settlement, but there are some problems in which time is a potent factor. We certainly propose to use it with patience as well as with firmness.

I have now covered, so far as I wish to at the moment, the immense variety of events in the world-wide scene which spreads around us. I have tried to do justice to those large issues in which we are in agreement with the policy pursued by the late Government. I have also tried to emphasise the urgent need of a complete and searching examination and review and, where necessary, the recasting of methods by which right decisions in major policy have been impaired by wrong methods or faulty execution.

The process of examining the enormous expenditure on defence in all its forms in order while doing our duty to spend this money and spend the rest more effectively will continue without rest or pause until we meet again. I hope then, with the help of the Ministers responsible for the Service Departments, to be able to make a more precise and definite statement than it is possible for me to do after only six weeks' examination of this immense and tangled field.

[. . .]

The Prime Minister: May I ask the indulgence of the House to intervene for a very few moments before my right hon. Friend the Secretary of State for War replies to the particular questions that have been asked?

I should not like – if the House would permit me – the speech of the late Minister of Defence[1] to go without its due and proper acknowledgement from this side of the House. We have our party battles and bitterness, and the great balance of the nation is maintained to some extent by our quarrels, but I have always felt and have always testified, even in moments of party strife, to the right hon. Gentleman's sterling patriotism and to the fact that his heart is in the right place where the life and strength of our country were concerned.

Tonight, he has made a speech which was the most statesmanlike, if he will allow me to say so, as I have heard him make in this House in these days that we have gone through. He has surveyed the whole field in terms from which I do not think we should differ.

We have our differences, and, when we were in Opposition, it was our duty to point out the things that we thought were not done right, and it is equally his duty, and that of those who sit with him, to subject us to an equally searching examination. I am so glad to be able to say tonight, in these very few moments, that the spirit which has animated the right hon. Gentleman in the main discharge of his great duties was one which has, in peace as well as in war, added to the strength and security of our country.

Anthony Eden to Winston S. Churchill
(*Churchill papers, 2/517*)

6 December 1951
Secret
PM/51/143

General Eisenhower telephoned to me at lunch-time today to say that when in Rome he had made plain to me that he did not expect us to play a direct part within the proposed European Defence Community. At the same time, he did hope that we would do all we could to encourage the others in it to get on with the job. From what some French Ministers had said to him lately, they were now arguing that not only were we not in the plan, but that we did not want it.

[1] Emanuel Shinwell.

2. Anything you could say to counteract this, and any encouragement you could give to closer union on the European Continent in general, would be most helpful.

3. I mentioned to General Eisenhower our contemplated visit to Paris. He was delighted and he said he could imagine nothing more useful at this moment.

David Hunt: recollection
('On the Spot', pages 71–3)

7 December 1951

One of the first speeches that I heard him make in the House after becoming Prime Minister has stuck in my mind, not because it was particularly eloquent but because it illustrates another of Churchill's qualities: his magnanimity, combined with good nature and a sense of fairness. It is not likely to find a place in a Churchillian anthology, in fact it is a rare example of a speech entirely unprepared; but I found it both just and moving, and an illumination of the spirit of British parliamentarianism. I had accompanied him to the House for a debate on Defence on 6 December 1951. I sat in the officials' box to hear him make the opening speech, so that I could check it against the prepared text, and remained until the end in case he wanted information in a hurry. He was at that time still Minister of Defence, an office he had assumed, with fond memories of 1940, as soon as he became Prime Minister. The closing speech for the opposition was made by his Labour predecessor, Emanuel Shinwell (now Lord Shinwell). Just before Antony Head, Secretary of State for War, rose to wind up the debate for the Government I was surprised to see the Prime Minister on his feet again. Having asked the indulgence of the House for speaking twice he said:

> I should not like – if the House would permit me – the speech of the late Minister of Defence to go without its due and proper acknowledgement from this side of the House. [. . .][1]

The house was stirred. Going back in the car to Number 10 after the debate ended Churchill harked back to the subject. 'I am glad I said that about Shinwell,' he said, 'he well deserved it. There's a lot of good in that Shinwell. He's a real patriot. During the war he and Bevan' – and he laid a thunderous emphasis on the second syllable, to be sure of distinguishing his aversion from the admired Ernest Bevin – 'were more or less playing the part of the opposition, but I always said there was a great difference between them. When things were going badly for us that Be-van used to look quite pleased

[1] Speech reproduced above (pp. 94–108).

but Shinwell looked miserable. Yes, there's a lot of good in Shinwell, and I'm glad I took the chance of saying something about him.' This assessment of the late Labour Minister of Defence was, as a matter of fact, quite in line with official opinion, but I found it engaging and instructive that the leader of the Conservative Party was prepared to acknowledge it both privately and publicly. Next morning there was a gracefully-expressed note of thanks from Shinwell, and the first trickle of what became a flood of protests from Conservatives. Churchill had no doubt borne in mind but disregarded the fact that at that time Shinwell was a great bugbear of the party having made, while still in office before the election, a very provocative remark about them which had featured in many large headlines. For the next week or so the letters of complaint continued to arrive, from individuals and from local branches of the party, some violent and some plaintive, as though the writers could not imagine how their hero had fallen into this strange error. Churchill was robustly impenitent, and the more that people protested the more certain he felt that he had spoken well.

Cabinet: conclusions
(Cabinet papers, 128/23)

7 December 1951 Prime Minister's Room, House of Commons
Secret
12 p.m.
Cabinet Meeting No. 15 of 1951

[...]
2. The Prime Minister said that his attention had recently been drawn to the fact that the cost of using the SS *Gothic* for the forthcoming Royal Visit to Australia and New Zealand was likely to total £1,100,000. The cost of hiring the vessel would be about £600,000. The cost of converting it, and re-converting it after the end of the Visit, had originally been estimated by the Admiralty at £139,000, but this estimate had been progressively increased and now stood at £550,000. It had been suggested that the Governments of Australia and New Zealand should be asked whether they were willing to bear some part of this expenditure.

After discussion it was agreed that it would be inexpedient to suggest to the two other Commonwealth Governments at this stage that they should bear a share of this cost. The Cabinet considered, however, that on the occasion of Royal Visits in the future the question of sharing the cost should be raised at the outset with the other Commonwealth Government or Governments concerned.

Ministers also expressed concern about the extent to which the cost of the work on the SS *Gothic* had exceeded the original estimate.

The Cabinet –
- (1) Agreed that the Governments of Australia and New Zealand should not at this stage be asked to bear any part of the cost of using the SS *Gothic* for the Royal Visit.
- (2) Invited the First Lord of the Admiralty to establish by means of a formal inquiry the reasons for the heavy expenditure involved in the use of the SS *Gothic* for the Royal Visit, and to report the results of this inquiry to the Cabinet.

3. The Cabinet considered a memorandum by the Foreign Secretary (C(51)40) on the situation in Egypt.

The Foreign Secretary said that the Commanders-in-Chief had asked for powers to detain, to try and to punish Egyptian terrorists in the Canal Zone. The grant of the full powers for which they had asked was likely to lead to the establishment of Military Government in the area, and this would give rise to the serious difficulties outlined in paragraph 6 of his memorandum. He therefore recommended that the Commanders-in-Chief should be authorized to detain Egyptian terrorists indefinitely, but should not for the present be empowered to try or to punish them. Administrative preparations should, however, be made for the introduction of Military Government in the Canal Zone; and, if the situation had not improved by the time these preparations were completed, a stern warning could then be given to the King of Egypt that drastic measures might have to be taken.

The Foreign Secretary also recommended that the Cabinet should not authorize the application of economic sanctions to Egypt, and, in particular, that the existing restrictions on the movement of oil from Suez to Cairo should not be increased.

The Cabinet were informed that the Chiefs of Staff supported the recommendations made in C(51)40. In addition, however, they recommended that the Commanders-in-Chief should be authorised to disarm Egyptian police, if they thought that the local situation demanded it.

The Cabinet were also informed that the Egyptian Government were now withdrawing all Egyptian officers from military courses in this country. It was suggested that it might have a salutary effect on the Egyptian Government if Egyptian officers were invited to withdraw from military courses in the United States. This suggestion might be made to the United States Government and any other of our friends who had Egyptian officers under training.

The Cabinet –
- (1) Approved the recommendations in paragraph 11 of C(51)40.
- (2) Invited the Chiefs of Staff to instruct the Commanders-in-Chief, Middle East, in the terms proposed in paragraph 10 (a) and (b) of C(51)40 and, in addition, to inform them that they were authorised in the last resort to disarm Egyptian police if they considered that the local situation made this necessary.

(3) Invited the Foreign Secretary to suggest to the United States Government that they might demand the withdrawal of Egyptian students from military courses in the United States, and to make a similar suggestion to any other friendly country in which Egyptian officers were now undergoing military training.

[. . .]

Winston S. Churchill: speech
(Churchill papers, 2/336)

7 December 1951   Harrow School

I have always taken a liking for this song 'The Island' (but I had forgotten all about it, and when eleven years ago – that is to say the twelfth occasion when I have been here – when eleven years ago I came here in 1940 I asked that it should be sung; but it could not be found, or at any rate not in time) because of these words at the end of the verse about the Spanish Armada:

But snug in her hive, the Queen was alive,
And Buzz was the word in the Island.

These were the days when 'buzz' was the word in the island; and if Dibdin[1] had been alive he could easily have put in another verse to his long story of our history. A great writer Dibdin. There is a whole book of his poems which will repay study. Very few people know the words of 'Rule Britannia'. I remember going on board a ship in the war, at Arromanches, and not one of them knew the words. If they had been Harrow boys they would have known the words; they would have known a lot of words. I do try to press on you the great attractive value of your songs. Not only do they bring you all together, but the words of Bowen[2] and Howson[3] have a beautiful simplicity and expression, a correct choice and balance combined with fine simple thought. All these songs constitute one of the greatest possessions that any famous school or community can have and one of the means by which life is prolonged – its collective life is prolonged – from one generation to another. I thank you very much always for letting me come and for singing to me so beautifully. And I thought our substitute, who filled the gap in an emergency, was magnificent, if he will allow me to say so. He must have felt 500 faces or more found him, and he did full justice to the occasion.

Now I should like to say to you that this is the twelfth time I have been here

[1] Thomas John Dibdin, 1771–1841. Actor, dramatist, and songwriter.
[2] Edward Ernest Bowen, 1836–1901. Asst master at Marlborough College, 1858. Master at Harrow School, 1859–1901. Wrote the Harrow school song, 'Forty Years On' (1872) and *Harrow Songs and Other Verses* (1886).
[3] Edmund Whytehead Howson, 1855–1905. Schoolmaster at Harrow.

and the tenth I have had the pleasure of being here as the Head Master's guest. It is a long time you know. We shall be becoming four-yearers three times over. School life is short compared with these twelve times I have come here. As you know, for a long time at the beginning of the War I was Prime Minister and then I had a long holiday and you were always very kind to me then and looked after me and let me come down and sang to me to while away the time. Now the term has begun again, a very severe and hard term, I can assure you. The hours are very long, the lessons are very hard. The arithmetic – that two and two make four, that one – and also the subtraction, are very very hard indeed; and we do not know quite, yet, what form the examinations will take. But they are going to be most severe examinations, not only into the performance of our predecessors but also into our own performance. We earnestly hope to pass the examination by a lot of swotting, if that is the right word. I must not say 'sapping' here for that is the Eton word. No toil and labour and effort we can give will be grudged. We shall 'tolly-up' (I beg your pardon) so far as is allowed by the regulations and we shall do our utmost, by every means which honour and fair play allows, to show up favourably in our papers at the examination; and not only to show up good papers, but to have the brains and wits behind to enable us to give good guidance when we go out into the world.

We have had our electioneering. Now we are trying to get together because we are one country in a very great and anxious situation, with fifty million people living in this small island and only growing a little more than half, say three-fifths, of our food; and everyone in whose veins British blood flows must make it the purpose of his life to see that we remain a free, progressive, cultured community, with a chance for all, fair play for all, moving forward into future generations and able to hold our own with independent force and strength in the vast world which grows up every year around us.

I thank you very much for singing to me tonight, I have enjoyed it very much indeed and I shall now return to my work of preparation for the examination which I mentioned to you.

Now we have a special *exeat*, yes an *exeat*, a few weeks' holiday at Christmas, and we shall return from that I am sure refreshed and braced. You will have a holiday, too, but I hope you will not have half as many holiday tasks as we shall have to do in ours.

James Thomas to Winston S. Churchill
(Premier papers, 11/64)

7 December 1951

The Service Ministers have decided that it would be useful for them to meet together from time to time to discuss non-operational matters on which co-ordinated Ministerial views are needed. In this way we hope to save much correspondence by settling the smaller issues among ourselves or by clarifying the larger ones before presenting them to you.

We aim to have the first of such meetings next week. Others will take place as business requires.

I thought you would wish to know of this arrangement.

Winston S. Churchill to Paul Reynaud
(*Premier papers, 11/73*)

7 December 1951
Private

Dear Monsieur Reynaud,

Thank you very much for your letter of November 29.[1]

You will by now perhaps have seen the statement I made in Parliament yesterday. You were also well aware of my views from our private talks in Paris. I have never contemplated the abolition of the French Army. On this you should see my speech in moving the resolution at Strasbourg to which you have referred; 'France must revive again her famous Army.' We must not lose sight of the military realities.

Winston S. Churchill to R. A. Butler
Prime Minister's Personal Minute M.133c/51
(*Premier papers, 11/132*)

7 December 1951

Could you let me have a brief interim report on what has happened at your Financial Committees? Bridges could put it down I am sure. I only want to see the salient points. Tomorrow would be time enough.

Winston S. Churchill to R. A. Butler
Prime Minister's Personal Minute M.139c/51
(*Premier papers, 11/88*)

8 December 1951
Personal and Secret

I was surprised to read the statement about the cuts in Education which fill so large a part of the newspapers today. This ought not to have been published until the Cabinet had considered the matter. I was not aware that your

---

[1] Reproduced above (pp. 83–4).

committees were going to authorize announcements of this character without Cabinet authority. Moreover, the timing was unfortunate and looks as if we had waited till Parliament was up.

I am very much in favour of these economies in many branches, but the timing should be considered, and it might be well to make the whole lot at once rather than give special prominence to a single branch. I must ask that all such proposed announcements shall be brought before the Cabinet in good time. Let me know what other similar announcements you have. The matter can be discussed at the 11.30 a.m. Cabinet on Tuesday.

Winston S. Churchill to Florence Horsbrugh[1]
Prime Minister's Personal Minute M.137c/51
(Premier papers, 11/88)

8 December 1951
Personal and Secret

I was surprised to read the announcement which you made after Parliament had risen about the cuts in Education. No such statement should have been issued by you without Cabinet authority. The timing seems also to have been most unfortunate. Pray let me have your explanation.

Florence Horsbrugh to Winston S. Churchill
(Premier papers, 11/88)

8 December 1951

Your minute of 8 December 1951.

I profoundly regret my error of judgment in authorizing the issue yesterday of the Departmental Circular to Local Authorities on Educational Expenditure which was in the newspapers this morning.

I offer you my unqualified apology.

To explain but not excuse myself:

The Circular was submitted for my approval last Wednesday, after it had been agreed with the Treasury. Its purpose was to give guidance to the Local Authorities. The preparation of their estimates of educational expenditure in 1952/3 is already far advanced. Both the Chancellor of the Exchequer and I regarded it as urgent to secure that those estimates should be appreciably reduced below the forecast figure.

The Circular announced no change in educational policy, and in no way prejudices any future decision the Government may wish to take.

---

[1] Florence Gertrude Horsbrugh, 1889–1969. MBE, 1920. MP (Cons.) for Dundee, 1931–45; for Manchester Moss Side, 1950–9. Minister of Education, 1951–4. CBE, 1939; GBE, 1954.

December 1951

Winston S. Churchill to Florence Horsburgh
Prime Minister's Personal Minute M.141c/51
(Premier papers, 11/88)

9 December 1951

Thank you for your minute.[1]

I have no doubts about the policy but the timing was bad and the Cabinet should have been consulted. You are always free to circulate a paper to the Cabinet on your departmental work, and you have only to ask Sir Norman Brook to be summoned on any point connected with your department that you desire to raise.

Winston S. Churchill to Sir Norman Brook
Prime Minister's Personal Minute M.145c/51
(Premier papers, 11/64)

9 December 1951

I do not remember that the Service Ministers met together, apart from Defence Committee Meetings, during the war. Let me know what the practice was.

Sir Norman Brook to Winston S. Churchill
(Premier papers, 11/64)

10 December 1951

Your minute M.145(c)/51 of 9th December. During the war the Service ministers did not meet together, apart from the Defence Committee meetings.

In peace-time, however, it is convenient for the Service Ministers to meet to discuss matters of common concern, many of which do not require reference to the Defence Committee or the Cabinet. The following are examples of the kind of subject which can usefully be handled in this way:

    Re-engagement bounties
    Courts-martial procedure
    Education of Service children
    Widows' pensions
    Re-settlement of ex-Regulars in civilian life
    Medical treatment of Servicemen on leave.

(The Chiefs of Staff meet separately. Meetings of the three Service Ministers would be the counterpart to those meetings of the Chiefs of Staff. They would in no sense reduce the authority or the scope of the Defence Committee.)

[1] Reproduced above (p. 115).

When there is a separate Minister of Defence, he would preside over these meetings. Meanwhile, however, you need not concern yourself with such matters as these, which the Service Ministers can discuss among themselves. They must meet on such subjects from time to time. If they meet in a formal Committee this has the advantage that the proceedings will be recorded and it will be easier for you to keep yourself informed of what is going on and to direct, if necessary, that particular matters be referred to the Defence Committee or the Cabinet.

Winston S. Churchill to Harold Parker
Prime Minister's Personal Minute M.148c/51
(Premier papers, 11/75)

10 December 1951

Page A. It would be very helpful if even in rough terms the existing strength of the French Army could be set forth. Several days could be allowed for this, but do not communicate with Paris. Give simply the information available here. Intelligence certainly ought to know.

Page B. How is the £76 million divided between 1951 and 1952? Is it deductible from the total figures of our estimates, or additional thereto?

Page C. What do you mean by 'the bid'? Do you mean request?

Page C (1).[1] Surely figures for April 1, 1951, are misleading? Eight and a half months have passed since then. This applies to all three Service returns. How do we stand at December 1?

Page D.[2] Explain to me the use to which these small arms are put. Do the Air squadrons assume responsibility for the local protection of their airfields (a) at home, and (b) abroad.

I note that 34,000 vehicles are available for 237,000 Regulars, i.e. 1 to every 7 men. I usually reckon it as 1½ men, i.e. over 50,000 men.

Page E, para. 1.[3] Again, how is the £71 million divided between 1950 and 1951? And why is so little asked for as £5 million for the 1952 programme?

I note on Page F[4] that we are distributing 527 aircraft to other countries including the re-arming of both Pakistan and India, presumably to fight one another.

Appendix A. The total of nearly 9,000 aircraft seems to bear no relation to reality. Columns (a) and (b) amount to only 2,250.

---

[1] 'The defence position on April 1, 1951, stating strengths and stocks of principal items of equipment and munitions.'
[2] Headed 'Other Important Items' under the main heading reproduced in the preceding footnote.
[3] Headed 'The value of equipment for the Royal Air Force, promised by the United States under their Mutual Defence Assistance Programme for 1950 and 1951'.
[4] Headed 'Jet Aircraft for NATO Countries'.

118   December 1951

Winston S. Churchill to Lord De L'Isle and Dudley
Prime Minister's Personal Minute M.149c/57
(Premier papers, 11/75)

10 December 1951

Please let me have the nearest figures you can get to the position on December 1, and generally correct this document[1] by the position on that date. If you prefer November 1, that will do, but evidently these returns are out of date. I should like to have these figures in time for our Meeting.

Please also distinguish between 'establishment' and 'strength'.

I shall quite understand that your figures cannot be complete or final.

Antony Beauchamp[2] to Winston S. Churchill
(Churchill papers, 1/50)

10 December 1951

Dear Mr Churchill,

I have sent your Stereo Realist camera to Sergeant Murray[3] who knows how to work the camera. It might be a good opportunity for him to get some third dimensional pictures of you and your voyage in the *Queen Mary*, and in Canada and the United States.

I hope it will provide a unique historical record and a really unusual way of documenting your activities for your own personal interest.[4]

Cabinet: conclusions
(Cabinet papers, 128/23)

11 December 1951
Secret
11.30 a.m.
Cabinet Meeting No. 16 of 1951

1. The Prime Minister referred to the circular on expenditure which the Ministry of Education had issued to local authorities at the end of the previous week. The timing of this had been unfortunate. The Government should aim at announcing all their proposals for curbing expenditure at one time, when

[1] Cabinet Paper No. 28 of 1951, reproduced above (p. 57–8).
[2] Antony Beauchamp Entwistle, 1918–57. Married, 1949, Sarah Churchill.
[3] Edmund Murray. Married, 1947, Beryl Hafliger. Metropolitan Police Special Branch Officer. Churchill's bodyguard, 1950–65.
[4] Churchill's Private Office drafted the following response: 'Thank you so much for sending me the Stereo Realist camera. It will indeed be useful, and I am sure it will give me a lot of fun.' Churchill indicated that he wanted a fuller letter.

Parliament was sitting. No further announcements of policy affecting major items of expenditure should be made without the authority of the Cabinet.

The Cabinet –

Took note of the Prime Minister's statement.

[. . .]

7. The Foreign Secretary informed the Cabinet that the United States Ambassador[1] had enquired whether the Prime Minister intended, during his forthcoming visit to Washington, to ask for financial aid from the United States. The visit would follow shortly after the United Kingdom's payment of the first instalment of the interest on the American loan, and the Ambassador thought it would be preferable that the question of financial aid should be settled either before or after the Prime Minister's visit.

The Prime Minister said that it was not his intention to ask for financial aid in the course of his discussions in Washington. He would ask for American assistance in the form of materials and equipment, for the purpose either of assisting our defence programme directly or of assisting our exports and thus furthering the defence programme indirectly. In this connection he attached great importance to steel. We should try to secure a decision on financial aid before the end of the year; but, if this proved impossible, the question should be left over until after his visit to the United States.

The Cabinet –

(1) Took note of the Prime Minister's statement.

(2) Agreed that the intention of the Government to pay the first instalment of the interest on the United States loan should be announced before Christmas.

8. The Prime Minister read to the Cabinet a letter which he had received from Field-Marshal Montgomery[2] on the subject of the European Army. The Field-Marshal considered that it was impracticable in present political circumstances to fuse the armies of the European countries into a single force under single direction; and that, although the French were in favour of attempting to do so because they were apprehensive of the creation of a German National Army, it was impossible by these means to produce an effective military force. The Field-Marshal was strongly in favour, however, of a European

---

[1] Walter Sherman Gifford, 1885–1966. Educated at Harvard University. Clerk, Western Electric, 1905–11. Chief Statistician, AT&T, 1911–16. Married, 1916, Florence Pitman: two children (div. 1929); 1944, Augustine Lloyd Perry. US Official Adviser to Council of Defense, 1916–18. Controller, AT&T, 1918–19; Vice-President of Finance, 1919–23; Executive Vice-President, 1923–5; President, 1925–48. US Official Director on Unemployment Relief, 1931–2. Ambassador to UK, 1950–3.

[2] Bernard Law Montgomery, 1887–1976. Educated at St Paul's School. On active service, 1914–18 (despatches, DSO). Maj.-Gen., 1938. Commanded 3rd Div. (retreat to Dunkirk), 1940; 8th Army (North Africa, Sicily, Italy), July 1942 to Jan. 1944. Knighted, 1942. C-in-C, British Group of Armies and Allied Armies, northern France, 6 June 1944 (Normandy landings). Commanded 21st Army Group, northern Europe, June 1944 to May 1945. FM, 1944. Commanded British Army of Occupation on the Rhine (BAOR), 1945–6. Viscount, 1946. Deputy Supreme Allied Commander, Europe, 1951–8.

Army made up of units maintaining their national character and spirit but integrated under one United Nations Command. He would not recommend that the United Kingdom Government should at present participate in the attempt to build up a European Army; but he thought they might indicate that in their view integration of national units into a European Army was right while attempts at fusion were wrong.

The Prime Minister informed the Cabinet that he had told Field-Marshal Montgomery that he was in general agreement with these views.

The Foreign Secretary said that the French Government had to take into account the strong body of feeling in France against the re-creation of a German Army. It was also important to keep in mind the effect of these plans on the Soviet Government: they were likely to regard the creation of a German national army as more provocative than any of the steps so far taken in building up the defence of Western Europe. And they would certainly be disturbed by any proposal which seemed to foreshadow the admission of Germany into the North Atlantic Treaty Organisation.

Progress of Defence Programme: minutes
(Premier papers, 11/75)

11 December 1951
Top Secret
6.30 p.m.
Progress of Defence Programme Meeting No. 1 of 1951

In opening the discussion the Prime Minister said that at this preliminary meeting only a general survey would be possible. It was clear from the reports submitted to him that, if this island was to be effectively defended, the production of the latest types of fighter aircraft must be given first priority over exports, civilian needs, and other defence needs, including the other needs of the RAF. Despite this a substantial saving would have to be made on the money at present asked for.

The Secretary of State for Air agreed that modern fighter aircraft were the most urgent need of the RAF. He recognised, however, that some delay in re-equipping RAF squadrons with modern types was inevitable. The aircraft programme was part of a carefully integrated plan designed to build up the strength of the Air Force in a specified time. Airfields and other works requirements and training equipment were an essential part of the plan and must be kept in step with aircraft production. The output of the most critical items, the F.3 and the Swift fighters, and the Canberra and Valiant bombers, could not be substantially increased by cutting back another part of the programme.

The Chief of the Air Staff[1] emphasized our obligations to NATO. We

---

[1] John Cotesworth Slessor, 1897–1979. RFC, 1915–18 (despatches, wounded, MC). Director of Plans, Air Ministry, 1937–41. Air Commodore, 1939. AVM, 1941. OC No. 5 Bomber Group, 1941–2.

alone had undertaken to contribute a tactical bomber force to General Eisenhower's forces. We regarded our contribution to those forces as part of the defence forces of the United Kingdom. The set back in production was severe. If nothing was done to remedy it our contribution to the 'Medium Term Defence Plan' was likely to be 20 Canberra bombers instead of the promised 200. We knew when the re-armament programme was undertaken that we should be dependent for a while on obsolescent aircraft. At present we should have largely to rely for the air defence of the country against the invader on American fighters, 100 of which were already here. In reply to questions about the possibility of getting more fighters from the USA, or of getting those promised sooner, the Chief of the Air Staff said we had asked for more, but the Americans had not felt able to supply them. They had, however, promised substantial reinforcements on the outbreak of war. He did not think the prospects of persuading them to change their minds were very good in view of their commitments in Korea, their obligations to other NATO countries which had no production capacity of their own, and the set back in American production. It might, however, be possible to persuade them that the common cause would be better served if they stationed more aircraft on this side and fewer on their own side of the Atlantic. It was hoped that the report of the 'Wise Men' who were about to conclude their discussions in Paris would include a recommendation to this effect.

There was now no chance of achieving the full £4,700m programme by 1954. It was vitally necessary to review our strategic priorities to ensure that we got first what we needed most. In the meantime we must not dislocate production by attempting to hasten the production of new types of aircraft at the expense of the old. The labour force must be kept in being until production lines could be switched to new types. Moreover, whilst 'obsolescent' aircraft might be ineffective against the MIG 15, they might well be effective against hostile bombers.

The Minister of Supply said that although there were other obstacles to the achievement of the programme, the shortage of labour – both skilled and unskilled – was the chief immediate difficulty. 25,000 extra workers were wanted at once in addition to the 160,000 already engaged in the production of aircraft. Another 135,000 would be needed by the time production reached its peak. To get them the aircraft programme and its essential ancillaries, such as ammunition and Rotor,[1] must be given effective priority over all other demands.

The selective control of engagement would be of great assistance. A

Asst CAS (Policy), Apr. 1942 to 1943. CB, 1942. AOC-in-C, Coastal Command, Feb.–Dec. 1943. KCB, 1943. Air Mshl, 1943. C-in-C, RAF, Mediterranean and Middle East, Jan. 1944 to 1945. Air Member for Personnel, 1945–7. Air Chf Mshl, 1946. Mshl of the RAF, 1950. CAS, 1950–2.

[1] 'Rotor': reactivation of WWII radar stations and construction of new surface and underground bunker stations. At the time, this was the largest defence capital project ever undertaken, with a total budget of £51.5 million.

short designated list of vital projects should be drawn up and all concerned instructed to ensure that these projects received super priority. The total impact on the export trade would be relatively small, though a considerable demand for labour would occur in certain difficult areas such as Coventry, Preston, Chorley, and Swynnerton.

The following points were made in discussion:
(1) Modern aircraft and essential equipment for them were much more complex now than they were during the last war. It took 4,000 machine hours to make an F.3 or an Avon jet engine, whereas a Hurricane took only 500 machine hours and a Merlin engine 600. Nevertheless, the labour force in the aircraft industry seemed unduly large in relation to the output, and this might repay investigation.
(2) The possibility of relieving the labour difficulty by letting subcontracts in Northern Ireland and elsewhere was being actively pursued, but the shortage of skilled labour placed a limit on the possibilities. There might be useful spare capacity in the motor car industry if steel supplies to the industry were to be cut.
(3) Before the needs of the RAF could be given absolute priority, it would be necessary to take into account the demands – on the metal using and building industries in particular – of the other Services and the American air force in this country.
(4) An analysis should be made by categories of the men in the RAF in this country with a view to cutting the 'tail'.
(5) There was a prima facie case for investigating the Services requirement of 12,000 tons of sheet steel a quarter for ammunition boxes.
(6) A list should be prepared of items such as IFF, radio and radar apparatus which the Americans might be asked to produce for us in relief for our own programme. They were already being asked to extend the scope of 'end item aid' to components and accessories.
(7) We already had a rocket assisted jet fighter. The jet assisted rocket was an idea still on the drawing board.

The Prime Minister:
(1) directed that overriding priority over export, civil and other defence needs, should be given to the production of the latest types of aircraft, ammunition for them, and operation Rotor;
(2) invited the Secretary of State for Air to prepare
  (i) a comprehensive statement of the case for supplying us with more fighter aircraft from America;
  (ii) an analysis by categories of the men employed in the RAF;
  (iii) a list of the items which the Americans might make available to us in relief of our own production programme;
(3) invited the Minister of Supply to prepare
  (i) an analysis of the labour force in the aircraft industry, showing

the cost in labour, materials and money of the production of a typical modern fighter and bomber;
(ii) an explanation of the requirement of 12,000 tons of steel a quarter for ammunition boxes.

Progress of Defence Programme: minutes
(Premier papers, 11/70)

12 December 1951
Top Secret
11 a.m.
Progress of Defence Programme Meeting No. 2 of 1951

The Prime Minister asked how the provision for the Admiralty estimates for 1952–53 compared with the provision in the current year and with the probable out-turn for the current year.

Sir John Lang[1] replied that the original estimate in 1951–52 was £278.5M. This was raised to £305M when the £4,700M programme was introduced but it was probable that only £279M would be spent in the current year. The present estimate for 1952–53 was £402M and of this £42M might be attributed to the rise in prices.

In reply to a question by the Prime Minister, it was explained that Vote A for 1952–53 was 151,000 and the Royal Fleet Reserve 20,000. For the financial year 1939/40 Vote A was about 130,000, but the effective bearing at the beginning of that year was about 120,000. The strength of the active and reserve fleet in 1939 was 344 vessels, not including mine sweepers. The comparable figure in 1951 was 375.

The Prime Minister then asked for an account of the programme of new construction for 1952–53. The Controller[2] replied that the programme consisted of one prototype third rate anti-submarine frigate of 900 tons, capable of a speed of 26 knots, which would cost rather less than half a million pounds; one prototype anti-E boat frigate for use in coastal waters; 4 fast battery driven submarines, which would cost £1⅓M and 4 X craft midget submarines, which

---

[1] John Gerald Lang, 1896–1984. 2nd Div. Clerk, Admiralty, 1914. Lt, Royal Marine Artillery, 1917–18. Married, 1922, Emilie J. Goddard: one child (d. 1963); 1970, Kathleen Winifred Goddard. Asst Principal, Admiralty, 1930; Principal, 1935; Asst Secretary, 1939; Principal Asst Secretary, 1942; Under-Secretary, 1946; Secretary, 1947–61. Chairman, Bettix Ltd, 1961–71. Principal Adviser on Sport to the Government, 1964–71.

[2] Michael Maynard Denny, 1896–1972. On active service during WWI. Assistant and Deputy Director of Naval Ordnance, Admiralty, 1937–40. Cdr, HMS *Kenya*, 1940–2. CoS to C-in-C Home Fleet, 1942–3. CBE, 1944. Cdr, HMS *Victorious*, 1944–5. DSO, 1945. RAdm., 1945. Flag Officer (Destroyers), Mediterranean Fleet, 1947–9. VAdm., 1948. Lord Commissioner of Admiralty, 3rd Sea Lord and Controller of the Navy, 1949–53. Adm., 1952. C-in-C Home Fleet, and C-in-C Eastern Atlantic (NATO), 1954–5. Chairman, British Joint Services Mission, Washington DC, and UK representative on standing group of NATO Military Committee, 1956–9.

would cost about £110,000 each. The purpose of the submarines was to patrol in enemy waters in order to deal with enemy submarines at the source. No fast submarines were currently under construction other than those which were being converted from the old T class. These were capable of a speed of 17½ knots under water. The submarine was at present the only effective blockading vessel.

The programme of new construction for 1952–53 included no cruisers, no fleet carriers and no capital ships. It was proposed to complete eight Daring class destroyers but not to start any new ones. Work would be continued on the *Ark Royal*, on four Hermes class carriers and on the *Majestic* (which was intended for Australia). 85 small ships, mine sweepers, were also to be laid down in 1952–53. The coastal mine sweepers would cost somewhat less than one third of a million pounds fully equipped and the inshore mine sweepers about half this amount. The latter was capable of a speed of 10 knots when dragging and 15½ knots when not dragging. Great importance was attached to the anti-mine measures by the Admiralty. Our submarines were capable of laying a maximum of 24 mines each.

Other elements in the new construction programme were boom defence vessels, to replace the wartime vessels now out of date, two fleet tugs, 16 assault landing craft, three surveying motor launches and eight motor boats, capable of a speed of 42 knots. The total cost of the programme at present prices was about £42M. This was spread over several years and the amount due in the first year 1952–53 was in the neighbourhood of £4M.

In reply to a question what ships were due to be delivered to the Admiralty in 1952–3, the Controller said there would be one or possibly two light fleet carriers, at least six, and possibly all of the eight Daring class destroyers, seven or eight of the new coastal mine sweepers and two motor torpedo boats.

The Chancellor of the Exchequer commented that the Admiralty's requirements appeared to be moderate and they had made a considerable contribution in response to his campaign for economy. The fact remained, however, that our resources were not sufficient to meet Service programmes of this magnitude. There must be a substantial reduction in the claims of the Services, particularly on the metal-using industries. The Treasury had in mind a figure of £407M for production for all three services in 1952–53.

Similarly we could not meet the demands of the Services for their works programmes. Even if money were available, structural steel and other materials were not. It was clear that considerable cuts would have to be made.

The Controller said that, if cuts had to be made, it should be done by deferring certain orders and, in effect, spreading the three year programme over a longer period.

Other points raised in discussion were:
    1. The annual requirement of steel for the Navy would be about 300,000 tons spread fairly evenly over the year. The Services'

consumption of a rather large quantity of steel on ammunition had previously been lost on account of unsatisfactory packaging.

2. A great deal of the expenditure on production had been attributed to material and equipment other than ships. The total figure included not only radar, aircraft and stores and materials for maintenance but also such items as clothing and the payment of dockyard repair staff.

3. Our present stocks of oil fuel were 4 million tons, i.e. about the same as at the end of the war. We had 6 million tons at the outbreak of war in 1939 and the wartime expenditure was about 7 million tons a year.

4. The Admiralty provision of £19M for works in 1952–53 was no more than the equivalent at present prices of the £15½M included in the current year's estimates. A cut would mean that there would be no new works at all and much retardation of works which had made progress during the current year. The original estimate was £25M. This has been cut by the Admiralty to £19M.

5. The provision for underground storage for oil in the Mediterranean (at Malta) which was expected to cost £1M to 1½M in 1952–53 might be considered acceptable because it did not represent entirely a drain on this country's resources of material and labour.

6. A separate report was in preparation on what coastal aircraft could do to help in the detection of hostile submarines.

7. There was little we could do in 1952–53 to improve our defences against the mine and the submarine since the ships we were building to cope with these menaces took two or three years to produce.

8. The Americans had about 200 destroyers and no frigates. They had built no carriers lately but were just laying down a great new carrier with a displacement of 70,000 tons. This had a Catapult with a 400 foot runway. We could achieve the same result using our catapult with a 250 foot runway and a carrier of 55,000 tons displacement. Arrangements were being made for our catapult to be demonstrated to the Americans.

9. Although the cost of the three year programme was now expected to be in the neighbourhood of £5,200M, whereas the printed estimates were based on the £3,600M programme, the actual monetary expenditure would be considerably less than this amount in view of the short-fall which had occurred in production, The original estimate in the production element of the £4,700M programme was £2,000M. Owing to rise in prices this was now up to over £2,200M.

10. The increase in civilian staff as compared to 1939 was explained by increase in activity on production, research and development, by the increased complements of warships and by the Admiralty's

assumption of responsibility for naval aviation. The housing of a considerable part of the staff at Bath was also expensive both in manpower and in money, however desirable for other reasons.

11. The chief items which the Admiralty had asked for from the United States were 50 airborne early warning aircraft. They would prepare a full list of items for inclusion in the Prime Minister's brief.

The Prime Minister said it was clear that the Service programmes would have to be scaled down in view of the shortage of materials and the pressure of other claims on our resources. He would write to the First Lord of the Admiralty asking him to consider what modifications he would wish to introduce into his programme if cuts of dimensions to be specified in the letter had to be imposed. The consequences of these modifications would then be reviewed.

Progress of Defence Programme: minutes
(Premier papers, 11/71)

12 December 1951
Top Secret
5.30 p.m.
Progress of Defence Programme Meeting No. 3 of 1951

The Prime Minister opened the discussion by referring to the Army estimate for 1951/2 as laid before Parliament on the basis of the £3,600m defence programme. This amounted to £418m. Under the £4,700m programme this was increased to £483m. The actual expenditure was now expected to be £432m. The provisional estimate for 1952/3 was £611m, an increase of £179m on the money expected to be spent this year. He asked the Secretary of State to explain why so much more was wanted.

The Secretary of State for War said that the main factors accounting for the increase were the need to make all existing forces more efficient, the necessity to replace vehicles, ammunition and other equipment expended in Korea, Malaya and the Middle East and the general rise in prices.

The Chancellor of the Exchequer said the country could not support the additional burdens which would be placed on it by this and the other Service programmes. The War Office were contemplating an expenditure in 1952/3 of £286m on production, £40m on works and £285m under other Votes. The maximum which the economy could stand was £215m on production, and £30m on works. The other Votes might also have to be cut, but the principal necessity was to reduce the load on the engineering, metal using and building industries.

The Prime Minister said that it seemed to him that the War Office would have to be content with a budget of £500m.

It was pointed out that the money provided for purposes other than production and works was not capable of very great adjustment unless the numbers of men in the Army were cut, since it consisted largely of elements such as pay and food. The Secretary of State stressed the political objections to reducing amenities and CIGS[1] said that the economies of this kind would be bad for morale and discourage recruiting.

The Prime Minister drew attention to the proposed expenditures during 1951/4 of about £100m on vehicles. This not only meant a serious strain on labour and capacity which might be devoted to exports or to other Service needs, but also implied that about 375,000 men would be needed to look after the vehicles. Was there not a serious risk that the effective fighting power of the Army would be dangerously diminished?

It was explained that the Army had been living on its fat since the end of the war and was now dependent on worn out vehicles which had to be kept serviceable at a great cost in money and manpower. This year for the first time new vehicles were to be bought. Of the 249,000 vehicles it was proposed to provide for the Army 85,000 were of ordinary commercial types. For mobilisation requirements of commercial type vehicles, the army would rely on requisitioning, but 40,000 a month for three months was the most that could be hoped for from that source. 75,000 of the vehicles had multiaxial drives which were essential for cross country work, 32,000 were combat vehicles and many of the rest were specialised for military purposes. There had been many cuts in divisional transport during the last two years. Our provision was on a much less lavish scale than that of the Americans, and was not much greater than that of the Russian mobile divisions. All our divisions were mobile. Quality was all we had to rely on against the Russian superiority in numbers.

The Minister of Supply added that the General Service vehicles for the 1952/3 programme were already being manufactured and there would be nothing to be gained by cancelling the orders, and much to be lost both in money and industrial efficiency. Export markets might be found for some frustrated Service orders.

The Chancellor of the Exchequer said that from a discussion he had that afternoon with Mr Batt,[2] the head of the American Economic Cooperation Administration Mission in London, it appeared that there might be a prospect of getting vehicles from America. This was being looked into. The Secretary

---

[1] William Joseph Slim, 1891–1970. Known as 'Bill'. Lt-Col., 1938. Col., 1939. Brig.-Gen., 1939. CO, 10th Indian Bde, 1939–41. Wounded, 1941. Brig. General Staff, British troops in Iraq, 1941. Maj.-Gen., 1941. GOC 10th Indian Div., Syria, 1941–2; Burma Corps, Burma, 1942; XV Indian Corps, Burma, 1942–3. Lt-Gen., 1942. CBE, 1942. DSO, 1943. GOC 14th Army, Burma, 1943–5. KCB, 1944. CB, 1944. Gen., 1945. C-in-C, Allied Land Forces South-East Asia, 1945. GBE, 1946. Commandant, Imperial Defence College, 1946–8. CIGS, 1948–52. FM, 1949. GCMG, 1952. Governor-General and C-in-C of Australia, 1952–60. GCVO, 1954. KG, 1959. Viscount, 1960.

[2] William Loren Batt, 1885–1965. Educated at Purdue University and University of Pennsylvania. President, SKF Industries Inc., 1923–50. Vice-Chairman, War Production Board, 1941–5. Chief of Economic Cooperation Administration Mission in Great Britain, 1950–2.

of State for War said that it would be helpful if the Americans would let us have spare parts for the American Vehicles we already held.

Other points made in the discussion were as follows:
(1) The allocation in the 1952/3 estimates of £40m for works included £5½m for housing, which was part of the national building programme.
(2) The Americans could help, if they were willing to do so, by providing trailers for our 25 pounder guns, anti-tank weapons and in other ways by relieving the strain on our own production capacity.
(3) It would be advantageous if the team of experts on small arms visited Canada while the Prime Minister was in the United States in case there was an opportunity of resuming discussions with the Americans on the subject of standardisation.
(4) Since cuts had to be made in the Army estimates, the retardation of orders for equipment was a lesser evil than the reduction of manpower.

The Prime Minister:
Invited the Secretary of State for War
(a) to prepare a list of the most vital items which we might ask the Americans to supply;
(b) to consider the issue of some form of uniform to the first 10,000 recruits to the Home Guard, and
(c) to arrange for a team of experts on the .280 rifle to be available in Canada at the end of December.

Winston S. Churchill to Anthony Eden
Prime Minister's Personal Minute M.151c/51
(Premier papers, 11/162)

12 December 1951

Either we want Duff[1] to do it or not.* If 'Yes', it should be a cordial invitation. If no cordial invitation is forthcoming we should let him alone.

* Sir Duff Cooper to take Chair at Conference of 'Central and Eastern European Commission'.

---

[1] Alfred Duff Cooper, 1890–1954. Known as 'Duff'. Educated at Eton and New College, Oxford. Entered FO, 1913. On active service, Grenadier Guards, 1917–18 (DSO, despatches). MP (Cons.) for Oldham, 1924–9; for St George's, Westminster, 1931–45. Financial Secretary, War Office, 1928–9, 1931–4. Financial Secretary, Treasury, 1934–5. PC, 1935. Secretary of State for War, 1935–7. 1st Lord of the Admiralty, 1937–8. Minister of Information, 1940–1. British Representative, Singapore, 1941. Chancellor of the Duchy of Lancaster, 1941–3. British Representative to French Committee of National Liberation in Algiers, Jan.–Aug.1944. Ambassador to France, 1944–7. Knighted, 1948. Viscount Norwich, 1952.

Cabinet: conclusions
(*Cabinet papers, 128/23*)

13 December 1951
Secret
11 a.m.
Cabinet Meeting No. 17 of 1951

[...]

2. The Prime Minister said that the broadcast which he had been proposing to make on 22nd December had been described in the Press as a Party political broadcast. It would be a mistake to revive political controversy immediately before his visit to Washington, and it might be better to postpone the broadcast until after his return.

In discussion there was general agreement that an authoritative statement should be made before Christmas about the gravity of the situation which had confronted the Government when they took office. It was further agreed that this statement could not be made effectively within the limits imposed on Ministerial broadcasts to which the Opposition had no right of reply.

The Prime Minister undertook to give a broadcast talk on 22nd December, as previously planned, and agreed that this could be regarded as a political broadcast to which the Opposition would have a right of reply.

[...]

Henry Hopkinson[1] to Winston Churchill
(*Premier papers, 11/153*)

13 December 1951
Personal

Dear Prime Minister,

As you are leaving for Paris on Sunday, I thought it might be useful for you to have my impressions of the last week at Strasbourg during which I have been leading the British Delegation. On the whole I think that in spite of the disturbing tone of the press reports the position at the end of the Assembly was better than we had at one time expected.

After I arrived we turned our attention to economic matters and other

---

[1] Henry Lennox D'Aubigne Hopkinson, 1902–96. 3rd Secretary, Washington DC, 1924–9. 2nd Secretary, FO, 1929–31; Stockholm, 1931–2; Cairo, 1934–8. Asst Private Secretary to Foreign Secretary, 1932–4. 1st Secretary, Athens, 1938–9. War Cabinet Secretariat, 1939–40. Private Secretary to Permanent Under-Secretary of State, FO, 1940–1. Diplomatic Adviser to Minister of State, Middle East, 1941–3. Minister Plenipotentiary to Portugal, 1943–4. CMG, 1944. Deputy High Commissioner to Rome and Political Adviser to Allied Commission, Italy, 1946–50. MP (Cons.) for Taunton, 1950–6. Secretary of Overseas Trade, 1951–2. PC, 1952. Minister of State, Colonial Affairs, 1952–5. Baron Colyton, 1956. Chairman, Anglo-Egyptian Resettlement Board, 1957–60.

technical topics which took away some of the heat. However, the imminent arrival of the four Foreign Ministers leading up to the resumed General Affairs Debate on Monday naturally led to speculation.

As Duncan will have told you, things, boiled up a day or so before at the dinner given for him by the European Movement where Spaak[1] and Reynaud, who seemed to be working hand in hand, bitterly attacked the British Government's attitude particularly in relation to the European Army. Duncan again explained our position.

All later political discussions in the Assembly centred on this question. Although there was no specific resolution down on the European Army it was referred to in almost every speech and also in recommendations and resolutions proposing alternative forms of a political authority. Everyone recognised that Britain would not federate. One or two of the more extreme Federalists called for a full political authority for Europe without Britain. Others put forward plans for intermediate schemes to which it was hoped we could adhere.

You will no doubt have seen the speeches of the four Foreign Ministers including that of Van Zeeland.[2] He implied that Belgium would not accept a supra-national political authority for the European Army and put forward an alternative plan obviously designed to enable us to come in. When the General Affairs Debate was resumed later that afternoon, it was quite clear that there had been a change of mood in the Assembly. Several speakers, including a Belgian of Spaak's own party as well as a French supporter of Schuman, said in effect that they did not want a political authority without Britain. The extreme Federalist recommendation was rejected and those which it was hoped would leave the door open for us were adopted.

The real objection of the Benelux countries to the supra-natural authority in the European Army was clearly that it would keep us out. I also think that the majority of other French delegates in the Assembly would be unwilling to go into a European Army with Germans and Italians alone.

When the debate ended, the general feeling seemed to be that the Foreign Ministers would make no progress on the point at their meeting the following day. Many people hoped that a compromise solution would emerge from your meeting with the French Prime Minister[3] next week.

Had it not been for Spaak's outburst on the last day the Assembly would I

[1] Paul-Henri Charles Spaak, 1899–1972. German POW, 1916–18. Educated at Université Libre de Bruxelles. Married, 1922, Marguerite Malevez: two children (d. 1964); 1965, Simone Dear. Belgian Minister of Transport, 1935–6. Minister of Foreign Affairs, 1936–8, 1939–45 (in exile), 1945–7, 1954–7, 1961–6. PM, 1938–9, 1946, 1947–50. President, UN General Assembly, 1946–7. President, Parliamentary Assembly of Council of Europe, 1949–51. Secretary-General of NATO, 1957–61.
[2] Paul van Zeeland, 1893–1973. A Director of Belgian National Bank, 1926; Deputy Governor, 1934. PM of Belgium, 1935–7. President, Co-ordinating Foundation for Refugees, 1939. In exile in England, 1940. President, European League for Economic Cooperation, 1946–9. Belgian Minister of Foreign Affairs, 1949–54.
[3] René Pleven.

think have closed on a more amicable note. Spaak had given no indication of his intention to resign and his decision may partly have been accounted for by domestic politics. But I think he has sincerely convinced himself that the only course now is for the Continental countries to go ahead with some form of federation on their own and has made himself the leader of the federal element in the Assembly. The violence of his speech may also have been partly due to the very provocative attitude of Gordon Walker[1] who led the Socialist group after Glenvil Hall went home and showed a remarkable lack of tact and courtesy.

In conclusion I would say that I feel certain that Monsieur Schuman must be aware of the reservations felt by the majority of the Assembly regarding further progress without Britain. It is quite possible that this may have some effect on his attitude when you meet him in Paris.

Winston S. Churchill to Anthony Eden
Prime Minister's Personal Minute M.153c/51
(Premier papers, 11/153)

13 December 1951

This is a good and carefully thought out letter.[2] I am naturally distressed at the way things have gone at Strasbourg. We seem in fact to have succumbed to the Socialist Party hostility to United Europe. I take the full blame because I did not feel able either to go there myself or send a message. You also know my views about the particular kind of European Army into which the French are trying to force us. We must consider very carefully together how to deal with the certainly unfavourable reaction in American opinion. They would like us to fall into the general line of European pensioners which we have no intention of doing.

I think Boothby's letter is very good and sober.

---

[1] Patrick Gordon Walker, 1907–80. Educated at Christ Church, Oxford. Married, 1934, Audrey Muriel Rudolf: five children. MP (Lab.) for Smethwick, 1945–64; for Leyton, 1966–74. Parliamentary Under-Secretary of State for Commonwealth Relations, 1947–50. Secretary of State for Commonwealth Relations, 1950–1. Foreign Secretary, 1964–6. Secretary of State for Education and Science, 1967–8. Baron, 1974. Member of European Parliament, 1975–6.

[2] Letter of Dec. 3 from Julian Amery and six other members of the Conservative Delegation to the Consultative Assembly.

Winston S. Churchill to Anthony Eden
Prime Minister's Personal Minute M.154c/51
(Premier papers, 11/112)

13 December 1951
Personal and Secret

Please see telegram from Tokyo, CAB 465.

Obviously the Communists are manoeuvring with the United States in order to gain time. The question is For What? The six months parleying have enabled the Chinese Communists to add sixty thousand to their strength; to build up their artillery, and above all to let the Russians teach them how to fly the Russian planes. The United Nations' position is actively and relatively far worse than it was six months ago. We may be grateful that we have only a small say in these matters. I am glad we do not bear the responsibility of having to guess the Communist motives. There can however be no doubt that so far time has been almost entirely on their side.

Winston S. Churchill to Anthony Eden, R. A. Butler, General Lord Ismay, Lord Cherwell and Sir Norman Brook (for others concerned)
Prime Minister's Personal Minute M.157c/51
(Premier papers, 11/160)

15 December 1951

I attach copies of the report of Sir Ian Jacob's[1] enquiry into the inter-Allied machinery for concerting the defence effort of the Western world.

I should be obliged if you would study this and let me have your views and recommendations. You will doubtless arrange to confer with Sir Ian Jacob if there are points in the report which you wish him to amplify or explain.

Sir Norman Brook will arrange to collect for you the views of the others (the Service Ministers and the Chiefs of Staff) who were informed that this enquiry was in progress.

---

[1] Edward Ian Claud Jacob, 1899–1993. 2nd Lt, RE, 1918. Military Asst Secretary, Committee of Imperial Defence, 1938. Lt-Col., 1939. Col., 1943. Military Asst Secretary to the War Cabinet, 1939–45. CBE, 1942. Retired with rank of Lt-Gen., 1946. Knighted, 1946. Controller, European Services, BBC, 1946–7; Director of Overseas Services, 1947–51; Director-General, 1952–60. Chief Staff Officer to Minister of Defence, and Deputy Secretary to Cabinet, 1952. Jacob had been temporarily released from his duties at the BBC to undertake this report for Churchill.

Anthony Eden to Winston S. Churchill
(Premier papers, 11/153)

15 December 1951
Secret and Private
PM/51/148

Your minute M153c/51 of the 13th December about Strasbourg.[1]

2. Certainly it has, I think, been unfortunate for our country that the Strasbourg discussions have been going on at this time. They have, I fear, done something to confuse and dim the leadership in foreign policy which I hoped we had regained in Paris and Rome.

3. I am afraid that I do not agree with your estimate of Boothby's letter. He mentions, and by implication supports, 'the creation of an organic union of Europe under British leadership'. This sounds all right but what does it mean?

4. It can only mean that we are being asked to merge ourselves in a European federation. But as you yourself said in the Defence Debate we cannot merge ourselves in schemes like the Pleven Plan for a European Defence Community. We can only associate ourselves with them as closely as possible.

5. We can merge ourselves wholeheartedly in associations for common purposes among the European Governments, when control remains in the hands of Governments. We have done this in the OEEC. We have done it in NATO.

6. The trouble at Strasbourg was that we were being urged to come right in to European federative schemes. To my mind we must stoutly refuse to do anything of the sort, however severe the criticisms from Spaak, Reynaud, and the rest at Strasbourg. And we must face possible criticism from the Congressmen. It would indeed be fantastic if the test for American military assistance was not our defence effort but our readiness to merge in a European Federation.

7. I would define our policy as follows:

First, we want a united Europe. There is no doubt about that, or our sincerity.

Second, there are two ways in which His Majesty's Government can foster and strengthen the uniting of Europe:

(i) We can and will continue to play an active part in plans for uniting national efforts on an intergovernmental basis;

(ii) We will also give all help and encouragement to the continental European countries when they wish to form federal organs among themselves. And though we cannot merge ourselves in such federal organs, we will always try to find the most practicable and useful means of establishing close relations with them. This is what we are doing in the case of the Schuman Pool, and may do on behalf of the Pleven Plan.[2]

[1] Reproduced above (p. 131).
[2] On Dec. 16 Churchill wrote at the bottom of the page: 'I feel we are in general agreement.'

134   DECEMBER 1951

L. S. Amery¹ to Winston S. Churchill
(*Premier papers, 11/162*)

17 December 1951

My dear Winston,

I think you have been kept in touch through Randolph with what is happening about the Eastern European Conference of the European Movement which is to take place from January 21st to 24th, the cost of which is being defrayed jointly by United Europe and by Beddington-Behrens² who is organizing the Conference. I have agreed to take the Chair at the Conference and at the Albert Hall Meeting on 'Freedom and Liberty for all Europe' on the 24th at which Randolph will be one of the chief speakers.

All the leading political leaders of the countries behind the Iron Curtain like Gafencu,³ Dimitrov,⁴ Ossusky,⁵ etc. will be coming, as well as Western Europeans such as Reynaud, Ramadier,⁶ de Menthon,⁷ Guy Mollet,⁸ Spaak,

[1] Leopold Charles Maurice Stennett Amery, 1873–1955. Known as 'Leo'. A contemporary of Churchill at Harrow. Fellow of All Souls College, Oxford, 1897. Manchester *Guardian* correspondent in the Balkans and Turkey, 1897–9. Served on editorial staff of *The Times*, 1899–1909. MP (Cons.) for South Birmingham (later Birmingham Sparkbrook), 1911–45. Intelligence Officer in the Balkans and eastern Mediterranean, 1915–16. Asst Secretary, War Cabinet Secretariat, 1917–18. Parliamentary Under-Secretary, Colonial Office, 1919–21. 1st Lord of the Admiralty, 1922–4. Secretary of State for the Colonies, 1924–9. Secretary of State for India and Burma, 1940–5.

[2] Edward Beddington-Behrens, 1897–1968. Educated at Christ Church, Oxford, and University of London. On active duty in WWI, 1915–18. Regimental officer in Belgium campaign and at Dunkirk, 1939–45. Chief Organiser, Commonwealth Conference of European League for Economic Co-operation, 1951; of Central and Eastern European Conference, 1952. CMG, 1953. Knighted, 1957.

[3] Grigore Gafencu, 1892–1957. Educated at Geneva and Paris. Editor and publisher of *Argus*, 1924. Elected to Romanian Parliament (National Peasant Party), 1928. Foreign Minister, 1938–40. Minister to the Soviet Union, 1940–1. Represented Romania in post-war peace talks, 1947. Member of Romanian National Committee, 1949–52.

[4] Georgi Mihov Dimitrov, 1903–72. Known as 'Gemeto'. Member of Bulgarian Agrarian National Union (BANU) Party, 1922. Organized peasant revolt and imprisoned, 1923. Educated in Sofia and at University of Zagreb, 1929. Campaigned against Bulgarian alignment with Axis powers, 1941. Headed pro-Allied Bulgarian National Committee, 1941–4. Leader of BANU, 1944; expelled from party, 1945. Founded anti-Communist Agrarian Committee, 1947. Assisted in founding Bulgarian NATO company, 1951.

[5] Štefan Osuský, 1889–1973. Moved to US, 1906. Doctor of Jurisprudence, 1916. Vice-President of Slovak league, 1916. Director of Czecho-Slovak press agency in Geneva, 1917–18. Czechoslovakia's diplomatic representative in UK, 1919–20. Member of Reparations Commission, League of Nations, 1921–32. Chairman, Supervisory Commission, 1922–36. Ambassador to France, 1921–39. Minister of Czechoslovak Government-in-Exile, 1940. Prof. at Colgate University, New York, 1945. Member, Council of Free Czechoslovakia, 1948.

[6] Paul Ramadier, 1888–1961. Opposed Vichy regime of Marshal Philippe Pétain. Member of French Resistance, WWII. PM of French Fourth Republic, 1947. Memorialized in Yad Vashem in Jerusalem, Israel.

[7] François de Menthon, 1900–84. Capt., 1939. Member of French Resistance. Minister of Justice, French Government-in-Exile, 1943–5. Attorney-General of France, 1945. Mayor of Menthon-Saint-Bernard, 1945–77. Member, French National Assembly, 1946–58. President, of Parliamentary Assembly of the Council of Europe, 1951–4.

[8] Guy Mollet, 1905–75. Educated at Le Havre. Member of French Section of Workers International

and a strong German delegation including Carlo Schmidt,[1] Brentano,[2] the Mayor of Berlin,[3] etc.

When the Economic Conference of the European Movement was held here some time ago the Labour Government, in spite of its luke-warmness on the whole subject, had Alexander[4] to speak at their opening session and also gave a reception to the delegates. As you created the whole European Movement and are its Honorary President I hope you will be able to arrange for some member of the Government to welcome the delegates on the opening day and also for some kind of Government reception.

The whole underlying idea of the Conference is to remind the countries behind the Iron Curtain that they are not forgotten and that we look to their peaceful reunion with the rest of Europe at some time or other. But great stress will be laid on making it clear that there is no idea of winning them back to Europe by force.

As I am writing to you I might add that at a meeting of the European Economic League at Brussels on Saturday I heard a good deal about the disillusionment of the Continent with our attitude at Strasbourg. I found, on the other hand, that they eagerly accepted, as an alternative to the idea of pulling us out of the Commonwealth into Europe, the conception of Europe working closely, particularly in the economic field, with the Commonwealth as a whole. It seems to me that by laying stress on that wider conception we get away from the Continental notion that we use the Commonwealth as an excuse for a negative attitude.

(SFIO) party. Joined French Army, 1939. Member of French Resistance, WWII. Elected to French National Assembly, 1945. Secretary-General of SFIO, 1946. Deputy PM, 1946, 1951. Minister for European Relations, 1950–1. Represented France at the Council of Europe. Vice-President of Socialist International, 1951–69. PM, 1956–7. Minister of State, 1958.

[1] Carlo Schmidt, 1896–1979. Educated at University of Tübingen. On active service for Germany, 1914–18. Judge, 1927. Privatdozent at University of Tübingen, 1930–40. Legal counsel of *Oberfeldkommandantur* (commander of occupied region), Lille. Member of Social Democratic Party (SPD) of Germany, 1947–70. Member of German Federal Parliament, 1949–72; Vice-President, 1949–66, 1969–72. Proponent of German–French reconciliation. Member of Parliamentary Assembly of Council of Europe, 1950–60, 1969–73.

[2] Heinrich von Brentano di Tremezzo, 1904–64. Educated at Giessen and Munich. Lawyer in Darmstadt, 1932–43; in Hanau, 1943–5. Helped to found Christian Democratic Union (CDU), 1946. President of Christian Democratic Union/Christian Social Union (CSU) Coalition, 1947. Served on Parliamentary Council that drafted the Basic Law for the Federal Republic of Germany, 1948–9. Elected to first Federal Bundestag, 1949. Parliamentary leader of CDU/CSU, 1949–55, 1961–4. Advocate of European unity. President of Schuman Plan Committee, organizing European Economic Community, 1952–3. Foreign Minister, 1955–61.

[3] Ernst Rudolf Johannes Reuter, 1889–1953. 'Free Berlin' spokesman and leader following Berlin blockade, 1948–9. Mayor of West Berlin, 1948–53.

[4] Harold Rupert Leofric George Alexander, 1891–1969. Educated at Harrow and Sandhurst. On active service, 1914–18 (wounded three times, despatches five times, DSO, MC). Lt-Gen. Commanding I Corps, 1940 (despatches). GOC Southern Command, 1940–2; Burma, 1942; Middle East, 1942–3. Knighted, 1942. C-in-C, 18th Army Group, North Africa, 1943; Allied Armies in Italy (15th Army Group), 1943–4. FM, 1944. Supreme Allied Commander, Mediterranean Theatre, 1944–5. Viscount, 1946. KG, 1946. Governor-General of Canada, 1946–52. Earl Alexander of Tunis, 1952. Minister of Defence, 1952–4. OM, 1959. Author of *The Alexander Memoirs* (1962).

On the army position for instance I pointed out that in both world wars the armies of the Commonwealth had played their decisive part in the European theatre. Could they really expect us to be inside a European army and then find Canadian, Australian or South African forces left outside or even attached to the American army? They at once saw the point and readily accepted it.[1]

Winston S. Churchill to Members of the Cabinet
(*Premier papers, 11/270*)

17 December 1951
Top Secret
Progress of Defence Programmes Paper No. 1 of 1951

PROGRESS OF DEFENCE PROGRAMMES

My proposals for reducing the Service Estimates are contained in a Minute of 15th December (below) which I addressed to the Service Ministers and the Minister of Supply. I will consider the Service Ministers' suggestions for bringing their programmes within the limits proposed at a meeting on Thursday, December 20th, at 3.0 p.m.

At our meetings earlier in the week we discussed each of the Service programmes separately. In the light of those discussions I have now reviewed the three Estimates as a whole. As they stand at present they total £1,547 millions. It is evident that the national economy could not bear so great a burden. We must aim at cutting down the total by at least £250 millions.

2. I divide this between the three Services as follows:

	Reduction £ millions
Admiralty	
Reduce from 402 to 330	72
War Office	
Reduce from 611 to 500	111
Air Ministry	
Reduce from 534 to 456	69
	252

3. *Production.* Within the totals given in paragraph 2, we must aim at reducing the provision for production from £716 millions to £551 millions (on the basis of September 1951 prices). The allocation of this £551 millions will be:

	£ millions
Admiralty	161
War Office	200
Air Ministry	190

---

[1] Churchill wrote to Duncan Sandys on Dec. 20: 'Please advise.'

Of the total allocation for production not more than £440 millions will be spent in the metal-using industries, allocated as follows:

	£ millions
Admiralty	130
War Office	140
Air Ministry	170

4. *Work Services.* Within the totals given in paragraph 2, we must aim at reducing the provision for Work Services from £175 millions to £129 millions. The allocation of this £129 millions will be:

	£ millions
Admiralty	14
War Office	30
Air Ministry	85

As regards new works in the United Kingdom, the allocation for the purposes of the Investment Programme (in terms of September 1951 prices) will be:

	£ millions
Admiralty	7
War Office	11
Air Ministry	35
Ministry of Supply (direct)	23

The Air Ministry allocation will not include expenditure on further instalments of the work for the United States Air Force provided that the United States will provide the steel needed and meet the bulk of cost in dollars.

5. I attach as an Appendix a table setting out the provisional Estimates of the three Services and the revised figures which I now propose.

6. I ask each of the Service Ministers to consider at once the implications of these reductions, and to frame the best proposals that can be devised for bringing his programme within these limits. The object must be to get the best value, in terms of fighting strength, for the reduced expenditure. This is an opportunity for ingenuity and resource to screw the most out of what we can afford.

7. I will consider the results of these enquiries with all the Ministers concerned at a meeting to be held on Thursday, December 20th at 3 p.m. I look to the Ministers to let me have their proposals in advance of that meeting – at latest by the evening of Wednesday, December 19th.

APPENDIX

	Provisional Estimates 1952–53 £ millions	Proposed Revisions
ADMIRALTY		
Works	19	14
Production	208	161
Research and Development	15	15
All other	149	140
	*391	330
WAR OFFICE		
Works	40	30
Production	286	200
All other	285	270
	611	500
AIR MINISTRY		
Works	116	85
Production	222	190
All other	196	190
	534	465

* Later increased to 402.

Anthony Eden to Winston S. Churchill
(Churchill papers, 2/517)

18 December 1951
PM/51/151

On the 7th December the Cabinet approved in principle the proposal made in my Paper C(51)36 of the 3rd December that in the case of the war criminals for whom we are responsible in the British Zone of Germany, the period of pre-trial custody should be reckoned towards sentences. The Cabinet took note that, before this was announced, I would send you a list of the war criminals who would be released and of those who would not be released as a result of adopting this proposal.

2. The lists, which have come from Germany, are attached. The first, namely those war criminals who will qualify for release, includes 46 names. You

will see that the well-known names (e.g. Manstein,[1] Kesselring,[2] Mackensen,[3] Falkenhorst,[4] which are starred, appear on the second list of 146 names, that is to say, the list of those who will remain in prison. Their offences were set out in the enclosure to a brief sent to you before Dr Adenauer's visit. This was to be expected because the first list is that of the prisoners who are serving the shorter sentences. If however the Cabinet approve the proposals which I am circulating for dealing with the general question of war criminals in the contractual settlement with the Federal Republic, all these cases could be considered in an orderly way by an Advisory Clemency Board, comprising neutral and German as well as British membership.

3. The last three names on the first list may have to be transferred to the second list since there is still some doubt about how their period of pre-trial custody ought to be counted.

4. The timing of the public announcement of our decision to release these war criminals is important. I propose to send instructions to Germany for action to be taken about the 22nd or 23rd December. Dr Adenauer expressed the hope that these people could be let out before Christmas.

5. At the time when the announcement is made our publicity will make it plain that the step is not a sop to the Germans, but is an administrative action designed to bring about fair and equal treatment.

6. You will also have seen a note which I have circulated to my colleagues about how the period of pre-trial custody was considered at the trials and in the subsequent review of sentences. This arises from the Cabinet Conclusions on December 7th.

---

[1] Erich von Manstein, 1887–1973. Entered German Army, 1906. Maj.-Gen., 1936. Lt-Gen., 1938. Gen., 1940. CoS to Gen. Gerd von Rundstedt, 1939. Planned Hitler's invasion of France through Ardennes Forest, 1940. Cdr, 11th Army, 1941. FM, 1942. Dismissed, 1944. Captured by British, 1945. Tried and convicted of war crimes, 1953. Author of *Lost Victories* (1955).

[2] Albert Kesselring, 1885–1960. On active service with Bavarian Foot Artillery, 1914–16 (Iron Cross); posted to General Staff, 1917. Chief of Luftwaffe General Staff, 1936–7. Air Gen., 1938. Cdr, Luftflotte 1, 1939–40; Luftflotte 2, 1940–3. FM, 1940. C-in-C South, 1941–5. C-in-C West, 1945. Tried for war crimes and sentenced to death; sentence commuted to life imprisonment, 1947. Released, 1952.

[3] Friedrich August Eberhard von Mackensen, 1889–1969. CoS, German 14th Army, 1939–40. Col-Gen., 1943–4. Responsible for Roman massacre of 24 Mar. 1944. Convicted of war crimes, Rome, 1947; death sentence commuted. Released, 1952.

[4] Nikolaus von Falkenhorst, 1885–1968. Entered German Army, 1903. CoS, 1935. Commanded 21st Army Corps in invasion of Poland, 1939. Commanded invasion of Norway, 1940. Dismissed, 1944. Tried for war crimes and sentenced to death, 1946. Released, 1953.

December 1951

Cabinet: conclusions
(Cabinet papers, 128/23)

19 December 1951
Secret
11 a.m.
Cabinet Meeting No. 18 of 1951

1. The Prime Minister gave the Cabinet an account of the discussions which he and the Foreign Secretary had held with French Ministers and with General Eisenhower during their visit to Paris on 17th and 18th December. The visit would, he thought, be of benefit to Anglo-French relations: in particular, it should have removed any French apprehensions lest their interests should be overlooked in the talks which he and the Foreign Secretary would shortly be having in Washington. It had also been valuable to have a free exchange of views with the French Ministers about the European Army. He had been able to make plain, in private conversations, his disappointment at the shape which the European Army was assuming under the Pleven Plan: but, as the United Kingdom was not to be a member of the European Defence Community, he had not felt able to press these technical points too far. The communiqué which had been issued at the end of the talks had made it clear that the United Kingdom Government favoured the creation of a European Defence Community, though they could not join it, and that they were ready to associate themselves with it as closely as possible in all stages of its political and military development. This should forestall any further suggestion that the delay in securing agreement to the creation of a European Army was due to the unhelpful attitude of the United Kingdom Government.

The Cabinet took note of the Prime Minister's statement.

[. . .]

Sir Vincent Tewson[1] to Winston S. Churchill
(Premier papers, 11/86)

19 December 1951

Dear Prime Minister,

SCHOOL AGE

Our General Council at their meeting today noted with some concern the answers which have recently been given by yourself and the Minister of Education to questions on the subject of the school age. They regret that you were

---

[1] Vincent Tewson, 1891–1981. 2nd Lt, 1917. Lt, 1919. MC, 1918. CBE, 1942. General Secretary, TUC, 1946–60. Knighted, 1950. President, International Confederation of Free Trade Unions, 1951–3.

unable to disclaim forthwith any intention on the part of the Government to lower the school leaving age or to raise the age of entry to school.

The General Council share your concern as to the general economic situation in which we find ourselves and the difficulties we face in regard to manpower, supplies, and finance. They have publicly declared their readiness to co-operate in seeking appropriate solutions for these problems.

But I have to say that in the view of the General Council a reduction in the school life of our children would be a highly inappropriate solution and one which they would strongly deprecate. From a material standpoint it would be the falsest economy. From the point of view of human rights and equality of opportunity it would be a disastrous blow.

We trust that you can take early steps to allay the serious and widespread fears which have been aroused as the result of the recent parliamentary exchanges on this subject.

Sir Norman Brook: note
(Premier papers, 11/313)

20 December 1951

Mr Harriman[1] asked if he could see the Prime Minister while he was in Paris. He gave no indication of the subjects which he wished to discuss but it was thought that he might wish to speak about UK coal production or possibly, the reorganisation of NATO.

Mr Harriman came to see the Prime Minister at the Embassy at 6.30 on 18th December and stayed with him, alone, for an hour. The Prime Minister subsequently told me that they had had no conversation about coal production – Mr Harriman had not raised the matter, and the Prime Minister had not thought it necessary to take any initiative in discouraging the suggestion of a European Coal Board. Nor, I gather, had Mr Harriman said any more about the reorganisation of NATO. The conversation had been general, and had ranged over a number of topics, which were then in the forefront of the Prime Minister's mind, e.g. the European Army, the course of the discussions with French Ministers, the terms of the communiqué which was to be issued at the end of the talks and the forthcoming visit to Washington. On this last topic

[1] William Averell Harriman, 1891–1986. Married, 1915, Kitty Lanier Lawrence (div. 1928); Marie Norton (d. 1970); 1971, Pamela Digby. Chairman of the Board, Merchant Shipping Corp., 1917–25; Union Pacific Railroad, 1932–46. Member, Business Advisory Council, Dept of Commerce, 1933–40. Roosevelt's emissary (Special Representative) in London, to negotiate Lend-Lease arrangements, March 1941. Accompanied Lord Beaverbrook on his mission to Moscow, with rank of Ambassador, 1941. On Combined Production and Resources Board, London, 1942. US Ambassador to Soviet Union, 1943–6; to UK, 1946. US Secretary of Commerce, 1946–8. Special Asst to President Truman, 1950–1. Chairman, NATO Commission on Defence Plans, 1951. Director, Mutual Security Agency, Oct. 1951–Jan. 1953. Asst Secretary of State, Far Eastern Affairs, 1961–3. US negotiator, Limited Test Ban Treaty, 1963; Vietnam peace talks, Paris, 1968–9.

the Prime Minister had told Mr Harriman that he was intending to ask for 1.5 million tons of steel. Mr Harriman had apparently shown no special surprise at this figure. He had said that this request would have to be negotiated with Mr Charles Wilson,[1] the Director of the Defence Production Authority; but he had promised that, for his part, he would make it clear to the appropriate authorities in Washington that further substantial supplies of steel would be the greatest practical contribution which the United States could make towards the UK economy. In general, Mr Harriman had promised to give all possible assistance to the Prime Minister in the Washington negotiations and had invited the Prime Minister and his Ministerial colleagues to call on him for any help that he could give.

Winston S. Churchill to King George VI[2]
(Premier papers, 11/270)

20 December 1951

Sir,

The basis on which I am discussing the Estimates of the Armed Services for 1952–53 with my colleagues is set out in a Paper which I think Your Majesty should see.[3] I enclose a copy. I am continuing my discussions today.

With my humble duty
I remain
Your Majesty's faithful
and devoted Servant

Anthony Eden to Winston S. Churchill
(Churchill papers, 2/517)

21 December 1951
Secret
PM/51/152

Your minute of M157c/51 of December 15th,[4] about Sir Ian Jacob's report on his enquiry into the inter-allied machinery for concerting the defence effort of the Western world.

---

[1] Charles Edward Wilson, 1886–1972. Born in Bronxville, NY. President, General Electric Co., 1940–2, 1945–50. Vice-Chairman, War Production Board, 1942–4. Chairman, President's Committee on Civil Rights, 1946–7. Director, Office of Defense Mobilization, 1950–2.

[2] Albert Frederick Arthur George, 1895–1952. Second son of King George V. Educated at Royal Naval Colleges, Osborne and Dartmouth. Lt RN, 1918. Succeeded his brother as King, Dec. 1936. Crowned (as George VI), May 1937.

[3] Reproduced above (pp. 136–8).

[4] Reproduced above (p. 132).

2. I see one major objection to Jacob's proposals. He proposes in paragraph 2 of his report:
- (a) that there should be a Permanent Representative of each member state – but he does not say to whom he would be responsible at home;
- (b) that the representation at any particular session should vary according to the agenda or the desires of the members – presumably selected from a number of different Ministers.

3. To my mind this is an example of a tendency, which has grown alarmingly during the last few years, to disperse the handling of international relations among a multiplicity of Ministers. International relations are the concern of Foreign Ministers, and I really must insist that, in our proposals for the reorganisation of NATO, it should be clear that the responsibility rests with the Foreign Secretary. This is certainly the present practice in other NATO countries.

4. Such a result could be achieved by laying down as a rule that, when a British Minister attends the Council, it is the Foreign Secretary who attends, and that it is for him to say whether he needs the assistance of a Ministerial colleague. I am sure that there will be many instances in which such assistance will be required, and I should not hesitate to call for it. But on many matters, including most of those concerning defence, I should hope that you would feel me perfectly competent to handle the matter on behalf of His Majesty's Government with advisers from the Departments concerned.

5. This is the rule I should hope that we would follow in this country. I would then expect that a similar practice would be generally adopted in NATO. Acheson, from what he told me in Rome, is very much of my mind. Unless the members of NATO (we are shortly to be fourteen) impose some such rule on themselves, I see no way of reducing the enormous number of Ministers and advisers who crowd the Council chamber and render any negotiation or indeed discussion impossible.

6. If this general rule is accepted, I see no objection to Jacob's proposal that the North Atlantic Council should be in permanent session and that each member state should appoint a permanent representative. The representative in our case should, in my view, continue to be an official, and a member of the Foreign Service, who would receive his instructions, as he does at present, from the Foreign Secretary.

7. I agree generally with the other recommendations in Jacob's report. I attach particular importance to the proposed creation of a new Economic and Production Board, which would be placed alongside the headquarters of the organisation. I also think it important to draw a clear distinction, as Jacob suggests, between the functions of this NATO board, which will deal with the financial, economic and production problems arising from NATO, defence, and the functions of OEEC, which relate to the economic problems

of Europe only and have no reference to defence. It is important to make it clear to our European allies, both inside and outside of NATO, that we still consider that the OEEC should be maintained and supported as an independent body for the performance of the functions described above.

8. Finally, you know that I wish to maintain the headquarters of the organisation (the Council with its new economic and production board) in London, leaving the Standing Group in Washington. I think we should fight hard for this. But we shall have a stern battle. Harriman and others prefer Paris. London is the true Atlantic capital.

9. There is another wider consideration to which Jacob rightly draws attention. That is that the organisation of defence in peace should be such that it could easily be adapted to be the organisation which would be required in war. I think that a reform on the lines proposed by Jacob would give the best possible results from this point of view.

10. If you agree generally, we can take the question up on these lines with the Americans when we go to Washington.

James Thomas to Winston S. Churchill
(*Premier papers, 11/159*)

21 December 1951
Top Secret and Personal
Guard

A paper written in July by the late Director of Naval Intelligence, Vice Admiral Longley-Cook,[1] has just been brought to my notice. It was shown to Mr Attlee by my predecessor, Pakenham,[2] in the autumn. Mr Attlee was very interested in it but did not pursue the matter in view of the imminent General Election.

I feel that I should let you see a copy of this document before your visit to America; it is a long one, but I also attach a summary. I must add that this

---

[1] Eric William Longley-Cook, 1898–1983. Entered RN, 1914. On active service, HMS *Prince of Wales*, 1914–18. Lt, 1919. Lt-Cdr, 1927. Capt., 1938. Cdr, HMS *Caradoc*, 1939–40. Deputy Director of Training and Staff Duties, 1940. Deputy Director of Gunnery and Anti-Aircraft Warfare, 1941. Cdr, HMS *Argonaut*, 1942–3. Capt. of the Fleet, Mediterranean Fleet, 1943; East Indies Fleet, 1945. DSO, 1945. CoS, Home Fleet, 1946–8. Director of Naval Intelligence, 1948–51. RAdm., 1948. CB, 1950. Vice-Adm., 1951.

[2] Francis Aungier Pakenham, 1905–2001. 2nd son of 5th Earl of Longford (killed in action at Gallipoli in 1915). Educated at Eton and New College, Oxford. Worked in Conservative Party Economic Research Dept, 1930–2. Lecturer in Politics, Oxford University, 1932. Personal Assistant to Sir William Beveridge, 1941–4. Parliamentary Under-Secretary of State, War Office, 1946–7. Chancellor of the Duchy of Lancaster, 1947–8. Minister of Civil Aviation, 1948–51. 1st Lord of the Admiralty, 1951. Succeeded his brother as Earl of Longford, 1961. Lord Privy Seal, 1964–5, 1966–8. Secretary of State for the Colonies, 1965–6. KG, 1971.

paper has never been formally considered by the Admiralty and contains only the personal views of its author.

May I ask you to return the paper when you have perused it? All other copies were ordered to be destroyed some months ago.[1]

Winston S. Churchill: broadcast
('Winston S. Churchill, His Complete Speeches', volume 8, pages 8314–18)

22 December 1951

THE STATE OF THE NATION

Tonight, my friends, it is my duty to tell you the broad truths of our national life and policy as they strike me on shouldering the burden again. I shall try to do so without regard to party propaganda and without seeking popularity at the public expense. I have but twenty minutes so I hope you will not reproach me for leaving out anything I have not time to say. The Conservative Party have now assumed control and bear responsibility for trying to make things better. During the eight weeks since I received His Majesty's Commission the new Government has been hard at work examining the state of the nation as we are now able to find it out. Six years of Socialist rule and the last two years of class warfare and party fighting have divided our strength and absorbed our energies. When we came in we found the country on the verge of insolvency. Our resources had been used up. The barrel had been scraped. There was nothing more that could be found without doing severe and unpopular things. That was why there was a General Election.

Let us look at the whole scene. It is quite certain that we cannot keep fifty millions alive in this island if they are divided half and half and electioneering against one another all the time. We have had more than two years of electioneering. You cannot say it is the fault of one party or the other. It is the way in which our free and time-honoured constitution has worked in this crucial and it may be tragic period in our history. One thing is plain. It can't go on if we are to go on. It certainly can't go on if we are to hold our rank among the nations or even if we are to keep ourselves independent.

His Majesty's present Government intend, if we can, to bring electioneering to a full stop. This is not the time for party brawling. Of course, we shall answer attacks made upon us and give back as good as we get. But we shall do what we believe is right and necessary for the country in its present crisis according to our convictions, without being dominated by the idea of winning

---

[1] Churchill responded on 9 Jan. 1952: 'It is the usual Communist approach to British intellectuals. A sharp eye should be kept upon the writer' (Prime Minister's Personal Minute M.7/52).

or losing votes. We do not seek to be judged by promises but by results. We seek to be judged by deeds rather than by words. After six years we have a right to have a fair try, not for the sake of any class or party but to surmount the perils and problems which now beset us. To do this we require not only resolve and design but time, and we think that we have not only the right to claim time but the power to take it.

The differences between parties in this island are not so great as a foreigner might think by listening to our abuse of one another. There are underlying unities throughout the whole British nation. These unities are far greater than our differences. In this we are unlike many countries and after all it has pretty well soaked into the British nation that we all sink or swim together. Take the Social Services. These have been built up during the past hundred years by each succeeding Conservative, Liberal and latterly Socialist Government. Take foreign affairs and national defence. Nine-tenths of the British people agree on nine-tenths of what has been done and is being done and is going to go on being done.

I paid my tribute in the House of Commons to the work of the Labour Government in their resolute defiance of Communism, in their close association with the United States, in their establishment of national service and in their attempt to form a solid front in Western Europe against aggression. We respect the memory of Ernest Bevin for the work he did, and I am certain he could not have done his work without the help and guidance in some degree which the Conservative Party gave him.

But now we have got to face the fact which not merely the Government or the Tory Party or the Socialist Party but all of us have got in front of us tonight. If a train is running on the wrong lines downhill at sixty miles an hour it is no good trying to stop it by building a brick wall across the track. That would only mean that the wall was shattered, that the train was wrecked and the passengers mangled. First you have to put on the brakes. The Chancellor of the Exchequer has already done that and the train is coming under control and can be stopped. Then the engine has to be put into reverse. We have to go back along the line till we get to the junction. Then the signalman has to switch the points and the train has to be started again on the right line, which, I am telling you beforehand – please remember it – is uphill all the way. On an ordinary railway this might cause quite a long delay. In the vast complex evolution of modern life and government it will take several years. We require at least three years before anyone can judge fairly whether we have made things better or worse.

We hear much talk of our Election promises. Let me read you what I said as Leader of the Conservative Party the last time I spoke to you on 8 October at the beginning of the General Election. Here are my words:

We make no promises of easier conditions in the immediate future. Too much harm has been done in these last six years for it to be repaired in a few months. Too much money has been spent for us to be able to avoid another financial crisis. It will take all our national strength to stop the downhill slide and get us back on the level, and after that we shall have to work up.[1]

Now, that is the warning I gave before you voted; and I have told you the same in other words tonight after you have voted.

Let me tell you what we found on taking over. First food. Our food supplies were slender. Our meat stocks were lower than they have ever been since 1941, during the crunch of the war and the U-boats. We shall be quite willing to take the blame if we fail, but let me make it clear that the price-rises and the cuts now being enforced are the legacy we received from those who during six years of peace have tried to buy the food for this island under wartime controls and through Government planners. They aimed at restriction. They got scarcity. It is not possible for us to recreate by a gesture the smooth-working trade process of food purchase that existed before the war. This can only be a gradual operation. We repudiate every scrap of responsibility for the state of things which has brought hardships upon the public this Christmas, and for other discomforts and shortages which may fall upon us in the coming months. It is only after a reasonable time has been allowed that the blame or credit for the quantity, quality and price of food and for the other methods of distribution can fairly be placed upon us.

But the dominant problem is how to pay our way. In the year 1951 the United Kingdom has failed by over £500 million to earn the money to pay other countries for what we have bought from them. In the month of October before we took office, our gold and dollar reserves fell by about £115 million or at the rate of nearly £1,400 million a year. This was the result not only of our own over-spending, but also of the over-spending of other countries in the sterling area. Yet at that time, the total reserves were little over £1,000 million. Unless this rate of loss could be reduced, we were within a few months of national bankruptcy and having to choose between charity, if we could get it, and starvation. Of course, whoever had got in at the last Election would have had to deal with this dire challenge not only to our standard of living, but to our life. I am sure that no British Government of either party would have failed to take very hard measures. The responsibility for meeting this crisis falls on us. We had no responsibility for bringing it about, but we are sure we can master it; and we shall not shrink from any measure, however unpopular, for which our duty calls. I must make it plain that if the late Government had called Parliament together at the end of August, and told them the facts, and

[1] Broadcast reproduced above (pp. 2177–82).

if they had then taken even the emergency steps which we took in our first few days of office in November the sharpness of our crisis would have been definitely reduced.

The emergency measures which we have already taken are only part of the process of slowing down the train, and getting it under control. There is still more to be done before we can go forward on the right lines. When Parliament meets in January we shall be ready with a list of fresh proposals. Many of them will be unpleasant and I have no doubt that they will excite the loudest outcry from all those bitter politicians and writers who place party scores in front of national solvency. The nation must remember that these are the men – or the kind of men – who have brought us to our present pass. But we are resolved to do all that is necessary, first to clear the ground and then to rebuild on solid foundations the strength and prosperity of our people and our industries. It will be a long task. It will not be an easy one. But we shall persevere.

At the General Election much party capital was made by calling me 'a warmonger'. That was not true. Now that I am at the head of the Government I shall work ardently in harmony with our allies for peace. If war comes it will be because of world forces beyond British control. On the whole I do not think it will come. Whatever happens we shall stand up with all our strength in defence of the free world against Communist tyranny and aggression. We shall do our utmost to preserve the British Commonwealth and Empire as an independent factor in world affairs. We shall cherish the fraternal association of the English-speaking world. We shall work in true comradeship for and with United Europe. It may be that this land will have the honour of helping civilization climb the hill amid the toils of peace as we once did in the terrors of war.

What we have to face now is a peril of a different kind to 1940. We cannot go on spending as a nation or as individuals more than we can make and sell. We cannot go on counting upon American aid apart, that is to say, from the work of allied defence and rearmament, in order to make ourselves comfortable here at home. We cannot fail in our duty to what is called 'the sterling area', that great grouping of countries to whom we are the banker; we cannot fail by becoming a burden upon them. We must not plunge into further indebtedness to our Colonial Empire. All these are stern and grim facts which will not be changed by speeches of leading articles or canvassing or voting. There they are. Now we must meet them.

I have nothing to propose to you that is easy. A certain number of unpleasant things have been done already. They are only the beginning of what lies ahead. We are resolved to make this island solvent, able to earn its living and pay its way. Without this foundation not only do we lose our chance, and even our right to play our part in the defence of great causes, but we cannot keep our people alive. If we cannot earn our living by the intense exertions of our strength, our genius, our craftsmanship, our industry, there will be no time to emigrate the redundant millions for whom no food is grown at home; and we have no assurance that anyone else is going to keep the British Lion as a pet.

My friends, Mr Eden and I have just returned from France. We wanted our French friends to feel that we meant to be good friends and allies, and that we welcomed the measures which the French have taken to bringing Germany into the new European system and to end their age-long quarrel from which both these valiant races have suffered so much, and have brought so much suffering upon the rest of the world. You will remember that at Zurich in 1946 I appealed to France to take Germany by the hand and lead her back into the European family. I rejoice at the progress which has been made since then.

In a week we are to cross the Atlantic. I wish the United States and Canada too to have the feeling that we here are determined and also able to put our house in order and to play our full part throughout the international scene and that given the time we need we have the power to do so. I do not want to attach any exaggerated hope or importance to my visit to Washington. My wish and object is that we should reach a good understanding over the whole field so that we can work together easily and intimately at the different levels as we used to do. You must not expect the Americans to solve our domestic problems for us. In rearmament and in the North Atlantic Treaty Organization we have immense and intricate affairs in common, and I want to make sure that we can help each other as much as possible and in the best way.

My friends, my twenty minutes are finished, and I have only time to wish you from the bottom of my heart a happy Christmas in your homes, a Christmas inspired by hope – high hope – and unconquerable resolve for the New Year. Good night, and good luck to you all.

Winston S. Churchill to Lieutenant-General Kenneth McLean,
for the Chiefs of Staff Committee
Prime Minister's Personal Minute M.166c/51
(Premier papers, 11/56)

23 December 1951
Most Secret

Owing to the fact that the arrangements for the movement of the 6th Armoured Division to Germany were too far advanced for me to stop them I approved the completion of the movement and thereby accept responsibility for the decision.

2. A weekly report is to be made to the Minister of Defence on the progress of imparting a combatant value to the 249,000 soldiers training, etc., in the United Kingdom. I also want a note on the financial aspects, but do not delay motion on this account.

3. I am glad that the CIGS is raising the seven extra battalions. Pray let

me have a note on the cost. Pray let me also have a full account of the plan, namely the establishment and locations of the battalions, their names, etc. Can you not make these into three mobile defence brigade groups? What artillery is available? It need not be mechanically mounted, so the guns can be towed behind tractors or even lorries. What other units would be required for such formations?

4. I should be glad to receive the answer to the above minute at least in outline before I leave.

Winston S. Churchill to Sir Vincent Tewson
(*Premier papers, 11/86*)

24 December 1951
Private and Confidential

Dear Sir Vincent Tewson,

I thank you for your letter of December 19,[1] and I note what you say about any alteration in the school age. It is quite true that I have been looking into this as into a great many other matters arising out of the three years rearmament scheme and our present difficulties. I have been for some years past impressed with the overcrowding due to the shortage of accommodation in the schools and the defective education resulting therefrom. I had never contemplated any permanent change, but only a possible three years suspension till the schools catch up the pupils and the armament drive is over. I have not yet received any reports on the subject.

As you know nothing could in any case be done, even on a temporary basis, without legislation, which would certainly be most controversial. Meanwhile I did not feel I ought repeatedly to be asked at Question Time in Parliament to issue general disclaimers on this or many other matters. When I get back from America I hope to have a talk with you and some of your colleagues whom I know and whose opinion and advice I value.

Duncan Sandys to Winston S. Churchill
(*Premier papers, 11/75*)

24 December 1951

TANKS

In the event of war, tanks will no doubt be needed in large numbers. At the moment, our Centurion is the best tank in the world. The Americans have

---

[1] Reproduced above (p. 140).

nothing in production equal to it. In fact they have been enquiring whether we would be willing to accept from them a substantial order for Centurions with which to equip NATO forces (including possibly American units).

Our present production programme provides for the manufacture of some 600 tanks in 1952/3 and about 1,000 in 1953/4. Of the 600 to be produced next year 100 had always been earmarked for the Canadians, leaving 500 for the British Army. However, as a result of the cut in the service estimates decided upon last week, the War Office have felt obliged to reduce their demand to 350. They propose to sell the balance of 150 to the United States.

It is not my concern to advise as to how the tanks we produce should be used. But it is my responsibility to ensure that our tank-making capacity is developed on a sufficient scale to meet the demands which are likely to be made upon us in war. This can only be done by placing increased orders now.

Provided that tanks were given the same super-priority as aircraft, we could probably turn out some 800 Centurions in the year 1952/3 and at least 1,500 in 1953/4. If for financial reasons the British Army could not afford the units to man the additional tanks, these might either be held in store as a war reserve or be sold to the Americans to help swell our dollar export trade.

I therefore, recommend:
(a) That we should, over the next two years, make as many tanks as possible of the Centurion type or better, up to a maximum of say, 3,000.
(b) That the same super-priority should be given to tank production as has been given to aircraft; and
(c) That the question of the disposal of any balance which the Army cannot afford to accept should be left over for decision later.

Konrad Adenauer to Winston S. Churchill
(*Premier papers, 11/166*)

25 December 1951

As the year draws to its close I send you, Mr Prime Minister, my sincere and cordial good wishes and beg you to believe that, inspired by our fruitful discussions in London, I will in the coming year also do everything in my power to consolidate the confident relationship between our two Governments and thereby to make a contribution to the establishment of peace in a free world.

Winston S. Churchill to Anthony Eden
Prime Minister's Personal Minute M.180c/51
(Premier papers)

25 December 1951

Thank you very much for drawing my attention to this series of telegrams. On the whole I am against the Chinese Communists but I agree with you in doubting whether Dulles'[1] line of opposition is the right one. Let us talk about this on the voyage.

Winston S. Churchill to Antony Head and Sir William Slim
Prime Minister's Personal Minute M.182c/51
(Premier papers, 11/75)

26 December 1951

See minute of Minister of Supply attached.[2]

We must have full production of Centurion tanks or a better type during the next two years and the same priority is to be accorded to them as is given to jet aircraft. Other expenses must be reduced accordingly. The disposal of these tanks between the British Army, NATO and other exports can be settled later. Pray report on this by the 28th.

Duncan Sandys to Winston S. Churchill
(Premier papers, 11/162)

26 December 1951

You have asked for my comments on Mr Amery's letter[3] about the Eastern European Conference convened by the European Movement in January in London.

Mr Amery makes two requests, namely:

(1) That a Cabinet Minister should welcome the delegates at the opening of the Conference; and
(2) That the Government should give an official reception for the delegates;

---

[1] John Foster Dulles, 1888–1959. Legal Counsel to US Delegation to Versailles Peace Conference, 1918. Chief Foreign Policy Adviser for Republican Presidential Nominee Thomas Dewey, 1944, 1948. Helped draft Preamble to UN Charter, 1945. US Delegate to the UN, 1946, 1947, 1950. Secretary of State, 1953–9.

[2] Reproduced above (pp. 150–1).

[3] Reproduced above (pp. 134–6).

The Labour Government did both these things when the European Movement held its last conference in London in 1949. The present Government could not decently do less.

Winston S. Churchill to Antony Head and Sir William Slim
Prime Minister's Personal Minute M.184c/51
(Premier papers, 11/75)

26 December 1951

Further to my minute[1] about top priority for Centurion tanks the Ministry of Supply should be asked how the increase in cost could be saved by reducing the number of soft-skinned vehicles whether four wheel or two wheel drive. It is here that the economy should be made.

Winston S. Churchill to Lieutenant-General George Erskine[2]
Prime Minister's Personal Telegram T.113c/51
(Premier papers, 11/91)

27 December 1951
Operational Immediate
Personal
Confidential
DEF 269

It would be better for you to keep to a minimum communiqués and interviews with the Press at the present time. There is no need to explain everything.

---

[1] M.182c/51, reproduced above (p. 152).

[2] George Watkin Eben James Erskine, 1899–1965. Known as 'Bobby'. QMG., Eastern Command, 1937–9. CO, 2nd Battalion, King's Royal Rifle Corps, 1940–1; 69th Bde, 1941–2. Brig.-Gen., 1942. GOC 7th Armoured Div., Jan. 1943 to Aug. 1944. Maj-Gen., 1944. Head SHAEF, Belgium, 1944. Deputy CoS, Allied Control Commission, Germany, 1945–6. Lt-Gen., 1946. GOC Hong Kong, 1946; Egypt, 1949–52. GOC-in-C Eastern Command, 1952–3. Gen., 1953. C-in-C East Africa (Kenya), 1953–4. GOC-in-C Southern Command, 1955–8. Director-General, Territorial Army, 1946–9. ADC General to the Queen, 1955–8. Retired, 1958. Lt-Governor and C-in-C, Jersey, 1958–63.

154   December 1951

Winston S. Churchill to Anthony Eden
Prime Minister's Personal Minute M.186c/51
(Premier papers, 11/162)

27 December 1951

When the European Movement held its Conference in London in 1949 the Labour Government arranged for the delegates to be welcomed by a Cabinet Minister and they gave an official reception for them.

Pray consider whether we should not follow the same course when the Movement meets from January 21–24.

Anthony Eden to Winston S. Churchill
(Churchill papers, 2/517)

27 December 1951
PM/51/157

You will remember how pleased General Eisenhower was with our communiqué in Paris and that I asked him whether he could give it a fair wind the next day. I understood that he would do this, but actually he has said nothing of the kind.

Meanwhile, the American press continues to suggest that General Eisenhower wants us in the European Army and that we are the recalcitrant party. This applies even to such well-informed papers as the *New York Times* and the *Christian Science Monitor* and no doubt the more anti-British elements, which are not quoted in the attached summary, are busy on a more violent theme.

In the circumstances I thought that you should see the last press summary received here.

Randolph S. Churchill to Winston S. Churchill
(Churchill papers, 2/130)[1]

27 December 1951

My dearest Papa,

This is to wish you Bon Voyage. I am sure you will have a success. It is not the interest of the Administration that any hint of disagreement should emerge. You have much to give & doubtless much to receive. I foresee the British Lion being a greater pet than ever! Winston and Arabella[2] have enjoyed

---

[1] This letter was handwritten.
[2] Arabella Spencer-Churchill, 1949–2007. Daughter of Randolph Churchill and his second wife, June. Educated at Fritham School for Girls and Ladymede School. Married, 1972, Jim Barton (div.):

being at Chequers as much as I have. It is indeed generous of you to have had the Trust make these settlements on them. It will be a great help to have the income for their upbringing & education & a constant comfort to think that they will start life with this provision. I think it wonderful that your marvellous literary industry in the six years after the war should cast its protection round these young lives for so many years to come. Bless you.

Anthony Eden to Winston S. Churchill
(*Premier papers, 11/162*)

29 December 1951
PM/51/159

Your minute of the 27th December about a conference of the European Movement.[1]

2. This conference is being organized by the Central and Eastern European Commission. It was the subject of Shuckburgh's[2] letter of the 10th December to Pitblado[3] and my minute to you of the 14th December. You will have seen from the latter that I do not think that His Majesty's Government as such should be associated with this conference, which is not really a conference of the European Movement but of an organisation of refugees affiliated with it.[4]

Winston S. Churchill to Sir Edward Bridges
Prime Minister's Personal Minute M.193c/51
(*Premier papers, 11/270*)

29 December 1951

By what date have the revised Service Estimates to be approved in detail? I should like to give a day to each on my return after the 20th. Will that be early enough?

In the meanwhile they should be carefully examined in order to make sure that efficiency has not been needlessly sacrificed.

---

one child; 1987, Ian 'Haggis' McLeod: one child. In the early 1970s, she played a major role in the establishment of the annual Glastonbury Festival.

[1] M.186c/51, reproduced above (p. 154).

[2] (Charles Arthur) Evelyn Shuckburgh, 1909–94. Educated at Winchester and King's College, Cambridge. Entered Diplomatic Service, 1933. Private Secretary to British Ambassador to Egypt. FO, 1947. Private Secretary to Secretary of State for Foreign Affairs, 1951–4. British Permanent Representative to North Atlantic Council, 1962–9. Ambassador to Italy, 1966–9.

[3] David Bruce Pitblado, 1912–97. Educated at Emmanuel College, Cambridge. Principal Private Secretary to PM, 1951–6. Permanent Secretary, Ministry of Power, 1966–9; Ministry of Technology, 1969–70. CVO, 1953. KCB, 1967.

[4] Churchill wrote: 'As you wish. I am sorry we cannot go as far as the Socialists in this Eastern matter.'

December 1951

Clementine Churchill to Winston S. Churchill
(Churchill papers, 1/50)[1]

29 December 1951
To be opened by Mr Churchill only

Chartwell

My darling – do not be angry with me – But first – do you not think it would be wiser to give Duncan a smaller post – Sec of State for War is so very prominent – then do you think it wise to have him working immediately under your orders as Minister of Defence. If anything were to go wrong it would be delicate & tricky – first of all having to defend your son-in-law & later if by chance he made a mistake having to dismiss him –

Forgive me I think only of your welfare, happiness and dignity.

John Colville: diary
('The Fringes of Power', page 637)

30 December 1951

RMS *Queen Mary*, Southampton

Lord Mountbatten[2] came from Broadlands to dine and talked arrant political nonsense: he might have learned by heart a leader from the *New Statesman*. The PM laughed at him but did not, so Pug Ismay thought, snub him sufficiently. He caused much irritation to the Chiefs of Staff. I escorted Mountbatten off the ship. As we walked down the corridor he put his arm on my shoulder and said: 'Without you, Jock, I should feel no confidence, but as you are back I know all will be well.' It was, of course, intended as a friendly remark, but flattery, especially when so exaggerated, makes one wonder why one should be thought so naive.

---

[1] This letter was handwritten.

[2] Louis Francis Albert Victor Nicholas of Battenberg (His Serene Highness Prince Louis of Battenberg), 1900–79. Known as 'Dickie'. Second son of Prince Louis of Battenberg (Churchill's 1st Sea Lord, 1911–14), who in 1917 was created Marquess of Milford Haven and assumed the surname of Mountbatten. Naval Cadet, 1913–15. Midshipman, 1916. Cdr, 1932. Naval Air Div., Admiralty, 1936. Capt., 1937. Commanded HMS *Kelly*, 1939 (despatches twice). Chief of Combined Operations, 1942–3. Acting Adm., 1943. SACSEA, 1943–6. Viscount Mountbatten of Burma, 1946. Viceroy of India, 1947. Earl, 1947. Governor-General of India, 1947–8. SACMED, 1953–4. 1st Sea Lord, 1955–9. Adm. of the Fleet, 1956. CDS, 1959–65. Murdered by IRA terrorists, 27 Aug. 1979, while fishing in a boat on a lake in the Irish Republic.

Admiral Lord Louis Mountbatten: diary
('Mountbatten, A Biography', pages 502–3)

31 December 1951   RMS *Queen Mary*, Southampton

[Churchill] then turned to me and said, 'I think you should be careful about (garbled) anti-American attitude. The Americans like you. They trust you. You are one of the few commanders that they would willingly serve under. You will throw all that away if they think you are against them!'[1]

I replied that I was very fond of all my American friends, and that individually I thought they were a charming people; but, taken as a corporate mass, they were immature, and if they were allowed their own way they would probably take a course which would not only destroy this country but would ultimately end in the destruction of their own system. [. . .]

He then said: 'I am very sorry to hear you express such Left-Wing views. I think you should try and avoid expressing any political opinions. Your one value as a sailor is that you are completely non-political. Take care you remain so!'

I pointed out that I had always been completely non-political. [. . .] I had never been known to make any political remarks, but that I could not see that expressing the hope that he would be able to guide the Americans in such a way that our own country would not be destroyed could possibly be regarded as Left-Wing.

My impressions of this grand old man are that he is really past his prime. He was very deaf and kept having to have things repeated to him. He quoted poetry at great length. He went through the whole of the verses of 'Rule Britannia' and 'It's All Quiet Along the Potomac'. He was very sentimental and full of good will towards me. He kept telling me what a friend he was of mine and of my family.

Winston S. Churchill to Konrad Adenauer
(Premier papers, 11/166)

31 December 1951

Thank you so much for your telegram.[2] I send you in return my very best wishes for the New Year. I too am confident that our recent meeting will lead to increasing co-operation and understanding between our two countries in the years to come and so help to safeguard the peace.

---

[1] Mountbatten was against tying British foreign policy to that of the United States.
[2] Reproduced above (p. 151).

Winston S. Churchill to James Thomas
Prime Minister's Personal Minute M.200c/51
(Premier papers, 11/64)

31 December 1951

I promised to send you my considered views about your proposal, made in your minute of December 7,[1] for meetings of Service Ministers.

The Defence Committee is the main forum in which the Service Ministers will share in the collective discussion of military policy. This is the instrument through which the Prime Minister and Minister of Defence will discuss with the Service Ministers, other Ministers directly concerned and the Chiefs of Staff military matters of importance which concern more than one Service.

The Minister of Defence will hold separate meetings with the Chiefs of Staff to discuss strategic and operational questions. Similarly, the Minister of Defence may find it convenient to hold separate meetings with the Service Ministers to discuss administrative questions which are of common concern to the three Services but are not of such importance that they must be brought before the Defence Committee itself. The Minister of Defence, from his central position, will determine the best distribution of business between Staff Conferences with the Chiefs of Staff, meetings with Service Ministers and the Defence Committee.

I approve the appointment of a Service Ministers' Committee, with the composition and terms of reference shown in the attached notice. For the present I do not propose myself to preside over meetings of this Committee, and you will take the Chair on my behalf. I shall rely on you during this period to keep me generally informed of the work of the Committee and to see that it does not attempt to deal with any matters which could more suitably be handled by the Defence Committee itself.

---

[1] Reproduced above (pp. 113–14).

January 1952

General Dwight D. Eisenhower to Anthony Eden
(Premier papers, 11/373)

2 January 1952
Immediate
Confidential
No. 22030

I am grateful for the Prime Minister's cable. He knows, of course, that I was delighted with the press statement he made at the end of his Paris visit. The trouble, if any, is that apparently some of the Benelux people thought that the tone was influenced mainly by his consideration for his hosts. I met with the six Foreign Ministers on Saturday night and emphatically stated my agreement with the position of the British Government. M Schuman took the occasion to reinforce my statements in this regard. It seemed to be the opinion of the Ministers that if their people could be certain that I was correct about the British position, then there should be no real trouble on that score. As you probably know, the Ministers took a long step in approving a practical approach to the business of political and economic federation, and this also, I hope, will get several enthusiastic boosts from the British.

Please tell the Prime Minister that I am delighted with the news that he sent me through Monty.[1] Also convey to him my warm greetings, and of course I extend to the entire party my hope that you are having a good voyage and some semblance of a rest.

---

[1] Probably concerning the prospects for a European Army.

JANUARY 1952

Evelyn Shuckburgh: diary
('Descent to Suez', pages 31–4)

5–9 January 1952

Arrival in New York. We got off the *Queen Mary* on to a cutter and bounced across rather choppy water in the rain, feeling as if we were about to be thrown to the lions. A tremendous reception on shore with bands and flags and troops, marred by the wholly undisciplined behaviour of hundreds of cameramen who swarmed all over and all around the scene. While Winston and AE were standing to attention for the National Anthems, there were cameramen shouting 'Look this way, Mr Churchill', '*Please*, Mr Eden', and so on. My old friend Jack Simmonds[1] is the head of Protocol and responsible for looking after us.

As we drove from the docks to the airport, the roads were lined with Irish placards saying: 'Go home Churchill', etc. A very comfortable flight to Washington in the President's aircraft and a really well-organized reception there. My hairdresser in London afterwards said he saw me on television descending from the aircraft. Shook Truman's hand and drove off with Acheson and AE to Blair House (where the President is living – the White House being under repair) for the President's lunch. I was left outside and found I had no car to get me to the Embassy. After some telephoning, the State Department provided one. A negro driver very interested in that curious anomaly England.

I attended most of the meetings with Truman in the White House Annexe. Thought him a very cheerful and nice man, though performing an act of continuous hearty efficiency, romping through the agenda with a loud, gay voice. He was quite abrupt on one or two occasions with poor old Winston and had a tendency, after one of the old man's powerful and emotional declarations of faith in Anglo-American co-operation, to cut it off with a 'Thank you, Mr Prime Minister. We might pass that to be worked out by our advisers.' A little wounding. I was impossible not to be conscious that we are playing second fiddle. Our own side (including AE, Lord Cherwell and Lord Ismay) were a good deal concerned by the PM's readiness to give away our case, both in regard to the Far East and on raw materials. On the latter subject, when we were trying to get steel in return for tin and some other metals, but were known to be unable to meet the Americans over copper, Winston electrified us by himself raising the question of copper, just at the point when agreement was about to be reached without it. He gave quite a little lecture on the need to develop copper production in the British African colonies, and appeared to be under the impression that he was addressing the British Cabinet. The American officials bravely and loyally extracted us from this difficulty.

The President's offices are decorated in the worst possible taste. The walls are covered with the most frightful cartoons of Mr Truman and relics of his

[1] John F. Simmons, 1892–1962. Chief of Protocol of the United States, 1950–7.

past political campaigns, and the main feature of his study – apart from the Stars and Stripes – is an enormous television set which I was offered the privilege of seeing in action by one the negro guards.

US–UK discussions: minutes
(*Cabinet papers, 21/3057*)

5–8 January 1952   Presidential Yacht *Williamsburg*
Virginia

President Truman and Mr Acheson asked Mr Churchill for his views on Russia.

2. Mr Churchill said there was fear in the Kremlin. The Russians had feared our friendship more than our enmity. This was now beginning to change. Risks were very great in 1948 at the time of the Berlin Air Lift. Now the risks were a little less. Mr Churchill did not expect a deliberate attack by the Soviets in 1952. On the other hand, the Soviets had not lost much. Since the end of the war they had gained half Europe and all China without loss.

Mr Churchill referred to the great decision made by the President when South Korea was invaded by the North Koreans. The whole affair had been a heavy cost to the United States. They had suffered 100,000 casualties. The great result, however, had been the new rearmament policy of the United States. Which was now well on in the second year of heavy rearmament. Mr Churchill pointed out that Britain, too, was doing her best. Now the free world was not a naked world, but a rearming world.

The United States had made the sacrifices and the effort in the Far East. Britain had interests in that part of the world. Mr Churchill looked on Hong Kong as a little Formosa. He promised to aid the United States as far as was possible. He did not think China had gone permanently Communist, but we had to deal with what was before us. Mr Churchill felt inclined to give aid in resisting any further aggression.

So far as the Middle East was concerned, Mr Churchill felt that if the present conference could have taken place a year before, there would have been no Persian or Egyptian difficulties like those of the moment. He asked the United States to give Britain moral assistance in Persia: we must both play one hand there. Our position in Egypt was not one of imperialism but of international duty. The proposal of the Four Powers to Egypt was an act of genius. Mr Churchill hoped the United States would be willing to back up our position by sending a Brigade perhaps, as a symbol, to the Canal Zone. If they would do so, everything would be cleared up quite quickly. Everyone else would fall in behind this.

3. Mr Acheson replied that the Americans concurred with the views expressed by Mr Churchill on Russia. Fear was the primary motivating force

in Russian policy. Fundamentally the régime lived in fear about their ability to maintain and exercise full control over their own people. In a secondary way they feared possible attack from outside. If this were so, one major element of our policy must be not to create such vast forces as might precipitate a desperate reaction by the Russians. On the other hand, we had to do enough to stop all easy triumphs. The problem was to translate this view into military terms.

Mr Acheson thought there were three principal questions at the present time confronting us in Europe. First, there was the solution of the problems about Germany. This centred around the French desire to put restrictions on German military production. If we could get over that, then satisfactory agreement with Germany was possible. Secondly, there was the creation of a European Army. Mr Acheson thought this effort would succeed or fail within forty days. At the present moment France, Germany and Italy were agreed on what they wanted to do. The three Benelux countries, Holland, Belgium and Luxembourg, did not agree with the three large countries. The problem before us was how to induce the three little countries to stop holding up progress by the three big countries. The prospect now opening up was no less than a re-creation of the Empire of Charlemagne. Thirdly, there was the report of the Three Wise Men.[1] If we could get it accepted for 1952, that would be a great stride forward. It was not necessary now to deal with 1953 and 1954. Mr Acheson stressed how completely, in his view, these three issues hung together.

Mr Acheson said about the Middle East that, if there was one place in the world where the theory of Karl Marx seemed to work, it was in this region. There were vast populations living in poverty. There was no middle class or very little of it. Governments were corrupt. They were liable to be, or to be thought to be, under the control of foreign Powers. In this situation the Kremlin need make no move; everything was ideal for them without any intervention. Our problem was how we could deflect the present course of events. He felt that the British prescription was to hold firm. He asked himself whether holding firm would do. He doubted it. That raised the problem of what more was wanted.

In the Far East Mr Acheson felt that policy about China must be pragmatic. It must depend upon what China is going to do. There was, for example, the present build-up on the borders of Indo-China. We had to make up our minds. We must decide whether South-East Asia was worth fighting for. If it was, how could effective resistance be offered. These were very grave questions. He thought we could not find solutions now on the main Far Eastern problems. We must explore each other's minds and then decide in a pragmatic way as circumstances arose.

4. Mr Eden said he agreed with Mr Acheson that there really was now an element of unity in Europe. That it existed was largely due to the policies

---

[1] Nickname for the Temporary Council Committee.

and help of the United States. In this matter the position of Britain raised no difficulties. The difficulty centred round the three Benelux countries, whose views were half-way between those of France, Germany and Italy on the one hand, and those of Britain on the other. Mr Eden believed that the difficulties of the Benelux countries could be met if they could see and believe that the full Atlantic story was a continuing one. He hoped that it might be possible to say something to this effect during the present meetings.

He felt that Russia faced a great deal of uneasiness in her satellites. There was more activity among the satellites against the régime than there was Communist activity within the free countries of Western Europe. He felt that these troubles in the satellites were something on which we could play, but it was important not to play it up too fast and too far: there was the risk of encouraging and stimulating something which we could not back.

Mr Eden agreed with much of what Mr Acheson had said about the Middle East. One of the elements in the picture was the economic help which the United States was pouring out. Britain was also doing something. The cardinal factor in the whole Middle East was the relation between Israel and the Arab States, and in this the central issue was the Arab Refugees. No real answers could be reached until something effective had been done on this refugee problem. He felt that all the present Middle Eastern problems were bound up with the great question of the Middle East Command. If we could get that into being, then all our efforts would be co-ordinated, whereas now they were inevitably diffuse.

In the Far East, South-East Asia was at present the most dangerous area. The French could handle Indo-China if it did not become a second Korea with major Chinese intervention. If this happened, there would have to be major decisions. The French could not do it by themselves. How much would it cost to meet the situation and what would the consequences be?

Returning again to Russia, Mr Eden said that he believed that, partly because of the policies and actions of the United States, partly through other circumstances, the Russians were for the time being on the defensive. We had the initiative. It was important to keep on the move. He felt that the next move should be the Austrian Treaty.

5. Mr Snyder,[1] in the course of a general reference to financial problems, said that they could not be dealt with just as so many immediate difficulties. It was necessary to look beyond the present and try to discover how to prevent these recurring crises.

6. Mr Lovett pointed out that expenditure on defence had been $19.2 billion in 1951, but it was now at the rate of $3.3 billion a month. He expected to spend

[1] John Wesley Snyder, 1895–1985. Head, St Louis Loan Agency, Reconstruction Finance Corp., 1937–43. Executive Vice-President, First National Bank of St Louis, 1943–5. Director, Office of War Mobilization and Reconversion, 1945–6. US Secretary of the Treasury, 1946–53. US Governor, International Monetary Fund, 1946–53. Adviser, US Treasury, 1955–69.

$44 billion in fiscal year 1952. In fiscal year 1953 defence expenditure was likely to reach $60 billion. The Americans proposed through this expenditure to establish a broad industrial base for the defence effort, and to do this without destroying the tax base of the country or an adequate supply of consumers' goods. There were some who thought this programme could not be achieved. Mr Lovett thought it could. They would have a force of 3.7 million men in 1953. This force would be fully equipped and modernised by 1955. They were busy putting in additional facilities for all the basic materials needed in war production, for example, aluminium. The effect of what they were doing could be judged in this way: the off-take of aluminium for defence was now 43 per cent of all domestic production but in twelve months' time total production would have expanded so much that the off-take for defence would be only 25 per cent of the whole. He gave the further illustration that at present they had one tank building plant in operation which was working flat out. What they were aiming at was four tank construction plants which would be operating on a 40-hour week and therefore capable of very rapid expansion of output if the need ever came. He reminded the meeting of the heavy call on equipment made by the Korean operations. The Americans had seven full Divisions in Korea and two in Japan; in addition there were ten South Korean Divisions. So far the Americans had shipped complete equipment for thirteen Divisions. Apart from this the divisional equipment of six Divisions had been lost. It must be remembered that each set of divisional equipment cost approximately $400 million.

7. Mr Harriman said that he agreed that the Kremlin was off balance. He felt that what was happening in Europe was of the greatest importance. During his residence there he had found what a very great respect Britain enjoyed in Western Europe. At the present time there was a great urge for unity. The Western Europeans felt they lacked support in this from Britain. It was a question of Britain's attitude: what was needed was that Britain should cheer them forward. Mr Harriman fully supported the wider conception of the Atlantic Community and he was in full sympathy with the position of Britain. At the moment the important things were to encourage the initiative of France and to cement the present degree of agreement between France and Germany which he felt could only be called 'fantastic'. In all this it was encouragement from Britain that was needed. If it could be given, it would make it much easier to get support in the Congress for all the actions promoting continental unity.

8. Lord Cherwell took up the main point made by Mr Snyder. He said the value of money had gone down. The cost of our imports had risen greatly but our reserves had not. The result was that small fluctuations, for example, whether the United States was buying for stockpiling or not, could make a crisis for us. He felt that we could do a lot to lessen or cure such crises if we could co-ordinate the policies which we both followed in buying materials up and down the world. He also placed special emphasis on Britain's need for steel.

JANUARY 1952 165

9. President Truman ended the discussion by saying that it seemed to have put all the problems on the table.

ANNEX A
Trade with China

In the course of the discussion on the *Williamsburg*, President Truman expressed to the Prime Minister in rather strong terms the opinion that British ships were carrying large quantities of strategic material to China. Enquiries were made of the State Department as to what the President had in mind, and the following memorandum was then handed to the United Kingdom delegation:

At President Truman's direction I[1] submit this memorandum following the discussion between the President and Mr Churchill, with ourselves present, held on Saturday night, 5th January, aboard the Williamsburg, on the subject of China trade.

The President expressed himself as seriously concerned over indications that the United Kingdom was continuing to give substantial assistance to Communist China through trade in strategic and other materials from British sources or carried on British flag vessels.

The information furnished the President by the Chief of Naval Operations,[2] upon which he based his remarks, is as follows:

Between 1st July, 1950, and 30th November, 1951, a total of at least 167 British-registered and British-owned merchant ships have engaged in trade with Communist China. The total gross tonnage of these ships is over 1 million. British-controlled shipping accounted for over half of the non-Communist registered shipping tonnage in the China trade in this period.

There are at least 163 ships registered in other non-Communist countries which were, between 1st July, 1950, and 30th November, 1951, engaged in trade with Communist China. The total gross tonnage of these ships is slightly less than 1 million.

Over the period stated above, the monthly average of voyages of British ships engaged in the China trade has been forty-eight. Since mid-summer there has been a reduction in the number of monthly voyages of these ships. In September there were thirty-six, in October thirty-one, and in November thirty. This decrease in British-owned tonnage is partially offset by an increase in communist flag traffic to China, especially Polish. Communist

---

[1] Acheson.
[2] William Morrow Fechteler, 1896–1967. Educated at US Naval Academy, 1916. Served on battleship *Pennsylvania*, 1916–18. Bureau of Navigation, 1942–3. Cdr, 7th Fleet Amphibious Group 8, 1944–5. Asst Chief of Naval Personnel, 1945. Cdr, Battleships and Cruisers, Atlantic Fleet, 1946–7. Deputy Chief of Naval Operations, 1947–50. Adm., 1950. C-in-C, Atlantic and US Atlantic Fleet, 1950–1. US Chief of Naval Operations, 1951–3. C-in-C, Allied (NATO) Forces, Southern Europe, 1953–6.

charters of British-registered shipping to handle normal trade to India and South America has released Polish flag vessels for the China trade. In addition, continuing Communist ship purchases are being employed almost exclusively in China trade.

We estimate that Communist China imported a minimum of 600,000 short tons per month by ship during 1951. This compares with an estimated monthly eastbound capacity for the Trans-Siberian Railroad of 670,000 short tons.

Although the voyages of British-registered and owned ships in the China trade have decreased in the last few months, British citizens have sold to the Soviet *bloc* at least twelve ships through intermediaries. Negotiations are believed to be currently under way for the sale of at least four others.

Regardless of whether the cargo, which is being delivered to China by sea, comprises material which directly contributes to the war effort, it is clear that the interdiction of this sea-borne traffic would have a serious and probably critical effect on the Chinese economy which would, of course, directly affect China's war-making potential. In the absence of a sea-borne traffic, China could not import more than a very small part of the equivalent tonnage by overland routes. The major route is, of course, the Trans-Siberian Railroad, which is probably now already operating to near capacity.

I would appreciate it if the appropriate authorities of your Government could look into the situation and take such measures as appear suitable in the circumstances.

ANNEX B
Trade with China

United Kingdom Memorandum prepared in
Reply to the United States Memorandum (Annex A)

On 8th January, the Secretary of State handed to Mr Eden a Memorandum arising out of a discussion between the President and the Prime Minister on board the *Williamsburg*, on the subject of trade with China in British ships. A joint fact-finding Group consisting of United States and United Kingdom representatives has now been authorised to investigate and, if possible, reach agreed conclusions on the volume and relative importance of goods reaching China by sea and by land. This Group will report its conclusion to the United States and United Kingdom Governments, but in the meantime, the following observations on Mr Acheson's Memorandum may be made.

2. While fully determined to prevent the supply to China of goods of strategic value, His Majesty's Government have always, for reasons of which the Department of State is aware, been opposed to the imposition of an embargo on *all* trade with China. In their view it is not the volume of sea-borne trade

which is important but its content. In view of the export controls exercised by members of the United Nations, particularly by the NATO countries, the proportion of strategic goods reaching China by sea must be very small.

3. There has not yet been time to check the figures given in the Secretary of State's Memorandum for ships of British and other non-Communist registers trading with China, but there is no reason to doubt them. They include some which, after arriving at Chinese ports in ballast, collect cargoes of *e.g.*, rice for India, which are important to the free world; other sail from Japanese ports.

4. As regards goods of non-British origin carried from non-British ports, the available evidence shows that the amount of goods (if any) carried to China in British ships must be negligible. His Majesty's Government would support action by the United Nations to prohibit the carriage of strategic goods in the ships of member States, but are not willing to take unilateral action to this effect.

5. In his Memorandum the Secretary of State says that Communist charters of British registered shipping have released Polish Flag vessels for the China trade. This appears to imply that the United Kingdom should altogether prohibit the chartering of British vessels to Communist countries even for 'normal trade'. Such action would be tantamount to economic warfare against the Soviet *bloc*, which the United Kingdom is not willing to contemplate. The total number of Polish-controlled vessels engaged in the carriage of goods to China is only about fifteen.

6. Of the British ships quoted as being engaged in China trade during September, October and November, 1951 (a total of ninety-seven voyages is quoted), only eleven were ocean-going and of these, ten sailed to China in ballast.

7. As regards the sale of ships to Communist countries, the Paris East–West Trade Group agreed in November 1950 that member countries would not export to the Soviet *bloc* ships over either 7,000 gross tons or 12 knots speed capacity, without prior consultation within the Group. A British proposal to embargo such exports altogether was rejected. Since then (except for one 13½-knot 3,000-ton ship under the Anglo-Polish Trade Agreement) no British dry-cargo ship over either limit has been sold to the Soviet *bloc*. As regards sale to non-Communist buyers with subsequent resale to the Soviet *bloc*, all transfers of British ships to foreign owners are controlled by statute and sales to possible intermediaries are closely watched, in particular sales to registers of convenience. The only case known of resale of a ship over 7,000 tons or 12-knots capacity, was the sale in October 1950 of the 7,100-ton 10-knot *Amelia Earhart* to a Panamanian Company in Hong Kong, which was followed in November 1951 by a sale through another Panamanian Company to Poland. One smaller ship, the *London Statesman* (5,100 tons and 11 knots) had a similar history. The United Kingdom has, of course, no power to control the sale of ships other than those wholly owned by British subjects, *i.e.*, British ships.

8. The United Kingdom estimate of Chinese imports by sea is in the region of 200,000 to 300,000 tons per month, rather than the 600,000 tons per month mentioned in the Secretary of State's Memorandum. Nor does the United Kingdom believe that the cessation of imports, even if complete, from the free world would affect the course of Chinese military operations on the present scale in the short term.

US–UK discussions: minutes
(Cabinet papers, 21/3057)

7 January 1952   The White House
Top Secret
11 a.m.
Plenary Meeting No. 1

I. ECONOMIC POSITION OF THE UNITED KINGDOM

Mr Churchill said that a statement was to be made that day by the Government of the United Kingdom showing that for the quarter ending 31st December, 1951, there would be a deficit in the balance of payments of $940 million. Moreover, the forecast of the future position indicated that the United Kingdom gold and dollar reserves, which at present stood at $2.3 billion, would drop by June, 1952, to $1.4 billion, in spite of the remedial measures which the Government had taken immediately after they had assumed office at the end of October. The position gave cause for grave anxiety, but it was the duty and the intention of the United Kingdom Government to take upon themselves the responsibility for ensuring the livelihood of the British people. They had no intention of asking for assistance or favours in carrying out this responsibility. They would impose whatever measures of economy were necessary for this purpose. The rearmament programme was, however, in a somewhat different category. The United Kingdom had put in hand a rearmament programme for the common cause against aggression and the spread of Communism. It followed that the rearmament programme of the United Kingdom was of interest to the United States, and any assistance which the United States could give towards its completion would be welcomed. The previous Government had originally proposed a three-year programme of the value of £3.6 billion. They had hoped that in the achievement of this programme help to the extent of £550 million would be forthcoming from the United States. Subsequently, they had increased this programme to a total of £4.7 billion. This had been done without any promise of direct aid from the United States, but in the expectation of an equitable sharing of the economic burden of rearmament between the North Atlantic Powers. The United Kingdom rearmament programme, originally valued at £4.7 billion, would now cost £5.2 billion. This increase was entirely due to the rise in prices and would not result in any increase in power. In practice, in the first year of this rearmament programme there had been lags in production which would make it impossible to attain the first year's target. This had given some temporary and immediate relief, though it would be largely offset by the rise in prices. It was, however, the intention of the United Kingdom to make the maximum possible contribution to common defence against aggression and Communism.

President Truman said that the military and domestic budgets of the United States were very large and gave cause for anxiety. The United States Government were most anxious to obtain the co-operation of the United Kingdom in creating a position of strength from which it would be possible to negotiate with the Soviet Union and to enforce peace. There were difficult areas in the world where the co-operation of all the North Atlantic Treaty powers was necessary. He was thinking of Korea, Indo-China and the Near East. In the supply of raw materials, he thought that the United Kingdom might be able to give some assistance to the United States which would help them to overcome the limitations which were now imposed upon their production and industrial capacity.

Mr Churchill said that the United Kingdom were in urgent need of increased supplies of steel, both for the rearmament programme itself and for the export trade on which the whole economy of the United Kingdom relied. He thought that the United Kingdom might assist the United States to secure the supplies of tin which they needed by means which would avoid the price being raised against them. Some 20,000 tons of tin might be made available in this way. He did not suggest that this was necessarily an equal exchange for the steel which the United Kingdom required from the United States – a figure of 11 million tons. This would be put to good use for rearmament and other purposes. He also hoped that deliveries of finished equipment from the United States might be increased. He was aware that unfavourable comparisons had been drawn between coal production in the United Kingdom and in the United States. The United Kingdom Government were determined to take all practicable measures to increase coal production, by offering special incentives to miners, by the provision of additional houses, and by the introduction of foreign labour. It was not easy to persuade miners to accept the importation of foreign labour, but every effort was being made to do so.

Mr Charles Wilson[1] said that he was much encouraged by what the Prime Minister had said about tin. The United States were also in great need of copper, nickel and aluminium. He hoped that the inevitable lag in the first year of a rearmament programme, to which the Prime Minister had referred, might enable the United Kingdom to give some help in the supply of these metals over the next nine months. At the end of that period the United States

[1] US Director of Defense Mobilization.

would be in a better position to meet its own demands. The United Kingdom requirement for steel was large, and he could not say how far it would be possible to meet it until the requirement had been broken down into types of steel. If, for example, the United Kingdom wanted large supplies of steel plate in the next six months, it would be very difficult to meet that demand. Other types it might perhaps be possible to supply with some sacrifice.

Lord Cherwell said that he wished to emphasise the dangerous position created by the low level of United Kingdom reserves. These were now worth only one-quarter of the pre-war reserves in respect of purchasing power. They were also much smaller in relation to the volume of transactions in sterling. As a result any fluctuations in world prices upset the whole economic equilibrium of the United Kingdom. There was a constant risk of recurrent crises provoking loss of confidence and a run on sterling. For this reason it was most necessary that those responsible for the sterling and dollar areas should work closely together and should concert policies and purchases so far as possible with a view to preventing these violent fluctuations. The United Kingdom must export in order to live. We were in fact exporting two-thirds more than we did before the war and importing less; but still we were not in sight of the economic equilibrium which would alone make it possible to fulfil our rearmament programme satisfactorily.

Mr Eden said that we had run into trouble with our rearmament programme largely because we had set a high target and tried to reach it with great speed. Our effort compared favourably with those of our European neighbours.

President Truman proposed that these questions should be discussed in further detail as follows:
   (a) The economic and financial questions could be considered at a luncheon which Mr Snyder was giving the following day;
   (b) The raw materials questions could be studied by a group of experts who would meet at 2.30 that afternoon.
The reports of these two groups could be considered at a later Plenary Session.

II. ORGANISATION OF THE WEST FOR DEFENCE

Mr Churchill said that he wished to raise two particular points:
   (a) The reform of NATO.
   (b) The Report of the Temporary Council Committee.

Reform of NATO

Mr Eden said that United Kingdom Ministers had formulated some proposals for the reform of the North Atlantic Treaty Organisation. They believed that there should be a body in permanent session with effective powers of decision, and that the Council Deputies should be abolished. The Council should be served by a stronger international staff under a Secretary-General, or

Director-General if the latter title was preferred. Responsibility for the organisation of the work of the Council should not be divided, as at present, between the Chairman and the Secretary-General, but should rest exclusively with this Director-General. The Chairmanship of the Council would be changed each year, and the main work of the Organisation would be in the hands of the Director-General. He had been disturbed at Rome to find that meetings of the Council were attended by as many as 400 people. He was most anxious that Foreign Ministers should have opportunities to meet together, with one or two advisers, to discuss their common problems. This procedure had been followed with success in the past at meetings of the League of Nations Council. He thought that the work at meetings of the North Atlantic Council might be broken down and remitted to separate meetings of Foreign Ministers, Defence Ministers, and Financial Ministers; the results of these discussions could then be reported, and if necessary discussed further, at a session of the Council. He also proposed that a single Economic and Production Board should replace the existing Defence Production Board and the Financial and Economic Board. The whole civil side of NATO should have permanent headquarters; and he hoped that this would be London.

Mr Acheson said that these proposals seemed to be very similar to those favoured by the United States. He was anxious that the civil side of NATO should be concentrated in one place, and that the international staff should work together under a single head. He would prefer that economic and financial questions should be studied, not by a separate Economic and Production Board, but by a standing committee of the Council itself. He was disturbed by the present system of a rotating Chairmanship. Under this system there might come a time when for a series of years the Chairmanship would be in the hands of weak Powers. He wondered, therefore, whether the Director-General might not act as the permanent Chairman of the Council. If that were considered difficult, the rotation rule might still apply to full meetings of the Council, but the Director-General might preside over meetings of the permanent group. On the location of the headquarters, he felt that the claims of Paris, which already had some of the agencies of NATO, ought to be carefully considered. He thought it important that the civil side of NATO should co-operate very closely with General Eisenhower's headquarters.

Mr Harriman said that the Temporary Council Committee were recommending increased responsibilities for the military side of NATO – the Military Committee, the Standing Group and SHAPE – with particular regard to supply and logistic questions.

Mr Lovett said that it was essential for SHAPE to have a sound logistic backing and any organisation for NATO must provide this.

Mr Harriman said that the future of OEEC needed consideration. If duplication of staffs was to be avoided, OEEC and NATO must be alongside one another.

Mr Eden said that he would like to consider the American proposals further; particularly the suggestion that the Director-General might be Chairman of the Council or of the Permanent Group.

President Truman and Mr Churchill agreed that Mr Eden and Mr Acheson, together with their official advisers, should study further the proposals made by the United Kingdom and the United States and report back to a plenary session.

Report of the Temporary Council Committee

Mr Harriman explained that the TCC Report was now being studied by military and other staffs and that there was no final United States view on it at the present time. Member Governments had been asked to make their comments by the middle of January. When these were received, the Temporary Council Committee would meet again and submit proposals for decisions by the North Atlantic Council at their meeting in Lisbon.

Mr Churchill said that he welcomed the report of the Temporary Council Committee, and he was glad to have this opportunity of expressing his appreciation of the very valuable contribution which Mr Harriman had made to its work. The report emphasised the extent to which completion of the United Kingdom rearmament programme depended upon the covering of the United Kingdom dollar deficit. The great burden which the United States were bearing on behalf of the free world was a matter of universal admiration. The United Kingdom would continue to make the biggest contribution of which they were capable. The second World War had swallowed up our reserves and resources and we still had to impose restrictions and restraint upon the 50 million inhabitants of the British Isles. We had been greatly helped by the generosity of the United States; but we, in our turn, had made substantial loans and payments to others. The point of paramount importance was that we should, in all our economic difficulties and in all our efforts to increase our strength, have close, frank, and continuous consultation with the United States.

President Truman said that between 1866 and 1914 the British, French and Germans had invested about £100 billion in the United States. These resources had been used up during the 1914–18 war. During the second World War, the United States had made a contribution to their Allies of $450 billion, and since the War they had contributed a further $60 billion. There were obviously political and financial difficulties in continuing aid on this scale. So far as he was concerned, he could not over emphasise the importance which he attached to friendship between the United States and the United Kingdom and the British Commonwealth.

JANUARY 1952 173

US–UK discussions: minutes
(*Premier papers, 11/161*)

7 January 1952 The White House
5 p.m.

ATOMIC ENERGY

President Truman opened by saying that as President he had a special responsibility and powers with respect to the strategic air plan and atomic weapons. Nevertheless, in the exercise of these powers he was tied by very considerable legislative halters. Nor was his legislature under such good control as that in the United Kingdom.

He could assure the Prime Minister that he was just as reluctant as His Majesty's Government to see the atomic weapon used and he hoped that the time would never come when he might have to give the decision to wipe out a whole population not in the fighting line. Nevertheless, this feeling would not prevent his taking the decision if and when it proved to be necessary. In any case, those countries 'lined up' with the United States should be consulted first.

Mr Lovett, at the President's invitation, said that discussions had already taken place in outline between the military authorities on both sides with regard to the concepts of the military use of the weapon. The advent of the tactical war head meant that the President might not in future face quite the same problem. As regards the legislative restrictions, they recognised the problem but in present circumstances it was virtually impossible to expand co-operation beyond the broad military aspect just described. Legislation had been under consideration to modify this position, but in present conditions had had to be shelved.

He regarded it as inevitable that in World War III the atomic bomb would have to be used, but there was no question of British bases being used without British consent. They were making arrangements to give Mr Churchill a briefing on the strategic air plan before he returned to England.*

Mr Churchill said that this was a long story and he had brought the original documents with him. We could have started a project in Canada but in the end it had been agreed that the United States should undertake it and he thought British moral pressure had been useful to President Roosevelt in encouraging him to spend £500 million on what was in fact a gamble. This was, however, history and there was now a new situation. He had no reproaches to make, and would have no objection to the facts in regard to atomic relations being known.

He appreciated that the Americans had a law which they could not easily alter. Now, however, he found, on taking office, that his predecessors had constructed a bomb and it was proposed to test this in Australia. He did not ask the President to embark on an amendment of the United States law but he thought there must be a possibility of mutual help within the provisions of the law. Lord Cherwell was his interpreter on these subjects and he would like him to discuss this possibility.

President Truman said that his great interest in this matter was to make it work for peace. He was in sympathy with the idea of the discussions proposed by the Prime Minister but it must be understood that the rather hysterical feeling in America on this subject limited his power to act independently.

Mr Churchill said that all he asked was that the President should say that he wished for the maximum co-operation within the limits set by the McMahon Act. President Truman agreed.

Mr Churchill said there was another matter connected with intelligence which he would like General Bedell-Smith[1] to discuss with Lord Cherwell and Sir Roger Makins.[2] It might be contrary to the United States law to give us certain information about the United States effort but this should not apply to an exchange of information about Russia. He would like all this to be gone into with Mr Lovett and, if necessary, the Atomic Energy Commission.

President Truman said that this seemed to him a good sense.

Mr Churchill said that as regards the strategic and tactical use of the weapon he would be very glad to have a briefing, as proposed, from Mr Lovett and General Bradley.[3] He wanted to form a view about the atomic war and its character. If ever they came to a conference with the Russians, which broke down, he would not like the immediate sequel to be an atomic conflict. He thought there should be some intermediate stage such as an intensified cold war. In considering the outbreak of an atomic war, they must consider two

[1] Walter Bedell Smith, 1895–1961. Known as 'Beetle'. Served during WWI with 4th Infantry Div. (US) in France; commissioned 1st Lt in the Regular Army. Adjutant, 12th Infantry Bde, 1922. At the outbreak of WWII, appointed Secretary of the US JCS and American Secretary of the Anglo-American CCS. Went to England in 1942 as CoS to Gen. Eisenhower, with whom he remained to war's end. Laid the basis for negotiation of Italian armistice of 1943; arranged surrender of German forces in the west, May 1945. US Ambassador to Soviet Union, 1946–9. Director of Central Intelligence (head of the CIA), 1950. Retired from Army and as DCI, 1953. Under-Secretary of State, 1953–4; involved in creation of the National Security Agency.

[2] Roger Makins, 1904–96. Entered FO, 1928. In Washington DC, 1931–4. Acting 1st Secretary, 1939. Adviser on League of Nations Affairs, 1939. Acting Counsellor, 1940. Asst to Minister Resident, Allied HQ, North-West Africa, 1942–5. Deputy Under-Secretary of State, FO, 1948–52. Knighted, 1949. Ambassador to US, 1953–6. Joint Permanent Secretary to the Treasury, 1956–9. Chairman, UK Atomic Energy Authority, 1960–4. Baron, 1964.

[3] Omar Nelson Bradley, 1893–1981. Married, 1916, Mary Elizabeth Quayle (d. 1965); 1966, Esther 'Kitty' Buhler. Instructor at US Military Academy, West Point, 1934–8. Chief of Operations Section, G-1, War Dept General Staff, 1938–40. Asst Secretary of General Staff, Office of the Chief of Staff, War Dept, 1940–1. Commandant, Infantry School, 1941–2. Commanding Gen., 82nd Div., Feb.–June 1942; 28th Div., June 1942 to Feb. 1943. Personal Representative in the Field for C-in-C US North African Theater of Operations, Feb.–March 1943. Deputy Commanding Gen., II Corps, Mar.–Apr. 1943. Commanding Gen., II Corps, Apr.–Sep. 1943. C-in-C, 1st Army Group (UK), Oct. 1943 to July 1944. Commanding Gen., 1st Army, 1943–4. C-in-C, 12th Army Group, Aug. 1944 to July 1945. Administrator for Veteran Affairs, 1945–7. CoS, US Army, Feb. 1947 to Aug. 1949. Chairman of JCS, 1949–53.

aspects. First, if the Americans heard that the Russians had started across the North Pole, they would have to act and there would be no hindrance to this from the side of His Majesty's Government. On the other hand, if it should rest with the United States to bring the situation to a head, then there should be consultation.

The President said that British bases would certainly not be used without British consent.

Mr Churchill asked whether there would be any objection to publishing this.

President Truman replied that he did not think so, but Mr Lovett interjected that the matter should be talked over.

Mr Churchill welcomed the extension of atomic bases to North Africa, but suggested that it would only be fair to the French to refrain from encouraging their difficulties with the local population. He welcomed the establishment of bases in Cyrenaica and also the presence of the Carrier fleet in the Mediterranean. He was even glad that they were encouraging Spain to provide bases. Franco was of no consequence; the point was to dilute the pressure on the United Kingdom and divide the horrors of war so far as possible by dispersion.

Mr Acheson referred to the Tripartite Security Group which had reported to Governments in the summer of 1951 and whose recommendations had been accepted by the United States Government, but not yet by the French and British. In discussion, it transpired that the Atomic Security discussions, to which Mr Acheson referred, had concerned the United Kingdom, the United States, and Canada.

Mr Eden said that he would look into the matter, but meanwhile certain action was being taken.

Mr Churchill asked if it would help if we stiffened up our anti-Communist procedure. It was proposed that this should be done on its merits, but he was anxious that it should not appear to be done under United States pressure. A decision had been taken, but some details of the procedure were still under consideration by the Cabinet. It was intended to provide a more severe scrutiny of holders of key positions in the administration, not only of those engaged in the atomic energy field.

President Truman said that this would help very much.

Mr Churchill said that it was his feeling that a man engaged by the Government for lucrative employment should be prepared and should be made to answer questions on oath. If he told lies in answer to the questions, he should be prosecuted for perjury, not merely sacked.

Mr Eden said he was anxious to make it clear that in all this the main decision had already been taken.

There followed a short discussion of French security and it was agreed that this was very bad.

Mr Lovett said he wished to make it clear that the amendments to the

McMahon Act permitted specific arrangements for the exchange of highly-classified information if there was commensurate advantage for the United States and if arrangements for security were definitely considered adequate. Subject to these conditions, only the design of weapons was excluded and there was some opportunity to expand co-operation. The main obstacle had lain in the cases of Fuchs,[1] Pontecorvo,[2] MacLean,[3] &c.

Mr Churchill observed that the Americans had had theirs, too, and the Canadians.

Lord Cherwell said that in some matters, co-operation would actually contribute to greater security.

Mr Matthews[4] enquired whether the new British security measures applied to future employees in the atomic energy field or to existing staff as well.

Mr Eden said that it would apply to all staff.

The President concluded the discussion by saying he thought both sides understood each other and their aim should be to achieve as good an understanding as possible within the limits set them.

* This was done in the Pentagon on 15th January.

[1] Emil Julius Klaus Fuchs, 1911–88. From 1947 to 1949, leaked to Soviet Union British nuclear intelligence regarding British and US development of the H-bomb. Confessed to being Soviet spy and sentenced to 14 years' imprisonment, 1950. Married, 1959, Grete Keilson.

[2] Bruno Pontecorvo, 1913–93. Left Italy for Paris after Mussolini began targeting the Jewish population, 1936. Moved to US, 1940; to England, to work in Atomic Energy Research Laboratory, 1948. Defected to Soviet Union from Helsinki, Finland, 1950. Suspected of sharing military secrets with the Soviets, but never formally charged with espionage.

[3] Donald Duart Maclean, 1913–83. Educated at Trinity Hall, Cambridge. Entered Diplomatic Service, 1935. In Western Dept of FO, 1935–8. 3rd Secretary, Paris, 1938–40. 2nd and later 1st Secretary, Washington DC, 1944–8. Head of Chancery, British Embassy in Cairo, 1948. Head of American Dept, FO, 1951. Defected to Soviet Union, 1951.

[4] Harrison Freeman Matthews, 1899–1986. Known as 'Doc'. Born in Baltimore, Md. US Naval Reserve, 1918. Studied at Ecole Libre des Sciences Politiques, Paris, 1922–3. Secretary, Budapest, 1924–6. 3rd Secretary, Bogotá, 1926–9. Asst Chief, Div. of Latin American Affairs, 1930–3. 2nd Secretary, Havana, 1933; 1st Secretary, 1933–7. 1st Secretary, Paris, 1937–40; Consul, 1938–40. 1st Secretary, Vichy, 1940–1. Chargé d'Affaires and Adviser to Gen. Eisenhower, London, 1941–3. Chief, Div. of European Affairs, 1943–4. Director, Office of European Affairs, 1944–7. Representative, Combined Civil Affairs Commission, CCS, 1945. Ambassador Extraordinary and Plenipotentiary to Sweden, 1947–50; to the Netherlands, 1953–7; to Austria, 1957–62. Deputy Under-Secretary of State, 1950–3. Chairman, US Section of Permanent Joint Board on Defense for the US and Canada, 1962–8.

JANUARY 1952 177

US–UK discussions: minutes
(Premier papers, 11/161)

7 January 1952 The White House
5 p.m.
Plenary Session No. 2

I. THE RIFLE

President Truman said that the United States Government were particularly concerned to achieve standardisation of weapons for the free world, and he had thought that a useful start could be made with the rifle.

Mr Lovett said that the Press of both countries had magnified out of all proportion the difference of opinion between the United States and the United Kingdom about the rifle. Nevertheless it was likely to be the verdict of public opinion that, if the two countries could not reach agreement on a small matter like the rifle, they were unlikely to reach agreement on more important issues.

Mr Pace[1] said that, in spite of various tests, British and American technicians had so far been unable to agree on the best round and rifle. In any case, the United States could not contemplate, at the moment, any change of calibre and were obliged to continue for some years with the MI rifle and the .30 round. He thought that some progress might be made towards standardisation by a compromise under which the British might use the T 65 case which was now in production on a small scale. Simultaneously, however, joint efforts should be made by the British and Americans to find the best possible rifle for standardisation in the future.

Mr Churchill said that it was dangerous to change the calibre of a rifle unless a really long period of peace was in prospect. Armies must exist upon a large pool of rifles. The United States possessed a very large pool of .30 rifles and the United Kingdom a considerable pool of .303 rifles. For the moment, when circumstances were critical, each of the two countries would be well-advised to continue to operate on these two pools. Joint efforts should, however, be made, as suggested by Mr Pace, to develop a better rifle and achieve true standardisation of rifle and bullet. This would take some time and need not be done hurriedly. He himself thought there was much virtue in the new British .280 rifle and he proposed to start production of these rifles on a very small scale. In two or three years there might

---

[1] Frank Pace, Jr, 1912–88. Educated at Princeton and Harvard Universities. Asst District Attorney, 12th Judicial District, 1936–8. General Attorney, Arkansas Revenue Dept, 1938–40. Served in Army Air Corps during WWII. Executive Assistant to Postmaster General, 1946–8. Asst Director, Bureau of the Budget, 1948; Director, 1949–50. Secretary of the Army, 1950–3. Chairman of Defense Ministers Conference, NATO, 1957–60. Member, President's Foreign Intelligence Advisory Board, 1961–73. Chairman of the Board, Corporation for Public Broadcasting, 1968–72.

be perhaps 20,000 or 30,000 .280 rifles with which specialist soldiers like paratroopers and commandos would be equipped.

Sir William Slim said that, as the United States did not contemplate the production of a new rifle and round for some ten or fifteen years, it was not possible for the British to agree in advance that the right calibre would eventually be .30. The joint tests and experiments which were now to be made in the development of a new rifle should not therefore be conducted on the assumption that .30 was the best calibre.

Mr Pace said that he saw merit in the limited production of the .280 rifle to which the Prime Minister had referred. This would allow this rifle to be properly tested in practical operations. In the meantime, he agreed that both countries would have to live on their own pools of existing rifles and try to reach agreement on the best standardised rifle and round for the future. It was most important that a decision on these lines should be carefully presented to the public. It could be announced that the British and the Americans would now undertake joint tests for the development of the best possible rifle and round for the future: in the meantime, the Americans could not give up their existing rifle and for that reason the British had agreed not to proceed with the production of the new .280 rifle except on a very limited scale for experimental purposes.

President Truman and Mr Churchill said that an agreed statement should now be drawn up on the lines agreed in discussion for issue to the public.

II. ATLANTIC COMMAND

Mr Lovett said that it was the view of the United States Government that discussions on the appointment of a Supreme Commander for the Atlantic should not be further prolonged. Immediate agreement to this appointment was needed both for the efficient preparation of defence and because the divergence of opinion between the Americans and the British had become a matter of public concern. It was expected that in the next world war the enemy would have six times as many submarines as the Germans had at the start of the last war. The development of anti-submarine defences and the assurance of logistic support for Western Europe and for American forces in Europe could be satisfactorily accomplished only by the creation of a centralised command. This centralised command would in no way interfere with British control in British home waters.

Mr Churchill said that he was not convinced of the need for this appointment. He had had great experience through the two world wars of the danger of submarine warfare in the Atlantic Ocean. The life of Great Britain and of the Western European countries depended upon the security of the sea lines of communication across the Atlantic Ocean. For this reason the British had necessarily developed effective techniques to ensure their own survival. In the last war the British had defeated the submarine threat in 1943 at a time when,

JANUARY 1952

by agreement, the main American naval effort was being made in the Pacific. In his view, control of the Battle in the Atlantic must in practice be exercised by the First Sea Lord and the United States Chief of Naval Operations, and there was no need for a Supreme Commander with a large headquarters. He might, however, be prepared to agree that the First Sea Lord and the Chief of Naval Operations should exercise this control under the authority of the Standing Group, and that there should be in addition a naval adviser to the Standing Group, who might be called 'The Admiral of the Atlantic', to make plans for the Standing Group and to decide any differences of opinion between the First Sea Lord and the Chief of Naval Operations which were too urgent to allow time for submission to the Standing Group and Heads of Governments. He was grateful for the efforts which had been made to meet his point of view, viz., that the First Sea Lord would have control in British waters inside the 100 fathom line. But he did not feel that this went far enough. He had hoped that he would be released from the agreement entered into by the previous United Kingdom Government.

President Truman said that he also held strong views on the question of unified command. It seemed to him that a Supreme Commander for the Atlantic was as necessary as a Supreme Commander for Europe. Efficient control could not be exercised by committees of six or more persons.

Admiral Fechteler said that the method of meeting the submarine threat in the next war, which involved attacks upon submarines at their bases and not at the moment when they had reached their targets, made it essential to have unified control. He did not think that the headquarters required for a Supreme Commander, Atlantic, need be very large. He had worked out the requirement and had found that the necessary staff could easily be accommodated in existing buildings. He reminded the meeting that this was a question which could not be settled by the British and Americans alone, but was subject to the approval of all the North Atlantic Treaty Powers who, with the exception of the United Kingdom, had already approved the proposals for the appointment of a Supreme Commander.

Mr Churchill said that it was the United States and the United Kingdom who would make the real contribution in navies and in shipping to the Battle of the Atlantic. He would be glad to consider further the operational aspects of this Battle. In his mind, the threat of mines was even greater than the threat of submarines.

President Truman and Mr Churchill agreed that this question should be deferred for further consideration.

Kay Halle:[1] notes on second plenary meeting
('The Irrepressible Churchill', pages 288–9)

7 January 1952

In January, on this first visit to Washington after becoming Prime Minister a second time, the European Defence Force was under discussion and exploration by all sides, especially the proposal that national uniforms should be scrapped in favour of a new European one.

WSC: (*to Secretary of Defense Robert Lovett*): Oh, no! That would be a sludgy amalgam.

and

At another of these Potomac conferences, arguments arose over failure to agree about a standard rifle for the NATO forces. One meeting took place at the British Embassy.

Field Marshal Sir William Slim: Well, I suppose we could experiment with a bastard rifle – partly American – partly British.

WSC: Kindly moderate your language, Field Marshal, it may be recalled that I am myself partly British, partly American.

and

During the same talks on various NATO Army and Navy Commands, WSC noticed Secretary of Defense Robert Lovett fixing him with his banker's eye.

Mr Lovett: Mr Churchill, who is going to command in the English Channel? I am told it was determined in Rome.

WSC: Thank you for that crumb, Mr Lovett. I suppose the President and I should issue a joint communiqué that naval traffic in the Potomac will be under the supervision of the US Navy?

US–UK discussions: minutes
(*Premier papers, 11/161*)

8 January 1952   The White House
11 a.m.
Plenary Session No. 3

I. – MIDDLE EAST
A. – *Middle East Command*

Mr Churchill said that he wished to take this opportunity of making clear the extent of British interest in the Middle East. The changed constitutional position of India and Pakistan and the loss of the Indian Army had affected

---

[1] Katherine Murphy Halle, 1903–97. Born in Cleveland, Ohio. Daughter of Blanche and Samuel Horatio Halle. Educated at Smith College and Cleveland Institute of Music. Served in OSS during WWII. Wrote *The Irrepressible Churchill* (1966).

the British attitude towards the Suez Canal and the Middle East generally. Communications with Australia and New Zealand could be maintained round the Cape of Good Hope. The British had lost their direct interest in Persia, for the time being at any rate, and Palestine was now an independent State. The British remained in Egypt to perform an international duty and not because the retention of Egypt was part of British Imperial policy. The maintenance of free passage through the Suez Canal could not be regarded as a purely British responsibility. He was, therefore, most anxious that the principles of the Four-Power Pact should be put into operation as soon as possible. If the Turks and Greeks preferred to be in General Eisenhower's command, he was ready to accept that, as long as the Turks were willing to contribute at least a token force to the Middle East command. If the other parties to the Four-Power Pact would also contribute forces to the Middle East Command, he felt that the trouble in Egypt would soon be brought to an end, and the British would be able to make more forces available to Europe or to the United Kingdom itself, which was at present without adequate defences. If it was desired that a British officer should be nominated as Supreme Allied Commander in the Middle East, that would be acceptable; but he wished to emphasise once again that the British remained in Egypt from a sense of international duty and for no other reason.

Mr Acheson said that the political circumstances made it desirable to establish an Allied command in the Middle East as soon as possible, but in the first place Turkey and Greece should be absorbed into NATO. This process should be separate from the creation of a command in the Middle East and should precede it.

General Bradley said that the United States Chiefs of Staff had come to the conclusion that Turkey and Greece should be included in General Eisenhower's southern command under the direct command of Admiral Carney.[1] Although this was not militarily sound, it was the only way to make a start: a better arrangement might be made at a later stage.

Sir William Slim said that the British Chiefs of Staff were now prepared to accept this proposal. It was militarily unsound and extended General Eisenhower's southern flank much too far. In war the system would almost certainly have to be changed; but this seemed, at the moment, the only way of satisfying the Turks and the Greeks. The Turks continued to insist that they were a European Power, but from a geographical point of view they were in fact an essential part of the Middle East. It was, however, most important that the Turks should contribute some forces to the Middle East Command. When Turkey and Greece had been included in Admiral Carney's Command, there

---

[1] Robert Bostwick Carney, 1895–1990. Educated at US Naval Academy. Flag Secretary to Adm. Louis R. de Steiguer; trained anti-submarine protection forces, 1941. Commanded USS *Denver*, 1942–3. RAdm., CoS to Adm. William Halsey, 1943. VAdm. and Chief of Naval Operations, 1946–50. Adm. and Cdr, 2nd Fleet, 1950. Chief of Naval Operations, 1953.

would have to be a strong link between that Command and the Middle East Command. That might perhaps be provided by making the Commander of the Turkish front the Deputy of the Commander in the Middle East. The exact form of this link would have to be worked out later.

General Bradley was doubtful whether agreement would be secured to a link on the lines proposed by Sir William Slim.

President Truman said that he was glad to note the close coincidence of British and American views in this respect, and he hoped that British and American policy on all Middle Eastern questions could be closely co-ordinated.

B. – *Egypt*

Mr Acheson said that he had started conversations with Mr Eden on the Egyptian problem. They hoped to arrive at some Four-Power agreement on the basis of a fresh approach to the King of Egypt. It was, however, clearly understood that King Farouk[1] could not expect any recognition of his assumed title of 'The King of Sudan', unless he agreed to self-determination for the Sudanese; no disturbance of the present régime; and acceptance of the Four-Power proposals with regard to Egypt. He thought that the Four-Power proposals could be restated in a form likely to make a greater appeal to the Egyptian people; and that this revision should now be put in hand so that they should be ready for presentation when the appropriate moment arrived.

Mr Eden said that the moment must be carefully chosen. At present, the King was not ready for an approach of this kind. As a result of the present meeting it might be stated in the communiqué that agreement had been reached between the United Kingdom and the United States Government on policy towards Egypt without specifying what that policy was. It might also be possible to repeat our joint adherence to the general principles of the Four-Power proposals. He must, however, make it clear that it would not be possible to give the King of Egypt exactly what he wanted with regard to the Sudan. Egypt had repudiated the Condominium Agreement and claimed exclusive sovereignty over the Sudan. This could not be accepted, but some formula might perhaps be found on the basis of the Condominium Agreement. He thought that the communiqué might also state that the Americans and British had reached agreement on the Command question.

President Truman and Mr Churchill agreed that suitable statements should be included in the communiqué about the identity of views on Middle East policy.

C. – *Persia*

Mr Eden acknowledged the assistance that he had received from Mr Acheson and the State Department over the Persian problem. The present

---

[1] Farouk, 1920–65. Born in Cairo. King of Egypt from 1936; overthrown 26 July 1952. Died in exile in Rome, 18 Mar. 1965, after being poisoned by Ibrahim al Baghdady, who was sent by Gamal Abdel Nasser.

position was that the International Bank had given the Persian Government a forecast of terms which might be proposed for restarting the oil industry. These proposals had received an unsatisfactory response from the Persian Prime Minister, but the International Bank would continue their efforts. Meanwhile, some heads of agreements, with particular regard to the price of oil, might be worked out between United Kingdom officials and the State Department for the guidance of the International Bank.

Mr Acheson agreed that the International Bank would require some guidance, not only on the substance of their proposals but also on procedure in negotiation. The Persian Prime Minister was a difficult and evasive negotiator.

Mr Eden said that, although the British were quite willing to attempt negotiations with the present Persian Prime Minister, he thought that if these negotiations failed it might be necessary to try to secure a change of Government in Persia.

President Truman and Mr Churchill agreed that our policy towards Persia should be as closely co-ordinated as possible and that this close co-ordination should be made known to the public.

II. – KOREA

General Bradley explained, with the aid of maps, the various phases of the operations in Korea and the progress of the armistice negotiations. In answer to Mr Churchill, he said that he thought the Chinese troops had been reinforced during the course of the armistice talks, but he was still satisfied that the United Nations forces would be able to hold approximately their present positions in the event of a Chinese offensive, provided that United Nations Air Forces had liberty to extend the area of their operations, not only on the other side of the Yalu River, but also against air-fields in other parts of China.

Mr Acheson said that M Vyshinsky had now proposed that the Korean armistice talks should be transferred to the Security Council in Paris. The object of this manoeuvre was probably to broaden the discussion on the Far East in order to divide the Western Powers. It was clear that the Chinese had ceased to take the armistice talks seriously. They attended the meetings in a spirit of levity and no end to the negotiations was in sight. It was, however, the aim of the United States and the United Kingdom Governments to seek a political settlement in Korea before any broader discussions on the Far East were undertaken. There should be firm agreement that the armistice talks were military talks only. When they were concluded, the United Nations should be invited to appoint a commission of representatives of six or seven nations to discuss with all the Governments concerned the basis for a political settlement in Korea. There was in practice not very much hope in achieving the unification of Korea. The South Koreans, nevertheless, attached great importance to unification and would never accept the division of the country at the 30th parallel. A satisfactory agreement had now been concluded between all members of the United Nations concerned on the issue of a warning statement about the extension of hostilities in the event of a serious breach of any armistice which might be concluded. There had, however, up to date been no agreement on what practical steps could then be taken to deal with the situations arising from such a breach. The Americans had had in mind an extension of bombing outside Korea, but they had no thought of bombing civil populations in China. They had also in mind the possibility of stopping all imports to China. China existed equally upon rail and sea imports, though no doubt the rail imports were strategically more important. The cessation of sea imports would undoubtedly hurt the Chinese economy. He recognised that no decisions should be reached on these points at the present meeting.

III. – FAR EAST AND SOUTH-EAST ASIA

Mr Acheson said that in January 1950 the United States Government had thought that it might be possible to base policy upon the possibility of a divergence between Chinese and Russian Communism. They no longer thought it reasonable to base policy upon this possibility. It was necessary to proceed step by step towards the formulation of a general policy to China. It would be contrary to British and American interests, in his opinion, to allow Formosa to fall under the domination of the Communists. The United States Government would continue to support Chiang Kai-shek[1] in Formosa, in spite of the weakness and corruption of his régime. He wished, however, to make it clear that they had no intention of persuading the Japanese to recognise Chiang Kai-shek as having any sovereignty over continental China. They key to the position in the Pacific was Japan. It was essential to build up Japanese strength and save Japan from Communism. It was for that reason that the President had pressed for a generous treaty with Japan and had agreed to the conclusion of the Pacific Pact. Finally, on the general question of relations with Communist China, Mr Acheson said that the previous Government in the United Kingdom had approached this question as though they were in diplomatic relations with the Chinese People's Government. In fact, there were no effective diplomatic relations between the United Kingdom and that Government. It would be easier to formulate a joint policy if this were recognised. As regards Indo-China, discussions would continue with the British and French with a view to recommending an agreed course of action.

Mr Churchill said that he had been much moved by the readiness of the United States to shoulder the major burden in Korea and in the Far East. It

---

[1] Chiang Kai-shek, 1887–1975. Joined Sun Yat-sen's Revolutionary Party in 1907. Member of Revolutionary Army in Shanghai on outbreak of Chinese Revolution, 1911. Served at Chinese General Headquarters, 1918–20. Visited Soviet Union to study its military and social systems, 1923. Founder and Principal, Whampoa Military Academy, Canton, 1924. Member of General Executive Committee of Kuomintang, 1926. C-in-C, Northern Expeditionary Forces, 1926–8. Chairman of State, and Generalissimo of all fighting services, 1928–31. Resigned, 1931. Director-General of Kuomintang Party, 1938. Chairman of Supreme National Defence Council, 1939–47. President of Republic of China, 1948–75.

was painful to contemplate the lists of American casualties incurred in Korea. He was most anxious to help the Americans in any way possible and would be glad to know where this help was needed. He agreed that British relations with Communist China were a mere fiction; but it would be difficult for the United Kingdom Government to withdraw their recognition now, particularly when armistice talks were going on in Korea. He agreed that, in spite of the weakness and corruption of Chiang Kai-shek's régime, it would be wrong to leave his three or four hundred thousand followers in Formosa to be massacred by the Communists. He was glad to have Mr Acheson's assurances on the questions of Japanese relations with Chiang Kai-shek; he thought that any arrangement made between them might be considered as temporary only.

Mr Eden said that policy towards China could not be based on the assumption that a wedge could be driven between Peking and Moscow. He agreed with Mr Acheson's appreciation of M. Vyshinsky's manoeuvres in Paris. He understood that the latest proposal was that the Korean armistice talks should be carried on, not by the Security Council, but by the Four Great Powers. This was clearly an attempt to embarrass us and he endorsed Mr Acheson's view that the first stage should be military armistice talks; the second stage, a political settlement for Korea to be discussed by interested parties; and the last stage, a discussion of a general settlement in the Far East. It was difficult to see a solution to the problems of South East Asia, although he thought that this should be considered as part of one single problem which embraced the whole of the Far East. While the Americans had shouldered the major burden in Korea, there would be serious consequences for France and the United Kingdom if the Chinese Communists made an incursion into Indo-China. The loss of Indo-China and subsequently Malaya would have grave consequences, both political and economic, for France and the United Kingdom.

Mr Churchill emphasised the effect of the war in Indo-China upon the position in Europe. It was a constant drain upon the French Army, with the result that France remained militarily weak in Europe and therefore more apprehensive about the arming of Germans.

President Truman and Mr Churchill agreed that discussions should continue with a view to formulating an agreed British and American policy in the Far East and South-East Asia.

JANUARY 1952

Brien McMahon[1] and Winston S. Churchill: notes of a conversation
(Premier papers, 11/291)

8 January 1952
Top Secret

The Prime Minister talked with the Senator Brien McMahon after lunch today about atomic energy.

2. The Prime Minister showed the Senator the original copies of the Quebec Agreement, the Hyde Park Agreement, the Declaration of Trust and the Tripartite Agreement of November 1945 between Mr Truman, Mr Attlee and Mr Mackenzie King. He expressed his disappointment that the purpose of these agreements had been frustrated by the United States legislation. Senator McMahon explained that the agreements had not been disclosed to the Congress before the McMahon Act had been passed.

3. The Prime Minister informed the Senator of the proposal to test the British atomic weapon in Australia. The Senator expressed his disappointment at this decision. He had hoped that we would agree to a test in Nevada as this would be notable evidence of cooperation between the two countries. The Prime Minister explained why he considered it better to continue with the test in Australia. Cooperation between the two countries would be on much better terms once we had shown our ability to fire an atomic bomb, assuming that the test was successful.

4. Senator McMahon added he did not think that a large forward step in Anglo-American cooperation on atomic energy was possible before next November. But under the amendment to the Act which bore his name there was a wide area in which immediate progress was possible. He understood that the Atomic Energy Commission took a more optimistic view about the possibility of cooperation under the amendment than did the Defense Department. His own view was that it should make cooperation possible over 90 per cent of the field. He expressed the hope that Lord Cherwell would be able to have some discussion with the Atomic Energy Commission. The Prime Minister mentioned Mr LeBaron[2] and said he understood that he was rather stiff in these matters. The Senator replied that the Prime Minister was correctly informed.

5. The Prime Minister gave the Senator an idea of the size of the United Kingdom programme. He regretted that United States legislation had made so large an undertaking necessary. The Senator said he would like representatives of the Atomic Energy Commission to go over to the United Kingdom

[1] Brien McMahon, 1903–52. American lawyer and politician. Educated at Fordham University and Yale Law School. US Senator (Dem.) for Connecticut, 1942–52. Helped found Atomic Energy Commission, 1946.

[2] Robert F. LeBaron, 1891–1983. American atomic scientist. Educated at Union College and Princeton University. Chairman of Military Liaison Committee to Atomic Energy Commission, Dept of Defense, and Asst to Secretary of Defense, 1949–54.

and see the programme so that they could come back and report that there were matters on which the United Kingdom could be of help to the United States. The Prime Minister said that it would be better to wait until after the bomb had been tested. On the one hand, there would be criticism that we were giving the Americans all our information without getting anything in return, and on the other, if by any chance the test was unsuccessful, there might be American criticism to the effect that we had misled them into giving us information which, on the basis of an unsuccessful test, they might not have been willing to supply.

6. Senator McMahon expressed a desire to meet Lord Cherwell and the Prime Minister said that such a meeting should be arranged.

US–UK discussions: minutes
(*Premier papers, 11/161*)

8 January 1952 The White House
5 p.m.
Plenary Session No. 4

I. – RAW MATERIALS

Mr Fleischmann[1] reported the results of the special working group on raw materials as follows:

(a) Tin

The United Kingdom would sell 10,000 tons of tin to the United States at $1.18 per lb. In addition an understanding had been reached that the United Kingdom would make available an additional 10,000 tons of tin during 1952 at a price between $1.18 and $1.25, the exact price to be settled later. The public announcement of this agreement would be confined to the first 10,000 tons only, in order to avoid price exploitation.

(b) Aluminium

The United Kingdom would make available to the United States a loan of 5,000 tons of aluminium per quarter for the last three quarters of 1952. This aluminium, together with the 10,000 tons already made available to the United States, would be repaid before July 1953 provided that the new American production schedule allowed this. This further loan of aluminium would be made possible by a diversion of Canadian contracts.

---

[1] Manly Fleischmann, 1908–87. American attorney. Born in Hamburg, NY. Educated at Harvard and University of Buffalo. Asst General Counsel to President Roosevelt's War Production Board, 1941–3. Served with OSS, 1943–5. Private practice, 1945–50. Defense Production Administrator and National Production Administrator, 1951–2.

(c) Steel

The United States should supply the United Kingdom with 1.25 million long tons of steel during the calendar year 1952. The types of steel to be supplied would be subject to further discussion, and the time of deliveries would be subject to American direction. Deliveries would be spread as evenly as possible, but it was unlikely that an even flow of 100,000 tons per month could be maintained. From this total supply of steel there would be deducted the deliveries of steel already made in late 1951 and early 1952. These might amount to 100,000 tons.

Mr Churchill asked whether the United Kingdom had been able to offer any contributions of copper or nickel.

The following points were made in answer to Mr Churchill's question:
(i) Lack of coal and problems of transportation made it difficult to secure any rapid increase in the production of copper in Rhodesia. The United Kingdom was, however, taking all possible measures to increase supplies of copper, and would consider further a suggestion made by Mr Charles Wilson that the United Kingdom should supply brass strip for armament purposes. This would assist not only United States production, but also the dollar position of the United Kingdom.
(ii) The United States were not asking the United Kingdom for supplies of nickel. Joint efforts would be made to get the International Materials Conference to recognise the importance of British and American requirements for nickel, on the grounds that these two countries were bearing the main burden of defence.

Mr Churchill said that the agreement reached had very great importance for the United Kingdom, in respect of both the rearmament programme and the export programme. He suggested that there might be advantage in holding further discussions on the supply of metals between representatives of the United States, the United Kingdom, and Canada.

II. – EUROPEAN DEFENCE COMMUNITY

Mr Churchill said that the United Kingdom Government fully supported the formation of a European Army, though he could not say that he personally approved the details of the Pleven Plan. He thought that that system had been too much dictated by current European views on federation. He had no objection to federation so long as it was understood that the United Kingdom would not participate in it. The United Kingdom would, however, do everything possible to further the formation of a European Army, and the French Government and General Eisenhower had both expressed themselves as satisfied with the position taken by the United Kingdom Government at the end of the talks in Paris in December. He agreed that the European Army offered the only method of integrating German forces in the defence forces of Western Europe, and without the support of the Germans he doubted if Western Europe could be successfully defended. He would be very ready to do anything further which might assist in the creation of this Army.

Mr Acheson confirmed that the Americans had no wish to urge the United Kingdom to join the European Defence Community. He would, however, like the full support of the United Kingdom Government in convincing the Benelux countries, and particularly the Dutch, that the present proposals for a European Defence Community should be accepted. The Benelux countries had taken an opposite view to the French, Germans, and Italians in this matter, and wanted to see a much looser association. The Dutch, in particular, had certain fears which, with the aid of the British, it should be possible to dispel. There was, in practice, no alternative method of including the Germans in the defence of Europe. The Dutch were mistaken in supposing that the United States would lose interest in Europe once the European Defence Community had been created. They also feared that the French and Germans would dominate the European Defence Community; but this danger could be avoided by a system of voting which gave the Benelux countries an effective voice. The Dutch thought that the United Kingdom might join the community if it were organised on a looser basis, and it would be most helpful if the United Kingdom Government could make it clear to the Dutch that on this point also they were mistaken. Nor was it true that Dutch participation in the European Defence Community would result in their bearing a heavier burden of the cost of German rearmament. The Dutch also feared that as a partner in the Community they would obtain smaller supplies of equipment from the United States. This was not so. Nor would there be any curtailment of the Dutch defence programme at the dictation of the European Defence Community. The Dutch programme would continue to be subject to review by NATO.

Mr Eden paid tribute to the work done by the United States Government and by General Eisenhower towards the creation of a European Army, without which there was no chance of including Germans in the defence of Europe. The United Kingdom Government would certainly help in trying to dispel the fears of the Dutch. The fact was that any looser association would increase French fears of German domination and German fears that they would not be treated as equals. The Dutch, like the British, were seafaring people and attached importance to the conception of an Atlantic community. It would therefore be helpful to emphasise that the Atlantic community was an enduring concept and that the European Defence Community was simply something within that wide concept.

Mr Churchill said that, in all these discussions on the organisation of a constitutional system, the main object should not be forgotten. What was needed was loyal divisions who would fight shoulder to shoulder in the defence of Europe. He sometimes wondered if the sacrifice of nationality which the

European Defence Community implied would not damage the loyalty of the soldiers.

General Bradley said that he appreciated Mr Churchill's point, but that experience in Korea had shown that sixteen different countries could fight with great distinction for a cause rather than for their own national territories. He thought that there was no reason to fear a lack of morale in the European Army.

III. – REFORM OF NATO

Mr Acheson reported that United States and United Kingdom officials had discussed the proposals for the reform of NATO. It appeared from these discussions that there was a substantial measure of agreement on the proposals which might be put forward for consideration at the next meeting of the North Atlantic Council. The one substantial difference of opinion was on the location of the NATO headquarters. This could be discussed further in the Council Deputies.

Mr Eden suggested that the United States and United Kingdom Governments should now send instructions to their Deputies in London to pursue the agreed proposals with the other Deputies. The United Kingdom Government were still anxious that the Headquarters of NATO should remain in London which, in his view, was appropriate as an Atlantic capital.

IV. – PRODUCTION POSSIBILITIES

Mr Harriman said that, if the United Kingdom defence production programme had to be spread forward, it seemed desirable that the items to be delayed should be selected with due regard to the common interests of the two countries. At the moment the Americans had little idea of the details of the United Kingdom production programme. But they would be glad to examine it, in consultation with representatives of the United Kingdom Government, with a view to discovering whether there were any ways of spreading it forward to the common advantage. A working group might be set up for this purpose.

President Truman and Mr Churchill agreed that a special joint working group should be set up for this purpose.

Clementine Churchill to Winston S. Churchill
(Churchill papers, 1/50)[1]

8 January 1952

My darling Winston,

It is now ten days since I said goodbye to you at Waterloo Station. It makes me very happy to feel how well things are going and shaping. I will tell you

---

[1] This letter was handwritten.

how I have been occupied. I returned to Chequers on the Sunday morning after you left and continued to entertain the remainder of our Christmas Party. On the 2nd I returned to No. 10 since when I have had pleasant contacts with Randolph. He is terribly disappointed over Southport. And yesterday I returned from spending a delightful weekend with Mary and Christopher at the Farm. I inspected Page's Cottage which has been beautifully renovated for the new bailiff's wife. I also visited your tropical fish who are well and full of colour. Today I'm giving a luncheon party:
  Harry Crookshank
  Harold & Dorothy Macmillan[1]
  Sir Edward Bridges
  Lady Cynthia Colville[2] (Jack's mother) and Johnnie[3] your nephew & Mary Churchill.[4]

I'm looking forward to staying with the Harveys[5] in Paris. I go by Ferry on Sunday night the 13th returning the following Wednesday night. This is rather a dry catalogue like the pages of an engagement book torn out but I send you my dear love and thoughts.

Your devoted

*Text of communiqué issued on 9th January, 1952,
at the conclusion of the first four plenary sessions*
(Cabinet papers, 21/3057)

9 January 1952

The President and the Prime Minister held four meetings at the White House on 7th and 8th January, 1952. The Prime Minister was accompanied by the Foreign Secretary, Mr Anthony Eden, by the Secretary of State for Commonwealth Relations, Lord Ismay, and by the Paymaster General, Lord Cherwell. The President's advisers included the Secretaries of State, Treasury, Defense, Mr Charles E. Wilson, and Mr W. Averill Harriman. The visit of

---

[1] Dorothy Evelyn Cavendish, 1900–66. Married, 1920, Harold Macmillan: four children.

[2] Helen Cynthia Milnes, 1884–1968. Married, 1908, George Colville. Woman of the Bedchamber to Queen Mary, 1923–53. DCVO, 1937. DBE, 1953.

[3] John George Vanderbilt Henry Spencer-Churchill, 1926–2014. Married, 1951, Susan Mary (div. 1961); 1961, Athina Livanos (div. 1971); 1972, Rosita Douglas (div. 2008); 2008, Lily Mahtani. Lt, Life Guards, 1946; Capt., 1953. Council member, Winston Churchill Memorial Trust, 1966–2014. 11th Duke of Marlborough, 1972. Chairman, Martini & Rossi, 1979–96. Chairman, Badminton Conservation Trust, 1997–2001.

[4] Susan Mary Hornby, 1929–2005. Married, 1951, John Spencer-Churchill (div. 1961): three children.

[5] Oliver Charles Harvey, 1893–1968. Educated at Malvern and Trinity College, Cambridge. On active service in France, Egypt and Palestine (despatches), 1914–18. Entered Foreign Office, 1919. Married, 1920, Maud Annora. 1st Secretary, Paris, 1931–6. Counsellor, and Principal Private Secretary to successive Secretaries of State for Foreign Affairs, 1936–9, 1941–3. Minister to Paris, 1940. Asst Under-Secretary of State, 1943–6. Knighted, 1946. Deputy Under-Secretary of State (Political), 1946–7. Ambassador to France, 1948–54. Baron, 1954.

Mr Churchill and his colleagues also afforded opportunities for a number of informal meetings.

At the end of the talks the President and the Prime Minister issued the following announcement:

> During the last two days we have been able to talk over, on an intimate and personal basis, the problems of this critical time. Our discussions have been conducted in mutual friendship, respect and confidence. Each of our Governments has thereby gained a better understanding of the thoughts and aims of the other.
>
> The free countries of the world are resolved to unite their strength and purpose to ensure peace and security. We affirm the determination of our Governments and peoples to further this resolve, in accordance with the purposes and principles of the United Nations Charter. The strong ties which unite our two countries are a massive contribution to the building of the strength of the free world.
>
> Under arrangements made for the common defence, the United States has the use of certain bases in the United Kingdom. We reaffirm the understanding that the use of these bases in an emergency would be a matter for joint decision by His Majesty's Government and the United States Government in the light of the circumstances prevailing at the time.
>
> We share the hope and the determination that war, with all its modern weapons, shall not again be visited on mankind. We will remain in close consultation on developments which might increase danger to the maintenance of world peace.
>
> We do not believe that war is inevitable. This is the basis of our policies. We are willing at any time to explore all reasonable means of resolving the issues which now threaten the peace of the world.
>
> The United States Government is in full accord with the views expressed in the joint statement issued in Paris on 18th December, 1951, at the conclusion of the Anglo-French discussions. Our two Governments will continue to give their full support to the efforts now being made to establish a European Defence Community, and will lend all assistance in their power in bringing it to fruition. We believe that this is the best means of bringing a democratic Germany as a full and equal partner into a purely defensive organisation for European security. The defence of the free world will be strengthened and solidified by the creation of a European Defence Community as an element in a constantly developing Atlantic Community.
>
> Our Governments are resolved to promote the stability, peaceful development, and prosperity of the countries of the Middle East. We have found a complete identity of aims between us in this part of the world, and the two Secretaries of State will continue to work out together agreed policies to give effect to this aim. We think it essential for the furtherance of our

common purposes that an Allied Middle East Command should be set up as soon as possible.

As regards Egypt, we are confident that the Four-Power approach offers the best prospect of relieving the present tension.

We both hope that the initiative taken by the International Bank for Reconstruction and Development will lead to a solution of the Iranian oil problem acceptable to all the interests concerned.

We have discussed the many grave problems affecting our two countries in the Far East. A broad harmony of view has emerged from these discussions; for we recognise that the overriding need to counter the Communist threat in that area transcends such divergencies as there are in our policies toward China. We will continue to give full support for United Nations measures against aggression in Korea until peace and security are restored there. We are glad that the Chiefs of Staff of the United States, the United Kingdom, and France will be meeting in the next few days to consider specific measures to strengthen the security of Southeast Asia.

We have considered how our two countries could best help one another in the supply of scarce materials important to their defence programmes and their economic stability. The need of the United Kingdom for additional supplies of steel from the Unites States, and the need of the United States for supplies of other materials including aluminium and tin, were examined. Good progress was made. The discussions will be continued and we hope that agreement may be announced shortly.

We have reviewed the question of standardisation of rifles and ammunition in the North Atlantic Treaty Organisation. Neither country thinks it wise at this critical time to take the momentous step of changing its rifle. In the interest of economy, both in time and money, we have agreed that the United States and the United Kingdom will continue to rely upon rifles and ammunition now in stock and currently being produced. In the interest however of eventual standardisation, we have also agreed that both countries will produce their new rifles and ammunition only on an experimental scale while a common effort is made to devise a rifle and ammunition suitable for future standardisation.

The question of the Atlantic Command is still under discussion.

Throughout our talks we have been impressed by the need to strengthen the North Atlantic Treaty Organisation by every means within our power and in full accord with our fellow members. We are resolved to build an Atlantic Community, not only for immediate defence, but for enduring progress.

194   JANUARY 1952

Sir John Colville: recollection
('The Fringes of Power', page 638)

9 January 1952

On January 9th we listened to the President address Congress on the State of the Union and then went by train to New York. Before we left the Embassy the Prime Minister, at Sir Oliver Franks'[1] request, agreed to address the staff assembled in the garden. When he walked out on to the terrace for this purpose, he gasped with astonishment. In front of him, filling the entire garden, was a crowd not, as he had expected, of some fifty or sixty people, but, including wives and children, the best part of a thousand. The service departments in particular were grossly overmanned. He addressed the huge gathering most affably, but he instructed me to procure a detailed list of the officers attached to the Embassy. I did so when we returned to London and discovered that there were, amongst many others, forty-seven lieutenant-colonels and forty-three wing commanders. Evidently nobody had given thought to reducing the vast staffs established in a war which had ended six and a half years previously. The Prime Minister then issued a peremptory order, in his capacity as Minister of Defence, and a drastic reduction was effected.

General George C. Marshall[2] to Winston S. Churchill
(Churchill papers, 2/144)

9 January 1952

My dear Mr Churchill,

Mrs Marshall and I appreciated very much the handsome card with Holiday Greetings from Mrs Churchill and yourself. We felt honoured to receive it.

I thought you would be interested to know that nearby Pinehurst where we are spending the winter there was quite an elderly lady[3] who sent word she wished to see me because of my friendship with a niece of hers who had died several years ago. When I reached the house, expecting to talk about the

[1] Oliver Sherwell Franks, 1905–92. Fellow and Praelector, Philosophy, Queen's College, Oxford, 1927–37; University Lecturer, 1935–7. Prof., Moral Philosophy, University of Glasgow, 1937–45. Temporary Civil Servant, Ministry of Supply, 1939–46; Permanent Secretary, 1945–6. CBE, 1942. KCB, 1946. Provost, Queen's College, Oxford, 1946–8; Worcester College, Oxford, 1962–76. British Ambassador at Washington, 1948–52. PC, 1949. GCMG, 1952. Baron, 1962. OM, 1977. KCVO, 1985.

[2] George Catlett Marshall, 1880–1959. 2nd Lt, US Infantry, 1901. On active service in France, 1917–18; Chief of Operations, 1st Army; CoS, 8th Army Corps. ADC to Gen. Pershing, 1919–24. CoS, US Army, 1939–45. Chairman of the newly created JCS Committee to advise the President on strategy, 1941–5. Advocated the principle of 'Germany First' in Anglo-American military priorities. Representative of the President (Truman) to China with rank of Ambassador, 1945–7. Secretary of State, 1947–9. Architect of the Marshall Plan to rebuild shattered economies of Europe. Secretary of Defense, 1950–1. Nobel Peace Prize, 1953.

[3] Bertha Jenks. See letter of Feb. 3, reproduced below (pp. 250–1).

niece, I found that she had only one subject and that was yourself. She had been collecting photographs, sketches and articles about you for a great many years and her friends, knowing of her interest, had sent her many presents such as miniature busts of you. I am being accurate in saying that for an hour and a half she talked of nothing else, never mentioning the niece. So when we returned home I took the liberty of sending her your Christmas card because I knew she would be overjoyed to add it to her collection.

I may see you before you have an opportunity to read this letter.

With hope that this strenuous trip is not tiring you greatly and looking forward to the pleasure of seeing you on the 17th.

Winston S. Churchill to R. A. Butler
(Premier papers, 11/21)

12 January 1952
Confidential
No. 30

I send to you and to your Commonwealth colleagues[1] my warm wishes for the success of your very important meeting. I am very sorry that I cannot be in London to greet them personally. We all face grave and difficult decisions but we have together overcome greater difficulties in the past and I do not doubt that between us we shall again succeed.

UK–Canada joint Cabinet meeting: conclusions
(Premier papers, 11/161)

14 January 1952　　　　　　　　　　　　　　　　　　　　　　　　　　　　Ottawa
11 a.m.

1. The Prime Minister[2] welcomed Mr Churchill and his colleagues. The Government of Canada felt that any matters that were of concern to the Government of the United Kingdom were also of concern to them as the welfare of the people of the two countries was so intimately related. They were particularly pleased, therefore, to have this opportunity of exchanging views. The Government of Canada had also been pleased that Mr Churchill and his colleagues had been able to visit the United States at this time to strengthen the ties between that country and the United Kingdom which were of such fundamental importance for all the countries of the Commonwealth. The

---

[1] The Commonwealth Finance Ministers.

[2] Louis Stephen St Laurent, 1882–1973. Educated at St Charles College and Laval University. President, Canadian Bar Association, 1930–2. MP (Lib.) for Quebec East, 1942–58. Minister of Justice, 1942–5. Secretary of State for External Affairs, 1945–8; PM of Canada, 1948–57.

members of the Canadian Cabinet would be glad to hear any comments that Mr Churchill might feel it proper to make relating to his discussions in the United States and concerning problems of common concern.

2. The Prime Minister of the United Kingdom referred to his visit to Ottawa ten years before. He was gratified to be able to meet again with the members of the Privy Council of Canada of which he had, since that time, been a member. He would be glad to discuss any matters they might wish to raise.

ATOMIC WEAPONS

3. Mr Churchill stressed the importance of the development and improvement of atomic weapons during the period when the relative strength of western countries in conventional weapons would not be adequate to afford them protection. The Labour Government in the United Kingdom had made progress in the development of an atomic bomb and the first one produced in the United Kingdom would be tested in Australia during the summer. If it was successful, production could proceed. Apart from its intrinsic importance a successful British bomb might have a substantial influence on the readiness of the United States to exchange information on atomic development. He was very anxious to see an equality of knowledge with the United States which would lead to a more ready exchange of technical information.

4. The Prime Minister suggested that detailed discussion on atomic energy questions might be left to Lord Cherwell and Mr Howe.[1]

POLICY TOWARD THE SOVIET UNION

5. Mr Churchill said that the policy was to preserve peace or at least a *modus vivendi* with the USSR of as long a duration as possible. This could only be secured from strength. Agreements with the USSR could not be secured on any other basis. The strength of the West was being developed through the North Atlantic Treaty Organisation. It was hoped that NATO would not be limited solely to preparations for defence but that it might develop into a lasting grouping of Powers which would produce a new effectiveness for the United Nations. The present did not appear to be a propitious time to enter into talks with the USSR but the United Kingdom would be ready at any time to respond to any genuine advance from the Soviet side.

A deterrent factor in the present dangerous situation was that war would be extremely unpleasant for both sides. Both would suffer what they dreaded most at the outset: Europe would be overrun and the USSR would be blasted by atomic weapons in all its vital points. This gave some assurance that peace could be maintained. It seemed certain that at best there would have to be a prolonged period of cold war. That, however, was much better than catastrophe.

[1] Clarence Decatur Howe, 1886–1960. Canadian Minister of Transport, 1936–40. Minister of Munitions and Supply, 1940–4. Minister of Reconstruction, 1944–8. Minister of Trade and Commerce, 1948–51. Minister of Defence Production, 1951–60.

JANUARY 1952   197

6. The Prime Minister enquired whether Mr Churchill thought that the apparent concessions made by M. Vishinsky at the United Nations in relation to the banning of atomic weapons and the possibility of inspection gave indication of desire on the Soviet side to see some progress.

7. Mr Churchill felt it would present a difficult problem if the Soviet Union were to offer to accept our conditions for the control of atomic weapons since the West was not sufficiently strong at present to do without the protection that their possession afforded. It was the vast superiority of the United States in atomic weapons and the technical improvements they had achieved, that provided a decisive deterrent at present. It was doubtful, however, that the USSR would be prepared to allow *bona fide* and continuous inspection since it would too greatly lift the veil they kept over their affairs.

8. Mr Eden said he thought the Vishinsky concessions did represent a positive move. The Western nations would have to expect more of these moves. They were indicative of a growing anxiety on the part of the Soviet Union.

9. Mr Churchill said that there was, perhaps, some significance in the Soviet emphasis on the development of fighter planes rather than of bombers. It was a defensive emphasis which revealed anxiety and suggested that fear was an important factor in Soviet actions.

THE FAR EAST

10. The Minister of National Defence[1] said he would be interested to hear the views of the United Kingdom Ministers on the position in the Far East, particularly on the prospects in Korea. He felt that the six months of discussion on a cease-fire in Korea had left the United Nations in a much weaker position relatively than when the talks began. The United States commanders in Korea thought that the Chinese genuinely desired a cease-fire. On the other hand, the Prime Minister of Japan[2] was of the opinion that the Communists would not accept one. He thought they would attempt to prolong the present discussions. Even if a cease-fire were achieved, it was not apparent how the United Nations were going to extricate themselves from Korea.

11. Mr Eden expressed general agreement with Mr Claxton's comments. He found it equally difficult to see how the Korean episode was to be resolved. He had felt some surprise in the discussions in Washington at the confidence of the United States authorities in their capacity to deal with any possible military developments in Korea next spring.

It was difficult to forecast developments in other parts of South-East Asia. There was no reliable evidence that an extension of hostilities in Indo-China

[1] Brian Brooke Claxton, 1898–1960. Educated at McGill University. On active duty, 1914–18 (DCM). KC, 1939. MP (Lib.) for St Lawrence–St. George, 1940–54. Parliamentary Assistant to Canadian PM, 1943–4. Minister of National Health and Welfare, 1943–6. Minister of National Defence, 1946–54.
[2] Yoshida Shigeru, 1878–1967. Educated at Tokyo Imperial University. Entered Foreign Ministry, 1906. Minister to Sweden, Norway, and Denmark, and Vice Foreign Minister, 1928–30. Ambassador to Great Britain, 1936–9. Foreign Minister, 1945. PM, 1946–7, 1948–54.

was imminent. There had been a number of reports of preparations by the Chinese but all had been contradicted by other sources. Some of the reports might be instigated by the Chinese Nationalists. He had been pleased that the President of the United States in his Message on the State of the Union had explicitly warned China against the possible consequences of further aggression. He had tried to follow that up in his own speech in New York. The French felt that they could hold their position in Indo-China if there were no major aggression as in Korea. If there were any such move they would want the United Nations to take action.

12. The Secretary of State for External Affairs[1] said that he was disturbed by M. Vyshinsky's statement in Paris in which he claimed that the United States had moved Chinese Nationalist's divisions to Burma and other South-East Asian countries. If any new Communist move were being contemplated, this was the sort of propaganda preparation that might be expected.

13. Mr Churchill pointed out that ten of the best United Nations divisions were tied up in Korea, and ten French divisions in Indo-China. The addition of that strength to Western Europe could make a very substantial difference. At the present time, there was not one complete division in the United Kingdom. There were, however, some 250,000 troops in military schools and depots in the United Kingdom, and these were now being armed and trained so that they would have some combatant value in an emergency. He meant to secure that the United Kingdom looked more like the back of a hedge-hog than the paunch of a rabbit. If the Chinese attacked Indo-China it would be necessary for the United Kingdom to reconsider its recognition of the Communist Government of China.

14. Mr Pearson asked what divergencies there now were between the United Kingdom and the United States on policy in the Far East.

15. Mr Eden said that there were now only two points of divergence, viz., the United Kingdom recognition of the Chinese People's Government and the proposed treaty between Japan and the Chinese Nationalists. The first was little more than a formal point and the United States Government were not now seriously concerned about it. The second was more troublesome. The United States Administration apparently felt very strongly that, in order to satisfy Congressional opinion, they must announce that as soon as the Japanese Peace Treaty was ratified Japan would conclude a treaty with the Chinese Nationalist Government in respect of Formosa. The United Kingdom Government agreed that, once she had achieved her independence, Japan would be free to do as she wished in this matter; but they would have preferred that no public announcement of her intentions should be made in advance. They would not, however, continue to press their objections upon the United States Government.

[1] Lester Bowles Pearson, 1887–1972. Known as 'Mike'. Canadian Ambassador to US, 1944–6. MP (Lib.) for Algoma East, 1948–68. Secretary of State for External Affairs, 1948–57. President, UN General Assembly, 1952. PM of Canada, 1963–8.

16. Mr Churchill said that, as regards Korea, he was glad that the United States Government were now consulting more fully with other Governments which were contributing to the United Nations Forces.

17. Mr Pearson said that seventeen countries had now accepted the draft of the warning declaration about the consequences of a major breach of the of the armistice terms in Korea.

18. Mr St Laurent pointed out that acceptance of the draft declaration would still leave unsettled a number of important questions on which decisions would have to be taken by the countries contributing to the United Nations Forces in Korea.

19. Mr Churchill said that the United Kingdom Government were anxious to avoid raising small points of disagreement with the United States on Far East questions, as they were conscious that the brunt of the military effort in that area was being borne by the United States. In the Middle East, where the United Kingdom were carrying the major part of the load, he hoped that the United States could be persuaded to give some support and assistance. Even token assistance would be valuable. The United Kingdom were carrying out an international responsibility in maintaining free right of passage through the Suez Canal.

MIDDLE EAST

20. Mr Eden said that in his discussions in Washington he had agreed with the United States Secretary of State that the Four-Power proposals should be revised and made ready for presentation in a new form possibly including something about the Sudan. It could then be indicated to King Farouk, at the appropriate moment, that these proposals were available for presentation to a Government likely to accord them a favourable reception.

21. Mr Churchill said that in so far as the oil dispute in Persia was concerned, the policy of the United Kingdom Government was to salvage what they could from the wreck. Britain could get her oil from elsewhere, but she needed the foreign exchange which she had earned from the Persian oil. Permanent loss of this source of revenue would mean a serious addition to the balance of payments difficulties of the United Kingdom.

22. Mr Eden said the International Bank had put forward certain proposals which were acceptable to the United Kingdom but had not yet found favour with Dr Mossadegh. There seemed to be some possibility, however, that Mossadegh might eventually agree to something along the lines of these latest proposals. In any event it seemed clear that they were the sort of proposals that would afford Mossadegh the best opportunity to reach a compromise with the United Kingdom without losing face provided, of course, he were disposed to do so. Throughout the protracted discussions and negotiations on this problem Mossadegh had shown himself to be an extremely shrewd bargainer. The United Kingdom Government had to ensure that any treatment given Persia should not be generous to the point where it would prejudice

the future of oil concessions held elsewhere by the United Kingdom and the United States. If a satisfactory price could be negotiated, the United Kingdom might be ready to forgo any claim it might have for compensation. Dr Mossadegh might, however, prefer to stress the compensation feature since it would then be easier for him to reduce or eliminate British control and influence.

EUROPE

23. Mr Churchill said that General Eisenhower had made it abundantly clear that he did not expect United Kingdom military units to join the European army. He was quite content that the United Kingdom should make appropriate military contributions to the NATO forces, of which the European army was part. Mr Churchill thought it not only unnecessary but unworkable that United Kingdom forces should be merged in the European army. He did not see how any Prime Minister of the United Kingdom could contemplate sending six British divisions to the European army in the knowledge that none of these divisions would ever stand shoulder to shoulder in the line. There were very real difficulties. He fully appreciated that the doctrine of European federation appealed strongly to the sense of logic of the French. He himself felt that the United Kingdom should offer every encouragement to the concept of European federation without, however, losing sight of the fact that it was in the interests not only of the United Kingdom, but of international peace that the United Kingdom should maintain her strong Commonwealth ties rather than become an integral part of a European federation.

24. Mr Eden pointed out that when the present United Kingdom Government took office, the plans for a European army had already been under discussion for nine months. If the new United Kingdom Government had joined in the discussions at that stage, every detail of the proposed arrangements would have been thrown open for renegotiation and this would have caused further substantial delays.

25. Mr Churchill thought it unfortunate that the Labour Government had decided not to participate in the conferences on the Schuman Plan and the European army.

As a general comment, he felt that the principle of the Grand Alliance had much to commend it, primarily because, as became evident during the Second World War, it enabled several sovereign States to work in the closest harmony without any suggestion that one country might be the vassal of another.

ATLANTIC COMMAND

26. Mr Churchill said that, in his opinion, British shipping would face greater dangers in a future war than in the last. Enemy submarines would be much more numerous, faster and armed with even more deadly weapons than before. Anti-submarine vessels would have to be much faster craft, which could not be improvised after war had broken out. Even greater than the submarine

danger was probably the mine threat. There had been developed new types of suction mines which were impervious to magnetic minesweeping. These could be dropped rapidly in large numbers and it was difficult to see at this time what effective measures could be taken against them.

The United Kingdom's dangers were much greater than those of the United States or Canada. If the United Kingdom failed to keep its ports open it could not survive. For North America the loss of the battle in the Atlantic would mean the loss of the campaign in Europe. For the United Kingdom it would mean extinction. It was for this reason that he had made every effort to impress on the Americans that it was a matter of practical necessity that the United Kingdom should retain complete naval control in the Eastern Atlantic at the reception end. Executive control of the battle and the convoys should be exercised in the eastern half of the Atlantic by the First Sea Lord and in the western half by the United States Chief of Naval Operations. On almost every occasion they would work in complete harmony. If any differences should arise between them, these could be resolved by the Standing Group who could be advised on policy by an Admiral of the Atlantic. He was, however, most strongly opposed to the creation of a Supreme Allied Commander, Atlantic. He was gratified to hear that some members of the Canadian Government shared his views on this question.

27. Mr Churchill said that Canada was to be congratulated on the growth of its Navy. It was building up one of the leading navies in the free world. He hoped that Canada, with its expanding resources, would continue to cherish the naval tradition, as it had been cherished for so long in the United Kingdom. A strong Canadian Navy would be of great value, not only for purposes of local defence, but also as a link between North America and Europe.

28. Mr Churchill thought that, while the Western countries were becoming stronger, they were not yet necessarily safer. The greatest danger would come in the period just before their strength became really effective. If the Russians made war, they were more likely to do so as a result of miscalculation than by reason of an 'incident'. In this view the odds were against a war this year, although no one could make an accurate forecast.

The Russians had greatly improved their position by bringing large portions of Europe and all of China under their control without loss to themselves. They might, therefore, think it best to continue as at present. Their leaders appeared to fear war and atomic bombing since these would undermine their control over their people. They seemed more interested in maintaining their power internally than anything else. If, at a later date, the West desired to intensify the 'cold war' it might possibly do so by taking steps to make more information available to the Russian people. The West would be in increased danger if there were the slightest sign that the NATO countries were not pursuing their defence plans with determination.

ECONOMIC SITUATION

29. Lord Cherwell said the Americans had been anxious to obtain additional supplies of aluminium. Canada's willingness that the United Kingdom should divert to the United States some of their Canadian supplies of aluminium had made it possible to persuade the United States to allocate to the United Kingdom considerable quantities of steel which would be of great value, both for rearmament and for exports. It was vitally important to maintain United Kingdom exports. For the United Kingdom gold and dollar reserves had fallen seriously in 1951 and it was going to be very difficult to stop them from continuing to decline in the next six months.

30. Mr Churchill said that his Government had been faced with a grave financial situation on assuming office. The sterling area was running a large deficit with the dollar area, with Europe and with the rest of the world. The rearmament programme of £4.7 billion would now cost £5.2 billion owing to increased prices. His Government was, however, not going to be afraid to take the unpopular steps that were necessary if national solvency were to be regained. He felt that, if the need for further stringencies were put squarely to the people of Great Britain, they would accept the measures required by the situation. He did not propose to ask for outside help for the purpose of enabling the people of the United Kingdom to avoid discomfort. Rearmament was, however, a different matter: for it was designed to serve the common cause. He was ready to seek external aid to help forward the United Kingdom defence programme. The assistance which the Americans were providing would be a great help to the rearmament effort and the export drive.

31. Lord Cherwell said that cuts could only be made in domestic consumption, to the defence programme or in exports. Consumption had already been cut to the bone. Some of the rearmament programme would have to be postponed.

32. Mr Churchill said that he now expected the United Kingdom rearmament programme to take four rather than three years to complete. In the circumstances, his Government was concentrating its efforts on such essential elements of the programme as new types of aircraft and tanks.

33. Mr St Laurent enquired whether there was any likelihood of the United Kingdom being able to reduce its unrequited exports.

34. Mr Churchill said that it was hoped to make some progress in this direction but that his Government's hands were tied to some extent by arrangements made since the close of the war.

During the war, he had been of the opinion that the United Kingdom should hold itself free to put in a counter-claim against the sterling balances which had been accumulated by countries which had been preserved by British troops from being overrun by the enemy.

35. Mr Howe said that the imbalance in Canadian–United Kingdom trade would have been less if Canada could have placed larger orders in the United

Kingdom for heavy equipment which had been going to countries in the sterling area.

36. Mr St Laurent said that he and his colleagues had greatly appreciated Mr Churchill's review of the world situation. The Canadian Government realised that the greatest possible efforts must be made by the Western countries in order to achieve the results that were essential to all.

37. Mr Churchill said that he was most grateful to Mr St Laurent and the other members of the Canadian Government for their kindness. The meeting of the four members of his Cabinet with the Canadian Cabinet had been a memorable event.

38. It was agreed that a brief communiqué (annex) should be issued to the press at the conclusion of the meeting. This would indicate that the discussion had ranged over the world situation with particular emphasis on the North Atlantic alliance, and that the exchange of views had revealed a complete understanding between the representatives of the two countries.

Winston S. Churchill: speech
('Winston S. Churchill, His Complete Speeches', volume 8, pages 8320–3)

14 January 1952   Banquet given by the Canadian Government
Ottawa

I am indeed honoured that you should receive me with so much kindness. I came here first more than fifty years ago to give a lecture about the Boer War. A little later on I was Under-Secretary of State for the Colonies when Sir Wilfred Laurier[1] came to England, and I saw a lot of that august Canadian statesman. He brought with him a young secretary named Mr Mackenzie King.[2] I made a lifelong friendship with him and I shared my grief with all Canada, and indeed the free world, at his death after so many years of faithful and skilful service to the great causes which we uphold today.

The Prime Minister of Canada and his Cabinet have welcomed me and my colleagues, who are one-quarter of the British Cabinet, not only with Canadian hospitality but with that sense of true comrades facing difficulties together, which often makes it possible for these difficulties to be overcome. I am very glad to see here also my old friend, Mr George Drew,[3] and I am truly sorry that I cannot now visit Toronto, where I have been invited to receive a

---

[1] Henri Charles Wilfrid Laurier, 1841–1919. Married, 1868, Zoe Lafontaine. MP (Lib.) for Drummond–Arthabaska, 1874–7; for Quebec East, 1874–1919. PM of Canada, 1896–1911.

[2] William Mackenzie King, 1874–1950. Born in Ontario. Entered Canadian Government as Minister of Labour, 1909. Leader of Liberal Party of Canada, 1919. Leader of the Opposition, 1919–21, 1930–5. PM of Canada, 1921–30, 1935–48. Secretary of State for External Affairs, 1935–46. OM, 1947.

[3] George Alexander Drew, 1894–1973. Premier of Ontario, 1943–8. MP (Tory/Progressive Cons.) for Carleton, 1948–57. Leader of the Opposition, 1948–56. Canadian High Commissioner to UK, 1957–64.

Degree. Mr Drew is the Leader of the Opposition. Well, I have been a Leader of the Opposition too. In a free country one is always allowed to have an Opposition. In England we even pay the Leader of the Opposition a salary of £2,000 a year to make sure that the Government is kept up to the mark. I have no doubt Mr Attlee, whom you welcomed less than a year ago, will devote himself to his constitutional task with the zeal which, under totalitarian systems, might well lead him to Siberia or worse. However, we in the free nations have our own way of life, and are able to keep separate, except perhaps at Election times, those things which affect the life of the State from those which decide what party gets into office.

It is ten years almost to a week since I last came to see you in Ottawa. That was indeed a memorable occasion for me with all the burdens I had to bear. It was also an inspiring but formidable moment in the war. With the entry of the United States into the struggle, the pathway to victory seemed, and in fact was, open and sure. But I bore in my heart and conscience the knowledge, which I could not share with you, of immense, shattering disasters which were about to fall upon us throughout the East, as the inevitable consequence of the Japanese onslaught in vast regions where we were weak and ill-prepared to meet it. I knew and could feel beforehand, the heavy blows that must fall upon us, and the peril of Singapore, the Dutch East Indies, Burma and India itself. I had no feeling of self-reproach because between the fall of France in 1940 and Hitler's invasion of Russia in 1941, it had taken Britain and the British Empire fighting alone – every scrap of our life and strength – to keep the flag of freedom flying, until we were joined by mighty allies. But while I spoke to you gaily and confidently and was sure that final victory would be gained I felt like one about to come under the lash wielded by a strong and merciless arm.

I knew that many months must pass before the United States Navy could regain the control of the Pacific Ocean. We, with your gallant Canadian help, had to fight the Battle of the Atlantic against the U-boats, whose attack was ever-growing in strength and skill, and who were about to take their greatest toll along the American seaboard. An almost unbroken series of misfortunes and defeats lay before us, until the Battle of Alamein, won by your famous Governor-General[1] and General Montgomery, and the concerted descent upon North-West Africa by General Eisenhower's Anglo-American Army, until these great events and great men turned the tide once and for all.

What is the scene which unfolds before us tonight? It is certainly not what we had hoped to find after all our enemies had surrendered unconditionally and the great world instrument of the United Nations had been set up to make sure that the wars were ended. It is certainly not that. Peace does not sit untroubled in her vineyard. The harvests of new and boundless wealth which science stands ready to pour into the hands of all peoples, and of none perhaps more than the people of Canada, must be used for exertions to ward

---

[1] FM Lord Alexander.

off from us the dangers and unimaginable horrors of another world war. At least this time I have no secrets to guard about the future. When I came last time I could not tell. Now I do not know. No one can predict with certainty what will happen.

All can see for themselves the strange clouds that move and gather on the horizons. But this time at any rate we are all united from the beginning. We all mean to stand by each other, here, in Canada, in the United States, in Britain, in Western Europe, all of us, are united to defend the cause of freedom with all our strength and by that strength we hope to preserve unbroken the peace which is our heart's desire.

I have spoken tonight a good deal about the past. Edmund Burke[1] said: 'People will not look forward to posterity who never look backward to their ancestors.' The past is indeed the only guide to the future. But it is the future which dominates our minds. A great future is yours in Canada.

The two world wars of the terrible twentieth century have turned the economic balance of power from the Old World to the New. It is certain that Europe could not have survived without the moral and material help which has flowed across the ocean from Canada and the United States. Now we have the North Atlantic Treaty which owes much to Canadian statesmanship and to the personal initiative of Mr St Laurent. The treaty is the surest guarantee not only of the prevention of war but of victory, should our hopes be blasted.

So far this solemn compact has been regarded only in its military aspect, but now we all feel, especially since our visit to Washington, that it is broadening out into the conception of the North Atlantic community of free nations, acting together not only for defence but for the welfare and happiness and progress of all the peoples of the free world. For this we need to do all in our power to promote United Europe and the design of a European Army, including Germany. I have long been an advocate of both of these ideas. We shall do all in our power to help them to success. That does not mean that Great Britain will become a unit in a federated Europe, nor that her army, which is already in line upon the Continent and which will grow steadily, will be merged in such a way as to lose its identity. We stand with the United States, shoulder to shoulder with the European Army and its German elements, under the Supreme NATO Commander to face whatever aggression may fall upon us.

It was only ten weeks last Friday that I accepted His Majesty's Commission to form a Government in the United Kingdom. We have hardly yet had time to learn the full facts of our economic position. But what we saw at first sight convinced us of its gravity. By reducing our imports by £350 million and other measures we strove to arrest the evils which were advancing and descending

---

[1] Edmund Burke, 1730–97. MP (Whig) for Wendover, 1765–74; for Malton, 1774, 1780–94; for Bristol, 1774–80. Author and editor of *Annual Register* (1758–88). Author of *Thoughts on the Cause of the Present Discontents* (1770); *On American Taxation* (1774); *Conciliation with the Colonies* (1775); *Reflections on the Revolution in France* (1791); *Letters on a Regicide Peace* (1795–7); *Letter to a Noble Lord* (1796). Regarded as the philosophical father of modern conservatism.

upon us. We do not want to live on our friends and relations but to earn our own living and pay our own way so far as the comforts and standards of the British people are concerned. We gave all our strength to the last ounce during the war and we are resolved to conquer our problems now that it is over. The ordeal which lies before us will be hard and will not be short. We shall not shrink from any measures necessary to restore confidence and maintain solvency, however unpopular these measures may be.

Prime Minister, you have spoken about the Crown in terms which express our deepest feelings. No absolute rules can be laid down. But on the whole it is wise in human affairs and in the government of men, to separate pomp from power. Under the long-established constitutional monarchy of Britain and of the Commonwealth the King reigns but does not govern. If a great battle is lost Parliament and the people can turn out the Government. If a great battle is won crowds cheer His Majesty. Thus, while the ordinary struggles, turmoils and inevitable errors of healthy democratic government proceed, there is established upon an unchallenged pedestal the title deeds and the achievements of all the Realms and every generation can make its contribution to the enduring treasure of our race and fame. You spoke, Mr Prime Minister, of the Crown as the symbol of our united life, and as the link between our vigorous communities spread about the surface of the globe. But perhaps you will allow me tonight to pass from the constitutional to the personal sphere. Besides the Crown there is the King. We have a truly beloved King. In constitutional duty he is faultless. In physical and moral courage he is an example to all his peoples. We are proud to pay him our tribute. This is no formal salute of loyalty, but the expression of our intense natural impulse. Here in Canada you have had what may be called a wonderful visit. HRH Princess Elizabeth and her husband[1] have travelled the length and breadth of what you will not mind my styling 'The Great Dominion'. They have left behind them a long and lasting trail of confidence, encouragement and unity.

I claim here, in Ottawa, that tonight we make a valiant and, I believe, unconquerable assertion of the spirit of our combined identity and survival. We have surmounted all the perils and endured all the agonies of the past. We shall provide against and thus prevail over the dangers and problems of the future, withhold no sacrifice, grudge no toil, seek no sordid gain, fear no foe. All will be well. We have, I believe, within us the life-strength and guiding light by which the tormented world around us may find the harbour of safety, after a storm-beaten voyage.

This year will see the Eighty-fifth Anniversary of Canada's Confederation. A magnificent future awaits Canada, if only we can all get through the present hideous world muddle. When I first came here after the Boer War these mighty lands had but five million inhabitants. Now there are fourteen.

---

[1] Philip Mountbatten, 1921–. Son of Prince Andrew of Greece and Denmark and Princess Alice of Battenberg. Educated at Royal Naval College. Married, 1947, Elizabeth Windsor. Prince Consort, Duke of Edinburgh, Earl of Merioneth and Baron Greenwich, 1952–.

When my grandchildren come here there may well be thirty. Upon the whole surface of the globe there is no more spacious and splendid domain open to the activity and genius of free men, with one hand clasped in enduring friendship with the United States, and the other spread across the ocean both to Britain and France. You have a sacred mission to discharge. That you will be worthy of it, I do not doubt. God bless you all.

Winston S. Churchill to Lord Swinton
Prime Minister's Personal Telegram T.20A/52
(Premier papers, 11/270)

14 January 1952
Emergency
Secret
No. 47

1. I had always intended that the additional points and expansions for which I pressed should be met by other economies on the general field.[1] This does not seem to have been done.

2. I shall be telegraphing further about the 27,000 increase in manpower for the Air Force which seems out of proportion to the increases in fighting planes.

Kay Halle: recollection
('The Irrepressible Churchill', pages 243–4)

15 January 1952

Much has been made of his zest for drink. He disliked cocktails ('I liked wine, both red and white, and especially champagne,' he wrote in one of his early works, and 'a small glass of brandy' and 'whisky in a diluted form'), but he liked to be thought a two-bottle man in the tradition of Pitt.*

WSC: (travelling by train with 'the Prof' (Lord Cherwell), his 'human slide rule'): Prof! How many pints of champagne in cubic feet have I consumed in 24 years at the rate of a pint a day and how many railway carriages would it fill?

The 'Prof' (after rapid calculation): Only a part of one.

WSC: So little time and so much to achieve.

* William Pitt, 1759–1806, 'the Younger Pitt'; Prime Minister at twenty-four; known as one of England's greatest Prime Ministers – and as a 'two-bottle man' for the quantities of port he consumed, and which killed him.

[1] Regarding Service Estimates: see Churchill to Members of the Cabinet, 17 Dec. 1951, reproduced above (pp. 136–8).

JANUARY 1952

Sir Henry Tizard[1] to Winston S. Churchill
(*Premier papers, 11/380*)

15 January 1952
Secret

You may like to know that the DRP Committee has for some time been issuing a series of Progress Reports on special subjects. I enclose a list of these Reports, together with their dates of issue. You have already seen and commented on No. 12.

Report No. 13 dealing with the present position of Guided Weapons is in preparation and will be issued very shortly.

Copies of these Reports should be available in your office but additional copies can be provided if you wish. Some of them, of course, are a little out of date now but the information provided by Reports Nos. 1, 2 and 8 has been brought, up-to-date in my full paper on Sea Communications in War, copies of which have already been sent to you. Additional information on other Reports to bring them more up-to-date can be provided if you wish.

During 1952 the Committee will be issuing Reports on the following subjects:

 Armoured Fighting Vehicles
 Naval Aviation
 Biological Warfare
 Signal Communications
 Air Navigation and Bombing Systems
 Infantry and Field Artillery Weapons

These Progress Reports were issued by direction of the Defence Committee in May, 1949.

Sir John Colville: recollection
(*'The Fringes of Power'*, *pages 639–40*)

15–19 January 1952

On the 15th we left by train for Washington and on the 17th the PM made a great speech to Congress, which I attended on the floor of the House. Lord

---

[1] Henry Thomas Tizard, 1885–1959. Educated at Westminster School, Magdalen College, Oxford, and Imperial College, London. Lecturer in Natural Science, Oxford, 1911–21. Royal Garrison Artillery, 1914; RFC, 1915–18. Lt-Col., and Asst Controller of Experiments and Research, RAF, 1918–19. Permanent Secretary, Dept of Scientific and Industrial Research, 1927–9. Rector, Imperial College, 1929–42. Chairman, Aeronautical Research Committee, 1933–43. Knighted, 1937. Member of Council, Ministry of Aircraft Production, 1941–3. President of Magdalen College, Oxford, 1942–6. Chairman, Advisory Council on Scientific Policy and Defence Research Policy, 1946–52.

Knollys,[1] Bill Elliot[2] and other Embassy people present thought it had had a chilly reception; but we were quite wrong. Congress reacted slowly, but the subsequent praise was generous – except at home where the Labour Party asserted that the PM had committed us to a more active part against China.

Churchill had been still in bed putting the finishing touches to his speech when Sir Roger Makins came into the room to say the cars were at the door and we ought already to be leaving for the Capitol. In the Prime Minister's speech it was essential to refer to Britain's contribution in the Korean War, which had been raging since 1950. 'If the Chinese cross the Yalu River, our reply will be – what?' 'Prompt, resolute and effective,' suggested Roger Makins on the spur of the moment. 'Excellent,' said Churchill. He wrote these words in the text of his speech, got up, dressed and reached the Capitol with two minutes to spare.

It was these words with no special significance except to declare that the Allies would react strongly to such an attack, which the Labour Opposition interpreted to mean that an atomic bomb would be used. Such a thought had not crossed Churchill's mind nor, I believe, President Truman's.

We returned to New York on the 19th and though the PM caught a cold which prevented a triumphal drive down Broadway, we had a gay time. [. . .]

Winston S. Churchill: speech
('Winston S. Churchill, His Complete Speeches', volume 8, page 8323)

16 January 1952   Washington DC

BECOMING A MEMBER OF THE
SOCIETY OF CINCINNATI

I regard this as a most memorable day in my crowded life, and you have conferred on me an honour which I deeply value. I treasure the eagle and diploma and will hand them to my descendants. As history unfolds itself, by

---

[1] Edward George William Tyrwhitt Knollys, 1895–1966. Educated at New College, Oxford. Page of Honour to King Edward VII, 1904–10; to King George V, 1910–11. On active service as an observer for RCC during WWI. DFC, Order of the Crown of Belgium, Croix de Guerre. MBE, 1918. Succeeded his father as 2nd Viscount Knollys, 1924. Local director, Barclays Bank, Cape Town, 1929–32. KCMG, 1941. Governor and C-in-C, Bermuda, 1941–3. Chairman, British Overseas Airways Corp., 1943–7; Director-General, 1946–7. Representative to International Materials Conference (Washington DC), 1951–2. GCMG, 1952. Chairman, Vickers Ltd, 1956–62. Chairman, English Steel Corp., 1959–65. Chairman, Employer's Liability Assurance Corp., 1960. FRSA, 1962.

[2] William Elliot, 1896–1971. On active service, 1914–18 (despatches, DFC and bar, 1918). Secretary, Night Air Defence Committee, 1940. CBE, 1942. Director of Plans, Air Ministry, 1942–4. AOC RAF Gibraltar, 1944; Balkan Air Force, 1944–5. Asst Chief Executive, Ministry of Aircraft Production, 1945–6. Knighted, 1946. C-in-C, Fighter Command, 1947–9. ADC to King George VI, 1950–2; to the Queen, 1952–4. Chairman of British Joint Services Mission, Washington DC, and UK Representative on the Standing Group of the Military Committee of NATO, 1951–4. GCVO, 1953.

strange and unpredictable paths, we have little control over the future and no control over the past. It therefore seems to me that when the events took place which this society commemorates I was on both sides in the war between us and we.

I remind you that many of the most famous English statesmen have taken the side of the colonists. I have been refreshing my memory during the morning by reading the elder Pitt, and I quote: 'If I were an American, as I am an Englishman, and foreign troops were landed in my country, I would never lay down my arms – never, never, never.' These are the kind of words which roll along the centuries and play their part in wiping out the bitterness of former quarrels and in effacing the tragedies that have occurred, so that we remember battles only to celebrate military virtues of those who took part on both sides.

I am proud of my American ancestry. I think it wonderful that I should have the honour to rejoice in that fact, while at the same time I have never failed in my constitutional duty to my own country. I hope that this honour will be of help to those forces – they are in my opinion irresistible – which are drawing the two countries together in order that we may defend freedom.

Sarah Beauchamp to Winston S. Churchill
(Churchill papers, 1/50)[1]

16 January 1952   The White House

Darling Papa,

We are staying here at the Blair House at Miss Truman's[2] invitation to hear you speak to Congress today.

We have also been invited to dine tonight with the Achesons.

We would have let you know all this before – but only knew it ourselves yesterday – though plans to hear you speak were made by Margaret Truman a week ago.

We will look forward to seeing you at luncheon today & tonight, but more properly in New York as I know you will be surrounded and busy – this just brings you my love, and to let you know how thrilled and happy we are to be here. Wow my darling. Much much luck. Your speech in Ottawa was wonderful. All my love.

PS. It would be nice when you see her, if you would thank Margaret for arranging everything so happily for us.

---

[1] This letter was handwritten.
[2] Margaret Truman, 1924–2008. Daughter of President Harry S Truman. Educated at George Washington University, 1946. Married, 1956, Clifton Daniel.

January 1952

R. A. Butler to Winston S. Churchill
Prime Minister's Personal Telegram T.22/52
(Premier papers, 11/21)

16 January 1952
Priority
No. 298

My Commonwealth colleagues assembled today in London have asked me to convey to you their warm thanks for your personal message[1] wishing success to our meeting. We are all very sorry that you are not here and we wish you a safe and speedy return. I know that Mr Holland,[2] the New Zealand Prime Minister, and Sir Arthur Fadden,[3] as well as others of the Finance Ministers who are staying on after the meeting, are greatly hoping for an opportunity to talk with you on your return.

You will be pleased to hear that we are having a private meeting with the Commonwealth Ministers tomorrow in the Treasury Board Room.

Winston S. Churchill to Lord De L'Isle and Dudley and Sir Norman Brook
Prime Minister's Personal Minute M.11/52
(Premier papers, 11/82)

17 January 1952

Thank you for your explanation issued to the Press about the crash of the prototype 'Valiant'. I am glad the crew escaped. I suppose we have lost a quarter of a million pounds. This is a heavy blow to all that line of Air thought who argue that Britain should plunge heavily on the largest class of Air bombers. The Americans will do this, and also have the things to carry. We should concentrate not entirely but far more on the fighter aircraft we need to protect ourselves from destruction. I am not at all comforted by the assertion that you are going to make a lot more 'Valiants', even though you may avoid repetition of this initial disaster.

---

[1] Of Jan. 12, reproduced above (p. 195).
[2] Sidney George Holland, 1893–1961. Born in New Zealand. Married, 1920, Florence Beatrice Dayton. Entered father's engineering business, 1912. Joined NZEF, 1915. New Zealand MP (Nat.) for Christchurch North, 1935–46; for Fendalton, 1946–57. Leader of Opposition, 1940–9. Minister of Finance, 1949–54. PM of New Zealand, 1949–57. PC, 1950. Minister of Police, 1954–6.
[3] Arthur William Fadden, 1894–1973. MP (Country Party) for Darling Downs, 1936–49; for McPherson, 1949–58. Treasurer of Australia, 1940–1, 1949–58. PM of Australia, 1941.

Dean Acheson: recollection
('Present at the Creation', pages 601–2)

17 January 1952

THE ATLANTIC COMMAND

On January 17, Mr Churchill for the third time addressed a joint and crowded session of the Congress, an experience that, as he said, was 'unique for one who is not an American citizen'. That honor, too, would be conferred on him by an admiring Congress. On the evening of his address my wife and I gave a dinner and reception for him at Anderson House with all the pomp and glitter we could muster. The next day we held our last meeting of the visit and faced the issue of the Atlantic Command.

The meeting was to take place in the afternoon. The British group spent the morning at the Pentagon, where Lovett briefed them on our nuclear armament and provided luncheon. While Mr Churchill went back to the British Embassy for a nap, the soldiers and sailors, including the jaunty Scottish First Sea Lord, Admiral Sir Rhoderick Robert McGrigor, drafted a joint communiqué in effect ratifying the earlier NATO decisions. Without Mr Eden, who had returned to London, or Mr Churchill who was with the President, a shaken British group joined us in the Cabinet Room. Mr Churchill had read their draft communiqué in the President's anteroom, torn it up, and tossed the pieces into the air. 'Hurricane warnings along the Potomac', said Admiral McGrigor.

Our two chiefs entered and the President brusquely announced the business of the meeting as the uncompleted subject of the Atlantic Command. Then followed one of Mr Churchill's greatest speeches, unfortunately unrecorded and lost. Only phrases remain with me. For centuries England had held the seas against every tyrant, wresting command of them from Spain and then from France, protecting our hemisphere from penetration by European systems in the days of our weakness. Now, in the plenitude of our power, bearing as we did the awful burden of atomic command and responsibility for the final word of peace and war, surely we could make room for Britain to play her historic role 'upon that western sea whose floor is white with the bones of Englishmen'.

As the majestic speech rolled to its conclusion, a note came from Sir Oliver Franks across the table, warning me to be 'very, very careful'. The best course seemed a preclusive one, to get the floor and hold it until some opening appeared. A whispered request to the President gave me what no one else wanted. I praised the Prime Minister's matchless statement and sympathized with his unwillingness to accept what he had publicly opposed and still thought wrong. He nodded vigorously. All of us on occasion, I went on, had had to weigh continuing opposition against a distasteful course to the point of impeding a broader purpose of which we approve. He nodded even more vigorously. I asked the President to let some of us – mentioning Ambassador Franks and Secretary Lovett, the two admirals, Air Chief Marshal Sir William Elliot, and General Bradley – retire to bring in a suggestion. Mr Churchill agreed.

When we reached the President's office, Admiral Fechteler burst into protest against this endless talk, until suppressed by his military colleagues. We had nearly botched the operation, I pointed out, by trying to get the Prime Minister to endorse Attlee's approval, for the British Government, of the command and commander. If allowed to continue his disagreement with it, there was a good chance that he would no longer block its execution. It was worth trying. A draft communiqué along those lines was quickly drafted and typed. I was to read it and no one would say more. Handing one copy to the President and one to the Prime Minister, I read it with what my children in their early school days called 'expression', bearing down on the words italicized and sliding over the others.

For an interminable minute the Prime Minister studied the paper; then, looking across at the President, he said, 'I accept every word of it.'

Winston S. Churchill: speech
('Winston S. Churchill, His Complete Speeches', volume 8, pages 8323–9)

17 January 1952　　　　　　　　　　　　　　　　　　　　　　　　Washington DC

ADDRESS TO THE UNITED STATES CONGRESS

This is the third time it has been my fortune to address the Congress of the United States upon our joint affairs. I am honoured indeed by these experiences which I believe are unique for one who is not an American citizen. It is also of great value to me, on again becoming the head of His Majesty's Government, to come over here and take counsel with many trusted friends and comrades of former anxious days. There is a lot for us to talk about together so that we can understand each other's difficulties, feelings and thoughts, and do our best for the common cause. Let us, therefore, survey the scene this afternoon with cool eyes undimmed by hate or passion, guided by righteous inspiration and not uncheered by hope.

I have not come here to ask you for money to make life more comfortable or easier for us in Britain. Our standards of life are our own business and we can only keep our self-respect and independence by looking after them ourselves. During the war we bore our share of the burden and fought from first to last, unconquered – and for a while alone – to the utmost limits of our resources. Your majestic obliteration of all you gave us under Lend-Lease will never be forgotten by this generation in Britain, or by history.

After the war – unwisely as I contended, and certainly contrary to American advice – we accepted as normal debts nearly £4,000 million sterling of claims by countries we had protected from invasion, or had otherwise aided, instead of making counter-claims which would at least have reduced the bill to reasonable proportions. The £1,000 million loan we borrowed from you in 1946, and which we are now repaying, was spent, not on ourselves, but mainly in helping others. In all, since the war, as the late Government affirmed, we have lent or given to European or Asian countries £1,300 million in the form of unrequited exports. This, added to the cost of turning over our industry from war to peace, and rebuilding homes shattered by bombardment was more than we could manage without an undue strain upon our life-energies for which we shall require both time and self-discipline to recover.

Why do I say all this? Not to compare our financial resources with yours – we have but a third your numbers, and much less than a third your wealth. Not to claim praise or rewards, but to convince you of our native and enduring strength, and that our true position is not to be judged by the present state of the dollar exchange or by sterling area finance. Our production is half as great again as it was before the war, our exports are up by two-thirds. Recovery, while being retarded, has been continuous, and we are determined that it shall go on.

As I said at Fulton in Missouri six years ago, under the auspices of President Truman, 'let no man underrate the abiding power of the British Commonwealth and Empire. Do not suppose we shall not come through these dark years of privation as we came through the glorious years of agony, or that a half century from now you will not see seventy or eighty millions of Britons spread about the world and united in defence of our traditions, our way of life and of the world causes which you and we espouse. If the population of the English-speaking Commonwealth be added to that of the United States, with all that such co-operation implies, in the air, on the sea and all over the globe, and in science, industry and moral force, there will be no quivering precarious balance of power to offer its temptation to ambition or adventure.'[1] I am very glad to be able to say the same to you here today.

It is upon this basis of recovery, in spite of burdens, that the formidable problem of the new rearmament has fallen upon us. It is the policy of the United States to help forward in many countries the process of rearmament. In this, we, who contribute ourselves two-thirds as much as the rest of Europe put together, require your aid if we are to realize in good time the very high level of military strength which the Labour Government boldly aimed at, and to which they committed us. It is for you to judge to what extent United States' interests are involved; whether you aid us much or little we shall continue to do our utmost in the common cause. But, Members of the Congress, our

---

[1] Speech of 5 Mar. 1946, reproduced in *The Churchill Documents*, vol. 22, *Leader of the Opposition, August 1945 to October 1951*, pp. 227–35.

contribution will perforce be limited by our own physical resources, and thus the combined strength of our two countries, and also of the free world, will be somewhat less than it might be. That is why I have come here to ask, not for gold, but for steel; not for favours but equipment, and that is why many of our requests have been so well and generously met.

At this point I will venture, if I may, to make a digression. After a lot of experience I have learned it is not a good thing to dabble in the internal politics of another country. It's hard enough to understand one's own. But I will tell you something about our British politics all the same. In our island we indulge from time to time in having Elections. I believe you sometimes have them over here. We have had a couple in twenty months, which is quite a lot, and quite enough for the time being. We now look forward to a steady period of administration in accordance with the mandates we have received. Like you we tend to work on the two-party system. The differences between parties on our side of the Atlantic, and perhaps elsewhere between British parties, are often less than they appear to outsiders. In modern Britain the dispute is between a form of Socialism which has hitherto respected political liberty, on the one hand, and on the other hand, free enterprise regulated by law and custom. These two systems of thought between political opponents, fortunately overlap quite a lot in practice. Our complicated society would be deeply injured if we did not practise and develop what is called in the United States the bi-partisan habit of mind, which divides, so far as possible, what is done to make a party win and bear in their turn the responsibility of office, and what is done to make the nation live and serve high causes.

I hope here, Members of Congress, you will allow me to pay a tribute to the late Senator Vandenberg.[1] I had the honour to meet him on several occasions. His final message in these anxious years gave a feeling that in this period of United States leadership and responsibility, all the great Americans should work together for all the great things that matter most. That at least is the spirit which we shall try to maintain among British leaders in our own country. And that was the spirit which alone enabled us to survive the perils of the late war.

But now let me return to my theme of the many changes that have taken place since I was last here. There is a jocular saying: 'To improve is to change; to be perfect is to have changed often.' I had to use that once or twice in my long career. But if that were true everyone ought to be getting on very well. The changes that have happened since I last spoke to Congress are indeed astounding. It is hard to believe we are living in the same world. Former allies have become foes. Former foes have become allies. Conquered countries have been liberated. Liberated nations have been enslaved by Communism. Russia,

---

[1] Arthur Hendrick Vandenberg, 1884–1951. Educated at University of Michigan. Married, 1918, Hazel Harper Whittaker. Editor, *Grand Rapids Herald*, 1906–28. US Senator for Michigan, 1928–51. US Representative to UN General Assembly, 1945. Rep. Senate Conference Chairman, 1945–7. Chairman, Senate Committee on Foreign Relations, 1947–9. President pro tempore, Senate, 1947–9.

eight years ago our brave ally, has cast away the admiration and goodwill her soldiers had gained for her by their valiant defence of their own country. It is not the fault of the Western Powers if an immense gulf has opened between us. It took a long succession of deliberate and unceasing works and acts of hostility to convince our peoples – as they are now convinced – that they have another tremendous danger to face and that they are now confronted with a new form of tyranny and aggression as dangerous and as hateful as that which we overthrew.

When I visited Washington during the war I used to be told that China would be one of the Big Four Powers among the nations, and most friendly to the United States. I was always a bit sceptical, and I think it is now generally admitted that this hopeful vision has not yet come true. But I am by no means sure that China will remain for generations in the Communist grip. The Chinese said of themselves several thousand years ago: 'China is a sea that salts all the waters that flow into it.' There's another Chinese saying about their country which is much more modern – it dates only from the fourth century. This is the saying: 'The tail of China is large and will not be wagged.' I like that one. The British democracy approves the principles of movable party heads and unwaggable national tails. It is due to the working of these important forces that I have the honour to be addressing you at this moment.

You have wisely been resolute, Members of the Congress, in confronting Chinese Communist aggression. We take our stand at your side. We are grateful to the United States for bearing nine-tenths, or more, of the burden in Korea which the United Nations have morally assumed. I am very glad that whatever diplomatic divergencies there may be from time to time about procedure you do not allow the Chinese anti-Communists on Formosa to be invaded and massacred from the mainland. We welcome your patience in the armistice negotiations and our two countries are agreed that if the truce we seek is reached, only to be broken, our response will be prompt, resolute and effective. What I have learnt over here convinces me that British and United States policy in the Far East will be marked by increasing harmony.

I can assure you that our British hearts go out in sympathy to the families of the hundred thousand Americans who have given their lives or shed their blood in Korea. We also suffer these pangs for the loss of our own men there, and not only there but in other parts of Asia also under the attack by the same enemy. Whatever course events in Korea may take in the near future, and to prophesy would be difficult – much too difficult for me to embark upon it – I am sure our soldiers, and your soldiers, have not made their sacrifice in vain. The cause of world law has found strong and invaluable defence, and the foundations of the world instrument for preserving peace, justice and freedom among the nations have been defended and strengthened. They stand now, not on paper but on rock.

Moreover, the action which President Truman took in your name, and with your full support in his stroke against aggression in Korea, has produced consequences far beyond Korea; consequences which may well affect the destiny of mankind. The vast process of American rearmament in which the British Commonwealth and Empire and the growing power of United Europe will play their part to the utmost of their strength, this vast process has already altered the balance of the world and may well, if we all persevere steadfastly and loyally together, avert the danger of a Third World War, or the horror of defeat and subjugation should one come upon us. Mr President and Mr Speaker, I hope the mourning families throughout the great Republic will find some comfort and some pride in these thoughts.

Another extraordinary change has taken place in the Far East since I last addressed you. Peace has been made with Japan; there indeed I congratulate you upon the policy which in wise and skilful hands has brought the Japanese nation from the woe and shame of defeat in their wicked war back to that association with the Western democracies upon which the revival of their traditions, dignity and happiness can alone be regained and the stability of the Far East assured. In the anxious and confused expanses of South-East Asia there is another sphere where our aims and interests, and those of the French, who are fighting bravely at heavy cost to their strength in Europe, may find a fertile field for agreement on policy. I feel sure that the conversations we have had between our two Foreign Secretaries – between Mr Eden and Mr Acheson – men whose names and experience are outstanding throughout the world, will help to place the problems of South-East Asia in their right setting. It would not be helpful to the common cause, for our evils all spring from one centre, if an effective truce in Korea led only to a transference of Communist aggression to these other fields. Our problems will not be solved unless they are steadily viewed and acted upon as a whole in their integrity as a whole.

In the Middle East enormous changes have also taken place since I was last in power in my own country. When the war ended the Western nations were respected and predominant throughout these ancient lands, and there were quite a lot of people who had a good word to say about Great Britain. Today it is a sombre and confusing scene; yet there is still some sunshine as well as shadow. From the days of the Balfour Declaration I have desired that the Jews should have a national home, and I have worked for that end. I rejoice to pay my tribute here to the achievements of those who have founded the Israelite State, who have defended themselves with tenacity, and who offer asylum to great numbers of Jewish refugees. I hope that with their aid they may convert deserts into gardens; but if they are to enjoy peace and prosperity they must strive to renew and preserve their friendly relations with the Arab world without which widespread misery might follow for all.

Britain's power to influence the fortunes of the Middle East and guard it from aggression is far less today, now that we have laid aside our Imperial responsibility for India and its armies. It is no longer for us alone to bear the whole burden of maintaining the freedom of the famous waterway of the Suez Canal. That has become an international rather than a national responsibility. I welcome the statesmanlike conception of the Four-Power approach to Egypt, announced by the late British Government, in which Britain, the United States, France and Turkey may share with Egypt in the protection of the world interests involved, among which Egypt's own interests are paramount.

Such a policy is urgent. Britain is maintaining over fifty thousand troops in the Suez Canal Zone, who again might be well employed elsewhere, not for national vainglory or self-seeking advantage, but in the common interest of all nations. We do not seek to be masters of Egypt; we are there only as the servants and guardians of the commerce of the world. It would enormously aid us in our task if even token forces of the other partners in the Four-Power proposal were stationed in the Canal Zone as a symbol of the unity of purpose which inspires us. And I believe it is no exaggeration to state that such token forces would probably bring into harmony all that movement by which the Four-Power policy may be made to play a decisive part by peaceful measures, and bring to an end the wide disorders of the Middle East in which, let me assure you, there lurk dangers not less great than those which the United States has stemmed in Korea.

Now I come to Europe where the greatest of all our problems and dangers lie. I have long worked for the cause of a United Europe, and even of a United States of Europe, which would enable that Continent, the source of so much of our culture, ancient and modern, and the parent of the New World, to resume and revive its former splendours. It is my sure hope and conviction that European unity will be achieved, and that it will not ultimately be limited only to the countries at present composing Western Europe. I said at Zurich in 1946 that France should take Germany by the hand and lead her back into the family of nations, and thus end a thousand-year quarrel which has torn Europe to pieces and finally plunged the whole world twice over into slaughter and havoc.[1]

Real and rapid progress is being made towards European unity, and it is both the duty and the policy of both Great Britain and her Commonwealth, and of the United States, to do our utmost, all of us, to help and speed it. As a forerunner of United Europe there is the European Army, which could never achieve its necessary strength without the inclusion of Germany. If this necessary and urgent object is being achieved by the fusion of the forces of the Continental nations outside what I have called in former times, the Iron Curtain, that great operation deserves our fullest support. But, Members of Congress, fusion is not the only way in which the defence of Western Europe can be built. The system of a grand alliance such as has been created by the

---

[1] Speech of 19 Sep. 1946, reproduced in *The Churchill Documents*, vol. 22, *Leader of the Opposition, August 1945 to October 1951*, pp. 458–61.

North Atlantic Treaty Organization is no bar to the fusion of as many of its members as wish for their closer unity. And the United States, British and Canadian troops will stand, indeed are already standing, shoulder to shoulder with their European comrades in defence of the civilization and freedom of the West. We stand together under General Eisenhower to defend the common cause from violent aggression.

What matters most is not the form of fusion, or melding – a word I learned over here – but the numbers of divisions, and of armoured divisions and the power of the air forces, and their weapons available for unified action under the Supreme Commander. We, in Britain, have denuded our island of military formations to an extent I have never seen before, and I cannot accept the slightest reproach from any quarter that we are not doing our full duty, because the British Commonwealth of Nations, spread all over the world, is not prepared to become a State or a group of States in any Continental federal system on either side of the Atlantic. The sooner strong enough forces can be assembled in Europe under united command the more effective will be the deterrents against a Third World War. The sooner, also, will our sense of security, and the fact of our security, be seen to reside in valiant, resolute and well-armed manhood, rather than in the awful secrets which science has wrested from nature. These are at present, it must be recognized – these secrets – the supreme deterrent against a Third World War, and the most effective guarantee of victory in it.

If I may say this, Members of Congress, be careful above all things, therefore, not to let go of the atomic weapon until you are sure, and more than sure, that other means of preserving peace are in your hands. It is my belief that by accumulating deterrents of all kinds against aggression we shall, in fact, ward off the fearful catastrophe, the fears of which darken the life and mar the progress of all the peoples of the globe. We must persevere steadfastly and faithfully in the task to which, under United States leadership, we have solemnly bound ourselves. Any weakening of our purpose, any disruption of our organization would bring about the very evils which we all dread, and from which we should all suffer, and from which many of us would perish.

We must not lose patience, and we must not lose hope. It may be that presently a new mood will reign behind the Iron Curtain. If so it will be easy for them to show it, but the democracies must be on their guard against being deceived by a false dawn. We seek or covet no one's territory; we plan no forestalling war; we trust and pray that all will come right. Even during these years of what is called the 'cold war', material production in every land is continually improving through the use of new machinery and better organization and the advance of peaceful science. But the great bound forward in progress and prosperity for which mankind is longing cannot come till the shadow of war has passed away. There are, however, historic compensations for the stresses which we suffer in the 'cold war'. Under the pressure and menace of Communist aggression the fraternal association of the United States with Britain and the British Commonwealth, and the new unity growing up in Europe – nowhere more hopeful than between France and Germany – all these harmonies are being brought forward, perhaps by several generations in the destiny of the world. If this proves true – and it has certainly proved true up to date – the architects in the Kremlin may be found to have built a different and a far better world structure than what they planned.

Members of the Congress, I have dwelt today repeatedly upon many of the changes that have happened throughout the world since you last invited me to address you here and I am sure you will agree that it is hardly possible to recognize the scene or believe it can truly have come to pass. But there is one thing which is exactly the same as when I was here last. Britain and the United States are working together and working for the same high cause. Bismarck once said that the supreme fact of the nineteenth century was that Britain and the United States spoke the same language. Let us make sure that the supreme fact of the twentieth century is that they tread the same path.

Randolph S. Churchill to Winston S. Churchill
(Churchill papers, 1/51)

17 January 1952

Perfect radio reception your magnificent masterly meaty speech.[1]

Anthony Eden to Winston S. Churchill
Prime Minister's Personal Telegram T.30/52
(Premier papers, 11/91)

18 January 1952
Immediate
Secret and Personal
No. 360

Speech came over splendidly and has been well received here. It has been specially valuable in putting the British standpoint on the big issues and in asserting our independence.

2. I am afraid, however, that there may be questions about our public invitation to America to come into Egypt now, in advance of any agreement. I hope that the United States Government can be dissuaded from making any public refusal.

---

[1] Churchill telegraphed back: 'Thank you so much. Papa'.

JANUARY 1952 221

US–UK discussions: minutes
(Premier papers, 11/161)

18 January 1952   The White House
3 p.m.
Plenary Session No. 5

I. – ATLANTIC COMMAND

Mr Churchill said that earlier in the day he and Mr Lovett had presided over a further meeting on the Atlantic Command. A full discussion had taken place but, unhappily, no agreement had been reached. He recognised that this was a matter on which final decisions could only be taken by the North Atlantic Council; but he would be sorry if it became necessary for the United Kingdom and United States Governments to refer to the Council for decision a matter on which they had failed to reach agreement among themselves. Open disagreement between the two Governments in the Council could not fail to weaken their position. Before assuming office he had expressed strong views about the Atlantic Command; and the discussions in which he had participated in Washington had not convinced him that he was mistaken in those views. In any statement which might now be made on behalf of the two Governments he must have regard to the views which he had previously expressed; and from this point of view he was not content with the draft communiqué which had been prepared as a result of the meeting held earlier in the day. During his visit to Ottawa, he had been assured that the Canadian Government were in sympathy with his views on this question and would be prepared to contemplate a revision of the arrangements originally approved by NATO. He agreed that planning and preparatory work for operations in the Atlantic should go forward on the basis of those arrangements; and, so long as it was made clear that he had not withdrawn his objections to those arrangements, he was content that they should continue in force until such time as they were changed by a further decision of the North Atlantic Council.

President Truman said that he was sorry that it had not yet been found possible to reach agreement on this subject. He was most anxious that the appointment of a Supreme Commander, Atlantic, should not be further delayed; and he had hoped that, as a result of the discussions which had taken place, it might now be possible to proceed with this appointment.

Mr Acheson suggested that it might be possible to find a form of announcement acceptable to Mr Churchill if greater emphasis was laid on the points on which agreement had been reached and if it was also made clear that the Prime Minister had not withdrawn his objections of principle to the original arrangements. He indicated the lines along which such an announcement might be framed. Mr Churchill suggested that some of his advisers might confer with Mr Acheson with a view of formulating a draft statement on the lines indicated.

After this consultation had taken place, Mr Acheson submitted the following draft communiqué for consideration by President Truman and Mr Churchill:

> The President and the Prime Minister with their advisers have had several discussions relating to the arrangements about the Atlantic Command recommended by NATO and accepted by the late Government of the United Kingdom. As a result of their discussions they agreed that His Majesty's Government and the United States Government would recommend to NATO certain alterations in the arrangements designed to extend the United Kingdom Home Command to the 100-fathom line. They also agreed on the desirability of certain changes which would provide greater flexibility for the control of operations in the Eastern Atlantic. These changes, however, do not go the full way to meet the Prime Minister, while not withdrawing his objections, expressed readiness to allow the appointment of a Supreme Commander to go forward in order that a command structure may be created and enabled to proceed with the necessary planning in the Atlantic area. He reserved the right to bring forward modifications for the consideration of NATO, if he so desired, at a later stage.

This draft was approved without alteration by President Truman and Mr Churchill. A joint communiqué in these terms was subsequently issued to the press.

II. – POLICY TOWARDS SOVIET UNION

Mr Churchill said that in present circumstances he would not be in favour of proposing a meeting with the leaders of the Soviet Union to review the major questions outstanding between Russia and the West. A different situation would, however, arise if at any time the Soviet leaders indicated that they were prepared to make a genuine effort to reach an understanding with the democracies. If that situation arose, and a meeting were held, it would in his view be most important to avoid proceeding upon the assumption that, if the conference broke down, war would then be inevitable. He would wish to interpose between the breakdown of such a conference and total war an intermediate stage in which there would be an intensification of the cold war. In that stage the democracies would make an intensive effort to bring home to all people behind the Iron Curtain the true facts of the world situation – by broadcasting, by dropping leaflets and by all other methods of propaganda which were open to them. He believed that the leaders in the Kremlin would fear such a revelation of the truth to the masses whom they held in their grip. And it might well be that, under the pressure of an intensive propaganda campaign on these lines, the conference might be resumed with greater hope of success. Mr Churchill suggested that detailed methods for conducting such

January 1952

a campaign might profitably be studied in advance by those concerned with these matters in the United States and the United Kingdom.

President Truman said that his advisers had already given some thought to this possibility and he was willing that it should be further studied in consultation with the United Kingdom authorities. He was in principle in favour of spreading knowledge of the truth among the people behind the Iron Curtain. He had never closed his mind to the possibility of holding a meeting with the Soviet leaders, although he agreed that the time was not ripe for such a meeting. Though he had made it clear that he was not prepared to go to Moscow, he had indicated that he would be ready at any time to meet Marshal Stalin in the United States. This invitation had not been accepted; and he doubted whether the Soviet leaders were genuinely anxious to come to an understanding at the present time.

III. – RAW MATERIALS

Mr Churchill said that he had been glad to learn that agreement had now been reached on the details of the arrangements for mutual assistance between the United States and the United Kingdom in steel, tin and aluminium. A formal agreement had been signed earlier in the day; and a public announcement had been issued during the afternoon.

IV. – ATOMIC ENERGY: PUBLICATION OF SECRET WARTIME AGREEMENTS ON TECHNICAL CO-OPERATION

Mr Churchill said that this was not a matter which he had wished to bring up formally but he wanted to mention it to the President. He himself would like to see these documents published.

President Truman replied that, in his opinion, it would not be wise to publish these documents while international discussions were proceeding about the control of the atomic weapon. But he had met a difficulty in that Senator Vandenberg's son[1] was anxious to publish his father's diaries and these contained passages relating to these transactions which were unfortunately inaccurate. He was hoping to prevent the publication of these passages, but, if he was unsuccessful, then of course Mr Churchill would be free to publish on his side.

V. – TECHNICAL CO-OPERATION ON ATOMIC ENERGY

Lord Cherwell informed the President of his talks with Mr Gordon Dean[2] and of the arrangement that specific cases would be put forward to the Atomic Energy Commission to test the possibilities of co-operation under

---

[1] Arthur Hendrick Vandenberg, Jr, 1907–68. Born in Grand Rapids, Mich. Educated at Dartmouth, 1928. Served in USAAF, 1941–5. Served on Gen. Eisenhower's personal staff as his Executive Assistant, 1952. Appointments Secretary to President Eisenhower, Nov. 1952 to Jan. 1953.

[2] Gordon Evans Dean, 1905–58. Chair, US Atomic Energy Commission, 1950–3. Executive, General Dynamics, 1955.

the amendment to the McMahon Act. If this procedure was unsuccessful, further consideration could be given after November to the amendment of the law.

President Truman said that this procedure was the only one to adopt. There was no prospect of amending the law in the present session of Congress.

VI. – CONCLUDING REMARKS

President Truman said that it he and his advisers had greatly appreciated the talks which they had had with Mr Churchill during his visit to the United States.

It had given great pleasure to welcome Mr Churchill to Washington. Their conversations had been most valuable and fruitful.

Mr Churchill said that it had given him great pleasure to renew his personal contacts with President Truman and members of his Administration. Apart from specific decisions which had been taken, the conversations had provided an opportunity for a valuable exchange of views on a wide range of problems which were of concern to both Governments. He was sure that, as a result of this visit, the partnership of the two countries would be greatly strengthened.

Winston S. Churchill to Anthony Eden
Prime Minister's Personal Telegram T.31/52
(Premier papers, 11/91)

18 January 1952
Immediate
Secret
No. 203

I showed your telegram No. 360[1] to the President this afternoon. He said that they were not proposing to make any statement nor would they do so except after consultation with us. Acheson said he had refused to receive the Egyptian Ambassador at Washington this afternoon.

---

[1] T.30/52, reproduced above (p. 220).

Record of a conversation
(Premier papers, 11/161)

19 January 1952

ADMISSION OF BRITISH OFFICERS TO
UNITED STATES NATIONAL WAR COLLEGE

At a dinner at the British Embassy on 18th January at which Mr Averell Harriman and the United States Joint Chiefs of Staff were present on the American side and the Ambassador, the First Sea Lord and Air Chief Marshal Sir William Elliot, among others, on the British side, the Prime Minister raised the question of the exclusion of British officers from the National War College and other American staff colleges.

2. The Prime Minister said that he greatly regretted this development which was not in keeping, in his view, either with the position which the United Kingdom occupied in Western defence or with the relationship between the two countries.

3. General Collins[1] said that this decision had been forced upon the United States Administration by pressure from the French and other allies in the United States. It was owing to the state of French security that it was not possible to admit French officers to the War College. On the other hand, France occupied a key position in the defence of Western Europe and it was essential to encourage them and raise their morale by every means possible. Open discrimination in favour of the United Kingdom had a bad effect on this morale. He regarded this as a superficial matter; the reality was that the United Sates had a relationship with the United Kingdom of a kind which they had with no other country. General Vandenberg said that the American Joint Chiefs of Staff dealt with their opposite numbers and with Sir William Elliot in the frankest possible manner. Sir William Elliot agreed that he had access to the American Chiefs of Staff at any time on any subject.

4. The Ambassador observed that we had been accepted in the War College and had been turned out of it. He suggested that the matter could have been handled in such a way as to leave us in the College and tell others that as soon as their security and standing warranted it they would be admitted. The First Sea Lord said the important point was that British and American officers should get to know each other and acquire the habit of working together at formative points in their careers. Co-operation was good at the top level but it had to be fostered as each new generation came along.

5. General Collins said that he was sorry that we had taken this matter in this way. He did not regard it as one of any significance and perhaps it might

---

[1] Lawton Collins, 1896–1987. US Military Academy at West Point, 1913–17. Company Cdr, 22nd Infantry Rgt, 1917. Instructor, Army War College, 1938–40. CoS, VII Corps, 1941. Lt.-Gen., 1945. VCS, US Army, 1949–53. Special representative of US in Vietnam, 1954–5.

have been handled differently. But now that we were not in the War College, it was quite impossible as far as he was concerned, to let in the British again without letting in the French, and that we should have to wait until we could both be let in together.

6. The Prime Minister repeated his disappointment at this attitude which was not at all in harmony with his view of the relationship between the two countries. He would not pursue the matter further. He was glad to think that it was possible to have a frank and open talk on such a matter.

7. General Collins and Admiral Fechteler then said that they thought a broader point was involved. The United States, against its will, had assumed a responsibility for world leadership and for the first time in their history they were having to organise an alliance. They were not experienced in this task and they might make mistakes, but they did feel that the policy implied that there should not be an open discrimination in favour of any one of the members of the alliance. They agreed that in practice there would always be a special relationship with the British, but this should not be an open relationship. General Vandenberg agreed and said that he wished to maintain a special relationship with the British Chiefs of Staff but that it must be maintained 'under the counter'.

8. Mr Harriman said that he and his colleagues knew that the United Kingdom was the only ally on which the United States could rely and that the British were therefore regarded as being in a special position. But he supported the point of view expressed by the Joint Chiefs of Staff. This was a new enterprise on which the United Kingdom had embarked. There was a problem of binding together the alliance. He felt that the United Kingdom and United States should handle this problem together, but it did involve the avoidance of open discrimination.

9. The Prime Minister said that in his view the realities of the situation which Mr Harriman had referred to should be openly recognised and accepted. He did not see why the United Kingdom should be treated like the other members of the alliance. The measures of conscription and the organisation of the territorial army which had been introduced by the Labour Government, would result in the United Kingdom having the finest land army that it had ever had in time of peace. He begged the Joint Chiefs of Staff not to under-rate the position and military strength of the United Kingdom.

10. The conversation then turned to other matters.

Winston S. Churchill to Clementine Churchill
(Baroness Spencer-Churchill papers)[1]

20 January 1952

My Darling,

Sir Roger Makins is flying home today and I send this line with him to tell you how much you have been in my thoughts and how much I love you.

I have just finished what seems to be the most strenuous fortnight I can remember, and I am staying quiet here for forty-eight hours to recover. I never had such a whirl of people and problems, and the two speeches were very hard and exacting ordeals. Now I sail for home going on board QM midnight 22.

Beatrice Eden[2] came to dinner last night. She seems as young and attractive as she was when I saw her last eight or ten years ago. She gave no intelligible explanations of her mental attitude though she tried very hard to do so. She says Anthony has no heart – She does not seem to have much herself. She is coming over to England in March. She is a real puzzle.

You will have seen what the papers say about my 'Mission'. The enclosed cutting which Bernie[3] gave me is fair and informative. I am far from sure about the future in the Far East – or indeed elsewhere. No one can tell what is coming. I still hope we shall muddle along to greater strength.

The Presidential Election is now going to amuse the Americans for the next nine anxious months. They in their turn will have the dose we have swallowed in the last two years. But I supposed the Russians have their troubles too. I hope so anyway.

I look forward so much to seeing you next Monday week. Let us dine alone at No, 10. Tender love my darling Clemmie.

Your ever loving husband
W
[Drawing of a pig]

Sarah is looking lovely, and Miss Truman and she seem to have made good friends.

---

[1] This letter was handwritten.
[2] Beatrice Helen Beckett, 1905–57. Married, 1923, Anthony Eden (div. 1950): three children.
[3] Bernard Mannes Baruch, 1870–1965. Born in South Carolina, the son of a Jewish doctor who had emigrated from East Prussia in the 1850s. A self-made financier, he became a millionaire before he was 30. As Chairman of the US War Industries Board from 3 Mar. 1918 until the end of the war, in almost daily communication with Churchill (then Minister of Munitions). Accompanied President Wilson to Paris Peace Conference, 1919. One of Churchill's hosts on the latter's visits to the US, 1929, 1931. From 1946 to 1951, US Representative on Atomic Energy Commission. Presented his private archive to Princeton University in 1964: it contained 1,200 letters from nine Presidents and 700 communications from Churchill.

Winston S. Churchill to Anthony Eden and R. A. Butler
Prime Minister's Personal Minute M.8/52
(Premier papers, 11/270)

20 January 1952

Your 370 of January 18.

I have been so hard pressed here that I have no chance of dealing in any further detail with the financial proposals of the Service Departments. I have however two points in my mind.

Paragraph 3, last sentence. You do not seem to include Centurion tanks. It seems to me vital that the Ministry of Supply build if possible the full thousand, and that this tank production should be included in the first priorities. We shall have plenty of time to settle how many we can keep ourselves, and whether we should sell more to the Canadians or indeed the Americans, for they are considered the best tank in the world. It takes two years to make a tank. There are so many other things that can be improvised in an emergency. Please do not do anything to prevent this full priority being accorded in the estimates. We can talk it over later.

2. About the Air Force. They ask for 36,000 more men, now reduced to 27,000. This ought to be most carefully scrutinized. How many more fighting and bombing aeroplanes do they propose to have on the establishment on the average throughout this year compared to last year? Where a new aeroplane replaces an obsolescent one there ought not to be any need for more men. Also, our squadrons are only 16, while an American squadron as part of a Wing carries 25. It might be much more economical to increase the strength of our squadrons rather than make new ones, with all staff and 'underfoots' which the Air Council is always expanding. I really think they ought to be made to handle whatever new aeroplanes go to them this year with the same outfit of ground staff as at present. This at least seems to me the weakest point in their very heavy bill. Someone ought to go through their Vote A in detail and make them justify every extra man. A cut of 10,000 men at £500 a year would mean a saving of £5 million. This is surely much better business than cutting school meals to save a quarter of that amount.

3. The American CAS talked to me about Operation 'Jujitsu'.[1] I really do not think we ought to run the risk of a definite breach of the Soviet frontiers at the present moment. We should be taking too much upon ourselves if we assume this very difficult and not apparently very urgent task. Anyhow, I have said no.

4. I will send you further telegrams from the ship as I study the different Estimates. [. . .]

---

[1] 'Jujitsu': reconnaissance operation undertaken by RAF at the request of USAF Strategic Air Command. British pilots flew state-of-the-art Canberra jet bombers over the USSR to identify potential targets for nuclear strikes. The programme ran sporadically between spring 1951 and autumn 1952.

Winston S. Churchill to Lord De L'Isle and Dudley
Prime Minister's Personal Minute M.9/52
(Premier papers, 11/4)

20 January 1952
Secret

1. I spoke to you and to Sir John Slessor about the rocket fighter aircraft. This is shot up to 40,000 feet by a rocket apparatus, but its life in the top air is too short for effective action against raiding bomber squadrons. I was told that therefore the Company making them (which I understand is the Hawker Siddeley Company) was trying to find a suitable rotary engine which, added to the vol. plane, would give a period of effective service in the high air. Even 20 minutes might be decisive. I was told this was not making good progress, and here was the hitch.

I attach great importance to this idea of the rocket ascent of the aeroplane, and I am told that mass production of such fighters would be easy and comparatively cheap. All this was explained to me by Squadron-Leader Duke,[1] when he commanded 615 (County of Surrey) Squadron, RAAF. He has now had to go back to his Company as the other test pilot was killed a few months ago.

2. Now over here I was shown a diagram of an American jet bomber which is shot off the ground and carried to a great height by a rocket attachment, and then cruises forward on its normal jet propulsion. If this could be applied to fighter aircraft, it would solve the problem of making a suitable rotary engine. We could then get up on the rocket, and cruise and kill on the jet.

I should be glad if you would give this matter your personal attention, and let me have a short report about how it all stands. The Americans say there is an enormous increase of range in getting to the high altitude by rocket impulsion. I am as you know deeply concerned at the present scantiness of our fighter aircraft.

---

[1] Neville Frederick Duke, 1922–2007. Born in Tonbridge, Kent. Joined RAF as a cadet, 1940. Top Allied ace in the Western theatre with 27 confirmed kills. Began work as a test pilot, 1945. Set world air speed record, 1946. Retired from test work after spinal injury in 1956.

Winston S. Churchill to Sir Walter Monckton[1] and Lord Swinton
Prime Minister's Personal Minute M.12/52
(Premier papers, 11/75)

20 January 1952

In my examination of the defence production programme I was disturbed to learn of the serious lag in the production of the latest types of aircraft (the Canberra bomber, the F.3 and F.4. and Swift fighters, and the Valiant medium bomber), 20 mm. ammunition, and the equipment for Operation Rotor (i.e. the radar chain). I agreed that the essential needs of these programmes should now be given priority over other defence needs and over essential civilian objectives such as exports.

I understood that the short-fall on these programmes was due largely to shortage of labour in particular areas. I should be obliged if you would consider, in consultation with the Minister of Supply, what practical administrative measures can be taken to overcome this shortage and whether any action, e.g. allocation of materials, is needed to make the priority fully effective.

Pray let me have a report on this on my return.

Winston S. Churchill to Duncan Sandys
Prime Minister's Personal Minute M.13/52
(Premier papers, 11/75)

20 January 1952

I have considered your various minutes suggesting the grant of overriding priority for a number of items in the defence production programme. I am satisfied that, if we sought to give overriding priority over so wide a range, we should defeat our own objects. All our experiences in the last war proved that a system of priorities can be effective only if it is applied within a very narrow field.

At our meetings on the Service Estimates, I agreed that overriding priority might be given to the latest types of aircraft, 20mm. ammunition, and Operation Rotor, because I understood that the lag in these programmes was due mainly to the shortage of labour. The special priority must be limited to these three items in the Air programme. I have asked the Minister of Labour and the Chancellor of the Duchy of Lancaster to consider, in consultation with you, what practical administrative measures can be taken to overcome this shortage of labour and whether any other action, e.g. allocation of materials, is needed to make this priority effective.

[1] Walter Turner Monckton, 1891–1965. Legal adviser to Prince of Wales during Abdication Crisis, 1936. KCVO, 1937. KCMG, 1945. MP (Cons.) for Bristol, 1951–7. Minister of Labour and National Service, 1951–5. Minister of Defence, 1955–6. Paymaster General, 1956–7. Viscount, 1957. Chairman, Midland Bank, 1957–64. GCVO, 1964.

Meanwhile, any statement which you may make to the Aircraft Advisory Council should, I consider, be limited to a promise that every effort will be made to provide the additional labour required in order to carry through the approved programme for the latest types of aircraft, 20mm. ammunition, and operation Rotor.

Winston S. Churchill to Clementine Churchill
(Baroness Spencer-Churchill papers)[1]

21 January 1952

Darling,

It is splendid (as I cabled) that you will meet me at Southampton. The arrangements are being made accordingly. It is possible we may have to motor to London as the train may have to wait for the other passengers. I have only one piece of urgent business which I may have to settle before starting either by train or car. This may settle itself beforehand. The enclosed telegram to Tommy Lascelles will explain the possible urgency.

I have let myself in for a Parade through the streets of New York to the Mayor's Parlour tomorrow (Tuesday) to receive a gold medal. Unfortunately the weather has turned <u>icy</u>. (Yesterday warm and muggy.) I have the beginning of a cold. This is a tiresome problem. I shall however have to follow Charles's directions. But if I cancel there will be great disappointment! Such is life nowadays. I am so glad you reminded me about the Ronnie Trees, I have been so hunted that I had forgotten them, and they have only today returned from Washington. They are coming to dine.

Sarah was really very good yesterday. In the opening, it is all in the Hall brothers Christmas Card Trade Advertisement programme of the Television. She does four a month – one of which is all her own acting. The fee is $2,000 each time! All this may broaden out considerably. She seems very happy and is looking beautiful.

I shall indeed be delighted to get home. I never remember three weeks taking so long to live, although it has been all kindness and compliments.

With fondest love
Your loving husband
W
[Drawing of a pig]

---

[1] This letter was handwritten.

Winston S. Churchill to Anthony Eden and R. A. Butler
Prime Minister's Personal Telegram T.32/52
(Premier papers, 11/91)

21 January 1952
No. 31

Am deeply shocked by murder of American nun in Egypt. Opinion here considerably aroused. Surely time has come to restrict or withdraw financial facilities granted to Egypt on day to day basis which they cannot claim as of right.

Sir Norman Brook to Winston S. Churchill
(Premier papers, 11/155)

21 January 1952

The Temporary Council Committee of NATO (Mr Harriman's Committee) have asked for comments on their Report as early as possible and not later than 22nd January. Our comments on the economic part of the Report have been sent in by the Chancellor of the Exchequer. The Report also includes recommendations about the availability and readiness of the forces of each NATO country and we must send in our comments on these so far as they affect the United Kingdom.

2. The recommendations on United Kingdom forces have been examined by the Chiefs-of-Staff who have submitted the attached report for your approval as Minister of Defence.

3. The recommendations on force contributions can be accepted within the limits of approved policy by which we are to carry on the £4,700 million programme, though its completion will be delayed beyond 1954.

4. The answers suggested to recommendations on increased strengths, additional peace-time training of reserves and equipment priorities are equally in line with approved policy.

5. May I inform the Ministry of Defence that the attached reply may be sent to the Temporary Council Committee in answer to their request for the comments of the United Kingdom Government on the military recommendations in their report?[1]

---

[1] Churchill wrote on this document: 'As proposed'.

JANUARY 1952 233

Winston S. Churchill to Clementine Churchill
(Churchill papers, 1/50)

23 January 1952

Started very comfortably. Temperature normal in the morning. Cold will take another day or two. Am staying in bed almost entirely. Much love.

Anthony Eden to Winston S. Churchill
Prime Minister's Personal Telegram T.44/52
(Premier papers, 11/91)

24 January 1952
Immediate
Secret
No. 4

The situation in the Canal Zone has deteriorated seriously in the last few days. General Erskine has already had to cordon off sectors of Ismailia in order to search for terrorists and arms. This has produced a warning from the Egyptian Government that these measures will be resisted by force. There has been no resistance so far. General Erskine has now decided that he must exercise authority already given him to disarm the Egyptian auxiliary police in Ismailia. This operation will start early tomorrow morning.

2. His Majesty's Ambassador at Cairo has warned us that these measures may result in the Egyptian Government taking violent anti-British steps and that there may be anti-British disturbances resulting in danger to British and other foreign lives. In that event it would be necessary to lay on 'Rodeo'[1] and he has asked that it should be put at much shorter notice for the next week.

3. I discussed the situation this evening with the Chiefs of Staff. We have agreed that 'Rodeo' should be put at 48 hours notice.

4. I will let you know immediately of any further developments.[2]

---

[1] 'Rodeo': Plan to protect the lives of British and foreign nationals in Cairo and Alexandria. See T.63/52, reproduced below (pp. 237–8).
[2] Churchill responded: 'I fully approve the action you have taken' (T.45/52, *Premier papers, 11/91*).

January 1952

Winston S. Churchill to Anthony Eden and R. A. Butler
Prime Minister's Personal Telegram T.48/52
(Premier papers, 11/270)

24 January 1952
Emergency
Secret and Personal
No. 4

I have not had time till today to read series of telegrams and papers you have sent me about retrenchment. I greatly appreciate all the work that my colleagues have done. Nevertheless, I must say that I think it falls far short of what is necessary. The Service estimates have been out by nearly £200 million, on an original total of £1,547 million. The Civil Estimates on an original figure of £1,957 million, are to take a cut of only £47 million. At this distance it seems to me to be a mistake to use all our arguments about emergencies and to produce something which does not in fact cover the need.

2. The dominant problem facing us is the deficit in the balance of payments. This cannot be cured only by cutting imports, though of course every million pounds reduction is an immediate gain. But far better is to increase exports. The cut in service and civil estimates should be made in such a way as to increase the material manpower available for making things for export.

3. I consider that the civil estimates should show a further reduction of at least £50 million, and softwood for housing is not the one that should be picked as the largest victim.

4. As regards the service estimate I have already suggested that the RAF should be required to abate their man-power demand. Consider that fifteen thousand men should be struck from these demands, and that the Air Force should be made to pilot and service the maximum number of new machines we can give them by severe and intelligent reorganisation of their staff. I have also suggested that we should make as many Centurion tanks as we can. If we have any to spare we can sell them for dollars. The best contribution which the War Office could make would be a further curtailment of their demand for other vehicles. They were proposing to spend £100 million on lorries. If half of these resources were devoted to exporting motor cars, Rootes[1] informs me that the total export of cars could be greatly increased.

5. Looking at it all from a distance and not having had the advantage of listening to your discussion, it seems to me that what is being arranged might give us the worst of both worlds. I recognise that another great measure of the

---

[1] William Edward Rootes, 1894–1964. Married, 1916, Nora Press (div. 1951): two children; 1951, Ruby Joy Ann Peek. On active service, 1915–18. Founder and Chairman, Rootes Ltd, 1917–64. Chairman of Motor Vehicles Maintenance Advisory and Supply Council, Ministry of Supply, 1941–2. Knighted, 1942. Chairman, Dollar Exports Council, 1951–64. Engineering Advisory Council, Board of Trade, 1947–62. Baron, 1959.

economy can be taken at the time of the budget. I still hope Rab that you will put yourself in the position where you will have the widest possible latitude of choice. If we show in our estimate that we are sincere and effectively acting to cut expenditure, our financial probity would not be impugned by carrying forward the whole of the surplus of 1951/1952 into the year 1952/1953 instead of putting it into the new sinking fund. I should like to see what precedents there are for this. War-time needs have certainly been pleaded before for such action, and cold war may also be valid. With such margin and such a highly proven spirit of economy and reduction of expenditure in hand, we might well be able to grapple in the budget with the still greater problem of food subsidies, compensated in part by larger improved family allowances, and by reducing taxation give other incentives to production.

James Thomas to Winston S. Churchill
(Premier papers, 11/200)

26 January 1952

Just before Christmas, the Secretary of the Ministry of Defence explained to you that an Opinion of the Law Officers of the late Government had cast doubt on the validity of the powers under which the War Office and the Air Ministry were retaining time-expired regulars in the Service and the War Office had called up reservists, both measures having been taken for the Korean emergency. The Law officers also mentioned 'many uncertainties' about the powers of large-scale recall of Class Z and other reservists on mobilisation, which ought to be cleared up by legislation.

2. In a minute of 25th December, you said you had no objection to drafting a Bill with appropriate variants, the matter to be considered by the Cabinet on your return.

3. The process of drafting the Bill has thrown up some important issues of policy. The Service Ministers' Committee invited me to submit them to you.

4. It had been intended that the proposed Bill should be a short one of three or four clauses. It now seems that a Bill to provide or confirm the required powers over all the classes of reservists, etc., concerned will run to ten or twelve rather detailed clauses. On the other hand, Parliamentary Counsel advises that the two main objectives of the Bill, that is, to validate past and present continuing irregularities and also to put beyond reasonable doubt the powers needed for any future 'cold war' emergency or for a major mobilisation, could be covered by a two or three clause Bill, leaving the clearing up of the less important matters for another Bill later.

5. There will be difficulty in promoting a Bill which might make considerable inroads on Parliamentary time in an already crowded legislative programme. While the Second Reading debate on either a long or a short Bill

of the kind proposed might not be very different in scope, the time required in the Committee and Report stages of a short Bill should be considerably less.

6. Once a Bill, long or short, is tabled, it must in our view be passed into law with all possible speed, as it will have exposed to Parliament and the public the irregularities which have been committed.

7. A first draft of a short Bill for the present purposes is attached: it could probably be tabled in the House within a week or so. The preparation of the larger and more comprehensive Bill and getting it ready for First Reading might take three or four weeks.

8. There would be considerable advantage in dealing with the matter in one comprehensive Bill. This cannot be introduced for some time. The delay would involve some risk of Parliamentary or legal challenge of the past and current action of the Service Departments, and if another emergency occurred (e.g. in Egypt) a quick Bill to legalise retentions and call-up measures would be necessary. The extent of the risk of Parliamentary challenge is difficult to assess but it must be recognised that the views of the late Law Officers are known to certain members of the late Government.

9. If HM Government consider that the risks should not be taken, there will be no alternative to a short Bill. It would be necessary to introduce and pass this Bill at once, however short Parliamentary time might be.

10. The comprehensive Bill (or the second Bill if a limited short Bill were introduced now), because it must deal with the continuing liability of Z Class and similar reservists, will inevitably raise by implication the liability of National Servicemen under the 1948 Act. These men begin completing their period of reserve liability in July 1954. The Government must declare its intentions on this before the end of 1953 – the powers to call up under this Act expire with that year unless renewed by Order-in-Council. There would be advantage in dealing with all these matters concurrently provided that the Government feel that the risks involved in delay can be accepted.

11. The courses open are thus:
   (a) a short Bill now, followed by a supplementary Bill later:
   (b) a comprehensive Bill, introduced in 1952/53 Session, with a view to its becoming law as soon as possible in that Session:
   (c) a comprehensive Bill, introduced concurrently with, or as part of, any legislation that may be required in 1953/54 Session to deal with the future of National Service reservists.

Chiefs of Staff to Winston S. Churchill
Prime Minister's Personal Telegram T.63/52, OZ 666
(Premier papers, 11/91)

27 January 1952
Operational Immediate
Top Secret
DEF 478

The following is our appreciation of the situation in Egypt as at midday, 27th January.

OPERATION 'RODEO'

1. Present plans to protect the lives of British and foreign nationals in Cairo and Alexandria (Operation 'Rodeo') are based on the assumption that the Egyptian Army will not be actively hostile. This operation is at 48 hours' notice.

NEW FACTORS

2. (a) Both the King and the Egyptian Army have now turned against us and the Commanders-in-Chief believe the Egyptian Army would almost certainly resist 'Rodeo' and abandon Cairo and Alexandria to extremist elements.

(b) At present the Egyptian Army has control of the situation in Cairo and Alexandria is quiet.

(c) The steps we have taken and the quite unexpected resistance of the Egyptian police in Ismailia have increased the tension and our potential commitments in the Canal Zone.

(d) It seems likely that the Egyptian Government will order the expulsion of a proportion of British nationals from Egypt. At the moment it appears that they may be sufficiently in control of the situation to do this without danger to British lives, but the situation remains uncertain.

POSSIBLE ACTION

3. In the new circumstances, the Commanders-in-Chief consider, and we agree, that 'Rodeo' would not have the effect of protecting the lives of British nationals but might well achieve the reverse.

4. British nationals in the Delta are hostages to fortune, and we should therefore be forced to acquiesce if the Egyptian Government orders the expulsion of our nationals and appears capable of carrying this out in an orderly manner. Should the Egyptian Government insist on deporting only a limited number of these nationals, we may have to consider the evacuation of the remainder so as not to perpetuate the present situation.

5. The forced evacuation of British nationals from Egypt would be a great fillip to Egyptian morale and might be interpreted as the first step to

a complete withdrawal. It is therefore important that if deportation occurs we should make it unmistakeably clear that we intend to stay in the Canal Zone and to keep open the Suez Canal for international traffic.

6. One result of this policy may be that we shall have to accept the most undesirable commitment of military government to the Canal Zone. Our hold over the oil supplies to Cairo and our position across the supply lines of the Egyptian forces in Sinai puts us in a strong bargaining position to force the Egyptians to continue civil government in the Canal Zone.

7. No doubt retaliatory measures such as those in para. 6 above and others will have to be considered by HMG, but it is important that they are not enforced until the evacuation of British nationals is complete.

8. Should the expulsion of British nationals be accompanied by a serious loss of British lives, we shall have no alternative but to launch 'Rodeo' even against resistance by the Egyptian Army accepting the risks involved. The following factors will have to be taken into account:

 (a) We have no doubt of our ability to defeat the Egyptian Army in the field, but the Ismailia operations showed that the Egyptians are capable of putting up serious resistance to our entry into the built-up areas of Cairo and Alexandria.

 (b) The departure of forces for 'Rodeo' would leave us dangerously weak in the Canal Zone.

 (c) There is an Egyptian Brigade at Kantara and two more in Sinai, and if we weaken ourselves unduly in the Canal Zone, we have to reckon with this additional threat.

9. We are examining the measures necessary for the evacuation of British nationals from Egypt by sea and air.

10. A squadron of Lincoln bombers arrives in the Canal Zone tomorrow which can, if necessary, be employed against Egyptian forces outside populated areas.

11. Our strategic reserve is now committed in Egypt, and there is little prospect of our being able to return it to the UK in the near future. We are unable at present to reinforce Egypt or to deal with any other emergency that may occur until a new strategic reserve has been built up. This will involve embodiment of Territorial Infantry formations.

Winston S. Churchill to Sir Edward Bridges
Prime Minister's Personal Minute M.20/52
(Premier papers, 11/176)

29 January 1952

What is the total financial saving on the reduction of forty in the subordinate staff?[1] What is the total saving in the primary staff? Let me know about the outstations. What is the cost of the outstations compared with Whitehall?

David Pitblado to Paul Beards[2]
(Premier papers, 11/112)

29 January 1952

Dear Beards,

When the Prime Minister read your Secretary of State's paper on winter Clothing in Korea (C (52)6) he asked what was a 'parka'. We explained this to him in general terms but I should be grateful for a short definition.

Winston S. Churchill: speech
(Hansard)

30 January 1952   House of Commons

ANGLO-AMERICAN CONVERSATIONS

I should myself have thought that it would have been more for the convenience of the House not to delay the important debate on the financial and economic situation which must follow on yesterday's statement by the Chancellor of the Exchequer and I should myself have liked to present my whole case, the whole case, to the House in its proper setting during the course, or at the opening, of the debate we are to have on foreign affairs next week. However, in deference to the wishes expressed by the Opposition, to which it is always my desire to concede every possible point, I will try to clear up a few points about the recent American visit of myself, my right hon. Friend and other Ministers in another place, and to deal with those points which, though not urgent, are the subject of misunderstanding or misrepresentation and have already figured upon the Order Paper of the House.

---

[1] At the Ministry of Defence HQ.
[2] Paul Francis Richmond Beards, 1916–93. Educated at Queen's College, Oxford. Entered Home Civil Service, 1938. On active service during WWII, 1940–4. Asst Private Secretary to PM, 1945–8. Principal Private Secretary to Secretary of State for War, 1951–4. Asst Under-Secretary of State, Ministry of Defence, 1964–9. Retired, 1970.

I was led to cross the Atlantic by my conviction that, in view of all that is going on in all continents, it was important for His Majesty's new Government to establish intimate and easy relations and understandings with the President and the governing authorities of the United States. I also thought it important to try to give the impression to the American people that we rejoice in their effort to defend the cause of world freedom against Communist aggression and penetration and that we will aid them in this purpose, which is also ours, with all our strength and goodwill.

My hon. Friend the Member for Morecambe and Lonsdale (Sir I. Fraser[1]) asked me a Question on the Order Paper today about the Joint Atlantic Command. I remain unconvinced of the need for the appointment of a Supreme Commander and I think that the method adopted in the last war afforded the most practical foundation for maintaining the traffic across the Atlantic in time of war. I was, however, confronted with the agreements which had been made and announced during the term of the late Government and with the fact that these agreements could not be altered except by discussions in the North Atlantic Treaty Organisation. I felt it would be very unfortunate if a protracted argument arose between us and the United States in this wide audience, and I have therefore been forced to accept in principle the situation as it was left to me.

The House will be aware, however, from the communiqué which was issued after my last meeting with President Truman on 18th January that I was able in my discussions in Washington to introduce into the Atlantic Command proposals certain alterations which will provide great flexibility in the Command of the whole Atlantic sphere and will also ensure that there is the fullest cooperation between the Commanders-in-Chief of the Eastern Atlantic and the Home Station, both of whom will be British officers. The Commander-in-Chief of the Home Station will be directly responsible to the Admiralty for the safe arrival and the dispatch of the convoys upon which our survival and the survival of any armies in Europe which the United States may have sent necessarily depend.

As an example of the greater degree of flexibility achieved in our discussions, I may say that it has been arranged that the new Supreme Commander will send instructions to his area commanders which will enable them to support adjoining commands in operations throughout the Atlantic and in British home waters without constant reference to himself. Further, His

---

[1] William Jocelyn Ian Fraser, 1897–1974. Educated at Marlborough and Sandhurst. 2nd Lt, 1st Battalion, King's Shropshire Light Infantry, 1915. Attached to 4th Battalion, Gloucestershire Rgt, 1916. Shot through the head during Battle of the Somme, losing sight in both eyes, 23 July 1916. Capt., 1918. Chairman of Council of St Dunstan's, 1921–74. Member, London County Council, 1922–5. MP (Cons.) for St Pancras North, 1924–9, 1931–7; for Lancashire, Lonsdale, 1940–50; for Morecambe and Lonsdale, 1950–8. Knighted, 1934. A Governor of the BBC, 1937–9, 1941–6. National President of British Legion, 1947–58. CH, 1953. Baron, 1958. Author of *Whereas I Was Blind* (1942) and *My Story of St Dunstan's* (1961).

JANUARY 1952 241

Majesty's Government, with the full agreement of the United States, are putting forward to the North Atlantic Treaty Organisation an amendment to the existing command boundaries so as to extend our Home Command to the westward as far as the one-hundred-fathom line. The right hon. Gentleman[1] will remember that I mentioned that to him at the beginning of this controversy many months ago.[2] The one-hundred-fathom line has many advantages; among others, it broadly corresponds to the limits within which moored mining is profitable and was a very well-known feature in all our affairs in the war.

I can also state, subject to these amendments, that His Majesty's Government are prepared, in the interests of NATO unity, to agree to the appointment within that organisation of an American Supreme Commander and a British Deputy Supreme Commander.

The choice of the officer whose name has been announced today, Admiral McCormick,[3] is one which should ensure the highest confidence among all members of the Atlantic Organisation.

I now come to the question of the war in Korea, the prolongation of the truce negotiations there, with the possibility of their break-down or breach after a settlement had been made, and the attitude we should adopt in that event towards the Chinese Communists whom we have recognised, but who have not entered into relations with us. As we all know on both sides of the House, we can recognise many people of whose conduct we do not entirely approve.

In discussing these matters, we must first of all bear in mind always, I think, the fact that the contribution by Britain and the British Commonwealth to the war in Korea is less than one-tenth of the forces employed; and while our losses, for which we grieve, have amounted in killed, wounded and missing, to nearly 3,000, similar American losses are over 105,000, or thirty-five or forty times as great. So there should be no party differences on the reasons why we are in this war. It was entered upon by the late Government with our full support, and it is authorised and sustained by the United Nations.

I was most anxious, therefore, that we should make the United States Government feel that we meant to be their good comrades at the council board, as our Commonwealth Division and Naval and Air Forces have proved themselves to be in the field of action.

The House is aware that for six months negotiations for a truce have been going on between the United States and the Chinese Communist Government. We do not know whether the negotiations – (Hon. Members: – 'The United Nations'.) – what did I say? – (Hon. Members: 'The United States'.) – between

[1] Emanuel Shinwell, former Minister of Defence.
[2] See Churchill: speech, 19 Apr. 1951, reproduced in *The Churchill Documents*, vol. 22, *Leader of the Opposition, August 1945 to October 1951*, pp. 2046–7).
[3] Lynde Dupuy McCormick, 1895–1956. On active service, 1914–18. Married, 1920, Lillian Addison Sprigg: two children. RAdm., 1942. VAdm. 1947. Adm., 1950. Vice-Chief of Naval Operations, US Navy Dept, 1950; Supreme Allied Commander, Atlantic, NATO, 1952–4.

the United States on behalf of the United Nations – (Hon. Members: 'Hear, hear'.) – we have a lot of things to quarrel about and we need not add to them – between the United Nations and the United States and the Chinese Government will be spun out indefinitely or whether a conclusion will be reached, or whether, after that conclusion has been reached, the Chinese Communists will break their engagement and take any advantages which might be open to them. Neither do we know whether a truce in Korea might not be reached only as a means of transferring Communist strength to the frontiers of French Indo-China or Malaya. This important aspect must be borne in mind.

The whole hypothetical question of what should be done, should a truce be made only to be broken, had been discussed before we left for America between the United Kingdom and the United States and the other Governments who have fighting forces in the field. It was agreed that clearly a very serious situation would arise in such an event as a breach of the truce; and various contingencies had been examined without any definite or formal commitments being entered into.

No change was made in the situation while we were in the United States. In fact, the matter did not figure to any large extent in our discussions. I do not feel it would be an advantage to go into the details of the discussions which took place before we left upon our voyage, those discussions about what we should do, or should not do, in the event, first of a truce being reached, and secondly of it being broken. It is not wise, when a war is going on, to tell everything always to everybody, including the enemy. I suppose I may call them the enemy – they are shooting our soldiers – but including, shall we say, the other side. I think they may sometimes be left with something to guess about.

I thought it better, therefore, when I was invited to address the American Congress – which I regarded as a very great honour for this House, one in which the Leader of the Opposition has also shared – to speak in general terms of the action we should take in the event of a breach of the truce, and I used the words, 'prompt, resolute and effective'. I do not believe they were bad words to use. Certainly, if one is dealing in general terms, they are better than 'tardy, timid and fatuous'. I certainly did not mean to suggest that the words, 'prompt, resolute and effective' represented any new designs or decisions arrived at during our visit –

Mr John Paton[1]: May I ask the right hon. Gentleman – (*Interruption.*) – this is very important –

Mr Churchill: They do not represent any new decisions arrived at during our visit.

Mr Paton: Or before, in the preliminary conversations?

Mr Churchill: I said there had been discussions, but there had been no final or definite commitment, and that is the position now.

---

[1] John Paton, 1886–1976. Editor of British socialist newspaper *New Leader*. MP (Lab.) for Norwich, 1945–50; for Norwich North, 1950–64.

JANUARY 1952

Mr Paton: A gentleman's agreement —

Mr Churchill: But they do express frankly and fully the spirit in which we shall face our difficulties together.

I will now turn to some of the larger issues which are in the background of all thought upon the Korean campaign. At the outset, eighteen months ago, I was personally disquieted by seeing, as I told the House at the time, the attention and resources of the United States being diverted from the main danger in Europe to this far-distant peninsula in the China Seas. But we must recognise that the United Nations have gained authority by the fact that unprovoked aggression has been met by armed force, and that the rule of law which we seek to establish has not lacked either will-power or resources.

This is of extreme importance. The ruin of the League of Nations, out of which so many disasters came, was because this will-power was lacking. It is also a fact that the stimulus of the fighting in Korea has developed to a degree otherwise impossible the re-armament of the free world, and, above all, of the United States. As I said to Congress, the balance of the world has been altered by the decision of President Truman, with the approval of the United Nations, to make this bold American stroke against aggression, in support of which we have all followed.

At the same time, when the main dangers are so much nearer home, we do not want to see ourselves tied down or entangled in a war in Korea — still less in a war in China. That would indeed, as General Bradley so forcibly said, be the wrong war, in the wrong place, at the wrong time.

Mr Sydney Silverman: And on the wrong side.

Hon. Members: Traitor!

Mr Churchill: That, I think, is a very candid revelation by the hon. Member that he thinks that we ought to be on the side of the Chinese Communists against the United Nations.

Mr Silverman: I do not raise a point of order, which might have been prompted by some of the remarks which have been made by some hon. Members opposite — I do not think they are worth noticing — but I want to say to the right hon. Gentleman that what I intended to convey was, that in any war in China, the issue of which would be whether the present Government should remain in power or whether Chiang Kai-shek should replace it, which would be the inevitable result of our taking part in those circumstances in a war in China now, it would not merely be the wrong enemy, the wrong war, the wrong time and the wrong place; it would also, in my opinion, be the wrong side.

Mr Churchill: I did not refer to General Chiang Kai-shek. I remember a time in the war when he was one of the great heroes and held to be the representative of the new Asia, and when he inspired marked enthusiasm in the hon. Gentleman because of his strenuous efforts to separate India from the British Crown. But everyone has his day, and some days last longer than others. I am glad that the hon. Gentleman has indicated that he was referring only to an inter-Chinese question, because I do not wish to burden him with any further responsibility than he already bears.

Mr Silverman: The right hon. Gentleman will bear in mind that this whole question is complicated by the fact that the United States of America still recognises Chiang Kai-shek as the Government of China, whereas we do not, and that, therefore, if this country were in these circumstances to find itself involved in an extension of the war to China, it would be a war in which one of the issues, and perhaps in many ways the most important issue, would be whether the Government of China recognised by the Government of the United States or the Government of China recognised by the Government of the United Kingdom would win. In such a war we should find ourselves ranged on the wrong side.

Mr Churchill: Of course, the hon. Gentleman is to be complimented upon the assiduity and attention with which he studies the daily newspapers; and many other Members of the House do the same. But no issue has arisen as to the question of employing General Chiang Kai-shek on the continent. What I have said and repeat is that he and those who fought with him against the Communists and have taken refuge upon the island of Formosa should not be invaded and massacred there while the United Nations Forces possess such overwhelming naval superiority.

I said 'the wrong war, in the wrong place, at the wrong time'. I entirely agree with those forcible remarks of General Omar Bradley. The facts are so serious that they ought not to be overlooked. There are, shall we say, the equivalent of 10 divisions, including a most important part of the American Army and our one Commonwealth division, in Korea, and we do not know how long they will have to stay there.

General Juin,[1] the French General, said in his recent visit to the United States that but for the Communist attacks in Indo-China the French Army in Europe could be ten divisions stronger. If those were at home, it would presumably enable France to take a more confident view about the development of a German army, which is of the utmost importance to the problem. However, let us count the diminution of the French Army in Europe as ten divisions; that is certainly a moderate estimate.

Then there are the British Forces which are spread about the East and Far East resisting Communist menace or other forms of Communist-inspired

---

[1] Alphonse Pierre Juin, 1888–1967. GOC, 15th Motorized Infantry Div., 1939–40. POW, 1940–1. Appointed Cdr of French troops in Morocco by Pétain, 1941. Gen., 1942. C-in-C, North Africa, 1942–3; Allied Forces, Central Europe, 1953–6. Resident-General of Tunisia, 1943; of Morocco, 1947–51. GOC Corps Expéditionnaire Français, Italy, 1943–4. Chief of National Defence Staff, 1944–7. Member, Supreme War Council, 1948–54. Inspector-General of the Army, 1951–3. CoS, Combined Armed Forces, 1951–3. President, CoS Committee, 1951–3. Marshal of France, 1952.

disorder, in Hong Kong, in Malaya and to some extent in the Canal Zone of the Middle East. These amount to at least six divisions, far more costly in resources to maintain than if they were at home or in Europe.

This makes a numerical total of twenty-six divisions, but the equivalent in war power measured by divisions employed in Europe might well be thirty or even thirty-five. And all this is withdrawn from the European front, where the Atlantic Treaty Powers have so far only been able to deploy – that is a better word than concentrate – on this enormous front a very much smaller force. But for these pressures and assaults in the Far East, in South East Asia and the Middle East, forces would exist to form a front in Europe against what are called the 176 Soviet divisions of which we have been given timely warning by the former Minister of Defence, an enormous force far superior to anything we have. I think those divisions are not numerically comparable to the United Nations divisions or the Atlantic Treaty divisions but they are far superior in total.

If we had fifty divisions deployed to protect the civilisation of Europe, including Germany, at the present time, as we should have but for the ones which are detached all over the world, the Atlantic Treaty Powers would not be forced, as they are now, to rely so disproportionately on the immense and ever-growing American superiority in the atomic bomb, and there would be a chance of establishing a calmer atmosphere, and those conditions might well lead, if we were blessed by heaven, to at least a make-shift settlement lasting perhaps for a good many years.

But the men in the Kremlin, who have many anxieties of their own to face, may at any rate at this moment compliment themselves not only on having subjugated or brought into their Communist grip half Europe and all China, but on having pegged down in far-distant areas around the globe a much greater force than the Atlantic Powers have so far been able to gather to defend the civilisation of the West; and they may pride themselves on the fact that they have done all this without losing a single soldier in Russian uniform.

I leave this sombre spectacle, which I feel it is absolutely necessary to place before the House: actions and words cannot be judged except in relation to what is always the uppermost feeling in one's mind – anxiety. I leave this spectacle to return to the Korean front.

I do not think we have gained security during this long period of haggling and wrangling which has gone on at Panmunjom. Apart from anything else, the Chinese Communist Government, whose troops were being slaughtered at the rate of about forty to one by the United Nations Forces, and who had a terrible mass of wounded and invalids flung back upon them far beyond their resources to handle, have, since the Soviet suggestion of a cease-fire and truce negotiations, reestablished what is called their 'face'. That, I believe, is a technical term, a term of art which has great vogue in China, and they have since been bargaining all this time on equal terms with the representatives of the United Nations.

We still hope that an agreement will be reached. We still hope that, being reached, it will be kept. I think we have secured a better chance for the reaching of an agreement by making it plain that the United States and Britain are working together in true comradeship, and that in the event of a treacherous renewal of the war they will together take 'prompt, resolute and effective action'.

We have improved the chances of a settlement and limited the risks of a spread by making this declaration instead of giving the impression that we were disunited and taking small points off one another. I am sure that the way to play into the hands of those who direct the Communist menace from the centre would be to magnify differences between Britain and the United States and that nothing would be more likely than that to lead to renewal on a larger scale of the local war in Korea.

My own thoughts are never long absent from the European front and I was, therefore, very glad to have the opportunity in Washington of making it clear that the English-speaking world are acting together in true loyalty and unity and are resolved to bring the local events in the Far East into their proper relationship to our predominating danger in Europe.

Apart from the turmoil in the Far East and in South-East Asia, there are the troubles in the Middle East and Egypt. I have never had the feeling that we should make a bargain with the United States that if we worked smoothly with them in the Far East they should do the same for us in the Middle East. I think this should not be the subject of a bargain. Both cases should be dealt with on their merits, and both cases are pretty strong when looked at on their merits. It is certain that if Britain and the United States are known to be acting together, the difficulties will by that very fact be substantially reduced and the possibilities of peaceful arrangements will be greatly strengthened.

It is certain also that the main interest of the Communist oligarchy in the Kremlin is to provoke or at least to suggest divergencies between us. That, I think, should not be overlooked even in our debates in this House. On the other hand, the fact of simultaneous or concerted action between us and the United States becoming apparent will be beneficial to both of us and even more beneficial to the free world as a whole.

No more hopeful course has yet been suggested for the Middle East than the approach to all its problems in the spirit of the Four Power proposals. This was the policy of the late Government, for which they deserve the fullest credit, and we have given it immediate, cordial, sustained and determined support. Now that we no longer have available the former Imperial armies which existed in India, the burden of maintaining the control and security of the international waterway of the Suez Canal is one which must be more widely shared.

It is upon an international basis that the most hopeful solution of our Middle Eastern difficulties will be reached, and I trust that all the Powers concerned will play their part, working together and sharing the burden and responsibilities for the peace and security of the Middle East. It may be some time before that is achieved, but that should clearly be our aim and goal.

I have today been able only to deal with three points all relating to specific Questions which have been put on the Paper, but I think that they were the three points which were perhaps most uppermost in the minds of hon. Gentlemen. There are, of course, a number of other issues upon which the House should receive information. These I shall reserve for our debate next week, when Members will have the fullest opportunity of interrogating the Government upon any points of doubt or difference which may exist between us.

I am very much obliged to the House for the patient hearing which they have given me, and I hope that we may now pass to the urgent and most important business of the day.

Winston S. Churchill to Anthony Eden
Prime Minister's Personal Minute M.21/52
(Premier papers, 11/91)

30 January 1952
Private *and* Personal

I think we should be very careful lest in our desire to have an easier settlement in Egypt we do not take account of the degree of atrocity committed by the Egyptians in the murders and massacres in Cairo. The horrible behaviour of the mob puts them lower than the most degraded savages now known. Unless the Egyptian Government can purge themselves by the condign punishment of the offenders and by the most abject and complete regrets and reparations I doubt whether any relationship is possible with them. They cannot be classed as a civilized power until they have purged themselves. Pray talk to me tomorrow morning if you are not in agreement with this line of thought.

Here is a Government against whose democratic foundations much may be said which is at this moment guilty of the vilest deeds. The main situation is in my opinion altered by these new facts.

JANUARY 1952

Nikólaos Plastíras[1] to Winston S. Churchill
(Premier papers, 11/179)

31 January 1952 Athens

Excellency,

Wishing to show their gratitude to the gallant sons of your country who fell fighting on Greek soil in defence of the cause of freedom and to pay a fitting tribute to their memory, the Greek people have raised in Athens, by public subscription, a Memorial to the soldiers of Great Britain, Australia and New Zealand who lost their lives in Greece.

This task, with the approval and support of the Government, was carried through by a committee of eminent personalities under the chairmanship of a Cabinet Minister.

The Memorial will be inaugurated on April 25th, 1952.

The Greek Government have decided to invite, as representatives, a British disabled soldier and one relative of the soldiers fallen in Greece, to be present as their guests.

The Greek Government and I personally should be very glad if His Britannic Majesty's Government and your Excellency would kindly agree to send also a representative to attend the ceremony of the unveiling of this Memorial which shall witness to posterity the common ideals of our People and their comradeship in arms.

I avail myself of this opportunity to renew to Your Excellency the assurances of my highest consideration.

[1] Nikólaos Plastíras, 1883–1953. Entered Greek Army, 1903. On active service in Balkan Wars of 1912–13. Led unsuccessful coup against Sofoklis Venizelos, 1933. PM of Greece, 1945, 1950, 1951–2.

February 1952

David Hunt to Winston S. Churchill
(*Premier papers, 11/86*)

1 February 1952

You will remember that you wrote,[1] on Christmas Eve, to Sir Vincent Tewson, in reply to a letter from him about the school age. You said in it that you hoped to have a talk with him when you got back from America.
Would you like me to try to arrange a meeting?[2]

Winston S. Churchill to R. A. Butler
Prime Minister's Personal Minute M.24/52
(*Premier papers, 11/125*)

2 February 1952
Secret

How much would it cost in next year's Budget if the Purchase Tax were removed from all articles included in the cost of living index?

---

[1] Letter reproduced above (p. 150).
[2] Churchill wrote at the bottom of the page: 'not yet'.

Emery Reves[1] to Lord Camrose[2]
(Churchill papers, 4/63)

2 February 1952

Dear Lord Camrose,

Several American reviewers of Volume V expressed their doubts as to whether Mr Churchill will be able to complete his 'Memoirs' now that he is back in office. This rumour has spread all over Europe and some of my publishers, particularly those who issued the work on a subscription basis, are rather worried. They have to answer many questions from booksellers, and they have asked me to authorise them to deny this rumour, and to reassure their public that the sixth and last volume is already in an advanced stage, so that it is certain that the work will be completed.

When I last saw Mr Churchill, just before the elections, he shewed me the proofs of Volume VI and told me that it was 60% ready and that he will complete it for publication whether he was returned to office or not.

I should be most grateful if you would kindly let me know whether it is proper for me to authorise European publishers to deny the American press rumours and to reassure the public that the sixth and last volume is already in an advanced stage, and that it is certain that the 'Memoirs' will be completed and the last volume published in time.

Bertha Jenks[3] to Winston S. Churchill
(Churchill papers, 2/144)

3 February 1952   North Carolina

My dear Mr Churchill,

When General Marshall brought me, as a gift from you, not only your photograph but that delightful *Painting as a Pastime*[4] I was overwhelmed with gratitude and wonder. I always shall be! Why should a more than 'elderly woman' quite unknown to you and at such an important time in your busy life, be so honoured? If it is because those keen eyes of the General could see how many years I have tried, to the limit of my ability, to understand and profit by your unique comprehension of human nature and its relation to diplomacy,

---

[1] Emery Reves, 1904–81. Founded Cooperation Publishing Service, 1933. Winston Churchill's literary agent, 1937. Naturalised as British subject, 1940. Married, 1964, Wendy Russell.

[2] William Ewart Berry, 1879–1954. Newspaper proprietor. Founded *Advertising World*, 1901. Editor-in-Chief, *Sunday Times*, 1915–36. Chairman, Financial Times Ltd, 1919–45; Allied Newspapers Ltd, 1924–36. Baron Camrose, 1929. Chief Proprietor and Editor-in-Chief, *Daily Telegraph* and *Morning Post*, 1936–54. Principal Adviser, Ministry of Information, 1939. Viscount, 1941. One of Churchill's close friends and from 1945 a principal financial adviser; in 1946, negotiated the sale of Churchill's war memoirs and also the purchase of Chartwell by a group of Churchill's friends and its conveyance to the National Trust.

[3] Bertha Wells, 1869–1957. Married George J. Jenks: two children.

[4] See Marshall to Churchill, Jan. 9, reproduced above (pp. 194–5).

I plead guilty. Arthur Krock,[1] of our *New York Times*, insists you had a Fairy Godmother. I have read and shall 'always save the documents in evidence' as proof that you were a Fairy Godfather to Franklin Roosevelt. Charm, what we call 'education' and great personal courage are not enough; the wisdom to use them properly is a gift Godparents too often neglect. Yours didn't. I suppose history is made by words, the psychological reaction to which can only be guessed when they are first spoken.

Words such as Liberty, Equality, and especially in my country, 'the Pursuit of Happiness'. In your recent address to our Congress you quoted Bismarck[2] as saying – undoubtedly, many times to that 'Willie'[3] who 'was so green he believed everything Bismarck told him' – that 'the supreme fact of the Nineteenth Century was that England and the United States spoke the same language'. They still do but with what a difference! Otherwise I might be able to thank you, as I would like to do, and assure you that I, also, and with all my heart hope the supreme fact of the Twentieth Century will be, that we tread the same path. Congratulations to your Parliament on its last vote of confidence which proves that 'England never was and never will be through with you' and apologies – if you ever have time to read thus far – for being so verbose even though I am always your faithful, grateful pupil.

Winston S. Churchill to Anthony Eden and Lord Salisbury
Prime Minister's Personal Minute M.29/52*
(Premier papers, 11/183)

4 February 1952

1. Nations should speak to nations on a high level. The attempt of the victors to educate the vanquished is not likely to alter the main current of events although it may supply a considerable number of jobs for extremely well-meaning people. Treating Germany as an equal and as a friend and ally; welcoming her to NATO; dropping all the foolery about using Heligoland for bombing practice, and a number of other points I could mention, would be gestures comprehended by all Germans, and would gain far more in a few months than this expensive education would do in years.

2. Indeed there seems to be a much stronger case at the moment for French education, to lift their country back to its former position. I do not gather you have any scheme for this.

3. If our main policy and attitude towards Germany does not convince

---

[1] Arthur Bernard Krock, 1886–1974. Married, 1911, Marguerite Polly (d. 1938); 1939, Martha Granger. Journalist, *New York Times*, 1927–67. Won three Pulitzer Prizes: 1935 (Correspondence), 1938 (Correspondence) and 1951 (Special Citation). Presidential Medal of Freedom, 1970.

[2] Otto von Bismarck, 1815–98. Prussian statesman known for unification of Germany, 1871. Minister President of Prussia, 1862–90. First Chancellor of the German Empire, 1871–90.

[3] Wilhelm Friedrich Ludwig von Hohenzollern, 1797–1888. King of Prussia, 1861–88. First Emperor of Germany, 1871–88.

the German people that we wish them well and welcome them back to the family of Europe and to their place in the world these educational centres may at any time become mere targets for hostility. In any case the proportion of good which they can do in a population of seventy million, actuated by most vehement external and internal pressures, is not worth the money it costs our overtaxed, hard-pressed island. I will gladly talk the matter over with the Foreign Secretary.

* Reference: Note by Foreign Secretary (FS/52/2) of 19 January 1952, on educational expenditure in Germany.

Winston S. Churchill to Harry Crookshank and Patrick Buchan-Hepburn
Prime Minister's Personal Minute M.30/52
(Premier papers, 11/270)

4 February 1952

What is the need to have a Defence White Paper? It would involve disclosing a great deal of unsatisfactory stuff for which we are not responsible. So much is printed nowadays that very little makes any impression at all on the parliamentary or public mind. I should think it much better to wait until there is a general demand.

Please remember that we are going to have an astoundingly early Budget and prolonged economic, financial rambles thereupon. The House will be gorged not hungry. Let me know your views.

Winston S. Churchill to Harry Crookshank and Patrick Buchan-Hepburn
Prime Minister's Personal Minute M.34/52
(Premier papers, 11/200)

4 February 1952

Here is another case* involving new and controversial legislation. We seem to have got on all right without it since it was asked for before Christmas. There are hopes that the situation in Egypt is improving. Will you talk it over with the First Lord on the basis we do nothing this year. If however you both think it is necessary then the right course is for a short Bill now and no other legislation till 1953/4 or better.

* Reference: Minute from First Lord on powers to recall Reservists etc.[1]

[1] Reproduced above (pp. 235–6).

FEBRUARY 1952

Winston S. Churchill to Sir Harold Parker
Prime Minister's Personal Minute M.35/52*
(Premier papers, 11/380)

4 February 1952

I cannot read all these reports at once but you should make a short summary, one page, of the first four. Let me have it in the course of next week.

* Sir Henry Tizard's minute of 15 January 1952 regarding DRP Committee Progress Reports.[1]

Cabinet: conclusions
(Cabinet papers, 128/24)

5 February 1952
Secret
11 a.m.
Cabinet Meeting No. 10 of 1952

1. The Prime Minister said that he had been concerned to see, in reports of a Press Conference which the Home Secretary had held on the previous day, references to the delivery of new sirens for sounding air-raid warnings. He thought it unwise that the public should be alarmed by undue publicity about civil defence preparations at this stage.

The Home Secretary said that the purpose of his Press Conference had been to stimulate recruiting for the civil defence services, which were seriously below their peace-time establishment. It was unfortunate that the newspapers had given such prominence to his remarks on the subject of equipment. He had no intention of obtruding upon public attention the arrangements which were being made to complete the air-raid warning system.

2. The Prime Minister drew attention to Press reports of the decision to raise the normal age of retirement of established civil servants. This decision had been presented in the Press in a manner which made it seem inconsistent with the steps which the Government were taking to reduce the size of the Civil Service.

The Chancellor of the Exchequer said that the Staff side of the national Whitley Council had conveyed this information to the Press prematurely and without his knowledge. He had demanded, and had received, the Staff side's apologies for their action. The timing of the disclosure was admittedly unfortunate. The policy was, however, sound and consistent with the current movement towards an extension of the working life of the population generally. It was also consistent with the policy of reducing Civil Service numbers;

[1] Reproduced above (p. 208).

for this should be achieved by dispensing with younger temporary staff who could be absorbed into other employment.

The Prime Minister said that he hoped that all Ministers would in future bear in mind the desirability of mentioning to the Cabinet, before any public announcement was made, any executive decisions which were of general importance or were likely to attract widespread publicity.

[. . .]

Cabinet: conclusions
(Cabinet papers, 128/24)

6 February 1952
Secret
11.30 a.m.
Cabinet Meeting No. 11 of 1952

The Prime Minister informed the Cabinet of the grievous news that His Majesty The King had died in his sleep at Sandringham during the previous night.[1] The Cabinet had been summoned at once to authorise the immediate action which had now to be taken.

The Cabinet agreed that the meeting of the Privy Council to proclaim the Accession of the new Sovereign should be held at 5 p.m. that day. When the House of Commons met at 2.30 p.m. they would be informed of the Demise of the Crown. The sitting would then be suspended until the Accession Council had been held. Thereafter, the House would meet again for the sole purpose of enabling the Speaker to take the oath of allegiance and to swear in such other Members as were present. Arrangements would be made for other Members of the House to take the oath on subsequent days. Similar arrangements would be made in the House of Lords. No tributes would be paid to His late Majesty in Parliament until the following week, when Addresses would be moved. The ordinary business of Parliament would not be resumed until after the Funeral.

The Cabinet then discussed the question of the return of the new Sovereign from Kenya. It was felt that She would wish to return at once by air. After discussion the Cabinet decided not to offer any advice to the contrary.

The Cabinet agreed that messages of condolence should be despatched on their behalf to The Queen and to the Queen-Mother.[2] These messages were drafted, approved by the Cabinet and despatched.

The Cabinet invited the Lord Chancellor, the Home Secretary and the

---

[1] Churchill had rung up Eden that morning, prefacing the news with: 'Anthony, imagine the worse thing that could possibly happen' (*Finest Hour*, No. 135, Summer 2007).
[2] Elizabeth Angela Marguerite Bowes-Lyon, 1900–2002. Married, 1923, Prince Albert Windsor, later King George VI. Duchess of York, 1923–36. Queen Consort, 1936–52. Queen Mother, 1952–2002.

FEBRUARY 1952 255

Commonwealth Secretary to consider the form of the Accession Proclamation, and to report to a further meeting of the Cabinet to be held that afternoon.

The Cabinet invited the Prime Minister to broadcast to the nation on the following evening on the death of His late Majesty.

It was agreed that for the present Ministers should not attend any public banquets or similar functions.

The Prime Minister undertook to inform the Leader of the Opposition of the points of procedure which had been decided by the Cabinet.

Cabinet: conclusions
(Cabinet papers, 128/24)

6 February 1952 Prime Minister's Room
Secret House of Commons
2.45 p.m.
Cabinet Meeting No. 12 of 1952

1. The Cabinet had before them a note by the Secretary of the Cabinet (C(52)22) covering alternative drafts of the Proclamation declaring the Accession of the new Sovereign. The first of these was in the traditional form. Its wording was not wholly in accord with present constitutional conditions in the Commonwealth. Thus, it referred to 'the Imperial Crown', which was an expression likely to be associated with the Indian Empire; it referred to 'Ireland' and not to 'Northern Ireland'; and it included references to 'British Dominions' which would not be welcomed by some of the other members of the Commonwealth. Moreover, it was cast in a form in which it could not be signed by the representative of India which, though remaining a member of the Commonwealth, no longer owed allegiance to the Crown. The second draft was designed to avoid these difficulties.

After discussion the Cabinet reached the conclusion that it would in any event be necessary to make some departures from the traditional form of the Proclamation, for instance by omitting the word 'Imperial' in the reference to the Crown, and by substituting 'Northern Ireland' for 'Ireland'. It would also be desirable to include some reference to the Sovereign's position as 'Head of the Commonwealth'. In these circumstances it seemed preferable that the Proclamation should follow the form of the second draft annexed to C(52)22, which was more consonant with the current constitutional relationships between the various parts of the Commonwealth.

After further discussion the following draft was approved:

'Whereas it hath pleased Almighty God to call to His Mercy our late Sovereign Lord King George the Sixth of Blessed and Glorious Memory by whose Decease the Crown is solely and rightfully come to the High and Mighty Princess Elizabeth Alexandra Mary: We, therefore, the Lords Spiritual and Temporal of this Realm, being here assisted with these of His late Majesty's Privy Council, with representatives of other members of the Commonwealth, with other Principal Gentlemen of Quality, with the Lord Mayor, Aldermen and Citizens of London, do now hereby with one Voice and Consent of Tongue and Heart publish and proclaim that the High and Mighty Princess Elizabeth Alexandra Mary is now, by the Death of our late Sovereign of Happy Memory, become Queen Elizabeth the Second, by the Grace of God Queen of this Realm and of all Her other Realms and Territories, Head of the Commonwealth, Defender of the Faith, to whom Her lieges do acknowledge all Faith and constant Obedience, with hearty and humble Affection; beseeching God, by whom Kings and Queen do reign, to bless the Royal Princess Elizabeth the Second with long and happy Years to reign over us.'

The Cabinet – Invited the Lord President to arrange that the Proclamation of the Accession of the new Sovereign should be made in the form set out above.

2. The Cabinet discussed suggestions for the meetings of Parliament and other arrangements during the period before the funeral of His late Majesty.

The Prime Minister said that the new Sovereign was returning to this country by air and was expected to arrive on the following afternoon. The Cabinet agreed that the Prime Minister, accompanied by several of his Ministerial colleagues and by the Leaders of the two Opposition Parties in the House of Commons, should meet Her on Her arrival at London Airport.

It was proposed that the second part of the Accession Council should be held on 8th February. On that day flags would not be flown at half-mast.

In discussion it was suggested that the body of His late Majesty might be brought on 11th February from Sandringham to Westminster Hall, where it might lie in state until 15th February, and the Funeral might take place on that day. In that event it would be appropriate that the Addresses should be moved in both Houses of Parliament on 11th or 12th February. Parliament should not resume their normal business until 19th February.

The Cabinet invited the Chancellor of the Exchequer, together with the Home Secretary, the Minister of Health, the Minister of Labour and the President of the Board of Trade to consider to what extent places of work should be closed on the day of the Funeral of His late Majesty, both in London and in other parts of the country.

Winston S. Churchill: broadcast
('Winston S. Churchill, His Complete Speeches', volume 8, pages 8336–8)

7 February 1952 London

KING GEORGE VI

My friends, when the death of the King was announced to us yesterday morning there struck a deep and solemn note in our lives which, as it resounded far and wide, stilled the clatter and traffic of twentieth-century life in many lands and made countless millions of human beings pause and look around them. A new sense of values took, for the time being, possession of human minds and moral existence presented itself to so many at the same moment in its serenity and its sorrow, in its splendour and in its pain, in its fortitude and in its suffering.

The King was greatly loved by all his peoples. He was respected as a man and as a prince far beyond the many realms over which he reigned. The simple dignity of his life, his manly virtues, his sense of duty alike as a ruler and a servant of the vast spheres and communities for which he bore responsibility – his gay charm and happy nature, his example as a husband and a father in his own family circle, his courage in peace or war – all these were aspects of his character which won the glint of admiration, now here, now there, from the innumerable eyes whose gaze falls upon the Throne.

We thought of him as a young naval lieutenant in the great Battle of Jutland. We thought of him, when calmly, without ambition, or want of self-confidence, he assumed the heavy burden of the Crown and succeeded his brother, whom he loved, and to whom he had rendered perfect loyalty. We thought of him so faithful in his study and discharge of State affairs, so strong in his devotion to the enduring honour of our country, so self-restrained in his judgments of men and affairs, so uplifted above the clash of party politics, yet so attentive to them; so wise and shrewd in judging between what matters and what does not. All this we saw and admired. His conduct on the Throne may well be a model and a guide to constitutional sovereigns throughout the world today, and also in future generations.

The last few months of King George's life, with all the pain and physical stresses that he endured – his life hanging by a thread from day to day – and he all the time cheerful and undaunted – stricken in body but quite undisturbed and even unaffected in spirit – these have made a profound and an enduring impression and should be a help to all. He was sustained not only by his natural buoyancy but by the sincerity of his Christian faith. During these last months the King walked with death, as if death were a companion, an acquaintance, whom he recognized and did not fear. In the end death came as a friend; and after a happy day of sunshine and sport, and after 'good night' to those who loved him best, he fell asleep as every man or woman who strives to fear God and nothing else in the world may hope to do.

The nearer one stood to him the more these facts were apparent. But the newspapers and photographs of modern times have made vast numbers of his subjects able to watch with emotion the last months of his pilgrimage. We all saw him approach his journey's end. In this period of mourning and meditation, amid our cares and toils, every home in all the realms joined together under the Crown, may draw comfort for tonight and strength for the future from his bearing and his fortitude.

There was another tie between King George and his people. It was not only sorrow and affliction that they shared. Dear to the hearts and the homes of the people is the joy and pride of united family; with this all the troubles of the world can be borne and all its ordeals at least confronted. No family in these tumultuous years was happier, or loved one another more, than the Royal Family around the King.

My friends, I suppose no Minister saw so much of the King during the war as I did. I made certain he was kept informed of every secret matter; and the care and thoroughness with which he mastered the immense daily flow of State papers made a deep mark on my mind. Let me tell you another fact. On one of the days, when Buckingham palace was bombed, the King had just returned from Windsor. One side of the courtyard was struck, and if the windows opposite out of which he and the Queen were looking had not been, by the mercy of God, open, they would both have been blinded by the broken glass instead of being only hurled back by the explosion. Amid all that was then going on – although I saw the King so often – I never heard of this episode till a long time after. Their Majesties never mentioned it, or thought it of more significance than a soldier in their armies would of a shell bursting near him. This seems to me to be a revealing trait in the Royal character.

There is no doubt that of all the institutions which have grown up among us over the centuries, or sprung into being in our lifetime, the constitutional monarchy is the most deeply founded and dearly cherished by the whole association of our peoples. In the present generation it has acquired a meaning incomparably more powerful than anyone had dreamed possible in former times. The Crown has become the mysterious link – indeed, I may say, the magic link – which unites our loosely bound but strongly interwoven Commonwealth of nations, States and races. Peoples who would never tolerate the assertions of a written constitution which implied any diminution of their independence, are the foremost to be proud of their loyalty to the Crown.

We have been greatly blessed amid our many anxieties, and in the mighty world that has grown up all around our small island – we have been greatly blessed that this new intangible, inexpressible but for practical purposes apparently, an all-powerful element of union should have leapt into being among us. How vital it is, not only to the future of the British Commonwealth and

Empire, but I believe also to the cause of world freedom and peace which we serve, that the occupant of the Throne should be equal to the august and indefinable responsibilities which this supreme office requires. For fifteen year King George VI was king; never at any moment in all the perplexities at home and abroad, in public or in private, did he fail in his duties; well does he deserve the farewell salute of all his governments and peoples.

My friends, it is at this time that our compassion and sympathy go out to his Consort and widow. Their marriage was a love match with no idea of regal pomp or splendour. Indeed, there seemed to lie before them the arduous life of royal personages denied so many of the activities of ordinary folk and having to give so much in ceremonial public service. May I say, speaking with all freedom, that our hearts go out tonight to that valiant woman with famous blood of Scotland in her veins who sustained King George through all his toils and problems and brought up, with their charm and beauty, the two daughters who mourn their father today. May she be granted strength to bear her sorrow. To Queen Mary, his mother, another of whose sons is dead – the Duke of Kent[1] having been killed on active service – there belongs the consolation of seeing how well the King did his duty and fulfilled her hopes, and of always knowing how much he cared for her.

Now I must leave the treasures of the past and turn to the future. Famous have been the reigns of our Queens. Some of the greatest periods in our history have unfolded under their sceptres. Now that we have the Second Queen Elizabeth, also ascending the Throne in her twenty-sixth year, our thoughts are carried back nearly 400 years to the magnificent figure who presided over, and in many ways embodied and inspired, the grandeur and genius of the Elizabethan Age. Queen Elizabeth the Second, like her predecessor, did not pass her childhood in any certain expectation of the Crown. But already we know her well, and we understand why her gifts, and those of her husband, the Duke of Edinburgh, have stirred the only part of our Commonwealth she has yet been able to visit. She has already been acclaimed as Queen of Canada: we make our claim, too, and others will come forward also; and tomorrow the proclamation of her sovereignty will command the loyalty of her native land and of all other parts of the British Commonwealth and Empire.

I, whose youth was passed in the august, unchallenged and tranquil glories of the Victorian Era, may well feel a thrill in invoking, once more, the prayer and the Anthem, 'God Save the Queen!'

---

[1] George Edward Alexander Edmund, 1902–42. Duke of Kent, 1934–42. Married, 1934, Princess Marina of Greece and Denmark: three children.

R. A. Butler to Winston S. Churchill
(Premier papers, 11/125)

8 February 1952
Secret

You asked[1] for the cost of removing Purchase Tax from all articles included in the cost of living index.

It is difficult to be precise about this, but the Customs estimate that the yield of tax from the articles actually specified in the index is something over £100 millions, out of a total revenue from Purchase Tax of over £300 millions a year.

Most of the articles, however, are specified simply as typical examples of the various kinds of expenditure. For example one of the articles is a 60 watt electric lamp, but this is there simply as a typical example of electric light fittings generally and of course we could not remove Purchase Tax from this without at the same time removing it from a wide range of such fittings. Looking at the matter in this way, I should think it would probably cost the Exchequer about £200 millions to eliminate completely the effect of Purchase Tax on the index.

I shall naturally have more to say about Purchase Tax generally, but I would prefer to leave this until we have our talk on Budget as a whole.

Winston S. Churchill to Duncan Sandys
Prime Minister's Personal Minute M.39/52
(Premier papers, 11/80)

11 February 1952

Now that the Army have made a substantial cut in their demand for lorries for the coming year, I hope it will be possible to use the capacity and steel that will not now be required for the Army to make vehicles for export. Sir William Rootes told me in New York that provided prices did not rise unduly any extra cars for which steel could be found could easily be sold in the United States.

Pray let me have a short note on the effect of the Army's reduction in demand for lorries on our export of cars.

I am sending a copy of this minute to the President of the Board of Trade.

---

[1] M.24/52, reproduced above (p. 249).

Winston S. Churchill to Sir Norman Brook
Prime Minister's Personal Minute M.40/52
(Premier papers, 11/176)

11 February 1952

Pray see the attached from Sir Edward Bridges. I was much struck on leaving Washington to see the great numbers of Officers, particularly Air Force Officers, who are retained on the Military Missions at Washington and no doubt also in New York. Military Attachés also are retained although their duties are done largely by the Military Missions. Let me have a complete list on one page of the organization of these Military Missions, including civilians, and also of the Military Attachés with their personal staffs. We cannot afford any unnecessary dollar expense.

Winston S. Churchill: speech
(Hansard)

11 February 1952   House of Commons

MOTION FOR ADDRESS AND MESSAGE OF SYMPATHY

I have read with attention the speeches made on the demise of the Crown during the present century, beginning with the end of an epoch on the death of Queen Victoria.[1] Mr Balfour,[2] Mr Asquith,[3] and Mr Baldwin,[4] as Prime Ministers or Leaders of the House, discharged the duty which falls on me today. I was a Member of the House on all those occasions and I shall follow, in what I say, the example of those eminent men.

I have three Motions to propose which, though they will be put separately from the Chair, should be read all at once, and I shall confine what I have to say in support of them, in accordance with precedent, within the compass of a single speech.

---

[1] Alexandrina Victoria, 1819–1901. Daughter of Edward, Duke of Kent; granddaughter of King George III. Queen of the United Kingdom of Great Britain and Ireland, 1837–1901; Empress of India, 1876–1901. Married, 1840, Albert of Saxe-Coburg-Gotha (d. 1861): nine children.

[2] Arthur James Balfour, 1848–1930. Educated at Eton and Trinity College, Cambridge. MP (Cons.) for Hertford, 1874–85; for Manchester East, 1885–1906; for the City of London, 1906–22. PM, 1902–5. First Lord of the Admiralty, 1915–16. Foreign Secretary, 1916–19. Lord President of the Council, 1919–22, 1925–9. Earl, 1922.

[3] Herbert Henry Asquith, 1852–1928. Married, 1877, Helen Melland (d. 1891); 1894, Emma Alice Margaret Tennant. MP (Lib.) for East Fife, 1886–1918; for Paisley, 1920–4. Home Secretary, 1892–5. Liberal Imperialist during Boer War. Chancellor of Exchequer, 1905–8. PM, 1908–16. Resigned Liberal leadership, 1926. Earl of Oxford and Asquith, 1925.

[4] Stanley Baldwin, 1867–1947. Educated at Harrow and Trinity College, Cambridge. MP (Cons.) for Bewdley, 1908–37. Financial Secretary, Treasury, 1917–21. President of the Board of Trade, 1921–2. Chancellor of the Exchequer, 1922–3. PM, 1923–4, 1924–9, 1935–7. Lord President of the Council, 1931–5. Earl, and KG, 1937.

First, there is the Address to the Queen. I beg to move: That an humble Address be presented to Her Majesty to convey to Her Majesty the deep sympathy felt by this House in the great sorrow which she has sustained by the death of the late King, Her Majesty's Father, of Blessed and Glorious Memory; To assure Her Majesty that His late Majesty's unsparing devotion to the Service of His Peoples and His inspiring example in the time of their greatest peril will always be held in affectionate and grateful remembrance by them; To express to Her Majesty our loyal devotion to Her Royal Person and our complete conviction that She will, with the Blessing of God, throughout Her Reign work to uphold the liberties and promote the happiness of all Her Peoples. We shall also resolve as follows: That a Message of condolence be sent to the Queen Mother tendering to Her the deep sympathy of this House in Her grief, which is shared by all its Members, and assuring Her of the sincere feelings of affection and respect towards Her Majesty which they will ever hold in their hearts. Then there is the Motion for a message to Queen Mary: That a Message of condolence be sent to Her Majesty Queen Mary tendering to Her the deep sympathy of this House in Her further affliction and assuring Her of the unalterable affection and regard in which Her Majesty is held by all its Members. All the three Prime Ministers or Leaders of the House whom I have cited reviewed the history of the reign that had ended and paid their tribute to the former occupant of the Throne. The reign of Queen Victoria had lasted over 63 years. It is now nearly 115 years since she assumed the Crown. King Edward VII[1] did not complete the tenth year of his reign; King George V[2] reigned for 25 years and our late lamented Sovereign for 15.

With the end of the Victorian era we passed into what I feel we must call 'the terrible 20th century'. Half of it is over and we have survived its fearful convulsions. We stand erect both as an island people and as the centre of a worldwide Commonwealth and Empire, after so much else in other lands has been shattered or fallen to the ground and been replaced by other forces and systems.

When King Edward VII, so long familiar to his generation as Prince of Wales, passed away, both Mr Asquith and Mr Balfour dwelt upon his labours for the cause of peace in Europe, and many called him 'Edward the Peacemaker'. But only four years after his death we were plunged in war by forces utterly beyond our control.

King George V succeeded to a grim inheritance; first, to the fiercest party troubles I have ever seen and taken part in at home, and then to the First World War with its prodigious slaughter. Victory was gained, but the attempt to erect,

---

[1] Albert Edward, 1841–1910. Eldest son of Queen Victoria. Married, 1863, Princess Alexandra. Succeeded as King Edward VII, 1901.

[2] George Frederick Ernest Albert, 1865–1936. Second son of King Edward VII and Queen Alexandra. Became heir to the throne on death of his elder brother Albert Victor, 1892. King of the United Kingdom and British Dominions and Emperor of India, 1910–36.

in the League of Nations, a world instrument which would prevent another hideous conflict, failed. The people of the United States realise today how grievous was the cost to them, in life and treasure, of the isolationism which led them to withdraw from the League of Nations which President Wilson[1] had conceived and which British minds had so largely helped to shape.

The death of King George V, in January, 1936, was followed in less than a year by the abdication, on personal grounds, of King Edward VIII,[2] and the Sovereign whose death we lament today then succeeded his brother. No British monarch in living memory had a harder time. It is true that the party and constitutional quarrels about the House of Lords and Ireland seemed more violent under King George V than those which we have had among ourselves since, but the greatest shocks fell upon our island in the reign of King George VI.

His first three years were clouded by the fears of another world war, and the differences of opinion, and indeed bewilderment, which prevailed about how to avert it. But the war came and never in our long history were we exposed to greater perils of invasion and destruction than in that year when we stood all alone and kept the flag of freedom flying against what seemed, and might easily have proved to be, overwhelming power.

The late King lived through every minute of this struggle with a heart that never quavered and a spirit undaunted; but I, who saw him so often, knew how keenly, with all his full knowledge and understanding of what was happening, he felt personally the ups and downs of this terrific struggle and how he longed to fight in it, arms in hand, himself.

Thus passed six more years of his reign. Victory again crowned our martial struggles, but our island, more than any other country in the world, and for a longer period, had given all that was in it. We had victory with honour and with the respect of the world, victor and vanquished, friend and foe alike.

Alas, we found ourselves in great straits from the exertions which we had made, and then there came, in the midst of the ordeals of the aftermath and of the problems which lay about us, a new menace. The surmounting of one form of mortal peril seemed soon only to be succeeded by the shadow of another. The King felt – as the Leader of the Opposition, who was his first Minister for so long, knows well – the fresh anxieties which thronged up against us and the disappointment that followed absolute triumph without lasting security or peace.

Though deeply smitten by physical afflictions, he never lost his courage or faith that Great Britain, her Commonwealth and Empire, would in the

---

[1] Thomas Woodrow Wilson, 1856–1924. President, Princeton University, 1902–10. Governor, New Jersey, 1911–13. US President, 1913–21.

[2] Edward Albert Christian George Andrew Patrick David, 1894–1972. Prince of Wales, 1910–36. Succeeded his father as King Edward VIII, Jan. 1936. Abdicated, Dec. 1936. Duke of Windsor, 1936. Governor of the Bahamas, 1940–5.

end come through. Nor did he lose hope that another hateful war will be warded off, perhaps to no small extent by the wisdom and experience of the many realms over which he ruled. As I have said, his was the hardest reign of modern times. He felt and shared the sufferings of his peoples as if they were his own. To the end he was sure we should not fail; to the end he hoped and prayed we might reach a period of calm and repose. We salute his memory because we all walked the stony, uphill road with him and he with us.

Let me now speak of his Consort, the Queen Mother, to whom our second Motion is dedicated. The thoughts of all of us go forth to her. It was with her aid that King George was able to surmount his trials. Let no one underrate what they were. To be lifted far above class and party strife or the daily excitements of internal politics, to be restrained within the strict limits of a constitutional Sovereign – in his case most faithfully upheld – and yet to feel that the fate and fortunes of the whole nation and of his realms were centred not only in his office but in his soul, that was the ordeal which he could not have endured without the strong, loving support of his devoted and untiring wife and Consort. To her we accord, on behalf of those we represent, all that human sympathy can bestow.

The third Motion is addressed to Queen Mary, who has now lost another of her sons, one killed on active service, the other worn down in public duty. May she find comfort in the regard and affection which flow to her from all who have watched and admired her through these long years when her example has inspired not only her family, but all the British people.

The House will observe in the Royal Proclamation the importance and significance assigned to the word 'Realm'. There was a time – and not so long ago – when the word 'Dominion' was greatly esteemed. But now, almost instinctively and certainly spontaneously, the many States, nations and races included in the British Commonwealth and Empire have found in the word 'Realm' the expression of their sense of unity, combined in most cases with a positive allegiance to the Crown or a proud and respectful association with it. Thus we go forward on our long and anxious journey, moving together in freedom and hope, spread across the oceans and under every sky and climate though we be.

So far I have spoken of the past, but with the new reign we must all feel our contact with the future. A fair and youthful figure, Princess, wife and mother, is the heir to all our traditions and glories, never greater than in her father's days, and to all our perplexities and dangers, never greater in peace-time than now. She is also heir to all our united strength and loyalty. She comes to the Throne at a time when a tormented mankind stands uncertainly poised between world catastrophe and a golden age. That it should be a golden age of art and letters, we can only hope – science and machinery have their other tales to tell – but it is certain that if a true and lasting peace can be achieved, and if the nations will only let each other alone, an immense and undreamed of prosperity with culture and leisure ever more widely spread can come, perhaps even easily and swiftly, to the masses of the people in every land.

Let us hope and pray that the accession to our ancient Throne of Queen Elizabeth II may be the signal for such a brightening salvation of the human scene.

Cabinet: conclusions
(Cabinet papers, 128/24)

11 February 1952   Prime Minister's Room
Secret   House of Commons
5 p.m.
Cabinet Meeting No. 15 of 1952

The Cabinet considered what advice should be offered to The Queen regarding the date of Her Coronation. The Precedents pointed to a date in the early summer of 1953. It was to be hoped that by then conditions might be more settled than they seemed likely to be in 1952. If the Coronation took place in 1953, it might be possible for The Queen, if she so wished, to visit Australia and New Zealand in the winter of 1952–1953. The Minister of Works said that there would be a great difficulty in making the necessary building preparations at Westminster Abbey for a Coronation in 1952.

The Cabinet –
1. Asked the Lord Chancellor to verify that there would be no constitutional objections to a Royal Visit to other Commonwealth countries, if desired by Her Majesty, in advance of the Coronation.
2. Invited the Prime Minister in ascertaining Her Majesty's wishes, to indicate their preference for holding the Coronation in the early summer of 1953.

2. The Cabinet had before them a memorandum by the Lord Chancellor and the Secretary of State for Scotland[1] (C(52)26) suggesting that the Coronation Stone should be replaced in the Coronation Chair in Westminster Abbey.

The Cabinet favoured this proposal but thought that, before any announcement was made, it would be desirable to consult through their Leader certain prominent Scottish Members of the Opposition. Similar consultations had taken place previously on matters concerning the Stone.

The Cabinet –
1. Approved in principle the proposal to restore the Stone of Scone to Westminster Abbey.

---

[1] James Gray Stuart, 1897–1971. 3rd son of the 17th Earl of Moray. Educated at Eton. On active service, 1914–18 (MC and bar). MP (Cons.) for Moray and Nairn, 1923–59. Entered Whips' Office, 1935. Deputy Chief Whip, 1938–41. PC, 1939. Government Chief Whip, 1941–5. Chief Opposition Whip, 1945–8. Secretary of State for Scotland, 1951–7. Viscount, 1959.

2. Invited the Prime Minister to seek the comments of leading Scottish members of the Opposition on this proposal.

3. The Cabinet had before them a memorandum by the Secretary of State for War inviting them to decide whether the Imperial War Graves Commission should proceed with their plans for a modest memorial at Dunkirk at a cost of some £23,000 or should erect there at more substantial cost a national memorial commemorating the Dunkirk operation.

The Secretary of State for War said that, as the site which had been selected was on the sea front, any memorial which included a garden as had been previously suggested by the Cabinet, must have a surrounding wall to retain the soil. A design had therefore been prepared for a national memorial which took the form of a courtyard surrounded by cloisters and enclosing a Garden of Remembrance. The cost to the public of erecting a memorial to this design would be about £77,000.

The Cabinet were disposed to favour the erection of a national memorial in preference to the more limited project of a small archway designed to commemorate those soldiers who fell in the 1939–40 Campaign and had no known graves. They did not, however, wish to authorise a grant for this purpose in the current economic circumstances.

The Cabinet – Deferred their decision on the nature of the memorial to be erected at Dunkirk; and invited the Secretary of State for War to bring this matter before them again in the summer of 1953.

4. The Cabinet were informed that an atomic bomb of British manufacture was to be exploded in Australia under test conditions during the summer. All the arrangements for this test had now been concluded with the Australian Government and the party in charge of it were shortly due to leave for Australia. Some information about the experiment had already found its way to the Press, and it was desirable that an official announcement should be made at an early date.

The Prime Minister said that no time should now be lost in settling the terms of the announcement, in consultation with the Australian Government, and arranging for its simultaneous release in this country and in Australia. The Paymaster-General undertook to make arrangements accordingly.

Winston S. Churchill to Bernard Baruch
(Churchill papers, 2/210)

13 February 1952

My dear Bernie,

I have been meaning and trying to find a moment to write to you ever since my return to this country.

I cannot tell you how much it meant to me to be with you, and in such

FEBRUARY 1952 267

peace and comfort, my dear friend. As you well know, these visits, although I am treated everywhere with the greatest kindness, are a heavy load; and to have a few days in such pleasant company and surroundings does more to refresh and strengthen me than anything else. Thank you so much for all your care for me, and for my party.

My cold now has been vanquished. I worked in bed most of the time on the ship, and did not leave my quarters at all. There was plenty to do, but except for one day, we had a very smooth passage.

We have sustained a terrible loss in the death of King George VI, who was a devoted and tireless servant of his country, and these are sad days indeed. But I am sure that in his daughter we have one who is in every way able to bear the heavy burden she must now carry.

I hope that all goes well with you, and with Elizabeth, and that you are benefitting from the rest and sunshine of South Carolina.

Once more, dear Bernie, my deepest thanks for your great kindness and hospitality.

Winston S. Churchill to Clement Attlee
(Premier papers, 11/252)

13 February 1952

My dear Attlee,

The approach of the Coronation is sure to raise once more the issue of the Scone Stone, and I am therefore in favour of a firm decision being taken and made public. Before taking such a step I think it appropriate to acquaint you with my intention and to seek your agreement to the course which we have in mind, so that controversy may as far as possible be limited.

As you know, the Stone is at present in the custody of the Dean of Westminster,[1] but it has not been put back in the Coronation Chair since the theft on Christmas Day, 1950.[2] Last December the Dean of Westminster asked that the Government should announce their intentions soon and said that he

[1] Alan Campbell Don, 1885–1966. Educated at Magdalen College, Oxford. Married, 1914, Muriel Gwenda McConnell. Vicar, Norton-by-Malton, Yorkshire, 1917–21. Provost, St Paul's Cathedral Church, Dundee, 1921–31. Chaplain and Secretary to Archbishop of Canterbury, 1931–41. Chaplain to the King, 1934–46; to the Speaker of the House of Commons, 1936–46. Canon of Westminster, 1941–6. Rector, St Margaret's Church, Westminster, 1941–6. Dean of Westminster, 1946–59. KCVO, 1948.

[2] The Stone of Scone is an oblong block of red sandstone that for centuries was used in the coronation of the monarch of Scotland. On 25 Dec. 1950 four Scottish students from the University of Glasgow stole the stone from Westminster Abbey and took it back to Glasgow. During the journey it broke into two pieces and had to be repaired. In Apr. 1951 the stone was recovered from Arbroath Abbey, a place of significance in the coronation of Scottish kings of old, and returned to Westminster. In 1996, the House of Commons voted to return the stone to Scotland: it arrived at Edinburgh Castle on Nov. 30, St Andrew's Day. It currently rests alongside the crown jewels of Scotland in the Crown Room.

was most anxious the Stone should be replaced in the chair without delay. I cannot myself see that anything will be gained by postponing a decision.

I therefore propose to advise The Queen that the Stone should be restored to the Coronation Chair at a suitable date after the Funeral of the late King. I consider that its replacement, which would not be accompanied by any ceremony, might appropriately be the subject of an arranged Question and Answer in the House of Commons.

I hope you will agree that this matter, which is of such close concern to the Crown, should not be one for Parliamentary dispute. If so, perhaps you will let me know whether you are in accord with the course I propose.

Winston S. Churchill to Sir Edward Bridges
Prime Minister's Personal Minute M.50/52
(Premier papers, 11/295)

13 February 1952

I have now been able to consider the future organisation for Atomic Energy. The importance of this matter from both the military and civil points of view demands exceptional treatment. The present arrangements have, as stated in the resolution carried in the House of Lords on 5 July 1951, had grave drawbacks. But it may be possible to leave the matter under direct Government control if there is a new approach, coupled with special provision to provide elasticity and avoid delay in getting decisions.

The most satisfactory solution in present circumstances would be to place the whole organisation immediately under the Prime Minister: but I realise that this would cause accounting difficulties. I therefore propose that the Minister of Supply's functions under the Atomic Energy Act should be transferred to the Minister of Defence. Though geographically it should remain where it is at present the Directorate of Atomic Energy would become a self-contained block in the Ministry of Defence: it would also be necessary to make provision for most of the common services now rendered to the Directorate by the other Branches of the Ministry of Supply.

I do not think that any problems will arise even when the Minister of Defence is no longer the Prime Minister. I propose that Ministerial direction should, subject to the formal responsibility of the Minister of Defence, be exercised by Lord Cherwell so long as he is in the Cabinet. He will report to me. Lord Cherwell will answer questions in the Lords and I shall do so in the Commons. The accounting responsibility will be with the Secretary to the Ministry of Defence.

Pray let me know whether you see any difficulties in these proposals and confirm that the change could be achieved by Order-in-Council under the Ministers of the Crown (Transfer of Functions) Act.

I will then discuss the proposals with the Minister for Defence (Designate).

FEBRUARY 1952

Cabinet: conclusions
(*Cabinet papers, 128/24*)

14 February 1952
Secret
5 p.m.
Cabinet Meeting No. 17 of 1952

1. The Prime Minister informed the Cabinet that the Coronation was likely to be held in the spring of 1953. It was understood that the Government of Australia and New Zealand would probably prefer that The Queen should postpone her visit to those countries until after her Coronation. The Royal Visit to Australia and New Zealand might therefore be made in the autumn of 1953.

[. . .]

4. The Cabinet had before them a memorandum by the Foreign Secretary (C(52)32) recommending the resumption of negotiations with Egypt on defence questions and on the Sudan.

The Foreign Secretary said that, if we could reach an agreement with the Egyptian Government involving their participation in the Middle East Command and the grant of full facilities to allied forces in time of war or of threat of war in the Canal Zone, we might be able to arrange, not only to retain in Egypt the technicians needed for the maintenance of the base, but also to maintain indefinitely a small combatant force in the Canal Zone. It might be necessary, however, to contemplate basing the major part of our force elsewhere in the Middle East, perhaps at Gaza or in Jordan. He sought authority to embark on the first three stages of the negotiations set out in Annex I to C(52)32, involving agreement to resume discussions, the formulation of an agreed agenda and the issue of a joint communiqué.

In discussion the following points were made:

a) The British base in the Canal Zone was the largest military base in the world and included costly accommodations, maintenance facilities and stores. A substantial transfer of the base to another part of the Middle East would be extremely costly, and the Chancellor of the Exchequer asked that he should be kept in touch with this aspect of the negotiations. No accommodation or facilities at present existed in Gaza, where there were large numbers of Arab refugees who would have to be moved before we could transfer forces there. We should not commit ourselves to maintaining the Canal Zone base by the use of civilian staff only, since civilians would not accept present living conditions in the Zone.

b) The Prime Minister saw serious objection to the suggestion that we should contemplate the removal of the British mobile land forces from the Canal Zone within a period of one year. Recent experience had demonstrated our power to maintain our position in Egypt, and he did not think we should relinquish it until our forces were replaced by adequate allied forces under a Middle East Command. He therefore suggested that we should make no immediate offer of withdrawal, but should keep this in reserve as a possible means of bringing pressure to bear on our Allies to induce them to share with us the responsibility of defending the international waterway. Even if satisfactory plans could be made for Four-Power defence of the area with Egyptian co-operation, it would probably be impracticable for us to leave the Zone with a year.

In discussion it was pointed out that paragraph 2(d) of C(52)32 did not contemplate that we should withdraw our troops from the Canal Zone unless a prior settlement satisfactory to us had been reached on all the other outstanding questions relating to the defence of the Middle East.

c) The Foreign Secretary said that, not only were we committed to the re-opening of discussions with the Egyptian Government, but we had at the present time a more favourable opportunity to resume negotiations than any that was likely to occur again. The present Government in Egypt might, if we delayed, be replaced by one much less well-disposed to us.

The Cabinet –
1) Invited the Foreign Secretary to authorise Her Majesty's Ambassador in Egypt, if this became necessary to embark on Stages I and II of the negotiations outlined in Annex I to C(52)32.
2) Invited the Foreign Secretary, in the light of their discussion to reconsider the wording of the draft communiqué set out in Stage III of that Annex; and agreed to resume on 18th February their discussion of the communiqué and of the remaining proposals in C(52)32.

In Annex II to C(52)32 were set out two alternative suggestions regarding the attitude which we should adopt to Egyptian claims concerning the Sudan. Under the first proposal we should hold that the all-Sudanese Parliament which was to be elected should decide the question of King Farouk's nominal sovereignty; that the elections for the Parliament should be observed by an International Commission and that the Egyptian Government should send a representative to the Sudan, although there was to be no interference by Egypt in the steps being taken towards Sudanese self-Government or in the freedom of the Sudanese to settle their own future.

In discussion it was suggested that the International Commission proposed in the first of these alternatives, to observe the conduct of Sudanese elections should consist of representatives only of Egypt the United Kingdom and the Sudanese. Wider representation might create an embarrassing precedent in relation to the colonies.

The Cabinet –
3) Agreed that in further negotiations with the Egyptian Government the attitude of the United Kingdom Government towards the Sudanese question should be that suggested in the first paragraph of Annex II to C(52)32.

[. . .]

Winston S. Churchill to Lord Woolton
(Churchill papers[1])

16 February 1952

I have on several previous occasions complained and drawn the attention of the Conservative Central Office to the fact that I think it highly improper for leaflets and advertisements about the publication of various books written by me to be distributed with Party literature.

I was sorry therefore to see, the other day, an advertisement of the new edition of my book, *Lord Randolph Churchill*, amongst other Party pamphlets. It is inappropriate to use the machinery and money of the Party for what people may think is an effort by me to push the sale of my own books. I hope a disclaimer may be issued saying that this was done without my being informed, and the leaflets be withdrawn.

General Lord Ismay to Winston S. Churchill
(Premier papers, 11/369)

16 February 1952
Top Secret

The following is a brief record of your discussion at Chartwell on Saturday, 16th February, with the Chief of Air Staff, Sir William Elliot, and myself.

1. INFRASTRUCTURE

One of the most important things to be decided at Lisbon is the various national contributions to the next instalment of Infrastructure – towards airfields, communications and operational Head-quarters on the Continent – particularly airfields. Eisenhower has insisted that it is vital as a complement to his operational plan that he should have firm decisions on this matter from the Atlantic Council, so that at least the necessary initial work can be put in hand.

2. You agreed that, in order, by example, to induce the Continent countries to make their contribution and ensure that some progress is made, we ought to

---

[1] The file number for this document cannot be established.

guarantee to contribute a token sum of the order of £5 million; but of course, there would have to be consultation with the Chancellor of the Exchequer.

Note: I am getting in touch with the Chancellor with a view to discussing the above with him before I leave for Lisbon.

2. NATO REORGANIZATION

There are two points about this on which, though we shall not have to come to a decision on them at Lisbon, I asked for your views:

a) The location of the central organization of NATO – Paris or London. On this your ruling was that we should press most strongly for London.

b) Whether the permanent head of the organization should be a Secretary General, on the lines of Trygve Lie, or a Director-General – something more like a civilian counterpart of Eisenhower, and what nationality he should be.

On this we agreed that the vital thing is to get the best possible man for the job.

3. MEDITERRANEAN COMMAND

On this matter there looks like being an impasse on the professional level at Lisbon –

a) The Americans will not accept our solution of a British Commander-in-Chief, Mediterranean responsible to the Standing Group and charged with the control of sea communications both to Eisenhower's southern flank and to the Middle East.

b) We will not accept their solution of a British Commander-in-Chief, Mediterranean under Eisenhower.

c) They are now suggesting a compromise under which all Allied Naval forces in the Mediterranean, except the British, will be under Eisenhower, and the British Fleet and Air Forces and their bases in the Mediterranean will be left to operate independently to control British sea communications to the Middle East.

This is obviously a military absurdity. You agreed that on the professional level we should dig our toes in and refuse to agree to what we regard as militarily unsound, and that the issue should be discussed on the Ministerial level at Lisbon.

4. ACTION AGAINST CHINA

A dangerous difference of opinion has revealed itself between the British and American Chiefs of Staff, on which the Chief of Air Staff expressed the view that it would be necessary for the Foreign Secretary to speak to Mr Acheson while they were together in Lisbon.

The point is that the Americans are agreed with us that a useful deterrent, either to the breach of an armistice or to further aggression elsewhere in the Far East – notably Indo-China – might be to make a statement to the Chinese that in either case their aggression would be met by Allied defensive measures not necessarily confined to the actual area of the Chinese attack.

The difference of opinion is on what we should in fact do if such a statement were made but ignored by the Chinese and further aggression ensued –
    a) The American view is that we should
        i) institute a naval blockade of the China coast.
        ii) Undertake widespread bombing of Chinese communications and mining of their rivers. They agreed that such action could not save Tongking or Hong Kong. Their stated object is 'to reduce the capability of China for further aggression in all areas and to reduce the profitability of exploitation of areas of aggression'.
    b) The British military view is that we should confine air action to bombing of rail communications, airfields, etc. in China, leading to the areas of aggression, not therefore widespread bombing over China.

We also consider that naval blockade would be quite ineffective unless we also took action against Russian shipping and ports in the Far East, to this we are opposed.

We are opposed to general war against China or to action which we feel might (almost involuntarily) involve Soviet Russia and lead to global war.

You agreed with these views. The American view is clearly very different from that expressed by the Foreign Secretary in the Foreign Affairs Debate on the 5th February. In view of the serious implications of such a divergence of policy, you agreed to speak to Mr Eden on this before his departure for Lisbon.

Winston S. Churchill to Anthony Eden
Prime Minister's Personal Minute M.61/52
(Premier papers, 11/91)

17 February 1952

Sir Ralph Stevenson's telegram No. 379 of February 15, third paragraph.[1]

I cannot quite understand this paragraph. I did not know we were going to bring in openly large reinforcements. On the contrary I thought we were letting some people go home and putting off our Rodeo preparations at a longer notice. What does the Ambassador mean by saying if the troops themselves could be brought in quickly by air, etc. we might 'get away with it'? The

---

[1] The paragraph reads: 'It is, of course, the case that we do not want to be openly bringing in large reinforcements just at the moment when we are preparing to open negotiations. But if the troops themselves could be brought in quickly by air, without any publicity whatever, we might get away with it. (I presume that their transport and heavy equipment could come by sea without attracting much attention.)'

idea that our negotiations would be hindered by our having sufficient forces on the spot is I am sure mistaken.

Winston S. Churchill to Colonel Malcolm Stoddart-Scott[1]
(Premier papers, 11/229)

17 February 1952

Dear Stoddart-Scott,

I have considered carefully your suggestion that I should invite General Eisenhower to address Members of both Houses of Parliament, and do not think it would be wise for me to do so.

General Eisenhower is Commander-in-Chief serving a number of nations and if he were to speak in London he might feel obliged to speak in other capitals as well.

I understand that it would be possible for further groups of MPs to visit General Eisenhower at SHAPE. This would give an opportunity for him to address them, which I am sure they would greatly value.

Cabinet: conclusions
(Cabinet papers, 128/24)

18 February 1952
Secret
12 noon
Cabinet Meeting No. 18 of 1952

1. The Cabinet's attention was drawn to reports that some change might be made in the Family name of the Queen's children and their descendants. The Cabinet were strongly of the opinion that the Family name of Windsor should be retained; and they invited the Prime Minister to take a suitable opportunity of making their views known to Her Majesty.[2]

[. . .]

5. The Cabinet considered a memorandum by the Foreign Secretary

---

[1] Malcolm Stoddart-Scott, 1901–73. Educated at University of Leeds. Lt, RAMC, 1939–45. Married, 1940, Elsie Mary Parkinson: two children. OBE, 1945. MP (Cons.) for Pudsey and Otley, 1945–50; for Ripon, 1950–73. Knighted, 1957. Hon. Col., Mobile Defence Corps, 1957–60.

[2] Early in the royal marriage HRH Prince Philip argued that the family should name be Mountbatten rather than Windsor. At the time of her accession, the Queen's pleasure was to retain the name Windsor. In 1960 an accommodation was reached by the Privy Council, which declared that the name Mountbatten-Windsor would apply to male-line descendants of the Queen without royal styles and titles. Members of the Royal Family do not usually use a surname, but some descendants of HM the Queen with royal styles have used Mountbatten-Windsor when a surname has been required for legal or other purposes.

(C(52)43) covering draft instructions to Her Majesty's Ambassador in Cairo on the resumption of negotiations with Egypt. Cabinet's discussion on the 14th February,[1] comprised (i) a draft telegram containing a revised text of the communiqué which might be issued jointly by the two Governments when agreement to resume negotiations had been reached; and (ii) a draft despatch setting out the results which we might hope to see emerge from the negotiations in respect both of defence and of the Sudan.

The Cabinet considered first the text of the suggested communiqué. The discussions were there described as being held 'with a view to reaching a defence settlement and an agreement regarding the Sudan'. The Foreign Secretary said that he would prefer that the communiqué should mention only defence, because of the risk of creating the impression that the future of the Sudan was being settled without proper consultation with the Sudanese. If it proved necessary to make any reference to the Sudanese problem, it might suffice to say that the discussions were being held 'with a view to reaching a defence settlement and agreement on other outstanding issues'. But Her Majesty's Ambassador should be asked to seek fresh instructions if a reference to defence alone was not acceptable to the Egyptian Government.

The Cabinet –

1) Agreed that Her Majesty's Ambassador should be instructed, if negotiations were resumed, to endeavour to obtain agreement on a joint communiqué which made no reference direct or indirect to the Sudan.

2) Subject to the conclusion 1) above, approved the terms of the draft telegram in Annex A of C(52)43.

A discussion followed on the draft despatch in Annex B to C(52)43, in the course of which the following points were made:

a) The line of approach to the Egyptian Government laid down in this draft was in its main essentials in harmony with the Four-Power proposals. It was intended to provide for the evacuation of British forces from the Canal Zone base only if it was agreed that the base should be made available to an Allied Middle East Command.

b) It was proposed that any agreement under which we relinquished possession of the Canal Zone base should apply only to the fixed installations, such as buildings, and not to movable equipment or stores.

c) The Prime Minister saw objection to the proposal in paragraph 8 (2) of the draft despatch, which involved handing over the base installations to the Egyptian Government as a preliminary to their being made available to the Allied Middle East Command. He thought that we should be in a position of dangerous weakness, after we had

[1] See Cabinet: conclusions, Feb. 14, para. 4, reproduced above (pp. 269–71).

handed over the installations to the Egyptians, if the Four Power arrangements didn't come into operation at once. He would much prefer an arrangement by which our responsibility was transferred directly to the Middle East Command. It might indeed be best to insist on Four-Power negotiations at the outset and on an agreement by which Egypt would be associated on terms of equality with the other Powers in the Middle East Command as a prior condition of any arrangement affecting the Canal Zone base.

d) On the other hand it was pointed out that the purpose of the paragraph to which the Prime Minister had drawn attention, as of the rest of the despatch, was to link evacuation of British forces from the Canal Zone and the handing over of the military base to the Egyptian Government with satisfactory arrangements for the use of the base by Middle East Command. The reason for transferring the base to the Egyptian Government in the first instance was that it was on Egyptian territory and none of the other Powers who would be concerned in a Middle East Command had at present any right to hold or use military property in Egypt.

The Foreign Secretary said that his present proposals preserved our position at least as fully as the Four-Power proposals put to the Egyptian Government in the summer of 1951, under which no foreign forces were to be stationed in Egypt without the Egyptian Government's agreement. While it would be possible to refrain from entering into direct negotiations with the Egyptian Government and to insist instead on Five-Power talks, he must remind the Cabinet that the Egyptians seemed more likely to be willing to make a satisfactory settlement with us alone in the first place than with the Four Powers, and also that in Four-Power discussions with them we should be likely to find ourselves under dangerous pressure to make unwise concessions, particularly in relation to the Sudan. He thought it preferable to begin with direct talks between ourselves and the Egyptians and urged that these should begin at once; we should otherwise be open to the criticism of having missed a valuable opportunity and the position of the present well-disposed Egyptian Government would be seriously weakened.

The Cabinet –
   3) Agreed to resume consideration of C(52)43 at a further meeting later in the day.

FEBRUARY 1952 277

Cabinet: conclusions
(*Cabinet papers, 128/24*)

18 February 1952
Secret
10 p.m.
Cabinet Meeting No. 19 of 1952

[...]

2. The Cabinet resumed their discussion of the Foreign Secretary's memorandum (C(52)43) covering draft instructions to Her Majesty's Ambassador in Cairo on the resumption of negotiations with Egypt.

The Prime Minister said that he had been considering what changes could be made in the draft despatch set out in Annex B of C(52)43 in order to meet the points which he had raised in the Cabinet's discussions earlier in the day. He now suggested that sub-paragraphs (1)–(4) of paragraph 8 of the draft should be recast as follows:

'(1) If agreement can be reached upon the establishment of an Allied Middle East Command, with Egypt's participation as a founder member therein, only such British land forces would remain in Egypt as were considered by the Supreme Allied Commander, Middle East, in agreement with the Egyptian military authorities, to be necessary to sustain the Egyptian land forces available for the defence of Egypt and the maintenance of the international waterway of the Suez Canal.

(2) Her Majesty's Government would welcome the opportunity of withdrawing other forces which the emergency has compelled them to move to the Canal Zone.

(3) The Egyptian armed forces will assume the task of providing for the security from land and air attack, and for the local safeguarding, of the Allied military base and the Suez Canal. In this they will be aided by such forces as the Allied Middle East Command may consider necessary. The important military base installations on the Suez Canal will pass under the Allied Middle East Command, of which Egypt will be a founder member, provided that all stores and munitions, including machine tools, which have been provided at British expense will remain British property to be disposed of as circumstances may require in the common interest, Great Britain being credited with any contribution made at her expense.

(4) The United Kingdom will retain in Egypt such technical and administrative personnel as are required to maintain at a state of operational readiness British military equipment held in the Allied military base.

(5) The overall direction of the air defence will be vested in the Allied Middle East Command, operating through an Allied Air Defence Organisation. This shall be stationed in Egypt together with any necessary

personnel, including troops for their defence, which may be considered by the Supreme Allied Commander, Middle East, in agreement with the Egyptian military authorities, to be necessary to supplement the Egyptian air forces and ground protection forces available.'

He also suggested that sub-paragraph (9) of paragraph 8, and the whole of paragraph 9, should be deleted.

The Foreign Secretary said that, while he was content with the framework of the rearrangement proposed by the Prime Minister, he felt bound to warn the Cabinet that, if the negotiations were to succeed, it would be necessary to make certain further concessions to the Egyptians which had been included in his original draft despatch. In order to reach an agreement, he thought we should have to give a definite undertaking that, once an Allied Middle East Command was established, we would withdraw from Egypt, within a specified period, all British land forces which were not required by the Allied Commander. He also thought that we should have to give an assurance that British military technicians at the base in the Canal Zone would be progressively replaced by British civilians or by Egyptians, and a similar assurance that British air forces would eventually be replaced by Egyptians, as the latter became fully efficient. He therefore suggested the following amendments of the Prime Minister's revised text of this part of the despatch:

(i) In the new sub-paragraph (1), after 'therein' delete the words 'only such British land forces would remain in Egypt as were' and insert: 'Her Majesty's Government will progressively withdraw from Egypt, within a limited period to be determined, all British land forces save those which are'.

(ii) In the new sub-paragraph (3), delete the words 'In this they will be aided by such forces as the Allied Middle East Command may consider necessary'.

(iii) At the end of the new sub-paragraph (4), add the following sentence: 'These personnel will so far as possible be replaced by British civilian technicians and wherever practicable by Egyptian personnel trained in the handling of British stores and equipment'.

(iv) In the new sub-paragraph (5), for the second sentence substitute the following: 'The Egyptian Government will permit the stationing in Egypt of such Allied air forces and ground protection forces as may be considered by the Supreme Allied Commander, Middle East, in agreement with the Egyptian military authorities, to be necessary to supplement the Egyptian air forces available. These Allied forces will be replaced by Egyptian units and personnel progressively as sufficient of the latter can be trained and equipped to the requisite standard.'

In the discussion which followed the Foreign Secretary made it clear that it was not his intention that Her Majesty's Ambassador in Cairo should offer all these concessions at the outset of his negotiations. The purpose of this part of the draft despatch was to let the Ambassador know, for his guidance, how far the United Kingdom Government would be prepared to go in order to reach an agreement with the Egyptian Government. The Foreign Secretary thought it important that we should lose no time in reopening negotiations as soon as the Egyptians were ready to do so; for the present Government in Egypt were not in a strong political position and, if they fell, they were likely to be succeeded by Ministers who would be less disposed to reach a friendly agreement with us. Although he believed that the concessions which he had indicated would have to be made in the end, if an agreement was to be reached, he was content that Her Majesty's Ambassador should restrict himself in his opening conversations to proposing an agenda for the talks and the issue of a joint communiqué in the terms already approved by the Cabinet. He could then report the results of this initial conversation before going further.

The Cabinet agreed that the Foreign Secretary should send to Her Majesty's Ambassador in Cairo a despatch in the terms of the draft in Annex B of C(52)43, subject to the amendments proposed by the Prime Minister. In this he should make it clear that paragraph 8 of the despatch represented the kind of agreement which we should like to make, and at which he should aim in his later discussions with the Egyptian Government. The Foreign Secretary should say, however, that the Cabinet recognised that some further concessions might have to be made to the Egyptians and would be prepared, if necessary, to make the concessions indicated in the amendments shown in paragraphs (i)–(iv) above. These, however, were being mentioned to the Ambassador at this stage for his guidance only, and they should not be communicated to the Egyptian Government without further authority from the Cabinet. The Ambassador should open the discussions by proposing an agenda for the talks (as set out in paragraph 6 of the draft despatch) and the issue of a joint communiqué in the terms approved by the Cabinet at their meeting earlier in the day. He should report the results of this preliminary conversation and await further instructions before proceeding with his discussions.

The Cabinet –

Invited the Foreign Secretary to instruct Her Majesty's Ambassador in Cairo in the sense indicated above.

Winston S. Churchill to John Maclay[1]
Prime Minister's Personal Minute M.64/52
(Premier papers, 11/17)

19 February 1952

I have read in the newspapers this morning about the imposition of a service charge on passengers arriving at airfields in this country. Please inform me why you did not bring your proposal to charge this levy before the Cabinet.

John Maclay to Winston S. Churchill
(Premier papers, 11/17)

19 February 1952

The answer to your minute about the passenger service charge is that the new charge raises only about £200,000 per annum, that there are numerous precedents for a charge of this kind – both in other countries and in the shipping world – and that it was agreed between the Chancellor of the Exchequer and myself after discussion at the Economic Policy Committee's Sub-Committee on the Economic situation (EA(E)(51) 5th Meeting). In the light of the foregoing it did not occur to me that it might be desirable to take the matter to the Cabinet.

The State, of course, provides the aerodromes to which the airlines, British and foreign, operate and also provides the many highly technical navigational aids which enable the airlines to fly through our congested air spaces and land in practically all weathers with a high degree of safety and regularity. The only charge at present made for these costly facilities is the landing fee, which recoups only about one-third of the cost of providing them. Thus, at present there is a substantial subsidy to all commercial aircraft, British and foreign, landing in this country and it has always been the acknowledging aim to eliminate this subsidy in the long run.

In view of the serious financial position of the country, I have recently been strongly pressed by the Chancellor of the Exchequer to reduce this subsidy by increasing the charges and as commercial flying is now making steady progress, both in the volume of traffic carried and financially, I agreed with him to raise an additional £200,000 per annum by imposing a charge of 5/- to 7/6d for each passenger landing in this country from abroad. The charge is, of course, very small in relation to the fare – e.g. 7/6d compared with a return

---

[1] John Scott Maclay, 1905–92. Educated at Winchester College and Trinity College, Cambridge. Married, 1930, Betty L'Estrange Astley. MP (Nat. Lib.) for Montrose, 1940–50; for Renfrew West, 1950–64. Member, British Merchant Shipping Mission, Washington DC, 1941; Head of Mission, 1944. CMG, 1944. Parliamentary Secretary, Ministry of Production, 1945. Minister of Transport and Civil Aviation, 1951–2. PC, 1952. Minister of State for Colonial Affairs, 1956–7. Secretary of State for Scotland, 1957–62. CH, 1962. Viscount, 1964. Lord-Lieutenant of Renfrewshire, 1967–80. KT, 1973.

FEBRUARY 1952 281

fare of about £175–£250 to or from New York, and 5/- compared with a return fare of £12–£15 to or from Paris. About half of the total will fall on British airlines, the other half on foreign.

I should add that this is one of a number of economies to the taxpayer being made which will reduce the total Estimate for civil aviation by about one-third in 1952/3 compared with that for 1951/52.[1]

Cabinet: conclusions
(Cabinet papers, 128/24)

20 February 1952   Prime Minister's Room
Secret   House of Commons
4 p.m.
Cabinet Meeting No. 20 of 1952

1. The Prime Minister informed the Cabinet that it was the Queen's Pleasure that the Coronation should take place in May 1953.

The Cabinet –
   (1) Agreed that the Commonwealth Relations Office should verify that this date presented no difficulties for other Commonwealth Governments.
   (2) Invited the Home Secretary to arrange for a public announcement to be made as soon as possible after the replies of the other Commonwealth Governments had been received.

2. The Prime Minister said that it was The Queen's Pleasure that She and Her descendants should continue to bear the Family name of Windsor. A draft proclamation to this effect should be prepared and submitted for Her Majesty's approval. Before this was promulgated The Queen's Private Secretary would notify Her decision to the Governments of other Commonwealth countries through Her Majesty's personal representatives in those countries.

The Cabinet –

Invited the Lord Chancellor, in consultation with the Home Secretary and the Law Officers, to prepare and submit to the Cabinet a draft proclamation declaring that The Queen and Her descendants would continue to bear the Family name of Windsor.

[. . .]

---

[1] Churchill wrote at the bottom of the page: 'You should at least have asked the Cabinet Secretary whether the question should be brought before the Cabinet or not. He would have reported to me. I do not like to read of additional imposts of a controversial nature in the newspapers.'

February 1952

Winston S. Churchill to Matrika Koirala[1]
(Premier papers, 11/225)

21 February 1952

Your Excellency,

I write to acknowledge the receipt of your letter,[2] delivered to me personally by His Excellency the Nepalese Ambassador in London,[3] in which you inform me of your appointment as Prime Minister and Foreign Minister of Nepal with effect from November 16.

I am indeed glad to receive this assurance of good will and I know that the Government of Nepal will continue to maintain the excellent and most friendly relations which have existed between our two countries for so long, and which have been proved, on so many occasions, to the great benefit of both Nepal and of the British Commonwealth.

I have the honour to be, with the highest consideration,

Your Excellency's obedient Servant.

House of Commons: Oral Answers
(Hansard)

25 February 1952

ATOMIC ENERGY TESTS, AUSTRALIA

Mr R. J. Mellish[4] asked the Prime Minister if he will make a statement on the intended visit of Ministers to Australia to view the intended atomic energy experiment in that country.

The Prime Minister: No Ministers will be visiting Australia to view the test of the United Kingdom's atomic weapon there.

Mr Mellish: Is the right hon. Gentleman aware how glad we all are to hear that?

Mr Emrys Hughes:[5] Will the Prime Minister invite a delegation of the

---

[1] Matrika Prasad Koirala, 1912–97. First President of the Nepali Congress, 1950–2. PM of Nepal, 1951–2, 1953–5. Nepali Ambassador to US, 1961–4.

[2] Of 23 Nov. 1951, which informed Churchill of his appointment as PM and Foreign Minister of Nepal. The concluding paragraph read: 'I avail myself of this opportunity to assure Your Excellency that it will be my earnest endeavour to carry out the Government in a democratic way, and to further strengthen the friendly ties so happily subsisting between our two countries for more than a century.'

[3] Shanker Shamsher Jang Bahadur Rana, 1909–79. Born in Kathmandu. Maj.-Gen., 1927. Director General, Public Works Dept, 1936–43; Roads and Railways Dept, 1946–7; Police Dept, 1947–9. KBE, 1946. Gen., 1948. ADC Gen. and CoS to the PM, 1948–9. Ambassador to UK, France, US and the Netherlands, 1949–54. GBE, 1949.

[4] Robert Joseph Mellish, 1913–98. On active service, 1939–45. Maj., 1945. MP (Lab.) for Rotherhithe, 1946–50; for Bermondsey, 1950–82. Minister for Public Building and Works, 1967–9. Parliamentary Secretary to the Treasury, 1974–6; Labour Chief Whip, 1969–76. Baron, 1985.

[5] Emrys Hughes, 1894–1969. Educated at City of Leeds Training College. Editor, *Forward*, 1931–46.

Christian churches, headed by the Archbishop of Canterbury,[1] to see the explosion of this infernal machine and to report progress?

The Prime Minister: I am not quite sure about that. Anyhow, as the whole of the preparations were made by the right hon. Gentleman opposite, when he was Prime Minister, perhaps the hon. Member for Ayrshire, South (Mr Emrys Hughes), would ascertain from him whether he desires a delegation of Christian churches to examine the infernal machine for which he has accepted responsibility.

Mr Emrys Hughes: On a point of order. In view of the complete evasiveness of that answer, and owing to the fact that I was no more responsible for the last Government than the Prime Minister was responsible for Mr Neville Chamberlain[2] I beg to give notice that I will raise this matter at the earliest possible opportunity on the Adjournment.

Winston S. Churchill: speech
(Hansard)

26 February 1952   House of Commons

VOTE OF CENSURE[3]

The Prime Minister (Mr Winston Churchill): When I learned the text of the Motion which has been put upon the Order Paper and saw that it took the unusual form of a personal Vote of Censure upon me I am bound to say that I did expect that some more serious attempt to frame and sustain charges would have been made than we have heard from the right hon. Gentleman the Member for Lewisham, South (Mr H. Morrison). I have hardly ever listened – from a skilled Parliamentarian – to such a weak, vague, wandering harangue which at no point touched the realities or which was so largely composed of

---

MP (Lab.) for South Ayrshire, 1946–69. Married, 1947, Nan Hardie. Author of *Winston Churchill in War and Peace* (1950), *Pilgrim's Progress in Russia* (1957), *Portrait of a Politician* (1962), *Sir Alec Douglas-Home* (1964), *Parliament and Mumbo-Jumbo* (1966), *The Prince, the Crown, and the Cash* (1969), and *Sidney Silverman: Rebel in Parliament* (1970), along with a variety of socialist anti-war pamphlets.

[1] Geoffrey Francis Fisher, 1887–1972. Ordained priest, 1913. Headmaster, Repton School, 1914–32. Bishop of Chester, 1932–9. Bishop of London, 1939–44. Archbishop of Canterbury, 1945–61. Knighted, 1953. Baron, 1961.

[2] (Arthur) Neville Chamberlain, 1869–1940. Educated at Rugby and Mason College, Birmingham. Lord Mayor of Birmingham, 1915–16. Director-General of National Service, 1916–17. MP (Cons.) for Birmingham Ladywood, 1918–29; for Edgbaston, 1929–40. Postmaster-General, 1922–3. Paymaster-General, 1923. Minister of Health, 1923, 1924–9, 1931. Chancellor of the Exchequer, 1923–4, 1931–7. Leader of the Conservative Party, 1937. PM, 1937–40. Lord President of the Council, May–Nov. 1940.

[3] 'Churchill's account of decisions taken by the previous Government aroused fierce controversy. The text of the proceedings from *Hansard* does not, however, convey the uproar and anger of the Opposition at what was regarded by them as an unworthy debating device' (Rhodes James, *Winston S. Churchill, His Complete Speeches*, vol. 8, p. 8342). The motion was defeated 311 to 284.

quotations of all kinds, some of his own, and none selected with a view to proving or sustaining any effective case.

I shall in due course – I hope I shall not too long detain the House – deal with the attack which is made upon me today, but if I had to confine myself to those aspects of it which have been dealt on by the right hon. Gentleman I am bound to say I should find myself very short of material with which to reply.

I wish, first of all, to draw the attention of the House to the agreement we reached in Washington about the atomic bomb. We reached an agreement about its not being used from the East Anglian base without British consent. This agreement states in a formal and public manner what had already been reached as a verbal understanding between the late Prime Minister and President Truman.

We felt, however, that it would be an improvement if the position were made public and formal, and I expect that will be the general opinion. A much more important atomic development is now before us. I was not aware until I took office that not only had the Socialist Government made the atomic bomb as a matter of research, but that they had created at the expense of many scores of millions of pounds the important plant necessary for its regular production. This weapon will be tested in the course of the present year by agreement with the Australian Government at some suitable place in that continent.

This achievement is certainly a real advantage to us and when I informed the Americans in Washington of the position which had been reached quite a new atmosphere was created on this subject. I was interested to read in the newspapers on Monday week the following statement by Senator MacMahon, the author of the MacMahon Act of 1946 which, under extreme penalties, forbade all sharing of secrets with Great Britain or other countries:

> 'The achievement of an atomic explosion by Great Britain, when an accomplished fact, will contribute to the keeping of the peace because it will add to the free world's total deterring power. This event is likely to raise in still sharper focus the problem of atomic co-operation between ourselves and Great Britain. The British contributed heavily to our own war-time atomic project. But due to a series of unfortunate circumstances the nature of the agreements which made this contribution possible was not disclosed to me and my colleagues on the Senate special atomic energy committee at the time we framed the law in 1946. Now we may consider rethinking the entire situation with all the facts in front of us.'

This is a very important declaration. We must now await the result of the experiment in Australia. While paying all credit to the late Government and their scientists for the action which they have taken I must, as an old Parliamentarian, express my surprise that a full and clear statement was not made of this policy to Parliament, especially in view of the immense sums of money which were voted by this House without their having any clear appreciation of what was being done. There was no reason why Parliament in time of peace should not have been made fully aware, not, of course, of the technical details, but of the large scale new departure in policy adopted on so grave a matter.

The Conservative opposition would certainly have supported the Government, as we did on so many other of their measures of defence, and their majority would no doubt have been overwhelming. Nevertheless, they preferred to conceal this vast operation and its finances from the scrutiny of the House; not even obtaining a vote on the principle involved, while, at the same time, with Machiavellian art, keeping open the advantage of accusing their opponents of being warmongers.

Mr C. R. Attlee (Walthamstow, West): I really cannot let those statements pass. We have carried on precisely the same policy on the advice of our experts and advisers with regard to the publicity of these atomic matters. I was ready at all times to see the right hon. Gentleman, and I always understood that his closest confidant, Lord Cherwell, was fully informed of all these matters. I do not know why he had not told me about it, and as for the Americans not knowing what we were doing, we were telling them every possible thing in order to get their co-operation.

The Prime Minister: The right hon. Gentleman will no doubt have various opportunities of making full statements upon all this topic, but it does seem to me that some of the late Government's followers hardly relished their success in this sphere. I notice, indeed, a certain sense of disappointment with the statement that the achievement which has been made could not be wholly attributed to us. Indeed, the right hon. Gentleman the Leader of the Opposition is in the position of one who 'did good by stealth and blushed to find it fame'.[1] Before the whole story passes from life into history he will have to do a good deal of blushing in the explanations which he will have to make to some of his followers.

This remarkable episode is a good prelude to the argument I shall now deploy in reply to the new move in the Socialist warmongering accusation, of which the right hon. Gentleman's Motion is the latest expression. I am complimented by the fact that the official Opposition's Vote of Censure should concentrate its gravamen on me. It is not the first time I have incurred the wrath of the Socialist Party. (Hon. Members: 'Nor of the Tories.') I remember that in March, 1946, a Motion condemning a speech I made at Fulton was put on the Order Paper by just over 100 Socialist Members of Parliament, including seven who subsequently became Ministers. Here is the relevant part of the Motion:

'That this House considers that proposals for a military alliance between the British Commonwealth and the United States of America for the purpose of combating the spread of Communism, such as were put forward in a

[1] From Alexander Pope, *Epilogue to the Satires*.

speech at Fulton, Missouri, by the right hon. Gentleman the Member for Woodford, are calculated to do injury to the good relations between Great Britain, the United States and the USSR, and are inimical to the cause of world peace. . . .'

That Motion was never debated. On the contrary, the policy which I outlined at Fulton five years ago has since been effectively adopted both by the United States and by the Socialist Party. Two years later, by the Brussels Pact, and in the following year by the North Atlantic Treaty, the whole substance and purpose of what I said was adopted and enforced by the Socialist Government, and today we all respect the foresight and wise courage of the late Mr Ernest Bevin in helping to bring those great changes about.

Now, today, the Opposition have adopted a position of protestation that there should be no war with China. We agree with them about the importance of avoiding such a war, but I seem to have a recollection that there was some trouble about the Chinese going into Korea, which began 15 months ago, and that the Chinese Communists and their North Korean allies killed and wounded more than 100,000 Americans and nearly 3,000 of our own men, and that they lost themselves what has been estimated at over 1,250,000 killed and wounded. Even half that number would be quite a lot. One reads, too, in the papers every day about fighting that is going on even now with the Chinese. Apparently, however, according to the mentality of the Socialist Party, which only five months ago supported all this devastating struggle in Korea, nothing matters unless we call it 'war'. Apparently the important point is: What is it to be called? As long as it is not called 'war' the high condition of moral idealism of the Socialist movement is in no way impaired.

Hundreds of thousands of men may fall mangled and torn by bomb, bayonet, bullet or grenade; whole areas of Korea may be devastated in the advances and retreats of the opposing armies; 35,000 dead may be picked up in front of a single American division; our own men may have killed many times their number in deadly fighting; but, whatever happens, it must not be called 'war'. (Hon. Members: 'Rubbish.') It is not the fact, but it is the name that counts. What a strange political philosophy. 'No war. Peace in our time' – that is what the Socialists said when they themselves were responsible, in conjunction with other nations, for using deadly modern weapons to share in the slaughter of a million or more Chinese and North Koreans. It is difficult to imagine such a process of self-delusion and mental obliquity.

But whatever has been going on in Korea in the last 18 months is war, even though they choose to call it a 'collective police operation'; and it is a war entered upon by the Socialist Government, and waged by them, side by side with other members of the United Nations. Since we have been in office the truce negotiations, begun eight months ago, have continued, and the slaughter of the Chinese has abated. A comparative calm rests on the blood-soaked front, and the Socialist Party can turn their energies, I have no doubt with a measure of relief, from being war wagers to calling other people warmongers.

I made it plain a month ago, in my first speech on my return from America, that I was opposed to action that would involve us or our Allies of the United Nations in a war in China. I drew the attention of the House to General Omar Bradley's statement which I will now quote exactly – (Hon. Members: 'Another quotation.') – for I was not quite accurate before. Verify your quotations is a good maxim. This is the quotation:

> 'We would be fighting the wrong nation in the wrong war and in the wrong place.'

Mr Christopher Mayhew[1] (Woolwich, East) *rose* –

The Prime Minister: We did not interrupt the right hon. Gentleman the Member for Lewisham, South (Mr H. Morrison), who has just sat down, and I really must ask for an opportunity of unfolding my case. I must remind the House that I have never changed my opinion about the danger of our getting involved in China. When the Chinese first came into Korea, after the Russian-instigated attack by the North Koreans, I said in the House – (An Hon. Member: 'Another quotation.') What did the hon. Gentleman say? Oh, I beg pardon. I thought it might have been an intelligent point. I said on 30th November, 1950:

> 'The plan would evidently be to get the United States and the United Nations . . . involved as deeply as possible in China, and thus prevent the reinforcement of Europe and the building up of our defensive strength there to a point where it would be an effectual deterrent. It is one of the most well-known – almost hackneyed – strategical and tactical methods, to draw your opponent's resources to one part of the field and then, at the right moment, to strike in another. Military history shows countless examples of this and of variants of it. Surely, however, the United Nations should avoid by every means in their power becoming entangled inextricably in a war with China'. – (Official Report, 30th November, 1950; Vol. 481, c. 1335.)[2]

I have never departed from those views in any way, either publicly or privately. I also endeavoured when I spoke here a month ago to show the danger which was arising in Europe by the dispersion of so many British, American

---

[1] Christopher Paget Mayhew, 1915–97. President, Oxford Union, 1936. Gunner, Surrey Yeomanry RA; served in BEF, 1939–40. Maj., 1944. MP (Lab.) for South Norfolk, 1945–50; for Woolwich East, 1951–74. Under-Secretary of State, FO, 1946–50. Labour Party TV representative, 1951–64. Labour Party Parliamentary Under-Secretary of State for Defence, 1964. Member, Liberal Action Group for Electoral Reform, 1974–80. Baron, 1981. Chairman, National Association for Mental Health, 1992–7.

[2] Reproduced in *The Churchill Documents*, vol. 22, *Leader of the Opposition, August 1945 to October 1951*, pp. 1950–7.

and French divisions in Asia as a result of acts of aggression which the Soviet Government had promoted without losing a single soldier in Russian uniform. This made it clear that I disagree profoundly with the kind of statements, some of which have been read to us this afternoon, which have recently been made in the United States by various prominent Americans engaged in the impending Presidential Elections. I am not going to mention names. It is not for us to be drawn into American politics. Her Majesty's Government deal with the United States Government of the day, and with them our relations are very good indeed.

But let me now give the House some account of what happened about Korea under the late Government, and also since we have become responsible. The reason why I have to use guarded language instead of simple facts is that if military action, like, for instance, bombing, were referred to precisely, it would reveal what had been agreed and might therefore expose British and American airmen to extra danger. There is nothing I should like better than that all the relevant documents on this subject should be published. But that is not possible while fighting is going on or may be resumed on a large scale. I will give the House the fullest account I can at this present time. On several occasions in the last year the United States asked the British Government what military action they would agree to if certain things happened. Questions were addressed to the late Government and later to Her Majesty's present advisers. On the first occasion in May of last year, before the truce negotiations began, the right hon. Gentleman the late Foreign Secretary replied to an inquiry that His Majesty's Government had decided that in the event of heavy air attacks from bases in China upon United Nations forces in Korea they would associate themselves with action not confined to Korea.

Mr Aneurin Bevan (Ebbw Vale): On a point of order. Is the right hon. Gentleman quoting directly from Cabinet papers? If he is, then I move that the papers be laid. If, as I understand, the right hon. Gentleman is making references to discussions inside the previous Cabinet, then he is in order in doing so. If he is quoting, then he must lay the papers, and I so move.

The Prime Minister: I am not quoting at all. I am carefully avoiding making any quotations on that account, but I am undoubtedly entitled in defence of our own position, which has been subjected to this shameful attack, to place the House in possession of the facts as far as that can be done.

[...]

The Prime Minister: We now come in the narrative which I am giving Parliament to the change of Government in this country. The General Election took place and Her Majesty's present advisers became responsible. The question was put to us by the United States: What would happen if a truce were agreed upon and then treacherously broken by the Chinese, greatly to the loss and disadvantage of the United Nations' armies, and if heavy fighting were resumed on a large scale? This involves one hypothesis on top of another, and on the whole it does not seem very likely to happen, especially if, as we hope, peace negotiations follow the present truce. Nevertheless, when allies or members of a common body like the United Nations are working together, the one who bears nine-tenths of the burden may well ask the others what they would do in certain circumstances, and Her Majesty's present Government agreed that it would be prudent to make clear that serious consequences would follow the breach of the terms of an agreed truce.

As I have already said today, and as I pointed out when I spoke a month ago, it is not possible, while military operations are going on, to state either positively or negatively exactly what those consequences might be. But let me make it clear that we conformed, in principle, to the policy of our predecessors. Indeed, in some respects it might be said that we did not commit ourselves even as far as they had done. Nevertheless, the action to which we agreed, like that of the Socialist Government before us, fully justified the description which I gave to Congress of being 'prompt, resolute and effective'. The dispatch in which our policy was set forth was approved by the Cabinet in December, and various communications were sent to other members of the Commonwealth. All this happened before my right hon. Friend the Foreign Secretary and I set out for Washington.

It is a fact that we did not discuss the matter further at any conferences in Washington with our American colleagues. They did not raise it, and we had received no answer to our reply. It is absolutely true therefore to say, as in the words of the Opposition Motion, that we adhered to the policy followed by the late Administration with regard to the Korean conflict and the relations between Great Britain and China. It is not true to say that I in any way departed from this position. There is no truth in the suggestion that any secret or private arrangements were made or any change of policy agreed upon, formally or informally, actual or implied, by me or my right hon. Friend the Foreign Secretary, on these issues during our visit to the United States.

Having told the House these facts, some of which evidently surprised them, let me come to the address which I was invited to deliver to the Congress of the United States. I am very glad that the House wished to have this document circulated to them and that it should have been examined with so much attention. I cherish the hope that it will be found, as time passes, not to have been injurious to British and American relations which are, of course, all-important to our survival here at home and to the part we can play in averting a Third World War. It is the design and intense desire of the Soviet Union and its satellites and all its associates and fellow-travellers in many lands to drive a wedge between the British and American democracies and everything which tends to consolidate the mighty forces of the English-speaking world, upon which the hopes of United Europe also depend. Anything that secures that unity must be considered a service not only to freedom but to peace.

I must ask the indulgence of the House – if there is any of it left at the end of this statement, though I hope some of the excitement has worn off as we go along – to let me present the background in my mind to what I said to Congress, for which I have been criticized by the official spokesman of the Opposition, the late Foreign Secretary. It was certainly no easy task, in the present circumstances of bitterness here at home and during election year in the United States, to choose the points on which to dwell. In July last, when I was a private person, a delegation of the American Senate, which had been sent round many countries, came to London, and during their visit they asked to see me, and I received them in my home. I was impressed by the fact that this powerful body was greatly disturbed by the anti-American feeling which they thought existed in the House of Commons. So I said to them: 'Do not be misled. The anti-American elements in Parliament are only a quarter of the Labour Party, and the Labour Party is only a half of the House. Therefore, you may say that one-eighth at the outside give vent to anti-American sentiments. The Labour Party as a whole, and the Government of the day, supported by the Conservative Party in this matter, are whole-heartedly friendly to the United States, and recognize and are grateful for the part they are playing in the world and of the help they have given to us.'

This was the message which I tried to give to Congress when I spoke, and in so doing I felt I was speaking – I hoped I was speaking – for the great majority of the present Parliament. Today, however, I must say that the attitude of a fraction of the late House of Commons and apparently of a larger proportion of the present House of Commons and the mood and temper which this Vote of Censure which the right hon. Gentleman has moved personally upon me implies, can be made use of throughout the United States by Isolationist forces and by the anti-British elements which form a powerful minority throughout the great Republic. I say to those former Ministers whose records lie behind them and who have put their names to this Motion: Beware lest in petty manoeuvres about the leadership of the Socialist Party you do not injure causes to which you have pledged your honour and all our fortunes.

I had no wish or need to proclaim any new policy to Congress because, so far as policy is concerned, in Korea and China, we were only following in accordance with our own convictions the policy entered into and long pursued by our predecessors. But I hoped by my visit to the United States, first to establish an intimacy and an atmosphere of goodwill in the high circles that rule in Washington which would make it much easier in the future to deal with problems as they arise. I also felt a keen sympathy with the American people in their losses, and in having so many of their men serving so far away from home. I hoped also to give the Congress and people of the United States something of a glow and sense of our abiding friendship for them, and of our gratitude to them for all they have done for us, and for the causes which we also are resolved to serve with all our strength. On the whole I cannot feel, in spite of this party challenge, that I have failed in what I sought to do.

[. . .]

Mrs Castle:[1] I would like to thank the right hon. Gentleman and to ask him in all seriousness if, as he says, he made no new commitment additional to the one made by the late Government he can tell us why it has been widely reported in the United States responsible Press that there has been a change of policy in relation to Korea as a result of the right hon. Gentleman's visit to the United States.

The Prime Minister: I am afraid that it is very difficult always to follow with complete accuracy all the movements represented in our own Press here at home, and I really cannot undertake to have a similar mastery of the mighty Press of the United States. But what I have stated here is a fact – that I made no new commitment in this field of foreign affairs of any sort or kind.

However, there are a few points of detail in this meticulous heresy hunt on which I will touch. The right hon. Gentleman the Leader of the Opposition complained in his speech the last time we debated this matter that I had used the word 'United States' more often than I had used the words 'United Nations'. Surely, when speaking to the American Congress, whose troops have contributed nine-tenths of the fighting power and whose casualties are twenty times as great as all the other members of the United Nations put together, it would not be unnatural that I should speak of them and of their sacrifices. But technically I have a right to speak of the United States as a prime factor because it is their commander who, under the United Nations, is the head of the Unified Command provided by the United States Government over all the forces employed. It only shows the limited and lopsided character of the Socialist trend of thought that they should complain that I did not deny the United States, in their own Assembly, the honour which belongs to them of being the supreme agent and chosen leader of the world instrument against Communist aggression.

The Leader of the Opposition admitted the other day that he agreed with what I had said to Congress about Formosa. This is what I said:

'I am very glad that, whatever diplomatic divergences there may be from time to time about the procedure, you' – that is, Congress – 'do not allow the Chinese anti-Communists on Formosa to be invaded and massacred from the mainland.' It is the only thing that one could say about Formosa which could be agreed on both sides of this House and on both sides of the Congress of the United States, and, indeed, on both sides of the Atlantic Ocean. I thought it was rather a good selection – almost a bull's-eye. The fact that I selected it was, by implication, adverse to other statements which could be made on the subject and was, I believe, so understood and accepted by the great majority of my audience on that occasion.

Finally, I have been accused of speaking with two voices on different sides

[1] Barbara Castle, 1910–2002. MP (Lab.) for Blackburn, 1945–50; for Blackburn East, 1950–5; for Blackburn, 1955–79. PC, 1964. Minister for Overseas Development, 1964–5. Minister of Transport, 1965–8. Secretary of State for Employment, 1968–70. Secretary of State for Health and Social Services, 1974–6.

of the Atlantic. That is not true. I speak with the same voice, I can assure hon. Members – the one to which they are having the opportunity of listening today. Wherever I speak, everything that I say on these occasions will no doubt be immediately reported or broadcast in the fullest manner on both sides of the Ocean. I am not conscious of the slightest change of thought or conviction on these important issues, and I do not retract a word that I have used on either occasion, here or on the other side, on our foreign outlook and policy.

Let me then sum up. First, there is no change in our policy towards the United States, towards the United Nations or towards the war in Korea. Secondly, on the circumstances which might justify action not confined to Korea, we have only followed and conformed to the policy for which the late Government were responsible and for which no two men were more personally responsible than the right hon. Gentleman the Leader of the Opposition and the right hon. Gentleman who has just spoken to us and who has thought it compatible with his personal candour and public behaviour to move this Motion. Thirdly, I believe that on both sides of the Atlantic we are convinced, as I have argued since the beginning of these troubles, that nothing could be more foolish than for the armies of the United States or the United Nations to become engulfed in the vast areas of China, and also that few adventures could be less successful or fruitful than for Generalissimo Chiang Kai-shek to plunge on to the mainland. Fourthly, if the truce is made only to be broken, a very grave situation will arise in which we must act as good comrades to our American and other United Nations friends and as a loyal member of the United Nations Organization. In this case, our action, like that contemplated by our predecessors, will be 'prompt, resolute and effective'.

Finally, the prospects of a truce being reached and respected in Korea will depend to a large extent upon the unity between Great Britain and the United States being proved to be not only unbreakable but growing stronger, and the attempts of all who seek to weaken or divide us being repulsed and condemned as they will be tonight by the House of Commons.

C. P. Wilson[1] to Winston S. Churchill
(Churchill papers, 1/54)[2]

26 February 1952

Dear Mr Churchill,

Thank you very much for arranging for me to be admitted to the House to hear the debate on the Vote of Censure.

May I say how much I appreciated your masterly address and how glad I was to be present at such a crushing and devastating disposal of your detractors.

---

[1] Ear, nose and throat specialist at Middlesex Hospital, London, and Churchill's throat doctor.
[2] This letter was handwritten.

February 1952

Lord Woolton to Winston S. Churchill
(*Premier papers, 11/38*)

26 February 1952

There is some difference of opinion concerning the proper description of Prince Charles[1] in the Prayers of the Church of England and the Church of Scotland.

By agreement with the Archbishop we had agreed that he should be described as the Duke of Cornwall. Lyon King of Arms,[2] however, has pointed out that as the Duke of Cornwall does not rank in the Peerage of Scotland, the Prince should be described as the Duke of Cornwall and Rothesay. The Secretary of State for Scotland is pressing this issue.

I understand that Scottish opinion feels that in view of the fact that The Queen is regarded as Queen Elizabeth II although there has never been a Queen Elizabeth of Scotland, that this compromise would mean much to Scottish opinion.

I withdrew the matter from the Privy Council last Friday because I did not want Her Majesty to be disturbed by any dispute. I understand from the Queen's Secretary that Her Majesty is not anxious for any change, but in view of the persistence of the Secretary of State for Scotland, I thought I ought to refer the matter to you. It is of some urgency since the Prayers have to be altered and the Church of England is pressing for a decision.

I have given the matter a great deal of consideration over the weekend and my advice would be not to introduce a Scottish title. If you also take this view I shall proceed straight away with the Order in Council to this effect.

I may add that the Moderator of the Church of Scotland[3] was consulted at an early stage and raised no objection to the title 'Duke of Cornwall'.

---

[1] Charles Philip Arthur George, 1948–. Eldest child of Queen Elizabeth II and Prince Philip. Educated at Cambridge University. Prince of Wales, 1958. Served in RAF, 1971–7. Married, 1981, Diana Spencer (div. 1996): two children; 2005, Camilla Parker Bowles.

[2] Thomas Innes of Learney, 1892–1971. Genealogist to Priory of Scotland in the Order of St John, 1947–70. Lord Lyon King of Arms, 1945–69. President, Scottish Ecclesiological Society, 1957–60. GCVO, 1967. Marchmont Herald of Arms, 1969–71.

[3] George Johnstone Jeffrey, 1881–1961. Educated at Glasgow University, 1903–7. Served in the Scottish Churches Huts during WWI, 1914–18. Minister of West High Kirk, 1920–8. Minister of Sherbrooke St Gilbert's Church 1938–51. Moderator, General Assembly of Church of Scotland, 1952–3. Editor, *The Sacramental Table*, 1954.

February 1952

Winston S. Churchill to Lord Woolton
(Premier papers, 11/38)

27 February 1952
NOT SENT

The issue was presented to me as <u>either</u> the Duke of Cornwall <u>or</u> Rothesay. Of course I was in favour of Cornwall; England must come in sometime. I mentioned it on this basis to The Queen in my Audience and Her Majesty seemed quite agreeable to Cornwall. However the matter should now be put forward on the new basis of Cornwall <u>and</u> Rothesay. I see no harm whatever in the two together.*

*After discussion with Lord Woolton the Prime Minister did not send this minute.

Cabinet: conclusions
(Cabinet papers, 128/24)

27 February 1952
Secret
11 a.m.
Cabinet Meeting No. 22 of 1952

1. In speaking in the Foreign Affairs debate in the House of Commons on the previous day the Prime Minister had made certain disclosures about the attitude adopted by the previous Government towards the proposal that, if heavy air attacks were launched from Chinese bases on United Nations troops in Korea, the air forces of the United States should undertake retaliatory bombing against those bases. This had provoked a demand that the relevant documents should be laid before Parliament; and some Members of the Opposition had assumed that the Prime Minister had derived his information from the Cabinet papers of the previous Administration. The Prime Minister said that his statement had in fact been based on Foreign Office telegrams and despatches, which for this purpose were in quite a different category from Cabinet papers. As, however, he had not purported to quote the telegrams textually, he did not think he was under any obligation to lay them before Parliament. In discussion it was suggested that it might be inexpedient to do so.

[. . .]

Winston S. Churchill to Lord Swinton
Prime Minister's Personal Minute M.79/52
(Premier papers, 11/75)

27 February 1952

1. I could not agree to any delay in the vital elements of the Defence programme. I have myself proposed and enforced important reductions upon what was proposed by our Socialist predecessors. Concentration with the highest priority on the latest forms of aircraft and upon Radar and Centurion tanks is imperative. The Centurion tanks may themselves be a great dollar winner. Meanwhile we have them under our lee.

2. I agree with you that there must be no abuse of all powerful symbols.[1]

I should welcome a detailed note from the Treasury suggesting more precise definition. I am well aware of the danger of departments using 'first priority' to brush everything else out of the way. Perhaps you will let me have something on these lines.

James Thomas to Winston S. Churchill
(Premier papers, 11/57)

27 February 1952

I should like to draw your attention to COS (52)136, which discusses means of meeting SACLANT's proposals for his staff, and the Minutes of COS (52)31st Meeting Item 4. When I approved the tabling of this paper it was my view that the matter should be considered at the highest level rather earlier than is implied by Conclusion (f) of the minutes to which I have referred.

I am sending a copy of this note to the Foreign Secretary.

Winston S. Churchill to Field Marshal Lord Alexander
Prime Minister's Personal Minute M.82/52
(Premier papers, 11/57)

28 February 1952

This[2] is a good example of the extraordinary 'bloated' staffs in which the United States indulge. I hope we can keep ours to a reasonable level and have quality and authority rather than jobs and numbers.

---

[1] Swinton had proposed that symbols could be used to identify defence contracts and sub-contracts to automatically entitle contractors to special preference in obtaining labour, components and raw materials.

[2] Thomas to Churchill of Feb. 27, reproduced immediately above.

FEBRUARY 1952

Lord Cherwell to Winston S. Churchill
(Premier papers, 11/369)

28 February 1952

NATO REPORT ON SOVIET AND NATO ECONOMIC
AND MILITARY STRENGTHS

Though very long, this NATO report contains some interesting information: I do not know how far we can trust the figures quoted which are, I gather, averages of the estimates made by the various intelligence services of the NATO powers.

The report certainly makes sombre reading. If the figures are right the Russian air force is very much larger than NATO's is likely to be for a very long time. Moreover their aircraft output seems to be twice that of the USA and ourselves combined – though it is true that the only US figures available to us are out-of-date and American production is now rising rapidly. The Russians will continue to have very many more divisions than the NATO Powers (147 as against 24). Though their net divisions contain two-thirds the number of men, it is alleged that the fire power of a Soviet net division is as great as that of a British net division. The Soviet gross division seems to be about half the strength of a British gross division.

I have tried to summarise the information given in this report, and other information which may be of interest to you, in the charts and tables in the attached album. If you want anything else, we can try to obtain it for you and include it in the album.

Cabinet: conclusions
(Cabinet papers, 128/24)

29 February 1952
Secret
11 a.m.
Cabinet Meeting No. 24 of 1952

The Foreign Secretary said that, on the previous day he had, with the Prime Minister's concurrence, arranged for the Leader of the Opposition and Mr Herbert Morrison, MP, to see a selection of the Foreign Office telegrams on which the Prime Minister had based his statements, in the Foreign Affairs debate on the 26th February, regarding the attitude of the previous Government towards retaliatory bombing against Chinese bases.[1] He had now learned that another member of the late Government had been given access,

---

[1] Reproduced above (pp. 283–92).

February 1952

in his old Department, to a wider selection of documents bearing on this question. In a matter of this kind independent action by a number of different Departments might have embarrassing consequences; and he suggested that Departments might now be instructed that former Ministers should not be given access to documents of this kind without prior reference to the Secretary of the Cabinet who would, as required, consult the Prime Minister or other Ministers concerned.

The Cabinet endorsed this suggestion, and took note that the Prime Minister would arrange for directions to be given accordingly.

The Prime Minister said that there seemed to be some confusion in the press about the extent to which a Government in office had access to the papers of an earlier Administration. There was a clear distinction between Cabinet papers, which were not made available to members of a succeeding Administration of a different political complexion, and the executive documents, *e.g.*, telegrams and despatches, which must be available to Ministers in office for the purpose of ensuring continuity in the conduct of public business. He was arranging for some guidance to be given to the press on this question; and in this he would take the opportunity of making it plain that his statements in the recent Foreign Affairs debate had been based on the facts contained in Foreign Office telegrams.

[. . .]

March 1952

Sir Norman Brook to Members of the Cabinet
(Premier papers, 11/601)

March 1952[1]
Confidential

ACCESS BY FORMER MINISTERS TO CABINET AND OTHER OFFICIAL PAPERS

The Prime Minister has directed that all applications by former Ministers to see Cabinet or Cabinet Committee papers issued to them while they were in office should be referred to me.

2. Applications by a former Minister to see Departmental memoranda, telegrams, dispatches, etc., prepared, during his period of office, in the Department over which he presided may be granted on the authority of the Departmental Minister or the Permanent Head of the Department, provided that the papers do not affect the interests of other Departments. Applications to see Departmental files which concern other Departments, or contain papers prepared by other Departments, should be reported to me so that I may consult the other Ministers concerned and report to the Prime Minister if necessary.[2]

---

[1] No day given in original document.
[2] Churchill minuted Brook on Mar. 4: 'Ought not the Government to stipulate that they also claim the right to see papers of this character called for from the past by Opposition Members? Otherwise they may not be informed of some question that is raised. Whether we should exercise that right in all cases is another matter' (Prime Minister's Personal Minute M.89/52, *Premier papers, 11/601*).

March 1952

Anthony Eden to Winston S. Churchill
(*Churchill papers, 2/517*)

2 March 1952
Top Secret
PM/52/18

DEFENCE OF THE FALKLAND ISLANDS

I have seen your minute to the Chiefs of Staff of the 20th February and their reply of the 22nd February, together with the additional note enclosed in Ewbank's[1] letter of the 26th February.

2. I quite agree that the Chiefs of Staff's revised recommendation, providing for a detachment of Royal Marines to be embarked in the frigate which is to be kept in the vicinity of the Falkland Islands, should meet our requirements very well. It will no doubt be easy to arrange that the Marines are in evidence at Port Stanley from time to time.

Winston S. Churchill to Enoch Powell[2]
(*Premier papers, 11/247*)

2 March 1952
Confidential and Personal

Dear Powell,

You wrote to me on February 27th about the Duke of Edinburgh being present in the Peers' Gallery during debates in the House. It seems to me a good thing that His Royal Highness should understand how our Parliamentary affairs work and I should myself think that Members of both Parties would be glad to see him do so. There is no true comparison with Prince Albert's[3] presence on a similar occasion in 1846 since in those days the contact of the Crown with political issues was more direct than it is today.

---

[1] Robert Withers Ewbank, 1907–81. GSO I, War Office, 1942–4. Cdr, RE, 50 Northumbrian Div., 1944–6. DSO, 1945. Col. Quartermaster (Movements) War Office, 1946–9. Secretary, Chiefs of Staff Committee, Ministry of Defence, 1951–3. CoS, British Army Staff, Washington DC, 1954–6. Director of Movements, War Office, 1956–8. CB, 1957. CoS, HQ Northern Army Group, 1958–60. Commandant, Royal Military College of Science, 1961–4. KBE, 1964. President, Officers' Christian Union of GB, 1965–76.

[2] (John) Enoch Powell, 1912–98. Educated at Trinity College, Cambridge. Prof. of Greek, University of Sydney, 1937–9. Capt., General Staff, 1940–1. Maj., 1941. Lt-Col., 1942. Col., 1944; Brig,, 1944. MP (Cons.) for Wolverhampton South West, 1950–74; (Unionist) for South Down, 1974–87. Married, 1952, Margaret Pamela Winston. Financial Secretary, Treasury, 1957–8. Minister for Health, 1960–3. Shadow Secretary of State for Defence, 1965–8.

[3] Francis Albert Augustus Charles Emmanuel, 1819–61. Prince Consort and husband of Queen Victoria of Great Britain. Father of King Edward VII.

March 1952

Winston S. Churchill to Anthony Eden
Prime Minister's Personal Minute M.87/52
(Premier papers, 11/112)

3 March 1952

As you know I have for some time past felt that the position in Korea had greatly deteriorated owing to the recovery the Communists have made, not only of 'face' by negotiating on equal terms, but by improving their Air Force and artillery.

It now appears from Bouchier's[1] telegram of March 1, para. 8, that they have also made strong fortified lines.[2] This gives a very different picture from that presented to us at Washington by Omar Bradley.[3]

Winston S. Churchill to Dean Acheson
(Premier papers, 11/160)

3 March 1952
Private and Personal

1. After much thought I have come to the conclusion, in which Mr Eden concurs, that our best candidate for the NATO Secretary-General would be Mr Hector McNeil.[4] You must know him well because of his long service as Minister of State at the UNO Conferences, where he kept our end up on all occasions and must have gathered much experience. He has been five

---

[1] Cecil Arthur Bouchier, 1895–1979. Graduated from RAF Staff College, Andover, 1930. HQ RAF India, 1931–2. Formed and commanded Indian Air Force, 1932–5. Air Ministry, 1942. Cdr, No. 11 (F) Group, 1943–5. Commanded fighter umbrella, Normandy landings, 1944 (CB). AOC No. 221 Group, Burma, 1945; British Commonwealth Air Forces during occupation of Japan, 1945–8; No. 21 Group, Swinderby, Lincs, 1948–9. Personal Representative of British COS to Gens MacArthur, Ridgway and Clark throughout Korean War, 1950–3.

[2] Para. 8 reads: 'It would seem that there is very little we can do about it but to await with patience the next move of the Communists. The Communist forces over the past six months have dug themselves well into deep bunkers and tunnels stretching across the peninsula to a depth of some twenty miles behind the battlefront. They realise as of course we must realise that we are not now negotiating from the same position of military strength as we were at the beginning of the armistice talks when the enemy forces were hard pressed and indeed in a bad way. Thus in conditions of complete military stalemate there is little we can do except in the air and by sea to bring military pressure upon the enemy except at a cost of incurring a very high casualty rate to our own forces.'

[3] Eden wrote on the bottom of this minute: 'I fear so. All that we can set against this is that we too have made strong fortified lines. But I understand that the American troops in them are not of the quality of their tried divisions. Meanwhile I don't know what to make of this latest Soviet move, insisting upon themselves as one of the supervising neutrals. It looks less and less as if the Communists wanted a settlement; maybe they don't want a renewal of the war either. Acheson, when I last saw him in Lisbon, still believed the chance to be in favour of an armistice.'

[4] Hector McNeil, 1907–55. Member (Lab.) of Glasgow Town Council, 1933–6, 1937–8. MP (Lab.) for Greenock, 1941–55. Parliamentary Under-Secretary of State for Foreign Affairs, 1945–6. PC, 1946. Minister of State for Foreign Affairs, 1946–50. Vice-President, UN General Assembly, 1947. Secretary of State for Scotland, 1950–1.

years Minister of State in the Bevin tradition, and also Secretary of State for Scotland, and a Privy Councillor and member of the Cabinet. I understood you favoured a political figure to an official, and here is one whom I can recommend.

2. Mr Gifford told me this morning that the American reaction to this proposal was unfavourable. Please tell me the kind of objections you have. It would be an advantage, though this was not my reason, to the bi-partisan character so necessary for us in NATO and foreign policy to have an ex-Minister from the Labour Party. I do not of course know whether McNeil would feel able to accept.

3. I was very glad to hear from your Ambassador that you liked my speech in the Foreign Affairs debate.

Winston S. Churchill to Members of the Cabinet
(Premier papers, 11/253)

3 March 1952
Confidential

CABINET: PROCEDURE
PARLIAMENTARY PRIVATE SECRETARIES

Parliamentary Private Secretaries occupy a special position which is not always understood by the general public, either at home or abroad. They are not members of the Government, and should be careful to avoid being spoken of as such. They are Private Members, and should therefore be afforded as great a liberty of action as possible; but their close and confidential association with Ministers necessarily imposes certain obligations on them, and has led to the generally accepted practice set out in the following paragraph.

2. Parliamentary Private Secretaries should not make statements in the House or put Questions on matters affecting the Department with which they are connected. They should also exercise great discretion in any speeches or broadcasts which they make outside the House, taking care not to make statements which appear to be made in an official or semi-official capacity, and bearing in mind at the same time that, however careful they may be to make it clear that they are speaking only as Private Members, they are nevertheless liable to be regarded as speaking with some of the authority which attaches to a member of the Government. Generally they must act with a sense of responsibility and with discretion; and they must not associate themselves with particular groups advocating special policies.

3. Only exceptionally, and then with the express authority of his Minister, may a Parliamentary Private Secretary be shown papers of the Cabinet or its Committees or other secret official papers. The information given to them

should be limited to what is strictly necessary for the discharge of their Parliamentary and political duties.

Nigel Nicolson[1] to Harold Nicolson
('The Later Years', pages 222–3)

3 March 1952

I have already witnessed many a stirring scene, the best of which was the Foreign Affairs debate last Wednesday. Herbert Morrison spoke for an hour so badly that people shuffled and groaned. It made a deplorable effect, and Winston's case was won before he got up. He started off pugnaciously and then pretended to go dull on us. 'I must ask for the patience of the House', he said, 'if I go back a bit to the record of the last Government.' Everybody relaxed, feeling that we knew all this past-history already and needn't listen. Then suddenly he lifted his head and brought out this story about Attlee having agreed to bomb the Chinese airfields.[2] There was pandemonium. I was sitting directly opposite Attlee. He was sitting hunched up like an elf just out of its chrysalis, and stared at Winston, turning slowly white. The Labour benches howled – anything to make a noise to cover up the moment of shock. Winston sat back beaming. Bevan – a most charming, dangerous man – did his best to launch a counter-attack, but it was too late. We had won. I was sitting in the smoking-room afterwards with Cranborne[3] when Winston came up to us, with a cigar and a glass of brandy. 'It was a great day,' he said, 'a great triumph, and I am glad that you joined us in time to witness it.'

How much better he is in the House than on a platform! How he loves it! He is looking white and fatty, a most unhealthy look, you would say, if he were anyone else, but somehow out of the sickly mountain comes a volcanic flash.

---

[1] Nigel Nicolson, 1917–2004. Son of Harold Nicolson and Vita Sackville-West. Officer Cadet Reserves, Grenadier Guards, 1939–45. Bde Intelligence Officer. Capt., 1942. MBE, 1945. MP (Cons.) for Bournemouth East and Christchurch, 1952–9. Author of *Portrait of a Marriage* (1973); *Alex: The Life of Field Marshal Earl Alexander of Tunis* (1973); and *Mary Curzon* (1977). OBE, 2000.

[2] See speech of Feb. 26, reproduced above (pp. 283–92).

[3] Robert Edward Peter Gascoyne-Cecil, 1916–2003. Educated at Eton. Served in Grenadier Guards, 1937–46. Took part in invasion of Normandy, 1944. Military assistant to Harold Macmillan, Resident Minister in North Africa, 1944–5. Viscount Cranborne, 1947–72. MP (Cons.) for Bournemouth West, 1950–4. Succeeded his father as 6th Marquess of Salisbury and entered the House of Lords, 1972.

Winston S. Churchill to Duncan Sandys
Prime Minister's Personal Minute M.92/52
(Premier papers, 11/75)

5 March 1952

I do not agree to the abandonment of the tank expansion programme especially as we are selling five hundred to the United States and could sell five hundred more at very good prices.

Para. 4.[1]

You do not say how much you would save by excluding tanks. I am not prepared to advise the withdrawal of the priorities but only to make sure by regulations and administration that they are not used unfairly.

Antony Head to Winston S. Churchill
(Premier papers, 11/7)

5 March 1952

You asked about a leader entitled 'The Army's April Fools' in the *Manchester Guardian* of 3rd March.

During and after the war non-commissioned officers held war substantive rank. All those NCOs who stayed on after the war were well aware that one day war substantive rank would cease. We have held on to it for a long time and the change over to normal substantive rank has for long been the subject of investigation and discussion in the War Office. After consultation with Commanding Officers and NCOs the solution of this problem was announced to the Army as long ago as last October. By and large the change over to normal substantive rank gives absolute security to those selected, while the remainder continue to hold their temporary rank so long as they hold an appointment which justifies it. The number of such appointments has not been decreased.

All this is a very complicated matter and the Press, notably the *Manchester Guardian*, have tended to misinterpret it. I would like to give you an example to explain how it works.

[1] Para. 4 read: '4. The Ministry of Supply consider that, if the system is to be effective, all sub-contractors should be able to identify contracts relating to the selected items by the use of a symbol in conjunction with the contract number and that this symbol should automatically entitle them to the same preference in obtaining components or raw materials from their suppliers as it will confer on main contractors. They do not consider there is any serious danger of abuse of these arrangements. They propose to make it clear that the preference should not be exercised unless it is essential in order to secure the item in time and they are prepared to make spot checks and to investigate cases of suspected abuse. They consider that without the use of a symbol, which facilitates verification of the entitlement, there is more rather than less danger of abuse. Moreover they state that their staff resources make it impossible for them to operate effectively any system that is not automatic, in view of the very large numbers of minor sub-contractors who will be affected.'

Suppose an infantry battalion has an establishment of, say, 35 sergeants. Nevertheless for reasons which I will explain they may well have 60 men belonging to the battalion, who hold the rank of sergeant. None of these 60 sergeants has true security within his rank because up till now none of them has been given true substantive rank. Under the present scheme 35 of these men will become sergeants and they cannot then drop their rank. None of the remaining 25 sergeants is given substantive rank but all continue to wear stripes and be paid as sergeants provided their job holds the rank. You will ask: 'Why is there such a discrepancy between the establishment (35) and the number of sergeants (60)?' The answer lies in the very large commitment which the Regular Army has for providing instructors, NCOs for the Territorial Army, cross postings, etc.

The men now being granted substantive rank are selected on a consideration of previous service, qualifications and efficiency.

I am sending a copy of this minute to the Minister of Defence.

Winston S. Churchill: speech
(Hansard)

5 March 1952   House of Commons

The Prime Minister (Mr Winston Churchill): I beg to move, 'That this House approves the Statement on Defence, 1952 (Command Paper No. 8475)'.

Although I feel that it will be in the general convenience that I should make this statement, I can no longer speak as Minister of Defence. On the day when I accepted the late King's Commission to form a Government, I proposed the appointment of Lord Alexander to this office, and His Majesty was greatly attracted by the proposal. It was necessary, however, to obtain the assent of the Canadian Government and to enable them to make all necessary arrangements in due course.

I had foreseen this delay, even if Lord Alexander were willing to accept so onerous a task. In the meanwhile, I welcomed the opportunity of surveying again this scene, which six years ago I knew quite well, and noting the many changes which had taken place in the interval. I will now, Sir, on handing over these duties, commend this White Paper, which has been circulated for some days, to the attention of the House.

I must, however, put on record certain reserves which are necessary. It takes a long time, and much Departmental work, as right hon. Gentlemen opposite know, to prepare documents of this kind, and, for reasons which the House will understand, we had to hasten its presentation to Parliament. Meanwhile, events move constantly forward. Even the present Service Estimates and the White Paper now before us, must be subject to unceasing scrutiny to eliminate all waste and, of course, production may be affected by the non-delivery of machine tools and by the shortage of dollar purchasing power.

I shall not occupy the House at any length with the Amendment which I have heard that the Ministers mainly responsible in the late Parliament for the conduct of our armaments – conduct good or bad – have placed on the Paper. We said something like this about them last year and we shall certainly not be offended by any opinion they may form of us. Our opinion, however, was based upon several years' experience of their methods. Theirs can only be a guess, and I trust will not be a hope.

While we criticised the mistakes they made from time to time, and above all their repeated changes – vacillations, I think, was the word that was used – in the periods of compulsory National Service – now up, now down, now up again – we always gave them support in all necessary measures for national security. They always knew they had us with them if it ever came to a vote against their own tail. I do not suggest that we were with them yesterday morning. But this must have been a great help to any Government carrying on the business of the nation, especially as they were able at the same time to accuse us of seeking war and armament expansion whenever an election came along.

I hope that the Division which, I understand, we are to have tonight will not mean that the Socialist Party intend to revert to their pre-war practice of voting against necessary measures of defence, as they did against conscription before the war, and that they will at any rate consider themselves as bound to give general support to measures for which they themselves were originally responsible.

I will now endeavour to give some general account of the British defence position as I leave it. When I spoke to the House on defence at the beginning of December, I mentioned that there would certainly be a lag in carrying out the £4,700 million programme to which the late Government had given their support, and which they had increased from their original £3,600 million programme introduced earlier in the same year. This has manifested itself in a shortfall in 1951–52 of £120 million, as is shown in the White Paper.

After the £3,600 million programme was proposed by the Socialist Government, they accepted an interim offer of 112 million dollars of aid from the United States of America in respect of machine tools. They had, indeed, stipulated for much larger help and relied on securing it in due course through the so-called 'burden-sharing exercise' then agreed in principle with the Americans. We are to receive this 112 million dollars progressively as machine tools are delivered, and delivery is only just beginning, but we hope it will be completed in about 15 months' time.

Meanwhile the £4,700 million programme on which we are now engaged has not received aid on a scale in keeping with the defence burden undertaken by the late Prime Minister or with our needs. Following the recent studies of the Temporary Council Committee – the 'three wise men', as they are sometimes called – the United States Government have allotted to us a sum of 300 million dollars, none of which has yet been received. There is no question of reproaches on either side, but the fact remains, as I have foreshadowed, that the re-armament programme is much more likely to be carried out in four years than in three. Had it been carried out in three years as originally planned, the cost through the rise in prices would have been not less than £5,200 million. Of course, spread over a longer time the impact is less severe, but the total will be larger because of the added cost of the longer maintenance.

I should, however, be misleading the House if I led it to suppose that the delay which has taken place is due only to a shortfall in earnings by contractors for various reasons. We have pursued a definite policy of giving a somewhat higher measure of priority to materials needed for exports. The grave financial crisis under which we are labouring supplies more than sufficient explanation for this decision. We depend upon exports to purchase the imports of food and raw materials without which we can neither re-arm nor live as a solvent economic society.

The expenditure set forth in the White Paper on Defence, and the Estimates of the three Service Departments which will shortly be brought before the House, represent the utmost that we can do during the present year; and it is certainly much more than any other country in the free world, except the United States of America, has attempted.

I am not suggesting that it is sufficient for our safety in the event of war, and I rely on the rapidly growing and already overwhelming power of the United States in the atomic bomb to provide the deterrents against an act of aggression during the period of forming a defensive front in Western Europe. I hope and I believe that this will deter; but, of course, I cannot make promises or prophecies, or give guarantees. I accept responsibility only for doing all that was possible, having regard to the state of our defences and economic position when, after an interval of more than six years, the Conservative Party resumed office 19 weeks ago.

My first impression on looking round the scene at home in November as Minister of Defence was a sense of extreme nakedness such as I had never felt before in peace or war – almost as though I was living in a nudist colony. When the 6th Armoured and the 3rd Infantry Divisions had left the country in pursuance of orders given or policies decided upon in the days of the late Administration, we had not a single Regular combat formation in the country; and although a seaborne invasion does not seem likely in view of our and Allied naval power in surface ships, I thought it right to take what precautions were possible against paratroop descents, and I spoke, as the House may remember, about the importance of our showing the back of a hedgehog rather than the paunch of a rabbit to any unfriendly eye that might contemplate our island from above.

There were at that time a quarter of a million – 249,000 was the exact figure – of officers and men in depôts and training centres of many kinds. Most of these men, though uniformed British soldiers, had little combatant organisation or value. They were engaged in preparing and maintaining the considerable Forces which had been spread about the world, in Europe, Asia and Africa. I considered it imperative to impart a combatant value to this potentially powerful body of British soldiers costing at least £400 a year each. Rapid progress has been made with this policy. All these men are now supplied with rifles and machine guns and with ammunition, and they are organised into effective fighting groups which now comprise 502 mobile columns.

These Forces are not, indeed, of the efficiency of the units on the Continent and overseas. Nor do they need to be. They are capable of giving a good account of themselves and of imposing a considerable deterrent upon any airborne adventure by being able to kill or capture the ones who land. The process has been greatly strengthened by the sailors ashore and the Air Force ground men, who also make important contributions. I am told by the weekly reports for which I called that morale is high, and that all ranks understand and have welcomed the reality and importance of their new duties, and that they like to feel that they are guarding their homes and their fellow countrymen as well as learning or teaching.

About two months ago, on the same line of thought, we started registration for the Home Guard. Since then 30,000 men have registered. This result is solid so far as it goes, but we still need many more volunteers. It may well be that many who have joined have felt that the likelihood of war has somewhat receded, and they think they can make up their minds later on. They must be careful not to leave it too late. If war should come, it will be with violent speed and suddenness, and here at home, with almost all our Regular Army overseas, we must rely to an unusual extent on the Home Guard. Enough resolute men must be armed and ready to aid all the other forms of protection against raids, descents and sabotage.

Although I had felt unable at first sight to provide the Home Guard with uniforms, and even with greatcoats or boots, I decided upon consideration to draw upon our mobilisation reserves to the extent necessary to clothe at least the first 50,000. My successor may do better later on. I have directed the War Office to place, as speedily as possible, all orders for which their Estimates provide in the coming year with the clothing trade, in which a certain amount of unemployment and under-employment, especially in Northern Ireland, had begun to appear.

Thirdly, we have been able, by a severe combing of the tail – not the tail I mentioned just now, but nevertheless a very desirable and necessary process – to produce seven more Regular second battalions of famous regiments which had been imprudently disbanded. I would not use the word 'imprudently' if I had not long studied all the economic advantages of the Cardwell system, with a battalion abroad and a battalion at home, and an inter-flow of reserves and reinforcements between them. These battalions now raised, in one of which the hon. Member for Ayrshire, South (Mr Emrys Hughes) took so much interest – the Black, what was it?

Mr Emrys Hughes (Ayrshire, South): The Black Watch.

The Prime Minister: I thought it was the 'Black Welsh'. These will become effective units, and during the present autumn will give us at least a couple of Regular brigade groups to work with the numerous mobile columns I have already mentioned, and to go to any point of special danger in this island.

The expense involved in these changes is not great, and the gain in defensive and deterrent power resulting from them is out of all proportion to their cost in money. I hope the House will greet these measures with approval in that limited sphere of our dangers to which they are necessarily restricted. There is no doubt – honour where honour is due – that the Socialist policy of compulsory National Service in time of peace will enable Britain to create a much better and stronger Army than was ever possible before. Right hon. Gentlemen opposite need not look too unhappy about it. We supported the late Government in this important decision, including their last step of raising the term of service to two years. Of course, the fruits of such a system only mature gradually. The yearly production of more than 100,000 well-trained reservists, representing the highest physical qualities of British manhood, will not only give us reserves for the Regular Army on mobilisation of fine quality, but will also provide for the creation of a Territorial Army which, when mobilised, will be far superior in efficiency and readiness at the outbreak of war to anything that was previously possible.

The disturbed condition of the world compels us to maintain outside Europe the equivalent of nearly six Regular divisions, as well as the equivalent of five divisions, including three armoured divisions, which we now have on the Continent. As soon as a sufficiency of modernised equipment can be provided we shall have available for service abroad or at home a total of 22 divisions which are of a much more complex character than anything known in the late war, and a considerable proportion of which will be armoured.

In the Centurion tank we have what many good judges believe to be the best tank now in service, and one which is in keen demand in Commonwealth and friendly countries. Not only is it of high military value, but it may also at times become a useful dollar-earning export. The plants which are being developed to make the Centurion tank will readily adapt themselves to the improved patterns which are on the way.

Before Christmas I spoke of the very heavy burden which distant foreign service throws upon our military organisation, and of the 30,000 men always in the pipe-line back and forth. A very real and important economy in the true sense would be introduced into our military system if we could increase the number of men serving for three or four years with the Colours. There is no question of our prolonging the compulsory term of military service, as was industriously suggested at the General Election by those who were enjoying our support in their military policy.

Mr Herbert Morrison (Lewisham, South): Who suggested it?

The Prime Minister: We have, however, started an active voluntary recruitment –

Mr Morrison: Who said it?

The Prime Minister: I hope hon. Gentlemen opposite will not say this has not all been made clear to them.

Mr Morrison: Who said it? The right hon. Gentleman, in telling his tale, has made an allegation. I am asking him who said this, and when?

The Prime Minister: We are very glad to see the right hon. Gentleman on his feet again. Much of the difficulty – (Hon. Members: 'Answer'.) – much of the difficulty we are suffering from –

Mr Morrison: Who said it?

The Prime Minister: Much of the difficulty – (Hon. Members: 'Answer'.) I have only a little time. Much of the difficulty we are suffering from –

Hon. Members: Answer.

Mr Speaker: Order. If hon. Gentlemen require an answer they must keep silent for it.

The Prime Minister: Much of the difficulty we suffer from on these occasions is that the leading men avoid making the charges, but a whispering campaign is started throughout the lower ranks and even the lowest ranks, which is a greater advantage to the statesmen who sit on the Front Bench opposite.

Mr A. C. Manuel (Ayrshire, Central):[1] Down in the mud again.

Mr R. T. Paget[2] (Northampton) rose –

The Prime Minister: I do not wish to be drawn into an altercation with the hon. and learned Gentleman because it may not be generally known that his grandfather was the author of a very famous book to which I have always paid the most careful attention and in which he clears one of my forebears of a lot of disagreeable charges.

Everyone knows the kind of campaign which was run, suggesting that we intended to increase the length of National Service. (*Interruption.*) I am so glad to be able to excite a sense of shame. (*Interruption.*) We really must get back to the laborious administrative details to which I had hoped to confine myself. (Hon. Members: 'Tell the truth.') Let me remind the House that we are not on

---

[1] Archibald Clark Manuel, 1901–76. Railway engine driver. MP (Lab.) for Central Ayrshire, 1950–5, 1959–70.

[2] Reginald Thomas Paget, 1908–90. Educated at Eton and Trinity College, Cambridge. Called to the Bar, 1934. Lt, RNVR, 1940–3 (invalided). MP (Lab.) for Northampton, 1945–74. Hon. Secretary, UK Council of European Movement, 1954. Master, Pytchley Hounds, 1968–71. Life Peer, 1974.

any account going to increase the compulsory term. We have, however, started an active voluntary recruitment.

Mr E. Shinwell (Easington): We started it.

The Prime Minister: I am delighted to share any credit which can be found with the right hon. Gentleman, but I must always be careful not to pay him too many compliments because his friends below the Gangway call that fulsome, and he himself might easily ask me some rude questions to put himself 'on side'.

Mr Shinwell: I am not going to ask the right hon. Gentleman any rude questions. All that I am seeking to do is to ask him to give us the facts about this new measure for voluntary recruitment. I interjected to say that the right hon. Gentleman's Government did not start this. It was, in fact, started by the late Government. The right hon. Gentleman may make a song and dance about it, but I ask him just to tell the truth.

Mr H. Morrison: Not again.

The Prime Minister: I have no desire to state anything but what is the truth. (Hon. Members: 'Oh.') Nor do I intend to. I say we have, however, started – we, the British nation, have, however, started – an active voluntary recruitment with incentives in pay for short Regular engagements of three or four years, particularly designed to attract National Service men and those about to be called up. This is making good progress. In the Air Force about 43,000 young men have taken these engagements in the past two years. In the three months – the right hon. Gentleman talked about telling the truth and he may have a bit of it – since the Army opened a similar engagement, we have gained about 1,000 from serving National Service men, and over 8,000 from civil life.

Mr Sydney Silverman (Nelson and Colne): Unemployment has been rising the whole time.

The Prime Minister: I thought that the right hon. Gentleman was going to claim all the credit for this. Now the hon. Gentleman comes in to take it away from him.

The latter are young men who would otherwise have been called up for National Service in the near future. They were not expecting to be unemployed. They were expecting to be called up by conscription in the near future. Instead of being called up, they take on this long service and have beneficial pay. This is a most helpful development in our Army organisation, and really, one might say, worth its weight in gold when one thinks of the cost of moving men to and fro from here to Hong Kong. That is all I am going to say about the Army this afternoon.

When the Navy Estimates are introduced tomorrow, the First Lord will give a full account of the naval position. (Hon. Members: 'Hear, hear.') That is not until tomorrow. Vote A at 147,000 is about the same as when I introduced the Navy Estimates of 1914. When I then introduced them it was 146,000. When

I returned to the Admiralty at the beginning of the Second World War, Vote A was at 129,000. The growth of the Naval Air Arm more than accounts for the increase. As in the past, Vote A comprises mainly long-service men with valuable, important high-class reserves – that great background and foundation of hereditary seamen, generations going back to generations, gathered round our great seaports and towns, furnishing us with a magnificent supply of youth, sustained by the tradition of their fathers.

The volume of new construction is, of course, less in tonnage than in 1914, and much less than in 1939. But whereas a ton of new construction for, let us say, destroyers – that very vital element – cost in 1914 £150 a ton and in 1939 £325 a ton, the present new construction, with all the improvements and apparatus vital to modern efficiency, and with all the decline in the purchasing power of money, costs £700 a ton – that is to say, nearly five times as much. The whole maintenance and organisation of the Royal Navy has also become vastly more complex and expensive than in former times. I am by no means satisfied with the progress so far made in pruning and purging. Nevertheless, the enormous increase in complexity is a dominating factor – I admit that.

There is, of course, no potentially hostile surface battle fleet afloat. The Russians have three old battleships, about 20 cruisers, and a considerable annual building programme; but all the surface navies which exist on the waters of the world are comprised and are being woven together in the North Atlantic Treaty Organisation. As large vessels take a long time to build, it is not likely that this situation will be altered in, let us say, the next five years.

None the less, the Royal Navy has three main threats to meet, each of which, if successful, would affect our survival in this island. I will state them in their order of gravity as they affect us – the mine; the U-boat – for that is what I call potentially hostile submarines, distinguishing between a wicked weapon used for wrong purposes and the honourable use of the submarine in the ordinary course of naval business; it is a good thing to separate them – (*Interruption.*) – I thought that would appeal to the hon. Member for Nelson and Colne (Mr S. Silverman) – and the threat from the air, ever-growing in its shore-based power.

It is upon improving and augmenting our resources to withstand these threats that our new construction and research of all kinds is in fact concentrated. Anti-mine and anti-U-boat measures absorb the overwhelming proportion of our new construction and material development. They also dominate our training, which includes constant anti-U-boat and minesweeping exercises. Here we also welcome the new shore mine-watching forces now being raised from men in civilian rig, who may well be as valuable to the Royal Navy and to the life of the island as are sailors afloat.

The House, I feel, may be assured that when the new frigates and minesweepers come into service they will be a proof of the perennial British ability to produce novel designs of high performance. From all that I have been able to learn and understand as a member of the Institution of Naval Architects – (*Laughter.*) – honorary, of course; I have made a few suggestions from time to time – I think the constructive Department of the Admiralty are entitled to take pride in their inventiveness and modernity.

The difficulty is not only design or quality in these spheres of anti-U-boat and anti-mine warfare. It is numbers that count, and every improvement, however necessary, in speed or apparatus is the enemy of numbers. I think that progress is being made on right lines in what are necessarily reconciliations of opposing needs. I spoke just now about the threat from the air. This threat, of course, cuts both ways, and the important fleet of aircraft carriers which already exists and is developing, as well as the expanding range of shore-based aircraft, is a vital factor in coping with mining and U-boat attack.

However, do not let anyone suppose that the problems have been solved or that these two dangers – the mines and the U-boat – present themselves in a less fateful form to us, or less important to the United States, than at the beginning of the Second World War. On the contrary, the dangers are greater, and the means of coping with them by rapid improvisations of civilian craft, like yachts and trawlers, are no longer effective against the new fast U-boat types, of which, however, the Soviets have, happily, at present only a few.

Our aircraft carrier fleet is also a powerful defence. The newest aircraft carrier has just now come into service.

Mr Emrys Hughes: What did it cost?

The Prime Minister: It bears the name of the *Eagle*, descended from her original namesake, commissioned in the first Elizabethan era.

Mr Emrys Hughes: What did it cost?

The Prime Minister: I shall be revealing no technical secrets if I say that the design and construction of the new *Eagle* are of a very different kind from those of her ancestor, for fashions have changed in all sorts of ways in this as in other spheres. The expense is no doubt very much greater.

Mr Emrys Hughes: It cost £15 million.

The Prime Minister: Why make these attacks upon the Front Bench opposite? Surely the hon. Member for Ayrshire, South, might leave to the Government the necessary task of defending themselves against the Opposition instead of making this flank attack upon his right hon. Friend who formerly represented the Admiralty in this House. To spend £15 million on an aircraft carrier – good gracious; fancy if the Tories had done a thing like that!

I now come to the third great Service. It is our air power which causes me the most anxiety. Deliveries of modern aircraft are seriously behind the original programme, which, in consequence, has had to be revised. As the result, the Air Force, though maintaining its size, is not being re-equipped with modern machines as rapidly as it should be.

Our greatest need is for modern aircraft in the squadrons. For example, we have no swept-back wing fighters in service, such as the American F.86

and the Russian MIG15. It is true, as the leader of the Opposition said in our debate last December, that it is not unnatural in this competition of types for one nation temporarily to outstep its rivals. It is rather unfortunate, however, if war should come at a moment when the enemy has a great advantage in modernity. It is not a good arrangement to have the highest class of air pilots and all the personal staffs required and for them to have only second-best weapons to fight with.

Mr S. Silverman: Will the right hon. Gentleman give way?

The Prime Minister: No, Sir. I prefer to deal with this in my own way. The problem of when to change from existing production to an improved type is not a new one. It has occurred in all countries during the increasingly rapid improvement of weapons in the last hundred years. It has never occurred with the same significance as in the air forces, which must always be to some extent in a state of flux.

I recognise the difficulty of the position, but the late Government, who are so critical in their anticipations of our ability, certainly did not produce good solutions. Here, as in other spheres, our inheritance leaves much to be desired. It is now that decisions taken soon after the war press upon us. If, indeed, all that was then forecast had come to pass, our problems would be simpler, but the appearance of the MIG15 in Russian squadrons in 1949, which the Russians now have in great numbers, marked a considerable advance in aeronautical design. This has falsified many predictions.

The ordering of new types off the drawing board, with all the risks that attend such decisions, can help in part but cannot itself fill the gap, which is too large for safety. This gap now faces us as a consequence of estimates which events have now disproved.

We are making great efforts to advance the production of the new Hawker fighter and also of the Swift, another first-class aeroplane designed to fill the same day-interceptor role. These types are much newer than the Soviet MIG15, but I must make it clear that we shall not have in the Service in the near future, or, indeed, for some time, anything like adequate numbers of these superior modern fighters. It will require intense exertions to build up production to the necessary level, and also to gain and keep a lead in design.

I have directed that super-priority should be given to the production of the latest and best types of fighter aircraft. This does not mean that everything else is to be knocked about in their exclusive interest. The assertion of priorities, without the necessary refinements of application, might well be most injurious to production as a whole. I have seen undue assertion of priorities do harm in both world wars. The whole subject is far better understood now than it was even during the last war, and in this light I affirm that the first need of our defence is the re-arming of the Royal Air Force with weapons worthy of their daring and skill.

The expansion of the number of aircraft in the front line of the Royal Air

Force, or the improvement in their quality, must not mean an equal increase in its overall manpower. A longer period of training is, however, now necessary, not only for pilots and navigators but for some of the technical ground trades. The training organisation of the Royal Air Force to produce in good time the necessary men is advancing. The response to the new trade structure, which was introduced a year ago and designed to offer a career with proper opportunities of advancement, has so far met with a most promising response. I am sure that the right hon. and learned Member for Rowley Regis and Tipton (Mr A. Henderson[1]), whose father[2] I knew so well, will be very gratified, as he was responsible for that.

As I said in reply to a Question a few days ago, the other Commonwealth countries are kept informed of the defence plans of the United Kingdom and are consulted whenever any of our commitments are likely to be of particular concern to them.

Canada is, of course, a member of the North Atlantic Treaty Organisation. But we must make sure that our contacts grow ever closer. The House will welcome the announcement made recently by the Canadian Minister of National Defence that, as part of the North Atlantic system of mutual help, we are to receive in due course from Canada a number of high-class fighter aircraft. F.86 is the label given to them. The frames will be made in Canada, the engines in America and the Royal Air Force will fly them. These aircraft will be a welcome addition to our strength at home and in Europe. – *(Interruption.)* – I think I said that the negotiations were begun under the right hon. and learned Gentleman the Member for Rowley Regis and Tipton.

Mr Arthur Henderson (Rowley Regis and Tipton): And they were completed, if I may say so.

The Prime Minister: May I not share with him in this event? It is far from me to wish to grasp any credit from anyone. Not even the late Foreign Secretary will say that I wish to rob him of any claim of his share in foreign affairs.

The Prime Minister of Australia[3] has today announced to the Australian

---

[1] Arthur Henderson, 1893–1968. On active service, 1914–18. Called to the Bar, 1921. MP (Lab.) for Cardiff South, 1923–4, 1929–31; for Kingswinford, 1935–50; for Rowley Regis and Tipton, 1950–66. KC, 1939. Joint Parliamentary Secretary of State for War, 1942–3. Financial Secretary, War Office, 1943–5. Parliamentary Under-Secretary of State, India Office and Burma Office, 1945–7. PC, 1947. Minister of State for Commonwealth Relations, 1947. Secretary of State for Air, 1947–51. Baron, 1966.

[2] Arthur Henderson, 1863–1935. Apprenticed as a moulder; later active in the trade union movement. MP (Lab.) for Barnard Castle, 1903–18; for Widnes, 1919–22; for Newcastle-upon-Tyne East, 1923; for Burnley, 1924–31; for Clay Cross, 1933–5. Chief Whip, Labour Party, 1914, 1921–4, 1925–7. President of the Board of Education, 1915–16. Paymaster-General, 1916. Member of Lloyd George's War Cabinet, Dec. 1916–Aug. 1917. Home Secretary, 1924. Foreign Secretary, 1929–31. President of the World Disarmament Conference, 1932–3.

[3] Robert Gordon Menzies, 1894–1978. Born in Jeparit, Victoria, Australia. Established himself as leading constitutional lawyer prior to entering Victorian Parliament in 1928. MP (United Aus.) for Kooyong, 1934–66. Attorney-General, 1934–8. Minister for Industry, 1934–9. PM of Australia, 1939–41, 1949–66. Minister for Coordination of Defence, 1939–42. Minister for Information and Minister for Munitions, 1940. Leader of the Opposition, 1943–9. KG, 1963.

Parliament at Canberra that his Government have decided to send a fighter wing to the Middle East to operate with the Royal Air Force in that area. The wing will consist of two squadrons of the Royal Australian Air Force and should be ready to leave Australia for the Middle East next June. The actual station of the wing in the area will be decided later on. One possibility is Cyprus.

I know that I shall be expressing the views of all parties in the House when I say that we warmly welcome this further practical contribution by Australia to the defence of the free world and of the interests of the British Commonwealth. We shall be very glad to have these Australian squadrons working with us in the task of defending the Middle East against external aggression should any occur.

I have not attempted this afternoon to deal either with the general problem of European defence or the still wider issues represented by what I think we have got sufficiently habituated to call NATO. We shall have a debate at the end of the month when the fruitful outcome of the Lisbon Conference and other questions larger than those comprised in the White Paper can be discussed.

But I should like before I sit down, if the House will permit me, to repeat in substance what I said before upon the reason why I do not believe that war is imminent or inevitable, and why I believe that we have more time, if we use it wisely, and more hope of warding off that frightful catastrophe from our struggling, ill-informed, bewildered and almost helpless human race.

I am glad to find that the words I used two years ago in this House still express my thoughts. This is what I said:

> There never was a time when the deterrents against war were so strong. If penalties of the most drastic kind can prevent in our civil life crime or folly, then we certainly have them here on a gigantic scale in the affairs of nations. . . . The penalties have grown to an extent undreamed of; and at the same time, many of the old incentives which were the cause of the beginning of so many wars, or features in their beginning, have lost their significance. The desire for glory, booty, territory, dynastic or national aggrandisement; hopes of a speedy and splendid victory with all its excitement – and they are all temptations from which even those which only fight for righteous causes are not always exempt – are now superseded by a preliminary stage of measureless agony from which neither side could at present protect itself. Another world war would begin by both sides suffering as the first step what they dread most. Western Europe would be overrun and Communised. . . . On the other hand, at the same time, Soviet cities, air fields, oil fields and railway junctions would be annihilated; with possible complete disruption of Kremlin control over the enormous populations who are ruled from Moscow. Those fearful cataclysms would be simultaneous, and neither side could at present, or for several years to come, prevent them. Moralists may

find it a melancholy thought that peace can find no nobler foundations than mutual terror. But for my part, I shall be content if these foundations are solid, because they will give us the extra time and the new breathing space for the supreme effort which has to be made for a world settlement.[1]

That is what I said two years ago, that is what I am not ashamed to repeat here now.

I thank the House for its courtesy and kindness to me. The interruptions which have occurred will not be deprived of the plea that they were unprovoked, for we have our own system of public business and of discussing our affairs across the Floor of the House while dealing with grave matters.

In conclusion, the House will realise that I cannot claim that the estimates and schemes presented in the White Paper go as far as the proposals of the Socialist Government. This is partly due to physical causes, which invariably delay large re-armament programmes, but it is also due to the present Cabinet's decisions to increase the emphasis on exports at the expense of the speed of the re-armament programme.

The motives which inspired the Leader of the Opposition, the former Minister of Defence, and the Service Ministers of those days, to embark upon this great scheme of re-armament, are creditable to their military zeal, but it was a scheme loosely and hastily framed and declared, and only five months intervened between the £3,600 million plan and its being superseded by that of £4,700 million. Moreover, they did not take sufficient account of the serious financial situation into which they were moving and of which we are today the anxious legatees. It is a curious commentary on British politics that it should fall to a Conservative Government in the face of dire financial stress to have to reduce or slow down the military defence programme and expenditure on which the Socialist Government had embarked and to which they had committed the nation.

We must, however, be governed by realities, and while trying our utmost to carry out the programme we must not mislead the country into expectations beyond what its life energies can fulfil.

---

[1] Speech of 28 Mar. 1950, reproduced in *The Churchill Documents*, vol. 22, *Leader of the Opposition, August 1945 to October 1951*, pp. 1702–12.

MARCH 1952 317

Cabinet: conclusions
(Cabinet papers, 128/24)

7 March 1952
Secret
11 a.m.
Cabinet Meeting No. 27 of 1952

1. The Prime Minister said that strong feelings had been expressed in the House of Commons on the previous day about the increases in bus fares and railway fares in the London area. He had therefore suggested to the Secretary of State for Co-ordination of Transport, Fuel and Power and the Minister of Transport[1] that he should issue without delay an announcement on the lines discussed by the Cabinet on the previous day, making it clear that the Government had no responsibility for these increases. The terms of the proposed announcement were read to the Cabinet. It included the statement that the Minister of Transport proposed to make a reference to the Central Transport Consultative Committee on the alteration of fare stages.

The Cabinet –

Invited the Prime Minister to arrange for the immediate issue of an announcement on the increase in passenger transport fares, in the terms of the draft which had been read to the Cabinet.

[. . .]

Anthony Eden to Winston S. Churchill
(Churchill papers, 2/517)

7 March 1952
Secret
PM/52/19

I have been looking into the documents which constitute the late Government's commitments in respect of extended operations in Korea. They are, as you know, Foreign Office telegrams and papers, not Cabinet Papers. I am quite sure that if you should be pressed to lay them before Parliament, the right course would be to refuse on the ground that publication would not be in the public interest.

2. The following are my reasons for this view:

(1) Details valuable to our opponents in Korea and to the Soviet

---

[1] Alan Tindal Lennox-Boyd, 1904–83. Educated at Christ's Church, Oxford. Lt, RNVR, 1940–3. MP (Cons.) for Mid Bedfordshire, 1931–60. Parliamentary Secretary, Ministry of Aircraft Production, 1943–5. Minister of State, Colonial Office, 1951–2. Minister of Transport and Civil Aviation, 1952–4. Secretary of State for the Colonies, 1954–9. Viscount, 1960. Director, Royal Exchange, 1962–70.

Government would be revealed, which you were careful not to divulge in your statement in the House on the 26th February.[1]

(2) It is not possible to make clear Her Majesty's Government's commitments without revealing in full the proposals made by the United States Government. For this the United States Government's consent would be necessary; and would almost certainly be withheld. Indeed, Acheson has already expressed to Oliver Franks the hope that he will not be involved in demands for disclosure of documents or agreements in Washington.

(3) To set out the United States Government's proposals and Her Majesty's Government's replies side by side, as would be necessary, would reveal to a most undesirable extent the important differences of policy between the Americans and ourselves.

(4) The disclosures would affect the United States Government, on whom the main responsibilities and risks in Korea rest, much more than ourselves, who are only one of a number of partners in the enterprise.

Anthony Eden to Winston S. Churchill
(*Churchill papers, 2/517*)

8 March 1952
Secret
PM/52/21

GERMAN CONTRACTUAL NEGOTIATIONS
SECURITY SAFEGUARDS

As you know, controls over the German armaments industry were discussed at my meeting with Acheson, Schuman and Adenauer last month. This has been one of the most difficult issues in the whole negotiation.

2. Adenauer agreed in London in effect that war material under the following heads should not be produced in 'exposed strategic areas of the European Defence Community' (i.e. Germany). These are contained in the so called 'short list', as follows:

Atomic, biological and chemical weapons;
Long-range and guided missiles;
Military aircraft;
Naval vessels other than minor defensive craft.

3. Other military equipment (set out in a 'long list') will be covered under a clause in the EDC treaty which prohibits manufacture unless the EDC

[1] Reproduced above (pp. 283–92).

Defence Commission places orders. There is no implication that items in this long list will be restricted to non-exposed strategic areas.

4. The Admiralty have now asked that 'influence mines'[1] should be covered by the short list under 'guided missiles'. They had not previously asked that they should be. These mines were previously listed among various items of naval equipment between torpedoes and Asdics[2] in what has now become the 'long list'.

5. Now that all has been agreed in London and Lisbon with Acheson and Schuman and, subject to the definitions, also with Adenauer, it is extremely difficult to see how this can be done. We have tried, but the United States High Commissioner will not even consider our proposal, which he regards as a breach of faith and contrary to the London and Lisbon agreements. The United States Naval Authorities in Washington have refused to support us. Our own High Commissioner[3] in Germany considers our position very weak.

6. I simply do not see what more can be done. The Americans are against us, and a further effort will seriously delay – perhaps even upset – the arrangements which we have so laboriously reached with Schuman and Acheson, and collectively with Adenauer. I have received a serious warning from Bonn that any prolonged delay in our negotiations may jeopardise the whole contract. I know that these mines are a grave risk – but there remains the safeguard that they cannot be made in Germany without the consent of a majority of the EDC Commission.

7. It is most unlikely that there will be a majority in the EDC in favour of the manufacture of 'influence mines' in Germany. We should be able to maintain close contact with the non-German members of the EDC through naval and other channels and ensure that the importance of this matter to them and to us is not overlooked. The only circumstances in which the Germans would be likely to make these mines for use against us would be if they moved over to the Soviet bloc, but in that event, no restrictions imposed now would be worth anything. Indeed, the German Contract is designed to provide precisely against this risk and the Chiefs of Staff view throughout these negotiations has been that the successful conclusion of the Contract should not be jeopardised.

[1] Mines triggered by the passing motion of a ship or submarine, rather than by direct contact.

[2] 'Asdic': term (derived from 'Anti-Submarine Division') for sonar detection device used by Allied escorts throughout WWII.

[3] Ivone Augustine Kirkpatrick, 1897–1964. On active service, 1914–18 (wounded, despatches twice). Diplomatic Service, 1919. 1st Secretary, Rome, 1930–2. Counsellor, Berlin, 1933–8. Director, Foreign Div., Ministry of Information, 1940. Controller, European Services, BBC, 1941. Joined PWE Policy Committee, Feb. 1942. Deputy Commissioner to Inter-Allied Control Commission in Germany, 1944–5. Asst Under-Secretary of State, Foreign Office, 1945; Deputy Under-Secretary, 1948; Permanent Under-Secretary (German Section), 1949; Permanent Under-Secretary of State, 1953–7. Knighted, 1948. British High Commissioner for Germany, 1950–3. Chairman, Independent Television Authority, 1957–62.

8. I should be grateful for early decision. Agreement is being held up in Bonn meanwhile.

9. Copy of this goes to First Lord.

Anthony Eden to Winston S. Churchill
(*Churchill papers, 2/517*)

8 March 1952
Personal
PM/52/22

NATO SECRETARY GENERAL

I send you this record of a difficult talk.[1] We are really up against a difficult problem of personality. What weight do we attach to this appointment? Is it worthy of our best? The Americans clearly think it is and do not want to take anything short of that. Yet how can I ask you to part with any of your leading colleagues at this time. Maybe we could have a word about it on the telephone. I ought to try to see the Ambassador again tomorrow. We may be doing serious damage to NATO if we cannot settle this business by the time they meet again next Wednesday.

Anthony Eden to Winston S. Churchill
(*Churchill papers, 2/517*)

8 March 1952

Sir,

I had a long and serious conversation with the American Ambassador this afternoon about the Secretary-Generalship of NATO.

2. Mr Gifford said that after he had asked to see me for a general talk about the situation, he had received the attached message from Mr Acheson which was on the same line as he had intended to speak to me.

3. The Ambassador said that he thought that the differences between us on the question of the appointment really arose from a different conception as to its importance. In reply to some questions from me probing this point, the Ambassador admitted, if a little reluctantly, that the consensus of opinion in NATO now was that the Secretary-General should be an Englishman. There was no doubt that Europe wanted to feel that this key post was filled by a leading personality from these Islands. The Ambassador went on to explain that the Americans felt that they had given of their best to NATO with Eisenhower in command in the Field and Harriman to represent them on the

---

[1] Reproduced immediately below.

TCC were examples of this. In their view it was essential to the future of the world that NATO should be preserved. It was the basis of American efforts in Europe. Upon its military and political organisation depended our chance to build up enough strength to meet the Soviet danger and to avert war. In their scale of things therefore it was almost impossible to exaggerate the importance of this work.

4. This point of view was re-expressed by the Ambassador at different stages in our conversation and was his last word as he left.

5. I asked the Ambassador to tell me frankly whether the objection to Kirkpatrick was in any way personal – if so, we had better know it. Mr Gifford emphatically denied this. He said that Kirkpatrick had many gifts, though he might be a little lacking in personality, but he was not of the stature for which they were seeking. I said that, after all, he was on a level with McCloy,[1] both excellent High Commissioners in Germany, to which the Ambassador replied that they would not consider McCloy as suitable for this task.

6. After some discussion of names, I said that what it amounted to was that the Americans really wanted us to give NATO one of the three or four top people in this country in the political world and, of course, they were to be found, so far as our party at least was concerned, in the Cabinet. The Ambassador said that this was so and it was with this in mind that they had mentioned such names as Alexander, Ismay or Oliver Lyttelton.

7. We then discussed the possibility of somebody filling the appointment for a relatively short period, say six months, in order to get the machine going and create the necessary confidence in NATO in this critical year. The Ambassador wondered whether it was possible to second somebody for that period and he spoke of Pearson in this connexion. I said that I did not see how a Foreign Secretary could leave his post for as long a period as that and neither of us thought this a really satisfactory solution.

8. There is no doubt that the American Government are also troubled by the fact that, after a successful meeting at Lisbon, the boat is losing much way in the rough seas of the failure to appoint the NATO Secretary-General. This worries them all the more at a time when they are trying to get the appropriations they need from Congress on a very large scale to meet the military needs of the NATO countries and to build up towards our target of 50 divisions in Europe. The Ambassador mentioned that the press was not being helpful in either country. The Ambassador referred, in particular, to the *Manchester Guardian* which he said contained a most deplorable article making the utmost of our difficulties.

---

[1] John Jay McCloy, 1895–1989. Born in Philadelphia. Educated at Harvard University. Asst Secretary of War during WWII. Responsible for the internment of Japanese Americans in 1942. Thrice refused to approve bombing of the railway lines leading to Auschwitz, 1944. High Commissioner for West Germany, 1947–52. Chairman, Council on Foreign Relations, 1953–70. Member, *Foreign Affairs* Editorial Board, 1953–89.

Walter Gifford to Anthony Eden
(*Churchill papers, 2/517*)

8 March 1952
Confidential

Dear Anthony,

I have been asked to deliver the following personal message to you from the Secretary of State:

'We are very much disturbed at the situation which has developed with regard to the appointment of a Secretary General of the North Atlantic Treaty Organization and believe it very important that you and we fully appreciate each other's point of view and reach an understanding on this matter. The purpose of this message is to try to make our attitude clear and to see where we go from here.

In Lisbon I thought that you and I both believed that the man selected for the appointment of Secretary General should be a man of the highest ability, reputation and prestige. These qualities were summed up in the phrase "Ministerial rank". I kept stressing these qualities in the Foreign Ministers' meeting because of the profound conviction that the person selected must give direction to the North Atlantic Treaty Organization and bring to it the same calibre of leadership on the civilian side as General Eisenhower has given in the military field. It seemed to me that unless we got a man capable of doing this, rather than even the most capable official, we would in large part nullify the objective of the North Atlantic Treaty Organization reorganization to which we all agreed at Lisbon and to which we attach the greatest importance.

While believing that the qualities of the candidate were more important than his nationality, we have fully recognized the sacrifice involved for you on the decision to move the North Atlantic Treaty Organization headquarters from London to Paris.

It was with these thoughts in mind that we took a strong and, I thought, helpful position in getting agreement that we should try to get Sir Oliver Franks to take the appointment. We felt that he possessed all the qualities for which we were searching, and it was a matter of deep disappointment to us that he did not find it possible to accept.

When Sir Oliver indicated his unavailability we were happy to agree on Mr Pearson who, in turn, proved not to be available. In our desire to be helpful and consistent with the standards which we were trying to set in this matter we then suggested Lord Alexander and Malcolm MacDonald.[1]

---

[1] Malcolm John MacDonald, 1901–81. Educated at Bedales and Queen's College, Oxford. MP (Lab.) for Bassetlaw, 1929–31; (Nat. Lab.) 1931–5; for Ross and Cromarty, 1936–45. Parliamentary Under-Secretary, Dominions Office, 1931–5. PC, 1935. Secretary of State for Dominion Affairs, 1935–8, 1938–9; for the Colonies, 1935, 1938–40. Minister of Health, 1940–1. High

When this suggestion did not prove to be practicable, we felt that we should turn to Mr Stikker[1] who was the remaining person of 'Ministerial rank' mentioned in Lisbon who was still available. We understood that at one point the choice of Mr Stikker had the approval of your Government and it was again a source of real disappointment to us when his name was not accepted.

Certain problems arose for us in connexion with your suggestions of Sir Edwin Plowden,[2] for whom we have high regard, as well as Sir Ivone Kirkpatrick, who in spite of his qualities does not, in our opinion, meet all the criteria which we have set.

I know how great a sacrifice it would be asking to suggest that a man high in your Government should be made available. Therefore, I do not suggest it but say only that if Oliver Lyttelton or Lord Alexander were available, we should be most happy. Perhaps the same difficulty for you would not arise in connexion with Lord Portal,[3] who is not now, as I understand it, in the Government. He also would seem to us to possess the high degree of leadership which the gentlemen mentioned could bring to this important work.

If it should prove that no man of such outstanding calibre and reputation is available, we should perhaps consider turning to a solution of separating the position of Vice Chairman of the Council from that of Secretary General. I am aware that sentiment toward a solution of this kind already exists particularly among some of our Continental colleagues. For our part we would come to such a solution with great reluctance since it would not only mean the abandonment of our concept of the job which we still feel is the correct one, but would also inevitably reopen the whole question of the functions and terms of reference of the Secretary General, thereby further

---

Commissioner, Canada, 1941–6. Governor-General of Malaya, Singapore and British Borneo, 1946–8. Commissioner-General for South-East Asia, 1948–55. High Commissioner, India, 1955–60. Governor-General of Kenya, 1963–4; High Commissioner, 1964–5. British Special Representative in East and Central Africa, 1965–6; in Africa, 1966–9. OM, 1969.

[1] Dirk U. Stikker, 1887–1979. Educated at University of Groningen. Worked in banking and industry, 1922–48. Director of Heineken International, 1935–48. Founded Party for Freedom and Democracy, 1946. Member, First Chamber, States General, 1946–8. Minister of Foreign Affairs, 1948–52. Ambassador in London, 1952–8. Permanent Representative of the Netherlands to North Atlantic Council and OEEC, 1958. Secretary General of NATO, 1961–4.

[2] Edwin Noel Auguste Plowden, 1907–2001. Educated at Pembroke College, Cambridge. Married, 1933, Bridget Horatia Richmond. KBE, 1946. KCB, 1951. Chairman, Atomic Energy Authority, 1954–9. Baron, 1959. Chairman, Treasury Committee of Inquiry, 1959–61. GBE, 1987.

[3] Charles Frederick Algernon Portal, 1893–1971. Known as 'Peter'. On active service, 1914–18 (despatches, DSO and bar, MC). Seconded to RFC, 1915. Maj. commanding 16 Sqn, 1917. Air Ministry (Directorate of Operations and Intelligence), 1923. Commanded British forces in Aden, 1934–5. Instructor, Imperial Defence College, 1936–7. Director of Organization, Air Ministry, 1937–8. Air Member for Personnel, Air Council, 1939–40. AOC-in-C, Bomber Command, Apr.–Oct. 1940. Knighted, July 1940. CAS, Oct. 1940 to Nov. 1945. Air Chf Mshl, temp. 1940; permanent, 1942. Mshl of the RAF, 1944. Baron, 1945. Viscount, 1946. OM, 1946. KG, 1946. Controller, Atomic Energy, Ministry of Supply, 1946–51. Chairman, British Aircraft Corp., 1960–8.

delaying a decision which in the interests of our whole enterprise should be taken at once.

I should be most grateful to have your thoughts on this tangled subject. I am most eager that we should come to a meeting of minds about it. Do you agree that we should try to do this before the matter again comes before the Deputies?

Thank you for your kind message to me on my statement regarding Malaya.

I have been distressed to hear that you have been laid low by the grippe and hope that you are now entirely well again.

With warm regards.'

Winston S. Churchill to Field Marshal Lord Alexander
Prime Minister's Personal Minute M.102/52
(Premier papers, 11/226)

8 March 1952

The Admiralty had on December 31, 1951, 2,327,000 tons of oil fuel for the Navy in the United Kingdom. This is more than in any of the five years 1940–1944 inclusive. They now ask to add in 1952 enough to raise their total in the United Kingdom alone to 2,850,000, producing a world wide total of 4,400,000. There is no military excuse for such a demand upon us. 2,850,000 is far greater than was required by a much larger Fleet opposed to the German, Italian and Japanese Navies during the five main war years. There is no justification for any increase on the present Admiralty reserves either in the United Kingdom or abroad. I am astonished that such a demand should have been put forward at a time when we have, as Lord Leathers mentioned, far more tankers than we had in the late war, when we have virtually no surface navy to contend with, when all other navies of the world are on our side, and when the character of a future war tends to be decisive in the first few months. They have no right to ask for a single ton addition to their reserves at home or abroad. If you agree with this, their 1952 demands should be cut down by 533,000 tons on their home fuel alone. There is a good case for making them draw on their reserves till they reach the average home stock of 1,806,000 on which we fought the war. I should, however, be content if no more oil fuel is added to reserve for all Services stocks for 1952, making a total of 3,072,000.

Will you please look into this. It only shows the liberties that were taken with the previous Administration. It would be more prudent to have a larger reserve of wheat, and this we must consider when we see the harvest.

Winston S. Churchill to Anthony Eden
Prime Minister's Personal Minute M.103/52
(Premier papers, 11/91)

9 March 1952

What exactly is the picture you make to yourself of the position if we evacuate our forces from the Canal Zone? What powers will remain to the Allied Military Commander if he has no fighting troops, and if the Egyptian Army has been more strongly armed by us? Who is to protect the international waterway of the Canal, the three hundred million pounds' worth of stores, etc., accumulated in the base, the British Air Force and airfields, and indeed his own Headquarters? Are all these to be entrusted to a rearmed and strengthened Egyptian Army which may at any time come under the control of a Wafd[1] or other hostile Egyptian Government? Have we to contemplate the great cost of a move to Gaza or Jordan as part of the evacuation? Is this to take place before the taking over by the Four Powers together with the Egyptians, they being the fifth (or first)? You say in paragraph 7, sub-section (c): 'Such withdrawal (of British troops) would, of course, be subject to any future agreement which might be reached between the Supreme Allied Commander, Middle East, and the Egyptian military authorities. . . .' Is the SAC to be instructed that he need not be responsible for the safeguarding of any of the interests and objects mentioned above, but is to entrust them to the Egyptian Army, of which his Command could only be nominal and exercised on sufferance?

I am most anxious to see our forces in Egypt reduced, but before we place ourselves and the Canal and all our interests at the mercy of the Egyptians, we ought at least to have a Treaty comprising the Four Powers, and until that is done the SAC ought not to be deprived of the necessary minimum of force in the Canal Zone. Neither ought we to commit ourselves without much more detailed examination to building the enormous new establishments which have been suggested as alternatives.

By your firmness and the use of British strength at great expense, we have vastly improved our bargaining position, which, after all, was only to ask that the Treaty you made should be kept. Why then are we reduced to begging for leave, from a non-representative Government and a Parliament adjourned or dissolving, to give them all that Nahas Pasha[2] ever asked? When you brought this matter up at the Cabinet on February 14, you indicated that the chance

---

[1] The Wafd (Hizb al-Wafd) was a popular Egyptian liberal nationalist political party, which reached its apogee between 1919 and the 1930s. It was instrumental in developing the 1923 constitution and supported moving Egypt from dynastic rule to a constitutional monarchy with power devolved to a nationally elected parliament. The Wafd did not survive the July 1952 Egyptian revolution.

[2] Nahas Pasha, 1879–1965. PM of Egypt, 1928, 1930, 1936–7, 1942–4, 1950–2. Helped found Arab League, 1944. Signed Anglo-Egyptian Treaty of 1936.

might be lost for ever if decision was not taken at once. A month has passed and things have got steadily better, and our relative strength has grown. Why then is there to be all this urgency of concluding an agreement which sacrifices our work of so many years and our power of discharging our international duty? An unfriendly Egyptian Government, once you have withdrawn your troops and have no force of power behind you, can repudiate any engagement entered into. I beg you to think of all this.

I cannot think it a good policy to hasten to make an agreement with this fragile Palace Government which will deprive us of all means of securing the observance of the agreement if, as you apprehend, a hostile Government may soon come. I am sure there are forces in the Conservative Party which will be deeply stirred by our moral surrender and physical exodus. We must have the maintenance of the international waterway of the Canal by the Four Powers, plus Egypt, before we strip ourselves of power.

Winston S. Churchill to Anthony Eden
Prime Minister's Personal Minute M.104/52
(Premier papers, 11/171)

9 March 1952

It should certainly not be decided without reference to the Minister of Defence.[1]

I should myself consider that a check vigilantly exerted through the EDC would be sufficient in view of the argument you use in Paragraph 7.

Would it not be possible to have a private understanding with Adenauer on this unfortunate omission.

I am having copies of the relevant minutes sent to Lord Alexander. I wonder whether you could not have a word with the First Lord yourself.

Winston S. Churchill to Anthony Eden
Prime Minister's Personal Minute M.111/52
(Premier papers, 11/601)

9 March 1952

There is certainly no need and no demand for further publication at present.[2] It may well be, however, that in a year or so publication might be harmless and even helpful.

---

[1] In response to PM/52/21, reproduced above (pp. 318–20).
[2] In response to PM/52/19, reproduced above (pp. 317–18).

Winston S. Churchill to Field Marshal Lord Alexander
Prime Minister's Personal Minute M.109/52
(Premier papers, 11/7)

9 March 1952

The Secretary of State for War should surely produce a satisfactory answer which could be published to this very damaging article, though without referring specifically to it.[1] The answer should not be too long and I should like to see it before it is put out.

It is a pity to let such misapprehensions and such misrepresentations gain uncorrected currency.

Anthony Eden to Winston S. Churchill
(Churchill papers, 2/517)

10 March 1952
Top Secret
PM/52/24

Your minute No. M.103/52[2] about Egypt does not seem to me to take account of the fact that we shall be bound to get out of the Canal Zone anyway in 1956 in the absence of some new agreement. If we have to leave, this would mean withdrawing not only our troops but also the stores in our base and leaving the base installations behind. We have not been able to discover any alternative site for the base, although there are alternative places for our combatant troops. My purpose is therefore to make a new agreement while we can. This was the purpose of the four-Power proposals of last October, leading to the establishment of an Allied Middle East Command.

2. In making such an arrangement we have to take account of the true facts of the position. These are, first, that our lease is up in 1956; secondly, that our present Treaty does not give us what we need, since it does not provide for the existence of the great base which was created during the war and which is now our main interest; thirdly that the internal position in Egypt has become more precarious and dangerous.

3. The Four-Power proposals do not specifically provide for the stationing of foreign troops on Egyptian soil, and in fact it has always been recognised that there is no chance of securing Egyptian agreement at present to the stationing of land forces of other nations in Egypt in time of peace. Nor indeed is there likely to be any question of this, since neither the Americans, nor the French, nor the Turks, have shown the smallest indication that they would be willing to provide such forces for Egypt. The Four-Power proposals do provide

[1] See Head to Churchill of Mar. 5, reproduced above (pp. 303–4).
[2] Reproduced above (pp. 325–6).

the outline of a plan of cooperation and a Command organisation which could control those forces anywhere in the Middle East which were placed at its disposal. We propose that this organisation, which would include Egypt, and with which other Middle Eastern States would be associated, will be set up <u>before</u> the actual withdrawal of British combatant troops from Egypt is completed.

4. The main Egyptian contribution to this scheme would be cooperation in the maintenance of the Middle East base. We hope that Egypt would agree that British technicians should be retained in it, while Egyptian troops would probably have to take over guard duties. This base would provide the means of sustaining all the forces of ourselves and our Allies in the Middle East in time of war, and it is thus that we should hope to protect the Suez Canal. There would also have to be an Allied air defence organisation in Egypt, to protect the base. These arrangements should of course run on <u>after 1956</u>.

5. I do not suggest that these arrangements are ideal, but I think that the time has now come when we have to make the best agreement we can with Egypt. The true alternatives are not between remaining as we are or making some other equally good or better arrangement, but between making the best arrangement that we can or finding ourselves involved in a commitment greater than we can bear.

6. I am convinced that we shall not reach an agreement unless we are willing to agree to the principle of evacuation. The net result of the last five months has been to bring Egypt to the verge of anarchy. The present Egyptian Government is the best we can possibly hope for. Its position is precarious and its continuance in power depends on its ability to clip the wings of the Wafd. To do this, it needs some helpful move by us, and it needs it soon. Time, I am convinced, is not on our side.

7. If we merely seek to hold the Canal Zone by force, we must expect sooner rather than later a revolution in Egypt. This will mean disturbances in the Delta on a far larger scale than on January 26th, with inevitable loss of many British lives and interests. We may be compelled to reoccupy the Delta towns, which will place upon us an administrative commitment which we cannot possibly afford in terms either of men or money. We must expect that all our commercial interests in Egypt will be lost. As for the base, our military authorities already admit, that, under the conditions prevailing during the last five months it would be useless from an operational point of view if war came, since our entire resources have been devoted to maintaining ourselves, and we have not had enough to spare to maintain the bases. Moreover, we should have no troops for the defence of the Middle East, since they would all be required to hold the position in Egypt.

8. In the circumstances foreseen, we could not expect continued support in the international field from our friends. The American are pressing us strongly to come to an agreement. It is therefore literally true to say that the

consequences of a failure to reach agreement with Egypt, or still more, failure even to put forward a reasonable offer to the Egyptians, are incalculable. There can be no doubt however that the damage to British interests and prestige would be immense. The plain fact is that we are no longer in a position to impose our will upon Egypt, regardless of the cost in men, money, and international goodwill both throughout the Middle East and the rest of the world.

If I cannot impose my will, I must negotiate. This is the best Government we have yet had with which to do so.

Winston S. Churchill to Sir Edward Bridges and Sir Norman Brook
Prime Minister's Personal Minute M.114/52
(*Premier papers, 11/295*)

10 March 1952

ATOMIC ENERGY

Lord Cherwell is to be responsible and act directly under me. All necessary accommodation and authority is to be given to him in the Ministry of Supply. The accounting will continue to be done by the Ministry of Supply. The Ministry of Supply is to house the establishment and make such arrangements as Lord Cherwell finds convenient. Any difference between Ministers should be reported to me.

Lord Cherwell to Winston S. Churchill
(*Premier papers, 11/295*)

10 March 1952

ATOMIC ENERGY

I have just seen a copy of the minute on Atomic Energy which has apparently been sent to Edward Bridges and Norman Brook. It is absolutely different from the one you dictated yesterday. Instead of transferring the organisation to the Ministry of Defence as agreed, it leaves everything just as it is in the Ministry of Supply.

As set out in my minute, at perhaps inordinate length, this arrangement is inadequate and has in practice proved unworkable. I will not repeat the arguments which I thought had convinced you yesterday, as I still hope that the change is due to some misapprehension.

If so, perhaps your original minute could be substituted so that a draft Order in Council could be prepared transferring the atomic energy organisation to the Ministry of Defence.

Winston S. Churchill to Lord Swinton, Field Marshal Lord Alexander,
Peter Thorneycroft,[1] Duncan Sandys, Sir Edward Bridges and Sir Norman Brook
Prime Minister's Personal Minute M.120/52
(Premier papers, 11/75)

10 March 1952

1. The principles and procedure set forth in the Ministry of Defence Paper of February 23 and summed up in Paragraph 13 should be adopted without further delay. The use of a symbol proposed in Paragraph 4[2] and referred to in Paragraph 6(a) is approved by me. I should like further explanation of 6(b),[3] but I am inclined to the 'automatic right' with vigilance to guard against abuse.

2. The Minister of Supply will be responsible for the administration of these super-priorities and will furnish monthly reports to the other Ministers concerned and to the Cabinet. The results if not agreed can be discussed at the Cabinet.

3. The priority is to extend to Centurion tanks which are at once a valuable export and a necessary protection. We must arrange to have a practical option whether to sell or use at a later stage, though this need not be formalized with our customers. It is essential to increase both the plant and the output of Centurion tanks and other modernized tanks, so as to supply if necessary a thousand to the United States (600 are already arranged). I am distinctly of the opinion that the first contingent of the Territorial Army divisions should be armed as soon as possible with Centurions. Preliminary models for training should be issued to them well in advance of the full supply.

4. The Ministry of Defence has made exertions and sacrifices of their programme in order to aid the financial and export position. No further delay can be accepted in carrying out the policy proposed by the Ministry of Defence.

5. This directive is operative from today, but should be brought before the Cabinet on Thursday if there are any objections.

---

[1] Peter Thorneycroft, 1909–94. MP (Cons.) for Stafford, 1938–45; for Monmouth, 1945–66. Parliamentary Secretary, Ministry of War Transport, 1945. President of the Board of Trade, 1951–7. Chancellor of the Exchequer, 1957–8. Minister of Aviation, 1960–2. Minister of Defence, 1962–4. Secretary of State for Defence, 1964. Baron, 1967.

[2] See M.92/52, reproduced above (p. 303 n.1).

[3] 'Whether sub-contractors should have an automatic right to preferential treatment by their suppliers of raw materials and components, or whether the onus should be on them to prove their case to departments locally, who would be responsible for taking administrative action.'

March 1952

David Hunt to Winston S. Churchill
(*Premier papers, 11/112*)

10 March 1952

You wanted to know when this warning statement on Korea was likely to be issued to the public. It is not possible to give a definite answer as it will not be issued until after an Armistice has been signed in Korea. The proposal is that within twenty-four hours of the signature of the Armistice, the representatives of the nations with Forces in Korea should sign this warning and send it to the Secretary-General of the United Nations and simultaneously issue the text to the Press.

Winston S. Churchill to President Harry S Truman
(*'Defending the West, The Truman–Churchill Correspondence', page 192*)

11 March 1952

You will no doubt have seen what has been happening over here and I am sure you will be interested in the Budget. Our defence programme is already somewhat spread out. It is not certain that even with a struggle we shall be able to fulfil it. I quite understand you have difficulties as well as we. When I was over with you there was much talk of 'offshore purchases' which could help the NATO front and enable us to fulfil our programme.

It would be possible for me to arrange for Canberra and Venom aircraft of the latest types now being made by us in the United Kingdom to be delivered to the United States and distributed by you to NATO wherever Eisenhower thought they could be most useful.

If as I hope, you think these ideas are worth pursuing I suggest that our people should talk to Mr Battle[1] in London and that Franks should discuss the matter with Averell Harriman.

[. . .]

A memo follows.*

---

* Aide-mémoire dated 12 March presented a detailed proposal for the United States to accept several hundred aircraft from the UK for use by NATO in order to ease Britain's balance of payments problem.

---

[1] Lucius Durham Battle, 1918–2008. Served with US Navy in Pacific during WWII. Special Assistant to the Secretary of State, 1949–53. 1st Secretary, American Embassy, Copenhagen, 1953–5. Secretary to Lord Ismay at NATO, Paris, 1956. Vice-President of Colonial Williamsburg, 1957–60. Executive Secretary, State Dept, 1960–2. Asst Secretary for Education and Culture, 1962–4. US Ambassador to Egypt, 1964–7. Asst Secretary of State for Near East and North Africa, 1967–8.

Winston S. Churchill to Anthony Eden
Prime Minister's Personal Minute M.115/52
(Premier papers, 11/112)

11 March 1952

I quite agree to the text of the warning,[1] but surely whether to issue it immediately after signing the Armistice should depend upon the circumstances and atmosphere at the time. It would be rather odd to put it out the day after we had officially kissed and made friends. I expect however that the conditions will be such as to make the publication appropriate.

Winston S. Churchill to Lord Cherwell
Prime Minister's Personal Minute M.118/52
(Premier papers, 11/295)

11 March 1952
Private

ATOMIC ENERGY

With reference to your Minute of March 10.[2] This was done to give you more power by avoiding putting the accountancy under the Ministry of Defence. You can see this from Bridges's Minute, which says that 'legal difficulties might follow from any arrangement under which the responsibility of the Minister of Defence was purely formal. . . . Where powers are vested by statute in a particular Minister, they can be validly exercised only under that Minister's authority and on his responsibility.' I can give directions to the Ministry of Supply which I can no longer give to the Ministry of Defence. I meant this to be an improvement in my Minute, with the object of giving you a freer hand. I think you might only be getting out of the frying pan into the fire.

By all means talk it over with me. Meanwhile I have told Bridges and Brook to suspend action.

Field Marshal Lord Alexander to Winston S. Churchill
(Premier papers, 11/23)

11 March 1952

A Commonwealth Advisory Committee on Defence Science on which all the members of the Commonwealth are represented was set up after the war. It meets every two or three years. Its terms of reference are:

[1] See immediately preceding document.
[2] Reproduced above (p. 329).

(i) to promote scientific research relating to defence in all fields which may be furthered by Commonwealth collaboration;

(ii) to keep under review machinery for Commonwealth liaison in defence science including methods of exchange of scientific staff.

Though in practice the field of discussion has been limited by security restrictions since India and Pakistan became members, the Committee is valuable as a forum for exchanging scientific ideas within the Commonwealth and in stimulating research on non-secret subjects of special interest to defence. The last meeting was held at Cambridge in July 1950.

The Indian Government has now issued an official invitation for the next meeting to be held in India in January or February 1953. The idea has already been approved unofficially by all member countries. Lord Ismay was consulted when the proposal was first discussed and he welcomed the idea of holding a meeting in India. I agree with this view.

I propose to invite the Commonwealth Relations Office to reply that HMG accepts the invitation to attend the next Commonwealth Advisory Committee on Defence Science meeting in India in 1953.

I am sending a copy of this minute to Lord Ismay.

Cabinet: conclusions
(Cabinet papers, 128/24)

12 March 1952
Secret
11 a.m.
Cabinet Meeting No. 29 of 1952

1. The Prime Minister informed the Cabinet that, with his approval, Lord Ismay had undertaken to accept appointment as Secretary-General of the North Atlantic Treaty Council. The Cabinet would, he knew, share his regret at losing Lord Ismay's services as a member of the Government; but they would wish him success in the important office which he was now to assume.

The Marquess of Salisbury would become Secretary of State for Commonwealth Relations and would in addition continue to act as Leader of the House of Lords. In this latter capacity he would have the assistance of the Chancellor of the Duchy of Lancaster, who for this purpose would in future attend more regularly the meetings of the Cabinet.

[...]

334

Winston S. Churchill to Commonwealth Prime Ministers
Prime Minister's Personal Telegram T.86/52
(Premier papers, 11/160)

12 March 1952
Immediate
Secret
B No.5

I have felt obliged to accede to the strongly expressed wishes of the North Atlantic Treaty Organisation (NATO) powers that Lord Ismay should be appointed their Secretary-General.[1] I have only done so because it is of overriding importance to the future of the Organisation that this new post should be held by a statesman of tried skill and capacity.

It is with reluctance that I see Lord Ismay leave the Commonwealth Relations Office and this is a heavy sacrifice to me personally. He himself relinquishes with the greatest disappointment an Office which he had found so congenial and which was so well suited to his talents. He goes solely from a sense of duty, under pressure which neither he nor I could resist.

The Queen has agreed to appoint Lord Salisbury as his successor. In view of his long experience in our joint concerns and his knowledge of Commonwealth affairs I am confident you will feel this is a good choice.

Defence Committee: minutes
(Cabinet papers, 131/12)

12 March 1952   Prime Minister's Map Room
Top Secret   Ministry of Defence
4.30 p.m.
Defence Committee Meeting No. 1 of 1952

1. ROYAL NAVAL BASE AT SIMONSTOWN

The Committee had before them a memorandum by the Secretary of State for Commonwealth Relations (D (51) 4) on the future of the Naval Base at Simonstown.

The Commonwealth Secretary said that, when the South Africans had raised this question in 1951, the Labour Government had asked for an unqualified assurance that the facilities of the Base would be available to the Royal Navy both in peace and in war. The South Africans, while making no difficulties about our use of the Base in peace, had been unwilling to say more, as regards its use in war, than that it would be available to us in any war in which they were themselves engaged. They had, however, made it

[1] The position was first offered to Sir Oliver Franks, who declined it.

clear that they would not remain neutral in a world war against Communist Russia, and they had accepted firm commitments to assist in the defence of the Middle East in such a war. As it was our assumption that in any world war the foreseeable future Russia would be our principal enemy, the Commonwealth Secretary thought that we could now go forward with these negotiations on the basis of the assurance which the South Africans were prepared to give. He suggested that in further discussions we should concentrate on the practical problems involved in creating conditions in the South African Navy which would in due course make transfer of the control of the Base a practical possibility. While the discussions would have to be conducted on the footing that we were prepared in principle to contemplate the gradual transfer of control, we should make it a cardinal point of the negotiations that no transfer should take place until the South African Navy were fully competent to take care of the Base.

The First Lord of the Admiralty said that, as the South African Government did not seem to be pressing for the negotiations to be reopened, he had hoped that the question could be still further delayed. If, however, it was necessary to resume negotiations on the general lines proposed by the Commonwealth Secretary, we should have to insist for political reasons on a clear guarantee that the prospects of the coloured craftsmen and apprentices employed at the Base would not be prejudiced by the transfer.

The Prime Minister said that he was not persuaded that it was necessary to reopen the question of Simonstown. The South African Government were not pressing for an answer, and we had a legal right of perpetual user on which we could justifiably stand firm. It was strategically necessary for the Royal Navy to have base facilities in Simonstown in any major war, and perhaps more particularly in a war in which South Africa was neutral. Simonstown was an essential link in Imperial communications and there was no obvious alternative to it. He was in favour of taking no fresh initiative in this matter; and, if it was raised by the South African Government, he would resist, on the basis of our legal rights, any proposal for transfer without an unqualified assurance that facilities would be available to us in both peace and war.

The Committee –
1) Agreed that no action should be taken to reopen the negotiations with the South African Government about the transfer of the Naval Base at Simonstown.
2) Invited the Secretary of State for Commonwealth Relations, and the Minister of Defence to discuss with the United Kingdom High Commissioner,[1] on his forthcoming visit to London, the state of South African feeling on this question.

[1] John Helier Le Rougetel, 1894–1975. Educated at Cambridge University. Served in Army, 1914–19. MC, 1917; Bar, 1918. Entered Diplomatic Service, 1920. Married, 1925, Mary Penrose-Thackwell. CMG, 1943. KCMG, 1946. Ambassador to Persia, 1946–50; to Belgium, 1950–1. High Commissioner, South Africa, 1951–5.

2. PROVISION OF OCCUPATION FORCES IN KOREA

The Committee had before them a report by the Chiefs of Staff (D (51) 3) on the question of a Commonwealth contribution to an Occupation Force in Korea.

The Chief of the Imperial General Staff said that, if an armistice were concluded in Korea, it would probably be politically necessary for the Commonwealth to make some contribution to the Occupation Force which the United Nations would wish to leave in South Korea. The Chiefs of Staff recognised that this political need would have to be met, in spite of the scarcity of forces to meet our many commitments, and they believed that there would be some positive military advantage in keeping in being a cohesive Commonwealth Force. The Commonwealth Division was generally acknowledged to be the best Division in Korea. The proposed composition of the Commonwealth contribution to an Occupation Force was stated in D (51) 3. It would be supported from the Commonwealth Base in Japan and every effort would be made to keep down the overheads, in spite of the great distance from the United Kingdom.

The Prime Minister agreed that it was right to examine this question and to have a plan in readiness. The proposals put forward by the Chiefs of Staff could be discussed, without commitment, with the other Commonwealth countries and with the United States.

The Committee –
  (1) Approved the proposals set out in D (51) 3 as a basis for discussion with the other Commonwealth countries concerned and with the United States authorities.
  (2) Invited the Secretary of State for Commonwealth Relations to open discussions with the other Commonwealth countries concerned.
  (3) Agreed that, subject to the concurrence of the Commonwealth countries, the proposals should be used as a basis for discussion with the United States authorities.

3. WAR RESERVES

The Committee considered certain aspects of the strategic stockpile of war reserves.

(a) Oil

The Prime Minister said he had been disturbed by the large demands which were being made by the Admiralty for stocks of fuel oil. On the figures supplied to him the Admiralty seemed to be aiming at stocks greater than those which they had held before and during the last war. It was surprising that this should be thought necessary at a time when there was no hostile Navy in existence comparable with the German Navy, when our own refining capacity had been greatly increased and our fleet of tankers was greater than ever before.

The First Lord of the Admiralty said that more accurate figures had now been drawn up and would be supplied to the Prime Minister. These showed that the total stocks of oil fuel, at home and overseas, were lower than they were in July 1939.

The Chief of the Air Staff said that at the present time we held only four weeks' reserves of jet aviation fuel calculated at intensive rates. The Air Ministry were making every effort to bring their stocks up to a three months' reserve.

The Committee –
(1) Took note that the First Lord would supply the Prime Minister with further figures of the stocks of oil fuel for the Navy.
(2) Agreed that stocks of aviation jet fuel should be built up to a three months' reserve as rapidly as possible.

(b) Wheat Stocks

The Prime Minister said that the Cabinet had provisionally decided to reduce the level of wheat stocks gradually over the next few months to the equivalent of ten weeks' consumption, and to review the matter again in the light of our own harvest for 1952. He would like to hear the views of the Chiefs of Staff on this point.

The Chief of the Imperial General Staff said that the threat to our sea communications and to our ports at the beginning of a war was so great and so difficult to combat that the burden of imports at this time should be reduced to the barest minimum.

The Paymaster-General pointed out that a run-down in stocks to ten weeks during June and July was not a very serious risk, seeing that the advent of the harvest would put the stocks up again to twenty-six weeks. In his opinion the important point was that the financial and economic risk was inescapable in 1952, whereas the risk of war remained at least doubtful.

The Committee –
(3) Agreed that it was strategically desirable to maintain a level of wheat stocks equivalent to three months' consumption.
(4) Agreed to recommend to the Cabinet that a final decision to reduce wheat stocks below that level should be postponed until April, when it might be easier to forecast both the financial prospects and the risks involved from the point of view of our preparedness for war.

(c) General War Reserves

The Chief of the Air Staff said that the Chiefs of Staff had put in hand an examination of the general position of our war reserves with the object of arriving at some common policy.

The Prime Minister said that the report of this examination should be most valuable and he hoped it might be made available within a few weeks. It was essential that we should know what stocks of general war reserves would give us security over a period of three to six months' war.

The Committee –
(5) Invited the Chiefs of Staff to submit in three weeks' time the results of their review of war reserves.

4. PROTECTED ACCOMMODATION FOR GOVERNMENT STAFFS

The Minister of Defence undertook, at the request of the Prime Minister, to examine the state of plans for the provision of protected accommodation for the Government staffs in war and the proposals for extending this accommodation.

5. THE EGYPTIAN BASE

The Chief of the Imperial General Staff said that to hold the Middle East it was necessary to have a Base in Egypt. This Base would only be effective if the Egyptians were cooperative; and it might become necessary, in order to gain the cooperation of Egypt, to withdraw the fighting troops from the Canal Zone in peace and to find alternative accommodation for them elsewhere. Various alternatives had been considered, but in none was any permanent accommodation available, and regular troops could not be required to live permanently in tents in peacetime without serious prejudice to recruitment. It seemed to him important that, if alternative locations had to be found, they must be places to which we had a legal right. Otherwise, we should find ourselves beset, as we were in Egypt, by political agitations. For the Air Force, Cyprus would be a satisfactory location. For the Army, he considered that there would be solid advantages in the choice of Gaza. It might be possible in any negotiations with Egypt over the withdrawal of forces from the Canal Zone to obtain legal rights to station troops in Gaza. The consent of Israel would also have to be obtained. It was true that Gaza at present had no port and no amenities, but it was a good location for a covering force for the defence of the Middle East and was sufficiently close to the Canal to enable us to exert pressure on Egypt for the proper control of our Base.

The Prime Minister said that he had no wish to see the British Forces evacuated from the Canal Zone, and he still hoped that it might be possible to prevent this. Nevertheless, as the Treaty ran out in 1956, it was prudent to consider alternatives, and he thought that the Chiefs of Staff should work out a detailed plan, with an estimate of the cost, for stationing British Troops in Gaza and Cyprus.

The Committee –

Instructed the Chiefs of Staff to work out in detail the provision of alternative locations for the fighting troops which might in certain circumstances have to be withdrawn from the Canal Zone.

6. THE SECRETARY-GENERAL OF NATO

The Prime Minister said he knew that the Committee would wish to offer their congratulations and good wishes to the Secretary of State for Commonwealth Relations, who had accepted the important and arduous appointment of Secretary-General of the North Atlantic Treaty Organisation.

Winston S. Churchill to Julian Sandys
(Churchill papers, 1/52)

12 March 1952

My dear Julian,

I am so sorry not to have had time to read your imaginative sketch until now. Several of the outrages you prophesy have already happened, but without the serious consequences following them. It seems to me very good practice for you to write such things. They show how closely you are following what is taking place.

I do not like the expression 'some new excuse for aggressing us'. To 'aggress' is not a verb in common use. Also, when you say 'Egyptian troops invaded the Sudan', I wonder how they got there so quickly? You should look at the map. In your report of what I am supposed to say, you attribute some rather colourful oratory to me. Still, I suppose I have used most of these words at some time or another.

Winston S. Churchill to R. A. Butler and Lord De La Warr[1]
Prime Minister's Personal Minute M.126/52
(Premier papers, 11/19)

13 March 1952

1. The Postmaster General's proposal* is melancholy but conforms to the usual style of charging more and giving less. In our statement of policy, ten thousand civil servants were said to be reduced. How many of them were ordinary postmen, and what was the reduction in the Post Office? It is quite easy to make up numbers by sacking the ordinary rank and file just because they are called civil servants.

2. A second question arises about how much the Treasury is getting out of the Post Office. I should like to have more clear figures on this. In my day

---

[1] Herbrand Edward Dundonald Brassey Sackville, 1900–76. Known as 'Buck'. Succeeded as 9th Earl De La Warr, 1915. Chairman, National Labour Party, 1931–43. Elected to the Other Club, 1935. Lord Privy Seal, 1937–8. President of the Board of Education, 1938–40. Chairman, Agricultural Research Council, and Director of Home Flax Production, 1943–9. Postmaster-General, 1951–5.

as Chancellor, I made about £15 millions a year for the revenue. I was much ashamed of this on the grounds that the Post Office ought not to be used as an instrument of taxation. Now, however, there are many nationalized industries, and the tendency will be to use all of them to exploit the ordinary citizen.

3. The Postmaster General proposes very serious restrictions, and I should like to know how much the Chancellor of the Exchequer is getting out of the process. You will, I hope, both forgive me for presenting what would be the reaction – if he knew the facts – of the man in the street. By all means bring it up on Tuesday.

* Proposed statement by Postmaster General on curtailment of postal services to secure economy in PO staff.

Cabinet: conclusions
(Churchill papers, 128/24)

13 March 1952
Secret
11 a.m.
Cabinet Meeting No. 30 of 1952

[...]

2. The Prime Minister informed the Cabinet that the War Office proposed, in agreement with the Government of Northern Ireland, to raise ten Home Guard battalions in Northern Ireland. For the present these would take the form of cadres of fifty men to a battalion. When the Home Guard Bill had been before Parliament in the autumn, it had been suggested that Northern Ireland should be excluded from its scope; and the proposal to raise these battalions would certainly be criticised in Parliament. Some protests and misrepresentation in the Irish Republic must also be expected. Despite this, however, the Cabinet agreed that the proposal should go forward.

The Cabinet – Authorised the Secretary of State for War to proceed with his proposal to raise units of the Home Guard in Northern Ireland.

[...]

4. The Cabinet had before them a note by the Prime Minister (C(52)50) covering a memorandum on the supply of arms to India and Pakistan.

The Prime Minister drew attention to the risk that these two countries might use the arms supplied to them for war against one another. We should then bear a grave responsibility. And we should not in any event receive any valuable return for these supplies, since their cost would be debited against the sterling balances held by India and Pakistan.

The Commonwealth Secretary said that he thought it most unlikely that there would be war between India and Pakistan. It was not for this purpose that they needed arms, but for the legitimate purpose of defending their vulnerable frontiers. If we continued to send them such equipment as we could, we should increase thereby the chance that in any future world war they would ultimately be found fighting on our side. If we declined to supply them they would buy equipment for dollars at the expense of sterling area reserves and would in time come increasingly to use United States types of equipment. This would close an important long-term market to us. While, therefore, we should not denude ourselves of needed equipment and must regard the claims of India and Pakistan as second to those of the older members of the Commonwealth and of foreign countries with which we had firm defence agreements, we should, nevertheless, continue to send them such supplies as we could.

In discussion the Cabinet were informed that, because of our own needs, we were having to delay the supply to India and Pakistan of Sea Fury and Seafire aircraft which had been promised to them. We could, however, supply some Spitfires if these would be acceptable. Lincoln bombers could not be made available to Pakistan for some years, but some offer of older types of bomber might be made. In general it should be our policy to continue to make limited supplies of equipment available on a scale sufficient to prevent India and Pakistan from turning to United States sources. The suggestion that £2½ million worth of Army equipment might be supplied in the next twelve months was probably optimistic.

The Cabinet – Agreed that, subject to the points made in the discussion, military equipment should continue to be supplied to India and Pakistan on the lines proposed in the memorandum annexed to C(52)50.

5. The Prime Minister had directed that priority should be given to the production of a limited number of specified types of defence equipment, viz., the latest types of aircraft, ammunition for aircraft, the Radar chain and Centurion tanks. The Ministry of Defence had worked out, in consultation with the Departments primarily concerned, the procedure to be followed in order to give effect to this priority. They recommended that the priority should also extend to Gannet naval aircraft, in addition to the types mentioned by the Prime Minister, to guided weapons and to certain specific items of the anti-mine programme. Departments were agreed upon the procedure save on two points, viz. (i) whether the contracts carrying this priority should be identified by symbol below the level of main sub-contractors; and (ii) whether sub-contractors should have a right to preferential treatment in the supply of raw materials and components.

The Chancellor of the Exchequer and the President of the Board of Trade said that, if the use of the priority symbol were extended to sub-contractors, there would be serious interference with the production of civil supplies, especially in the engineering industry, and consequent loss of production for export which, in the current crisis in our balance of payments, was no less important than defence production. They would therefore prefer that the sub-contractors should be denied the use of the priority symbol and should be left to ask the Departments concerned to assist them to overcome any difficulties which they might encounter in obtaining the necessary materials and components for these contracts.

In discussion it was pointed out that this alternative had two main disadvantages; first, it would mean waiting until difficulties arose before any action could be taken to meet them and, secondly, it would involve a substantial increase in staff. Experience in the early years of the last war had, it was true, demonstrated that a system of priorities had great disadvantages as compared with a comprehensive system of allocation; but in current peace-time conditions it would be impracticable to introduce a full allocation system and, that being so, there was no certain means of ensuring preferential treatment for specified items of defence production other than a system of priorities extending to sub-contractors.

The Minister of Supply said that he would do everything practicable to avoid the abuse of this system by sub-contractors. He would institute a system of sample checks in order to verify that the symbols were being properly used; and, since the abuse of the system by one firm would damnify others, he hoped to be able to enlist the support of industry in supervising and enforcing it.

In discussion the following points were also made –
  (a) The Prime Minister had proposed the enlargement of the industrial capacity available for the production of Centurion tanks. The Minister of Supply said that the existing capacity would suffice for the programmes now contemplated; and the creation of additional capacity would conflict seriously with exports. It was agreed, after discussion, that no further capacity need be provided at present for the production of Centurion tanks.
  (b) The Minister of Supply confirmed that the priority procedure would not be applied to the production of firms manufacturing obsolescent types of aircraft.
  (c) It was agreed that the priority procedure should apply to the production of both 20-mm and 30-mm ammunition for aircraft.

The Cabinet –
  (1) Approved the immediate introduction of the procedure devised by the Minister of Defence, in consultation with the other Departments concerned, for ensuring priority for the production of a limited number of specified types of defence equipment, and agreed that this should be applied to the latest types of aircraft, 20-mm and 30-mm ammunition for aircraft, equipment required for the Radar chain, guided missiles, certain specified items of the anti-mine programme, and the existing programme of Centurion tanks.
  (2) Agreed that this procedure should extend to sub-contracts, and

that sub-contractors should be authorised to secure, by the use of a special symbol, preferential treatment in the supply of raw materials and components.

(3) Invited the Minister of Supply to take all practicable steps to ensure that this procedure was not abused by sub-contractors; and asked him to submit monthly reports to the Cabinet on the working of the scheme.

[. . .]

7. The Cabinet had before them a memorandum by the Foreign Secretary (C(52)73) recommending that British troops in Libya should be stationed in cantonments away from the main towns, that this policy should be applied immediately in Benghazi and that arrangements for its more general application should be set in hand without delay.

The Minister of State[1] said that anti-British elements in Libya were making political capital out of the presence of British troops in Benghazi and other towns; and that, unless we gave early practical proof of our intention to apply the policy recommended by the Foreign Secretary, we should jeopardise our chances of negotiating a favourable treaty giving us the right to maintain troops in Libya for a substantial period of time.

The Prime Minister said that, while the whole future of the British garrison in the Middle East remained uncertain, it seemed unjustifiable for the Government to commit themselves to substantial expenditure in constructing permanent quarters for British troops in Libya. He would be reluctant to endorse at the present time the long-term policy outlined in C(52)73.

In further discussion it was suggested that the immediate need would be met if the War Office were able to move some troops from Benghazi and evacuate some of the premises which they occupied there; and for this purpose a Military Accommodation Board might be appointed, as recommended in paragraph 11 of C(52)73, to ensure that some of the buildings occupied by British troops in Benghazi were evacuated by 15th April. This might suffice to create favourable conditions for the treaty negotiations.

The Cabinet –

(1) Invited the Secretary of State for War to appoint a Military Accommodation Board, as recommended in paragraph 11 of C(52)73, which would meet in Benghazi and arrange for the early removal of British troops from some of the buildings which they now occupied there.

(2) Agreed to defer their consideration of the long-term policy recommended in C(52)73.

(3) Invited the Minister of Defence, after consultation with the Chiefs of Staff, to submit to the Prime Minister a report on the location

---

[1] Selwyn Lloyd, Minister of State at FO.

of the British garrison, and future troop movements, in the Middle East.

[. . .]

Sir David Maxwell Fyfe to Winston S. Churchill
(*Premier papers, 11/26*)

13 March 1952

1. I recently agreed at the instance of the Foreign Secretary to refuse admission to the United Kingdom to foreign delegates coming to attend the International Women's Day conference held last weekend. The grounds on which I was urged to do this are that the organization holding the conference is affiliated to the Women's International Democratic Federation, which is a Communist dominated body used as an instrument of the so-called 'peace' propaganda conducted by the Soviet against the policies of the Western democracies. Mr Driberg[1] is asking a Question about the refusal today and I propose to defend my decision on these grounds.

2. I have also decided, in agreement with the Foreign Secretary, to inform the World Federation of Scientific Workers that I will not admit foreigners to attend a meeting of the Executive Council of the Federation later this month. The President of this body is Professor Joliot Curie,[2] the Vice-President Professor Bernal,[3] the Secretary J. G. Crowther,[4] and it is dominated by Communists.

3. I am being asked a Question today in which it is suggested that I should ban a Communist sponsored British Youth Festival which is to be held near Sheffield at Whitsun. In reply I propose to say that I have no power to ban the gathering, but that I will not give facilities to foreigners to attend it.

4. That policy of refusing admission to foreigners coming to meetings organised by bodies which can fairly be regarded as instruments of Soviet propaganda, seems to be not inconsistent with continuing to allow foreign

[1] Thomas Edward Neil Driberg, 1905–76. Educated at Lancing College and Christ Church, Oxford. Joined Communist Party aged 15. From 1928, worked on the *Daily Express*, where he became the widely read columnist 'William Hickey'. MP (Lab.) for Maldon, 1942–59; for Barking, 1959–74. Expelled from Communist Party, 1941. Took Labour Whip, 1945. Chairman of Labour Party, 1957.

[2] Frederic Joliot-Curie, 1900–58. Educated at Ecole Supérieure de Physique et de Chimie Industrielles de la Ville de Paris. Asst to Marie Curie, 1925. Married, 1926, Irène Curie. Awarded the Nobel Prize in Chemistry, jointly with his wife, 1935. Prof., College de France, 1937. French High Commissioner for Atomic Energy, 1945. Oversaw construction of France's first atomic reactor, 1948. Relieved from government positions for being a Communist, 1950. Stalin Peace Price, 1951. Chair of Nuclear Physics, the Sorbonne, 1956.

[3] John Desmond Bernal, 1901–71. Educated at Cambridge University. Researcher, Davy Faraday Laboratory, 1923–7. Lecturer in Crystallography, Cambridge University, 1934–7. FRS, 1937. Prof. of Physics, University of London, 1937–63; of Crystallography, 1963–8.

[4] James Gerald Crowther, 1889–1983. Technical books representative for Oxford University Press from 1924. Science correspondent for *Manchester Guardian*, 1927–49. Regular contributor to BBC broadcasts, 1940–7. Director, Science Committee, British Council, 1941–6.

delegates from behind the Iron Curtain to come to meetings of reputable organisations in this country. For example, I should propose to continue the policy of admitting persons from Iron Curtain countries who are invited to attend the annual conferences of trade unions, and against whom there are no objections on personal grounds.

Winston S. Churchill to Sir David Maxwell Fyfe
Prime Minister's Personal Minute M.124/52
(Premier papers, 11/26)

14 March 1952

Your Minute of March 13.

This only reached me after you had taken your action and replied to the Question. Naturally I shall support you in what you have done. I think, however, it would be well to clarify Cabinet thought upon the somewhat complicated issues. Perhaps you would prepare a short paper on the subject. On principle I am against the Communists.

Winston S. Churchill to Nikólaos Plastíras
(Premier papers, 11/179)

14 March 1952

My dear Excellency,

I was deeply touched to learn from your letter of January 31[1] of the plans of the Greek Government to unveil a memorial on April 25, 1952, dedicated to the soldiers of the United Kingdom, Australia and New Zealand who fell in Greece during the last war. This is an act which will be acclaimed by all my countrymen. It will recall to them the gallant defence of Greece by her heroic people, in days when Greece and the British Commonwealth were alone in confronting the whole might of the enemy.

I have appointed the Right Honourable the Earl of Halifax,[2] KG, OM, to represent Her Majesty's Government in the United Kingdom and myself at the ceremony. He will bear with him the warmest wishes of Her Majesty's

---

[1] Reproduced above (p. 248).
[2] Edward Frederick Lindley Wood, 1881–1959. Educated at Eton and Christ Church, Oxford. MP (Cons.) for Ripon, 1910–25. Parliamentary Under-Secretary of State for the Colonies, 1921–2. President of the Board of Education, 1922–4. Minister of Agriculture, 1924–5. Baron Irwin, 1925. Viceroy of India, 1926–31. KG, 1931. President of the Board of Education, 1931–4. Succeeded his father as 3rd Viscount Halifax, 1934. Secretary of State for War, 1935. Lord Privy Seal, 1935–7. Lord President of the Council, 1937–8. Foreign Secretary, 1938–40. Ambassador in Washington DC, 1941–6. Earl of Halifax, 1944. British delegate to San Francisco Conference, 1945; attended the first sessions of the UN. Resigned as Ambassador, 1946. OM, 1946. Author of *Fullness of Days* (1957).

Government and of the peoples of these islands for the prosperity of your country and the final obliteration of the ravages left by war.

Antony Head to Winston S. Churchill
(*Premier papers, 11/7*)

15 March 1952

I am referring to your personal minute M.109/52 addressed to the Minister of Defence.[1]

I attach a draft statement which we propose to issue to the Press concerning the promotion of warrant officers and NCOs to substantive rank.

I have sent a copy of this minute to the Minister of Defence.

I would mention that in addition to this hand out I had a luncheon party last Tuesday, 11th March for all the military correspondents at which I explained this matter in some detail. I think they all then understood the effect of this new policy including the military correspondent of the *Manchester Guardian*.

DRAFT STATEMENT

No ranks granted to Warrant Officers and NCOs since the outbreak of the war in 1939 have been permanent.

The War Office promised some two years ago that they would, as soon as possible, re-introduce permanent promotion.

Specifically, last October, by which time all Warrant Officers and NCOs knew the permanent rank which they would receive, the Army was told that these permanent ranks would be introduced on the 1st April, 1952. Paid acting rank would also be granted to any man doing a job higher than his permanent rank.

The main effect of the measure will be to give security in their rank to the majority of regular Warrant Officers and NCOs.

The permanent ranks granted to a small proportion of Warrant Officers and NCOs will be lower than the ranks they are at present holding but if they are doing a job which carries a higher rank they will, as has been indicated, receive paid acting rank.

---

[1] Reproduced above (p. 327).

March 1952

Winston S. Churchill to Peter Thorneycroft
Prime Minister's Personal Minute M.138/52
(Premier papers, 11/283)

16 March 1952

This article in the *Sunday Dispatch* should show you the dangers into which we are running by these large exports of rubber to Russia. Could you fill in the figures of the remaining months of 1952.

Does this sudden expansion in exports to Russia spring from any decision on your part, or is it simply the working out of previous Socialist decisions?

John Colville: diary
('The Fringes of Power', page 643)

16 March 1952

At 6.00 we all went to a film (*Edward and Caroline* – French and admirable) at Chartwell, where we dined afterwards. W liked Meg (who was petrified of him) and told me he found her charming indeed. He is worried about Egypt, where he thinks Eden is throwing the game away; irritated with the Prof who is being tiresome about atomic matters; and disturbed by the thought that the old-age pensioners may suffer in consequence of an otherwise admirable Budget.

Winston S. Churchill to Sir Edward Bridges
Prime Minister's Personal Minute M.143/52
(Premier papers, 11/295)

17 March 1952

The Minister of Supply suggests the following alternative.[1] It certainly has the advantage of being shorter.

'Under the Prime Minister, the Paymaster General is responsible for directing policy and development on Atomic research and production. He will preside at the Atomic Energy Council and will deal with this subject in the House of Lords. The Minister of Supply will remain statutorily responsible for the administration of Atomic energy matters, and will answer questions on this subject in the House of Commons which do not require the attention of the Prime Minister.'

---

[1] See Cherwell to Churchill, Mar. 10, and Churchill's reply of Mar. 11 (M.118/52), both reproduced above (pp. 329, 332).

March 1952

Harold Macmillan to Winston S. Churchill
(*Premier papers, 11/153*)

17 March 1952
Private and Personal

It would be affectation for me to conceal my sense of disappointment at the course of the discussion at last Thursday's Cabinet on the future of the Council of Europe and European unity generally.

My own feelings are not of great importance. But I ought to let you know the growing sense of confusion and dismay of those who have worked with you, in and out of the House of Commons, in support of the European movement.

From affection and respect, few of them tell you what they feel. But they tell me; and I think you ought to know.

These people do not understand the continued opposition of the Foreign Office, in big and small things alike, to the whole movement.

This appears just as strong under your administration as under the previous one.

All this seems quite inconsistent with the pronouncements made by you, and by the Foreign Secretary, when in opposition, on such questions as the Schuman Plan and the European Army, and with the conduct of the Conservatives at Strasbourg under your leadership.

Meanwhile, by a strange paradox, the Labour Party (I am informed) is moving towards the position which we formerly held.

I am told that many of them now support the conception of a European Army on the lines which you first put forward.

This view is likely to be expressed in the debate. If it were to take the form of an official amendment, it might prove embarrassing.

I have always felt that the American conception of a Federated Western Europe, without Britain and the Commonwealth, was wrong and contrary to our long-term interests.

It will probably fail; its success might be just as dangerous.

The recent resolutions of the French Assembly seem to provide an opportunity for us to come into European institutions on our own terms – that is, in accordance with your original conception.

The new Russian move only underlines the need.

I am not persuaded that our membership of NATO is enough. That organisation already separates us from most of the Commonwealth. If the EDC proposals should come into being they will separate us from our most important Continental neighbours. As I see it, it is only by adding the leadership of Europe to our natural leadership of the Empire that we can bring to bear, through an expanded NATO, the influence on world affairs which should be ours. It is no longer a case of choosing between the policies of Marlborough and Bolingbroke, but of combining them.[1]

Winston S. Churchill to Field Marshal Lord Alexander
Prime Minister's Personal Minute M.140/52*
(Premier papers, 11/23)

17 March 1952

Will it not be difficult to have this meeting in India when we do not trust the Indian or Pakistani Governments in subjects of special interest to Defence. How can you draw the line between secret and non-secret?

As long as this can be made merely as civility it helps to explain the sense of our all being together but may it not be ruptured in practice by the feeling that we are not trusting each other in secret matters as we certainly ought not to do.

* Reference: Commonwealth Advisory Committee on Defence Meeting in India in 1953.

Field Marshal Lord Alexander to Winston S. Churchill
(Premier papers, 11/23)

18 March 1952

Your minute M.140/52 of 17 March about the meeting of the Commonwealth Advisory Committee on Defence Science in India.

I agree that there are difficulties about this but I think that for the following reasons we ought to accept the Indian invitation.

(1) The invitation has already been received from India and the Indians know that the other members of the Committee have all expressed, informally, their acceptance of the invitation. It would therefore be extremely difficult for us to refuse at this late stage.

(2) The kind of subjects that will be discussed will be meteorological problems, questions in connection with clothing and food and hot and cold weather testing. These are all scientific matters of very real interest to Commonwealth countries which do not involve any security risks.

[1] Churchill minuted Eden: 'Please let me have your comments on this letter and enclosure' (M.146/52, *Premier papers, 11/153*). Churchill then wrote back to Macmillan: 'Thank you very much for your paper, which I have referred to the Foreign Secretary. I doubt if we can do any more than he is now planning.' Macmillan, during his premiership from 1957 to 1963, pushed for Britain to be admitted to the European Economic Community (EEC), but France ultimately vetoed Britain's official bid to join in 1963. Britain would not succeed in joining the EEC until 1973.

(3) All members of the Commonwealth fully realise that we only disclose secret defence information on the 'need to know' basis and that our assessment depends on the contribution which each individual member is making to the overall Commonwealth defence programme.

(4) The meeting serves the useful purpose of bringing together the various Commonwealth representatives, and in particular it brings together the Pakistanis and Indians in the presence of other Commonwealth representatives.

(5) I have already given instructions that the proposed agenda should be submitted to me before the conference takes place.

In view of the above points I hope that you will be prepared to approve the proposal that HMG should accept the invitation.

Cabinet: conclusions
(*Churchill papers, 128/24*)

18 March 1952
Secret
11 a.m.
Cabinet Meeting No. 31 of 1952

1. The Prime Minister raised the question whether members of the Government should not take an active part in the forthcoming municipal elections in London.

In discussion it was pointed out that, traditionally, members of the Cabinet did not normally speak in by-elections, and that Ministers above the rank of Parliamentary Secretary did not normally speak in local government elections. If the Government made any substantial departure from this practice at the forthcoming London elections, they would be expected later in the year to give similar support to Conservative candidates in the local government elections in other parts of the country and there would be great practical difficulty in doing this at a time when Parliament was sitting.

The Prime Minister felt, however, that the present circumstances were somewhat exceptional; and the Cabinet agreed that the Home Secretary should speak in the London elections in his capacity as President of the London Municipal Society. They also agreed that a number of junior Ministers should speak in these elections. They invited the Chief Whip to make arrangements accordingly.

[. . .]

7. The Prime Minister said that he was concerned lest the present Government should be held responsible for the recent increases in bus fares and railway fares in the London area. These were causing widespread discontent,

MARCH 1952

and he wished the public to understand that they resulted directly from the policy of nationalisation which had been pursued by the Labour Government. With this in view he had suggested to the Minister of Transport that he should add, to his reply to a Parliamentary Question by Air Commodore Harvey, MP,[1] about the withdrawal of special fares for shift workers, a paragraph in the following terms:

'All these rules were made and all those who are enforcing them were appointed by the late Government and they are a definite feature in the nationalisation policy. We are considering how and when changes can be made which will secure that workmen working on a night shift can again obtain workmen's travel tickets.'

In discussion it was pointed out that nothing should be said on behalf of the Government which would reflect upon the impartiality of the Transport Tribunal, which was a judicial body enjoying the powers, rights and privileges of the High Court. Moreover, it would not be right to imply that the appointment of the Tribunal was one of the features of the nationalisation policy adopted by the late Government, for similar functions had been exercised for some time previously by the Railway Rates Tribunal set up under the Railways Act, 1921. For the reasons indicated in the paper by the Secretary of State for Coordination of Transport, Fuel and Power (subsequently circulated as C(52)84), it was important that a clear distinction should be made in this matter between the position of the British Transport Commission and that of the Transport Tribunal.

Air Commodore Harvey had now withdrawn his Question; but, if it were reinstated, it would be inexpedient to make any statement in reply which might imply that the special concessions for shift workers might be restored. The system of workmen's fares which had previously been in force in the London area had been full of anomalies; and there was much to be said for the view that the withdrawal of shift workers' tickets was in principle a sound reform.

After further discussion, the Cabinet –

1) Invited the Minister of Transport to continue to take every suitable opportunity of impressing it upon public opinion that the responsibility for the recent increase in passenger transport fares did not rest with the present Government.

2) Agreed that, if Air Commodore Harvey, MP, should again put down his Question about the withdrawal of shift workers' tickets, the answer should include a sentence in the following terms: 'All the relevant statutory provisions and all the functions exercised by the British Transport Commission result from the legislation introduced

---

[1] Arthur Vere Harvey, 1906–94. Educated at Framingham College. RAF, 1925–30. Director, Far East Aviation Co. Ltd, 1930–5. Adviser, Southern Chinese Air Forces, 1932–5. Sqn Ldr, Surrey Sqn, 1937–44. MP (Cons.) for Macclesfield, Cheshire, 1945–71. Baron, 1971.

by the late Government and are a definite feature in the nationalisation policy.'

[. . .]

Anthony Eden to Winston S. Churchill
(Premier papers, 11/153)

18 March 1952
Private and Personal
PM/52/26

Thank you for your minute M.146/52 and for sending me Harold Macmillan's letter and enclosure.[1]

2. I have just come from talking to the Foreign Affairs Committee on this and other subjects and I have never known the Party so unanimous except for Hinchingbrooke[2] who takes a rosier view of the Russian Note[3] than anyone else. No doubt the Whips will report to you on this meeting.

3. You will have seen that the first French reaction to our paper is distinctly favourable (see Paris telegram No. 157). The Italian Ambassador[4] has also told me that he thinks it will appeal to his Government. I expect the Dutch likewise to be attracted by the idea. We shall have to see how it goes. Naturally we cannot ram the plan down other people's throats.

4. What Macmillan's paper seems to me to ignore is that so much of Europe wants to federate. We cannot do so but I consider that it would not be right – or good policy – to try to stop the others. On balance I had rather see France and Germany in confused but close embrace than at arm's length, even though we think we can better influence events that way.

---

[1] Reproduced above (pp. 348–9).

[2] Alexander Victor Edward Paulet Montagu, 1906–95. Known as 'Hinch'. Styled Viscount Hinchingbrooke, 1916–62. MP (Cons.) for South Dorset, 1941–62. On active service in France, 1940. Founded Tory Reform Committee, 1943. President, Anti-Common Market League, 1962–84. Succeeded his father as 10th Earl of Sandwich, 1962; disclaimed the title, 1964. Member of Conservative Monday Club. Wrote *Essays in Tory Reform* (1944); T*he Conservative Dilemma* (1970).

[3] Document dated 10 Mar. 1952 from Andrei Gromyko, Soviet 1st Deputy Minister of Foreign Affairs, to the representatives of the UK, France and the US, outlining provisions for the creation of a unified, democratic and neutral Germany. The proposed terms stipulated the withdrawal of all armed forces of the occupying powers, the liquidation of all foreign military bases in Germany, and a prohibition on Germany entering into a coalition with any power militant against Germany during WWII. It allowed Germany to rearm and also stated that free, democratic elections would be established. It called for a four-power conference for the purpose of agreeing to these terms. Owing to western and West German resistance to the proposals, the conference never took place.

[4] Manlio Giovanni Brosio, 1897–1980. Barred from Italian politics in 1920s and 1930s for opposition to Fascism. Deputy PM and Minister of Defence, 1945–7. Italian Ambassador to Soviet Union, 1947–51; to the UK, 1952–5; to the US, 1955; to France, 1961–4. Secretary-General of NATO, 1964–71.

Winston S. Churchill to Charles Eade[1]
(Premier papers, 11/283)

18 March 1952
Private and Personal

My dear Eade,

I am sure you would like to know the true facts and figures of the Rubber exports to Russia. No increase is being allowed on what was accepted by the Americans in previous years. Only arrears of 18,000 are being made up. The mistake of your correspondent was due to the fact that the Rubber had gone from London instead of direct from Singapore.

Winston S. Churchill to Raymond Triboulet[2]
(Premier papers, 11/671)

18 March 1952

Dear Monsieur Triboulet,

I am obliged to you for your kind letter of March 6 inviting me to attend the commemoration at Arromanches of the landing of the allied troops in Normandy of June 6, 1944. It would be very agreeable to me to re-visit Normandy for this purpose, but I regret the pressure of my public duties at that time will render it impossible

I should be glad if you would express to your colleagues my very best wishes for the success of the celebrations.

---

[1] Charles Stanley Eade, 1903–64. Deputy Editor, *Sunday Graphic*, 1933–6; *Daily Sketch*, 1936–8. Editor, *Sunday Dispatch*, 1938–57. Editor of five volumes of Churchill's wartime speeches and the three-volume compilation *The War Speeches* (1952–3). At this time he was also engaged on a classic work on Churchill's character, talents, many faces and hobbies, titled *Churchill by His Contemporaries* (1953).

[2] Raymond Triboulet, 1906–2006. French journalist, 1930s. Mobilized, 1939; taken prisoner, 1940; repatriated, 1941. Member of French Resistance. Secretary, Departmental Committee of Liberation of Calvados, 1944. Inspector, Rhineland-Palatinate, 1946. Deputy for Calvados, 1946. Founding member of Rassemblement du Peuple Française, 1947. Chairman, Social Republicans, 1956. Minister of Veteran Affairs, 1955. Dept of Veteran Affairs, 1959–66. President, French Committee of the Pan-European Union, 1973–87. Member of the Academy of Moral and Political Sciences, 1979. Delegate of the Academy at the Annual Public Meeting of the Five Academies, 1988. President of the Academy, 1991.

March 1952

Defence Committee: minutes
(Cabinet papers, 131/12)

19 March 1952
Top Secret
11.30 a.m.
Defence Committee Meeting No. 2 of 1952

Prime Minister's Map Room
Ministry of Defence

1. SOUTH-EAST ASIA

The Committee had before them two memoranda by the Chiefs of Staff:
D(52)4: on the action which might be taken in the event of an open Chinese aggression in South-East Asia;
D(52)5: on the action which might be taken to deter the French from withdrawal from Indo-China, and on the action which should be taken in the event of a French withdrawal.

Action in the Event of Overt Chinese Aggression in South-East Asia

The Chief of the Imperial General Staff said that the Chiefs of Staff were concerned at the difference of opinion which had arisen between them and the American Chiefs of Staff on the action to be taken in the event of further aggression by the Chinese in South-East Asia. The Americans would like to extend the area of conflict beyond the actual point of aggression by bombing ports and communications in areas immediately adjacent to the battle front, though this might, if necessary, include the bombing of Chinese territory. The problem was now under discussion in Washington between the Pentagon and the State Department, and the Chiefs of Staff hoped that, as soon as Mr Acheson was ready to hold politico-military discussions with us in Washington, the British representatives in these discussions might be instructed to follow the line recommended by the Chiefs of Staff.

The Prime Minister said that in his view a blockade of China would be futile if it did not include Soviet ports. This would bring about a direct challenge to the Soviet Government, with consequences which no one could foretell. On the other hand, the bombing of Manchurian communications or air bases would not, in his judgment, raise the decisive issue. It would be effective in stopping supplies sent to the Chinese Communist forces in Korea, whether they came by land or sea. Similarly, air attacks on the communications from China to French Indo-China delivered from the Philippines might be effective. It would be silly to waste bombs in the vague inchoate mass of China, and wrong to kill thousands of people for no purpose. This was the view which Her Majesty's Government had previously expressed, and there should be no question of our departing from it. He agreed that British representatives in any discussions with the Americans should follow this line.

The Committee –

(1) Took note of the existing state of discussions regarding Allied policy in South-East Asia in the event of overt Chinese aggression.

(2) Agreed that when the politico-military discussions were held with the Americans, the British representatives should be authorised to take the line indicated in paragraphs 8–10 of D. (52)4 and developed by the Prime Minister in the Committee's discussion as recorded above.

(3) Invited the Secretary of State for Commonwealth Relations to keep the Governments of the older Commonwealth countries informed of our views and of the action which we proposed to take.

Action in the Event of a French Withdrawal from Indo-China (D. (52)5)

The Prime Minister said that there were solid reasons why the French should withdraw from Indo-China and he personally believed that they would. The return of large French regular forces from Indo-China to Europe would substantially increase the capacity of Western Europe to defend itself. The Committee should, however, consider the effect of a French withdrawal upon our own position in South-East Asia.

The following points were made in discussion:

(a) The loss of Indo-China to Communism would probably result sooner or later in the establishment of Communist regimes in Siam and Burma. That would bring the Communist threat to the borders of Malaya. The first effect of the loss of Indo-China would possibly be an intensification of bandit activity in Malaya, though it was questionable how far the resources of the bandits would allow large increases of effort. The direct threat of a Chinese Communist attack upon Malaya could only develop later, perhaps after two years, and might never develop at all.

(b) Plans should, however, be made to meet the possible development of this threat. These should be directed towards ensuring that we could seal off Malaya from Communist infiltration and attack, by occupying the Songkha position, which was in Siamese territory. To hold this position against a full-scale Chinese attack would need two to three divisions; but for its initial occupation it would suffice to move one division from convenient positions close at hand in the North of Malaya.

(c) It would be easier to carry out this move, when the time came, if the Siamese Government were friendly. Moreover, anything which could be done to keep an anti-Communist Government in power in Siam would help to avert the danger. The Minister of State[1] said that the Foreign Secretary was preparing a paper on this point.

---

[1] For Colonial Affairs, Alan Lennox-Boyd.

(d) The view of the Chiefs of Staff was that, unlike Hong Kong, Malaya was defensible against a full-scale Chinese attack. If, in the meantime, the internal position in Malaya was cleared up, it would be easier to find the resources to resist aggression from without; but little improvement in the internal situation could be expected for at least a year. In an extreme emergency some assistance in the defence of Malaya could be looked for from Australia and New Zealand; but the most urgent need was the expansion of the Malayan Regiment, on which a paper was being prepared for the Defence Committee.

(e) Apart from strategic considerations, the loss of Indo-China, Siam and Burma would cause grave difficulties in maintaining the supply of rice to the population of Malaya, and the possibilities of building up a stockpile should be examined.

(f) It would not be possible for the United Kingdom to offer the French any practical assistance in the defence of Indo-China. Moreover, to urge the Americans to increase the scale of their financial aid to France would be inconsistent with our argument that the small amount of American aid to the United Kingdom took no account of our vast defence effort and ought to be increased.

The Prime Minister said that it was too early to assume the worst. There might be many developments in the world situation before a real threat to Malaya developed. The Americans, for example, might conclude that the time had arrived for straight talking with the leaders of the Soviet Union. The result of straight talking might be an intensification of the cold war, or even the start of open war; on the other hand, it might lead to a general pacification of the world, including the Far East and South-East Asia. It would, therefore, be wrong to commit ourselves at this stage to preparations for the defence of Malaya against a possible threat in the future. It would, however, be prudent to make plans, without expenditure of money or resources, on the lines suggested by the Chiefs of Staff. These plans could then be brought back to the Defence Committee for consideration. Meanwhile, there should be an interchange of views on the whole subject with the Americans, and the older Commonwealth Governments should be kept informed.

The Committee –

(4) Took note of the indications that the French might be contemplating a withdrawal from Indo-China, and of the serious situation that would follow from this.

(5) Invited the Foreign Secretary to initiate an urgent interchange of views and information with the United States authorities on this problem, taking account of the point noted in paragraph (f) above.

(6) Instructed the Chiefs of Staff to prepare plans against the development of a threat to Malaya, and to submit these to the Defence Committee.

MARCH 1952   357

(7) Invited the Secretary of State for the Colonies to put in hand an examination of the possibilities of building up a stockpile of rice for Malaya.

(8) Invited the Secretary of State for Commonwealth Relations to keep the Governments of the older Commonwealth countries informed of our views.

[...]

5. RUSSIAN SUBMARINE STRENGTH

The Prime Minister said he would be glad to receive from the Admiralty an estimate of Russian submarine strength, both actual and potential. He was particularly interested in the number of fast submarines now possessed by the Russians, or likely to be available to them in the future. The threat from submarines and mines in the next war would be far greater than any possible threat from surface ships.

[...]

Cabinet: conclusions
(Cabinet papers, 128/24)

20 March 1952
Secret
11.30 a.m.
Cabinet Meeting No. 32 of 1952

[...]

6. In reply to a question by the Prime Minister, the Minister of Agriculture[1] said that the pig population in this country had now been raised to a level approximately equal to that of the years immediately preceding the war. If adequate supplies of coarse grains continued to be imported, it should be possible to raise the annual home production of pig meat to about 600,000 tons in 1955–56.

The Minister said that there was a risk that a smaller acreage would be sown to potatoes this spring. There was at present a substantial glut of potatoes from last year's crop, and farmers had no assurance of being able to secure the labour required to lift a heavy crop in the autumn. These two

---

[1] Thomas Lionel Dugdale, 1897–1977. Joined Royal Scots Greys, 1916. On active service, 1916–18. Capt., 1923. Maj., Yorkshire Hussars (Yeomanry), 1927. MP (Cons.) for Richmond, Yorkshire, 1929–59. Parliamentary Private Secretary to Stanley Baldwin, 1935–7. Lord of the Treasury, 1937–40. Deputy Government Chief Whip, 1941–2. Vice-Chairman of Conservative Party, 1941–2; Chairman, 1942–4. Bt, 1945. Minister of Agriculture and Fisheries, 1951–4. UK Delegate, Council of Europe and Western European Union, 1958–9. Baron, 1959. Chairman of Political Honours Scrutiny Committee, 1961–76; of North of England Advisory Committee for Civil Aviation, 1964–72.

considerations, coupled with the high cost of sowing potatoes, might have the result that a smaller acreage would be sown. The Prime Minister said that no opportunity should be lost of encouraging the growing of potatoes, not only by farmers, but by smallholders. He also suggested that vigorous steps should be taken, by publicity and otherwise, to ensure that full use was made of the abundant supplies of potatoes which were currently available.

The Cabinet –

Took note of these statements.

[. . .]

Winston S. Churchill to Lord Cherwell
(Premier papers, 11/295)

20 March 1952

My dear Prof,

I do not see how it is possible to move the Atom staff (over 11,000) from the administrative care of the Ministry of Supply to that of the Ministry of Defence. At the Ministry of Supply they have all the support of the vast machinery for contracts, accountability, security, etc. The Ministry of Defence is not an administrative Department. At least half a dozen sub-branches would have to be set up there to deal with all that is done in the broad sweep of the Ministry of Supply. The Atomic Vote would be isolated and every shilling would have to be accounted for separately. I understood from you that this would be a great disadvantage. It will also be argued that transference to the Ministry of Defence implies only a warlike use of Atomic Energy.

Under the arrangements I am making, and which are set out on the sheet enclosed, you will have the fullest power to guide and direct with my authority and constant access to me on all the practical steps which must be taken in the next critical six months, while at the same time not being burdened with contracts, the management of the working staff, accountancy and all these alternative matters, in which Sandys is quite ready to serve you.

There remains the delicate question of security. Who will be blamed if another Fuchs or Pontecorvo turns up? I am sure it is better for Sandys to be responsible for carrying out in the Ministry of Supply the general system which had been approved by the Cabinet on the advice of the Home Secretary.

Anthony Eden to Winston S. Churchill
Prime Minister's Personal Telegram T.96/52
(Premier papers, 11/153)

20 March 1952
Immediate
Personal
No. 168

Paris

I have been greatly heartened by the helpful and sympathetic response of the European Ministers assembled here to our proposals for the future of the Council of Europe. I think we have gained a valuable initiative without departing from reality. Even the Swedes, who are averse to any formal association with Western European Defence, have agreed to join in careful study of our suggestions.

2. An open dispute about the Saar was also avoided thanks to the admirable last minute efforts by Schuman and Adenauer, who have agreed to go further into the problem together with the Saar Government. This is most satisfactory.

3. On the whole I think we can be well content. Things have gone better than we could have expected.

4. I am seeing Eisenhower tomorrow and I shall tell you more when we lunch on Saturday.

Lord Cherwell to Winston S. Churchill
(Premier papers, 11/139)

21 March 1952

Harrod[1] makes four main proposals:

1. We should buy the whole gold output of the sterling area on long-term contract, and possibly subsidise it.

These suggestions are worth examining, but I do not think there is nearly so much to be gained as Harrod suggests. The total gold output of the sterling area is about $500 million a year, but the bulk is already used to help balance the area's accounts with the rest of the world.

2. We should revalue sterling so as to get higher dollar prices for our exports.

When our textile exporters are finding it hard to sell at existing prices, I think this is going too far. While I believe we should get the best prices we can

---

[1] Henry Roy Forbes Harrod, 1900–78. Married, 1938, Wilhelmine Cresswell. Educated at King's College, Cambridge. Tutor in Economics at Christ Church, Oxford. Oxford University Lecturer in Economics, 1929–37, 1946–52; Reader in Economics, 1952–7. In Churchill's Statistical Branch, 1940–2. Statistical Adviser to the Admiralty, 1943–5. UK Economic Adviser to IMF, 1952–3. Knighted, 1959.

for our exports, and maintain the £ at $2.80, I am sure it may well be that to raise it to, say, $3.50 would soon lose us markets and greatly encourage speculation against sterling.

3. <u>We should make non-resident sterling convertible at once, if necessary by blocking part of the sterling balances.</u>

Without complete blocking, I am afraid that whatever was left free would immediately be converted into dollars.

As you know, I was always in favour of dealing firmly at the end of the war with the Indian and Middle East balances which in my view were grossly exaggerated. But these have now been drawn on heavily. What remains forms only a relatively small part of our total liabilities, and we have already agreed to release the bulk of it as part of the Colombo Plan. The main part of the balances now consists of sterling earned by the Colonies and other overseas countries in perfectly genuine trade. To block these merely to suit our convenience would cause the greatest resentment and probably the break-up of the Sterling Area.

4. <u>We should cut our investment by £500–£700 million a year, especially in manufacturing industry.</u>

I believe we should do all we can to economise in many forms of investment, for example, road schemes, and to limit the need for investment in industry and in power generation, by working double-shifts and by sensible electricity tariffs. But I am sure that it would be folly to attempt a cut of anything like the size Harrod suggests.

Last year we added some £900 million to the nation's stock of equipment and buildings. Harrod's proposal would put a stop to most of this. As you once said, we must not risk consuming our seed-corn.

I do not think it is true to say that we have created an excessive manufacturing power employed on unrequited exports. It is true that we have repaid doubtful debts to India and Middle Eastern countries at much too high a rate. But in total we have imported <u>more</u> goods and services than we have exported, not less.

This is proved by our balance of payments which has shown a large deficit since the war as follows:

	£ million
1946	− 344
1947	− 545
1948	− 28
1949	+ 6
1950	+ 238
1951	− 516
	−1189

In fact we have enjoyed unrequited imports financed by the Colonies, North America and many other countries who have lent to us or have given us grants. Moreover, we now need a surplus for several years to come in order to rebuild our gold reserves.

Harrod argues that we have a higher proportion of our population engaged in manufacturing than the Americans. But this is bound to be so. They get most of their food and raw materials out of their own soil. We have to get most of ours from other countries, and to pay for them we have to make a large quantity of manufactures over and above our own needs.[1]

R. A. Butler to Winston S. Churchill
(Premier papers, 11/197)

21 March 1952

You asked for the comments of the Minister of Labour, Minister of Supply and myself upon the Paymaster General's Minute of 12th February about the importance of working double shifts in industry.

The attached report by a Committee of officials was prepared at my request, and its conclusions are endorsed by the Ministers concerned (Minister of Labour, President of the Board of Trade, Minister of Supply, Minister of Food and the Minister of Works[2]). I, too, accept the conclusions of the report, and have agreed to send it on to you for your approval.

The only proposal for immediate action is that the Departments concerned should, when examining proposals for licensing new building or the import of machinery, make it a rule to investigate whether new capacity could be saved by means of double-shift work.

In general, there are considerable difficulties about trying to get any widespread extension of double-shift work in present circumstances. There is no simple answer to the question whether or not such a wide extension of shift work would, as a long term object, be desirable. There are, however, cases in which double-shift working is practicable and would be of advantage, and in general, industry is alive to the possibilities.

[1] Churchill wrote on May 18: 'There are many points in this which strike me. I can well believe that we have created a manufacturing power employed on unrequited support and producing inevitably a deficit in imports. Let me know your views before I send it to the Chancellor' (M.144/52, *Premier papers, 11/139*).
[2] David McAdam Eccles, 1904–99. Educated at Winchester and Oxford. Married, 1928, Sybil Dawson (d. 1977); 1984, Mary Hyde. Ministry of Economic Warfare, 1939. Ministry of Production, 1942–3. Economic Adviser, HM Ambassadors at Madrid and Lisbon, 1940–2. MP (Cons.) for Chippenham Division of Wilts, 1943–62. PC, 1951. Minister of Works, 1951–4. KCVO, 1953. Minister of Education, 1954–7, 1959–62. President of the Board of Trade, 1957–9. Baron, 1962. Trustee, British Museum, 1963–99; Chairman of Trustees, 1968–70. Viscount, 1964. Chairman, Anglo-Hellenic League, 1967–70. Paymaster-General, 1970–3. President, World Crafts Council, 1974–8. CH, 1984.

I hope you will agree that this has been a useful examination, and will confirm the conclusion which we have reached as to the proposal for immediate action.[1]

Winston S. Churchill to President Chaim Weizmann
(Chaim Weizmann papers)

21 March 1952

My dear Weizmann,

I have today received the oranges and Jaffa grapefruit which you have sent me, and I hope, my dear friend, that you will both accept my warmest thanks for this magnificent gift.

Charles Eade to Winston S. Churchill
(Premier papers, 11/283)

21 March 1952

Dear Prime Minister,

I am grateful to you for the trouble you have taken in writing to me[2] about the *Sunday Dispatch* story on rubber exports to Russia and for explaining the point about supplies from Malaya and London.

I have since read Mr Peter Thorneycroft's reply to a question in Parliament regarding these exports and note his statement that 'the matter is being kept under very close watch'.

One point has been brought to my attention since last Sunday. Last April, *Associated Press*, America's leading news agency, circulated a story that Mr James Currie,[3] Commercial Counsellor to the British Embassy, had announced that <u>no more</u> rubber would be shipped to Russia and Communist China from Singapore.

It seems that he must have been misquoted but I cannot trace that any official correction of *Associated Press*'s statement has ever been published and I feel that it might have caused some confusion both here and in America in view of the fact that since that date 6,697 tons of rubber have been sent from Malaya to Russia direct.

---

[1] Churchill wrote: '<u>Urgent</u>. Lord Cherwell, please comment.'
[2] Letter of Mar. 18, reproduced above (p. 353).
[3] James Currie, 1907–83. UK Commercial Counsellor to US, 1949–52; to Denmark, 1952–6. Consul-General, São Paulo, 1956–62; Johannesburg, 1962–7.

March 1952

Winston S. Churchill to Lord Cherwell
Prime Minister's Personal Minute M.159/52
(Premier papers, 11/4)

22 March 1952

I send you De L'Isle and Dudley's comments on your paper,* and I mentioned to you the other day the films of guided missiles which I was shown. It could I am sure be arranged by the Ministry for you to see them in London at your convenience. Perhaps you will give me a short summing up of the interesting discussion these papers contain.

* On rocket propulsion for fighters.

John Colville: diary
('The Fringes of Power', pages 643–4)

22–23 March 1952

Drove to Chequers with the PM. Meg was invited for the weekend and other guests were the Salisburys, the Alexanders and the Soameses. Lord Montgomery and the Prof came to luncheon on Sunday – Monty, mellow and in good form but, as ever, trying to lobby the PM about matters in which he is but slightly interested (this time Greece and Turkey) or on which he hardly thinks Monty an expert. The PM is angry, almost to breaking point, with the Prof who is digging in his toes over the control of atomic energy. In the long gallery on Sunday night, after the rest had gone to bed, he told Christopher and me that the programme of the Tory Party must be: 'Houses and meat and not being scuppered.' He didn't feel quite happy about the latter though he does not himself think war probable unless the Americans lose patience. As he subsequently added, perhaps 'not being broke' is going to be our major difficulty and preoccupation.

Quite favourably impressed by Alex this time. He is not original or clever, but I thought he showed common sense on most things, even though he usually took the obvious line. Surprisingly he feels strongly about class distinction: he loved Canada for its absence and is alarmed by it in his own Brigade of Guards.

Winston S. Churchill to Gwilym Lloyd George
Prime Minister's Personal Minute M.170/52
(Premier papers, 11/149)

24 March 1952
Top Secret

Please translate these money figures into tons of food stocks taking April 1949 as a standard, and let me know where the principal commodities stand:
(a) when we took over, and
(b) today.

Winston S. Churchill to Anthony Eden
Prime Minister's Personal Minute M.168/52
(Premier papers, 11/93)

24 March 1952
Secret and Personal

1. The announcement of an Egyptian General Election raises all the most important issues open thereabouts. Hilaly[1] will no doubt try to beat the Wafd by declaring that King Farouk and his Government appeal to the electors on the two main principles that we evacuate Egypt and make Farouk King of the Sudan. There is therefore no difference in principle between him and the Wafd. He will be asking for exactly the same as Nahas attempted by violence to procure. He does not however wish to be drawn into violence, and both he and Farouk and all the forces that they can control are profoundly alarmed at the danger of anarchy and bloodshed in Cairo and Alexandria.

2. The shock that the recent outrages in Cairo gave to Egyptian society and to the status of Egypt as a civilized country are the dominant factors in their minds. They must greatly fear a Wafd success.

3. We for our part would prefer a Farouk–Hilaly victory at the poll. The question arises, should we therefore give up all we have been fighting for in order to help them to win their election. The differences between the two contending parties means to us giving way quietly and politely if Farouk wins, or, having to face a renewal of the violence which we suffered and repelled at the hands of Nahas.

4. Personally I do not see, if the worst comes to the worst, why we should fear this second alternative. We should only be back where we were when we took office; but the Egyptians, whether Farouk or Nahas predominates, will be

---

[1] Ahmed Naguib el-Hilaly, 1891–1958. Educated at Khedival Law School. Chancellor of the Niyaba, 1931. Education Minister, 1934–6. Joined Wafd Party, 1938. Served in Cabinet of Mustafa al-Nahhas, 1937–8, 1942–4. Left Wafd Party, 1951. PM, 1952. Banned from politics following Egyptian Revolution of 1952.

suffering every increasing pressure and it may well be that out of their strife and resulting weakness Farouk will be forced to come to terms with us, and take all necessary measures to preserve order.

5. I do not think that we should in any case give up the Treaty rights which we possess and which we have the power to enforce, before the Election takes place. We should stay where we are in the Canal Zone and await events with composure and resolution. There are barely six weeks before the election and it would not be possible, even if it were advisable to reach an agreement with Farouk to enable him to win the Election. If we have to pay as the price all that we have been and are contending for, we do not risk much by waiting to see what happens.

Meeting: minutes
(Premier papers, 11/287)

24 March 1952   Cabinet Room
4 p.m.

Present:
    Prime Minister
    Lord President
    Secretary of State for Co-ordination of Transport, Fuel and Power
    Attorney General[1]
    Minister of Transport
    Sir Gilmour Jenkins[2]
    Sir Cyril Birtchnell[3]
    Mr D. B. Pitblado

1. The Minister of Transport reported that Lord Hurcomb[4] had investigated

---

[1] Lionel Frederick Heald, 1897–1981. Educated at Christ Church, Oxford. Married, 1923, Flavia Forbes: two children (div. 1928); 1929, Daphne Constance Price: three children. Called to the Bar, Middle Temple, 1923. Junior Counsel, Board of Trade, 1931–7. RAF, 1939–45. Governor, Middlesex Hospital, 1946–53. MP (Cons.) for Chertsey, 1950–70. Knighted, 1951. Attorney-General, 1951–4. PC, 1954. Retired, 1970.

[2] Thomas Gilmour Jenkins, 1894–1981. Educated at London University. Commissioned in Royal Garrison Artillery, 1914–18. Married, 1916, Evelyne Mary Nash. MC, 1918. Board of Trade, 1919; Asst Secretary, 1934; Principal Asst Secretary, 1937. 2nd Secretary, Ministry of Shipping, 1939. CB, 1941. Deputy Director-General, Ministry of War Transport, 1941–6. Knighted, 1944. Permanent Secretary, Control Office for Germany and Austria, 1946–7. KCB, 1948. Permanent Secretary, Ministry of Transport, 1947–53; Ministry of Transport and Civil Aviation, 1953–9.

[3] Cyril Augustine Birtchnell, 1887–1967. Joined HM Customs, 1906. Ministry of Transport, 1920. Member of League of Nations Permanent Commission on Road Traffic, 1927. Principal Asst Secretary (Road Transport), 1940; Deputy Secretary, 1947. British member of Executive Board of European Inland Transport Organisations, 1945–6. Knighted, 1949.

[4] Cyril William Hurcomb, 1883–1976. Entered Post Office, 1906. Permanent Secretary, Ministry of Transport, 1927–36. Knighted, 1929. Director-General, Ministry of Shipping, 1939–41; Ministry of War Transport, 1941–7. Chairman, British Transport Commission, 1947–53. Baron, 1950.

the case of Mrs Hill. She had had three-month licences for a period of 18 months for distances varying between 40 and 100 miles. At present there was less work in the area and some of the Road Haulage Executive lorries were idle. This was why the Permit had not been renewed.

The Prime Minister said, and it was agreed, that this was an example of the process of continuing nationalisation, going on despite the Government's policy. Lord Leathers explained that it was going on under the Act and that decisions on new policy were necessary before the trend could be reversed.

2. The Minister of Transport further reported that the number of cases in which Permits had not been continued since the 25th October was 160. Of these 3 had been revoked and the remainder not renewed. Of the remainder there had been no application in 109 cases. The number of cases in question was therefore about 51. The Prime Minister was surprised at the small number involved in view of the many reports of unjustices and the strong feeling which existed in the Party.

3. There was some discussion on the Paper before the Cabinet tomorrow. It was agreed that if broad decisions of policy were taken by the Cabinet it would be possible to take steps to prevent cases like that of Mrs Hill continuing. To enable a general direction to be made it would not be necessary to introduce legislation. It would be sufficient that there should have been a definite announcement of the intention to introduce legislation and its broad scope. It was indeed possible that Lord Hurcomb would be able to prevent hard cases arising in the interim period without such a direction, though he might on the other hand need to prevent the possibility of the Commission being attacked for not carrying out the Act.

4. The possibility of having a short Bill was discussed since the full Act reforming Transport would take some time to draft and to get through the House. It was however agreed that a one-clause Bill imposing such a standstill on the revocation of licences would be right and that it would be easier to work under a direction.

It was agreed that the Minister of Transport should draft, discuss with Lord Leathers and Lord Woolton, and send to the Prime Minister before the Cabinet tomorrow,

    (a) the draft of a possible public announcement after the Cabinet approved the proposals in C (52)83, and

    (b) the draft of a general direction to the Transport Commission.

If these were agreed it would be possible for Lord Leathers and the Minister to see Lord Hurcomb, who as yet knew nothing of the Government's proposals. The situation could be discussed with him and it might be possible to persuade him to proceed on the lines the Prime Minister wished – which would cover the case of Mrs Hill – without an announcement or a direction. There would be some advantages in avoiding too early an announcement, both because it would be better not to announce the Government's policy in too great detail before appropriate consultations had taken place, and also because it would be difficult to work the Road Haulage Executive after its winding up had been announced since those concerned would naturally be trying to leave for continuing work.

House of Commons: Oral Answers
(Hansard)

24 March 1952

ATOMIC ENERGY

Sir I. Fraser asked the Prime Minister whether he will permit Parliamentary observers to attend the atom bomb test in Australia.

The Prime Minister (Mr Winston Churchill): The arrangements for this test are under consideration with Her Majesty's government in Australia: but I can hold out no expectation that Parliamentary observers will be able to attend.

Sir I. Fraser: Can my right hon. Friend say if Parliamentary observers went to the tests in the Pacific which the Americans arranged?

The Prime Minister: I cannot, without notice, say what arrangements took place in the tests in the Pacific: but, at any rate it would not affect the substance of the answer I have just given to my hon. Friend.

Mr C. R. Attlee: May I ask if the right hon. Gentlemen does not recollect that there were two Members of this House, one belonging to his party and one to mine, who did attend these tests?

The Prime Minister: I am very much obliged to the right hon. Gentlemen for refreshing my memory upon this matter, and indeed furnishing me with information, but I have nothing to add to what I said.

Mr Attlee: May I ask whether that was not a useful precedent? Perhaps the right hon. Gentlemen will consult one of the members of his own Government, in the Admiralty, who was one of the representatives?

The Prime Minister: I should be very much obliged for any assistance of that character.

Mr G. R. Strauss:[1] asked the Prime Minister whether he has now decided if any adjustments should be made in the existing statutory responsibility of the Minister of Supply for work on atomic energy: and if he will make a statement.

The Prime Minister: In view of the fact that important experiments are to be made in the autumn of this year, I have felt that this is not the appropriate

---

[1] George Russell Strauss, 1901–93. MP (Lab.) for Lambeth North, 1929–31, 1935–50; for Vauxhall, 1950–79. Member, London and Home Counties Traffic Advisory Committee, 1936. Parliamentary Secretary to Minister of Aircraft Production, 1942–5. Minister of Transport, 1946–7. Minister of Supply, 1947–51. PC, 1947. 'Father of the House', 1974. Baron, 1979.

moment to make radical changes in the existing arrangements or to create a new organisation on a long-term basis. It has therefore been decided to make no change for the present in the statutory responsibility of the Minister of Supply in regard to atomic energy. As indicated, however, in my reply of 15th November, to the hon. Member for Gloucestershire, West (Mr Phillips Price),[1] the Paymaster-General will continue to advise me on atomic energy questions and to exercise general supervision over work in this field.

Mr Strauss: Is the Prime Minister aware that the decision not to alter the administrative set-up and responsibility which has existed during the past four years is considered, anyhow by some of those responsible for the development of this work during that period, as being a very wise one?

The Prime Minister: A very wise one? I thank the right hon. Gentleman for his compliment, which is also a compliment to himself.

Cabinet: conclusions
(Cabinet papers, 128/24)

25 March 1952
Secret
11.30 a.m.
Cabinet Meeting No. 33 of 1952

1. The Cabinet's attention was drawn to the increasing unemployment in the textile and clothing industries. It was estimated that about 10 per cent of the labour force of these industries was either unemployed or working less than full time. In many of the areas affected these workers could not yet be absorbed into defence production.

In discussion it was suggested that further orders should be placed in these areas for clothing for the Armed Forces and the Civil Defence Services. The Cabinet agreed that this possibility should be urgently examined. They recognised, however, that only a limited relief could be obtained by these means, and that it would be necessary to consider other measures which would have more lasting and more widespread effects. The Chancellor of the Exchequer would consider these, in consultation with the Minister of Labour and the President of the Board of Trade.

The Cabinet –
    1) Invited the Minister of Defence and the Home Secretary to consider urgently what further orders could be placed for clothing for the Armed Forces and the Civil Defence Services with a view to relieving the unemployment in the textile and clothing industries.
    2) Took note that the Chancellor of the Exchequer would consider,

[1] Morgan Philips Price, 1885–1973. Educated at Harrow and Trinity College, Cambridge. MP (Lab.) for Whitehaven, 1929–31; for Forest of Dean, 1935–50; for West Gloucestershire, 1950–9.

with the other Ministers concerned, what further measures could be taken to alleviate this situation.

[. . .]

Winston S. Churchill to Anthony Eden
Prime Minister's Personal Minute M.171/52
(Premier papers, 11/116)

25 March 1952

I presume we are agreed that so far as we have any say in the matter, no United Nations prisoner of war shall be handed back to the Communists against his will. I understand a lot of them are being allowed to slip away and disappear. This may be a tactful process, but the principle of handing back by force seems to involve both honour and humanity.

Duncan Sandys to Winston S. Churchill
(Premier papers, 11/277)

25 March 1952

You asked for my comments on the Paymaster-General's Minute about structural steel.

2. I entirely agree that existing safety factors on constructional steel-work could be reduced without danger, and that the most effective way of enforcing economy is for the Ministry of Works to refuse to issue licences for buildings whose structural design involves the use of more steel than is necessary.

3. The Ministry of Supply and the steel industry are doing their utmost to increase supplies of re-inforcing materials and we hope that by June the rate of production will meet current demands.

Anthony Eden to Winston S. Churchill
(Churchill papers, 2/517)

27 March 1952
PM/52/31

Thank you for your minute about Egypt (M.168/52).[1] Here are my thoughts.

If we reach agreement with Egypt on terms acceptable to us and them, then:

---

[1] Reproduced above (pp. 364–5).

1) There is a good chance the Egyptian Government will survive and friendly relations develop;
2) It will enable us to withdraw most of our forces instead of having to keep more than 70,000 men in the Canal Zone to deal with the Egyptians;
3) It will have a helpful influence on the whole of the Middle East, including Persia;

If we cannot reach agreement, the results we must expect are:
1) The present Egyptian Government will fall and be replaced by a Wafd or other extremist government;
2) We shall revert to the situation of January last;
3) Valuable British assets will be in the gravest danger;
4) There will be increased difficulties for all British interests throughout the Middle East;
5) There will be no Middle East defence plan and we shall suffer increasing embarrassment with the United States;
6) We must be ready to face constant conflict to maintain our position and calls to occupy Cairo and Alexandria to save British lives.

Winston S. Churchill to Sir Norman Brook
Prime Minister's Personal Minute M.177/52
(Premier papers, 11/268)

27 March 1952

The American expression 'Top Secret' should not be adopted by us. Secrecy is not to be measured by altitude. If it were so many might think that 'Bottom Secret' would be more forceful and suggestive. It would be good and correct English to say 'Most Secret'. I hope this may be adopted.

Lord Moran to Winston S. Churchill
(Premier papers, 11/495)

27 March 1952

My dear Prime Minister,

To save you reading through my long speech, this is the substance of what I said:

EXPENDITURE

The *Daily Telegraph* says that the House was deeply impressed when I asked: 'Where are we going unless we make a stand against this expenditure?' But my argument was simple. Expensive new techniques and new drugs like

Aureomycin are being discovered at short intervals and they must be incorporated in the Health Service because they save lives. Therefore the expenditure is bound to rise steadily, with no ceiling, unless there is economy elsewhere. The economy must either be lowering of standards or putting a charge on something in the Service. Of these the hotel charge and the Denmark arrangement about drugs have nothing against them except that they may lose votes.

ADMISSIONS OF GENERAL PRACTITIONERS TO THE HOSPITALS

The *Daily Telegraph* devotes all its leader to this, and the *Times* also supports it. It costs no money, except a small amount in salaries to clinical assistants. With Health Centres it would transform the education of the general practitioner. As it is he works as an individual and gets more and more rusty as years pass. He would work say two afternoons a week as a clinical assistant in a hospital, and much of the rest of his time would be in a Health Centre. At present you have got 6,000 consultants working in ideal conditions, and 20,000 practitioners working under conditions which are scientifically unsound.

REMUNERATION OF SPECIALISTS

The last government undertook to pay the general practitioners and specialists in terms of 1938 money, and the difference between 1938 money and the present time is called betterment. The betterment given to general practitioners by Mr Justice Danckwert[1] was 100 per cent. At present the consultants are only getting 20 per cent betterment. The obligation on the government is exactly the same for the specialists as for the general practitioners, and it would be much more economical for the government to settle the question now than to allow it to drag on and go to arbitration.[2]

Anthony Eden to Winston S. Churchill
(Churchill papers, 2/517)

31 March 1952
PM/52/33

Your minute M.171/52: Prisoners of war in Korea.[3]

We have fully supported the Americans in their efforts to find a way to avoid having to hand back any prisoners of war to the Communists against

---

[1] Harold Otto Danckwerts, 1888–1978. Educated at Winchester, Balliol College, Oxford, and Harvard University. Called to the Bar, 1913. On active service in WWI with East Riding of Yorkshire Yeomanry and Machine Gun Corps (despatches). Justice of Chancery Div. of High Court of England and Wales, 1949. Lord Justice of Appeal in Court of Appeal of England and Wales, 1961. PC, 1961.

[2] Churchill wrote in the margin: 'I reason the consultants would I'm sure accept less than 100 per cent.' He then responded on Apr. 11: 'Thank you so much for sending me a note on your speech. I have read it with attention and have forwarded it to the Minister of Health.'

[3] Reproduced above (p. 369).

their will. We do not know whether any Chinese or North Korean prisoners are being allowed to slip away and disappear.

2. We are mercifully not at the point where an armistice in Korea could be obtained only at the price of agreeing to force some prisoners to return to Communist territory. The humanitarian argument does not work only one way because we must not forget the fate of our own men whose release can be brought about only by an armistice.

3. Meanwhile, there are some grounds for hoping that the recent proposal for secret sessions to discuss the exchange of prisoners may lead to an acceptable compromise. The first of these sessions took place on March 25th.

4. If the secret sessions should yield no result and we are faced later with the problem of a possible breakdown of the talks over the issue of voluntary repatriation I should want to discuss the position with you. I naturally agree that it revolts the conscience to contemplate the forced return of prisoners who would go, not to freedom, but to slavery or death.

Winston S. Churchill to Peter Thorneycroft
Prime Minister's Personal Minute M.185/52
(Premier papers, 11/198)

31 March 1952

1. Reference Hansard for March 26, Column 467, fifth paragraph.[1] Let me have a report on this suggestion, which might perhaps be some help.

2. What other proposals are you making to cope with growing unemployment in the textile trade? In particular let me have in outline any alternations of the purchase tax which would be helpful.

---

[1] Christopher Soames made the following statement in Parliament on Mar. 26:

'The United Nations General Assembly has recently approved a three-year programme of relief for those refugees costing £80 million, of which some £25 million is to be spent in the first year. Of the £25 million the United States Government have offered to contribute the dollar equivalent of £17 million, and our Government will contribute some £4 million. Could not some of this money be spent on providing clothing for those unfortunate people who are in such dire need of it? Could not the orders for this clothing be placed in Lancashire?

I would suggest to my right hon. Friend that he makes representations to the Foreign Secretary that, say, £2 million worth of clothing be ordered and paid for out of the United Nations fund. Divided among 850,000 people, £2 million is not a very large sum. It is something just over £2 per head per year on clothing. It could be paid for either out of this country's contribution to the United Nations fund, or, better still, it could be regarded as a purchase by the United States, and paid for out of their contribution to the fund, and we should then receive payment in dollars for the clothing.'

April 1952

Sir Edward Bridges to Sir Norman Brook
(Premier papers, 11/268)

1 April 1952

I am told that you would like my recollections of the origin of the phrase 'Top Secret'.[1]

At the beginning of the last war there was no common standard for grading of papers in Government Departments of Whitehall. Such security regulations as existed were mainly confined to such matters as preventing entry to Government Departments and sabotage in industrial establishments.

It was certainly after the Norway Campaign – the despatch of which was a secret known all over London for a fortnight before it sailed – though it may have been later – that the Cabinet Office, in order to be in a position to give effect to the PM's injunctions about greater security, started on the attempt to arrive at a single, common standard about circulation of papers on really secret matters. And this, of course, entailed a common definition throughout Whitehall of papers from the secrecy point of view. The attempts to bring all Departments into line met with violent resistance. But before long it became evident that the right system was a four-tier system:

    Most Secret – as it was then called;
    Secret;
    Confidential; and
    Restricted.

It took a long time to get this settled. I rather think that before we had finally settled the internal problem, the same question of a common standard arose between the Americans and ourselves. The Americans had a three-tier system, the tiers being called, I think:

    Secret;
    Confidential; and
    Restricted.

---

[1] See M.177/52, reproduced above (p. 370).

Their 'Secret' corresponded with our 'Most Secret' and with the greater part of our 'Secret'.

The difficulties of working with the Americans without a common standard in this matter were very considerable. The difficulty arose from the fact that it was necessary to have an Anglo-American understanding that documents of the top grade of secrecy were encyphered in top secret cyphers and were handled after receipt in the appropriate way. The basis for this was a common standard for grading papers. The difficulties of working with the Americans would have been greatly enhanced if we had not been able to reach a settlement on this matter. If my recollection is right, we had prolonged discussion with the Americans and found great difficulty in coming to terms with them. It appeared that their greatest objection was to use of the term 'Most Secret', which – to their way of thinking – implied that papers which were called 'Secret' were not really secret at all.

In the end we had to send a delegation to Washington to argue the matter. The leader of the Delegation, Mr Buckley of the Cabinet Office, eventually managed to persuade the Americans to adopt our four-tier system as right on merits, by using the argument that what we described as 'Most Secret' referred so to speak to the papers which were kept in 'the top drawer of the cupboard in which the secret files were kept'.

'Top' is not, therefore, used as an adverb. 'Top Secret' was intended as a telescoped way of describing the 'top layer of secret papers', thereby overcoming the American objection to 'Most Secret'. It was from this that the expression 'Top Secret' arose, which in some mysterious way overcame the American reluctance to adopt our four-tier system.

I have a clear recollection that having got agreement with the Americans at the conference on this business I submitted the matter to Mr Churchill, who gave instructions that all Departments should henceforth work on the four-tier system and that the top tier should, in future, be called 'Top Secret' and not 'Most Secret'.

This is dictated without reference to papers and I cannot vouch for its accuracy in all details. But I think you will find that the story is substantially right.

On merits, there need be no difficulty so far as I see of re-adopting 'Most Secret' instead of 'Top Secret' where the domestic circulation of papers is concerned. But I am not sure exactly how we should stand with the US Defence Department on this matter and I would imagine that this would need to be looked into.

APRIL 1952 375

Cabinet: conclusions
(Cabinet papers, 128/24)

1 April 1952
Secret
11.30 a.m.
Cabinet Meeting No. 35 of 1952

[...]

10. The Cabinet considered a memorandum by the Foreign Secretary (C(52)98) reporting the stage which had been reached in the attempt to resume negotiations with the Egyptian Government on defence and the Sudan.

The Foreign Secretary said that the Egyptian elections had been postponed and the Government had come some way to meet the conditions which we had prescribed for the resumption of negotiations. There were now some indications that the Egyptians were anxious to find a basis for a settlement, and HM Ambassador had suggested that he might return to London for consolations. The Foreign Secretary did not wish him to return unless there was a reasonable prospect that negotiations would be opened in the near future. The memorandum which had been circulated to the Cabinet set out a formula which, subject to some doubt about the concluding phrase in paragraph 1, the Egyptians were now prepared to accept as a basis for the resumption of negotiations.

The Cabinet's discussion turned largely on the proposal, in paragraph 2 of C(52)98, that this formula should be accompanied by a statement, which we should place on record either in a letter or in the minutes of the first meeting, that it was our understanding that, as regards defence, the negotiations would be resumed on the basis that 'the Egyptian Government were now prepared to accept the military consequences involved in their determined intention to defend the Canal Zone and thus to play their part in the defence of the Middle East'. The Minister of Defence thought that the wording of this paragraph was not sufficiently precise to commit the Egyptians to full participation in an Allied Middle East Command. The Egyptians might take it to mean that, if they undertook themselves to defend the Canal Zone, this would relieve them of all responsibility for playing any further part in an Allied scheme for the defence of the Middle East. He therefore proposed that a further sentence should be added to make it clear that this commitment would involve active association with their Allies in the defence of the Middle East and the provision of the necessary facilities in Egypt. The Foreign Secretary said that he was prepared to delete the word 'thus' from the formula in paragraph 2 of C(52)98: this would go some little way to meet the view put forward by the Minister of Defence; but he had grave doubts whether the Egyptians would be willing to accept the additional words which the Minister had suggested. The Prime Minister said that he would himself prefer that no statement on the lines of this paragraph should be placed on record at the outset of the negotiations; but the Foreign Secretary explained that the purpose of doing so was to draw the Egyptians into some form of commitment to associate themselves with a Middle East Command on the lines of the Four-Power proposals.

In further discussion the Prime Minister expressed his reluctance to accept any agreement which involved withdrawing British troops from Egypt until the security of the Suez Canal and the British base was assured by the establishment of an international system backed by sufficient force. The Foreign Secretary, on the other hand, said that under the Four-Power proposals for an Allied Middle East Command, which was the only international system which had so far been suggested, none of the other Powers concerned would station forces on Egyptian territory in time of peace; and he was satisfied that no Egyptian Government would conclude an agreement which provided for land forces of the United Kingdom or any other foreign Power to be stationed in Egypt in peace. The Allied Middle East Command was no more than a command structure which, in peace, would be backed in the main by Egyptian land forces and British air forces and base technicians; but this, in his view, would afford a substantial safeguard, since the Egyptians were most unlikely to encroach upon base installations which were maintained under the control of an Allied Command.

The Chancellor of the Exchequer said that on economic grounds it was undesirable to risk any open breach with the Egyptian Government at the present time. Egypt's financial position was now so precarious that it would shortly become necessary to make some new arrangement to make further sterling resources available to her.

The Cabinet – Agreed to resume their discussion on C(52)98 at their next meeting on 3rd April.[1]

Field Marshal Lord Alexander to Winston S. Churchill
(*Premier papers, 11/226*)

1 April 1952

ADMIRALTY OIL FUEL STOCKS

I have discussed the questions raised in your minute M.102/52 of 8th March[2] with the First Lord of the Admiralty and his Advisers, and I attach a copy of a full report on the subject which the First Lord has sent to me.

In my view, if the money is available, there are good reasons for adding 400,000 tons to the reserve in 1952/53, but, at my suggestion, the First Lord

---

[1] In the event, discussion was resumed on Apr. 4. See Cabinet: conclusions of this date, reproduced below (pp. 379–80).

[2] Reproduced above (p. 324).

April 1952

has agreed that a decision should be deferred until July when the economic prospects may be a little clearer. I therefore suggest that we should review the position again in July.[1]

Cabinet: conclusions
(Cabinet papers, 128/24)

3 April 1952
Secret
11.00 a.m.
Cabinet Meeting No. 36 of 1952

[...]

4. The Prime Minister said that after further discussion it had been agreed that, instead of a formal Proclamation, Her Majesty should make a declaration to the Privy Council to the effect that She and her children would bear the name of Windsor. He had now submitted formal advice to Her Majesty in this sense. The terms of this Declaration would be published in the *Official Gazette*.

The Cabinet –

Took note of the Prime Minister's statement.

[...]

Sir Norman Brook to Winston S. Churchill
(Premier papers, 11/268)

3 April 1952

I share your dislike of the term 'Top Secret'[2] and I wish that we had never had to adopt it. In point of fact, however, it was introduced with your approval in 1944. We had found it essential to have common Anglo-American standards of security classification, and the Americans refused to employ the term 'Most Secret' which we then used: our adoption of 'Top Secret' was the price which we had to pay for American acceptance of the four-tier system and standard definitions. Since then this standard system, including the term 'Top Secret', has been adopted by the other Commonwealth countries and also by the North Atlantic Treaty Organisation. We now have so many dealings on

---

[1] Churchill minuted his Private Office on Apr. 11: 'Does this mean that they asked for 800 thousand tons in addition to the existing reserves and are not content to drop it to 400 thousand and that the 400 thousand is to be reviewed in July? Let me know.' His office responded on Apr. 15: 'The First Lord of the Admiralty is not challenging the Cabinet decision of March 7 that the increase in stocks should be reduced from 800,000 tons to 400,000 tons. In view of the balance of payments position, however, he proposes, at the suggestion of the Minister of Defence, to defer any action to acquire this oil until July. Lord Alexander proposes that there should be a further review in July before any action is taken.'

[2] See M.177/52, reproduced above (p. 370).

secrecy subjects with other Commonwealth countries and with North Atlantic Treaty Powers that it would be highly inconvenient, for civil as well as Service agencies, to operate two different systems of security classification – one for domestic use and the other for international business. It would involve, not only a major upheaval, but serious loss of efficiency if we now sought to revert to the old term 'Most Secret'.[1]

I attach, in case you should wish to refer to it, a detailed note by Sir Edward Bridges on the origins of this term.[2]

Winston S. Churchill to Field Marshal Lord Alexander
Prime Minister's Personal Minute M.190/52
(Premier papers, 11/49)

3 April 1952

I do not understand how and when the anticipated Russian threat against the Middle East would eventuate. Obviously there would be a global War and no part of it can be considered except in relation to the whole. The Soviet Armies would in 1952 and 1953 move swiftly forward to the ocean, subjugating the capitals of Western Europe. This process might take a month or six weeks. There would no doubt be certain citadels like Switzerland or bridgeheads from which the evacuation of the United Nations troops might be possible. But nothing would stop the general roll forward of the overwhelming mass of the Soviet Armies.

2. However at the same time the United States atomic bombing attack would fall upon the Soviet regime. This ought to paralyse all communications between their advancing armies and the central Government, except wireless messages. In addition there would be the effects explained to me at length at the Pentagon of the application of the programme of atomic assault on the industries, communications, oilfields, etc., of Soviet Russia.

3. After these two processes had presented themselves fully we should (if still surviving) be able to take a new view. I do not see where 'the anticipated Russian invasion of the Middle East', and presumably Northern Africa, comes in. If Soviet Russia is shattered as an organic military force in the first three months of the War she will certainly not be in a position to cross the Sinai Peninsula and play about in the Western Desert. The whole proportion of events in the Middle East is petty compared to the terrible decisions which would be reached at the outbreak of the War. If the American atom attack succeeds it should be possible to destroy by ordinary bombing the railway and other communications through Persia and Syria. Turkey also will be fighting hard and

---

[1] Churchill wrote on this minute: 'I surrender.'
[2] Reproduced above (pp. 373–4).

will not be easy to traverse quickly. I should like to have full particulars of the picture which the Chiefs of Staff make about the Middle East. On what day after the outbreak of the War is a serious Russian invasion of Syria, Persia, Palestine and Egypt expected? What numbers of invaders are involved? What do they do when they get there, and what do we suffer compared with what will be happening elsewhere?

4. It is of course important to prevent infiltration into the Middle East in time of peace and to preserve a semblance at least of military power. But the idea of a heavy Russian invasion of the Middle East and across the Suez Canal into Egypt, Libya, Cyrenaica and Tripoli is to my mind absurd. The best defence of the Middle East would be an overwhelming Air Force in Cyprus sustained by the necessary anti-submarine and air carrier forces. No surface fleet exists, even in imagination, for the American, British, French and Italian Navies to fight.

5. As it is already decided that the Commando Brigade should go to Malta and they begin to leave in 48 hours this movement cannot be interrupted. The movements of the other units should be the subject of discussion at the Defence meeting.

Cabinet: conclusions
(Cabinet papers, 128/24)

4 April 1952
Secret
11.30 a.m.
Cabinet Meeting No. 37 of 1952

[...]

6. The Cabinet resumed their discussion of the Foreign Secretary's memorandum (C(52)98) on the formula to be used as a basis for resuming negotiations with the Egyptian Government.

The Foreign Secretary said that since the Cabinet's previous discussion on 1st April the prospects of securing a resumption of the negotiations had not improved. He saw only two possible means of preventing the deadlock from continuing. One was to summon to London, for discussions, both Her Majesty's Ambassador at Cairo and the Governor-General of the Sudan. The other was for him to go himself to Cairo and Khartoum for consultations.

The Prime Minister said that, of these alternatives, he would greatly prefer the first. For himself, however, he was not persuaded that we had much to gain by pressing for the resumption of negotiations on the basis suggested. In his view the first need was to demonstrate to the Egyptian Government and people that we were not to be turned out of the Canal Zone by force or by threats. The show of force which we had recently made had produced good results; and he believed that still further advantages might be secured by making it clear that we were not in any hurry to abandon our rights under the existing Treaty. Our second objective should be to convince the United States Government that effective international arrangements would have to be made for safeguarding the security of the Suez Canal after the expiration of the present Treaty. It should be made clear to the Americans that we were not prepared to go on carrying this burden alone, and that they would have to take their share in fulfilling this international obligation. In this lay the best hope of persuading Egypt to join in an international organisation which would serve, not merely to protect the Canal, but to safeguard the security of the Middle East.

The Foreign Secretary said that it was his aim to guide the negotiations along lines which would draw the Egyptian Government into accepting a commitment to enter into international arrangements for the defence of the Middle East and, at the appropriate stage, to seek to enlarge the discussions by associating with them the Governments of the United States, France and Turkey. It was, however, clear that the Egyptian Government would not enter at the outset into multilateral negotiations with the four Powers; and it was for this reason that he proposed to start the discussions on a bilateral basis. The formula set out in C(52)98 was designed solely for the purpose of getting the negotiations started. The Cabinet should, however, understand that no agreement would be concluded unless the Egyptians could be persuaded in the discussions to accept some sort of share in an international organisation for the defence of the Middle East.

After further discussion the Prime Minister indicated that he would be prepared to agree that an attempt should be made to resume the negotiations with the Egyptian Government on the basis of the formula set out in paragraph 1 of C(52)98, if the Foreign Secretary would withdraw his suggestion for a unilateral declaration of our aims in the terms set out in paragraph 2 of that memorandum. The Foreign Secretary said that it had been his objective, in putting forward the suggestion in paragraph 2, to make plain our intention that Egypt should associate herself with an international organisation for the defence of the Middle East. He was, however, content to withdraw that suggestion, if the Prime Minister so desired.

The Cabinet –

Authorised the Foreign Secretary to seek to reopen negotiations with the Egyptian Government on the basis of the formula set out in paragraph 1 of C(52)98 on the understandings (i) that no unilateral declaration by the United Kingdom Government would be made in the terms of paragraph 2 of C(52)98, and (iii) that we should, if necessary, be ready to accept an Egyptian statement regarding the Sudan on the lines indicated in paragraph 3 of C(52)98.

April 1952

Winston S. Churchill to R. A. Butler,
Peter Thorneycroft and Gwilym Lloyd George
Prime Minister's Personal Minute M.194/52
(Premier papers, 11/151)

6 April 1952

I saw on Friday Mr James Duncan[1] who is Chairman of the Canadian Dollar–Sterling Trade Board. He said that he had been made anxious by the decision to cut off all imports of cheese from Canada into this country. He said that this had 'a worrying air of finality about it'. In 1948 some 150 million lbs. of cheese were imported from Canada into this country. Last year this figure had been cut down to 27 million lbs. and this year it has been decided to cancel it completely. He thought it much better if the door of trade were kept ajar, even if the imports amounted to only a small figure like 10 million lbs.

Winston S. Churchill to R. A. Butler
Prime Minister's Personal Minute M.197/52*
(Premier papers, 11/8)

6 April 1952

I should very much like to see Mr Menzies on other matters and it would be inadvisable on general grounds to discourage him from coming. Unless you have anything further to urge I propose to send the telegram.

* Reference: Proposed visit of Mr Menzies to this country.

Winston S. Churchill to Field Marshal Lord Alexander
Prime Minister's Personal Minute M.198/52
(Premier papers, 11/91)

6 April 1952

1. Let me know broadly how much more it costs to keep our existing garrison in the Canal Zone in Egypt than it would to keep them:
   (a) in Europe
   (b) in England.
We have to pay for them anyhow.
2. Let me have a short description of the stores in Egypt – e.g.:
   (a) how much are arms and ammunition,

[1] James Alexander Lawson Duncan, 1899–1974. On active service, Scots Guards, 1917–20, 1940–5. MP (Cons. Unionist) for Kensington North, 1931–45; (Lib. Unionist) for South Angus, 1950–64. Bt, 1957.

(b) how much clothing and other supplies,
(c) how much plant in the workshops.

Surely a great deal of this plant would be useful here at home. Pray have the matter looked at from the point of view of what we could save from the wreck.

Winston S. Churchill to Anthony Eden
Prime Minister's Personal Minute M.201/52
(Premier papers, 11/91)

6 April 1952
Personal and Secret

About Egypt. There are three additional points that I should like you to consider.

1. There is no question of our reducing our total military forces in the next few years, and the difference between the cost of maintaining the troops in Egypt as compared with in Europe or England is not great. I am having it worked out.

2. We are asked to confide all to a Treaty to be made by a Government which may easily be turned out at the elections. The Treaty which you made with Nahas was 'unilaterally' repudiated by him six months ago. What guarantee is there that when we have moved all our forces from their present positions, which hitherto have stood the test of violence, there will not be another 'unilateral' repudiation?

3. What troubles me deeply and what I really cannot understand is that we are giving <u>everything</u> into Egypt's power and have nothing in return, nor any means of securing the fulfilment of any understanding.

Winston S. Churchill to John Maclay
Prime Minister's Personal Minute M.203/52
(Premier papers, 11/288)

7 April 1952

Let me have a list of decisions of this character[1] which you have taken since you came into Office and also of any pending either on appeal or otherwise. Did you consult Lord Leathers in this case and do you as a rule consult him on similar cases. I understand that you are sending him a statement of the principles on which these licences are at present awarded or refused. When I

---

[1] The Licensing Authority in East Anglia had refused to renew some existing direct coach licences for weekend travel from RAF camps. It appears that Maclay had endorsed their position, prompting Churchill's frustration and this intervention.

receive this I will send you my comments. Meanwhile I wish you to inform me of anything, the announcement of which is pending, or of any case on which you now have to give a decision.

Winston S. Churchill to Lord Leathers
Prime Minister's Personal Minute M.205/52
(Premier papers, 11/287)

7 April 1952

When are you ready to present your proposals for the Transport Bill? It is necessary that decisions on principle should be taken before we separate.[1]

The essence of our policy is, I understand, as follows:

It does not matter whether the nationalized railways show a deficit though of course every possible economy should be used in their administration. What is important is that the public should have the best transport service on the roads which can only be furnished by private enterprise. It is necessary that the railways should be properly maintained. For this purpose the Road Transport should bear a levy and this it can do owing to the greater fertility of private enterprise. On an altogether lower level of importance some control must be reserved over 'picking out the plums' and preventing competition of independent road haulage companies from becoming anti-economic. Under a free system there will of course be natural corrections.

2. What economies in personnel in the Bond Haulage staff do you contemplate making as a result of your legislation? Let us know how many there are now in all these licensing authorities. What is their cost?

3. It cannot be expected of course that any contribution from Road Transport will meet the probable deficit on the railways including as their total does, the interest payable to the expropriated and compensated railway shareholders. This loss must continue to be borne by the State and illustrate the disadvantage of nationalisation.

John Colville to Sir Oliver Harvey
(Premier papers, 11/671)

7 April 1952
Confidential

My dear Ambassador

Thank you for your letter of the 3rd April about the D-Day Commemoration at Arromanches.

---

[1] For the Easter recess.

The Prime Minister is considering the possibility that he and Mrs Churchill might after all be able to make the trip. He would arrive by destroyer from Portsmouth and return by air. However, before committing himself in any way, Mr Churchill would like to know what the programme would be. I wonder if you could let me have a rough idea of this without raising Monsieur Triboulet's hopes too high in advance.

John Colville: diary
('The Fringes of Power', page 633)

8 April 1952

Trouble with the Ministry of Transport which has been brewing for long came to something of a head. The PM wants to denationalise road haulage as quickly as possible. Personally I think that undoing what the last government did, in the certain knowledge that they will re-do it when next they come into power, is folly; and this applies more to iron and steel than to road transport.

There is also trouble with Eden over the Egyptian situation, the PM wishing to take a much stronger line with the Egyptians than Eden does. The latter is rather discredited in the PM's eyes at present. I don't myself quite see how he can prove a very good successor to Winston when he has no knowledge or experience of anything except foreign affairs.

Winston S. Churchill to Robert Menzies
Prime Minister's Personal Telegram T.104/52
(Premier papers, 11/8)

8 April 1952
Secret
Cypher
Immediate
No. 65

My colleagues and I would greatly welcome an opportunity of making personal contact with you again. There are a number of topics on which personal discussion might be fruitful. We are wondering therefore whether you could pay us a short visit in the near future.

If you could come here for even a few days we should be delighted to see you. So far as we are concerned we can, I think, leave the choice of dates with you during the next three weeks.

Anthony Eden to Winston S. Churchill
(*Premier papers, 11/153*)

9 April 1952
PM/52/39

COUNCIL OF EUROPE

The first part of this year's session of the Consultative Assembly of the Council of Europe opens in Strasbourg on 26th May and will last for approximately one week. The second part of the session will be held in September.

2. We have been asked by the Secretary-General for the names of the United Kingdom representatives and their substitutes. We should, therefore, now make arrangements for the appointment of our delegation.

3. I assume we shall not wish to make any change in the number of representatives drawn from each party, and that the delegation will consist, as was the case last November, of 9 Conservatives, 8 Labour and 1 Liberal, with 4 substitutes for each of the major parties and 1 Liberal substitute. I attach a suggested list of names for the Conservative delegation, which has been agreed with the Chief Whip. You will no doubt wish to consult Mr Attlee and Mr Clement Davies[1] about Labour and Liberal representation.

4. The past practice has been for nominations to be made by party leaders and for the Prime Minister subsequently to announce the composition of the full Delegation in the House. I suggest that we should continue to follow this practice. I have suggested that Mr Nutting[2] should lead the delegations because our proposals will be before the Assembly.

5. I am sending copies of this minute to the Minister of Health and the Chief Whip.

Council of Europe
Conservative Delegation to Consultative Assembly
May, 1952

Representatives:
    Mr Anthony Nutting
    Mr Julian Amery[3]

---

[1] Clement Davies, 1884–1962. MP (Lib.) for Montgomeryshire, 1929–62. Leader of the Liberal Party, 1945–56. President, Welsh Liberal Federation, 1945–8; Parliamentary Association for World Government, 1951.

[2] Harold Anthony Nutting, 1920–99. Educated at Eton and Trinity College, Cambridge. Entered Leicestershire Yeomanry, 1939. In Foreign Service, 1940–5. Married, 1941, Gillian Lenora Strutt (div. 1959): three children. MP (Cons.) for Melton, 1945–56. Parliamentary Under-Secretary of State for Foreign Affairs, 1951–4. Minister of State for Foreign Affairs, 1954–6. PC, 1954.

[3] (Harold) Julian Amery, 1919–96. Son of L. S. Amery. Educated at Eton and Balliol College, Oxford. A war correspondent in the Spanish Civil War, 1938–9. Attaché, British Legation, Belgrade (on special missions in Bulgaria, Turkey, Romania and the Middle East), 1939–40. Sgt, RAF, 1940–1. Commissioned, and transferred to the Army, 1941. On active service in Egypt, Palestine and the Adriatic,

April 1952

Mr Robert Boothby
Mr Hamilton Kerr[1]
Mr Montgomery Hyde[2]
Lord John Hope[3]
Mr Charles Mott-Radclyffe[4]
Lady Tweedsmuir[5]
A Peer (to be nominated by Lord Salisbury)
Substitutes:
A Peer (to be nominated by Lord Salisbury)
Mr Iain Macleod[6]

1941–2. Liaison officer (behind German lines) to the Albanian resistance movement, 1944. Churchill's Personal Representative with Generalissimo Chiang Kai-shek, 1945. Unsuccessful Parliamentary candidate (Cons.) for Preston, July 1945. MP (Cons.) for Preston North, 1950–66; for Brighton Pavilion, 1969–92. Married, 1950, Catherine, daughter of Harold Macmillan. Parliamentary Under-Secretary of State, War Office, 1957–8; Colonial Office, 1958–60. PC, 1960. Secretary of State for Air, 1960–2. Minister of Aviation, 1962–4; of Public Building and Works, 1970; for Housing and Construction, 1970–2. Minister of State, FCO, 1972–4. In 1948, published his Albanian recollections, *Sons of the Eagle*. Biographer of Joseph Chamberlain's career from 1901 to 1914 (in succession to J. L. Garvin). Life Peer, 1992.

[1] Hamilton William Kerr, 1903–74. Flying Officer, RAF, 1939; Flt Lt, 1941. MP (Cons.) for Oldham, 1931–45; for Cambridge, 1950–6. Parliamentary Secretary at Admiralty, 1937–8; at Air Ministry, 1942–5; to Minister of Health, 1945; to Harold Macmillan, 1954–6. Bt, 1957.

[2] Hartford Montgomery Hyde, 1907–89. Educated at Sedbergh and Queen's University, Belfast. Called to the Bar, Middle Temple, 1934. Lecturer in History, Oxford University, 1934. Private Secretary to Marquess of Londonderry, 1935–9. Asst Censor, Gibraltar, 1940. Commissioned into Intelligence Corps, 1940. Military Liaison and Censorship Security Officer, Bermuda, 1940–1. Asst Passport Control Officer, New York, 1941–2. British Army Staff, US, 1942–4. Maj., 1942. Member, Allied Commission for Austria, 1944–5. Lt-Col., 1945. Asst Editor, Law Reports, 1946–7. Legal Adviser, British Lion Film Corp. Ltd, 1947–9. MP (Ulster Unionist) for North Belfast, 1950–9. Prof. of History and Political Science, University of the Punjab, Lahore, 1959–61.

[3] John Adrian Hope, 1912–95. Son of Victor Alexander John Hope, 2nd Marquess of Linlithgow. Educated at Eton College and Christ Church, Oxford. Served in WWII (despatches). MP (Cons.) for Midlothian and Peebles Northern, 1945–50; for Edinburgh Pentlands, 1950–64. Under-Secretary for Foreign Affairs, 1954–6. Joint Parliamentary Under-Secretary, 1957–9. PC, 1959. Minister of Works, 1959–62. Baron Glendevon, 1964.

[4] Charles Edward Mott-Radclyffe, 1911–92. Educated at Eton and Balliol College, Oxford. Served in Diplomatic Service (Athens and Rome), 1936–8. Commissioned, Rifle Bde, 1939. Member, Military Mission to Greece, 1940–1. Liaison Officer, Syria, 1941. MP (Cons.) for Windsor, 1942–70. On active service, Middle East and Italy, 1943–4. Parliamentary Private Secretary to Secretary of State for India (L. S. Amery), Dec. 1944 to May 1945. Junior Lord of the Treasury, May–July 1945. Cons. Whip, 1945–6. Chairman, Cons. Parliamentary Foreign Affairs Committee, 1951–9. Knighted, 1957. Capt., Lords and Commons Cricket, 1952–70.

[5] Priscilla Jean Fortescue Buchan, 1915–78. Married, 1934, Arthur Lindsay Grant (d. 1944); 1948, Baron Tweedsmuir. MP (Cons.) for Aberdeen South, 1946–66. Delegate to Council of Europe, 1950–3; to UN General Assembly, 1960–1. Joint Parliamentary Under-Secretary of State of Scotland, 1962–4. Baroness, 1970. Minister of State, Scottish Office, 1970–2; at FCO, 1972–4. PC, 1974.

[6] Iain Norman Macleod, 1913–70. Educated at Gonville and Caius College, Cambridge. Professional bridge player, 1935–52. Commissioned 2nd Lt in Duke of Wellington's Rgt, 1940. Married, 1941, Evelyn Hester Mason: two children. Staff College, Camberley, 1943–4. Maj., 1944. Member, Conservative Parliamentary Secretariat, 1946–8; Conservative Research Dept, 1948–50. MP (Cons.) for Enfield West, 1950–70. Minister of Health, 1952–5. Minister of Labour and National Service, 1955–9. Secretary of State for the Colonies, 1959–61. Leader of House of Commons, 1961–3. Chancellor of Duchy of Lancaster, 1961–3. Chancellor of the Exchequer, 1970. Editor of *The Spectator*, 1963–5.

Mr David Renton[1]
Major Tufton Beamish[2]

Henry Channon: diary
('Chips', page 467)

9 April 1952 House of Commons

Could there be any more nauseating performance than that of half a hundred hale young Socialists howling at Mr Churchill, jeering at his pronouncements and even at his entrances and exits into the House, taunting him with his advanced age and growing deafness? The man who may be the wrecker of the Tory Party, but was certainly Saviour of the civilised world? It happened again today. However in the 1922 secret Committee he had a rapturous reception, and stood the strain of speaking and answering questions well for over an hour.

Cabinet: conclusions
(Cabinet papers, 128/24)

9 April 1952
Secret
11.30 a.m.
Cabinet Meeting No. 40 of 1952

1. The Cabinet had before them a memorandum by the Foreign Secretary (C(52)122) reporting that the Egyptian Foreign Minister had accepted a revised formula, in the terms set out in the memorandum, as a basis for resumed negotiations with the Egyptian Government.

The Foreign Secretary said that the first paragraph of this formula was in the terms which had already been approved by the Cabinet. The second paragraph was somewhat different from the earlier draft; but it implied that in the negotiations we should put forward our point of view regarding the defence of the Canal Zone, and it would thus enable us to press our view of the arrangements which should be made for the defence of the Middle East generally. The third paragraph, regarding the Sudan, represented a marked

---

[1] David Lockhart-Mure Renton, 1908–2007. Educated at University College, Oxford. Called to the Bar, Lincoln's Inn, 1933. Member of General Council of the Bar, 1939. In Royal Artillery, 1940–4. President, British Military Court at Tripolitania, 1945. MP (Nat. Lib.) for Huntingdonshire, 1945–79. QC, 1954. PC, 1962. KCB, 1964. Chairman, National Liberal Party, 1964–8. Baron, 1979. President, Association of Conservative Peers, 1998.

[2] Tufton Victor Hamilton Beamish, 1917–89. Educated at Sandhurst. 2nd Lt, Royal Northumberland Fusiliers, 1937; Capt., 1945. MP (Cons.) for Lewes, 1945–74. Married, 1950, Janet McMillan Stevenson (div. 1973); 1975, Pia McHenry. Baron, 1974. Author of *Must Night Fall?* (1950) and *Half Marx* (1970).

improvement; for it involved the Egyptian Government in full recognition of the right of the Sudanese people freely to decide their future status. If the revised formula were accepted, it would not be made public at this stage, though an agreed statement would doubtless be issued to the effect that negotiations were being resumed.

The Cabinet's discussion turned on the wording of the second part of paragraph (ii) of the formula. The Prime Minister felt that the references to the arming of Egyptian forces, 'in order that Egypt might fulfil her determined intention to defend' the Canal Zone, were open to objections similar to those advanced in the Cabinet's discussion on the 4th April against the proposed unilateral declaration by the United Kingdom, which had been similarly worded. It seemed to him that we ought not at the outset of negotiations, of which the purpose was to achieve five-Power arrangements for the defence of the Middle East as a whole, to appear to accept the suggestion that Egypt was to assume sole responsibility for the defence of the Canal Zone.

The Foreign Secretary pointed out that this paragraph of the formula did not go beyond recognizing the right of the two Governments to discuss their respective points of view. He welcomed the reference to the arming of Egyptian forces, since the Egyptian Army had always been the most co-operative element in the country and it would be wise to invite their continued support. The paragraph might, however, be amended by deleting the words 'in order that Egypt may fulfil her determined intention to defend this area'.

The Cabinet –

Authorised the Foreign Secretary to approve the text of the formula for resumption of negotiations with Egypt as set out in C(52)122, subject to the deletion of words following 'Egyptian forces' in paragraph (iii).

[. . .]

Lord Cherwell to Winston S. Churchill
(*Premier papers, 11/149*)

10 April 1952
Top Secret

The attached food chart shows how our total food stocks have changed since the beginning of 1948 and gives you, I think, a fair summary of the information in the Minister of Food's minute. If you wish, we can let you have the charts showing the movement of individual food stocks for the past few years and the stocks which it is hoped we shall hold at the end of this year.

As regards individual stocks, we are in a better position now than we were a year ago for all commodities except butter. Our stocks are also larger than when we took over, except for wheat and meat which always drop during the winter months; and here the fall in stocks was less this winter than last. We

April 1952

plan to keep our food stocks at roughly the present level during 1952, a fall in stocks of some commodities (mainly wheat and sugar) being balanced by a rise in stocks of other commodities (including, we hope, wheat, butter, and tea).

Our situation seems to be about as satisfactory as our balance of payments position will permit.[1]

Peter Thorneycroft to Winston S. Churchill
(Premier papers, 11/151)

10 April 1952

Your Minute M.194/52.[2]

The decision to cut off all imports of Canadian cheese was conveyed on February 9th to the Canadian Government. The Canadian Government instructed their Commercial Counsellor in London to protest through the channel of the United Kingdom/Canada Continuing Committee on Trade and Economic Affairs and to suggest that a cut of only 50% would be more appropriate. A reply was sent on 2nd March saying that 'The United Kingdom Government have carefully considered the Canadian Government's request, but they regret that they are unable to modify their decision not to buy any Canadian cheese this year. This conclusion has been reached only after very full examination of the possible alternative import cuts.' Since this has not evoked any response, it may be inferred that the Canadian Government have accepted the necessity of our decision.

While any relaxation would naturally be very well received in Canada both by the Government and by the producers, and would, of course, be welcome on general grounds of Anglo-Canadian trading relations I understand that the Chancellor would be most reluctant to make any relaxation of our recent dollar cuts so soon and I do not feel therefore that Mr Duncan's intervention at this stage gives any ground for reopening the matter.

Winston S. Churchill to Duncan Sandys and David Eccles
Prime Minister's Personal Minute M.213/52
(Premier papers, 11/277)

10 April 1952

I am glad to learn that you have already taken steps to insist on economical design before granting building licences and to increase supplies of reinforcing

---

[1] Churchill responded on Apr. 12: 'Thank you very much for your minute and diagram of April 10. We seem to be better off than we were in 1948. I have sent your paper and diagram to the Minister of Defence. I will return it to you with his comments' (Prime Minister's Personal Minute M.232/52).

[2] Reproduced above (p. 381).

material in order to save structural steel. It now seems that steel supplies may become even more critical and I hope you will press these, and other measures, forward as quickly as possible.

I understand that there are difficulties in obtaining immediate revision of existing building standards as these are controlled through local authority bye-laws. You should nevertheless seek to obtain any acceptable revisions which will save steel as quickly as possible.

Winston S. Churchill to Members of the Cabinet
(*Cabinet papers, 129/51*)

10 April 1952
Top Secret
Cabinet Paper No. 119 of 1952

MINISTERIAL RESPONSIBILITY FOR ATOMIC ENERGY

I circulate, for the information of the Cabinet, the following Directive which I have issued, after consultation with the Paymaster-General and the Minister of Supply, regarding their respective responsibilities for Atomic Energy matters.

This is a confidential Directive issued for the guidance of Ministers and senior officials concerned; and none of its contents will be made public without specific approval by the two Ministers concerned and myself.

Directive

Final responsibility for all major decisions on atomic energy rests with the Prime Minister.

2. The Paymaster-General is responsible for advising the Prime Minister and the Cabinet on policy matters relating to atomic energy. He will preside over an Atomic Energy Board comprising the senior officers of the project. Subject to any directions by the Prime Minister or the Cabinet, the Paymaster-General will take all Ministerial action required in regard to research, development, production, the provision of buildings and technical facilities for those purposes, appointments of staff (within the ceilings approved by the Treasury) and the allocation and supervision of their duties, and all other matters concerning atomic energy which are not specifically entrusted to the Minister of Supply by the Prime Minister.

3. On all matters within his sphere of responsibility the Paymaster-General will deal directly with the officials of the Ministry of Supply concerned and will issue such instructions as he may consider necessary. The Paymaster-General will keep the Minister of Supply informed of any important decisions taken by him.

4. The Minister of Supply will be entirely responsible for day to day administration in regard to contracts, staff management, accounting questions, security and public relations and such other matters relating to atomic energy as the Prime Minister, on the advice of the Paymaster-General, may from time to time entrust to him. Within this sphere, the Minister of Supply will be responsible for taking any administrative action which may be asked for by the Paymaster-General to give effect to policy decisions taken by the latter.

5. The Minister of Supply will answer Parliamentary Questions on Atomic Energy matters in the House of Commons other than those which the Prime Minister may decide to answer himself.

6. The Minister of Supply will have no responsibility for any matters other than those specifically entrusted to him by the Prime Minister.

7. Subject to the above, the Minister of Supply will formally retain the powers and duties conferred upon him by Statute in regard to atomic energy matters, and will have full access to all information connected with this subject.

Winston S. Churchill to Sir Harold Roper[1]
(Premier papers, 11/234)

10 April 1952

My dear Roper,

Thank you for your letter of March 20 in which you suggest the amalgamation of the National Assistance Board and the Ministry of National Insurance.

I am always on the look out for opportunities to amalgamate Departments but I do not think we could at present amalgamate these two, but we shall keep in mind the possibility of doing some local work in common.

Most of the work of the National Assistance Board in assessing need is necessarily conducted in the applicants' home and the fusion might therefore fail to provide absolute secrecy.

---

[1] Harold Roper, 1891–1971. Educated at Blundell's School and Sidney Sussex College, Cambridge. On active service, 1914–18. MC, 1918. Knighted, 1945. MP (Cons.) for North Cornwall, 1950–9.

House of Commons: Oral Answers
(Hansard)

10 April 1952

ATOM BOMB TEST (PRESS CORRESPONDENTS)

Lieut.-Colonel Bromley-Davenport[1] asked the Prime Minister whether he is now in a position to state what arrangements will be made for the attendance of the Press at the test of the United Kingdom atomic weapon which is to take place this year.

The Prime Minister: After consultation with Her Majesty's Government in the Commonwealth of Australia, Her Majesty's Government in the United Kingdom have decided that it will not be practicable for Press correspondents or any unofficial observers to be present at the test. Arrangements will, however, be made to give out the fullest suitable information after the test has taken place.

Winston S. Churchill to Anthony Eden
Prime Minister's Personal Minute M.219/52
(Premier papers, 11/153)

11 April 1952

1. I have signed the necessary letters.*

2. I notice Boothby is placed below Amery on the list which is not alphabetical in order, and Boothby is senior.[2]

3. There is a rumour in the Assembly of Boothby being chosen to fill Spaak's place. I do not see that we have any reason to discourage it unless it would entail absences unpaired. Let me know what you think.

*To Mr C. Attlee and Mr C. Davies.[3]

---

[1] Walter Henry Bromley-Davenport, 1903–89. Educated at Malvern College. Entered Grenadier Guards, 1922. Commanded 5th Battalion Cheshire Rgt, 1940. MP (Cons.) for Knutsford, 1945–70. Conservative Junior Whip, 1948–51. Deputy Lt of Cheshire, 1949. Knighted, 1961.

[2] See PM/52/39, reproduced above (p. 385).

[3] Reproduced below (p. 394).

April 1952

Winston S. Churchill to R. A. Butler
Prime Minister Personal Minute M.221/52
(Premier papers, 11/197)

11 April 1952

Your minute and report of March 21 about double-shift working.[1]

1. I certainly think the enquiry has been valuable. I am glad you have accepted the proposal that, before granting licences Departments should investigate the possibility of saving new building or the import of machinery by double-shift working.

2. Another point has been suggested to me by Lord Cherwell. In building new capacity for defence work it is the aim to plan for single shifts in peace to allow expansion in war by working double-shifts. This has advantages but is costly, especially if the machinery may soon become obsolete. It might be worth having an enquiry to see what savings could be made.

Winston S. Churchill to R. A. Butler
Prime Minister's Personal Minute M.227/52
(Premier papers, 11/130)

11 April 1952

I understand that there can be long delay in converting earnings of foreign exchange into sterling. Might it not greatly help our reserves in the critical months ahead if it were made obligatory to turn the money in, or give adequate reasons for not doing so, within three months of shipment?

I also gather from the newspapers that there are considerable opportunities for evasion of exchange control. Should we not stop this even if it means an increase in the number of officials, or what could in more normal times be considered unreasonable interference with commercial freedom.

Please let me have a report at your convenience.

---

[1] Reproduced above (pp. 361–2).

Winston S. Churchill to Field Marshal Lord Alexander
Prime Minister's Personal Minute M.226/52
(Premier papers, 11/55)

11 April 1952

1. Para. 4.[1] How is it that when all our formations are out of the country there is no barrack accommodation available? Is everything taken up by the schools and training colleges with their 249 thousand men? If we are forced to evacuate Egypt, where is it proposed these troops should go? How is it there is no accommodation in Germany? The Germans had a very large Army before the War and they must have had ample barracks, etc.

2. Would not these stores if transported home or to other points in the 'infra-structure' dumps be a substitute for the new stores we are making at great expense, and would there not be a corresponding economy? How much would the 120 thousand tons of shipping cost for two years? Lord Leathers, who should be asked, can no doubt give this figure and say where the shipping could be found. I was under the impression there was spare shipping available.

Winston S. Churchill to Clement Davies
(Premier papers, 11,153)

12 April 1952

My dear Davies,

As you know the first part of this year's session of the Consultative Assembly of the Council of Europe opens on May 26 and will last about a week. We propose that the United Kingdom Delegation should, as previously, consist of nine Members of the Conservative Party, eight of the Labour Party and one of the Liberal Party. We also think that there should be four Conservative substitutes, four Labour substitutes and one Liberal substitute.

I should be obliged if you would let me have the names of a Liberal representative and a Liberal substitute. I will then write to them in accordance with the usual practice and invite them to serve as representatives of the United Kingdom Parliament.[2]

---

[1] Of Alexander's minute to Churchill of Apr. 10: '4. There is not enough accommodation for the Canal Zone garrison either in the United Kingdom or Germany. It would cost about £15m. to provide temporary accommodation, and about £50m. to provide permanent accommodation in either place, and it would be extremely difficult to get the work done in any reasonable period.'

[2] An identical letter was sent to Clement Attlee.

April 1952

Robert Menzies to Winston S. Churchill
Prime Minister's Personal Telegram T.105/52
(Premier papers, 11/8)

12 April 1952
Secret
Cypher
Immediate
No. 230

Your telegram to Commonwealth Government No. 65 of 8th April.[1]

I greatly appreciate your message and cordial invitation, which I am anxious to accept, for there are several matters on which personal consultation would I am sure be fruitful. But there are difficulties of time table.

2. On 1st May we have our important Loan Council Meeting with the State Premiers, in the preparation for and conduct of which my presence is essential. The questions involved this year are all important to our internal economy. On 6th May the House meets and I should see it well launched before going away. Under these circumstances I could leave here on 17th May travel via America to clear up in Washington one or two points which would concern my talks with you in London and arrive London 24th May remaining for a fortnight.

3. To leave here almost immediately would be quite impracticable in any event for matters such as imports and exports, dollars and sterling, defence supply, Middle East Command, and the position in South East Asia, all of which I would wish to discuss cannot be made the subject of effective preparation in a few days.

4. Should my proposed time table be agreeable I suggest that we could make an announcement of my visit in general terms on Wednesday next 16th April (your morning paper time) indicating that I will proceed to London as soon as practicable after the meeting of the Commonwealth Parliament.

5. If it were indicated at your end that import restrictions would be among the things discussed, that might help you on the home front.

6. Please inform Sir Thomas White.[2]

---

[1] T.104/52, reproduced above (p. 384).
[2] Thomas Walter White, 1888–1957. Educated at Moreland State School, Australia. Joined Citizen Military Forces, 1902. 2nd Lt, 1911. Lt, 1912. Capt., 1913. Capt., Australian Imperial Force, 1915. On active service, 1915–18 (despatches twice). DFC, 1919. Maj., 1922. Lt-Col., 1926. MP (United Australia Party) for Balaclava, 1929–45, (Lib.) 1945–51. Minister for Trade and Customs, 1932–8. Minister for Air, 1949–51. Minister for Civil Aviation, 1949–51. Australian High Commissioner to the UK, 1951–6. KCB, 1952.

Winston S. Churchill to Robert Menzies
Prime Minister's Personal Telegram T.106/52
(Premier papers, 11/8)

12 April 1952
Secret
Cypher
Immediate
No. 294

Your telegram No. 230.

We are delighted to know that you will be able to visit us and your proposed timetable is entirely agreeable. It will be good to see you again and I have no doubt that we shall be able to make real progress on a number of subjects.

I agree that we should make an announcement for the Press for our morning papers of Wednesday 16th April and suggest that it might be on the following lines: 'On the cordial invitation of Mr Churchill, Mr Menzies is paying a visit to the United Kingdom towards the end of May to renew old contacts. During his visit he will take the opportunity to discuss matters of common concern to both Governments.' We would not propose to say more in Press announcement but we are sure to be asked whether discussions will include import restrictions and we would say 'Yes'.

Winston S. Churchill to Field Marshal Lord Alexander
Prime Minister's Personal Minute M.231/52
(Premier papers, 11/149)

12 April 1952
Top Secret

You may be interested to see the attached.[1] They seem to be above the 1948 level which was certainly a more dangerous year than this. Kindly return the file with your comments or corrections which your department may make.

---

[1] Food Stocks Index, prepared by Lord Cherwell and sent to Churchill on Apr. 10 (see letter of that date reproduced above, pp. 388–9).

Winston S. Churchill to Anthony Eden
Prime Minister's Personal Minute M.235/52
(Premier papers, 11/168)

13 April 1952
Private and Personal

I do not think at first sight that the Soviet refusal for UNO to supervise the elections[1] should necessarily end the story, if they are willing that the Four Powers – Russia, America, Britain and France – should supervise the voting. This is three to one against the Russians, and nothing would result if they do not satisfy the other three Powers.

I am not at all clear on the general question, but I had this feeling that the Four Powers is a more manageable way of doing things than UNO. Also it fits in with our other ideas.

Turn this over in your mind.[2]

Winston S. Churchill to Anthony Eden
Prime Minister's Personal Minute M.237/52
(Premier papers, 11/116)

15 April 1952

It is, as I have written before, a matter of honour to us not to force a non-Communist prisoner of war to go back to be murdered in Communist China. This is not a matter of argument, but one of the fundamental principles for which we fight and, if necessary, die. Bouchier's telegram shows a taint of pro-Communism. Indeed it is so redolent that I wonder whether he is not playing irony. Why, for instance, had he 'hoped' that they would all wish to go back to the Communists? (See para. 2.)[3] Why is he disappointed that a great

---

[1] The impending elections in Egypt, where the government had just been dismissed by the Egyptian monarch. The elections were never held owing to the Nationalist coup.

[2] Eden responded on Apr. 16: 'We shall be discussing this fully in Cabinet. I certainly agree that we should look at all aspects of the problem. I do not think there is any particular hurry about sending a reply to the Russians' (PM/52/40, *Churchill papers, 2/517*).

[3] Paragraphs 2 and 3 of Bouchier's telegram of Apr. 15 to the Chiefs of Staff read:
'2. Request following information be treated great discretion. Earliest indications are that the number of Communist prisoners who are electing not repeat not to be repatriated back to the Communists is a much larger total than we had hoped would result. This in spite of the fact that those Communist prisoners who so far have flatly refused to be repatriated have each been told that we cannot feed them indefinitely and that their future on our side of the Iron Curtain is most uncertain. They have also been told that the Communist authorities already officially know the names of all Communist prisoners of war we hold and that if they refuse to be repatriated they will probably never see their homeland or their families again. And moreover that it is possible that the Communist authorities may indeed take retaliatory action against their families.

3. In spite however of us making it as tough and as frightening as possible for the Communist prisoners to refuse to be repatriated back nevertheless the earliest indications are that a large percentage are refusing to be repatriated in spite of our stern warnings and the obvious risks to their own families in China.'

many of them think this would be odious? Why should he be worried lest the number who do not wish to go back to the Communists are 'too large a total for the Communist authorities to stomach?' Of course, he may only be talking the conventional jargon into which they have got, but if these are his sincere options, he is an insult to the British employment or uniform.

Cabinet: conclusions
(Cabinet papers, 128/24)

16 April 1952
Secret
5.30 p.m.
Cabinet Meeting No. 43 of 1952

6. The Prime Minister said that in pursuance of the Cabinet's decision of 8th April he had advised The Queen to select a date for the Coronation between 29th May and 6th June, 1953. Her Majesty had decided that the Coronation should be held on Tuesday, 2nd June, 1953.

The Cabinet –

(1) Took note that Her Majesty's Coronation would take place on 2nd June, 1953.

The Prime Minister said that the Coronation Committee of the Privy Council, when appointed, would probably need some guidance from the Government regarding the scale of the arrangements to be made for celebrating the Coronation. He proposed that a small Ministerial Committee should be appointed to consider this in detail and to make recommendations to the Cabinet. It would be convenient that this Committee should be composed of Ministers who would be members of the Coronation Committee. The Chancellor of the Exchequer should be a member of the Ministerial Committee; but, while he was occupied with business arising from the Finance Bill, he might be represented at its meetings by another Treasury Minister.

The Cabinet –

(2) Appointed a Committee consisting of the Lord Privy Seal (Chairman), the Home Secretary, the Chancellor of the Exchequer and the Minister of Works to consider and report to the Cabinet what guidance should be given on the scale of the arrangements to be made for celebrating Her Majesty's Coronation.

Winston S. Churchill to Field Marshal Lord Alexander
Prime Minister's Personal Minute M.236/52
(Premier papers, 11/226)

16 April 1952

There is no question of the Admiralty having any additional oil, neither the 800,000 tons nor the 400,000, without a Cabinet decision. I hope you will press for this at the right moment.[1]

Chiefs of Staff: memorandum
(Premier papers, 11/367)

16 April 1952
Secret
Defence Committee Paper No. 9 of 1952

BLACKOUT POLICY

The Air Defence Committee have recently re-examined the influence of blackout in the Air Defence of the United Kingdom, and for the reasons set out in the paper at Annex, they have concluded that a degree of blackout would be an essential contribution to our Air Defence. They consider that the blackout regulations need not be so meticulously restrictive as they were in the last war; the main purpose of the blackout would be to obscure the recognisable pattern of lighting on the ground and so prevent visual navigation and visual bomb-aiming by the enemy.

2. We are entirely in agreement with this conclusion of the Air Defence Committee.

3. Last war experience demonstrated that an effective blackout cannot be introduced at short notice. At the outset we were dangerously unprepared, and if we are not to be caught unprepared again, the necessary planning must be done in peace.

Recommendation

4. Whether or not financial approval can now be given to the various measures required, we recommend that the need for a degree of blackout in war should be affirmed in principle now, in order to give impetus and guidance to Civil Defence planning.

---

[1] See Alexander to Churchill, Apr. 1, reproduced above (pp. 376-7).

Winston S. Churchill to Anthony Eden
Prime Minister's Personal Minute M.241/52
(Premier papers, 11/116)

17 April 1952

Paragraph 6 of attached telegram.[1] I hope we have informed the Americans that we could not approve of sending prisoners-of-war back to the Communists against their will.

Winston S. Churchill to Peter Thorneycroft
Prime Minister's Personal Minute M.245/52
(Premier papers, 11/285)

19 April 1952

Your note to the United States.*

I do not remember this having been brought before the Cabinet. The Foreign Office inform me that they were not consulted. Please let me know how this stands.

*Regarding tariffs on British goods.

Winston S. Churchill to Anthony Eden
Prime Minister's Personal Minute M.251/52
(Premier papers, 11/285)

21 April 1952

I understand that the British memorandum on Tariffs which was published in Saturday's Press was delivered to the State Department on 10th April without your knowledge or that of the President of the Board of Trade.

Please report to me forthwith how this occurred. The intention to present a note on a matter of this political significance should surely have been brought to the attention of the Cabinet.

[1] Para. 6 of Bouchier's telegram of Apr. 16 to the Chiefs of Staff read:
'6. Thus this is the moment when Washington has to decide whether for political reasons it is still essential for us to continue in our present stand that the repatriation of all prisoners of war must be on no other than a purely voluntary basis. Because after we have informed the Communists of the results of the census we have taken there can be no going back on our part. In other words if we are to drop our existing inflexible stand that repatriation of all prisoners of war must be on a voluntary basis, this is the moment for us to do it. If we do not do it now we shall have to go through with it to the end. In making their decision I have no doubt that Washington will consider the possibility of the Communists retaliating in kind and submitting to us a list of United Nations prisoners of war in their hands who they may allege have similarly refused to be repatriated back to us. I think this is a distinct possibility as indicated at paragraph ten of my yesterday telegram.'

April 1952

Winston S. Churchill to Lord Leathers
Prime Minister's Personal Minute M.253/52
(Premier papers, 11/287)

21 April 1952

More than three weeks have passed since you said it would take the draughtsmen two months or more to draft a Bill on the lines of the White Paper. What progress has been made since then? If, for instance, we could have the Transport Bill in six weeks, that might not be inconvenient, as the Budget and other matters still occupy us fully. We could also give a Second Reading to the Steel Bill if convenient. But in my opinion the Transport Bill is more urgent.

President Chaim Weizmann to Winston S. Churchill
Prime Minister's Personal Telegram T.113/52
(Premier papers, 11/186)

21 April 1952   Tel Aviv

Relying on your sympathy with Israel's struggle for consolidation and development and your wise and far-sighted statesmanship, I take the liberty of invoking your assistance in enabling us to meet one of our most pressing needs. What is at stake is the financing of our oil supply, which comes through a British company and is the lifestream of our whole economic system. Our trusted and competent financial adviser and special representative, Mr David Horowitz,[1] who is now in London, has put before the Chancellor of the Exchequer certain proposals for assistance by credits which Mr Butler, despite his personal goodwill, has been unable to accept in view of his present difficulties. Mr Horowitz is now approaching Mr Butler again with a more modest request. If even this limited help is denied us, our position will be grave indeed. Far be it from me to under-estimate the difficulties with which Britain herself is contending, but I know, and rejoice to know, that despite them, Britain is finding means to uphold her good name, safeguard her interests, and contribute to international stability in the vital area of the Middle East, by maintaining her position in the Suez Canal, by bearing her share in the financing of the re-settlement of Arab refugees and by continuing her grants-in-aid to the Hashemite Kingdom of Jordan. I feel confident that you will see the wisdom of including in the system of British Middle Eastern interests a certain measure of aid to Israel, which we are seeking, not by way of a free gift or non-recoverable expenditure, as in the cases I have just mentioned,

---

[1] David Horowitz, 1899–1979. Born in Galicia. Moved to Palestine, 1920. Director of Economic Dept of Jewish Agency for Israel. Member of Jewish Agency delegation to UN, 1947. Director General of Israeli Ministry of Finance, 1948–52. Founded Bank of Israel, 1954. Governor of Bank of Israel, 1954–71. Chairman of Advisory Council and Advisory Committee of the Bank of Israel, 1971–9.

but by credits on a moderate scale to be completely repaid, partly in dollars. By authorising such assistance you will, I believe, be helping to create a valuable asset for Britain's future in this corner of the world in terms of Israel's gratitude, and strengthening the ties between our countries which, after the tragic separation of recent years, have now been so auspiciously renewed.

Our old friendship and your staunch support of our cause embolden me to address this personal appeal to you.[1]

Anthony Eden to Winston S. Churchill
(Premier papers, 11/116)

22 April 1952
PM/52/43

Your minute M.241/52 of the 17th April: Prisoners-of-war in Korea.[2]

2. As recently as April 2nd, Her Majesty's Embassy in Washington impressed on the State Department 'that before any irrevocable decision was taken on the prisoner-of-war issue we should expect to be consulted'.

3. Since I last wrote to you on the 31st March,[3] the United Nations Command have taken a census of prisoners in our hands, and this census shows that only 70,000 Communist prisoners out of the 132,000 wish to be repatriated. This information has been passed on to the Communists. First reactions by the Communists are, as was to be expected, unfavourable, but we have not yet reached deadlock, nor have we exhausted the possibilities of compromise. We might, for example, have a fresh census of those unwilling to go back and this new census could be taken either by a team of neutrals with observers from each side, or by the International Red Cross.

4. The position is therefore broadly the same as when I last wrote to you. If the Communists really want an armistice, the outcome of the present exchanges may be a compromise acceptable to us without offence to our conscience. If, however, deadlock is reached, we shall have to take a definite stand and make our views known to the Americans. Meanwhile, the Americans know that we expected to be consulted before they take a final decision, and I think we can leave it at that for the moment.

---

[1] Churchill responded the next day: 'Thank you for your telegram. I will at once look into this matter and let you know if there is anything we can do' (T.114/52).
[2] Reproduced above (p. 400).
[3] Reproduced above (pp. 371–2).

April 1952 403

Anthony Eden to Winston S. Churchill
(*Churchill papers, 2/517*)

22 April 1952
PM/52/44

COUNCIL OF EUROPE

Your minute M.219/52.[1]

The election of a new President is entirely a matter for the Assembly. I agree with you that we need not discourage the idea that Boothby should be asked to fill Spaak's place.

2. As regards pairing, there is no reason to suppose that Boothby, if elected, would be absent in Strasbourg for any longer than he would be as a member of our delegation.

3. As President, however, he would be entitled to have a substitute to sit and vote in the Assembly in his place. This means that we should have to send an additional person to Strasbourg during Assembly sessions if we wish to keep our delegation at full strength. This arrangement is purely optional and one which we need not accept if it is likely to involve us in further difficulties over pairing.

4. I am sending a copy of this minute to the Chief Whip.

Winston S. Churchill: speech
(*'Winston S. Churchill, His Complete Speeches', volume 8, pages 8365–6*)

23 April 1952   House of Commons

SIR STAFFORD CRIPPS

Since we met yesterday we have learned of the death of a statesman of national pre-eminence who had long served with distinction in the House of Commons, and it is in accordance with recent precedents that I should attempt to pay some tribute, necessarily brief and inadequate, to his memory. Stafford Cripps[2] was a man of force and fire. His intellectual and moral passions were so strong that they not only inspired but not seldom dominated his actions. They were strengthened and also governed by the working of a powerful, lucid intelligence and by a deep and lively Christian faith. He strode

---

[1] Reproduced above (p. 392).
[2] Richard Stafford Cripps, 1889–1952. Educated at Winchester. Barrister-at-law, 1913. Served with Red Cross, France, 1914. Asst Superintendent, Queen's Ferry Munitions Factory, 1915–18. KC, 1927. Knighted, 1930. Solicitor-General, 1930–1. MP (Lab.) for East Bristol, 1931–50; for South-East Bristol, 1950. Ambassador to Russia, 1940–2. Lord Privy Seal and Leader of the House of Commons, 1942. Minister of Aircraft Production, 1942–5. President of the Board of Trade, 1945. Minister of Economic Affairs, 1947. Chancellor of the Exchequer, 1947–50.

through life with a remarkable indifference to material satisfaction or worldly advantages. There are few members in any part of the House who have not differed violently from him at this time or that, and yet there is none who did not regard him with respect and with admiration, not only for his abilities but for his character.

His friends – and they were many, among whom I am proud to take my place – were conscious, in addition to his public gifts, of the charm of his personality and of the wit and gaiety with which he enlivened not only the mellow hours, but also the hard discharge of laborious business in anxious or perilous times. In all his complicated political career he was the soul of honour and his courage was proof against every test which the terrible years through which we have passed could bring.

Having sat with him in the wartime Cabinet, which he joined in 1942 and of which he was always a member – or, as we called it in those days, a constant attender – I can testify to the immense value of his contributions to our discussions. There was no topic I can remember – no doubt right hon. Gentlemen opposite have longer experiences of their own – on which he did not throw a clarifying light and to which he did not often bring a convenient and apt solution. Most of us have in our memories the distinction with which he filled the great office of the Exchequer and how easily he explained and interpreted the problems of finance. We all could not always agree with his policy, but everyone was grateful for his exposition.

As a master of words and dialect both in the law and Parliament, he had also a most practical and organizing side to this nature. During the First World War he managed a small arms factory, and its excellence and efficiency were brought to my notice when I was Minister of Munitions. It was this that prompted me to offer him the most complex business of the Ministry of Aircraft Production in the Second World War, after he ceased to lead this House, and I have very little doubt that his conduct of it was not only the most helpful to our interests but highly congenial to his nature. His was a mind that fastened itself as easily upon small as upon great things, and to him detail was not a burden but, often, a relief.

One of the most recent precedents for the intervention I am making today was when the House paid its tribute to Oliver Stanley,[1] who, like Stafford Cripps, was in our own time a member for Bristol. Both had qualities which will long be cherished in that famous city, where they were so well known.

---

[1] Oliver Frederick George Stanley, 1896–1950. Educated at Eton. On active service, France, 1914–18 (MC, despatches). Maj., 1918. Called to the Bar, 1919. MP (Cons.) for Westmorland, 1924–45; for Bristol West, 1945–50. Parliamentary Under-Secretary, Home Office, 1931–3. Minister of Transport, 1933–4. Minister of Labour, 1934–5. PC, 1934. President of the Board of Education, 1935–7. President of the Board of Trade, 1937–40. Secretary of State for War, Jan.–May 1940. Secretary of State for the Colonies, 1942–5.

It is not for me in these few words to attempt to epitomize the place which Stafford Cripps will bear in the history of our life and times, or of his contribution to their political philosophy; but that, as a man, he had few equals in ability or virtue will be generally affirmed by his contemporaries, and that he brought an unfailing flow of courage, honour, and faith to bear upon our toils and torments will be attested by all who knew him and, most of all, by those who knew him best.

Our hearts go out to the noble woman, his devoted wife, who through these long months of agony, mocked by false dawns, has been his greatest comfort on earth. To her we express profound sympathy, and we trust that she may find some solace in the fact that Stafford's memory shines so brightly among us all.

Anthony Eden to Winston S. Churchill
(Churchill papers, 2/517)

23 April 1952
PM/52/45

Your minute No. M.251/52 of the 21st April.[1]

The memorandum on tariffs which was given to the State Department and subsequently published was dealt with at a comparatively junior level in the Foreign Office.

2. It was not referred to higher authority on the ground that the action lay within the ambit of existing policy; that the memorandum was confidential and not intended for publication; and that the officials of the State Department who were dealing with this matter had informed Her Majesty's Embassy in Washington that it would be helpful to them if they were to receive a memorandum on these lines.

3. As a result of the enquiries which have been made, I do not think that the failure to refer a matter of this importance to higher authority will recur.

4. I am sending a copy of this minute to the President of the Board of Trade.

---

[1] Reproduced above (p. 400).

April 1952

R. A. Butler to Winston S. Churchill
(Premier papers, 11/130)

24 April 1952

You sent me a minute on 11th April (M.227/52)[1] asking for a report on two Exchange Control points.

DELAYS IN SURRENDER OF PAYMENTS FOR EXPORTS

This question has been raised and looked into from time to time. It was last raised by Mr Gaitskell[2] in the House and answered by the Minister of Health in debate (Hansard 31st January, 1952 Col. 484). I have not seen evidence of any long delays in surrendering foreign exchange: the great majority of exports are paid for promptly. To make earlier payment compulsory would not be effective because we have no sanction against the foreign purchaser, and it might well lose us export orders. Three months would be an unreasonably short time for goods which have to reach the remoter destinations.

EVASIONS OF EXCHANGE CONTROL

It is true that Exchange Control can never be wholly effective so long as travel is open to all and there is no postal censorship. But the vast majority of UK residents still obey the rules, and Customs and Immigration Officers at the ports, as well as the Bank of England and Treasury enforcement staff, do their best to make evasion difficult. I do not think that additional staff would achieve anything worth while but I have purposely refrained from cutting Customs staff as much as I should otherwise have done, in order to safeguard the control.

You may have seen references to cheap sterling traffic, by which for example foreigners buy Sterling Area products and sell them for dollars to the US. This is a wide question. We cannot hope to control this traffic by greater supervision here because the offenders are mostly abroad. We do what we can, but it is bound to continue so long as the pound is inconvertible.[3]

---

[1] Reproduced above (p. 393).
[2] Hugh Todd Naylor Gaitskell, 1906–63. Educated at New College, Oxford. Married, 1937, Anna Dora Frost. MP (Lab.) for Leeds South, 1945–63. Ministry of Fuel and Power, 1946–7. Minister of Fuel and Power, 1947–50. Chancellor of the Exchequer, 1950–1. Shadow Chancellor of the Exchequer, 1951–5. Leader, Labour Party, 1955–63. Leader of the Opposition, 1955–63.
[3] Churchill wrote to Lord Cherwell: 'Please Comment'.

APRIL 1952

Private Office: note
(*Premier papers, 11/606*)

24 April 1952

D.(52)10
CIVIL DEFENCE PREPAREDNESS

The Home Secretary reports that by the end of 1954 there should be, on present plans, a good nucleus of trained part-time volunteers, a reasonably adequate communication system and an air-raid warning system capable of giving at least some minutes warning. The evacuation of the priority classes could be carried out and people in the blitzed areas provided with food and cooking facilities. But the fire and rescue services will still be seriously under strength; there will not be adequate supplies of equipment; there will be a grievous shortage of emergency water supplies for fire fighting. And there will be practically no provision of shelter of any kind.

A mere decision of policy to accelerate Civil Defence preparations would not enable all the deficiencies to be made good in two years, but the Home Secretary suggests that even a modest start would be worthwhile.

Winston S. Churchill: speech
('*Winston S. Churchill, His Complete Speeches*', volume 8, pages 8366–8)

25 April 1952 Albert Hall
London

GRAND HABITATION OF THE PRIMROSE LEAGUE

It is a great pleasure for me to preside once again at your annual celebration and to do so this time as head of a Conservative and National-Liberal Government. (*Cheers*) I am glad to hear that the work of the Primrose League is proceeding successfully throughout the country. There never was a time when this was more important or when the great causes for which we stand were more in need of steadfast and ardent support. Now, when we are passing through a period of effort and sacrifice, is the time for the utmost energies of the Primrose League to be exerted.

Her Majesty's Government is trying its best to undo the harm of six years of Socialist rule which have brought us to the verge of national bankruptcy and left to us a hard task to get back to the high road, stony and uphill though it may be, by which alone we can recover our position in the world and revive the moral and economic strength of our island society. Mr Attlee would not have had the General Election when he did but for the fact that he knew he would leave his successors a burden which he himself feared to bear. We have accepted the responsibility, not for what has been done in the past, not for what strikes over into the present from the past, but for doing our utmost to put things right even though, as we all know, the process must be long, painful and in many ways unpopular.

The steps we have taken so far have already brought a definite improvement in our international position. Mr Eden's conduct of foreign affairs and Mr Butler's courageous and comprehensive Budget have won universal recognition abroad among our friends and widespread agreement at home. Time must be required for the severe cuts we had to make in our consumption and expenditure to bring about their full results. It is my belief that in three or four years we shall be able to present to our fellow-countrymen a situation in which world peace will be more secure and British solvency firmly re-established. More than that, it is our faith, based upon resolve, that there will be a sense of improvement in conditions here at home which will be apparent throughout all classes of our fellow-countrymen.

Meanwhile, we are confronted in Parliament by an Opposition, which regardless of the reproach that falls upon them for the plight into which they have brought the nation during their long reign of power, seeks only to gain party advantage by opposing the necessary steps we are forced to take to remedy the evils that they largely, and even sometimes consciously created. We shall not be turned from our course by their clamour or obstruction. They are themselves most bitterly divided on the main issues of the day and the struggle for the leadership of their party is going on. They try to heal or conceal these differences as much as possible by spitting out their spite upon us. I cannot remember a time – and my experience is a very long one – when public difficulty and party strife have both risen to such heights together.

Very often a common sense of the dangers of the country has caused an abatement of party strife, but in this case we still seem to be living in an electioneering atmosphere, and it is only by long, steady, faithful and skilful administration that we shall get into the cooler and calmer atmosphere – so necessary to enable our country, by natural fruition, to attain its highest expression. Here let me say how much we owe to the Conservative Members of the House of Commons – and I see here my friend Sir Ian Fraser – who, by their regular attendance on all occasions, especially at long night sittings, have enabled us to maintain an average majority double that which we gained at the polls. I hope that you will carry this impression away with you to your homes and constituencies. Conservative organizations throughout the country should recognize the services which their Members are rendering, and the great severity which Parliamentary life has for the time assumed.

It does not follow, however, that these harsh conditions will rule indefinitely. Once it is realized and proved that threats and bullyings do not deter us from our national duty, that we care nothing for abuse, except from people we respect, that the Government are proceeding upon a large design which unfolds itself step by step, and has to be proved, not by mere assertion but by results, to be serving the national interest, a more agreeable temper may prevail in the House of Commons. This, however, is only a hope of mine, based upon the saying that trees do not grow up to the sky. Anyhow, whatever happens, we are not afraid to face it. We are not asking for any favours; we shall do our duty not for any party or class or interest in the nation, but for the country as a whole. We shall do our duty without fear or favour and we are confident that so long as we maintain that attitude and are seen by the nation to be doing so, we shall be suffered to carry out our difficult task.

Among the Members of the House of Commons, or Government, who do their hardest work, none stand out with more distinction than my friend the Home Secretary. In the arduous discharge of his duties (both national and party) he is second to none. On Monday he will explain to the House of Commons the measures which we have taken, and are going to enforce, to protect the travelling public and Londoners from the needless series of annoyances and deprivations which the Socialists – by their legislation – have cast upon them. We wish him good luck in this task. I only regret that ill-health will not enable Mr Maclay, the Minister of Transport, to introduce the Motion we have placed upon the Order Paper of the House of Commons. But in the Home Secretary we have a Cabinet Minister who knows every aspect of this story, not only what has been made public, but what lies ahead in the near future, and we shall await with the greatest interest his opening of the debate on Monday. We are very fortunate in having him with us here today, and it is with confident anticipation that I now call upon him to address you.

Winston S. Churchill to John Cashmore[1]
(Churchill papers, 1/52)

25 April 1952

My dear Mr Cashmore,

It has given me much pleasure to receive your letter of April 2, and to read the most kind words you used in your speech at the unveiling ceremony of the plaque on the house where my Mother was born in Brooklyn. Such expressions of friendship and goodwill, and the fact that my Mother's birthplace will ever be remembered in the Borough of Brooklyn, are most agreeable and a source of pride to me. Pray accept my thanks for all of your kindness.

---

[1] John Cashmore, 1895–1961. Aide to general manager of New York Edison Co. Member, New York State Assembly, 1923. Borough President of Brooklyn, 1940–61. Delegate to Democratic National Convention, 1948, 1952, 1956, 1960.

April 1952

John Colville: diary
('The Fringes of Power', page 646)

26–27 April 1952

Went to Chartwell for the week-end. The PM plans to sack Lord Woolton and make 'Mr Cube' (Lord Lyle)[1] Chairman of the Tory Party. He also revealed to me a private project for getting the Queen Mother made Governor General of Australia. We went through the Honours List during the week-end and I was pleasantly surprised to find the PM amenable to my views on most points.

On Sunday evening Lord[2] and Lady Donegall[3] came bringing a Russian film called *The Fall of Berlin*. Russia, it seems, won the war single-handed and now breathes nothing but peace.

I gave Christopher Soames a lecture on not appearing to have too much of the PM's ear. It is dangerous for his future. I like him increasingly, though his manners can be coarse. Brendan Bracken,[4] with whom I had a drink the other day, says that Eden is violent against Christopher.

Evelyn Shuckburgh: diary
('Descent to Suez', page 41)

27 April 1952

Drove up from home in the Sunbeam in the morning and worked with AE at his flat. AE tells me that the Party are more and more concerned about the conduct of the Government, especially Winston's lack of grip and the fumblings of the Leader of the House. All reports show that the Government has lost a great deal of support. The trouble is lack of co-ordination on the home front and for this Lord Woolton is to blame. Jock Colville says he is becoming slower and more ineffective every day. Jock said, incidentally, that he had been

---

[1] Charles Ernest Leonard Lyle, 1904–54. Educated at Harrow and Trinity Hall, Cambridge. MP (Cons.) for West Ham, Stratford, 1918–22; for Epping, 1923–4; for Bournemouth, 1940–5. Knighted, 1923. Chairman of Tate & Lyle, 1928–37; President, 1937–54. Baronet, 1932. Baron, 1945. Known as 'Mr Cube' in reference to his campaign using the eponymous cartoon character against the Labour Government's plans to nationalise the sugar industry.

[2] Edward Arthur Donald St George Hamilton Chichester, 1903–75. 6th Marquess of Donegall, 1904. Educated at Eton and Christ Church, Oxford. Wrote for *Sunday Dispatch*, *Sunday News*, and *Sunday Graphic*. Married, 1943, Gladys Jean Combe (div. 1968); 1968, Maureen McKenzie. DJ for BBC, 1949.

[3] Gladys Jean Combe, 1900–?. Married, 1943, Edward Chichester (div. 1968).

[4] Brendan Bracken, 1901–58. Chairman, *Financial News*, 1928. MP (Cons.) for North Paddington, 1929–45; for Bournemouth, 1950–1. Elected to the Other Club, 1932. PC, 1940. Parliamentary Private Secretary to PM, 1940–1. Managing Director, *The Economist*, 1940, 1941. Minister of Information, 1941–5. First Lord of the Admiralty, May–July 1945. Chairman, *Financial Times*, 1945. Viscount, 1952.

astonished to find, when discussing the question of CH for E. M. Forster,[1] that Winston had never heard of him and had not read *A Passage to India*. Some concern about the PM's health. It is announced that he has a bad cold.

After finishing our work we waited half an hour in the street for Robert Carr[2] and his wife who were to drive AE down to Binderton. Great patience was displayed.

High Wood was looking beyond words beautiful this weekend. The beeches coming out, bluebells in the woods, all our new trees and shrubs bursting forth and tulips and blossom everywhere.

Winston S. Churchill to Anthony Eden
Prime Minister's Personal Minute M.258/52
(Premier papers, 11/116)

28 April 1952

Yours of April 22.[3]

I have for some time felt that this question raised the largest issues. The Americans have now definitely pronounced, as I hoped and thought they would, against handing over prisoners of war to the Communists against their will. I have read the latest telegrams on the subject and quite agree with your asking for about twenty-four hours delay in order to communicate with the Dominions. I do hope there will be no question of our differing from the Americans on this point of moral principle as I think the consequences might be very far reaching. On the other hand a fresh census of those unwilling to go back by a team of neutrals with observers from each side or by the International Red Cross would be all right provided that you can get the Americans to agree. Perhaps you will tell us about the petition at the Cabinet tomorrow.

---

[1] Edward Morgan Forster, 1879–1970. Educated at King's College, Cambridge. Author of *A Room with a View* (1908), *Howards End* (1910) and *A Passage to India* (1924). OM, 1969.

[2] Leonard Robert Carr, 1916–2012. Educated at Westminster School and Gonville and Caius College, Cambridge. Married, 1943, Joan Kathleen Twining: three children. MP (Cons.) for Mitcham, 1950–74; for Carshalton, 1974–6. Parliamentary Private Secretary to Iain MacLeod, 1951–5. Secretary of State for Employment, 1970–2. Lord President of the Council and Leader of the House of Commons, 1972. Home Secretary, 1972–4. Baron, 1976.

[3] PM/52/43, reproduced above (p. 402).

Winston S. Churchill to Anthony Eden
Prime Minister's Personal Minute M.257/52
(*Premier papers, 11/233*)

28 April 1952

Some time ago I found Drayson[1] next to me in the smoking room and I urged him most strongly not to go with the British Delegation to the Conference[2] and after a good deal of argument he promised me that he would not do so. It is true however that at the end he said would there be the same objections to his going privately during the Easter Recess and I said that I thought there was a great difference between his going as a member of this delegation and as a Member of Parliament paying a visit to Russia. I thought the point at issue was the Conference not what a Member of Parliament should do in his own time if the law permits. When I saw that he had gone and had got there while the Conference was sitting and thus mixed himself up with it I thought he had treated me unfairly and had not fulfilled the promise which he gave. I meant him to keep quite clear of the Conference and thought that that was what he meant to do. By all means scold him; I will re-inforce if the opportunity occurs.

Winston S. Churchill to Lord Blandford[3]
(*Churchill papers, 2/187*)

29 April 1952
Private and Confidential

My dear Sunny,

Thank you for your letter about the question of fox-hunting in Germany.[4] Alas, I cannot agree to make representations to the Federal Chancellor.

We are trying to complete the contractual negotiations with Western Germany which are vital to Western defence, and we are pressing the Germans to give way on a number of much more important issues which we have closely

---

[1] George Burnaby Drayson, 1913–83. Educated at Borlase School. Member of the Stock Exchange, 1935–54. Married, 1939, Winifred Heath (div. 1958): one child; 1962, Barbara Radomska-Chrzanowska. Royal Artillery, 1942–3. MP (Cons.) for Skipton, 1945–79. Member of Expenditure Committee, 1970–4.

[2] International Economic Conference in Moscow.

[3] John Spencer-Churchill, later the 11th Duke of Marlborough.

[4] Blandford had written: 'The German Federal Parliament are reputed to be bringing in a law forbidding [fox hunting] and when the ~~Peace Treaty~~ Continued Agreement is signed we come under their law. [. . .] The main trouble seems to be the shooting interests; they claim we disturb their hens and game, which is of course absurd. I think they really are being rather bloody minded about it, and they just don't want us to have our fun. Once again please forgive me for bothering you' (*Churchill papers, 2/187*). Churchill wrote a further note on the matter, which stated: 'Do the Germans really object to fox-hunting by British troops in Lower Saxony? If they do, it should be stopped. You may occupy a country but that does not give you unlimited freedom to indulge in sports which annoy the inhabitants' (*Churchill papers, 2/187*).

at heart. This is not a moment at which it would be right to make a fuss about the foxes.

It was nice to hear from you. I hope all goes well.

Cabinet: conclusions
(Cabinet papers, 128/24)

29 April 1952
Secret
11.30 a.m.
Cabinet Meeting No. 47 of 1952

[...]

5. The Foreign Secretary reported that little progress was being made in the conversations which he had been holding with Amr Pasha,[1] the Egyptian Ambassador in London. It seemed impossible to find a formula which would be acceptable to both sides regarding the Egyptian claim to sovereignty over the Sudan. The Foreign Secretary read to the Cabinet a new draft which he had prepared for this purpose. In this he had gone as far as he could to meet Egyptian susceptibilities, while safeguarding the essential rights of the Sudanese. He proposed that Her Majesty's Ambassador in Cairo should present this on his return to Egypt at the end of the week; but he had little hope that it would prove acceptable to the Egyptian Government. If nothing came of his latest attempt to find a basis on which he could resume discussions with the Egyptian Government with a view to negotiating a new agreement on defence and the Sudan, we should have to try to arrive at some *modus vivendi* by which we could retain our existing position in Egypt for the time being.

In discussion the following points were made:
(a) The Foreign Secretary undertook to arrange for his latest formula about the Sudan to be circulated to other members of the Cabinet so that he could take into account any other comments which any of them might wish to offer.
(b) The Minister of Defence suggested that it might be helpful at this stage in the negotiations to suggest the appointment of an Anglo-Egyptian Military Committee to consider ways and means by which we could assist in training and re-equipping the Egyptian Army. This might give encouragement to the Egyptian Army, who were known to be well disposed towards us, and its activities might be welcome to other friendly elements in Egypt.
(c) The Prime Minister hoped that no opportunity would be lost of

---

[1] Abdelfattah Amr, 1909–88. Known as 'F. D. Amr Bey', 'Amr Bey', or 'Amr Pasha'. Born in Asyut Governorate, 1909. Egyptian diplomat to England, 1928. Men's British Open Champion (Squash), 1933, 1934, 1935, 1936, 1937, 1938. Ambassador to London, 1945–52.

bringing home to the United States Government our unwillingness to continue indefinitely to carry alone the international burden of safeguarding the security of the Suez Canal. The Foreign Secretary said that, while he would continue to keep this in mind, he was unlikely to make much impression on the United States authorities at the present time, since they were disposed to think that he should have been ready to make further concessions about the Sudan for the purpose of reaching an agreement with the Egyptian Government.

The Cabinet –

Took note of the Foreign Secretary's statement and of the points raised in discussion.

[. . .]

May
1952

Winston S. Churchill to Lord Leathers
Prime Minister's Personal Minute M.262/52
(Premier papers, 11/175)

1 May 1952

1. How many and what questions require the Minister's[1] quasi-judicial decision? How many are:
   (a) pending
   (b) are likely to arise in the next month?
2. To what extent would it be possible to delay decisions on these?
3. Is there anything that must be settled by the Minister in his quasi-judicial capacity in the next month?
4. If his decision is delayed what action can be taken?

Winston S. Churchill to Lord Simonds
Prime Minister's Personal Minute M.263/52
(Premier papers, 11/175)

1 May 1952

Please see the Treasury Solicitor's note at 'A' and let me have your opinion.[2]

I have also asked the attached questions of the Ministry of Transport. The answers will be, I think, that a rapid accumulation of minor decisions is inevitable; they even talk of 70 already.

---

[1] The Minister for Transport, John Maclay, who was unwell at this time.
[2] The note read: 'I think it might be possible to use the powers contained in the Ministers of the Crown (Transfer of Functions) Act, 1946, to transfer by Order in Council to another Minister of the Crown the functions of the Minister of Transport. Such an order could be revoked on the present Minister's recovery and the functions transferred back to him.'

May 1952

Sarah Beauchamp to Winston S. Churchill
(Churchill papers, 1/50)[1]

1 May 1952

Darling Papa,

Thank you so much for sending me a message to read at the celebration of Israel's 4th birthday. They were thrilled, and I enjoyed myself, as I found quotes from your speech in 1921 when you planted a tree at the Hebrew University on Mount Scopus – and also from your speech to Congress this year. Speaking is really quite easy that way!

Some weeks ago Antony & I attended the ceremony for the unveiling & dedicating of a plaque on the house where your mother was born in Brooklyn.

It was a charming ceremony with lovely speeches of tribute to your beautiful Mama and to yourself, and I as proud granddaughter unveiled the plaque with the President of the Borough. About 1000 people crowded into the narrow street & there were lots of children all let out of school for the half day.

I thanked them on your behalf & said that I knew you would have been touched at their kind tributes to your mother & yourself & would be anxious to see the plaque the next time you visited these shores.

For the rest I have been busy at my television series.[2] It is getting better, but we still have a long way to go before I am satisfied, though our 'rating' is good, & I was given a citation by the students of a college for 'maintaining good standards of presentation & performance on television'!!

As Mummie has probably told you, we will be home in July for the summer & Autumn. I am enclosing a press account of the dedication of the plaque to your mother – although I'm sure they sent you everything. Also I want you to see Antony's latest feature in McCalls Magazine.

I think it is rather fun – & the picture of Margaret Truman very fine & a really amazing likeness – my likeness of course. Was a little retouched (no jokes please!)

Since President Truman's withdrawal – most people feel certain – even the Democrats, that it will be General Eisenhower, although Taft[3] is (unfortunately I think) a strong runner up. The Democrats seem to have no one really who excites anybody – unless they produce a dark horse.

Antony & I were thrilled by your wonderful victory in the Foreign debate – *Time* magazine gave a wonderful account of it. No party deserved a beating more – for the horrible way they fought the election –

---

[1] This letter was handwritten.
[2] *The Hallmark Hall of Fame*, which Sarah hosted 1952–4.
[3] Robert Alphonso Taft, Sr, 1889–1953. Educated at Yale College and Harvard Law School. Attorney with Maxwell and Ramsey, 1913–17. Married, 1914, Martha Wheaton Bowers: four children. Legal adviser, Food and Drug Administration, 1917–18. Legal adviser, American Relief Administration, 1918–19. Formed law partnership Taft, Stettinius and Hollister, 1924. Member (Rep.) of Ohio House of Representatives, 1920–30; Ohio Senate, 1930–2. US Senator, 1938–53. Senate Majority Leader, 1953. Unsuccessful candidate for Republican nomination for President, 1952.

Do hope you are well & <u>not</u> getting tired – Please give Duncan & Diana & Mary & Christopher our love and of course Mummie – but I will be writing to her –

We are in correspondence with Randolph & hope very much that something exciting may come out of his interviews with Tito[1] & de Gasperi[2] –

Much much love darling

Papa – yours very loving
Sarah

P.S. I can't draw me' anymore!

PPS. Antony sends his fondest regards & wishes to you.

Winston S. Churchill to Gwilym Lloyd George
Prime Minister's Personal Minute M.264/52
(Premier papers, 11/149)

1 May 1952
Top Secret

Thank you for your Minute of March 31 about food stocks. Please let me have further information on:

1. how our stock of the principal commodities today, and at the end of 1952 on the present programme, will compare with the stocks which we had in 1939 and during the war.

2. how far the stocks we hold are genuine reserves and how far they represent simply what we need to keep supplies moving at current consumption levels.

---

[1] Josip Broz Tito, 1892–1980. President of League of Communists of Yugoslavia, 1937–80. Federal Secretary of People's Defence, 1943–53. President of Federal Executive Council, 1943–63. Marshal of Yugoslavia, 1943–80. Federal Secretary of National Defence, 1945–53. President of Yugoslavia, 1953–80. Secretary-General of Non-Aligned Movement, 1961–4.

[2] Alcide de Gasperi, 1881–1954. Editor of *La Voce Cattolica*, 1905; of *Il Trentino*, 1906. MP (Popular Political Union of Trentino) in Austrian Reichsrat, 1911–18. Co-founder, Italian People's Party, 1919. Member of Chamber of Deputies for Trentin and South Tirol, 1921–6, 1946–54. Married, 1922, Francesca Romani: four children. Arrested and imprisoned for opposition to fascism, 1927; released, 1928. Cataloguer, Vatican Library, 1929–43. Co-founder, Christian Democracy Party, 1943; Secretary, 1944–6, 1953–4; President, 1946–54. Minister of Foreign Affairs, 1944–6; of Italian Africa, 1945–53; of Interior, 1946–7; of Foreign Affairs, 1951–3. PM, 1945–53. President of European Parliament, 1954.

Field Marshal Lord Alexander to Winston S. Churchill
(Premier papers, 11/367)

1 May 1952
Secret

D(52)9 – BLACKOUT POLICY[1]

You asked for my views on this paper and what it involved in actual deeds this year. I have deferred a reply till the paper had been considered by the Defence Committee at their meeting yesterday.

2. The object of the Chiefs of Staff's paper was to obtain the Defence Committee's approval in principle of the need for a blackout in a future war so that detailed planning could proceed. Until the nature of the blackout required has been examined in more detail it is impossible to say what positive measures can be taken now. It is not proposed to stockpile blackout materials at the present time.

3. The Defence Committee –
   (i) confirmed in principle the need for a degree of blackout in war;
   (ii) invited me and the Home Secretary to arrange for a joint examination of the nature of the blackout to be made by the Air Defence Committee and the Civil Defence Joint Planning Staff, and agreed that the results of this examination should be reported to the Defence Committee.

4. Action is being taken accordingly.

Winston S. Churchill: broadcast
('Winston S. Churchill, His Complete Speeches', volume 8, pages 8368–72)

3 May 1952   London

THE CONSERVATIVES' FIRST SIX MONTHS

At the Cup Final this afternoon I couldn't help taking a great deal of interest in the work of the goalkeepers. There seemed to be something – or several things – in common with their job as with that of Prime Minister. I only hope that as Prime Minister I may do as well as both the goalkeepers did this afternoon.

My theme, my friends, tonight, may be called 'The First Six Months'. It is in fact almost exactly six months since the Conservative Party became responsible for managing British affairs. But our first six months cannot be judged apart from the background of the previous six years. Mr Attlee's Government

---

[1] Reproduced above (p. 399).

had a hard time in their last two years of office. They had to live between General Elections with a majority of only six. They were able to pursue a firm foreign policy of resistance to aggression abroad, and to set on foot a very large rearmament programme at home, because, and only because, they could count, for these purposes, on the support of a Conservative Opposition nearly as strong as they were themselves.

But the results of their six-year record of extravagance and waste, of over-spending and of living upon American money had brought us all within sight of a dead stop. National insolvency was what stared us in the face when we took over. The Socialist fault is two-fold: first, that when they saw and felt what was happening they did not take any of the necessary measures to preserve our solvency because these would lose them votes; and secondly, that having been defeated, they are trying to make all the party capital they can out of the difficulties they left their successors, which they themselves had been unable to face.

We knew well at the General Election that hard trials and problems would await us if we won. For this reason, speaking with the authority of Leader of the Conservative Party, I gave a solemn warning in my broadcast of October 8, a fortnight before the polls, while the Election fight was in full vigour, and this is what I said:

> We make no promises of easier conditions in the immediate future. Too much harm has been done in these last six years for it to be repaired in a few months. Too much money has been spent for us to be able to avoid another financial crisis. It will take all our national strength to avoid the downhill slide and after that we shall still have to work up.[1]

That is what I said, before the votes were counted. It is from that starting-point that I claim that our first six months should be judged. I must admit that when we took office we found things much worse than we knew or expected. At the time of the General Election we were spending abroad at the rate of £800,000,000 a year more than we were earning: and if hard and decisive action had not been taken, there and then, when we came into power, by the new Chancellor of the Exchequer, Mr Butler, and followed throughout what is called the Sterling area, its whole reserve and our whole reserve of gold and dollar securities would have been exhausted by the end of this summer. For an island of fifty million people, which grows only enough food for thirty million, and has to buy its raw materials wherewith to earn its living from all over the world, that would have been a shocking disaster, causing far more privation and hardship than all the cuts we have made or are likely to make in imports.

These, my friends, have already been severe. We have cut no less than

[1] Reproduced in *The Churchill Documents*, vol. 22, *Leader of the Opposition, August 1945 to October 1951*, pp. 2177–82.

£600 million from our purchases abroad, and other unpleasant remedies like raising the bank rate have been taken. The full effect of these acts of national self-denial and self-restraint has not yet been felt. The medicine is bitter, and the taste lingers; while the cure, on the other hand, has only just begun. If I tell you some favourable facts I hope you will not exaggerate them or think that we are out of our troubles. On the contrary, we cannot yet claim that we are paying our way in our foreign purchases.

There is, however, an improvement. We are not eating up our limited resources so fast. Here are some figures. The average monthly loss of our reserves for the last three months of 1951 was $311 million. In January it was $299 million. In February $266 million; in March only $71 million. So much for the first quarter of 1952. The April figure will be better still and the pace at which we were going downhill has greatly slackened. If our present progress continues, and is not upset by world misfortunes, we ought, before the end of the year, to be paying our way. After all, that is only what every household – every man and woman in the land – has to do, to preserve their self-respect and independence. Another favourable sign is that the reputation of the pound sterling abroad has improved. The devaluation from which we suffered in 1949 was a heavy blow. It meant that we had to send out more exports for less imports. We trust, up to the present at any rate, so far, that we have saved the country from a repetition of this.

Up to this moment I have been talking only about our buying power abroad. If we lose that we should be like a swimmer who cannot keep his head above water long enough to get a new breath. (No fun at all!) But the same kind of evils happen here inside the country when prices and wages and profits continue to chase each other up in a fantastic spiral. That simply means that the money we earn buys less and less. We have not, so far, overtaken this evil and peril. We are swimming against the stream trying to keep level with a bush on the bank. We shall persevere faithfully to the utmost of our strength, but a truly national effort is needed to make headway.

It was my hope, when I became responsible, that just as we in Opposition had supported what was done in the national interest in foreign policy and defence by the Labour Government, so they would help in matters at home which were national rather than party. For this reason, after taking office, I wanted to get out of the electioneering atmosphere and make sure that our whole national strength was available for the matters of survival with which we are confronted.

We are in the strange position that, although four-fifths of each of the great parties agree about four-fifths of the things that ought to be done at home and abroad, and although if the worst happened we should all sink or swim together, we seem to be getting ever more bitterly divided as partisans, and Mr Attlee even talks of another General Election. I cannot think of anything worse for any country, and this country above all other countries, than to have a General Election every year, and for us all to dwell in constant violent party strife, trying to set one half of the people against the other, bidding against each other for votes, and with no Government capable of doing the unpopular things that have to be done. Even in quiet and easy times it would be a very poor service to true democracy. Now, in our crisis and peril, it would be lunacy.

The date of a General Election does not, however, rest with Mr Attlee, or with the Leader of the Opposition whoever he may be, or may be going to be. We have the will, and I believe we have the power, to continue for another three or four years of steady, calm and resolute Government at home and abroad, making our mistakes – who does not? – but devoting our life-effort to what we believe is the national interest; and we ask to be judged by results and by deeds rather than by words, and for a fair time to bring them about.

In our general policy, we are trying our best to encourage effort and enterprise and to evoke the creative genius of the British race. We think it is a good thing to 'set the people free' as much as possible in our complicated modern society – to set them free from the trammels of State control and of bureaucratic management. Of course, everything cannot be done at once, or even in six months. But quite a lot has been done already. And more will be apparent as the months unfold.

Next month the burden of PAYE will be lifted off the shoulders of another two million of our people and sixteen million in all benefit from tax relief. The harder they work the more they will benefit. But with incentives to the strong there must also march compassion for the weak and poor. The addition which will be made in the autumn to old age and all other insurance benefits will be a real relief if the cost-of-living can be controlled. We pledged ourselves that we would undo, as far as was possible, the harm and waste arising from the nationalization of steel and of road transport. Transport is more urgent than steel. Steel is being managed by the same competent hands which in later years have made it the foremost factor in our export industries. Our Bill is already drafted, and will be presented to Parliament this year. But it is in the reform of our transport system that I believe the most fertile hope of a genuine economic and social improvement is possible. The action we have taken on fares has shown our resolve to keep State industries under proper control and to protect the ordinary public from the rigid workings of the official machine.

In other fields, some minor fields, some larger, we have promptly accepted the recommendations of the Cotton Import Committee that spinners should be allowed the choice of buying their cotton from private sources. All the trade in timber is now in private hands. We have done our best to throw off some of the more irksome and needless restraints that have been laid upon the nation in these past years. We thought that you had carried your identity cards about long enough. We did not see why boys and girls should not take the General Certificate examination at the age their teachers thought they could pass it.

But it is over housing that the most definite advance has taken place. We in the Conservative Party have always held and always promised that housing should have first place in our social programme. We have given it first place. And already there are welcome results. The figures for the first three months of this year announced yesterday by Mr Macmillan, the Minister of Housing, are certainly heartening to us all. They will bring hope to thousands on the waiting lists. They should provide encouragement to the fine efforts of the building industry. And – may I say? – they have given keen pleasure to us in the Government and our supporters as we push our way through the tangles of the times, and the ill-will of those who created many of the difficulties. In the first quarter of this new year, nearly 10,000 more houses were completed, nearly 30,000 more houses were building; and more than 15,000 more houses were begun than in the same period of last year. Nor are the houses all of one type. There are both more for letting and more for sale; more council houses and more privately built houses. Notice please, my friends, the word 'more'; that is our watchword in housing: 300,000 a year we proclaimed as our target. There is a bull's-eye we mean to hit. Of course, all our hopes of making things better at home depend upon keeping the peace. The fear of another world war casts its dark shadow upon every land on both sides of 'the Iron Curtain' that divides mankind. I have the feeling that this fear is becoming universal and that it is sinking deeper into all human hearts, and from that I draw the hope that all will in the end come right. If the shadow were lifted, an age of prosperity would dawn upon the masses of every race and nation. We have anxious years to endure, but I cannot believe that the danger of world war is as great as it was a year ago, or that the last six month have not seen an improvement. If that proves true, no one, I assure you, will rejoice more than those who in this country were so wickedly accused by their political opponents of seeking war when the present Parliament was being chosen. The wise and skilful conduct of our foreign affairs by Mr Eden, the increasing defensive strength of the free countries, and their growing intimacy have made things safer.

Our cause is sacred: peace and freedom. The way for us in Britain to serve this cause is plain. There are linked together the three circles I have often described. First, the British Empire and Commonwealth of Nations growing in moral and physical strength. Secondly, the irrevocable association of the English-speaking world around the great Republic of the United States. Thirdly, the safety and revival of Europe in her ancient fame and long-sought unity. In all these circles we in this hard pressed but unvanquished island have a vital part to play, and if we can bear the weight we may win the crown of honour.

May 1952

Winston S. Churchill to Gwilym Lloyd George
Prime Minister's Personal Minute M.269/52
(Premier papers, 11/148)

4 May 1952

Can you let me have a return <u>in tons</u> showing the amount of meat consumed in any one year in Britain, pre-war and 1945–1951 inclusive. How does the consumption this year to date compare?

An alternative figure should also be presented showing the effect of the increase of population. This need not delay the rest of the return.

Winston S. Churchill to John Maclay
(Churchill papers, 6/2)

5 May 1952

My dear Maclay,

I deeply regret to receive your letter of May 3 tendering your resignation of the Offices of Minister of Transport and Civil Aviation. Owing to the pressure of decisions imposed on you in a quasi-judicial capacity as Minister of Transport and not easily transferable to another Minister I feel I have no choice but to accept it.

I can only hope that your recovery will not be long delayed as your work in this important and difficult post has been most valuable.

John Colville: diary
('The Fringes of Power', pages 646–7)

6 May 1952

Tonight I went with the PM to dine with the Massiglis[1] at the French Embassy. The others at dinner were Eden, Alexander, General Juin and Gérard André[2] also Madame M[3] who couldn't bear to be out of it but left us at the end of dinner. General Juin was inhibited by his bad English. The PM said Germany must be given fair play: if France would not co-operate we, America and Germany must go forward without her. He wanted to see British,

---

[1] René Massigli, 1888–1988. During WWI, served in French Foreign Service. Secretary General, Conference of Ambassadors, 1920–31. Exiled to Turkey, 1938–40, where he served as Ambassador. Commissioner for Foreign Affairs, 1943–4. Ambassador to Great Britain, Sep. 1944 to Jan. 1955. Secretary-General, Quai d'Orsay, 1954–6.

[2] Gérard André, Minister at French Embassy in London.

[3] Odette Isabelle Boissier, 1907–?. Married, 1932, Rene Massigli.

American, German and French contingents march past him at Strasbourg, each to their own national songs; in creating international unity, national marching songs could play a great part.

When Juin said that General Koenig[1] had now gone into politics the PM, looking at Alexander, said far be it from him to run down soldiers turned politician. Look, he said, at Napoleon. Wellington, too, I ventured. No, he replied, Wellington was a politician turned soldier. A totally invalid statement.

Alexander, next to whom I sat, said to me that war was a tradition among men. As Clausewitz[2] had put it, it was a way of pursuing national policy 'by other means'. But he thought the atomic bomb might well put a stop to all that: it might be the end of war by making war impossible. He thought, too, that now was the time to show an imaginative policy to Germany: we should lose all if we niggled.

Massigli said that Pinay,[3] the new French PM, had come to stay. He believed a new political stability was dawning in France.

R. A. Butler to Winston S. Churchill
(*Premier papers, 11/186*)

6 May 1952

You asked for comments of the Foreign Secretary and myself on the telegram which you received from President Weizmann on 21st April asking for a loan.[4]

I have consulted with the Foreign Secretary and our joint views are set out in the memorandum attached.

We should be glad to know whether the course of action proposed in paragraph 6 of the memorandum meets with your approval.[5]

[1] Marie Joseph Pierre François Koenig, 1898–1970. CoS, 1st Free French Div., Syria, 1941. Brig.-Gen., 1942. CO, 1st Free French Bde, North Africa, 1942. Asst GOC, 1st Free French Div., 1942–3. Maj.-Gen., 1943. Deputy Chief, National Defence Staff, 1943–4. Lt-Gen., 1944. French Liaison Officer to SHAEF, 1944. C-in-C, Free French Forces in Great Britain, 1944; Forces Françaises de l'Intérieur, 1944–5; French Occupation Force, Germany, 1945–9. Military Governor of Paris, 1944–5. Gen., 1946. GOC, French Army of the Rhine, 1945–9. Inspector-General, Forces of North Africa, 1949–51. Vice-President, Supreme War Council, 1950–1. Minister of National Defence, 1954, 1955. Marshal of France (posthumous), 1984.

[2] Carl von Clausewitz, 1780–1831. Cavalry officer, Prussian Army, 1792–1831. Officer, Imperial Russian Army, 1812–13. Officer, Russian–German Legion, 1813–15. Director, Prussian Staff College, 1815–30. Author of *On War* (1832).

[3] Antoine Pinay, 1891–1994. Married, 1917, Marguerite Fouletier: three children. Member of Chamber of Deputies, 1936; Senate (Independent Radicals), 1938. Helped found a conservative political party, the National Centre of Independents and Peasants (CNIP), 1951. Minister of Public Works, Transport, and Tourism, 1950–2. PM, 1952–3. Minister of Finance and Economic Affairs, 1952–3. Minister of Foreign Affairs, 1955–6. Interim Minister of Public Works, Transportation and Tourism, 1958. Finance Minister, 1958–60.

[4] T.113/52, reproduced above (pp. 401–2).

[5] Churchill wrote on this minute: 'Para 6 is really all you need read. [. . .] I am vy sorry no help can be given.'

MAY 1952 425

Clementine Churchill to Winston S. Churchill
(Premier papers, 11/8)

6 May 1952

How would it be if we invited the Menzies to come for the weekend at Chequers on Saturday the 7th of June till Monday? (The day before you are by way of going to Arromanches, but I think you would be back in time.)

I have ascertained that the Menzies are likely to be here over this weekend. If you agree to this, we can have the Whitsuntide Recess quietly at Chartwell, and we could ask a small party of people to meet the Menzies on Saturday the 7th of June.

I think it would be a good thing if this could be planned out as soon as you are able to decide, out of civility to the Menzies, and also it would be more comfortable if we knew what our plans were going to be. If the Menzies know we are not going to invite them over to Whitsuntide they will no doubt make a plan of their own.

Cabinet: conclusions
(Cabinet papers, 128/24)

7 May 1952
Secret
11.30 a.m.
Cabinet Meeting No. 50 of 1952

[...]

4. The Cabinet considered a memorandum by the Foreign Secretary (C(52)141) reporting that after a date not later than June 1953 the local costs of British forces stationed in Germany would cease to be met by the Germans. These costs were estimated at about £130 million a year in foreign currency. The immediate action proposed by the Foreign Secretary was to send a message to the United States Secretary of State warning him of the serious effect of our having to bear these costs, and asking for his support in insisting on the maintenance of a German contribution adequate to cover our costs until June 1953.

The Chancellor of the Exchequer emphasized the gravity of the situation disclosed in the memorandum. He was preparing for the Cabinet a paper reviewing our economic and financial prospects and our capacity to carry out the obligations which we had undertaken. This would show that our overseas military commitments in Germany, the Middle East and the Far East were ten times greater than they had been before the war, when we had the help of the Indian Army in meeting them. While he believed that the situation could be held for the next six months, the long-term outlook was very grave. He thought that the burden of occupation costs in Germany should be taken into account in a comprehensive review of our military commitments.

Discussion then turned upon the measure of the local costs of the British forces in Germany. It was suggested that, when the time came for us to assume the burden of these costs, it ought to be possible to reduce the total below the estimated figure of £130 million. It seemed likely that the Germans had been placing an inflated value on some of the services which they supplied to the Occupation War Office. On any basis, the present cost per man in Germany seemed surprisingly high. Against this, it was pointed out that present costs included capital expenditure on married quarters and other requirements which would have been largely completed before the summer of 1953. Amenities for troops stationed abroad could not be cut below a certain point without serious effects upon recruiting.

The Prime Minister said that great care must be taken to avoid any public statement which might imply that we were likely to break our pledges to NATO by reducing our forces in Germany. This would have the gravest possible effects on the whole structure of Western defence and would shock public opinion in the United States. At the same time, it was essential that the minimum figure for the local costs of the British forces in Germany should be firmly established, and that all unnecessary expenditure should be eliminated. A small Committee should be appointed to examine these costs and to indicate means by which they might be reduced, say, to £70 million a year.

The Cabinet –

1) Authorized the Foreign Secretary to send a communication to the United States Government on the lines of the draft in Annex A of C(52)141.

2) Appointed a Committee (consisting of the Minister of Defence, the Paymaster-General, the Chancellor of the Duchy of Lancaster and representatives of the Foreign Secretary and the Chancellor of the Exchequer) to examine in consultation with the Service Ministers the estimated local costs of the British forces in Germany after June 1953 and to report to the Cabinet on the implications of reducing them to a figure of £70 million a year.

5. The Cabinet had before them a note by the Lord President (C(52)143) covering a further redraft of the proposed White Paper on Broadcasting.

The Lord President said that paragraphs 6 to 10 and paragraph 18 of the White Paper had been redrafted, in the light of the Cabinet's previous discussion, in order to indicate that Parliament was not now being asked to take a decision of principle in favour of sponsored television. The new draft stated merely that the Government did not propose to ask Parliament to commit themselves to the continuation of the exclusive broadcasting rights of the BBC and would leave the question of the licensing of private broadcasting of television to be determined by Parliament when the establishment of private stations became practicable. This change would be unwelcome to some Government supporters; but, in view of the probable criticisms of those who wished to maintain the Corporation's monopoly, it seemed unlikely that Government supporters would actually vote against it. Paragraph 37 of the White Paper had also been redrafted for a different purpose, viz., to exclude the obligation on the part of the Corporation to consult the Government on wages and kindred matters.

In discussion it was agreed that paragraph 7 of the draft White Paper should be amended (i) by deleting the second sentence, which might be read to indicate that the question of licensing private broadcasting might be deferred for as long as the ten-year life of the new Charter; and (ii) by making it explicit that the Government's intention not to ask Parliament to commit themselves to the continuation of the exclusive privilege of the Corporation related to television and not to sound broadcasting.

Opinion in the Cabinet favoured the changes made in the White Paper; but the Cabinet felt that before they reached a final conclusion it would be well that there should be further consultation with Government supporters who had shown interest in the problem.

The Prime Minister said that he would wish the Home Secretary to present the Government's proposals in debate in the House of Commons.

The Cabinet –

1) Invited the Lord President, in association with the Home Secretary and the Postmaster-General, to consult further with Government supporters on the policy towards broadcasting embodied in the draft White Paper annexed to C(52)143.
2) Agreed to reach a final decision in the light of these consultations on 13th May, with a view to the issue of the White Paper within a few days thereafter.

[...]

Gwilym Lloyd George to Winston S. Churchill
(*Premier papers, 11/148*)

8 May 1952
PM 52/10

The attached statistical tables give the information about meat consumption for which you asked me in your minute of 4th May (Serial No. M.269/52).[1]

Table I shows the annual consumption for the specified periods.

Table II shows the consumption in the first 4 months of this year as compared with the first 4 months of the two previous years. Forecasts of the

[1] Reproduced above (p. 423).

level of supplies for the whole of this year are very tentative, but if present expectations are fulfilled, the total meat consumption in 1952 will be about 1,500,000 tons.

Table III shows the consumption of meat per head of population in pre-war years and the period 1945–1951.

Table I
Annual Consumption in United Kingdom, Pre-war and 1945–1951

	Pre-war average 1934–38	1945	1946	1947	1948	1949	1950	1951
			Thousand tons					
Total Consumption	2108*	1706	1696	1636	1583	1533	1853	1362

Table II
Consumption in period January–April 1950, 1951, 1952

	1950	1951	1952
		Thousand tons	
Consumption in 4 months: Jan–April	650	368	468

Table III
Consumption in lbs. per head per year

	Pre-war average 1934–38	1945	1946	1947	1948	1949	1950	1951
			lbs. per head per year					
Consumption per head	98.8	75.2	76.5	72.6	68.5	68.5	82.2	59.9

* In order to provide the same supplies of meat per head for the present population, 2,250,000 tons would be needed as compared with the pre-war supplies of 2,108,000.

Winston S. Churchill to Charles Eade
(*Premier papers, 11/283*)

8 May 1952

My dear Eade,

In your letter of March 21[1] about a *Sunday Dispatch* story on rubber exports to Russia, you mentioned a report by the *Associated Press* that the Commercial

---

[1] Reproduced above (p. 362).

Counsellor to the British Embassy in Washington had announced that no more rubber would be shipped to Russia and Communist China from Singapore.

As you supposed the Commercial Counsellor was misquoted. What he in fact said was that no rubber could thenceforth be shipped from the United Kingdom, Malaya or Singapore to a destination other than the Commonwealth, Ireland and the United States without an export licence. The *Los Angeles Examiner*, which has an anti-British record, chose however to report this statement without mentioning the important qualification 'without an export licence'. It is true that no correction was issued by the Embassy. Had it been, it would doubtless have been subject to further misrepresentation.

Winston S. Churchill to Arthur Deakin[1]
(Premier papers, 11/474)

8 May 1952

My dear Mr Deakin,

You wrote to me on the 2nd May about the breakdown in the negotiations between the Service Departments and the Central Workers Union of Malta in relation to the wage claim presented by the Union. I understand that the final offer made to the Union was to increase the cost of living bonus to 30s. a week as from the 1st April and to pay a lump sum of £14 6s. 0d. per man. This offer was made subject to acceptance of certain conditions, two of which concerned the important subject of the machinery by which any future wages dispute should be adjusted. This represented a very considerable advance over what the Services had previously been prepared to do and I know from Sir Walter Monckton that you did your best to help towards an adjustment upon this footing. I still hope that the Union may eventually accept the Government's latest offer. In the meantime payments on the basis of the increase of the cost of living bonus to 30s. a week will be made with effect from 1st April, and the question whether, on consideration, the Union could not accept the lump sum with the conditions, can stand over for the time being. I am particularly anxious that some machinery should be devised to avoid similar difficulties in the future and I hope that you will be able, by your advice to the Maltese Union, to help towards this result.

I should be grateful if you would treat this letter as confidential until the Government's intention to take the action I have described has been announced.

---

[1] Arthur Deakin, 1890–1955. General Secretary, Transport and General Workers' Union, 1945–55. General Secretary, TUC, 1945–55; Chairman, 1951–2.

Winston S. Churchill to President Chaim Weizmann
Prime Minister's Personal Telegram T.122/52
(Premier papers, 11/186)

9 May 1952
Priority
Secret
No. 172

My colleagues and I have given long and anxious consideration to the proposal made with eloquence and force on your behalf by Mr Horowitz.[1] We fully recognise the extent of Israel's present difficulties but we very much regret that our own remain so great that we cannot meet your request. We have reached this decision with the greatest reluctance and are still anxious to do all that may lie within our power to help you. In particular, if you cannot so arrange your expenditure as to pay for your oil in United States dollars other than those received as Grant-in-Aid, we would suggest that you should, with our support, again approach the United States Government for permission to use Grant-in-Aid dollars for this purpose. We should also be ready to support you in any approach you may find it necessary to make to the United States Government for further assistance to tide you over your present difficulties. Please let me know of any steps you would like me to take in connexion with these suggestions.

Winston S. Churchill to Sir Norman Brook
Prime Minister's Personal Minute M.275/52
(Premier papers, 11/148)

10 May 1952

We really must have a discussion in Cabinet before Whitsuntide on the food budget. Will you confer with Lord Woolton, the Minister of Food, the Minister of Agriculture and the Chancellor of the Exchequer. Papers ought to be circulated by the Department concerned. I am greatly shocked at the fact that our people are eating little more than half the meat they ate in 1939.

---

[1] See T.113/52, reproduced above (pp. 401–2).

May 1952

Winston S. Churchill to Field Marshal Lord Alexander
Prime Minister's Personal Minute M.279/52
(Premier papers, 11/171)

10 May 1952

I have read Paragraph 3 of D (52) 4th Meeting.[1] It seems to me a very serious decision for us to authorise the Germans to make atomic weapons. If they are on the right side in any future war they will get all the advantage of the vast American production. It is not likely that any contribution they could make themselves would appreciably alter the situation, especially limited as proposed, in the next few years. Surely however much alarm would be created by the announcement that we had authorised and approved their embarking on the atomic field. To sum up, there would be no appreciable gain to NATO or Germany but considerable public alarm.

Winston S. Churchill to Lord Leathers
Prime Minister's Personal Minute M.285/52
(Premier papers, 11/175)

11 May 1952
Private

1. I should like you to read the attached note which has been prepared for me and let me know after you have had a look round how you feel about the accumulation of quasi-judicial responsibilities upon you as Minister.[2]

2. The first category of the paper (marked 'A' in red) has caused the most trouble. Until the railways were nationalised in 1947 no serious difficulties arose in what were decisions between different types of private enterprise. When however the railways were taken over by the State the bias of the 1930 Act to protect the railways against road transport became in the hands of a Socialist Minister a definite measure of partisan policy to make the railways a success no matter at what cost or inconvenience to non-nationalised road

---

[1] This paragraph read:
'Security Controls in Germany. The Committee had before them a memorandum by the Foreign Secretary (D(52)15) asking the opinion of the Committee on the extent of the controls to be applied to the production of atomic energy and guided missiles by the Germans in Germany.
Atomic Energy: The Foreign Secretary said that it was already agreed that there should be a complete prohibition on the production of atomic weapons by the Germans. They were, however, not prohibited from some form of development work in atomic energy. The Federal Chancellor had previously asked that the Germans should be allowed to make 2,000 grammes of nuclear fuel in a year. This was a good deal more than was being made by any other country in Western Europe except the United Kingdom. The Chancellor had, however, now said that he would accept a limit of 500 grammes, subject to review in three years and to the Germans being able to obtain isotopes from the United Kingdom or elsewhere.'

[2] During Maclay's illness Leathers temporarily took on his duties, though not his formal position, as Minister of Transport.

transport. When we took office a number of cases became highly controversial and some of the decisions taken by the Minister in harmony with the 1930 Act were the subject of great publicity and complaint.

3. It seems to me that some general principles should be laid down by the Minister for dealing with these cases in the interim period before,
    a) a new Road Haulage Bill is passed, and
    b) the amendments that will be needed in the 1930 Act next year.
Our policy is:
    <u>First</u>, not to strangle the expansion of road transport in the interests of making nationalised railways pay.
    <u>Secondly</u>, to preserve the railways in the most efficient form possible for the indispensable though diminishing duties they discharge.

4. I should like to know from you how serious you feel will be the burden of your decisions and how much of them can be settled by their falling into particular categories and, finally, whether the burden upon you is too heavy. You will have a great deal of work to do in the House with the important measures impending this year and next and you must not let yourself be over-burdened by the personal discharge of quasi-judicial functions. I shall look forward to hearing from you.

Winston S. Churchill to Lady Lytton[1]
(Lytton papers)

11 May 1952

Dearest Pamela,

I have had some enquiries made about the 'German Democratic Report'. It looks as though the copy which was sent to you was one of the large number which are being sent free and apparently unsolicited to various people in this country and the United States.

I do hope we can meet soon, I am much hunted by politics. We are reaping where others sowed. Presently we shall reap our own crop.

Winston Churchill to Winston S. Churchill and Clementine Churchill
(Churchill papers, 1/51)[2]

11 May 1952

Dear Grandpapa and Grandmama,

Thank you very much for taking me out, it was great fun. We saw a film

---

[1] Pamela Frances Audrey Plowden, 1874–1971. Married, 1902, Victor Bulwer-Lytton: two children.
[2] This letter was handwritten.

last night called *Elusive Victory* it was about the MCC against the Australians, at cricket. We have been playing sports, cricket begins tomorrow.

I hope Nicholas[1] and everyone else are well. I am having great fun. Swimming begins next month, everyone is looking forward to it.

Winston S. Churchill to Winston Churchill
(Churchill papers, 1/51)[2]

12 May 1952

My dear Winston,

I was so pleased to get your letter this morning and to learn your news. It was very nice having you at Chartwell though only for a flash; and I hope you were not too tired by the excursion. Tell me how your Master received the book I ventured to send him. I hope he was not offended by my peace offering – though I do not know him.

Please carry on this correspondence with your ever loving grandfather,

Winston Churchill to Winston S. Churchill
(Churchill papers, 1/51)[3]

13 May 1952

Dear Grandpapa,

Thank you very much for your letter. The Headmaster was very pleased with the book and thanks you very much for it.

I am playing lots of cricket and having lots of fun. The swimming[4] has just been painted, and is going to be filled soon.

My uncle, Capt. Digby[5] took me out yesterday and we went on the river.

Please give Nicholas my love, and can I have a few stamps please.

Hope you are well,

---

[1] Arthur Nicholas Winston Soames, 1948– . Educated at Eton College and Mons Officer Cadet School. Married, 1981, Catherine Weatherall (div. 1988: one child); 1993, Serena Smith: two children. Lt, 11th Hussars, 1967–72. Equerry to the Prince of Wales, 1970–2. Asst Director, Sedgwick Group, 1976–82. MP (Cons.) for Crawley, 1983–97; for Mid Sussex, 1997– . Parliamentary Private Secretary to Minister of State for Employment, 1984–5; to Secretary of State for the Environment, 1987–9; to Secretary of State for Trade and Industry, 1989–90. Parliamentary Secretary, Ministry of Agriculture, Fisheries and Food, 1992–4. Minister of State for the Armed Forces, Ministry of Defence, 1994–7. Shadow Defence Secretary, 2003–5.

[2] This letter was handwritten.

[3] This letter was handwritten.

[4] swimming pool.

[5] Edward Henry Kenelm Digby, 1924–2018. Brother of Pamela, Randolph Churchill's first wife. Educated at Eton, Trinity College, Cambridge, and Royal Military Academy, Sandhurst. Capt., Coldstream Guards. Married, 1952, Dione Sherbrooke: three children. 12th Baron Digby, 1964. Lord Lieutenant of Dorset, 1984–99. KCVO, 1999.

Cabinet: conclusions
(Cabinet papers, 128/25)

13 May 1952
Secret
11 a.m.
Cabinet Meeting No. 52 of 1952

[. . .]

2. The Minister of Defence made a report to the Cabinet on his visit to Paris to discuss with the French Minister of National Defence technical questions affecting the association of British forces with the forces of the European Defence Community. These discussions had been conducted in a frank and friendly atmosphere; but the French seemed obsessed with the logistical difficulties of joint military operations by forces drawing their supplies from different countries, and they had evidently not yet overcome their disappointment at our unwillingness to become full members of the European Defence Community. Agreement had now been reached, however, on the practical step of initiating joint staff discussions on methods of associating the British forces with the forces of the Community in matters of training, administration and supply.

In discussion attention was drawn to news reports that units of the future German forces might receive training in this country. The Minister of Defence said that no such statement had been made in the course of his conversations in Paris. There might be opportunities of correcting this misrepresentation in the forthcoming debate in the House of Commons on Foreign Affairs.

The Cabinet –
Took note of this statement by the Minister of Defence.
[. . .]

Winston S. Churchill to Field Marshal Lord Alexander
Prime Minister's Personal Minute M.288/52
(Premier papers, 11/369)

13 May 1952

I cannot pretend to have read this lengthy document[1] but Lord Cherwell's brief summary conveys, I believe, its pith. As it emerged before you took Office I send it to you in order that you may have it in mind. I may say that I assume as a working hypothesis for myself about 80 Soviet Divisions immediately ready. I credit them with 50 or 60 atomic bombs. I believe they greatly, and rightly, fear the American atomic attack as explained to me by the Pentagon

---

[1] NATO report on respective Soviet and NATO strengths.

MAY 1952 435

– so far as they know it. It may be that the mining and Soviet U-boat attack on our ports and transatlantic communications would be very severe during the first three months. I do not however see how the U-boats are going to be refuelled and if their Soviet bases and also the Soviet airfields are destroyed by American atomic attack, great relief might be found thereafter. It is therefore most important to have at least six months' supplies of all vital needs. We have got, of course, to dispose of all Soviet parachutists who land in Britain. After the first phase the war may go forward in a broken-backed condition in various theatres apart from Europe, which would be overrun. The position of Russian armies in Europe after their central Government had largely broken down and their communications with their homeland were severed, would indeed be peculiar. It might be that an arrangement could be come to on a non-Communist basis with the Russian Generals.

Defence Committee: minutes
(Cabinet papers, 131/12)

14 May 1952 Prime Minister's Map Room
Secret Ministry of Defence
11.30 a.m.
Defence Committee Meeting No. 5 of 1952

1. CIVIL DEFENCE AND WAR PLANS OF CIVIL DEPARTMENTS

The Committee had before them the following papers:
D(52)14: Third Annual Report by the Defence (Transition) Committee on the State of War Plans and Preparations.
D(52)10: By the Home Secretary on Civil Defence Preparedness.
D(52)18: By the Home Secretary on Financial Considerations Affecting Civil Defence Preparedness.
D(52)19: By the Minister of Defence on Industrial Mobilisation.

The Home Secretary, referring to D(52)10, drew the attention of the Committee to the weakness of civil defence preparations. Even the most urgent measures approved by the Chiefs of Staff as a direct contribution to the Armed Forces (listed in the Appendix), were falling behind owing to the restrictions on capital expenditure and on production. On the credit side, he hoped that by the end of 1954 there would be a satisfactory number of part-time volunteers trained in a system universally acknowledged to be excellent; a satisfactory network of communications, though not fully protected; an air-raid warning system; and plans for the evacuation of the priority classes. On the other hand, the fire and rescue services would be far under strength; there would be no whole-time civil defence workers and no equipment for them; no provision would have been made for hospital expansion, and little for the care of the homeless or for emergency water supplies, and little protection would have been provided for vital industry. Finally, there would be no public shelters, except those which were still available from the last war. Plans were being made on the assumption that there might be six months' warning period of war, but even this six months would not enable civil defence preparations to be completed. He therefore hoped that a firm figure might now be fixed for expenditure on civil defence, so that effective plans could be made accordingly. The present figure, allotted within the rearmament programme to civil defence, amounted in all to £316 million; but if this sum was to be spent in the time allotted, there would have to be a sharp rise in the expenditure in 1953 and 1954, and he doubted whether in present circumstances this was a realistic assumption to take. Apart from this need for a firm figure for expenditure, he was particularly anxious to see the early establishment of an experimental civil defence mobile column which would be centrally controlled and would work with the military in areas subjected to particularly severe attack. For this experiment he only needed, in the first instance, about 150 men, which the Army were willing to provide, and accommodation for them in army huts on a site which he already had.

In discussion the following points were made:
    (a) The six months' warning period to which the Home Secretary had referred was a planning assumption only. If Departments were told to plan on the assumption that war might break out at any moment without warning, they would have to aim at having all their plans and preparations permanently ready for immediate application. This was clearly impracticable. On the other hand, if they were allowed to assume a longer period of warning, there was a risk that they would neglect or postpone preparatory work which should be done well in advance of the imminence of war.
    (b) The measures listed in the Appendix to D(52)10 had been selected for urgent completion because they would help to reduce the effectiveness of enemy attack and were also linked with aggressive measures to destroy and divert the enemy's attack. The list included the experimental civil defence column to which the Home Secretary had referred, and blackout measures which were now under consideration by a committee of officials. The object of these blackout measures was, not to achieve a complete system of blackout, but so to arrange the pattern of lighting that the enemy would be confused and deceived.
    (c) Proposals would be made separately through the Minister of Defence to the Prime Minister about the provision of protected accommodation for essential Government staffs in war, based on the assumption that the seat of Government would remain in London. The problem of providing shelter for the population of London,

MAY 1952 437

other than the priority classes which were to be evacuated, had not been tackled. The Minister of Works suggested that, as a modest start, those erecting in London new buildings of more than, say, four storeys might be obliged by regulation to provide a basement covered with reinforced concrete.

(d) The Committee were informed that the Chancellor of the Exchequer was preparing a report for the Cabinet which would attempt to estimate how much the national economy could afford to devote to defence as a whole. At the same time, the Chiefs of Staff were preparing a new strategic appreciation, which would help to settle priorities in the provision of offensive and defensive equipment of all kinds. When these two reports were ready, it would be easier to judge the best allocation of the money available between all the differing needs of defence.

The Prime Minister, summing up the discussion, said that, while he appreciated the Home Secretary's anxiety about his responsibilities for civil defence, he doubted whether it would be justifiable to devote to civil defence large sums of money which could be more profitably used in active defence measures, which would be a more effective deterrent to war or, if the worst came, more valuable in the early stages of a war. He was not convinced that all the special measures included in the Appendix to D(52)10 would really make a valuable contribution. Certainly, the full development of an air-raid warning system was essential. A complete blackout was not necessary, though deceptive lighting would be useful. In many areas it should be possible to provide protected war rooms in buildings similarly used in the last war. The experimental mobile column was certainly something which could be done at little cost and this should go forward. In general, he was disposed to think that very large expenditure could be incurred on civil defence without any proportionate reduction of the military effectiveness of enemy air attack; and, although it would be wise to do enough to create an impression of activity in civil defence, care must be taken to avoid spending large sums of money on measures which would pay no dividend. He agreed that any firm allocation of money to civil defence must await consideration of the reports by the Chancellor of the Exchequer and the Chiefs of Staff.

The Committee –

(1) Took note of the Third Annual Report by the Defence (Transition) Committee (D(52)14).
(2) Took note of the memorandum by the Home Secretary on Civil Defence Preparedness (D(52)10).
(3) Took note of the report by the Minister of Defence on Industrial Mobilisation (D(52)19).
(4) Agreed that a firm decision on civil defence expenditure must await consideration of the report by the Chancellor of the Exchequer on

the financial resources likely to be available for defence, and of the new strategic appreciation by the Chiefs of Staff.

(5) Authorised the Home Secretary to proceed with the creation of an experimental mobile civil defence column.

[. . .]

Cabinet: conclusions
(Cabinet papers, 128/25)

15 May 1952
Secret
11 a.m.
Cabinet Meeting No. 53 of 1952

[. . .]

7. The Cabinet considered a memorandum by the Foreign Secretary (C(52)155) regarding a recommendation by the Consultative Assembly of the Council of Europe that a conference of European and Commonwealth countries should be convened to discuss the possibility of a closer economic association between Western Europe and the sterling area.

Discussion showed that the Cabinet were fully agreed on the desirability of discouraging this project for a conference on methods of promoting closer economic cooperation between Europe and the Commonwealth. There were, however, some differences of view on the detailed reasons for rejecting this project, which were set out in Annex B of C(52)155; on the extent to which other Commonwealth countries should be encouraged to maintain general liaison with the Council of Europe; and on the tactics to be followed in dealing with this particular recommendation of the Consultative Assembly.

Some Ministers, whilst accepting the Foreign Secretary's conclusion, were unwilling to endorse all the arguments in support of it which were set out in Annex B of C(52)155. They felt, in particular, that some of the statements in paragraph 3 of that Annex about the commercial interests of the United Kingdom were open to argument; and they thought it would be premature to take any final position on those points while the general question of commercial policy, with particular reference to the General Agreement on Tariffs and Trade, was under consideration by Ministers.

The Commonwealth Secretary said that he was impressed by the arguments set out in this Annex. In his view any attempt to create an economic association between Western Europe and the sterling Commonwealth would be likely to prejudice Commonwealth unity. Indeed, he thought it would be dangerous to suggest that, because of our position in Europe, the other Commonwealth countries should cultivate a close association of any kind with the Council of Europe. He feared that the effect of our pressing such a suggestion upon them would be to increase the likelihood that some of them might turn towards the United States.

The Prime Minister said that, while he would certainly deprecate any project for economic association between Europe and the sterling Commonwealth, he saw no reason to discourage other Commonwealth Governments from showing interest in the work of the Council of Europe. Political leaders in many Commonwealth countries had welcomed this movement towards European unity, as a valuable factor in preserving world peace; and as those countries had twice been involved in a world war originating in Europe, they would be ill-advised to disinterest themselves wholly from European affairs.

On the tactics to be followed if this recommendation was discussed at the forthcoming meeting of the Committee of Ministers of the Council of Europe, it was suggested that it would be inexpedient to ask the Consultative Assembly for a more explicit statement of the type of association which they had in mind. After discussion it was generally agreed that it would be unwise to refer the matter back for further consideration by the Assembly, since it was unlikely that any detailed proposals which the Assembly might formulate would be any more acceptable to us. The Commonwealth Secretary said that he would prefer that the Committee of Ministers should be invited to reject this recommendation outright. The preponderant view in the Cabinet was, however, that it would be wiser for the Foreign Secretary, if the matter came up for discussion at all, to point out its difficulties and to suggest that its further discussion should be adjourned.

The Cabinet –
  (1) Agreed that, if this proposal for closer economic association between Western Europe and the sterling Commonwealth came up for discussion at the forthcoming meeting of the Committee of Ministers of the Council of Europe, the Foreign Secretary should not suggest that it should be referred back for further consideration by the Consultative Assembly but, after pointing out its difficulties, should seek to secure that its further discussion should be adjourned for as long as possible.
  (2) Authorised the Commonwealth Secretary to inform other Commonwealth Governments of the line which the Foreign Secretary was proposing to take on this question at the forthcoming meeting of the Committee of Ministers.

The Cabinet considered the reply which the Prime Minister was proposing to give to a Parliamentary Question by Mr Geoffrey de Freitas,[1] MP, asking whether it was still the Government's policy to enable the House of Commons

---

[1] Geoffrey de Freitas, 1913–82. Barrister-at-Law, Lincoln's Inn. MP (Lab.) for Central Nottingham, 1945–50; for Lincoln, 1950–61; for Kettering, 1964–79. Parliamentary Secretary to PM, 1945–6. Under-Secretary of State for Air, 1946–50; at Home Office, 1950–1. President of Assembly, Council of Europe, 1966–9. Vice-President, European Parliament, 1975–9.

to debate the proceedings of the Council of Europe. While he agreed that Parliament ought to be able to review those proceedings, he would himself prefer that they should normally be discussed in the context of a general foreign affairs debate.

The Prime Minister said that, in deference to the Foreign Secretary's views, he would refrain from accepting any definite commitment at the present stage. But the Conservative Party, when in Opposition, had undertaken at Strasbourg that the House of Commons would review the Council's proceedings, and they had been willing to use Supply Days for that purpose. He did not think it would be consistent, when in Office, to decline as a matter of principle to find Government time for such a debate.

The Cabinet –

(3) Took note that the Prime Minister would state, in reply to this Question, that it was still the policy of Her Majesty's Government to do everything possible to enable the affairs of the Council of Europe to be debated in the House of Commons.

[...]

John Colville: diary
('The Fringes of Power', page 647)

15 May 1952

Tonight the PM and Mrs C gave a farewell dinner for the Eisenhowers at No. 10, on the eve of his departure from SHAPE to become a candidate in the Presidential Election. There were thirty-two to dinner, including most of the war-time Chiefs and the present Service Ministers – Alexanders, Tedders,[1] Alanbrookes, Portals, Jumbo Wilson,[2] Attlees, etc. Both the PM and Ike made admirable speeches. When Ike left he said that if he were elected he would pay

---

[1] Arthur William Tedder, 1890–1967. Educated at Whitgift and Magdalene College, Cambridge. Colonial Service (Fiji), 1914. Married, 1915, Rosalinde Maclardy (d. 1943): three children; 1943, Marie Black. On active service, RFC, France, 1915–17, and Egypt, 1918–19 (despatches thrice). Commanded 207 Sqn, Constantinople, 1922–3; Royal Navy Staff College, 1923–4; No. 2 Flying Training School, 1924–6. Director, RAF Staff College, 1921–9. Director of Training, Air Ministry, 1934–6. AOC RAF Singapore, 1936–8. Director-General, Research and Development, Air Ministry, 1938–40. Deputy AOC-in-C, RAF, Middle East, 1940–1; AOC-in-C, RAF, Middle East, 1941–3. Knighted, 1942. Air Chf Mshl, 1942. AOC-in-C, Mediterranean Air Command, 1943. Deputy Supreme Cdr (under Gen. Eisenhower), 1943–5. Baron, 1946. CAS, and 1st and Senior Air Member, Air Council, 1946–50. Chairman, British Joint Services Mission, Washington DC, 1950–1. Chancellor, University of Cambridge, 1950–67.

[2] Henry Maitland Wilson, 1881–1964. Known as 'Jumbo'. On active service in South Africa, 1899–1902; on the Western Front, 1914–17 (despatches, DSO). GOC-in-C, Egypt, 1939; in Cyrenaica, 1940; in Greece, 1941; in Palestine and Transjordan, 1941. Knighted, 1940. C-in-C, Allied forces in Syria, 1941; Persia–Iraq Command, 1942–3; Middle East, 1943. Supreme Allied Cdr, Mediterranean Theatre, 1944. FM, 1944. Head of British Joint Staff Mission, Washington DC, 1945–7. Baron, 1946.

MAY 1952   441

just one visit outside the USA – to the UK – in order to show our special relationship. The atmosphere could not have been more cordial – though things almost started badly with neither the PM nor Mrs C knowing that it was white tie and decorations.

John Colville: diary
('The Fringes of Power', page 647)

16 May 1952

Went to Chartwell this evening. Alone with the PM who is low. Of course the Government is in a trough, but his periods of lowness grow more frequent and his concentration less good. The bright and sparkling intervals still come, and they are still unequalled, but age is beginning to show. Tonight he spoke of coalition. The country needed it he said, and it must come. He would retire in order to make it possible; he might even make the demand for it an excuse for retiring. Four-fifths of the people of this country were agreed on four-fifths of the things to be done.

Lord Moran to Winston S. Churchill
(Premier papers, 11/495)

16 May 1952

My dear Prime Minister,
Thank you for your letter and enclosure.

Expenditure – I was only concerned as a doctor to explain to the laity in the Lords that the constant discovery of expensive new drugs and procedures – life savers – made economies inevitable. I recognized that, provided that the efficiency of the service was unaffected, the particular charges made must be governed by political expediency. The suggestion I made for cutting the fifty millions spent yearly on drugs was not original; it is the practice of two democracies. The Minister's rather trivial criticism of this procedure seems to overlook the fact that it has been found to work in Australia and Denmark.

Remuneration of Specialists – I am afraid I fail to follow the Minister's argument. The facts are not in dispute.

    (i) The Labour Government appointed two Spens[1] committees to consider what ought to be the remuneration of (a) general practitioners,

---

[1] William Spens, 1882–1962. Educated at Rugby and King's College, Cambridge. Fellow of Corpus Christi College, Cambridge, 1907–52; Master, 1927. Married, 1912, Dorothy Theresa: three children. Vice Chancellor, Cambridge University, 1931–3. Regional Commissioner for Civil Defence, Eastern Region, 1939–45. Chairman, Governing Body of Rugby School, 1944–58.

(b) specialists, in the new health service, 'with due regard to what have been the financial expectations of specialist practice in the past'.

(ii) In both the Spens practitioner committee and in the Spens specialist committee, their May 1948 report was based on Professor Bradford Hills'[1] investigation into the income tax returns of the net incomes of specialists and general practitioners before the war. Incomes earned in the year 1938–39 were taken because the committee decided that social and economic conditions were not yet sufficiently stable to justify taking a post war year.

(iii) The committee did not feel competent to translate these pre war incomes so as to produce corresponding incomes today. It was decided therefore to 'frame its recommendations in terms of 1939 value of money. . . . We leave to others the problem of the necessary adjustments to present day values of money'. The difference between 1939 values and 1950 values is called 'Betterment'.

(iv) The exact figure of betterment was in dispute until it was referred to arbitration. This led to Mr Justice Danckwert's award.

(v) The Spens recommendations were accepted by the Government, including betterment, and both specialists and general practitioners joined the service on that understanding.

I think the Minister cannot have been aware of these facts when he proposed that instead of honouring a commitment entered into by the Labour Government (a commitment already met in case of the practitioners) the Ministry should, if and when the specialists protest, embark on a theoretical dispute 'on the basis of proper relationship between the remuneration of general practitioners and that of specialists'.

Remuneration of Specialists 'Unduly generous' –

When the Minister says that 'in many quarters' the remuneration of specialists was felt to be 'unduly generous', he is not apparently in touch with informed opinion or indeed with the facts.

The feeling to which he refers was based on:

(a) The BMA, after the Bill became law, launched a skilful propaganda campaign in the course of which it was insinuated that general practitioners had had a raw deal in comparison with specialists. The BMA was careful not to mention that the remuneration in both cases had been decided in precisely the same manner; namely by a statistical investigation into the income tax returns for one year of specialists and general practitioners respectively, conducted by the

---

[1] Austin Bradford Hill, 1897–1991. Prof. of Medical Statistics, London School of Hygiene and Tropical Medicine, University of London, 1945–61; Dean, 1955–7. Hon. Director of Statistical Research Unit, Medical Research Council, 1945–61. President, Royal Statistical Society, 1950–2. FRS, 1954. Knighted, 1961.

same individual, Bradford Hill, and forwarded to the two committees which had the same chairman, Sir Will Spens.

(b) The BMA was supported by the Vice-Chancellors. As long ago as 1913 a Royal Commission recommended that whole-time Professors of Medicine, Surgery and Obstetrics should be appointed. This was implemented in 1919. These professors were paid £2,000 per annum. Immediately the non-medical faculties got up in arms. Why should a professor of medicine be paid £2,000 and a professor of history only £1,000? But the Government of the day recognised that it was a question of supply and demand, and for more than thirty years their decision has been endorsed by successive governments. Nevertheless when the awards system was introduced, the Vice-Chancellors seized the opportunity to refloat the old controversy, in the course of which frequent visits were made to Sir Stafford Cripps at the Treasury. It is the Vice Chancellors the Minister has in mind when he talks of 'Representatives in University Circles'.

When the Bill became law the BMA continued to agitate for its revision; they threatened that the doctors would retire from the service unless their demands were met, and preparations were made for a strike, including a fighting fund. The specialists, though they intensely disliked certain aspects of the Act, felt that it was the law of the land and that they must make the best of things and help to work it. It is a new and disturbing doctrine that those who protest and prepare to strike against an Act of Parliament should be rewarded for their intransigence.[1]

John Colville: diary
('The Fringes of Power', page 647–8)

17 May 1952

A heatwave. I lunched alone with W who recited a great deal of poetry. While he slept in the afternoon I bathed in the swimming pool, and then we drove for two hours to Chequers. On the way he dictated notes for a speech to wind up the transport debate next Wednesday. He says he can only dictate in a car nowadays. His theme seems a good one: the nationalisation by the socialists of only 41,000 vehicles was for doctrinaire, not practical motives, and they need 80,000 people, including 12,000 clerks, to run them. Private owners (of transports for hire) to a total of 800,000 have been driven to the most uneconomic measures to survive. When he had finished he said to me: 'It is a great mistake to be too mechanically minded in affairs of State.'

---

[1] Churchill minuted Minister of Health Ian Macleod on May 29: 'Please give your personal attention to this and see what you can do. I attach much importance to Lord Moran's views' (M.70/53).

At Chequers were Lord Montgomery, Duchess of Devonshire (Moucha),[1] Antony and Dot Head,[2] Marques and Marquesa de Casa Valdes[3] and their pretty daughter Maria.[4]

The men sat up till 2.30 gossiping about strategy and Generals in a lively manner.

John Colville: diary
('The Fringes of Power', page 648)

18 May 1952

Heatwave intensified. Worked with W all the morning; sat on the lawn and gossiped most of the afternoon: walked on the monument hill (the whole party went, notwithstanding all the picnickers) after tea. Monty in role of grand inquisitor: how did the PM define a great man? Was Hitler great? (PM said No – he made too many mistakes). How could PM maintain that Napoleon was great when he was the Hitler of the nineteenth century? And surely the great religious leaders were the real great men? The PM said their greatness was indisputable but it was of a different kind. Christ's story was unequalled and his death to save sinners unsurpassed; moreover the Sermon on the Mount was the last word in ethics.

Monty has become a mellow, loveable exhibitionist; tamed but lonely and pathetic. He is not afraid of saying anything to anybody. But Maria de Casa Valdes scored (to Monty's great delight) when she asked him: 'But you tell me you don't drink, and you don't smoke: what *do* you do that is wrong? Bite your nails?'

Winston S. Churchill to Sir David Maxwell Fyfe
Prime Minister's Personal Minute M.292/52
(Premier papers, 11/30)

19 May 1952

I see that you are reducing the number of prison wardens in pursuit of the economy campaign. But the number of convicts has more than doubled since before the war. Pray let me know how this stands.

---

[1] Evelyn Emily Mary Petty-FitzMaurice, 1870–1960. Married, 1892, Victor Christian William Cavendish. Mistress of the Robes to Queen Mary, 1910–16, 1921–53. Viceregal Consort of Canada, 1916–21. GCVO, 1937. Duchess of Devonshire, 1950. JP for Derbyshire. Dame of Justice, Order of St John of Jerusalem.

[2] Dorothea Ashley-Cooper, 1907–87. Daughter of Anthony Ashley-Cooper, 9th Earl of Shaftesbury. Married, 1935, Antony Henry Head, 1st Viscount Head: four children.

[3] Félix Juan Valdés Armada, 1900–82. 3rd Marquis of Casa Valdés. Married, 1925, María Teresa Ozores Saavedra (1902–83): three children.

[4] María Valdés y Ozores, 1929–?. Married Jaime Mariátegui y Arteaga: 11 children.

May 1952

Sir David Maxwell Fyfe to Winston S. Churchill
(Premier papers, 11/30)

20 May 1952

The Treasury directed[1] as an economy measure that the Prison Staff (including all grades, administrative, executive, clerical and prison warders) should be reduced from 6064 (the staff in post on 1st October, 1951) to 6014 on the 30th June, 1952.

In order to ensure that the ceiling fixed by the Treasury was not exceeded by too rapid an increase in the rate of recruitment to the warder grade the Prison Commission found it necessary to give notice to some 34 temporary warders (of whom 13 were re-engaged pensioners aged 61 and over – the normal retiring age being 55). It is thus not true, as reported in the press, that notice has been given to every prison officer who had remained in the service after reaching the usual retiring age.

In view of the rapid and alarming growth in the Prison Population the Prison Commissioners are reopening with the Treasury as a matter of urgency the ceiling fixed for their staff and will press the Treasury to allow them a sufficiently high ceiling to enable them to have a reasonably minimum of prison warders.

I hope that I can count on your support if necessary.[2]

John Colville: diary
('The Fringes of Power', page 648–9)

20 May 1952

This evening Brendan, with whom I had a drink, was very gloomy about the Government's prospect, doubtful about W's ability to go on and highly critical of R. A. Butler whose financial policy he has been attacking vigorously in the *Financial Times*.

Anthony Eden to Winston S. Churchill
(Premier papers, 11/156)

21 May 1952
Top Secret
PM/52/55

You should know that there is a difficulty over the procedure to be followed in Western Europe if a Russian attack seems imminent.

---

[1] Churchill wrote in the margin: 'You are responsible unless you appeal to the Cabinet.'
[2] Churchill wrote at the bottom of the page: 'On no account reduce the number of prison warders while the prison population is rapidly increasing. I am also shocked about the "3 in a cell" condition.'

2. We have always taken the view that the decision to call an 'alert' (which presupposes a time of international tension, when measures contemplating imminent war might themselves have grave consequences) cannot be left to military commanders alone but must have political approval. The Emergency Defence Plan prepared by SHAPE, on the other hand, authorises military commanders in certain circumstances to declare alerts on their own responsibility. The Standing Group, to whom SHAPE submitted the Plan, have failed to discuss it because the US member is without instructions from his Government. In the absence of any response from the Standing Group, SHAPE have made the Plan effective as an interim measure, although they realise that there may be political implications to be considered by the North Atlantic Council.

3. We have now agreed to a private exchange of views with the Americans, which we hope will lead to an early discussion of the SHAPE Plan by the Standing Group. The British member will then insist that the question of 'alerts' should be referred to the North Atlantic Council in view of its political implications. When the question comes before the North Atlantic Council, ministerial approval will be sought (perhaps through the Defence Committee) for the instructions to be sent to the United Kingdom Permanent Representative.[1]

4. This minute has been prepared in consultation with the Ministry of Defence, and I am sending a copy of it to Alexander.

John Colville: diary
('The Fringes of Power', page 649)

21 May 1952

Transport debate in House of Commons. W who spoke fifth made a good impression, but I cannot help feeling it is both wrong and foolish to denationalise transport and steel, however doctrinaire may have been the motives of the late Government in nationalising them. When the Labour Government get back they will be renationalised and this political game is not only unsettling for the economic life of the country but a blow to the constitutional 'Gentleman's Agreement' that one Government did not normally set about undoing the work of its predecessor. It is clear that a large element in the Tory party feel the same.

---

[1] Churchill wrote here in the margin on May 25: 'How long will this take? Shall we be able to agree about the "Alert" before the "Attack" occurs?'

May 1952

Winston S. Churchill: speech
(Hansard)

21 May 1952   House of Commons

TRANSPORT (GOVERNMENT POLICY)

I am sure that the House welcomed the tone and spirit of the speech which the hon. Member for Bradford, East (Mr McLeavy)[1] has just delivered. I should like to assure him that nothing is nearer to our wishes than to consult the Trades Union Congress, and particularly the important union that he mentioned, upon matters of this kind which have so close a contact with immediate affairs. The course we are taking will give plenty of opportunity for such consultation. If the answer was only a formal one in December last, it was because these matters were in a state of flux and consideration, and because the Government must at least make up their own mind and see clearly what their main line of advance must be before they go hawking their ideas around in all quarters. But the course that we are taking now will give ample opportunity. That is why we have brought out this White Paper – good or bad. It is brought out now in plenty of time to enable opinions to be collected and expressed from all quarters, friendly and unfriendly. The White Paper is, I think, a guide rather than a rule. It expresses our aims and policies, but it is capable of being influenced and affected by public opinion and by the consultations we shall have.

The right hon. Gentleman the Member for Lewisham, South (Mr H. Morrison), also complained that the Transport Commission have not been consulted fully beforehand. Considering how much they were affected by our declared intention to denationalize road haulage – an intention declared so plainly that, if we had not acted upon it, we should have been taunted from that side of the House with going back on our promises – it was not, in the circumstances, really quite possible to consult with these appointees of the late Government about all the details of altering the legislation on which they depended and which they were administering. We have looked at it from a different angle, but, now that the facts are known and our policy has been brought forward in the White Paper, we shall, of course, welcome consultations with Lord Hurcomb and his colleagues, and I trust that they will continue to give us their assistance in arriving at the best solution possible.

The right hon. Member for Lewisham, South, is a curious mixture of geniality and venom. The geniality, I may say after a great many years of experience, is natural to himself. The venom has to be adopted in order to keep on side with the forces below the Gangway. Some parts of his speech were unexpectedly moderate, but, obviously, he had thought it necessary to

---

[1] Frank McLeavy, 1889–1976. MP (Lab.) for Bradford East, 1945–66. Baron, 1967.

prepare the way, as I often see hon. Gentlemen doing, in putting himself on good terms below the Gangway by saying a number of things in which I know he does not believe and of which I am sure he is ashamed. The right hon. Gentleman accused me of being cowardly in asking my right hon. Friend to open the debate.

There is another thing which the right hon. Gentleman said which I thought was rather unworthy of him, and that was when he said that we did not know and we did not care what happened to the 80,000 workers employed. I should have thought that, apart from all questions of philanthropy and good comradeship, decent humanity and even self-interest would have actuated a Government in that matter, but we shall, in fact, embody in our action the exact clauses – Sections 98, 101 and 102 – of the Socialist Government's Act of 1947, which deal with compensation and pensions. Nobody ever dreamed that any contrary course would be adopted.

The right hon. Gentleman went on to use a really insulting taunt. He said that we were under some sort of obligation to the Road Haulage Association. We are under no such obligation of any kind; not at all. They have never even been consulted in the matter. It is quite true that they had an agitation in the country, and that some of us agree with what they said, but our association with them is entirely non-existent in any form at all, and in no way compares with the close association in so many ways of the party opposite with the Co-operators,[1] without whose influential counsel I doubt very much whether 'C' licences would ever have existed at all.

I have been drawn into this question on which I speak tonight because it transcends ordinary Departmental measures, and is a part of the main policy of Her Majesty's Government. It illustrates more clearly than almost any other example the fallacy of doctrinaire nationalization, as opposed to the fertility of regulated private enterprise. Therefore, it really represents, as was complained of by the Liberals, the doctrinaire division, the great division in principle, between the two principal parties in the State and the two sides of the House. I should like to say that no step has been taken by me without the approval of the Cabinet. The decision to intervene on the suddenly announced increased transport charges – the increase of fares – was the result of a five-hour Cabinet meeting on this subject on the Thursday before Easter, when the full legal rights of the Government of the day were examined, set forth and explained to us by the Law Officers and the Lord Chancellor. The Cabinet left the drafting of the communiqué and the timing of its issue and publication to me. That was the extent of my personal action, though I had and have very strong opinions upon what should be done.

---

[1] The reference is probably to the Salter Committee, chaired by Arthur Salter, which sat in 1932; its report, delivered in 1933, directed transport funding policy for decades to follow.

Leaving these current issues, let me say that we felt it our duty, in accordance with the public pledges that we have given, to reverse the legislation of the previous Government about road haulage.

This was not in a spirit of mere contrariness. We are convinced that a very considerable and needless injury was done to the national economy by the compulsory acquisition by the State of a section, only numerically a small section, of road transport, and we are sure that the arrangements which we propose to make will be a real help to public convenience and, consequently, to general recovery in these critical years.

This White Paper – I quite agree that I am not its author, and I dare say, in some ways, it has the defects which attach to a document which has been many times considered and in which many minds and many hands have played their part in arriving at the complete agreement – and the Bill which is being founded upon it have been the result of prolonged Cabinet study, beginning as soon as the Government was formed in November last. The Ministry of Transport, under the ex-Minister, whose loss through ill-health we greatly regret, worked in the closest harmony with Lord Leathers whose long proved practical business efficiency was of so much service to us in the war.

I have seen it suggested that this White Paper was a hurriedly produced document. In fact, it has been before the Cabinet for several months, and this is, I think – I am sure – the fifth edition. (*Interruption.*) We are stating our opinion, good faith and sincerity against all hon. and right hon. Members have to say on the other side. When we became aware that the denationalization of road transport was even more urgent in the public interest than that of steel, we decided to lay this White Paper before Parliament, in order to carry the House with us and to do just what I have said, to profit by the movement of opinion on this intricate subject without in any way weakening our main purpose.

The draftsmen have long been engaged upon the Bill, and we propose that it should be brought before the House in July. Meanwhile, we shall carefully reflect on well-grounded criticism, and, of course, consult the Transport Commission, as I have already replied to the hon. Member for Bradford, East.

It has been suggested that there was no need to sell back to private enterprise the nationalized road haulage vehicles. It is no doubt true that the simple raising of the mileage of the 'A' and 'B' licences from twenty-five to even as little as forty miles would expose the Road Haulage Executive to destructive competition, plunging them into a growing deficit, affecting, in its turn, the British Transport Commission as a whole. The twenty-five-mile limit is the radius. Therefore, it is really fifty miles, and to lift that to sixty or even to forty would be to make an enormous difference, and it is quite clear that if we had taken that course it would have produced a much less smooth and speedy method than the one we propose in the White Paper and which we intend to embody in the Bill.

The Amendment dwells, first, upon the 'properly integrated' transport system which it alleges we are seeking to destroy. This is no true description of the present system of operating the road and rail services under the Transport Commission. The Railway Executive and the Road Haulage Executive are operated as separate entities, and the road undertaking can quite easily be disposed of separately. A transport system, whether 'properly integrated' or not, exists to serve the community, and must be judged not by its quality of integration, but by the quality of its service to the public.

The 1947 Act is not a 'properly integrated' system. It has not led to a more speedy or efficient service or to one more ready to adapt itself to the varied and often urgent practical requirements of trade and industry. That is the position in which we found ourselves. But we need not exaggerate the magnitude of the actual physical step we are taking. Some figures, with which I agree, were mentioned by the right hon. Gentleman. Altogether, there are nearly a million vehicles on the roads which are involved. Of these numbers only about a twentieth part have been nationalized – 41,000, and then there are the 14,000 which rest with the railway companies, but I am speaking of the 41,000 – and all the rest are run by private enterprise under 'A', 'B' and 'C' licences.

We propose to transfer back that twentieth part from the State to the private user, or, if you like, to the general public. That is our intention. Our hope and our belief is that the liberation of this small though important part of our road transport will enable goods and services to be interchanged over the whole area of road transport in an easier, more flexible and more convenient manner than at present, and in our struggle to earn our livelihood and thus win survival in the modern world this is a factor which cannot be set aside.

It would be a wrong thing to complicate, hamper and often frustrate the whole organization and flow of road transport just for the sake of allowing one section of it – albeit important long-distance – to remain under State management at the cost of imposing a vast mass of restrictions on all the rest. This is the case which we submit to the House and which will be argued out by all the processes of Parliamentary discussion when the Bill is in due course presented to the House. We believe, rightly or wrongly but sincerely, that a thoroughly bad arrangement is going forward now. Take, for instance, the 'C' licences. Forty-one thousand road vehicles, apart from the 14,000 of the railways, are nationalized and are run by the State for general purposes. Under 'C' licences alone over 800,000 are run by private people carrying their own goods without limit of distance, but allowed to carry only their own goods, so that the late Government, as I said, did not dare to abolish this right or privilege.

It is, of course, often a wasteful process to run an enormous number of vehicles which are restricted in this way. Many of them only carry half their full load on many journeys and many more, nay a vast majority, come back empty. Think of the petrol, and tyres, the wear and tear of the vehicles; the labour lost in driving them; the resultant overcrowding of the roads. This is a point which is not novel. It has often been made in debates in the House, and most frequently by Members of the party opposite. Socialist Members who have spoken in that sense must face fairly and squarely the reason for what is being done and what has happened.

Industrialists with their mind properly on costs – profit if you will – would not have taken the expensive course of operating under 'C' licences if they could have got from nationalized long-distance transport the facilities which industry and production need and are well entitled to expect. When the late Government, for reasons which I have described, exempted the 'C' licences and nationalized 41,000 important long distance vehicles and restricted to a 25-mile radius the 110,000 free haulage vehicles operating under 'A' and 'B' licences, they condemned the overwhelming proportion of our road transport to what everyone can see is a thoroughly wasteful misuse of our hard-pressed resources. It is indeed remarkable that the consequence of the Government nationalizing so small a section of the road vehicles has been to double the 'C' licences. Before the war there were fewer than 400,000, mostly short-distance delivery vans; now there are over 800,000. In the last four years nearly half the owners of the road transport have sought to escape becoming dependent upon the Government, and have chosen instead to put up with these obviously unsound economic conditions under which 'C' licence holders work, like going often with half loads and many returning quite empty.

Is this a party question? I do not think it is, because many misgivings were felt on that side of the House and we feel them here. Can we really afford to hamper ourselves in this extraordinary manner? Think of it. Four hundred thousand, or 350,000, more road vehicles working only for private ownership – not private enterprise, because enterprise is crippled – rather than undergo the inconveniences of an inferior service in an economic sense offered by the State. What is the use of talking about a properly integrated system of transport, when the great change which has so far resulted has been this enormous increase of between 350,000 and 400,000 'C' licence road vehicles? No one ought to be content with a thing like that going on. There is an argument – I think it is a bad argument; nevertheless, it is a classic Socialist argument – for forcing every load to be carried by the method chosen by the State.

There is an argument – which I am venturing to present this evening – for setting free this small section under State control and allowing it to be merged in a general harmonious system of regulated private enterprise. Surely, today, although we differ on the remedy, we might agree we are now having the worst of both worlds. I will make allowance for the fact that the scheme of the party opposite has not reached its full conclusion. But let us just look at these 41,000 vehicles under the Road Haulage Executive. I am coming to the railway aspect presently. I must apologize for detaining the House and I will curtail my remarks as much as possible, but I feel we owe it to Parliament and the nation to show that what we do is out of no mere mood of partisanship or desire to undo what was done but because we firmly believe that we can produce by the process of liberation a beneficial accretion to our national wealth.

The 41,000 vehicles are about, as I have said, a twentieth of the road transport in question today. They are an eighth part only of those which have sprung into being under 'C' licences while the nationalized 41,000 vehicles were being taken over. It was pretty hard on people who had for many years run small but efficient businesses – the man driving the van and the wife keeping the accounts – that often happens – when their vehicles were acquired under the 1947 Act.

True, they were paid a large sum – £30 million – for the goodwill they had built up. (An Hon. Member: 'A fair price.') I suppose at a fair price, the party opposite were responsible. Still, many of them bitterly resented the treatment they received, and a proportion of the smaller people took their share of the £30 million compensation and have now left the country for the Dominions and the Commonwealth.

The taking of these vehicles over was a harsh and unreasonable thing to do, even though the Socialist Government, in accordance with their hitherto correct principles of compensation, paid out this large sum of money. I say 'hitherto' because I shall have a word to say about that later. It pleased nobody except the politicians pursuing the theme of nationalization. Here was the variegated field of road transport, all of which had grown up naturally, responding from day to day to the laws of supply and demand, and corrected by the penalties constantly operative which befall private enterprise when it is unsuccessful. Here it was before us. This represented the end of a long process of the survival of the fittest.

What have we now? We have the 800,000 private vehicles under specialized ownership which forbids them to touch any goods but their own. We have 50,000 under the 'A' licences and 60,000 under the 'B' licences, and against all this vast field of privately owned transport 41,000 nationalized vehicles to be managed by the Road Haulage Executive. Let us just see how they have managed their sphere. I make all allowances for their difficulties. The fact remains that the 41,000 nationalized road vehicles, apart altogether from those who drive them and keep them, and apart also from over 6,000 operating and maintenance clerical staff, require a headquarters and have set up a headquarters and administration staff of no fewer than 12,000 clerical and administration personnel. The exact figure I have been furnished with is 12,348.

I am told that the Road Haulage Executive staff of 12,000 which has sprung into being costs more than £6 million a year. I am told that is probably many times as much money as would be needed if these 41,000 vehicles were allowed once again to be merged in the general system of road transport. The whole of this vast apparatus has been brought into being to manage a twentieth of the road haulage vehicles of the country. This lies upon us as a dead weight and is an unnecessary burden upon our intimate communications which are a vital factor in our economic life. The question we have to ask is why should this have been done, and, if it has been done, why should it go on?

Now we come to the railways. I have never been shocked by the idea of nationalizing the railways. In fact, I believe I proposed it on my own before almost all the Members of the House had even thought about going to Parliament. I am by no means sure I have been right. It is no part of my case that I am always right.

Anyhow, we have to face the facts. The railways are and will remain nationalized, and the Tory Party will do their utmost to make them a great, living, lasting success in the vital, though limited, sphere that is open to them. If we wanted to do the most idiotic thing that we could conceive, it would be for our countrymen to divide themselves into two gangs, one lot backing road transport and the other backing rail, and trying to fight a political battle on that intimate and delicate, and in some respects tormented, front.

There is no development of road transport which can replace the services rendered by the railways. There are immense classes of traffic which only the railways can carry. There are important classes of non-remunerative traffic which must be carried. There are military needs – and I do not mean only definite military needs; this country cannot possibly get on in time of war by road transport alone, however great its development may be. There are military needs, as the right hon. Member for Lewisham, South said in a thoughtful passage of his speech the other day, which only the railways can fulfil.

We accept the nationalization of the railways. We do not mean to see them let down or maltreated in the vital and indispensable service they have given us. I do not look upon the railways – I rather echo the eloquent words of my right hon. Friend the Minister of Transport – and the harbour and port authorities connected with them, as a purely commercial business. I have a feeling that associates them with the defensive services of our island. Well do we remember how, in all their various ways, the railwaymen and their comrades stood by us in all the trials through which we made our way in the war.

There are, no doubt, great opportunities for improving the administration of the railways. Decentralization, we hope, will yield fruits. Anyhow, it will bring about a revival of the old stimulus of competition – or disinterested competition, if you like. This, while not hampering the making of *Bradshaw* or the *ABC*, gave everyone employed a feeling of *esprit de corps*.

Then there is the levy on road transport of £4 million a year – not much to put upon the broad backs of liberated and free road transport; once set free, they will take it in their stride – but at least, the levy meets the actual purchase price of the goodwill and it will increase in the future only as new traffic is taken over from the railways. In this it offers them a solid security without hampering private enterprise road transport at all. Thus we believe that road and rail, Socialist and Tory, and even Liberals – although I fear they regard it as very essential to their position to find fault with whatever is done – might all live happily together in this field to the advantage of everyone.

I ventured to put these points before the House because I am anxious that hon. Members should appreciate with how much care, zeal and earnestness we on this side of the House have worked to try to remedy the evil plight into which we have got, in a manner which will be conducive to the public advantage. But there is one grave issue to which I must refer before I conclude, and that is the threat to renationalize road haulage without paying fair compensation. The right hon. Member for Lewisham, South, did not like the word 'threat'. He called it a public duty and an act of decency. I admit that he somewhat toned down the statements which we have recently heard from less responsible members of his party and, I think, from their party organ. Nevertheless, the words he has used today deserve very careful attention and must be most carefully studied.

Hitherto, British Socialist policy has been to nationalize what industries they thought fit and to pay reasonable compensation to the owners and shareholders. This is a matter of principle in which they differ from the Communist Party. That and the maintenance of political liberty are the two main points of difference. I should not like to see them weaken those barriers at all. To establish the principle of confiscation, even though it was preceded by a threat – I beg pardon, by an act of decency – would be a departure from what has hitherto been a fundamental practice, and it would undoubtedly affect the whole aspect of our laws. If persons acting in good faith under the full authority of the Crown and Parliament are to be dispossessed without compensation, or with inadequate or unfair compensation, a new era will open. Of course, one Parliament may change or reverse the legislation of another. That is what we are going to do when we reach the month of July. It is quite a different thing to violate the broad equities of legal or commercial transactions. It would not only affect our credit in many directions, but the constitutional authority of Parliament itself would be impugned.

Mr H. Morrison (Lewisham, South): The right hon. Gentleman heard my speech. I said nothing to justify these observations. I said that we would pay compensation which, in all the circumstances of the case, would be fair, but that we must be fair to the community as well as to individuals, and that while we were against confiscation of private property we were equally against, and must protect the community against, the confiscation of public property. The right hon. Gentleman's interpretation is not justified at all.

The Prime Minister: I am very glad to hear any reassurances of that kind, and I am willing to accept them for what they are worth. But we should certainly not be afraid to join issue with the party opposite on this ground. If the threat or act of public duty were taken seriously it would, of course, affect the value of the national property which we propose to sell. That will not deter us from proceeding with our policy. It would mean, however, that the purchasers might get it very cheap because of this new element of risk, and that the State would be the loser, perhaps by a large sum. The responsibility will not rest with those who are pursuing a constitutional and Parliamentary course with the full right and authority of the House of Commons, but it will rest with those who, by an unprecedented and non-constitutional action, will be inflicting a serious injury upon the nation for the undoubted advantage of private individuals who will get national property very cheap. The more these sales are prejudiced by this kind of talk in which the right hon. Gentleman and his party have been indulging, the more that evil will take place. It would seem, I should have thought, at any rate, only common prudence for the Opposition to wait and see what the situation and condition of the transport industry is before committing themselves, what may be long in advance, to steps hitherto accepted only by the Communist Party.

We believe that in less than the lifetime of this Parliament the benefits of a liberated road transport system, combined with the successful administration of the British Railways, may make it seem a very wrong and foolish thing to renationalize the road transport in a future Parliament. Thus the threat which is now made will be proved to have been vain and idle.

It might not, however, prevent it from having cost the State many millions of pounds and enabling individual purchasers to secure national property far below its value. I am sure that this has been carefully considered by the Leaders of the Opposition. I see evidences of it today, and the right hon. Gentleman's eagerness to interrupt me to express his position is a sign of grace in the matter; but, nevertheless, much harm may already have been done. Never, however, in any circumstances would we be justified in surrendering in the teeth of such a challenge the undoubted rights of Parliament to legislate as it chooses.

To sum up, we believe in both road and rail transport. We believe that they should be helped by both parties to play their vital part in the internal economy of our hard pressed society. We do not think that the levy on road transport will hamper its development and imperative expansion. We regard the temporary retention of the twenty-five-mile limit for certain classes of vehicles as no more than a lever and spur to the whole process of liberating road transport from its present tangle and restrictions. We have no intention either of cramping the full, natural expansion of road transport or of disinteresting ourselves in the future of the railways. We believe that a far better service will be available for the public as a result of the policy we are determined to pursue than what they would get if matters were simply allowed to drift.

21 May 1952

ISRAEL (LOAN REQUEST)

Mr Wyatt asked the Prime Minister whether he will make a statement on the letter he recently sent to the President of Israel informing him that Her Majesty's Government were not prepared to make a loan requested by the Government of Israel.

The Prime Minister: President Weizmann recently sent me a message asking that Her Majesty's Government should agree to make Israel a loan of £5 million in order to finance Israel's purchases of oil during the next six months. Her Majesty's Government gave this request the most careful and sympathetic consideration, but despite our understanding of the difficulties with which Israel is faced, we felt compelled to inform the President that the gravity of our own economic situation precluded us from making a loan.

Mr Wyatt: Could I ask the Prime Minister to reconsider this matter, because Israel plays an extremely important part now in the affairs of the Middle East and it is important that we should maintain our influence there? Is it not a fact that it was proposed that a large part – I think one-quarter of this loan of £5 million – should be repaid in dollars, which would give it an attraction to us from a commercial point of view?

The Prime Minister: I can assure the hon. Gentleman that it was only with the greatest regret that I bowed to what I was convinced were the commanding facts of the situation.

Mr Shinwell: But as very little assistance has been rendered by Her Majesty's Government, in opening up the Haifa refinery and assisting Israel to obtain supplies of oil, would not the right hon. Gentleman consider this matter? Will he have regard – there is no doubt that he will – to the military and defence aspects involved?

The Prime Minister: Yes, Sir. I have for a long time considered this matter of great importance, but every step has to be taken by the Government with great care in order not to complicate still further the situation in these quarters.

Mr Shinwell: Has the right hon. Gentleman observed that the United States Government has now decided to render arms assistance to Persia, apparently without consulting Her Majesty's Government? If the United States Government can render assistance to Persia, in view of what happened some time ago, surely Her Majesty's Government can render some assistance to Israel?

The Prime Minister: I sincerely think that all those matters ought carefully to be borne in mind.

Mr Wyatt: Is not the nub of this matter the re-opening of the Iraqi pipe-line, and did not the Prime Minister, when in opposition, say that his Government would carry out a strong policy on these matters, and these difficulties we have had with these other States in the Middle East would be cleared up? Could he tell us why the Iraqi pipeline has not been opened?

The Prime Minister: I do not think I could do so without a definite Question being put on the Paper. The complications of all these oil questions are considerable, and they are multiplied when the foreign diplomatic aspect is also involved.

Major Legge-Bourke[1]: Would my right hon. Friend give an assurance that before this matter is reconsidered he will do everything which lies in his power to get the co-operation of the Israeli Government in preventing frontier incidents affecting the Arabs?

The Prime Minister: I do not really think I am called upon to make any particular statement on that subject. That question should be put to the Foreign Secretary. It is with very deep regret that I have been convinced that it is not possible for us to give aid.

Mr Dalton:[2] Is the right hon Gentleman still open to re-conviction on this matter?

The Prime Minister: I am still open to reason, and it is because of reasons piling up one on top of the other that I have drawn the conclusion which was against my personal wishes, but that sometimes happens in life.

Mr George Porter:[3] May I ask the Prime Minister if, in determining the situation in regard to this particular request, full consideration was given to the considerable loss of trade which would have ensued to this country in regard to the previous discussions concerning a loan for Israel?

The Prime Minister: Yes, Sir. All these matters were taken into consideration.

---

[1] Edward Alexander Henry Legge-Bourke, 1914–73. Educated at Eton and Royal Military College, Sandhurst. Joined Royal Horse Guards, 1934. Married, 1938, Catherine Jean Grant: three children. Maj., 1944. MP (Cons.) for Isle of Ely, 1945–73. Chairman, 1922 Committee of Conservative backbenchers, 1970–2.

[2] Edward Hugh John Neale Dalton, 1887–1962. Educated at Eton and King's College, Cambridge. Called to the Bar, 1914. On active service in France and Italy, 1914–18. Reader in Commerce, University of London, 1920–5; Reader in Economics, 1925–6. MP (Lab.) for Camberwell, 1924–9; for Bishop Auckland, 1929–31, 1935–59. Parliamentary Under-Secretary, FO, 1929–31. Chairman, Labour Party National Executive, 1936–7. Minister of Economic Warfare, 1940–2. President of the Board of Trade, 1942–5. Chancellor of the Exchequer, 1945–7; resigned over a Budget leak, 1947. Minister of Town and Country Planning, 1950–1. Baron, 1960.

[3] George Porter, 1883–1974. MP (Lab.) for Leeds Central, 1945–55.

MAY 1952

House of Commons: Official Report
(Hansard)

21 May 1952

Lieut.-Colonel Lipton[1] asked the Prime Minister whether he will depute the Paymaster-General to observe the forthcoming atomic test in Australia.

The Prime Minister (Mr Winston Churchill): As stated in my reply to the hon. Member for Bermondsey (Mr Mellish) on 25th February, no Ministers will be visiting Australia to view the test of the United Kingdom atomic weapon there.[2]

Lieut.-Colonel Lipton: Does the Prime Minister really favour the discharge at such long distance of the responsibilities of the Paymaster-General in the field of atomic development? Would it not, perhaps, be in the public interest to ensure that, as between the Paymaster-General and the forthcoming explosion, there should be a somewhat closer contact?

Lieut.-Colonel Lipton asked the Prime Minister which other Governments have been invited to send observers to the forthcoming atomic test in Australia.

The Prime Minister: None, Sir.

Lieut.-Colonel Lipton: Is it not desirable, at a time when the economic and other relationships between the Commonwealth countries are more disrupted than ever it has been, that, in this respect at any rate, they should be brought into consideration which would enable Commonwealth observers to be present, if not Australian observers too? – May I ask if the Prime Minister will condescend to answer that question, because it seems that Commonwealth relations are involved to some extent? If he is not interested in the matter, then, of course, he need not answer the question.

The Prime Minister: It was after full consideration of all those points that I gave my somewhat comprehensive answer, 'None, Sir'.

Mr Emrys Hughes: asked the Prime Minister to what extent the safety of bird and animal life has been considered in relation to the atomic weapon tests that are to be carried out at the Montebello Islands, Australia.

The Prime Minister: The report of a recent special survey showing that there is very little animal or bird life on the Montebello Islands was one of the factors in the choice of the site for the test of the United Kingdom atomic weapon.

I should add, however, that an expedition which went to the islands 50 years ago reported that giant rats, wild cats and wallabies were seen, and these may have caused the hon. Member some anxiety. However, the officer who explored the islands recently says that he found only some lizards, two sea eagles and what looked like a canary sitting on a perch.

---

[1] Marcus Lipton, 1900–78. Educated at Merton College, Oxford. Member, Stepney Borough Council, 1934–7. Served in British Army during WWII. Lt-Col., 1945. MP (Lab.) for Brixton, 1945–74; for Lambeth Central, 1974–8.

[2] See House of Commons: Oral Answers, Feb. 25, reproduced above (pp. 282–3).

Mr Hughes: Will the Prime Minister tell us whether any competent officer will go on this expedition? Is he aware that there are still civilised people in this country who are interested in bird and animal life? Will he get some report which will satisfy civilised human beings that no unnecessary destruction of wild life will take place?

The Prime Minister: Certainly. I think everything should be done to avoid the destruction of bird life and animal life and also of human life.

Cabinet: conclusions
(Cabinet papers, 128/25)

22 May 1952
Secret
11 a.m.
Cabinet Meeting No. 55 of 1952

[...]

5. The Cabinet had before them a memorandum by the Chancellor of the Exchequer (C(52)166) reviewing the economic situation and describing the policy which he proposed to follow in order to regain economic stability and to build up a strong, free and prosperous country. The memorandum summarised the causes of our economic weakness, viz., the loss of capital wealth during the war and the deterioration in the terms of trade; the increase in social expenditure and in standards of amenity at home; the growing cost of defence; and the pressure on our overseas account resulting from our present liabilities, the need to build up our reserves and the need for overseas investment. It then reviewed the main economic and financial problems which had to be solved, viz., the management of sterling as a world currency; the limitation of our overseas commitments to correspond with our economic strength; the control of imports and the encouragement of exports, especially of coal; the control of internal inflation, the limitation of Government expenditure, the control of investment and the review of the resources devoted to defence production.

The Chancellor of the Exchequer said that there were indications that the recent improvement in our overseas account might not be maintained. Unjustified criticisms of our financial and fiscal policy in some sections of the Press were having an adverse effect on confidence. Steps were being taken to counter this. He thought that among the suggestions for action made in C(52)166 the most urgent were those for Ministerial review of (i) the possibility of diverting from defence production to exports some part of the capacity of the metal-using industries and (ii) our overseas expenditure on military purposes and in support of our foreign policy.

The Colonial Secretary said that, while he was in general agreement with the Chancellor's memorandum, he thought that it laid too much stress on increasing the export of highly-developed manufactured goods which were difficult to sell and too little on increasing the production and export of raw materials both at home and in other parts of the Commonwealth. We must of course export the products of our skill and craftsmanship but we must not neglect primary production at home (*e.g.* steel) or the long-term prospects of restoring an economic balance between the dollar and the non-dollar world by further development of the resources of the Commonwealth.

The President of the Board of Trade supported this view and suggested that it should be kept in mind in the forthcoming study of commercial policy. We must recognise that, if we were to buy less from dollar sources, we must also expect to sell less to dollar countries. This would increase the importance of developing production in the Commonwealth and trade exchanges with it. He attached great importance to the proposal in paragraph 9 of C(52)166 that the needs of the export trade should not be subordinated, as at present they were, to any other objective.

The Prime Minister said that there should be no interference with the special priority accorded to certain types of arms production.

The Minister of Supply said that, outside that limited field, he was at present proceeding on the basis that in those industries with which he was concerned production for defence and for export should rank as of equal importance. Production of the less essential types of defence equipment could be slowed down if the Cabinet should so desire, though a switch to production for export would take some little time to bring about. He was already considering in which directions engineering exports could most readily and most profitably be expanded, and he would report to the Cabinet on the means of doing this with the least damage to the defence programme.

The Cabinet –

Agreed to resume their examination of the economic situation at a later meeting.

General Dwight D. Eisenhower to Winston S. Churchill
(Churchill papers, 2/217)

22 May 1952

Dear Prime Minister,

If I had been given a wish how I would spend my last night in England before saying farewell, I could not have had it fulfilled in all respects so completely as I did at your dinner party last Thursday.

Mrs Eisenhower and I thank you and Mrs Churchill most sincerely for your great kindness in giving a dinner in our honor. It was indeed a privilege to be present at such a distinguished gathering of old and trusted friends with you at their head. It was for me a memorable evening of friendship and understanding.

I need hardly tell you how much I appreciate the high honor which you have recommended should be bestowed on Brigadier Gault.[1] I realize full well that, aside from the Brigadier's worthiness, this is another example of your never-failing friendship, which has been one of my most heartwarming experiences during the past ten years. I value and treasure my good fortune.

With my best wishes and warm personal regard,

Lord Quickswood[2] to Winston S. Churchill
(Premier papers, 11/119)

22 May 1952

My dear Winston,

I venture to write to suggest to you that Ellis (L. S.) Amery should be made a peer. When your Government of '45 left office, his son[3] was about to be hanged for treason, which naturally made the offer of a peerage to the father impossible. But it is one of the advantages of capital punishment that the family are freed, at any rate after a few years, from the connection with the culprit's crime. I don't know whether you read the private paper which Amery wrote about his son, but I thought it both touching and in a large measure convincing. I suggest, therefore, that Amery's previous tenure of Cabinet office for many years, which would normally have qualified him for a peerage, should now be remembered, and the customary honour be bestowed on him.

As I am writing, I cannot help saying that I do not understand why the Allies do not release all those prisoners of war who hate the Communists so much that they will not go back to be under them, and having released them the Allies could cheerfully consent to the Communists' demand for the repatriation of prisoners, since only prisoners who liked the Communists would remain. I do not think there is any international law which prevents a government releasing any prisoner of war it pleases. I suppose these poor anti-Communist people want to go either to Formosa or to Japan, and in this case, they might be helped on their journey.

I am very well and very cheerful, for I live in perfect tranquillity, which is what all my life I have desired. My eyesight does not allow me to read, and aided by the wireless and an ingenious talking book contrivance, I do not find the handicap so intolerable as one might expect. Oddly, it affects my

---

[1] James Frederick Gault, 1902–77. Educated at Eton and Trinity College, Cambridge. Served with Scots Guards during WWII. Military Assistant to Gen. Eisenhower, 1944–5. Col., 1944. OBE, 1946. Brig., 1950. Military Assistant, Supreme Commander Allied Powers in Europe, 1951–3. KCMG, 1952.

[2] Hugh Richard Heathcote Gascoyne-Cecil, 1869–1956. Known as 'Linky'. Educated at Eton and University College, Oxford. MP (Cons.) for Greenwich, 1895–1906; for Oxford University, 1910–37. 'Best man' at Churchill's wedding, 1908. Provost of Eton, 1936–44. Baron Quickswood, 1941.

[3] John Amery, 1912–45. Sought to recruit a British force among POWs to fight alongside the Germans, 1942–4. Captured by Communist partisans and returned to England, 1945. Arraigned for treason and pleaded guilty. Hanged, 1945.

writing far more than my reading, and as you will see my signature suffers in consequence, for I cannot see at all what I am doing at the moment though afterwards I can read the signature which I have written.

I have always been impatient of what is called 'nature' in respect to illness and infirmities, and I utterly deny that it is divine, though it is just conceivable that it may be angelic, for one can imagine incompetent but well-intentioned angels. It seems more likely to be the subliminal self, which is always doing silly things; but as I say, notwithstanding nature, I am very well and happy.

Winston S. Churchill to Lord De L'Isle and Dudley
Prime Minister's Personal Minute M.294/52
(Premier papers, 11/209)

23 May 1952

The power of the Secretary of State is best wielded from his desk.

I am much concerned at the economics which will have to be made in the Air Force, and am sure that considerable reductions in expenditure and manpower can be achieved without in any way preventing the increase in fighting power which has been so much neglected in the past.

How much will this very extensive tour cost? I agree that if you go at all it would be well to include Australasia. Who would you take with you? You would want an officer of medium rank and high quality, able to help you in effecting substantial reductions in redundant air ground staff. Of these places that you wish to visit the ones most affecting our major problems are Malta, Habbaniyah, Cyprus, Cyrenaica and Tripolitania. Singapore and Kuala Lumpur have been already visited by Mr Lyttelton but you would have to go through them anyway.

Winston S. Churchill to Roy Welensky[1]
(Churchill papers, 6/2)

23 May 1952

Dear Mr Welensky,

I quite understand your regret that Mr Lennox-Boyd should have left the Colonial Office for the Ministry of Transport but you can be assured that his transfer from there to take full charge of an important Department of State

---

[1] Roy Welensky, 1907–91. Employed with Rhodesia Railways, 1921; Chairman of Broken Hill Branch, 1933. Member, Northern Rhodesian Legislative Council, 1938. Formed Northern Rhodesian Labour Party, 1941. Proposed federation of Rhodesia. Member, federal legislature (United Federal Party), 1953. Rhodesian Minister of Transport, 1953–6. PM of Rhodesian Federation, 1956–63. Moved to England, 1981.

does not mean in any way a lessening of the Government's interest in the Colonies. On the contrary the importance of the Colonies, particularly the economic importance to which you refer, is fully recognised by Her Majesty's Government.

I am confident that, as Minister of State under Mr Lyttelton, Mr Hopkinson will be a worthy successor to Mr Lennox-Boyd.

John Colville: diary
('The Fringes of Power', page 649)

23 May 1952

W, who had been at Chartwell all day, came up to speak at a Tax Inspectors' dinner with a speech almost entirely written by me. This is indeed a sign of advancing senility – and it wasn't nearly as good as the one I wrote for him at Ottawa.

Lord Cherwell to Winston S. Churchill
(Premier papers, 11/270)

23 May 1952

RAF MANPOWER

At present we have in the RAF about 1600 operational aircraft i.e. nearly 200 less than originally planned. The detailed distribution by types and by commands is shown in the album of Defence Charts which I send you regularly.

The Ministry of Supply expect to produce about 1300 operational aircraft in 1952/53 and more in future years; but we are using many of them to replace obsolete types; moreover about one quarter of the aircraft in squadrons are written off every year for one cause or another. The Secretary of State hopes that the front line strength will rise to 2130 over the year and to about 3000 by March 1955. It is to meet this increase of 92% that he asks for an increase in manpower above the March 1952 figure of 33%.

At present we have about 160 men in the Air Force per operational aircraft. If the increase is granted this number would fall to 110 per aircraft in March 1955. Towards the end of the last war we had something like 120–130 per aircraft.

As the economic position seems to be developing it appears unlikely, unless big cuts are made elsewhere, that the Air Force will be able to afford all the aircraft being produced and the surplus (which, no doubt, would not include any of the 'super-priority' types) may have to be sold abroad, as with the

Centurion tanks. If this is so, there seems no case for increasing the manpower ceiling above the 297,500 men and women given in the Defence White Paper. A decision to allow such an increase should therefore in my view await our discussions next month on the size of our future defence effort.

I attach a chart summarising the statistics given in the Appendix to the Secretary of State's minute.

Winston S. Churchill to Sir William Strang
Prime Minister's Personal Minute M.303/52
(Premier papers, 11/168)

25 May 1952

Please send me to No. 10 by tomorrow afternoon the substance of the Potsdam decisions as the Soviet Government claim them.

Winston S. Churchill to Commonwealth Prime Ministers
Prime Minister's Personal Telegram T.129/52
(Premier papers, 11/35)

25 May 1952
Confidential
Y No. 217

We should be thinking about the arrangements for the next meeting of Commonwealth Prime Ministers. The last such meeting was held in January 1951 and there has been a general understanding that it would be desirable if these meetings took place at intervals of two years or so. Accordingly the next meeting would be due some time next year.

2. It seems to me that the most suitable date would be immediately after the Queen's Coronation in June, 1953, when it is to be hoped that all Commonwealth Prime Ministers will be in London. It would probably in any case be difficult to find any other time which would be equally convenient to all concerned.

3. I should contemplate that the meeting if it is held would be one of Prime Ministers similar to those in 1951 and earlier years since the end of the war with a similar scale of attendance. The meeting would afford an opportunity for a full and frank exchange of views on broad questions of common concern, chiefly in relation to the international situation.

4. I should be grateful if you would let me know at your earliest convenience whether you are in agreement with the above suggestions and whether you would accept an invitation to take part in such a meeting. Details of the

precise arrangements and agenda could be settled nearer the time. We should of course hope that as on previous occasions those taking part in the meeting would be guests of the United Kingdom Government.

5. In view of Southern Rhodesia's interest in the matters likely to be discussed I propose as in 1951 to extend an invitation to Sir Godfrey Huggins[1] to be present.

Winston S. Churchill to Lord Quickswood
(Premier papers, 11/119)

25 May 1952

My dear Linky,

How nice it is for me to hear from you[2] but I am very sorry to hear of your failing eyesight. You seem however to be well equipped with information about the depressing scene which we have reached at the end of our stormy pilgrimage.

I offered Leo Amery a Viscountcy in the last New Year List but he declined on account of Julian's Parliamentary career. If there should be reform of the House of Lords which enables Peers to enter the Commons if they wish he would no doubt change his mind and the offer is still open. He is certainly entitled to it by his long Ministerial service. He is marvellously well preserved though as you know often wrong in his views.

I am putting your point about the prisoners-of-war to the Foreign Office and will let you know what they say. It is of course a matter primarily for the Americans.

---

[1] Godfrey Martin Huggins, 1883–1971. Born in Kent. Migrated to Southern Rhodesia, 1911. GP and surgeon (on active service, RAMC, France, 1916–17). PM of Southern Rhodesia, 1934–53. Knighted, 1941. Viscount Malvern, 1955.

[2] Letter of May 22, reproduced above (pp. 461–2).

Winston S. Churchill to Anthony Eden
Prime Minister's Personal Telegram T.128/52
(Premier papers, 11/373)

25 May 1952
Immediate
Confidential
No. 670

The phrase 'for so long as it is practicable and necessary for them to do so' ought not in any circumstances to be published.[1] This is almost like saying 'so long as it pays'. Please be careful about it, I know this is not what you mean or stand for.

2. The phrase 'so long as it can effectively achieve its objectives' in paragraph 2 of Foreign Office telegram No. 648 to Wahnerheide is equally open to criticism. It seems to reserve the right to quit when things go badly. I should advise a simpler version 'with all their faith and strength'.

3. There is no difference between us in thought, but the phrases might become deadly.

Winston S. Churchill to Lord Cherwell
Prime Minister's Personal Minute M.297/52
(Premier papers, 11/270)

25 May 1952

I do not want anything done to stop the increase of serviceable machines but I do not consider that they need to be manned by such large numbers of ground personnel.[2] If it be true that in the last war we had 120–130 to each aircraft, could we not make the Air Ministry conform to this standard? What then would be the economy in manpower between this and the 150–160 as now asked for?

Perhaps you would draft a minute on this point.

---

[1] Eden proposed to write Dr Stikker the following letter: 'Her Majesty's Government in the United Kingdom have repeatedly made it clear it is their hope that the association of parties to the North Atlantic Treaty will be of an enduring character. For their part, they will maintain their membership of the North Atlantic Alliance for so long as it is practicable and necessary for them to do so.'

[2] See Cherwell to Churchill, May 23, reproduced above (pp. 463–4).

May 1952

Sir William Strang to Winston S. Churchill
(*Premier papers, 11/168*)

26 May 1952
PM/WS/52/57

Your minute No. M.303/52 of the 25th May.[1]

In their latest note the Soviet Government make in effect three claims in relation to the Potsdam Agreement. The relevant passages in the Soviet note are marked in the annexed copy.

(1) The Contractual Agreements with the German Federal Republic constitute a 'separate agreement' and are thus a violation of the Potsdam Agreement which 'laid responsibility for the preparation of a peace treaty on the four Occupying Powers'.

Comment

The Potsdam Agreement stated 'The Council of Foreign Ministers shall be utilised for the preparation of a peace settlement for Germany to be accepted by the Government of Germany when a Government adequate for the purpose is established.'

But the Contractual Agreements are not a peace treaty. Allied rights in regard to the preparation of such a treaty are specifically reserved. The Soviet Government stated in their first note that the peace treaty should be worked out 'with the participation of' an all-German Government'.

(2) In determining the rights to be enjoyed by an all-German Government pending signature of a peace treaty the four Powers must be guided by the Potsdam Agreement.

Comment

The Potsdam Agreement laid down the political and economic principles to govern the treatment of Germany during 'the initial control period'. The chief of these were: Allied supreme authority exercised through a four-power Control Council; demilitarisation; decentralisation; reparation; punishment of war criminals.

The Soviet Government now appear to be maintaining (though again their meaning is not clear) that this control machinery designed for the initial control period should be reimposed after the formation of an all-German Government and maintained until the peace treaty. The Western Powers, on the other hand, have held that any all-German Government must have the necessary freedom to exert its authority throughout Germany and to take part in full freedom in the negotiation of a peace treaty.

(3) In working out a peace treaty the four Powers should be guided by the Potsdam Agreement, in particular on the question of Germany's frontiers.

Comment

---

[1] Reproduced above (p. 464).

The Potsdam Agreement stated that the final delimitation of the Polish–German frontier should await the peace settlement. Pending that settlement the territories East of the Oder and the Western Neisse should be under the administration of the Polish State. The city of Königsberg and the adjacent area were transferred to the Soviet Union pending the final settlement of territorial questions at the peace settlement, and the Western Powers agreed to support at that settlement the final transfer of the area to the Soviet Union.

The Soviet Government claim that the territorial provisions of the Potsdam Agreement were a final settlement and cannot be changed. The Western Powers have maintained that the matter cannot be finally settled until the peace treaty.

Winston S. Churchill: speech
(Hansard)

28 May 1952   House of Commons

KOREA (MILITARY SITUATION)

The Prime Minister: With your permission, Mr Speaker, and that of the House, I should like to make a statement on the military situation in Korea.

Since the armistice talks began last July, there has been a great change in the military position in Korea. The Communist forces have taken full advantage of the lull in the fighting to reinforce, re-organise and re-equip their armies. The size of the force in the field against the United Nations Command is not far short of one million men, compared with a total of just over 500,000 last July. Although the number of enemy formations has been increased, this reinforcement has largely consisted of building existing units up to full strength. The fresh troops are mainly Chinese.

At the same time, the enemy's strength in armour and artillery has steadily mounted. They are now believed to have over 500 tanks and self-propelled guns. There have been large increases in the numbers of anti-aircraft and anti-tank guns, heavy mortars and field artillery. Rocket launchers have also made their appearance.

Despite our air superiority over the immediate battle area, the enemy have also been able to build up large stocks of all types of supplies during the past ten months. There has been a marked increase in the size of the enemy air forces, which have about 1,800 aircraft compared with some 1,000 aircraft last July. About a thousand of these aircraft are jet fighters, mostly MIG 15s.

There is no evidence at present of an imminent enemy attack, but with their reinforcements, the Communists are now in a position to launch a major offensive with little warning and could maintain the initial pressure of their attacks for some time. The United Nations Forces have not been idle during the last 10 months. They now hold the most strongly defended line that they have ever occupied across the peninsula and they are, of course, backed by strong close support air forces.

Ground operations have only been on a small scale since last July, but the United Nations Air Forces carry out regular heavy attacks against enemy positions. These air forces are playing a very important part in limiting the enemy's chances of launching a successful offensive. Their chief task is to put out of action and keep unserviceable the major North Korean airfields capable of being used for jet fighter operations. As an example of their success, our accurate night bombing made the Communists abandon their effort to base jet fighters on three new airfields, which they constructed in the Sinanju area last autumn, and on two other airfields, which they had enlarged to accommodate jet aircraft. The result of these operations has been that the United Nations has air superiority over the immediate battle area. A large proportion of the Chinese aircraft are still stationed in Manchuria. The lack of forward airfields would seriously handicap them if they attempted to carry out a sustained air offensive.

The other main objective of the attacks by our air forces is to disrupt the flow of supplies to the enemy, to limit their troop movements and destroy their supply areas. The success of these attacks has severely restricted rail traffic in North Korea and has forced the enemy to limit vehicle movement almost entirely to the hours of darkness.

Ground operations in Korea consist at present of reconnaissance patrols and probing attacks. Our Forces hold strong defensive positions, strengthened by field fortifications, wire and mines and the Communists have also strengthened their defences. Patrolling is active and determined on both sides.

The Communists have launched a number of attacks of up to regimental strength, supported by heavy concentrations of artillery and mortar fire. These attacks have been contained by United Nations Forces and in almost all cases any ground lost initially has subsequently been regained. In this static situation, the United Nations Command is taking every opportunity to relieve units for rest and re-training.

Ships of the Royal Navy are operating on both the west and east coasts of Korea and serving with them are units of the Australian, Canadian and New Zealand navies. A force, including two British light cruisers and one British aircraft carrier, maintains command of the Yellow Sea and patrols the west coast of North Korea between the Gulf of the Yalu River and the Han River estuary, thus cutting all enemy sea communications between China and North Korea and between North Korea and the battle area.

This force also prevents the enemy from invading the numerous islands lying off the west coast which are held and used by our Forces. Guns of our naval units also regularly engage enemy troops and other military targets on this coast. Our aircraft carrier provides coastal reconnaissance and daily air strikes against enemy targets on the mainland and gives close support to the army when required.

British destroyers are frequently engaged in vigorous and effective action off the North Korean coast. Her Majesty's ship *Charity* was recently straddled by four enemy guns while supporting American minesweepers in the Taedong estuary. She promptly returned the fire and knocked out three of the four enemy guns.

Although they have not recently been engaged in heavy fighting, troops of the Commonwealth Division take part daily in patrols and probing attacks, and they have maintained their reputation of being in the highest rank of the divisions in Korea. They are occupying one of the most vital defensive positions of the Allied line across the peninsula covering the approaches to the capital city of Seoul. There are Canadian, Australian, New Zealand and Indian units in addition to our own in the Division and their team-work under the most stringent conditions has proved an outstanding success.

The Royal Air Force squadron of Sunderland flying boats continues to take an active part in the anti-submarine and shipping patrols which ensure the security of the sea lines of supply between Japan and Korea. A number of RAF fighter pilots have been serving with American squadrons and they have acquitted themselves with distinction during their tour of duty. South African and Australian squadrons have also been playing their part in United Nations air operations.

So far this year the losses suffered by the United Kingdom forces have been sixty-eight officers and men killed and 168 wounded; four are prisoners of war and four are missing. Our total casualties since the beginning of the war in June, 1950, now amount to 3,250 – 513 killed, 1,601 wounded, 939 prisoners of war and 197 missing. Her Majesty's Government wish to express their sincere condolences with the bereaved and with those who have been and are anxious about the wounded, missing and prisoners.

I am sure that the House will wish to record the admiration we must all feel at the bearing of all ranks in the trying conditions in Korea. We can only hope that a satisfactory armistice and peace settlement will soon crown the efforts they have made.

I have also to inform the House that my noble Friend the Minister of Defence has received an invitation from General Mark Clark[1] to stay with him in Tokyo and visit the battle-front in Korea. I think it is most desirable that this

---

[1] Mark Wayne Clark, 1896–1984. On active service with US Army, 1917–18. CoS for US ground forces in England (for European operations), 1941–2. Cdr, 5th Army, Anglo-American invasion of Italy, 1943, and capture of Rome, June 1944. Hon. knighthood, 1944. US High Commissioner and Commanding Gen., Austria, 1945–7. Deputy to Secretary of State, 1947. Gen., 6th Army, 1947–9. Chief of Army Field Forces, 1949–51. Supreme Cdr, UN Command, 1952–3. President, The Citadel, 1954–65.

invitation should be accepted. Lord Alexander proposes to go to the Far East at an early date. On his return a further statement will, of course, be made to the House.

[. . .]

With regard to the general situation, I should have thought what I have said to the House sufficiently sustained the right hon. Gentleman's contention that the situation is very grave. It is very grave, but the United Nations Commander, the American general on the spot,[1] believes that the United Nations are capable of holding a violent offensive should it be made against them on the breakdown of the peace negotiations.

No one can pronounce about battles before they are fought, but that is the view that is taken by the military authorities of the United States who furnish, I think, nine-tenths or more of the troops engaged with the enemy – that should not be forgotten – and who are responsible for taking the necessary measures.

What those measures would be I cannot presume to forecast at all, but I feel that during the last ten months we have been engaged in truce making under extraordinary conditions. I do not think there has ever been any will to peace on the side of the enemy, who were suffering so heavily when the truce was begun and who have certainly improved their position in the meanwhile.

The reason why we have not made a statement on the military operations is that no operations were going on apart from the air forays and the patrolling which I have described and which has also been fully reported in the newspapers. Of course, once the truce breaks down, if it should, and large-scale military operations begin, then much more frequent statements will have to be made to Parliament.

Mr Shinwell: In view of the protracted nature of the armistice negotiations, would not the right hon. Gentleman agree that a case can be made out for the summoning of a United Nations conference –particularly of the nations participating in the Korean affair on the United Nations side – to consider the whole situation? Would it not be desirable that such a conference should be held?

The Prime Minister: That is really a question which might well await the return of my right hon. Friend the Foreign Secretary. It is not a purely military question by any means.

Mr Driberg: Can we have an assurance that when the Minister of Defence is in Tokyo he will fully discuss the question of the possibility of having British representation at the truce talks and also the question of the conduct of the prisoner of war camps on Koje Island and, if possible, will visit the British troops who are now taking part in guarding those camps?

The Prime Minister: Lord Alexander and General Mark Clark are great

[1] Gen. Mark Clark.

personal friends. As everyone knows, General Mark Clark commanded an army under the supreme command of General Alexander. They are trusted friends who know a great deal about the subjects with which we are now concerned. I think that it would be a great advantage that they should talk all matters over freely between them, but I certainly would not presume to attempt to prescribe beforehand exactly how and in what way and to what extent they should deal with particular matters.

Mr Hollis:[1] Can the Prime Minister tell the House anything about Communist guerrilla activities in South Korea?

The Prime Minister: I have not any information on that, without notice.

Mr A. Henderson: As a very large number of trained and experienced pilots are required to maintain a front line strength of 1,000 jet aircraft, can the Prime Minister say whether there is any evidence of the nationality of the pilots?

The Prime Minister: Certainly the Chinese seem to be picking it up very quickly.

Mrs Castle: Further to the question asked by my hon. Friend the Member for Maldon (Mr Driberg), is the right hon. Gentleman aware that what is worrying the House is the lack of reliable information available to us about the prisoner of war camps and about the screening of prisoners, and that we are anxious that there should not only be talks between the Minister of Defence and his colleague over there but that there should be, as a result of his visit, a full, factual report to the House on these points, which are most obscure at the moment?

The Prime Minister: I am sure that there is a great deal of concern over a lot of things that have happened in Korea. Everyone – no one more than our Allies in America – has not been by any means contented with the course which these events have taken. However, these matters are now receiving the concentrated attention of the Government principally concerned – the United States Government – which is acting for the United Nations and, I must again remind the House, which has the overwhelming majority of the Forces employed. Further measures are being taken and I think it would be wrong if the other nations who are contributing token forces, in many cases, to the United Nations armies, leaving the main bulk of the work to be done by the United States, did not take their part in this difficult question of the handling of the prisoner of war camps. It may well be that they will all make a valuable contribution, not only in forces, but in policy.

Lieutenant-Colonel Elliot: Is not my right hon. Friend also aware that, although the House is distressed about the situation in the prisoner of war

---

[1] Maurice Christopher Hollis, 1902–77. Educated at Eton and Balliol College, Oxford. Prof. of History, Stonyhurst College, 1925–35. Visiting Prof., University of Notre Dame, Ind., 1935–9. RAF intelligence officer during WWII. MP (Cons.) for Devizes, 1945–55. Parliamentary commentator for *Punch*, 1955.

camps, it would not be correct to say that that is what is mainly troubling us? It is the grave general situation which has been disclosed, and which we hope will be discussed with the commanders in Tokyo.

The Prime Minister: Certainly.

Mr Harold Davies[1]: Does the right hon. Gentleman realise that the House is getting less information on the Korean situation than his equally great predecessor Mr Gladstone was giving the House in the time of the Crimean War? Does he also realise that we on this side of the House could not throw our weight into any major activity there without the information being before us? Will he, therefore, for the sake of the House, insist that the Minister of Defence supplies us with the information on the situation on Koje Island and at Pusan?

The Prime Minister: I am afraid I have not got at my fingers' ends the exact part which Mr Gladstone took in the Crimean War; it was even before my time. There really have been no military operations on a large scale going on. Truce talks have been going on and, therefore, there has not been that regular military information which would be very right and proper in other circumstances, and which will, I can assure the House, be freely and fully given should we not, unfortunately, reach the conclusion of a lasting truce.

Sir R. Acland[2]: Can the Prime Minister tell us anything about the work of the United Nations Civil Administration Command in Korea, the number and condition of civilian refugees in their care, who are alleged by reliable reports to be very numerous and in very bad conditions; and whether the British personnel take any share in the work of this Command? Could that also be considered by the noble Lord during his visit?

The Prime Minister: If the hon. Gentleman will put a Question on the Order Paper, I will see what information on this matter is at our disposal.

Mr Cocks[3]: Can the Prime Minister say where this great mass of material, including jet planes and self-propelling guns, came from?

Sir Waldron Smithers[4]: Moscow.

The Prime Minister: Although there are movements ever being made in aerial locomotion, it would be premature to suppose that they came from the moon.

---

[1] Harold Davies, 1904–85. MP (Lab.) for Leek, 1945–70. Joint Parliamentary Secretary of Social Security, 1966–7. Special Envoy of the PM on Peace Mission to Hanoi, 1965.

[2] Richard Thomas Dyke Acland, 1906–90. MP (Lib.) for Barnstaple, 1935–40; (Lab.) for Gravesend, 1947–55. 15th Bt, 1939. Senior Lecturer, St Luke's College of Education, 1959–74.

[3] Frederick Seymour Cocks, 1882–1953. Author of *The Secret Treaties* (1918), denouncing British policy during WWI. MP (Lab.) for Broxtowe, 1929–53. Member, Joint Select Committee on Indian Constitutional Reform, 1933–4; All-Party Committee on Parliamentary Procedure, 1945–6. Leader, All-Party Parliamentary Delegation to Greece, 1946. CBE, 1950.

[4] Waldron Smithers, 1880–1954. Member of London Stock Exchange. MP (Cons.) for Chislehurst, 1924–45; for Orpington, 1945–54. Knighted, 1934.

Mr Nicholson[1]: Could my right hon. Friend give us any information about contacts with the United States? Am I right in thinking that we are bound to make these inquiries through the State Department, and, if that is the case, could not some more direct channels be arranged?

The Prime Minister: Of course, all the regular contacts through the Foreign Office and the State Department continue, but we are in very close personal relationships with the leaders in the United States, and can at any time, if we desire, address them directly. My right hon. Friend the Foreign Secretary has been from hour to hour, during the last anxious days, in close personal contact with Mr Acheson, and it must not be thought at all that matters rest upon the routine contacts established through diplomatic channels.

Mr Nicholson: The Prime Minister has misunderstood the drift of my question. Is he aware that even the State Department finds difficulty in eliciting this information owing to internal American conditions, and would it not be more convenient to us to have more direct contact with the Pentagon?

Mr Emrys Hughes: Is the Prime Minister aware of the great disquiet in this country, expressed recently by the Archbishop of York,[2] about the widespread use of the napalm bomb, which is indiscriminately burning up villages, including women and children, schools and orphanage buildings, and so on? Is it not time that the Government realised that there is a great volume of opinion in this country that we should complete a withdrawal from Korea, because the war there can no longer be described as anything like an international police action, but as one of the most cruel and futile wars in history?

The Prime Minister: The napalm bomb is a question on which carefully considered answers have been given by my hon. Friend, and the whole matter was considered by the Cabinet in relation to the conditions of warfare now prevailing. As to the general case of the war in Korea, that occurred before we had to bear the burden of public office, but very prompt and courageous action was taken by the Labour Party, who were then the Government, and who gave immediate support to the United States, and thus a grave act of aggression was confronted with effective physical force.

---

[1] Godfrey Nicholson, 1901–91. MP (Cons.) for Morpeth, 1931–5; for Farnham Div., Surrey, 1937–66. Bt, 1958.

[2] Cyril Forster Garbett, 1875–1955. Educated at Keble College, Oxford, and Cuddesdon Theological College. Curate of St Mary, Portsea, 1900–9; Vicar, 1909–19. Bishop of Southwark, 1919–32; of Winchester, 1932–42. Clerk of the Closet to the King, 1937–42. PC, 1942. Archbishop of York, 1942–55. GCVO, 1955.

MAY 1952

John Colville: diary
('The Fringes of Power', page 649)

30 May 1952

The country is in a bad way. It is difficult to see how our economic ills can be cured and at the moment nothing that is done seems to be more than a short-term palliative. The remedy for 50 million people living in an island which can maintain 30 million and no longer leads the world in industrial exports or in capital assets invested abroad is hard to find. Harold Macmillan said to me at the Turf[1] yesterday that he thought development of the Empire into an economic unit as powerful as the USA and the USSR was the only possibility. At present this seems to be neither pursued nor envisaged.

The Government is in a bad way too. Their popularity has fallen owing to bad publicity, rising prices and a silly policy of denationalisation. Winston is, I fear, personally blamed both in the country and by his own party in the House. Mrs Churchill does not think he will last long as Prime Minister.

Winston S. Churchill to Lord Leathers
Prime Minister's Personal Minute M.307/52
(Premier papers, 11/287)

30 May 1952
Secret

1) I had a talk with Mr Menzies about my ideas of helping the nationalized railways while setting road transport free. He said that he had had the same problem to face in Australia, and that he had solved it in exactly the way I have in mind. The expression he used was to me suggestive. He had told the Treasury to 'write over twenty millions from the railway capital debt to the national debt'. He has told all this to the Chancellor of the Exchequer. This of course is only a matter of book-keeping. That is all I have in mind. The Treasury is now responsible for making good any deficiency in the earnings which affect the annual payment of twenty-eight millions. Therefore this affects our credit as much as if it were part of the national debt. There would be no alteration in our credit as the result of a mere transference form one account to another.

2) I am anxious to know how you think my wish could be given effect. The twenty-eight millions represent a permanent annual payment on over 1100 millions of shares, which were absorbed. How could the amortization be planned of this vast bulk of capital? Or should we simply reduce it by (say) transferring three or four hundred millions of the realized Budget surplus,

[1] The Turf Club, a gentlemen's club in central London.

and making a corresponding reduction in the twenty-eight millions annual payment?

3) I do not see clearly the details, but something like this is I am sure necessary if Trade Union opinion is to be carried along. Supposing, for instance, nine or ten millions could be struck off the twenty-eight and added to the levy and the improvements of decentralization, it might give the railway a real, buoyant future, without harsh treatment of existing employees.

4) You told me that in your plan for making the railways pay effectively, you would presently cut out a lot of slow trains and replace them with bus services, and that you had thought these bus services should be run by the railways. What are you doing with the previously railway-owned road services? Are they to go back to the railways or not?

5) I am very glad to see the Bill in print, and look forward to receiving the revised edition in a few days. The draftsmen have done a fine piece of work as the result of my personal appeal to them, and the gloomy tales of our not being able to get the Bill till late July surely belong to the past. Intense work must be done upon the revised text. I am looking forward to it being brought into the House early in July.

6) I am sending a copy of this Minute to the Minister of Transport.

Winston S. Churchill to Field Marshal Lord Alexander
Prime Minister's Personal Minute M.308/52
(Premier papers, 11/49)

30 May 1952
Secret

Although I have not yet seen the COS paper there are a few points which have already emerged from our discussions in Cabinet.

(1) Your suggestion of totally dropping out the manufacture of obsolete weapons like heavy anti-aircraft guns was admirable. I earnestly trust you have some others items like this.

(2) I did not like the idea of scrapping the 3rd Division and using the men to replace the German tails of our existing Divisions in Germany. I would not hesitate to run the risk of the Germans fighting loyally on our side against Russian-Communist invasion of their hearths and homes. But to abolish a Divisional formation to replace them would really by cutting down the teeth for the sake of the tail. We greatly need a formed Division in our Island. Indeed I was deeply concerned when the 3rd and 6th Divisions were sent abroad, leaving us with no strategic reserves in hand.

(3) I am sure the artillery ammunition programme can be greatly reduced. We cannot imagine a repetition of the heavy prolonged bombardments of World War I or even the much lesser expenditures of World War II, in a War

in which guided missiles and atom rockets will be the new and perhaps the dominating factor.

(4) I am sure that the intake of national service recruits should be reduced and that exports should have the apprentices they need. I do not think the Air Force ought to increase its demand for groundsmen beyond the 110 per machine in the late War. I do not know how much such a restriction would yield. I have been for some time in correspondence with S of S for Air on this subject. The formation of an Immediate Reserve of air groundsmen should not be difficult. 20 per cent?

(5) The Navy must also again be scrutinized. It is certainly not necessary to maintain the larger surface ships, which have no enemy to meet, at the present high level of crews.

(6) On broader matters it is surely not necessary in peacetime to keep the combatant units in Germany at absolutely full strength. An Immediate Reserve should be formed for them which on mobilization could reach them in ten days. I would rather have more formations and the power to fill them from our growing Z Reserve.[1] However this is a matter on which I have no fixed opinion and I should welcome discussion.

---

[1] The Class Z Reserve, first authorized on 3 Dec. 1918 and composed of recently discharged soldiers who met certain requirements, was established as a way for the British army to recall trained soldiers quickly in the event of continuing hostilities with Germany after WWI. It was abolished on 31 Mar. 1920 but reintroduced after WWII.

June 1952

Winston S. Churchill to Lord Leathers
Prime Minister's Personal Minute M.310/52
(Premier papers, 11/175)

1 June 1952

Your minute of May 15.

I am not at all convinced about setting up a public committee.* We can of course have any kind of departmental or inter-departmental committee we like in order to help us make up our minds and explore the subject. But in a matter of this very sharp controversy I do not yet see how a public committee could be formed unless both sides were represented upon it. Do you consider that this would simply lead to a deadlock? Let me have your idea of 'an independent committee to take evidence in public'. Who would be the members you have in mind? I fear the other side will say they are packed from our point of view.

* To inquire into road and rail fares.

Winston S. Churchill to Iain Macleod
Prime Minister's Personal Minute M.311/52
(Premier papers, 11/28)

3 June 1952

What is the truth behind the report in the *Daily Express* of May 29 about the changes introduced at Broadmoor by the Board of Control?

Sir David Maxwell Fyfe to Winston S. Churchill
(Premier papers, 11/294)

4 June 1952

In view of the recent discussion at the Defence Committee I forward a note on the anticipated effect of Atom bombing prepared in consultation with my Chief Scientific Adviser. I hope that you may be interested in the views expressed.

1. Atom bombs are differentiated from 'conventional' weapons in two main ways – (a) the radiological effects and (b) the scale of damage and casualties which they are capable of causing.

2. As regards the radiological effects, the <u>immediate</u> effects are only one of the factors (the others being blast and heat-flash) which cause casualties. The possibility of <u>continuing</u> effects has been greatly exaggerated; on the basis of available experience and scientific theory there is no reason to think that so-called radioactive contamination would persist to any appreciable extent from a bomb burst at or about the height used for the two bombs dropped over Japan; it is true that some persistent radioactivity would result from a low burst but (i) this is operationally less probable and (ii) in any event the radioactive area could be detected and it would probably be possible for it to be entered after a few hours for short periods without risk.

3. The effects of blast and heat-flash would be (i) destruction of or damage to buildings etc., (ii) wide-spread fires (iii) fatal or other casualties either directly caused or resulting indirectly from (i) and (ii). It is considered that within a radius of half to three quarters of a mile from ground zero, the devastation would be very great and even if there were survivors in shelters in this area rescue and fire-fighting operations might be impracticable. But beyond that radius the effects rapidly diminish and a point is soon reached at which the conditions are comparable with those which we experienced in World War II though the area affected would be larger.

4. It has been estimated that it would take three atom bombs to produce something like the damage and casualties caused by the Allied raids on Hamburg in July/August 1943. It must be recognized however that the concentration into a short space of time of the effects of an atom bomb as compared with the spread of the 'Hamburg' attacks over several days would greatly increase the difficulties of any civil defence organisation.

5. There is no technical difficulty in providing measures of protection or mitigation of the effects of atom bombs comparable with those which were taken in World War II; the problems of fire fighting and rescue of trapped casualties, for example, would (outside the area of complete devastation) be the same; shelter for the public could be provided which would be comparable with that of World War II[*] and structural protection for essential

plant etc., could similarly be provided; and other measures of treatment and relief could be organised on the same lines as before.

6. It is no doubt true that these measures would be less effective than those of the last War if only because of the operation of the time factor, but it is thought that they would have a considerable degree of effectiveness if the scale of attack did not become too heavy. It is not possible to predict what number of atom bombs would constitute an insupportable scale of attack.

7. It is clearly impossible to base civil defence policy on the assumption that the scale of attack will be insupportable and it is suggested that the only possible basis for policy is that such efforts should be made as will satisfy public opinion that all practicable measures are being taken; this does not mean that the public should be led to expect that heavy damage and casualties can be avoided, but that efforts should be so planned and directed, with due regard for priorities, as to ensure a reasonable measure of mitigation. The result of any other policy might well be that public morale would break at an early stage in war and by breaking destroy the will to win of the Armed Forces.

8. It is not suggested that this policy would justify at present a concentration of effort on civil defence inconsistent with our economic position, but it is suggested that any resources which can be spared for the support of well conceived measures of civil defence would make an effective contribution to the general defence of the United Kingdom.

* It was not the normal object of shelter policy to give protection against direct hits or near misses; even the inadequate Japanese shelters stood up well at half a mile from the atom bomb and in some cases at shorter distances.

Iain Macleod to Winston S. Churchill
(Premier papers, 11/28)

5 June 1952

Your Minute No. M.311/52 of 3rd June.[1]

1. The proceedings reported are part of a campaign launched by the Prison Officers' Association to discredit the Board of Control. Their motives are:
    (a) By suggesting that security arrangements generally have been impaired by the Board of Control, to prevent the blame for Straffen's[2] escape from attaching to an individual member of the

---

[1] Reproduced above (p. 478).
[2] John Thomas Straffen, 1930–2007. Diagnosed a mental defective, 1940. Committed to Hortham Colony, 1947. Transferred to a lower-security agricultural hostel in Winchester, 1949, for good behaviour; returned to Hortham, Nov. 1950, after he began stealing again. Murdered two girls, 1951;

Union. The escape has in fact been found to be due primarily to the default of the attendant in charge of Straffen.

(b) To strengthen their case in a current wage claim.

2. A fuller report of the proceedings, given in the *Daily Telegraph* of 29th May, quotes Bell, one of the Broadmoor officers, as saying that Dr Hopwood,[1] Medical Superintendent of Broadmoor, had been 'deprived of much of his power'. Dr Hopwood has made the following comment on this:

'With regard to the general management of the institution, the security, care and treatment of patients, control of staff, etc., my powers have been in no way curtailed since the Board of Control have been managing Broadmoor. In conclusion, I can only express my sincere regret that officers from Broadmoor should have made statements of so irresponsible and misleading a character.'

3. The total staff in post at Broadmoor today is higher than on 1st April, 1949, when the Board of Control took over the management.

4. A detailed note on the points referred to in the *Daily Express* report is attached. I am quite satisfied that we have a good answer to these and similar attacks, but I have felt debarred from making any public comment till the Scott Henderson[2] Committee have reported.

Lieutenant-General Sir Ian Jacob: note
(*Premier papers, 11/118*)

6 June 1952

The Prime Minister gave me the following instructions:

1. During the absence of the Minister of Defence the Prime Minister would handle all important Defence matters that could not await the Minister's return.

2. Departmental matters in the Ministry of Defence would be handled by the Parliamentary Under-Secretary of State.[3] If the Prime Minister brought

---

arrested and committed to Broadmoor psychiatric hospital, 1952. Escaped Broadmoor and murdered another girl, 1952. Sentenced to death, reprieved and sentence commuted to life imprisonment, 1952. Confined in Wandsworth Prison, 1952–6; Horfield Prison, 1956–8, 1960–6; Cardiff Prison, 1958–60; Parkhurst Prison, 1966–8; Durham Prison, 1968–?. Died in Frankland Prison, 2007.

[1] Joseph Stanley Hopwood, 1886–1971. Medical Superintendent at Broadmoor, 1937–51.

[2] John Scott Henderson, 1895–1964. Educated at Airdrie Academy and London University. Served in WWI with Royal Dublin Fusiliers and RASC, 1914–19. Ministry of Health, 1920–7. Secretary, British Delegation to International Sanitary Conference, Paris, 1926. Secretary, Inter-Departmental Committee on Optical Practitioners Bill, 1927. Called to the Bar, Inner Temple, 1927; Bencher, 1952. Recorder of Bridgwater, 1944; of Portsmouth, 1945–62. Chaired several committees of inquiry, including that of 1952 established to report and recommend on the security arrangements at Broadmoor.

[3] Evelyn Nigel Chetwode Birch, 1906–81. Served in WWII. Lt-Col., 1944. MP (Cons.) for Flintshire, 1945–50; for West Flint, 1950–70. OBE, 1945. Parliamentary Under-Secretary of State, Air Ministry,

to the Cabinet any matter affecting the Ministry of Defence the Parliamentary Under-Secretary should attend the Cabinet meeting.

3. The Prime Minister would continue to address minutes to the Service Ministers. He would also address minutes to the Ministry of Defence where they should be dealt with by the Parliamentary Under-Secretary of State, Sir Harold Parker or General Jacob as might be appropriate. The Prime Minister's minutes addressed to the Chiefs of Staff would go to them direct.

4. The Prime Minister hoped that the Chiefs of Staff Paper on Global Strategy would be available as soon as possible. If there were differences of opinion it would be better for the Chiefs of Staff to express these, than to spend additional time on trying to reach a compromise.

5. The Prime Minister would hold meetings with the Chiefs of Staff as necessary in the Prime Minister's Map Room.

Winston S. Churchill to Lord Cherwell
Prime Minister's Personal Minute M.312/52
(Premier papers, 11/294)

8 June 1952

Pray comment on this.[1]

There is nothing in the footnote to page 2 which I have marked in red. A single 'direct hit' by an ordinary bomb might inflict destruction within a circle of 150 yards diameter. When the direct hit covers a mile and a half the 'directness of the hit' or the 'nearness of the miss' lose much of their meaning. How much bigger in square mileage is a circle of one and a half miles diameter than one of three hundred yards diameter?

I shall have much more to say about this.

What are the chances of hitting with modern gadgets from so high up?

Winston S. Churchill to Gwilym Lloyd George
Prime Minister's Personal Minute M.315/52
(Premier papers, 11/147)

8 June 1952

I am sorry that you have not been able to do anything for the small bakers. Please explain to me the meaning of the passages underlined on page 2 of the

---

1951–2; for Ministry of Defence, 1952–4. Minister of Works, 1954–5. PC, 1955. Secretary of State for Air, 1955–7.

[1] Maxwell Fyfe's minute of June 4, reproduced above (pp. 479–80).

attached memo.¹ What is the 'safety limit' and what form would the 'risks of abuse' take? What is the 'temptation' which you fear? I quite agree we could not incur any heavy additional cost.

Winston S. Churchill to Iain Macleod
Prime Minister's Personal Minute M.316/52
(Premier papers, 11/28)

8 June 1952

You should not commit yourself in public upon the question of whether Broadmoor etc. should be under the Home Office or the Ministry of Health until the matter has been considered by the Cabinet.² Every Department naturally tries to keep as wide a sphere as possible for itself. But this Departmental *esprit de corps* should not be allowed to prejudice the decision to which we must come in due course.

I gather that the precautions at Broadmoor are being appreciably strengthened. This is to the good but in itself implies a criticism upon the system which had been allowed to develop. Where murderers are concerned the safety of the public, especially in the neighbourhood, must claim priority.

Winston S. Churchill to Gwilym Lloyd George and Sir Thomas Dugdale
Prime Minister's Personal Minute M.325/52
(Premier papers, 11/146)

8 June 1952

I do hope we are not going to have a glut of fruit this year and no sugar to make jam. It would be worth while making some exertions and running some risks for this. Please let me have a report and then bring it up in Cabinet.

---

¹ On the Bread Subsidy, of which the relevant passage read as follows:
'7. The bread subsidy is at present running at about £13¾ million a year and increases in wages and other costs are likely to raise this figure to some £15 million before long. This is very close to the safety limit for a subsidy of this kind, for there are real risks of abuse if the temptation is put too high. To accept the proposals of the Master Bakers for special treatment of the small baker would cost about £1½ million in the first instance, but this would certainly lead the industry as a whole to press – as even the Master Bakers are now doing – their claim to an increase in the general rate of profit allowed on bread baking which would cost a further £3 million. As I have shown, I do not consider that such additions to the subsidy would be justified on merits and they would certainly bring the total subsidy to a level involving risks of abuse.'
² See Macleod's minute of June 5, reproduced above (pp. 480–1).

Winston S. Churchill to Anthony Eden and Field Marshal Lord Alexander
Prime Minister's Personal Minute M.327/52
(Premier papers, 11/8)

8 June 1952

I have read the report* of the meeting with Mr Menzies at the Ministry of Defence on June 3. I only make three comments:

1. On Page 3 – I had supposed that the Gaza project would involve great expense and would be no substitute for the effective defence of the Canal. The Egyptians also can hardly be expected to facilitate what is in my opinion intended to be a pistol pointed at their heads.

[. . .]

3. Section 6, para. 3 – I do not think we should be well advised to press as Lord Alexander suggests for a share in controlling the operations and policy in Korea. We should ask to be kept fully informed but not necessarily consulted except on matters like air retaliation already specified. We have only one division out of ten and it would be a pity for us to seek and assume direct responsibility.

* MV(52)5th Meeting.

Winston S. Churchill to Lord Quickswood
(Premier papers, 11/119)

8 June 1952

Dear Linky,

I enclose a reply from the Foreign Office[1] to your suggestion about prisoners-of-war in Korea. I think there is a lot in what they say. Would you let me have the letter back in due course?

> My dear Colville,
>
> You wrote to me on the 26th May enclosing an extract from a letter which the Prime Minister had received from Lord Quickswood[2] suggesting the release of non-Communist prisoners of war in South Korea and the repatriation of all the remainder.
>
> For your own information, we think that there is, in theory, something to be said for Lord Quickswood's idea. It is true that Article V of the 1949 Prisoner-of-war Convention appears to contemplate by inference that prisoners of war will be kept under the actual care of the capturing power from the time of capture to that of 'release and repatriation'. Moreover,

[1] Letter from Michael Wilford to John Colville, May 30.
[2] Reproduced above (pp. 461–2).

the capturing power might well pretend to have 'released' prisoners, whom it had in fact unlawfully liquidated. On the other hand, the whole Convention is, of course, founded on the assumption that the capturing power will want to detain the prisoners in order to deprive the other belligerent of their services. The power to detain and confine is a right of belligerents and in principle it is difficult to see why if they do not want to exercise it – or cease to want to – they should be under any compulsion to do so. The real object of the Convention is to secure for prisoners certain treatment on the assumption that they will in fact be kept in confinement.

In practice, however, it would have been difficult for the United Nations Command to adopt the expedient suggested by Lord Quickswood since, even before the prisoner-of-war lists were exchanged at Panmunjom in December, 1951, the United Nations Command had regularly furnished the International Committee of the Red Cross with the names of all prisoners taken, for onward transmission to the Communists. Moreover, it was not until the prisoners were screened in April that the United Nations Command had any firm idea of the number who would oppose repatriation by force. The first public statement of the principle of 'voluntary repatriation' in relation to the Korean conflict was made by the United Nations Command in January this year.

The United Nations Command are in fact proposing to release after an armistice about 40,000 South Korean civilians who have been impressed into the North Korean forces. The Communists have reluctantly accepted this. It would, however, be another matter to extend this release to those of the genuine North Korean and Chinese soldiers, comprising the 132,000-odd prisoners on the list handed to the Communists in December, 1951, who do not wish to return to China or North Korea. Moreover, if this were done, the Communists might easily retaliate by 'releasing' a certain number of United Nations prisoners held in North Korea, which of course means that they would disappear and never be heard of again.

We consider that the United Nations Command, having gone so far in insisting that the Communists accept the principle of 'voluntary repatriation', can only keep trying to achieve an armistice on the general basis of the offer they made to the Communists on the 28th April, which the Foreign Secretary explained in detail in his statement of the 7th May.

I leave it to you to decide how much of this can be passed on to Lord Quickswood.

Winston S. Churchill to Alan Lennox-Boyd
Prime Minister's Personal Minute M.317/52
(Premier papers, 11/287)

8 June 1952

You mentioned to me a great number of questions with which you were about to be bombarded. Surely many of these could be answered by the formula 'All these matters must await the presentation of the Bill to the House.' Let me know how this strikes you.

Lord Quickswood to Winston S. Churchill
(Premier papers, 11/119)

10 June 1952

My dear Winston,

Thank you for sending me the very interesting letter, which I return. It is news to me that so many as 130,000 do not wish to go back to China, and one wonders why. I thought it was only a comparatively small number of four or five thousand who had conspired against the Communist Government and were afraid of punishment. Such might be dealt with, I think, in the way I suggested, but I really do not know why the 130,000 who are merely reluctant to go back and are not afraid of being hanged, should be considered. We cannot keep them all going on for ever because of their preference for one climate rather than another. I should therefore release prisoners who are afraid of punishment, but nobody else, and consent thereafter to the Communists' demands.

I do not think the quotations from the 1949 Prisoners-of-War Convention really stand in the way. They were written obviously without contemplating such a situation as now exists, or the difficulty of repatriating people against their will. Treaties should always be interpreted in accordance with their strict wording. They are not Acts of Parliament.

JUNE 1952 487

Cabinet: conclusions
(*Cabinet papers, 128/25*)

10 June 1952
Secret
11.30 a.m.
Cabinet Meeting No. 58 of 1952

[...]

4. The Cabinet had before them a memorandum by the President of the Board of Trade (C(52)182) reporting (i) that, owing mainly to falling prices, the additional defence orders which were to be placed with the object of relieving unemployment in the textile areas would now cost only about £16.5 million, compared with the £20 to £25 million promised; and (ii) that the share for Northern Ireland was unlikely to exceed £1.9 million. The President therefore proposed that additional orders should be placed to the value of some £6.5 million, of which £1.5 million would be for hosiery and £5 million for cotton and woollen goods not covered by the £4,700 million rearmament programme; and that union cloth should be substituted for cotton in appropriate specifications with the object of increasing Northern Ireland's total share of the orders to £3.4 million.

The following aspects of the problem were covered in the Cabinet's discussion:

(a) Total Scale of Orders to be Placed

The Chancellor of the Exchequer said that in his view orders totalling £20 million at present prices, which would be equivalent to between £25 and £27 million at the prices ruling in April, would suffice to implement the Government's undertaking. He thought that the figure of £20 million could most suitably be made up by adding to the programme £1½ millions' worth of hosiery and £2 millions' worth of cotton and woollen goods.

As against this it was pointed out that the Government undertaking had mentioned £25 million as the upper limit, and that if the orders were restricted to the lower limit of £20 million the programme might well be criticised as inadequate, particularly by those Government supporters who had urged the more drastic remedy of abolishing the purchase tax on textiles.

(b) Northern Ireland

Unemployment in Northern Ireland had reached serious levels, and special measures should be taken to alleviate it. While unemployment in Great Britain as a whole was 2.2 per cent, and in the textile areas about 4.8 per cent, the corresponding figures for Northern Ireland were 10 per cent, and 22.8 per cent.

The Chancellor of the Exchequer said that, even so, he could not regard it as business-like to spend an additional £300,000 on union cloth, for purposes for which cotton would suffice, and thereby involve the Ministry of Health in a supplementary estimate.

The Minister of Supply suggested that additional orders for canvas goods might offer an alternative means of helping Northern Ireland without incurring avoidable extra expenditure. This would not give immediate relief, since it was in the linen industry that unemployment was most severe, but it should be possible to include at least some orders for canvas in the Northern Ireland share.

(c) Scotland

Concessions to Northern Ireland inevitably stimulated pressure by Scottish interests for a share in the orders. It was true that the unemployment figure for Scotland (3.3 per cent) was little worse than the figure for Great Britain as a whole, but some linen firms in Scotland were threatening to close down or to introduce short-time working.

It was agreed that it should be possible to place some orders, for example, for canvas, in Scotland.

(d) Coronation Uniform

The Secretary of State for War mentioned a proposal to issue blue No. 1 dress to Army formations taking part in the Coronation celebrations at a cost of about £600,000. These uniforms, which would comprise both wool and cotton, would later be re-issued more widely to units of the Regular Army for ceremonial and walking-out dress.

It was agreed that, subject to more detailed examination as part of the current review of the general scale of expenditure on the Coronation, this proposal might be found suitable to form part of the proposal additional programme of textile orders.

The Prime Minister, summing up the discussion, said that the preponderant view in the Cabinet clearly favoured the general approach to this problem outlined in C(52)182, though there might be room for adjustment of the details. The Chancellor of the Exchequer said that he regretted that the Cabinet should think it necessary to go beyond an expenditure of £20 million and to authorize the purchase of the more expensive union cloth in substitution for cotton.

The Cabinet –

(1) Approved in principle the proposals put forward in C(52)182.
(2) Invited the President of the Board of Trade, in consultation with other Ministers concerned, to consider the detailed questions of allocation involved, including the nature of the orders to be placed in Northern Ireland; the amount of hosiery orders to be placed; and the proportions of woollen and cotton goods to be ordered.

In the course of the discussion The Prime Minister said that, apart from special measures to meet the situation in the textile industries, the Government should make plans well ahead against the possibility of more widespread unemployment as a result of a trade recession. Early consideration should be given to the measures which might be taken to avert such unemployment, including such public works projects as the reclamation of marginal land, highway development and the construction of a Severn barrage. This problem should be examined by a small Committee of Ministers, who should put constructive proposals before the Cabinet.

The Chancellor of the Exchequer said that a certain measure of short-term unemployment was an inevitable accomplishment of the transfer of workers to the armament and export industries, and care would have to be taken to ensure that any public works projects, some of which would in any case involve the use of materials badly needed for rearmament and export purposes, did not delay these movements of labour.

The Cabinet –

(3) Invited the Prime Minister to appoint a small Ministerial Committee, under the Chairmanship of the Chancellor of the Duchy of Lancaster, to formulate and submit to the Cabinet plans for checking any tendency towards widespread unemployment.

[...]

Winston S. Churchill: speech
('Stemming the Tide', pages 298–300)

11 June 1952 Press Association Luncheon
Savoy Hotel, London

The Press Association plays an important part in our national life by presenting from minute to minute the news about all kinds of things happening all over the world. You have two important guides in your difficult task: first, that your presentation should be factual and unbiased, and secondly, that it should preserve a true sense of proportion. Both these conditions have been observed in a high and increasing degree during the eighty-four years of your honourable service. It is because what you offer us is so valuable – indeed irreplaceable – that your responsibilities are heavy. Without your help the public would be uninformed; without your integrity they would be misled. You have also since the war had to exercise a discrimination never previously forced upon a National Press. As the world grows more complex and as time and space contract year by year, the news increases in volume and variety. But newsprint shrinks at least as fast. You have therefore to strike the balance between what people want to read and what you think they ought to know. Many will feel that you strike a fair balance, and I believe you will continue to resist temptations to diminish fact for the sake of sensation, or twist truth to serve partisanship.

Last week I watched the Trooping the Colour and our young Queen riding at the head of her Guards. I thought of the history of the past and the hopes of the future. Not only of the distant past – it is barely ten years since we upheld on our strong, unyielding shoulders the symbols, the honour and even perhaps the life of the free world. Certainly no one of British race could contemplate such a spectacle without pride. But no thinking man or woman could escape the terrible question: on what does it all stand? It does indeed seem hard that the traditions and triumphs of a thousand years should be challenged by the ebb and flow of markets and commercial and financial transactions in the swaying world which has sprung up and is growing ever larger around us, and that we have to watch from month to month the narrow margins upon which our solvency and consequently our reputation and influence depend. But fifty million islanders growing food for only thirty millions, and dependent for the rest upon exertions, their skill and their genius, present a problem which has not been seen or at least recorded before. In all history there has never been a community so large, so complex, so sure of its way of life, posed at such dizzy eminence and on so precarious a foundation. Lands and nations whom we have defeated in war or rescued from subjugation are today more solidly sure of earning their living than we, who have imparted our message of Parliamentary institutions to the civilized world, and kept the flag of freedom flying in some of its darkest days.

Around us we see the streets so full of traffic and the shops so splendidly presented, and the people, cheerful, well-dressed, content with their system of Government, proud, as they have a right to be of their race and name. One wonders if they realize the treacherous trapdoor on which they stand. I would not say this to you if it was not your duty to expose any facts, however unpleasant, to them. Britain can take it.

To speak like this is not to cry despair. It is the Alert; but it is more than the Alert; it is the Alarm. We have never been beaten yet and now we fight not for vainglory or imperial pomp, but for survival as an independent, self-supporting nation. It has often been said we were approaching national bankruptcy in October last after our two years orgy of electioneering, and certainly the figures to prove it can all be produced. But any British Government, worthy of the name, called upon to bear the burden would have taken severe, unpopular measures of one kind or another to ward off the obvious and imminent peril. In wartime we were confronted with extreme decisions. There was nothing we would not have done for our life and cause. In time of peace happily we work under more limited conditions both in risks and in remedies. The dangers do not present themselves to the mass of the people in the same acute and violent manner as in the days when London was being bombed. Now the crisis is different in form, but as it seems to me, scarcely less fateful. Moreover there is this outstanding difference between the perils of war and of peace. In war we were united, now in peace we find ourselves torn apart by quarrels which bear no relation to our dangers, and, while we brawl along, our thought and action are distracted by a vast superficial process of reciprocal calumniation. We have to live our life from day to day and give back as good as we get, but I warn you that without an intense national realization of our position in all parties and by all classes, we shall find it very hard to reach that security without which all that we have achieved, all that we possess and all our glories may be cast away.

If I were not sure that the vital forces in our race, not only in this island, but throughout the British Empire and Commonwealth of Nations, have only to be aroused to conquer, I would not use these hard words. I use them to you because they may be a guide in the discharge of your responsible duties and also because, through your Agency, they may command the attention of our countrymen here and across the oceans. Thanks to the unpopular measures that have already been taken by the Chancellor of the Exchequer, we have reached in the last six months a position of equipoise. Our head is above water. It is not enough to float. We have to swim and we have to swim successfully against the stream. We are holding our own. That is a considerable return for the sacrifices which our people are having to make. But we cannot be satisfied with that. We must not only pay our way. We cannot be content to live from hand to mouth and from month to month in this world of change and turmoil. We must create, by long and steady systems of trade and exchange throughout our Empire and Commonwealth and throughout the wider world, reserves of strength and solvency which enable us to rise solid, steadfast and superior, above the waves of cosmopolitan speculation. Thus and thus alone can we stand firm and unbroken against the winds that blow.

Winston S. Churchill to George Woodcock[1]
(Premier papers, 11/474)

11 June 1952

Dear Mr Woodcock,

Thank you for your most interesting letter of April 16 about Malta, which has been carefully considered by the Departments concerned.

As you probably know the Maltese Government has now made certain requests for financial aid over a wide field from Her Majesty's Government and a delegation of Maltese Ministers is in London at the moment discussing these requests with the Minister of State for Colonial Affairs and the Departments concerned. The views which the General Council of the Trades Union Congress have formed as a result of Mr Deakin's visit to Malta will be very helpful to the Minister of State. In view of the fact that these discussions are

[1] George Woodcock, 1904–79. Married, 1933, Laura McKernan. Civil Servant, 1934–6. Secretary to TUC Research and Economic Dept, 1936–47. Asst General Secretary, TUC, 1947–60; General Secretary, 1960–9. Member, Royal Commission on Taxation of Profits and Income, 1950. Vice-Chairman, National Savings Committee, 1952–75. Member, Committee on the Working of the Monetary System, 1957. Member, National Economic Development Council, 1962–9. Member, Royal Commission on Trade Unions and Employers' Associations, 1965–8. Chairman, Commission on Industrial Relations, 1969–71.

now in progress, and of the Constitutional position of Malta, you will not expect me to comment in detail on the General Council's suggestions, which cover much the same field. I am, however, attaching a memorandum which sets out the comments of the Service Departments on the specific points which concern them on pages four and five of your letter.

I should be obliged if you would express to Mr Deakin the Government's appreciation of his most valuable work in Malta.

MEMORANDUM BY THE SERVICE DEPARTMENTS ON CONDITIONS OF EMPLOYMENT IN MALTA

(a) It is the policy of the Service Departments to provide for full consultation with recognised representatives of their employees in Malta, and, as the Trades Union Congress will be aware, the recent wage claim has been fully discussed with representatives of the Malta General Workers Union. The wages policy of the Service Departments in Malta will continue to pay due regard to the practice of local good employers as a whole. This policy does not of course imply any direct relation between conditions in the United Kingdom and conditions at bases overseas, but it is in principle the same as the fair wages policy of Her Majesty's Government in the United Kingdom.

(b) It is not the policy of the Service Departments automatically to reduce the number of their employees in Malta, or elsewhere, to compensate for increases in staff costs, but as the amount of money for the Services is limited the Departments must always take into account the level of staff costs in any particular place in deciding how much employment they can afford to provide there, and this may require reductions in numbers employed when wages or other staff costs rise.

(c) Opportunities for promotion to higher posts for Maltese employees are in fact provided. For example, on the industrial side in the Dockyard all posts up to and including Chargemen are open to suitable local candidates, and a number of Maltese apprentices are brought to the United Kingdom each year to complete their training in a Home yard where, if they are good enough, all the opportunities open to a Dockyard apprentice trained in the United Kingdom are open to them also. All the Services make the maximum possible use of local labour and this policy will be continued.

(d) If the reference here is to the difference in some respects between conditions of service in Malta on one hand and in the United Kingdom on the other, the point has already been covered in (a) above.

(e) Consultation between the Service Departments, with a view to co-ordinating policies on wages and other conditions of service in Malta, is the accepted practice.

June 1952

Winston S. Churchill to Sir David Maxwell Fyfe
Prime Minister's Personal Minute M.329/52
(Premier papers, 11/42)

12 June 1952

From the paper attached to your minute of June 5 I see that the Treasury are unwilling to agree to your proposal for the appointment of a Director-General of Civil Defence Operations. I think that it would be best for you to argue this out with the Chancellor of the Exchequer and see if you can reach agreement before the matter comes before the Defence Committee or Cabinet. This is the usual practice.

Winston S. Churchill to Winston Churchill
(Churchill papers, 1/51)

12 June 1952

My dear Winston,

Thank you so much for your letter of May 13.[1] I am very glad the Head Master was pleased with the book. I send you some sets of Luxembourg stamps which have been sent to me in case they may be of interest and I have told my Private Office to look out for any that come to us in the ordinary way.

The racing season has opened not badly for us. Although we have no beloved Colonist II, Pol Roger and Loving Cup[2] have both distinguished themselves. Your Father came with me to the races at Windsor last Thursday but Non Stop only ran third.

We begin tomorrow our last session of Parliament before the summer holidays. It is a nine week stretch and I expect there will be a good many late nights.

With much love dearest Winston
Your loving grandfather

---

[1] Reproduced above (p. 433).

[2] Both horses were acquired in 1949. Pol Roger had his best season in 1952–3, winning three times. Loving Cup had her only win in 1952, and was retired to Newchapel as a broodmare.

June 1952

Jack Binns to Winston S. Churchill
(Premier papers, 11/136)

13 June 1952

WORKING MEN TORIES

Sir,

Excuse us writing but we thinks you should know. First we can't understand why you did not bring out a white paper and put before the nation and all our mates on the Labour side the mess you had to face when you took over. If you put the facts widely about and exposed the weakness of the mess Labour made it would have given a different verdict at the local elections. We are always being told at our factories and by shop stewards what a mess you have made of it and if you had had any exposure of the Labour rule you would have made it. This argument has influenced the great mass and even some of our lads who were Tories are now Labour. They have swallowed the pill. We and they won't accept our argument. They say if Churchill had anything to expose he would have done it and given details. So sir to put things straight do expose with all your might what mess the Labour party left you to face. Your government is being blamed for all this mess. Make the exposure broadcast so all can know the facts. These they do not know. If you don't we fear Labour will have a walkover of an election, as Labour lies are swallowed. So broadcast the facts and expose Labour lies.[1]

Winston S. Churchill to Sir Norman Brook and Lieutenant-General Sir Ian Jacob
Prime Minister's Personal Minute M.330/52
(Premier papers, 11/49)

13 June 1952

As soon as I have studied the Chiefs of Staff Paper* I propose to hold a series of committee meetings at No. 10 beginning next week, in order to inform myself more fully upon it.

*Global Strategy.

---

[1] Churchill forwarded this letter to Lord Swinton on June 16, adding: 'What has been done about the statements that we agreed were to be prepared on the condition when we took over? This is a very impressive letter on the subject' (M.338/52).

June 1952

John Colville: diary
('The Fringes of Power', pages 306–7)

13–15 June 1952

I spent the weekend at Chartwell. Last Friday and Saturday I went racing with the PM at Lingfield. On Saturday evening Lord Cherwell and Bill Deakin[1] came to stay. We did little work, but W was in better form than of late, though still depressed. He told me that if Eisenhower were elected President, he would have another shot at making peace by means of a meeting of the Big Three. For that alone it would perhaps be worth remaining in office. He thought that while Stalin lived we were safer from attack than if he died and his lieutenants started scrambling for the succession.

He also elaborated his theme of 'the commodity sterling dollar'[2] – an international medium of exchange based on the world price of, say, fifteen commodities over a period of three years. This year, for instance, the years chosen would be 1948, 1949, 1950; next year 1949, 1950, 1951; and so on. The Prof said that such a scheme had possibilities if the Americans would lend it their support and their material backing.

Feeling wearied by the prospects of the future I wrote the following in the early hours of the morning:

It is foolish to continue living with illusions. One may bury one's head in the past, reading James Boswell[3] or the privately printed letters of Labouchere[4] to Lord Rosebery[5]; or one may talk of forcing reality on the people by a

---

[1] Frederick William Dampier Deakin, 1913–2005. Known as 'Bill'. Educated at Westminster School, 1926–30. Studied for six months at the Sorbonne, 1931, then at Christ Church, Oxford, 1931–4: BA Hons, 1st class, Modern History. Taught in Germany, 1934–5. Fellow and Lecturer at Wadham College, Oxford, 1936–49. Research Assistant to Churchill, 1936–9. 2nd Lt, RA (TA), 8 July 1939. Served with Queen's Own Oxfordshire Hussars, 1939–41. Special Operations, War Office, 1941. British Military Mission to Tito, 1943. DSO, 1943. Lt-Col., 1943. Married, 1943, Livia Stella Nasta. 1st Secretary, British Embassy, Belgrade, 1945–6. Director of Researches for Churchill, 1946–9. Warden of St Antony's College, Oxford, 1950–68. Author of *The Brutal Friendship*, a study of the relationship between Hitler and Mussolini (1962). Knighted, 1975. Published an account of his wartime experiences in Yugoslavia, *The Embattled Mountain* (1971).

[2] A Churchill concept since at least 8 Oct. 1933, when James Roosevelt paid a visit to Chartwell. Churchill drew an intertwined pound and dollar sign which he referred to as the 'Sterling Dollar', and said: 'Pray bear this to your father from me. Tell him this must be the currency of the future.' Roosevelt asked: What if his father wished to call it the dollar sterling? 'It is all the same,' Churchill replied (Kay Halle, *The Irrepressible Churchill*, pp. 7–8).

[3] James Boswell, 1740–95. Educated at University of Edinburgh. Married, 1769, Margaret Montgomerie: five children. 9th Laird of Auchinleck, 1782. Author of *The Life of Samuel Johnson, LL.D.* (1791).

[4] Henry Labouchere, 1831–1912. MP (Lib.) for Windsor, 1866; for Middlesex, 1867; for Northampton, 1880–1906. His magazine *Truth* ran a series of attacks on Churchill, for impropriety, when Churchill was a cadet at Sandhurst.

[5] Archibald Philip Primrose, 1847–1929. Educated at Eton, Brighton and Christ Church, Oxford. 5th Earl of Rosebery, 1868. Married, 1878, Hannah de Rothschild (d. 1890): four children. Under-Secretary of State for Home Dept, 1881–3. First Commissioner of Works, 1885. Lord Privy

slump with the accompaniment of hunger and unemployment and the consequent acceptance of a lower standard of living. But the facts are stark. At the moment we are just paying our way. A trade recession in America will break us; the competition of German metallurgical industries and the industrialisation of countries which were once the market for our industrial products will ruin our trade sooner or later and sap the remaining capital on which our high standard of living is based.

It costs too much to live as we do. The price of keeping a man in hospital is more than £700 a year. To send an individual to settle in the Commonwealth costs £1,000 a head.

What can we do? Increasing productivity is only a palliative in the face of foreign competition. We cannot till sufficient soil to feed 50 million people. We cannot emigrate fast enough to meet the danger, even if we were willing to face the consequent abdication of our position as a great power and even if there were places for two-fifths of our population to go.

The British people will face war or the threat of invasion with courage. It yet remains to be seen if they will accept a lower standard of living.

Lord Cherwell sees hope in the union of the English Speaking World, economically and politically. He thinks that just as the Scots complained of Union with England but ended by dominating Great Britain, so we in the end should dominate America. He thinks that Roosevelt, had he lived, and Winston, had he remained in power in 1945, might have led us far along the road to common citizenship. They often spoke of it. But now England, and Europe, distrust, dislike and despise the United States.

Some pin their faith in the development of the Empire as a great economic unit, equal in power to Russia and the USA. We have left it late. Ambitious efforts, such as the groundnuts scheme, have failed.

It is easier for the old. Their day is almost over. Meg and I hope for a child in November. It should be easier for him or her if neither hunger nor nuclear fission cut life short, because the child will grow into a new world. We are the transitional generation, who have climbed to the watershed and will soon look down the other side, on a new world. It will be wiser neither to think nor to speak too much of the past.

The Prime Minister is depressed and bewildered. He said to me this evening: 'The zest is diminished.' I think it is more that he cannot see the light at the end of the tunnel.

Nor can I. But it is 1.30 a.m., approaching the hour when courage and life are at their lowest ebb.

Seal, 1885. Foreign Secretary, 1886, 1892–4. Chairman of London County Council, 1889–90. PM, 1894–5. Leader of the Opposition, 1895–6.

Bill Deakin to Winston S. Churchill
(Churchill papers, 4/24)

14 June 1952

A meeting[1] was held at 27 Hyde Park Gate on 11 June between Pownall,[2] Allen,[3] Deakin and Kelly.[4] The following points were discussed:

1. Maps. Pownall has all maps ready with the exception of two, which Deakin is obtaining from the Foreign Office.

2. Appendices. These have now been checked by Pownall, and Deakin is having a final read over the weekend.

3. Deakin reported that he has discussed the chapter on the Second Quebec Conference with Lord Cherwell, and that between them they are drafting an insertion on the Morgenthau Plan. With this exception, Book XI was thought to be in an advanced state.

4. Certain minor corrections were made to Book XII, Chapter 11, 'The American Interregnum', and Chapter 12, 'The German Surrender'. Deakin has re-constructed part of the former chapter.

Book XII, Chapter 13. It was agreed to write in a short narrative of the events leading up to the fall of Trieste. Deakin to do.

A further meeting of the syndicate will be held in about three weeks to consider further progress on Book XII.[5]

---

[1] About the sixth and final volume of Churchill's *The Second World War*.

[2] Henry Royds Pownall, 1887–1961. Entered Army, 1906. On active service, 1914–18 (DSO, MC). Director, Military Operations and Intelligence, War Office, 1938–9. CGS, BEF, 1939–40. Knighted, 1940. Inspector-General, Home Guard, 1940. GOC, British Forces, Northern Ireland, 1940–1; in Ceylon, 1942–3. VCIGS, 1941. C-in-C, Far East, 1941–2. GOC-in-C, Persia, 1943. CoS to Supreme Allied Cdr, South-East Asia, 1943–4. Churchill's principal aid on military aspects of war memoirs, 1945–55. Chief Commissioner, St John's Ambulance Brigade, 1947–9. Chancellor, Order of St John, 1951.

[3] George Rolland Gordon (Peter) Allen, 1891–1980. Educated at United Services College. Lt, 1912. OBE, 1919. Lt Cdr, 1920. Cdr, 1926. Married, 1928, Alicia Lilian Griffin Eady. Deputy Director, Trade Div., Admiralty, 1939–42. Capt., 1941. Special Service, HMS *Quebec*, 1942–3; HMS *President*, 1944–7. DSO, 1943. CSO to RAdm. Force 'G', HMS *Odyssey*, 1943–4 (despatches). CBE, 1944. Commodore, 1945. Author of *Victory in the West*, vol. 1, *The Battle of Normandy* (1962).

[4] Richard Denis Lucien Kelly, 1916–90. Educated at Marlborough and Balliol College, Oxford. Surrey and Sussex Yeomanry, 1939–40. Indian Mountain Artillery, India and Burma, 1941–5. Called to the Bar, *in absentia*, Middle Temple, 1942; Bencher, 1976; Emeritus, 1987. Married, 1945, Anne Marie Anderson (div. 1954). Archival and literary assistant to Churchill during preparation for publication of *The Second World War* and *A History of the English Speaking Peoples*, 1947–57. Published an abridgement of Churchill's *The Second World War* (1959); *The Ironside Diaries, 1939–40* (1962). Recorder, Crown Court, 1972–80.

[5] On June 17 Churchill wrote on this letter: 'Thank him very much.'

June 1952

Winston Churchill to Winston S. Churchill
(*Churchill papers, 1/51*)[1]

15 June 1952

Dear Grandpapa,

Thank you so much for the letter and the stamps, they are the best I have got; I have given them to the Headmaster to keep for me till the end of the term in case I loose them.

I have been swimming today, the pool was very warm. I have been playing lots of cricket, I like wicket-keeping very much. I hope everyone's well. We break up on the 29th July.

Winston S. Churchill to Sir Norman Brook
Prime Minister's Personal Minute M.332/52
(*Premier papers, 11/49*)

15 June 1952

I am reading the Chiefs of Staff Appreciation[*] which reached me last night. I do not know what meetings will be necessary with them until I have annotated it.

2. What I am anxious to examine myself are the possibilities of substantial reductions in obsolete weapons and superfluous ammunition, as well as the maintenance of present numbers, so far as possible, in the Air Force, although new types of machines are being introduced, the complements of surface ships of the Navy, and the intake into the Army, especially questions relating to apprentices, and any other possible reductions in the rearmament expense in order to stimulate the export trade. This is the practical task.

3. Meanwhile I should be glad if the Foreign Secretary presided over the discussions of the various economic issues raised in the latest series of papers. He would of course be welcome at any of the meetings I hold myself.

[*] On Global Strategy.

---

[1] This letter was handwritten.

Winston S. Churchill to Sir Edward Bridges
Prime Minister's Personal Minute M.333/52
(Sir Martin Gilbert papers)

15 June 1952

All departments should be directed to deal with dates in official correspondence or statements either as 'the 20th of April', or 'April 20'. The former is better for speaking. '20th April', or '20 April' should not be used.

Sarah Beauchamp to Winston S. Churchill
(Churchill papers, 1/50)[1]

16 June 1952   New York

Darling Papa,

Antony and I are so happy that Mummie will join us in Italy for a holiday.[2] We will take good care of her, and all be home by August 3rd latest. We are longing to see you. I hope you liked the film of Randolph. We think it could be a really wonderful series.

The two first films were made a little impetuously – but if it goes, we will be well organised in the future.

When he speaks without notes he has a wonderful personality, a warm human quality and a fine wind. He will have to look after his voice and diction though.

We are busy packing and finishing up everything. I have two more shows to do – and then we are free!

The newspapers print gloomy things everywhere. I hope you find some solace, in the comfort that your presence brings.

---

[1] This letter was handwritten.
[2] On July 7 Clementine travelled with Mary, Duchess of Marlborough, to Monte Catini for a stay at a health spa.

June 1952

Winston S. Churchill to Florence Horsbrugh
Prime Minister's Personal Minute M.337/52
(Premier papers, 11/84)

16 June 1952

This is an interesting cutting,[1] and as you know the speakers fully represent my view. Please give me a brief report showing:

How many classes are there in England where the pupils number over 30, over 40, and over 50;
How many boys and how many girls;
How many pupils there are between the ages of 14 and 15;
What would be the saving if the leaving age became optional to the parents at 14.

Would it be possible to organise evening classes for pupils between 14 and 15 on, say, three days a week, with a substantial additional payment to teachers who took them? When will the school building programme enable all classes to be reduced to 30, (a) on the present basis, and (b) if the optional leaving age were reduced to 14? Is it not a fact that the quality of the education has definitely deteriorated through the size of the classes and the undue mingling of the ages?

Pray let me have objective answers on these points.

John Colville to Evelyn Shuckburgh
(Premier papers, 11/541)

16 June 1952
Top Secret

Dear Shuckburgh,

The Prime Minister has asked me to find out how the number of Soviet citizens employed by the Soviet Government in their Embassy in London and in any ancillary Missions compares with the total number of British subjects employed in our Embassy in Moscow. If we allow more Soviet citizens here than we have British subjects in Russia, has the possibility been considered of insisting that the Russians employ no more in London than we need to employ in Moscow?

---

[1] Article from *The Scotsman*, 16 June 1952: 'Cut Leaving Age to 14: Highland School Teachers' Plea'. To summarize: a teacher, Mr W. J. Clark, pleaded at the annual general meeting of the Educational Institute of Scotland 'that the school leaving age be reduced to 14 until sufficient staff and adequate accommodations were available to cope with the increase in pupils consequent on the raising of the age limit to 15'. Raising the age limit, he argued, had the adverse effect of overcrowding the classrooms and overworking the teachers, thus leading to deterioration in the quality of education.

JUNE 1952

Field Marshal Lord Alexander to Winston S. Churchill
Prime Minister's Personal Telegram T.136/52
(Premier papers, 11/118)

16 June 1952
Immediate
Secret and Personal
No. 1004

I have just returned with my party from Korea after a very informative and interesting visit to the battle front lasting two full days. I visited the Commonwealth Division and a ROK Division and the American 45 Division besides various other ancillary units and Headquarters.

My impressions are favourable. I consider that the organization of the front is sound and on the right lines. The soldiers are in good heart and morale excellent. The front positions are well chosen resting on naturally strong defensive terrain, well dug in wired and mined. Behind which there is another good natural position called the Wyoming lines also well prepared and wired. A third position known as Kansas line several miles to the rear is equally well prepared for defence if necessary. The arrangements for air support and artillery support are well organised. Communications in the form of new roads are well planned.

To sum up I am happy about the defensive strength of the United Nations front which I consider strong enough to withstand a mass assault. However there is one weakness namely the army commander should have one corps at least in mobile reserve. He cannot at the moment achieve this without unduly extending the divisional fronts. General Van Fleet[1] is aware of this weakness.

2. Visited Koje island and prisoners of war. Great energy has been displayed here and their new arrangements are sound. Consequently there should be no trouble in the future.

3. Interviewed President Syngman Rhee[2] and spoke frankly with what results I do not know. Record of interview follows. Have been most warmly welcomed by Americans who could not have been more friendly and cooperative.[3]

[1] James Alward Van Fleet, 1892–1992. Born in Coytesville, Fort Lee, NJ. Attended West Point, 1911. Graduated and commissioned 2nd Lt, 1915. 1st Lt, 1916. Capt., 1917. Maj., 1920. Lt-Col., 1936. Col., 1941. Brig.-Gen., 1946. Maj.-Gen., then Lt-Gen., 1948. Gen., 1951. Served in WWI, WWII and Korean War. Three Silver Stars, two LOMs, three Bronze Stars, three Purple Hearts, three DSCs, four DSMs.

[2] Syngman Rhee, 1875–1965. Educated at George Washington University (BA), Harvard University (MA) and Princeton University (Ph.D.). Helped form Independence Club, 1896. President, Korean Provisional Government, 1919–21, 1925. Married, 1934, Franziska Donner. President, Republic of Korea, 1948–60. Forced to resign, 1960. In exile, Hawaii, 1960–5.

[3] Churchill responded on June 17: 'Your reconnaissance has already done much good and you have avoided many pitfalls. All our colleagues send warmest wishes for continuance of good luck' (T.137/52).

JUNE 1952

Anthony Eden to Winston S. Churchill
(*Churchill papers, 2/517*)

16 June 1952
Confidential
PM/52/63

Your minute M.318/52 referred to certain of the German Military Commanders now held as war criminals.

We still hold Kesselring and Manstein. But Rundstedt[1] is not under arrest and was never brought to trial in view of his bad state of health.

The total number of war criminals detained in the British Zone of Germany has gone down very much in recent months. Last December the total was 191. At the end of this week it will be 131. This reduction is due to:
> (a) The Cabinet's decision of last December that the period spent by each war criminal in custody before his trial should be counted towards the sentence he was serving.
> (b) The exercise of clemency as part of a Clemency Review which is still going on.
> (c) The normal expiry of sentences.

The plan which we eventually agreed with Adenauer as part of the German Contract differs from our previous plan only in one respect. Instead of the Germans taking over the custody of the war criminals, the Three Powers will continue to be responsible for custody until such time as the Germans can overcome certain legal difficulties and take it over themselves. But the plan itself has not fallen through.

Briefly, a Mixed Board is to be set up consisting of three German representatives and one representative of each of the Three Powers. The Board will make recommendations on clemency or reduction of sentence. Clemency will be exercised by the convicting power. A unanimous recommendation by the Board will be binding.

Of course, this arrangement cannot begin to work until the Contract is ratified by all Four Powers. But we are determined that no time should be lost after that. Indeed, we have already chosen the British member of the Board. Once the Board starts work, we can be sure that the cases of Kesselring and Manstein will be among the first to be put to it.

Until that time, I do not see how we can get Kesselring and Manstein out of prison. We could only do so by giving them exceptional and privileged treatment. I am opposed to this. We must not imply that we no longer have

[1] Karl Rudolf Gerd von Rundstedt, 1875–1953. Served in Imperial German Army, 1893–1918; German Army, 1918–38. Retired with rank of General. Rejoined army, 1939: Cdr, Army Group South, Polish campaign; Army Group A, invasion of France, 1939–40. FM, 1940. Dismissed by Hitler following German retreat from Rostov, 1941. Recalled and appointed C-in-C in the West, 1942. Dismissed after Allied invasion of Normandy, 1944. Recalled as C-in-C West, Sep. 1944. POW, 1945–9. Witness for German High Command, Nuremberg Trials, 1946.

confidence in the justice of our war crimes procedure and sentences. To do so would be to cast a doubt upon the whole system which is now the subject of agreement in the German Contract. We must therefore apply general principles with absolute impartiality towards all the prisoners, whatever their rank and notoriety.

At present Kesselring is due to be released in May 1959 and Manstein in May 1953. Selwyn Lloyd[1] has been carefully into Manstein's case. We had hoped that it might be possible to arrange his release on grounds of ill-health. But it is clear that the state of his health would not justify it under any of the normal rules.

When agreement was reached with Adenauer about the terms of the Contract on war criminals, he appealed to the Three Powers to do their best to speed up releases in the period before the Contract comes into force. A new method of computing pre-trial custody will lead to a few releases. Apart from this, the Clemency Review which is now going on can be expected to lead to further releases. I cannot say how many because each case has to be examined in detail and on its merits. Kesselring's and Manstein's cases have already been examined and no grounds for the exercise of clemency could be found. We recently had a meeting with the Chief Judge of the Occupation Courts in Germany about the Clemency Review. We hope to exercise clemency in all cases where a fair and even a generous application of general principles justifies it. As you know, the late Government was nervous about exercising clemency in more than a few cases. Our people in Germany who are conducting the Review are quite aware that this inhibition has been removed.

Peter Thorneycroft to Winston S. Churchill
(Premier papers, 11/263)

17 June 1952
Top Secret

1. My attention was recently drawn to two cases where individuals known to have had close associations with Communists hold appointments on statutory bodies for which the Board of Trade is responsible. I have come to the conclusion that no action need be taken in either case, but I feel that I ought perhaps to report the circumstances to you.

---

[1] John Selwyn Brooke Lloyd, 1904–78. Educated at Fettes College and Magdalene College, Cambridge. Called to the Bar, 1930. Member, Hoylake Urban District Council, 1932–40. Reserve officer, 1937. 2nd Lt, 1939. Capt., 1939. Bde Maj., 1939. Maj., 1941. Lt.-Col., 1942. OBE, 1943. Deputy CoS to 2nd Army, 1944. Acting Brig.-Gen., 1945. CBE, 1945. MP (Cons.) for Wirral, 1945–76. KC, 1947. Minister of State for Foreign Affairs, 1951–4. Minister of Supply, 1954–5. Minister of Defence, 1955. Foreign Secretary, 1955–60. Chancellor of the Exchequer, 1960–2. Leader of the House of Commons, 1963–4. Lord Privy Seal, 1963–4. Baron, 1976.

2. Dr Joan Robinson[1] (a daughter of the late General Sir Frederick Maurice[2]) has been a part time member of the Monopolies Commission since its inception. She holds extreme left wing views, and not only attended the recent Moscow Economic Conference but was active in persuading other economists to attend. But the Security Service – who, at my instance, have recently reassessed their information about her – are satisfied that she is not a member of the Communist party or a fellow traveller in the sense of a person who deliberately refrains from joining the party in order to be better able to further its objects. In any event she proposes, for purely personal reasons, to resign from the Commission in August. It seems to me that the best course will be to let this resignation take its course, but to do nothing in the matter in the meantime, especially as, to remove her, I should have to be satisfied, under the legislation that she was 'unfit to continue in office'.

3. A rather more difficult case is that of Professor P. M. S. Blackett,[3] who is a part-time member of the Board of the National Research Development Corporation, the body which was created in 1948 to further the development and commercial exploitation of inventions made by Government Research Staff. Professor Blackett was appointed to the Board in 1949 and his appointment was renewed for a further period of three years by my predecessor in September last – but only after prolonged consideration of his position and reference to the then Prime Minister.

It is a matter of common knowledge that Professor Blackett is closely associated both in his domestic life and in his scientific work with known active Communists. The Security Service report confirms, however, that he is not himself a member of the party and states that there is indeed some evidence that he is deliberately dissociating himself from extreme left wing politics. But the factor which weighed most with my predecessor, in deciding to reappoint him – and which I myself regard as decisive – is that in his capacity as a member of the Board Professor Blackett would in fact not be dealing with

---

[1] Joan Violet Maurice, 1903–83. Educated at Girton College, Cambridge. Married, 1926, Austin Robinson: two children. Asst Prof. of Economics, Cambridge University, 1928; Junior Asst Lecturer, 1931; Lecturer, 1937; Reader, 1949. Member, British Academy, 1958. Elected Fellow of Newnham College, 1962. First female Fellow of King's College, Cambridge, 1979. Author of *The Economics of Imperfect Competition* (1933); *An Essay on Marxian Economics* (1942); *The Production Function and Theory of Capital* (1953); *Accumulation of Capital* (1956); and *Exercises in Economic Analysis* (1960).

[2] Frederick Barton Maurice, 1871–1951. Married, 1899, Helen Margaret Marsh. Entered Army, 1892. Col., 1915. Director of Military Operations, 1915–18. Maj.-Gen., 1916. Knighted, 1918. Principal, Working Men's College, St Pancras, 1922–33. Prof. of Military Studies, London University, 1927. Principal, Queen Mary College, London University, 1933–44.

[3] Patrick Maynard Stuart Blackett, 1897–1974. Educated at Royal Naval College, Osborne; Britannia Royal Naval College, Dartmouth; and Magdalene College, Cambridge. Served in RN, 1914–18. FRS, 1933; Royal Medal, 1940. President of the Royal Society, 1965. Prof. of Physics, Birkbeck College, University of London, 1933–7; University of Manchester, 1937–53; Imperial College of Science and Technology, 1953–65. Director, Operational Research, Admiralty, 1942–5. Nobel Prize for Physics, 1948. Author of *Fear, War, and the Bomb, The Military and Political Consequences of Atomic Energy* (1948), and *Atomic Weapons and East/West Relations* (1956). CH, 1965. OM, 1967. Baron, 1969.

JUNE 1952 505

work involving information of security value or work which would add significantly, if at all, to the information available to him as a physicist working in a British University. The Corporation handles no secret matters or matters relevant to defence. Its primary purpose is to circularise details of public inventions as widely as possible to industry. I would add that the Chairman of the Corporation, Sir Percy Mills,[1] strongly advocated Professor Blackett's reappointment as being one of the most useful and constructively-minded members of the Board.

4. Here again, I am satisfied that, in view of the considerations summarized in the preceding paragraph, I should not be justified in taking action to remove Professor Blackett from the Board.[2]

Cabinet: conclusions
(Cabinet papers, 128/25)

19 June 1952
Secret
11.30 a.m.
Cabinet Meeting No. 61 of 1952

[. . .]

2. The Foreign Secretary said that he had been considering in the light of reports from the Minister of Defence and the Minister of State on their mission to Korea, what arrangements could be made to ensure that we were kept more closely and continuously informed on military and political developments in Korea. Some dissatisfaction was being expressed in Parliament about the existing arrangements. He didn't think it would be advisable to press at this stage for British representation on the delegation conducting the armistice negotiations: this would be taken to imply a lack of confidence between ourselves and the Americans. He also saw difficulty in securing ourselves a larger political role in Korea, though he would discuss with the United States Secretary of State the possibility of our appointing a more senior diplomatic representative with the South Korean Government. A more promising possibility was the integration of British officers in the Headquarters of the United Nations Command. The Minister of Defence had

[1] Percy Herbert Mills, 1890–1968. Born in Thornaby-on-Tees. Educated at Barnard Castle School. Married, 1915, Winifred Mary Conaty: two children. Controller-General of Machine Tools, 1940–4. Knighted, 1942. Head of Production Division, Ministry of Production, 1943–4. President of Economic Sub-Commission of British Element of Control Commission for Germany, 1944–6. KBE, 1946. President, Birmingham Chamber of Commerce, 1947–8. Chairman, National Research Development Corp., 1950–5. Baron, 1952. Minister of Power, 1957–9. Paymaster-General, 1959–61. Minister without Portfolio, 1961–2. Deputy Leader of House of Lords, 1960–2. Viscount, 1962.

[2] Churchill responded on June 22: 'I sent your minute of June 17 about two people known to have close association with Communists to the Home Secretary and he and I agree with your conclusions' (M.347/52).

reported that the United Nations Commander, General Mark Clark, had himself suggested the appointment of a British Deputy Chief of Staff for operations in Korea; and, if the United States Government could make a statement welcoming the introduction of some British officers, this would be helpful in allaying public anxiety in this country. If the Cabinet approved, the Minister of Defence might be asked to discuss this suggestion with the United States military authorities in Washington, with a view to stimulating an initiative on their part.

The Chief of the Imperial General Staff said that the Chiefs of Staff had been quite satisfied with the military direction of operations and also with the handling of the military side of the armistice negotiations. They did not favour the establishment of an integrated Allied Headquarters: the introduction into the Headquarters of a number of comparatively junior British officers would have no effect on military policy. They were, however, ready to fall in with the suggestion that a British Deputy Chief of Staff should be appointed. This officer would fit into the existing organisation and would not require a British staff.

The Prime Minister said that the United Nations had entrusted the conduct of the Korean campaign to the United States; and we should be well-advised to avoid a position in which we shared the responsibility without the means of making our influence effective. The difficulties that had arisen in Korea were political rather than military and our influence could be exerted most effectively by the Foreign Secretary in his dealings with the United States Government.

In further discussion there was general agreement with the limited proposal for the appointment of a British Deputy Chief of Staff. The Cabinet considered that this should be a United Kingdom officer, rather than an Australian or Canadian.

The Cabinet

1) Invited the Foreign Secretary to inform the Minister of Defence that they would welcome the appointment of a British Deputy Chief of Staff for operations in Korea, and to ask him to discuss this proposal with the Canadian Government and subsequently with the United States military authorities.

2) Invited the Foreign Secretary to instruct Her Majesty's Ambassador in Washington to inform the Prime Minister of Australia of this proposal during the course of his visit to Washington.

[. . .]

June 1952

John Colville: diary
('The Fringes of Power', pages 651–2)

20 June 1952

I again went to Chartwell, alone with the PM, but joined by Norman Brook in the evening.

After we had fed the fish – indoor and out* – and driven away the horses which were eating the water lilies in the lake, we had lunch together. W greatly exercised by the economic prospects. He said: 'I can assure you it is the most horrible landscape on which I have ever looked in my unequalled experience.' But when champagne and brandy had done their work he talked of the Chamberlain family – Joe[1] the greatest of the three; Austen,[2] generous and gallant but whose whole work came to nothing; Neville who wasn't above scheming to ruin Baldwin at the time of the Duff Cooper–Petter[3] election in the St George's Division of Westminster so that Neville might profit by his fall.

After the usual film, Christopher and Mary dined and Norman who wanted to talk confidentially about the weak position of sterling and suggest changes in the Government, was irked because Christopher would not leave us. However he did tell the PM that Woolton should give up the Home Affairs Committee and that Eden should take it over, relinquishing the FO. The PM also thinks Eden should have a change but says he is 'Foreign Officissimus' and doesn't want to go.

* Apart from his outdoor ponds, full of large golden orfe, Churchill established in his working library at Chartwell tanks full of brightly-coloured small tropical fish, each tank supplied with an elaborate oxygen apparatus. Feeding the fish was a frequent diversion from serious work.

[1] Joseph Chamberlain, 1836–1914. Educated at University College School. Married, 1861, Harriet Kenrick (d. 1863): two children; 1868, Florence Kenrick (d. 1875): four children; 1888, Mary Crowninshield Endicott. Mayor of Birmingham, 1873–6. MP (Lib.) for Birmingham, 1876–85; for Birmingham West, 1885–1914. President of the Board of Trade, 1880–5. President of Local Government Board, 1886. Secretary of State for the Colonies, 1895–1903. Chancellor of the University of Birmingham, 1900–14. Leader of the Opposition in the Commons, 1906.

[2] (Joseph) Austen Chamberlain, 1863–1937. Educated at Rugby and Trinity College, Cambridge. MP (Cons.) for Birmingham West, 1892–1937. Chancellor of the Exchequer, 1903–5. Unsuccessful candidate for Conservative Party leadership, 1911. Secretary of State for India, 1915–17. Minister without Portfolio, 1918–19. Chancellor of the Exchequer, 1919–21. Lord Privy Seal, 1921–2. Foreign Secretary, 1924–9. KG, 1925. 1st Lord of the Admiralty, 1931. Half-brother of Neville Chamberlain.

[3] Ernest Willoughby Petter, 1873–1954. Designed and built one of the first British motor cars, 1894. Unsuccessful Parliamentary candidate (Cons.) for Bristol North, 1918 and 1923; for St George Div., Westminster, 1931. President, British Engineers' Association, 1923–5. Knighted, 1925.

JUNE 1952

Winston S. Churchill to Oliver Lyttelton and Gwilym Lloyd George
Prime Minister's Personal Minute M.344/52
(Premier papers, 11/144)

20 June 1952

When Mr Joseph Chamberlain was Colonial Secretary he introduced a striking feature into our life, 'the banana on the street barrow'. I suggest to you that you try to make a plan for this. There was a Liverpool merchant called Jones,[1] long since dead, who ran a line of ships especially for the banana trade during the particular season of the year. The banana is a valuable food for the people as well as being a variation. I am sorry that it seems to have vanished from the scene.

Lord Swinton to Winston S. Churchill
(Premier papers, 11/136)

20 June 1952

I have discussed your minute M.338/52 of June 16th[2] with the Chancellor of the Exchequer.

After you saw the '22 Committee some months ago the Research Department circulated to Conservative Members of Parliament a full brief on the financial mess we found and some other topics as a background to the Budget.

Some time ago the Chancellor and Lord Cherwell went through a lot of material provided by Government Departments; though voluminous, the material was of varying value and not always convincing, as there was a good deal of disparity between what was found in the various departments.

I said to you yesterday that I did not think the present moment was a convenient time to bring out an official statement, and I find that the Chancellor fully agrees. When we have finished the review of the state of the nation, we shall have to produce an authoritative statement on the present situation, the measures we decide to take and the road ahead. That, I think, will be the right time to show that we have accomplished in stopping the rot since we came into office, and in doing so, to re-state the situation we found how rapidly it was deteriorating, and what we have achieved. In the meantime, on the Chancellor's advice, which I like, I propose to do this. I will get all the material looked at and tabulated by Fife Clark.[3] When Fife Clark has got on a bit with this,

---

[1] Alfred Lewis Jones, 1845–1909. Manager, African Steamship Co., 1871. Founded Alfred L. Jones & Co., 1878 (dissolved, 1879). Partner, Messrs Elder, Dempster & Co., 1879. Credited with reviving trade in the Canary Islands by exporting bananas to England. Co-founder, Liverpool School of Tropical Medicine, 1899. KCMG, 1901. Chairman, Liverpool Institute of Tropical Research, 1903. Honorary Fellow, Jesus College, Oxford, 1905.

[2] Reproduced above (p. 494 n.1).

[3] Thomas Fife Clark, 1907–85. Principal Press Officer, Ministry of Health, 1939–49. Controller,

I will ask Fraser[1] of the Research Department and Chapman-Walker of the Central Office to have a shot at preparing a booklet which sets out all the facts. This would be a party publication and would be available to all party workers. I hope you will agree that this is the best way of tackling the job.

Winston S. Churchill to Duncan Sandys
Prime Minister's Personal Minute M.345/52
(Premier papers, 11/542)

20 June 1952

I wish for full and clear information about the steel now being used for ammunition for artillery. I did not understand how it was that the figures which have been approved as requirements should be brushed aside by you without reporting the fact that you could not execute them. Pray inform me exactly what tonnage of steel has been used and what types of projectile produced by the Ministry of Supply quarter by quarter in the last twelve months, assuming June 30 as the last date and filling these last few days in by estimate. In view of the Chiefs of Staffs' recent paper it is quite clear that the extravagant scale of reserves which are the only figures with which I have been furnished is obsolete. What scale are you working to, and what military authority is behind it? We cannot afford to waste steel. Any that we can save in ammunition as judged by the Chiefs of Staff, and not being suitable for export purposes would be available for the Housing programme <u>which cannot in any circumstances be cut.</u>

You should submit to me a draft return of your general distribution of the principal materials actually used in production quarter by quarter. If you send me the form I will see whether it gives me the information I require. This quarterly report, which should not exceed two pages of print, should be furnished to such members of the Cabinet as I specify every quarter.

Home Publicity, Central Office of Information, 1949–52. Adviser on Government Public Relations, 1952–5.

[1] Richard Michael Fraser, 1915–96. Born in Nottingham. Educated at King's College, Cambridge. Served with RA, 1939–45. Capt., 1941. Maj., 1941. Married, 1944, Elizabeth Chloe Drummond: two children. Lt-Col., 1945. Worked at Conservative Research Dept, 1946–74: Joint Director, 1951–9; Director, 1959–64; Chairman, 1970–4. CBE, 1955. Knighted, 1962. Deputy Chairman, Conservative Party, 1964–75. Director, Glaxo Holdings, 1975–85. Director, Whiteaway Laidlaw Bank Ltd, 1981–94.

June 1952

Sir Edward Bridges to Winston S. Churchill
(Sir Martin Gilbert papers)

20 June 1952

Your minute M.333/52 of 15 June 1952[1] enjoins, if I understand it, that except where a long form of words is used, such as is suitable for speaking ('the 20th of April'), Departments should always put the day after the month ('April 20'); and that the form '20th April' or '20 April' should be discontinued.

This is a matter of style or convention only and you won't mind my saying with all respect, that your first thoughts on this occasion, seem to me difficult to sustain and that there is at least as much to be said for the opposite conclusion to the one you have reached.

I attach a memorandum, based largely on information obtained from the British Museum.

NOTES ON DATES
(derived from material provided by the British Museum)

1. The practice of dating documents and letters in the Middle Ages was to put the day of the month first. This followed the Latin system, 'XVIT die Junii'.

2. This continued to be the normal practice in official and private communications throughout the 16th century, even when the date was written in English 'the XVIIth (or 17) of June'.

3. The newspapers, from the earliest, seem to have adopted the other form, i.e. June 17, 1952.

4. It would seem that by the 18th century the newspaper habit of putting the month first was often used in private letters; but that the older system, i.e. the day first, has persisted in official and legal documents.

Merits

1. The following occurs in the rules for compositors and readers at the Oxford University Press, 1950:

'As to the form May 19, 1862, Sir James Murray says, "This is not logical: 19 May 1862 is. Begin at day, <u>ascend</u> to month, <u>ascend</u> to year; not <u>begin</u> at month, <u>descend</u> to day, then <u>ascend</u> to year."'

2. To put the month between the day of the month and the year avoids confusion. Thus June 20 might mean 20th June or June 1920 or 1820.

3. Again, if the date is given all in figures (17.6.52) (as in your Minute M.333/52) the month appears a matter of course in the middle. Is it not better always to stick to the same order?

4. If you write June 17th, 1952 you have to use an otherwise unnecessary comma.

5. There is at present a very great measure of uniformity instead of putting

---

[1] Reproduced above (p. 499).

the day before the month in official documents. To upset this would cause a wholly disproportionate use of time.

Suggested Conclusions

1. The difference of practice is several centuries old, but the practice of putting the day of the month first
   a) is older than the other form;
   b) is the practice more consistently followed in the Government and official documents ever since the Middle Ages.
   c) is on the whole less likely to lead to confusion.

2. If uniformity in this matter is needed (about which I am not frightfully enthusiastic) the better course is to reaffirm the long continued practice that in official documents the day of the month should be put first.

3. If you do this, whether you write '20th April' or '20 April' when you come to speak it you would naturally say 'the 20th of April', and I am not sure that I see the need to prescribe this last as a form to be used on certain occasions in official documents or statements.

Winston S. Churchill to Admiral of the Fleet Sir Rhoderick McGrigor
Prime Minister's Personal Minute M.348/52
(Premier papers, 11/57)

22 June 1952

Your Minute of June 20 about the Commander-in-Chief, Mediterranean's Plans for stopping U-boats getting out of the Black Sea.

You say at 'A' '. . . until the Bosphorus and Dardanelles have been overrun and secured'. How many weeks do the Chiefs of Staff say should be allowed for this? What numbers of troops would it require?

Winston S. Churchill to Lord Quickswood
(Premier papers, 11/119)

23 June 1952

My dear Linky,

Thank you for your letter.[1] I am afraid that there was an ambiguity in the Foreign Office letter — I enclose the relevant paragraph.[2] 132,000 is the total number of prisoners-of-war on the list given to the Communists last December. 70,000 of these do not refuse to be repatriated, those who object to repatriation numbering 62,000.

I have been following these issues very closely. It is a matter of principle

[1] Of June 10, reproduced above (p. 486).
[2] Paragraph in letter enclosed with Churchill to Quickswood, June 8, reproduced above (p. 485), beginning: 'The United Nations Command are in fact proposing to release . . .'.

and honour to us not to force prisoners-of-war to return to the Communists to their own danger. I am sure that we must stand to this moral principle. I myself would have liked to see some of the non-communists being allowed to slip away and disappear but there are obvious difficulties in this being done on any large scale while exchange of prisoners is a matter of negotiation. A lot of our own prisoners in their hands might disappear too.

Cabinet: conclusions
(Cabinet papers, 128/25)

24 June 1952
Secret
11.30 a.m.
Cabinet Meeting No. 62 of 1952

[. . .]

5. The Prime Minister said that statements on their mission to Korea should be made simultaneously by the Minister of Defence in the House of the Lords and by the Minister of State in the House of Commons. The Minister of Defence should have an opportunity for consultation and discussion before making his statement, and both statements should therefore be made on 1st July. He would give notice of this intention in reply to a Question in the Commons that afternoon.

The Cabinet –
    1) Invited the Minister of Defence and the Minister of State to make statements in Parliament on 1st July on their mission to Korea.

The Prime Minister said that he was to be asked in the House of Commons that afternoon whether he had any statement to make about the bombing attacks which had been delivered upon the power stations on the Yalu River. This action by the United Nations air forces might give rise to the suspicion that a more aggressive policy was being adopted as a result of the visit of the Minister of Defence. He therefore wished to make it clear that the decision to undertake this attack was within the competence of the United Nations Commander and that the United Kingdom Government had not been consulted in advance. He would stress the fact that this attack did not reflect any change of policy. It would be helpful if he could say that similar attacks had taken place in the past. The Foreign Office should take immediate steps to verify this, in consultation with the Ministry of Defence.

The Cabinet –
    2) Took note of the general line which the Prime Minister proposed to adopt in his statement in the House of Commons on the bombing of power stations on the Yalu River.

[. . .]

Winston S. Churchill to Commonwealth Prime Ministers
Prime Minister's Personal Telegram T.139/52
(Premier papers, 11/22)

25 June 1952
Immediate
Secret
W. No. 106

COMMONWEALTH ECONOMIC CONFERENCE

I and my colleagues in the United Kingdom Government are becoming more and more convinced that there is an urgent need for a Commonwealth Economic Conference. Economic problems are pressing severely upon many Governments of the Commonwealth. The outlook for the balance of payments is causing great anxiety in all countries of the sterling area. There is danger of a recession in world trade. Standards of living, levels of employment, and the position of sterling are threatened.

2. These, I fear, are not mere temporary troubles. On the contrary, I think the only sound assumption to make is that a period of severe economic difficulty of some years' duration lies ahead. We are no longer clearing up the debris of the war. We have reached the point at which we need to think out afresh the fundamental policies to guide our economies for a considerable time to come. Our separate Governments can either work out independently different policies for meeting the threats to the prosperity of their own countries, or we can meet together to try to concert our policies to the benefit of all. If we do not develop a common economic strategy there is a great danger that each of us, in trying to save his own economy, may in various ways inflict lasting damage upon the economies of other members of the Commonwealth.

3. In recent years, many meetings of Commonwealth Ministers have been held on individual aspects of our common economic problems. The meetings of Commonwealth Finance Ministers have been particularly valuable. But the scope of our consultations should now, I feel, be broadened. We need to know one another's minds and to concert our various plans over the whole field. This would involve a survey of major economic and financial policies, of Commonwealth development, and of commercial and commodity policy. Unless we are to frustrate one another's endeavours, we need to develop so far as we can a common outlook towards issues arising in certain international institutions, especially the International Monetary Fund, the International Bank, the General Agreement on Tariffs and Trade and the Economic and Social Council of the United Nations. We also need to consider proposals which are being made in the Council of Europe and the Organisation for European Economic Co-operation for closer association between our economies and those of the countries of Western Europe. Among all these problems

I would place primary emphasis upon reaching the greatest possible measure of agreement, and indeed, I should hope, an identity of view, first upon the steps, throughout the whole field of economic policy, necessary to strengthen sterling and to achieve early convertibility; and second, upon the measures we need to take to develop more rapidly the resources of the Commonwealth, especially of foodstuffs.

4. As these are matters of such great moment and moreover transcend in all our countries the sphere of responsibility of an individual Minister, it is my earnest hope that you would yourself attend such a Commonwealth Economic Conference if you possibly could. I have already invited you to come to London for a meeting of Prime Ministers after the Coronation next June. But I feel strongly that we cannot wait until then to come to closer grips with our economic difficulties, many of which are becoming increasingly urgent. Moreover, I am impressed with the importance of discussions with the United States President and Administration as soon as possible after the American Election and before views in Washington have crystallised. It is most desirable that a Commonwealth Economic Conference should precede discussions with the United States Government.

5. I therefore propose to you that we should arrange to hold such a Conference in the second half of November in London. If you agree, I would propose that the preparations for the Conference should be undertaken by a body of senior officials drawn from as many Commonwealth countries as are willing to make them available for this purpose.

6. I should like to put this proposal to you as a matter of first importance. I shall be most grateful if you will let me have an early expression of your views.

Cabinet: conclusions
(Cabinet papers, 128/25)

26 June 1952
Secret
11.30 a.m.
Cabinet Meeting No. 63 of 1952

1. The Prime Minister welcomed the Minister of Defence on his return from Korea and expressed the Cabinet's congratulations on the success with which he and the Minister of State had conducted their mission. He suggested that the two Ministers should make a full report to the Cabinet on 30th June.

The Cabinet briefly reviewed the discussion which had taken place in the House of Commons on the previous day about the bombing attacks on power stations on the Yalu River. The Foreign Secretary said that, while he would continue to support the action of the United States Government in authorising the United Nations Commander to make this attack, he proposed to make it clear in private conversation with the United States Secretary of the State that the United Kingdom Government thought they ought to have been consulted in advance and would expect to be so consulted on any future similar occasion. The Prime Minister agreed that this would be justified, but stressed the importance of avoiding any public statement which might be taken to imply that there was any divergence of view on this matter between the Governments of the United Kingdom and the United States.

[...]

John Astor[1] to Winston S. Churchill
(Premier papers, 11/113)

26 June 1952

Dear Prime Minister,

As a Back-Bencher who is concerned at the inability of the Conservative propaganda machine to explain the Government's actions in the last few months, I would trespass on your time in drawing your attention to one simple aspect of propaganda that I submit could do much over a period of time to restore confidence in our Party. I refer to Ministerial broadcasts, as opposed to Party Political broadcasts.

I submit that it should be the rule rather than the exception for Ministers to give short factual broadcasts when new Regulations and Orders are about to come into force, or when a complicated international situation has arisen.

As an example, I feel that a Treasury Minister might have explained, to great effect, the Income Tax Reliefs which recently came into force. Similarly, a description by the Minister of State or the Minister of Defence of his recent visit to our troops in Korea would not only be immensely popular, but informative. Such broadcasts would primarily give the impression that Conservative Ministers were taking the public into their confidence, and taking a human and personal interest in the public. Secondly, a clearer picture of our intentions and the reasons for our actions, and a clarification of the details of these actions could be given to the public. In addition, we would discover which of our Ministers had a natural aptitude for broadcasting – a factor which is not unimportant at Election times.

I submit that it is preferable even to explain unpopular legislation by broadcasts rather than to remain silent about it.

[1] John Jacob Astor V, 1886–1971. Educated at Eton and New College, Oxford. Served in 1st Life Guards, 1906. Olympic Gold Medal, Men's Doubles in Rackets, 1908. ADC to Viceroy of India, 1911–14. Capt., 1913. On active service, 1914–18. Married, 1916, Violet Mary Elliot-Murray-Kynynmound: three children. Maj., 1920. Lt-Col., 5th Battalion Home Guard, 1940–4. Purchased *The Times*, 1922; Chairman, 1922–59. Alderman, London County Council, 1922–5. MP (Cons.) for Dover, 1922–45. Chairman, General Council of the Press, 1953–5. Baron, 1956.

With all respect, I feel that those responsible for our propaganda have under-estimated the power of the radio, have misjudged the inevitable perplexity and obscurity of Government decisions to the ordinary man-in-the-street, and have miscalculated the desire of the public to have the Government's actions explained.

I would further suggest that if a Minister turns out to be particularly popular on the air, it might well be possible and advantageous to use him frequently as an Interpreter for the Government's actions.

In conclusion, I would offer one further point. Television is fast taking the place of the wireless, and it seems essential for our Party to discover and train some Party leaders who have a natural aptitude for television, so that in due course they can be used to full effect.

I hope you will consider these suggestions, as I feel that many of our supporters, who at present are more dissatisfied with our propaganda than with our actions, would welcome these broadcasts.

Winston S. Churchill to Consuelo Balsan[1]
(Churchill papers, 1/50)

27 June 1952

My dear Consuelo,

I have now finished reading your book, which I think is a very graceful and readable account of a vanished age. I am sure it will command wide attention and interest.

I think the chronology requires a little further study. If you got someone to put the dates on the margin opposite each event, you could then see where the pack might be shuffled with advantage. Chronology is not a rigid rule and there are many occasions when a departure from it is a good thing. Nevertheless, I think it true to say that chronology is the secret narrative.

The only serious point that strikes me is your references to Henry Asquith and Margot.[2] These, I feel, would cause pain and anger to their children who are alive, which I am sure you would not like. It would be easy to tone down the reference to Mr Asquith. I would not put in the story of your dining with him so soon after Raymond[3] was killed in action, nor do I think you will want

---

[1] Consuelo Vanderbilt, 1877–1964. Married, 1895, Charles Richard John Spencer-Churchill, 9th Duke of Marlborough (div. 1921): two children; 1921, Jacques Balsan. Author of *The Glitter and the Gold* (1952).

[2] Emma Alice Margaret Tennant, 1864–1945. Known as 'Margot'. Married, 1894, Herbert Henry Asquith: five children.

[3] Raymond Herbert Asquith, 1878–1916. Educated at Winchester and Balliol College, Oxford. Fellow, All Souls College, Oxford, 1902. Called to the Bar, 1904. Junior Counsel, British Wreck Commission Inquiry into the sinking of RMS *Titanic*, 1912. 2nd Lt, 16th Battalion, London Rgt, 1914. Killed in action during the Battle of the Somme, 1916.

to leave in the account of Margot's behaviour when she was your guest at Crowhurst.

As I have read so many proofs in earning my own livelihood, I have marked a few casual corrections which I noticed, but these are by no means complete.

The last chapter makes a very moving end to your tale, and the title is brilliant.

With my best love.

July 1952

Cabinet: conclusions
(Cabinet papers, 128/25)

1 July 1952
Secret
12 noon
Cabinet Meeting No. 64 of 1952

1. The Prime Minister invited the Cabinet to consider what should be said, in the debates that day in both Houses of Parliament, about the development of arrangements made for consultation and liaison between the United Nations Command in Korea, the United States Government and other Governments contributing forces to Korea.

In discussion the following points were made:

(a) Although it was true that there were no satisfactory arrangements in Tokyo for giving political advice to the Supreme Commander, it would be unprofitable to put forward in debate inconclusive suggestions for remedying this defect. An admission that the weakness existed but that no measures had yet been taken to remedy it would serve to fortify the arguments of the Opposition. It was the general view of the Cabinet that no reference should be made in the forthcoming debates to the question of developing arrangements for giving political advice to the Supreme Commander in Korea.

(b) The appointment of a British Commonwealth military officer as Deputy Chief of Staff to the Supreme Commander had been suggested by the United States Government, and accepted by Canada, Australia and New Zealand. South Africa had not yet given formal agreement, but had raised no objection. This officer would be under the orders of the Supreme Commander and would owe allegiance and loyalty to him. He could not, therefore, act as a direct link with the British Chiefs of Staff and the United Kingdom Government. On the other hand, the Supreme Commander was anxious to make this appointment, if an officer could be made available, and would undoubtedly tend to seek his advice on matters on which the United Kingdom Government might be expected to hold strong views. This officer could also establish efficient liaison intelligence machinery, through which it should be possible for the United Kingdom Government to obtain better and more authoritative information of developments in Korea. The view of the Cabinet was that the balance of advantage lay in announcing forthwith that a British Commonwealth Military Officer would be made available for appointment as Deputy chief of Staff to the Supreme Commander in Korea.

The Cabinet –

Agreed that the Prime Minister, the Minister of Defence and the Minister of State, in their statements to Parliament that afternoon, should make no reference to the development of arrangements for giving political advice to the Supreme Commander in Korea, but should announce that a British Commonwealth Military Officer would be made available for appointment as a Deputy Chief of Staff to the Supreme Commander.

[. . .]

Lord Cherwell to Winston S. Churchill
(*Premier papers, 11/294*)

1 July 1952
Secret

I gather from our bombing experts that in war conditions and with their present equipment, they think that the probable error in bombing from great heights would be about 1,000 yards.[1] If the target was within say 200 miles of the aircraft's base the error could be reduced to about 300 yards by using radio beams. They hope to improve on these figures if new ideas can be put into practice but this will take some years.

Atom bombs can, of course, vary enormously in size from the equivalent of 5,000 tons of TNT to that of 100,000 or even 200,000 tons. The Civil Defence people believe, probably rightly, that a 20,000 ton equivalent atom bomb would cause complete destruction of buildings over a circle 1½ miles in diameter. This circle would cover an area of 1¾ square miles or 175 times that of the circle of 200 yards diameter in which a 10 ton block-buster would cause similar destruction.

The general view seems to be that the air burst atom bomb will be more effective than one bursting on the ground, against most types of target. It is said that the air burst bomb would cause most of the demolition by blast, whereas

---

[1] See M.312/52, reproduced above (p. 482).

if it burst on the surface an atom bomb would waste much of its energy evaporating the ground on which buildings had already been completely destroyed. On the other hand, there is very little radioactive contamination from an air burst atom bomb whereas one exploded on the surface would make the ground unhealthy for quite a number of days.

On all these questions of the effect of atom bombs we have comparatively little precise information at present although I hope we shall be able to get much more from the Americans next year if all goes well. Without this information, we can only make the best estimate possible and opinions differ considerably. I, personally, am by no means sure that a concrete shelter with a roof 3 or 4 feet thick at ground level would not stand up to an air burst of a 20,000 ton equivalent atom bomb 1,000 ft. above. The pressure from the burst of the bomb would fall upon the ground as well as the shelter and much of its energy might be absorbed in sinking the shelter and the surrounding ground as a whole.

Winston S. Churchill: speech
(Hansard)

1 July 1952 House of Commons

THE KOREAN WAR

One would hardly have thought from the interesting and in many ways excellent speech to which we have listened that a vote of censure was being moved against Her Majesty's Government. Indeed, it seemed to me that the whole emphasis and bias of the speech was directed against the extremists in the right hon. Gentleman's[1] own party and was intended to teach them a lesson in the elementary facts of the situation, and that what was left over of the censure by that process, which was considerable, was directed, I regret to say, against the United States. We, the Government of the day – whose fate and fortune turn upon the issue of this evening's debate and Division – had hardly a word of criticism directed against us. The only point with which I will deal fully, was that we ought to have been better informed. Let us look into that in the course of our discussions.

---

[1] Philip John Noel-Baker, 1889–1982. Educated at Haverford College, Pa., and King's College, Cambridge. Married, 1915, Irene Noel: one child. 1st Commandant, Friends' Ambulance Unit, France, 1914–15. Adjutant, 1st British Ambulance Unit for Italy, 1915–18. Olympic Silver Medal, 1500 metres, 1920. Served in League of Nations Secretariat, 1919–22. Prof. of International Relations, University of London, 1924–9; lecturer, Yale University, 1933–4. MP (Lab.) for Coventry, 1929–31; for Derby, 1936–50; for Derby South, 1950–70. Parliamentary Secretary, Ministry of War Transport, 1942–5. Delegate, UN Preparatory Commission, 1945. Secretary of State for Air, 1946–7. Member, British Delegation, UN General Assembly, 1946–7. Secretary of State for Commonwealth Relations, 1947–50. Minister of Fuel and Power, 1950–1. Nobel Peace Prize, 1959. Baron, 1977.

JULY 1952   521

I was very much interested in the right hon. Gentleman's retrospect, which reminded one of a great many things which are so easily forgotten in this bewilderingly busy period. No one, I agree with him, can attempt to form a true opinion about the question now before us without looking back. I shall not attempt to go over all the ground he went over of the wartime decisions and so forth, but I think we should look back on the recent sequence of events.

While the Communists were prospering in their aggression, as he reminded us, they brushed aside all proposals for a parley, and, in the three months from April to June, a great change took place. They suffered nearly 400,000 casualties against 50,000 suffered by the United Nations Forces, including those of South Korea. This was a great change and the Communist Government in China had what is called in that part of the world 'lost face'. Their demoralisation was profound and widespread and that was no doubt why we had the Soviet proposal for an armistice of 23rd June, 1951.

The White Paper gives a very full account of all that has happened since – nearly a year's negotiations during which the Chinese Communists steadily recovered their 'face' by negotiating and arguing with the utmost – I almost said truculence, but let me use a neutral term – vigour with the United Nations. What they had lost in the field they recovered at the haggling table at Panmunjom. At the same time, as the House has already been told, they restored strength and order to their armies, doubled their size to nearly a million and made elaborate defensive works and lines of underground approach which would permit them to make an attack on a great scale.

If we compare the position today with what it was a year ago, we can see how shrewd and how well-timed was the Russian request for an armistice and how heavy has been the cost to the American armies who are bearing nine-tenths of the burden and the brunt of the war in Korea. It is said that the United States Forces have had 32,000 casualties in the bickering on the front during these armistice negotiations. We ourselves have had 1,200.

I was told that the armistice period had been costing the United States £4,500,000 a day and the British about £50,000 a day over and above the ordinary upkeep of their troops in both cases. That has been the rate of expenditure during the year of armistice and in the end we are about half as well off as we were in the beginning.

Anyone who attempts to read the details of the armistice negotiations in the White Paper may well be tempted to ask themselves in justice whether his own patience is equal to that of our negotiators. Certainly every possible concession has been made by the representatives of the United Nations to make an agreement with the Communists who were military pulp at the time they began the talks. The right hon. Gentleman told us of a number of concessions which have been made. We have not been conscious of any desire on the part of the Chinese Communists and those who guide and direct them to come to a friendly conclusion. It was not likely that they would have such wishes when they were gaining so much at every dilatory step they took and with every month that passed.

The future which lies before us in this sphere is indefinite. This armistice negotiation is in itself only intended to lead up to a truce and the truce, if acted upon, is to lead to discussions about peace, which may be equally prolonged. All the time the immense expenditure of the United States will continue. I am not at this moment arguing the rights or wrongs of the world issue; I am only arguing that due consideration should be given – nothing I say here conflicts with the arguments of the right hon. Gentleman – by the sympathisers with the Chinese Communists and by the British nation as a whole to the monumental patience, breaking all previous human records, which has been displayed by the American Government and people in discharging their duty to the United Nations. I defy anyone to show any other historical example which can equal it.

We in this country are all convinced that it would be a great mistake, with Europe in its present condition, for the United Nations or the United States, which is their champion, to be involved in a war with the Communist Government inside China. I have repeatedly emphasised the danger of such a development. But do not let us blind ourselves to the terrible cost that is being paid for their patience by the people of the United States.

I think we ought to admire them for the restraint which they have practised, instead of trying to find fault with them on every occasion. There might easily come a time, especially during a Presidential election, when a very sharp reaction of emotion, even of anger, might sweep large sections of the American people, and when any candidate for the Presidency who gave full vent to it would gain a very considerable advantage.

We here have suffered our own losses, too, in this year of negotiation. Our casualties have been a 25th part of those of the United States, and in money a 90th part, but I think it is a very dangerous thing for this country – much though we mourn and regret these losses – making so comparatively small a contribution, although greater than any of the other United Nations members, to overpress its claims and complaints against those who are bearing almost the whole burden and who, as I have said, have shown patience beyond all compare.

I can only hope that the American people will not suppose that the House of Commons is unfriendly to them or that we are simply naggers and fault finders. They have their own political and election quarrels and understand the process full well, and I can assure them that the same sort of thing is going on over here in the Socialist Party, with its internal disputes about leadership –

Mr Ellis Smith[1]: And in the Conservative Party.

Mr Churchill: – and as they are experiencing themselves in America. Above

---

[1] Ellis Smith, 1896–1969. On active service, 1914–18. MP (Lab.) for Stoke, 1935–50; for Stoke-on-Trent South, 1950–66.

all, I hope we shall not concern ourselves with American party politics and that they will make all the necessary allowances for the struggles and rivalries going on on the benches opposite.

Let me come to the Motion of censure on the Paper. We have all watched with attention, mitigated by occasional fatigue, the twirls, twitchings and convulsions which are taking place on the Front Bench opposite, and it may well be that they will feel a sense of relief in putting their differences to the test of a Division in the House as well as those which, I understand, take place in other quarters.

But there is a Motion of censure. As I said, nearly all of the speech of the right hon. Gentleman dealt with the United States, their generals, speeches they have made, and so on. We do not control the speeches which they make. But what does the complaint and censure against the Government amount to? It is that we have not sufficiently been considered by the United States, in spite of the visits that were paid to them by so many Ministers earlier in the year.

I have never denied the overwhelming contribution which the United States is making. Still, as the Foreign Secretary has said, we think that, as the second contributor to the United Nations campaign, although our contribution was so small, nevertheless we should have been consulted, or at least informed, before the bombing of the power stations in North Korea. Yet it cannot be disputed that these power stations were legitimate military targets. They supplied electric power to the military workshops and repair depots maintained by the enemy underground and in railway tunnels. They served also for the radar warning system operated by the enemy. That they were military targets cannot be disputed.

Some may ask why this particular moment was selected for the attack. According to the answer that I was given when I made that inquiry, air operations cannot be undertaken without reference to the weather conditions. Korea suffers from heavy monsoon rains in July and August, and it was necessary, if these attacks were to be made, and made successfully, that the operation should be carried out before the heavy cloudy weather set in. (*Interruption.*) I have been asked to give an explanation, and that is the information which I have been given.

One of the plants bombed lies on the frontier between Korea and Manchuria, and sends some of its output into Manchuria. This has certainly raised a matter of principle and was not, in my view, a decision of military routine. As we were not informed, we could not know. Therefore, although technically aimed at Her Majesty's Government, the censure of the official Opposition, as I said, really falls upon the United States.

[. . .] many difficulties have been settled at Panmunjom by concessions, mainly on the part of the United Nations, but in the early months of this year the exchange of prisoners, of which we held 132,000 and the Chinese Communists 12,000, became the crucial issue. There is a great deal about this in the White Paper, which I trust hon. Members will have perused, and the facts disclosed should be shown in their true light. What is a prisoner of war? He is a man who has tried to kill you and, having failed to kill you, asks you not to kill him.

Long before the Christian revelation, the world had found out by practice that mercy towards a beaten enemy was well worth while and that it was much easier to gain control over wide areas by taking prisoners than by making everyone fight to the death against you. Julius Caesar gained far more by his clemency than by his prowess. We therefore are much in favour of encouraging prisoners to surrender by giving them good treatment, and the United Nations' command have voluntarily accepted the principles of the Geneva Convention.

In my opinion, in the present electioneering atmosphere across the Atlantic there might well be Isolationists who would take such threats at their word and say, 'Let the British take their troops away and let us conduct the affair ourselves. We could easily replace their division with one of ours in Europe.' There are many Americans who think that China is more important than Europe. It certainly would be a great misfortune if that line of thought were to prevail. Indeed, it might easily lead to the ruin of the whole European structure of defence which is being built up with so much effort and sacrifice and would expose us all to mortal danger not only of war but of destruction.

Everyone knows our main policy and that is in full accord with the United States. At all costs avoid being sprawled about in China. That is and has always been our basic policy. That could not have been expressed more forcibly than by President Truman himself in his broadcast in April, 1951.

I was, I think, the first in this House to suggest, in November, 1949, recognition of the Chinese Communists. I thought at that time that the Americans had disinterested themselves in what had happened in China, and as we had great interests there and also on general grounds, I thought that it would be a good thing to have diplomatic representation. But if you recognise anyone it does not mean that you like him. We all, for instance, recognise the right hon. Gentleman the Member for Ebbw Vale (Mr Bevan). But it is just at the time when things are disagreeable between countries that you need diplomatic relations.

But there is one thing which usually severs diplomatic relations, and that is the shedding of blood on a large scale by war-like action. It is remarkable that in spite of the fact that the Chinese have in no way responded to our diplomatic gesture and have, on the contrary, treated us with scorn and have shed the blood of our own soldiers and that of our Allies, we should not only continue – our Government has continued the policy of the previous Government – to accord them diplomatic recognition but, if we followed the advice of the party opposite, we would make it a major effort of policy to persuade the United States, with their 20,000 dead, to do the same while the fighting is actually going on.

I have endeavoured – no, not to answer the right hon. Gentleman the Member for Derby, South, because in the main I have only been preaching his theme by a parallel method. I can see hardly a point of difference between us, except that he has to do his best to move a vote of censure. We ask the House to cast this censure back upon those who have moved it. The attitude towards the United States of many of the Socialists below the Gangway is devoid alike of wisdom and of prudence. We denounce their wanton and reckless conduct, seeming to care nothing for the peace and freedom of the world and the safety of this island; and there is no one who cannot feel ashamed at the deference which has to be paid to them by their leaders on the Front Bench opposite.

Henry Channon: diary
('Chips', page 461)

1 July 1952

Winston spoke on Korea and the recent bombings, and the divided Socialists tried to turn the Debate into a Censure Motion. But the old lion, coolly dressed in light grey trousers, and a short coat, fairly pulverised his attackers; rarely has he been more devastating; perhaps he is aware of the growing Tory discontent.

Sir Esler Dening[1] to Foreign Office
(Premier papers, 11/111)

2 July 1952
Priority
Secret
No. 1110

My telegram No. 1082: Korea.

I had the American Ambassador[2] and General Mark Clark to dinner last night to meet Mr Malcolm MacDonald and we had some conversation about Korea. The General asked me if I had any news about the debate in the House of Commons and I said I did not expect to hear until today. In our

[1] Esler Maber Dening, 1897–1977. Staff Assistant to Adm. Lord Louis Mountbatten, 1940–5. British Political Representative in Tokyo, 1950–1. Ambassador to Tokyo, 1952–7. Knighted, 1955.
[2] Robert Murphy, 1894–1978. Born in Milwaukee, Wisc. Cipher Clerk, American Legation, Bern, 1917–21. US Consul, Paris, 1930–6. President Franklin D. Roosevelt's personal representative in North Africa, 1941–3; in Italy, 1943–5. US Ambassador to Belgium, 1949–52; to Japan, 1952–3. Asst Secretary of State for International Organization Affairs, 1953. Asst Secretary to Deputy Under-Secretary for Political Affairs, 1953–5. Deputy Under-Secretary for Political Affairs, 1955–6. Personal representative of President Dwight D. Eisenhower during 1958 Lebanon crisis. Under-Secretary of State for Political Affairs, 1959. Retired, 1959. Chair, Intelligence Oversight Board, 1977–8. Author of *Diplomat Among Warriors*, 1964.

conversation after dinner the General reverted to the bombing of the power stations and reiterated that he did not know the decision until after Lord Alexander had left. He had agreed to the appointment of a British Deputy Chief of Staff and expected any day now that names would be submitted to him. He referred to the secrecy necessary in mounting an operation such as that which took place to bomb the power stations. There was always the difficulty that if too many people got to know of it it would leak out, which would be disastrous. With the appointment of a British Deputy, who would know about operations before they happened, he hoped that in the future Her Majesty's Government would be in a position to say that they had been consulted and that they approved the operations. He did not like the idea of a political adviser on his staff.

2. We went on to talk about the armistice negotiations and here, I am afraid, the American Ambassador displayed the cloven hoof. He brushed aside the notion that communistic face had to be saved on the prisoners of war issue. When MacDonald and I tried to argue that the Communists had to consider their prestige in the rest of Asia, where their aim was to increase fear and respect for their power, Murphy made some very hostile remarks about India and implied that there was no reason to consider Asian susceptibilities. Altogether he made a bad impression both on MacDonald and on me, and I cannot help wondering whether his counsels with General Mark Clark are likely to be very wise or to lead in the right direction.

[. . .]

Winston S. Churchill to Sir William Strang
Prime Minister's Personal Minute M.355/52
(Premier papers, 11/111)

3 July 1952

This is a disturbing telegram.[1] The passage marked 'A'[2] shows the dangers of the steps we have taken in accepting the invitation to appoint an officer who will be on General Mark Clark's staff and not free to report to us and yet whose presence will give the General a right to say that we have been 'consulted'. Thus we have a more direct responsibility without real power.

Paragraph 2. I do not agree that the American Ambassador could 'display the cloven hoof' in not being keen enough to 'save the Communist face'. It is amusing, however, that this Ambassador should be Murphy. I expect his views about India were very different ten years ago.

[1] No. 1110, reproduced immediately above.
[2] From the first paragraph, beginning 'He referred to the secrecy necessary' and ending 'idea of a political adviser on his staff'.

JULY 1952 527

Sir William Strang to Winston S. Churchill
(Premier papers, 11/116)

3 July 1952
Confidential
PM/WS/52/65

KOREA

Your minute M.356 of July 3rd.[1]

'Basis of Paragraph 51'

During the winter there had been discussion at Panmunjom between the two Delegations to the Armistice Talks about the 'voluntary' or 'non-forcible' repatriation of prisoners. The Communists did not wish to see any reference to either principle included in the final armistice document.

2. In March the UN Delegation suggested that the prisoner-of-war issue should be solved by releasing and repatriating prisoners whose names were on lists to be exchanged and checked by the other side before the signature of the armistice.

3. A provision to this effect is included in the draft Armistice Agreement and this was the 'basis of paragraph 51' referred to in your minute. It was in fact an attempt to avoid formal admission by the Communists that large numbers of their prisoners would not return. The proposal entailed, however, the preparation of new lists of prisoners held by the UN Command, so that all the prisoners whose names were on these lists could be repatriated. It seemed in March as if the Communists would tacitly accept this way out of the difficulty. It was the shock of discovering that so many of their prisoners (and in particular a high proportion of the Chinese prisoners) would not go back that led the Communists to attack the 'screening operation'.

'Paragraph 3 of Tokyo Tel. No. 1021'

4. General Harrison,[2] the leader of the UN Command Delegation, believes that an armistice is possible if we can find a formula which will
  (a) secure the return of our own men;
  (b) safeguard our principle of no forcible repatriation; and

[1] In which Churchill had asked for clarification on the meaning of certain sections in FO telegrams.
[2] William Kelly Harrison Jr, 1895–1987. Graduated from West Point, 1917. Served in France during WWI, 1918. War Dept General Staff, 1939–42. Asst Commanding Gen., 78th Infantry Div., 1942; 30th Infantry Div., 1943–6. Commanding Gen., 2nd Infantry Div. 1945–6. Executive for Administrative Affairs and Reparations, GHQ for Supreme Allied Powers, Japan, 1946–7; CO, 1947–8; Chief of Reparations Section, 1948. Chief of Armed Forces Information and Education Div., 1948–50. Deputy Commanding Gen., 8th Army in Korea, 1951–3. Member, Korean Armistice Delegation, 1952–3. CoS, US Far East Command, 1953–4. C-in-C, US Caribbean Command, 1954–7.

(c) avoid compelling the Communists to admit publicly and formally that many of their men refuse to go back.

5. He doubts whether the Communists can afford to take part in any screening or to recognise the results of any screening.

6. He thinks that a new approach will be necessary. He has been turning over in his mind the possibility of suggesting to the Communists that they should sign the armistice, return all our prisoners whom they hold, take back all the prisoners we hold whose names are on the lists which we will give them, and then allow the Communists to complain that our lists are incomplete but that as 'peace-loving nations' they will not continue the war in order to liberate by force the remaining prisoners who are 'illegally and forcibly detained by the United Nations'.

7. He thinks that in this way we might get an armistice and have our men back, whilst the Communists would not have publicly admitted that any of theirs had refused to return, but would have a propaganda line to use for internal consumption in China. On our side we would, of course, have a very good answer to that propaganda line inasmuch as we could invite neutral observers to South Korea to satisfy themselves that we were not in fact illegally and forcibly detaining any Communist prisoners.

8. In essence, therefore, General Harrison's idea is that we should not try to persuade the Communists to participate in an interrogation process but that we should try to get them in practice to accept the results, whilst leaving them a way to retreat to explain to their own public why fewer men have come back than they had lost, and for this purpose to put the blame on the United Nations.

9. I should add that when we in the Foreign Office first heard of this proposal (which has not yet been submitted formally to Washington by General Harrison) the Foreign Secretary commented that he thought this would in effect be an agreement to disagree, and would leave unresolved the serious doubts and misgivings which had divided public opinion here. The Foreign Secretary thought moreover that there were obvious disadvantages in deliberately courting a charge of 'illegal and forcible detention'.

Winston S. Churchill to Field Marshal Lord Alexander
Prime Minister's Personal Minute M.360/52
(*Premier papers, 11/111*)

3 July 1952

PROPOSED APPOINTMENT OF A BRITISH DEPUTY
CHIEF OF STAFF TO GENERAL MARK CLARK'S HEADQUARTERS

The British Officer will be responsible to the United Nations Supreme Commander and should not impart any secret information to Her Majesty's Government except with his approval. He will however receive guidance from Her Majesty's Government about their views and will seek opportunities of acquainting the Supreme Commander with them as the occasion serves. Neither consultation nor information are involved in the appointment except in so far as the Supreme Commander desires. Her Majesty's Government therefore accept no more direct responsibility for the conduct of operations otherwise than as arranged with the United States Government.

Evelyn Shuckburgh to John Colville
(*Premier papers, 11/541*)

3 July 1952
Secret

Dear Colville,

In your letter of the 16th June[1] you asked about the relative strength of Soviet Embassy and ancillary organizations in London and of our Embassy in Moscow.

2. The present figures are:

	Work Members (excluding locally-engaged staff)
British Embassy in Moscow	56
Soviet Embassy and Consulate in London	98
Soviet Trade Delegation and other commercial organizations	53

There is as you see, a very wide disproportion.

3. We have at various times considered, at departmental level, the possibility you refer to: that the Russians should be allowed to employ no more in London than we need to employ in Moscow. For the following reasons, however, the idea has not been followed up:

(i) Legal advice has been that it is in general for the sending Government to determine what is a convenient and necessary size for its

---

[1] Reproduced above (p. 500).

Mission in a foreign country. This is in fact the line we took when the Bulgarian and Hungarian Governments took steps in 1949 and 1950 respectively to restrict the size of our Missions. We have felt, therefore, that we should not limit the numbers of foreign Embassy, Legation or Consular staffs unless:

(a) the foreign Government concerned had already limited the size of the UK Mission in their country, or

(b) the composition or size of the Mission were such as to make it clear that a number of its members were there for some diplomatic relations in their various aspects, political, commercial and military. (In 1950 we did in fact freeze the number of Soviet Service Attachés in the UK at 13, the Legal Advisers considering that this action could be justified on the basis of (b)).

(ii) The Board of Trade have always resisted suggestions that the size of the Soviet Trade Delegation should be reduced. They point out that given Soviet methods of business and the pattern of our trade with the Soviet Union, there must, if we are to trade with the USSR at all, be a Trade Delegation in this country, and, for the work it has to do, its numbers are not, in the Board of Trade's opinion, excessive.

(iii) Although the Soviet Embassy in London is bigger than ours in Moscow and the Polish Embassy is bigger than our Embassy in Warsaw, the staff of our Missions in the Satellite countries as a whole is larger than that of the Satellite missions in London. The approximate figures are:

	Staff in London	Staff of HM Missions
Poland	64	44
Czechoslovakia	26	29
Bulgaria	8	20
Hungary	15	28
Roumania	13	20
Total	126	141

Lord Cherwell to Winston S. Churchill
(*Premier papers, 11/542*)

3 July 1952
Top Secret

I understand that the services originally said they would require for the first year of the war the enormous quantities of ammunition which were quoted to you (for example 17 million rounds for 3.7-inch AA guns). The Minister of Supply was worried that there was nothing like the capacity needed to produce munitions at such a rate, or even at the reduced rate required if we got considerable American imports. These figures have not as yet been submitted for Cabinet or Defence Committee approval. Presumably they will be reduced in consequence of the new view of the course of the war taken by the Chiefs of Staff.

The table you have now sent me gives the orders actually placed as part of the existing rearmament programme, which the Minister is trying to fulfil, apparently with fair hopes of success.

It is very difficult for me to express a view as to whether these orders from the services should be cut down in view of the new ideas adopted by the Chiefs of Staff. Everything depends, for instance, on whether our troops are still fighting on the Continent or are back in this country after the first month or two of violent conflict when we expect the war to drag on in a 'broken-backed' condition.

I submit comments on a few types of ammunition as illustrations, but it is of course impossible to go through the whole table.

We have now about $7^{3}/_{4}$ million rounds of 25 pdr ammunition in stock which would be sufficient to provide about 10,000 rounds a gun for the 11 regular divisions. If we required this to last only a couple of months our stocks would be ample but if a considerable number of guns are still in the line, they would probably consume a good many rounds every month. In Korea our troops, who had on average 56 guns, fired off about $^{3}/_{4}$ million rounds in the year before the truce talks began, i.e. about 1100 rounds a gun per month.

For the 20 pdr gun in the modern Centurion, forecast deliveries this year are 400,000 rounds. Stocks are very small as the gun has only recently come into use. If we have 2,000 tanks carrying 20 pdrs by March 1953, there will be only 200 rounds a tank which is definitely very low, even if the war only lasts a very short time.

Our stocks of 3.7-inch AA ammunition are about $4^{3}/_{4}$ million rounds which is roughly equivalent to the amount we used in the whole of the 1940/41 blitz. If we are reckoning on a short war we can probably reduce production – at present 55,000 a month – to the lowest level consistent with keeping the production line running. In the Minister's table it is stated that we are now using 2,000 tons of steel a month for this ammunition and its boxes. This seems very high, as the steel used in the shell would only account for 600 tons a month. In this form of ammunition at any rate it must be possible to save steel and reduce the burden on the metal-using industries.

JULY 1952

Winston S. Churchill to Harry Crookshank
Prime Minister's Personal Minute M.364/52
(Premier papers, 11/235)

4 July 1952

I do not feel that the Steel Bill as now settled will in fact rouse the passions of a highly controversial measure, although no doubt the Opposition will oppose and obstruct it. Steel policy resolves itself into Supervision and Ownership. As regards Ownership, the difficulty of finding buyers will limit the extent to which denationalisation can be carried out in practice for a number of years. The Supervision proposals are not only in harmony with the Trade Union paper of two years ago and enjoy the support of Mr Lincoln Evans,[1] but in fact they extend the State supervision in some respects even beyond the bounds of the present law. They should end duality and conflict in the Steel Industry and they command the support of the Steel Federation. They are in reality a national and not a partisan solution which unites free enterprise and State supervision in a manner wholly agreed by the principal parties concerned. I cannot feel that we should abandon the policy to which we are profoundly pledged, desert the Steel Federation after they have so fully accepted the principle of State supervision and control, and accept defeat upon what is one of the principal manifestations of our theme.

I do not believe that at the present time any such appeals to the other side as are suggested in your note would be received except as a signal of surrender. It would, I believe, be violently resented by the mass of the Party, who would be completely stultified before the electorate, and it would leave Ministers with no footing but a desire to retain office and solve the financial problem by doing unpopular things.

Winston S. Churchill to Field Marshal Lord Alexander
Prime Minister's Personal Minute M.365/52
(Premier papers, 11/75)

4 July 1952

You should I think circulate your Minute as a Cabinet Paper.[2] I do not see how we can take any decision until we get the Costing and Steel papers which are being prepared. But a full statement must be made before the end of July on decisions of policy which have been taken. I shall probably have to make a statement myself in the Economic Debate in which I will deal

[1] Lincoln Evans, 1889–1970. Member, Iron and Steel Board, 1946–8. General Secretary, Iron and Steel Trades Confederation, 1946–53. Member, Economic Planning Board, 1949–53. Deputy Chairman, British Productivity Council, 1952–3. Member, BBC General Advisory Council, from 1952.
[2] Reproduced immediately below.

with the Defence aspect. This should be spread over more time rather than reduced in compass.

Sir Norman Brook to Members of the Cabinet
(Premier papers, 11/75)

4 July 1952
Secret
Cabinet Paper No. 225 of 1952

By direction of the Prime Minister I circulate a copy of a minute from the Minister of Defence.

PRIME MINISTER FROM MINISTER OF DEFENCE: MINUTE OF 2ND JULY, 1952

At this morning's meeting of the Defence Committee, the Service Ministers and the Minister of Supply drew attention to the need for an early statement of Government policy on defence production. They pointed out that it was already becoming known, particularly to the aircraft industry, that considerable readjustments of programme work were contemplated. Indeed, discussions had had to be started with the firms making Canberras to indicate to them that they were unlikely to get follow-up orders. It will soon become known, too, that considerable sales of equipment are being negotiated.

2. Great efforts have been made over the last 18 months to accelerate production programmes, to bring in new capacity, and, generally, to stimulate industry to the maximum efforts in rearmament. The effect of cutting back orders, of changing capacity over to production for export, and of other similar measures, will be very bad indeed unless a clear statement is made of Government intentions and policy. All the steam will go out of the effort if industry is left to draw what will probably be quite wrong conclusions from administrative acts and actions consequent upon a policy which has not been explained to them.

3. May I suggest that the situation should be discussed at Cabinet early next week. In the meanwhile thought can be given to the scope of any Government statement, and the method to be followed in making it.

Winston S. Churchill to Antony Beauchamp
(Churchill papers, 1/50)

5 July 1952

My dear Anthony,

I have now read your letter of June 29, and find it very agreeable and interesting. You do not, however, say what you actually suggest about television. Do you suggest that I should be televized for presentation in the United States, or for presentation in this country, or both? It would not be wise for me to intervene in American politics at this juncture, but I am not entirely adverse to the idea of being televized making a speech or in a dialogue for this country. [. . .] I cannot, however, commit myself to anything.

Winston S. Churchill to Lord De L'Isle and Dudley
Prime Minister's Personal Minute M.367/52
(Premier papers, 11/209)

5 July 1952

I hope you will limit your tour to the Middle East, namely, Malta, Habbaniyah, Cyprus, Cyrenaica, Tripolitania, etc. and the Egyptian bases. Let me know how many Squadrons are based in these Middle East stations compared to those in the Far East, excluding Australasian squadrons.

If you go to the Middle East I think you should use a Service plane.

Winston S. Churchill to Duncan Sandys
Prime Minister's Personal Minute M.366/52
(Premier papers, 11/542)

5 July 1952

Thank you for your papers* which I am keeping. The draft quarterly return seems suitable. Let me have it for the quarter ending June. I can tell better whether it gives me the information I want when the actual figures are presented. I send you a minute[1] by the Paymaster-General on which pray comment. It seems to me that we ought to slow down the 3.7" AA Shell. What will be the economy in steel and in money if we limited steel allotments to this type to say two thousand tons a quarter? Would this be enough to keep the plant ticking over?

Please return the Paymaster-General's note.

* On artillery ammunition – steel being used.

---

[1] Reproduced above (pp. 530–1).

Gwilym Lloyd George to Winston S. Churchill
(Premier papers, 11/661)

5 July 1952
PM 52/16

BUTTER AND MARGARINE

The Cabinet is already aware that the butter ration will have to be reduced by 1 ounce in August. When I met the Chancellor of the Exchequer with other Ministers on the 30th June to discuss the Import Program, I explained that I could offset this forthcoming reduction in the butter ration by an increase of 1 ounce in the margarine ration. This was accepted by my colleagues.

Although we shall have to reduce the butter ration by 1 ounce on August 10th, I shall be able, therefore, to announce an increase of 1 ounce in the margarine ration at the same time.

I think it would be advantageous to announce these ration changes in the House and I should be grateful for your approval to make such an announcement on, say, Wednesday, July 9th.

Winston S. Churchill to Gwilym Lloyd George
Prime Minister's Personal Minute M.370/52
(Premier papers, 11/661)

6 July 1952

Your Minute PM 52/16.

I like your approach. It is always better to tell the British people that things will be bad and then they turn out not so bad than to tell them things will be good and they turn out not so good. But they are shockingly ill fed at the present time. Certainly make the announcement you propose.

Winston S. Churchill to Sir William Strang
Prime Minister's Personal Minute M.371/52
(Premier papers, 11/548)

6 July 1952

Nearly all Foreign Office telegrams are much too long and add very little to our knowledge. They all have to be encyphered and decyphered, which must be a heavy charge upon the public. Can nothing be done to make the writers at each end realize how little help they give to the country by pouring out words as if they were writing articles for the weekly newspapers? Nearly everything contained in these telegrams could have been sent by despatch in the air mail bag. Surely it is time for another warning to posts abroad to practise brevity and concentrate thought in telegrams.

Winston S. Churchill to Sir William Strang
(Premier papers, 11/116)

6 July 1952
Secret

I do not like it at all.[1] I agree with Mr Eden. We must not grovel, but they may stew. The bombing (inside Korea) may be salutary.

Jawaharlal Nehru[2] to Winston S. Churchill
Prime Minister's Personal Telegram T.146/52
(Premier papers, 11/22)

6 July 1952
Secret
No. 854

I am grateful to you for your message which your Acting High Commissioner in Delhi[3] communicated to me on the 27th June.[4] My colleagues and I have given careful consideration to your proposal to have a conference of Commonwealth Prime Ministers in the second half of November in London. I appreciate fully that the troubles we have to face are not likely to pass soon and that we have to look ahead and fashion our basic economic policies for a considerable time to come. Indeed it is with this object in view that our Planning Commission has been giving the most earnest consideration to our economic problems. I realise also that though we may have independent policies, we should always endeavour to cooperate with each other in so far as this is possible. Circumstanced as we are in India we are faced with the urgent

---

[1] See PM/WS/52/65, reproduced above (pp. 527–8).

[2] Jawaharlal Nehru, 1889–1964. Educated (like Churchill) at Harrow. Barrister-at-law, Inner Temple, 1912. Member, All-India Congress Committee, 1918–47. President, Indian National Congress, 1929. Imprisoned by the British several times for his political activities and calls for non-cooperation. Vice-President, Interim Government of India, 1946. PM of India from 1947 until his death. Both his daughter, Indira Gandhi, and his grandson, Rajiv Gandhi, were subsequently Prime Ministers of India; both were assassinated.

[3] Joseph John Saville Garner, 1908–83. Principal Private Secretary to Secretary of State for the Dominions, 1940–3. Senior Secretary, High Commission, Canada, 1943–6. Deputy High Commissioner, Canada, 1946–8. CMG, 1948. Asst Under-Secretary of State for Commonwealth Relations, 1948–51. Deputy Under-Secretary for Commonwealth Relations, 1950–1, 1953–6. Deputy High Commissioner, India, 1951–3. Acting High Commissioner, India, 1952. KCMG, 1954. High Commissioner in Canada, 1956–61. Permanent Under-Secretary of State for Commonwealth Relations, 1962–8. GCMG, 1965. Head of Diplomatic Service, 1965–8. Baron, 1969.

[4] T.139/52, reproduced above (pp. 513–14).

necessity of increasing our production and ensuring fairer distribution and thus raising the standards of the people of our country and relieving unemployment. The immediate problem that we have to tackle is the land problem which is of primary importance in a country which is basically agricultural. We have at the same time to increase our industry and our social services. Though our problems may be somewhat different from the problems of other nations of the Commonwealth, we have always endeavoured to profit by the views and experience of other Commonwealth countries and particularly the United Kingdom.

I have welcomed the meetings of Commonwealth Prime Ministers because this helps us in understanding each other's viewpoints and in promoting cooperation between the different member-nations of the Commonwealth. It is because of this that I gladly welcomed and accepted your invitation to the Prime Ministers' conference in June 1953. It is, however, with regret that I find myself unable to accept the present invitation to a conference in November next. That is just the time when our Parliament will be meeting and considering matters of great importance to us. My presence then in India will be very necessary. About that time also the General Assembly of the United Nations will be meeting in New York and this Assembly, as you are no doubt aware, will be dealing with matters of vital importance. I should like to be present in my headquarters and in Parliament then to keep in touch with all these developments.

In the event of the Prime Ministers' conference being held in November, as you have suggested, we will be glad to send an observer and my Government and our Parliament will further consider any problem on which we can make a useful contribution for mutual good.

Winston S. Churchill to Lord Swinton and Thomas Fife-Clark
Prime Minister's Personal Minute M.372/52
(Premier papers, 11/113)

6 July 1952

I think the suggestion that the BBC should be asked to arrange debates between Junior Members of the Government and their predecessors in the same office deserves to be explored and I should be glad if you will so proceed.

I hope you will also keep in mind Mr J. J. Astor's suggestion about Ministerial broadcasts[1] on suitable occasions, as well as the importance of selecting Ministers and Members of the House who have an aptitude for television.

Pray report to me.

---

[1] See letter of June 26, reproduced above (pp. 515–16).

538   July 1952

Winston S. Churchill to J. J. Astor
(Premier papers, 11/113)

7 July 1952

My dear Astor,

Thank you for your letter of June 26[1] which I find interesting.

I agree in principle with what you say about Ministerial Broadcasts, and I shall keep your proposals in mind during the coming months. The only difficulty I can see at present is that if Ministerial Broadcasts are too frequent, or if their subject matter is controversial, the Opposition will claim the right to reply and the BBC may well be disposed to agree. I doubt whether, in any case, the BBC would agree to a member of the Government giving a Ministerial Broadcast on a subject outside his field of Ministerial responsibility, just because he was a particularly effective broadcaster. We can and shall do everything possible to persuade the BBC to be co-operative, but we cannot coerce them or use them for purely Party purposes.

I agree with what you say about television, as indeed with the purpose of your letter as a whole and I am obliged to you for your clear statement of the problem.

Winston S. Churchill to Sir William Strang
Prime Minister's Personal Minute M.374/52
(Premier papers, 11/116)

8 July 1952

I could not agree without protest to forcible repatriation of the 14,000 Chinese prisoners. They are the pith of the matter. The island plan and the impartial re-screening are quite defensible.

John Colville to Winston S. Churchill
(Premier papers, 11/541)

8 July 1952

Neither the Foreign Office nor 'C'[2] are in favour of cutting the Soviet Embassy in London down to the numbers we have in Moscow. Amongst their reasons are:

1) The Russians have never sought to limit the size of our Embassy

---

[1] Reproduced above (pp. 515–16).
[2] John Alexander Sinclair, 1897–1977. Midshipman, RN, 1914–16. OBE, 1940. Deputy Director of Military Operations, 1941. Commandant RA, 1st Div., 1942. Director of Military Intelligence, 1944–5. CB, 1945. Col. Commandant RA, 1952–62. Chief of SIS ('C'), 1953–6. Knighted, 1953.

July 1952   539

(although two of the satellites have and we took counter action).

2) We have restricted the number of Service attachés but the Board of Trade do not think that the Trade Delegation and Commercial organisations are excessive.

3) However much we restricted the number of Soviet officials, the Government would still have here all the agents whom they require.

'C' says that a larger representation in Moscow would not help his service and that the size of the Soviet Embassy in London does not affect him though it may well be a source of inconvenience to MI5 (Sir Percy Sillitoe).[1] The Joint Intelligence Committee are examining the whole subject. Would you like to await an account of their report before taking further action?

Winston S. Churchill to Clementine Churchill
(Churchill papers, 1/50)

8 July 1952

Delighted to hear of your safe arrival. My very best love to you both.[2] Mind you take it easy darling. I hear Italy is very hot.

Air Chief Marshal Sir John Slessor to Winston S. Churchill
(Premier papers, 11/46)

9 July 1952
Top Secret

The First Sea Lord has asked me to answer your Minute dated 6 July on the subject of attack by US atom bombers on Soviet U-Boat mining bases.

2. These objectives are not yet included in US air plans except in that of the US carrier-borne aircraft in the Mediterranean, for which plans are understood to exist for dealing with U-Boat bases in the Black Sea.

3. I have discussed the subject with Admiral McCormick (SACLANT) and General Le May[3] (Strategic Air Command), with particular relation to the

---

[1] Percy Joseph Sillitoe 1888–1962. Joined British South African Police, 1908. Served in German East Africa campaign, 1914–18. Married, 1920, Dorothy Mary Watson: two children. Chief Constable of Chesterfield, 1923–25; of East Riding of Yorkshire, 1925–26; of Sheffield, 1926–31; of Glasgow, 1931–43; of Kent, 1943–6. CBE, 1936. Director-General, Security Service (MI5), 1946–53. KBE, 1950. Published an autobiography, *Cloak without Dagger* (1955).

[2] Clementine was accompanied by her daughter Mary.

[3] Curtis Emerson LeMay, 1906–90. Born in Columbus, Ohio. Educated at Ohio State University. Commissioned 2nd Lt, US Army Air Corps, 1930. Married, 1934, Helen Estelle Maitland: one daughter. Bombardment Cdr 8th Air Force, 1942–4; 21st Bomber Command, Marina Islands, 1945. Head, US Strategic Air Command, 1948–57. Gen., 1951. Vice-Chief of Staff, US Air Force, 1957–61; Chief of Staff, 1961–5. Vice-Presidential candidate with George Wallace, American Independent Party, 1968.

bases in the Arctic and Baltic. VCAS[1] also emphasized the importance of these bases as objectives to the US Naval Staff during a recent visit to Washington.

4. The tendency is for the USAF to say they are the business of the US Navy; while McCormick said he had not yet got the resources to do the job. When I last spoke to him, however, during his recent visit, he told me he was meeting Le May shortly to discuss the problem. He is fully alive to its importance. I pointed out to him that we have some extremely highly trained crews in Bomber Command who could do this job if they gave us the bombs.

5. I have told Sir William Elliot that I want to discuss the matter with the American acting CAS and with Admiral Fechteler during my forthcoming visit to Washington.[2] I raised the subject today with General Ridgeway,[3] in connection with the security of his sea line of supply, and suggested that a message from him to the US Chiefs of Staff timed to coincide with my visit, expressing his concern with this problem, might be useful. He took the point well.

6. I will let you know on my return what progress I make. I am afraid this is one of the many matters in which co-operation between the US Navy and Air Force is woefully lacking.

7. I have sent a copy of this minute to my Secretary of State and the First Sea Lord.[4]

Clementine Churchill to Winston S. Churchill
(Churchill papers, 1/50)

9 July 1952

My darling Winston,

Yesterday's *Times* has just reached us announcing Eisenhower's initial success at Chicago. I hope it is an augury. Mary and I have started our 'cures'.[5] They begin at 7.30 in the morning at a palatial establishment surrounded by a lovely garden. We drink 5½ pints of very nasty tepid water (3 different kinds). This takes til 9 o'clock because you have to sip very slowly and allow at least 10 minutes between each glass. It's really quite difficult to swallow them

---

[1] Ralph Alexander Cochrane, 1895–1977. Assisted in creation of Royal New Zealand Air Force, 1936–7. CoS, Royal New Zealand Air Force, 1937–9. Air ADC to the King, 1939–40, 1949. AOC, No. 3 Bomber Group, 1942; No. 5 Bomber Group, 1945. KBE, 1945. AOC-in-C, Transport Command, 1945–7; Flying Training Command, 1947–9. KCB, 1948. GBE, 1950. VCAS, 1950–Nov. 1952. Air ADC to the Queen, 1952.

[2] Churchill wrote in the margins here: 'Yes'.

[3] Matthew Bunker Ridgway, 1895–1993. Educated at West Point. Married, 1917, Julia Caroline Blount: two children (div. 1930); 1930, Margaret Wilson Dabney (div. 1947); 1947, Mary Princess Anthony Long: one child. Lt-Col., 1940. Col., 1941. Maj.-Gen., 1942. Lt-Gen., 1945. SACEUR, 1952. CoS, US Army, 1953–5.

[4] Churchill wrote at the bottom of the page: 'Please report further in due course.'

[5] At a Spa at Montecatini Terme, Tuscany.

because they are slightly nauseating! Then back to breakfast after which a delicious [. . .] bath and massage. This brings you to nearly luncheon time. After luncheon 2 hours in bed and then further walks in another garden! Then dinner and walk in the brightly lit little town and then bed!

It's very very hot but we are bearing up. The right temperature for the cure is 80°–85° as all the pores must be open but 95°–100° is a bit too much.

The flowers are lovely and strangely enough it's not at all burnt up. There are crickets and frogs who keep up a constant chorus. The food is delicious but great moderation is enjoined. We cannot see any English anywhere, but there are a few Americans – some very agreeable friends of Consuelo's, Mr and Mrs Cutting, Mr Henry May[1] who was staying at the same time as us with the Duke and Duchess[2] of Windsor at Antibes.

I wonder if Sarah and Antony have started for Italy. It would be better to wait till it has cooled down a bit.

Sir Norman Brook to Winston S. Churchill
(*Premier papers, 11/49*)

9 July 1952

You asked me to let you see how I was proposing to express the conclusion reached at last night's meeting on the adjustment of the defence production programmes.

My record of this is attached.

The Prime Minister, summing up the discussion, said that the Service Departments were now estimating the cost of the Forces to be provided in accordance with the new strategic appreciation submitted by the Chiefs of Staff in D(52)26. He asked that, in working out these estimates, the Services should assume that a limit of £500 millions a year would be set to their demands on the metal-using industries. This total £500 millions should be divided between the Services in accordance with strategic needs and not, as in GEN. 411/2, on the basis of a percentage cut on each Service. He did not ask at this stage that production by the metal-using industries for civil defence and infrastructure should be included within this limit of £500 millions. On the other hand, the Services should realise that, after their

[1] Henry Farnum May, 1915–2012. American historian. Born in Denver, Colo. Married, 1941, Jean Louise Terrace (d. 2002): two children; 2002, Louise Brown. Instructor of History, Lawrence College, 1941–2. Japanese language translator, US Navy Reserve, 1942–5. Associate Prof., Scripps College, 1947–9. Visiting Associate Prof., Bowdoin College, 1950–1; Prof. of History, University of California, Berkeley, 1952–80. Retired, 1980.

[2] Wallis Warfield, 1896–1986. Daughter of Teakle Wallis Warfield of Baltimore, Md. Married, 1916, Earl Winfield Spencer (div. 1927); 1928, Ernest Aldrich Simpson (div. 1937); 1937, Edward, Duke of Windsor, formerly King Edward VIII. Duchess of Windsor, 1937–86. Resident in Bahamas, 1940–5; in France from 1945.

plans had been worked out on this basis, further reductions might be made if it were found that particular items had been included which, on further examination, Ministers considered to be extravagant or unnecessary. The figure of £500 millions should be accepted as a firm guide for one year only. The costing of the Forces recommended by the Chiefs of Staff was, however, proceeding on a three-year basis; and it should therefore be possible to show what burden would be imposed on the metal-using industries in the second and third years if expenditure in the first year was limited to £500 millions.

The Meeting:

Invited the Minister of Defence to arrange for the current work on the costing of the Forces recommended in D(52)26 to be completed on the lines laid down by the Prime Minister, and to submit the results for discussion by Ministers as early as possible in the following week.

Chiefs of Staff: report
(Premier papers, 11/49)

10 July 1952

DEFENCE POLICY AND GLOBAL STRATEGY
Introduction

The Aim of this Report

1. In this report we examine allied strategic policy. We suggest how the present policy should be modified to take into account factors which have arisen since it was established and the United Kingdom £4,700 million rearmament programme initiated. The chief of these factors are the notable increase in United States atomic power and the economic situation.

[. . .]

Section VII – Need for a Co-ordinated Allied Strategy – World-Wide

A Co-ordinated Strategy

69. We are impressed by the need for a more coherent direction of the world-wide campaign by the Free World, not only to meet the demands of the Cold War, but also to prepare for war should it come. So far the efforts of the Allies have been concentrated largely on NATO which has tended to absorb most of their attentions. A start has been made in the Far East with the ANZAM region planning and the Pacific Pact. In the Middle East, efforts are being made to set up a Defence Organisation. Generally, however, all these efforts at co-ordination have been piecemeal and have lacked central

direction. Overall strategic direction exists solely in the Standing Group in Washington, which covers NATO planning only, and this is both a reflection and a cause of United States' preoccupation with the NATO concept to the exclusion of some other equally important strategic areas elsewhere.

70. The first step to obtain more coherent direction would be to reach agreement between the United States and the United Kingdom on the need for such central direction; but France, in spite of her weakness and inefficiency, is nevertheless a world Power with a considerable stake in the Far East and in Africa, and must ultimately be associated with any world-wide system of defence co-ordination. We therefore suggest that the allied aim should now be to establish a tripartite body under which each theatre would have its own defence organisation designed specifically to meet its own peculiar needs and problems.

[. . .]

Winston S. Churchill to Jawaharlal Nehru
Prime Minister's Personal Telegram T.147/52
(Premier papers, 11/22)

11 July 1952
Priority
Secret
W. No. 111

Your telegram No. 854.[1]

I thank you very much for your message of July 5 and I can well understand the difficulties which prevent you coming yourself. I realize fully all the problems you have before you and I wish you all success in solving them. We shall do everything we can to help you and Pakistan but I am sure you realize that we too are engaged in a struggle for life. Please do not hesitate to keep in personal touch with me.

Winston S. Churchill to Lord Leathers and Alan Lennox-Boyd
Prime Minister's Personal Minute M.377/52
(Premier papers, 11/287)

11 July 1952

I hope you are having all the press comments on the Transport Bill studied in order to see whether we can learn anything from their gruntings.

Let me have a report at your convenience.

---

[1] T.146/52, reproduced above, dated July 6 (pp. 536–7).

July 1952

Winston S. Churchill to Clementine Churchill
(Baroness Spencer-Churchill papers)

11 July 1952

My darling Clemmie,

Yr '1700' feet letter was vy welcome and I look forward to an account of how you are & what it is all like. I see a picture in the papers wh I enclose. You certainly look 'relaxed'. Are you playing Okla[homa] w Mary? I do hope the weather is not too bad. Here it is cooler & cloudy.

Another week of toil is over & I am off to Chartwell in an hour. How I wish I were going to find you there! I feel a sense of loneliness and miss you often, and wd like to feel you near. I love you vy much my dear sweet Clemmie. But I am sure you needed the 'Off Duty' break to recover buoyancy & resilience. I am most anxious to get yr report.

The Shane Leslies[1] come Sat. for luncheon & I am polishing off the Lew Douglas's[2] at the same time. I am told he is far from well. Last night Gen Ridgeway dined. I think he is a vy good man.

We have changed our Parly time table, rising July 31 returning October 14 to wind up the Session, reopening the new Session Nov 4 when we shall push the Transport & Steel Bills through. We shall only get a month at Christmas – but it is good to look forward to 10 weeks recess <u>now</u>.

It is a vy bleak outlook – with all our might majesty dominion & power imperilled by having to pay the crashing Bills each week. I have never seen things so tangled & tiresome. But we must persevere.

I am relieved at Ike's progress over Taft. Once the American election is over we may be able to make real headway. Either Ike or the Democrat wd be all right. A Taft–MacArthur[3] combine wd be vy bad.

I send this scribble by Sarah who is starting today & will send it to you from Rome. She brought Margaret Truman and & Mr Snyder's daughter[4]

---

[1] John Randolph Shane Leslie, 1885–1971. Author and lecturer. Churchill's first cousin. Son of Sir John Leslie and Leonie Jerome. Educated at Eton and King's College, Cambridge. Received into the Catholic Church, 1908. Unsuccessful Parliamentary candidate (Nationalist) for Derry City, 1910. Married, 1912, Marjorie Ide: three children (d. 1951); 1958, Iris Carola Laing. Served in British Intelligence in the US, 1915–16. Editor, *Dublin Review*, 1916–25. Succeeded his father as 3rd Bt, 1944.

[2] Lewis Williams Douglas, 1894–1974. Born in Bisbee, Ariz. Educated at Massachusetts Institute of Technology, 1916. On active service in WWI. 2nd Lt, 1917. Instructor, Amherst College, 1920. Married, 1921, Margaret 'Peggy' Zinsser: three children (d. 1974). Representative (Dem.) in Arizona House of Representatives, 1923–5; in US House of Representatives, 1927–33. Director of the Budget, 1933–4. Principal and Vice-Chancellor, McGill University, Montreal, Canada, 1938–9. Deputy Administrator, War Shipping Administration, 1942–4. US Ambassador to UK, 1947–50. Director, General Motors Corp., 1944–65. Head of Government Study of Foreign Economic Problems, 1953. Member, President's Task Force on American Indians, 1966–7.

[3] Douglas MacArthur, 1880–1964. On active service, 1917–18 (twice wounded). CoS, US Army, 1930–5. FM, Philippine Army, 1936. Retired, 1936. Returned to active duty, 1942. Supreme Allied Cdr, South-West Pacific Area, 1942–5. Hon. knighthood, 1943. C-in-C, US forces, Far East Command, 1943–51. Supreme Cdr, Allied Powers in Japan, 1945–51. C-in-C, UN forces in Korea, 1950–1.

[4] Edith Cook Snyder, ?–1999. Known as 'Drucie'. Daughter of Secretary of the Treasury John

to luncheon two days ago. All went off nicely. I will write again over the week end. Give my love to Mary Marl[borough] and believe me always yr devoted loving husband.

Winston S. Churchill to Sir William Strang
Prime Minister's Personal Minute M.382/52
(Premier papers, 11/116)

12 July 1952

In my view there can be no question of forcing any Chinese prisoners-of-war to go back to Communist China against their will. These are the ones, above all others, who carry with them the moral significance, as the ones who had opted for us would certainly be put to death or otherwise maltreated.

Winston S. Churchill to Lieutenant-General Sir Ian Jacob
Prime Minister's Personal Minute M.384/52
(Premier papers, 11/49)

14 July 1952

I have read and noted the expurgated version of the Chiefs of Staff paper on Defence Policy.

I do not agree with the last two lines in paragraph 69 on page 16.[1] What other strategic areas are equally important to Western Europe? I suggest the deletion of the words 'some other equally'.

Winston S. Churchill to Lord Leathers and Alan Lennox-Boyd
Prime Minister's Personal Minute M.386/52
(Premier papers, 11/287)

14 July 1952

You have no doubt been studying the newspapers at their very superficial crabbing: particularly *The Times*, the *Manchester Guardian* and the *Economist*. Please consider these criticisms and let me know if they suggest any changes to you. It might even be well for the Minister of Transport, if he feels inclined, to talk it out with Mr Crowther[2] of the *Economist* and get him to say what he

---

Wesley Snyder. Close friend of Margaret Truman. Married, 1950, John Ernest Horton, who liaised between Hollywood producers and the Pentagon.

[1] Reproduced above (pp. 542–3).

[2] Geoffrey Crowther, 1907–72. Joined staff of *The Economist*, 1932; Editor, 1938–56. Ministry of Supply, 1940–1; of Information, 1941–2. Deputy Head of Joint War Production Staff, Ministry of Production, 1942–3. Chairman, Central Advisory Council for Education, 1956–60.

would do himself. They are the most conceited paper in the world and one remedy for conceit is cross-examination.

We have not made our counter case sufficiently. I tried to in a speech which I made in the House.[1] It is the million vehicles all restricted and fettered for the sake of the forty thousand nationalised on whose management twelve thousand men sit at their desks at a cost of six or seven million a year. The only thing we seek is truth and the public convenience and well-being. ~~One must not be too proud to pick up a cue even from a sweep.~~ It would be a good thing to see these three Editors, or whoever they designate, separately. We have plenty of time before the autumn.

Winston S. Churchill to Sir David Maxwell Fyfe
Prime Minister's Personal Minute M.387/52
(Premier papers, 11/606)

15 July 1952

The Defence Committee accepted your suggestion that further thought should now be given to the effect on civil defence planning of the report by the Chiefs of Staff on defence policy (D(52)25). I have asked the Minister of Defence to discuss with you the assumptions which you should take for this fresh review of civil defence planning and preparations. You will wish to have the help of other Ministers concerned with the various aspects of civil defence, and I think it would be useful if a standing Committee of the Cabinet were now constituted to handle civil defence problems. You should preside over this Committee, and you might have with you:

>Secretary of State for Scotland
>Minister of Housing and Local Government
>Minister of Food
>Minister of Transport
>Minister of Works
>Financial Secretary, Treasury.[2]

Others concerned, such as the Ministers of Education, Fuel and Power, should be invited to attend for discussion of matters affecting their apartments. The Committee will receive guidance from the Defence Committee as required; and I look to you to see that the Defence Committee are informed from time to time on the progress of your Committee's work.

I had occasion recently to ask about the progress of the plans for the evacuation of children and invalids from London in war. I hope you will give early

---

[1] Speech of May 21, reproduced above (pp. 447–55).
[2] John Archibald Boyd-Carpenter, 1908–98. Educated at Balliol College, Oxford. Called to the Bar, 1934. MP (Cons.) for Kingston-on-Thames, 1945–72. Financial Secretary to the Treasury, 1951–4. Paymaster-General, 1962–4. Baron, 1972.

attention to this on your Committee. I rely on you to keep me informed on all matters of importance.

Defence Committee: minutes
(Cabinet papers, 131/12)

16 July 1952　　　　　　　　　　　　　　　Prime Minister's Map Room
Secret　　　　　　　　　　　　　　　　　　　　　Ministry of Defence
11.30 a.m.
Defence Committee Meeting No. 9 of 1952

1. APPOINTMENT OF A DEPUTY CHIEF OF STAFF FOR KOREA

The Committee had before them a Minute from the Minister of Defence to the Prime Minister (D(52)33) suggesting that the Defence Committee should approve draft instructions (attached to the Minute) from the United Kingdom Chiefs of Staff to the Deputy Chief of Staff in Korea.

The Prime Minister said that the danger of making this appointment was that the powers and functions of the Deputy Chief of Staff would be misunderstood and misinterpreted, and that the Government would be thought to have assumed additional responsibilities for the war in Korea and to have obtained a more powerful influence upon its conduct. This was not at all the case. If a British Deputy Chief of Staff were appointed, he would be responsible to the United Nations Commander and to him alone. It was, therefore, of the utmost importance that any announcement about this appointment should make these facts unmistakably clear. If the Government wished to make representations on the conduct of the war in Korea they would do so, as at present, direct to the President of the United States on particular occasions or to the United States Joint Chiefs of Staff.

In discussion the following points were made:

a) The United Nations Commander himself asked that a British Officer should be appointed as his Deputy Chief of Staff, but his request was subject to the agreement of the Governments of the United Kingdom and the United States, and it would, therefore, be possible to defer the appointment for further reflection. On the other hand, Parliament certainly expected that the appointment would be made and hoped for a statement on the subject before the summer recess.

b) Although the Deputy Chief of Staff could not himself act as a liaison between the United Nations Commander and the United Kingdom Chiefs of Staff, his presence at Headquarters should make it easier for United Kingdom liaison officers to perform their duties. Air Vice-Marshal Bouchier had completed two years in his appointment as representative of the United Kingdom Chiefs of Staff, and the Chiefs of Staff were considering recommending his replacement by an officer of lower rank. The Chiefs of Staff were preparing draft instructions for this liaison officer, which they would like to discuss with the United States Chiefs of Staff before they were issued, in order to ensure that it was clearly understood that there was a precise distinction between the functions of the Deputy Chief of Staff and of the liaison officer. The Minister of State said that he thought that it would be a mistake to reduce the rank of the Chiefs of Staff's representative at the present time, and that liaison should be left in the hands of this representative rather than in the hands of a team of attachés.

c) The Commonwealth Secretary suggested that the draft instructions to the Deputy Chief of Staff should make it clear that he was a Commonwealth officer and that his appointment had been agreed, not only by the United Kingdom Chiefs of Staff, but by the Chiefs of Staff of Australia, New Zealand, Canada and South Africa also.

d) There was general agreement that paragraph 2 of the draft instructions should be omitted. This seemed to imply that the Deputy Chief of Staff would receive constant military and political advice on United Kingdom and Commonwealth views, which he would have discretion to pass on to the United Nations Commander. In fact he would not be the channel for this advice, which would continue to be sent through the United States Chiefs of Staff in Washington.

The Prime Minister said that before any decision was taken he wished to discuss the whole matter with the Foreign Secretary. In the meantime, however, the draft statement which he might make in Parliament should be prepared. This statement should describe carefully the limited functions of the Deputy Chief of Staff.

The Committee –

Invited the Minister of Defence to submit to the Prime Minister a draft statement which he might make in Parliament, if it was decided to proceed with the appointment of a Commonwealth officer as Deputy Chief of Staff for Korea.

[. . .]

George Ward[1] to Winston S. Churchill
(*Premier papers, 11/123*)

17 July 1952

Dear Prime Minister,

When I was staying with you at the Chequers recently, we discussed the film *The Sound Barrier*[2] and you asked me to arrange with Sir Alexander Korda[3] to see the film and let you have my comments on it. I have now seen it and I took with me experts from the Air Ministry and the Ministry of Supply.

We all thought that it was one of the best films we had ever seen from an entertainment point of view and that technically it was nearly perfect. I have only one or two very small criticisms.

I thought it was a pity that the brother had to be killed on his first solo in a light training aircraft. In my experience, which is confirmed by our experts here, this is a very rare occurrence indeed, since a pupil is never sent solo until his instructor is quite sure that he is fit to do so. Moreover, he is trying so hard that the carelessness which causes so many accidents is absent on his first solo. I could not help feeling that this incident in the film would not help RAF recruiting.

After the first 'Prometheus' crashed, the second one was built in the short period between the birth and the christening of the baby and while the designer was on holiday at Bognor. This is surely super-priority at its best!

There was a small error in timing connected with the trip to Cairo. When they returned to England in the Comet they read of the death of Geoffrey de Havilland,[4] whereas he was in fact killed long before the Comet was even built.

It may interest you to know every type of aircraft when flying at sonic speeds becomes nose-heavy as shown in the film. The Venom, for example, rolls over on its back while the Hunter becomes slightly tail-heavy but suffers no 'juddering' whatever. In any case the Hunter will have power controls.

Of course we now know considerably more about the sonic problem than we did even as short a time ago as when the film was made.

---

[1] George Reginald Ward, 1907–88. Educated at Christ Church, Oxford. In RAF, 1932–7, 1939–45. MP (Cons.) for Worcester City, 1945–60. Parliamentary Under-Secretary of State, Air Ministry, 1952–5. Parliamentary and Financial Secretary, Admiralty, 1955–7. Secretary of State for Air, 1957–60.

[2] Produced and directed by David Lean, 1952.

[3] Alexander Korda, 1893–1956. Educated at Budapest University. Film producer in Budapest, Vienna, Berlin, Hollywood and Paris. Founder and Chairman, London Film Productions Ltd, 1932. British subject, 1936. Founded Alexander Korda Productions, 1939. Made 112 films, including *The Scarlet Pimpernel* (1934), *The Third Man* (1949) and *Richard III* (1956). Knighted, 1942.

[4] Geoffrey Raoul de Havilland, Jr, 1910–46. Son of English aircraft designer Sir Geoffrey de Havilland, founder of the de Havilland Aircraft Company. Test pilot for de Havilland Aircraft Company, 1937–46. Conducted test flights for Havilland prototypes such as the 'Mosquito' and 'Vampire'. OBE, 1945. Died while carrying out high-speed tests of de Havilland DH 108 'Swallow', Sep. 1946.

Winston S. Churchill to George Ward
Prime Minister's Personal Minute M.395/52
(*Premier papers, 11/123*)

19 July 1952

Your note of July 17 about *The Sound Barrier*.

You should go and see Sir Alexander Korda and talk over your suggestions. Personally I do not see why the brother should not be killed in the early stage. The emphasis has to be made and I am sure the RAF can take it. But have a talk with him, and encourage the presentation of the film.

Winston S. Churchill to Sir Norman Brook and Lieutenant-General Sir Ian Jacob
Prime Minister's Personal Minute M.397/52
(*Premier papers, 11/133*)

19 July 1952

Please remember that it looks as if I shall have to make a speech in the Economic Debate (probably on the second day) which will express the main features of our further policy of remodelling the defence programme. I must base myself upon the material provided and I shall be very much obliged if you will try to draft a brief for me on which I can prepare the speech. This ought to be with me by Friday next. Mr Sandys' draft of July 10 is an admirable foundation but we must now go further and the Defence Ministry's point of view must be incorporated.

You will also have seen Lord Cherwell's grave paper. I have asked him and General Jacob to discuss this together on Monday to arrive if possible at a common conclusion.

Winston S. Churchill to Dominion Prime Ministers
Prime Minister's Personal Telegram T.152/52
(*Premier papers, 11/49*)

19 July 1952
Top Secret and Personal
No. 55

I have asked our High Commissioner/Acting High Commissioner to hand to you personally a copy of a Report which the United Kingdom Chiefs of Staff have just completed on Defence Policy and Global Strategy. You will see that this is a most important paper. It will be a key document in our consideration of defence policy and it will form the basis for important reviews of different sectors thereof, including in particular reviews of the planned build-up of

United Kingdom forces and of our defence production programmes. We shall wish to keep in close touch with the Canadian, Australian, New Zealand and South African Governments as these studies progress.

We should greatly welcome your views on this Report. If there are any special points on which you have immediate comments to offer we should be glad to learn them as soon as possible and without necessarily waiting for your full consideration of the Report as a whole.

I know that you would agree that it is of the first importance that we should try to reach agreement with the United States on allied global strategy and the Report is accordingly being made available to the United States Administration and the United States Joint Chiefs of Staff.

You will appreciate the specially Top Secret nature of this document and I would ask you to ensure that its security is most strictly preserved and knowledge of it confined to the smallest possible circle. Naturally however we would expect that you will wish to show it to your Chiefs of Staff.

Winston S. Churchill to Anthony Eden
Prime Minister's Personal Minute M.398/52
(Premier papers, 11/111)

21 July 1952

I send you herewith the draft statement about the representative on Mark Clark's Staff. The matter will be finally decided by the Cabinet tomorrow. I still think that it is liable to criticism as being 'much ado about nothing' and 'parturiunt montes, etc.'[1] Moreover I fear that we shall be held to be sharing responsibility more directly than we do now or need to do. Lastly the prospects of a Truce in Korea have improved according to Bouchier, whose telegrams are certainly informative and well written. I did not know at the time that the Chiefs of Staff were opposed to this appointment. In all the circumstances I should prefer to say we do not propose to take advantage of General Mark Clark's friendly offer upon full consideration of all the circumstances. Or; in view of the new hope of a favourable outcome of the Truce negotiations it would be premature to make the appointment at the present time. I hope you will agree to one or other of these courses with any amendments you may suggest.

---

[1] From Horace's *Epistle to the Pisones* (*Ars Poetica*), l. 139: 'Parturiunt montes, nascetur ridiculus mus' ('The mountains are in labour, and a ridiculous mouse will be born').

Anthony Eden to Winston S. Churchill
(*Churchill papers, 2/517*)

21 July 1952
Secret
PM/52/78

Your minute M.398/52 about the Deputy Chief of Staff at General Mark Clark's headquarters.

2. I do not see how we can now change our plans. I do not think that we shall in practice be any more committed by this appointment than we are at present, provided that the statement is made in succinct terms, indicating plainly that the Deputy Chief of Staff will be responsible solely to General Mark Clark. I agree with you that the original statement was much too long.

3. If we were to change our minds now it would be very confusing for the House of Commons and for public opinion in this country and the Commonwealth. Apart from the change of order, counter-order, disorder, it might be suggested that there was some new discord in Anglo-American relations.

4. With regard to the truce negotiations, Bouchier's reports are usually optimistic. I am not yet satisfied that the prospects have improved.

5. I attach a suggested redraft of the statement which I think makes all the essential points without superfluous wording.

6. I am sending a copy of this minute to the Secretary of State for Commonwealth Relations and the Minister of Defence.

Winston S. Churchill to Lord De L'Isle and Dudley
Prime Minister's Personal Minute M.399/52
(*Premier papers, 11/2*)

21 July 1952

This seems a very serious rate of casualties for an aircraft* which has been in service for nearly two years. How do these figures compare with other types? Out of how many pilots have the losses last year and this year been borne?

*Jet aircraft.

July 1952

Winston S. Churchill to Clementine Churchill
(Baroness Spencer-Churchill papers)[1]

21 July 1952   Chartwell

My darling one,

    The end of the Session is approaching and will give relief to a vy harsh & worrying strain. Inside our circle we toil continuously at plans to pay our way. The problems are baffling & bewildering because of their number & relationship. What to cut, & all the hideous consequences of the choice. Food, Arms, Housing? or all three? Indeed we were left a dismal inheritance! Beneath all the party malice there is a realization of the facts. But the nation is divided into 2 party machines grinding away at one another with tireless vigour.

    Anthony's absence adds to my burdens. He has had a steep dose of jaundice & has lost a stone & a half. His doctor wants him to rest for another week & I am pressing him to do so. Salisbury has been vy tiresome – frail health, private business and combined with these a defeatist frame of mind. However I hope to bring things to a satisfactory close.

    It will be a welcome change to have a lull – brief tho that must be.

    Bernie comes here next Friday for a long week end, when I have an important speech to prepare & much to settle: but Mary & Christopher will help & I expect all will pass off well.

    The sun is shining & the weather bright & cool. The gardens are lovely. (They are to be opened on the 23rd as you know). The fish are doing well, (seven baby black Mollies) I have managed to get a good long week-end (Thursday night to Monday afternoon).

    I am afraid the gt heat of Italy may have been a burden to you my darling. I do hope that when you join with Sarah & Anthony you will not do too much & that cooler breezes will blow. I am expecting you back about August 10. I miss you vy much & am often lonely & depressed. Your sweet letter wh reached me yesterday was a joy. I have been wondering how to draw a Clem Pussy Bird ever since. I enclosed a daring attempt. Tender love my dearest.

---

[1] This letter was handwritten.

Field Marshal Lord Alexander to Winston S. Churchill
(Premier papers, 11/271)

22 July 1952
Top Secret

APPLICATION OF NEW SECURITY PROCEDURE TO MEMBERS OF THE ARMED FORCES

The Cabinet decided at their meeting on 27th February, 1952, that those holding key posts, including those involving access to classified atomic energy information, should be subject to a new security procedure (CC(52)22nd Conclusions).

This procedure is of a positive and open character. The individual has to fill up a questionnaire about his antecedents and answer a specific question designed to force him to admit any Communist associations. On the basis of his replies further enquiries are made to satisfy the Head of his Department that he is suitable for employment on exceptionally secret work.

The discussion in Cabinet on 27th February did not specifically mention members of the Armed Forces serving in key posts. I have discussed this matter with my Service colleagues. They are loath to undertake any unnecessary work and it is pointed out that a considerable amount of information is already available about officers.

On the other hand unless we extend positive vetting to Service personnel we may not be able to rely on getting all the information we require from the Americans. Moreover, serious difficulties would arise in those cases where two people had access to the same highly secret information and one, a civilian, was subject to positive vetting whilst the other, a member of the Armed Services, was not.

These considerations are appreciated by my Service colleagues and I propose to inform them and the Minister of Supply that the positive vetting procedure should be applied to Service personnel in their Departments filling key posts. We shall naturally interpret key posts reasonably strictly.

JULY 1952 555

Cabinet: conclusions
(Cabinet papers, 128/25)

22 July 1952
Secret
11 a.m.
Cabinet Meeting No. 71 of 1952

[...]

6. The Cabinet had before them a note by the Prime Minister (C(52)250) covering a draft statement prepared by the Minister of Defence on the proposed appointment of a Deputy Chief of Staff to the United Nations Commander in Korea. A revised draft statement, prepared by the Foreign Secretary, was circulated at the meeting.

The Prime Minister said that the appointment of a Commonwealth officer as Deputy Chief of Staff to the United Nations Commander in Korea would be held to give us more responsibility for the conduct of the operations without any increase in our power to influence it. The Foreign Secretary thought, however, that it would be a mistake to abandon the proposal, which had first been put forward by the United Nations Commander himself.

The Cabinet examined the two draft statements before them and the following points were made –

(a) It was unnecessary to repeat in the statement the text of the instructions which were to be given to the officer appointed as Deputy Chief of Staff.

(b) The statement should make it clear that Her Majesty's Government accepted no more responsibility for the conduct of operations than they had at present as a member of the United Nations, who had entrusted to the United States Government the conduct of the Korean operations on their behalf. It should also be made clear that the channel for consultation about Korea would continue to be between our representatives in Washington and the United States Government and military authorities there.

(c) The statement, revised on the lines agreed in discussion, should be made in the House of Lords by the Minister of Defence, and in the House of Commons by the Parliamentary Secretary to the Ministry of Defence, as part of the statement which was to be made on 28th July on the military situation in Korea.

The Cabinet –

(1) Approved the appointment of a United Kingdom officer as Deputy Chief of Staff at the Headquarters of the United Nations Commander in Korea.

(2) Invited the Minister of Defence to arrange for statements to be made in both Houses of Parliament as agreed in discussion.

[...]

Cabinet: conclusions
(*Cabinet papers, 128/25*)

23 July 1952
Secret
11.30 a.m.
Cabinet Meeting No. 72 of 1952

1. The Cabinet were informed that during the previous night there had been a *coup d'Etat* in Cairo by a group of military officers who had now assumed complete control over the city and had opened parleys with the Government in Alexandria. The leaders of the group had announced that they were not concerned with foreign relations and aimed only at suppressing corruption within the country. They had, however, made it clear to the British Embassy that they would offer organised resistance to any British intervention. The Embassy had already asked the British military authorities in the Canal Zone to give them notice in advance before taking any military action, in view of possible political consequences. The Foreign Secretary might wish to go further and ask that there should be no military intervention without specific authority from London.

The Minister of Defence said that he hoped that a reasonable discretion would be left to the local Commanders, who could be trusted to avoid any appearance of taking sides in a domestic Egyptian dispute.

The Prime Minister said that in present circumstances any movements of British troops in Egypt should be as unobtrusive as possible.

The Cabinet –
Took note of these statements.

[. . .]

5. The Cabinet had before them a memorandum by the Minister of Defence (C(52)253) on the estimated cost of the rearmament programme up to the year 1955–56 and the load which this would impose on the metal-using industries.

The Prime Minister said that he had already discussed with some of his colleagues the possibility of reducing the load of the defence production programme on the metal-using industries in order to free more resources for export. They had provisionally agreed that in the calendar year 1953 this load should in no circumstances exceed £500 million, and that every effort should be made to reduce it towards £450 million by means which would facilitate the expansion of engineering exports. Further meetings of Ministers would have to be held during the six weeks to consider what assumptions could be taken about the level of defence expenditure in the years after 1953, with regard both to the defence load on the metal-using industries and also to the Budgetary consequences of defence expenditure as a whole. In the meantime, the Supply Departments, without imposing any general standstill on orders for production in 1954 and later years, should avoid prejudging by any abnormal ordering the decision which Ministers would have to take in the coming weeks.

The Chancellor of the Exchequer said that he must warn the Cabinet that, in his view, it was quite unrealistic to suppose that the country could support the rising burden of defence expenditure outlined in paragraph 3 of C(52)253. He calculated that, if expenditure on civil defence, atomic energy and other defence preparations were added, the total cost of defence in 1954–55 would amount to half the total budget. He believed that means would have to be found of preventing defence expenditure from rising much above the level of 1952–3.

The Minister of Defence said that an increasing load on the metal-using industries was a natural and inevitable consequence of a rearmament programme. If a flat level of expenditure were imposed, no sufficient provision could be made for the introduction of new types of equipment, since a large proportion of allotted capacity of the metal-using industries would have to be devoted to the maintenance and replacement of existing types of equipment. If the total size of the Forces was to be reduced, there would have to be a complete review of commitments – not only peace-time commitments in the cold war, but also obligations in the North Atlantic Treaty Organisation (NATO) in the event of war. It was difficult to see where our efforts in the cold war could be relaxed, and substantial curtailment of our NATO commitments would impair the spirit of the Alliance.

In discussion the following points were made:

(a) If the defence load on the metal-using industries were limited to £500 million a year or less over the next three years, the Services would be denied improved equipment which was essential to their efficiency in war. The load must increase on a rising curve until re-equipment was completed, and the curve would then flatten out or decrease. On the other hand, this made it the more important that the curve should start at a point which would leave some scope for the engineering industry to accept increased orders for export.

(b) The conflict between the demands of defence and of exports upon the metal-using industries could not be resolved, and no firm plan adopted for either, unless some total figure for the limitation of the defence load were fixed for some years ahead. Otherwise it would be impossible to avoid sudden variations in the rearmament programme and wasteful cancellations of contracts.

(c) If the total size of the forces remained constant, the imposition of a flat level of expenditure, whether in money or in the use of metal, would fall largely upon new production. If the total size of the forces were reduced, then the corresponding reduction in maintenance would permit some new production for re-equipping the smaller forces. On the other hand, smaller forces could not fulfil all existing cold war commitments and obligations to NATO. The Prime Minister said that he would like to see an analysis for each Service of the load imposed on the metal-using industries for (i) maintenance, (ii) new production.

(d) The Minister of State said that the Foreign Secretary felt that any review of the demands of the defence programme upon the national economy would offer no sound basis for judgment unless it was accompanied by a review of the demands made upon the economy by the housing programme and other social services. The Chancellor of the Exchequer pointed out that considerable cuts had already been imposed on civil investment, social services and consumption and he was seeking to impose more.

The Prime Minister said that no decisions could be reached at this stage on this level of defence expenditure over the next three years, but examinations should immediately be put in hand in accordance with the provisional decisions to which he had referred at the outset of the discussion. In the meantime, he and the Chancellor of Exchequer, when speaking in the forthcoming debate on the economic situation, would be careful to avoid prejudging the level of defence expenditure over the next three years.

The Cabinet –

Agreed to resume their discussion on the defence programme at a later date.

Winston S. Churchill to Commonwealth Prime Ministers
Prime Minister's Personal Telegram T.155/52
(Premier papers, 11/22)

23 July 1952
Immediate
Secret
W. No. 119

I have now received replies from yourself and all other Commonwealth Prime Ministers to my message of the 25th June,[1] which show general agreement with my proposal for a Commonwealth Economic Conference of Prime Ministers in London in the latter half of November. All Prime Ministers other than Dr Malan and Pandit Nehru have indicated their hope to attend themselves for the whole or part of the Conference. Dr Malan and Pandit Nehru, who find special difficulty in attending in person at that time have stated that their countries will be represented. In view of the range and depth of the questions to be discussed we should welcome the presence of other Ministers

---

[1] T.139/52, reproduced above (pp. 513–14).

whom Prime Ministers may wish to have with them to cover the various fields of discussion.

2. Some replies have emphasised the importance of the preparatory work of officials and that the precise date of the Conference must depend on progress in this direction. Adequate preparatory work is, indeed, an essential condition of the success of the Conference; but it seems to me most important for the reasons given in paragraph 4 of my earlier message (my telegram W. No. 106 of 25th June), that we should arrange to have this work completed in time to allow the conference to open before the end of November. My colleagues and I are already working hard on the problems as we see them, in order to be able to send you our ideas for the agenda as soon as possible.

3. I would suggest that the 25th November would be a suitable date for the opening of the Conference and that the preparatory discussions among our officials should commence on 22nd September. The officials should press ahead as rapidly as possible with their work so that, on their return home, Ministers will have adequate time to study the results of these discussions before the Conference opens.

4. In view of Press speculations, I think we should make an early announcement that the Conference is to take place. An announcement at this stage cannot refer in other than general terms to the purpose of the Conference, but I do not believe that it should be delayed until we have agreed on the details of the agenda. I should propose that a statement on the lines of a message which I am sending you separately (see my immediately following telegram) should be made in Parliament here on 29th July.

5. I should be glad to learn, if possible by Monday, 28th July, whether you agree that the conference should open on 25th November, and whether a statement on the lines suggested would be acceptable to you. If so, I shall inform you in advance when the statement would be made so that announcements can be issued, if desired, in all Commonwealth countries at about the same time. I should also be glad to learn in due course whether the date suggested for the meeting of officials is convenient.

560

Winston S. Churchill to Sidney Holland
Prime Minister's Personal Telegram T.154/52
(*Premier papers, 11/22*)

23 July 1952
Immediate
Secret
No. 280

Thank you for your most helpful reply to my message of the 25th June, about the proposed Commonwealth Economic Conference of Prime Ministers.[1] You will have received my further message to yourself and the other Commonwealth Prime Ministers telling you of the response I received to my invitation.

2. I well understand the inconvenience you will suffer from yet another journey to London, and the strain that the recurrent absence from New Zealand and[2] yourself and other Ministers imposes upon your Cabinet.

3. I attach the fullest weight to your expression of concern lest the outcome of the Conference may fall short of the high expectations that will be publicly aroused. I had myself given careful thought to this point before I decided to suggest that the Conference should take place. That there is some risk from exaggerated expectation of spectacular results cannot be denied, but I suggest that we should not allow ourselves to be deterred by this thought in view of the urgency of the problems which demand our attention. I need hardly assure you that I shall see that everything we can do here in advance of the Conference to ensure its success is done, and I know that we can rely on the fullest co-operation from New Zealand during the preparatory meeting of officials in London.

4. I have noted your desire to be home before Christmas and see no reason to suppose that the Conference will not end in good time for this. We shall certainly keep your wishes in mind in making the final Conference arrangements.

[1] T.139/52, reproduced above (pp. 513–14).
[2] Error for 'of'.

Winston S. Churchill to Commonwealth Prime Ministers
Prime Minister's Personal Telegram T.156/52
(Premier papers, 11/22)

23 July 1952
Immediate
Secret
W. No. 120

Some little time ago I communicated to my fellow Prime Ministers in the Commonwealth a proposal that we should meet in London in the latter part of November to discuss together the many pressing issues of financial, commercial and economic policy which are common to our several countries, and to develop a constructive approach to the economic problems of the free world. I am glad to be able to inform the House that my fellow Commonwealth Prime Ministers have agreed that such a meeting will be timely and useful and that it will open on 25th November. The Prime Ministers of South Africa and India have told me that, while they themselves would unfortunately have special difficulty in attending the Conference at the time proposed, their countries will be represented. All other Commonwealth Prime Ministers, including the Prime Minister of Southern Rhodesia,[1] hope to be present themselves for the whole or part of the Conference.

Arrangements will also be made for the representation of the Colonial territories.

The Conference will be preceded by preparatory discussions between officials and Commonwealth countries.

I shall give the House further information on the subject in due course.

Winston S. Churchill to Field Marshal Lord Alexander
Prime Minister's Personal Minute M.402/52
(Premier papers, 11/271)

23 July 1952

Your minute of July 22 about the application of new security procedure to members of the armed forces.[2]

We must be careful to respect The Queen's Commission.

I was not aware of this new danger and I should like to discuss the matter with you before a decision is taken.

---

[1] Garfield Todd, 1908–2002. Educated at Glen Leith Theological College and University of the Witwatersrand. Married, 1932, Jean Grace Wilson: three children. Moved to Southern Rhodesia, 1934. Missionary, 1934. MP (United Rhodesia Party) in colonial Parliament, 1948. PM of Southern Rhodesia, 1953–8.

[2] Reproduced above (p. 554).

Winston S. Churchill to Field Marshal Lord Alexander
Prime Minister's Personal Minute M.404/52
(Premier papers, 11/51)

23 July 1952
Most Secret

I presume General Jacob has shown you Field Marshal Montgomery's FM/67 of July 18.[1] Of course there is no possibility of our reaching in the next two or three years anything like the target of ninety-seven divisions. Indeed it is questionable whether any rapid or effective increase on the present strength will be possible. We certainly cannot do <u>more</u>, if indeed we can maintain the present strength. With the cost of military forces in the free countries at its present level per man and per ton of steel, it seems that no practical scheme of matching the Soviet forces exists, or has ever existed, even if we reduce those forces, as I imagine we should, to perhaps a third of their present exaggerated strength.

2. All the economies which Montgomery suggests would not, when put together, meet the demands of the Chancellor of the Exchequer, supported as they are by hard facts. Indeed it may well be that the supply and equipment of the large numbers of troops he asks for on, say, the thirtieth and the sixtieth days of mobilization, would be utterly beyond our power.

3. On the other hand there is the immense improvement in power and accuracy of the American Atomic Bomber Offensive, which is our only hope of peace or victory.

4. I think it would be wise for you and the Chiefs of Staff to have a talk with Field Marshal Montgomery about it and let him know, for his own secret information, what the real position is. There is no immediate hurry about this. No doubt opportunities will occur in the next few weeks.

5. Furthermore I cannot feel it would be useful to raise the whole question of our European front, such as it is, until the American Presidential Election has been decided. Then indeed we shall have to come to grips with the whole problem. Meanwhile it would be most unwise to disturb the minds of our European allies.

---

[1] This paper has since been destroyed.

Winston S. Churchill to Lieutenant-General Sir Ian Jacob
Prime Minister's Personal Minute M.403/52
(Premier papers, 11/203)

23 July 1952

How many recruits do you propose to draw in the next twelve months into National Service from Agriculture? How many recruits is the War Office <u>at present</u> planning to take in the years 1952/3, 1953/4, 1954/5, and 1955/6 from the nation?[1]

Cabinet: conclusions
(Cabinet papers, 128/25)

24 July 1952
11 a.m.
Cabinet Meeting No. 73 of 1952

[...]

8. The Cabinet considered a memorandum by the Chancellor of the Exchequer (C(52)249) recommending further adjustments in the investment programme for 1953.

The Chancellor of the Exchequer said that the demands of the Departments for building in 1953 totalled £110 million of new building in excess of the programme for 1952. This would involve an unwarrantable diversion of resources from exports. He considered that the limit for new building work in 1953 should not exceed £900 million, but he was prepared to take the risk of allowing a figure of £933 million, which might be achieved if all Departments would accept a 5 per cent reduction on the allocations hitherto proposed. This would mean a lower housing programme, but he thought it would be difficult to justify the cuts proposed in defence works and other programmes if no cut were made in housing. If no money limits were imposed on the building programmes, it was certain that building resources would be diverted to inessential purposes and probably that much work would be started which, for lack of material could not be finished.

The Minister of Housing and Local Government said that the foundations for the houses to be built in 1953 were already laid and that unless contracts were cancelled and materials withheld, 260,000 houses would be built in that year. If expenditure on housing in 1953 were limited to £395 million, the

---

[1] Lt-Gen. Jacob sent Churchill the following figures:
    1952 – 173,000;
    1953 – 139,000;
    1954 – 139,000;
    1955 – 134,000.

resources now employed on the programme would not be transferred to other building work: the sole result would be that productivity would decrease and the momentum of the programme would be lost. The political effects would also be serious: the public, as well as the building industry, would be greatly discouraged. He was therefore unwilling to agree to any reduction in the housing target for 1953. The programme for 1954, to which he was not yet committed, could be reviewed in November. It should be possible to include in that a much larger number of houses of new designs which would secure great economies in imported materials, and it was his aim to build in 1954 as many as 300,000 houses with no more timber than was being used for 230,000 houses in 1952.

In discussion the following points were made:

(a) The Minister of Housing and Local Government said that, whatever decisions were reached he hoped that the investment programme would not be made public. The publication of these limits on the various sectors of the building programme could not fail to cramp the expansion of productivity in the building industry. There was general agreement with the view that the programme should not be made public.

(b) The Prime Minister said that in his view it would be unwise to curtail the housing programme in the critical year 1953. If the momentum was lost in that year, it would be more difficult to achieve the economies planned for 1954 by the use of novel designs.

(c) It was suggested in paragraph 9 of C(52)249 that the housing programme should in future be brought within the starting-date control operated by Regional Building Committees. The Minister of Housing and Local Government said that this procedure was inappropriate for single houses but he was ready to agree that it should be applied to large housing schemes. He was also willing to co-operate in special interdepartmental discussion of the building problems of particular areas, such as Coventry, where it appeared that building resources were being drawn into housing work at the expense of productive industry or other projects of national importance.

(d) The President of the Board of Trade said that the imposition of a further cut on new building for manufacturing industry was not consistent with the efforts which were being made to expand exports. He hoped that manufacturing industry might be allowed a total of £100 million, which was less than his original demand.

The Prime Minister said that he thought it would be wrong to accept any reduction in the housing programme for 1953. The target of 260,000 houses should be retained, but within that target every effort should be made to reduce the use of building labour and imported materials. The reductions proposed in C(52)249 for other building programmes might be accepted as a general guide, subject to a margin not exceeding £10 million, which would give the Chancellor of the Exchequer some discretion in judging additional demands for work of particular importance, *e.g.*, the manufacturing industry devoted to the export trade.

The Cabinet –
(1) Agreed that the limitations imposed by the investment programmes should not operate to prevent the Housing Ministers from reaching their target of completing 260,000 houses in 1953.
(2) Subject to Conclusion (1), approved in principle the reductions in the investment programme proposed by the Chancellor of the Exchequer in C(52)249, as a general guide to the distribution of building resources in 1953.
(3) Authorised the Chancellor of the Exchequer to discuss with the President of the Board of Trade and other Ministers concerned the possibility of increasing the limits proposed in C(52)249 by an amount not exceeding £10 million for projects likely to assist in redressing the adverse balance of payments.

[. . .]

Winston S. Churchill to Field Marshal Lord Montgomery
(Premier papers, 11/51)

24 July 1952
Private

My dear Monty,

Thank you very much for your paper of July 18,[1] which I will have duly considered. I do not myself think any change should be made before the result of the American Presidential Election is known. We should only disturb our European allies. We must all just go on doing the best we can.

Antony Head to Winston S. Churchill
(Premier papers, 11/201)

24 July 1952

Mr Shinwell suggested that National Service should be reduced to 18 months. You asked me what the effect of such a change would be in terms of our money and manpower. I have had it worked out and the result is as follows:
(a) the reduction in the numbers of men serving with the colours would be about 58,450 (including 1,050 officers).
(b) the reduction in the cost of the Army would be about £17M a year.

---

[1] This paper has since been destroyed.

Winston S. Churchill to Antony Head
Prime Minister's Personal Minute M.405/52
(Premier papers, 11/201)

25 July 1952

I had hoped you were going to give me a more helpful note about Shinwell's proposals, bringing out the effect on the training of the Army and the character of the units, especially the difficulties of relief on foreign service, the pipe-line and so on, showing that there were many additional causes of expense or loss which it would be hard to make good. You should make the strongest case you can against this most improvident proposal. I hope you can have this done for me today. What you sent me is very little good.

Winston S. Churchill to Field Marshal Lord Alexander
Prime Minister's Personal Minute M.409/52
(Premier papers 11/111)

25 July 1952

Would it not be well to let Bouchier continue as he is for a few weeks, so as not to give the appearance of having made a change in the liaison arrangements? When Shoosmith[1] has taken up his duties it would be quite proper to relieve Air Marshal Bouchier.

Sir Ralph Stevenson to Foreign Office
('Descent to Suez', page 22)

27 July 1952
Priority
Secret

Farouk's abdication has been received without excitement here, but general feeling is of satisfaction.

No news of any reaction throughout the country, and I see no reason why we should have any trouble.[2]

---

[1] Stephen Newton Shoosmith, 1900–56. Educated at Royal Military Academy. Married, 1938, Kathleen Mary Noad: two children. Commissioned, Royal Artillery, 1920. Staff College, 1936. Served during WWII. Asst Military Secretary, War Cabinet, 1941. Col., 1946. Maj-Gen, 1949. Deputy Chief of Staff, UN Command, Japan, 1952–4. Cdr, US Legion of Merit, 1954.

[2] Churchill wrote on his copy of this telegram: 'They have lost their King!' Farouk's baby son, Ahmed Fuad, was proclaimed King Fuad II, but Egypt was now governed by Naguib, Nasser and the Free Officers. On 18 June 1953, the revolutionary government announced the abolition of the monarchy, ending 150 years of the Muhammad Ali dynasty's rule, and Egypt was declared a republic.

Field Marshal Lord Alexander to Winston S. Churchill
(*Premier papers, 11/51*)

28 July 1952
Top Secret

Reference your minute M.404/52.[1] I have seen Field Marshal Montgomery's paper FM/67 of July 18th. As you will have perceived, the Field Marshal's paper reflects our thinking here, and it is the first move in the process of trying to get NATO forces planned on a realistic basis. The Chiefs of Staff have recently had a talk with Field Marshal Montgomery, but will certainly be seeing him again in the next few weeks.

2. I do not think that anything is likely to emerge in a concrete form before the Presidential Election, though, as you know, CAS will be trying to get the US Chiefs of Staff to begin thinking in line with us. There will certainly be no question of disturbing the minds of our European Allies. The Field Marshal's paper is being kept to a strictly limited Anglo/American circle.

Cabinet: conclusions
(*Cabinet papers, 128/25*)

29 July 1952
Secret
11.30 a.m.
Cabinet Meeting No. 74 of 1952

[...]

2. The Prime Minister questioned the expediency of the arrangement by which the members of a Parliamentary Delegation which was to visit Canada during the recess were to fly there together in a single aircraft. It was pointed out that this aircraft had been placed at their disposal by the courtesy of the Canadian Government, and it might be embarrassing to decline that offer; and that, even if the Delegation crossed the Atlantic by sea, they could not avoid substantial use of air transport during their stay in Canada. The Commonwealth Secretary undertook, however, to consider whether any alternative arrangements could be made which would reduce the risk to which the Prime Minister had drawn attention.

3. The Cabinet had before them a memorandum by the Minister of Defence (C(52)248) presenting the arguments for and against the granting of an amnesty for men who had deserted from the Armed Forces during the last war.

The Prime Minister said that, in his view, it was a grievous thing that, seven

---

[1] Reproduced above (p. 562).

years after the end of the war, a large number of war-time deserters should still be living in this country as outcasts and outlaws. After the First World War an amnesty had been granted after four years. He had received many expressions of reproach and indignation from the public on this matter. On reflection he did not wish to press the suggestion that an amnesty should be declared in connection with the Coronation; but he felt very strongly that the existing position should not be allowed to continue indefinitely. Amnesties had already been granted by Canada, Australia and South Africa; and it was inhuman to condemn so many men to live the lives of outlaws under assumed names.

In discussion there was some support for this view. On the other side it was strongly contended that the Government should not, by an amnesty, appear to condone the serious crime of deserting from the Forces in time of war. Some Ministers thought it would be specially dangerous to do this at a time when men were being drafted abroad for operations in Korea and Malaya.

The Cabinet –

Agreed to resume their discussion of C(52)248 at a later meeting.

[. . .]

5. The Cabinet had before them a memorandum by the Foreign Secretary (C(52)247) and a joint memorandum by the Secretary of State for Co-ordination of Transport, Fuel and Power, the First Lord of the Admiralty and the Minister of Transport (C(52)255) dealing with the effect upon the delimitation of territorial waters of a judgement given by the International Court at The Hague in the Anglo-Norwegian fisheries case.

The Foreign Secretary said that the principles enunciated in this judgment would enable countries to delimit their territorial waters from a 'base line' joining headlands and outlying islands or rocks. Norway, Iceland, Sweden and France had already adopted this method, which resulted in a substantial extension of territorial waters, and Denmark was under great pressure to follow suit. If these countries, as seemed likely, gave a wide and liberal interpretation to this new method, our fishing interests would suffer. If we adopted this new method, we should be in a position to influence other countries to apply a reasonable interpretation, and it would enable us to exclude foreign fishing fleets from our own fishing grounds – e.g., the Moray Firth. It would also enable us to make effective representations to the Mediterranean Powers, who at present insisted upon a six-mile limit for their territorial waters.

In discussion the following points were made:

(a) A great extension of territorial waters would limit our exercise of belligerent rights in war and increase the opportunities for unfriendly Powers to interfere with our shipping in peace. It would hamper the operations of the Royal Navy in war in keeping hostile coasts under observation and clearing minefields. In general, it was to the advantage of a great maritime Power to keep free of territorial control as large an area as possible of the sea and of the air above it.

(b) The White Fish Authority were in favour of adopting the new method. The Scottish fishing interests, which had long suffered from the incursions of foreign fishing fleets into the Moray Firth, were anxious that immediate advantage should be taken of The Hague Court judgment to exclude these fleets. On the other hand, it was pointed out that a base-line drawn across the Moray Firth would extend to seventy-eight miles; and, if we claimed that as reasonable, it would be difficult to argue against similar interpretations by other countries.

(c) It would be useful if, before a final decision were taken, the views of the Governments of the United States and of other Commonwealth countries were ascertained.

(d) The International Law Commission of the United Nations was now studying the questions, but it was doubtful if they would give any decision until late in 1953. If we took no action until their decision was made, other countries would adopt the new method and we should have lost the opportunity of influencing them in in their interpretation of it.

The Cabinet –

(1) Invited the Minister of Defence, in consultation with other Ministers concerned, to examine further the military significance (in peace, in a precautionary state, and in war) of the new base-line method of measuring territorial waters, and to report to the Cabinet.

(2) Invited the Foreign Secretary and the Commonwealth Secretary to ascertain what views were held on this question by the Governments of the United States and of other Commonwealth countries.

[. . .]

Winston S. Churchill to Anthony Eden
Prime Minister's Personal Minute M.414/52
(Premier papers, 11/392)

30 July 1952
Secret

I notice in the newspapers that Neguib[1] uses the expression that the Sudan and Egypt should work together 'against the common enemy'. This seems to me a fairly clear indication of his views.

---

[1] Mohamed Naguib Yousef Qotp Elkashlan, 1901–84. Born in Khartoum, Anglo-Egyptian Sudan. Educated at Royal Military Academy, Cairo. Entered Egyptian military, 1919. Maj.-Gen., 1950. A figurehead for the Free Officers movement which led the overthrow of the Egyptian constitutional monarchy in 1952. (The abolition of the monarchy ultimately took effect in June 1953.) Minister of War and Navy, 1952–3. PM of Egypt, 1952–4. President, 1953–4. Forced to resign by Nasser in 1954.

Winston S. Churchill: speech
(Hansard)

30 July 1952

THE ECONOMIC POSITION

The Prime Minister (Mr Winston Churchill): There is no doubt that our financial and economic position has improved substantially in the first six months of this year as the result of the considerable measures taken since we became responsible. Nevertheless, at the beginning of June my right hon. Friend the Chancellor of the Exchequer informed his colleagues that the margin of safety was not sufficient. He asked for a further effort to restore the balance between exports and imports by substantial economies, and he asked that these should be effective in the last six months of the present calendar year.

The Chancellor convinced us that a new and strenuous effort was necessary and urgent. Since then we have been engaged upon a severe scrutiny of our resources, unusual at this time of the year. The first objective was to find economies in imports and improvements in exports which would yield their results within the short period specified. This made the task particularly difficult because of the limited sphere of economies which come to hand in so short a time.

This involved a mid-summer overhaul of our expenditure in a good many fields. It was, however, a special and a short-term study, and it is in no way a substitute for the detailed, long-term examination of the estimates which usually begins in November and is the foundation of the Budget for the coming year; that is to say, the financial year 1953.

What we sought to achieve was a stronger protection for our gold and dollar reserves which at less than 1,700 million dollars, leave us too much at the mercy of unfavourable episodes outside these shores or in the immense sterling area of which we are the bankers. We are therefore now apprising the House and the world of a further tightening up and consolidation of our resources on a scale which, taken with all that has gone before, should not in any way be underrated.

I thought that the Chancellor's speech yesterday was somewhat ill-treated, both here and out of doors, considering the commanding position which he has made for himself in Parliament and the immense load he has had to bear. I have helped him all I could in those efforts to further economies and he has been successful to a remarkable degree. I am told of differences between us. I was not aware that any existed – (Hon. Members: 'Oh'.) – but they are certainly nothing like the differences between a contented cat purring over a substantial meal – including a second helping – and the ravenous jaguar who, six weeks ago, was prowling round our spending Departments in search of prey. I think that if my right hon. Friend found reasons for satisfaction yesterday, he may well justify himself by the very remarkable economies which he has effected by his influence and by his pertinacity at this period of the year.

Let me summarise shortly what he told us yesterday. Imports of unrationed foods will, in the second half of this year, amount to only three-quarters of what they were in the same period in 1951. That is a cut of 25 per cent. Imports of raw materials and manufactures will be even more drastically reduced. Pulp and paper imports, for example, will be less than half of what they were in the second half of 1951, and imports of manufactured goods will be reduced by 40 per cent. Exports of coal will be sharply increased in the remaining months of the year.

Mr Hugh Gaitskell (Leeds, South): I wonder whether the Prime Minister would clear up one point –

The Prime Minister: Today it is the desire that speeches should be kept as short as possible –

Mr Gaitskell: I do not want to interrupt the right hon. Gentleman, but I should be obliged if he would tell us whether the import cuts which he has just mentioned constitute new decisions, adding further to the total of import cuts which the Chancellor announced in his Budget statement.

The Prime Minister: Well, I am giving the facts as I gathered them from the speech my right hon. Friend made yesterday. (Hon. Members 'Answer'.) Exports of coal, as I said, will be sharply – (Hon. Members: 'You do not know?') I do not mind at all being interrupted. I think the habit of disorderliness which I have noticed on the benches opposite recently only shows what guilty consciences hon. Members have. The aim at the end of the year – (Hon. Members: 'Answer'.) – the aim at the end of this year – (Hon. Members: 'Answer'.) I will not answer a question if I do not choose. You distinguish yourselves by denying me a fair hearing. (Hon. Members: 'Answer'.) I could not have been making a simpler or plainer statement of what was said of our policy yesterday as announced by the Chancellor of the Exchequer.

By increased sales of military equipment we expect to earn another £10 million this year. All this was said yesterday, and then it was argued that no effective statement had been made. As a matter of fact – (*Interruption.*) I am not apparently allowed to adduce and define the statement to show that that assumption which has been so impatiently made by hon. Gentlemen opposite is as devoid of foundation as many of their other dogmas.

These measures to strengthen our reserves and to increase confidence in our resolve to maintain solvency must not be viewed by themselves alone. Apart from their beneficial effect upon the United Kingdom economy, they are the preliminary to the economic conference of the Commonwealth Prime Ministers which I announced to the House yesterday and which is to open here on 25th November. At this conference the whole position of the sterling area will be searchingly reviewed and we shall enter upon the discussions all the stronger for the action we are taking now.

Various questions were asked yesterday about the conference. It will be a meeting of Prime Ministers and, in accordance with custom, I shall preside. But I shall, of course, have the help of my colleagues who are directly concerned with the special matters under discussion. The preparations for this conference concern a number of Ministers, including particularly the Foreign Secretary, the Secretary of State for Commonwealth Relations, the Chancellor of the Exchequer and the President of the Board of Trade. These preparations, which are already in hand, are being supervised on my behalf by the Foreign Secretary in his capacity as Deputy Prime Minister.

The Chancellor of the Exchequer spoke yesterday mainly about the civil economy. It falls to me to speak more at length about defence. One of our greatest problems in the hard discussions which we have had has been that of finding means by which, despite our economic difficulties, we can still maintain a defence effort in accordance with our duties and our needs. We shall not weaken in our resolve to do our utmost in the defence of the free democracies. We reaffirm our determination to stand fast with the Commonwealth, with the United States and our other Allies, in resisting the encroachments of Communism. In particular, in the West, we are resolved to stand shoulder to shoulder with the United States and our Allies in Europe in resisting any aggression.

But there can be no assurance of lasting military strength without a firm economic foundation, and no defence programme can stand without the economic resources to carry it through. The defence programmes must be kept within the limits of our economic strength. The right hon. Gentleman the Member for Leeds, South (Mr Gaitskell) seemed to suggest that no review or revision of our armament scheme could be undertaken by us except in conjunction with all the other Allied Powers.

I trust indeed that we shall continue to set an example to the European States and no doubt when the meetings of NATO take place in the autumn we shall all discuss together our common affairs and how we have got on. But to suggest, as the right hon. Gentleman did, that we have no right to make necessary or even beneficial changes in our own military organisation and expenditure without a general meeting of all the NATO Powers would be an abrogation of our rights and an alteration of our ordinary practice such as I have not hitherto seen in peace or war.

Let me now look back a little. Two years ago, after the outbreak of the war in Korea, the Socialist Government, with praiseworthy zeal but little study, announced a re-armament programme of £3,600 million to cover both new equipment and the maintenance of the Forces, spread over three years. Five months later, for reasons which were not made clear at the time, they raised this figure to £4,700 million. Now, by the decline in the purchasing power of the pound, it would be about £5,400 million.

The original £4,700 million at the old prices was divided by the late

Government in their three-year plan as follows: 1951, £1,250 million; 1952, £1,531 million; 1953, £1,694 million, making a total for the three years of £4,475 million, to which they added £225 million for civil defence and stock-piling, thus making up the total of £4,700 million.

I pointed out, however, in December that it would not be possible to complete so vast a scheme in the period prescribed. There are the inevitable time-lags which may be put, in the first two years, at between 10 per cent and 20 per cent. In the first year, 1951, actual expenditure amounted to only £1,132 million as compared with the programme figure of £1,250 million. In the current year, 1952, we expect, though this is nothing more than a very speculative estimate, to spend £1,462 million against the forecast of £1,531 million made by our predecessors. I thought that the House might like to have these figures in their minds.

Nevertheless, had we not made a considerable slowing down of the programme to which we had been committed, spreading it into the fourth year, the total bill for these three years would have been far above £4,700 million. Actually, on our present decisions and calculations, we and our predecessors, allowing for the price increase, which has been continuous, will have spent in the three years a sum not far short of the £4,700 million originally proposed.

But, through the time-lag and increased costs, there will be a short-fall in the results achieved in the first three years. Our resources are not expanding at the rate we need to enable us to recover in any period which can be foreseen the position which we held before the war. As a contribution to the immense new burden of the re-armament plan, we are receiving in this year, 1952, about £175 million from the United States; but this is quite different from the £400 million or £500 million a year enjoyed by the late Government before the arms programme was begun, in loans or gifts from the United States and, to a lesser extent, from Canada and the Commonwealth. It must never be forgotten that this foreign aid, on which the Socialist Government lived for its whole tenure of power, virtually made good the loss of foreign investments that we suffered at the beginning of the war. Now we are facing the increased burden without having either the one or the other. Now we are striving to repay the American loan with interest.

All these facts might well, I think, be taken into consideration by all fair-minded people friendly to Britain and her survival. If this cold war ordeal is to continue – and it certainly does not rest with us –we must organise our defences on lines which do not require a constantly expanding expenditure of money and materials over an indefinite period. Within those boundaries, very great improvements and economies, in the true sense of a higher fertility, will be possible, and it is to this that the Ministry of Defence, under Lord Alexander, whose knowledge in all these matters is of the greatest value to us, and the three great Service Departments, are now devoting their unremitting attention.

The original programme was conceived by the late Government in the mood of the crisis which came upon them when the Korean war began. Many of the resources and much of the equipment in hand at the end of the war had been improvidently dispersed or destroyed. Virtually no new equipment had been provided. For five years the Forces had lived on vanishing war stocks, and there was a heavy lee-way to make up.

Re-armament was such a violent reversal of the policy previously pursued that many errors in the programme were inevitable. Since we assumed office nine months ago, we have made a comprehensive review of defence policy and strategy, and we are now engaged in reshaping the original programme so as to bring it into accord with the results of our new assessment of the position.

There are two requirements to be met. First, we have to take account of the ceaseless technical developments which affect our preparations for a world war, should such a disaster come upon us. In the two years that have passed since the original programme was launched, some weapons, on which immense sums were to be spent, have become obsolescent, and new types and devices of a greatly improved character have come into view. These technical advances have resulted in changes in military tactics, and, in turn, changes of emphasis as between the various sectors of the defence production programme.

Immense strides have been made by the United States, not only in their stockpile of atomic weapons, but in the power of atomic weapons, and in the range and accuracy of their delivery. All this is reinforced by the advent of new aircraft which profoundly affect the tactics of air warfare, and anti-air defence. Remarkable progress has also been made in our own development of guided missiles, or guided rockets, as was mentioned by the Minister of Supply the other day. On the other hand, the development, such as it may be, of the atomic weapon by Russia is a factor which, though unknowable, we must increasingly bear in mind.

At sea, we have to be prepared to meet new and faster types of U-boat and novel methods of mining. All these developments change the picture of the likely course and character of a future war, and many consequential changes are enforced upon the scale and pattern of weapons and equipment required.

We must not think of a possible third world war in terms of the first, or even the second, of these vast human catastrophes. The days of prolonged artillery bombardment, of immense and almost stationary armies, had vanished before the Second World War came. The expenditure on ammunition in the future may be far less than in the Second World War, and merely to proceed on the previous conventional lines would be to squander our military treasure and our strength.

These developments have affected the views of our military experts on the character and course of any future struggle, and this process of change continues, and even accelerates, with the remorseless march of the science of human destruction.

The second requirement we may have to meet is the continuance of armed peace or cold war, as forecast by the right hon. Gentleman the Member for Lewisham, South (Mr H. Morrison), for a prolonged period. The technical developments which I have just mentioned will not help us much in that. It is by more conventional armaments, mainly, in fact, by the infantry soldier serving in so many parts of the world, that we have to make our current contribution towards security against Communist encroachment.

The need to maintain this kind of military strength in peace must be balanced against the other need to ensure that, if war comes, we shall be able to meet the first intense phase with all its new inventions. I do not doubt that, if the party opposite had continued in power, they would also have been impelled by these developments to review and recast their original scheme, which we supported.

To sum up this part of the argument, I would say that, allowing for the time-lag on the one hand, and the increase of costs on the other, we shall in four years have spent more on re-equipment than was proposed by the late Government for three. But the improvements in types of weapons will have enabled many practical economies and reductions to be made in the original programme with a positive increase in war power. Had that original programme been allowed to continue in its expanding course after the third year, the expenditure would have risen enormously beyond our power to bear.

I will repeat in a varied form what I have said before – that a period of rearmament follows the rule: first year, nothing; the second, not much; the third year, more than you can pay for. With the great complexity of modern weapons, and particularly of aircraft, this rule must now to be extended into the fourth and even the fifth year.

If we had followed up to its logical conclusion the defence programme which we found descending upon us when we took office, in 1954 or 1955 we should have been exposed to enormous increases in expenditure, unforeseen, so far as we know, at the time when the programme was originally launched, and utterly beyond our economic capacity to bear. Even if we had not been called upon at this time to make new efforts to stimulate exports and to reduce the investment programme and social expenditure at home, it would, in any event, have been necessary to grip the whole position in order to prevent the automatic growth of defence expenditure from rising in the third, fourth and fifth years far beyond the limits of our economic strength.

It must be remembered that the process of re-armament is a continuous one. Modern weapons take two or three years to make. Modern aircraft take four or even five years. It is wasteful to the highest degree to spend many months retooling factories for re-armament and moving labour for that purpose, and then, while the weapons are still good and current, to break them up and disperse the labour. Very good reasons must be shown in every case where contracts are modified or cancelled with heavy costs in compensation and ineffectual employment of skilled labour.

It is the continuity of what we were committed to that I am drawing to the attention of the House. Therefore, although we are varying the programme, for the reasons which I have explained, it is still essentially the programme shaped and put forward by the late Government at a time when the right hon. Member for Ebbw Vale (Mr Bevan) was one of its leading Members. Indeed, had he remained responsible, he, and others associated with him, would have had to make some of the changes which we are now making. But in view of the programme on which he helped to launch us, and the great mass of contracts already placed before he left office, he has every right to share the credit, as he shares the responsibility, for what was in the main a timely and patriotic decision.

So far I have been dwelling on finance. Money, however, is not the only limiting factor in re-armament. Steel and its companion products impose absolute limits, alike on our solvency and on our security. We are importing more than a million tons of steel and pig iron this year, and prospects of an improvement in our outlook next year are not unfavourable. Perhaps that is an under-statement. I hope so. If so, the under-statement may be set against any errors in the opposite direction which I may be considered to make.

The problem is how exactly the steel available after domestic needs are met should be allocated between defence services and exports, for without a sufficiency of exports, as the House knows and as I have so often said, a collapse of our economic and financial life would overwhelm us. It cannot be dogmatically stated that defence should have absolute priority over exports, or vice versa. Our supply of steel and various other metals is limited, and it would be equally foolish for the Government to lay it down that either armaments or exports should have an unlimited call on them at the expense of the other. Demands on these materials by those engaged in manufacturing goods for exports have to be carefully weighed one at a time – weighed carefully against our individual defence requirements – and we hope and believe that we can, with patience strike a balance which will build up our defences without endangering our solvency.

What applies to steel applies also to the transfer of industrial capacity throughout the metal-using and engineering industries. This diversion of resources from defence to the export drive is just as necessary for our military strength as for our daily lives. Not to make it would be to plunge into bankruptcy. It seems, therefore, and it is true to say, that priority is given to exports over defence, but the sphere in which such transfers will be fruitful is a limited one, and there will still be left a very heavy quantity of steel for the defence programme.

This process is going on now. Every case is being considered on its merits.

I am not going to publish exact figures on these matters; we have no parallel information from Soviet sources. But I may say that, broadly speaking, the decisions we have reached after months of intensive labour will alter the pattern of defence production in a way which will limit its demands on the engineering industry, and in the coming years set free a valuable part of its capacity for the expansion of our civil exports.

Mr Aneurin Bevan (Ebbw Vale): How much?

The Prime Minister: I cannot possibly estimate how much.

Mr Bevan rose –

The Prime Minister: The right hon. Gentleman is going to have an opportunity, I believe, of speaking later in the debate, so I hope he will allow me to complete my argument.

Mr Bevan: Perhaps the right hon. Gentleman would give way.

The Prime Minister: Very well.

Mr Bevan: I asked the Chancellor yesterday whether he would give us the figure of the reduction, if any, in the arms programme, and the right hon. Gentleman said he was leaving it to the Prime Minister to tell the House what he wanted to tell the House about defence today. Has the right hon. Gentleman no figure in his mind at which priorities are to become exercisable? If the priorities for exports run ahead too far, at what figure will they be arrested for the defence programme?

The Prime Minister: Well, I have no intention whatever of trying to anticipate the study which will be given to these matters in their final form in the November examination.

Mr Harold Davies (Leek): Have the Government not done anything? Nothing has been done.

The Prime Minister: After all, I am in possession of the House, and I am perfectly entitled to take that course.

Mr Davies: We have had two speeches from the Government with nothing in them.

The Prime Minister: No doubt the hon. Gentleman will later try to catch Mr Speaker's eye.

Mr Davies: There was nothing in them about what we have been waiting for.

The Prime Minister: I have been endeavouring to show the general tendencies which are modifying and affecting our policy in re-armament, but I am certainly not in a position to say how these will affect the estimates of expenditure for next year, or even for the course of this year.

There is, however, one section of steel to be transferred from armaments to exports which will I am sure, interest the House, if only from its paradoxical character. I mean the export of armaments to friendly and allied countries. It may indeed seem odd, when we are straining to re-arm that we should be willing to sell armaments to others. It was suggested yesterday that it would be better to starve the armaments plants and turn instead for all exports to civil production. I think the right hon. Gentleman was one of those who raised that point. This would indeed be imprudent. Moreover, armaments are, in these uneasy days, best sellers; they find ready and profitable market.

But the savings and efficiency that come from mass production, and the advantage of having the plants kept at their full compass, with all that that means for reserve power in the plants and in the pipeline should war come, is so great that in this time of stringency we feel fully justified in making contracts with Canada, with the United States, or with other countries for the supply of tanks and aeroplanes which will thus form a valuable addition to our high-grade exports, and at the same time enable our parent plants to develop their full strength.

Mr Percy Shurmer[1] (Birmingham, Sparkbrook): They are obsolete.

The Prime Minister: The price we pay is, of course, that some weapons that we make in this time of need will go abroad, though care will be taken not to deprive our front line of its essential requirements. I feel keenly the responsibility of this decision, but I find myself in the fullest agreement with the Minister of Defence, the Foreign Secretary and the Chancellor, with whom I have so long pondered upon these and similar matters. I feel myself in full agreement in believing that the export of a certain proportion of our munitions will be a feature in the growth of our munition plants, as well as an aid to our trade balance. Moreover, it will strengthen our friends and Allies throughout the Commonwealth and NATO.

We are now, as I have explained, approaching the third year where expansion of our armament programme is beginning to come into full swing, and when, if the process is not to get out of control, effectual limits must be assigned to its demands. It will be necessary for all three Fighting Services to divide their budgets between the maintenance of existing forces and new and improved equipment. At the Admiralty we have always considered maintenance and new construction as separate features. But this is less easy in the Army, where manpower has been in former times the outstanding factor. In the Air Force, which is a newcomer to the first place in our defence, the pressure of new types and superior inventions is intense.

The worst thing that happened to the Air Force since re-armament began was the failure to take the steps needed to accelerate the arrival of the newest and finest types of aircraft. This is now being remedied under, what I venture to call, super-priorities. For the sake of this, it will be necessary to reduce the maintenance charge in the existing Air Force by ceaseless economies in the overheads, or what perhaps may be called in this connection 'the under-foots'. The key figure of all Air Force administration is the number of men required to keep a fighting aeroplane and its pilot and crew in the air. In the late war

---

[1] Percy Lionel Edward Shurmer, 1888–1959. MP (Lab.) for Birmingham Sparkbrook, 1945–59.

this rose to 112. At present it is, according to Air Force figures, 113 but with the expansion of the Air Force it is planned to reduce it to 95.

Of course, the new types of aircraft which are coming into service, and more so those that await us in the future, require many refinements of care both in the training of the crews and the maintenance of the machines. The rule must, however, be that every man on the strength of the Air Force must be judged by his contribution to our flying, fighting strength. The provision and skilled use of the latest types must, above all things, remain at the head of the list. It might well be that the number of air personnel could be reduced without detriment by a system of what I have called in the past 'immediate Reserves'.

In the Navy before the First World War we created an 'immediate reserve' several thousand strong of highly-skilled men, sailors and mechanics, who were held ready to come up if called upon in a precautionary period, without, or in advance of, any general calling out of the Reserves. This system still exists in the Navy and has been applied in the Army. It may prove a great help to the Royal Air Force at present juncture.

In the Army the obvious way of reducing maintenance is to reduce numbers, and the question always arises where to strike the balance between a smaller number of men, fully trained and highly equipped, and a larger number at a lower level of training and equipment. The intake of men into the Army next year will be about 30,000 fewer than this year. The explanation of this is that a decrease is taking place in the number of Regular non-commissioned officers who train the new entry. These non-commissioned officers are departing to civil life, as they have a right to do, and the War Office do not feel that they can handle the full intake without some loss of efficiency. This misfortune will incidentally reduce the cost of maintenance. It will, however, have very little effect on the need for new equipment which is required for the existing trained formations.

Mr F. J. Bellenger (Bassetlaw):[1] Are we to understand that the Regular Army content is to be reduced, or the National Service intake?

The Prime Minister: No the National Service intake will be reduced.

Lieut.-Colonel Lipton: How?

The Prime Minister: I am assured that there is no difficulty about that. I do not desire to go too much into detail on these matters.

Mr Alfred Robens (Blyth):[2] As the National Service intake is to be reduced,

---

[1] Frederick John Bellenger, 1894–1968. Started work as a tea-packer at the age of 14. Later a boy messenger in the Post Office. Enlisted, Aug. 1914. Active service, Royal Artillery, 1914–18 (twice wounded). 2nd Lt, 1916. Conservative member, Fulham Borough Council, 1922–8. MP (Lab.) for Bassetlaw from 1935 until his death. Capt., Royal Artillery, 1939–40 (including retreat to Dunkirk). Financial Secretary, War Office, 1945–6. Secretary of State for War, 1946–7.

[2] Alfred Robens, 1910–99. Educated at Manchester Secondary School. Official of Union of Distributive and Allied Workers, 1935–45. Married, 1937, Eva Powell: one adopted son. MP (Lab.) for Wansbeck, 1945–50; for Blyth, 1950–60. Governor, Queen Elizabeth Training College for the

does that mean that there is now to be a study of the deferment of call-up?

The Prime Minister: That question ought to be put to the Secretary of State for War. I have answered five questions and I will answer no more questions at this juncture. (Hon. Members: 'Oh'.) Five is quite a lot. Even if the right hon. Gentleman holds up his hand like a boy at school, I will not defer to his wishes.

Mr Robens: May I pursue my point?

The Prime Minister: In the third year of re-armament, namely, 1953, a very heavy fertile crop of new equipment will be coming along. At this point may I say that I was astonished at the suggestion made by the late Minister of Defence, the right hon. Member for Easington (Mr Shinwell), in a speech at Rugby on 12th July, that the period of compulsory National Service should be reduced from two years to 18 months. It would hardly be possible to adopt a more improvident course. The fighting units of our Army today are almost all overseas, at least one-half are in the far-off foreign stations of the Middle East, Malaya and Korea, and in all of these there are rather more National Service men than Regulars.

The final six months of their two years' service is of the utmost value, since their efficiency as soldiers will by then have reached its peak. It is during these last six months that a man really begins to gain that degree of training and morale on which so much depends. Indeed, we are today relying on many of those fine young men to play their part in junior leadership, and many National Service junior officers and non-commissioned officers are to be found in our fighting units abroad. To reduce the period of service would aggravate in the most wasteful manner our movements problem. A very large number of men, over 30,000, would be permanently and completely out of action travelling to and fro in the pipeline.

In the Middle East, for instance, the rate of reinforcement would rise from 24,000 a year, on the two years' system, to 35,000 a year on the 18 months' system. In Korea it would rise from 5,500 a year to over 12,000. The saving in cash of about £17 million by the reduction of service would bring a loss of 58,000 men, which would grievously injure the Army structure built up at such heavy cost. Moreover, from the saving of £17 million on Estimates which are over £450 million, there would have to be deducted the cost of extra transport.

There is one further argument which should not be overlooked, and which the right hon. Gentleman I think should not overlook.

Mr E. Shinwell (Easington): Is the right hon. Gentleman arguing with me?

Disabled, 1951–80. Baron, 1961. Chairman, National Coal Board, 1961–71. Chancellor, University of Surrey, 1966–77. Director, Times Newspapers Ltd, 1967–83. Chairman, Vickers Ltd, 1971–79. Chairman, St Regis International, 1976–81. Chairman, Alfred Robens Associates, 1984–99. Published *Engineering and Economic Progress* (1965), *Industry and Government* (1970), *Human Engineering* (1970) and *Ten Year Stint* (1972).

JULY 1952

The Prime Minister: We have been pressing our friends on the Continent, in France and the Benelux countries, to raise their service to two years. Belgium has already adopted it. Such a step is absolutely necessary to the recreation of the French Army, with its heavy burden of foreign service. If we were to step back now and reduce our service, it is certain that the hopes of NATO would fail.

How, then, should we without casting doubts upon our sincerity reduce our two years' period of service at this present critical juncture in the build-up of a Western defence organisation? It is not long since the right hon. Gentleman was himself pressing this view on the House. It was as recently as 30th May in the present year.

Mr Shinwell: Will the right hon. Gentleman give way?

The Prime Minister: I will certainly give the right hon. Gentleman time to get up when I have finished this point. I am taking a lot of trouble with him because I am most anxious that some of the good things that he has done shall not be entirely swept away from his credit account. As recently as 30th May, speaking in this House, he said: '. . . there is not a high military authority in this country or associated with NATO or elsewhere who does not agree that, even if all the equipment were provided in the build-up of the Western defence organisation, it will not serve our purpose in the event of aggression unless the period of National Service which we have imposed upon ourselves is accepted by the other countries.' – (Official Report, 30th May, 1952; Vol. 501, c. 1814.) That is what the right hon. Gentleman said on 30th May. Yet on 12th July – not six weeks later – he urged that our period of National Service should be reduced to 18 months. What an example to set.

Mr Shinwell: I cannot do it just now for obvious reasons, but one of these days I will take trouble with the right hon. Gentleman and explain to him exactly the reasons we decided upon a two years' period of National Service. Might I remind him that at the time we did so we said that this was a temporary measure? That is the first point.

The second point is this. When he talks about the difficulty that would present itself in our cutting down the period of National Service, he should have regard to the fact that there are many existing commitments which will in due course be reduced. Let me give him one example and then I will sit down, because I do not want to argue with him at this stage. Just now we have nearly three divisions in the Middle East, far more than ever we had in peace-time before. One of these days we shall be able to reduce the number of divisions in the Middle East and then, as we have a vast number of trained reserves, we shall be able to reduce the period of National Service. Let the right hon. Gentleman argue against that.

The Prime Minister: I am sorry that the right hon. Gentleman should deprive himself of the consistency of his policy, because, as I have shown, up to 30th May he was strongly in favour of the maintenance of the two-year system – and the credit of introducing it is due to him – but now he turns to this new proposal – which I consider to be alike dangerous and unthrifty – for, I suppose, highly complicated reasons connected with the movement of opinion in the party opposite.

Mr Shinwell: Will the right hon. Gentleman give way for one moment?

The Prime Minister: I cannot give way again.

Mr Shinwell: That is a shocking and disgraceful thing to say. The right hon. Gentleman should be ashamed of himself.

Mr Deputy-Speaker (Sir Charles MacAndrew): Order.

Mr Shinwell: The right hon. Gentleman has given way.

Mr Deputy-Speaker: Order. The Prime Minister is sitting down because I am standing up. If the Prime Minister does not give way, right hon. Gentlemen must remain in their seats.

Mr Shinwell: The right hon. Gentleman ought not to have said that. It is disgraceful. He should be ashamed of himself.

The Prime Minister: The French have a saying that it is the truth that wounds.

Mr Shinwell: It was a disgraceful thing to say. The Prime Minister does not give anybody any credit. I will deal with him next Monday.

The Prime Minister: Why not on Sunday evening?

Yesterday, I was surprised to see the right hon. Gentleman the Member for Leeds, South standing so smiling and carefree at the Despatch Box as if he had no responsibility for the shocking and shameful state to which our finances were reduced during his tenure of the Exchequer. When a Minister has in a single year brought his country from the best position it had held since the war to the verge of bankruptcy, and when he has left to his successors heart-tearing problems to face and solve, I wonder indeed that he should find nothing to do but mock and jeer at the efforts that others make to clear up the confusion and disorder that he left behind him. Indeed, I almost think it is a pity that he ever escaped from Winchester.

Let me also say in answer to him and to that shining star of television, my hon. Friend the Member for Aberdeenshire, East (Mr Boothby), whose rays were turned upon me last night – I very much regret not having heard his speech – that I do not take back a word I said in describing, not the immediate crisis, for that we are dealing with, but the general financial economic position of our country.

My resolve is that the people should realise how different is their position from that of all other Western communities; 50 million of us here standing at a level of civilisation not surpassed in the world, and yet barely able to earn our living and pay our way, and dependent for the food of two-fifths of our people on how we can do this in this vast swirling world.

Tragic it is indeed. (*Laughter.*) Why is there laughter? Surely it is not a party matter. (*Interruption.*) Hon. Gentlemen opposite cannot get much by shouting

JULY 1952 583

me down. Tragic indeed is the spectacle of the might, majesty, dominion and power of the once magnificent and still considerable British Empire having to worry and wonder how we can pay our monthly bills. I fully admit I am tortured by this thought and by the processes which I see around me, and I shall do everything in my power – (Hon. Members: 'Resign!') – to bring home to the mass of our race and nation the sense of peril and the need for grave and far-reaching exertions.

Cabinet: conclusions
(Cabinet papers, 128/25)

31 July 1952
Secret
11.30 a.m.
Cabinet Meeting No. 75 of 1952

[...]

6. The Cabinet had before them memoranda by the Lord Chancellor (C(52)262) and the Attorney-General (C(52)263) reporting the results of the examination which they had made, in pursuance of the request made by the Cabinet on 24th June, into the question whether the Government were committed to according privileges and immunities to the international organisations listed in an earlier memorandum by the Foreign Secretary (C(52)191).

The Attorney-General said that he had confined himself to the question whether the Government were under a legal obligation to accord these privileges, and he was of opinion that such an obligation could be shown to exist in respect of only three of these organisations.

The Lord Chancellor said that he had felt obliged to take a somewhat broader view of the question. He had thought it inappropriate in considering international commitments which were not enforceable by any court of law, to confine himself to strictly legal obligations: he had felt impelled to take account also of political and moral obligations. He could not therefore advise the Cabinet to draw a distinction between agreements which the United Kingdom Government had ratified and agreements which had been signed on behalf of the Government but had not been formally ratified. If that course were followed it would have the result, for example, that we should withhold these privileges from the North Atlantic Treaty Organisation, though the agreement defining them had in that instance been drawn up on our initiative by a committee over which our own representative had presided. His conclusion was that the Government were under a clear obligation to accord the agreed privileges to all these organisations, save only the one which had not yet been established.

The Prime Minister said that he greatly deplored the extension of diplomatic immunity contemplated by these agreements. The advantages conferred on the international staffs would tend to encourage the proliferation of these international agencies, of which there were already too many. If it was necessary to honour the commitments accepted in this matter by the previous Government, he hoped that the Foreign Secretary would do his utmost to prevent the establishment of still more international agencies to which similar privileges might have to be accorded.

In further discussion attention was drawn to the point made in paragraph 2 of C(52)262, that the agreements would have the effect of limiting to some extent the privileges which could otherwise be claimed at common law by national representatives attending the meetings of these international organisations. Those members of the Government who, when in opposition, had in both Houses of Parliament criticised the grant of these privileges to these international organisations would find their position easier if this point were more clearly explained when the matter came before Parliament again.

The Cabinet –

(1) Agreed that Her Majesty's Government should now accord to the international organisations listed in Annex III of C(52)191 the privileges and immunities prescribed in the agreements concluded by the respective organisations.

(2) Authorised the Foreign Secretary to present the Orders in Council required for this purpose, as set out in Annex III of C(52)191.

(3) Asked the Foreign Secretary to give them early notice of any new proposal to extend similar immunities and privileges to other international agencies.

[...]

Winston S. Churchill to Clementine Churchill
(Baroness Spencer-Churchill papers)

[Undated, July 1952]

Max[1] dined with me at No. 10 the other night. We were alone and I had a very agreeable talk. He is very anxious to order the lift to be got ready to put in, so that whenever it is convenient we can have the carpentering done. I told him of your plan to move my studio upstairs and refit the drawing room as of yore.

[1] William Maxwell Aitken, 1879–1964. Known as 'Max'. Canadian financier and newspaper proprietor. MP (Cons.) for Ashton under Lyne, 1910–16. Knighted, 1911. Canadian Expeditionary Force Eye-Witness in France, May–Aug. 1915; Canadian Government Representative at the Front, Sep. 1915 to 1916. Bought *Daily Express*, his largest-circulation newspaper, Dec. 1916. Baron Beaverbrook, 1917. Chancellor of the Duchy of Lancaster and Minister of Information, 1918. Minister for Aircraft Production, 1940–1. Minister of State, 1941. Minister of Supply, 1941–2. Lord Privy Seal, 1943–5.

I still hold to my plan of closing Chartwell from the end of October until the beginning of May and using Chequers meanwhile for weekends and Christmas. This would be the time to put in the lift & move my studio up.

When Chartwell house is closed it would be convenient to me to have Wellstreet Cottage as a pied a terre, if I come down on Friday or Friday night. Any furniture lacking could easily be taken from my room at Chartwell.

They showed me the plans, which you discussed with the Ministry of Works, for reviving the State Rooms and dining room at No. 10, and I told Jock he might write to you about them. There are a few minor improvements the Ministry of Works suggest. I think it is a brilliant conception and should be done in the public interest, as it is a great pity these rooms are not available for use. We really ought to have them for the Coronation year. Look at all the distinguished people I have had to entertain in our poor little attic. I am sure they are surprised at the difference between the accommodation and the menu.

The only time the changes can be made is during the ten weeks holiday. Once finished, this would not commit you to using them until you felt inclined. There would be no need for more servants, except perhaps one in the kitchen, as the State Rooms would continue to be cleaned as at present. However I think the structural changes should be made in the Recess and we could stay where we are until you felt able to move down.

Winston S. Churchill to Clementine Churchill
(Baroness Spencer-Churchill papers)

[Undated, July 1952]

My Beloved One,

No letter yet from remote Cattini.

I send you the enclosed notes and plans. I don't want you to be worried about them. The changes in structure at No. 10 must be begun in the first week of August, but everything can go on as it is at present till you feel like moving down.

Yr letter of 8th[1] has just arrived from London. The temperature seems vy high. I do hope it will not 'sizzle' you for long. Let me know how it goes on.

I have a lot of troubles here with the money shortage & the inevitable cuts. Also <u>Steel</u> is not agreed by all. Bobbety is difficult & uncertain. But I expect we shall get away all right for the Ten Weeks interlude – holiday it will not be for your devoted loving husband.

[Drawing of a pig]

---

[1] Reproduced above, dated July 9.

August
1952

Clementine Churchill to Winston S. Churchill
(Churchill papers, 1/50)[1]

1 August 1952   Capri

My Darling,

At last we have got hold of the *Daily Telegraph* with a report of your speech[2] which I thought good and necessary. What atrocious interruptions form the Opposition. Now in the calm of the recess, the alterations you announced will be calmly carried out.

Yesterday we visited the neighbouring island of Ischia. It is not dramatic like Capri, but more convenient for daily life. It is four times as large and very fertile and has numerous little bays. It is an old volcanoe, extinct I hope and think. Like Montecatini it is an important thermal station with mud baths, radioactive waters and so on.

We were taken there by a pretty and intelligent Capri Duchess in her speed boat. She has also a husband, four children, two villas in Capri and one in Ischia, a lover, an apartment in Rome, and everything else needed to make life pleasant and convenient!

King Farouk is here and the Islanders are rather cross about it; as last year when he was honeymooning in Capri he behaved very arrogantly.

I'm longing to see you darling and will come back soon.

                                                                                     Your loving Clemmie
                                                                                     [Drawing of a cat]

---

[1] This letter was handwritten.
[2] Of July 30, reproduced above (pp. 570–83).

Winston S. Churchill to Clementine Churchill
(*Churchill papers, 1/50*)

1 August 1952

Session finished. Off to Chartwell. Nellie[1] coming. I need rest. Delighted with your letters. Monty comes night of 16th for christening next day. Let me know your plans. Fondest love.

Winston S. Churchill to Antony Head
Prime Minister's Personal Minute M.418/52
(*Premier papers, 11/202*)

4 August 1952

When about a month ago in the War Room at a Defence Committee meeting I suggested that there might have to be cuts in the numbers of the Army, and you said that in any case there was going to be a reduction, I thought of 33,000. This was not accurate as the figures you give in paragraph 3 show.* 1952 is the only exceptional year and the others all vary round 125,000. I think that you or the CIGS mentioned the birth rate on this occasion. At any rate it was with this in my mind that I considered the various explanations given.

* Your minute of 31 July 1952 on National Service intake in Army.

Winston S. Churchill to Clementine Churchill
(*Baroness Spencer-Churchill papers*)[2]

4 August 1952

My darling one,

With intense relief I have got back here with ten weeks before Parl meets again. The last month has been vy trying. But now we have a chance to survey the scenes and to try to make better plans. We have saved about £125 m from the torturing exchange and have taken another step to solvency. It seems hard indeed that we should get no credit for saving the country from Bankruptcy. And even that will require prolonged vigilance. Anthony Eden is back & I have

---

[1] Nellie Hozier, 1888–1957. Clementine Churchill's sister. Served as a nurse in Belgium, 1914. Captured by the Germans, Aug. 1914, but released almost immediately. Married, 1915, Col. Bertram Romilly (1878–1940: Egyptian Camel Corps, 1914–17; Chief Instructor, Cairo Military School, 1925–8).

[2] This letter was handwritten.

felt his absence vy much. He looks thin & is I fear frail. Still we shall have a holiday – or at least a change.

Rain has come & the arid fields are freshened. Yr croquet lawn is the greenest spot for miles. The Magnolia is just beginning its beautiful crop. I see a wealth of buds & several are trying to climb in to my window. Yr garden is looking lovely & so is yr terrace. I think you will be pleased with all you see.

Nellie cd not come on account of Giles[1] & the baby.[2] But I have Randolph & Arabella (the latter in the Tower room). The Prof is here & is full of thought & wisdom. Patrick[3] speaks this Sunday night.

On my way down here from London I went to a cocktail party given by Betty[4] at her Chelsea house. The Q Mother was there also Princess Margaret[5] & Diana DC[6] & her son Julian[7] & his fiancé[8] to whom he will be married on Tuesday. She seems vy beautiful. They are going to the Lac de Garde (that auberge across the lakes wh Diana likes so much). I advised Correzze if it were too hot on the lakes. I am sending him two vols of Marlborough as a token.

The row between Attlee & Bevan is flaring up vy nicely & it is a pleasure to see the newspapers full of Socialist splits instead of only our shortcomings. It was vy disreputable of the Opposition leaders not to vote for their own German Treaty to wh they were pledged in the plainest terms.

Duncan has done vy well & is recognised by all to have won his position as a leading figure on our side.

It is too hard for any horses to be galloped, but we hope to have some races in Sept. & Oct. The fish (indoor & out) are well & pretty. I feed them all myself. The labour is not unwelcome, after too much politics.

Darling I thought yr letter about Tiberius & the ants most interesting. I

---

[1] Giles Samuel Bertram Romilly, 1916–67. Educated at Wellington College and Oxford University. Married, 1949, Mary Ball-Dodd. Correspondent for *Daily Express* on Spanish Civil War and WWII. POW, 1940–5 (escaped with the help of Dutch officers). Author of *The Privileged Nightmare* (1952).

[2] Edmund Humphrey Samuel Romilly, 1951–2018. English barrister and writer. Married Deborah Bowker. Author of *Skinner* (2006), *The Barn* (2006) and *Victims: A Tale of Betrayal and Revenge* (2014).

[3] Patrick Buchan-Hepburn.

[4] Elizabeth Vere Cavendish, 1897–1982. Known as 'Betty'. Eldest daughter of Lord Richard Cavendish and Lady Moyra Beauclerk. Married, 1915, Robert Gascoyne-Cecil, Viscount Cranborne: three sons. Styled Marchioness of Salisbury, 1947.

[5] Margaret Rose, 1930–2002. Only sibling of Queen Elizabeth II. Born Glamis Castle, Scotland. Married, 1960, Antony Armstrong-Jones, 1st Earl of Snowdon (div. 1978): two children.

[6] Diana Olivia Winifred Maud Manners, 1892–1986. Daughter of 8th Duke of Rutland. Married, 1919, Alfred Duff Cooper (later Viscount Norwich). After her husband's death in 1954 she was known as Lady Diana Cooper.

[7] John Julius Cooper, 1929–2018. Educated at Upper Canada College, Eton, University of Strasbourg and New College, Oxford. Writer for RN, 1947–9. Married, 1952, Anne Frances May Clifford (diss. 1985): two children; 1989, Mollie Philipps Sherfield. Entered FO, 1952. Viscount Norwich, 1954. 3rd Secretary, British Embassy, Belgrade, 1955–7. 2nd Secretary, British Embassy, Beirut, 1957–60. Worked in FO (1st Secretary from 1961) and in British Delegation to Disarmament Conference, Geneva, 1960–4. Chairman, British Theatre Museum, 1966–71. Chairman, Venice in Peril Fund, 1970–92. Chairman, Colnaghi, 1992–6.

[8] Anne Frances May Clifford, 1929–. Artist. Married, 1952, John Julius Cooper (diss. 1985): two children.

expect you have really enjoyed yr stay at Capri. It certainly sounds lovely. I look forward to yr report on the Blue Grotto.

Forgive these disjointed scribblings wh I send by the bag to meet you in Rome on Tuesday.

I love you so much & miss you & long for your return. We will just do nothing but sit & purr.

Your ever loving & devoted husband,
W
[Drawing of a pig]

Give much love to Sarah

Winston S. Churchill to Lord Swinton
Prime Minister's Personal Minute M.422/52
(Premier papers, 11/113)

5 August 1952

On second thoughts I am rather shy about these Junior Ministers' broadcasts.[1] Why should they be given precedence over their departmental chiefs? Why should the Socialists have the advantage of putting up quite irresponsible people to cross-examine our Under Secretaries? It is not a fair contest anyway. Their people can say anything that is popular, and ours in reply will be limited not only by Government policy but by how far they are entitled to be the exponents of it.

The first case that came along was for an Under Secretary of the Foreign Office to have a duel with Aneurin Bevan on Foreign Affairs. Do we really want this? Are we not giving Bevan an advertisement which he does not deserve?

I am afraid I did not see all the difficulties when you put up the proposal.

Please do not go any further with it until after we have had a talk.

Sir David Maxwell Fyfe to Winston S. Churchill
(Premier papers, 11/29)

5 August 1952

1. You may like to glance at the Criminal Statistics for England and Wales for 1951 which have just been published. I enclose a copy.

2. The picture shown by these statistics is on the whole a gloomy one. In particular:

    (a) The number of indictable offences known to the police was 13.7%

---

[1] See M.372/52, reproduced above (p. 537).

higher than in 1950, and the number of persons found guilty of such offences was 14.5% higher than in 1950.[1]

(b) The following table shows how the increase in the number of persons found guilty of indictable offences was distributed among the main types of offence:

receiving	22%
larceny	19%
sexual offences	13%
breaking and entering	5%
violence against the person	2%
fraud and false pretences	2%[2]

(c) The number of persons found guilty of non-indictable offences in 1951 was 3.5% higher than in 1950.[3]

(d) Following are the most important increases in the numbers of persons found guilty of non-indictable offences:

prostitution	15%
drunkenness	13%
neglect or ill-treatment of children	10%
malicious damage	10%[4]

3. There are a few more satisfactory features to be set against these rather depressing facts.

(i) The number of persons found guilty of offences against Defence Regulations was 22% lower in 1951 than in 1950.

(ii) There was a decrease of 23% in the number of persons found guilty of robbery. The main offence included under this heading is robbery with violence, the only offence of violence which was punishable by corporal punishment up to 1948. In the age group 21–30 there was a decrease of 41% compared with the figure for 1950.

(iii) The number of offenders under 21 who were sentenced to imprisonment fell from 1,382 in 1950 to 1,214 in 1951.

4. The general and continuing increase in crime gives cause for much concern, and I fear that the figures for the first part of 1952 do not show signs of improvement.

5. It is true that the better recording of crime by the police has led to a paper increase in the number of offences compared with the years before the war. Moreover, it is believed that the public are now more ready to report minor offences than they used to be and recent increases in police strength have made it easier for them to do so. But after making all allowances for these factors there can be no doubt that many forms of crime have substantially increased.

---

[1] Churchill wrote in the margin: 'How many!'
[2] Churchill wrote: 'numbers please'.
[3] Churchill wrote: 'How many!'
[4] Churchill wrote: 'numbers'.

6. I have been consulting chief officers of police and others as to possible reasons for this increase. I think that there can be little doubt that to a large extent it is a symptom of a general decline in standards of honesty and morality. There is no easy solution; but I am exploring various suggestions, and contemplate that it will be desirable to consult among others the Judges, the Churches, and leaders of labour with a view to tackling the problem on a wide front. I do not want to trouble you now with a detailed list of steps which might possibly be taken, but I will consult you later when my proposals have taken more definite shape.

Winston S. Churchill to Sir David Maxwell Fyfe
Prime Minister's Personal Minute M.423/52
(Premier papers, 11/29)

6 August 1952

I would be much obliged if you could give me this statement with the actual numbers. Percentages are most misleading and to me almost useless. The growth of the prison population should surely also be included. Owing to the non-infliction of corporal punishment not only for the offences for which it was previously legal the Judges are imposing far heavier sentences and the prisons are overcrowded to a startling and dangerous degree. Pray let me have at your leisure a further statement.[1]

Winston S. Churchill to Anthony Eden
Prime Minister's Personal Minute M.424/52
(Premier papers, 11/392)

7 August 1952

Surely it would be very dangerous to use the bait of rearming the Egyptian forces or improving their equipment in the hopes that they will take a reasonable view about making our forces withdraw from Egypt in spite of our Treaty rights? I believe it is an Eton custom to make parents of pupils pay for the birch!

---

[1] Maxwell Fyfe sent Churchill an amended version on Aug. 18.

Anthony Eden to Winston S. Churchill
(*Churchill papers, 2/517*)

7 August 1952
Secret
PM/52/86

You asked me whether our Embassies in Cairo and Tehran had arms. (Your personal minute No. M.415/52.)

2. HM Embassy in Cairo have a variety of small arms, including four Bren guns, 2" Mortars and tommy-guns and tear gas, sufficient to arm the equivalent of two platoons, and a planned operation for their use in emergency. At one point on January 26th last the Ambassador sent the Army a signal saying 'We are standing by to repel boarders'; and his staff are in fact confident that they could have given the boarders a warm reception.

3. I am enquiring about the position in Tehran.

Winston S. Churchill to Lord De L'Isle and Dudley
Prime Minister's Personal Minute M.425/52
(*Premier papers, 11/2*)

7 August 1952

I do not question the achievement but I am concerned at the sacrifice.[1] One fatal accident to every sixteen jet pilots in eighteen months is formidable. All these young men face a sixteen-to-one chance of death in eighteen months. How does this compare with ordinary life? Is there any difficulty in obtaining volunteers? It seems to me there would be a case for treating service of this kind as if it were Active Service. I am not entirely convinced that the comparison with the training figures in the height of the War makes sufficient allowance for the risks which then had to be taken. In enquiring about these matters I in no way underrate the honourable, indeed glorious, spirit which evidently prevails.

---

[1] See M.399/52, reproduced above (p. 552).

Anthony Eden to Winston S. Churchill
(Premier papers, 11/392)

8 August 1952
Secret
PM/52/87

In your minute M.414/52[1] you drew attention to the expression General Neguib was reported to have used that the Sudan and Egypt should work together 'against the common enemy', meaning us.

2. The Newspaper report to which you referred was quoting a Sudanese newspaper not always well disposed to us, which had had a telephone interview with the General. He may therefore have been misquoted.

3. The phrase 'the common enemy' is used by the Moslem Brotherhood, among whose ranks are many of Neguib's supporters. It could therefore have been used by him, but these hostile expressions have become commonplaces of Egyptian public expression and are not the result of considered opinion.

4. While we can expect General Neguib, like anyone else in public life in Egypt now, to work to remove British influence from the Sudan and British forces from the Canal Zone, it would be a mistake to assume that his and Aly Maher's[2] regime will be radically anti-British from the start. Indeed, over the past ten days there have been a number of reassuring signs, which I do not think are designed solely to lull us into a sense of false security.

Anthony Eden to Winston S. Churchill
(Premier papers, 11/392)

9 August 1952
PM/52/88

Your minute M.424/52 about Egypt.[3]

We will not let them have this equipment just yet anyway. Even if we did so, I doubt if they would make the mistake of trying to push our forces into the Egyptian equivalent of Ducker![4]

---

[1] Reproduced above (p. 569).
[2] Aly Maher Pasha, 1882–1960. Director, Egyptian Royal Law School, 1923. Chief of the Royal Cabinet, 1935–6. PM of Egypt, 1936, 1939–40, 1952. Retired, 1952.
[3] Reproduced above (p. 591).
[4] 'Ducker': the Harrow School swimming pool.

John Colville: diary
('The Fringes of Power', page 653)

11 August 1952

Returned from Chartwell after a long week-end. I have been particularly slothful about this diary of late, partly because it has been such a hot summer.

The session ended in heated feelings, partly engendered by the Government's forecast of important decisions to announce, coupled with their failure in the event to do so – and one of the worst speeches I have ever heard W make about defence.

Now the Churchills are at Chartwell. Just before he went (Mrs C being at Capri) W took Meg and me to see *The Innocents*, a stage version of Henry James'[1] *The Turn of the Screw*. He got a great welcome but embarrassed us by being unable to hear and asking questions in a loud voice.

Philip's[2] Dragon *Orthos* sank under him at Cowes last Saturday; King Farouk has abdicated;[3] the Persian situation deteriorates with the return of Moassadeq to power; Anthony Eden and Clarissa Churchill[4] are engaged. Clarissa, who was at Chartwell for the week-end, is very beautiful but she is still strange and bewildering, cold if sometimes witty, arrogant at times and understanding at others. Perhaps marriage will change her and will also help to calm the vain and occasionally hysterical Eden. W feels avuncular to his orphaned niece, gave her a cheque for £500 and told me he thought she had a most unusual personality.

Thomas Fife-Clark to Lord Swinton
(Premier papers, 11/113)

12 August 1952

Re the Prime Minister's minute about junior Ministers' broadcasts,[5] I should like to have a word with you about this on your return. I doubt whether Lord Woolton has yet had a chance of discussing the 'Opposite Numbers' idea with the BBC, and certainly the BBC proposal that Mr Aneurin Bevan should debate foreign affairs with the Under-Secretary of the Foreign Office cannot arise from our proposal, which is intended to secure for the Government the

---

[1] Henry James, 1843–1916. US novelist. Born in New York City. Educated at Harvard Law School. Took British citizenship, 1915. OM, 1916. Published many novels, plays and non-fiction works including *The Portrait of a Lady* (1881), *The Turn of the Screw* (1898) and *The Ambassadors* (1903).

[2] Philip Mountbatten, Duke of Edinburgh.

[3] Farouk abdicated on July 26. See Stevenson to Foreign Office, July 27, reproduced above (p. 566).

[4] Clarissa Churchill, 1920–. Daughter of Winston Churchill's brother Jack. Married, 1952, Anthony Eden (as his second wife).

[5] See M.372/52 and M.422/52, reproduced above (pp. 537, 589).

advantages of Ministerial representation while at the same time protecting it from the risk of being 'out-gunned'.

The position very shortly is this. The BBC would naturally like to have Ministers — if possible senior Ministers — as radio and TV contestants with Opposition representatives. But Broadcasting House, in arranging these debates, seems to be concerned rather more with providing public entertainment than public information; and its idea is always to get a contest in which one side gets well beaten — for preference, massacred.

It is an interest of the Government to have Ministers to speak for it instead of back-benchers who have neither adequate knowledge nor proper authority (probably this would broadly suit the Opposition also, since they could put up ex-Ministers against Ministers and they are as tired of their Foots[1] as some people are on the other side of the Boothbys). On the other hand it has been assumed — and I think this is right — that there are good reasons why senior Ministers, even if they could spare the time, should not be exposed to 'off the cuff' debate in public. The main aim of the 'Opposite Numbers' idea therefore is to make use of junior Ministers but to ensure that (1) they are reasonably well matched; (2) the debates take place on subjects and with opponents assuring the highest possible standards of responsibility.

On (1), we must copy the BBBC rather than the BBC, and make sure that a nine-stone-seven contestant is not put up against a fourteen-stone man. This is assured by the 'Opposite Numbers' proposal, since if the BBC accepted it, it would be quite impossible for either the BBC or the Opposition to wangle the matchings — you can set down now, of course, the junior Ministers the Government would choose and the Opposition members which occupied those very posts in the last Government.

On (2), it is of course inevitable that the Opposition has the advantage of irresponsibility, but it has less advantage if its spokesman in any debate has occupied the post in a State Department now held by his opponent, who can of course remind him of that fact and quote his own actions or statements when in that office.

Unless the BBC offered protection on those lines, the Government would be well advised not to expose any Ministers to the risks of these debates. But I still feel that the 'Opposite Numbers' idea is well worth exploring — it will of course need careful consideration before detailed discussion with the BBC — because the Government is suffering quite severely under the present system

---

[1] Michael Mackintosh Foot, 1913–2010. Born in Plymouth, Devon, brother of Sir Dingle Foot. Educated at Wadham College, Oxford. Editor, *Evening Standard*, 1942 to July 1943; *Tribune*, 1948–52, 1955–60. MP (Lab.) for Plymouth Devonport, 1945–55; for Ebbw Vale, 1960–83; for Blaenau Gwent, 1983–92. Secretary of State for Employment, 1974–6. Leader of the House of Commons, 1976–9. Lord President of the Council, 1976–9. Deputy Leader of the Labour Party, 1976–80. Leader of the Opposition (Labour), 1980–3. Oldest sitting member of the House of Commons, 1987–92.

of selection of BBC speakers. Moreover, I am sure that it will become more and more difficult, as TV develops, to keep Ministers out of these debates, without losing points to public opinion. If Ministers are to take part, a controlled and systematic method of selection on the lines suggested is much to be preferred to any ad hoc catch-as-catch-can method which is bound to give too much power to the BBC and sometimes to produce results which from the Government's point of view will be both surprising and damaging.

Winston S. Churchill to James Thomas
(Premier papers, 11/355)

13 August 1952

It was decided not to hold reviews of the Navy, Army and Air Force on account of the expense, nearly a quarter of a million, which would have been caused thereby. There is no reason however why ships of the Royal Navy in the Home Fleet should not gather in the Solent, display bunting and if convenient allow visitors on board (or even do this at their various ports). This ought not to cost anything as the ships are in commission and have allowance in fuel for their normal movements. There is no need to issue a communiqué today and the second proposed answer[1] is not true. I shall be glad to see you before I leave tomorrow afternoon for the country.

Anthony Eden and Clarissa Eden to
Winston S. Churchill and Clementine Churchill
(Churchill papers, 2/216)

14 August 1952

We are still so overcome by your overwhelming kindness which has made this the most perfect day for us.[2] Thank you and bless you both.[3]

---

[1] '(2) that with the fleet distributed as it is, all over the world, and the situation so uncertain, it is impossible to make any plans at the present time. The Admiralty are however watching the situation' (Colville to Churchill, 13 Aug. 1952, *Premier papers, 11/355*).

[2] Anthony Eden and Clarissa Churchill were married on this day.

[3] The Churchills responded: 'We too have enjoyed it so much. All good luck, Winston and Clemmie'.

Winston S. Churchill to Lieutenant-General Sir Ian Jacob
Prime Minister's Personal Minute M.437/52
(Premier papers, 11/255)

15 August 1952

The first two names are not well chosen.* 'Bombshell' would excite alarm among people who were not meant to be aware of its meaning. 'Blarney' is disrespectful to the troops engaged.

I wrote a minute on the subject of these names during the war, I think early in 1942. This might be studied.[1]

*Names given to Operations forming part of main 'Rodeo' operation.

Winston S. Churchill to Lieutenant-General Sir Ian Jacob
Prime Minister's Personal Minute M.438/52
(Premier papers, 11/201)

15 August 1952
Personal and Secret

Let me have a cold-blooded factual view of Mr Shinwell's proposals to reduce the National Service period to 12 or 18 months. He re-iterates that he knows what he is talking about, and considering that he was the Ministerial author of the two years Service and has on several occasions shown patriotic inclinations I should like to know whether he has any foundation for his views. For instance have the Chiefs of Staff or the Army Council altered their opinions, or have they any misgivings about the decisions for which they were responsible? Has he any backing in truth or fact for his new modifications? I hesitate, having watched him for the last twelve years in Parliament, to believe that he is simply thinking of the obvious political advantages he might reap in the internal Socialist Party conflict. If there is any official support for what he now says I should like to know. I am sure it would be a mistake of the first order to drop the two years period.

John Colville: diary
('The Fringes of Power', page 653)

15–18 August 1952

Meg and I spent the week-end at Chartwell. Montgomery was the other guest, with his persistent but oddly endearing egotism (even on the croquet

[1] See D.(Q)4/3 of 8 Aug. 1943, reproduced in *The Churchill Documents*, vol. 18, *One Continent Redeemed*, p. 2218.

lawn). He and I and Sarah were godparents to Jeremy Soames,[1] christened in Westerham Church on Sunday, 17th. On the 18th Christopher and I shot duck at Sheffield Park and lunched there; in the evening Churchills, Soameses and Colvilles went to see *The Yeomen of the Guard* at Streatham. The PM was received with immense acclamation by the audience.

Winston S. Churchill to President Harry S Truman
Prime Minister's Personal Telegram T.162/52
(Premier papers, 11/237)

16 August 1952
Immediate
Personal and Secret
No. 3362

In Anthony's absence I am taking charge of the Foreign Office correspondence.

I am concerned about the Alton Jones[2] visit to Musaddiq after his personal interview with you. If it came about that American oil interests were working to take our place in the Persian oil fields after we have been treated so ill there, this might well raise serious controversy in this country. We are doing our utmost to bear the heavy load, and do not possess the bi-partisan support of the Opposition, which we gave the late Government in foreign and defence affairs. We are also helping all we can in Korea. No country is running voluntarily the risks which we are, should atomic warfare be started by Soviet Russia.

I hope you will do your best to prevent American help for Musaddiq, either governmental or commercial, from becoming a powerful argument in the mouths of those who care little for the great forward steps towards Anglo-American unity in the common cause which you and I have worked for so long.

With kind regards and many thoughts.

Winston

---

[1] Jeremy Bernard Soames, 1952–. Grandson of Winston Churchill. Educated at Eton. Married, 1978, Susanna Keith: three children.

[2] William Alton Jones, 1891–1962. President of Cities Service Corporation (now CITGO), 1940–53. Major contributor to the war effort. Invited by Iranian PM Mossadeq to Iran to advise the government on the operation of the Iranian oil industry, Aug. 1953. Killed in an airplane crash on his way to join Eisenhower on a fishing trip.

Winston S. Churchill to Sir Norman Brook
Prime Minister's Personal Minute M.439/52
(Premier papers, 11/257)

16 August 1952

1) Please find out whether the Minister of Defence or the Minister of Supply have been consulted upon this business.* Why is it, if it were necessary to consult me at all, was this left until matters were so far advanced that they could not be stopped without causing much disturbance.

2) The idea of stimulating, through an inspired article, information both true and false, so mixed up as to be deceptive, to any particular newspaper, is not one hitherto entertained in time of peace. Certainly no departure from the principle that the Government tells the truth or nothing should be made except upon direct Ministerial responsibility as an exception in the public interest.

3) It is impossible now to prevent or postpone publication, as the Sunday papers are already largely in print. It may be no harm will come. If however the other newspapers complain (a) that the *Sunday Express* has been unduly favoured, or (b) inquire whether the Official Secrets Act is not involved, the statement should be made either by the newspaper or from the Ministry of Defence that the article in question was submitted beforehand to the security authorities who saw no reason to object to it.

* Article in the *Sunday Express* on testing the Atomic weapon.

Winston S. Churchill to Sir Vincent Tewson
(Premier papers, 11/474)

16 August 1952
Private

Dear Sir Vincent Tewson,

In your letter of June 18 you said that the General Council would wish to pursue the comments made by the Service Departments on Mr Woodcock's earlier letter.

The Departments concerned would be glad to have discussions with you about the position in Malta, and the First Lord of the Admiralty will be getting into touch with you. Such discussions would provide an opportunity for you to exchange views in confidence and would not, of course, take the place of negotiations through the usual machinery between representatives of the Departments and the Maltese Unions.

Winston S. Churchill to John Selwyn Lloyd
Prime Minister's Personal Minute M.441/52
(Premier papers, 11/392)

19 August 1952
Secret

1. I have never agreed in principle to our evacuation of the Canal Zone before the expiration of the Treaty, and then only if satisfactory arrangements are made, which may take place at any time, for the four-power association with Egypt, and if you like with Egypt in the van, for the defence of the famous international waterway.[1]

2. The Gaza project which is mentioned in the newspapers is not bearable by us, and it would involve anything around £100 to £120 millions expenditure to make a proper habitable base for a mobile armoured division and a brigade group. There is no question of this being done. Moreover the immense mass of stores and plant we have in the Canal Zone cannot be cast away to the Egyptians and left to their good faith or goodwill.

3. When the Cabinet discussed these matters earlier in the year all the acceptances by Egypt of the substantial points to which we hold were presumed to be an essential part of our position.

4. I am quite sure that we could not agree to be kicked out of Egypt by Nahas, Farouk or Neguib and leave our base, worth £500 millions, to be despoiled or put in their care, and to make another highly costly establishment at Gaza or elsewhere. It would be far better to clear out of the whole show in the Middle East, after bringing home and selling what materials we have got. Since we took office we have followed out the resolute policy of the late Government and have not hesitated to fire at Ismailia and elsewhere the decisive volley. How different would the position have been if the late Government had not flinched from doing this at Abadan.

5. I am not opposed to a policy of giving Neguib a good chance provided he shows himself to be a friend. I hope he will do something for the fellaheen,[2] but we must not be afraid of him or be driven by the threats of cowards and curs from discharging our duty of maintaining the freedom of the Suez Canal for all nations until we can hand it over to some larger, more powerful combination.

---

[1] On 23 Sep. 1945, the Egyptian Government demanded the modification of the 1936 Anglo-Egyptian treaty to terminate the British military presence in Egypt, and also to allow the annexation by Egypt of the Anglo-Egyptian Sudan. In 1950 a new Wafd government was elected which in Oct. 1951 unilaterally abrogated the treaty. In 1954, the UK agreed to withdraw its troops from Egypt; the withdrawal was completed in June 1956, before the Suez crisis.

[2] 'Fellaheen': Arabic term for agricultural labourers in the Middle East and North Africa.

Winston S. Churchill to John Selwyn Lloyd
Prime Minister's Personal Minute M.443/52
(Premier papers, 11/237)

17 August 1952

All this is not without hope but surely we would make a great mistake if at this moment when Musaddiq may be about to yield we relieved him from his burdens by lifting the restrictions on exports to Persia or transfers of Persian sterling. If we do this or do not attempt to restrain the United States from giving Musaddiq an immediate grant of 10 million dollars, we are simply giving him the power to carry on. All these things are difficult to judge but in my view we should hold such bargaining power as we have in our hands until we see the next move. The pressure has got to work on Musaddiq. We may throw everything away in relieving him at a critical and may be decisive moment.

All these things are a matter of judgement and luck. I am for sitting on the safety valve firmly for as long as we can; anyhow for a little longer. I am not afraid of the arguments about Communism in Persia. Perhaps not so afraid as is Musaddiq tonight. I should advise the Cabinet on Wednesday to hold firm and stubborn. The Cabinet paper should be prepared on these lines. We have not got much so far by bolting.

Winston S. Churchill to Lord Swinton
Prime Minister's Personal Minute M.442/52
(Premier papers, 11/113)

18 August 1952

I am not at all convinced by Mr Fife-Clark's minute of August 12.[1] The BBC should be discouraged from making such a feature of these particular debates on political issues. It is a form of entertainment which is bound to be the disadvantage of the Government of the day for the reasons mentioned in my minute of August 5.[2] Backbenchers should be used by us wherever it is unavoidable, and should be carefully picked for the purpose.

Television is a different matter. Here I think several Cabinet Ministers should take a part. The Chancellor has already done very well and Mr Eden told me he was going to do one. There are several others who should be effective.

---

[1] Reproduced above (pp. 594–6).
[2] M.422/52, reproduced above (p. 589).

President Harry S Truman to Winston S. Churchill
Prime Minister's Personal Telegram T.164/52
(Premier papers, 11/237)

18 August 1952
Immediate
Secret and Personal
No. 1551

I have your message of 16th August[1] and understand your concern over the Jones visit to Persia. However, Jones impressed me favourably and was emphatic about his desire to be helpful in facilitating a British–Persian oil settlement. He seems to be sincere in his belief that resumption of large-scale oil operations in Persia is impossible without the cooperation of the AIOC[2] and said he would emphasise this to Musaddiq. As we told Sir Oliver Franks, Jones plans to talk to the AIOC people after seeing Musaddiq. As we see it, there are two problems:

(1) An agreement must be reached with the Persians on the amount of Compensation due the AIOC, and
(2) means must be found to enable Persia to pay this sum out of oil revenues.

I think there is a good chance Jones can be helpful on the second problem. First of all, he will again explain to Musaddiq the facts of life in the oil industry and the need of dealing with the AIOC. Secondly, if the latest Persian proposals lead to an agreement with the company for the sale and distribution of Persian oil, Jones may be able to help the Persian Government resume production and refining processes so that there will be oil for the AIOC to buy and market.

If Jones can work out something it might be useful, since, with the political temper in Persia as it is, I think there is no possibility that British management as such would be allowed to return and take charge of the oil fields or refinery. By the same token, no other foreign interests could take the place in Persia which the AIOC formerly held, and I am certain the American oil companies understand this.

I need not tell you that we have not the slightest wish to profit by your present difficulties. We will do everything possible to avoid even the appearance of this.

On the wider issues, I am hopeful that you will be able to take up Musaddiq's most recent proposals in a broad and conciliatory spirit. Our reports make me think there is no chance that this or any other Persian Government can come forward with anything better, and the danger which would be

---

[1] T.162/52, reproduced above (p. 598).
[2] Anglo-Iranian Oil Company, a British firm, had controlled the extraction and marketing of Iranian oil since 1933.

involved in missing this opportunity seems to me too great to be risked. It looks to me as if time is running out for us.

In particular, I hope you will be willing to accept the Persian nationalisation law. I see no possibility of any agreement if you include in the Court's terms of reference any question of the validity of the law, which seems to have become as sacred in Persian eyes as the Koran. This need not of course prevent you, during the arbitral proceedings, from maintaining the validity of the 1933 Concession and claiming damages for its unilateral abrogation. Dean Acheson sent a message to Eden along this line on 12th August. If Persia goes down the communist drain, it will be little satisfaction to any of us that legal positions were defended to the last. The strategic consequences of the loss of Persia to the West and the possibility therein of gradually losing the great bulk of the Middle East with its oil resources to the Soviets are too obvious to mention. Such a disaster to the free world would undoubtedly also place a strain on general Anglo-American relationships not pleasant to contemplate.

It is my earnest hope that we can avoid these misfortunes and move forward together in the common cause. I think you know how much Anglo-American unity means to me.

With warm regards
Harry

Cabinet: conclusions
(Cabinet papers, 128/25)

20 August 1952
Secret
3.30 p.m.
Cabinet Meeting No. 77 of 1952

[...]

6. The Cabinet considered a memorandum by the Minister of Defence (C(52)278) proposing a system of tax-free educational allowances for officers and men in the Armed Forces who were liable to be moved frequently from one place to another, whether at home or abroad. The object of these allowances would be to enable Service parents to send their children to boarding schools.

The Minister of Defence and the Secretary of State for War said that there was greater need for some such system now that so large a proportion of the Army was serving overseas. Officers in the middle ranks were finding it increasingly difficult to provide for the education of their children, and many of them were leaving the Services on that account. It was false economy to spend large sums on training officers and then, for the sake of a relatively small additional expenditure, allow them to leave the Services because, in the middle ranks, they could not afford to provide for their children's education.

The Prime Minister said that Service parents were not alone in this difficulty: all middle-class parents were finding it increasingly difficult to send their children to boarding schools by reason of the high level of taxation. The proposal in C(52)278, though it might cost a small amount of money, raised a large question of principle. Was it right that the effects of high taxation should be mitigated, by tax-free allowances, for particular sections of the community who were paid by the State? Should not the Government aim rather at reducing taxation to a level which would enable people to meet their obligations out of taxed incomes?

The Chancellor of the Exchequer agreed that he could not consider in isolation the difficulties which Service parents found in providing boarding education for their children. Members of the Colonial Services had similar difficulties, on which he had recently been approached by the Colonial Secretary. And representations had also been made to him, on behalf of the public schools, regarding the difficulties of middle-class parents generally. He was disposed to view this problem sympathetically, but he must look at it as a whole. The solution might be found to lie, not in the grant of tax-free allowances to public servants, but rather in some form of income-tax relief in respect of expenditure on children's education.

The Cabinet –

1) Took note that the Chancellor of the Exchequer would confer with the Minister of Defence and the Colonial Secretary on the extent to which any plans which he might be able to devise for assisting parents to provide boarding education for their children would meet the special problems of parents in the Armed Forces and the Colonial Services.

2) Invited the Minister of Defence to arrange for the Prime Minister and the Chancellor of the Exchequer to be provided with statistical evidence of the extent to which serving officers in the middle ranks were leaving the Armed Forces because they were unable to provide for the education of their children.

[...]

August 1952

Field Marshal Lord Alexander to Winston S. Churchill
(Premier papers, 11/115)

20 August 1952

NAPALM BOMBING IN KOREA

At an informal discussion with Sir William Elliot, General Bradley said that it had been brought to his notice that an impression was gaining weight in certain journalistic circles in Washington and New York that the British were becoming very critical of the use of the Napalm bomb by the United Nations' Air Forces in Korea. This was causing some concern to himself and his colleagues. General Bradley fully realised that Parliamentary Questions on this subject did not necessarily reflect the general British view, but the impression was gaining ground that this feeling of uneasiness was also held in official circles in Whitehall.

2. In order to forestall newspaper articles expressing these views, which were now being prepared and which would harm Anglo-American relations, General Bradley wished to be able to make an 'off the record' statement that there was no foundation for the belief that the British Government were critical of the way the Napalm bomb is being used in Korea. He would like to be able to say that the British Government were in agreement with and supported the use of this weapon as at present employed.

Draft 'Off the Record' Statement for General Bradley on the British Attitude to the Use of Napalm Bombs in Korea

The British Government has given us no grounds for believing that they are critical of the use of napalm in Korea. The attitude of the British Government has always been that they do not claim to decide the air operations which the Supreme UN Commander carries out within Korea though they would expect to be consulted before the atom bomb was used.

Napalm is a modern development of flame-throwing weapons which have long been used in warfare. The British Service authorities regard it as a legitimate and useful weapon for use against military targets, particularly tanks and strong points. I believe the British Government like our own, would wish to avoid unnecessary loss of life and suffering among civilians such as might result from the use of napalm or any other weapon in crowded urban areas. And it is the practice of the UN Command in Korea to give due warning to civilians to evacuate the vicinity of military objectives in urban areas.

Winston S. Churchill to President Harry S Truman
Prime Minister's Personal Telegram T.165/52
(Premier papers, 11/237)

20 August 1952
Priority
Personal and Secret
No. 3403

1. Thank you so much for your deeply considered reply.[1] Why do not we send a joint telegram Personal and Secret to Musaddiq? It is true we could not sign it with our Christian names because he has not got one. Nevertheless if we could agree to say 'If you Musaddiq will do (a) (b) and (c), we two will do (x), (y) and (z)', and if this could be put down shortly it might be a help to our common interests. If you think well of this idea, shall I try my hand at a draft or will you?

2. We are dealing with a man at the very edge of bankruptcy, revolution and death but still I think a man. Our combined approach might convince him. The alternative is the United States taking on the burden of being indefinitely blackmailed by Persia to the detriment of her greatest friend. It will be worse for you even than for us if what is called Persia thinks that she can play one off against the other.

Winston S. Churchill to President Harry S Truman
Prime Minister's Personal Telegram T.166/52
(Premier papers, 11/237)

20 August 1952
Immediate
Personal and Secret
No. 3419

I thought it might save time if I sent this draft to you which expresses our view of the policy we might perhaps put forward together.

Following are my ideas of a possible joint message:

If the Persian Government will agree to

(i) the submission to the International Court of the question of the compensation to be paid in respect of the nationalisation of the enterprise of the Anglo-Iranian Oil Company in Persia and the termination of the 1933 Concession Agreement having regard to all the claims and counter-claims of both parties

---

[1] T.164/52, reproduced above (pp. 602–3).

(ii) appoint suitable representatives to negotiate with the AIOC arrangements for the flow of oil from Persia to world markets,

then

(a) the United Kingdom Government will agree on behalf of the AIOC to the submission to arbitration set out in (i)
(b) the United Kingdom Government will relax certain of the restrictions on exports to Persia and on Persia's use of sterling
(c) the United States Government will make their immediate grant of $10 million to the Persian Government
(d) the United Kingdom Government will arrange for the AIOC to take their part in the negotiations set out in (ii).

When agreement on the submission under (i) and (a) has been completed, (ii), (b), (c) and (d) will become operative.

Thus far the message.

The form of words in (i) is not meant to be a precise formula for the reference to the Court. I do not think there will be any difficulty in our accepting the nationalisation law as a fact. The terms of reference must not, however, prevent us from maintaining, as you put it, the validity of the 1933 Concession and claiming damages for its unilateral abrogation.

I should hope that further aid from the United States would be conditional on the progress of (ii) and (d).

When delivering the message the United Kingdom and United States representatives should point out that the negotiations under (ii) and (b) stand no chance of success unless the anti-British and anti-United States campaign in Persia has been stopped.

President Harry S Truman to Winston S. Churchill
Prime Minister's Personal Telegram T.167/52
(Premier papers, 11/237)

21 August 1952
Immediate
Personal and Secret
No. 1588

I want you to know that I am personally grateful for the fine message you sent me last evening. I consider its contents a great step forward in the solution of a problem which seems fraught with grave danger to the interests of our two countries. I shall be happy to give your latest proposal my support, and to assist in every way we can to convince the Iranian Government that it is in their interest to accept this offer.

Our physical separation complicates the problem of a joint message. Furthermore, I am concerned lest the enemies of the West in their propaganda, seize on such an approach as evidence that our two nations are 'ganging up' on Iran. The most logical procedure seems to me to have each of us send a message to Musaddiq, but so drafted as to clearly indicate consultation and agreement between us. I would much prefer this procedure and hope you can agree. My suggestions for drafting are attached in Annex A. In agreeing with you as I have above, I wish to point out certain matters which I believe will continue to merit your personal attention:

(1) If we are successful in this approach, the type of representation of AIOC for the scheduled talks will be of utmost importance. I earnestly ask your consideration of the appointment of a highly qualified and preferably well-known representative of your Government to be in fact the AIOC representative. I would be extremely reluctant to join in the approach if I felt that future negotiations would be conducted on anything but the broadest possible point of view in the interests of our Governments.

(2) Musaddiq's request for immediate financial assistance from the United Kingdom Government seems to have been met only partially. If you can see your way clear in finding additional and immediate funds, that would be of great importance. We have in the past suggested, as an approach to this problem, that you make immediate arrangements to lift and make payment against the oil now stored in the tanks, and Mr Eden, in his message to Mr Acheson of August 9th indicated that advances in respect to oil lifted could be made after satisfactory terms of reference of the arbitration had been agreed upon.

(3) In agreeing to your proposal, I assume that the wording of paragraph (ii), in which you spoke of the arrangements for the flow of oil, refers to the distribution problem. As you know, I consider that unfortunately it is not any longer a matter for discussion as to whether AIOC would produce oil or operate the Abadan refinery. We would probably both have to stand ready to offer our assistance to the Iranian Government in its arrangements for the efficient future operation of the oil industry in Iran, if requested to do so.

(4) I hope in drafting the message you would send you will be able to rearrange points so as to avoid specific mention of 'termination of the 1933 Concession Agreement'. Henderson[1] has informed us in

---

[1] Loy Wesley Henderson, 1892–1986. US diplomat. Born in Rogers, Ark. Educated at Northwestern University. Served with American Red Cross, 1919–21. US Foreign Service as Vice-Consul, Dublin, 1922; Queenstown, 1923. 3rd Secretary, Riga, Latvia, 1924–7. 2nd Secretary, Kovno, Lithuania, 1927–30. Eastern European Affairs, Dept of State, 1930–3. 2nd Secretary, American Embassy, Moscow, 1934; 1st Secretary, 1935–8. Asst Chief, European Affairs Bureau, 1938–43. US Ambassador to Iraq, 1943–5. Head of Near Eastern Affairs Bureau, 1945–8. US Ambassador to India, 1948–51; to

the past that direct reference to this matter might place Musaddiq in a difficult position with some of the more extreme elements of the Nationalist Front. Perhaps this could be avoided by the deletion of this phrase and the substitution of 'having regard to the legal position of the parties existing at the time of nationalisation'.

(5) The matter of handling publicity on this deserves consideration. With so many unfortunate leaks these days, I think we should both use every precaution to keep our approach secret until we discover how Musaddiq would like the matter handled. I think perhaps only he can judge whether immediate publicity would be helpful or harmful.

(6) Of course, I am certain you understand our agreement in this particular matter does not limit the freedom of action of either of our Governments in the future to meet situations not now known. I believe in these critical times we will both want to maintain our freedom to judge each situation as it occurs, and on what we believe to be the merits of the case.

I wish again to express my appreciation for your message which I consider to represent a statesmanlike approach to an extremely difficult problem.

John Selwyn Lloyd to Winston S. Churchill
(Premier papers, 11/301)

21 August 1952
Secret
PM/MS/52/98

The State Department have been having some preliminary discussion with us on the line to be taken about Korea at the meetings of the United Nations Organisation which begin on the 14th October next.

Their ideas are
1. a General Assembly Resolution
    a. praising the gallantry of the United Nations troops
    b. approving the conduct of the Armistice negotiations
    c. approving the stand taken on no forcible repatriation of prisoners of war
    d. instructing the President of the Assembly to transmit the resolution to the Chinese and North Korean Governments.
2. On receipt of the report of the President (whether or not there have been replies) the Additional Measures Committee of the Assembly should meet and recommend the imposition of a total embargo (details set out in Annex I).

Iran, 1951–4. Deputy Under-Secretary of State, 1955–60. Prof. and Director, Center for Diplomacy and Foreign Policy, American University, 1961–8.

3. The General Assembly on receipt of this recommendation from the Additional Measures Committee should pass a resolution, inter alia, calling upon states to sever, limit or refuse to enter into diplomatic relations with the aggressors in Korea, and recommending all states to take the actions recommended by the Additional Measures Committee.

The propositions that we should sever diplomatic relations with Communist China and impose a total embargo are contrary to our present policies. In my view they are dangerous courses which might cause a general war in the Far East, and it is out of the question for us to endorse them so far ahead, if ever.[1]

I should like to authorise Sir Oliver Franks to say at once to the State Department that these proposals are at present quite unacceptable to us.

I must make it clear that these ideas have not yet been put to United States Ministers who may not agree with them. Nevertheless I feel that we should leave their officials in no doubt as to our attitude.

Do you agree with this course?

ANNEX I

The General Assembly might recommend that every state prohibit all direct or indirect exports, re-exports, trans-shipments to, and imports from, Communist China and North Korea, and impose the following ancillary controls:

1. Prohibit vessels and aircraft of its registry from proceeding to Communist China or North Korea.
2. Prohibit the use of free ports within its territorial jurisdiction for the trans-shipment of any goods to or from Communist China or North Korea.
3. Prohibit the sale or charter of vessels and aircraft to the Chinese Communist regime or to the North Korean authorities, or to their nationals, or to any person or entity acting for them.
4. Deny bunkering and port facilities to vessels owned or controlled by the Chinese Communists or North Koreans, and to vessels of any nationality believed to be proceeding to or from Communist China or North Korean ports.
5. Prohibit the insurance or reinsurance within its territorial jurisdiction of vessels included in paragraph 4 and of all cargoes destined to or proceeding from Communist China or North Korea.
6. Block all assets and sterilize all gold resources of the Communist Chinese and North Korean regimes and of persons subject to their control; suspend all payments to these regimes or to persons subject to their control; prohibit loans, credits, and capital flotations likely to benefit these regimes or persons subject to their control.

---

[1] Churchill wrote in the margin: 'No'.

August 1952

Winston S. Churchill to John Colville
(*Premier papers, 11/50*)

21 August 1952

Who are the Admirals, and of what nationality, commanding 'Cincleastlant' and 'Cincaireastlant'? And what nationality is 'Comsubeastlant'?

John Colville: diary
('*The Fringes of Power*', *pages 653–4*)

22–25 August 1952

Again to Chartwell with Meg, this time alone with the Churchills except for Horatia Seymour[1] and in glorious sunny weather. There is a slight drama. W has persuaded Truman to join with him in sending a message, signed by them both, to Mossadeq in Tehran about the Persian oil question. W himself did it and the FO oil people agreed. It is the first time since 1945 that the Americans have joined with us in taking overt joint action against a third power. Fear of ganging up has hitherto prevented them. But Anthony Eden, completing his honeymoon in Lisbon, is furious. It is not the substance but the method which displeases him: the stealing by Winston of his personal thunder. Moreover, should Eisenhower be elected President of the USA in November – an event thought to be decreasingly probable – there will be further trouble on this score, because W has several times revealed to me his hopes of a joint approach to Stalin, proceeding perhaps to a congress in Vienna where the Potsdam Conference would be reopened and concluded. If the Russians were uncooperative, the cold war would be intensified by us: 'Our young men,' W said to me, 'would as soon be killed carrying truth as death.'

Meg and I spent all September at Mertoun.[2] When I returned to London at the end of the month I accompanied the Prime Minister to Balmoral where he went in his capacity as Prime Minister at his own suggestion. The Queen and Prince Philip, who had a very young party staying with them, may have been a little reluctant, but the visit went off well and was in the event enjoyed by both sides, although Winston (aged nearly seventy-eight and not having touched a gun for years) complained to me on the way home that he thought he should have been asked to shoot!

---

[1] Horatia Seymour, 1881–1966. A bridesmaid at Churchill's wedding, 1908.
[2] His brother-in-law's house in Berwickshire.

Winston S. Churchill to Field Marshal Lord Alexander
Prime Minister's Personal Minute M.449/52
(Premier papers, 11/115)

22 August 1952
Secret and Personal

I do not like this napalm bombing at all. A fearful lot of people must be burned, not by ordinary fire, but by the contents of the bomb. We should make a great mistake to commit ourselves to approval of a very cruel form of warfare affecting the civilian population. Napalm in the war was devised by us and used by fighting men in action against tanks and against heavily defended structures. No one ever thought of splashing it about all over the civilian population. I will take no share in the responsibility for it. It is one thing to use Napalm in close battle of ground troops, or from the air in immediate aid of ground troops. It is quite another thing to torture great masses of unarmed people by it.

The statement[1] about giving 'due warning to civilians to evacuate', etc., is not worth much. If people have to go to their work every day and live in their homes, they have not much choice of dwelling. My own feeling is that Napalm ought not to be used in the way it is being done by the American Forces. This is I am sure the overwhelming feeling of the House of Commons, but I do not take my opinion from them. I certainly could not agree to our taking any responsibility for it, otherwise than in the general duty of serving with and under the United Nations Commander.

Winston S. Churchill to Foreign Office
Prime Minister's Personal Minute M.447/52
(Premier papers, 11/541)

22 August 1952

I do not think we should allow any more of them here than they allow of our people over there.[2] Let me have comparative tables. The question of the facilities accorded should also be considered relatively. We ought not to take everything lying down.

---

[1] Draft circulated by Lord Alexander, reproduced above (p. 605).
[2] On this subject, see Colville to Churchill, July 8, reproduced above (pp. 538–9).

John Selwyn Lloyd to Winston S. Churchill
(Premier papers, 11/114)

22 August 1952
PM/MS/52/100

A procedure has been worked out with the Japanese Foreign Office whereby the two sailors if they are given bail should be returned to the Royal Navy and removed from Japanese jurisdiction.[1] In effect we and the Japanese Foreign Office would be conniving at an obvious abuse of normal legal processes. It would lead to violent anti-British propaganda fostered by the Opposition in Japan.

2. The Japanese Foreign Office have tried to be helpful in devising a procedure. They have stated orally that they fully understand that if the men are bailed they will never be returned to Japanese custody. They have, however, refused to accept confirmation in writing of this understanding.

3. The disadvantage of taking no action is that the men's sentences may be confirmed by the Appeal Court and they may have to remain in prison until we can negotiate their release as part of the settlement of the status of British Service men in Japan. It is possible that we may be blamed for not getting the men out by the means now suggested.

4. On the other hand in the absence of any documentary proof of the proposed arrangement there is in my view a probability that it will be repudiated by the Japanese Foreign Office when the row starts in Japan. The blame will be laid solely on the British Government. We shall be accused of bad faith and it may damage our good name. The incident might also have a prejudicial effect upon the future treatment of British subjects by Japanese Courts.

5. It is an unfortunate dilemma. My own feelings on the whole are that we should not be party to a process whereby the British guarantor and the two sailors should be prevented by official action from keeping their word unless we have written confirmation of the Japanese Government's agreement to the whole business.

6. We should of course do all we can by other means to secure the men's release.

7. I should be grateful for your views.

---

[1] Two drunken British sailors assaulted and robbed a Japanese cab driver, and were sentenced by the Japanese authorities to five years' hard labour. Owing to ambiguities about Japanese jurisdiction over British occupying forces, however, the sentence was commuted and the sailors released.

Winston S. Churchill to John Selwyn Lloyd
Prime Minister's Personal Minute M.450/52
(Premier papers, 11/114)

23 August 1952

When is the Court of Appeal going to deal with this case? I think the argument is strong for letting events take their course while continuing our pressure for the release of the two sailors. Merely to get them out a fortnight or three weeks earlier it would not be worth while to expose ourselves to a charge of breach of faith. You ask for my views. I should go on protesting and let things drag for the present. This does not mean that we should not keep continued pressure upon Japan to release these two men.

Winston S. Churchill to John Selwyn Lloyd
Prime Minister's Personal Minute M.451/52
(Premier papers, 11/392)

23 August 1952

I hope that it is understood that I am not prepared in any circumstances that I can foresee in the near future to commit myself to expenditure which may shortly rise to more than £100 million for the creation of a new base at Gaza. The idea that Sir R. Stevenson seems to have about the cabinet position on this point is erroneous. Our ambassador should be acquainted with this view.

Winston S. Churchill to President Harry S Truman
Prime Minister's Personal Telegram T.168/52
(Premier papers, 11/237)

23 August 1952
Immediate
Secret and Personal
No. 3503

All that I have ventured to suggest to you about Musaddiq was on the basis of a joint approach. I thought that it might do good if we had a gallop together such as I often had with FDR. There is little doubt that a brief, cogent, joint telegram would be far more effective than a continuance of a futile parleying which has got us no further in all these months.

2. Our 'physical separation' did not prevent such methods in the war. However, there was often a fear of our being accused of 'ganging up' and this hampered necessary action, for instance about the Warsaw massacre in

August, 1944. I do not myself see why two good men asking only what is right and just should not gang up against a third who is doing wrong. In fact I thought and think that this is the way things ought to be done.

3. I see that your Government on July 31st actually proposed a joint approach with us to Musaddiq. This was a fine idea which might prevent him or anything else that turns up in Persia from thinking they can play one of us off against the other.

4. From the United States' point of view I should have thought it would be a most unprofitable course to pay Persia indefinite sums of money in order that she should not become Communist. It does not follow that even far larger sums than the 10 million dollars you have mentioned would avert these dangers. Also the fact that blackmail pays and that those who behave the worst make the largest profits will not have a good effect over all the vast area of your own oil interests in the Persian Gulf and Iraq. I therefore hoped that a strong note could be sounded now by both of us together. It was on this basis that I proposed and could defend further concessions on our part. It is not that I fear criticism here, though that would be troublesome, but it is because I believe that your name and mine at the foot of a joint telegram would be an effective assertion of right over wrong. Please see what you can do.

5. All my personal regards and many thanks for your consideration and courtesy

Winston S. Churchill to John Selwyn Lloyd
(Premier papers, 11/301)

23 August 1952

I think we take a great responsibility considering our relatively small contribution in taking too stiff a line with the United States who are bearing practically all the burden. It is very easy to talk about 'causing a general war in China'[1] like the Socialists told us we would have a world war if we had fired the necessary volley at Abadan. I do not regard Communist China as a formidable adversary. Anyhow you may take it that for the next four or five years 400 million Chinese will be living just where they are now. They cannot swim, they are not much good at flying and the Trans-Siberian railway is already overloaded. I do not see how they can get to us except in South-East Asia and Hongkong. We might put the point to the Americans about Hongkong. I am in favour if necessary of interruption by air of key points on the communications between Communist China and Indo-China, Malaya, Siam, etc. This, I believe, can easily be done. When you think how much the Chinese are costing us, and the American twenty times more, in Malaya I cannot feel that

[1] See Selwyn Lloyd to Churchill, Aug. 21, reproduced above (pp. 609–10).

the measures proposed by the United States should be incontinently turned down. I think the Chinese might well be made to feel as uncomfortable as they make us.

However, this is a matter I should like the Foreign Secretary to consider in the light of these remarks and then perhaps he would bring it before the Cabinet. I do not want to take a decision in his absence. In the late war I never believed in the power of China. I doubt whether Communist China is going to be the monster some people imagine.

Anyhow as long as we do not send American or United Nations troops into China or transport Chiang Kai-shek's people there nothing very serious can happen in China. Do not let us be too hard on the Americans in this part of the world.

Winston S. Churchill to John Selwyn Lloyd
Prime Minister's Personal Minute M.448/52
(Premier papers, 11/48)

23 August 1952

This is a serious business to spring up out of a sham fight arranged by the military.[1] We are told that the admirable ardour of the Danes will be cooled or even quenched by any alteration in this programme. But what is their ardour when expressed in terms of armed force? Their opinion ought not to involve great powers in what might be serious incidents.

2. So far as I can remember Bornholm was one of the very few places which the Russians showed good faith by evacuating. We should be very foolish to teach them that they have made a mistake for the sake of four hundred Danes being landed there for a few days. The British attitude should be 'No Bornholm'. This is a policy I wish to be pursued. The idea that the Americans would break with Britain because we do not want to have a sham fight by four hundred Danes on Bornholm seems to me to impugn their sense of proportion.

---

[1] In Sep. 1952, NATO forces were to take part in a large-scale military exercise in the Baltic Sea called 'Mainbrace'. Churchill considered the exercise unnecessarily provocative to the Soviet Union.

August 1952

Winston S. Churchill to George Ward
Prime Minister's Personal Minute M.453/52
(Premier papers, 11/2)

23 August 1952

No doubt all this is judicious.[1] However twelve lives lost in fourteen days of these gallant, highly-trained expert airmen is a grave fact. How does it compare with losses in the United States? Give me figures not percentages at this stage. How does it compare with losses of white officers in Malaya or Korea? Has nothing been done about a decoration in time of peace for these men who are really in action?

Winston S. Churchill to James Thomas
Prime Minister's Personal Minute M.454/52
(Premier papers, 11/50)

23 August 1952

As they[2] all seem to be British their ugly code names do not matter much. I approve.

Winston S. Churchill to Duchess of Marlborough[3]
(Churchill papers, 1/52)

23 August 1952

My dear Mary,

I am enchanted with the beautiful, sharp little knives you have sent me. They make tough meat seem tender, and tender meat delicious!

I am sending you sixpence, so that the knives do not cut our friendship.

PS. I have also signed the two books.

---

[1] On this subject, see M.399/52 of July 21 and M.425/52 of Aug. 7, reproduced above (pp. 552 and 592).
[2] 'Cinceastlant' (Commander-in-Chief Eastern Atlantic), 'Cincaireastlant' (Commander-in-Chief Air Forces Eastern Atlantic) and 'Comsubeastlant' (Commander Submarine Force Eastern Atlantic).
[3] Alexandra Mary Cadogan, 1900–61. Married, 1920, John Spencer-Churchill, later 10th Duke of Marlborough: five children.

President Harry S Truman to Winston S. Churchill
Prime Minister's Personal Telegram T.169/52
(Premier papers, 11/237)

24 August 1952
Immediate
Personal and Secret
No. 1611

Like you I want very much to see our two Governments reach full agreement on the Persian problem and to see us put, at the earliest practicable date, an offer before Musaddiq in an effort to settle the present dispute.

In view of your strong feelings on the matter, and the fact that we are in agreement that this approach limits neither you nor me nor our Governments to particular courses of action in the future, I agree to join with you in a common message to the Prime Minister of Persia.

I have re-studied our messages to each other and your Government's latest views on my six points, which Sir Oliver Franks has given us. While I am disappointed that action by your Government cannot be more immediate on the question of financial assistance to the Persian Government, I am prepared to proceed in the hope that the course of action upon which we are in concert may succeed. Since days are slipping away which we can ill afford to lose, I suggest a draft which I would be willing to sign.

I propose a very short cover message jointly from you and me which would have attached to it the substantive points of the proposal.

For the covering message I suggest the following: 'We have reviewed the messages from our two Embassies in Persia regarding recent talks with you, as well as your communication of 8th August, 1952 to Her Majesty's Government. It seems clear to us that to bring about a satisfactory solution to the oil problem will require prompt action by all three of our Governments. We are attaching proposals for action which our two Governments are prepared to take and which we sincerely hope will meet with your approval and result in a satisfactory solution. We are motivated by sincere and traditional feelings of friendship for the Persian nation and people and it is our earnest desire to make possible an early and equitable solution of the present dispute.'

In view of the comments of your Government, it seems to me that the following could well be used for the text of the attached annex.

'(1) There shall be submitted to the International Court of Justice the question of compensation to be paid in respect of the nationalisation of the enterprise of the Anglo-Iranian Oil Company in Persia, having regard to the legal position of the parties existing immediately prior to nationalisation and to all claims and counterclaims of both parties.

'(2) Suitable representatives shall be appointed to represent the Persian Government and the Anglo-Iranian Oil Company in negotiations for making arrangements for the distribution of Persian oil to world markets.

'(3) If the Persian Government agrees to the proposals in the foregoing two paragraphs, it is understood that:
   (a) Representatives of the AIOC will seek arrangements for the movement of oil already stored in Persia, and as agreements are reached upon price, and as physical conditions of loading permit, appropriate payment will be made for such quantities of oil as can be moved;
   (b) Her Majesty's Government will relax restrictions on exports to Persia and on Persia's use of sterling, and
   (c) The United States Government will make an immediate grant of $10,000,000 to the Persian Government to assist in their budgetary problem.'

I believe you and I are substantially in accord on the offer that should be transmitted to Musaddiq and I am extremely eager to have it made without further delay. If you have other ideas as to drafting, I suggest you notify me immediately as to exact wording of the changes you would desire so that we may promptly produce an agreed text.

With warm regards.[1]

Winston S. Churchill to President Harry S Truman
Prime Minister's Personal Telegram T.172/52
(Premier papers, 11/237)

25 August 1952
Immediate
Secret
No. 3519

I am delighted we are in such close agreement. I will gladly sign the Truman–Churchill cover message.

2. Barring one drafting point in the Annexe, which we are mentioning to the State Department, we hope it and the message can be delivered to Musaddiq tomorrow at latest. It would surely be best for our two representatives in Tehran to take it personally together.

3. There are two points which do not alter the text of the message but which should be agreed between the United States and British Governments and kept for record, namely:

---

[1] Churchill responded quickly: 'Not a minute shall be lost. Cabling tomorrow' (T.170/52).

(a) It is vital to us that, as mentioned in your No. 1, of the annexe, the International Court of Justice should be the tribunal on compensation.

(b) It would be against the interests both of the United States and Great Britain if the Persians got better terms for their oil than other oil-producing countries who have kept their agreements.

Winston S. Churchill to Anthony Eden
Prime Minister's Personal Telegram T.173/52
(Premier papers, 11/237)

25 August 1952
Immediate
Secret and Personal
No. 325

You will see from the telegrams which the Foreign Office are sending you that I have had a try with Truman over Persia. Your people seem quite content with the result so far. Looking forward to your return on Wednesday.

President Harry S Truman to Winston S. Churchill
Prime Minister's Personal Telegram T.174/52
(Premier papers, 11/237)

25 August 1952
Immediate
Secret and Personal
No. 1621

I am gratified that we are agreed on the contents of a joint message to Dr Musaddiq. I accept the change you suggest in paragraph 2 of your message of the 25th.[1]

I am telegraphing Ambassador Henderson tonight to be prepared to go ahead in concert with Middleton[2] just as soon as Middleton receives your instruction.

I agree to the point you make in paragraph 3(A).

---

[1] T.172/52, reproduced above (pp. 619–20).

[2] George Humphrey Middleton, 1910–98. Educated at Magdalen College, Oxford. Entered Consular Service as Vice-Consul, Buenos Aires, 1933. Vice-Consul, Asunción, 1934–5; New York, 1936–9. Consul, Lemberg, 1939; Cluj, 1939–40; Genoa, 1940; Madeira, 1940–3. 2nd Secretary, Washington DC, 1944; 1st Secretary, 1945–7. CMG, 1950. Counsellor, British Embassy, Tehran, 1951; acting Chargé d'Affaires, 1951–2. Deputy High Commissioner, Delhi, 1953–6. Ambassador to Lebanon, 1956–8; to Argentina, 1961–4; to United Arab Republic, 1964–6. KCMG, 1958. Political Resident in Persian Gulf, 1958–61. Chief Executive, British Industry Roads Campaign, 1969–76.

With respect to paragraph 3(B), I of course agree that it is in the interests of both of us that the basis negotiated for the future flow of Persian oil not be such as to dislocate arrangements elsewhere in the Middle East. There are of course so many complex considerations of volume, quality, location, relation to compensation, and the like, that the variable factors make it difficult to judge the comparability of any two arrangements. Naturally, we should want to look at concrete proposals before we could judge their effect and reasonableness.

I want to thank you for your understanding in handling this difficult problem.

I have high hopes that a solution can be reached.

With best regards.

Anthony Eden to Winston S. Churchill
Prime Minister's Personal Telegram T.175/52
(Premier papers, 11/237)

26 August 1952
Emergency
Dedip
Secret
No. 275

Your telegram No. 325 of the 25th August.[1]

I should have been glad of an opportunity to examine and discuss these proposals in detail.

2. In particular I feel concerned as to how paragraph 3(b) of Foreign Office telegram No. 3519 to Washington[2] is covered by the existing proposals to Musaddiq. Will not the effect of this offer to him be to hand over the fate of our oil interests not only in Persia but everywhere else, to the findings of the Hague Court?

3. I shall be in London by 3 p.m. on Wednesday. Can reply not wait till then?

[1] T.173/52, reproduced above (p. 620).
[2] See para. 3(b) in Truman's draft message, contained in T.169/52 (reproduced above, p. 619).

Winston S. Churchill to Anthony Eden
Prime Minister's Personal Telegram T.176/52
(Premier papers, 11/237)

26 August 1952
Immediate
Dedip
Secret and Personal
No. 331

I am sure you need not be worried about the Persian business. Matters became urgent when after seeing Truman big American oil man departed for Persia. This was what made me act directly on Truman. Cabinet approved and all your people at the Foreign Office are I think pleased. Fred Leathers is enthusiastic and the Company have been informed and seem all right. Lloyd will explain to you on the telephone the point of detail which you mentioned. All are agreed we must go forward now. Of course if Musaddiq refuses all is off but we shall have the Americans with us in the new situation. I will ring you at the Foreign Office tomorrow evening after you have read the correspondence. Could you and Clarissa by any chance come down here Thursday luncheon time. We can put you up.

Winston S. Churchill to Field Marshal Lord Alexander
Prime Minister's Personal Minute M.457/52
(Premier papers, 11/257)

26 August 1952

Your Ministry includes, I understand, a Directorate concerned with the techniques which we evolved during the war for misleading the enemy about our future plans and intentions.

2. The experience of these strategies which we gained in the war should not, of course, be thrown away: knowledge of the old techniques should be kept alive, and it may be that new methods may usefully be evolved. But it is a nice question how far this weapon should actually be used in the time of peace at any rate for peacetime purposes. It may be a different matter to use these methods for concealing our military plans in operational theatres like Korea and Malaya.

3. How large an organization is maintained for this purpose? What is its cost? What is the scope of its present activities? Is it limited mainly to the concealment of military operations, or is it open to any Department which may become aware of its existence to ask for its services? Is it EQ staff only, or has it local organisation as well?

4. Let me have the main facts, and also your personal views on the extent to which these activities are permissible in time of peace.

Winston S. Churchill to Anthony Eden
Prime Minister's Personal Minute M.458/52
(Premier papers, 11/392)

26 August 1952

The more I read the news from Egypt the more I like the Neguib programme which I hope Ali Maher will express in the constitutional form. We ought to help Neguib and Co. all we can unless they turn spiteful. It is most important that we should not appear to be defending the landlords and Pashas against the long overdue reforms for the fellaheen. We are never going to get anything out of the Wafd or the Moslem Brotherhood. But there might well be a policy, in which the United States would join, of making a success of Neguib. The Sudan luckily does not come much into the story at the moment.

Winston S. Churchill to Louis St Laurent
Prime Minister's Personal Telegram T.178/52
(Premier papers, 11/49)

26 August 1952
Top Secret and Personal
No. 121

I send you a copy of a report, submitted to me by the United Kingdom Chiefs of Staff, on the discussions which the United Kingdom Ambassador and Chief of the Air Staff had in Washington at the end of last month on the Report by the Chiefs of Staff on Defence Policy and Global Strategy.

I was glad to find that the United States Administration and Joint Chiefs of Staff are so well in accord with our own views. The Chief of the Air Staff also reported on his talks in Ottawa with Mr Pearson and the Canadian Chiefs of Staff from which I was pleased to learn that in Canada too there is close agreement on these major issues.

May I ask you to treat this document with the same care as the Report on Defence Policy and Global Strategy and similarly to restrict knowledge of it to the smallest circle?

624   August 1952

Winston S. Churchill to Prime Ministers of Australia, New Zealand and South Africa
Prime Minister's Personal Telegram T.179/52
(Premier papers, 11/49)

26 August 1952
Top Secret and Personal

In my message sending you a copy of the Report by the United Kingdom Chiefs of Staff on Defence Policy and Global Strategy I said that I was making the Report available to the United States Administration and the United States Joint Chiefs of Staff. The United Kingdom Ambassador and the Chief of the Air Staff, who visited Washington at the end of last month, have had some discussions on the Report with the United States authorities concerned, and I send you a copy of the report which the Chiefs of Staff have submitted to me on these discussions. I was glad to find that the United States Administration and Joint Chiefs of Staff are well in accord with our own views. May I ask you to treat this document with the same care as the Report on Defence Policy and Global Strategy and similarly to restrict knowledge of it to the smallest circle?

Winston S. Churchill to Anthony Eden
Prime Minister's Personal Minute M.460/52
(Premier papers, 11/48)

27 August 1952

I am still convinced that we ought not to let sham fights and military exercises bring us to the verge of such grave and delicate matters.[1] Why should Admiral Brind make such a fuss about recasting his plans? Plans often have to be recast in war at very short notice, and a change now might be a valuable experience for these distended Staffs.

Eliahu Elath[2] to Foreign Ministry, Tel Aviv
(Government of Israel Archives)

27 August 1952
Secret

David Sarnoff[3] lunching privately with Churchill yesterday discussed at length his impressions visit Israel. Sarnoff had earlier seen me and accepted

[1] On this subject, see M.448/52, reproduced above (p. 616).
[2] Eliahu Elath, 1903–90. First Israeli Ambassador to US, 1948–50. Ambassador to UK, 1950–9. President of Hebrew University, 1962–8.
[3] David Sarnoff, 1891–1971. Jewish Russian–American pioneer in broadcasting industries. Born in Uzlyany, Russian Empire. Emigrated to United States, 1900. Married, 1917, Lizette Hermant: three children. Founder, National Broadcasting Corporation, 1926. Marconi Wireless Telegraph Co. of America, 1906–19. Radio Corp. of America, 1919–70; President, 1930–70. Retired, 1970.

number my suggestions for incorporation his presentation to PM which included following points:
1. Israel most reliable and determined democracy ME and western democracies will strengthen own positions that area by strengthening her.
2. Israel's army young brave and as high spirited as in great days their victory over Arabs. Provision more arms equipment will make them formidable force entire area second only to Turkey.
3. Israel desires peace enable her devote main energies resources to developing country and integrating new immigrants for which she needs and deserves material assistance her friends everywhere.
4. So long as no peace reached with neighbours Israel must stay prepared for second round. Unilateral British allied military assistance to Arabs without equal simultaneous support Israel bound increase danger second round with inevitable detrimental effect on Mideastern and world security. Thus while actively supporting Israel's desire for peace especially with Egypt, Britain must extend to Israel every military supply facility extended to Arabs while conditioning latter on Arab undertaking not use such supplies against Israel and acceptance Israel's proposal non-aggression pact.

According Sarnoff Churchill showed much interest asking many questions different aspects Israel's life including personalities especially PM. He agreed importance strengthening Israel every respect as 'good and reliable investment' for western democracies. Explaining Britain's economic difficulties prevent her doing much for Israel, Churchill promised nondiscrimination including military supplies. He stressed HMGs interest Israel Arab peace and declared his support idea non-aggression pact but remained vague about what they could do to promote it. Expressing satisfaction Egypt's defeat by Israel Churchill said he had 'not much use' for Egyptians and had little faith their capacity put own house in order. His is ready however give Naguib his chance and prepared wait another three months in hope of situation clearing before taking final decision further policy towards Egypt and related problems. Churchill said American Mideastern policy could be useful and effective only if USA Government agrees send token force Suez and take full share British responsibilities area he complained his repeated suggestion this effect been rejected by Washington.

On general situation Churchill said did not expect Russia start world war and would like discuss general settlement personally Stalin. Suggested Sarnoff on return USA should use influence pro more better understanding between USA Britain especially on ME.

Sarnoff highly pleased conversation feels Churchill sincerely friendly Israel and ready help us. Thinks conversation great contribution cause. I expressed our gratitude.

Winston S. Churchill to President Harry S Truman
Prime Minister's Personal Telegram T.180/52
(Premier papers, 11/237)

28 August 1952
Immediate
Secret and Personal
No. 3581

Anthony has now returned and we have considered together the very lengthy account which our representatives have given of their three and a half hour talk with Musaddiq. I feel that they should have presented our very carefully considered message and withdrawn as soon as possible with all diplomatic courtesy. It is clear, however, from the account they give that Musaddiq (repeat Musaddiq) feels very acutely the pressure of a United States–British message from us both. Though we have not yet received the comments of our two representatives, our immediate view is that the message should now be presented and published immediately this has been done. We have decided to offer what is right and fair. Let the world judge.

2. Anthony is seeing Mr Gifford this afternoon.

President Harry S Truman to Winston S. Churchill
Prime Minister's Personal Telegram T.181/52
(Premier papers, 11/237)

28 August 1952
Immediate
Secret and Personal
No. 1645

Thank you for your message of this morning. After reading the account from our representatives of the fantastic conversation which they had with Musaddiq, I personally feel that they acted wisely in temporarily withdrawing our message until they could seek further advice. Furthermore, I consider their drafting changes well-advised, although I would suggest that on the first point the following wording would be preferable:

> 'There shall be submitted to the International Court of Justice the question of compensation to be paid in respect of the nationalisation of the enterprise of the Anglo-Iranian Oil Company in Persia. The validity of the Nationalisation Law shall not be brought into question by either party. The Court in deciding the question of compensation shall take into consideration claims and counter-claims of both parties. If it should appear that the two parties in preparing their respective claims and counter-claims have

different views with regard to the legal situation prevailing in Persia prior to Nationalisation, the Court shall be at liberty to decide for itself what the situation was.'

I understand that you would prefer not to adopt the suggested changes. If you insist, I shall stick to our original text and agree that our representatives in Tehran be instructed to present our proposal formally to Dr Musaddiq. Our proposal is a fair one and its publication will serve to clarify the complicated issue in the oil dispute. I would strongly urge you, however, to give sympathetic consideration to the proposed changes, which I am convinced would make our public position even better. Whatever version is adopted, I believe that the message should be made public immediately after delivery in London, Washington and Tehran. The State Department will concert with your Foreign Office on the time of delivery and the release of the text and will suggest a line which we intend to take in explaining the message to the press.[1]

Winston S. Churchill to Lord Beaverbrook
(*Churchill papers, 2/211*)

28 August 1952

We are looking forward so much, dear Max, to coming on the 8th and I hope to be able to get a fortnight or so without interruption.[2] I can always fly back for a day to these toils. Please let me know your own movements between now and the 8th. I should so much like to see you. We shall be here or in London all the time. Please ring me.

Field Marshal Lord Alexander to Winston S. Churchill
(*Premier papers, 11/115*)

28 August 1952

I have had your minute M.449/52[3] about napalm bombing considered by the Chiefs of Staff and they are concerned about the position which may arise if we are unable to agree to General Bradley saying something which will dispel the idea that we are not in agreement with the Americans on this question. General Bradley will undoubtedly revert to the subject and we shall

---

[1] 'It was not until 24 Sep., nearly a month later, that Mossadeq replied to the joint communication from Truman and Churchill. It was at this juncture, however, that British and U.S. policy came to differ on the continuation of this joint approach, with Churchill and Eden wanting to continue along that path and with Truman and Acheson viewing the continuation of that approach as unwise' (Sand, *Defending the West*, p. 202).
[2] Churchill was referring to a planned trip to Lord Beaverbrook's villa, La Capponcina.
[3] Reproduced above (p. 612).

have to send Sir William Elliot some definite instructions on the line he is to take.

I understand that the American Press are trying to work up a case to prove that there is disagreement between the British and American Governments on the use of napalm, which may culminate in an article which would be most damaging to Anglo-American relations. Unless something is done to dispel the impression that there is a serious disagreement between us everyone will assume that the Press criticism is justified.

The Americans think that napalm is a legitimate and effective weapon of war, and the Chiefs of Staff agree with them. We ourselves used it in the last war against the Japanese and Germans and hold reserves for use in a future war. Both Australian and South African squadrons have been using it in Korea.

We have no reason to believe that the Americans have used napalm against anything other than legitimate military objectives. The spate of Communist propaganda about the bomb suggests that it has been a very effective weapon.

In drafting the proposed 'off the record' statement the Chiefs of Staff have used as their guide your message to General Bradley in Telegram No. I.J.20 of 3rd July, but the draft could, of course, be modified in detail if you think it is necessary. I feel, however, that it is most desirable that we should allow General Bradley to say something which will be sufficiently definite to dispose of the idea that there is a serious difference of opinion between ourselves and the Americans on this subject.[1]

Winston S. Churchill to Field Marshal Lord Alexander
(Premier papers, 11/115)

28 August 1952
NOT SENT

Your minute of August 28.

I do not see how Press articles and jabber of that kind compares with splashing about this burning fluid on the necks of humble people living where they have to. We are a subordinate factor in the UN operations in China. I do not suggest a protest at the present time but I am not going to take any direct avowed responsibility – nor will the House of Commons – for the undiscriminating use of napalm not in warfare between fighting men but to torture civilian populations. There is nothing doing in all this I can assure you. I do not mind at all if the American Press complain that I am not loyal to the napalm stunt. The most we can do is to let them go on and say anything.

[1] Churchill responded on Aug. 30: 'My opinion is unchanged. By all means bring it up at Cabinet if you wish. There does not seem to be any immediate hurry' (Prime Minister's Personal Minute M.466/52).

AUGUST 1952 629

Even this will cause serious trouble. I am quite willing to telegraph to General Bradley myself and show him where we stand if you think that this would be worth while. Anyhow there must be no approval by any British Government of which I am head. By all means bring it up at Cabinet if you wish. There does not seem to be any immediate hurry.

Anthony Eden to Winston S. Churchill
(Churchill papers, 2/517)

29 August 1952
Confidential
PM/52/104

In your minute M.452/52 of the 23rd August to the Minister of State, you reverted to the question of German war criminals.

2. May I first explain what war criminals we hold and then what arrangements about war criminals are contained in the Contract with Germany?

3. We now hold only 128 war criminals in the British Zone. Last December our total was 191. The 128 will shortly be reduced to 15 as a result of clemency recommendations which I have made or am about to make to the Queen. Over and above this, I am recommending clemency in the case of General von Mackensen. I am sending you a separate reply to your earlier minute M.318/52 covering his case and those of Field Marshals Manstein and Kesselring. This was delayed by my absence in Portugal. I shall be considering a number of other clemency submissions which will be reaching me in the coming weeks. The process of reduction in the above numbers is therefore continuous.

4. The figures which I quote above show how great has been the recent reduction in numbers. There is therefore no possibility of our releasing 'several hundred' war criminals, as you suggest. The majority of the prisoners now remaining in our hands are real thugs, convicted on charges of ill-treating or killing Allied prisoners-of-war or persons held in concentration camps. Dr Adenauer has said that he does not want us to let such criminals out. The clemency cases which it is now my distasteful responsibility to consider are therefore mostly those where the prisoner was almost certainly a ruffian but where the evidence admits of some doubt. I attach a memorandum of one such case, typical of many, where I have nevertheless recently decided to recommend clemency. As there have already been many reviews in past years, submissions recently put to me are among the most promising ones for clemency. You can judge therefore the type of crimes committed by the majority of the remaining 100 or so prisoners in our charge, whose claims for clemency are inevitably less strong.

5. You speak, however, in your minute of the war criminals who held high

command. I attach a list of the members of the German armed forces whom we now hold. You will see that there are only 15 in all and only 4 who could be described as having held high command: several of the 15 are SS men. Of these, I am recommending clemency in the case of Mackensen. Kesselring and Manstein have been released on parole. And I shall be considering clemency shortly in one further case.

6. The arrangements about war criminals in the German Contract were set out in my minute to you PM/52/63 of the 16th June.[1] The arrangements with the Germans have not fallen through. If the Mixed Board, for which the Contract provides, considers that any prisoners ought to be let out, the Board will make a recommendation accordingly to the Power which convicted the criminal. The unanimous recommendation will be binding on that Power.

7. The above remarks refer only to the war criminals whom we ourselves hold. Wahnerheide telegram No. 986 Saving, which provoked your minute, referred to the war criminals held by the Americans. I am not of course responsible for what the Americans are doing. But you may like to know that the present number of war criminals held by the Americans in Germany is about 350. The number held by the French in Germany is about 112. The French also hold a certain number in France.

8. In general, I am as anxious as you to reduce the number of war criminals whom we hold, so far as this can decently be done. But I hope you will agree with what I said in my minute of the 16th June, that clemency can properly be exercised only in cases where a fair and even a generous application of general principles justifies it. If I were to go further than this, I should not only be doing wrong, but I should be doing what Dr Adenauer has specifically asked me not to do.

Anthony Eden to Winston S. Churchill
(Churchill papers, 2/517)

29 August 1952
Confidential
PM/52/105

Since I sent you my minute PM/52/63 of the 16th June[2] there have been some new developments about the German military commanders whom we hold as war criminals.

2. Kesselring was let out of prison last month to undergo an exploratory operation. The operation has shown that he has cancer of the throat. Kesselring is now being kept on sick leave. A report on his condition will be produced

[1] Reproduced above (pp. 502–3).
[2] Reproduced above (pp. 502–3).

in a short time. If, as his Doctor believes, his illness seems likely to prove fatal, we shall release him on the grounds of ill health.

3. Manstein is to be released on parole for an eye operation. He is being given sick leave for a period of six weeks, which will be extended if his condition justifies it. Judging from what happened when Manstein had a similar operation some years ago, his sick leave may last for a considerable period. In any case, he is due to be released for good in nine months' time.

4. Thus Kesselring and Manstein are now both out of prison and will probably not go back. These two Generals are the main cases that agitate German public opinion. We are told by our people in Germany that, from this point of view, the important thing is that they should be out of prison. Whether they are out on parole or out for good is a point of less importance.

5. The only other army Generals whom we hold (there are two SS Generals) are Mackensen and Falkenhorst. I have examined Mackensen's case and am recommending to the Queen that he be released as an act of clemency.

6. Falkenhorst's case will be examined shortly.

7. Less than twenty members of the German Armed Forces are now held by us in prison. This number will be reduced by the release of Mackensen and, at least temporarily and probably permanently, by the release on parole of Kesselring and Manstein. Recommendations for clemency in respect of certain of the German military prisoners of lower rank are also being examined.

Winston S. Churchill to President Harry S Truman
Prime Minister's Personal Telegram T.182/52
(Premier papers, 11/237)

29 August 1952
Immediate
Secret and Personal
No. 3611

Thank you so much for your most helpful message of yesterday.[1] We are explaining to the State Department and to Mr Gifford our views about the proposed changes in the joint message. I feel sure you will understand our strong feelings against any changes at this stage.

---

[1] T.181/52, reproduced above (pp. 626–7).

Winston S. Churchill to Duchess of Kent[1]
(Churchill papers, 2/197)

31 August 1952

Madam,

At the Court last month I mentioned that I had a very small compact aluminium painting box which I would be honoured to lend to Your Royal Highness for your journey to Malaya. It was made especially for me by a Cuban gentleman and I think that you will be astonished at its small size and ingenuity. Quite large scale canvasses may be mounted as well as the cards which it contains. It of course forms its own easel and painting table all being self-contained. If this may tempt Your Royal Highness I will send it round by someone who can show you or one of your attendants how to set it up.

I think it would be a great mistake for Your Royal Highness to go to Malaya and all these places without being able to put down the vivid colour impressions which I am told they give.

I remain Your Royal Highness'
devoted and obedient servant,

---

[1] Marina, 1906–68. Born in Athens to Prince Nicholas of Greece and Denmark and Grand Duchess Elena Vladimirovna of Russia. Married, 1932, George Edward Alexander Edmund, Duke of Kent (d. 1942): three children. First Chancellor, University of Kent at Canterbury, 1963–8.

September 1952

Anthony Eden to Winston S. Churchill
(*Churchill papers, 2/517*)

1 September 1952
Secret
PM/52/108

I have seen your minute of the 26th August (M.459/52) to the Minister of State about our preliminary discussions with the State Department on the line to be taken over Korea at the forthcoming meeting of the General Assembly.

2. I feel that the American proposals would cause us the gravest difficulty.

3. A general embargo on trade with China would be against the economic interests of the United Kingdom, would mean the ruin of Hong Kong, and, if it was to be effective, would have to include the Soviet-controlled ports of Port Arthur, Dairen and Vladivostok, as well as Soviet and satellite shipping; there would thus be a very serious risk of such a blockade leading to a third World War.

4. The severance of diplomatic relations with Communist China would not harm or frighten the Communists, but would lose us the listening-post represented by our Embassy in Peking, which still has value.

5. The American draft resolution also seems to me to go unnecessarily far in tying the hands of the United Nations Command negotiators at Panmunjom by giving the maximum publicity to the prisoner of war issue, which we believe can only be solved as we wish by removing the limelight from it.

6. The American proposals are certain to meet with wide opposition in the General Assembly. The views of the Australian Government are very much in line with my own, as you will see from the summary of a telegram from Canberra to Spender[1] which was shown to us in confidence by Australian House.

[1] Percy Claude Spender, 1897–1985. Born in Darlinghurst, Sydney. KC, 1935. MP for Warringah, Ind. 1937–8, United Australia Party, 1938–44, Liberal Party of Australia, 1945–51. Assistant to the Treasurer, then Acting Treasurer, 1939–40. Treasurer, 1940. Minister for the Army, 1940–1. Member, Advisory War Council, 1940–5. Minister for External Affairs and Minister for External Territories, 1949–50. Vice-President, 5th General Assembly of the UN, 1950–1. Australian Ambassador to US, 1951–8. KBE, 1952. Vice-President, Australian delegation to UN, 1952–6; President, 1956. KCVO, 1957. Elected to the International Court of Justice, The Hague, 1958; President of the Court, 1964–7.

Very similar views have been expressed by the South African Government. Indeed, I very much doubt whether the Americans have much hope of getting the necessary two-thirds majority for resolutions along the lines proposed.

7. We certainly should not be in the forefront of the opposition to the Americans, but the essential thing is to avoid an open Anglo-American disagreement while the Assembly is sitting, as happened over the resolution naming China as an aggressor.

8. If therefore, as I very much hope, you approve the general lines of the foregoing train of thought, I should like to instruct our Delegation in New York to speak informally to their American opposite numbers in that sense as soon as possible.[1]

David Eccles to Winston S. Churchill
(Premier papers, 11/277)

1 September 1952

Your Personal Minute No. M.213/52 of 10th April about economy in building steel.[2]

You may care to know of the steps which have been taken to secure a better use of steel in building. A committee was formed of the Heads of the Works Directorates of my Department and of the Service Departments to concert economies in Defence building. Their report has been favourably received and should lead to important savings.

For the benefit of the building industry in general the Building Committee has arranged to issue a series of Steel Economy Bulletins. The first will appear tomorrow. The idea is to lay down simple standards of economy, and to see that Licensing Authorities refer to these standards before they allocate steel to particular building projects.

As you are aware, one of the most effective ways of making steel go further is to employ reinforced concrete in place of structural sections. The supply of reinforcing material has been inadequate, but, with the help of the Minister of Supply, the position is now considerably better.

---

[1] Churchill responded on Sep. 3: 'Proceed as you propose; but don't let us fall out with US for the sake of Communist China.'

[2] Reproduced above (pp. 389–90).

James Thomas to Winston S. Churchill
(*Premier papers, 11/355*)

2 September 1952
Secret

I am sorry to reopen the question of a Coronation Naval Review after the Cabinet decided against it but I feel I ought to let you know that there is growing evidence from Commonwealth countries, from foreign Naval Attachés, from shipping companies and from agencies dealing with foreign tourists, as well from the Press, that a Review is expected.

As you know, a Naval Review is so traditional a feature of Coronations that it is becoming increasingly difficult to stall on these questions without giving the reason for omitting it next year. Our questioners suspect that it is economy and warn us that, important though economy is, they do not consider it is a reasonable answer in this particular case.

I should be very grateful if you could look at these figures again. We are not spending £200,000 on uniforms as the Army is doing and our expenditure will be divided between £30/40,000 on oil and fuel and another £50,000 on ammunition, fireworks, stores, etc. Some of this represents consumption of existing stores which may or may not be replaced immediately and the whole of the expenditure will be found from Navy Votes at whatever figure it is fixed. The net effect of this would be that we should have only a little less of everything in the locker than we should otherwise have had.

The alternative offered by the Cabinet of illuminating ships at home ports and opening them to visitors is no real alternative. It is nothing like the same spectacle and it provides no answer to the quite strong foreign interest in a Review and on Coronation Day the ships would be dressed and probably illuminated anyway.

What the Navy want is an opportunity to pay respect to their Queen in person and so do the Merchant Navy. They cannot troop the Colour or stage a fly-past like the other two Services and a Review is their only chance of seeing the Queen.

I am sure you will also realise the psychological value of a Review next year after the strong way in which the country has reacted to our troubles with the Americans over the Atlantic and Mediterranean Commands.

There is no need to tell you after your many years at the Admiralty what a disappointment for the Navy it will be at having no opportunity to pay this traditional homage.

Cabinet: conclusions
(*Cabinet papers, 128/25*)

4 September 1952
Secret
3.30 p.m.
Cabinet Meeting No. 78 of 1952

[. . .]
11. The Chancellor of the Duchy of Lancaster said that increases in the prices of bacon, butter, margarine, sugar and cheese were to come into force early in October at the same time as the increase in family allowances, pensions, &c., allowed for in the Budget. This arrangement would now coincide with the difficulties which were being encountered with the engineering unions, who had decided to impose a ban on overtime and piece-work. It was hoped, however, that, with the help of the Ministry of Labour, a settlement of the dispute in the engineering industry might be obtained, on the basis of some modest increase in wages. It was likely that this settlement would be made more difficult if, in the course of negotiation, an announcement were made that there was to be a further increase in food prices. He felt, therefore, that it might be wise to postpone this increase for a further two months.

In discussion the following points were made –

(a) The increase in the price of bacon would enable home-produced gammon to be sold at the low price of 8s per lb. It was estimated that the profit made on the sale of gammon could be used to reduce the total weekly increase in food prices, resulting from the Budget, from 1s 6d to 1s 3d per head.

(b) If increased prices were to take effect at the beginning of October, discussion with the trade would have to begin on 11th September and, even without any formal announcement by the Minister of Food, the price increases would then become public knowledge.

(c) While a postponement in price increase for two months might possibly facilitate negotiations with the engineering unions, there was no certainty that at the end of two months there would not be some other reason for still further delays.

The Prime Minister said that the loss of overtime would much reduce the wages of men employed in the engineering industries and he was by no means convinced that the ban would in fact be imposed. In any case, he hoped that a settlement would be found by which the employers would agree to some small increase in wages. He felt therefore that it would be inappropriate to postpone the increase in food prices, which had been carefully timed to take place when the increased family allowances, pensions, &c., came into force. Consultation with the trade should therefore go forward as proposed, though any official announcement to the Press should be delayed as long as possible, and should be carefully devised to make plain the advantages which the increases in family allowance, pensions, &c., conferred, and the lower rate of increase in food prices which was now possible.

The Cabinet –

Agreed that increases in food prices should take place as planned at the beginning of October, that consultations with the trade should proceed, but that any official announcement of the increases should be delayed as long as possible and should emphasise the compensating advantages referred to in discussion.

Winston S. Churchill to Sir David Maxwell Fyfe
Prime Minister's Personal Minute M.471/52
(Premier papers, 11/28)

5 September 1952

I am somewhat concerned at the present position about Straffen.[1] He was reprieved because he was a lunatic. Now he is to serve a life sentence as a criminal, which means that he may be released after fifteen years. It is difficult to see the logic of this. I should have thought that, in view of the decision which you took to reprieve him as a lunatic, he should go to the asylum and be detained at the Royal Pleasure. The fact that you do not send him there may be taken as an admission that security conditions do not prevail at Broadmoor. If there are proper security conditions, what is the reason for treating a lunatic, whom you have reprieved, as if he were a convict criminal?

We must I think discuss this matter in Cabinet before Parliament meets.

Winston S. Churchill to Anthony Eden
Prime Minister's Personal Minute M.472/52
(Premier papers, 11/392)

6 September 1952

A decent fellow* – on our side. That is why he is being kicked out. But I do not see what we can do.

*Prince Mohamed Aly[2] (reference telegram Cairo to FO No. 1306).[3]

[1] See Macleod to Churchill, June 5, reproduced above (pp. 480–1).
[2] Mohammed Ali Tewfik, 1875–1955. Younger son of Khedive Tewfik I, nephew of King Fuad I. Paternal uncle of King Farouk I of Egypt. Born in Cairo. Studied in England ages 11. Chief Regent of Egypt, 1936–52. Exiled to Switzerland after military coup, 1952.
[3] The relevant paragraph from Ralph Stevenson's FO No. 1306 reads: 'His Royal Highness sent an urgent message to me asking me to call on him this morning. I found him even more despondent than usual. He said that despite assurances received from the Prime Minister, General Neguib had not been to call on him. This fact (coupled with other information which he has received about the attitude of

September 1952

Winston S. Churchill: speech
('Winston S. Churchill, His Complete Speeches', volume 8, pages 8402–8)

6 September 1952 Woodford

THE GOVERNMENT'S TASKS

Parliament is having a holiday. That is a very good thing for the House of Commons. I have rarely seen it more jaded in the fifty years I have served there. Those who value the strength of our Parliamentary institutions will realize that nothing weakens them more than for the House of Commons to go on bickering and biting and barking, with only short intervals all the year round, with everybody tired of their scenes and nobody reading their Debates. For the House of Commons to keep its influence and authority with the nation, definite pauses are needed so that the Members can recover their physical and mental strength, and make good contacts with their constituents, while Ministers are able to take a more general view of their problems, and while the life, work and thought of the country can go forward in a calmer and quieter mood. I have therefore exerted myself to procure for Parliament a ten-weeks' break, from which they will return I trust with new health and strength, and better poised to discharge their duties.

There is another reason which I must not forget for Parliament having a holiday. We felt it would be a good thing for the Opposition to have a little leisure to think over their political position, and arrive at some more coherent form of thought, and consistent line of policy. Something better than class warfare is surely needed at a time when parties are so evenly balanced that it is really like setting one-half of the nation against the other. As I have said, four-fifths of both parties agree on four-fifths of what should be done and after all we all sink or swim together on our perilous voyage into the unknown future. It certainly was a fine thing to see the great trade unions pronounce so clearly upon the need of building up the defence of Britain as one of the United Nations of the free world, and I hope that our policy of rearmament within the bounds of national solvency will also commend itself to sensible men and women throughout the country. Wise statesmanship has also been shown at Margate on the vital question of wage restraint, so important to the success of our renewed export drive. The action of the TUC will do much to assist the Government in its all-out attack on the cost of living. In asking for wage restraint, I want to emphasize that we do not in any way wish to limit the earnings of any section of the working population. On the contrary, it is

---

the military junta towards him) has convinced him that the army is definitely hostile to him and that there is no future for him in this country. He went on to say that he had decided definitely to seek the protection of Her Majesty's Government and to request them to ensure that he will be able to leave Egypt and reside abroad for the present, taking with him about £E.100,000.'

our aim to encourage the highest possible level of earnings in every industry, provided these swim upon increased output and efficiency.

British trade unionism is a national institution, representing much that is solid in our island character, and I have always urged Conservative wage-earners, of whom we have so many millions, to join their unions and take an active interest in their work. The increasing association of employees and wage earners with business and industry, through joint consultation, profit-sharing and varied forms of co-partnership, certainly opens paths we should not hesitate to tread.

There is also a larger reason why Parliament should have substantial periods of repose. The strength and character of a national civilization is not built up like a scaffolding or fitted together like a machine. Its growth is more like that of a plant or a tree. The British oak, on which for centuries our Navy depended, grows slowly and noiselessly without headlines or sensation and no one should ever cut one down without planting another. It is very much easier and quicker to cut down trees than to grow them. In cases where bad, oppressive laws warp the free development of human society much cutting down may be needed and sometimes the forest itself has to be cleared. Great work was done by the Liberal and Conservative Parties in the nineteenth century, but the twentieth century with its terrible events has brought us problems of a different order, not many of which can be solved merely by passing Acts of Parliament.

In order that the business of Parliament shall be properly planned, it is desirable that the principal Bills of the session should be introduced before Christmas, and this requires long months of preparation and drafting beforehand. As we did not become responsible till the end of October, and were hardly formed as a Government till the middle of November, it was not, in any case, possible to bring in the measures we announced in the King's Speech until much later in the session. We had also to face at the very outset of our task the grave financial crisis, with its imminent danger of national bankruptcy. It was the fear of having to cope with this which had forced our predecessors to have a General Election. I will presently speak to you about the measures we have taken to restore our solvency and build up our reserves. But they certainly dominated our thoughts and action during our first few months of power. The solemn event of the demise of the Crown involved a further suspension of normal Parliamentary business, and for these reasons it was not possible for us to pass into law this session the two principal measures to which we have pledged ourselves, namely, the denationalization of road transport and of the steel industry. The delay, however, has enabled both these complicated problems to be studied with deep attention, and both these measures will be introduced in the new session in November and will, I have no doubt, be passed into law before it ends next year.

I will first speak to you about the Transport Bill. This is a measure designed to restore vitality and flexibility to our road transport system, as well as to improve and strengthen the working of our national railways. It is not generally realized what a small part of our road transport has been taken over by the State. Only 41,000 lorries had been acquired, out of a total of over a million mercantile road vehicles. For this twenty-fifth part of our road transport an enormous centralized overhead organisation has been set up at a very heavy cost and with far-reaching powers. I have no doubt that all the 12,000 officials, apart altogether from the ordinary management, did their best to manage the 41,000 vehicles.

I was, however, astonished to learn that over 800,000 vehicles are run under 'C' licences and still more that these 'C' licences have risen by 300,000 since the 1947 Act. Now what is a 'C' licence? It means that the lorry or vehicle can only be used to carry the goods of its owner. This means that a very considerable portion of our road transport wastes its strength in one way traffic, and consumes labour, petrol and machinery in processes which cannot be reconciled with sound economy and good housekeeping. It also means that the alternative service offered by the State vehicles did not attract this enormous number of users. Surely in times like these, when we have to do everything in our power to promote the vitality and efficiency of British industry, we cannot afford this waste. This startling increase in 'C' licences – which has not merely taken place in the small delivery van type of vehicle but also in the large types capable of carrying heavy loads – is the best indication of how dissatisfied traders are with the road services provided by the British Transport Commission. It is our belief that a vehicle in the hands of a private haulier, able to carry anyone's goods and allowed to cater in free competition for the public need, is a more flexible and efficient instrument than it can be in the hands of a vast, unwieldy, centralized public corporation, for whose sake other hauliers must be hampered and restricted. And by the cheaper rates which we hope to see being offered, we trust that the increase in these 'C' licensed vehicles will be halted.

Another part of our proposed measure liberates the railways from some of the ancient statutory fetters which prevent their competing, as they would wish, with road transport. Thus in both spheres – railway and road transport – we are setting free the capacity to provide cheaper transport. Of course a question like this has got to be debated by Parliament, but I am sure any responsible Government trying to expand the productive energies of our country would have been wrong to leave our road transport to suffer the unnatural direction and restriction to which it was being subjected for the sake of Socialist theory.

We do not think there will be any difficulty in transferring the 41,000 vehicles back to private ownership, thus making the interchange of goods between man and man throughout our island, more smooth, more easy and more fertile to the public welfare. That at any rate is what we are going to do. I claim that these measures, on which we shall concentrate next session are inspired solely by the resolve to make things go better for the advantage of all. I will go further. I claim that we have been actuated by no thought but to bring our country out of the troubles of peace as we did out of the perils of war.

We have also tried to increase the incentive to active and skilful labour. In Mr Butler's first Budget, two million wage-earners were exempted altogether from income tax, in order to produce more in the hard times through which we are passing. Another form of incentive is the possibility of having, and still more of owning, a home of your own where a family can live and grow and have its own front door, which none may pass except by invitation or with proper warrant. Insufficient and bad housing is a hindrance to production, and this is especially true in times of rearmament and change. More than that, it is destructive of happiness and morality and a reproach to a Christian nation. Some of our political opponents used to mock us because we have set before ourselves as our goal a rate of building 300,000 houses a year. We meant to reach our goal and we are already making steady progress towards it, under the skilful and broad-minded management of Mr Harold Macmillan, the first Cabinet Minister of Housing. He has been helped by his able Parliamentary Secretary, Mr Marples,[1] and by his colleagues, Lord Swinton, the Minister of Materials, and Mr Eccles, the Minister of Works. All this is going forward well. The rigid ratio upon private building has been removed. Today local performance will decide the local programme. The more the local authorities build, the more they will be allowed to build. Builders and their men – including bricklayers – need have no fear they will work themselves out of their job. Measures have been taken to improve the supply of bricks, cement and tiles. New methods are being devised which, while maintaining essential standards, may enable us to build British homes with British materials and so, while increasing the number of houses, lessen the burden upon our imports from overseas. This will take time; but when you see how British genius shines in the design of aircraft, in which we have for the moment out-matched the world, we may be hopeful that in a year or two novel and beneficent improvements in housing may be achieved. Anyhow we are resolved to persevere. We have also a right to be encouraged that 19,000 more houses were built in the first half of this year than in the first half of 1951. This should surely be a matter for general rejoicing.

Finance is the worst of our problems. Ten months have passed since the Socialist Government recoiled from the consequences of their long administration and sought the refuge of a General Election. I must again remind you that before the poll I said in a broadcast:

---

[1] Alfred Ernest Marples, 1907–78. Married, 1937, Edna Harwood (div. 1945); 1956, Ruth Dobson. Capt., Royal Artillery, 1941–4. MP (Cons.) for Wallasey, 1945–74. Postmaster-General, 1957–9. Minister of Transport, 1959–64. Baron, 1974.

We make no promises of easier conditions in the immediate future. Too much harm has been done in these last six years for it to be repaired in a few months. Too much money has been spent for us to be able to avoid another financial crisis. It will take all our national strength to avoid the downhill slide, and after that we shall have to work up.[1]

When we took office I found that we were in a far worse plight than I had feared. We were spending abroad more than £800 millions a year beyond what we earned. Our gold and dollar reserves were draining away. To go on like that would be to plunge into national bankruptcy. That means we should have been unable to buy the food and raw materials from abroad in order to eat and work. It ought not to be forgotten that we took office in the shade of bankruptcy and that unless prompt measures had been taken we should have sunk into ruin and famine. How then do we stand as this summer draws to an end? We have not hesitated to do many unpopular things. Our imports have been drastically cut. The first steps to curtail and control detrimental expenditures have already been taken. The rates of interest at which money can be borrowed have been raised. Intense efforts are being made to stimulate our exports, even to some extent at the cost of our rearmament.

Thus we may now forecast that we in this island will in the second half of this year, after taking credit for defence aid, be in general balance with the non-sterling world, and that the whole sterling area will be in balance with the rest of the world. Do not forget that, apart from the American contribution to our rearmament effort, we are now supporting ourselves. We have none of that American Loan and Marshall Aid – 400 millions a year – which our predecessors enjoyed and used up so lavishly. We are not living on the United States; nor are we abusing them in spite of receiving their aid.

The Chancellor of the Exchequer has had a remarkable success in the first stage of restoring our world solvency. He has not feared to face a torrent of abuse, ill-deserved in itself, and especially shabby because of the guilty quarters from which it comes. I should be misleading you if I led you to suppose that greater efforts were not needed. We have got our head above water. Our future task is to swim up against the stream. Fifty millions in this island only grow the food for thirty. We can only buy for the other twenty by sending the things across the oceans which our Commonwealth and foreign customers need and desire. We must improve our balance of trade. We must strengthen our reserves of dollars and gold. That is what we are going on perseveringly to do. It is by results that we seek to be judged, and time will be needed for the results to be achieved.

We have had one heavy loss, which I think might have been avoided by courage and firmness. We have been robbed by violence of the Persian oil

[1] Reproduced in *The Churchill Documents*, vol. 22, *Leader of the Opposition, August 1945 to October 1951*, pp. 2177–82.

industry, which we created, and from which Persia derived such great benefit. I was happy to join President Truman in presenting new proposals to Dr Mossadeq for solving the deadlock resulting from our expulsion from Abadan. These are fair and reasonable proposals and were put forward upon the authority of the British and American Governments. I trust they will be given the attention which their constructive character and serious purpose should command. It is a good thing for all the world to see our two countries in agreement and working together. It quite reminds me of the great times not so long ago. We are all watching with keen interest the Presidential election in the United States. Democracy works by different methods in the great Republic from those we are accustomed to over here. But there are two things about which there is no doubt. The first is that the American system has produced two candidates for the Presidency who are in character and ability two of their finest men; and the second is that, whichever wins, the United States will not abandon the mission of leading the free nations in resistance to Communist aggression, and that the solid foundations of the English speaking world will grow broader and deeper and stronger, as the years roll by.

Then there is steel. This vital industry was nationalized by the Socialist Party last spring. But, apart from expropriating the shares of the previous owners, there was not time for any extensive damage to be done in the few months which intervened before the general election. Fortunately we got into power in time to preserve the separate identity and independence of the great steel companies, whose world-wide reputations and trade connections constitute such important national assets. Thanks to the directions given by the Minister of Supply, Mr Duncan Sandys, immediately the Conservative Government came in, any undesirable interference by the State Corporation in the management of the companies was effectively prevented. By this action the position was held pending the introduction of a Bill. This will be presented to parliament early in the new session in November.

Our detailed proposals were published last July in a White Paper, and have met with a most favourable reception from fair-minded people both inside and outside the industry. Unlike the Socialist Act of nationalization, our scheme for steel is not based upon political doctrine and theory. On the contrary, like all Conservative policies, it is founded upon practical needs and experience. The system of organization and supervision which we propose has been progressively evolved by the industry itself over the last twenty years. And in its general conception it follows closely the view expressed by the TUC in its well-known report on the public supervision of industry. A more practical means of public control, they said, would be a tripartite board of control on the lines of the former Iron and Steel Board, which was composed of representatives of employers, trade unions and consumers. That is precisely what our scheme sets out to do.

We feel entitled to ask that our proposals should be viewed against this background of common thought and experience. If they are examined in this spirit, we believe that, subject to improvements of detail, which we shall be glad to consider, our scheme will be found to offer the best basis for a lasting and workable solution to the problems which confront the steel industry. Meanwhile the industry has not been standing still. Its great companies under their experienced managements, have continued to make progress in output and efficiency. Our home production of steel this year is running at the rate of nearly half a million tons more than in 1951 and it is expected to increase by an even greater amount next year.

Our opponents say, 'If you want the country to work together, why do you bring in these controversial measures to undo the work of your predecessors?' It would not have been right to repeal either the Transport or Steel Nationalization Acts merely to undo the work of our opponents, or to condemn a doctrine which we deem fallacious. In the case of Transport we are confronted with an evil position, detrimental to the interests of the general public and to the efficient running of our industrial life. We are sure that a definite easement and improvement will be achieved, from which the whole country and all classes will be the gainers. It is that object alone which makes us undertake this heavy labour. In the case of steel, the main step we are taking in reconciling State supervision and control with free enterprise is one which springs as much from the minds of trade unionists as from employers and is really the culmination of a very long period of growth and progress in an industry which, for sixty years, has not been the cause of any serious trade dispute.

Winston S. Churchill to James Thomas
Prime Minister's Personal Minute M.475/52
(Premier papers, 11/355)

7 September 1952

As the Cabinet were already consulted and gave a decision on this matter,[1] you will have to lay your case before them again. It must be made clear that there will be no military or Air Force reviews, on account of the immense expense involved.

You should prepare a programme of a Naval Review, I presume at Spithead, showing how the expense is to be accounted for. Why cannot they pay for the fuel out of their ordinary fuel allowance? Surely it does not cost very much to fire the ordinary salutes with blank cartridges. Why are more stores used up when the ships are lying at anchor at Spithead than if they were lying at anchor elsewhere? As to fireworks, what actually do you propose? If you can so arrange it that no extra charge is involved, except for fireworks, I should advise the Cabinet to approve.

[1] See Thomas's minute of Sep. 2, reproduced above (p. 635).

Sir David Maxwell Fyfe to Winston S. Churchill
(Premier papers, 11/28)

8 September 1952

I have received your minute of 5th September (M.471/52).[1] Straffen was reprieved, not as a lunatic, but because he was sufficiently mentally defective not to be fully responsible for his crimes.

When a murderer is reprieved on the ground of mental defect he is normally sent by order of the Home Secretary to the Rampton State Institution for Mental Defectives from which he cannot be discharged without the consent of the Home Secretary and from which he would not be discharged unless the Home Secretary were satisfied that this could be done safely. There is no question of considering the release of a mental defective merely because he has been detained for so many years.

In view of the apprehension about Straffen, I decided that in the first instance he should be detained in a prison which the public accepted as secure and that the question of his transfer should be postponed for the present. But this does not in any way imply that I think that he should be considered for discharge after a certain number of years. Indeed, as I told the Cabinet on 4th September, I have recorded on Straffen's file the opinion that unless there is a marked change in his mental state, he should not be released at all.

Sarah Beauchamp to Winston S. Churchill
(Churchill papers, 1/50)[2]

8 September 1952

Darling Papa,

Just a line to wish you a happy and sunny holiday with lots of painting.
You <u>do</u> deserve it – Wow and much much love from us both.

Your loving Sarah

---

[1] Reproduced above (p. 637).
[2] This letter was handwritten.

Major Sir Desmond Morton[1] to Winston S. Churchill
(*Churchill papers, 4/62*)[2]

9 September 1952

Dear Winston,

Thank you very much for sending me a copy of *Closing the Ring*. No comment from me will be of much value to you; but I cannot help declaring my conviction that in the circumstances of those days of which you treat, there is no single occasion on which you could have done other than you did. Your critics after the event – and they are but few – are pitifully unaware of the limitations placed sometimes upon your better judgement by persons and events beyond your control. This book, as indeed the earlier volumes, should enlighten them if they are men of good will.

I am not pretending to have read already the book which arrived yesterday on my office table. I read the American Edition some months ago, sent me by a kind friend and ex-colleague in the USA.

Thank you again and for Heaven's sake, or at least for that of this country, do look after yourself.

Winston S. Churchill to Anthony Eden
Prime Minister's Personal Minute M.479/52
(*Premier papers, 11/237*)

11 September 1952

I hope no encouragement will be given to any idea of our paying any money to Persia beyond what was contained in our proposed settlement.

---

[1] Desmond John Falkiner Morton, 1891–1971. On active service, 1914–18. Met Churchill in the field while Churchill was painting, 1916. Shot through the heart at Battle of Arras, Apr. 1917, but survived. MC. ADC to Sir Douglas Haig, 1917–18. Head of Committee of Imperial Defence's Industrial Intelligence Centre, 1929–39. Member of Imperial Defence Sub-Committee on Economic Warfare, 1930–9. CMG, 1937. Personal Assistant to Churchill throughout WWII. CB, 1941. KCB, 1945. Member, UN Economic Survey Mission, Middle East, 1949. Ministry of Civil Aviation, 1950–3.

[2] This letter was handwritten.

September 1952

Anthony Eden to Winston S. Churchill
(*Churchill papers, 2/517*)

13 September 1952
PM/52/115

COMMONWEALTH CONFERENCE

We have now completed our preliminary guidance to officials for their meetings with their Commonwealth colleagues. The issues are very complicated but I think that we are starting on the right lines.

2. I had useful talks with Pearson yesterday. The Canadians are sending a strong official delegation and clearly intend to make a constructive effort to get the results.

3. I hope the sun shines. I am off to Strasbourg tomorrow afternoon.

Winston S. Churchill to Bill Deakin
(*Churchill papers, 4/365*)

15 September 1952

I return you the Dulles account which is of course far too detailed for my purposes. I assume that the draft of Chapter VI is written in the light of it. If there are any differences let me know. Also if you want me to read any particular passages mark the draft and keep it for my return.

You will note on page 6 the addition I have made. When the chapter is printed I will ask General Marshall the full history of this passage. It looks as if the President had told Marshall to draft a severe reply and then wrote the last sentence in himself. If so it is probable that it was the last powerful impulse of his life. This however can await further information.

Page 7. Let me see the insulting phrases which I quoted and which are not printed here.

Page 9. Stalin to me. Para. 2 must be considered with Norman Brook in spite of the eight years that have passed.

Page 10. I do not want to bring Roosevelt's death into this chapter. It reads very well and the telegrams tell their own tale far more impressively than any narrative however good.

September 1952

Winston S. Churchill to Private Office
(Premier papers, 11/250)

21 September 1952

GERM WARFARE.

I want a report from the Ministry of Defence and if possible from Lord Cherwell about this. The Communists continue to charge the United States with having spread plague germs throughout China for many months past. The *Daily Worker* should be studied carefully and also the Dirty Dean.[1] I think this is a good example of how the Communists use lies and make them truths or facts by repetition. I am rather thinking of taking this up myself in a world broadcast but I must be on very firm ground beforehand. I cannot see that the United States attempted to destroy the population of China by spreading plague bacilli. People think they can deal with this by pooh-poohing it, but the lie goes on. I thought it might be good perhaps for me to deal with it on behalf of the free world.

Get this all on the move before I return and let me know where we are.

Lord Cherwell to Winston S. Churchill
(Premier papers, 11/250)

25 September 1952

I understand you have asked for a report on germ warfare propaganda and would like comments on this subject from me. I have not had time to go into this in detail but my present general view is as follows:

The Communists in the East evidently have been suffering from serious epidemics resulting from lack of hygienic precautions and medical care. No doubt it occurred to them that they could escape responsibility and at the same time make useful anti-America propaganda by attributing these epidemics to American germ warfare.

It would of course be extremely easy for them to fake evidence going to show this had occurred. Anybody can photograph containers which could have carried insects or the like, and groups of insects, and say the two are causally connected with some aircraft that may have been heard passing in the night. No normal mind would consider such suspect pieces of evidence as valid proofs.

[1] Hewlett Johnson, 1874–1966. Educated at Owens College, 1894; Wycliffe Hall, Oxford, 1900; Wadham College, Oxford, 1904. Ordained priest, Church of England, 1904. Vicar of St Margaret's, Altrincham, 1908. Hon. Canon, Chester Cathedral, 1919. Rural Dean of Bowdon, 1923. Dean of Manchester, 1924. Dean of Canterbury, 1931–63. Stalin International Peace Prize, 1951. Wrote autobiography *Search for Light* (1968). Known as 'the Red Dean of Canterbury' owing to his support for the Soviet Union and its allies, he believed the claims by the communist newspaper the *Daily Worker* (whose board he chaired, 1959–66) that the US was using biological weapons against the Chinese.

Curiously enough the Communists have paraded insects reputedly infected with cholera which they assert rapidly produced outbreaks of disease. As has been pointed out, these things are nonsense from a scientific point of view. Cholera is a waterborne disease and is not carried by insects, and plague is only spread to humans when the rats which carry the plaguey fleas have died in such numbers that the fleas are reduced to adopting human hosts. Other similar examples of equal absurdity have been mentioned in the press. It is strange that the Communist propagandists should be so stupid as to allow allegations of this sort to be put forward when any competent biologist must know they are rubbish. It shows either that they are extremely ignorant or extremely careless in faking their evidence.

Incidentally, in opposing this propaganda I doubt whether it is wise to say, as *The Times* has done, 'No one in the West believes for a moment that the Americans, or any other people of the United Nations, have ever considered using so vile a method of warfare.'

I will try to get some more information from our own experts and will keep you informed of anything I may find out.

Cabinet: conclusions
(Cabinet papers, 128/25)

26 September 1952
Secret
11.30 a.m.
Cabinet Meeting No. 81 of 1952

1. The Prime Minister drew attention to newspaper criticism of the recent ordinances made by the Government of Kenya for the purpose of checking the activities of a secret society known as Mau Mau.

The Colonial Secretary said that, before approving these ordinances, he had satisfied himself that the members of this society who had been guilty of crimes of violence could not be brought to justice by the ordinary processes of law. He had not, however, approved all the proposals which had been submitted to him by the Government of Kenya and, so far as possible criticism in Parliament was concerned, he would have no difficulty in showing that the special powers conferred by these ordinances were less drastic than some which had been approved during the period of office of the Labour Government.

In further discussion the suggestion was made that a show of military force might assist the civil authorities in Kenya in preserving law and order. The Colonial Secretary said that he would consider this suggestion and the Minister of Defence undertook to enquire whether a small force would be sent from Egypt for this purpose, if required.

The Cabinet –

Took note of the Colonial Secretary's statement.

2. The Minister of State said that Dr Musaddiq had now sent a formal reply to the joint message from President Truman and the Prime Minister on the Persian oil dispute. This reply was wholly unsatisfactory. The fact that it was addressed only to the Prime Minister suggested that Dr Musaddiq still hoped to deal separately with the two Governments and to play one off against the other; and this made it all the more important that the joint Anglo-American approach to the problem should be preserved. There would be every advantage in sending a short joint reply to this message, even if this had to be supplemented by a more detailed British note refuting some of the arguments advanced in Dr Musaddiq's message.

The Prime Minister expressed his preference for a brief reply on the general lines that Dr Musaddiq's arguments could not be accepted and that his message made no contribution towards a reasonable settlement of the dispute. Every effort should be made to induce the United States Government to stand firm on the offer made in the joint message to which President Truman had set his name.

The Cabinet –

Invited the Minister of State to prepare a draft reply to Dr Musaddiq's message on the lines indicated in the discussion and, after consultation with the Foreign Secretary to submit this for the Prime Minister's approval.

3. The Commonwealth Secretary said that, despite the representations made to him by the Foreign Secretary, the United States Secretary of State continued to insist that the United Kingdom could not be associated in any way with the Council established under the Tripartite Treaty between the United States, Australia and New Zealand for the preservation of peace and security in the Pacific on the ground that this would make it impossible to resist similar applications from other countries. This ignored the fact that the United Kingdom was the only other country which would immediately go to the assistance of Australia and New Zealand if they were attacked. The Governments of Australia and New Zealand had, however, accepted the view of the United States Government and, if we continued to press our claim, we should risk a further rebuff. This did not mean that we should feel precluded from stating in Parliament our reasons for claiming that we should be associated with the Council and our disappointment that our claim had not been conceded. Dr Evatt's[1] criticism of our exclusion could not fail to embarrass the Australian Government.

[1] Herbert Vere Evatt, 1894–1965. Born in Australia. Member (Lab.) New South Wales Legislative Assembly, 1925–9. KC, 1929. Justice of High Court of Australia, 1930–40. Attorney-General and Minister for External Affairs, 1941–9. Australian Advisory War Council, 1941–5. Australian War Cabinet, 1941–6. Australian Representative in UK War Cabinet, 1942, 1943. Australian Member of Pacific War Council, 1942–3. Deputy PM of Australia, 1946–9. Leader, Australian Delegation, UN General Assembly, 1946, 1947. Chairman, UN Palestine Commission, 1947. Leader, Parliamentary Labour Party, Australia, 1951–60.

The Prime Minister said that he greatly regretted the Australian acquiescence in this attempt by the United States to usurp our special position in relation to Australia and New Zealand, particularly when he recalled our promise in the late war that we would divert our forces from the Middle East if Australia were attacked by Japan. He was disposed to send personal messages about this to the Prime Ministers of Australia and New Zealand and possibly also to the Australian Foreign Minister.

The Cabinet –

Took note that the Prime Minister would communicate personally with the Prime Ministers of Australia and New Zealand on this question.

[. . .]

5. The Minister of State recalled that on 18th September the Cabinet had agreed in principle that some measure of credit should be offered to the Argentine as part of a general agreement providing for our requirements of meat. The Ministers concerned had subsequently agreed, after consultation with Her Majesty's Ambassador in Buenos Aires,[1] that up to £10 million of credit should be offered in the first instance.

The Lord President said that he was doubtful whether this would be sufficient. It was vital that these negotiations should be brought to a successful conclusion, and if this could be achieved speedily it might be possible to avoid reducing the present meat ration even in December. If our initial offer of credit was refused we ought at once either to increase it or to express willingness to buy more meat than was at present contemplated and pay for part of it in advance.

On the other hand, it was pointed out that the present state of our reserves obliged us to pay careful regard to the short-term prospects for our balance of payments and that the grant of credit to Argentina was bound to affect these adversely.

The Prime Minister said that the timing of any reduction that might have to be made in the meat ration in December would need careful consideration. The Minister of Food would doubtless submit to the Cabinet in due course his proposals about Christmas food generally.

[. . .]

---

[1] William Henry Bradshaw Mack, 1894–1974. Educated at Trinity College, Dublin. Served in WWI (RA) in France and Flanders, 1916–19. Entered FO and Diplomatic Service, 1921. Served at Istanbul, Berlin, FO, Cairo, Prague, Vienna, Rome and Paris. Head of French Dept, FO, 1940. British Civil Liaison Officer to Allied C-in-C North Africa, 1942. Deputy Commissioner (Civil), Allied Commission, Austria, 1944. Political Representative, Austria, 1945. Political Adviser to British High Commissioner and GOC-in-C British Troops, Austria, 1945. HM Minister to Austria, 1947–8. Ambassador to Iraq, 1948–51; to the Argentine Republic, 1951–4.

SEPTEMBER 1952

Defence Committee: report
(Cabinet papers, 131/12)

29 September 1952
Top Secret
Defence Committee Paper No. 41 of 1952

THE DEFENCE PROGRAMME
Report by the Chiefs of Staff

In paragraph 140 of our report on Defence Policy and Global Strategy (D(52)26), we wrote:

'The reductions which we recommend in the build-up and equipment of the forces can be undertaken only by incurring real and serious risks. These risks are only justifiable in the face of the threat of economic disaster.'

We would like to recapitulate the background to the present Defence Programme upon which we are embarked, and to draw attention to the reasons which caused us to write these words.

2. The objects of our Defence Programme can be summarised as follows:
   (a) To provide the forces required to protect our world-wide interests in the Cold War.
   (b) To build up, with our Allies in the North Atlantic Treaty Organisation (NATO), forces of a strength and composition likely to provide a reliable deterrent against aggression.
   (c) To make reasonable preparations for a hot war should it break out.

The requirements of both (b) and (c) above entail the modernisation of our weapons and equipment which, for the five years following the end of the war, fell increasingly below the standard called for in modern war.

3. The main conclusion in our report on Defence Policy and Global Strategy was that, provided the deterrents of atomic war and adequate forces on the ground in Europe were properly built up and maintained, the likelihood of war would be much diminished and we could in consequence ease our economic position by accepting a smaller and slower build-up of forces, equipment and reserves for war. We also recommended that preparations for war should be primarily directed to the requirements of the first few intense weeks, little provision being made for more long-term requirements.

4. Following through this line of thought, we were able to adjust the Defence Programme so as to spend considerably reduced resources on the second and third of the objects set out in paragraph 2 above. We could not recommend any reductions in the requirements of the first object – that is to say, the requirements of the Cold War – because our world-wide commitments are at present inescapable, as can be seen from the paper circulated to the Cabinet by the Foreign Secretary (C(52)202).

5. The reductions in the build-up of our forces for NATO which we recommended were a matter of grave concern to us, because they would cause us to fall far below the contribution which we had undertaken to provide, and might have most unfortunate effects upon the determination and cohesion of the Alliance. We hoped, however, to mitigate the effects of these reductions by convincing first the authorities in the United States and then our other Allies in NATO that the real strength of the Alliance would not be impaired because there would still exist the powerful deterrent in the shape of atomic air power and adequate forces at immediate readiness on the Continent. Nevertheless our proposals were founded upon certain assumptions which could only be matters of opinion and might not be thought convincing by our Allies. We therefore felt it necessary to warn Her Majesty's Government of the risk that they would be running if they accepted our recommendations, and this we did in the sentence quoted at the outset of this paper. We have since held discussions with the American Chiefs of Staff, at which our whole strategic thought was exposed and fully thrashed out. The American Chiefs of Staff are in general agreement with our views on the longer term. But they rate higher than we do the likelihood of war in the near future and regard 1954 as a dangerous year. They are not wedded to the longer term goals set at Lisbon, but they are insistent that every effort should be made to build up the largest possible land and air forces in Europe in the next two years. They think we have over-estimated the effect of atomic air power on Russia in that period, though they are not unanimous on that point. Our warning as to the risks involved even in our Global Strategy proposals is therefore reinforced by the views of the American Chiefs of Staff, with whom the State Department is in general agreement.

6. Turning to the other fields, our recommendations had a serious effect on our war potential in the Middle East. We proposed that as soon as a settlement could be reached in Egypt our Middle East garrisons should be reduced to a level adequate only to meet Cold War requirements, and that we should rely in an emergency on the possibility of rapid reinforcement from the United Kingdom and elsewhere. We made these recommendations, not because we believed they were militarily sound, but because it was only in the Middle East that we could see any way of reducing, in the fairly near future, our overseas expenditure. The reductions could not be made without risk to our position in that most important area, but we considered that the demands of NATO and of the Cold War in the Far East must take precedence if economic necessity forced a curtailment of our effort.

7. It must not be thought that the proposals we made in our Global Strategy paper for the size and scope of the Rearmament Programme would have given us, at the end of three years, forces with full modern equipment backed by adequate reserves. Under our plan it would not be until 1958 – nearly eight years from the beginning of the Rearmament Programme

– that re-equipment and modernisation would have reached a reasonably satisfactory level.

8. This short summary will be sufficient to indicate why it is that we hold to our view that nothing less than the measure of rearmament that we proposed in our report on Defence Policy and Global Strategy should be accepted by Her Majesty's Government. We do not underestimate the importance of restoring our economic position if we are to hold our full status and influence as a major partner of the United States in world affairs. But this in itself will be insufficient unless we can also maintain our position as a strong military power, not only in NATO but also in the Middle East and Asia. Our standard of living stems in large measure from our status as a great power, and this depends to no small extent on the visible indication of our greatness, which our forces, particularly overseas, provide.

9. We have examined most carefully what the effect on our plans would be of the fixing of lower levels of expenditure. The outcome of this examination, which has been most thoroughly carried out under our authority by a Committee under the chairmanship of Mr R. R. Powell,[1] is set out in full detail in the annexed report. We do not propose to attempt to summarise still further what is there revealed. We simply put forward the following comments.

10. The effects of accepting in full the requirements of Exercise I, both on budgetary figures and on the use of the metal-using industries, is such that we could not possibly, on military grounds, recommend its acceptance. Not only would the build-up of our forces be still further reduced, but a satisfactory measure of rearmament would be postponed until somewhere about the year 1961. A rearmament programme on such terms is a misnomer. Still less could we recommend the adoption of Exercise II.

11. With regard to the load on the metal-using industries, we would like to point out that rearmament involves the ordering and manufacture of very large quantities of engineering products. It is quite out of the question in the first two or three years of rearmament for the load thrown on the metal-using industries to remain level from year to year. It is bound to rise as production gets into its stride. After the third or fourth year the load may level out. It will only fall if rearmament is carried through at a quick enough rate. The longer it is spread over, the higher the load on the metal-using industries will remain. Any attempt to cut down too low, or to level off in the first years, the load on the metal-using industries, can only result in hamstringing rearmament.

12. Our next comment relates to those items now included in the three-year Defence Budget which inflate it but do not in any way add to the effectiveness of our defence. These are fully set out in paragraphs 5 and 6 of the annexed

[1] Richard Royle Powell, 1909–2006. Educated at Sidney Sussex College, Cambridge. In Civil Service, 1931–3; Admiralty, 1934. Civil Service adviser to Adm. Bruce Fraser, 1944. CMG, 1946. CB, 1951. Knighted, 1954. Deputy Secretary, Ministry of Defence, 1950s. Member, Strath Committee, 1955. Secretary to Board of Trade, 1960–8. KCB, 1961. GCB, 1967. Chairman, Alusuisse, 1969–84.

report. The sums involved are very large and give an erroneous idea of the size of the true Defence Budget.

13. Finally, we would draw particular attention to Section VIII of the annexed report which deals with End-Item Aid. With the best will in the world, we do not see how any increased reliance can be placed on American equipment to take the place of what we now propose to make for ourselves. Indeed, it is very far from certain that military aid in any form will be forthcoming after 1954. Even if a new United States Administration were to agree to continue or increase End-Item Aid, the source of supply would be so uncertain, the maintenance difficulties so great, and the conditions attached to it so restrictive, that it would be dangerous to base our plans upon it to an extent more than is already unavoidable.

14. In conclusion we would urge Her Majesty's Government to accept the proposals we have made as a result of our review of Defence Policy and Global Strategy. We do not claim that no reductions or deferments whatever can be accepted from the revised costs of our plan, and we are ready to co-operate to the full in seeking ways of making economies, provided they do not disrupt the general scale of the programme. But we should be failing in our duty if we did not submit our advice that reductions in defence expenditure to the figures we were instructed to consider are unacceptable on military grounds, and involve the taking of risks which we cannot believe to be justified in the present state of international relations.

Winston S. Churchill to President Harry S Truman
('Defending the West, The Truman–Churchill Correspondence', page 202)

29 September 1952

You will no doubt have already seen the lengthy message which Mossadeq sent me in reply to our joint telegram. Anthony and I have prepared a draft answer for your consideration. Evidently his hope is to avoid our approach. It seems for this very reason all the more important that we should continue together. Britain has suffered by Persian depredations losses which I am told may amount to six million pounds sterling a year across the dollar exchange. We cannot I am sure go further at this critical time in our struggle for solvency than the proposals which you agreed were fair and just. It seems also to me, if I may say so, that it would be a hard prospect for the American taxpayer to have to bribe Persians (and how many others?) not to become communists, once this process started it might go a long time in a lot of places. Naturally I have thought a great deal about the danger of a revolution and Soviet infiltration or aggression. I may of course be wrong but as I at present see it I do not feel that it will happen that way in the near future. Anyhow it seems far more likely that Mossadeq will come to reasonable terms on being confronted with a continued Truman–Churchill accord. I earnestly hope therefore that we can send him a message from us both on the line of this draft.

Cabinet: conclusions
(Cabinet papers, 128/25)

30 September 1952
Secret
5 p.m.
Cabinet Meeting No. 82 of 1952

[. . .]

5. The Cabinet were informed that the Prime Minister had sent a personal message to President Truman (No. 4087 to Washington) accompanying the draft of a joint reply to Dr Musaddiq's message (No. 4088 to Washington).

The Foreign Secretary said that the President was absent from Washington on an election tour, and the State Department's first response to this message had been discouraging. He had thought it advisable to send at once a strongly-worded reply combating the State Department's attitude.

The Prime Minister said that we must do all in our power to maintain a joint Anglo-American pressure on the Persian Government, though in the last resort we had no means of preventing the United States Government from financing Dr Musaddiq in the hope of preventing Persia from going Communist.

The Cabinet –

Took note of these statements.

[. . .]

October 1952

Cabinet: conclusions
(Cabinet papers, 128/25)

1 October 1952
Secret
11 a.m.
Cabinet Meeting No. 83 of 1952

[...]
4. The Cabinet had before them a memorandum by the Minister of Housing and Local Government (C(52)299) outlining a short-term policy of relaxing rent control for the purpose of encouraging the owners of house property to carry out essential repairs.

The Prime Minister said that any legislation amending the Rent Restriction Acts must be so designed as to bring no financial benefit to landlords; it must be made evident that the Government had no other purpose than to increase the number of habitable houses. The Labour Party, in a recent pamphlet, had admitted that the controlled rent of some houses did not provide an income sufficient to maintain the property in a proper state of repair, and that tenants would benefit by some amendment of the Acts which would enable a proportion of the rent to be spent on the improvement and maintenance of the dwelling. There might therefore be a political opportunity in the coming session to pass amending legislation which could fairly be represented as designed to increase the national stock of habitable houses.

The Minister of Housing said that the scheme outlined in his memorandum had been framed with this in view. It would not bring any additional profit to owners of house property. It would, however, serve the national interest by helping to prevent existing houses from falling further into disrepair.

In discussion there was general support for the scheme outlined in C(52)299. The Chancellor of the Exchequer said that he accepted the scheme in principle, and he undertook to communicate to the Minister of Housing certain comments on technical aspects of the scheme connected with income tax and assessment for rates. He observed, however, in the final paragraph of the

Minister's paper, a reference to slum-clearance: he could not agree that any new programme of slum-clearance should be added to the existing housing programme.

The Cabinet –
1) Approved in principle the scheme outlined in C(52)299 for amending the Rent Restriction Acts.
2) Invited the Minister of Housing to work out this scheme in further detail, in consultation with other Ministers concerned, and to proceed with the preparation of amending legislation.

[. . .]

6. The Prime Minister recalled that on 19th June the Cabinet had agreed that no Service Reviews should be held in connection with the Coronation in 1953. This decision had been taken on the assumption that heavy expenditure would be involved; but he had recently been informed that a Naval Review could be held without any additional cost beyond that of a firework display and the charter of a liner in which distinguished visitors could steam round the Fleet. He thought that the matter might be reconsidered on this basis: there need be no question of corresponding Coronation Reviews by the other two Services.

The Cabinet –

Invited the First Lord of the Admiralty to consider whether arrangements could be made to hold a Naval Review at the time of the Coronation without incurring special expenditure otherwise than on the two particular items mentioned by the Prime Minister.

President Harry S Truman to Winston S. Churchill
Prime Minister's Personal Telegram T.188/52
(Premier papers, 11/237)

2 October 1952
Immediate
Secret
No. 1869

I do not believe that a joint reply to Musaddiq's note would be wise. I had hoped that our reasonable and fair joint offer, which seemed to meet Musaddiq's principal points of difficulty, would break the log jam. I am now convinced that Musaddiq will not, and believes he cannot (if he is to survive), accept this solution. The situation in Iran has deteriorated so far that he is threatened by the extremists who will not have it. To lock ourselves into this offer by a joint reply reasserting it, seems to me to so constrict our future relations with Iran as to preclude any influence or action which might help to save the country. I believe that pressure will not save it by bringing Musaddiq to reason but will hasten its disintegration and loss.

We both want to accomplish the same results in Iran – to prevent a Communist take-over and to preserve the moral and legal rule of just compensation for property taken.

There seems very little that any reply as such can accomplish except to keep the record straight. I can understand, too, your belief that you must answer the accusations made against British action in Iran. So I think that if this Government replies at all it should do so separately. We are thinking of something along lines which Mr Acheson will show to Sir Oliver.

Winston S. Churchill to Lord De L'Isle and Dudley
Prime Minister's Personal Minute M.497/52
(Premier papers, 11/43)

5 October 1952

I should like a very short considered report on the results.* I am afraid I shall not be able to attend at Biggin Hill.

* Exercise 'Ardent'.[1]

Winston S. Churchill to Lord Cherwell
Prime Minister's Personal Minute M.498/52
(Premier papers, 11/250)

5 October 1952

What do these records amount to?[2] Do not let their study interfere with more important work. I want to know however whether there is any truth in the story* or whether it is one of those Soviet lies which become truths after continuous repetition.

* Germ warfare campaigns.

---

[1] 'Ardent': the largest air-defence training exercise in the UK since WWII up to that point. Took place 4–5 Oct. 1952. Its object was to subject UK air defences to likely wartime operations. Aircraft flew several thousands of sorties to test defences and methods of attack. Canberras and Sabres were used for the first time. Other participants were Anti-Aircraft Command, the Royal Navy Air Arm, and US and NATO air forces. The code name continued to be used, most recently in the 'Ardent Sentry' exercise of June 2019.

[2] See Cherwell's minute of Sep. 25, reproduced above (pp. 648–9).

Randolph S. Churchill to Winston S. Churchill
(Churchill papers, 1/51)[1]

9 October 1952

My dear Papa,

Your office twice rang me up to find out what train I was taking to Scarborough. I naively supposed that this was so that we would, if convenient, go on the same train. But when I rang you up you made it very plain that you did not want me on the same train as yourself. I have since learnt that this was not due to a desire for privacy for composing your speech (as you told me) but obviously for sheer distaste for my presence in your entourage.

In these circumstances you will scarcely be surprised to learn that I am not coming to Scarborough.

Winston S. Churchill: speech
('Winston S. Churchill, His Complete Speeches', volume 8, pages 8410–18)

11 October 1952   Conservative Annual Conference, Scarborough

THE FIRST YEAR

Twelve years have passed since in the crisis of the war I was chosen Leader of the Conservative Party, as our chairman has reminded you, but this is the first time I have had the honour to address our Annual Conference as Prime Minister. I do so this afternoon with feelings of growing confidence and hope for our party and, what is far more important, for our country. I believe we may fairly claim that there is a definite improvement in British affairs at home, and also in our position in the world and that this has taken place since we became responsible. As has been made plain by the Ministers who have addressed you, we do not seek to be masters, but to serve supreme causes: the maintenance of world peace founded on strength, the unity of the British Empire and Commonwealth, of which our island is still the heart, and the preservation of national solvency without which all our power and reputation would be cast away.

We have been in office for almost exactly a year. That is not a long time in which to change the course or the aspect of our complicated modern life. No doubt we have made mistakes, especially, it is said, in propaganda. I would rather make mistakes in propaganda than in action. Events are the final rulers and time is needed for them to make their pronouncements clear. Still, it would be best to have no mistakes at all. I do not speak this afternoon in any complacent mood. I can assure you we will try to do better. I wish indeed I

---

[1] This letter was handwritten.

could promise that we should solve all the problems that lie before us. We can only try our best for the interests of the nation as a whole. Although we live in a period of keen and even bitter party strife on narrow margins, the country split in twain, and although an intellectual and moral gulf separates us in doctrine from those who try to reduce us to a Socialist State – in spite of all that – we are an ancient and neighbourly race. There are an awful lot of British folk, and perhaps in Yorkshire I may even be allowed to say English folk, who think much the same way about an awful lot of things. I can assure you that we have no thought nor wish, nor indeed could we have any personal or party interest, but to bring about British recovery and be helpful to all our fellow-countrymen.

When we took office last October we were plunging into national bankruptcy at a rate of £800 millions a year. Large further inevitable increases in expense impended upon us. These could in many cases only be avoided by a wholesale scrapping of much of the costly effort already made. We therefore had to face the full impact of rearmament at a time when the £400 millions a year of American and Canadian aid from loan or gift, on which British Socialism had lived, came to the end. Thus we inherited the quadruple onrush of Social Services growing automatically, of rearmament getting into its full stride, of the end of the American bounty, and of rapidly approaching insolvency in our overseas payments. Here was the grievous and menacing combination which the Chancellor of the Exchequer has striven and is striving so manfully to conquer. And that is the task in which it is our duty to give him all possible aid and not flinch before abuse from those who are themselves directly responsible for the hazardous plight in which they left us. It is said reap where you have sown. That is a hard rule, a stern rule and we accept it. But we are not now reaping where *we* have sown, we are reaping where others have sown, where they have sown weeds as well as grain. We have to hold firmly to our duty, and stand resolutely together, persevere along right lines and then we shall be able to reap where we have sown ourselves, and by that we shall be ready to be judged.

We have two hard tasks before us. The first and the less difficult is to maintain and improve our position as a party in the House of Commons and in the confidence of the electors. We owe a debt to our Members of the House of Commons who, by their admirable attendance, often at serious sacrifice have enabled us with an overall majority of only sixteen to average thirty in all the 230 divisions we have had since the new Parliament began. I hope the constituents of all these Members will make them feel how much they appreciate the effort and sacrifice which they have made, without which our business might indeed be in sorry confusion. And here we must not fail to pay a tribute to the excellent discharge of their strenuous task by the Chief Whip and his devoted colleagues. He has done a fine job. If we can maintain this high standard and also improve our propaganda and public relations service, as I hope we may, we shall have created that solid political foundation upon which our second and larger task – our national recovery – must stand.

Here indeed the problems tower menacing and inscrutable above us. The Socialist Government during their six years of power, spent every last penny they could lay their hands upon, including, as I have said, over £2,000 millions or more borrowed or begged from the United States whom they now abuse, and from the Dominions. We have stood on our own feet, independent, apart from military aid for the common cause of the free world.

In the last year of the Socialist rule they committed us to an enormous three year programme of rearmament, first, of £3,600 millions, increased a few months later by – what calculations I do not know – to £4,700 millions. On patriotic grounds and because of our loyalty to the cause of the free world and the United Nations the Conservative Opposition supported this well meant though loosely and hurriedly framed policy. Now in the first year the expense of a munitions programme is of course comparatively little. Plants have to be altered, factories re-tooled, and skilled labour trained or re-disposed.

But in the present year, 1952, and still more next year, what was started so light heartedly on a finance already heavily strained by years of reckless extravagance and waste, in the third year, next year all this comes to fruition, requiring ever more expenditure and skilled manpower and eating ever more steel and other raw materials. That is what we have to face and the Socialist Party who knew quite well what they were leaving behind them should not be allowed to forget these facts. They tell us we have broken our promises. Well that can only be proved by time. It would be more true to say that the Socialist predictions of the General Elections have already in many cases been falsified. What was the first thing they promised us if a Conservative Government was elected? War. Churchill, the warmonger, would plunge us into war. Only a year ago that was what they were using. Well, it has not happened yet. On the contrary there is a general feeling in the world that on the whole the danger of world war has receded since we became responsible.

We politicians have all, I think, been honoured by the presence among us as a member of our party and as Minister of Defence of a great military commander, Field Marshal Alexander, whose name will shine in history. I was struck by the pith of the point which he made when he said:

> 'Always remember that many of those who now say that rearmament is no longer necessary are the very same people who, during the General Election, put forward the idea that there would be another war if Mr Churchill became Prime Minister.'

I wonder what is the answer to that. Anyhow that Socialist slander and libel, and the whispering campaign, which may have cost us fifty seats, is as dead as a doornail. Our opponents have got to think of another lie for next time. And, as they are now realizing, really paying lies, upon which the whole

Socialist Party can unitedly agree, are rather hard to find. Do not let us hurry them too much.

There was another Socialist prophecy which has been proved false. At the election the nation was threatened by the Socialist Party machine with mass strikes of a political character if they elected a Conservative Government according to their rights. This prediction has not come true. The trade union leaders (I shall have to refer to them later) have set an example to Socialist political agitators in the firmness with which they have denounced the idea of using the strike weapon to effect constitutional changes. Such a threat which the Communists and their fellow-travellers in or out of the House of Commons freely use would be a challenge to the whole life of Parliamentary democracy, as it has so slowly been built up among us, and all that has been built up across the centuries. The foundations of Parliamentary democracy would be overthrown by the use of the strike weapon for political and constitutional purposes.

But now let me come to a more concrete point you will have in your minds. I do remember last time I was with you two years ago the explosion of the feelings in our Party – 'mob rule' the Socialists called it (they ought to know) – in favour of a target of 300,000 houses a year. 'What an absurd proposal,' cried the Socialist organs. 'Do you really think that if Aneurin Bevan can only build 200,000 houses in a year there is any other statesman in the world who could surpass him?' I believe, or at least I have heard it said, that there is not nowadays the same unanimous agreement, even in his own party or in his party within his own party, there is not the same unanimous agreement about his genius, or even about his character. Certainly I think that among the hundreds of thousands of couples who seek a home, with its own front door, where they can rear a family of valiant Britons, there is more hope in Mr Harold Macmillan and his energetic lieutenant, Mr Marples, and other Ministers like Mr Eccles and Lord Swinton, who are all involved in this special team, there is more hope that they will achieve what we have in hand than there ever was in the ambitious demagogue who called one half of his fellow-countrymen 'vermin'.

I will, at that point, leave the Socialists and their predictions to stew in their own juice and turn to the field of constructive, positive action. It is our intention, when Parliament meets, to introduce and carry the repeal of both the Transport and Steel Nationalisation Acts. We do not doubt that we shall be able to accomplish our purpose. Of course, as the oldest child of the House of Commons – or shall I say, the one who has spent the longest time in the cradle of parliamentary government – I do not take the view that every Bill must be rammed through Parliament exactly in the form that the Cabinet of the day thinks fit. I believe in parliamentary discussion and I hold strongly that the elected representatives of the people, and the House of Lords, in its relation established by the Parliament Act, should both share in the shaping of legislation. We are not like the Czar, or the Kaiser, or Hitler, or Lenin, or Stalin, or a lot of others of the same brand, who utter ukases or other decrees which cowed assemblies, elected by swindling and intimidation, have to endorse and swallow. We are not like that. Lots of people have a say in what happens here and I hope that may long be so. It is not necessarily a humiliation to a Government to defer to the House of Commons feelings and to genuine sense established in debates, provided that it does not sacrifice any moral principle or inflict injury or injustice on the public. Nevertheless, making all allowance for what I have said, I am confidently able to assure you that Road Transport and Steel will be de-nationalized before we are a year older, and that subject to the necessary State supervision they will continue in freedom indefinitely, before a Socialist administration has the power or thinks it worth while to disturb or assail them again. I put this plainly before you because in the last session the demise of the Crown and other difficulties made it impossible for us to carry these important measures; but we are resolved in every way that they should be on the Statute Book before the next Session of Parliament is over.

Now let us look at these two proposals, and the reasons for them. Why do we wish to repeal the Transport and Steel Nationalization Acts? I can assure you that it is not for party spite or out of mere contrariness. It is because we believe profoundly that a more flexible, fertile, virile and growing industry can be restored, serving for the interchange of goods and services between the British people and also, by this fact, aiding our export trade. If I were not convinced that this was true I would not pursue or advise my colleagues to pursue either measure. Rather than do what we had become convinced was unwise, I would not hesitate to ask release from the pledges we have given in opposition. Of course, it is better to be both right and consistent. But if you have to choose – you must choose to be right. I declare, therefore, that we are sure that the British people as a whole will have a better time and a better chance with steel as we propose it and with the reorganization and liberation of our transport, giving a chance to the nationalized railways, which we accept and which we mean to make the utmost success, and also for steel a better chance than under the present rigid regulations which were made for the sake of party politics and for fallacious doctrine in which many of those who pronounced them have lost faith. That is why we go forward on our course.

Now take transport. Who can be satisfied with the confusion and restriction in which it now lies? The whole of our road transport system is obstructed and distorted for the sake of keeping nationalized 41,000 vehicles managed by an overhead staff of 12,000 officials. (Did I say 12,000? I beg Mr Morrison's pardon, I should have said 11,919. I accept his correction. I hope it will be a comfort to him. He must need some cheering up nowadays.) But the fact remains that for the sake of giving a national road monopoly to these 41,000 vehicles, thousands of small hauliers have had their livelihood taken from them, and those who have been allowed to retain their property are cramped within a twenty-five-mile radius. Yet so unsatisfactory is the service of the 41,000 vehicles, owned by the State, that what are called 'C' licences have gone up from 300,000 to 800,000 since the Nationalization Act in spite of the fact that they are only allowed to carry their owner's goods, and often return half empty or quite empty.

Think of the waste involved in this. It is – I offer this to my political opponents – the quintessence of private ownership made uneconomic by law. More than that, they are not even 41,000 vehicles at work in the State monopoly. In the last year they have fallen off by 3,000 and yet for the sake of these remaining 38,000 vehicles all the others on the road or which would like to go on the road are to be held in one form of strait-jacket or another. Now this is one of the evils we set out to cure, and it is my firm hope that we may render the whole movement of traffic, the interchange of goods and services between one man and another in this island quite definitely more easy and elastic than what now prevails, and thus make a contribution, only one of many that is needed, to our productive efficiency, at this most critical time. So much for transport.

Then there is steel. If ever there was an industry which was unsuitable for nationalization, it was this vital business of steel production. The degrees of damage which nationalization can do vary from industry to industry. It is one thing to apply it to public services like railways, gas, electricity. But the harm to our economy is incomparably greater when nationalization is turned upon an industry like steel, whose products in the form of materials or manufactured goods, are exported in great quantities and have to hold their own against the keenest competition throughout the world. Unlike the Socialist Act of Nationalization, our scheme for steel is not based upon political doctrine and theory. On the contrary as all or at any rate most Conservative policies ought to be, it is founded upon practical needs and experience. The system of organization and supervision which we propose has been progressively evolved by the industry itself over the last twenty years. And in its general conception it follows closely the views expressed by the Trades Union Congress in its well-known report on the public supervision of industry. In that report the TUC made it clear that they did not regard nationalization as being the only or necessarily the best method of securing for the State an effective say in industry. A more practical form of supervision they said, would be through a tripartite board of control on the lines of the former Iron and Steel Board, which was composed of representatives of employers, trades unions and consumers. That is precisely what our scheme sets out to do. We feel entitled to ask that our proposals should be viewed in this setting of common thought and experience. If they are examined in this spirit, we believe that subject to improvements in detail which we shall be glad to consider, our scheme will be found to offer the best basis for a lasting and workable solution of the problems which confront the steel industry. And let me give this warning to our opponents, and to everyone.

Any loss of efficiency or blunting of initiative in the steel industry may only too easily price our exports out of foreign markets and may strike a fatal blow at our engineering industries, upon whose overseas sales we, all of us, not Conservatives only – all parties – the whole country, rely to balance our external trade. Happily, as you may remember, we got into power just in the nick of time to save this great industry from disaster. Although the Socialists took over the shares of the steel companies, they did not have time, in the few months between nationalization and the change of government, to upset seriously the practical working of the industry.

One of the first acts of the Conservative Minister of Supply, Mr Duncan Sandys, was to direct the State Corporation not to interfere with the structure of the companies or their management without the Government's consent. This has effectively preserved the identity of the companies, famous throughout the globe as they are as symbols of British efficacy, and had maintained their experienced leadership. We have in fact by prompt action held the position pending de-nationalization. The Bill to de-nationalize steel will be presented to Parliament next month. Apart from criticisms of detail, our plan as set forth in the White Paper has been very favourably received, both inside and outside the steel industry, and we go forward with the encouragement that we have wide support among those who know the industry and desire its wellbeing. Meanwhile steel itself is not standing still. The foresight and enterprise of the companies enabled them to make plans at the end of the war to expand our pig-iron steel production. These schemes were set on foot long before nationalization, and in spite of its menace, are now bearing fruit. New blast furnaces and more pig-iron swell the output of our steel. We confidently expect that Britain's output of steel next year will beat the previous all-time record. And let nobody be misled by the humbug we shall no doubt hear that all this was the result of a few months' nationalization. It is, on the contrary, a vindication of years of preparation under free enterprise which was rescued only just in time by the expulsion of the Socialists from power.

I have not attended your Conference, though I have followed it with diligence. We had a striking speech yesterday from Mr Mawby,[1] a trade unionist, who reminded us that Mr Pollitt,[2] speaking in Moscow, had said that the trade unions in this country are going to be used as a political pawn in Soviet aggrandisement or words to that effect. Mr Mawby, you will remember, warned us against the danger of the unions becoming a tool of any party in our country. There is a great force in what he says.

Two years ago at Blackpool I pointed out to the trade union leaders how

---

[1] Raymond Llewellyn Mawby, 1922–90. Married, 1944, Carrie Aldwinckle: two children. MP (Cons.) for Totnes, 1955–83. Asst Postmaster-General, 1963–4. During the 1960s, he provided information to the Czech Socialist Republic in exchange for monetary compensation.

[2] Harry Pollitt, 1890–1960. Secretary, Hands Off Russia Movement, 1919; National Minority Movement, 1924–9; Communist Party of Great Britain, 1929–56.

much harder would be their task in dealing with a corporate Socialist State like Russia with its totalitarian structure than with present day employers who have to get on with their people in the long run or hand over their business to someone else. We owe a great deal to the trade unions. They are an institution in our land, an institution given its original Charter of Rights by the Conservative Party. I regret that many of them have been misled by what is the undoubted fallacy of Socialism and that they show an undue bias towards the Socialist Party. Would they not be wise to concentrate upon looking after the interests of their own members in all the processes of collective bargaining which on the whole work well? Everyone must, however, recognize the quality, character and courage of the trade union leaders. We do not agree with them on doctrine, as I have said, nor on the part they should play in domestic politics, but we respect them, and there is no doubt the country could not get on without them. And after all the Conservatives or Tories (I am certainly not afraid of that word Tory) have the matter in their own hands. Today at least one-third of the trade union members vote Conservative. Why should we stop there? All Conservative wage-earners should join their trade unions and attend the branch meetings as regularly as the Communists do. But I do not suggest that they should attend in order to try to capture trade unions' political influence for our party, but in order that their force should primarily be concentrated upon the relations between employers and employed, and should in addition aid and explore those large issues of profit-sharing and co-partnership which may play so fruitful a part in our hard-pressed national life. We know they are our party opponents. But there is no aspect of our social policy that our successful, capable and tactful Minister of Labour, Sir Walter Monckton – or if need be I myself – would not readily discuss with responsible leaders of the TUC. I hope, therefore, that whatever fighting there may be will be conducted with the minimum of interference in the efficient earning of their daily bread by the entire mass of the British people.

You heard on Thursday last our Deputy Prime Minister, Mr Eden set forth in weighty words the broad conceptions and purposes which we pursue in the vast sphere of foreign affairs in which his experience and world-wide repute are of great value to us all. In the main these conceptions are a continuance of the policy which, under the late Mr Bevin and with the loyal support of the Conservative Opposition, was followed during his long tenure of power. It will indeed be a pitiful exhibition if the leaders of the Labour Party desert the causes to which they committed the nation, just because they ceased to be Ministers of the Crown. I do not believe myself that the bulk of them will do so, though a hard time no doubt lies before them. It may well be a case where virtue will have to be its own reward.

The foundation of our policy is a true and honourable comradeship with the United States, in defence of the life of the free world against the immense aggression and ceaseless infiltration of Communist Imperialism. This has already since the war dominated half Europe and all China without the loss of a single soldier in Russian uniform, and at the present time, the oligarchy in the Kremlin, wielding autocratic power far exceeding that exercised by any Czar in the old and bygone days, controls armies in Europe at the present time far beyond any which we and our Allies have been able to gather together. We intend to persevere faithfully and resolutely in strengthening the ties of friendship and kinship which have brought us into such effective alliance with the great English-speaking Republic across the Atlantic Ocean. On this the future peace of the world and the survival of its freedom depend. This does not mean, as Mr Eden indicated to us, that we find ourselves always in complete agreement with our American allies or that we should hesitate to press our view on matters about which we differ. I certainly never hesitated during the war to put our case strongly to them, and very often succeeded in having our views accepted to what, in the end, was found to be advantageous to the common cause. But we shall certainly not fall into the snare laid for us by the Soviet Government and their Communist adherents and fellow travellers here or in other countries, and allow any breach in the effective harmony of thought and action between Britain and the United States which is the mainstay of all we hold dear.

Most of us are watching from day to day the Presidential Election in the United States. Democracy works by different methods in the Great Republic from those to which we are accustomed over here. But there are two facts about which there is no doubt. The first is that the American system has produced two candidates for the Presidency who are, in character and ability, two of their finest men; and the second is that whichever of them wins, the United States will not abandon the mission of leading the free nations in resistance to Communist aggression and that the underlying unities of the English speaking world will grow broader, and deeper, and stronger as the years roll by. This has been a memorable meeting of the Conservative Party at Scarborough. It has come at a time of difficulty and strain, both at home and abroad. The sober realization of all our members that they must face the real facts of British life, grim though they be in many ways, and not fear passing gusts of unpopularity in the discharge of our duty to the nation as a whole – that resolution is outstanding in our minds. That has been the keynote of the Conference. It needs no background such as might well be found at Morecambe of what other parties have done to command the attention and respect of all who cherish the enduring strength of Britain. Her Majesty's Government are grateful to those who have sustained them by their confidence and loyalty, and we shall go forward on the uphill march with our willpower stimulated by the wish to be worthy of your respect.

I have used the word 'memorable' about our Conference. Let us also endow it with lasting effect. The Recruiting Campaign which Lord Woolton (whose absence we so much regret) has launched may well bring enduring reinforcement to our party's strength. Let us march forward with our sturdy lions, jaunty lions – yea, unconquerable lions – enrolling our members as we go. So many people believe in us and vote for us who remain silent between elections. We need the encouragement and help of their declared fellowship in our grand design to restore Britain to freedom and to reviving fame.

Winston S. Churchill to Private Office
(*Premier papers, 11/127*)

12 October 1952

Look up the precedents for loans for Defence Programmes in time of peace. I am sure there was a big Naval Programme, for which a Navy Loan was quoted. I think it may mean going back to the '80s or '90s.

Let me know what the National Debt is and what it has been reduced to since the War – I mean the regular National Debt.

Winston S. Churchill: speech
('*Winston S. Churchill, His Complete Speeches*', *volume 8, pages 8418–19*)

14 October 1952 Pilgrims' Dinner, Savoy Hotel

NATO

We all regret the absence from our dinner this evening of Lord Halifax, whose career as British Ambassador to the United States added lustre to his long record of eminent service. Tonight we have a distinguished gathering at the Pilgrims' Dinner.[1] You will note, by the way, that in this well-known and long-known island we have succeeded for nearly a thousand years in preventing any invaders from coming in. But you should also note – as pilgrims – that we have never prevented any from going out – not even in the *Mayflower* – and speaking as a Briton I must admit that some quite good ones have gone out. But now larger syntheses (if I may use the kind of learned jargon which is fashionable) are bringing together by forces, which are primarily moral and intellectual, all the individuals and all the nations who would die rather than submit to Communist rule. But there is no reason why the free world should die. On the contrary, it has only to remain united and progressive not only to survive, but to preserve its right to live in its own way without the need of another hideous catastrophe.

Here tonight we have two of our famous British commanders, Alex and Monty. I am sure that in their separate spheres that are going to do all in their

---

[1] The Pilgrims of Great Britain and Pilgrims of the United States are sister societies, founded in 1902, which encourage Anglo-American good fellowship.

power to help our guest of the evening, General Ridgeway, to carry out the enormous task which he has undertaken. General Ridgeway had a predecessor. I am afraid that I might get into trouble if I told you his name. All I will say is that those who understand the work he did in Europe will ever remember it with thankfulness. We are fortunate indeed that General Ridgeway has come to our aid in this critical period with his record in the war and in Korea as soldier and statesman.

We have also been forced to spare from the Cabinet Lord Ismay – his international status prevents my using his pet name – who is doing the same sort of thing for NATO as he did for me in the war – to make all things go as well as possible between the military and the politicians and to weave together many diverse elements into the harmonious structure of a machine capable of giving decisions for millions of men.

All down the ages many and varied, but not always wholly successful, have been the expedients which have tried to bring the nations together in peace or war. It may be that NATO, our shield against war, can also unite us for peace. There are hopeful stirrings in Europe today, most of which find their inspiration directly or indirectly in the leadership which NATO has given. From small beginnings who can tell what blessings they may bring us? Come what will, at the present time it is in NATO that wise men in Europe and America will do well to place their trust as a benevolent combination of the free peoples for their defence against mortal danger.

Our policy, the policy of the English-speaking world, the policy of NATO, and of all who prefer Parliamentary democracy with its many defects – never concealed – to totalitarian rule wherever it comes from, our policy is by hard sacrifice and constant toil to increase the deterrents against an aggressor. I can assure you tonight that we shall do our utmost, short of going bankrupt, to increase these deterrents and also to convince the other side that we are planning no assault on them.

We all hate and fear war. Let me tell you why in my opinion, and it is only an opinion, not a prophecy, a third World War is unlikely to happen. It is because, among other reasons, it would be entirely different in certain vital respects from any other war that has ever taken place. Both sides know that it would begin with horrors of a kind and on a scale never dreamed of before by human beings. It would begin by both sides in Europe suffering in this first stage exactly what they dread the most. It would also be different because the main decisions would probably come in the first month or even in the first week. The quarrel might continue for an indefinite period, but after the first month it would be a broken-backed war in which no great armies could be moved over long distances. The torments would fall in increasing measure upon the whole civilian population of the globe, and Governments dependent upon long distance communications by land would find they had lost their power to dominate events.

These are only a few of the grave facts which rule our destinies; but we can be sure that this proved and experienced General of the United States Army, whom we welcome here tonight as our guest of honour, will do his utmost for our common cause, and it is with sincere feelings of hope that I support our President in asking you to drink the health of our distinguished guests at these tables tonight, and first and foremost of General Ridgeway.

Cabinet: conclusions
(Cabinet papers, 128/25)

14 October 1952
Secret
11 a.m.
Cabinet Meeting No. 85 of 1952

[. . .]

8. The Cabinet had before them a memorandum by the Chancellor of the Exchequer (C(52)328) suggesting a modification of the local loans procedure.

The Chancellor of the Exchequer said that, under Section 1 of the Local Authorities Loans Act, 1945, local authorities must borrow from the Exchequer through the Local Loans Fund unless authorised by the Treasury to do otherwise. The practical effect of this provision was that, apart from what they were authorised to borrow on private mortgage, local authorities were able to meet all their needs of capital through the Local Loans Fund. For each year since 1948–49 loans made by the Government from the Fund had exceeded the provision made in the Budget, the probable excess for the present financial year being estimated at about £100 millions. He now recommended that the section should be allowed to expire on 31st December by omitting it from the forthcoming Expiring Laws Continuance Bill, and that local authorities' borrowing from the Fund should in future be limited to the sum provided for this purpose in the Budget, supplemented as necessary by mortgage loans and by issues of stock by authorities of recognised credit standing. Local authorities' expenditure would continue to be controlled as at present through the machinery of the investment programme, but the necessity for the larger authorities to resort to the market for a proportion of their capital needs might be expected to make them rather more cautious in their plans. While the practical effects of the proposed change would be limited, it would be likely to strengthen both Government credit and public confidence.

The Minister of Housing and Local Government said that he did not question the advantage of shifting part of the burden of local authorities' loans from the Local Loans Fund to the capital market, but he was doubtful about the method which the Chancellor proposed to adopt for effecting this. There did not appear to be anything in the wording of Section 1 of the Local Authority Loans Act, 1945, which would prevent the Treasury from allowing and, indeed, helping a small number of the larger authorities to float issues of stock. By proceeding on such lines the Government might secure their object without making any change in the existing law. He also wished the Cabinet to understand that the proposed change would have no restrictive effect upon local authorities when they planned their capital expenditure. Of the total investment programme of local authorities, amounting to £476 millions during the present financial year, all but some £2 millions represented projects carried out at the instance of Government Departments and under their control through the machinery of the investment programme. Further, the creditworthiness of even the larger local authorities was not what it formerly had been. Expenditure on housing, which amounted to nearly £400 millions out of their total programmes, was incurred by no less than 1,500 separate housing authorities, very few of whom would be able to raise money on the market.

The Prime Minister said that some means must be found of preventing the capital expenditure of local authorities from exceeding the provision made for it in the Budget. The Chancellor should discuss his proposals in detail with the Minister of Housing before submitting the matter again to the Cabinet for decision.

The Cabinet –

Invited the Chancellor of the Exchequer to discuss the proposals in C(52)328 with the Minister of Housing and thereafter to submit the matter again to the Cabinet.

[. . .]

Winston S. Churchill to Queen Elizabeth II
(Premier papers, 11/246)

14 October 1952

Mr Churchill with his humble duty to The Queen begs to submit for Your Majesty's approval a proposal for the position to be given to the Duke of Edinburgh at the Opening of Parliament.

The Lord Chancellor has prepared a note on the precedents and the law, of which Mr Churchill encloses a copy in the belief that it will be of interest to Your Majesty and to His Royal Highness. In the light of this memorandum the following arrangements would seem appropriate on the 4th of November and on future occasions. The Duke of Edinburgh would accompany Your Majesty in the procession from the Robing Room to the Parliament Chamber. In the Chamber there would be a single throne for Your Majesty which would be placed in the middle alcove and there would be a chair of state placed for His Royal Highness in the alcove on the left of the throne. The Duke would

OCTOBER 1952 673

conduct Your Majesty to the throne and then take his seat on the chair of state.

This procedure would follow precedent in being similar to that used in the reign of Queen Victoria both before and after Prince Albert was made Prince Consort in 1857. Mr Churchill trusts that it will be acceptable to Your Majesty.[1]

R. A. Butler to Winston S. Churchill
(*Premier papers, 11/127*)

16 October 1952

I understand that you have asked for information on two points.[2]

(a) What precedents exist for the raising of loans for defence in time of peace?

Apart from loans for military and naval <u>works</u> between 1893 and 1905, the precedents are:

(i) Defence Loans Acts, 1937 and 1939.

Each act authorised borrowing of £400 million. The conception was that rearmament would involve heavy expenditure for a few years, followed by a lower level thereafter, and the loans were designed to equalise the Budget charge over a longish period. (The objective of Budget policy in those days was to secure a moderate surplus above the line. The 'below the line' items were insignificant.) The total issues under these Acts until they were rendered inappropriate by the war were £685 million.

(ii) Armed Forces (Housing Loans) Act, 1947.

Borrowing of £40 million was authorised for the building of houses. There were two reasons for this arrangement. The defence total was then limited to a ceiling figure within which the service departments found it difficult to finance housing. When the houses would be suitable for civilian occupation if the military left (and it was only in such cases that borrowing was permitted by the Act), it was thought reasonable to allow them to borrow just as local authorities borrow for housing. The arrangement is still in operation.

(b) What is the amount of the 'regular' national debt and by how much has it been reduced since the end of the war?

I am not quite sure what you mean by 'regular' national debt.

The total national debt on 31st March, 1952 was £25,890,000,000 as compared with £23,636,000,000 on 31st March, 1946, i.e. an increase of £2,254,000,000. But this increase is more than compensated for by the fact

[1] Her Majesty approved.
[2] See Churchill to Private Office, Oct. 12, reproduced above (p. 669).

that the 1952 figure includes £4,127,000,000 and the 1946 figure includes £731,000,000 of loans offset by assets (i.e. loans to local authorities; loans for purchase of the coal mines, to the Exchange Equalisation Account, etc.).

If loans offset by assets are excluded, the national debt has been reduced by £1,142,000,000 in the six years to 31st March, 1952.[1]

Winston S. Churchill to Randolph S. Churchill
(Churchill papers, 1/51)

16 October 1952

My dear Randolph,

I was so sorry that you did not feel able to come to Scarborough. When, in response to your call, I telephoned you, I thought it was all settled and that you would be with us at 9 o'clock. You could also have seen the Woodford delegation the next day, and we could have come back together. I am always nowadays much worried while making up a speech, and wished to be as much alone as possible on the journey down.

I am very much concerned about your health. What doctors are you consulting? If I were you I should have a thorough cure, even if it took a couple of months. There must be effective remedies nowadays. Pray let me know about this.

Randolph S. Churchill to Winston S. Churchill
(Churchill papers, 1/51)[2]

16 October 1952

My dear Papa,

Thank you for your letter. You seem to be indifferent to my reasons for not coming to Scarborough. I certainly do not wish to labour them. But I don't want them to be overlooked, still less to be misunderstood.

In your letter you say 'I am always nowadays much worried while making up a speech, and wished to be alone on the journey.' I can't actually recall any occasion when I have disturbed you when composing. Anyway, much though I rejoice in being in your company, particularly on great political outings, I have long abandoned any thought of ever proposing my presence to you either at your home or in public.

But – since there is no point in my writing to you at all unless I am frank – may I say that it has been a growing source of grief to me that ever since you first became Prime Minister you have repeatedly made it clear to me – and to

---

[1] Churchill wrote at the bottom of the page: 'Eleven hundred and forty-two millions! Not so bad.'
[2] This letter was handwritten.

others – that you no longer have that same desire for my company in private or in public which between 1923 and 1940 was the chief delight and pivot of my existence.

I recognize that when we are together these days I often say things of a provocative character. I assure you that I often try hard to avoid this. But I, who was once honoured by an intimacy with you which few have experienced, find it impossibly hard to sit at your table and prattle platitudes. Instead I attempt a paradox and, in the place of the tolerant comprehension I knew, my portion is snubs and insults, flouts and jeers, cries of 'shut up' which you never address to anyone else and which no one else would ever address to me. And all of this, mark you, when we are talking on an abstract topic like politics.

I have said that I know that I often say provocative – and needlessly provocative – things. (Such is often the tendency of spirited children with their parents.) Often, too, I indulge in cynicism and irony – doubtless in a clumsy fashion. But where, except at your table and at your feet did I learn to think that these were the most enjoyable vehicles of political talk and that levity and frivolity and unexpected heterodoxy were the proper terms in which the tiny minority who are interested in politics, to the exclusion of all else, should discuss their own peculiar brand of 'shop'?

I realize too that you regard me as a failure and that you cannot disguise this view entirely successfully from other people. Failure is of course a relative term and I should have thought that if you ever had time to cast an eye over the children of your political contemporaries you could scarcely regard my failure as absolute. My view, for what it's worth, is that I am not a failure in any terms. Perhaps I will be, but I haven't started yet. In any case the love of one friend for another cannot be affected by worldly success or failure.

What happened about Scarborough would not have been significant or important except that it followed on a score of similar, though partially veiled, incidents in the last few years. I have no wish to recall them. But when one is repeatedly disregarded, rejected and snubbed by the person one loves most in the world one's sensitivity forms a scar tissue of pride and arrogance which seems to protect the injury, not only from others, but (by self-deception) from oneself. But there are some calculated, cold-blooded, open rebuffs which only those of the meanest spirit can overlook.

If we are ever to be friends again (and I cherish this hope above all others in this world) you must, please, understand what you did to me last week. For otherwise you cannot possibly understand the basic cause of my unhappiness and disenchantment which make me in your eyes, and in those of many others, such an awkward customer.

It would never have occurred to me to suggest that I should journey with you to Scarborough. (Fifteen years ago I would have; but those golden days of our friendship and instinctive understanding are now nothing but precious memories – more irrevocably etched in my mind than any other experience.)

Of course if you had proposed it I should have been overjoyed. But when one afternoon I came home to find that your office had twice telephoned to ask what train I was taking to Scarborough my heart was filled with joy. Fool that I was, the idea never brushed my mind that the only purpose of the enquiry was to ensure that we should travel on separate trains. (And, what is so droll is that if you had not been at such pains to arrange this it would have happened anyway: I have never been a safe-creature.)

So, the following morning I rang you up. You were busy and called me back a few moments later. I asked you what train you were taking. After first establishing that you understood that I was taking the three o'clock, you said that you were taking the two o'clock. You added that I should not change my plans as you wished to be alone to work on your speech. I naturally accepted this. But I'm bound to say that I felt dunched. 'In my Father's house there are many mansions.' There's also lots of room in a private car; and still more on an express train.

This was a pretty hard knock. Far apart from my own feelings this odious situation was inevitably apparent to three other members (at least) of our family and also to your secretaries — not to speak of mine. But an additional laceration was to be drawn across the wounds of my pride. I was soon to learn that your desire for privacy (which you think worth repeating, even after this event, in your letter) was nothing of the sort. It was a simple desire for my absence.

Since I have never, and especially not in recent years, ever tried to thrust myself upon you this was for me a bitter moment in which, willy nilly, I had to face and accept something which had been creeping up on me for twelve years and which now could only be disregarded by a supreme act of moral cowardice.

I have no boats to burn. They have all mouldered, it seems, on the beaches long ago. I don't pretend to be an acute judge of human nature or character — least of all of my own. But of this I am sure: I have changed much less in the last ten years than you have.

In one thing I have never changed or faltered — my absolute love, devotion, and loyalty to you. At this moment I love you more than any man or woman I have ever met. I don't think that anything you could say or do to me or anyone else could make more than a dent in the whole hearted admiration I have for you and which, despite everything, has grown with the years.

Can't you understand the maladjustment, the frustration, yes even (recently) the jealousy that urges the bile of resentment when one's love is scorned as worthless and the person one loves scarcely troubles to hide from friend or foe the indifference or hostility which he feels?

All this permeates the fabric of our relationship. Usually a father and son get on well; (it is an easier relationship than marriage) and, if their interests happen to lie in the same direction, the relationship is that of partners. (Before the war this was virtually achieved.) Now all is changed to a horrible degree. And nothing will be improved by humbug.

Frankly I see no point in our continuing to meet as we have done since the war. The situation is only aggravated when we meet, as we do, occasionally, formally, half-heartedly, almost as a duty and with manifest misgiving on both sides.

What is odd, which I don't think you have noticed – I think Mamma has – is that both before and since the war we have always got on much better in public than in private. The very few times we have been on a jaunt together since the war – Metz, Luxembourg, Strasbourg, Plymouth – never a cross word. It is not for nothing that I coined the 'mot' about myself: 'Randolph should never be allowed out in private.'

I believe that a single episode with Anthony Eden in the Mediterranean (about which you were much too busy to understand the psychological background) has convinced you that I am wholly unfit to be in your company when persons of consequence are present. You assume that the rows we have in private would inevitably be duplicated in an even more painful fashion if outsiders were there. In fact this is the contrary of the truth.

I am confident that you will not do me the injustice of interpreting the foregoing as a plea to be invited to meet your colleagues. Many of them I meet most harmoniously and some of them are my close friends.

But the fact that I am never invited when you have any official guests shows the world as well as myself how low a view you take of me. God knows, I don't wish to come to your table, either when you are alone or with company, on the basis that it is a painful duty for you – a doubtful treat for me.

I should not repine if I only saw you five or six times a year provided that on those occasions you showed me, as in earlier days, your trust and affection which, with all my faults, I do not think I have deserved to forfeit.

From the time I was a school-boy I have followed your fortunes in good times and bad. Except for money, over which you have always been supremely generous, I don't think that I have ever asked you for anything. I ask something now: that you should try to understand me as I am (and not as you imagine I am or think I ought to be): that you should try once more to show me the love and trust which you brought me up to expect and value above all else in this life; and that if these two requests are too hard of fulfilment you will at least believe that not one word in this letter is intended as a reproach or even a self-justification. The only object of this excruciating exercise has been to try to explain to you some of the reasons for the wayward conduct and profound unhappiness of your devoted son,

Randolph.

PS. It is wrong of me to impose so long a letter on you. I can only hope that is it not so difficult to read as it was to write.

Lord Cherwell to Winston S. Churchill
(Premier papers, 11/250)

16 October 1952

The Foreign Office notes are mainly concerned with statements that the Communists have made, and their refutation.[1] The Foreign Office states quite clearly that there is no truth in the charges and they are trying to ensure that these do not gain acceptance by constant repetition.

I myself would not believe there was an iota of truth in the charges, even if no official denials had been issued. This is also the view of our germ warfare experts. Quite elaborate studies have been made as to what diseases and methods of spreading them could be used from the air, and only two so far seem to show the slightest promise. The disease the Communists charged the Americans with using did not include either of these until Needham[2] went out recently with other Communist scientists to 'investigate'; one of them was then mentioned, amongst many others of an absurd nature. This may have been chance, or Needham may have heard that it was a possibility.

The wild nature of the Communist charges, together with the innumerable inconsistencies in the statements of the American airmen and the lack of valid evidence from fanatics like Needham and the Dean of Canterbury, has, I believe, led all reasonable British scientists to discredit the whole of the Communist case.

If you wish I can give you more details of work which has been done on these questions.

P. G. Oates[3] to Clementine Churchill
(Premier papers, 11/204)

17 October 1952

The Prime Minister has agreed to inaugurate the War Memorial to members of both Houses of Parliament and servants of the two Houses who died in the war.

The ceremony is to be at 12.15 p.m. on November 12 in St Stephen's Hall. The Memorial takes the form of stained glass in the Great South Window and those taking part in the ceremony will be seated below the window in

---

[1] See M.498/52, reproduced above (p. 659).
[2] Noel Joseph Terence Montgomery Needham, 1900–95. Educated at Gonville and Caius College, Cambridge. Director, Sino-British Science Co-operation Office, Chongqing, 1942–6. First Head, Natural Sciences Section, UNESCO, Paris, 1946–8. George Sarton Medal, 1961. President of the Fellows of Gonville and Caius College, 1965; Master, 1966. Established Society for Anglo-Chinese Understanding, 1965. Fellow, British Academy, 1971. J. D. Bernal Award, 1984. Fukuoka Asian Culture Prize, 1990. CH, 1992.
[3] Peter Geoffrey Oates, 1919–2007. Asst Principal, Ministry of Transport, 1946–51. Private Secretary to PM, 1951–4.

St Stephen's Porch at the top of the steps which go down into the Hall.

The Duke of Wellington[1] on behalf of the joint Parliamentary War Memorial Committee is inviting the wives of the Party Leaders in both Houses and of the Speaker and the Lord Chancellor to attend the ceremony. Seats will be provided in St Stephen's Porch near to those to be occupied by those taking part in the ceremonial. The Duke has asked me to enquire whether you would like to be present.

The Prime Minister will speak for about 10 minutes and the whole ceremony will last about 20 minutes.[2]

Winston Churchill to Winston S. Churchill
(Churchill papers, 1/51)[3]

18 October 1952

Dear Grandpapa,

Thank you very much for the money you gave me. We had a film last night; it was a detective story. Grandmama sent me two lovely books and a cake. There were two football matches yesterday, we won both. I am sorry that I am so late in writing. It's alright at school but I am longing for the holidays. I hope you are well.

Lots of love

Winston S. Churchill to Anthony Eden
Prime Minister's Personal Minute M.510/52
(Premier papers, 11/231)

18 October 1952

Mr Leather[4] has no authority from me to make any such statements.* Some of them are quite sensible but I never made them to him, or, still less, authorized him to utter them on my behalf. He has, in my opinion, behaved improperly. Do you think any action should be taken?

* That PM would visit Washington in March 1953.

---

[1] Gerald Wellesley, 1885–1972. Educated at Eton. Joined Diplomatic Corps, 1908. 3rd Secretary, Diplomatic Service, 1910–17; 2nd Secretary, 1917–19. Married, 1914, Dorothy Violet Ashton: two children. Fellow, Royal Institute of British Architects, 1921. Fellow, Royal Society of Arts, 1935. Lt-Col., Grenadier Guards, 1939. On active service, 1939–45. Succeeded as Duke of Wellington, 1943. KG, 1951.

[2] Clementine Churchill replied on Oct. 18: 'Yes, I would very much like to be present.'

[3] This letter was handwritten.

[4] Edwin Hartley Cameron Leather, 1919–2005. Born in Toronto, Canada. Served in 1st Canadian Parachute Battalion, WWII. Parachuted into Normandy on D-Day. MP (Cons.) for North Somerset, 1950–64. Knighted, 1962. Governor of Bermuda, 1973–7. KCMG, 1974. KCVO, 1975.

Anthony Eden to Winston S. Churchill
(Churchill papers, 2/517)

21 October 1952
Personal and Secret
PM/52/125

Your personal minute M.512/52.

Before I saw your minute I had already approved a Cabinet Paper about releasing fifteen obsolescent jet aircraft to Egypt. You will not yet have seen it.

2. Israel has already been offered a like number. So have one or two Arab States. You have often told me that you had some hopes of Neguib. This small instalment against the payments on account for much larger numbers which Egypt has already made does not seem to raise the big issues brought up in your minute. Let us discuss these separately.

Cabinet: conclusions
(Cabinet papers, 128/25)

21 October 1952
Secret
11.30 a.m.
Cabinet Meeting No. 87 of 1952

1. The Prime Minister said that the forthcoming by-election at High Wycombe was of such importance that the Cabinet should consider whether it warranted a departure from the tradition that Cabinet Ministers did not speak in by-elections.

Discussions showed that it was the general view of the Cabinet that on this occasion an exception should be made from the normal rule. It was agreed that it would suffice if one member of the Cabinet spoke in the High Wycombe election; and the Chief Whip was invited to make arrangements accordingly.

The Cabinet also agreed that no change should be made, by reason of this by-election, in the arrangements already made for Party political broadcasts for the current quarter.

2. The Cabinet considered memoranda by the Lord Chancellor (C(52)321 and 345) and the Chancellor of the Exchequer (C(52)334) regarding the need to increase the remuneration of Judges of the High Court.

The Lord Chancellor said that it was clear, from preliminary consultations which he had held, that there was general agreement among his colleagues that some improvement should be made in the financial position of the Judges. The main question for decision by the Cabinet was the method by which this should be done. There seemed to be a general disposition against granting an increase in salary; and the choice seemed to be to lie between granting a tax-free allowance in addition to the existing salary, or providing that some part of the existing salary should be free of tax.

The Prime Minister said that a High Court Judge was in a unique position, and was not to be compared with the holder of any other office in public service. This had been marked by the quite exceptional level of the salary fixed in 1832. The position and respect thus accorded to the Judges had enabled them to maintain, throughout a hundred years and more, the unrivalled reputation of the English Bench for integrity and impartiality of judgment. This was a national asset which the Conservative Party should feel honoured to uphold. It could not be maintained if leading barristers were unwilling to accept appointments to the Bench or, even worse, if Judges should feel obliged for financial reasons to resume practice at the Bar. There was in his view an overwhelming case for putting the Judges well beyond the possibility of financial embarrassment, and he thought that the proper course was to arrange that £2,000 of a Judge's salary should be free of all taxation. This would follow the precedent created by the Labour Government, who had arranged for £4,000 of the Prime Minister's salary to be free of tax.

The Chancellor of the Exchequer said that this tax concession to the Prime Minister was based on the expenses which he necessarily incurred in the performance of his official duties. It was admitted that the Judges had no necessary expenses connected with their work which would afford anything like the relief which it was desired to give them. Under the existing law the Board of Inland Revenue had no authority to grant tax-free allowances to the Judges of anything like the amount which the Lord Chancellor and the Prime Minister now had in mind. If a tax concession of this order was to be made, if would have to be authorised by special legislation. The Judges would then be the only members of the community to enjoy a substantial tax-free allowance quite unrelated to the expenses necessary for the performance of their duties. Might they not feel that this placed them in a somewhat invidious position?

It was the general view of the Cabinet that a concession of this kind could be justified, especially if it were authorised by specific legislation, on the ground that the Judges occupied a unique position in the community.

The Cabinet were informed that the Secretary of State for Scotland, who was unable to be present, wished to put forward a claim on behalf of the Scottish Judges, not merely that they should receive a tax concession comparable to any granted to the English Judges, but also that their remuneration should be brought more closely into line with that of the English Judges.

The Cabinet –
  (1) Agreed in principle that remuneration of the Judges should be improved by arranging for a proportion of their existing annual salary to be exempted from all taxation; took note that legislation would be required for this purpose; and invited the Lord Chancellor

and the Chancellor of the Exchequer to work out a detailed scheme and submit it for final approval by the Cabinet.

(2) Invited the Lord Chancellor to discuss with the Secretary of State for Scotland how corresponding concessions could best be made to the Judges of Scottish Courts.

[. . .]

7. The Prime Minister said that Ministers should take note of public comment on the proposed arrangements for the Coronation. It would be helpful if the Minister of Works would circulate a paper setting out the main points of criticism and the arguments in favour of the arrangements proposed.

The Cabinet's discussion turned mainly on the question whether the Coronation ceremony within the Abbey should be televised. In their earlier discussions on this point the Cabinet had been influenced by the importance of avoiding unnecessary strain for Her Majesty and upholding the sanctity of the ceremony. Some Ministers felt that this decision might be reviewed in the light of the serious public disappointment which it had caused.

The Cabinet –

(1) Invited the Minister of Works to circulate a paper setting out the arguments in favour of certain arrangements for the Coronation which were now the subject of public criticism.

(2) Invited the Prime Minister to arrange for the question of televising the Coronation ceremony within the Abbey to be reviewed by a small group of Ministers, in consultation with the Archbishop of Canterbury, the Earl Marshal[1] and the Dean of Westminster.

[. . .]

Winston S. Churchill: speech
(Hansard)

23 October 1952   House of Commons

ATOM BOMB TEST, AUSTRALIA

The Prime Minister: With your permission, Sir, I shall now make a statement in answer to Question No. 45, asked by my hon. Friend the Member for Morecambe and Lonsdale (Sir I. Fraser).

The object of the test was to investigate the effects of an atomic explosion in a harbour. The weapon was accordingly placed in HMS *Plym*, a frigate of 1,450 tons, which was anchored in the Monte Bello Islands.

Conditions were favourable and care was taken to wait for southerly winds

---

[1] Bernard Marmaduke Fitzalan-Howard, 1908–75. Succeeded as 16th Duke of Norfolk and Earl Marshal, 1917. Served in Royal Horse Guards, 1931–3; 4th Territorial Army Battalion, 1934. Married, 1937, Lavinia Mary Strutt: four children. Maj., 1939.

so as to avoid the possibility of any significant concentration of radio-active particles spreading over the Australian mainland.

Specimen structures of importance to Civil Defence and to the Armed Services were erected at various distances. Instruments were set up to record the effect of contamination, blast, heat flash, gamma ray flash and other factors of interest.

The weapon was exploded in the morning of 3rd October. Thousands of tons of water and of mud and rock from the sea bottom were thrown many thousands of feet into the air and a high tidal wave was caused. The effects of blast and radio-active contamination extended over a wide area and HMS *Plym* was vaporised except for some red hot fragments which were scattered over one of the islands and started fires in the dry vegetation.

Very soon after the explosion two naval officers undertook the dangerous task of flying helicopters over the heavily contaminated lagoon where *Plym* had lain. This was in order to take samples of the water so that its radio-activity could be measured. After a longer interval, scientists and Service personnel in protective clothing entered the contaminated area to examine the effect and to recover records.

Technical descriptions of the performance of the bomb cannot, of course, be given. It may, however, be said that the weapon behaved exactly as expected and forecast in many precise details by Dr W. G. Penney,[1] whose services were of the highest order. Scientific observations and measurements show that the weapon does not contradict the natural expectation that progress in this sphere would be continual.

To give some idea of the character of the explosion perhaps I might say this: normal blood temperature is 98⅖ degrees. Many of us go over 100 degrees. When the flash first burst through the hull of *Plym* the temperature was nearly 1 million degrees. It was, of course, far higher at the point of explosion.

The explosion caused no casualties to the personnel of the expedition. No animals were used in the test. Apart from some local rats which were killed, no mammals were seen in the affected area and such birds as there were had mostly been frightened away by the earlier preparations.

Her Majesty's Government in the United Kingdom wish to express their indebtedness for all the help received from Australia. Not only did the Australian Commonwealth allow us to use their territory for the test, but all branches of their Government, and particularly the Navy, Army and Air Force, gave

---

[1] William George Penney, 1909–91. Atomic scientist and leading figure in Britain's nuclear programme. Educated at Royal College of Science, London University; PhD, 1935. Asst Prof. of Mathematics, Imperial College of Science, London, 1936–45. Scientist, Ministry of Home Security and Admiralty, 1940–4. Principal Scientific Officer, DSIR, 1944–5. Chief Superintendent, Armament Research, Ministry of Supply, 1946–52. Director, Atomic Weapons Research Establishment, Aldermaston, 1953–9. Member for Weapons R&D, UKAEA, 1954–9; Member for Research, 1959–61; Deputy Chairman, 1961–4; Chairman, 1964–7. Rector, Imperial College of Science and Technology, 1967–73.

us most valuable collaboration in the preparation and execution of this most important experiment.

All those concerned in the production of the first British atomic bomb are to be warmly congratulated on the successful outcome of an historic episode and I should no doubt pay my compliments to the Leader of the Opposition and the party opposite for initiating it.

Sir I. Fraser: Can my right hon. Friend say whether any new scientific knowledge has emerged which will lead to improved weapons or to a speedier use of nuclear fission in industrial matters?

The Prime Minister: I have carefully considered the terms of the statement I have made to the House, and I do not wish to add to them at the present moment.

Mr Shinwell: May I ask the right hon. Gentleman whether the United States authorities have asked for information about the results of the test, and whether, if it is intended to furnish them with information, it will be on the basis of reciprocity?

The Prime Minister: The original arrangements made in the war were, of course, on the basis of strict equality and reciprocity. Those results were superseded by other arrangements after the war. We have conducted this operation ourselves, and I do not doubt that it will lead to a much closer American interchange of information than has hitherto taken place – than has taken place in the last two years – but I do not wish to make any statement on the subject.

Mr Emrys Hughes: Is the Prime Minister aware that the note of flippancy which crept into his statement will appal many people who visualise what would happen to us in this country if an atomic bomb were dropped in the Port of London? Is it not now quite clear that this country is in enormous danger and that the atom bomb ought to be exported to America?

The Prime Minister: I think that this raises very large issues. There is no question of flippancy in what I say. I am only stating the facts. One may be confronted with very terrible facts – we live in a very terrible age – but there is no reason why we should lose our spirits.

Mr Beswick:[1] Would the Prime Minister not agree that the bombs which the Americans originally exploded would not have been possible had it not been for the contributions of Dr Penney, and furthermore, would he not agree that Dr Penney himself would not have helped create the weapon which was exploded in Australia had it not been for his experience in the laboratories of the United States? If we are to have further progress in this matter, in the civil and military field, would it not be better if we could get the closest possible

---

[1] Frank Beswick, 1911–87. Joined RAF, 1940. MP (Lab.) for Uxbridge, 1945–59. Parliamentary Secretary, Ministry of Civil Aviation, 1950–1. Baron, 1964. Parliamentary Under-Secretary of State, Commonwealth Office, 1965–7. Government Chief Whip, House of Lords, 1967–70. PC, 1968. Chief Opposition Whip, 1970–4. Minister of State for Industry, 1974–5. Deputy Leader, House of Lords, 1974–5. Chairman, British Aerospace, 1976–80.

co-operation between the United States and ourselves, and will he do all that he possibly can to facilitate that co-operation?

The Prime Minister: There are a very large number of important people in the United States concerned with this matter who have been most anxious for a long time that Britain should be kept better informed. This event will greatly facilitate and support the task which these gentlemen have set themselves.

Mr S. Silverman: Can the right hon. Gentleman tell the House approximately what was the total cost of this experimental explosion, and will he bear in mind that to some of us it is no comfort at all to realise that both the major parties in the State are equally responsible for this colossal folly?

The Prime Minister: I do not know that we are equally responsible. We took the matter up at the point at which it was left to us. It seems to me that the problem is one which faces us all equally. Even if one sits below the Gangway, one does not escape the responsibility.

Mr Silverman: What about the cost?

The Prime Minister: As to the cost, I have said before, as an old Parliamentarian, that I was rather astonished that well over £100 million should be disbursed without Parliament being made aware of it. I was a bit astonished. However, there is the story, and we now have a result which on the whole, I think, will be beneficial to public safety. As for the future, I think we must be guided by the precedents established under the last régime as to detailed accounts and the way in which the expenditure is recorded.

Cabinet: conclusions
(Cabinet papers, 128/25)

23 October 1952
Secret
11 a.m.
Cabinet Meeting No. 89 of 1952

[...]

2. The Prime Minister drew attention to the strength of the views expressed in the debate in the House of Lords on the previous day in favour of restoring corporal punishment as a penalty for crimes of violence. He thought it would be unwise for the Government to close their minds to the possibility of restoring this penalty if the case for doing so were fully established and public opinion hardened in favour of it. There had been a great increase in crime and the prisons were overcrowded: the problem of prison administration would be eased if, through having discretion to impose corporal punishment the courts sentenced fewer offenders to long terms of imprisonment.

The Lord Chancellor said that, since corporal punishment was abolished in 1948, the incidence of offences for which it could then be imposed had in fact decreased. The demand voiced in the House of Lords debate that it should be available as a penalty for all crimes of violence involved reverting not merely to 1948 but substantially to 1827, when felonies were punishable by death and misdemeanours by whipping. In reply to the debate he had taken the line that, before corporal punishment was restored, the Act of 1948 should be given a longer trial and Parliament should be satisfied first that corporal punishment would be an effective means of checking the increase in violent crime and, secondly, that no other penalty would be equally effective.

The Prime Minister said that it would be useful if, at some convenient opportunity, the Cabinet held a fuller discussion on this question.

The Cabinet – Invited the Home Secretary to circulate a memorandum which would serve as a basis for discussion on the question of corporal punishment as a penalty for crimes of violence.

[. . .]

Winston S. Churchill to Bill Deakin
(Churchill papers, 4/74)

25 October 1952

My dear Bill,

As I mentioned to you some months ago, there will be no more group work on the book after this month, as I shall not be able to do anything on it until just before it is published. At this stage I do not know when that is likely to be, or whether indeed it will be published while I am in office. However I hope you will not mind if I write to you, should anything crop up on it in the meantime.

Thank you very much indeed for all your help to me during these past years. I greatly value the work you have done.

PS. I am hoping to see you and Pussy[1] one day when we get into the new Session.

---

[1] Livia Stela Nasta, 1916–2006. Known as 'Pussy'. Secretary, Ministry of Cooperation, Bucharest, 1939. Fled Romania, 1941. Secretary, Sqn Ldr, RAF 2nd Photographic Reconnaissance Unit, Heliopolis, Egypt, 1941. Joined SOE, 1942. Married, 1943, William Deakin.

October 1952

Winston S. Churchill to Sir Norman Brook
Prime Minister's Personal Minute M.519/52
(*Premier papers, 11/34*)

26 October 1952

I think the answer[1] on Tuesday might be something on these lines:

'Although I am willing to answer these questions the House must understand that there are many points connected with the Coronation of which the Prime Minister or the Cabinet are by no means the sole or even the decisive judges. According to precedent and custom the arrangements are made by the Coronation Commission, which have representatives of all Parties of the Commonwealth countries and various high functionaries upon it, including the Earl Marshal, who has special hereditary duties. The Chairman is the Duke of Edinburgh. I cannot therefore, on behalf of myself and my colleagues, accept direct or undue responsibility for the conclusions which are reached, after much careful thought, and have no aim but the public welfare and happiness in the many realms owing allegiance to the Crown, while preserving the traditions of our ancient monarchies.

In practice proposals are made by the Coronation Joint Committee presided over by the Earl Marshal. It is not practicable for all the members of the Commission to be members of this Committee, but all are consulted in the sense that they are informed of what the Committee have proposed and have full opportunity to make comments before these conclusions are ratified by the Coronation Commission. In the case of the announcement made last week, no comments or dissent had been received from any of the members of the Commission, who had been asked to make any such observations before July 21. It is not therefore correct to say that the Commission had not been consulted on the announcement, which was made in due course by the Earl Marshal.

However matters of this complex character, with many novel features, may well be reviewed as the event approaches. It appears, for instance, that television requires no lighting additional to what would be provided for black and white films, and less lighting than is required for colour films. It therefore does not seem that there is any practical or technical reason for differentiating between the television and the filming. There is I feel a broad general opinion in this country at least – though, as I have said, I accept no personal responsibility, and I certainly do not claim to be its judge

---

[1] To the questions asked by Lt-Col. Lipton, MP (Lab.) for Brixton on Oct. 23: 'What advice was tendered by Her Majesty's Government in connection with the arrangements for televising the Coronation ceremony?' and 'Is the Prime Minister aware that it is reported that the advice of the Cabinet was sought; that the ban on television has caused bitter disappointment to a very large number of loyal subjects; and will he, therefore, be so kind as to make representations, either to lift or to modify the ban so that this historic national occasion is not unnecessarily marred by a wide-spread sense of grievance?'

– that the modern mechanical arrangements should enable the many millions of people outside the Abbey to see what is seen by the congregation of notables in the Abbey. I am speaking of the general congregation and not of course of what is seen by the high ecclesiastical dignitaries and state functionaries, whose duties require them to be close to The Sovereign. It is not thought that in practice it will be difficult to carry this principle into effect, mainly that the world can see what the congregation in the Abbey see and hear. Certainly it would be unfitting that the whole Ceremony, not only in its secular but also in its religious and spiritual aspects, should be presented as if it were a theatrical performance. I do not think the problem, approached on these lines, is by no means insoluble.

I believe it would be for the public advantage if the Coronation Commission were to consider any new report which later knowledge and reflection permit the Earl Marshal's Committee to make to them. More than that I do not feel entitled to say this afternoon, and I am sure it would not be in the public interest that Parliament should become an active debating centre for issues of this character. Above all, let me make it clear that the responsibility rests collectively with the Coronation Commission, one of whose duties it is to ensure that The Queen herself is not brought into any form of controversy.'

Winston S. Churchill to Members of the Cabinet
(Cabinet papers, 129/56)

27 October 1952
Confidential
Cabinet Paper No. 367 of 1952

TELEVISION AT THE CORONATION

I am concerned at the public disappointment caused by the announcement that there would be no television of the Coronation east of the Screen in Westminster Abbey. Together with certain of my Cabinet colleagues I have discussed this matter informally with the Archbishop of Canterbury, the Earl Marshal and the Queen's Private Secretary. As a result I am satisfied that the earlier decision should be reviewed and that, subject to The Queen's approval and convenience, some parts of the actual ceremony within the Screen should be televised.

2. I commend the following principles for consideration by the Cabinet:
    (i) No differentiation should be made between those parts of the ceremony to be televised and those to be filmed.
    (ii) The anointing of The Queen, the Prayer of Consecration and

the Sacrament itself should be excluded from both the films and television.
(iii) No 'close-up' views of The Queen should be photographed, filmed or televised at any stage of the ceremony.
(iv) Subject to (ii) and (iii) above, facilities to televise the proceedings beyond the Screen should be granted, on the general understanding that television should furnish no more intimate a view than that which would be available to a spectator seated east of the Screen in the Abbey.
(v) Permission to televise should be subject to approval by the appropriate authorities of the technical arrangements for the placing of the cameras and the handling of the transmission.

3. If the Cabinet endorse these principles, I will so inform the Earl Marshal who would, after consulting the Coronation Joint Committee, seek the approval of the Coronation Commission and the Coronation Committee of the Privy Council for a suitable submission to The Queen.

4. I take this opportunity to make it clear that, contrary to reports which have appeared in the Press, the earlier recommendation of the Coronation Joint Committee against the use of television east of the Screen was submitted in writing to all the members of the Commission and of the Committee of the Privy Council on 15th July, 1952. It was accompanied by a covering note to the effect that in the absence of comment by 21st July it would be assumed that the Commission and the Committee approved the recommendation.

Winston S. Churchill to Queen Elizabeth II
(Premier papers, 11/36)

27 October 1952

Mr Churchill with his humble duty to The Queen begs to advise Your Majesty that at the Opening of Parliament on November 4 it would be appropriate to make the formal Declaration on the Protestant Accession to the Throne. The form of this Declaration is prescribed by the Accession Declaration Act of 1910 in the following terms:

'I, – , do solemnly and sincerely in the presence of God profess, testify and declare that I am a faithful Protestant, and that I will, according to the true intent of the enactments which secure the Protestant succession to the Throne of my Realm, uphold and maintain the said enactments to the best of my powers according to law.'

In 1937 His late Majesty was advised to make this Declaration omitting the words 'of my Realm' on the ground that they did not take account of the independent status of the Dominions which had been affirmed by the Statute of Westminster. Mr Churchill considers that on the present occasion Your Majesty would do well to follow the precedent established by King George VI.

Mr Churchill feels that Your Majesty will Yourself wish to decide whether to use the title 'Elizabeth' or 'Elizabeth the Second' in the opening words of the Declaration.[1]

Cabinet: conclusions
(Cabinet papers, 128/25)

28 October 1952
Secret
11 a.m.
Cabinet Meeting No. 90 of 1952

[. . .]

6. The Cabinet had before them a memorandum by the Prime Minister (C(52)367)[2] suggesting that the Coronation Commission should be invited to review their earlier decision that no facilities should be given for televising the Coronation ceremonies east of the Screen in Westminster Abbey.

The Prime Minister said that he had been concerned at the public disappointment caused by this decision and, together with certain of his Cabinet colleagues, he had discussed the matter informally with the Archbishop of Canterbury, the Earl Marshal and The Queen's Private Secretary. As a result, he suggested that the decision might now be reviewed on the basis of the principles which he had set out in paragraph 2 of his memorandum. He did not think it would be possible to defend against public criticism a decision which discriminated between the televising and the filming of the ceremony. The spiritual parts of the proceedings should be excluded from both the films and television, but the other proceedings within the Screen might, he thought, be televised on the general understanding that no more intimate a view would be given than that which would be available to the average person seated within the Screen.

The Prime Minister also read to the Cabinet the draft of a statement which he was proposing to make in the House of Commons that afternoon in reply to Questions on this matter.[3]

In discussion there was general support for the principles set out in the Prime Minister's memorandum C(52)367. The Cabinet were, however, informed that the technical problems of televising the proceedings within the Screen had not yet been fully explored, and that it might be unwise to give

---
[1] Her Majesty gave her approval and noted in the last paragraph her preference for 'Elizabeth' over 'Elizabeth the Second'.
[2] Reproduced above (p. 688–9).
[3] M.519/52, reproduced above (pp. 687–8).

the impression that this amount of television would be allowed until it was certain that all the technical difficulties could be overcome. It was agreed that words should be added to the statements which the Prime Minister was to make in the House of Commons that afternoon in order to safeguard the possibility that the televising of the ceremony might have to be further curtailed on account of technical difficulties. In this connection it was also agreed that additional lighting within the Screen, whether for television or for colour film, should not be permitted to an extent which would impair the dignity of the proceedings.

The Cabinet –

(1) Invited the Prime Minister to ask the Earl Marshal to move the Coronation Commission to review, in the light of the principles set out in paragraph 2 of C(52)367, their earlier decision that no part of the Coronation ceremony within the Screen at Westminster Abbey should be televised.

(2) Took note with approval of the statement in this matter which the Prime Minister was proposing to make that afternoon in the House of Commons; and invited the Commonwealth Secretary to make a corresponding statement in the House of Lords.

The Cabinet had before them a note by the Prime Minister (C(52)353) covering a minute by the Earl Marshal seeking guidance on proposals for allocating seats in Westminster Abbey at the Coronation. Under this plan it was proposed that, in order to provide places for representatives of other Commonwealth countries and of Trade Unions, the seats available for Members of the House of Lords and of the House of Commons should be restricted to 880 and 650 respectively; that the general body of Peers and Members of the House of Commons should ballot for seats; that Peers successful in the ballot should be allowed to be accompanied by the Peeresses or Dowager Peeresses; and that Members of the House of Commons successful in the ballot should be allowed to be accompanied by their spouses.

In discussion it was suggested that, if 650 seats were available for Members of the House of Commons, it might be preferable that any Member should be allowed to claim a seat as of right and that the balance should be available for wives of Members to be selected by ballot. A similar arrangement could perhaps be adopted for the general body of Peers. The Minister of Works might provide special facilities on the route of the procession for Members of both Houses of Parliament who were not given seats in the Abbey.

Some arrangement would also have to be made for determining the extent to which Trade Union representatives should be accompanied by their wives; but the best course there might be to allot a definite number of seats for Trade Union representatives and leave it to the Trade Union Congress to determine which of the representatives chosen could be accompanied by their wives.

Comment was made on the large numbers of seats which it was proposed to allot to members of the Civil Services and Fighting Services. It was pointed out that these Services were now much larger than they had been in 1937. On the other hand, they included a larger number of Knights Grand Cross, for whom separate provision was to be made in the Abbey. It was thought that on this account there was scope for some further reduction in the number of seats allotted to the Services.

The Cabinet –

(3) Invited the Minister of Works to make, in the light of their discussion, a critical analysis of the proposals set out in C(52)353 for the allocation of seats in Westminster Abbey and to submit this, together with his recommendations, to the Prime Minister.

The Cabinet had before them a memorandum by the Minister of Works (C(52)358) setting out the main arguments for and against certain aspects of the Coronation arrangements which had been the subject of public comment.

The Cabinet discussion turned on the plans for providing seats along the route of the Coronation procession. Comment was made on the high charges which were being made for accommodation in private buildings along the route. The Cabinet recognised that it would be impracticable to regulate these charges by any system of price control, and that public action to check extortionate charges must be limited to increasing as far as possible the number of seats to be provided by public authorities. The proposed extension of the outward route should be of value from this point of view.

The cost of erecting Government stands along the route would be even higher than had been expected and, if the full cost was to be recovered from seat-holders, the charges would have to be at least £6 for a covered seat and £4 for an uncovered seat. Some of the Commonwealth High Commissioners in London were inclined to suggest that these prices were too high, particularly as some of them had made tentative arrangements on the basis of earlier, and lower, estimates of the charges which were likely to be made. The Cabinet agreed, however, to maintain the principle that the United Kingdom Exchequer could not be expected to make any contribution towards the cost of erecting these stands – though other Commonwealth Governments and organisations like the Trades Union Congress, who took over whole stands from the Ministry of Works at the full cost, would be free, if they chose, to sell the seats at lower prices and make up the difference themselves.

The Cabinet –

(4) Took note of this memorandum by the Minister of Works.

[. . .]

Winston S. Churchill to Anthony Eden
Prime Minister's Personal Minute M.522/52
(Premier papers, 11/90)

28 October 1952
Private

1. I think it a pity to tie up the five jets[1] with compensation for the Turf Club murders. (This I suppose will be paid out of sterling balances.) The five jets like the £5 million is defensible as a gesture to show our general friendliness to the regime or Neguib. All the point is taken out of it if it is tied up to some minor, if serious, grievance we have with the Egyptians. Nothing is often achieved between countries by making small bargains.

2. To me the greatest issue in this part of the world is not deserting Israel. She is only getting a quarter of the jets which it is proposed to give to various Arab states apart from the five promised to Egypt. There might have been something in opening the Canal to Israelite trade and to foster a more friendly feeling between Egypt and Israel by the growing influence we may establish with the Egyptians. But the Turf Club murders compensation seems to me irrelevant to the large emotional issues which are dominant.

Winston S. Churchill to Clement Attlee
(Premier papers, 11/34)

28 October 1952

My dear Attlee,

In view of our discussions after Question time today I send you a copy of the paper which was sent on July 15 from the Secretary of the Coronation Commission[2] to you and Morrison. You will notice that on Page 7, Paragraph 5, it is distinctly stated that the Committee's view that television should be restricted to the processions west of the Choir Screen was fortified by the knowledge that the problem had recently been considered by the Cabinet and that the views of the Cabinet were similar to those which were expressed. This fact was also made public in the Duke of Norfolk's communiqué issued on October 20 in which he said that the decision of the Coronation Joint Executive Committee had been made 'with the consent of

[1] See Eden to Churchill, Oct. 21, reproduced above (p. 680). Churchill appears to misremember the number of aircraft: the following telegram Eden sends to Stevenson in Egypt refers to 15 jet aircraft, not five (PREM 11/90).

[2] Robert Uchtred Eyre Knox, 1889–1965. War Office Secretariat, 1912–14. On active service, 1914–16 (DSO, despatches, severely wounded). War Office, 1918–19. Treasury, 1920. Private Secretary to Permanent Secretary to the Treasury, 1928–39. CVO, 1933. Secretary, Coronation Commission, 1936–7. KCVO, 1937. Secretary, Political Honours Scrutiny Committee, 1939–65. Secretary, Coronation Commission, 1952–3. KCB, 1953.

the Coronation Commission and after receiving the advice of the Cabinet'.

I had not seen the public communiqué and did not feel I had authority without consultation to reveal the opinion of any members of the Coronation Commission or the Coronation Committee of the Privy Council. Otherwise I would of course have said that the Cabinet's agreement with the recommendations had already been made public by the Earl Marshal.[1]

Winston S. Churchill: speech
('Winston S. Churchill, His Complete Speeches', volume 8, page 8421)

28 October 1952   Unveiling of a Commemorative Panel
                                                          Westminster, London

...[2] It is inspiring to sit in the chair of Gladstone, but the precedent of the age at which Gladstone retired might well, if I did not issue some word of reassurance, have a serious effect on morale in many places. (*Laughter.*)

(Editor's Note:[3] Concerning the building of the new House of Commons, Mr Churchill said): I hold strong views, which the Leader of the Opposition shares. I laid down the principle, which was thought very odd outside this country, that on no account must the chamber be big enough to contain all its members. That principle has been carried out to the satisfaction of all who have thus been enabled to speak with a considerable audience facing them, instead of rows of empty writing desks. On the other hand, it is right that the Press Gallery has been given more roomy and convenient accommodation than formerly.

The important function that the Press Gallery has to discharge is to give a fair and truthful representation of what has passed in the House of Commons. In my lifetime, I have seen the reporting of the debates in Parliament sink a great deal as a factor in our public life. Far less space is given to it in the newspapers, but apart from that, the debates are not read with as great attention as they used to be, by a far smaller audience, 50 years ago, when I first cast my eyes on this scene of strife and turmoil.

This diminution makes the work of parliamentary reporters more important because the selective faculty comes into play far more.

The tradition that misrepresentation should be avoided has been very largely upheld. Those who carry on the important duties of the Press Gallery are tenants of a clean and honourable estate through which the food and fertilization of the minds of the country are well supplied.

---

[1] Attlee responded: 'Thank you so much for sending me a copy of the report of the Coronation Committee. I recall now that I saw this but the particular point with regard to television escaped my attention.'

[2] The text was truncated by the editor of *His Complete Speeches*, Robert Rhodes James.

[3] Note added by the editor, Robert Rhodes James.

OCTOBER 1952

Cabinet: conclusions
(Cabinet papers, 128/25)

29 October 1952
Secret
11 a.m.
Cabinet Meeting No. 91 of 1952

[...]

7. The Cabinet considered a memorandum by the Foreign Secretary (C(52)369) on the question of resuming defence negotiations with the Egyptian Government.

The Foreign Secretary said that, since this problem was last considered by the Cabinet, there had been several significant changes in the situation. Turkey had come into the Middle East as a firm Ally, and some progress was being made towards the establishment of the Middle East Defence Organisation. The new régime in Egypt offered a better prospect of a satisfactory agreement than we had had for some time past. Financial and strategic considerations suggested that British military strength in the Middle East might be less, in peace and in war, than had previously been assumed. In the light of these new facts the Minister of Defence and the Chiefs of Staff were reviewing afresh the whole of our defence policy in the Middle East; and it should be our aim to defer the resumption of formal defence negotiations with the Egyptian Government until that review had been completed. He proposed to instruct HM Ambassador in Cairo accordingly. It might, however, prove impossible to avoid any discussion with the Egyptians on defence questions; and he therefore proposed to authorise the Ambassador to be guided in any interim discussions by the principles set out in paragraph 8 of his memorandum. These were, briefly, (i) that we should not for the present withdraw any troops from the Canal Zone – though at a later stage, if we were satisfied that defence discussions were making real progress and that operation Rodeo (for the protection of British lives in Cairo and Alexandria) would no longer be required, we would start withdrawing troops which had been sent in earlier in the year to reinforce the normal garrison; (ii) that we should seek to maintain our base though, as part of a general agreement, we would be ready to entrust its custody to the Egyptians; (iii) that we should be prepared to set up an Anglo-Egyptian Air Defence organisation; (iv) that Egypt should undertake to give us and our Allies in the Middle East Defence Organisation full military facilities in time of war or imminent threat of war; and (v) that any new defence agreement would be regarded as superseding the Anglo-Egyptian Treaty of 1936.

The Chief of the Imperial General Staff said that the Chiefs of Staff fully agreed that we should seek to defer the resumption of defence negotiations with Egypt until we had completed our review of defence policy in the Middle

East. Meanwhile, however, the Chiefs of Staff were inclined to favour action which might strengthen the new Egyptian Government which, they believed, was more likely to take a realistic view of defence problems than its predecessors had been. They favoured a limited supply of arms, including jet aircraft, to Egypt. They were also prepared to begin the withdrawal of the British reinforcements which had been sent to the Middle East at the time of the disorders in Egypt at the beginning of the year. They now thought it most unlikely that need would arise to carry out operation Rodeo: moreover, while the present Egyptian Government remained in office, it was doubtful whether we should be able to undertake that operation with the troops at our disposal.

The Minister of Defence endorsed these views, and recommended that an early start be made in withdrawing some of the troops which had been sent to reinforce the British garrison in the Middle East. Should we not make a start, for example, by withdrawing the 16th Parachute Brigade from Cyprus? The Foreign Secretary said that he would like to know what HM Ambassador in Cairo thought about this before any final decision was taken.

The Cabinet –
  (1) Agreed that we should seek to defer the resumption of defence negotiations with the Egyptian Government until the review of defence policy in the Middle East had been completed, and invited the Foreign Secretary to inform HM Ambassador at Cairo accordingly.
  (2) Authorised the Foreign Secretary to instruct HM Ambassador at Cairo that, if in the meantime he found it necessary to engage in any discussion with the Egyptians on defence questions, he should be guided by the principles set out in paragraph 8 of C(52)369.
  (3) Invited the Foreign Secretary to consult further with the Minister of Defence regarding the proposed withdrawal of the 16th Parachute Brigade from Cyprus after HM Ambassador at Cairo had been given an opportunity to say what effect this movement might have on the Egyptian Government.

In connection with the discussion recorded above, reference was made to the proposal to move the British Headquarters organisation in the Middle East from the Canal Zone to Cyprus. The Minister of Defence and the Secretary of State for War said that a great deal of constructional work would have to be carried out before this move could be begun, and it was most desirable that authority should be given to put this in hand without further delay. The cost of completing the whole transfer would be very large; but this would be spread over a number of years and it was only the preliminary work for which authority was now being sought.

The Prime Minister asked whether it was feasible to sanction any part of this plan until more was known about the future strength of our garrison in the Middle East. Large issues of policy were still undetermined. He himself still hoped that it might be possible to persuade the United States to take some share of the responsibility for safeguarding the Suez Canal as an international waterway, so that we could hand over our responsibilities in Egypt to an international organisation in which the United States and ourselves would both play some part. It was surely too early to take final decisions about the size of the military organisation to be established at Cyprus. He also wished to have some further information about the disposal of the stores and equipment now in the British base at Tel el Kebir.

In further discussion it was suggested that some work could be put in hand in Cyprus without prejudice to the larger issues of defence policy in the Middle East, which could not be finally settled for some months to come.

The Cabinet –

(4) Invited the Minister of Defence and the Chancellor of the Exchequer to consider to what extent authority could now be given for the commencement of constructional work for a military Headquarters establishment in Cyprus, without prejudicing the decisions yet to be taken on the larger issues of defence policy in the Middle East, and to submit proposals for consideration by the Cabinet.

(5) Took note that the Secretary of State for War would submit to the Prime Minister a note on the disposal of the stores and equipment now in the British base at Tel el Kebir.

Christopher Soames to Winston S. Churchill
(Premier papers, 11/126)

30 October 1952

You asked me to put on paper the theme of the thoughts you expressed last night about taxation relief.

1. In all probability the cuts which the Government will be bound to make during the coming year will adversely affect the cost of living. For example, food subsidies and rents either of privately-owned houses or of Council houses.

2. In the last Budget the Chancellor relieved entirely from direct taxation a further two million people, and there are now only fourteen million who are paying any income tax at all.

3. A reduction of income tax given as a result of savings made on, for example, food subsidies, would not therefore in any way mitigate the effect of the resultant rising cost of living on the average wage-earner. The Government would therefore certainly be faced with large-scale wage increase demands.

4. If the cost of living rises it will be virtually impossible not to grant considerable wage increases. The object therefore must be not to allow the cost of living to rise any more than is necessary. There are many articles included in the cost of living index which still carry purchase tax. Would it

not therefore be possible to mitigate any rise in the cost of living brought about by a cut in food subsidies, by taking off all this purchase tax element within the cost of living index? You would like to obtain a list of goods included in the cost of living index, together with the amount of purchase tax which each item carries. You would then be able to see to what degree the cost of living index could be reduced by the abolition of all purchase tax on goods contained in it.

Winston S. Churchill to Anthony Eden
Prime Minister's Personal Minute M.526/52
(Premier papers, 11/392)

30 October 1952

I should be glad to know what your view is about this, especially the last sentence, '. . . without a political success he thought there might well be a revolution in Egypt.'[1] I was under the impression one had already occurred.

Their demands seem to be getting down to a dead-level scuttle by us.

Winston S. Churchill to Oliver Lyttelton
Prime Minister's Personal Telegram T.202/52
(Premier papers, 11/190)

30 October 1952
Immediate
Secret and Personal
No. 715

If you deem the presence of the two Socialist MPs a danger to Kenya the Governor is of course free to send them home. The Cabinet would, I am sure, support you as the situation is very different from when their expedition was considered. You have full freedom to decide.

---

[1] The final passage of the FO's telegram to the British delegation in Cairo read as follows: 'Allen's impression was that Amin was a tough customer who spoke throughout this long and very frank conversation with great confidence. Amin made it quite plain that the economic situation in Egypt was so bad that without economic help and (even more important) without a political success he thought there might well be a revolution in Egypt' (29 Oct. 1952, No. 1690).

Oliver Lyttelton to Winston S. Churchill
Prime Minister's Personal Telegram T.203/52
(Premier papers, 11/190)

31 October 1952   Kenya
Immediate
Secret and Personal
No. 686

Your telegram No. 715.

Thank you for your typically generous and helpful telegram. So far Brockway[1] and Hale[2] are no more than a nuisance, and are not doing themselves any good. But, of course, the situation may change at any time and although I shall try to avoid using your and the Cabinet's authority, it is valuable to have it in reserve. Situation quiet, but we still have a long way to go.

[1] Archibald Fenner Brockway, 1888–1988. Joined staff of *Examiner*, 1907. Sub-editor, *Christian Commonwealth*, 1909. Sub-editor, *Labour Leader*, 1911; Editor, 1912–17. Married, 1914, Lilla Harvey-Smith: two children (div. 1945); 1946, Edith Violet King: one child. Joined Independent Labour Party, 1920; Organising Secretary, 1922; General Secretary, 1928, 1933–9. Chairman, No More War Movement and War Resister's International, 1923–8. Member, Executive of Labour and Socialist International, 1926–31. MP (ILP) for East Leyton, 1929–31 Joined Labour Party, 1950. MP (Lab.) for Eton and Slough, 1950–64.

[2] Charles Leslie Hale, 1902–85. Member, Leicestershire County Council, 1925–50. Married, 1926, Dorothy Ann Latham. MP (Lab.) for Oldham Division of Lancashire, 1945–50; for West Division of Oldham, 1950–68. Freedom of Oldham, 1969. Baron Oldham, 1972.

November
1952

Winston S. Churchill to Anthony Eden
Prime Minister's Personal Minute M.528/52
(Premier papers, 11/298)

1 November 1952

The suggestion which the Turks made to General Odlum[1] at the beginning of paragraph 3 seems to me quite unfounded.[2] The Soviets would not be likely to give up their opportunity of obtaining the great prizes available to them from a major invasion of Western Europe for the sake of gaining the Bosphorus, the Suez Canal and the Persian Gulf. They may have enough troops to do both, but the Suez Canal and the Persian Gulf would take much longer than the advance through Germany into France. Meanwhile the full force of the atomic attack would develop on the war making capacity of Russia and her communications.

---

[1] Victor Wentworth Odlum, 1880–1971. Educated at University of Toronto. Served in Canadian military, 1900–24, 1940–1. On active service, Boer War, 1899–1900; WWI, 1914–18; WWII, 1940–1. Maj., 1914. Brig.-Gen., 1918. Maj.-Gen., 2nd Canadian Div., 1940–1. Canadian High Commissioner to Australia, 1941–2. Ambassador to China, 1942–6; to Turkey, 1947–52.

[2] Para. 3 of Cabinet Paper No. 362 of 1952 by Eden reads: 'Turning to the general strategic picture, General Odlum said that the Turks saw themselves in the centre of the stage. They believed that they were in the front-line and would bear the brunt of the Soviet attack which was certainly to be directed, not so much on Western Europe, as on the Bosphorous, the Suez Canal and the Persian Gulf. They despised all their neighbours, Arabs, Greeks and Italians alike, and had no opinion of their will or capacity to resist aggression. They were not prepared to enter into any commitments towards such neighbours from which they themselves could not possibly derive any advantages in return. The only people they took seriously were the Americans and ourselves. Their approach to the problem of Middle East defence was essentially realist. If plans were made which provided for the allocation of, say, ten outside divisions for the defence of the Middle East, the Turks on their side would be prepared to allocate forces for service in the area; but at present they did not see where those ten divisions would come from. The United Kingdom forces in Egypt were too small; they knew that no American forces were allocated to the area; and they doubted the ability of the Commonwealth to make up the deficiency. If, however, we could convince the Turks that forces would be forthcoming, then it would be easy to do business with them, and we should find them willing to cooperate in defence plans.'

Winston S. Churchill to Prince Bernhard[1]
(Churchill papers, 2/180)

3 November 1952

Sir,

I received with gratification Your Royal Highness's telegram of good wishes on my birthday. Alas I have not yet reached the distinction of 78 years and shall not do so until November 30! I shall however carry forward Your Royal Highness's good wishes to that date and I am sincerely touched that you should have thought of my birthday.

Field Marshal Lord Alexander to Winston S. Churchill
(Premier papers, 11/6)

3 November 1952
Confidential

You have asked why General Ridgway and Field Marshal Montgomery told the Chiefs of Staff privately that it would be inadvisable to extend Admiral Brind's tenure of Command in the North. The reason is because they do not consider that he has made a success of the organisation and running of a combined Allied Headquarters. They have nothing against him personally, and he gets on very well with the Norwegians and the Danes, but they feel that he should be succeeded as soon as possible by someone who has a better understanding of High Allied Command.

Winston S. Churchill: speech
(Hansard)

4 November 1952   House of Commons

DEBATE ON THE ADDRESS

I naturally join with the Leader of the Opposition in the compliments which he has paid, in a long-established custom, to the hon. Members who have proposed and seconded the Address in reply to the Gracious Speech. I am bound to say that I think they both gave us the feeling of having lived fully up to the high standard observed on these occasions and attained, almost without exception, by all three parties in any period which my lengthy recollection can recall. I admit that I do not go back so far as the reign of Queen Victoria in 1837, but at any rate my hon. and gallant Friend the Member

---

[1] Bernhard Graf von Biesterfeld, 1911–2004. Educated at University of Lausanne, Switzerland, and Friedrich-Wilhelm University, Berlin. Married, 1937, Princess Juliana Wilhelmina of the Netherlands. Prince Consort, 1948–76. Founder and First President, World Wildlife Fund, 1962–76.

for Berwick and East Lothian (Major Anstruther-Gray[1]) may comfort himself that his seconder[2] managed to get through his ordeal with distinction. Now we have had a speech, as is customary on these occasions, from the Leader of the Opposition, and I can only hope that the moderation and sobriety of his statement will not expose him to any undue risk among his own friends. I am sure I may offer him my congratulations on his being able to address us from those benches as stroke and not, to quote the term he has just used, from the tow-path.

The Gracious Speech refers in several important passages to foreign affairs. I do not propose to deal with these today, except to say that in the main we have hitherto preserved continuity in foreign policy, and I do not know of any new marked disagreement which has arisen between the two main parties up to the present time. We shall all, no doubt, have a clearer view of the whole situation after the result of the election – I mean, of course, the one in the United States – is known. It has now, I understand, been arranged that the debate on Thursday will be devoted to the foreign situation and to defence, and my right hon. Friend the Foreign Secretary will take part in the debate before he flies the next day to New York to attend the United Nations' meeting. I shall, therefore, confine myself this afternoon to the tangles and disputations of the domestic field. Let me, however, say from a business point of view that the debate on the Address will occupy the remainder of the present week and will, it is hoped, be brought to a conclusion in the early part of next week. Under your guidance, Mr Speaker, we shall endeavour to arrange the debate, whether on Amendments or otherwise, in accordance with the general wish of the House.

We propose that Private Members should enjoy their rights in respect of Bills and Motions in the same manner as last year, including the right to bring in Bills under the Ten Minutes Rule. Perhaps I may now give notice that my right hon. Friend the Leader of the House will tomorrow propose a Motion naming twenty Fridays on which Private Members' Bills and Motions will have precedence. It is proposed that the first of the Private Members' days should be Friday, 28th November.

No mention has been made in the Speech in regard to various features of legislation which are under consideration. As we move on we shall be able to see our way more clearly on the long pilgrimage through public business. We have made no mention in the Gracious Speech of legislation about the

---

[1] William John St Clair Anstruther-Gray, 1905–85. Educated at Eton and Christ Church, Oxford. Commissioned, Coldstream Guards, 1926–30. MP (Unionist) for Lanarkshire Northern, 1931–45; for Berwickshire and East Lothian, 1951–66. Parliamentary Private Secretary to John Colville, 1931–9. Married, 1934, Monica Helen Lambton: two children. On active service, Coldstream Guards, WWII (MC). Asst Postmaster-General, 1945. Bt, 1956. Deputy Speaker, House of Commons, 1959–64. Chairman of Ways and Means, 1962–4. Baron, 1966.

[2] Henry Alfred Price, 1911–82. Married, 1938, Ivy May Trimmer: two children. MP (Cons.) for West Lewisham, 1950–64.

preservation of historic houses, for it has seemed best to confine the Speech to Measures of first importance, but we hope to proceed with a Measure on this subject when time permits. This would apply to some of the other topics to which the Leader of the Opposition has referred.

Compared with this time last year, almost to a day, the Parliamentary situation in the House of Commons gives a definite impression of greater stability. We no longer feel that we are dwelling in the advent of another General Election. Right hon. Gentlemen opposite ought to cheer that; I am anxious to give as much reassurance as I possibly can. The strength and unity of the forces supporting Her Majesty's Government have been proved, and we do not doubt our ability to carry the legislation mentioned in the Gracious Speech, and in particular to pass into law the two important rectifying Measures of transport and steel.

Mr E. Shinwell (Easington): Wrecking Measures?

The Prime Minister: Rectifying Measures. Part of the process of cleansing the Statute Book is a definite element in any general scheme of rectification. We do not doubt, I say, our ability to carry these Measures, which were leading issues at the General Election, into law. Both these Bills will be presented to the House tomorrow.

One of the complaints made against us is that we ought not to introduce controversial legislation at a time like this, with such a small majority, especially in Coronation year. I wonder what would have been said by the right hon. Gentleman – by the same mouths – if we had not introduced these two Bills. What a howl of broken pledges and broken promises would have gone up. It is quite true that we are keeping our promises, as hon. Members opposite will find out. This is not the sole reason for proposing these Bills. Neither is it true that we are only giving expression to the ideological differences between the free enterprise system, to which we hold, and the foolish, as we deem it, system of Socialism. These reasons, powerful and valid though they may be, would not give sufficient warrant in themselves for the effort we are making to repeal these Acts of nationalisation. It is only because we believe on the merits that these changes are necessary and will be beneficial to the general and modern economy of our harassed island that we press them forward at the present time.

The story of steel nationalisation since the war must be viewed in its completeness. This was an act of nationalisation which the late Government, with all their power, considered with the greatest misgiving. We know very well the alternative solutions which many of their wisest leaders hankered after. On the other hand, it was evident that it was in the interest of the extreme elements of the right hon. Gentleman's party to force steel nationalisation on the Government and the country, because the frontiers of the steel industry are so undefined, so vaguely defined, that by nationalisation they could break into many other fields, and thus smudge at one stroke the whole page of British industry. I was looking for the former Minister of Supply,[1] but he seems to be missing at the moment. I venture to quote what he said in moving the Second Reading of the Iron and Steel Bill in 1948. He said:

> 'This great reform removes from the private sector of our economy to the public, the industry which is the citadel of British capitalism.'

He is himself very well circumstanced to defend that citadel from every point of view. (Hon Members: 'Cheap'.) We consider that the nationalisation of the steel industry in the circumstances in which it was brought about was a wrongful and needless act of partisan politics. The fact that the final step to bring it into operation was taken at the time of our entry into the Korean War and of the Socialist rearmament policy may well excite curiosity as to whether it was part of a deal in the party to persuade the Left Wing to do their duty by the country.

We had a debate the other day upon this subject of steel, and the Minister of Supply explained in friendly terms why the new Measure for regulating steel ought not to be regarded with hostility by the Labour Party. The right hon. Gentleman the Member for Lewisham, South (Mr H. Morrison) had to turn down his appeal. I am sure that was not due only to its consideration on the merits. It is an illustration of a fact, which will become more evident from day to day, that the leaders of the Front Bench opposite can only hold their position by giving renewed and repeated signs of their extremism, which in their hearts they abhor. We do not intend to vie with them in partisanship on this issue. The Bill which we are presenting to the House has the purpose of securing the widest opportunity for initiative and enterprise within the industry, coupled with the necessary measure of public supervision in the interests of the nation as a whole, on the lines of the Trades Union Congress report. We are all the more confident in the solution we propose in that it is based upon practical experience over many years and is the next logical step in the constitutional evolution of this primary basic industry.

We hope – hope springs eternal in the human breast, and so, I say, we hope – that whatever differences of political approach there may be, the Bill will at least be judged on both sides of the House by the one primary test, namely, how it will help the iron and steel industry to maintain and further develop its productivity. (Hon Members: 'Hear, hear'.) All right, hon. Gentlemen opposite take me at my word. I assure them that if they act up to that principle we shall not fall behind it on this side of the House.

Mr Shinwell: Hon. Members opposite should cheer up.

The Prime Minister: The right hon. Gentleman should restrain his enthusiasm until he comes to speak on defence.

---

[1] George Strauss.

Now I come to transport. No one underrates the difficulties and complications which the present century has brought to every country in the constant adjusting and readjusting of road and rail transport. Since we rose for the Summer Recess, we have given long and continuous study to the many difficult questions that have been opened. When the Bill is published tomorrow, the changes that we have made will be seen. I am sure that prolonged discussion has been beneficial. Personally, Mr Speaker, I am always ready to learn, although I do not always like being taught, but I shall not attempt to foreshadow the proposals which will be brought before the House tomorrow. Today it will be sufficient and appropriate to deal with the obvious difficulties and confusion of the situation as we found it on taking office. Everyone must be conscious of the evils which exist and which we inherited – the restriction in one form or another of some nineteen-twentieths of our vehicles for the sake of the 41,000 to be nationalised, the indefinite maintenance of the twenty-five miles limit, the growth of 'C' licences, which have risen by 339,000 to a total of 826,000 since the Transport Act became law on 1st January, 1948. It is a very remarkable fact that people should prefer to be bound only to carry their own goods, with all the restrictions that that involves, rather than avail themselves of the advantages of nationalised transport.

The failure of the 41,000 vehicles, of which I believe only 35,000 are working at the present time, is certainly not due to any lack of sincerity or zeal on the part of those who operate them. They have tried sincerely to meet the public need, but the mere fact that this enormous expansion in other forms of restricted transport has come into play is surely one which Parliament might, without partisanship, gaze at in thought. We all live in one country, and there is no harm in thinking about a thing like that. Then there is the millstone round the neck of the railways – the terrible fact of the £300 million or something like that. (*Interruption.*) I am a very old supporter of the nationalisation of the railways, and hon. Members opposite must take me with my past and all, but I am bound to say that to hang this millstone round the neck of the nationalised railways was a very formidable event. (Hon. Members: 'What millstone?') The £300 million on which interest has to be earned. I am well aware that the party opposite has always adhered to the principle of compensation. That was perfectly right, but in choosing the moment which involves this enormous burden, this permanent dead weight hanging round the necks of the railways, they took a very grievous step. It may undoubtedly be that, had they not done so, and had the railways not been nationalised, the shareholders would have had to go home and nurse their grievances and many of their losses. This is what happens under the capitalist system. Now there has been fixed round the necks of the railways, by law, this permanent burden of £300 million.

Mr Herbert Morrison (Lewisham, South): rose –

The Prime Minister: I will give way in a minute. On top of all this –

Mr Morrison: What £300 million?

The Prime Minister: On top of all this – (*Interruption.*) I will not give way yet. (*Interruption.*) I shall certainly take my time. On top of all this is the number of restrictions on the railways' freedom in the matter of charges, dating from the days when, having swallowed the canals, they were really a monopoly.

Mr Morrison: In connection with compensation to the railways, the Prime Minister has referred to £300 million as a millstone. Will he be kind enough to say what he means by '£300 million' and to what it refers?

The Prime Minister: It was the price paid to the shareholders.[1]

Hon. Members: No.

Mr James Callaghan[2] (Cardiff, South-East): Will the Prime Minister take it from me that the price paid to the shareholders was in the region of £1,100 million to £1,200 million and that the annual interest which is payable to the shareholders is between £30 million and £40 million?

The Prime Minister: I have not those figures in my notes, but to have to pay £30 million to £40 million a year constitutes a very heavy millstone tied round the necks of the British Railways. (*Interruption.*) I was merely asking at that moment for a glass of water.

The Gracious Speech mentions a third important Measure relating to the Town and Country Planning Act, 1947. Again, I will not anticipate its provisions but will offer a few introductory remarks.

Mr G. Lindgren[3] (Wellingborough): Three hundred million pounds.

The Prime Minister: I remember the old days, which were my young or younger days, when the taxation of land values and of unearned increments in land was a foremost principle and a lively element in the programme of the Radical Party to which I then belonged. But what is the situation which presents itself to us today? In those days we had the spectacle of valuable land being kept out of the market until the exact moment for its sale was reached, regardless of the fact that its increased value was due to the exertions of the surrounding community. Then we had the idea that, if those obstructions could be cleared out of the way, free enterprise would bound forward and small people would have a chance to get a home, or to improve their existing homes, and many other things besides. But here at the moment we have the exact opposite.

---

[1] Randolph Churchill noted in *Stemming the Tide*, which he edited, that Churchill intervened later in the debate to explain that through a mistake in his notes he had misled the House. The compensation to the former stockholders was £900,000,000 on which the annual interest was nearly £30,000,000.

[2] (Leonard) James Callaghan, 1912–2005. MP (Lab.) for Cardiff South, 1945–50; for Cardiff South East, 1950–83; for Cardiff South and Penarth, 1983–7. Parliamentary Secretary, Ministry of Transport, 1947–50; Admiralty, 1950–1. Foreign Secretary, 1974–6. PM, 1976–9. Leader of the Labour Party, 1976–80. Father of the House, 1983–7. KG, 1987. Baron, 1987.

[3] George Samuel Lindgren, 1900–71. MP (Lab.) for Wellingborough, 1945–59. Parliamentary Secretary, Ministry of National Insurance, 1945–6; Ministry of Civil Aviation, 1946–50; Ministry of Town and Country Planning, 1950–1; Ministry of Housing and Local Government, 1951; Ministry of Transport, 1964–6; Ministry of Power, 1966–70. Baron, 1961.

The problem which now confronts us directly and urgently is that of the £300 million, established by the 1947 Act, and also the development charge. (*Interruption.*) Before hon. Gentlemen opposite work themselves up into a rage, I would remind them that the 1947 Act was based upon the Report of the Uthwatt[1] Committee of 1942, which was accepted in substance by the Coalition White Paper of 1944. So we are all in it together. I might remind hon. Gentlemen opposite that we are all in quite a lot of things together. The White Paper proposed a once-for-all payment, not strictly speaking compensation, for loss of development value at 1939 prices. That is the origin of the £300 million to the landowners which is payable under the 1947 Act. The foundation of the 100 percent development charge is, no doubt, the 80 percent included in the Coalition Government White Paper. Any man, however modest his means – and a very great number of very small owners are involved in this – must pay this very heavy price in addition to the cost of building anything in times when everything is becoming more expensive, although at a definitely less rapid rate than was the case under the previous Administration.

The result of the development charge or betterment charge is that it has become a direct deterrent upon enterprise and production and has brought a lot of it to a standstill. We may ask ourselves, is that what we want now? If ever there was a subject which might be considered calmly and coolly without partisanship by both parties, who are both concerned in what has been done in the past and are also concerned in what emerges in the future, it is here in this Measure that will come before us this Session. The logic of the Uthwatt Report may be impeccable, and both parties yielded to it and are involved, but in practice the result has been unhappy. To pay out £300 million next year, as the Act requires, would put money into the pocket of many who have no intention of ever exercising development rights and who suffered no loss. The ordinary small landowner also does not understand the theory that he must buy back potential development rights. The process is unenforceable except by the drastic use of compulsory powers. Before the end of the month the Government's full proposals on this subject will be presented to the House of Commons, and I trust that they may receive fair consideration in view of the association of both parties for over eight years in this extremely difficult and baffling situation.

I have dealt now with the three principal Measures, steel, transport and the one I have referred to dealing with the development charge under the Town and Country Planning Act. I do not want to keep the House too long. (Hon. Members: 'Go on.') Hon. Members opposite are not getting so much out of

[1] Augustus Andrewes Uthwatt, 1879–1949. Legal Adviser to Ministry of Food, 1915–18. Treasurer of Gray's Inn, 1939–40; Vice-Treasurer, 1941. Judge of Chancery Div., High Court of Justice, 1941–6. Chaired Committees on Responsibility for Repair of Premises Damaged by Hostilities (1939), on Liability for War Damage to the Subject Matter of Contracts (1939), on Principles of Assessment of War Damage to Property (1940), on Compensation and Betterment (1941), the last of which reported in 1942 and dealt with public control of the use of land. Baron, 1946.

it as they try to encourage themselves into thinking they are. I come to the position which we occupied a year ago. When we succeeded hon. Gentlemen opposite a year ago we were moving into bankruptcy and economic ruin at a hideous pace. There is no doubt that any Government called upon to bear the burden would have had to take prompt and severe measures, many of which would have been unpopular, in order to avert the disaster which was imminent. Hence the General Election.

The right hon. Gentleman the Leader of the Opposition the other day derided us for saying that we are doing our best. He said if that were true it was the strongest argument for turning us out. The justice and even the decency of such a remark can only be judged in relation to the facts. A year ago we were certainly in a crisis of the first magnitude. Our taxation, especially on wealth, was and still is the highest in the world. Our reserves drained by the war have been spent with lavish hands, and many schemes of social welfare have been set on foot which increase normally and almost irresistibly every year. The fall in the purchasing power of money, or in other words the rise in the cost of living, was increasing rapidly. (Hon Members: 'And still is'.) It is still increasing, but not so rapidly. On the top of all this was this new re-armament programme, which, in principle, we supported, and which had been launched and was getting into its stride. We had to face, on taking over, not only a gigantic expenditure, but many formidable increases which have not reached fruition but have become inevitable. No one pretends that we have yet mastered that problem. We have warded off imminent catastrophe by many painful measures, and we are strengthening our margin of safety. On the whole, no one can doubt our position is better, actually and relatively, than it was a year ago. We always said we could be saved, but that several years of resolute policy and steady administration would be needed. We should also remember that during the first five years of Socialist rule £2,000 million of sterling was received mainly from the United States of America in loans or gifts. At £400 million this more than equalled the loss we suffered in the early part of the war in income from foreign investments. We have had none of this since we took office, except the earmarked payment to aid our rearmament programme. It ill becomes those who after six years of power, power unequalled by any Government in this country in time of peace, and who are responsible in no small measure for the evils and dangers by which we are surrounded, to mock us when we say we are doing our best.

As a result of the measures we took, the United Kingdom recovered so far that in the first half of this year we achieved a small surplus, even before counting the defence aid received from the United States. Further, as a result of the Conference of Commonwealth Finance Ministers held in January, the position of the sterling area as a whole has also improved, and we confidently expect it to balance with the outside world in this second half of 1952. Since the end of June the monthly figures of our gold and dollar reserves have also shown improvement. We must not judge, of course, by a single month's figures, but it is true that the October results published today are the best since April, 1951. Hon. and right hon. Members opposite must not look gloomy when a thing like that comes along. They should rejoice as we rejoice, even though, as I have said, a single month's returns cannot be taken as a criterion or indication. These encouraging results are merely signs that we are able to enjoy what the Chancellor of the Exchequer has rightly called a breathing space in our task of putting our overseas finances on to safer and sounder foundations. It is not enough merely to balance our accounts and so pay our way. We have debts to repay, and the future holds many risks and many unknowable factors. The only way to provide for all this is, of course, to expand our overseas trade by an all out effort to increase our exports. It will be the Government's primary endeavour not only to keep this objective before the country, but to foster the conditions under which it can be most easily and swiftly achieved.

Naturally, we are disappointed at the decline in production, which the Leader of the Opposition also deplores. The shortage of steel has been having a restrictive effect, but the steel is coming along, and we are looking forward to an increase in our production of steel. The prospect for the textile and clothing industries appears to be improved, and we hope to see an increase in output and employment. Unemployment in those industries is already tending to fall, and elsewhere it remains very low. The total unemployment remains below 2 percent of the vast number of persons employed. There are also signs of a more mobile state in our economy. One welcome sign is the flow of manpower to the mines. Another sign, equally welcome, in view of our need to divert exports to dollar markets, is the recent increase in our exports to Canada. Our economy has been able to adapt itself to the stresses and strains of outside influence, in spite of the fact that these adjustments take time. We believe that events will show, both externally in our trade balance and internally in our domestic production, that our policy has been justified. That more might have been done is a field in which there may be argument, but at any rate we have tried our best, and we have so far made definite and indisputable progress.

Her Majesty's Government attach the greatest importance to the Conference of Commonwealth Prime Ministers which will open in London at the end of this month. It has not been called, like so many others in recent years, to examine immediate steps for escaping from a crisis already upon us. Indeed, since the meeting of Commonwealth Finance Ministers in January, things appear to have improved. The object now is to try to chart a course to a more secure future in which recurring crises will not occur. That is the end which we all seek, and as a means to that end we shall survey the economic and financial problems which are common to all our several countries, and shall consider any possible steps which will strengthen Sterling and help us to move towards the goal, accepted by the Commonwealth Finance Ministers, of a world in which trade will be free to move unhampered by the controls and arrangements which at present restrict it. The Government look forward keenly to welcoming our Commonwealth colleagues in London – not the Government only, but all parties – and to discussing with them these issues, which are of such great importance to every citizen of every country and to the Commonwealth as a whole, and to the great part which the British Commonwealth of Nations has yet to play in the wider world outside.

Defence Committee: minutes
(Cabinet papers, 131/12)

5 November 1952 Prime Minister's Map Room
Top Secret Ministry of Defence
11.30 a.m.
Defence Committee Meeting No. 11 of 1952

The Committee had before them –
(i) A memorandum by the Chiefs of Staff (D(52)45) pointing out the serious consequences of accepting limiting defence expenditure in 1953–54 to the figure of £1,570 millions now proposed by the Chancellor of the Exchequer;
(ii) A memorandum by the Minister of Defence (D(52)46) stating that he would not be justified on military grounds in accepting a lower limit than the figure of £1,645 millions to which he had already reluctantly agreed;
(iii) A memorandum by the Minister of Supply (D(52)47) calling attention to the serious effects of reducing the programme of research and development.

The Committee were informed that, before the figure of £1,645 millions had been put forward as a minimum requirement, a most rigorous examination had been made into the needs of all three Services and all the less essential administrative and ancillary services had been reduced to a minimum. The further cut now proposed by the Chancellor of the Exchequer was bound to result in a decrease in the fighting power of the Services. There was no escape from the cost of maintaining existing forces and, therefore, when that cost had been reduced to the minimum, any further reduction must be at the expense of improving equipment and readiness.

The Minister of Defence said that in these circumstances he hoped that the Committee could approve the figure of £1,645 millions for 1953–54 and could indicate the scale of expenditure on which plans could be based for the two following years. Although he understood that no firm commitment could be made at this stage in respect of expenditure in that further period, man-power and production planning would be impossible unless some

NOVEMBER 1952   711

planning assumptions were authorised about the level of future expenditure on defence.

In discussion the following points were made:

(a) There was a possibility that, if negotiations for the setting up of a Middle East Defence Organisation were successful, there might be some reduction in the number of United Kingdom forces maintained in the Middle East. If one division could be withdrawn, there would be some saving in overseas expenditure, but the net saving would not be considerable unless the division were disbanded. If that were done, there would still be no strategic reserve in the United Kingdom.

(b) There seemed little chance of reductions in overseas commitments in any other part of the world, although, if the German contribution to the defence of Western Europe became a reality and increased at a steady rate, some reduction in the number of British forces in Germany might be considered in the future.

(c) Although the budgetary figure for defence must remain an important factor in the economic stability of the country, the urgency of reducing the load of the defence programme on the metal-using industries now seemed to be rather less than had previously been thought. It had hitherto been assumed that this would allow a corresponding expansion of engineering exports, but it appeared that the engineering industries were finding increasing difficulty in marketing their exports, owing to high costs, and might be unable to make fully effective use of capacity released from defence work.

(d) The Prime Minister expressed surprise at the extent of the cut in fighting power brought about by the comparatively small cut in money which the Chancellor of the Exchequer now proposed. Would it not be possible, in order to meet the Chancellor of the Exchequer, to impose a further cut on the administrative and ancillary services? He could not accept the idea that the latest types of fighter aircraft, to which super-priority had been given, should be selected for reduction. The policy for the expansion of the medium bomber force would also have to be examined. It was pointed out in reply that drastic cuts had already been made in the less essential requirements before the Minister of Defence had proposed the figure of £1,645 millions. It was inevitable that any cuts below that figure must fall upon new equipment and the size of the fighting formations. Of the total Defence Budget, three-quarters was devoted to the maintenance of the forces and one-quarter to new equipment. Any reduction in the Air Ministry programme must mean either fewer new types of aircraft or not enough men to operate the aircraft. The Army was obliged to maintain large training organisations to deal with the National Service intake and large numbers of men in transit to different overseas theatres. Any reduction in the number of men in the Army must in these circumstances lead to a reduction in the number of fighting formations.

(e) It was suggested that, if the likelihood of war had receded, it was difficult to defend a Defence Budget of such magnitude for a protracted period of peace. It was argued, on the other hand, that a cold war – which in certain areas of the world meant active operations – was already in progress and that in any event the equipment of forces to act as a deterrent was not very different from the equipment of forces to take part in a war. Savings were already being made in the provision of reserves.

(f) The Chancellor of the Exchequer said that he had been surprised by the assessment now made by the Chiefs of Staff of the effect of accepting the budgetary figure he proposed. The consequences were graver than he had been led to expect. If expenditure on defence had to be retained at the figures proposed by the Minister of Defence, he would have to re-examine the distribution of the economic resources of the country. Too much of our economic resources were being absorbed in unproductive commitments like defence and housing at a time when exports were falling and increased productivity was essential. He would circulate a paper to the Cabinet.

The Prime Minister said that it would be necessary for the Cabinet to settle before the end of the week the size of defence expenditure in 1953–54, so that the information required by the NATO Annual Review could be provided in time. It would, however, be impossible for the Cabinet to reach firm decisions on the scale of defence expenditure for the two subsequent years. He agreed that some indication of this must be given so that a general design and pattern of defence could be worked out, but before this was done he would wish to examine more closely the effects of cuts in expenditure upon the fighting power of the Services. He was not yet satisfied that every possible reduction had been made in administrative and ancillary services, or that the three Services were obtaining the best value for their expenditure.

The Minister of Defence and the three Service Ministers emphasised that it was their considered view, after full and detailed examinations, that the fighting power of the Services could not be maintained if the budgetary figure proposed by the Chancellor of the Exchequer was adopted.

The Committee –

Took note that the Prime Minister would invite the Cabinet to determine on the 7th November the amount of defence expenditure in 1953–54, and to indicate their views on the general pattern of defence expenditure in the two following years.

November 1952

Oliver Lyttelton to Winston S. Churchill
Prime Minister's Personal Telegram T.205/52
(Premier papers, 11/190)

5 November 1952   Kenya
Immediate
Personal and Confidential
No. 697

Brockway and Hale are proving a complete flop. Hale's arrival sans collar, tie and socks was ill received by all sections of opinion here. Brockway has a strong police escort constantly on roads and we have succeeded in keeping him in a dust cloud.

Situation in Kenya is on the whole quiet but not yet settled. I will give you a full report as soon as I get home.

Winston S. Churchill to President-Elect Dwight D. Eisenhower
(Premier papers, 11/572)

5 November 1952

General Eisenhower,

I send you my sincere and heartfelt congratulations on your election. I look forward to a renewal of our comradeship and of our work together for the same causes of peace and freedom as in the past. Writing.

Sir Norman Brook to Winston S. Churchill
(Premier papers, 11/545)

5 November 1952

SUDAN
(C(52)388)

The Egyptian Government's comments upon the draft self-government Statute for the Sudan suggest that they may wish to exclude the possibility of the Sudan eventually applying for membership of the British Commonwealth. This is clearly a matter to which further thought must be given. Other Commonwealth Governments would have to be formally consulted if any such application were made.

Would it not be well for the Cabinet to ask the Foreign Secretary and the Commonwealth Secretary to consider what our attitude would be if such an application were made?

Meanwhile, the Foreign Secretary proposes to send a non-committal reply

714   NOVEMBER 1952

to a letter he has received from Mr Omar, the Secretary of the Sudan Party, which (though it is neither large nor influential) favours the Sudan joining the British Commonwealth. The kernel of the draft letter is in this sentence: 'It is not possible for Her Majesty's Government in the United Kingdom at this time to express any opinion about the form which that relationship' (i.e. between the British and Sudanese peoples) 'should take'.

President-Elect Dwight D. Eisenhower to Winston S. Churchill
Prime Minister's Personal Telegram T.206/52
(Premier papers, 11/572)

6 November 1952
Immediate

Dear Winston,
    Thank you very much for the typically generous sentiments expressed in your cable.[1] I shall look forward to receiving your letter and I too look forward to a renewal of our cooperative work in the interests of a free world.

Cabinet: conclusions
(Cabinet papers, 128/25)

7 November 1952
Secret
11.30 a.m.
Cabinet Meeting No. 94 of 1952

The Cabinet had before them the following memoranda on the defence programme:
    C(52)316 and D(52)46: by the Minister of Defence.
    C(52)320 and C(52)393: by the Chancellor of the Exchequer.
    C(52)394: by the Service Ministers.
    D(52)45: by the Chiefs of Staff.
The Minister of Defence said that, when he took office in March 1952, the planned defence programme for 1953–54 was estimated to cost £1,838 million and that for 1954–55 £1,916 million. The Chiefs of Staff had then set in hand a radical review of strategy and their conclusions had been approved in principle at the beginning of July. The forces needed to support this strategy were then costed at £1,719 million for 1953–54, £1,777 million for 1954–55 and £1,790 million for 1955–56. In view of the difficulties of the financial situation he had then insisted upon further drastic cuts in the programme

---

[1] Reproduced above (p. 713).

which had brought the figures for these three years down to £1,645 million, £1,688 million and £1,698 million respectively. He could, therefore, claim that he had reduced the programme very substantially since the early part of the year, and the reduction was in fact even greater than it seemed owing to the rise in costs and the additional items which were now to be included in the Service Estimates. He was satisfied that it would be impossible to fulfil all our overseas commitments and our obligations to our Allies in the North Atlantic Treaty Organisation (NATO) if the budgetary figure in 1953 were reduced below £1,645 million.

The Chancellor of the Exchequer said that, while he was grateful for these reductions in the programme, the figure now put forward by the Minister of Defence as the minimum was more than the country could afford. He had himself advanced from the figure of £1,550 million, which he had first proposed, and he was now prepared to accept a figure in the neighbourhood of £1,600 million for 1953, provided that a radical review of the future pattern of our defence effort was undertaken at once, with regard not only to strategic needs and foreign commitments but also to economic and financial factors. Within the figure of £1,600 million he was prepared to agree to a load on the metal-using industries of £480 millions in 1953. The financial position of the country and the fall in productivity made it impossible to contemplate a rising curve of defence. It was already clear that he would be faced with a very difficult budgetary position in the spring. He was prepared to recommend severe cuts in civil expenditure, which would involve substantial retrenchment in the social services. He indicated to the Cabinet some of the main proposals which he would have to bring forward under this head. But, even if they were all approved, the savings thus secured would do no more than offset the increase in defence expenditure for which the Minister of Defence was asking. He would thus be left with no means of enabling industry to increase its productivity and competitive power; and we should then be faced with the prospect of diminishing exports and greater financial instability which must, in turn, undermine our defence effort.

In discussion the following points were made:
(a) The Service Ministers said that, as explained in C(52)394, any further reduction below the £1,645 million proposed by the Minister of Defence must diminish the fighting strength of the Services. All possible economies in the administration of the Services had already been taken into account and the allocation of less money to the defence programme could only result in fewer fighting formations and a reduced supply of new equipment. The Secretary of State for Air said that it would mean, for example, that the withdrawal of a number of operational squadrons from the Middle East and Far East Air Forces would have to be put in hand immediately. The Prime Minister said that he was not fully satisfied on this point

and would wish to examine the organisation of the three Services in greater detail once the budgetary figure for 1953–54 had been fixed.

(b) The Minister of Supply pointed out that failure to plan a firm production programme over three years might well lead to waste of money through compensation for the cancellation of orders. The curtailment of the defence programme had already forced him to cancel certain orders for tanks and aircraft, the production of which he had made every effort to accelerate less than a year ago. The Prime Minister said that every effort should be made to avoid having to pay compensation for the cancellation of contracts for valuable equipment. He would be glad to have a detailed report on this from the Minister of Supply.

(c) The figure of £1,645 million proposed by the Minister of Defence was based on existing wage rates in the engineering industry. If, as seemed likely, these were increased, there would be a corresponding increase in the total cost of defence production in 1953, which might possibly amount to £15 million. The Chancellor of the Exchequer agreed that the additional cost arising from this wages award would have to be added to the figure finally approved by the Cabinet that day for defence expenditure in 1953.

(d) In arriving at his figure the Minister of Defence had assumed that the United Kingdom costs in Germany would not exceed £30 million. It was possible that this was an optimistic assumption. The Chancellor of the Exchequer agreed that, if German costs exceeded £30 million, the Service Departments should not be required to find the surplus by savings on other parts of their Vote. Other means of financing any such surplus would have to be found.

(e) The President of the Board of Trade said that he was prepared to accept a defence load of £480 million on the metal-using industries in 1953, on the understanding that he and the Minister of Supply would be free to consider, firm by firm, what transfers could effectively be made from defence work to exports. He believed, however, that the general level of defence expenditure contemplated by the Minister of Defence was higher than the national economy could bear, and that greater efforts would have to be made to reduce Government expenditure, both civil and military, so that industry could be enabled to increase exports. It was the view of several Ministers that to accept a defence budget beyond what was economically wise at the present stage might well lead to a still lower figure for defence in subsequent years. It was therefore vital to the success of the rearmament programme that the right figure for defence should be determined now.

(f) The Foreign Secretary said that a decision on the defence budget for 1953–54 was urgently needed in order that NATO could complete its annual review. Any drastic reduction of expenditure at this stage would severely shake the confidence of our Allies in NATO. But he fully agreed that, once the 1953–54 figure had been fixed, an exhaustive review should be undertaken on the lines suggested by the Chancellor of the Exchequer. He could not foresee any large reductions in our oversea commitments, although he still hoped that it would be possible to come to some arrangement with Egypt and other interested Powers which would enable us to make economies in the Middle East. In this connection it was suggested that it would be helpful if a distinction could be made between the cost of temporary commitments (e.g., in Korea and Malaya) which might be expected to diminish or disappear and that of our more lasting commitments in respect of NATO and the re-equipment of our Forces.

The Prime Minister, summing up the discussion, said that the Cabinet might fix a sum of £1,610 million for the defence budget for the financial year 1953 on the understanding that this figure did not include any additional cost arising from the current claim for a wages increase in our engineering industry or any increase in United Kingdom costs in Germany over the £30 million at present allowed for this. Such a decision would allow the necessary submission to be made to NATO for its annual review – though he would wish to examine in detail the incidence of this further cut upon the three Services. He was most anxious that there should be no substantial reduction in the fighting strength of the Services, and he still hoped that the cuts could be made in such a way as to avoid destroying fighting formations or curtailing the production of the latest types of equipment. A radical review of the defence programme for subsequent years should be undertaken against a comprehensive background of our strategy, our oversea commitments and our financial and economic position.

The Cabinet –

(1) Decided that defence expenditure in the financial year 1953 should be fixed at £1,610 million calculated at existing prices, and that this figure should not be held to include any additional cost arising from the current wages dispute in the engineering industry, or from any increase in United Kingdom costs in Germany above the £30 million already allowed for this.

(2) Agreed that in the financial year 1953 the load of defence production on the metal-using industries should not exceed £480 million.

(3) Invited the Minister of Defence to arrange for the necessary information based on the decisions in Conclusions (1) and (2) above to be

given to NATO with the least possible delay; and to discuss further with the Prime Minister the effect which this limit of expenditure in 1953 would have on the organisation of the three Services.

(4) Took note that the Prime Minister, in consultation with the Foreign Secretary, the Chancellor of the Exchequer and the Minister of Defence, would put in hand a radical review of the pattern of our defence effort in the years after 1953.

James Thomas to Winston S. Churchill
(Premier papers, 11/219)

7 November 1952

I am afraid I misled you this morning when you asked what ships we had off Korea as I thought that our cruisers had been relieved, at the moment, by Commonwealth cruisers. I found on my return to the Admiralty that I was wrong and in Japanese waters we have today:

1 aircraft carrier
2 cruisers
1 hospital ship
2 destroyers
2 frigates

2. You asked specifically about the Fleet in Japanese waters but you may also like to know the strength of the Far East Fleet as a whole. In addition to the ships mentioned above there are:

5 destroyers
7 frigates
6 ocean minesweepers
1 aircraft maintenance ship
1 HQ ship

(Plus Fleet Train and coastal and inshore minesweepers)

Normally there would be a third cruiser but HMS *Belfast* has just come home and HMS *Newfoundland* has not yet joined.

3. The Korean contribution varies from time to time and I apologise for making the mistake about the cruisers.

4. You may also be interested to hear that to keep a carrier in the Far East involves, roughly, one-quarter of our naval aviation effort.

Winston S. Churchill: speech
(Churchill papers, 2/336)

7 November 1952
Harrow School

I almost thought I had got off. But after all you must not expect too much good luck when you are present on a thirteenth occasion. An awful lot isn't it? This is the thirteenth time I have had this honour and great comfort and pleasure of coming here, in war and peace, in office and out of it – we're back again now – to be cheered by your singing to me. The thirteenth time I have been here! And one of the difficulties which attach to such an anniversary is how difficult it is to find anything new to say, because although generations of Harrow boys who have listened to me these thirteen years have changed there is after all a certain limit to the number of topics which are suitable.

The first thing that comes into my mind tonight, and will come into all yours, is our delight in seeing Lord Alexander here. We are also very glad to have him in the Government. It is not often that ordinary politicians feel themselves strengthened and sustained by the presence of a man of action who has gained great fame in battles in the field in the cause of freedom against the enemy. I am delighted that he should be here this evening, and much gratified. But is comparatively junior to me. He came long after I left. I was here in Mr Amery's time. He was a Monitor. I remember he wielded the cane – in theory at any rate – in those far off days. Well, we try to keep going. Presently we are going to sing 'Forty Years On', but that is no good to Leo and me. I don't know how far we shall have to extend it, but sixty years is more like it.[1] If you should hear that particular word when it comes to our turn to sing you will understand the reason why.

Now my friends I have always preached the gospel of the Harrow Songs. Wonderful! You have only got to learn them all by heart – it isn't much – to have a vocabulary of true simplicity which is bound to be of real service to you in life. These two writers, Mr Bowen and Mr Howson, I was here with both of them. I was here when these songs were almost entirely written. They certainly have rendered enormous service to the School. Compare the Harrow songs to the river song. A river is merely a facility for drainage. The other is an inspiration of all kinds. But you should love your Songs and you should learn them off by heart and you should sing them from your heart, and they will come back as they say themselves in 'Songs' which we began with. They will come back all your life, carrying you back to the days when all the future was open to your endeavour and sacrifice and opportunity to serve your country. I am sure they will be the greatest possible help.

Now I wish to tell you that you must not suppose that the troubles of Britain are over because from the last two terrible wars that have shaken and rent the

---

[1] In 1954, Harrow added a new verse to mark Churchill's 80th birthday. It began: 'Sixty years on, though in time growing older, Younger at heart you return to the Hill.'

world in the twentieth century we have emerged victorious without shame of any kind either in the making or the fighting of those struggles. You must not imagine that these struggles are over. On the contrary, you may feel that in the world which has grown so much vaster all around us and towers up above us, we in this small island have to make a supreme effort to keep our place and station, the place and station to which our history and our traditions and our undying genius entitle us. A great effort is required, and you to whom much of the future belongs will play your part in this proud, equal, free, democratic England. You have a chance to make a contribution, each of you and all of you together, to put into practice the spirit of all you learn here, which is repeated in your songs; it may well play its part in enabling the old country, this famous island, the scene of so much, to have an important effect upon the progress, freedom, honour of the world in the future, as she has in the past.

I thank you very much, Mr Baldwin,[1] for having given me this opportunity to say a few words tonight.

Winston S. Churchill to James Thomas
Prime Minister's Personal Minute M.532/52
(Premier papers, 11/219)

8 November 1952

What is the annual cost of this Fleet including the third cruiser HMS *Newfoundland*?[2] Apart from the vessels what is the number of men and the cost of the naval base installations which are required?

Winston S. Churchill to Harry S Truman
('Defending the West, The Truman–Churchill Correspondence', pages 203–4)

8 November 1952

Dear Harry,

I have felt shy of obtruding myself on you while all this battle was on and all my best friends in the US were fighting one another. We tried to follow with discerning eye all the movements of the troops in the field. It must have been very exciting for those engaged. Our island is unhappily too small for any really full-sized whistle stop tour but I am studying the plan with attention in case which is unlikely I should have a next time. I hope to come over some time next year and look forward to seeing you again if only in my capacity as an Honorary Doctor of Civil Law of Westminster College, Fulton, Missouri.

---

[1] Robert Maurice Baldwin, 1897–?. Lt, WWI. History and French teacher at Harrow School, 1922–57.
[2] See Thomas's minute of Nov. 7, reproduced above (p. 718).

Let me however meanwhile express my gratitude to you for all you have done for our common show. I am very glad we had that final gallop together.

Harry S Truman to Winston S. Churchill
('Defending the West, The Truman–Churchill Correspondence', page 204)

12 November 1952

Dear Winston,

I can't tell you how very much I appreciated your cable of November eight, which was forwarded to me by Sir Oliver Franks. The whistle stop tour on my part didn't work out as well this time as it did before. I think the people were voting for their great military hero because the majority in the House and Senate is very narrow and a great many members of the House and Senate were elected in the states that went for the General. If you come to the United States at any time I certainly do want to see you and have a visit with you. I'll never forget the pleasant time we had when we received the degrees at Westminster College.

John Colville: diary
('The Fringes of Power', pages 654–5)

9 November 1952

I have not written this for many weeks, partly from laziness, partly because living in flats, with a shared writing table, militates heavily against keeping a diary. I have been to Chartwell numerous weekends, but although much has been said and a few things done there is nothing especially noteworthy. However, I do record that last Wednesday evening, November 5th, after Eisenhower's victory in the American Presidential Election had been announced, Winston said to me: 'For your private ear, I am greatly disturbed. I think this makes war much more probable.'

He (W) is getting tired and visibly ageing. He finds it hard work to compose a speech and ideas no longer flow. He has made two strangely simple errors in the H of C lately, and even when addressing the Harrow boys in Speech Room last Friday what he said dragged and lacked fire. But he has had a tiring week, with speeches, important Cabinet decisions, etc., so that I may be unduly alarmist.

On Friday, November 7th, Ashley Clarke[1] lunched with me at the Turf and

---

[1] Henry Ashley Clarke, 1903–94. Educated at Pembroke College, Cambridge. Entered Diplomatic Service, 1925. Head of Far East Dept, FO, 1942–4. Minister to Portugal, 1944–6; to France, 1946–9. CMG, 1946. Asst Under-Secretary, Foreign Office, 1949–50; Chief Clerk, 1949–53; Deputy Under-Secretary, 1950–3. KCMG, 1952. Ambassador to Italy, 1953–62. GCVO, 1961. GCMG, 1962. Governor of the BBC, 1962–7.

offered me the post of Counsellor and head of Chancery in Washington next summer if I can escape from No. 10 then.

Dreadfully tied up with the Coronation arrangements.

Meg's baby, approaching delivery, has turned the wrong way up and now the right way up again. It appears to be a most energetic child.

Winston S. Churchill: speech
('Stemming the Tide', pages 361–5)

10 November 1952   Guildhall

LORD MAYOR'S BANQUET

My Lord Mayor, Your Excellencies, My Lords, Ladies, and Gentlemen: When I came to your Banquet a year ago our Government had only just been formed and we had to face with a slender, and it might well have been a precarious, majority not only the partisanship of our opponents, but a task, the full magnitude of which was becoming every day more plain. We were moving into bankruptcy at an alarming rate. Only prompt, vigorous and unpopular action could gain us the breathing space necessary to place our affairs upon a sound foundation. By severe exertions we have gained the breathing space, but it will require several years of sober and persevering government to restore our financial and economic strength, without which our nation cannot play an effectual part, during this twentieth century of storm and tumult and terrible wars, in the vast world which has grown up around us.

I should not wish tonight to exaggerate our achievements. I am content with the modest plea that we have tried our best with no other aim but the common interest of the whole people. We are still only at the beginning of our task, and it may well be that disappointments and set-backs will afflict us. They will not, however, conquer us. We are encouraged by the fact that both at home and abroad there is a feeling that our position has definitely improved; that we are recovering our strength; that danger of a Third World War seems to have receded, and that our national solvency has been freed from immediate peril. We are also cheered by a confident feeling that, no matter how much we are abused by our opponents, if we do our duty faithfully and without fear, we shall get fair play from the British people.

There has been an Election lately in the United States which we have all watched with unflagging attention. For me, I must admit it has been painful to see so many of my best friends over there and comrades in war and peace fighting one another with all the ardour which we associate with party politics and democracy. Nothing like that could have happened under the Soviets or their satellite states. There all is presented with glacial decorum. One party only is allowed, and majorities are presented of 98 per cent. What I always wonder at is how the remaining 2 per cent are persuaded to deny their votes to the mighty oligarchy who hold their lives and every detail of their daily life in its grasp. Are they rewarded, or are they punished, and if punished, does this take place beforehand or afterwards? After all, it would be a very serious thing if any of these elections produced a hundred per cent result. That might easily lead the capitalist world to doubt whether actually all had been fair and square. They might even suggest that the whole performance was humbug, enforced by iron discipline. Personally I prefer the kind of thing that happens at British and American Elections, even though I must admit there ought, in both countries, to be some lucid intervals between them.

At any rate there was one thing about the American Election which gave us great comfort here and throughout the Commonwealths who together are partners in the English-speaking world. Both candidates were the finest figures American public life could present. Both were worthy of the highest traditions of the Great Republic which is now so valiantly sustaining the freedom of the world. With full confidence I express, in your name here tonight, our salutations to General Eisenhower and our assurance that, to the utmost limit of our strength, we will work with him for those great causes which we have guarded and cherished in ever greater unity as the generations have rolled by.

I did not wonder at all that the President-Elect, in the brief period before his inauguration, wished to visit Korea to view the scene with his own experienced and discerning eye. There is no doubt that the absorption of so large a proportion of American and United Nations resources in the Far East is to the advantage of Moscow and of the Communist Movement as a whole. That was why the Kremlin ordered the original aggression to begin; and that is why (after President Truman had effectively marshalled the United Nations to repel it) the so-called 'truce talks' have been dragged out over more than a year. It is a convenient way of dispersing the strength of the free world and preventing, or at least delaying, the building up of a secure defence against the subjugation of Western Europe.

For these reasons I have always been anxious to bring the conflict in Korea to an end as speedily as possible and to keep it within the strictest limits while it lasts. That is my view today, but there is one thing it is never worthwhile doing. That is to purchase peace at the price of dishonour. It would be dishonour to send thousands of helpless prisoners-of-war back by force to be massacred by a Chinese Communist Government which boasts that it has actually rid itself of two millions of its own people. All history shows that such bargains, though they may afford a momentary relief, have to be paid for on a far larger scale later on. Every kind of reasonable proposal has been made by the Allies and there can be no doubt that it has so far been the policy of Moscow, for reasons which are obvious, to prevent an agreement from being reached. All these are matters of grave concern. I turn to another scene.

A year ago, in the closing days of the late Government and following on the retreat from Abadan, our forces in Egypt were subjected to an outbreak of murderous attacks at the instigation of the Wafd Party led by Nahas Pasha. The Socialist Government ordered strong reinforcements to the Canal Zone and resisted these unprovoked outrages. They also put forward the statesmanlike conception of a four-power approach to Egypt in which Britain, the United States, France and Turkey should share with Egypt in the protection of the world interests involved in maintaining the freedom of the famous waterway of the Suez Canal. We continued the policy of our predecessors and after a few months the terrorist campaign – in which the Egyptian Army did not join – was quelled.

In July there was a revolution in Egypt rather similar to that of the young Turks in Turkey many years ago, as a result of which a distinguished Egyptian soldier became, for the time being, virtually a military dictator. I have visited Egypt at frequent intervals under varying circumstances during the last fifty-four years. I am bound to say that I felt much sympathy with the new hope aroused by General Neguib, that the shocking condition of the Egyptian peasantry under the corrupt rule of former Egyptian Governments would be definitely improved. We are anxious to help the new Government and to negotiate with them on friendly terms. We understand their point of view and we hope they will understand ours.

We are not in Egypt for imperialist motives or self-seeking mastery or advantage, but in the common interests of all nations and to discharge what has become an international rather than a national responsibility, and we have no intention of being turned from our duty. I hope indeed that negotiations may reach a happy conclusion, as they may well do if only they are inspired by a sense of mutual responsibility and seek the preservation of interests most important to the peace and safety, not only of Egypt, but of the whole anxious area of the Middle East.

There is another country I must mention at this moment. Those of us who have been Zionists since the days of the Balfour Declaration know what a heavy loss Israel has sustained in the death of its President, Dr Chaim Weizmann. Here was a man whose fame and fidelity were respected throughout the free world, whose son was killed fighting for us in the late war, and who, it may be rightly claimed, led his people back into their promised land, where we have seen them invincibly established as a free and sovereign State.

All our safety and the hopes of bringing the world – gradually, it may well have to be – out of its present oppressive and ruinous plight, rest upon the preservation of friendship, alliance, and growing unity between Great Britain and her Commonwealths and the USA. In what is called NATO – the North Atlantic Treaty Organization – of which Lord Ismay is the Secretary General – we have the most effective instrument ever prepared to resist aggression in the Western hemisphere. We have also the Council of Europe. NATO embraces all active, living movements towards the unity of the free nations of Europe, in which I have always felt the hopes of a lasting peace reside.

The organization of NATO does not exclude the Mediterranean and here we are very glad to welcome during the year the membership of Greece and of Turkey. Both these ancient and virile races have repudiated the Communist conception of society. I am very glad to remember the help I was instrumental in winning for the Greeks during the great crisis of their fate in the winter of 1944. I had the pleasure only the other day of receiving the Prime Minister of Turkey,[1] and of learning from that strong-minded statesman of the fearless outlook of modern Turkey and of their readiness to play a full part in our general organization of defence.

Six years have passed since I said at Zurich that France should take Germany by the hand and lead her back into the family of nations, and thus end the thousand-years' quarrel which has torn Europe to pieces and finally plunged the whole world twice over into slaughter and havoc.[2] There can be no effective defence of European culture and freedom unless a new Germany, resolved to set itself free from the ghastly crimes of Hitlerism, plays a strong and effective part in our system. Any man in Germany or France or Britain who tries to hamper or delay that healing process is guilty of undermining the foundations upon which the salvation of all mankind from war and tyranny depends.

Every addition to the strength of NATO increases the deterrents against aggression on which our hopes and convictions stand. It is for this that our Foreign Secretary, Mr Eden, strives, as did Mr Bevin before him. It was for this that General Eisenhower, under President Truman's administration, undertook his solemn task in Europe, to which General Ridgway, our new and trusted commander, has now succeeded, It is to this that Mr Schuman, the Foreign Minister of France, and the German Chancellor, Dr Adenauer, have devoted their remarkable wisdom and their courage. Time alone can prove whether final success will reward these earnest, faithful efforts. Terrible would be the accountability of those in any country who, for petty, narrow, or selfish ends, weakened the common cause by stirring bygone passions, hates and tragedies.

A year ago I said here, in this famous Guildhall, that Britain stood erect, calm, resolute, and independent.[3] What report should I make tonight? Surely it is that we have gained both in strength and in purpose. Britain is loyal to her faith: to her belief in the principles of the United Nations and in the dignity of the individual: and to her determination to see, with all her Allies, a true and

---

[1] Adnan Menderes, 1899–1961. Educated at American College, Izmir, Turkey. Married, 1929, Fatma Berin Yemişçibaşı: three children. MP (Republican People's Party), 1930–45. Expelled from RPP, 1945. Co-founded Democratic Party, 1946. PM of Turkey, 1950–60.

[2] See speech of 19 Sep. 1946, reproduced in *The Churchill Documents*, vol. 22, *Leader of the Opposition, August 1945 to October 1951*, pp. 458–61.

[3] Speech of 9 Nov. 1951, reproduced above (pp. 31–4).

lasting settlement among the nations. With this faith, and in this high companionship, we shall march forward undaunted by danger, unwearied by toil.

Lord De L'Isle and Dudley to Winston S. Churchill
(Premier papers, 11/43)

10 November 1952
Secret

It will be some time yet before the lessons of Exercise 'Ardent' can be fully analysed, but we can now draw some conclusions from it which are significant in relation to our knowledge of the Russian Air Force.

2. As far as peacetime conditions allow, the Exercise provided a realistic test for the air defences, and enabled Bomber Command to try out a number of new tactics and techniques. The activity over the five days of the Exercise was on a scale comparable with the peak periods of the Battle of Britain; there was not a single serious accident.

3. The Exercise showed a welcome improvement in the efficiency of the air defences; the interception rate against conventional bombers was most impressive. It has, however, emphasised once again the need to press ahead with current developments, particularly with:

(a) the new swept-wing fighters – the Hunter, Swift and Javelin;
(b) the air to air guided weapons which will give the fighter a much better chance of <u>destroying</u> the bomber when it has been intercepted;
(c) the strengthening of the control and reporting system;
(d) defensive radio warfare.

All these matters are in hand, but on present form it will be 1955 before we can hope to see the full results. An improved experimental type of radar which was tried out on a small scale proved very successful.

4. Our existing defences should be able to deal successfully with the current types of Russian piston engined bombers – their best is a similar aircraft to the American B.29. Against jet bombers of the Canberra type, which now form part of the Russian bomber force, and until the improvements listed above are well advanced we are very vulnerable.

5. The problem of an adequate interception and kill rate is largely one of numbers. We shall never have enough modern fighters to get a sufficiently high rate, when atom bombs are included in the attack, unless we can do something to reduce the attack at its source – i.e. the bases in Russia. This task, for which the smaller atom bomb is specially suitable, is among the first priority for the bomber force, of which the development must proceed in step with that of the fighter defences.

6. 'Ardent' has confirmed that our present ideas about air warfare, both in defence and attack, are sound. Its main lessons are:

(a) We must strive to get adequate quantities of the new aircraft and equipment into the air defence system at the earliest moment in order to hold our present advantage.

(b) We must hasten the development of the bomber striking force.[1]

James de Rothschild[2] to Winston S. Churchill
(Churchill papers, 2/199)[3]

10 November 1952

My dear Winston,

Or perhaps on this occasion I should prefer to say my dear Prime Minister.

I have just listened to you and watched you on our TV set and I feel that I really must write and tell you how enchanted I was with your appearance and with what you said.

I have not seen you in action now for nearly 7 years (save perhaps at the Jockey Club meeting) and seven years is a cycle in man's life.

But my dear Winston, you have not changed, the same voice, the same appearance, the same fire and the same cool logic.

I was particularly touched and want to thank you personally for what you said about Weizmann; it will mean a lot to the many thousands & tens of thousands of Jews, it will mean a lot to those who are their friends, also perhaps to those who like them less.

Winston S. Churchill to R. A. Butler
(Churchill papers, 2/181)[4]

10 November 1952

My dear Rab,

I send you my condolences on the death of your Father.

I know what it was to me to lose my Father, although I had seen him so little. I revered and admired him from a distance, except for a few glittering occasions. I have striven to vindicate his memory.

But you had the comfort and joy of long years of mature intimacy. And he the even greater satisfaction to a parent of watching the unfolding of your career.

Time rolls along, but I feel both you and he have been blessed by Fortune.

---

[1] Churchill wrote at the bottom of the page: 'This depends upon what we settle with the new President about the priority of targets.'

[2] James Armand Edmond de Rothschild, 1878–1957. Educated in Paris and at Cambridge University. On active service, 1914–18. Maj., Royal Fusiliers, 1918. A prominent Zionist. MP (Lib.) for Isle of Ely, 1929–45. Joint Parliamentary Secretary, Ministry of Supply, 1945.

[3] This letter was handwritten.

[4] This letter was handwritten.

Cabinet: conclusions
(*Cabinet papers, 128/25*)

11 November 1952
Secret
11.30 a.m.
Cabinet Meeting No. 95 of 1952

[. . .]

2. The Minister of Transport said that in view of opposition to the proposed development of Gatwick Airport which was showing itself, especially among Government supporters, the Cabinet might wish to review their decision of 29th July. He suggested that for this purpose he should circulate a memorandum, in the form of a draft White Paper, explaining the Government's attitude on all aspects of the matter. This would set out the Government's intentions in regard to civil airfields in the London area generally; would explain why it was necessary to develop an alternative civil air terminus to London Airport and why Gatwick had been chosen for this purpose in preference to nearly 50 other possible sites; would disclose the Government's attitude towards suggestions that long-distance airline services should terminate at airfields well outside the London area from which passengers would be conveyed to London by helicopter; and, finally, would explain how it was expected that a substantial proportion of the cost of developing Gatwick would be offset by the release of no less than four of the seven civil airfields at present retained in the London area. If, on the basis of such a document, the Government were to reaffirm their decision that Gatwick should be developed, a local enquiry might thereafter be held into the local aspects of the project, for example the exact siting of the runways.

The Minister of Housing and Local Government said that it was important to avoid a situation in which representatives of his Ministry, holding a local enquiry, were expected to deal with questions of national policy connected with the proposed development of Gatwick Airport which it would not be within their competence to answer. He, therefore, supported the Minister's proposal.

The Prime Minister welcomed the proposed submission of a draft White Paper but said that he was by no means convinced that it would be right for the Government to reaffirm and make known for a second time their decision to develop Gatwick Airport before allowing local interests to express their views through some form of public enquiry.

The Secretary of State for Air said that he would wish to be associated with the preparation of the proposed White Paper.

The Cabinet –
Invited the Minister of Transport, in consultation with the Secretary of State for Air and other Ministers concerned, to prepare and submit to the

Cabinet the draft of a White Paper setting out in full the case for developing Gatwick Airport as an alternative civil air terminus to London Airport.

Took note that, in the announcement which he would shortly be making of impending changes in ration scales, the Minister of Food would not include any statement about the winter level of the weekly meat ration.

[. . .]

Winston S. Churchill to Lord De L'Isle and Dudley
Prime Minister's Personal Minute M.536/52
(Premier papers, 11/76)

11 November 1952

I am still not clear about the jet airplanes, about seventy-five of which are being sold in the Middle East. What exactly are they? When were they completed? How much is their value? How is it that we do not want them ourselves? Are all our squadrons, including auxiliary squadrons, equipped with these or better jets? When will the actual deliveries be made?

Winston S. Churchill to President-Elect Dwight D. Eisenhower
Prime Minister's Personal Telegram T.211/52
(Premier papers, 11/572)

12 November 1952
Immediate
Confidential
No. 4811

Thank you for your letter of November 8th. You were certainly right not to reply to the *Sunday Pictorial*, which like the *Daily Mirror* of the same firm uses its large circulation in a mischievous manner. They are our version of McCormick. They were the spreaders of the 'war-monger' lie, which did us much harm, and for which I made them apologize and pay damages in an action for libel. Of course, it would have been a great score for their correspondent if he could have got a word from you.

2. I am very glad that you are going to Korea. You will probably have seen what I said at the Guildhall on the subject on November 10th.[1] I also received a message from Omar saying that you would be glad if one of our officers could meet you out there. We have a good Lieutenant-General (Shoosmith) on Mark Clark's Staff, who is well apprised of our point of view.

---

[1] Speech reproduced above (pp. 722–6).

John Colville to Winston S. Churchill
(Premier papers, 11/351)

12 November 1952

You asked me about the sentence which could be imposed on Craig,[1] the murderer of the Croydon policeman. As he is under 18 he cannot by law be hanged. He can and doubtless will be sentenced to be detained during Her Majesty's pleasure.

In theory this could be a heavier sentence than that imposed on an adult murderer who for one reason or another was not hanged. The adult would be sentenced to life imprisonment which means 20 years and, in practice, a good deal less. A juvenile can be imprisoned indefinitely. What actually happens is that the length of an adult unhanged murderer's sentence depends on the nature of the murder – some being undoubtedly worse than others – while the length of time during which a juvenile is detained depends more on the development and personality of the murderer rather than on the crime. Sometimes small children commit murders; and it may in certain cases be thought right to let them out very soon. As for Craig, it would depend on the prison Governors' assessment of his character and development at what stage he was released. It might be a few years, but if he was thought to be still dangerous it might be a good many. I gather the Home Office believe that after 12 years' imprisonment a man's character deteriorates to such an extent that he is often more dangerous than he was before. It follows that they usually try to release people before this deterioration sets in.

John Colville to Winston S. Churchill
(Premier papers, 11/351)

13 November 1952

You asked 'Can nobody be sentenced to penal servitude for any offence if only 16?'

The position is that penal servitude was abolished in 1948 and there is now only simple imprisonment. A Court of Summary Jurisdiction (i.e. a Magistrates' Court) cannot sentence anybody to imprisonment under the age of 17. A Court of Assize or Quarter Sessions cannot sentence anybody to imprisonment under the age of 15. Furthermore the Act demands that no Court shall impose imprisonment on anyone under 21 unless the Court decides that there is no other appropriate method of dealing with the offender. If it does so decide, it shall state its reasons.

Murder, as I said in my previous minute, is in a different category. Anybody

---

[1] Christopher Craig, 1936– . Convicted of murder, 1952; imprisoned, 1952–63.

under 18 convicted of murder is sentenced to be detained during Her Majesty's pleasure and the length of their sentence really depends on the Home Secretary.

Winston S. Churchill to Anthony Eden
Prime Minister's Personal Telegram T.215/52
(Premier papers, 11/323)

15 November 1952
Secret
No. 12

Am very glad you are seeing Ike on Wednesday. It would be good if he could stop in London on his way back from Korea. We should be proud to welcome him. I should greatly like a talk with him but he must of course consider American public opinion.

2. Your speech[1] was very good and as usual we think alike.

Winston S. Churchill to Foreign Office
Prime Minister's Personal Minute M.543/52
(Premier papers, 11/207)

17 November 1952

Surely there can be no question of Israel being asked to give up the Negeb, as its development might afford the only means of sustaining their great population of refugee immigrants?

Sir William Strang to Winston S. Churchill
(Premier papers, 11/207)

19 November 1952
Confidential
PM/52/137

Your Minute M.543/52 about the Negeb.

2. We have of course not asked the Israelis to give it up, and can foresee no circumstances in which we should be justified in doing so. We consider the Arab claim to be unrealistic and we recognise Israel's need of an area in which her population can expand and which, once developed, may be a source of wealth to the country.

---

[1] The reference is most likely to Eden's speech of Nov. 6 in the Commons on Foreign Affairs and Defence.

3. In any case, the Israelis would never agree to the cession of an area which appeals to their pioneering spirit and on which they are expending great efforts to make it habitable and to discover minerals.[1]

Winston S. Churchill to Duke of Windsor
(Premier papers, 11/32)

19 November 1952

Sir,
    The Chancellor of the Exchequer will be very glad to have the honour of a visit from Your Royal Highness tomorrow, Thursday. If your Private Secretary rings up his or mine, a time can easily be arranged. There is a Cabinet in the morning. I should think after Questions in the afternoon would be most suitable. I think the meeting can do nothing but good.
    About the Coronation. I thought Your Royal Highness's suggestion about the statement which you would make when convenient or necessary to American reporters was excellent. I have consulted the Lord Chancellor upon it, and he says that you would be quite right in stating that 'it would not be in accordance with constitutional usage (or 'precedent') for the Coronation of a King or Queen of England to be attended by the sovereign or former sovereign of any State and that for any departure from such usage (or 'precedent') there has been a special reason which does not apply in the present case.' I should myself have thought that the first part of the sentence was sufficient. It is certainly a most dignified reply.
    It was a great pleasure to me to have a talk yesterday, and I hope Eric's pheasants were up to the mark this morning.

With my humble duty
I remain
Your Royal Highness's faithful servant.

Winston S. Churchill to Sir Alan Lascelles
(Premier papers, 11/32)

19 November 1952

My dear Tommy,
    I send you a copy of a letter I have sent to the Duke of Windsor upon his wise suggestion of not coming to the Coronation. I think he is quite right, and that his attitude is becoming. I am so glad he is lunching with The Queen and the Duke of Edinburgh today.

---

[1] Churchill wrote on this minute: 'I am glad we are in full agreement.'

About the transfer of funds, I am telling the Chancellor of the Exchequer that I think it would be generally in accordance with the public interest if the Duke were able to make himself a home in France. After all it is his own money, and all we have to do is to assent to the transfer.

You are welcome to show this letter to The Queen.

Cabinet: conclusions
(Cabinet papers, 128/25)

20 November 1952
Secret
11.30 a.m.
Cabinet Meeting No. 99 of 1952

[. . .]

8. The Cabinet had before them memoranda by the Home Secretary and the Secretary of State for Scotland (C(52)386 and 387) on the question of corporal punishment as a penalty for crimes of violence.

The Prime Minister said that he was not attracted by the suggestion, put forward in the Home Secretary's memorandum, that a Royal Commission or Departmental Committee should be appointed to make a further enquiry into this question. He would prefer that the Government should hold themselves free to introduce legislation restoring corporal punishment if at any time it became clear that there was a sufficient body of public support for this course to make it possible to pass the necessary legislation through Parliament. Corporal punishment, if it were reintroduced, should be avoidable as a penalty for all crimes of violence or brutality; and he did not exclude the possibility that this penalty might be reintroduced on an experimental basis, for a period of not more than five years, at the end of which it could be seen whether there had been an appreciable decrease in the crime for which it was made available. He thought that, if a plebiscite could be held on this question, the majority of the people of this country might be found to be in favour of reintroducing this penalty.

The Home Secretary said that he recognised that there was widespread public anxiety about the increase in the number of crimes involving violence. But robbery with violence was the only such crime for which the penalty of corporal punishment had recently been available, and it should be remembered that the incidence of this particular offence had in fact decreased since that penalty was withdrawn in 1948. The increase in crimes of violence had been in other offences, for which the penalty of corporal punishment had not been available for nearly 100 years. He had little doubt that the proper remedy was to build up the strength of the police forces, which were now far below establishment in all our principal cities. He himself was doubtful whether the Government would be justified in promoting legislation on this subject without a further enquiry which would take account of post-war conditions. But the Cabinet should in any event consider the political difficulties of introducing legislation to restore corporal punishment: there seemed to him to be little prospect of passing such a measure through the House of Commons if, as he believed, the Labour Party would oppose it and at least one-fourth of the Government's supporters would be unwilling to vote for it.

The Secretary of State for Scotland said that a majority of Scottish Members in the House of Commons would be opposed to the restoration of corporal punishment.

In further discussion it was pointed out that, since the two memoranda were circulated, a Member who had obtained a high place in the ballot for Private Members' Bills had indicated his intention to introduce a Bill to restore corporal punishment as a penalty for crimes of violence. The Second Reading of this Bill, which would be taken in February, would provide a convenient opportunity to test public opinion on this question and to obtain a free expression of the views of the House of Commons. Though the Government would be expected to indicate their views, the issue could properly be left on that occasion to a free vote of the House.

The Cabinet –

(1) Decided not to proceed further at present with the suggestion for a further enquiry into the question of corporal punishment as a penalty for crimes of violence.

(2) Agreed that Members of the House of Commons should be encouraged to express their views on this question, in a free vote, on the Second Reading in February of the Corporal Punishment Bill which was shortly to be introduced by a Private Member.

(3) Agreed to consider at a later meeting what views should be put forward on the Government's behalf in the debate on that Bill.

Winston S. Churchill to Anthony Eden
Prime Minister's Personal Telegram *T.222/52*
(Premier papers, 11/111)

22 November 1952
Personal and Secret
Immediate
No. 1034

1. Am making the following changes which will be announced Tuesday morning. Bobbity[1] to LPC. Philip[2] to Secretary Commonwealth. Fred[3] has accepted Duchy.[4] This will enable him to convalesce at leisure and also enables me to meet Bobbity's wishes. Salter[5] will take over Materials in the Commons. Maudling[6] will succeed him. As a minor consequential change Patrick[7] presses strongly for Profumo[8] to follow Maudling. I like this idea and so does ALGB.[9]

2. Peter Thorneycroft will be in bed till Christmas but Philip will represent the Board of Trade and hold the Duchy till December 15 when Bobbity vacates Commonwealth.

3. This arrangement has been welcomed by Bobbity, Philip and Rab.

4. I had hoped you would be back today but I quite understand the importance of being able to feel that everything in human power has been done about the prisoners in Korea and to end the war there. The Tass Agency reports this evening, if correct, make it clear the Kremlin want the war to go on. At least you can say we have done our best.

Looking forward much to your return.

[1] Lord Salisbury.
[2] Lord Swinton.
[3] Lord Woolton.
[4] Chancellorship of the Duchy of Lancaster.
[5] James Arthur Salter, 1881–1975. Transport Dept, Admiralty, 1904. Chairman, Allied Maritime Transport Executive, 1918. Knighted, 1922. Director, Economic and Finance Section, League of Nations, 1919–20, 1922–31. Prof. of Political Theory and Institutions, Oxford University, 1934–44. MP (Ind.) for Oxford University, 1937–50; (Cons.) for Ormskirk, 1951–3. Parliamentary Secretary, Ministry of Shipping, 1939–41; Ministry of War Transport, 1941. Head of British Merchant Shipping Mission, Washington DC, 1941–3. PC, 1941. Deputy Director-General, UNRRA, 1944. Chancellor of the Duchy of Lancaster, 1945. Minister of State for Economic Affairs, 1951–2. Minister of Materials, 1952–3. Baron, 1953. Head of Special Economic Mission to Iraq, 1954..
[6] Reginald Maudling, 1917–79. Educated at Merton College, Oxford. Married, 1939, Beryl Laverick. Called to the Bar, Middle Temple, 1940. MP (Cons.) for Barnet, 1950–74; for Chipping Barnet, 1974–9. Parliamentary Secretary to Minister of Civil Aviation, 1952. Economic Secretary to Treasury, 1952–5. PC, 1955. Minister of Supply, 1955–7. Paymaster-General, 1957–9. President of the Board of Trade, 1959–61. Secretary of State for the Colonies, 1961–2. Chancellor of the Exchequer, 1962–4. Home Secretary, 1970–2.
[7] Patrick Buchan-Hepburn.
[8] John Profumo, 1915–2006. Known as 'Jack'. Commissioned 2nd Lt, Royal Armoured Corps, 1939. MP (Cons.) for Kettering, 1940–5; for Stratford-on-Avon, 1950–63. OBE, 1944. Parliamentary Secretary, Ministry of Civil Aviation, 1952–7. Married, 1954, Valerie Hobson. Parliamentary Under-Secretary of State for the Colonies, 1957–8. Under-Secretary of State for Foreign Affairs, 1958–9. Minister of State for Foreign Affairs, 1959–60. Secretary of State for War, 1960–3. CBE, 1975.
[9] Alan Lennox-Boyd. The 'G' appears to be an error.

NOVEMBER 1952

Anthony Eden to Winston S. Churchill
(Premier papers, 11/111)

23 November 1952

Thank you so much for telling of the changes. Among the juniors the promotion of Maudling and Profumo seems to me admirable.

I am encouraged by your last paragraph. We still have hopes of agreement, at least amongst all except the Russians, on an improved Indian resolution. But the Americans have suddenly published inaccurate accounts of our discussion which I fear will only make their own position more difficult. There is strong support for our view amongst the Commonwealth and European delegations. I am confident too that many Americans share this. It was voiced to me emphatically by Lew Douglas, whom I happened to see last night. He is of course in touch with our new friend.

Duke of Windsor to Winston S. Churchill
(Premier papers, 11/32)

23 November 1952

Dear Winston,

I have been giving further thought to the matter of the statement you, the Lord Chancellor and I agree could be made to the Press with regard to my not attending the Coronation.

Should this valid reason for my absence from Westminster Abbey next June 2nd be given, I must be assured that the principle upon which it is based be not violated.

In other words I feel it would be only right and proper that I be protected from the possibility of the presence in the Abbey of any person or persons falling within the category or 'the sovereign or former sovereign of any State'. I have in mind such people as Leopold[1] of the Belgians, Umberto[2] of Italy, and Peter[3] of Yugoslavia. This you could do as Prime Minister by 'advising' against such a possibility.

The chances of any of these former monarchs being invited would, I imagine, be remote. On the other hand I know you will readily appreciate how

---

[1] Leopold III, 1901–83. Educated at Eton. Married, 1926, Princess Astrid of Sweden (d. 1935): three children; 1941, Mary-Lilian Baels: three children. King of Belgium, 1934–50. Captured by German forces, 1940. Deported to Germany, 1944. In exile, 1945–50. Abdicated, 1951.

[2] Umberto II, 1904–83. Educated at Royal Military Academy, Turin. Married, 1930, Princess Marie José of Belgium: four children. Mshl, 1942. Lt-Gen. of the Kingdom, 1944. Succeeded as King Umberto II, May 1946. Abdicated, June 1946.

[3] Peter II, 1923–70. King of Yugoslavia, 1934–45. Evacuated Yugoslavia following German invasion of 1941. Married, 1944, Princess Alexandra of Greece and Denmark. Deposed by Yugoslavia's Communist Constituent Assembly, 1945.

quickly I could be held up to ridicule were a statement made the substance of which would become meaningless in the event of such an eventuality arising. Nor, do I believe, would you wish such a thing to happen.

It has also occurred to me that in order to avoid any possible misrepresentation, in which the Press so freely indulge, the statement be issued by the Earl Marshal. From the powers vested in him by the Crown with regard to all State ceremonial, he is the constitutional authority for everything connected with the Coronation ceremony. Any statement made by the Earl Marshal therefore would be official as opposed to personal if it emanated from me.

The statement I suggest could read as follows:

'The Duke of Windsor will not be present at the Coronation in Westminster Abbey on June 2nd 1953 because it would not be in accordance with constitutional usage for the Coronation of a King or Queen of England to be attended by the Sovereign or former Sovereign of any State.'

I regret having to bother you further with this matter, but it is a delicate one, and has been aggravated by the wide interest and speculation it has evoked in the Press. You did not seem to be aware of this unpleasant publicity when I told you about it last week. It is no fault of mine; no one resents it more than I do. Unfortunately it all stems from my family's uncompromising attitude towards the Duchess and I which causes the rekindling of this controversial subject as headline news with each and every Royal public occasion.

With the Duchess's and my warm regards.

Cabinet: conclusions
(Cabinet papers, 128/25)

25 November 1952
Secret
11 a.m.
Cabinet Meeting No. 100 of 1952

[...]

6. The Cabinet had before them memoranda by the Chancellor of the Exchequer and the Secretary of State for Air (C(52)415 and C(52)422) on the provision of married quarters for the United States Armed Forces in the United Kingdom.

The Chancellor of the Exchequer said that he thought it desirable that some further provision should be made for married quarters for members of the United States Armed Forces stationed in the United Kingdom. He had contemplated that 5,000 pre-fabricated timber houses might be erected by private companies who would make their own arrangements for finance and would receive a guarantee for rents for at least five years. A scheme on these lines would bring in about $6 millions a year by way of rent and an additional $10 millions a year as a result of the extra expenditure which would be incurred by the families living in these houses. He recognised, however, that there would be considerable difficulty about selecting sites and he was prepared to agree that in the first place the Secretary of State for Air should arrange for this to be examined in detail in consultation with the other Departments concerned.

In discussion the following points were made –
  (a) The scheme proposed by the Chancellor of the Exchequer was profitable, would make use of pre-fabricated houses which were available for sale, and would not interfere with the housing programme. It was, however, desirable that sites should be selected which would not entail the provision of additional water and sewerage schemes.
  (b) The Secretary of State for Air said that he feared that the creation of American communities with their higher standard of living might cause criticism and discontent among English communities in their neighbourhood. The additional married quarters should therefore be established to the greatest possible extent within the confines of United States airfields or, failing that, on land owned or held on requisition by the Air Ministry. He hoped that no further commitment would be entered into until the sites had been selected.

The Prime Minister said that the presence of United States Forces in the United Kingdom was an essential feature in the cold war and it was possible to defend on this ground the provision of reasonable amenities for the United States Forces. The first step should be the selection of sites on the lines suggested by the Secretary of State for Air. Continuous effort should be made to preserve friendly relations between the United States Forces in this county and their English neighbours and he would be glad to hear from the Secretary of State for Air what was being done for this purpose.

The Cabinet –
  (1) Agreed in principle that help should be given in the provision of married quarters for the United States Armed Forces in the United Kingdom on the general lines suggested by the Chancellor of the Exchequer.
  (2) As a first step invited the Secretary of State for Air to arrange for an interdepartmental committee of officials, representing the Departments affected, to carry out a selection of the sites on the basis indicated in the Cabinet's discussion.
  (3) Took note that the Secretary of State for Air would report to the Prime Minister what arrangements were being made to foster good relations between the United States Armed Forces in the United Kingdom and their English neighbours.

[. . .]

Winston S. Churchill to Field Marshal Lord Alexander
Prime Minister's Personal Minute M.551/52
(Premier papers, 11/764)

25 November 1952

Mr Bevan has on several occasions asserted that we have increased the Rearmament Programme since we took over. This is of course because many projects, started under the £4,700 million programme, only came into full activity after the change of government and no doubt some have not come into full activity yet. I should like some figures to be prepared which show what the £4,700 million programme would have been in the current year if we had not made reductions and if we had not sold munitions abroad; and also for the next year 1953/54. There is also the increase of prices due to the continued fall in the purchasing power of the £. My own impression (not founded on any calculations) is that the 1952/53 Estimates, with supplementaries, of the whole Rearmament Programme, as designed by the late government would have been (say) £1,800, or £300 million more than the present estimates. So also proportionally the 1953/54 Estimates, if not handled by us, might well have reached a total of (say) £1,700 or £1,800 million. We have, therefore, effected net reductions of _ million in 1952 and _ million in 1953/4. In other words the Socialist rearmament programme of £4,700 million would in fact have passed, in the first three or four full years of its life, £6,000 or £7,000 million. Owing to our compression, correction and revision it will not cost more than (say) £5,500.

All these figures are of course purely suggestive but I feel that I should like to see the real ones in order that this part of our case may be fully made.

President-Elect Dwight D. Eisenhower to Winston S. Churchill
(Churchill papers, 2/217)

25 November 1952

Dear Winston,

Mrs Eisenhower[1] and I send our heartiest good wishes and congratulations on your Birthday anniversary Sunday.

May your celebration be filled with joy and herald the start of another year of brilliant and inspired devotion to your country and mankind.

Our warmest regards to you and Mrs Churchill.

---

[1] Mamie Geneva Doud, 1896–1979. Married, 1916, Dwight D. Eisenhower: two children. First Lady, 1953–61.

Chiefs of Staff Committee: minutes
(Premier papers, 11/45)

28 November 1952
Top Secret
12.15 p.m.
Chiefs of Staff Meeting No. 17 of 1952

The Chief of the Air Staff and The First Sea Lord outlined to the Prime Minister proposals which had been provisionally agreed in the Standing Group in Washington on Mediterranean Command, the Iberian area, and the striking Fleet Commander in the North Atlantic.

The Prime Minister said that the primary task of the United States Carrier Forces in the Mediterranean was to co-operate with the US Air Forces in the strategic attack to paralyze Russian movements. The major strategic air attack must be under United States command. He agreed, therefore, that the US carrier force was best directed by SACEUR. He understood that the proposal now was to appoint a Commander-in-Chief, Mediterranean and Black Sea, who would be a British officer, under SACEUR. He hoped that the C-in-C, Mediterranean, would be able to do his duties in the Middle East. General Ridgway, in giving him orders, would have to take into account his responsibility towards the Middle East. He appreciated that the French would have an area in the Western Mediterranean, but hoped that convoys passing through this area would not need to change escorts.

The Chief of Staff explained that the C-in-C, Mediterranean, would be responsible only for coordinating the movements of the US Carrier Forces in the Mediterranean, but not for command of their operations, which would be exercised by SACEUR through C-in-C, South. The responsibilities of the C-in-C, Mediterranean, towards the Middle East were fully safeguarded, since, in the agreement, he was responsible for the 'support of adjacent commands'. The C-in-C, Mediterranean, would be responsible for co-ordinating escorts for convoys throughout the Mediterranean.

The Prime Minister said that it was of first importance on the outbreak of war to send submarines into the Black Sea to prevent amphibious operations against Turkey. We must seal the Bosporus and prevent the enemy issuing into the Mediterranean. He was most anxious that the Turks should be given all available information on modern mines, and that they should be made to feel confident that we could make amphibious landings on the Turkish coast impossible and could prevent the escape of Russian ships from the Black Sea.

The First Sea Lord said that the C-in-C, Mediterranean, would, immediately on his appointment, be tackling these problems, on which some progress had already been made in discussions with Admiral Carney.

Continuing, the Prime Minister said he was glad that the problem of command in the Arctic and North Atlantic had been satisfactorily agreed. It was our task to assist the operations of the American Carrier Forces: but he agreed that the movements of these forces must be co-ordinated by the British C-in-C, EASTLANT.

The Chiefs of Staff explained that in the Iberian area, the status quo was to continue for the time being, but that Allied Staff Officers were to be integrated into the Headquarters of the British Commander at Gibraltar. They had agreed that SACLANT should explore the facilities for a Headquarters in Lisbon, but believed that this examination would show the futility of the proposal to spend large sums in setting up a new HQ in LISBON when there was already in being a working HQ with adequate communications in Gibraltar.

The French were anxious to establish a sub-area off the Moroccan shores under the French Naval Commander at Casablanca. They saw no objection to this proposal, provided that the sub-area was under the British C-in-C, EASTLANT.

The Prime Minister said that the Chief of the Air Staff and First Sea Lord had had a most successful mission to Washington. At one time he did not wish to have command committed to that area. He originally wanted command of the Atlantic. The position was now quite different; the United States had the command in the Atlantic, and strong American forces had been sent into the Mediterranean. He was therefore prepared now to accept a British Commander in the Mediterranean.

The proposals made in Washington were good and had his full agreement. A minute to this effect should be sent to the Foreign Secretary, and the Chiefs of Staff should tell their representative in Washington to inform the United States Joint Chiefs of Staff and Standing Group members of HMG's approval at once. He hoped that he would be able to announce the agreement on Mediterranean command before Parliament rose.

The Chiefs of Staff explained that an announcement could be made as soon as the NATO Council had agreed to it in Paris; probably about the 17th of December.

The Prime Minister:

a) Invited the Chiefs of Staff to transmit, as soon as possible, British agreement on the Washington proposals to the United States Joint Chiefs of Staff and Standing Group representatives.

b) Invited Sir Nevil Brownjohn[1] to prepare a minute to the Foreign Secretary on the outcome of his discussions with the Chiefs of Staff.

---

[1] Nevil Charles Dowell Brownjohn, 1897–1973. Educated at Malvern College and Royal Military Academy, Woolwich. Joined RE, 1915. MC, 1917. Married, 1929, Isabelle White: one child. OBE, 1941. CB, 1944. Deputy Military Governor, Control Commission for Germany (British Element), 1947–9. Vice-QMG, 1949–50. CMG, 1949. VCIGS, 1950–2. KCB, 1951. Chief Staff Officer, Ministry of Defence, 1952–5. Col. Commandant, Corps of RE, 1955–62. QMG, 1956–8. GBE, 1957. ADC to the Queen, 1957–8.

Winston S. Churchill to Anthony Eden
Prime Minister's Personal Minute M.554/52
(Premier papers, 11/44)

28 November 1952
Secret

I have discussed with the Chiefs of Staff the provisional agreements on Naval Commands made in Washington by the Chief of the Air Staff and the First Sea Lord. I think them very satisfactory. The Chiefs of Staff are instructing their representative in Washington to inform the American Chiefs of Staff and members of the Standing Group that we agree to the proposals. I hope that this will prevent second thoughts in America and that your message to Schuman will help to overcome any misgivings on the part of the French.

Winston S. Churchill to James Thomas
Prime Minister's Personal Minute M.555/52
(Premier papers, 11/478)

28 November 1952

Your Private Secretary's letter of November 27. You say 7,600 Naval Fleet Reservists have been recalled for 18 months' service. How many have been recalled in each of the years since 1950? How many 'juniors' in each of the above years were recalled?

2. There is a great difference between calling men up for seven days' training every second year and calling up others for 18 months' continuous service regardless of their employment and regardless whether they are married or single. On what principle is this selection made of men who have to suffer this altogether exceptional hardship in time of peace? I trust you will give your personal attention to this matter.

Evelyn Shuckburgh: diary
('Descent to Suez', page 62)

28 November 1952

PM has told Clarissa he wants to give up. She says he is looking for an opportunity and Anthony must be gentle with him. Must let him go to America. Today he begged Anthony to let him go 'as privately as possible'. 'Only one speech'. AE is tempted. It might be the way out. But Winston is worried that AE is so deep in foreign affairs and not preparing.

Winston S. Churchill to David Eccles
Prime Minister's Personal Minute M.557/52
(Premier papers, 11/357)

30 November 1952

I have seen your minute of November 25 about the allocation of seats to Members of the House of Commons in Westminster Abbey.

I certainly think that a ballot should be avoided. I hear that a very rough preliminary canvas has shown that about one fifth of the Members on our side would definitely prefer to see the procession outside and that rather more than another fifth are doubtful. If it is possible to adopt some or all of the expedients suggested in my Private Secretary's letter of November 25, we may hope that a substantial proportion of the waverers will be encouraged to choose seats outside.

I think that for the present we might let the Cabinet's proposal of 1,710 seats for the Lords and Commons, of which 910 would be for the Lords, go forward to the Commission. If, in the event, the House of Commons require a few more seats than those provided in their allotment, I should be willing to see the Earl Marshal and ask his help in obtaining them, if necessary at the expense of some of the other categories.

Winston Churchill to Winston S. Churchill
(Churchill papers, 1/51)[1]

30 November 1952

Dear Grandpapa,

Many happy returns of yesterday.[2] I did not know that it was your birthday until I saw it in the papers, but I hope you got the telegram. There are sixteen more days left this term. Yesterday there was a conjurer who came here, he was very good. And day before that was the 'merit half holiday' which is a half holiday for boys who have done well in their work during the term. On Wednesday there will be a 4th XI match which I hope to play in. Give my love to grandmama, please. I hope you are well.[3]

---

[1] This letter was handwritten.
[2] It seems young Winston made a mistake with the date.
[3] Churchill wrote back: 'Thank you so much darling.'

December 1952

Sir Norman Brook to Winston S. Churchill
(Premier papers, 11/487)

3 December 1952

MOVE OF THE MIDDLE EAST HEADQUARTERS
(C(52)382)

In this paper the Minister of Defence sets out the arguments for agreeing now in principle that the Middle East Headquarters should be transferred to Cyprus and that such preliminary work should be put in hand as can be done without committing the Government to a decision on the ultimate size of the Headquarters or of the forces to be retained in the Middle East theatre.

2. The Foreign Secretary endorses the Minister's view that the most that we should be able to retain in Egypt under any defence settlement would be a base and its associated air defence. We have no right under the 1936 Treaty to keep the Headquarters in Egypt at all.

3. The Minister's proposals are based on the assumption that we shall retain in the Middle East a force of one division and 160 aircraft, as recommended by the Chiefs of Staff in their paper on Global Strategy. Even if we were compelled to reduce our strength in the Middle East still further there would still have to be a headquarters for the area though possibly a smaller one. The only decision on general defence policy that would be prejudged by approval to transfer the Headquarters to Cyprus is that we should in any circumstances keep some forces in the Middle East theatre.

Combined Cabinet and Commonwealth Prime Ministers' meeting: conclusions
(Cabinet papers, 128/25)

4 December 1952
Secret
11.30 a.m.
Cabinet Meeting No. 102 of 1952

Mr Churchill said that it was for him a unique experience and privilege to preside over a Cabinet meeting attended by so many Prime Ministers and other Ministers from other countries of the Commonwealth.[1] In considering the many grave problems which confronted them they would be encouraged by the knowledge that their combined influence was capable of affecting the course of world events. They would all welcome a review by Mr Eden of the main features of the international situation.

Mr Eden said that in Germany, through which ran the dividing line between East and West, Dr Adenauer was working strenuously to bring the Federal Republic into the closest possible association with Western Europe. His greatest difficulty was the failure to reach an agreement with the French over the Saar. At an earlier stage agreement had almost been reached on the basis of German acceptance in principle of the permanent autonomy and 'Europeanisation' of the Saar. It had not proved possible, however, to provide adequately for the economic needs of France, to whom Saar coal was vital in order to maintain the balance of the Schuman Plan. The results of the recent elections had created an atmosphere more favourable to a settlement and there would be further discussions while Ministers were in Paris for the meeting of the North Atlantic Council in the following week. Dr Adenauer was genuinely anxious for a settlement and the election results should have strengthened his position *vis-à-vis* the more extreme opinion in Germany.

Relations with Russia, in respect of Germany, were settling down on the basis of Russian consolidation in the east and Russian acceptance of our consolidation in the west. This position, though it could not be called satisfactory, had certain advantages to all parties, not excluding the Germans themselves. The Russians doubtless believed that they were better able to withstand a protracted 'cold war' than were the Western Powers, and it must be expected that they would exploit all the difficulties of the Western Powers and any differences of view between them which might reveal themselves.

The recent executions of political leaders in Czechoslovakia were thought to be due partly to the failure of the Government's economic programme

[1] Louis St Laurent (PM of Canada); Sidney Holland (PM and Minister of Finance, New Zealand); Dudley Senanayake (PM and Minister of Defence and External Affairs, Ceylon); Nicolaas Havenga (Minister of Finance, South Africa); Robert Menzies (PM of Australia); Khwaja Nazimuddin (PM and Minister for Defence, Pakistan); Sir Godfrey Huggins (PM and Minister of Defence, Southern Rhodesia); Sir Chintaman D. Deshmukh (Minister for Finance, India).

and partly to personal rivalries within the local Communist Party. It was possible that M Clementis[1] had had ambitions to follow Marshal Tito's example, but this was not true of M Slansky[2] who was an orthodox Communist. He was also a Jew, but there was no conclusive evidence of anti-Semitic motives behind the recent events in Prague, though Russia was undoubtedly opposed to Zionism because of its appeal to Jews to leave their countries of domicile for Palestine. The recent events in Prague had given rise to serious apprehensions in Hungary.

There appeared to be a reasonable prospect that the European Defence Community treaty would be ratified by Germany before the end of the year. Dr Adenauer hoped for a clear majority when the Bundestag voted upon it at the end of the present week. It seemed unlikely that the Federal Court would intervene and there was a fair prospect that a majority would be obtained later in the Bundesrat.[3] The prospects of ratification by France were more uncertain. M Pinay's Government was becoming weaker and the French were keenly apprehensive of the effect of the war in Indo-China upon the relative strengths of the French and German elements in the proposed European Army. The French Government would undoubtedly welcome some move by the United Kingdom in the direction of closer association with the Community but we had already gone as far as we could short of full membership. We should continue to discourage any suggestion that the cohesion of the Community should be loosened in order to make our participation possible and to do everything in our power to persuade the French Government to ratify the Treaty. If the European Defence Community were not formed, it would be difficult to avoid the admission of a national German army to the forces of the North Atlantic Treaty Organisation (NATO). This alternative, though it might well be preferable militarily, would not be politically agreeable to the French.

Mr Churchill said that, while he agreed that this should be our policy, he would not be unduly disturbed if the present plans for a European Defence Community were not carried into effect. It had still to be shown that an international army could be an efficient instrument in spite of differences of language and weapons between participating contingents. And he doubted whether the soldier in the line would fight with the same ardour for an international institution as he would for his home and his country.

Mr Eden said that there was no real prospect of a Treaty for Austria, as the

---

[1] Vladimír Clementis, 1902–52. Educated at Charles University, Prague. Joined Communist Party of Czechoslovakia (CPC), 1925. Married, 1933, Leda Pátková. MP (CPC), 1935–8. Expelled from CPC, 1939; readmitted, 1945. Deputy PM, 1945–8. Minister for Foreign Affairs, 1948–50. Arrested, 1951. Executed, 1952.

[2] Rudolf Slánský, 1901–52. Joined CPC, 1921. Member, National Assembly, 1935–8. In Soviet Union, 1938–44. General Secretary, CPC, 1946. Arrested, convicted of Titoist activities and executed, 1952.

[3] Literally, 'Federal Council': the legislative body that represents the sixteen *Länder* (federated states) of Germany at the national level.

Russians clearly intended to stay there so long as the Western Powers remained in Germany. There had, however, been an improvement in Austria's relations with Yugoslavia.

The Western Powers' relations with Yugoslavia continued to grow closer but the differences between Yugoslavia and Italy over Trieste persisted. At the time of his visit to Belgrade Marshal Tito had been willing to accept a permanent division of the free Territory on the basis of Zone A (including the city of Trieste itself) going to Italy and Zone B to Yugoslavia. The United States Government had been unwilling to press Italy to accept a settlement on these lines, and they were now in favour of urging Yugoslavia to give up Capodistria in Italy. It seemed to him unwise, particularly in view of the impending Italian elections, to encourage Italy to look for further concessions by Yugoslavia which we were in no position to enforce. He was therefore trying to keep matters in suspense until the new United States Government had assumed office.

The recent visit to London of the Turkish Prime Minister and Foreign Minister[1] had been very successful and relations with that country were now more cordial than they had been for many years. The full co-operation by Turkey, on which we could now rely, would be of great assistance to us in connection with the many problems arising in the Middle East.

Mr Eden said that the main difficulties with Egypt were the future of the Sudan and the revision of the Anglo-Egyptian Treaty. Since the abdication of King Farouk the Sudan problem had become somewhat easier, since General Neguib had abandoned the demand for the unity of the Sudan and Egypt under the Egyptian Crown. Satisfactory progress was being made towards the holding of elections in the Sudan, but there remained the particular difficulty of the Southern Sudan. This was much less advanced than the North and might possibly develop separatist tendencies; and we therefore thought it important that the Governor-General should retain special powers over it for some time to come. It was likely that the Egyptians could be brought to agreement with us on this point. An Electoral Commission would then be appointed, consisting of representatives of the United Kingdom, Egypt, the Sudan, the United States and, he hoped, India. Subsequently an Advisory Commission would be set up, consisting of representatives of the United Kingdom, Egypt, the Sudan and, he hoped, Pakistan; and ultimately the way would be open to self-determination for the Sudan. The form of constitution which the Sudan would adopt could not, of course, be foreseen, but he hoped at any rate that she would be bound by Treaties to the United Kingdom and to Egypt.

---

[1] Mehmet Fuat Köprülü, 1890–1966. Educated at School of Law, Darüfünun. High school teacher, 1910–13. Prof. of Turkish literary history, 1913. Under-Secretary, Ministry of Education, 1924. President, Turkish History Council, 1927. Dean, Faculty of Arts, Istanbul University, 1933. MP (Republican People's Party), 1935–46. Co-founded Democratic Party, 1946. MP (Democratic Party) 1946–57. Foreign Minister, 1950–6. Joined Freedom Party, 1957.

On defence questions progress was less satisfactory. General Neguib claimed that he could not discuss defence with us until we had left the Canal Zone, but he might shortly adopt a more conciliatory attitude. It would be difficult for us to contemplate abandoning the Base and all the valuable installations which we had created in Egypt before we had any assurance that satisfactory alternative arrangements would be accepted.

Mr Churchill said that the previous Government in the United Kingdom had proposed a seven-Power plan for the protection of the Canal Zone. This had not been acceptable to Egypt. But we would certainly not be forced out of the Canal Zone until some satisfactory alternative method of protecting the international waterway could be found. He still hoped that other countries would be persuaded to contribute token forces to an international garrison. At the moment, we were keeping 70,000 soldiers in the Canal Zone and that was a burden which we could not carry indefinitely. He was therefore most anxious to find some method of sharing the burden with others or, if that were impossible, of finding some means of controlling the area from a remoter base. Cyprus was an attractive alternative, and the establishment of a base there would be welcomed by Turkey, which would play a great part in delaying any attempted Soviet invasion of the Middle East.

Mr Eden said that the accession of Turkey to the North Atlantic Treaty Organisation had changed the whole problem of Middle East defence. He also hoped that we should conclude a Treaty with Libya which would give us certain strategic facilities. It might well be possible to devise a successful form of defence for the Middle East, based on Turkey, Cyprus and Libya. Nevertheless, he had not given up hope that General Neguib might be more forthcoming on defence problems. The General's main difficulty was that the economic position of Egypt was weak; the standard of living had fallen since his *coup d'état*, and his own political position was weakened in consequence.

Mr Eden expressed his gratitude to Australia, New Zealand and South Africa for the practical assistance which they were giving in the formulation of plans for the defence of the Middle East.

Our relations with other Arab States were very satisfactory and Syria had recently asked us to conclude a Treaty with her. Relations with Jordan and Iraq were good. Iraq was receiving £60 millions a year in return for oil concessions and was using this money on sound schemes for development. The military *coup d'état* in Iraq[1] was probably a façade behind which Iraqi politicians remained in control and was not a radical military revolution, as it was in Egypt.

The only real difficulty which had arisen with the Arab States was the

---

[1] The Iraq Communist Party organized strikes in Basra and Baghdad in Aug. and Oct. 1952. In Nov. the Regent, Faisal II's uncle, installed as PM Gen. Nureddin Mahmud, who introduced martial law and stifled dissent. In May 1953, Faisal II became an adult and assumed responsibilities as King. In 1958, Army officers overthrew the monarchy and murdered the royal family.

encroachment of Saudi Arabia on the small Trucial Sheikdoms, where we enjoyed considerable oil concessions. We should have to resist this and it might be necessary to increase the size of the levies employed by these Sheikdoms. It was easy to justify resistance to King Ibn Saud's[1] claims, since in point of fact the standard of living in the Sheikdoms was a good deal higher than in Saudi Arabia.

In Persia a split seemed to be developing in the National Front. Kashani,[2] the most extremist of the Nationalist leaders, was moving towards co-operation with the Tudeh Party in opposition to Musaddiq and the more moderate members of the National Front. This conflict might soon come to a head, but he could not foresee whether it was likely to assist towards a settlement of the oil problem. The United States Government were still anxious for a settlement. He believed that General Eisenhower had found rather too severe the terms under which we had insisted that the problem should be submitted for arbitration by the Hague Court. Although we were not in fact expecting to get a very large sum in compensation, we had thought it necessary to our case that the terms of compensation should be fixed on a fair basis by an international tribunal. General Eisenhower also seemed to be considering the possibility of increasing the offer of American financial assistance from $10 millions to $30 millions.

The situation in Malaya had improved, but matters had grown worse in Indo-China. If the French were unable to maintain their position in Indo-China, there was a grave danger that Communism would spread throughout Burma and Siam and reach the frontiers of India and Malaya. The United States were giving substantial financial and material help to the French in Indo-China. The main danger was the possibility of direct intervention by China, but that, on the whole, he thought unlikely.

In Japan there was a danger of future difficulties, even though the present Government was anti-Communist. The population was increasing at the rate of one million persons per year, and the attraction of developing close trading relations with China was very great.

General Eisenhower had told him that the sole object of his visit to Korea was to make a military review. Some American opinion was in favour of using Japanese forces in the Korean war, but this would be strenuously resisted by the Government of South Korea. Hardly less welcome would be the introduction of Chiang Kai-shek's forces into Korea, and in practice there were only two divisions which could be made available. He did not think that General

---

[1] Abdul Aziz ibn Abdurrahman el Feisel Al Saud, 1880–1953. Known as 'Ibn Saud'. Born in Riyadh, a member of the Wahhabi dynasty. Exiled as a child by the Turks. Led a Bedouin revolt to regain Riyadh, 1902. King of Hejaz and Nejd, 1926–32; of Saudi Arabia, 1932–53.

[2] Sayyed Abu'l-Qāsem Kāšāni, 1877–1962. Exiled from Iran, 1893. Elected to Iranian Constituent Assembly (Majles-e mo'assesān), 1925. Leading political cleric, 1941–53. Arrested by British forces, 1944; released, 1945. Arrested, 1946; released, 1947. Arrested and exiled in Beirut, 1949; returned, 1950. Re-elected to the Majles, 1950. Arrested, 1956; released, 1956.

Eisenhower supported either of these two suggestions. There seemed to be only two possible courses to follow in Korea – either to continue to hold the present position, equipping and organising South Korean forces as fast as possible, or to undertake a major military operation with the object of destroying the Chinese Army in Korea. The latter course would mean the provision of additional American divisions which General Eisenhower would find politically difficult.

In general our object in the Far East must be to divide China and the Soviet Union, and it was particularly for this reason that he welcomed the recent Indian resolution on Korea in the General Assembly of the United Nations. The support which the resolution had received was a remarkable tribute to this Indian initiative. In his efforts to secure its adoption he had received most valuable help from Mr Pearson, the Canadian Foreign Minister, and from the representatives of other Commonwealth countries. It would not be possible to accept a cease-fire in Korea until agreement had been reached on the prisoners of war question. If we did so before then, it was very doubtful if we should ever recover our own prisoners of war and the enemy would also have opportunities to build up his air power unobserved.

In conclusion Mr Eden said that it remained a cardinal point in the foreign policy of the United Kingdom Government to retain and develop the closest possible co-operation with the United States. He had found General Eisenhower insistent that one of his chief aims was to co-operate with the Commonwealth and with France, and he had in general been greatly encouraged by the appointments in the new United States Administration which had so far been indicated by General Eisenhower.

In the discussion which followed, the representatives of other Commonwealth Governments expressed their appreciation of Mr Eden's valuable survey of the international situation. Tribute was also paid to Mr Eden's skill in the conduct of foreign policy. Mr Menzies said that there was widespread appreciation of the courage and competence with which Mr Eden faced his heavy responsibilities; and he himself believed that the improvement in international relations which was discernible over the last twelve months owed much to the knowledge, perception and wisdom which Mr Eden had shown in the discharge of his duties as Foreign Secretary. Mr Holland said that at the current meeting of the Assembly of the United Nations he had had personal experience of the great influence which Mr Eden exercised in international affairs. There was no doubt that the wide support which had eventually been secured for the Indian resolution on Korea was due in no small measure to his personal influence and diplomacy.

In further discussion the following particular points were raised:
- (a) Mr St Laurent said that the initiative which India had taken in the United Nations discussion on Korea had given great encouragement to all Commonwealth Governments. The large number of States

which had eventually supported that resolution was an encouraging demonstration of the strength and solidarity of democratic feeling throughout the world.

(b) Mr Hayenga[1] said that the general objectives of United Kingdom foreign policy had the full approval and support of the South African Government, who were resolved to do everything in their power to prevent a third world war. Though South Africa was being somewhat roughly treated in the United Nations at the present time, it should not be forgotten that South Africans were fighting in Korea to uphold the stand which the United Nations had taken against aggression.

(c) Mr Holland recalled that New Zealand had also made her contribution towards the United Nations Forces in Korea. Though she was a small country she would always do her utmost to help those who were seeking to preserve world peace. When he had last been in London it had been suggested that New Zealand should contribute to the British garrison in the Middle East, and he was glad to be able to say that a New Zealand contingent had now arrived in Cyprus.

(d) Sir Chintaman Deshmukh[2] said that, although there had recently been some improvement in international relations generally, the situation in Indo-China and Korea continued to give cause for grave anxiety. He agreed with Mr Eden that it was unlikely that the Chinese would intervene directly in Indo-China: he thought they would be reluctant to add to the commitment which they had already undertaken in the north. He could see no easy or quick solution of the difficulties in Indo-China, and he feared that the United States would have to be asked to continue for some time the support which they were giving to the French in that theatre. One could not help wondering for how long the Americans would be willing to carry this heavy burden. In Korea also a heavy responsibility rested on the United States, and there seemed no alternative but to persevere on the lines indicated in the resolution which the Indian Government had brought forward in the United Nations Assembly. Any policy which entailed an extension of the area of the conflict in Korea would involve very great risks; and he had agreed with Mr Eden that a cease-fire pending negotiations would give

---

[1] Nicolaas Christiaan Havenga, 1882–1957. Born in Fauresmith, South Africa. MP for Fauresmith, 1915–41; for Ladybrand, 1948–54. Defected from United Party and became leader of Afrikaner Party during 1943 election. Minister of Finance, Union of South Africa, 1924–39, 1948–54.

[2] Chintaman Dwarakanath Deshmukh, 1896–1982. Educated at Jesus College, Cambridge. Married, 1919, Rosina Arthur Wilcox (d. 1949): one child; 1949, Padma Vibhushan Durgabai Bennuri (d. 1981). Liaison Officer, Reserve Bank of India, 1939; Secretary, Central Board, 1939–41; Deputy Governor, 1941–3; Governor, 1943–9. Member, Board of Governors, International Monetary Fund, 1946–56. Indian Minister of Finance, 1950–6. Chairman, India University Grants Commission, 1956–61.

the Chinese an opportunity to build up their strength on land and in the air. India had fewer illusion than was sometimes supposed about the policies and intentions of her northern neighbours.

Mr Churchill agreed that it would be a grave mistake to take any course which would widen the area of conflict in Korea. It was the considered policy of the United Kingdom Government that these operations should be confined within the frontiers of Korea itself.

(e) Mr Nazimuddin[1] said that, while he fully supported the resolution on Korea which India had moved in the United Nations Assembly, resolutions alone would not suffice to bring the hostilities in Korea to an end. He was alarmed at the degree of success which the Soviet Government had attained in their cold-war policy of weakening in advance the nations which, if the time came, would seek to withstand an open aggression by Russia. The strength of the French was being sapped in Indo-China. In Malaya and elsewhere the resources of the United Kingdom were being subjected to severe strain. In Korea the United States were suffering casualties and loss which even they were finding it hard to bear. These tactics were subjecting the democracies to great strain. While he could not say what counter-moves should be made, he thought that no opportunity should be lost of consolidating the forces of the democracies and putting them in a position to offer a more effective resistance if aggression should come. In particular, any outstanding differences between them should be resolved without delay so that, if open aggression occurred, they could meet it united and strong.

Mr Eden said that it was true that the operations in Korea were imposing a great strain on the United States; but, as against this, it should be remembered that President Truman's decision to meet the aggression in Korea had resulted in a very great strengthening of the United States Forces and a vast defence production programme which had substantially increased the military power of the western democracies.

In conclusion, Mr Churchill said that he had welcomed this opportunity for an exchange of views on questions of foreign policy. He suggested that this might be supplemented by a similar meeting in his Map Room, where the Minister of Defence could give a corresponding review of defence policy. The representatives of other Commonwealth Governments gladly accepted this suggestion.

---

[1] Khawaja Nazimuddin, 1894–1964. Born in Bangladesh. Educated at Trinity Hall, Cambridge. Member of Bengal Legislative Assembly, 1923–9. Married, 1924, Shah Bano Ashraf. Reorganized Muslim League in Bengal, 1935; Head, 1943. Education Minister of Bengal, 1929. Representative on Governor's Executive Council, 1929. Minister of Agriculture, Bengal, 1934; Home Minister, 1937–41; Chief Minister, 1943. Governor-General of Pakistan, 1948–51. PM of Pakistan, 1951–3.

Finally Mr Churchill suggested that a suitable communiqué might be issued to the Press to let it be known that the leaders of the Commonwealth Delegations had met together with the Cabinet for a general exchange of views on the international situation. Mr Menzies suggested, and it was agreed, that it might be stated in this communiqué that the representatives of the other Commonwealth countries had placed on record their appreciation of the conduct of the foreign policy of the United Kingdom Government and their recognition of its contribution towards the preservation of world peace.

Winston S. Churchill: speech
(Hansard)

4 December 1952
House of Commons

MOTION OF CENSURE[1]

The Prime Minister (Mr Winston Churchill): I have today to deal with a Motion of censure, and therefore I hope I shall be pardoned if I do not confine myself entirely to the uncontroversial methods which I usually practise. Let me in the first place begin by offering my congratulations to the Leader of the Opposition who left the sharp, harsh language of the Motion behind and launched out into a general parade of all those topics which are usually a subject of discussion in our constituencies. Taking all that he said together, one must feel that he made a scathing denunciation of the Government, and I earnestly hope that that may be considered sufficient and that he will not be left at the post, as it were, when the right hon. Gentleman the Member for Ebbw Vale (Mr Bevan) resumes his role of virtuous indignation reinforced with the abuse for which he is celebrated.

It is a remarkable fact that, if we look at the terms of the Motion, the first occasion for 10 months in which the Opposition have moved a formal Motion against the present Government is on terms of a purely technical matter in the conduct of the House, and which has no bearing whatever upon the daily lives of the people or the march of events. No censure is urged on the manner in which the Government conduct their affairs in these anxious times either at home or abroad, and Her Majesty's Government may congratulate themselves upon the success of their administration. The country has no reason to rejoice on the feeble, barren absence of constructive thought on the part of the Opposition.

---

[1] 'That this House regrets that Her Majesty's Government is dealing with the Business of the House incompetently, unfairly and in defiance of the best principles of Parliamentary democracy and the national interest, and records the view that this is in part brought about by the efforts of Ministers to force through measures, unrelated to the needs of the nation, for which they have no adequate support in Parliament or the country' (*Hansard*). The motion was defeated 304–280.

Mr Attlee: May I remind the right hon. Gentleman that only a few weeks ago we were on the debate on the Queen's Speech. Therefore, it would be inappropriate to cover the ground we amply covered then.

The Prime Minister: I should have thought that, in view of the interval that has occurred, the right hon. Gentleman might well have thought of some variants to the general indictment which we all remember he threw upon us then. I am quite sure the right hon. Gentleman did his best, and he had every reason to do his best. We shall have the opportunity of seeing how this works out before we get to the end of the day. I should like to look back a little on the course of events in order rightly to judge this Motion on the Paper. On Tuesday last we were expecting a strong, vigorous debate upon the Steel Bill. At the end of Questions, when we were about to take this important discussion, the Adjournment of the House was moved about a tragic incident in Kenya,[1] and, after some vehement discussion, this was permitted by Mr Speaker.

I was sorry that the Opposition should have concentrated upon this single point in the difficult and harrowing scene in East Africa. I thought I made a fair and reasonable offer to the Opposition, namely, to give them a whole day for the debate on East Africa. It would have protected the Second Reading of the Steel Bill from violent interruption, which would have been so much better than focusing public attention by debate and by, as it then seemed, a Division on party lines upon the action of two or three young police officers who, with only 20 native police, were confronted with 2,000 tribesmen with long knives. Upon the nerve and decision of these officers at a critical moment much depended. Had they not acted with resolution, the whole detachment of police would have been torn to pieces, even if they had fired every bullet they possessed. When there is such a state of affairs as exists in Kenya, it would be most dangerous to undermine the confidence of subordinate officers.

Mr R. T. Paget (Northampton): Is a discussion of events in Kenya in order on this Motion?

Mr Deputy-Speaker (Sir Charles MacAndrew): I thought the opening speech was fairly wide. I did not stop it, and I do not see any reason to stop this now.

The Prime Minister: I am only discussing this particular episode in Kenya in order to draw the attention of the House to what actually happened before the proceedings on Tuesday night. I am giving the House my own feelings at the time. When there is such a state of affairs as in Kenya, I thought myself that, if there were a debate and Division on this matter, we might rupture and break the nerve of these young people, and we might well find that great

---

[1] In late 1952 the Mau Mau, a banned rebel organization of the Kikuyu tribe, initiated open revolt against British rule in Kenya. A state of emergency was declared by the Governor and violent conflict ensued. In the incident referred to here, police had fired upon 2,000 tribesmen armed with blades.

disasters and bloodshed would follow. Not only might there be a massacre, but the whole structure of Government might be weakened. All the settlers throughout this scattered country would be in mortal peril. (*Interruption.*) Hon. Members opposite will give me credit for not being afraid of interruptions or noise. It even would be much easier to be shouted down continually or booed down, because I have not the slightest doubt I could obtain publicity for any remarks I wish to make, even if they are not audible in the House.

It was this desire to debate the matter which made us make what I thought was a generous offer of a whole day's debate. However, the Opposition persisted and obtained the Adjournment. Then we came to the Steel Bill – I am showing the background in which the count was sought – which we have been told was so important – a terrible Bill of reaction. But what happened? There could have hardly been a greater contrast between the House excited in the arguments about the Adjournment on the Kenya episode and the scene at the Second Reading of the Steel Bill. Not only had the debate been wantonly disturbed and interrupted by the Opposition –

Mr John Hynd[1] (Sheffield, Attercliffe): Am I correct in understanding that the debate was interrupted in order to discuss Kenya because the Chair considered that that was an urgent matter of vital public importance, and in that case is not the right hon. Gentleman criticising the Chair?

Mr Deputy-Speaker: It was not I who gave the decision, and I do not think the right hon. Gentleman was criticising the Chair.

Mr Sydney Silverman (Nelson and Colne): The right hon. Gentleman has just said in the hearing of all of us that the interruption to which he refers, namely, the debate on the special adjournment of the House under Standing Order No. 9, was a wanton interruption. If it were a wanton interruption, the reflection would not be upon my right hon. Friends but upon the Chair which allowed the wanton Motion to be moved.

Mr James Griffiths[2] (Llanelly) rose –

Mr Deputy-Speaker: Let me take one at a time. It is the House that gives permission.

Hon. Members: No.

Mr J. Griffiths: Further to that point of order. Is it not a fact that on that day, when I moved the Adjournment of the House and Mr Speaker accepted it, the Colonial Secretary himself said the matter was important? He made a statement to the House on that Tuesday, in reply to a Private Notice Question, because it was of urgent public importance.

Mr Deputy-Speaker: I think that that is a different incident.

---

[1] John Burns Hynd, 1902–71. Clerk, National Union of Railwaymen, 1925–44. MP (Lab.) for Sheffield Attercliffe, 1944–70. Chancellor of the Duchy of Lancaster, 1945–7.

[2] James Griffiths, 1890–1976. Educated at Betws Board School. Married, 1918, Winifred Rutley: four children. President, South Wales Miners' Federation, 1934–6. MP (Lab.) for Llanelli, 1936–70. Minister of National Insurance, 1945–50. Chair, Labour Party, 1948–9. Secretary of State for the Colonies, 1950–1. Deputy Leader, Labour Party, 1955–9. Secretary of State for Wales, 1964–6.

The Prime Minister: I am certainly not making any reflection at all upon the Chair.

Mr Silverman: Then withdraw the word 'wanton'.

The Prime Minister: I will not withdraw the word 'wanton' or any other word I use.

Mr Silverman: On a point of order. The right hon. Gentleman has said that he will not withdraw the word 'wanton'– (Hon. Members: 'Under the hon. Gentleman's instructions'.) – although it is perfectly clear that, under the Ruling you have just given, Sir, the word 'wanton' could only be an attack on the Chair. (Hon: Members: 'Nonsense'.) There is only one occupant of the Chair, and I understand it to be you, Sir, and not the dozen or so answering Members opposite. The point I put to you is this, that to call that Motion or debate 'wanton' is a reflection on the Chair, without whose permission the Motion could not have been moved, and if that is so, I suggest to you that it is your duty in the Chair in this House to keep every Member of the House strictly within the rules of order even if it be the Prime Minister himself, and not to discriminate between Members. (Hon. Members: 'Oh!') Therefore, I say it is your duty – I submit to you with respect – to call upon the Prime Minister to withdraw the offending word.

Mr Deputy-Speaker: If my duty is at fault, it will be discussed on Monday. I do not want to say anything about that now. In order to raise a Motion under Standing Order No. 9, a Member has to get the leave of the House, which he got, and that is all I have to say on the matter.

Mr Attlee: Further to that Ruling. It is quite true that he has to get the leave of the House, but it is Mr Speaker who says whether it is a matter of definite urgent public importance. That is a Ruling as to the nature of the subject.

Mr Deputy-Speaker: That is how it arises, but I do not see that 'wanton' is necessarily directed to that.

Mr F. Beswick (Uxbridge): Do I understand it to be your Ruling, Mr Deputy-Speaker, that Mr Speaker would give permission for a debate in this House which can be properly described as a 'wanton' subject?

Mr Deputy-Speaker: Mr Speaker allowed the matter because it was urgent, public and definite. The Prime Minister did not use the word against Mr Speaker at all. He used it against the subject.

Mr Jack Jones[1] (Rotherham): Not only did he refuse to withdraw the word 'wanton', but the Prime Minister went on to say that nor would he withdraw any other word he used. May I have an assurance that, while we on these back benches are confined to the rules of the House, the Prime Minister shall not have rules of his own?

Mr Deputy-Speaker: If the Prime Minister uses un-parliamentary words I shall stop him.

---

[1] John Henry Jones, 1894–1962. Known as 'Jack'. Educated at Bangor University. On active service, 1914–18. MP (Lab.) for Bolton, 1945–50; for Rotherham, 1950–62.

The Prime Minister: I hope I shall be allowed a measure of free speech. I thought it was perfectly understood that the Chair interpreted the rules of the House. Those who put these rules into motion, and those who, when opportunity is given to them, cry for action – they are the ones who take the actual responsibility. And it is to them, and to them alone, the word 'wanton' applies. I have got a lot to say, and I shall have to keep the House several hours if we go on at this rate. Nothing will induce me to be frustrated in unfolding the argument – not even sham points of order.

Let me recall the House to the point I had reached in the argument. I said that the Adjournment of the House was given, that the debate on the Iron and Steel Bill, which, we had been told, was very important indeed – (Hon. Members: 'Who said so?') – was to be interrupted at 7 p.m. We could not have had a greater contrast between the House, excited by the Adjournment on the Kenya episode, and the scene at the beginning of the Second Reading of the Iron and Steel Bill. Not only had the debate been interrupted, but it had been made to extend to 1 a.m. instead of ending at 10 p.m. But not only that. There appeared to be a strange lack of interest on the subject on the part of the Opposition.

Mr Ivor Owen Thomas[1] (The Wrekin): Where were the Prime Minister's men?

The Prime Minister: Rarely have I seen such a change of mood in the House. The Opposition Members trooped out in all directions, and a quiet, half empty House was left to listen to the debate on a Measure which, we were told, was such a flagrant example of reactionary legislation. Nothing could more clearly vindicate the Government in allocating only two days to the debate on the Second Reading of the Iron and Steel Bill than the lack of interest – and, I may say, of argumentative power – shown throughout the proceedings by the Opposition. (*Interruption.*) I am going through what happened on Tuesday.

We now reach the Adjournment at 7 p.m. on Kenya. I was very glad that the Opposition, or the responsible Members of it, on second thoughts did not force a party Division on the conduct of those young officers in their terrible ordeal, and that the right hon. Gentleman asked leave to withdraw the Motion. That shows how much better advised he and his colleagues would have been to have accepted my offer – (Hon. Members: 'No'.) – yes – of a whole day's debate on the general question, on which, I understand, a reasoned Amendment could have been moved – and I understand is even now under discussion. After all, we all have common interests and responsibilities in Kenya, and the situation which has come to a head there grew up mainly in

---

[1] Ivor Owen Thomas, 1898–1982. Conscientious objector, 1918. Educated at Central Labour College, London, 1923–5. Member, National Union of Railwaymen, 1925–45, 1955–8. Councillor (Lab.), Battersea Metropolitan Borough Council, 1928–45. Married, 1929, Beatrice Davis: one child. MP (Lab.) for The Wrekin, 1945–55.

the six years of Socialist administration. Certainly there was widespread relief – and it was not confined by any means to one side of the House – when the ill-timed Motion for the Adjournment –

Mr Beswick: Ill-timed?

The Prime Minister: – was withdrawn. I am going on with the story. Hon. and right hon. Gentlemen must look at how things strike other people, even if they do not agree.

It was with a sense of anti-climax when, at 10 p.m., we returned to the interrupted and mutilated debate on the Iron and Steel Bill. Again the Chamber was nearly deserted as the debate proceeded. I wish here and now to express my regret at the failure of the Government to maintain a quorum. The contrast between the stormy debate about Kenya, and the excitement it caused, and the curious apathy with which the de-nationalisation of the iron and steel industry is received by the Socialist Party –

Mr A. C. Manuel (Central Ayrshire): There was not one Tory in the House at 10 p.m.

The Prime Minister: That is not an excuse, but I must say –

Mr George Chetwynd[1] (Stockton-on-Tees): On a point of order. When the debate on the Steel Bill was adjourned at 7 p.m. the last speaker – (*Interruption.*)

Mr Deputy-Speaker: Order. I cannot hear the point of order unless hon. Members keep quiet.

Mr Chetwynd: The last speaker was from this side of the House. When the debate was resumed at 10 p.m., Mr Speaker had again to call on this side of the House for another speaker because there was no hon. Member opposite to speak. In those circumstances, is the Prime Minister entitled to make the remark he just made about the position in that debate?

Mr Deputy-Speaker: There is no point of order about that.

The Prime Minister: There was – (*Interruption.*) I remain wholly unaffected by this discourtesy and interruption, because I know that nothing can possibly do more harm to hon. Gentlemen opposite than shouting down, and breaking down if they can by repeated interruption, the Minister who is responding to an official Motion of censure. Do not, I beg of them, imagine that this distresses me, except by contemplation of their conduct.

There was a sense of anti-climax, and I express my regret at the failure of the Government to maintain a quorum, but it was due to the contrast between the stormy debate –

Mr I. O. Thomas: We have heard that.

The Prime Minister: I am telling the House what happened. It was due to

---

[1] George Roland Chetwynd, 1916–82. Educated at King's College London. Married, 1939, Teresa Reynolds Condon. Enlisted in Royal Artillery, 1940. Commissioned, Army Education Corps, 1942. MP (Lab.) for Stockton-on-Tees, 1945–62. Parliamentary Private Secretary to Chancellor of Duchy of Lancaster, 1948–50; to Minister of Local Government and Planning, 1950–1. Delegate to Consultative Assembly, Council of Europe, 1952–4. Member, North-East Advisory Committee for Civil Aviation, 1964.

the contrast between the stormy debate about Kenya and the apathy on the Iron and Steel Bill. As I said, this is not an excuse. It is, however, an honest explanation of the error we made in thinking that all faction was over for the night. I am confessing quite plainly that we were in error. But what was the conduct of the Opposition? Only four of their Members were present at the time – (Hon. Members: 'No'.) – only four of their Members were present – (Hon. Members: 'No'.). The Opposition must not be afraid of argument; do not be afraid of what is coming; brace yourselves to bear it.

Only four of their Members were present in the Chamber at the time the count was taken. The hon. Member who moved the count has since stated that there were over 100 Socialist Members in the House at the time. Well, I do not know how many there were, but there were certainly more than would have been necessary to maintain a quorum. However, I quite agree that no responsibility to maintain a quorum rests on the Opposition. Nevertheless, they remained in hiding, these large numbers, or posted in the Lobbies or corridors to dissuade their colleagues from entering the Chamber. This must have taken a lot of planning and organisation – almost as much, perhaps, as was needed to alter the method of electing their 'Shadow Cabinet' in order to isolate the right hon. Member for Ebbw Vale (Mr Bevan).

If we failed to keep a House, it was a bona fide accident which is regretted. That the House was counted out was the result of an elaborate and deliberate manoeuvre which had no regard for the importance of the Iron and Steel Bill, or for the dignity of the House. It was wholly inconsistent with the demands put forward by the Opposition for more time for the de-nationalisation Measure. It showed their love of faction for faction's sake, and the hollowness of their objections to the iron and steel de-nationalisation Bill.

I am glad to put these two Parliamentary events before the House and the country: first, the rejection of my offer for a whole day to debate the Kenya situation rather than an Adjournment debate on a particular episode; and secondly, the elaborate scheme worked out on the back benches opposite, but later blessed by the authority of the Front Bench, for getting the House counted out. The Opposition in neither case considered the public interest. They preferred sensationalism and excitement, and a needless spoiling of our debate on iron and steel.

Mr S. Silverman: What did the right hon. Gentleman's people do?

The Prime Minister: I have already said that we regret that we did not keep a quorum. I have already explained that the reason was that after the other debate on Kenya had been concluded there was – (*Interruption.*) Well, if hon. Gentlemen opposite will not listen I will not interrupt my own speech.

I have gone at some length and in full detail into the sequence of events which led to the count and to the House being counted out against our responsibility, on which the Opposition have based their demand for a Motion of censure, which we have naturally accorded at the earliest possible moment.

The consequences of this Socialist misbehaviour involved the House in an exhausting all-night sitting, which turned out very badly for the Opposition. In a long series of Divisions they were defeated by majorities far outranging the normal and greatly improving the Government's average majority. They were far above the normal or what we received from the electors.

Mr I. O. Thomas: Where was the right hon. Gentleman?

The Prime Minister: I will be perfectly frank with the House. I was better employed in sound slumber on that occasion. I was, of course, paired. If I had not taken some of these precautions I should not have sufficient strength to sustain the ordeal to which I am now being subjected.

The Opposition were beaten in this long series of Divisions. They have shown that they do not really regard the de-nationalisation of the iron and steel industry as an important or, indeed, highly controversial Measure, and this will be a valuable guide to us in considering the amount of time to be given to its later stages.

Here let me pay my tribute to the Leader of the House and the Chief Whip, who have been the subject of so much abuse. Both my right hon. Friends were in their places at the count, and I have already expressed my regret that a quorum was not maintained. But I repudiate with conviction the charge that the management of Parliamentary business this Session, or indeed since the new Parliament met, has been in any way unequal to the very difficult duties entrusted to these two Ministers.

The word 'incompetence' is used in the censure Motion. (An Hon. Member: 'Wanton incompetence'.) I think that is a contradiction in terms. This rude word is not an expression of opinion which need be treated with the slightest respect. It is only a yelp of anger from men who have been beaten thoroughly in all their manoeuvres, however disreputable. Not only have Her Majesty's Government been the victors in over 250 Divisions, but they have had throughout these Divisions a majority almost double what it is on paper. Is that incompetence?

When this Parliament first met, just over a year ago, the Opposition challenged us twice on Amendments to the Address. Our actual majority is only 16. On the first occasion we had a majority of 38, and on the second 37, or more than double. Is that incompetence? In the Division on the Christmas food supplies, we had a majority of 37. Was that incompetence? In February, the Opposition tried a snap Division on an Adjournment debate on the resignation of the Chairman of the Iron and Steel Corporation. Our majority was 47. Is that incompetence?

On the question of fares, in April, we had a majority of 44. Was it incompetence that we had a majority of 64 in the debate on food? Was it incompetence that on the Steel Bill we had a majority of 36 a week ago? Was it due to incompetence that the business for last week was finished at the time originally proposed, or that the business for this week will be disposed of with equal precision? On the contrary, our success, which has been the cause of so much anger, is due not only to the competence of the Ministers concerned but to the vigour and exertions of a united party.

The present indications seem to show that public opinion is hardening in favour of Her Majesty's Government. It may well be that this tendency will be strengthened by the exhibitions we are having and by the frustration from which the Socialist Party – or Labour Party, as I call them when I mean to be polite – rent and torn with their bitter internal quarrels, is so obviously suffering.

A year ago, their party managers thought that our majority was too small for the Government to have any real expectation of long life or of being able to undo the harm and bear successfully the grievous burden we inherited. It was prophesied by the high expert Socialist authorities that by-elections would soon reduce that majority. Mr Morgan Phillips,[1] whose competence I should be the last to assail, in a broadcast on 2nd November of last year said – and I will read this to the house: 'If we cannot cut into the Government's majority in by-elections in the next 12 months, I will eat my hat.' The 12 months are over, so what is going to happen? Let me say that I do not think that such an unpalatable ordeal is needed at a time when the Christmas season is upon us and there will be other things to eat. I have always been an advocate of magnanimity in victory, and so far as the Government and their supporters are concerned, I wish formally to announce that we give Mr Phillips complete release from his obligation. We will not even occupy time in asking whether his mistake was due to his competence or incompetence.

This brings me to another point to which I must draw the attention of the House, namely, the treatment by the Opposition of the mass of routine legislation without which the administration of national affairs would be brought to a stop. Take the Expiring Laws Continuance Bill. I have looked into what has happened since the war. I find that in 1945 1 hour 9 minutes were taken on it; in 1946, 1 hour 21 minutes; in 1947, 1 hour 9 minutes – through all stages; in 1948, 2 hours 51 minutes, and in the second Session in 1948–49, 53 minutes. In 1950–51 the time taken was 2 hours 44 minutes; in 1951–52, 2 hours and 41 minutes – the average of all this being 1 hour and 49 minutes. In this particular Session, we have had to give 14 hours and 33 minutes, or eight times the average for the previous years.

Mr Alfred Robens (Blyth): Will the right hon. Gentleman look into the history of the Gas Bill?

The Prime Minister: That is a tempting subject – the Gas Bill. The right hon. Gentleman has given great study to it, which he will no doubt benefit by now that he is in opposition.

---

[1] Morgan Walter Phillips, 1902–53. Born in Aberdare, Glamorgan. Secretary, Caerphilly divisional Labour Party, 1923–5. Secretary, Labour Party in West Fulham, 1928–30; in Whitechapel, 1934–7. General Secretary, Labour Party, 1944–61.

I wish to speak, if I may, in reply to the Leader of the Opposition, who moved the Motion of censure. He said on 6th November of last year, 'The Opposition will be vigilant but not factious. We shall not oppose merely for the sake of opposition . . . the Press expect a much higher standard of public service from Socialists than they do from Conservatives. They suggest that it would be quite wrong for anyone in this House to indulge now in the kind of tactics which were indulged in during the last Parliament. They expect something altogether better from us, and they are quite right.'– (Official Report, 6th November, 1951; Vol. 493, c. 67.) This was a boast of a much better performance and a much higher standard which was as little fulfilled by the Opposition as were Mr Morgan Phillips's expectations which induced him to undertake such formidable forfeits.

I now come to the Public Works Loans Bill. Here again the time spent in the last six years has been 35 minutes, 46 minutes, 46 minutes, 50 minutes, 21 minutes, and, in 1950–51, 1 hour and 22 minutes, an average of 47 minutes for all that period, the bulk of which we were in Opposition. But on this last occasion, it is 8 hours and 39 minutes, or nearly 12 times the previous average. More time has been spent in this present Session on that Bill than in the previous six. (*Interruption.*) I do not pretend that I have never tried to delay the proceedings of the House, but this is a matter which is designed to affect our conduct of a Bill.

Mr Aneurin Bevan (Ebbw Vale) rose –

The Prime Minister: Cannot you let your right hon. Friend have the afternoon, anyhow? As the right hon. Gentleman is so lonely, I will treat him with chivalry.

Mr Bevan: I am very grateful to the right hon. Gentleman for giving way. I just wanted to understand his argument, as I am under an obligation to reply. Is he rebuking his hon. Friends behind him for the speeches they made in those debates?

The Prime Minister: I was not reproaching any of my hon. Friends behind me but trying to throw rebukes upon those who are in the wrong this afternoon. It seems to me that it is quite clear that with this process of a handful of Members, unable and unwilling to divide the House, nevertheless delaying the whole process of legislation, they could produce a situation different from any which has hitherto confronted Parliament.

The hope of the Opposition is to hold up our de-nationalisation Measures. We cannot accept the words of the Motion that these Measures are not related 'to the needs of the nation'. On the contrary, we should never have faced the trouble and burden of this legislation if we were not convinced that not only were we redeeming our pledges – and who would have mocked us if we had not done so? – but that we were notably improving the conditions on which the fertility and prosperity of our trade and production depends.

I am finishing in a minute; I will not keep hon. Members under such a vocal strain for too long. I do not want to make them so hoarse that they cannot even continue the debate. But we must now contemplate this Motion of censure, and the use of normal routine business to produce deadlocks, in their larger setting. The abusive language of the right hon. Gentleman's Motion, the harsh epithets, may no doubt be dismissed with any attention it deserves, but the Motion of censure and the tactics now being employed against Her Majesty's Government in the circumstances I have described must be viewed against the general political background.

We have had two General Elections in little more than two years. Each has resulted in Parliamentary majorities far smaller than are required for the convenient course of Parliamentary business. The Standing Committees are no longer the help and relief to the House of Commons that they were. A far greater portion of our business must be conducted in the whole House. That is only one of the factors which adds to the very heavy burden imposed upon Members of all parties, but so far borne, as the figures show, with greater success by Her Majesty's Government. We feel that we are in a definitely stronger position, both in the House and in the country, than we were a year ago, but I cannot feel that it would be in the national interest to have another General Election, even though it would seem that we should improve our position, and not suffer at any future election – and hon. Members opposite should pay attention to this – the serious injury which was inflicted upon us by what is now admitted to be the warmonger lie.

The country needs a period of steady, stable administration to recover from its maltreatment, as we say, but anyhow from the extreme exertions and disturbance in the preceding six years; to undo some of the work that was then done and to ward off, as we are trying to do, bankruptcy; and to strengthen and broaden the foundations of peace. I have repeatedly said that we ask to be judged by deeds not words, by results not promises; and time and perseverance are needed for these.

We do not believe that it is in the power of the party opposite to prevent us from doing what we conceive to be our duty. If we act, as we shall do, in a resolute manner, we shall make it clear to our opponents that artful dodges and dull methods of delay – (An Hon. Member: 'Obstruction'.) – I am rather careful about the word obstruction; I have looked it up, but its permissibility has carefully to be considered – cannot bring the House of Commons to a standstill; or else, if that failed, it would be the prelude to a succession of General Elections contrary to the principle of the Quinquennial Act. If we can show that a Government, even with a majority as moderate as our own, can in fact do several years' good and faithful work, we shall have rendered a historic service to Parliamentary government.

We are much encouraged by what has happened so far and by the failure of the Opposition to mask their own internal feuds by uniting in hysterical and violent abuse of their opponents. Their conduct throughout this Parliament in our opinion has been reprehensible in a high degree. Far from moving a Motion of censure on Her Majesty's Government, they should shake and shiver in their shoes with shame.

Winston S. Churchill to Winston Churchill
(*Churchill papers, 1/51*)

4 December 1952

My dearest Winston,

I thought you would like to have, on the morning of their issue, these first stamps of Queen Elizabeth II's reign. I think they will make an interesting addition to your collection.

PS. Your letter of November 30 has just arrived. Thank you so much for it and its good wishes. When am I going to see you?

James Thomas to Winston S. Churchill
(*Premier papers, 11/478*)

4 December 1952

The answers to the questions asked in your Personal Minute of 28th November[1] are:

Numbers of Royal Fleet Reservists recalled for eighteen months' service –
    1951   ...   4,400, including 1,700 juniors.
    1952   ...   3,200, including 1,400 juniors.[2] (Also includes the last batch of about 1,000 who have now received recall notices and will report for duty early next month.)

2. In addition to these numbers we called up 660 reservists for the Korean emergency in 1950, of which 260 were juniors. As I informed you in my minute dated 5th September, and as announced in the press, no more men will be recalled from the Royal Fleet Reserve.

3. By 'juniors' we mean non-supervisory ratings under Leading Rates. All these reservists, however, are already trained with many years of experience.

4. Korea and the subsequent measures of increased preparedness decided upon by the Government created a sudden need for large numbers of additional skilled ratings for particular billets. Retentions of time-expired men alone were insufficient and given the limited content of the Royal Fleet

---

[1] M.555/52, reproduced above (p. 742).
[2] Churchill wrote to Thomas the next day: 'Let me know how the 1,400 juniors are employed. As you are not going to call up any more why is it necessary to impose hardship on a small number?' (M.562/52).

Reserve we had not an unrestricted field of choice in dealing with individual cases if the build-up of the active fleet was to fulfil the policy of HMG. By retaining time-expired men and recalling Royal Fleet Reservists we were able to restrict the period of extra service to eighteen months.

5. In determining our selection of ratings to be recalled, we decided not to recall any man in the last six months of his reserve engagement and all recalled reservists were invited to represent hardship at once on receiving recall notices. Sympathetic consideration has been given to such appeals, not only in cases of family distress or hardship but in those of serious interruption of study or on personal business grounds where the means of livelihood might be endangered by call-up. While requests by employers for exemption of reservists from recall have generally been refused, some period of deferment has been allowed where this would ease the employer's difficulties. The reservist's employment has, of course, been safeguarded by the Reinstatement in Civil Employment Act, 1950.

Winston S. Churchill to William Ross[1]
(Premier papers, 11/238)

5 December 1952
Private

Dear Mr Ross,

I thought your remark on December 3 was a misquotation. The expression is 'to say Bo (as in Bo-Peep) to a Goose', and not 'Boo'. I find this confirmation of my view

> 'A Scholard, when just from his college broke loose,
> Can hardly tell how to cry Bo to a Goose.'
> Swift, Grand Question Debated, line 157
> (1729).

I thought that you would like to know. I must also point out that I should be anyhow a gander.

---

[1] William Ross, 1911–88. Educated at Glasgow University. Schoolteacher, 1932–9. Served in India, Burma, Singapore and Ceylon, 1939–45. MP (Lab.) for Kilmarnock, Ayr and Bute, 1946–79. Secretary of State for Scotland, 1964–70, 1974–6.

Winston S. Churchill to Duke of Windsor
(*Premier papers, 11/32*)

5 December 1952

Sir,

I have delayed replying to Your Royal Highness's letter of November 23[1] until I could assure you definitely that there neither is nor will be any question of a former Sovereign, such as King Peter of Yugoslavia or King Leopold of the Belgians, being invited to the Coronation. This I am now able to do.

I should not, however, be in favour of the Earl Marshal issuing a formal statement on this subject. I feel that the statement which you suggest will come with force and dignity from Your Royal Highness personally, in reply to any questions which may be addressed to you. Any Press enquiries received by the Earl Marshal or Buckingham Palace would of course be given a similar answer.

Winston S. Churchill to Antony Head
Prime Minister's Personal Minute M.560/52
(*Premier papers, 11/487*)

5 December 1952

Your Annex A to your minute of November 3.

In my opinion you should aim at reducing the total of these figures to one third.

The General Headquarters should be reduced from 696 to 300. Let me have the details of the Command Secretaries, Civilian Department. What is a Command Secretary; is he the Private Secretary of the Commander in Chief? If so why does he require 39 officers and officials under him?

Royal Navy Headquarters 93. This should be reduced to 25. Why indeed can it not be done all from Malta?

What are 'the British Middle East Office (political and military divisions)' which apparently require 56 persons? Let me have the details and their salaries.

Joint Signal Unit and Communications Board 609. Let me have on a separate sheet the exact composition of this. We must not let ourselves be led into undue expenditure by vague talk of all our vital communications with the Middle East.

What does Sub Area HQ 29 mean? Let me have a list.

GHQ Group (mainly administrative) 361. Observe please that apart from all the other functionaries the 4,202 require 361 administrative details. Let me have this man for man.

---

[1] Reproduced above (pp. 736–7).

What is this Car Company of 256?

Provost and Field Security. It seems off that all these highly picked, carefully chosen Staff Officers and their assistants require Provost and Field Security protection in addition to the Car Company etc. of 37.

What is the difference between Wireless Troops and the Joint Signal Unit?

What are the small units contained in the 187?

Evelyn Shuckburgh: diary
('Descent to Suez', page 66)

8 December 1952

Asked AE: how he got on over the weekend at Chequers. He said to Winston that he must know something of his plans. PM made a solemn Winstonian speech to the effect that his intention was, when the time came, to hand over his powers and authority with the utmost smoothness and surety to Anthony. AE said yes – but the point was when would that be? A whole minute of silence, then, 'Often I think there are things I could say, speeches I could make more easily if I were not Prime Minister.' Then another long silence. AE said the position regarding leadership in the House could not be maintained. Crookshank not competent. But the net result was no clear indication.

Winston S. Churchill to Duncan Sandys
Prime Minister's Personal Minute M.564/52
(Premier papers, 11/764)

8 December 1952

I have approved a letter from the Chancellor of the Exchequer to you about Supplementary Estimates, but please give me a short explanation why you underestimated in this extraordinary manner.

Winston S. Churchill to Winston Churchill
(Churchill papers, 1/51)

10 December 1952

My dear Winston,

The Director of the Administration of Posts, Telegraphs and Telephones in Luxembourg has sent me some more new Luxembourg stamps. I thought you would like to have them for your collection.

I am so glad you enjoyed the cake.

Congratulations on winning your match the other day.

December 1952

William Ross to Winston S. Churchill
(Premier papers, 11/238)[1]

11 December 1952

Dear Prime Minister,

Thank you for your letter of the 15th. I must seek, however, acquittal of the suggestion of misquotation – much more serious offence than that of Parliamentary misbehaviour.

For more than a hundred years before Swift, and two hundred years since, the expression 'bo to a goose' has been in common use, and subject to the natural variations of time and dialect.

I have never heard it used in Scotland otherwise than 'Boo to a goose'. Jamieson's Scottish Dictionary noting the expression adds, 'This is probably the same term with the Scots "bo" or "boo" used to excite terror.' Further, the Scottish National Dictionary lists 'BO, BOO' together.

As an ex-schoolmaster I congratulate you on the aptness of your confirmatory quotation. Personally I would have preferred yet another variation. As the writer – Bridges[2] – resorted to synthetic Scots it may have been a recognition of the dialect difference:

> 'I dare for the honour of our house
> Say boo to any Grecian goose.'
> (Homer Travestied Bk VII Page 20)
> 1762

When I alluded to the expression in the House, I had as I said, someone else in mind. If doubt lingers one thought comforts.

As I recollect the historic days of 1940–41 when this scholar forsook his classes for more boisterous and immediate tasks, I remember too that it was the geese that saved the Capitol.[3]

---

[1] This letter was handwritten.

[2] Thomas Bridges, c.1710–75. English writer of parodies and dramatic works. The quoted work is *A Burlesque Translation of Homer* (1762).

[3] Churchill responded on Dec. 17: 'Thank you very much for your kind letter, which leaves me in your debt. We shall certainly not quarrel on the differing usage of "Boo" and "Bo" north and south of the Tweed.'

Defence Committee: minutes
(Cabinet papers, 131/12)

11 December 1952   Prime Minister's Room
Top Secret   House of Commons
5.30 p.m.
Defence Committee Meeting No. 12 of 1952

1. ATOMIC ENERGY PROGRAMME

The record of this discussion is included in a Confidential Annex.

2. THE FUTURE OF ANZAM

The Committee had before them a memorandum by the Chiefs of Staff (D(52)48) describing the development of the ANZAM concept and its relationship with ANZUS.

The Minister of Defence explained that ANZAM (Australia, New Zealand and Malaya) was a geographical area embracing also Indonesia, Borneo and New Guinea and a large area of the South-West Pacific. The concept was that in this area Australia should take the lead in initiating defence plans and should discuss these with the United Kingdom and New Zealand. In war the military control of operations in the area would be in the hands of the ANZAM Chiefs of Staff, consisting of the Australian Chiefs of Staff and a representative each of the United Kingdom and New Zealand Chiefs of Staff. ANZUS (The Pacific Security Treaty between the United States, Australia, and New Zealand) was quite a different conception. It was not related to a geographically-defined area and the ANZUS Powers were free to concern themselves with events in the ANZAM region. Moreover the boundary of the American Commander-in-Chief, Pacific, embraced the whole of the ANZAM region. We might to some extent offset our exclusion from ANZUS by inviting American observers to join us in ANZAM.

The Prime Minister said that it would be better to hear the views of the Prime Ministers of Australia and New Zealand before coming to any conclusion on the line we should adopt. He therefore proposed that an opportunity should be taken on the following day for a discussion between these two Prime Ministers, himself, the Commonwealth Secretary and the Minister of Defence. He knew that Mr Menzies and Mr Holland were anxious to come to some arrangement which did not exclude the United Kingdom from discussions about an area in which they had important interests.

The Committee –

Took note that the Prime Minister, the Commonwealth Secretary and the Minister of Defence, would discuss the relationship of ANZAM and ANZUS with the Prime Ministers of Australia and New Zealand on the following day.

[. . .]

4. DEFENCE NEGOTIATIONS WITH EGYPT

The Committee had before them a memorandum by the Chiefs of Staff (D(52)50) proposing a basis for defence negotiations with Egypt. The memorandum proposed that an essential condition of any negotiations should be the participation of Egypt in a Middle East Defence Organisation, and propounded in the Annex some variations of concessions which might be made to Egypt to win her support and at the same time to retain the facilities of the base.

The Foreign Secretary said that he agreed in principle with the proposals made by the Chiefs of Staff. He was most anxious that the basis of negotiations should be agreed with the Americans before any approach was made to the Egyptian Government. He therefore proposed that he and the Minister of Defence should discuss the proposals with the United States Secretary of State while they were in Paris and try to enlist his support.

The Prime Minister agreed that this should be the first step. The Americans should be made to understand that we could not support indefinitely the burden of keeping 70,000 soldiers in the Canal Zone. Other countries must be made to share this burden. The speed with which operations would move in the next war had an effect upon the value of retaining a large and elaborate base in the Canal Zone.

The Committee –
1) Approved in principle the basis of defence negotiations with the Egyptians proposed by the Chiefs of Staff in their memorandum D(52)50.
2) Took note that the Foreign Secretary and the Minister of Defence would discuss these proposals with the United States Secretary of State during their forthcoming visit to Paris.
3) Authorised the Commonwealth Secretary to send the memorandum by the Chiefs of Staff to the Governments of the older Commonwealth countries and keep them informed of the negotiations in Paris.

TOP SECRET
CONFIDENTIAL ANNEX TO D (52)12TH MEETING
1. ATOMIC ENERGY PROGRAMME

The Committee had before them two memoranda by the Paymaster-General:
(i) A memorandum on plutonium output (D(52)51) requesting approval in principle for the doubling of the present output in the United Kingdom;
(ii) A memorandum (D(52)52) requesting approval for an atomic bomb trial in October 1953, in the Australian desert 300 miles north-west of Woomera, with the object of finding out the maximum content

of the isotope 240 which could be tolerated in plutonium used for military purposes.

The Paymaster-General said that the Chiefs of Staff had asked that, for military purposes, the output of the plutonium in the United Kingdom should be doubled within four years. To meet this need two further atomic piles would be required. These would be different in design and more economical than the existing piles. It was hoped that they would be *net* producers, and not consumers, of electric power; and, if this proved to be so, it would be a significant step in the development of the civil use of atomic energy. The cost of the work would be about £25 million spread over four years. The cost in the first year would be small, perhaps not exceeding £1 million. An essential prelude to this project was an atom bomb trial to find out the maximum content of the isotope 240 which could be tolerated in plutonium used for military purposes. If a place in the Australian desert 300 miles north-west of Woomera could be made available for this trial, it could take place in October 1953. It would take much longer and cost more to mount another trial at the Monte Bello Islands. The Australian Prime Minister would have to be asked for permission to undertake this trial, and the general arrangements and sharing of costs would have to be agreed between the Governments of Australia and of the United Kingdom.

The Prime Minister said that he was quite ready to agree to an atom bomb trial in October 1953 and would write to the Prime Minister of Australia about this. The trial would undoubtedly add to our knowledge of atomic energy. He was not, however, prepared to agree to the doubling of the output of plutonium in the United Kingdom until he had had an opportunity to discuss with the new United States Administration the question of cooperation in atomic energy. It had always been his understanding that the United States, whose production of atom bombs would far exceed ours for many years to come, would be willing to supply us with atom bombs for our use. It was true that the McMahon Act and the attitude of the present United States Administration had prevented any satisfactory cooperation up to date, but he felt sure that the success of the test at the Monte Bello Islands and the change of Administration in the United States would alter the American attitude. It would certainly be unwise to embark upon costly expansion until a further approach had been made to the Americans. The delay involved would be small.

The Minister of Supply suggested that it would save time and anticipate the possible failure of negotiations with the United States if it were now decided that the design stage of the new piles could proceed. It could be made clear that no building commitments should be entered into without further authority.

The Committee:
    1) Approved the holding of an atom bomb trial in October 1953 and invited the Prime Minister to ask the Prime Minister of Australia for

his consent to the use for this trial of a place in the Australian desert 300 miles north-west of Woomera.

2) Invited the Paymaster-General to submit, with estimates of cost, precise proposals for proceeding with the design stage of two new piles, on the understanding that there would be no commitment to erect those piles, before a further approach had been made to the new United States Administration on the subject of cooperation in atomic energy projects.

John Colville to Sir Norman Brook
(Premier papers, 11/541)

12 December 1952
Secret

The Prime Minister has been expressing considerable interest in the question of retaliation against the Soviet and Satellite Governments for the victimization, both financial and otherwise, of our Diplomatic Missions in the countries concerned.

I learn from the Foreign Office that the Home Affairs Committee are shortly to be asked by them to find a place in the legislative programme for a Bill on Diplomatic Immunities. This Bill would empower HMG to withhold all diplomatic immunities from those members of the staff of a foreign Mission who are not on the Diplomatic list, to the extent that such immunities are withheld from our own non-diplomatic staffs in the countries concerned. It would perhaps also include a provision to enable HMG to demand exit visas from representatives of those countries which demand exit visas for our own diplomats.

Mr Churchill has asked to be kept informed of the progress of this Bill, and so I should be obliged if you would ask the Home Affairs Committee Secretariat to keep us informed of developments and, in due course, to let us know when it is estimated that such a Bill could be presented to Parliament.

Winston S. Churchill to Field Marshal Lord Alexander
Prime Minister's Personal Minute M.563/52
(Premier papers, 11/478)

12 December 1952

I am no longer prepared to agree to the recall of the final three thousand men for eighteen months' service unless it can be shown in each case that the man recalled is a key man. I send you herewith some correspondence I have had by minute with the First Lord on the subject of the recall for eighteen months' service of three or four thousand reservists.[1] These men are of course liable to a week's training each year, and there is no hardship in this but in time of peace to call a man up for an additional spell of eighteen months is a measure of great severity which, in my opinion, is not warranted by the world situation.

Winston S. Churchill to Field Marshal Lord Montgomery
Prime Minister's Personal Minute M.570/52
(Premier papers, 11/6)

12 December 1952

Your minute of December 10.*

Will not the appointment of a British General Officer have the effect of making it almost certain that we shall not get an admiral in this important command hitherto held by Admiral Brind. The work of a military representative on General Ridgway's staff is nothing like as important to us as the Naval command of this area with all its contacts with the Baltic, South Norway etc. The matter must be looked at as a whole.

*On appointment of General Mansergh.[2]

John Colville to Winston S. Churchill
(Premier papers, 11/6)

12 December 1952

I read your minute M.570/52 to Lord Montgomery.

He said that he did not himself think there was any danger of our losing the naval Command in consequence of General Mansergh's appointment. Up till now the position has been that there was a British Admiral, a British General and an American Air commander, the British Admiral being No. 1. All that is now intended, according to Field Marshal Montgomery, is that General Mansergh should step into Admiral Brind's place and a British Admiral should take the place General Mansergh has hitherto held, the American airman of course retaining his post. He said that this was General Ridgway's philosophy

[1] M.555/52 and Thomas's reply, reproduced above (pp. 742, 764–5).

[2] Maurice James Mansergh, 1896–1966. Midshipman, 1914. On active service, Dardanelles, 1915. A specialist in navigation. Executive Officer, HMS *Rodney*, 1936–7. Asst Director of Plans, Admiralty, Jan.–May 1939. Director, Trade Div., Admiralty, May 1939 to Nov. 1941. CBE, 1941. Deputy Asst CNS (Trade), 1941. CoS to Allied Naval C-in-C, Allied Expeditionary Force, Normandy, 1944–5. Commodore, 15th Cruiser Sqn (in action in northern Adriatic), 1945. Senior Naval Officer, Haifa, 1946. RAdm., 1946. 5th Sea Lord and Deputy CNS (Air), 1949–51. C-in-C, Plymouth, 1951–3. Deputy C-in-C, Allied Forces Northern Europe, 1951–3; C-in-C, 1953–6. Knighted, 1952.

and he was himself sure that there would be no question of the Naval Officer being anything but an Englishman.

The Field Marshal said he was telling Lord Alexander that this was his view.

I think you should see (below) the letter which his COS wrote to General Gruenther[1] on Nov 29.

Field Marshal Lord Montgomery to Winston S. Churchill
(Premier papers, 11/6)

12 December 1952

1. The British refusal to agree to the Press release about the appointment of Mansergh as C-in-C at Oslo is causing irritation here. A British Admiral will eventually be needed as COMNAVNORTH but if the British make this a blackmail condition to be included in the announcement our prestige in the NATO Defence Organisation will suffer serious damage.

2. I would point out that SHAPE action in the matter is based entirely on the Chiefs of Staff letter to Gruenther dated November 29 and the present British attitude is a reversal of the terms of that letter.

3. Can you help me in the matter and get British agreement today to the announcement?

Field Marshal Lord Montgomery to Winston S. Churchill
(Premier papers, 11/6)

12 December 1952

I apologize for using the word 'blackmail' in my letter to you, but that is how it is regarded here and I thought I should let you know.

Winston S. Churchill to Field Marshal Lord Montgomery
(Premier papers, 11/6)

12 December 1952

I do not accept your description of this proposal.

---

[1] Alfred Maximilian Gruenther, 1899–1983. Educated at US Military Academy, West Point. 2nd Lt., Field Artillery, 1918. Married, 1922, Grace Elizabeth Crum: two children. Capt., 1935. Maj., 1941. Lt-Col., 1941. Brig.-Gen., 1942. Maj.-Gen., 1943. Deputy Cdr, US forces in Austria, 1945–6. Deputy Commandant, National War College, 1946–7. Director, Joint Staff/JCS, 1947–9. Lt.-Gen., 1949. Four-star Gen., 1951. CoS, SHAPE, 1951–3. SACEUR/C-in-C, US European Command, 1953–6. Retired, 1956. President, American Red Cross, 1956–64.

DECEMBER 1952 775

Meeting with Australian and New Zealand Prime Ministers: minutes
(Cabinet papers, 130/86)

12 December 1952   No. 10 Downing St
Secret
6 p.m.

ANZUS AND ANZAM

Mr Churchill said that he was most anxious to find a solution of the problem caused by the exclusion of the United Kingdom from Anzus. He and Mr Eden had been disturbed by reports of the proceedings of the Anzus Staff Planners, which seemed to show that Anzus was seeking to extend its scope throughout the Pacific theatre, including South East Asia. It was not reasonable that such planning should go forward without the direct assistance of the United Kingdom and perhaps of France whose interests were closely involved. Anzam, which was a closely defined geographical area and did not include the Americans, was no sort of substitute. The real object must be to create a central machinery of control for the whole Pacific area, including South East Asia, consisting of representatives of Australia, New Zealand, the United States and the United Kingdom. So long as that reality could be achieved, the outward forms were of comparatively small importance. He had great hopes that General Eisenhower would understand this point clearly, and he would be very willing to put it to him but in doing so must feel assured that he had the full support of Australia and New Zealand. In recent months he had found even the present United States Administration much more forthcoming, and they had shown great readiness to meet our point of view over the organisation of Saclant, the elimination of Iberlant and the proposed base at Lisbon and finally over the Mediterranean Command, where they were now ready to accept a British Admiral as Commander-in-Chief of the whole area under the general supervision of Saceur. He felt confident that this forthcoming attitude would be even more in evidence when General Eisenhower became President.

Mr Menzies emphasised the close and intimate interest of Australia in the problems of the South West Pacific and South East Asia. They had of course an equal interest in security against a resurgence of Japanese power and that was the reason why they had welcomed the Pacific Security Pact (Anzus). He recalled that Mr Dulles had originally discussed proposals for an Offshore Pact, in which Japan and the Philippines and perhaps Indonesia would also be included. His idea had been that Continental subjects involving the interests of other Powers would not be discussed. Mr Menzies said that he had made it clear that Australia could not enter a Pact which included Japan, and that he regarded the Philippines as a mere liability. The Americans had then proposed the Anzus Treaty and, with the full agreement of Mr Attlee's Government, Australia and New Zealand had accepted the offer. Attempts had then been made by Australia and New Zealand to persuade the United States Administration to accept the association of the United Kingdom with Anzus, either as a member or as an observer. The Americans had understood the special interest of the United Kingdom but had feared that, if any concession were made France and the Philippines and others would also clamour for the same rights. That would have meant the end of any effective planning and a grave danger to security of information.

Mr Menzies said that Australia, like the United Kingdom, would welcome some machinery for comprehensive military planning throughout the Far East including South East Asia. The security of Malaya was of the utmost consequence to Australia. Australia would therefore support any approach which Mr Churchill felt willing to make to the new United States Administration. Clearly that should be the first course of action. Mr Churchill would have great influence with the new President, and in any approach he made could take it for granted that he had the fullest possible support from Australia and New Zealand.

If, nevertheless, the new President found it impossible to arrive immediately at a wholly satisfactory solution, Mr Menzies thought that it would be quite possible to proceed by stages. The first step would be to give reality to Anzam planning. The second step would be to make the Americans realise the significance of Anzam. The third step would be to arrange a system of liaison on a high military level between Anzus and Anzam. It would then follow as a natural consequence of this procedure that the planning done in Anzus and Anzam separately should fall into the hands of a join Anzus/Anzam Committee.

Mr Holland said that he supported all the proposals made by Mr Churchill and Mr Menzies. He felt, however, that he must make clear the position of New Zealand. New Zealand had entered into commitments for sending a Division with air and naval support to the Middle East in war. In terms of manpower this was a commitment of 235,000 men, or ten percent of the whole population of New Zealand. The result was that there would be nothing left for home defence. It was essential, therefore, that New Zealand should have a Security Pact with the United States and Australia. They had signed this Pact with the full agreement of Mr Attlee's Government in the United Kingdom. In consequence there was some resentment felt in New Zealand that criticism of Anzus seemed sometimes to imply that New Zealand had done something disloyal to Great Britain in signing this Pact. Nothing surely could be further from the truth. He agreed that the Anzus machinery left a good deal to be desired, but he did not think the principle underlying the Anzus agreement ought to be the subject of criticism. He was convinced that a satisfactory machinery, leading to a marriage of Anzus and Anzam, could be achieved on the lines suggested by Mr Menzies. He had had some discussions with two American Admirals in Honolulu and he had found them most willing to undertake planning exercises with Australia and New Zealand and also with the United Kingdom. This sort of thing could be prelude to joint machinery for the control of the whole Pacific theatre, including South East Asia. He thought it quite insufficient to press for the admission of the United Kingdom as an observer in Anzus. This would be beneath the dignity of the United Kingdom which must be a full partner in Far Eastern planning.

Mr Churchill said that he had been much encouraged by the discussion which had shown complete understanding with regard to certain fundamental propositions, which he would in due course discuss on a friendly basis with the new President of the United States.

It was agreed by the three Prime Ministers that a communiqué in the following terms should be issued to the Press for publication in the morning newspapers of Monday 15th December.

'The Prime Ministers of the United Kingdom, Australia and New Zealand took the opportunity, provided by the Commonwealth Economic Conference, to discuss the situation in the Pacific and the problems of South East Asia. They reached complete understanding with regard to certain fundamental propositions which will, in due course, be the subject of friendly discussion with their Allies, the United States.'

Lord Moran to Winston S. Churchill
(Churchill papers, 1/54)

13 December 1952

My dear Prime Minister,

I have started a high temperature this morning and as it is probably a cold I don't want to risk infecting you. I shall be all right in a day or two.

I gathered yesterday that there were plans for a journey at the end of the month. I think a holiday is very much indicated. What I am not happy about is the long flight. It is true that just as warm water reduces the risk of bathing, so a pressurized cabin does mitigate the effects of flying. Nevertheless in our present state of knowledge of the relations between the circulation in the superficial vessels under the skin and the deep circulation, we just don't know the precise risk. In the event of any slight circulatory weakness drugs can be given which, if they are given at once, help considerably. One could use these in the air but because of the above-mentioned uncertainty one would be happier using them on the ground.

Is it at all possible to arrange a holiday which avoids these uncertainties?

In any case, whatever you decide I hope you will take me with you because I might be able to help.

Randolph S. Churchill to Winston S. Churchill
(Churchill papers, 1/51)[1]

13 December 1952

My dearest Papa,

We must decide in the next few days the title for the new book of Speeches. The following have been suggested by Cassell's.

A New Start
Stemming the Tide[2]
Against the Stream
A Matter of Survival
Fight for Survival
Perils of Peace
Holding Our Own
Effort and Sacrifice
Shouldering the Burden

None of them are very inspiring, but I thought the last the best. Perhaps you can suggest something better?

Your loving son.

Randolph S. Churchill to Winston S. Churchill
(Churchill papers, 1/51)[3]

14 December 1952

My dearest Papa,

Further to my letter of yesterday I have stumbled upon what I believe to be a much better title for the book:

'Uphill All the Way'

It is a phrase from the first broadcast you made after the last Election.[4] It admirably describes the task of the nation and of His Majesty's Government.

The sentence which could be printed on the fly-leaf is as follows: '. . . the train has to be started again on the right line, which, I am telling you beforehand – please remember it – is uphill all the way.'

Your loving son,

---

[1] This is the first written communication between Randolph and his father since their quarrel two months earlier. WSC had not replied to Randolph's distraught letter of Oct. 16 (reproduced above, pp. 674–7), in order to avoid fanning the dispute. Martin Gilbert notes of this letter and the one below that 'Churchill replied at once, all hint of quarrel gone' (*Winston S. Churchill*, vol. 8, *Never Despair*, p. 784).

[2] Churchill placed a mark next to 'Stemming the Tide'.

[3] This letter was handwritten.

[4] Reproduced above (pp. 145–9).

Robert Boothby to Winston S. Churchill
(*Churchill papers, 2/181*)[1]

14 December 1952
Personal

Dear Prime Minister,

I feel impelled to write you a line to say what a very great privilege and pleasure it was for me to dine once again at Chartwell in your company. It took me back to the old care-free days when I was your Parliamentary Private Secretary, and there seemed to be no cloud on the horizon; and on to the fateful days when the cloud was no bigger than a man's hand, and there was still time to save the sum of things.

It was in November 1934 that you invited me to be one of the six signatories of the amendment to the Address which declared that 'the strength of our national defence, and especially of our air defences, is no longer adequate to secure the peace, safety and freedom of Your Majesty's faithful subjects,' and to speak in the subsequent debate. I shall be proud of that as long as I live. They are all flinging mud at old Baldwin now, but in those days you were almost alone in facing the facts and telling the truth. The battle was lost, and with it our civilization; but it is good to have taken part in it on the right side, and under your leadership.

I do hope I am not now the cause of any embarrassment to you. I have had a long and hard struggle for survival, but I see the light at the end of the tunnel; and, thanks to you, I have been able to do some work at Strasbourg which may one day bear fruit. I have no grievances.

All good wishes for Christmas and the New Year.

This letter, of course, requires no answer.

Winston S. Churchill to Randolph S. Churchill
(*Churchill papers, 1/51*)

15 December 1952
Personal

Dearest Randolph,

Thank you for your letters of December 13 and 14.[2] I rather think STEMMING THE TIDE is the best, but SHOULDERING THE BURDEN is a good second. Let us have a word about it when we meet at the children's party on Friday.

'Uphill all the way' is a cry of pain.

Your loving Father,

---

[1] This letter was handwritten.
[2] Reproduced above (p. 778).

Antony Head to Winston S. Churchill
(*Premier papers, 11/591*)

15 December 1952

There are at present 88 Militia battalions formally in existence. They were placed in a state of suspended animation in 1923. They were not disbanded at that time because it was thought that there might possibly be some role for them in the future; but experience has shown that the Militia as such is no longer required in any way as part of our Armed Forces.

The old Militia, which had been in existence since the 17th Century, ceased to exist in 1921. At that time the Special Reserve was given the title of Militia. This was done when you were Secretary of State for War so that the Militia which we now propose to disband is the old Special Reserve of our time.

There seems little or no point in keeping these battalions in existence as they contain no other ranks and only one officer, Lord Shaftesbury,[1] who is an Honorary Colonel. I shall, of course, tell him what I propose to do before any public announcement is made.

The practical effect of formal disbandment would be to enable plans to be made to deal with the regimental funds of these battalions.

I thought you would like to know about this before I took any further steps. I have sent a copy of this minute to the Minister of Defence.[2]

Duncan Sandys to Winston S. Churchill
(*Premier papers, 11/764*)

16 December 1952

You asked me to explain why my Department had spent more in this financial year than was allowed for in its original estimates.

After taking into account the effects of the recent revision of the defence programme, it is likely that this Department will exceed its approved expenditure of £835 million by about £57 million.

This is accounted for as follows:

(a)	Refunds to Service Departments	£9 million
(b)	Import duty paid on steel	£7 million
(c)	Textile relief programme	£7 million
(d)	Defence super-priority	£13 million

---

[1] Anthony Ashley-Cooper, 1869–1961. Succeeded as Earl Shaftesbury, 1886. Military Secretary to Governor of Victoria, 1895–8. Chamberlain for the Princess of Wales, 1901. Commanded North Irish Horse, 1902–12. KCVO, 1906. Chamberlain to Queen Mary, 1910–22. CBE, 1919. GCVO, 1920. PC, 1922.

[2] Churchill responded on Dec. 17: 'Please give me a return of the regimental funds of these battalions and what use you propose to make of them' (M.574/52).

(e)	Underestimate of progress payments to be made on production programme of £528 million	£14 million
(f)	Increases in cost of transport, wages, and raw materials	£7 million
	Total	£57 million

Thus, £16 million (items (a) and (b)) are purely bookkeeping debits which are offset by credits in the accounts of other Ministries. £20 million (items (c) and (d)) are the direct result of Cabinet decisions taken after the estimates had been published and, like the extra £14 millions of progress payments, will correspondingly reduce the size of the defence bill in subsequent years.

Only £7 millions (due to increased costs over which we had no control) of the £57 millions excess expenditure in fact involve any extra charge upon the Exchequer.

I enclose a copy of my reply to the Chancellor of the Exchequer which explains the reasons for the Supplementary Estimates more fully.

Cabinet: conclusions
(Cabinet papers, 128/25)

16 December 1952
Secret
11.30 a.m.
Cabinet Meeting No. 105 of 1952

[. . .]

3. The Cabinet had before them a memorandum by the Minister of Supply (C(52)424) recommending that the scheme under which certain defence orders had been brought forward for the purpose of relieving unemployment in the clothing and textile industries should not be regarded as completed.

The Minister of Supply explained that the total value of orders actually placed under the scheme was likely to be about £20–5 millions, as compared with the figure of £23 millions approved by the Cabinet on 10th June and with the expenditure limits of £20–£25 millions originally announced in Parliament. Unemployment in the clothing and textile industries had dropped from 183,000 in May to 67,000 in October and short-time working had been considerably reduced.

The Cabinet – Approved the recommendation made in C(52)424.

Winston S. Churchill to James Thomas
Prime Minister's Personal Minute M.575/52
(Premier papers, 11/478)

17 December 1952

You say that you can now reduce the number of Reservists to be recalled to something less than a thousand (probably 750 to 800). From what is this reduction made? I presume from the final three thousand men for eighteen months' service. If this is so it is a substantial measure. Let me know exactly what were the final three thousand men, i.e. how many were described as 'juniors' and how many were key men or 'men particularly wanted because of their previous experience'. Let me know in what month this final three thousand were to be called up, dividing between juniors and the rest.

It is an act of great severity in time of peace to call up a small number of men for such a prolonged period of service as eighteen months. Most of them were I expect under the impression when they accepted £18 a year bounty that their liability did not extend beyond the annual or biennial week's training. Suddenly they find themselves booked for eighteen months. This surely should be kept for an emergency and would be quite justified in that case. I should have thought their recall in time of peace should be on the same footing as the Immediate Reserve. I am very much in favour as you know of the principle of the Immediate Reserve but the essence of it is a bona fide emergency. This does not exist at the present time.

The complaints in the cuttings I sent you have not been referred to in your minute.

Pray let me have this further information at your convenience.

Cabinet: conclusions
(Cabinet papers, 128/25)

18 December 1952
Secret
11.30 a.m.
Cabinet Meeting No. 106 of 1952

[. . .]
4. The Cabinet resumed their discussion of a memorandum by the Minister of Defence (C(52)248) on the question whether an amnesty should be declared for men who had deserted from the Armed Forces during the war.

The Prime Minister said that he found great difficulty in accepting the arguments against a general amnesty for deserters. It was not in the national interest that these men should continue to live the lives of outcasts and outlaws. Nearly eight years had passed since the end of the war, and he could not accept the view that desertion should never be condoned. The national rejoicing at the time of the Coronation would provide a suitable occasion for an act of mercy towards these men.

Discussion showed that opinion in the Cabinet was divided on this question. The Service Ministers, supported by some members of the Cabinet, expressed the firm conviction that an amnesty for deserters would be taken as implying that desertion in war was no longer regarded as the most serious of military crimes, and would lead to increased desertion from the Armed Forces at a time when very large numbers of men were serving overseas in circumstances which imposed the most disagreeable duties upon them. The numbers who would benefit from an amnesty, now estimated as not more than 2,000 were not so large as to justify this risk to the general discipline of the Forces. No true comparison could be drawn with circumstances after the 1914–18 War, when the Services were much smaller and were not engaged in active military operations.

The majority of the Cabinet, on the other hand, doubted whether the effect on Service discipline would be as severe as the Service Ministers foresaw, and thought it was outweighed by consideration of mercy and by the disadvantage of driving these deserters and their children into criminal habits by branding them as outlaws. If the amnesty were granted in connection with the Coronation of a new Sovereign, no man now serving in the Forces could be led thereby to expect that, if he deserted, his offence would be condoned if he escaped detection for a few years.

The Prime Minister, summing up the discussion, said that the balance of the opinion in the Cabinet seemed to be in favour of recommending that Her Majesty should grant some form of amnesty for men who had deserted from the Armed Forces in the war as a special act of clemency in the year of her Coronation.

The Cabinet –
(1) Invited the Minister of Defence to consider what procedure should be adopted for extending clemency to men who had deserted from the Armed Forces in the last war.
(2) Took note that the Prime Minister would take steps to ascertain informally whether Her Majesty would wish such an act of clemency to be associated directly with her Coronation.

The Cabinet also considered a memorandum by the Home Secretary and the Secretary of State for Scotland (C(52)436) on the question whether an amnesty should be granted to civil prisoners on the occasion of the Coronation.

The Home Secretary said that this would necessarily involve unfairness between one prisoner and another and, for the reasons indicated in the memorandum, could not be applied at all to various classes of prisoner. He and the Secretary of State for Scotland were agreed that it would be inexpedient to recommend an amnesty or other form of special clemency for civil prisoners on the occasion of the Coronation.

The Cabinet –
> (3) Agreed that no recommendation should be made for the exercise of special clemency towards civil prisoners on the occasion of the Coronation; and authorised the Home Secretary and the Secretary of State for Scotland to make a public announcement to this effect.

[. . .]

6. The Cabinet had before them memoranda by the Prime Minister (C(52)447) and the Foreign Secretary (C(52)444) on the alternative courses of action now open to the United Kingdom Government in the fisheries dispute with the Iceland Government.

The Prime Minister said that the Government of Iceland were not justified in using the judgment of the Hague Court in the Anglo-Norwegian fisheries dispute as a ground for depriving our trawlers of the free access to Faxa Bay, which they had enjoyed for half a century, in order to promote the interests of Iceland's own inshore fishermen. It was satisfactory that, in spite of the ban on landings of fish from Iceland, we had obtained our normal supplies for the last two months; but, if the restrictions imposed on our trawlers around the coast of Iceland were extended to other traditional fishing grounds, the threat to our fish supplies would become serious. If we now referred the dispute to the International Court, which might appear to the Cabinet to be the least objectionable course, the ban on landings was likely to be maintained while proceedings in the Court were pending and in progress, since there was no means of coercing the trawler owners and skippers in the matter. Moreover, the Court's ultimate judgment might well prove unfavourable to our cause.

One view expressed in discussion was that the United Kingdom Government might refrain from taking any special action in the matter for the time being. We could explain once again to the Government of Iceland that the ban on landings represented a spontaneous reaction by our fishing interests, over whom the Government had no control. The closing of the English market to Icelandic fish might well be the best deterrent to discourage others from following Iceland's example. If we adopted this course we must expect retaliation against our exports to Iceland.

Other Ministers were, however, inclined to favour referring the dispute to the International Court. The Icelanders' interpretation of The Hague Court ruling in the Anglo-Norwegian fisheries case was exceedingly wide and went beyond what the Court itself had intended.

The Court might welcome an opportunity of narrowing the interpretation placed in practice upon its earlier ruling.

The general view of the Cabinet was that, on balance, we should be wise to refer the dispute to the International Court, and that, in doing so, we ought if possible to be able to say that, if the Government of Iceland withdrew their restrictions on our trawlers pending a decision by the Court, the ban on landings of Icelandic fish in this country would be similarly lifted.

The Cabinet –
(1) Agreed in principle that Her Majesty's Government should refer the Iceland fisheries dispute to the International Court of Justice.
(2) Invited the Minister of Agriculture and Fisheries to obtain from the trawler owners and skippers concerned the necessary assurances to enable Her Majesty's Government to inform the International Court that, if the restrictions on our trawlers imposed by the Government of Iceland were raised pending a decision by the Court, the ban on landings of Icelandic fish in this country would also be lifted.
(3) Invited the President of the Board of Trade to examine the possibility of revoking the open general licence for the import of fish from Iceland and of imposing quota restrictions should such measures prove eventually to be necessary.

[. . .]

Charles de Gaulle[1] to Winston S. Churchill
(Premier papers, 11/164)[2]

20 December 1952
Translation

Dear Mr Churchill,

I wish you to know that my most sincere wishes go to you, to yours and to noble and valiant England at this Christmas of a cruel epoch.

Although at the present time her greatness, of which formerly advantage was taken, is now questioned you know how to remain great yourself. And so my friendship and admiration are faithful to you.

I ask you to present to Mrs Churchill my respectful greetings and wishes to which my wife joins her warm wishes and memories. To you, Mr Churchill, my devoted sentiments.

---

[1] Charles de Gaulle, 1890–1970. On active service on the Western Front, 1914–16 (thrice wounded; despatches). POW, 1916–18 (five attempts to escape). Commanded 4th Armoured Bde, 5th Army, 1939; 4th Armoured Div., 1940. Under-Secretary for War and National Defence, 1940. Chief of the Free French (later President of the French National Committee), London and Brazzaville, 1940–2. President, French Committee of National Liberation, Algiers, 1943. President, Provisional Government of the French Republic, and head of its armed forces, 1943–6. PM, 1958–9. President, 1958–69.

[2] This letter was handwritten in French.

Randolph S. Churchill to Winston S. Churchill
(*Churchill papers, 1/51*)[1]

21 December 1952

My dearest Papa,

Your princely Christmas present[2] fills me with gratitude which I scarcely know how to express. It is immensely welcome not only on material grounds but as a renewed expression of your affection. Thank you from the bottom of my heart.

Your loving son

James Thomas to Winston S. Churchill
(*Premier papers, 11/159*)

21 December 1952
Top Secret and Personal
Guard

A paper written in July by the late Director of Naval Intelligence, Vice Admiral Longley-Cook,[3] has just been brought to my notice.[4] It was shown to Mr Attlee by my predecessor, Pakenham,[5] in the autumn. Mr Attlee was very interested in it but did not pursue the matter in view of the imminent General Election.

I feel that I should let you see a copy of this document before your visit to America; it is a long one, but I also attach a summary. I must add that this paper has never been formally considered by the Admiralty and contains only the personal views of its author.

May I ask you to return the paper when you have pursed it? All other copies were ordered to be destroyed some months ago.

[1] This letter was handwritten.
[2] A substantial cash gift.
[3] Eric William Longley-Cook, 1898–1983. Entered RN, 1914. On active service, HMS *Prince of Wales*, 1914–18. Lt, 1919. Lt-Cdr, 1927. Capt., 1938. Cdr, HMS *Caradoc*, 1939–40. Deputy Director of Training and Staff Duties, 1940. Deputy Director of Gunnery and Anti-Aircraft Warfare, 1941. Cdr, HMS *Argonaut*, 1942–3. Capt. of the Fleet, Mediterranean Fleet, 1943; East Indies Fleet, 1945. DSO, 1945. CoS, Home Fleet, 1946–8. Director of Naval Intelligence, 1948–51. RAdm., 1948. CB, 1950. Vice-Adm., 1951.
[4] The Longley-Cook Report drew attention to three factors that could influence British policy: the Kremlin's reluctance to fully commit the USSR to war; the chance of a preventative war against the USSR launched by the US; and the likelihood of a long-drawn-out struggle between the western democracies and the USSR, which could not be solved by immediate warfare.
[5] Francis Aungier Pakenham, 1905–2001. 2nd son of 5th Earl of Longford (killed in action at Gallipoli in 1915). Educated at Eton and New College, Oxford. Worked in Conservative Party Economic Research Dept, 1930–2. Lecturer in Politics, Oxford University, 1932. Personal Assistant to Sir William Beveridge, 1941–4. Parliamentary Under-Secretary of State, War Office, 1946–7. Chancellor of the Duchy of Lancaster, 1947–8. Minister of Civil Aviation, 1948–51. 1st Lord of the Admiralty, 1951. Succeeded his brother as Earl of Longford, 1961. Lord Privy Seal, 1964–5, 1966–8. Secretary of State for the Colonies, 1965–6. KG, 1971.

Cabinet: conclusions
(Cabinet papers, 128/25)

22 December 1952
Secret
4 p.m.
Cabinet Meeting No. 107 of 1952

1. The Cabinet had before them a memorandum by the Foreign Secretary (C(52)450) on the attempt of the Saudi Arabians to extend their influence into the territories of the Trucial Sheikdoms in the Persian Gulf.

The Foreign Secretary said that this policy of encroachment had been encouraged by our failure to protect our interests at Abadan. These States along the western shore of the Persian Gulf, with their large potential resources of oil, were of great importance to us, and it was most desirable that positive steps should be taken to deter the Saudi Arabians from further incursions. It was doubtful whether Ibn Saud would accept our offer of arbitration, though there was some reason to suppose that the Americans might support this course. If he did not, it seemed necessary that we should make some show of force in the area, and take steps to build up the military strength of these small States to enable them to protect themselves. He understood that the Chiefs of Staff could make some small British force available in the near future, and he recommended that action should be taken concurrently to increase the Trucial Oman Levies to a total of 300 or 400 men, and to provide a cadre for a force of 200 men for the Sultan of Muscat.

In discussion the following points were made –

(a) A cruiser (HMS *Ceylon*) and a frigate would be in the Persian Gulf from mid-January to mid-February and thereafter two frigates would be there. Twelve RAF armoured cars could be sent from Iraq in mid-January, and one squadron of Vampires could also be sent for short periods. It would take about a month to concentrate this small force.

(b) British forces could not remain indefinitely in the area, and an immediate start should therefore be made with the building up of the local levies. Consideration might also be given to the possibility of employing the Aden Levies.

The Prime Minister said that it was clear that as an immediate step there should be some concentration of British forces in the area. He hoped that it would be possible to send in stronger forces than those suggested in the discussion. At the same time measures should be put in hand to build up the local levies, and the Colonial Secretary should examine the suggestion that the Aden Levies should also be used. This concentration of forces should take place as unobtrusively as possible.

The Cabinet –

(1) Invited the Foreign Secretary to renew his offer to submit these

frontier disputes to arbitration, and to ask the United States Government to press Ibn Saud to accept this offer.

(2) Approved in principle the early movement of suitable British forces to the Trucial Sheikdoms and the initiation of measures to build up the strength of the local levies.

(3) Instructed the Chiefs of Staff, in consultation with the Foreign Office and Colonial Office, to set in hand the action to give effect to Conclusion (2) above and to examine the possibility of using the Aden Levies in this area.

[. . .]

Winston S. Churchill to Antony Head
Prime Minister's Personal Minute M.585/52
(Premier papers, 11/591)

28 December 1952

These are substantial sums,* carefully saved and guarded, and if they are to be sequestrated and redispersed they should be surely devoted to preserving regimental, and territorial esprit-de-corps. Please keep me informed.

* Regimental funds held in trust for various Militia Battalions.

Winston S. Churchill to Lord Moran
(Churchill papers, 1/54)

29 December 1952

My dear Charles,

Thank you so much for your letter.[1] I think I will take a chance, as the visit is not official in any way.

I have asked Juler[2] to come at 9.50 on Tuesday morning, because the eye is being a nuisance and it would be very nice if you could look in around the same time. I have a Cabinet at 11.30.

I am most grateful to you for your generous offer.

---

[1] Reproduced above (p. 777).
[2] Frank Anderson Juler, 1880–1962. Leading British ophthalmologist. Educated at Trinity College Cambridge and St Mary's Hospital, Paddington. Served in European war, of 1914–19. Col., RAMC, 1916–19. Surgeon-Oculist to HM Household, 1936–52. President, Ophthalmic Section, Royal Society of Medicine, 1942–4. Vice-President, Faculty of Ophthalmologists, 1946–7. CVO, 1947. President, Ophthalmological Society of UK, 1948–50. Extra Surgeon-Oculist to HM Household, 1952–62.

Winston S. Churchill to Charles de Gaulle
(Premier papers, 11/164)[1]

29 December 1952

My dear de Gaulle,

I was moved by the inspiring words of your letter to me of December 20.[2] I am grateful to you for what you write about England. We are indeed living in a cruel epoch for the world. But I still believe that Truth and Freedom will survive.

Mrs Churchill wishes me to thank you for your very kind messages to her, and we both send you and Madame de Gaulle,[3] our warmest wishes for a Happy New Year.

Cabinet: conclusions
(Cabinet papers, 128/25)

30 December 1952
Secret
11.30 a.m.
Cabinet Meeting No. 108 of 1952

[. . .]

2. The Foreign Secretary said that there were indications that the new United States Administration might seek to free their hands in dealing with the Korean situation by repudiating President Truman's declaration that the Formosa Straits would be neutralised. Their object would be to allow raids to be made from Formosa against the Chinese mainland or against neighbouring islands held by Chinese Communist forces. It would be represented, no doubt, that these raids might take some of the pressure off the French in Indo-China. From the military point of view he thought that such raids would be of little value and were unlikely to be welcomed by the French, who were most anxious to avoid provoking large-scale Chinese intervention in Indo-China and were chiefly in need of additional money and equipment with which to organise Vietnamese forces. From the political angle there would be great disadvantage in taking this limited and unproductive step. He would therefore seek to dissuade the new United States Government from taking it, at any rate until there had been an opportunity for full Anglo-American discussion on the whole Far Eastern situation.

The Prime Minister said that in his forthcoming visit to the United States

---

[1] This letter was handwritten.
[2] Reproduced above (p. 785).
[3] Yvonne Charlotte Anne Marie Vendroux, 1900–79. Married, 1921, Charles de Gaulle: three children.

he would point out to General Eisenhower that, although we had no intention of evacuating Egypt under duress, it was beyond our strength to maintain permanently a force of 70,000 men in the Canal Zone. He would press for some effective assistance from the United States in this area.

The Foreign Secretary said that the Americans might be more willing to co-operate in a Joint Air Defence Organisation in the Middle East and to contribute some air forces to it. That seemed at the moment to be the best hope of getting American help in this area. It might be worth reminding the Americans that, as their investments in the Middle East now totalled no less than $726 million, it was to their advantage to support our Middle Eastern policy in the same way as we had supported the French in North Africa.

The Foreign Secretary said he did not propose to inform the United States Government in advance of our plans for British troop movements and for the development of local levies in the Persian Gulf area and in the Trucial Sheikdoms. It would be better to put these measures in hand and to explain their purpose to the Americans after they had been taken.

[. . .]

4. The Prime Minister said that he had been surprised to learn that it was proposed to allow the Egyptians to draw £10 million of their blocked sterling balances at the beginning of 1953. He had hoped that, as had been done twelve months previously, this release would be delayed and held as a useful card in negotiations over the Sudan and over defence. He had certainly expected that this would be fully discussed in Cabinet before any decision was made.

The Chancellor of the Exchequer said that the release of sterling balances to Egypt was controlled by the Sterling Releases Agreement made with the Egyptian Government in July 1951. Under this Agreement £5 million could be released whenever Egypt's free sterling holdings totalled less than £45 million. These holdings were now down to a figure of £6 million and the release of the £5 million available in 1953 had been made in advance as a result of the Cabinet decision in September 1952. The Agreement also provided for the annual release of £10 million. This could be made in the course of any one year, but was normally made at the beginning of the year. In 1952 the release had been delayed until April owing to the grave political situation in Egypt and the disturbances in the Canal Zone. In the autumn of 1952 the political situation had become easier and negotiations with General Neguib's Government were more promising. Accordingly, an undertaking had been given at that time that, if there were no unforeseen developments, the release of £10 million for 1953 would be made at the beginning of the year. From the United Kingdom point of view the Agreement was most satisfactory. Without it, Egypt would be able to draw freely upon her total sterling balances, which amounted to £179 million. A refusal to honour the Agreement or to allow any drawings from sterling balances would shake world confidence in sterling and was incompatible with the position of the United Kingdom as the banker for the sterling area. It was, moreover, of importance to United Kingdom trade that the economy of Egypt, which was now in a perilous condition, should receive some support and, even though Egypt would pay for United Kingdom imports with these sterling balances, that was better than the cessation of all trade. The matter had not been brought to Cabinet since it had been regarded by both the Treasury and the Foreign Office as the routine working of a contractual arrangement.

The Prime Minister said that he found it difficult to regard this as a routine matter. The releases already made had not improved the attitude of the Egyptian Government towards the United Kingdom; and, while it was right that international agreements should be kept, it was possible to make exceptions where the other party to an agreement had repudiated a treaty as Egypt had done.

The Cabinet –

(1) Took note that £10 million of Egypt's blocked sterling balances would be released in January, 1953, in accordance with the Sterling Releases Agreement of July 1951.
(2) Invited the Chancellor of the Exchequer to bring before the Cabinet any proposal for further releases of Egypt's sterling balances.

[. . .]

John Colville: diary
('The Fringes of Power', page 657)

30 December 1952

The Prime Minister, Mrs Churchill, Mary and Christopher Soames and I left Waterloo at 7.30 p.m. bound for Southampton and the *Queen Mary*. We dined on the train and talked of many things, from the War of 1812 to the future of Pakistan. We went on board about 9.45 and occupied a series of eminently luxurious cabins.

John Colville: diary
('The Fringes of Power', pages 657–8)

31 December 1952

We sailed at 10.15 a.m. I worked with the PM for most of the morning and lunched *en famille* in his dining-room, with the usual gastronomic excellence associated with these liners. At Cherbourg we sent off a bag. Christopher and I had a Turkish bath.

Sir Roger and Lady Makins[1] to dinner. The PM said he thought the recent treason trials in Prague, with so many Jews among the condemned, indicated that the Communists were looking towards the Arab States, Persia and North Africa and were deliberately antagonising Israel. He also said he would preach to Eisenhower the vital importance of a common Anglo-American front 'from Korea to Kikuyu and from Kikuyu to Calais'.

Saw the New Year in at a somewhat amateurish ceremony in the main lounge.

Winston S. Churchill to Anthony Eden
Prime Minister's Personal Minute M.589/52
(Premier papers, 11/541)

31 December 1952

We think alike on this ill-natured action.[2] We should take advantage of it to effect marked reduction in the staff of our Moscow Embassy.

Could you not at the same time think out some further reductions that should be enforced upon the Russian Embassy and Commercial Mission in London, and also some restrictions on their movements? There would be no need to link this action directly with the incident in Moscow. It should stand on its own merits, but I dare say conclusions would be drawn.

Winston S. Churchill to James Thomas
Prime Minister's Personal Minute M.592/52
(Premier papers, 11/478)

31 December 1952

I am not satisfied with the present position about the recall of Reservists for eighteen months' service when no 'emergency', such as is intended to govern such measures, exists. To take a man from his employment and family for so long a period is an abuse or misuse of the powers governing the Royal Fleet Reserve. It is all the more invidious when the numbers concerned are so small. I hope therefore you will be able to make me detailed proposals for a substantial reduction in those already called up, and call no more up in present conditions.

Meanwhile please inform me how you deal with hard cases.

---

[1] Alice Brooks Davis, –1985. Daughter of Dwight Davis, after whom the Davis Cup tennis competition was named. Married, 1934, Roger Makins, during his three-year assignment in Washington DC.
[2] See Colville to Brook, Dec. 12, reproduced above (p. 772).

January
1953

John Colville: diary
('The Fringes of Power', page 658)

1 January 1953

A quiet day on board with sunshine and smooth seas. We all lunched and dined in the Verandah Grill. During the evening Winston told me several things worth remembering. He said that if I lived my normal span I should assuredly see Eastern Europe free of Communism. He also said that Russia feared our friendship more than our enmity. Finally he lamented that owing to Eisenhower winning the presidency he must cut much out of Volume VI of his War History and could not tell the story of how the United States gave away, to please Russia, vast tracts of Europe they had occupied and how suspicious they were of his pleas for caution. The British General Election in June 1945 had occupied so much of his attention which should have been directed to stemming this fatal tide. If FDR had lived, and had been in good health, he would have seen the red light in time to check the American policy: Truman, after all, had only been a novice, bewildered by the march of events and by responsibilities which he had never expected.

Winston S. Churchill to Members of the Cabinet
(Premier papers, 11/49)

January 1953
Top Secret
Proof

The following notes are an attempt to forecast the opening phases of a potential third World War, should our efforts to avert it fail during the next eighteen months:

(1) It should be assumed that the initiative will rest with the Soviets, who will thus have the advantage of striking the first blow, never of so much importance as in the atomic age. The advantages of Surprise to the weaker Power in

atomic weapons will probably outweigh the need of having everything ready on the ground and at sea.

(2) The eighty Russian Divisions on the European front are always in a high state of preparedness, and mobility, and we cannot expect any warning signs of troop movements during the month before. Their overwhelming superiority in the European theatre would justify a few days' delay, or 20 per cent short of full mobilisation, before the actual advance Westward was begun. We cannot therefore expect any warning data from the ground troops.

(3) The Naval preparations may be far more tell-tale, as the Soviets must expect an obliterating attack on their submarine and mining bases within a few hours, or at the outside days, of Zero. The whole of their naval war depends upon their U-boats and mining craft being at sea before their atomic blow has drawn its retaliation. Indeed they may well be in their ocean war stations, with supply vessels, beforehand. Most careful watching arrangements should be developed both by Air and Intelligence. It would be worth while trying to mark down all the Soviet U-boats and minelayers from week to week.

(4) Whatever reconnaissance of the Russian airfields is possible should of course be organised and in any period of expected danger photographs of the airfields would be of the highest importance both to us and the Americans. I should expect to be consulted beforehand as in the case of Ju-Jitsu.

(5) I doubt whether the Soviet would begin war as the result of an accident or incident. It is safer to assume that they will act on a settled plan. The question of what would be their best time of year requires persevering thought. The first World War began on 4th August and the second on 3rd September. These dates may have been chosen because of politics rather than season. It would seem that the harvest will be of greater consequence to the Russians under modern conditions. Their collective farming agriculture is upon an oil-drawn tractor basis. If the oil-fields and oil-storage centres can be destroyed or seriously damaged in the first fortnight of the war, the means of reaping the harvest might be destroyed with the certainty of famine a year later. This line of Soviet thought would seem to make October and even November more dangerous months to us than August. All this should be worked out.

(6) On the other hand, we must make up our minds what are the most dangerous months for Russia under atomic air attack. In which months does the weather give them most protection – August–September or October–December? (Both inclusive.) Anyhow, from the end of July till the end of November would seem to be the most dangerous season and vigilance should be toned up for it.

SECTION II

(7) Proceeding on the assumption that 1st October, 1952, or 1953 might be Zero, let us consider what would happen. There are two alternatives: (*a*) That we have indication beforehand, and (*b*) complete surprise. Dealing with

(*a*) first: If the Americans were sure that a major attack were imminent they might well decide to attack first with the atomic bomb. This might destroy the concentrations of aircraft on Soviet airfields carrying the atomic weapon. If this were so they would probably give us at least 48 hours' notice. Alternatively we might be aware of menacing Soviet dispositions on the sea and on the airfields, even perhaps some data from the armies, and a period of tension might arise warranting the introduction of the '*Alert*'. We should not be shy, if substantial evidence of danger is forthcoming, to order the Alert. If nothing happened we could always say it was an exercise. Indeed it might be well to have skeleton Alert exercises proclaimed beforehand as such, in order that the real one – if nothing happened – would be easily explainable.

(8) A real Alert would involve:
- (a) All the necessary precautions, like putting the 250,000 troops in the Island into the highest mobility possible, calling out the Home Guard, and mobilising our Ack-Ack resources.
- (b) Corresponding measures for the 'Alert' of the Air and Naval forces and the calling out of all Immediate Reserves that had been created. It would not be necessary in the 'Alert' period to call up the mass of ordinary Z Reservists.
- (c) Every effort should be made to evacuate children and invalids from London. I presume a detailed plan has already been made. If not, it should be done forthwith.
- (d) The evacuations from London of the Staffs not needed in the capital for war conditions. These should be limited to about 7,000, and for these adequate atom bomb accommodation should be provided. This accommodation should be put in good order without delay, and questions of ventilation, &c., should be dealt with.

(9) We should of course fight it out in Whitehall, although it is the bull's-eye, because the best bomb-proof shelter and the only concerted centre of Government lies there. Preparation should be made not only for the bomb-proof accommodation of the 7,000 approved Staff, but against the descent in the Parks of up to 5,000 hostile paratroops. It would be necessary on the Alert to have three or four thousand men well armed, additional to the 7,000 already mentioned. Are there any shelters under Wellington Barracks? No preparation need be made for the Parliament. They had better be dispersed until we see how the first shock goes. The Sovereign and the Royal Family would move out of the capital probably to Windsor or the neighbourhood.

(10) Supposing, however, the surprise is complete, and the Soviet Government begin atomic bombing attack on East Anglia and the seat of Government in Whitehall, how much notice should we get? Our radar on the continent and at home and on the coasts should give perhaps half an hour. Plans should be worked out for what everyone is to do on the alarm signal being given. It must be understood that these arrangements cannot prevent immense destruction

of life. It is hoped, however, that a nucleus of command control can be preserved, and also that an alternative secondary skeleton command can be established somewhere within 50 miles of London.

John Colville: diary
('The Fringes of Power', pages 658-9)

3 January 1953

[. . .]
After dinner, in the Verandah Grill, I was left alone with the PM and fired at him about thirty questions which he might be asked at his press conference on arrival in New York. He scintillated in his replies, e.g.:

Qn: What are your views, Mr Churchill, on the present stalemate in Korea?
Ans: Better a stalemate than a checkmate.

Qn: How do you justify such great expenditure on the Coronation of your Queen, when England is in such financial straits?
Ans: Everybody likes to wear a flower when he goes to see his girl.

Qn: Is not British policy in Persia throwing Persia into the hands of the Communists?
Ans: If Britain and America refuse to be disunited, no ill can come.

And there were many others as good or better. I wished so much I had had a microphone.

John Colville: diary
('The Fringes of Power', pages 659-60)

5 January 1953

Docked in New York at 8.15 a.m. pandemonium let loose. Mr Baruch, high dignitaries, low officials, Embassy people, pressmen swarmed on board. The PM saw the press in the Verandah Grill and answered questions well; but perhaps less well than the night before last.

When we disembarked we went to Baruch's flat and thence I drove to Henry and Mimi Hyde's[1] house on E 70th Street, where I am staying.

General Eisenhower arrived amid the flashing of bulbs at 5.00 p.m. and greeted W with: 'Well, the one thing I have so far learnt in this damned game of yours is that you have just got to have a sense of humour.' After a blinding photographic session, Baruch and I withdrew leaving the two to talk of many things (papers about which I deposited on a table beside W).

---

[1] Marie Emily de la Grange, 1919-83. Known as 'Mimi'. Born in Paris. Emigrated to US, 1939. Editor, broadcasting section, French Div., Office of War Information, London and New York. Married, 1941, Henry Baldwin Hyde: two daughters.

Returned for dinner at which Eisenhower, Baruchs (father, son[1] and daughter), Sarah, Christopher, Mr and Mrs C and Miss Navarro[2] were present. Winston said that a protoplasm was sexless. Then it divided into two sexes which, in due course, united again in a different way to their common benefit and gratification. This should also be the story of England and America. Ike talked about Cleopatra's Needle (how the Egyptians raised it), the charm of the Queen, the intelligence of the Duke of Edinburgh, and a few war-time indiscretions.

After dinner I listened to the PM and the President elect talking: Winston made one or two profound observations. For instance, 'I think you and I are agreed that it is not only important to discover the truth but to know how to present the truth'; and (apropos of the recent treason trials in Czechoslovakia) 'That they should think it good propaganda is what shows the absolutely unbridgeable gulf between us.'

Bernard Baruch, next to whom I sat at dinner, told me that he thought European unity, in some striking form, was essential if America was not to tire of her efforts – and only Winston (who, he said, was deaf to his pleas on the subject) could bring it about. England now had three assets: her Queen ('the world's sweetheart'); Winston Churchill; and her glorious historical past. I said there was a fourth: her unrivalled technical ability. But his pleas for rapid action were met by the following remark of Winston's: 'It may be better to bear an agonising period of unsatisfactory time.... You may kill yourself in getting strong enough.'

John Colville: diary
('The Fringes of Power', page 660)

6 January 1953

A day of unrelenting activity. After a hideous morning, during which Mrs C and Mary left for Jamaica, I lunched at the Knickerbocker Club with Gladwyn Jebb.[3]

At 2.30 I went to the Commodore Hotel with a letter and Cabinet Paper

---

[1] Bernard M. Baruch Jr, 1903–92. Educated at Milton Academy and Harvard. Married, 1932, Winifred Beatrice Mann. Member of the New York Stock Exchange, 1928–36. Served in RN during WWII.

[2] Elizabeth Navarro. Long-time secretary and nurse to Bernard Baruch, who left a large part of his wealth to her.

[3] Hubert Miles Gladwyn Jebb, 1900–96. Educated at Eton and Madgalen College, Oxford. Diplomat in Teheran, 1924. Asst Under-Secretary to Minister of Economic Warfare, 1940. Head of Reconstruction Department, 1942. CMG, 1942. Counsellor, FO, 1943. Acting Secretary-General, UN, 1945–6. FO Adviser to UN, 1946–7. CB, 1947. KCMG, 1949. British Ambassador to UN, 1950–4. GCMG, 1954. Ambassador to France, 1954–60. Grand Croix de la Légion d'Honneur, 1957. Baron, 1960. Member of the European Parliament, 1973–6. Vice-President, European Parliament Political Committee, 1973–6.

for Ike from the PM. Ike kept me twenty minutes talking about Persia, and John Foster Dulles was with him too, in a rather bare hotel room which is his office until he moves to the White House on January 20th. He was very genial and talked a great deal. Has a bee in his bonnet about 'collusion' with us: is all in favour of clandestinely but not overtly. Dulles said little, but what he did say was on our side. Ike struck me as forceful but a trifle naive.

At 6.00 John Foster Dulles came for a conversation with PM. He brought with him Winthrop Aldrich,[1] the new American Ambassador in London. He began by saying that 1953 was a critical year: if the new administration did not get off to a good start, and the American people lost faith in it, who could say what might happen. W said that he, for his part, thought nothing should be done for some four months: 'the trees do not grow up to the sky'; we should let events in many places – Korea, Persia, Egypt – take their course and see where we found ourselves. At this point I left them. Subsequently W told me what passed and I made a record for the FO.

Winston S. Churchill to Anthony Eden
Prime Minister's Personal Telegram T.2/53
(Premier papers, 11/392)

6 January 1953
Immediate
Personal and Top Secret
No. 7

Two talks lasting four hours most friendly and intimate. Dulles today and Eisenhower again tomorrow. About the formal visit, he mentioned February 20th, saying, 'that would give us a month'. This would seem to suit us. No need for any announcement yet.

2. Eisenhower's outlook on AB favourable. He said he had in 1945 and 1946, used all his influence to prevent the McMahon Act and urged that good faith between the Allies, not the legal interpretations of documents, was required. When I showed him my original agreement he seemed deeply impressed. He had never seen it before. He said that when he took over he would write me a formal letter asking for a copy. There can be nothing but good in this. I told him of our plans to go ahead making the new piles and our own missiles. He seemed to like it. Evidently he would favour exchange of information, and my own feeling is that we might easily get a supply from the United States meanwhile. This would make up for the loss of time caused by the McMahon Act. These are not his words by my impressions.

[1] Winthrop Williams Aldrich, 1885–1974. Educated at Harvard University and Harvard Law School. Married, 1916, Harriet Alexander: six children. Lt, US Naval Reserve, 1917–18. President, Chase National Bank, 1930–53; Chairman of Board of Directors, 1934–53. US Ambassador to UK, 1953–7.

3. About Persia, he said he had understood from you that we had attached no conditions to The Hague arbitration, but afterwards he showed you that we had. I pointed out the danger of the United States weighing in with blobs of money at a time when hope of settlement hung in the balance. He seemed to agree. I am showing him C(53)1,[1] which does not seem to me bad.

4. About Egypt, he was astonished to hear that we had 70,000 men there. I made it clear this could not go on indefinitely. There were better uses, both for the troops and the money. I urged the importance of British and American policy having the same focus, though from different angles. The international waterway ought to be protected. He had not heard about any American suggestion for air squadrons.

5. On Middle East questions and also generally he said that we should work together but there should be 'no collusion'. Contacts should be maintained underground. I said sometimes Anglo-American joint action carried great advantages, even if publicity was undesirable in many cases. I explained in familiar terms my abhorrence of the idea that Britain and the Commonwealth was just one among other foreign nations. The English-speaking world was the hope. We had 80 million whites, which added to their population was the foundation of all effective policy. He took it very well. I think what he meant by 'no collusion' was 'no public collusion'. I don't like this line of thought.

6. I told him about Anzus and Anzam, and said that the two Prime Ministers wished that I should open the matter to him. He seemed surprised that we were not to have even an observer, but said surely Australia and New Zealand would tell us all that went on. He had evidently not previously considered the stresses which the public exclusion of the United Kingdom aroused. I am leaving him a short memorandum in suitable terms of the report of our meeting with the two Prime Ministers. It has occurred to me that perhaps matters might be solved by a British staff officer being taken on publicly, (repeat publicly), by Australia or New Zealand in order to keep us informed. Thus there would be no addition to membership, but clear proof we were informed and able to advise. Pray think of this and let me know. It might suit his mood.

7. He seemed to think much more of the Arabs then of the Jews. Who could the Jews trade with if not with their Arab neighbours? Must they live always on voluntary subscriptions from co-religionists? When I pressed that he should not make the French task in North Africa more difficult by seeming to favour the Moors, etc., he talked about the general principles of racial equality which animated the United States. I said that countries which had no colonies always took very lofty views, just as countries which only had one colour were very much against a colour bar. The French had done a

---

[1] A memorandum of 1 Jan. 1953 by Anthony Eden entitled 'Persia'.

great work in North Africa, and this was no time to add to their burdens. We pressed it no further.

8. He is strongly in favour of the existing EDC plan and army being carried through, and only in the last resort using NATO as the means of incorporating a German army. I said we had done and would do everything to help EDC, but there must be a German army one way or the other. He agreed. We argued about the quality of an EDC army, in which, as you know I have not much faith. He then voiced a view which is prevalent here, namely that the United Kingdom has lost interest in United Europe and though he admitted that we could not be expected to join a continental federation, urged that we should try to lend real encouragement and inspiration to the EDC conception, both military and economic. I said you had tried your best and would go on and so would I. He seemed very keen on building up the front in Europe, and told me with great pleasure about the American arms grant of 400 million dollars being paid in full, as is announced today.

9. About Korea, he would evidently like to do something new, and when I deprecated the blockade of China, he did not respond. There is a very powerful feeling here that America is bearing the whole brunt of the prolonged stalemate while Britain and Europe are content to let it go on for ever at American expense. Baruch also says there is a deep and growing feeling in the United States that matters must be brought to a head and perhaps not only to a local head. Certainly it would be very silly to try to stop the Korean war by a blockade or by our de-recognising Red China. These steps would not alter the course of events but only make an outcry. I do not think the United States have any plan apart from doing something or other. Although Eisenhower did not express any of these views I urged that on this and indeed on other matters it would be wise to take a few months and let us pool our brains meanwhile. He liked this idea. I will let you know more tomorrow.

John Colville: diary
('The Fringes of Power', pages 661–2)

7 January 1953

Wrote a document about Anzus and Anzam for the PM to give Ike this evening.

At 4.30 the Duke of Windsor, Duchess of Windsor, Mrs Luce[1] (a beautiful woman shortly to be appointed American Ambassador in Rome on account

---

[1] Ann Clare Boothe, 1903–87. Married, 1923, George Tuttle Brokaw (div. 1929); 1935, Henry 'Harry' Robinson Luce: one child. War Correspondent, *Life*, 1939–40. Congresswoman (Rep.) for Connecticut's 4th District, 1943–7. US Ambassador to Italy, 1953–6; to Brazil, 1959. Member, President's Foreign Intelligence Advisory Board, 1973–7. First woman recipient of Sylvanus Thayer Award, West Point, 1979. Presidential Medal of Freedom, 1983.

of Luce's support of the Republicans in the recent Election), Mrs Philip Reid,[1] Mr Swope,[2] Sarah and another Baruch daughter came to drinks. Mrs Luce tried to cross-question W about the Tory antagonism to Chiang Kai-shek, but W (a) thought she said *socialist* (b) wasn't playing! The Windsors would not go, and Eisenhower arrived at 5.00. So Ike and Winston went to another room. The only remark of Ike's I overheard was: 'we must not make the mistake of jeopardising big things by opposition to little'. This seems to be one of the bees in his bonnet.

The PM told me, after Ike had left, that he had felt on top of him this time: Ike had seemed to defer to his greater age and experience to a remarkable degree. I made a record of what W told me had transpired.

Governor Dewey[3] came to dinner. The others present were Baruch, WSC, Christopher and myself. For a lawyer Dewey seemed to have a remarkably inaccurate memory for dates and places, but otherwise he talked well and made himself agreeable. All was quiet until towards the end of dinner John Foster Dulles arrived, by invitation. He had come, at Ike's suggestion, to say what he felt about a project of W's for not returning to England in the *Queen Mary* on January 23rd but remaining another fortnight in Jamaica, going to Washington for three or four days on February 1st or 2nd, being joined there by Rab (who would stay on for the economic discussions arising out of the recent Commonwealth talks) and returning home on February 7th. Dulles said he thought this would be most unfortunate, whereupon W sat up and growled. He explained that the American public thought W could cast a spell on all American statesmen and that if he were directly associated with the economic talks, the fears of the people and of Congress would be aroused to such an extent that the success of the talks would be endangered. W took this very reasonable statement ill, but Christopher and I both took pains to assure Dulles afterwards that we thought he was absolutely right.

Irritated by this, W let fly at Dewey after dinner and worked himself into a fury over certain Pacific Ocean questions. Christopher and I again applied soft soap subsequently. We told Dewey that a sharp debate was the PM's idea of a pleasant evening and assured him that he would only have spoken thus to a man whom he trusted and looked upon as a friend.

But, alas, this was not so. W was really worked up and, as he went to bed,

---

[1] Helen Miles Rogers, 1882–1970. Born in Appleton, Wisc. Secretary to Elisabeth Mills Reid, wife of US diplomat Whitelaw Reid, 1903–14. Married, 1911, Ogden Mills Reid: three children. Owner and President of *New York Herald Tribune*, 1947–53. Fellow, American Academy of Arts and Sciences, 1950.

[2] Herbert Bayard Swope, 1882–1958. War Correspondent, New York *World*, 1914–16; Chief Correspondent, Paris Peace Conference, 1919; Executive Editor, 1920–9. Pulitzer Prize, 1917. Lt Cdr, US Navy, 1918. Assistant to Bernard Baruch, War Industries Board, 1919. Member, International Press Commission, 1919. In retirement, 1929–42. Consultant to Secretary of War, 1942–6.

[3] Thomas Edmund Dewey, 1902–71. Born in Owosso, Mich. Asst US Attorney, Southern District of New York, 1931; Acting US Attorney, 1933. Special Prosecutor, New York City, 1935–7. District Attorney, New York County, 1937–43. Governor (Rep.) of New York, 1943–54. Republican candidate for US Presidency, 1944, 1948. Attorney in private practice, 1955–71.

said some very harsh things about the Republican party in general and Dulles in particular, which Christopher and I thought both unjust and dangerous. He said he would have no more to do with Dulles whose 'great slab of a face' he disliked and distrusted.

For what it is worth my impressions of the leading New Men is that they are well intentioned, earnest, but ill informed (which can be remedied) and not very intelligent – excepting Dulles – (which cannot). Ike in particular I suspect of being a genial and dynamic mediocrity.

John Colville: diary
('The Fringes of Power', pages 661–2)

8 January 1953

[. . .]

The President arrived for dinner at 9.00.[1] Others at the dinner party were: Dean Acheson, Snyder, Averell Harriman, General Marshall, General Bradley, General Bedell Smith, 'Doc' Matthews, the Ambassador,[2] the PM, Kit Steel,[3] Sir E. Hall Patch,[4] ACM Sir William Elliot, Christopher, Dennis Rickett.[5]

I sat between General Bradley and 'Doc' Matthews. We had very agreeable conversation until the PM and the President decided to hold the table. This happened after the PM had, quite wrongly, proposed the Queen's health. The President later said, quite rightly, that this was for him to do and so we had to drink it twice.

There was some talk about Stalin. Truman recalled how at Potsdam he had discovered the vodka Stalin drank for toasts was really weak white wine, and how when WSC had said the Pope would dislike something, Stalin had answered 'How many divisions has the Pope?' W said he remembered replying

[1] The party was now in Washington DC.
[2] Walter Gifford.
[3] Christopher Eden Steel, 1903–73. Known as 'Kit'. Entered Diplomatic Service, 1927. Asst Private Secretary to Prince of Wales, 1935–6. Served on diplomatic missions to Rio de Janeiro, Paris, The Hague, Berlin and Cairo. Secretary to Minister Resident in the Middle East, 1942–5. British Political Officer, SHAEF, 1945. Political adviser to C-in-C, Germany, 1947. Minister, British Embassy, Washington DC, 1950–3. Knighted, 1951. UK Permanent Representative, North Atlantic Council, 1953–7. Ambassador to West Germany, 1957–63.
[4] Edmund Leo Hall-Patch, 1896–1975. Asst Secretary of the Treasury, 1935–44. CMG, 1938. Asst Under-Secretary of State, FO, 1944; Deputy Under-Secretary of State, 1946–8. KCMG, 1947. Chairman, Executive Committee, OEEC, 1948. GCMG, 1951. UK Executive Director, IMF and IBRD, 1952–4. Chairman, Standard Bank, 1957–62.
[5] Denis Hubert Fletcher Rickett, 1907–97. Educated at Oxford University. Treasury official, and personal assistant to Sir John Anderson, to 1945. Principal Private Secretary to PM Clement Attlee, 1950–1. Economic Minister at British Embassy in Washington DC, 1951–4. Head of UK Treasury and Supply Delegation, 1951–4. 3rd Secretary, HM Treasury, 1955–60; 2nd Secretary, 1960–8. Vice-President, IBRD, 1968–74.

JANUARY 1953   803

that the fact they could not be measured in military terms did not mean they did not exist.

After dinner Truman played the piano. Nobody would listen because they were all busy with post-mortems on a diatribe in favour of Zionism and against Egypt which W had delivered at dinner (to the disagreement of practically all the Americans present, though they admitted that the large Jewish vote would prevent them disagreeing publicly). However, on W's instructions, I gathered all to the piano and we had a quarter of an hour's presidential piano playing before Truman left. He played with quite a nice touch and, as he said himself, could probably have made a living on the stage of the lesser music-halls.

When he had gone, the political wrangle started again, this time between W (unsupported) and Dean Acheson (supported by Harriman, Bedell Smith and Matthews). The main bones of contention were the European Defence Community, which the PM persists in describing as 'a sludgy amalgam' infinitely less effective than a Grand Alliance of national armies, and the situation in Egypt where Acheson and Co have far greater hopes of General Neguib (our last hope, they say) than has W. The Americans, apart from Truman and Marshall, stayed till 1.00 a.m. I had an uneasy feeling that the PM's remarks – about Israel, the EDC and Egypt – though made to the members of an outgoing administration, had better have been left unsaid in the presence of the three, Bradley, Bedell Smith and Matthews, who are staying on with Ike and the Republicans.

Winston S. Churchill to Anthony Eden and R. A. Butler
(Premier papers, 11/422)

8 January 1953
Immediate
DEDIP
Top Secret
No. 34

My telegram No. 7 from New York.[1]

1. Eisenhower opened yesterday with much vigour about direct contacts with Stalin. I was quite welcome to go myself if I thought fit at any time. He thought of making it plain in his inauguration speech that he would go to, say Stockholm, to meet him, if Stalin were willing. Evidently he did not want Britain. 'That would involve asking France and Italy.' I said would he not be wiser to keep to generalities in his inauguration speech and wait till he could survey the whole scene at leisure and have all official information,

---

[1] T.2/53, reproduced above (pp. 798–800).

before taking plunges. There was no battle going on, and as a General he could afford to wait for full reconnaissance reports. This applied to everything. The election was over; he had four years certain power. Why be in too great a hurry? He seemed much impressed by this line of argument, but I do not know what he will do. He and others around him are still in their electioneering mood and thinking in headlines and pronouncements. To him and the others I have urged, 'take a few months to get into a calmer atmosphere and learn the facts.' They are not kept informed by State Department. Neither Eisenhower nor Dulles had seen the American message about Persia. Both were steadied by its evident complexity and care. Baruch, who has a good deal of influence, talks in the same strain to them.

2. Dulles promised me no action would be taken in Korea without consulting, or at least telling, us beforehand. He spoke of 'the fall' as the time when they might make a considerable concerted effort to end the stalemate. Dulles will come over and have full talks with us about all these plans, for which I promised careful unprejudiced consideration.

3. Dulles came back last night, 7th January, and joined Dewey and me at dinner. Dewey proposed a scheme for a Pacific Treaty between all Pacific powers including the Philippines, Formosa, and the like, excluding (repeat excluding) Great Britain. I said I would denounce such a plan scathingly. Dulles then gave a long account of the negotiations leading up to the Anzus Treaty, and how the Labour Government had made no objection to it at all. I explained our point of view. Dewey, who is thoroughly friendly, then said that if I objected so strongly, he would let his baby, i.e. the Pacific Treaty, die. In fact I could consider it dead. On the spur of the moment he said that an alternative plan might be for the United Kingdom and the United States to make a joint declaration (comparable to our guarantee to Poland in 1939) that if Communist China attempted to occupy Indo-China, Burma or any other countries in the Pacific Area, we and the Americans would declare war.

4. I tell you all this to show you the rough weather that may well lie ahead in dealing with the Republican Party who have been twenty years out of office; and I feel very sure we should not expect early favourable results. Much patience will be needed.

5. I am sailing home 23rd January. I presume you will be sending out experts in advance of the February Conference (see paragraph 1 of my previous telegram), to explain at length what is in our minds, so that when Rab, or Rab and you, arrive, they will have had time to think about it all. It might well be that Rab should come in front of you.

6. All the above is for you and Rab alone. Am now flying in the Sacred Cow[1] to Washington in dense cloud. Tomorrow Jamaica.

7. Many congratulations on your excellent broadcast.

---

[1] Nickname for the Presidential plane.

Sir Roger Makins to Anthony Eden
(Foreign Office papers, 371/103517)

10 January 1953 British Embassy, Washington DC
Secret
No. 11

Sir,
I accompanied the Prime Minister on his visit to President Truman on the afternoon of January 8th. We were received at the main entrance to the White House by the President who was accompanied by the Secretary of State, Mr Dean Acheson, the Secretary of Defense, Mr Lovett, the Secretary of the Treasury, Mr Snyder and Mutual Security Administrator Mr Averell Harriman. After the President and the Prime Minister had been photographed on the White House steps, we proceeded upstairs where we were welcomed by Mrs Truman and Miss Margaret Truman.

2. We then went to the President's study and remained in conversation for over an hour. The talk ranged widely. It began with some reminiscence about the Prime Minister's speech at Fulton. The Prime Minister said that he had been taken to task by prominent Americans on the grounds that this speech was premature. He had replied that there was not much point in being a prophet unless one was premature. There was some discussion about the decision to use the atomic bomb. The President and the Prime Minister agreed that this decision had been fully justified, and that it had saved possibly hundreds of thousands of Allied lives since it had given the Japanese an excuse for surrendering, which enabled them to save face. It was probably due to this decision that the Russians had not reached the Channel in the post-war years. The President said that the most difficult decision he had had to take during his presidency was the decision about Korea, which he had made in an aeroplane returning from Missouri. The Prime Minister said that the importance of this decision was not just a local one, but lay in the fact that it had led to the rearmament of the United States, which now constituted the greatest strength of the free world.

3. The Prime Minister said that he had been much impressed by the President's State of the Union message and that his remarks addressed to the Russians on the subject of atomic energy were well chosen. He was particularly struck by the warm reference which the President had made to General Eisenhower. Mr Truman said that he had worked very hard on this message. As regards General Eisenhower, there would be no trouble with him, though personally he had to admit that he preferred him as a General than as President.

4. Mr Churchill asked about the recent explosion of the atomic weapon at Eniwetok, and the President said he understood that the power of the bomb tested had been as much in advance of the Hiroshima bomb, as that had been in advance of the TNT bomb.

5. There was some discussion on the relative rate of production of aircraft in the Soviet Union and in the United States. Mr Churchill said that he thought some of General Vandenberg's remarks on this subject were misleading. Mr Lovett agreed and said that they were directed towards the Department of Defense rather than to the general public in a determined attempt to secure the full appropriation for which the Air Force had asked. The position was that as far as modern types of aircraft were concerned the United States of America had equalled the monthly rate of Soviet production and they would pass the Soviet production rate of jet engines in February. He also said that the ratio of MIGs shot down in Korea to American losses was sharply improving last month. Mr Lovett drew attention to the size of the American defence effort. The expenditures of the Department of Defense were greater than those of the nineteen largest corporations in the United States and the personnel employed in the armed services in the Defense Department were greater than those employed in all the public utility services of the United States.

6. After some reference to Persia, where it was agreed that there seemed now some hope of a settlement, and to the Commonwealth Economic Conference, the Prime Minister formally thanked the President for the manner in which he had always worked with him in friendly partnership. Mr Truman responded in a similar vein and said that he would never forget the kindness which had been shown his daughter Margaret during her visit to England. Mr Churchill expressed the hope that Mr Truman would visit England soon after he had laid down his office.

7. At the conclusion of the conversation the President conducted the Prime Minister to the steps of the White House, where another photograph was taken.

8. This was a most friendly and cordial meeting, and I have endeavoured to convey some of its flavour in this brief record. The President and his advisers, who are clearly still smarting from their election defeat, were touched by the manifest courtesy and attention shown to them by the Prime Minister in their closing days of power. I am sure that his action will be noted and remembered with gratitude in the Democratic ranks.

Margaret Truman: recollection
('After the Presidency', Life Magazine, 1 December 1972, pages 69–70)

10 January 1953

During our last weeks in the White House, Prime Minister Churchill arrived for a visit. My father gave him a small stag dinner to which he invited Secretary of Defense Robert Lovett, Averell Harriman, General Omar Bradley, and Secretary of State Dean Acheson. Everyone was in an ebullient mood, especially Dad.

Without warning, Mr Churchill turned to him and said: 'Mr President, I hope you have your answer ready for that hour when you and I stand before St Peter and he says, "I understand you two are responsible for putting off those atomic bombs. What have you got to say for yourselves?"'

Robert Lovett asked: 'Are you sure, Prime Minister, that you are going to be in the same place as the President for that interrogation?'

Mr Churchill said: 'Lovett, my vast respect for the Creator of this universe and countless others gives me assurance that He would not condemn a man without a hearing.'

Mr Lovett: 'True, but your hearing would not be likely to start in the Supreme Court, or, necessarily, in the same court as the President's. It could be in another court far away.'

Mr Churchill: 'I don't doubt that, but, wherever it is, it will be in accordance with the principles of English Common Law.'

Dean Acheson then spoke up: 'Is it altogether consistent with your respect for the Creator of this and other universes to limit His imagination and judicial procedure to the accomplishment of a minute island, in a tiny world, in one of the smaller of the universes?'

Mr Churchill: 'Well, there will be a trial by a jury of my peers, that's certain.'

Mr Acheson: 'Oyez! Oyez! In the matter of the immigration of Winston Spencer Churchill, Mr Bailiff, will you empanel a jury?'

Each guest accepted an historic role. General Bradley decided he was Alexander the Great. Others played Julius Caesar, Socrates and Aristotle. The Prime Minister declined to permit Voltaire on his jury – he was an atheist – or Cromwell, because he did not believe in the rule of law. Then Mr Acheson summoned George Washington. That was too much for Mr Churchill. He saw that things were being stacked against him:

'I waive a jury, but not habeas corpus.'

They ignored him and completed the selection of the jury. Dad was appointed judge. The case was tried and the Prime Minister was acquitted.

During this visit Mr Churchill confessed to Dad that he had taken a dim view of him as President when he had succeeded Franklin Roosevelt. 'I misjudged you badly,' the Prime Minister said. 'Since that time, you, more than any other man, have saved Western civilization.'

JANUARY 1953

Winston S. Churchill to Lord Cherwell
(Churchill papers, 4/379)

10 January 1953   Jamaica
Secret

My dear Prof,

Can you let me have a record of the progress made in the last three or six months before the experiment in the Mexican Desert? What did the Americans tell us? I do not recollect that the Cabinet or the Defence Committee were ever informed that matters were so imminent. You have added 'British consent to the use of the weapon had been given on July 4.' When was this decided by the Cabinet? What was the actual detailed procedure by which this decision was taken? I am not making a case about this in any critical sense, but I really must know the details. Had I known that the Tube Alloys were progressing so fast it would have affected my judgment about the date of the General Election. Please consult Norman Brook and let me have the best information you can awaiting me on my return. We will have a talk about it then.

I have had a dreadful flurry of business in New York and Washington, both with Republicans and Democrats. There are lots of difficulties ahead. Now I am resting in this pleasant but rather warm and today cloudy Island. We had a very rough flight here. Clemmie and the others send their greetings to you.

John Colville: diary
('The Fringes of Power', page 66)

11 January 1953

Not good weather. Lord Beaverbrook to luncheon. He spoke very disparagingly of Anthony Eden. Then all drove to the Brownlows'[1] house, Roaring River, for drinks. The PM (who last night said he would give £10,000 to be back at Chartwell) is cheering up a bit.

---

[1] Peregrine Francis Adelbert Cust, 1899–1978. On active service, 1914–18. Married, 1927, Katherine Kinloch: three children (d. 1952); 1954, Dorothy Power (d. 1966); 1969, Leila Joan Watson. Baron Brownlow, 1927. Personal Lord-in-Waiting to King Edward VIII, 1936. Parliamentary Private Secretary to Lord Beaverbrook, 1940. Staff Officer, Bomber Command, 1941; to Deputy CoS, 8th Air Force, 1943–4.

John Colville: diary
('The Fringes of Power', pages 646–7)

12 January 1953

Bathed by myself at Laughing Water Beach (a superb mixture of salt and fresh water against a background of golden sand and waving palms). A golden retriever stole my towel.

Went with Christopher and Mary to lunch with Lord Brownlow, whose house is marvellous (with lovely furniture brought from Belton, wide verandahs and a spreading view of the park and the sea beyond). His daughter, Caroline Cust[1] (vivacious and agreeable), his son Edward[2] and a painter called Hector Whistler[3] were there.

After dinner, *en famille* at Prospect, W attacked Christopher and me violently for criticising one of his literary assistants. I told him, after the tirade, that I thought he had been guilty of the most unprovoked aggression since September 1939. He said of Ike that he was 'a real man of limited stature' – which, I think, about sums the new President up.

Everybody very nicely says they wish I were not going home so soon and W's goodnight words were: 'If I didn't admire Meg so much, I wouldn't allow you to go.'

Sir Roger Makins to Anthony Eden
(Foreign Office papers, 371/103517)

12 January 1953
Priority
No. 49

Following is gist of article by Reston[4] in *New York Times* of 12th January. (Begins).

Acheson appealed to the Prime Minister to provide more leadership in Western Europe and the Middle East. Acheson's thesis was as follows: Unusual progress had been made towards greater unity in the Middle East and Western

---

[1] Caroline Elizabeth Maud Cust, 1928–2015. Mayoress of Grantham, 1950–1. Married, 1954, John Arthur Partridge (div. 1973).

[2] Edward John Peregrine Cust, 1936– . Director, Hand-in-Hand Fire Office, 1962–82. Married, 1964, Shirlie Edith Yeomans. High Sheriff of Lincolnshire, 1978–9. Baron, 1978. OStJ, 1997. CStJ, 2000.

[3] Reginald Hector Whistler, 1905–78. Educated at Victoria College, London School of Architecture and Slade School of Art. Illustrated *When Poland Smiled* (1940) and *The Prime Minister* (1973).

[4] James Barrett Reston, 1909–95. Reporter, *Dayton Daily News*, 1932–3; Associated Press, 1934–7, (in London) 1937–9. Married, 1935, Sally Fulton: three children. Reporter, *New York Times*, London Bureau, 1939–41; Washington Bureau, 1941. US Embassy press officer, London, 1942. Personal Assistant to the publisher, *New York Times*, 1943–4; Washington Bureau, 1944–53; Chief Washington Correspondent, 1953–64. Associate Editor, *New York Times*, 1964–8; Executive Editor, 1968–87.

Europe, but at the present moment the efforts to create a European army and political union in Western Europe had slipped back. There seemed at least a chance to reach agreement with Persia and Egypt. These situations required bold leadership from the United States and Britain, particularly from the latter during the transition here. This was an historic moment when bold decisions might produce historic results.

2. 'The official view here is that the British are overrating their strength in the Middle East and underestimating the danger in both Egypt and Persia. It is also felt here that Mr Churchill, with his love of guards' brigades and his lack of enthusiasm for international armies, has hampered the formation of the European army by a lukewarm diplomacy in both Paris and Bonn. Apparently Mr Acheson did not ask the British to reconsider their decision against joining the European army, but felt that Mr Churchill could do more in the future than he has in the past toward urging the French and Germans to create the European army.'

3. Bradley and Harriman supported Acheson. Acheson said that failure by the United Kingdom to act boldly in the Middle East might prove as unfortunate for the United Kingdom as its rigid policies towards the American colonies in the 18th Century.

4. The Prime Minister responded, 'without enthusiasm: he defended his policy in Europe and the Middle East, but apparently agreed with Acheson that events in both areas had now reached a decisive point'. In the British view, United States officials are unduly alarmed about Persia. The British have been less willing to make concessions about the Sudan than the State Department would approve. There is some evidence that a compromise may be possible over Persian oil, a compromise solution also seems more likely with Egypt if the British will make certain concessions in the Sudan. United States official quarters fear that if too much time is wasted on details with Egypt, the larger opportunities of a compromise may be lost.

5. Acheson did not imply that the Eisenhower administration would retreat from present policies in Europe and the Middle East, but he seemed to think that in the present critical period they would be preoccupied with questions of organisation in Washington.

Sir Roger Makins to Anthony Eden
(Foreign Office papers, 371/103517)

12 January 1953
Priority
Confidential
No. 50

The Prime Minister's visit.

It will not surprise you to know that some of the conversation at the dinner here on January 8th at which the Prime Minister, President Truman, Mr Acheson and others were present, has now appeared in the press. My immediately preceding telegram contains the gist of an article by Reston in the *New York Times* of 12th January.

2. I understand that Reston got the material for this article at a dinner party at which one of the Americans present at the dinner here gave the account which appears in the article. It is a most accurate account of Acheson's remarks.

3. We are refusing to comment in reply to press enquiries. State Department are taking the line that these conversations were private and that they have therefore nothing to say.

Winston S. Churchill: statement
(Churchill papers, 2/204)

14 January 1953

The death of Edward Marsh[1] is a loss to the Nation and a keen personal grief to me. Since we began working together at the Colonial Office in 1905, we have always been the closest friends. Apart from and above his distinguished career as a civil servant he was a master of literature and scholarship, and a deeply instructed champion of the Arts. All his long life was serene and he left this world I trust without a pang and I am sure without a fear.

---

[1] Edward Howard Marsh, 1872–1953. Educated at Cambridge University: 1st Class, Classical Tripos, 1893; Senior Chancellor's Medal for Classics, 1895. Clerk, Colonial Office, 1896. Asst Private Secretary to Joseph Chamberlain, 1900–3; to Alfred Lyttelton, 1903–5; to Winston S. Churchill, 1905–15, 1917–22, 1924–9; to H. H. Asquith, 1915–16; to Duke of Devonshire, 1922–4; to J. H. Thomas, 1924, 1929–36; to Malcolm MacDonald, 1936–7. Trustee, Tate Gallery, 1937–44. Chairman, Contemporary Art Society, 1937–52.

Evelyn Shuckburgh: diary
('Descent to Suez', pages 73–4)

16 January 1953

[. . .]

Jock Colville back from Jamaica came to see me. He described the PM's talks with Eisenhower and Dulles and in particular the 'three-pronged plan for the fall' which Dulles outlined for settling the Korean issue. Winston has this in his head and will report to Cabinet on return. Ike asked if Winston saw any objection to his meeting Stalin alone. Winston said, 'I would have objected strongly during the war when our contribution in forces was about equal. Now I don't mind. But don't be in a hurry. Get your reconnaissance in first.' Winston seems to have been unfavourably impressed with the brashness and impatience of the Republican leaders. According to Jock, he spoke once of his own plans, only to say, 'I think Anthony should have it, but I have not decided when.'

Winston S. Churchill to Field Marshal Lord Alexander
(Premier papers, 11/392)

17 January 1953
Immediate
Top Secret and Personal
No. 16

You will remember that when Neguib became dictator about six months ago, our army in Egypt was put at 48 hours' notice to carry out extensive offensive operations, involving the occupation of cities. No one seemed to doubt our ability to do this at the time. I do not suggest that any such far reaching measures should be taken now, but please report to me whether the very large army we have in the Canal Zone is capable of resisting any attack, either by terrorists, or by the Egyptian army, or both. I presume you are taking every measure to alert your forces and bring them into the highest readiness to defend themselves, if attacked.

Evelyn Shuckburgh: diary
('Descent to Suez', page 74)

19 January 1953

Went to Buckingham Palace to see Alan Lascelles. I was surprised to be told, 'if Winston were to die tomorrow there is no doubt at all the Queen would send for Anthony. But by the end of the year there will be doubt, if present trends continue. There might be at least 50 per cent opinion in the party and in the City by that time in favour of Butler.' Adeane[1] confirmed this. I expressed astonishment and am unconvinced.

AE obviously feels that this sort of thing is growing. He is very depressed this evening. He doesn't think the Old Man will ever go. There are more attacks on him by the Beaverbrook press. There is no doubt that Rab is coming along very fast. I myself heard him answering Questions in the House today and was much impressed. I suddenly thought of myself in the character of Griffith (nurse to Katharine of Aragon in *King Henry VIII*) consoling my master in his loss.

Lord Cherwell to Winston S. Churchill
(Churchill papers)

20 January 1953

My dear Winston,

Just a line to thank you for your letter.[2] I am glad to hear that you are having a good time and trust you have not been overdoing the bathing.

I am getting together the facts and dates concerning the matter to which you referred. The complete story will, I hope, be ready for you when you return.

With best wishes to you all for a pleasant voyage home,

Lord Cherwell to Winston S. Churchill
(Churchill papers, 4/379)

28 January 1953

As requested in your letter I attach a note showing the principal events leading up to the dropping of the atomic bombs at Hiroshima and Nagasaki.

---

[1] Michael Edward Adeane, 1910–84. Educated at Eton and Magdalene College, Cambridge. Married, 1939, Helen Chetwynd-Stapleton: two children. Page of Honour, 1923–7. ADC to Lord Bessborough, 1934; to Lord Tweedsmuir, 1934–6. Asst Private Secretary to King George VI, 1945–52. Knighted, 1946. Private Secretary to Queen Elizabeth II, 1953–72. PC, 1953. Baron, 1972.

[2] Reproduced above (p. 808).

I think this account answers all the questions you asked – if you want further details I will try to unearth them.

EVENTS LEADING UP THE USE OF THE ATOMIC BOMB, 1945

On March 21, 1944, Sir John Anderson[1] suggested that the Tube Alloys programme should be mentioned to the Service Ministers and to the other Ministers concerned but you minuted 'I do not agree.' Sir John Anderson was perturbed by your decision and I am fairly certain that in the spring of 1945 he made another attempt to persuade you to bring the matter to Cabinet and that I supported him. No papers bearing on this can however be found. In the event, it seems, the question was never discussed at Cabinet or in the Defence Committee.

2. In September 1944 Sir John Anderson minuted you annexing a report which included the information that a bomb (equivalent to 20,000–30,000 tons of TNT) would 'almost certainly' be ready by August 1945. On my return from America in November 1944, I gave you further details about the work they were doing and said that it was hoped a bomb would be ready some time the following summer.

3. In the winter of 1944/5 so far as I recollect I mentioned to you that some doubts had arisen about the initiation of the detonation of the plutonium bomb but that there was no anxiety about the U.235 bomb. But I well remember telling you in the spring of 1945 that I thought the successful explosion of a bomb was 90 to 95% certain but that the people actually working on it considered it 99% certain.

4. In April 1945 Lord Wilson telegraphed to Sir John Anderson that the Americans proposed to make a full scale test in the desert in July and to drop a bomb on the Japanese in August and I told you about this.

5. On May 2 Sir John Anderson minuted you that he had had some details from Lord Wilson of the American intentions for the operational use of the bomb and requested your approval of his proposal that Lord Wilson should tell General Marshall that you had been consulted and would want to be kept informed. On May 21 you agreed that Wilson should speak to Marshall 'in a tactful and friendly way'; you thought that the machinery for reaching a joint decision would emerge from this talk. Discussions took place and it was agreed that in order to fulfil the Quebec Agreement the concurrence of

---

[1] John Anderson, 1882–1958. Educated at Edinburgh and Leipzig Universities. Secretary, Ministry of Shipping, 1917–19. Knighted, 1919. Chairman, Board of Inland Revenue, 1919–20. Joint Under-Secretary of State in Government of Ireland, 1920. Permanent Under-Secretary of State, Home Office, 1922–32. Governor of Bengal, 1932–7. MP (Nat. Gov.) for the Scottish Universities, 1938–50. Lord Privy Seal, 1938–9. Home Secretary and Minister of Home Security, 1939–40. Lord President of the Council, 1940–3. Married, 1941, Ava Bodley Wigram, widow of Churchill's leading informant on German rearmament in the 1930s. Chancellor of the Exchequer, 1943–5. Chairman, Port of London Authority, 1946–58. Member, BBC Gen. Advisory Council, 1947–57. Viscount Waverley, 1952. OM, 1957.

HMG should be recorded at a meeting of the Combined Policy Committee.

6. On June 29 Sir John Anderson reminded you of the American intentions about which I had told you. In this minute he requested authority to instruct our representatives to give the concurrence of HMG in the decision to use the bomb against the Japanese. You initialled this minute on July 1. On July 4 Lord Wilson formally gave the concurrence at a meeting of the CPC.

7. A minute from Rickett to Sir John Anderson's Secretary dated July 2 reads:

'Lord Cherwell told me this evening that in initialling the Chancellor's minute of the 29th June on the Operational Use of TA, the Prime Minister had wished it to be understood that he would expect to discuss this matter with President Truman at "Terminal",[1] though he was anxious that nothing should be done by us to retard the use of the TA weapon.'

8. A report on discussions at Potsdam records:

'Mr Stimson[2] described the results of the recent test to the Prime Minister and the Prime Minister confirmed the agreement given by Field Marshal Wilson at a meeting of the Combined Policy Committee to the use of the weapon within the next few weeks against the Japanese.'

9. It must be remembered that until the actual explosion in the desert in New Mexico there was great scepticism in military and political circles about the efficacy of the new form of explosive. Certainly nobody thought it would end the war. And in fact it is doubtful to what extent it did so. As you know it has now been proved that the Japanese asked the Russians to convey an offer accepting the Potsdam terms of unconditional surrender to the Allies on August 2. The Russians did not pass on this message. Had they done so, it might well be that the bombs on Hiroshima and Nagasaki would not have been dropped. Whether the fact that they were dropped did more than induce the Japanese to make a direct offer of surrender to the Americans is therefore questionable.

10. In retrospect it seems unlikely that the atom bombardment could have forced the Japanese to surrender before the planned invasion of the Home Islands in November 1945, had they not – unknown to us – been already at the point of collapse. For the Americans could not have dropped much more than two bombs a month for the rest of the year. But of course the Japanese did not know this.

---

[1] 'Terminal': code name for the Potsdam Conference, held July–Aug. 1945.
[2] Henry Lewis Stimson, 1867–1950. Admitted to the Bar, 1891. Secretary of War, 1911–13. Col., American Expeditionary Force, France, 1917–18. Governor-General of the Philippines, 1927–9. Secretary of State, 1929–32. Member, Permanent Court of Arbitration, The Hague, 1938–48. Secretary of War, 1940–5.

January 1953

Clementine Churchill to Winston S. Churchill
(Churchill papers, 1/50)[1]

28 January 1953 RMS *Queen Mary*

When you have read the following note please destroy or seal it up marking it 'Private', I would not like the Secretaries to see it.

About 2 months ago I mentioned to you that Miss Hamblin[2] had been in our employment over 20 years. (She is now between 45 and 50.) I am sure you would like to make some provision for her in your will in the form of a legacy or a pension. (If a legacy) I would suggest £1000. I have left her in my will £500. I write this in case I should die before you and that in your many activities and preoccupations she might be forgotten.

Should I survive you and you had perhaps forgotten to include her in your will I would increase the amount in my will.

But I think she would like to be remembered by you. She is deeply devoted to your interests and to you personally.

Chiefs of Staff: memorandum
(Cabinet papers, 131/13)

28 January 1953
Top Secret
Defence Committee Paper No. 3 of 1953

LIKELIHOOD OF GENERAL WAR
WITH THE SOVIET UNION UP TO THE END OF 1955

Our last report on the likelihood of war with the Soviet Union, written in November 1951, dealt with the period from that date to the end of 1954. We concluded that:

(a) The Soviet Government would not wish to start a total war in the period under review.

(b) So long as the West was weak in conventional armaments the Soviet Government would continue to exploit this weakness, principally by cold war methods, but also by local aggression should the opportunity arise. There was still a danger that total war might result from some situation that obliged the Western Powers to take military action against Soviet forces.

---

[1] This letter was handwritten.
[2] Grace Ellen Hamblin, 1908–2002. Educated at Crockham Hill Church of England school, near Chartwell, and at secretarial training college. Began secretarial work for Churchill in 1932. Worked as No. 2 to Mrs Pearman, 1932–8. Secretary to Mrs Churchill, 1939–66. In charge of secretarial and accounts work at Chartwell, 1945–65. OBE, 1955. Administrator at Chartwell for the National Trust, 1965–73. Secretary to the Churchill Centenary Exhibition, 1974.

(c) Provided it was made perfectly clear that in the event of Soviet aggression the Western Powers would not hesitate to wield their overwhelming superiority in atomic weapons, that superiority would continue to be a powerful deterrent.
(d) We could not, however, exclude the possibility that Western rearmament would lead the Soviet Government to believe that a Western attack was intended and therefore to start or provoke a total war before it became effective. We believed that such a danger existed then and would continue through the period covered by our paper.
(e) Provided the Western Powers combined resolution with restraint there should be no total war during that period.

2. The considerations on which these conclusions were based are summarised below.

<u>Our View of Soviet Policy</u>

3. We believed, and still believe, that the aims of Soviet policy are:
(a) To preserve and strengthen the Stalinist regime in the Soviet Union.
(b) To consolidate and protect the Soviet Orbit.
(c) To spread the revolution to other countries and eventually to establish a world order of Communist states under the leadership of the Kremlin.

Since Communists hold that the capitalist and imperialist world will decay of itself, our view has been that the Soviet Government's programme of world revolution is a long-term one and that they intend if possible to achieve their aim without a total war, using their armed forces as a threat to support successive steps of subversion and of aggression by proxy rather than committing them to direct aggression. We thought last year that they would have been supported in this view by events in the Middle East and by the strains to which the economy of Western Europe was being subjected through rearmament. A fuller statement of our understanding of the fundamental long-term principles of Soviet foreign relations is given in our report of 11th December, 1950.

<u>Military Considerations</u>

4. We thought that, in view of the immense resources of the United States, including their capacity for producing atomic weapons, it was unlikely that the Soviet Government would at that time consider themselves strong enough to bring a war with the Western Powers to a successful conclusion.

5. In addition there were a number of specific reasons which made us think that during the period under review the Soviet leaders would wish to avoid a total war. These were:
(a) The risk of large-scale atomic attack on the Soviet Union and of the tactical use of atomic weapons against the Soviet armed forces.
(b) Their relatively small stock of atomic bombs.

(c) The difficulties of delivering these bombs effectively in the United States, their strongest opponent.
(d) Their doubts as to the ability of the Soviet economy, until it had been expanded, to sustain a prolonged major war and withstand Allied air attacks.
(e) The comparatively undeveloped state of their air defences.

Likely Soviet Action

6. We believed therefore that the Soviet Government would seek to avoid a major war, but would continue to build up their military strength, and, in pursuit of their aim of hastening the decay of the West, would seize every opportunity of disrupting the Western alliance and of extending their own influence by subversion or local aggression.

Danger of Unintentional War

7. Action by the Soviet Union such as that described in the preceding paragraph might lead to war, without either side having originally intended to start it, if the Western Powers felt obliged to take military action against Soviet forces.

Danger of the Soviet Union Starting a 'Preventive' War

8. The Soviet Government might consider the growth of NATO and the scale of Western rearmament to be direct threats to the security of the Soviet Union and might decide that their best course was to start a war before Western rearmament became effective.

Western Reactions

9. The best insurance against a war arising from either of the circumstances described in the two preceding paragraphs would be the exercise by the Western Powers of a policy of resolution combined with restraint.

Developments Since Our Last Report

10. We have now re-examined the above views in the light of developments, both in the political and military fields, in the year since our last report was written, and have carried our estimate forward to the end of 1955.

Political Development

11. Our general estimate of Soviet policy has been supported by statements by Soviet leaders, particularly those made in connection with the 19th Congress of the All-Union Communist Party held in Moscow in October 1952, and by a recently published article by Stalin on the 'Economic Problems of Socialism in the USSR'. These have suggested that the Soviet Government continue to be preoccupied with basic economic developments in the USSR:

that they continue to be convinced that the capitalist world is inherently unstable and that this instability can be successfully exploited by the Communist world organisation; and that they are confident that the Soviet Union can stand the economic strain of a prolonged period of tension better than the West. Although Communist propaganda against American preparations for a new war has continued, Stalin's own recent statements do not suggest that he regards a Western attack on the USSR as inevitable in the near future.

12. Despite the growth of Western power as exemplified in the development of NATO, proposals for an integrated Europe and the proposed rearmament of Germany and Japan, world developments in 1952 have not been altogether unsatisfactory for the Soviet Union. Military operations in Korea, Indo-China and Malaya, with their drain on Western resources, drag on. Other countries in South-East Asia are far from stable and, if the Viet Minh were to succeed in Indo-China, might well pass into the Communist camp. The Communists achieved an unexpected success in the Indian elections. Relations between India and Pakistan continue unsettled. In the Middle East the debacle at Abadan has lowered British prestige and the continuance of Dr Musaddiq's Government has increased the danger of Communist rule in Persia and has had repercussions elsewhere. In Egypt the coup d'état has started a ferment which might prove beneficial, but which equally, by upsetting the old order, might make the Communist task easier. There is unrest in French North Africa, Kenya and the Union of South Africa. The Western attempt to organise the defence of the Middle East has not so far met with much success. The European Defence Community Treaty has not yet been ratified and Franco-German differences have increased. The economic problems of the West continue and doubtless bulk large in Soviet eyes.

13. There is reason therefore to believe that on the whole the Soviet Government will have been encouraged by the difficulties of the West to think that in the long run their present policy will cause the balance of world power to shift decisively in their favour without a war.

14. It is also significant that, despite their subversive and aggressive activities in many spheres, whenever the Soviet leaders have been faced with a situation carrying a serious threat of conflict with the United States, e.g., in Korea and in Berlin, they have acted with great caution.

<u>Military</u>

15. Despite advances made by the Soviet Union and the Satellites in the past year, we consider that the considerations described in paragraphs 4 and 5 above still hold good. We believe that Soviet air defence technique remains relatively ineffective, particularly at night or in bad weather, but the quality of Soviet radar equipment is improving rapidly. We also consider that it will still be difficult to deliver atomic bombs accurately on the United States even in 1955. Such attacks would be likely to require the large-scale use of one-way

missions, on which we do not believe the USSR would be prepared to expend a large part of its strategic bomber force. We believe that the Soviet leaders still doubt the ability of the Soviet economy, until it has been further expanded and dispersed, to sustain a long major war in the face of Allied air attacks. As a result of recent announcements they must also assume that the United States has now developed an even more powerful weapon of mass destruction, the so-called 'hydrogen bomb'. (Whilst the construction of a comparable bomb must presumably be a high-priority objective for the USSR, it is reasonable to assume that, during the period of this review, American supremacy in this field will be substantially unchallenged.)

16. It is true that these deterrents may become less effective as the Soviet Government build up their own stockpile of atomic bombs and improve their ability to deliver them, and as they strengthen their economy and improve their air defences. On the other hand, the catastrophic nature of modern atomic warfare should act as a restraining influence so long as the West retains its striking power.

Danger of Deliberate War

17. We conclude that on balance the Soviet Government will have been encouraged by political events to believe that they can achieve their aim without deliberately resorting to war, and that they will still be deterred from doing so by the relative military situation and particularly by their relative inferiority in atomic weapons. We believe therefore that they are unlikely to resort to war as a deliberate act of policy in the period under review.

Other Ways in which War Might Break Out

18. There still remain, however, the dangers of an 'unintentional war' and a 'preventative war' (paragraphs 7 and 8 above).

Dangers of Unintentional War

19. The Soviet Government are already engaged in a continuing conflict with the non-Communist world, in which we believe they will seize every opportunity of extending their influence by subversion or local aggression. Such a situation necessarily carries a continuing risk of local collisions, which could lead to general war. The points of special danger may vary from time to time. The most serious at present is Korea. Another, less immediately dangerous, is the exposed Western position in Berlin. A further new factor is the policy of the Chinese Government, whose army and air force have greatly improved during the past few years and whose actions could now materially affect the danger of general war.

20. We believe that the Soviet Government will probably continue to try to avoid taking up positions from which it will be difficult to withdraw. We also think it unlikely that the Chinese Government will embark on any further

deliberate aggression while the Korean war continues. Yet so long as Communism, whether under Soviet or Chinese leadership, retains its dynamic pressure to expand, there is always a danger that this pressure might produce a situation where the Western Powers, however unwillingly, and contrary to Communist expectations, felt obliged to take military action. In the period under review this danger is likely to exist particularly in the Middle East and South-East Asia. It would be increased by a series of Western reverses.

Danger of a Preventive War

21. If, as Western power grows, the Soviet Government became convinced, e.g., by Western strategic dispositions, that the West was planning an imminent attack on them, they might themselves move first and attack at the moment which they judged most favourable to them; this danger may become more serious as time goes on. We cannot exclude this possibility, particularly in view of the suspicion and isolation of the Soviet leaders and the possibility that the reports which they receive about the policies of the Western Governments are biased or incorrect. It is important, therefore, while building up Western strength, to avoid not only any single action which would convince the Soviet leaders that they were going to be attacked, but also, so far as is consistent with necessary Western plans, any series of individually less provocative actions which would have the same cumulative effect. Nevertheless, it is at least as important not to give the impression of Western weakness through our anxiety to avoid provocation.

Relative Danger of any Particular Year

22. It is impossible to foresee at what time the danger of miscalculation leading to an 'unintentional war' might be greater than at others. It is also impossible, and indeed dangerous, to attempt on grounds of relative military advantage to point to any year as one of particular danger, since the question turns on so many unpredictable considerations. These include the views of the Soviet leaders on the relative importance of various arms, the armament expansion or re-equipment programme in the Soviet *Bloc*, the rate of Allied build-up, Soviet estimates of Allied strength and efficiency and Soviet assessment of the political situation, such as the internal stability or weakness in the countries on the Soviet line of advance. None of these can be forecast.

Conclusions

23. Our conclusions are as follows:
    (a) The Soviet Government will still wish to avoid starting a general war in the period under review.
    (b) They will, however, continue to conduct an unremitting struggle against the Western Powers by every means open to them which they calculate can stop short of general war.

(c) Provided it continues to be made perfectly plain that in the event of Soviet aggression the Western Powers will not hesitate to use their superiority in atomic warfare, that prospect will continue to be the chief military deterrent.

(d) While we consider that general war is on the whole unlikely in the period under review, we cannot exclude the possibilities:
  (i) that general war might result unintentionally from some situation that obliged the Western Powers to take military action against the Soviet Union or China, contrary to the latter's calculations;
  (ii) that, as Western power grows, the Soviet Government might become convinced, e.g., by Western strategic dispositions, that the West was planning an imminent attack on them, and decide to attack first.

We believe that these dangers exist now, and will continue during the period covered by this paper.

(e) It is not possible to assess whether war is any more or less likely in any specific year in the period under review.

(f) We remain convinced that it is by combining strength and unity with resolution and restraint that the Western Powers can best hope to avoid a general war.

Recommendations

24. We recommend that the Defence Committee should:
  (1) Take note of our conclusions above.
  (2) Agree to the transmission of this Memorandum to the United States Joint Chiefs of Staff.

R. McGrigor
J. Harding[1]
W. Dickson[2]

---

[1] Allan Francis John Harding, 1896–1989. Educated at King's College, London. On active service, WWI (MC). CO, 1st Battalion Somerset Light Infantry, 1939–40. GSO I, Middle East Command, 1940. Brig., General Staff, Western Desert Force, 1940–1 (CBE, DSO). Brig., General Staff, XIII Corps, 1941–2. Deputy Director of Military Training, Middle East Command, 1942. Deputy CoS, Middle East Command, 1942. GOC, 7th Armoured Div., North Africa, 1942–3 (wounded). GOC, VIII Corps, 1943. CoS, 15th Allied Army Group, Italy, 1943–4. GOC, XIII Corps, Italy, 1945. GOC-in-C, Southern Command, 1947–9. Legion of Merit, 1948. Gen., 1949. C-in-C, Far East Land Forces, 1949–51. ADC General to the King, 1950–2. C-in-C, British Army of the Rhine, 1951–2. CIGS, 1952–5. Governor and C-in-C, Cyprus, 1955–7. Baron, 1958.

[2] William Dickson, 1898–1987. RNAS, 1916–18. Transferred to RAF, 1918. Air Ministry, 1923–6. Cdr, RAF Station, Hawkinge, 1935–6; Nos 9 and 10 Groups, Fighter Command, 1942–3; Desert Air Force, 1944. Director of Plans, Air Ministry, 1941–2. Russian Order of Suvarov, 1944. KBE, 1946. VCAS, Air Council for Air Ministry, 1946–8. GCB, 1953. CAS, 1953–6. Chairman, CoS Committee, 1956–9. Chief of Defence Staff, 1958–9. President, Royal Central Asian Society, 1961–5.

JANUARY 1953   823

Evelyn Shuckburgh: diary
('Descent to Suez', page 75)

29 January 1953

But when the Prime Minister got back and AE went round to see him at noon today, Jock Colville came round to me in a great state of agitation. He said there was going to be a row. He had gone overnight to Southampton and travelled up with the PM. The latter was in a rage against AE, speaking of 'appeasement' and saying he never knew before that Munich was situated on the Nile. He described AE as having been a failure as Foreign Secretary and being 'tired, sick and bound up in detail'. Jock said that the Prime Minister would never give way over Egypt. He positively desired the talks on the Sudan to fail, just as he positively hoped we should not succeed in getting into conversations with the Egyptians on defence which might lead to our abandonment of the Canal Zone. Jock, who has hitherto sided strongly with the PM over this Egypt question, seemed seriously concerned. He said, 'The only hope is that Neguib will behave so badly that our two masters will see eye to eye.' In other words, the hope is that the talks will fail, which is Winston's hope.

I told only William Strang about this and spent the lunch-hour wondering what might have happened at the interview and in the subsequent lunch which the Churchills had with the Edens. In the event, AE told me, nothing happened at all. There was no confrontation. The conversation was quite amicable but equally no decisions taken. These two always shy away from a quarrel at the last moment.

[. . .]

President Dwight D. Eisenhower to Winston S. Churchill
(Premier papers, 11/1074)

29 January 1953   The White House

My dear Prime Minister,

I have asked Secretary Dulles and Mr Stassen[1] to convey to you and your colleagues my warm personal greetings. I am very glad that they will have the opportunity of visiting London during their trip to Europe and to talk to you and your associates. I shall always remember with pleasure my own visits to the United Kingdom and the cordial and warm reception I invariably received there. I am sure that the visit of Secretary Dulles and Mr Stassen will be equally pleasant and profitable.

---

[1] Harold Stassen, 1907–2001. Married, 1929, Esther Gladys Glewwe: two children. Governor (Rep.) of Minnesota, 1939–43. Enlisted in US Navy, 1943. Asst CoS to Adm. William Halsey, 1943–5. President, University of Pennsylvania, 1948–52. Director, Mutual Security Agency and Foreign Operations Administration, 1953–8. Special Asst to the President for Disarmament Policy, 1955.

The purpose of the trip undertaken by Secretary Dulles and Mr Stassen is to obtain first-hand information about the problems which we and our NATO partners face in pursuing our common goals of peace, security, and economic health. The passage of time has reinforced my conviction that this joint enterprise is one of the most important developments in modern history, because it is clear that our combined strength is far greater than the sum total of its individual parts. It is for this reason that I have watched with great satisfaction the far reaching steps which have been taken towards the integration of the European community, and I retain the most fervent hope that the continental European nations will continue to move forward toward a more complete unity.

In particular, I have been impressed by the support which your government has given to the creation of a European defence community. I believe that your continued support and encouragement are of the utmost importance in the successful completion of this great undertaking which will lay a more solid foundation for peace and progress throughout the free world.

I wish to express my personal admiration for your vital contribution to European unity and Atlantic cooperation, and to assure you that my government will continue to cooperate in every practicable way to advance the mutual interests of our respective peoples.

I enjoyed our recent talks in New York, and hope that you have had a pleasant and restful stay in Jamaica.

Winston S. Churchill: speech
(*'The Unwritten Alliance', pages 1–2*)

30 January 1953

WESTMINSTER ABBEY APPEAL

We are met here today for a purpose for which we believe that at least a million people throughout the English-speaking world will be happy to give a pound and perhaps repeat the process; and others less wealthy will be proud to join with their friends in giving a pound. That is what we are asking for today – a million pounds from a million people. We have one gift already; the Queen is the first subscriber. The purpose is to save from decay and ruin Westminster Abbey, in the famous words of Macaulay:[1] 'That temple of silence and reconciliation where the enmities of twenty generations lie buried.'[2]

Westminster Abbey is not only an active centre of our religious faith, but the shrine of nearly a thousand years of our history. Founded by King Edward

---

[1] Thomas Babington Macaulay, 1800–59. Scottish historian, essayist, parliamentarian and poet. Baron, 1857. Author of *Lays of Ancient Rome* (1842) and *The History of England* (1848).
[2] From Macaulay's essay on Warren Hastings (1843).

the Confessor¹ it presents the pilgrimage of our race, and has been in many ways the focus of our island life. Here all may see the panorama of our various fortunes, from the triumph of a Norman conqueror through the long succession of sovereigns who, in good or evil days, in glory and tragedy, safety and peril, unity and strife, have formed the chain of our ancient monarchy, until now we are looking forward to the moment next June when the Crown of St Edward will be set upon the head of our young and beautiful Queen Elizabeth the Second.

But the Abbey has not only been associated with the Coronation of all our sovereigns. The Chapter House across the way sheltered over a period of many generations the vigorous beginnings of that system of representative and Parliamentary government which has spread far and wide through so many lands. For us in the British Empire and Commonwealth of Nations the Abbey must be considered not only as the embodiment and enshrinement of our long record, but as a living spring of hope, inspiration, and unfailing interest wherever the English language is spoken in any quarter of the globe. Today we stand where, in the words of Kipling,² 'The Abbey makes us one.'³ I speak in the Jerusalem Chamber, where, as Shakespeare⁴ tells us, Henry V tried on the Crown while his dying father slept, and where the Star Chamber achieved its variegated reputation. In the Abbey itself are the tombs and monuments of famous men, from Norman and Plantagenet kings to the Unknown Warrior of the First World War. In Macaulay's words: 'In no other cemetery do so many citizens lie within so narrow a space.'

We in our day have come through many perils but we have been helped and sustained by that sense of continuity which finds no other symbol more commanding than this historic edifice which links the past with the present and gives us confidence in the future. Shall we in this valiant generation allow the building to moulder under our eyes? Both the monuments and the stonework of the centuries are falling into decay. The soot of London must be cleaned away if we are to prevent the stones from crumbling. The structure must be restored. The Choir School, with its long tradition of musical excellence, must be given security and an assured income must be provided for the daily work of maintenance.

Our generation would indeed be held to shame by those who come after us if we failed to preserve this noble inheritance. I ask those whom my words may reach, in Great Britain, in the Commonwealth, and across the oceans, to join me in sending the Dean of Westminster their one pound contributions so that the glorious memories that have come down to us may be preserved as

---

¹ Edward, 1003–66. King of England, 1042–66. Commenced building Westminster Abbey between 1042 and 1052.

² (Joseph) Rudyard Kipling, 1865–1936. Anglo-Indian writer. Nobel Prize in Literature, 1907.

³ Actually 'The Abbey makes us We': from 'The Native-Born' (1894).

⁴ William Shakespeare, 1564–1616. English playwright and poet. Author of 38 plays, 154 sonnets and two long narrative poems.

the treasures of generations yet to come. All the pounds should be sent to the Dean of Westminster, whose address, I may mention, is Westminster Abbey, London.

Cabinet: minutes
(Cabinet papers, 130/83)

30 January 1953
Secret
4.15 p.m.
Gen.421/Meeting No. 2

Ministers had before them a note by the Foreign Secretary (reproduced in the Annex to these minutes) setting out the various courses of action open to Her Majesty's Government in response to the latest Egyptian move in the negotiations for an Anglo-Egyptian agreement on the future of the Sudan.

The Foreign Secretary said that of the possible courses he preferred that set out in paragraph 4(c) of his note, viz. that we should tell the Egyptians that we could not accept their proposals and that the only way of resolving the differences between the Co-Domini was to arrange for early elections in the Sudan so that a Sudanese Parliament could pronounce on the outstanding issues. (These were (i) whether the Governor-General should retain special responsibility for the Southern Provinces and, if so, whether his exercise of this responsibility should be subject to an Egyptian veto; and (ii) whether the replacement of British by Sudanese officials must be completed before the Sudan became entitled to exercise the right of self-determination.) If his colleagues agreed that this was the wisest course to take, he proposed that before any communication was made to the Egyptians the Governor-General should first see the leaders of the Sudanese political Parties and try to persuade them to support our proposal. Although he thought that this attempt should be made he feared that it was not likely to succeed. The Sudanese political Parties had come to terms with the Egyptians in the hope that this would enable them to get the Egyptians out of the Sudan; and they were evidently under the mis-apprehension that a Sudanese Parliament, once it had been elected, would be able to alter the terms of any previous agreement with the Egyptian Government. In fact, however, this was not so: the agreement, if concluded, would be an Anglo-Egyptian agreement and, as such, outside the competence of the Sudanese Parliament. It would certainly be right to attempt to bring this point home to the Sudanese political leaders. But it must be recognised that some of them saw in the proposed agreement an opportunity to get both the British and the Egyptians out of the Sudan, and to achieve complete freedom to manage their own affairs. There was therefore the risk that, if we persisted in the proposal set out in paragraph 4(c) of the memorandum, some of the

Sudanese political parties would boycott the elections and we should fail in the attempt to create a Parliament fully representative of the Sudan as a whole.

In discussion Ministers agreed that, despite the risks involved, the wisest course was that proposed by the Foreign Secretary in paragraph 4(c) of his memorandum.

The Prime Minister said that he had been reviewing the general state of our relations with the new Egyptian Government and he was strongly of the opinion that we should now show greater firmness in all our negotiations with them. When General Neguib had first come to power it had seemed right to adopt a more conciliatory attitude, and even to offer some concessions, in the hope of strengthening his position. Recently, however, his public utterances had become increasingly hostile toward this country; and it was now evident that he was seeking to retain his political influence by pandering to those sections of Egyptian opinion which demanded the early and unconditional evacuation of British troops from Egypt. The time had come to make it clear that we were not prepared to make concessions in order to appease these sections of the Egyptian public. As regards the Sudan, we should not lightly cast away all the benefits which British administration had conferred on the Sudanese people; nor should we allow the Sudanese to be trapped by Egyptian promises which were unlikely to be fulfilled. We should take our stand on the argument that it should be left to a properly elected Sudanese Parliament to decide how far the Sudanese people still required the safeguards provided by the special powers of the Governor-General and the continued assistance of British officials. If the Egyptians were unwilling to accept this solution, negotiations for an Anglo-Egyptian agreement could be broken off: this was as good a ground as any on which to break off the talks.

Similarly, on the defence negotiations, we could take our stand on the 1936 Treaty and keep our troops in the Canal Zone until 1956. If an attempt were made to dislodge us by force we could doubtless give a good account of ourselves. And if there were widespread disorders in Egypt, we could no doubt do something to protect the lives of the British communities in Cairo and Alexandria.

The Minister of Defence said that there was no doubt that, with the troops already available there, we could deal with any attack which the Egyptians might make on our position in the Canal Zone. Our strength there was sufficient to repel, not only guerilla activities, but any assault which could be mounted by the Egyptian Army. Different considerations would arise if we had to undertake operations outside the Canal Zone. There was presumably no question of attempting a complete military occupation of Egypt: for that, substantially larger forces would be required. It might, however, be necessary to undertake operations in Cairo and Alexandria for the protection of the British communities there. The original plans for these operations had been compromised and it would no longer be possible to relieve the British community in Alexandria by sea. This meant that there would be rather longer delay before effective help could reach the British in Alexandria. It would also be necessary, if these operations had to be mounted, to fly in an additional battalion to the Canal Zone; and a battalion of the Green Howards now in this country was held at 96 hours' notice for this purpose. It should not, however, be assumed that these operations would necessarily have to be undertaken, even if an attempt were made to dislodge the British forces from the Canal Zone. Since Neguib's advent to power the general state of discipline and public order in Egypt had improved, and it was less likely that British lives in Cairo and Alexandria would be threatened by outbreaks of mob violence.

The Minister of Defence added that it was of great importance that, in the present state of uncertainty, the Americans should withhold the supply of military equipment for which the Egyptians had asked; for the items to which they had attached the highest priority (machine guns and armoured cars) would be of special value to them in the sort of fighting which could be expected if they should make an attempt to force the evacuation of British troops from the Canal. The Foreign Secretary said that the United States Government had now undertaken to delay the delivery of this equipment.

The Prime Minister said that since his return he had discussed with the Foreign Secretary whether we should, in present circumstances, allow the delivery of any of the jet aircraft which had been promised to Egypt in pursuance of the Cabinet's decision of 23rd October. He had ascertained that only four of these aircraft were due for immediate delivery; and, as this was so small a number, he agreed that the balance of advantage lay on the side of allowing them to be handed over to the Egyptians in pursuance of the earlier agreement. No more were due to be delivered for about a month and the Cabinet could consider later in the light of developments whether these further deliveries should be suspended.

The Meeting – Agreed that in the current negotiations with the Egyptian Government on the future of the Sudan the Foreign Secretary should take the line indicated in paragraph 4(c) of the annexed memorandum; and took note that the Foreign Secretary would in the first instance instruct the Governor-General of the Sudan to do his utmost to persuade the Sudanese political Parties to support this course.

JANUARY 1953 829

Cabinet: minutes
(*Cabinet papers, 130/83*)

31 January 1953
Secret
12.30 p.m.
Gen.421/Meeting No. 3

Ministers had before them the telegram which the Foreign Secretary had sent to the Governor-General of the Sudan (Foreign Office telegram No. 122 of 30th January) in pursuance of the decision reached at their meeting on the previous day.

They also had before them a number of telegrams which had been received meanwhile from Cairo and Khartoum, viz:

From Cairo	Nos. 186, 189 and 190 dated 30th January
	No. 193 dated 31st January.
From Khartoum	Nos. 65, 66 and 67 dated 30th January.

These telegrams suggested that the potentialities of the situation were even more serious than had appeared at the meeting on the previous day. Thus, HM Ambassador in Cairo represented, in paragraph 3 of his telegram No. 186, that unless we reached early agreement with the Egyptian Government, we should before long be faced with the choice of a forcible reoccupation of the Delta or an ignominious withdrawal from the Canal Zone. The Ambassador also said, in his telegram No. 193, that there would be an 'explosion' in Cairo as soon as the Egyptians learned of the consultations which the Governor-General had been authorised to hold with the Sudanese political Parties. By this he evidently meant, not an outbreak of disorder, but a violent change in the atmosphere in which the Anglo-Egyptian discussions on the future of the Sudan were being conducted. In his earlier telegram No. 189 he had stated that there had been a considerable improvement in the atmosphere, as a result of his latest meeting with the Egyptians, and that a spirit of compromise still existed.

The Governor-General of the Sudan, on the other hand, was convinced that the Egyptians did not want to conclude an agreement on the Sudan and were prolonging the negotiations in order to delay the holding of elections until the autumn. If the negotiations were to break down, it was in our interests that the break should come soon; and, in his telegram No. 67, he indicated the action which he thought we should then take in order to regain the initiative. This included the immediate dispatch of a battalion of infantry and a squadron of aircraft to Khartoum. In his telegram No. 66 he recommended that arrangements should at once be made to enable a battalion to be flown to Khartoum from the Canal Zone at short notice.

In discussion Ministers agreed that these telegrams afforded no grounds for modifying the conclusions which they had reached at their meeting on the previous day, but they showed the urgency of bringing the Anglo-Egyptian discussions to a head and the importance of being prepared to take immediate and effective action if there were a breakdown in those discussions. The first need was to ascertain whether the Sudanese political Parties could be persuaded to support our suggestion that the main issues outstanding between ourselves and the Egyptians (viz., the safeguards for the Southern Provinces and the replacement of British officials) should be left for decision by the Sudanese Parliament and that for this purpose there should be early elections for a Parliament which would represent the Sudan as a whole. The Governor-General should be urged to expedite the consultations which he had been instructed to hold with the Sudanese political Parties. HM Ambassador in Cairo should also be informed that we had every right to consult the Sudanese in this way and that we proposed to do so, despite the effect which he thought this might have on the Egyptians. It might be that the Egyptians would break off the discussions on hearing that we had consulted the Sudanese in this way. Alternatively, if we could rely on a reasonable amount of Sudanese support, we could insist that the two outstanding issues should be reserved for decision by a Sudanese Parliament and could ourselves break off the negotiations if we failed to persuade the Egyptians to accept that view. Our aim should be, by one means or another, to bring the Anglo-Egyptian negotiations to a head as quickly as possible, so that elections could be held in the Sudan before the rainy season.

The question of reinforcing the British troops in Khartoum and of taking the other measures suggested in Khartoum telegram No. 67 would not arise until the negotiations with the Egyptians had broken down. Ministers agreed, however, that the necessary steps should be taken at once to ensure that reinforcements could be flown promptly to Khartoum if that situation arose. The Prime Minister said that, if there were to be a show of force, we should run less risk of trouble if we were able to make a demonstration of overwhelming strength; and for that reason he would prefer that two battalions rather than one should in those circumstances be sent to Khartoum, in addition to the squadron of aircraft which had been suggested. He believed that, apart from steadying the situation in the Sudan, a demonstration of that kind might have a salutary effect on General Neguib. The Minister of Defence said that the troops in the Canal Zone were already at 96 hours' notice for possible operations there, and they would be able at short notice to send forward one (or, if necessary, two) battalions to Khartoum so long as arrangements were made to replace these immediately from the United Kingdom.

The Meeting –
    (1) Invited the Minister of Defence to instruct the Commander-in-Chief, Middle East Land Forces,[1] to be ready at short notice to dispatch

---

[1] Brian Hubert Robertson, 1896–1974. On active service, WWI, 1914–18. MC, DSO, 1919. Managing Director, Dunlop South Africa Ltd, 1935–40. Asst Quartermaster, General East African

JANUARY 1953   831

one (and, if necessary, two) battalions and one squadron of aircraft to Khartoum on the basis that these battalions would be replaced immediately from the United Kingdom. All precautions should be taken to prevent the Egyptians from learning the destination for which these troops were being held ready.

(2) Invited the Foreign Secretary (i) to instruct the Governor-General of the Sudan to expedite the consultations which he had been asked to hold with the Sudanese political Parties, and (ii) to inform HM Ambassador in Cairo that these consultations must go forward, notwithstanding the effect which they might have on the Anglo-Egyptian negotiations.

Command, 1940–1; General 8th Army, North Africa, 1941–2. Commandant, Tripoli, 1942. CBE, 1942. Deputy Adjutant and Quartermaster, General 8th Army, North Africa, 1942–3. Chief Administration Officer, 15th Army Group, Italy, 1943–4; Allied Armies, Italy, 1944. KCVO, 1944. Chief Administration Officer, 15th Army Group, Italy, 1944–5. Chief, Central Commission, Germany, 1945–7. Deputy Military Governor, British Zone, Germany, 1945–7. KCMG, 1947. Military Governor, British Zone, Germany, 1947–9. British High Commissioner, Allied High Commission, Germany, 1949–50. GBE, 1949. ADC General to the King, 1949–52. C-in-C, Middle East Land Forces, 1950–3. ADC General to the Queen, 1952. GCB, 1952. Retired, 1953. Chairman, British Transport Commission, 1953–61. Baron, 1961. Director, Dunlop PLC, 1961–9.

February
1953

Winston S. Churchill to Air Marshal Lord Portal
(Churchill papers, 2/195)

2 February 1953
Confidential

My dear Peter,

Thank you for your letter of January 26. I am indeed glad that Winston is to be your Page at the Coronation and am delighted that you should have invited him. Randolph is to be a Gold Staff Officer so that, thanks to you, there will be three generations of my family in the Abbey.

[. . .]

President Dwight D. Eisenhower to Winston S. Churchill
(Premier papers, 11/1074)

2 February 1953   The White House
Personal and Confidential

Dear Winston,

Over the weekend, I had your cable referring to our intention of relieving the Seventh Fleet of responsibility for defending China.

Of course, I have no means of knowing what will be the effect of this order if the Communists are determined to hunt for any excuse in order to justify some indefensible action on their part. Your message made a point of the fact that no great military advantage would result from our decision. This is likely true. But there is a very definite psychological point involved – even self-respect. The United States is in the peculiar position of battling Chinese Communists in Korea; while, at the same time, under the old order, of accepting the humiliating position of defending Communist China against a possible attack.

You may be right in your guess that the United Nations will, initially at least, disapprove of our decision. Nevertheless, I am making it quite clear in my statement that we intend nothing aggressive – that we were just tired of being dupes.

No one could be more desirous than I of developing a common political attitude among the Western nations with respect to our Asiatic problem. Never will you or your associates find anything but the greatest of sympathy from us in our effort to reach logical common attitudes and policies in that region. But, to save me, I cannot see why any of our friends have a right to expect of the United States that it maintain such an anomalous attitude as was required of us under the original order.

I assure you again that there is nothing belligerent in my feeling – in fact, there is possibly in this whole world not a less belligerent person than I am!

This message is nothing but a personal communication. It is not, of course, a part of the diplomatic exchanges between the British Government and the United States Government. But it is my understanding that you and I hope to maintain, even if only intermittently, a personal correspondence, which will provide opportunity to help clarify intentions, and explain reasons for decisions, when this seems appropriate.

With warm personal regard,
As ever,
Eisenhower[1]

Cabinet: conclusions
(Cabinet papers, 128/26)

3 February 1953
Secret
11 a.m.
Cabinet Meeting No. 6 of 1953

[. . .]

2. The Prime Minister said that he had considered, in consultation with the Chancellor of the Exchequer, what reply he should give to the deputation from the Liberal Party on the question of electoral reform. He believed that there might be a case at some later stage for considering the introduction of proportional representation in the larger cities. But the experience of other countries suggested that proportional representation increased the difficulties of securing stable government; and this was certainly not a favourable moment for experiments in electoral reform.

There was general agreement with this view.

The Cabinet –

Took note that the Prime Minister would give no encouragement to the

[1] After this letter, Eisenhower always signed himself, when writing to Churchill, as 'Ike', 'DE', or 'Ike E.'.

proposals of the Liberal Party for experiments in electoral reform. . . .

[. . .]

5. The Cabinet had before them a note by the Prime Minister (C(53)39) covering a draft letter to the Leaders of the Opposition Parties inviting them to co-operate in a three-party conference on the reform of the House of Lords. This draft had been prepared by the Lord President in pursuance of the Cabinet's decision of 30th December.

The Prime Minister said that it had been suggested that he might discuss this matter with Leaders of the Labour Opposition before these invitations were sent. He was reluctant to do this for he had good reason to believe that the Labour Party would urge that the conference should be postponed until late in the life of the present Parliament. From the point of view of fulfilling the pledges which they had given at the election, it was better that the Government should issue the invitations and have them declined, rather than find themselves in the position of being prevented, by the results of preliminary consultations with the Labour Party, from taking any overt step to convene the conference.

The Commonwealth Secretary said that it was also desirable that he should be able to say, in the debate in the House of Lords that afternoon on Lord Simon's[1] Bill for the creation of life Peers, that these invitations were about to be issued.

The Cabinet –

Invited the Prime Minister to write to the Leaders of the Opposition Parties, in the terms of the draft annexed to C(53)39, inviting them to co-operate in a three-Party conference on the reform of the House of Lords.

[. . .]

Cabinet: conclusions
(Cabinet papers, 128/26)

5 February 1953
Secret
11 a.m.
Cabinet Meeting No. 7 of 1953

[. . .]

5. The Prime Minister said that the conclusions reached by the Cabinet on 14th January about the Latin version of the Royal Title had been reported

---

[1] John Allsebrook Simon, 1873–1954. Educated at Fettes and Wadham College, Oxford. MP (Lib.) for Walthamstow, 1906–18; for Spen Valley, 1922–31, (Nat. Lib.) 1931–40. Knighted, 1910. Attorney-General, with a seat in the Cabinet, 1913–15. Home Secretary, 1915–16; resigned in opposition to conscription. Maj., RAF, serving in France, 1917–18. Foreign Secretary, 1931–5. Home Secretary, 1935–7. Chancellor of the Exchequer, 1937–40. Viscount, 1940. Lord Chancellor, 1940–5.

to him before a formal submission had been made to Her Majesty. It had seemed to him that the words '*Britanniarum et Ceterorum Regnorum Suorum et Terrarum Regina*' would strike harshly upon English ears, and he had asked the Lord Chancellor to consider whether a less cumbrous version of this part of the Title could not be devised. The Lord Chancellor had now recommended the following alternative: '*Britanniarum Regnorumque Suorum Ceterorum Regina*'.

The Prime Minister said that this alternative seemed to him to be preferable. For himself, however, he regretted the necessity for a Latin version of the Title. The days were long past when Latin had served as a means of communication between peoples of different races; and the English language was today spoken or understood by a large proportion of the population of the civilised world.

The Cabinet —

Agreed that, subject to Her Majesty's pleasure, the Latin version of the new form of the Royal Title for use in the United Kingdom should be: Elizabeth II, *Dei Gratia Britanniarum Regnorumque Suorum Ceterorum Regina, Consortionis Populorum Princeps, Fidei Defensor.*

[. . .]

Lord Cherwell to Winston S. Churchill
(*Premier papers, 11/388*)

6 February 1953

You asked me to let you know whether there was any truth in the reports about there being Communists among Rhodes Scholars.[1] I have made one or two discreet enquiries at Oxford and the position appears to be as follows:

There are two separate accusations that have been made.

First that the Communists have secured the election to scholarships of Party members. This is, I am sure, absurd; the fact that selection is by 56 separate committees in the USA would foredoom any such attempts — if they were ever made — to failure. Sir Carleton Allen,[2] who was Warden of Rhodes House from 1931 to 1952, told me that he did not think that any of his American Rhodes Scholars had been Communists.

The second accusation made is that the Communists are approaching Rhodes Scholars and inviting them to join the Communist party or University organisations with Communist leanings. There is, I gather, no Communist club in the University but there are several extreme Left-Wing organisations which

---

[1] The Rhodes Scholarship is an international postgraduate award for students to study at the University of Oxford. Established in 1902, it was the first large-scale international scholarship programme.

[2] Carleton Kemp Allen, 1887–1966. Served with 13th Middlesex Rgt during WWI. Prof. of Jurisprudence, Oxford, 1929–31. Oxford Secretary to Rhodes Trustees and Warden of Rhodes House, Oxford, 1931–52. Knighted, 1952.

I dare say the Communists control and it may well be, and probably is, true that Rhodes Scholars are sometimes invited to join them. But undergraduates are continually being approached to join every conceivable type of political, religious and cultural society, and I think it very unlikely that the Communists are running a campaign specially directed against Rhodes Scholars.

Winston S. Churchill to President Dwight D. Eisenhower
(Premier papers, 11/1074)

7 February 1953
Personal and Confidential

My dear Ike – if I may so venture,

I was so glad to get your letter of February 2,[1] and to feel that our private correspondence will continue apart from the regular official communications. I hope you believe that I understand all the reasons that led to your declaration. If it had been necessary, I would have explained to the House of Commons the distress of millions of Americans whose relations are under fire in Korea because of the prolonged stalemate, and the apparent association of the United States Seventh Fleet with the security of the Communist country that is firing on them. I feel it in my bones, and it grieves and stirs me every day. If you could find time to read Anthony's speech, which I enclose, you will see how earnestly he put this aspect before the House; and there was no doubt that it is fully accepted by all except perhaps an eighth of the Members, and most of them would come into line on a grave issue. What I do hope is that where joint action affecting our common destiny is desired, you will let us know beforehand so that we can give our opinion and advice in time to have them considered. Now that you are in the saddle and can deal with long term policies, this ought to be possible. Anthony and I are resolved to make our co-operation with the United States effective over the world scene. I am sure that you will not hesitate to tell him frankly all your thoughts on these matters when you see him. He will know mine.

Let me know if I should send you the facsimile of my agreement with Roosevelt about the atomic bomb. When we talked you said you would like it, but maybe you have found one in your own archives. I am hopeful that now that we are making the bomb ourselves, we could interchange information to mutual advantage.

I am very glad it is all arranged for Anthony and Rab Butler to come over next month. I shall stay here myself and mind the shop.

Dulles asked if we still see difficulties about Alton Jones and his 'grease monkeys'. We do. Public opinion here would not understand why the United

---

[1] Reproduced above (pp. 832–3).

States should help Musaddiq to get even part of Abadan going before he has settled his accounts with us. It is hard enough already to keep Musaddiq running down the course and the appearance of a new face would most probably make him shy off just when your Ambassador Henderson is doing his best to get him over the jump. You were kind enough at my request to hold hard so that Henderson should have every chance of success in the present negotiations.

I am sure you will realize that in these matters I do not wish to ask favours of the United States but only action or inaction for our mutual advantage.

Winston S. Churchill to President Dwight D. Eisenhower
(Premier papers, 11/1074)

9 February 1953

My dear Mr President,

Thank you very much for your letter of January 29[1] and for your kind greetings.

We have been very glad to have your Secretary of State and Mr Stassen with us for a short visit, and I am sure that the discussions which they had with the Foreign Secretary and myself and some of our colleagues were most valuable to both sides.

We entirely agree with you about the paramount importance of the North Atlantic Treaty Organisation, on the strength of which our whole future depends. A good deal of attention was given during our talks with Mr Dulles to the problem of the European Defence Community. We were able to tell Mr Dulles of our most recent communication to the six Powers about our military association with these. We hope that this will lead to really close practical co-operation and also help to solve the immediate problem of securing French ratification. We agreed to urge our Dutch friends to ratify the Treaty at the earliest opportunity without necessarily waiting for the French and the Germans to ratify.

We shall be discussing these questions with the French Ministers this week. We have certain ideas for equally close co-operation with the HHC in the political field. You can rely upon us to continue to give every support and encouragement to this great undertaking. I have noted with great pleasure the successful talks Mr Dulles has just had in Bonn with the Federal Chancellor and I am sure they will be a great help to Mr Adenauer in completing German ratification.

I need hardly assure you of our determination to work as closely as possible with your Government in all matters affecting our common interests.

[1] Reproduced above (pp. 823–4).

Collaboration within the wider society of the Atlantic community is indeed essential to the attainment of our goals of peace, security and prosperity.

Winston S. Churchill to James Thomas
Prime Minister's Personal Minute M.11/53
(Premier papers, 11/355)

9 February 1953

What about my suggestion of an additional ship carrying paying passengers at, say, £50 a head?[1] Might this not give you a good profit? Otherwise, proceed as you propose.

I was sorry you could not come at the weekend, and hope you are better.

Defence Committee: minutes
(Cabinet papers, 131/13)

11 February 1953   Prime Minister's Map Room
Top Secret   Ministry of Defence
11.30 a.m.
Defence Committee Meeting No. 2 of 1953

[. . .]

2. THE SITUATION IN THE CANAL ZONE

The Prime Minister said that he feared that, when General Neguib had concluded an agreement on the Sudan, he would do his utmost to be rid of all British forces in Egypt, so that he would then be free to exert pressure upon the Sudan by bribery and other means to seek unity with Egypt. He thought it necessary that we should have some positive plans to defeat military action by the Egyptians against our forces in the Canal Zone and some means by which we could negotiate from strength a further agreement with Egypt about the base. He suggested that we might insist that the cost of removal from the Canal Zone should be charged against Egypt's sterling balances. If this point were maintained, Egypt would be more ready to conclude an agreement which did not entail this financial burden. He thought also that the least sign of military activity, whether by the Egyptian Army or by guerilla forces against us, would be sufficient justification for rounding up and disarming that part of the Egyptian Army which was located in the Sinai Peninsula. This would be an effective card in negotiations, and would carry with it far fewer disagreeable responsibilities and commitments than the occupation of

---

[1] The reference is to liners hired for the accommodation of guests at the Naval Review planned as part of the Coronation celebrations.

Cairo and Alexandria, which would inevitably lead to action against mobs and bloodshed among civilians.

In discussion the following points were made:
- a) The Chancellor of the Exchequer said that he would wish to reserve his position on the blocking of Egypt's sterling balances, since that would affect the trade relationships between Egypt and this country. There would, however, be no further release of sterling balance for Egypt this year, as Egypt had received all that was allowed under the terms of the agreement.
- b) The Chiefs of Staff confirmed that it would be a practical military operation to cause the surrender of that part of the Egyptian Army which was in the Sinai Peninsula, either by direct action or by stopping supplies. If the main Egyptian Army launched an attack upon our forces in the Canal Zone – which seemed very unlikely – there would be no great difficulty in defeating it.
- c) The plans which existed allowed for a rescue operation to be carried out in Cairo and Alexandria in case of further attacks against British and friendly nationals in these two cities. If it became necessary to occupy these places permanently there would be a need for further reinforcements.
- d) The object of negotiations with Egypt would be to arrive at an agreement by which the base would be retained in the Canal Zone and would continue to serve as the maintenance base for all British forces in the Middle East. It was hoped that the agreement would allow for the retention of 5,000 British Service personnel to look after the base, but, although these men would have their personal arms, they would not be organised in combat units.

The Prime Minister said that he would like the Chiefs of Staff to prepare for him a short note showing the plans which existed for positive action in the Canal Zone in the face of provocation. He hoped that the Minister of Defence would be able to explain these to the Cabinet at a meeting later that day, when he might also refer to a suggestion previously made by him that we should give a military guarantee to the Sudan against external attack.

The Committee –
1) Instructed the Chiefs of Staff to prepare a note giving the outline of existing plans for action in the Canal Zone in the event of further provocation.
2) Invited the Minister of Defence to be ready to explain the position to the Cabinet later that day.

3. THE DEFENCE OF MALAYA

The Committee had before them a memorandum by the Chiefs of Staff (D(53)1) pointing out that it might become necessary to occupy the Songkhla position on the Kra Isthmus at short notice if Chinese forces invaded Tonkin, or if Siam turned Communist after a French evacuation of Tonkin or the whole of Indo-China.

In discussion the following points were made:

a) If it became necessary to occupy the Songkhla position the decision would have to be taken at very short notice, as the opportunity for occupying the position at small cost would be fleeting. As the operation involved entry into Siam's territory without invitation or notice, it was of the utmost importance that secrecy should be maintained. There would, on the other hand, be considerable advantage if the President of the United States and his military advisers were made aware of our intentions and signified their support.

b) It would be premature to judge the effect of this action upon our intentions with regard to the defence of Hong Kong. There was now evidence that the Americans attached greater importance to our retention of Hong Kong and might in certain circumstances be willing to assist us in its defence.

c) The Prime Minister said that, if the need arose, it would be better to provide the reinforcements need to occupy the Songkhla position by sending the Second Division from Germany and replacing it in Germany with a territorial division. It would be far more difficult to send territorial formations to South-East Asia than to send them to Germany.

d) The Colonial Secretary said that, as the Cabinet would have to take a quick decision if this situation arose, he thought it would be wise to warn them of the possibility in advance. The Prime Minister suggested that he should make a short oral statement to the Cabinet on the subject, and that thereafter a small group of Ministers could be set up to watch the progress of events on the Cabinet's behalf and to direct any further planning that was required.

The Committee –

1) Took note of the memorandum by the Chiefs of Staff (D(53)1) and agreed that the Australian and New Zealand Chiefs of Staff should be informed of its contents.

2) Took note that the Colonial Secretary would make a statement to the Cabinet, and that thereafter the Prime Minister would set up a special committee of Ministers to deal with this problem.

4. SITUATION IN KOREA

The Prime Minister said that he had much sympathy with the desire of the Americans to break the stalemate in Korea and he had suggested on his recent visit that, if they wished to propose any plans for accomplishing this, they should discuss them with us – allowing plenty of time for consultation before the plans were to be put into operation. He hoped that the Minister of Defence and the Chiefs of Staff would consider themselves what decisive action might be taken to bring the war in Korea to a successful conclusion.

The Minister of Defence said that he had considered this problem and would be ready to propose the scope and outline of operations which might prove decisive. An opportunity might be found for him to explain these views to the President of the United States at some later date.

5. THE LIKELIHOOD OF GENERAL WAR WITH THE SOVIET UNION UP TO THE END OF 1955

The Committee had before them a memorandum by the Chiefs of Staff (D(53)3)[1] assessing the likelihood of a general war with the Soviet Union up to the end of 1955.

There was general agreement with the conclusions reached by the Chiefs of Staff.

The Committee –
1) Took note of the memorandum by the Chiefs of Staff (D(53)3).
2) Agreed that it should be shown to the United States Joint Chiefs of Staff.

Cabinet: conclusions
(Cabinet papers, 128/26)

11 February 1953 Prime Minister's Room
Secret House of Commons
6.30 p.m.
Cabinet Meeting No. 9 of 1953

1. The Foreign Secretary recalled that on 3rd February the Cabinet had approved the text of a telegram to Her Majesty's Ambassador in Cairo setting out their requirements on the two major points then outstanding in the negotiations with the Egyptian Government on the future of the Sudan, viz., safeguards for the Southern Provinces and control over the replacement of British officials in the Sudan. As a result of his further discussions with the Egyptian Government the Ambassador had now obtained satisfaction on both these points. The latest draft of the proposed Agreement included safeguards for the Southern Provinces which were acceptable to the Governor-General of the Sudan; and it provided that the replacement of British officials should be subject to review, if necessary, by an International Commission. Having thus secured acceptance of the conditions laid down by the Cabinet, the Ambassador had provisionally arranged to initial the final text of the Agreement on

---

[1] Of Jan. 28, reproduced above (pp. 816–22).

the following day. The Foreign Secretary had considered whether this could be delayed for a day, in order to give the Cabinet longer time in which to examine the final text. But the Egyptians would not be willing to sign the Agreement on a Friday, which was their Sabbath, and signature on a Saturday would involve publication some time before an announcement could be made in Parliament. The choice, therefore, lay between authorising the Ambassador to initial the Agreement on the following day, or postponing its conclusion until early in the following week. The Foreign Secretary was reluctant to accept so long a postponement; for the Egyptian Government were subject to strong pressure to adhere to the agreement which they had concluded with the Sudanese political parties, and any delay on our part at this stage involved the risk that they would withdraw some of the concessions which we had extracted from them in the negotiations. The Sudanese were determined not to lose this opportunity of concluding an agreement which included Egypt's renunciation of her claim to sovereignty over the Sudan – a claim which all previous Governments in Egypt had maintained since 1819. The draft Anglo-Egyptian Agreement which had now been evolved was much more satisfactory, from our point of view, than the agreement which the Egyptians had made with the Sudanese political parties some months ago; but that agreement equally involved Egypt's renunciation of her claim to sovereignty over the Sudan, and the Sudanese would certainly insist on standing by that if we lost the present opportunity of concluding a more satisfactory agreement on an Anglo-Egyptian basis. In that event, we should find ourselves opposed by both the Egyptians and the Sudanese, and we should be powerless to prevent them from going forward on the basis of their earlier agreement.

The Prime Minister said that he was gravely concerned about the reception of the proposed Anglo-Egyptian Agreement by public opinion in this country. He had received disturbing reports of a discussion on this subject which had been held by the Foreign Affairs group of Government supporters in the House of Commons. All but a very small minority of those present at this meeting had been highly critical of the Government's handling of the Sudan situation. There seemed to be a widespread anxiety about this among Government supporters; and, from what he had heard, he doubted whether the Foreign Secretary's proposals would command a sufficient measure of support in the Conservative Party. He feared that the proposed Agreement would be represented as an ignominious surrender of our responsibilities in the Sudan and a serious blow to British prestige throughout the Middle East. He believed that it would be sharply criticised by the Press. It seemed likely to involve the Government in serious political difficulties, which would doubtless be exploited to the full by the Opposition. He would, therefore, prefer that no decision should be taken until early in the following week, by which time it would be easier to forecast the probable reaction of public opinion in the country.

In discussion it was pointed out that the proposed Agreement was the logical outcome of the long-standing promise to confer on the Sudanese people the rights of self-government and self-determination. The expectation had been held out to the Sudanese that they would achieve self-government by the end of 1952. It was against this background that the terms of the proposed Agreement would have to be defended to public opinion in this country. And it would be much easier to defend the Agreement which we had now negotiated with the Egyptians – including, as it did, satisfactory safeguards for the Southern Provinces and reasonable provision for the replacement of British officials in the Sudan – than be forced to accept the much less satisfactory arrangement which the Egyptians had negotiated with the Sudanese political parties behind our backs. There was no doubt that the latest draft of the Anglo-Egyptian Agreement was a great improvement on that: several valuable concessions had been extracted from the Egyptians in negotiations during the past few weeks. Nothing would now be gained by delay. Apart from the risk that the Egyptians might withdraw some of the concessions which they had made, it was in our interests that the negotiations should not be drawn out any longer; for it was most desirable that the Sudanese elections should be held before the onset of the rainy season, and this could not be done unless the preliminary arrangements were completed by the end of February.

At the same time, the Cabinet recognised the importance of satisfying Government supporters, before any public announcement was made, that the balance of advantage lay on the side of concluding an Anglo-Egyptian Agreement in the terms now proposed. There was undoubtedly a great deal of misunderstanding and uncertainty on this question among Government supporters in the House of Commons. The Foreign Secretary had originally proposed to authorise Her Majesty's Ambassador in Cairo to initial the Agreement on the following morning, and to explain its provisions to a private meeting of Government supporters in the early afternoon before making a public announcement about it in Parliament. It was, however, the general view of the Cabinet that it would be preferable for the Foreign Secretary to explain the position to a representative meeting of Government supporters interested in foreign affairs, and to satisfy himself that he would be able to command their support in the course which he proposed, before the Cabinet finally decided to authorise the conclusion of the proposed Agreement. In order to avoid delay, this meeting might be held that evening.

The Cabinet –
(1) Invited the Foreign Secretary to explain the proposed Anglo-Egyptian Agreement on the Sudan to a representative meeting of Government supporters interested in foreign affairs to be held at 9.30 p.m. that evening.
(2) Agreed to take a final decision on this question later in the evening when the Foreign Secretary had reported the results of the meeting to be held in accordance with Conclusion (1) above.

[. . .]

February 1953

President Dwight D. Eisenhower to Winston S. Churchill
('The Churchill Eisenhower Correspondence', page 23)

12 February 1953

Dear Winston,

I shall write you at length another time, but meantime I wanted to send you this note to thank you very much for your letter of the seventh.[1]

I read Anthony's speech with great interest and thought it was fine. We are looking forward to his visit.

With warm personal regard,

Cabinet: conclusions
(Cabinet papers, 128/26)

17 February 1953
Secret
11 a.m.
Cabinet Meeting No. 12 of 1953

[...]

2. The Cabinet had before them a memorandum by the Foreign Secretary (C(53)17 Revise) on the resumption of defence negotiations with Egypt, which they had previously considered on 14th January, and a further memorandum by the Foreign Secretary (C(53)65) summarising some of the main arguments in favour of seeking an agreement on the lines indicated in his earlier memorandum.

The Cabinet first discussed the nature of the proposed agreement outlined in C(53)17 Revise. It was emphasised that what was contemplated was a general settlement comprising –

(i) a phased withdrawal of British troops from Egypt;
(ii) maintenance of the military base in the Canal Zone in peace under conditions which would enable us and our Allies to have immediate use of it in war;
(iii) an Anglo-Egyptian organisation for the air defence of Egypt;
(iv) Egypt's participation in a Middle East Defence Organisation; and
(v) a programme of military and economic assistance to Egypt by the United Kingdom and the United States.

In discussion the following points were made:

(a) These proposals should be presented as five interdependent elements in a single settlement. In particular, our offer to withdraw British troops from Egypt would be dependent on Egyptian acceptance of the other proposals.

---

[1] Reproduced above (pp. 836–7).

(b) Special importance was attached to the second and fourth of these proposals. It was essential that we should receive effective assurances that the base in the Canal Zone would be readily available to us in a future war. For this purpose it was most desirable that we should secure Egyptian agreement to those conditions set out in Case 'A' on page 7 of C(53)17 Revise. Neither Case 'B' nor Case 'C' would give us a sufficient certainty of being able to make effective use of the base in war. It was also important that the British technicians and others who would run the base installations in peace should be members of the Armed Forces entitled to wear uniform and to carry personal arms. If this point could be secured, we might even be content to accept rather smaller numbers than those suggested in paragraph 4 of Case 'A'.

(c) As regards the fourth proposal, the proposed Middle East Defence Organisation must be something more than a paper plan. We should not agree to withdraw our troops from the Canal Zone until the Egyptians had given practical proof of their readiness to make this Organisation a reality. The withdrawal of British troops from Egypt could not be defended against political criticisms in this country unless it were possible to present the Middle East Defence Organisation as an imaginative and practical alternative to the continued maintenance of a British garrison in the Canal Zone.

(d) If we were to satisfy the French and the other maritime nations of the world that free passage through the Suez Canal would continue to be safeguarded, we must be able to show that some satisfactory alternative would be substituted for the protection hitherto afforded by the presence of British troops in Egypt.

(e) Much would turn on the international character of the organisation proposed for planning the defence of the Middle East. The United States should be closely associated with this from the outset. The precise composition of the Middle East Defence Organisation would, however, need careful thought. In particular, were there not difficulties in including all the Arab States while excluding Israel? Might this not be regarded as a concentration of power against Israel? On this point the Foreign Secretary said that an association including the United States and the United Kingdom could not reasonably be regarded by Israel as an association hostile to their interests.

(f) In connection with the point noted in the preceding paragraph the Foreign Secretary drew attention to a telegram from Amman (No. 92 of 16th February) reporting a proposal of the Jordan Government that a British brigade might be permanently stationed in Jordan. In discussion it was pointed out that this might have considerable advantages for us, both strategic and financial; and that it need not be assumed that Israel would necessarily be hostile to it. The Cabinet agreed, however, that no final decision should be taken on this proposal at the present time.

The Cabinet next considered the procedure for resuming the defence negotiations with Egypt.

The Prime Minister said that in his view the first need was to assure ourselves that we should have the full sympathy and support of the United States Government in the approach which we were proposing to make. We were not asking them to give us any military assistance in Egypt at the present time: we ourselves had ample forces there to deal with any situation which might arise. But they should understand that we were not prepared to be bullied or cajoled into withdrawing our troops from Egypt unless we secured in return satisfactory alternative arrangements on the lines indicated in C(53)17 Revise. These would together form a settlement which we could accept; but they must be taken as a whole and we should not be prepared to see them whittled away in the course of negotiation. He would wish to be satisfied, by an exchange of personal messages with the President, that the United States Government would give their whole-hearted support to an attempt to reach an agreement with the Egyptians on this basis. Secondly, he was doubtful whether the British and American Ambassadors in Cairo should be left to handle by themselves the next stage in these negotiations. These were after all, defence negotiations; and he would prefer that two prominent military figures, one British and one American, should handle them jointly with the two Ambassadors. Field Marshal Sir William Slim would be a very suitable person to lead the British side of the negotiating team, if Her Majesty were willing to allow him to defer taking up his appointment as Governor-General of Australia and the Australian Government could be persuaded to agree to this. He hoped that President Eisenhower might be persuaded to nominate someone like General Bedell Smith or General Ridgway to represent him in the discussions. With two such military men, working in association with the two Ambassadors, an impressive weight of Anglo-American influence would be brought to bear on the Egyptians.

The Foreign Secretary and the Commonwealth Secretary warmly supported the Prime Minister's proposals for handling the next stage of these negotiations.

The Cabinet –
  (1) Reaffirmed their approval of the papers annexed to C(53)17 Revise as a basis for the resumption of defence negotiations with Egyptian Government.
  (2) Approved the Prime Minister's proposal that the next stage of the conversations in Cairo should be undertaken by leading military figures, one British and American, in association with the British and American Ambassadors.

FEBRUARY 1953 847

(3) Took note that the Prime Minister would take steps to ascertain whether Her Majesty would be willing that the Australian Government would be asked to agree that Field Marshal Sir William Slim should defer taking up his appointment as Governor-General in Australia so that he might first undertake this special duty; and that, subject to Her Majesty's pleasure, the Prime Minister would put this suggestion in a personal message to the Prime Minister of Australia.
(4) Took note that the Prime Minister would send a personal message to President Eisenhower inviting him to co-operate, in the manner outlined in the discussion, in a joint Anglo-American approach to the Egyptian Government.
(5) Agreed that, until an understanding had been reached with the United States Government on the procedure now envisaged, no indication should be given to the Egyptian Government on the basis on which we were prepared to resume the defence negotiations.

[. . .]

Winston S. Churchill to Sir Robert Menzies
Prime Minister's Personal Telegram T.6/53
(Premier papers, 11/704)

18 February 1953
Cypher
Emergency
Personal and Top Secret
No. 12

We have been considering most anxiously in Cabinet here how best to conduct the critical negotiations in Egypt over the Middle East Defence Organisation and the whole future of the Suez Canal. In all these matters you are as deeply interested as we are, both by old comradeship in the two world wars and by our common interests.

We feel, as I am sure you do, that a sound and lasting settlement of all our problems in the Middle East, centring on and radiating from Egypt, is the most urgent and perhaps the most vital element in allied policy and strategy for world peace.

In this, the interests of your country and ours are vitally linked, but it is also essential that we should carry with us the wholehearted co-operation and support of the United States Government, with whom we have reached a considerable measure of agreement at the official level.

After mature consideration in Cabinet we have agreed that I should propose personally to President Eisenhower with all the influence I can bring to bear that the representation of the United Kingdom and United States should be reinforced by the strongest military personalities we can both supply. I am therefore proposing to the President that we should both nominate as our negotiators, in association with our Ambassadors, two military men of the highest standing, who, by their prestige and their personal capacity, will carry the greatest possible weight. If, as I hope, the President agrees, this will present to Egypt and the whole Middle East, a united front of the greatest strength and ability.

We are all agreed that, on the Commonwealth side, there is no man who, in knowledge, prestige and capacity, could match Field Marshal Slim for this most important task.

I have spoken with the Field Marshal who, with characteristic selflessness said, that if it is the considered opinion of both our Governments that this is the best service he can render, he is ready to undertake the task. He will only do so from an over-riding sense of duty, and not without your full concurrence.

I know well the temporary difficulties this involves for you. The Field Marshal is expected to leave by ship next week. All arrangements are made for his reception and inauguration in Australia. A delay in his arrival has many inconveniences. I trust however that you will agree the disadvantages are over-ridden by the critical situation in the Middle East, and the unique service he can render to both our countries at this time. You and I have taken some critical decisions together before.

If you agree, we must also plan in the interim period to avoid publicity. There could not, of course, be any murmur of this until, as I hope, President Eisenhower has agreed, both with the general proposition and with the appointment of his own military representative of equal standing with the Field Marshal. I would therefore propose that it should be announced that the Field Marshal has temporarily postponed his departure. This should not give rise to serious comment.

If all goes according to plan, then a full announcement would be made that, with the concurrence of your Government, the Field Marshal has undertaken to lead the Commonwealth team in the Egyptian negotiations. This, I feel sure, would be equally welcomed in your country and mine. It would involve a temporary and I believe short postponement of the actual date on which he will assume his position as Governor-General.

While, of course, it will be for you to submit to Her Majesty the proposals necessary to give effect to the plan I am putting to you, I am, as United Kingdom Prime Minister, explaining to The Queen the whole of the plan we have in mind so that, as is my duty, Her Majesty may know the whole mind of Her Government in this country, while, of course, safeguarding entirely your position and the advice which you will tender to Her.

I feel that this is a decision at once important and hopeful which we have to take and I sincerely trust that our minds may be in accord and that we may go forward together.

Winston S. Churchill to President Dwight D. Eisenhower
(Premier papers, 11/1074)

18 February 1953
Private and Confidential

My dear Friend,

[. . .] I now write to you about the Suez Canal and MEDO.

(1) We reached an agreement with the late United States Administration about the minimum arrangements necessary before we began to withdraw our forces. I do not know the level on your side which our discussions with your people had reached; Acheson and Bradley certainly knew. The talks took place here between December 31 and January 7 and the conclusions were set out in agreed papers copies of which I enclose. I have given my assent to these plans, epitomized on page 11, paragraph 1, in the five sub-heads a, b, c, d, and e, and in A in the Appendix on page 7, because of the enormous advantages which might flow from our joint action.

(2) There is no question of our seeking or needing military, physical, or financial aid from you. Alex assures me that our forces in the Canal Zone are in ample strength to resist any attack, and even if necessary, in order to prevent a massacre of white people and to rescue them, to enter Cairo and Alexandria, for which all preparations have been for some time at 96 hours' notice. Moreover, nearly half the effective Egyptian Army, about 15,000 men, stands on the Eastern side of the Canal watching Israel. They could be easily forced to surrender, perhaps indeed merely by cutting off supplies. As for Egypt herself, the cutting off of the oil would, as you know, exercise a decisive effect. There is therefore no question of our needing your help or to reinforce the 80,000 men we have kept at great expense on tiptoe during the last year. The advantages of our working together on the lines agreed with your predecessors are so great that a successful result might be achieved without violence or bloodshed and without exposing you to any military obligation.

(3) We feel however that our Ambassador, Stevenson, requires to be guided by one of our strongest military personalities. The Socialist Government sent Field Marshal Slim out there in 1949 and 1950, and he did extremely well in his visits. He has profound knowledge of the military situation and was indeed until recently responsible as CIGS for advising us upon it. I am sure you know him well. He would head our delegation if the Australian Government will agree to postpone for a few weeks his assumption of their Governor-Generalship. If not, it might be Slessor or Portal or Tedder, as the Air has a lot to say. I wonder whether you would consider favourably placing a first class American military figure with Ambassador Caffery?[1] You have

---

[1] Jefferson Caffery, 1886–1974. Educated at Tulane University. Admitted to Bar of Louisiana, 1909. Secretary of Legation, Caracas, 1911; Stockholm, 1913; Teheran, 1916. Special Representative of State Dept, Permanent Inter-allied Commission on Treatment and Training Disabled Soldiers and

many versed alike in policy and defence.

(4) Thus we should present to the dictator Neguib an agreed plan which represents far-reaching concessions on our part, sustained by Britain and the United States and by outstanding representatives thoroughly soaked in the Middle East problem. This would, I am sure, give the best chance of making a tolerable arrangement for MEDO without a renewal of Anglo-Egyptian strife. Let me repeat that if all fails the United States would in no circumstances be involved in military operations.

I shall be most grateful if you will let me know what you think of these ideas.

Cabinet: conclusions
(Cabinet papers, 128/26)

19 February 1953
Secret
11.30 a.m.
Cabinet Meeting No. 13 of 1953

[. . .]
7. The Cabinet had before them a memorandum by the Lord Chancellor (C(53)62) on the question whether special legislation was required to authorise the changes proposed in the form of the Coronation Oath.[1]

The Prime Minister said that he was impressed by the legal and constitutional arguments set out in this memorandum. Those who were advocating the passage of special legislation on this subject had evidently failed to appreciate the change in the constitutional position which had been brought about by the enactment of the Statute of Westminster. Legislation by the Parliament at Westminster would not now suffice; and it was clear that, in the time now remaining before the Coronation, it would not be possible to arrange for each member State of the Commonwealth to pass legislation sanctioning the changes to be made in the form of the Oath. The Government could base themselves upon this practical consideration, whatever constitutional arguments might be deployed in any public controversy on this question. A Parliamentary Question on this point would have to be answered in the House of Commons in the course of the following week; and, while the oral answer might be brief, he thought it would be advisable to publish in the Official Report a reasoned statement of the legal and constitutional considerations which the Government had taken into account in reaching their decision.

Sailors, 1917–22. Counsellor, US Embassy, Tokyo, 1923; Berlin, 1925. Minister to El Salvador, 1926; to Colombia, 1928. US Ambassador to Cuba, 1934; to Brazil, 1937; to France, 1944–9; to Egypt, 1949–55. Married, 1937, Gertrude McCarthy.

[1] The proposed changes added Pakistan and Ceylon to, and removed Northern Ireland and India from, the list of governed Possessions and Territories.

In discussion there was general support for the views expressed by the Prime Minister.

The Cabinet –

(1) Agreed that no special legislation should be introduced to authorise the changes proposed in the form of the Coronation Oath.

(2) Invited the Lord Chancellor, in consultation with the Home Secretary and the Commonwealth Secretary, to prepare a statement of the legal and constitutional considerations on which this decision was based in a form suitable for publication in the Official Report.

The Cabinet had before them a note by the Commonwealth Secretary (C(53)68) covering a draft of the message which would have to be sent to other Commonwealth Governments if the Coronation Committee of the Privy Council should wish to proceed further with the suggestion that the Speaker of the House of Commons should do homage to Her Majesty in the Coronation ceremony.

In discussion it was pointed out that this suggestion, like that for the introduction at Westminster of legislation authorising changes in the form of the Coronation Oath, paid insufficient regard to the independent position of the other member States of the Commonwealth. The Coronation ceremony was to a considerable extent a Church of England Service and its special emphasis on English institutions could be defended so long as its traditional character remained unaltered. But once innovations were suggested, equal regard would have to be paid to the position of the other independent member States of the Commonwealth, and no new procedures affecting them could properly be introduced except with the agreement of all Commonwealth Governments. This particular suggestion should have been put forward, not to the Coronation Committee, but to the Coronation Commission on which the other Commonwealth Governments were represented.

The Cabinet –

(3) Took note that the Lord Chancellor would seek to ensure that the Coronation Committee would proceed no further with the suggestion that the Speaker of the House of Commons should do homage to Her Majesty in the Coronation ceremony.

The Cabinet had before them a memorandum by the Foreign Secretary (C(53)61) setting out his recommendations regarding the order of precedence to be observed among the representatives of foreign Powers at the Coronation.

The Cabinet –

(4) Subject to the point noted above, approved the order of precedence suggested in C(53)61 for the representatives of foreign powers at the Coronation; and invited the Foreign Secretary to advise the Lord Chamberlain accordingly.

[. . .]

Winston S. Churchill to President Dwight D. Eisenhower
('The Churchill Eisenhower Correspondence', page 27)

20 February 1953

I sent you yesterday by air an important letter about Egypt.[1] I was so glad to hear today that your Government endorse the agreement we reached with your predecessors in January. I shall be very grateful for an early answer.

Anthony Eden to Winston S. Churchill
(Premier papers, 11/432)

20 February 1953
PM/53/9

You enquired about American intentions as to the repudiation of secret wartime agreements.

2. The Republicans said in their election platform that they would repudiate all secret commitments 'aimed at Communist enslavement'. The attached extract from the President's State of the Union Message was evidently meant to fulfil this pledge. It is very widely drawn and could cover many things (e.g. Sakhalin, the Kuriles, Manchuria, Polish frontier, Konigsberg, Germany). Dulles's somewhat conflicting comments during his visit to Europe did little to clarify what was meant. It is now clear that the Administration, whatever they may earlier have had in mind, do not intend to repudiate any particular agreement, but to propose a general resolution in Congress which will purport to fulfil their election promise with the minimum of embarrassing consequences.

3. HM Ambassador has been shown the draft. It condemns Soviet domination of other peoples against their will, rejects 'unjustified applications and interpretations of international agreements' and asserts the right of all peoples to life, liberty and the pursuit of happiness. Both the President and Dulles have indicated in their press conferences this week that their aim is to make clear, in a general but dramatic way, America's disapproval of enslavement and their desire that the 'captive peoples' should be liberated. In putting forward a resolution of their own, the Administration are trying to keep control of Congress, where a number of much more specific proposals have been brewing. It remains to be seen whether this attempt will succeed.

4. Dulles has told the Press that, since no agreements are to be repudiated, no other Governments are affected. Congress may of course get out of hand. Similarly, the Administration may later feel emboldened to denounce specific commitments. But there seems no reason to expect that we shall be pressed to take action ourselves, and indeed I have told the House that we should not follow suit.

[1] Reproduced above (pp. 847–8), dated Feb. 18.

EXTRACT FROM PRESIDENT EISENHOWER'S STATE OF THE UNION MESSAGE

'Our policy, dedicated to making the free world secure, will envision all peaceful methods and devices – except breaking faith with our friends. We shall never acquiesce in the enslavement of any people in order to purchase fancied gain for ourselves. I shall ask the Congress at a later date to join in an appropriate resolution making clear that this Government recognises no kind of commitment contained in secret understandings of the past with foreign governments which permit this kind of enslavement.'

Winston S. Churchill to Anthony Eden
(Premier papers, 11/392)

20 February 1953

I thought we were agreed that it would be best to maintain silence and let Neguib make his demands. These then could be confronted with the Anglo-American proposals which if they could be made jointly and with the theme we have planned, might put him in a grave fix. Now you are warning him not to put forward demands which we cannot accept. This is the reverse of what I thought should be our course. This military Dictator is under the impression he has only to kick us to make us run. I would like him to kick us and show him that we did not run.

I like paragraph 2 but not 1 and 3.[1] Unless you can show that we have imposed our will upon Neguib you will find it very difficult to convince the Conservative Party that the evacuation of the Suez Canal Zone conforms with British interests or British prestige.

James Thomas to Winston S. Churchill
(Premier papers, 11/355)

21 February 1953

The difficulty I envisage over your suggestion[2] that the Government should charter a liner for guests who would pay a substantial amount for the privilege of being present at the Naval Review is that no steamship company would willingly charter a ship to the Government for a profit-making scheme: it would prefer to handle the business itself. The Ministry of Transport experienced

---

[1] Para. 1 expressed the hope that the Egyptian Government would not demand the evacuation of British forces. Para. 2 stated that while the British accepted the principle of evacuation they did not intend to evacuate on terms that the Egyptian government was likely to accept. Para. 3 stated that the British must discourage any Egyptian attempts to demand an evacuation of British forces.
[2] Of Feb. 9, reproduced above (p. 838).

considerable difficulty in finding shipping companies prepared to let us have any liners for Government guests, because such charters would deprive them of profitable opportunities for the use of their accommodation.

2. Even if a liner were available for the purpose we should have to decide who should be a free guest and who should be a paying guest. Admittedly, anyone who may be accommodated in HM Ships will have to pay something towards the journey to and from Portsmouth but it will be a trivial sum compared with the cost of a place in a liner. It would, therefore, be most embarrassing to have to suggest that some should pay a large sum while others were accommodated free or at a more or less nominal cost.

3. Another invidious distinction would be that the ship carrying paying guests would be moored in the line and would thus not enjoy the privilege of the Government guest ships of following the Royal Yacht through the lines:[1] there could be no question of including in the royal cavalcade a vessel in which the accommodation had been let on a more or less commercial basis.

4. I have consulted the Treasury and the Ministry of Transport. They agree with this reply.

5. I hope you will agree on reflection that this plan should not be pursued.[2]

Winston S. Churchill to Anthony Eden
Prime Minister's Personal Minute M.23/53
(Premier papers, 11/432)

22 February 1953

Your minute PM/53/9.[3]

I do not think that you and I should be compelled to linger under this vague but implied censure of having made agreements involving enslavement, etc. The facts of what happened at Yalta should be disclosed, namely that the arrangements were made between the President and Stalin direct. We were only informed of them at our parting luncheon, when all had been already agreed, and we had no part in making them. But it is true that we did not wish to separate ourselves from our two Allies at that moment when great battles impended on the Western Front and no conclusion could be foreseen to the war with Japan. I am told that Stettinius[4] revealed in his book that he

[1] Churchill wrote in the margin: 'No'.
[2] Churchill minuted Thomas on Feb. 24: 'As you make such heavy weather about it the idea must be dropped' (M.26/53).
[3] Reproduced above (pp. 852–3).
[4] Edward Reilly Stettinius, Jr, 1900–49. Born in Chicago. Married, 1926, Virginia Gordon Wallace: three children. Chairman, Finance Committee, US Steel, 1934; of the Board, 1938. Chairman, War Resources Board, 1939. Chairman, National Defense Advisory Commission, 1940. Director, Priorities Board and Priorities Div., Office of Production Management, 1941. Supervised Lend-Lease programme. Special Assistant to the President, 1941–3. Under-Secretary of State, 1943–4. Secretary

himself had not been consulted, although he was Secretary of State. Your people might look up what is said. As head of the British delegation I am not prepared to leave the matter where it is. You will remember that Dulles, at my luncheon, said he would have no objection to our stating the facts.

Winston S. Churchill to President Dwight D. Eisenhower
('The Churchill Eisenhower Correspondence', page 27)

22 February 1953

I am sending you the text of a statement* about Field Marshal Slim which we propose to issue tomorrow or on Tuesday a few hours after the Australian Government have announced that his assumption of office as Governor-General is temporarily postponed. It has been necessary for the Australians and ourselves to take this course as Slim was due to sail for Australia on Tuesday.

We have not, of course, referred in any way to your participation, for which we so greatly hope.

* The proposed statement announced a request by the British to the Australian government for Slim to be permitted to postpone his assumption of office in order to participate in the negotiations with the Egyptian government.

Winston S. Churchill to President Dwight D. Eisenhower
('The Churchill Eisenhower Correspondence', pages 27-8)

23 February 1953

At Menzies' request I have agreed to defer British announcement sent with my message of 22nd February until we have your reply. Meanwhile publicity is being confined to a general statement that Slim is postponing his departure for Australia in order to be available to us for consultations about the Middle East.

Amended text follows. Timing has been very difficult owing to Slim having to disembark his baggage today which must give rise to speculation. Also I did not know about George Washington's Birthday, for which I send my sincere apologies.*

* George Washington's birthday, February 22, was a public holiday in the United States.

---

of State, Dec. 1944 to 1945. Accompanied Roosevelt to Yalta Conference, 1945. Led US delegation to San Francisco Conference, 1945. First US delegate to the UN, 1946. Published *Roosevelt and the Russians: The Yalta Conference* (1949).

Winston S. Churchill to James Thomas
Prime Minister's Personal Minute M.25/53
(Premier papers, 11/453)

23 February 1953

ADMIRAL OF THE FLEET THE KING OF GREECE[1]

How will it be for him to visit Portsmouth to have his Union flag hoisted with the appropriate ceremonies. He will be here for about a week. If you and your Board agree you might perhaps suggest it tomorrow at luncheon.

2. Thank you so much for your letter about the past, which I shall carefully preserve. It is a pity that Baldwin's biographer did not know about it.

Winston S. Churchill to Field Marshal Lord Alexander
Prime Minister's Personal Minute M.24/53
(Premier papers, 11/392)

23 February 1953
Top Secret

1. This paper seems to assume that the Egyptian forces are really effective fighting men. I am not convinced that this is so, or that the operation of obtaining the surrender of the 8000 men, including training units, should be so serious as is made out. The advantages of procuring this surrender by a comparatively bloodless action would be very great and might exercise a highly beneficial effect upon the situation in Cairo. At any rate these cautious forecasts should not prevent alternative plans being prepared for rounding up the Eastern detachment.

2. It seems to me an unreal assumption that the Egyptian infantry division and 'the equivalent of one armoured brigade' (? devoid of modern tanks) are a danger. At any rate the Egyptians might be as shy of attacking a prepared front with inferior numbers and artillery as we seem to be about rounding up the 8000 Egyptians East of the Canal. I hope the first contacts will increase Egyptian timidity and reduce our own.

3. The paper does not make clear whether the dispositions and actions proposed for us are to be simultaneous with 'Rodeo' as modified. Surely this is fundamental? I should greatly prefer to see a purely defensive attitude towards the West, for which I am sure we have overwhelming strength, and a swift

---

[1] Paul of Greece, 1901–64. Born in Athens, third son of King Constantine I. Trained as naval officer; joined British Royal Naval Academy in Dartmouth. Entered Greek Royal Naval Academy, 1920. Crown Prince of Greece, 1922. Exiled with Royal Family, 1924. In exile, worked as an apprentice mechanic in Britain. Returned to Greece, 1935. Married, 1938, Princess Frederika of Hanover. King of Greece, 1947–64.

collection of the 8000 men to the East. How far are the Egyptian 8000 separated from the two brigades who are facing the Israelites, and what transport have they to move these two brigades swiftly to reinforce the 8000? I do not like the idea of beginning by bombarding the 8000 from ground and air. At any rate, it requires further consideration. There is something to be said for a bombardment which keeps the 8000 motionless and in hiding while armoured cars and a few tanks surround them effectively. This would give them a good excuse to surrender. To bombard from a motionless British front unable to advance looks like useless bloodshed.

4. Let me have the exact Field state of the Army in the Canal Zone. The figure of 80,000 has frequently been mentioned. I presume our whole army is equipped with rifles, whether the men are employed in combat formations or not. Let me know, in as much detail as possible, the division made in these forces, and whether there are any unarmed men.

5. Paragraph 4. The problem of guarding prisoners is one which should surely be discharged by the very large numbers of men not included in the mobile formations. No prisoners should be released either to the East or to the West of the Canal. As soon as violence is used upon us, good cages should be made. There must be any amount of room in the large area comprised within our lines. How many days' rations have our troops got? If there are insufficient food supplies, every effort should be made without delay to increase them. If the prisoners became a burden they, or some of them, could surely be moved to Aden? I do not contemplate more than 30,000 prisoners.

6. I should be very glad to discuss these points with you. I did not much like the document.

Anthony Eden to Winston S. Churchill
(Premier papers, 11/373)

23 February 1953
Secret
PM/53/11

JOINT MILITARY PLANNING WITH THE GERMAN AUTHORITIES

Military preparations for the defence of Western Europe have suffered from the postponement of the entry into force of the Bonn Conventions and of the European Defence Community Treaty. General Ridgway (Saceur) is anxious to make all possible arrangements in advance, so that, when the Treaties are eventually ratified, they may be put into effect without further delays. He has now arranged that his subordinate commanders in Germany should open discussions with the Blank Office (the shadow German Ministry of Defence) for the deployment of the future German contingent to the European Defence Forces.

2. We must be careful not to give the impression that we are carrying out any of the provisions of the European Defence Community Treaty in advance, as this might jeopardize ratification in France. But there are the following strong reasons for agreeing to Saceur's present request:
 (i) present Western defence plans are based upon the raising of German troops and we must save as much time as possible by planning in advance;
 (ii) advance German military planning has already gone a long way and it is desirable to associate ourselves with it in order to find out what is going on and to influence developments in good time;
 (iii) the Americans agree to Saceur's request, and the French, who have recently shown some initiative in pressing for preparations in Germany, also favour it, provided they are satisfied that it will not become public and make difficulties for them at home.
3. The Chiefs of Staff and the Minister of Defence see no objection to the proposed discussions with the Germans. The British Commanders in Chief have therefore been authorized to take part in them, on condition that the Allied High Commission also participates, so that proper political control can be retained. I have just heard that the SHAPE delegation arrived in Bonn earlier than had been expected and that the talks were to begin on the 19th February.[1]

Cabinet: conclusions
(*Cabinet papers, 128/26*)

24 February 1953
Secret
11.30 a.m.
Cabinet Meeting No. 14 of 1953

[. . .]
2. The Foreign Secretary said that a good deal of damaging information had been obtained by the examination of the documents seized on the arrest of Werner Naumann[2] and his associates. There was evidence that members of this group had maintained contacts with Fascist sympathisers in other countries, and that one at least of their number had established contact with the Russians. It was hoped that the examination of the documents would shortly

---

[1] Churchill wrote at the bottom of the page: 'I like it all. Two if not three years have been lost through French nationalism.'

[2] Werner Naumann, 1909–82. Educated at University of Breslau, Poland. Joined Nazi Party, 1928. Chief, Propaganda Office, Breslau, 1937. Personal aide to Joseph Goebbels, 1938. Under-Secretary and Chief of the Minister's Office, Ministry of Public Enlightenment and Propaganda, 1942; State Secretary, 1944; Minister, 1945. Arrested by the British Army, 1953: charged with infiltrating West German political parties.

FEBRUARY 1953 859

have reached a point at which sufficient evidence could be made available to the German Federal Government to enable them, if they chose, to bring criminal charges against some of the members of the group.

Meanwhile, protests were being made in this country against the decision of the British authorities in Germany to withhold from Naumann facilities for private consultation with his legal adviser. This decision was being called in question by Sir Hartley Shawcross,[1] MP, in a letter published in *The Times* that morning, and by Lord Simon, in a Question which he was proposing to ask in the House of Lords that afternoon. This matter was in a sense *sub judice*, since both sides had appealed to higher legal authority against the decision of the British judge that Naumann should be allowed to see his legal adviser in the presence of the registrar of the court. It should be possible to avoid Parliamentary controversy over that aspect of the matter while that appeal was pending. For the rest it could be stated that Naumann was being held in custody merely for the purposes of interrogation; that there was no intention of holding him indefinitely for this purpose; and that, if any charges were preferred against him, he would be given full facilities for consultation with his legal adviser.

The Prime Minister said that every effort should be made to avoid Parliamentary controversy over this, especially as we hoped to be able in the near future to transfer to the German authorities the responsibility for dealing with these men.

The Cabinet –

Took note of these statements, and invited the Foreign Secretary to arrange that questions about the grant to Naumann of facilities for consultation with his legal adviser should be handled on the lines indicated in the Cabinets discussion.

[...]

6. The Colonial Secretary said that the Judicial Committee of the Privy Council had rejected the application of Lee Meng[2] for leave to appeal against the death sentence imposed upon her in Malaya. He had asked the British authorities in Malaya to ensure that the Ruler of Perak[3] was made aware of the strong arguments against exacting the death penalty in this case, and he hoped that it would be commuted to a sentence of imprisonment. Were the Cabinet agreeable that in this event we should accept the offer of the

[1] Hartley William Shawcross, 1902–2003. Called to the Bar, Gray's Inn, 1925. KC, 1939. Chief Prosecutor for UK at International Military Tribunal, Nuremberg, 1945–6. OBE, 1945. Knighted, 1945. MP (Lab.) for St Helens, 1945–58. Attorney-General, 1945–51. PC, 1946. Baron, 1959. Chairman, International Advisory Council, Morgan Guaranty Trust, 1967–74. GBE, 1974.
[2] Lee Meng, 1926–94. Also known as 'Lee Ten Tai'. Born in Guangzhou, China. Joined Communist Party, 1942. Arrested by British authorities, July 1952, for possession of hand grenade; sentenced to death, 1953. Sentence commuted to imprisonment. Released, 1964.
[3] Sultan Yussuf Izzuddin Shah Ibni Almarhum Sultan Abdul Jalil Karamatullah Nasiruddin Mukhataram Shah Radziallah, 1890–1963. Sultan of Perak, 1948–63.

Hungarian Government to exchange Mr Edgar Sanders[1] for Lee Meng and proceed with the necessary practical arrangements?

The Prime Minister said that he had grave doubts about the wisdom of proceeding with the proposed exchange. It must be assumed that it would be impossible to conceal the connexion between the two releases. The cases were not in any way comparable, and the whole transaction was likely to have the appearance of a somewhat disreputable deal with the Communists. Once we lent ourselves to these practices, it was difficult to know where they might lead. Communist Governments would certainly have no scruple in arresting other British subjects and holding them as hostages, if they thought that they might be able thereby to extract concessions from us. Were there not other means of applying pressure to the Hungarian Government with a view to securing Mr Sanders's release?

The Foreign Secretary said that strong commercial sanctions had already been applied, and it was doubtless these which had led the Hungarian Government to obtain the permission of the Soviet authorities to make their offer to exchange Mr Sanders. He doubted whether anything more could be done to persuade them to release Mr Sanders without some countervailing concession. He would, however, consider the matter further in the light of the views which the Prime Minister had expressed; and would see whether there was any different proposal which he could put to the Cabinet.

The Cabinet –

Agreed to resume their discussion of this matter at their next meeting.

[...]

Field Marshal Lord Alexander to Winston S. Churchill
(Premier papers, 11/392)

24 February 1953

Instructions have been sent to CIGS, who will be in Fayid tomorrow night, to discuss with the Commanders-in-Chief, Middle East, the points which you have raised in your Personal Minute M.24/53.[2] Immediately on his return, the Chiefs of Staff will submit a further note to you; and I suggest that then you might like to have a discussion with them.

2. In the meantime, I would like to say that the plans which were submitted to you were made to meet a rather different situation to that which you now envisage. They were designed to bring great pressure on the Egyptians and thus to make them see reason as rapidly as possible: but to avoid unnecessary conflict with the Egyptian forces, so as not to prejudice the chance of

---

[1] Edgar Sanders, 1906–?. Arrested by Hungarian authorities, Budapest, 1949; charged with espionage and sentenced to 13 years in prison. Pardoned, 1953.
[2] Reproduced above (pp. 856–7).

obtaining their subsequent co-operation in running the base. I do not think that the Commanders-in-Chief overestimate the fighting effectiveness of the Egyptian forces; indeed, I am sure that they are confident of being able to defeat them very rapidly, if they can be brought to action.[1]

President Dwight D. Eisenhower to Winston S. Churchill
(Premier papers, 11/704)

25 February 1953
Top Secret

I read your personal letters regarding Egypt with great interest and confess with some concern; however, as you know, we are in general accord with the agreed position arrived at during the January conference in London. I would rather not make final decision on the other matters you mention, such as military representation during Suez discussions, until Dulles and I have had an opportunity to discuss the entire problem with Eden, who I understand arrives next Wednesday.

As you know, I have highest regard for Slim and personally feel his participation in discussions will have good and stabilizing effect.

With warm regards, as ever, your old friend.

Winston S. Churchill to President Dwight D. Eisenhower
(Premier papers, 11/704)

25 February 1953
Personal and Confidential

1. I had a talk with Aldrich when he delivered your message this morning. The time factor is important to me and Menzies as Slim is needed in Australia by the end of April, but of course if you so prefer, the decision can await Eden's talks with you and Dulles.

2. I am sure you will consider my suggestion in relation to Ridgway's front now so advantageously extended to Turkey. All the Egyptian theatre lies behind Ridgway's right wing and if cast away might be a source of weakness to the whole position in Western Europe. The Canal of course is a lateral communication in the whole potential front which I believe you would wish to see sustained southward from the North Cape to Korea. Our British interest in the Canal is much reduced by the post-war changes in India, Burma, etc., and we got on all right round the Cape for a long time in the War. I cannot regard it as a major British interest justifying the indefinite maintenance of eighty

---

[1] On Feb. 27, Churchill wrote on this minute: 'I await the Report.'

thousand British troops at immense expense. There are lots of places where they could be used better or the money saved.

3. On the other hand we are not going to be knocked about with impunity and if we are attacked we shall use our concentrated strength to the full.

4. It seems to me that you might by standing with us in the approach to Neguib on the lines on which we have agreed bring about a peaceful solution in the truest harmony with the military and moral interests of the anti-Communist front. This is no question of British Imperialism or indeed of any national advantage to us, but only of the common cause. If an Anglo-American team, military and diplomatic, puts our agreed plan firmly to Neguib all may come well without bloodshed, and other blessings would flow from the success of this decisive accord. Please think of a potential regrouping of forces as a part of your bitter problem in Korea.

5. We were very pleased to see the line Ambassador Caffery has taken since your hand was on the tiller.

6. Please talk everything over with Anthony, including the atomic point I made to you. I hope that he can be shown the same kind of picture I was given at the Pentagon last year.

7. Every good wish,

Your much older friend.

Cabinet: conclusions
(Cabinet papers, 128/26)

26 February 1953
Secret
11 a.m.
Cabinet Meeting No. 15 of 1953

[. . .]

9. The Prime Minister said that he had now received from President Eisenhower a reply to the personal message which he had sent inviting his co-operation in the next stage of the defence negotiations with Egypt. President Eisenhower had reaffirmed his acceptance of the documents annexed to C(53)17 Revise as a basis for an Anglo-American approach to the Egyptian Government. But, on the suggestion that a military representative of the United States should be associated with Field Marshal Sir William Slim in the next stage of the negotiations in Cairo, he had said that he would prefer to reserve his final decision until he had had an opportunity for personal discussion with the Foreign Secretary during his forthcoming visit to Washington.

The Prime Minister read to the Cabinet the text of the reply which he had sent to this message.

The Cabinet –

Took note of this exchange of messages between the Prime Minister and President Eisenhower regarding the resumption of defence negotiations with the Egyptian Government.

[...]

12. The Prime Minister said that the Foreign Secretary and the Chancellor of the Exchequer were leaving that evening on their mission to Washington, where they would be broaching with the United States Administration the financial and economic plans which had been evolved at the Commonwealth Economic Conference. These discussions, though preliminary and informal, might well prove to be of crucial importance for the future prosperity, not of this country alone, but of the whole of the free world. He knew that his Cabinet colleagues would desire him to express on their behalf their good wishes to the Foreign Secretary and the Chancellor of the Exchequer for the success of their mission.

The Cabinet warmly endorsed the Prime Minister's statement.

John Colville to Winston S. Churchill
(Premier papers, 11/432)

27 February 1953

In connection with the Yalta Treaty, Sir William Strang has asked me to point out to you the following:

During the Presidential campaign quite strong language was used by the Republicans about the immorality of the Yalta Treaty and the responsibility of the Democrats and President Roosevelt in particular. By implication these charges might have been extended to you and the Coalition Government in this country.

However once the campaign was over, the President and Mr Dulles made obvious efforts to damp down these charges and the reference to the matter in the message on the State of the Union was moderate in tone. The resolution now proposed is still more moderate and it seems that the Republicans are trying to shift the emphasis from condemnation of the Russians for distorting the intentions of the Agreement. Moreover from Mr Dulles' statement before the Congress Foreign Affairs Committee yesterday (see attached extract from *The Times*) it looks as if the Republicans intend to use this matter as a platform for their new policy of 'Containment Plus'. This means barring the way to further Russian advances combined with an offensive based on propaganda and psychological warfare.

Strang feels it is possible that a statement by you in the House at this stage might embarrass Eisenhower personally if he is trying to water down the declarations on this matter which were made during the Presidential campaign. He does not want to suggest that you should not make a statement but would merely like you to be aware of what the Foreign Office think is the trend of Republican policy in this matter.

Winston S. Churchill to Dr William Hall[1]
(*Westminster College papers, M/1*)

28 February 1953

Dear Dr Hall,

Thank you for your letter of February 11, from which I am interested, and highly complimented, to know that you are setting aside a room in the new library building at Westminster College to bear my name, and to contain mementoes connected with myself.

I have the most vivid recollections of my visit to Westminster College and of all the kindness with which I was received there. I would much like to be able to do as you suggest and send you one of my paintings for the Churchill room. So many distinguished people and organizations make the same request to me, however, that I find I cannot accede to them. Were I to agree in one case I feel there would be no end to it. I am so sorry to disappoint you, but I hope you will excuse and understand me.

When the copy of *The Sinews of Peace* arrives I shall of course be glad to sign it for you.

Meanwhile I hope you will accept, as an addition to your collection, a photograph which I have signed and which I send with my good wishes to all at Westminster College.

Winston S. Churchill to Field Marshal Lord Alexander
Prime Minister's Personal Minute M.37/53
(*Premier papers, 11/377*)

28 February 1953

1. We had better have a talk about this at the next Defence Committee Meeting. I thought it was very silly to have a French officer in Command of the sea considering that outside the Mediterranean they have only a flotilla and a few cruisers. It is also questionable whether Juin should be Commander-in-Chief Europe. The French have done their best out of their fear of Germany to stop the creation of an effective front against Russia. Juin, though he is quite a good man, has made many verbal mistakes.

2. The word 'initially' is used a great deal in your minute. How long is it proposed that a Frenchman should Command the sea, land and air forces of

---

[1] William Webster Hall, 1884–1973. President of Westminster College, MO, 1948–54.

Central Europe? What are the parts of Europe in which the sea forces will be principally employed?

3. About the air. It may well be that by giving a nominal post of high dignity to an American Officer a British Commander will be able to have effective control. This has happened before. I share your confidence in Air Marshal Sir Basil Embry,[1] but see the line of attack mentioned in the *Daily Worker* today. This may be taken up by others.

---

[1] Basil Edward Embry, 1902–77. Joined RAF, 1921. DSO, 1938. Wg Cdr, 1938. Served in France and Norway, 1939. Bar to DSO and second bar to DSO, 1940. Shot down and captured by German Army in occupied France but escaped to England via Spain and Gibraltar, 1940. AOC RAF Wittering, 1940. Gp Capt., 1941. AVM, 1943. CB, 1945. DFC and third bar to DSO, 1945. Director-General of Training, 1945. KBE, 1945. Awarded Order of Dannebrog, Cdr 1st Class, by Danish Government, 1947. AOC-in-C, Fighter Command, 1949–53. KCB, 1953. C-in-C, Allied Forces Central Europe, 1953–6. GCB, 1956.

March 1953

Winston S. Churchill to Anthony Eden
Prime Minister's Personal Telegram T.27/53
(Premier papers, 11/554)

3 March 1953
Emergency
Confidential
No. 33

Cabinet discussed American complaints against British shipping and trading practices with China this morning.

2. It was agreed that you may speak on following lines to the President or Mr Dulles:

(a) <u>Trade</u> We already have very comprehensive list of goods whose export from this country and from the Colonies is banned. If it can be shown that there are goods of strategic importance to China not covered by existing list, we will certainly add them. But in that case we look to the Americans to support us in ensuring that other members of the Paris Group come into line. It is for other countries to match what we are doing already before we can fairly be asked to do more.

(b) <u>Shipping</u> There may have been a very few cases of strategic cargoes of non-British origin being carried to China among mixed cargoes in British ships. Extent of this has been grossly exaggerated. Nevertheless we shall take steps to prevent this happening in future. For this purpose we are prepared to institute voyage licensing forbidding British ships to carry specified goods, and we will join with the United States Government in persuading the other maritime powers to follow suit.

In practice, for working purposes, list of goods given to masters will have to be readily identifiable. Again, for practical reasons it may not be possible to apply voyage licensing system to small ships less than, say, 1,000 tons. United States Administration will

of course realise that these new measures cannot be fully effective without steps in some cases involving legislation being taken by certain Colonial Governments.
(c) Measures are in force to stop ships, whether friendly or Soviet bloc, carrying strategic cargoes for China being bunkered at British ports.
(d) Denial of bunkers at non-British ports (including Commonwealth ports) depends on cooperation not only of the oil companies themselves but of the local governments. This will therefore require consultation with governments concerned. We expect United States Government to join with us in making representation to foreign Governments. In the case of Commonwealth Governments (e.g. Ceylon and Pakistan) Her Majesty's Government will take initiative.
(e) <u>Stores</u> Apart from bunkers, non-British ships call at British ports for stores, minor repairs etc. As leading maritime nation we could not contemplate interfering with established merchant shipping customs. It may be possible by administrative means to impose inconveniences on non-British ships in transit through British ports if they are carrying strategic cargoes for China, but beyond this we cannot go. Unlike the oil trade, which is in the hands of a few companies, it is difficult to control miscellaneous supplies through small chandlers.
(f) <u>Hong Kong</u> As we understand it, American complaint is not that Hong Kong based or registered ships are carrying strategic goods to China but that they are being used for purposes of Chinese coastal cabotage trade in non-strategic commodities. System of voyage licensing which we are proposing to introduce for all United Kingdom and Colonial registered ships will go a long way to stop any loopholes which may exist in regard to strategic materials. About Hong Kong registered ships carrying non-strategic cargoes, it is, as we see it, an advantage rather than a disadvantage that they should remain on the British Register. In this way, unless they continue to operate in legitimate trades only, their owners and masters will be liable to prosecution and in extreme cases it would be within our power to requisition them. It should be noted that under the Merchant Shipping Acts there is no provision for striking ships off the British Register.

3. It is agreed that if you are tackled by the press on arrival you should say:
   (a) that Her Majesty's Government are fully supporting United Nations policy in regard to trade with China;
   (b) that we already have a very comprehensive list which ensures that no goods of strategic importance are exported to China from the United Kingdom or from British Colonies;

(c) existing measures to prevent bunkering of ships carrying strategic goods to China are being tightened;
(d) that we are always ready to deal with anomalies or loopholes as they arise or come to our notice;
(e) that these are matters which will no doubt be discussed with the Administration in Washington.

4. There has been some publicity about the Finnish tanker *Wiima* on charter to Soviet bloc which left Constanza for China with a cargo of kerosene (which could be used as jet fuel). She has for some days delayed at Singapore because master fears interference by Nationalists if he tries to go on. She has received no bunkers. We are encouraging the master's fears.

Winston S. Churchill: speech
(Hansard)

5 March 1953   House of Commons

DEFENCE

The Prime Minister: I am afraid that I cannot guarantee to conform to the shorter limits you mentioned, Mr Speaker, for I feel that the House must approach this debate in its proper setting and it is necessary for this purpose that I should recapitulate – I can do no more – the salient features of our post-war story. In the first years of peace, we reduced our Forces from the dizzy heights of war-time to a little over 700,000 men, and our military expenditure to under £700 million. In 1946 the Labour Government, with our full support, decided that we must continue National Service in peace-time. There was some hesitation originally as to the proper period of whole-time service, but by 1st January, 1949, when the Act came into operation, it had been fixed at 18 months.

In the early summer of 1948 came the coup d'état in Czechoslovakia, which made a profound impression on everyone's mind, and was followed by the attempted blockade of Berlin. This was broken by the airlift. There was great international tension. No major re-equipment programme was, however, put in hand, and we continued, to some extent, to live on our stocks; but in the summer of 1950 the wanton, no doubt, inspired, act of aggression by the North Koreans on South Korea occurred. As a result, under the authority of the United Nations organisation, most of the countries in the free world felt that they should shoulder the burden both of a major rearmament programme and the maintenance of much larger forces.

The right hon. Gentleman the Leader of the Opposition, in January, 1951, who had already increased the period of National Service to two years, announced the final plans of the late Government, which are now conveniently referred to as the £4,700 million three years' programme. This was a bold and a necessary act, and, to a great extent, still dominates our domestic position. Even if events have proved that it was over-optimistic – hastily thought out – that does not detract from the statesmanship and courage of the Measure.

We on this side of the House gave our prompt and unwearying support to the policy as a whole, even at a time of sharp political disagreement on minor matters. It was, of course, hoped in many quarters that, as a result of a three years' effort in many countries, above all in the United States, the forces of the free world, and among them our own, could be built up and re-equipped and that, thereafter, there would be a substantial drop in defence expenditure with consequential relief to our economy now so grievously overweighted by taxation.

The re-armament programme, like all others of its kind, was slow in getting into its stride. At this time last year it was concluded that by the end of the financial year, 1952, expenditure would have risen very steeply. It was in the light of the original delay and of the pent up and cumulative rise in the cost of the programme in its second year that we decided that it must be rolled forward and spread over at least a fourth year. We have now had the opportunity of beginning a more thorough review of the whole programme, both in strategic thought and in the light of our financial position. This was not possible, I think, to the same degree at an earlier period either in our tenure or that of those who preceded us.

What is called the cold war – which is not a legal term – continues. What we are faced with is not a violent jerk, but a prolonged pull. We must create forces which can play a real part as a deterrent against aggression and also can afford some measure of defence should war come.

I regret that we were not able to accept the Opposition's proposal to substitute the words 'takes note of' for the word 'approves' in the Motion which we are putting to the House. The circumstances differ in many respects from those of March, 1950. I shall not take up time in a debate when so many important subjects can be raised by arguing this matter of procedure in detail, although I have looked it all up. The reason for our decision is that there is today one outstanding point of principle at stake on which the Government are bound to make their position clear to our allies and others by vote as well as by words.

The maintenance of the system of two years National Service is, according to our judgment, vital to the security of our country and to the discharge of our obligations overseas. It is vital to our influence in the struggle of the United Nations to avert a general war and to the practical efficiency of our fighting Services, particularly the Army and the Air. I shall deal with some of these aspects in the course of my remarks. I wish to say now that we should regard a decision to reduce the two-year period at this critical but formative, grave but not unhopeful moment as a mistake and as a disaster of the first order. The brute fact that we had not the courage – we the Government – to express our convictions at this juncture would, in our opinion, be an act unworthy of the dignity of the Parliament we serve which could in no way be compensated for by an appearance of unity where, perhaps, it does not exist.

I do not quarrel with the terms of the Amendment which the Opposition have placed on the Order Paper. The first part recognises very clearly the policy of the Government and in no way evades responsibility for the decision of our predecessors to re-arm on the largest scale and at the utmost speed possible. About the terms and obligations of National Service we are following their example, so far as the period for which we are now seeking powers is concerned. The original Act covered five years and also provided for its extension, if necessary, by Order in Council. We are availing ourselves of this in proposing to extend its operation for another five years. The House will be asked later this year to pronounce a positive affirmation of this period.

That does not mean that the House is asked to commit itself to a prolongation of the two-year service during the whole of a five-year period. That must depend on the course of events, which, at the present moment, give no ground for expecting an early reduction. On the contrary, for the reasons I have mentioned, and to some of which I shall recur, this is a testing time for the free world, and any sign of weakening purpose would undermine what good has already been done by both parties at heavy cost to everyone. But the measures which we should in due course take in no way prevent the Government, this or any other, from reducing the two-year period at any time if they feel it can safely be done. And they can reduce it without legislation. It cannot be increased without legislation, but it can be reduced by an Order in Council at any moment this may be thought fitting by any Ministry which may bear the responsibility.

Where, then, is there the need for an annual affirmative Resolution? The procedure of the House provides ample and recurring opportunities of challenging the Government of the day upon this or any other clear-cut issue, and of bringing it to the test of debate and of Division. There is the debate on the Address; there are all the facilities which the House uses for debate and vote upon any Motion it may wish to discuss; there is the annual debate on defence; there are the Services' Estimates; and various other occasions. On any one of these the matter could be raised, threshed out, a Division could be taken, whether to terminate the two-year system or produce, in the words of the Opposition Amendment, an 'affirmative Resolution' in its favour. The issue remains continually in the hands of the House.

If we were to extend the period only year by year, as suggested, we believe that it would discourage our friends abroad and might well encourage the other ones. Above all, there would be uncertainty – uncertainty when so many aspects of daily life are affected – the daily life of great numbers of people is affected. Every year rumours, and the agitations following upon them, would spread: 'There is going to be a big reduction.' This would affect everyone who thought he was likely to be called up. Still more, it would make it difficult for the Service Departments to plan on a coherent and thrifty basis. For us at this stage – responsible Ministers – to shrink from definite approval of the two-year system would spread uncertainty throughout the Services, and would be, in our opinion, at the present time in no way justified by the international position. We must, therefore, persist in asking for the word 'approves'.

If I may make a brief diversion, I have thought for several years that it would be greatly to the advantage of France as well as ourselves to have a two-year period of military service. This would enable them to revive the strength of the French army in Europe and render possible their valiant efforts to maintain their Empire. When I mentioned this to French statesmen, while I was a private person, some months ago, they contended that they drew from their population a much larger proportion of men for service in the armed forces than we did, and that our exemptions for one reason or another made a selective cut in our intake which profoundly reduced our defensive effort. This is, in fact, not so. The only permanent deferments we make are for miners and seamen and certain agricultural labourers.

Mr Emrys Hughes (South Ayrshire): And clergymen.

The Prime Minister: In a typical age-group these amount to not more than 8 per cent of the total numbers registered for military service. About 30 per cent more are deferred after registration in order to complete apprenticeships or other training, but these are called to the Colours three or four years later, when their training is finished, and, it may be, their capacity to render service greatly improved.

I did not convince my French friends two years ago, nor did the right hon. Member for Easington (Mr Shinwell) when he said, just about a year ago, how strongly he had urged the French and the Benelux countries to adopt the two-year system. But there is no doubt in my mind that at the present time two years' service would produce for France – I hope that they will not mind my trespassing on their own affairs, but we have worked together for so many years that I think I may – as it does for Britain, much more efficient and convenient Forces to meet home and overseas commitments.

Mr Speaker, let us envisage – an unpleasant and overworked word which here, Sir, might find, I think, its proper place – the practical and physical effects of a reduction from 24 to 18 months. We estimate that on 1st April the active strength of our Forces will be about 880,000, of which about 310,000 will be National Service men. A reduction in the length of National Service by six months would mean that the National Service element in the Forces would be reduced by about 75,000. But this is the least part of the consequences.

The increase in the length of National Service has stimulated the new short-service Regular engagements introduced so advisedly in 1950 by the Air Ministry and in 1951 by the War Office. This is a very remarkable development. During 1952, nearly 70,000 men – 66,880 men to be exact – who would have been called up for National Service or who had actually commenced such service volunteered for the new three or four year short Regular engagement. The value of this is enormous. We get well-trained soldiers. We get a supply of non-commissioned and commissioned officers. We get strong cadres, frameworks, which make all the difference, or a great deal of difference, to whether troops fight well or badly should war come.

At the present time, the total Regular strength is about 540,000 men compared with 420,000 three years ago. I am talking of the Army. If the period of National Service were reduced we could not hope to continue to receive the improved numbers of volunteers for the Regular Army which we do at the present time. Over a period of three or four years, the total injury to the character and quality of our Forces, apart from numbers, would really be measureless. It astonishes me that the right hon. Gentleman the Member for Easington does not understand what was the best thing he ever did. I hope he will, and try to distinguish it from the worst thing he might possibly do.

Let me emphasise the effect on the Forces of cutting six months from the period of National Service. It is during the last six months of his service that a man becomes a well-trained soldier. Very likely he is an NCO or has gained a commission. I am told that a reduction from 24 to 18 months would strike from the Army over 10,000 corporals and lance-corporals and about 1,800 young officers who have come up from the ranks. Perhaps we may call them all the flower of our military youth. This ill-timed and ill-aimed stroke would not reduce the intake of the National Service men nor the number needing to be trained. There would be no saving in training overheads. The total number in the Army would be less. The proportion in the training establishments would be larger, and the general result undoubtedly inferior.

But look at the effects of such a change upon our overseas obligations at the present time, when all our divisions are abroad, spread about the world, many engaged in some form of warfare. To cut six months off National Service would reduce the period which National Service men could spend in Korea from 11 months to five, in Malaya, from 16 months to 10, and in the Middle East, from 19 months to 13. Thus, if we are to continue to discharge our present commitments – so far accepted by all parties and not directly relevant to our debate today – the use of National Service men in the most distant theatres would simply mean more movement and less result. Many thousands more men would be in the pipeline, doing no good to themselves or anybody else at either end in the meanwhile.

This waste of manpower would require the more extensive use of Regulars in the more distant theatres. This would have a deterrent effect on the voluntary extensions of service in the Regular Army, which I explained a few minutes ago, and which the party opposite have agreed and which has been so highly advantageous. The French are suffering from this acutely, but have not yet found a remedy.

I have dealt with the consequences to the British Army. The effect on the Royal Air Force would, in general, be very similar. However, I am strongly of the opinion that the members of non-flying personnel in the Royal Air Force must be the subject of continued scrutiny with a view to any saving which will not detract from efficiency

Another important feature in the White Paper is the addition of five years on the Reserve of the commitments of National Service men under the post-war conscription Acts of the late Government. This is indispensable if we are to have our vitally necessary Reserve kept at an adequate strength. Otherwise, the Z and G Reserve would slowly fade away. They are actually fading away.

Neither the new reservists who will already have completed their two years' service and their three-and-a-half years in the Territorial and other Forces, nor the Z and G Reservists who fought in the late war will be required to discharge any commitments except in periods of the gravest war emergency. They will have to let their Service Department know where they are and what they are doing in civil life, which is most important to any general mobilisation, but they will not be required for training. Not to take the step which we are now proposing would mean either the total lack of a Reserve or the imposition of further sacrifices upon the Z men. This would be most unfair. So far from adding to our claims upon the Z and G Reservists, we are now proposing to give them marked relief. Their loyal response to their recall by the late Government for refresher training in 1951 and by us in 1952 was most helpful to the country. We now have the good news for them that in the absence of any sudden darkening of the world scene we do not propose to call up any more for refresher training, and secondly, that after 45 we make no further call upon them.

When I came into office, 16 months ago, I was startled and concerned with the condition of home defence, especially against large-scale attacks by paratroops. I felt naked as I had not felt at any time in the recent war. We had moved, or it had been decided to move, all our divisions out of the island. I did not cancel these movements, and, therefore, I accept inherited responsibility. However, we took important measures. There were 250,000 men in uniform here who, at that time, were entirely absorbed in training or administrative duties of one kind or another. As I explained to the House, I considered it my first duty as Minister of Defence, as I then was, to impart a combative value to this large body of proud and capable youths and men.

Continuous progress has been made. Weapons and ammunition were issued. Motor cars were made available. Every man in uniform was made to feel that he had to fight to the death for the sake of his native land and the protection of his fellow-countrymen. Over 450 mobile columns have been formed, and plans have been made, and exercises conducted, at very small expense comparatively, to enable these columns to concentrate rapidly on any point where we should be subjected to an air descent.

Still, the fact remains that we have not got a single combatant division in this country. This is another aspect of what I said just now: our whole formed or regularly organised Army is abroad. This shows how great is the need to improve our fighting strength at home. No other country is voluntarily running the risks to which we have subjected ourselves. They are, however, I think, appreciably diminished by the measures we have taken.

There is another aspect which may be borne in mind, though I should be shy of dwelling too much upon it. The farther east, speaking of the European scene, the effective front line is drawn in Western Europe, the greater is our protection not only from paratroop attack but also from air bombing with all its measureless features, especially in the early days of a conflict.

However, it seems to me at the moment that one of the really vital processes of national survival is the development and expansion of the Home Guard. So far its growth has not been in any way adequate to our needs or our dangers. The Home Guard is an indispensable aid to the Territorial Army, because it helps in the defence of airfields and takes over vulnerable points and so forth in the hour of peril. Until an adequate Home Guard is in being and on a far stronger scale than we have so far attained, the Territorial Army, instead of preparing for rapid mobilisation, would be largely scattered over the country carrying out local defence.

The men who have joined the Home Guard are of first-class quality; but we need many more of them. There are 9,000 officers, but only 20,000 men who have as yet enrolled. This is not a quarter of what we need. Any man who is a Z reservist and under 45, although he has a Reserve liability, should write to the War Office. There are many reservists whose present occupation suggests that they would not be called up in war-time, but they might volunteer and play their part in the defence of hearth and home around where they are working and carrying out probably very skilled and specialised functions.

I make my appeal to all parties in the House to help in every way in encouraging enlistment in the Home Guard, not as a measure of panic or alarm but as a bringing into play of a new, effective and necessary element in our system of home defence.

I must now warn the House that I am going to make an unusual departure. I am going to make a Latin quotation. It is one which I hope will not offend the detachment of the old school tie and will not baffle or be taken as a slight upon the new spelling brigade. Perhaps I ought to say the 'new spelling squad', because it is an easier word. The quotation is, 'Arma virumque cano', which, for the benefit of our Winchester friends, I may translate as 'Arms and the men I sing.' That generally describes my theme.

Mr Hugh Gaitskell (Leeds, South): Should it not be 'man', the singular instead of the plural?

The Prime Minister: Little did I expect that I should receive assistance on a classical matter from such a quarter. I am using the word 'man' in a collective form which, I think, puts me right in grammar.

Let me now come to arms, about which I believe there is no classical dispute. Here let me again embark on some generalisations. Ever since we took office, the Government have been pursuing the twin but divergent objectives of financial solvency and military security. Solvency is valueless without security, and security is impossible to achieve without solvency. Whichever way one turns, one does not like the look of it. On the other hand, by the adjustments that we have made and the spreading out which was inevitable, we have tried to bring our military expenditure within the limits of what we can afford. I say 'tried' because, even after the adjustments have been made, it can be argued that we are still devoting a disproportionately large slice of the nation's economic effort to defence production.

Mr Harold Davies (Leek): Hear, hear.

The Prime Minister: We feel that very much indeed. Even in the absence of the Chancellor of the Exchequer, it does not pass from our minds. But I would face criticism on that score rather than lay ourselves open to the charge of not bearing our full share with our allies or, indeed, of failing to set an example to Europe in the defence of the free world. No one with knowledge of the facts of our economic situation could challenge our claim that the effort we are making on defence is the absolute maximum of which we are capable, and that any further substantial diversion of our resources from civil to military production would gravely imperil our economic foundations and, with them, our ability to continue with the rearmament programme. (Hon. Members: 'Hear hear'.) There are a frightful lot of things we are all agreed about.

Over and above our own rearmament, we are developing a substantial export trade in arms to other countries. Nearly all of this is in the form of what are called 'off-shore' purchases by the United States for NATO or purchases by the Commonwealth and Western European countries. Let me emphasise that these exports of arms are over and above not what we want, but the maximum expenditure which we are financially able to afford for the re-equipment of our own Forces. We should like to rearm some of our own formations more rapidly, but we do not withhold modern weapons from our own troops in order to sell them to other countries. In so far as there is retardation apart from technical delays, it is because we cannot afford to spend more on ourselves. This is a serious and unpleasant fact which I do not hesitate to state to the House.

There are, of course, on the other hand, solid compensating advantages even in the military sphere. The value of these exports adds not only to our balance of payments, but also to our military strength. In these times of rapid scientific progress when new and improved weapons are being constantly evolved, one of the most vital factors in the nation's preparedness for war is the possession of an adequate and flexible armament industry capable above all of speeding expansion.

By making arms for others in addition to those we make for ourselves, we are enabled to build up a war potential substantially greater than we could otherwise achieve. In the event of hostilities the existence of this extra war production capacity, fully equipped with machine tools and manned up with skilled and experienced labour, would provide us with an important armament reserve of inestimable value. In short, the sale of arms to other countries has three most valuable compensations. It increases our own war potential; it increases our export earnings; and seven-eighths of it, which goes to the Commonwealth and Europe adds to the military strength of the free world as a whole.

There is one field in our export of arms which should be more clearly illuminated this afternoon. I mean the furnishing of jet aircraft to Egypt, to the other Arab States and to Israel. All this is on a very small scale, and so far as it has been carried out it fulfils contracts entered into in the time of our predecessors when, no doubt, circumstances were somewhat different. Nevertheless, we must not forget that there was a war four years ago between Israel and the four Arab States, including Egypt if that is the correct description, and that a truce has been established on a somewhat precarious basis but that no peace has been made. We must, therefore, be very careful, even on the small scale on which we are supplying aircraft, not to alter in any appreciable way the balance between the sides. I can assure the House that this principle will be observed.

About the export of jet aircraft to Egypt, 43 were sent in the time of our predecessors and we have agreed while the negotiations about the future are in progress not to interrupt the supply. Four more have gone. I can assure the House that this addition to Egyptian air power makes no difference to our overwhelming air superiority in those regions. I wanted to deal with this matter this afternoon although it is a little outside the scope of the White Paper, but I felt that the House ought to understand very clearly the position which Her Majesty's Government takes up.

As a result of the Government's strategic review, the types and quantities of weapons and ammunition to be produced have been more precisely related to the kind of war or wars which we might have to fight in various parts of the world. This has enabled us to make considerable economies in many directions. To some extent these economies have reduced our overall defence expenditure and eased the strain upon the metal-using industries to which we look for the needed expansion in our export trade. To some extent, also, these economies have made it possible, while keeping within the limits of what we can afford, to re-direct money saved to the production of other more urgent or vital items of defence equipment.

The period of gestation required for the production of a complicated, modern weapon, as we all know, is a fairly long one. Even, therefore, in the case of weapons and aircraft already in production, the results of changes which we have decided upon do not in most cases affect the pattern of deliveries for about 12 months. In the case of weapons still in the development stage, the cycle is, of course, much longer. I can assure the House that within these limits of our economical and technical resources our material rearmament is making good headway.

As I stated a year ago, the production programme when we took over was a long way behind the forecasts of the late Government, whose estimates made in haste or, shall I say, in emergency consultations – I do not wish to be controversial – were necessarily, in many cases, unrealistic. I do not blame them for that. They tried their best. Defence production can be divided into three stages. The first stage is of research and development. Over most of this field work is proceeding well and results are extremely encouraging. The third and last stage is what is called flow production. In older days at the Ministry of Munitions it used to be called mass production, but flow production is probably the more accurate term. The flow production of weapons means those weapons whose design has been more or less finalised. The rate of deliveries of aircraft and equipment of this class is in most cases satisfactory and up to expectations.

Between the stage of development and the stage of flow production there is an intermediate stage in which, in order to save time, production has to be started notwithstanding the fact that the design is not fully settled. During this stage modifications in design have to be introduced both in the tooling-up period and even later in the period when production has already started. With the growing rapidity of new inventions and in consequence of the increasing rapidity of obsolescence, the practice of going into production off the drawing board, which still remains a risk, is becoming almost a normal procedure.

The time taken to cure defects which reveal themselves in the tests and trials of prototype aircraft and specialised military equipment varies greatly from case to case. It is not, therefore, possible to generalise about the progress in this intermediate stage. I can assure the House that we will seek tirelessly the correct solution of this ever-varying problem, and that we are very much aware of the importance, both of designing new weapons and of getting them as rapidly as possible into the hands of the troops. It is an issue which changes from month to month and it is not a new one. It has always been a question when we should go on producing in the regular way and when we should turn to experiment with something new. Never has this process been so rapid, so tense, giving such opportunities for making mistakes, as it is at the present time.

I am grateful to the House for the attention with which it has listened to me. I have confined my speech almost entirely to the limits of the White Paper and have not sought to sail out on to the sullen and unpredictable oceans of human destiny on which this modest document floats. The policy we are pursuing may claim, and ought, I think, to command, the loyal and friendly support of all parties, for all are deeply and gravely committed on all the broad principles involved. The more united is the decision of the House the better will it be for our country, provided that we are not led or lured away from plain, clear-cut expressions of our duty. That is the reason why I have moved the Motion.

President Dwight D. Eisenhower to Winston S. Churchill
('The Churchill Eisenhower Correspondence', pages 29–30)

5 March 1953

Dear Winston,

I have studied your recent telegram[1] and will discuss the whole subject with Anthony whom I hope to see this evening.* I am sure the conversations here with Foster Dulles and other members of this government will be mutually profitable.

*Anthony Eden visited Washington with R. A. Butler, March 4–7, 1953.

Anthony Eden to Winston S. Churchill
Prime Minister's Personal Telegram T.29/53
(Premier papers, 11/431)

5 March 1953
Immediate
Secret
No. 460

At my conversation with the President, Dulles was present for part of the time and the Ambassador throughout. Ike began with an affectionate reference to yourself and then plunged at once into a discussion on the Middle East. He was extremely worried about the position in Persia. He said that as a result of Henderson's intervention in favour of the Shah,[2] his position with Musaddiq had been much weakened and that there was a definite possibility that he might be given his passport. He seemed to feel that a rupture of relations between the United States and Persia would be intolerable and must be prevented at any price. He thought that in any case it might be necessary to recall Henderson and send another United States representative who was less compromised. He himself made the point that it would be undesirable to make any settlement with Persia which would undermine the agreements with

[1] Of Feb. 25, reproduced above (pp. 861–2).
[2] Mohammad Reza Pahlavi, 1919–80. Crown Prince of Iran, 1926. Married, 1939, Fawzia Faud (d. 1948); 1951, Soraya Esfandiary-Bakhtiary (d. 1958); 1959, Farah Diba. King of Iran, 1941–67. Crowned Imperial Majesty, Shah of Iran, 1967. Exiled, 1979.

other oil producing countries but recognising this he seemed ready to bring pressure to bear on the American oil companies and to go to considerable lengths to keep Musaddiq in power, since he regarded him as the only hope for the West in Persia. Dulles said that he was certain that Musaddiq would turn down the latest Anglo-American offer and the President remarked that in this event he would like to send to Persia a man in whom the Persians had confidence, with authority to make the best arrangement he could to get the oil flowing again. He had in mind Mr Alton Jones who was his personal friend and had his unreserved confidence. He said the American people would never be brought to understand the need to make sacrifices in the Middle East and that the consequences of an extension of Russian control of Persia, which he regarded as a distinct possibility, would either involve the loss of the Middle East oil supplies or the threat of another world war. I suggested that Russian control of Persia, if it were ever achieved, would not necessarily involve the control of other Middle East oil supplies and that they could not benefit from Persian oil resources but only deny them to the West where they were not needed any longer. The President said that his experts had told him that a pipeline could be built from Abadan to the Caucasus in a matter of a couple of years. I several times emphasised the effect on other countries of a bad agreement with Persia. While the President accepted this he seemed obsessed by the fear of a Communist Persia. Musaddiq has evidently again scared the Americans.

2. We then turned to Egypt. The President agreed with me that it was essential to maintain the base in Egypt and that if we were to evacuate the Canal Zone before making a Middle Eastern defence arrangement we should be exposing ourselves to Egyptian blackmail. In contrast to Dulles he was clear and firm on this point. I put it to him strongly that Egypt was the key to Middle East defence but that if we were to secure a satisfactory agreement we must act together. I pressed him repeatedly to send a military adviser to Cairo to work with Slim. He seemed finally to agree with this. His difficulty was to find a suitable officer. But he said that he would consider the possibility of sending General Hull[1] (the Deputy Chief of Staff and an entirely suitable man) accompanied by a personal message to Neguib stressing the importance which he attached to the setting up of an effective defence organisation in the Middle East and the securing of a base on the canal.

3. The President then turned to the problem of Israel and to his anxiety to bring about peace between Israel and the Arabs. He asked me whether I thought there was any hope of this before a defence arrangement was reached. I replied in the negative but added that if we could reach agreement with

---

[1] John Edwin Hull, 1895–1975. Asst CoS, War Dept General Staff, 1942–6. Director of Operations Div., War Dept, 1944–6. Commanding Gen., US Army Forces Pacific, 1946–8. Director, Weapons Systems Evaluation Group, Secretary of Defense, 1949–51. Deputy CoS for Administration, US Army, 1951. Vice-Chief of Staff, US Army, 1951–3. C-in-C, UN Forces Far East, 1953–5.

Egypt we should be better placed to use our influence for peace with Israel. He thought, however, that progress towards the Middle East defence organisation would have to be accompanied by assurances of support for Israel.

4. Towards the end of the conversation I expressed my anxiety to try to reach an agreed policy with him in the Middle East during this visit. The President thought that this would be possible and asked me to go over the ground with Dulles, preparatory to a further talk with him on Friday. I shall do this and shall hope to make progress. The prospects in regard to Egypt seem fairly hopeful but I foresee the greatest difficulty in regard to Persia.

5. The President could not have been more friendly and said that he wanted to have more than one further talk with me while I was here.

Defence Committee: minutes
(Cabinet papers, 131/13)

6 March 1953
Top Secret
11.30 a.m.
Defence Committee Meeting No. 4 of 1953

1. PROPOSED LOAN OF A DESTROYER TO PAKISTAN

The Committee considered a Memorandum by the First Lord of the Admiralty (D(53)13) proposing to meet a Pakistani request for a destroyer by offering them Her Majesty's Ship *Chivalrous* on loan for three years, subject to the ship being returnable on demand in the event of an emergency.

The First Lord of the Admiralty and the Commonwealth Secretary pointed out that the Indian Navy was considerably stronger than the Pakistani Navy and that it seemed desirable to redress this balance.

The Prime Minister said that in view of impending constitutional developments in Pakistan he would be most reluctant to make any unconditional gifts or loans of military equipment to Pakistan at the present time. Similarly, regarding the three frigates which were due shortly to be handed over to India, he thought that we should first obtain from the Indian Government a satisfactory assurance of their support in our negotiations with Nepal regarding the future recruitment of Gurkhas. He was prepared to accept any risk that Pakistan or India might turn to the United States for their military requirements.

The Chief of the Air Staff[1] said that the air base at Mauripur, near Karachi, was of great importance to us as a staging post. At present our rights at Mauripur were extended year by year only. It might be that we could make use of Pakistan's desire for a destroyer as a bargaining counter to improve our own positon at Mauripur.

[1] William Dickson.

The Committee —

Invited the First Lord of the Admiralty, in consultation with the Secretary of State for Air and the Commonwealth Secretary, to reconsider the proposals for lending naval vessels to India and to Pakistan, on the basis that no further loans should be made without some compensating concession such as Indian assistance in securing satisfactory arrangements for the future recruitment of Gurkhas and facilities from Pakistan for the continued use of Mauripur as a staging post for a period of years.

[. . .]

3. ACQUISITION OF A RUSSIAN MIG 15

The Chief of the Air Staff informed the Committee of developments which had taken place since the arrival in Bornholm of a Russian MIG 15 aircraft, which had been flown in by a Polish pilot who had sought asylum in Denmark. This aircraft was believed to be a MIG 15; it was virtually undamaged and was capable of being flown off again.

The British Air Attaché in Copenhagen[1] had flown at once to the spot and had already obtained some valuable information about the aircraft. Technical RAF experts were proceeding to Copenhagen in the hope that the aircraft would be detained and made available for detailed examination.

The following points were made in discussion:
  a) The Danish Government were showing some reluctance to allow experts to examine the aircraft. The Danes, in view of their exposed position, were anxious to avoid giving offence to the Soviet Union.
  b) There were, however, precedents for detaining stranded aircraft. For instance, the Russians had held a British Meteor for ten days and its pilot three weeks.

The Prime Minister stressed the importance of using our influence to facilitate technical examination of the aircraft by United States as well as British experts.

The Committee —

Invited the Minister of State to bring all possible pressure to bear on the Danish Government to enable full advantage to be taken of this opportunity of carrying out a thorough technical examination of the MIG 15 which had landed in Bornholm.

4. KENYA

The Chief of the Imperial General Staff said that he had recently returned from Kenya, where he had toured the whole of the troubled area. He had submitted a report (D(53)12) which, he understood, would be considered by Ministers in the following week at a meeting which the Colonial Secretary could attend.

---

[1] F. R. Jeffs.

His main conclusion was that, unless comprehensive measures were taken urgently to restore confidence, both to the British farmers and to the Kikuyu, the trouble would spread and we should be faced with a growing and costly commitment, as had happened in Malaya. On the other hand, if we were to send reinforcements without delay, it should be possible to restore security and confidence within a comparatively short time. He therefore recommended the very early despatch to Kenya of one Infantry Brigade Headquarters and two British Infantry Battalions, and also a small number of aircraft. These reinforcements could be provided from the United Kingdom; it would not be wise to find them from the Canal Zone at this juncture. He sought approval to make the preliminary arrangements, so that the men concerned could be inculcated and sent on embarkation leave without delay.

In discussion there was a general agreement with the proposal to send these reinforcements to Kenya.

The Commonwealth Secretary emphasised the good effect which this would have in Nyasaland and Northern Rhodesia, particularly in the context of Central African Federation.

The Prime Minister asked whether helicopters could not be used in Kenya. The Committee were informed that the few helicopters available were of a type unsuitable for operation at the considerable height of the Kenya plateau. Arrangements were, however, in hand to send to Kenya a few Harvard aircraft, to supplement the light aircraft which were already in use, and further transport aircraft could be provided from Aden. The Prime Minister stressed the importance of making a display of air power over the heads of the Mau Mau. The more often they saw an aircraft overhead, the more they would feel that all their movements were under observation.

The Committee –

1) Authorised the Secretary of State for War to proceed forthwith with the necessary arrangements to enable one Infantry Brigade Headquarters and two Infantry Battalions to leave the United Kingdom for Kenya as soon as possible. Movement should not commence until the confirmation of the Cabinet had been obtained early in the following week.

2) Agreed that, subject to confirmation by the Cabinet, arrangements should be made for the early despatch to Kenya of three Harvard aircraft from Rhodesia and further transport aircraft from Aden.

5. DEFENCE OF THE UNITED KINGDOM: RISK OF PARACHUTE ATTACK

In connection with the discussion recorded in the preceding Minute the Prime Minister suggested that a study should be made of the possibilities of parachute attack on this country and of the means of dealing with such an attack. Would it be practicable for a potential enemy, from existing bases, to drop something of the order of 20,000 parachutists in this country? What warning might we expect? At what points were parachutists most likely to be dropped? It might be assumed that, in order to get the benefit of surprise, the enemy might be ready to launch such an attack even in circumstances in which the troop-carrying aircraft could not make a safe return. This study should be made under three possible hypotheses: (i) a surprise attack without notice; (ii) an attack during the first three days of war; and (iii) an attack after the end of the first week of war.

The Committee –

Invited the Chiefs of Staff to arrange for a study to be made of the possibility of parachute attack on this country on the lines indicated in the discussion.

Winston S. Churchill to Anthony Eden
Prime Minister's Personal Telegram T.30/53
(Premier papers, 11/431)

6 March 1953

1. Many thanks for your telegrams. Of course I am eager for definite news about Egypt. Neguib has kept very quiet since the name of Slim was mentioned but every day's delay makes the Australian end more difficult. I don't know Hull but any sensible American military man would be acceptable. The great thing is that we make a joint approach with a quadruped delegation on the basis of Capital A[1] with no whittling away.

2. I thought it right to do the civil by Stalin[2] and no more. This was evidently your feeling.

3. All good wishes.

Anthony Eden to Winston S. Churchill
Prime Minister's Personal Telegram T.31/53
(Premier papers, 11/431)

6 March 1953
Priority
Secret
No. 475

We had a full discussion this morning with Mr Dulles and his advisers on European issues. This was on the whole the most encouraging exchange of views I have yet had with the new Administration. There is no important divergence anywhere in our European policies. The Americans feel considerable impatience with the French and are not prepared to make any more

[1] Probably an error for 'Case A'.
[2] Stalin died of a cerebral haemorrhage on 5 Mar. 1953.

piecemeal concessions. They clearly thought we had offered all we should, for the present at least. At the same time Mr Dulles did not exclude the possibility of an extension of the NATO period[1] if this was the only means of securing French ratification.[2] For the time being, however, the United States Government wish to leave the French to themselves, and to press for ratification of EDC agreements by all the other signatories. This seemed to me sensible tactics and I said so. Records of this discussion and on Trieste and other matters will follow.

2. The Far Eastern discussion went very well. The Americans were clearly gratified by our efforts to meet the problem of trade with Communist China, which aroused much public feeling here. We hope to include passages in our communiqué which will reassure their legitimate anxieties.

3. Tonight Dulles, Bedell-Smith and others came to dine at the Embassy and I had the opportunity for a long talk with Bedell-Smith. He was clearly preoccupied about Persia and the President's close friendship with Alton Jones. He said that he had done all he could to delay action by Alton Jones to send a number of technicians into Abadan to start up the lubricating plant. But the United States Government had no powers to restrain Alton Jones, and he did not know how to persuade the President to use his personal friendship with Alton Jones to hold him back any longer. I said that I understood that in fact the lubricating plant was already working at Abadan, and that all the Persians needed was a few spare parts. If this were true, it would be much less damaging if the Americans were to send, as quietly as might be, a few bits of machinery, than if American technicians were to arrive in Abadan. Our American friends must understand the use that would be made of the arrival of Americans in our refinery and the criticism which would be levelled both against them and against Her Majesty's Government, that Americans were working in stolen British property. I could not believe that for the sake of allowing a few technicians to travel to Abadan it was worth risking serious Anglo-American discord.

4. General Bedell-Smith agreed with all this, and said he had done his utmost to persuade the President but without avail. He thought that the only hope was that I should put the matter frankly to him tomorrow with all the emphasis I could command.

5. General Bedell-Smith then raised the question of Saudi Arabia and Buraimi. He said that he had had a very difficult time with Emir Feisal,[3] who has complained that he was under strong pressure from his father, who

---

[1] The reference is to the period of time before the envisaged replacement of international cooperation through NATO by EDC–American cooperation. In the event, France failed to ratify the EDC in Aug. 1954.

[2] Of the EDC agreements.

[3] Faisal bin Abdulaziz Al Saud, 1906–75. Son of King Ibn Saud, first monarch and founder of Saudi Arabia. Minister of Foreign Affairs, 1930–60, 1962–75. PM, 1954–60, 1962–75. King of Saudi Arabia, 1964–75.

had recited numerous British infringements of the Stand-Still Agreement. Bedell-Smith added that no doubt we had a similar list of complaints against Saudi Arabia. Moreover, after the unhappy consequences of American intervention in Persian affairs, he was most reluctant to give any advice about Buraimi. All the same could we not find some other term for the arbitration we had offered? That word seemed to be unacceptable to Ibn Saud. Could not we find some Arabic equivalent?

6. I said that I knew of none and that in any event our offer of arbitration was fair and all we could offer. In fact, it would be easy for us without any infringement of the Stand-Still Agreement to cut Buraimi off from outside supplies. I thought that this was what we ought to do. General Bedell-Smith would have heard of the attempted Saudi incursion many miles within British protected territory. We had dealt with this. General Bedell-Smith replied that the Saudis had been loud in their complaints about our military intervention, but he accepted that we were well within our rights. His attitude was that, while the Americans were supporting us loyally in our demand for arbitration, they were acutely embarrassed by the Saudi attitude and by the pressure which Ibn Saud is clearly exercising upon them by the threat to their oil supplies. This is Persia in reverse. We agreed that both in our conversations with Dulles and Bedell-Smith tomorrow, and later with the President, we must make a supreme effort to reach understanding on all these Middle Eastern problems which are in danger of wrecking Anglo-American understanding throughout this area.

Winston S. Churchill to Anthony Eden
Prime Minister's Personal Telegram T.32/53
(Premier papers, 11/431)

6 March 1953
Personal and Secret

I was most interested in your telegram No. 475. Egypt is our Number One and you might consider whether the President's special view about Alton Jones could not be met if we got a good arrangement about Neguib in return. Of course it would be better to have both but nobody can blame us about Persia. I like all you say about the French. The two year service went through quite easily.

All good luck.

Anthony Eden to Winston S. Churchill
Prime Minister's Personal Telegram T.33/53
(Premier papers, 11/431)

6 March 1953
Emergency
Dedip
Top Secret
No. 479

We had a long and at times difficult discussion this morning about Egypt, first with Dulles, Bedell Smith, Aldrich and others, and later with the President and those I have named. The Americans have two preoccupations. They feel some reluctance to enter these discussions from the very beginning, particularly if there is no clear invitation to them to do so. The President was emphatic that he could not gate-crash, and that there must be some form of invitation, he suggested from the Egyptians and later agreed from us both. On this preliminary problem the President eventually said that he would be satisfied with some indication that the British and Egyptian Governments would be ready to accept American participation. We agreed that there was a locus standi for this, in that the package proposals include MEDO and the re-equipment of the Egyptian Army, which would come mainly from American sources.

2. Much more difficult was the American reluctance to commit themselves in advance not in any circumstances to go beyond Case A. They repeatedly emphasised that they thought case A represented an American as well as a British interest, and that they would go all out with us to try to get it. Bedell Smith said that the American Chiefs of Staff greatly preferred A, and when I remarked that we could not accept a Persian type of negotiation again, both he and later the President said that we must not doubt their sincere determination to get A if by any means they could. If however A was unobtainable, they did not wish from the start to exclude B, and later to be told by us that they were pressing us to concessions we did not want to make.

3. As a result, I think the choice before us is clear. Either we can go ahead on our own with their good will, and Americans would have no objection to this course, but without American participation, limiting our discussions strictly to A, or we can get American participation in a real effort to obtain A, so long as we do not specifically exclude modifications to it in the direction of B.

4. My immediately following telegram sets out the best arrangement I can persuade the President and Dulles to accept. I am quite sure that we cannot get American participation in this negotiation on any other terms. The President is fully alive to the importance of having a base available in Egypt in time of war. For that reason he wants to get as near as he can to A, because we can then be certain that the base would be immediately available.

5. If we can accept this proposal, the President has promised that General

Hull, Deputy Chief of Staff, would be available for at least six weeks, and will be ready to begin work on Monday. I do not know him, but in the Ambassador's judgment and that of Bedell Smith, there is no better choice. It would clearly be of great advantage to us to have so high-ranking an American officer in the negotiations.

6. My own judgment is that on balance we should be infinitely better placed with full American participation from the start on these terms than in attempting to negotiate by ourselves on the side-lines. The Americans are as alive to the urgency of opening the negotiations as we are.

7. If you are with me that to negotiate in these conditions is much better than to attempt the task alone, I must clinch the matter before I leave Washington. I am seeing the President again on Monday morning at 10 o'clock Washington time, and can, I believe, finally dispose of the whole business then if I can have your assent.

8. The President made two other points in the course of this discussion. First, while his administration agree in principle with the MEDO plan, they do not wish to be committed to the details of the organisation which we worked out with the previous administration, pending further study. I accepted this, but said that it was urgent that any amendments should be agreed rapidly, since our negotiators would need to know what the MEDO proposals were early in their talks with Neguib.

9. Secondly, both the President and Dulles spoke of the importance of getting peace between Israel and the Arab States. I promised them our full cooperation in such an endeavour, and suggested that the timing of such a move might well be after our joint negotiations with Egypt had made some progress. The Americans agreed that it might then be possible to open the idea with Neguib.

10. The President said that while he was committed to the supply of arms to Egypt, he did not wish to finance an Egypt/Israel arms race. He said that he thought that it would be necessary to give some assurances to the Israelis. Perhaps a reaffirmation of the 1950 Tripartite Agreement would be sufficient for this purpose.

11. As regards the best tactics for securing Egyptian assent to American participation in the early stages of the talks, which are on the basis of the Anglo-Egyptian treaty, I should be grateful for Sir R. Stevenson's advice by Monday morning.

Anthony Eden to Winston S. Churchill
Prime Minister's Personal Telegram T.36/53
(Premier papers, 11/431)

7 March 1953
Immediate
Top Secret
No. 487

When we turned to subject of Persia Dulles said that Henderson had asked at last moment for publication of statement to be once more postponed until the situation in Tehran clarified. Dulles made it quite clear that if present offer was not accepted by Persians negotiation for a general oil settlement should be put on one side. There would then remain the problem of dealing with Persia and trying to keep her economy just alive. The Americans suggested this should be done by allowing marginal dealings in oil and by reactivating the lubricating plants at Abadan, using for this purpose American technicians.

2. I argued that if the Americans were convinced that Persia must be given some help to prevent her going Communist, it would be far better to do this discreetly by direct financial help rather than by encouraging small sales of oil or starting up the lubricating plant with American commercial or technical assistance. The latter would be admittedly a gesture. It seemed to me impossible to have American technicians in Abadan without the fact becoming known and the publicity might be very damaging to Anglo-American relations. Even small sales of oil would break the common front on this issue and endanger our joint agreements in other oil-producing countries. Mr Aldrich said emphatically that the major American oil companies were unanimously opposed to Jones' proposal to send technicians. It emerged in the course of discussion that Jones would no longer be keen on sending these technicians if he had not given his word to Musaddiq to do so, and that even as it was he would do whatever the President asked him to do. It was left that Bedell-Smith would see Alton Jones next week. Mr Dulles later said that in his opinion it was not worth the risk of upsetting Anglo-United States relations. He had told Bedell Smith to discourage Jones and subsequently authorised Aldrich to do the same. So, although we were not given a positive assurance, my impression is that the technicians will not go.

3. Apart from the Jones affair, which all admitted was of minor importance, the President once more voiced his deep concern over the general Persian position. He repeated that he could not tolerate a situation in which the American Mission was turned out completely and that we must all try to think out some imaginative way of making some new approach to the Persian problem which would prevent the country being taken into the Soviet orbit.

4. The President kept repeating that we could not do nothing. I said that

I thought it unlikely that Musaddiq would link himself up with the West, but he was equally reluctant to join the East. He wanted to stay in the middle. This had been Persian policy for two thousand years and I saw no reason to suppose that it would change now. Dulles said that he thought it was difficult to draw up a precise course of action and that we should have 'to play it by ear'. I think he accepts the position that the wisest course would be for the Americans to keep Musaddiq going by dribbling out cash grants, if he rejects the oil settlement.

5. The difficulty of this situation remains that the Americans are perpetually eager to do something. The President repeated this several times. I reminded him that in response to American pressure we had modified our terms over and over again for a Persian settlement. For my part, I had many times felt in the last two years, that if we could just stay put for a while, the chances of settlement would be improved.[1]

Winston S. Churchill to Anthony Eden
Prime Minister's Personal Telegram T.38/53
(Premier papers, 11/431)

7 March 1953
Immediate
Top Secret, Private and Personal
No. 1077

Your telegram No. 479.[2]

The Americans propose first not that we should both jointly address Neguib, but that we should ask him for an invitation to them. Secondly, in effect, should this be forthcoming, they will work with him to beat us down from A to B and so on. We could certainly not do worse than this by going into the business on our own, I trust with their proffered goodwill. After our earnest interchanges with them they could hardly do less than this.

2. In the circumstances I am sure we had better go on alone and be grateful for any help they may give us. We have all the force, all the risks to run, all the concessions to offer, all the blame to take in British public opinion. I had thought they would come along with us and, without involving themselves in any commitment or expense, help us in our modest demand on which they and their predecessors had already agreed. It was for this reason that I made my appeal to Eisenhower. If we cannot be united in a definite demand on the Egyptian dictator, there can obviously be no joint action, but only resolute British action within the limits already agreed.

3. A further telegram follows giving in full views agreed with Alexander,

[1] Churchill telegraphed back: 'I like all you say, especially the last sentence' (T.37/53).
[2] T.33/53, reproduced above (pp. 886–7).

Slim, Swinton, Selwyn Lloyd and Strang. Surely we have not yet got Eisenhower's last word.

Winston S. Churchill to Anthony Eden
Prime Minister's Personal Telegram T.39/53
(Premier papers, 11/431)

7 March 1953
Immediate
Top Secret and Personal
No. 1078

My immediately preceding telegram.
The following was the considered opinion of the meeting.

1. We cannot accept less than A with possibly some latitude on actual numbers.

2. Rather than accept less we would prefer to negotiate alone.

3. Slim would be unwilling to undertake negotiations on other terms. His independent appreciation is contained in my immediately following telegram.

4. All we are asking for under A is the minimum which the United States rightly insist on in any base they use anywhere in the world.

5. Case B is impossible. Under B British officers and men would be employed in Egyptian installations under Egyptian command and control. Neither the United States nor we have been subjected to this in Europe.

6. If we cannot get A the whole plan is not worth while and falls to the ground.

7. Lord Alexander felt sure that the President, himself a soldier, would appreciate the validity of all this and would himself refuse to take less where American military interests were concerned.

8. We cannot believe that your telegram is the President's last word. We sincerely trust there will be a joint approach on the above conditions and that there will be no punctilio about waiting for an invitation from Egypt. Endless time affecting Australia would be wasted over this. See also Stevenson's telegram No. 430 with which we entirely agree.

9. If we can act firmly together on these lines we are confident we can settle the Egyptian question and go far to securing all the Middle East.

Winston S. Churchill to Anthony Eden
Prime Minister's Personal Telegram T.40/53
(Premier papers, 11/431)

7 March 1953
Immediate
Top Secret and Personal
No. 1079

My immediately preceding telegrams.

Field Marshal Slim's view with which I agree is that the minimum requirement to enable a base in Egypt to function is that, while the area would be under Egyptian Command, the actual depots, installations and stores must be under British command and control. This would be completely analogous to the position of United States bases in the United Kingdom or other foreign countries (including Saudi Arabia) and to our base in Belgium. Our attitude can surely be explained to the Americans by asking them what would be their reaction to a proposal that the British should take over command and technical control of their bases in the United Kingdom. They might also be asked if they would be prepared to see their important post-strike air base with all its valuable stores at Abusueir handed over to Egyptian control.

2. Under case A there would still be ample opportunity for handing over to the Egyptians certain of the depots and installations, or parts of them.

3. In Field Marshal Slim's view, if the Americans will not agree to negotiate on the principle of our keeping command and technical control of our own depots, he would rather not have American direct participation in negotiations.

4. If a joint approach were eventually found possible the Field Marshal says how glad he would be to work with General Hull whom he knows well.

Winston S. Churchill to Anthony Eden
Prime Minister's Personal Telegram T.42/53
(Premier papers, 11/431)

8 March 1953

My telegrams 1077, 1078, 1079.

However matters shape themselves in Egypt, we must reserve the right to remove the valuable stores which are not fixtures. We really cannot afford to throw away such large sums of money.

2. The following approximate figures have been given to me:

Army
   Movable   ... £210 millions
   Fixed   ... £200 to £300 millions

RAF
    Movable   ... £60 to £65 millions
    Fixed   ... £25 millions
    Navy   ... Negligible

Anthony Eden to Winston S. Churchill
Prime Minister's Personal Telegram T.43/53
(Premier papers, 11/431)

8 March 1953
Emergency
Dedip
Top Secret
No. 511

Your telegrams Nos. 1077, 1078, 1079.

Dulles left for New York at lunchtime yesterday so I asked General Bedell Smith to come to see me this morning.

2. We went over the whole ground again when I explained your anxieties and gave him Field Marshal Slim's view on minimum requirements. I also gave him your view as set out in paragraph five of your telegram 1078 and Alex's also. General Bedell Smith, whose attitude was most understanding and helpful throughout, said at once that the Americans had not been keen to enter into this negotiation at the outset. Indeed, there had been considerable discussion about this, both on receipt of your telegram to the President and since I had been here. It had been largely as a result of strong pressure by General Bedell Smith and others, who believed that best results could only be obtained by a joint Anglo-American approach, that the Americans had been willing to make the offer of General Hull's services.

3. We then got down to a discussion of objectives. Bedell Smith was emphatic that the Americans wanted, and would do everything in their power to obtain, Case A as set out in your paper. General Hull was the best choice they could possibly have made of a negotiator and Bedell Smith had already been over the whole ground carefully with him.

4. We then took up second sentence of paragraph eight in Case B. Bedell Smith thought that it should be perfectly practicable for the stores and heavy workshops to be kept in a standby condition in Egyptian hands with the assistance of Allied supervisory and technical staff. Bedell Smith recognized that communications would be a serious problem. But we would be keeping some of our own personnel in the base area and this would surely be one of their chief tasks. He would have thought it quite possible to have a system of joint inspection in order to make sure that the workshops and installations were

kept in reasonable repair. Equally, guards would have to be employed to make sure that vital components were taken care of.

5. General Bedell Smith quite understood that there might be certain depots and installations which must be kept under our control while others passed to Egyptian control. It was impossible for us here to determine the relative scale of this, but it was just the kind of thing which could be readily determined by men of the standing of Field Marshal Slim and General Hull, working together on the spot.

6. But Bedell Smith's position was essentially this. We would both work hard for Case A. The implications of Case B were declared to be in the document that it should be possible to reactivate the base within sixty days. From his own experience the experts often over-estimated how long such an operation took. For instance, they were told it would take thirty days to build the first two track railway bridges over the Rhine. Actually it had taken eleven days and a few hours. It might be that if we could not get Case A in its entirety we could get an arrangement which would be materially better than Case B and which would result in its being possible to reactivate the base within a much shorter time. Moreover, even if the whole base could not be reactivated at once, some part of it could probably be brought into working order, from the beginning. Therefore, there were in fact quite a number of varying possibilities between Case A and Case B. These Field Marshal Slim and General Hull would be able to assess on the spot.

7. I have no doubt that General Bedell Smith and the President and all concerned are really anxious to help us in these negotiations. It is all the more important to bring them along when we bear in mind that in Congress and elsewhere are powerful forces who want the United States to pursue an independent policy in the Middle East. I am myself absolutely convinced that a joint Anglo-American approach with the Americans in at the beginning, in the spirit in which General Bedell Smith and General Hull want to help, gives us far and away the best chance of getting a satisfactory result. If we attempt to go ahead without them, the Americans will be on the side lines and the Egyptians will be appealing to them just the same. We should not have the help of General Hull on the spot, nor would the Americans be committed to a negotiation. In those circumstances the chance of getting Case A would surely be negligible.

8. General Bedell Smith said that he would brief General Hull in the sense that he should not agree to a settlement which would not (repeat not) allow the reactivation of the base in war at very short notice. Thus we should have the best prospect, on the basis now proposed for United States participation, of obtaining in effect what we require. It would not, however, be possible, according to Bedell Smith, to get any amendment of the terms of reference.

9. I urge therefore that I may be authorized to go ahead and close with the President tomorrow on this basis.

Winston S. Churchill to Anthony Eden
Prime Minister's Personal Telegram T.46/53
(Premier papers, 11/431)

9 March 1953
No. 1091

You cannot clinch on the basis of your long telegram. If you have to see the President tomorrow at ten a.m. Washington time, please hand him the following personal and private telegram from me.

Begins.

My dear Friend,

We are neither unable nor afraid to deal with Neguib alone. We ask nothing from you in men or money. If you feel morally justified in coming with us on Case A it may save our being attacked with resultant bloodshed but we are not asking favours of any kind. We hope that we can go forward together as comrades and allies, it being understood that we ask no physical contribution. If this is impossible we do not wish that you should be mediators. In no circumstances will HMG abandon the United Nations crusade in Korea. We must ask ourselves the question, do we want to work for a costly indefinite stalemate both in the Middle East and the Far East? Cannot we help each other to reach conclusions agreeable to world peace at both ends.

2. If on consideration you do not feel you can go in with us now in Egypt we had much better do the best we can ourselves hoping for and counting on your good will. Ends.

I should be glad if as background you would show the President the three telegrams Nos. 1077, 1078 and 1079, which so far, I gather, have only reached him indirectly.

Winston S. Churchill to Anthony Eden
Prime Minister's Personal Telegram T.47/53
(Premier papers, 11/431)

9 March 1953
Immediate
Secret
Personal and Private
No. 1092

I am so sorry for all your worries and troubles but we have them here too. I would gladly have flown out but I did not want to get in your way. I wish you all success.

2. The Trinity House will be ready for you on your return. Clemmie and I send our love to Clarissa.

Anthony Eden to Winston S. Churchill
Prime Minister's Personal Telegram T.48/53
(Premier papers, 11/431)

9 March 1953
Emergency
Top Secret
No. 518

I am much distressed by your telegram No. 1091 and hope that you will be able to consider matter further before our ten a.m. meeting Washington time.

I am convinced that the Americans are sincere in believing that we take too literally classification of Case A and Case B and that there are number of variants between them, which could meet our essential needs.

We can assume that no modification of Case A can be made to which two Generals do not agree. I will seek assurance on this basis tomorrow.

If I can get this I would urge most strongly that we proceed on Anglo-American basis. I gravely fear the consequences of failure to act together on Anglo-American relations, not only in Middle East but in wider spheres. Our failure to agree will inevitably become apparent and public.

In view of this I must ask that you and my colleagues will further consider whether you cannot approve the line I suggest.

Winston S. Churchill to Anthony Eden
Prime Minister's Personal Telegram T.50/53
(Premier papers, 11/431)

9 March 1953
Emergency
Top Secret
No. 1095

Your telegram No. 518.

I see great danger in the Americans coming with us without our having agreed with them beforehand. This would give them virtually sole power at the Conference. If they differ from us on some decisive point the negotiations would break, with America and Neguib on one side in opinion at least and we, with all the risks and burdens, alone on the other. This would be much worse than their watching with good will from outside.

2. I have never considered Case A as being intrinsically perfect. It represents a halting point at the end of our long retreat.

3. In your No. 518 you say 'We can assume that no modification of Case A could be made to which the two Generals to do not agree. I will seek assurance on this basis tomorrow.' If you can get this assurance it will alter the picture. We should be freed from the feeling that there is no point where the Americans and we will ever make a stand together in the negotiations.

4. I suggest you make this request at your meeting with the President at 10.0 a.m. today, Monday, Washington time. When I hear from you that you have got this assurance I will support the proposal. I am calling a Cabinet for this evening.

5. I still think you might find it helpful to show Ike my personal message to him contained in my telegram No. 1091, but do what you think best.

Anthony Eden to Winston S. Churchill
Prime Minister's Personal Telegram T.51/53
(Premier papers, 11/431)

9 March 1953
Emergency
Top Secret
No. 523

Your telegram No. 1095.

I had a good talk with the President on Egypt. He spoke very fully about the necessity of having workable base in Egypt. He wants to get a base which is workable in peacetime (case A) and will strive for this. If we cannot get it, then we must have a base which can be reactivated as soon as possible after the outbreak of war and in no event in less than two months. In the second case he spoke firmly of the necessity of keeping certain installations and depots under British technical supervision and control. But our two soldiers in his opinion should be allowed to judge the technical conditions which are necessary to achieve this objective, and he thinks that they should have latitude to make modifications in the optimum plan which they both agree. Reference to plan B in the terms of reference to Slim and Hull should be so interpreted.

2. I read to the President the 'package' proposals contained in Foreign Office telegram No. 1100 and he thought they were good, but in paragraph A he would speak of the 'earliest possible' rather than the 'immediate' reactivation of the base on the understanding recorded in the preceding paragraph of this telegram.

3. I can assure you that both the President and Bedell Smith are perfectly clear about the issues involved and on what is required for an operational base in Egypt.

4. The President said he would send a personal message to Neguib by General Hull who has already begun work setting out his position and interest in these defence negotiations.

5. This telegram deals only with the immediate points. I had one and a half hours with the President and further records follow.

Anthony Eden to Winston S. Churchill
Prime Minister's Personal Telegram T.53/53
(Premier papers, 11/431)

9 March 1953
Emergency
Top Secret
No. 524

My telegram No. 523 was read out by Her Majesty's Ambassador to General Bedell Smith on the conclusion of our meetings this morning. He agreed that this accurately set out the position we had reached. If, as I devoutly hope, these arrangements are acceptable, the next step is the joint approach by the two Ambassadors to the Egyptian Government of which Caffery has already been warned (see my telegram No. 495).

2. I am leaving for New York in an hour, and you will no doubt send the necessary instructions to Her Majesty's Ambassador Cairo repeating to Washington, so that this joint step can be taken as soon as possible.

3. Hull is ready to start the moment the Ambassadors give the all clear, will fly direct to Cairo by special aircraft.

4. Americans at one time suggested that conversations should start without waiting for Hull's arrival. I deprecated this because of my mistrust of Caffery

which they understand and, while acutely conscious of the time factor, they have agreed to wait for Hull.

Anthony Eden to Winston S. Churchill
Prime Minister's Personal Telegram T.54/53
(Premier papers, 11/431)

9 March 1953
Emergency
Top Secret
No. 529

My telegram No. 523.
Additional Points on Egypt in Discussion with President.
The President emphasized that we must leave enough men to exercise sufficient control of the installations in the base, but he thought the figures in Case A might be a little high.
2. While the President showed a desire for generally improved relations with the Arabs, he is alive to the opportunity that successful negotiations with Egypt may afford for a settlement with Israel. Peace between Arabs and Jews ranks high among American desiderata.
3. Bedell Smith said that he had been in close touch with the Israelis recently. The Israeli military incursions into Jordan had made a deplorable impression in Washington and he had made the strongest representations to the Israel Government both about this and the transfer of the capital to Jerusalem. He thought the first had had some effect, but was less confident about the second.

Anthony Eden to Winston S. Churchill
Prime Minister's Personal Telegram T.55/53
(Premier papers, 11/431)

9 March 1953
Priority
Secret
No. 532

The President showed considerable concern about the future of Japan. He said he did not see how she could live economically without some trade with China. From this arose a discussion of such questions as the barter between Ceylon and China over rice and rubber. I assured him that our ships would not carry that rubber but I pointed out that there was a close relation between Ceylon's need for rice and Japan's need for trade. The President made it clear that in his mind some arrangement must be found by which Japan could trade with China in commodities which would give the communists the least strategic advantage.

2. I said that this was generally our position in regard to trade with China. The President distinguished the United Kingdom from Japan on the ground that we were not dependent for our livelihood on trade with China while Japan was. I said that while this might be true of the United Kingdom it was not true of Hong Kong. He accepted this. I also pointed out that whatever might be said about the Ceylon deal it would at least ensure additional supplies of rice in South East Asia, and that this was the first defence in that area against Communism. The President assented. He remarked that one of the mistakes which had been made in the Philippines was that they had neglected to increase their rice supplies. I said that the crop was not profitable enough and we both agreed that efforts must be made to increase it wherever we could in South East Asia.

Cabinet: conclusions
(Cabinet papers, 128/26)

9 March 1953 Prime Minister's Room
Secret House of Commons
10 p.m.
Cabinet Meeting No. 17 of 1953

The Cabinet had before them a number of telegrams from the Foreign Secretary reporting the results of his discussions with President Eisenhower on the suggestion that the next stage of the defence negotiations with the Egyptian Government should be undertaken in Cairo by an Anglo-American team comprising military as well as diplomatic representatives of the two Governments.

The United States Administration were prepared to support the proposals outlined in the documents annexed to C(53)17 Revise as a basis for the next stage of the negotiations, but they had at first been reluctant to participate directly in the negotiations. As a result of the Prime Minister's personal message to the President, and the conversations which the Foreign Secretary had held in Washington, the Administration had been brought to agree that a joint Anglo-American approach offered the best prospect of success; and the President had promised that General Hull, Deputy Chief of Staff of the United States Army, would be made available at short notice to join the United States Ambassador in Cairo in the negotiations. Difficulties had then arisen over the conditions on which we should insist regarding the maintenance in peace of the military base in the Canal Zone. While the Americans agreed that we should do our utmost to persuade the Egyptians to accept the conditions laid down in Case 'A' in the papers annexed to C(53)17 Revise, they were reluctant to commit themselves in advance to the view that nothing less than Case 'A' could be accepted. If it were found that the Egyptians could not be persuaded to accept this, they did not wish to exclude from the outset consideration of Case 'B' or of some compromise lying somewhere between the two. The Prime Minister had feared that the position of the British negotiators would be seriously weakened if the American attitude on this point remained uncertain. If there were any risk that the Americans would not support us on some condition regarding the maintenance of the base which we thought essential for our future security, it would be better that we should enter upon the negotiations alone. He had conveyed his anxieties to the Foreign Secretary in a series of messages despatched during the two previous days, and had urged the Foreign Secretary to press for satisfactory assurances on this point in his final interview with the President which had taken place earlier that day.

The Cabinet now had before them a telegram from the Foreign Secretary (Washington telegram No. 523 of 9th March) giving a preliminary report on this interview. This showed that President Eisenhower fully shared our anxiety to secure Egyptian acceptance of the conditions set out in Case 'A', and that his representatives would be instructed to do their utmost to secure agreement on the acceptance of those conditions. If, however, this attempt should fail, he recognized that the alternative arrangements must be such that we could resume the use of the base as soon as possible after the outbreak of war, and that for this purpose we should insist on the need for keeping certain of the installations and depots under British technical supervision and control. He also agreed that no modification of the conditions under Case 'A' should be made unless they were acceptable to both the British and the American military representatives in the negotiations.

In discussions the following points were made:
    (a)   Field Marshal Sir William Slim said that in his view there was some scope for minor concessions under Case 'A', so long as there was no infringement of the principle that the essential depots and installations should remain under British command.

    It was agreed that, before opening their discussions with the Egyptians, the British and American negotiators should first agree upon the minimum conditions regarding the maintenance of the base which should in no circumstance be compromised. Field Marshal Slim undertook to draw up a note of these in consultation with the Minister of Defence.

    (b)   It would be wise to remind the United States Government once again that the five main proposals outlined in C(53)17 Revise were to be treated in the negotiations as an interdependent whole. There could be no question of our agreeing to withdraw British troops from the Canal Zone unless the Egyptians accepted the other proposals.

MARCH 1953   901

(c) The Government would face political difficulties in defending to their supporters any agreement involving the withdrawal of British troops from Egypt before the expiration of the Anglo-Egyptian Treaty in 1956. But those difficulties would be greatly reduced if the withdrawal could be presented as part of a general Middle East settlement carrying the full support of the United States Government. The fact that we had acted in concert with the Americans would also be a great help in justifying an agreement to Australia and other Commonwealth countries.

The Prime Minister, summing up the discussion, said that his anxieties had been relieved by the assurances which the Foreign Secretary had been able to obtain in his final interview with President Eisenhower. He was specially glad to know that the President appreciated the need for keeping the vital depots and installations in the base under British supervision and command. If this point were stressed, if the Americans were reminded that the five proposals were to be treated as interdependent parts of a single settlement, and if it was clearly understood that no modification of the conditions in Case 'A' would be made without the concurrence of both the British and American military representatives, the Foreign Secretary could, he thought, be authorized to make final arrangements for a joint Anglo-American approach to the Egyptian Government on the basis which he had discussed with the President.

The Cabinet endorsed the Prime Minister's view.

The Cabinet –

(1) Approved the terms of a telegram (subsequently despatched as Foreign Office telegram to New York No. 153 of 9th March) informing the Foreign Secretary that, on the understandings to which the Prime Minister had referred, the Cabinet agreed in principle that a joint Anglo-American approach should now be made to the Egyptian Government on the basis which he had discussed with President Eisenhower.

(2) Invited the Commonwealth Secretary to inform the Prime Minister of Australia of the outcome of the discussions which the Foreign Secretary had held in Washington regarding the suggestion that an American military officer should be associated with Field Marshal Sir William Slim in the next stage of the defence negotiations with Egypt.

(3) Authorised the Commonwealth Secretary to inform the Governments of all the older Commonwealth countries of the basis on which a joint Anglo-American attempt was now to be made to secure a comprehensive defence settlement with Egypt.

Winston S. Churchill to Anthony Eden
Prime Minister's Personal Telegram T.56/53
(Premier papers, 11/431)

9 March 1953
Immediate
Dedip
Top Secret and Personal
No. 153

Thank you for your No. 523.
Cabinet considered this tonight.
We were particularly glad to hear that the President understood the need for keeping vital depots and installations under British technical supervision and control, which we assume to mean British command.
We await your further report of your talks with the President. Meanwhile we agree in principle that we and the Americans should go ahead on the basis of the package proposals which you have agreed with the President and on the understanding that no modification of Case A can be made to which the two Generals do not agree.

Anthony Eden to Winston S. Churchill
Prime Minister's Personal Telegram T.57/53
(Premier papers, 11/431)

9 March 1953
Priority
Top Secret
No. 531

My telegram No. 523.
The tenor of my long discussion with the President, at which Her Majesty's Ambassador and Bedell Smith were present, could not have been more friendly or more satisfactory. At the same time the President clearly had it in mind that we ought to trust him in the general handling of his policy and not ask for detailed assurances on specific points. He made it quite plain that he regarded Britain as his principal ally and that Canada ranked next. He had every intention of working along with us both on all the issues of the day.
2. The President said that of course he felt the American constitutional system was the best in the world (this with a smile) at the same time British ministers had certain advantages in the control of their legislature which the President of the United States did not possess. We would know the limits of his own powers in relation to Congress. He had always to bear this in mind. While therefore he could not give us specific undertakings he could not conceive

of any circumstances except one of extreme emergency when he would not consult us. He then referred to the particular case of Korea. He did not carry in his head the precise conditions on which the United States had command of the United Nations forces, but it was quite clear to him that before any new step of a major character was taken in Korea, whether a military operation or otherwise, there must be consultation.

3. A lot of this comment arose from our discussion about the use of the atomic bomb. The President said that in his opinion the idea that the atomic weapon was of a totally different character from other weapons was 'out-moded thought', particularly now that the United States had so many of them. He said for instance, 'I suppose you would want me to consult you before I dropped a block buster anyway'. He therefore deprecated attempts to deal with it in isolation. In view of his constitutional position, he thought it would be 'treasonous' on his part to give a binding assurance to us that he would consult us in all circumstances about the use of the atomic weapon. But it would also be 'treasonous' if he were not to consult with his two strongest allies on these grave matters if the time factor in any way permitted. No doubt we would adopt the same attitude in regard to the use of our atomic weapon. He realised very well the exposed position that the United Kingdom was in. He preferred to think, not in terms of specific undertakings in isolated matters, but rather in terms of constant consultation with us as world conditions deteriorated. I replied that we did clearly distinguish between an immediate retaliation in the face of an attack by atomic bombs and consultation before their premeditated use. The President accepted this and added that he hoped we did not think that he was reckless or that his administration was composed of irresponsible people.

Anthony Eden to Winston S. Churchill
Prime Minister's Personal Telegram T.60/53
(Premier papers, 11/431)

10 March 1953 New York

Emergency
Dedip
Top Secret
No. 127

Your telegram No. 153.

Understanding between us and the Americans is contained in my telegram No. 523. There is nothing I can do to that, and no interpretation I can give to it.

2. If my telegram No. 523 is acceptable to the Cabinet, I hope there will be

no further delay in so informing Washington. Her Majesty's Ambassador tells me that the Americans are awaiting Her Majesty's Government's acceptance of the proposals set out in my telegram No. 523 before instructing Caffery to join in the approach to the Egyptians.

3. General Hull is ready to start, and of course cannot do so until the Ambassadors have cleared the ground.

Winston S. Churchill to Anthony Eden
Prime Minister's Personal Telegram T.61/53
(Premier papers, 11/431)

11 March 1953
Immediate
Top Secret
No. 170

Your telegram No. 127. Our telegram No. 153 expressed Cabinet outlook and was not intended to delay action. As you will see we sent Stevenson No. 510 which is an all-clear. This remains the position and Makins should so inform the Americans.

2. But see No. 438 from Stevenson, paragraph 2. I understood that Hull would be the opposite number of Slim who will head our delegation. It now appears he is only to be 'a military adviser' to Caffery. Stevenson most loyally points out that this does not seem in harmony with the last five lines of paragraph 1 of your Washington 523. I hope you can put this right with Dulles, Bedell or the President before you leave. In any case Slim will be the leader of our delegation and in view of the agreement we have reached about the accord of the two military members it would surely be odd for Hull not to be on the same level as Slim.

3. I agree with you that all this is urgent. I was hoping to get Slim away Sunday at latest, thus we might have a talk *à trois* before-hand Saturday afternoon.

4. For your information I will send you (later) a note which Slim wrote after yesterday's Cabinet. (See my second immediately following telegram.)

5. See also the Foreign Office draft of a communiqué which is being sent you. Let me know what you think of it.

6. Cabinet accepted your and Rab's view about Japan trade which though orthodox will be unpopular. No reduction in estimates for adult education and we agreed to jump the fence as Rab wishes on sugar. Have telegraphed this to Rab.

7. Looking forward to your return. Hope you are not working too hard and that you have received my personal message and that all is well with your party.

8. Let me know whether you showed Ike my Personal to him about Egypt contained in my telegram No. 1091.

9. Please see my following Personal telegram to the President and if you agree send it on. (Contained in my immediately following telegram.)

Winston S. Churchill to President Dwight D. Eisenhower
Prime Minister's Personal Telegram T.62/53
(Premier papers, 11/422)

11 March 1953
Immediate
Dedip
Top Secret
Personal and Private
No. 171

I am sure that everyone will want to know whether you still contemplate a meeting with the Soviets. I remember our talk at Bernie's when you told me I was welcome to meet Stalin if I thought fit and that you intended to offer to do so. I understand this as meaning that you did not want us to go together, but now there is no more Stalin I wonder whether this makes any difference to your view about separate approaches to the new regime or whether there is a possibility of collective action. When I know how you feel now that the personalities are altered I can make up my own mind on what to advise the Cabinet.

2. I have the feeling that we might both of us together or separately be called to account if no attempt was made to turn over a leaf so that a new page would be started with something more coherent on it than a series of casual and dangerous incidents at the many points of contact between the two divisions of the world. I cannot doubt you are thinking deeply of this which holds the first place in my thoughts. I do not think I met Malenkov[1] but Anthony and I have done a lot of business with Molotov.[2]

3. I am so glad to have reached an agreement about joint negotiations in Egypt. Kindest regards.

---

[1] Georgy Maksimilianovich Malenkov, 1902–88. Enlisted in Red Army, 1919. Joined Communist Party, 1920. Staff Position on Organizational Bureau (Ogburo), Central Committee of the Soviet Communist Party, 1924–39; full member, Ogburo, 1939–52. Head of Communist Party Cadres Directorate, 1939. Candidate member, Politburo, 1941–6; full member, 1946–57. Chairman, Council of Ministers, 1953–5. Failed in attempt to overthrow Khrushchev, 1961: expelled from Communist Party and exiled.

[2] Vyacheslav Mikhailovich Molotov, 1890–1986. Joined Bolsheviks, 1906. Educated at St Petersburg Polytechnic. Secretary, Central Committee of Ukrainian Bolshevik Party, 1920–1. Responsible Secretary, Russian Bolshevik Party, 1921–2. Full Member, Ogburo, 1921–30. Full Member, Secretariat, 1921–30. Candidate Member, Politburo, 1921–6. Full Member, Presidium, 1926–57. Chairman, Council of the People's Commissars, 1930–41. Minister of Foreign Affairs, 1939–49, 1953–6. First Deputy Chairman, Council of Ministers of the Soviet Union, 1942–57.

Sir Gladwyn Jebb to Anthony Eden
(Premier papers, 11/422)

12 March 1953
Personal and Top Secret
No. 162

Your telegram No. 16.

Dulles asked me to call this evening and gave me a copy of the reply which the President is sending through the United States Embassy in London to the Prime Minister's message[1] in your telegram No. 17. The text is contained in my immediately following telegram.

2. Dulles asked me to let you have the following additional comments. The President had already been giving thought over the weekend to the problem posed by the Prime Minister and he also wanted to find some way to start a new page. But he was not at all clear as to how he should go about it. Proposal to call a Four Power meeting had been considered and rejected. The President and Dulles felt that the new Soviet regime would not be ready for such a move and were therefore likely to follow the same line as the previous one. Dulles believed that there were two notes from the West still unanswered and he felt that some weeks might be spent arguing over an agenda. In the meantime the plans for Europe would become unsettled and no progress would be made, for example with EDC, since the European countries would be waiting for something to come out of the meeting. As there was no real ground for expecting that anything would in fact come out of it, the President had turned down the idea of suggesting a meeting.

3. He was now pondering the possibility of issuing a statement in simple language to the effect that he stood ready to work for a better world, to avoid the diversion of resources to non-productive purposes; and to raise the standard of living everywhere. The general object would be to express the hope that the post Stalin era would be better than its predecessor. Nobody on the American side had a very clear idea of what to say or how to say it, and various people were now trying their hands at drafts.

4. All Dulles could tell me positively was that the President was thinking along the lines that it would be desirable to say something of this kind either to the press or in some more formal statement. If you had any ideas or suggestions to contribute Dulles would be very grateful.

5. I thanked Dulles very much for this information which I said I would communicate to you immediately. I expressed the personal view that it all sounded very sensible.

6. I am leaving it to you to repeat this telegram to the Foreign Office.

[1] Reproduced immediately above.

President Dwight D. Eisenhower to Winston S. Churchill
(*Premier papers, 11/1074*)

12 March 1953
Top Secret

Dear Winston,

The subject raised in your message of today[1] has been engaging our attention here for some days. We are convinced that a move giving to the world some promise of hope, which will have the virtues of simplicity and persuasiveness, should be made quickly. A number of ideas have been advanced, but none of them has been completely acceptable.

At our meeting in New York I by no means meant to reject the possibility that the leaders of the West might sometime have to make some collective move if we are to achieve progress in lessening the world's tensions.

However, even now I tend to doubt the wisdom of a formal multilateral meeting since this would give our opponent the same kind of opportunity he has so often had to use such a meeting simultaneously to balk every reasonable effort of ourselves and to make of the whole occurrence another propaganda mill for the Soviet. It is entirely possible, however, that your Government and ourselves, and probably the French, should agree upon some general purpose and program under which each would have a specific part to play.

I am sure that Foster Dulles will attempt to keep in rather close touch with Anthony regarding possibilities and any tentative conclusions we may reach.

Winston S. Churchill to Lord Beaverbrook
(*Beaverbrook papers*)

15 March 1953

My dear Max,

You very kindly invited me to Cap d'Ail for the Easter holidays, and it would have given me the greatest pleasure to come, especially if you were there as host. However, I fear I cannot manage to get away from England. In the first place I have two horses running on Easter Saturday and two more on Easter Monday whose fortunes are of great interest to me. But more seriously the Budget comes on immediately after the recess and this affects our affairs so much that I feel bound to be in constant touch with Rab, so I am going to stay at Chartwell with a number of grandchildren. I do hope you will give me another invitation later in the year.

The lift is in full working order and I am sure it will be a great relief to me

---

[1] T.62/53, reproduced above (p. 905).

if I go on living. Thank you so much for your very kind thought and for the care and skill with which it has been carried into effect.

Do not fail to let me know when you come to England for there are lots of things to talk about. We seem to have been having a pretty rough time lately. Hardly a week passes without some unusual misfortune. The Larne packet, the floods,[1] the poor soldiers and their wives flying to Jamaica.[2] The new Soviet Government shooting down our airplane and killing six men.[3] Neguib, Mussadiq and all the rest. However I am going to welcome Tito on Monday. I hope you are enjoying yourself too.

PS. Clemmie has just shown me your most kind letter to who she has cabled a reply.

President Dwight D. Eisenhower to Anthony Eden
(Premier papers, 11/431)

16 March 1953   The White House

Dear Anthony,

Thank you very much for your nice message, which was sent to me by Sir Roger Makins.

I was really disturbed this morning to find that the question I had personally raised about the planned Joint Conference in Cairo had obviously not been successfully answered. You will recall I expressed a reluctance to get publicly involved in the initial phases of this matter until the United States could be assured of the agreement of General Naguib – preferably an official invitation from him – to participate in the negotiations.

It seems to me that we should have been able to achieve this. Now we are told that the proposal – apparently coming jointly from our two governments – is not acceptable. I feel we have been clumsy.

This brings to mind again my concern over the way we present to the world the picture of British–American association, which association in our joint view will mean so much to progress in the development of collective security and to the best interests of the whole free world, including, of course, ourselves.

---

[1] On 31 Jan. 1953 a storm sank the ferry *Princess Victoria* in the North Channel as it sailed from Stranraer to Larne, with the loss of 132 lives. That same night, extreme weather conditions across the North Sea resulted in exceptionally high storm tides, displacing 30,000 persons across the UK and also devastating Belgium and the Netherlands.

[2] On 11 Apr. 1953, a Caribbean International Airways flight carrying members of the RAF among its passengers crashed into the sea, killing 13 with one survivor. These were the first fatalities in the history of commercial flying in Jamaica.

[3] On 12 Mar. 1953, a Soviet MiG15 fighter shot down a British Avro Lincoln four-engine bomber in the Hamburg–Berlin air corridor, provoking international condemnation.

We must, by all means, avoid the appearance of attempting to dominate the Councils of the free world. This, I think, is just as necessary as is the prior study of common problems, by joint effort, before we go into multilateral conferences. Over the past decade I have had some experience, in the military field, with international conferences. I am certain that nothing infuriates an individual in one of these meetings so much as an insinuation or implication that he may be representing a country, whose convictions, because of some national reason, are not really important. I know, for example, that the French frequently feel that the United States and Britain are guilty of power politics on this point, and they resent it fiercely. (You remember the Malta Conference!) At the same time their willingness to go along with us is tremendously important; not only because of their responsibility in the Indo-China war but because of their central, key position in Western Europe.

I am repeating these thoughts merely so that you and your associates will not forget the conviction we hold that our two nations will get much further along towards a satisfactory solution to our common problems if each of us preserves, consciously, an attitude of absolute equality with all other nations, in every kind of multilateral conference in which we jointly participate.

I am, of course, hopeful that the Egyptian tangle will be straightened out and that we can get forward with our negotiations. The proposed plan, if adopted, will operate to the advantage of Egypt and is in keeping with their just claims to sovereignty and equality. It will likewise give the free world assurance that the Canal will remain available for use. I feel certain that no justifiable criticism of the plan itself can be made; consequently it is doubly important that the methods we use do not defeat it.

I once had a very wise commander who would use a very simple illustration to point out to me the difference between 'command' and leadership. Maybe you can try it sometime on some of your associates and assistants, just as I do on mine. It goes:

'Put a piece of cooked spaghetti on a platter. Take hold of one end and try to push it in a straight line across the plate. You get only a snarled up and knotty looking thing that resembles nothing on earth.

Take hold of the other end and gently <u>lead</u> the piece of spaghetti across the plate. Simple!'

I did not mean to get into a long letter like this in acknowledging your nice note, but in conformity with our agreement to unload our minds when we feel like it, I send this on to you.

Cabinet: conclusions
(Cabinet papers, 128/26)

17 March 1953
Secret
11 a.m.
Cabinet Meeting No. 20 of 1953

[. . .]

7. The Prime Minister read to the Cabinet the draft of a statement which he was proposing to make in the House of Commons that afternoon on the circumstances in which a bomber aircraft of the Royal Air Force on a training flight from Yorkshire to Berlin, had been shot down by Russian fighters on the borders of the Eastern and Western Zones of Germany. In the concluding sentence of this statement the Prime Minister proposed to say that should Soviet aircraft stray into the British Zone of Germany 'every effort will be made to warn them and to avoid loss of life'. In discussion some doubt was expressed about the expediency of implying, as this sentence did, that in the last resort we might fire on a Soviet aircraft which persisted, despite warnings, in flying over the British Zone. It was suggested that, if our statement implied this, it would be twisted by the Soviet Government to suit their purpose. On the other hand it was argued that, whatever statement was made, the Soviet Government would misrepresent it if it suited their purpose to do so.

After discussion it was agreed that the final sentence of this statement should be amended to read: 'Should Soviet aircraft stray into our Zone, every effort will be made to warn them and, by following the procedures normally used by nations at peace, to avoid loss of life.'

[. . .]

Winston S. Churchill to President Dwight D. Eisenhower
Prime Minister's Personal Telegram T.71/53
(Premier papers, 11/1074)

19 March 1953
Immediate
Top Secret
Personal and Confidential
No. 1280

My dear Friend,

I am very sorry that you do not feel that you can do much to help us about the Canal Zone. Naturally I am glad that we are broadly speaking agreed upon the merits and upon what we must get. I know that we can count on your goodwill. A month has passed since I wrote my first letter to you and I fear it will be impossible for us to keep Field Marshal Slim any longer from his task in Australia. I hope however that though you may not be able to help us positively it will not look as if the United States is taking sides against us. I am like the American who prayed 'Oh Lord, if you cannot help me don't help the bear.' It would be a very great pity if differences about the method of approach were represented as differences of policy between our two countries and still worse if they became public.

2. We are discharging an international duty and are resolved not to be bullied any further by Neguib either in the Canal Zone or in the Sudan. I have reached my limit. We are neither unable nor afraid to deal with Neguib by ourselves. But even if we have to continue keeping 80,000 troops in the Canal Zone I assure you that in no circumstances will Her Majesty's Government abandon the United Nations crusade in Korea. At present we seem to be heading for a costly and indefinite stalemate both in the Middle East and the Far East instead of helping each other to reach conclusions agreeable to world peace at both ends.

3. Tito seems full of commonsense. He is definitely of opinion that the death of Stalin has not made the world safer, but he believes that the new regime will probably feel their way cautiously for some time and even thinks there may be divisions among them. Malenkov and Beria,[1] he says, are united but Molotov is not so closely tied. Anthony and I are doing all we can to urge him to improve his relations with the Italians and also with the Romans. He is very anxious about what would happen if he were attacked all alone. We have said we do not think a local war in Europe is likely or even possible. He was not therefore in particular danger. I pointed out to him the risks we had shown ourselves ready to run by having an American Bomber base in this Island. The point did not seem to have occurred to him.

President Dwight D. Eisenhower to Winston S. Churchill
(Premier papers, 11/1074)

19 March 1953 The White House
Top Secret

Dear Winston,

I am a bit puzzled as to the real meaning of your recent note to me. By no means have I, or my associates, indicated or implied that we are not in

---

[1] Lavrentiy Pavlovich Beria, 1899–1953. Joined Bolsheviks, 1917. Member, Cheka (secret police), 1920. Deputy Head, Georgian Cheka, 1922. Head, Georgian OGPU (secret police), 1926. Secretary, Communist Party of Georgia, 1931. Secretary, Communist Party of Transcaucasia, 1932. Member, Central Committee of the Communist Party of the Soviet Union, 1934. Deputy Head, NKVD, 1938; Head, 1938–46. Commissar General for State Security, 1941. Deputy Chairman, Council of People's Commissars, 1941. Full Member, Politburo, 1946–53. Executed, 1953.

agreement with your Government in what you are trying to do in the Canal Zone. On the contrary, Anthony and I reached a clear understanding of what we should strive to get under the various alternatives laid down by the staff, and both of us were very clear that the offer we would be making would be so fair to the Egyptians that we hoped it could not possibly be rejected.

While he was here, I raised one question involving procedure. The question was: 'How does the United States get into this consultation?'

It was obvious that no one had thought very much on this point and it was recognized a very awkward situation could result for our representative, and, indeed, for the negotiations themselves, if an American should show up without some prior invitation and agreement between the principals, namely, your Government and the Egyptian Government.

My point is this: If the United States walks into a conference with you, against the wishes of the Egyptian Government, then the only obvious interpretation would be that our two governments, together, are there to announce an ultimatum. An uninvited guest cannot possibly come into your house, be asked to leave, and then expect cordial and courteous treatment if he insists upon staying.

So far as I know, this is the only point that has blocked the initiation of the conference. But until it is ironed out, I do not see how we can possibly get into it.

I am sure that Anthony will confirm to you that I expressed exactly these sentiments to him when he was in my office.

Please be assured that I have no idea that either of us should be bullied by Naguib. We have objectives in common and they are vital objectives, so vital indeed that I do not think we should be inflexible on procedure.

I am much interested in what you say about Tito. I am glad that you and Anthony have been urging him to improve his relations with some of his neighbors.

Cabinet: conclusions
(Cabinet papers, 128/26)

20 March 1953
Secret
11.30 a.m.
Cabinet Meeting No. 21 of 1953

1. The Secretary of State for Air said that it was now established that the RAF bomber aircraft which had been shot down by Russian fighters over Germany was itself unarmed and had received no warning of attack. It was true that the Russians had collected some rounds of ammunition from the wreck, but these were some odd rounds which had been left in the aircraft by

mistake. The aircraft was certainly off its course and the crew had apparently either been unable, or neglected, to establish their position by the use of radio aids. In either case there appeared to have been a breach of flying discipline. It was normal practice to use Lincoln bombers on these training flights over Germany with the object of testing the efficiency of our radar screen. These flights were undertaken by skilled crews who thereby gained important navigational experience.

The Prime Minister said that this latest information confirmed the truth of the preliminary statement which he had made in the House of Commons. It was, however, likely that there would be further public criticism of this form of training.

In discussion reference was made to the Russian suggestion of a conference on the regulation of flying near the Zonal boundaries in Germany. It was agreed that this suggestion should be accepted, but that before the discussions began our own technical case should be carefully prepared and agreement reached with the Americans on the line to be adopted. It was also agreed that the Air Staff representatives at the discussion should be accompanied by a member of the Staff of the United Kingdom High Commissioner in Germany in view of the political issues involved.

The Cabinet –
   (1) Agreed that the Russian suggestion of a conference on the regulation of flying near the Zonal boundaries in Germany should be accepted.
   (2) Invited the Foreign Secretary and the Secretary of State for Air to prepare the instructions for the United Kingdom representatives at the conference.

2. The Cabinet were informed that opposition to the Judges' Remuneration Bill was developing among members of all Parties in the House of Commons. The Labour Party had given notice of a motion for the rejection of the Bill. Some Liberals intended to support a motion which, while endorsing the principle that the remuneration of Judges should be improved, would deprecate the method of tax-free allowance which was proposed in the Bill. Among Government supporters there were divided opinions on the best method of improving the Judges' remuneration. A number of Conservative Members had expressed disapproval of the proposal for a tax-free allowance, but there were indications that others would feel similar objections to proposals for a substantial increase in the gross salaries of Judges. In these circumstances it was doubtful whether it would be practicable to proceed with the present programme of carrying the Second Reading of both the Bill and the Financial Resolution in the House of Commons on 26th March.

The Chancellor of the Exchequer said that most of the objections which were now being raised to this Bill had been set out in the paper (C(52)334) which he had circulated to the Cabinet on 14th October. He believed that the

Cabinet would now be compelled to consider other methods of improving the Judges' remuneration. He was at present disposed to favour an increase of gross salary combined with a travel allowance. If that method were adopted, it might not be possible to confer on all the Judges a net benefit equivalent to the tax-free allowance of £1,000 a year proposed in the present Bill. Ministers clearly needed further time in which to consider alternative methods of carrying out this policy and to justify their proposals to their supporters in the House of Commons. It might therefore be wise to defer Parliamentary discussion of the Bill until after Easter.

The Prime Minister said that the Government must adhere firmly to the principle that the remuneration of the Judges should be improved. So long as they maintained that principle they could afford to listen to arguments about the method by which effect should be given to it. He himself still believed that the method proposed in the Bill was the most convenient; but he would be ready to accept an alternative method which commanded a wider measure of support among Conservative Members in the House of Commons so long as it conferred roughly the same net benefit on the Judges as they would have derived from a tax-free allowance of £1,000 a year. He thought that the Government would show weakness if they deferred all Parliamentary discussion of this question until after Easter. He would prefer that the matter should be debated on 26th March as previously planned and that the House of Commons should then be asked to take a decision on the point of principle. The choice of method could, if need be, be left over for further discussion and brought up for final decision after the Easter recess.

There was general agreement with the Prime Minister's view. Further discussion turned on the best tactics for separating the questions of principle and of method. It was ultimately agreed that the most convenient course would be to move the Second Reading of the Bill on 26th March as previously planned, but to indicate at the outset of the debate that the Financial Resolution would be allowed to stand over until after Easter. It could then be made clear that the decision on the Second Reading would be treated as a decision on the principle of improving the Judges' remuneration, and that the method by which this should be done would be left open for further discussion of the Financial Resolution. Meanwhile the Prime Minister would explain the position to the Executive of the 1922 Committee. The Cabinet recognised that if, as a result of the discussions, they decided to adopt a different method of improving the Judges' remuneration, the necessary changes in the form of the Financial Resolution might be so substantial that the Speaker might rule that a fresh Bill should be introduced.

The Cabinet –
  (1) Agreed that the Second Reading of the Judges' Remuneration Bill should be taken in the House of Commons on 26th March but that proceedings on the Financial Resolution should be deferred until

March 1953

after the Easter recess so that further discussions might be held with Government supporters about the method by which the Judges' remuneration should be improved.

(2) Invited the Prime Minister, in moving the Second Reading of the Bill, to make it clear that the Government were at that stage asking the House of Commons to pronounce only on the principle of improving the Judges' remuneration and were not committed to giving effect to that principle by the method proposed in the Bill.

(3) Took note that the Prime Minister would take steps to see that this position was explained, before the Second Reading debate, to Government supporters in the House of Commons.

(4) Invited the Chancellor of the Exchequer to consider alternative means of conferring on the Judges a net benefit approximately the same as that which they would have derived from the provisions of the present Bill.

[. . .]

4. The Cabinet were informed that the reinforcements which were to be despatched to Kenya, in accordance with their decision of 10th March, were due to leave this country by air on 30th March and to arrive in Kenya on 7th April. Fayid and Khartoum were among the intermediate points at which the aircraft carrying these troops would land to refuel.

The Prime Minister said that it was convenient that these staging points were being used. It might be useful, when the time came, to keep some of these troops for a few days in Khartoum, where their presence might have a salutary effect on public opinion both in the Sudan and in Egypt. This advantage could be secured at slight cost if it imposed only a short delay on their arrival in Kenya. The Foreign Secretary should keep this possibility in mind. Meanwhile, the Minister of Defence could consider whether any special arrangements would need to be made to enable these troops to prolong their stay in Khartoum for a short period, though care must be taken to ensure that no rumour of this possibility should reach the Sudanese or the Egyptians.

The Foreign Secretary undertook to keep this possibility in mind and to consult further with the Minister of Defence if it was desired that any of these troops should remain for a few days in Khartoum on their way to Kenya.

[. . .]

Winston S. Churchill to Field Marshal Lord Alexander
Prime Minister's Personal Minute M.53/53
(Premier papers, 11/392)

23 March 1953
Secret

In view of the sharpening of the situation in the Canal Zone and Neguib's threats it would, I think, be wise to have at least one Brigade available for reinforcements. I suppose this could be found from Germany. I gathered from reports you have made me that it is not likely to be needed. Still, it is always well to be prepared especially if secrecy, particularly of destination, can be preserved.

Cabinet: conclusions
(Cabinet papers, 128/26)

24 March 1953
Secret
11.30 a.m.
Cabinet Meeting No. 22 of 1953

1. The Prime Minister said that on the previous day he had discussed with the Executive of the 1922 Committee the Government's proposals for handling the Judges' Remuneration Bill. He had been impressed by the strength of their opposition to the Bill. Though they were ready to agree in principle that the Judges' remuneration should be improved, they were very critical of the proposal to do this by the grant of a tax-free allowance. It became clear from the discussion that the Government would find great difficulty in carrying the Second Reading of the Bill on the basis contemplated by the Cabinet in their discussion on 20th March;[1] and, after consulting the Lord Privy Seal, the Prime Minister had come to the conclusion that they must postpone the Parliamentary proceedings on the Bill until after Easter in order that they might have more time in which to discuss with their supporters the method by which the Judges' remuneration should be improved. Later in the evening he had learned the news of this decision had reached the Press, and he had therefore issued a formal announcement to the effect that the Second Reading of the Bill would be postponed until after the Easter recess.

The Cabinet endorsed the Prime Minister's conclusion and his action in announcing it.

The Lord Privy Seal said that he would have to make a statement in the House of Commons that afternoon about the alteration in the business for

---

[1] See Cabinet: conclusions, Mar. 20, reproduced above (pp. 912–15).

26th March. He would take that opportunity of making it clear that the Government still considered that an increase in the Judges' remuneration was overdue and that they would proceed with legislation in due course. It was for consideration whether he should say that the extent of the increase should be that declared in the Bill. For, if a different method had to be adopted, it might not be possible to secure for the Judges the same net benefit as they would have derived from the tax-free allowance proposed in the Bill. After discussion it was agreed that the Lord Privy Seal should refer to the Government's determination to secure an increase in the Judges' remuneration 'of the order proposed in the Bill'.

The Cabinet –
  (1) Took note that the Second Reading of the Judges' Remuneration Bill would be postponed until after the Easter recess.
  (2) Invited the Lord Privy Seal to make a formal announcement to that effect in the House of Commons that afternoon.
  (3) Took note that the Prime Minister would arrange for further discussions to be held with Government supporters after the Easter recess on the method by which the remuneration of the Judges should be improved.

[. . .]

Winston S. Churchill: speech
(Hansard)

25 March 1953

THE DEATH OF QUEEN MARY[1]

I beg to move, that an humble Address be presented to Her Majesty to express the heartfelt sympathy of this House in the great sorrow which Her Majesty has sustained by the death of Her Majesty Queen Mary, and to condole with Her Majesty on this melancholy occasion; to assure Her Majesty that we shall ever hold in affectionate and grateful remembrance the love which Queen Mary inspired in all peoples of this land and her devoted service to their welfare, and that we share fully in the universal feeling of sympathy with Her Majesty in her grievous loss. The address to the Crown which it is my sorrowful duty to propose is no mere formal expression of sympathy from this House. Queen Mary, by her personality, her example and her bearing over so many years, had endeared herself to the whole people of these islands and throughout the vast regions of the Commonwealth and Empire.

---

[1] Victoria Mary, 1867–1953. Only daughter of Mary Adelaide, Duchess of Teck (a granddaughter of King George III, and Queen Victoria's first cousin), and Francis, 1st Duke of Teck. Married, 1893, George, Duke of York, later King George V.

There has not, in living memory, been a figure more widely known or more universally honoured. Wherever she went, she was assured of an applause which sprang from a deep-seated affection and respect. She looked a Queen: she acted like a Queen: her death leaves a void in our hearts and in the life of the nation – a void which it will be hard indeed to fill.

Sir, when King George V came to the Throne he was confronted almost immediately by political and constitutional problems of a gravity and complexity which has fortunately been unequalled in the history of the Monarchy in recent times. Hardly had these been surmounted, or partly surmounted, when they were overwhelmed by the fury of the First World War. During these unceasing ordeals, in which the King acquitted himself so wisely and so well, he was immeasurably strengthened by the support and comfort for which he could always look to Queen Mary.

As the years went by she had to endure many personal sorrows, including the sudden death of three of her five sons. But she never allowed either personal sorrow or public anxiety to interrupt the discharge of her duties and her obligations. With a tireless energy far outstripping those many years younger, she devoted herself to carrying out functions which never exceeded her patience or lost her keen interest.

In many spheres, particularly those connected with the arts, she acquired a knowledge which the experts admired and often envied. Her lively interest in the theatre was a source of real encouragement to the gifted generation of actors and actresses whom we are fortunate to possess. It may sometimes have been thought that Queen Mary, brought up in an age of conventions more rigid than those that now find acceptance, was intolerant of the changes which she lived to see. This was far from the truth. One of the most remarkable qualities she possessed was her lack of prejudice, and the welcome which she spontaneously gave to young people and to new ideas.

I am sure that the House will be unanimous in wishing to record its sympathy not only with Her Majesty the Queen, to whom I ask that this Address may be forwarded, but also with Queen Mary's surviving children, the Duke of Windsor, the Duke of Gloucester[1] and the Princess Royal,[2] and with her brother, Lord Athlone,[3] whom she so dearly loved and whose long record of service to the Commonwealth and Empire was always a source of special pride and pleasure to her.

[1] Henry William Frederick Albert, 1900–74. Educated at Eton and Trinity College, Cambridge. 2nd Lt, KRRC, 1919. Lt, 10th Royal Hussars, 1921. Capt., 1927. Duke of Gloucester, 1928. Col.-in-Chief, Gloucestershire Rgt, 1935. Married, 1935, Alice Montagu Douglas Scott: two children. Joined BEF, 1939. Chief Liaison Officer, GHQ Home Forces, 1940. Lt.-Gen., 1941. Gen., 1944. Governor-General of Australia, 1944–7. FM, 1955.

[2] Victoria Alexandra Alice Mary, 1897–1965. Married, 1922, Henry George Charles Lascelles: two children.

[3] Alexander Augustus Frederick William Alfred George, 1874–1957. Educated at Eton and Royal Military College, Sandhurst. 2nd Lt, 7th Queen's Own Hussars, 1894. Lt, 1899. Capt., 1900. DSO, 1901. Married, 1904, Princess Alice of Albany: three children. Maj., 1911. Lt-Col., 1915. Earl of Athlone, 1917. Governor-General, Union of South Africa, 1923–8; of Canada, 1940–6.

Winston S. Churchill: broadcast
('Winston S. Churchill, His Complete Speeches', volume 8, pages 8464–5)

25 March 1953

I have been asked to say just a few words upon the sad event which fills our thoughts this evening. Men and women of all ages, in all the lands owing allegiance to the Crown, have sorrowing hearts to-night. Queen Mary was loved and revered far and wide, as perhaps nobody has been since Queen Victoria. During six reigns, far longer than most people can remember, she has moved among us with the poise and the dignity which, as age drew on, made her a figure of almost legendary distinction.

How few of you listening to me to-night can recall a time without Queen Mary, and even those who never saw her will feel a deep and sincere pang at the passing of this last link with Queen Victoria's reign. When she was born Napoleon III[1] ruled in France and Palmerston[2] had only recently ceased to be Prime Minister of this country. Railways were comparatively new; electric light and the internal combustion engine were unknown. She knew Gladstone[3] and Disraeli;[4] her grandfather[5] was the son of George III.[6] Yet she lived into this atomic age, through the two fearful wars, which cast almost all the thrones of Europe to the ground, and rent but also transformed the world.

The chasm which scientific invention and social change have wrought between 1867 and 1953 is so wide that it requires not only courage but mental resilience for those whose youth lay in calmer and more slowly-moving times to adjust themselves to the giant outlines and harsh structure of twentieth century history. But Queen Mary did not cling to the insubstantial shadows of what had been. She moved easily through the changing scenes. New ideas held no terrors for her. Dispassionate in judgment, practical in all things, she was also far too much interested in the present to be unduly prejudiced by the past.

She died in the knowledge that the Crown of these realms, worn so gloriously by her husband, and her son, and so soon to be set with all solemnity on the head of her granddaughter, is far more broadly and securely based on the people's love and the nations will than in the sedate days of her youth, when rank and privilege ruled society. I hope she realized that her sympathy, her influence and example played a notable part in all this, and that it was for these services the British peoples, with their keen and seldom-erring instinct, placed and held her so high in their affections.

---

[1] Charles-Louis Napoléon Bonaparte, 1808–73. President of 2nd French Republic, 1848–52. Emperor of France, 1852–70.

[2] Henry John Temple, 1784–1865. PM, 1855–8, 1859–65. 3rd Viscount Palmerston, 1802.

[3] William Ewart Gladstone, 1809–98. PM, 1868–74, 1880–5, 1886, 1892–4.

[4] Benjamin Disraeli, 1804–81. PM, 1868, 1874–80. Lord Privy Seal, 1876–8. Leader of the House of Lords, 1876–80.

[5] George Augustus Frederick, 1762–1830. Prince Regent, 1811–20. King George IV, 1820–30.

[6] George William Frederick, 1738–1820. King George III, 1760–1820. Married, 1761, Charlotte of Mecklenburg-Strelitz.

Queen Mary will long live mellow and gracious in all our memories, and in the annals of these tumultuous times. We pray that she may now rest in peace. Good night.

Sir Norman Brook to Winston S. Churchill
(Premier papers, 11/369)

25 March 1953

NATO ANNUAL REVIEW
(D(53)14)

The long-term problem raised in paragraphs 20–24 of this paper is difficult – but it is becoming increasingly urgent.

The problem is, briefly, how to persuade NATO that in calculating their forces requirements they should consider, not what is required to defeat a Russian attack, but what is required to deter the Russians from making one.

We are at once confronted with the difficulty that there is in NATO no very effective means of reconciling military 'requirements' with political and economic possibilities. It is the duty of military authorities to say what forces would be required to repel an enemy attack. It is no part of their duty to assume the responsibility for assessing the likelihood that he will make an attack, or for accepting the risk of being somewhat less than fully prepared to meet it. These are the responsibilities of political authorities.

In our own domestic affairs we have means of applying political judgment to military estimates of requirements. It is accepted without question that the final judgment rests with the political authority. But the processes of adjustment are eased by the fact that the Chiefs of Staff, as the Government's professional advisers on military matters, sit with Ministers in the Defence Committee and on occasion in the Cabinet.

In NATO we have not yet evolved corresponding procedures for knitting together the civil and the military sides of the Organisation. The procedures followed are much more likely to lead to a situation in which the military authorities seem to be the final judges of the forces which Governments ought to provide, and Governments appear to be failing in their duty if these military requirements are not met in full. And, to make matters worse, NATO commanders are free to make public pronouncements about the force levels which they believe to be necessary.

The problem posed in this part of the paper will not be solved until some means have been found to establish in NATO the same supremacy of political decision over military advice as is ensured to us domestically by our constitutional arrangements. Lord Ismay, I know, has had this problem much in mind; but I do not think he has yet found means of solving it. One of the difficulties is that, although the Council is in form the supreme political authority in NATO, the permanent representatives on the Council are officials not Ministers and the Ministers do not meet often or long enough to establish a corporate spirit.

The specific suggestion made by the Minister of Defence is that we should discuss with the Americans how best to relate NATO force requirements to the 'deterrent' theory. I recognize that we shall not get very far with this unless we can carry the Americans with us. But I wish I could be sure that they would see as clearly as we do that these are matters on which military authorities advise and political authorities decide. As we know that Lord Ismay has been giving some thought to this, certainly in its procedural aspects and probably on the question of substance also, might it be wise to have some consultation with him in the first instance before broaching the subject with the Americans? He may well have had some talk about this with President Eisenhower during his recent visit to Washington.

Sarah Beauchamp to Winston S. Churchill
(Churchill papers, 1/50)[1]

26 March 1953 New York

My darling Papa,

I was very sad – indeed quite stunned to hear of Queen Mary's death – I knew she had been in poor health – but somehow I thought she would live still longer. Your speech and your emotion were very moving I hated to see you sad and sombre.

I didn't catch the actual broadcast, but the station that relayed it is sending me a transcription.

It is always extremely moving how much, and how sincerely, the newspapers report the Royal Family's joys and misfortunes. You would think it was their Queen!

Everything goes well here. I come home to play in all Antony's films April 27th and will stay the inside of two weeks. Then back here to finish up this season. It has gone increasingly well. Some things we do are really quite good.

I was talking to Rupert Allan[2] today (Mummie will tell you about him) he is writing and editing articles on the coronation here for *Look* magazine. From what he told me I think they will be well informed – and very warm. Since he is a friend and would not use anything without permission, I told him – without context – of your saying (misquoted I'm afraid) but the gist and sentiment remained – 'Everyone should wear a buttonhole when they go

[1] This letter was handwritten.
[2] Rupert Allan, 1913–91. Naval intelligence officer, journalist, magazine editor, Rhodes Scholar and Hollywood publicist. Press agent for Marilyn Monroe.

to see their best girl.' Even not said quite correctly, it moved him profoundly. 'That's it,' he said that's what would really describe the coronation spirit of England to Americans. 'May I use it?' I said I would write and ask you if he might quote you as having said this at sometime, to complement his article. I hope you let him – I feel it really expresses the right spirit and all of the feeling.

If yes, or no, will you have Jock or someone write to me by return.

Sorry this is a scribble – but I write on the spur of the moment and wish to catch the post. Much much love to Mummie and the family and much much to you darling Papa.

Your loving Sarah.

PS. I have a small terrace only 2ft wide. A family of pigeons have made their home in a small planted tub tree! I am thrilled – to date one awkward adolescent, one new egg!

Love again S.

Winston S. Churchill to Anthony Eden
Prime Minister's Personal Minute M.54/53
(Premier papers, 11/544)

26 March 1953

I was in full agreement with you about Selwyn Lloyd going to the Sudan but hope that he will not get mixed up in Canal Zone negotiations, which should be undertaken when the moment comes by a military representative vice Slim and Her Majesty's Ambassador.

Winston S. Churchill to R. A. Butler
Prime Minister's Personal Minute M.56/53
(Premier papers, 11/355)

27 March 1953

The Cabinet decided, subject to your agreement and mine, that guests of the Government to the Naval Review should all be treated in the same way about their fares as well as their fare. I am sure this rule should hold throughout, and cover even those guest MPs unsuccessful in the ballot who will <u>only</u> go from HM ships instead of on a liner.

If you are in agreement with this, will you kindly communicate with the Admiralty.

Winston S. Churchill to Sir Alan Lascelles
(*Churchill papers, 4/63*)

28 March 1953

My dear Alan,

The sixth and last volume of my History of the Second World War will be published before the end of the year. I held it back until after the Presidential election in the United States, and since then I have gone over it again and taken out any critical references to General Eisenhower which, now that he is President, might conceivably damage Anglo-American relations. Stalin's death has now removed my last remaining doubts about the expediency of publishing this volume, and I hope to bring it out in the autumn.

I should like to reproduce in it two messages which I sent to His late Majesty – one after I had watched the landing in the south of France, and the other from Moscow. I enclose the text of these two messages.

If Her Majesty were pleased to give her consent to my publishing these messages in my final volume, I should be greatly obliged. Would you be good enough to take Her pleasure on my behalf.

Winston S. Churchill to Anthony Eden
(*Premier papers, 11/422*)

28 March 1953
Most Private

The news you gave me is most favourable.[1] We should certainly say at once to the Americans that we hope talks at Panmunjom should be reopened at once. If they agree this would be a considerable event.

It is for you to judge whether you need to recall your Ambassador in Moscow[2] for consultations. I should have thought that he knows nothing that you do not know and direct talks between you and Molotov was the important interim objective. It is not the fault of our Moscow Ambassador that he plays no part, but rather the Soviet system of reducing them all to mouthpieces. If you announce that he has been called home in consultation you would in my opinion only be emphasising an official machinery which has long ceased to work. It would however attract a great deal of attention and many people would think that you have not got a view of your own upon the subject. What

---

[1] The Korean People's Army had captured several British diplomats when it overran Seoul in 1950; they were released, and returned to Britain, in 1953. Among them was the MI6 agent and later Soviet spy George Blake, who became a Communist during his imprisonment in North Korea.

[2] Alvary Douglas Frederick Trench-Gascoigne, 1893–1970. 2nd Lt., Cavalry Dragoons, 1914. 2nd Secretary, FO, 1925–33; 1st Secretary, 1933–9. Consul-General for Tangier Zone and Spanish Zone, Protectorate of Morocco, 1939–41. Embassy Counsellor, 1941–6. British Political Representative in Japan, 1946–51. KCMG, 1947. GBE, 1951. British Ambassador to Soviet Union, 1951–3.

is there you can tell him to ask for an Audience about that you cannot telegraph direct to Molotov? I see no advantage in procedure for procedure's sake. If you liked it I could send something like the following to Molotov.

> Begins. Greetings. I was so glad to learn from Eden about your action in seeking the release of British diplomatists captured in North Korea. You have also suggested reciprocal release of wounded and resumption of talks at Panmunjom. All this is agreeable to our minds and we are talking to our American friends about it. What I should like to see most of all would be for you and Eden, who have had so many long and famous contacts for our two countries, to have another friendly and informal meeting. This might perhaps be at Vienna. I also wondered whether it might not arise out of any broader political aspects of the talks between General Chuikov[1] and Kirkpatrick about arrangements to prevent another aeroplane disaster. Such talks however they originated might lead us all further away from madness and ruin, but even if nothing much came out of it I can't see that any of us would be worse off. Churchill. Ends.

Let me know what you think about this sort of approach. I do not want an interview between Gascoigne and Molotov, but between Molotov and you. At a later stage if all went well and everything broadened I and even Ike might come in too.

Anthony Eden to Winston S. Churchill
(Premier papers, 11/422)

28 March 1953
Top Secret

    Your message of 3.45 p.m. today.

    Your para. 1. I agree. A message had already been sent to the Americans in this sense.

    Your para. 2. The recall of our Ambassador at Moscow. Of course this is not a question of procedure for procedure's sake. It has only occurred to us that if we were to send a message to Moscow it would be useful if the Ambassador could have been personally briefed as to our purpose. He could then have returned to deliver it. Admittedly there would be some publicity, but I should not have thought it would be considered wrong for me to consult Her Majesty's Ambassador at a time like this. A decision on this matter is not of the first importance but it must be taken by tomorrow or he cannot arrive back in time to see me before Easter.

---

[1] Vasily Ivanovich Chuikov, 1900–82. Joined Red Army, 1918. Cdr, 40th Rgt, 1919. Commanded Soviet army in Central Berlin, 1945. Chief, Group of Soviet Forces in Germany, 1949–53. Cdr, Kiev Military District, 1953–60. Chief of Soviet Armed Forces and Deputy Minister of Defence Forces, 1961–72.

Much more complicated and serious than this is whether we should attempt a meeting between Molotov and myself and if so what topics we could discuss. The Annexe gives the few issues which we have been able to discover which are exclusively Anglo-Soviet. As you will see it is very thin. Admittedly once we met we could talk of other topics. But what are they? The most important are:
(a) The Korean War.
(b) Germany.
(c) Austria.

As to (a). I think the Americans would have a legitimate grievance if we entered into talks on Korea with the Russians in their absence. Theirs is so much the largest share.

As regards Germany it is Adenauer who would be most anxious. A discussion of Germany's future without his being present must do him great harm. Moreover in the next month or two he will have completed ratification of the EDC and even the French should be nearing the same decision. Austria is essentially a Four Power problem.

This new Russian trend is potentially dangerous. It looks as though the Russians like Neguib have decided to change their tactics. Neguib thought he could do better for Egypt by abandoning the sterile slogan of sovereignty and the unity of the Nile Valley and by agreeing to self-Government and self-determination for the Sudan in the hope that he could then go into the Sudan and win over the Sudanese for Egypt. Perhaps now the Russians are recognizing that the only effect of their rigid and intransigent and aggressive policy is to promote the building up of the West morally and materially against them. They may think that they may more successfully disintegrate the anti-Communist front and bring the neutrals over to their side by a policy of moderation and concession in minor matters and perhaps in some major matters too. We have in the past been pretty sure that the Russians would not let us down by performing embarrassing conciliatory manoeuvres. It looks as if this is no longer so. Their peace propaganda will now have some more substance in it. Our own tactics will have to be to respond as freely as we can without surrendering vital positions like the North Atlantic Treaty. In this we may find the French to be very weak vessels.

My conclusion therefore is that we ought to have a full talk about all this (including your message to Molotov) as soon as possible. You may like to ask some colleagues. If so I have no objection. I am available at any time tomorrow (except after the Service until about 5.30 p.m.)

Would you agree to lunch here tomorrow?

ANNEX

1. Soviet Government agrees to extend the Anglo-Soviet Temporary Fisheries Agreement of 1930.

2. Soviet Government agrees to restore a diplomatic rate for the rubal.

3. Mrs Hall[1] (the last remaining Soviet Wife) and her child should be allowed to leave the Soviet Union to join her Husband.

4. Soviet Government agrees to submit to arbitration in the United Kingdom the claim of the Tyne Improvement Commissioners for damages of about £700 against the Soviet steam-ship *Rzhed* which has been outstanding since 1946.

5. Bundock[2] should be included in the reported amnesty.

Winston S. Churchill to Anthony Eden
Prime Minister's Personal Minute M.58/53
(Premier papers, 11/544)

29 March 1953

Foreign Office telegram to Khartoum No. 425. Today's Mau Mau atrocities in Kenya show the urgency for getting troops there. At the same time there are advantages in staging a battalion en route for a few days at Khartoum and thus imprinting upon the minds of the Egyptian dictators the fact that we can quite easily cut them off entirely from the Sudan out of which they hope to talk, bribe, and swindle us. If this can be done incidentally, it is worth considering. But Mau Mau have priority.

Sir Alan Lascelles to Winston S. Churchill
(Churchill papers, 4/63)

30 March 1953   Buckingham Palace
Personal and Private

My dear Prime Minister,

I have laid before The Queen your letter of the 28th March.[3]

Her Majesty is very glad to approve your reproducing in the sixth volume of your book the messages to The King, dated August 17th 1944 and October 16th 1944, of which you were good enough to send copies.

The only comment, which The Queen asked me to report to you, was that the fourth paragraph of the October 16th message seemed to her rather rough on the Poles. The Queen wondered if your reference to the Lublin delegates ought not, in the interests of international amity, to be toned down a bit.

---

[1] Mrs Hall was a Russian woman who married a British service member. Stalin blocked her (and twenty other women's) exit visas, trapping them in the USSR. She was permitted to emigrate in 1953.

[2] George Bundock, 1922–? Radio operator who was working in the British Embassy in Moscow when in 1948 he was sentenced *in absentia* by the Soviet authorities to 18 months' imprisonment for, 'an offence against a Russian girl'. Britain, believing any trial would be only for show, kept him safely in their embassy for five years until he was granted amnesty in 1953.

[3] Reproduced above (p. 923).

May I on my own account point out that in your typescript there is an error in the last line but one on page two? The word 'out' should be 'our'. I have checked this with The King's copy of your note, which I have in front of me.

John Colville to Winston S. Churchill
(*Premier papers, 11/422*)

30 March 1953

Mr Eden, who thinks it an excellent thing that you should be seeing Mr Aldrich tonight and discussing with him the draft telegram to Eisenhower, asks me to say that he hopes that you will not talk to Mr Aldrich about the Russian question (apart from the fact that Gascoigne is being brought home for consultations) because he feels that at this stage it would be better that the Americans should not know what we are thinking on this issue.

Winston S. Churchill to Anthony Eden
Prime Minister's Personal Minute M.61/53
(*Premier papers, 11/422*)

30 March 1953
Private

I asked Aldrich to come to see me tonight. I showed him the draft answer I had prepared to Ike. He reminded me that he had not seen Ike's message as it was sealed. I had not recalled this. I showed it to him. He agreed that he ought not in fact officially to have seen either: both were purely personal.

He thought my message could do no harm and even good. He would like to be able to back it up himself without saying he had seen it. He said that apart from any direct contacts I had with the President, he ought to be trying to bring pressure upon Dulles, whom he always referred to as Foster. (Apparently there was some joke about dull, duller, Dulles.) I think it would be a good thing if you had a talk to him on the lines on which we are agreed so that he can perhaps a little later begin feeding Dulles (Foster) and feel he, Aldrich, is in the show. He thinks Ike is much influenced by someone in the State Department and that 'no gate-crashing' came from there – perhaps by a Byroade,[1] (though he did not mention the name.) I think it would be good for you to bring him

---

[1] Henry Alfred Byroade, 1913–93. Educated at US Military Academy, 1933–7. Army Corps of Engineers, Hawaii, 1937–9. On active service in China–Burma–India theatre, 1937–44. Deputy Chief and Acting Chief, Asiatic Theater section, for Army CoS, 1944–5. Brig.-Gen., 1946. Military Attaché to Gen. Marshall, 1946–7. Director, Office of German Affairs, Dept of State, 1949–52. Asst Secretary of State for Middle East, South Asia and Africa, 1952–5. US Ambassador to Egypt, 1955–6; to South Africa, 1956–9; to Afghanistan, 1959–62; to Burma, 1963–8; to Philippines, 1969–73; to Pakistan, 1973–7.

in on our side. Unless you have later misgivings I will send my telegram sometime tomorrow.

I got your note not to talk to him on Russia before our meeting. However he raised the point of our communiqué and asked whether it was merely a matter of routine that our Ambassador was coming home. I said no, but as we had just entertained Tito and you were going to Greco and Turko it was necessary to show some interest in friendly gestures by Russia.

Winston S. Churchill to Harry S Truman
('Defending the West, The Truman–Churchill Correspondence', pages 209–10)

30 March 1953

My dear Harry,

I am proposing to publish this year the sixth and last volume of my *History of the Second World War*. This will cover the period from the launching of 'Overlord' to the Potsdam Conference; and the second part of the volume will enter upon the period of your Presidency.

I am naturally anxious to follow the method which I have adopted in earlier volumes, and to reproduce the text of some of the personal messages which I sent to those with whom I was associated in the strategic control of the war. I prefer to be judged by what I wrote at the time, rather than rely on present narrative and argument which is liable to be influenced by after-events.

In order that I may be able to tell my story in this way, I should like to reproduce the text of a dozen personal messages from you which came to me during this period. A list of these, together with the text of each is attached.

I should be obliged if you would allow me to reproduce in full the text of these few personal messages from you. If you would prefer that they should not be published textually, I can readily turn them, by paraphrase, into narrative form. But, as I have said already, for myself I prefer to rest on the actual words which I used at the time; and I dare say that you also will prefer that these messages should be printed as they were sent.

I must soon put this volume into its final shape for the publisher. I should be grateful therefore if you could look through the enclosed texts and let me know your views.

I see that you are writing a book yourself. Pray let me know if there is any point on which I can be of assistance.

With all good wishes.

April 1953

Cabinet: conclusions
(Cabinet papers, 128/26)

1 April 1953
Secret
11 a.m.
Cabinet Meeting No. 24 of 1953

[...]

10. The Prime Minister said that he would be making a statement in the House of Commons that afternoon about the resumption of the armistice talks in Korea. The proposals now made by the Chinese Communist Government for an exchange of sick and wounded prisoners, and their apparent readiness to consider thereafter arrangements for the disposal of other prisoners of war, was a welcome step towards breaking the present deadlock and might be an indication of a genuine desire to conclude an effective armistice in Korea. We should be careful not to appear to discourage such overtures as these, though we should continue to handle them with all due caution.

The Prime Minister said that in this statement he would take the opportunity to comment on the patience and foresight which the Foreign Secretary had shown, since assuming office, in all the negotiations which he had undertaken, in the United Nations and elsewhere, with a view to achieving an effective armistice in Korea.

[...]

Winston Churchill to President Dwight D. Eisenhower
Prime Minister's Personal Telegram T.76/53
(Churchill papers, 6/3)

5 April 1953
Priority
Secret, Personal and Private
No. 1531

Anthony and I have been thinking a good deal as we know you have also about the apparent change for the better in the Soviet mood. I am sure we shall be in agreement with you that we must remain vigilantly on our guard and maintain all that process of defensive rearmament from which any real improvement must have resulted. We think, as I am sure you do also, that we ought to lose no chance of finding out how far the Malenkov régime are prepared to go in easing things up all round. There seem certainly to be great possibilities in Korea and we are very glad of the steps you have taken to resume Truce negotiations.

2. For our part we are sending our Ambassador back to Moscow with instructions to try to settle with Molotov a number of minor points which concern Britain and Russia alone and have caused us trouble in the last few years. None of these are of major importance: they include such matters as the recent Soviet notice of intention to terminate the Temporary Anglo Soviet Fisheries Agreement of 1930, the cases of certain individual British subjects in Russia, exchange rates and restrictions on movements. Talks on them may give us some further indication of the depth of the Soviet purpose. We shall of course gladly keep your people informed of how we progress.

3. It may be that presently the Soviets will make overtures for some form of direct discussion of world problems whether on a Four Power basis or in some other manner. I assume of course that we shall deal in the closest collaboration with any such overtures if they are made.

4. I am sending you today a reply to your letter of the 19th about Egypt.[1]

Winston S. Churchill to President Dwight D. Eisenhower
(Premier papers, 11/1074)

5 April 1953

My dear Friend,

1. Thank you so much for your letter.[2] You know the importance I attach to our informal interchange of thoughts.

2. Of course my Number One is Britain with her eighty million white

---

[1] Reproduced above (pp. 910–11).
[2] Of Mar. 19, reproduced above (pp. 911–12).

English-speaking people working with your one-hundred-and-forty million. My hope for the future is founded on the increasing unity of the English-speaking world. If that holds, all holds. If that fails no one can be sure of what will happen. This does not mean that we should seek to dominate international discussions or always try to say the same thing. There are some cases however where without offending the circle of nations the fact that Britain and the United States took a joint initiative might by itself settle a dispute peaceably to the general advantage of the free world.

3. It was for this reason that I hoped that Anglo-American unity in Egypt and also in the Levant including Israel, would enable us without bloodshed to secure our common military and political interests. I did not think it would have been wrong for Slim and Hull with our two Ambassadors to have presented the package to Neguib and then seen what he had to say about it. This was on the basis that you would not be asked by us to contribute money or men to any fighting if things went wrong as they may well do now.

4. However, you have decided that unless invited by Neguib, who like all dictators is the servant of the forces behind him, we cannot present a joint proposal. We therefore have to go on alone. I think however that the fact that Britain and the United States are agreed upon what should be done to preserve an effective base there seems as far as it has gone, already to have had a modifying and helpful influence. Mere bluster by Neguib has not so far been accompanied by any acts of violence.

5. There is a view strongly held on the Opposition side of Parliament that we ought to abandon Egypt altogether. It is argued that the interests in the Middle East which we bear the burden of defending are international and NATO interests are far more than British. The post-war position of India, Pakistan and Burma makes the Suez Canal in many ways more important to them than to us. Even in the War, as you will remember, for three years we did without the Suez Canal. We can keep our contacts with Malaya and Australasia round the Cape as we did then. We could maintain our influence in the Levant and Eastern Mediterranean from Cyprus and our interests in the Persian Gulf from Aden. The great improvement of the right flank of the Western Front achieved by the Yugo-Tito-Greeko-Turko combination has made the danger of a physical Russian attack upon Palestine and Egypt definitely more remote in distance and therefore in what is vital namely in (Capitals) TIME. It is pointed out that if we brought our troops home and under their rearguards our worthwhile stores valued at about £270 million and also cancelled the £200 million so-called sterling debts (incurred in defending Egypt in the War) we should experience great relief.

6. If your advisers really think that it would be a good thing if we washed our hands of the whole business I should very much like to be told. It is quite certain that we could not justify indefinitely keeping eighty thousand men over there at more than £50 million a year to discharge an international task in

this area. If with your influence this burden could be largely reduced the great international Canal could continue to serve all nations, at any rate in time of peace, without throwing an intolerable burden upon us. It is for these reasons which have nothing to with Imperialism that I persevere.

7. As all this seems to have something to do with history in which we have both occasionally meddled, I am sure you will not mind my putting the matter before you as I see it.

Winston S. Churchill to Randolph S. Churchill
(Churchill papers, 1/51)

6 April 1953

Dearest Randolph,

Many thanks for sending me this. I have added a few notes and queries.

The practical cause of Lord Randolph's[1] rise, apart from the House of Commons, was his mastery of the National Union of Conservative Associations, which had great power in those days. On this Lord Salisbury came to terms. The fact that my Father went on a four months' visit to India in 1884/5 was no doubt a proof of the office Lord Salisbury had led him to expect.

Your loving Father,

President Dwight D. Eisenhower to Winston S. Churchill
(Premier papers, 11/422)

7 April 1953   The White House
Personal and Secret

Dear Winston,

Just before your letter of April fifth[2] reached my desk, I learned that Anthony is to undergo a major operation. Please convey to him my warm greetings and my most prayerful wishes for his early recovery. I have a great respect for his wisdom and integrity; the free nations cannot spare his sound counsel in these parlous times.

It would be difficult for me to find a single line in your letter with which I disagree, even if I were minded to look for such an opportunity. The convictions expressed in my former letter to you merely paralleled the old proverb about leading a horse to water. I assume that Neguib wants, above all else, to remain in power in Egypt. To do that, he has to have a large proportion of

---

[1] Randolph Henry Spencer Churchill, 1849–95. 3rd son of 7th Duke of Marlborough. Secretary of State for India, 1885–6. Leader of the House of Commons and Chancellor of the Exchequer, June 1886. Resigned in Dec. 1886 and held no further political office.

[2] Reproduced above (pp. 930–2).

the population with him. To satisfy the population's intense emotionalism with respect to national prestige, he must appear always to be treated in the world's councils as a <u>complete equal</u>. Consequently, a meeting on his own territory should be arranged, if possible, by <u>his</u> invitation.

If this is to be brought about, then we need really skilful negotiators to get him to realize how big he would look to his own people if he should issue an invitation and both of our governments should accept.

As to abilities of our own Ambassadors – either yours or ours – in Egypt, I know nothing. They may be quite skilful and imaginative; likewise they may be the reverse. In any event, our two Ambassadors went to see Neguib and were rebuffed. This is the unpleasant fact that must be taken into consideration as we lay plans to go further.

Possibly one way, now, to go about the affair is for your own representatives to start negotiations with Neguib and, when there arises in those negotiations the question of additional arms for Egypt – which might in part be provided by us – the question of America's interests and the conditions on which these arms would be furnished, would seem to create a natural opening for an invitation of our representatives to the conference. As quickly as we should receive any kind of intimation of welcome, General Hull would be on his way.

Our general agreement with you as to the things that ought to be done in that area and our readiness to do our best in bringing these things about, stand just as they did when we so expressed ourselves to Anthony during his visit.

But we are convinced that if your government and ours should press Neguib with some sort of ultimatum to the effect that he had to come into a conference with the two of us or we would simply walk out and desert the region, then he would have no recourse but defiance. He would realize, of course, that as a result he might eventually go under. But he would calculate that, by acceptance, he would go under without delay.

There is another subject of vital interest to us both and concerning which I have spoken to you a number of times. It is the need, in Europe, for uniform progress on the Common Defense Plan and for greater political and economic unity. In recent weeks I have been consulting with official and unofficial representatives from some of the countries in Western Europe. Almost without exception, they have said that a more emphatic <u>public</u> endorsement by Great Britain of these projects would be helpful, particularly in securing the support of the Socialist Party in France, which is more or less the key to that country's probable action. Permit me to say again that I should very much like to see you seize some appropriate opportunity to make a major address on the general subject of greater European military and economic unity, stating in your own inimitable and eloquent way the things that <u>you have already announced that Britain is ready to do</u> in support of these purposes. Such might just happen to be the decisive influence.

Anthony Eden to Vyacheslav Molotov
(*Premier papers, 11/422*)

8 April 1953
Priority
Secret
No. 171

Sir A. Gascoigne has already told you how pleased Her Majesty's Government and I are at the action you have taken about the British civilian internees in North Korea, in response to my appeal to you.

I am encouraged by this to ask myself whether there are further questions directly arising between our two Governments on which progress might now be made. Sir A. Gascoigne will tell you what questions I have in mind. You for your part may have other matters, also arising directly between you and us, which you would like to see disposed of. If so, please do not hesitate to let us know.

I hope that you will allow Sir A. Gascoigne, who knows my mind on these various topics, to discuss them fully and frankly with you. I feel sure that you will share my view that, if we can settle them, this will do much to effect the improvement in our general relations which I am confident we both have at heart.

The Prime Minister asks me to send you his greetings and good wishes.

Sir Alvary Gascoigne to Winston S. Churchill
(*Premier papers, 11/540*)

8 April 1953
Confidential
No. 54

SOVIET UNION: QUARTERLY REPORT
JANUARY–MARCH 1953

Sir,

I have the honour to transmit to you herewith a report for the first three months of 1953.

2. A quarter which began with the 'doctor's plot',[1] took in its stride Stalin's death and his succession by Malenkov and ended with Chou En-lai's[2]

---

[1] Campaign organized by Stalin which resulted in the dismissal and arrest of many doctors and officials. Following Stalin's death, the new Soviet leadership dropped the case, the evidence for which was soon declared to have been fabricated.

[2] Zhou Enlai, 1898–1976. First Premier, People's Republic of China, 1949–76. Foreign Minister, 1949–58. Chairman, National Committee of the Chinese People's Political Consultative Conference, 1954–76. Vice-Chairman, Communist Party of China, 1956–66, 1973–6.

acceptance of the voluntary repatriation of Korean war prisoners, has claims to be historic. The apparent departure from attitudes which, while Stalin was alive, seemed immutable, is astonishing enough. But even more remarkable is that the process of change should have been initiated before he was cold in his grave and by men whom we still have no reason to suppose were not, while he was alive, anything but his devoted associates.

3. Yet we still know much too little to see these developments in perspective. In the foreign field the war of position seems for the time at least to be evolving into a war of movement, whether because the new leaders have decided that Stalin's policy was too dangerous for them to follow or because they think they can gain more by behaving with suppleness where his system suffered from over rigidity. The new departures have been limited in scope, but have followed each other in quick succession. Their rapidity, again, places in an even more interesting light the events surrounding and immediately preceding Stalin's death and underlines the fact that with it a new page has been opened in Soviet history.

I have, &c.
(For the Ambassador),
Paul Grey[1]

Winston S. Churchill to Le Pacha El Hadj Thami El Glaoui[2]
(Premier papers, 11/353)

8 April 1953

My dear Excellence,

I understand that you are going to be in England at the time of the Coronation this summer. If this is the case, I should be happy if you would care to watch the Royal Procession on June 2 as my personal guest. I hope that you will be able to accept, and in any case I look forward to seeing you when you come to this country.

---

[1] Paul Francis Grey, 1908–90. Educated at Christ Church, Oxford. Married, 1936, Agnes Mary Weld-Blundell: three children. Entered Foreign Service, 1943; served in Rome, 1933; in Rio de Janeiro, 1944. Head of South-East Asia Department, FO, 1947–9. Counsellor, Embassy in Portugal, 1949–50. CMG, 1951. Minister in USSR, 1951–4. Asst Under-Secretary for Foreign Affairs, Information and Culture, 1954–7. Ambassador to Czechoslovakia, 1957–60. Ambassador to Switzerland, 1960–4. KCMG, 1963.

[2] Thami El Glaoui, 1879–1956. Appointed Pasha of Marrakech, 1912–56. Deposed Sultan of Morocco, 1953; pardoned by the Sultan, 1955.

President Dwight D. Eisenhower to Winston S. Churchill
(Premier papers, 11/429)

9 April 1953
Secret

Dear Winston,

Thank you very much for your cabled message[1] which reached me this morning. I feel sure that you will find our thinking on the subject largely paralleling your own. We feel that it is entirely possible that you will realize your hope of exploring further into the sincerity of the Soviet intentions through your impending negotiations with them on fisheries and so on.

I am considering the delivery of a formal speech, with the purpose of setting concretely before the world the peaceful intentions of this country. I would hope to do this in such a way as to delineate, at least in outline, the specific steps or measures that we believe necessary to bring about satisfactory relationships with resultant elimination or lowering of tensions throughout the world. These steps are none other than what our governments have sought in the past. I have been working on such a talk for some days and will soon be in a position to show it to your Ambassador, who will of course communicate with you concerning it. While I do not presume to speak for any government other than our own, it would be useless for me to say anything publicly unless I could feel that our principal allies are in general accord with what I will have to say. I am particularly anxious that this be true of Britain, and I think it also necessary to check with France and, as regards Germany, with Adenauer who arrives here tomorrow.

This whole field is strewn with very difficult obstacles, as we all know; but I do think it extremely important that the great masses of the world understand that, on our side, we are deadly serious in our search for peace and are ready to prove this with acts and deeds and not merely assert it in glittering phraseology. This presupposes prior assurance of honest intent on the other side.

Winston S. Churchill to President Dwight D. Eisenhower
(Premier papers, 11/429)

9 April 1953
Private and Personal

My dear Ike,

The sixth and last volume of my History of the Second World War was finished before I took office again and will be ready for publication, here and in the United States, towards the end of this year. It deals with the period from

---

[1] T.76/53, reproduced above (p. 930).

the launching of 'Overlord' down to the Potsdam Conference – a period of almost unbroken military success for the Allied arms but darkened by forebodings about the political future of Europe which have since been shown to have been only too well founded.

It contains, of course, a good many references to yourself, and I am writing to ask whether you would like to see these before the book comes out. I know that nothing which I have written will damage our friendship. But, now that you have assumed supreme political office in your country, I am most anxious that nothing should be published which might seem to others to threaten our current relations in our public duties or impair the sympathy and understanding which exist between our countries. I have therefore gone over the book again in the last few months and have taken great pains to ensure that it contains nothing which might imply that there was in those days any controversy or lack of confidence between us. There was in fact little controversy in those years; but I have been careful to ensure that the few differences of opinion which arose are so described that even ill-disposed people will be unable to now to turn them to mischievous account.

I think therefore that you can be confident that the publication of this final volume will do nothing to disturb our present relationship. And I can imagine that, in these first few months of your new responsibilities, you will not find much time to turn back to those 'far-off things and battles long ago'. If, however, you would prefer to have seen, before publication, those passages which refer directly to yourself, I will gladly have the extracts made and sent to you.

Anthony Eden to Sir Robert Howe
(*Premier papers, 11/544*)

9 April 1953
Immediate and Confidential
No. 503

It is not clear to me how Egyptian propaganda is thought to have doubled in intensity in the last month. Is this by means of newspapers, broadcasts, or bribery? We cannot prevent the first two, though you could presumably ban newspapers if they were subversive of public order. If you have any evidence of the third, I should be ready to instruct Her Majesty's Ambassador at Cairo to take this up with General Neguib. Meanwhile we are doing everything we can by positive means, e.g. broadcasts, to counter Egyptian propaganda to set up and we hope shortly what amounts to an information office.

2. We do not repeat do not agree that it is not now up to the Sudan Government to take steps to counteract this propaganda. It is, we think, primarily for the Sudan Government to do their utmost to ensure that the Sudanese get

a fair deal, and in this they can count on our full support. There are several ways of doing this, some negative and some positive. Among the latter are the exposure of the falsity of Egyptian allegations, and the removal of grievances exploited by the Egyptians, where this can be safely done.

Winston S. Churchill to Sir Robert Howe
Prime Minister's Personal Telegram T.82/53
(Premier papers, 11/544)

10 April 1953
Personal and Secret
No. 513

I am glad to telegraph you for the first time. You will have received Foreign Office telegram No. 503. Considering the methods Cairo have used and will certainly continue to use, there is surely no reason why all our faithful officials in the Sudan should not tell the people who trust them where their real interests lie. We must not take it all lying down. Pray do not hesitate to telegraph me.

Winston S. Churchill to President Dwight D. Eisenhower
Prime Minister's Personal Telegram T.80/53
(Premier papers, 11/429)

10 April 1953
Immediate
Dedip
Personal and Secret
No. 1596

1. Thank you so much for sending me an advance copy of your proposed speech. This is indeed a grave formidable declaration. You will not I am sure expect me to commit Her Majesty's Government to the many vital points with which it deals except to say that we are as ever wholly with you in the common struggle against Communist aggression.

2. I believe myself that at this moment time is on our side. The apparent change of Soviet mood is so new and so indefinite and the causes for it so obscure that there could not be much risk in letting things develop. We do not know what these men mean. We do not want to deter them from saying what they mean. Hitherto they have been the aggressors and have done us wrong at a hundred points. We cannot trade their leaving off doing wrong against our necessary defensive measures and the policy which such action demands and has procured.

April 1953

3. Nevertheless great hope has arisen in the world that there is a change of heart in the vast, mighty mass of Russia and this may carry them far and fast and perhaps into revolution. It has been well said that the most dangerous moment for evil Governments is when they begin to reform. Nothing impressed me so much as the Doctors[1] story. This must cut very deep into Communist discipline and structure. I would not like it to be thought that a sudden American declaration has prevented this natural growth of events.

4. All this comes to a particular point upon Korea. I was hoping that at least we should secure at this juncture a bona fide, lasting and effective truce in Korea which might mean the end of that show as a world problem. Indeed if nothing more than this happened everyone would rejoice. I hope you will consider what a tremendous score it would be for us all if we could bring off this truce. It seems to me very unlikely that the terms you require for the later political settlement of Korea as set out in your statement would be accepted as they stand by the other side. I fear the formal promulgation of your five points at this moment might quench the hope of an armistice.[2]

5. Anthony and I have in mind important comments we could make on your text but we are not putting them forward now, as we hope our arguments will persuade you to bide your time. We cannot see what you would lose by waiting till the full character and purpose of the Soviet change is more clearly defined and also is apparent to the whole free world. I always like the story of Napoleon going to sleep in his chair as the battle began saying 'wake me up when their infantry column gets beyond the wood'.

6. In Anthony's unfortunate but temporary illness I have had to take over the Foreign Office. But this telegram is addressed to you as part of our personal correspondence. I am, however, showing it to Makins and Aldrich.

7. Pray let me know what you decide. Kindest Regards.

Winston S. Churchill to Members of the Cabinet
(Cabinet papers, 129/60)

10 April 1953
Secret
Cabinet Paper No. 124 of 1953

ATOMIC ENERGY ORGANISATION

I circulate for the consideration of my colleagues an interim report by the Committee on the future of the Atomic Energy Organisation under the

---

[1] See above (p. 934 n.1).

[2] Eisenhower's terms were: (1) cessation of hostilities; (2) exchange of prisoners; (3) free elections in the reunited part of Korea and American economic aid to all parts of Korea, North and South; (4) a neutral zone in North Korea along the Yalo River; (5) withdrawal of all foreign troops.

940   April 1953

Chairmanship of Lord Waverley, which was established in accordance with the decision taken by the Cabinet on 14th January (CC(53)2nd Conclusions, Minute 9).

Committee on Atomic Energy Organisation
Interim Report

We were appointed by the Prime Minister —

'To devise a plan for transferring responsibility for Atomic Energy from the Ministry of Supply to a non-Departmental Organisation and to work out the most suitable form for the new Organisation, due regard being paid to any constitutional and financial implications.'

2. We have had a preliminary exchange of views with representatives of the Treasury (Sir Edward Bridges, Sir Bernard Gilbert,[1] Sir Thomas Padmore[2] and Mr G. P. Humphreys-Davies[3]); of the Ministry of Defence (Mr R. R. Powell, Deputy Secretary, and Sir Frederick Brundrett,[4] Deputy Scientific Adviser); and of the Ministry of Supply (Sir James Helmore,[5] Permanent Secretary). We have also had oral evidence from the following officers who are responsible under the Minister of Supply for various aspects of atomic energy; General Sir Frederick Morgan,[6] Controller of Atomic Energy; Sir

---

[1] Bernard William Gilbert, 1891–1957. Educated at St John's College, Cambridge. Joint Second Secretary of the Treasury, 1944–56.

[2] Thomas Padmore, 1909–96. Principal Private Secretary to Chancellor of the Exchequer, 1943–5; 2nd Secretary, 1952–62. KCB, 1953. Permanent Secretary, Ministry of Transport, 1962–8. GCB, 1965.

[3] George Peter Humphreys-Davies, 1909–85. Educated at New College, Oxford. Asst Principal, Admiralty, 1932. Treasury, 1934. Married, 1935, Barbara Crompton: three children. Private Secretary to PM, 1936–8. Under-Secretary, Treasury, 1949–56. Deputy Secretary, Ministry of Supply, 1956–60.

[4] Frederick Brundrett, 1894–1974. Educated at Sidney Sussex College, Cambridge. Served in RNVR, WWI. Scientific Staff, Royal Naval Signal School, 1919–37. Married, 1920, Enid James: one child. Principal Scientific Officer for HQ of Royal Naval Scientific Service in London, 1937; Superintending Scientist, 1940; Asst Director, 1941; Deputy Director, 1943; Chief, 1947. Knighted, 1946. Deputy Chairman, Defence Research Policy Committee, 1950; Chairman, 1954. Deputy Scientific Adviser, MoD, 1950–4. Honorary Scientific Adviser to Ministry of Civil Aviation, 1953–9. Chairman, Air Traffic Control Board, 1959–74. Chairman, Naval Aircraft Research Committee of the Aeronautical Research Council, 1960–6. Civil Service Commissioner, 1960–7.

[5] James Reginald Carroll Helmore, 1906–72. Educated at New College, Oxford. Entered Board of Trade, 1929. Private Secretary to President of the Board of Trade, 1934–7. Secretary, Board of Trade Representative in Washington DC, WWII. Under-Secretary, Board of Trade, 1946; 2nd Secretary, 1946–52. Permanent Secretary, Ministry of Materials, 1952. Permanent Secretary, Ministry of Supply, 1953–6. KCB, 1954.

[6] Frederick Edgworth Morgan, 1894–1967. GSO II, Army HQ India, 1932–5. GSO II, War Office, 1936–7. Deputy Asst Military Secretary, War Office, 1937–8. GSO I, 3rd Infantry Div., 1938–9. CO, 1st Support Group, 1st Armoured Div. (France), 1939–40. Brig.-Gen., Staff, II Corps, 1940–1. GOC 55th Infantry Div., 1941–2. GOC I Corps, 1942–3. CoS to Supreme Allied Cdr, 1943–4. Deputy CoS to SHAEF, 1944–5. Head of UNRRA in Germany, 1945–6. Col. Commandant, RA, 1948. CB, 1943; KCB, 1944. Controller of Atomic Energy, 1951–4; of Nuclear Arms, 1954–6.

John Cockcroft,[1] Director, Atomic Energy, Production; Sir William Penney, Chief Superintendent, High Explosives Research.

3. We have carried our discussions to the point at which it is clear that the main problems with which we shall have to deal are:
- (a) The position of Ministers in relation to the new Organisation and, in that connection, the determination of the best methods of reconciling the practical efficiency of the various plants and establishments with the ultimate responsibility of Ministers to Parliament.
- (b) The procedure for providing the new Organisation with the necessary finance and the system of financial control.
- (c) The devising of means which will ensure that the standards of security observed in the new Organisation are not less effective than those at present in force.
- (d) The provision of suitable safeguards for the interests of existing staff who are to be asked to transfer to the new Organisation.
- (e) The relations of the various Atomic Energy Establishments and Plants to each other and to the Headquarters of the new Organisation.
- (f) The status of the Establishments which are engaged on atomic weapon research and on the production of parts such as weapons; and the relation of those Establishments so far as they may be brought within the new Organisation to the Defence Departments and the Ministry of Supply.
- (g) The special difficulties of the interim period during which legislation is being prepared and passed and administrative preparations are being made for the building up of the new Organisation.

4. None of the departmental representatives with whom we have discussed these problems has suggested to us that any of them are insoluble. And indeed we are now satisfied that it is completely practicable to devise a plan which will include reasonable solutions to all these issues. Many of the problems, however, call for further close and detailed investigation, much of which can only be carried out effectively at the various plants and establishments. We are not therefore in a position to commit ourselves in respect to the most suitable form for the new Organisation, or for the transfer of responsibility to it, until we have been freed to carry on investigations on the spot. Such examination

---

[1] John Douglas Cockcroft, 1897–1967. Educated at St John's College, Cambridge. Entered Army, 1915. Lt, 1918. Married, 1925, Eunice Crabtree: six children. Fellow, St John's College, 1928. Along with Ernest Walton, succeeding in splitting the atom. Supervisor in Mechanical Sciences, St John's College, 1931. Director of Research, Mond Laboratory, 1935. FRS, 1936. Prof. of Natural Philosophy, 1939. Asst Director of Scientific Research, Ministry of Supply, WWII. Chief Superintendent, Air Defence Research Development Establishment, 1941. Director, Atomic Energy, Production, 1946–58. Knighted, 1948. Nobel Prize in Physics, 1951. President, Institute of Physics, 1954–6. Master of Churchill College, Cambridge, 1959.

will inevitably lead to some publicity and possibly to embarrassing questions which we understand that the Government may wish to forestall. We therefore hope that the Government will now be prepared to take such steps as they think fit to set us free to make all such enquiries as appear necessary to us, including visits to any of the establishments.

5. In the event of the Government's deciding, in the light of this report, to announce publicly at this stage a decision in principle to transfer responsibility for atomic energy to a non-Departmental Organisation, we would urge that such announcement should include a general undertaking that the interests of the existing staff will be fully safeguarded.

Waverley
J. H. Woods[1]
W. A. Akers[2]

Winston S. Churchill to General Lord Ismay
Prime Minister's Personal Minute M.74/53
(Premier papers, 11/548)

10 April 1953

Can nothing be done to reduce the length of telegrams like this.* When you consider how much it costs to telegraph it and all the cyphering and de-cyphering it is a serious matter. Could I know what this telegram cost including the cyphering and de-cyphering. There seems to be nothing in it which could not have come by airmail.

* From UKHC Australia No. 238 of 5 April 1953 re: ANZAM.

---

[1] John Harold Edmund Woods, 1895–1962. Served with 22nd Battalion, Royal Fusiliers during WWI (wounded). Principal Asst Secretary, HM Treasury, 1940–3. CB, 1943. Permanent Secretary, Ministry of Production, 1943–5; Board of Trade, 1945–51. KCB, 1945. Member of Economic Planning Board, 1947–51. GCB, 1949. Member of Waverley Committee on Atomic Energy, 1953.

[2] Wallace Akers, 1888–1954. British physical chemist. Director of Tube Alloys project, 1941–5. CBE, 1944. Knighted, 1946. Director of Research, Imperial Chemical Industries, 1946–53.

President Dwight D. Eisenhower to Winston S. Churchill
Prime Minister's Personal Telegram T.85A/53
(Premier papers, 11/1074)

11 April 1953
Immediate
Dedip
Personal and Secret
No. 1618

Dear Winston,

I deeply appreciate your offer to allow me to go over certain excerpts from your forthcoming book, and I am grateful for your expressed anxiety to avoid saying anything that could possibly hurt our relations either directly or indirectly. Although I am so pressed at the moment that I could not go over them personally, Bedell Smith, who, as you know, was my constant companion in the days of which you are now writing, would be glad to perform this service for me. His current position as our Under-Secretary of State also makes him peculiarly sensitive to any possible expressions of thought that could have a jarring effect upon our mutual relations. Consequently, if you will send the excerpts to Bedell he will go over them and return them to you at the earliest possible moment.

With regard to your concern about the speech that I must give on 16th April, I have a considerable sympathy with your point that we must be careful to avoid anything that would make the Russians retreat into their shell, if they are, in fact, sincere in extending certain feelers for peace. Nevertheless, the time has come in this country when something must be said by me on the whole subject, and of course it cannot be a meaningless jumble of platitudes. I shall consequently soften the parts concerning Korea, and change certain other expressions so that there can be no misinterpretation of our position to be fully and completely receptive of any peace proposals, while at the same time never letting down our guard. I think we must all realize it is primarily our own growing and combined strength that is bringing about a change in the Russian attitude, and that if this is a sincere change we must not be lulled into complacency just as surely as we must not be belligerent or truculent. That is the attitude for which I shall strive in this talk.

As for the matter of timing, of course no one can accurately gauge the probable influence of an early statement as opposed to a later one. However, since I am obligated beyond any possibility of withdrawal to making a speech on this general subject, I suggest that you cable at once any comments that you and Anthony may wish to make after reading what I have had to say in this message. While I cannot agree in advance to be guided by all of them, I shall certainly consider them prayerfully.

April 1953

Winston S. Churchill to President Dwight D. Eisenhower
Prime Minister's Personal Telegram T.86/53
(Premier papers, 11/1074)

12 April 1953
Immediate
Dedip
Secret
No. 1616

1. Thank you so much for your very kind message. I do not seek any share of responsibility in the speeches you make to the United States although they play so vital a part in the fortunes of the world. You may be sure that we shall stand by you on fundamentals. The question of timing did however press upon me. It would be a pity if a sudden frost nipped spring in the bud, or if this could be alleged, even if there was no real spring. I do not attempt to predict what the Soviet change of attitude and policy, and it seems to me of mood, means. It might mean an awful lot. Would it not be well to combine the re-assertions of your and our inflexible resolves with some balancing expression of hope that we have entered upon a new era. A new hope has, I feel, been created in the unhappy, bewildered world. It ought to be possible to proclaim our unflinching determination to resist Communist tyranny and aggression and at the same time though separately, to declare how glad we should be if we found there was a real change of heart and not let it be said that we had closed the door upon it.

2. Since you kindly invite me to make a few detailed comments I venture to append a few suggestions. (See my immediately following telegram.)

3. I have to make a speech on the 17th and hope to use the theme 'we are firm as a rock against aggression but the door is always open to friendship'.

4. About the book. I am delighted that Bedell should vet it for you and I will communicate with him.

5. Anthony's operation[1] this morning is reported to have been completely successful and absolutely necessary.

---

[1] To remove gallstones.

Winston S. Churchill to President Dwight D. Eisenhower
Prime Minister's Personal Telegram T.87/53
(Premier papers, 11/1017)

12 April 1953
Immediate
Dedip
Secret
No. 1617

My immediately preceding telegram.

These are my comments:

1. No reference is made to the North Atlantic Treaty Organization while great stress is laid upon the EDC. Would it not be well to place EDC within the wider scope of our developing North Atlantic Community?

2. There is also no reference to the problem of China and the Far East generally. Could not this be covered by adding to your paragraph about Korea some words about the need to find a basis for future peace in the whole Far Eastern area?

3. Thirdly we are not sure what is meant about the 'reunited part of Korea'. Does it mean South Korea and North Korea less the neutral zone? In considering such a 'neutral zone' much would depend upon the width.

4. In your section about armaments the thought behind paragraph 2 is new to me.[1] As you alone produce at least three times the Soviet steel production this would not be likely to suit their fancy.

5. Sub-paragraphs 3 and 4 about the control of Atomic Energy are I presume a continuance of the position which Bernie Baruch's Committee took up in 1946 and on which we have rested ever since and must continue to rest.

6. Finally I am entirely with you on not letting Adenauer down. He seems to me the best German we have found for a long time.

---

[1] Eisenhower had suggested limiting the total production for military purposes of certain materials across all nations.

April 1953

Winston S. Churchill to President Dwight D. Eisenhower
Prime Minister's Personal Telegram T.91/53
(Premier papers, 11/1074)

13 April 1953
Immediate
Secret
No. 1632

I thought that now Slim is no longer available the best man to replace him in our negotiations with the Egyptians would be General Sir Brian Robertson, Commander-in-Chief, Middle East Land Forces. I am sure you know him well. The Ambassador will lead our delegation with Robertson as his co-delegate. Therefore if, as I still hope, you can join us at a later stage, Robertson will be in almost exactly the same position as Hull. Robertson is being relieved of his Command for this purpose a month earlier than would otherwise have been the case.

2. This announcement will be made on 16th April, and will be preceded on 15th April by an invitation from us to the Egyptians to open negotiations. I intend that there shall be a definite and formal opening. We hope this will be before the end of April.

Sir Robert Howe to Winston S. Churchill
Prime Minister's Personal Telegram T.93/53
(Premier papers, 11/544)

13 April 1953   Khartoum
Personal and Secret
No. 275

Your telegram No. 513.[1]
Thank you very much for your telegram.
The problem of countering Egyptian action here is one of great difficulty, on which the Foreign Secretary knows my mind. The Governor-General is the agent of both the British and Egyptian Governments and in principle cannot therefore take that partisan attitude which any propaganda or counter-propaganda demands. Moreover the recent Anglo-Egyptian Agreement is based on the principle of building up a free and neutral atmosphere in the Sudan pending self determination, which again precludes the administration from overtly taking sides during the transitional period. Our guiding principle here must primarily be to keep the ring on that account for the Sudanese themselves and to protect them as much as possible.

---

[1] T.82/53, reproduced above (p. 938).

On the positive side there is little we can do within the above limits, but all the influence which we have here, and it is very great, will be directed towards convincing the Sudanese where their real interests lie. This influence must be largely exercised privately and unofficially by any and every British subject here and this is being done.

On the other side there is the unending strain of press and radio propaganda from Cairo and lavish bribery. Concrete evidence of this latter is impossible to obtain, but one can see signs of it in the way of living of the pro-Egyptian Sudanese here. The leader of the Mahdist Party[1] tells me that he knows that Egypt is prepared to pay £10,000 for every seat at the elections for the National Union Party.

Then there are the propaganda visits of Egyptian personalities. It does not help us here, whenever we take strong action against these gentry, such for example as Salah ed Din,[2] to be asked to back down, on the plea that 'Neguib's face must be saved' or 'it would greatly assist in improving the atmosphere for military talks in Cairo' (reference Cairo telegram No. 643).

Our best propaganda here is to stand firm against such Egyptian efforts, where necessary applying such sanctions as we have. Every successful action of this kind by the administration gives an immeasurable gain for British prestige. But we must have your support.

Winston S. Churchill to Lord De L'Isle and Dudley
Prime Minister's Personal Minute M.83/53
(Premier papers, 11/355)

13 April 1953

If you only require an additional £500 and are prepared to invite and transport all Members of Parliament from London as official guests there is no need for you to bring the matter before the Cabinet again.

---

[1] Sayed Abdallah Khalil, 1892–1970. Born in Omdurman, Sudan. Served in Egyptian Army, 1910–24; Sudan Defence Force, 1925–44. Helped found pro-Mahdist Umma Party, 1945. Formed close political relationship with Robert Howe. Leader of Legislative Assembly and Executive Council, 1948. Elected to Parliament, 1953. PM and Minister of Defence, 1956–8.

[2] Salah ed Din Nasr, 1920–82. Head of Egyptian General Intelligence Directorate, 1957–67.

Cabinet: conclusions
(Cabinet papers, 128/26)

14 April 1953
Secret
11.30 a.m.
Cabinet Meeting No. 26 of 1953

1. The Prime Minister reported to the Cabinet the latest proposals for resuming defence negotiations with the Egyptian Government. It had now been arranged that, when the negotiations were resumed, Her Majesty's Ambassador in Cairo would be supported by General Sir Brian Robertson, who would for this purpose relinquish his military command in the Middle East a few weeks earlier than he would otherwise have done. General Robertson had been brought back to London for consultations; and it was now hoped that the negotiations would open in Cairo on 27th April. This plan fitted in with the possibility of the United States joining with us later, on the original model.

The Prime Minister was anxious that our conditions, as formulated in the instructions which were to have served as the basis for the proposed Anglo-American approach, should be plainly stated to the Egyptians at an early stage; and he preferred on this account that there should be a formal opening of negotiations which would be distinct from normal diplomatic exchanges. His conversations with General Robertson had confirmed him in this view. He had therefore instructed our negotiators to proceed on the basis that it was the Egyptians who desired to resume the negotiations; that the discussions should begin with a formal meeting at which both sides would state their views; and that our case should be developed on the lines indicated in the instructions which had been drawn up for the purpose of the proposed Anglo-American approach. It would be announced in advance that the discussions were to be opened on 27th April.

The Prime Minister also said that he was instructing our negotiators to do their utmost to secure Egyptian agreement to the proposal that British troops retained in the base installations in the Canal Zone should wear uniform and carry personal arms. He thought it specially important that these men should not be left unarmed and open to arrest by Egyptian police if, for instance, trouble arose about the Sudan. If they wore uniform and carried personal arms they could not be molested by the Egyptians without military action which would constitute an act of war.

Discussion showed that the Cabinet were in agreement with the action taken by the Prime Minister.

The Cabinet –

(1) Endorsed the decision that General Sir Brian Robertson should be

April 1953 949

associated with Her Majesty's Ambassador in Cairo in the renewed defence negotiations with the Egyptian Government.

(2) Approved the instructions which the Prime Minister had given regarding the manner in which these negotiations were to be opened.

[...]

President Dwight D. Eisenhower to Winston S. Churchill
(*Premier papers, 11/429*)

14 April 1953
Secret

Dear Winston

Thank you very much for your prompt reply[1] to my cablegram.[2] I agree with the tenor of your comments and shall certainly strive to make my talk one that will not freeze the tender buds of sprouting decency, if indeed they are really coming out.[3]

John Selwyn Lloyd to Winston S. Churchill
(*Premier papers, 11/422*)

15 April 1953

You may like to know that on March 30th Mr Robert Boothby, MP had a long conversation with M Zhivotovski,[4] a Third Secretary of the Soviet Embassy. The conversation took place in Mr Boothby's flat over tea, as he had been unable to accept M Zhivotovski's invitation to luncheon.

2. The conversation ranged fairly widely, but dealt chiefly with Europe. After some preliminary exchanges, during which Mr Boothby explained forcefully that the coup d'état in Czechoslovakia and the Korean war had been the principal factors in starting Western re-armament, the conversation turned to Germany. Mr Boothby asked whether the Russians now proposed permanent partition as the solution to the German problem. M Zhivotovski replied: 'That would be a permanent threat to peace, and it is now too late to go back to Potsdam.' He then asked whether the United Kingdom would take the lead in proposing a Four-Power conference at the highest level. Mr Boothby replied

---

[1] T.86/53, reproduced above (p. 944).
[2] T.85A/53, reproduced above (p. 943).
[3] Churchill replied: 'Thank you so much for your last message. All good luck' (*The Churchill Eisenhower Correspondence*, pp. 45–6).
[4] Georgi Mikhailovich Zhivotovski.

that, whereas he had no doubt that the Prime Minister and the Foreign Secretary would go anywhere if there were any chance of achieving something it would be necessary to obtain some prior agreement on the general lines in advance, which must be obtained by preliminary diplomatic exchanges. M Zhivotovski's comment, according to Mr Boothby, was 'I don't see what good diplomatic exchanges can do in this case. The problem is too complicated. It can only be settled round a table by the men at the top.' From this remark it occurred to Mr Boothby that the Russians do not in fact know what to do next about Germany. M Zhivotovski then asked about Strasbourg and Mr Boothby explained the aims of the so-called Strasbourg Economic Plan.

3. In general, Mr Boothby gained the impression, from his discussion with M Zhivotovski, that the Soviet authorities, at least on the official level in the Embassy, are in some doubt over what is going on and some uncertainty over what they should do next.

4. Mr Boothby has accepted an invitation from M Zhivotovski and expects to lunch with him towards the end of this week. He will no doubt let us know what happens. In general, the Foreign Secretary is not in favour of trying to do business with the Soviet Embassy at the present time through unofficial contacts. In consequence, while Mr Boothby has been thanked for the information he has sent us, no attempt has been made to 'brief' him for his next meeting.[1]

John Colville to Evelyn Shuckburgh
(Premier papers, 11/422)

16 April 1953

My dear Shuckburgh,

The Prime Minister saw Mr Gromyko[2] this morning in order, as acting Secretary of State for Foreign Affairs, to take leave of him on his departure for Moscow. The conversation was confined to generalities and nothing of any substance was said by Mr Gromyko apart from a broad wish that the present improvement in the situation should continue. Mr Churchill gave Mr Gromyko a bound copy of one of his books.

After Gromyko left Mr Churchill telephoned the American Ambassador in order to tell him of the visit and to ask him to assure the United States Administration that it had been purely formal in nature and had no other

---

[1] Churchill wrote: 'Noted'.
[2] Andrei Andreyevich Gromyko, 1909–89. Senior Instructor, Institute of Economics, Moscow, 1936–9. Counsellor, Soviet Embassy, Washington DC, 1939–43. Ambassador to the US, 1943–6; to the UK, 1952–3. Permanent Representative of Soviet Union to UN, 1946–8. 1st Deputy Minister of Foreign Affairs, 1949–57. Minister of Foreign Affairs, 1957–85. 1st Deputy Chairman of the Council of Ministers, 1983–5. Member of Supreme Soviet, 1985–8.

significance. Mr Aldrich did not know that Mr Gromyko was giving up the Embassy here and that Mr Malik[1] was taking it over.

Winston S. Churchill to Sir Robert Howe
Prime Minister's Personal Telegram T.94/53
(Premier papers, 11/544)

16 April 1953
Personal and Priority
No. 533

Your telegram No. 275.[2]

My colleagues and I hold that there is a great deal which the British members of the Sudan Administration can and should do to counteract Egyptian propaganda and pressure upon the Sudanese. Please let me have a detailed analysis of the means used by the Egyptians. Meanwhile I think that your attitude should be as follows:

2. The Administration should defend themselves strongly when attacked by the Egyptians. They should do everything they can to encourage the Sudanese to stand up for themselves in every way. I agree that, except when members of the Administration are attacked, they must preserve an appearance of impartiality, since they are the servants of both co-domini. But I cannot believe that a great deal cannot be done to unmask Egyptian intrigues. It is above all the most important to seek out and expose bribery.

3. Her Majesty's Government will support you in this. We are already taking certain positive steps to ensure that our policy is made known to the Sudanese. We shall continue to bring home to them our continuing interest in the Sudan. We cannot physically prevent the Egyptians spreading propaganda by overt means, for example by radio. But you may rely on us to support you in such measures as are judged necessary to control Egyptian activities in the Sudan. We have for example given you full support over the prevention of visits to the South. We must be resolute to resist Egyptian encroachments.

---

[1] Yakov Alexandrovich Malik, 1906–80. Born in Kharkov, Ukraine. Educated at Simon Kuznets Kharkiv National University of Economics and Soviet Institute for Foreign Affairs, University of Moscow. Counsellor, Soviet Embassy, Japan, 1939–42. Ambassador to Japan, 1942–5. Deputy Foreign Minister, 1946–8. Ambassador to UN, 1948–52, 1968–76; to UK, 1953–60. Deputy Foreign Minister, 1960–80. Chairman, Africa Dept, Soviet Ministry of Foreign Affairs, 1968–76. Twice awarded the Order of Lenin and the Order of the Red Banner of Labour.

[2] T.93/53, reproduced above (pp. 946–7).

Winston S. Churchill to John Selwyn Lloyd
Prime Minister's Personal Minute M.84/53
(Premier papers, 11/544)

16 April 1953

In the draft telegram to Sir Robert Howe about the treatment of the British Administration in the Sudan, which you sent me for approval this morning, you mentioned that the Sudanese elections are to be postponed. I am surprised that the first intimation that I have received of this grave and unexpected change of plan should be in a passing reference in a telegram. I thought that the holding of early elections was one of the main advantages we expected from the Sudan Agreement. It was certainly among the principal arguments which were put forward for accepting the Agreement. The Cabinet should be given a full report about this new departure.

Winston S. Churchill: speech
('*Winston S. Churchill, His Complete Speeches*', volume 8, pages 8465-70)

17 April 1953   Scottish Unionist Association Annual Meeting
Green's Playhouse, Glasgow

THE GOVERNMENT'S RECORD

It is eighteen months ago this very day that I last spoke in Glasgow on the eve of the General Election. We were returned in October, 1951, with an overall majority in the House of Commons of only sixteen. It was feared by many of our friends and hoped by most of our opponents that a government commanding such a slender majority could not look forward to any long or useful life. Now after eighteen months of responsibility Her Majesty's Government have acquired an increasing sense of strength and power. It is usual for governments, especially those who are compelled by the public need to do unpopular things, to lose public support in the first stage of their administration. We have a right to be encouraged by the fact that the opposite has happened to us.

The by-elections and the reports we receive from many quarters show that we are gaining an increasing measure of confidence and that we are definitely stronger now than we were when we started on our uphill road. Thanks to the exertions of our Members in the House of Commons we have in practice secured majorities more than double our nominal figure to carry forward our legislative programme and our administrative reforms.

Let me express my thanks to all of you Scottish Unionists for the continued efforts you have made to sustain that public good will and understanding upon which we rely for our continued efficiency. Here I should like to pay tribute to the devotion and duty which our Scottish Unionist Members have shown in the House of Commons. Upon them, operating far from their home base, constant and regular attendance to support the Government in debate and in division night after night, has imposed specially heavy burdens. They all look very well here to-night in spite of it all.

We Conservatives and Unionists fought the General Election mainly on the maintenance of peace through strength. We fought on the restoration of sound finance, on which prosperity, continued full employment and our social services all alike depend. We declared our resolve amid much derision, to aim at the target of three hundred thousand houses a year. And finally, we urged the return to a freer enterprise society, involving the reduction of bureaucratic restrictions and controls, and a general limiting of the growing power of the state over the individual.

Our Socialist opponents on the other hand, having exhausted the few constructive ideas on which their movement was founded and having discredited the nationalization of industry, and being already deeply divided and bewildered about what to do next, tried to win a majority by arousing fear. A new world war would come upon us; I shall before I sit down return to this.

There would be unemployment on a great scale. Mr Robens,[1] the former Minister of Labour, speaking only a year ago, predicted that there would be a million unemployed by the end of last year. Actually, even at the worst period of the winter, the total unemployed did not reach half that figure, and was less than what the Socialist Government when in office had adopted as their full employment obligation. The latest figures are the most encouraging and the fall of 55,000 in unemployment between January and March was the biggest for this period in any post-war year except 1951. In March the total was 397,000 or less than one in fifty of the total number of employees.

It was prophesied that there would be widespread industrial unrest. In fact, however, the number of days lost in industrial disputes was more than a hundred thousand fewer in 1952, the first full year of Conservative office, than in the year's average during the last year's Socialist Rule.

A very good understanding and relationship has grown up between Her Majesty's Government and the trade unions under the wise and sympathetic guidance of our Minister of Labour, Sir Walter Monckton. The trade union leaders have shown a high sense of responsibility, and have declined to allow the permanent interests of the wage-earners to become the sport of party

---

[1] Alfred Robens, 1910–99. Official of Union of Distributive and Allied Workers, 1935–45. Manchester City Councillor, 1942–5. MP (Lab.) for Wansbeck, 1945–50; for Blyth, 1950–60. Parliamentary Private Secretary to Minister of Transport, 1945–7. Parliamentary Secretary, Ministry of Fuel and Power, 1947–51. Minister of Labour and National Service, 1951. Governor, Queen Elizabeth Training College for the Disabled, 1951–80. Shadow Foreign Secretary, 1955–6. Baron, 1961. Chairman, National Coal Board, 1961–71. President, Advertising Association, 1963–8. Director, Bank of England, 1966–81. Chairman of Vickers, 1971–9.

politics. Very wise words were spoken yesterday by Mr Tom O'Brien,[1] the Chairman of the TUC at their Scottish gathering at Rothesay. They should be studied by serious-minded men of every party and of no party.

I regard the trade unions as one of the outstanding institutions of our country. At least a third of the trade unionists are Conservatives. I have urged all Conservatives concerned to join them, to attend their meetings, and take a keen interest in their policy. This is not because I expect that the trade unions will become supporters of the Conservative fortunes of their country, whichever of the two great political organizations is in office. Above all, they stand as a bulwark not only against Communism but against those fellow-travellers whose activities are so mischievous and prominent at the present time.

Lastly – among major points – the voters were told that a Conservative Government would slash social services and ruin the welfare state. It is not Conservatives who would destroy the welfare state. It is national bankruptcy that would be its ruin. It is by warding off national bankruptcy that we cherish and protect our social services in the creation of which we and in former times the Liberals have played an overwhelming part. In spite of our grave financial problems we have improved the benefits under the various social insurance schemes, and we are actually spending more than the Socialists did on education, health, and housing. When I addressed you in October, 1951, you may remember that I dealt at some length with housing. Failure to grapple with housing was one of the biggest blots on the record of the late administration. I expressed my belief that by leaving party politics out of it and by allowing enterprise and ingenuity to play their part under conditions of flexibility, a Conservative and Unionist Government would bring a substantial relief to the housing needs of the nation, in spite of the priority we should have to give to rearmament. You can now judge how far we have redeemed the pledge I then made.

Last year we built in Britain close on two hundred and forty thousand houses. I made you a further pledge. Realizing that bad as was the housing situation in England and Wale, it was worse in Scotland, I said that a Unionist Government would see that in the allocation of housing resources Scotland's needs were given their full share. Last year in Great Britain as a whole the number of houses completed rose by nearly a quarter over 1951. In Scotland the increase was more than a third. The total of houses completed in Scotland last year – just under thirty-one thousand – was the highest recorded since records began over thirty years ago. It beat even the pre-war 1938 total by more than four thousand. The returns for the early months of this year show that there is no falling off from that high achievement.

---

[1] Thomas O'Brien, 1900–70. General Secretary, National Association of Theatrical and Kine Employees, 1932–70. MP (Lab.) for Nottingham West, 1945–59. Representative to the American Federation of Labor, 1946. President, TUC, 1953. Chairman, Trades Councils' Joint Consultative Committee, 1953–70.

We must not slacken in our high endeavours. We cannot be content until local authorities have resumed their pre-war Conservative drive against the slums. Also we must tackle the problem of the older houses which are falling out of repair. It is good that so many new houses are being put up, but there will always be a housing shortage and overcrowding if we allow the older houses to become unfit for use. These solid facts are answers to the untruthful panic-mongers' charges and prophecies which misled many people at the General Election, but which are now coming home to roost with those who scattered them forth. Nothing encourages us in our long and anxious task more than that these facts are confidently being recognized by our fellow-countrymen.

When we took over eighteen months ago the financial position was grim and grave in the last degree. For six years the Socialist Party had ruled the land with more power for good or ill than any Government I have even seen in peacetime. They had enjoyed in loans and gifts from Canada and the United States more than two thousand million pounds of aid and subsidy. They had maintained war taxation at a higher rate than any country in the free world, and yet at the end of it all they saw national bankruptcy approaching with hideous strides. In the fourth quarter of 1951 we lost more from our gold and dollar reserves than we had ever lost before in any quarter. If our reserves had continued to fall at the same rate as they were falling when we took over, they would have disappeared entirely by the middle of 1952. In the second half of 1951 we spent abroad as a nation nearly four hundred million pounds more than we earned.

Our international financial position was almost as dangerous because of the internal inflation that had been steadily undermining the value of the pound since 1945. During the six years of Socialist rule the pound lost nearly a third of its value and when they were dismissed by the electors the national finances seemed to have passed almost out of control.

Had this mismanagement continued we should have been hard put to it to buy our food; and our factories would have stood idle for want of raw materials. The change of Government came only just in time. The claim which I assert here to-night is that we have already made things solidly better. But here is no resting point. We may draw breath for a moment and look around, but then forward with perseverance and fortified resolve.

Last Tuesday I went to the House of Commons to hear the Budget. It was a memorable occasion. It was the first Budget since the war without any new taxes. The Chancellor of the Exchequer, Mr Butler, gave a full account of the improvement in our world position; how much further we were from national bankruptcy than a year ago and still further than eighteen months ago. You may remember he took over from Mr Gaitskell. This old school tie, left-wing careerist may rightly claim to have been worst Chancellor of the Exchequer since Dr Dalton. Mr Butler not only described the progress we had made by sound finance, including doing a lot of things that were hard and unpopular, but after this he actually unfolded a long list of taxes which he was not putting on but taking off, not piling up but cutting down.

From where I sat I had a fine view of the faces of our Socialist opponents and could watch their expressions as the story unfolded. It was quite painful to see their looks of gloom and sorrow when any fact was stated which was favourable to our country and its prospects. They frowned and scowled and hung their heads until I thought some of them were going to break into tears. However, we are far from being out of the woods yet, and when warnings were given by the Chancellor of the disappointments that had occurred or dangers that lie ahead, it was wonderful to see how quickly they cheered up. Their eyes twinkled, their faces were covered with grins not only of mirth but of mockery. However, on the whole they had a bad time and there was much more for them to bemoan and bewail than for them to jibe and jeer at. They had to face our plans for doing away with sugar rationing and making sugar more plentiful. After all we are the only country in the world to have kept on rationing sugar and yet I have been told we won the war.

Then Mr Butler restored the initial allowances on new equipment for our factories and farms. No doubt he did this because he thought they would be better able to compete in the export market and help us to earn our living instead of begging and borrowing from the Americans. They didn't seem to like it at all, especially as they had to support it. With the same idea of regaining independence in mind the Chancellor went on to announce the ending of the excess profits levy next year. But worse was yet to come. The purchase tax was cut by a quarter. And then there was that awful thing about making it easier for families to keep their aged and dependent relatives. This really seems to show preference for quite old-fashioned family ties – instead of all the new dreams of the Utopian State in which our Socialist friends indulge, where everyone queues up equally and is looked after more or less by the officials. No wonder they were upset. But the culminating point, the climax, the top notch, was hit when Mr Butler perpetrated his most insulting and malevolent deed. He took sixpence off the income tax. I never take pleasure in human woe, and yet I must confess I wish you had been there with me to see the look of absolute misery and anger which swept across the crowded faces opposite. Sixpence off the income tax! Class favour to over thirty millions of people. What shocking Tory reaction. Only nine shillings in the pound left for the income tax collector!

How could anyone tell that in future years more atrocities like this might not be committed? And what about the two million people at the bottom of the income tax scale who last year were actually freed by Mr Butler from income tax altogether? They were let off last year so there is nothing more for them this year. They just have to go on being let off. What a shame! The Socialists went off and held an indignation meeting at which they were so distressed that they actually had to appeal to Mr Aneurin Bevan (whom most of them hate with an intensity unusual in our British political life) to come to their aid and spend the weekend – excluding, I hope, the Sabbath – thinking out all the rudest things to say to us on Monday night.

But the strangest incident of all in the reception of the Budget is that the Opposition, if I may judge by their official newspaper, should try to combine the accusation that we are inflicting a real hardship on the people with the other charge that we are going to spring an election upon the country in order to improve our voting strength by Budget popularity. It has never been in our thoughts to spring any election – the third, it would be, in just over three years – upon the country. We came in to do a job. It was a hard job but we said we would do our best to do it. We shall be judged by the job we had to do and by the way we have done it. Our aim is deeds, not words: results, not promises. For this the nation do not need an electioneering crisis with all the bitter antagonisms on which it feeds. We need a greater spirit of unity and a stronger sense of stability in our public affairs. Of course with our very small majority if it became impossible for the Government to fulfil its programme a different situation would arise. But it is hoped that this may be avoided and a definite period of stability, confidence, and recuperation be granted to this overburdened island after all she has done for others and all we have gone through ourselves.

Think of our position in the world. On a highly artificial foundation we have brought into being in this island fifty million people, and they have grown accustomed to enjoy a standard of living equalled in few other countries. Indeed we have gone far ahead of most others in the development of our social services. This year we are spending eighty million more than ever before on these services. On top of all that we have undertaken the heaviest defence burden this country has ever shouldered in time of peace. What does this all rest upon? What is it that keeps us going? We live and survive solely by the efforts of free enterprise industry. That was as true under the Socialist Government as it is today.

The importance of the Budget Mr Butler introduced on Tuesday is that it marks a profound change in attitude towards enterprise. We are done with the Socialist policy of discouragement by ever-mounting taxation, multiplying controls, and the ever present threat of nationalization. We turn a more hopeful page. The first aim of the Chancellor is to lighten the burden on industry and of course on agriculture, and to make them more productive by greater incentives and fewer restrictions. The surest way to make life safer for the weak is to liberate and stimulate the energies of the strong, and the ingenuity of the bold, and the neighbourliness and good housekeeping of us all.

But the most effective panic-charge at the General Election was that a vote for the Unionist Conservative Party was a vote for war. We were war-mongers. I was the chief war-monger. I have no doubt that the Socialists gained many seats by this cruel and wicked falsehood. But what has happened since? By adhering firmly to our policy of peace through strength we have helped so far as it lay in our power all those forces in the world which make for an enduring peace. And now suddenly mighty events far beyond our control but in harmony with our highest hopes have made their mark on the life of the world. New men have obtained supreme power in Moscow and their words and gestures, and even to some extent their actions, seem to betoken a change of mood. We cannot yet tell what this means. We cannot measure how deep is their purpose or where the process they have set on foot will lead them.

Is there a new breeze blowing on the tormented world? Certainly sudden hopes have sprung in the hearts of peoples under every sky. We live in a time when science offers with blind prodigality to mankind the choice between a golden age of prosperity and the most hideous form of destruction. When at the end of the war eight years ago the three victorious powers met in Berlin all this lay before us. I could not understand why Soviet Russia did not join with the Western Allies in seeking a just and lasting treaty of peace. Instead this immense branch of the human family was led into the morasses of measureless ambition for the triumph and expansion not only of Communist doctrines but of Communist control. It was only gradually that the Western world became aware of their new danger and several hard years had to pass before they even began to regain their united power. Many grievous things have happened to many valiant and ancient nations and heavy burdens of toil and fear have been laid upon the backs of mankind.

Now it may be that another chance will come. Perhaps indeed it has come. We cannot tell. The future is inscrutable. But as so often happens the path of duty is clear. We must not cast away a single hope, however slender, so long as we believe there is good faith and goodwill. It is for these reasons that we in Britain, and I doubt not throughout the British Empire and Commonwealth of Nations, have welcomed the massive and magnificent statement made yesterday by President Eisenhower. He has set forth the range of practical issues which divide the world. He has declared the resolve of the free nations, headed and sustained by the giant power of the United States, not to weaken their defensive measures until an honourable settlement is reached. But he has closed no door upon sincere efforts to reach a true world peace. We give him our resolute and wholehearted support and we will do our utmost to work in the closest concord with the great republic of which he is the chosen chief. There are many famous countries with whom we are friends and allies but it is my faith that it is in the abiding fellowship and brotherhood of the English-speaking world that the best hopes reside both for securing peace today and for the broadening future of mankind.

House of Commons: Oral Answers
(Hansard)

20 April 1953   House of Commons

WORLD PEACE (PRESIDENT EISENHOWER'S DECLARATION)

Mr H. Morrison (by Private Notice) asked the Prime Minister whether he has any statement to make on Her Majesty's Government's policy regarding the declaration on international affairs made by President Eisenhower on Thursday last.

The Prime Minister (Mr Winston Churchill): Sir, I have already welcomed the bold and inspiring initiative by the President of the United States of America. In his declaration he seeks to find means of establishing world peace on a genuine and enduring basis. Her Majesty's Government, and probably all the countries of the free world, will be glad to associate themselves with his sincere expression of those ideals and aims to which we all subscribe.

I was glad to see that the acting Leader of the Labour Party and the former Foreign Secretary, according to the report in the *Daily Herald* of 17th April, seems to share these views. I cannot do better than read the words he is reported to have used – I am quoting from the *Daily Herald*: 'The British people,' said the right hon. Gentleman, 'in common with enlightened people all over the world, will welcome this most important statement. It is exactly the plan that was so enthusiastically endorsed by the Labour Party Conference – the World Plan for Mutual Aid – which I introduced on behalf of the National Executive. What is needed now is a forthcoming response from all governments so that the road will be open to a new era of peace, progress and ultimate world prosperity.' They were very well chosen words. I hope, therefore, that at this momentous juncture we shall not be hampered by party controversy. It seems to me that patience is needed rather than haste. In my opinion, no one can measure the extent or purpose of the change which has become apparent in the Soviet mood or even perhaps in their policy. I repeat what I said at Glasgow on Friday; no single hope, however slender, should be cast away. Time may well be needed to enable a sure judgement to be made.

I did not read President Eisenhower's speech as a challenge nor should I expect the Soviet Government to give an immediate categorical reply to the many grave and true points which his remarkable and inspiring declaration contained. It is, of course as yet too soon to consider any relaxation of our efforts for collective defence.

I trust that nothing will be said here or elsewhere which will check or chill the processes of good will which may be at work and my hope is that they may presently lead to conversations on the highest level, even if informal and private, between some of the principal Powers concerned.

There is, however, one sphere which claims priority because it is both practical and urgent. The establishment of a sincere and honourable truce in

Korea, with due regard for other Asiatic countries affected, would not only be of the highest value in itself but it might also open the door to further priceless advances towards that general easement of the world situation from which a real and lasting peace might come. We should, therefore, all rejoice at the steps that are being taken to resume the parleys at Panmunjom.

I do not wish to say more today except to assure the House that the whole subject holds the first place in the thoughts and attention of Her Majesty's Government.

Mr Morrison: On behalf of the Opposition, may I welcome the statement made by the Prime Minister which, I think, commands our general acquiescence and support. In the meantime, let us hope that all the statesmen of all the Western democracies will be equally cooperative and forthcoming, and let us hope that nobody will say anything which is liable to discourage the somewhat improved atmosphere of the international situation. It would be our wish that Her Majesty's Government should be forthcoming on any practicable means of improving the international situation, and we are glad that the Prime Minister has represented that spirit in the answer which he has given this afternoon.

Mr Younger:[1] While we all welcome President Eisenhower's speech and statement of United States' policy, may I ask the Prime Minister whether he is aware that some us feel that the United Kingdom has a slightly different perspective on some of these problems, particularly those of the Far East, and whether he will, therefore, consider making a contribution at a very early date by making a statement of United Kingdom policy which, of course, we should not expect to be in conflict with President Eisenhower's statement but which would at any rate be supplementary to it, perhaps clarifying certain important points?

The Prime Minister: I understand that we shall probably have a debate on foreign affairs on the 29th of this month, but I would rather not endeavour to forecast precisely beforehand the lines which any remarks I might have to make should take.

Mr Strachey:[2] Would not the Prime Minister consider making a statement now that, if and when an armistice has been successfully concluded in Korea, Her Majesty's Government would favour the seating of the Chinese Government on the Security Council of the United Nations?

---

[1] Kenneth Gilmour Younger, 1908–76. Educated at Winchester and New College, Oxford. Called to the Bar, Inner Temple, 1932. Married, 1934, Elizabeth Stewart: two children. MP (Lab.) for Grimsby, 1945–59. Parliamentary Private Secretary to Minister of State for Air, 1945–6. Chairman, UNRRA Committee of Council of Europe, 1946. Parliamentary Secretary, Home Office, 1947–50. Minister of State, FO, 1950. Acting Foreign Secretary, 1950. PC, 1951. Shadow Home Secretary, 1955. Chairman, Howard League for Penal Reform, 1960–73. KBE, 1972.

[2] John Strachey, 1901–63. Educated at Eton and Magdalen College, Oxford. Married, 1928, Esther Murphy (div. 1933); 1933, Celia Simpson. Wg Cdr, RAFVR. MP (Lab.) for Aston, 1929–31; for Dundee, 1945–50; for Dundee West, 1950–63. Under-Secretary of State, Air Ministry, 1945–6. PC, 1946. Minister of Food, 1946–50. Secretary of State for War, 1950–1.

The Prime Minister: I think it might even hamper the movement of events in Korea towards an effective truce if I were to try to lay down conditions or make offers at the present time.

Mr Irvine:[1] Is it not a fact that the President's statement does not make entirely clear how far the liberation of the satellite countries and certain other matters are to be prerequisites of American mutual aid? Will the Prime Minister ask for clarification of that vital point, so that the whole matter may be usefully considered in the House?

The Prime Minister: I am sure it would not be in the interests which we all have at heart for me to attempt to go into details on these matters at the present time.

Several Hon. Members rose –

Mr Speaker: I think we are having a debate in a short time. These matters ought to be considered and then discussed in the debate.

Sir Robert Howe to Winston S. Churchill
Prime Minister's Personal Telegram T.98/53
(Premier papers, 11/544)

20 April 1953   Khartoum
Personal and Confidential
No. 297

Your telegram No. 533.[2]

A detailed analysis of the Egyptian methods of propaganda follows immediately by bag.

2. You may be assured that administrators are doing, and will continue to do, everything possible within legal limitations to combat Egyptian propaganda and intrigue.

3. The Umma[3] are prepared to take a strong line with Egypt over this propaganda, and in addition to action described in my telegram No. 283 they are sending Abdel Rahman Ali Taha[4] and Dr Ali Bedri[5] to Cairo tomorrow to protest in person against the use of Egyptian money.

The Umma leader[6] feels now that they have been deceived by Neguib and his men, and unless the Egyptian propaganda and bribery stops, it seems likely

---

[1] Arthur James Irvine, 1909–78. Educated at Edinburgh Academy and Oriel College, Oxford. Called to the Bar, 1935. Secretary to Lord Chief Justice, 1935–40. MP (Lab.) for Liverpool Edge Hill, 1947–78. QC, 1958. Knighted, 1967. Solicitor-General for England and Wales, 1967–70. PC, 1970.

[2] T.94/53, reproduced above (p. 951).

[3] The Umma Party of Sudan, one of the two nationalist parties, which supported taking gradual steps towards nationhood.

[4] Faisal Abdel Rahman Ali Taha. Educated at Universities of Khartoum and Cambridge (PhD Cambridge, 1973). Published multiple books and articles regarding Sudanese–Egyptian border conflicts.

[5] Ali Bedri, 1903–87. Member of Sudan Legislative Assembly and Minister of Health, 1949–54. Fellow, FRCP, 1952.

[6] Sayed Khalil (see p. 947 n.1 above).

that they will abandon all pretence of cooperation and friendship with Egypt, and they would no doubt be followed by SRP.

4. The situation is thus developing more hopefully but as I said in my telegram No. 295 we should let Umma play the hand in their own way for the present. We are in close and friendly touch with them and will give them any help and support they need.

Winston S. Churchill to Vyacheslav Molotov
Prime Minister's Personal Telegram T.99/53
(Premier papers, 11/422)

20 April 1953
Immediate
Secret, Private and Personal
No. 228

I hope you will look at the statement I made in the House today. I asked Gromyko to give you my good wishes, which no doubt he has done.[1]

Winston S. Churchill to John Selwyn Lloyd and Sir William Strang
Prime Minister's Personal Minute M.91/53
(Premier papers, 11/554)

20 April 1953

If Anglo-United States relationships are to be 'most seriously affected' by the movement of a single ship[2] this would indeed be a silly result after we have done our best. The State Department ought not to say such things.[3]

2. What would happen if we did forcibly detain the ship and exactly how would this have to be done physically?

---

[1] Molotov responded on Apr, 23: 'I thank you for your kind wishes. Sir A. Gascoigne at your request transmitted to me the text of your speech in Parliament, which will be studied by me with due attention. Allow me to extend to you from Moscow my very best wishes' (T.106/53, No. 290).

[2] The Finnish tanker SS *Wiima*: see T.27/53, reproduced above (pp. 866-8), para. 4.

[3] Strang's minute of Apr. 18 reported: 'Two days ago, the United States Ambassador received instructions to press HM Government to detain the ship, if the negotiations for purchasing the cargo failed. The State Department pointed out that the ship was in British territorial waters and that, if we let her go, the effect in America would be most serious for Anglo-United States relations' (PM/WS/53/50).

Winston S. Churchill to John Selwyn Lloyd and Sir William Strang
Prime Minister's Personal Minute M.94/53
(Premier papers, 11/465)

20 April 1953

DRAFT AIDE MEMOIRE TO ISRAEL

I think this should be strengthened. Israel is the most powerful fighting force in the Middle East and may come in very handy in dealing with Egypt if Neguib attacks us. We ought never to have allowed the obstruction in the Suez Canal of oil for Haifa. Pray let me have a more vigorous draft. If necessary I will see the Israel Ambassador myself. The late Mr Bevin, who had a strain of anti-Semitism in his thought, put the Foreign Office in on the wrong side when Israel was attacked by all the Arab States.

Winston Churchill to President Dwight D. Eisenhower
Prime Minister's Personal Telegram T.101/53
(Premier papers, 11/429)

21 April 1953
Immediate
Dedip
Secret and Personal
No. 1751

My dear Friend,

Thank you very much for your letter of 7th April[1] about Egypt on which I am pondering. I conveyed your message to Anthony who was cheered by it. He is having a hard time but is progressing. As you know, we are having our first meeting with the Egyptians on the 27th and nothing will be agreed to by us except as part of a 'package' settlement.

2. Your speech about Russia was well received here by all Parties. I append my statement and that made by Herbert Morrison in reply. No dissent was expressed in any part of the House.

3. I should like to know what you think should be the next step. Evidently we must wait a few days for their reply or reaction. It is not likely that the Soviets will agree about the release of the Satellites or unified Korea. There will, however, be a strong movement here for a meeting between Heads of States and Governments. How do you stand about this? In my opinion the best would be that the three victorious Powers, who separated at Potsdam in 1945, should come together again. I like the idea you mentioned to me of

---

[1] Reproduced above (pp. 932–3).

Stockholm. I am sure the world will expect something like this to emerge if the Soviets do not turn your proposals down abruptly.

4. If nothing can be arranged I shall have to consider seriously a personal contact. You told me in New York you would have no objection to this. I should be grateful if you would let me know how these things are shaping in your mind.

Sir William Strang to Winston S. Churchill
(Premier papers, 11/554)

22 April 1953
Secret
PM/WS/53/60

Your Minute M.91/53[1] about the Finnish Tanker SS *Wiima*, which is in Singapore with a cargo of kerosene for communist China.

2. If the Master of the ship applies for port clearance the only delay the Governor can impose would be about twelve hours to enable a contraband search to be conducted. Unless this revealed an infringement of the law, he would have no power to withhold port clearance and could not instruct the harbour police to prevent departure.

3. To prevent the vessel leaving or if, the vessel having left, we wished to stop it getting to China, there would be no alternative but the use of force by the Navy. Any such action would be a war-like act and inconsistent with our policy of not maintaining a blockade of China.

4. I do not believe that the United States Government have any real expectation that we would go to such lengths.

5. If the vessel leaves Singapore, she will be shadowed by the Navy for a sufficient distance to determine her probable destination: e.g. South China, or some other port such as Djakarta. Any information thus obtained will be passed to the Americans. The Americans have been told this.

Winston S. Churchill: speech
('Winston S. Churchill, His Complete Speeches', volume 8, pages 8471–3)

23 April 1953 St George's Day Dinner

ENGLAND

You do me great honour tonight by inviting me to your dinner and by the kindness with which you have welcomed me here. I am proud to come here and be the guest of the Honourable Artillery Company – a City company but

---

[1] Reproduced above (p. 962).

April 1953 965

not a limited liability company. Not that there's anything wrong with British enterprise and business if it is given half a chance. Still, the qualities which have been possessed and paraded before history by the two members who are here tonight who gained the Victoria Cross, belong to the unlimited liability sphere of city action.

I'm very glad indeed to meet here again my cherished friends – I might say my cherished affinities of the Great War, Brookey,[1] Andrew Cunningham,[2] and Peter Portal – what a difference this last war was to the kind of thing that happened in the First World War. All the collisions and divisions between the politicians and the military men. They didn't exist and it was fortunate for us indeed that they didn't – there was no such thing as division and I always look back and cherish my association with these highly capable and resolute companions who shaped and planned the line we should take in so many difficult and perilous situations.

You have said, Lord Alanbrooke, that the 'pug' – I beg your pardon, Lord Ismay – is not here tonight. He is, I trust, equally well employed in Paris, but I cannot let our wartime association be mentioned without referring to the debt we all owe to Dudley Pound,[3] whom I found one of the greatest sailors with whom I worked in the many anxious months over many varied years at the Admiralty.

Now I must say something about the artillery. I've had very little help from our Chairman because he was mostly on the bow and arrow; after that we got to the musketoon and the tripod, and there was the period when our artillery really came boldly out on to the battlefield. George Bernard Shaw[4] – if I remember – said about Napoleon[5] that his dominant theme and master thought was 'Cannons kill men' – well, I must say that rather struck in my mind and in August 1941, on my way to Placentia, where we signed the North Atlantic Pact, I had a little time to think about things, and I did write in a memorandum 'Renown awaits the commander who first in this war restores artillery to its prime importance upon the battlefield' from which it had been ousted by heavily armoured tanks.

It was left, I think, to General Montgomery in the Battle of Alamein to

[1] FM Lord Alanbrooke.
[2] Andrew Browne Cunningham, 1883–1963. On active service, RN, 1914–18 (DSO and two bars). VAdm. Commanding Battle Cruiser Sqn, 1937–8. DCNS, 1938–9. Knighted, 1939. C-in-C, Mediterranean, 1939–42. Head of British Admiralty Delegation, Washington DC, 1942. Naval C-in-C, Expeditionary Force, North Africa, 1942. C-in-C, Mediterranean, 1943. Adm. of the Fleet, 1943. 1st Sea Lord and CNS, 1943–6. Baron, 1945. Viscount, 1946.
[3] Alfred Dudley Pickman Rogers Pound, 1877–1943. Entered RN, 1891. Torpedo Lt, 1902. Capt., 1914. 2nd Naval Assistant to Lord Fisher, 1914–15. Flag Capt., HMS *Colossus*, 1915–17. On Admiralty Staff, 1917–19. Director of Plans Div., 1922. Cdr, Battle Cruiser Sqn, 1929–32. 2nd Sea Lord, 1932–5. Knighted, 1933. C-in-C, Mediterranean, 1936–9. Adm. of the Fleet, 1939. 1st Sea Lord and CNS, 1939–43. OM, 1943.
[4] George Bernard Shaw, 1856–1950. Joined Fabian Society, 1884. Married, 1898, Charlotte Payne-Townshend. Nobel Prize in Literature, 1925. Author of, including many other works, *Pygmalion* (1912), *Saint Joan* (1923), *The Intelligent Woman's Guide to Socialism and Capitalism* (1928).
[5] Napoléon Bonaparte, 1769–1821. 1st Consul of France, 1799–1804. Emperor of France, 1804–15.

show the power of a thousand or more guns all firing in a regular system to enable an army to advance. These are important things and the story doesn't stop here. I can't tell you all that's going to happen. I'm not sure if you'll all be quite so good and artillery will necessarily play such a large part in the battles of the future as it did in the battles of the past. It may well be that guided missiles and all kinds of modern intruders of that character may take a little of the light off the practical value and power of the field gun.

But nothing will ever deprive the Honourable Artillery Company and those who have served in the Royal Regiment of their share in bearing forward the burden which fell upon their generation. Forever the honour will be theirs, the traditions will go on. But now I have to speak about St George's Day.

It is twenty years since I had to speak on this toast of England and on St George's Day – twenty years – it's a long time, and I did try to see what would have happened if St George had lived twenty years ago, and really it does apply very much to what might happen if he lived today. I said St George would arrive in Cappadocia accompanied not by a horse but by a Secretariat. He would be armed not with a lance but with several flexible formulas. He would, of course, be welcomed by the local branch of the League of Nations Union – or I ought to alter that to be correct and say of the United Nations Union. He would propose a conference with the dragon – a round table conference – no doubt it would be so much more convenient for the dragon's tail. He would make a trade agreement with the dragon. He would loan the dragon a lot of money. The maiden's release would be referred to Geneva (it would now be to New York), the dragon observing all his rights meanwhile. Finally, the dragon would be photographed with St George.

Now, I do not think there's anything very much wrong with that passage although twenty years have passed, but there are a few things I would like to mention about England. I'm not boasting but I would like to say that here no one questions the fairness of our Courts of Law and Justice. We have our own way of life, that is so. Here no one thinks of persecuting a man on account of his religion or his race. Here everyone, except the criminals, looks on the policeman as the friend and servant of the public. Here we provide for poverty and misfortune with more compassion, in spite of all our burdens, than any other country. Here we can assert the rights of the citizen against the state or criticize the government of the day without failing in our duty to the Crown or our loyalty to the Queen.

If I am not detaining you too long, there are two points I would like to make. One is our weakness. Our weakness is that there are always a certain number of English people who wake up every morning – very brainy they are – they wake up and they look all round over the fields and they think, 'Now what is there we can find belongs to our country that we can give away?' or 'What is there we can find that has made our country great that we can pull down?' Well, that is the question they ask themselves and that is our weakness – they are very brainy and they have done us a great deal of harm.

On the other hand, England has a quality which no one should overlook. England, like nature, never draws a line without smudging it. We lack the sharp logic of some other countries whom in other ways we greatly admire – in our climate, the atmosphere is veiled, there are none of these sharp presentations, and although we have our differences – especially as in a few minutes I have to go back to the House of Commons – I won't say are slaves to differences, but at any rate present the point of view which we hold. We have our differences but they do not divide us as they do in nearly all the other countries of the world. There is a great underlying spirit of neighbourliness and there is without a doubt a very strong common sense of our national unity and life which, though it doesn't help us in the small matters with which we have to deal from day to day, may well be our salvation in our troubles.

Nothing can save England, if she will not save herself. If we lose faith in ourselves, in our capacity to guide and govern, if we lose our will to live, then, indeed, our story is told. If, while on all sides foreign nations are every day asserting a more aggressive and militant nationalism by arms and trade – if we remain paralysed by our own theoretical doctrines or plunged in the stupor of after-war exhaustion – but this is twenty years ago, this is not new – indeed, all that the croakers predict will come true and our ruin will be certain and final.

But why should we break up the solid structure of British power founded upon so much help, kindliness, and freedom? Why should we break it up for dreams which may some day come true but now are only dreams, or it may be nightmares? We ought as a nation and Empire – you won't mind my mentioning that word? – I didn't get shouted down when I said it twenty years ago tonight – Empire, we might, we ought, to weather any storm that blows at least as well as any other existing system of human government.

We are at once more experienced and more truly united than any people in the world. It may well be, I say, that the most glorious chapters of our history are yet to be written. Indeed, the very problems and dangers that encompass us in our country ought to make English men and women of this generation glad to be here at such a time. We ought to rejoice at the responsibilities with which destiny has honoured us and be proud that we are the guardians of our country in an age when her life is at stake. I have lived, since then, to see our country accomplish, achieve her finest hour and I have no doubt that if this spirit of England continues, there is no reason at all why twenty years hence someone may not stand at the table of this ancient company and speak in the sense of pride and hope in which I have ventured to address you tonight.

Henry Channon: diary
('Chips,' page 474)

23 April 1953

I had just put Mollie Buccleuch[1] in the Gallery to hear Winston and Bevan speak, when there was a storm of gibs and ribaldy and noise. One Socialist . . . shouted out 'Bloody lie'. The Speaker tried in vain to restore order: Bevan looked at poor, plain Florence Horsbrugh and hailed her with the words 'That's the face that sank a thousand scholarships'. Later, when Winston got up to leave the Chamber the squawking Socialists rudely shouted 'Good night' at the old man. The PM, surprised, turned and, with his little mocking bow, blew kisses to the Opposition, who were somewhat startled by this response.

Winston S. Churchill to Michael Creswell[2]
Prime Minister's Personal Telegram T.102/53
(Premier papers, 11/392)

23 April 1953
Priority
Dedip
Secret
No. 847

We must not be too easily worried by speeches made by members of a usurper government most anxious about their own position. If they are rude while we remain polite this would help us when the conference opens. There should be no question of British 'provocation' by Egyptian words. The more abusive and insulting they are the easier it will be for us to take a calm line and also, if need be, a strong one. Pray take this message as a guide in your outlook.

---

[1] Vreda Esther Mary Lascelles, 1900–93. Known as 'Mollie'. Married, 1921, Walter Montagu Douglas Scott: three children.

[2] Michael Justin Creswell, 1909–86. Educated at Rugby and New College, Oxford. Entered Foreign Service, 1933. 3rd Secretary, Berlin, 1935–8. 2nd Secretary, Madrid, 1939–44; Athens, 1944; FO, 1944–7. Counsellor, Tehran, 1947–9; Singapore, 1949–51. Minister, British Embassy, Cairo, 1951–4. CMG, 1952. Ambassador to Finland, 1954–8; to Yugoslavia, 1960–4; to Argentina, 1964–9. Senior Civilian Instructor, Imperial Defence College, 1958–60. KCMG, 1960.

APRIL 1953

Winston S. Churchill to Sir William Strang
Prime Minister's Personal Minute M.103/53
(Premier papers, 11/465)

23 April 1953

ISRAEL AND THE EGYPTIAN NEGOTIATIONS

I don't understand why we should be so alarmed about all this. I do not mind it being known here or in Cairo that I am on the side of Israel and against her ill-treatment by the Egyptians. The idea of selling Israel down the drain in order to persuade the Egyptians to kick us out of the Canal Zone more gently is not one which attracts me. We have probably got to have a showdown with Neguib, and Israel will be an important factor both Parliamentary and military. We must not throw away any important card we have in our hand.

2. The latest secret information shows how dangerous it would be to let things drag on while Neguib uses Nazi Germans to teach the Egyptian Army and the terrorist auxiliaries sabotage and guerrilla warfare.

3. Mr Creswell need not go on protesting against abusive speeches and anti-British propaganda and then seeming to be gratified by vague promises that it will be mitigated. Let us leave them alone till the Conference opens and then confront them with our present overwhelming force and resolute intention to work on the basis agreed with the Americans. All their blustering only strengthens our case. Our aim is to avoid bloodshed but this will not be achieved by our being disturbed by words.

4. Please redraft in this spirit.

Winston S. Churchill to Sir William Strang
Prime Minister's Personal Minute M.104/53
(Premier papers, 11/540)

23 April 1953

Moscow telegram No. 277 of the 21st of April. All this is interesting and may be important. Let me have your view briefly on what the purges in Georgia signify. Are you glad to read about them or sorry? and will they be more agreeable to Beriya or to Malenkov?

Sir William Strang to Winston S. Churchill
(Premier papers, 11/540)

23 April 1953
PM/WS/53/61

Your personal minute No. M 104/53 of April 23 about the purges in Georgia.

1. You probably know that Georgia has been a cause of worry to the Central Government in Moscow for some time past. About a year ago the collective farm system broke down fairly widely in the Republic. Later the Russian press said that nepotism and exploitation for personal interest were rife there. It is not surprising that Georgia should have been made the scene of one of the stiff purges which were in progress during the last days of Stalin. Now that he is no more, it is equally natural that there should have been whitewashing, as in the case of the Kremlin doctors.

2. All this is satisfactory from our point of view. We have often thought that the Central Government have been worried about conditions in some of the Constituent Republics. It is satisfactory to have this confirmed.

3. As between Beriya and Malenkov, I should say that Sir A. Gascoigne's summing up in paragraph 7 of his telegram No. 277 is about right. The new leaders need to keep together for the present. If Beriya is thought to need to be exculpated for the time being, it is natural that this should be arranged. Sir A. Gascoigne in paragraph 6 of his telegram No. 282 (a copy of which is attached) does not share the view of his colleagues in Moscow that Beriya is being attacked by Malenkov. However, if the time comes when the leaders do begin to fall out among themselves, recent events in Georgia would no doubt be held against Beriya.

4. I hope that we may hear more of similar developments elsewhere within the Soviet Union. Though we have nothing official at present from Moscow, you will have seen a report in today's *Times* about a reshuffle in Latvia. The local Ministry of State Security changed hands there in March.

Winston S. Churchill to Sir William Strang
Prime Minister's Personal Minute M.107/53
(Premier papers, 11/554)

24 April 1953
Secret

Your minute PM/WS/53/60 of April 22.[1]
I am quite content with this if nothing more can be done. My anxiety

---

[1] Reproduced above (p. 964).

was aroused by the words 'the effect in America would be most serious for Anglo-United States relations' in paragraph 3 of your minute of April 18.[1] I gather from paragraph 4 of your minute of April 22 that this is no longer your view. If so, nothing special needs to be done.

Foreign Office to Tel Aviv
(Premier papers, 11/465)

24 April 1953
Immediate
Confidential
No. 155

[. . .]

Mr Churchill wishes to assure His Excellency that Her Majesty's Government will always give friendly and active study to anything the Israel Government may have to say about the many interests common to the two Governments and to exchange views wherever their interests are directly affected. They entirely understand how much concern the Israel Government must feel in the matters raised in the Ambassador's Note and the Israel Government may rest assured that Her Majesty's Government will always be mindful of Israel's interests.

President Dwight D. Eisenhower to Winston S. Churchill
(Premier papers, 11/421)

25 April 1953   The White House
Top Secret

Dear Winston,

I am glad to learn from your message of April 22[2] that Anthony is progressing and hope he will soon be completely restored.

Your comments about the reception of my recent speech were most welcome and I warmly appreciate the support contained in your statement in the House of Commons and Mr Morrison's reply.

As to the next step, I feel that we should not rush things too much and should await the Soviet reply or reaction longer than a few days. There is some feeling here also for a meeting between Heads of States and Governments, but I do not think this should be allowed to press us into precipitate initiatives. Premature action by us in that direction might have the effect of giving the Soviets an easy way out of the position in which I think they are now placed. We have

---

[1] The relevant passage is reproduced above (see p. 962 n.3).
[2] T.101/53, reproduced above (pp. 963–4), dated Apr. 21.

so far seen no concrete Soviet actions which would indicate their willingness to perform in connection with larger issues. In the circumstances we would risk raising hopes of progress toward an accommodation which would be unjustified. This is not to say, of course, that I do not envisage the possible desirability at an appropriate time that the three Western Powers and the Soviets come together. We should by all means be alert.

My thinking concerning personal contact at this moment runs somewhat along the same line. The situation has changed considerably since we talked in New York and I believe that we should watch developments for a while longer before determining our further course. However, if you should find it necessary for some special and local reason to seek a personal contact, we would hope for as much advance notice as you could possibly give us.

President Dwight D. Eisenhower to Sir Winston S. Churchill[1]
('The Churchill Eisenhower Correspondence', page 48)

25 April 1953

This morning I read that you have become a member of the Order of the Garter. My most sincere congratulations both to the Order and to the new member. I am delighted to hear that Anthony is better. To him also my warm regard.

Lord Ivor Churchill[2] *to Sir Winston S. Churchill*
(Churchill papers, 1/53)[3]

26 April 1953   Hampshire

My dear Winston,
I felt I must write on an occasion of such universal rejoicing even if I add [. . .] to the burden of your post bag.

Of all the Tributes none gave me more pleasure than the *Times* leader which seemed to extract the heart of the matter in uncommonly felicitous language which led me to reflect upon what joy my father[4] would have derived

---

[1] Churchill had declined the Garter from George VI in 1945, deeming it inappropriate on the morrow of his rejection at the general election. Eight years later he capitulated, and was appointed a Knight of the Garter on 24 Apr. 1953.

[2] Ivor Charles Spencer-Churchill, 1898–1956. Second son of Churchill's cousin 'Sunny', 9th Duke of Marlborough. Educated at Eton and Magdalen College, Oxford. On active service, 1917–18 (Lt, RASC). In 1947, after his marriage to Elizabeth Cunningham, he lived at Rogate, Hampshire, in the next village to Churchill's friend Paul Maze, the painter.

[3] This letter was handwritten.

[4] Charles Richard John Spencer Churchill, 1871–1934. Churchill's cousin. Known as 'Sunny'. Succeeded his father as 9th Duke of Marlborough, 1892. Paymaster-General of the Forces, 1899–1902. Staff Capt. and ADC to Gen. Hamilton during South African War, 1900. Under-Secretary of State

from the lustre you have shed upon the family name. No one estimated your potentialities more highly than he and a favourite theme of his was to speculate upon your chances of attaining political immortality.

To one who shared his convictions and who has lived to see their realization, this culmination is the more moving in that it unites the present with the past. I send you both this expression of my pride and affection and may you both be spared many years in which to reap the marriage you deserve.

Yr affec cousin,[1]

Sir Winston S. Churchill to General Bedell Smith
Prime Minister's Personal Telegram T.110/53
(Premier papers, 11/554)

27 April 1953
Immediate
Secret
No. 1827

What do you suggest we should do about the Finnish ship? I am assured that all legal methods are exhausted. They have the law on their side. This is quite a different case from sending arms to Egypt. Here we are actually asked to break the law and custom of the sea about the ships of a friendly power. Let me know your view. Meanwhile we will go on doing all we can to delay the ship.

Sir Norman Brook to Members of the Defence Committee
(Premier papers, 11/645)

28 April 1953
Top Secret
Defence Paper No. 26 of 1953

CONCLUSIONS OF A STAFF CONFERENCE HELD BY THE
PRIME MINISTER AT CHEQUERS ON SUNDAY, 26TH APRIL, 1953

The attached note on the conclusions of a Staff Conference held on Sunday, 26th April, 1953, is circulated for consideration by the Committee at their meeting to be held on Wednesday, 29th April, at 11.45 a.m.

---

for the Colonies, 1903–5. Lt-Col., Queen's Own Oxfordshire Hussars, 1910. An original member of the Other Club, 1911. Employed at War Office as a Special Messenger, 1914–15. Joint Parliamentary Secretary, Board of Agriculture and Fisheries, 1917–18.

[1] Churchill responded: 'Thank you so much dear Ivor. I loved yr father & I rejoice in yr friendship.'

JOINT NOTE PREPARED BY THE CIGS AND CAS AND APPROVED BY THE PRIME MINISTER OF THE CONCLUSIONS REACHED AT A STAFF MEETING HELD BY THE PRIME MINISTER AT CHEQUERS ON SUNDAY, 26TH APRIL

(Attended by Prime Minister, Lord Alexander, CIGS, CAS, and Sir William Strang)

1. Reinforcements for the Canal Zone

You affirmed your decision that no reinforcements from Malta or elsewhere should be sent to Commanders-in-Chief, Middle East. They will not be changed without reference to you.

2. Rodeo

You expressed your strong distaste for this operation, which is shared by the Chiefs of Staff, and decided that the Commanders-in-Chief, Middle East, should not be held responsible for the safety of British subjects beyond their control in Egypt, though plans for Rodeo should be kept up to date.

3. Sudan

You decided that in the event of serious trouble in Egypt which the Cabinet might conclude amounted to a state of war, we should at once reinforce Khartoum with two Infantry battalions and appropriate air forces, disarm the Egyptian battalion there, and resume full control of Sudan.

4. Malaya

You accepted the CIGS's view that the Songkhla (Singora) position is the best for the defence of Malaya against invasion by land. You agreed that Her Majesty's Government must seize and hold that position immediately if the security of Malaya on the landward side was in danger as a result of events in Indo-China or Siam. The plan should be prepared in detail now.

5. Indo-China

You decided that in view of possible developments in Egypt, and our many commitments elsewhere, we could not afford to dissipate any of our resources, or prejudice the mobility of our air and land forces by lending any of our limited air transport resources to the French for use in Indo-China. This may, however, require reconsideration by the Cabinet at a later stage.

APRIL 1953

Cabinet: conclusions
(Cabinet papers, 128/26)

28 April 1953
Secret
11.30 a.m.
Cabinet Meeting No. 29 of 1953

1. The Prime Minister drew attention to a newspaper report of the reply sent by the Soviet Foreign Minister to a proposal, made by the Congress of the Peoples for Peace, for the conclusion of a peace pact between the Soviet Union, the United States, the United Kingdom, France and Communist China. M Molotov had said that there was no dispute or unsettled issue which could not be settled peaceably on the basis of mutual agreement between the countries concerned, they were ready to cooperate with the Governments of other States in strengthening world peace and security.

The Prime Minister said that, if there was to be any such meeting of Great Powers, he would prefer that it should be limited to the Soviet Union, the United States, and the United Kingdom, who could take up the discussion at the point at which it had been left at the end of the Potsdam Conference in 1945. It was in any event unlikely that the United States Government would be willing to be represented at any such meeting which included representatives of Communist China.

In discussion it was pointed out that proposals for a Five-Power peace pact had formed part of Communist propaganda for some time past; and that M Molotov had done no more than endorse a proposal to this end submitted by the Congress of the Peoples for Peace, which was a Communist-controlled organisation. More significance could have been attached to his statement if it had been made, of his own initiative, in an official offer to the other Governments concerned.

The Cabinet agreed that it would be premature to draw any conclusions from this announcement, and that it would be unnecessary for the government to volunteer any public statement about it at this stage.

[. . .]

John Selwyn Lloyd to Sir Winston S. Churchill
(Premier papers, 11/554)

28 April 1953
Secret
PM/MS/53/83

You asked us to consider whether a warship might be stationed near it, and if the *Wüma* attempted to leave the warship might instruct it not to do so.

The *Wiima* has been kept under close surveillance by a number of naval vessels in turn. This has probably helped to discourage the Master from wanting to leave. If the *Wiima* tried to leave without having first obtained port clearance from the harbour authorities, we should be within our rights in preventing it. However, if the Master applies for port clearance, all that we can do is carry out a search for contraband and to ensure, through examination by the Surveyor General of Ships, that her papers and the ship itself are in order. If so, then port clearance could not legally be withheld. If in that event a naval vessel were to order the ship not to leave, this order could not be enforced without breaking the law and custom of the sea. As we are not prepared to do this, I do not believe that such an order would help. If it were ignored, it would not do our position any good.

Defence Committee: minutes
(Cabinet papers, 131/13)

29 April 1953   Prime Minister's Map Room
Top Secret   Ministry of Defence
11.45 a.m.
Defence Meeting No. 7 of 1953

[. . .]

3. THE MIDDLE EAST

The Committee had before them a note by the Secretary (D(53)26) setting out the conclusions of a Staff Conference which the Prime Minister had held on 26th April, 1953, with the Minister of Defence, the Chief of the Imperial General Staff, the Chief of the Air Staff, and Sir William Strang.

The Committee discussed the conclusions reached at this Staff Conference under the following headings:

   (i)   reinforcements for the Canal Zone;
   (ii) Operation 'Rodeo';
   (iii) the Sudan.

Reinforcements for the Canal Zone

The Conference had reaffirmed the decision that no reinforcements from Malta or elsewhere should be sent to the Canal Zone without reference to the Prime Minister. Orders to that effect had already been sent to the Commanders-in-Chief, Middle East.

The Chief of the Imperial General Staff said that Operation 'Rodeo' was now at 7 days notice. He explained that it was inherent in the plans for this operation that the Royal Marine Commando Brigade should be moved from Malta to the Canal Zone when the notice was shortened to 96 hours.

The Committee –
(1) Endorsed the conclusion of the Staff Conference, noting that instructions to this effect had already been sent to the Commanders-in-Chief, Middle East.
(2) Instructed the Chiefs of Staff to ensure that the notice for Operation 'Rodeo' should not be shortened below 7 days without reference to Ministers.

Operation 'Rodeo'

The Conference had noted the risks involved in this operation, and had considered that, although plans for the operation should be kept up to date, the Commanders-in-Chief, Middle East, should not be held responsible for the safety of British subjects in Egypt who were outside their control.

The Prime Minister said that he hoped we should not have to embark on this difficult and dangerous operation. If we had to undertake it, we should do so only if the Egyptians had first attacked us in the Canal Zone. In the event of our having to undertake operations against hostile mobs in Egypt, full use should be made of tear gas, adequate stocks of which should be maintained in the Canal Zone.

In discussion the following points were made:
(a) The Government would incur serious political criticism if British civilians were massacred in Egypt, and no British forces were sent to their assistance. But this had to be balanced against the disadvantages of allowing British forces to become embroiled with Egyptian mobs on Egyptian territory, in which event numbers of Egyptian civilians would undoubtedly be killed.
(b) British civilians were probably in less danger under General Neguib's régime than under the previous régime in Egypt. Furthermore, General Neguib must know of our plans to intervene in the Delta to save British lives, and it was to his own advantage to ensure that we were not provoked to intervene. The British subjects themselves were probably in the best position to judge the likelihood of danger and were always free to leave Egypt if they so wished. It would be inexpedient to start evacuating those who were not considered essential.

The Committee –
(3) Endorsed the conclusion of the Staff Conference, noting that the Chiefs of Staff would keep the plans for Operation 'Rodeo' up to date in case the operation became inevitable.

The Sudan

The Conference had concluded that, in the event of serious trouble in Egypt amounting to a state of war, we should at once reinforce Khartoum with two infantry battalions and appropriate air forces, disarm the Egyptian battalion there, and resume full control of the Sudan.

The Prime Minister said that firm action in the Sudan might offset the damage to our prestige in the Middle East which would result from an unsatisfactory solution in Egypt. He considered that we should be ready at short notice to reinforce Khartoum, to disarm the Egyptians, and to resume full control of the country, thereupon proceeding with the elections as quickly as possible.

The Minister of State said that it would be preferable if the Egyptians could be provoked into denouncing the recent Anglo-Egyptian Agreement on the Sudan rather than that we ourselves should do so. He wondered whether one British battalion already in the Sudan would not be adequate for our requirements.

The Chief of the Imperial General Staff said that, in the circumstances envisaged, he would prefer to build up the garrison to a brigade by the addition of two infantry battalions. Provided we held Khartoum and the Sudan Defence Force remained loyal, the Egyptians could do nothing to embarrass us unduly. They had no means of staging overland operations, nor was their air force of any consequence. The War Office had plans for sending the two reinforcing battalions to Khartoum.

The Minister of Defence considered that we could well handle the situations which might develop concurrently in Egypt and the Sudan, provided Operation Rodeo was not also being carried out.

The Committee –
(4) Endorsed the conclusion of the Staff Conference, noting that the War Office and Air Ministry already had plans for reinforcing Khartoum at short notice with two infantry battalions and appropriate air forces.

[. . .]

5. TREATMENT OF RETURNING PRISONERS OF WAR FROM KOREA

The Committee considered a memorandum by the Minister of Defence (D(53)27).

The Minister of Defence said that a difficult situation had arisen in connection with the return of the first batch of United Kingdom ex-prisoners of war exchanged in Korea. Out of this batch of thirty-two men, who were expected to arrive in the United Kingdom on 1st May, five were believed to be pro-Communist. Furthermore, at least one of these five was suspected of having cooperated actively with Communists; for example, he had broadcast on the Peking radio and had written letters to Mrs Monica Felton[1] and to

---

[1] Monica Felton, 1906–70. PhD, London School of Economics, 1934. Member (Lab.) of London County Council, 1937–46. Chairwoman, London County Council Supplies Committee, 1939–41. Ministry of Supply, 1941–2. Clerk, House of Commons, 1942–3. Asst Secretary, Women's International Democratic Federation, North Korea, 1951. Stalin Peace Prize, 1951.

the *Daily Worker*. The first question was whether the five men believed to be pro-Communist should be subjected to further interrogation; it was not at present intended to detain any of them on their arrival in the United Kingdom. The second question concerned the man who had cooperated actively with the Communists: it might be thought desirable to warn the press about this man who, though he was being repatriated with sick and wounded prisoners, had never, in fact, been either wounded or sick.

In deciding what should be done about these five men it should be realised that there would be much larger numbers returning, after an armistice had been concluded, who had cooperated with the Communists to an objectionable degree.

The Prime Minister said that it would be preferable to take no action at all against the five men on their return to the United Kingdom. Nor should anything be done about the man suspected of having cooperated actively with the Communists except to provide evidence in order to discredit him if he started airing his views in public. People in this country could be relied upon to treat with contempt any subversive activities that these men might indulge in. It would be useful, however, to obtain full details concerning their families and general way of life in case it subsequently became necessary to take any action against them. As regards the larger number of pro-Communist ex-prisoners of war that might eventually return to the United Kingdom, we could decide what was best to be done in the light of our experience in dealing with the first five such men.

The Committee –

Agreed that no action should be taken in respect of those members of the first batch of the United Kingdom ex-prisoners of war to arrive in the United Kingdom from Korea who were believed to be pro-Communist, unless it became necessary to discredit them if they attempted to spread Communist propaganda.

Sir Winston S. Churchill to John Selwyn Lloyd and Sir William Strang
Prime Minister's Personal Minute M.117/53
(Premier papers, 11/554)

29 April 1953
Private

Your minute PM/WS/53/83[1] marked 'A' by me in red.[2]

I am not convinced that we have not more powers of delay. Take for instance the following time-table.

Monday morning the Master applies for port clearance. There is a

---

[1] Reproduced above (pp. 975–6).
[2] The second half of the second paragraph.

considerable delay at the office which gives this authority and on Tuesday afternoon notification is given that we will carry out a search for contraband. It will be unfair to disturb the Surveyor General of Ships so late in the day, when no doubt he is resting. On Wednesday morning he will then visit the ship. He must make a most thorough search. He ought to spend at least half a day in looking through half the ship. If he is obstructed or urged to hasten in any way, he must raise this point with the Fort Authority and the Master should be invited to attend on the Thursday some time, when a most patient and courteous hearing should be given to him. An invitation to Luncheon would be appropriate at this point. However, when the difficulty about the speed at which the search for contraband is to be carried out has been resolved the Surveyor General should go back and continue the search. That carries us well on late Friday. It may be that some point of doubt or difficulty will arise and if so that must be referred to higher authority.

When this procedure has been exhausted the final decision should not be given by the Port Authority until I have been consulted here as serious issues of international policy are involved. The telegrams about this should be despatched not earlier than Sunday. I shall do my best to attend to the matter in due course, but there is a great deal of pressure at the moment and it may well be three or four days before I am able to give a decision.

That carries us to Thursday week. In the meanwhile port clearance must not be given and a war vessel should lie alongside *Wiima* continuously, making it perfectly clear that we should not allow the anchor to be raised or the cable slipped without our permission. If this were done the ship should be stopped, using no more force than is necessary, and a crew put on board in order to assert the control of the Fort Authority.

And again, in the event of anything so serious happening, it would be necessary to consult Her Majesty's Government, the whole matter being put to me. At such a stage I should certainly bring it before the Cabinet. However, if we miss the Thursday's Cabinet the matter would have to stand over until the Thursday following as I could not agree that the emergency was sufficient to disturb Ministers engaged on so many other important tasks.

I should hope that these indications will give you something to play about with.

2. Sir A. Noble's[1] telegram No. 56 of April 27 shows that while all the above is going on we may, if thought necessary or desirable, persuade Finnish sailors to leave the ship. Pray give us an estimate of the cost likely to be involved in this and in transporting them home in a comfortable manner. Anything under £5,000 is at your disposal. Of course it might be more effective to deal with

---

[1] Andrew Napier Noble, 1904–87. Educated at Oxford. Married, 1934, Sigrid Michelet. Counsellor, British Embassy, Buenos Aires, 1945–7. Asst Under-Secretary of State, FO, 1949. HM Minister, Helsinki, 1951–4. Ambassador to Poland, 1954–6; to Mexico, 1956–60; to the Netherlands, 1960–4. Author of *Centenary History, OURFC* (1969) and *History of the Nobles of Admore and of Ardkinglas* (1971).

the Master if he wished to be repatriated. At any rate, if he were to try to engage a foreign crew this obviously raises general issues affecting the Government of Singapore and not merely the Naval authorities, and on this I should wish to be consulted. Nor can I feel that in matters of this consequence and urgency I should not have to consult the Cabinet, already pressed with such business.

PS. Please draft a telegram to Singapore putting in a few lines the point I have outlined expansively here.

May
1953

Sir Winston S. Churchill to Field Marshal Lord Alexander and John Selwyn Lloyd
Prime Minister's Personal Minute M.119/53
(Premier papers, 11/544)

1 May 1953
Secret

I agree that it would be better that Howe should not come back through Cairo. If, for reasons of travel, he has to come through Cairo he should not pay a courtesy call on Neguib unless specially invited to do so by Neguib. Let me know before any decision is taken and give me a draft of the amended telegram you would send. The initiative should come from the Egyptians in view of the snub we received from them last year.

I agree to your proposals about my reply to Cairo No. 724.

Sir Winston S. Churchill to John Selwyn Lloyd
Prime Minister's Personal Minute M.124/53
(Premier papers, 11/645)

1 May 1953

Mr Joy's[1] telegram No. 103 from Saigon. Please advise on whether the King[2] should stay or not. The situation may be changing with the arrival of French reinforcements.

2. Mr Joy's telegram is difficult to understand. In paragraph 2 he thinks the situation will be 'brighter' if the King flees from Luang Prabang, but in paragraph 3 he is putting MacDonald's draft into 'temporary cold storage',

---

[1] Michael Gerard Laurie Joy, 1916–93. Educated at Winchester and New College, Oxford. Served in the Army, 1940–6. MC, 1945. Entered FO, 1947. Private Secretary to Permanent Under-Secretary of State, 1948–50. Served in Saigon, 1950–3. Married, 1951, Ann Félise Jacomb: four children. In Washington DC, 1953–5; Imperial Defence College, 1956; FO, 1957–9. Counsellor of State, 1959. In Addis Ababa, 1959–62; Stockholm, 1962–4; Cabinet Office, 1964–6; FO, 1966–8. CMG, 1965.

[2] Sisavang Phoulivong, 1885–1959. King of Luang Phrabang, 1904–45; of Laos, 1946–59. Succeeded by his son, who reigned until the country was taken over by the Pathet Lao, Jan. 1975.

MAY 1953   983

Paragraph 4 also seems inconsistent with paragraph 2. Please clarify the point in a short note.

I certainly agree that MacDonald's draft should be held up for the present.

Sir Winston S. Churchill to John Selwyn Lloyd and Sir William Strang
(Premier papers, 11/645)

1 May 1953

Foreign Office telegram No. 346 from New York.

The French are naturally afraid of being 'Dutched out' of Indo-China by the same sloppy United Nations methods as lost Indonesia. On the other hand they will not take the only step which could restore their position, namely two years' military service and sending conscripts to the Front. France cannot be a great nation, still less an overseas Empire, without a good French Army. A strong French Chamber breeding Prime Ministers by the score and the Deputies having splendid fun in politics is no substitute for the hard simple decisions which they have to take to remain a great power. All they have done in the last four years is to delay the formation of a German Army because they are not able to form one of their own.

Sir Winston S. Churchill to Sir Gladwyn Jebb
Prime Minister's Personal Telegram T.115/53
(Premier papers, 11/789)

2 May 1953
Dedip
Secret
No. 420

Thank you very much for your congratulations, and also for your letter of April 24. Are you sure we are doing justice to the loyal Chinese who were cut off on the Burmese Front by the Communist conquest of China. This is temporary, and China will long outlive it. It would be very shabby of the Americans to desert Chiang Kai-shek, whom Roosevelt rammed down my throat in the war, and of whom they despaired too soon because of the corruption which General Marshall felt in his régime. I did not like the American support of Chiang when he represented their wish to get us out of India, but I am not hostile to him now and certainly consider that we should not try to force the United States to betray him. It is in my opinion a matter of honour with the United States to preserve an asylum in Formosa for those who have fought against the Communization of China. This does not mean that I would not at the right moment agree to or even propose the recognition of

Communist China as the result of an armistice in Korea, but this could only be done if Formosa remained a refuge for those with whom the United States and ourselves were Allies in the war. I do not mind arrangements being made to take the Chinese troops cut off in Burma to Formosa if it can be done. Perhaps however things will broaden out in a bad way in Siam and they may come in handy where they are. [. . .]

Sir Winston S. Churchill to John Selwyn Lloyd and Sir William Strang
Prime Minister's Personal Minute M.129/53
(Premier papers, 11/645)

2 May 1953

LUANG PRABANG AND THE KING'S EXODUS

Now that we have refused rightly to send aircraft, I do not see what ground we have to advise the French about whether the King should be urged to stay or go. I should like to know what is their wish, but it is really for them to decide. You will have seen my other minute on the difficulty of understanding Mr Joy's telegram.[1] If in fact he has held up the MacDonald message and not acted on Sir William Strang's telegram, there is a lot to be said for his doing nothing more.

Sir Winston S. Churchill to Antony Head
Prime Minister's Personal Minute M.132/53
(Premier papers, 11/645)

2 May 1953

There are a lot of things happening which we rightly view with anxiety. I do not think these anxieties would be diminished by our becoming involved in the immense regions concerned. I am glad the Americans are sending some transport aircraft to the French, but I think we were quite right not to dissipate further our own limited and over-strained resources. It is not much use setting forth vague but natural desires without having some practical plans for giving effect to them. I doubt very much whether a direct communication by me to the President at this juncture would produce effective results. He would probably reply: 'We, like you, are greatly concerned at the whole situation, and have already sent some aircraft. We should be very glad to know what you feel able to do.' The root of the evil in Europe and in Indo-China is the French refusal to adopt two years' national service, and send conscripts abroad as we

---

[1] M.124/53, reproduced above (pp. 982–3).

do. Their political infirmities have prevented them from doing this and they have so weak an army that they can neither defend their own country nor their Empire overseas. They have however been successful in delaying the formation of a German army for three or four years, thus weakening NATO and all that it stands for.

I am sending a copy of this Minute to the Minister of Defence.

Sir Winston S. Churchill to Lady Lytton
(Lytton papers)

3 May 1953

Dearest Pamela,

Thank you so much for yr lovely letter. No congratulations were more welcome than yours. I took it because it was the Queen's wish. I think she is splendid.

I am sorry that the Garter stirs poignant memories in yr mind of dear Victor[1] and valiant Antony.[2] You have indeed had fearful blows to bear in life. Still courage and beauty have conquered all.

I do hope yr recovery is now complete. I did not like the cough when I came to see you, but how [. . .] you were, in yr charming home!

With my best love,
Yours devotedly,

Sir Winston S. Churchill to Sir Roger Makins
(Premier papers, 11/421)

4 May 1953
Immediate
Dedip

My immediately following telegram contains the text of a message to President Eisenhower. Please deliver this to him without comment. It is for your eye alone in the Embassy.

---

[1] Victor Alexander George Robert Bulwer-Lytton, 1876–1947. Educated at Eton and Trinity College, Cambridge. Married, 1921, Pamela Frances Audrey Plowden: two sons. Admiralty and Marine Affairs, 1916–20. PC, 1919. Under-Secretary of State for India, 1920–2. GCIE, 1922. Governor of Bengal, 1922–7. GCSI, 1925. Viceroy and Acting Governor-General of India, 1925. Chairman, League of Nations Manchurian Commission, 1931–2. KG, 1933.

[2] Edward Antony James Bulwer-Lytton, 1903–33. Educated at Eton and Oxford University. Education Dept, Central Conservative Office. MP (Cons.) for Hitchin, 1931–3. Joined RAAF, 1932. Died in plane crash, 1933.

Sir Winston S. Churchill to President Dwight D. Eisenhower
Prime Minister's Personal Telegram T.117A/53
(Churchill papers, 6/3)

4 May 1953
No. 1962

I thought of sending something like the following to Molotov: BEGINS: I had hoped that you and Eden might soon be having a talk about things as you know each other so well, but his unfortunate illness will prevent this for some time. I wonder whether you would like me to come to Moscow so that we could renew our own war-time relations and so that I could meet Monsieur Malenkov and others of your leading men. Naturally I do not imagine that we could settle any of the grave issues which overhang the immediate future of the world but I have the feeling that it might be helpful if our intercourse proceeded with the help of friendly acquaintance and goodwill instead of impersonal diplomacy and propaganda. I do not see how this could make things worse. I should of course make it clear beforehand that I was not expecting any major decisions at this informal meeting but only to restore an easy and friendly basis between us such as I have with so many other countries. Do not on any account suppose that I should be offended if you thought the time and circumstances were unsuitable or that my thought and purpose would be changed. We have both of us lived through a good lot. Let me know how you and your friends feel about my suggestion. ENDS.

The sort of date I have in mind would be three or four days in the last week of May. All good wishes.

President Dwight D. Eisenhower to Sir Winston S. Churchill
(Premier papers, 11/421)

5 May 1953
Immediate
Dedip
Top Secret
No. 973

Dear Winston,

Thank you for yours on May 4 giving me the lines of a message you are thinking of sending to Molotov. Dulles and I have considered it deeply and since you sought my views I must say that we would advise against it.

You will pardon me I know, if I express a bit of astonishment that you think it appropriate to recommend Moscow to Molotov as a suitable meeting place. Uncle Joe used to plead ill health as an excuse for refusing to leave territory under the Russian flag or controlled by the Kremlin. That excuse no longer applies and while I do not for a minute suggest that progress toward peace should be backed by mere matters of protocol, I do have a suspicion that anything the Kremlin could misinterpret as weakness or over eagerness on our part would militate against success in negotiating.

In my note to you of April 25[1] I expressed the view that we should not rush things too much and should not permit feeling in our countries for a meeting between heads of states and governments to press us into precipitate initiatives. I feel just as strongly now as I did ten days ago that this is right, and certainly nothing that the Soviet Government has done in the meantime would tend to persuade me differently. I do not feel that the armistice negotiations are going well and this to me has been the first test of the seriousness of Communist intentions. Far from there having been any Communist actions which we could accept as indications of such seriousness of purpose the *Pravda* editorial repeats all the previous Soviet positions and we are now faced with new aggression in Laos.[2]

But in my mind the most important considerations are the results which might be expected to flow from such a personal contact and the effect of such a meeting on our Allies, the free world in general, and the Russians themselves. It would of course finally become known that you had consulted me, and it would be difficult for me to explain the exact purpose of the visit. Beyond this failure to consult the French would probably infuriate them, especially when the situation in Indo-China is hanging in the balance. If they were consulted in advance, the result would almost certainly be a proposal for a four-party conference, and this, I am convinced, we are not ready for until there is some evidence, in deeds, of a changed Soviet attitude.

Many would expect dramatic and concrete achievements from a personal visit to Moscow by the Prime Minister of Great Britain. Whatever you said publically about the purposes of your solitary pilgrimage, I suspect that many in the Far East as well as the West would doubt that you would go all the way to Moscow merely for good will. I feel this would be true in this country, and the effects on Congress which is this week taking up consideration of our Mutual Defence Program and extension of our reciprocal trade act, would be unpredictable. It seems to me that in this crucial period when the Soviet peace offensive is raising doubts in people's minds, the thing we must strive for above all other is to maintain mutual confidence among the members of NATO and other free nations and to avoid any action which could be misinterpreted. Naturally the final decision is yours, but I feel that the above factors are so important that I should in all candor and friendship lay them before you.

[1] Reproduced above (pp. 971–2).
[2] On Apr. 25 *Pravda* editorialized in favour of continuing Stalin's foreign policies. On Apr. 26 objections were raised by the Communists at Panmunjom over exchanges of prisoners. During spring 1953 three divisions of Vietminh forces led by Gen. Giap crossed into Laos to harass French forces in the Plain of Jars.

Cabinet: conclusions
(Cabinet papers, 128/26)

5 May 1953
Secret
11.30 a.m.
Cabinet Meeting No. 30 of 1953

1. The Prime Minister said that at their meeting on 29th April the Defence Committee had decided that, in view of our limited resources, we must refuse a French request for the loan of transport aircraft for use in Indo-China. Since then, however, he had been told that we were holding a number of suitable aircraft in reserve against the possibility that we might have to resume the air-lift into Berlin. If this were so, it might be more difficult to continue to refuse this French request.

In discussion it was suggested that such transport aircraft as were available in this country might be needed for our own military purposes if an emergency arose requiring the reinforcement of British troops in the Middle East or in South-East Asia. It was also said that there was some reason to believe that the French themselves had transport aircraft available which they had not yet sent to Indo-China.

The Cabinet –
Invited the Minister of Defence and the Minister of State to enquire further into the points which had been raised in discussion and to report the result of their enquiries to the Prime Minister.

[. . .]

6. The Prime Minister said that he had been asked for a reply to the representations, made by a deputation from leading members of the Labour Party which he had received on 1st April, in favour of increased remuneration for Members of the House of Commons. He was being asked, in particular, whether the Government were willing to propose that this question be examined by a Select Committee. He remained convinced that any proposal to raise Members' salaries at this juncture would be strongly opposed by a majority of Government supporters, and he therefore preferred that the Opposition should be left to take the initiative in raising the matter publicly. He also thought that the pressure for an increase in Members' salaries might possibly be relieved by encouraging the discussion of means of easing the strain on Members by adjustments in the procedure of the House. Such a discussion on questions of procedure might disclose possibilities of increased allowances for Members, e.g., for postage, and other facilities which might lessen the demand for an increase of salary. He proposed to reply to the Opposition Leaders on those lines, and to point out that it was open to them to raise the matter on one of their Supply Days.

In discussion the Cabinet were informed that the Opposition had now

MAY 1953 989

agreed to the appointment of a Select Committee to enquire into the amenities available for Members in the Palace of Westminster.

The point was also made that, in the interests of Party discipline, Government supporters should not be encouraged to put forwards suggestions for improving the present arrangements for pairing: the discussion of this matter could best be handled through the usual channels.

The Cabinet –

Took note that the Prime Minister would ascertain the views of the Chancellor of the Exchequer and the Lord Privy Seal on the terms of the reply which he proposed to send to the representations made on behalf of the Labour Party in favour of increased remuneration for Members of the House of Commons.

[...]

Meeting held at No. 10 Downing Street: notes
(*Premier papers, 11/421*)

6 May 1953
Top Secret
10.30 p.m.

Present:
    Prime Minister
    Chancellor of the Exchequer
    Secretary of State for Commonwealth Relations
    Minister of State
    Sir William Strang
    Mr Pitblado

1. Correspondence with President Eisenhower

A reply had been received from President Eisenhower (Washington telegram No. 973 of May 5) to the Prime Minister's message of May 4.[1] The Prime Minister discussed with his colleagues what line should now be adopted. They considered and approved a draft message to the President and the Prime Minister authorised its despatch through HM Ambassador in Washington (sent as telegram No. 2019 of May 6).

2. Egypt

The Prime Minister informed his colleagues of a conversation with the United States Ambassador that morning, in the course of which the US Ambassador had informed him that the State Department proposed to submit a revised arms list to the Egyptian Embassy in Washington that day. The State Department had taken the line that there were a number of stages

---

[1] Both reproduced above (pp. 986–7).

to pass through before any question of implementing the programme arose and that the US Government would have complete freedom to hold back or refuse delivery. The Prime Minister had expressed to the Ambassador his surprise and regret that the US Government should take this step at the present stage in the Egyptian negotiations and subsequently the Ambassador had at his request asked the State Department not to hand the list to the Egyptian Embassy pending receipt of a message from the Prime Minister to Mr Dulles. The State Department had agreed.

The Prime Minister showed his colleagues a draft message which he had prepared to Mr Dulles.[1] They entirely agreed with the line proposed.

The Prime Minister authorised the despatch of the message with two amendments suggested by the Minister of State through HM Ambassador in Washington (sent as telegram No. 2018 of May 6).

Sir Winston S. Churchill to President Dwight D. Eisenhower
Prime Minister's Personal Telegram T.120A/53
(Premier papers, 11/421)

6 May 1953
Immediate
Dedip
Top Secret
No. 2019

Thank you for your telegram of May 5.[2] According to my experience of these people in the War we should gain more by good will on the spot by going as guests of the Soviets than we should lose by appearing to court them. This was particularly the case when Anthony and I spent a fortnight in Moscow in October, 1944. I am not afraid of the 'solitary pilgrimage' if I am sure in my heart that it may help forward the cause of peace and even at the worst can only do harm to my reputation. I am fully alive to the impersonal and machine-made foundation of Soviet policy although under a veneer of civilities and hospitalities. I have a strong belief that Soviet self-interest will be their guide. My hope is that it is their self-interest which will bring about an easier state of affairs.

2. None of the four men who I am told are working together very much as equals, Malenkov, Molotov, Beria and Bulganin[3] has any contacts outside

---

[1] Reproduced below (p. 994).
[2] Reproduced above (pp. 986–7).
[3] Nikolai Alexandrovich Bulganin, 1895–1975. Joined Bolsheviks, 1917. In the Cheka, 1918–22. Director of electricity supply in Moscow, 1927–31. Chairman, Executive Committee of the Moscow Soviet, 1931–7. PM, Russian Republic, 1937. Deputy PM, Soviet Union, 1938, 1947–50. Minister for Armed Forces, 1947–9. Minister of Defence, 1953–5. Premier of the Soviet Union, 1955–8.

Russia, except Molotov. I am very anxious to know these men and talk to them as I think I can frankly and on the dead level.

3. It is only by going to Moscow that I can meet them all and as I am only the Head of a Government not of a State I see no obstacle. Of course I would much rather go with you to any place you might appoint, and that is I believe the best chance of a good result. I find it difficult to believe that we shall gain anything by an attitude of pure negation and your message to me certainly does not show much hope.

4. I will consult with my colleagues upon the position and your weighty adverse advice. At any rate, I will not go until after your Budget has been settled by Congress which would mean my delaying till after the Coronation and about the end of June. Perhaps by then you may feel able to propose some combined action. I deeply appreciate the care and thought you have bestowed on my suggestion.

5. I have also today telegraphed as acting Foreign Secretary to Foster Dulles about the United States offering arms to Egypt at this critical juncture.[1] I presume this telegram will also be laid before you. With kind regards.

Defence Committee: minutes
(Cabinet papers, 131/13)

6 May 1953   Prime Minister's Map Room
11.30 a.m.   Ministry of Defence
Defence Committee Meeting No. 8 of 1953

[. . .]
2. Measures to Maintain our Position in Egypt

The Committee considered a report (D(53)25) by the Chiefs of Staff setting out a number of military measures which the Commanders-in-Chief, Middle East, regarded as essential to maintain our position in the Canal Zone in the event of further serious trouble with Egypt, particularly in the context of a breakdown of the current defence negotiations. The Chiefs of Staff were seeking approval in principle to these measures, so that, when the time came, Her Majesty's Government might authorise their implementation without delay.

The Secretary of State for War pointed out that the measures recommended by the Commanders-in-Chief carried with them considerable consequences in so far as the Army was concerned. If Operation Rodeo was forced upon us, the long-term commitments would be serious; as indeed would be the consequences of having to impose Military Government in the Canal Zone.

---

[1] Reproduced below (p. 994).

The Commonwealth Secretary said that it would be unnecessary at this stage to tell the Governments of the older Commonwealth countries the detailed measures which we contemplated taking in certain circumstances, but it would help us to carry them with us in the event, if he were able to inform them of our intentions if and when it appeared that action on our part in the Canal Zone was imminent. He would, before taking any such action, consult the Prime Minister. He reminded the Committee that both Australia and New Zealand had air force units stationed in the Middle East – but outside the Canal Zone. We were under agreement not to move these units without the consent of their respective Governments.

The Chancellor of the Exchequer said that the paper implied that the Commanders-in-Chief, Middle East, had already been authorised to put certain measures into operation in the Canal Zone at their discretion (Annex to D(53)25, Column (b), and D (52) 7th Meeting, Minute 4). He would have thought that such measures as these should not be adopted without the knowledge and approval of the Cabinet.

In discussion the following points were made –

(a) Serious trouble might arise suddenly in the Canal Zone. In such circumstances the Commanders-in-Chief on the spot must be able to take such measures as were essential for the safety of their own forces. They had already been informed that the powers delegated to them were to be exercised only after Ministerial decision or, in the event of sudden and serious emergency, in circumstances of such immediate and obvious menace as to make it impossible to await fresh Cabinet authority (Annex to D(53)25, Column (d), Serials 1 to 4). In practice it was most unlikely that the Cabinet would be unaware that such a situation was impending and, when signs of trouble appeared, they would be able to review the position.

(b) A number of incidents had recently occurred in the Canal Zone. A summary of these should be circulated to the Defence Committee and also forwarded to the Governments of the older Commonwealth countries.

The Committee –

(1) Took note of the report by the Chiefs of Staff.

(2) Invited the Commonwealth Secretary to consult the Prime Minister before informing the Governments of the older Commonwealth countries of the measures contemplated by the Commanders-in-Chief, Middle East (Annex to D(53)25).

(3) Invited the Minister of State to circulate to the Defence Committee a summary of the incidents, involving British forces, which had recently occurred in the Canal Zone; and invited the Commonwealth Secretary to keep the Governments of the older Commonwealth countries informed of such incidents.

3. Israel and Middle East Defence

The Committee considered a memorandum by the Chiefs of Staff (D(53)21) on Israel's part in the defence of the Middle East.

The Prime Minister said that the Chiefs of Staff were anxious to secure the co-operation of Israel in the defence of the Middle East, not only on account of its geographical position, but because the Israelis were potentially the best military material in the area. A Military Mission had visited Tel Aviv in October 1952 and had had exploratory talks with the Israelis. The Chiefs of Staff wished to have further discussions with them, but considered that before doing so it was necessary to secure American agreement to our policy, as we should have to look to the United States to finance the equipment of Israeli forces and defence works. They therefore asked for authority to hold secret discussions with the Americans with the object of securing their support for the general policy proposed in their memorandum. This was largely based on the strategic requirements in a war with Russia, and it was therefore proposed that the Israelis should make their major fighting contribution in the air. Israel would be reluctant to establish anything but a balanced force, since their main preoccupation was the defence of their soil against invasion by their neighbours. Moreover, the fear of stronger Israeli forces would constitute a useful deterrent against Egyptian aggressive aspirations and the possibility of such forces being built up would be a useful factor in our present negotiations with the Egyptian Government.

In discussion the following points were made –

(a) The internal economy of Israel was unsound and any outside support that could be given to enable her to build up her forces would be of advantage.

(b) The discussions which our Military Mission had already held with the Israelis had gone as far as they could be taken until we had secured American support for our policy, since we should have to look to the Americans to provide Israel with the arms and equipment she would require.

(c) It was generally agreed that our aim should be to strengthen the armed forces of Israel generally, but without undue emphasis on her contributions in the air, and that we should continue negotiations to this end. We should inform the United States Government of the policy we were adopting with the object of obtaining their support.

The Committee –

(1) Agreed that our aim should be to help Israel build up her armed strength, not only for her own defence, but also as a contribution to a settled situation in the Middle East.

(2) Invited the Minister of State, in consultation with the Minister of Defence, to arrange for this policy to be explained to the United

States Government and to seek their support in providing the arms and equipment that Israel would require.

Sir Winston S. Churchill to John Foster Dulles
('Foreign Relations of the United States, 1952–1954', vol. IX, pages 2060–1)

7 May 1953
Secret
Priority

1. I have just heard from Aldrich that you are proposing to give the Egyptian Embassy in Washington today a list of arms and equipment which you would eventually be prepared to supply to the Egyptians. I have been following this matter very closely myself and I had hoped that you would be able to postpone any offer to the Egyptians.

2. I know that the first of the equipment will not be supplied for ninety days but this is a moment when the negotiations have reached a temporary breakdown. We have confined ourselves to the case agreed between us and the United States both under the late and the present American Administrations. We hope indeed that the negotiations may be resumed and I am sure you would greatly regret it if your intervention with an offer of arms contributed to a complete breakdown and this was followed by bloodshed on an indefinite scale. I cannot understand what can be the urgency of your presenting the list to the Egyptians or sending them the weapons. I trust therefore that you will reconsider your proposal. Surely you could in any case refrain from coming to a decision until after you yourself have had an opportunity in the next few days of seeing things on the spot and judging the situation at first-hand.

3. Apart from the above we have definite information that quite a number of German Nazis, possibly even the notorious Remer,[1] have actually been engaged by Naguib and are training the Egyptian Army and irregulars in guerrilla and sabotage operations. Do you wish to give them American arms as well at a moment when so much hangs in the balance and when we are faithfully working on a joint plan about the Suez Canal on the case agreed between us?

---

[1] Otto Ernst Remer, 1912–97. Commissioned, German Army, 1932. Served during WWII. Arrested plotters of 20 July 1944 assassination attempt on Hitler. POW, 1945–7. Founded far-right Socialist Reich Party, 1950 (banned, 1952).

John Foster Dulles to Sir Winston S. Churchill
('Foreign Relations of the United States, 1952–1954', vol. IX, page 2061)

8 May 1953

I have received your personal message of May 7, 1953 regarding the arms and equipment which we indicated to the Egyptian Government they can buy in this country. In consideration of your strong feeling of concern, I have instructed the Department again to delay delivery of the list until after I have had the opportunity to assess the situation in Cairo. However, after discussion with the President, we feel that it may not be possible to continue these dilatory tactics without serious consequences in our relations with Egypt and charges of bad faith. Therefore, I am leaving the situation here in such shape that, if it seems desirable, I can say at Cairo that the decision to submit the list had already been taken prior to my departure. I want to be in this position so that such action, if it is to be taken, cannot be interpreted as approval or disapproval of any Egyptian viewpoints I may learn at Cairo.

President Dwight D. Eisenhower to Sir Winston S. Churchill
(Premier papers, 11/421)

8 May 1953   The White House
Secret

Dear Winston,

I like to have your letters.

Your latest one to me[1] was on the subject of your possible visit to Moscow. I gave you my frank comments, and these included the views of my principal advisers, such as Foster Dulles and others. I did try to make it clear that I recognized very clearly your right to make your own decision in such matters. Certainly I share one simple thought with you – this thought is that I would not admit that any consideration of protocol or of personal inconvenience had any slightest weight as compared to a possible chance of advancing the cause of world peace. My own comments to you were addressed solely and exclusively to the possible effects of your projected visit on friends – and others not so friendly.

As of the moment, I am far more concerned in the specific trouble spots of the world. Korea, of course, there still is. Alongside of it we must place in our concern Southeast Asia – with especial emphasis on the new invasion in Laos – and the frustrating situations in Iran and Egypt. This makes no mention of the famine conditions in Pakistan and the still unsettled quarrel between that country and India over the Kashmir problem.

---

[1] T.120A/53, reproduced above (pp. 990–1).

I know that some of our people had talks with your Mr Butler about a possible new approach to the Iranian affair. In my own official family, George Humphrey[1] was very hopeful that he might be of assistance in getting that situation straightened out, but now he tells me that a letter from Mr Butler rejects the suggestion we had to offer. This was the offer involving the suggestion that a number of our major oil companies might buy out British interests and start afresh in that region. Mr Humphrey reported to me that your Government felt it very unwise to make any further attempts to settle the Iranian problem, even through the expedient of selling out to a group of commercial companies.

Of course I do not know for certain that we here could have made the necessary arrangements to have permitted these companies to go ahead without the risk of prosecution under our anti-trust laws, but it is disturbing to gain the impression that your Government now considers the situation absolutely hopeless and believes that it would be preferable to face the probability of the whole area falling under Russian domination than to look for a new approach. We appreciate, of course, your concern for proper respect for contracts in the world; we thoroughly understand your conviction that anything that could be interpreted as additional retreat on your part might set loose an endless chain of unfortunate repercussions in other areas of the globe. Nevertheless, I still regard that area as one of potential disaster for the Western world.

Foster showed me your communication about the Egyptian affair. It is possible that I have not thoroughly understood the background in which should be viewed the existing impasse. I was told that some very protracted negotiations between the Egyptians and ourselves, looking toward the supply to them, by us, of a meager quantity of arms, had been held up for a long time pending a satisfactory solution of the Sudan problem. I understand that by agreement with your Government, we were to proceed with that transfer of a small amount of equipment (finally reduced to about five million dollars worth) upon the satisfactory completion of that agreement. It is my impression that the Egyptians knew of this general intention on our part.

Later, when there began to appear in press reports some intemperate remarks – even threats – by the Egyptian authorities against our British friends, we began to drag our feet on fulfilling our part of the bargain. The Egyptians, of course, have pressed us again and again on the matter, and we get a bit embarrassed because of their right to charge us with failure to carry out an agreement. We can, of course, adopt the attitude that, because of some of their extraordinary and threatening statements, we are compelled to make certain that they do not intend to use these arms against our friends. In fact, it

---

[1] George Magoffin Humphrey, 1890–1970. Educated at University of Michigan. Practised law, 1912–17. Married, 1913, Pamela Stark: three children. At M. A. Hanna Co., 1917; President, 1929–52; Hon. Chairman and Director, 1957. Chairman, Business Advisory Council for US Dept of Commerce, 1946. Secretary of the Treasury, 1953–7.

is my impression that we have long since done this. It is, however, quite difficult to refuse even to talk about the matter or to go so far, for example, as to decline to allow the Egyptian officials to see a list of the kind of articles that would be available. I believe that the initial items to be transferred involved only such things as helmets and jeeps.

Now, of course, we can continue to drag our feet for a while. But I do most deeply deplore having gotten into a positon where we can be made to feel like we are breaking faith with another government. It is possible that some years ago we may have been too hasty in promising to include Egypt among those countries to whom we would give some help in preparing necessary defense forces, but that is water long over the dam.

With respect to this particular item, we will at least do nothing further until after Foster has had his talk with Naguib. While it is possible that some hopeful break will develop out of that meeting, I must say that I am extremely doubtful.

As of this moment I still think that we have no recourse except to continue the steady buildup of Western morale and of Western economic and military strength. This is the great 'must' that confronts us all, but whenever you have an idea – even a piece of one – that might suggest the possibility of us diminishing the burdens that we are compelled to lay upon our collective peoples, please let me know about it. I should certainly like to ponder it.

I hope my comments do not offend – I assure you again I welcome yours.

Won't you please convey to Anthony my very best wishes and the earnest hope that he will soon be returned to full health?

With warm regards to your good self.

Sir Winston S. Churchill to Michael Creswell
(Premier papers, 11/392)

8 May 1953
Immediate
Secret and Personal
No. 938

Just take it calmly. After the necessary civilities let Dulles come to you.

2. Do not stop necessary military precautions but keep them as unostentatious as possible. We should not fire unless fired upon.

Sir Winston S. Churchill to Sir Ralph Stevenson
Prime Minister's Personal Telegram T.123/53
(Premier papers, 11/392)

10 May 1953
Priority
Secret
No. 951

I give you full authority to deliver a warning immediately it becomes necessary and if possible before a major organised clash occurs. I suggest and approve the following wording –

BEGINS.

(a) An organised attack made on members of Her Majesty's forces by Egyptians who are or have been members of the Egyptian armed forces, or by persons known to be trained or armed by the Egyptian forces would be regarded by Her Majesty's Government as tantamount to an act of war.

(b) British forces would therefore be obliged to use all necessary means in their own defence.

(c) Anyone found bearing arms and not in uniform would be liable to penalties in accordance with the customs of war.

ENDS.

I fully support you in the action you deem necessary. Do not delay delivering your warning from the moment you and General Robertson consider it necessary to the safety of Her Majesty's forces.

Sir Winston S. Churchill: speech
(Hansard)

11 May 1953   House of Commons

FOREIGN AFFAIRS

The House has already shown its deep concern and regret for the severe illness of the Foreign Secretary,[1] whose condition, though continually improving, involves his absence for several months from the office in which he has unsurpassed experience.

The Prime Minister has always to watch the course of foreign affairs with close attention, and there are many and recent precedents for his taking

---

[1] On 12 Apr. 1953, a routine gall-bladder operation went unexpectedly awry when Eden's bile duct was accidentally cut, necessitating two critical follow-up operations, the second of which involved an extended leave of absence from the FO. The damage could not be fully repaired, however, and Eden would suffer from occasional bouts of fever and ill-health for the rest of his life.

charge of the Foreign Office in such circumstances. My knowledge, such as it is, is not mainly derived from books and documents about foreign affairs, but from living through them for a long time. I hope, with the assistance of the Minister of State and of the two Under-Secretaries, to discharge these duties until the Secretary of State has recovered. It is only if I find the burden more than I can bear that I shall ask for relief, but, naturally, I shall be grateful for any consideration which the House will give me.

This afternoon, we have to survey a field so vast and varied that it is not possible to do more in the space which I could rightly claim than to deal with the salient features, and even for that a severe process of selection and compression is required. My right hon. and learned Friend the Minister of State, who will speak tomorrow, will be able to supplement the account that I can give today.

Let me, first of all, touch factually upon some of the more rapidly moving scenes as they present themselves to us at this moment. Our immediate aim is, of course, the conclusion of a truce in Korea. I doubt very much whether there could be any agreement at the present time on a united Korea. Terrible injuries have been done to each other by the North and South Koreans, but, even if both sides only stood still where they are now, and ceased fire and tried to replace the foreign troops in the country by Korean forces – even if only that happened, time might once more prove to be a healer, especially in ravaged countries when given a revival of prosperity and help in repairing the really fearful damage. Therefore, I should be very content with even a truce or a cease-fire for the moment.

We all desire a settlement of the prisoners of war dispute at Panmunjom. The wonder is that it has been kept alive so long. There is only one vital point, namely, that a prisoner of war cannot and should not be forcibly repatriated against his will. That issue has involved many months of wearisome discussion, but it is now no longer an obstacle. The question of the conditions governing the exchange of prisoners has really been reduced to terms which no longer involve any difference of principle. All that now remains is methods and procedure. Both sides have made numerous concessions, and the United Nations representatives have themselves suggested at least half-a-dozen alternatives.

It is obvious that, if at any time, there is a wish among the Communists to reach an agreement as between rational human beings, the matter could be instantly, or almost instantly, settled. It has also been made plain – abundantly plain – that, if there is no wish to settle, endless and inexhaustible variants can be proposed. So far as we are concerned, we readily accepted the idea that Switzerland or Sweden or India or Pakistan should take over the task of handling in an honourable manner the 40,000 or 50,000 prisoners who fear to go home.

Now, a proposal has been made by the Communists that five Powers – Poland, Czechoslovakia, Switzerland, Sweden and India – shall all deal together with the problem. This involves much complication, but, at the same time, the claim that all the prisoners concerned shall be moved from their present camps to other distant countries has been dropped. I must remind the House, as I have done several times, that the United States, as mandatory for the United Nations, has borne nineteen-twentieths of the burden in blood and treasure. The matter is not one which we have either the right or the responsibility to decide, but it is our duty, without separating ourselves from our great ally, to express our opinion frankly and plainly to them as occasion offers. I certainly feel that this new proposal requires patient and sympathetic examination, and there is no reason known to me at present to assume that it may not form the basis of an agreement, provided always that it is put forward by the Communists in a spirit of sincerity.

During the last few weeks, we have watched with much anxiety the deterioration of the position in Indo-China. I am glad to say that, so far as my information goes, it is less serious than was at one time assumed, and that the measures taken by the French, together with the approach, or, indeed, the arrival, of the rainy season, will probably give a lull of several months. I ought to say that, in my opinion – I am venturing to offer my opinion – the sudden advance of elements of the Viet-minh forces, or their foraging parties, towards the Siamese frontier ought not to lead us to conclude that it is a Soviet-inspired move inconsistent with the new attitude of the Soviet Government. This may unhappily prove to be the case, but also it might well have arisen from local circumstances and impulses, and from plans made many months ago and now, perhaps, reversed. We should at least not be over hasty in drawing a conclusion in an adverse sense.

Now I come to Egypt, a long way nearer to our scenes of activity, and here I think it will be well to trace the recent sequence of events. Within a week of the evacuation of Abadan, the Wafd Government of Egypt announced that they would repudiate one-sidedly – unilaterally, if you prefer it – the Treaty of 1936 which remains valid in its present form until at any rate 1956. It may well be that they did not realise what a weak position that put them in juridically and internationally, and, indeed, in common decency. We undoubtedly retain the legal advantages which go to a nation affronted by an act of bad faith.

When this happened eighteen months ago, the then Prime Minister, now Leader of the Opposition, and the then Foreign Secretary, although in the midst of the election, gave very stiff orders to the British troops on the Canal to defend themselves and make preparations to protect British civilians from outrage and massacre. A kind of guerrilla war immediately broke out, and this is what we inherited when, on 25th October, 1951, we became responsible.

By the end of January, 1952, these attacks upon our Forces, which had been heavily strengthened under the decision and in accordance with the decisions of the late Government, with which we were in full accord, were brought to an end by a rather rough episode in Ismailia. There were some shocking mob murders in Cairo, but there was no more fighting. At the end of July of last year an officer of the Egyptian Army, with a band of military associates, expelled King Farouk and made himself, or was made, without any electoral foundation, dictator of Egypt. Power has since rested with the military junta.

One of the disadvantages of dictatorship is that the dictator is often dictated to by others, and what he did to others may often be done back again to him. There has followed a period of tension in Egypt during which the new dictator and his comrades have found it convenient, or necessary, to gain as much popularity as possible by the well-known process of 'taking it out of the British'. This process was confined to wordy warfare until about the beginning of last month, April, since when a number of minor acts of violence causing the loss of several lives has taken place.

In November of last year, General Neguib and the ruling junta in Cairo asked us to begin negotiations with them on our evacuation of the Canal Zone and of the important and very costly base which has been established there wholly at our expense during and after the war. We were quite ready to talk over the whole position with General Neguib or his representatives, in a friendly manner. Naturally, we do not wish to keep indefinitely 80,000 men at a cost of, it might be, over £50 million a year discharging the duty which has largely fallen upon us, and us alone, of safeguarding the interests of the free nations in the Middle East, and also of preserving the international waterway of the Suez Canal.

If agreeable arrangements can be made to enable this latter service and also the solid maintenance of the strategic base to be discharged by agreement with Egypt, it would mean a great saving of our men and money. This, let me point out, is not an Imperialist or Colonial enterprise by the British, but it is for purposes with which every member of NATO from the North Cape to the Caucasus and also the countries of the East and Middle East are directly concerned.

It was the Egyptian monarchy which, in 1951, denounced the 1936 Treaty, and it was the Egyptian dictatorship which in November last sought the Conference. We have not accepted the repudiation of the Treaty, but we have willingly agreed to the Conference. However, before meeting the Egyptian delegates, we thought it better to come to an understanding between the United States as the leading world Power about the indispensable minimum conditions for preserving these international objects I have described.

These conditions, while fully respecting Egyptian sovereignty, must enable the base to be maintained in such a condition that in the event of a Third World War it could, if needed, function effectively in good time throughout the Middle East. After careful and thorough discussions with the American authorities, both military and civil, under the Truman Administration, we reached conclusions on the necessary conditions.

I do not propose to describe in detail this afternoon these conditions. Suffice it to say that if accepted in good faith they would render possible the reduction of the British Forces in the Canal Zone from 80,000 to a small fraction of that number. There would be left technical personnel discharging their functions with the good will of the Egyptian monarchy, republic, oligarchy, dictatorship, or whatever it may turn out to be.

It was agreed with Mr Truman's Administration that we should act together to carry forward this policy. When, after the Presidential election, President Eisenhower came into power all this matter was reviewed. I am not authorised to state this afternoon the form of agreement which was reached. In March, however, we proposed to the Egyptians that the British and United States delegates should meet them and discuss the position. The Egyptians, however, did not wish to meet us both together in the discussion, and the United States deferred to their wish while holding themselves ready at any time to join the discussions if invited by Neguib.

We, the British, therefore went into conference with the Egyptians on 27th April, a fortnight ago. We had intended some time ago to ask Field Marshal Slim to join with our Ambassador in presenting our case, which is largely military technique. His need to be in Australia made it necessary for us to substitute another military authority. In General Robertson we have found a representative of the highest professional knowledge and of varied political experience in the administration both of the Middle East and earlier of the British Zone in Germany. It was in these circumstances that negotiations began.

We did not, let me repeat, seek these negotiations. We complied with the Egyptian desire for them. They asked for them and they have now – to quote the violent outpourings of General Neguib reported in today's newspapers – washed their hands of them. Let me here say that I have hitherto had no personal communication with General Neguib, as is stated in some newspapers this morning, and nothing in the nature of an ultimatum has come from Her Majesty's Government or their delegation. It is more likely that the outburst springs from a desire to impress Mr Foster Dulles, who has arrived in Cairo today. If, at any time, the Egyptians wish to renew the discussions we are willing, and if they would renew them both with us and with the United States, that would be still better. In the meanwhile, no action so far as I can see is called upon from us.

Of course, if the boastful and threatening speeches of which there has been a spate in the last few months, and, in some instances, even in the last few hours, were to be translated into action and our troops in the Canal Zone were to be the object of renewed attacks by saboteurs or even by the Egyptian Army, which is being aided and trained by Nazi instructors and staff officers in unusual numbers, and our soldiers were being killed, we should have no choice – I am sorry to say this to the House, but we must face facts – but to defend ourselves. I am advised that we are entirely capable of doing this without requiring any physical assistance from the United States or anyone else. Our hope is that negotiations will be resumed. In the meanwhile, we may await the development of events with the composure which follows from the combination of patience with strength.

I come now to the main position in Europe. The dominating problem is, of course, Germany. If our advice had been taken by the United States after the Armistice with Germany, the Western allies would not have withdrawn from the front line which their armies had reached to the agreed occupation lines unless and until agreement had been reached with Soviet Russia on the many points of difference about the occupation of enemy territories, of which the occupation of the German Zones was, of course, only a part. Our view was not accepted and a wide area of Germany was handed over to Soviet occupation without any general settlement among the three victorious Powers.

After the interrupted Potsdam Conference, which the right hon. Gentleman the Leader of the Opposition attended in two different capacities – with my entire contentment, at any rate so far as his first capacity was concerned – the Russia of Stalin took a very hostile line to the Western allies. Stalin found himself resisted from a very early stage by the firmness and tenacity of the late Ernest Bevin, who marshalled and rallied democratic sentiment strongly against this new movement of Russian Soviet ambitions. All the tragic and tremendous events of the last eight years followed in remorseless succession. As the result, the immense and formidable problem of Germany now presents itself in an entirely different aspect.

The East of Germany – more than one-quarter of her population and one-third of her territory, has fallen into great misery and depression and has a powerful and well armed, Soviet-organised, Communist German, military force of over 100,000 men. The question of the German–Polish frontier was specifically reserved at Potsdam for the general peace treaty which, to put it mildly, seems no nearer now than it was then.

We, with the United States, and France, have entered into a new and remarkable relationship with Western Germany. The policy of Her Majesty's Government is to adhere most faithfully in the spirit as well as in the letter to our agreements with Western Germany. Dr Adenauer may well be deemed the wisest German statesman since the days of Bismarck. I have greatly admired the perseverance, courage, composure and skill with which he has faced the complex, changing, uncertain and unpredictable situations with which he has been ceaselessly confronted. Strong as is our desire to see a friendly settlement with Soviet Russia, or even an improved modus vivendi, we are resolved not in any way to fail in the obligations to which we have committed ourselves about Western Germany. Dr Adenauer is visiting us here in a few days, and we shall certainly assure him that Western Germany will in no way be sacrificed or – I pick these words with special care – cease to be master of its own fortunes within the agreements we and other NATO countries have made with them.

Then there is France. As I have urged for several years, there is no hope for the safety and freedom of Western Europe except by the laying aside forever of the ancient feud between the Teuton and the Gaul. It is seven years since, at Zurich, I appealed to France to take Germany by the hand and lead her back into the European family. We have made great progress since then. Some of it has been due no doubt to the spur to resist the enormous military strength of Soviet Russia, but much is also due to the inspiring and unconquerable cause of United Europe. We have Strasbourg and all that it stands for, and it is our duty to fortify its vitality and authority tirelessly as the years roll on.

We have the Organization for European Economic Co-operation, which has done such beneficent work in consolidating the material strength and sense of unity of European countries; we have the European Payments Union and there is also the European Coal and Steel Community, on which I believe we have observers. Finally, we have, or rather we sincerely hope before long to have, the European Defence Community, so long delayed but also so intensely needed. This will form an essential component of a progressively developing North Atlantic Organization.

The military position of France is one which may well, however, cause serious anxiety in the English-speaking world. This is not mainly because of its effect in Europe – since whatever our fate there we are in the line together; it is not mainly because of that – it is rather because of its effect on the French position and policy in the far-reaching regions they are seeking to defend.

The Americans invite the French to bring their case in Indo-China before UNO where probably a favourable vote at the moment could be found. The French, as I understand from my own observation, hesitate to do so because they know that thereafter their system in Indo-China would be brought under the continuous survey of UNO. As most of the members of UNO have no colonies they are apt to take a rather detached view about those who have. Hence the French hesitation to invoke the machinery of UNO.

But surely if France wishes to preserve the authority and life of the French Union without any associations with UNO she should take more effective steps herself. If, today, the French had the same military system that the Socialist Government set up in Great Britain – what I may call the Shinwell system – namely, two years' military service and the power to send National Service men or conscripts abroad beyond Europe, they would, I believe, have had much less difficulty in maintaining their positions in Indo-China and could also have developed a far stronger army in defence of their own soil in line with their allies. The fact that they have hitherto found themselves unable to take these kinds of military measures has exposed them to great difficulty.

Where do we stand? We are not members of the European Defence Community, nor do we intend to be merged in a Federal European system. We feel we have a special relation to both. This can be expressed by prepositions, by the preposition 'with' but not 'of' – we are with them, but not of them. We have our own Commonwealth and Empire. One of the anxieties of France is lest Germany, even partitioned as she is now, will be so strong that France will be outweighed in United Europe or in the European Defence Community. I am sure they could do a lot, if they chose to make themselves stronger. But, anyhow, I have always believed, as an active friend of France for nearly 50 years, that our fortunes lie together.

Certainly we have, since the end of the war, guaranteed five times under the various NATO and EDC agreements, under the Dunkirk Treaty and the Brussels Treaty, to help to the utmost of our strength defend France against aggressive attack. Quite a lot – five times; and not as a result of any party decisions, but with the general assent of the British nation. We also declared our abiding interest in building up the strength and integrity of the European Defence Community. We have offered close links with its institutions and its forces. This ought to restore the balance and remove fears that Western Germany will preponderate in the combined organization.

Let me, if I may, go into some detail for a few moments on our part in the European Defence Community. We accept the principle that there is a specially close relationship between ourselves and the EDC. In anticipation of the coming into effect of the EDC Treaty we are already working out with the members of the Community the measures that will be necessary, both on the military and on the political side. On the military side we will ensure effective and continuous co-operation between our forces and those of EDC. In the air we shall be ready when the European Air Force is fully established to exchange officers for command and training and to co-operate in many other ways. There will also be close association between the armies and the navies. On the political side we intend to consult constantly and earnestly about problems of common concern. That is our policy as it was the policy of our predecessors.

I feel bound also to place on record from another angle what we have done so far. We have stationed our largest military force with the French on the Continent. We have the strongest armoured force which exists between the Elbe and the Rhine. We have very intimately associated all our air forces. We have placed our troops in Europe under the command of General Ridgeway, the NATO Commander-in-Chief. And should war come he can move our divisions about, after reasonable consultations such as we had in the late and preceding world wars, in accordance with strategic requirements or even tactical requirements.

What more is there, then, that we could give, apart from completely merging ourselves with the European military organization? We do our best for them. We fight with them under the orders of the Supreme Commander. On the Continent we share their fate. We have not got a divisional formation in our own island. No nation has ever run such risks in times which I have read about or lived through, and no nation has ever received such little recognition for it.

We shall continue to play a full and active part in plans for the political, military and economic association of Western Europe with the North Atlantic Alliance. That is, I think, a perfectly sober and reasonable statement of our position in regard to the European Defence Community.

I cannot, however, leave French problems, about which I have perhaps spoken with a frankness which I think my long friendship entitles me to do, without reaffirming our devotion to the life and fame of France. France was our enemy for centuries but our ally in the worst struggles we have either of us endured. No one should ever forget the glorious but fearful sacrifices made by France in the First World War when, with her then static population of 39 million, she suffered the loss of two million of the flower of her race. We rejoice to see every revival of French strength and influence, and all the counsel which I venture to offer them as their oldest friend in Britain, springs from my admiration for the part they have played in the glory and the culture of Europe.

I move over these maps – because that is what one has to do in one's mind. When we consider the security of Europe we must not overlook a most important development in the last year – the new relationship between Yugoslavia, Greece and Turkey. These nations are on the right flank of the front in Europe, and their agreement greatly strengthens the whole system of allied defence. It also has reactions on the defence of the Middle East which are highly beneficial.

The inclusion of Turkey among the NATO powers has, of course, an important influence upon the Arab States and generally with the Moslem world. We trust that the wisdom of the Arab States may lead them to ever closer association with the Western allies, with whom they have so many ties of common interest and mutual security.

Another most important factor in the Middle East is the State of Israel. Ever since the Balfour Declaration of 1917 I have been a faithful supporter of the Zionist cause. I have, of course, had periods of deep pain when shocking crimes were committed against our officers and men by the extreme factions in this intense and complex Jewish community. But when I look back over the work they have done in building up a nation, in reclaiming the desert, in receiving more than half a million refugees hunted by terror from Europe alone, I feel that it is the duty of Britain to see that they get fair play and that the pledges made to them by successive British Governments are fulfilled.

Fortunately for them they have formed the best Army in the Levant and, as the House will remember, they successfully repulsed the combined attack which was made upon them by their neighbours and Egypt four years ago. It is very unfortunate that no peace has been made between them and the Arab States, with whom their fortunes are interwoven. Nothing that we shall do in the supply of aircraft to this part of the world will be allowed to place Israel at an unfair disadvantage.

We earnestly hope that the problem of Arab refugees will receive continuous attention and that the unfortunate and, particularly, peculiarly untimely bickering which has broken out between Israel and Jordan will be brought to an end with mutual advantage to both sides. I had a lot to do with the interests and the formation of both these States more than 30 years ago, and I believe that they have both great services to render each other by living together as good neighbours.

I had hoped very much that King Abdullah[1] and Mr Weizmann – two men I knew and honoured greatly – might have come together, but death has removed one and assassination the other. But perseverance and good neighbourliness is not a policy with which anyone can find fault. Therefore, I hope and trust that the Arab States will come to peace with Israel, and I earnestly pray that the great Zionist conception of a home for this historic people, where they live on the land of their ancestors, may eventually receive its full fruition.

The supreme event which has occurred since we last had a debate on foreign affairs is, of course, the change of attitude and, as we all hope, of mood which has taken place in the Soviet domains and particularly in the Kremlin since the death of Stalin. We, on both sides of the House, have watched this with profound attention. It is the policy of Her Majesty's Government to avoid by every means in their power doing anything or saying anything which could check any favourable reaction that may be taking place and to welcome every sign of improvement in our relations with Russia.

We have been encouraged by a series of amicable gestures on the part of the new Soviet Government. These have so far taken the form of leaving off doing things which we have not been doing to them. It is, therefore, difficult to find specific cases with which to match their actions. If, however, any such cases can be cited they will certainly be examined by Her Majesty's Government with urgency and sympathy. On this subject I will now, however, venture to make some general observations which, I hope, will be studied with tolerance and indulgence.

It would, I think, be a mistake to assume that nothing can be settled with Soviet Russia unless or until everything is settled. A settlement of two or three of our difficulties would be an important gain to every peace-loving country. For instance, peace in Korea, the conclusion of an Austrian Treaty – these might lead to an easement in our relations for the next few years, which might in itself open new prospects to the security and prosperity of all nations and every continent.

Therefore, I think it would be a mistake to try to map things out too much

---

[1] Abdullah I bin al-Hussein, 1882–1951. First King of Jordan. Born in Mecca. Commanded Arab Eastern Army in Arab Revolt, 1916–18. Refused kingship of Iraq, 1920. Emir of Transjordan, 1921–46. Helped the British occupy Syria and Iraq during WWI with his army, the Arab Legion. King of Jordan, 1946–51. Assassinated while visiting Jerusalem in 1951. Succeeded by his eldest son, Talal.

in detail and expect that the grave, fundamental issues which divide the Communist and non-Communist parts of the world could be settled at a stroke by a single comprehensive agreement. Piecemeal solutions of individual problems should not be disdained or improvidently put aside. It certainly would do no harm if, for a while, each side looked about for things to do which would be agreeable instead of being disagreeable to each other.

Above all, it would be a pity if the natural desire to reach a general settlement of international policy were to impede any spontaneous and healthy evolution which may be taking place inside Russia. I have regarded some of the internal manifestations and the apparent change of mood as far more important and significant than what has happened outside. I am anxious that nothing in the presentation of foreign policy by the NATO Powers should, as it were, supersede or take the emphasis out of what may be a profound movement of Russian feeling.

We all desire that the Russian people should take the high place in world affairs which is their due without feeling anxiety about their own security. I do not believe that the immense problem of reconciling the security of Russia with the freedom and safety of Western Europe is insoluble. Indeed, if the United Nations organisation had the authority and character for which its creators hoped, it would be solved already.

The Locarno Treaty of 1925 has been in my mind. It was the highest point we reached between the wars. As Chancellor of the Exchequer in those days I was closely acquainted with it. It was based upon the simple provision that if Germany attacked France we should stand with the French, and if France attacked Germany we should stand with the Germans.

The scene today, its scale and its factors, is widely different, and yet I have a feeling that the master thought which animated Locarno might well play its part between Germany and Russia in the minds of those whose prime ambition it is to consolidate the peace of Europe as the key to the peace of mankind. Russia has a right to feel assured that as far as human arrangements can run the terrible events of the Hitler invasion will never be repeated, and that Poland will remain a friendly Power and a buffer, though not, I trust, a puppet State.

I venture to read to the House again some words which I wrote exactly eight years ago, 29th April, 1945, in a telegram I sent to Mr Stalin:[1]

> There is not much comfort (I said), in looking into a future where you and the countries you dominate, plus the Communist Parties in many other States, are all drawn up on one side, and those who rally to the English speaking nations and their associates or Dominions are on the other. It is quite obvious that their quarrel would tear the world to pieces, and that all

[1] T.675/5, reproduced in *The Churchill Documents*, vol. 21, *The Shadows of Victory, January–July 1945*, pp. 1197–1202.

of us leading men on either side who had anything to do with that would be shamed before history. Even embarking on a long period of suspicions, of abuse and counter-abuse, and of opposing policies would be a disaster hampering the great developments of world prosperity for the masses which are attainable only by our trinity. I hope there is no word or phrase in this outpouring of my heart to you which unwittingly gives offence. If so, let me know. But do not, I beg you, my friend Stalin, underrate the divergencies which are opening about matters which you may think are small to us but which are symbolic of the way the English-speaking democracies look at life.

I feel exactly the same about it today.

I must make it plain that, in spite of all the uncertainties and confusion in which world affairs are plunged, I believe that a conference on the highest level should take place between the leading Powers without long delay. This conference should not be overhung by a ponderous or rigid agenda, or led into mazes and jungles of technical details, zealously contested by hoards of experts and officials drawn up in vast, cumbrous array. The conference should be confined to the smallest number of Powers and persons possible. It should meet with a measure of informality and a still greater measure of privacy and seclusion. It might well be that no hard-faced agreements would be reached, but there might be a general feeling among those gathered together that they might do something better than tear the human race, including themselves, into bits.

For instance, they might be attracted, as President Eisenhower has shown himself to be, and as *Pravda* does not challenge, by the idea of letting the weary, toiling masses of mankind enter upon the best spell of good fortune, fair play, well-being, leisure and harmless happiness that has ever been within their reach or even within their dreams.

I only say that this might happen, and I do not see why anyone should be frightened at having a try for it. If there is not at the summit of the nations the will to win the greatest prize and the greatest honour ever offered to mankind, doom-laden responsibility will fall upon those who now possess the power to decide. At the worst the participants in the meeting would have established more intimate contacts. At the best we might have a generation of peace.

I have now finished my survey of the world scene as I see it and as I feel about it today. I express my thanks to the House for the great consideration with which I have been treated. I hope I have contributed a few thoughts which may make for peace and help a gentler breeze to blow upon this weary earth. But there is one thing I have to say before I end, and without it all the hopes I have ventured to indulge would be utterly vain. Whatever differences of opinion may be between friends and allies about particular problems or the general scale of values and sense of proportion which we should adopt, there is one fact which stands out overwhelmingly in its simplicity and force. If it is made good every hope is pardonable. If it is not made good all hopes fall together.

This would be the most fatal moment for the free nations to relax their comradeship and preparations. To fail to maintain our defence effort up to the limit of our strength would be to paralyse every beneficial tendency towards peace both in Europe and in Asia. For us to become divided among ourselves because of divergences of opinion or local interests, or to slacken our combined efforts would be to end for ever such new hope as may have broken upon mankind and lead instead to their general ruin and enslavement. Unity, vigilance and fidelity are the only foundations upon which hope can live.

Sir Winston S. Churchill to Sir Alvary Gascoigne
Prime Minister's Personal Telegram T.129/53
(Premier papers, 11/422)

11 May 1953
Secret
No. 275

Do not worry any more for the moment about the packet of small things we are asking the Russians to do. They were put together rather in the hopes that the discussion of them might make an excuse for an Eden–Molotov talk. That alas is no longer possible for some months.

2. Let me know if there are any reactions to what I said in the House today.

Sir Winston S. Churchill to Sir Ralph Stevenson
Prime Minister's Personal Telegram T.128/53
(Premier papers, 11/392)

11 May 1953
Immediate
Secret
No. 963

You should certainly warn the British Community that those with no pressing reason to remain in Egypt should leave. If they elect to stay, their choice must be made on their responsibility.

2. You have authority to send home at public expense the families of your staff.

Sir Robert Howe to Foreign Office
(*Premier papers, 11/544*)

12 May 1953
Immediate
Confidential
No. 357

There is considerable speculation among the Sudanese about the effects of the breakdown of the Canal negotiations on the future of the Anglo-Egyptian agreement of February 12.

2. It is already being suggested by NUP[1] that the British will take the opportunity to repudiate the Agreement and to delay self-government in the Sudan. To meet such rumours I am issuing this evening the statement contained in my immediately following telegram en clair.

3. It would be of great value in steadying opinion here and in scotching Egyptian and NUP rumour-mongering if a statement could be made in the House of Commons at the earliest opportunity reaffirming Her Majesty's Government's intention of carrying out the Agreement to the full, whatever the outcome of the Cairo negotiations.

4. It is obviously important, that if there is to be any breakdown in the working of the Agreement of February 12 it should come, and plainly be seen to come, from the Egyptian action.

Sir Robert Howe to Foreign Office
(*Premier papers, 11/544*)

12 May 1953   Khartoum
Immediate
No. 358

My immediately preceding telegram. Following is text of statement.

(Begins):
It is natural that at this time of uncertainty, over the future of the negotiations in Cairo on the Suez Canal Base, there should be some speculation in the Sudan about the possible effects of a breakdown in these negotiations on the working of the Anglo-Egyptian Agreement of February 12 on the Sudan.

I wish to make it quite clear that, for its part, the Sudan Government will continue to carry out the Agreement to the full and in particular will adhere strictly to the arrangements made by the Electoral Commission for the holding of parliamentary elections.

(Ends)

[1] National Unionist Party of Sudan, later renamed the Democratic Unionist Party.

John Nicholls[1] to Sir William Strang
(Premier papers, 11/421)

12 May 1953
Secret

We have not yet heard what the Soviet press has said today about the Prime Minister's speech.[2] In all probability no more was said than was carried on Moscow radio – namely, 'The Prime Minister of England, Churchill, deputizing for the Foreign Secretary, Eden, during his illness made a speech in the House of Commons today on foreign policy.'

2. Monitoring reports so far received show that the East German radio mentioned various passages in the speech which were relatively favourable to the Soviet Union, while the Soviet radio in Austria used it to demonstrate the extent of Anglo-American contradictions.

3. So far as our own propaganda is concerned, we are confining ourselves to making known the text of the speech and quoting press comment on it. I should be very grateful for any guidance you can give me as to presentation overseas. If, for instance, it was desired to build up the references to some form of guarantee on the Locarno model (without of course suggesting that the references amounted to a formal proposal in this sense) we could no doubt contribute quite a lot.[3]

Sir Alvary Gascoigne to Sir Winston S. Churchill
(Premier papers, 11/429)

12 May 1953
Confidential
No. 91

THE SUPPOSED FOREIGN POLICY OF THE USSR –
'A POLICY OF PEACE AND INTERNATIONAL COLLABORATION'

Sir,
With reference to my despatch No. 73 of 28th April enclosing a translation of the *Pravda* reply to President Eisenhower's speech of 16th April, I have

---

[1] John Walter Nicholls, 1909–71. Educated at Malvern and Pembroke College, Cambridge. Entered FO, 1932. 2nd Secretary, 1937. OBE, 1941. 1st Secretary, 1942. Counsellor, 1946. CMG 1948. Asst Under-Secretary of State, 1951–4. British Ambassador to Israel, 1954–7; to Yugoslavia, 1957–60; to Belgium, 1960–3; to South Africa, 1966–9. KCMG, 1956. Deputy Under-Secretary, FO, 1963–6. GCMG, 1970.

[2] Reproduced above (pp. 998–1010).

[3] Sir William Strang wrote to Churchill on May 5: 'I take it that you would wish to allow your speech to speak for itself.' Churchill responded: 'Yes'.

the honour to enclose a translation of an article by A. Nikonov[1] published in *Kommunist* No. 7 of 1953 under the title 'The Foreign Policy of the USSR – a policy of peace and international collaboration'.

2. The article repeats nearly all the statements made in *Pravda*'s reply to President Eisenhower. It also quotes Stalin on the inevitability of war between the imperialist Powers. Its chief interest, however, lies in the connexion it establishes between the *Pravda* leader of 25th April and the general theory of the peaceful co-existence of Communist and non-Communist States.

3. Nikonov points out that Communist theory presupposes a period of co-existence while the first Communist State is consolidating and developing its strength in conditions of capitalist encirclement. If peace can be preserved, the development of the Communist State is faster and better balanced. The experience of thirty-five years of the co-existence of the Soviet Union and the capitalist countries has shown that peaceful relationships are possible between the two systems. The Communists believe, according to Nikonov, that capitalism will disappear sooner or later. But they also believe that this will only happen when the time is ripe. The working of the laws of history as manifested in the development of the national liberation movement is not to be ascribed to Soviet foreign policy. The aim of which is the maintenance of peace and of normal trade relations with all countries.

4. This policy, according to Nikonov, is not based on any illusions about the attitude of the capitalist world towards the USSR. It does not assume that the enemies of communism will one day renounce their hostility. Soviet confidence in the possibility of maintaining peace is based on the steadily growing economic and political might of the Soviet Union. It also takes into account the desire of certain capitalist groups to establish mutually advantageous economic relations with the USSR and the other countries of the Socialist camp, and the fact that for a capitalist State war with the USSR is more dangerous than war with another capitalist State. Moreover, the capitalists themselves realise, for all their propaganda about Soviet aggressiveness, that Soviet policy is one of peace and that the Soviet Union will not attack the capitalist countries.

5. The foregoing is the theoretical basis to which Nikonov relates the individual aspects of policy listed in the *Pravda* leader. He asserts that the policy of peace and friendship preached by the Soviet Union is not a temporary or fleeting phenomenon. It is an organic part of the Soviet State, which subordinates its foreign policy to its internal policy, and which has sought for peace in order that it might transform Russia from a backward, agrarian country into a mighty Socialist Power. The Soviet-planned economy suffers from no crises, and freedom from crises means that its Government has no need

---

[1] Aleksandr Nikonov, 1918–95. Born in Latvia. Minister of Agriculture, Latvia, 1951–61. President of All-Union Academy of Agricultural Sciences, 1984–92. Director, Agricultural Institute in Moscow, 1990–5.

of military adventures. The Soviet Government has established equality of rights and friendly relations between the nations within the Soviet frontiers, and would like to see these principles observed throughout the world. The support it gives to the workers of the capitalist and colonial countries cannot be described as the export of revolution. The mother of revolution is imperialism, though certain capitalist statesmen cannot or will not understand this. Far from exporting revolution, the Soviet Government has always stood for the preservation of peace, for international collaboration and for the development of businesslike relations with all countries, irrespective of their social systems. Any statements to the contrary are false. But the Soviet Government's wish for peace does not mean that it will negotiate on other than equal conditions, or that it can be influenced by threats or talk of a 'firm policy'. Soviet policy is based on the basic interests of the Soviet people and on the preservation of peace and security.

6. As regards the States of Eastern Europe, the Soviet Government 'supports these countries in their lawful wish to defend their national independence and sovereignty'. 'The Communist Party and the Soviet Government, the whole Soviet people consider it their sacred duty to preserve and further consolidate the greatest achievement of the workers – the camp of peace, democracy and socialism.' On this point Nikonov writes in the same sense as the *Pravda* leader, but is more categorical in his terms.

7. For the rest, Nikonov repeats what *Pravda* said about China, Korea, Germany and Austria.

8. Nikonov, writing as a contributor to *Kommunist*, does not carry anything like the weight of the *Pravda* leader. But the publication of his article in the principal theoretical journal of the Central Committee is evidence of official approval for his attempt to show the connexion between the present Soviet appeals for a relaxation of international tension and the general theory of peaceful co-existence. The doctrine and the underlying strategy of the new Soviet Government in foreign affairs appear to be those which prevailed under Stalin's rule.

9. I am sending copies of this despatch to Her Majesty's Representatives in Washington, Paris, Vienna, Wahnerheide, Tokyo, Peking, Helsinki, Warsaw, Prague, Bucharest, Budapest and Sofia.

Defence Committee Meeting: minutes
(Cabinet papers, 131/13)

13 May 1953   Prime Minister's Map Room
Top Secret   Ministry of Defence
11.30 a.m.
Defence Committee Meeting No. 9 of 1953

1. FIVE-POWER CONFERENCE ON SOUTH-EAST ASIA
(Previous Reference D(52)12th Meeting, Minute (3))

The Committee considered a Report by the Chiefs of Staff (D(53)28) on the results of a preliminary conference of representatives of the United States, France, Australia, New Zealand and the United Kingdom which had been held at Pearl Harbour during the second week of April 1953 to discuss machinery for Five-Power military planning in respect of the South-East Asia theatre.

The Minister of Defence said that the results of this conference had been encouraging. A properly representative group had now been set up to study future plans in South-East Asia, and this would go a long way to remove the difficulties arising from our not being represented in ANZUS.

The proposals for the future procedure of the Five Power Conference were designed to initiate planning studies in the context of further major Chinese aggression in the area. These studies would be undertaken entirely without commitment to Governments. The purpose of this restriction was to avoid the possibility of contracting new commitments in South-East Asia. However, in view of the current situation in Indo-China there was an urgent need for the co-ordination of military plans to counter further Communist advances. In approving the Report of the Pearl Harbour meeting, the Chiefs of Staff had therefore recommended that the studies on the provision of assistance to friendly forces in Siam, Malaya and Burma which were at present contained in the third group of priorities for planning studies, should be raised to the first group. They also suggested that the terms of reference of the Staff Agency might be extended to permit planning studies to be undertaken, without commitment to Governments, to counter further Communist aggression or infiltration in the area, in addition to actual Chinese aggression.

In discussion the following points were made:
(a) Even with proviso that planning studies would be undertaken without commitment to Governments, an extension of the terms of reference to include measures against Communist aggression or infiltration might lead to political complications, particularly as it was difficult to prove that the Chinese were in fact behind the Communist move in South-East Asia. Once the planning studies were under way their scope could probably be extended without prior amendment of the terms of reference.

(b) Grave decisions would have to be taken before any of the action falling in the second category of planning studies, concerning the use of Chinese Nationalist Forces and the seizing of a beachhead on the Chinese mainland, was taken. It might even be considered unsound to institute planning studies on such subjects at all and they should certainly be undertaken only in the context of further Chinese aggression. The proposal of the Chiefs of Staff to raise certain studies in the third priority into the first priority would, however, have the effect of deferring the planning studies in the second priority.

The Committee –
(1) Took note with the approval of the results of the preliminary discussion of the Five-Power Staff Agency held at Pearl Harbour from 6–10th April, 1953.
(2) Approved in principle the instruction set out in D(53)28 for future action in the Five-Power Staff Agency.
(3) Agreed that the planning studies to be undertaken should be in the context of future Chinese aggression and that the terms of reference for the Staff Agency should not be extended to include further Communist aggression or infiltration in South-East Asia.

2. THE STATE OF WAR PLANS AND PREPARATIONS
(Previous Reference D(52) 5th Meeting, Minute 1)

The Committee had before them:
(i) The Fourth Annual Report by the Defence (Transition) Committee (D(53)23); and
(ii) A memorandum by the Minister of Defence (D(53)22) covering a report by the Joint War Production Committee.

The Minister of Defence said that these two Reports described progress made in war plans and preparation by Civil Departments and changes which had taken place in war planning for defence production since the two Committees had reported on these subjects in April 1952. Neither of these reports called for any decisions and he proposed that the Committee should merely take note of the situation they described.

The Committee –

Took note of the situation in the Fourth Annual Report by the Defence (Transition) Committee (D(53)23) and the Report by the Joint War Production Committee attached to D(53)22.

3. THE CORONATION NAVAL REVIEW

The First Sea Lord said that, while all the ships required for an immediate emergency in the Canal Zone or the Delta were remaining at their stations, the remainder of the Mediterranean Fleet had begun their journey home for the Coronation Naval Review. The Commanders-in-Chief, Middle East, had expressed themselves as satisfied that they would have adequate naval strength to cope with any situation likely to arise in the Mediterranean Fleet in the near future. In these circumstances he asked the Committee to confirm the Admiralty's decision that the ships from the Mediterranean which were due to take part in the Naval Review should proceed to this country as planned.

The Committee –

Invited the First Lord of the Admiralty to proceed with planned arrangements for the return of HM Ships from the Mediterranean Station for the Coronation Naval Review.

4. MEASURERS TO MAINTAIN OUR POSITIONS IN EGYPT
(Previous Reference: D(53)8th Meeting, Minute 2)

Captain Maude (Military Intelligence Directorate, the War Office) gave the Committee an intelligence appreciation of the military situation in Egypt. During the past month there had been a steady pattern of movement of Egyptian units designed to counter the British intervention in the Delta. For instance, the main roads between Cairo and the Canal Zone were now covered; the Egyptian garrison in Qantara East had been strengthened; extensive defences were being prepared on the east bank of the Canal between Port Said and Ismailia, with a Battalion Group guarding the El Firdan bridge, and various units had moved out from Alexandria and Cairo to unknown destinations during the last few days.

The general pattern of rail movement between the Delta and Sinai had recently shown an increase in the quantity of supplies moving eastwards to Sinai, with an increase in troop movement westwards from Sinai to the Delta.

Certain interesting features of recent Egyptian preparations were (i) that 4,000 Auxiliary Police had left Cairo last weekend, and large numbers of these were thought to be moving into the Canal Zone – it was the Auxiliary Police who had caused so much trouble in 1951; (ii) that some 1,000 members of the Moslem Brotherhood, in armed bands of 40 to 50 under German leaders and in civilian clothes, seemed to be preparing to take independent action, whether or not the Egyptian armed forces intervened; and (iii) that various para-military units were likely to operate in civilian clothes.

The Secretary of State for War drew attention to the danger of widespread sabotage in our base installations in the Canal Zone. We had already removed a number of suspicious Germans from our installations. In this connection, the Moslem Brotherhood gangs represented a particularly sinister threat.

The Prime Minister said that the recent Egyptian military movements did not necessarily imply a hostile intent. They appeared to be deploying their troops defensively to counter 'Rodeo'. He thought that the Egyptians might not use their armed forces against us unless and until we had entered the Delta. He considered that, if we were to arrest any of the German leaders of the Moslem Brotherhood gangs, we should detain them and not merely expel them from the Canal Zone.

The General Situation

The Prime Minister said that Mr Dulles' statement in Cairo was very favourable to ourselves (Cairo to Foreign Office telegrams Nos. 786 and 787). He was thinking of bringing this statement to the notice of the House of Commons, in order to emphasize the extent to which the Americans shared our point of view.

The Prime Minister referred to a personal telegram (Cairo Telegram No. 790 of 12th May) which he had received from General Robertson in Cairo. He said that he was not inclined to recall General Robertson for consultation at this juncture, since this might look as though we had accepted that the negotiations had finally broken down.

Operation 'Rodeo'

The Prime Minister said that the latest intelligence from Egypt confirmed him in the view that it would be unwise to undertake Operation 'Rodeo' prematurely; for it would involve a wide dispersal of our limited forces. However, if civilians were murdered in Cairo or Alexandria, a new situation would have arisen: a situation in which we would presumably have a strong outside support for vigorous action. The Prime Minister said that he wished to be informed of the detailed plans for the defence of Her Majesty's Embassy in Cairo against a mob attack.

The Committee –
(1) Invited the Minister of State to inform the Prime Minister of the plans for the defence of Her Majesty's Embassy in Cairo against mob attack.

Isolation of the Egyptian Armed Forces in Sinai

The Secretary of State for War explained the practical difficulty that would arise in isolating the Egyptian armed forces – approximately 3 Brigades – in Sinai. There were 200,000 refugees in the Gaza area requiring 3,000 tons of food monthly, provided by UNRWA. Stocks of food for these large numbers were sufficient to last until the end of July, and the stocks were kept close to the Egyptian Army supply depots and readily accessible to the Egyptians, who themselves administered the refugees. So far no solution had been devised of feeding the refugees and at the same time starving out the Egyptian Army.

Emergency Measures in the Canal Zone

The Secretary of State for War reminded the Committee that the Commanders-in-Chief, Middle East, had already been authorized to implement, when they thought it necessary to do so, measures 1 to 4 set out in the Annex to D(53)25. They had now asked that the remaining measures (5 to 19 inclusive) should be approved in principle, so that there would be the minimum delay if it became necessary to ask Ministers to authorize any of these measures. There was a general agreement that this approval in principle should now be given.

The Committee –
- (2) Invited the Chiefs of Staff to inform the British Defence Co-ordination Committee, Middle East, that Ministers had approved in principle Measures 5 to 19 inclusive in Annex to D(53)25 on the clear understanding that no executive action would be taken to implement any of these measures without further authority from London.

Civil Affairs Measures in Egypt

The Committee considered a memorandum by the Secretary of State for War (D(53)29) seeking authority from the War Office to take certain preparatory measures for the institution of Military Government in the Canal Zone (Measure 17).

The Secretary of State for War recommended that the preparatory measures set out in his memorandum should now be taken. There were at present some 400,000 civilians in the Canal Zone, of whom some 160,000 were likely to remain in the event of serious trouble with Egypt. Many of these were necessary for the normal life of the Canal Zone. That being so, we should have to feed them, as food supplies from the Delta might be cut off. In addition we should have to feed the other Europeans in the Zone. We had in the Canal Zone today only four days' stocks for the local inhabitants.

In discussion the following points were made:
- (a) The War Office should arrange to send out to the Canal Zone five senior civilians for key posts to study the civil affairs plans.
- (b) For security reasons, it would be unwise at this juncture to approach the 80 lower-grade civilians who would be needed.
- (c) Stockpiling of the necessary food, as set out in D(53)29, should be put in hand forthwith.

The Committee –
- (3) Invited the Secretary of State for War to implement all the measures recommended in D(53)29, except that the 80 lower-grade civilians should not yet be approached.

Move of the Commando Brigade from Malta to Egypt

The Minister of Defence said that, on his instructions, the Chiefs of Staff had ordered the move of the Commando Brigade from Malta to Egypt. Subsequently, the Governor of Malta had strongly recommended that one of the three Commandos should remain in Malta because of the possibility of civil disturbance there.

In discussion it was pointed out that there were other units in Malta who would be suitable and available for internal security duties. The Commandos would be better employed in the Canal Zone.

The Committee –
- (4) Confirmed the instructions already issued to the effect that the complete Commando Brigade should move from Malta to the Canal Zone.

Sir Winston S. Churchill to Sir Robert Howe
Prime Minister's Personal Telegram T.134/53
(Premier papers, 11/544)

13 May 1953
Immediate
Dedip
Secret
No. 595

Your telegrams Nos. 357 and 358 (of May 12).[1]

You should have asked me about your statement before you published it. I do not see how people can work together unless they consult when there is time.

Sir Robert Howe to Sir Winston S. Churchill
Prime Minister's Personal Telegram T.135/53
(Premier papers, 11/544)

13 May 1953
Immediate
Secret
No. 359

Your telegram No. 595.

I have been given no information whatever about the progress of the Cairo negotiations which are of course liable to have immediate repercussions here. This makes it necessary for taking action often at very short notice and in the present case a delay of even 24 hours would have greatly reduced the effect and value of the statement.

I am and must remain the sole judge of the necessity to encounter urgent local action in the interests of public tranquillity. Otherwise my position

---

[1] Reproduced above (p. 1011).

becomes impossible. Experience here over the last ten years bears this out time and again.[1]

Cabinet: conclusions
(*Cabinet papers, 128/26*)

14 May 1953
Secret
12 noon
Cabinet Meeting No. 31 of 1953

[...]

8. The Prime Minister informed the Cabinet of the latest developments in the defence negotiations with the Egyptian Government. A deadlock had been reached over the arrangements for technical supervision of the base installations in the Canal Zone, and the negotiations were in effect suspended. Meanwhile provocative speeches were being made by Egyptian Ministers and sporadic attacks on British troops and property in the Canal Zone were increasing. It was known that about 1,000 members of the Muslim Brotherhood had been organized into parties of 50, each under German leadership, for the purpose of undertaking sabotage and guerilla activities in the Canal Zone. The Defence Committee had considered the situation and had authorised certain precautionary measures, including the dispatch of some reinforcements from Malta. It would, however, be unwise to launch the operation for protecting British lives and property in Cairo and Alexandria unless civilians in those cities were clearly seen to be in imminent danger. The Defence Committee would continue to keep a close watch on developments.

In discussion the following points were made –

(a) General Robertson had recommended that for the present no initiative should be taken by us to secure the resumption of the negotiations. His latest message to the Prime Minister was read to the Cabinet (Cairo telegram No. 790 of 12th May).

(b) The United States Secretary of State, who was now visiting Cairo, had made a helpful statement about the attitude of his Government towards the objectives of the negotiations. The Cabinet considered whether it would be expedient to bring this specially to the notice of Parliament. It was recognised, however, that a Parliamentary statement about it would provoke numerous questions designed to elicit any points of difference between the United States and United Kingdom Governments; and, after discussion, it was decided that

---

[1] Churchill wrote on this telegram: 'No answer'.

on this account it would be preferable not to volunteer any further statement at the present time about the attitude of the United States Government toward the negotiations.

(c) The British military authorities in the Canal Zone would be under increasing pressure to provide information to Press representatives. The Minister of Defence undertook to consider, in consultation with the Minister of State, whether they should be provided with further expert assistance in dealing with the Press.

The Cabinet –

Took note of the Prime Minister's statement and of the points raised in the Cabinet's discussion.

Field Marshal Lord Alexander to Sir Winston S. Churchill
(Premier papers, 11/392)

14 May 1953
Top Secret

SITUATION IN EGYPT

The Chiefs of Staff think it very necessary that the Commanders-in-Chief, Middle East, should be told the general lines on which you are thinking. They are not at present aware that you do not intend to order 'Rodeo' except in the last resort, nor do they appreciate the importance which you place on securing the position in the Sudan, in the event of a complete break with the Egyptians.

2. They have submitted to me the attached telegram and asked for authority to despatch it. You will notice that its contents are for the personal information of the Commanders-in-Chief themselves.

3. I agree that it is essential to keep the Commanders-in-Chief informed of what is in our minds, so that their actions are in tune with your policy. I should be grateful, therefore, for your authority to despatch the telegram.

Sir Roger Makins to Anthony Eden
(Foreign Office papers, 371/103527)

14 May 1953
No. 1036

Washington DC

Following is the text of a statement issued to the press by the State Department yesterday evening.

'Prime Minister Churchill's statement concerning a high level conference with the Soviets is a further manifestation of his own high purpose and of the fervent desire of all the peoples of the Free World to achieve a just and lasting peace.

Such a peace is a goal towards which we and our Free World allies are devoting our constant effort so that we might help all peoples toward better standards of living.

Recently President Eisenhower stressed his willingness to do all within his power to ameliorate international tensions and to meet the other side halfway when, and if, there is concrete evidence that such a meeting would produce positive results.

The President indicated in his speech of April 16 those places in Asia and Europe towards which we should look for such evidence.

Indeed, at the present time, negotiations at Panmunjom and pending negotiations with respect to Austria afford opportunity for the Soviets to demonstrate the sincerity of their avowals about the peaceful settlement of major international issues.

Such a demonstration would help to pave the way towards a high-level conference.'

Sir Winston S. Churchill to Field Marshal Lord Alexander
Prime Minister's Personal Minute M.143/53
(Premier papers, 11/392)

15 May 1953

Remember that 'Rodeo' leaked to the Egyptians. I am afraid that once anything goes out to Fayid all the Staffs of the three Services are informed, or get to hear of it. Give me the names of the three officers commanding the Army, Air and Navy at Fayid. I should not mind their being personally informed. At this stage however no one else should know. There is time to do it by airmail letter which avoids bringing in another large area of people concerned with cyphering and de-cyphering.

General Nevil Brownjohn to Sir Winston S. Churchill
(*Premier papers, 11/392*)

16 May 1953

The names of the officers commanding at Fayid are:
Air Chief Marshal Sir Arthur Sanders[1] who is Chairman of the Defence Co-ordination
General Sir Cameron Nicholson[2]
Rear-Admiral G. H. Stokes,[3] Flag Officer Middle East who represents Lord Mountbatten at Fayid.

I do not think it necessary for Lord Mountbatten at Malta to be informed.

I think, however, that Sir Thomas Rapp[4] who is Head of the British Middle East Office and advises the Commander-in-Chief on the political aspects should also be informed. I would propose to send one copy to Sir Arthur Sanders and instruct him to inform his colleagues.

Sir Winston S. Churchill to Field Marshal Lord Alexander
Prime Minister's Personal Minute M.144/53
(*Premier papers, 11/392*)

16 May 1953

I consider the General should be the responsible Commander-in-Chief and head of the defence co-ordination. After all, it is he who has the great mass of men under him and on whose decisions the greatest loss of life depends. This idea of the Services taking it in turn has no foundation in good sense. This can only be settled according to the character of the campaign. In this case the

[1] Arthur Penrose Martyn Sanders, 1898–1974. Educated at Haileybury and Royal Military College Sandhurst. Joined RFC, 1916; entered RAF, 1918. Director of Ground Defence, Air Ministry, 1940–2. CBE, 1942. CB, 1944. KBE, 1946. AOC-in-C, British Air Forces of Occupation, Germany, 1947–8. Air Mshl, 1948. VCAS, 1948–50. Air Chf Mshl, 1951. DCAS, 1950–2. KCB, 1952. C-in-C, Middle East Air Force, 1952–3. ADC to the Queen, 1954–5. GCB, 1955. Retired from RAF, 1956.

[2] Cameron Gordon Graham Nicholson, 1898–1979. Served with Army in WWI, 1915–18 (MC and bar); in WWII (DSO and bar). CO, Battle of Kasserine Pass, 1943. Cdr, 44 Indian Armoured Div., 1943–4; 2 British Div., 1945–6. Director of Artillery, War Office, 1946. GOC-in-C, West Africa Command, 1948–51; Western Command, 1951–3. C-in-C Middle East Land Forces, 1953. Adjutant-General to the Forces, 1953–6. ADC General to the Queen, 1954–6. Retired, 1956.

[3] Graham Henry Stokes, 1902–69. Educated at Royal Naval College, Dartmouth. Naval Cadet, 1919–25. Lt, 1925–38. Cdr, 1938–42. Commanded various destroyers. Capt., HMS *Devonshire*, 1950. RAdm., 1952. Senior British Naval Officer and Flag Officer (Liaison) Middle East, 1952–4. Retired, 1954.

[4] Thomas Cecil Rapp, 1893–1984. Educated at Cambridge University. Served in WWI, 1914–18. Acting Vice-Consul, Port Said, 1920. Married, 1922, Dorothy Clarke. Vice-Consul, Cairo, 1922; Rabat, 1927. Consul, Sofia, 1931; Moscow, 1932; Zagreb, 1936. Consul-General, Zagreb, 1939–41; Tabriz, 1943–4; Salonika, 1944–5. Captured and interned in Germany, 1941–3. Head of British Economic Mission to Greece, 1946–7. Ambassador to Mexico, 1947–50. Head of British Middle East Office, Cairo, 1950–3.

preponderance is overwhelmingly military, while the Air and the Navy play subordinate parts.

I am agreeable to those mentioned in General Brownjohn's minute being given all the information.

Sir Winston S. Churchill to Field Marshal Lord Alexander
Prime Minister's Personal Minute M.145/53
(Premier papers, 11/613)

16 May 1953

I should be obliged if you would let me have a critical analysis of the French military system in relation to their immediate needs at home and in the East.

The period of 18 months' service, however completely enforced, does not give them the kind of Army they need for the tasks in hand. A very large number of partly trained conscripts are available, who overcrowd the divisional and other formations. Am I right in thinking they have no large training depots? In the event of full mobilization, what exactly would occur? Would not the fighting formations be choked with masses of reservists in addition to the training of the annual intake of conscripts?

As no conscripts are allowed to be sent, say, to Indo China, do they not have to draw upon the cadre personnel, NCOs and specialists, to the detriment of their combat formations? Is it true that the great majority of officers employed in Indo China are St Cyrians[1] because those promoted from the conscript intake are not allowed to go? Do not these and other points mentioned grievously affect the efficiency of their home Army as well as denying the necessary rank and file to Indo China? When these points are put to French Ministers, they reply by simply quoting the larger numbers they call up for 18 months compared with our system. How far is this true? I think myself they overstate their case, but anyhow it would be better to have fewer men in a period of service which rendered their movement abroad possible and which relieved the undue strain of the comparatively few divisional formations. I should like a detailed comparison of the British and French demands upon the population. Can you show me the establishment of a French regular combat division and its British counterpart (a) in peace and (b) when mobilised for war?

Please let me have also the system that prevails in North Africa. Are conscripts allowed to be sent there?

Finally, let me have the French Army establishment of divisions and other units, schools and training colleges, technical training institutions (a) in peace and (b) in mobilisation. How do they compare with us in the arrangements

---

[1] The Special Military School of St Cyr is the premier military academy in France. Since its establishment by Napoleon in 1802, it has been responsible for the education of French officers in the art of war.

they make for the proper proportion of technical experts and specialists, which of course grows every year greater owing to the greater complexity of weapons? How for instance does their radar compare in numbers and length of training with ours?

Sir Winston S. Churchill: note
(Churchill papers, 4/58)

16 May 1953

A NOTE ON THE PLAINTIFF'S SOLICITORS' LETTER AND
ON COUNSEL'S OPINION

1. Counsel is not apprised of the basic circumstances. The reason why General Dorman-Smith[1] was removed was not because he was responsible for the operational decisions connected with the military disasters at Gazala and Tobruk. His solicitor states that he had no official part in operations till the 25th of June. It is surely absurd to suggest that the fact that he was removed could be attributed to his part in operations, which never existed and was known by all concerned never to have existed. Nor is there anything in Chapter 26[2] which connects him with such matters, any more than with earlier misfortunes recorded in earlier Chapters.

2. Neither is it true that his removal mentioned on page 416[3] was 'only superseded as a necessary consequence of changes occasioned by the short-comings of others'. It was the considered opinion of my advisers, after extensive consultation on the spot, that he was personally unsuited to his position as Deputy CGS. The decision to remove him was based upon their view, with which I concurred, that his influence and personality were detrimental to the confidence which those we consulted in the Army had in the High Command. This was an honest opinion formed after wide and careful enquiries and by my own personal impressions gathered on the spot, both of his personality and of his relationship with other Generals.

3. I have no doubt that Lord Alanbrooke, who as CIGS was my chief responsible adviser, would testify in a similar sense, and other responsible evidence is no doubt forthcoming.

[1] Eric Edward Dorman-Smith, 1895–1969. Educated at Uppingham School, Rutland, Royal Military College, Sandhurst, and Staff College, Camberley. Married, 1927, Estelle (div.); 1949, Eve Nott: two children. 2nd Lt, 1st Battalion Northumberland Fusiliers, 1914. Capt., 1916. Instructor, Royal Military College, Sandhurst, 1924–7. Maj., 1931. Lt.-Col., 1937. Col., 1938. Acting Maj.-Gen., 1942. Acting Brig.-Gen., 1942. Deputy CGS, 1942. Retired, 1944. Changed his name to Eric Edward O'Gowan, 1948.

[2] Of *The Hinge of Fate*, vol. 4 of *The Second World War*. Chapter and page nos refer to the 1st edn (London, Cassell, 1951).

[3] Citing Churchill to Attlee of 6 Aug. 1942, reproduced in *The Churchill Documents*, vol. 17, *Testing Times, 1942*, pp. 1041–2.

May 1953

4. With regard to Chapter 29, pages 465–466,[1] about the condition of the Army and the lack of confidence in the previous High Command, I have no doubt that Field-Marshals Alexander and Montgomery would testify to the accuracy of paragraph 2 of my minute of August 21. For this condition General Dorman-Smith had a measure of responsibility for the undue part he sought to play or was believed to be playing in influencing the decisions of his Chief during the time he was 'Chief Operations Officer'. This, I understand, is not an official military title (check), and was used by Dorman-Smith to cover decisions far beyond those which fall to the sphere of Deputy Chief of Operations. For these decisions General Auchinleck[2] is of course formally responsible, but the impression was widespread that his Staff Officer in the improvised Staff he had taken with him to the front was taking far too much upon himself and that this caused resentment and loss of confidence throughout the High Command.*

* The above Note was dictated by Sir Winston Churchill from memory and of course without being considered in its legal aspects.

Sir Winston S. Churchill to Sir David Eccles
Prime Minister's Personal Minute M.146/53
(Premier papers, 11/357)

18 May 1953

It is important that the bridge by which Peers and Members of parliament are to go from Westminster Abbey to the Houses of Parliament should be in position at least three days before the Coronation in order that careful tests may be made of its safety.

During these three days weights equivalent to the maximum weights which it is expected to bear on Coronation Day at any one time should be applied to the structure by a small and selected number of men. This might be achieved by wheeling or pulling heavy weights over the bridge on small trolleys. On the day of the Coronation guards should be posted at the entrance to the bridge to ensure that not too many people cross at the same time.

[1] Citing Churchill to Attlee, for the War Cabinet, of 21 Aug. 1942, reproduced in *The Churchill Documents*, vol. 17, *Testing Times, 1942*, pages 1102–4.
[2] Claude John Eyre Auchinleck, 1884–1981. Known as 'The Auk'. Entered Indian Army, 1903. On active service in Egypt and Aden, 1914–15; Mesopotamia, 1916–19 (DSO, 1917); North-West Frontier of India, 1933, 1935. Deputy CGS, Army HQ, India, 1936. Member, Expert Committee on the Defence of India, 1938. Commanded Anglo-French ground forces, Norway, May 1940. Knighted, 1940. C-in-C, Southern Command, 1940; India, 1941, 1943–7; Middle East, 1941–2. FM, 1946.

Sir Winston S. Churchill to Oliver Lyttelton
(Prime Minister's Personal Telegram T.150/53)
(Premier papers, 11/544)

18 May 1953

I hope all goes well with you. I have no special mission for you at Khartoum, but of course if you can find a few hours it would be well to have a talk with the Governor-General and a few of his leading men, including General Scoones,[1] Chick[2] and Riches.[3]

Denis Kelly to Sir Winston S. Churchill
(Churchill papers, 4/58)

19 May 1953
Private

1. I have been reflecting on our conversation the other night about Dorman-Smith. As I understand the law, you can put up three defences at the same time, namely:
> (1) Your remarks are not defamatory.
> (2) If they are, they are still true ('Justification').
> (3) Even if they are not true, you honestly believed them ('Fair Comment').

2. <u>Defence No. 1</u>
The judge decides whether your remarks are capable of being defamatory, and I agree with your counsel that he would probably think they might be. But the jury could still 'laugh it out of court', i.e. say that the words were not in fact defamatory. They could do this without hearing any of your defence at all.

3. If the judge ruled that the remarks might be defamatory, and the jury refused to stop the case, then you have <u>Defence No. 2</u>, namely that the words, though defamatory, are true. If you can convince the jury of this, then he cannot win. You would have to prove that the public interest compelled his

---

[1] Reginald Laurence Scoones, 1900–91. Educated at Wellington College and Royal Military College, Sandhurst. Bde-Maj., Cavalry Bde, Cairo, 1939. GSO II Western Desert Corps, 1940. GSO I War Office, 1941. Cdr, 254 Tank Bde, Burma, 1943. Deputy Director, Military Training, 1945. Asst Cdr, Sudan Defence Force, 1947–50. Maj.-Gen., 1950. Cdr British Troops Sudan, and Commandant Sudan Defence Force, 1950–4.

[2] Alfred Louis Chick, 1904–72. Entered Sudan Civil Service, 1930. Asst Financial Secretary, 1943–6. Deputy Financial Secretary, 1947–8. Financial Secretary, 1948–53. KBE, 1952. Fiscal Commissioner, Nigeria, 1953. Chief of Mission, International Bank Mission to Malaya, 1954. Chairman, White Fish Authority, 1954–63.

[3] Derek Martin Hurry Riches, 1912–97. HM Consul, Kabul, 1948–51; Jedda, 1951–2. Trade Commissioner, Khartoum, 1953. Attached to Imperial Defence College, 1955. Returned to FO, 1955. Counsellor, Head of Eastern Dept, 1955. Ambassador to Libya, 1959–61; to the Congo, 1961–3. Retired, 1963.

removal. This would take a lot of research but is far the best line if it can be established. Hearsay would not suffice. Eye-witnesses of his work and unsuitability are necessary.

4. Your <u>Defence No. 3</u> is that Lord Alanbrooke, General Jacob and other important people advised you that he ought to be relieved and that you honestly accepted their opinion. This is called 'fair comment' and should not be difficult to prove.

5. If he brings the action in England, the court might, before allowing him to start the case, make him deposit a sum of money to pay your costs in case he lost. This is because he resides out of the jurisdiction. I am not sure if this applies to Southern Ireland, but your counsel could tell you. If he brought the action in Southern Ireland, you would have to go there and give evidence yourself. He could also bring an action in both places.

6. I gather he is a drunkard and a crank, and I personally feel that the best course is a bare acknowledgment of his letter. If this does not stop him, someone who has influence over him should tell him privately to shut up. Perhaps Lord Ismay or General Pownall could advise here.

7. This is not a formal legal opinion. The only people entitled to give this are such counsel and solicitor as you may choose to instruct. I merely offer these reflections in my personal capacity based on such knowledge of the law as I possess.

Cabinet: conclusions
(Cabinet papers, 128/26)

19 May 1953
Secret
11.30 p.m.
Cabinet Meeting No. 32 of 1953

[. . .]
4. The Prime Minister referred to the slow progress of the armistice talks in Korea and the growing impression that the United States authorities were adopting an unduly stiff attitude towards the proposals put forward by the Chinese. In this connection he drew special attention to a message from Her Majesty's Ambassador in Washington (Washington telegram No. 1052 of 18th May) from which it appeared that the opposition to some of the Chinese proposals had come mainly from Syngman Rhee, the President of the South Korean Republic. This message stressed the fact that South Korean troops now outnumbered the United Nations forces in Korea and that objections raised by Syngman Rhee must be given due weight.

The Prime Minister said that this consideration must be taken into account in any assessment of the conduct of the armistice negotiations.

The Cabinet –
Took note of the Prime Minister's statement.
[...]

Helenus Milmo:[1] opinion
(Churchill papers, 4/58)

19 May 1953

In my opinion the passages complained of in the letter of Messrs Louis CP Smith & Co. dated the 1st May, 1953 are defamatory of their client, the former Brigadier Dorman-Smith who now appears to have changed his name to O'Gowan. Briefly, when read as a whole, they convey that General Dorman-Smith was relieved of his post as Deputy CGS, not because a change became necessary through no short-coming of his own, but for the very reason that he had shown himself unequal to the job with which he was entrusted.

In the event of Brigadier O'Gowan implementing his threat of proceedings for libel the action will not be a simple one to defend; but far from suggesting that the claim should be compromised, I am of the opinion that it must be strenuously resisted. In the first place the delay which has occurred since publication does not suggest that the proposed Plaintiff has any great confidence in his cause; secondly, any display of weakness in the face of this threat would be well calculated to encourage others who appear in unfavourable light in this, or any of the other volumes of *The Second World War*, to launch proceedings for libel against Sir Winston and the publishers.

There are two possible defences to the proposed action, justification and fair comment. I am not in a position to express any view as to whether the heavy onus of proving a plea of justification could be discharged. Suffice it to say that the task would be an extremely difficult one, more particularly if no clear cut incident indicating incompetence or worse could be established against the Plaintiff.

The subject-matter of the alleged libel is manifestly of public interest and the basis of a plea of fair comment would be that the reason which caused Sir Winston and his colleagues to relieve General Dorman-Smith as Deputy CGS were matters of opinion. The task of the defence would be to prove not that the view of General Dorman-Smith as DCGS taken by Sir Winston and expressed in the book was the correct view, but that it was the view which Sir Winston and his advisers in Cairo honestly formed.

[1] Helenus Padraic Seosamh Milmo, 1908–88. Educated at Trinity College, Cambridge. Called to the Bar, Middle Temple, 1931. Married, 1933, Joan Frances Morley (d. 1978): five children; 1980, Anne Brand. Civil Assistant, General Staff, War Office, 1940–5. QC, 1961. Judge of High Court of Justice, Queen's Bench Div., 1964–82.

MAY 1953 1031

A plea of fair comment will involve the defence in having at an early stage in the action to deliver full particulars of the facts and matters upon which the comments alleged to be fair are based. I draw attention to this because I apprehend that it may prove a troublesome matter to unearth at this stage the detailed material upon which Sir Winston made the decision that General Dorman-Smith should.[1]

I would point out that if it be the fact that General Dorman-Smith was only superseded as a necessary consequence of changes occasioned by the short-comings of others and that it was not the considered opinion that he bore some share of responsibility for the failure of the High Command in the Near East, this action will in my opinion succeed.

Sir Roger Makins to Foreign Office
(*Premier papers, 11/421*)

19 May 1953
Immediate
No. 1058

Responsible British informants reported today that Prime Minister Churchill was in informal touch with the Soviet Union with the idea of arranging a Big Three parley to insure world peace. The informants, who insisted upon anonymity, said Churchill's move has met with Russian approval, and if all goes well it will not be long until the Russians invite Britain and the United States to join in an early Big Three meeting somewhere between Moscow and Washington. American leaders are being kept informed about the informal British–Russian contacts. The proposal for a heads of state meeting – among Malenkov, Eisenhower and Churchill – is expected to come formally from the new Soviet Ambassador to Britain, Jacob Malik, within the next three weeks or so if there is no sharp change in the international situation. The backstage Anglo-Soviet discussions have taken place through normal diplomatic channels.

Harry S Truman to Sir Winston S. Churchill
(*'Defending the West, The Truman–Churchill Correspondence', pages 210–11*)

20 May 1953

Dear Winston,

As I told you in my communication from Coconut Island, I have tried to get to my files and I find that they are not in shape for me to get into them at the

---

[1] Sentence incomplete in original.

present time because the man from the National Archives has not appeared on the scene yet.

I am working on a historical volume covering the period from 1935 to 1952, particularly the seven years and nine months while I was President and I am hoping that I can use the text of the cables to which you refer. I would suggest that you paraphrase these cables for the reason that I can't get at the originals at the present time. It is perfectly all right for you to paraphrase them and use them but I hope you won't publish the text as yet. I would like to do it as a joint affair when I get around to the point of making publication of my own – then we can simultaneously release the exact text if that is satisfactory to you.

I hope everything is going well with you and I congratulate you on that 'Sir' before your name.

Please remember me to Mrs Churchill. Mrs Truman and Margaret join me in wishing you the best of everything.

President Dwight D. Eisenhower to Sir Winston S. Churchill
(Premier papers, 11/520)

20 May 1953
Top Secret
Personal

This confirms our telephone conversations this afternoon and this evening. I have informed Paris that you are in agreement with me in connection with Rene Mayer's[1] suggestion. Pursuant to our understanding, you in London and I in Washington will make an announcement simultaneously with Mayer's appearance before Parliament at approximately 6 p.m. Paris time tomorrow substantially as follows: 'Our three governments have been in consultation with the view of holding an informal high level meeting between the United States, Great Britain and France. We have agreed that such a meeting is desirable at a date convenient to all of us. A primary purpose will be further to develop common viewpoints with these friends on the many problems that must be solved cooperatively so that the cause of world peace may be advanced.' It is understood between us, and I have conveyed to Mayer our understanding, that this proposed meeting is not in any way to be tied to Four Power talks with the Soviet Union or to be considered as preliminary thereto. I have informed Mayer that a tentative acceptable place of meeting would be Bermuda and a

---

[1] René Joël Simon Mayer, 1895–1972. Educated at University of Paris. On active service, WWI (Croix de Guerre). Entered French Civil Service, 1919. Married, 1921, Denise Bloch: two children. Deputy Attorney-General, 1923–8. Director, Railroad Company of Northern France, 1928–32; Vice-President, 1932–8. Commissioner for Communications and the Merchant Marine, French Committee of National Liberation, 1943–5. Minister of Public Works and Transportation, 1945. General Commissioner for German Affairs, 1945–6. Minister of Finance, 1947–8, 1951. PM of France, 1953. President, High Authority of the European Coal and Steel Community, 1955–8.

date sometime after June 15 would be agreeable to both of us. The arrangements, particularly with regard to any time or place of meeting, are to be developed later.

Sir Winston S. Churchill to President Dwight D. Eisenhower
Prime Minister's Personal Telegram T.157/53
(Premier papers, 11/520)

21 May 1953
Emergency
Secret
No. 2158

I will make the following statement in the House of Commons about 3.30 p.m. (BST).

President Eisenhower has expressed a wish for a personal meeting with M Mayer and myself on June 17 to discuss our common problems. Her Majesty's Government feel that such an exchange of views could only be of advantage at the present time. It has been agreed that Bermuda, where an American Base lies, would be a suitable meeting place. The 17th of June is a convenient date to the President and so far as Her Majesty's Government are concerned it will enable the discussions with the Commonwealth Prime Ministers to be completed in accordance with the plans we have already agreed with them. All arrangements are being prepared accordingly and a similar announcement in the French Chamber is, I believe, being made today.

Sir Roger Makins to Foreign Office
(Premier papers, 11/520)

21 May 1953
Immediate
Confidential
No. 1084

Following is text of United States guidance.

'The announcement at the White House of a meeting, probably to be held in Bermuda in the latter weeks of June, among the President, the Prime Minister of the United Kingdom and the Prime Minister of France, again demonstrates the desire of the leading nations of the free world to coordinate their strength in order to promote the cause of peace. The meeting is an entity in itself, it does not (repeat not) constitute a commitment to engage in a high level conference with the new régime in the USSR. Furthermore, the meeting does not constitute evidence that existing policies with regard to major national issues will inevitably be changed. Any speculation that specific matters will be discussed should be scrupulously avoided. Major emphasis should be placed on the theme that the meeting provides an opportunity to develop common views on many problems requiring cooperative solutions in order that progress may be made toward a true and lasting peace. A meeting should reinforce the basic unity that exists and has always existed among the Powers involved. Such basic unity must be invigorated through frank discussion and maintained by genuine understanding. The initiative, the vitality and the purpose of the free world all will be advanced at the meeting.'

Sir David Eccles to Sir Winston S. Churchill
(Premier papers, 11/357)

21 May 1953

Your Personal Minute M.146/53.[1]

The Bridge has been designed for a superimposed load of 100 lbs. per square foot and each span will be tested in the makers' works by loading with 200 men which is approximately equal to 20% overload. A transverse load equivalent to the wind pressure will also be applied simultaneously. The men will mark time and march across the bridge. Vertical and horizontal deflections will be recorded.

I hope you will agree that these tests are adequate, because a test on the site three days before the Coronation would mean erecting and dismantling, holding up the traffic, and a good deal of expense.

I will certainly see that the bridge is not overloaded during use.[2]

---

[1] Reproduced above (p. 1027).
[2] Churchill wrote at the bottom of the page: 'You are responsible.'

May 1953

Cabinet: conclusions
(Cabinet papers, 128/26)

21 May 1953
Secret
12 p.m.
Cabinet Meeting No. 33 of 1953

1. The Colonial Secretary reported to the Cabinet the impressions which he had formed during his recent visit to Kenya.

The main favourable factors were that the disaffection had not spread to any significant extent from the Kikuyu to other tribes; that the number of Kikuyu abandoning their Mau Mau allegiance was greatly increasing; that the authorities were receiving a much greater volume of intelligence about Mau Mau movements; and that the recruiting of loyal Kikuyu to Home Guard units was proceeding satisfactorily. On the other hand the Mau Mau were now operating in much larger gangs. Although this was to our advantage so far as they could be engaged by the military or by regular police, the larger gangs represented a serious threat to the smaller Home Guard posts.

The Colonial Secretary said that the situation had improved greatly since his previous visit. The European community were regaining confidence in the local Government, and the atmosphere generally was much improved. If the authorities could now give a fresh impetus to their activities and if, in particular, a few more British Troops could be provided, order might be fully restored in a few more months.

Meanwhile there were serious delays in disposing of the criminal charges awaiting trial by the courts, and the more extreme elements in the European community were demanding the application of the methods of summary justice. He was not prepared to meet this demand, but he had arranged with the local Government for the establishment of a system of emergency assizes to deal with these cases under a slightly simplified procedure.

The Prime Minister said that care should be taken to avoid the simultaneous execution of any large number of persons who might be sentenced to death by these courts. Public opinion in this country would be critical of anything resembling mass executions. The Colonial Secretary said that there would be no question of executing anyone who had not been tried and convicted on a capital charge by due process of law. But he would seek the advice of his Cabinet colleagues, if any question arose of carrying out simultaneously death sentences imposed on more than, say, twelve persons.

The Cabinet –

Took note of this statement by the Colonial Secretary.

2. The Prime Minister said that President Eisenhower had spoken to him on the telephone at a late hour on the previous evening and had expressed a wish for an early personal meeting with him and the Prime Minister of France.

This suggestion had been made at the instance of the French Government who desired that, if it were accepted, a simultaneous announcement should be made in the three capitals in the afternoon of 21st May. In the course of the conversation it was provisionally agreed that the meeting, if held, might take place in Bermuda on or soon after 17th June.

The Prime Minister had at once called into consultation the Lord President, the Chancellor of the Exchequer, the Commonwealth Secretary and the Minister of State. They had all agreed that it would be right to accept this invitation. The Prime Minister had therefore confirmed in a further telephone conversation with the President his willingness to attend such a meeting; and he had obtained The Queen's permission to leave the country for this purpose. Other Commonwealth Governments had been informed. It was proposed that an announcement should be made to Parliament that afternoon.

In discussion warm approval was expressed for the Prime Minister's prompt acceptance of President Eisenhower's proposal.

The Cabinet –

Endorsed the action taken by the Prime Minister in accepting this invitation to attend a meeting with President Eisenhower and the Prime Minister of France, and expressed their gratification at the choice of Bermuda as the place for this meeting.

Sir Winston S. Churchill to Anthony and Clarissa Eden
(*Churchill papers, 2/216*)

21 May 1953

After Shuckburgh[1] had brought me the news I saw Horace Evans[2] and Cattell[3] on Tuesday night on the question of Anthony going to Boston in about a month. I had asked Lord Moran to come to advise me not on the medical aspects of the case but on the policy as it affected the medical profession. He took a day to think things over and then wrote the enclosed paper which is sagacious. On the whole I think his conclusion was that Anthony's decision should turn on whether he felt he would like a change of doctors and environment. He considers Cattell outstanding in every way though equally competent men exist in England.

---

[1] Probably about the further surgical intervention that would be necessary following the botched operation of Apr. 12. See p. 944 n.1 above.
[2] Horace Evans, 1903–63. Educated at Liverpool College and London Hospital Medical School. Married, 1929, Helen Aldwyth Davies: two children. Asst Director, Medical Unit, 1933–6. Asst Physician, London Hospital, 1936–47; Full Physician, 1947–63. Physician to Queen Mary, 1946–53, and to King George VI, 1949–52. Board of Governors, London Hospital, 1962–3.
[3] Richard Barley Channing Cattell, 1900–64. Educated at Mount Union College and Harvard University. Married, 1952, Agnes Campbell Matsinger: five children. In US Army Medical Corps, World War I. Clinical Staff, Lahey Clinic, 1927–53; Director, 1953–62.

As I have been asked to express a view I would say this: 'If Anthony feels he would like the new man I will try to arrange for Cattell to come over here to do the operation and stay at least a fortnight. There is a Prime Minister's Fund which can be used in exceptional cases so the expense need be of no worry to you. If however Cattell cannot manage to operate anywhere but in his own setting at Boston and if Anthony feels a strong inclination to using him I recommend he should not hesitate to cross the Atlantic travelling by sea.'

All my love to both of you.

President Dwight D. Eisenhower to Sir Winston S. Churchill
(Premier papers, 11/520)

22 May 1953
Top Secret

Dear Winston,

I apologise for getting you on the telephone at an hour that must have been inconvenient for you. However, I felt it necessary to cable an answer promptly to Mr Mayer, and I certainly wanted to make no kind of suggestion on the matter of a personal meeting without prior consultation with you. Because Anthony was in the hospital, I knew of no one else to talk to except yourself.

Your cable[1] reached me the first thing this morning. I am delighted that you are stressing the importance of a friendly, informal talk among the three of us because of its own value. I agree with you that a lot of good ought to flow from such a meeting.

As we cabled you late last evening, I was mistaken as to the duration of my mid-June trip to the western part of the country. It will be possible for me to reach Bermuda on the evening of the 15th, provided that date will be convenient also for you and Mr Mayer. Incidentally, one of the reasons that I suggested our state of Maine as a suitable meeting place is because of the lovely weather there this time of year.

I assume that the three governments will be communicating among themselves concerning detailed arrangements for the conference. My personal thought is that each delegation should be quite small. I hope that the three top men can practically limit themselves to friendly discussion and informal conversations. I am personally restive if not irritable under the restrictions of formal agenda. I understand, of course, that each of us should have one or two associates along so that detailed matters can be studied and put into proper form for any action we may find it desirable to take.

I particularly like the idea of the three of us bringing along our wives,

[1] T.157/53, reproduced above (p. 1033).

which in my opinion would increase the value of the meeting as a symbol of the friendship existing among us.

With warm regards, as ever,

Field Marshal Lord Alexander to Sir Winston S. Churchill
(Premier papers, 11/613)

22 May 1953

I am having the critical analysis made of the French military system for which you asked in your minute of 16th May,[1] but as this will take some little time to prepare, I am sending you an interim reply to some of the questions raised in your minute.

2. The French Army has no primary training units such as we have. The whole of a conscript's training is done within units of active divisions. This means that at any one time a large number of the men in the combat divisions are not adequately trained to fight. Further a large part of the energies of every fighting formation is permanently devoted to the elementary training of the conscript; therefore, no division can carry out adequately its cycle of unit and formation training.

3. On mobilisation, the active units throw off all conscripts with less than four months' service, who go to reserve formations. They are replaced in the active units by reservists. The intake of reservists into divisions in Germany would be on about the same scale as in our own divisions; but there is no doubt that the French divisions would be faced at a critical time with the disorganisation of conscripts leaving and reservists joining.

4. Primarily because the law prohibits the sending of the conscript outside Europe and North Africa, unless he volunteers, 25% of French regular officers and 40% of the regular NCOs are serving in Indo-China. Almost all the officers serving in Indo-China are from St Cyr or from other sources of regular recruitment, whereas many of our junior officers in the Far East are national service officers. The French, in fact, assert that the equivalent of a year's output from St Cyr become casualties there annually.

5. The effect of this is that far too high a proportion of regular junior leaders, both officers and NCOs are fighting in Indo-China. Thus the active units of the Army in Europe and North Africa are seriously short of the young regular instructors which are so essential for efficient training in all its stages.

6. The confidential reports of our observers at recent French exercises have commented on the poor state of training of French divisions. The unsound organisation of conscript training and the shortage of regular instructors are two of the main factors contributing to this.

---

[1] M.145/53, reproduced above (pp. 1025–6).

7. Our information about the French national service arrangements indicates that they call up larger numbers than we do in this country. The main reasons for this are that they accept a lower medical standard than we do and they do not exempt from service, miners, agricultural workers and merchant seamen. On the other hand, their conscripts serve for a shorter period than our national servicemen, at the same time more men in this country from the national service field take on short regular engagements. I am having a detailed comparison prepared of the British and French demands on the population. This will show the percentages of the youth of the two nations actually with the colours at any one time.

Sir Winston S. Churchill to Sir Roger Makins
Prime Minister's Personal Telegram T.160/53
(Premier papers, 11/520)

22 May 1953
Immediate
Confidential
No. 2171

Your telegram No. 1083.[1]
Considering how well everything seems to have gone in Congress and how general is the agreement here it seems a pity to issue guidance which is sure to leak out and have the effect of whittling away the importance of the conference on which many hopes are based. Would it not be better to say that the meeting is for talking over between friends some of the obvious difficulties of the world situation with no agenda and no commitments beforehand.

2. We are not issuing any guidance to our people. Considering that we do not meet for nearly a month and that Korea will have come to a head in a few days there really is no need to refer to that especially as we are in virtual agreement with each other about it. (See my telegram No. 2170.)

Sir Winston S. Churchill to Sir William Strang
Prime Minister's Personal Minute M.152/53
(Premier papers, 11/544)

22 May 1953

Why cannot the Mahdi[2] come home without stopping at Cairo.

[1] A brief covering telegram to No. 1084, reproduced above (pp. 1033–4).
[2] Abd al-Rahman al-Mahdi, 1885–1959. Muslim leader of the Mahdist Party in Anglo-Egyptian Sudan. Political moderate who supported Sudanese independence and a republican government for Sudan. KBE, 1926.

President Dwight D. Eisenhower to Sir Winston S. Churchill
(Premier papers, 11/1074)

23 May 1953

I have carefully considered your message in reply to discussions which Bedell-Smith had with representatives of Her Majesty's Embassy on the Korean Armistice Negotiations. I feel that the position Bedell set forth was eminently reasonable especially in view of the fact that we are the parties who are resisting an unprovoked aggression. I had hoped his proposals could have provided the basis upon which we all could have taken a final stand. It is essential that a firm unified stand be taken if the Communists are to be convinced that the United Nations will never forsake the principle of non-forcible repatriation, either in statement or in fact. Upon this there can be no possibility of misunderstanding. The matter has been thoroughly discussed and considered by members of my administration and with Congressional leaders in the light of your message. Although we have grave doubts concerning the conviction of some of the Allies that we can depend upon a simple majority vote we are prepared also to agree to such a voting formula for the Commission provided that the Terms of Reference for the Commission are such as to ensure beyond any reasonable doubt that coercion and force will not be used against the prisoners. This is not a question of detail or procedure but involves the integrity of the basic principle for which we have so long fought and stoutly defended.

The Terms of Reference and basic procedures which will be set forth by the United Nations Command at Panmunjom on May 25 will be clear, simple, and essential for the maintenance of the principle upon which we are all agreed. If an armistice is to be obtained upon any acceptable basis it will be essential that the Communists clearly understand that there can be no deviation from the essential elements of the position to be taken by the United Nations Command. Any sign of weakening in our unity or resolve would again be exploited by them to the disadvantage of all of us. I am sure that you will appreciate that any failure on the part of our principal Allies fully to support the position so clearly reasonable and fair and going so far to meet the views of those Allies would have most adverse effects upon American public and Congressional opinion at this critical time.

With respect to Syngman Rhee's attitude I quite agree that we cannot allow him to dictate policy to our two countries. Yet I beg of you not to forget that Korea is the one place where we have an inspired resistance by the peoples themselves to the Communist enemy. The Koreans are valiantly resisting in numbers that far exceed the combined contributions from all of us. The inspiration for that struggle largely comes from President Rhee.

I believe that a prompt public and unequivocal statement that the United Kingdom was fully consulted and fully supports the position which the United Nations Command is taking in the forthcoming Executive Sessions would assure an armistice promptly, if in fact the Communists want one on the basis acceptable to us.

Field Marshal Lord Montgomery to Sir Winston S. Churchill
(Premier papers, 11/369)

24 May 1953

1. I have very strong views on the matter of sending a British Brigade from BAOR to Schleswig-Holstein. From the military point of view it is completely unjustifiable. If by any unfortunate chance war should break out it would gravely weaken the British position in Germany and would result in losing two battles instead of winning one. The fact that a British Brigade was north of the Kiel Canal would have no possible effect on the battle for Denmark.

2. The Danish morale is at present very low. This is chiefly because the Danish Government is weak and has not the courage to take a firm line about NATO. The Danish nation is not properly geared for war and the government has not got the courage to see this is put right.

3. I agree that something should be done to give confidence to Denmark in these difficult times. But it is no good pretending that this British Brigade would meet the case in war.

In my view the proper line to take would be to initiate planning for a line of communication on the northern flank which would allow of Denmark being quickly reinforced from outside sources in wartime. For instance a United States Marine division is available under the Supreme Commander and it has always been my view that the proper place for its quick employment would be to land it in Jutland. It is also conceivable that a British Territorial Army division might possibly have to go to Denmark, but this could only be done if the situation in Denmark could be held for at least a month or six weeks.

4. I therefore do not agree with paragraph 10 of the minute by Selwyn Lloyd dated May 18, 1953. I would recommend that the correct action is to initiate immediately the necessary planning for a line of communication to admit of quick reinforcement of Denmark in time of war. This should not involve the addition of any infrastructure at present; the action should purely be limited to a plan of a possible future line of communication on the northern flank.[1]

---

[1] Churchill minuted Selwyn Lloyd on May 26: 'You should see the attached minute from Field Marshal Montgomery. I am much impressed by Lord Montgomery's arguments. I really do not feel that it is a good way of animating a weak Government to disperse further our meagre forces. Please consult the Minister of Defence bringing Lord Montgomery's minute and my comments to his attention' (M.166/53).

Sir Winston S. Churchill to President Dwight D. Eisenhower
Prime Minister's Personal Telegram T.172/53
(Premier papers, 11/1074)

24 May 1953
Confidential
No. 2197

Thank you for your most kind message of May 22.[1] I am very glad your plan has gone off so well in both our countries.

I hope to attend the Naval Review on the 15th but would be able to fly to Bermuda that night arriving the following day. If you could arrive on the evening of the 16th the 17th could be the nominal day for the beginning of our talks if the French can agree.

I like all you say about having very few people, no formal agenda and the three top men talking two and three together about our affairs. Clemmie is looking forward greatly to coming. My present idea is that we should all three stay in the Mid-Ocean Golf Club. I have received high reports of this and Winthrop Aldrich thought you would probably be attracted by it. I do not (repeat not) play golf any more so I shall bring my paint-box. I think that the three of us with our personal staffs – say 8 to 10 each, might stay here while other officials of the delegations will be accommodated separately in suitable hotels. The three of us would have separate accommodation in the Club with our own separate dining arrangements where we would entertain each other as convenient. The main room at this hotel would be suitable for any more formal meetings at which I should certainly invite you to preside as you are the Head of the State and we are only politicians.

The Governor, Sir Alexander Hood,[2] will give an official dinner at Government House. About reporters I think that the Press of all three countries should be asked to choose a limited delegation of not more than say 30 in all, including television representatives.

The people I shall bring with me besides Clemmie will be two Private Secretaries; perhaps Sir Norman Brook, the Cabinet Secretary; Makins from our Washington Embassy and one or two Foreign Office experts particularly on the Far East.

If arrangements on these lines are agreeable to you I will suggest them to the French. I am looking forward so much to seeing you. With kindest regards.

---

[1] Reproduced above (pp. 1037–8).
[2] Alexander Hood, 1888–1980. Educated at George Watson's College and University of Edinburgh. House Surgeon, Royal Infirmary, Edinburgh, 1910–11. Lt RAMC, 1912. On active service during WWI, 1914–18. CBE, 1939. Maj.-Gen., 1941. Director-General, Army Medical Services, 1941. Governor and C-in-C, Bermuda, 1949–55. KCVO, 1953.

May 1953

Sir Winston S. Churchill to Sir Stephen Pierssené[1]
(Premier papers, 11/473)

24 May 1953

Let me have a short note on the Socialist proposal to nationalise all rented land. What is the argument for differentiating against rented land?

Sir Winston S. Churchill to James Thomas
Prime Minister's Personal Minute M.162/53
(Premier papers, 11/496)

24 May 1953

About Naval Cadets I hold the opinion that the most important thing is prolonged vocational training such as is necessary to make a Naval officer of the type upon which we have hitherto relied. Four years period should be the rule though there may be exceptions. This would mean the bulk of the Cadets going to Dartmouth at thirteen, and working together there. The best arrangements possible should be made to secure the best type for entry irrespective of class. If any preference is shown it should be for the sons of Naval officers. All the above is of course without prejudice to the University or Public Schools entry and entry from the lower deck. Let me have a short paper on this showing where you and the present Board stand. A thousand words should be enough.

President Dwight D. Eisenhower to Sir Winston S. Churchill
('The Churchill Eisenhower Correspondence', pages 62–3)

26 May 1953

Dear Winston,

I appreciate your suggestions for the Bermuda meeting.[2] Needless to say, the proposal for the three of us to stay at the Mid-Ocean Golf Club is personally appealing. However, may I suggest that even though we do not order our lives to meet press reaction, we are meeting on very serious matters, and consequently one of the hotels would seem to be preferable to the golf club as a meeting place. The other arrangements you outline seems eminently satisfactory.

I am glad that we are in agreement that our delegations should not be large and I will let you know as soon as I have talked to Foster and made up

---

[1] Stephen Herbert Pierssené, 1899–1966. Lt, Queen's Rgt, 1922. General Director, Conservative and Unionist Central Office, 1945–57. Knighted, 1953.

[2] See T.172/53, reproduced above (p. 1042).

my mind on the composition of our group. With regard to press representation I think we would have considerable difficulty in limiting ourselves to the extent you suggest. But isn't this a matter which can be discussed further by our appropriate people?

While I am most grateful for your thought in inviting me to preside at the formal meetings, it seems to me that as our host you should preside at the opening, at least.

It would still be impossible for me to arrive on the evening of the 16th provided that proves practicable for the French which I seriously doubt.* We asked our people in Paris whether they thought Mayer's commitment to be in Turkey at that moment would create the same obstacle to a mid-June meeting for a new government as it did for the old. Ambassador Dillon[1] reported over the weekend that the visit of the French Prime Minister and the Foreign Minister to Ankara is now scheduled from June 23 to June 27, inclusive, and that June 29 seemed the earliest date at which the new Prime Minister could reach Bermuda unless the Turkish visit is again postponed. I should not like to press the French to postpone this again.

I see no objection to your inquiring directly of the French whether they think they could meet the mid-June date, although I hardly think that the present Ministers will feel that they can commit the future Prime Minister before he is selected and obtains parliamentary investiture.

Mamie and I are looking forward to seeing you both.

*On May 22, 1953, Mayer lost a vote of confidence in the French National Assembly. Efforts to form a new government were unsuccessful until Laniel formed a government on June 26, 1953.

Sir Winston S. Churchill: speech
('Sir Winston S. Churchill, His Complete Speeches', volume 8, pages 8485–6)

27 May 1953   St Stephen's Hall
                                                           Westminster

COMMONWEALTH PARLIAMENTARY ASSOCIATION LUNCHEON

In this hall of fame and antiquity, a long story has been unfolded of the conflicts of Crown versus Parliament, and I suppose we are most of us within a hundred yards of the statue of Oliver Cromwell.[2] But those days are done.

[1] Clarence Douglas Dillon, 1909–2003. Educated at Harvard University. Married, 1931, Phyllis Chess Ellsworth: two children (d. 1982); 1983, Susan Sage. Vice-President and Director of Dillon, Read & Co., 1938–41. In US Navy during WWII. Chairman, Dillon, Read & Co., 1946–53. US Ambassador to France, 1953–7. Under-Secretary of State for Economic Growth, Energy, and the Environment, 1958–9. Under-Secretary of State, 1959–61. Secretary of the Treasury, 1961–5.

[2] Oliver Cromwell, 1599–1658. Led Parliamentary forces, 1648–9. Co-signatory, order to execute King Charles I, 1649. Lord Protector of the Commonwealth of England, Scotland and Ireland, 1653–8.

The vehement passionate moral and intellectual forces that clashed in tragic violence three hundred years ago are now united. It is no longer a case of Crown versus Parliament, but of Crown and Parliament.

In our island, by trial and error, and by perseverance across the centuries, we have found out a very good plan. Here it is. 'The Queen can do no wrong.' Bad advisers can be changed as often as the people like to use their rights for that purpose. A great battle is lost. Parliament turns out the Government. A great battle is won. Crowds cheer the Queen. We have found this a very commanding and durable doctrine. What goes wrong passes away with the politicians responsible. What goes right is laid on the altar of our united Commonwealth and Europe.

Here today we salute fifty or sixty parliaments and one Crown. It is natural for Parliaments to talk and for the Crown to shine. The oldest here will confirm me that we are never likely to run short of Members and of Ministers who can talk. And the youngest are sure they will never see the Crown sparkle more gloriously than in these joyous days.

Of course some envious people say we want to have it all ways at once. That may well be true. We seek the best of all worlds and certainly we have got the pick of this one. It is always dangerous to make comparisons about forms of government. We accept the principle that everyone should have what they like, but there can be no harm in my saying we like very much what we have got. Still, we recognize that others may prefer different solutions.

We must be very careful nowadays – I perhaps all the more because of my American forbears – in what we say about the American Constitution. I will therefore content myself with the observation that no Constitution was ever written in better English. But we have much more than that in common with the great republic. The key thought alike of the British constitutional monarchy and the republic of the United States is the hatred of dictatorship. Both here and across the ocean, over the generations and the centuries the idea of the division of power has lain at the root of our development. We do not want to live under a system dominated either by one man or one theme. Like nature we follow in freedom the paths of variety and change and our faith is that the mercy of God will make things get better if we all try our best.

I suppose it is because I have served Her Majesty's great-grandfather, grandfather, father, and now herself, that I have been accorded the honour of expressing our thanks this afternoon to her for her Royal presence here. Well do we realize the burdens imposed by sacred duty upon the Sovereign and her family. All round we see the proofs of the unifying sentiment which makes the Crown the central link in all our modern changing life, and the one which above all others claims our allegiance to the death. We feel that Her Gracious Majesty here with us today has consecrated her life to all her peoples in all her realms. We are resolved to prove on the pages of history that this sacrifice shall not be made in vain.

Cabinet: conclusions
(Cabinet papers, 128/26)

27 May 1953
Secret
3 p.m.
Cabinet Meeting No. 34 of 1953

1. The Prime Minister referred to the public announcement which he had issued on the previous day to the effect that the latest proposals made in the armistice talks on Korea on behalf of the United Nations Forces had the complete support of the United Kingdom Government and had been prepared by the United States Government after consultation with the United Kingdom Government and other Governments concerned. President Eisenhower had said that he would welcome some such indication of our support for these proposals; and the Prime Minister had felt that the statement was one which he could issue without prior reference to the Cabinet.

The Cabinet –
Endorsed the action taken by the Prime Minister in issuing this statement.

2. The Prime Minister referred to recent comments by members of the United States Congress on the extent to which British ships were engaging in trade with Communist China. He hoped that it would be possible to deny the particular allegation that Chinese Communist troops had been carried in a British ship.

The Secretary of State for Coordination of Transport, Fuel and Power said that he was investigating this allegation. It was conceivable that this use might have been made of some ship which had been chartered by Chinese Communist interests some years ago on bare-boat terms and was still flying the British flag though outside British control. He hoped to be able to show that this was not so and he would submit a report to the Prime Minister as soon as possible.

The President of the Board of Trade said that, as regards the shipment of strategic goods to China, we could show that we were exercising a more effective control than any of the European countries.

The Prime Minister asked that a draft statement should be prepared on both points and held in readiness for use at the appropriate moment to rebut criticisms made in Congress.

The Cabinet –
Invited the Minister of State to arrange for a draft statement rebutting recent American criticisms of British activities in the China trade to be prepared in consultation with the Departments concerned and submitted for consideration by the Cabinet.

3. In continuation of their discussion of 21st April the Cabinet were informed of certain measures which had been put in hand to counteract Egyptian propaganda in the Sudan during the period before the holding of the Sudanese elections.

There was some reason to hope that the Sudanese political parties might become disillusioned about Egypt's willingness to respect the future independence of the Sudan.

The Cabinet –

Took note of these statements.

4. The Prime Minister said that he had asked the Secretary of State for War to arrange for a sufficient number of officers and men of the Royal Welsh Fusiliers to be moved from Jamaica to Bermuda in order to provide a guard of honour and perform other duties during his forthcoming meeting with President Eisenhower and the Prime Minister of France.

The Secretary of State for War said that, if these troops had to proceed to Bermuda by sea, they would be unable to play their part in the Coronation celebration in Jamaica. He therefore proposed that they should be moved by air after those celebrations were over. He would arrange for the movement to be carried out in modern aircraft provided by the British Overseas Airways Corporation.

The Cabinet –

Agreed that these troops should be moved from Jamaica to Bermuda by air as proposed by the Secretary of State for War.

[. . .]

Sir Winston S. Churchill to President Dwight D. Eisenhower
Prime Minister's Personal Telegram T.178/53
(Premier papers, 11/ 1074)

28 May 1953
Secret
Immediate
No. 2236

Yours of the 27th. The official name is Mid-Ocean Club. I put 'Golf' in to attract you. Actually the golf links are around this otherwise admirable hotel. Any arrangements agreeable to you can easily be made. Formal meetings could be held at Government House and I would open the proceedings only by asking you to preside. This follows the Yalta precedent if that is still a help.

2. It now looks as if the French uncertainties may impose a much longer delay upon our meeting. I like the idea of Reynaud coming as he knows the story and has lived through it. He is quite right to demand some security of tenure. Nevertheless I feel the delay is unfortunate.

3. I will cable you again as soon as the French situation clears. Meanwhile I am making all preliminary arrangements.

4. I hope that our declaration of support will be of help at Panmunjom.

5. Let me thank you warmly for your kindness in responding so readily to Makins' suggestion about Anthony's aircraft. The doctors have today decided

he should leave on the 5th and as the Canadian government aircraft already here is going back on that date this will be the easiest course. Please allow me to mention your kind offer when the arrangements are announced. All good wishes.

Sir Winston S. Churchill to Sir Roger Makins
(Premier papers, 11/420)

28 May 1953

Your no. 1130.

I do not think it would be a good thing for the United States to make an approach to Moscow at this juncture and I think it would be taken as a sign of weakness there. It would be quite a different thing for me to send a Personal and Private message to Molotov and indeed I had thought of doing this anyhow. My message would be in effect. BEGINS. You will no doubt have seen about the Bermuda conference. I am hoping that it may result in bridges being built not barriers between East and West. It would I am sure be a help if this Panmunjom prisoners-of-war business were got out of the way. ENDS.

Sir Winston S. Churchill to President Dwight D. Eisenhower
Prime Minister's Personal Telegram T.179/53
(Premier papers, 11/1074)

28 May 1953
Immediate
Secret, Private and Personal
No. 2247

In the talk between Bedell and Makins on May 23 the idea was mentioned that perhaps United States might make some approach to Moscow to help agreement at Panmunjom. I don't know how it all passed, but since the matter has been discussed I hope you won't mind my giving you my opinion. I think it would be a pity for the United States to make an approach to Moscow at this juncture and that it would only be taken by them as a sign of weakness. You are the overwhelmingly powerful figure in the ring and we are supporting you in your effort to make the Communists accept.

2. It would be quite a different thing for me to send a personal and private message to Molotov and indeed I had thought of doing this anyhow. My message would be in effect –

BEGINS. You will no doubt have seen about the Bermuda Conference. I am hoping that it may result in bridges being built not barriers between

East and West. It would I am sure be a help if this Panmunjom Prisoners of War business were got out of the way. ENDS.

3. The position would then be the United States maintaining a formidable front and Britain, bound to them by unbreakable ties, giving a friendly hint. Let me know how you feel about this.

4. I am so glad to read just now your remarks about Taft's speech.[1] I look back with dark memories to all that followed inch by inch upon the United States's withdrawal from the League of Nations over 30 years ago. Thank God you are at the helm.

Sir Winston S. Churchill to Oliver Lyttelton
Prime Minister's Personal Minute M.167/53
(Premier papers, 11/475)

28 May 1953

I cannot wait to see Mr Borg Olivier.[2] I should advise him to go privately to the place we have reserved for him in Westminster Abbey and to take your advice about the other points raised. Of course if he will not be presented to The Queen by <u>you</u> his appearance at the luncheon would be an intrusion. If after all the trouble we have taken he threatens to go back to Malta we should help in every way. I do not wish to be troubled with this matter again and leave it for you to decide. On no account let The Queen be burdened with any aspects of it.

Lord Stafford[3] to Sir Winston S. Churchill
(Premier papers, 11/477)

28 May 1953

My dear Prime Minister,

Lord Rosebery tells me that he was discussing with you the other day the difficulties which trainers are experiencing in getting a reasonable deferment from Military Service for their apprentices.

[1] Sen. Robert Taft, a prominent isolationist in the 1930s, argued that the US should cease to work with the UN in Korea. President Eisenhower publicly disagreed with Taft on this point.
[2] Giorgio Borg Olivier, 1911–80. Born in Valletta, Malta. Educated at Lyceum, Malta, and Royal University of Malta. Elected to Council of Government, 1939; to Legislative Assembly, 1947. Minister for Public Works and Reconstruction and Minister of Education, 1950. PM of Malta, 1950–5, 1962–71. Leader of Opposition, 1955–8, 1971–7. Minister of Economic Planning and Finance, 1962–71. Minister of Foreign and Commonwealth Affairs, 1965–71. Resigned from Parliament, 1977.
[3] Basil Francis Nicholas Fitzherbert, 1926–86. Educated at Ampleforth College. Baron Stafford, 1941. Lt, Scots Guards, 1944–8. Married, 1952, Morag Nada Campbell: six children. North Staffs Branch, Institute of Marketing, 1955–76. Member, North Staffordshire Sporting Club. Local Director, Barclays Bank Ltd (Birmingham), 1976–82. Retired, 1982.

The trouble, as no doubt he pointed out to you, is that the period of Military Service usually comes just as the boy is at a light weight and starting to ride a few winners. Unless he can get a reasonable period of deferment his whole career as a jockey is likely to be ruined, because he cannot take full advantage of the early promise which he shows as an apprentice, and by the time he returns from the Army he is probably forgotten.

I wonder whether it would be possible to arrange that apprentices who find themselves in this situation could be granted deferment until, say, after their 21st birthday.

I think it has one other advantage from the point of view of the Minister of Defence, inasmuch as the lads which would come to him after their 21st birthday would probably be of a more reasonable physique for the Services.

I should be most grateful if you would have this point of view put forward to the right quarter. I know it will have the support of my two co-Stewards.

Michael Fraser to David Pitblado
(Premier papers, 11/473)

29 May 1953

Dear Pitblado,

In a minute dated 24th May,[1] the Prime Minister asked Sir Stephen Pierssené for a short note on the Socialist proposal to nationalise all rented farm land. As this is a policy matter, Sir Stephen passed it to me, and I now send you two copies of a memorandum on the subject.

NATIONALISATION OF RENTED FARM LAND

1. Mr Bevan outlined his proposal for nationalisation of rented farm land in *Reynolds News* on 11th January, 1953.

> 'I would take over all rented agricultural land so that the State could provide for the cultivator those functions which were formerly provided by the best landlords . . . it does not mean that the State would cultivate the land directly, except in a few instances where ranching might be suitable. What it should mean is a new flow of capital to the land under conditions which guarantee increased production of the sort we require.'

2. These proposals appeared again, in more detail, in *Tribune* on 1st May, 1953.

> 'Private ownership of the land has failed . . . the old landlord system has broken down and nothing has been put in its place. Since the start of the

---

[1] Reproduced above (p. 1043).

MAY 1953 1051

great agricultural depression 60 years ago, the landowners have done much less than is needed to maintain buildings, to force through land draining schemes, to provide capital needed for re-equipment. Public money has been pumped into the industry . . . something has been achieved – but nothing like enough. No real plan for British agriculture is possible so long as the landlords collect the rents. . . . The nationalisation of rented land would make possible guaranteed prices plus efficiency. It would enable the farmer to get on with his job and give him a new landlord who fulfilled his part of the bargain.'

Co-operative Party Policy

3. In February, 1953, a special report on 'Public Ownership of Land' was issued by the National Committee of the Co-operative Party.

'From its inception, the Co-operative Party has accepted the principle of public ownership of land (Para. 2). . . . The transfer of the ownership of the land into public hands need not be accomplished in one sweep. In our view it would be preferable, as the first step, to transfer to public ownership all land for which rent is paid to landowners other than public owners (Para. 28). . . . Forty per cent. Of the cultivated land in this country is owner-occupied. These farmers would be untouched by such a measure as is proposed. Only where farm land is held on lease would there be a transfer of the ownership (Para. 33).'

Labour Party Policy

4. On 31st March, 1953, it was reported that Socialist leaders had been unable to come to a decision on the proposal to nationalise all rented farm lands. At a meeting of the Labour Party Executive at the end of April, the proposal was rejected on a vote, although Mr Attlee had himself spoken in favour of it. In speeches in the country both Mr Stokes[1] (29th January, 1953) and Sir Hartley Shawcross (3rd May, 1953) have opposed the proposal on grounds of cost and administrative complication. According to the latest reports, Mr Bevan is still trying to have the proposal included in the forthcoming Labour Party policy statement. If it is not included, an amendment may be moved at the Margate Conference in September.

ARGUMENTS FOR DIFFERENTIATING AGAINST RENTED LAND

5. Mr Bevan's argument is that the landlord system has failed, insufficient capital has been provided and production has not increased as it should. By

[1] Richard Rapier Stokes, 1897–1957. On active service, RA, 1915–18 (MC and bar). Unsuccessful Parliamentary candidate (Lab.), 1935. MP (Lab.) for Ipswich from 1938 until his death. A persistent critic of the conduct of the war, 1940–5. Minister of Works, 1950–1; Minister of Materials, 1951.

making the State the landlord, capital could be provided where and when needed and efficiency ensured.

6. The Co-operative Party justify the proposal on the same grounds and regard it as the first step towards public ownership of all land.

7. The fact that it would be politically, as well as practically, easier to expropriate a relatively limited number of landlords, rather than a very large number of owner-occupiers, no doubt also has some influence.

President Dwight D. Eisenhower to Sir Winston S. Churchill
(Premier papers, 11/520)

30 May 1953
Secret

Dear Winston,

The Mid-Ocean Club is perfectly satisfactory to me, especially since it appears that each of us can have a few of his principal people around him. I will deem it an honour to share the Mid-Ocean Club with you and our French confrere. Incidentally, I hope that there will be no objection to my bringing along with Mrs Eisenhower her mother[1] and her woman companion. Could you let me know on this point? Of course, the overflow part of the American Governmental delegation will be stationed on our air base in Bermuda.

I earnestly hope to keep my entire official delegation down to something on the order of a dozen to fifteen, but I cannot greatly influence the size of the press, radio, and photographers sections. These people, of course, travel under their own steam and secure their own accommodations without specific governmental approval. A great proportion of the foreign press representatives stationed in Washington will insist upon going and, of course, the American press will want to be heavily represented. I imagine that they soon will be trying to reserve every hotel in Bermuda for their operations, and I am frank to say that I do not know how we can do anything at this end to control this matter. In fact, it is possible that we would not want to control it for the reason that I should think it would be best for all of us that the entire world was saturated with information that we were enjoying a friendly, informal, and profitable get-together.

[1] Elivera Mathilda Carlson Doud, 1878–1960. Married, 1894, John Sheldon Doud: four children.

Field Marshal Lord Montgomery to Sir Winston S. Churchill
(*Churchill papers, 2/143*)[1]

30 May 1953

My dear Winston,
　On Monday 8th June Clemmie is going with me to the Palace Theatre to see *The Glorious Days*. It is a play which projects you into the past very cleverly. It is at 7.30 p.m. and I am calling for Clemmie in my car at No. 10 at 7.15 p.m. I have the Royal Box and we shall be alone: no one else.
　Do please come with us. It will be quite easy for you and very restful; just the three of us in the Box. And you would be back in No. 10 soon after 10 p.m.
　I am sure you need a few moments relaxation in your very strenuous life.
　I knew Reynaud would not be approved by the French Assembly. I think we had a bet of 1/- on it at Chartwell!!

Sir Winston S. Churchill to President Dwight D. Eisenhower
Prime Minister's Personal Telegram T.182/53
(*Premier papers, 11/520*)

30 May 1953
Immediate
Secret
No. 2268

My dear Friend,
　Your message of the 30th.[2]
　1. I am so glad the Mid Ocean Club will suit you. I am assured it is the best pick and as it is stated to hold 80 guests there should be plenty of room. It will be splendid if Mrs Eisenhower's mother and companion will come too.
　2. My official circle will be kept very small like yours. I agree with you that the Press cannot be limited. Sir Norman Brook, the Secretary of the Cabinet and about to become a Privy Counsellor, will look after details for me and keep any member of your staff you nominate fully informed on any points that arise. I am sure you do not want to be bothered with detail.
　3. I am glad about the message to your Ambassador in Moscow. I shall send Molotov a telegram on my own responsibility on the lines I mentioned to you.
　4. About the date. The French delay in forming a Government may be considerable and anyhow they have their Turkish function on the 23rd or 24th. It looks to me that that the 29th may well have to be our target. Let us try to keep four or five days for our stay. I was sorry about Reynaud whose attitude was manly and patriotic.

[1] This letter was handwritten.
[2] Reproduced above (p. 1052).

Sir Winston S. Churchill to Sir Walter Monckton
Prime Minister's Personal Minute M.173/53
(Premier papers, 11/477)

30 May 1953

Please give this consideration as I think endless harm, though on a small scale, is being done.[1] If necessary you should see Lord Rosebery and Sir Humphrey de Trafford[2] and discuss the matter with them.

John Colville: diary
('The Fringes of Power', pages 713–14)

31 May 1953

The newspapers are saying that the lavishness, the popularity and the magnificence of the Coronation are due to the inspiration of Sir W. Churchill. Some Labour supporters doubtless think he will have an election on the emotional proceeds. All this is far from the case. Indeed he thinks it is being overdone, particularly by the newspapers, and he has had little or nothing to do with the preparations. But it is certainly a gay time and the country has gone wild with delight, showing its enthusiasm by decorations which are far more elaborate than those of 1937.

Meg and I, living temporarily at Chobham, have neither the energy nor indeed the strength to go to all the parties and the celebrations to which we have been invited. We went to the Coronation Ball at the Albert Hall on Wednesday last, May 27th, after a dinner party of sixteen at 10 Downing Street (WSC resplendent in his Garter, with the diamond star that belonged to Castlereagh); and on Friday (after I had spent an agreeable but exhausting twenty-four hours alone with W at Chartwell) we went to the Household Brigade's Ball at Hampton Court. That was a splendid affair. The whole Palace was floodlit and the fountains were surrounded by massed flowers. Every man wore a tailcoat and decorations, the Knights of the Garter in knee breeches. Almost every woman wore a tiara and a dress worthy of the occasion. We danced in the Great Hall and supped in the orangery. A world that vanished in 1939 lived again for the night, which obliged by being a fine and balmy one. The Queen dancing with the Duke of Edinburgh and looking as beautiful as the people imagine her to be, stopped to ask us how her goddaughter[3] did and

[1] See Lord Stafford's letter of May 28, reproduced above (pp. 1049–50).
[2] Humphrey Edmund de Trafford, 1891–1971. Prominent English racehorse owner. Educated at Oratory School and Royal Military College, Sandhurst. Married, 1917, Cynthia Cadogan: four children. Lt., Coldstream Guards; on active service during WWI (MC, 1916). Bt, 1929. Steward of the Jockey Club, 1934–7, 1944, 1951. High Sheriff, Herts, 1945–6.
[3] (Elizabeth) Harriet Colville, 1952– . Godchild of Queen Elizabeth II. Married, 1976, David James Bowes-Lyon: four children.

whether she was yet out of control. She must, I thought, have wished she lived at Hampton Court rather than Windsor.

On Saturday and Sunday we recovered, with the help of some strenuous gardening, and eschewed the garden party at Hatfield with the prospect of so much before us in the coming week. Meanwhile in London Coronation fever grew, the crowds milling through the streets to see the banners and the arches, to catch a glimpse of the arriving celebrities among whom the most famous, such as Nehru and General Marshall, pass for nothing among so many. Practically all traffic was stopped and the police were near to being overwhelmed. Never has there been such excitement, never has a Monarch received such adulation, never has so much depended on the weather being kind for the great day.

June 1953

Sir Winston S. Churchill to Field Marshal Lord Montgomery
(Churchill papers, 2/143)

1 June 1953

My dear Monty,

Thank you so much for your invitation to attend the theatre party on Monday, June 8. I should like to come but I am not sure if I will be able to do so. May I therefore leave it open?

I enclose my debt of honour. I am sorry that it did not go the other way.

Gwilym Lloyd George to Sir Winston S. Churchill
(Premier papers, 11/661)

1 June 1953
PM 53/4

You will be glad to know that improved supplies of butter will make it possible for me to raise the ration on June 14th.

The increase will bring the ration up from 3 ozs. to 4 ozs. and will last for twelve weeks.

I propose to announce this change on June 4th.[1]

---

[1] Churchill noted: 'Vy good'.

Sir Winston S. Churchill: broadcast
('Sir Winston S. Churchill, His Complete Speeches', volume 8, page 8487)

2 June 1953

THE CORONATION OF QUEEN ELIZABETH II
AN INTRODUCTION TO A ROYAL BROADCAST

We have had a day which the oldest are proud to have lived to see and the youngest will remember all their lives. It is my duty and honour to lead you to its culmination. You have heard the Prime Ministers of the Empire and Commonwealth pay their moving tributes on behalf of the famous states and races for whom we speak. The splendours of this second of June glow in our minds. Now as night falls you will hear the voice of our Sovereign herself, crowned in our history and enthroned for ever in our hearts.

Let it not be thought that the age of chivalry belongs to the past. Here at the summit of our world-wide community is a lady whom we respect because she is our Queen and whom we love because she is herself. 'Gracious' and 'noble' are words familiar to us all in courtly phrasing. Tonight they have a new ring in them because we know they are true about the gleaming figure whom Providence has brought to us and brought to us in times where the present is hard and the future veiled.

It is our dearest hope that the Queen will be happy and our resolve – unswerving – that her reign shall be as glorious as her devoted subjects can help her to make it. We pray to have rulers who serve, for nations who comfort each other, and for peoples who thrive and prosper free from fear. May God grant us these blessings. The Queen.

Anthony Montague Browne:[1] recollection
('Long Sunset', pages 173–4)

2 June 1953

The Coronation was the apotheosis of WSC's love and reverence for the Crown. Dressed for the part, in the unique and bizarre uniform of the Lord Warden of the Cinque Ports, and with his Orders and medals, he was an unforgettable sight. The Duke of Wellington had lent him the Iron Duke's 'Great George' part of the Garter Regalia, and accompanied by CSC he

[1] Anthony Arthur Duncan Montague Browne, 1923–2013. Pilot, RAF, 1941–5. Entered Foreign Service, 1946. Resident Clerk, FO, 1947–9. 2nd Secretary, British Embassy, Paris, 1949–52. Married, 1950, Noel Evelyn Arnold-Wallinger (div. 1970): one child; 1970, Shelagh Macklin Mulligan. Seconded as Private Secretary to PM, 1952–5; as Private Secretary to Sir Winston Churchill, 1955–65. Counsellor, Diplomatic Service, 1964. CBE, 1965. Seconded to HM Household, 1965–7. Director, Columbia (British) Productions, 1967–77. Wrote *Long Sunset: Memoirs of Winston Churchill's Last Private Secretary* (1995). KCMG, 2000.

drove in the Royal procession in a horse-drawn carriage. He caused a certain amount of confusion when, on the return from Westminster Abbey, the horses became over-excited near Admiralty Arch and he ordered the coachman to pull out of the procession. [. . .]

I had been invited to be a Gold Stick – an usher in the Abbey – but had declined. I don't quite know why. The cost of acquiring full-dress diplomatic uniform? (I had the Court sword.) An innate distaste for elaborate ceremonial? A dislike of getting up at 4 a.m.? Probably just a curmudgeonly nature, and a feeling that such showy rejoicing did not fit in with our lamentable national decline.

The Prime Minister gave a number of grand parties, to one of which he invited the Glaoui, the Pasha of Marrakech. He was a picturesque old bandit, a true war-lord of the Atlas in his younger days, but with a sinister reputation when it came to dealing with his opponents. After dinner a few of us set out from Number Ten to watch the firework display from the Air Ministry roof. Downing Street was blocked by a jolly and friendly crowd, and when they spotted the Prime Minister in the first car, they began to rock it, while he grinned at them benevolently. The Glaoui later misunderstood the crowd's mood. To my consternation, he put his hand inside his robe and I saw the butt of an automatic pistol emerging. 'No, no, Excellency!' I shouted; politely holding his arm, 'these are very nice people.' He looked doubtful but subsided.

He had a pretty miserable Coronation in other ways. His seat for the procession was in an uncovered stand; and he had to walk there in pouring rain from the Savoy. He had been invited to a garden party at Blenheim Palace and, assuming that it was in London, had left for it at 5 p.m., eventually arriving at Woodstock just as the waiters were clearing up the last crumbs. And finally, the gold and emerald crown he had bought as a present for the Queen had to be returned under the strict Palace protocol rules.[1] Cartier had valued it at £13,000. Most of the emeralds were flawed.

My most vivid memory of the Prime Minister's feelings for the Queen is seeing him gazing with great tenderness at a charming photograph she had given him, with a warm inscription. It showed her laughing and happy as she returned from the Opening of Parliament. 'Isn't she a winner?' he said.

---

[1] See Churchill to Le Pacha El Hadj Thami El Glaoui, June 14, reproduced below (pp. 1112–13).

JUNE 1953 1059

Sir Winston S. Churchill to Vyacheslav Molotov
Prime Minister's Personal Telegram T.183/53
(Premier papers, 11/420)

2 June 1953
Secret and Personal

I am now acting Foreign Secretary during Mr Eden's illness and am very glad to re-open my former contacts with you. You will no doubt have seen about the Bermuda Conference. I am hoping that it may result in bridges being built not barriers between East and West. It would I am sure be a help if this Panmunjom prisoners-of-war business were got out of the way. Please do not hesitate to telegraph direct and personally to me whenever you feel inclined. All good wishes.

Vyacheslav Molotov to Sir Winston S. Churchill
(Premier papers, 11/420)

3 June 1953
Translation
No. 45A

I thank you for your message which M Gascoigne passed to me on the 2nd of June. I hope that you already know our opinion on the Bermuda meeting, and so far there are no visible grounds for changing this opinion. As regards Panmunjom, as is known, the outcome of this matter does not depend on us. Nevertheless, we can state with satisfaction that the path to a successful conclusion of the negotiations has already been marked out. I am grateful for your proposal that I should address you directly when necessary. I beg you, too, in future so long as you carry out the duties of Secretary of State for Foreign Affairs, in all necessary cases, to use the same form of direct address to me. I take this opportunity to ask you to convey to Mr Eden my good wishes for his speedy recovery.

Meeting of Commonwealth Prime Ministers:[1] minutes
(Cabinet papers, 133/135)

3 June 1953
Secret
3 p.m.
Prime Ministers Meeting No. 1 of 1953

1. OPENING STATEMENT

Sir Winston Churchill welcomed the other Commonwealth Prime Ministers. This was a memorable gathering on an occasion which all would treasure in their memories. It gave an opportunity to survey the wide prospect of world affairs and to see on how many matters Commonwealth Governments were agreed: he was confident that these were far more numerous than those on which they might disagree. He was deeply honoured to have the privilege of presiding at this gathering.

The object of the Meeting was to see how best the members of the Commonwealth should dispose of affairs which concerned them all. Their cherished ideals of freedom and peace were threatened and the facts of the world situation must be faced. He felt that members of the Commonwealth should be able to get round any points of difficulty which lay between them and that unity would grow among them.

2. PROCEDURE
Agenda for the Meeting

It was proposed that the Meeting should discuss Soviet Foreign Policy and Western Europe that afternoon; the Far East and South-East Asia on 4th June; the Middle East on 5th June; unfinished political business and the communiqué on 8th June; and economic affairs, after a statement by Mr Butler, on 9th June.

Mr Menzies said that it would be difficult to dispose of some of these items in one session and it might be necessary in some cases to continue discussion at a later one. But he agreed that it would be possible to do this at the session on 8th June which was set aside for unfinished political business and the communiqué.

The Meeting –

Accepted the proposed agenda for the Meeting and invited the Secretary to circulate it.

---

[1] The Prime Ministers of Australia, Canada, Ceylon, India, New Zealand, Pakistan, South Africa, and Southern Rhodesia were in attendance.

Publicity

It was proposed that Sir Winston should undertake the duty of handling the press on behalf of the Meeting as a whole. A short formal communiqué would be issued each day and a full communiqué at the end of the Meeting.

It was explained that this would not prevent Prime Ministers from seeing press representatives if they so desired. It was designed merely as a matter of convenience to protect them from being unduly harassed by press representatives.

The Meeting –
Accepted the proposals for handling press during the Meeting.

3. Foreign Policy of the New Soviet Régime

Sir Winston Churchill said that after Stalin died he had been struck by the hope that a change had occurred in Russia. He was not particularly impressed with the changes in external policy which had so far manifested themselves, but the repudiation of the doctors' arrest had seemed to him significant. It meant that the whole Russian people had to think on one day the opposite to what they had been required to think on authority the day before. He did not pretend to know the extent of any changes in Soviet policy, but he felt that if all held together in the anti-Communist front and strengthened their unity no risk would be run in trying to ascertain how important these changes were and to reach some settlement with Russia. We should do all we could to avoid a drift into war when perhaps there had been a change in Soviet policy, and he had already advocated making quite sure that the Soviet Government had no intention of changing their policies before the steps now taken by them were disregarded. So long as the members of the Commonwealth were united, they could retain their influence on the policy of the United States, to whom the free world owed so much, and he believed that they would be able to carry the United States with them in seeking a period of *détente*, about which he was not without hope.

The Soviet Government must have their own anxieties about a future war. Though they had the power to overrun much of Western Europe they must know that their central government machinery, their communications and their war potential would be shattered by atomic attack. A future war would differ from any experienced before, for both sides would suffer at the start the worst that they both feared. When he spoke of accumulating deterrents against Russia, he did not mean deterrents against the Russian people but deterrents against the Communist régime. The development of atomic warfare would deter the régime, since it would face them with the certain loss of power to wage modern war within a few months of its start. The mighty ocean of land in Russia and Siberia would quickly become uncontrollable and, once the peoples realised that they were free to do as they liked and could no longer be controlled by the central machinery of Soviet Government, they might show their preference for living happily by themselves without allegiance to a unified Soviet state.

There therefore seemed to be no risk in seeking to find out what lay behind the policy of the new Soviet régime. If their actions were a trick to deceive the rest of the world, this would quickly be discovered, but there should be a sincere examination of what he hoped was a new situation. The effort should be made even if there was a risk that it might not succeed. The British people would not fight in a future war with a good conscience if they thought that there had been a possibility of a change in the Soviet attitude which had not been followed up.

Sir Winston Churchill said that in making this examination of Soviet intentions and policies he was willing to risk disappointment, diplomatic rebuff or accusation of being a false prophet. The members of the Commonwealth should hold together and try to find out what the signs amounted to. The best way to proceed seemed to be, as he had suggested in his recent speech, to have an informal talk with the Soviet leaders. This would not be a conference to settle every point of difficulty, but there might be some settlements which would lead to an easier period and there could be further talks as time went on. Time should be allowed to play its part. The free countries had time to wait so long as they did not weaken in their resolve.

Dr Malan agreed that it was important to discover what really was behind the recent Soviet change of attitude. They had always pretended that they had every reason to fear Western aggression, but was this really what they were afraid of or were they merely uncertain whether they would be prevented from spreading Communist domination throughout the world?

Sir Winston Churchill said that the Russians could not possibly be afraid that the western allies could overpower them on the ground, since Soviet forces were vastly greater than those of the West. But the Kremlin undoubtedly did fear the results of the use by the Western Allies of the overwhelming atomic power in the hands of the United States.

Mr Mohammed Ali[1] said that the need was to discover whether there had been a change of mood in the Kremlin or only a change of tactics. This might be put to the test by discussing, for example, the Austrian peace treaty. He agreed that it was desirable for a high-level conference to be held to test the underlying motives of present Russian policy by an exchange of ideas. As regards to the proposal to hold a preliminary Three-Power meeting at

---

[1] Sahibzada Mohammad Ali Bogra, 1909–63. Educated at Presidency University, Calcutta. Married Begum Hamida Mohammad Ali: two children; 1955, Aliya Saddy. Party worker, Muslim League, 1930–7. Member, Bengal Legislative Assembly, 1937. Chairman of Bogra District, 1938–42. Parliamentary Secretary to Chief Minister, 1943–6. Minister of Health, Finance, and Local Government, 1946–7. Pakistan Ambassador to Burma, 1948–9. High Commissioner of Pakistan to Canada, 1949–52. Ambassador of Pakistan to US, 1952–3, 1955–9. PM of Pakistan, 1953–5. Minister of Defence, 1953. Minister of Foreign Affairs, 1954–5, 1962–3.

Bermuda, he was apprehensive lest this would give the impression that the three Allied Powers were intent on formulating a common policy against the Russians before a Four-Power meeting took place. At least the Russians should not be given any excuse to cause a breakdown in the Four-Power discussions on the ground that the previous Three-Power meeting had prejudiced their position. He agreed that it was necessary and right that the United States, the United Kingdom, and France should agree a common line first, but he had wondered if this could not be done without a formal and fully publicised conference.

Mr St Laurent said that when he had originally heard about the Bermuda meeting he had hoped it would lead to a subsequent meeting with the Soviet Union. The announcement of the Bermuda meeting itself had already had a very good effect in showing the world that there was no serious difference of view between the Three Allied Powers concerned; and it was certainly necessary to hold such a conference with the President of the United States before any approach was made to the Soviet Government, since it would be necessary to persuade the President that a Four-Power meeting was worthwhile. It was also desirable, whatever the disadvantages might be, to include the French in the Bermuda meeting, since it was right that one of the Continental Powers should be represented. Care should be taken to avoid the impression that the Bermuda meeting was an attempt to concert action against the Soviet Government; but, if the Russians wished to provide themselves with an excuse for causing a breakdown in a subsequent Four-Power meeting or to refuse to take part in one, they would not find it difficult to invent some other pretext.

Sir Winston Churchill said that after his recent speech in the House of Commons, when he had said that he thought a meeting with Russia should be held, the President of the United States had himself suggested a Three-Power meeting as a preliminary. This had now been agreed but was unlikely to take place before the end of June. He believed that a meeting with the Russians with the object of 'building bridges and not barriers' was the right aim, but it would be necessary first to persuade the President of the United States that such a meeting without conditions was desirable. The present attitude of the United States Government was that they were prepared to move nearer to our point of view. In any event he believed a personal meeting with the President of the United States was the only satisfactory method for reaching the desired measure of agreement.

Mr Nehru welcomed the proposal for a high-level conference with the Russians and agreed that it should be kept on an informal basis without previous conditions. He also agreed that it was necessary first to hold the Bermuda meeting. This should be held as soon as possible in order to clear the way for the even more important Four-Power meeting with the Russians. One of the main objects of the Bermuda meeting would be to reach agreement on the method of approach to a Four-Power meeting, since Sir Winston Churchill believed it should be without previous conditions or commitments, which was undoubtedly right, while President Eisenhower at present appeared to think otherwise.

The recent change in Soviet policy certainly seemed to offer a better opportunity for achieving peace and preventing war. While efforts should be made to discover the motives behind this Russian policy, at the same time, whatever those motives might be, advantage should be taken of the situation now presented. It seemed clear that Russia did not want a war, at least in the foreseeable future, though she undoubtedly would like to achieve the results of war without having to resort to one. It was, however, an extreme over-simplification of a highly complicated situation, to present the problem as one of Communism versus anti-Communism. There were large areas of the world, particularly in Asia, where the outlook of the people was governed by factors which lay outside that simple definition. There were considerable nationalist movements and a desire for collective political freedom leading, it was hoped, to an increased measure of individual freedom. In those countries it was very difficult to convince people that they should give up their nationalist aspirations or their desire for freedom, while attempts were made to protect them from a Communist menace, which was by no means apparent in their particular area. It was, moreover, very difficult to appear as a liberating force if the anti-Communist world continued to offer willing support to certain individuals who in fact had no representative power and whom history had now passed by – e.g. Chiang Kai-shek and Syngman Rhee. He thought there was too great a tendency to look upon the whole problem from the military point of view and to forget the psychological factors affecting large masses of people, especially in Asia.

Sir Winston Churchill said that he had been deeply interested in what Mr Nehru had said. Chiang Kai-shek had fought on our side against Japan, and the United States attached great importance to maintaining his position. His view was that they had an obligation in honour not to hand him over to the Communist authorities in China, and should continue to protect him in Formosa. There ought to be no question of allowing him to operate on the mainland, and it appeared that the de-neutralisation of Formosa had had no untoward consequences.

Mr Nehru agreed that there could be no question of handing over Chiang Kai-shek to Communist China.

Sir Winston Churchill added that neither he nor the Opposition in the House of Commons had realised the part that Mr Syngman Rhee had been playing in the armistice negotiations in Korea nor the full difficulty of the position in which the United States had thereby been placed; his influence had been behind the views which General Harrison had had to express. It had to be remembered that Mr Syngman Rhee had been returned to power by the efforts of the United States with the approval of the United Nations, and that he was now supported by twenty divisions of well-armed and well-trained troops. Nevertheless, the United States should be able to persuade him to agree to an armistice, if one were attained as a consequence of the proposals that had now been put forward as a result of our talks with the United States. He was, moreover, not perhaps as powerful as he thought himself to be. He depended almost entirely on the support of the United States and it would be easy to overrate the importance of the attitude which he had taken up. But it was natural that the United States should not wish to pick a quarrel with him, since they would want him to be responsible for the administration of South Korea when peace was concluded.

Mr Menzies sought more information on the state of opinion within the present United States Administration. He had been profoundly disturbed at the growth of McCarthyism, a movement that was whipping up anti-Communism by means of denunciation and inquisition; despite its extravagance and lack of balance, it might well lead to a revival of isolationism in certain parts of the United States. The United States had been isolationist in outlook until the middle of the First World War and had thereafter lapsed again into a state of isolationism which not all the ability of President Roosevelt had been able to dissipate until the attack on Pearl Harbour had swung the balance in favour of a policy of intervention; everything possible should be done to avoid stimulating resurgent isolationism.

In these circumstances he thought that it would be a mistake to engage in talks with Russia without preliminary discussions of an informal kind with the United States, and he was therefore in favour of holding the Bermuda meeting; it would be surprising if it proved impossible to discover a common approach with which to embark on a Four-Power meeting. But without previous consultation there was a grave danger that in the course of the talks differences between the United States and the other Western participants might arise which would prove fatal to the Western cause.

He agreed that Russia did not desire a war but would do all that she could to advance her own interests short of war; her strategy was to keep the democratic countries guessing and under stress, in the hope that under the pressure of inflation their peoples would tire of paying for defence, and demand new governments which would be ready to meet Russia on Russia's own terms. If we refused to engage in talks with Russia except on predetermined conditions, the cold war would last long enough to destroy the Governments of all those round the table and Russia would be left with the sum of the advantages that had accrued to her as a result of it.

Dr Malan said that he would like to get at the back of the minds of those in power in Russia. Did they really fear that they would be overpowered by the Western countries or were they more concerned to preserve opportunities for spreading the doctrine of Communism in other countries? It was fundamental that each country should be allowed to adopt the system of government to which it gave preference. If we could assure the Russians that we had no wish to interfere with the system of government they had chosen and that we were not opposed to Communism as such but only to its aggressive form, we should find that we had gone a long way to disperse the fears which Russia entertained for her safety in her own boundaries and sphere of influence. But there would be no disagreement that aggression and subversive propaganda must be resisted.

There could be no objection, in general, to tripartite discussions with the United States and France and every possible means should be explored in order to secure peace on honourable conditions. He therefore supported the proposal to hold the Bermuda meeting and Sir Winston Churchill's suggested attempt to come to some agreement with Russia. It would, however, be necessary to determine how far to proceed in negotiations with Russia. He recalled the reported denunciation by President Eisenhower of the Yalta and Potsdam Agreements and referred to the difficult problem of determining how far the satellite governments were under the domination of Russia against their will and how far they now aspired to freedom. Such problems as these might well obstruct all attempts to reach agreement in talks with Russia.

Other points of difference, for example the admission of Communist China to the United Nations and a solution of the Korean war, on which he hoped that agreement would soon be reached, were subsidiary when viewed against the world situation. If we did not in any way threaten Russia in regard to her own ideology inside the Soviet Union but made it clear that we were prepared to resist altogether any aggression on her part, then it would be right to explore with our friends all possible methods of achieving peace.

Sir Winston Churchill said that there must be an interval between the conclusion of peace in Korea and the admission of Communist China to the United Nations. We had recognised the People's Republic of China, though they had not recognised us. The United States, however, felt differently, since they had suffered immense casualties and borne the main burden of the Korean war. He would not wish to press the matter for the present, but he did not reject as a solution that the two Chinas should both be members of the United Nations. For the moment, however, the United States should not be pressed to consider this question.

Mr Holland said that he had found Sir Winston Churchill's statement most helpful. There was general support in New Zealand for the proposed Bermuda meeting which, it was hoped, would perhaps lead to discussions with the leaders of the Soviet Union. The real fear about the Soviet Union was that a small incident would lead to a sudden invasion of Western Europe by the Russian army. This was always a possibility, even if the danger of a deliberately planned war had receded. The death of Stalin was not a reason for suddenly trusting the intentions of the Soviet Union, but it was, nevertheless, wise to give the present Soviet leaders the credit for good intentions. On his journey through the United States he had recently had conversations with the President, the Vice-President[1] and with General Bedell Smith, Under-Secretary of State, and he well understood the fears and hesitations of the United States. In these circumstances he thought it particularly important to give the Soviet Union concrete evidence of the unity which existed between the Commonwealth and the United States and not to shrink from expressions of this unity because other people chose to interpret them as 'ganging up' against the Soviet Union. The methods of Senator McCarthy[2] and the support which he seemed to have in the United States were undoubtedly matters for concern, but he hoped that in spite of this we could avoid emphasising our differences with the United States or insisting upon points which we knew would be unacceptable, like the admission of Communist China to the United Nations. President Eisenhower had assured him that he saw no reason for any major differences of view between the United States and the Commonwealth. He would like to suggest that this meeting of Commonwealth Prime Ministers might contribute much to the strength of President Eisenhower's position and might demonstrate forcibly to the Soviet Union the unalterable friendship which existed between the Commonwealth and the United States by sending a message to the President assuring him of the support of all Commonwealth Prime Ministers for the meeting in Bermuda, making it clear that Commonwealth opinion would be represented there by the Prime Minister of the United Kingdom and adding a general expression of the goodwill which the Commonwealth felt for the United States.

Sir Winston Churchill said that he would like to consider Mr Holland's suggestion further. If any message were to be sent to the United States, it might also include an expression of hope that the Bermuda meeting would lead to discussions with the leaders of the Soviet Union and a general *détente* but that, if it did not, our feelings of unity with the United States would not in any way be impaired.

Mr Senanayake said that the whole world had welcomed the change in Soviet internal policy and the apparent desire of the Soviet Union for peace and friendship with other countries. How far this was a sincere change of heart was a question which could not be pursued unless it were put to a practical test, for example by open discussion with the leaders of the United States, the United Kingdom and France. It had always been accepted that the Russian revolution had been intended to lead to revolution throughout the

[1] Richard Milhous Nixon, 1913–94. Educated at Whittier College and Duke University School of Law. Married, 1940, Thelma Catherine Ryan: two children. Representative (Rep.) for California's 12th Congressional District, 1947–51. Senator (Rep.) for California, 1951–3. Vice-President of the US, 1953–61. President of the US, 1969–74.

[2] Joseph Raymond McCarthy, 1908–57. Educated at Marquette University Law School, 1930–5. Judge, Wisconsin 10th Judicial District, 1939–42. Maj., US Marines, 1943–5. US Senator for Wisconsin, 1947–57. Married, 1953, Jean Kerr. Chair of Senate Government Operations Committee, 1953–5.

world. That intention might now have been changed. On the other hand, the apparent changes in policy might be nothing but a tactical manoeuvre. He felt sympathy with Mr Nehru's views on the division of the world between nations which were communist and those which were anti-communist. That was an over-simplification, which perhaps sometimes denied us the support of countries which were in fact friendly disposed. Yugoslavia was an example of this, and he thought that different treatment of the Chinese Communist Government in the early stages might have yielded better results. He would welcome an approach to the United States, and he was particularly anxious that President Eisenhower's suggestion for the devotion of resources to peaceful development programmes in backward countries should be actively pursued. He feared that there were certain elements in the United States which believed that the peaceful solution of problems and the consequent reduction of armaments would lead to a dangerous economic recession which might prove even worse than the present tense international situation. He supported Mr Nehru's views about countries which desired to achieve political freedom and felt inclined to embrace communism as a means to that end. It was necessary, however, in plans for the granting of greater political freedom, to avoid leaving power vacuums which would only be filled with communism.

Sir Godfrey Huggins said that he had listened with interest to the arguments put forward in discussion and that he agreed with the main thesis of talks with the United States and France, leading to an informal discussion with the leaders of the Soviet Union.

Mr Nehru said that he agreed with Mr Holland's conception of a friendly approach to the United States and, indeed, he felt that our approach to all countries should be friendly. Sometimes differences of opinion made that difficult, but it was still the object which should be pursued. He agreed with Dr Malan who had put forward the doctrine of no interference with forms of government in other countries. But a great many of the troubles in the world had in fact arisen from political or economic interference by one country with another. He feared very much that, if the United States affirmed in advance that one of their objects was to disturb the existing form of government in the satellite countries or in China, no progress could be made in the settlement of disputes. The United States were most anxious to receive evidence of good faith from the Soviet Union and from Communist China; but Communist China and the Soviet Union were equally anxious to receive similar evidence from the United States. Russia had undergone two German invasions, and there was no doubt that the basis of much Russian policy was the fear of a third.

Mr Nehru said that he had had recent talks with Mr Dulles, the United States Secretary of State, and he had regained the impression from him that he feared that the problems of peace would be even more difficult than those of the present state of cold war. Four years ago he had heard Mr Dulles say that war settled nothing and that the country which could make the greatest economic advance would win any competition for power and create public opinion in its favour. There was no doubt in his mind that war-like preparations were throwing a strain on the economy of the Soviet Union which was interfering with progress in raising the standard of living of the Russian people.

On the question of admitting Communist China to the United Nations, Mr Nehru said that he recognized that it would be impossible at the moment and that it would have no meaning if it were suggested to the United States. Nevertheless, the refusal to admit Communist China into the United Nations had led to many evils, including the war in Korea, and a reversal of that refusal was an essential part of any settlement in the Far East.

4. COMMUNIQUÉ

The Meeting agreed to issue the following communiqué to the press —

'The first plenary session of the Meeting of Commonwealth Prime Ministers was held at 10 Downing Street this afternoon. It was attended by the Prime Ministers of the United Kingdom, Canada, Australia, New Zealand, South Africa, India, Pakistan, Ceylon and Southern Rhodesia. The Prime Ministers began their general discussion of the international situation. This will be continued at their meeting tomorrow afternoon.'

Meeting of Commonwealth Prime Ministers: minutes
(Cabinet papers, 133/135)

4 June 1953
Secret
3 p.m.
Prime Ministers Meeting No. 2 of 1953

1. FAR EAST AND SOUTH-EAST ASIA

Mr Selwyn Lloyd said that any survey of the Far East must start with Korea. It was believed that there were three points outstanding between the United Nations and the Communists in the truce negotiations. The first was the introduction into South Korea of armed contingents from the nations comprising the repatriation commission. We thought it a mistake to bring in troops from Poland, Czechoslovakia or Sweden: the Swiss could not provide troops, and we hoped that any troops introduced would come from one country only. The second point was the future of those prisoners who refused repatriation. It was intolerable to condemn them to indefinite captivity, and the new proposal of the United Nations accorded with the Indian resolution of last December.

The third point of difference was on the detailed methods of handling the prisoners who refused repatriation. It seemed, however, that the new United Nations proposals were being fairly well received by the Communists. Their request for secrecy was a favourable sign.

If a truce was agreed, we were pledged to refer the Korean question to the United Nations. But the General Assembly was not a suitable body to deal with it, and it seemed preferable to transfer the problem to the political conference envisaged in the draft armistice agreement. The composition of the political conference would present some difficulties, but in order that it might have a useful outcome Russia, Communist China, North and South Korea should certainly be represented. It would be for discussion who the other members should be. We were pledged to discuss in this conference the future of Korea. The resolution of the General Assembly of October, 1950, specified unification as our aim but, though unification was desirable in theory, it was hardly practicable in the immediate future. But we should try to see that any economic help given for the rehabilitation of Korea was given to the whole country; this might lead in due course to unification. The political conference would also have to discuss the withdrawal of foreign troops from Korea. In any arrangements we made for withdrawal of foreign troops we would have to ensure that South Korea was restrained from attacking North Korea.

It was clear that both sides attached different meanings to the phrase '*et cetera*', which had been added to the proposed agenda for the political conference. The Chinese Communists and North Koreans hoped that all Far Eastern problems would be discussed, but the United States disagreed. It seemed best to wait and see how the work of the conference developed. If it showed that it was capable of handling the Korean problem, it might be a suitable forum for the discussion of the wider problems of the Far East. The first of these wider problems was Chinese representation in the United Nations and our present policy was that, while fighting continued in Korea, there could be no question of supporting the claims of the Chinese People's Government. The United Kingdom Government held no dogmatic view about representation of the Chinese People's Government in the United Nations when the Korean war ended. The United States were opposed to it, but a compromise might be found by which, if the Chinese People's Government became a member of the Security Council, the Nationalist Government might also be allowed to remain in the United Nations as representing Formosa. The People's Government would probably have to be given the permanent seat on a *de facto* basis. But any firm conclusion would at this stage be premature.

If the Korean truce negotiations broke down, there would be an entirely new situation, and it was essential that those countries with troops in South Korea should consult together before a decision was reached on the next stage.

The view was held by some that, if there was a truce in Korea, the Chinese People's Government would transfer their troops to reinforce Vietminh. The front against Communism was stabilised in Korea, but it was very fluid in South-East Asia. In Indo-China the French disliked any outside interference in their conduct. But what seemed to be lacking was a broader political basis for the Associated States[1] and more effective methods for training Vietnamese forces. The efforts of the French were frequently criticized, but it should be remembered that 25 per cent of their regular officers and 40 per cent of their regular NCOs were in Indo-China, though if the French adopted a two-year conscription period their difficulties would be much less.

In Siam the prospects were now more promising than they had been. It seemed that the Siamese might be capable of organising their defence against Communism. The question had arisen of referring to the Security Council the inviolability of the Siamese frontiers; the French had been opposed to this action, but the United States were in favour of it although they were now advocating delay. There seemed to be advantage in the United Nations accepting responsibility for the Siamese frontiers, but it was undesirable at this stage to have a debate in the United Nations which might make more difficult the conclusion of a truce in Korea. Our general policy in Siam should be to stimulate the Siamese will to resist Communist attack.

The United Nations debate on the presence of Chinese Nationalist troops in Burma had turned out well and did credit to the Commonwealth representatives. So long as these troops were in Burma the Communists had an excuse for intervention. The method of their withdrawal had now to be worked out.

Mr Selwyn Lloyd said that the most important aim in the Far East was to get peace in Korea but, if there were peace, he feared that the Communists would increase their pressure in South-East Asia and members of the Commonwealth should concert their efforts to show that they were prepared to meet it.

Mr Lyttelton said that there had been a great change in the Malayan situation; the numbers killed by terrorists were now less than one-quarter of the road deaths in the Malayan Federation. We had two main objectives: to carry on operations against the terrorists and to win over the population. The Chinese were now coming over to our side with enthusiasm. This was partly due to the success of Operation 'Service', the aim of which was to get the population to understand that the police were their friends. We wanted to create a united Malaya, but the Chinese and the Malayan populations, different in language, religion and customs, did not readily mix. The Chinese were getting a firm hold on commerce but the Malayans, under the present constitution, had the predominant political power.

Although the end of the activities of the terrorists could not be foreseen, they were now so reduced that it could be said that Malaya was at peace,

[1] The Associated States of Laos, Cambodia and Vietnam was a grouping formed in 1949. These three countries remained subordinate to the French, but experienced greater internal independence. Cambodia was granted full independence in 1953 and Laos and Vietnam followed shortly thereafter.

and there were no major anxieties except that of Communist influence from outside. If Indo-China were overrun or Siam dominated by the Communists, there were two dangers to Malaya. There would be a serious rice crisis and, although increased cultivation of rice was being encouraged, sufficient supplies could not be provided if the supplies from Indo-China and Siam were cut off through Communist influence in the next 18 months. If Communists established themselves on the northern frontier of Malaya, our efforts to curb the activities of terrorists in Malaya would be made much more difficult.

Sir Winston Churchill emphasised the vital part played by Malaya in the economy of the Commonwealth. The marked improvement which had now taken place was due in great measure to the skill, enthusiasm, and shrewd political sense of the High Commissioner, General Sir Gerald Templer.[1]

Korea

Mr Nehru agreed that the entire situation in the Far East was governed by whether or not a truce in Korea was successfully negotiated. It was quite clear that neither side would be in favour of the indefinite captivity of prisoners of war who did not wish to be repatriated, but there might well be differences over the method of putting an end to such captivity. The object, therefore, should be to get the principle agreed, leaving it to later discussions to decide how to implement it. The forum in which such problems should be discussed was a difficult matter, since the Chinese People's Government were perfectly entitled to object to such discussions taking place in the United Nations, of which they were not members. The proposed political conference would perhaps be the best place in which to settle such problems and he agreed with Mr Selwyn Lloyd that such a conference would be of little value unless Russia and the Chinese People's Government, as well as North and South Korea, were represented. It must be remembered by all nations concerned that, until it was settled, the problem of a seat for the Chinese People's Government in the United Nations would continue to be before them, and the recent United States Senate resolution stipulating that under present conditions no support should be given to the Chinese People's Government's claim to a seat was ill-timed, even though it did refer specifically to the present situation. The Government of the United States were not alone in having to take account of the views of their parliament, press and public opinion.

As regards the question of introducing armed contingents into South Korea, India had been much embarrassed by the pressure from both sides to provide a contingent. The fact was that India was reluctant to do so, but

[1] Gerald Walter Robert Templer, 1898–1979. Educated at Wellington College and Royal Military Academy Sandhurst. 2nd Lt, Royal Irish Fusiliers, 1916. Lt, 1918. Capt., 1928. Maj., 1938. Col., 1941. Acting Maj.-Gen., 1942. Acting Lt-Gen., 1942. Field Cdr, Italy, 1943–4. Maj.-Gen., 1945. KMG, 1946. Director, Military Intelligence, 1946–8. VCIGS, 1948–50. KBE, 1949. GOC-in-C, Eastern Command, 1950–2. GCB, 1951. Col., Royal Horse Guards, 1951–62. British High Commissioner, Malaya, 1952–4. GCMG, 1955. CIGS, 1955–8. FM, 1956.

she had, nevertheless, intimated that, provided there was general agreement to such a course, she would be prepared to play her part in accordance with her capacity and policy; she would not attempt to send a contingent to South Korea unless such agreement was reached.

Should the present truce negotiations break down, many problems would of course arise, and he agreed that these would call for further careful consultations. But he was afraid that in that event there might be a tendency on the part of the United States to resort to increased and widespread military operations which might well seriously increase our subsequent difficulties.

Sir Winston Churchill said that if the truce did break down there would probably be a demand by the United States for a vigorous impulse to active operations and this would have to be considered if and when it arose. It must be remembered that the United States bore nineteen-twentieths of the military and financial burden of the United Nations in the Korean war. There were, however, certain indications of a slight easing in the general situation; for example, Chou En-lai had sent a friendly telegram concerning Her Majesty's coronation.

Mr St Laurent agreed with Mr Selwyn Lloyd that it would not be practicable to achieve a unified Korea immediately after a truce. If, as a result of a truce, both North and South Korea could be included in rehabilitation schemes, then this would be the best way of encouraging unification.

Lord Alexander said that he did not believe that with their present forces the enemy were strong enough to break through in Korea. If truce negotiations broke down, then there would either be a stalemate, with the present forces stabilised in their present positions, or the United States would build up the South Korean forces to a strength of 20 divisions, which would allow United Nations ground troops to be withdrawn over a period. The present front of approximately 140 miles could be held by 20 South Korean divisions, but the United States would still have to support them with air forces and, to a less extent, with naval forces. In such an event, it seemed quite possible that the Communists would realise that their continued support of active operations in Korea no longer paid a dividend since they had ceased to contain United Nations troops in Korea. This would presumably make for a more favourable atmosphere for further peace negotiations.

Syngman Rhee had said from time to time that, if the United Nations withdrew from Korea, he would advance and occupy North Korea with his own South Korean forces. It was, however, clear that if he attempted to do this he would fail. In the north of Korea the front would widen to as much as 300 miles and this would be beyond the capabilities of 20 divisions. In any case he was very doubtful whether the South Korean divisions, who had been trained by the United States, were sufficiently loyal to be prepared to undertake such an operation.

He explained that the South Korean army had been built up gradually;

battalions had first been trained in United States divisions and now the South Koreans had regiments and divisions of their own, commanded by their own officers, but so far serving in United States army corps. They had also recently obtained their own artillery. They made good soldiers, but were short of capable senior officers; this might prove to be a further argument against a successful advance into North Korea, since a South Korean higher command might be unequal to such an operation. For some time to come at least he expected that the United States would agree to leave a senior officer in command who would also co-ordinate the supporting air and naval forces, themselves under the command of United States officers.

From a purely military point of view an attractive operation would be to advance about 100 miles from the present position to the 'wasp's waist' of Korea, where the front would be shortened by nearly 50 miles and fewer troops would accordingly be required. To undertake such an advance, however, would require an additional 5 fresh divisions, and it would be necessary to accept casualties amounting, perhaps, to between 30,000 and 40,000.

On the whole, therefore, the most favourable course, if the truce negotiations broke down, seemed to be to hold fast on the present United Nations positions and to concentrate on building up the South Korean forces so that United Nations ground forces could be withdrawn. He thought that by that time the United Nations would not bear direct responsibility for the operations.

Mr Nehru said that in that case he supposed that the United Nations would naturally have to withdraw their political support from South Korea.

Mr Menzies wondered whether United States opinion would allow the United Nations to adopt the course favoured by Lord Alexander. He had gained the impression that the United States would not be prepared to go on supporting a war in Korea indefinitely and would very soon reach the point of deciding to step up operations so as to reach a conclusion. Should the United States insist on such a course, many serious problems would arise, and he hoped that before any decisions were made an opportunity would be taken at the Bermuda meeting to discuss the future intentions of the United States with President Eisenhower himself. It was also highly desirable to discover what Syngman Rhee's intentions really were in view of the extremely awkward political problems that would arise if he tried to occupy North Korea himself.

He agreed that there could be no question of permitting the admission of Communist China to the United Nations so long as fighting was taking place. If peace were concluded, however, the question of her admission would become a live issue, and he hoped that, when the occasion arose, arrangements would be made for the Commonwealth countries to consult together and concert their policies.

Sir Winston Churchill said that he was confident that our contacts with the United States were such that they would take no big step without first consulting us. Although our contribution to the United Nations forces in Korea was small when compared with that of the United States, the United States set considerable store by our moral support of their actions and were exceedingly sensitive to our criticisms. They were likely to afford us far more consultation than our contribution entitled us to, if we wielded our considerable influence with tact and friendliness.

He thought it not unlikely that the United Nations would follow the policy adopted by the United States, since the latter were bearing so very high a proportion of the burden of the war, more particularly if genuine efforts for peace had failed and in view of the fact that the war had been begun by North Korea.

One great world fact had emerged from the Korean conflict; the United States was now the most heavily armed nation in the world. Russia undoubtedly possessed far greater armies than the United Kingdom and Western Europe and could, if she wished, advance a long way across Western Europe; but she would be immediately exposed to a blasting attack on her communications, arsenals, oilfields, railways and bridges. In such circumstances, the Kremlin would no doubt think twice before unleashing a war.

Mr Holland expressed appreciation of Mr Selwyn Lloyd's survey of the situation in the Far East.

The negotiations in Korea were complicated by the fact that two parties were facing one another as equals and there was no conqueror to impose terms on the vanquished. General Cassels,[1] who had lately relinquished command of the Commonwealth Division, had stated on a visit to New Zealand six months ago that neither the United Nations nor the Communist forces were capable of making any great advance.

Mr Holland thought that Syngman Rhee's attitude was most unsatisfactory and advocated taking a strong line with him; Syngman Rhee appeared confident that he would continue to receive the support of the United States if his policies led him into trouble, but, if his venture failed, Korea would be lost and the way would lie open for an advance by the Communists into South-East Asia.

He expressed surprise that the Russians had not made available to the North Koreans a number of submarines, which could have played havoc with the shipping of supplies to the United Nations forces in Korea.

In the course of his journey through the United States Mr Holland had formed the view that the United States would not be prepared to tolerate a stalemate. He could understand their opposition to having members of the forces of Communist countries behind their lines, and he thought it not

---

[1] Archibald James Halkett Cassels, 1907–96. DSO, 1944. CBE, 1944. Maj.-Gen., 1948. GOC 1st British Commonwealth Div. in Korea, 1951–2. KBE, 1952. Commander, 1st Corps, 1953–4. Director-General, Military Training, War Office, 1954–7. GOC-in-C, Eastern Command, 1959. C-in-C, British Army of the Rhine and NATO Northern Army Group Commander, 1960–3. GCB, 1961. FM, 1968.

unreasonable that the United Nations should take to themselves the final decision on the future of the prisoners of war, if other methods failed: certainly the Communists could not be allowed to be judges in their own cause. He failed to see how the United States could be expected to make any further concessions and he agreed with Mr Menzies that there must be a gap after which action would succeed negotiation. We should let the United States know that we supported them now.

He had one further point to make; did the military authorities make the best negotiators? Should they not be given some political assistance?

Sir Winston Churchill said that he was hopeful that the Indian Government would be prepared to allow four to five thousand troops to go to Korea. It was a great compliment to India that more than any other country in the world she found herself trusted by both sides; she should not now hold back. At the same time it was out of the question to allow her to bear the whole financial burden, and she would find that we were ready to give her our support.

As he had pointed out the previous day, General Harrison had been influenced by the attitude adopted by Syngman Rhee and he had perhaps been too harshly judged. There was now, however, more hope of a settlement. If these hopes were disappointed, courage still remained.

South-East Asia

Lord Alexander said that the French had 64 French battalions in Indo-China, not all of them from Metropolitan France, but with officers and, to a large extent, NCOs from the French Metropolitan Army; in addition, they had raised 50 Vietnamese battalions, though it must be recognised that the Vietnamese did not make such good soldiers as the South Koreans. Their tactics were, however, in his view, misconceived, and there was the danger that they had adopted a defensive mentality based on the fortress points which they had constructed beyond the perimeter round Saigon. Moreover, they did not appear to have succeeded in obtaining the support of the local population nor to have given them much political hope for the future. On the other hand, Vietminh maintained light forces in Vietnam and Laos, collecting rice and recruits and spreading propaganda; it was unlikely that they could stage a major attack until after the monsoon.

Mr Nehru said that an appeal by Siam to the United Nations seemed to have little meaning. No one was invading Siam and it was very unlikely that the People's Republic of China would invade Indo-China, Siam or Burma. China had her own internal problems to settle and invasion would lead to widespread war which she would wish to avoid. The spread of Communism by infiltration was another matter; but Communism had little hold in a country which was plentifully supplied with rice.

South-East Asia should be examined from a long-term point of view, and we should not continually be thinking only of immediate problems. At the end of the war no country had been so popular in China as the United States and now it was most hated. The United States must therefore have followed a wrong policy. This was a lesson which should make us examine the broader issues of policy in order to keep the peoples of South-East Asia on our side and to avoid mistakes of which our opponents took advantage. The United States had carried the burden of the Korean war, but this should not blind us to the possibility that their policies might bring the wrong results and entangle them more and more in difficulties. The French in Indo-China had failed to take account of political aspirations and they were unlikely to succeed in doing more than hold the position against the Vietminh. There was no likelihood that they could restore the situation unless they took more thought for the wishes of the people. It was even doubtful whether they could rely on Vietnamese troops, which might go over to the other side if they were not given something to fight for.

Mr Selwyn Lloyd had referred favourably to the United Nations resolution on the withdrawal of Chinese Nationalist troops from Burma. But it had not yet brought any concrete results. Mr Dulles had told him that Chiang Kai-shek would not take steps to remove the troops and that the United Nations could not help further. These troops had grown in number from 3,000 to 12,000 in two or three years. They were equipped with new weapons and they were supplied by air across Siam from Formosa. They were stationed near the border of Siam and could easily leave Burma if they wanted to. They were committing aggression in Burma and looting and killing the Burmese people. They were a constant embarrassment to the Burmese Government and the Communists in Burma were taking full advantage of their presence to further their own cause. This was itself an invasion of Burma. The Chinese Communists might have invaded Burma to attack these Nationalist troops, but they had not done so because they did not want a war. He doubted, therefore, if they were likely to transfer troops released from Korea to Indo-China, Siam or Burma. They had no shortage of man-power and, if they wished to invade Indo-China or Burma, they could easily do so now while they still had an army in Korea.

He did not think that there was any fear of Communist invasion of South-East Asia in the foreseeable future. If, however, we concentrated our attention on the possibilities of immediate war and based our policies on that fear, supporting unpopular régimes, we would lose our grip of the entire situation. We should rather take a longer view. The spread of Communism could only be countered by recognising the dynamic rise of nationalist aspirations among peoples who were now politically conscious, and by taking account in our policies of their desire for independence.

Sir Winston Churchill said the Mr Nehru had given the Meeting much to think about. We had been conscious of the problem of the Chinese Nationalist troops in Burma for a long time. We would be very glad to see them leave Burma and we should do all we could to get them out.

2. COMMUNIQUÉ

The Meeting agreed to issue the following communiqué to the press –

'At their meeting this afternoon the Commonwealth Prime Ministers continued their review of the international situation, with particular reference to the Far East and South-East Asia.'

John Selwyn Lloyd to Sir Winston S. Churchill
(Premier papers, 11/540)

4 June 1953
Confidential
PM/MS/53/193

When the Finnish Prime Minister[1] came to see me on June 1, I asked him his opinion of the changes in Russia. He said that Finland did not get a great deal of information about what was going on inside Russia. He himself, however, had been to Moscow for Stalin's funeral and he had heard over and over again whilst he was there phrases like 'we must prevent any panic'. He thought that there had been genuine fear on the part of those in control that Stalin's death would give rise to general upset. He thought that that explained their anxiety to be nice to everyone.

2. With regard to the doctors' plot and the Georgian leaders, he thought that both stories had some secret background which would not be disclosed for many years to come. He did not believe that the Russian objective had changed. He was certain that they did not mean war, but he was equally certain that they would seek to extend their domination by every other means. He thought that these other means were easier and more likely to be successful and that the USSR must be very satisfied to see the Western powers straining their economies at the present time. He thought that from this economic strain the Soviet expected large dividends.

---

[1] Urho Kekkonen, 1900–86. PM of Finland, 1950–3, 1954–6. President of Finland, 1956–82.

Sir Winston S. Churchill to President Dwight D. Eisenhower
Prime Minister's Personal Telegram T.190/53
(Premier papers, 11/1074)

4 June 1953
Immediate
Secret
No. 2298

In the course of my talk with the Turkish Prime Minister and his Foreign Secretary on Monday, June 1, the Prime Minister said that they had just received a telegram from Ankara to the following effect:

Molotov had sent them a most friendly message saying that in 1945 Georgia and Armenia had made substantial territorial claims to Turkish territory in settlement after the war and also that the USSR had claimed military control of the Bosphorus and Dardanelles. Molotov now wished to assure the Turkish Government that these demands no longer formed part of Soviet policy and should be considered as withdrawn.

2. The Turkish Prime Minister asked me what I thought of this. I said that it showed how wise Turkey had been to join the NATO front. The Turkish Prime Minister replied that this was exactly the impression he and his colleagues had sustained. I then said that of course it might be either part of a plan to divide the allies or, as we should all hope, part of a new Soviet policy to have a détente and easier relations all round. The course for all of us seemed simple, namely, while welcoming any improved change of heart, to hold firmly together and to our present policy. He appeared to agree cordially with this.

John Selwyn Lloyd to Sir Winston S. Churchill
(Premier papers, 11/540)

4 June 1953
Secret
PM/MS/53/195

You should I think know that the Parliamentary Leader of the Indian Communist Party, Mr Gopalan,[1] recently returned from the Soviet Union where he has spent some months ostensibly on grounds of health. He gave Mr Nehru his interpretation of recent developments in Soviet Foreign Policy. He was in Russia at the time of Stalin's death and for some weeks afterwards.

2. Mr Gopalan's view was that the new Soviet Administration had not changed Stalin's basic foreign policies. The trends which had developed since

[1] Kunnathu Puthiyaveettil Rayarothu Gopalan, 1906–97. Member, Kerala Pradesh Congress Committee, 1937–40. Member, Malabar District Board, 1939. Founding member, Communist Party, Kerala, 1940. Imprisoned, 1940, 1948–51. Member of Kerala State Assembly, 1957–60, 1965–8.

his death had been decided by Stalin himself and were part of a general policy prepared after the Party Congress last year. The only difference was that the public formulation of these policies by the present Soviet rulers differed from Stalin's personal style.

3. Mr Gopalan had made public statements to the above effect, which had been much criticized by other Indian Communists. These found it more convenient to argue that the new rulers of the Soviet Union had turned over to a more peaceful and co-operative policy. Mr Gopalan was quite definite that Soviet world aims had not altered, although Stalin had decided before his death that it would be wiser to proceed more cautiously and to lay more emphasis upon the possibility of peaceful co-existence between Communist and non-Communist States.

4. The source of the above information is the former Home Secretary to the Government of India, who was until recently specially concerned with Communist questions. He is on a short visit to Europe in his present capacity as Commerce Secretary. He was speaking in strict confidence to a member of this Department, who worked very closely with him in Delhi.

5. I am sending a copy of this minute to Lord Swinton.

John Selwyn Lloyd to Sir Winston S. Churchill
(Premier papers, 11/544)

4 June 1953
Secret
PM/MS/53/189

I had a satisfactory two hour conversation with the Mahdi on Thursday last. The Umma Party is reaching the end of its patience with Egyptian misbehaviour in the Sudan, and I think that there is more than an even chance that the Umma will denounce their agreement of last November with Neguib.

2. I will not weary you with the full record of the conversation, which I am circulating to the Cabinet, but the Mahdi appeared to accept my points. He was more forthcoming than in Khartoum in March.[1]

---

[1] Churchill wrote on this minute: 'What about Howe? I am with him on Saturday morning.'

John Selwyn Lloyd to Sir Winston S. Churchill
(*Premier papers, 11/544*)

5 June 1953
Personal
Confidential

I have had two conversations with Sir Robert Howe. He also came to the luncheon party which I gave for the Mahdi. He is a difficult man to make out – he seems to take up a negative attitude to almost everything.

2. I think I have convinced him that the Sudan Government have got to shake themselves out of their neutralism. I would suggest that you should speak to him forcibly upon that matter.

3. I see no reason why he should go back to the Sudan in the immediate future. Luce[1] is doing very well without him. Also, I think it is useful to have Howe in England until we see what the next fortnight brings between the Umma Party and the Egyptians. I suggest that he remains here on his Coronation visit but ready to return to Khartoum at short notice.

4. With regard to Howe's future, a successor would have to be appointed by the Egyptian Government on the nomination of Her Majesty's Government. This presents difficulties at the moment. It may be easier to deal with this when a Sudanese Parliament has been elected, and if it comes out for independence of Egypt. Therefore Howe should remain Governor-General for the time being.

Winthrop Aldrich to Sir Winston S. Churchill
(*Premier papers, 11/1074*)

5 June 1953
Secret

My dear Sir Winston,

I have been asked to deliver the following messages about Bermuda to you. The first is a letter from the President, while the second is a supplementary note from Foster Dulles.

> 'Dear Winston: I fully agree with you that June 29 should be our target date for Bermuda and that the meeting should last about four days. Foster will of course come with me and he will be accompanied by a small group of advisers, generally corresponding to the group which Makins has indicated

[1] William Henry Tucker Luce, 1907–77. Private Secretary to Governor-General of Sudan, 1941–7. OBE, 1947. Governor, Blue Nile Province, Sudan, 1951. Adviser to Governor-General of Sudan on Constitutional and External Affairs, 1953–6. CMG, 1954. KBE, 1956. Governor and C-in-C, Aden, 1956–60. KCMG, 1957. GBE, 1961.

will accompany you. Douglas MacArthur II,[1] who is Counsellor of the Department of State, will be the opposite number of Norman Brook and will coordinate details for us. Brook can get in touch with him at any time.

I understand through Makins that your view is that the purpose of the meeting should be announced as one of a general exchange of views and that it will be informal and without official agenda. I agree with this. Regarding your suggestion that there be no daily press briefings, I do believe there will have to be some sort of daily briefing of the press by the three press officers, even if not much of substance is handed out. In fact, I think it would be good for the press to know that we are getting along well together. I am instructing my people to discuss the substance and the timing of the announcement as well as press arrangements with our representatives here, and of course this as well as other matters such as the June 29 date will have to be coordinated with the French.

My plane will be flying to Bermuda about mid-June, returning the following day, and Makins might desire to send Gore-Booth[2] or some other representative on this short trip for a preview of preliminary arrangements.

As Makins is accompanying you, I will probably have to invite Ambassadors Aldrich and Dillon, but these two and any additions that we may have to make would not impose on your hospitality, as they can be accommodated at our air base in Bermuda.

With warmest regards, (signed) Ike.'

'Supplementing the President's telegram, we intend to avoid here giving any public impression that arrangements regarding Bermuda are finalized while a French Government is in process of formation. We hope you will think it appropriate to adopt the same attitude so as to avoid giving possible offense at this sensitive moment.

The President intends, unless you see serious objection, to invite three or four members of Congress to be his personal guests at the Bermuda base during the conference. It would be made clear that while they might participate in social occasions, there would probably not be any formal conference proceedings at which they would be expected to participate except possibly to appear at the final conference after the communiqué has been agreed. Dulles.'

---

[1] Douglas MacArthur II, 1909–97. Named after his uncle, Gen. Douglas MacArthur. Educated at Yale University. Married, 1934, Laura Louise Barkley. 1st Lt, 6th Field Artillery, 1935. Served at Canadian Consulate, Vancouver, 1935–7; French Embassy 1937–42. Councillor, Foreign Service Office, 1953–6. Ambassador to Japan, 1956–61; to Belgium, 1961–5; to Australia, 1967–9; to Iran, 1969–72. Asst Secretary of State for Legislative Affairs, 1965–7.

[2] Paul Henry Gore-Booth, 1909–84. Educated at Eton and Balliol College, Oxford. CMG, 1949. Director-General of British Information Services in US, 1949–53. Ambassador to Burma, 1953–7. High Commissioner to India, 1960–5. KCVO, 1961. GCMG, 1965. Permanent Under-Secretary, FO, 1965–8; FCO, 1968–9. Baron, 1969.

Sir Winston S. Churchill to John Selwyn Lloyd
Prime Minister's Personal Minute M.184/53
(Premier papers, 11/540)

5 June 1953

If the Soviet plan is to work the ruin of the Western Powers by straining their economies why would they seek a détente now? This would only mean that the Western Powers would reduce the strain on their economies and go a little easier. I suppose the answer would be that they are only doing it to tide over the shock of Stalin's death.

Obviously the Finnish line, not for the first time, is vitiated by contradiction.

Sir Winston S. Churchill to President Dwight D. Eisenhower
Prime Minister's Personal Telegram T.193/53
(Premier papers, 11/1074)

5 June 1953
Immediate
Confidential
No. 2310

Our Ambassador in Paris tells me that M Parodi,[1] Secretary General to the Ministry of Foreign Affairs, has telephoned to say that he has been in touch with M Bidault[2] and with the Secretariat of the President of the Council. These both agree that subject to a reserve about the constitutional position, June 29 would be acceptable. Parodi said that although there was no French Government he would take it upon himself to say that arrangements could go ahead accordingly for that date.

2. In these circumstances I am making all arrangements for starting our talks on the 29th. I shall leave on the 27th and arrive in Bermuda the 28th so that I can receive you.

---

[1] Alexandre Parodi, 1901–79. Civil servant, French Labour Ministry, 1926–? Married, 1931, Anne-Marie Vautier: two children. Asst Secretary-General, National Economic Council, ?–1941. Member, Free French Resistance, 1942–5. Minister of Labour, 1944–6. French representative, UN Security Council, 1946–9. Secretary-General, Foreign Ministry, 1949–56. NATO Representative, 1956–7. Ambassador to Morocco, 1957–60. Vice-President, State Council, 1960–71. Member, World Court, 1964–71.

[2] Georges-Augustin Bidault, 1899–1983. Founded Catholic Association of French Youth and anti-Fascist newspaper *L'Aube*, 1932. Entered French Army, 1939. In French Resistance, 1941. Foreign Minister, French Provisional Government, 1944, 1946. President of France, 1946. Minister of Foreign Affairs, 1953–4.

JUNE 1953

Meeting of Commonwealth Prime Ministers: minutes
(Cabinet papers, 133/135)

5 June 1953
Secret
3 p.m.
Prime Ministers Meeting No. 3 of 1953

1. KOREAN TRUCE NEGOTIATIONS

Sir Winston Churchill said that the latest news showed that there was now promise of a successful outcome of the Korean truce negotiations. He had heard that Mr Syngman Rhee was not making serious difficulties. Before the last United Nations proposals had been put to the Communists the United Kingdom had been consulted, and the United States had accepted four out of the five points we made. We had been able to play our part in improving the atmosphere of the negotiations and, if they succeeded, all members of the Commonwealth would share the credit. If a truce was made, the main burden of the work would rest on India. There was a universal opinion that India was better qualified than any other country to play this part, but she would not be expected to carry the whole financial burden herself or to provide all the physical resources required.

2. MIDDLE EAST

Sir Winston Churchill said that he wished to place the main issues of the Egyptian problem before the Meeting. The Suez Canal was not now so important for our strategy as it used to be, for we had lived without it for three years in the last war and the character of a future war would be such that atomic attacks against Russia would precede any Russian invasion of Africa across the Sinai peninsula or any attempt at domination of the Near East. It might well be that after the first few months of war there would be a change in the strength of the two sides which would make it difficult for the Russians to conduct war over long distances. But we must, nevertheless, secure the maintenance of the Suez Canal and of the Canal Zone base.

The United Kingdom was accused by some of pursuing imperialist or colonialist policies in Egypt. We had a proud imperial and colonial record of which we were not ashamed, but it was unfair to apply these adjectives to our policy in Egypt. British troops were in Egypt for international reasons, in the interests of the free world, to maintain the waterway of the Suez Canal and to secure the base. Without the base an effective defence of Africa would not be assured.

After we abandoned Abadan the Egyptians had started to insist upon British withdrawal from Egypt, and when General Neguib seized power these demands increased in violence. Last November we had started discussions

with the United States about the value of the base to the free countries and to the North Atlantic Treaty Organisation. We had agreed with them that proposals on the following lines should be put to General Neguib:
  (i) The Canal Zone would be handed over to Egypt and the base area would be placed under Egyptian Control. Within this base existing depots and installations would be retained and would be run and controlled on the analogy of our base in Belgium or the United States base in the United Kingdom.
  (ii) The depots and installations would act as a working maintenance base for a proportion of the Middle East Land Forces in peace.
  (iii) The Royal Navy would retain equipment in Egypt for the defence of ports and maintain it under British supervision and have the use of the existing commercial oil storage facilities and pipe-lines.
  (iv) The Army would retain not more than 5,000 personnel to run these installations and the Royal Air Force not more than 2,000 for the same purpose.
  (v) There would be an integrated Anglo-Egyptian air defence organisation.
  (vi) An Allied-manned staging post would be maintained in Egypt.
  (vii) If the Egyptians could be persuaded to accept these conditions in peace-time, the allies would be assured of having a working maintenance base in peace, which they would return to and operate immediately in war and which would be protected by an efficient air defence system.

It was our intention that the 7,000 troops whom we wished to maintain in Egypt to take care of the base should be armed with personal weapons only for their own defence; they would not be in any sense an organised military force capable of offensive action. These proposals entailed no impairment of Egyptian sovereignty and would relieve the United Kingdom of the immense burden of maintaining 80,000 men in the Canal Zone at a cost of some £50 millions a year. Nothing less than these proposals would secure the interests of the Commonwealth and of the North Atlantic Treaty Organisation in the Eastern Mediterranean.

General Neguib had then asked for a conference to which request we had willingly agreed. We proposed that a series of technical committees should examine in detail the various aspects of the problem, such as the maintenance of the base by technicians and the phased withdrawal of British troops. Our view was that we could not settle any one of these topics separately from the others, but the Egyptians insisted that we should agree to a declaration that we would withdraw from Egypt before the topics could be discussed. We could not accept this and the talks were broken off.

General Neguib was now being pressed by the Egyptians to show how he would make good his promises to drive us out of Egypt. We were sticking to our proposals, which we had agreed with the United States, but were willing to resume discussions at any time. We wanted no control of Egypt, but we must see that the Canal and the base were protected. We would only be too glad to remove our troops and so reduce our financial burden, but we were not going to accept any solution of the problem at the expense of British humiliation: there was no question of yielding to an ultimatum.

It was in the interests of the United States to maintain the waterway of the Suez Canal and to secure the base for the protection of the Middle East but, though they supported our intentions and Mr Dulles had been not unhelpful, they had been unwilling to brush aside Egyptian objections to their participation in the discussions.

The United Kingdom had had cause many times in the past to be grateful for military assistance given by other members of the Commonwealth but we did not at this moment need military help in Egypt. We had a strong army there and if attacked it would defend itself with good conscience and with justification.

We had defended Egypt against Mussolini[1] but at the end of the war we found ourselves faced with a debt of £250 millions. We did not put in a counter-claim for defending them and the debt was now being paid back in instalments. The cost of the depots and installations in the base was now some £300 millions and the replacement value of stocks in them at the moment was estimated at about £200 millions. We could not afford to lose these vast sums.

Sir Winston Churchill said that the principle of not abandoning our interests in Egypt had been agreed with the United States. We only wished to discharge international functions with no affront to Egyptian sovereignty and, if any other country was willing to help us in discharging these functions, we would be very glad to share our burden: but we would not be ordered out of Egypt and in the meantime we would wait and see. Things might well improve.

Mr Mohammed Ali said that, if the new Russian gesture was a change of tactics rather than of policy, there might well be less pressure in Europe but more in the vulnerable countries of the Middle East and South-East Asia. Pakistan was interested to ensure that both the Middle East and South-East Asia were peaceful and secure. The Egyptian dispute affected the whole Arab world and undermined the standing of the United Kingdom in the Middle East. If agreement could be reached with General Neguib, it would be to the good of the whole area.

There was a fear that the Russians sought world domination and an outlet to the Persian Gulf. The Arab world must find unity against Communist aggression and so long as there were disturbances in the countries of the Middle

[1] Benito Amilcare Andrea Mussolini, 1883–1945. In Royal Italian Army, 1915–7. Leader of National Fascist Party in Italy, 1919–45. PM, 1922–43. Deposed by King Victor Emmanuel III, 1943. Leader of Italian Social Republic, 1943–5. Executed near Lake Como by Italian partisans, Apr. 1945.

East the international cause was not served. These disturbances gave rise to anti-British and anti-American feelings and must be settled.

Apart from the Egyptian dispute there were also the oil dispute between the United Kingdom and Persia and the uneasy state of relations between Israel and the Arab world; the existence of large numbers of Arab refugees posed a particularly difficult problem. It was important that all these disputes would be settled with the utmost despatch so as to gain the general co-operation of the countries of the Middle East in the defence of freedom. In fact the strategy of the Soviet Union was likely directed against the weakest link, which was the Middle East. This link must, therefore, be strengthened.

Sir Winston Churchill said that he could give complete assurance that Her Majesty's Government had nothing but good feelings towards the Arab world, and indeed our record supported this; for example, we had supported the attainment of freedom from French control by both Syria and the Lebanon and we had the closest possible ties with Transjordan, where General Glubb[1] and the Transjordan Frontier Force provided great security. We also had very good relations with Iraq and had originally been responsible for establishing the present dynasty there. At the same time we would not allow Israel to be crushed by the Arab countries surrounding her, though equally we certainly should not support Israel aggression against the Arabs. All we desired was that Israel should have her rightful chance to live in peace and be accorded fair play.

Mr Mohammad Ali said that, if the United Kingdom could publically announce the fact that she would never support any attempts by Israel to expand beyond her rightful territories, then such a statement would go a very long way towards removing the distrust of British intentions which was unfortunately at present in the minds of some Arab peoples.

Lord Alexander said that the object of maintaining a base in Egypt in time of peace was to enable us to use it in war. Such a base was a highly complex structure consisting of docks, wharves, roads, railways, hospitals, oil pipe-lines and storage installations, workshops &c., all of which were required for the operation of large forces in war. The present base had taken three and a half years to install at a cost of £300 millions; it contained £200 millions worth of equipment including 14,000 trucks and 700,000 tons of stores. Even under the proposed arrangements we should of course continue to be dependent on Egyptian labour, and it was perfectly true that the base could not be maintained under these conditions without the goodwill of the Egyptian people. He believed, however, that they were friendly to us at heart but that this friendship had been undermined by the subversive influence of Egyptian politicians. There was no question of impairing Egyptian sovereignty any more than

---

[1] John Bagot Glubb, 1897–1986. Known as 'Glubb Pasha'. Educated at Cheltenham College. OBE, 1924. Brig. in Transjordan's Arab Legion, 1930; Cdr, 1939–56. Married, 1938, Muriel Rosemary Forbes: five children. CMG, 1946. Formed Jordanian National Guard, 1951. KCB, 1956.

United Kingdom sovereignty was impaired by the presence in this country of the United States bases. We only wanted in Egypt the same rights that we had afforded the United States in England and which the Belgians had afforded us in their country.

Mr Holland wondered whether, if it took 80,000 British troops to defend the base at present, it would be possible for 7,000 to do so should the Egyptians at some future date decide to abrogate any new agreement that was drawn up. Did the settlement proposed offer us the measure of security which would enable us to use the base in war?

Sir Winston Churchill said that we had already obtained a large measure of United States support for our proposals for a new agreement. Provided these satisfied Egyptian feelings and continued to have United States support, he felt that it was unlikely that the situation would again deteriorate to the point at which the Egyptians would repudiate an agreement.

Mr Menzies said that at present we had 80,000 troops in Egypt to defend a position which was generally regarded as a purely national one. If we were to alter this situation and reduce the burden on the United Kingdom, while at the same time ensuring the security of the Egyptian base, then effective co-operation with the United States was essential. Egypt regarded the Suez Canal as a national waterway. It was not. The Suez Canal and its surroundings represented a vital area in the event of war and its defence could not be entrusted to the Egyptians alone. The facts were that, first, the Suez Canal was an international waterway of immense importance and, secondly, the base was vital to the security of the free world in the event of a global war. These two considerations made it quite clear that, provided our proposals gave us the minimum of safety and recognised the Canal as an international waterway, we should stand on them; but would the United States persevere in their support? It was one thing for the Egyptians to renounce the 1936 Treaty, but it would be quite a different matter for them to renounce any new agreement which they might make with the United Kingdom backed up the United States. The proposals were, he considered, reasonable and realistic as long as United States collaboration was assured.

As an illustration of the peculiar way in which the minds of Egyptian politicians worked, he described a discussion he had had some two years ago with the then Egyptian Foreign Secretary.[1] The latter had stated that the evacuation of the British from Egypt was an article of Egyptian faith and must be carried through, but at the same time he had admitted that in the event of war Egypt would be unable to defend herself and would require the British to re-establish the base again with miraculous speed.

It was, therefore, of paramount importance that we should persuade the Egyptians to realise that the Suez Canal was an international and not a

---

[1] Muhammad Salah al-Din Bey. Egyptian Foreign Secretary, 1950–2.

national waterway. Provided the United States would take an equally realistic attitude, then the terms of the proposals, which had been outlined by Sir Winston Churchill, could be defended and we should stand by them.

Sir Winston Churchill said that he was prepared to defend before the world an agreement reached with the Egyptians with the support of the United States Government. He would not be able to say the same if he allowed the proposals that had been made to be whittled away by further concessions.

Both India and Pakistan had a great interest in the free flow of traffic through the Suez Canal and any interference with this flow would prove detrimental to the great trade which, he trusted, the Indian Peninsula would continue to have with the countries of Europe.

Mr Nehru said that all were interested in seeing the dispute between the United Kingdom and Egypt settled satisfactorily, in a way which involved neither side in national humiliation; its continued existence gave rein to nationalist feelings which might spread over other parts of Africa with no good results. If no settlement were arrived at, it would be little consolation to realise that one had been in the right and one's opponent in the wrong. He agreed that some speeches by Egyptian leaders had been offensive and irritating and scarcely conducive to a settlement. But however difficult these leaders might be to deal with, they were in power and the régime appeared popular; to attempt to deal with anyone else could only strengthen its position. He had seldom come across a more pleasant and friendly sort of person than General Neguib, who seemed to be the last person to make difficulties in negotiation.

It seemed to him the points in dispute were few. The United Kingdom proposals recognised Egyptian sovereignty and allowed for the phased withdrawal of troops. It would not be gainsaid that some technical personnel would be required to service the installations and the only personnel competent to do this in the foreseeable future were those who were there at present; in this respect he understood that the sole point of argument was the manner by which the orders should be transmitted to them. If that were so, it seemed that the points of difference were so small that it would be extraordinary if they proved insoluble.

For the United Kingdom to obtain her objectives in Egypt it was necessary for her to retain the friendship of the people; the base would be of no value if set in the midst of a hostile population. Furthermore, if a future war took the course outlined by Sir Winston Churchill, no question of an attack on the Suez Canal would arise in the early stages, and the whole nature of the war and of the defence of the area would require to be thought out afresh. In peacetime there should be no difficulty in placing the Suez Canal under the control of some form of international company, established without impairment of the sovereignty of Egypt; in time of war some new agreement might be needed. Too much store, therefore, should not be placed on the defence of the base and the Canal.

He hoped that the present difficulties between the United Kingdom and Egypt would not have an adverse effect upon the recently concluded settlement on the Sudan, which had been a great step in a forward direction.

He did not know what the ultimate intentions of the United States were, but it appeared that they were not entirely in accord with the United Kingdom point of view. He would not like to see an agreement forced on Egypt by the superior power of the United Kingdom and the United States Governments, regardless of the consequences. He had himself no positive suggestions to make and, while the policy of wait and see might be justified on its merits, he feared it would not lead to results. Indeed, if no positive steps were taken, the situation might well grow worse.

Sir Winston Churchill said that it must not be forgotten that in the past a whole series of concessions had been offered to Egypt without any result. There was no intention of waiting for ever, though he was prepared to wait for six months or a year. While he would be glad to have further talks with the Egyptians at any time, he would never agree to evacuate Egypt in the face of their threats. He hoped that General Neguib would before long change his view.

Dr Malan explained the particular interest which the Union of South Africa took in the Middle East. If the dispute with the Egyptian Government was confined to the occupation of a part of Egypt by United Kingdom forces, then South Africa would be content to regard the settlement as a matter for the United Kingdom and Egypt alone. The problem was, however, much wider than that, and South Africa, which had assumed commitments in concert with other countries throughout Africa and war-time commitments in the Middle East itself, viewed with deep concern the continuation of the Egyptian dispute. Egypt was the gateway into Africa and unsettled conditions in that country weakened the security of the whole African continent. Moreover, there was no doubt that the Soviet Union was unfortunately also interested in Africa and for that reason kept a close watch on events in Egypt. The security of the Canal was of universal interest; it had a particular interest for South Africa, because the alternative route between East and West lay round the Cape. The ideal to aim at would be some form of international control over the Canal shared between Egypt and other interested countries. Finally the security of a military base in the Canal Zone was vital to South African interests; and South Africa, in company with other Commonwealth countries, had already undertaken commitments for the defence of the Middle East in war which would be quite valueless if there were no efficient base from which to conduct operations. A settlement of the Egyptian dispute was, therefore, as important to the countries of Africa as to the countries of Europe.

Mr St Laurent said that Canada regarded Egypt as one of the potential trouble spots in the world at the present time and was, therefore, most anxious that a settlement should be reached. On the strategy for bringing about this settlement he would not wish to offer an opinion. He felt that the root of the problem was to persuade the Egyptian Government that, for reasons which none could escape, the matters under dispute were of international concern; and he hoped that Mr Nehru and Mr Mohammed Ali would try to convince General Neguib of the truth of this and would impress upon him that there was no question of the United Kingdom wishing to impair in any way the sovereignty of Egypt.

Mr Senanayake agreed that an early settlement was vital. The value of a base in the Canal Zone depended to a large extent upon the co-operation of the Egyptians and their feelings of hostility must, therefore, be allayed by one means or another. It was difficult to estimate the strength of General Neguib's position, but his own impression on a recent visit had been that General Neguib enjoyed a large measure of popular support. The fact that both he and previous Egyptian Governments had insisted continuously upon the evacuation of British troops seemed to show that Egyptian public opinion was united on this point. It was difficult to tell what attitude General Neguib would adopt towards the British proposals, since he understood that he had refused to discuss them unless there was first of all a declaration that the withdrawal of British troops would start at once.

Sir Winston Churchill said that he was most grateful for the advice and encouragement of his colleagues. All the points which they had made would be carefully weighed and the United Kingdom would do its best to keep in close touch with the other countries of the Commonwealth on the development of the situation in Egypt. He would be most grateful if Mr Nehru and Mr Mohammed Ali would do their best, without of course offering to act in any way as mediators, to convince General Neguib of the soundness and the firmness of the present British proposals.

3. COMMUNIQUÉ

The Meeting agreed to issue the following communiqué to the press:

'At their meeting this afternoon the Commonwealth Prime Ministers continued their review of the international situation. After taking note of the latest developments in the armistice talks in Korea, they held a general discussion on the problems of the Middle East.'

4. NEXT MEETING

It was agreed that the next meeting should take place on Monday, 8th June, at 11.30 a.m. in Conference Room 'D' in the Cabinet Office. The meeting would be concerned with completing outstanding business and approving a final communiqué.

President Dwight D. Eisenhower to Sir Winston S. Churchill
(Premier papers, 11/1074)

6 June 1953

I have received your message with reference to Bermuda date.[1] We shall proceed correspondingly from this side subject to the consideration pointed out by Foster yesterday that we must in the last analysis be prepared to accommodate ourselves to the French situation and not seem to put them under external pressures as they are solving their governmental problem at home.

I look forward to our meeting.

David Pitblado to Sir Winston S. Churchill
(Premier papers, 11/356)

6 June 1953

SERVICE AT ST PAUL'S
TUESDAY, JUNE 9[2]

You and Lady Churchill are asked to arrive at St. Paul's not later than 10.45a.m. The Queen arrives at 10.50. You will be seated in the front row on the left-hand side directly below the Lectern. A Verger will conduct you to the Lectern for the reading of the Lesson.

The Lesson has been printed in the special Form of Service, and since it omits certain verses a copy of the printed sheet will be laid on the open Bible. You wished to read it during the weekend. It is flagged in the copy below. You will see that the ending of the Lesson is at the top of the next page.

THE LESSON
Ephesians VI 10–18 and 23 and 24

Finally, my brethren, be strong in the Lord, and in the power of his might. Put on the whole armour of God, that ye may be able to stand against the wiles of the devil. For we wrestle not against flesh and blood, but against principalities, against powers, against the rulers of the darkness of this world, against spiritual wickedness in high places. Wherefore take unto you the whole armour of God, that ye may be able to withstand in the evil day, and having done all, to stand.

Stand therefore, having your loins girt about with truth, and having on the breastplate of righteousness; and your feet shod with the preparation of

---

[1] T.193/53, reproduced above (p. 1083).
[2] The Coronation Thanksgiving Service for Queen Elizabeth II, traditionally held a week after the monarch's coronation.

the gospel of peace; above all, taking the shield of faith, wherewith ye shall be able to quench all the fiery darts of the wicked. And take the helmet of salvation, and the sword of the Spirit, which is the word of God; praying always with all prayer and supplication in the Spirit, and watching thereunto with all perseverance and supplication for all saints.

Peace be to the brethren, and love with faith, from God the Father and the Lord Jesus Christ. Grace be with all them that love our Lord Jesus Christ in sincerity. Amen.

Meeting of Commonwealth Prime Ministers: minutes
(Cabinet papers, 133/135)

8 June 1953
Secret
11.30 a.m.
Prime Ministers Meeting No. 4 of 1953

1. FINAL COMMUNIQUÉ

The Meeting considered the draft of a final communiqué which had been handed round.

Sir Winston Churchill proposed that the Meeting should settle the final form of the communiqué at the end of the last plenary session on Tuesday, 9th June. It would be issued to the press on the evening of that day, for publication on Wednesday, 10th June. The reference to the Korean armistice negotiations would have to be altered, as it had now been heard that an agreement on the exchange of prisoners of war had been signed. A paragraph on economic affairs would also have to be settled at the end of the session on 9th June.

In discussion of the draft communiqué the following points were made:

(a) Some reference to European problems should if possible be included, and the Meeting agreed that in the later stages of their discussion on the following day they would exchange views about Europe. In the meantime a few lines might be included in a revised draft of the communiqué.

(b) It would be more appropriate and effective if references to the Bermuda meeting could precede references to relations with the Soviet Union. There was a general hope that the Bermuda meeting would in fact lead to discussions with the leaders of the Soviet Union and, although this could not be stated precisely in a communiqué since it was by no means certain that the United States accepted this view, the order in which the references were made – first to the Bermuda meeting and then to relations with the Soviet Union – would give a sufficient indication of Commonwealth hopes.

(c) Mr St Laurent suggested that a reference should be made to our wish that the outstanding issues in the Middle East should be settled in such a way as to respect the sovereignty of the countries of that area. He thought that an assertion of this kind would help in the negotiations with Egypt.

(d) Mr Nehru said that the objective of any reference to the Middle East must be to further the prospect of a satisfactory settlement with Egypt. It was particularly important not to miss chances of bringing this settlement about, now that the international atmosphere had been much improved by the success of negotiations in Korea. He wondered, therefore, if it was wise to emphasise the military value of the Canal and of the base, and the use of the base in the war. Would not that make it more difficult for the Egyptians to ask for a resumption of negotiations? In reply, Sir Winston Churchill said that evidence of the support of the whole Commonwealth for the present British proposals would be a powerful inducement to the Egyptians to resume negotiations. If, on the other hand, the Egyptians felt that there was disunity between members of the Commonwealth, there was a grave danger that the Egyptians would preserve in obstinacy and resort to bloodshed. He was, therefore, most anxious that something positive should be included in the communiqué. If nothing more than platitudes could be said, then it would be better to say nothing at all.

The Meeting –

(1) Agreed that officials should meet that afternoon at 3 p.m. to prepare a new draft of the final communiqué in the light of the discussion.

(2) Agreed to discuss the final communiqué at their meeting on Tuesday, 9th June.

2. KOREA

Sir Winston Churchill said that the Meeting would no doubt rejoice at the news that an agreement on the exchange of prisoners of war had been signed in Korea. He thought that the suggestions which the United Kingdom Government had put to the United States had made a valuable contribution to this result. The part played by Mr Nehru himself and by the Republic of India had been of special importance, and he assured Mr Nehru that the United Kingdom would do all in its power to help India in the new duties which would now fall upon her.

Mr Nehru said that, in his view, the advice offered by Sir Winston Churchill and the United Kingdom Government had contributed powerfully to this achievement, and he wished to offer his sincere congratulations.

3. EUROPE

Mr Menzies said that time had not so far allowed any discussion of the problems in Europe, and he hoped that before the Meeting broke up an opportunity would be found for an exchange of views.

Mr Nehru supported this suggestion. He pointed to the conflict of fears which prevailed in central Europe – the fear of Soviet aggression on the one hand and the fear of resurgent German militarism on the other.

Sir Winston Churchill said that a German army in some form or other was an essential part of an effective defensive system for Western Europe. What the Soviet Union would like to see was a united Germany forming a vacuum in the middle of Europe. That was a proposition which would have to be resisted. The plight of Czechoslovakia was evidence enough of the dangers of this type of solution. He would be happy to develop his views on Europe in the later stages of the Meeting on the following day; in the meantime a few lines on Europe could be included in the draft communiqué which was to be prepared that afternoon.

4. NEXT MEETING

Sir Winston Churchill suggested that on the following afternoon the Meeting should consider first the economic situation which would be expounded by Mr Butler, then the problems of Europe and, finally, the draft communiqué which was to be submitted to them. He regretted that Dr Malan would not be able to be present at that meeting, and he expressed the gratification which all felt at having had the advantage of his presence during the discussions.

It was agreed that the next Meeting would be held at 10 Downing Street on Tuesday, 9th June, at 2.30 p.m., to discuss (i) the economic situation, (ii) the problems of Europe and (iii) the communiqué.

Meeting of Commonwealth Prime Ministers: minutes
(Cabinet papers, 133/135)

9 June 1953
Secret
2.30 p.m.
Prime Ministers Meeting No. 5 of 1953

[. . .]

2. FINAL COMMUNIQUÉ
(Previous Reference: PMM (53) 4th Meeting, Minute 1.)

The Meeting resumed their discussion of the final communiqué and considered a note by the Prime Minister of the United Kingdom covering a fifth draft of the communiqué, and a draft paragraph on economic affairs.

A number of verbal amendments were made.

Mr Nehru said that he could not accept paragraph 5 on Western Europe as it was now drafted. India was not associated with the North Atlantic Treaty Organisation and she was not in the European system. He was deeply interested in the general peace of Europe, but he could not commit himself to a hope that the European Defence Community with its proposed German contingent would be established at the earliest possible date. This would involve a change in India's policy of non-alignment. India did not wish to be dissociated from Europe, but she felt that there were other ways in which she could better help Europe than by lining up with the North Atlantic Treaty Organisation.

Mr Menzies said that the communiqué gave a clear expression of opinion on the problems of the Middle East and it would create a most unfortunate impression if no specific reference was also made to the hopes of Prime Ministers concerning the recent developments in Western Europe. The European Defence Community was just as important for the defence of democracy as was the security of the Middle East.

Mr Mohammed Ali agreed that the communiqué would lack balance if a paragraph on the Middle East were included but no comparable reference were made to Western Europe.

Sir Winston Churchill said that it would be better to say nothing about Western Europe than to show that there was no unanimity of opinion. But this was a critical time for Europe and it was very important that the Meeting should express the hope that the European Defence Community would be established at the earliest possible date. He agreed with Mr Menzies that a mere reference to a review of recent developments in Western Europe would be inadequate. The European Defence Community would make a great contribution to the united effort of the democracies to secure Western Europe, and if the Meeting could not give a clear expression of their hopes the cause of peace would suffer.

After further discussion it was agreed that the second sentence of paragraph 5 should be amended to say that the Commonwealth countries associated with, or interested in, the North Atlantic Treaty Organisation expressed the hope that the European Defence Community would be established at the earliest possible date.

The Meeting –

Approved the draft of the final communiqué subject to the amendments agreed in discussion.

3. CONCLUDING SPEECHES

Mr St Laurent said that he wished on behalf of all the other Prime Ministers to express his appreciation of the hospitality of Sir Winston Churchill and the United Kingdom Government. His feeling was deeper than could easily be expressed in words. It had been most valuable to have this opportunity of discussing their common problems. There were many difficulties in the world but hopes were now brighter.

Sir Winston Churchill said that he was greatly honoured to find round him in this famous capital the representatives of all the members of the Commonwealth. He was deeply gratified that, after making all allowances for differences of outlook, they had found it possible to express a united opinion on the work of the Meeting: this could only have a beneficent effect throughout the world.

The nations of the world had the power to tear themselves in pieces in a matter of months. If we could stave off these dangers we would give to the toiling millions the chance of reaping the fruits of science in a larger, safer and better way of life than had ever been offered or dreamed of. We had done something to bring about a better world which would cast off fear and make the proper use of the gifts which nature had provided.

On behalf of Her Majesty, and of his colleagues, he wished to thank the other Prime Ministers for their gratitude, courtesy and kindness. We would all preserve throughout our lives the memory of these talks, whose sole object was to benefit mankind.

He hoped that all would have prosperous journeys home. It might not be long before we foregathered again in more hopeful circumstances. He was proud to have been associated with this Meeting.

Sir Winston S. Churchill: speech
(Hansard)

9 June 1953   House of Commons

KOREA (TRUCE TALKS)

The Prime Minister: With permission, Sir, I will now answer these five Questions.

As the House is aware, on 8th June the Armistice Delegations at Panmunjom signed the agreement on the question of prisoners of war. This agreement followed quickly the revised proposals which were put forward by the United Nations Command on 25th May with the support of Her Majesty's Government. We are satisfied that the arrangements now agreed will ensure that no prisoner of war is repatriated by force.

Two points of substance which were outstanding when I made my last statement on 21st May have been settled to our satisfaction. India will be invited to provide the forces to take custody of prisoners under the Neutral Nations Repatriation Commission. Prisoners who refuse to be repatriated will not be detained beyond 120 days, after they have been transferred to the custody of the Commission. The other provisions of an armistice agreement have already in the main been agreed for many months past. Thus nothing ought now to stand in the way of the conclusion of an armistice except the necessary administrative arrangements, which I trust may be soon completed.

I will venture to repeat again for the third time to the House what I said a month ago upon our relationship with the United States about Korea: '. . . the United States, as mandatory for the United Nations, has borne nineteen-twentieths of the burden in blood and treasure. The matter is not one which we have either the right or the responsibility to decide, but it is our duty, without separating ourselves from our great ally, to express our opinion frankly and plainly to them as occasion offers.' – (OFFICIAL REPORT, 11th May, 1953; Vol 515, c 888.) This was well received in Washington and generally throughout the United States. We made a number of suggestions to the United States Government. These were most attentively considered. They were discussed on several occasions not only with our Ambassador but with representatives of the members of the British Commonwealth who have combatant forces in Korea who were invited by the State Department to attend the meetings. In the result, we found ourselves in complete accord on the new proposals to be made at Panmunjom. We thought it right, in view of this, to make public our intention to support the United States along these lines in any way that might be desirable or necessary.

When this statement was issued, events moved rapidly to the agreement to which I have just referred. Under the decisive guidance of President Eisenhower a result has been achieved which, unless new disappointments occur, will be of high value in itself on all sides, and also important in relation to the world position.

Perhaps I may make one further observation which rather concerns ourselves here. I do not feel that full justice has been done by us here – I include myself – during the last few months to the difficulties to which General Clark and General Harrison were subjected, not only by Communist obstinacy but also by the attitude – not very apparent to us – of the South Korean Government under Mr Syngman Rhee. One must remember that it was the policy of the United States to build up a strong, well-armed, efficient South Korean Army which would in course of time relieve them of the heavy burden they have been carrying. This army has for some time been a factor of growing importance.

In my opinion, these American Generals, whose names I have given, most faithfully sought to bring hostilities to an end in terms compatible with the honour of the Allied Powers acting under the authority of the United Nations, but all the time they had to consider the reactions which might occur in the powerful South Korean forces which they were creating and had to a large extent created. I think it is only fair to say that, because I did not appreciate the full aspect of this myself. We must never be unjust to people who do their very best.

The House will recall that the draft Armistice Agreement provides for the summoning of a political conference where serious issues remain to be discussed; that is, after the prisoner of war business has been settled and after an armistice has been reached, there is then this political conference. It would be unwise to assume that many difficulties do not lie ahead. But I feel we may regard what has already happened as constituting a definite step forward towards the goal we all seek.

Mr Henderson: In welcoming this statement of the Prime Minister, I am sure that I speak on behalf of all my right hon. and hon. Friends when I offer him our congratulations on the consistent part that Her Majesty's Government have played in bringing about a solution of this very difficult problem, and I am sure the Prime Minister would be the first to acknowledge the valuable contributions that have been made by the various Commonwealth Governments, especially the Government of India. May I ask him, on another point, with regard to the agreement itself, whether the various declarations of President Syngman Rhee indicate that the South Korean Government will be a party to the agreement and the truce that will follow?

The Prime Minister: I do not know at all what the answer could be, but, on the whole, I expect it would work out all right in the end, having regard to the very great power and clear, decisive policy of the United States.

In reply to the other point, certainly I would like to acknowledge the contributions made by other Governments. We have been following out, in the main, the sort of line that I am sure would have been taken by the party to which the right hon. and learned Gentleman belongs – by the Front Bench opposite. The matter only came to a head after all this long period of delay. I think that if we are going to make acknowledgements we should remember my right hon. Friend and Foreign Secretary who influenced the United Nations very much towards giving great emphasis to the Indian influence as a means of solving these difficulties. I am sure we all wish him God's help in the ordeal which he is going to face.

Mrs Castle: While warmly welcoming the progress so far made towards an armistice, may I ask the right hon. Gentleman whether he would agree that the Chinese Communists have made fundamental concessions in these negotiations on principle, without which an armistice could not have been possible; and, in view of this hopeful evidence of a co-operative attitude, will Her Majesty's Government now take the initiative towards a wider settlement by pressing upon the United States Government the urgency of admitting the Peoples' Government of China to the United Nations?

The Prime Minister: I think all this could have been settled many months ago if the Chinese Government had not, for reasons which I cannot measure, shown no desire to bring these matters to a conclusion.

Mr Hughes: Does the Prime Minister agree that after this great success the next great step forward should be the recognition by the United Nations of the China Government in Peking, and will he say what steps he will take to bring about that desirable event?

The Prime Minister: The course which we are following has a lot of fences in it, and I really think it is better to jump them one at a time.

Mr Nicholson: Is my right hon. Friend aware that though events have taken a more favourable turn latterly, they have left in their train a considerable deterioration in Anglo-American relations and a failure in the United States to understand our point of view? Will he take an early opportunity to direct his unparalleled prestige towards an amelioration of those relations?

The Prime Minister: That raises a lot of issues, but I certainly feel that we have an absolute right to put our views forward, and we have done so, not with disadvantage to anyone. I also feel deeply indebted to the United States, who have borne the burden for so long and who were joined by the members of the late Government at the time of the invasion of Korea. I do not think there is any real difference between us on the main principles involved.

Mr Donnelly:[1] Will the right hon. Gentleman bear in mind that the best way to improve Anglo-American relations is for us always to speak frankly, as he has already done? Amongst all the general congratulations which have been offered to the right hon. Gentleman today, will he express his hope that this – to use his own words – is just the end of the beginning and that many

---

[1] Desmond Louis Donnelly, 1920–74. served in RAF, 1939–46. Lecturer, RAF Staff College, 1945–6. Editor, *Town and Country Planning*, 1946–9. Director, Town and Country Planning Association, 1948–50. Married, 1947, Rosemary Taggart: three children. MP (Lab.) for Pembrokeshire, 1950–70. Political columnist, *Daily Herald*, 1960–3. Chief political correspondent, *News of the World*, 1968–70.

great events will follow, in which there will be just as great a readiness by people on the other side of the Iron Curtain to see our point of view as there has been by people on this side of the Iron Curtain to express the views of China when it has been unpopular to do so?

The Prime Minister: We should always look forward with eagerness to opportunities of speaking frankly, but I think the time must be well chosen.

Mr Noel-Baker: The Prime Minister spoke of the political conference which is to follow the signing of the truce and the many great problems it must face. If I understand the matter rightly, the first step is for the Assembly of the United Nations to be convened again by its President, Mr Pearson, of Canada. Should we rightly assume that it will be the Assembly which will decide the composition and the terms of reference of the political conference, on behalf of the United Nations?

The Prime Minister: We have just met after a holiday and we have a considerable period of the Session before us. Therefore, I think I may fairly ask for notice of that somewhat complicated series of hypothetical questions.

Sir Winston S. Churchill to General George C. Marshall
(Churchill papers, 2/144)

10 June 1953

My dear Marshall,

I send you herewith the picture I mentioned to you and your wife the other day. It was painted in January 1951 in the Atlas Mountains at a place called Tinherir. The river which flows boldly out of the mountains soon comes to its end in the Sahara. It was shown at the Royal Academy last year.

Sir Winston S. Churchill to General Nevil Brownjohn
Prime Minister's Personal Minute M.196/53
(Premier papers, 11/341)

10 June 1953

Please see the attached minute which I have received from Sir William Strang in reply to my minute of June 8 of which a copy is also attached.

Paragraphs 2 and 3 give no indication of the difference between establishments and fighting strength. Please let me have the establishment of a British Division including the proportion of reward Services and Corps troops.

My own feeling is that a Chinese 'Army' is about the equivalent of a strong British Division. What is meant by a 'weak British Corps'? I am asking about establishments not fighting strengths.

What is the total establishment of the Commonwealth Division in Korea?

President Dwight D. Eisenhower to Sir Winston S. Churchill
(Premier papers, 11/1074)

11 June 1953
Top Secret

From my discussions with Foster about the findings of his recent trip, I am particularly concerned about Egypt. While I wish to talk to you personally about this matter in Bermuda, there seems to me a real danger that the situation there will not hold that long without further action.

I was happy to hear that you agree with Foster's statement of our position on May 12, 1953 at Cairo. He reaffirmed that position in his radio report to the American public on June 1. I fully concur in his views.

From Foster's personal observation and from all other reports which reach me, I have come to the conclusion that some step should be made soon to reconcile our minimum defense needs with the very strong nationalist sentiments of the Egyptian Government and people. It appears that it is not possible to conclude a settlement on the basis of Case A in its entirety, despite its desirability from a military point of view. As we had agreed when it was thought we might negotiate side by side, there may have to be some concessions which will permit a quick start on withdrawal of UK troops and produce adequate if not ideal arrangements for maintenance of the base. Department of State is sending to American Embassy London a formula which illustrates what we have in mind and which your staff can examine if you so desire. To assist further with this problem, if you desired and if it proved helpful with the Egyptians, I would be prepared to assign US technicians to participate in the maintenance of the base.

In addition to the question of maintenance there is, of course, the problem of assuring availability of the base in time of need. Pending more formal arrangements, a private undertaking by Egypt that the base would be made available in case of general war to the Arab states and to the Allies of the Arab states might serve the purpose. You could invoke our treaties with Jordan and Iraq and we might also be able to utilize our special relationship with Saudi Arabia.

Also, on the conclusion of agreement on evacuation and the future maintenance of the base, Neguib might publically invite the United Kingdom and the United States to help develop the defense of Egypt, including training and equipping of Egyptian forces. In response to this initiative, we could jointly negotiate the necessary formal defence requirements of the West, as well as assistance to Egypt. The results of these negotiations could be made public. Meanwhile, as I think you know, Foster, at your request, is presently deferring any arms aid to Egypt.

Once agreements of the nature described were reached with the Egyptians, we would be prepared to insist uncompromisingly on their being carried out in good faith. This determination could be made unequivocably clear to the Egyptians.

I am sorry to bother you with this before we can talk together at Bermuda but the possible danger from the situation to us all is so much on my mind that I intrude these ideas at this time in accordance with the spirit which has animated our full and frank exchange of views.

ENCLOSURE

In order to clarify certain points of misunderstanding that have arisen in recent discussions between Egypt and the United Kingdom, the following memorandum of understanding is hereby agreed and constitutes the terms of reference for the 'base committee':

To draw up plans for the transfer of the present military base in the Canal Zone to Egyptian control and for keeping it in working order and use so that it may strengthen the area by continuing to supply forces outside Egypt and be available for immediate use in the event of hostilities endangering the peace and security of the area.

Recommendations will be made regarding the installations and the equipment within the base area and the equipment in the base under the following considerations:

(A) That the Egyptian Government, in exercise of its sovereignty over the base, will undertake by the agreement to insure the security of British property therein.

(B) That the present level of depot stocks may be maintained but not increased except by consent of the Egypt Government.

(C) That the British experts needed shall be limited to the absolute minimum numbers required for the efficient operation of the installation and the maintenance and current withdrawals and additions of British equipment left in the base.

(D) That arrangements will be proposed for the training of Egyptian personnel to replace British personnel utilized for the above purpose within a minimum period to be agreed upon between the two delegations. At the end of this period British personnel will no longer be stationed within the base area, except as may be agreed to at that time by the Egyptian Government. It is understood that at the end of the above time period British inspectors may be attached to the staff of the UK Ambassador to Egypt and will be allowed to inspect Egyptian maintenance of British-owned supplies in the base and examine the measures taken by the Egyptian base commander to carry out British directions regarding the maintenance and disposition of such supplies, equipment and facilities.

(E) It is understood that channels from London affecting the above matters will be to the United Kingdom Military Attaché attached to the United Kingdom Embassy in Egypt. These instructions will be forwarded to the Egyptian base commander through such channels as the Egyptian Government may prescribe, it being realized that efficiency and speed of communication is of the utmost importance in matters of this nature.

(F) That any arrangements proposed above shall not be inconsistent with Egyptian sovereignty nor with British ownership and use of the property concerned.

(G) That the Egyptian Government is conscious of the responsibility placed upon it as custodian of the base area, the purpose of which is to deter aggression against the Middle East as a whole, to supply forces beyond Egypt's borders and to increase the defenses of Egypt itself including the Suez Canal waterway. The Egyptian Government recognizes and has no intention of interference with the right of the British Government to direct the shipment of its equipment and supplies in the base to areas and forces outside Egypt.

(H) That the committee will not concern itself with the duration in time of the arrangements which it proposes. This will be determined by the two delegations.

James Thomas to Sir Winston S. Churchill
(*Premier papers, 11/355*)

11 June 1953

You spoke to me this morning about the statements in the press that bright colours should not be worn by ladies at the Naval Review.

2. I find that this recommendation is contained in the Coronation Review Orders issued jointly by the Commanders-in-Chief, Home Fleet and Portsmouth. This only applies to guests on board HM Ships and not to the liners. The reason for this expression of hope by the Commanders-in-Chief is evidently because they do not wish to spoil the general impression that the ships companies paraded on board will give to the Queen. This general impression could, indeed, be much marred by loud contrasts in colour. The guests on board HM Ships are there by special invitation and I do not think it is too much to invite them to try and conform as far as possible to the general appearance.

3. I feel it would be a great pity for the Admiralty to embroil themselves with the press in giving explanations which I understand are fundamentally well appreciated by reasonable people.[1]

---

[1] Churchill responded on June 13: 'I cannot see what harm it would have done to state that this only applied to Admiralty guests on naval vessels' (M.204/53).

Peter Thorneycroft to Sir Winston S. Churchill
(Premier papers, 11/604)

11 June 1953

COTTON: IMPORTING AND MARKETING ARRANGEMENTS[1]

The Minister of Materials and I circulated a paper (C(53)164) to the Cabinet on the 6th June about future purchasing arrangements for cotton.

2. For the reason explained in paragraph 5 of the paper, it is necessary to make an announcement on or before the 16th June about the arrangements for the 1953–54 buying season. As it will not be possible for the memorandum to be taken at the Cabinet before the 16th June, I have confirmed from the Chancellor of the Exchequer, the Chancellor of the Duchy of Lancaster, and the Minister of Labour that they are in agreement with the proposals in it – namely that we should announce forthwith that the Government agrees that the purchasing arrangements for the 1953–54 buying season should be those recommended by the Review Committee, which are, broadly, a continuance of the current procedures subject to some technical changes. (The Raw Cotton Commission has agreed to operate on that basis.)

3. Accordingly, I propose to make an announcement on the above lines in answer to a pre-arranged Question in the House on the 16th June.

4. Though the subject of cotton purchasing arrangements is always capable of arousing political controversy I do not think that this announcement of the interim arrangement is likely to do so. It has in any event the support of a Committee representative of all sections of the cotton industry including the Liverpool and Manchester Cotton Associations.

5. I ought to add that I shall still hope to have an opportunity of discussing with my colleagues at some convenient time after the 16th June the longer term problems referred to in C(53)164 so that I can have the benefit of their advice before the consultations proposed in paragraph 8 of that paper are taken.

Lord Cherwell to Sir Winston S. Churchill
(Premier papers, 11/604)

12 June 1953

COTTON: IMPORTING AND MARKETING ARRANGEMENTS

You may remember that when this last came up to the Cabinet (in February) I was not very happy about the proposals.

[1] Churchill wrote at the top of the page: 'Lord Cherwell, please comment.'

The fundamental trouble is that we are trying to run a scheme half-way between complete Government trading (which we want to get rid of) and complete private freedom, with the Liverpool Cotton Exchange reopened (which we cannot yet risk because of our still precarious balance of payments).

The scheme involves the use of public funds to cover the risks of private traders; and it reduces our power in the event of an American recession to save dollars by discriminating against US cotton without damaging our non-dollar trade.

But it hardly seems possible to go back on the scheme at this stage and I see no alternative to accepting the proposal of the President of the Board of Trade.

General Sir Brian Robertson to Sir Winston S. Churchill
(Premier papers, 11/1074)

12 June 1953
Immediate
Secret
No. 2378

The proposals in the 'formula'[1] are scarcely distinguishable from the proposals which the Egyptians made to us and which we rejected 4 weeks ago. We have already had in substance from General Neguib what we are now offered by the Americans.

2. Mr Dulles said to me that it might be necessary to move towards Case 'B'. These proposals represent something which is very little better than Case 'C'. I have already given you my views as to why I consider that we should reject Case 'B' and it follows that in my opinion these proposals are quite unacceptable.

3. I may be too optimistic but I believe that we could get an agreement which retains the essentials of Case 'A' provided that resumption of discussions is not too long delayed, and that you can accept certain concessions of form to pander to Egyptian conceit. I am prepared at any time to amplify my ideas on this point.

4. However I am now fearful lest these latest United States proposals should reach the ears of the Egyptians. I should have no chance then of getting a better agreement out of them. For this reason I hope that you will lose no time in telling the President that you are unwilling to make an agreement on these terms.

5. The assistance of American technicians in the Base would be a complication, but it might have considerable political advantages. I suggest that this

---

[1] See 'Enclosure' in Eisenhower to Churchill of June 11, reproduced above (pp. 1103–4).

offer by the President should be acknowledged with thanks but without commitment as yet.

6. I do not consider that the 'private undertaking' mentioned in the 4th paragraph of the President's letter would be nearly good enough. A future Egyptian Government could very easily disclaim responsibility for any such private undertakings. Incidentally I suggest that it would be difficult to satisfy Parliament and public opinion on this very important point of 'reactivation' if you had nothing except a private understanding which you would be debarred from disclosing.

7. While the United States Government seem prepared to accept conditions for the base which are most unsatisfactory in our view, the great importance which they attach to the organization of a MEDO is revealed in paragraph 5 of the President's message. Whatever its political value, MEDO will have no real military value, will be no substitute for the Base, and incidentally will in no way counteract the effect on British prestige of accepting these proposals on the Base.

John Colville: diary
('The Fringes of Power', pages 716–17)

12 June 1953

On Friday, 12th, I escaped the Banquet to the Queen at the Guildhall and went to Chartwell. On the following day Tommy Lascelles drove down to tell the PM and me of Princess Margaret's wish to marry the recently divorced Peter Townsend[1] – a pretty kettle of fish.

The Prime Minister's first reaction after Lascelles had left was to say that the course of true love must always be allowed to run smooth and that nothing must stand in the way of this handsome pair. However, Lady Churchill said that if he followed this line he would be making the same mistake that he made at the abdication.

This gave me an opportunity of asking him what he had really intended at the abdication. Had he contemplated the possibility of Mrs Simpson as Queen of England? He said that he had certainly not. He was, however, loyal to the King whom he wrongly believed to be suffering from a temporary passion. His scheme, and that of Lord Beaverbrook, had been to frighten Mrs Simpson away from England. When she was gone he hoped the King would retire to Windsor and 'pull up the drawbridge, post Lord Dawson of Penn at the front

[1] Peter Wooldridge Townsend, 1914–95. Born in Rangoon, Burma. Served in RAF, 1933–56. DFC, 1940. Sqn Ldr, 1940. Wg Cdr, 1941. DSO, 1941. Married, 1941, Rosemary Pawle: two children (div. 1952); 1959, Marie Luce Jamagne: three children. Commanded No. 85 Sqn RAF, 1940–1; RAF Drew, 1942; No. 605 Sqn RAF, 1942; RAF West Malling, 1943–44. Equerry to King George VI, 1944–52. CVO, 1947. Deputy Master of HM Household, 1950. Equerry to the Queen, 1952–3. Gp Capt., 1953. Romantically involved with HRH Princess Margaret, 1953. Air Attaché, Brussels, 1953–6.

gate and Lord Horder at the back gate', and let it be announced that he was too ill to undertake public business.

Winston said that great measures were taken to frighten Mrs Simpson away. Bricks were thrown through her windows and letters written threatening her with vitriol. 'Do you mean that you did that,' I said, aghast. 'No,' he replied, 'but Max did.'

Years afterwards I told this story to Lord Beaverbrook who said that he certainly did not, but it was possible somebody from the Daily Express *might have! He also said that whereas it was probably true that Winston's principal motive had been loyalty to the King, his had been that it was all a lot of fun.*

I omit accounts of the lavish balls and other festivities which followed the Coronation – the Naval Review, magnificent fireworks at a great Windsor Castle ball, visits to Sutton to stay with the Sutherlands and many other purely social activities, all of them in sparkling contrast to the constraints of the previous years and seeming to usher in a period of prosperity and relaxation. They may have been, for a privileged few, the bubbles on the surface; but the surface itself was for the next ten years much less troubled than would have seemed credible twelve months previously.

One of the last emblems of austerity to vanish was sugar and sweet rationing. Churchill had, against the advice of the Minister of Food, insisted that this be abolished before the crowds assembled, from home and abroad, for the Coronation. He was warned that such action might lead to a chaotic shortage. In fact, by the autumn of 1953, there was a glut of sugar.

Sir Winston S. Churchill to President Dwight D. Eisenhower
Prime Minister's Personal Telegram T.197/53
(Premier papers, 11/1074)

12 June 1953
Immediate
Secret
Personal and Private
No. 2377

My dear friend,

I look forward to a good talk about Egypt when we meet in Bermuda. Meanwhile, I think I must send you at once my first reactions to the new formula suggested in the message which I have just had from you.[1]

2. In the hope of reaching agreement with you and your predecessor we went over all this ground before and agreed to make a number of concessions to the Egyptian point of view. Our object in these discussions was not to obtain

---

[1] Reproduced above (pp. 1102–4).

military or financial aid from the United States, but only their moral support in what we hoped would be a joint approach to the Egyptian dictatorship. However, you decided to defer to Egyptian objections to your representatives, including General Hull, taking part in the discussions. Since then we have been disappointed not to receive more support particularly in Cairo from your Government in spite of the numerous far-reaching concessions which we made in our joint discussions with you.

3. We went forward alone, having made clear to you that we did not seek United States mediation or arbitration. The Egyptian dictatorship presently 'washed their hands' of the discussions, timing it no doubt to fit in with Mr Foster Dulles' visit. We are quite ready to resume the talks if they should intimate a wish to do so. This could be no humiliation to them as the meeting place is under their roof. Nothing however has happened: the campaign of threats and abuse of the most violent character to which we have been for many months subjected has not been followed by any action except a few murders. Latterly there has been a decline in the campaign of threats and abuse, and this no doubt is due to the fact that the Egyptian people have lost faith in its sincerity and consider it all bluff for political purposes, or are hoping for some help from the United States. We propose to await developments with patience and composure. If a further approach is made to us to resume discussions, we shall comply without, however, any change in principle in the terms on which we had decided and to which we understood you had in the main agreed. I should have no objection to your advising the Egyptians to resume the talks, provided of course they were not led to believe that you were whittling us down, or prepared to intervene in a matter in which the whole burden, not nineteen-twentieths but repeat whole burden, falls on us, and about which I thought we were agreed. After all there are other bases conceded for mutual security in other countries not even established by formal treaty – for instance yours in the United Kingdom.

4. If at the present time the United States indicated divergence from us in spite of the measure of agreement we had reached after making so many concessions, we should not think we had been treated fairly by our great Ally, with whom we are working in so many parts of the globe for the causes which we both espouse. If as the result of American encouragement at this juncture or a promise or delivery of arms, Dictator Neguib is emboldened to translate his threats into action, bloodshed on a scale difficult to measure beforehand might well result, and for this we should feel no responsibility, having acted throughout in a sincere spirit for the defence not of British but of international or inter-Allied interests of a high order.

5. As I have said I look forward to talking these matters over with you in Bermuda. Meanwhile I watch the progress of events with the closest attention.

6. I asked General Robertson, who with our Ambassador has been conducting the negotiations and is now in London, for his opinion. My immediately

following telegram contains the note he has written.[1] I send it to you although it was not drafted for your eye, and I wrote my own cable before seeing it.

7. I am sending you a separate message about other events.

Sir Winston S. Churchill to President Dwight D. Eisenhower
Prime Minister's Personal Telegram T.198/53
(Premier papers, 11/1074)

12 June 1953
Immediate
Secret
Personal and Private
No. 2381

My dear friend,

1. Our Egyptian correspondence seems to add a greater urgency to our meeting at Bermuda. On the other hand the French vacuum continues and our Ambassador in Paris reports that we may well have to wait for a fully functioning French Government until the 22nd, and I suppose they would like to have some discussion among themselves after that. Then there is the Fourth of July which I presume would require your presence at home. I will come any time but it seems doubtful whether the Big Three including the one who perhaps ought to be called the Unknown Quantity can meet before the end of the first week of July or perhaps even later. In the meantime there is this controversy about Egypt, the developments in the Far East and Adenauer's fortunes at the German elections, on all of which it is urgent that you and I should reach agreement.

2. I really think we should both make it clear to the French that we are going to meet as proposed on the 29th for which all arrangements have been made. Might this not be a spur to the French or at the least teach them a lesson?

President Dwight D. Eisenhower to Sir Winston S. Churchill
(Premier papers, 11/520)

13 June 1953

Dear Winston,

I am concerned about the continuing French cabinet crisis. According to the best guess of my people and assuming that he will get his vote and investiture, André Marie[2] cannot be expected to have his cabinet formed and

---

[1] Reproduced above (pp. 1106–7).
[2] André Marie, 1897–1974. Served in French Army, 1916–18. Member or French National Assembly for Seine-Inférieure, 1928–41, 1945–62. Under-Secretary of State, 1933. Rejoined Army as Capt.

June 1953 1111

functioning before the end of next week at best. This would give our French friends only a short week to take stock of their situation and to review their policies before joining us at Bermuda. I do not believe that this would contribute to the general lines of agreement which I hope will result from our talks. I therefore suggest that our ambassadors inform the French Government that we fully appreciate their difficulties and propose to postpone our meeting at Bermuda by two weeks to give them ample time to settle their internal problem and to prepare for our meeting.

I believe the French would appreciate this initiative on our part and that it should yield dividends when we meet.

When one takes into account the possibility that André Marie may fail in his attempts to form a government, the above course of action seems even more advisable.

Sir Winston S. Churchill to Peter Thorneycroft
Prime Minister's Personal Minute M.203/53
(Premier papers, 11/604)

13 June 1953

I think it a pity this could not come before the Cabinet on Wednesday 17th.[1] What is the special sanctity of June 16. If it is a fixed public date I agree that you should proceed as you propose in view of the great measure of agreement among the Ministers concerned and those you have consulted. I enclose you a note by the Paymaster General[2] who seems to be in agreement with you.

Sir Winston S. Churchill to Winston Churchill
(Churchill papers, 1/51)

13 June 1953

Dearest Winston,

I thought you would like these Coronation stamps which have just been issued and were sent to me by the Postmaster General.

I hope you enjoyed the coronation; you certainly looked very smart in your outfit. I have had a very busy time but hope to get down to Chartwell this weekend. Four cygnets hatched out, two of which unfortunately died but the others are very pretty and swim about on their mother's back.

(Reserve), 1940. Captured and imprisoned, 1940–1. In French Resistance, 1942–3. Captured and imprisoned, 1943–5. Minister of Justice, 1947–8, 1948–9. PM of France, 1948. Deputy PM, 1948–9. Minister of Education, 1951–4.

[1] See Thorneycroft to Churchill of June 11, reproduced above (p. 1105).

[2] Reproduced above (pp. 1105–6).

I hope you are enjoying yourself. Write to me sometime and let me know what you are doing.

Sir Winston S. Churchill to President Dwight D. Eisenhower
Prime Minister's Personal Telegram T.200/53
(Premier papers, 11/1074)

14 June 1953
Confidential
No. 2399

Your telegram No. 1238.
We are certainly prepared to help in transporting Indian troops to Korea. Nehru will I am sure be very willing to help. I have told him it would mean 5,000 men. He said he had passed this to his Commander-in-Chief in India. I do not know whether he would choose Cariappa[1] but I am confident he will do his best to find a good man.

Sir Winston S. Churchill to Le Pacha El Hadj Thami El Glaoui
(Premier papers, 11/353)

14 June 1953
Private and Confidential

My dear Glaoui,
I have told The Queen of your most generous wish to present to Her Majesty the magnificent golden diadem, set with emeralds and diamonds, which you brought with you to London and, at the same time, to give the Duke of Edinburgh a golden sheathed dagger made at Marrakesh.

Her Majesty is most sensible of your kind intentions and has commanded me to express to you her very sincere thanks for them. She has however, instructed me to explain to you the strict rule she has made about accepting presents on the occasion of the Coronation. Her Majesty was offered gifts by the people of Canada and of many of her Dominions, but she firmly decided only to accept presents from Heads of States on this particular occasion. The Queen therefore feels that, grateful though she is for all that you have proposed, both she and the Duke of Edinburgh must be allowed to decline the gifts. There have, as you know, also been certain political repercussions in

[1] Kodandera Madappa Cariappa, 1899–1993. Known as 'Kipper'. Born in Madikeri, Kodagu, India. Educated at Presidency College, Chennai, and Imperial Defence College, Camberley. 2nd Lt., 1920. Lt., 1921; Capt., 1927. Staff Capt., 1936. Married, 1937, Muthu Machia: two children (d. 1948). Maj., 1938. Second-in-Command, 7th Rajput Machine Gun Battalion, 1942. Asst QMG, 1943. Brig., 1944. OBE, 1945. Maj.-Gen., 1947. C-in-C, Indian Army, 1949. Retired, 1953. Indian High Commissioner to Australia and New Zealand, 1953–6. FM, 1986.

Morocco arising from your known desire to give a present to The Queen and these must necessarily reinforce the considerations which Her Majesty has had to take into account.

I have no doubt that as an old and valued friend of this country you will fully understand the reasons which have inspired Her Majesty to take this decision with which I am myself in accord.

I am arranging for the Foreign Office to return to you, by safe hand, the beautiful diadem and dagger.

Admiral Lord Louis Mountbatten: recollection[1]
(The Rt Hon. Sir Winston S. Churchill Society, Edmonton, Alberta)

15 June 1953

I brought some 20 of my ships in the Mediterranean to the Coronation Naval Review and Winston said, 'Dickie, you must come and see me. I wish to talk to you about the Dardanelles.'

At that time I was Allied Commander for NATO, but knowing he was very busy, I did not go anywhere near him. He did not forget. He sent for me. He was sitting alone in the Cabinet room. He had got rather deaf, and in front of him he had the latest form of a rather elaborate hearing aid, and some sort of amplifier.

He held up his hand for me not to speak. He plugged in his earphones, put them on, switched on the amplifier, tapped it once or twice, and for a quarter of an hour he held forth about what I ought to do about the Dardanelles. When it was finished he took off his headphones, switched off the amplifier, and said, 'Now what have you got to say to that?'

I picked up the headphones, I switched on the amplifier, and I gave it to him back. I said, 'If you will put that on I will tell you.'

---

[1] From a speech given by Lord Mountbatten on 11 Apr. 1966.

1114   JUNE 1953

Sir Winston S. Churchill to President Dwight D. Eisenhower
Prime Minister's Personal Telegram *T.203/53*
(Premier papers, 11/1074)

16 June 1953
Immediate
Dedip
Secret, Personal and Private
No. 2420

My dear Friend,
  I have just had a long talk with Winthrop Aldrich and I was delighted to hear from him all the friendly things you said about me and our close relationship in the face of so many baffling problems.
  2. About Bermuda. Our telegrams of the 12th and 13th[1] evidently crossed and I suppose we were both waiting to hear from each other. André Marie has accepted and my information from our Embassy in Paris is that he may well be accepted by the Chamber on Thursday, the 18th; that Bidault would be his Foreign Secretary; that the foreign policy would be very much what Mayer and he were pursuing and that therefore there would still be time for them to make the 29th, as you proposed to me when the 15th failed. I am told that the Quai d'Orsay have not received any suggestion from the United States that the date should be again put off, and that they have not made any request themselves, and also that they are going on with the arrangements for the journey of the French representatives to Bermuda. I hope therefore we may await what happens in Paris on the 18th and 19th before offering a further delay.
  3. It seems to me that the imminence of this date, the 29th, will help André Marie to get his vote because there is deep concern in French circles lest their failure to form a Government should prevent their formal recognition by our two countries as being one of the Big Three.
  4. Of course if they fail again or if the new Premier asks for a little more time you and I could consider that together. I hope however that we should not go beyond an extra week, say Tuesday, July 7. I have my problems too and Parliament rises on July 31. It would leave me very little time to get back after the Conference and put the case resulting from our decisions to them if we did not meet before the 15th. Moreover the world anxiously awaits the result of our mission and no-one is more worried than Dr Adenauer, with his elections pending in the last days of August.
  5. I am still hoping for the 29th and all my plans and also arrangements in Bermuda have been made for the 29th. I trust therefore we can keep our

---
[1] Reproduced above (pp. 1108–11).

options open till we see what happens in Paris on Thursday the 18th. Please let me know your wishes at your earliest convenience.

Jack Ward[1] to Sergey Dengin[2]
(*Premier papers, 11/673*)

18 June 1953   Wahnerheide
Immediate
Confidential
No. 555

As Commandants of the French, British and United States sectors of Berlin and in the name of the Allied High Commission, we[3] desire to express our grave concern over events which have taken place in Berlin in the past few days.

We condemn the irresponsible recourse to military force which had as its result the killing or serious wounding of a considerable number of citizens of Berlin, including some from our own sectors.

We protest against the arbitrary measures taken by the Soviet authorities, which have resulted in the interruption of traffic between the sectors and free circulation through Berlin.

We formally deny that Willy Goettling,[4] executed after a travesty of justice, was an agent provocateur under the order of the intelligence service of a foreign Power. His condemnation to death and his execution, on an empty pretext, appear to us as acts of brutality which will shock the conscience of the world.

As the highest Soviet authority in the Soviet sector of Berlin you share with us the responsibility of guaranteeing the well-being and the freedom of the people of Berlin. We therefore demand in the interest of Berlin as a whole that the harsh restrictions imposed on the population be lifted immediately and that free circulation within Berlin be re-established.

---

[1] John Guthrie Ward, 1909–91. Known as 'Jack'. Educated at Pembroke College, Cambridge. Member of UK delegation, Moscow Conferences, 1943–5, and Potsdam Conference, 1945. High Commissioner in Germany, 1951–4. Ambassador to Argentina, 1957–61; to Italy, 1962–6. GCMG, 1967.

[2] Sergey Dengin, 1900–89. Commandant of Soviet Zone, Berlin, 1950–3.

[3] French zone: Pierre Manceaux-Démiau; British zone: Charles Coleman; American zone: Thomas S. Timberman.

[4] Willy Goettling, ?–1953. Resident of West Berlin executed by Soviet authorities in 1953 for alleged espionage and civil disruption.

Sir Winston S. Churchill to Sir William Strang
Prime Minister's Personal Minute M.215/53
(Premier papers, 11/673)

19 June 1953

1. Telegram No. 555 from Wahnerheide. I am surprised that they should have issued this protest without informing us beforehand. Do you consider Sir I. Kirkpatrick should remain on leave at so critical a moment? Is it suggested that the Soviet should have allowed the Eastern Zone to fall into anarchy and riot? I had the impression that they acted with considerable restraint in the face of mounting disorder.

2. See also telegram No. 126 from Berlin which I had not read till later.[1]

President Dwight D. Eisenhower to Sir Winston S. Churchill
(Premier papers, 11/1074)

19 June 1953
Top Secret

Dear Winston,

Thank you very much for your prompt response[2] to my recent message on Egypt.[3] There are certain passages in your reply which I fail to understand, but I believe it more profitable to leave these for the personal talks we anticipate in Bermuda.

I was interested to note that Robertson feels that agreement might be reached which would retain the essentials of Case A, providing there is reasonably prompt resumption of discussions and that some adjustments are made to meet Egyptian sensibilities.

As you know, I personally believe that the best interests of all of us will be served if friendly discussions are promptly resumed in Cairo. Obviously, however, it would be worse than futile to resume those talks unless you and I are absolutely clear as to the minimum objectives we hope to attain, and have some reason to believe that these would not be rejected out of hand by the Egyptians. Perhaps our March agreement on the type of base arrangement to be sought, which you mention, would serve the purpose. If my memory serves me correctly, the negotiators were to have flexibility between arrangements which would insure a working base in peace which would be immediately operable in event of war, and one which would require 60 days for reactivation.

[1] Churchill noted specifically the following paragraph: '(d) Russian troops (and indeed also Volkspolizei) have throughout acted with marked restraint and moderation and have clearly been under instructions to use minimum of force, presumably in the hope of salvaging as much as possible of the new SED policy introduced on June 9.'
[2] T.197/53, reproduced above (pp. 1108–10).
[3] Reproduced above (pp. 1102–4).

Won't you please dismiss any thought of us, here, seeming to assert any agreed position or exhibiting weakness. Foster's statements in Cairo and his notification to the Egyptians that they cannot get arms as long as you and they are disagreed should reassure you on this.

Sir Winston S. Churchill to Anthony Nutting
(Premier papers, 11/427)

19 June 1953

My dear Nutting,

In my speech of May 11[1] I said 'This would be the most fatal moment for the free nations to relax their comradeship and preparations. To fail to maintain our defence effort up to the limit of our strength would be to paralyse every beneficial tendency towards peace both in Europe and in Asia. For us to become divided among ourselves because of divergencies of opinion or local interests, or to slacken our combined efforts, would be to end for ever such new hope as may have broken upon mankind and lead instead to their general ruin and enslavement.'

The policy of Her Majesty's Government is to do their utmost to bring about the creation of the European Defence Community at the earliest possible date and to do all they can to support it and associate themselves with it. I hope that you will make this clear beyond doubt in Strasbourg, both in public speeches and in private conversation. We have very distinguished members of our Party in the British Delegation including, as you remind me, Boothby, Amery, John Hope, Beamish, Longden,[2] Goschen[3] and McMillan Bell.[4] I hope that they, too, will take every occasion to let it be known where we stand on this issue.

---

[1] Reproduced above (pp. 998–1010).

[2] Gilbert James Morley Longden, 1902–97. Born in Durham. Enrolled in Army Officers' Emergency Reserve, 1938. Called up into Durham Light Infantry, 1940. MBE, 1945. MP (Cons.) for South West Hertfordshire, 1950–74. UK Representative to Council of Europe, 1953–4. UK Delegate to UN, 1957–9. Knighted, 1972. Wrote *A Conservative Philosophy* (1947), *One Nation* (1950), *Change Is Our Ally* (1954), *A Responsible Society* (1959) and *One Europe* (1969).

[3] John Alexander Goschen, 1906–77. 2nd Lt Grenadier Guards, 1926. ADC to Governor of Madras, 1931. Served in WWII. Lt-Col., 1944. OBE, 1944. British Military Mission to Greece, 1945–7. Succeeded as 3rd Viscount, 1952. Captain, Yeomen of the Guard, 1962–4, 1970–1. Chief Opposition Whip, House of Lords, 1964–70. KBE, 1972.

[4] Ronald McMillan Bell, 1914–82. Secretary and Treasurer, Oxford Union Society, 1935. President, Oxford University Conservative Association, 1935. Called to the Bar, 1938. Served in RNVR, 1939–46. MP (Cons.) for Newport, 1945; for South Buckinghamshire, 1950–74; for Beaconsfield, 1974–82. QC, 1966. Member, Select Committee on European Legislation, 1974–82. Member of Court of the University of Reading, 1975–82. Knighted, 1980.

1118   June 1953

Sir Winston S. Churchill to President Dwight D. Eisenhower
Prime Minister's Personal Telegram T.204/53
(Premier papers, 11/1074)

19 June 1953
Immediate
Dedip
Secret and Personal
No. 2454

My dear friend,

1. I was very glad to get your message of the 18th about Egypt.[1] I look forward to a good talk with you about the problem at Bermuda. Thank you especially for your final paragraph. I did not mean to suggest anything to the contrary in my cable, as I have absolute confidence in American goodwill and fair play.

2. The French and Bermuda. Marie has failed. These recurring delays are very painful to me and very bad for world affairs. You and I have quite a lot of things which concern us both on which our public agreement would be helpful all round. Could we not both tell the French that we two shall be meeting on July 8, and hope they will join us?

This would enable me to receive you at any time convenient to yourself on the 7th with the Guard of Honour of the Welsh Regiment which I have brought from Jamaica. The Conference could start the next day, the 8th. Such a message would, I believe, help to clinch matters in the French Chamber. Every day's delay before we meet is unfortunate and it would be a disaster if our meeting did not take place. Uncertainty and bewilderment are growing in Europe every day, and Adenauer's election draws near.

3. I was very glad to read Foster Dulles' statement about Syngman Rhee's violation of the United Nations agreement.[2] I shall do all I can to keep Parliament in step with you on these lines. There will be a lot of trouble if the war goes on while Syngman Rhee remains in office.

4. I shall be grateful if you would let me know about Bermuda at the earliest moment, and also let me know when you receive this.

---

[1] Reproduced above (pp. 1116–17).
[2] On June 18, Syngman Rhee released 25,000 POWs. Dulles warned him that he must abide by UN authority in ending the war, or else 'another arrangement' would be necessary.

Winthrop Aldrich to Sir Winston S. Churchill
(Premier papers, 11/520)

20 June 1953

My dear Sir Winston,

The President has requested me to deliver the following two messages to you on the Bermuda meeting:

(First)

'Dear Winston: I have put off attempting a definitive reply to you regarding a date for our Bermuda talks, because of the uncertainty of the French situation. I know that Foster has kept you advised of our thinking through Roger Makins. Now the latest effort to form a French government under Marie has failed and I suppose we cannot anticipate a government before the latter part of next week, which would be only a day or two before the Prime Minister and Foreign Minister would presumably have to leave if we hold to the 29th. It seems to me unrealistic to think that under these circumstances we can have a responsible and authoritative French government to talk with at Bermuda on the 29th. I am reluctant to proceed without them or with only token French representation, because many of the matters on which we should reach an understanding involve the French. I have particularly in mind such matters as firming up on EDC and also arriving at some clear understanding of how the French propose to deal with the situation in Indo China. This touches both of us deeply – you because of your Malayan problem – us because we are already footing much of the bill, and because what happens there has a great bearing on the off-shore position, including the Philippines and Japan.

Under the circumstances, I suggest we should advise the French government that we are postponing our Bermuda conference until July 13. I am very reluctant to do this, as I know you are, but I really see no practical alternative.

Another consideration is the extremely awkward turn that Rhee has given the Korean situation. We do not know yet what this may portend – whether it is a single gesture of defiance, following which he will go along in efforts to repair if possible the damage and make an armistice possible, or whether he is determined to prevent any armistice. I fear the latter.

Foster and I must give this matter close attention for a few days and from that standpoint a little delay on Bermuda could be put to good advantage by us in relation to Korea. Please let me know as soon as convenient how your own thoughts are running on this matter.

Faithfully yours, Ike.'

(Second)

'Dear Winston: Your message just reached my office.

First, with respect to Bermuda. This morning I sent you a message suggesting the thirteenth, but I can easily make the eighth if that is more convenient for you. Consequently, we shall count on arriving there on the seventh, with work to start on the eighth, and will notify the French of this intent. This, however, does not preclude the possibility that either you or I may be faced with some circumstance that again will require modification of our plans. I hope that will not be the case, because I quite agree with you that we should have a meeting, and I sincerely trust that the fixing of this kind of date may sufficiently accommodate the French.

The Korean business is indeed difficult. There can be no question as to the soundness of your observation about the trouble we shall have if the war goes on and Syngman Rhee remains in his present office. It is remarkable how little concern men seem to have for logic, statistics, and even, indeed, survival; we live by emotion, prejudice, and pride.

With warm regards, Ike.'

Sir Winston S. Churchill to President Dwight D. Eisenhower
Prime Minister's Personal Telegram T.204A/53
(Premier papers, 11/1074)

20 June 1953

The following is only a thought of my own. Syngman Rhee arrested or dismissed from office. British send an extra brigade from Egypt to Korea.

Sir Winston S. Churchill to President Dwight D. Eisenhower
Prime Minister's Personal Telegram T.206/53
(Premier papers, 11/1074)

20 June 1953
Immediate
Secret
No. 2482

1. Thank you so much for your latest telegram. I shall sail in the *Vanguard* to arrive Bermuda on the 6th and welcome you on the 7th. The more we can make it clear this date is a fixture the better will be the chances of a French Government. I must again emphasize my own difficulties in further indefinite delay.

2. You may like to see the directive about EDC (attached) which I have sent to our Conservative delegates at Strasbourg.

3. Clemmie and I are looking forward so much to meeting you and your family party.

All good wishes in these troublous times.

Sir Winston S. Churchill to President Dwight D. Eisenhower
Prime Minister's Personal Telegram T.206/53
(Premier papers, 11/1074)

20 June 1953
Immediate
Confidential
No. 2483

Following is directive dated June 19, 1953 referred to in my immediately preceding telegram.

In my speech of May 11[1] I said 'This would be the most fatal moment for the free nations to relax their comradeship and preparations. To fail to maintain our defence effort up to the limit of our strength would be to paralyse every beneficial tendency towards peace both in Europe and in Asia. For us to become divided among ourselves because of divergencies of opinion or local interests, or to slacken our combined efforts, would be to end for ever such new hope as may have broken upon mankind and lead instead to their general ruin and enslavement.'

The policy of Her Majesty's Government is to do their utmost to bring about the creation of the European Defence Community at the earliest possible date and to do all they can to support it and associate themselves with it. I hope that you will make this clear beyond doubt in Strasbourg, both in public speeches and in private conversations.[2]

---

[1] Reproduced above (pp. 998–1010).

[2] President Eisenhower responded on June 23: 'Thank you very much for your several messages. I am particularly delighted to read the instruction that you have sent to your delegation at Strasbourg. I have always felt certain that an emphatically stated British position on this point would be most effective. At different times you have given all of the assurances that seemed to be necessary or appropriate, but many people have doubted British enthusiasm. I shall be looking forward to seeing you on the 7th.'

Sir Roger Makins to Sir Winston S. Churchill
Prime Minister's Personal Telegram T.208/53
(Premier papers, 11/1074)

21 June 1953
Immediate
Dedip
Secret
No. 1303

I also gave the President personally this morning the message about Bermuda contained in your telegram No. 2482.

2. He said that he certainly agreed to set July 8 as the target date, but he still seemed a bit hesitant about the possibility that there would be no French Government. He regarded it as imperative that there should be at least token French representation especially in view of the EDC and the Indo-China situations. I replied that I was sure you agreed with this, but that you felt it essential to set a date by which a French representative must be produced. We could not wait about for the French indefinitely. I think he now quite accepts this. He observed that the French had a caretaker government who could come if necessary.

3. On EDC he said he often wished that you would make one of your great and 'booming' speeches in its support. He felt that the Europeans had a tremendous regard for the political maturity of Great Britain and they were still hanging back because they were doubtful about our attitude.

Sir Winston S. Churchill to President Dwight D. Eisenhower
Prime Minister's Personal Telegram T.209/53
(Premier papers, 11/1074)

21 June 1953
Immediate
Secret
No. 2488

I have received the following messages from Sir Oliver Harvey in reply to a 'buck-up' telegram I sent him about the Bermuda rendez-vous.

I conveyed your message to Parodi this morning. French authorities had received similar communication from Washington. M Bidault has replied that they agree.

I am therefore making all arrangements to leave here in the *Vanguard* on the night of June 30 and look forward to receiving you on the 7th in Bermuda. My projected movements will be published here tomorrow Monday.

As military questions are sure to crop up between us I should like to bring

Alex with me and, as I wished to talk over with you atomic matters and a document I showed you when we met last January, to bring the Professor i.e. Lord Cherwell. He explains things to me I cannot otherwise understand. I do not suppose you have any objection to this addition to my party. It would not in any way impede our separate private talks.

Sir Roger Makins to Sir Winston S. Churchill
Prime Minister's Personal Telegram T.210/53
(Premier papers, 11/1074)

21 June 1953
Immediate
Top Secret
Deyou
No. 1034

I saw the President this morning and gave him your message.

2. On Rhee he sympathised with your desire but said emphatically that any change must come or appear to come from within. He felt strongly that the Western Powers who had intervened in Korea to uphold freedom and democracy must not be seen to be setting up a puppet government. He had given much thought to this. He had some hope that there were elements in South Korea who understood that their country was wholly dependent on the United States for its reconstruction and future support and that they would exert influence. I asked him whether something would not be done through the South Korean Army. He seemed to think the Army might in fact make a move.

3. As to additional British brigade the President observed that this would have a gainsaying effect in the United States.

4. Finally he said he would not answer your message today but would reflect further upon it. He entirely agreed that the matter should be kept in closest secrecy. Any hint that such a thing was under discussion could have most serious effect.

5. The President was in excellent form and very friendly.

6. I understand very confidentially that the President and some of his advisors have in fact already discussed at length ways and means of dealing with Rhee and that there are also unconfirmed indications that a military coup in Korea is being prepared.

7. The President did not raise the time-factor involved in the move of the British Brigade but this may come up later. I suppose there is no possibility of bringing troops from Hong Kong Garrison rather than from Egypt.

Sir Winston S. Churchill to General Cyril Coleman[1]
(Premier papers, 11/673)

22 June 1953
Immediate
Dedip
Secret
No. 168

I cannot see how you reconcile the 2nd, 3rd and 5th paragraphs of Mr Ward's telegram No. 555[2] with the admirable factual accounts you have been giving us in your telegrams but most precisely I complain of the contrast with Paragraph 2 of your No. 126, see especially (d) Quote Russian troops (and indeed also Volkspolizei) have throughout acted with marked restraint and moderation and have clearly been under instructions to use minimum of force, presumably in the hope of salvaging as much as possible of the new SED policy introduced on June 9 Unquote.

2. If the Soviet Government, as the occupying Power, were faced as you have described with widespread movements of violent disorder they surely have the right to declare Martial Law in order to prevent anarchy and if they acted in your words of No. 126 'with marked restraint and moderation' this is no reason for making the statements contained in No. 555. We shall not find our way out of our many difficulties by making for purposes of local propaganda statements which are not in accordance with the facts.

Sir Winston S. Churchill to Jack Ward
(Premier papers, 11/673)

22 June 1953

I send you a copy of a message I have sent to General Coleman.

2. I still consider that in view of the above you should have referred the declaration put forward in No. 555 to me before associating yourself with it.

3. I am glad that you 'succeeded in defeating the American desire to insert in the statement words which would have implied that the Allies approve of the riots'. It would indeed be a poor service to the German people, with whom I have the deepest sympathy, to provoke them into revolt against overwhelming power which might easily have been used and may still be used with the 'restraint' of which General Coleman writes.

[1] Cyril Frederick Charles Coleman, 1903–74. Commander, 4th Battalion, Welch Rgt, 1941–4. OBE, 1944. DSO, 1945. Cdr, 160th Infantry Bde, 1947–8. GOC, South-Western District and 43rd (Wessex) Infantry Div., 1949–51. CB, 1950. Commandant, British Sector, Berlin, 1951–4. CMG, 1954. CoS, Northern Army Group, 1954–6. GOC-in-C Eastern Command, 1956–9. KCB, 1957. Col., Welch Rgt, 1958–65. KStJ, 1964.
[2] Reproduced above (p. 1115).

JUNE 1953

President Dwight D. Eisenhower to Sir Winston S. Churchill
('The Churchill Eisenhower Correspondence', page 79)

23 June 1953

I should like you to know that I have personally approved the proposal which I have asked Foster to make to Roger Makins that the United States, British and French Governments invite Pug Ismay to come to Bermuda in his capacity as Secretary General of NATO. This step would demonstrate to the world the solidarity of the North Atlantic Alliance in a highly effective and dramatic way. Furthermore, I am sure you will agree that Pug's informal advice, counsel and comradeship will be of great value to us.

President Dwight D. Eisenhower to Sir Winston S. Churchill
('The Churchill Eisenhower Correspondence', pages 79–80)

23 June 1953

Dear Winston,

Circumstances have arisen which make it inadvisable for me to bring Mamie and her mother to Bermuda. This I regret very much but it cannot be helped. Mamie is very disappointed to miss this fine opportunity to visit with Clemmie.

On the evening of 23 June 1953, during a dinner for de Gasperi, Churchill had another stroke. He was moved to Chartwell after the June 24 Cabinet meeting.

Sir Winston S. Churchill to President Dwight D. Eisenhower
Prime Minister's Personal Telegram T.211/53
(Premier papers, 11/1074)

24 June 1953
Immediate
Secret, Private and Personal
No. 2555

I am very sorry about Mamie but Clemmie will come all the same in a private capacity.

2. I am bringing Alex and the Prof with me. We all hope to have a good rest during the voyage although we shall be in full contact both ways.

3. I am holding three battalions and an Artillery regiment at short notice in Hong Kong 'to reinforce General Mark Clark's Army in any action that may

be required of them by the United Nations'. Let me know whether you would like this made public. I did not quite understand what 'gainsaying' meant, but presume you meant it would stave off adverse criticism in the United States.

Am looking forward so much to seeing you.

Cabinet: conclusions
(Cabinet papers, 128/26)

24 June 1953
Secret
11.30 a.m.
Cabinet Meeting No. 36 of 1953

1. The Prime Minister suggested that instructions should be given to a brigade in Hong Kong to be ready to move to Korea if the situation required it. There would be no commitment to move this Brigade, but he thought that the act of putting it under orders to be ready would help to sustain the United Nations decisions in Korea and would strengthen the hands of the Americans. Meanwhile, it was important that the Commonwealth division in Korea should not find itself isolated with a South Korean division on each of its flanks. On one side at least it should be flanked by an American division.

The Minister of Defence said that a Brigade Headquarters, two infantry battalions and a regiment of artillery could be brought to a state of readiness in Hong Kong. If shipping were available, it would take about two weeks to complete the move to Korea. An additional battalion, drawn from the ten battalions at present constituting the Commonwealth division, could be added to this Brigade on its arrival in Korea. He would check the present position of the Commonwealth division. During his visit to Korea about a year ago it had been placed between two American divisions.

The Cabinet –

Agreed that instructions should be given to a Brigade in Hong Kong to hold itself ready to move to Korea on receipt of further orders.

[. . .]

3. The Prime Minister referred to the message addressed to him by the Federal Chancellor of Western Germany about the events in Berlin and the need to restore unity and freedom to the whole German people. He intended, in reply to Dr Adenauer's message, to refer to the practical proposals put to the Soviet Government in the Note from the Western Powers of 23rd September, 1952, which provided for the organisation and holding of free German elections, for the subsequent formation of a free all-German Government and for the eventual negotiation of a peace treaty with that Government. He would add to the reply some complimentary reference to the efforts made by Dr Adenauer in pursuit of the task which he had defined in his message as one

of restoring 'unity and freedom to the whole German people in such a way that they may serve the peace of Europe'.
[. . .]

Sir Winston S. Churchill to Jack Ward
(Premier papers, 11/673)

24 June 1953
Emergency
Confidential
No. 493

My immediately following telegram contains text of answer to be given in the House of Commons this afternoon about Germany. It is not yet certain whether I shall give this answer or whether it will be given by Minister of State. In any case, I have approved it myself.

2. Please inform Federal Government. If answer as delivered in House of Commons varies from text in my immediately following telegram, you will be informed at once.

3. You should explain that answer may be delivered before Dr Adenauer can receive my reply to his personal message of June 21. My reply will be on lines indicated in the answer, making three main points:
   (a) reaffirming the practical proposals for German reunification in freedom set forth in the Western note to the Soviet Government of September 23, 1952;
   (b) reaffirming my intention, as stated in my speech of May 11,[1] to adhere faithfully to our agreements with Western Germany;
   (c) ending with a tribute to courage and steadfastness of Berliners.

4. Terms of answer set out in my immediately following telegram were of course decided upon before receipt of Paris telegram No. 235 (of June 23). Her Majesty's Ambassador in Paris should therefore inform M René Mayer of substance of answer and of lines on which I propose to reply to Dr Adenauer. Sir O. Harvey should express the hope that French reply to Dr Adenauer will be on the same general lines.

5. Her Majesty's Ambassador in Washington should inform United States Government in the same sense.

---

[1] Reproduced above (pp. 998–1010).

Sir Winston S. Churchill to Jack Ward
(Premier papers, 11/673)

24 June 1953
Emergency
Confidential
No. 494

My immediately preceding telegram.
Following is text of reply.

(Begins.)
According to my information, the events in Berlin last week were preceded by strikes and demonstrations at many points in the Eastern Zone of Germany against the repressive Communist régime. In Berlin itself a spontaneous protest strike on June 16 developed on the following day into a widespread demonstration against the East German administration.

When late on June 17 the authority of the East German Administration had broken down completely, the Soviet occupation authorities moved three divisions of troops into East Berlin, imposed martial law and took firm measures to restore order. Although the Russians appear to have behaved so far with restraint, a number of East Berlin citizens have been killed or wounded. In addition a West Berlin citizen has been summarily executed, and at least seven people have been killed and over a hundred wounded in the Western sectors by shots fired from East Berlin. All communications between East and West Berlin were severed with serious results upon the life and economy of the City. In fulfilment of their duty to protect the interests of the population, a firm protest was made by the three Allied Commandants to the Soviet Representative in Berlin on the evening of June 18.

Since the weekend, the situation in East Berlin appears to be gradually returning to normal. The Soviet and Allied authorities in Berlin are now in touch regarding the early resumption of communications. The picture of events in the Eastern Zone as a whole is not yet clear.

So far as we are aware, no British subjects have been involved.

Contrary to Soviet allegations, these demonstrations were neither provoked by, nor directed from the West. In expressing their sympathy for those who have suffered and admiration for their courage, Her Majesty's Government must equally counsel prudence and restraint so that further bloodshed and suffering may be avoided.

The Prime Minister has received a personal message from the German Federal Chancellor appealing to Her Majesty's Government to do all in their power to realise the unity and freedom of the German nation.

He intends to inform Dr Adenauer in reply that Her Majesty's Government are in full accord with the spirit of this message. We have frequently made clear that our aim is a Germany reunited in freedom. We believe that the only way to achieve this is on the basis of the practical proposals contained in the note of the three Western Powers to the Soviet Government of September last year, but to which no reply has yet been given. The resolution passed in the Bundestag on June 10 shows that this is the policy of the German Government Coalition and also of the Social Democratic opposition.

Meanwhile I repeat that Her Majesty's Government are resolved to adhere most faithfully in the spirit as well as in the letter to their commitments to Western Germany, and that Western Germany will in no way be sacrificed or cease to be master of its own fortunes within the agreements we and other NATO countries have made with her. (Ends.)

Sir Winston S. Churchill to Jack Ward
(Premier papers, 11/673)

24 June 1953
Immediate
No. 497

My immediately preceding telegram.
Following is text of reply to Dr Adenauer's message.

(Begins):
In reply to your message of June 21 about recent events in East Germany, I would invite Your Excellency's attention to the statement being made in the House of Commons today. I fully agree with you that recent events in Berlin and in East Germany have again demonstrated the urgent necessity for enabling Germany to be reunited in conditions of freedom and in conditions which promote peace throughout Europe. You refer to the Bundestag resolution of June 10. This seems to me to conform to the practical proposals put to the Soviet Government in the Western note of September 23, 1952. These provide for the organisation and holding of free German elections, for the subsequent formation of a free, all-German Government and eventually for the negotiation of a peace treaty with that Government. I believe that these proposals provide the only basis for achieving our common aim of a Germany reunited in freedom. It is my hope that the Soviet Government may see their way to negotiate with the Western powers on such a basis.

Meanwhile, Her Majesty's Government are resolved, as I said on May 11, to adhere most faithfully in the spirit as well as in the letter to our agreements with Western Germany which will in no way be sacrificed nor cease to be master of its own fortunes within the agreements we and other NATO countries have made with her. These agreements establish beyond doubt our continuing interest in Berlin.

The courage and steadfastness of the people of Berlin over a period of years have earned the admiration of us all. But that courage must continue and go hand in hand with patience and restraint so that further bloodshed may be avoided.

I take this opportunity to put on record my high regard for your personal efforts to restore unity and freedom to the whole German people in such a way that they may serve the peace of Europe. (Ends).

John Colville to R. A. Butler
(R. A. Butler, 'The Art of the Possible', pages 169–70)

25 June 1953

I write, very sorrowfully, to let you know quite privately that the PM is seriously ill[1] and that unless some miracle occurs in the next 24 hours there can be no question of his going to Bermuda and little, I think, of his remaining in office.

You must have noticed what befell him after the De Gasperi dinner on Tuesday. It was a sudden arterial spasm, or perhaps a clot in an artery, and he has been left with great difficulty of articulation although his brain is still absolutely clear. His left side is partly paralysed and he has lost the use of his left arm. He himself has little hope of recovery.

His courage and philosophic resignation are beyond praise and admiration and Lady Churchill, too, is heroic.

I have not as yet told anybody but a few of his intimate friends and among his colleagues yourself, Lord Salisbury and the Prof – though I am keeping Tommy Lascelles fully informed. Therefore although the PM certainly wants you to know the position, I hope you will keep the whole matter strictly private for the time being. I will let you know how things progress.

President Dwight D. Eisenhower to Sir Winston S. Churchill
('The Churchill Eisenhower Correspondence', page 80)

25 June 1953

Dear Winston,

I am still chasing the word 'gainsaying' back and forth across the ether

---

[1] Churchill had suffered another stroke on June 23.

waves of the Atlantic. Certainly I have never been guilty of using such a ten shilling monstrosity.

Sir Winston S. Churchill to Shunichi Matsumoto[1]
(Premier papers, 11/468)

25 June 1953

Sir,

I have the honour to refer to Your Excellency's letter of June 10 conveying a message from your Prime Minister.

I shall be obliged if Your Excellency would kindly transmit to Mr Yoshida[2] the following reply:

> I received with pleasure Your Excellency's kind message regarding the visit to this country of His Imperial Highness Crown Prince Akihito.[3] I trust he found his stay amongst us both agreeable and profitable. Her Majesty's Government and the British people were glad and honoured to be afforded this opportunity of meeting His Imperial Highness during a visit which I feel sure will have contributed greatly to Anglo-Japanese understanding.

I have the honour to be, Sir,
Your Excellency's obedient servant,

Field Marshal Lord Montgomery to Sir Winston S. Churchill
(Premier papers, 11/370)

26 June 1953

My dear Prime Minister,

I am disturbed at the present state of the game in NATO. I do not think Ridgway understands it; but he leaves SHAPE on 17 July, on which day Gruenther takes over.

I have written the attached memorandum for Gruenther and I gave him a copy of it yesterday. It sets out the problem as it appears to me and gives the

---

[1] Shunichi Matsumoto, 1897–1987. Japanese Vice-Minister of Foreign Affairs, 1942–4, 1945–52. Ambassador to French Indochina, 1944–5; to UK, 1952–5. Member, House of Representatives of Japan, 1955–63.

[2] Shigeru Yoshida, 1878–1967. Member, Japanese legation, Paris Peace Conference, 1919. Minister to Sweden, Norway and Denmark, 1928. Deputy Foreign Minister, 1928–30. Ambassador to Italy, 1930–6; to UK, 1936–8. PM of Japan, 1946, 1948–54. Member, Diet of Japan, 1954–63. Wrote 159 works in six different languages, including *The Yoshida Memoirs, the Story of Japan in Crisis* (1957–83) and *Japan's Decisive Century, 1867–1967* (1967).

[3] Akihito, 1933–. Born in Tokyo, Japan. Educated at Gakushuin University, Tokyo. Invested as Crown Prince of Japan, 1952. Married, 1959, Michiko Shoda: three children. Succeeded to the Chrysanthemum Throne, 1989.

general lines on which the answer may be sought. I have given a copy to Pug Ismay.

I would be most grateful if you will read the memorandum and would discuss it with Ike at your conference with him in Bermuda.

MEMORANDUM ON THE PRESENT STATE OF THE GAME IN NATO
BY FIELD MARSHAL MONTGOMERY: 26 JUNE 1953

1. The affairs of the defence organisation of NATO are approaching a crisis. Some very tough decisions lie ahead of political chiefs and Governments, and it is essential they should receive clear and sound professional advice from military chiefs.

The purpose of this memorandum is to suggest the form that the military advice should take.

The Problem in Outline

2. Nations cannot continue to carry much longer the present enormous defence budgets.

The situation today is that the economic ceilings are being approached and in some cases exceeded.

Next year we shall see certain nations having to reduce the armed forces that they have been building up in accordance with the short term aim.

It is clear that rearmament is near its peak and will soon level off: we may even find that a decline sets in as regards active forces maintained 'in being' in peace time.

3. We have been working on a short term aim to try and create, by an anticipated date, sufficient forces 'in being' to act as a deterrent against war and to be able to defend the peoples and territories of the NATO nations if we were attacked.

It is clear that we have now got to build on a long term basis <u>as well as</u> trying to complete the short term aim, and that the two must be carefully synchronized. A new approach to the problem is therefore needed.

The New Approach

4. The whole object of the new approach to the problem must be to get national war machines so geared that nations can handle any emergency for the next 25 to 30 years ahead, without damaging their peace time economies.

From a purely military point of view this involves finding the correct balance between active and reserve forces, and also creating an organisation which will produce <u>effective and well trained</u> reserve forces quickly after mobilisation.

5. What are the minimum air, sea and land forces that we must maintain 'in being' in peace in order to ensure survival in the opening clashes, and what further forces are needed in reserve and by when are these required to be ready for battle?

We must set the sights high. We want an organisation that will enable nations to spring to arms quickly at any time behind the shield. In the past the first step has always been to insist on large land armies as the first essential in any defence organisation; this attitude is not in keeping with modern times or with our particular problem. The land forces should be limited to the minimum required to safeguard our vitals against the first onslaught.

6. In our case, air power and sea power are essential. If we lose control of the seas, Europe falls since it must be supplied in war time almost entirely from across the Atlantic. If we cannot hold our own in the air, Europe falls.

We want, also to determine the minimum land forces necessary to hold the situation until nations can spring to arms, get their reserves into action, and get their national war machines into gear. The bulk of these land forces must be produced in the first instance by the nations of continental Europe.

It must be realised that the more we are forced to rely on reserve forces, the more we require a good logistic and movement organisation which will enable us to move reserves and supplies at will. We must be able to push stuff around freely and quickly.

7. The final organisation that we adopt must be in full accord with practical realities and economic possibilities.

Main Reasons for Our Present Troubles

8. We have reached the present difficult position because of a failure on the part of political and military authorities to reach agreement on certain fundamental issues, and indeed to face up to practical realities. Apart from that, the military approach as regards 'forces' has always been to ask Supreme Commanders to say what forces they want; their replies ignore the economic factor. It is not possible to produce the large forces that are demanded, and they could not be maintained over many years of cold war even if they were produced by a tremendous effort which reduced certain nations to bankruptcy.

We must not bury our heads in the sand, and ignore facts. We must get a realistic approach if we want to succeed.

The Realistic Approach

9. The new approach must be based on the following fundamental principles.
 A. <u>A global strategic concept is essential before we can plan the defence of the free world against aggression.</u>
It is ignominious to say that we can never reach agreement on this point. So far, it may not have been possible because agreement is sought <u>on every detail</u>.

We want a global strategic concept on the <u>broadest</u> lines; details can be tackled later as planning progresses. It is no answer to say that NATO is not geared to consider global problems. The problem <u>is</u> global; the solution must therefore be based on a global concept. For example, we need to obtain agreement as to the relative importance of the three main theatres of war: Europe, the Middle East, and the Far East.

Certain nations are faced with the inescapable need to reduce their active forces and they need to decide very soon which theatre must bear the brunt of the cuts. This is a decision which affects the USA, the UK, France, NATO, and the British Dominions.

B. <u>In military planning, do not let us get bogged down in discussions on imponderables.</u> We shall get no progress if we start by saying that the atomic bomb solves all our problems, or that we can win the war solely by strategic bombing, etc. That may, or may not, be the case. The effect of the atomic bomb will of course be very great; it may upset certain tactical conceptions of past days; it may enable us to redress the balance of power between ourselves and the Russians in both the strategical and tactical fields.

But none of the present claims about its use can be proved; they are imponderables. Also, we have reason to believe that the Russians have the bomb, and have the ability to deliver it.

We <u>can</u> say that our use of the atomic weapon will have a retarding effect on the enemy movement westwards; but we cannot say how great that retardation will be.

The correct concept is that of
'the hammer and the anvil'.

The hammer is the strategic air offensive. The anvil is the tactical land/air forces holding the enemy in the vital sectors of the 'free-world front'.

C. <u>NATO Commanders must be given the political aim and strategical policy, in some detail.</u>

It is not sufficient merely to say that the aim is to defend the peoples and territories of the NATO nations.

What areas are vital?

What are the broad principles on which the defensive organisation is to be built in order to achieve the aim?

And so on.

D. <u>NATO Commanders must be told by their political chiefs what forces they can have to achieve the aim.</u>

Up to date, NATO Commanders have been asked what they want and have consistently demanded the impossible.

The members of the Military Committee must take some responsibility for balancing what is desirable and what is possible. They know the facts and the problem; they must recommend to Governments what forces shall be given to Commanders in the field.

The possible forces must be given on a progressive build-up, and on a sure basis which can be relied on not to change as the years go by, e.g. it must be in full accord with the practical realities and economic possibilities.

E. <u>NATO Commanders must then be ordered to plan the conduct of their</u>

operations, in case of attack, in accordance with the forces they are told will be available in the opening stages of the war.

They must of course be told what reserve forces they can be given later, and when these can be expected.

These forces will no doubt be less than those they think they ought to have. This is always the case in war.

They must fight their battles accordingly.

An Example to Explain Para. 9 e.

10. As an example of Para. 9 E, I outline below the problem in the Central European Command.

11. Our potential enemy has great superiority initially on the ground and in the air; and science has given an aggressor the power to strike a heavy blow without much warning.

The Western nations will never be able to afford to keep 'in being' in peace the forces necessary to meet and defeat a heavy blow <u>on their frontiers</u>.

On purely military grounds we must fight as far East as we dare; we want the additional airfields, radar cover, and depth to air defence which this policy would give us. The point is, how far dare we go with our limited forces and to what extent can we push this policy without running the risk of defeat in detail.

In 1956, or in any foreseeable future, it will be sheer wishful thinking to imagine we can fight on the line of the Elbe. We will never have sufficient land forces 'in being' in peace to justify forcing a major conflict so far East. To do so would invite defeat in detail.

12. If the blow comes our active forces must survive, and they must somehow gain time for nations to spring to arms behind the shield.

They can do these two things only by fighting a withdrawal battle in the first instance. How far back they would have to withdraw would depend on a variety of factors, and planning to determine the answer must be realistic.

The underlying principle must be to cover the deployment of reserve forces and ensure their coming into the line of battle in good order; they must not be used to plug holes.

How far west we shall have to withdraw to unite with the reserve forces, and then fight and win a united battle, will disclose itself in the event.

But the final position must not be further back than astride the Rhine. <u>Once we let the enemy over the Rhine in strength, that is the end.</u>

Summary of the Crux of the Problem

13. Defence expenditure has in most cases reached the peak compatible with sound economies; in some cases the peak has been passed.

14. The 'long haul' policy must be applied to all aspects of defence. That means a long term plan (25 years) to balance security and economic stability.

15. Security means having sufficient active and potential strength to avoid losing a war.

16. If war comes, the superior war potential of the free nations must win in the end, provided they are not overwhelmed before they can develop their full war potential.

17. The crux of the problem, therefore, is how to gain that time at the minimum cost to the peace economies of the free nations, i.e. how to survive the initial onslaught.

18. The political/economic problem is:

'what must the free nations retain in their possession or control (territories, sea bases, air bases, routes, etc.) to survive in a fit state to build up their war potential'?

19. The military problem is:

'what is the best and cheapest means of making sure of retaining the answer to para 18 above'?

20. In producing the answer to the military problem, the main points for decision will be:

    (a) The proper balance between sea, air and land forces.
    (b) The right balance between active and reserve forces.
    (c) The correct balance between combat forces and logistic support.

Suggested Action to be Taken

21. First. The new approach must be put over to the President of the USA, and the Prime Minister of the UK. If they will back it whole-heartedly, the other nations will follow.

Second. The principals of the Standing Group (USA, UK, France) must meet and agree on an outline plan for the new approach.

Third. The Standing Group must be ordered to go to Paris and work out the plan in detail, in close cooperation with Lord Ismay and his Council of Permanent Deputies; this may take up to two months or more. The Standing Group must stay in Paris till an agreed plan is produced. We must get the Standing Group to Paris.

Fourth. Agreement is necessary as to what forces can be given to NATO Commanders – who must then do the best they can with those forces, planning their operations accordingly.

The Alternative

22. The only alternative is failure in the cold war, with all that such failure would entail.

Unless some action as is outlined above is taken, all our past efforts will be largely stultified.

Sir Winston S. Churchill to President Dwight D. Eisenhower
Prime Minister's Personal Telegram T.212/53
(Premier papers, 11/520)

26 June 1953

1. You will see from the attached medical report the reasons why I cannot come to Bermuda.[1] I am as bad as the French. We think the Conference should be postponed. Meanwhile Lord Salisbury could fly to Washington at any time convenient to you in the next fortnight and would put our point of view and establish that intimate Anglo-American contact which is the keystone of our policy.

2. Let me know your reactions. No announcement will be made till tomorrow, Saturday.

3. Thanks for your gainsaying telegram. Every good wish.

President Dwight D. Eisenhower to Sir Winston S. Churchill
Prime Minister's Personal Telegram T.213/53
(Premier papers, 11/520)

26 June 1953
Emergency
Deyou
Secret
No. 1366

Dear Winston, I am deeply distressed to learn your physicians have advised you to lighten your duties at this time and that consequently you will be unable to come to Bermuda for our talks.

I look upon this only as a temporary deferment of our meeting. Your health is of great concern to all the world and you must therefore bow to the advice of your physicians. With best wishes from your friend,

---

[1] The report read: 'The Prime Minister has had no respite for a long time from his very arduous duties and is in need of a complete rest. We have therefore advised him to abandon his journey to Bermuda and to lighten his duties for at least a month' (Moran, *The Struggle for Survival*, p. 437). The original draft, written by Lord Moran, specifically mentioned 'a disturbance of the cerebral circulation' as the primary reason for the mandatory period of rest.

Queen Elizabeth II to Sir Winston S. Churchill
(Gilbert, 'Never Despair', page 852)[1]

26 June 1953

I am so sorry to hear from Tommy Lascelles that you have not been feeling too well these last few days.

I do hope it is not serious and that you will be quite recovered in a very short time.

Our visit here is going very well and Edinburgh is thrilled by all the pageantry. We have been lucky in having fine weather, but I fear that it is now raining after a thunderstorm.

With all good wishes,
Yours very sincerely,[2]

Mary Soames: diary
('Clementine Churchill', page 435)

27 June 1953

Saw Papa – felt wretchedly gloomy. There are nurses now, and he cannot walk, or use his right hand much. In the afternoon he had a fall – but beyond the jolt – no damage.

Mary Soames: diary
('Clementine Churchill', page 435)

28 June 1953

Today he is gayer. . . . Lord M says there is a distinct improvement. It's so difficult to tell people when they ring up – Because when he's down – we're down – And when he's cheerful our spirits too, revive. . . . Mama is truly marvellous – tender, considerate, thinking of everyone's comfort. Unblinded by hope or fear – she teaches us all.

---

[1] This letter was handwritten.

[2] Churchill's response to the Queen is missing from the record. Lord Moran summarized it as follows: 'He showed me his reply which more than rose to the requirements of the occasion. Written only five days after his stroke, it seemed to me a remarkable document with its poise, proportion and sense of detachment. I took heart that he could do so much. In his letter he recalled the circumstances in which he had been stricken down; he spoke of his plight as he lay in bed as if it had happened to someone else; he told Her Majesty that he was not without hope that he might soon be about and able to discharge his duties until the autumn, when he thought that Anthony would be able to take over' (*The Struggle for Survival*, pp. 440–1).

Field Marshal Lord Montgomery to Sir Winston S. Churchill
(*Churchill papers, 2/143*)[1]

28 June 1953

My very dear Winston,

I am greatly distressed that you are not too fit. Do get well and return to steer the ship. There is much to be done as you will see from the paper I sent you on 26 June on the present state of the game in NATO.[2]

Can I come and see you at Chartwell? I could come next Sunday 5th July, or 7th or 8th July. Please let me know.

Cabinet: conclusions
(*Cabinet papers, 128/26*)

29 June 1953
Secret
12 noon
Cabinet Meeting No. 37 of 1953

1. The Chancellor of the Exchequer said that the Prime Minister was suffering from severe over-strain and was in need of a complete rest. His doctors had advised him to abandon his proposed journey to Bermuda and to lighten his duties for at least a month. The Bermuda Meeting had therefore been postponed, with the concurrence of the United States and French Governments.

During his absence the Prime Minister would continue to receive the more important official papers, and decisions on major questions of policy would be referred to him. The Minister of State would handle the day-to-day business of the Foreign Office, but would consult as required with the Lord President, who would assist the Prime Minister in the conduct of foreign policy. The Chancellor of the Exchequer would preside over the meetings of the Cabinet; and he and the Lord Privy Seal would share any questions in the House of Commons on matters of general Government policy.

The Cabinet –
  (1) Took note of the arrangements for the conduct of public business during the Prime Minister's absence.
  (2) Placed on record their deep regrets at the Prime Minister's absence and asked the Chancellor of the Exchequer to convey to him on their behalf an expression of their sincere sympathy and good wishes.

[. . .]

---

[1] This letter was handwritten
[2] Reproduced above (pp. 1131–6).

July 1953

Sir Winston S. Churchill to President Dwight D. Eisenhower
(Churchill papers, 6/3)

1 July 1953
Most Secret and Personal

My Dear Ike,

It was indeed kind of you to send me such a nice letter. I am so sorry to be the cause of upsetting so many plans. I had a sudden stroke which as it developed completely paralysed my left side and affected my speech. I therefore had no choice as I could not have walked with you along the Guard of Honour of the Welch Regiment complete with their beautiful white goat, whose salute you would I am sure have acknowledged. Four years ago, in 1949, I had another similar attack and was for a good many days unable to sign my name. As I was out of Office I kept this secret and have managed to work through two General Elections and a lot of other business since. I am therefore not without hope of pursuing my theme a little longer but it will be a few weeks before any opinion can be formed. I am glad to say I have already made progress. I have not told anybody these details which are for your eyes alone.

Meanwhile I am sure you and Foster will like Salisbury. He holds all my view on Egypt and the Sudan very strongly and I think his idea of bringing General Robertson with him next week is a very good one. I still hope that he and Hull and our two Ambassadors may jointly meet the Egyptian Dictator and that Agreement may be reached on the general basis of Case A. If we could say that you are satisfied with the arrangements for the security of the Base and with the discharge of our international duty, it would make a solution easier and better looking. I wish I could have talked to you about all this and could convince you that we are only doing our duty. However I have great confidence that Salisbury, whom I have known for so many years and admired ever since he resigned from Chamberlain's Government with Anthony Eden, will put our case to you in firm but agreeable terms.

I had never thought of a Four Power meeting taking place till after EDC was either ratified or discarded by the French and I thought November would be the sort of time. Adenauer and Bonn seem to be moving towards a united Germany and now they speak of a Four Power Conference with approval.

I thought Senator Wiley's[1] assumption that the Russian change of policy is only due to fear among a trembling remnant of gangsters and felons 'cringing in the Kremlin' goes too far in assessing a situation where these 'cringing' people could at any moment march to the Rhine in a month and to the sea in two months, and where if they do not wish to play the full stake themselves they can stir, bribe and arm the Chinese to throw Indo-China, Siam and Burma into immense disturbance. It is this feeling that makes me so anxious that before we reject all hope of a Soviet change of heart we should convince our peoples that we have done our best. After all, ten years of easement plus productive science might make a different world. I have no more intention than I had at Fulton or in 1945 of being fooled by the Russians. I think however there is a change in the world balance, largely through American action and re-armament, but also through the ebb of Communist philosophy, which justifies a cold-blooded, factual study by the free nations while keeping united and strong.

I am venturing to send you some papers about the Duke of Windsor which I hope you will find time to consider. Also I am today sending Bedell the chapters in my last volume which refer to you and to some divergencies of view between us. They will probably be published in October though whether I shall still remain in Office is unpredictable.

Clemmie sends greetings to you and Mamie. She was much looking forward to our excursion.

Sir Winston S. Churchill to General Walter Bedell Smith
(Churchill papers, 4/52)

1 July 1953

I was very glad to know that the President had asked you to examine on his behalf those parts of my final volume which make reference to him. We lived through much together in those years, and there is no one whose opinion I would value more on my treatment of the very few differences of judgment which arose between me and Eisenhower at that time.

There has been so much going on this summer that I have not been able to write to you earlier about this. But I now send you with this prints of the following chapters:

[1] Alexander Wiley, 1884–1967. Educated at Augsburg College, University of Michigan and University of Wisconsin Law School. District Attorney for Chippewa County, 1909–15. US Senator (Rep.) for Wisconsin, 1939–63. Chairman, Senate Judiciary Committee, 1947–9; Senate Foreign Relations Committee, 1953–5.

Book 1 Chapter IV Attack on the South of France
         Chapter VI Italy and the Riviera Landing
         Chapter VIII Alexander's Summer Offensive
         Chapter XIII Liberation of Western Europe
         Chapter XVII Counter-Stroke in the Ardennes
Book 2 Chapter V Crossing the Rhine
         Chapter VIII Western Strategic Divergences
         Chapter XI The Final Advance

These contain all that you need consider. Some of them make few references to the President, but I send you the Chapters as a whole so that you may see the context in which they occur. Others – namely Chapters IV, VI and VIII of Book 1 on 'Anvil' and Chapters VIII and XI on the closing phases of the campaign in Europe – deal with the larger strategic issues on which we were to some extent at variance. These differences cannot be wholly concealed or glossed over. They belong to history. And the final judgment on them will be made by the historians of the future. Meanwhile, I hope you will think that I have handled them fairly and with not intent to prejudge the verdict of history. These differences did not then disturb my respect and regard for the President, and the publication of this account of them will not, I think, lead others to misjudge or under-rate the confidence and mutual trust on which our current relationships are founded.

In some of these Chapters I have reproduced the text of messages sent to me by Eisenhower. I cannot, of course, publish these without his express consent. I look to you to draw his special attention to these and to ask whether he is willing that I should publish them.

For myself I cannot think that the publication of these Chapters will do any damage to the cause of Anglo-American relations which we all have so much at heart. But, if you have any doubt about any passage in them, please do not hesitate to express it.

PS. There is a point which you will both like in Chapter IV. Your relationship to your Chief and his to you was a model. See page 10.[1]

---

[1] In *The Second World War*, Churchill wrote of the British opposition to the South of France attack: 'Bedell Smith, on the contrary, declared himself strongly in favour of this sudden deflection of the attack, which would have all the surprise that sea-power can bestow. Eisenhower in no way resented the views of his Chief of Staff. He always encouraged free expression of opinion in council at the summit, though of course whatever was settled would receive every loyalty in execution' (*The Second World War*, vol. 6, *Triumph and Tragedy*, p. 61).

General George C. Marshall to Sir Winston S. Churchill
(Churchill papers, 2/144)[1]

1 July 1953

My dear Mr Prime Minister,

With a world flooding you with expressions of concern, affection and sympathy there is not much that I can add. I do want you to know that you are deeply in our thoughts very deeply and constantly.

I am the more concerned because I have seen you ill or convalescing and you are a hard patient to hold down to a careful regime. Please do be careful, a patient in the full meaning of the word. You are too vastly important to the world to take any risks.

Field Marshal Lord Montgomery: memorandum
(Premier papers, 11/370)

2 July 1953
Private and Top Secret

POLITICAL FACTORS AFFECTING THE PRESENT STATE OF THE GAME IN NATO

1. On the 26th of June I wrote a memorandum[2] on the present state of the game in NATO; that Paper dealt almost entirely with military factors.

In this memorandum I have attempted to deal with certain political factors as they appear to me.

The German Problem

2. The political and military situation in Europe is dominated by the problem of Germany.

Post-war Europe is the consequence of the meeting of the armies in the centre of Europe in the Spring of 1945.

Since that date we have had two Europes, East and West, and the dividing line goes through the middle of Germany. The result today is that a partitioned, dismembered and disarmed Germany lies in the middle of a great array of powers – North America, Europe and Russia. And Germany is herself a great power.

3. The present condition of Germany cannot be permanent. If it is to be permanent, then there can be no lasting peace in the world.

4. We therefore arrive at the conclusion that a united Germany is essential. There are many people in Germany today who are working for German

---

[1] This letter was handwritten.
[2] Reproduced above (pp. 1131–6).

unity. These realize that once Western Germany is armed and taken into the bosom of the Western Allies, German unity will be put back for a very long time. Indeed, my view is that once Western Germany is armed by us and integrated into the Western fold, a united Germany will be achieved only by fighting. Many Germans believe this, and they include Dr Adenauer – he told me himself.

5. The currents of opinion in Western Germany against rearmament are being heavily backed by the Russians. Dr Adenauer is most anxious about the whole matter.

We have definitely got to face the fact that we may not see the German contribution to Western Defence that we have been led to expect.

And we know that without a German contribution all our present military plans fall to the ground.

Our aim in the past

6. When it became clear in the 1945/46 that a united Germany was not possible as an immediate aim, the Allies initiated a policy of trying to get Western Germany integrated into the bosom of the West. Later, it was decided to arm the Western Germans

The Bonn Government agreed with this policy, while still retaining the long term aim of unification. The policy was – integration first, then work for unification, the whole being a German state incorporated in the Western bloc.

7. This aim still remains, and indeed it must. But it is now becoming doubtful if it will be achieved.

8. We may well find that we finish up with a unified and neutral Germany lying between the Communist East and the Democratic West.

If this should happened the free world would be in grave danger.

Possible Russian moves in the future

9. Russia will work hard for a unified and neutral Germany.

In order to bring this about and to get this Germany looking East, Russia may well offer to return to the German nation their former territories lying to the East of the Oder; this would mean sacrificing the Poles, which of course Russia would do.

10. It is not impossible that Russia may withdraw her forces from Eastern Germany altogether. The West would then be in a difficult position and might well have to evacuate Western Germany. There is no room in France or in the Low Countries for the American and British forces now in Germany and they would most probably have to be withdrawn to their own countries.

11. This would produce a very difficult situation politically and it would also necessitate a complete recasting of military plans for Western Defence. It would no longer be possible to base our defence plans on the barrier of the Rhine, and the defensive battle would have to be fought on the frontiers of the Western powers.

12. If these moves were carried out by Russia and the West was obliged to fall into line, the Communist East would be well placed in the cold war. The score would be 40–love against us.

What are we to do about it?

13. If the military subject matter of my paper of 26 June is combined with the political factors outlined in this present memorandum, it is clear that any soldier must view the future with grave misgiving.

If events should move in the general direction outlined above, all our work on military security during the past five years falls to the ground; we would have to begin again.

14. In all our previous calculations we have always, so far as I am aware, discarded as 'unthinkable' the idea of a neutral Germany.

I suggest that this unthinkable idea has now got to be regarded as a very distinct possibility.

15. We must use all political and diplomatic means at our disposal to get a neutral Germany looking Westwards and not Eastwards.

In this connection we must have something to offer.

We should concentrate on financial and economic considerations and on measures which will get a good flow of trade going between Germany and the West.

We must be skilful in propaganda, showing that we have something to offer and that there is a worth-while future for the Germans in linking their country to the West.

16. We must also begin a serious examination of the military implications of a neutral Germany – a sovereign state evacuated by our forces. This is a frightful problem and it has never even been considered.

The European Army concept would of course collapse. The sole reason for the concept was to make it practicable to get an armed Western Germany to take part in Western Defence, and this does not seem likely to happen.

17. So great would be the danger for the nations of Western Europe, that they would have to unite far more closely than they have found it possible to do in the past.

Their only hope would be unity and solidarity.[1]

The only alternative would be to disappear one by one into the Communist fold.

18. The attitude of the United Kingdom to the danger would require most careful consideration.

Without robust UK leadership, I doubt if the nations of Continental Europe would survive – which would be catastrophic for Britain.

---

[1] Churchill wrote in the margin here: 'And the Atom bomb'.

Conclusion

19. It is clear that the future holds possibilities which could have unpleasant results. We are going to face in the near future a period of far greater difficulty that we have experienced since 1945. Terrific problems are arising and they will need tough decisions.

The problems will need all the courage, wisdom, understanding and unity of the West – far greater than has been shown in the past.

In particular, United States and British leadership will call for great wisdom and great understanding.

Harold Macmillan: recollection
('Tides of Fortune', pages 516–18)

2 July 1953

On 2 July I had been summoned to Chartwell and arrived before dinner.

When I went into the sitting room, only Lord Moran was there. He told me that he was very satisfied – more than satisfied – at the progress made. But he feared that I might be rather shocked at PM's appearance, although he was much better in the last two days.

My first impressions were of astonishment that a man who had suffered such a calamity could show such gaiety and courage. During dinner, and until he went to bed, just after 11 p.m., his talk seemed much the same as usual. The atmosphere was not oppressive, but almost lively. Early in the dinner he said to me:

'You know, I have had a stroke. Did you know it was the second? I had one in 1949, and fought two elections after that.' He then described how he had gone from Strasbourg to Lord Beaverbrook's villa in the South of France and had had a seizure after bathing. He said his arm was almost restored and his leg much better. There were certainly times, at and after the dinner when I thought he was putting on an act – but it was a jolly brave one, anyhow.

Many times in the evening I was nearer to tears than he, for never had I more admired his extraordinary strength of will. Our talk covered a wide range:

We discussed the possibility of a Dissolution; death and Dr Johnson's fear of it; Buddhism and Christianity; Pol Roger – a wine, a woman and a horse; and many other topics.

But he soon turned to Germany and Europe:

He had read my papers and was grateful. His mind was not fully made up. He felt that now the time was getting on and we must await the German elections, and the French decision on EDC. But he did not despair. He hoped the Americans would agree to talk with the Russians.

He knew of course that Eden would not be fit to take up duty until the autumn, but he was awaiting his return in August with impatience.

After Churchill had gone to bed I learned the full story of this terrible week:

The attack was at the Gasperi dinner – on Tuesday June 23rd. It was slight and the PM was got off to bed. Lord Moran could not be got till the next morning. (Churchill) got to the Cabinet room without too much difficulty and got through the Cabinet meeting without disclosing what had happened. (I certainly noticed nothing beyond the fact that he was very white. He spoke little, but quite distinctly. I remember that he called to me 'Harold, you might draw the blind down a little, will you?' I also noticed that he did not talk very much.)

After the Cabinet, Churchill was still anxious to go to the House and answer questions, but he was dissuaded from doing so. The next day he left for Chartwell.

He got much worse – the clot seemed to grow and his arm and leg movements got worse. It seems, therefore, not to have been a sudden incapacitating paralytic stroke, but something which began fairly gently and grew steadily worse.

On Friday, Butler and Salisbury had gone to Chartwell and it was decided to issue the announcement on Saturday at 3 p.m. However, on the Saturday his condition deteriorated and the end seemed near.

Then he rallied – and has been getting steadily better since Monday or Tuesday. On Monday he was telephoning and so on. Today I could see his state – a sick but a very gay man.

Butler and Salisbury took a heavy responsibility in agreeing to what was undoubtedly the wish of the Prime Minister and the members of his family that the medical bulletin should be issued in a comparatively hopeful form. However, I felt that they were fully justified. It was only fair that Churchill should have a few weeks to make up his mind.

He has two courses. He can go on till October and then hand on to Eden. Or he can go on till October – and then, if he is all right – go on 'till the pub closes'. It is clear that the old man has this in mind. Out of chivalry to Eden and in repayment of all that he owes him, he must not hand over to Butler, unless he feels in conscience unable to serve the Queen efficiently in the essential work of the First Minister. To do this it is not necessary to walk or make speeches – I mean, for a few weeks.

Lord Salisbury to Members of the Cabinet
(*Premier papers, 11/425*)

3 July 1953
Secret
Cabinet Paper No. 187 of 1953

FOREIGN MINISTERS' MEETING IN WASHINGTON:
POLICY TOWARDS THE SOVIET UNION AND GERMANY
MEMORANDUM BY THE ACTING SECRETARY OF
STATE FOR FOREIGN AFFAIRS
General

1. My colleagues may like to have the following account of my general approach to the Washington meeting next week, with special reference to two of the main topics which I shall be discussing with Mr Dulles and M Bidault. These are (a) policy towards the Soviet Union, and (b) the problem of Germany and the connected problem of the strengthening of Western Europe. Our tripartite talks will also no doubt cover such important Far Eastern questions as the Korean peace settlement and the future of Indo-China and there will perhaps be some reference in tripartite meetings to the Austrian question. On these latter issues, however, our policies are clear and well known to my colleagues. I do not therefore propose to touch upon them in this paper. Mr Dulles wishes to discuss with me separately the question of Egypt and on this I am circulating a separate paper.

Object of Washington meeting

2. One of our main objectives is to maintain the initiative in foreign affairs flowing from the Prime Minister's speech of 11th May,[1] and to satisfy public opinion here and elsewhere that the unavoidable postponement of the Bermuda meeting of Heads of Governments will not delay our joint efforts to reduce international tension and to compose, or at least ease, existing differences. It is therefore my hope that we may at Washington, without pressing the Americans too hard at the moment, at least clear the way for a possible high-level meeting with the Soviet leaders, perhaps later in the year. An essential preliminary to such a meeting is, however, the coordination of Western, and more especially Anglo-American policy on the main questions of the day.

---

[1] Reproduced above (pp. 998–1010).

It is also most important to demonstrate to the world, and more especially to Europe, the continued unity and firmness of purpose of the three Western Powers, and their readiness to continue to make the sacrifices essential for the joint defence of the free world. If all goes well, this should be one of the main results of the Washington meeting.

Policy towards the Soviet Union

3. There is a broad agreement between the three Western Powers, and indeed between all the North Atlantic Treaty Powers, on the interpretation of Soviet policy, internal and external, since the death of Stalin. Internal changes, although perhaps less spectacular than some Soviet external moves, are likely to prove more important in the long run. They amount so far to more incentives and less repression for the Soviet population. Although the present 3 or 5-man Directorate seem to be in control, they lack collectively and individually Stalin's prestige, and the internal situation is clearly less stable than it was under his absolute authority. While we should not fall victims to wishful thinking, there are even possibilities of the situation developing in such a way as seriously to weaken, or at any rate to modify the character of, the Soviet régime. In the external field there have been many steps to reduce the international tension, although without affecting basic Soviet long-term policies. These steps can be explained by (i) a desire on the part of the new rulers to acquire popularity and to establish their internal position free from external worries; (ii) fear of America (the atom bomb, industrial potential, and possible impatience); and (iii) a desire to weaken and divide the Western world. The most important gesture so far has been Russian support for an armistice in Korea, but broadly speaking these gestures (for list see Annex), although significant, do not yet amount to much more than 'leaving off doing things which we have not been doing to them'. It is by no means clear that the present Soviet rulers are anxious or ready for serious negotiations on current problems; but it is to our advantage on grounds of policy and public relations alike to test out what may prove to be a new situation in Russia. At the best we might over a period obtain a settlement of some problems; if no more, we might prolong the present relaxation in international tension and we might well learn more about the real intentions and capabilities of the present Soviet leaders.

Anglo-American differences about the Soviet Union

4. The main difference between ourselves and the American Administration is that the Americans, no doubt partly influenced by their different domestic situation, have hitherto wanted to let events behind the Iron Curtain develop further before embarking upon any high-level talks. There also seems now to be a new and more dangerous American tendency, which has its roots in the Republican election campaign and was illustrated in a recent statement by Mr Dulles, to interpret the situation behind the Iron Curtain as already

very shaky and therefore to advocate new although unspecified measures to encourage and even promote the early liberation of the satellite countries. It is my intention to resist American pressure for new initiatives of this kind. A policy of pinpricks is calculated to exasperate the Russians and is most unlikely to help the unhappy peoples of the occupied countries. The last thing we want to do is to bait the Russian and satellite Governments into taking violent measures against them. The growing strength of the West is likely to be the best stimulus to the morale of the subject peoples. We must of course keep the spirit of freedom alive in Eastern Europe, but we should also counsel prudence and restraint. In this, judging by his Press Conference this week, we should have the support of the President. It is also my intention to try to persuade Mr Dulles that high-level talks with the Russians, of the exploratory and informal character advocated by the Prime Minister, held in due time and after proper preparation might do good and could do no harm, and that it would be a great mistake to take the responsibility upon ourselves of disappointing public expectations about such talks. It should be possible to count on French support on both these issues.

5. We must, of course, bear in mind the continuing danger of a highly armed Russia, which is moreover relevant also to Mr Dulles' policy of pinpricks. The Soviet Government never disarmed after the war, and in the years between 1945 and now have succeeded in modernizing the Soviet forces to a point where they rival the forces of the West in quality, and greatly outstrip them in number. The Russian industrial potential has kept pace with this military development. It is possible that Stalin's successors may decide to ease up on the pace of military production and industrial development, but even a significant easing up would still leave Russia with an expanding economy and advanced armaments programme. We must thus count on being faced by a clearly powerful military threat. It would be a mistake to suppose that, if the Soviet Government made some adjustments in their external policy, they would automatically go over to a policy of disarmament. It follows that, even if a *détente* in relationships could be produced as a result of a four-Power meeting, it would still be necessary for the Western Powers to maintain a policy of collective defence and rearmament. In this view, we should be supported by the Americans.

Germany: the key problem in Soviet relations with the West

6. The Soviet attitude on the Austrian Treaty, which President Eisenhower last April coupled with Korea as test cases of Soviet intentions, suggests that no real progress can be made in easing relations with the Soviet Union in Europe without a discussion of the German problem. Public opinion in Europe as well as in Germany will not easily be satisfied unless this has at least been attempted. The basic approach of the Soviet Union and of the Western Powers to Germany has been not dissimilar. Each side has been equally afraid

of the resurgence of a strong Germany allied to, or likely to fall under the influence of, the other party. There is also a fear, certainly held in France, and shared by the Russians, of the re-emergence of a strong, independent and reunified Germany. The main struggle between the Soviet Union and the Western Powers since the final breakdown of the Potsdam arrangements in 1947–48 has therefore been for future control of Germany. The three Western Powers, in occupation of nearly three-quarters of the area and the populations of post-Potsdam Germany, and with a successful record of political and economic rehabilitations behind them, have so far had much greater success than the Russians. But this success is still precarious and too dependent upon the personality of the German Federal Chancellor, Dr Adenauer.

Alternative Soviet policies towards Germany

7. There are broadly two possible alternative Soviet policies towards German – (i) defensive, and (ii) expansionist. The defensive policy hitherto followed has been to write off the Federal Republic as an outpost of Western capitalism and to strengthen Soviet control of East Germany as another satellite State, while maintaining Soviet troops on the Elbe and keeping a potential stranglehold upon the Western Allies in Berlin. The alternative expansionist Soviet policy would be to abandon the Communist regime in Eastern Germany, allow genuinely free elections and gamble upon the resulting all-German Government being weaned away from association with the West in the hope that it would sooner or later fall under Russian domination. While we must always be prepared for a Soviet move from the first to the second policy, there has been no sign so far that the Russians are in fact prepared to make what they must regard as a major gamble, since they would then be running the risk that they would merely have added another 18 million anti-Communist Germans to the Federal Republic and so to the strength of the West. They would also have set a dangerous precedent of retreat in Eastern Europe. The recent rioting in Berlin and in the Soviet Zone has been a warning to them of the danger of an apparently more liberal policy.

Western policies towards Germany

8. United Kingdom policy, which is part of a tripartite policy conducted in concert with the Americans and with the French through the agency of the Allied High Commission, has been to work for the earliest possible association of the Federal Republic with Western Europe with the aims of (i) ending the old Franco-German feud, (ii) providing the essential German addition to the Western defence system, and (iii) preventing the revival of dangerous German nationalism. This policy is embodied in the Bonn Conventions and the European Defence Community (EDC) Treaty of May, 1952. It is fully supported by the present German Chancellor and a majority in the Federal Republic. As

the Prime Minister made clear on 11th May and subsequently, it remains our firm policy that these Treaties, which we ourselves have ratified, should come into force at the earliest possible date. While working for this immediate aim, we also have the long-term aim of reuniting the Soviet Zone with the Federal Republic. Any other policy would forfeit German goodwill, run counter to historic facts and confront us indefinitely with the dangers of Russian troops on the Elbe and of our own precarious position in Berlin. Reunification can however only be achieved safely and in conditions of freedom on the basis of genuinely free elections throughout the four Zones of Germany followed by the formation of a free, all-German Government with whom to negotiate a peace treaty. This policy, laid down in the Allied note to Moscow of 23rd September, 1952, has the support of all German parties other than the Communists, as was shown by the Bundestag resolution of 10th June, 1953. This dual policy was most recently set out in the Prime Minister's message to the Federal Chancellor of 24th June.[1] The exchange of notes with the Russians in 1952 showed that, while opposed to the association of the Federal Republic with the West, the Russians were not prepared to offer terms for German reunification acceptable to the West or to the Germans themselves.

Dr Adenauer's position and policy

9. A relatively new factor with the German situation is that, although the Federal Republic remains technically occupied, Dr Adenauer's Government is now de facto a partner of the three Western Allies with an effective voice in our counsels and with the acknowledged right to constant consultation on German questions. The admitted success of Dr Adenauer's internal policies and the progress he has made in changing Germany's international status and in the field of Western integration (the Coal and Steel Community, the European Defence Community and the European Political Community) would normally have assured his success in the elections at the end of August. It is a major United Kingdom and Western interest that he should succeed. The possibility of four-Power negotiations or of some new Soviet move for German unity, coupled with the electric effect of the recent risings in East Berlin and throughout the Soviet Zone, have however introduced a dangerous element of uncertainty into the German electoral scene. Hence the necessity for the reaffirmation of our existing policies in the Prime Minister's message to Dr Adenauer of 24th June, which was fully endorsed by President Eisenhower and the French Prime Minister. It is, I suggest, of great importance to Dr Adenauer that these policies should be reaffirmed yet once more and that Western unity on that basis should be openly proclaimed after the Foreign Ministers' meeting in Washington. Since the German Socialists are campaigning against Dr Adenauer on a programme of early four-Power talks

---

[1] Reproduced above (pp. 1128–9).

for German reunification, it is essential that any four-Power talks should be delayed at least until after the German elections have been completed in early September. This view will no doubt be strongly held by the American Government, and we can agree with them on it.

Uncertainties in Europe

10. The existing uncertainties, to which I have referred above as being especially dangerous in Germany owing to the forthcoming elections, are also widespread throughout Western Europe. The EDC and similar schemes for European integration are by no means universally popular in France or elsewhere. In France there has long been a fear that Western Germany as a partner would be likely to dominate the Six-Power Communities in Western Europe, and this fear will no doubt be intensified if there is any prospect that the Federal Republic is likely to expand into a reunified Germany. Progress therefore is being held up. France in particular is waiting to see where four-Power talks will take place and, if so, whether they will result in German reunification, and the whole momentum towards Western European integration and towards the strengthening of the Western defensive system through EDC has for the time being been lost. The key to this situation is in France, and we and the Americans must make every effort to bring the French to accept their responsibilities by ratifying the EDC Treaty as soon as possible in the autumn. (We ourselves have done all we can to this end through undertakings of United Kingdom political and military association which have been found acceptable by all six EDC Powers.) As explained in paragraph 11 below, much the best position from which to negotiate with the Russians would be with the EDC Treaty in force. But in the present state of French opinion, it may well be that we shall fail to get any definite undertakings out of the French Government. In that case the momentum in Western Europe will probably not be regained until a real effort has been made by the West to hold four-Power talks and perhaps not until such talks have actually taken place, unless it can clearly be shown that the Russians have prevented them. We and the Americans would then have to consider whether four-Power talks should not be held before ratification of the EDC Treaty. Clearly, however, they should not take place until well after the German elections.

11. It would be greatly preferable if we could embark on four-Power talks with a united Europe at our back and with Western Germany safely anchored to Western Europe, i.e. <u>after</u> the EDC Treaty has been ratified. The chief Soviet objective at four-Power talks will be to undermine European unity, hold up the integration of Germany into the West, and prevent the ratification of the EDC Treaty. The ideal programme therefore would provide that the four-Power talks would only take place after the German elections have been held, and after the EDC Treaty has been ratified. As a matter of tactics it would be wise to announce to the world at the conclusion of the three-Power

meeting that this is what we are aiming at, even though we may privately have reservations about the possibility of attaining it.

Possible alternative policies towards Germany

12. While the French will argue for delaying ratification of the EDC Treaty and the Americans for a more 'positive' policy towards the liberation of Eastern Germany and of Eastern Europe generally, I do not expect to find Mr Dulles or M Bidault in disagreement with the continuation of our present German policies as summarized in paragraph 8 above which also have the full support of Dr Adenauer. It is, of course, always open to the Russians to accept our offer of September 1952 and to take their chance on genuinely free elections throughout Germany. If they do so, we shall clearly have to agree to discussions, as we and Dr Adenauer would otherwise lose all German support and support of public opinion in many other countries. But we should be careful to negotiate on the basis clearly laid down last year after the very thorough exchange of notes with the Russians, i.e. that the first problem is how to organize free elections, the second to hold such elections, the third the formation of a free all-German Government, and only then could we proceed to the negotiation of a peace treaty with that Government, which would involve such major questions as frontiers and the withdrawal of Soviet and Western troops. We should also have to maintain the position we have firmly held hitherto that a reunited Germany must be free to associate itself with the West.

13. It may, however, be argued that there must be some alternative to our present German policy of anchoring the Federal Republic firmly within the Western world through the EDC as a prelude to the eventual reunification of Germany, which can after all only be achieved in agreement with the Soviet Union. There are indeed two alternatives:

(1) direct German membership of the North Atlantic Treaty Organisation (NATO). It is however entirely premature to propose this at this stage. It is not desired by Dr Adenauer himself and it would be even less acceptable to France than the EDC solution. We hold it however in reserve should the EDC solution finally fail.

(2) the neutralisation of a reunited Germany. This would no doubt be the easiest way to reach agreement with the Soviet Union. But apart from the majority of the German people it would be highly dangerous for the West. A neutralised Germany with no ties with the West would, if disarmed, soon fall a prey to Russia. If armed, as proposed last year by the Russians, it would soon fall back into the traditional German policy of balancing East against West, or, still worse into a modern variant of Rapallo under which the Germans would attempt to regain their lost Eastern territories by aligning themselves with the Soviet Union. Before long such a Germany might be little better than a Soviet satellite and the balance of power

JULY 1953 1155

in Europe would have been fatally shifted to our disadvantage. We should have lost the essential German contribution to the NATO and Western defence. American troops, removed from Germany, would soon be out of Europe altogether. We could only contemplate such a solution if all else had failed and we were compelled to rely for our future self-preservation upon our confidence in the good intentions of a Soviet Union, which had thus become the actual or potential master of the whole of Europe.

Consultation with our Allies

14. It is clearly important to carry with us not only the Germans but also our NATO allies, and more especially the inner circle of the Brussels Treaty Powers. In addition, some degree of consultation is also desirable with Yugoslavia, if only to prevent the fear that the three Great Powers are deciding their affairs over their heads. I intend therefore to concert with Mr Dulles and M Bidault the most effective methods to ensure such consultation.

Conclusion

15. I hope therefore that my colleagues will agree that our major objectives at Washington should be:
   (1) to confirm and reaffirm publicly existing policies towards Germany;
   (2) to continue to support Dr Adenauer in his pursuits of these policies;
   (3) to press the French to go ahead as fast as possible with ratification of the EDC and Bonn Treaties, as providing (a) the safest policy towards Germany, and (b) the necessary basis of strength from which to negotiate effectively with the Soviet Union; and to reaffirm publicly after the Washington meeting that this is our policy;
   (4) to discourage Mr Dulles from any dangerous new initiatives intended to provoke early liberation movements behind the Iron Curtain as distinct from continued support and encouragement of a spirit of independence and resistance to Communism;
   (5) to agree upon the necessity for maintaining and strengthening the military defences of the West, more especially through the NATO; this also needs reaffirmation;
   (6) to persuade the Americans to keep the door open for high-level and informal four-Power talks.

Sir Winston S. Churchill to Lord Salisbury and Sir William Strang
(Premier papers, 11/373)

6 July 1953

In his masterly and comprehensive survey of the European scene Lord Salisbury has arrayed many facts with which I am in full agreement. I wish, however, to assign prominence and priority to some of the objects we have in view, though, alas, not in hand.

EDC is our immediate policy. The French have succeeded in delaying for several years the beginning of a German Army by this elaborate logical device. Its ratification must be the prelude to the holding of a four-Power Conference, though not to the declaration of our desire that one should be held.

Will the French ratify EDC and if so when. I have heard they would like to delay it by one device and another until next year, when new reasons for delay may be discovered. In my opinion we and the Americans should demand ratification before the end of October. We should warn them that if this is refused or does not occur we shall propose a new NATO Treaty in which no Power would have a veto on the inclusion of a German contingent. This would be formidable pressure on the French and is the most powerful lever at our disposal to induce them to comply and thus abandon the method of taking everything and giving nothing which they have followed since their rescue.

With either EDC or a reformed NATO (with or without France's formal adhesion) we should be in a far better position to talk to Russia than if the present indefinite delay continued. The prospect of a substantial German Army as a part of NATO, through EDC is a profound and legitimate anxiety in Russia. Let us therefore, as our first aim, persuade the French to ratify EDC in October. This could and should be coupled with a declaration of willingness for a four-Power Conference before the end of the year.

These are objectives which we can certainly pursue at Washington without serious division of British opinion. Whether we can achieve them now or not is doubtful; at any rate we must try. If the French remain recalcitrant we should not hesitate to make a joint declaration with the United States that we will meet Russia in conference. If the United States refuses we should reserve our freedom. A friendly conversation between Great Britain and Soviet Russia, even if isolated, would be watched with intense interest and hope and might well lead to an easement in the world tension. Anyhow there could be no meeting before the end of the German Elections.

Whatever happens about EDC or NATO, and however Adenauer fares at the Elections we shall have to face very soon the problem of German unity. A pregnant paper has been written on this subject by Field Marshal Lord Montgomery. Nothing will turn the German people from unity and Adenauer himself, although a loyal partisan of EDC, is being forced every day to emphasize it more. However the Election goes all the German Parties will be ardent

for unity. This is surely coming upon us and coming all the quicker from a French desertion of EDC. We must face the fact that there will always be 'a German problem' and 'a Prussian danger'. I am of opinion that a united, independent Germany would not become allies of Soviet Russia. Three facts stand forth –
1. The character of the German people rises superior to the servile conditions of the Communist world.
2. They have had a potent object in the fate of the Eastern Zone and millions of witnesses will exist for many years to testify to the horrors of Communist rule, even exercised by Germans over Germans.
3. The hatred which Hitler focused against Bolshevism is strong in German hearts.

The eyes of Germany are turned against Soviet Russia in fear, hate and intellectual antagonism. For France there is only contempt and pity. What is Alsace-Lorraine compared with Silesia and the Western Neisse in Russian hands? <u>I am sure that Germany will not, in the next 20 years, join with Russia against the West or lose her moral association with the Free Powers of Europe and America.</u> That, at any rate, is the basis from which we ought to consider our terrible problem.

The Russians have, however, certain very powerful bribes to offer. First, the unity of Germany through the release of the Eastern Zone after free elections. Second, a readjustment of the frontiers at the expense of Poland. We shall need all our skill so to steer events that we get as much credit for any future advantages Germany may gain as do the Soviets.

Happily, there is no need to initiate any detailed discussion of the future of Germany at Washington and no hope of reaching agreement upon it. The Americans no doubt contemplate in their hearts that in a war between the United States and the Soviets they would make a firm and lasting alliance with the German people. What must not be forgotten by us, and will I hope be remembered by the Soviets, is the safety of Russia against another Hitlerite invasion. It is along these lines of thought that, without prejudice to other things I have set down, our minds might adventurously travel. Of course, the solution is a real UNO where all are bound to aid the victim and attack the aggressive invader. Here is of course the supreme solution, a true World Instrument of peace. For the present I have only two practical points in Europe – the early ratification of EDC followed by a four-Power Conference. The whole policy being simultaneously announced.

President Dwight D. Eisenhower to Sir Winston S. Churchill
(Premier papers, 11/1074)

6 July 1953 The White House
Secret and Personal

Dear Winston,

I shall, of course, keep completely secret the character of your illness. I am cheered to note that you are very hopeful, but of course I agree that your doctors must make the final judgement on the question of your return to full duty. My prayers are with you.

While I have met Lord Salisbury only once or twice – and then very briefly – I am quite sure that I shall come to share your high opinion of him. Everything I have ever heard about him leads me to such a conclusion. Foster knows him and has the highest regard for him.

In the Egyptian affair we, of course, always have wanted to obtain a solution that would conform as nearly as possible to Case A. However, we have recognized the probability that some concessions would have to be made to Egyptian pride and spirit of nationalism. And so, in our thinking we established Case B as representative of a minimum position, and have hoped for an agreement that would be somewhere in between these two cases – as near, of course, to Case A as possible.

We shall certainly be ready to talk to Lord Salisbury about the matter. In laying out a program looking toward a settlement, we earnestly believe it would be a grave error to ignore the intensity of Egyptian popular feeling. Dictators can never afford to cease striving for popularity; I think that the methods by which they normally come to power inspire them with a feeling of great personal insecurity. In Egypt, if Naguib thought that the population wanted him to be conservative and reasonable, we would have no trouble whatsoever. As it is, I think he feels he is sitting on a lid that covers a seething desire to throw out every foreigner in the country. In other words, he believes that any formula found for the solution of this problem must have appealing features for the Egyptian population – otherwise he will find himself happy indeed to join another Egyptian exile, now in Italy.

It is possible that whatever difference there may be in our respective approaches to this whole Egyptian affair springs out of our differing estimates of the flexibility that Naguib feels is available to him in negotiation. We believe that he is very definitely a prisoner of local circumstances of which the most important is Egyptian nationalism, and consequently he will act and react in accordance with them.

I note with interest your thought about a four-power meeting and French action on the EDC. If the French Parliament should reject it, I cannot possibly overemphasize the adverse effect such action would have on public opinion in this country. Our people and our Congress are getting exceedingly tired of aid programs that seem to them to produce no good results. They believe earnestly that only closer union among the nations of Western Europe, including Western Germany, can produce a political, economic and military climate in which the common security can be assured. Personally I think our people are right on this point – but the important fact is that they most earnestly believe they are right. As a consequence, if they find their judgments and convictions completely ignored by the principal NATO country in Western Europe, it will indeed take genius to keep our people from washing their hands of the whole affair. To my mind that kind of result would be catastrophic for us all.

Not for one moment do I believe that I am overstating the adverse results in this country that would follow failure of the EDC to achieve French and other Western European endorsement. On the contrary, we are already suffering because of dilatory tactics heretofore pursued in the region. Soon we are to present to the Congress a request for appropriations to support the Mutual Security arrangements in Western Europe, and we are going to have a lot of trouble with those who believe that Europe has no intention of unifying or of adopting EDC.

I have sent messages both to Holland and Belgium urging early ratification so as to bring additional pressure on France. I have done this not because I want to interfere in anybody else's business, but because I know what it means in this country. This also is the reason why I continue to ask every personal and official friend that I think I have in Europe to get in and help. Possible alternatives to NATO's and EDC's success are too alarming to contemplate. If this country should return, no matter how reluctantly, to a policy of almost complete isolationism, or at the very least, to a 'Western hemisphere only' philosophy of security and interest, then Heaven help us all.

As to your comments on some of our Senatorial speeches, you should be no more disturbed by what some of our extremists say from the public platforms of this country, than we are by what your Mr Bevan occasionally directs at us or at the world situation. Both Foster and I are determined to give the Soviets every possible opportunity to convince the world they have had a change of heart. Moreover, we do not believe you are fooled by the Russians. Finally, no one would be more anxious than we to develop any practical arrangement that would lead toward easing of tensions and a measurable degree of disarmament. But such an arrangement must, above all else, carry its own guarantee of good faith and fulfilment.

Some days ago I replied to your question about the Windsor papers. I brought the matter to the attention of Bedell, who, as you will recall, was with me when I first came into contact with the affair. He shares my convictions expressed in my former letter, and I am hopeful that the matter will be settled with decency, justice and finality.

Again my assurances that we are looking forward to our talks with Salisbury, while we continue to hope for your early return to health and vigor.

Anthony Nutting to Sir Winston S. Churchill
(Premier papers, 11/427)

7 July 1953

My dear Prime Minister,

Thank you for your letter of July 5 enquiring how your letter about EDC was received at Strasbourg.

Unfortunately the general political debate was postponed at the last minute so that I had no opportunity of referring to the letter in a speech. I did however send a copy of it to each Conservative Member of our Delegation. The results of this were varied in effect, though in all cases salutary. Those who want the EDC to go through were encouraged and those who do not were somewhat more restrained than usual in giving vent to their views.

I am most grateful to you for taking this trouble.

Sir Winston S. Churchill to General George C. Marshall
(Churchill papers, 2/144)

9 July 1953

My dear Friend,

Thank you so much for your letter,[1] which touched me a great deal. I am now getting on well, and I am really resting at Chartwell, and doing as little work as possible.

I hope all goes well with you. It was most agreeable to see you again, and I trust it will not be too long before your next visit.

Sarah Beauchamp to Sir Winston S. Churchill
(Churchill papers, 1/50)[2]

9 July 1953

Darling Papa,

This is just to tell you how much I love you. I know you know but I have to tell you again. It is in these moments when you feel down that you are never more magnificent.

I never realise more fully the genius of your spirit than when I see you in a 'tough spot,' and see your wisdom and humour and philosophy, and above all your command of the situation. It helps me to be near you. I wish I could do something more than just love – to help you regain completely your strength. But it is joyful and merciful to know that you will. I know it is slow – be patient.

[1] Reproduced above (p. 1143).
[2] This letter was handwritten.

The improvement in the 8 days I have been home has been miraculous. Try not to fret – I know that although you have laid aside your work – you have much on your mind but remember the most important thing is your health – remember how deeply you are loved and needed not only by the world – but by us – including your loving and devoted Mule.[1]

[Drawing of a mule]

Anthony Eden to Sir Winston S. Churchill
(Churchill papers, 2/216)[2]

10 July 1953

Rhode Island

My dear Winston,

It has been most heartening to hear steadily improving reports of your progress from Jock & Harold Macmillan – I look forward to hearing the latest news from Bobbety tomorrow. Clarissa and I have felt wretchedly far away during this time and I want so much to get home and to see you again.

However, we are dutifully fulfilling our period of convalescence here, but have decided, since doctor approves, to fly home at the end of it, leaving here on 25th.

This is an ideal place in which to gain strength. We are and have been alone in the house, except for Nicholas who stayed a few days before returning to Canada & home, which he will reach before us. We have contrived – or rather Clarissa has – to keep out of local social life, and our only visitors to date have been the Giffords who spent the day with us yesterday, and Roger Makins and his wife who were staying near by.

The weather is perfect; it seems to rain only at night. We walk in the garden in the morning, and visit the beach in the evening when there is nobody there. Clarissa swims and I paddle.

But I am really gaining strength, even though weight takes a little time to come back.

The Beria development is intriguing.[3] Cannot be injurious to us anyway, as far as I can see, which is not very far in this obscure scene.

---

[1] Churchill replied: 'Darling Sarah. I have thought very much about you though we are still very far apart. Looking forward so much to seeing you at Christmas.'

[2] This letter was handwritten.

[3] On June 26, Beria was forced out of office in a scheme orchestrated by Nikita Khrushchev, who had secured the support of other powerful figures in the Party. Malenkov announced on July 10 that he had been 'dismissed'. In fact, he had been arrested on June 26. On Dec. 23 he was tried by a special session of the Supreme Court of the Soviet Union with no defence counsel and no right of appeal. Found guilty of treason, terrorism and counter-revolutionary activity dating back to 1919, he was sentenced to immediate execution. According to the widow of the general who carried out the execution, Beria pleaded on his knees for mercy. He was shot through the forehead by Gen. Pavel Batitsky, who had to stuff a rag into Beria's mouth to silence him. (See Richard Rhodes, *Dark Sun, The Making of the Hydrogen Bomb*, New York, 1995, p. 523.)

Clarissa is well and I think really enjoying herself here, after trying the trying vigil of Boston. Love from us both to you and Clemmie, and with luck we shall see you in about a fortnight's time.

Meanwhile every good wish.

Lord Salisbury to Foreign Office
(Premier papers, 11/425)

10 July 1953　　　　　　　　　　　　　　　　　　　　　　　Washington DC
Immediate
Secret
No. 1460

Informal tripartite talks began this afternoon under the impact of the news of Beria's fall. While Mr Dulles and M Bidault were inclined to speculate unduly upon its exact significance, we all reached the satisfactory conclusions formulated by Mr Dulles himself:
(1) that recent events in the Soviet Union and satellite countries did not call for any alteration of existing policies. They had proved their worth, were producing dividends and should be pursued.
(2) That while we must keep hope alive among the satellite populations by propaganda and example, we should not provoke revolt and should rely upon spontaneous action. Both accepted my suggestion that our methods should be
   (a) The evidence of the growing strength and unity of the West and
   (b) Restatement of our aims and principles, and that we should avoid pinpricks and irritants.

2. Speaking after Mr Dulles and M Bidault, I explained our general programme for reaffirming and vigorously pursuing existing Allied policies towards Germany, NATO and the EDC with a view to an eventual high level, informal Four Power meeting after
   (a) the German Elections
   (b) a possible high level Three Power meeting and
   (c) entry into force of the Bonn and EDC Treaties
and expressed the strong hope that all this would be clearly reflected in the Washington communiqué. Recent events, such as Beria's fall, seemed to strengthen rather than weaken the case for carrying out this programme.

3. M Bidault, while showing no enthusiasm for a Four Power meeting and emphasising its difficulties and dangers, argued strongly that no progress was possible on the EDC until French Parliamentary and public opinion had been convinced that no other solution was possible. He, therefore, favoured an early Four Power meeting with a clear time limit and on a specific agenda restricted

to the terms for German reunification set out in the Allied Note of September 23, 1952 and the Bundestag Resolution of June 10 last. His suggestion clearly was that such a meeting would fail and that he could then secure French ratification of the EDC.

4. Mr Dulles had meanwhile listed the subjects on which practical decisions were required in Washington as follows:
   (1) Estimate of developments in the Soviet Union;
   (2) Attitude to unrest behind the iron curtain;
   (3) German reunification and its bearing on the German elections;
   (4) An Austrian treaty;
   (5) The EDC;
   (6) A high level Four Power meeting perhaps preceded by another Three Power meeting;
   (7) Method and substance of consultation with our associates (e.g. NATO and Germany).

When pressed for his reactions to my programme for a high level meeting and to a statement on this in the communiqué he indicated that his final view on this would depend on whether the three Western allies had first reached agreement upon policy towards Germany. Without this any Four Power meeting would be dangerous.

5. I was encouraged by this as subsequent exchanges, to which I contributed a full statement of our views on German integration with the West and on eventual German reunification, did not suggest any basic differences between us on this key problem. There was also agreement that we should issue a declaration from Washington solemnly reaffirming our German policies. We shall consider tomorrow drafts which Mr Dulles is circulating, and also a letter delivered to him today from Dr Adenauer for consideration by the three Foreign Ministers advocating an invitation to the Russians to attend Four Power talks on the basis of our proposed programme for German reunification. Text will be telegraphed separately.

5. (sic) Mr Dulles suggested, and M Bidault and I agreed, that if such a Four Power meeting took place Austria as well as Germany would have to be on the agenda.

6. Today's meeting closed with a brief discussion of the EDC, which will be completed later. M Bidault argued very strongly that, while his Government was firmly behind the EDC and hopeful of securing the necessary Parliamentary majority this autumn, any attempt to secure its passage now before a Four Power meeting had been held on German reunification would be doomed to failure. I pointed out the obvious danger of meeting the Russians with the EDC still ahead of us, as they would concentrate all the discussion upon this. There was no alternative solution to the EDC and I could not, at this stage, accept the argument that EDC ratification must come after Four Power talks. Mr Dulles definitely supported me, pointing out that the whole prestige of

President Eisenhower and his Administration was committed to the EDC solution. Any failure would have most unfortunate effects upon Congress and upon American public opinion. He and Mr Stassen had earlier warned M Bidault that the Foreign Aid Bill shortly to be reported back after consultations between the House and the Senate would allow the appropriations for the six EDC countries to go forward only on condition that the President would have to resubmit the whole matter to Congress if there were no EDC in existence when the material aid came out of the pipeline some eighteen to twenty four months hence. The Administration had had to work hard even for this concession as the original proposal had been to freeze the money until the EDC was in being. Mr Dulles did not, however, come out strongly against a preliminary Four Power meeting on Germany, more especially as this proposal now has Dr Adenauer's endorsement, and in subsequent private conversation with me he expressed sympathy for M Bidault's parliamentary difficulties.

7. Mr Dulles informed us that Dr Blankenhorn[1] had arrived in Washington today without American agreement or invitation. We all agreed that his mission was a mistake and was embarrassing for us as no NATO countries are similarly represented here behind the scenes. We agreed also that our consultations with Dr Adenauer should be carried out through the Allied High Commission and not through Dr Blankenhorn.

8. Our discussions on all these subjects are to continue tomorrow. Today's meeting should, therefore, be regarded as a preliminary exchange of views of an informal nature with no decisions reached or hard positions taken up by any of us. While undoubted progress was made, there are three very real difficulties before us:

(a) the idea of a Four Power conference with a specific German agenda favoured by M Bidault, Mr Dulles and Dr Adenauer is a different thing from the exploratory high level meeting we had in mind;

(b) the timing of such a conference would presumably be shortly after the German elections and would squeeze out a high level Three Power meeting of the Bermuda type;

(c) M Bidault will clearly find it very hard to meet us on the ratification of EDC as a necessary preliminary to talks with the Russians.

I should, however, prefer to postpone expressing any considered views on all this until we have reflected further and further and had further discussions tomorrow.

[...]

---

[1] Herbert Blankenhorn, 1904–91. Entered German Foreign Office, 1929. Joined Nazi Party, 1938. Head of Foreign Office, 1943. Head of Political Div., West German Foreign Office, 1950–5. West German Ambassador to NATO, 1955–8; to France, 1958–63; to Italy, 1963–5; to UK, 1965–70.

Lord Salisbury to Foreign Office
(*Premier papers, 11/419*)

11 July 1953   Washington DC
Immediate
Secret
No. 1461

My telegram No. 1460, paragraph 5: Tripartite Talks in Washington. Following is text of Dr Adenauer's letter.

'The Foreign Ministers' meeting in Washington will deal primarily with the question of Germany.

Please submit to the meeting the following proposal of the Federal Government:

I. A conference of the Four Powers on the German question should meet in the fall at the latest.

II. The basis of the talks should be the following five points which were adopted by the German Bundestag at its session of June 10, 1953:

1. Holding free all-German elections. Free elections require the creation of a free political atmosphere before, during and after elections. Effective guarantees of such a free atmosphere through international control should likewise be the subject of the Four-Power conference.

2. Formation of a free government for all Germany.

3. Conclusion of a peace treaty freely negotiated with this Government.

4. Settlement in this peace treaty of all territorial problems still pending.

5. Guaranteeing the freedom of action of an all-German Parliament and an all-German Government within the framework of the principles and purposes of the United Nations.

III. The European Defence Community should be the basis of a security system which would take into consideration the security needs of all European nations, including the Russian nation. This system should be integrated in the system of general disarmament and security within the framework of the United Nations which President Eisenhower proposed in his address of April 16 of this year.

Accept, Excellency, the assurances of my most distinguished consideration.'[1]

---

[1] Colville wrote to Shuckburgh on July 27: 'The Prime Minister would like to know what are the views of the Foreign Office about Dr Adenauer's proposal, outlined in III of Washington telegram No. 1461 of July 11.' Shuckburgh replied on July 31: 'The short answer is that the Foreign Office are working on this suggestion of Dr Adenauer's, which we regard as a helpful and constructive contribution. It is in fact a development of the Prime Minister's own suggestion for a Locarno-type settlement put forward in his speech of May 11. In his speech winding up the Foreign Affairs Debate on July 22 (Hansard, Columns 510 and 12), Mr Nutting indicated that we regarded the EDC in much the same light as Dr Adenauer. Lord Salisbury has given even more direct support to Dr Adenauer's general conception in his speech in the House of Lords on July 29 – see Columns 1033 and 1034 in Hansard' (*Premier papers, 11/373*).

Sir Winston S. Churchill to Lord Salisbury
Prime Minister's Personal Telegram T.218/53
(Premier papers, 11/425)

11 July 1953
Secret
Personal
No. 2772

Your long and deeply interesting telegram No. 1460.

I hope you will not let the communiqué grow into a bristling hedge of conditions. Bidault's argument that we must have a Four Power Conference hoping for a breakdown in order to help EDC through the French Parliament is lamentable. The Americans ought to do justice to what is happening in Russia and to the many favourable events which have occurred. Above all nothing should be said to discourage Malenkov in his efforts for moderation and arm his domestic enemies against him. Russia is entitled to feel assured that she will not be the victim of another Hitler attack. This is all in accordance with UNO and we are all already bound to resist the aggressor and aid the victim of aggression. As these conditions are not likely to occur for many years, it costs us little to offer security against them, and thus find something to say which strengthens the forward movement of peace forces in the Soviet Union. All good wishes.

Sir Winston S. Churchill to Lord Salisbury
Prime Minister's Personal Telegram T.219/53
(Premier papers, 11/425)

12 July 1953
Immediate
Top Secret and Personal
No. 2779

The Cabinet must of course decide about the postponement of EDC which they will do tomorrow. I do not myself object, though I think that the threat of a Four Power meeting might have been helpful to French Parliamentary intrigues, to Western security and to Soviet compliance. We should certainly not let a delay in EDC, which has only been used by the French to obstruct the creation of a German Army, stand in the way of a meeting with Russia. That is what the people here want and what, if rightly shaped, might give the greatest hopes now.

2. The kind of Four Power meeting which Dulles and Bidault evidently have in mind is intended to bring about a breakdown and would very likely leave us where we were or even worse. Nevertheless if you bring back a Four Power meeting with you, this will be very welcome here.

3. We need not settle the exact character and composition now. For you to have a meeting of Dulles, Bidault, and Molotov, does not look a very cheerful prospect, especially if you have a long and detailed agenda. In the war all our principal meetings were attended both by heads of Governments and (repeat and) Foreign Secretaries. The latter did the work and the former expressed the mood. I hope therefore you will keep both the agenda and the composition in a non-rigid form. Let us know how and in what terms you propose to make the suggestion to the Soviet.

4. I am a little struck by Adenauer's paragraph II (3) in No. 1461[1] about a conclusion of a peace treaty freely negotiated with the German Government. It ought not to be entirely overlooked that we won the war on the basis of unconditional surrender. I do not press the point, and as you know I am very friendly to the Germans. Still I think this aspect of complete equality between victors and vanquished is one that should not remain unnoticed.

5. I greatly sympathize with you in the extreme difficulties of your task. Anyhow, try to bring home a frank and friendly offer to Russia for a Four Power talk.

General Walter Bedell Smith to Sir Winston S. Churchill
(*Churchill papers, 2/217*)

14 July 1953

My dear Prime Minister,

I read your manuscript with the same feeling of being near you and of actually hearing your voice that your writings always give me. There are no specific deletions which I could justly urge in view of the form of your presentation. I must confess, however, that it grieves me a little that you have thought it necessary so strongly to champion[2] 'Anvil'.

It is true that there were differences of view regarding this operation and that these differences need not be concealed or glossed over. But the fact is that very strong and convincing counter-arguments in favor of 'Anvil' could be presented, and after all we have victory as a final argument.

General Eisenhower in his book confined himself to a simple statement of the considerations pro-and-con 'Anvil'. His views at the time were those of an Allied theater commander who had been directed by his Governments to enter the Continent of Europe and strike at the heart of Germany. As your narrative shows, these views were shared by senior British officers associated with him, and these officers certainly represented a respectable segment of 'responsible British opinion', or at least of Britain's military opinion. Moreover, in the

---

[1] Reproduced above (p. 1165).

[2] Churchill wrote in the margin here: 'challenge?'. Smith responded on July 21: '"Challenge" is correct. I do hope that you are beginning to feel completely fit again. Things are not quite the same unless you are in the saddle and riding hard. Faithfully, Bedell' (T. 226/53, *Churchill papers, 2/217*).

case of Anvil the ultimate decision was made by the statesmen and not by the soldiers.

Your place in history is monumental and your previous books have, to my opinion at least, been completely objective in their approach to all strategic problems. I fear that such a strong presentation may result in another 'Americans vs British' controversy. I have taken the liberty of underlining a few phrases and sentences which it seems to me might be made somewhat less positive.

The President had already told me that he had no slightest objection to your reproducing the text of any messages which he had exchanged with you and which in your judgement should be published. Therefore, I did not ask him for any special authority in the case of those included in these paragraphs.

Sir Winston S. Churchill to Lord Salisbury
Prime Minister's Personal Telegram T.220/53
(Premier papers, 11/419)

16 July 1953
Immediate
Secret and Personal
No. 3

I am proposing to send the following as one of my private and personal messages to the President, but think it right to let you see it first. I think you did very well in the face of Dulles and Bidault.

Following is text of message.

BEGINS. Personal and Private from Prime Minister to President Eisenhower.

Please consider at your leisure whether it might not be better for the 4-Power meeting to begin, as Salisbury urged, with a preliminary survey by the Heads of Governments of all our troubles in an informal spirit. I am sure that gives a much better chance than if we only come in after a vast new network of detail has been erected. Moreover, Bidault made it pretty clear he wanted the meeting to break down in order to make a better case for EDC before the French Chamber, whereas it would have been a great advantage to go plus EDC with friendly hands in strong array. Above all, I thought that you and I might have formed our own impression of Malenkov, who has never seen anybody outside Russia. After this preliminary meeting we might have been able to set our State Secretaries to work along less ambitious, if more hopeful, easier lines than we now propose. I am very sorry I was not able to make this appeal to you personally as I had hoped.

2. I have made a great deal of progress and can now walk about. The

doctors think that I may be well enough to appear in public by September. Meanwhile, I am still conducting business. It was a great disappointment to me not to have my chance of seeing you. ENDS.¹

Lord Salisbury to Sir Winston S. Churchill
Prime Minister's Personal Telegram T.221/53
(Premier papers, 11/419)

16 July 1953
Emergency
Secret
No. 4

Your telegram No. 3 of July 16.

Warmest thanks for kind things you say about my efforts over the Four-Power talks, and also for letting me see the proposed telegram to the President, with reference to a possible Four-Power meeting at the highest level, prior to the proposed meeting of Foreign Ministers.

2. I am bound to tell you that I am afraid that such a proposal will be quite unacceptable to them. I had a long conversation with Dulles on the subject. He told me that the President's objections to the idea, which are personal to himself and do not derive from the State Department, are based on his conception of the high character of his office. He believes that it would not be right constitutionally for him as President, any more than for a King, to be involved in detailed negotiations, and maybe wrangles, with the Soviet Government. A formal appearance at the end of a negotiation, to lend lustre to an agreement, would be possible, but no more. I understand that his views on this subject are violent.

3. You may wish to take account of this in deciding whether or not to send your message. I should add that I found the President, to my surprise, very strongly anti-Russian, far more so than Dulles.

John Colville: diary
('The Fringes of Power', page 671)

19 July 1953

By way of contrast lunched at Stratfield Saye to look at a house which the Duke of Wellington offers to let to us. We thought it most attractive.

Went to Chartwell for dinner as R. A. Butler was to be there, with his

¹ Churchill sent this message to President Eisenhower on July 17 (T.222/53, No. 2876, *Premier papers*, 11/1074).

speech for the foreign affairs debate. W much improved in powers of concentration. He did a little work before dinner (including approval of my draft reply to a tricky PQ about the Regency Act – made tricky by the Pss Margaret–Townsend explosion); he sparkled at dinner; and after dinner he went carefully and meticulously through Rab's speech.

Drove back to London with Rab, who is very, very smooth, though oddly enough an agreeable companion. He says he will serve loyally under Eden and that anyhow some of the Conservative Party might not want him (Rab) as PM because of Munich. We discussed potential troubles when Anthony Eden returns next week fully expecting that he is shortly going to form a new administration. But there is no certainty that the PM intends to give up: on the contrary I surmise that he still hopes to bring off some final triumph, like Disraeli at the Congress of Berlin in 1878, and perhaps light the way to the end of the Cold War. Rab says he hopes his end will be like that or, if it cannot be so, like Chatham's[1] end.

Sir Winston S. Churchill to Lord Beaverbrook
(Beaverbrook papers)

19 July 1953

My dear Max,

You see that whereas the Press magnates as a class are to be hanged on the 'Victory' yardarm, Lord Beaverbrook is picked out by name as one whom on personal grounds Deakin would be sorry to see figure in this massacre. This is a marked compliment.

The cartoon will do him harm & Bevan good.

Cummings[2] is a master of black & white: but he has a queer streak in his nature.

President Dwight D. Eisenhower to Sir Winston S. Churchill
(Premier papers, 11/419)

20 July 1953   The White House
Secret

Dear Winston,

Many thanks for your letter of July 17.[3] First of all, let me say how greatly I rejoiced at the report of your improved health. Your own country, and indeed

---

[1] William Pitt, 1708–78. Known as 'Pitt the Elder'. Earl of Chatham, 1766. PM, 1766–8. Died a month after collapsing during a speech he was making in Parliament.
[2] Arthur Stuart Michael Cummings, 1919–97. Educated at Chelsea School of Art. Cartoonist for *Daily Express*, 1949–90; for *Sunday Express*, 1958–98; for *Daily Mail*, 1990–2. OBE, 1983.
[3] See T.220/53, reproduced above (pp. 1168–9).

the world, can hardly spare you even in semi-retirement. Therefore, I am delighted that you expect to emerge in full vigor by September.

With regard to the Foreign Ministers meeting, I had, through Foster, kept in close touch with it and I gained the impression that the programming of a 4-power meeting was along lines agreeable to you. Indeed, this was the program which I would have presented to you at Bermuda had we been able to meet there. I have the feeling that it could be somewhat dangerous for us to meet with the Russians and talk generalities, at least unless and until it became apparent, through action in relation to Germany and Austria, that they seriously want to get on to a dependable basis with us.

I like to meet on a very informal basis with those whom I can trust as friends. That is why I was so glad at the prospect of a Bermuda meeting. But it is a different matter to meet informally with those who may use a meeting only to embarrass and to entrap. I would prefer to have our Foreign Ministers be the ones to make the first exploration on a limited and specific basis. Furthermore, as President I am very restricted by our Constitution when it comes to leaving the country because I cannot in my absence appoint any Acting President. I have to carry with me all of the paraphernalia of government.

I was very glad to get acquainted with Salisbury when he was here and I have the impression our Foreign Ministers got along well together. Their final communiqué surely showed that close unity and friendship prevail between our countries.

Again, I say, I eagerly look forward to your public reappearance.

Sir Winston S. Churchill to Sir Norman Brook
(Churchill papers, 4/392)

21 July 1953
Private

My dear Norman Brook,

Here is Bedell's answer about the Eisenhower references.[1] I should be grateful if you would give me your opinion on the points mentioned. We certainly might meet the bulk of them, though it is not possible for me to conceal my aversion to 'Anvil'. To be quite just one ought to emphasise how much 'Anzio' took the place reserved at Teheran for 'Anvil'.

What a funny typing error to write 'champion' for 'challenge'!

I think we have now got all the necessary permits and I propose, if you think this is so, to let Camrose have the text in a few days for serial publication after October. This will give a good interval for further correction and improvement, and perhaps other things may settle themselves.

It gives me much pleasure to address this letter with my own hand.

[1] Reproduced above (pp. 1167–8).

July 1953

Sir Norman Brook to Sir Winston S. Churchill
(*Churchill papers, 2/217*)

22 July 1953

Dear Prime Minister,

Thank you very much for your letter of yesterday.

I have read Bedell Smith's letter and I have looked again at the two Chapters concerned – Chapters IV and VI of Book I. I have also read against what Eisenhower said in his own book about this difference of opinion on 'Anvil'.

You cannot be expected to gloss over your dislike of 'Anvil' or your attempts to stop it. The differences of view about it were fully disclosed in Eisenhower's own book (pages 308–312). Not only did he set out the arguments for and against, as Bedell Smith says; but he also made it plain that you took one view and he took another.

Nor should you conceal your view that, looking back, you were right. It is not fair to say, as Bedell Smith does, that the victory was 'a final argument' in favour of 'Anvil'. Your case is that 'Overlord' could have succeeded without 'Anvil' which, by drawing off resources, prevented Alexander from exploiting other and additional possibilities in Italy and the Balkans.

The fact is that Eisenhower was arguing from the point of view of a theatre commander, concerned only with the battle in North West Europe. You were looking at this then, and are writing of it now, from a wider strategic angle. Bedell Smith says that Eisenhower's views were supported by senior British officers on his staff: this is not surprising, as their responsibilities were also limited to the campaign in North West Europe. But the British Chiefs of Staff, with their wider strategic responsibilities, supported your view. It is significant that Eisenhower should have said in his book that on this point 'the United States Chiefs of Staff, following their usual practice, declined to interfere with the conclusions of the commander in the field' and left it to him to argue with you. This is tantamount to saying that the United States Chiefs of Staff abrogated any strategic interest in any European theatre except the North West.

I conclude therefore that you should not consider for a moment making any major changes in these two Chapters – and that you need not be disturbed by Bedell Smith's general comments. It would, however, be tactful to make some verbal changes in the passages to which he has drawn particular attention; and I do not think that the book would be harmed by making the changes which he evidently has in mind. I attach a separate sheet showing how you could give effect to his particular points. I also attach a draft which may be of some help to you in framing a reply to his letter.

* * *

I confirm that all the necessary permissions for Volume VI have now been obtained. The Queen has given permission for the publication of the War

Cabinet documents which you are proposing to include in this Volume. Her Majesty has also given her consent for your proposed publication of the two messages to King George VI. Official permission has been obtained for your proposed publication of messages to other Commonwealth Prime Ministers. Truman's messages have, I understand, been paraphrased in accordance with his request. And the paraphrases required to safeguard cypher security have all been included. Thus, so far as official consents are required, the way is clear for you to hand over the text, as you propose, for serial publication after October.

Evelyn Shuckburgh: diary
('Descent to Suez', pages 91–2)

24 July 1953

S[1] spent the day preparing his speech for the House of Lords debate next week, when he will be able for the first time to defend his Washington agreement himself. Great arguments between him and the rest of us as to the line he should take. He wants in effect to say that he tried to get top-level four-power meeting on the Churchill recipe but that his allies would not have it. We think this wrong, (a) because it suggests that he was unsuccessful in his mission, (b) because it gives the impression that Winston's great initiative has been smothered by the Americans, and (c) because it is negative and apologetic in regard to the offer which *has* been made to the Russians. We want to suggest that the three powers considered how best to forward Winston's initiative in the light of the actual situation (including Winston's own illness, the French political crises, the fall of Beria and the riots in Eastern Germany) and came to the conclusion that the meeting now proposed was the best first step, a top-level meeting later on being not excluded; that this is a test of whether the Russians want accommodation and that we should now await expectantly their reply. Admittedly S's version is more straightforward, but less politic and characteristic of him.

The more I think of it, the more I disapprove of WSC fostering this sentimental illusion that peace can be obtained if only the 'top men' can get together. It seems an example of hubris which afflicts old men who have power, as it did Chamberlain when he visited Hitler. Even if you do believe in the theory, surely you should keep this trump card in your hand for emergency and not play it out at a time when there is no burning need, no particularly dangerous tension (rather than the reverse) and your opponents are plunged in internal struggles and dissensions. It is hard to avoid the conclusion that WSC is longing for a top-level meeting before he dies – not because it is wise or

[1] [Lord] Salisbury.

necessary but because it would complete the pattern of his ambition and make him the Father of Peace as well as of Victory. But it would do no such thing unless he were to make sacrifices and concessions to the Russians which there is no need to make, in return for a momentary and probably illusory 'reduction of tension'. After that splendid achievement he would die in triumph and we should all be left behind in a weaker position than before. I also object in principle to the idea that when a particular negotiation does not succeed or a particular problem proves intractable it must be because your negotiator or Ambassador is not senior and important enough. All through the birth of NATO this doctrine had full rein. Every time Foreign Ministers met and failed to agree on how much money to pool for defence they turned with relief to the appointment of a higher-level committee or a more powerful superman who, they hoped, might make the decision for them.

John Colville: diary
('The Fringes of Power', page 672)

24 July 1953

Lunched alone with W at Chartwell. He is now amazingly restored, but complains that his memory has suffered and says he thinks he probably will give up in October or at any rate before the Queen leaves for Australia in November. Still very wrapped up with the possibility of bringing something off with the Russians and with the idea of meeting Malenkov face to face. Very disappointed in Eisenhower whom he thinks both weak and stupid. Bitterly regrets that the Democrats were not returned at the last Presidential Election.

Sir Winston S. Churchill to Lord Salisbury and Sir William Strang
Prime Minister's Personal Minute M.245/53
(Premier papers, 11/497)

24 July 1953
Secret

I am somewhat concerned about the Russian objection to the Mediterranean Fleet visiting the Marmora. Pray let me have advice on this. I am wholeheartedly with the Turks and I am committed to them about the Dardanelles. Nevertheless I should not like the Russian gesture of amity to Turkey made about two months ago to encounter anything like a rebuff. What could be done? Would there be any use in sending a few ships to visit Sebastopol or Odessa as a purely courtesy visit. Would that upset things with the Turks and make them think we were simply carrying on any secrets we had learned from them to the Russians who they have every reason to fear. Would it not perhaps be better to arrange a visit to Soviet ports in three or four months time? Anyhow some friendly message should be sent to the Soviet. Please advise me.

Sir Winston S. Churchill to Lord Camrose
(Camrose papers)

26 July 1953
Private

My dear Bill,

Mr Crisp[1] seems to be active again, and *The People* seems to be interested. Perhaps you will have a word with me when a chance offers. My own feeling is that nothing need be done except to warn any would-be purchaser we know of that copyright is reserved.

THE PEOPLE
SUNDAY, JULY 26, 1953.
WINSTON ASKED HIM 'MAKE ME SOME MONEY'

A man who once dealt in millions and who was asked by Churchill to 'make some money' for him, is now planning to sell a hundred private letters from the Premier to supplement the £5 allowance he receives from the Stock Exchange Benevolent Fund.

Charles Birch Crisp was a name known in high society 50 years ago. He gave lavish parties. Ambassadors feted him because he was able to raise millions of pounds for their countries.

One of his friends was a young man named Winston Churchill. The two exchanged many personal and intimate letters.

Now Mr Crisp, 85, has decided to sell the letters after a fruitless attempt to raise a loan from the Prime Minister.

'I sent the letters by runner to Sir Winston,' Mr Crisp told me, 'and mentioned that if he cared to lend me a little money it would be appreciated.

'Sir Winston was unable to help and eventually I had the letters back. Now they are at the auctioneers. I hope to get at least £500 for them. That would be most useful.'

Mr Crisp brewed me a cup of tea and then searched vainly for a saucer to match. He has no servants. Once he had dozens.

'In the old days,' he mused, 'Sir Winston left me to invest money for him when he was hard up.

---

[1] Charles Birch Crisp, 1867–1958. Born in Bristol. Financier who had managed the young Churchill's investments. Conservative running mate with Churchill for Oldham during the 1900 general election.

'He wrote me letters in the best Churchillian tradition thanking me for performing miracles on his behalf.'

Mr Crisp began as a 5s.-a-week office boy. Within a few years he was raising millions for China in a business loan.

Sir Winston S. Churchill to Lord Camrose
(*Churchill papers, 4/392*)

26 July 1953
Secret

My dear Bill,

I send you herewith Norman Brook's comments and statement upon Volume VI in the light of Bedell Smith's letter, which I also enclose for your convenience.[1] Kindly return both of these.

Kelly will present to your Secretary, Mr Rees,[2] one complete master copy to date on Friday, July 31. Will you tell the printer how many copies you want printed. This constitutes the formal delivery of the last volume, which is now 'all clear' with the authorities concerned. I do not wish the serials to begin until the end of October. Meanwhile in August and September I will give the text a final read. I do not think, however, that much alteration will be necessary, as it has been so carefully revised during the last two years. I reserve my rights, however, as to what we have called Overtake corrections and improvements.

Thank you very much for the letter I have received from the *Daily Telegraph*, and its enclosure.

It was very nice seeing you on Wednesday. I think I am making steady progress.

John Colville: diary
(*'The Fringes of Power', page 672*)

27 July 1953

At Chequers. Anthony and Clarissa Eden came to luncheon, the former thin and frail after his three operations but in good spirits. He is, of course, thinking above all of when he will get the Prime Ministership, but he contrived to keep off the subject altogether today and to talk mainly of foreign affairs. He thinks the fall of Beria three weeks ago may have been a defeat for moderation. The signs, flimsy though they be, do seem to point that way.

---

[1] Both reproduced above (pp. 1172–3, 1167–8).
[2] Douglas Rees.

Gave Winston *Candide* to read. He has had a surfeit of Trollope's political novels.

Today the Korean War ended – after months of infuriating haggling over the terms of the armistice.

Sir Winston S. Churchill to Lord Bracken
(Churchill papers, 2/215)

27 July 1953

My dear Brendan,

The following points should be borne in mind.[1]

First, we were joint candidates in a long and hard fight in which we made friends.

Secondly, his position and standing fully entitled him to be considered for a candidature at the Carlton Club.

Thirdly, but quite unconnected with this, he wrote to me as an active stockbroker, suggesting that he should be allowed to make an investment for me. I sent him a thousand pounds and he bought some shares in what was called the Anchor Syndicate. Presently I needed the money and asked him to sell the shares, if necessary at a loss. I think this amounted to several hundred pounds. I never received the slightest financial assistance or advantage from him, and my transactions were on a purely business basis.

The complications about Oldham arose from its being a double-barrelled seat, and my quarrelling with the Conservative Party and with Chamberlain, though not personally, about Free Trade. He admits that I own the copyright of all the letters, if indeed copyright holds after so long as fifty years has passed.

I do not authorise you to show these letters to anyone or to ask any favours from *The People* or any newspaper on my behalf. It will be a great nuisance if I have to take legal proceedings but I shall certainly not hesitate to do so if copyright is violated or anything of a libellous nature is suggested.

I send you also some of his letters which have been unearthed and which must be read in context with the correspondence.

When four years ago he appeared to be in distress he talked of using the letters in a Memoir he was writing and later on selling. I sustained the impression in the correspondence that he had the idea that he could extract money from me by this process. It therefore was quite impossible for me to help him as I would have done in a small way as a friend. Later he sent me all the originals back but apparently expected me to pay him several hundred pounds. I refused to do this. He then asked for the originals back and I sent them all to him.

---

[1] See Churchill to Camrose regarding Crisp, July 26, reproduced above (pp. 1175–6).

What I do not understand is the purpose of *The People*'s article. I heard some time ago that he was trying to get them to buy the letters, but I thought they had dropped it on account of the copyright difficulty. The passage which appeared in *The People* on Sunday is very offensive and falls little short of a suggestion of blackmail. I am sorry for the poor old man. He is 85, bankrupt, and dependent on the Stock Exchange Benevolent Fund for a pittance.

I send you the whole bundle of correspondence, including my last letter to Bill. I think it reads connectedly. Do not let it out of your possession.

Sir Winston S. Churchill to General Walter Bedell Smith
(Churchill papers, 2/217)

27 July 1953
Private

My dear Bedell,

I am greatly obliged to you for giving such prompt attention to the chapters of my final volume which you undertook to read on the President's behalf. I can well imagine that your new duties leave you with very little leisure and it was good of you to find time to discharge this additional task so quickly.

The differences of view which arose over 'Anvil' are matters of history. As you say, they cannot be glossed over. They are in fact well known – and General Eisenhower described in his own book how the two of us were at variance over this. Looking back on it from this calmer point of time I cannot conscientiously say that I now think I was mistaken. Indeed I believe firmly that I was right. I also believe that our difference of views was due very largely to the fact that, while General Eisenhower was concerned only with the campaign in Northwest Europe, it was my duty to survey a much wider strategic scene. I think that I have contrived to bring this out in my book; and I certainly hope that people will infer from it that the differences between us are explained, to some extent at any rate, by differences in responsibility and point of view.

I do not think it would be right to try to blur this part of my story – and I am sure you would not ask me to do so. But I should be very sorry to think that I had unnecessarily provoked, by too sharp a phrase here and there, useless controversy over the Anglo-American strategic divergence of the past. With this in mind I have looked again at the passages to which you drew my particular attention, and I can readily agree to change all of these in the direction which you desire. In point of fact I am proposing in most cases to delete entirely the words which you found somewhat too positive in tone. I hope that with these alterations the book may be agreeable. The last thing I would wish is to publish anything which might damage those close and friendly relations with my American comrades which I prize so highly.

Sir Walter Monckton to Sir Winston S. Churchill
(Premier papers, 11/477)

28 July 1953

You minuted me on 30th May[1] about the possibility of deferring the call-up of apprentice jockeys until after their 21st birthday.

I have since seen Sir Humphrey de Trafford and the Stewards of the Jockey Club on this question. At present, under a scheme based on the apprenticeship arrangements in racing and agreed by the representative organisations in the industry, apprentice jockeys can normally get deferment up to the age of 20. I should be on difficult ground if I were to make any change in the scheme except on the basis of an agreed recommendation from all the representative interests. I have, therefore, suggested to Sir Humphrey de Trafford that as a first step the Jockey Club should call a meeting with the trainers and the trade union concerned in an endeavour to agree proposals which would eventually be put to me. Sir Humphrey de Trafford has promised to act on this suggestion.

---

[1] M.173/53, reproduced above (p. 1054).

August 1953

John Colville: diary
('The Fringes of Power', pages 672–3)

31 July–4 August 1953

To Chequers again. Lord Beaverbrook came on Friday night, in disgrace because of an unpleasant cartoon of Lord Salisbury in the *Daily Express*. Winston has seen more of Lord B since his illness than at any time since he formed the present administration. Junor,[1] of the *Evening Standard*, told me when I lunched with him last Wednesday, that the Labour Party saw in an (imaginary) split between W and the rest of the Cabinet over four-power talks with Russia their best propaganda line for many a day. The *Daily Express*, because of Lord B's hatred of Lord Salisbury (and of the nobility in general) seems to be playing roughly the same hand. However, at Chequers Lord B's charm soon thawed the resentment – though Winston had the Visitors' Book removed so that Lord B's signature should not be visible when Lord Salisbury arrived next day!

The Edens, the Salisburys, Meg, Mary, and Christopher were there for the weekend. Randolph, Sarah and Duff Cooper came over on August Bank Holiday. The underlying interest was twofold. First of all the two invalids: Winston and Eden. The latter was burning with the big question-mark: 'When do I take over?' The former had told me in private that if asked he would say that the more he was hustled, the longer he would be. However, Eden (warned by Patrick Buchan-Hepburn, Brendan and, I expect, Rab – with all of whom I have discussed the problem in recent weeks) said nothing. He looked very frail and probably realises he must first prove that he will be fit to be PM himself.

The second drama is our attitude toward Russia. Winston is firmly hoping for talks which might lead to a relaxation of the Cold War and a respite in

---

[1] John Donald Brown Junor, 1919–97. Educated at Glasgow University. Commissioned in Fleet Air Arm, 1940. Married, 1942, Pamela Welsh: two children. Reporter, *Daily Express*, 1948–51; Asst Editor and Chief Leader Writer, 1951–3. Deputy Editor, *London Evening Standard*, 1953. Editor, *Sunday Express*, 1954–86. Knighted, 1980. Columnist, *Mail on Sunday*, 1990–7.

which science could use its marvels for improving the lot of man, and, as he put it, the leisured classes of his youth might give way to the leisured masses of tomorrow. Eden is set on retaining the strength of NATO and the Western Alliance by which, he believes, Russia has already been severely weakened. W is depressed by Eden's attitude (which reflects that of the FO), because he thinks it consigns us to years more of hatred and hostility. Still more depressing is that Lord S. says he found Eisenhower violently Russophobe, greatly more so than Dulles, and that he believes the President to be personally responsible for the policy of useless pinpricks and harassing tactics the US is following against Russia in Europe and the Far East.

On Sunday I went with W to Royal Lodge where he had an audience of the Queen. He said that he had told her his decision whether or not to retire would be made in a month when he saw clearly whether he was fit to face Parliament and to make a major speech to the Conservative Annual Conference in October. He also asked, and received, permission to invite Eisenhower here on a State Visit in September or October. He has learned from Winthrop Aldrich (US Ambassador) that Eisenhower would do this for him but for nobody else – after he retired there would be no question of it. It would be a great event, because US Presidents seldom if ever go abroad and none has been here since Woodrow Wilson at the end of World War I.

Meg and I left Chequers on Tuesday, August 4th.

Sir Winston S. Churchill to President Dwight D. Eisenhower
Prime Minister's Personal Telegram T.230/53
(Premier papers, 11/1074)

3 August 1953
Immediate
Dedip
Top Secret, Personal and Private
No. 3102

My dear Friend,

Winthrop Aldrich brought me your very kind messages and enquiries last week when he visited me. I am making continual progress and have almost got back my full mobility. By the end of August I hope to be in fairly good condition bar accidents.

2. Winthrop conveyed to me the great news that you might perhaps find it possible to come to London for a talk about things with me. This would indeed be a memorable event and the enthusiasm which it would incite would make us all the stronger amid the difficulties which lie around and ahead.

3. I told The Queen about this yesterday and Her Majesty was very pleased indeed and would return from Balmoral to welcome you at Buckingham

Palace during your stay. Would some time in the last week in September or the first in October be convenient to you and Mrs Eisenhower? If so, the procedure for the visits of Heads of States will be set in motion.

4. We have not had the honour of a visit from the President of the United States since Woodrow Wilson came in 1918, thirty-five years ago, and this new proof of Anglo-American friendship and goodwill would make a profound impression all over the world.

Evelyn Shuckburgh: diary
('Descent to Suez', pages 94–5)

4 August 1953

S told me all about the weekend at Chequers. He formed a poor impression of AE's state of health. Thought him 'fragile'. PM in no mood to discuss retirement and they did not raise it. Jock Colville went so far as to speak of Winston carrying on until June 1954 when the Queen comes back from Australia (AE says that the PM himself said he was very tired and feeling worse, but that his 'ménage' (Jock, Soames, etc.) came in like attendants in an oriental court, flattering him and assuring him that he was perfectly all right and fit to carry on for ever.) But S thinks the situation very serious for the Government and hinted that if AE is not well enough to take over in October other arrangements will have to be made. The Opposition will not refrain, when Parliament meets again, from complaining at the part absence and incapacity of the Government's two chief men. He is also disturbed, as we all are, by the interference in foreign policy. The suggestion that Ike might be willing to come to England has now been passed to the PM by the United States Ambassador and Winston has sent an enthusiastic invitation. He realizes now that Ike will not meet the Russians so he will try to get 'authorization' to meet Malenkov by himself in Zurich for an all-round friendly discussion of all questions at issue. Apart from the certainty that Eisenhower could not agree; that M would not come and that such a meeting would give heart attacks to all the Western nations, it has rather absurd internal implications. It would place the future relationship with Russia on a personal basis between him and Malenkov precisely at a moment when he himself is likely to quit the stage. It would be rather like the speech of 11 May[1] only a hundred times worse. Frank Roberts[2] takes the view that that speech destroyed the first real success we have had in our diplomacy in recent years. NATO policy had produced results, the Russians

[1] Reproduced above (pp. 998–1010).
[2] Frank Kenyon Roberts, 1907–98. Entered FO, 1930. Desk Officer, Central Dept, 1937–40. Chargé d'Affaires, Czechoslovakia, 1943. British Minister in Soviet Union, 1945–7. Principal Private Secretary to Secretary of State for Foreign Affairs, 1947–9. UK Deputy High Commissioner in India, 1949–51. Knighted, 1953. Ambassador to Yugoslavia, 1954–7; to Soviet Union, 1960–2; to Federal Republic of Germany, 1963–8.

were disturbed at troubles at home, riots in Germany, and were toying with small concessions. All we had to do was to sit tight and 'believe it when we see it'. Into this the PM, for reasons dictated by the pattern of his own life, threw a life line to the Russians and confusion into our camp.

It seemed that the old man is now changing his ideas on Egypt. He has come round to thinking that we must have an agreement to evacuate the Canal Zone and seems to have dropped his precious idea that we could not possibly go until a lot of people had been killed. The main stumbling point now is the period of the agreement. We are asking for ten years. We would take five years with consultation at the end and provision that the agreement would remain in force another five years unless an alternative can be worked out. Most privately the PM has said he would take five years as a last resort, but S thinks the Tory Party will be difficult over this.

Sir Winston S. Churchill to Lord Salisbury
Prime Minister's Personal Minute M.257/53
(Premier papers, 11/419)

6 August 1953

I suggest a few amendments to this very lengthy paper with the general purport of which I agree. It is I fear an example of the ocean of verbiage upon which we are now likely to embark, as a result of the Dulles–Bidault impulsion. It may well be that the American contribution will be even longer and that its object will be to prove that there is no change in the Soviet outlook and that we must just jog along indefinitely as we are doing. This may be true. Alas!

2. I think the Cabinet should consider this paper (with or without my amendments) on Monday. The Chancellor of the Exchequer has just telephoned to me that this is his view. I will try tomorrow morning to put a few thoughts down for your consideration and perhaps for circulation to the Cabinet. Let me repeat that in substance I approve the course you are taking.

3. I supposed you read *The Times* article on Beria and Malenkov on the 5th. It affected my view about them both. Malenkov's position seems very weak and his treatment of his colleague for a hundred days very shabby even by Communist standards. I would certainly not go into politics in Russia.

John Colville: diary
('The Fringes of Power', pages 674–5)

6–9 August 1953

At Chequers again. Meg, Nanny and Harriet came over for the day on the 9th and I drove them home. On the 8th, Lord Salisbury, Rab Butler and

William Strang came for a meeting at 12.00 noon about the reply from Russia to the three-power note sent after the Washington Conference. The PM took the meeting in the Hawtrey room, the first time he has presided at a meeting since the Cabinet on the morrow of his stroke. The line he had proposed was accepted: namely to ask the Americans a lot of questions and leave them the burden of drafting the answer: this in spite of contrary and long-winded drafts prepared by the FO. The old man still gets his way: usually because it is simple and clear, whereas the 'mystique' of the FO (as Selwyn Lloyd calls it) tends to be pettifogging and over detailed. After the meeting we had a most agreeable luncheon party, the PM in sparkling mood. He said that all his life he had found his main contribution had been by self-expression rather than by self-denial. And he has started drinking brandy again after a month's abstinence. Apart from his unsteady walk, the appearances left by his stroke have vanished, though he still tires quickly. However Lord Moran told me he thought there might be another stroke within a year. Indeed it was probable.

On the afternoon of the 8th Monty came for the weekend. I walked up Beacon Hill with him (the weather for the last week has been gorgeous). He volunteered the opinion that Frank Roberts was a menace to the country with his 'rigid constipated mentality'. After dinner we talked, the PM, Monty and I, till late about the two world wars. Monty and the PM said the Americans had made five capital mistakes in the military field in the last war:

    i. They had prevented Alexander getting to Tunis the first time, when he could easily have done so.

    ii. They had done at Anzio what Stopford[1] did at Suvla Bay: clung to the beaches and failed to establish positions inland as they could well have done. The PM said he had intended it to be a wholly British expedition.

    iii. They had insisted on Operation 'Anvil', thereby preventing Alexander from taking Trieste and Vienna.

    iv. Eisenhower had refused to let Monty, in 'Overlord', concentrate his advance on the left flank. He had insisted on a broad advance, which could not be supported, and had thus allowed Rundstedt to counter-attack on the Ardennes and had prolonged the war, with dire political results, to the spring of 1945.

    v. Eisenhower had let the Russians occupy Berlin, Prague and Vienna – all of which might have been entered by the Americans.

Monty told me he had got Ridgway sacked from SHAPE. He had gone off to America specifically to tell Ike that this was necessary and had found Ike alive to the fact. But Ridgway, who had been made American Chief of Staff, still thought he had been promoted and not sacked!

[1] Frederick William Stopford, 1854–1929. Commissioned, Grenadier Guards, 1871. Capt., 1884. Maj., 1885. Lt-Col., 1894. Col., 1896. CB, 1898. KCMG, 1900. KCVO, 1909. GOC IX Corps, Gallipoli, 1915. Relieved of command, Aug. 1915. KCB, 1921.

He inclines to agree with Lord Salisbury about Ike's present political ineptitude but says he is the prisoner of Congress.

Sir Winston S. Churchill to Lord Salisbury
(Premier papers, 11/419)

7 August 1953

1. It must be remembered that the Note to Russia prepared in Washington owed its character to American and French initiative and that the Acting Foreign Secretary tried his best to procure a different policy. Would it not therefore be better to cast any communication we may make in some interrogative form? Thus we should place the full burden of responsibility where it rightly belongs, namely with those who had the power. This might lead to considerable shortening of our paper and make it less a positive statement of our opinion than a desire to know how the Americans propose to meet the fairly obvious manoeuvre which their own and French manoeuvres have produced from the Soviet. We should then have the advantage of pointing out any weaknesses or errors which we might discern in their statement of opinion and our influence upon the official rejoinder note might then be greater.

2. I see it stated in the Press that a Committee of the three Allied nations concerned is to draft the reply to the Soviets. Thus we are already descending below the Foreign Secretaries' level and falling into the lengthy mechanical process of trying to reach compromise by deputies or officials. It is suggested that Paris should be the centre where this triple official level meeting should take place. Considering that M Bidault does not conceal his hope ~~that the procedure adopted at Washington~~[1] that the Four-Power meeting of Foreign Secretaries would break down and thereby strengthen his hand for carrying EDC through the French Parliament at some time in the indefinite future it does not seem that Paris has any special claim to be chosen as the centre where this unavoidable work has to be done.

3. My own feeling is that we should in the first instance deal entirely with the Americans and assume that they have the leadership and should help them both by stating our view and by asking pertinent questions of how they would deal with this or that difficulty. It is only when we have reached the best possible agreement with Washington that we should jointly or simultaneously submit our opinions to the Soviet. This need not take long; the Kremlin who have only themselves to consult took three weeks to answer our note and we being three may reasonably claim at least as long as that.

4. To sum up I think we might ask Washington what sort of answer they propose and then see how we can improve upon it by suggestion and comment.

---

[1] The struck-through words and phrases reflect Churchill's own amendments to this letter.

I regard the Foreign Office paper as a most able document but on reflection I am doubtful whether we need at this stage lay our views at such length before them. We are in no position to accuse the Soviets of 'bad-faith' when we know that our triple note proposing the Four-Power Conference of Foreign Ministers on Germany and Austria is was very likely to lead to a break down and thus afford Bidault after a long delay greater possibility of carrying EDC through the French Parliament. The Soviets are replying to one manoeuvre by another. I fear we are moving into a course of propaganda manoeuvring on both sides likely to end in failure. I do not think we should be well advised in all circumstances to seek the leadership.

Since I wrote the foregoing I have read the American message.

The position seems to me to have been decisively changed by the American telegram (No. 1727 from Washington). Obviously if they are ready to accept a Four-Power Conference <u>as a step following the Russian reply</u>, we could not stand out against it especially as Adenauer also has favoured the idea of a Four-Power talk. It is really a meeting without an agreed agenda. I am sure that your telegram ought to be reviewed in the light of this very important American decision. Nor indeed do I see any need for haste for a day or two. It would surely be sufficient to thank them and say we are considering the position. After all, there is nothing in your very excellent telegram that should not be known to anyone who has studied the subject.

I should be at your disposal tomorrow morning if you cared to come down here bringing Strang, and I would ask Rab to come too. If necessary I could come up myself.

Record of a meeting[1]
(Premier papers, 11/419)

8 August 1953   Hawtrey Room
Top Secret   Chequers
12 noon

The purpose of the meeting was to discuss the action to be taken on the Soviet Note of August 4 sent in reply to the parallel notes of the British, French and United States Governments, dated July 15.

The Prime Minister had proposed that our comments to the United States should be in interrogative form. We should ask a number of questions and allow the United States Government to take the initiative in drafting a further communication to the Soviet Government. On this we should then be free to make such comments as we thought fit.

Lord Salisbury and Mr Butler agreed that this was the best course to adopt.

[1] In attendance: Sir Winston S. Churchill, Lord Salisbury, R. A. Butler, Sir William Strang and John Colville.

The Foreign Office would draft a telegram to Washington on these lines and it would be submitted to the Cabinet and to the Prime Minister before dispatch.

The Prime Minister said that we should not press the United States to accept the terms or the agenda put forward by the Russians, but refusal to accept these terms need not prejudice a 4-Power Meeting such as was widely desired in all countries. Lord Salisbury added that the three Governments had put a fair proposition to the USSR, but the Soviet reply included certain provisions which could not possibly be accepted and which the Western Powers could not even be expected to consider. This should be made clear to the British public.

The Chancellor of the Exchequer said that the course now proposed met the objections he had felt towards the original draft telegram to Washington, but he was still a little uneasy about the method of presenting to the British public at home the unpalatable probability that effective 4-Power talks were now unlikely to take place. He thought that the eventual way out of the difficulty might be 'a return to UNO' where international discussions at a high level could take place with the greatest measure of satisfaction to all parties in this country. The Prime Minister enquired whether the Security Council might not at a convenient stage be able to appoint a Sub-Committee of its leading members to discuss some of the topics with which a Four-Power Conference was at present expected to deal.

President Dwight D. Eisenhower to Sir Winston S. Churchill
(Premier papers, 11/1074)

8 August 1953
Top Secret

Dear Winston,

I am afraid either that Winthrop misinterpreted a little wishful thinking on my part, growing out of disappointment at not being able to see you in Bermuda, or that you may have misunderstood him. The fact is that I am scheduled for a number of inescapable commitments during the foreseeable future and it would be impossible for me to leave the country. I am trying to get a partial vacation during the coming weeks, but even this will be heavily interspersed with business.

It was very gracious of the Queen to respond as she did to the idea of a possible visit by Mrs Eisenhower and me. We both appreciate this most sincerely and we are equally grateful for the warmth of the welcome you promised me.

I am delighted that your progress toward complete recovery continues so steadily. Please insure that it continues rapidly and without interruption.

With warm personal Regards, as ever.

Sir Winston Churchill to R. A. Butler and Lord Salisbury
(Premier papers, 11/419)

10 August 1953

1. So far no amplification or contradiction of telegram No. 1727 has been received from Washington but today Mr Dulles is reported to be flying home. It would surely be prudent to wait a few days for him to return as he may well make considerable changes in No. 1727.

2. I do not disagree with most of the points set out in the Foreign Office draft. They are many of them so obvious that it is hard to believe they do not occur to the State Department. I am glad to see they are now couched in an interrogative form.

3. Still it seems to me we have to run a needless risk in sending a telegram which undoubtedly reads as if we were progging the Americans into sharper controversy with the Russians than they have themselves proposed. Mr Dulles may take advantage of this new attitude of Britain and confront us with proposals which would lead to the loss of the Four-Power talks. It would cause a shock here if it leaked from the United States that we had prompted the more severe attitude of the United States. We have nothing to lose and much to gain by waiting for a few days when we may be sure of what is their final reaction to the Soviet reply. If Mr Dulles adheres to No. 1727 it may be necessary to bring the points mentioned in the Foreign Office draft, or some of them, before him. But let us be sure of their position before we try to stiffen them up. It is a great advantage to be able to wait till the full facts are before us without losing any of our power to advise, or running the risk of being accused of stirring up the United States against Russia.

John Colville: diary
('The Fringes of Power', page 675)

12 August 1953

At Chequers again, alone with the PM and Norman Brook. Talk about reconstituting the Cabinet. Possibly Eden Leader of House and Lord President, Salisbury Foreign Secretary; or Harold Macmillan Foreign Secretary, Eccles Minister of Housing, Patrick Buchan-Hepburn Minister of Works. But all depends on W's own future and he gives himself till the end of September to decide.

Much talk about Russia: the PM still inclining to think we should have another shot at an understanding. He said, 'We must not go further on the path to war unless we are sure there is no other path to peace.'

Wrote a Cabinet Paper, which the PM accepted about the Windsor Papers (relating to the Duke's activities in Spain and Portugal in 1940). The PM still set on suppression.

August 1953

Sir Harold Nicolson: diary
('Harold Nicolson, Diaries and Letters', volume 3, page 244)

12 August 1953

I go to Lime Grove and dub my television obituary of Winston. It rather amuses me. We go through it five times before we get it right.*

* This recording was televised twelve years later, on Sir Winston's death in January 1965.

Sir Winston S. Churchill to Lord Beaverbrook
(Churchill papers, 2/211)

12 August 1953
Private and Personal

My dear Max,
You will be glad to know I am making continual progress, and have strong hopes of being able to do the Margate Conference on October 9 and attend the House of Commons when it meets. I have not been able to make up my mind about any plans for going abroad, being content to live one day after another at Chartwell or Chequers. The last week has been lovely. It is rather necessary for me to be on the spot at a time when so much, including my own small affairs, hangs in the balance.

For your eye alone: I have not absolutely excluded the idea of going to Washington in the last fortnight in September if progress continues good. There are a lot of things I might say in a talk with Ike. At any rate I hope you will not alter your own plans or inconvenience yourself in any way because of me. It is most kind of you to have made me such an attractive offer.

I have decided to bring the whole Windsor question before the Cabinet in the course of the next month. Jock has kept me well informed about your views, and I see the force of what you say about not giving it a sounding board. Still, I am not yet resolved to give up my attempt to prevent Government publication.

I have just returned to Chartwell, and shall go back to Chequers on the 21st or 22nd.

John Colville: diary
('The Fringes of Power', page 675)

14–15 and 17 August 1953

At Chartwell. PM coming round towards resignation in October. Says he no longer has the zest for work and finds the world in an abominable state wherever he looks. Greatly depressed by thoughts on the hydrogen bomb. He had a nightmare on Thursday dreaming that he was making a speech in the House of Lords and that it was an appalling flop. Lord Rothermere[1] came up to him and said, 'It didn't even *sound* nice.'

He made a good pun at luncheon on Monday. We were talking about a peerage for Salter, who is to be removed from the Ministry of Materials. Christopher asked whether he could not also get rid of Mackeson[2] from Overseas Trade, but said he didn't merit a peerage. 'No', said W, 'but perhaps a disappearage'.

Sir Winston S. Churchill to Sir Pierson Dixon[3]
Prime Minister's Personal Minute M.273/53
(Premier papers, 11/548)

15 August 1953

The length of all telegrams seems to have increased very greatly in the last few weeks. Is this so or not? How does the weekly verbiage compare with two months ago?

Sir Pierson Dixon to Sir Winston S. Churchill
(Premier papers, 11/548)

18 August 1953
Confidential
PM/PD/53/287

Your minute M.273/53 of August 15 about the length of telegrams.

In June the average length of code and cypher telegrams, both to and from the Foreign Office, was 116 groups. This figure was the lowest since the war for telegrams in either direction. In July the figures rose to 126 groups for inward telegrams and 138 groups for outward telegrams. This was a period of abnormal diplomatic activity, and some rise in the telegram figures was to be

---

[1] Esmond Cecil Harmsworth, 1898–1978. Educated at Eton. Married, 1920, Margaret Hunam Redhead: three children (div. 1938); 1945, Charteris O'Neill (div. 1952); 1966, Mary Ohrstrom Murchison: one child. In Royal Marine Artillery, 1917. ADC to PM at Paris Peace Conference, 1919. MP (Union.) for Isle of Thanet, 1919–29. Chairman, *Daily Mail* and General Trust Ltd, 1932–71. Chairman, Newspaper Proprietors Association, 1934–61. 2nd Viscount Rothermere, 1940.

[2] Harry Ripley Mackeson, 1905–64. Educated at Rugby and Royal Military Academy, Sandhurst. Joined Royal Scots Greys, 1925. Adjutant, 1933–5. Bde-Maj., Egypt, 1938–40. Married, 1940, Alethea Cecil Chetwynd-Talbot: two children. GSO I, 1940–2. Cdr, Armoured Bde, UK, France and Belgium, 1942–4. MP (Cons.) for Hythe, 1945–50; for Folkestone and Hythe, 1950–9. Lord of the Treasury, 1951–2. Secretary for Overseas Trade, 1952–3.

[3] Pierson John Dixon, 1904–65. Known as 'Bob'. Principal Private Secretary to Foreign Secretary, 1943–8. CB, 1948. Ambassador to Czechoslovakia, 1948–50. KCMG, 1950. Deputy Under-Secretary of State, FO, 1950–4. Permanent Representative to the UN, 1954–60. GCMG, 1957. Ambassador to France, 1960–4.

expected. Even so, they compare favourably with the averages for the whole of 1952 (139 and 146 groups respectively). In the first two weeks of the present month, the averages dropped to 125 groups for telegrams in both directions.

2. I attach a copy of our most recent circular enclosing telegram statistics. The table at the bottom of page 5 shows that steady progress has been made in recent years in combating verbosity. But we are not satisfied and will not relax our efforts to cut down the length of telegrams still further.

Cabinet: conclusions
(Cabinet papers, 128/26)

18 August 1953
Secret
5 p.m.
Cabinet Meeting No. 49 of 1953

[...]

2. The Cabinet had before them a memorandum by the Lord President (C(53)232) outlining the further instructions which he was proposing to send to the United Kingdom Delegation in Cairo.

The Lord President said that there were three outstanding points in the defence negotiations on which the Delegation thought they would be obliged to make some concessions if any agreement was to be reached with the Egyptians. It had become clear that the Egyptians would not accept an agreement for an initial period of five years continuing thereafter until a satisfactory regional defence organisation had come into being; and that they would only consider a fixed period beyond three years if we were prepared to reduce below 4,000 the number of British technicians to be left in the base. The Delegation believed that a ten-year agreement might be secured if we were to agree to run down the numbers of technicians on the following lines:

(i) 4,000 to stay for three years after the withdrawal of combatant troops (*i.e.*, for 4½ years after the date of the agreement);
(ii) the numbers to be reduced to 3,000 over the following two years;
(iii) the parties to consult then on the numbers to stay for the remaining 3½ years – failing agreement, the technicians would be withdrawn, but we should retain the right to inspect our stores and installations.

In other respects the Delegation would adhere to Case A, particularly as regards control of our own technicians, their right to wear uniform and to carry personal weapons, the control of our property in the base and the retention of staging rights to which the Air Staff attached importance as a link with the Far East. It was already agreed that a joint Anglo-Egyptian Air Defence Organisation would no longer be included in Case A.

On the question of access to the base, the Lord President said that the

Egyptians had held out strongly against allowing this either in the event of a major war or an attack on Persia or Turkey. It was difficult to find any satisfactory definition of a major war and it might be preferable to rely on some alternative formula referring to action by the United Nations. He therefore proposed that the Delegation should put the following formula to the Egyptians:

> 'In the event of the United Nations action to resist an act of aggression, or the event of an attack on any Arab country by an outside Power, the base area shall be at the full disposal of the United Kingdom. An attack on Turkey shall be regarded as an attack on an Arab country for the purposes of the Agreement. In the event of an attack on Persia, or in the event of a threat of an attack on any of the above-mentioned countries, there shall be immediate consultation between the United Kingdom and Egypt.'

The period for the withdrawal of British troops was estimated by the Chiefs of Staff at eighteen months from the date of the agreement and the Delegation expected that there might be some difficulty with the Egyptians over this. At present, however, it was not a point in the negotiations; it would be a practical matter for discussion when the negotiations were completed. Equally, the American interest in the base at Abu Sueir was a separate question.

In discussion the following points were made:

(a) The new proposal for the duration of the agreement had the grave disadvantage that it provided no guarantee that any British technicians would be left in the base after $6\frac{1}{2}$ years, and thereafter the base would not be of substantial use to British forces deployed elsewhere in the Middle East. Could we not arrive at some agreement by which the progressive reduction of British technicians was somewhat slower and made dependent on an efficient system of training Egyptians in substitution? It might, for example, be possible to persuade the Egyptians to agree that, in the last $3\frac{1}{2}$ years of a ten-year agreement, one or two thousand British technicians should be allowed to remain. The Lord President agreed to consider this proposal.

(b) The right of inspection after the withdrawal of British technicians might well be used with advantage; but the fact remained that, as there was no prospect of a long agreement, efforts would have to be made during the period of the agreement to remove valuable stores and movable installations from the base.

(c) The duration of the agreement would have an effect upon plans for the redeployment of British forces elsewhere in the Middle East. Was it worth incurring the expense of the redeployment if there was no guarantee that the base in Egypt would be available for the maintenance of these forces after $6\frac{1}{2}$ years?

(d) It was only at Abu Sueir, which had been developed for the Americans, that American technicians could be militarily useful. The Secretary of State for Air said that he would send the Lord President a note on the position at Abu Sueir and on any other points which particularly affected the Royal Air Force.

The Prime Minister said that it was the view of the Cabinet that the United Kingdom Delegation in Cairo should have discretion to negotiate on the terms proposed by the Lord President in C(53)232. They should, however, be reminded that we still hoped that firm dealing would result in a better agreement than that now proposed.

The Cabinet –

Authorised the Lord President to instruct the United Kingdom Delegation in Cairo on the lines proposed in C(53)232; but took note that he would first reconsider the proposals for reducing the numbers of British technicians in the light of the suggestions noted in paragraph (a) above.

[...]

8. The Cabinet had before them a note by the Lord President (subsequently circulated as C(53)236) covering:
   (i) a United States draft of a reply to the Soviet note of 4th August regarding the suggestion for a Four-Power Meeting of Foreign Ministers to discuss the future of Germany and Austria;
   (ii) a telegram from Her Majesty's Ambassador, Moscow, commenting on a further Soviet note of 15th August making new proposals regarding the future of Germany; and
   (iii) a Foreign Office draft of a reply to the Soviet Government which took into account the proposals made in this later Soviet note.

The Lord President said that the second Soviet note was plainly designed to influence the forthcoming election in Germany, and it might now be necessary that the Western Powers should reply to the first note before the elections. He awaited Dr Adenauer's final views on that point. He still considered, however, that the aim of the reply should be to secure the holding of a Four-Power Meeting, and he thought that the American draft was unduly controversial both in tone and in content. From that point of view it was fortunate that the American draft had been prepared before the second Soviet note had been received; and he hoped that the Foreign Office draft, which took account of that second note, might be adopted as the basis for the drafting work which was now to be undertaken in Paris by officials of the three Governments. He proposed two small changes in paragraphs 2 and 3 of the draft, viz. (i) that the opening words of paragraph 2 should be amended to read: 'In their note of August 4 the Soviet Government made the suggestion that . . .'; and that the second sentence of paragraph 2 should be transferred to the end of paragraph 3. Subject to these changes he commended the draft for approval by the Cabinet.

In discussion it was agreed that the Foreign Office draft was greatly to be preferred to the American and that every effort should be made to secure that it should be adopted as a basis for the drafting discussions which were about to be held in Paris.

The Prime Minister said that he was apprehensive about the statement in paragraph 4 of the draft that 'a peace treaty can only be negotiated with a free all-German Government . . . enjoying freedom of action in internal and external affairs'. If a unified Germany were allowed to achieve this degree of freedom before the conclusion of a peace treaty she would have nothing further to gain from such a treaty except the rectification of frontiers. Was this consistent with her unconditional surrender in 1945? Germany was still, after all, a defeated, divided and occupied country. Would it not be wiser to omit the words which referred to 'freedom of action in internal and external affairs'?

The Lord President said that a substantial measure of independence had already been given to Western Germany, which was no longer treated as an occupied country; and we should not wish to give the impression that we subscribed to the Soviet thesis that the Germans were still subject to dictation by the Powers to which they had surrendered in 1945. He was under the impression that the phrase 'enjoying freedom of action in internal and external affairs' had been used in earlier statements about Germany's future; and, if this were so, great suspicion would be caused if we now used a comparable phrase from which those words were omitted.

In further discussion reference was made to a statement in a note addressed to the Soviet Government on 25th March, 1952, that 'the all-German Government should be free both before and after the conclusion of a peace treaty to enter into associations compatible with the principles and purposes of the United Nations'. It was pointed out that this statement was qualified by the reference to the principles and the purposes of the United Nations. It was also suggested that similar statements contemplating freedom of action in external affairs from a German Government before the conclusion of a peace treaty might have been made in a context assuming the different matter to make such a statement in the unqualified terms used in the present draft.

It was the general view of the Cabinet that the words 'and itself enjoying freedom of action in internal and external affairs' should be deleted from paragraph 4 of the draft unless it were found that similar words had been used, without qualification, in earlier statements on the position of an all-German Government in the period before the conclusion of a peace treaty.

The Cabinet –

   (1) Invited the Lord President to review, in the light of their discussion, the wording of paragraph 4 of the draft reply to the Soviet notes of 4th and 15th August on the proposal for a Four-Power Meeting on the future of Germany.

   (2) Subject to conclusion (1) above, agreed that the draft prepared by the

Foreign Office would serve as a valuable basis for the forthcoming discussions with officials of the United States and French Governments regarding the terms of the reply to be sent to the Soviet notes.

9. The Commonwealth Secretary said that there had had been some serious rioting in Colombo following a general strike organised by the local Communist parties. The Ceylon Government feared that there might be further outbreaks of violence, and they had asked our High Commissioner in Colombo[1] whether, if the situation deteriorated and a formal request for assistance were made, naval landing parties from Her Majesty's ships now at Trincomalee could be made available to operate in aid of the civil power.

Opinion in the Cabinet was divided on the response which should be made to any such request. Some Ministers thought it of special importance that nothing should be done to blur the responsibility of the Ceylon Government for maintaining law and order. Others thought that prompt assistance rendered by United Kingdom forces, at the request of the Ceylon Government, would serve to demonstrate the readiness of members of the Commonwealth to help one another in time of difficulty. The Cabinet were reminded that United Kingdom troops had on two occasions operated in aid of the civil power in Newfoundland, when that territory was a self-governing Dominion.

The Cabinet's conclusion was that, if a situation arose in which the Ceylon Government found it necessary to ask for assistance by the United Kingdom's troops, naval landing parties from Her Majesty's ships already in the neighbourhood might be made available primarily for the purpose of guarding our own defence installations in the Island. The landing of these detachments would have some steadying effect, and their deployment to guard our own installations would free Ceylonese troops for other duties.

The Cabinet –

Invited the Commonwealth Secretary to give guidance to the United Kingdom High Commissioner in Colombo on the lines indicated in the Cabinet's discussion.

---

[1] Cecil George Lewis Syers, 1903–81. Educated at St Paul's and Balliol College, Oxford. Entered Dominions Office, 1925. Asst Private Secretary to Secretary of State for Dominion Affairs, 1930–4. Married, 1932, Yvonne Allen: one child. Private Secretary to PM, 1937–40. Asst Secretary, Treasury, 1940. Deputy UK High Commander, Union of South Africa, 1942–6. Asst Under-Secretary of State, Commonwealth Relations Office, 1946–8. Deputy Under-Secretary of State, 1948–51. High Commissioner for the UK in Ceylon, 1951–7. Doyen of Diplomatic Corps, Ceylon, 1953–7. Secretary, University Grants Commission, 1958–63.

August 1953

Sir Winston S. Churchill to Henry Laughlin[1]
(Churchill papers, 4/14)

22 August 1953

I cannot guarantee Ninth for absolute final but I will try to give you the minimum wordage of every chapter in each volume and if any additions are made they will be balanced by other omissions. Moreover you have a certain margin at the end of each chapter. This should enable page-proof setting to be completed. I hope this will meet your difficulty. Kelly is preparing the minimum wordage list, which will reach you by airmail. I hope you and Book of Month will make the inside margins sufficiently wide even at the expense of outside page margins. It is so inconvenient not to be able to open a book easily and many publishers now cut the inner margin unduly. A quarter of an inch would be ample. I am so glad you like the volume.

Sir Winston S. Churchill to Pamela Churchill[2]
(Churchill papers, 1/51)

24 August 1953

My dear Pamela,

Thank you so much for sending me Winston's report. I think it is very good. I have kept a copy and am sending you back the original. I am preparing to encounter Winston in '*attaque*'. When are we going to meet?

Cabinet: conclusions
(Cabinet papers, 128/26)

25 August 1953
Secret
3 p.m.
Cabinet Meeting No. 50 of 1953

[. . .]

4. The Lord President gave the Cabinet a brief account of the loyalist revolution in Persia, which had resulted in the overthrow of Dr Musaddiq's government. There was reason to believe that, if this military *coup d'etat* had not succeeded, a Communist revolution would have been attempted; and it

---

[1] Henry Alexander Laughlin, 1892–1978. President of Houghton Mifflin Co., 1939–77. Responsible for the publication in the US of Hitler's *Mein Kampf* as well as Churchill's *The Second World War*.

[2] Pamela Digby, 1920–97. Daughter of 11th Baron Digby. Married, 1939, Randolph Churchill (div. 1946); their son Winston was born at Chequers in 1940. Subsequently married Leyland Hayward (1960; d. 1971), and then Averell Harriman (1971). Took US citizenship, 1971. US Ambassador to Paris from 1993 until her death.

was in our interests that General Zahedi's[1] Government should become more firmly established since, with the disappearance of Dr Musaddiq, a Communist régime was now the only alternative. The new Persian Government would stand in immediate need of financial assistance from abroad. The United States would probably be disposed to offer this; and, unless we were prepared to sacrifice all prospect of re-establishing British influence in Persia, we should be well-advised to join with them in extending financial assistance to the Persians and in seeking an early solution of the Anglo-Persian oil dispute.

The Prime Minister endorsed this view. In present circumstances it would be easy for the Americans, by the expenditure of a relatively small sum of money, to reap all the benefits of many years of British work in Persia. He therefore hoped that the task of supporting General Zahedi's Government might be undertaken on an Anglo-American basis.

The Chancellor of the Exchequer said that he would deprecate any hasty offer of a loan to General Zahedi. It could be repaid only in oil; and the Anglo-Iranian Oil Company, having developed other sources of supply, were now less interested in securing a resumption of the flow of oil from Persia. It would be premature to offer a loan to a Government which had not yet resumed diplomatic relations with us. And we might find it embarrassing to be lending money to Persia when we were obliged to refuse applications for development loans from friendlier countries in the Middle East and even from our partners in the Commonwealth. He suggested that we should in the first instance ascertain the views of the United States Government, and that any offer of financial help which we might give should in some way be made conditional upon a satisfactory settlement of the oil dispute.

The Cabinet –

Invited the Lord President to consider further, with the Chancellor of the Exchequer, the possibility of rendering some financial assistance to the new Persian Government, and to ascertain what were the intentions of the United States Government in this regard.

[. . .]

6. The Lord President reported the latest developments in the defence negotiations with the Egyptians. There now seemed to be some prospect of obtaining an agreement within the limits of the concessions approved by the Cabinet at their meeting on 18th August.

The Prime Minister said that the United Kingdom Delegation in Cairo had done well. They should be encouraged to maintain the firm attitude which they had shown.

---

[1] Fazlollah Zahedi, 1892–1963. Educated at Iranian Military Academy. Company Cdr, 1915. Brig.-Gen., 1917. Military Governor, Khuzestan Province, 1926–32. Chief of National Police, 1932–41, 1949–50. Imprisoned, 1942–5. Inspector of Military Forces, 1945–9. Senator, 1950–1. Minister of the Interior, 1951. Minister of Foreign Affairs, 1953. PM of Iran, 1953–5. Iranian Ambassador to UN, 1955–63.

The Secretary of State for War said that we could be more certain of being able to complete the withdrawal of our combatant troops from the Canal Zone within the suggested period of 18 months if further progress could be made with the preparation of military installations in Cyprus. The Prime Minister said that there should be no acceleration of this work until an agreement had been reached with the Egyptians.

The Cabinet – Took note of these statements.

[. . .]

Sir Winston S. Churchill to Lord Salisbury
Prime Minister's Personal Minute M.282/53
(Premier papers, 11/497)

25 August 1953
Secret

NAVAL VISIT TO THE SOVIET BLACK SEA PORTS

I do not press it now but, in any case, it could not be made on a smaller scale than the recent visit to Constantinople. That would be worse than nothing.

Sir Winston S. Churchill to General Walter Bedell Smith
(Churchill papers, 2/217)

25 August 1953

My dear Bedell,

In my final read I have made some alterations in Chapters IV and VI as you last saw them. You will see that I have cut out from VI, at the bottom of page 10, the quotation from Ike and my argument against it. I have also cut out Mark Clark's statement on page 13 and I have cut down the Smuts' quotations so that they do not bear on the 'Anvil–Dragoon' controversy. I have also put in a summing up of my own. The changes which I have made do not appreciably alter the balance of the story. The differences of view which arose over 'Anvil–Dragoon' are matters of history and, as you say, they cannot be glossed over. But I have softened some of the sharp edges here and there, and I have deleted or modified all the phrases to which you drew particular attention in the earlier version.

I enclose copies of the original version which was sent to you earlier and of the final version. Unless I hear to the contrary I shall go ahead.

Evelyn Shuckburgh: diary
('Descent to Suez', pages 99–100)

26–27 August 1953

All this week we are trying to conduct our foreign policy through the PM who is at Chartwell and always in the bath or asleep or too busy having dinner when we want urgent decisions. He has to be consulted about drafting points in the reply to the Soviets; about every individual 'intelligence' operation (which he usually forbids for fear of upsetting the Russians); about telegrams to Persia and Egypt. We are constantly telephoning minutes and draft telegrams down to Chartwell. After many minutes and arguments he has consented not to insist upon a full-scale naval visit to Sebastopol. This idea occurred to him as a means of offsetting British and American naval visits to Turkey which the Russians have complained about. There are inspired stories in the evening papers that the PM is engaged in forming a new Government for the autumn with AE as a sort of Deputy – described in the *Standard* as 'Personal Assistant to Sir Winston' and Leader of the House. Monckton is tipped for Foreign Secretary, mainly because he has recently lunched at Chartwell.

I went over to see Monckton one day this week at the Ministry of Labour in St James's Square to talk about the 'Windsor' papers – captured German documents which show how the Germans tried to get hold of the Duke in 1940 when he was in Portugal. M described what a terrible time he had in 1940 persuading the Duke and the Duchess to get on board ship for the Bahamas, and how she was persuaded that the British would murder him, etc. He said one must always remember how completely at sea a king is, who has always been surrounded with advisers and had the best opinions constantly available to him, when he finds himself alone. . . . M seems to have an affection for the Duke and none for her. He sent me back to the FO in his car as there was a tropical downpour.

Cabinet decided – feebly and under pressure from the PM – to try to suppress the Windsor papers. There is sure to be a row with the historians who will regard this as tampering with history. The PM and Salisbury are to see the British editor, Miss Lambert, and try to 'persuade' her. She has already threatened to resign if her historian's conscience is assailed. We shall see.

Salisbury very concerned at having to continue as Acting Foreign Secretary for two reasons:

(1) He does not approve of our line in recognizing Red China and will not want to be responsible for pressing for her admission to the United Nations;

(2) he disapproves of the PM's policy of trying to get a top-level meeting with the Russians. He says it is one thing to be a member of the Cabinet and to refrain from opposing such policies but quite another to be the responsible Minister.

Now I see why AE gets so little active support in Cabinet when he is fighting the PM's bright ideas.

September 1953

Sir Winston S. Churchill to Lord Salisbury
Prime Minister's Personal Minute M.285/53
(Premier papers)

2 September 1953

I do not think it surprising that the Russians have refused to come to a Conference about the Austrian Treaty. A settlement about Austria before a settlement about Germany would be disturbing to their general position. It is always well to try to put oneself in the other man's view point. If I were in the Kremlin, and even if I were well intentioned, I would not think that a settlement with Austria would be a good prelude to German negotiations.

Lady Churchill to Sir Winston S. Churchill
(Churchill papers, 1/50)[1]

3 September 1953

My darling Winston,

It was sweet of you to ring me up last night & to say loving & forgiving words to me. I would like to persuade you to give up Doncaster & Balmoral. <u>First Doncaster</u>. You will be watched by loving but anxious & curious crowds. It would be rather an effort to keep up steady walking. It may be a longish way to the Paddock & there will be much standing about. Altho' you sit in the Queen's Presence in intimate Court Circles, if you sat in public when she was standing it would be noticed. <u>Then Balmoral</u>. You are improving steadily though slowly, but I fear you are not up to a night in the train and so on yet. And you don't want to have a set-back before the Margate Speech; but rather you must husband your strength for that important event, & for Parliament. Doctor Barnett who has just been to see me (& diagnoses cracked ribs) says

---

[1] This letter was handwritten.

that the improvement in you will (or may if not arrested by fatigue) continue for 2 years.[1]

I will be with you this afternoon.

Lady Churchill to Mary Soames
(Mary Soames, 'Clementine Churchill', page 437)

5 September 1953

I am sad about Papa; because in spite of the brave show he makes, he gets very easily tired & then he gets depressed – He does too much work & has not yet learnt how & when to stop. It just tails off drearily & he won't go to bed. He *is* making progress, but now it is imperceptible. If no setback occurs the improvement can continue for 2 years. . . . I expect you have seen from the newspapers the tremendous 'va-et-vient' of ministers. Papa enjoys it very much. Incidentally they are even more tired than he is by the sitting over the dinner table till after midnight! . . .

Cabinet: conclusions
(Cabinet papers, 128/26)

8 September 1953
Secret
11.30 a.m.
Cabinet Meeting No. 51 of 1953

[. . .]

2. The Cabinet had before them a memorandum by the Parliamentary Under-Secretary of State for Foreign Affairs (C(53)249) describing the present state of defence negotiations with Egypt.

The Prime Minister said that it now seemed possible that we could come to some agreement with Egypt on the outstanding points in the negotiations – the number of technicians, the duration of the agreement and the availability of the base; but great care would be needed in presenting any such agreement to Parliament and the public. The omission of any reference to freedom of transit through the Suez Canal would certainly attract criticism, as it was the popular belief that this was the main purpose of our military base in the Canal Zone.

General Sir Brian Robertson said that there were still several obstacles

---

[1] On Sep. 11, Churchill disregarded his wife's advice and travelled to both Doncaster and Balmoral as guest of the Queen.

to the conclusion of a defence agreement. Thus, the Egyptians had not yet agreed that British technicians in the base should wear uniform; they had not accepted our view of the numbers of British technicians to remain after three years; they had not agreed that it would take eighteen months to withdraw British forces; and they had not undertaken to go beyond a five-year agreement. He thought, however, that they might be induced to accept a seven-year agreement made up of (i) eighteen months for the withdrawal of combatant troops; (ii) three further years with 4,000 technicians; (iii) two-and-a-half years with a smaller number of technicians or inspectors. They would agree to any form of words which made the reactivation of the base dependent upon action by the United Nations to resist an act of aggression or upon an attack on any member of the Arab Mutual Security Pact. They would not, however, agree to automatic reactivation in the event of attacks on Turkey or Persia. He thought it probable that the Egyptians would agree to some reaffirmation, perhaps in the preamble of the agreement, of their existing obligations for allowing freedom of transit in the Suez Canal, but he did not think they could be induced to include in the agreement any extension or variation of these obligations.

In discussion the following points were made:
- (a) It was likely that we should need the help of the United States in persuading Egypt to accept the points still in dispute. The United States might be less willing to lend this support if we sought to include in the agreement any full definition of future rights of transit though the Suez Canal. They were particularly sensitive on this point because of their own position with regard to the Panama Canal.
- (b) The opinion was expressed that, even if no absolute settlement of the Suez Canal problem could be included in the defence agreement with Egypt, there would be some advantage in getting into the preamble of the agreement some general formula about freedom of transit through the Canal. This would go some way towards reassuring public opinion in this country, and it would open the way for fuller negotiations at a later stage in which all interested maritime Powers might take part.

The Cabinet −
- (1) Agreed that there no longer seemed to be any serious objection of principle to the conclusion of a defence agreement with the Egyptian Government on the general lines now envisaged by the United Kingdom Delegation in Cairo, as outlined in C(53)249, if some suitable reference to the Suez Canal could be included in the preamble to such an agreement.
- (2) Appointed a Cabinet Committee consisting of −

Lord Privy Seal (Chairman)
Commonwealth Secretary
Colonial Secretary
Minister of Transport
Parliamentary Under-Secretary of State for Foreign Affairs

Together with Lord Leathers and General Sir Brian Robertson, to make recommendations on the points still outstanding in the defence negotiations with Egypt and to consider, in particular, the possibility of including in the preamble to the agreement an appropriate formula about the international rights of passage through the Suez Canal.

(3) Agreed to consider the report of the Cabinet Committee at their next meeting.

The Cabinet considered a note by the Secretary of the Cabinet (C(53)246) covering a memorandum by the Chiefs of Staff on the measures that would be needed if the situation in the Canal Zone deteriorated.

The Minister of Defence said that, although the situation in the Canal Zone had become easier during the past year, there was always the danger that the Egyptian Government might stimulate hostile activities against British troops. Experience had shown that widespread security measures were needed to deal effectively with outbreaks of violence and that these measures might have to be put into force at very short notice. The Chiefs of Staff had therefore recommended that the Cabinet should delegate authority to the Prime Minister, the Acting Foreign Secretary and the Minister of Defence, to bring into force the military measures in Egypt which would be needed in an emergency. They suggested also that, if the situation in the Canal Zone deteriorated, there might be advantage in issuing a formal warning to the Egyptian Government about the maintenance of law and order.

The Prime Minister said that he did not think it necessary for the Cabinet to do more than take note of the points raised by the Chiefs of Staff in their memorandum. If the situation did in fact deteriorate, it might well be desirable to issue a formal warning to the Egyptian Government, and at that point it might also be necessary to authorise the Commanders-in-Chief in the Middle East to put in hand widespread security measures; but this situation could be faced when it arose. If the situation deteriorated so rapidly that a full Cabinet could not be summoned to consider it, the Prime Minister would take upon himself the responsibility for giving the necessary instructions. It should not be forgotten that there were economic and financial sanctions which could be applied to Egypt without having recourse to active intervention by British forces. It was open to us to block Egypt's sterling balances and to control the flow of oil to Cairo.

The Chancellor of the Exchequer pointed out that Egypt's use of sterling was already controlled by a severe sterling release agreement. So long as there was hope of a successful conclusion to the defence negotiations, it would be better not to depart from this agreement. On the other hand, he did not wish at the present stage to consider increasing the extent of economic and financial aid to Egypt, as suggested by Her Majesty's Chargé d'Affaires in Cairo.[1] That was a question which could be further discussed as the defence negotiations proceeded.

The Cabinet –

(4) Took note of the memorandum by the Chiefs of Staff (C(53)246).

3. The Cabinet had before them a memorandum by the Minister of Defence (C(53)245) seeking approval of the main features of a proposed new Defence Agreement with the Government of Burma.

The Minister of Defence said that the Burmese Government wished to replace the present Defence Agreement (Cmd. 7240 of 1947), which was due to expire on 3rd January next, by a new agreement on the lines of the draft annexed to his paper. The main change would be the substitution of a British instructional team, to help with the training of Burma's armed forces, for the existing Services Mission, whose functions were advisory. Burma would continue to procure military material from this country, but her requirements would no longer be scrutinised by British military representatives in Rangoon. The value of the proposed agreement would be insignificant from a narrow military point of view, but on wider strategic, political and economic grounds the Chiefs of Staff favoured its conclusion. The Burmese would meet the cost of all that they received under an agreement, and the position of our instructional team should be acceptable provided that it was not made subject to Burmese control.

The Parliamentary Under-Secretary of State for Foreign Affairs said that the draft agreement annexed to C(53)245 represented the most which the Burmese Government hoped to obtain from an agreement, and it should be possible to make the terms of any new agreement more acceptable to us during the course of negotiation.

The Secretary of State for War said that it was particularly important that the Burmese should be pressed to concede sufficiently attractive terms of service to enable us to staff our instructional team by volunteers including, if necessary, retired officers and men. He would be most reluctant to agree that the team should be staffed to any extent by means of compulsory posting.

The Prime Minister said that, in spite of Burma's unsatisfactory record, the balance of advantage appeared to lie on the side of retaining, if possible, this link with her armed forces. The size of the proposed instructional team should not, however, exceed the size of the existing Mission.

The Cabinet –

[1] Michael Creswell.

Agreed that negotiations should be undertaken with the Government in Burma for the conclusion of a new Defence Agreement on the general lines proposed in C(53)245.

4. The Cabinet considered a memorandum by the Lord President (C(53)247) discussing the line which should be taken by the United Kingdom Delegation if the question of China's representation at the United Nations were raised at the forthcoming session of the General Assembly.

The Parliamentary Under-Secretary of State for Foreign Affairs said that, since this memorandum was circulated, Her Majesty's Ambassador in Washington had discussed the matter with the United States Secretary of State. Mr Dulles was unwilling to accept our suggestion of a resolution postponing consideration of this question until the Assembly had been able to consider the position in the light of developments resulting from the establishment of a Political Conference on Korea. It seemed likely that, despite our representations, he would continue to favour a resolution postponing consideration of this question for a further year. This was the formula which had been adopted in earlier years, when Chinese Communist troops were fighting against United Nations forces in Korea; and public opinion in this country would expect that some account should now be taken of the fact that an armistice had been concluded. It was therefore proposed that, if the Americans insisted on bringing forward a resolution in those terms, we should abstain from voting. But our Delegation would be in a more difficult position if some other Delegation put forward, as an amendment, an alternative resolution on the lines of that which we had ourselves suggested to the Americans. In that event it might perhaps be difficult for us to abstain from voting on the amendment.

The Prime Minister said that he strongly endorsed the statement, in paragraph 5 of C(53)247, that it would be unwise to subject Anglo-American relations, so soon, to a second strain comparable to that which arose from our proposal that India should be a member of the Political Conference on Korea. We should be well-advised to go to great lengths to avoid any further cause of Anglo-American misunderstanding at the present time. It was natural that, after all the losses and suffering which they had endured in the Korean war, the Americans should feel reluctant to see Communist China take her seat in the United Nations; and we should make due allowance for the strength of this feeling, which was not likely to be influenced by considerations of logic or expediency.

In discussion it was agreed that we should avoid voting against the Americans on this question on this occasion. Further attempts should be made, between now and the opening of the Assembly, to find some compromise formula which both we and the Americans could support. The Americans might perhaps be willing to accept a resolution which would have the effect that consideration of this question would be postponed for one year or until there had been a settlement of outstanding issues in Korea, whichever was the earlier. If, however, these attempts should fail and the Americans brought forward a resolution proposing postponement for one year, we should abstain from voting. If some other Delegation should bring forward a resolution on the lines indicated in paragraph 2 of C(53)247, and the Americans decided to vote against it, we should also abstain from voting; for we must avoid a situation in which we and the Americans voted in opposite lobbies on this question.

The Cabinet –
(1) Invited the Parliamentary Under-Secretary of state for Foreign Affairs to continue the search for a form of resolution regarding Chinese representation in the United Nations which could be supported by both the United Kingdom and the United States; and asked him, in particular, to ascertain whether the United States would support a resolution postponing this question for one year, or until there had been a settlement of outstanding issues in Korea, whichever was the earlier.
(2) Agreed that the United Kingdom Delegation at the General Assembly should be instructed that they should in no circumstances vote against the United States Delegation on this issue; that they should not vote in favour of a resolution postponing consideration of this question for a full year; and that they should abstain from voting in any circumstances in which this became necessary in order to avoid an open conflict of view with the United States Delegation.

[. . .]

6. The Parliamentary Secretary, Ministry of Labour,[1] informed the Cabinet of the latest developments in the strike called by the Electrical Trades Union. A further attempt was to be made, at a meeting at the Ministry of Labour that afternoon, to secure agreement between the two parties to the dispute; but this was unlikely to succeed and, if it failed, a Court of Enquiry would at once be appointed to make a report on all the relevant facts. It did not follow, however, that this would necessarily bring the strike to an end.

The Prime Minister welcomed the proposal to appoint a Court of Enquiry. He thought it important that there should be a full public exposure of the new and sinister techniques adopted by this Union, in calling out on strike selected workers in undertakings of special importance to the national economy. These innovations might with advantage be debated in the House of Commons, when Parliament re-assembled, even though the strike was then over.

The Cabinet –

Took note of these statements.

[. . .]

---

[1] Harold Arthur Watkinson, 1910–95. Served with RNVR during WWII. MP (Cons.) for Woking Div. of Surrey, 1950–64. Parliamentary Private Secretary to Minister of Transport and Civil Aviation, 1951–2; to Ministry of Labour and National Service, 1952–5. Minister of Transport and Civil Aviation, 1955–9. Minister of Defence, 1959–62. Viscount, 1964.

Sir Winston S. Churchill to Antony Head
Prime Minister's Personal Minute M.296/53
(Premier papers, 11/487)

10 September 1953

Your paragraph 2.[1] Let me have the establishment in units of the Infantry Division in question. What is the difference between an Armoured Brigade and an Armoured Brigade Group?

2. Let me have the establishment of Joint Headquarters.

3. I should have thought that the earliest to move would be the Guards and Infantry Brigades since this would mean the minimum of paraphernalia and the maximum of men coming home. Instead you pick a Commando Brigade which one could have thought would have stayed towards the end to cope with unexpected events.

4. Let me have the establishment of a Field Regiment. I presume it is three batteries of four guns and about 170 men per battery. What is the calibre of the guns and the weight of shell?

5. What is the difference between a Regiment (of Artillery) and a Field Regiment?

6. In paragraph 3 you describe the garrison at Cyprus as one Infantry Brigade and Joint Headquarters but in paragraph 4 one Field Regiment and one Field Engineer Regiment are to be moved to Cyprus in the first movement. Please explain this. Also in Libya: in paragraph 3, one Armoured Brigade and in paragraph 4 One Armoured Regiment, one Field Regiment and one Field Engineer Regiment. Are these additional units or components of one Armoured Brigade?

7. Let me have the establishment of the Survey Engineer Regiment. Why is it included in the Cyprus Infantry Brigade?

8. Finally how many officers and men are to reach the UK in 18 months? How many are to reach Cyprus and how many Libya? How many is the present actual total strength?

9. If you give me these facts I shall be able to see the picture more clearly.

---

[1] Para. 2 of Head's minute read: 'At the Present moment we have in the Middle East: One Infantry Division; One Infantry Division less one Brigade; One Independent Parachute Brigade Group; One Armoured Brigade Group.'

September 1953

Sir Winston S. Churchill to Alan Hodge[1]
(*Churchill papers, 4/27*)

11 September 1953
Private and Confidential

Thank you so much for all the trouble you have taken and the most valuable suggestions you have made.

Of course I cannot give necessary attention to this project until my burdens in other directions are lightened and I do not yet know when that will be. The final grasping of Volume I, of which I sent you a copy, is not a work which can be combined with my present duties. I should however like you very much to interest yourself in the enterprise and I shall look forward to another talk with you and with Brendan.

I have today put together what has been written on the Tudor period, with which I am far from content. If you will kindly piece it together I will have it reprinted for what it is worth. It can then be the basis for further study. You could also note many omissions which exist, but it is not worth spending time upon.

Meanwhile I send you a paper on the story of the Common Law with which a great deal of pains was taken at the time, and is I believe a good factual authority. I should be glad if you would look it through and consider whether the part applicable to Volume I, namely to the end of Galley 627, would be better interleaved reign by reign or period by period, or whether it should not be woven into a general chapter of its own. I am afraid it is one to which many readers would not devote the necessary attention. The theme of the growth of our Common Law which is the inheritance of the English-speaking Peoples as a whole, must however run through the story. It will take some art to tell this tale to others than lawyers who know much of it already.

It will be great interest to me to immerse myself in this work without the violent distractions which filled the years 1938/9, and I hope I may have your company and perhaps that of some of your friends in browsing about these extensive pastures.

---

[1] Alan Hodge, 1915–79. Married, 1938, Beryl Pritchard (div. 1943); 1947, Jane Aiken: two children. Asst Private Secretary to Minister of Information, 1941–5. Editor of *The Novel Library*, 1946–52. Joint Editor of *History Today*, 1951–79. Churchill's principal research assistant for *A History of the English-Speaking Peoples* from 1953.

Cabinet: conclusions
(Cabinet papers, 128/26)

16 September 1953
Secret
5 p.m.
Cabinet Meeting No. 53 of 1953

1. The Cabinet had before them memoranda by the Lord Privy Seal (C(53)254) and the Lord President (C(53)257) on the outstanding issues in the negotiations for a Defence Agreement with Egypt.

The Lord President said that the prospects of concluding an Agreement now appeared to be reasonably good but it was essential that the terms of any Agreement should prove acceptable to Government supporters. Of the two main outstanding issues, one concerned the duration of the Agreement and the number of technicians to be allowed at the various stages. Hitherto, we had been unwilling to go below ten years and the Egyptians had not gone above five. General Robertson now believed that he could obtain six-and-a-half years and that in certain circumstances the Egyptians might be induced to accept a seven-year Agreement made up of –

(a) 18 months for withdrawal of combatant troops;
(b) 3 further years with 4,000 technicians;
(c) 2½ years with a smaller number of technicians and inspectors.

He considered that seven years was the minimum period likely to be acceptable to Government supporters in Parliament and the country and that our delegation should be instructed to reduce their minimum requirement to seven years but no further.

The Prime Minister said that in the circumstances we must be content with a seven-year Agreement but we must also be prepared to face a breakdown of the negotiations on this issue, if necessary.

The Lord Privy Seal said that the second main issue on which a Cabinet decision was required concerned freedom of navigation through the Suez Canal. The Committee under his chairmanship which had considered this matter recommended that our delegation should be instructed to secure Egyptian agreement to the inclusion in the preamble to the Defence Agreement of a clause in the following terms:

'Recognising the economic, commercial and strategic importance of the Suez Canal as an International waterway and being agreed as to the necessity of preserving and upholding the principles of freedom of navigation set forth in the international Convention at present governing the use of the Canal;'

and that it should be made clear to the Egyptian negotiators that we wished also to see a suitable article included in the body of the Agreement.

Discussion showed that the Cabinet adhered to their view that some reference to this matter should be included in the Defence Agreement. They considered that the suggested clause for inclusion in the preamble would be very suitable for this purpose. They agreed that the essential need at this stage was to secure Egyptian agreement to the inclusion of such a clause in the preamble. Placed there it would have sufficient legal validity to be used later as the basis for a complaint to the International Court if Egypt should disregard her obligations and it would pave the way for a subsequent multilateral approach to Egypt by the main maritime Powers.

The Lord President said that our chances of reaching final agreement with the Egyptians on terms that were acceptable to us would be enhanced if we were able to enlist general American support or at the very least, by making abundantly clear the limits beyond which we were in no circumstances prepared to go on the main outstanding issues, prevent the United States Ambassador in Cairo from again raising false hopes among the Egyptians.

The Prime Minister said that he would consider whether he should follow up any approach which the Lord President might make to Mr Dulles for this purpose by a personal message to President Eisenhower. It might well be, however, that, in spite of all our efforts, it would not prove possible to reach an acceptable Agreement with the Egyptians; if this should happen, we must not flinch from the consequences. If, on the other hand, an Agreement was finally concluded, we must make sure that we reaped the full advantages to be derived from it, including the greatest possible reduction in our military forces in the Middle East.

The Minister of Defence said that, if an Agreement should materialize, he would share the Prime Minister's desire to effect the greatest possible reduction in our forces in the Middle East consistent with the maintenance of our prestige and influence in that important area. The exact disposition of the forces that remained was a matter to be considered later.

The Commonwealth Secretary welcomed the proposal in paragraph 7 of C(53)257 to communicate our minimum requirements on the main outstanding issues also to the Governments of India, Pakistan and Iraq.

The Chancellor of the Exchequer said that there were also important financial aspects of the proposed Agreement with Egypt which must in no circumstances be allowed to go by default.

General Sir Brian Robertson said that special arrangements had recently been made to ensure that these aspects of the Agreement were adequately handled during the remaining stages of the negotiations.

The Prime Minister said that the Cabinet would wish to record their appreciation of the services which General Robertson had already rendered in this matter and their good wishes to him for the successful conclusion of negotiations.

The Cabinet –

SEPTEMBER 1953   1211

(1) Agreed that our delegation in Cairo should be instructed:
   (a) to propose to the Egyptians a seven-year Agreement on the lines of 'X' above;[1]
   (b) to secure Egyptian assent to the inclusion in the preamble to the Agreement of a clause in the terms set out at 'Y' above[2] and to indicate that we should also wish to see a suitable article included in the body of the Agreement.
(2) Approved the draft formula regarding the availability of the base set out in Annex B to C(53)254.
(3) Invited the Lord President to seek American support for our final proposals to the Egyptians.

2. The Commonwealth Secretary reported that, in spite of the efforts made by the Prime Minister and himself, Pakistan was determined to become a Republic, and that the Constituent Assembly, which would meet on 22nd September, would take decisions accordingly. Thereafter the Government of Pakistan would almost certainly ask that Pakistan as a sovereign independent Republic should continue full membership of the Commonwealth. This was a matter on which application would have to be made to all members of the Commonwealth, but he assumed that the Government of the United Kingdom would agree to it if, as seemed likely, this proved to be the general wish. The fact was that, although many prominent Pakistanis were anxious to continue to recognize the Crown, there was an overwhelming popular feeling in Pakistan in favour of a Republic.

3. The Prime Minister said that this was the last meeting of the Cabinet at which Lord Leathers would be present. He knew that the Cabinet would share his regret at losing the services of Lord Leathers, which had been of the greatest value both to the present Government and to the Coalition Government during the war.

Field Marshal Lord Alexander to Sir Winston S. Churchill
(Premier papers, 11/487)

16 September 1953

REDEPLOYMENT OF BRITISH TROOPS IN THE MIDDLE EAST

You asked for my comments on paragraph 3 of Foreign Office telegram No. 378 from Ankara.[3]

[1] Referring to points (a), (b) and (c) above.
[2] Referring to quotation above beginning 'Recognising the economic, commercial and strategic importance ...'.
[3] Para. 3 read: '[The Secretary-General] explained that the Prime Minister's misgivings had no concern in the necessity of these facilities being granted. The Prime Minister was, however, apprehensive lest evacuation of British forces from the Canal Zone would make more difficult, or at least delay,

2. In May this year a conference (Emerald Green) was held between the representatives from our Army and Air Headquarters in the Middle East and the NATO Land Forces Command for South East Europe about the practical requirements for Turkish Ground Forces and Middle East Land Forces. It was there agreed that GHQ, MELF should inform the Turks about their requirements for stock-piling in Turkey in the vicinity of the Aleppo–Mosul railway in peace and for use of the railway in war.

3. The Turkish Prime Minister has expressed doubts about the effect of our redeployment from the Canal Zone on the movement of British troops in war to the north-east passes between Persia and Iraq. The Counsellor's purpose was to reassure the Turks that redeployment need not affect our plans for forward deployment in war.

4. It seems to me important at this stage that we should not let the Turks think that we are backing out of our responsibilities in the Middle East, including the support of their right flank. I consider, therefore, that the Counsellor's statement was on the right lines, although it was perhaps unfortunate that he went so far as to say that the bulk of our troops would remain in the Middle East.

5. It is the present recommendation of the Chiefs of Staff that if we make an agreement with the Egyptians involving the withdrawal of combatant troops from the Canal Zone, we should retain one armoured division in the ME. The speed with which forces could be deployed in N Iraq in war will depend on whether we are able to locate the armoured brigade in Jordan in peace.

Lord Butler: recollection
('The Art of the Possible', page 171)

17 September 1953

At the end of September I heard from Anthony who was in Athens at the conclusion of a yachting trip round the Greek islands. He thanked me for my help during this taxing time and added, 'I really feel well now and hope to be a passenger in the boat no longer.' By the same post I had a letter from my niece, Jane Portal, who was at Cap d'Ail with Winston as his secretary. She said, 'The PM has been in the depth of depression. He broods continually whether to give up or not. He was exhausted by Balmoral and the Cabinets and the journey. I sometimes feel he would be better engaged on his *History of the English Speaking Peoples* which is already very remarkable. He greatly likes

---

the dispatch of British Forces to the northern Iraq passes on the outbreak of hostilities. Counsellor said that whatever plans may be made for re-deployment of British troops [? gp. omitted] evacuation from the Canal Zone, the bulk of them would doubtless remain in the new Middle East area, and it need not be assumed that their new locations would be such as to delay the moving of forces to northern Iraq in the event of hostilities.'

your messages telling him all the news and you are in high favour. He is preparing a speech for the Margate conference but wonders how long he can be on his pins to deliver it. He has painted one picture in tempera from his bedroom window.'

Sir Winston S. Churchill to Field Marshal Alexander of Tunis
Prime Minister's Personal Minute M.298/53
(Premier papers, 11/487)

18 September 1953

I certainly think the Counsellor's statement was unfortunate. The actual policy will require early decision should an agreement be reached with Egypt. I should like to know the establishment of the Armoured Division in question. I have always understood the expression of 'locate' to mean 'to find' but in para. 5 it is used as if it meant 'stationed'.

Sir Winston S. Churchill to Lady Churchill
(Baroness Spencer-Churchill papers)[1]

18 September 1953   Cap d'Ail

Darling,

All is beautiful & sunlit here. There is a sense of peace & quiet. Nothing but your presence is lacking. The children swim & I have plunged in *Coningsby*. I am going to have a smack at a canvas this afternoon. There is no scarcity of official papers – but I know how to melt them into an easy existence as Honorary Mayor of Cap d'Ail!

Fondest love Darling do not worry about anything for a space, but think again about coming here when the children leave.

I have written to the Queen[2] & send you a copy (secret)

With all my love
Your loving Husband

Sir Winston S. Churchill to Paul-Henri Spaak
(Premier papers, 11/1338)

21 September 1953

Dear M Spaak,

Thank you for your letter of September 4 inviting me to attend the Congress

---

[1] This letter was handwritten.
[2] Letter excerpted in Martin Gilbert, *Winston S. Churchill*, vol. 8, *Never Despair, 1945–1965*, pp. 886–7.

to be held at The Hague. I regret that the pressure of my duties makes it impossible for me to accept your invitation.

You know, however, that Her Majesty's Government support the efforts of the six countries to strengthen the unity of Europe. These efforts have already led to the setting up of the European Coal and Steel Community and the European Defence Community, with both of which Her Majesty's Government wish to be closely associated. We in the United Kingdom are watching with sympathy and interest the endeavours of the European Defence Community countries to crown this structure with a six-power Political Community for Europe. I am sure the Hague Congress, which is to discuss this project under your guidance, will make an enlightened contribution to these studies.

Sir Winston S. Churchill to Lady Churchill
(Baroness Spencer-Churchill papers)[1]

21 September 1953

My darling one,

The days pass quickly & quietly. I have hardly been outside the garden, & so far have not had the energy to paint in the sunlight hours. Maugham[2] who lunched yesterday said that we had left it late in the year to come here. But the climate is mild and cheerful, but for one downpour & thunderstorm. I do not think I have made much progress tho as usual I eat, drink & sleep well. I think a great deal about you & feel how much I love you. The kittens are very kind to me, but evidently they do not think much of my prospects. I have done the daily work and kept check on the gloomy tangle of the world, and I have dictated about 2000 words of a possible speech for Margate in order to try & see how I can let it off when it is finished to a select audience. I still ponder on the future and don't want to decide unless I am convinced.

Today I went into Monte Carlo and bought a grisly book by the author of *All is quiet on the Western Front*.[3] It is all about concentration camps, but in good readable print, which matters to me. It is like taking refuge from melancholy in horror. It provides a background. I have read almost ¾ of *Coningsby*, but the print was faint and small. I am glad I did not have to live in that artificial society of dukes & would-be duchesses with their Tadpole & Tapers. I think it would be interesting to write a short condensed account of the Victorian

[1] This letter was handwritten.
[2] William Somerset Maugham, 1874–1965. British writer. Educated at King's School, Canterbury, and Heidelberg University. Married, 1917, Syrie Wellcome: one child. Served in Red Cross, WWI. Entered British Secret Intelligence Service, 1916.
[3] Erich Maria Kramer, 1898–1970. Reversed his surname for his pseudonym, Remarque. Served during WWI (wounded twice). Author of *All Quiet on the Western Front* (1929) and *Spark of Life* (1952), which was about conditions in the concentration camps.

political scene. There were so many Governments & so many swells jostling each other for the minor jobs of Court & Office. No doubt we picked the best period to wander in.

Esmond H[1] came to luncheon yesterday and was very friendly & not a bit vexed about poor Randolph's performance[2] – published <u>verbatim </u>as you have no doubt seen in the Bevanite rag. Kitty L[3] has been quite ill and cannot yet walk. I shall try to go to see her – though I don't relish the prospect of all those steps! O'Brien the TUC President has been here today. He is a sensible man and I gave him a good dose of Tory Democracy – quite as good a brand as your Liberalism.

Forgive this scrawl in bed with a tiny Biro. I can do better, but I so rarely write to you with my own paw. <u>Please continue to love me</u> or I shall be very unhappy. I suppose you and Nellion[4] will now be off to Stratford to enjoy *Richard III* and *Twelfth Night*. I doubt if I shall stay much beyond the present week. Write me about it all. I long to hear from you. Burn this scribble. It is worse than I really am.

Ever your loving & as yet unconquered
[Drawing of a pig]

PS. Once more all my love & with a better pen – like the one you gave UJ & he told me he always wrote in pencil. If Beria has escaped he will be much better value than Mrs Maclean![5]

Lady Soames: recollection
('Clementine Churchill', pages 437–8)

22 September 1953

Max Beaverbrook had offered the loan of La Capponcina at Cap d'Ail, and Winston, Christopher and I flew out there on 17th September. Clementine did not come with us – Winston was now so much better she felt she could entrust him to us, and she and Nellie went off for a few days sightseeing and theatre-going in Stratford. From La Capponcina I reported truthfully, if rather sadly:

---

[1] Esmond Harmsworth, Viscount Rothermere.
[2] In a speech at a Foyle's literary luncheon at the Dorchester, Randolph, inebriated, asked why a rich man like the press baron Lord Rothermere (his former employer) needed to 'prostitute' himself by printing details about the private lives of public figures, which Randolph described as 'pornography for pornography's sake'.
[3] Katherine de Vere Beauclerk Lambton, 1877–1958. Married, 1896, Henry Charles Somers Augustus Somerset (div. 1920): three children; 1921, William Lambton (d. 1936).
[4] Nellie Romilly.
[5] Melinda Marling, 1916–2010. Married, 1940, Donald Maclean: three children. Secretly left Geneva in Sep. 1953 for Moscow, to join her husband, who had disappeared from the FO in 1951.

Papa is in good health – but alas, low spirits – which Chimp and I are unable to remedy. He feels his energy and stamina to be on an ebb tide – He is struggling to make up his mind what to do. I'm sure you know the form – you have been witnessing it all these months . . .

He thinks much of you & wonders what you are doing . . .

Chimp & I are having a lovely time – bathing – reading – cards & we love being with Papa – only we yearn to be able to do more than be the mere witnesses (however loving) of his sadness . . .

Sir Winston S. Churchill to Lady S. Churchill
(Churchill papers, 1/50)

23 September 1953

Have at last plunged into a daub. Hope you have got my letter. Much love.

Lord Tryon[1] to John Colville
(Premier papers, 11/464)

23 September 1953

My dear John,

I have been informed that the present system of Queen's Plates for racing in Ireland is really out of date, as the amount of money given compares unfavourably with the other races on the programme. Consequently the races do not get many entries or runners.

I attach a list of the various prizes given from the Civil List. This is quite out of proportion to prizes given for racing in the Commonwealth, as Canada, Australia, South Africa, India and Ceylon receive Cups and other prizes amounting to a total of about £350 a year, so that Eire is receiving more than the whole of the Commonwealth although the Irish Republic has left it altogether.

Mr Attlee was approached about this when he was Prime Minister in 1948, but thought the time was not appropriate to alter it.

The Queen approves a suggestion I have made, that we should cut out all the small Plates except for the £197.6.2d. to Down Royal in Northern Ireland, and give one Plate of 500 Sovs. to the Curragh. This would result in a good

---

[1] Charles George Vivian Tryon, 1906–76. ADC to Governor-General of Canada, 1933–4. Married, 1939, Etheldreda Josephine. Baron, 1940. DSO, 1945. CO, 5th Guards Bde, 1945–6. Asst Keeper of the Privy Purse, 1949–52. Keeper and Treasurer to the Queen, 1952–71. KCVO, 1953. Cdr, Legion of Honour, 1960. KCB, 1962. GCVO, 1969. Permanent Lord in Waiting to the Queen, 1971. PC, 1972.

saving for the Civil List, which is always in need of retrenchment, and would I am sure in many ways make a more worthwhile contribution. Even then it would be roughly the same in total to the prizes given to all the Commonwealth countries (including Northern Ireland) added together.

Could you please let me know if the Prime Minister would agree?

Doreen Pugh[1] to John Colville
(Premier papers, 11/464)

24 September 1953

I have looked into the correspondence in 1948. Sir Ulick Alexander[2] approached us about withdrawing the King's Plates at the time Ireland was becoming a Republic. Mr Attlee consulted Lord Rugby,[3] the first United Kingdom Ambassador, who was in this country. Lord Rugby, who was very interested in Irish racing, thought that to withdraw the Plates at that moment would be considered as being done through pique and would offend the section of the population most friendly to this country. Mr Attlee therefore advised that, while it was by no means necessary that these payments should be continued indefinitely, a considerable interval should be allowed to elapse before they were stopped. His late Majesty entirely agreed with this view.

Five years have now passed and in any case the action proposed would leave one better race associated with The Queen.

Lady Churchill to Sir Winston S. Churchill
(Churchill papers, 1/50)[4]

24 September 1953

My darling Winston,

By the time you get this letter Christopher & Mary will have left you, & Jock & Meg will have arrived to keep you company.

Your letter[5] reached me only this morning; as of course when you are not

---

[1] Doreen Pugh, 1925–. Churchill's secretary during the last decade of his life.

[2] Ulick Alexander, 1889–1973. Comptroller of the Household of the Duke and Duchess of Kent, 1928–36. Financial Secretary to the King, 1936–7. Keeper of the Privy Purse, 1936–52. Extra Equerry to the King, 1937–52. GCVO, 1948. PC, 1952. GCB, 1953.

[3] John Loader Maffey, 1877–1969. Entered Indian Civil Service, 1899. Private Secretary to Viceroy, 1916. Chief Political Officer with forces in Afghanistan, 1919. Knighted, 1921. Chief Commissioner, North-West Frontier Province, 1921–3. Governor-General of the Sudan, 1926–33. Permanent Under-Secretary of State. Colonial Office, 1933–7. UK Representative in Eire, 1939–49. Baron Rugby, 1947.

[4] This letter was handwritten.

[5] Reproduced above (pp. 1214–15).

here[1] there are no cars going & coming. I wish my dearest that you did not feel so sad and melancholy. I feel at our age it takes a little time to become acclimatized to the soft relaxing air of the Riviera. It would probably be good if you could be there a month, but that's not possible.

It will be lovely to welcome you back & I am making all arrangements for us to spend the weekend of Friday October the 2nd or Saturday the 3rd at Chartwell; as I know that is what you would like.

I expect Mary and The Chimp have told you that tomorrow Friday they are dining with me at Downing Street & then we all three go down to Chartwell where I am to be their guest for this weekend. I shall of course sleep & breakfast in the big house as they have not got a spare bed-room.

The Stratford visit was very pleasant – I did not think the acting first rate but the words are sufficient, But Alas! One could not always hear them – this is I think a sad fault.

Randolph lunched here & is with me now. I don't think he has my idea of what we all think of his ill-natured blunder. He is such good company when in a good mood & we have played highly competitive croquet both yesterday & today which we both enjoyed.

I'm sending you a letter from him – I will come with you to Margate on Saturday the 10 a.m. The following Monday I'm going to stay with the Ismays in Paris.

All my love Darling,
Your devoted
[Drawing of a cat]

Randolph S. Churchill to Sir Winston S. Churchill
(Churchill papers, 1/51)[2]

24 September 1953

My dearest papa –

Just a line to say that I hope you are having a happy holiday & are recharging your batteries successfully. Mamma with whom I have played croquet the last two days is very well. She tells me you have started work on your Margate speech. It looks as if it will be an easy conference after the comrades' meeting the week before.[3]

All my deepest love and devotion
Your loving son

---

[1] i.e. in London.
[2] This letter was handwritten.
[3] The Labour Party Conference at Margate, Sep. 28 to Oct. 2.

Sir Winston S. Churchill to Lady S. Churchill
(Baroness Spencer-Churchill papers)[1]

25 September 1953   Cap d'Ail

My Darling,

Mary & Christopher leave now & will carry this to you. I shall follow on the 30th. It was very nice talking on the telephone to you tho' I found it so difficult to hear. The weather was perfect yesterday but today is cloudy. I have taken the plunge in painting and certainly feel the necessary vigour & strength to be as bad as I used to be. This is a relief because it is a great distraction and a little perch for a tired bird.

We had the Minister of the Interior[2] here yesterday and about 20 local notables & gave them & their wives champagne. It went off all right. The Minister said he was for a German Army. I think their Govt. feels stronger now that Guy Mollet, & the Socialists have rallied to EDC. But there is not much life in the Latin Republics. Nothing could be more comfortable than this villa, and all arrangements are perfect. I have only left the garden twice, and the days pass very quickly. I continue to resolve my fate. As usual there seems to be something to be said on both sides. It is rather like a Home Secretary pondering about his own reprieve.

I am so glad you are going down to Chartwell tonight. Do write me the news about it all – including the little yellow cat, with whom I thought I was making progress thanks to grouse.

I do hope my darling that you have found the interlude restful and pleasant. I must admit I have had a good many brown hours. However the moment of action will soon come now.

I wish you were here for I can't help feeling lonely.

                                                             Your ever loving husband
                                                                    [Drawing of a pig]

PS. I have begun *Père Goriot* in French.

---

[1] This letter was handwritten.
[2] Léon Martinaud-Déplat, 1899–1969. Member, French Radical Party. Minister of Justice, 1952–3. Minister of the Interior, 1953–4.

SEPTEMBER 1953

Sir Winston S. Churchill to Lord Beaverbrook
(Churchill papers, 2/211)

26 September 1953   Cap d'Ail

Dear Max,

I have had a very good ten days here, and I shall have enjoyed your princely hospitality for a fortnight when I return on Wednesday the 30th. I have successfully made a plunge back into painting and have produced something which has at any rate vigour in it. Alas, it is raining today, but as Randolph puts it well in a letter he has written me, I am recharging my batteries. We had the French Minister of the Interior, the Prefect of the Alpes Maritimes,[1] and the Mayors of Nice[2] and Cap d'Ail to tea as you saw on Thursday, and everything passed off agreeably. Christopher and Mary left for home yesterday, having, I think, really enjoyed themselves. Christopher would of course have liked to gamble at the Casino, but you cannot do much with £10. I have not been near the rooms, though I must admit they are a temptation. Your Chef is magnificent in the food he presents, and we have lapped your special champagne with great advantage. Albert has managed things splendidly and I cannot tell you how good it was of you to deprive yourself of his services for my benefit. He tells me he has been with you for 32 years. Certainly a lot of things must have happened in that time. I suppose he was on duty on the night that you persuaded Bonar[3] to go to the Carlton Club! I have been reading for amusement the first volume of my *History of the English Speaking Peoples* written fifteen years ago. I think it will entertain you one of these days. Certainly there has always been plenty going on. On the whole I think I would rather have lived through our lot of trouble than any of the others, though I must place on record my regret that the human race ever learned to fly.

A word on serious matters. I think you ought to be careful about your opposition to a German army. Although armies are no longer the instruments by which the fate of nations is decided, there is certainly going to be a German army and I hope it will be on our side and not against us. This need in no way prevent, but may on the contrary help, friendly relations with the Bear.

I plan to return on the afternoon of Wednesday the 30th, and should not be sure of arriving before seven o'clock. I have heard that you are flying to Canada that night. I should like so much to see you before you go; do let me know your timetable.

Once more thanking you for all your kindness

[1] Henry Soum.
[2] Jean Médecin, 1890–1965.
[3] Andrew Bonar Law, 1858–1923. Born in Canada. Brought to Scotland aged 12. MP (Cons.) for Glasgow Blackfriars, 1900–6; for Dulwich, 1906–10; for Bootle, 1911–18; for Glasgow Central, 1918–23. Parliamentary Secretary, Board of Trade, 1902–5. Cons. Leader in House of Commons, 1911. Secretary of State for the Colonies, May 1915 to Dec. 1916. Chancellor of the Exchequer, 1916–19. Lord Privy Seal, 1919–21. PM, 1922–3. Two of his four sons were killed in action in WWI.

Sir Winston S. Churchill to Lady Churchill
(Churchill papers, 1/50)

26 September 1953

Thanks so much for your dear letter.[1] Alas another rainy day. Love.

Sir Winston S. Churchill to Randolph Churchill
(Churchill papers, 1/51)

26 September 1953

Thank you for your letter.[2] Am recharging. Love.

Sir Winston S. Churchill to Lord Beaverbrook
(Churchill papers, 2/211)

26 September 1953

Mary almost swallowed by an octopus but the Chameleon in the Dining Room caught two flies at dinner last night. Jock and Meg have arrived. All having a lovely time and most comfortable.

Sir Winston S. Churchill to Lord Tryon
(Premier papers, 11/464)

27 September 1953   Alpes Maritimes
Private

My dear Tryon,

I have seen your letter to Jock of September 23 about The Queen's Plates.[3]

I am very doubtful about this. It is almost the only link remaining and was put on the Civil List with, I suppose, corresponding provision for that purpose. I would suggest that the matter should be reconsidered every year.

I remember my old nurse[4] told me when I was a child about a little boy

---

[1] Reproduced above (pp. 1217–18).
[2] Reproduced above (p. 1218).
[3] Reproduced above (pp. 1216–17).
[4] Elizabeth Anne Everest, 1833–1895. Born in Kent. A children's nurse, employed by Lord Randolph Churchill from 1875 to 1893. Known by Winston and Jack Churchill as 'Woom' and 'Woomany', she was Churchill's principal confidante from his earliest years until her death. In his novel *Savrola*, published in 1900, Churchill wrote of the hero's nurse: 'She had nursed him from his birth upwards with a devotion and care which knew no break. It is a strange thing, the love of these women. Perhaps it is the only disinterested affection in the world. The mother loves her child; that is maternal nature. The youth loves his sweetheart; that too may be explained. The dog loves his master; he feeds him; a man loves his friend; he has stood by him perhaps at doubtful moments. In all these are reasons; but the love

who when a scaffolding fell was left on the top of a very tall chimney with no means of coming down. His Father shouted to him, 'unravel thy stockings and let them down'. This he did and presently pulled up a cotton thread which in its turn pulled up a light cord and finally a rope ladder, by which he reached the ground again safely. I incorporated this in my philosophy of life.

The only hope in the case of Ireland is that the South will woo the North by offering to re-enter the circle of The Crown. Time is on our side.

No changes are to be expected immediately in the Commonwealth, except in Pakistan, which is not for the better. (I am not thinking of running any of my horses in the Pakistan Derby next year.)

I am convinced that the change now proposed would stir up the whole issue out of all proportion, and artificial political demonstrations might be worked up; whereas now if The Queen ever had a horse running in Ireland it would get a great welcome.

The idea of increasing the major prize at the expense of some of the smaller ones rears another aspect and might be talked over privately with Irish racing authorities. A thousand would look better than a Monkey.[1]

---

of a foster-mother for her charge appears absolutely irrational. It is one of the few proofs, not to be explained even by the association of ideas, that the nature of mankind is superior to mere utilitarianism, and that his destinies are high.'

[1] 'Monkey': slang for £500.

October 1953

Chiefs of Staff: memorandum
(Cabinet papers, 131/13)

1 October 1953
Top Secret
Defence Committee Paper No. 45 of 1953

LIKELIHOOD OF GENERAL WAR WITH THE SOVIET UNION
UP TO THE END OF 1955
Introduction

Our last report[1] on the likelihood of general war with the Soviet Union, which covered the period up to the end of 1955, was written in December 1952. Its conclusions were:
  (a) The Soviet Government will still wish to avoid starting a general war in the period under review.
  (b) They will, however, continue to conduct an unremitting struggle against the Western Powers by every means open to them which they calculate can stop short of general war.
  (c) Provided it continues to be made perfectly plain that in the event of Soviet aggression the Western Powers will not hesitate to use their superiority in atomic warfare, that prospect will continue to be the chief military deterrent.
  (d) While we consider that general war is on the whole unlikely in the period under review, we cannot exclude the possibilities:
    (i) that general war might result unintentionally from some situation that obliged the Western Powers to take military action against the Soviet Union or China, contrary to the latter's calculations;

---

[1] Defence Committee Paper No. 3 of 1953, reproduced above (pp. 816–22).

(ii) that, as Western power grows, the Soviet Government might become convinced, e.g., by Western strategic dispositions, that the West was planning an imminent attack on them, and decide to attack first.

We believe that these dangers exist now, and will continue during the period covered by this paper.

(e) It is not possible to assess whether war is any more or any less likely in any specific year in the period under review.

(f) We remain convinced that it is by combining strength and unity with resolution and restraint that the Western Powers can best hope to avoid a general war.

2. Shortly after that report was written Stalin died, and since then there have been a number of important developments in the Soviet orbit. It is too early yet to assess the full significance of these events but in this report we examine whether they offer any grounds for modifying the conclusions set out above.

Recent Developments

3. The most important developments since Stalin's death have been the following, which are not listed in any particular order:

(a) The reorganisation of the Soviet Government and the emphasis on collective leadership.

(b) The measures taken by the new Soviet Government to make their regime more acceptable to the ordinary Soviet citizens; and the minor concessions made to lower international tension. These include, for example, the emphasis on the rights of the individual, the concessions to non-Russian minorities, the resumption of diplomatic relations with Yugoslavia and Israel, and the renunciation of territorial claims in Turkey.

(c) The riots and unrest in Eastern Germany.

(d) A change of economic policy in E Germany and Hungary which will apparently slacken the pace of collectivisation and industrialisation.

(e) Political and economic concessions in E Germany and Austria and to a certain extent in some of the Satellites.

(f) The downfall of Beria, with its implications that the Soviet Army has strengthened its position vis-à-vis the MVD.

(g) The conclusion of an armistice in Korea.

(h) Malenkov's speech at the closing session of the Supreme Soviet, in which he announced plans for improving the supply of consumer goods, a change in agricultural policy, and an apparent levelling of defence expenditure.

(i) The first experimental Soviet thermo-nuclear explosion.

Bearing of Recent Events on Likelihood of War

4. There is nothing in these events to show that the basic aims of Soviet policy have changed. The Soviet budget includes a large increase in the miscellaneous vote but we do not yet know whether this reflects any significant change in economic policy. The changes in Hungary and East Germany appear to have been made because of local economic and political difficulties and probably denote no change in the long-term policy of integrating the Satellite economies with that of the USSR and of improving the military strength of the *bloc* as a whole. Despite the apparent levelling of defence expenditure, there has been no sign of any reduction in the military strength of the Soviet Union or of any slackening in the militarisation of the Satellites, except in E Germany. Soviet atomic capabilities are steadily growing; it is estimated that their stock of fission bombs is now of the order of 150–200. They have recently claimed to have achieved an experimental thermo-nuclear explosion, and we have reason to believe that this statement is literally true. This does not necessarily mean, however, that they now possess an operational weapon. Politically there is nothing to show that the Soviet attitude has altered on any fundamental issue or that the long-term Soviet aim is no longer to achieve a Communist world under the leadership of the Kremlin.

5. There are nevertheless certain broad inferences to be drawn from the events set out in paragraph 3 which suggest not only that the Soviet Government still wish to avoid starting a general war but that temporarily at least they will be more careful than before not to run the risk of precipitating the unintentional war described in paragraph 1 (d) above. These inferences are:

    (a) Since Beria's fall, there have been no outward signs of a struggle for power, although this should not be taken to mean that the present form of Government by Committee has already achieved complete stability. The emphasis on 'collective leadership' remains. The relative strength of the organs of power are unknown, but the Army seems to have improved its position vis-à-vis the MVD, and to be giving its support to the Party. There is no reason to suppose that the Soviet leaders, unless they fall out further, will be unable to retain full control of the country, but it seems likely that there are powerful cross-currents of opinion beneath the surface of Soviet leadership. While these persist, the Soviet Government may feel it necessary to maintain a more cautious attitude in foreign policy than was the case when Stalin was alive.

    (b) Accordingly, Stalin's successors are not in a position to pursue Stalin's policies, which involved heavy pressure on the Soviet peoples and a high degree of tension in international relations. They may also have felt that more flexible policies would produce better results both at home and abroad.

(c) The unrest in East Germany may have caused the Soviet Government to revise their views on the security of their lines of communication in the event of general war. This is not a consideration which of itself would deter them from going to war but it would clearly help to induce them to be more cautious.

6. On the other hand, the Soviet leaders must be aware that there is strong pressure in some quarters for the West to adopt a more forward policy towards the Soviet Union, designed to take advantage of its present uneasy situation. The Soviet leaders may even partially believe their own propaganda that the riots in East Germany were planned and fomented by the West. They may therefore be apprehensive of some Western initiative, particularly in the Satellites, and be liable to react with ill-considered vigour to any Western move which they considered provocative. These feelings may tend to offset any more cautious trend such as that described in paragraph 5 above, though on balance we believe that a more cautious mood will prevail.

7. There remains the possibility that unresolved problems in the Far East might lead to a war in that area which sooner or later might involve the USSR and develop into general war. There are no indications that the Chinese intend to resume the fighting in Korea or, on the other hand, to make use of the truce there to start fighting elsewhere or increase their intervention in Indo-China.

Relative Danger of any Particular Year

8. In our last report we concluded that it was not possible to assess whether war was any more or any less likely in any specific year of the period under review. There has been no new intelligence bearing on this problem since our report was written, but it has been suggested that, as the atomic capabilities of the Soviet Union and the West increase, the likelihood of war will diminish correspondingly.

9. It is argued in support of this theory that, as we near and reach the point when either side could destroy the other and when war might well result in the annihilation of both, neither will risk a deliberate war and neither will allow itself to be drawn into war by a process of 'chain reaction' in a time of crisis.

10. It can, however, equally well be argued that, as the atomic power of both sides grows, so will the temptation to strike the first blow, and that this will increase the dangers inherent in any such crisis.

11. We cannot assess whether either of the conflicting arguments described above is more valid than the other. The fear of atomic attack is, and will remain, a major deterrent, and we adhere to our view that war is unlikely. But we cannot say whether the growing atomic potential of both sides will make it more or less unlikely.

OCTOBER 1953 1227

Conclusions

12. We see no reason to alter any of the conclusions of our last report, except that we believe the Soviet Government, temporarily at least, will be more cautious in the conduct of their cold-war struggle against the West. While this trend continues, the danger of war developing form a series of miscalculations will be smaller than it was.

Recommendation

13. We recommend that the Defence Committee should take note of our conclusion above.

(signed) R. McGrigor
J. Harding
W. F. Dickson

Sir Winston S. Churchill to Raymond Triboulet
(*Premier papers, 11/671*)

1 October 1953

Dear Monsieur Triboulet,

Thank you for your letter inviting me to take part in the 10th anniversary commemoration of the landings in Normandy. I should like to be able to be present but I fear that this may not be possible. I should like, if you agree, to consider the matter further next spring when I shall have a better idea of the pressure of my public engagements at that time.

Cabinet: conclusions
(*Cabinet papers, 128/26*)

2 October 1953
Secret
11.30 a.m.
Cabinet Meeting No. 54 of 1953

[. . .]

2. The Lord President said that our final proposals for a defence agreement had been put to the Egyptians in accordance with the Cabinet's decision of 16th September. It seemed unlikely that the Egyptians would accept them. They were now making difficulties even on points on which there had previously seemed a good chance of reaching agreement. Thus, they were unwilling to accept the inclusion, in the preamble of the agreement, of a reference to

freedom of transit through the Suez Canal; they were challenging the right of British troops in the Base to wear uniform; and they were raising objection to the proposal that the Base should become available in the event of United Nations action to resist an act of aggression. He thought it would be unwise to offer any further concessions to them at this stage and, subject to the Cabinet's views, he proposed to intimate that the proposals now communicated to them represented our last word.

The Chief of the Imperial General Staff said that British troops in the Base must wear uniform when on duty, though they might, if desired, wear some distinctive shoulder-title. There was no reason why they should not wear civilian clothes off duty, and there might be some advantage in making it a rule that they should not wear uniform when visiting Egyptian towns off duty.

The Prime Minister agreed that we should make no further attempt to compromise with the Egyptians. Government supporters would find it difficult to accept the concessions already made, but they would be more likely to regard them favourably if it could be explained, when Parliament reassembled, that we had informed the Egyptians of our final terms for a settlement and that we were holding firmly to these.

The Cabinet –

Authorised the Lord President to make it clear to the Egyptians that the proposals recently made to them in pursuance of the Cabinet's decision of 16th September represented our final terms for a defence agreement and that we were not prepared to make any further concessions.

[. . .]

Sir Winston S. Churchill to Anthony Eden
(*Churchill papers, 2/216*)

2 October 1953
Private

Chartwell

My dear Anthony,

I hope you will not overwork yourself by trying to read up all the back papers, and that you will take over from Bobbety in a leisurely way. I am sure he will be delighted to help, and he certainly has got his teeth into the detail. I think also the machine is working very well. For some time I have been watching it very carefully, and have had the feeling that we are getting into a smoother period in international affairs. The important thing for you (and me) is to make a good impression on the Margate Conference and upon Parliament when we meet. I hope you will give first place in your thoughts to your speech next Thursday, and I should myself much like to see any draft beforehand so as to shape my own remarks accordingly. I also think that when Parliament meets there will have to be a Foreign Affairs Debate which may well take a

October 1953

couple of days. In this case I would speak either the first or the second day as you wished, and I think it would be very good for Nutting to wind up. I am sure we have got a thoroughly good case if we all stand together. I am sorry that Bobbety has after all decided not to publish his excellent communiqué.

Take your own time also about lightening the burden. There is no need for public statements on this part of the business. It was a great pleasure to me to see you in your place today, and I am sure it was right that you should resume your high office on Monday as we have arranged.

Love to Clarissa.

Lord Tryon to Sir Winston S. Churchill
(Premier papers, 11 / 464)

3 October 1953

Dear Prime Minister,

Thank you for your letter of the 27th September.[1]

Captain Charles Moore, The Queen's Racing Manager, who is himself a Steward of the Irish Turf Club, and a Director of the Irish National Stud, has discussed the matter of The Queen's Plates with the Irish Racing Authorities. They have suggested that it would be most generous if The Queen would make up the stake for The Whip to £600 added; it is at present only £105. The other small Plates at the Curragh which are really out of date would then be abolished, but all the Plates at the small country meetings would be retained, the one for Down Royal being increased from £197 to £300.

As these proposals emanated from the beneficiaries, I hope that you will be able to agree to them. I am sure the small boy will in due course get his rope ladder as a result.

Cabinet: conclusions
(Cabinet papers, 128 / 26)

6 October 1953
Secret
11 a.m.
Cabinet Meeting No. 55 of 1953

1. The Prime Minister said that since the Cabinet's discussion on 3rd October there had been much speculation in the Press about the Government's plans for dealing with the political situation in British Guiana.[2] As

---

[1] Reproduced above (pp. 1221–2).

[2] In Apr. 1953, the People's Progressive Party had won the first general election in Guiana under the new constitutional arrangements introduced that year. The British, fearing a Marxist revolution,

a result, the element of surprise had now been lost; and, that being so, he thought that an official announcement should at once be issued stating that the Government intended to take all necessary steps to restore law and order and to prevent the establishment of a Communist régime in the Colony. Other Commonwealth Governments and interested foreign Governments should also be informed without delay of the action which we were proposing to take and the reasons for it.

The Prime Minister added that the fact that the Commander-in-Chief of the America and West Indies Station[1] had himself sailed in the cruiser which was carrying the troops from Jamaica to British Guiana, and the statement which he had made to the Press on his departure, might have contributed towards the undue Press publicity which had been given to this movement.

The Cabinet –
 (1) Agreed that an official announcement should now be made regarding the Government's plans for handling the political situation in British Guiana, and invited the Colonial Secretary to submit a draft announcement for the Prime Minister's approval.
 (2) Invited the Colonial Secretary to concert with the Foreign Office and the Commonwealth Relations Office arrangements for informing other Commonwealth Governments and interested foreign Governments of these plans and of the reasons which had made it necessary to put them into operation.
 (3) Took note that the First Lord of the Admiralty would submit to the Prime Minister a report on the action of the Commander-in-Chief, America and West Indies Station.

[. . .]

John Colville to Lord Tryon
(Premier papers, 11/464)

7 October 1953

My dear Charles,
The Prime Minister asks me to thank you for your letter of the 3rd of October about the Queen's Plates in Ireland.[2] Sir Winston has expressed his views on the subject, but as the Irish racing authorities are content with the

---

deployed troops to Guiana. Eventually the new constitution was suspended and an interim government installed.
 [1] John Felgate Stevens, 1900–89. Educated at King's College, Cambridge. Midshipman, 1918. Married, 1928, Mary Gilkes: three children. At Staff College, 1930. Cdr, 1933. Capt., 1940. Director of Plans, Admiralty, 1946–7. Commanded HMS *Implacable*, 1948–9. RAdm., 1949. Director of Naval Training, 1949–50. CoS to Head of British JSM, Washington, 1950–2. Flag Officer, Home Fleet Training Sqn, 1952–3. C-in-C, America and West Indies Station, and Deputy SACLANT, 1953–5.
 [2] Reproduced above (p. 1229).

rearrangement proposed, he would not wish to press his views any further and is quite willing to acquiesce with the redistribution.

Sir Winston S. Churchill to President Dwight D. Eisenhower
Prime Minister's Personal Telegram T.257/53
(Premier papers, 11/1074)

7 October 1953
Immediate
Deyou
Top Secret and Personal
No. 3892

My dear Friend,

I have not troubled you with telegrams lately although there are so many things I should like to talk over with you. I feel it would be a great advantage if we could meet, especially now I have Anthony back. The idea has occurred to me of a meeting at the Azores, which is not much farther away for you than for us. I am sure the Portuguese would help in every way. Also I could send a ship. It would have to be next week as our Parliament meets on the 20th. If you could spare a couple of days between the 15th and the 18th inclusive (say the 15th and 16th) we might be able to clear up a great many things. I would bring Anthony with me and hope you would bring Foster. This would be much easier for me and Anthony, who are both convalescents, than for us to fly to Washington with all the business and publicity that would involve. About the French, we should have a much better talk together alone as most of the topics concern our two countries. But if you wished them to come, and they could and would come to the Azores that would be all right. In this case it would be a good thing if Laniel[1] came along with Bidault.

2. I hope you will not mind my putting this suggestion to you. If you find it impossible Eden and I will be at the British Embassy, Washington, within the dates mentioned.

---

[1] Joseph Laniel, 1889–1975. PM, French Fourth Republic, 1953–4.

President Dwight D. Eisenhower to Sir Winston S. Churchill
(Premier papers, 11/892)

8 October 1953
Secret

Dear Winston,

It is good to know that you have Anthony back with you. Hope both of you are feeling fit.

As for the suggested talk, you have picked a week that is completely impossible for me. I leave Washington the night of the 14th and have five public engagements between that time and the early morning of the 20th, when I plan to be back here. So it is not only impossible for me to go to the Azores but likewise I cannot be in Washington during the period you mention.

While Foster had planned to be with me in Texas on the 19th when I meet the President of Mexico,[1] it would be possible for him to break that engagement and, consequently, could be here for the weekend of the 18th–19th if you and Anthony could fit this into your program. If you could stay through the 20th, I could personally participate in the discussions on that day, but not earlier.

So far as the French are concerned, it seems to me quite clear that, if we meet any place, an invitation to them would be inescapable. We believe that Laniel is doing a good job, and I think it would be best for both you and us to make the gesture of an invitation. If they accept, there would still be plenty of opportunity at such a meeting for bi-partisan talks between us, while if the French would find it impossible to attend, they would still be complimented by our thought of them.

All of these suggestions, of course, have no point in the event that my personal situation destroys whatever value you might see in the visit. Possibly you would want to send Anthony here by himself from the 15th to 18th because of this circumstance. Foster (and) his associates would welcome him.

I would appreciate hearing from you on this as soon as possible since if you can come, I would like to give the French as much advance notice as possible.

---

[1] Adolfo Tomás Ruiz Cortines, 1890–1973. Born in Veracruz, Mexico. Educated at Instituto de Veracruz and Colegio de los Jesuitas. Director, Mexico City, 1935–44. Governor of Veracruz, 1944–51. President of Mexico, 1952–8.

Cabinet: conclusions
(Cabinet papers, 128/26)

8 October 1953
Secret
6 p.m.
Cabinet Meeting No. 56 of 1953

1. The Cabinet considered the latest developments in British Guiana.

The Colonial Secretary said that it had hitherto been intended that, as soon as British troops were deployed in the territory, the Governor[1] should take the following action:
 (i) assume emergency powers under the Order-in-Council made at Balmoral on 4th October;
 (ii) remove the Ministers' portfolios under the emergency powers;
 (iii) publish a statement of Her Majesty's Government's policy and announce the intention to suspend the constitution;
 (iv) arrest the leaders of the People's Progressive Party.

Suspension of the constitution could not be effected without Parliamentary action at Westminster and must, therefore, await the reassembly of Parliament. Under the emergency powers now available, however, the Ministers could in the meanwhile be relieved of their responsibility, although they would technically remain Ministers so long as the constitution remained in force.

The Royal Welch Fusiliers had now landed at Georgetown. Their reception had been friendly and the situation in the town was entirely calm. In these circumstances the Governor had urged that, while action under (i)–(iii) above should be taken as planned, no arrests should be made unless there were further developments in the situation. He (the Colonial Secretary) remained of the opinion that there was ample justification for immediate arrests, but he agreed that it would be inexpedient to make the arrests at the present moment, when there had been no public disorder in the Colony. He had, therefore, with the Prime Minister's approval, instructed the Governor to proceed with the action summarised in (i)–(iii) above but to await developments before making any arrests and, if possible, to refer to him before making them (Colonial Office telegram No. 78 to Sir A. Savage of 8th October).

The Prime Minister said that he had no doubt that this was the right course. Removal of the Ministers' portfolios and suspension of the constitution could be abundantly justified on the ground that Ministers had been given a fair trial but had demonstrated that their management of the Colony's affairs could only lead to its ruin. It would, however, be very much harder to justify arresting and detaining men who would of necessity remain Ministers for the time

---

[1] Alfred William Lungley Savage, 1903–80. Entered Home Civil Service, 1920. Married, 1931, Doreen Hopwood: two children. CMG, 1948. Governor and C-in-C, Barbados, 1949–53; British Guiana, 1953–5. KCMG, 1951. Crown Agent for Overseas Governments, 1955–63.

being if they were not to be charged with any specific offence and conditions in the Colony remained quiet.

There was general support in the Cabinet for the course which it was now proposed to follow, although it was recognised that this might well make it necessary for the troops to remain in the territory for a longer period. It was also recognised that, if the Ministers were left at liberty after being relieved of their functions, they would be likely to make as much capital as they possibly could out of the position and might seek to stir up disaffection by agitation and possibly strike action. While it was agreed that it would not be politic to arrest them at the moment, Ministers considered that they should not be allowed indefinitely to flout the Government of the Colony and Her Majesty's Government before the eyes of the world.

The Minister of Defence asked whether the battalion of Argyll and Sutherland Highlanders which was about to leave this country for Georgetown should still proceed thither or be diverted to Jamaica, and whether the move of the battalion of the Gloucestershire Regiment, which was due to sail from Liverpool on 14th October for Jamaica, should be cancelled.

The Cabinet –
    (1) Endorsed the instructions sent to the Governor of British Guiana in Colonial Office telegram No. 78 of 8th October.
    (2) Agreed that the projected move of the Argyll and Sutherland Highlanders to Georgetown should proceed on the understanding that they could be diverted to Jamaica *en route* if the development of the situation in British Guiana appeared to justify this course.
    (3) Agreed that no overt action should be taken for the time being in regard to the proposed move of the First Battalion of the Gloucestershire Regiment to Jamaica, on the understanding that the position should be reviewed in three to four days' time.

[. . .]

Sir Winston S. Churchill to President Dwight D. Eisenhower
Prime Minister's Personal Telegram T.259/53
(Premier papers, 11/892)

9 October 1953
Immediate
Deyou
Top Secret and Personal
No. 3966

My dear Friend,

Thank you so much for all the thought that you have given to this matter. In view of your engagements, it does not look as if the meeting I had hoped for with you can be arranged immediately. I am very sorry, as there are so many things I would like to talk over with you quietly and at leisure. I earnestly hope a chance may come in the not too distant future.

Anthony has another suggestion, namely, that Foster should come over here for a tripartite talk with us and Bidault. We feel that this could be most useful, for the Far East as well as for European affairs. Anthony is cabling direct to Foster.[1]

John Colville: diary
(*'The Fringes of Power'*, pages 679–80)

9–10 October 1953

On October 9th I went to Margate with W for the Conservative Conference. He made a big speech the following day and did it with complete success. He had been nervous of the ordeal: his first public appearance since his stroke and a fifty-minute speech at that; but personally I had no fears as he always rises to occasions. In the event one could see but little difference, as far as his oratory went, since before his illness.

Meanwhile a sudden scheme for a meeting with the President at the Azores next week (we going in *Vanguard*) has been turned down by Eisenhower. The blunt truth is that E does not want to meet him as he knows he will be confronted with a demand for a conference with the Russians which he is unwilling to accept. W was for pursuing the matter but was stopped by a chance remark of mine on Friday evening when I said to him, 'What subjects are you going to discuss when you get there?' It suddenly dawned on him that everything he might say to the President would necessarily be met with a negative response and that on other topics, such as Egypt, he (W) would have nothing to offer but criticisms and complaints of the US attitude. To bring the President 1,000 miles for that seemed discourteous and unfair.

Eden, who though still thin looks a great deal better, also had his success at Margate. On the surface he seems resigned to W remaining in power (W told me, after his speech, that he now hoped to do so until the Queen returned from Australia in May). There are two potential causes of friction: (i) Egypt. If W and Eden fall out over that – assuming the Egyptians agree to our terms – W would have the support of the Conservative Party against Eden but not of the Opposition. (ii) A visit to Malenkov. Here W would have the support of the country and the Opposition against Eden, backed by the Foreign Office and a section of the Conservatives. W thinks a meeting, of an exploratory kind,

---

[1] Eisenhower telegraphed Churchill on Oct. 10: 'Foster has gone away for the weekend but as soon as he can be contacted you will hear further from us. I am sure he will be most sympathetic but I do not know what are the detailed commitments on his calendar for the near future' (T.260/53). The Foreign Ministers' meeting was duly arranged for Oct. 16–18 in London.

might do good and could do no harm. The FO think it might lead to appeasement and would certainly discourage our European allies who would relax their defence efforts if even the shadow of a detente appeared. The Foreign Office and the USA are at one in thinking that Russia's slightly more reasonable attitude of late is due less to Stalin's death than to the success of our own constant pressure and increased strength,

On Saturday night we got back to London from Margate and I dined at No. 10 with W and Clemmie and Duncan and Diana Sandys. W very elated by his success, but more tired than one might have hoped.

At this stage I abandoned keeping a diary, in the main because living in the country, and above all moving to a new home at Stratfield Saye, absorbed such energy as might otherwise have been left to me by the end of the day. I did, however, keep detailed accounts of two more journeys to America, which were written at the time.

Anthony Eden: diary
(Robert Rhodes James, 'Anthony Eden, A Biography', page 371)

10 October 1953

Talk with W this morning for over an hour, having first seen Sir Horace[1] who seemed well pleased.

Made it clear to W that I was ready to serve in any capacity, but he made it evident he wanted me to stay on at FO. Asked him about plans & he said he wanted to try himself, first in Margate & then in the House. Have some doubts as to how that will go physically. Some talk of the international situation & he seemed to accept conclusion that latest Soviet answer showed little desire for talks at any level (but he admitted he hadn't read it!). We also spoke of Bobbety's desire for younger men in govt. & I told him this was (a) widespread complaint. He made no comment, but clearly doesn't want any changes now.

Bobbety & I & Rab dined with W in evening. Long talk, almost entirely on Foreign Affairs. It was difficult at times. W didn't like my lack of enthusiasm for May 11th speech.[2] He kept emphasizing its popularity to which I replied that I was not contesting that. Later Bobbety pulled him up very sharp – even

[1] Horace Anthony Claude Rumbold, 1911–83. Known as 'Tony'. Educated at Eton, Magdalen College, Oxford, and Queen's College, Oxford. 3rd Secretary, FO, 1935–7. Married, 1937, Felicity Ann Bailey: four children (div. 1974); 1974, Pauline Graham Baddeley. 2nd Secretary, Washington DC, 1937. Succeeded his father as 10th Bt, 1941. FO, 1942. On staff of Resident Minister, Mediterranean, 1944. 1st Secretary, 1945; in Prague, 1947–9. Counsellor, British Embassy in Paris, 1951–3. CMG, 1953. Principal Private Secretary to Foreign Secretary, 1954–5. Asst Under-Secretary of State, FO, 1957. British Minister in Paris, 1960–3. KCMG, 1962. Ambassador to Thailand and UK Representative on the Council of SEATO, 1965–7. Ambassador to Austria, 1967–70. KCVO, 1969.

[2] Reproduced above (pp. 998–1010).

angrily – when the former thought his loyalty to W had been impugned. I had to make it clear that I did not regard four power talks at the highest level as a panacea. He maintained that in the war it was only the Stalin Roosevelt Churchill meetings that had made our Foreign Secretaries' work possible. I said this was not so, nor was it true that to meet without agenda was the best method with Russians. I believed they liked to have an agenda which they could chew over well in advance. Our most productive meeting with them had been with (Cordell) Hull[1] at Moscow in 1943 before Teheran when we had used just these methods about Second Front, creation of UNO, Austria etc. This had let to Teheran meeting. Anyway the important question was 'what next?' On this W appeared to have no ideas. A depressing evening.

Sir Winston S. Churchill: speech
('Winston S. Churchill, His Complete Speeches', volume 8, pages 8489–97)

10 October 1953 Margate, Kent

CONSERVATIVE PARTY CONFERENCE

I am sure you are all relieved by the news from British Guiana. Sufficient forces to preserve peace and order have now been safely landed and indeed widely welcomed by the people they have come to protect. It is always a difficult problem to decide at what point Communist intrigues menace the normal freedom of a community, but it is better to be in good time than too late.

The attitude of the Opposition here at home is remarkable. They say, 'There ought to be a debate in Parliament.' Well, what is Parliament for if it is not to discuss such matters and to make sure that the freedom, prosperity, and happiness of a British colony is effectively preserved? We shall certainly seek opportunities in both Houses to present to them the case as we see it and to invite their approval of what we have done.

I am very glad that this conference yesterday expressed so decidedly its confidence in Mr Oliver Lyttelton who has so many troubles to bear, a large proportion of which were inherited from the late administration.

It is now nearly two years since the Conservative Party became responsible for the government and guidance of Britain. Two years is not a long time in human affairs. But it is nearly half the span of a Parliament and I think it is our duty to take stock of our position and to present to our friends and supporters in the National Union the main features of what we have done and what we are trying to do. If I compare our work with that of our predecessors to their disadvantage, it is not because I wish to raise ill-feeling and faction but

---

[1] Cordell Hull, 1871–1955. Member of US Congress for Tennessee, 1907–21, 1922–31. Senator, 1931–3. Secretary of State, 1933–44. Nobel Peace Prize, 1945. Published *The Memoirs of Cordell Hull* in 1948.

rather to gain encouragement and strength for the future – for our future and for the future of our country.

Certainly we have tried very hard to make our administration loyal, sober, flexible, and thrifty, and to do our best to be worthy of the anxious responsibilities confided to us. We have tried to be worthy of the confidence and energy of our Members of Parliament and of the great political organization which sustains them in the constituencies. Never in its long history has it been so lively and efficient and never more free from class interests or personal motives.

Great reforms have taken place in the organization of the Conservative Party, and the Young Conservatives who carry with them so much of the hope of the future are making immense strides forward.

We salute Lord Woolton, our Chairman, now that he has recovered from the long and dangerous ordeal through which he has passed since we separated at Scarborough. I don't at all wonder at the joy with which he has at all your meetings been welcomed here. And I am sure I speak for this whole Conference in sending greetings to our Ulster Unionist friends who are about to hold their General Election. Ulster's loyalty to our country is famous. They kept the life-line open in the war. Now we wish Lord Brookeborough[1] all success in his resolve to keep Ulster strong, prosperous, and free within the United Kingdom.

We are a Party met together on a party occasion and we have to fight as a Party against those who oppose us and assail us. But faction is not our aim. Party triumphs are not our goal. We think it a high honour to serve the British people and the world-wide Commonwealth and Empire of which they are the centre.

We are sure of our cause and not without some satisfaction at our performances.

We are not electioneering. We have a deep respect for public opinion but we do not let our course be influenced from day to day by Gallup Polls, favourable though they may be. It is not a good thing always to be feeling your pulse and taking your temperature: although one has to do it sometimes, you do not want to make a habit of it. I have heard it said that a Government should keep its ear to the ground but they should also remember that this is not a very dignified attitude.

When I spoke at Glasgow to the Scottish Unionist Association and opinion was said to be very favourable to us, six months ago,[2] I did not hesitate to say

---

[1] Basil Stanlake Brooke, 1888–1973. Succeeded his father as 5th Bt, 1907. On active service in WWI (despatches). Married, 1919, Cynthia Mary Sergison: three sons (d. 1970); 1970, Sarah Eileen Bell. CBE, 1921. Asst Parliamentary Secretary to Minister of Finance, 1929–33. PC Northern Ireland, 1933. Minister of Agriculture, 1933–41. Minister of Commerce and Production, 1941–5. PM of Northern Ireland, 1943–63. Viscount Brookeborough, 1952. Air Commodore, Ulster Maritime Support Unit, RAAF, 1960–73. MC, 1961. VAdm. of Ulster, 1961–73. KG, 1965.

[2] Speech of Apr. 17, reproduced above (pp. 952–8).

that there would be no General Election this year (unless the behaviour of the Opposition rendered the course of Parliamentary business impossible). I have rarely heard at a public meeting a more sonorous wave of assent than this declaration received from the serious and representative Scottish audience which I was then addressing.

Let me now repeat what I said then, that we have no intention of plunging the nation into electioneering strife this year, and indeed so far as my immediate knowledge is concerned that applies to next year too. We have to do our duty. That is what is expected of us. We have to do our work, our job. We have to do it or try to do it with all our lives and strength. We seek to be judged by deeds, not words, and we claim the time necessary to convince our fellow-countrymen that the progressive Conservatism of Tory democracy has an honourable part to play in the history of our native land and will play that part during a period when difficulties are many and resources strained, and danger broods none too far away.

Do you know that I think danger is farther away than when we went into harness? Certainly the sense of crisis in our world relations is less than it was two years ago, and we hope that if we persevere recovery from the convulsions of the past and barriers against their recurrence will grow surer and firmer as the clattering months roll by.

Take our finances. Surely they come first to our minds, for it is not much use being a famous race and nation with institutions which are the envy of the free world and the model of many states, if at the end of the week you cannot pay your housekeeping bills. I see the Chancellor of the Exchequer. He deserves our admiration and the respect of our fellow-countrymen. No one has tried harder to handle and solve the intricate problems left by nearly six years of war and more than six years of Socialist Government.

We are not out of the wood yet, but we have the feeling of increasing strength, and certainly we have far larger reserves. Two years ago we were sliding into bankruptcy and now at least we may claim solvency. There is something more to aim at. Solvency must be the stepping-stone of independence. (Mr Butler spoke of that on Thursday.) We are no longer living on loans or doles, not even from our best friends. I care above all for the brotherhood of the English-speaking world, but there could be no true brotherhood without independence, founded as it can only be on solvency.

We do not want to live upon others and be kept by them, but faithfully and resolutely to earn our own living without fear or favour by the sweat of our brow, by the skill of our craftsmanship and the use of our brains. And do not let us underrate the strength and quality of British industry and inventiveness. The task of maintaining 50,000,000 people in this small island at a level superior to the average European standards might indeed appal a bold man. But when the life and death of our country is at stake we have sometimes found ways and means of helping one another which no other society has been able to surpass, in peace or in war. Let us make sure that Tory democracy is a fountain of activity and hope to our race and age.

And what about 300,000 houses a year? I remember well at Blackpool three years ago how you clamoured for a tremendous effort and an audacious target and how a gust of passion swept the hall as we proclaimed the goal of 300,000 houses a year. I remember also how we were mocked by the Socialist Ministers and told we were promising the impossible.

One can quite understand how a politician who thinks more than half his fellow-countrymen are vermin cannot feel much enthusiasm for providing them with homes. 'Homes for vermin' can hardly seem an inspiring theme for the Socialist Party. 'Soak the Rich' and 'Jobs for the Boys', they seem to have a much more cheerful smack about them. But we persevered and now this second year at least 300,000 houses to let or sell will actually be built. Moreover we are building more schools than ever before – and there is the man who did it.[1] A fine piece of work for which his countrymen will always respect him and they will also respect the capable building industry and makers of building materials who have served the nation well.

Nor must we forget those vigorous and practical ministers who helped him – Sir David Eccles and Mr Marples, who has stayed away through modesty. But the building of houses, new houses, by itself is not enough. Old houses must be kept in repair. Our Socialist friends are always reminding us that both the repair of old and the building of new houses count equally. One cannot succeed without the other.

Now the building of new houses was difficult and the repair of old houses might well be unpopular, so our opponents stinted the old and neglected the other. We are well aware of the responsibility that falls upon us for the maintenance and improvement of houses which the conditions of war and war-time rent restrictions have robbed of their natural means of renewal.

We must not be deterred from tackling this problem because of the prejudice excited by the word 'landlord'. The community, the nation, as represented by the local authorities, is often the biggest landlord and charges often the highest rents. We must look at the facts. Funds must be drawn in from renewed private investment as well as supplemented by the state to enable dwellings which are falling or which are in danger of falling into decay to be repaired, renewed, and fitted with modern requirements. And apart from these the work of slum clearance, on which the Tory Government before the war was so busily engaged, must be resumed on an effective scale.

Well, what about meat? Even red meat! Lord Woolton cannot any longer be derided for what he said because it has been made good. But they tell us that if there is more meat in the shops it is only because the prices are so high and the people so poor that it cannot be bought.

---

[1] Harold Macmillan.

Now I am always very chary about loading a speech with percentages. I like the simplest forms of statement. I have had this matter very carefully examined, and this is the fact which I have been furnished with by our Food Minister, Mr Gwilym Lloyd George. He is rapidly and skilfully reducing his Ministry and his officials. And also, we must all recognize, adding to his own stature thereby. But he found time to work me out this fact which I asked for because I knew it would be plain and simple and could be well understood even by collective ideologists (those professional intellectuals who revel in decimals and polysyllables).

Personally I like short words and vulgar fractions. Here is the plain vulgar fact. In the first two years of Tory Government the British nation has actually eaten 400,000 tons more meat, including red meat, than they did in the last two years of Socialist administration. That at any rate is something solid to set off against the tales we are told of the increasing misery of the people – and the shortage of television sets.

The conference debate on agriculture was most important. We quite understand that the derationing of various foods as abundant supplies become available means that new methods must be found to give farmers the confidence and security they have and they need. We must see that the farmers have assurance against the wide fluctuations of world food prices.

Her Majesty's Government adhere to the principles of the 1947 Agriculture Act and the system of guaranteed prices remains and will remain, though sometimes in a changed and more flexible form than at present. This indeed was contemplated when the 1947 Bill was introduced.

I thought it right and proper to give this definite assurance because I know that a great deal of anxiety is felt in the farming community at the present situation which is inevitable when freedom is being resumed upon the one hand, and the absolute necessity of their having an assured market on the other. I notice that Mr Attlee a little while ago drew attention to all the litter in the parks. I do not know whether you found any doodles when you arrived here. Some of them are well worth keeping. I sat beside him for six years in the war and I frequently possessed myself of one or two of these papers and I have no doubt they are very useful and very necessary. He had to put up with a lot of trouble in this hall last week and a more confused and incoherent spectacle has rarely been witnessed on occasions of this kind. I feel I can speak with full sympathy and without falling out with any of my Conservative friends.

The lessons and experiences of the last few years are having their effect on both parties in the state. Nothing is more clear than that many large and important sections, who hitherto believed implicitly in collectivism, are altering their opinion. The fallacy of the nationalization of all the means of production, distribution, and exchange, which we used to be assured was the eldorado of the working man – that fallacy has already become obvious to millions. There are now grave doubts about the theory of nationalization and even more disagreements about its practice.

The trade unions and co-operatives are organizations in daily contact with reality. They are not hunting for votes and political notoriety, but facing facts. There is anxiety among them lest for the sake of political slogans the practical interests of the large masses for whom they are responsible or with whom they are concerned will be endangered. A few years ago nationalization was among Socialists the cure-all for social and economic difficulties – now, keep this to yourselves, there is a general feeling that it is an utter flop.

The Conservative Government have adopted a sensible and practical policy towards what we found on becoming responsible. For the success of those industries like coal mining and railways which we felt must remain nationalized we have done and will continue to do our very best. But steel and transport which had been so harshly struck at we have liberated just in time. It will be proved in the next two years that this is greatly to the public advantage and convenience.

You will remember how last year at Scarborough you were deeply concerned that we had not succeeded in passing either of these two de-nationalization Bills, and how I assured you of our resolve to do so. It has been a remarkable feat with our small majority to overcome all the resistance and obstruction with which we were confronted. We owe a debt to the Leader of the House and to the Chief Whip and his able colleagues for their efficient management of Parliamentary business, and above all we owe a debt, every one of us, to our Members who made so many personal and physical sacrifices to sustain and maintain the strength and stability of our Government. And let me make a personal appeal to you on this point. I trust that the Associations in all the constituencies, in spite of the extra and ever-increasing efforts which are required from them, will do their utmost to lessen the strain upon their Members while the Party fight is so sharp and the burden which they carry so heavy.

But to return to nationalization, there is no doubt that it has been proved a failure, hampering the competitive power of our industry, rendering an inferior service to the public and weakening the just and necessary influence of the trade unions by confronting them not with private employers but with the power of the state. All this is an illustration of the inherent fallacy of Socialism as a philosophy. But our opponents have another theme on which they greatly count – I mean class warfare and the exploitation of jealousy and envy.

This, of course, is a very serious feature of our national life, and we are striving to cure it not only by argument, but as Tory democracy has always sought to do, by tireless endeavour to maintain and raise the standards of life and labour and to provide ever-widening opportunities for all to bring aid and comfort to the weak and poor.

The trade unions play an important part in our national life. We are not seeking to bring them into the Conservative Party, but we are asking – I have asked for some time – we are asking all Conservative wage earners to join trade unions and take an effective part in their daily work. I have often said that the trade unions should keep clear of both parties and devote themselves solely to industrial matters. At the present time, however, I must admit they are doing very useful work where they are in restraining the featherheads, crackpots, vote-catchers, and office-seekers from putting the folly they talk into action.

Our Conservative principles are well known. Lord Salisbury in his very kindly speech opening our proceedings touched upon them broadly. We stand for the free and flexible working of the laws of supply and demand. We stand for compassion and aid for those who, whether through age, illness, or misfortune, cannot keep pace with the march of society. We stand for the restoration of buying and selling between individual importers and exporters in different countries instead of the clumsy bargainings of one state against another, biased by politics and national feelings as these must necessarily be.

We have made great advances in restoring this method of active, nimble, multiple private trading which should be allowed to flourish so long as the necessary laws against the abuses of monopoly are vigilantly enforced. We are for private enterprise with all its ingenuity, thrift, and contrivance, and we believe it can flourish best within a strict and well-understood system of prevention and correction of abuses. We are against state trading except in emergencies.

I am sure it is much better for the consumer to buy his food or raw materials from a private trader, who has to make a profit by good management and shrewd business or go into bankruptcy and out of business. That is much better than to use large numbers of salaried officials who, if they make a blunder and lose millions or hundreds of millions, have only to mark up the prices to the public or send in the bill to the House of Commons.

In a complex community like our own no absolute rigid uniformity of practice is possible. But we here speaking of Party causes and Party principles must make it clear, as Lord Salisbury did, that we are on the side of free enterprise with proper safeguards against state monopoly in the hands of officials.

Now I come to the vexed and formidable sphere of foreign affairs, and we all rejoice to see Mr Eden recovered from his cruel six months of pain and danger, and able to bring his unrivalled experience and knowledge to bear upon the problem which haunts all our minds – namely, finding a secure foundation for world peace.

I too have thought a great deal about this overpowering problem which hangs so heavily on the daily lives of every one of us. My prime thought at this moment is to simplify. We have lived through half a century of the most terrible events which have ever ravaged the human race. The vast majority of all the peoples wherever they may dwell desire above all things to earn their daily bread in peace. To establish conditions under which they can do this and to provide deterrents against aggression are the duties confided by the heart's desire of mankind to the United Nations. Our first duty is to aid this world instrument loyally and faithfully in its task.

But the world also needs patience. It needs a period of calm rather than vehement attempts to produce clear-cut solutions. There have been many periods when prompt and violent action might have averted calamities. This is not one of them. Even if we entered on a phase only of easement for five or ten years that might lead to something still better when it ended. So long as the cause of freedom is sustained by strength, beware of that, never forget that, and guided by wisdom it might well be that after those five or ten years improvement would be continued on an even larger scale. Patience.

In Mr Attlee's speech here a week ago there were several sensible statements on foreign policy. There was one that struck my attention particularly, when he said that in all international matters it was well to remember there was a limit to what could be done by one government. But I view with some concern the attitude which the Bevanite faction and some others of his Party are adopting not only against the United States but against the new Germany. Mr Robens, a former Minister of Labour – the man who predicted that we should have a million unemployed by last Christmas (that shows you what his judgment is worth even on questions where he has a right to speak as an authority) – Mr Robens argued at Strasbourg that there must be no German army as a part of the European Defence Community for five years.

There are no doubt some Socialist politicians who hope to win popularity both by carping and sneering at the United States and by raising hostility to the new Germany. Of course, it is vital to maintain ever strengthening ties of friendship with the United States. It would also be a great disaster if Germany were needlessly made an enemy of Britain and the free world against her will. It is nearly four years ago since I said that Western Europe could never be defended against Soviet Russia without German military aid. Mr Attlee denounced that statement as irresponsible. But a year later he and his colleagues committed themselves and all of us to the arrangements for European defence which involved the creation of twelve German divisions.

We inherited these arrangements and pledges – which we supported at the time – which involve British good faith from our predecessors, the very men who, some of them because they are not in office, think they are entitled to cast aside the work that they have done and the position to which they have committed us all.

At the present time the Soviet Armies in Europe, even without their satellites, are four times as strong as all the Western allies put together. It would indeed be an act of unwisdom to weaken our efforts to build up a Western defence. It would be madness to make our heavily-burdened island take up an attitude which if not hostile was at any rate unsympathetic both to the United States and to the new Germany which Dr Adenauer is building, and yet all the time for us to remain bound by the treaties which the Socialists have made to defend friendly European Powers who are incapable of maintaining themselves alone.

I am sure that the decisions taken by the Socialist Government, which were supported by us at the time and are now being carried forward steadfastly and soberly by Her Majesty's Government, constitute the best chance – and indeed I think it is a good chance – of getting through this awful period of anxiety without a world catastrophe.

We at any rate are going to adhere faithfully to them, and do our utmost to promote the formation of the European Army, with a strong contingent of Germans in it. We, like the Americans, shall maintain our forces in Europe, thus restoring the French balance of equality with our new German associates. If the European Defence Community should not be adopted by the French, we shall have no choice in prudence but to fall in with some new arrangement which will join the strength of Germany to the Western allies through some rearrangement of what is called NATO. You must not mind my putting these things plainly to you because I have had a life of experience in the matter and I am bound to say that I feel that every word that I am now saying gives us the best chance of securing the peaceful development of the world. Five months ago, on 11 May, I made a speech in the House of Commons.[1] I have not spoken since (the first time in my political life that I have kept quiet for so long). I asked for very little. I held out no glittering or exciting hopes about Russia. I thought that friendly, informal, personal talks between the leading figures in the countries mainly involved might do good and could not easily do much harm, and that one good thing must lead to another as I have just said.

This humble, modest plan announced as the policy of Her Majesty's Government raised a considerable stir all over the place and though we have not yet been able to persuade our trusted allies to adopt it in the form I suggested no one can say that it is dead.

I still think that the leading men of the various nations ought to be able to meet together without trying to cut attitudes before excitable publics or using regiments of experts to marshal all the difficulties and objections, and let us try to see whether there is not something better for us than tearing and blasting each other to pieces, which we can certainly do.

Her Majesty's Government (as Mr Eden and Lord Salisbury told you on Thursday) still believe we should persevere in seeking such a meeting between the Heads of Governments.

The interest of Britain and of Europe and of the NATO alliance is not to play Russia against Germany or Germany against Russia, but to make them both feel they can live in safety with each other in spite of their grievous problems and differences. For us who have a very definite part in all this, our duty

---

[1] Reproduced above (pp. 998–1010).

is to use what I believe is our growing influence both with Germany and with Russia to relieve them of any anxiety they may feel about each other.

Personally I welcome Germany back among the great Powers of the world. If there were one message I could give to the German people as one, a large part of whose life has been spent in conducting war against them or preparing to do so, I would urge them to remember the famous maxim: 'The price of freedom is eternal vigilance.' We mustn't forget that either.

When in this same speech I spoke about the master thought of Locarno I meant of course the plan of everybody going against the aggressor, whoever he may be, and helping the victim large or small. That is no more than the United Nations was set up to do. We are told the Locarno Treaty failed and did not prevent the war. There was a very good reason for that. The United States was not in it. Had the United States taken before the First World War or between the wars the same interest and made the same exertions and sacrifices and run the same risks to preserve peace and uphold freedom which I thank God she is doing now, there might never have been a First War and there would certainly never have been a Second. With her mighty aid I have a sure hope there will not be a third.

One word personally about myself. If I stay on for the time being bearing the burden at my age it is not because of love for power or office. I have had an ample share of both. If I stay it is because I have a feeling that I may through things that have happened have an influence on what I care about above all else, the building of a sure and lasting peace.

Let us then go forward together with courage and composure, with resolution and good faith to the end which all desire.

Cabinet: conclusions
(Cabinet papers, 128/26)

13 October 1953
Secret
11.30 a.m.
Cabinet Meeting No. 57 of 1953

[. . .]

5. The Colonial Secretary said that the situation in British Guiana still remained quiet. The Governor feared that there might be outbreaks of incendiarism, but this had not yet been attempted on any considerable scale. Mr Jagan,[1] the spokesman of the dismissed Ministers, had expressed a wish to

---

[1] Cheddi Jagan, 1918–97. Educated at Queen's College, Georgetown and Northwestern University, Chicago. Married, 1943, Janet Rosenberg: two children. Treasurer, ManPower Citizens' Association, 1945–6. Elected to Legislative Council (Ind.) for Central Demerara, 1947. Chief Minister, British Guiana, 1953, 1961–4. President of Guyana, 1992–7.

come to London for discussions with the Colonial Secretary, but he had been told that he should in the first instance see the Minister of State for the Colonies, who was due to arrive in Georgetown on 19th October.

The Prime Minister said that no great harm would be done if Mr Jagan came to this country and were seen to be associating with Communists here; but it would hardly be appropriate for the Colonial Secretary to receive him immediately after he had been dismissed from office.

The Colonial Secretary said that the Opposition were anxious that the situation in British Guiana should be debated as soon as Parliament reassembled. He proposed to present a White Paper on 20th October: this would obviate the need for any statement before the debate, which was to be held on 22nd October. From soundings which he had taken he believed that, in view of the attitude of the dismissed Ministers towards the trade union movement in British Guiana and of their association with the World Federation of Trades Unions, the Labour Opposition in the House of Commons would not be united in condemning the action which the Government had taken in this matter.

The Cabinet –

Took note of the Colonial Secretary's statements, and invited him to submit to the Prime Minister the draft of his proposed White Paper on the situation in British Guiana.

[. . .]

Sir Winston S. Churchill to Lady Churchill
(Baroness Spencer-Churchill papers)[1]

13 October 1953

My Darling,

I do hope you are enjoying yourself. The French are not pleased with me; nor indeed did I expect them to be. But I don't think they will revenge themselves on you. The pug will certainly approve. Duffie will be adverse.

The Kitten[2] is behaving admirably & with its customary *punctilio*! Rufus is becoming gradually reconciled. Generally the domestic situation is tranquil.

French St Farm has been bought by Cromer[3] for ten thousand. This is a gt relief to me. The Nobel Literature prize is said to be worth £11,000. I don't think the Swedish Amb[4] wd have rung up asking for an appointment at 4 p.m.

---

[1] This letter was handwritten.
[2] Named 'Margate' by Churchill, after the location of his most recent speech.
[3] George Rowland Stanley Baring, 1918–91. Educated at Eton and Trinity College, Cambridge. Private Secretary to Marquess of Willingdon, 1938–40. On active service in WWII, 1939–45. Governor of Bank of England, 1961–6. Ambassador to US, 1971–4. Earl of Cromer, 1953.
[4] Bo Gunnar Rickardsson Hägglöf, 1904–94. Swedish Ambassador to UK, 1948–67; to France, 1967–71.

on Thursday afternoon to announce the award to me unless he was pretty sure it wd be all right. However we must not count our chickens before they are hatched. Dulles–Bidault arrive Thursday. I am giving D dinner that night & B luncheon on Friday. Five or six only. Then Chartwell for Sunday.

I was lonely last night Pitblado dined. I am reading *The Dynasts* & getting into it.

A long good Cabinet this morning. It is curious how much less formidable things look round the Cabinet Table, than they do in the newspapers.

With all my love my beloved Clemmie from
Your devoted husband

I am writing in bed after a good sleep & Camrose is coming to dinner.

[Drawing of a pig]

Defence Committee: minutes
(Cabinet papers, 131/13)

14 October 1953
Top Secret
11.30 a.m.
Defence Meeting No. 13 of 1953

[. . .]
5. Likelihood of General War with the Soviet Union
(Previous Reference: D(53)2nd Meeting, Minute 5)

The committee considered a memorandum by the Chiefs of Staff (D(53)45)[1] submitting a further appreciation of the likelihood of general war with the Soviet Union in the period up to the end of 1955.

The First Sea Lord said that a similar appreciation had been made in December 1952. The Chiefs of Staff had thought it desirable to review this in the light of Stalin's death and the events immediately following it. They had not, however, found any reason to modify the general conclusions reached in their earlier appreciation. They still considered that general war was on the whole unlikely in the period up to the end of 1955.

The Minister of Supply suggested that the conclusion to be drawn from this report was, not so much that war was unlikely during the period under review, but rather that it was impossible to estimate the likelihood of war during that period. He thought it would be unfortunate if the impression gained ground among Government Departments that the possibility of an early outbreak of war could be dismissed.

The Prime Minister said that he was in agreement with the conclusions

---

[1] Reproduced above (pp. 1223–7).

reached by the Chiefs of Staff. He thought it was true that the possibility of major war had receded slightly. He was not shaken in this opinion by Russia's recent support of Yugoslavia in the Trieste dispute; this, he thought, was designed solely for the purpose of undermining the domestic position of Marshal Tito within Yugoslavia. At the same time he thought it would be unwise to give any wide currency to this appreciation by the Chiefs of Staff. In particular, he deprecated the suggestion that it should be communicated to the United States authorities – it was unnecessary for us to do anything which might encourage them to reduce the level of their defence expenditure. And public statements by Ministers about the likelihood of war should be made sparingly and with caution.

The Committee –

(1) Took note of the report by the Chiefs of Staff (D(53)45) on the likelihood of general war with the Soviet Union up to the end of 1955.
(2) Agreed that this report should not be communicated to the United States Chiefs of Staff.

[. . .]

Cabinet: conclusions
(Cabinet papers, 128/26)

15 October 1953
Secret
11 a.m.
Cabinet Meeting No. 58 of 1953

[. . .]

4. The Cabinet had before them memoranda by the Foreign Secretary (C(53)281) and the Minister of Defence (C(53)282) on the stage reached in the defence negotiations with the Egyptian Government.

The Foreign Secretary said that both parties to the negotiations in Cairo now felt that the time had come to bring the discussions to a head and the next meeting between them, which was to be held within the next few days, would evidently be decisive. The United Kingdom Delegation had asked for final instructions regarding the attitude which they should adopt at this meeting. They believed that, if they then declined to make any further concessions, the Egyptians would break off the negotiations. There seemed, however, to be a reasonable chance of securing an agreement if we were willing to go a little further to meet the Egyptians on some of the points to which they attached special importance. The concessions which, in the opinion of the Delegation, should suffice to secure an agreement on principles were set out in the Appendix to C(53)281.

The Foreign Secretary said that he was disposed to instruct the Delegation to continue their efforts to secure an agreement on principles. The Cabinet accepted the Foreign Secretary's view and proceeded to consider the various points enumerated in the Appendix to C(53)281.

(a) Duration. It was agreed that we should insist on an agreement lasting for seven years.

(b) Withdrawal of Troops. It had been suggested that we might offer to complete the withdrawal of combatant troops in fifteen months (instead of eighteen months) from the date on which an agreement came into force.

The Minister of Defence said that this would be practicable if withdrawal began immediately agreement on principles had been reached. In that event, however, the withdrawal would have to be so planned that we should retain in Egypt until the final agreement was reached enough troops to enable us to hold our position if negotiations broke down on details. It would also be important that the movements made in this initial phase should not be such as to weaken our bargaining position.

The Cabinet agreed that on the basis indicated by the Minister of Defence the Delegation might be authorised to agree that withdrawal would be completed within fifteen months of the date on which the agreement came into force.

(c) Number of Technicians. It was agreed that we must continue to insist on a total of 4,000 British technicians for the first $4\frac{1}{2}$ years of the agreement.

The Minister of Defence said that military requirements would be satisfied if in the following $1\frac{1}{2}$ years we could retain in the Base a minimum number of 2,500 technicians. In the last year of the agreement we should ask for a minimum number of 1,000 technicians, excluding the small numbers required by the Royal Air Force in connection with their staging facilities at Abu Sueir, though our negotiators might be authorized in the last resort to reduce this figure to 750.

The Cabinet agreed that the proposals put forward by the Minister of Defence should be communicated to the United Kingdom Delegation in Cairo.

(d) Availability. The Foreign Secretary suggested that the Delegation should be authorised to put forward a new formula regarding the availability of the Base for war purposes. This would provide that the Base would be made immediately available to us in the event of (i) an attack by an outside power on Egypt; or (ii) an attack by an outside power on any member of the Arab Mutual Security Pact; or (iii) a recommendation by the United Nations that the Base should be made available in the event of aggression or threat of aggression. It would also provide that in the event of a threat of attack on any member of the Arab Mutual Security Pact, Iran or Turkey there should be immediate consultation between the United Kingdom and Egypt.

The Cabinet agreed that the Egyptians should be pressed to accept the revised formula suggested by the Foreign Secretary.

(e) Uniform. The Foreign Secretary said that he was not content with the proposal which our Delegation had suggested regarding the wearing of uniform by British technicians in the Base. He would, however, be willing that they should suggest to the Egyptians a formula in the following terms:

'British personnel in the Base will normally dress as follows. When at work: overalls or shirts and shorts, with rank distinctions. At other times: plain clothes. They will be entitled to wear the uniform of the Service to which they belong and to carry a weapon for their personal protection.'

The Prime Minister said that he saw no reason to include in the agreement this description of the working dress of British technicians in the Base. He proposed that the formula for inclusion in the agreement should be as follows:

'Within the Base installations and in transit between them British personnel will be entitled to wear the uniform of the Service to which they belong and to carry a weapon for their personal protection. Outside the area of the base they will wear plain clothes.'

Our Delegation might be authorised to inform the Egyptians orally that the British technicians when at work would normally wear overalls or shorts and shirts with rank distinctions. This statement should, not, however, be included in the formal agreement itself.

The Cabinet accepted the proposal put forward by the Prime Minister.

(f) Air Facilities. The Cabinet were informed that agreement had already been reached with the Egyptians regarding the provision of staging facilities at Abu Sueir. The Secretary of State for Air said that this would secure the essential requirements of the Royal Air Force in peace. The Cabinet should, however, understand that, with the failure of the original proposals for Anglo-Egyptian arrangements for the air defence of the Base, we had no assurance that the airfields would be maintained in such a condition that the Royal Air Force would be able to operate from them soon after our re-entry into the Base in war. This would greatly reduce the potential military value of the Base in war.

(g) Organisation of the Base. The Cabinet agreed that the officer in charge of British technicians in the Base should have the title 'Senior British Officer, Canal Zone Base'.

The Prime Minister said that he was concerned about the attitude which some Government supporters were likely to adopt towards an Anglo-Egyptian defence agreement of the kind which the Cabinet were now contemplating. Some would be disposed to suggest that, sooner than accept an agreement on these lines, we should have sought to maintain our position in Egypt by force; and they would probably argue that, if a drastic military solution had been sought, it would have been possible thereafter to reduce the strength of the British garrison in Egypt to a figure well below the present level. He was himself inclined to think that this course could not have been followed unless the Egyptians had committed some flagrant acts of provocation which would have justified us in proceeding on the basis that something equivalent to a state of war had arisen in Egypt. If we had taken strong military action in a situation short of that, we should have lacked the support of the United States Government; and, if the dispute had been reported to the United Nations, we could not have expected that a decision would have been given in our favour. Matters having now gone as they had, he was prepared to agree that it might be the wiser course to seek an agreement on principles on the lines which the Cabinet had now approved. This should, however, be presented to the Egyptians as our last word; and he was anxious that no final agreement should be reached with them until Parliament had reassembled and Ministers had had an opportunity of explaining privately to Government supporters the situation which had now been reached. It was of great importance that Ministers should have that opportunity of preparing the way for the agreement, if it was to be concluded, and doing their utmost to reduce the risk of its being subjected to damaging criticism by their own supporters.

The Cabinet –

(1) Invited the Foreign Secretary to instruct the United Kingdom Delegation in Cairo that, at their next meeting with the Egyptians, they should attempt to secure agreement on principles with the limits indicated in paragraphs (a)–(g) above, but that no announcement indicating that final agreement had been reached should be made until Ministers had received a report of the results of that meeting.

(2) Took note that, as soon as Parliament had reassembled, the Chief Whip would arrange for the Prime Minister, the Foreign Secretary and the Minister of Defence to explain privately to Government supporters the stage which had been reached in these negotiations.

(3) Authorised the Lord Privy Seal, in consultation with the Foreign Secretary, to arrange for the Governments of the older Commonwealth countries to be informed of the further proposals which were now to be made to the Egyptians; and to consider what information should be given to other Commonwealth Governments, after the next meeting with the Egyptians, about the course which the negotiations had taken.

Sir Winston S. Churchill to Lady Churchill
(Baroness Spencer-Churchill papers)

16 October 1953

My darling one,

I am just off to Chartwell, but come back Sunday to give the Foreign Ministers a final luncheon. Their talks seem to be going all right, but there are a lot of tiresome things happening, & next Tuesday the Parlt meets again to help us.

It is all settled about the Nobel prize. £12,100 free of tax. Not so bad!

I think we shall have to go to Stockholm for a couple of days in December & stay with the King[1] & Queen[2] there.

I am writing in the Cabinet room & the little cat is holding the notepaper down for me. I miss you vy much. One night I had dinner in bed as I did not want anyone but you for company. I do hope you are enjoying yourself and finding the days interesting.

I am dining with Mary tonight & tomorrow and she lunches with me on a chicken pie on Saturday. Pamela C lunched w me yesterday. How agreeable she is! I had not seen her for years. She told me she had seen you at dinner at the Pugs.

Tender love my darling from yr devoted husband.

[Drawing of a pig]

President Dwight D. Eisenhower to Sir Winston S. Churchill
('The Churchill Eisenhower Correspondence', page 91)

16 October 1953

Dear Winston,

I am most happy to learn that you have been awarded the Nobel Prize for Literature. The Swedish Academy could have made no more fitting choice. Congratulations on yet another deserved tribute to your magnificent career.

---

[1] Oscar Fredrik Wilhelm Olaf Gustaf Adolf, 1882–1973. King Gustaf VI Adolf of Sweden, 1950–73.
[2] Louise Alexandra Marie Irene Mountbatten, 1889–1965. Born in Hesse, Germany. Enlisted with British Red Cross as a nurse during WWI. Married, 1923, Gustaf VI Adolf: one child. Queen Louise of Sweden, 1950–65.

October 1953

Sarah Beauchamp to Sir Winston S. Churchill
(Churchill papers, 1/50)[1]

19 October 1953   Los Angeles, California

Darling, <u>darling</u> Papa,

    I can't explain how this letter has taken so long. I wrote to you on the airplane that night, after leaving you, to thank you for our talk. It comforted me so much. But the letter was in pencil, and I meant to copy it out when I got to New York, but on arriving, as I wrote Mummie, I had to leave for Los Angeles at once. When the excitement of the first program was over – it seemed out of date. I am sorry for I had so wanted to tell you right away. Something of the feeling you had left me with. Your concern for me, and then your talking to me about the decision you had to make about your strength to carry on.

    Time has flown & you have made the decision that only you could make.

    It was the most wonderful news to read your Margate Speech[2] and know that not only must you feel well enough to go on, but that wisdom & resolve are undimmed.

    It was a simply exceptional Speech. It was a breath of hope to the world to see and hear you again. When I think of how you looked when I arrived back in England, and of the long, long months of climbing back to the top of the hill – I cried with pride. <u>Please please</u> now don't overdo it – since you pack more into a day than anyone else living – please heed the warning. Couldn't you for every period and concentrated effort – have an equivalent time of rest (rest, being for you – change, sleep, reading, bathing etc.) but I do feel you have to stop the <u>ceaseless</u> unremitting strain on yourself, if you want to achieve this last great triumph.

    If you try to measure wisely the strain you put on yourself, you will still find that you are a day's march ahead of anyone. <u>Please please measure the strain</u>. Everyone, everyone expresses the relief and joy that you are back at the helm. You must feel the concerted wish of so many many people willing and praying for your strength.

    I enclose a cartoon from the *Los Angeles Times* that made me smile. I think it will make you too, being now such an undisguised 'peace-monger'!

    I was <u>so</u> thrilled about the Nobel Prize. I'm glad it was for literature. You can win the Peace prize later – for you have proved more than once that the pen is mightier than the sword.

    Darling Papa, it is very pleasant here. Mountains and swaying trees and 'eternal summer' which I can do with for a bit. It is easier than New York – the strain and racket far less – for it is country. I love my little house – it is full of friends – never empty.

[1] This letter was handwritten.
[2] Reproduced above (pp. 1237–46).

Accept the truce between Antony and me. Do not work yourself into a hate against him. If I can not solve it, let me paint the picture.

I think I will know quite soon what I will do, but as yet, I do not know. The untying of a relationship is very difficult for me. A human relationship is like a rope to me. You meet, and start weaving strand by strand until you have a stout (?) cord between you, and the ending is the same for me – I cannot sever abruptly. I have to unravel the whole thing strand by strand. Severing sharply is probably braver and better, but I can't, I just can't, and the last strand of all, I cling to most tenaciously, whether I want it or don't want it. I never know. I only know I hate endings. I can't bear even to see guests leave a party I'm giving. I find myself following them down to the 'garden gate' imploring them to stay even though the party is over.

My heaven will be an airport with a one-way system. Just constant arrivals. There will be a departure platform (for people should always be free to go) but no one would ever use it – wow –

I hope to be back for Christmas in fact, I know I will be, not alas for your birthday – we have a big program the 29th (Richard II) and there is no plane fast enough to get me home in time.

The program has really 'come of age' at last. The longer time gives us greater opportunity. I enclose a list of plays and biographies we are doing these 13 weeks. It is quite a stride from a 15 mins interview show 2 years ago.

[...]

Much – oh so much love

Sir Winston S. Churchill to Lady Churchill
(Baroness Spencer-Churchill papers)[1]

20 October 1953

My darling,

Welcome Home! I am resting in bed, before my H of C reappearance & many questions. I am following the Margate plan including a Moran[2] wh he advised.

I do hope you have got the better of yr cold. If I am asleep when your arrive, it wd be good of you to leave till 2.30 when I dress for the House at 3. Questions 3.15. But probably I shall be awake longing to see you.

Tender love
[Drawing of a pig]

---

[1] This letter was handwritten.
[2] An amphetamine pill (Benzedrine), prescribed for Churchill by, and nicknamed after, Lord Moran.

Henry Channon: diary
('Chips', page 478)

20 October 1953

The long holidays are ended: and the House crowded, friendly and excited, met today. I have enjoyed my twelve week holiday. Weeks of Venetian bliss, Casanova adventures; of my Paul's[1] triumphs; Winston's illness; Anthony's recovery.

I lunched with the Austrians; where I found the Soames', Walter Lippman[2] and others. Mary Soames, who has become a ravishing beauty, drove me on to the House, where we saw Winston's long-awaited (and some prophesied never-to-be) return acclaimed. He seemed self-confident, though a touch deaf in spite of his hearing aid, but apparently more vigorous than before. But I doubt whether he can carry on for long. The added strain of the House of Commons will be too much.

Cabinet: conclusions
(Cabinet papers, 128/26)

22 October 1953
Secret
11.30 a.m.
Cabinet Meeting No. 60 of 1953

[...]

4. The Prime Minister said that he had been looking again at the proposed terms of reference for the Royal Commission on the certification and detention of mental patients, which the Cabinet had approved on 19th October. He thought that the wording should be adjusted so as to make it more clear that treatment without certification was not given without the consent of the patient.

The Cabinet –

---

[1] Henry Paul Guinness Channon, 1935–2007. Educated at Eton and Oxford. 2nd Lt, Royal Horse Guards (The Blues), 1955–6. President, Oxford University Conservative Association, 1958. MP (Cons.) for Southend West, 1959–97. Personal Private Secretary to Minister of Power, 1959–60; to Home Secretary, 1960–2; to First Secretary of State, 1962–3; to Foreign Secretary, 1963–4. Married, 1963, Ingrid Olivia Georgia Wyndham Guinness. Opposition Spokesman on Arts and Amenities, 1967–70. Parliamentary Under-Secretary of State, Dept of Energy, 1970–2. Minister for Housing and Construction, 1972–4. Minister of State, 1979–81; for the Arts, 1981–3; for Trade, 1983–6. Secretary of State for Trade and Industry, 1986–7; for Transport, 1987–9. Chairman, House of Commons Finance and Services Committee, 1992–7. Baron Kelvedon, 1997.

[2] Walter Lippmann, 1889–1974. Educated at Harvard University. Associate Editor, *The New Republic*, 1914–17. Asst to Secretary of War, 1917. Capt., US Military Intelligence, 1918. Editor, *New York World*, 1919–31. Special writer to New York Herald Tribune syndicate, 1931–62. Pulitzer Prize for International Reporting, 1962.

Agreed that he terms of reference for the Royal Commission on the certification and detention of mental patients should be amended by inserting, after the words 'to be treated', the words 'as voluntary patients'.
[. . .]

President Dwight D. Eisenhower to Sir Winston S. Churchill
(Premier papers, 11/423)

23 October 1953
Top Secret

Dear Winston,
    Foster tells me that you are seriously considering coming over here to join your old friend Bernie for a week in South Carolina. Of course, if you come I want very much to have a good talk with you. I assume that you would land initially in New York and from there would proceed to Carolina either by train or by plane. In either case I think the earliest and most convenient opportunity we could have for a talk would be for you to stop off with me for a day. If you could arrive in Washington so as to give us a full afternoon and evening together, we could start you on your way again at a reasonable hour the next morning. Of course, I should want you to spend the night at the White House and I could also put up a staff officer if one should accompany you. Quite naturally, we should hope that Lady Churchill would be with you.
    This I think would be better than having me attempt to come to South Carolina. You are familiar with the sometimes awkward arrangements that the security people make when the President goes to a strange place. In Washington, however, all this is routine and unobtrusive.
    Since our visit would be merely incidental to your longer stay in Carolina, I think it would be assumed by all our friends to be perfectly normal procedure and would awaken no particular comment or feeling of being left out.
    If you think there is any possibility of making such a visit, would you give me early indication of the approximate date you might consider so that I could keep my calendar completely free of other commitments.
    I was delighted at Foster's report of your almost miraculously quick and complete recovery. Also he brought a very gratifying report of how well the three Foreign Ministers had worked together.[1]

---

[1] Churchill responded: 'Thank you so much for your message. I have no plans at present and a lot is going on here. I quite understand all your difficulties and will not fail to let you know in plenty of time if anything comes into the sphere of possibility. I have never suggested the matter to Bernie.'

Sir Winston S. Churchill to James Thomas
Prime Minister's Personal Minute M.311/53
(Premier papers, 11/496)

24 October 1953

NAVAL CADET ENTRY

You have no reason to hurry a decision of this grave and complicated character. The Defence Committee must consider it and it must then be the subject of Cabinet discussion. You can perfectly well say that the matter is under active consideration. I do not think that any conclusion will be reached in the present Session.

Cabinet: conclusions
(Cabinet papers, 128/26)

27 October 1953
Secret
11 a.m.
Cabinet Meeting No. 61 of 1953

[...]
4. The Cabinet considered memoranda by the Minister of Food (C(53)298) and the Minister of Agriculture (C(53)299) on the arrangements to be made for the future marketing of home-produced meat and bacon after the end of meat rationing.

The Minister of Agriculture said that this was a difficult problem, which had been under discussion between the Departments concerned for some time past. In the last month, however, the National Farmers Unions (NFUs) had introduced a new factor into the situation by producing firm proposals of their own. They had come down strongly against any system of deficiency payments, and had formulated a scheme for the central purchase of livestock by a producers' Marketing Board, at pre-determined fixed prices, followed by re-sale in a free market. He doubted whether it would be possible to restore the farmers' confidence in the Government's agricultural policy unless some of the main principles underlying those proposals were accepted. He had therefore devised a plan (outlined in C(53)299) which, while avoiding some of the difficulties inherent in the proposals of the NFUs, preserved its main principles and, in particular, provided for the establishment of producers' Marketing Board. Many of the Government's present supporters were firmly pledged, as he was himself, to the principle of agricultural marketing boards, which had been a feature of the agricultural policy of the Conservative Government before the war. The farmers had now, however, become apprehensive that the

Government might abandon that principle, and he believed that their confidence in the Government would not be restored unless it were reaffirmed. The plan which he had outlined in C(53)299 would make it plain that the Government were prepared to encourage the establishment of producers' Marketing Boards. Further, by continuing the system of an assured market at pre-determined prices, it would provide the farmers with the security which they required. At the same time, by its provision for the re-sale of meat in a free market, it would redeem the Government's pledges to the meat traders and would restore freedom of choice to consumers. State trading by the Ministry of Food might, it was true, have to be continued during the interim period before the establishment of the producers' Marketing Board; but he hoped that the Board might be able to begin operations by the middle of 1955.

The Minister said that the farmers, remembering their experience after the end of the First World War, were genuinely nervous of the consequences of de-control. Their fears had been increased by their temporary difficulty in disposing of this season's crops, following the de-control of cereals; and they were on this account the more distrustful of the method of deficiency payments. It was these feelings which had led the NFUs to take such a firm stand against any proposals for the future marketing of meat which were based on the principle of deficiency payments – though it must be admitted that they were not yet aware of the suggestion that deficiency payments should be supplemented by a system of buttress prices.

The Minister of Food said that he was strongly opposed to the proposal that his Department should continue State trading in meat until such time as a producers' Marketing Board could be established with monopoly powers. During this interim period, under the plan proposed by the Minister of Agriculture, the Ministry of Food would be required to buy meat at fixed prices and re-sell it in a free market for what it would fetch. The Ministry would be unable to control the quality or the quantity of the meat offered by producers and would have to sell it to traders enjoying, for the first time for fourteen years, the right to refuse meat which they did not want to accept. This was a bad commercial proposition for any Government Department to undertake. Moreover, the meat traders would be bitterly opposed to this system and would therefore have every reason to increase the Department's potential losses. The producers would also have a positive incentive to increase them, since the initial amount of the Exchequer assistance to the new Marketing Board, when it was established, was to be determined by reference to the trading loss incurred by the Ministry in the last year before the establishment of the Board. Such a system would also make it necessary for the Ministry to continue to control meat imports and to engage in the bulk purchase of foreign meat during the interim period. Finally, there could be no assurance that this interim system could be brought to an end by the middle of 1955. A long and complicated procedure had to be complied with before a producers'

Marketing Board could be established. If therefore the Government adopted the plan proposed by the Minister of Agriculture, it seemed likely that the Ministry of Food would still be trading in meat, at heavy cost to the Exchequer, at the time of the next General Election. Monopoly trading in meat by a central agency was in fact open to very serious objections, as indicated in paragraph 10 of C(53)298. And, politically, it could be represented as a stage towards the nationalization of the meat trade.

The Minister said that the alternative plan which he had outlined in C(53)298 would further the Government's general policy of abolishing bulk purchase and State trading and would at the same time provide adequate means of fulfilling the Government's guarantees to the farmers. It would carry out the Government's pledge to restore to meat traders the business which had been taken from them at the beginning of the war. And it would restore freedom of choice to the consumer. It did not exclude the creation of a producers' Marketing Board, though it was not based on the principle of a single Board with powers of monopoly trading.

The Prime Minister said that he was impressed by the advantages of the plan put forward by the Minister of Food. It was in accord with the general theme of the Government's policy for relaxing controls and restoring free markets, and abandoning State trading and bulk purchase. At the same time it would honour the Government's guarantees to the farmers by way of an Exchequer subsidy based on the two principles of deficiency payments and buttress prices. The farmers could insist that the Government should carry out these guarantees; but it was for the Government to determine by what methods they should do so. He himself preferred that the public should pay through taxation such sums as were required to ensure the stability of British agriculture, and that the prices which, as consumers, they paid for home-produced food should be left to be determined by the operation of a free market.

The Chancellor of the Exchequer said that the present Government were not committed to the principle of producers' Marketing Boards with powers of monopoly trading. In the Agricultural Charter published by the Conservative Party in 1948 it had been stated that 'the basis of good marketing in the future should be producers' co-operation both through voluntary organisations and through statutory Marketing Boards'. It had clearly been contemplated that the method would vary according to the requirements of different commodities.

The Chancellor said that the Minister of Agriculture had removed some of the worst features in the proposals put forward by the NFUs, but even his modified scheme as outlined in C(53)299 seemed to be too ambitious. It would be highly dangerous to establish a single agency responsible for buying at fixed prices all home-produced meat, involving an annual turnover of about £300 millions, and for selling it for what it would fetch on a free market. He could not accept the unlimited liability which this would create for the Exchequer.

The scheme was unsound financially and, even if it were well received by the farmers in the first instance, it would expose the Government to damaging criticism in later years. On economic and financial grounds, there could be no doubt that the system of deficiency payments and buttress prices proposed by the Minister of Food was the better plan. But it would not be easy to persuade the NFUs to accept it. They were in a difficult mood, and were disposed to reject out of hand any scheme based on the principle of deficiency payments. Further thought should therefore be given to the means of presenting such a plan to the farmers. It might be helpful if their representatives were invited to co-operate from the outset in framing long-term arrangements for promoting efficient marketing. A Marketing Council might perhaps be established to consider the problems listed in paragraph 3 of the Appendix to C(53)298. But if, after further consideration, Ministers felt that it would be impossible to persuade the farmers' representatives to accept a plan on the general lines proposed by the Minister of Food in C(53)298, the alternative course would be to set up an independent committee of enquiry to consider the whole problem.

In further discussion the following points were made:

(a) The suggestion of an independent enquiry was open to two objections. First, criticism of the Government's agricultural policy had arisen largely from the delay in announcing plans for the future marketing of home-produced foodstuffs, and it was likely to increase if one of the most important aspects of this problem were now remitted for independent enquiry. Secondly, the appointment of a committee of enquiry would mean that the Ministry of Food would have to continue for a further year the existing system of State trading in meat.

(b) The Cabinet were informed that the Government of Northern Ireland supported the plan outlined by the Minister of Agriculture in C(53)299.

(c) The Secretary of State for Scotland said that the Government would have difficulty, both with the farmers and with many of their own supporters in Parliament, if they appeared to reject the principle of producers' Marketing Boards. On the other hand, it was argued that the creation of Marketing Boards with powers of monopoly trading was not a suitable remedy for universal application and, if pressed as such, would be strongly opposed by some Government supporters.

(d) The Government were under no less an obligation to fulfil their pledges to the meat traders than to carry out their undertakings to the farmers.

(e) Although the balance of the economic and financial arguments might lie in favour of the plan proposed by the Minister of Food in C(53)298, there would be serious political difficulty in securing its acceptance. It would be unwise to confront the NFUs with it as a firm Government decision. Further thought should be given to the possibility of making adjustments and additions which might make it more acceptable to the farmers and to certain sections of Government supporters in Parliament.

The Cabinet –

(1) Agreed that policy proposals for the future marketing of meat and bacon should be worked out on the general lines of the plan proposed by the Minister of Food in C(53)298.

(2) Invited the Chancellor of the Exchequer to discuss with the Ministers of Food and Agriculture and the Secretary of State for Scotland and other interested members of the Cabinet, what additions and adjustments could be made to that plan with a view to making it more acceptable to the farmers and, in particular, how a system of 'buttress prices' for meat and bacon would be operated in practice and how it could be reconciled with the provisions of Section 5 of the Agriculture Act, 1947; and also to consider how proposals on these lines could best be presented to the farmers' representatives and to Government supporters.

(3) Agreed to resume their consideration of this problem later in the week, in the light of the results of the discussions to be undertaken in pursuance of Conclusion (2) above.

[...]

Defence Committee: minutes
(Cabinet papers, 131/13)

28 October 1953
Top Secret
11.30 a.m.
Defence Committee Meeting No. 14 of 1953

[...]

3. Cadet Entry into the Royal Navy

The Committee had before them a memorandum by the First Lord of the Admiralty (D.(53)53) setting out the conclusions of a Committee appointed by him to advise on cadet entry into the Royal Navy; and proposing that the entry at sixteen years of age should be abandoned as soon as practicable and thereafter all Royal Navy cadets should be entered at about eighteen years.

The First Lord of the Admiralty said that on assuming office he had appointed a Committee to advise on the steps that should be taken to ensure an adequate supply of cadets to the Royal Navy. This Committee, composed of members of the Admiralty, naval officers and educational authorities, had recommended that a new form of entry at thirteen should be introduced but that the entry at sixteen should not be abandoned. The thirteen-year-old entry would, however, be subject to certain conditions. A substantial quota of vacancies would be reserved for boys from the grant-aided schools, the naval character of the College would be diminished with the day-to-day control in the hands of a civilian headmaster instead of a naval officer, and cadets would not be required to commit themselves to a naval career until they became eighteen. These conditions had raised a number of problems both political and educational and, as a result of discussions with the Minister of Education, Secretary of State for Scotland, Government supporters in the House of Commons and naval officers of both senior and junior ranks, he had come to the conclusion that the only way to provide officers of the standard required and in the right numbers was to enter all cadets at about eighteen. It was most important to reach a definite settlement which would be permanent and not likely to be revised by any succeeding Government.

The First Sea Lord said the pre-1947 thirteen-year-old entry, and in addition a special entry at eighteen was the best system from the naval point of view. The situation was, however, now different since only 40 per cent of the entry at thirteen would be open to general competition and 60 per cent reserved for State-aided schools with no latitude to adjust these percentages. Such an entry, in addition to the present entry at sixteen, would be entirely unsatisfactory, as those officers entered at thirteen from general competition would be gradually squeezed out. If the choice lay between entry at thirteen on the conditions proposed by the Committee and entry at eighteen, he would prefer the latter; but it would not give as good a result as the old mixture of entry at thirteen and eighteen.

The Minister of Defence said that he would welcome an opportunity of further discussion before any decisions were taken.

The Prime Minister said that he was deeply perturbed by the Admiralty proposal to limit the cadet entry to eighteen-year-olds. Life in the Royal Navy was quite different from that in the other two Services; the naval officer was required to spend much of his life afloat in conditions of discomfort, and his efficiency depended on his having a true sense of vocation. By entering cadets at thirteen, this extremely important vocational atmosphere was created. The educational aspect was not so important. He had himself introduced the special entry at the age of eighteen. It was successful because there was a steady stream of boys who had had a strong naval stamp put on them from their earliest days and were carried through by their intense vocational feelings. He still favoured the mixed entry; but in his opinion, restriction of entry to cadets of eighteen would be striking a death blow to the Royal Navy.

The Committee – Took note that the Minister of Defence would discuss further with members of the Board of Admiralty the proposals by the First Lord as set out in D.(53)53 and agreed to resume discussion thereafter.

Cabinet: conclusions
(Cabinet papers, 128/26)

29 October 1953
Secret
11.45 a.m.
Cabinet Meeting No. 62 of 1953

[...]
6. The Cabinet had before them a memorandum by the Secretary of State for War (C(53)258) on the future of the Home Guard.

The Secretary of State for War said that the time was approaching when those who had joined the Home Guard when it was first re-established would have to decide whether to extend their two year period of service or be discharged; and it was therefore necessary for the Government to decide their future policy. It might perhaps seem anomalous to maintain the Home Guard at a cost of £1,000,000 a year at a time when substantial reductions might have to be made in the size of the Army. On the other hand, the Commander-in-Chief Designate, United Kingdom Land Forces,[1] attached considerable importance to the maintenance of the framework of the Home Guard and it was also necessary to bear in mind the statements which Government spokesmen had made in defending the Home Guard against Opposition attempts to have it disbanded. Indeed, the issue had become in part a political one. If it should be decided to retain the Home Guard, the case for doing so must be effectively presented if recruiting was to be maintained.

The Minister of Defence said that the future of the Home Guard ought properly to be considered as part of the current review of defence expenditure generally. He had no doubt, however, that there was a good case for retaining in peacetime the nucleus of an organization which in atomic war might well have an invaluable part to play, particularly in assisting the civil defence services.

The Home Secretary said that disbandment of the Home Guard would have a discouraging effect on recruitment to the civil defence services, which were seriously under strength.

The Secretary of State for Scotland hoped that any announcement about the future of the Home Guard would include some reference to the part which it might play in assisting the civil defence services in war.

The Prime Minister said that it was clearly the view of the Cabinet that the Home Guard should be retained. The decision to retain it should be announced boldly.

[1] Miles Christopher Dempsey, 1896–1969. Served in both WWI and WWII. MC, 1918. Commanded 13th Bde BEF during the campaign in France, 1940. DSO, 1940. KCB, 1944. C-in-C Allied Land Forces in South East Asia, 1945–6. C-in-C Middle East, 1946–7. C-in-C (designate) UK Land Forces, 1951–6. GBE, 1956.

The Cabinet –

Authorised the Secretary of State for War to announce that it was the Government's intention the Home Guard should continue in being.

7. The Prime Minister said that, in accordance with the Cabinet's decision of 27th October,[1] two informal meetings of Ministers had been held to discuss the proposals for the future marketing of meat and bacon which had been outlined by the Minister of Food in C(53)298 and to consider how these could best be presented to the farmers' representatives and to Government supporters. These meetings had served to clarify some of the doubts expressed in the Cabinet's earlier discussion. In particular, it had been established that a system of buttress prices would not be inconsistent with the provision for minimum prices under section 5 of the Agriculture Act, 1947, though it would be necessary that in the first two years of the new scheme the buttress prices should not be lower than the minimum prices already declared for those years. In presenting this plan to the farmers and to Government supporters Ministers would have to make it plain that it did not imply any weakening of their support for the principle of producers Marketing Boards; and on this account it was now proposed that the announcement of these arrangements for meat marketing should be accompanied by a declaration that the Milk Marketing Boards would resume operations in 1954 over the whole range of milk products including liquid milk.

The Prime Minister said that the plan now proposed was outlined in a draft memorandum (C(53)302) which had been prepared by officials of the Departments concerned in the light of the discussions at the two informal meetings of Ministers to which he had referred. The choice before the Cabinet was whether, despite the political risks, they should go forward with this plan, which was consistent with their general policy of relaxing Government controls and freeing the economy, or whether they should continue State trading and delay the dismantling of the Ministry of Food while a public enquiry was made into the whole problem of meat marketing.

Discussion showed that there was general support in the Cabinet for the proposal to go forward with a plan on the general lines indicated in C(53)302.

The following points were raised in discussion of this plan:
    (a) It was suggested that, as a matter of presentation, the new price proposals should not be described as a 'deficiency payments' system. The principle of deficiency payments was unpopular with the farmers' representatives and with Government supporters. And this description also tended to obscure the new and important feature of buttress prices. The plan was in fact a dual-price system providing both collective and individual guarantees. Some short title should be devised which would bring out the true nature of the plan.

---

[1] See Cabinet: conclusions, reproduced above (pp. 1258–62).

(b) The Minister of Agriculture said that, if he was to refer to the possibility that a producers' Marketing Board might eventually be established with wide powers of trading in meat, he would wish to do so in more encouraging terms than those used in the last part of paragraph 16 of C(53)302.[1] He would like to invite the farmers' representatives to formulate proposals for a Meat Marketing Board with wider functions, and to promise them his assistance in working out such proposals.

The point was made that there were limits to the extent to which the Minister could properly assist one of the interested parties in working out proposals for a marketing scheme which, at a later stage, would require his Ministerial approval. It was his duty to consider, not only the interests of the producers, but also those of other parties affected by a marketing scheme, and at some stage of the procedure he had a semi-judicial function to discharge. It was, however, agreed that this consideration need not preclude the Minister from encouraging producers to formulate proposals for marketing schemes, since it was the declared policy of the Government that Marketing Boards should be established in appropriate cases.

In further discussion it was suggested that the invitation to the farmers' representatives to formulate proposals for a Meat Marketing Board could be given in more encouraging terms if it were made before, instead of after, the reference to the establishment of a Board which would develop the voluntary marketing of fatstock and exercise compulsory powers in respect of pigs sold for bacon curing.

This part of the statement should also be amended so as to make it clear whether the Board which would exercise compulsory powers in respect of bacon and pigs would also operate, on a voluntary or a compulsory basis, in respect of other livestock.

(c) The Minister of Agriculture suggested that further consideration should be given to the method of exercising Government control over the fixing of prices by Milk Marketing Boards. In his view this should be secured by directions given by the Agriculture Ministers under the Agricultural Marketing Act, even if it were necessary to amend the Acts for that purpose. He thought it preferable that this control should be exercised under these permanent Acts and not under temporary powers available to the Minister of Food under the Defence Regulations. This might affect the wording of paragraph 20 of C(53)302.

The Minister of Education said that, if the Milk Marketing Boards were to

---

[1] The last part of para. 16 read: 'It should be made clear to producers that it will be open to them to put forward proposals for a Marketing Board or Boards with wider functions in this field, which would have to be considered in the light of any difficulties of the sort mentioned in the preceding paragraph which the proposals might raise.'

operate the Welfare Milk Scheme, it might be desirable that they should also assume responsibility for the School Milk Service.

The Cabinet –
  (1) Approved in principle the proposals outlined in C(53)302 on the future marketing of meat and bacon and on the future operation of the Milk Marketing Boards.
  (2) Invited the Agriculture Ministers and the Minister of Food to consider further the particular points noted in paragraphs (a)–(c) above.
  (3) Asked the Lord Privy Seal, in consultation with the Agriculture Ministers, the Minister of Food, the Minister of Housing and the Chief Whip, to draw up a detailed programme and time-table for presenting these proposals to Parliament after preliminary consultation with Government supporters in the House of Commons and with representatives of the farmers and the food trades concerned; and invited him to submit this programme and time-table for the Prime Minister's approval.

November 1953

Sir Winston S. Churchill: speech
(Hansard)

3 November 1953   House of Commons

DEBATE ON THE ADDRESS

I thought the Leader of the Opposition chose very apposite words in which to pay the traditional compliments to the mover[1] and the seconder[2] of the Motion. It is always difficult to find new terms in which to express the broad general feeling of the House in this matter because, after all, it happens every year and most of the good points have been taken on bygone occasions.

I think I have been a witness of these proceedings longer than anyone else, and I certainly would not guarantee to think of something entirely new. This I can say, however; that the mover stated his case with simple force, and the seconder certainly earned fully the praise of the Leader of the Opposition, in that she will have a most valuable and important contribution to make to our discussions over the social and, particularly, the health spheres. At any rate, I am obliged to the right hon. Gentleman for the way in which he has referred to these, my two hon. Friends, and I am glad that all has started in such a quiet and nice and friendly spirit. I trust that I shall not be guilty of trespassing beyond those limits further than is necessary to place the realisation of the facts before the House.

The debate on the Address will continue for the rest of this week, I have to tell the House, and it is hoped that it will be completed early next week. It is our intention, Mr Speaker, under your guidance to arrange both the general debate, and the debate on any Amendments which may be tabled, so as to meet the wishes of the House. It is proposed that Private Members shall enjoy

---

[1] John Granville Morrison, 1906–96. Served with Royal Wilts Yeomanry, 1939–42. MP (Cons.) for Salisbury Div. of Wiltshire, 1942–64. Chairman, 1922 Committee, 1955–64. Baron Morgadale, 1964. Lord Lieutenant of Wiltshire, 1969–81.
[2] Edith Maud Pitt, 1906–66. OBE, 1952. MP (Cons.) for Edgbaston Div. of Birmingham, 1953–66. Joint Parliamentary Secretary, Ministry of Pensions and National Insurance, 1955–9. Parliamentary Secretary, Ministry of Health, 1959–62. DBE, 1962.

their rights in the matter of Bills and Motions in the same manner as in recent Sessions. Perhaps I may take this opportunity to give notice that my right hon. Friend the Leader of the House will tomorrow propose a Motion to provide that Private Members business should have precedence on 20 Fridays, the first of which will be Friday, 27th November.

The right hon. Gentleman referred to a few matters which are mentioned in the Gracious Speech, but not as fully as he would wish. He said that the question of Egypt was omitted. Well, the Egyptian negotiations were mentioned in the Prorogation Speech and there has been no development of importance since then, but there may be as time passes.

The Overlords came in for comment. I had no experience of being Prime Minister in time of peace and I attached more importance to the grouping of Departments so that the responsible head of the Government would be able to deal with a comparatively smaller number of heads than actually exists in peacetime. I think we had great advantage – although it may not be believed opposite – from the services of the three noble Lords, who did their very utmost to help forward the public service. On reflection, I have thought it better to revert to the proposal which the right hon. Gentleman himself recommended, namely, to hush it all up and manage it in the Cabinet.

That also applies in a certain sense to what the right hon. Gentleman said about atomic energy, for there too his record is one which, at any rate, may be taken as an example in some ways. He demands the control of atomic energy by the House, but we must not forget that when he was in office his Government spent more than £100 million without ever asking the House to be aware of what was going on. No doubt having been in office such a short time as we have, we have not yet learned all the tricks of the trade. The question of atomic energy being dealt with under Government authority by a corporation will be laid before the House next week when a White Paper and a draft Order in Council will be issued. They will give the House a very great deal of information upon a subject which, I must warn hon. Gentlemen, means quite hard reading, if one has to undertake a great deal of it.

I notice that both the mover and the seconder of the Motion and the Leader of the Opposition gave prominence in their remarks to the expression of their fervent good wishes to the Queen and the Duke of Edinburgh for the tremendous journey round the Commonwealth and Empire and round the world upon which they shortly will embark. Nothing like it has even been seen before in our history. There is no doubt of the welcome which awaits Her Majesty in Australia, New Zealand and all the other lands which give their loyalty and allegiance to the Crown, and through which she and her husband will travel. We all join together in wishing Her Majesty and the Duke God-speed on their journey and a safe return to her loyal and devoted subjects in these islands next May.

This is the third time that I have been called upon to follow the Leader of the Opposition in the debate on the Address in this present Parliament and two years have passed since we had a General Election. When are we going to have another? (Hon. Members: 'Tomorrow'.) It is always difficult to foresee, and rash to forecast, the course of future events. Still, for practical purposes, one has to try from time to time to weigh the probabilities and make the best guess one can. I do not hesitate to say that, viewing the political scene as it appears to me, it looks as if a General Election was further off this afternoon than it did two years ago.

It certainly is not the wish or intention of Her Majesty's Government to take advantage of any temporary fluctuation in public opinion in the hopes of securing an electoral victory. Two years ago many thought there might soon be another trial of strength, even within a twelve month, making three quarrelsome, costly, machine made tumults in less than three years. Now it is quite evident that different expectations prevail.

After all, we were elected for a five-year period under what is called the Quinquennial Act. I have always been in favour of the Quinquennial Act. In fact, 48 years ago, in 1905, I moved a Bill under the Ten Minutes Rule to establish the quinquennial period instead of the septennial, which was then the legal term. It seems to me that this 'quinquennial' strikes a happy medium between Parliaments which last too little and Parliaments which last too long.

We are not only a democracy but a Parliamentary democracy, and both aspects of our political life must be borne in mind. To have a General Election every year, as the Chartists proposed, would deprive the House of Commons of much of its dignity and authority. It would no longer be an Assembly endeavouring to find a solution for national problems and providing a stable foundation for the administration of the country, but rather a vote-catching machine looking for a springboard, in an atmosphere where party advantage and personal ambition would be by no means wholly excluded. There is no doubt, and I should like to put this general proposition to the House for their consideration, that elections exist for the sake of the House of Commons and not that the House of Commons exists for the sake of elections.

If this were true in former generations, it seems even more so in this cataclysmic 20th Century when everything is in flux and change and when, after the fearful exertions, sacrifices and exhaustions of two world wars, the element of calm, patient study and a sense of structure by both sides may render lasting service to our whole people and increase and consolidate their influence for good and for peace throughout the quivering, convulsive and bewildered world.

More especially is this true of a period in which the two-party system is dominant and about 14 million vote Tory and about another 14 million Socialist. (Hon. Members: 'Ah'.) I looked the figures up. I have not done anybody out of anything. The two-party system is dominant. It is not really possible to assume that one of these 14 million masses of voters possess all the virtues and the wisdom and the other lot are dupes or fools, or even knaves or crooks. Ordinary people in the country mix about with each other in friendly, neighbourly relations, and they know it is nonsense for party politicians to draw such harsh contrasts between them. Even in this House it is very difficult for the specialists in faction to prevent Members from getting very friendly with each other and worrying about their common difficulties and the grave strain and expense of modern Parliamentary life. We have at least that in common.

On the other hand, I am sure it would be a mistake if the possibilities of dissolution were removed altogether from the mind of Parliament. In some countries Parliaments cannot be dissolved, or can hardly be dissolved, until they have run their fixed term. It is an advantage of our system that, while we aim at five-year Parliaments – which, by etiquette, means four-and-a-half years – extraordinary situations may arise at home or abroad which justify or even compel a precipitate appeal to the country.

Nothing I say about our desires and intentions to allow this Parliament to run its lawful course is intended to exclude necessary constitutional action if events should require it. I have fought more elections than anyone here, or indeed anyone alive in this country – Parliamentary elections – and on the whole they are great fun. But there ought to be interludes of tolerance, hard work and study of social problems between them. Having rows for the sake of having rows between politicians might be good from time to time, but it is not a good habit of political life. It does not follow that we should get further apart by staying long together.

I am not suggesting that our goal is a coalition; that, I think, would be carrying good will too far. But our duties, as we see them, are varied and sometimes conflicting. We have to help our respective parties, but we have also to make sure that we help our country and its people. There can be no doubt where our duty lies between these two.

I am pleading for time, calm, industry and vigilance, and also time to let things grow and prove themselves by experience. It may sometimes be necessary for Governments to undo each other's work, but this should be an exception and not the rule. We are, of course, opposed, for instance, to nationalisation of industry and, to a lesser extent, to the nationalisation of services. We abhor the fallacy, for such it is, of nationalisation for nationalisation's sake. But where we are preserving it, as in the coal mines, the railways, air traffic, gas and electricity, we have done and are doing our utmost to make a success of it, even though this may somewhat mar the symmetry of party recrimination. It is only where we believed that a measure of nationalisation was a real hindrance to our island life that we have reversed the policy, although we are generally opposed to the principle.

Here, let me say, in passing from these general remarks, that I earnestly hope the appointment of Sir Brian Robertson as head of British Railways will be distinguished not only by marked improvements in their running, but also by a feeling among the railwaymen that an element of personal contact and leadership will be developed between the management and the men so that healthy pride may play its part in the success of these national services.

In his speech, the right hon. Gentleman referred briefly both to housing and to farming. I had thought beforehand that something like this might happen, so I collected a few remarks to make upon the subjects. I have heard some talk about our policy for the repair and improvement of houses being a Tory plot to put more money into the pockets of the landlords – What, not a sound! I hope that that will not be considered – I am encouraged by the way it is received – an exhaustive exposition of the problem. It would certainly be a premature judgment, for no attempt has yet been made to explain our plans. Before I sit down this afternoon White Papers, giving full schemes for England, Wales and Scotland, will be found in the Vote Office. My right hon. Friend the Minister of Housing and Local Government will unfold his scheme in detail during our debate tomorrow, and I shall not anticipate his explanation of its structure. (Hon. Members: 'Oh'.) But I am going to say a few words upon the subject.

We have claimed credit, as we have a right to do, for building at the rate of 300,000 new houses per year. We were frequently told, and have long known, that building new houses cannot by itself solve the urgent problem of providing homes for the people. If it were true that while 300,000 new houses were being built nearly as many were mouldering into ruin and a far larger number were devoid of modern conveniences, the gain of new building would be largely cancelled out. The Opposition have said that to us, and we concede it. The Minister of Housing and Local Government has produced – with immense work and months and months of discussion – what we believe is a practical, I will not say solution, but mitigation, of the problem.

We have to face the fact that $2\frac{1}{4}$ million houses were built 100 years ago and another $2\frac{1}{2}$ million are between 65 and 100 years old. Even the more modern ones require regular maintenance and repair. Surely this is a matter which ought to interest – and which I am sure will interest – the whole of any House of Commons elected on the basis of universal suffrage. I hope it will not be brushed aside. I can quite see, as far as I have got, that it is not going to be treated merely as a party matter. If when the White Paper has been studied and when my right hon. Friend has commended it to the House, the Opposition have a counter proposal, let them put it forward; we shall give it our earnest attention.

These are not the sort of questions which party Governments are usually anxious to tackle, but it cannot be allowed to drift any longer by any Government determined to do its duty. I would quote to the House some words spoken by an eminent and independent man, a life-long champion of Left-wing politics, highly regarded on both sides of the House, Mr Thomas Johnston.[1] He said last year at Stirling – I really must read this to the House: 'I venture once again to draw attention to the galloping disasters coming to us in the increasing obsolescence and decay of our existing housing structures being permitted – indeed rendered inevitable – I believe through sheer political cowardice. Private house proprietors and housing trusts are unable to provide repairs, much less improvements, owing to the high cost of materials. . . . To allow great national assets like that to crumble and disappear prematurely does not make sense; and when it is remembered that not only no repairs but no improvements can be effected, and that hundreds of thousands of tenants are condemned for all the years of their lives to live without even the ordinary decencies of a separate family water-closet or a bath, we can see that unless existing house assets are maintained and improved side-by-side with the provision of new houses, then not only will the house problem not be solved in our day and generation, but the financial and administrative position of our local authorities will become hopeless and impossible.' He concluded: 'This is not the occasion to outline remedies, but I suggest that the first and essential condition is that the repair and maintenance and improvement of housing be taken outside the orbit of partisan politics altogether.' We shall see how we get on, but let us start with that hope.

It must be realised that houses cannot be repaired without money, and where is that money to come from? Is it to be found by the State? Or is it to be new private investment by landlords? Or will both these processes be necessary? Is it quite certain that no adequate system of repairing millions of houses, let alone fitting them with baths and other basic modern requirements, will be brought into existence unless this Parliament takes effective action, and begins now.

Undoubtedly new burdens will fall upon the national finances, and this must be viewed with gravity at a time when our solvency and our independence of foreign aid, on which we count so much, stand foremost in our minds. On the other hand, we must not forget that our financial credit will be substantially enhanced by our coping with a problem which is known to have been outstanding for so long. Surely any fair and reasonable scheme for inducing private as well as public resources to be made available for these vital public purposes should not be curtly dismissed – I am sure it will not be curtly dismissed – by the House of Commons.

Would it be very wrong if I suggested, following the lines which Mr Tom

[1] Thomas Johnston, 1881–1965. Founder and Editor, *Forward*. MP (Lab.) for West Stirlingshire, 1922–4, 1929–31, 1931–45; for Dundee, 1924–9. Lord Privy Seal, 1931. Regional Commissioner, Scottish Civil Defence Region, 1939–41. Secretary of State for Scotland, 1941–5. Chairman, Scottish National Forestry Commissioners, 1945–8. CH, 1953. Director, Independent Television Authority in North-East Scotland, 1960–5.

Johnston indicated, that we might look into this together, with the desire to have more decent homes for the people counting much higher in our minds than ordinary partisan political gains and advantages for either side? War and its restrictions: aerial bombardment and its destructions: time and decay: potential improvements: all seem to make this matter worthy of the good will and mental effort of the House as a whole.

But this process will need time, time not only to pass the legislation but also to allow its effects to show themselves and to make people feel that benefits have been received which are welcomed by many thousands of families. Certainly we should not have embarked upon this policy to repair the crumbling homes and resume our work of cleaning up the slums unless we had intended to remain responsible long enough to be judged by results. With these introductory words, I commend the White Papers now in the Vote Office to hon. Members.

The Leader of the Opposition referred also to the farmers. The House knows that it is our theme and policy to reduce controls and restrictions as much as possible and to reverse if not to abolish the tendency to State purchase and marketing which is a characteristic of the Socialist philosophy. We hope instead to develop individual enterprise founded in the main on the laws of supply and demand and to restore to the interchange of goods and services that variety, flexibility, ingenuity and incentive on which we believe the fertility and liveliness of economic life depend. We have now reached a point when the end of war-time food rationing, with all its rigid, costly features and expensive staff, is in sight. For our farmers, the abandonment of controls will bring great opportunities.

In the agricultural field, however, another set, of arguments must be borne in mind. It is the policy of both parties in the State to sustain and increase home grown food on which this island depends so largely for a favourable trade balance and, in the ultimate issue, for its life. It is not an easy task to reconcile the beneficial liberation of our food supply from Government controls with that effective stimulus of home production which is vital. (*Interruption.*) Hon. Members want the good without the evil; that is often very difficult to solve.

It is necessary for the Exchequer to subsidise in one form or another, so as to bridge the gap between the price level reached in a free market on the one hand, and the price level necessary to sustain the welfare of the farmers on the other. Moreover, the gap must not only be bridged in the industry as a whole by maintaining average returns but we must also, in the case of what are called fat stock – a technical term covering a very considerable field – provide safeguards for individual transactions where necessary.

We have laboured patiently and arduously at the difficult problems of marketing and production, and we have reached conclusions which we shall submit to the House in another White Paper – I had better not get them mixed together – this very week. We believe that these will deal equitably and encouragingly with the producers without throwing an undue burden on the taxpayer or denying the consumer – and we are all consumers – the advantages of world abundance and of widening choice in so intimate a business as meals.

The Minister of Agriculture will deal with this complicated and not entirely non-political subject when he speaks later in the debate. But I can assure the House that we intend to help the farming industry to solve their difficulties by every means compatible with the general welfare of the community, which requires the maintenance of confidence throughout the agricultural industry and that increasing flow of food which is vital to the health and stamina of the nation.

I have mentioned the larger domestic issues, which were also mentioned by the Leader of the Opposition, on which our minds this Session will be set; may I say that while controversy lends life and sparkle to Parliamentary debates, the real honour belongs to any Member, wherever he sits, who can contribute constructive suggestions and thus directly serve the people as a whole?

We shall have another debate on foreign affairs in the near future, and I shall not attempt anything like a general survey today. Comparing the outlook now with two years ago, I think it would be true to say that it is less formidable but more baffling. The issues as they had shaped themselves in the days of our predecessors were clear-cut. The vast three-year re-armament plan was just getting into its stride. The war in Korea was still raging. General Eisenhower was organising Western Europe. A feeling of crescendo and crisis filled the air. Our Socialist Government, with the full support of the Conservative Opposition, were marching with our American allies in a vehement effort to meet the Soviet menace.

The main structure of this position is maintained, and no weakening in British purpose has resulted from the change of Government. Nevertheless, certain important events have happened which, rightly or wrongly, have somewhat veiled, and, it may be, actually modified the harshness of the scene. The fighting in Korea has shifted from the trenches to the tables. We do not know yet what will emerge from these stubborn and tangled discussions. But whatever else comes, or may come, as a result of the Korean war, one major world fact is outstanding. The United States have become again a heavily armed nation.

The second world event has been the death of Stalin and the assumption of power by a different régime in the Kremlin. It is on the second of these prodigious events that I wish to dwell for a moment. Nearly eight months have passed since it occurred and everywhere the question was, and still is asked, did the end of the Stalin epoch lead to a change in Soviet policy? Is there a new look?

I should not venture to ask the House, or any outside our doors to whom my words have access, to adopt positive conclusions on these mysteries. It may well be that there have been far-reaching changes in the temper and outlook of the immense populations, now so largely literate, who inhabit 'all the Russias', and that their mind has turned to internal betterment rather than external aggression. This may or may not be a right judgment, and we can afford, if vigilance is not relaxed and strength is not suffered again to dwindle, to await developments in a hopeful and, I trust, a helpful mood.

The only really sure guide to the actions of mighty nations and powerful Governments is a correct estimate of what are and what they consider to be their own interests. Applying this test, I feel a sense of reassurance. Studying our own strength and that of Europe under the massive American shield, I do not find it unreasonable or dangerous to conclude that internal prosperity rather than external conquest is not only the deep desire of the Russian peoples, but also the long-term interest of their rulers.

It was in this state of mind that six months ago I thought it would be a good thing if the heads of the principal States and Governments concerned met the new leaders of Russia and established that personal acquaintance and relationship which have certainly often proved a help rather than a hindrance. I still hope that such a meeting may have a useful place in international contacts.

On the other hand, one must not overlook the risk of such a four-Power conference ending in a still worse deadlock than exists at present. It certainly would be most foolish to imagine that there is any chance of making straight away a general settlement of all the cruel problems that exist in the East as well as in the West, and that exist in Germany and in all the satellite countries. We are not likely straight away to get them satisfactorily dealt with and laid to rest as great dangers and evils in the world by personal meetings, however friendly. Time will undoubtedly be needed – more time than some of us here are likely to see.

I am, of course, in very close touch with President Eisenhower, and my hope was that at Bermuda we might have had a talk about it all. I was sorry to be prevented by conditions beyond my control. We are at present looking forward to the four-Power conference of Foreign Secretaries, and we earnestly hope it will take place soon. If it leads to improvements those themselves might again lead to further efforts on both sides. We trust we shall soon have a favourable answer to our conciliatory invitation to the Soviet.

I have mentioned two dominant events that have happened in the last two years. But there is a third which, though it happened before, has developed so prodigiously in this period that I can treat it as if it were a novel apparition which has overshadowed both those I have mentioned. I mean the rapid and ceaseless developments of atomic warfare and the hydrogen bomb.

These fearful scientific discoveries cast their shadow on every thoughtful mind, but nevertheless I believe that we are justified in feeling that there has been a diminution of tension and that the probabilities of another world war have diminished, or at least have become more remote. I say this in spite of the continual growth of weapons of destruction such as have never fallen before into the hands of human beings. Indeed, I have sometimes the odd thought that the annihilating character of these agencies may bring an utterly unforeseeable security to mankind.

When I was a schoolboy I was not good at arithmetic, but I have since heard it said that certain mathematical quantities when they pass through infinity change their signs from plus to minus – or the other way round. I do not venture to plunge too much into detail of what are called the asymptotes of hyperbolae, but any hon. Gentleman who is interested can find an opportunity for an interesting study of these matters. It may be that this rule may have a novel application and that when the advance of destructive weapons enables everyone to kill everybody else nobody will want to kill anyone at all. At any rate, it seems pretty safe to say that a war which begins by both sides suffering what they dread most – and that is undoubtedly the case at present – is less likely to occur than one which dangles the lurid prizes of former ages before ambitious eyes.

I offer this comforting idea to the House, taking care to make it clear at the same time that our only hope can spring from untiring vigilance. There is no doubt that if the human race are to have their dearest wish and be free from the dread of mass destruction, they could have, as an alternative, what many of them might prefer, namely, the swiftest expansion of material well-being that has ever been within their reach, or even within their dreams.

By material well-being I mean not only abundance but a degree of leisure for the masses such as has never before been possible in our mortal struggle for life. These majestic possibilities ought to gleam, and be made to gleam, before the eyes of the toilers in every land, and they ought to inspire the actions of all who bear responsibility for their guidance. We, and all nations, stand, at this hour in human history, before the portals of supreme catastrophe and of measureless reward. My faith is that in God's mercy we shall choose aright.

Henry Channon: diary
('Chips', page 479)

3 November 1953

In the House, Winston, who had not been present at the Opening of Parliament this morning, rose amidst cheers, and it was immediately clear that he was making one of the speeches of his lifetime. Brilliant, full of cunning and charm, of wit and thrusts, he poured out his Macaulay-like phrases to a stilled awed house. It was an Olympian spectacle. A supreme performance which we shall never see again from him or anyone else. In 18 years in this honourable House I have never heard anything like it . . . then he sought refuge in the

Smoking Room and, flushed with pride, pleasure, and triumph sat there for two hours sipping brandy and acknowledging compliments. He beamed like a school-boy.

Sir Winston S. Churchill to Anthony Eden
Prime Minister's Personal Minute M.317/53
(Premier papers, 11/618)

3 November 1953

I put these notes down not for a speech but to review my own mental processes about EDC. We might have a word together later on in the week.

One thing is capital in my mind: no new engagements to France unless Germany, with a German Army, is also accepted as an Ally.

NOTES

I am sometimes told that I have weakened in my advocacy of a European Army to make some sort of front against the enormous forces gathered along or behind the Iron Curtain. There is no truth in this. I have always felt that a European front must be established and maintained and that this could never be done without a strong German contribution. The French however proposed a European Defence Community, on lines quite different from those I had contemplated. I had always thought of a Western defence force founded on the principles of a Grand Alliance and had always feared that the intermingling of individuals without regard to their nationality would not produce the fighting class qualities without which armies are a useless expense. However when the French developed their scheme and when no unit smaller than a division was contemplated I and my colleagues both in and out of office accepted this arrangement and have done our best to make a success of their plan, though we could not merge ourselves in it. We have made it clear how effectively we should be with it though not in it. In all these complicated discussions in which the logic of French ideas have leaned continuously towards a European Federation two or three years have been consumed, EDC has not been ratified and we have no German Army except the very powerful one created by the Soviet in the Eastern Zone. This delay has been injurious to our security and I was not a little surprised to read the account of the debate in the French Senate last week where an overwhelming majority declared themselves in favour of a European Army based on the principle of alliances instead of the [. . .] amalgam in creating which so much time has been spent. We should certainly take our part in such an army provided it contained French German and American forces. To do this would involve no more commitments than those entered into by both parties in our effort to further EDC by our close association, nor are our obligations any greater than they are under

NATO. The whole problem of Western defence has been centred in NATO with of course its German contribution. It is indeed melancholy to think of all the wasted time which could have been saved by the simple adoption of the well-tried principle of a Grand Alliance which has worked effectively in the past and the adoption of which I have consistently advised.

Sir Winston S. Churchill to President Dwight D. Eisenhower
Prime Minister's Personal Telegram T.266/53
(Premier papers, 11/1074)

5 November 1953
Emergency
Deyou
Top Secret, Personal and Private
No. 4538

My dear Friend,

The Soviet answer[1] puts us back to where we were when Bermuda broke down through my misfortune. We are confronted with a deadlock. So why not let us try Bermuda again? I suggest four or five days during the first fortnight in December.

We could then take stock of the whole position and I think quite a lot of people will be pleased that we are doing so. If you want the French, I am quite agreeable and it would be a good opportunity to talk to them about EDC, which surely we ought to get settled now. I hope you would bring Foster. Anthony is all for it and would come with me. It would be worth trying to make Laniel come with Bidault.

All the arrangements were very carefully worked out last time, and it only takes a word of command to put them all on again.

Let me know how this strikes you. I really think there will be a serious criticism if we are left gaping at a void.

---

[1] The Soviet Union proposed a five-power meeting, including China, on a broad range of issues, rather than the four-power meeting on the subject of Germany proposed by the US and UK.

November 1953

Lord Moran to Sir Winston S. Churchill
(*Churchill papers, 1/54*)

6 November 1953

My dear Prime Minister,

I have had a talk with MacKenna[1] about the Phenergan tablets (the greens), which you have just renewed from Martindale. You have been taking these now for several months, and we both feel that we ought to stop them because they may have a rather depressant effect of the circulation if taken too long. Their general sedative effect is so slight that I doubt whether it will be necessary to replace them. They were originally given because of the irritation. If, however, what you already take at night is not sufficient, then I will go into the matter.

The more I think of Tuesday's effort in the House, the more astonishing it seems from every angle.

President Dwight D. Eisenhower to Sir Winston S. Churchill
(*Premier papers, 11/418*)

7 November 1953
Top Secret

Dear Winston,

I am temporarily out of touch with Foster but I assume that within limits he could arrange his schedule to conform to whatever plans you and I might make.

Because of the negative character of the Soviet reply, there may be considerable value in a good talk between us and the French in order to survey the situation in which we now find ourselves. It would be necessary of course to avoid creating a false impression that our purpose in the meeting is to issue another invitation to the Soviets. There is nothing to be gained by showing too much concern over their intransigence and bad deportment and I believe that instead of relating our meeting to any Soviet word or act, past or future, we should merely announce that we are meeting to discuss matters of common interest. I feel that the presence of the French is almost an essential because of the EDC, Indochina and NATO problems in general, in which both you and we have such a great stake. My only reservation about our meeting would be

---

[1] Robert Merttins Bird MacKenna, 1903–84. Educated at Royal Navy College, Dartmouth, and Clare College, Cambridge. Married, 1927, Helen Todrick: two children (div. 1943); 1943, Margaret Hopkins: two children. Dermatologist, Royal Liverpool United Hospital, 1934–46. Specialist in Dermatology, Northern Command, 1940–1. Adviser in Dermatology and Asst Director of Hygiene, War Office, 1941–3. Dermatologist to British Army, 1943–5. Physician in charge of skin care, St Bartholomew's Hospital, 1946. Board member, St John's and St Bartholomew's Hospitals. Hon. Consultant in Dermatology to British Army, 1946–64. Dermatologist, King Edward VII's Hospital for Officers, 1946–72.

if it were some way seized upon as a pretext by opponents of EDC in France to delay ratification. This would be a tragedy for us all. Also, in view of the French presidential elections now scheduled for about mid December, I do not know whether the French would find it possible to attend such a meeting in early December. Of course if Laniel could not come, Bidault might attend. I assume you, as head of the host government, would issue the invitation to the French and inquire whether they could attend such a meeting.

In the event the French accept, my calendar does not leave me much leeway in choice of dates. I could reach Bermuda on the morning of December 4 and stay through the 7th, returning here on the morning of the 8th. It is also possible that I myself could arrive on the morning of the 11th returning on the 15th but in this case, Foster would be unable to come with me as the North Atlantic Council ministers meet in Paris on December 14–16 and Foster must leave Washington not later than December 12. I give you these possibilities only tentatively because I have yet to discuss it with Foster.

Foster should be back here by Monday morning, by which time you may be able to inform me as to the suitability of the periods I suggest before making any approach to the French. I think then we would have to agree quickly as to timing of the announcement so that danger of leaks can be eliminated.

Sir Winston S. Churchill to President Dwight D. Eisenhower
Prime Minister's Telegram T.267/53
(Premier papers, 11/1074)

7 November 1953
Emergency
Dedip
Top Secret
No. 4610

My dear Friend,

I am delighted you will come to Bermuda from December 4 till the morning of the 8th. Anthony and I will be there to receive you. If there are troubles in Trieste or elsewhere we shall probably be able to deal with them better all together than we could apart. The moment you clinch this I will invite the French. I am told the French presidential election does not take place till the 16th or 18th and that anyhow they will not ratify EDC before it happens. Thus there would be no delay of EDC through our meeting on the dates fixed. By all means let us merely announce that we are meeting to discuss matters of common interest. There are quite a lot of things I want so much to talk over with you and I thought we might both brace the French up on EDC. Time is short. I should be most grateful if you would give me the OK and we can settle it all with an agreed communiqué for Tuesday's newspapers.

President Dwight D. Eisenhower to Sir Winston S. Churchill
(Premier papers, 11/1074)

8 November 1953
Top Secret

Dear Winston,

If the French agree, and barring some consideration unknown to me which may occur to Foster, I am prepared to go ahead with the meeting on December 4th at Bermuda.

However, Foster will not return to Washington until the afternoon of Sunday, November 8th at the earliest. I beg of you to allow no whisper of our meeting to get out before 12 noon, Tuesday, November 10th Washington time. This will give me an opportunity to consult with Foster. I agree that we should then merely announce that the three of us are meeting to discuss matters of common interest.

In the meantime I would appreciate your ideas on the specific terms in which the announcement of the meeting would be framed. If the three of us are in agreement we could each make a simple statement to the above effect at any convenient time after 12 noon, November 10th Washington time.

I think it is most important that we should all set the same tone and that the announcement should not be misconstrued by world opinion, particularly in view of the conditions imposed by the last Russian note.

Sir Winston S. Churchill to President Dwight D. Eisenhower
Prime Minister's Personal Telegram T.269/53
(Premier papers, 11/418)

8 November 1953
Emergency
Dedip
Top Secret
Personal and Private

My dear Friend,

I am so glad that it is all fixed. I have telegraphed to the French emphasising secrecy. I will be host at the banquets and elsewhere but you must preside at any formal conference. I send you a draft announcement which I have also sent to the French. Let me know if you want any alterations. I will announce it as you suggest at 12 noon Washington time on Tuesday November 10th.

I am bringing my paintbox with me as I cannot take you on at golf. They say the water is 67 degrees which is too cold for me.

NOVEMBER 1953

Sir Winston S. Churchill to President Dwight D. Eisenhower
(Premier papers, 11/1074)

8 November 1953
Emergency
Dedip
Top Secret
No. 4637

Following is text of draft announcement:

'It has been decided to hold the three Power Conference at Bermuda which was planned for the beginning of July but had to be put off. President Eisenhower and Mr Dulles will represent the United States, M Laniel and M Bidault France, and Sir Winston Churchill and Mr Eden Britain. It is hoped to meet from December 4 to December 8 and various matters of common concern to the Three Powers will be discussed.'

Sir Winston S. Churchill to Joseph Laniel
Prime Minister's Personal Telegram T.268/53
(Premier papers, 11/418)

8 November 1953
Emergency
Dedip
Top Secret, Private and Personal
No. 1629

My dear Prime Minister,

The Soviet answer to our note puts us back to where we were when our intended meeting in Bermuda last July was cancelled through my illness. We are confronted with a deadlock. The time now again seems ripe for a meeting with yourselves and the Americans to survey the situation and discuss the many matters of common interest to us which are open. I therefore propose that we should meet at Bermuda from Friday December 4 until Tuesday December 8.

President Eisenhower favours this plan and expects to bring Mr Dulles with him. I hope that you and M Bidault will come from France and Mr Eden and I myself will be on the United Kingdom side.

Time is short and I should be much obliged if you can give me your reply with the least possible delay so that we may aim at an announcement, as President Eisenhower suggests, at 12 noon Tuesday Washington time. He emphasises the importance of secrecy and of not connecting the matter specifically with our recent correspondence with Russia. My immediately following telegram contains a brief draft announcement.

It will be easy to revive and adapt all the July arrangements. The climate is agreeable. I much look forward to my first meeting with you and to having the honour of being your host.

Cabinet: conclusions
(Cabinet papers, 128/26)

9 November 1953
Secret
12 p.m.
Cabinet Meeting No. 64 of 1953

[...]
2. The Prime Minister said that, in view of the unsatisfactory tone of the latest Soviet response to the proposal for a Four-Power Meeting on Germany, he had thought it would be valuable if the Heads of Governments of the United States, United Kingdom and France could meet, with the Foreign Ministers, to review the possibility of breaking the existing deadlock and to discuss the urgent problems which were of common interest to the three countries. He had therefore suggested to President Eisenhower that the project of the Bermuda Meeting, which he had been obliged to postpone in July, should now be revived. The President had favoured this plan, though he was unable to give a final answer until his Secretary of State returned to Washington. An invitation had therefore been sent to the French. It now seemed likely that definite agreement would be reached within the next 24 hours to hold this tri-partite Meeting in Bermuda from 4th–8th December. It might be possible to make an official announcement to this effect in the course of the following day.

The Cabinet –

Endorsed the initiative which the Prime Minister had taken to bring about an early meeting of Heads of Government of the United States, United Kingdom and France.

Sir Winston S. Churchill: speech
('Winston S. Churchill, His Complete Speeches', volume 8, pages 8506–8)

9 November 1953

The Lord Mayor's Banquet
The Guildhall, London

FOREIGN AFFAIRS

I am very glad to come again as Prime Minister to the Guildhall banquet and to pay my respects to the new Lord Mayor, whose father I knew before him when he held the same office, and also to compliment Sir Rupert De la

Bere[1] on the effective and skilful manner in which he has discharged the exceptionally difficult duties of the Coronation year. We in the House of Commons look forward to hearing his voice soon again. It is normally quite audible. I thank you, my Lord Mayor, for all the kind things you have said about me. I share your regrets, as I did with your predecessor, that we have not yet secured a Member for the City of London in the House of Commons.

I certainly feel the force of all you have said about the failure to make any effective efforts to repair the ruins which the war caused in the City. It is indeed a shocking sight and one can hardly think of a worse advertisement of British recovery and strength. But while I express sorrow I cannot accept guilt. The City was not very generously treated by our predecessors. I can find no sufficient explanation why they took London out of the class of blitzed cities which were granted special licences to rebuild their bombed centres.

The Conservative Government could not put everything right at once. In our two years seven millions pounds worth of licences have been given to the City. We now intend to issue more licences well ahead of starting date and to maintain a steady rhythm of rebuilding within the limits of the labour and material available. Our very capable Minister of Works, Sir David Eccles, is about to discuss with your authorities, my Lord Mayor, the choice of buildings for the next batch of licences and I trust that the assurance that rebuilding will go steadily forward will encourage owners to prepare their plans in advance so that no time is lost.

There is one thing at any rate that I rejoice to see – I can compliment you on having responded to the appeal which I made you two years ago and restored Gog and Magog to their traditional position from which Hitler had hurled them.[2] I think they look magnificent and they certainly remind us that English democracy fought its battles for freedom before the costly glories of the present century were gained.

It is the custom at this annual Guildhall banquet for the Prime Minister to speak about foreign affairs and I hoped that tonight we might have the advantage of having the Foreign Secretary here himself once again bearing his heavy burden. Alas he cannot get away, but I shall try my best not to add to it by anything I may say. Mr Eden and I have worked very closely together in and out of office for the last sixteen or seventeen years and we have nearly always found ourselves in spontaneous agreement. In fact I believe that if at any time in this long period we had been put at opposite ends of this spacious hall and separately asked for our opinion on some new point that had cropped up we should in nine cases out of ten have been found in broad agreement.

The world is certainly in an awful muddle now. It is very difficult to find

---

[1] Rupert de la Bère, 1893–1978. Capt., East Surrey Rgt: on active service, 1914–18. Joined RAF, 1918. MP (Cons.) for Evesham, 1935–50; for South Worcestershire, 1950–5. Sheriff of the City of London, 1941–2. Lord Mayor of London, 1952–3. Knighted, 1952.

[2] Speech of 9 Nov. 1951, reproduced above (pp. 31–4).

any part of it where a lot of people are not trying to be disagreeable to a lot of other people. More than eight years have passed since the Second World War ended in the unconditional surrender of all our foes and yet we seem no nearer a settled peace. Indeed many people think that the best we can do is to get used to the cold war like eels are said to get used to skinning. Others, and I am one of them, think there is an improvement and that time and patience and goodwill may bring about a real easement provided what we call the free world does not lose its unity or relax its precautions.

When I was young – a long time ago – the great Lord Salisbury,[1] as his distinguished grandson is proud to call him, presided over our part of the international scene. Those were the days when very few words were spoken in diplomacy and far fewer speeches were made. All the same quite important things were done and we lived through long years of dangerous tension between the great Powers in a very civilized fashion. I remember a saying I had in my youth: 'Every word of Daniel Webster[2] weighs a pound.' But that was before the days of television.

We modern politicians live in a clattering age where so much is said and so many things happen that I am sure some of you even here in the City of London find it quite difficult to take it all in. True wisdom is to cultivate a sense of proportion which may help one to pick out the three or four things that govern all the rest and as it were write one's own headlines and not change them very often.

Another old saying comes back to my mind which I have often found helpful or at least comforting. I think it was Goethe[3] who said, 'The trees do not grow up to the sky.' I do not know whether he would have said that if he had lived through this frightful twentieth century where so much we feared was going to happen did actually happen. All the same it is a thought which should find its place in young as well as old brains. But I am forgetting all about my speech on foreign affairs which I have come here to make to you and now I have hardly any time left. It would not be much use, my Lord Mayor, for you have this great company to drink a toast of 'Her Majesty's Government' if we all got turned out in the Division at ten o'clock. That would not be good for our health and perhaps not good for our country's health.

All speeches by responsible people on foreign affairs have to tread the narrow path between platitude and indiscretion, and to avoid both what the

---

[1] Robert Arthur Talbot Gascoyne-Cecil, 1830–1903. MP (Cons.) for Stamford, 1853–68. Secretary of State for India, 1866–7, 1874–8. Succeeded as 3rd Marquess of Salisbury, 1868.Secretary of State for Foreign Affairs, 1878–80. PM, 1885–7, 1900–2. Uncle of A. J. Balfour, his successor as PM, and father of Churchill's friends Lord Hugh Cecil and Lord Robert Cecil.

[2] Daniel Webster, 1782–1852. US Representative from New Hampshire, 1813–17; from Massachusetts, 1823–7. US Senator (Whig) from Massachusetts, 1827–41, 1845–50. US Secretary of State, 1841–3, 1850–2.

[3] Johann Wolfgang von Goethe, 1749–1832. German poet and polymath. Author of many works of poetry, drama, memoir, cultural commentary and natural philosophy.

French call 'clichés' and what the English call 'bloomers'. There are always a number of quite interesting things to say about foreign affairs, but it does not follow that the ones that are most interesting are those which it is always best to talk about.

There is, however, one place which I must mention tonight. I was sorry to read about the hostile demonstrations in Italy against Britain and the United States. British and American soldiers have been kept waiting at Trieste at heavy expense for more than eight years and all we wish to do is to take them away after helping the Italians and the Yugoslavs to come to a friendly arrangement together. Is that such a very wicked thing to do? I do not think that Britain and the United States should be abused and insulted by mobs, either Fascist or Communist, and I am very sorry the Italians and Yugoslavs are so angry with each other. Personally I have warm feelings toward both countries.

I remember making a very earnest appeal to Mussolini not to join Hitler against us when France collapsed in 1940. I could not persuade him. He thought we were finished. In fact we were only beginning. But I was deeply grieved to find Italy in the war against us. I did my very utmost to enable her to get on the right side again, and I lent nearly a dozen British warships to Russia for several years in order to preserve a good Italian fleet for Italy.

Now at the present time the British and Americans are acting together in Trieste and they are consulting each other constantly and are not at all unsure of their power and influence to bring about a good fair solution of the frontier dispute although it may take longer than we had hoped. We have, as Mr Eden said this afternoon in the House of Commons, full confidence in the Anglo-American commander General Winterton,[1] and we strongly advise partisans of either side in the disputed zones to keep quiet and behave in a law-abiding manner. Nothing would be easier than for the Anglo-American troops to steam away home. It would certainly be much harder to predict what would happen after that.

It is not because we had anything to gain for ourselves that we went there or that we stay there. We might of course give ourselves the Royal Humane Society medal and certainly we deserve it. Some people say their worry is about Anglo-American relations. I do not share their anxieties. After all we are both very free-speaking democracies and where there is a great deal of free speech there is always a certain amount of foolish speech. But any rude things we say about each other are nothing compared to what we both say about ourselves. It would be a pity if we thought about each other in terms of our

---

[1] Thomas John Willoughby Winterton, 1898–1987. Educated at Royal Military Academy, Woolwich. On active service, WWI, 1917–18. Married, 1921, Helen Cross: three children. Served in Burma, 1930–2; in WWII, 1939–45. Deputy Cdr, Allied Commission for Austria, 1945–9. British High Commissioner and C-in-C in Austria, 1950. Military Governor and Cdr, British/US Zone, Free Territory of Trieste, 1951–4.

local bugbears, and match one against the other. As this is a festive occasion I will not mention names.

Let us stick to our heroes John Bull and Uncle Sam. They were never closer together than they are now; not only in sentiment but in common interest and in faithfulness to the cause of world freedom. In fact it is the growing unity and brotherhood between the United States and the British Commonwealth of Nations that sustains our faith in human destiny. But we do not want to do it all alone. There is France, our cherished ally and the famous cultured state of Western Europe with whom we have so many ties. There is Germany with whom we have finished what might almost be called a second Thirty Years' War. It was fearful but it is finished.

There is no luxury so shameful and so costly as hatred and revenge. Ever since the fighting stopped I have striven for friendship with Germany and my dearest hope has been that France, who has been so terribly stricken, would have the honour of leading Germany back into the European family, and not the European family only, but the world family of free nations. That is a goal which may still be won. The policy of Her Majesty's Government is peace through strength, together with any contacts, formal or informal, which may be helpful. All this of course is founded, and can only be founded, upon the moral unity of the English-speaking world and its many allies who have vowed themselves to the cause of freedom, and have created the great alliance of NATO. All this stands and we all stand by it, with no thought of aggression against any country in the world.

Cabinet: conclusions
(Cabinet papers, 128/26)

10 November 1953
Secret
12 noon
Cabinet Meeting No. 65 of 1953

[. . .]

2. The Prime Minister said that the French Government had now accepted the invitation to attend the meeting of the three Heads of Governments which it was proposed to hold in Bermuda from 4th to 8th December. Rumours of this meeting had already been published in the Press, apparently as a result of premature disclosures in Paris. It had been agreed that an official announcement should be issued in the three capitals that afternoon.

The Cabinet –
Took note of the Prime Minister's statement.

[. . .]

President Dwight D. Eisenhower to Sir Winston S. Churchill
Prime Minister's Personal Telegram T.270/53
(Premier papers, 11/1074)

10 November 1953
Secret

Dear Winston,

This morning I was informed that the French have accepted the invitation sent to them by you. This apparently clinches the whole matter, and tomorrow at 12 noon we shall release from The White House the announcement that you suggested. However, I have just learned that there is some possibility that all of us may be pressed for an earlier release because the story has already apparently leaked in France. To us, this is a matter of indifference except that we want to be coordinated with you.

I do not know that I shall bring along my golf clubs, but I do hope that the entire period will not be one of such exhausting work that we shall be denied time for any recreation, to say nothing of a bit of thinking.

I should say that our meeting will in a sense be of itself an answer to one point in the latest Soviet note, which seriously objects to this kind of meeting between us. In any event, I am delighted that the earlier of the two periods I suggested is suitable for all because this will enable Foster to be with me at the party.

Sir Winston S. Churchill to Vyacheslav Molotov
Prime Minister's Personal Telegram T.271/53
(Premier papers, 11/420)

10 November 1953
Immediate
Deyou
Secret and Personal
No. 878

Now that the Bermuda Conference is on again I hope you will look up my private and personal telegram to you of June 2[1] about bridges being built, not barriers, between East and West. All good wishes.

---

[1] T.183/53, reproduced above (p. 1059).

Sir Winston S. Churchill to President Dwight D. Eisenhower
Prime Minister's Personal Telegram T.273/53
(Premier papers, 11/418)

12 November 1953
Immediate
Deyou
Top Secret and Personal
No. 4736

I am very glad it is all settled about Bermuda and I share your hopes that we shall not spend all our time on parade. The table, I presume, should be round.

I agree with you that there is no point in the Soviet complaint about 'collusion'. I always thought allies were expected to 'collude' and I have always had a great dislike for the expression 'ganging up' which has several times got seriously in my way. All the same I am, as I said last time in Parliament, hoping we may build bridges not barriers.

2. I should like to bring Lord Cherwell with me as I want to talk over with you our 'collusion' on atomics, etc. . . . Indeed it might strengthen the impression to which I gathered you were favourable, that our meeting was not simply an incident in the recent correspondence with the Soviets. He can always slip across to Washington after we have had a talk if you thought it convenient for him to see more of your people.

3. I plan to fly with Anthony the night of the 1st via Gander to Bermuda and we shall have a whole day to recuperate before receiving you on the 4th. The Welch Fusiliers with their Goat will form your Guard of Honour. The barbed wire to protect us from assassins or journalists is still standing as it was.

4. For your eye alone: I was so delighted to read what you said to the Press about Harry Truman. He is rather a friend of mine.[1]

Anthony sends his regards. With all my good wishes.

---

[1] Truman had been subpoenaed by the House Un-American Affairs Activities Committee, and when asked about this at a press conference, Eisenhower stated: 'Now, I think once before, before this group, I tried to make quite clear that I am not going to be in the position of criticizing the Congress of the United States for carrying out what it conceives to be its duty. It has the right, of course, to conduct such investigations as it finds necessary; but if you asked me, as I understood it, my personal reaction, I would not issue such a subpoena' (*American Presidency Project*).

Vyacheslav Molotov to Sir Winston S. Churchill
Prime Minister's Personal Telegram T.274/53
(Premier papers, 11/420)

12 November 1953

Your Ambassador, Mr Hayter,[1] has delivered to me your message today. Concerning the Bermuda Conference I can only repeat what I said on the 3rd of June last,[2] for you know our present attitude to this matter as well as our desire for a real removal of barriers between the West and the East.

Accept my best regards.

President Dwight D. Eisenhower to Sir Winston S. Churchill
Prime Minister's Personal Telegram T.276/53
(Premier papers, 11/418)

13 November 1953
Top Secret

Dear Winston,

Your cable[3] came just as I was leaving for Canada. By all means bring Lord Cherwell and I shall probably bring Admiral Strauss[4] with me. The two of them can have a good talk and then give you and me a briefing. I rather think it might be a good idea to have Ismay come out with us for a day if that could be arranged. Again his presence would serve a useful purpose both for us and for the public.

---

[1] William Goodenough Hayter, 1906–95. Educated at Oxford University. Entered Diplomatic Service, 1930. Served in Vienna, 1931; Moscow, 1934; FO, 1937, 1944; China, 1938; Washington DC, 1941. Married, 1938, Iris Marie Grey. Asst Under-Secretary of State, FO, 1948; Deputy Under-Secretary of State, 1957–8. CMG, 1948. HM Minister in Paris, 1949. KCMG, 1953. Ambassador to USSR, 1953–7. Warden, New College, Oxford, 1958–76.

[2] Molotov to Churchill, June 3, reproduced above (p. 1059).

[3] T.273/53, reproduced above (p. 1290).

[4] Lewis Lichtenstein Strauss, 1896–1974. Private Secretary to Herbert Hoover, 1917–19. Intelligence Officer, US Navy Reserve, 1925. On active naval duty, WWII. RAdm., 1945. Commissioner, Atomic Energy Commission, 1947–50; Chairman, 1950–8.

Sir Winston S. Churchill to President Dwight D. Eisenhower
Prime Minister's Personal Telegram T.277/53
(Premier papers, 11/418)

13 November 1953
Immediate
Depip
Top Secret and Personal
No. 4777

My dear Friend,

Pug will arrive on the 6th. We are keeping it quiet till nearer the date. He was much complimented that you wanted to talk to him.

I am taking a stiff line in the House on Monday about the two year military service.

With all my good wishes

Cabinet: conclusions
(Cabinet papers, 128/26)

13 November 1953
Secret
11.30 a.m.
Cabinet Meeting No. 66 of 1953

The Cabinet considered the arrangements for the debate, to be held in the House of Commons on 16th and 17th November, on the Order in Council extending the operation of the National Service Act for a further period of five years.

It had been agreed through the usual channels that on the first day of the debate discussion would be based on an Opposition motion, and that the vote on the Order in Council would be taken on the second day. The Opposition had now tabled a motion in the following terms:

> 'That this House, whilst accepting the necessity for national service in present circumstances, nevertheless considers that the time has now arrived when the period of service should be determined by Parliament on an affirmative resolution not less frequently than once a year.'

It was likely that some Members with pacifist views would force a division on this motion; but, if the Government were ready to accept it, it could be carried by an overwhelming majority. Even so, however, there was no assurance that the Labour Opposition would vote in support of the Order in Council on the second day. For, although their motion accepted 'the necessity for national service in present circumstances' and the Order in Council did no more than extend the principle of national service for a further five years, the Government would be obliged to make it clear in the debate that they saw no early prospect of reducing the period of service below two years and it was likely on that account that the Labour Opposition would feel able to do no more than abstain from voting in any division on the Order.

The Prime Minister said that he had at first been disposed to think that the Government might accept the Opposition motion. Parliament already had many opportunities to challenge in debate the period of national service, and it might be argued that the adoption of an affirmative resolution procedure would do no more than regularise the existing position. Moreover, the annual Army Acts were themselves a precedent for giving Parliament a regular annual opportunity to authorise the continuance of the obligation to a particular period of national service. It might well have been worthwhile to accept the principle of annual Parliamentary approval by affirmative resolution if the Opposition had been willing in return to give a positive vote, in the division on the Order in Council, in favour of extending national service for a further five years. This, however, they were unlikely to do. And the Service Ministers also feared that the adoption of a system of annual Parliamentary decision on the period of service would create an atmosphere of uncertainty about the future course of national service which might prejudice recruiting for regular service with the Armed Forces.

In discussion the Service Ministers reaffirmed the view that the Forces could not be maintained at the strength required to meet foreseeable commitments over the next few years unless the two-year period of national service were maintained. This was especially important as an incentive to induce national service men to accept a regular engagement for three years. The Government's acceptance of the Opposition motion would be widely interpreted as foreshadowing a change of attitude towards the period of national service. This would prejudice recruiting for regular service in the Forces, and it would also discourage our friends in the North Atlantic Alliance.

In further discussion it was pointed out that these and other arguments against the proposal for annual affirmative resolutions had been effectively deployed by the Prime Minister in his speech in the Defence debate in the House of Commons on 5th March.[1] The proposal now put forward in the Opposition's motion had then been embodied in a Labour amendment to the Government motion inviting the House to approve the Defence White Paper; and the Prime Minister had invited the House to reject that amendment. In view of the arguments then used against this proposal, it was bound to be assumed, if the Government now accepted it, that circumstances had changed since March. This, indeed, was implied by the phrase in the present motion that 'the time had now arrived' to adopt the system of annual review

---

[1] Reproduced above (pp. 868–78).

of the period of service. The impression would certainly be created that since March there had been some change in the international situation which justified a change of policy. This was not so in fact; and to give the impression that it was so would be inconsistent with the Government's general approach to the present international situation. Thus, in view of what had been said in the debate on 5th March, the Government now had no alternative but to resist this Opposition motion.

The Cabinet –

Agreed that, in the debate in the House of Commons on 16th November, the Government should invite the House to reject the Opposition motion proposing that the period of national service should be determined annually by Parliament by affirmative resolution.

Sir Winston S. Churchill: speech
(Hansard)

16 November 1953					House of Commons

NATIONAL SERVICE

It looks as if we are going to have a quiet afternoon. I can assure the House I shall not try unduly to dim the prospect of such an agreeable, becoming and unusual situation.

This debate arises from the request of the Opposition to have one day on a Motion of their own before proceeding to the more limited debate on the Order in Council on National Service, which will be moved tomorrow. We have carefully considered the terms of the Motion, and it is with regret that we find ourselves unable to support it. We should note, however, that the Motion begins by accepting the need of compulsory National Service in the present circumstances. That, and indeed all the actions of the Socialists and Labour Party on this subject of conscription since the late war, is remarkable when we consider the deep, latent prejudices which have always existed against compulsory military service in these islands.

I believe I myself in my young days spoke of 'the foul tyranny of conscription'. Little did I believe that I should live to see not only Liberals but Radicals, and not only Radicals but Socialists, voting for compulsory service, not only in time of war but actually after victory and in time of peace. It shows how the force of events bites deeply into all our thoughts, principles and prejudices, and, of course, we have lived through the most extraordinary convulsions recorded in human experience. There is no doubt at all that they have left their mark on all our minds in an almost irresistible fashion.

There are two points of outstanding importance which have to be borne in mind today. The first is to keep this tremendous question as far as possible above the level of domestic party politics, and thus present to the world a spectacle of national unity on the grave and fundamental issue of National Service for national defence. The second is to avoid, at this moment perhaps above all others, giving the impression that we have changed or weakened our policy in national and international defence from what we inherited from our Socialist predecessors, or from what we stated it to be ourselves earlier this year.

These sets of arguments are to a certain extent in conflict with each other, but only to a certain extent, and I shall hope in the short time in which I shall trespass upon the indulgence and attention of the House to try to show, as the right Hon. Gentleman has done to a large extent, the very limited character of the differences between us; also, secondly, notwithstanding the slightness of our differences, why we cannot adopt any change in the policy which we declared and voted upon in March in the sense of weakening it. Those are the two points, and I think that they both deserve careful weighing.

Let me first dwell upon the great measure of agreement which prevails between us. There is no doubt that the tremendous decision taken by the late Government five years ago, with our wholehearted support, to institute compulsory service for a five-year period and to embark upon an immense programme of rearmament, and the decision three years ago to increase the period of service from 18 months to two years – there is no doubt that these decisions have played a great part in preventing another major war, and certainly in building up the strength, security and unity of what we call the free nations. It has perhaps saved Western Europe from going the way of Czechoslovakia, and certainly it has increased enormously our influence amongst all the nations to whom we are allied.

History will not deny a high measure of credit to the British Labour Party, to the right Hon. Gentleman the Leader of the Opposition, to the late Mr Ernest Bevin and to the right hon. Gentleman the Member for Easington (Mr Shinwell), and to many others who sit on that bench and behind it this afternoon. This is all the more so because it was repugnant to many of their inclinations, and seemed in a way antagonistic to some of their ideals. In fact, the House of Commons five years ago revived, in spite of the bitter domestic controversy which was going on, the spirit which alone enabled us to save our lives and honour in the long years of war and for a while, with our Commonwealth and Empire, to keep the flag of freedom flying alone among the nations.

Now let us see what precisely are the differences which separate us in this debate, and that make it impossible for us to accept the terms of the Motion. They are exactly what I set out here on 5th March of this year and on which we voted in a Division. The House decided by a majority of 41 to adhere to the policy of the late Government, which was also our policy, and that is what we propose tonight. I do not want to exaggerate the importance of the Division tonight. After all, it is only repeating what happened nine months ago and it will, I trust, be followed by a united and overwhelming vote on the main issue tomorrow – if there is a Division at all, which I trust there will not be.

Both sides were agreed last Session, as they are now, about the necessity for compulsory National Service, but the Opposition wished that the period of service should be determined at least yearly on an affirmative Resolution, whereas we considered that the ordinary procedure of the House gave ample facilities for annual, or even more frequent review, and for the will and power of Parliament to assert itself at any time.

Perhaps the House will forgive me if I quote, I am afraid at some length, what I said on that occasion. It is comforting to be able to say things over again, not merely because it saves labour, but because it gives one an impression of conviction, of sincerity and of consistency. Because it is absolutely relative, I will now venture, if I may, to quote what I said:

> I do not quarrel with the terms of the Amendment which the Opposition have placed on the Order Paper. The first part recognises very clearly the policy of the Government and in no way evades responsibility for the decision of our predecessors to re-arm on the largest scale and at the utmost speed possible. About the terms and obligations of National Service we are following their example, so far as the period for which we are now seeking powers is concerned. The original Act covered five years and also provided for its extension, if necessary, by Order in Council. We are availing ourselves of this in proposing to extend its operation for another five years. The House will be asked later this year –

I said this nine months ago –

> to pronounce a positive affirmation of this period.

That is what we shall do tomorrow. I went on:

> That does not mean that the House is asked to commit itself to a prolongation of the two-year service during the whole of a five-year period. That must depend on the course of events, which, at the present moment, give no ground for expecting an early reduction. On the contrary, for the reasons I have mentioned, and to some of which I shall recur, this is a testing time for the free world, and any sign of weakening purpose would undermine what good has already been done by both parties at heavy cost to everyone. But the measures which we should in due course take in no way prevent the Government, this or any other, from reducing the two-year period at any time if they feel it can safely be done. And they can reduce it without legislation. It cannot be increased without legislation, but it can be reduced by an Order in Council at any moment this may be thought fitting by any Ministry which may bear the responsibility.
>
> Where, then, is there the need for an annual affirmative Resolution? The procedure of the House provides ample and recurring opportunities

of challenging the Government of the day upon this or any other clear-cut issue, and of bringing it to the test of debate and of Division.

In the debate on the Address the right Hon. Gentleman reminded us of the Army Annual Act. It begins by saying that, whereas it is illegal to maintain a standing Army in time of peace in this country, let us have five million men under compulsion – or words to that effect. And all goes off quite smoothly.

I said:

> There is the debate on the Address; there are all the facilities which the House uses for debate and vote upon any Motion it may wish to discuss; there is the annual debate on defence; there are the Services' Estimates; and various other occasions. On any one of these the matter could be raised, threshed out, a Division could be taken, whether to terminate the two-year system or produce, in the words of the Opposition Amendment, – that was the amendment of nine months ago – an 'affirmative Resolution' in its favour. The issue remains continually in the hands of the House.

I have nearly finished my quotation:

> If we were to extend the period only year by year, as suggested, we believe that it would discourage our friends abroad and might well encourage the other ones. Above all, there would be uncertainty – uncertainty when so many aspects of daily life are affected – the daily life of great numbers of people is affected. Every year rumours, and the agitations following upon them, would spread: 'There is going to be a big reduction.' This would affect everyone who thought he was likely to be called up. Still more, it would make it difficult for the Service Departments to plan on a coherent and thrifty basis. For us at this stage – responsible Ministers – to shrink from definite approval of the two-year system would spread uncertainty throughout the Services, and would be, in our opinion, at the present time in no way justified by the international position. – (Official Report, 5th March, 1953; Vol. 512, C. 570–1.)

That is pretty good, you know; but I have a point to add. I gave at that time many administrative reasons for the inconvenience and uncertainty of frequent changes, but I do not think that I need repeat them today. My plea to the House is simple. This is not the time even to toy with the idea of change. That is my case and my plea. Much though I welcome the great measure of unity –

Mr Attlee: Does not the point which the right hon. Gentleman has made there imply that the Government will not change because, if there is any thought of their changing, the military and people abroad would be in a state of uncertainty? The implication of the right hon. Gentleman's speech, therefore, is that two years will remain without any change.

The Prime Minister: No, not at all. What I said was that this was not the time even to toy with the idea of change. I by no means exclude the possibility of change, but this is by no means the time for us to advertise and ventilate that all over Europe and the United States.

Much though I welcome the great measure of unity that prevails between us on this question, and much though I would like to remove what is really not more than a technical difference of procedure, I fear that this would be interpreted alike by friends and others throughout the world as a definite change in our policy. The change would not be large enough to produce beneficial results, but without in any way lessening our dangers it would weaken the confidence that is felt in us by our allies and our influence among them. The phrase in the Motion . . . the time has now arrived . . . is really the reverse of the facts.

I thought that we were all agreed that our policy at present might be defined as, 'Peace through strength', but a change of this character, small as it would be, though it might be understood in its proper proportion by Hon. Members in all parts of the House, would have the effect abroad of being thought to be the beginning of a policy of 'Conciliation by weakness', which we regard as most dangerous to peace. Certainly that would do us immense harm both ways. The Communist world might say, 'There, the NATO forces are breaking up. The British have introduced the thin end of the wedge. Why should we make concessions when we have only to persevere to win?' And the greatest of our allies, the one without whom the safety of the free world would be doomed, might be quite needlessly disquieted. I do not want to dwell on that too much.

As I said, and repeat, Parliament is supreme and its procedure gives it numberless opportunities for expressing its view or making its will effective. But surely we could not choose a worse moment to suggest a change of policy than now, when so much is in the balance and when we are actually on the eve of a tripartite conference at Bermuda. I ask the House to consider that. This conference is not in order to weaken our forces or our resolves, but to discuss ways of strengthening them, both morally and materially, and at the same time – where it is not inconsistent – to study the ways of reassuring the other half of the world that we mean them no harm and repudiate all intention of aggressive action and will study the best methods and occasions of making easy practical contacts with them and, even if we cannot solve our major problems, thus reduce the world tension. That at least is the sort of thing that I hope may develop from our talks.

I am sure that there will be much more chance of a favourable atmosphere if the Foreign Secretary and I are known to represent a solidly united Britain, than if it is thought that we are playing about for party advantage over here on this great issue and using these trifling differences in Parliamentary procedure to set false hopes in motion. I therefore ask the House not to exaggerate the differences on procedure and to rest solidly on its existing rights and powers to review our military policy whenever it chooses; and above all not to choose this moment for making what looks like a change, however small, in what has so long been the solid policy of the country.

Cabinet: conclusions
(Cabinet papers, 128/26)

17 November 1953
Secret
11.30 a.m.
Cabinet Meeting No. 67 of 1953

1. The Prime Minister said that, when the Lord President assumed the responsibilities for atomic energy outlined in the recent White Paper (Cmd. 8986), the Minister of Works would answer on his behalf Questions in the House of Commons affecting those responsibilities. This arrangement could not, however, be brought into effect until the responsibilities were formally transferred on 1st January, 1954. In the meantime the Minister of Supply would continue to answer in the Commons all Questions on atomic energy matters save those affecting foreign policy or external relations, which, he hoped, would normally be answered by the Foreign Secretary.

2. The Prime Minister recalled that, in pursuance of the Cabinet's request of 19th October, Lord Cherwell had circulated a written report (C(53)303) on the results of the visits to Australia and the United States which he had undertaken earlier in the autumn. He had since received a further report from Lord Cherwell indicating that the Americans had now agreed to exchange information with us and with the Canadians on the effects of the explosion of atomic weapons of all types. Their agreement would be regularised by an amendment of the existing *modus vivendi* for the exchange of information between the United Kingdom, the United States and Canada, and the approval of the Congressional Committee and of the President had already been secured. The public announcement of this change would refer simply to an extension of co-operation and would not specify the exact nature of the new agreement.

The Cabinet –
Took note of these statements by the Prime Minister.

2. The Lord Privy Seal said that, in accordance with precedent, it was proposed that each House of Parliament should present a humble Address to Her Majesty on the occasion of her departure on her visit to Australia and New Zealand. The motions for these Addresses would be moved in both Houses on 19th November. The terms of the proposed Addresses were read to the Cabinet.

The Cabinet –

Agreed that Addresses in the terms proposed should be moved on 19th November, by the Prime Minister in the House of Commons and by the Lord President in the House of Lords.

3. The Foreign Secretary said that the Italian and Yugoslav Governments now seemed to be taking a somewhat less inflexible attitude towards the possibility of a Five-Power Conference on Trieste. The Yugoslavs had indicated that they were ready to attend a Conference, provided that in the meantime no administrative responsibilities in Zone A were transferred to the Italians. It would be difficult to persuade the Italians to accept this condition. He hoped, nevertheless, that means could be found of bringing both Italy and Yugoslavia to the conference table.

The Cabinet –

Took note of the Foreign Secretary's statement.

4. The Foreign Secretary said that he had received a message from the United States Government asking when we proposed to make the next move in defence negotiations with Egypt. He did not propose to answer this, as he had already made it clear to them that we thought it was for the Egyptians to make the next move. He had also been told that the Americans now wished to give economic aid to Egypt. He proposed to represent to them very strongly the inexpediency of doing this while the outcome of the defence negotiations remained uncertain. If they wished to discuss the Egyptian question with us, there would be a convenient opportunity for them to do so at the forthcoming meeting in Bermuda.

The Cabinet –

Took note of the Foreign Secretary's statement.

5. The Cabinet had before them a memorandum by the Foreign Secretary (C(53)318) on the United Kingdom's obligations under the Anglo-Jordan Treaty of 1948.

The Foreign Secretary recalled that on 29th October the Cabinet had agreed in principle that we should accept the invitation of the Jordan Government to send an armoured squadron to Ma'an in Eastern Jordan for training with the Arab Legion. Since then, however, relations between Israel and Jordan had become strained by reason of the frontier incident at Qibya, and he had decided that the move of this armoured squadron should be delayed until the Security Council had completed its discussions on the Qibya incident. He proposed that thereafter the squadron should be sent to Ma'an and that we should at the same time assure the Government of Israel that it would not be used for aggressive purposes against them but remind them of our obligations under the Anglo-Jordan Treaty. Apart from the despatch of this particular squadron, we had also to consider whether we should send additional forces to Jordan, either now or in the event of an attack by Israel. He thought that the best course would be to discuss with the Jordan Government, after the despatch of the armoured squadron to Ma'an, what further help we might be able to give in the event of an attack by Israel. Any action of ours should be sufficiently firm to deter Israel from an act of aggression and sufficiently forthcoming to prevent Jordan from invoking the terms of the Treaty and possibly precipitating the hostilities with Israel which we wanted to avoid.

In discussion the following points were made:
- (a) There was some risk that if we moved British forces into Jordan they might become involved in hostilities between Jordan and Israel. On the other hand, if the Israeli Government felt sure that we would do nothing to honour our Treaty obligations to Jordan, that might encourage them to attack Jordan.
- (b) Although a major act of aggression would be reported to the Security Council, that would not absolve us from our Treaty obligation to come immediately to the aid of Jordan in the event of war. If we sought to escape from these obligations by denouncing the Treaty, we should impair our influence with other Arab States. The Anglo-Iraq Treaty was of particular value to us, and we could not overlook our oil interests in other Arab countries of the Middle East.
- (c) The despatch of one armoured squadron for training with the Arab Legion might well have a steadying effect, but there would be little value in supplementing this with an additional battalion and four RAF squadrons, which would be ineffective in the event of major hostilities between Israel and Jordan. If war did break out, one infantry brigade group and one armoured squadron could be sent within a week, but further reinforcements could only come from the Canal Zone.

The Prime Minister said that the situation was one of grave potential danger and the Cabinet should consider it further. It was beyond our strength to carry all the burdens of trouble in the Middle East and he was inclined to think that this particular source of trouble concerned the United Nations more than it concerned the United Kingdom. In any case, we ought to know what the United States intended to do in the event of further trouble between Israel and Jordan. He agreed that no troops should be sent to Jordan until the Security Council had concluded its discussions on the Qibya incident. In the meantime, he would be glad to consider further the terms of the warning statement which we might make to the Israeli Government if it was finally decided to send an armoured squadron to Ma'an. He was impressed by the danger that by sending small forces we might merely provoke Israel. If we had to intervene at all, it would be better to use overwhelming force which could provide an effective deterrent.

The Cabinet –
- (1) Invited the Foreign Secretary to consider further (i) the terms of a warning statement which might be made to the Israeli Government, if it were decided to send the armoured squadron to Ma'an, in order

1302 NOVEMBER 1953

to discourage them from any aggression against Jordan; and (ii) the terms of the statement which might have to be made to the Jordan Government about our obligations under the Anglo-Jordan Treaty of 1948 if it were decided not to send any British forces to Jordan.

(2) Agreed to resume their discussion of this question on 19th November.

[. . .]

Defence Committee: minutes
(Cabinet papers, 131/13)

18 November 1953
Secret
11.30 a.m.
Defence Committee Meeting No. 16 of 1953

[. . .]

2. Cadet Entry into the Royal Navy
(Previous Reference: D(53)14th Meeting, Minute 3)

The Committee resumed their discussion of future conditions for cadet entry into the Royal Navy.

The Committee were informed that the Minister of Defence had, as requested, discussed this question with the members of the Board of Admiralty. As a result he was satisfied that naval opinion generally would favour a combination of entry at age thirteen and special entry at age eighteen, but would be strongly opposed to a system of entry at age thirteen which was subject to the conditions recommended by the Montagu Committee. The Board of Admiralty also thought it very important that the system of cadet entry should not be subjected to frequent change; and they understood that it was likely that a Labour Government would reverse any decision taken now to restore entry at age thirteen without the conditions recommended by the Montagu Committee. These considerations had led them reluctantly to the conclusion that the wiser course would be to abandon cadet entry at age thirteen and to rely on entry between the ages of 17½ and 19 as the main source of supply of naval officers.

The Prime Minister said that he would not himself be deterred from taking what he regarded as the right course by the fear that it might be reversed by a subsequent Government. He still adhered to the view which he had expressed at the Committee's previous discussion on 28th October.[1] He favoured the restoration of cadet entry at age thirteen, and he would be ready to accept the condition that a proportion of the entry must in future come from grant-aided schools.

---

[1] Reproduced above (pp. 1262–3).

In discussion it was pointed out that for the State-aided schools thirteen was an awkward age for entry into the Navy: the breaks in State-aided education came at the ages of eleven and sixteen. Emphasis was also placed on the need for a settled system of cadet entry, which would not be liable to frequent change. There was in fact good reason to believe that, if entry at age thirteen were now restored, a Labour Government would feel obliged to upset it. There was strong feeling on this subject in the Labour Party; and, if a future Labour Government had to go into this matter again, they might well be disposed to suppress Dartmouth altogether and rely wholly on lower-deck promotion for the supply of naval officers. On the other hand, a proposal to recruit naval cadets exclusively from youths between 17½ and 19 would be welcomed by the majority of Government supporters and, from informal soundings which had been taken, it seemed likely that this solution would prove acceptable to all Parties in the House of Commons. Age eighteen was the normal age for cadet entry in all other navies of the world, except those of Russia and Australia, which recruited their cadets at the ages of ten and fourteen respectively.

The Prime Minister said that he remained of the opinion that a combination of entry at age thirteen and special entry at age eighteen would be the best method of ensuring a satisfactory supply of naval officers. As, however, the Board of Admiralty were unanimously in favour of relying exclusively on special entry between the ages of 17½ and 19, he would not press his view further.

The Committee –
(1) Approved the proposals, put forward by the First Lord of the Admiralty in D(53)53, that cadet entry into the Royal Navy at age sixteen should be abandoned as soon as practicable and that thereafter all naval cadets should be entered between the ages of 17½ and 19.
(2) Authorised the First Lord of the Admiralty to take an early opportunity of announcing this decision in reply to a Parliamentary Question in the House of Commons.

Cabinet: conclusions
(Cabinet papers, 128/26)

19 November 1953
Secret
11.30 a.m.
Cabinet Meeting No. 68 of 1953

[. . .]

6. The Cabinet had before them a further memorandum by the Foreign Secretary (C(53)323) on the United Kingdom's obligations under the Anglo-Jordan Treaty of 1948.

The Foreign Secretary said that he favoured sending an armoured squadron to Jordan for training as soon as the Security Council had pronounced on the Qibya incident. Before this was done, it would be wise to give the Israel Government an assurance that neither these nor any other British troops would be used in Jordan for an aggressive purpose, and to take that opportunity of reminding them of our Treaty obligations to Jordan. It was more difficult to know what should be said at this stage to the Jordan Government. We might do no more than accept their invitation to send an armoured squadron for training in Jordan, without saying anything about its possible use in fulfilling our obligations under the Treaty. Alternatively, we might offer to discuss ways and means of fulfilling those obligations. In that event we should have to make the point that, if were to be able to discharge those obligations effectively, we should have to station an armoured brigade in Jordan in time of peace. We might thus secure their agreement to this in principle, while making it clear that its timing would turn on the outcome of our defence negotiations with Egypt.

The Chief of the Imperial General Staff said that, in the eventual redeployment of British troops in the Middle East, there would be strategic advantages in stationing an armoured brigade group in Jordan. It would be well placed in relation to the tasks which it would have to perform in a major way, and in peace it would serve to stiffen the Arab Legion. But, although this was a sound long-term objective, we could not at present afford the cost of constructing the permanent accommodation which such a force would require. For the moment, therefore, the Chiefs of Staff would prefer to do no more than send an armoured squadron to Jordan for training with the Arab Legion and to build this up, as resources allowed, to the strength of a regiment. If hostilities broke out again between the Jews and the Arabs and it became necessary for that purpose to send reinforcements to Jordan, the strength required would be one infantry brigade group and an armoured regiment, and a force of this strength could not be made available in Jordan within less than one month.

The Foreign Secretary said that, in view of this statement, if seemed preferable that our immediate communication to the Jordan Government should be kept within the limits proposed in paragraph 4 (i) of C(53)323, and that nothing should be said to them at this stage about the possible use of British troops to fulfil our obligations under the Anglo-Jordan Treaty.

In the discussion which followed there was general support for the first of the alternatives set out in paragraph 4 of C(53)323.

The Prime Minister repeated the view which he had expressed in the Cabinet's discussion on 17th November[1] that we should be careful to avoid a situation in which British troops became engaged in hostilities between Israel and Jordan.

---

[1] Reproduced above (pp. 1299–1302).

The Cabinet –
  (1) Agreed that, as soon as the Security Council had pronounced on the Qibya incident, an armoured squadron might be sent to Ma'an in Jordan for training with the Arab Legion.
  (2) Invited the Foreign Secretary to inform the Israel Government of this movement, before it took place, assuring them that British troops would not be used in Jordan for an aggressive purpose but reminding them of our obligations under the Anglo-Jordan Treaty.
  (3) Invited the Foreign Secretary to communicate with the Jordan Government, at the appropriate time, in the sense proposed in paragraph 4 (i) of C(53)323.

[. . .]

Sir Winston S. Churchill: speech
('Winston S. Churchill, His Complete Speeches', volume 8, pages 8513–14)

20 November 1953

MR CLEMENT ATTLEE

It is my agreeable duty to propose the health of a distinguished statesman, whom you, my Lord Mayor, and the Corporation of this City, have so rightly elected to honour. I could not pretend that he does not from time to time say things both in the country and in the House of Commons which do not command my wholehearted accord or that I am able to fit all his ideals quite tidily into a harmonious picture. But that may well be because of the flickering light which plays on the party and political scene and often leads to diverse opinions being formed about the same set of facts or even to disputes about the facts themselves. Of course there is one difference between us. I was at Harrow and he was at Haileybury. At Haileybury I understand he received certain marks of disfavour from the Headmaster in connection with the excessive jubilation with which he celebrated Mafeking Day. I will not however rake that up against him on this occasion especially when I remember that so far as the City of London was concerned you were all in it too.

He has however other qualifications which have commended him to wide circles in this country, and many that entitle him to the respectful tributes of all. He was wounded in the First World War in Mesopotamia. He fought at Gallipoli. He devoted many years of his life to philanthropic work and an intensive study of the institutions which are specially helpful to the weak and poor. He has been for more than six years Prime Minister of Great Britain, for most of the time with an overwhelming majority, and we must remember that he played the leading part in the formidable and costly rearmament programme including the establishment of National Service in time of peace and the culture of the atomic bomb which have enabled the nations of the free world to confront Communist aggression and perhaps clear the way for safer and smoother times.

But of course my bond with him is the fact that he was my colleague and comrade for more than five years through the grim and awful ordeal of the war, and that he acted as my Deputy with high loyalty and efficiency throughout the whole period when I bore the chief responsibility. It was in those days that I could refer to the Right Honourable Gentleman in public as I must admit I still very often think of him in private as my Right Honourable Friend.

History tells us that Coalition Governments in this country have not always been a success and often been unpopular, but the National Coalition Government which lasted from 1940 till 1945 is very generally believed to have done its job well; and it may be that future generations will deem it worthy of an honoured page in history. In those years it was indeed true that none was for the party and all were for the state. We worked together unconscious of the differences that had lain between us in the past and must surely divide us again in the future. We did not quarrel with the generals or with our allies, or with each other: we kept our rancour for the enemy on whom we turned it with all the force we could jointly gather. May it long remain the fundamental law of our country and a deep instinct of our nature that whatever may be our political quarrels and divisions, should mortal peril come we shall stand together for all that Britain and her causes mean to us, and indeed for mankind.

It is with sincere satisfaction that I propose this afternoon to this distinguished company the health of a statesman whom it is no mere term of art for me to describe as My Right Honourable Friend.

Cabinet: conclusions
(Cabinet papers, 128/26)

25 November 1953
Secret
11.30 a.m.
Cabinet Meeting No. 71 of 1953

1. The Prime Minister said that, in view of the strong feeling which had been aroused in the House of Commons by the announcement of the Government's decision on the retired pay of certain Service officers, the Cabinet should consider what further action was now required in this matter.

The Minister of Defence said that he adhered to the view that sooner or later the Government would find it necessary to make some concession.

The Chancellor of the Exchequer said that, at the Prime Minister's request, he had looked further into two aspects of the matter. First, it was clear that the Labour Party, during their period in office, had alike in public statements and in their pensions increase measures confined the scope of pension concessions to cases of hardship and had consistently refused to meet the claim of these retired Service officers. In their Pensions Increase Act of 1952 and in their decision on the claim of these retired Service officers the present Government were following this precedent. Secondly, these Service officers had derived advantage from the 1935 stabilisation to the extent of some 3 per cent to 4 per cent during the period from 1935 to 1939, but this advantage had thereafter been more than offset by subsequent rises in the cost of living. The Cabinet should also be aware that the deputation on behalf of senior retired Civil Servants which had been received by the Financial Secretary on 23rd November had made it clear that they would not be content with restoration of the cut resulting from the stabilisation of pensions but would continue to press for adjustment of pensions to the current cost of living.

If, however, his colleagues agreed with him that the strength of feeling in Parliament made some action imperative, he would be ready to explain the Government's attitude privately to Government supporters in the House of Commons. Such an explanation should, in his view, be on the lines that the Government recognised the strength of the Service officers' claim and very much hoped that the time would come when it could be met; that this would have to be accompanied by corresponding concessions to Civil Servants, which would involve legislation and a total outlay of some £400,000 a year; and that the economic situation ruled out the making of any such concessions at the present time in view of the risk of repercussions.

The Chief Whip said that, although no less than 76 of the 111 Members who had put their names to the motion criticising the Government's decision on this matter were Labour Members, opinion on the subject amongst Conservative back-benchers was extremely strong and the narrowness of the Government's present majority made it very desirable that early steps should be taken to explain the reasons for the Government's decision to its critics on the Government side of the House.

The Prime Minister said that it was clear that if the Government were to weaken on this issue at this juncture they would lay themselves open to the charge that they were sacrificing what they had publicly declared to be in the national interest and would be exposing themselves to further dangerous pressures. No time should be lost, therefore, in making it clear publicly that for the present at any rate there was no question of the Government's altering their policy, though that policy did not exclude the possibility that the issue might be reviewed after an interval if circumstances should then make it practicable to meet the claim.

There was general support for this view and for the suggestion that it would be opportune to remind Government supporters that, in spite of the apparent improvement in the country's position, the country's fortunes remained precariously balanced. In explaining the issue to Government supporters effective use might also be made of the evidence available that the support which Opposition Members were now giving to the claims of these Service Officers was likely to be followed by the fullest possible exploitation of any concession which the Government might be forced to make.

The Minister of National Insurance[1] confirmed that, while he recognised the strength of the Service officers' claim in principle, the present would be a particularly unfortunate time for meeting it, as the British Legion were inaugurating a campaign on behalf of war disability pensioners and the claims of old age pensioners always tended to be pressed at this time of the year.

The Cabinet –
  (1) Took note that informal guidance would be given forthwith to the Press to the effect that the Government adhered firmly to the decision on this matter which had been announced in both Houses of Parliament on the previous day.
  (2) Invited the Foreign Secretary and the Chancellor of the Exchequer to explain the Government's attitude on the matter to Government supporters, on the general lines suggested in discussion, at a meeting of the 1922 Committee to be held on the following day.

[. . .]

Cabinet: conclusions
(Cabinet papers, 128/26)

26 November 1953
Secret
11 a.m.
Cabinet Meeting No. 72 of 1953

[. . .]

2. The Prime Minister said that, from representations which had recently been made to him, it was clear that some of the Government's supporters in the House of Commons would be seriously disturbed if a defence agreement on the lines now envisaged were concluded with the Egyptian Government. These Members were not specially interested in the future of the Canal Zone Base: they were concerned that British troops should remain in Egypt to ensure the right of free transit through the Suez Canal. They would find it difficult to support any agreement which failed to safeguard the use of the Canal as an international waterway.

---

[1] Osbert Peake, 1897–1966. MP (Cons.) for Leeds North, 1929–55; for Leeds North East, 1955–6. Under-Secretary of State for the Home Dept, 1939–44. Parliamentary Under-Secretary to the Treasury, 1944–5. Minister of National Insurance, 1951–3. Minister of Pensions and National Insurance, 1953–5. Viscount Ingleby, 1956.

The Prime Minister said that the strategic importance of the Base, for peace or for war, was much less than it had formerly been; and, if the Egyptian Government rejected our latest proposals for an agreement, there was much to be said for starting afresh on an entirely new basis. Our essential requirements in the Middle East would be met if there were in Egypt an international base, containing a few thousand British troops, to which we could have access in time of war, and if we had one armoured division stationed elsewhere in the Middle East. He believed that, if we could obtain unequivocal American support in a fresh approach, the Egyptians might still be forced to concede our minimum demands.

The Foreign Secretary said that the Egyptians had hitherto been quite unwilling to join any international organisation for the defence of the Middle East, and he was doubtful whether they could be induced to adopt a different attitude on that point. He agreed, however, that there would be every advantage in exploring the possibility of securing stronger American support in any fresh approach to the Egyptian Government. An attempt should certainly be made to secure this in the forthcoming discussions in Bermuda.

The Cabinet –

Took note that at the Bermuda Conference the Prime Minister and the Foreign Secretary would seek to secure a firm promise of American support in a fresh approach to the Egyptian Government, to be made in the event of a breakdown in the current defence negotiations in Cairo.

[. . .]

Sir Winston S. Churchill to President Dwight D. Eisenhower
Prime Minister's Personal Telegram T.280/53
(Premier papers, 11/1074)

26 November 1953
Immediate
Deyou
Secret, Personal and Private
No. 5001

My dear Friend,

Do you think it would be a good thing if I asked Bernie Baruch to come and spend the night of the 8th with me at Bermuda as a personal guest? He is a wise friend of both of us and I should like to pay him a courtesy and return his hospitality. I will be guided entirely by you.

Looking forward so much to seeing you.

November 1953

Sir Winston S. Churchill: speech
(Churchill papers, 2/336)

27 November 1953   Harrow School

This year I am a fourteen-yearer.[1] More than any of you can say. It is astonishing how quickly time seems to go. I do remember coming down here at a rather tragic moment in our fortunes, our lives, in 1940, and it was suggested we should sing a few songs to keep up our spirits, and I have always found in the Harrow Songs a great source of inspiration. You cannot make a fresh speech every year, you know.

I certainly believe this book[2] is one of the most precious possessions that any school in this land has got. These two great men, Bowen and Howson – and the two musicians who gave them assistance – had wonderful gifts. As I have said to you before, there is a really complete vocabulary in the Harrow Songs and, if the words are learnt and pondered over and repeated in the mind, you will find they enrich the process of your thought. The spirit is very good, buoyant, lifting, to our minds and to our hearts.

And then there is this song 'The Silver Arrow'. I have never heard that before. But look at the third verse:

> Their spirit today is dead, men say –
> Dead as their stalwart frames –
> Their blood now runs in idler sons,
> Loving less manly games.

Well, I looked at the date of that song – 1910. We were just then to begin a most awful period of stress and struggle than we have ever gone through in this island, and never in its long history had our race proved more worthy of what we here sing than in those years of slaughter, when the flower of our youth was proud to be cut away.

It is remarkable that this thought should have taken its place in the Song Book because, at that moment, the aspirations of the writer were to be vindicated by the brushing aside of the aspersions which he had deliberately set down in this verse.

Well now, trials and tests of many kinds impend upon us. I do not myself think that they will be of the same kind as those which we have just gone through. I have a feeling that the problems of Britain will, nevertheless, be more trying in many ways. The simple path of duty which war presents is easier to follow than the many-sided obligations of modern society. Our mighty population of fifty millions in this small island should by their qualities of virtue and courage, and by their wit, their invention, their intelligence and

---

[1] Meaning this was his fourteenth visit to Harrow Songs. This was a nod to the language of Harrow, which uses the term 'yearer' to denote a boy's status in the school.
[2] The Harrow Song Book.

by their tireless industry, show the world that they can preserve a society which carries forward the ancient glories of the past and make good all the highest hopes of the future. We have a great part to play in the world.

I see you all round here today. I must say I said to the Head Master, 'I think they look bigger'. I used to feel quite a little boy when I was here. Five hundred faces was the spirit. But here today you all seem so strong. I do trust this will be vindicated by your action and that Harrow will continue to set an example of tolerance and wisdom and faithful self-sacrifice wherever the needs of our country require you. This is not a time for class prejudice or a time for those who have had exceptionally good fortune in their education to take advantage of it. They must render even more service and make even greater sacrifices, and that, I believe, the spirit of this institution will enable them to do.

I am most grateful to you for singing to me and to my friends. I have brought down several Old Boys with me. We have got a few of them in the Government now. But they were not picked because they came from Harrow. They made their way themselves.

We have great trials and burdens upon us at the present time. We are not in the least afraid. We are going to do our very utmost to do our best for our country. We have had some inspiration in the past and it is with high hopes that I come to you this afternoon and cast out upon the future expectations that we shall make good all along the line. But remember the unity of our country, although we may be divided by Party strife. Our greatness is that we value decent behaviour between man and man, and faithful service to our native land when its perils are dangerous.

Thank you very much for singing all those nice songs. And now we are to have some for which we hardly need the book to read. I thank you very much.

President Dwight D. Eisenhower to Sir Winston S. Churchill
Prime Minister's Personal Telegram T.281/53
(Premier papers, 11/1074)

28 November 1953

Dear Winston,

Of course ask Bernard Baruch to be your personal guest if you so desire. I do not see how his coming for night of 8th could be interpreted as having anything to do with the general meeting which will have terminated prior to his arrival, as I personally must leave Bermuda no later than early morning of the 8th, possibly even the evening of the 7th.

Cabinet: conclusions
(Cabinet papers, 128/26)

30 November 1953
Secret
12 noon
Cabinet Meeting No. 73 of 1953

[...]

3. In connection with the discussion recorded in the preceding Minute, the Prime Minister said that he had been considering the re-deployment of British troops in the Middle East. The point of cardinal importance was to obtain American agreement to a joint Anglo-United States plan which would effect the best disposition of forces in support of the North Atlantic Treaty Organisation and would reassure public opinion in the United Kingdom. He had sketched the outline of a possible plan, which was not dependent on our continued control and operation of the Canal Zone Base. He would ask the Minister of Defence to examine this plan.

The Cabinet –

Took note that the Prime Minister would invite the views of the Minister of Defence on his suggested re-deployment of British forces in the Middle East on the basis of an agreed Anglo-United States plan.

[...]

Sir Winston S. Churchill to Henry Luce[1]
(Churchill papers, 4/28)

30 November 1953
Private and Confidential

My dear Luce,

I have thought carefully about your letter of October 2.

The *English-Speaking Peoples* will consist, I think, of four volumes, the first ending with the Wars of the Roses and the Plantagenets at Bosworth. This you have seen, but it is of course capable of considerable improvement though it does not require much expansion. The second volume deals with the Tudors and the Stuarts, down to the fall of James II.[2] This is thought to be a lively tale, and of course the dawn of America and the New World breaks

---

[1] Henry Robinson Luce, 1898–1967. Born in China, the son of an American missionary there. On active service with US Army in France, 1917–18. Founder, Editor and Publisher of *Time* (1923), of *Fortune* (1929) and of *Life* (1935), becoming a multi-millionaire. Evolved the cinema programme *The March of Time* (1935). Organized United China Relief, 1940. His wife Clare Boothe Luce, a pre-war friend of Randolph Churchill, was later US Ambassador to Italy.

[2] James II of England and VII of Scotland, 1633–1701. Succeeded as King, 1685. Ousted from the throne by the 'Glorious Revolution' of 1688.

upon us here. The third volume will be the Age of Anne and the Hanoverians, down to the accession of Queen Victoria. In the background are the two great continental wars with Louis XIV[1] and Napoleon, and of course the War of Independence and the war of 1812. All this is done, but more recasting and additions are required. The last volume, as I foresee it now, is the reign of Queen Victoria which incidentally contains a 40,000 word account of the American Civil War. I took great pains about this, and have visited, as you know, nearly every battlefield in the United States. This volume will in any case take us to the end of the nineteenth century. I do not expect there will be any more as I begin to tread on my own tail of contemporary volumes. All the above was completed before the outbreak of the second world war. My present idea, subject to the unforeseeable, is to publish the first volume in the late autumn of 1954 or the Spring of 1955 and then one a year. I do not exclude the possibility of a new introductory essay on the lines you suggest in your fifth paragraph. We could consider later, if I am still at work the appropriate finale.

My only remaining financial interest in the book is the serial rights, together with cinema, TV, etc. In the course of the next few months I shall be able to group the material I have already prepared but which is not in its final array. I thought that, with your coloured illustrations that you carry to such a high standard in *Life*, you might be able to make a very remarkable presentation of this march through the centuries, with all its wonderful and famous dramatic episodes. All the main events are already dealt with. As far as the serials are concerned (in contrast to the perfecting and completion of a historical survey) I do not think that your interests would suffer if I did not live to see the end myself.

Perhaps you will let me know how you feel about all this, and what terms you offer, because I have to make my plans, and I am receiving various enquiries.

I am so glad that your staff are pleased with the sixth volume of the Memoirs. I have had quite favourable opinions expressed about it by those who have read it. I sent all the relevant passages to Eisenhower on account of his official position and my own. He entrusted the task of reading them to Bedell Smith, who is quite satisfied with them, although of course we did not always agree about strategy and tactics. I hope also that Truman will not be displeased.

You will I am sure not mind my saying that I certainly think in equity a further payment should be made by *Life* and the *New York Times* for the serials of Volume VI. This has undoubtedly proved a feature of first rate importance to you, and had I not been able to complete my tale, or had I compressed it into five volumes, you would have had, I suppose, to have paid a large sum of money to someone else to fill the gap. I must however repeat my thanks for the

---

[1] Louis XIV, King of France 1643–1715.

hospitality which you accorded me at Marrakech and elsewhere in the currency difficulties from which we suffer so much in England.

Sir Winston S. Churchill to Field Marshal Lord Alexander
Prime Minister's Personal Minute M.327/53
(Premier papers, 11/481)

30 November 1953

Lord Montgomery lunched with me on Saturday and suggested that the proper place for the Headquarters base in the Middle East would be Smyrna. This would of course merge our responsibilities in those of NATO and might be made the means of a link for action with the United States in the Egyptian settlement. It should be carefully considered. We could limit our Staff to the proportions used by the other NATO powers which I am assured are severely restrained. It might be possible to move some of the stock-in-trade of the Suez base which would be useful to NATO and we might obtain some credit from NATO funds. I intend anyhow to press upon Eisenhower the active and complete co-operation of Britain and the United States in winding up the Egyptian entanglement from which neither Britain nor the United States should be regarded as deriving any advantage. If they would give real and reasonable help our problems would be capable of speedier, simpler and above all more dignified solutions than now impend.

2. Following the CIGS's estimate of one division not exceeding 16,000 combatants and 4,000 white ancillaries, I have pictured to myself the following disposition:

    (a) Anglo-American and Egyptian air-base on the existing site under Egyptian sovereignty but with Britain and America in close and direct accord.

    (b) One Armoured brigade in Libya.

    (c) One Infantry brigade (no staff other than the strict brigade staff) in Cyprus.

    (d) One Armoured brigade divided equally between Palestine and Transjordania with the agreement of both as a security against aggression.

    (e) A small and suitable force somewhere in the Persian Gulf as a nucleus and gesture for the assertion of our interests in the oil, including the new discoveries. The Navy should participate.

4. Every detail must be worked out for the demolition of the sea-base at Suez. The sale and dispersion of the stores should be worked out in detail with the utmost rapidity. The workshops etc. should be scrapped. This should proceed with Anglo-American authority and with Anglo-American assent from the moment chosen without waiting for any agreement with Egypt with

whom negotiation should be broken off. Whether they get any remnants of assets from the base will of course depend on their behaviour and upon a new agreement being made between Egypt on the one hand and Britain and the United States on the other.

5. The troops surplus to the division allocated to the Middle East should be brought home to form our reserve. No attempt should be made to find employment in the Middle East for the disbanded Staff. New staffs should be limited to our representatives at Smyrna according to NATO scales to the Staff of the divisions dispersed as described in the Middle East, plus the minimum additional officers necessitated by the widely divided Commands.

6. As a part of this agreement the United States should join with Britain in finding, say ten millions, to provide for the refugees which we are at present keeping in the Sinai peninsula. A habitation must be found for them which they can work up and irrigate with Anglo-American aid.

Pray examine this, if possible today or tomorrow so that the picture may at least be somewhat more filled in. I have contented myself with drawing the main outlines.

December 1953

John Colville: diary
('The Fringes of Power', page 682)

3 December 1953   Bermuda

This morning went to the airport with the PM for the ceremony of receiving the French Prime Minister, M Laniel, and the Foreign Secretary, M Bidault. Last time this conference was proposed, the French could not form a Government and the meeting had to be postponed week after week until just as we were packing to leave the PM had his stroke.

Lunched in the PM's dining room at the Mid-Ocean with Eden, Cherwell, Brook, Bob Dixon and Christopher as the other guests. An undistinguished conversation. Rushed away to see the Governor and the Speaker of the Assembly,[1] both of whom are exercised over the colour question. There was a row because when the Queen was here last week no coloured guests were invited to the banquet at the Government House. The PM has insisted that two should be asked to the Governor's banquet tomorrow. This meant tampering with the precedence list (oh horror!) and leaving out three most important local guests. I solved the problem by dropping instead three of our delegation.

Bathed twice today in the limpid blue sea (temperature nearly 70 degrees) and dived by the rocks to look at black and yellow striped and fish shaped like melons.

Dinner with the PM, Prof, Lord Moran, Brook, Christopher and Pitblado. The PM got going well after dinner, but the room was too small and we were all but perishing from the heat. The PM said, 'It may be that we are living in our generation through the great demoralization which the scientists have caused but before the countervailing correctives have become operative.'

First prize to the Prof who began illustrating a point with the following words: 'I was told by a Russian waiter at Los Angeles in 1912 . . .'

Delicious balmy night and the noise of the tree frogs is far better than that of crickets. We sat outside on the terrace at midnight with no discomfort.

---

[1] John William Cox, 1900–90. Married, 1926, Dorothy Carlyle Darrell: three children (d. 1982); 1984, Joan Maitland Cooper. Member, House of Assembly, Bermuda, 1930–68; Speaker, 1948–68.

December 1953

John Colville: diary
('The Fringes of Power', pages 682–4)

4 December 1953

Went to a delegation meeting with N. Brook at the Castle Harbour Hotel and escaped in time to bathe before luncheon, while the PM, who had met Eisenhower and Dulles on their arrival at the airport, pirated the former and took him to lunch privately in his room. This greatly disturbed both Dulles and Eden who neither of them trust their chief alone. However, the PM seemed, from what he told me, to get a good deal out of Ike including some alarming information about tough American intentions in certain circumstances.

When Ike had left, the PM, Christopher and I walked to the beach and the PM sat like King Canute defying the incoming tide (and getting his feet wet in consequence) while C and I bathed naked and I swam out to fetch Winston some distant seaweed he wished to inspect.

At 5.00 there was the first Plenary Meeting, of which I made a record. There were memories of former conferences. The Big Three first sat on the porch in wicker chairs and were photographed in a manner reminiscent of Tehran. Then, when the conference started, all the lights fused and we deliberated by the light of candles and hurricane lamps as in Athens at Christmas 1944. After a turgid if quite intelligent speech by Bidault, the PM (who had not prepared anything to say) launched forth into a powerful disquisition on his theory – which he calls a 'double-dealing' policy – of strength towards the Soviet Union combined with holding out the hand of friendship. He spoke of contacts, trade and other means of infiltration – always provided we were united and resolute in our strength. Only by proving to our peoples that we would neglect no chances of 'easement' could we persuade them to go on with the sacrifices necessary to maintain strong armed forces. This, coming after an intransigently anti-Russian speech by Bidault ('the only decent Frenchman' as Evelyn Shuckburgh called him to me), upset the Foreign Office representatives except for Denis Allen[1] who thought the speech statesmanlike and constructive. Frank Roberts and Shuckburgh said it was a disaster. I gather Eden felt the same. But I think Allen was right.

Ike followed with a short, very violent statement, in the coarsest terms. He said that as regards the PM's belief that there was a New Look in Soviet Policy, Russia was a woman of the streets and whether her dress was new, or just the old one patched, it was certainly the same whore underneath. America intended to drive her off her present 'beat' into the back streets.

I doubt if such language has ever before been heard at an international conference. Pained looks all round.

[1] William Denis Allen, 1910–87. HM Diplomatic Service, 1934–69. Married, 1939, Elizabeth Helen Williams: one child. Deputy Commissioner General for South East Asia, 1959–62. Ambassador to Turkey, 1963–7. Deputy Under-Secretary, FO, 1967–9.

Of course, the French gave it all away to the press. Indeed some of their leakages were verbatim.

To end on a note of dignity, when Eden asked when the next meeting should be, the President replied, 'I don't know. Mine is with a whisky and soda' – and got up to leave the room.

Busy with Norman Brook doing the record of the meeting, while the PM, Eden, Cherwell and Lord Moran went to the dinner at Government House. We all (the rest of us) dined in the PM's private dining room where we thought the food would be a good deal better than in the Grill Room.

Sir Winston S. Churchill: note
(Premier papers, 11/418)

[Undated]

THE SATELLITE PROBLEM

We must say to Russia we will not help Germany to attack them, and to Germany that although no immediate solution is offered of the satellite problem we shall by no means abandon the cause of Poland, Czechoslovakia, etc. Germany therefore is not asked to abandon further effort, it clearly being understood that they must not attempt it by force. If they attempt it by force we will be against them.

Our position is that we have not accepted the present position as final or even tolerable.

'Locarno' means that while we do not abandon the case of the satellites we are determined not to allow Germany to alter the frontiers by War. This shows the limited character of our reassurances both to Germany and to Russia where the satellites are concerned.

Sir Winston S. Churchill: note
(Premier papers, 11/418)

[Undated]

TRADE

Aiming at an indefinite period of 'easement' with Russia founded on the prolonged maintenance or if possible increase of our strength, we should regard trade as the most valuable weapon at our disposal. The balance of military power will not be decisively affected by importations into Russia of a quasi or indirect military character. On the other hand exchange of goods and services must lead to infiltration from which goodwill, contacts of all kinds, and information about the way of life behind the Iron Curtain. There are also the usual arguments in favour of trade, namely that it is the way in which peaceful people earn their livelihood. If we are to make the full contribution we seek to do to the strength of NATO, we must refresh and extend our overseas trade in Russia. We can find a fertile field I am therefore for the widest possible trade with the Soviets in everything except actual weapons.

Bermuda Conference: minutes
(Premier papers, 11/418)

4 December 1953   Mid-Ocean Club
5 p.m.
First Plenary Meeting

1. PRESIDENT EISENHOWER'S PROPOSED ADDRESS TO THE UNITED NATIONS

At the outset of the Meeting the three Heads of Delegations and the three Foreign Secretaries met alone to hear a statement by President Eisenhower regarding a speech which he was proposing to make at the General Assembly of the United Nations in the following week.

2. PROCEDURE

Sir Winston Churchill expressed the hope that President Eisenhower, as the only Head of a State present, should preside over the Plenary Meetings of the Conference.

3. POLICY OF SOVIET UNION

President Eisenhower suggested that the first topic to be discussed should be the present policy of the Soviet Union and invited the French Delegation to express their views.

M Bidault said that M Laniel had asked him to speak on this subject. The French Government believed that after Stalin's death there had been a change of manner and of attitude in foreign affairs rather than a fundamental alteration of policy. He wished to speak first of the internal policy of the Soviet Government. Absolute figures rather than percentages were now available and, thanks to the speeches of Krushev[1] and Mikoyan,[2] it was now known

[1] Nikita Sergeyevich Khrushchev, 1894–1971. Joined Bolsheviks, 1918. Fought in the Russian Civil War, 1918–20. Member, Central Committee of the Communist Party of the Soviet Union, 1934. 1st Secretary, Communist Party of the Ukraine, 1938–49. Secretary of the Central Committee of the Communist Party, 1949–53. 1st Secretary of the Central Committee of the Communist Party, 1953–64. Premier of the Soviet Union, 1958–64.

[2] Anastas Ivanovich Mikoyan, 1895–1978. Joined Bolsheviks, 1915. Member, Central Committee of the Communist Party, 1923. People's Commissar for External and Internal Trade, 1926. Member,

that the Five-Year Plan was unlikely to bring about rapid improvements in the internal economic condition of the country. There were today less cattle in Russia than in the days of the Czar, in spite of an increase of 50 million in population: in 1955 the Soviet people would have to eat twice as much fish as meat and twice as much sugar as meat: only one metre of woollen textiles would be available per head each year and a Soviet woman would be able to buy a new dress once in every thirteen years. The decrease in contributions to compulsory loans, and the attempts to reorganise industry, were very meagre evidence of the other side and it should be noted that 70 per cent of Russian industrial labour was still employed in heavy industry. Therefore the French Government concluded that it would be some time before a condition of economic security and stability could be established in the Soviet Union. Thus, the raising of the Iron Curtain and freedom of travel were not immediate possibilities and the Soviet Government were bound to put greater accent on its external policy than on internal improvements. Indeed the only room for manoeuvre available to them was in external affairs.

As regards Soviet foreign policy, M Bidault said that there was still much which was obscure. We knew little with certainty about Russian relations with China or with the satellites which had recently taken place in Soviet diplomatic representation abroad, for example in China. The Kremlin's relations with China were of fundamental importance to them; but they might not be as easy as we supposed, particularly since Stalin's prestige, and the fear which his name engendered, had gone.

There was another aspect of Russian policy which appeared to represent a definite trend, namely the improvement of the Soviet Union's relations with her neighbours. This could be seen in the case of Turkey and, through the medium of Bulgaria, with Greece too. In Finland also there had been a noticeable playing-down of Communist activities. Since, however, this policy had produced few results, the Soviet Government had resorted to another kind of manoeuvre. Towards France, certainly, they had made gestures and appeals which were more or less veiled, or in some cases not veiled at all. Last July they had signed a Trade Agreement by which France obtained chrome, which was of high strategic value, without being expected to offer anything comparable in return. M Molotov had called on the French Ambassador in Moscow on 14th July; M Malenkov had gone out of his way, in his speech of 8th August, to recall the Franco-Soviet Pact: there had been hints that Southeast Asian problems could be solved by agreement; and there had been suggestions for talks on Germany. The intention was obvious. It was to foster the resentment of Frenchmen against Germany and to destroy the unity of those who were fighting for peace and freedom. While these overtures were being made to

---

Politburo, 1935–66. Member, State Defence Committee, 1942. Deputy Premier, 1946. Minister of Trade, 1953–5. 1st Deputy Premier, 1955–64. Chairman of the Presidium of the Supreme Soviet, 1964–5.

France, the Soviet Union continued its policy of being violently antipathetic to the United States. It was evident from the last Soviet Note that the Kremlin were trying to address each of the Three Powers separately rather than as a collective whole. Therefore, in M Bidault's view, the aim of the Soviet policy was clear. Whatever the surface modifications might be, there remained permanent the intention of the Soviet leaders to drive a wedge between the Western Powers and to undermine the North Atlantic Alliance.

M Bidault concluded by reading an extract from Malenkov's speech of 8th August to the effect that Imperialist circles feared a détente since this would put an end to the profits of armament manufacturers. M Malenkov had added the following sentence: 'Aggressive circles also realise that since, in the present conditions of international tension, the North Atlantic Pact is already torn by internal strife and contradiction, it would collapse entirely in the event of a détente.'

President Eisenhower thanked M Bidault for his interesting statement and said that he particularly appreciated the positive quality of its approach. Other Delegations might wish to comment on this statement or to put forward their own views.

Sir Winston Churchill said that he would prefer to reserve his comments on M Bidault's clear and broadminded statement until he had had an opportunity to study it. Meanwhile, he would venture to put forward his own preliminary views. The supreme question before them, which must underlie their judgment in a dozen spheres, was whether there was a 'new look' in Soviet policy. Had there been a deep change in the policy of the Soviet Union since the death of Stalin? Several of the points which M Bidault had made might suggest that such a change had occurred. Other parts of his statement might suggest that there had been no change of heart but only an ingenious variation of tactics. It must have been a great shock to the leaders of the Kremlin when, after the war was won and the future seemed at their feet, they found that owing to the resolute initiative and giant strength of the United States their hopes and plans were confronted by the formidable decision of the free world to rearm and to withstand the expansionist ambitions of the Soviet Union. At the end of 1945 they must have thought that they had only to press forward in order to carry Communism, and behind it Soviet Imperialism, to the shores of the Atlantic. Now they realised that this way was no longer open to them. When Stalin's regime ended, they may have seen an opportunity to reconsider their situation. They must have recognised that, if they persevered in their earlier policy, they would face a tremendous struggle. On reviewing the new situation and circumstances, they may well have concluded that the policy which they had followed since the Potsdam Conference now required recasting.

That, Sir Winston said, was the first reason which inclined him to give an affirmative answer to the question 'Is there a new look in Soviet Policy?' The second reason was that the promise of better economic conditions which had been dangled for years before the Soviet millions had not been fulfilled. And the Soviet people must be aware that, if policies were changed, a substantial improvement could be made in their economic condition. These two factors – the opposition to the Western Powers and the vast economic hopes of the Soviet people – may well have led to a definite change and outlook which would govern at any rate the actions of the Soviet leaders for some years to come. In these circumstances we must be sure that we did not dismiss too lightly the possibility that there might have been a 'new look' in Soviet policy. In assessing the position we must be mindful of two dangers – first, that we should be put off our guard; and second, that we should exclude altogether the possibility that there might have been a real change. Of course, if there had been such a change, it was due mainly to the strength and unity displayed by the Western Alliance. If the leaders of the three Western Powers had come to Bermuda to consider relaxing that strength, or allowing themselves to be divided or to forget the danger or imagine that it was past, they would be very foolish. Their only hope was to maintain their strength and unity and to persevere in a clear and resolute determination to defend the cause of freedom by all means in their power. It would be the extreme of criminal folly for the Western Powers to entertain any thought of relaxing their defence effort. But, if they were resolved to persevere in those efforts, then the second question (whether there had been any change in Soviet policy) was one which they ought to examine, within its limits, and one which ought to find its place in their survey of the world situation. Their first task was to convince them that the Western Powers would not reject any genuine approach which they might make. It would be a mistake to suppose that every Soviet move must be viewed only with suspicion. So long as we maintained our defensive precautions, we could afford to look at new Soviet approaches on their merits. The leaders of the Western Powers must be able to convince, not only themselves, but their peoples that no bona fide movement by the Soviets toward a détente, no genuine gesture on their part had been rebuffed or dismissed without due consideration. If they were vigilant for any sign of amendment or amelioration, while still maintaining their strength and unity, they would gain fresh power to guide their peoples and win a new hope of reaching a better situation.

Thus, he proposed for the West a twofold policy – to maintain their strength, but also to be ready to look, and even to run some risks in looking, for a better state of mind in the immense populations of the Soviet Union.

The British Parliament and people were ready to make every effort to maintain the strength of the North Atlantic Alliance, but their leaders would be better able to rally them to make those efforts if they could convince them that nothing had been brushed aside which offered any assurance or hope of improvement in international relations.

Sir Winston Churchill said that he was particularly anxious that no opportunity should be lost to improve contacts between the Western peoples and the

Soviet Union. The Russians had much more to fear from such contacts than we had. Infiltration behind the Iron Curtain was feared by everything that was bad in the Kremlin regime. But it could do us no harm. Trade would be a vehicle for this – as well as a means by which countries could live. We had nothing to fear from increased contacts and increased trade with countries behind the Iron Curtain; and he hoped that all these processes of infiltration would be developed and extended. It would be a mistake to assume too quickly that nothing but evil animated the hearts of the Soviet people, and that nothing but evil and peril to the world would come out this vast ocean of land which we understood so little.

In conclusion Sir Winston Churchill said that he might sum up his statement in this way. Improved contacts with the Soviet peoples; infiltration behind the Iron Curtain; increased trade leading to greater prosperity; ample reassurance that the Soviets would not again be exposed to the ravages of a resurgent German militarism; recognition that, while the present position of the satellites was not tolerable as a permanent condition, it was no part of our policy to try to change it by the method of a third world war – time and patience must play their part in that – these were the essentials of a balanced approach towards a better understanding between East and West. While it was true that 'hope springs eternal in the human breast', never was there an occasion when hope should be more modest and more restrained. It was beyond our power to cure all the world's ills. But we might aim at an easement. This, by stimulating prosperity and putting the peoples of the world in a more agreeable frame of mind, might carry us through a period of years until the time came when a better light might dawn on the international scene. But this would not come unless we continued meanwhile in the strongest and most resolute manner to maintain our defences and organization in the West. We must not risk throwing away the great work which had been already been achieved. If there were any suggestion that the Western Powers should mitigate their defensive efforts, he would not for one moment ask that the other side of the case should even be considered. If, however, we remained indissolubly united and preserved our strength, we might then cherish the hope that we should find a way towards a solution of our difficulties and a means of preserving the peace of the world.

President Eisenhower said that these statements by M Bidault and Sir Winston Churchill had raised vitally important issues which would doubtless recur in subsequent discussions throughout the Conference. He hoped that on the following day there would be an opportunity for Mr Dulles to state the views of the United States Government on these matters. Meanwhile, he would only say that he had been enlightened by both these statements. He had been encouraged by the note of confidence in M Bidault's statement. He had been intrigued by Sir Winston Churchill's hypothesis of a 'new look' in Soviet policy. He hoped that he had understood this correctly. He would be very ready to consider whether this was a new dress or the old dress with a new patch on it; but he hoped that no one was under any illusion that the woman wearing it had changed her profession. If that were understood, they could all examine Sir Winston's statement in order to see whether it afforded some ground for a fresh positive approach to this problem. But, for himself, he did not believe that there had been any significant change in the basic policy and design of the Soviet Union to destroy the capitalist system and the free world by force, lies and corruption.

4. COMMUNIQUÉ

The Heads of Delegations invited the three Foreign Ministers to settle the terms of a brief communiqué which might be issued to the Press on the day's proceedings. It was agreed that this should be as short as possible and should go no further than to indicate that the Delegations had held a general review of the world situation.

John Colville to Sir Winston S. Churchill
(Premier papers, 11 / 418)

4 December 1953

You should know that the Press were very discontented with the four-line communiqué which was given to them after the Plenary Meeting tonight. It is a long time since there has been a Conference such as this and they – in particular the Americans – have got into the habit of expecting much fuller daily reports. The three Press Officers who met some 200 Press representatives remained firm and refused to budge beyond what they were authorized to say.

It would ease matters greatly tomorrow if the Press Officers were authorized to say that you, the President and M Laniel will give a personal Press Conference at the end of the Meeting. I believe that you in any case intend to do this. An announcement of this intention tomorrow would give the journalists something to look forward to and prevent them being discontented and unruly.

John Colville: note
(Premier papers, 11 / 418)

5 December 1953

SUMMARY OF THE PRIME MINISTER'S REMARKS

Meeting the Chinese does not necessarily imply recognising them for any purpose other than identification. In war there are often parleys between enemies while they are in fact still fighting (c.f. the campaign of 1814). This is quite distinct from approval of the actions and policy of the other side or their recognition in the diplomatic sense.

John Colville: diary
('The Fringes of Power', page 684)

5 December 1953

To the British delegation suite at the Castle Harbour for a briefing meeting. Everybody greatly perturbed by the American attitude on (a) the prospects (b) their action, in the event of the Korean truce breaking down. This question has such deep implications that it is undoubtedly the foremost matter at the conference – though it has to be discussed behind closed doors with the Americans. No atomic matters can be talked about to the French who are very sensitive at having no atomic piles or bombs. The PM, Ike, Lord Cherwell and Admiral Strauss discussed the matter in the President's room from 11.30 till lunch time.

This afternoon, while standing on the beach, I talked to Douglas MacArthur of the State Department. He said that the French system was hopeless, though Bidault was doing all he could. If EDC (the European Defence Community: a plan for a European army) were not ratified, the American administration could ask for no appropriations from Congress and would have to reorientate their whole policy to Europe.

I did not go to the Plenary Meeting – leaving David Pitblado to do this. Instead I went with Christopher to Government House for a quarter of an hour as the Governor was giving a cocktail party.

We gave a dinner party at 'Out of the Blue' for Pug Ismay who arrived today. Meanwhile the PM and Eden were dining alone with Eisenhower and Dulles and were engaged in grim conversations about the truce in Korea. Eden was most particularly perturbed by this and by the effect on public opinion in England. There was also discussion of a draft speech, mainly on atomic matters, which Eisenhower wants to deliver next week at the General Assembly of the United Nations. Christopher read it aloud in the PM's bedroom, while I sat in a chair and the PM and Eden, still fully dressed in dinner jackets, lay side by side flat on the PM's bed. The Americans had of course gone to their own apartments by then.

John Colville to Sir Winston S. Churchill
(Premier papers, 11/418)

5 December 1953

At tonight's Plenary Meeting there may be an opportunity for you to say something which brings out the importance of the three Governments linking in their thought the problems of Communism in the East and the West. There are many points of agreement for all three but some divergence. The points of agreement could be listed as follows:

(a) We all want to prevent the further spread of Communism in the Far East and to get the Asiatic nations themselves to resist subversion and infiltration.
(b) We support French policy in Indo-China.
(c) We support United States policy in Japan, including controlled rearmament.
(d) We agree that Formosa must be defended against Chinese Communist attack.
(e) We are all agreed that a political conference in Korea is the essential first step before a Five-Power Conference.
(f) If Korea cannot be unified, South Korean independence must be supported.
(g) We think we can count on French and American support for our policy in Malaya.
(h) The Five-Power Staff Agency should be supported by all as the most effective organization for defence planning in the East. From it we might eventually develop machinery for an effective defence policy at political and military levels.

Points of Divergence

(a) Recognition of the Communist regime in China as an established fact (which does not mean approval).
(b) Communist China's claim to admission to the United Nations.
(c) We cannot indefinitely maintain trade embargoes at their present level.

Surely the important thing is to suggest that these problems are in reality closely connected with those facing us in Europe and to stress the importance of reaching agreement on action in the Far East (e.g. a common policy for building up the Five-Power Staff Agency) as effectively as we have united in Europe.

Sir Norman Brook and Sir Pierson Dixon asked me to put these points before you as they both feel the importance of looking at the Communist problem, both in the East and in the West, as a whole and of bringing this out at a Plenary Meeting if the opportunity occurred.

Since dictating the above I hear that Mr Dulles intends at this evening's meeting to continue yesterday's discussion and turn it to a discussion of the Far East.[1]

Bermuda Conference: minutes
(Premier papers, 11/418)

5 December 1953 Mid-Ocean Club
Secret
5 p.m.
Second Plenary Meeting

1. M LANIEL

President Eisenhower said that M Laniel was indisposed and his medical advisers had forbidden him to attend this meeting. He voiced the regrets of the United States Delegation and their good wishes for M Laniel's speedy recovery.

Sir Winston Churchill endorsed these sentiments on behalf of the United Kingdom Delegation.

M Bidault expressed thanks on M Laniel's behalf.

2. PROCEDURE

Sir Winston Churchill said that he had been disturbed to learn how much information had reached the Press about the proceedings at the Plenary Meeting the previous afternoon. Press representatives were aware, not only of the general drift of the discussion, but of actual phrases used; and it was evident that their information had been obtained from persons present in the Conference Room. The local newspapers, though they had handled it with discretion, plainly had full information about the course of the proceedings; and other newspapers, not yet available in the Island, would presumably have published similar stories. He felt bound to bring this to the notice of his colleagues and to ask that steps should be taken to prevent a repetition of these unauthorized disclosures.

President Eisenhower said that the Head of each Delegation should instruct all members of his staff that they should in future observe the strictest discretion in this matter. He also thought it would be helpful if three officials were at once appointed, one from each Delegation, to begin the preparation of the final communique. The appointment of such a group might reduce the pressure which newspaper representatives were bringing on other Delegation officials.

[1] The last paragraph was handwritten.

Sir Winston Churchill and M Bidault endorsed President Eisenhower's suggestions.

It was agreed that the following officials –
Mr Robert R. Bowie[1] United States Delegation
Mr W. D. Allen United Kingdom Delegation
M Seydoux[2] French Delegation
should be appointed to prepare a draft of the final communiqué and that they should hold their first meeting for this purpose that evening.

[. . .]

Lady Churchill to Sir Winston S. Churchill
(Churchill papers, 1/50)[3]

5 December 1953

My darling Winston,

Although this is my first letter, I have been thinking of you constantly since you flew away at midnight on December the 1st. A telegram has just come from you saying that 'the work is heavy'. I do pray that it will also be fruitful. The newspapers have very good photographs of you (looking well & jaunty) greeting Monsieur Laniel & later several others.

However, last Wednesday Diana's Doctor (Carl Lambert) took her up to Scotland to a Hospital near Dumfries which specializes in deep insulin treatment. She went by her own wish, and last night Duncan went up by the night train to spend the weekend with her. He returns tomorrow night & I shall see him on Monday before Mary and I leave on Tuesday for Stockholm. I am glad Diana has left the Nursing Home in London, I thought it rather melancholy & felt that nothing was being achieved & that it was merely marking time.

This afternoon I went to see Sydney Butler[4] at the Westminster Hospital. There is no facial disfigurement & it seems that in the terrible circumstances everything has gone as well as possible. But it will be a long time till she is well.

I have had several letters from guests saying how much they enjoyed your

---

[1] Robert Richardson Bowie, 1909–2013. Educated at Princeton University and Harvard Law School. Lt-Col., US Army, 1943–5. Special Assistant to Deputy Military Governor for Germany, 1945–6. Prof., Harvard Law School, 1946–55. General Counsel and Special Adviser to US High Commissioner for Germany, 1950–1. Asst Secretary of State, 1953–7. Founder and Director, Center for International Affairs, 1958–73. Deputy Director for National Intelligence, CIA, 1977–9.

[2] Roger Seydoux Fornier de Clausonne, 1908–85. Educated at University of Paris. Minister, French Ministry of Information and Cultural Services, 1952–4. French Ambassador to Tunisia, 1956. French Ambassador to Morocco, 1960–2; to UN, 1962–7; to Soviet Union, 1968–72.

[3] This letter was handwritten.

[4] Sydney Courtauld, 1902–54. Friend to Clementine Churchill. Married, 1926, Richard Austen Butler: four children. She was undergoing treatment for cancer, of which she died the following year.

Birthday Party. I hope you are being good attending to & following Charles' advice.

Tender love my darling

PS. I told Sydney how touched you were by her letter.

John Colville: diary
('The Fringes of Power', page 685–7)

6 December 1953

This morning everybody was in rather a state. First there is the momentous matter of last night's discussion* which far outstrips in importance anything else at the conference. Secondly there is EDC. The Americans are disgusted with the French but nevertheless convinced that EDC is the only alternative for them to withdrawing to the periphery of Europe. The French, wily diplomats that they are, have at least this card to play: Bidault and the Quai d'Orsay are all for EDC and have done everything possible to meet the American point of view. Therefore, say the Americans, it is the British who must satisfy the French Chamber of Deputies by guaranteeing to leave their troops on the continent for a defined number of years or even by actually joining the EDC. Thus it is we who are to suffer on account of French weakness and obduracy. Of course, the obvious is (i) we will keep our troops on the continent as long as the Americans agree to do so, (ii) we could not possibly get our Parliament and people, or the Commonwealth, to accept our actual membership of EDC.

The Prime Minister, when first I went to see him this morning, was engaged in writing to Ike approving, apart from one or two points, the text of his draft speech to UNO. I took it down to the beach to show Eden who was lying there with Dulles, engaged in a mixture of bathing and negotiation. Anthony Eden at once said that in view of what we knew from yesterday's private talks with the Americans, approval of the terms of the speech in all its aspects would make us accessories before the act. He proposed the insertion of a statement that in view of our exposed position, we had to make reservations. This the PM accepted and sent me down with the letter to give it to the President.

Eisenhower was in his sitting room, cross-legged in an armchair, going through his speech. He was friendly, but I noticed that he never smiled: a change from the Ike of war days or even, indeed of last January in New York. He said several things that were noteworthy. The first was that whereas Winston looked on the atomic weapon as something entirely new and terrible, he looked upon it as just the latest improvement in military weapons. He implied that there was in fact no distinction between 'conventional weapons' and atomic weapons: all weapons in due course became conventional weapons. This of course represents a fundamental difference of opinion between public opinion in the USA and in England. However, he said that America was prepared to be generous in the sacrifice of fissionable material to an international authority that she was willing to make.

I told him that a reference to 'the obsolete Colonial mold' contained in his draft speech would give offence in England. He said that was part of the American philosophy. I replied that a lot of people in England thought India had been better governed by the Viceroy and the British Government of India than at present. He said that as a matter of fact he thought so himself, but that to Americans liberty was more precious than good government.

W saw him for half an hour before lunch and he agreed to remove the obnoxious phrase about colonialism and to substitute for the United States being 'free to use the atomic bomb' a phrase about the United States 'reserving the right to use the atomic bomb'.

It has been a gloriously sunny day. I bathed twice and lunched out of doors.

After luncheon there was trouble because the Foreign Ministers had sent off to Adenauer the text of the proposed reply to the Soviet Government, accepting a conference at Berlin in January, without showing it to Ike or W (Laniel retired to bed yesterday with pleurisy and a temperature of 104 degrees). W remonstrated strongly with Eden and wanted to have left out the reference to German reunification, on the grounds that you couldn't confront the Russians at Berlin with both our determination that Western Germany should be an armed member of EDC *and* a demand that Eastern Germany be united to it. Eden enlisted the support of Dulles (even heavier and more flabby now than last January) and after pointing out that German reunification had figured in all the previous notes, and that Adenauer expected it, they won their case. In the confusion Frank Roberts, who was in a state of fury with the PM, was mistaken by the latter for one of Dulles' advisers and treated to a homily as such.

During the Plenary Conference, which centred on EDC and which again Pitblado attended, Christopher and I entertained to drinks at 'Out of the Blue' Alastair Buchan,[1] Wilson Broadbent (*Daily Mail*), Ed Russel, and one or two members of the delegation.

Dined at the 'Pink Beach' with Christopher, Ed Russel, and two particularly glamorous American women called Mrs Steele[2] and Miss Jinx Falkenburg.[3] The latter is the sister of the Wimbledon champion[4] and obviously a champion

[1] Alastair Francis Buchan, 1918–76. Commissioned in Canadian Army, 1939. Maj., 14th Canadian Hussars, 1944. Served in north-west Europe campaign, 1944–5. Asst Editor, *The Economist*, 1948–51; Washington Correspondent, 1951–5. Diplomatic and Defence Correspondent, *The Observer*, 1955–8. Director, Institute for Strategic Studies, 1958–69. CBE, 1968.
[2] Mildred Helen Shay, 1911–2005. American actress, appearing in several films in the 1930s. Married, 1934, Thomas Francis Murphy (div. 1935); 1936, Winthrop Gardiner (div. 1937); 1941, Geoffrey Steele: one child.
[3] Eugenia Lincoln Falkenburg, 1919–2003. Known as 'Jinx'. Well-known American actress and socialite. Married, 1945, Ted McCrary: two children.
[4] Bob Falkenburg, 1926–. Tennis player. Winner, Grand Slam Doubles, US Open, 1944; Wimbledon, 1947; Grand Slam Singles, Wimbledon, 1948. Founded Bob's Fast Food Chain.

herself in other ways. There is no doubt that American women are supreme in the art of flattering the male ego.

Dragged self away to return to the Mid-Ocean and put a thoughtful PM (unconscionably bored by a dinner given in his honour by the French) to bed. He said, as I have been feeling for the past forty-eight hours, that all our problems, even those such as Egypt, shrink into insignificance by the side of the one great issue which this conference has thrown up.

A snake runs away from you because it is frightened. But if you tread on its tail it will rear up and strike you. This is to me an analogy with Soviet Russia. I put it to Eden who agreed most heartily.

Before going to bed the PM told me that he and Ike had agreed to treat forcing through the ratification of EDC as a combined military operation. If it does not go through, the Americans do not agree with the PM that Germany must be invited to join NATO. On the contrary they talk of falling back on 'peripheral' defence, which means the defence of their bases stretching in a crescent from Iceland via East Anglia, Spain and North Africa to Turkey. This, in the PM's view, would entail France becoming Communist-dominated (and finally going the way of Czechoslovakia) while the Americans sought to rearm Germany sandwiched between the hostile powers of Russia and France. Frank Roberts thinks that we shall in the event just get over the EDC hurdle. If we don't, the PM intends to go all out to persuade the Americans to work for the Germany-in-NATO alternative. This is a precarious situation.

* The American inclination to use the atomic bomb in Korea if the Chinese came to the aid of the Communist North Koreans, a suggestion strongly resisted by Churchill and Eden.

Sir Winston S. Churchill: note
(Premier papers, 11/618)

6 December 1953

We are all agreed to try to press EDC through. President Eisenhower rejects the idea that if it continues to be indefinitely delayed an arrangement can be made to include a German Army in NATO. It must be EDC or some solution of a 'peripheral' character. This would mean that the United States forces would withdraw from France and occupy the crescent of bases from Iceland, via East Anglia, Spain, North Africa and Turkey, operating with atomic power therefrom in case of war. The consequence would be a Russian occupation of the whole of defenceless Germany and probably an arrangement between Communist-soaked France and Soviet Russia. Benelux and Scandinavia would go down the drain. The Americans would probably declare atomic war on the Soviets if they made a forcible military advance westward. It is not foreseeable how they would deal with a gradual though rapid and certain Sovietisation of Western Europe a la Czechoslovakia. It is probable that the process would be gradual so that Sovietisation would be substantially effective and then war come. Thus we should certainly have the worst of both alternatives.

If the United States withdraws her troops from Europe the British will certainly go at the same time. The approach of the Russian air bases and the facilities soon available to them west of the Rhine would expose us, apart from the bombing, rockets, guided missiles, etc., to very heavy paratroop descents. We must have all our available forces to garrison the Island and at least go down fighting.

The French should realise that failure to carry out EDC (unless they can persuade the United States to try the NATO alternative) would leave them without either any American or British troops in Europe, and that a third World War would become inevitable. It would be conducted from the American peripheral bases, and as the Russian Armies would be in occupation of Western Europe all these unhappy countries would be liable to American bombing of strategic points. Whatever happens Great Britain will continue to resist until destroyed. In three or four months or even less after the beginning of atomic war the United States unless outmatched in Air Power will be all-powerful and largely uninjured, with the wreck of Europe and Asia on its hands.

No one can guarantee that this unpleasant result may not occur even if we take the right course, and follow the 'peace through strength' policy. We should however at least have a chance of escaping the doom which now impends upon mankind.

Sir Winston S. Churchill to President Dwight D. Eisenhower
(*Premier papers, 11/1074*)

6 December 1953
Top Secret

You agreed at our talk on Saturday that you would look into the possibility of earmarking a certain number of atomic bombs and storing them in England, which could be used by our bombers in case of War. In order that this should be feasible it is essential that we should obtain as soon as possible the technical information necessary to enable us to fit them into our planes. The principal points on which we would require information are the weights, dimensions and fusing arrangements of your weapons and the methods of attaching them to and releasing them from the aircraft. Without this advance information it would almost certainly take many months to adapt our aircraft to carrying and dropping the bombs.

Would you be good enough to let me know what steps we can take to make this arrangement effective.

December 1953

Sir Norman Brook to Sir Winston S. Churchill
(Premier papers, 11/418)

6 December 1953

1. There are various points outstanding which we had wished to discuss bilaterally with the Americans:
   (i) Support in Anglo-Egyptian negotiations.
   (ii) United States military aid to Pakistan.
   (iii) Gibraltar and Cyprus.
   (iv) United States military aid to Iraq.
   (v) Sale of rubber and other strategic materials to China.

2. The only point of major substance in this list is the first – Egypt. On this Mr Eden has already had a satisfactory assurance from Mr Dulles privately but wants to get this confirmed at a more formal meeting. The rest are relatively quite small points.

3. Would you be willing that Mr Eden should deal with all the points in the above list on your behalf? There will be little time tomorrow; and he would be willing to try to meet Mr Dulles at about 10.30 p.m. this evening. Before arranging this he would like to know that you are agreeable.[1]

Sir Winston S. Churchill to President Dwight D. Eisenhower
(Premier papers, 11/1074)

6 December 1953   The Mid-Ocean Club
                                                              Bermuda

I think it is a very fine speech and tackles the terrible problems which confront us with your usual courage and candour. I think it will help toward the 'easement' of which I have sometimes spoken and it may well be that the contacts which may develop will be useful. It is a great pronouncement and will resound through the anxious and bewildered world.

Naturally I do not like what appears on page 11.[2] History will, I am sure, make a different appraisement.

About page 7.[3] I hope we may have some further talk, for I know you understand the reservations I have to make in the light of our exposed position. Circumstances, proportion and the fate of friends and allies would never, I am sure, be absent from your mind.

---

[1] Churchill wrote a note in the margin: 'I want to talk tomorrow Ismay or Ike about Egypt. Then with us four.'

[2] On p. 11 of his draft speech 'Atoms for Peace', Eisenhower referred to the 'obsolete colonial mould'. He did not include this phrasing in the final version of the speech.

[3] On p. 7 of the draft the statement appeared that the US was 'free to use the atomic bomb'. In the final version of the speech, this was amended to read that the US was 'reserving the right to use the atomic bomb'.

I am sending you privately a short note about the proposed international Atomic Energy Administration which Cherwell prepared for my eye.

Sir Winston S. Churchill to President Dwight D. Eisenhower
(Premier papers, 11/1074)

7 December 1953
Top Secret

We agreed, did we not, that Admiral Strauss and Lord Cherwell should compile a White Paper of the documents, and their linking together, which constitute the story of Anglo-American relations about the Atomic Bomb. You and I will then consider and discuss whether it will be helpful or not to publish. Personally I think it will be. We both desire a fuller interchange of intelligence and the fact that secrecy is evaporating through growth of knowledge between us, and alas between both of us and Soviet Russia, makes it desirable that we two should make the best joint progress we can. Your speech will, I think, encourage the new atmosphere. Cherwell and Strauss, I understand, take it that they should prepare the White Paper.

Sir Winston S. Churchill to President Dwight D. Eisenhower
(Premier papers, 11/1074)

7 December 1953

Thank you so much for your kind consideration of the points I felt it my duty to make. I have one more bearing on page 7. The last part of your speech will of course thrill the whole world and dominate opinion. Do you need to take the emphasis off it by a sentence or a phrase which will undoubtedly be fastened on by all the enemies of America and Britain at home or abroad.

Whatever you decide to say it should be made clear that it is your speech and your inspiration and that you take full responsibility for it. The fact that you have shown it to me and some of your friends beforehand is only an example of the intimate terms on which we work.

I have in my letter expressed to you my association with the spirit and mood of your new message about atomic material and whereas your speech is the result of long consideration and study I and Anthony have only had a brief opportunity to examine the problem which your courtesy allowed us.

You ought to see if you have not already done so the front page of today's *Washington Post*. We live under a system of Cabinet Government and not one of our colleagues has ever dreamed of the departure that you are going to make.

I am looking forward to half-an-hour with you around 10 a.m. tomorrow or any other time you send for me.

Bermuda Conference: minutes
(*Premier papers, 11/618*)

7 December 1953
Secret
Third Plenary Meeting

[...]

Mr Dulles said that M Bidault's full and clear presentation of the issues involved deserved the most careful consideration, and the United States Government would certainly study it with great attention. Meanwhile, he would make only two points. First, the United States would be the last to want to see a federation of continental Europe if it meant the disappearance of France as a great Power – a great Power not merely from the material point of view but even more as a source of that intellectual and spiritual inspiration which had contributed so much to the civilization of the world and not least to his own country. No Frenchman need be apprehensive on this issue: France was too precious to be submerged. Secondly, he wished to emphasize that the nations of Europe were not being confronted with steps which might lead to the disassociation of the United States from Europe. If the future of Europe were likely to be a sad repetition of the quarrels of the past, prudence might counsel such disassociation. But the creation of the EDC was designed to preserve a Europe with which the United States could continue to maintain close association. He was sure that this would at the right time be made absolutely clear by the United States Government.

Sir Winston Churchill said that he had imagined that, in discussing the creation of the EDC, the Conference would have had primarily in mind the future salvation of France. He would be sorry to think that the success or failure of the plan for EDC was to turn on the future of a few fields in the Saar Valley. This would indeed imply a sad lack of a sense of proportion. This project for the EDC was a French plan. France's allies and friends had done their best to help in working it out. Three years had been spent in the process, and during all that time the creation of a German army had been delayed. The critical moment was now approaching. Would the French Parliament accept the plan? If they were reluctant to do so, surely they should force themselves to face the grim alternative. For himself he had hoped that a second course was open, viz., the integration of a German national army into NATO. But, from what President Eisenhower had said on the previous day, it seemed that this might not be regarded as a practicable alternative. But, if EDC could not be created and a German army could not be incorporated in NATO, the situation would indeed be grave. For Western Europe could not be defended without a German contribution. And, if Europe itself could find no way of securing it, she would in effect be inviting the United States to fall back on a peripheral defence. This would have frightful consequence for Europe – which, even in peace, would be exposed to intensive Communist infiltration and, if war came, would immediately suffer the utter destruction of every aspect of its culture and civilization. If the United States were to withdraw their vital aid from Europe, British troops could not be kept their any longer – they would stay as long as, but no longer than, their American comrades. The Allied front in Europe was a protection to the United Kingdom; but, once it was broken by the withdrawal of United States troops, Britain would have to build up her defences in her own island. No country had made comparable sacrifices: though she had maintained compulsory military service for two years in time of peace, she had not even a brigade stationed at home – and that in a country which, before long, would be within range of heavy attack by Russian paratroops. This situation could only be tolerated while the front was held in Europe: if it were not held, we should have to concentrate on preparing to fight to the death in our own island. He begged that a matter like the future of the Saar should not be allowed to obscure a question which was one of life or death for the flaming spirit of France and for the Atlantic Alliance on which all hopes were now founded. Britain had offered to maintain very close links with the EDC. She could not offer any further military assistance. France, having devised this project and carried it thus far, would surely carry it through. The French Parliament should surely force themselves to face the alternative, so that they might see where their duty and their interests lay. The creation of an EDC was an essential step in preventing the outbreak of a third world war, which, if no front in Western Europe were held, would certainly sweep away all the culture, civilization and liberty which had been the pride of Europe for centuries. Britain had at least the barrier of the English Channel and, though she would be shattered, might escape subjugation. The EDC could be for France the equivalent of the Channel.

It was not to convince M Bidault that he spoke like this. He knew only too well that M Bidault had fought hard to establish the EDC and was ready to risk his political future and even his life in that cause. He urged him to persevere. But, if the plan for the EDC should fail, he would still work for the establishment of a German army, preferably within the NATO framework, as a contribution towards the defence of the West. And, if even that should fail, France could rest assured that British troops would stand in the line in Europe so long as American troops remained there.

President Eisenhower said that he would like to add a few comments. This had not been a debate on the merits of EDC. All present believed in it and wished to support it. But he had himself asked M Bidault to indicate what his difficulties were in getting the French Parliament to accept it. He was grateful to M Bidault for his clear presentation of the difficulties, and these would certainly be considered fully. But he also agreed with everything of what the Prime Minister had said about the gravity of the situation. He had himself asked for United States troops to be sent to Europe. The United States was not a fair weather friend. They did not intend to jump out of Europe. They knew that the EDC could not be created overnight. But the situation was serious. If EDC failed, the United States Government would of course consider every possible alternative. The reason why he had expressed doubts at the previous meeting about the inclusion of a German national Army in NATO was that he believed that neither France nor Germany wanted it and that it would therefore be an even more difficult solution than the creation of EDC.

In conclusion he deprecated any undue pessimism. He himself believed that EDC would go through. If it did, this would rapidly clear the whole atmosphere in Western Europe, and there would be a rapid inflow of strength with guarantees to all concerned. The plan for the creation of the EDC must succeed, nobody must even think of it in terms of failure.

Sir Winston S. Churchill to Anthony Eden
Prime Minister's Personal Minute M.330/53
(Premier papers, 11/418)

7 December 1953

I can find nothing in this communiqué which shows the slightest desire for the success of the Conference or for an easement in relations with Russia. We are to gang up against them without any reference to the 'Locarno' idea. The statement about Europe ends with the challenge about a united Germany in EDC or NATO, for which Russia is to give up the Eastern Zone. Many people would think that we were deliberately riding for a fall. Perhaps we are.

I understand this draft is to be submitted to us 5 p.m., and I hope it will be understood that it is only draft.[1]

Bermuda Conference: minutes
(Premier papers, 11/484)

7 December 1953
Secret
Fifth Plenary Meeting

1. EGYPT AND THE MIDDLE EAST

Sir Winston Churchill said that he did not wish to speak in any detail about the dangerous situation which at present existed between the Egyptian forces and the 80,000 British troops and airmen stationed in Egypt. If there were two full days still available to the Conference he could go fully into this. But there

---

[1] Eden wrote on this minute: 'I had not seen the draft until I came into the chair at 3 p.m. – I am doing my best with it, without much success. It is certainly still a draft. We have done 5 lines in an hour!'

was another aspect of the matter which was of world interest, namely the international significance of that great waterway, the Suez Canal. He felt that there should be unity in their determination to take every possible measure to preserve it against neglect and obstruction. He was not speaking of the closing of the Canal by hostile action in time of war by a nation other than Egypt: that would be very difficult to prevent, especially with the improved methods now available for such operations. But he thought we should attempt to place the Suez Canal on an international basis as worthy of respect as that of the Panama Canal. Such an achievement would do a great deal to stabilize the situation in the Middle East.

Sir Winston Churchill continued that if Her Majesty's Government could receive assurance from the President, that they had the moral support of the United States Government in their present negotiations with Egypt, these assurances might bring the current defence negotiation in Cairo to a reasonable conclusion and might prevent what was otherwise not impossible, namely serious fighting in the area.

Mr Eden said that in our negotiations with Egypt there were now only two major points outstanding. On neither of these could we make any further concession. The first related to the reactivation of the base; and we were willing to leave it to the United Nations to decide whether circumstances had arisen which justified this. The second was the question of uniforms. This was vital, not for reason of prestige, but because our technicians in the Canal Zone must have the same protection given to NATO personnel in other countries so that they could not be hauled before the local Courts. If the United States could give us solid support on these two questions when our Ambassador returned to Cairo in a fortnight's time, we still stood a fair chance of succeeding in negotiations.

Sir Winston Churchill emphasized that we could not allow our technicians to be arrested by the Egyptian police. If they were wearing uniform, action against them by the Egyptians would constitute an act of war.

Mr Eden thanked Mr Dulles for his assurance that no economic aid would be given to Egypt by the United States until the New Year, when a new appreciation of the situation could be made.

Mr Dulles said that the United States Government were certainly prepared to agree to hold up aid to Egypt until the New Year in the hope that this would help the defence negotiations; but he should make it clear that he had also indicated to Mr Eden that he did not think that this aid could be held up after the New Year.

M Bidault said that France had a great interest in the Suez Canal – moral, material and strategic. French supplies to Indo China were dependent on the canal. He was satisfied that we should base ourselves on the 1888 Agreement about navigation through the Canal, since he considered this Agreement to be of great importance to all countries which made use of this route for strategic and commercial purposes.

[. . .]

Bermuda Conference: minutes
(*Premier papers, 11/664*)

7 December 1953
Secret
Sixth Plenary Meeting

2. INDO-CHINA

M Bidault said that he would begin by describing the military situation in Indo-China. Vietminh had reached the ceiling of their numerical strength and were confronted by military stagnation. It was evidence of this that they now were setting up special tribunals to try men who would not submit to military service with the Communist forces. But they were also receiving increased support from China, in the form of signal and anti-aircraft equipment and other such supplies. The French on the other hand, had taken the unpopular step of sending out reinforcements from home; and the native forces established by Viet Nam continued to be built up. 54 supplementary battalions were being raised and furnished with United States equipment. There were limited cadres available for these new battalions but 34 were already formed and the remainder would be in action by the end of February. The Viet Nam regular army had also been increased by a division of 9 battalions and 13 artillery battalions. General Navarre[1] had adopted a new policy of yielding those parts of the territory which he did not choose to defend and concentrating on those which were important, instead of attempting to hold every inch of the ground. This gave the anti-Communist forces an increased power of manoeuvre. In general, the situation had greatly improved as compared with last year.

None of this would have been possible if Indo-China had not received aid from the United States in finance and in equipment. They had lent an aircraft carrier, the *Arromanches*, and fighter aircraft would soon be arriving from America. France was grateful for this timely aid.

The main effort was being made in the Red River delta, an area of Tonking where there were 2,000 inhabitants to the square mile and where it was difficult to distinguish the enemy from the ordinary people. Up to now the enemy

---

[1] Henri Eugène Navarre, 1898–1983. In French Resistance, WWII. Brig-Gen., 1945. Lt-Gen., 1952. 7th and final Cdr, French Far East Expeditionary Corps, First Indochina War, May 1953 to July 1954. Published *Agonie de l'Indochine* (1958).

had been infiltrating by night, so that there was one master by day and another by night. The French had now initiated action to ensure that there was only one master, both by day and by night. A number of offensive actions, with mysterious code-names, had been put in train. These had succeeded in stopping the offensive which the Viet Minh had intended to launch in Laos and in both the branches of the delta during the dry season. Vietminh had indeed intended this offensive to produce a final decision, and they had been thrown completely off their balance by General Navarre's harassing offensives.

The Viet Nam regular troops could not be supported financially by the country. Moreover, they must have French cadres. The 54 new supporting battalions also required such cadres on a more restricted scale, and it was proposed to bring them to a pitch of efficiency for undertaking mopping-up operations. Metropolitan France was making her full contribution to this war. There were 100,000 French troops in Indo-China, and every year the equivalent of one graduating class at St Cyr was wiped out. Without them the war would long since have been lost.

The order of operations intended by the military commander was first the delta, then Cochin China, Cambodia and finally Annam. The effects of a bad climate and also psychological effect on the French troops of being 8,000 kilometres from France had to be considered. Nevertheless the military situation in Indo-China was better than he had seen it before.

Turning to the political situation, M Bidault said that on July 3 M Laniel's Government had proclaimed the independency of the Associated States of Indo-China. This proclamation had involved certain risks. First, it might give the impression that independence for the Associated States was something new. This was an entirely false supposition, because the French had been following a consistent course since the end of the war. There was another danger. After the proclamation Bao Dai[1] had called a conference at Saigon at which many were present who were ready to ask for independence but not to fight for it. These had tried to suggest that independence must carry with it a complete break with France, and they had spoken of this at a time when French soldiers were shedding their blood for the real independence of the country. This conference had had serious consequences, both in France and in Indo-China. Bao Dai had done his best in the face of great difficulties. The question at issue for him was 'Is the French Union enough?' The search for an answer had brought him to the South of France, but he had been told that his place was in Indo-China. The idea held in some quarters that the French Union was a kind of prison was being fostered by Communists and by their nationalist allies. But France would uphold the flexible constitutional concept of the French Union. Thousands of Frenchmen were ready to travel 8,000 kilometres to fight for it.

[1] Nguyen Vinh Thuy, 1913–97. Known as 'Bao Dai'. Educated at Lycée Condorcet and Paris Institute of Political Studies. 13th and final Emperor of the Nguyen dynasty, 1926–45. Chief of State, Vietnam, 1949–55. Exiled, 1955.

M Bidault was confident that it would prevail, and would sustain the French effort in Indo-China.

Ho Chi Min[1] had recently made some proposals for a truce. They might perhaps have been drafted far from Indo-China because, for instance, it was noticeable that the first of them contained a statement of his opposition to EDC! The French Government had returned a reply which was meant to exclude negotiations. They insisted that true liberty for the citizens of Indo-China should be respected and to this Vietminh could never honestly agree. While negotiations with Ho Chi Min alone might be useless, France would not reject peace negotiations for Indo-China within an international framework, provided that it was a real international framework. It was essential that the Associated States should be represented. Without their agreement France would do nothing. The alternative of mediation would be expensive; moreover it was difficult to think of a mediator who would be acceptable to both sides. Another solution, negotiations with China, was out of the question because the Chinese would certainly not admit responsibility. Perhaps there might be Five-Power talks, provided always that the representatives of the Associated States were present. It was in any case indispensable that something should be done because the French people must not see before them an endless dreary plain on which they were expected to continue marching while elsewhere in the world hostilities ceased.

In conclusion, M Bidault repeated that nothing could or should be done to normalise political and commercial relations between France and China until the war in Indo-China had first been satisfactorily settled.

Sir Winston Churchill said that he would like to pay a heartfelt compliment to France for her valiant effort to preserve her Empire and the cause of freedom in Indo-China. He greatly admired the efforts which France was making: he was only sorry that the British had not been able to do the same in the vast subcontinent of India. It would be seen in 50 years' time what a great disaster our leaving India had been to the human race. France had done valiant work, not only in Indo-China, but also, if he might digress for a moment, in North Africa. He was greatly impressed by the way in which the French had cherished and nourished the civilisation which they had established there, and he hoped that all the Powers allied with France would give her their moral support in the difficult tasks which the French Government were tackling there with so much skill and resolution. Britain had a smaller, but costly and wearying, operation in Malaya. Conditions there were improving, but we had not the slightest intention of slackening our effort. It was a

---

[1] Nguyen Sinh Cung, 1890–1969. Known as 'Ho Chi Minh'. Born Kim Lien, French Indochina. Married, 1926, Zeng Xueming. Leader of the Viet Minh independence movement in WWII. Member, Political Bureau of the Central Committee, Communist Party of Vietnam, 1935–69. Minister of Foreign Affairs, 1945–6. PM, Democratic Republic of Vietnam, 1945–55; President, 1945–69. First Secretary, Central Committee of the Workers' Party of Vietnam, 1956–60; Chairman, 1951–69.

great mistake to suppose that the ancient powers of Europe had not made a valuable contribution to the countries of Asia, or that all that they had done in Asia was obsolete and should be cast away.

He would venture to offer one suggestion to the French Government, namely that there was great advantage in prolonging the period of compulsory military service, even if this were accompanied by a diminution in the total numbers of men available to the armed forces. Longer service and fewer men meant less demand on the nation and a higher quality in the forces. Britain had found great advantage in this, in meeting her overseas commitments; since it meant that there was scope for 'breeding the cadres', and a smaller turn-over of officers and men.

He wished to pay a sincere compliment to the French effort in Indo-China and to say again how much he wished he could pay a similar compliment to his own country about India. Many round the table, though not he himself, would live to see darkness descend on large areas of Asia because their people had thrown away all the help and the direction that Europe had offered them. This was an unpopular theme, but one to which he had given great thought and much of his energies throughout his life. In conclusion, he also expressed his gratitude to the United States for their far-seeing action in furnishing such generous and timely aide in Indo-China.

President Eisenhower said he wished to be associated with Sir Winston Churchill's compliment to the French on their campaign and also to pay a special tribute to General Navarre. As regards American aid, another aircraft carrier with 25 transport planes and several helicopters would soon be with them. He had found M Bidault's allusion to Five-Power talks a little cryptic. That phrase now had a very unpleasant connotation in the United States.

M Bidault said that he could dispel the President's anxieties on this point. He was not in favour of a Five-Power Conference on world affairs in general, as proposed by the Soviet Government. The French would be ready to accept a multilateral Conference to deal with South-East Asian problems alone, provided the Associated States were represented. He hoped that an international Conference on South-East Asia would be convened at the appropriate moment, but its composition must depend on the scope and objectives of its work.

3. EUROPE: SECURITY ASSURANCES

Sir Winston Churchill said that one of the difficulties in preparing for a Four-Power Meeting was to find something which might be gratifying to the Russians. This he was anxious to do, but the difficulty was that they had already taken everything that they could lay their hands upon. During the later phases of the War he had been much impressed by the deep feeling and desire of the Soviets for real protection against aggression from a new Hitler. He had sympathised with them in this and, if they had not been carried away by the opportunities of victory, it might well have been possible to find an acceptable means of re-assuring them. They had treated us ill for several years since then, but we should not on that account be unwilling to do what was just. He hoped that full assurance could be given to them, not only that our own defence organizations had no aggressive purpose, but that if they were wrongly attacked we would help and support them. He had tried to strike that note some months ago and thought that it could still be struck with advantage. What would have been right and fair if they had behaved well was also right and fair at a time when they might be inclined to behave less badly. He had also thought they should have freedom of access to the broad waters. As regards the satellites, he had never contemplated that we should commit ourselves to accepting the present position as permanent, but we ought to make clear that we should not attempt to correct it by force, though we hoped that time, patience, and good fortune would bring improvements. Nothing could be more unfortunate than to stir up trouble in the Satellites without the means of helping them: this would only lead to the strengthening of tyranny and untold suffering for the peoples.

Since the final communiqué of the Conference was to strike so many notes of strength, we could surely afford to strike one which would give at any rate some sense of wishing the Soviet no harm or even being ready to help them against unjustified assault and would indicate that the World Instrument would, as was intended, play its part on their side; on occasions when they were in the right. This would be only a very small counterpoise to our main effort of maintaining our defences.

M Bidault said that that it was desirable that Ministers should let it be known from time to time that they read what was prepared for them by their experts. Those who had met in Paris had produced a report which represented in value something worthwhile and in weight about half a pound. There were still some differences of opinion among the experts. He could say a good deal on the texts they had prepared but this would form part of the preparations for the Four-Power Meeting.

The Soviet Government like precise assurances and it was difficult to see what guarantees could be given or accepted from them which either side would consider adequate. The desire for such guarantees was not unnatural. For example there were strong natural boundaries between France and Spain but the French had crossed the Pyrenees many times over the centuries, and despite their long friendly relations it would not be unreasonable for Spain to ask for guarantees from France. But there would be great difficulty in evolving any multilateral agreement affording such guarantees to the countries of eastern and western Europe. He therefore believed that a solution must be sought on the lines of a unilateral declaration. Whatever satisfaction it might or might not give to the Soviets, it would help to demonstrate to public opinion in the West the objectives of their own Governments. The experts had suggested that Germany might declare that she renounced any resort to violence for the settlement of frontiers, and that the other countries should associate themselves with this declaration. Juridical objections had been raised but he was satisfied that under EDC it would be possible for each State to enter into obligations with the support of its partners.

In his view the French proposals were the best but he thought that no such proposal should be mentioned publicly at the present time and that even at the Four-Power Meeting it should be held in reserve until the appropriate moment.

Mr Dulles said that he himself had from time to time spoken in very much the same sense as had Sir Winston Churchill. But, as M Bidault had said, and the Paris discussions had shown, it was a most complicated task to translate these general sentiments into an actual plan.

As he remembered the Locarno idea, it had been a guarantee within a group of countries that they would join together to help any one of their number who was attacked, whether by one of themselves or from the outside. No one country was singled out as the danger to be guarded against. He thought it important that Germany should not now be so singled out. Some general formula would therefore be preferable. Sir Winston had spoken of guarantees against another Hitler, but he thought that the greatest factor in helping Hitler to power was the feeling among Germans that Germany had been singled out as a Power to be kept in a position of inferiority and subjection, and that Hitler could hold out to them a prospect of becoming once more a first-class Power. He hoped that the Paris studies would lead to results which would bring the benefits for which Sir Winston hoped.

Mr Eden said that he was somewhat concerned about the timetable at the Four-Power Meeting in January. The Soviet representative would certainly ask what had been intended by the general references already made to the possibility of some security assurance. The three Western Powers must be prepared to answer that question at the Meeting. Of the two methods of giving security assurances, all were now agreed that it would be impracticable to negotiate a multilateral agreement and that it would be necessary to proceed by way of a declaration. The declaration might take the form of repeating the sort of undertakings which had previously been given, e.g. in the North Atlantic Treaty. Alternatively, the German Government might be ready to volunteer a declaration which the others could endorse. Dr Adenauer had already made statements of this kind, and there seemed to be no reason why he should not be asked if he would be willing to do so again. If he were ready to volunteer a statement this would meet the fears which Mr Dulles had voiced, since it could not then be supposed that Germany had been forced to accept an inferior position. He hoped that further work would now go forward on this without delay. The experts who had recently discussed this matter in Paris, would be meeting again in the following week. They could prepare a communication designed to elicit Dr Adenauer's view, taking as a basis the Anglo-French draft which had already been drawn up.

Mr Eden's suggestion was approved.

Bermuda Conference: minutes
(Premier papers, 11/418)

7 December 1953   Mid-Ocean Club
Secret
10.15 p.m.
Seventh Plenary Meeting

COMMUNIQUÉ

The Meeting had before them a revised draft of the final communiqué, which had been prepared by officials in the light of the discussion at the meeting of Foreign Ministers held earlier in the day.

The meeting considered this draft paragraph by paragraph and various minor amendments were suggested and approved.

The discussion of substance turned wholly on one paragraph describing the exchanges of views which had taken place at the Conference on the subject of the European Defence Community (EDC). M Bidault said that he could not accept this paragraph in the form in which it had been drafted by the officials. He proposed that the paragraph should be amended to read as follows:

> 'The French Minister for Foreign Affairs reaffirmed the continuity of the French Government's policy in regard to the European Defence Community. The fulfilment of this policy depends on the solution of the problems with which France has long been faced. His statements were fully discussed; the three Governments will give them further detailed consideration at an early date.'

Mr Dulles and Mr Eden said that the second sentence of this revised paragraph would put their Governments in an embarrassing position. It implied that the French Parliament would not be willing to accept EDC unless other problems had first been solved and their Governments would be pressed to say precisely what those problems were. Moreover, it was well-known that in the earlier debates in the French Parliament there had been put forward, as pre-conditions of the acceptance of the EDC, various suggestions which were quite unacceptable to the United Kingdom and United States Governments; and the paragraph as now drafted did not specifically exclude any of these. It would certainly be suggested that among the conditions envisaged was the maintenance of British and United States forces on the continent of Europe.

For these reasons Mr Dulles and Mr Eden felt unable to accept this paragraph in the form proposed by M Bidault.

In the discussion which ensued various alternative formulae were put forward on behalf of the United Kingdom and United States Delegations; but none of these proved to be acceptable to M Bidault.

After prolonged discussion, M Bidault eventually said that he was inclined to propose, subject to M Laniel's approval, that the better course would be to omit this paragraph altogether.

Mr Eden withdrew from the meeting in order to explain to M Laniel the deadlock which had been reached and the suggestion which M Bidault had put forward with a view to ending it.

On Mr Eden's return, M Bidault said that M Laniel was unable to agree that the communiqué should include no reference to the discussions which had taken place at the Conference about the EDC. He therefore proposed that, in the place of the paragraph previously suggested by the French Delegation, there should be inserted the following sentence:

'The French Minister for Foreign Affairs explained the problems facing his Government in regard to the EDC.'

After some further discussion, Sir Winston Churchill and Mr Dulles said that they were prepared to accept this latest suggestion of the French Delegation.

The communiqué, in the form in which it was finally approved by the French, is reproduced as an Annex to these Minutes.

2. CONCLUSION OF CONFERENCE

President Eisenhower, who was due to make an important speech to the United Nations Assembly on the following day, had withdrawn from the meeting shortly before midnight. Before he left, Sir Winston Churchill thanked him for presiding over the Conference. He said that he felt sure that he was expressing the views of all Delegations in extending to the President their cordial thanks for the patient and skilful manner in which he had presided over their proceedings. For himself, he counted it an honour to have sat at these meetings under the Chairmanship of the President of the United States.

M Bidault warmly endorsed Sir Winston Churchill's expression of thanks to the President.

President Eisenhower, in expressing his appreciation of these remarks, said that he was gratified by the characteristically kind manner in which Sir Winston Churchill had referred to him.

ANNEX
COMMUNIQUÉ

The President of the United States, the Prime Minister of the United Kingdom and the President of the Council of Ministers of the French

Republic, accompanied by the Foreign Ministers of the three countries, met in Bermuda from December 4 to 7, 1953. At their meeting they discussed their policies regarding many parts of the world where their countries have obligations. On the conclusion of the Conference they issued the following statement:

I

Our meetings symbolized and confirmed the unity of purpose of our three countries. We found ourselves in accord on our analysis of the problems confronting us and have agreed on various measures essential for their solution.

Confident that our united strength is the best guarantee of peace and security we are resolved to maintain our joint efforts to perfect it. If the danger of aggression now appears less imminent, we attribute this to the mounting strength of the free world and the firmness of its policies.

We shall remain resolute in maintaining our solidarity and vigilant against efforts to divide us.

With their material and moral resources we are confident that the free peoples can provide both for their security and for their well being. We dedicate ourselves to work together towards these ends.

II

The North Atlantic Treaty is and will remain the foundation of our common policy. We discussed means of developing the defensive capacity of our Alliance. Lord Ismay, the Secretary General of the North Atlantic Treaty Organisation, was present at the conversations on this subject.

In the continuing development of a united Europe, including Germany, we see the best means of achieving greater prosperity, security and stability for its free peoples. We reaffirmed that the European Defence Community is needed to assure the defensive capacity of the Atlantic Community of which it will be an integral part. Within this framework it will ensure intimate and durable cooperation between the United Kingdom and the United States forces and the forces of the European Defence Community on the Continent of Europe. The French Minister of Foreign Affairs explained the problems facing his Government in regard to the European Defence Community.

We cannot accept as justified or permanent the present division of Europe. Our hope is that in due course peaceful means will be found to enable the countries of Eastern Europe again to play their part as free nations in a free Europe.

III

Our three Governments will lose no opportunity for easing the tensions that beset the world and for reassuring all nations that they have no cause to fear that the strength of the West will be invoked in any cause of wrongful violence. On the contrary it is the fundamental principle of the United Nations Organisation, which we serve, that the guarantees against aggression shall be universal in their application.

We are confident that if we remain strong, united and steadfast it will become possible gradually to solve the stubborn problems which have too long been unsettled.

In this spirit we have examined the latest note from the Soviet Government. We approved the text of our replies, which should lead to an early meeting of the four Foreign Ministers. Our hope is that this meeting will make progress towards the reunification of Germany in freedom and the conclusion of an Austrian State Treaty and thus towards the solution of other major international problems.

IV

We reviewed the situation in the Far East. The immediate object of our policy continues to be the convening of the political conference provided for in the Korean Armistice agreement. This would provide the means for reaching a peaceful settlement of the Korean question and for making progress in restoring more normal conditions in the Far East and South East Asia.

In Indo-China we salute the valiant forces of France and of the three Associated States of Indo-China fighting within the French Union to protect the independence of Cambodia, Laos and Viet Nam. We recognise the vital importance of their contribution to the defence of the free world. We will continue to work together to restore peace and stability in this area.

V

Our meetings have reinforced our solidarity, strengthened our resolve, and fortified our hopes. Confident in our common purposes and united in our views we shall persevere in our policies, whose sole aim is to foster and assure peace.

John Colville: diary
('The Fringes of Power', pages 688–9)

8 December 1953   Bermuda

This morning I strolled down to bathe with John Foster Dulles, who said that the presence of the French, and the constant need for interpretation, had greatly hampered the conference. Since it was the Americans who insisted on the French being invited, I thought this indeed ironical. The surf was heavy on the beach and Dulles was twice capsized.

The PM went to see Ike at 10.00 and told me that he said to him that the Americans sending arms to Egypt after January 1st would have no less effect in the UK than the British sending arms would have in the USA. The President, he said, took this seriously.

Eisenhower also told him that he was in favour of International Conferences provided there was no agenda *and* no communiqué. The press here (nearly 200 of them) are furious at the scanty information they have received. Alastair Buchan had the impudence to tell me that conferences such as this should be arranged for the convenience of the press.

The President left before lunch, and Bidault with Parodi and de Margerie[1] came to take leave of the PM before their departure. W said to Bidault that if he had been rough on the French it was not because he loved them less than formerly, but because he wanted to urge them to save themselves and not, in consequence of refusing EDC, to force the Americans to fall back on a 'peripheral' defence of Europe. It was not the French Government which was 'bitching' (a word de Margerie found difficulty in translating!) it all but the French parliamentary system. With this Bidault heartily concurred.

This evening the Speaker (Sir John Cox) gave a dinner for the House of Assembly in the Mid-Ocean – the Conference Room having rapidly been converted for the purpose. The PM was the principal speaker and did very well. The Governor, Sir Alexander Hood, was outstandingly eloquent; the Speaker outstandingly turgid.

I sat between two members of the Assembly. Bermuda has a parliamentary system in which there are no parties but each member votes according to his conscience. This is simplified by property qualifications for the franchise which means that out of the 35,000 inhabitants only 5,000 can vote. One of my neighbours was gravely annoyed that the PM should have insisted on two coloured men being asked to the banquet which the Governor had given for the Big Three. No black men had been asked to the banquet given for the Queen a fortnight ago and there had been a fuss both in the House of Commons and in the British press which had prompted the PM's action.

Sir Winston S. Churchill to Antony Head
(*Premier papers, 11/696*)

8 December 1953

I am in favour of a military enquiry in closed Court with subsequent report to the House of Commons. I am opposed to such wide terms of reference as 'the general conduct of the Army in Kenya.' It would, I should think be better

---

[1] Roland Jacquin de Margerie, 1899–1990. Educated at Ecole Libre des Sciences Politiques. ADC to Gen. Gamlin, Feb.–Mar. 1940. French Consul-General, Shanghai, 1940–4. Minister Plenipotentiary, 1949. Ambassador to the Vatican, 1956–9; to Spain, 1959–62; to Bonn, 1962–5. Conseiller d'Etat, 1965–70.

to make specific inquiries into the Griffiths[1] case, the KAR and any other occurrences to which the attention of the Tribunal will be directed.

Antony Head to Sir Winston S. Churchill
Prime Minister's Personal Telegram T.293/53
(Premier papers, 11/696)

8 December 1953
Emergency
Secret
No. 192

I have now received the proceedings of the Griffiths' Court Martial and today discussed with Cabinet the statement which I should make to the House. It was generally agreed that this should be made before the proceedings were placed in the library of the House of Commons and therefore it was felt that a statement should be made on Thursday December 10.

Evidence given in Griffiths' Court Martial indicates that irregularities were confined to the King's African Rifles. Nevertheless it was felt that any enquiry into the matter should cover all troops operating in Kenya both to satisfy public opinion and to clear the good name of the remaining units of the British Army in Kenya.

There are two choices as to the method of enquiry. First, an outside enquiry, second, a military court of enquiry.

The first has the disadvantage that no civilian can be compelled to given evidence and any soldier giving evidence in open court is warned that he may be subsequently prosecuted as a result of his evidence.

General Erskine wants to make a most scrupulous enquiry into all these matters with a view to further prosecutions wherever necessary. An open enquiry would make it much harder to follow up and prosecute those cases where such action seems necessary.

The disadvantage of the second course is that the House and the general public may be given the impression that the Army is trying to cover up what has happened in Kenya by holding a military enquiry in closed court. I think that criticism of the second method can be met by explaining the disadvantages of the first and by giving an undertaking to report to the House in the light of the findings of the military court of enquiry.

I therefore propose, and the Cabinet has provisionally agreed, that a military court of enquiry should be set up consisting of one Lieutenant General and one senior representative of the Army Legal Services sent from this country together with one Army representative in Kenya. Their terms of reference

---

[1] Gerald Selby Lewis Griffiths. Cdr, B Company, 5th Battalion, King's African Rifles, Chuka, Kenya. Court-martialled on charge of murdering a Mau Mau soldier, 1953; found not guilty.

would be to enquire into the general conduct of the Army in Kenya during operations against Mau Mau with special reference to the allegations made in the trial of Captain Griffiths.

With regard to Captain Griffiths the question of further prosecution is being urgently considered by legal advisers here and in Kenya but it will be impossible to make any statement on this subject on Thursday.

The Cabinet instructed me to ask for your comments on the action proposed above so that I should be able to make a statement on December 10.

President Dwight D. Eisenhower to Sir Winston S. Churchill
(Premier papers, 11/1074)

8 December 1953

Dear Winston,

As I depart from this lovely spot, I leave this note behind to thank you once again for acting as our host for a very interesting and, I hope, profitable conference. While my disposition had not always been equal to the pressures of some of the lectures, I think that I came through my first international conference – in a political role – in fairly good shape.

Give my love to Clemmie and all your nice family.

Lady Churchill to Sir Winston S. Churchill
(Churchill papers, 1/150)[1]

8 December 1953

My Darling,

Mary & I are leaving for Stockholm in ten minutes & I have just time to send a line for the bag which leaves this afternoon.

I hope that now the heavy work of the Conference is over you will have a little sunshine & rest before flying home. It's very hard to judge by the newspapers what has been achieved. The general impression is that the French have been as tiresome obstructive & odious as usual. I'm sure you were right to insist on this meeting. I long to see you Saturday.

---

[1] This letter was handwritten.

December 1953

President Dwight D. Eisenhower to Sir Winston S. Churchill
(Premier papers, 11/1074)

9 December 1953

Dear Winston,

The Goat's[1] soldierly deportment puts me to shame – you would suppose that after some forty years in the Army, I would not have embarrassed him so sadly.[2]

John Colville: diary
('The Fringes of Power', pages 689–90)

10 December 1953

Bathed in the morning and attended to the PM who was in a cantankerous frame of mind. I, too, was mentally dyspeptic.

In the afternoon drove with Norman Brook to St George's, the old capital, to see the beautiful seventeenth-century colonial style church, white without and roofed with delicious-smelling cedar beams within. The early colonial stone memorial tablets are particularly delightful. It is notable how many Governors and eminent citizens were carried off by yellow fever in comparatively early youth. Observed, with amusement, that the vain Lord Moran had contrived to have his signature, solitary on a large sheet of writing paper, inserted in the treasure chest, among seventeenth-century silver, with those of the Queen, Mr Eden and M Bidault.

Boarded the BOAC aircraft Canopus at 8.00 p.m. with the rest of the British delegation and the now recovered M Laniel. The PM, who didn't want to have to talk French, contrived to have him sent straight to his bunk on Lord Moran's advice, after arranging for him to dine before we left. Heavily drugged, the unsuspecting M Laniel went to sleep and did not disturb the dinner party on board.

The four-hour difference of time between Bermuda and London rather puts one out for eating and sleeping purposes.

John Priestman[3] stood on his head in the main cabin saying that he wanted to be first Englishman who had even done so in the mid-Atlantic.

[1] An actual goat. Mascot and member of the Welch Royal Fusiliers, holding the official rank of Lance Corporal.

[2] Churchill had written to the President: 'In explanation of the goat's refusal to accept the cigarette you offered him this morning I think I ought to point out that he was aware that smoking on parade is strictly forbidden.'

[3] John David Priestman, 1926–2009. Educated at Christ Church, Oxford. Served in Coldstream Guards, 1944–7. 3rd and 2nd Secretary, FO, Belgrade, 1949–53. Married, 1951, Nada Valić: four children. Asst Private Secretary to Anthony Eden, 1953–5. Joined Secretariat, Council of Europe, 1955; Head of Secretary-General's Private Office, 1961; Secretary, Committee of Ministers, 1966; Deputy Clerk, Parliamentary Assembly, 1968–71.

Sir Winston S. Churchill: speech[1]
('Winston S. Churchill, His Complete Speeches', volume 8, pages 8515–16)

10 December 1953

State Banquet, Town Hall
Stockholm

THE NOBEL PRIZE FOR LITERATURE

The roll on which my name has been inscribed represents much that is outstanding in the world's literature of the twentieth century. The judgment of the Swedish Academy is accepted as impartial, authoritative, and sincere throughout the civilized world. I feel we are both running a considerable risk, and that I do not deserve it. But I shall have no misgivings if you have none.

Since Alfred Nobel[2] died in 1896 we have entered an age of storm and tragedy. The power of man has grown in every sphere except over himself. Never in the field of action have events seemed so harshly to dwarf personalities. Rarely in history have brutal facts so dominated thought or has such a widespread individual virtue found so dim a collective focus. The fearful question confronts us: Have our problems got beyond our control? Undoubtedly we are passing through a phase where this may be so. Well may we humble ourselves and seek for guidance and mercy.

We in Europe and the western world who have planned for health and social security, who have marvelled at the triumphs of medicine and science, and who have aimed at justice and freedom for all, have nevertheless been witnesses of famine, misery, cruelty, and destruction before which pale the deeds of Attila[3] and Jenghiz Khan.[4] And we who, first in the League of Nations and now in the United Nations, have attempted to give an abiding foundation to the peace of which men have dreamed so long have lived to see a world marred by cleavages and threatened by discords ever graver and more violent than those which convulsed Europe after the fall of the Roman Empire.

It is upon this dark background that we can appreciate the majesty and hope which inspired the conception of Alfred Nobel. He has left behind him a bright and enduring beam of culture, of purpose, and of inspiration to a generation which stands in sore need. This world-famous institution points a true path for us to follow. Let us, therefore, confront the clatter and rigidity we see around us with tolerance, variety and calm.

The world looks with admiration and indeed with comfort to Scandinavia, where three countries, without sacrificing their sovereignty, live united in their

[1] Read by Lady Churchill in Winston's absence.
[2] Alfred Bernhard Nobel, 1833–96. Swedish businessman and chemist. Founder (in his will of 1895) of the Nobel Prizes.
[3] Attila (?–453). Leader of the Hun people of the Central Asian steppes who overran much of the former Roman Empire in the late fifth century.
[4] Genghis Khan (c. 1162–1227). Leader of the Mongol people of the Central Asian steppes who ruled a vast empire from his base in what is now Mongolia.

thought, in their economic practice, and in their healthy way of life. From such fountains new and brighter opportunities may come to mankind. These are, I believe, the sentiments which may animate those whom the Nobel Foundation elects to honour, in the sure knowledge that they will thus be respecting the ideals and wishes of its illustrious founder.

Sir Winston S. Churchill to Anthony Eden
(Premier papers, 11/700)

11 December 1953

OPERATION REDEPLOYMENT

The exit from all your troubles about Egypt, the Suez Canal, the Sudan, the Southern Sudan and later on in the Middle East will be found in deeds not words, in action not treaties. What security have we got that the Egyptians now breaking your Treaty of 1936 will keep any agreement you will make with them. On the contrary, it is almost certain that increasing bad blood will develop between us over the Sudan; that as our troops in the Canal Zone diminish in strength in carrying out the proposed agreement the Egyptian riots and petty attacks will continue or increase. We shall no longer have available the force to occupy Cairo, etc. All that will happen is that our troops would be tied up half way through their evacuation, and many in our own Party will be able to say 'we told you so', while the others mock.

2. Let me now tell you the action which, although apparently local, I believe would be comprehensive and decisive. Find some reason to send 2 battalions of infantry and 3 or 4 squadrons RAF by air to Khartoum. The Governor could perhaps claim that public order required it as a protection and of course make it clear that there is no going back on our bargain of self-government for the Sudan. This would merely be a temporary measure to enable the new government to be set up in an orderly manner. The thing is not to talk about this, but after close, secret, intimate study among a few <u>to do it</u>.

3. Once this sign of strength and action of policy and design has been shown all the Conservative troubles here would be quenched. The negotiations with Egypt would of course be broken off or lapse, but the evacuation would be declared and would begin none the less, and the redeployment of our troops to the extent of an Armoured Division or 4 Brigades in the Middle East and Cyprus could begin and proceed as fast as convenient. There would be a regular series of troop movements organised as if they were operations of war, yet we should be asking no favours and breaking no treaty and only taking security measures [. . .] while giving even more than the Egyptians had asked in the Canal Zone, that the Sudan should not be molested during its trial period of government.

4. The Egyptians should at the same time be told that all fresh additional expense caused by riotous attacks on our troops or rearguards and all damage done to the installations of the obsolescent base would be charged against their Sterling balances.

5. It would take say a month to plan and put this into operation, and meanwhile the Tory 'rebels' should be told to have confidence in the Government which has a plan. There is no alternative except a prolonged humiliating scuttle before all the world, without advantage goodwill or fidelity from those Egyptian usurpers to whom triumph is being accorded.

Sir Winston S. Churchill to Anthony Eden
Prime Minister's Personal Minute M.332/53
(Premier papers, 11/635)

14 December 1953

Your PM/53/344. On careful consideration I do not think an explanation by the three or four you mention to the Foreign Affairs Committee should be given on Wednesday afternoon. The arguments we should have to use are not dissimilar in principle to those for which Bevan will have to defend himself in the Debate on Thursday. Shinwell in the *Daily Telegraph* is taking an anti-scuttle line. I will therefore content myself with telling the 1922 Committee at Luncheon on Wednesday that they must have confidence that we are not animated by fear or weakness, but only by the need of making a better deployment of our forces, and that in any case we are not going to be in any hurry. You need not therefore send Alex home.

About Khartoum. I am impressed with the Mahdi's message. The hand must be played in such a way as to encourage him in the best way. There will be time enough to write to Howe.

I hope your work in Paris is going well.

Cabinet: conclusions
(Cabinet papers, 128/26)

14 December 1953	Prime Minister's Room
Secret	House of Commons
6.45 p.m.	
Cabinet Meeting No. 78 of 1953	

[. . .]

2. The Prime Minister said that it had been suggested to him that, before the Foreign Affairs debate on 17th December, there should be a meeting of the Conservative Party's Defence Committee at which Ministers concerned

could explain the military background to the policy which the Government were pursuing in the current defence negotiations with Egypt. He understood that such a meeting might well be attended by as many as 200 Government supporters and, if this was so, the suggestion seemed to him to have serious disadvantages. There would not be the same objection to the holding of a small private meeting at which the Minister of Defence, possibly with General Sir Brian Robertson, could explain the situation to four of five of those Government supporters who felt particularly strongly on this issue and who, it was known, might decide to table a motion upon it. He had agreed to speak at a luncheon arranged by the 1922 Committee on 16th December, and he might take that opportunity to assure Government supporters generally that the Government's policy in the negotiations was not in any way based on fear of what the Egyptians might do but on a realistic appraisal of our own interests, and he could appeal to them to have faith that the Government would continue to handle the situation with firmness and cool judgment. He could mention at the same time that steps were being taken to explain the military aspects of the problem, in confidence, to a small number of those who were concerning themselves most closely with the subject. In view of the many other important topics to be covered in the debate on 17th December it seemed unlikely that much time would be devoted on that occasion to the defence negotiations with Egypt. In any event those Government supporters who were dissatisfied on this issue hardly seemed likely to resort to extreme courses, at least on that occasion. When the Government's policy came to be fully debated in the House, he would be both able and anxious to expound the powerful military arguments which could be adduced in support of it.

In discussion there was support for the view that there was both widespread ignorance and dissatisfaction on this issue among Government supporters in the House of Commons and that, if a motion critical of the Government were tabled, it might well attract a number of signatures. There was no doubt that those Government supporters who were exercised about this matter held very strong views upon it, and could not necessarily be relied on to refrain from causing acute embarrassment to the Government. In these circumstances the situation could not adequately be met by explaining the military background to four or five of the more prominent Government supporters concerned. On the other hand, there were certainly objections to explaining even the facts underlying the Government's policy to as many as 200 Government supporters at this stage. If the meeting of Government supporters could be confined to members of the Party's Defence Committee, the number might possibly be restricted to about 80. Alternatively, it might be possible to arrange a private dinner, at which attendance might be restricted to about 30 Members. Such a gathering might be presided over by the Lord Privy Seal and addressed by the Minister of Defence. The Cabinet were informed that General Sir Brian Robertson had expressed his willingness to meet Government supporters during the first half of the present week and explain the situation to them, although he considered that, if he met any substantial number of Government supporters for this purpose, he ought also to offer to meet Labour Members.

The Prime Minister said that he was not convinced that the tabling of a motion by those Government supporters who were uneasy about the possible outcome of the negotiations with Egypt would seriously embarrass the Government. Indeed, the tabling of a motion and the support which would no doubt be forthcoming for it from Conservative Members would serve as a timely reminder to the Egyptian Government that the United Kingdom Government also had to consider Parliamentary and public opinion. At the same time, if it was the general view of the Cabinet that steps should be taken to try to arrange a meeting of modest size at which the military background to the defence negotiations could be explained to Government supporters, he would not wish to press his objections to that course.

The Cabinet –

Invited the Lord Privy Seal and the Chief Whip to explore further, and report to the Prime Minister upon, the possibility of arranging before the Foreign Affairs debate on 16th December a private meeting to be attended by a strictly limited number of Government supporters at which the military facts underlying the Government's policy in the current defence negotiations with Egypt could be explained by the Minister of Defence and possibly by General Sir Brian Robertson.

Sir Winston S. Churchill to President Dwight D. Eisenhower
(*Premier papers, 11/1074*)

14 December 1953
Top Secret
Private and Personal

My dear friend,

I am so glad that the Russians seem to be ready to give your far reaching scheme more reasonable consideration than first appeared.[1] Thank you for your letter, it was very pleasant seeing you again. All good wishes.

---

[1] In his 'Atoms for Peace' speech of Dec. 8 before the UN, Eisenhower called for less secrecy and more transparency regarding atomic weapons technology. The speech laid the ideological groundwork for the creation of the IAEA and the Treaty on Non-Proliferation of Nuclear Weapons. It can be read in full online at the websites of the IAEA and the Eisenhower Archive. On Dec. 9, Moscow Radio called Eisenhower's speech 'warmongering'.

December 1953

Sir Winston S. Churchill to President Dwight D. Eisenhower
Prime Minister's Personal Telegram T.308/53
(Premier papers, 11/1074)

16 December 1953
Emergency
Top Secret, Private and Personal
No. 5289

My dear Friend,

I have to tell the House of Commons tomorrow about our meeting and I send you a draft of what I have prepared on atomic affairs. I hope that you only need to send me an OK as time is so very short before I speak at 3.30 p.m. GMT tomorrow Thursday.

2. I have included nothing of what I shall say about our talks and interchanges upon your UNO Speech as I am giving full support to your inspiring lead and trying to persuade the Bear to stop growling. I shall make it clear that I no more write your Speeches than you write mine and I expect to stave off questions about the untruthful press rumours of which there have certainly been no lack.

3. I shall defend Foster for speaking frankly to the French in Paris about EDC. Anthony and I both believe the secondary reaction may be favourable.

President Dwight D. Eisenhower to Sir Winston S. Churchill
Prime Minister's Personal Telegram T.309/53
(Premier papers, 11/1074)

16 December 1953
Top Secret

Dear Sir Winston,

Just this minute I received your cable and immediately consulted with Admiral Strauss. He points out that the last sentence of your first paragraph is somewhat in error because the agreement on this point was firmed and announced here several weeks before the Bermuda talks took place.

Admiral Strauss also suggests that before you make your talk you consult again with Lord Cherwell about the final two sentences. He feels that Lord Cherwell might want you to be very general and indefinite in talking about a possible White Paper.

Having said all the above, I assure you that we have no objection to the paper.

Sir Winston S. Churchill: speech
(Hansard)

17 December 1953 House of Commons

FOREIGN AFFAIRS

The curious fact that the House prefers to give two days to the television White Paper and only one day to foreign affairs may be noted by future historians as an example of a changing sense of proportion in modern thought. It is, however, also a proof of how great a measure of agreement exists between our established parties on the present handling of foreign affairs. I shall not, therefore, need to consume much time in a debate which we are told may also have among its features the explanation of the right hon. Member for Ebbw Vale (Mr Bevan) of his latest journalistic activities, and, possibly, his further reproof at the hands of the right hon. Member for Easington (Mr Shinwell).

Our relations with the United States, the international structure of Europe, our attitude towards the mighty power of Russia, and even the future of atomic energy and atomic weapons must indeed be dealt with, but I shall try not to allow them to bulk too largely upon our limited and crowded time. My right hon. Friend the Foreign Secretary will wind up the debate and will endeavour, when he presents his general survey, to supply all the gaps or details which I may omit. He, too, must keep his eye on the clock.

The Egyptian question raises differences among all shades of opinion on both sides of the House. I do not feel any sense of hurry. When last I spoke on foreign affairs, on 11th May,[1] the Egyptians had broken off their formal conference with us and were indulging in a cataract of most offensive threats. I said on that occasion: 'Naturally, we do not wish to keep indefinitely 80,000 men at a cost of, it might be, over £50 million a year discharging the duty which has largely fallen upon us, and us alone, of safeguarding the interests of the free nations in the Middle East, and also of preserving the international waterway of the Suez Canal.' Further, on the same occasion, I said: 'Our hope is that negotiations will be resumed. In the meanwhile, we may await the development of events with the composure which follows from the combination of patience with strength.' That is what we have done. Since then, informal discussions have been resumed, but I made it clear at Bermuda that there was no prospect of any modification of our position. There has been this flood of insults and boasting and a constant stream of minor outrages; otherwise, no change has taken place. We remain convinced, however, that it is in our interests, military and financial, to procure a redeployment of our forces in North Africa and the Middle East.

---

[1] Speech reproduced above (pp. 1262–3).

On some future occasion I may, perhaps, be able to welcome an opportunity of dealing with this subject fully, but I shall not attempt to do so today. All that I can say is that our action will be based on a careful and faithful study of the merits of the problem, and will not be dictated either by the violence of our foreign enemies or by the pressure of some of our best friends. (Hon. Members: 'Oh'.) There is no vitality in a party unless there are differences of opinion. (Hon. Members: 'Hear, hear'.)

I was very glad to bring about the conference at Bermuda, although it was largely my fault that it was delayed for six months. I felt it most important that I should have long, intimate, secret talks with President Eisenhower, with whom I have worked on terms of close and growing friendship for over 11 years, about a lot of things which are easily settled if Britain and the United States understand one another and are in accord. We had some good talks.

I use the word 'secret', by which I mean that everything said is not the subject of what is called a 'handout' or even 'guidance' to the world Press every evening, or necessarily embodied in a communiqué at the end. The results of conferences or private talks of this character should be conveyed to Parliament in the regular manner – as I am doing now – and should also manifest themselves not so much in words as in policy and action and improved relations as the months go by. This is, no doubt, very hard upon the Press. Having earned my livelihood by writing for them from my youth up, I have keen sympathy for them, but I am afraid they have got to realise that the tendency for keeping the world Press out of international conferences between heads of States or Governments is likely to increase with the march of time.

Science confronts us with fearful problems, yet at the same time marvellous improvements in locomotion have rendered personal intercourse between responsible people easy and swift to an extent never known before. If such a meeting as we had at Bermuda – I travelled back in 11 hours of flying time – or as, I hope, we are going to have in Berlin next month could have taken place between Germany, Austria, France, Russia and ourselves in 1914, as Sir Edward Grey desired, after the murder of the Archduke[1] at Sarajevo, I believe, having lived through it all rather near the centre, that the First World War might have been, if not prevented, at any rate delayed, even though any communiqué published at the end of the conference would very likely have been both cryptic and platitudinous. This would not have applied in the same degree to the Second World War, because we were dealing with a ferocious maniac by whom the German nation, to its sorrow, had allowed itself to be gripped.

Now in every land the prime desire is for peace, not only in the hearts of the people, but I believe in the hearts, as it is certainly in the interests, of their

---

[1] Franz Ferdinand Carl Ludwig Joseph Maria, 1863–1914. Archduke of Austria-Este. Heir presumptive to the Austro-Hungarian throne, 1896. Assassinated by Gavrilo Princip, 28 June 1914, setting off the train of events that culminated in the outbreak of WWI.

Governments and rulers, and there will have to be many patient international conferences. The object of these will be to look at all we have in common as well as at our many differences. We must not expect too much of any of these conferences. We must cherish the hope of taking the nations out of the rut of machine-made haggling. Success will in all cases best be measured by easement rather than by headlines. I expect I shall be somewhat scolded for saying these things, but in old age popularity does not seem to be as important as in the days of youth, while, on the other hand, a little abuse on occasions may prove a necessary and invigorating stimulus.

With these introductory words, let me say that I went to Bermuda hoping to render ever more cordial and lively the vital relations between Britain and the United States. It would be a great pity if these were to be increasingly expressed in what I may call McCarthy–Bevanite terms. It would be very discreditable to the English-speaking world and disastrous to the whole world if this particular manifestation were to be regarded as other than a proof of our faith on both sides of the Ocean that in free communities free speech, however misused, can find its own correctives. It may be that the case I have mentioned will in the end prove the crowning example of the way democracy can overcome many of the necessary evils which it has to suffer in its progress.

At any rate, I can assure the House that the first object of the Bermuda Conference was to nourish Anglo-American friendship and co-operation; and that, I am sure, has been achieved. It was also a great pleasure to me and my right hon. Friend to welcome our French friends and to meet M Bidault again, and for me for the first time to make the acquaintance of M Laniel.

M Laniel's very clear statement on his return to France effectively disposed of a lot of gossip and rumours, quite unfounded, which appeared in some French newspapers. I do not need to refer to them today. I must make it clear, however, that I learned in Bermuda that if EDC were not ratified without undue delay by the French, the alternative solution of a wider NATO, including Germany, to which I had looked in this deplorable contingency, was likely to be beset by many difficulties, possibly by even fatal difficulties. There are many in the United States who share Dr Adenauer's objections to the creation of a German national army, and, of course, President Eisenhower attaches the utmost importance to the formation of a European Army on the lines worked out after so much discussion and delay, and to which he has given such important personal service.

It was evident that the question of what might happen if EDC were not accepted by the French had become for the time being unanswerable. I thought it my duty to give warning to our French friends at the conference of the gravity of the situation which might then occur. Germany must make her military contribution to the safety of Europe. We cannot, in any case, expect a robust and valiant people of 60 million to rest unarmed and defenceless in an unstable Europe for an indefinite period of time. These facts have got to be faced whether any of us in any country like them or not. All this has now been discussed in Paris. My right hon. Friend will be in a position to give a direct account to the House later in the debate of the work of NATO and the recent conference.

Mr Foster Dulles has stated in public the facts which were in my mind after having learned very plainly what the American position was. The phrase used by Mr Foster Dulles about the situation possibly having to be 'agonisingly reappraised' seemed to me most formidable. I must say personally that when the safety of France, indeed of Europe, depends upon the policy of the United States, all the possible consequences of abandoning EDC should be placed squarely before the French people. I should not like it to be slurred over as a matter of little importance. It is of vital importance.

I must make it clear, however, that at Bermuda I was not trying to convince M Bidault or M Laniel of the need for EDC; they are both ardent patriots who fought in the Resistance, and both have argued the case for EDC in the French Chamber. The French Chamber, divided into so many parties, with all their intricate convictions and rivalries, may well find it difficult to come to any decision in favour of the policy which was so largely their own idea and in the hopes of which the wider security of Western Europe has been delayed for over three years.

At Bermuda I made it clear that we should keep our troops on the Continent at least as long as the American troops were kept there. I am still hopeful of a favourable solution for our difficulties, and I do not propose this afternoon to expatiate more than I have done, which is only suggestively, upon the various gloomy possibilities which imagination can so readily suggest. Hon. Members in all parts of the House have, I am sure, given enough thought and study to these matters to be able to speculate about them for themselves, though I hope these will not be their only thoughts during the Christmas festivities.

We were very glad that the Russians had at last accepted our invitation to meet us on the problems of Germany and Austria early in the New Year. We had no difficulty in agreeing among ourselves that this meeting should be held in Berlin, as proposed by the Soviet Government, and we suggested that it should begin on 4th January. We have not so far received their reply.

I used the opportunity of the conference to emphasise the view which I expressed here on 11th May that the Soviet Union is entitled to assurances against aggression after what she suffered at Hitler's hands. I think I was successful in impressing upon my colleagues at Bermuda the justice and the advantage of such a course, even though Russian strength is so vast. It is my hope that from the Berlin meeting there may emerge some means of providing the Russians with a sense of security arising from other facts than mere force. The whole world is in need of that.

Apart from the formal meetings of the three Powers, we took the opportunity of holding informal bilateral talks on matters of concern only to two of us. There were talks between the Americans and the French and between ourselves and the French as well as talks between ourselves and the Americans. As was to be expected, much of our time was devoted to the discussion of current difficulties in the Far East and South-East Asia. It is no secret that in this part of the world there have been some divergences of policy between the Western Powers. We discussed such questions as trade with China, recognition of the Chinese Communist Government, the admission of China to the United Nations organisation, Korean problems and even such awkward personalities as Syngman Rhee and Chiang Kai-shek. I hope I shall not tempt hon. Members in any part of the House to ask questions which in the present circumstances it would not be in the public interest for me to answer.

However, I can assure the House that on all these difficult problems which have so often been discussed here and which play their part in questions and answers, we were very glad to have this opportunity of making our views clear to the United States Administration and were grateful to them for the attention with which they heard us, even when they did not entirely agree. It would certainly be a great gain if there could be a rather close alignment of policies in this part of the world, and I hope that at Bermuda we may have laid foundations on which we can build with advantage over the coming months.

We naturally did not overlook questions connected with Persia and Trieste. About Persia I have only a word to say, but it is easier for me to talk about it than it is for the Foreign Secretary, because he deserves a compliment on the subject. Old friends like Britain and Persia sometimes have estrangements, but it is not right that these should continue for longer than need be. I am sure, therefore, that the House would wish to express its pleasure at the resumption of diplomatic relations with Persia and will join me in paying tribute to the perseverance of my right hon. Friend which, together with good will in Teheran, has ended the breach which has wasted so much Persian and British wealth.

Now I come to Trieste, which we also examined in the tripartite talks. Let me first welcome the steps which the Italian and Yugoslav Governments have agreed to take to bring the situation on their common frontier back to normal. This we regard as a happy augury for the success of the efforts which the Foreign Secretary, in close collaboration with the American Secretary of State and the French Foreign Minister, has devoted to solving this stubborn problem. I have no doubt that, given time and good will, he and his distinguished colleagues will succeed in their task.

For what is our interest in this quarter? It is simply to withdraw our troops in conditions which will consolidate the forces of peace in that area and enable us to co-operate still more closely with our two friends whom this problem divides. We offered a solution which we thought both would accept. We are striving now to bring them to the conference table on mutually acceptable terms. It is our hope, and I think I might go so far as to say our expectation

– we have to be awfully careful in these foreign affairs, but I think I can say our expectation – that they may find a way of reconciling their national interests with the requirements of international peace.

I was asked a question on the next subject this afternoon, and I am now proceeding to answer it. I discussed with the President a number of points about the atomic problem affecting our two countries. Lord Cherwell made definite progress in the autumn when the Americans agreed to exchange information with us about the effects on various targets of atomic explosions. As they have made 43 atomic tests against our three, they have a great deal of knowledge of these matters, so that this agreement is of considerable value. I hope that it will soon be put into effect. It was what may be called ratified at Bermuda, but it was made beforehand, and I hope that it will soon be put into effect.

The other important matter we discussed was the exchange of information on intelligence matters. We hope to enlarge the area over which these exchanges can take place without in any way infringing the McMahon Act which has so often prevented co-operation between our two countries. It is this Act, of course, which sets limits to the exchange of technical information. But this is all getting into an easier atmosphere.

We in Britain have already discovered almost as much as our American allies, and it is probably true that our Russian fellow mortals – because that is what they are – may well know almost as much as either of us. At any rate, I hope that results will in due course become apparent which will bring Britain and the United States into closer, more agreeable and more fertile relationship upon atomic knowledge.

Secondly, the President and I have asked Lord Cherwell and Admiral Strauss, who are very good friends and may in some ways be considered opposite numbers, to prepare a record of the history of Anglo-American co-operation in the atomic field since the subject first cropped up during the war. When this compilation is completed, the President and I will consult together about publication, of course guided by our Governments.

The right hon. Gentleman the Leader of the Opposition need not be at all concerned, because I am sure it will be shown that any error which could be attributed to him in negotiations was eventually and largely repaired by the technical activities which he promoted, in spite of the parliamentary lapses which have entailed, and which, as one who admires the causes for which Hampden[1] died in the field and Pym[2] upon the scaffold, naturally cause me painful reflection. However, we are in many ways following the precedent he has set.

---

[1] John Hampden, 1595–1643. Leading politician and soldier in the Parliamentary cause before and during the English Civil War.

[2] John Pym, 1584–1643. Leading political figure in the Parliamentary cause before and during the English Civil War. Died in fact not on the scaffold but from illness, possibly cancer of the bowel.

After the President's arrival, in one of our earliest talks, he informed me of his intentions to deliver a speech to the United Nations on a new proposal for the future of atomic energy for industrial or for peaceful purposes. He gave me a copy of this document upon the policy of which many months of American thought in the highest circles had been concentrated. I asked his permission to show it to Lord Cherwell. Mr Dulles had already given a copy to my right hon. Friend.

When I had received Lord Cherwell's report – and I had only a very short time to do it in – I wrote to the President saying I welcomed his proposal, as I thought it ended a long period of deadlock and might afford an opportunity for contact with the Soviets on the highest level. I suggested one or two alterations, not of course in the theme but in the preliminary and surrounding matter. I discussed with the President, but I was not aware when he left Bermuda what alterations he would make.

While we were at Bermuda all sorts of statements were made by the Press, whose fertility and imagination were remarkable. On the one hand, I was charged with trying to prevent the President from making his speech and, on the other, with having largely written it for him. I brought home the two opposite efforts, published in the clearest terms, in case the House should manifest any interest in this form of public entertainment. I can assure the House that I would never presume to write a speech for the President – I have quite enough trouble to make up my own. I did not see any of the Press myself or attempt to correct their stories; I thought it better to reserve this simple factual account for the House.

I consider this speech of the President as one of the most important events in world history since the end of the war. A few weeks ago, I spoke to the House about the ever-increasing destructive power which has now come into human hands, and also about the almost limitless material benefits which science can for the first time give to a peaceful age. As I meditated on the President's proposals, limited though they are in scope, and shrouded in technicalities as they are for laymen, I could not help feeling that we were in the process of what might prove to be a turning point in our destiny. I fervently hope that the Soviet Government will not ignore this beam of light through much darkness and confusion. I am sure of the sincerity and altruistic good will by which it was inspired, and I trust that they will advance with the confidence to which their own strength entitles them along a path which certainly leads in the direction of expanding the welfare and calming the fears of the masses of the people of all the world.

Cabinet: conclusions
(Cabinet papers, 128/26)

18 December 1953
Secret
3 p.m.
Cabinet Meeting No. 80 of 1983

1. The Foreign Secretary said that there were some indications that the Egyptian Government might be contemplating a course of action hostile to our interests. This might possibly be the conclusion of a non-aggression pact with the Soviet Union, or further attacks upon our forces in the Canal Zone, or penal measures against British subjects living in Egypt. In this event it might be right to break off the defence negotiations and to stand upon our rights under the 1936 Treaty, which did not expire until 1956. We should then proceed in our own time with the re-deployment of our forces in the Middle East. He did not propose to give any advance warning to the Egyptian Government but simply to await further action on their part or further approaches for a resumption of defence negotiations.

The Cabinet –

(1) Took note of the Foreign Secretary's statement.

The Chief Whip reported that the explanations given by the Minister of Defence and the speech made by the Foreign Secretary in the debate on the previous day had failed to allay the anxieties of the group of Government supporters in the House of Commons who were concerned about the Government's Egyptian policy. They were not proposing to withdraw their motion and there was some reason to believe that they would continue to express public dissatisfaction with the Government's policy.

The Prime Minister said that he hoped that Conservative Members of Parliament would be dissuaded from accepting the invitation of General Neguib to visit Egypt at the expense of the Egyptian Government. It would be lacking in dignity to accept hospitality from a Government which had encouraged acts of hostility against British troops and indulged in abusive propaganda against this country. If government supporters wished to visit Egypt at their own expense that was a matter for them. He suggested that the Chief Whip should write to the Members concerned inviting them with the Prime Minister's authority to refrain from availing themselves of General Neguib's invitation.

The Cabinet –

(2) Invited the Chief Whip to make known to the Conservative Members of Parliament concerned the Cabinet's wish that they should not accept the hospitality of the Egyptian Government at this juncture.

[. . .]

John Foster Dulles to Sir Winston S. Churchill
Prime Minister's Personal Telegram T.311/53
(Premier papers, 11/618)

19 December 1953

Please advise Sir Winston Churchill my appreciation of his clear statement to the House on necessity of facing up to EDC.[1]

Sir Winston S. Churchill to President Dwight D. Eisenhower
Prime Minister's Personal Telegram T.310/53
(Premier papers, 11/618)

19 December 1953
Immediate
Top Secret, Private and Personal
No. 5334

My dear Friend,

1. I am very much worried at the idea of the grant of American economic aid to Egypt at a time when our differences with them are so acute. It would, I am sure, have a grave effect in this country on Anglo-American relations. The Socialist Opposition would use it to urge us to press for the inclusion of Red China in UNO and might class it with trade to that country upon which subject McCarthy's unjust charges are already much resented. The frontier of the Suez Canal Zone shows very much the same conditions of unrest and potential warfare as does the frontier in Korea. So much for the Opposition. On our Conservative side too we have a disturbed and increasingly angered section who could at any time cancel our modest majority. They would not, I think do that but the fact ought not to be ignored.

2. Whether in your policies and immense responsibilities you would get much help from a Socialist Government, I shall not attempt to predict, and it would not be my business anyhow. What I fear, however, is that the offended Conservatives might add their voices to that section of the Socialist Party who criticize the United States. In fact I think there would be a considerable outpouring which of course would be used in America by all who are hostile to the unity of action of the English-Speaking World. This would make more difficult the solving of those large problems which occupy your mind and in which I do all I can to help. I ask you to think over this particular proposal about Egypt with due regard to its setting in the general picture, which may be out of proportion to your interest or ours. We have not the slightest intention

[1] Churchill wrote to the British Embassy in Washington the following day: 'Will you please convey to Mr Dulles my thanks for his appreciative message. I am very glad I was a help to him. I send him my good wishes.'

of making any more concessions to Egypt after all we have done in these long negotiations, and fighting might easily occur at any moment.

3. I have had a nice message from Foster about the support which I gave to his blunt but salutary statement in Paris about the agonising re-appraisal. If EDC is repudiated by the French, I still think some variant of NATO will be necessary. After all, this meets the French objection to being in a European Association alone or almost alone with a much more powerful Germany. I think you would find it very difficult to make and get a good plan on the 'empty chair' basis.

4. Kind regards.

Sir Norman Brook to Sir Winston S. Churchill
(Premier papers, 11/597)

21 December 1953

TELEVISION

Now that both Houses of Parliament have approved the main principles outlined in the White Paper, the Government can afford to make some concessions on points of detail in the preparation of the Bill. After Christmas, consultations ought to be held with some at any rate of those who have taken a prominent part in this controversy. The BBC have offered their technical help and should be given an opportunity of stating their views: Lord Halifax and Lord Waverley may have points to raise: and the Leaders of the Opposition Parties might well be seen, now that the principles have been established. The Chancellor of the Exchequer, who has discussed this with me, feels that the Government could now adopt a more accommodating attitude on the detail.

2. All this can hardly be left to the Postmaster-General; it needs to be supervised by a senior member of the Cabinet.

The Chancellor of the Exchequer has handled this up to now; but he will be away for a month in Australia and would in any event wish to be relieved of this burden now that he has so much else on his hands.

I understand that the Lord President would be willing to undertake the task, if you so desired. He would certainly take a balanced view – for, while he has committed himself in the House of Lords to the principles of the Government's plan, he has no personal enthusiasm for commercial television.

3. I therefore suggest that you should appoint a small Cabinet Committee, under the Lord President's Chairmanship, to supervise the preparation of the necessary legislation.

In constituting this, you will have it in mind that the Assistant Postmaster-General will need the help of a Minister of Cabinet rank in handling the eventual legislation in the House of Commons. Apart from a speech by a senior member of the Government in the Second Reading debate, Mr Gammans will also need continuing help in the Committee Stage. I suggest that this should be given by some Minister not heavily burdened with other work – e.g. Mr Peake or Mr Macleod.

4. There was previously a Cabinet Committee on Television Policy under the Chancellor's Chairmanship. Its composition is shown in Annex A. But, if the Chancellor is now to give this up and a new House of Commons Minister is to be brought in, there is much to be said for wiping the slate clean and starting afresh. We are, after all, entering a new phase of this subject.

5. I therefore suggest that the new Cabinet Committee on Television might be composed as follows:
Lord President (Chairman)
Commonwealth Secretary
Minister of Pensions or Minister of Health
Postmaster-General
Financial Secretary, Treasury
Assistant Postmaster-General

6. If you agree with these proposals, you may care to send a Minute to Lord Salisbury on the lines of the attached draft (Annex B).

President Dwight D. Eisenhower to Sir Winston S. Churchill
Prime Minister's Personal Telegram T.314/53
(Premier papers, 11/1074)

21 December 1953
Emergency
Dedip
Top Secret
No. 2753

My Dear Winston.

You are so well aware of my convictions as to the necessity for sound and friendly Anglo-American relations that you must keenly realize the concern I feel over the sombre tone of your cabled message.[1]

Because it is a personal communication I am answering in the same fashion, without waiting to call together the State Department staffs which will be, of course, deeply interested in what you have to say. I shall hope to get this cable off to you the first thing Monday morning so that I may have your further observations on certain delicate phases of this matter.

In considering our common interests in various areas, I am, of course, anxious to take into consideration your particular political problems and to

[1] T.310/53, reproduced above (pp. 1367–8).

adjust our activities so as best to accommodate your position so long as this leads toward a satisfactory solution. We likewise have our political problems. For example our aid programme for the Mid-East was drawn up and was approved by the Congress on the basis that there would be a reasonable division of aid between Israel and Arab countries.

Since we have already made allocations to Israel we have little excuse to avoid moving in the case of the Arab countries, but as you know, at your request we have not only withheld military aid from Egypt, but have likewise postponed several times the initiation of economic aid.

You state that the Socialist opposition would be bitterly resentful of American economic aid to Egypt because of the American objection to trade with Communist China. It has been my understanding that Britain has continued to carry on trade in economic non-strategic items with Red China, and we do not now propose more with respect to Egypt than beginning to help develop its economy. Consequently, I am at a loss to understand the basis on which the Socialists could make a logical attack. You likewise mention that the opposition would resent any economic aid to Egypt so bitterly that they would urge you to press for inclusion of Red China in the United Nations. By implication this would seem to mean that if we do not (repeat not) extend economic aid to Egypt, you are prepared to stand firm with us in opposing the inclusion of the bloody Chinese aggressor into the councils of peaceful nations, at least until Red China withdraws her invading armies, ceases supporting the Indo-China war and begins to act like a civilized Government. Could you confirm this to me?

I assume, of course, that you are genuinely anxious to arrange a truce with Egypt and that the only remaining obstacles are the two points you mentioned to me at Bermuda, namely availability and uniforms. Now if we continue to press Egypt to accept your conditions on these two points, can we do so with the assurance that they can count on a settlement if they accept your position? You can well understand my anxiety to avoid asking our people to do everything in their power to bring about a settlement of this situation, including another postponement of economic aid, and then discover that we have been operating on a complete misunderstanding.

As I told you at Bermuda, I am most deeply sympathetic with your whole problem in the area, even though at times I have believed that different methods might have been more effective. I repeat that in our actual dealings with Egypt, we have gone to great lengths to meet your convictions and opinions. We certainly want to continue to do so. We think we proved that in Persia, and I hope we shall together make that effort seem worth while.

I know that you realize that there are in this country many people who believe that the United States has treated the Arab countries shabbily and, because parts of the Arab holdings are vital to the Western World, this segment of our citizenry asserts that we should work to improve our relationships with the Arab countries. But this Government had always refused to do this at the cost of anything we believed detrimental to Anglo-American best interests. In spite of outrageous and irresponsible criticism of each other on both sides of the Atlantic, American governmental policy and popular sentiment recognize the great value to the free world of keeping Anglo-American relationships co-ordinated with respect to the rest of the world and friendly as between themselves.

Now a word about EDC. I appreciate what you say about the 'empty chair' idea, and I am quick to agree. But I re-state my conviction that any, and I repeat any, projected alternative to EDC will present problems no less acute and difficult to solve. All the treaties made with West Germany and ratified in that country on the so-called contractual theory are based upon the premise that EDC will come into being. To scrap that work and to start again, particularly at a time when some dissatisfaction seems to be growing in West Germany and while increased Russian pressures are constantly exerted against our European friends, would be dangerous in the extreme. On the other hand, I believe that if we, and by we I mean you and I and the Governments we head, continue to press earnestly, sincerely and constantly for the enactment of EDC, we shall get it. I shall make another public statement on this matter as soon as France elects a President, and I shall continue to do so as opportunity presents itself.

I hope that you can find it possible to answer this personal cable promptly so that I can assemble the necessary staffs and go over this whole matter in detail. I assure you that I am prepared to meet locally any political difficulty in carrying out whatever arrangements we may make between ourselves for the common good of our two countries.

I realize that this is long and possibly a tedious cablegram. But it is quite necessary that there be the clearest kind of understanding between us if we are at one and the same time to operate together in some of these critical situations abroad and still be able to withstand any kind of political problem and criticism that can arise in our respective countries.

I shall look forward to early receipt of your comments.

Sir Winston S. Churchill to President Dwight D. Eisenhower
Prime Minister's Personal Telegram T.315/53
(Premier papers, 11/618)

22 December 1953
Emergency
Deyou
Top Secret, Private and personal
No. 5366

My dear Friend,

1. Thank you for all the thought you have given to my message. It is always difficult to explain the internal politics of one country to another and I have not succeeded this time. I did not say or mean that the Socialists would be bitterly resentful of American economic aid to Egypt at this juncture. Indeed on this narrow issue they might be more favourably inclined to your proposal than we are. They would however be able to press their strong views and feelings about China in an atmosphere much less favourable to the United States than now exists.

2. If the Egyptians accept our present terms, we shall certainly abide by them. But we do not think you ought to give them moral and material support while they threaten and assault our troops and conduct a campaign of hatred against us. No doubt the Egyptian issue seems petty to you in comparison with the other great questions, including China, confronting us both. It is nevertheless one which might well cause a deep and serious setback to the relations between America and Great Britain. That would certainly be a disaster for all.

3. Whether you take sides against us in Egypt or not will not affect the support which we have thought it right to give you over China. It will, however, make it more difficult for Anthony and me to help you in the Far East if we have to do it in the face, not only of Socialist opinion, but of general feeling of indignation throughout the country. I earnestly hope the United States Government will not so act as to let it be said that their intervention has wrecked any chances of agreement in Egypt and possibly has even caused bloodshed.

4. There are, however, few things we cannot do together. After all, we were your good comrades in the War. 50,000 British graves lie in Egypt and its approaches. We were virtually agreed together on the detailed proposals about the base and had we put them jointly to Neguib, all might well have been settled six months ago. Our being on opposite sides in the Mediterranean will gird on every enemy we have in common throughout the world.

I feel I should not be doing my duty if I did not let you know what I believe to be the truth of the matter.

5. About EDC. We shall, as I told you, do our utmost to press and persuade the French to ratify, and I still hope they may. But we must consider the alternatives if they fail and I am glad to know how your thought is moving. I will

write to you further about this when there is a respite from the French political confusion.

6. I thought it likely that the Soviet would take advantage of your valiant and wise attempt to take a step, albeit a small one, forward from the shrewd, Baruch deadlock. There are several not unhelpful things which they say and I still have hopes of progress if only we are content with small results for a beginning.

Sir Winston S. Churchill to Sir Norman Brook
Prime Minister's Personal Minute M.336/53[1]
(Premier papers, 11/597)

22 December 1953

Three Peers, two in the Cabinet; no Cabinet Minister from the Commons. This does not look suitable to deal with what is after all to be a House of Commons fight. Lord Salisbury has the whole atomic problem on him and is often ill. I think the Lord Privy Seal as Leader of the House would be better and a new eye might be welcome – say, Mr Sandys. The Home Secretary has been a key figure and he likes work. He should certainly be asked. I think the Minister of Health should be preferred to the Minister of Pensions. Otherwise I agree.

Record of a luncheon
(Premier papers, 11/668)

23 December 1953   Chequers

Present: The Prime Minister and Lady Churchill
           The Soviet Ambassador (Mr Malik)
           Mr Rodionov[2]
           Sir Walter Monckton
           Captain Soames
           Mr Colville

The Prime Minister proposed the toast of 'More cows and less cannons'. He impressed on Mr Malik that the world needed opportunities for peaceful scientific development which could only be brought about by the lessening of tension and decrease of armaments. His whole weight and influence in the years remaining to him would be thrown on the side of easement in the

---

[1] In response to Sir Norman Brook's minute of Dec. 21, reproduced above (pp. 1368–9).
[2] Georgiy Mikhailovich Rodionov, 1915–?. Chargé d'Affaires, Soviet Embassy in London, ?–1954. 1st Secretary, Soviet Embassy in London, 1954–?. Soviet Ambassador to New Zealand, 1956–60; to Ghana, 1962–6.

relations between East and West. But it was a mistake to think that everything could be done at once. Endless patience was required and we should be content with gradual improvements, growth of understanding and the removal of small difficulties. There was a great opportunity for this process to begin in Berlin and he hoped that the Russians would not allow themselves to be put off by difficulties which might arise, or to break off negotiations because of apparent obstacles. If they did have to break off, let it be understood that this should be only for a year and the process of amelioration should continue steadily.

The Prime Minister said that everybody agreed that Russia should be freed from the fear of another aggression such as that which took place in 1941. Russia had the right to be shielded[1] safeguarded against another Hitler. It appeared from Mr Malik's comments that there was evidently misunderstanding about the Locarno idea and that Mr Malik thought that America would not be associated with any security assurance. The Prime Minister told him that this was definitely not his idea.

The Prime Minister said that he looked upon trade as a most fruitful method of breaking down barriers. Mr Malik said that he agreed but his Commercial Adviser had informed him that while opportunities for increased trade were available, the Board of Trade's attitude was negative and unhelpful.

The Prime Minister emphasized the importance of taking seriously President Eisenhower's proposal for an atomic pool.[2] He knew that this was a genuine suggestion and not a propaganda move. It really was not a trap but only a move a sincere attempt to transfer something from the warlike aspect of atomic power to the industrial aspect and thus to move gradually from one pedal to the other. It was an example of his thesis that from small beginnings greater results might come. Mr Malik said that he did not think the proposed American contribution was nearly sufficient and he gave the Russian view of the various efforts which they had made since the war to bring about a reduction in both atomic and conventional weapons. The Russians were convinced that no distinction both types should be made between such weapons dealt with.

Throughout the conversation, which lasted until 4.0 p.m., Mr Malik reverted on several occasions to Russian distrust of American motives. He said that some people in America, realising the difficulty of dispersing their production surplus, thought that they could only retain a healthy economic system by retaining warlike preparation. He accused the American Government and people of aggressive intentions and said he had told Mr Baruch and other influential American businessmen they ought to thank God for Russia

[1] The struck-through words and phrases reflect Churchill's amendments to this record.
[2] President Eisenhower had proposed in his 'Atoms for Peace' speech of Dec. 8 the formation of an international group of nations for the purpose of co-operating in the non-military applications of atomic energy.

since they were able to ascribe all the evil things that happened in the world to the Soviet Union. Why was America spending so much on armaments? With Canada to the north and Mexico to the south, the Atlantic Ocean to the East, and the Pacific to the West, they had nothing to fear in the way of aggression. These armaments were evidently not therefore for defensive but offensive purpose. The Prime Minister replied that the Americans had arrived at the summit of power and only wanted to do what was right. Neither the Russians nor anyone else had anything to fear from American aggression.

The Prime Minister emphasized several times that England and America were indissolubly united and that there was no chance of splitting them. They were as close together, had as much in common, as the Ukraine and White Russia. Mr Malik said that this was too close. The Prime Minister made it clear, however, that he had used, and would continue to use, his influence to persuade the United States to lower the barriers which had been raised as a result of Russian activities in the years after the war. Mr Malik asked whether at Bermuda there had been any such lowering of these barriers. The Prime Minister said that there had been no obvious results, but that he did think he had convinced the Americans of the Russian right to security assurances.

The Prime Minister said that as regards the satellites (which Mr Malik preferred to have described as 'the popular democracies') we had no intention of attempting to change things by war. We could wait for ten years and see how things developed and how the population of these countries felt in the meanwhile. Mr Malik said, with particular reference to Poland, that what the Prime Minister felt about the indissoluble unity of England and America was no less true of the Soviet Union and Poland. In reality Russia did not wish to export revolution. Communism and capitalism were the internal affairs of each country and should be left to their own choice. He had tried to impress this on Americans for more than four years without any apparent success.

The Prime Minister ended by asking Mr Malik to tell Mr Molotov and his friends in Moscow that the Prime Minister had nothing but good and peaceful intentions towards them, that he wanted to see friendship grow and that he wanted to impress upon them the importance of a gradual policy of easement and the folly of expecting to put everything right at a single stroke. He did not himself believe that war was at all probable for the next 25 years. It was too horrible to contemplate what it would be if it came. Mr Malik agreed and said that this was what Russia had felt for many years past. They had only wanted to abide by the Potsdam Agreement, they had never had anything but peaceful intentions and it was only the Americans who had distrusted their ideas and brought about this fear of war. The Prime Minister corrected this view by a brief resumé of post-war events and said that the past should be used not as a burden but as guidance. What mattered was the future and the slow improvement, which all the peoples desired and which might lead in due course to a world in which the marvels of science and invention could be used for the benefit of all men.

President Dwight D. Eisenhower to Sir Winston S. Churchill
Prime Minister's Personal Telegram T.316/53
(Premier papers, 11/1074)

23 December 1953
Immediate
Dedip
Top Secret
No. 2776

Dear Winston,

I have your reply[1] to my message. We shall study it and you will hear further from us, probably through the State Department. Foster knows that I am anxious to find a way for us to conform as far as possible to your views on Egypt. Of course you know of our conviction that if we can together reach a prompt and completely successful arrangement with Iran, this will immeasurably strengthen our hands here at home against any opponent seeking to weaken our support of the efforts you are making to reaching a proper arrangement in Egypt.

Merry Christmas to you and yours.

Sir Winston S. Churchill to President Dwight D. Eisenhower
Prime Minister's Personal Telegram T.317/53
(Premier papers, 11/1074)

25 December 1953
Emergency
Deyou
Top Secret, Personal and Private
No. 5410

1. Many thanks for your reply of December 23.
2. I saw Malik yesterday before he returns to Moscow. I impressed two things on him. First, that your atomic proposal was no mere propaganda move but a sincere attempt to break the deadlock, and though on a small scale might well achieve invaluable results and also open fruitful contacts. Secondly, there was no chance of splitting the English-speaking world, though we use our common language to argue about a lot of things.

[1] T.315/53, reproduced above (pp. 1372–3).

3. Coty[1] has for long been a keen supporter of the European Movement and has frequently spoken in favour of EDC. I think we might easily have got someone worse. Anyhow, no-one can now say that Foster's outspoken warning which I supported has done any harm.

It seems that in France in order to get on you have to be unknown. It is different in our two democracies where a certain amount of publicity is not necessarily always a drawback.

4. Clemmie and I send our best wishes to you both for a happy Christmas.

Sir Winston S. Churchill to Lady Churchill
(Baroness Spencer-Churchill papers)[2]

25 December 1953   Chequers

My darling Beloved Clemmie,

I hope you will ask Brendan to invest this for you. It may come in handy on some Christmas I shall not see.

How wonderfully you have organised it all this time! With all my fondest love

Your devoted husband
[Drawing of a pig]

Sir Winston S. Churchill to Anthony Eden
Prime Minister's Personal Minute M.349/53
(Premier papers, 11/484)

28 December 1953
Secret and Private

1. You have spoken to me at times about our breaking off negotiations with Egypt and doing what we think best for ourselves on the basis of 'all bets being off'. My thought has been moving along these lines. This would of course take the form of a time limit telling the Egyptians that our proposed terms had been before them for some months now and that they would only remain open for acceptance for, say, a month more. There is no doubt that from the point of view of prestige the fact that we had delivered such a warning, even if it resulted in the Egyptians accepting our terms, would make it appear to the world and especially to other countries in the Middle East such as Iraq, that we had forced them to accept our terms. It might look as if it were a victory

---

[1] Jules Gustave René Coty, 1884–1962. Educated at University of Caen. District Councillor, 1907–19. Communal Council, Le Havre, 1908–19. Member, Conseil Général of Seine-Inférieure, 1913–42; Vice-President, 1932–42; Deputy, Chamber of Deputies, 1923–36; Senator, 1936–44, 1948–53. Minister of Reconstruction and Urban Development, 1947–8. President of France, 1954–9.

[2] This letter was handwritten.

for us instead of for the Egyptians. This would also be of some value in Parliament and indeed throughout the country.

2. On the other hand we have asked the Americans to withhold their aid to Egypt on the grounds that we have promised to stand by the terms we have offered should the Egyptians accept them. We must be careful not to give the impression of deceiving the Americans. Bearing this in mind I have thought out this suggested time-table.

    3. (a) On or before January 1 the Americans say they will not give any aid until the Egyptians accept the terms we have offered.

    (b) When Parliament meets you make an announcement that unless by the middle of February the Egyptians accept our terms all our offers will be withdrawn. Perhaps you might tell the Americans you intend to do this a few days before.

    (c) On February 15 we regain our freedom. All negotiations lapse and we act towards Egypt in accordance with what we think are our long-term interests and Redeployment.

4. Of course there are many things which may happen to derange this programme. But I do not see what we stand to lose by giving the notice. If the Egyptians accept our terms it will look as if we have forced them into it. If they do not, then we have regained our freedom and we will be free to think again.

5. If the Americans refuse to withhold their aid, a more difficult situation will arise, which we can judge when the time comes.

Cabinet: conclusions
(Cabinet papers, 128/26)

29 December 1953
Secret
3 p.m.
Cabinet Meeting No. 81 of 1953

1. The Chancellor of the Exchequer recalled that under the terms of the Agreement made in 1951 Egypt was entitled to draw £5 millions of her sterling balances on 1st January in each year. An additional £10 millions could be drawn in the course of the year, and this was normally transferred to the account of the Bank of Egypt at the beginning of each year. Failure to release the £5 millions on 1st January would involve a direct breach of an international agreement and a consequent loss of confidence in sterling. He would prefer that the £10 millions should also be released on 1st January. On a previous occasion we had withheld this release for several months and this device of delay could doubtless be adopted again. The Bank of England, who would handle the transaction, could find means of imposing a short delay; but the

Government would find it embarrassing to explain the delay and it could not be justified for long.

The Prime Minister said that he was most reluctant to see this money paid to Egypt at a time when she was showing such hostility to us. He was particularly embarrassed at the thought that this should be done when, with the Foreign Secretary's concurrence, he had been pressing the President of the United States to delay the grant of economic aid to Egypt. If we now released sterling balances, as proposed by the Chancellor of the Exchequer, we might lay ourselves open to the reproach that we were trying to win from the Egyptians favours which we wished to deny to the United States.

The Foreign Secretary said that the United States Administration would appreciate the difference between the two transactions. We should be repaying debt in accordance with an international agreement; but the United States were being asked to postpone giving new money for development projects in Egypt which would bring benefits to American engineering contractors. He agreed with the Chancellor of the Exchequer that to withhold the promised instalments of Egypt's sterling balances might lead to a loss of confidence in sterling. It might, in particular, prompt other Arab countries, notably Kuwait, to withdraw sterling balances which were not governed by any formal agreement.

Discussion showed that it was the general view of the Cabinet that the £5 millions due on 1st January should be released in accordance with the terms of the Agreement. The further £10 millions should, however, be withheld for a time until it became possible to judge more clearly the probable course of the defence negotiations and of our general relations with Egypt.

The Cabinet –
  (1) Agreed that £5 millions of Egypt's blocked sterling balances should be released on 1st January, 1954, in accordance with the Sterling Releases Agreement.
  (2) Took note that the Chancellor of the Exchequer would arrange with the Governor of the Bank of England to defer for as long as possible the release of the further £10 millions due in 1954.

The Prime Minister said that he thought the time had now come to bring to a head the defence negotiations with Egypt. He suggested that, unless the Egyptian Government agreed in the very near future to accept our latest proposals, we should declare that after a specified date these proposals would lapse and we should regard ourselves as free to make our own plans. We should then begin to carry out a vigorous and effective redeployment of our forces in the Middle East.

The Minister of Defence suggested that, if negotiations broke down, we should at once begin to dismantle the Base and remove from it everything which could be removed regardless of its value. This might well take a year. In the meantime we should not reduce our forces by degrees but should, at a time of our own choosing, withdraw them all at the same time in a carefully planned military operation. We should thus keep the initiative and deny the Egyptians any opportunity of attacking us during the withdrawal period.

The Foreign Secretary said that, though some Government supporters would welcome the breaking off of the defence negotiations, it was not to be assumed that they would also welcome the consequent withdrawal of our forces from Egypt. If we withdrew without an agreement, we should have lost the right of return and might have weakened our influence with other Arab States. It would certainly be possible to bring the negotiations to a head, as the Egyptians had refused to accept our formula for the reactivation of the Base and this was the most favourable breaking-point from our point of view. He would wish, however, to consider the various courses which were now open to us and the advantages and disadvantages of each.

The Cabinet –

(1) Agreed to resume their discussion of the defence negotiations with Egypt on the basis of a memorandum, to be circulated by the Foreign Secretary, summarising the advantages and disadvantages of the various courses now open.

[. . .]

Lord Bracken to Lord Beaverbrook
(Beaverbrook papers)

30 December 1953

I am lunching with Winston today who is in good fettle, but is, of course, very worried by the possibility of a crop of strikes during the coming year. The victory of the railwaymen who threatened to hold up all traffic at Christmas time has encouraged all other Unions to consider making use of the strike weapon.

January 1954

Cabinet: conclusions
(Cabinet papers, 128/27)

7 January 1954
Secret
3 p.m.
Cabinet Meeting No. 1 of 1954

[...]

2. The Cabinet had before them a memorandum by the Foreign Secretary (C(54)4) regarding a suggestion of the United States Government that their offer of military aid to Pakistan should be linked with the initiation of some military collaboration between Pakistan and Turkey, which might eventually be developed into a system of collective defence in the Middle East. The memorandum set out certain objections to this project and proposed that the United States Government should be discouraged from pursuing it in its present form.

The Prime Minister said that he was not opposed to this project on its merits. Indeed, if some military association were eventually built up between Turkey and Pakistan, this might turn out to our advantage. If we failed to reach a defence agreement with Egypt and disengaged our forces from the Canal Zone, the general direction of our redeployment in the Middle East would be to the northward. The creation of a new defence grouping in the northern part of this area would fit in with that movement. Nonetheless, he thought it highly undesirable that this project should be announced immediately before the Four-Power Meeting in Berlin. It could do nothing for the moment to increase the military strength of the West, and it was bound to be regarded by the Soviet Government as a provocative gesture. Its announcement at this moment was likely to increase Soviet suspicions of American intentions and might even be taken to imply that the Americans were not anxious to reach any agreement at the Four-Power Meeting. Public opinion, in this country and abroad, had high hopes of that Meeting; and, if it led to nothing, the responsibility for the breakdown should be clearly seen to rest with the Soviet Government. We at any rate should have no part in any action or announcement in advance of the Meeting which seemed calculated to impair what chances it had of procuring satisfactory results. These arguments should be forcibly presented to the United States Government.

In discussion attention was drawn to the fact that, although no official announcement had yet been made, much information about this project had already been published in the United States Press. This was bound to create an unfavourable impression on the Soviet Government. It would also alarm the Indian Government, who had objected to the proposed grant of military aid to Pakistan, and had been reassured on the basis that no military pact was in contemplation.

It was the general view of the Cabinet that every effort should be made to dissuade the United States Government from making any early announcement of the project. Our representations, should, however, be based not on any objection to the project in itself, but on the disadvantages of making, immediately before the Four-Power Meeting in Berlin, a gesture which the Soviet Government were bound to regard as provocative.

The Cabinet –

(1) Invited the Foreign Secretary to represent strongly to the United States Government that it would be most untimely to make, before the Four-Power Meeting, any announcement regarding a projected military association between Turkey and Pakistan.

(2) Invited the Foreign Secretary to make similar representations to the Turkish Government through Her Majesty's Ambassador in Ankara.[1]

[. . .]

---

[1] Alexander Knox Helm, 1893–1964. Educated at King's College, Cambridge. On active service in Palestine during WWI. Vice-Consul to Thessaloniki. 3rd Dragoman at Constantinople, 1924. Consul, Ankara. On staff in FO, 1930–7. Consul, Addis Ababa, 1937–9. On staff in British Embassy, Washington DC, 1939–42. Counsellor, Ankara, 1942–6. Minister to Hungary, 1947–9. Ambassador to Israel, 1949–51; to Turkey, 1951–4. Last Governor-General of the Sudan, 1954–5.

Anthony Eden to Sir Winston S. Churchill
(Premier papers, 11/608)

7 January 1954
Confidential
PM/54/1

TRIESTE
SUCCESSOR TO GENERAL WINTERTON

You will recall that in August last you agreed that General Winterton, the Commander of the British–United States Zone of Trieste, who is due to retire next March, should be succeeded by an American officer. We thought that it was time that the Americans should take their full share of the responsibilities, and of the odium, of this job, and that the appointment of an American would impress the Italians that Zone A of Trieste was a joint Anglo–United States responsibility.

2. When the decision of October 8 to withdraw from Zone A was announced, it was assumed that there would be no need to replace the Zone Commander. But it is now clear that we shall not be out of the Zone by Spring, nor is it possible to forecast exactly when the job of Zone Commander will come to an end. The question of a successor to General Winterton therefore again arises. In present circumstances, I doubt whether it would be wise to press the Americans to provide a new Commander. The Americans themselves seem by no means keen to take on the responsibility, and I feel sure that the appointment of an American would be represented by the Italians as being the result of the pressure which they have been exerting to have the British Commander replaced by an American. I would therefore propose to drop the idea of getting an American replacement for General Winterton.

3. It is then open to us (a) to prolong Winterton's appointment, or, (b) to select a new British officer. Winterton has acquitted himself satisfactorily in a difficult job, but I should see some advantage in his being replaced, when his time is up, by another British officer. It is quite impossible to foretell how much longer we shall have to remain in Trieste; it may be some time yet and once we start prolonging Winterton's appointment, it may be difficult to know where to stop.

4. I have consulted the Minister of Defence, who agrees. If you approve, the next step will be for the Chiefs of Staff to propose the name of a British officer to the United States Joint Chiefs of Staff. Our Chiefs of Staff might also suggest that, as soon as the Americans have accepted the British officer selected, a joint statement should be made announcing that Winterton was being relieved as a matter of routine on the expiry of his three years tenure of the appointment.

JANUARY 1954

Sir Winston S. Churchill to Sir Ivone Kirkpatrick
Prime Minister's Personal Minute M.5/54
(Premier papers, 11/598)

8 January 1954

It is not my desire to expand the circulation of telegrams to Ministers. No. 2793[1] was of peculiar importance and if it had been overlooked when it arrived it should have been appended to the important pink answer (which was sent me) and which meant nothing without 2793.

I have just got (last night) the Foreign Secretary's Cabinet Paper about Egypt. In view of the continuous correspondence we are having together about this urgent problem, you could have sent me a proof earlier. I do not wish to read typescript unless it is absolutely necessary, but when a document I am to see, and which is urgent, is printed it would be continent[2] for you to send me a proof copy.

Anthony Eden to Sir Winston S. Churchill
(Premier papers, 11/598)

9 January 1954

Your minute M.5/54 of January 8 to Sir Ivone Kirkpatrick.

I have noted your paragraph 1. Action has already been taken to ensure that your interest in such telegrams is not overlooked.

2. I have looked into the possibility of letting you have early proof copies of Cabinet Papers in which you are interested. I would have no objection but I am told that in these days the Cabinet Office seldom if ever print proof copies of my Cabinet Papers. It seems that these would take as long to produce as the final product which is sent to you at once by the Cabinet Office. Fair copies of the final draft version with my manuscript amendments are not made.

---

[1] Regarding US military aid to Pakistan and collaboration between Turkey and Pakistan.
[2] convenient.

Sir Winston S. Churchill to Randolph S. Churchill
(*Churchill papers, 1/51*)

9 January 1954

My dear Randolph,

Thank you very much for sending me your essay on Blenheim. I think it is very good, presenting its subject with style, quality and dignity. I should think the book would be popular with the growing company who like to look at the contrast between the past and the clatter of the present. I have also shown it to your Mother.

Lord Bledisloe[1] to Sir Winston S. Churchill
(*Premier papers, 11/582*)

11 January 1954
Private and Confidential

My dear Winston,

I venture (albeit an 'old stager', now in the 87th year, and yclept 'the GOM of British Agriculture') to send you the enclosed letter which appeared over my signature in the last week's issue of *Farmer and Stockbreeder*, for such consideration as you may deem it to merit. I have been a little unhappy for some months past about the feeling and insecurity that has developed among many of our more efficient farmers during the current period of transition from a highly protective agricultural policy to one of a freer economy and the growing criticism (not wholly unjustified) of the cost of home-raised food as an element in the 'vicious spiral' of wages and commodity prices. As I live in a semi-industrial area (represented politically by a Socialist MP) and as a practical farmer for 60 years who is making a fairly good profit out of it, especially out of winter milk, the price of which is in my opinion dangerously high, I can see 'Both sides of the picture' and am a little concerned about it.

---

[1] Charles Bathurst, 1867–1958. Farmer and agriculturalist. MP (Cons.) for South Wiltshire, 1910–18. Parliamentary Secretary, Ministry of Food, 1916–17; Ministry of Agriculture, 1924–8. Knighted, 1917. Baron Bledisloe, 1918. PC, 1926. Chairman, Royal Commission on the Land Drainage of England and Wales, 1927. Governor-General and C-in-C, New Zealand, 1930–5. Viscount, 1935. President, Empire Day Movement, 1937–45.

Sir Winston S. Churchill to Anthony Eden
Prime Minister's Personal Minute M.7/54
(Premier papers, 11/608)

11 January 1954

Your Minute PM/54/1.[1]

Had we been going to stay in Trieste for any length of time, I should have preferred your suggestion of an American bearing the burden. Now I understand all is indeterminate. But surely we expect to get out of Trieste in under a year or a year and a half? In these circumstances I do not see the advantage of changing Winterton, with his experience, for another British general who has to begin at the beginning. It looks like changing for changing's sake, and perhaps a concession to those who want to get rid of Winterton. In addition it will give the impression that we contemplate prolonged occupation. Anyhow I cannot see any disadvantage in prolonging Winterton's appointment, and it could stop either when the occupation stops or when we conclude that it will last so long as to make a new appointment necessary.

The matter is not anyhow of major importance.

Randolph S. Churchill to Sir Winston S. Churchill
(Churchill papers, 1/51)

12 January 1954

My dearest Papa,

I am now getting down in earnest to my difficult task of the Derby[2] biography. There is quite a lot of good material available, but I am very short of letters. Do you think you could let me have any letters of his in your possession? I would also like to have any files you have about the Privilege Case on India to which I shall certainly have to allude.[3]

[1] Reproduced above (p. 1383).

[2] Edward George Villiers Stanley, 1865–1948. Educated at Wellington College. Lt, Grenadier Guards, 1885–95. MP (Cons.) for West Houghton, 1892–1906. Postmaster-General, 1903–5. Succeeded as 17th Earl of Derby, 1908. Director-General of Recruiting, 1915. Under-Secretary of State, War Office, 1916. Secretary of State for War, 1916–18, 1922–4. Ambassador to France, 1918–20. Member, Joint Select Committee on the Indian Constitution, 1933–4. Subject of Randolph Churchill's biography, *Lord Derby, 'King of Lancashire', The Official Life of Edward, Seventeenth Earl of Derby, 1865–1948* (1959).

[3] 'On 17 June 1938 Duncan Sandys had sent Hore-Belisha the draft of a question which he wished to ask on London's air defences. As the question was clearly based on secret information, Hore-Belisha, with Churchill's approval, told Sandys to call on the Attorney-General, who told Sandys that unless he disclosed the name of his informant, he would be liable to prosecution under the Official Secrets Act. On June 29 Sandys informed the House that, in his capacity as a junior officer in the Territorial Army, he had received orders to appear in uniform before the Military Court of Inquiry. This he submitted, was a 'gross breach' of the privileges of the House. His submission

Diana was greatly touched that you came to Duff's Memorial Service and was much pleased that she ran into you.

Sir Winston S. Churchill to Randolph S. Churchill
(Churchill papers, 1/51)

12 January 1954

My dear Randolph,

Thank you for your letter. I think it would be best if you wrote to the Trust asking to be shown the documents relating to Lord Derby. I am sure they will agree, but it has to be settled formally on account of the constitution of the Trust. As soon as you have received their consent, I will ask Mr Kelly to look out the papers referred to.

Sir Winston S. Churchill to Sir Thomas Dugdale and Gwilym Lloyd George
Prime Minister's Personal Minute M.8/54
(Premier papers, 11/582)

13 January 1954
Urgent

I attach a letter[1] which Bledisloe has sent to me enclosing an article he wrote for the *Farmer and Stock Breeder*, and also an article I saw in *The Field* of January 7 which seems to pose some apt questions. I would be glad if you would comment on these.

It would seem that there is still considerable anxiety and disquiet in the farming world.

I am much concerned at what I hear.

---

was upheld, and a Committee of Privileges reported on the following day that a breach of privilege had indeed been committed. During the ensuing debate, Churchill commented caustically that an act devised to protect the national defence should not be used to shield Ministers who had neglected national defence' (Gilbert, *Winston S. Churchill*, vol. 6, *Finest Hour, 1939–1941*, p. 1106 n. 1).

[1] Reproduced above (p. 1385).

January 1954

Sir Winston S. Churchill to Anthony Eden
Prime Minister's Personal Minute M.9/54
(Premier papers, 11/664)

14 January 1954

It seems to me we might say something like the following to the Russians:

BEGINS. While we still think our view was reasonable we are willing to meet your wishes in the hopes it may enable our Conference to start in a good spirit. ENDS.

I do not fear any mockery that we have given way. As Bismarck said 'there are often international questions upon which the more sensible party gives way'. Indeed I believe it will strengthen your hands when we come to the real issues. As a very minor point my feeling is that one can get better treatment out of the Russians when you're on their ground than when they are on yours.[1]

Sir Thomas Dugdale to Sir Winston S. Churchill
(Premier papers, 11/582)

16 January 1954

I am not surprised at Lord Bledisloe's letter[2] or Mr Henriques'[3] article. I shall be surprised if there are not more in the same vein.

As I told the Cabinet on 6th October, farmers are bound to be anxious about the future. The State has been buying their main products at fixed prices for 14 years and that has given them cast-iron security. Now we are making a change, and until they have some experience of it they are bound to regard it as change for the worse. Instead of Whitehall telling them what to do they have to decide for themselves what the housewife will want to buy and try to produce it for her in the right quantity and quality and at the right price.

We are still underwriting the industry with our guarantees, and time will show that only the inefficient need have cause for anxiety; the efficient ones, who have been frustrated by controls up to now, will have every incentive to go ahead and make the most of the opportunities we are offering them. I think this is what Lord Bledisloe is really trying to say, although he perhaps does not see very clearly that if control is relaxed there is bound to be flexibility (not 'vacillation') for farmers to plan their own production. Mr Henriques seems to be hankering after Government direction at the same time as he ignores the

---

[1] In the margin, Churchill wrote: 'FO might verify this. It might be appropriate for Bonn.'
[2] Reproduced above (p. 1385).
[3] Robert David Quixano Henriques, 1905–67. Joined RA, 1926; served in TA, 1934–9. On active duty, 1939–45. MBE, 1943. Author of *Death by Moonlight* (1938), *No Arms No Armour* (1939), *Through the Valley* (1950), and *100 Hours to Suez* (1957).

JANUARY 1954 1389

information we have already given him, as, for example, the minimum prices we assure the farmers for eggs until 1956.

I am sure you will be glad to know that now the NFU leaders are getting the fresh air of freedom in their lungs they are deciding it is not so bad after all. Their Secretary and their Vice-President have both spoken this week on the need for whole-hearted co-operation with the Government. Their main concern, as well as ours, is to get the new schemes operating quickly.

I have agreed this with the Minister of Food.

Cabinet: conclusions
(Cabinet papers, 128/27)

18 January 1954
Secret
3.30 p.m.
Cabinet Meeting No. 3 of 1954

[...]
3. The Cabinet had before them memoranda by the Foreign Secretary on the general prospects for the Four-Power Meeting[1] at Berlin (C(54)13) and on the particular problem of security assurances (C(54)10).

The Foreign Secretary said that the arrangements for the meeting-places in Berlin had now been agreed on a basis which was reasonably satisfactory; but the difficulties raised over this augured ill for the success of the Meeting. The French Foreign Minister had drawn attention to the danger that the Russians would be led to suggest that in other matters the principle of parity between the East and the West should be applied. Any such suggestion would have to be firmly resisted.

The major issue of the Meeting would be the means of holding free elections in Germany. The Soviet Foreign Minister would doubtless argue that the two German Governments should be left to arrange these without any outside assistance or supervision. The Foreign Secretary said that he had it in mind to lay before the Meeting a constructive plan for the holding of these elections, which could serve as the basis of a practical discussion with the Russians. If they refused to accept it, this would be a useful propaganda point if the Meeting broke down.

The Russians would also exploit the failure of the arrangements for the exchange of prisoners in Korea as a pretext for urging an early Five-Power Meeting. They would argue that the release of prisoners by the United Nations Command, in spite of the Indian proposal that they should remain in captivity, was a breach of the armistice, and that this had made it more unlikely that

[1] Between Foreign Ministers.

practical results could be achieved by the proposed Political Conference on Korea.

The best that we could hope to secure from the Berlin Meeting was a further demonstration of the solidarity of the Western Powers, possibly an agreement that further technical work should be done on the German and Austrian questions with a view to further meetings of the Foreign Ministers and, in private conversations with M Molotov, a clearer indication of the real trend of Russian policy.

The Prime Minister said that the Cabinet would wish to extend their good wishes for the Foreign Secretary's success in these difficult negotiations.

The Cabinet –

Took note of C(54)10 and C(54)13 and of the statements made by the Foreign Secretary.

4. The Foreign Secretary said that the results of the recent meeting of the Arab League could not be gratifying to Egypt. Both Iraq and Jordan had shown themselves hostile to any form of neutralism and had reaffirmed the need for alliances with Western Europe. The Egyptians might well be apprehensive of losing the effective leadership of the League and falling back into a position of less importance, both politically and strategically. At the same time the internal position of the Egyptian Government might well be weakening. Their suppression of the Moslem Brotherhood was a sign of their isolation.

The Prime Minister said that in these circumstances he wondered if it would not be wise to set a time limit to the defence negotiations with Egypt by giving notice that after a certain date our offer would be regarded as withdrawn.

The Foreign Secretary said that this should certainly be considered. On the other side it was arguable that we should gain by allowing the differences of view between Egypt and the other Arab States to develop for a little longer. We should in any event wait for a few days to judge the effect of any representations which the United States Government might make to Egypt. He would have opportunities in Berlin of discussing the whole problem with the United States Secretary of State.

The Cabinet –

Took note of these statements.

5. The Cabinet had before them (i) a memorandum by the Foreign Secretary (C(54)18) proposing that we should suspend attempts to secure United States agreement to a 'short list' of goods which on security grounds should not be exported to the Soviet bloc and should consider instead, first with the Americans and then in the Paris Group,[1] the possibility of achieving substantial amendment of the existing lists by considering particular items and

---

[1] Established during the winter of 1949–50, the Paris Group was a trade control organization managed by COCOM under the OEEC (itself created in 1948 to implement the Marshall Plan), whose HQ was in Paris. Its purpose was to control trade between Western powers and Eastern, Communist powers.

removing those of less strategic importance; and (ii) a memorandum by the President of the Board of Trade (C(54)18) suggesting that further steps should be taken to secure agreement between Departments of the United Kingdom Government on the content of a 'short list' and that a further attempt should then be made to persuade the Americans to accept it, in discussions between Ministers of the two countries.

The Prime Minister said that increased trade with the Soviet bloc would mean, not only assistance to our exports, but greater possibilities for infiltration behind the Iron Curtain. Determined efforts should be made to persuade the United States Government to accept a new policy in this matter. The policy which he suggested was that we should in future deny to the Soviet bloc only goods of direct military value, and should no longer seek to prevent the export of goods which would help merely to strengthen their industrial economy. He considered that the existing lists should at once be revised on that basis.

In discussion the following points were made:

(a) The United States Government had hitherto resisted the substitution for the present lists of a 'short list' of that kind desired by the President of the Board of Trade. But it was known that Mr Stassen, Director of the United States Foreign Operations Administration, was anxious to take positive steps towards increased trade with the Soviet bloc, and it would be useful if he could be invited to come to this country for further discussions on this subject with United Kingdom Ministers.

(b) Before any discussions were held with Mr Stassen, agreement should be reached between the Departments of the United Kingdom Government on the list of goods which we were willing to see subjected to embargo. Up to date, there had been wide differences of opinion between the Departments concerned. The Defence Department had been anxious to prevent the export to the Soviet bloc of certain metals and some types of ships, which would be valuable to the development of the Soviet war potential.

(c) Some of these interdepartmental differences would be resolved if Ministers gave fresh policy guidance on the lines suggested by the Prime Minister. Though it might still be wise to prevent the export of goods which would directly increase the industrial war potential of the Soviet bloc, there seemed now to be insufficient reason to frame the prohibited list with the object of hampering the general development of the industrial economy of the Soviet Union and its satellites. A change of policy on those lines would permit the export of electric generating plant and other engineering products for which there was a considerable Russian demand.

(d) In considering the extension of trade with the Soviet bloc, regard should be paid to the criticisms made by Conservative leaders, when in opposition, against the action of the Labour Government in allowing the export to these countries of goods which might be of value to a potential enemy. Though there had been some change of circumstances since then, the criticisms should be borne in mind.

The Cabinet –
(1) Instructed the Secretary of the Cabinet to arrange that officials of the Departments concerned should at once revise the existing list of goods whose export to the Soviet bloc was at present subject to embargo, by applying the principle that we should in future deny to the Soviet bloc only goods of direct military value, and should present within a week a report covering the original and revised lists together with the arguments for and against the exclusion of any items still in dispute between Departments.
(2) Took note that the Prime Minister would appoint a Ministerial Committee to consider the report of the officials and to submit recommendations upon it to the Cabinet.
(3) Agreed to resume their discussion of this question when the report of this Ministerial Committee was available.

6. The Cabinet had before them a memorandum by the Lord President (C(54)15) regarding the final report of the House of Commons Select Committee on the Nationalised Industries (House of Commons paper No. 235).

The Lord President said that the Committee's main recommendation was that a standing Select Committee should be appointed with the duty of 'examining the reports and accounts of, and obtaining further information as to the general policy and practice of, the nationalized industries established by statute'. The Home Affairs Committee had favoured acceptance of this recommendation as offering the best means of keeping Parliament informed about the affairs of the nationalised industries. The recommendation in the report was for a standing Select Committee of the House of Commons only. The House of Lords had not yet considered the matter but, when they came to do so, were likely to press for a standing Joint Select Committee of both Houses. The Lord President therefore hoped that, when the report was debated in the Commons, the Government spokesmen would keep open the possibility of appointing a Joint Committee of both Houses.

In discussion the following points were made:
(a) The new Atomic Energy Corporation should not come within the scope of the standing Select Committee. Its exclusion could be defended on the ground that its annual receipts were likely for a considerable time to come to be 'wholly or mainly derived from monies provided by Parliament or advanced from the Exchequer'.
(b) The Iron and Steel Board should similarly be excluded from the scope of the standing Select Committee. The steel industry was in process of being denationalized.

JANUARY 1954   1393

(c) The Minister of Fuel and Power said that he had felt bound to represent to the Home Affairs Committee the possible dangers of appointing a standing Select Committee on the nationalized industries. He did not, however, wish to press his earlier objections to the establishment of such a body, particularly as it was now intended that it should have much more restricted terms of reference.

The Prime Minister, summing up the discussion, said that the balance of advantage was clearly on the side of taking this occasion to increase the opportunities for Parliamentary scrutiny and discussion of the conduct of the nationalized industries. In the forthcoming debate in the House of Commons on the Select Committee's report, the Government should announce that they accepted the Select Committee's recommendation in principle but wished to keep open the possibility of a Joint Select Committee of both Houses as a point which merited further consideration in the light of the views expressed in both Houses.

The Cabinet –
(1) Endorsed the recommendations in paragraph 14 of C(54)15.
(2) Agreed that the Atomic Energy Corporation and the Iron and Steel Board should be excluded from the scope of the proposed standing Select Committee on the nationalized industries.

[. . .]

Defence Committee: minutes
(Cabinet papers, 131/14)

20 January 1954
Top Secret
11.30 a.m.
Defence Committee Meeting No. 1 of 1954

[. . .]

2. REDUCTION OF COMMONWEALTH FORCES IN KOREA

The Committee had before them a memorandum by the Minister of Defence and the Commonwealth Secretary (D(54)5) suggesting that the other Commonwealth Governments concerned should be consulted on a proposal to approach the Government of the United States regarding a reduction in the size of the Commonwealth division in Korea.

The Minister of Defence said that it was contemplated that the Commonwealth division might be reduced by one brigade group. This could be done by withdrawing two British, one Australian and one Canadian infantry battalion, together with the one New Zealand field artillery regiment. He hoped that this suggestion could be accepted. Until we began to reduce our commitments we had no chance of building up a strategic reserve, or of keeping within the total expenditure on defence which the Chancellor of the Exchequer found it necessary to propose.

In discussion the following points were made:
- (a) In view of the many other difficult issues which we needed to discuss with the Americans at the present time, it would not be opportune to raise the question of reducing the Commonwealth division.
- (b) If we said nothing about our consideration of this problem to the Commonwealth Governments, there was a danger that one of them might raise it independently. It would, therefore, be wise to tell the Commonwealth Governments that we had considered the problem but did not think the moment opportune to make an approach to the United States.

The Prime Minister said that he would take the opportunity to mention the matter to the Canadian Prime Minister when he visited the United Kingdom in the near future. In the meantime, no approach should be made to the United States Secretary of State. The whole matter could be reconsidered in a month's time.

The Committee –
- (1) Authorised the Commonwealth Secretary to inform the Commonwealth Governments concerned that we had considered the possibility of reducing the strength of the Commonwealth division in Korea, but did not consider the time opportune to broach this possibility with the United States Government.
- (2) Took note that the Prime Minister would mention this matter to the Canadian Prime Minister during his forthcoming visit to the United Kingdom.
- (3) Agreed to resume their discussion of this question in one month's time.

[. . .]

Sir Winston S. Churchill to Lord Bledisloe
(Premier papers, 11/582)

20 January 1954

My dear Bledisloe,

Thank you very much for your letter of January 11[1] and for sending me your letter which was published in *The Farmer and Stockbreeder.* I can assure you that these matters are very present in our minds. I have sent a copy of your

---

[1] Reproduced above (p. 1385).

letter to the Minister of Agriculture and I am grateful to you for letting me know your views, which are based on so wide an experience of agriculture.

Cabinet: conclusions
(Cabinet papers, 128/27)

21 January 1954
Secret
11.30 a.m.
Cabinet Meeting No. 4 of 1954

[...]
3. The Foreign Secretary said that he had considered whether there might be an opportunity at the Four-Power Meeting at Berlin to raise the question of an expansion of trade with the Soviet bloc. He had, however, concluded that he could not open this question with the Russians until we had first reached agreement with the Americans on a revised list of goods whose export to the Soviet bloc was to be subject to embargo. If we went outside the limits of the present agreed list, we should be denied economic aid from the United States in accordance with the terms of the Battle Act.

The Prime Minister said that he would preside over a meeting of Ministers on 25th January to discuss the report by officials for which the Cabinet had asked on 18th January.[1] The Conclusions reached would be made known to the Foreign Secretary in Berlin.

[...]
6. The Prime Minister drew attention to the decision of the Egyptian Government to intensify their blockade of Israel. This would lead to increased interference with the passage of ships through the Suez Canal and the black-listing by Egypt of many ships of all flags trading with the Levant. The Israel Government were proposing to raise the matter in the Security Council and had asked whether they could count on our support, and that of the United States Government.

The Prime Minister said that he hoped we should give prompt and effective support to the Israel Government in this matter. In Parliament members of all parties would welcome an initiative designed to assert the rights of free transit through the Canal; and it would be convenient if we could transfer the emphasis, in our current differences with Egypt, from the Base to the Canal.

The Foreign Secretary said that he was anxious to gain support for Israel's protest against Egypt's interference with her trade. The Cabinet should realise, however, that the Egyptian Government had legal grounds for their

---

[1] See Cabinet: conclusions of Jan. 18, para. 5, reproduced above (pp. 1390–2).

actions, in that their war with Israel had not legally been terminated. It was therefore desirable that we should not take any public position in this matter until we had assured ourselves that we should have the support of some of the other maritime Powers. He had, in the first instance, approached the United States Government; and, as soon as he knew that they were willing to support Israel's complaint, he would take steps to verify that some of the other maritime Powers would be willing to take the same line. The Israel Government could then be informed that, if they raised the matter in the Security Council, they would have the support of the leading maritime Powers.

The Cabinet –

Invited the Foreign Secretary to continue to enlist the support of leading maritime Powers for the protest which Israel proposed to make in the Security Council against the decision of the Egyptian Government to intensify their blockade of Israel.

[. . .]

Sir Winston S. Churchill to Anthony Eden
(Premier papers, 11/701)

21 January 1954

My dear Anthony,

You said something to me the other day about my looking after Egypt in your absence. Certainly something like that will have to happen if the present strain continues. I cannot argue everything out over the telephone between London and Berlin and hold all the discussions which may be necessary in Cabinet subject to your detailed comment. You would, of course, be kept fully and instantly informed. In the main, however, the power of prompt action if needed by events must rest here.

You and I have never been more in harmony of feeling about the Egyptian problem than we are now. I therefore propose to you that I shall correspond directly with Stevenson and Howe, that Kirkpatrick and the head of the Egyptian Department[1] shall report regularly to me (I am available at all hours here), that I shall deal with all Egyptian Questions in the House of Commons and that unless you have expressed a contrary opinion I may assume your agreement in Cabinet decisions of an urgent character.

We have worked so long together and our affairs are so closely interwoven that I think it better to put things as I see them plainly down on paper instead of awaiting unforeseen crises.

With all good wishes for success in your tremendous mission and every resolve to defend you if it fails.

[1] Sir Ralph Stevenson.

Lord Woolton to Sir Winston S. Churchill
(Premier papers, 11/733)

22 January 1954

The American technique to which you refer is the one that the President has used and is called the 'teleprompter'. It shows the typescript of a speech, set out in large letters on a ribbon that goes from left to right directly under the lens of the camera, and gives the impression that the speaker is speaking without notes.

In practice I'm told that it isn't as good as it sounds, since the ribbon goes on at its regular speed and doesn't, therefore, allow for the normal variations of conversational talking.

There is not one in this country, and the BBC do not think they could get one, but from all I hear of it I don't think you would like it very much in any case.

At the Central Office we have a film that lasts for about 20 minutes, showing the various ways in which people have used television for politics. Probably the outstanding success was Max, who did a combination of reading and speaking without looking at his notes, and, as you will remember, made a great hit with it. I wonder if you would let us have the thing brought down to you at Chartwell.[1] So that you could see it. It would not take you long and it might interest you.[2]

Anthony Eden to Sir Winston S. Churchill
Prime Minister's Personal Telegram T.4/54
(Premier papers, 11/664)

24 January 1954
Priority
Confidential
Personal
No. 10

Preliminary moves have gone as well as could be expected. There is close unity between us and the Americans and French. Russians have made a few tentative approaches and so I am asking a small party of bears to dinner later this week. We have made all arrangements for keeping in touch with Adenauer so the stage is set. Weather cold and fine. Berliners are very friendly.

---

[1] Churchill wrote in the margin: 'Yes, next weekend'.

[2] Churchill was doing screen tests for television, a medium he despised. On Feb. 22, after reviewing the machine, Churchill wrote to Lord Woolton: 'I have decided not to attempt the performance on March 26 and I strongly recommend that you should try to persuade Mr Eden to undertake it. He will, I am sure, do it very well.'

January 1954

Sir Winston S. Churchill to Anthony Eden
Prime Minister's Personal Telegram T.5/54
(Premier papers, 11/701)

25 January 1954

I am glad things have opened fairly well.

In the Foreign Office replies about Egypt today I inserted the words 'These grave matters are engaging the constant attention of the Cabinet.' I will keep you informed.

The officials seem to have taken a big step forward in East–West Trade. I have had a check-up meeting this afternoon. There is a lot more difficulty in it than I thought.

Cabinet: minutes
(Cabinet papers, 130/99)

25 January 1954
Secret
4.30 p.m.
Gen. 454/1st Meeting

EAST/WEST TRADE

The Committee had before them a report (Gen. 454/1) by the Interdepartmental Working Party on Security Export Controls reviewing the lists of goods, embargoed to the Soviet bloc, against the principle provisionally accepted by the Cabinet on the 18th January, that we should in future deny to the Soviet bloc only those goods which were of direct military value.[1]

The Prime Minister said that by applying this principle the goods subject to embargo had been reduced from 263 to 98. The resulting list was doubtless open to improvement, but it showed that there were prospects of expanding trade with the Soviet bloc and thereby increasing not only our exports but our opportunities for infiltration behind the Iron Curtain. Practical prospects of increased trade with the Soviet bloc might prove a valuable factor in negotiations with the Soviet Union if the political discussions in Berlin proved abortive.

The Minister of Defence said that, while he shared the wish for an expansion of trade with the Soviet bloc, he must make it clear that on defence grounds he could not advise the free export of items which were likely to increase the war making capacity of the Russians by improving their technical knowledge and equipment. Moreover, it could not be assumed that goods

---

[1] See Cabinet: conclusions of Jan. 18, para. 5, reproduced above (pp. 1390–2).

exported to Russia would not be sent on to China and used in direct hostilities against the Western Powers.

In discussion the following points were made:
(a) The Minister of Defence and the Minister of Supply said that in their view the reduced list of embargoed items was too short. A good case could be made out on military grounds for including some additional items, e.g. some machine tools and some electronic and precision instruments.
(b) The officials had been unable to reach agreement on the question whether three particular items – tankers and whaling factories, four-wheel drive vehicles and marine diesel engines – should be classified as of direct military value.

Ministers agreed that tankers and whaling factories should continue to be subject to the embargo. Apart from the military arguments, it was thought to be economically unsound to sell these ships, as we should thus reduce our earnings in the carrying trade.

It was also agreed that large four-wheel drive vehicles should continue to be subject to the embargo. Smaller vehicles of this type (15 cwt. or less) should, however, be excluded from the embargo list.

Marine diesel engines could be used both for warships and for a large range of merchant ships. Efforts were now being made to restrict the definition, so as to embargo only those types of engine needed for naval and merchant vessels included on the embargoed list. It was agreed that, if this could not be done, the whole range of marine diesel engines should be included in the embargo list.

(c) The Minister of State, Foreign Office, said that it was very doubtful whether the United States Government could be brought to accept so drastic a reduction of the existing lists as was now being contemplated. American opinion was not ready for such a radical change of policy. The presentation of so short a list might defeat its object by causing American opinion to harden against any relaxation. He thought it would be wiser to proceed more gradually, while American opinion was developing. The President of the Board of Trade said that it was arguable that we should do better to put forward, in our discussions with the United States Government, a completely new policy as an aim towards which we should work. But the first need was for United Kingdom Ministers to formulate their own policy and to reach agreement on the content of a revised list.
(d) It would be easier to arrive at a practical policy if any revision of the list could show the measure of the trade value of particular items. There was no object in excluding from embargo a large number of items in which no trade was likely. On the other hand, if traders were to make any progress at all in negotiations with the Russians,

they must have some flexibility and must not find themselves tied down by long lists of restricted items. The Prime Minister said that he would like to see an analysis under about six main headings of the trade between the United Kingdom and the Soviet bloc in 1949 and in 1952.

(e) It was agreed that we should aim at the complete suppression of the second list of goods on which exports were controlled and restricted in amount. It would be preferable, if it were thought necessary, to transfer some items from this list into the list of embargoed goods. It would be of great help to traders to know that, if goods were not embargoed, they were entirely free.

(f) The Commonwealth Secretary drew attention to the close interest of Canada in this subject, particularly with regard to copper. Canada was the only Commonwealth country which was a member of the Paris Group, and therefore directly concerned. Any new policy which we adopted ought to be discussed with the Canadians before we made an approach to the United States.

(g) The Prime Minister said that he would like to see an analysis of the Soviet defence effort in terms of the various materials and metals which we felt it so important to deny them. Had they in fact enough of these vital materials to make their defence effort as overwhelming as it was generally held to be? The Minister of Defence undertook to submit a report to the Prime Minister on this matter.

After further discussion, the following conclusions were reached:

(1) The Interdepartmental Working Party on Security Export Controls should revise the reduced list of embargoes items set out in Appendix I of Gen. 454/1 by (i) taking into account the views of Ministers on the disputed items as recorded in paragraph (b) above and (ii) adding to the reduced list not more than say, 30 items which, though not of direct military value, had an indirect military importance of such significance as to justify their inclusion in the embargo list. Attention should be drawn to any item which was of substantial economic importance to the United Kingdom. The items excluded from the embargo list should be arranged in a rough order of trade importance. A report should be submitted to Ministers within a week.

(2) The President of the Board of Trade, in consultation with the Minister of Supply, should send the Prime Minister an analysis of trade with the Soviet bloc in 1949 and 1952.

(3) The Minister of Defence should submit to the Prime Minister an appreciation of the Soviet defence effort covering the point noted in paragraph (g) above.

JANUARY 1954 1401

Cabinet: conclusions
(Cabinet papers, 128/27)

26 January 1954
Secret
11.30 a.m.
Cabinet Meeting No. 5 of 1954

[...]

2. The Prime Minister said that over the coming months various Ministers would need to be in attendance at Standing Committees of the House of Commons which sat on Tuesday and Thursday morning, and he had been wondering whether it would not be convenient on this account to revert to the pre-war practice of holding one regular weekly meeting of the Cabinet on Wednesday morning. Additional meetings could be held, if required, on Monday or Thursday afternoon.

In discussion it was pointed out that the Scottish Grand Committee of the House of Commons met on Wednesdays and that, when business became congested, the other Standing Committees might need to meet on three mornings of the week, including Wednesday. For the time being, however, the balance of advantage lay on the side of holding the main Cabinet meeting on Wednesday morning.

The Cabinet –

Agreed that during the next few weeks they would aim at transacting their weekly business at a regular meeting on Wednesday morning, but invited Ministers to hold themselves free to attend an additional meeting, if required on Monday at 4.30 p.m.

3. The Prime Minister drew attention to a telegram from the Foreign Secretary (Berlin telegram No. 12 of 25th January) suggesting that the United Kingdom Government should review their attitude towards the proposal for a Five-Power Meeting on the problems of the Far East. It was clear that this proposal would be strongly pressed at the Berlin Meeting, and that the French would be embarrassed if their Western allies adopted a wholly unconstructive attitude towards it. The Foreign Secretary was now inclined to think that it might be wise to accept the proposal, if the Americans could be persuaded to agree to it.

The Prime Minister said that, if there was no prospect of making progress on Far Eastern questions either at Panmunjom or in the United Nations, it would be unreasonable to resist a proposal that these questions should be discussed at a Five-Power Meeting convened for that purpose. He hoped that the Foreign Secretary might be able to bring the Americans round to this opinion.

In discussion there was general agreement with the Prime Minister's view.

The Cabinet –

Took note that the Prime Minister would inform the Foreign Secretary that they were in full sympathy with his view that it would be inexpedient to resist a proposal for a Five-Power Meeting confined to Far Eastern questions and beginning with Korea, and hoped that he might be able to persuade the United States Secretary of State to fall in with this view.

4. The Prime Minister referred to the Cabinet's discussion of 21st January regarding the decision of the Egyptian Government to intensify their blockade of Israel.[1] He again stressed the importance of upholding the right of international passage through the Suez Canal and the Parliamentary advantages of putting this issue in the forefront of our differences with Egypt. He hoped, therefore, that no effort would be spared in enlisting the support of leading maritime Powers for the protest which Israel wished to make in the Security Council against the Egyptian decision to intensify the blockade.

The Minister of State said that this matter would be taken up with other maritime Powers as soon as a favourable response had been secured to the representations already made to the United States Government.

The Cabinet –

Took note of the position.

5. The Prime Minister said that it was important that we should retain the initiative in the current defence negotiations with Egypt. We were in some danger of giving the impression that we were allowing matters to drift. He would still like to be in a position to set a time limit after which the final proposals for a defence agreement which we had put forward in October would be regarded as withdrawn. But, before this could be done, the Cabinet must have decided on the alternative policy which they would follow if no agreement were reached. Some time must also be allowed for the United States Government to make their final representation to the Egyptians.

The Prime Minister suggested that a full review of the position should be made by the Cabinet at their next meeting, on the basis of a memorandum which could be circulated meanwhile by the Minister of State.

The Cabinet –

Agreed to discuss, at their next meeting, the various courses which would be open to the United Kingdom Government in the event of a breakdown in the current defence negotiations with Egypt.

[. . .]

---

[1] See Cabinet: conclusions of Jan. 21, para. 6, reproduced above (pp. 1395–6).

JANUARY 1954

Sir Winston S. Churchill to Anthony Eden
Prime Minister's Personal Telegram T.7/54
(Premier papers, 11/665)

26 January 1954
Immediate
Secret
No. 31

The Cabinet this morning warmly approved the proposal in paragraph 3 of your telegram No. 12 for a Five Power Conference confined, of course, to the Far East and beginning with Korea, and hope that you will be able to persuade Mr Dulles of the wisdom of supporting such a proposal.

Sir Winston S. Churchill to Anthony Eden
Prime Minister's Personal Telegram T.9/54
(Premier papers, 11/665)

27 January 1954
Immediate
Top Secret, Personal and Private
No. 40

Your telegrams Nos. 19 and 21.
Certainly it would be an advantage to postpone the Assembly[1] till you see how you get on at Berlin.

2. I hope you will continue to work for a Five Power Meeting strictly limited wherever it sits to the Far East. I find it hard to believe that any settlement can be reached about Germany. We must stand by the principle of a German contingent either to EDC or an amended NATO. This alone gives the West the chance of obtaining the necessary strength by creating a European or internationalized German Army but not a National one. I think we are bound in good faith to Adenauer to bring this about and we should in no circumstances agree to Germany being reduced to a neutralised, defenceless hiatus which would only be the preliminary to another Czechoslovakia process. I find it hard to believe that the Soviets will relinquish their grip on Eastern Germany if the above is true.

3. The great thing is to avoid a deadlock with all the disappointment and danger that would follow from it. For this purpose the institution of a Five Power Conference, as defined, could do no harm and might do much good. It involves no military weakening on our part and would prevent the sense of a renewed breakdown between East and West. Even if it did not meet till June

[1] The UN General Assembly.

its influence would be beneficial. It would keep alive the atmosphere of easement and friendly, or at least civil, relationships between the two sides while in no way injuring our fundamental theme, namely, 'peace through strength'.

4. I do not consider that seeking friendly relationships with Russia is contradictory to forming the strongest combination possible against Soviet aggression. On the contrary it may well be true that the Russians can only be friends and live decently with those who are as strong or stronger than they are themselves.

5. It seems to me that if the German question had to be suspended after everything possible had been done, the Five Power Far Eastern parley might play an invaluable part, as this would be held to be a Russian victory though it cost us nothing substantial. They might well then agree to a settlement about Austria. Of course, on the spot, you may have better hopes of a German settlement and it must be patiently explored. This is no time for despair about it. I am sure however it would make the world safer if the Five Power Conference including China, could be brought on to the scene as soon as possible, if only as a shock-absorber. I would much rather have the Five Power Conference about the Far East than have Red China before any proof of goodwill, admitted to UNO and so, I believe, would the Americans. After all to meet at an international Conference implies no condonation of the past but is only a practical measure to deal with the present and the future.

6. If you think it worthwhile to pray show this to Foster or tell him my views in conversation.

Anthony Eden to Sir Winston S. Churchill
Prime Minister's Personal Telegram T.10/54
(Premier papers, 11/664)

27 January 1954   Berlin
Immediate
Top Secret and Personal
No. 29

Thank you so much for your message. Things are more complicated tonight, Molotov's speech having apparently been more embarrassing to French and Americans than to ourselves. Will keep you posted.

January 1954

Lord Bracken to Lord Beaverbrook
(Beaverbrook papers)

27 January 1954

The Socialists are playing a very clever game by suggesting that many Tories want to push out Churchill. If he does resign they will set up a lot of maundering wailings about the wickedness of the Tories in parting from such a great leader.

The *Daily Mirror* is running a tremendous campaign against Churchill: it is a skilful compound of hatred, malice and greasy pity. This, of course, is their method of replying to Churchill's writ and the rough ride he gave the *Mirror* during the war. I don't know what effect this type of attack really has on the public. The most of the readers of the *Mirror* are either mentally adolescent or natural supporters of the Left.

Cabinet: conclusions
(Cabinet papers, 128/27)

28 January 1954
Secret
11.30 a.m.
Cabinet Meeting No. 6 of 1954

[...]

2. The Cabinet had before them a memorandum by the Minister of State (C(54)29) summarising the possible courses of action open to the United Kingdom in regard to the defence negotiations with Egypt.

The Minister of State said that since his memorandum was written the United States Ambassador in Cairo had officially urged the Egyptian Government to accept the terms which we had offered in October, and had said that until an agreement was reached no economic aid would be forthcoming from the United States (Cairo telegram No. 117). This was very satisfactory, though it was by no means certain that the Egyptian Government would heed this advice, and there were indications that they were unlikely to accept the clauses about the availability of the Base and the wearing of uniforms. The Foreign Secretary still felt that the best solution would be the conclusion of an agreement on the terms we had offered. If that proved impossible, the next best course would probably be to decide to liquidate the Base and redeploy our forces in our own time, but to maintain our rights under the 1936 Treaty and offer to submit to international arbitration any matters of disagreement about its revision.

The Prime Minister said that, if the Egyptian Government accepted our terms, we should be obliged to conclude an agreement. We must, however, decide on a positive alternative course in case the Egyptians refused the terms and broke off the negotiations, or delayed unduly a definite reply to our final offer. He thought that the best course of action in those circumstances would be that outlined by the Minister of State. We should have many valuable advantages if we took our stand on the 1936 Treaty. But, if this course were adopted, we should be obliged – unless the Egyptians attacked us – to begin to reduce our forces to the 10,000 which the Treaty allowed. Could we, for example, assume that a force of this size could hold both ends of the Canal so that we could safeguard the rights of free navigation and also preserve our power to control the supply of oil to the Delta?

The Minister of Defence said that with this small number of troops we could not hope to defend the whole Base area or secure rights of navigation through the Canal against open hostilities by the Egyptian army. Against intensified guerrilla activity we might be able successfully to remove some of the less heavy stores in the Base. And if the Egyptians gave us some cooperation, we could move more of these stores and in less time. The Egyptian army was believed to be short of ammunition and therefore unable to sustain hostilities for any length of time. On the other hand, hatred and bitterness were powerful factors in sustaining the morale of an army and it could not be assumed that the Egyptians would not fight well. In these circumstances the best military course would be to hold a perimeter round Suez, including one airfield. This could be done with the 10,000 troops organized as a small division less one brigade. The rest of the forces now in the Canal Zone would be redisposed in the Eastern Mediterranean area. In the event of difficulties at Suez a brigade could be flown in from Cyprus and an armoured brigade could enter Egypt from Libya. Reinforcements from the United Kingdom could use the port of Tobruk. The retention of Suez would enable us to control the supply of oil to the Delta and to secure the southern entrance to the Canal.

It was the general view of the Cabinet that this course of action offered considerable attractions. It would satisfy Government supporters. It might placate public feeling in Egypt, where it would be seen that the majority of British forces were being withdrawn from the Canal Zone. It was not, however, free from legal difficulty. For we had no rights under the 1936 Treaty to station this number of troops in Suez. If, therefore, we announced that we were taking our stand on the 1936 Treaty, how could we justify moving our troops into positions which, under that Treaty, we had no right to occupy? In the discussion which followed, the following arguments were put forward on this point:

(a) It was contemplated in the 1936 Treaty that British troops would be stationed in the Canal Zone for the purpose of ensuring free navigation through the Canal. We might argue that, without Egypt's cooperation, the small number of troops allowed us was insufficient to fulfil this object and that we had been obliged to move those troops into positions where they could at least accomplish a part of this purpose by securing the southern entrance to the Canal.

(b) The Egyptians had unilaterally denounced the 1936 Treaty and it could be argued that in these circumstances the other party to the Treaty must be free to make dispositions to protect its rights. We could argue that the creation of a defensive position at Suez was our only means of doing this. If, on the other hand, the Egyptian Government went back on their denunciation of the Treaty and said that they wished to revive it, we could offer to go to arbitration for its revision, and during this period we should redeploy our forces in the Middle East with the minimum loss of privilege.

The Prime Minister said that the problem was to reconcile the minimum military security of the 10,000 troops allowed by the 1936 Treaty with the other provisions of that Treaty. If we could solve this problem, we should be in a position to adopt a positive alternative course of action if the defence negotiations with Egypt were broken off for one reason or another. He suggested that a special Committee of Ministers should examine this problem and report back to the Cabinet.

The Cabinet –

Appointed a Committee consisting of –
    Lord Chancellor (in the Chair)
    Home Secretary
    Minister of Defence
    Secretary of State for War
    Secretary of State for Air
    Minister of Transport
    Minister of State

To give urgent study to the problem outlined by the Prime Minister, taking account of the points made in the discussion, and to report their conclusions to the Cabinet as soon as possible.

3. In the course of the discussion recorded in the preceding Minute the Minister of Transport said that we should be on the watch for a suitable opportunity to revive our proposal that the maritime Powers should jointly seek from the Egyptian Government firmer guarantees regarding the freedom of navigation through the Suez Canal. We had hitherto been unable to proceed with this proposal because the United States Government had been unwilling to join in a multilateral approach to the Egyptian Government on this subject while we were negotiating for a new defence agreement with Egypt. If those negotiations failed, this proposal might with advantage be revived.

The Cabinet –

Invited the Minister of State to keep under review, in consultation with the Minister of Transport, the timing of further representations to the United States Government regarding the proposal that the maritime Powers should jointly seek from the Egyptian Government firmer guarantees regarding the freedom of navigation through the Suez Canal.

[. . .]

General Lord Ismay to Sir Winston S. Churchill
(Premier papers, 11/771)

29 January 1954
Personal and Confidential

My dear Prime Minister,

Thank you so much for sending me a copy of Volume VI. I am not sure that it isn't the best of the lot. Everyone here to whom I have lent it has commented on the prophecy you made about the Soviet danger in your telegram to Truman on the morrow of VE-Day. It has proved horribly accurate.

I had a long talk with de Staercke[1] and the Dutchman on the NATO Council, van Starkenborgh,[2] about your idea that EDC should start off with an empty chair: but they were both positive that their respective Governments would not feel able to agree.

De Staercke has a number of other ideas which might help the business forward. He feels – perhaps too optimistically – that there is a good chance of French ratification if both America and ourselves could do just a little bit more in the way of guarantees. De Staercke added that he was, of course, at your disposal at any time that you wished to spare him five minutes. He could fly across at very short notice.

I have had a long talk with Gruenther about Soviet strength. The upshot was that he was quite sure that, even without a German contribution, we already have sufficient force to hold any attack by the Soviet with the troops that they have at present in the front line. In other words, there would have to be a build-up before they launched an all-out attack: and this would give us good warning.

---

[1] André de Staercke, 1913–2001. Educated at Catholic University of Louvain. CoS to Hubert Pierlot (PM of Belgium), 1942–5. Secretary of the Regent, 1945–50. Belgian representative, NATO, 1950–76.

[2] Jonkheer Alidius Warmoldus Lambertus Tjarda van Starkenborgh Stachouwer, 1888–1978. Married, 1915, Christine Marburg: two children. Entered Netherlands Diplomatic Service, 1915. Queen's Commissioner, Groningen, 1925–33. Envoy to Brussels, 1933–6. Governor-General, Dutch East Indies, 1936–42. Captured and imprisoned by Japanese, 1942–5. Ambassador to France, 1945–8. Dutch representative, NATO, 1950–6.

Lord Thurso[1] to Lord Beaverbrook
(Beaverbrook papers)

31 January 1954

It seems an age since we have met, but it is impossible to meet a mutual friend of ours without one of us asking 'How is Max? When did you see him last? What's he thinking about such & such or so and so?'

Accordingly, on Thursday night when Winston had insisted on putting me into the Chair at the Other Club (my first dinner out since my illness!) & we were all talking noisily with Winston at his gayest, the talk turned to you and Winston said 'as he's not here, Archie, write to him and tell him we're all thinking and talking about him.'

The one cloud over us was the loss of Duff[2] who had been at the previous dinner in one of his most amusing and controversial moods – a few days before he sailed. Winston spoke briefly and movingly of our loss.

---

[1] Archibald Henry Macdonald Sinclair, 1890–1970. Succeeded as 4th Bt, 1912. Second-in-Command (under Churchill) of 6th Royal Scots Fusiliers, Jan.–May 1916. Sqn Cdr, 2nd Life Guards, 1916–18. Maj., Guards Machine Gun Rgt, 1918. Private Secretary to Churchill, Ministry of Munitions, 1918–19. Churchill's Personal Military Secretary, War Office, 1919–21. Churchill's Private Secretary, Colonial Office, 1921–2. MP (Lib.) for Caithness and Sutherland, 1922–45. Secretary of State for Scotland, 1931–3. Leader, Parliamentary Liberal Party, 1935–45. Secretary of State for Air in Churchill's Coalition Government, 1940–5. Viscount Thurso, 1952.

[2] Sir Alfred Duff Cooper died unexpectedly on a sea voyage on 1 Jan. 1954. He was not yet 64 years old.

February
1954

Sir Winston S. Churchill: speech
(Hansard)

1 February 1954   House of Commons

ADOPTION OF A NEW ARMY RIFLE

This is an interesting controversy and it is one which, I think, is very properly made a subject of debate. Certainly the dispute is not one about which there should be ideological cleavages, party feeling, bad temper, or even insulting language.

We have a common interest in taking the right decision. No party interest is involved in any way, and I really do not think that the hon. Member for Aston (Mr Wyatt) should assume that he is in the presence of a villainous plot when all that has happened is that the best focusing of the latest and best expert advice we can obtain has governed the decisions which have been taken. The hon. Gentleman was fairly moderate this afternoon in what he said, but a week ago in *Reynolds News* he used this sort of language:

> Sir Winston Churchill announced the biggest betrayal of British designers and inventors in political history. It was also the shameful abandonment of the British soldier and of British interests.

The nearest he got to that today was to say that I was lacking in patriotism and guilty of dilatoriness.

I have only a fairly simple tale to tell this afternoon, but before I come to the tale I should like to make a few general observations arising out of what the hon. Gentleman said about the rapidity of fire. He said the new British rifle fired 80 shots as against 40 by the Belgian. As a matter of fact, these two rifles, if used on automatic gear, can fire at the rate of over 600 rounds a minute. Both can fire by semi-automatic gear, that is to say, self-loading but trigger-pulling for every shot, 50 or 60 rounds a minute. That is what I am advised is the case.

I doubt very much whether there is any real military advantage in these extraordinary rates. It seems to me incredible that a human being can give individual thought and aim to 50 or 60 decisions a minute. Even if a very highly trained expert soldier could achieve such a result in peace conditions, I am sure that the ordinary rank and file, especially in these short service days, would simply be wasting their ammunition if they tried to pull the trigger sixty times a minute. In the stress and excitement of battle, the soldier would be far more likely to fire away his limited amount of ammunition, the supply of which is always a main interest especially on the move in the front line.

It is remarkable and indeed odd that the more efficient fire-arms have become, the fewer people are killed by them. The explanation of this apparent paradox is simply that human beings are much more ingenious in getting out of the way of missiles which are fired at them than they are at improving the direction and guidance of these individual missiles. In fact, the semi-automatic and automatic rifles have already, in a certain sense, gained their triumph by largely putting an end to the very mass attacks they were originally devised to destroy.

But those are only general observations upon the point that it is, I think, an error to try to think only in purely technical terms, and that the practical usage and experience and qualities of the human being must be brought into all these questions of modern weapons with their ever-increasing improvements. One of the recurrent military problems of the last one hundred years had been the ever more rapid progress of scientific invention in all countries. In that condition the difficulty has been to choose the moment when to change from research and experiment in major weapons to what the French call *production en série* which, for the benefit of those who have studied ancient rather than modern languages, I will venture to translate as 'mass production'.

The period of transition, perhaps 10 years, in the rifle must be one of awkwardness and anxiety, but to have two different rifles in the Army at the same time is a serious disadvantage. To hold on to an obsolescent type too long may lead to disaster if war comes. On the other hand, to plunge into a new type too soon is to cut oneself off from the further improvements of invention which have now become perpetual.

I am not a technical expert, nor am I attempting to speak as one. I certainly should not have taken part in this discussion but for the fact that I was involved in it during the period when we sat on the other side of the House. I thought it was a mistake of the late Administration to take a plunge into the .280 rifle in April, 1951. That was not because it was not a very good one and a great advance on our well-proven but obsolete .303, but because we might find ourselves all alone with this new rifle for what at that time was mentioned to me as a 10-year transitional period at the very time when our supreme aim was the building up of a grand alliance and a common front between the nations of the free world.

Even if the .280 was the best rifle in the world, which we do not think it now is, I would rather that we were not the only country with it in a longer period of transition. When the various patterns of rifles are all so narrowly matched, it is wiser to keep company with the largest possible number of allies, but it would be a foolish boast to say that we had the best rifle in the world when we had in fact complicated and confused the whole standardisation of the allied arms on the common front, of which common front we form only about a quarter on the Rhine and about one-tenth on the whole NATO front.

To simplify and unify ammunition supply on a common front must be held to rank very high in military policy. It has been said that the general wins who makes the fewest mistakes, and it is very tiresome when ammunition is brought with difficulty and suffering to troops in mortal peril and it turns out to be the wrong kind. Therefore, when competing types are neck and neck, it may well be that standardisation claims priority.

Mr Woodrow Wyatt (Aston) *rose*.

Sir W. Churchill: The hon. Gentleman had better wait. He will get a chance later. Let me point out that when the decision to go into production with the EM2 in isolation was declared by the right hon. Gentleman the Member for Easington (Mr Shinwell) on 25th April, 1951, at that time the problem of finding a common type of ammunition had not been solved and the British pattern rifle had not been devised, as it now has been, to take the .300 round. Therefore, I asserted – this is the only reason I am speaking in this debate – that such policy was a great mistake, but I do not impute any evil motives to the right hon. Gentleman, and I am glad to feel with Pope that: 'To err is human; to forgive, divine.'

Mr E. Shinwell (Easington): Perhaps the right hon. Gentleman will forgive me instantaneously if I venture to interject and to remind him that, although provisionally a decision was taken on the date he mentioned, in April, 1951, we engaged in discussions at Washington with some of the other NATO countries much later in the year and were prepared to consider any suggestions made by the other countries, and it was only because of the American intransigence that we were unable to reach some agreement.

Sir W. Churchill: As I say, the fact remains that the right hon. Gentleman very authoritatively adhered to the .280 round at the time when no arrangements for production of a common round had been made.

The House might be interested to know how it came about that the .300 round was selected. In August, 1951, following an appeal by Canada, which was worried that Britain was what was called 'going out on a limb' with the .280 round, a Defence Ministers' Conference took place in Washington between Great Britain, the United States, Canada and France. At this conference the right hon. Gentleman, who was then Minister of Defence, offered to show the ammunition to NATO on trial. This offer was accepted, and the trials of our .280 round with American .300 round took place in September, 1951.

A vote was taken after the trials, at which the United States and France came down solidly for the .300 round, and Canada, while appreciating the efficiency of the .280 round, considered that the .300 round met all requirements.

Mr Shinwell: I am sorry to interrupt the right hon. Gentleman again, but we had better get the facts right. I was present at that Conference and took part in the negotiations. The position of the United States was as the right hon. Gentleman has stated, the position of France was that she had no opinion at all, and the position of Canada was as stated by the then, and, I think, present, Minister of Defence, Mr Brooke Claxton, that he was quite unconcerned about the size of the round or the type of rifle as long as Canada had the opportunity of producing whatever rifle or whatever round was decided upon.

Sir W. Churchill: All I say is that a vote was taken after the trials, and notwithstanding the vote, which I have described, the British representatives decided to adopt the .280 round and go ahead alone.

Mr Shinwell: Is the right hon. Gentleman suggesting that there was a vote of Ministers at that Conference?

Sir W. Churchill: No, Sir. Notwithstanding the fact that that was the opinion of the different countries at the Conference, it was decided to go on with the .280 round and to go ahead alone. This was a grave decision, and such was the position which we found when we came into office.

There is another aspect affecting the production of the rifle itself. Uniformity of type is not only important on the battlefield but the whole process of manufacture can be simplified and expedited if it is undertaken on a great scale by many allied countries at the same time. Above all, it was, and is, very important to us if possible to keep in step with the United States. Canada certainly never would have adopted a different round from that of the United States, but if both Canada and the United States were making the same rifle and round as Great Britain, that would be of enormous advantage. We should be in a really gigantic pool, meaning not only speed and ease of manufacture but vast reserves capable of transference between allies if the emergency of war rendered it necessary. It was these general reasons and not any claim to expert knowledge of the types involved that led me when in Opposition to intervene.

In October, 1951, when we became responsible, I, as the then Minister of Defence, reversed the right hon. Gentleman's decision of 25th April of that year to proceed with the .280 round and rifle in isolation. I take full responsibility today for that.

In January, 1952, I visited Washington and conferred with President Truman on the whole subject. I should have been perfectly ready to go forward with the .280 EM2 rifle if he would have agreed to adopt it for the American Army. But the overpowering need was to find a common round between us both, or, better still, a common round for NATO. It was not until September, 1953, that the common round was achieved.

Now I come back to the rifle and the reasons why the Belgian was adopted instead of the British. The British and Belgian rifles, both then of .280 calibre, were first tested in the United States in 1950. British and Canadian representatives were present. The conclusion then reached was that the Belgian rifle showed most promise for development. They were tested again in America in 1952, when the Belgian rifle was considered preferable to the British.

Meanwhile, trials were also taking place in Great Britain. In 1951, the Belgian and British rifles were compared — I am giving the information which is given to me by the War Office, and which has been most carefully sifted and examined — and the conclusion reached by the British Trials Board was that the Belgian rifle FN (*Fabrique Nationale*) was technically and most efficient on the score of dependability, functioning and accuracy. That was the view. I am not going into the specially technical aspects as to where they were almost neck and neck, but that was the view taken by the British Trials Board in 1951, and the right hon. Gentleman did say in one of his interventions this afternoon that he had begun to modify his views because of the later information which had reached him.

Mr Shinwell: I was at Washington and took part in the discussions about the rifle. We were not adamant about the round at Washington. We listened to the discussion, took part in it ourselves and came away from Washington with an open mind about the possibility of making modifications in the round, just the same as other people. This is the point I want to take up with the right hon. Gentleman, because it seems to me to be the most important point in these discussions: Are we to understand, from what the right hon. Gentleman had just said, that the British Trials Board, only a few months after they had decided that both the round and the rifle were the best yet produced, actually changed their minds to decide in favour of the Belgian rifle?

Sir W. Churchill: Yes, Sir. Various modifications were thereafter incorporated in the Belgian rifle, and, in 1953, it was subjected to further tests, when it was judged to meet our requirements.

Mr Wyatt: The Prime Minister is deliberately falsifying —

Sir W. Churchill: On a point of order. I demand an apology for that extremely discourteous remark. To say that a Minister dealing with a highly technical and complicated question and endeavouring to give the House information is deliberately falsifying his statements is, I think, unparliamentary in its character.

Mr Wyatt: If I have said anything that I should not have said, I naturally withdraw it and apologise, but I am afraid that in this matter the Prime Minister is endeavouring to put a very partial view on certain trials that have taken place and is not giving the whole truth about them. If I used one brief unparliamentary word to describe that, I am sorry and I withdraw it. May I now come back to the point?

Sir W. Churchill: I have given way once.

Mr Deputy-Speaker (Sir Charles MacAndrew): Order.

Mr Wyatt *rose* —

Sir W. Churchill: I do not know whether I am in possession of the House or not.

Mr Deputy-Speaker: Order. I understood that the Prime Minister complained of something that was said, and that he gave the hon. Member for Aston (Mr Wyatt) the opportunity to withdraw, which he has done. The Prime Minister has the Floor of the House, and unless he gives way the hon. Gentleman cannot rise.

Mr Wyatt: On a point of order. The Prime Minister gave way to me, and I began to say something to him, and he took violent objection. I was never able to say what I wanted to say. The point is this. The Prime Minister said that certain trials had taken place. What we are trying to find out is when, where and under whose auspices. The Prime Minister referred to two trials in America under American auspices, and we know that they were prejudiced against the British rifle, and, not unnaturally, gave a report unfavourable to the British rifle.

It is in the recollection of my right hon. Friend the Member for Easington (Mr Shinwell), of my right hon. Friend the Member for Dundee, West (Mr Strachey), and myself that other trials took place in 1951 in Britain which conclusively showed that the British rifle was the best. I am now trying to find out from the Prime Minister what was this other mysterious trial and where it took place, because nobody on this side of the House — and we were then the Government — ever heard of it. When and where did this trial take place?

Mr Head: This is a purely factual matter of some detail, and it is one about which I should be responsible for knowing something. In answer to the hon. Gentleman, there were two trials. First, the British technical board in April, 1951, made a trial after which their unanimous conclusion was that the FN rifle was efficient in all conditions in the point of view of dependability, functioning and accuracy. That was in 1951. In the same year a user trial took place, after which the verdict was three all. Those were the only two trials that took place with the two rifles in 1951.

Mr Shinwell: The more I listen to this debate, the more I am staggered at what the right hon. Gentlemen opposite have said. Either they have been badly briefed, or there is something very wrong with this business. I am wondering what is behind it. May I put this to the Prime Minister? Is the right hon. Gentleman aware that, when I went to Washington in 1951 — not in April, but much later in the year; I think it was September or October, but it was towards the end of the year — to conduct negotiations with the United States, French and Canadian representatives on the question of the rifle and the round, I was accompanied by men who were regarded as the best military experts in the country on small arms, and by no less a person than Lieut.-General Whiteley,[1] whose reputation, I think, is very high. If at that time I was advised by the War Office that this was the best rifle and the best round, and this was the advice of these military technical experts, supported by the Ministry of Supply experts – and I challenge the right hon. Gentleman the Minister of Supply to deny that; let him look up the records – if that was the way I was briefed, surely what the right hon. Gentleman has just said about the military experts changing their minds indicates that there is something very far wrong?

Sir W. Churchill: I understand that the right hon. Gentleman is going to wind up for the Opposition. I think he would be well advised to keep that lengthy speech for incorporation in his reply.

The right hon. Gentleman said that he was briefed by his experts and by the War Office. I, too, on these technical matters, have been most carefully briefed by them, and I have most carefully checked up, and I am not going to say what I do not believe to be true. I really do not think we should do well in a debate of this kind to start calling each other liars, or as near as we can get to it in Parliamentary language, and I shall certainly not myself be drawn into those depths this afternoon.

Mr C. R. Attlee (Walthamstow, West): We have just been given some information about what occurred in 1951, but the date or the month was not given. I should like to know what time of the year it was.

Mr Head: I did give the months; it was in April and May, 1951.

Sir W. Churchill: The conclusion reached in 1951 by the British Trials Board was that the Belgian FN was technically the most efficient on the score of dependability, functioning and accuracy. Various modifications were thereafter incorporated in the Belgian rifle, and, in 1953, it was subjected to further tests, and was then judged, in 1953, to meet our requirements.

The greatest objection to the isolated production of the .280 or EM2 at that time had been removed. The EM2 was now a .300, and we had achieved a common round among the NATO Powers. Those were great events, but, in the interval, the Belgian FN rifle, which had on several occasions over a long period of years been preferred by certain international expert boards had, in this interval, while we were reaching a common round, been still further improved. It was generally considered more suitable, and as far more likely to be widely adopted than any other competing weapon.

In these circumstances, on 30th October of last year, 1953, the Army Council, taking a different view from its predecessor two years before – (Hon.

---

[1] John Francis Martin Whiteley, 1896–1970. Educated at Royal Military Academy, Woolwich, and Staff College, Camberley. Commissioned 2nd Lt, RE, 1915. On active service, 1915–18, 1939–45. Married, 1929, Margaret Aline Anderson: two children. In War Office, 1935–8. Deputy Director of Organization, Middle East Command, 1940–2. CBE, 1941. Deputy CoS, Middle East Command, 1942–3; Allied Force HQ, North Africa, 1942–4. CB, 1943. Chief Army Instructor, Imperial Defence College, 1945. Commandant, National Defence College, Canada, 1947–9; Canadian Army Staff College, Canada, 1947–9. DCIGS, 1949–53. KCB, 1950. GBE, 1956.

Members: 'Hear, hear'.) – but not under pressure – taking a different view why, do hon. Members suppose? Because things had happened. (Hon. Members: 'Yes'.) – decided to recommend the adoption of the Belgian *Fabrique Nationale*, the Belgian rifle. On 4th November, 1953, the Secretary of State for War formally requested authority to proceed with its manufacture, and I should add, with the large-scale troop trial which is necessary. This was approved and supported by the Ministry of Defence, over which Earl Alexander then presided. I accepted his advice.

Mr H. Hynd (Accrington): Has he resigned?

Sir W. Churchill: I was Minister of Defence when the present Government began, and after a certain time my Noble Friend, Lord Alexander, became Minister of Defence. It has been quite a frequent event to happen with Governments that offices are changed during their continuance. I accepted this advice, which was given to me through the regular channels without any initiation by me, in my dilatory condition, as the hon. Member opposite said, after studying the papers and arguments submitted. The policy received final Cabinet approval on 1st December last. I gave the House, in answer to a Question on 19th January, the main reasons for that decision.

Let us look once more at the procedure in this case. The responsibility for deciding the intricate technical questions I have described rests in the first instance with the War Office, subject to the approval of the Ministry of Defence. The adoption of the Belgian FN rifle was formally proposed to me on the authority of both those departments. I was very glad to find that the weapon was in harmony with certain important practical and tactical conceptions to which my own lengthy experience has led me, but which I should not have dreamed of using as a ground for basing such far-reaching decisions of policy, or deciding such highly complicated matters.

Perhaps I may just mention that, because a lot of Members have experience of actual warfare, and they must know perfectly well that everything is not settled exactly by technical and mechanical considerations. For instance, while being fully up to date in ease and rapidity of fire, a rifle should be carefully safeguarded against too rapid expenditure of ammunition, leading to exhaustion of any supplies which soldiers, or platoons, or even companies, can carry to the front. This is at any rate partially achieved by preventing our new rifle being used as an automatic weapon, unless individual weapons have been specially converted by the field armourers on superior orders, for some particular contingency. The private soldier cannot do it himself. Thus the terrible danger of a convulsive grip pouring away hundreds of precious cartridges is averted. This is quite important, although I have not heard it mentioned.

Mr John Strachey (Dundee, West): That applies to both weapons.

Sir W. Churchill: I only say that that is one of the reasons why I personally like what I have been able to learn about this weapon. I do not pose as a technical expert, but I pose as a man capable of seeing what a disaster it would have been if we had gone for a round which no other nation in our alliance was sharing.

Secondly, the handiness and simplicity of the firing mechanism and the general maintenance of the weapon are deemed superior to the EM2; that is the advice I have received. Thirdly, although it is about 1lb heavier than the EM2, a fact which should not be overlooked, the FN is approximately the same weight as our present Lee–Enfield rifle, to which I have been so long accustomed. The troops have handled that for a long time. The Belgian FN is considered to be a more soldierly weapon on the march.

Mr George Wigg[1] (Dudley): Ah!

Sir W. Churchill: Why should the hon. Gentleman say that? I do not suppose the hon. Gentleman has carried a rifle very far.

Mr Wigg: I challenge the Prime Minister. I have carried a rifle further and longer than the whole of the Government Benches.

Hon. Members: Withdraw.

Sir W. Churchill: I do not withdraw at all. I see nothing invidious or insulting in speaking of the length of time that people have carried a rifle. Certainly not. I do not feel at all ashamed to say that the FN is a more soldierly weapon on the march and is more suited for use in manual exercises – (Hon. Members: 'Ah!') – which hon. Members opposite mock at, but which are very important for discipline and morale. I am assured that it is also easier to teach soldiers how to use this rifle, and that is important in these days of short service. Last, but not least, I repeat what hon. Gentlemen opposite so foolishly mock at, that the FN is a better weapon both with the bayonet and with the butt and is capable of giving confidence to a soldier in a mêlée.

Those are not the reasons for taking the decision. The fact that this rifle, chosen and recommended by the War Office and the Ministry of Defence, seemed to me to embody all those and many other important characteristics, gave me confidence in the wisdom of the professional advice I was receiving.

Mr James Callaghan (Cardiff, South-East): Have the Americans accepted it?

Sir W. Churchill: As hon. Gentlemen on that side of the House are always looking round in every controversy, even in this one about rifles, to try to find fault with the Americans, I suppose if I were to say that the Americans had accepted it, the hon. Gentleman would regard it as a further argument against the rifle.

I will sum up. I have been interrupted by about seven hon. Gentlemen on this occasion. Really, it is not usual to do so, especially on a matter so complicated and technical. What is trying to be worked up, I can see, is prejudice and

---

[1] George Edward Cecil Wigg, 1900–83. Served in Royal Tank Corps, 1919–37; in Army Educational Corps, 1940–6. MP (Lab.) for Dudley, 1945–67. Parliamentary Personal Secretary to Minister of Fuel and Power, 1945–7; to Secretary of State for War, 1947–50; to Minister of Defence, 1950–1. Opposition Whip, 1951–4. Paymaster-General, 1964–7. PC, 1964. Baron, 1967.

hostility and partisanship to cover up what was a gross and scandalous act of folly, namely, embarking on the .280 rifle before achieving a common round.

Mr R. T. Paget (Northampton): If the Prime Minister will not tell us whether the Americans have accepted the Belgian rifle, will he tell us whether anybody has accepted it? Have the French? Have even the Belgians? Are we not alone?

Sir W. Churchill: I am not in the least alarmed by being shouted at. In fact, I rather like it. The descendant of Paget's 'Examen' will, I hope, be very careful and precise in his facts, and be careful in not misrepresenting and misquoting and otherwise defaming other people. He was a great defender of my ancestor.

Mr Callaghan: Will the right hon. Gentleman –

Sir W. Churchill: I really did not know that the hon. Gentleman came into this. I saw the former Secretary of State for War, I saw the hon. Member for Aston (Mr Wyatt); the Leader of the Opposition has a great responsibility, and there is the late Minister of Defence. I thought that they would all have a claim to have a whack, but I do not see why, in a short debate like this, the hon. Gentleman cannot take his chance of rising when he is called.

I wish to conclude. I would have concluded long ago but for the extraordinary rowdiness and malice with which I have been received. I do not ask for any favours of any kind from hon. Gentlemen opposite, but I must say I think they show themselves very unsuited to have calm judgment on a complicated matter of this kind, although I must admit that the hon. Member for Aston did not allow his prejudices or malice against the Belgian rifle to prevent him from making a most remarkable score with it this morning. I hope he will live up to that principle, being a faithful seeker after truth, whatever use he makes of information he is able to obtain.

The British rifle was a fine piece of work, but it would have been fatal to adopt it in isolation, and in the three years that have passed the rival weapons have been continuously improved. We are very lucky to have escaped the isolated inheritance of the .280 calibre and to be able to stand on a general front as well as on a sound foundation.

Antony Head to Sir Winston S. Churchill
(Premier papers, 11/591)

2 February 1954

In your minute dated 28th December, 1952,[1] you asked to be kept informed on the dispersal of the regimental funds and chattels of the disbanded Militia Battalions of Infantry.

The law and practice relating to Charitable trusts require that these funds

---

[1] M.585/52, reproduced above (p. 788).

and chattels should be applied according to cy-pres doctrine,[1] and agreement has now been reached between the Charity Commissioners and the Army Council that the cy-pres application should be in the following order of priority:

(a) Firstly for equivalent purposes, on an equal basis in the Regular and Territorial Battalions of the Regiment concerned.

(b) Secondly for the relief of necessitous cases among personnel of the Regiment past or present, or their dependants. (This has been one of the purposes of many of the existing Trusts for a considerable time.)

In addition it has been agreed that the Trustees of these Regimental chattels should be given power to loan them to Home Guard Battalions where they are not needed by the Regular or Territorial Army Battalions.

The Lord Advocate's Department and the Clerk of the Crown, The Royal Courts of Justice, Ulster, are being informed of the agreement reached between the Charity Commissioners and the Army Council.

Sir Winston S. Churchill to John Selwyn Lloyd
Prime Minister's Personal Minute M.23/54
(Premier papers, 11/701)

2 February 1954

CAIRO TELEGRAM TO FOREIGN OFFICE NO. 133

It is not our intention to be blackmailed into weakening our position on the question of availability by serious incidents in the Canal Zone. I will raise this in Cabinet on Wednesday.

Peter Thorneycroft to Sir Winston S. Churchill
(Premier papers, 11/656)

2 February 1954

THE SAVOY HOTEL

I undertook to keep you informed of developments on the Savoy case.

2. The transfer by the Directors of the Savoy's assets in the Berkeley Hotel Company beyond the control of the Savoy shareholders raises a matter of substantial importance in Company law affecting the whole basis on which the

---

[1] The cy-pres legal doctrine states that when the original intent of a charitable trust becomes impossible or illegal to fulfil, the court will amend the terms of the trust so as to match the original intent as closely as possible.

existing Companies' system operates. I referred the case to the Law Officers for advice, and now attach a copy of their opinion. I would particularly draw your attention to the following extract from paragraph 6:

> 'If the object of the transaction was, as it would appear to be, to dispose of a valuable asset of the Company in such a way as to prevent the Company and its members from exercising control over its future use, it would in our opinion be "misfeasance or other misconduct". Indeed it might be held to be fraud on the ground that the Directors, in their endeavour to defeat existing or potential shareholders, could not have been acting honestly for the benefit of the Company.'

3. In these circumstances it is my statutory responsibility under the Companies Act to decide whether to appoint an Inspector to investigate the affairs of the Company.

4. I have discussed with the Chancellor what should be done, in the light of the Law Officers' opinion. He agrees that the Board of Trade should follow the normal course in cases where the question of an investigation under the Companies Act is raised. That is, to write to the Company, saying that there is a prima facie case for the appointment of an Inspector to investigate its affairs, and inviting the Directors to put forward any observations which they wish to make to enable the Board to consider the matter further.

5. A letter on these lines will be sent to the Company during the course of tomorrow.

Anthony Eden to Sir Winston S. Churchill
Prime Minister's Personal Telegram T.16/54
(Premier papers, 11/665)

3 February 1954
Immediate
Secret and Personal
No. 78

I have tried in my two dinner conversations with Molotov to penetrate a little his relations with Malenkov, having in mind our conversation. I must confess that I have not got very far. He has never once volunteered a reference to Malenkov himself and when I have done so, though perfectly correct in his comments, he has shown no particular enthusiasm. I do not mean to suggest by this that his relations with Malenkov are other than good, but it may be that they are less close personal friends than we know that Molotov and Stalin were.

2. Alternatively, it may be that Molotov regards foreign affairs as his own field and does not like suggestions from any quarter that Malenkov should be

brought into them directly and publicly. He clearly has a very free hand and has never even hinted in any of our talks, public or private, at the need for a reference home. I suppose he could be regarded now as the elder statesman of the Kremlin.

3. Hayter, who has now many contacts with the Russians, agrees with the above, especially paragraph 2, which he believes to be the correct explanation.

Cabinet: conclusions
(Cabinet papers, 128/27)

3 February 1954
Secret
11 a.m.
Cabinet Meeting No. 7 of 1954

[. . .]

2. The Prime Minister drew attention to a telegram from Her Majesty's Ambassador in Cairo (No. 133) suggesting that, in order to break the deadlock in the defence negotiations, he should be authorised to open further discussions with the Egyptians on the availability of the Base, provided that there were no further serious incidents in the Canal Zone. The Prime Minister said that these incidents should not be linked with the defence negotiations, and we should adhere to our final offer to the Egyptians. He agreed, however, that we must soon take steps to end the present deadlock. It was evident from the record of a conversation between Gamal Abdul Nasser[1] and a member of Her Majesty's Embassy that the Egyptians felt that time was on their side and that it was of no advantage to them to conclude an agreement. Our interests, on the other hand, were ill-served by a protraction of the negotiations, which would prevent us from making progress with the re-deployment of our forces and the building up of a strategic reserve. But, before we made any move, we must have a positive plan to put into operation if negotiations broke down, and he hoped that the Committee of Ministers which was considering this plan would report to the Cabinet without delay.

The Lord Chancellor said that his Committee were awaiting the formulation of a definite military plan which entailed obtaining information from the Commanders-in-Chief in the Canal Zone. He hoped they would be able to report to the Cabinet on 10th February.

The Minister of State said that he agreed that, until we had a positive alternative plan, it would be inopportune to open discussions with the Egyptians about the availability of the Base or any other points in the proposals which we had put to them in October. He thought, however, that, when a suitable

[1] Gamal Abdul Nasser, 1918–1970. Entered Egyptian Army, 1938. Lt-Col., 1952. Minister of the Interior, 1953–4. Deputy PM, 1954. President, 1956–70. PM, 1967–70.

time arrived for discussions, we might derive some advantage from offering an alternative formula about the availability of the Base which did not link it up in any way with action by the United Nations.

The Cabinet –

Agreed to resume their discussion on 10th February, on the basis of a report by the Cabinet Committee under the Chairmanship of the Lord Chancellor.

[. . .]

4. The Cabinet had before them memoranda by the Home Secretary (C(54)34) and the Chancellor of the Exchequer (C(54)37) on the possibility of restricting the number of coloured people seeking employment in this country and on the particular question of their employment in the public service.

The Home Secretary said that this problem should be considered in its true perspective. The total number of coloured people at present in this country was about 40,000, compared with 7,000 before the last war, and about 3,000 were entering the country each year. In June 1953 the number of coloured people registered as unemployed was 3,366 and 1,870 were in receipt of national assistance. Of 62 persons convicted in the Metropolitan Police District in the twelve months ending 31st August, 1953, of living on women's immoral earnings 24 had been coloured men. No further action to prevent the immigration of coloured people could be taken without legislation, which might take one of two forms. One possible course was to extend immigration control to all British subjects from overseas. Such an extension could not be confined to coloured people only. It would involve additions to the staff of the Home Office and the Ministry of Labour. The alternative course would be to take power to deport British subjects from overseas who were convicted of a serious criminal offence or found to be a charge on public funds. He recognised that a case could be made for measures to exclude or remove from this country the riffraff amongst British subjects from overseas, and the fact must be faced that at any time the occurrence of some shocking crime involving a coloured person might give rise to strong public feeling on the matter. There was already evidence of some racial feeling in those districts, for example in London, Liverpool and Manchester, where there were concentrations of coloured people. On balance, however, he did not believe that the problem had yet assumed sufficient proportions to justify legislation which would involve a reversal of our traditional practice and would antagonise liberal opinion. It had to be recognised that any action which the Government might take could be easily misrepresented as introducing a 'colour bar'.

The Commonwealth Secretary said that in all other Commonwealth countries except India and Pakistan there were legislative restrictions upon immigration of British subjects. Power to deport undesirable British subjects was available in all those countries. He thought it unlikely that opinion in other parts of the Commonwealth would be disturbed if powers were taken to deport from this country British subjects from overseas.

The Minister of State for Colonial Affairs said that in all the Colonies there was power to restrict entry, and to deport, British subjects from other parts of the Commonwealth. While the Colonial Office would be bound to raise strong objection to the imposition in this country of any restrictions based upon colour grounds alone, the assumption by the United Kingdom Government of power to deport on clearly defined grounds might well be found to be practicable.

The Prime Minister said that the rapid improvement of communications was likely to lead to a continuing increase in the number of coloured people coming to this country, and their presence here would sooner or later come to be resented by large sections of the British people. It might well be true, however, that the problem had not yet assumed sufficient proportions to enable the Government to take adequate counter-measures.

Some support was expressed for the view that the traditional practice in this matter might need modification in the light of changing conditions. Apart from the improvement of means of travel, the raising of standards in the Colonies made their inhabitants better adapted to European conditions and they were attracted to this country by the high level of its Social services. There were, moreover, sound arguments for the view that it was no longer incumbent on the United Kingdom to follow a policy more liberal than that in force in other Commonwealth countries and there might, therefore, be a case for assuming a power to deport from this country British subjects form overseas.

The Cabinet –

Invited the Commonwealth Secretary and the Colonial Secretary to submit a memorandum summarising the present powers of other Commonwealth and Colonial Governments to deport British subjects.

[. . .]

Field Marshal Lord Montgomery to Sir Winston S. Churchill
(Churchill papers, 2/142)[1]

3 February 1954

My dear Winston

Would you very kindly give me your advice about the enclosed.

Is it suitable that I should address the 1900 Club[2] one evening? I have never heard of it, but there is no reason why I should have. I could do it on Saturday 20th March. But I will not do so unless you approve.

Could you send your reply to this address. I am here till 15 Feb.

Please return enclosed letter.

I thought your speech about the rifle was superb!

[1] This letter was handwritten.
[2] A Tory gentlemen's club, founded in 1900.

Sir Winston S. Churchill to Field Marshal Lord Montgomery
(Churchill papers, 2/143)

5 February 1954

My dear Monty,

Thank you for your letter of February 2.[1] I should certainly decide against this. I do not see what you get out of making a confidential speech to the 1900 Club, though it is a very good body and would no doubt be greatly honoured. There would however be an immense amount of talk as to what you have said and the mere fact that it was confidential would lead to all kinds of fairy tales. Moreover it would be argued by the Socialist Party that you ought not to go to one side and not the other, whether confidentially or publicly. The Imperial Defence College would of course be quite a different matter.

There is however a meeting of the Other Club on the 25th where you would not have to make a speech at all but could converse agreeably to a small handful of your friends and admirers.

Sir Winston S. Churchill to Peter Thorneycroft
Prime Minister's Personal Minute M.30/54
(Premier papers, 11/656)

7 February 1954

With regard to the Savoy[2] I think you should consider the great provocation they have received and the fight they were making to preserve the character of their business. This should be set against legal technicalities. After all as soon as they realised they were infringing the law did they not withdraw the new Company and cancel it, so that no shareholders were in fact damaged? There will be a certain amount of sympathy in the House of Commons (not one side only) with the case of employees who had worked for 20 years in the Berkeley Hotel and were to be cleared out for the sake of a profit-making ramp by speculators.

It would be a good thing if you had a word with Lord Swinton who has strong views on the subject.

---

[1] Reproduced immediately above, dated Feb. 3.
[2] See Thorneycroft to Churchill of Feb. 2, reproduced above (pp. 1420–1).

Sir Winston S. Churchill to General Lord Ismay
(Premier papers, 11/771)

8 February 1954
Private and Secret

My dear Pug,

Thank you so much for your letter of January 29.[1]

The idea of the 'empty chair' is not mine but Foster Dulles' suggestion of filling the gap if EDC fails otherwise than by making a different variant of NATO to which the Americans, to my surprise, declared themselves opposed.

I have been thinking a lot about what you say in your last paragraph taken in conjunction with General Gruenther's speech of January 12, an extract of which I enclose. Does this mean that the Soviets have moved some of the Forces they had two years ago upon their Western Front eastward or northward into Russia? What changes have taken place in the last year or two in your and his estimate of their strength on our front? We used to talk of eighty divisions, but now I see that Monty mentions thirty. That would plainly not be enough to overwhelm our existing forces immediately.

That however is not the point I am immediately pursuing. I believe our safety would be enormously increased by a period of Alert before the actual outbreak. If the Soviets have not got a sufficient force on the spot to strike suddenly but would have to move considerable reinforcements towards us, this would assure the necessary Alert being given to our atomic apparatus.

When Gruenther used the word 'concentrate' which I have underlined, did he mean strategic reinforcement of the front opposite to us or merely a tactical concentration? I do not wish you to ask him personally but any information you can give me about the actual strength of the Soviets in the area menacing us compared to one and two years ago would be of interest to me.

The assurance of an Alert before a full-scale ground attack would be a great security against aggressive War by conventional means. This again might affect the probabilities of atomic surprise as the two must be linked together in the Soviet calculations.

[1] Reproduced above (p. 1408).

Sir Winston S. Churchill to Field Marshal Lord Alexander
Prime Minister's Personal Minute M.33/54
(Premier papers, 11/771)

8 February 1954

Could you let me have the best layout your Intelligence permits of the Soviet dispositions and deployment in relation to the Western Front:
(a) now
(b) one year ago
(c) two years ago

I have seen it stated that there have been large-scale movements of their forces both eastward and northward. I am thinking about the chances of an Alert for ground attack caused by necessary hostile concentration.

Sir Winston S. Churchill to Anthony Eden
Prime Minister's Personal Telegram T.21/54
(Premier papers, 11/665)

8 February 1954
Priority
Secret
No. 134

I think you are quite right to try your Far East Meeting. It is important to keep parleys afloat.

Sir Winston S. Churchill to Sir Norman Brook
Prime Minister's Personal Minute M.34/54
(Premier papers, 11/701)

8 February 1954

It should be considered whether the spectacle of large British withdrawals from Egypt would be so disagreeable to the Egyptians as to lead them to attack our troops and thus, ipso facto, impede our departure. It is at least possible they would like the process all except the last 10,000 remaining. If they attack us while we are withdrawing, our case for action is immensely strengthened. I do not myself, expect that an immediate outbreak of Egyptian hostility to delay our departure, is likely. We must consider a period of a year or eighteen months.

FEBRUARY 1954

Peter Thorneycroft to Sir Winston S. Churchill
(*Premier papers, 11/656*)

9 February 1954

Thank you for your minute of 7th February about the Savoy.[1]

I have not yet decided that there should be an investigation into the affairs of the Company;[2] but have simply invited the Company to put forward any observations they may have in order to enable me to consider whether an Inspector should be appointed.

I will naturally take fully into account the points that you make in your minute. I shall certainly talk to Lord Swinton; and should be glad to talk to you about the case, if you would like me to do so.

Defence Committee: minutes
(*Cabinet papers, 131/14*)

9 February 1954
Top Secret
11.30 a.m.
Defence Meeting No. 3 of 1954

[. . .]

3. STATEMENT ON DEFENCE, 1954

The Committee had before them a note by the Minister of Defence (D(54)10) covering a draft of the Statement on Defence, 1954, which was to be published as a Command paper on 18th February and debated in the House of Commons on 2nd March.

The Minister of Defence said that the draft statement had been adjusted to take account of comments made by the Departments concerned and he hoped that the general lines of the draft now before the Committee would be found satisfactory. He was anxious to get early approval, as the Parliamentary time-table made it necessary for the White Paper to be published on 18th February.

In discussion the following points were made:
    (a) Paragraphs 3, 4 and 5 of the Introduction might be held to be inconsistent with the hopes and efforts which we were making at the Four-Power Conference in Berlin. The Minister of State gave to the Minister of Defence a revised version of these paragraphs which

---

[1] Reproduced above (p. 1425).
[2] Churchill circled 'the affairs of the company' and wrote: 'What does this general phrase mean?'

was designed to retain their essential point, but to avoid embarrassment if the Berlin Conference were still in progress when the White Paper was published.

(b) If any impression were given in the White Paper that we intended to relax our defence effort and preparations, this would be seized upon by some other Commonwealth countries as a pretext for relaxing their own.

(c) The Home Secretary suggested that, in view of the attention drawn to the dangers of atomic air attack in paragraph 13, and the section devoted to Civil Defence in paragraphs 85–99, it would be logical to include some forward reference to Civil Defence in the last paragraph of the Introduction (paragraph 17).

The Prime Minister said that he had no doubt that we must maintain our defence effort; and we were in fact doing so. No other country had imposed two years' national service and undertaken so many commitments overseas that it had no formations available for the defence of its own territory. Ministers who had detailed comments to make on the draft Statement on Defence should send them to the Minister of Defence as early as possible, and a revised draft should be circulated for consideration by the Committee on Monday, 15th February.

The Committee:

(1) Approved in principle the draft Statement on Defence, 1954, attached to D(54)10.
(2) Invited Ministers to send detailed comments to the Minister of Defence by 3 p.m. on Thursday, 11th February.
(3) Agreed to conclude their discussion of the draft Statement on Defence, 1954, revised in accordance with Conclusion (2) above, at a meeting to be held on Monday, 15th February.

4. INTELLIGENCE ABOUT THE SOVIET ARMED FORCES

The Prime Minister said that he had been encouraged by the statement in a speech by the Supreme Allied Commander, Europe, to the effect that the Soviet Army was in no position to launch an attack upon Western Europe without further concentration of forces in the forward areas. Would not this involve large and obvious troop movements? If so, it should mean that we could expect a period of alert, during which we should have the opportunity to make further attempts to prevent war and at the same time to press on with vigorous preparations for it. He had asked the Minister of Defence to send him the latest intelligence reports about the disposition of the Soviet Armed Forces.

The Chief of the Imperial General Staff said that he believed that there were now about twenty-two Soviet divisions in Eastern Germany. Allied Forces in Western Germany had improved in quality and in equipment, and there was no doubt that the Soviet Union would have to reinforce their divisions in Eastern Germany and stock up airfields before they could launch an attack on Western Europe. This was, however, a process which might be undertaken gradually and unobtrusively, and it was, therefore, of the greatest importance to watch the movement of Soviet Armed Forces with close attention.

The Committee:

Took note that the Minister of Defence would send the Prime Minister the latest intelligence reports about the disposition of Soviet Armed Forces.

Anthony Eden to Sir Winston S. Churchill
Prime Minister's Personal Telegram T.24/54
(Premier papers, 11/701)

9 February 1954
Immediate
Secret and Personal
No. 122

I understand Cabinet will discuss Egypt on Wednesday and should like to be sure that you know my views.

2. I am more than ever convinced that of the choices before us the least evil is to reach an agreement with Egypt. All the alternatives seem to me to offer worse prospects from the point of view of prestige, military advantage and the economic burden.

3. The Egyptians seem now ready to come nearer to us on availability. The addition of Turkey and Persia would I think be of more practical value than the United Nations formula if not so general. The introduction of Turkey brings NATO into the picture and there was always the risk with United Nations that we might not have got a majority in Assembly.

4. As regards uniform, I assume that our main purpose is to secure the protection of our men. If the Cabinet took the view that this could be secured with a special dress with badges of rank as Chiefs of Staff have suggested, I would concur. An alternative has occurred to me that the Egyptians should recognise that the technicians are British soldiers, with the rights that belong to them as such and that we might then, in return, agree that British uniform shall not in practice be worn. The Egyptians would then recognise as part of the formal agreement that these men are entitled to the same protection, status and privileges as are normally accorded to the uniformed soldiers of a friendly power. This would give us a very strong position when we come to negotiate a 'status of forces' agreement. Perhaps this could be considered.

5. I want you to be in no doubt that my considered view is that we must make every possible effort to reach an agreement soon. I am ready to face any

section of the party in defence of this policy which I believe vital to the future of our relations in the Middle East.

6. I am sending copies of this message to the Lord Chancellor as Chairman of the Ministerial Committee which you have set up, and to Rab and Bobbety.

President Dwight D. Eisenhower to Sir Winston S. Churchill
(Premier papers, 11/1074)

9 February 1954   The White House
Personal

Dear Winston,

Recent reports that you have been on the firing range personally testing the merits of the new Belgian rifle would indicate that you are again in the very best of health. Needless to say, your friends here greet such indications with great joy.

My official reports from Berlin are not quite so discouraging as would be expected after reading some of the Molotov outbursts in the daily press. I grow weary of bad manners in international relationships. When abuse grows so flagrant as to include insult, false charges, and outright vituperation, I sometimes wonder whether we help our own cause by allowing the world to believe us meekly ready to sit quietly under such attacks for no other apparent reason than a desperate hope for a crumb of concession out of the propaganda feast the enemy enjoys at our expense.

The free nations' case must be better understood by the entire world – including ourselves. More and more I come to the conclusion that the salvation of liberty rests upon the unremitting effort of all of us to establish a solidarity among ourselves that in major objectives and purposes will remain firm against any assault. Such an association of free nations must be expanded as widely as possible, even to include very weak nations when those weak nations are exposed directly or indirectly to the threats and blandishments of the Soviets. We are deeply concerned of course with Indo-China, Iran and Egypt. But the entire Moslem world, India and Southeast Asia, as well as our European friends, are all important to us!

Such an association of nations must have clear political, economic and military objectives of its own; while avoiding all belligerence in its attitude, it must still be so firmly confident of its own security that it will have no reason to worry about the possibility that the stupid and savage individuals in the Kremlin will move against us in any vital way.

At the very best, of course, to produce such an association of nations will require the finest of leadership. To this we, the larger nations, must contribute. We must be generous, understanding, determined, and always faithful to our pledges. Tactics will vary. In some areas and on some subjects, we will have to use cajolery; in others, firmness. In some situations, some particular one of the principal countries of the coalition should take the lead in the conduct of negotiations; in others, another will have to assume the burden.

Of one thing I am certain. If we could get real unity of understanding and basic purpose among a few of the principal nations of the free world – including, of course, West Germany – it would not be long until the common security of all of us was vastly improved and the material fortunes of our countries would be advanced markedly and continuously.

The problem, of course, is to achieve much more than mere paper agreement. Our consortium[1] must rest solidly upon a common understanding of the Russian menace and in the clear conviction that only through unity, stubbornly maintained in the face of every inconsequential point of argument and difference between us, can these great things be achieved.

Of course there is no real reason for writing you such a letter as this. Not only do you understand these things better than I – in many instances I have absorbed my ideas from you. But I've been thinking a bit of the future. I am sure that when history looks back upon us of today it will not long remember any one of this era who was merely a distinguished war leader whether on the battlefield or in the council chamber. It will remember and salute those people who succeeded, out of the greatness of their understanding and the skill of their leadership, in establishing ties among the independent nations of the world that will throw back the Russian threat and allow civilization, as we have known it, to continue its progress. Indeed, unless individuals and nations of our time are successful – soon – in this effort, there will be no history of any kind, as we know it. There will be only a concocted story made up by the Communist conquerors of the world.

It is only when one allows his mind to contemplate momentarily such a disaster for the world and attempts to picture an atheistic materialism in complete domination of all human life, that he fully appreciates how necessary it is to seek renewed faith and strength from his God, and sharpen up his sword for the struggle that cannot possibly be escaped.

Destiny has given priceless opportunity to some of this epoch. You are one of them. Perhaps I am also one of the company on whom this great responsibility has fallen.

---

[1] consortium.

FEBRUARY 1954

Cabinet: conclusions
(Cabinet papers, 128/27)

10 February 1954
Secret
11 a.m.
Cabinet Meeting No. 8 of 1954

[. . .]
5. The Cabinet considered a telegram from the Foreign Secretary (Berlin telegram No. 120) commenting on the proposal for a Five-Power Meeting (Berlin telegram No. 113) which the United States Secretary of State had put forward at a private discussion between the four Foreign Ministers in Berlin. The Foreign Secretary had pointed out that in further discussion of this question it might be difficult to maintain the unity of the three Western Powers; but he had added that their main concern must be to prevent any appearance of disunity, even though that might mean that he would have to defend positions which fell short of what the United Kingdom alone might have been able to offer.

The Minister of State said that, in his view, the American proposal was unfortunately worded and unduly restricted in its scope. He hoped that it might be possible to persuade Mr Dulles to accept a modified draft. It was most important that the offer to hold a Five-Power Meeting should be kept open, even if its scope was restricted. He agreed with the Foreign Secretary, however, that we must avoid any appearance of disunity between the Western Powers.

The Minister of Housing emphasised the need to give support to the French Foreign Minister. It was now likely that no agreement would be reached on the unification of Germany and in these circumstances M Bidault, who had been firm in his support of the European Defence Community, would need all the help we could give him in persuading the French Parliament to proceed to its ratification. He was unlikely to find support for this course unless it was clear to French public opinion that he had not sacrificed French interests in Indo-China.

The Prime Minister said that the fact of a Five-Power Meeting would be more important than its form. If small results were obtained from Berlin, there would still be hope that something better might be obtained from a Five-Power Meeting, and it would be a point gained if the United States and the Chinese People's Government sat down at the same conference table. For these reasons he thought the Cabinet might tell the Foreign Secretary that he should do his best to secure a Five-Power Meeting, and that he need not feel obliged to defend every detailed argument used by the French and the Americans on particular points, though he should maintain the unity of the three Western Powers on all issues of principle.

The Cabinet –

Invited the Minister of State to send a message to the Foreign Secretary on the lines suggested by the Prime Minister.

6. When the Cabinet had considered on 28th January the possible courses which would be open to the Government in the event of a breakdown in the defence negotiations with Egypt,[1] they had been disposed to agree that the best alternative policy would be to wind up the Base in the Canal Zone, to re-deploy the British Forces in the Middle East in our own time, and in Egypt to stand on our rights under the Treaty of 1936. They had appointed a Committee of Ministers to consider the military and legal implications of such a policy.

The Cabinet now had before them a memorandum by the Lord Chancellor (C(54)45) presenting the conclusions of this Committee. The Appendix to this memorandum outlined the military plan recommended by the Chiefs of Staff, after consultation with the Commanders-in-Chief, Middle East, for carrying out such a policy. This envisaged that the Base would be wound up by clearing Tel El Kebir first and rolling up from the south. It would be two years before this process could be completed, and the Treaty force (of 10,000 ground troops and 2,000 RAF) would eventually take up their position in an area round Moascar/Abu-Sueir. They would there be adjacent to a land-force Treaty area, though not within it; and they would be in a position to control the bridges over the Suez Canal and the supply of black oil to Cairo. Their lines of communication, and their eventual line of evacuation, would be through Port Said. The project of a defended perimeter near Suez, which had been mentioned in the Cabinet's discussion on 28th January, had been abandoned – partly for legal reasons, but mainly because there was no accommodation for such large numbers of troops near Suez and it would not be justifiable to build it at this stage.

The Committee were satisfied that a reasonable legal defence could be put forward for this policy if it were challenged before an international tribunal during the two years that would necessarily be spent in winding up the Base and evacuating seven-eighths of the British Forces now in Egypt. We should be on strong legal grounds if we had announced that we were in process of evacuating the Base and reducing our troops to the numbers prescribed in the Treaty and if we had ensured that all our actions taken in Egypt thereafter were demonstrably directed towards that end. For we were clearly entitled to take a reasonable time to withdraw, and during that time we should be entitled to safeguard the security of our troops. It would not be necessary to announce in advance the precise positions which we expected to be occupying in 1956; and the question whether we could justify in law the positions actually occupied in 1956 would depend on the circumstances at that time.

---

[1] See Cabinet: conclusions of Jan. 28, reproduced above (pp. 1405–8).

In discussion of this alternative policy the following points were made:
 (a) This plan for winding up the Base could not be carried through successfully without Egyptian cooperation. Some of the British authorities in Egypt thought it unlikely that this cooperation could be secured if the policy had to be presented to public opinion in this country as a policy of standing on our rights under the Treaty of 1936.

 The Prime Minister said that it should not be assumed that the Egyptians would necessarily withhold their cooperation. If this plan were put into operation, it would be seen in Egypt that large numbers of British troops were being withdrawn; and the Egyptians might well feel that they need not offer active opposition to that part of the plan which provided for the evacuation of seven-eighths of the British forces now in Egypt. If, on the other hand, the Egyptians showed active hostility and resorted to violence, a new situation would be created in which it would be easier for us, both politically and militarily, to take a firmer line.

 (b) The Chief of the Imperial General Staff said that he was mainly concerned about the security of the small force of 12,000 which under this plan would eventually be concentrated in the middle of the Canal Zone, with no power to safeguard its communications with Port Said or Suez.

 The Prime Minister said that any military attack on this force would be regarded as an act of war which would justify us, not merely in reinforcing those troops, but in using air power in retaliation against the Egyptian forces.

 (c) If this policy were adopted, we should have to explain why we attached less importance than we had hitherto to the maintenance of an effective Base in the Canal Zone. It would have to be made clear that no Base could be effective in war without the cooperation of the local government and the availability of local labour. The policy would have to be presented simultaneously with the plan for the redeployment of our forces in the Middle East in areas where local cooperation was more likely to be forthcoming.

 (d) If this policy were adopted, it would probably be expedient that, in addition to any public announcement, we should also make our intentions plain in a secret communication to the Egyptian Government. This could go further than the public announcement: it could, in particular, make it clear that any interference with our withdrawal by organised Egyptian forces would be regarded as an act of war.

The Prime Minister, summing up this part of the discussion, said that further study should be made of the alternative policy outlined in C(54)45.

In particular, a detailed time-table should be prepared, showing the sequence of the military movements involved and their relation with the political steps which would have to be taken. For this purpose it could be assumed that the small British force of 12,000 which would eventually remain in Egypt under this plan need not be confined wholly within the areas prescribed in the Treaty for land forces.

The Cabinet then proceeded to discuss the prospects of securing a new defence agreement with Egypt.

The Lord Chancellor reminded the Cabinet that the alternative policy outlined in C(54)45 had been suggested as one which might be adopted only if the defence negotiations with Egypt came to nothing. He himself believed that the more satisfactory course would be to conclude a new defence agreement and he would be ready, if necessary, to make some further concessions to the Egyptians in order to obtain such an agreement.

The Prime Minister said that the terms which had been offered to the Egyptians in October had been presented as our final offer. It was on this basis that we had persuaded the United States Government to urge the Egyptians to accept them. And we had hitherto resisted all American suggestions that those terms should be modified with a view to making them more acceptable to the Egyptians. Were we now to give away, because of Egyptian intransigence, what we had been unwilling to concede in response to the suggestions of our American friends? This would surely weaken our bargaining position with the Egyptians. And it would certainly provoke criticism from Government supporters in the House of Commons.

The Minister of State said that we should certainly be on weak ground if we appeared to be offering concessions to the Egyptians at this stage. There was, however, some possibility of alterations in the October terms which would be to our advantage. Thus, on the clause regarding the availability of the Base in war, it had now been suggested that the Egyptians might be willing to accept a formula which included a reference to attacks on Turkey or Persia; and this would probably be preferable, from our point of view, to our own formula which in effect involved arbitration by the United Nations. On the wearing of uniforms by British technicians in the Base, we had less scope for varying our terms without appearing to make concessions to the Egyptians. But it was perhaps arguable that our essential needs would be met if the Egyptians could be brought to agree that these technicians, though not entitled to wear military uniform, would have the right of carrying personal arms and would be exempt from the jurisdiction of Egyptian courts.

In further discussion the Cabinet showed little disposition to compromise on the October terms, particularly on the clause asserting the right of British technicians in the Base to wear military uniform. It was argued that we should derive little long-term advantage from a defence agreement with Egypt if we seemed to have been forced to accept unsatisfactory terms under Egyptian pressure. An agreement concluded in that atmosphere would impair our influence in other countries in the Middle East.

The Cabinet —
(1) Agreed that no steps need yet be taken to bring to a conclusion the current negotiations for a new defence agreement with Egypt.
(2) Invited the Minister of Defence and the Minister of State to arrange for further study to be given to the details of the alternative policy outlined in C(54)45, and for a timetable to be prepared of the military and political action which would have to be taken under that policy.
(3) Agreed to resume their discussion at a later meeting, in the light of a report of the studies to be made in pursuance of Conclusion (2).

[...]

8. The Prime Minister said that the Governor of Kenya,[1] in considering whether he should recommend commutation of the sentence of death passed on a leader of the Mau Mau rebels known as General China,[2] should give due weight to the fact that it was now being claimed on General China's behalf that he had given himself up in response to the Government's offer of an amnesty. In view of the importance of convincing Mau Mau supporters generally of the reliability of this offer, might it not be advantageous to exercise clemency in General China's case, even though the Government did not in fact accept his claim to have surrendered under the terms of the amnesty? It appeared from paragraph 3 of the Governor's telegram No. 113 that he would be prepared to consider commutation in certain circumstances.

The Colonial Secretary said that on the facts there was no room for doubt. The judge who had tried General China had stated publicly that he did not believe that the rebel leader had given himself up in response to the surrender offer. On the question of expediency he was in full agreement with the Governor's view that commutation of the sentence would have a deplorable effect in Kenya, particularly among the Government's Kikuyu supporters, and would encourage the rebels to fight to the last in the belief that they would, even then, be treated with clemency. He did not share the Governor's view of the circumstances in which commutation of this sentence would be justified. There was, however, another case of a Mau Mau leader in which a claim that surrender had been made in response to the Government's surrender offer might possibly be established. In that event commutation of that sentence might be considered to be justified.

The Cabinet —

---

[1] Evelyn Baring, 1903–73. Governor of Southern Rhodesia, 1942–4. KCMG, 1942. High Commissioner of South Africa, 1944–51. KCVO, 1947. Governor and C-in-C of Kenya, 1952–9. GCMG, 1955. KG, 1972.

[2] Waruhiu Itote, 1922–93. Known as 'General China'. Served in KAR, 1942–6. Member, Kenya Africa Union, 1946–50. Leader of Mau Mau rebellion, 1950–4; captured by British forces, 1954.

Took note of the Colonial Secretary's view that commutation of the sentence passed on General China would not be warranted but that, where a claim to have surrendered in response to the Government's surrender offer could be clearly established by a Mau Mau leader, commutation of sentence might be justifiable.

[. . .]

11. The Cabinet had before them memoranda by the Prime Minister (C(54)39) and the Commonwealth Secretary (C(54)49) and a note by the Secretary of the Cabinet (C(54)48) about a proposal that The Queen, during her forthcoming tour of Ceylon, should visit the Temple of the Tooth at Kandy.

The Prime Minister said that, whereas the late Prime Minister of Ceylon[1] had been of the opinion that in all the circumstances The Queen should not visit the Temple, the present Prime Minister of Ceylon[2] was strongly in favour of such a visit and hoped that Her Majesty would be willing to observe Buddhist etiquette by removing her shoes when she entered the Temple. It has been ascertained that The Queen was anxious to meet the wishes of her Ceylonese subjects in this matter, and there did not appear to be any ground on which the Cabinet should consider tendering advice in a contrary sense.

The Cabinet –

Took note with approval of the Prime Minister's statement.

House of Commons: Oral Answers
(Hansard)

11 February 1954

CABINET PAPERS (ACCESS)

46. Mr Bellenger asked the Prime Minister whether he will define the rule governing the access to Departmental or Cabinet papers by former Ministers of the Crown.

The Prime Minister: So much general agreement was expressed on Tuesday that there is little for me to add. The rule is that a former Minister may refresh his memory of any Cabinet documents which were issued to him while in office.

Mr H. Morrison: Or Departmental papers?

The Prime Minister: There is no fixed rule about Departmental documents, but especially where the matter enters the field of political controversy,

---

[1] Stephen Senanayake, 1883–1952. Educated at St Thomas School, Mutwal. Managed family graphite mines. Elected to National House, 1942. Formed United National Party, 1946. Selected as first PM of Ceylon on the country's independence in 1948. Suffered a stroke while on horseback; d. Mar. 1952.

[2] John Lionel Kotelawala, 1895–1980. Educated at Christ's College, Cambridge, and Royal College, Colombo. Member, State Council of Ceylon, 1931. Minister for Communications and Works, 1935. Minister for Transport and Works, 1947. PM, Minister of Defence and External Affairs, 1953–6. Published *An Asian Prime Minister's Story* (1956). Knighted, 1965.

it would certainly be usual to give similar facilities in regard to Departmental documents seen by a Minister or used by him during his period of office. I may say that should any disagreement occur at any time on a Departmental issue the Prime Minister of the day, who is in charge of the Administration, should certainly be appealed to.

Mr Bellenger: I thank the right hon. Gentleman for that answer, but is he not aware that my right hon. Friend the Member for Easington (Mr Shinwell) was denied access to a Departmental document by a permanent official? Does he not deprecate that?

The Prime Minister: I have looked into that in some detail, and I have written to the right hon. Member for Easington (Mr Shinwell) a very lengthy letter, enclosing a bundle of documents. What happened was that there was a misunderstanding. There is no question that he had a right of access to the document in question, nor was it ever intended to deny it, nor was there any need to do so. So far as I can see it, this document in question, was utterly without significance. Had he said on the telephone, 'I wish to see the document' and requested to see it, he would have been invited to come and see it at the earliest possible convenience.

Mr H. Morrison: What did he say on the telephone?

The Prime Minister: I do not know what he said; but it was a *bona fide* misunderstanding. They told him there was nothing in the document, and they thought he did not insist on any sudden appointment being made to see it. I might explain that it is not customary to circulate a document. Access is given at the office, because when we are in private life we may not all have facilities for keeping documents. I think that this is much the best way to do it. But he had an absolute right to see that document and it was not intended in any way to challenge that right.

Mr Morrison: I am much obliged to the right hon. Gentleman for that assurance which, I think, now puts us right. I would only ask him whether he does not recall that in the long years in which he was Minister, and in the long years in which he was an ex-Minister, he himself has been very active in asserting his right to Departmental documents, and whether he will see that he will at least give us the same rights – (Hon. Members: 'The Prime Minister said so.') – the same rights as he has most vigorously asserted himself? If they had been denied to the right hon. Gentleman I can imagine the fury with which he would have addressed the Government from this Box.

The Prime Minister: I have paid some tribute to the manner in which the party opposite conducted this aspect of our affairs, and, as I said, we have every intention of continuing, as they did, to keep alive the easy tradition that has grown up. Occasions will occur when there will be disputes like this one by which the general tenor of our ways is maintained harmoniously. I beg the right hon. Gentleman the Member for Easington (Mr Shinwell) to wait until the letter I am sending him reaches him.

Mr Shinwell: I am glad to know that the right hon. Gentleman has communicated with me, but I have not yet received the letter. Is not much of what the right hon. Gentleman has said about this telegram business an after thought? Is not this a discovery made after the event? Is it not true to say, and quite factual, that the Department did not advise me at the time, when I asked for copies of the document, that they would have no significance? They only informed me about that very long afterwards. All that I asked for was a copy of documents which were relevant to the debate. I was told that I could not have copies. There was not even a suggestion that I could have access to a copy of the telegram if I came to the Department. That was never mentioned to me at the time.

The Prime Minister: In my letter and the enclosure which I am sending to the right hon. Gentleman there is a statement which was made by the persons who answered him at the end of the telephone. I think that one of them was his former private secretary.

Mr Shinwell: I am not complaining about that.

The Prime Minister: They certainly thought that the right hon. Gentleman was satisfied and was not pressing the matter further. Let there be no doubt on the matter of principle. If the right hon. Gentleman wishes to have that document he has the right to have access to it, and if he wishes to do so now he has the right.

Mr Bowles:[1] Would it not save a lot of trouble if back benchers also were allowed to see this document?

The Prime Minister: I think it might make a bad precedent. It certainly would cause no inconvenience if this particular telegram and the Ministerial comment upon it were made available, but I think it would be a bad precedent.

Peter Thorneycroft to Sir Winston S. Churchill
(Premier papers, 11/656)

11 February 1954

Your further minute of 10th February on the Savoy case.[2]

Section 165 of the Companies Act empowers the Board of Trade to appoint an Inspector 'to investigate the affairs of a company'. This phrase is therefore invariably used in Orders appointing Inspectors, but the Order usually goes on to specify the particular matters into which the Inspector should enquire. In this case – if an Inspector were to be appointed – the particular matters stated in the Order would be the formation of the new company and the transfer to it of the freehold of Berkeley Hotel property. It is the action of a Board of

---

[1] Francis George Bowles, 1902–70. Educated at University College London and London School of Economics. Solicitor, Pearl Assurance Co., 1925–47. MP (Lab.) for Nuneaton, 1942–64. Deputy Chairman of Ways and Means, 1948–50. Capt. of the Yeomen of the Guard, 1964–70. Baron, 1964.

[2] See Thorneycroft to Churchill, Feb. 9, reproduced above (p. 1428 and n.2).

Directors in transferring the assets of one company to another, without proper financial consideration accruing to the Shareholders of the former company and without their consent, which has caused such perturbation.

General Lord Ismay to Sir Winston S. Churchill
(Premier papers, 11/771)

12 February 1954
Private and Secret

My dear Prime Minister,
 Many thanks for your letter of 8th February.[1] I will try to answer your questions in the order that you have put them.
 The Soviets have not moved any significant forces from their Western front, either eastward or northward; nor have there been any significant changes in SHAPE's estimate of Soviet strength on our front in the last two years. This has always stood at 30 M-day divisions, and I do not know how the figure of 80 divisions crept in. It must have included satellite divisions or Soviet reserve divisions.
 Before dealing with the vital question of an alert period, may I give you some further figures. At the end of 1953, we had 18 M-day divisions facing 30 Russian M-day divisions. By M+30 our figure goes up to 33 divisions and the Russian to 100 Soviet and satellite divisions; but some of the satellite divisions are not first line troops. The 12 German divisions contemplated under EDC are, of course, not included in our order of battle, so you can see what an immense difference they would make.
 The above figures relate only to the central front: but the general impression is that the situation is slightly more favourable to us on the other fronts. The overall Russian peace-time strength is estimated at 175 divisions, of which only 30 that I have mentioned are outside Russia proper. Their believed dispositions are:

East Germany	22
Poland	2
Hungary	2
Austria	2
Roumania	<u>2</u>
<u>Outside Russia</u>	<u>30</u>
<u>Russia Proper</u>	145

 So much for figures. Now to return to your other questions. When Gruenther used the word 'concentrate', he meant tactical concentration not strategic reinforcement. I ought also to add that when he said that the 'shield' was

---

[1] Reproduced above (p. 1426).

sufficiently strong not to be overcome, he meant not to be overcome within the first two or three weeks. But the way I look at it is that the Soviets must realise that 18 good and ever improving divisions, plus atomic weapons, would not be easily brushed aside.

Now for the all-important question of an alert period. All here entirely agree that our safety would be enormously increased by a period of alert of, say, five to seven days, before the actual outbreak. With less than five to seven days warning, the curve of actual forces that we would require rises very steeply. Further, I am advised that this alert period would only be fully effective if:

(i) General mobilisation and all the other precautionary measures are taken at the very beginning of the warning: and
(ii) The decision to use non-conventional weapons is made before either side opens fire.

We have for some time been working away at the arrangements that are necessary to enable a general alert to be given at the earliest possible moment: but I confess that, however simple and sensible these arrangements may be, it will be very difficult to get Governments to take the plunge if and when the time comes. You remember what happened in the latter days of August, 1939. Our request that the precautionary period should be put into force on about the 20th August was met by the Cabinet of the day with the objection that it was vital not to send up the temperature and that only the very minimum precautions should be taken. If that could happen in the case of one Government, when Hitler's intentions were so completely obvious, how much more difficult it is going to be for fourteen Governments to take the plunge, when much is concealed behind an iron curtain.

Lady Churchill to Sir Winston S. Churchill
(*Churchill papers, 1/50*)[1]

13 February 1954

Winston,

I have read a second time this dynamic letter.[2]

I think Eisenhower looks to you for help.

It is a bitter disappointment, but alas, I fear he is right about the Russian menace.

But if only America were not so unsympathetic & indeed unhelpful to us over Egypt, India in the past & now the clumsy suggestion to Pakistan – we could go all in with her more easily. I wish you could see 'Ike'.

I think his letter is a tribute to you and is modest about himself.

[1] This letter was handwritten.
[2] From Eisenhower to Churchill of Feb. 9, reproduced above (pp. 1431–2).

Sir Winston S. Churchill to Winston Churchill
(Churchill papers, 1/51)

13 February 1954

My dearest Winston,

 I thought you would like to have these new stamps to put in your collection. They have only just been issued.

 I am also sending you the Table Plan of a Dinner I attended on Thursday – you will see that for the occasion I became Master Churchill!

 I hope you are well and enjoying yourself, & settling down at Eton.

Yr loving Grandfather

Sir Winston S. Churchill to Anthony Eden
Prime Minister's Personal Telegram T.34/54
(Premier papers, 11/665)

15 February 1954
Immediate
Secret and Personal
No. 208

 I see that you have agreed to 'end' the Conference on Thursday. Please consider whether you could not carry 'adjourn sine die'. It might make it easier to come together without all the pomp and ceremony, and also it would show that any contacts would endure. Moreover it strengthens the impression that there is no complete breakdown.

Sir Winston S. Churchill to Anthony Eden
Prime Minister's Personal Telegram T.35/54
(Premier papers, 11/665)

15 February 1954
Immediate
Secret
No. 222

 Another version: say au revoir and not goodbye.

 Your telegram No. 184 just arrived. I quite see the force of its last sentence.[1] All good luck.

---

[1] This read: 'We may well be faced at the last moment by an attempt on Molotov's part to represent our discussions on Germany as merely adjourned for a few months, so as to enable the opponents of EDC to argue that there is still hope of an alternative solution. We must avoid this.'

Winston Churchill to Sir Winston S. Churchill
(*Churchill papers, 1/51*)[1]

15 February 1954

Dear Grandpapa,

Thank you very much for the lovely stamps, they are most beautiful; thank you also for your letter. I wish I could see the cygnets.

Yesterday our 1st XI played Horris Hill 1st XI; they made 82 for 8 wkts declared and we made 93 for four wkts. At one moment we had six minutes in which to make ten runs to win. I am doing lots of swimming in the indoor swimming pool and having lots of fun. Longing to see you in the holidays.

Cabinet: conclusions
(*Cabinet papers, 128/27*)

17 February 1954
Secret
11 a.m.
Cabinet Meeting No. 9 of 1954

[. . .]

3. The Prime Minister drew attention to a telegram from Khartoum (Khartoum Telegram No. 28) reporting a speech made by the Prime Minister of the Sudan on the occasion of the anniversary of the signing of the Anglo-Egyptian Agreement. The speech was strongly biased in favour of Egypt, and contained statements to the effect that the Sudan would never consider herself free unless the Suez Canal was evacuated, and that Britain should realise that the time had passed for forcible occupation of other people's lands. These hostile sentiments would be ill-received in this country.

The Cabinet –

Took note of this statement.

4. The Minister of State said that the Four-Power Meeting in Berlin would be concluded before the end of the week. It was already clear that no agreement would be reached over Germany or Austria, but there was still a possibility of some agreement about a Conference on the Far East.

The Prime Minister said that, even though no decisions were reached, some advantage might accrue from the fact that there had been no violent disharmony in the conduct of the discussions and no lasting sense of frustration at their conclusion. The Cabinet would wish to have an early opportunity of hearing the Foreign Secretary's account of the Meeting; and, if it were convenient to him, the Cabinet might meet for that purpose on the afternoon of 22nd February.

---

[1] This letter was handwritten.

[...]

8. The Prime Minister drew attention to a telegram from the Governor of Kenya stating that there was now some possibility that General China might be ready to arrange for a substantial number of Mau Mau rebels to surrender under the conditions of the amnesty offer and that, if he were able to bring this about, this would justify the commutation of his sentence. The Prime Minister expressed the view that, once negotiations had been opened with General China on that basis, it would not be justifiable to execute the death sentence even if the negotiations failed.

The Colonial Secretary did not dissent from that view. He himself adhered to his original opinion that this sentence should have been carried into effect, despite any attempt by General China to purchase his life by an offer to give information or to procure the surrender of a number of his followers. But the exercise of clemency was a matter for the Governor's discretion, in which he did not propose to intervene.

The Cabinet –

(1) Took note of these statements.

The Cabinet considered a memorandum by the Colonial Secretary (C(54)50) recommending that more effective steps should be taken to neutralise the passive supporters of Mau Mau and, in particular, the large numbers of unemployed Kikuyu who had drifted into Nairobi. He proposed that the Governor of Kenya should be authorised to hold substantially increased numbers of these persons in detention and that, while under detention, they should be required to undertake useful employment. This course had been recommended despite the fact that it was thought to involve a technical breach of the Forced Labour Convention of 1930 and of the Convention on Human Rights adopted by the Council of Europe.

The Colonial Secretary said that, since his memorandum was circulated, the legal difficulties had been further discussed with representatives of the other Departments concerned. As a result it was now agreed that breach of the two Conventions could be avoided if the employment to be undertaken in the detention camps were in some way related to the emergency. It was therefore proposed that the regulation authorising compulsory employment should contain words to the effect that any person detained in a special detention camp might be usefully employed in work which, in the opinion of the officer in charge, would assist in bringing the emergency to an end. He proposed to instruct the Governor to make the regulation in this form. In these circumstances it would probably be unnecessary to pay market rates of wages for work undertaken by prisoners in the detention camps.

The Minister of Labour welcomed this modification of the proposal originally put forward in C(54)50. It would be much easier to defend this modified plan if it were challenged at an International Labour Conference or elsewhere.

The Cabinet –

(2) Approved the proposals for large-scale detention of Mau Mau

supporters in Kenya, and for requiring them to undertake useful employment while under detention, on the basis proposed in the discussion; and authorised the Colonial Secretary to instruct the Governor of Kenya accordingly.

[. . .]

Sir Norman Brook to Sir Winston S. Churchill
(*Premier papers, 11/601*)

19 February 1954

It was in 1934 that the present practice was adopted of asking Ministers not to take Cabinet papers away with them on vacating office. Since then the rule has been enforced with varying success. A few Ministers have insisted on taking some papers away with them; and a few former Ministers, who had left office before 1934, have declined to return papers in their possession. You will also remember that in 1945 you ruled that Ministers might take with them copies of War Cabinet papers and similar documents which they had written themselves. In general, however, the rule is pretty fairly established that Ministers will leave their papers behind on vacating office – on the understanding that they may thereafter have access to them at any time on application to the Secretary of the Cabinet.

On a change of Government involving a change of Party, Cabinet papers are not left in the Departments but are collected by the Cabinet Office – so as to ensure compliance with the rule that members of the Government in office may not have access to the political papers of a preceding Administration of a different political colour.

2. I understand that Mr Shinwell has also asked whether the rule is uniformly applied that a former Minister desiring access to a paper which he saw when in office must go for the purpose to his old Department or to the Cabinet Office. This is the general rule – for the reason, which you yourself gave in answering supplementary Questions on 11th February,[1] that in private life former Ministers may not all have facilities for keeping secret documents. But in the Cabinet Office we try to be as considerate as possible. If a former Minister wishes to see a number of documents, or a document which is readily available only in a bound volume, we usually ask him to call here. But I may sometimes send the papers to the House of Commons or to a private house by the hand of a member of my staff, who will show them to the former Minister and bring them back. Occasionally, when circumstances warrant it, I may send a loose copy of a paper by messenger asking that it may be returned to me as soon as it has served its purpose. But it is fair to say that our general rule

---

[1] See House of Commons: Oral Answers of Feb. 11, reproduced above (pp. 1438–40).

is to ask a former Minister to come here and to put a room at his disposal for the purpose.

Sir Winston S. Churchill to Sir Norman Brook
Prime Minister's Personal Minute M.35/54
(Premier papers, 11/601)

20 February 1954
Private

Thank you for your minute of February 19. There is an inevitable distinction in the case of documents written by the Minister himself, of which he may have retained a copy and the copyright. I was also allowed by the incoming Socialist Government in 1945 to take all my papers away, but I think I left a large number behind.

Cabinet: conclusions
(Cabinet papers, 128/27)

22 February 1954 Prime Minister's Room,
Secret House of Commons
4 p.m.
Cabinet Meeting No. 10 of 1954

1. The Foreign Secretary gave the Cabinet his impressions of the Four-Power Meeting in Berlin. One of the most noticeable features had been the extreme rigidity of the Soviet attitude towards European problems. There had been no yielding, even on Austria, where it might have been thought that the Russians could gain some public approval at little cost. This attitude was probably due to the fear that, if any concessions were made, others would at once be demanded. Thus, the Russians justified their retention of troops in Hungary because it was on their line of communication to Austria; and, if they had agreed to withdraw their troops from Austria, there would no doubt have been a demand for a withdrawal from Hungary. It had also been suggested that the dominating influence in Russian policies was now held by the military leaders, and that they had insisted that no positions in Europe should be sacrificed. If either of these explanations was correct, it was clear that Russian policy was dictated by a sense of weakness and was for that reason unlikely to change. He did not think, however, that the Russians had any real fear of the Germans in the immediate future or that they would regard the ratification of the European Defence Community (EDC) as a serious threat demanding some form of military counter-action. It was even possible that M Molotov had recognised that the EDC was itself an insurance against future German aggression. On

the other hand, there was no doubt that the Russians were genuinely alarmed by the development of United States bases throughout the world and by the large programme of airfield construction in Western Europe.

In general the discussions had not been marked by any bitterness and, even though little result had been achieved, there was no heightened tension in the relations between the Four Powers.

The relations between the Soviet Union and the Chinese People's Republic would need careful study. M Molotov had shown himself most anxious to reach agreement on a Five-Power Meeting at Geneva. His attitude on this had been much less rigid: he had been prepared to negotiate on it. Mr Dulles and M Bidault had formed the view that the reason for this was that since Stalin's death the Chinese Communists were less ready to accept advice from the Kremlin and that the Russians feared that the Chinese leaders, unless treated with care, might entangle the Soviet Union in dangerous commitments.

M Molotov had signally failed to cause any break or dissension among the Foreign Ministers of the three Western Powers. M Bidault had retained his resolution despite Russian blandishments and bullying. Mr Dulles had taken a considerable political risk in supporting the Five-Power Meeting at Geneva.

The Foreign Secretary said that the most urgent question was now the ratification of the EDC. In Berlin he had gained the impression from many Germans, from both political and business circles, that Western Germany was becoming impatient of the policy of the Western Powers. The Germans were once again growing prosperous, and with their prosperity had come a strain of arrogance. It was urgent, therefore, that France should ratify the EDC and that the Bonn Agreements, which had been concluded nearly two years ago, should come into force at an early date. He had had further discussions with M Bidault about United Kingdom association with the EDC and there were certain proposals which he would like to discuss with the Minister of Defence before they were considered by the Cabinet. We could not give the French an assurance that we would retain British forces in Germany on a pre-determined level, especially as it was certain that once the EDC had been ratified the Americans would reduce their forces in Germany. It might, however, be possible to find some means of earmarking for service with the EDC some British troops, perhaps an armoured brigade group. There were technical difficulties about this proposal, but he would like to consider it.

The Prime Minister said that he was not surprised or disappointed by the results of the Four-Power Meeting. The agreement to hold a Five-Power Meeting at Geneva meant that negotiations on Far Eastern problems would be continued. In Europe the Russian attitude should help the French Parliament to proceed to ratification of the EDC. Public disappointment at the lack of political agreement on Europe would be greatly offset if we could secure American agreement to an expansion of East/West trade. It would be evidence that we were continuing to try to find peaceful means of living side

FEBRUARY 1954   1449

by side with the Soviet Union. He agreed that the Foreign Secretary and the Minister of Defence should study further the suggestion that an armoured brigade group might somehow be attached to the EDC.

The Cabinet –
(1) Took note of the Foreign Secretary's statement on the Four-Power Meeting in Berlin.
(2) Took note that the Foreign Secretary and the Minister of Defence would consider methods of bringing about a closer association between the United Kingdom and the EDC and would report on this to the Cabinet.

[. . .]

Sir Winston S. Churchill: speech
(Hansard)

25 February 1954   House of Commons

THE BERLIN CONFERENCE

I am sure that the House will feel that the right hon. Gentleman the Leader of the Opposition has made a concise, massive, statesmanlike contribution to a subject which has caused much widespread heart searchings among all parties and throughout all parts of the country. I have on several occasions paid my tribute to the action which was taken by Ernest Bevin, by the right hon. Gentleman and by other leaders of the Labour Party in the crisis which Russian ambition and aggression after the war produced. It has helped us to keep our heads above water.

If the present mood of the Socialist dissentients – I prefer to use that word than 'rebels', being in a peaceful state of mind today – had ruled, between 1947 and 1951, the policy of the Government in power, it is very likely that the cause of the free nations might have been cast away. It does not follow either that peace would have been preserved.

In the main, we have carried forward the policy of the late Government, modifying it to suit the changing circumstances. But, in principle, there is nothing that we are now doing to which they are not committed and to which we were not committed by them and with them. That is why I think we can regard this matter – as, indeed, the atmosphere of the House proves – as one of national policy above the ordinary, healthy partisanship which exists.

Russia emerged from the war clad in the glory of the arms and the patriotism of her people. It was our hope that she would play one of the leading parts in the United Nations, and that the sense of unity among the victorious powers would guide the world. The course which the Soviets followed in the last eight years of Stalin's rule produced several tremendous results. Russia gained the power to hold Europe and its capital cities up to what is now called the Iron Curtain line under her authority.

This line began by running from Stettin to the southern end of the Adriatic. Its southern section has been modified by events in Yugoslavia, but no one can suppose that what has happened to Poland and Czechoslovakia, to Roumania, Bulgaria and Hungary will endure in permanence. I will speak about Austria, which is in a different category altogether, later on, but no solution is in sight at present for these subjugated States.

We have all rejected the use of aggressive force for this purpose. Time may find remedies that this generation cannot command. The forces of the human spirit and of national character alive in those countries cannot be speedily extinguished, even by large-scale movements of populations and mass education of children. Thought is fluid and pervasive, hope is enduring and inspiring. The vast territorial empire and multitudes of subjects, which the Soviets grasped for themselves in the hour of allied victory, constitute the main cause of division now existing among civilised nations.

On the other hand, Stalin's use of his triumph has produced some other results which will live and last, and which certainly would not have been seen in our time but for the Soviet pressure and menace. No one but Stalin, nothing but the actions of Russia under his sway, could have made that alliance and brotherhood of the English-speaking peoples, on which the life of the free world depends, come so swiftly and firmly into being. Nothing but the dread of Stalinised Russia could have brought the conception of united Europe from dreamland into the forefront of modern thought.

Nothing but the policy of the Soviets and of Stalin could have laid the foundations of that deep and lasting association which now exists between Germany and the Western world, between Germany and the United States, between Germany and Britain and, I trust, between Germany and France. These are events which will live and which will grow while the conquests and expansion achieved by military force and political machinery will surely dissolve or take new and other forms.

It is absolutely necessary that these facts, good or bad, should be realised by both sides, and that we should not fear to state them even to one another. I cannot bring myself to believe that men with such able minds as the Soviet rulers have not taken stock of the price they have paid, as well as of the possessions they have gained, by the Stalin policy. That, I am sure, exists in Russia; looking at the scene, they have become conscious that though they have gained much in worldly power they have lost much which would otherwise have been open to them. It was in this setting that the end of the Stalin regime and the arrival at the summit in the Kremlin of new men gave us all the hope that a new mood would rule in Russia and a new day would dawn for the people of the world, and also for the kindly, toiling, valiant people of Russia themselves.

The House will pardon me if I look back over the ground we have traversed since I addressed it on Foreign Affairs last May.[1] I suggested a small meeting between the heads of Governments without agenda, without Press, without communiqués, where full and frank talks could be indulged in and where the principals would not be oppressed by the ordeal – and it is an ordeal which few have experienced and no one should underrate – of playing on the world stage with every word studied, weighed and analysed, with every word liable to be misrepresented, torn from its context and used by vast, highly-organised machinery for propaganda purposes.

I thought that a simpler, more primitive meeting, at any rate as a preliminary, would be the best way of finding an answer to the question which everyone was then asking, but which few of us here are asking today: Has there been a significant change in Russian policy since the death of Stalin?

I was not able to go to the three-Power conference at Bermuda, planned last July, for reasons which I could not help, and, instead, there was a conference of the same Powers at Washington. It was there suggested that the Soviets should be invited to a meeting of Foreign Secretaries to deal with the problems of Germany and Austria upon a somewhat rigid agenda. In the various Notes that were exchanged it gradually became apparent that more flexibility was desirable, and more flexibility was obtained. Anyone can see the magnitude of the obstacles to be surmounted. We certainly were not able to give up EDC or NATO, or some variant between them without impairing our safety, and it did not seem that the Russians would be likely to give up their gains and conquests in Europe while they still held such an enormous superiority of military strength.

There is also a general point to be remembered here and elsewhere. When three or four great Powers are working together, no one of them can expect always to have his way, or often to have all of it. Each has to do what he can and not what he wishes. For my own part, I favoured the proposal sent to Russia for a conference for one overwhelming reason – I thought that any meeting with the Soviet Government under the new régime was better than no meeting at all. I still think so.

I do not regret this decision of the three Powers at Washington. I am sure it has been fully justified by the events which have now taken place at Berlin. Since the Washington meeting, seven months ago, several things have happened to make things easier. The agenda question and various matters of procedure were handled in a manner which prevented them from being an obstacle to discussion on the merits.

My right hon. Friend the Foreign Secretary prepared a very fair-minded plan for dealing with Germany on the basis of free elections as we understand them. The Locarno spirit, as I called it in May, was expressed in solid and solemn guarantees to Russia against any form of aggression. The only reason

[1] Speech of 11 May 1953, reproduced above (pp. 998–1010).

why these guarantees were not effective was because the military strength of Russia in what is called conventional warfare – a term which is coming into use – was so many times greater than that of the NATO Powers that she did not feel she needed any guarantees in any period which can now be foreseen. Still, I am glad that they were offered, and they certainly stand, and I believe they have played their part in reducing tension.

When my right hon. Friend the Foreign Secretary uses the word 'disappointment' about the conference, it is, no doubt, a modest and natural reaction after the prolonged and intense efforts he has made with so much skill and experience. Even if there is much that has disappointed us, and if very little that is definite has been agreed, it is certain that some real advantages have been gained.

I must say, Sir, that I think that this was a very remarkable conference. It has restored the reputation of such meetings after some very unfortunate examples. It was a very remarkable conference, where all the arguments on so many difficult points were interchanged with skill and tenacity and yet no offence was given. And new contacts have been established at various levels between important men; indeed, I believe it to be true that personal relations and comprehension of each other's point of view were improved as the great debate proceeded.

So far from the conference having proved a failure or a disaster it has actually made the discussion of all these questions less delicate and less dangerous than it was. Further meetings between those concerned are in no way prevented. Nay, one meeting which seemed hopelessly barred has been fixed. At Geneva, on 26th April, all the Powers directly concerned in the Far East will meet together.

This will include the meeting in high-level conference of Communist China and the United States of America. I have always understood the strong feelings in the United States against Communist China being admitted to the Assembly of the United Nations at a time when she was, in fact, engaged in a war against the decision of that body, in which war the United States was bearing nine-tenths of the burden. It would have worn the aspect of condonation of what the Assembly had proclaimed to be an act of aggression, and it would have condoned it before peace had been made.

I do not think it surprising that the people of the United States, who have sacrificed so much of their blood and have a large army still dwelling under severe conditions far away from home, should have wished to delay the entry of Communist China as a member of the Assembly until peace had been established. On the other hand, it seemed very unwise for the Allies not to meet the leaders of Communist China in negotiation for a peace.

There is nothing improper in belligerents meeting to discuss their affairs even while actual battles are going on. All history abounds in precedents. All the time that Napoleon was fighting his desperate campaigns in France in

1814 the International Council, composed of his representatives and those of the allies, were in constant conference at Chatillon-sur-Seine. I earnestly hoped that this meeting between the Powers directly concerned in Korea and the Far East would take place. Now it has been arranged. It has been arranged by the conference at Berlin and it will be held in a few weeks, and it has a better chance of producing fruitful results than the one at Berlin had. Here, at any rate, is one outstanding hopeful result of their labours for which we are grateful.

The most obvious disappointment at Berlin was, of course, the failure to secure the liberation of Austria by the signing of a treaty. No people have so little deserved their hard fate as the Austrians. I am sure that the Soviets would have been wise in their own interests to make this gesture of humanity. From a military point of view they could easily afford to do so, especially in the light of the far-reaching guarantees of the Western world against a renewal of German aggression. At any rate, I do not think we need regard this door as finally closed. I certainly do not feel inclined to take 'No' for an answer in this matter.

It would not be a case of making a bargain but a demonstration of moral strength on Russia's part which might be of enormous advantage to her. I always think that in these most difficult matters it is well to try to get into the mind of the other party and see the problem as they see it. It is that, I am bound to say, that gives me hope, though I hope that it will not be thought that I deceive myself or try to lead the House into foolish and vain ideas.

I feel a special responsibility about Austria because at the beginning of 1942, in a particularly bad moment for us, I gave a personal pledge. I made a speech in Downing Street to a delegation of Austrians in Britain led by Sir George Franckenstein,[1] whose memory is much respected here. In this, speaking with the full assent of a National Government and Parliament, I said: 'We remember the charm, beauty and historic splendour of Vienna, the grace of life, the dignity of the individual; all the links of past generations which are associated in our minds with Austria and with Vienna. . . . In the victory of the allies, Free Austria shall find her honoured place.'[2] That was in 1942. In 1943, as the Foreign Secretary reminded us, a Declaration affirming Austria's independence was signed by Britain, Russia and the United States. I am glad to be able to repeat that pledge on our part now. We still invite our allies of that perilous moment to join with us in making it good.

Let us make sure that we do not throw away any of the other advantages, minor though they be, which have been secured at Berlin. Patience and

---

[1] Georg Freiherr von und zu Franckenstein, 1878–1953. Born in Dresden, Germany. Educated at Vienna University. Married, 1939, Editha King: one child. Envoy Extraordinary and Minister Plenipotentiary to UK, 1920–38. GCVO, 1937. Naturalized British subject, 1938. Knighted, 1938.
[2] Speech of 18 Feb. 1942, reproduced in *The Churchill Documents*, vol. 17, *Testing Times, 1942*, pp. 281–2.

perseverance must never be grudged when the peace of the world is at stake. Even if we had to go through a decade of cold-war bickerings punctuated by vain parleys, that would be preferable to the catalogue of unspeakable and also unimaginable horrors which is the alternative. We must not shrink from continuing to use every channel that is open or that we can open any more than we should relax those defensive measures indispensable for our own strength and safety.

I do not feel that there is any incongruity between building up the strength of EDC and NATO and associating with it under the conditions which have been set forth a powerful German contribution, on the one hand, and faithfully striving for a workaday understanding with the Russian people and Government on the other.

There is one agency, at any rate, which everyone can see, through which helpful contacts and associations can be developed. The more trade there is through the Iron Curtain and between Great Britain and Soviet Russia and the satellites the better still will be the chances of our living together in increasing comfort.

When there is so much prosperity for everybody round the corner and within our reach it cannot do anything but good to interchange merchandise and services on an increasing scale. The more the two great divisions of the world mingle in the healthy and fertile activities of commerce the greater is the counterpoise to purely military calculations. Other thoughts take up their place in the minds of men.

Friendly infiltration can do nothing but good. We have no reason to fear it and if Communist Russia does not fear it, that, in itself, is a good sign. I was, therefore, very glad to read of the measure of success which attended the recent visits by British business men to Moscow. I do not suggest that at the present time there should be any traffic in military equipment, including certain machine tools such as those capable only or mainly of making weapons and heavy weapons. But a substantial relaxation of the regulations affecting manufactured goods, raw materials and shipping, which, it must be remembered, were made three or four years ago in circumstances which we can all feel were different from those which now prevail – a substantial relaxation would undoubtedly be beneficial, and beneficial in its proper setting, bearing in mind the military and other arguments adduced. We are examining these lists and will discuss them with our American friends.

My right hon. Friend the President of the Board of Trade has been for some time very active in this matter. I am speaking so far, of course, only of trade with Russia. We cannot relax restrictions on trade with China until a Korean or, perhaps, a wider Far Eastern peace has been established. But that is the prospect to which we hope the conference at Geneva will open the road.

Now I come to the main issue of the debate. Should Germany rearm, and under what authority? The hon. Member for Wednesbury (Mr S. N. Evans[1]) spoke yesterday of this with force and clarity, and the hon. Member for Shettleston (Mr McGovern[2]) made a speech which stirred the House deeply. In the First World War, Germany suffered little. Scarcely a yard of her territory was conquered in the battles. Her armies killed and wounded two or three times as many men as they lost themselves.

But this time she paid a terrible penalty. The right hon. Member for Lewisham, South (Mr H. Morrison) reminded us of this yesterday. Before the war ended the losses of Germany from bombing and other forms of warfare far exceeded ours, and the losses to her civilian population far exceeded ours. Her cities were shattered, great numbers of her civilian population were killed, and her soil was trampled mile by mile, her industries and shipping were destroyed.

For more than 40 years I have been living in relation to German power and watching the fearful drama from many varied and advantageous viewpoints. My deep feeling today is that the horrors of war have sunk deep into the German mind, and still deeper is the fear and hatred of Soviet domination.

Why, as my right hon. Friend the Foreign Secretary asked, should we try to make an outcast of this branch of the European family? The right hon. Gentleman the Leader of the Opposition spoke with force and understanding of this aspect. Like so many others, I have pondered over the proposal to create a united, neutralised, disarmed Germany, and it seems to me full of the gravest dangers.

My right hon. Friend the Foreign Secretary has described in powerful terms how it is loaded with danger. It astonished me that anyone can imagine the mighty, buoyant German race being relegated to a kind of no-man's-land in Europe and a sort of leper status –

Mr Percy Collick[3] (Birkenhead): No.

The Prime Minister: at the mercy, and remaining all the time at the mercy, of Soviet invasion and always permeated by Communist designs. It has been said from every quarter of the House that either they would make a national army of their own or they would share on a gigantic scale the fate of Czechoslovakia.

There is another reason for not throwing over the arrangements we have so long been working at for association with Germany. I do not wonder that

---

[1] Stanley Norman Evans, 1898–1970. On active service with Northumberland Hussars, 1914–18. Founded Stanley N. Evans, Ltd, 1919. MP (Lab.) for Wednesbury, 1945–56. Parliamentary Secretary, Ministry of Food, 1950. Leader, Parliamentary Delegation to Rhodesia, Nyasaland, Malta and Mauritius, 1951. Member, All Parliamentary Delegation to Soviet Union, 1954.

[2] John McGovern, 1887–1968. Worked as a plumber, 1909–29. Member, Glasgow Parish Council, 1929–31. MP (Lab.) for Glasgow Shettleston, 1930–59.

[3] Percy Henry Collick, 1899–1984. Asst General Secretary, Associated Society of Locomotive Engineers, 1940–57. MP (Lab.) for West Birkenhead, 1945–50; for Birkenhead, 1950–64. Joint Parliamentary Secretary, Ministry of Agriculture, 1945–7. Honorary Freeman of Birkenhead, 1965.

the public men on the Front Bench opposite, who have been concerned and responsible as Cabinet Ministers for so much of the work that has been done, should feel it a matter of honour not to break faith with Dr Adenauer. Dr Adenauer is, in my view, one of the greatest men Germany has produced since Bismarck. He is a sincere and convinced friend of the Western democracies. He has gathered together the German people out of the pit of ruin and chaos into which they had fallen, and from which they might not have escaped.

He is a strong champion of the European idea, for the sake of which he has persuaded the bulk of the German people to reject those ultra-nationalist conceptions which so often spring from the agony of defeat. He has staked his political existence upon the cause of Germany in Europe. That we should desert him now would be not only an unfair blow to him, but it might react upon the whole future mind of the German people to an extent to which no one can set limits.

I earnestly and hopefully hope that this will not become a matter of party and electioneering strife in this country. It would indeed be a melancholy event if the Labour Party, or any important section of them, were to seek to perpetuate the quarrels with Germany by reviving the awful memories of a recent past. Risks attend every course in the world. There could be no more needless multiplication of risks than to use the tragedies of the past to breed bitter hatred for the future. I trust that we shall leave the past behind us and allow new healing ties to grow across the grievous wounds.

While there is close association between Germany and the United States, we are strangely respected in Germany. Perhaps we are respected most, both in France and Germany, for what we ourselves are most proud of, namely, that we fought on alone against what seemed to many hopeless odds.

When I spoke in May, I had in mind a meeting like we used to have in the war of the heads of States and Governments, with the Foreign Secretaries, and I still think that this procedure should not be ruled out. It must be remembered that in May we were not discussing the details of a settlement, but only the revival of contacts between ourselves and the leaders of the Soviet Union, at a time when they presented a new regime to the world and when many hopes were raised in many lands.

I trust that we shall always hold the resource of a meeting of the heads of States and Governments in reserve. I am sure it is a good thing for people concerned in these great affairs to be on speaking terms. It would certainly be improvident to see that resource used lightly, and it would perhaps be disastrous to use it in vain.

Lastly, let me make it clear that there is no contradiction between our policy of building up the defensive strength of the free world against Communist pressure and against potential armed Soviet aggression and trying, at the same time, to create conditions under which Russia may dwell easily and peacefully side by side with us all.

On the contrary, I am sure that the British nation and our sister Commonwealths would find it difficult to go forward with the policy of increasing our military strength at such great sacrifices if they could not feel in their heart and conscience that everything in human power and prudence would be done, and was being done, to ward off the supreme catastrophe, and to try to build bridges and not barriers between Russia and the Western world.

It is in this two-fold policy of peace through strength – and also out of this policy – that wisdom and also honour reside. Peace is our aim, and strength is the only way of getting it. We need not be deterred by the taunt that we are trying to have it both ways at once. Indeed, it is only by having it both ways at once that we shall get a chance of getting anything of it at all.

Sir Winston S. Churchill to President Dwight D. Eisenhower
(Premier papers, 11/1074)

27 February 1954
Immediate
Top Secret
No. 785

I have not yet answered your letter of February 9[1] but do not think it is always in the forefront of my thoughts.

---

[1] Reproduced above (pp. 1431–2).

March 1954

Cabinet: conclusions
(Cabinet papers, 128/27)

1 March 1954　　　　　　　　　　　　　　　Prime Minister's Room,
Secret　　　　　　　　　　　　　　　　　　　House of Commons
6.30 p.m.
Cabinet Meeting No. 13 of 1954

1. The Foreign Secretary said that there had been a considerable number of casualties in the riots provoked by General Neguib's arrival in Khartoum for the opening of the Sudan Parliament. As a result, the opening of the Parliament had been postponed until 10th March and General Neguib would be returning to Cairo on the following day.

The Prime Minister said that he hoped the Cabinet would give serious consideration to the possibility of sending additional British troops to Khartoum to preserve law and order and to ensure that the progress of the Sudanese people to self-government was not hampered by outbreaks of violence. Two battalions and two RAF squadrons could easily be sent in from the Canal Zone. They could arrive by air within a few days and could be quartered in some convenient cantonment in the city. There would be no difficulty in keeping them supplied by air. Such a force would be in a position to repel any attempted invasion from Egypt by cutting the railway line across the desert. The move would be a useful preliminary to the redeployment of our forces in the Canal Zone, and would give us control of one important strategic point. It would not interfere with the redeployment of other forces to Cyprus, Jordan and Libya as already planned. He recalled that he had made a similar proposal to the Foreign Secretary at the beginning of December 1953.

The Foreign Secretary undertook to examine this suggestion urgently. A relevant consideration would be the extent of the Governor-General's continuing responsibility for law and order, and his duty, as the servant of both the Governments sharing the condominium, to seek assistance when he needed it from both the United Kingdom and the Egyptian Government. It was unlikely that any hostile move would be made from Egypt if British battalions were sent to Khartoum; but it was not to be assumed that their arrival would be welcomed by the Sudanese – even by the Mahdi's supporters or by those sections of the population which were favourable to the British.

The Foreign Secretary said that he would at once send a telegram to the Minister of State in Khartoum[1] asking for his appreciation of the situation and suggesting that he should remain in Khartoum until the opening of the Sudanese Parliament on 10th March.

The Cabinet –

(1) Took note that the Foreign Secretary would ask the Minister of State for an appreciation of the situation in Khartoum.

(2) Agreed to resume their discussion at a later meeting.

[. . .]

3. The Prime Minister read to the Cabinet a personal message from the Colonial Secretary (Kenya telegram No. 185) reporting that there were grounds for believing that General China, if his life was spared, might be able to secure the surrender of large numbers of Mau Mau rebels, not only in his own area, but throughout the country as a whole. If this was to be secured, it would be necessary to state publicly that those who surrendered would not be prosecuted, even though they had been wanted for murder; but it would be made plain that they would be liable to be detained for prolonged periods. The Colonial Secretary sought authority to proceed with this plan and to make the necessary announcement, despite the strong criticism which this was likely to evoke among white settlers in Kenya.

In discussion there was general agreement that the Colonial Secretary should be given full discretion to deal with this matter on the lines proposed in his telegram.

The Cabinet –

Invited the Prime Minister to inform the Colonial Secretary that they fully supported the proposal made in his telegram for securing, through the exercise of clemency in respect of General China, a widespread surrender of Mau Mau rebels in Kenya.

4. The Cabinet were informed that those Government supporters who were opposed to the Teachers' Superannuation Bill were now formulating proposals for consideration by the Government. It was desirable that they should receive some guidance, before their proposals were submitted, and it had been suggested to them that they should for this purpose consult with the Leader of the House of Commons and the Minister of Education. The Secretary of the

---

[1] Philip Adams, 1915–2001. Entered British Consular Service, 1939. Counsellor, Khartoum, 1954; Beirut, 1956; Chicago, 1963. Ambassador to Jordan, 1966–70; to Egypt, 1973–5.

National Union of Teachers[1] had also been informed that, if had any suggestions to put forward, he should communicate them to the Minister.

The Prime Minister said that, although he would have preferred to avoid Parliamentary controversy on this question, he was inclined to think that, in the circumstances as they had now developed, the Government's best course would be to show firmness in putting the Bill through.

The Cabinet –

Agreed to resume this discussion at a later meeting.

[. . .]

Sir Winston S. Churchill: speech
(Hansard)

2 March 1954   House of Commons

DEFENCE (GERMAN REARMAMENT)

I was a little surprised at the unusually strong and remarkably disproportionate language which the Leader of the Opposition used in referring to the Parliamentary Secretary to the Ministry of Defence. I am sure that the last thing in the world he wished was to be discourteous to the House. He has been here nearly three years in office and has never had an opportunity of presenting the Defence Estimates to the House. I thought that it would be quite all right if I came along at the end, especially as this really is an occasion when no real, serious passion is raging in the Chamber. When the right hon Gentleman says it was an insult to give the House accurate and precise information about the important changes in pay and pensions, I must say that I think we shall very seriously limit the freedom of our discussions if we are going to call such a very harmless and considerate ceremonial as that an insult.

This is not a good moment, I think, for us to quarrel on the broad issue of defence. I hope that it may be possible even at the last minute to avoid a mere partisan Division on defence as a whole. The Amendment as such is not quite the same. Still, I should be glad if this went off without a vote. There is nothing that is stated in the Amendment which could not be brought out and emphasised in the debates on the various service estimates, but tonight we are dealing with the general policy of the country at a time when our unity and composure should increase our moral influence among our allies.

I do not myself understand how the leaders of the Opposition can vote for the policy of arming the Germans and at the same time urge that we should

---

[1] Ronald Gould, 1904–86. Educated at Westminster College, London. Married, 1928, Nellie Denning Fish: two children (d. 1979); 1985, Evelyn Little. Asst Master, Radstock Council School, 1924–41. Headmaster, Welton County School, 1941–6. General Secretary, National Union of Teachers, 1947–70.

weaken our necessary counterpoise of strength. It will certainly be misunderstood abroad. Foreigners do not understand our party complications any more than we do theirs. The French will certainly think it odd that the leaders of the British Socialist Party should vote for German rearmament one week and British disarmament the next. I always thought that the French hoped that we should help to counterbalance the German contribution. It is not, of course, true, but now it will look to some foreign eyes as if the Leader of the Opposition is simply anxious to shuffle off some of our load on to France. That, I am sure, is not his aim, and I have taken every precaution to disclaim it on his behalf.

Now I come to the Amendment. I understand that it must have taken a lot of care in its composing, but that it was very carefully considered, that it slipped through quite placidly, with none of those shocks and disturbances which sometimes attend ordeals of this kind. The first two charges of the Amendment are very vague and general. It is only on the issue of two years' service that a precise challenge is made. It is made; it is not an inquiry, it is a challenge on the length of service. All right; I am in full agreement. Let me deal with the general charges first.

The situation today is not only critical, but it is very complicated. All is in flux – political, economic and, above all, scientific; all is in flux. Uncertainties, acting and reacting on each other, dominate the scene.

When I was a subaltern in India about 60 years ago, and was endeavouring to improve my education, I read a passage in Schopenhauer. It stuck in my mind. I will repeat it to the House, because it a little applies to the general situation.

> We look upon the present as something to be put up with while it lasts and serving only as the way towards our goal. Hence most people, if they glance back when they come to the end of life, will find that all along they have been living ad interim.

Everyone can weigh the truth of these words of the pessimistic philosopher, but there is no doubt that they very accurately describe the mood of the leaders of many countries, especially the military leaders, on the present position in defence. No sweeping, clear-cut, wholesale decisions are possible. The changes in the types of weapons are so rapid and continuous that if war should come at any time in the next decade, all the countries engaged will go into action with a proportion – a large proportion – of obsolete or obsolescent equipment, and they will fight each other with this as well as they can on the ground, in the air and on the sea. Changes there must be, but it is inevitable that the changes should be gradual, because you must go on living from day to day all the time you are improving. You have to go on living and trying to improve at the same time. It is very hard.

One thing I must say. The Opposition Amendment complains that we are spending too little on defence research. It says 'research'; that means research on defence. We are, in fact, planning to spend on defence research in this coming year almost exactly double the amount spent on research in 1951–52, the last year for which the Opposition were responsible. One may learn and improve one's outlook by learning, but one should be a little charitable of other people who are toiling along the same road by which one has made such progress.

There never was a moment when it was more difficult to decide when to quit research and experiment for mass production, or when there were more numerous examples of these baffling riddles. On the whole, I believe that in Britain the three Services, guided by the Ministry of Defence and aided by the Ministry of Supply, are pursuing a right and reasonable course. We all know the old jibe about the War Office always preparing for the last war. It would also be a mistake, on the other hand, for the War Office to be preparing for the next war but one. It would be folly to suppose that our Forces could be organised on the basis solely of what we think would be needed for what is called a pushbutton war in, say, 10 years' time. Moreover, the assumption that the sole purpose of armed forces is to fight a major war is a fallacy, and with no one is it more of a fallacy than with our country.

Our armed forces have to guard us during what we hope will be long years of peace and minor bickerings, and to maintain continuously a deterrent against aggression. It is therefore necessary that we should move gradually and not precipitately, keeping in mind the three ruling purposes, all of which go on together: to maintain law and order, to deter aggressors and to fight effectively for life if need should come.

We have argued so much about two years' service that I really do not want to plunge into that. It can all be talked over on the Army Votes – two years, 18 months, or some compromise between the two. There are certainly no new arguments. With our forces spread as they are about the world under the pressure of events, and with the European position so utterly undetermined, our whole military system would be thrown into confusion by such a reduction at the present time.

I cannot understand how the right hon. Member for Easington (Mr Shinwell) brings his mind and his character to this point, when we think that it was he who introduced it – and he knows how big a change it was – and when we think that it was he who reproached the French so severely, even in this Parliament, for limiting themselves to 18 months. I do not want to quarrel with the right hon. Gentleman tonight or to provoke him to interrupt me, but it really is difficult to find any reasons for his change of policy, except reasons which are at once obvious and uncomplimentary.

I was very glad to hear, I must say, the right hon Gentleman the Member for Dundee, West (Mr Strachey) – indeed, I always have agreeable recollections of Dundee – say that he disagreed with the suggestion that two years was not necessary now in the present circumstances, and that some alterations in our commitments would have to be made before any change of that kind could be brought about.

Then there is the burden of expense. We have to balance the burden of arms and of finance. No one denies the burden of expense. We have the Chancellor of the Exchequer, and he does not often allow matters to slip from our minds. If these two announcements made today were somewhat belated, it was not out of any discourtesy to the House, but only because for many months they have been the subject of long, persistent and careful argument and examination inside our own body, which is exactly what we are supposed to do.

I consider that the late Government rendered a national service in starting up re-armament when they did in harmony with the NATO Powers. But there is no doubt that if all the orders which they placed and the whole expansion which they planned had been allowed to reach their maturity, our financial position would be much more anxious than it is. We have, therefore, undoubtedly modified in important respects the scope and the rate of the Socialist re-armament plans. What about that?

In this we have taken serious responsibility. I think so. I am ready to bear my share of it. The Estimates this year are practically the same as last year, and the Estimates for the last two years are £400 million more in each year than those of the last year of the late Administration. But that is because what the late Administration sowed, although greatly pruned and reduced, has been growing naturally to its maturity, which is gigantic. Had we gone on with the whole re-armament scheme outlined in emergency by our predecessors, we should be nearer £2,000 million today than £1,600 million.

In this process we have been greatly helped by the wisdom and knowledge of Lord Alexander, by the friendly influence in which he has guided and helped the Service Ministers and the sense of proportion which he has gathered in a wide survey and experience of the world. All three Services have made vehement exertions to lessen their demands upon the taxpayer, and have achieved substantial savings in expenditure without a proportionate loss – I do not say without any loss – of war power.

I give full credit to the party opposite for the patriotic action which they took, and they ought to treat our policy, which is only a natural modification of theirs, with similar fair play. It would be a great pity if in this critical period we cannot at any rate have a general agreement on our defence policy. One could not choose a worse moment to show party divisions on vital defence matters or appear to the world to be relaxing our efforts.

We are, of course, strong enough to carry our own estimates ourselves. We do not ask for favours. But the appearance of disunity might throw away much that was gained by the late Administration. The forces which have worked and are working successfully for the consolidation of the peace of the world would, in my judgment, be seriously injured by the appearance of weakness or division in Britain. If there be a force in Russia which believes that the Stalin policy was mistaken, or at least overdone, they would be stultified if it could be said to them, 'See there the British are breaking up under the strain of re-armament.' Well, think a bit. It may cut both ways, but let us look at things even when they do not happen on our side. Weakness, I think, might be an inordinate danger to the cause of peace.

The result in Germany and France of our making a definite gesture of diminution and disarmament would be wholly bad, and we should be hampered at a time when we need all our influence with our American friends and allies to make them feel that Britain and the Commonwealth are a force not only for tolerance and patience, but also for vigilance and strength.

Frankly, I do not see how those opposite who last Thursday took so strong and decided a line in favour of arming Germany can consider withdrawing their support from the sober measures of prudence in defence which we are promoting after an immense amount of work and toil. I tell them solemnly that the policy introduced by the Socialists for rearmament and sustained by us has undoubtedly been largely responsible for the improvement in world tension that occurred in the last three years, and that any weakness and disunity in Britain, when she is known to be working for peace, will weaken her strength in the world to an extent out of all proportion to the money saved.

These matters are so grave that it is a serious national misfortune when they fall into the trough of party bickering, for the facts are then exaggerated on both sides. In carrying on an animated argument one side tends to exaggerate the danger, and the other to brush it away.

In order to make a good cause for rearmament many things have to be said which, though true and in our minds, might well be left to slumber as far as public controversy at the time is concerned. I think it would be a misfortune if, at the present time, we had to reiterate a long indictment against the Soviets for their policy since the war, and still more if in the course of discussion an undue feeling of anger and alarm was aroused, as it might well be when one dwells on Russia's overwhelming strength in conventional ground war in Europe and their power with and in China.

I think we ought to try to keep the temperature low, and to do what is necessary without having to restate facts which are only too well known by responsible people. I hope at least, that this aspect may be favourably considered by the House as a whole. I cannot think of anything worse than that the two parties should be divided, one recapitulating all the crimes of the Germans and the other stating the whole case against the Soviets. It would indeed be wrong to minimise our dangers, but neither is it helpful to world peace to have to rub them in all the time.

The House of Commons will add to its reputation, not only throughout the Commonwealth but also throughout the world, if it shows how superior it is to mere partisanship, and shows its power to settle vital issues without being drawn into national or anti-national ebullience. I think we can all think over this without having any quarrel with each other.

That remarkable military figure, General Gruenther, the Supreme Commander of the NATO Forces, made a speech last month which deserves study and consideration. It was mentioned also by my hon. Friend the Parliamentary Secretary to the Ministry of Defence. General Gruenther said that the strength which we have on the front from the northern tip of Norway to the eastern borders of Turkey, a distance of 4,000 miles, is from three to four times as effective as it was when General Eisenhower came to Europe, although there is no accurate arithmetical yardstick. But certainly the improvement is of that order of magnitude. He said, 'this air–ground team constitutes a very effective shield and it would fight very well in case of attack. We think it is of such strength that the Soviets do not now have in occupied Europe' – There he indicated on a map the satellite countries – 'sufficient air and ground forces to be certain of overwhelming this shield. Of course the Soviets can move additional forces to overwhelm that deficiency, but if they do we should be able to get some warning of an impending attack. As a result of that warning we ought to be able to increase our defensive strength considerably, in particular we ought to be able to alert our air forces.' It is very important. The hon. Member for Aston (Mr Wyatt) said – I must apologise to him because I was not here, but I was told what he said – that NATO was pathetically weak and that our shield in the West was only strong enough to make the Russians reinforce their ground forces before launching an attack. But that is the very point that constitutes the great improvement. It means that we may hope for a warning period or an alert. I attach the greatest importance to the creation of a warning period – I think I coined the word 'alert' at one time and introduced it into the method of air protection. A period of alert means not only that immense precautions can be taken for the saving of life from an atom bomb raid, but also that in that period – please remember this – before firing is opened, short though it may be, even only a week or two, final efforts can be made to avert the supreme catastrophe; avert it, perhaps, even by a revelation of the strength which the allied forces possess in the atomic field. At any rate, I can assure all parties in the House that an alert period means not only a sure and substantial minimisation of the massacre but an additional hope of averting the conflict itself.

It is remarkable and comforting to battlers for peace that the Soviets have not increased their armed forces in the deadly area concerned and have even reduced their air force in that area during the four years of allied rearmament. They are still vastly superior in numbers and with reserves certainly four or perhaps five times as great as ours, and they have no fear of invasion; but the idea that we should ever make our forces so strong that we should be able to invade Russia is so silly that it does not deserve to be mentioned to the House.

But the fact that we have to get in our heads is that the Soviet armies can afford to be cool and are able to be cool, and that is all that we in our preparations are seeking to be able to do at the present time.

Here I must mention that it is only by securing an alert period that we can be saved against a paratroop attack on a formidable scale, as we have no regular formations, not even a brigade in this island, and only depend upon those mobile columns and organisation of training forces which I set on foot on assuming responsibility. It is vital for us to be safeguarded against paratroop attack until at least the full power of the allied aid has come into being. As long as the Soviet paratroops are held at a considerable distance – I need not go into geographical details – their fighter aircraft have not got the range to escort their carrier aircraft to this island, and the slaughter that these last would suffer from our fighters would probably be regarded as prohibitive.

Holding the line of hostile paratroop attacks as far east as possible is indispensable to anything like the present arrangement of our forces which leaves us so weakly defended at home and enables us to make such a large contribution to the defence of other countries – the only country in the world that ever had two years' national compulsory service and not a brigade to defend its own land. It is a situation full of anxiety, but certainly not without honour.

These are the reasons why I attach such commanding importance to the alert safeguard against surprise which General Gruenther is working out and developing. It cannot be any menace to the safety of Russia, but is a great pad and interruption to the horrible dangers that dwell with us night and day if we think about things, and nothing must be done to deprive us of that.

We are only acting in prudence and moderation in bringing our Forces, which four years ago were almost non-existent, up to a level where, although it would be unwise to predict how long Western Europe can be successfully defended on the ground, there will be at any rate an alert period, the longer the better, before any irrevocable blow is struck.

What we are doing now in harmony with our allies is aimed only at securing the merciful interlude necessary for this modest but none-the-less invaluable security. It is, of course, utterly impossible for anyone to deal with these vast and various subjects in the course of a single day's debate. I have only tried to submit to the House a few thoughts, some of which at least I hope will be calming and not relaxing to effort. I should be relieved if the House, as I suggested earlier, left this general question of defence, without a Division and if the definite issue of two years' service has to be raised the Army Estimates are used for that purpose, for whatever attempts are made to explain it a Division on the principle of defence, perhaps with a narrow majority, would be a blow not so much to the strength of the Government as to the nation and, still more, I venture to submit, a blow to our influence for peace in the world in what is, it may well be, a most important year.

Question put, 'That the words proposed to be left out stand part of the Question.'

The House divided: Ayes, 295; Noes, 270.

Anthony Eden to Sir Winston S. Churchill
(*Premier papers, 11/1074*)

2 March 1954
Top Secret
PM/54/40

I have given further thought to the President's message to you of February 9[1] and I am ready to have a talk about it whenever you wish.

2. I find it very difficult to assess the real meaning of Ike's message. It may be that he is indulging in a general and informal 'thinking aloud' and that its implications are not serious, as another reading could make it.

3. I do not, however, feel sure about this. There is one phrase in the letter which cannot, I think, be allowed to pass unchallenged, be it only for the purpose of the record. This phrase appears in the last paragraph but one, namely the words: 'and sharpen up his sword for the struggle that cannot possibly be escaped'. Taken by themselves, these words could mean that the President thinks that a war with the Soviet Union cannot be escaped and that we should build up our armaments with that end in view. I should have thought that in any reply you would probably wish to use some form of words to deal with this passage. The following is only a draft, but I suggest it for what it may be worth:

'I agree especially with the grave words you use at the end of your letter about the faith which must inspire us in the struggle against atheistic materialism. I take it that you are referring there to the spiritual struggle. Otherwise your words might suggest that you believe war to be inevitable. I certainly do not think so and I am sure you do not either.'

---

[1] Reproduced above (pp. 1431–2).

President Dwight D. Eisenhower to Sir Winston S. Churchill
(Premier papers, 11/1074)

2 March 1954
Confidential

Dear Winston,

Thank you for your note.[1] Please do not trouble yourself about any need for replying to my letter of February 9th. I meant it as only an item in a friendly exchange of ideas that has extended now over a period of a dozen years. I think that possibly I was merely testing my thoughts against yours to determine whether we are as basically in agreement as I think we are.

With warm regards, as ever.

Sir Norman Brook to Sir Winston S. Churchill
(Premier papers, 11/587)

5 March 1954

You asked that the Cabinet should consider the Air Ministry proposal to extend the airfield at Scampton, near Lincoln, in Captain Crookshank's constituency.

There is no inter-departmental dispute about this. The dispute is between the responsible Minister and Captain Crookshank in his capacity as Member for Gainsborough. Is it right that a Member should be able to bring a constituency matter to the Cabinet merely because he happens to be a Cabinet Minister? I cannot myself remember an occasion when this has been done.

Captain Crookshank has appealed to you because he has failed to dissuade the Secretary of State for Air from proceeding with this project. Would it not be best that you should see the two Ministers and try to bring them to agreement – or, failing that, give your ruling? Alternatively, if you do not wish to adjudicate alone, you could invite two other Ministers to join you in hearing the parties to the dispute – Lord Alexander and Lord Salisbury might be suitable choices.

Either of these courses would I think be preferable to bringing the matter formally before the Cabinet.

---

[1] Of Feb. 27, reproduced above (p. 1457).

Sir Winston S. Churchill to Sir Norman Brook
Prime Minister's Personal Minute M.47/54
(Premier papers, 11/587)

6 March 1954

A Cabinet Minister's freedom to bring matters to the notice of his colleagues is not limited by whether the matter arises in his Constituency. Matters of great importance may arise anywhere. At any rate it is I who am bringing it before the Cabinet.

Sir Winston S. Churchill to Field Marshal Lord Alexander
Prime Minister's Personal Minute M.46/54
(Premier papers, 11/771)

7 March 1954
Top Secret

This is the letter I received in February from Lord Ismay.[1] You see how positively he expresses himself about the word 'concentrate' and that his interpretation of General Gruenther's speech is the opposite of what you gave me. I saw Montgomery yesterday who told me that your view was correct. After all he must know.

Please return Ismay's letter.

Sir Winston S. Churchill to President Dwight D. Eisenhower
(Churchill papers, 6/3A)

8 March 1954
Most Secret and Confidential

My dear Friend,

Thank you for your letter.[2] I am honoured by the kind personal things you say.

There is no difference between us upon the major issues which overhang the world, namely, resistance to Communism, the unity of the free nations, the concentration of the English-speaking world, United Europe and NATO. All these will and must increase if we are to come through the anxious years and perhaps decades which lie ahead of hopeful but puzzled mankind.

On the day that the Soviets discovered and developed the Atomic Bomb the consequences of war became far more terrible. But that brief tremendous phase now lies in the past.

[1] Of Feb. 12, reproduced above (pp. 1441–2).
[2] Of Feb. 9, reproduced above (pp. 1431–2).

An incomparably graver situation is presented by the public statement of Mr Sterling Cole[1] at Chicago on February 17. I have discussed these with my expert advisers. They tell me that the 175 ft. displacement of the ocean bed at Eniwetok Atoll may well have involved a pulverisation of the earth's surface three or four times as deep. This in practice would of course make all protection, except for small Staff groups, impossible. You can imagine what my thoughts are about London. I am told that several million people would certainly be obliterated by four or five of the latest H bombs. In a few more years these could be delivered by rocket without even hazarding the life of a pilot. New York and your other great cities have immeasurable perils too, though distance is a valuable advantage at least as long as pilots are used.

Another ugly idea has been put in my head, namely, the dropping of an H bomb in the sea to windward of the Island or any other seaborne country, in suitable weather, by rocket or airplane, or perhaps released by submarine. The explosion would generate an enormous radioactive cloud, many square miles in extent, which would drift over the land attacked and extinguish human life over very large areas. Our smallness and density of population emphasizes this danger to us.

Mr Cole further stated that Soviet Russia, though perhaps a year behind the United States, possessed the know-how and was increasing its production and power of delivery (or words to that effect). Moreover after a certain quantity have been produced on either side the factor of 'overtaking', 'superiority', etc., loses much of its meaning. If one side has five hundred and the other two hundred both might be destroyed. A powerful incentive to achieve surprise would be given to the weaker – what about Pearl Harbour. His natural fears would prey upon his moral and spiritual inhibitions (if indeed he was so encumbered).

When I read Mr Cole's widely reported speech, I was so surprised that its searing statements attracted so little comment. The reason is that human minds recoil from the realization of such facts. The people, including the well-informed, can only gape and console themselves with the reflection that death comes to all anyhow, sometime. This merciful numbness cannot be enjoyed by the few men upon whom the supreme responsibility falls. They have to drive their minds forward into these hideous and deadly spheres of thought. All the things that are happening now put together, added to all the material things that have ever happened, are scarcely more important to the human race. I consider that you and, if my strength lasts, I cannot flinch from the mental exertions involved.

I wondered, pondering on your letter, whether this was the background

---

[1] William Sterling Cole, 1904–87. Educated at Colgate University and Albany Law School. Admitted to New York Bar, 1929. Representative (Rep.) for New York's 37th Congressional District, 1935–44; for 39th Congressional District, 1945–52; for 37th Congressional District, 1953–7. Director-General of International Atomic Energy Agency, 1957–61. Chairman, US Congress Joint Committee on Atomic Energy, 1953–4.

which had forced you to express yourself with such intense earnestness. I understand of course that in speaking of the faith that must inspire us in the struggle against atheistic materialism, you are referring to the spiritual struggle, and that like me, you still believe that War is not inevitable. I am glad to think that in your spirit, as in mine, resolve to find a way out of this agony of peril transcends all else.

I entirely agree with Mr Cole's remarks that in this matter 'It is more sinful to conceal the power of the atom than to reveal it.' This would not of course mean one-sided imparting of secret knowledge. But perhaps we have now reached, or are reaching, the moment when both sides know enough to outline the doom-laden facts to each other.

Of course I recur to my earlier proposal of a personal meeting between Three. Men have to settle with men, no matter how vast, and in part beyond their comprehension, the business in hand may be. I can even imagine that a few simple words, spoken in awe which may at once oppress and inspire the speakers might lift this nuclear monster from our world.

It might be that the proposals which you made at Bermuda and which are accepted by the Soviets for parleys on this subject, could without raising the issue formally, give a better chance of survival than any yet mentioned. The advantage of the process you have set in motion is that it might prove the chances of settlement to the heart without at the same time bringing nearer the explosion we seek to escape.

Sir Winston S. Churchill to General Lord Ismay
(Premier papers, 11/771)

10 March 1954
Private

My dear Pug,
Recurring to your letter of February 12[1] you said:

'When Gruenther used the word "concentrate", he meant tactical concentration not strategic reinforcement. I ought also to add that when he said that the "shield" was sufficiently strong not to be overcome, he meant not to be overcome within the first two or three weeks.'

The opposite opinion was expressed to me by Alex who said:

'I agree with General Gruenther's view that the Allies now have a sufficiently strong and effective air/ground shield in Western Germany to force the Russians to concentrate additional air and ground forces in the forward areas, if they are to be certain of success in penetrating this shield.'

---

[1] Reproduced above (pp. 1441–2).

When I saw Monty on Sunday he told me that Gruenther definitely meant strategic reinforcement, thus confirming Alex's view. Monty certainly ought to know what Gruenther means. You might just clear this up for me as it plays a part in my thoughts.

Evelyn Shuckburgh: diary
('Descent to Suez', pages 145–6)

11 March 1954

Lovely spring morning and I walked to the office from Connaught Street – just over half an hour. Crocuses in full bloom in St James's Park.

AE was summoned to PM at 12.0, to talk about 'the future of the Government'. Great excitement. He said he had been expecting it, because Rab has at last succeeded in getting the Old Man to see the Budget problem, and the need for a plan for elections, etc. On return, he told me as follows, strictly in secret and no one else to know. PM said he had decided to resign in May – or end of summer at the latest (depending on his health). His only concern is to hand over as smoothly and effectively as possible to AE. He will not resign his seat in the House, but remain as a back bencher. As to timing, Harold Macmillan had told him it would be awkward for Ministers now steering Bills through the House if the change came before the summer recess. He recognized that this was nonsense when AE said so. They then discussed the question of the Budget and elections. PM asked AE whether he thought election should be this year or next. AE replied (as he had said he would) that he would like to have the option. PM had seemed impressed by this 'which showed that I had thought the matter over'. They both agreed that it was better not to decide until much nearer the autumn; it would not do to appear to be taking a snap election before the economic difficulties of next year set in; but perhaps the socialists would demand an election in the event of a change from Winston to Eden, in which case AE might well decide to have one this autumn. But that means WSC must go in May at the latest, so as to give him six months in office.

[...]

March 1954

Sir Winston S. Churchill to Sir Shane Leslie
(Churchill papers, 1/52)

12 March 1954

My dear Shane,

Sir James Dunn[1] came to see me yesterday and brought me the letters of mine which he had purchased from you. He has invited me to keep several of them which, as they deal with such very private family matters, I have done.

This morning I received your letter enclosing the original of one from our Grandfather, Leonard Jerome,[2] of which you had already sent me a very interesting extract. I am very much obliged to you for this gift which I shall value.

I should be glad to know whether you have many family papers, because if you were willing to dispose of them I might be able to purchase them from you. I should like to have them examined on my behalf, and if this were agreeable to you, I would send somebody over to see you in Ireland, and make me a report upon them.

Sir Winston S. Churchill to Sir David Eccles
Prime Minister's Personal Minute M.51/54
(Premier papers, 11/584)

14 March 1954

What is this you have been doing in the Parks? Let me have a special note. It is a dreadful thing to cut down a tree which has life in it.

Sir Winston S. Churchill to Sir Thomas Dugdale
Prime Minister's Personal Minute M.52/54
(Premier papers, 11/584)

14 March 1954

Let me have a short report on this. Are many more trees being felled than in previous years? Let me have a paper with figures.

---

[1] James Clement Dunn, 1890–1979. Born in New Jersey. On active service, US Navy, WWI. Chargé d'Affaires, Haiti, 1922–4. Chief of Protocol, 1928–30, 1933–5. Asst Secretary of State for European, Far Eastern, Near Eastern and African Affairs, 1944–6. US Ambassador to Italy, 1946–52; to France, 1952–3; to Spain, 1953–5; to Brazil, 1955–6.

[2] Leonard Walter Jerome, 1817–91. Born in New York. Educated at Union College, NY. Married, 1849, Clarissa Hall: four children (one of whom, Jennie, became Lady Randolph Churchill). Attorney and Wall Street financier. US Consul in Trieste, 1852–3.

Sir David Eccles to Sir Winston S. Churchill
(Premier papers, 11/584)

15 March 1954

Your personal minute M.51/54 about the felling of elms in Kensington Gardens.

For many years First Commissioners of Works have been advised to cut down and replant elms in the Royal Parks which have become dangerous. It is the nature of the tree to shed branches and to fall down as it approaches its two hundredth year. We lost thirteen in one night in November, 1952. Between 1948 and 1953 large boughs or whole trees caused damage or injury on seven occasions. One man and four women were injured, three seriously.

A year ago I consulted Kew, the Royal Botanic Garden, Edinburgh, and the Department of Forestry at Oxford University. They all advised me to test the trees in Kensington Gardens and to remove those shown to be dangerous. Examination, including boring by augers, showed that the great proportion of the Broad Walk elms was dangerous and some 200 more in other parts of Kensington Gardens (i.e. 400 out of a total of 3,500 trees). I told the House of Commons on the 15th July last that this test left me no choice but to cut down and replant the Avenue and to remove dangerous trees elsewhere. This work is now almost completed and no further felling will take place this Spring

The contractor added to the public alarm by leaving any sound timber on the ground until such time as it could be removed for sale. The rotten trunks and limbs he burned immediately. I estimate that well over three-quarters of the trees in the Broad Walk were dangerous, but all had to come down in order to replant a uniform avenue. Elsewhere only trees found to be rotten were cut down.

The replanting has started. The Avenue will be a double line of beeches and scarlet oaks and the individual trees removed from other parts of the Gardens will be replaced by a variety of species.

I knew quite well that this operation would distress many people but, like the felling of the Long Walk at Windsor, it had to be done.

I enclose extracts from the Press showing that there was a good deal of opinion on my side.[1]

---

[1] Churchill wrote at the bottom of the page: 'Thank you – a very good defence'.

MARCH 1954 1475

Cabinet: conclusions
(*Cabinet papers, 128/27*)

15 March 1954　　　　　　　　　　　　　　　Prime Minister's Room,
Secret　　　　　　　　　　　　　　　　　　　　House of Commons
5.30 p.m.
Cabinet Meeting No. 18 of 1954

1. The Cabinet had before them memoranda by the Foreign Secretary (C(54)99 and 102) suggesting a new approach to a defence agreement with Egypt.

The Foreign Secretary said that in the middle of 1953 the Egyptian Government had rejected the proposal that the Base in the Canal Zone should be made available in the event of a threat of aggression against Turkey or Persia. In the following October we had suggested to them the United Nations formula, which they had also rejected. They had now indicated that they would be willing to agree that we should be free to re-enter upon the Base in the event of a threat of aggression against Turkey. This was an important concession, not only because of the geographical position of Turkey, but because Turkey was herself a member of the North Atlantic Treaty Organisation. There was, therefore, now only one outstanding issue viz., the status of the British technicians in the base and their right to wear uniform and carry personal arms. The Egyptian Government might at any moment make it publicly known that they were prepared to accept our views on the availability of the Base and that the sole remaining issue was the wearing of uniforms. This would put us in an embarrassing position; for too many sections of opinion, in this country and abroad, it would seem unreasonable that we should decline on that ground alone to conclude an agreement. The Foreign Secretary said that in these circumstances he had once again reviewed the expediency of leaving in the Base 4,000 British soldiers, decreasing in numbers over a period of years. Whatever was agreed about their status, these men would in fact be hostages to fortune. He had therefore put forward, for the Cabinet's consideration, the alternative that the essential Base installation might be maintained by civilian contract labour. If this were found to be a practicable alternative, he would first instruct Her Majesty's Ambassador in Cairo to make it clear to General Neguib that he must take the necessary steps to restore confidence before there could be any defence agreement. The Egyptian Government must, in particular, undertake to observe the terms and the spirit of the Anglo-Egyptian Agreement on the Sudan and contribute to the orderly transfer of power in the Sudan by using their influence to ensure that the balance in the Governor-General's Commission was not upset. They must also refrain from unbridled attacks on Britain and on British public servants in the Sudan. Her Majesty's Ambassador would explain that, if General Neguib took the necessary action to secure this, we might be willing to conclude a defence agreement on the terms suggested i.e., that key installations and airfields in the Base should be maintained by civil contractors and that no British soldiers would remain there as technicians. In return for this concession, we should ask that the agreement should last for twenty years instead of seven, and that a rather longer time, probably two years, should be allowed for the withdrawal of all British troops.

In discussion of this proposal the following points were made:

(a) The Minister of Defence said that, from the military angle, there would be no practical objection to the employment of civil contractors for the maintenance of the Base installations and airfields. A similar system had been adopted with success in Libya. It would, however, be advisable to retain the right to send military inspectors to the Base at intervals to ensure that all was in order: these need not necessarily wear uniform.

(b) Care would be needed in drawing up the terms of the proposed contracts so as to ensure that the Egyptians accepted due responsibility for the care and maintenance of the Base, and did not interfere unreasonably with the work of the contractors.

(c) Under our original proposals the position of the British military technicians in the Base would have been anomalous and unsatisfactory. Though it would have been convenient, in presenting the plan to some sections of opinion in this country, to stress the fact that these would be soldiers, they would in fact have had no military value; and, as their numbers declined under the terms of the proposed agreement, they would have become hostages to fortune. From this point of view we should perhaps be on surer ground if we could abandon the pretence that these technicians were a military force. There was more realism in the new proposal that the Base should be maintained by civilian contractors.

(d) The view was expressed that men employed by civil contractors in the Base might be treated with less respect than military technicians and that, if no British troops remained there, the Egyptians would make less effort to maintain the Base in good order. Against this it was argued that it was in the Egyptian interest that the Base should remain efficient. In this connection the suggestion was made that, if it could be arranged that American as well as British civil contractors should take charge of installations, this would be a powerful guarantee that the Base would be properly cared for and would also have considerable political value.

(e) The new proposal would enable us to remove all our troops from Egypt. This would reduce our overseas military expenditure, and would enable us to redeploy our forces in the Middle East to better advantage. Moreover, on the new basis, we might hope to secure an agreement valid for twenty years instead of seven. And the provision for re-entry into the Base in the event of a threat of aggression against Turkey would be of particular value in linking the agreement with the North Atlantic Alliance.

(f) On the other hand, Ministers recognised that it might not be easy to justify to their supporters an agreement on the lines now suggested. Involving, as it did, the withdrawal of all British troops from Egypt, this could easily be represented as a complete surrender to the more extreme demands of the Egyptian Government. If, therefore, it were decided to go forward with this plan, its timing and presentation would need very careful consideration.

(g) In particular, it would be necessary to satisfy public opinion in this country that adequate safeguards were being provided for the right of international passage through the Suez Canal. The suggestion was made that appropriate provisions on this point might be included in the body of the new agreement. The Foreign Secretary pointed out that it would hardly be practicable to include binding provisions on this point in a bilateral agreement between ourselves and Egypt, since the subject was of close concern to a great number of maritime Powers, all of whom were parties to the original Suez Canal Agreement. It was admitted that the declaration about the Canal which the Egyptians had agreed to include in the preamble would, as a matter of law, impose on them a binding obligation.

(h) Whatever agreement was made with Egypt, we needed to re-deploy British forces in the Middle East in such a way as to enable us to maintain our prestige in that area and to exert effective power if Egypt failed to keep the agreement. Present plans contemplated the stationing of an armoured brigade in Libya, a brigade in Cyprus and, possibly, a brigade in Jordan. If a situation arose necessitating the re-entry into the Canal Zone by force, reinforcements would have to be sent from elsewhere.

The Prime Minister said that he felt great anxiety about the new proposal now put forward, both on its merits and because of the political criticism which it seemed likely to arouse. It was an essential part of the Foreign Secretary's proposal that confidence should be restored before any new defence agreement was concluded, and General Neguib was to be asked to give assurances of his good intentions. He himself found it difficult to repose any confidence in any promises which General Neguib might be induced to make. The Egyptian Government had in fact already undertaken, in the Anglo-Egyptian Agreement on the Sudan, to do the very things we should now be asking them to do as the price for a defence agreement. General Neguib himself was in no position to give satisfactory guarantees about the Sudan. The main sources of his power in Egypt were (i) the fact that his mother was Sudanese and that the Egyptians expected him to bring the Sudan under Egyptian control, and

(ii) the expectation that he would drive the British out of the Canal Zone and bring the Sudan under exclusively Egyptian influence. Although it was true that the question of uniform was not a good issue on which to break off the negotiations, it was a point of practical importance. If British soldiers employed as technicians in the Base were accorded the status of soldiers, that was some physical guarantee that the Base would not be neglected and an assurance that the Egyptians could not ill-use them without affording us an ample justification for intervening to protect them. If that physical guarantee were removed, nothing would be left but verbal promises on which it would be folly to rely. It would, no doubt, be easier and less costly to abandon both Egypt and the Sudan, but that would not be the end of our troubles. If Egypt were free to do as she pleased in the Sudan, there would almost certainly be a civil war from which we could not stand aside. It would be small consolation to point to the longer duration of the new agreement, since it was only too likely that there would be continuing causes for friction and finally for the repudiation of the agreement by Egypt. He was anxious to start moving some troops away from the Canal Zone as soon as possible, but we must first find some more solid and effective guarantees for the independence of the Sudan.

The Prime Minister therefore invited the Cabinet to consider, as an alternative policy, the possibility of launching a programme of positive action. Thus, we might break off the defence negotiations and embark on a definite plan of redeployment. An armoured brigade could be sent at once from the Canal Zone to Libya. A brigade could be sent to Khartoum in order to demonstrate in a practical matter our determination to ensure the independence of the Sudanese and to protect them from Egyptian interference. The troops remaining in Egypt could be redeployed in the manner best calculated to ensure their safety. Meanwhile we should do our utmost to promote effective multi-lateral action by the maritime Powers to assure the right of international passage through the Canal. He would like to examine a plan of this kind in greater detail with the Foreign Secretary and the Minister of Defence.

The Foreign Secretary said that, while he would be ready to consider an alternative policy on these lines, he was not convinced that the arrival of a British brigade in Khartoum would be welcomed by any of the political parties in the Sudan. There was at the moment no real justification for such a move, although there might be if the Governor-General found it necessary to declare a constitutional emergency.

The Foreign Secretary added that he had been impressed by the suggestion made in the discussion that we might associate American civil contractors in the care of the Base installations. He would like to put this to the United States Ambassador in London and ascertain his views. He would explain that, so long as the responsibility for safeguarding the Base rested on British troops, we should have to insist that their military status should be adequately safeguarded. We would, however, be prepared to consider the alternative

MARCH 1954 1479

proposition that the maintenance of the Base in peace should be entrusted to a civilian organisation if the Americans were prepared to share that responsibility with us. In that event, all British military personnel could be withdrawn from Egypt, though some arrangement would need to be made for British military inspectors to visit the Base in plain clothes from time to time in order to verify that the installations and equipment were being maintained in good order.

The Cabinet −
(1) Agreed to resume their discussion at a further meeting.
(2) Took note that in the meantime the Foreign Secretary would consult informally with the United States Ambassador in London on the suggestion that the maintenance of the Base installations in the Canal Zone might be undertaken in peace by an Anglo-American civilian organization; and that the Prime Minister would discuss further with the Foreign Secretary and the Minister of Defence the alternative policy of redeployment which he had suggested in the discussion.

[. . .]

Cabinet: conclusions
(Cabinet papers, 128/27)

16 March 1954
Secret
12 p.m.
Cabinet Meeting No. 19 of 1954

1. The Prime Minister said he had thought it necessary that the Cabinet should consider urgently the problems raised by the epidemic of poliomyelitis in Western Australia, where The Queen was due to arrive on 26th March for a visit lasting five days. The Queen's principal medical adviser, Sir Horace Evans, had recently been informed by the doctor accompanying Her Majesty on her tour that this epidemic was definitely increasing and was on a larger scale than had been experienced in Western Australia for some time. Sir Horace Evans himself considered that The Queen would incur only a slight risk, and that this could be reduced by taking sensible precautions about feeding and avoiding close contact with crowds. He had put forward a number of practical suggestions and had advised that The Queen and the Duke of Edinburgh should receive a second inoculation with gamma globulin, which might give immunity for a few weeks, when they arrived in Adelaide on their way to Perth.

The Prime Minister said that there seemed to be two main questions for consideration. First, what was the degree of risk to The Queen? Secondly, ought the visit to Western Australia to go forward, subject to the taking of all possible precautions, or would it be better abandoned? In his view The Queen would be reassured by the knowledge that the matter had been considered by the Cabinet and that their advice upon it was at her disposal if she should wish for it.

The Commonwealth Secretary said that such expert medical advice as was available to him was to the effect that the risk to The Queen's safety from poliomyelitis was very small – much less, indeed, than that which she was regularly running by air travel. No special precautions for the health of the Royal Family had been considered necessary in this country in 1947 or 1951, when there had been outbreaks of poliomyelitis of an intensity comparable with that of the present outbreak in Western Australia. According to this view The Queen could safely proceed with her tour as planned, provided that she observed such precautions as had been recommended by her medical advisers. One of Sir Horace Evans's suggestions was that it might be advisable for The Queen to live on the *Gothic* during her visit to Western Australia. This would be practicable if the *Gothic* could be stationed at Fremantle, which was a relatively short distance from Perth; but it was arguable that The Queen would run no greater risk if she were to stay in Government House at Perth, as arranged. Apart from the risk to The Queen's health, account should be taken of the increased danger which the population of Western Australia would incur through assembling in large numbers to celebrate The Queen's visit. On the other hand, the Cabinet should bear it in mind that, although they were entitled to concern themselves with any measures necessary to preserve The Queen's health or safety, the arrangements for her tour of Australia were a matter on which constitutionally she must look for advice primarily to Australian Ministers. He had, however, felt justified in sending a private telegram to the Governor of Western Australia[1] asking for information on a number of detailed aspects of the problem. He had also repeated this telegram to our High Commissioner in Canberra,[2] asking him for his views but making it clear that he did not wish to consult Mr Menzies at this stage.

In discussion the view was expressed that the fact that special precautions for the health of the Royal Family had not been considered necessary in this country in 1947 and 1951 was hardly relevant. The risks attendant upon a Royal Tour were of a quite special nature and called for special precautions,

---

[1] Charles Henry Gairdner, 1898–1983. CO, 10th Royal Hussars, 1937–40. GSO I, 7th Armoured Div., North Africa, 1940–1. Brig., Armoured Fighting Vehicles, Middle East Command, 1941. Deputy Director of Plans, 1941. CBE, 1941. GOC 6th Armoured Div., North Africa, 1941–2; 8th Armoured Div., 1942–3. Commandant, Staff School Haifa, Palestine, 1942. CoS, 15th Army Group, Italy, Feb.–Aug. 1943. Director, Armoured Fighting Vehicles, Army HQ India, 1943–5. Head of British Liaison Mission to Japan, 1945–6. British Representative to Gen. MacArthur, 1945–8. CB, 1946. KCMG, 1948. Governor, Western Australia, 1951–63; Tasmania, 1963–8. GBE, 1969.

[2] Stephen Holmes, 1896–1980. Served in WWI, 1916–19 (MC, 1918). Senior Secretary, Office of High Commissioner for UK in Canada, 1936–9. High Commissioner for UK in Australia, 1952–6.

even in a country where the population was less densely concentrated than in the British Isles.

The general view of the Cabinet was that, while the risk to The Queen from her forthcoming visit to Western Australia was probably not serious, it was desirable that the Australian Government should be made aware of the anxiety felt on this score by United Kingdom Ministers and of the support which they would give to any decision by the Australian Government either to cancel the visit or to impose such restrictions on it as might be considered wise in the interests of The Queen's safety or of the health of the inhabitants of the State.

The Commonwealth Secretary prepared a draft of such a message, to be sent by the Prime Minister to Mr Menzies. This was read to the Cabinet and was approved subject to amendments.

The Cabinet –

Invited the Prime Minister to telegraph to the Prime Minister of Australia about The Queen's forthcoming visit to Western Australia on the lines approved by the Cabinet in their discussion.

[. . .]

3. The Prime Minister drew attention to Press reports of a dispute over the sale of Hermes aircraft by British Overseas Airways Corporation (BOAC).

The Minister of Transport and Civil Aviation said that these reports were inaccurate and misleading. Nineteen of these aircraft had been put into service by BOAC in 1950, but had later been withdrawn as they had been replaced by Comets and Argonauts. Three had since been sold to Silver City Airways and negotiations were in progress for the sale of a further two to another charter company. There were grounds for believing that certain Labour Members of Parliament, having failed to achieve their object in the recent debate on the subject in the House of Commons, were endeavouring to obstruct the carrying out of the Government's policy by encouraging industrial resistance to it. So far, however, discussion had been confined to the workers' panel of the National Joint Council for Civil Air Transport and there had been no failure on the part of BOAC's employees to carry out the Corporation's instructions to them. The Corporation were, moreover, reasonably confident that, when the matter came before the National Joint Council itself on 19th March, they would be able to obtain the Council's acquiescence in the course of action which they wished to follow.

The Minister of Labour confirmed that there was evidence that a genuine fear of redundancy resulting from the withdrawal of Hermes aircraft was being exploited for political ends. The Trade Unions concerned were somewhat lacking in responsible leadership, but he had reasonable grounds for hoping that, when the matter came before the full National Joint Council, they would recognize and observe the normal limits of industrial action.

The Prime Minister said that he had brought this matter to the notice of the

1482   MARCH 1954

Cabinet because serious constitutional issues would arise if industrial action were successful in obstructing the execution of decisions taken by Parliament. The matter should continue to be closely watched.

The Cabinet –

Took note of these statements.

Cabinet: conclusions
(Cabinet papers, 128/27)

17 March 1954
Secret
11.30 a.m.
Cabinet Meeting No. 20 of 1954

[. . .]

4. The Cabinet resumed their discussion of the Home Secretary's proposal that a Royal Commission should be appointed to review the existing law relating to prostitution and homosexuality.

The Home Secretary restated the case for an enquiry which was outlined in his memorandum C(54)60 and had been developed in the Cabinet's earlier discussion on 24th February. His conclusion was that the prevalence of prostitution, particularly in London, and the unexplained increase in homosexual offences, constituted a serious social problem which the Government could not ignore; that, without support from the findings of an independent and authoritative enquiry the Government would not be in a position to promote legislation, or to take other measures, to deal with this problem; and that in these circumstances the only course open to them was to appoint a Royal Commission or other appropriate form of enquiry to examine the problem and to suggest appropriate remedies.

Discussion showed that some Ministers were still reluctant to agree to this proposal for the appointment of a Royal Commission.

The Prime Minister said that, in his view, the prudent course would be to take no action save to encourage a Private Member to introduce in the House of Commons, under the ten-minute rule, a Bill designed to prohibit the publication of detailed information of criminal prosecutions for homosexual offences. The Home Secretary said that he would be ready to submit to the Cabinet a memorandum examining the arguments for and against such restrictive legislation. But he pointed out that such legislation, even if it had the effect of allaying public anxiety about homosexuality, would make no contribution whatever towards a solution of the problem of prostitution. This, in his view, was the more urgent and obvious problem. He had no doubt that the proper remedy for it was to increase the penalty for soliciting and to dispense with the necessity of proving 'annoyance'; but he was satisfied – and in this

MARCH 1954   1483

he had the support of the majority of his Cabinet colleagues – that there was no prospect of passing legislation to make these changes in the existing law without the support of an independent enquiry.

The Cabinet –

(1) Invited the Home Secretary to submit a memorandum summarizing the arguments for and against legislation designed to restrict publication of the details of criminal prosecutions for homosexual offences.

(2) Agreed to resume, when this memorandum was available, their discussion of the proposal to hold a formal enquiry into the law relating to prostitution and to homosexual offences.

5. The Cabinet had before them a memorandum by the Home Secretary (C(54)97) seeking authority to appoint a tribunal under the Tribunals of Inquiry (Evidence) Act, 1921, to enquire into the administration of the Leeds City police force.

The Home Secretary said that there was mounting evidence of the unsatisfactory disciplinary state of the Leeds Police. During a three-year period ending in September 1952, the number of disciplinary cases in the force expressed as a percentage of its establishment had been no less than 16 per cent, compared with 6 per cent in Sheffield and only 2 per cent and 1.5 per cent in Birmingham and Bristol. Mr Diplock,[1] QC, who had reheard the cases of two police sergeants who had recently been sentenced to reduction in rank, had been unfavourably impressed with the credibility of a number of officers in the plain clothes branch of the force; and the Chief Constable of Leeds had himself admitted, in his evidence to the Royal Commission on Betting, Lotteries and Gaming, that to license ready-money betting offices would be to regularize what was already existing in fact in Leeds. The Watch Committee of the City Council had been clearly shown to be an unsatisfactory disciplinary body. He recognized that the course of action which he proposed would single out the Leeds Police for severe condemnation and would expose the Government to the criticism that the trouble was really due to their own failure to amend the betting laws. He was finding it increasingly difficult, however, to refrain from strong action which was being urged upon him by two Members for Leeds constituencies – one a supporter of the Government and one of the Opposition. Appointment of a Tribunal of Inquiry would require approval by a resolution of each House of Parliament.

The Prime Minister said that he was by no means convinced of the need to take this action, which would reflect gravely upon the Leeds City Council. Individual offenders in the City's police force had been duly brought to

---

[1] William John Kenneth Diplock, 1907–85. Educated at University College, Oxford. Barrister, Middle Temple, 1932. Married, 1938, Margaret Sarah Atcheson. Served in RAF, 1941–5. KC, 1948. Judge of High Court of Justice, Queen's Bench Div., 1956–61. Judge of Restrictive Practices Court, 1960–1. Lord Justice of Appeal, 1961–8. Baron, 1968.

judgment and the wiser course, in his view, would be to ensure that this process continued and that all possible administrative measures were taken to improve the state of discipline in the Force.

In discussion attention was drawn to the limited scope for administrative action by the central Government in a matter which was primarily the responsibility of the local authority concerned. At the same time ultimate responsibility remained with the Home Secretary and his position in Parliament would be vulnerable if he failed to take any measure open to him to improve the situation. On the other hand, it was recognised that the Government's position was seriously weakened by the fact that the unsatisfactory state of discipline in the Leeds Police could be said to be due largely, if not entirely, to the present state of the betting laws which the Government had so far shown no disposition to remedy on the lines recommended by the Royal Commission. It could be argued that the first step for the Government to take was to propose legislation to amend the betting laws.

The Cabinet –
   (1) Withheld their approval of the proposal to appoint a tribunal under the Tribunals of Inquiry (Evidence) Act, 1921, to enquire into the administration of the Leeds City police force.
   (2) Invited the Home Secretary to take all administrative measures open to him to secure an improvement in the state of discipline of the Leeds City police force.

[...]

Christopher Soames to Sir Winston S. Churchill
(*Premier papers, 11/668*)

17 March 1954

The Russian Chargé d'Affaires invited Mary and me to a film showing followed by supper last night. Two or three other Members of Parliament were present, and that was the whole part apart from Russians. The Chargé d'Affaires took me into a room alone and said that he was 'authorised to say' that if you were to suggest a meeting between yourself and Mr Malenkov it would be 'given favourable consideration'. I replied that if Mr Malenkov wanted to see you, why didn't he himself suggest a meeting? He replied that he was 'not authorized to comment on that'. I then asked whether he had any ideas about the time and place of such a meeting. He said he had no ideas about such details. He did not say that your invitation to Malenkov would be accepted; he only said it would be favourably considered.

March 1954

General Lord Ismay to Sir Winston S. Churchill
(Premier papers, 11/771)

17 March 1954

My dear Prime Minister,
Thank you for your letter of 10th March.[1]

I confess that I am very puzzled by the extract that you quote from my letter of 12th February. It was dictated verbatim from a note approved by Gruenther's Chief of Staff.[2]

I will check with Gruenther himself when he comes back from Washington in a week's time: but, in the meanwhile, I feel sure that his opinion is as follows:

'The Soviet have only 30 divisions outside Russia. They are unlikely to launch an attack on me unless these divisions are reinforced from Russia. But if they did so, my shield could hold them for two or three weeks.'

In other words, he agrees with the opinions expressed by Alex and Monty. So do I.

Sir Winston S. Churchill to Anthony Eden
Prime Minister's Personal Minute M.55/54
(Premier papers, 11/701)

18 March 1954

The CIGS wrote the enclosed* after I had a talk with him. It would enable redeployment to begin at any time without waiting for a reestablishment of 'coincidence'. I am not of course committed to the details but I am very anxious for deeds, not words, with the Egyptians.

I should like to talk it all over with you next week after my Tuesday speech, or tomorrow, Friday, morning if you like.

*Note about the Canal Zone Base.

---

[1] Reproduced above (pp. 1471–2).
[2] Cortlandt Van Rensselaer Schuyler, 1900–93. Educated at United States Military Academy. Married, 1923, Wynona Coykendall: two children (d. 1981); 1981, Helen Stillman. Brig.-Gen., 1942. US Military Representative to Allied Control Commission, 1944–7. Chief, Plans and Policy Group, Army General Staff, 1947–52. Maj.-Gen., 1952. Lt-Gen., 1954. CoS to Supreme Commander, SHAPE, 1954–9.

1486   March 1954

Sir Winston S. Churchill to General Sir John Harding
Prime Minister's Personal Minute M.56/54
(*Premier papers, 11/701*)

18 March 1954

I am very much impressed with your note on the Canal Zone Base and am much obliged to you for the promptness with which you have acted. Am I right in supposing that you do not need two Brigades in Cyprus in addition to the 15,000 troops (in Ismailia and Port Said) and the Brigade Group in Tripolitania? We will have another talk about it all next week. Meanwhile I am sending a copy to the Foreign Secretary.

Sir Winston S. Churchill to General Lord Ismay
(*Premier papers, 11/771*)

18 March 1954

My dear Pug,

Thank you so much for your letter of March 17. That is exactly what I thought and we are all agreed.

General Sir John Harding to Winston S. Churchill
(*Premier papers, 11/701*)

18 March 1954

CANAL ZONE BASE

In reply to your minute of 18th March, while we have 15,000 troops in the Ismailia–Port Said area it will not be necessary to maintain more than an internal security garrison of one infantry battalion or the equivalent in Cyprus.

To reinforce our troops in the Ismailia–Port Said area we should have plans ready to move any or all of the following formations:
    (a) The armoured brigade group or part of it by sea form Libya and Tripolitania.
    (b) The Commando Brigade by sea or air from Malta.
    (c) The Parachute Brigade by air from the UK.

These reinforcements plus action by our Middle East Air Force should be enough to enable us to defeat any attempt to drive us from our position.

If it were decided to withdraw our forces altogether from Egypt, or it became safe to reduce them, we should move one of the infantry brigade groups, the divisional headquarters and divisional troops from the Ismailia–Port Said area to Cyprus where with the armoured brigade group in Libya and Tripolitania, and the armoured squadron in Jordan, they would complete our permanent Middle East garrison of one armoured division.

It has never been our intention to have two brigades in Cyprus. An armoured division now has only one infantry brigade group.

Anthony Eden to Sir Winston S. Churchill
(Premier papers, 11/701)

18 March 1954
PM/54/49

Your minute M.55/54.[1] I have read the CIGS paper, which of course takes a different view from all the previous ones by the Chiefs of Staff.

2. So far as it deals with political forecasts, I would have important reservations to make. I certainly agree that the course of action he outlines 'may lead us into open conflict with Egypt', and if so, such conflict could not be limited to 15,000 men on our side, apart from all the consequences in Cairo and elsewhere.

3. In any event we must clearly await the Americans' answer which I hope to have over the weekend. I am considering a possible course of action to submit to the Cabinet should that answer be negative.

4. I may have to ask you to help me by having a Cabinet on Monday. I am sorry that I have to be in my constituency tomorrow, but I shall be available from Saturday lunchtime.

President Dwight D. Eisenhower to Sir Winston S. Churchill
(Premier papers, 11/1074)

19 March 1954
Top Secret

Dear Winston,

I have pondered over your letter.[2] You are quite right in your estimate of my grave concern at the steady increase in methods of mass destruction. Whether or not the specific possibilities of devastation that you mention are indeed demonstrated capabilities, the prospects are truly appalling. Ways of lessening or, if possible of eliminating the danger must be found. That has been my principal preoccupation throughout the last year.

It was after many weeks of thinking and study with political and technical advisers that I finally reached the conclusions which we talked over at

[1] Reproduced above (p. 1485).
[2] Of Mar. 8, reproduced above (pp. 1469–71).

Bermuda and which were embodied in my eighth of December address to the United Nations Assembly. As you are well aware, that plan was designed primarily as a means of opening the door of world-wide discussion – with some confidence on both sides – rather than as a substantive foundation of an international plan for the control or elimination of nuclear weapons. But honest, open technical discussions on an internationally supported plan to promote peaceful uses of this new science might lead to something much more comprehensive.

Since last December, we have been following up this matter as actively as its technical character permits. Foster had two or more talks with Molotov when they were at Berlin. We have a draft plan which, after consultation with your people and those of two or three other countries, will, I expect, be transmitted to the Soviet Union through diplomatic channels, as agreed, probably next week.

While there have been some indications that the Soviets might want to confuse the issues with extraneous political matters, on the whole it is encouraging that they so far seem prepared to accept businesslike procedures.

In its entirety the problem is one of immensity and difficulty, as you so graphically stated. But I repeat that I deem it important to make a beginning in an exchange of views, which, as you suggest, could open up new and more hopeful vistas for the future.

I doubt whether the project on which we are engaged would, at this moment, be advanced by the meeting of heads of government. In fact, I can see that such a meeting might inject complications. From our side, there is the question of France, which is very delicate at the moment. The Soviets have indicated that, if there were oral conversations, they would want to bring in the Chinese Communists.

My impression is that matters are in a reasonably good way, but that they require constant concern and vigilance and, I hope, frequent and intimate personal exchanges of views between the two of us.

President Dwight D. Eisenhower to Sir Winston S. Churchill
('The Churchill Eisenhower Correspondence', pages 127–8)

19 March 1954

Dear Winston,

I have studied carefully the proposals for relaxation of East–West trade controls which officials of your Government gave to our Embassy in London on March 1. I understand that these proposals have been personally approved by you.

As you no doubt realize, the United States Government has for some time been conducting a searching review of all aspects of East–West trade controls.

I can assure you that the United States is prepared to go a significant distance toward the contraction and simplification of those controls – objectives which we both share.

However, we do not believe we should go a great distance and so suddenly as the United Kingdom proposals suggest. To do so would be, I think, to go beyond what is immediately safe or in the common interest of the free world.

I appreciate the weight that must be given to the strong views in favour of decontrol that are held by the British public and by the British business community. I assume, however, that you equally realize the weight of public and Congressional opinion in the United States and the problems arising out of the Battle Act. It would be most unfortunate if pressures in either of our countries produced reactions adversely affecting Anglo-American relations – political, economic, and military – as well as the strength of the NATO coalition.

Ordinarily, I would not insert into our correspondence any matter of detail that properly belongs to our respective diplomatic services. But because your recent speech indicates that you have personally considered some of the included questions of the broad general subject, I feel a slight deviation from our normal practice is justified.

I feel strongly that the control system must continue to include equipment and raw materials of high war-potential significance, whether or not they have wide civilian use, where the Soviet bloc has a serious deficiency which it cannot overcome in a short time. However, there is room for discussion as to the scope and severity of the controls which should be applied under this principle.

Whereas the United Kingdom proposals would appear to eliminate International Lists II and III, I am convinced that there is an area in which quantitative restrictions are the most appropriate control mechanism. Of course, I recognize that it may be desirable to narrow substantially the area to which such controls need be applied, but I do not think we can scrap them altogether.

These seems to me to be the main difference between us. Although the gap appears to be wide, we have resolved greater differences before this to our mutual advantage and will do so again. I suggest, then, that we ask our responsible officials to meet together very soon, presumably with their French counterparts, and try to find the common ground on which we can continue jointly to provide constructive leadership to the Consultative Group.

Finally, I have two other suggestions to make. For one thing, I think it would be very useful if our representatives and subsequently the members of the Consultative Group, were jointly to examine and assess the meaning and direction of the Russians' new trade policy, including the much-publicized Russian profession of interest in consumer goods. Secondly, I think it would be advantageous for our representatives to explore ways and means by which the free world might exploit, in its relations with the Soviet bloc, any decision to relax existing controls.

General Lord Ismay to Sir Winston S. Churchill
(*Premier papers, 11/771*)

20 March 1954
Private

My dear Prime Minister,

Gruenther has returned from Washington earlier than I expected and I asked him to confirm the opinion expressed in my letter of 17th March.[1] He did so at once, but added 'as of now'. On my request for a translation of this condition, he summarised his position in the following sense:

> 'I do not believe that at the present time the Soviet would launch an attack on us with the forces they have outside Russia. But my views might change when —
> (i) The satellite divisions have trained into first-class troops: and
> (ii) The Soviet are in a position to deliver "much heavier stuff" by air.'

As regards the first condition, it seems questionable whether the Soviet would regard satellite forces, however efficient, as safe enough to be employed on anything but garrison or line of communications duties — at any rate at the beginning of the war.

The main point is, however, that Gruenther, Alex and Monty all think exactly alike on the present position.

Cabinet: conclusions
(*Cabinet papers, 128/27*)

22 March 1954 Prime Minister's Room
Secret House of Commons
5.30 p.m.
Cabinet Meeting No. 21 of 1954

[. . .]

2. The Foreign Secretary said that the United States Secretary of State had made an encouraging response to the suggestion that the maintenance of the Canal Zone Base in peace might be entrusted to a civilian organisation in which the Americans would take some share of responsibility. Mr Dulles had said that the United States Government were in principle prepared to cooperate in working out a solution along these lines, provided that this would not involve them in any new military commitment and that they would not be asked to participate in negotiations with the Egyptians unless they were asked to do so by the Egyptian Government. Mr Dulles had added that there were

---

[1] Reproduced above (p. 1485).

many technical and other aspects of the proposition which would have to be considered before a final decision was reached.

The Foreign Secretary said that, as he had made clear in his statement in the House of Commons that day, the defence negotiations with Egypt must be suspended until there was positive evidence that the Egyptians intended to take active and cooperative measures to improve the situation in the Canal Zone. Meanwhile, he proposed that he should explore, in consultation with the Americans, the possibility of handing over the maintenance of the Base to an Anglo-American civilian organisation.

The Prime Minister agreed that the details of an Anglo-American civilian organisation to maintain the Base might now be worked out further, in consultation with the Americans and without any final commitment. He would have preferred a definite rupture of the negotiations with the Egyptian Government, which would have enabled us to take our stand on the 1936 Treaty and to announce that we intended to redeploy the forces now located in the Canal Zone in accordance with our own interests. This redeployment could continue for about two years, at the end of which we should still have 15,000 troops in the Canal Zone in the region between Ismailia and Port Said. These troops, who would be able to ensure their own security, could remain until we had reason to place complete confidence in the promises of the Egyptian Government.

In discussion the following points were made:

(a) The Minister of Transport emphasised the importance of including in any agreement with the Egyptians an article about the freedom of navigation through the Suez Canal. The Foreign Secretary said that he doubted if it was possible at this stage to consider the inclusion of an article to this effect. There was already agreement on the inclusion of a statement in the preamble and this had sufficient legal validity.

(b) The redeployment of British troops in the Canal Zone would entail the gradual abandonment of parts of the Base, and if this were to start before the conclusion of an agreement it might invalidate the argument that the proper maintenance of the Base was one of the main reasons for seeking agreement with the Egyptian Government. It was pointed out, on the other hand, that some initial redeployment of forces might help to create those conditions of confidence without which no agreement was possible. This initial redeployment could be accompanied by a corresponding contraction and concentration of the Base.

(c) As the prospects declined of securing continuing payment of our occupation costs in Germany, it became increasingly important to obtain some relief in our overseas military expenditure in Egypt.

The Cabinet –

(1) Invited the Foreign Secretary to explore, in consultation with the Americans, detailed proposals for the maintenance of the Base installations in the Canal Zone by means of an Anglo-American civilian organization, and to report back to the Cabinet.

(2) Invited the Minister of Defence to report what initial steps could be taken to concentrate and contract the Base in the Canal Zone; and to recommend the phases of redeployment which could be carried out in parallel with this contraction.

[. . .]

4. The Prime Minister said that he was due to answer, in the House of Commons on the following day, a number of Questions designed to elicit the assurance that the United States Government would not use atomic weapons without prior consultations with the United Kingdom Government – especially in circumstances in which such action might provoke a retaliatory atomic attack on this country. He had been advised to reply, in effect, that he was satisfied with the existing arrangements for consultation between the two Governments on this and related matters. But, in view of the disclosures recently made by responsible United States authorities about the power of the hydrogen bomb, he was not sure that an answer on those lines would satisfy Parliament. He had therefore been considering whether he should preface this reply with a general statement on the strategic implications of the hydrogen bomb – disclosing no more information than had already been made public by the responsible authorities in the United States.

In discussion it was argued that the disclosures made about the effects of the hydrogen bomb had not as yet excited great public anxiety in this country. The public had probably assumed that, in the event of Russian aggression in Europe leading to general war, the Americans would use atomic weapons in retaliation; and they might not have paused to consider in detail the effects which such action would have on this country. They were more concerned with the risk that the Americans might use atomic weapons in limited operations, e.g., in Korea or in Indochina, and might thus precipitate a general war in which the Russians would retaliate by launching an atomic attack on this country. Parliament might therefore be more interested to know what assurances the United States Government had given that, if hostilities were resumed in Korea, they would not use atomic weapons without prior consultation with us. On this, although informal assurances had been given orally at the time of the Bermuda Meeting, it could not be publicly stated that the United States Governments were firmly committed to consult with us before taking action. On the other hand, the United States Secretary of State, in a recent Press conference, had stated in effect that his Government would not authorize the use of atomic weapons, without consultation with interested Allies, except for the purpose of self-preservation; and it would be reasonable for the Prime Minister to say, without being more specific, that he was satisfied with the understandings which had been reached with the United States Government on this point.

In further discussion the following points were made:

(a) A general statement on the strategic importance of the hydrogen bomb would certainly provoke a demand for a full debate. In this, questions would be raised – both on the detailed machinery for consultation between Governments, and on the preparations which we were making to meet the new risks involved – which the Government were not at present in a position to answer in detail.

(b) It was desirable that, at the appropriate moment, the public should be made aware of the full implications of the development of the hydrogen bomb. But the timing of this disclosure should be carefully judged. It would not in any event be easy to deal with a matter of this gravity within the limits of replies to Parliamentary Questions. It seemed preferable that the subject should be developed at greater length, at the appropriate moment, in a speech.

(c) Great care would be needed to check the development of a movement in favour of international agreement to prohibit the use of the hydrogen bomb or other atomic weapons. There could be no certainty that such an agreement could be effectively enforced. And, for some years at any rate, it would deprive the Western Powers of their main deterrent against Russian aggression in Europe.

(d) So far as concerned the use of atomic weapons in Europe, the United States Government had given a written undertaking that they would not launch an atomic attack from their air bases in this country without our agreement. This point should be given prominence in the reply to the Questions in the House of Commons.

The Prime Minister, summing up the discussion, said that it seemed better that the reply to the Questions for answer in the House of Commons on the following day should deal only with the extent to which the United States Government had undertaken to consult with us and other Allies before using atomic weapons, and need not be prefaced by any general statement on the effects of the hydrogen bomb. It would, however, be desirable that the answer should be designed to allay public anxiety and that it should, in particular, deal with the American use of East Anglian bases for an atomic attack. The question of a Government statement on the effects of the hydrogen bomb could be reserved for later consideration.

The Cabinet –

Took note that the Prime Minister would answer, in the light of their discussion, the Questions to be addressed to him in the House of Commons on the following day about the extent to which the United States Government had undertaken to consult the United Kingdom Government before using atomic weapons.

1494   March 1954

Sir Winston S. Churchill to President Dwight D. Eisenhower
Prime Minister's Personal Telegram T.50/54
(Premier papers, 11/1074)

24 March 1954
Immediate
Top Secret and Personal
No. 1135

My dear Friend,

Thank you for your message of March 19[1] about the relaxation of East/West trade controls. We shall be very glad to talk over with your representatives the points set out in your message and I would urge that the talks should take place as soon as possible. I agree that French representatives should also take part. I suggest that if possible our officials should be informed before the discussions begin what variations in terms of items your Government would wish to make to the revised list we have proposed.

Sir Winston S. Churchill to President Dwight D. Eisenhower
(Churchill papers, 6/3A)

24 March 1954
Private and Personal

My dear Friend,

Thank you very much for your letter about East/West Trade. As consultation and discussion between our two countries were urgent, I sent you my telegram of today's date. I now venture to put before you some of the wider considerations that have influenced my thought.

While doing all that is possible to increase our joint strength and unity, I am anxious to promote an easement of relations with Soviet Russia and to encourage and aid any development of Russian life which leads to a wider enjoyment by the Russian masses of the consumer goods of which you speak and modern popular amenities and diversions which play so large a part in British and American life. I hope that this process will lead to some relaxation of the grim discipline of the peoples of this vast land ocean of Russia and its satellites. Moreover, trade means contacts and probably involves a good deal of friendly infiltration which I think would be to our advantage from every point of view, including the military.

I am of course opposed to exportation to Russia of weapons or military equipment in a direct form, but I do not think this principle should be used to ban so many items because they might be used for military purposes in a

---

[1] Reproduced above (pp. 1487–8).

secondary or subsequent stage. Any advantage given by this would only be on a small and almost trivial proportion of Russian armaments, for the whole scale of East/West Trade is small and we should be dealing only with a percentage of a percentage. I do not think this ought to stand in the way of the widening of commercial intercourse so long as only conventional forms of equipment are concerned. On the contrary I believe that even in this limited military sphere we should, I think, gain as much or almost as much as we should lose.

Over and beyond that there are those hopes of a broadening of Russian life and relaxation of international tension which may lead to the reestablishment of a peaceful foundation for the tormented and burdened world.

How minute do all these military considerations, arising out of trade as limited, appear compared to the Hydrogen bomb and the rapid progress the Soviets are said to be making with it. There is the peril which marches towards us and is nearer and more deadly to us than to you. We may be sure that whatever raw materials or equipment is available to the Russians, whether from their own resources or from imports, the first priority will be given to nuclear expansion, just as at a former stage in Germany guns counted before butter. I fear, therefore, that even a total prohibition of all East/West trade would not impede the physical progress of these fearful forces. On the other hand there is the hope that the sense of easement may render more fruitful those tentative yet inspiring conceptions of which you told me at Bermuda and which your letter of March 19,[1] which I received yesterday and to which I will reply later, also so pregnantly deals.

I have not hampered this expression of my most anxious thought by expatiating on the well-known arguments about British trade in the present economic phase. I will merely mention the headings. If the United States will not let us pay for her goods by rendering reciprocal services and make a reasonable proportion of things your people want or might be attracted by, as is our deep desire, the present deadlock must continue. As the old tag says, those who do not import cannot export. I have learned all about these difficulties from my political youth up and am making no complaint. 'Off shore' purchase is a Godsend, but you are still in the position of having to give away on a vast scale with generosity and human patriotism what we should like to earn by hard work and mental exertion. The arrival of Germany and Japan in the world market make it necessary that we should open out our trade in every possible direction for we have to keep 50 million people alive in this small island as well as maintaining the greatest armaments next to your own in the free world.

As the proportions of our trade with Russia must in any case be on a minor scale for many years, I cannot rate the commercial aspect so highly as I do those I have mentioned above.

---

[1] Reproduced above (pp. 1487–8).

I enclose a copy of the telegram which I have agreed with my colleagues and which will by now have reached you.

Cabinet: conclusions
(Cabinet papers, 128/27)

24 March 1954
Secret
11.30 a.m.
Cabinet Meeting No. 22 of 1954

[. . .]
3. The Prime Minister said that he had received a personal message from President Eisenhower[1] in answer to our proposals for relaxation of the existing controls over trade with countries in the Soviet bloc. The President had indicated that, while the United States Government were prepared to go some way in contracting and simplifying these controls, he felt that the United Kingdom proposals went further than public and Congressional opinion in the United States would be able to accept. In particular, he considered that the controls should continue to extend to equipment and materials which were of high value to the Soviet war potential, and that quantitative restrictions should be retained as part of the mechanism of control. He had suggested that British, American and French officials should meet together soon and try to arrive at agreed proposals which could be submitted to the Paris Group. The Prime Minister said that he intended to accept this suggestion for an early meeting and to ask the President to indicate in advance what variations the Americans would like to see made in the proposals which we had put to them.

The Foreign Secretary said that it was possible that, when the President had received this reply, he would arrange for Mr Stassen to attend these official conversations. It would be useful if an early opportunity could be taken to make it clear publicly that the relaxations which we were proposing concerned only the countries in the Soviet bloc and were not intended to apply to trade with Communist China.

The Cabinet –

Took note of these statements by the Prime Minister and the Foreign Secretary.

[. . .]

---

[1] Reproduced above (pp. 1488–9).

March 1954

Queen Frederica of Greece[1] to Sir Winston S. Churchill
(Premier papers, 11/682)

24 March 1954   Athens

Dear Sir Winston,

In writing to you today I feel as if I have been advised to do so by our mutual friend General Smuts. He was, as you know, during the war years not only a friend but also adviser and teacher to me. I remember him always pointing out to all of us that the only man left who combined within himself the qualities of a statesman, as well as those of a great human being, was you, yourself. I therefore address myself today to the statesman with real insight, as well as to the great human with deep understanding.

My husband and I are beginning to get really worried about what is happening concerning Anglo-Hellenic friendship from a purely emotional point of view. A very small island called Cyprus[2] seems to become a cause for estrangement between Greece and England. This should not be. England and Greece have been emotionally linked together for a long time and their union has been based upon completely unselfish foundations. We proved this when we stood by you during the most dangerous hours in recent British history.

In Europe you had no other friends that were yet free to decide if they wanted to make your cause their own and thereby risk unconditionally all material values to keep those of the spirit sacred, or to give in as so many of our neighbors did, thus saving their skins but losing their souls.

We knew that your ideals were ours. We did not bargain and we stood by you alone in the South, as you were alone in the North. I believe that ours were the only people who gave flowers to the British soldier when he had to withdraw, thus bringing healing in defeat to the wounded pride of many a British soldier.

Our people love England. It is a love possible owing to a complete lack of a sense of inferiority. I have so often noticed in other countries who pretend to dislike England that in reality they suffer from an inferiority complex. Our people are a proud people, just and fair; therefore even in the face of misery, defeat, and an unknown future they could yet feel that the British Tommy had to leave Greece in order to come back again. So they gave him all they had to give, not minding what to-morrow might bring.

---

[1] Frederica of Hanover, 1917–81. Married, 1938, Prince Paul of Greece, who succeeded as King in 1947.

[2] The Cyprus Convention of 1878 gave Britain authority in Cyprus, which it annexed in 1914. Turkish Cypriots make up 18% of the population, and a separate Turkish zone became an issue at the time of this letter. The majority Greek Cypriot population pursued union with Greece. Cyprus was granted independence in 1960, but later the island was *de facto* partitioned into two main parts: the Greek part, 59% of the area, in the south and west, and the Turkish part in the remainder, administered by a self-declared Turkish Cypriot Republic.

But now, Sir Winston, the Greek spirit is really getting hurt owing to the categorical refusal to have any discussions upon the future of Cyprus.

Love such as our people always had for England is slowly but surely turning into bitter resentment. Our people feel that those great values that united us during History have not any more the same meaning for England as they have for Greece.

I know that politics are not based on emotion, but our people are a highly emotional people. They feel that truly and honestly they have played the game. That now it is England's turn to prove her friendship, sense of justice and fair-play.

The Greeks of Cyprus are Christians, Europeans as well as Greeks, out of whose spirit has come the ideals of Democracy and Freedom. Do you believe that our people could ever understand that Christians, Europeans, as well as Greeks, should remain Colonials during these modern times? You cannot make them understand that England, our England, could possibly think and feel like this about any Greek, in or outside of our own country. It is in this last-mentioned thought that our people feel justifiable bitterness.

I have put to you now the emotional side of the problem as far as our people are concerned. It is in no way exaggerated and is unfortunately continuously growing. Something must be done to save our union. It is a good one, the best there has ever been.

You may well ask, but is England's friendship less dear to you than Cyprus? I can only answer: England's friendship was dear enough for us to sacrifice ourselves and our Country in the same cause and for the same ideals that have been mutually ours for generations. But I point out that we are true to our ideals and to personal interest, as we have proved during the War. Should those ideals still remain true to you, then shall remain true forever the meaning of these words, 'Where England stands we stand, where England goes we go.'

The prestige of England for us 'foreigners' lies not in the greatness of her Empire, nor has it dwindled yet to the value of a small island, but it lies in the greatness of her spirit. And this spirit, Sir Winston, is still incorporated within yourself.

I appeal to you to help us keep the door open where an agreement between our two countries could yet be possible, so that we should not be forced to drag into the open before the profane eyes of the world our family quarrel. (Because so long as our spirit is the same it will remain a family quarrel.) All we want is an open door where discussions would be possible which might determine a gradual evolution of the Cyprus question to the satisfaction of our countries.

I remember that once before a discussion between you and me, which has never come before the public, has been of a great blessing to my Country. You understood our problem, you helped to bring General Marshall in contact with me, greater American aid was given to our army, and as a result of this meeting our troops, led by our present Prime Minister the then Commander-in-Chief

Field Marshal Papagos,[1] were able to achieve the first victory against communist aggression. I believe, therefore, that through your influence once again great mischief can be prevented.

I would so like to be able to privately and quite unofficially discuss this subject with you and with any one else whom you might suggest, so long as we can keep it out of the press and away from official documents and reports. But if it is not possible then this letter must remain the only hope that something might be done to keep the door open.

Would you please treat this letter as absolutely and completely confidential, as it is a purely personal letter and expresses our personal feelings and views.

My husband joins me in sending you our best regards and wishes.

Anthony Eden to Sir Winston S. Churchill
(*Premier papers, 11/593*)

25 March 1954
Top Secret
PM/54/53

USE OF AUSTRIAN MANPOWER IN THE EVENT OF WAR

I attach a paper on this subject prepared jointly by the Secretary of State for War and myself. You will see that we should like our diplomatic and military representatives in Vienna, in conjunction with their American and French colleagues, to discuss orally with certain trusted Austrian Ministers the highly secret arrangements set out in the last paragraph of the paper.

2. We have not thought it necessary to suggest putting this matter to the Cabinet, but copies of this minute and of the paper are being sent to the Chancellor of the Exchequer, who has no comment, and the Minister of Defence, who strongly supports. Unless you or they dissent, I should like to send early instructions to Her Majesty's Ambassador in Vienna[2] in the sense recommended.

[1] Alexandros Papagos, 1883–1955. Born in Athens. Educated at Brussels Military Academy. Commissioned 2nd Lt, Hellenic Army, 1906; Lt, 1911. On active service during Balkan Wars, 1912–13. Capt., 1913. Maj., 1916. Lt-Col., 1920. Col., 1923. Maj.-Gen., 1930. Deputy Chief of Hellenic Army General Staff, 1931–3. Inspector-General of Cavalry, 1933–5. Lt-Gen., 1935. Participated in military coup restoring Greek monarchy, 1935. Minister of War, 1935–6. CGS, 1936–40. On active service during WWII. C-in-C, Hellenic Army, Greco-Italian War, 1940–1. POW, 1941–5. Gen., 1947. FM, 1949. C-in-C, Armed Forces, 1949–51. Resigned from Army, 1951. Founded Greek Rally, 1951. PM of Greece, 1952–5.
[2] Geoffrey Arnold Wallinger, 1903–75. Educated at Clare College, Cambridge. Entered Diplomatic Service, 1926; on assignment in Cairo, Vienna, Pretoria and Cape Town, Buenos Aires and Nanking, and in FO, 1927–49. Married, 1939, Diana Peel Nelson: one child; 1950, Alix de la Faye Lamotte (d. 1956); 1958, Stella Irena Zilliacus. CMG, 1947. Minister to Hungary, 1949–51. Ambassador to Thailand, 1951–4; to Austria, 1954–8; to Brazil, 1958–63. KCMG, 1953. GBE, 1963.

Evelyn Shuckburgh: diary
('Descent to Suez', pages 153–4)

26 March 1954

The newspapers today say that the H-bomb explosion on 1 March was three times more powerful than the scientists themselves expected. In other words, it was out of control. Very great excitement everywhere about it, as if people began to see the end of the world. AE went over to talk to the PM, who was on the whole quite sensible – unlike *The Times* leader of this morning which proposes an immediate Churchill–Malenkow meeting as a sort of desperate throw. AE saw Sir William Haley,[1] editor of *The Times*, and tried to instil some calm into him. He also had a very unsatisfactory interview with Massigli, and his contempt for the French grows daily, as they twist and wriggle in the inexorable toils of EDC.

President Dwight D. Eisenhower to Sir Winston S. Churchill
(Premier papers, 11/1074)

28 March 1954
Top Secret

Dear Winston,
  Your letter of March 24[2] only reached me Saturday afternoon, the plane which brought it having been delayed. Consequently I did not have an opportunity to go over it with Harold Stassen before he left for London. However, Harold is fully informed of my views on this difficult and important matter. As I indicated in my earlier letter your proposals in this field seem to go a bit further than seems wise or necessary. However, it remains my hope that after Harold has explained the lines along which our thoughts are running, and when we pass from the general to the concrete, we shall be able to reach agreement.

---

[1] William John Haley, 1901–87. Educated at Victoria College. Sub-editor, *Manchester Evening News*, 1922; Director, 1930. Director-General, BBC, 1944–52. KCMG, 1946. Editor, *The Times*, 1952–66. Editor-in-Chief, *Encyclopaedia Britannica*, 1968–9.
[2] Reproduced above (pp. 1494–6).

MARCH 1954 1501

Cabinet: minutes
(Cabinet papers, 130/100)

29 March 1954　　　　　　　　　　　　　　　Prime Minister's Room
Top Secret　　　　　　　　　　　　　　　　　House of Commons
5.30 p.m.
Gen. 460/1st Meeting

1. HYDROGEN BOMB

The Meeting considered the draft of a statement to be made by the Prime Minister in reply to a number of Parliamentary Questions about the hydrogen bomb tests in the Pacific. Several detailed amendments were suggested in discussion of this draft.

The Prime Minister said that he thought it would be wise to preface his statement with a reference to the fact that the laws of the United States forbade disclosure of a great deal of information about these tests, that our own knowledge was therefore incomplete, and that any opinions which he might express on technical aspects of the tests were derived from British scientific advice and not from information divulged to us by the Americans. He proposed to refuse to answer supplementary questions on points of detail. He would explain that he had sought permission to answer the numerous questions on the Order Paper in a single statement because of the need in matters of such grave importance to weigh carefully the expressions used. If he had not covered all the points raised in the Questions, it was because he did not regard it as in the public interest to answer them.

The Prime Minister said that, if there was a request for an early debate, he would reply that there would be no opportunity before Easter. He was, however, willing to discuss with the leaders of the Opposition the advisability of having a debate at some later date. If some of the information which was available to the Government were disclosed to him in confidence, Mr Attlee would be in a better position to form a judgment whether it was in the national interest to have a debate in Parliament.

The Meeting –
(1) Took note that the Prime Minister would revise the draft statement in accordance with the amendments suggested in discussion and with his own proposals for introducing the subject,
(2) Endorsed the Prime Minister's proposals for handling supplementary Questions and for dealing with any demand for a debate in Parliament.

2. EGYPT

The Foreign Secretary said that a dangerous situation was developing in Egypt. Strikes might lead to a breakdown in the distribution of food and this would possibly be followed by serious riots. At present there was no sign that disturbances would be directed against foreign residents in Egypt, but there was nevertheless a danger that this might occur. He therefore proposed that the British troops in the Canal Zone should be put at 72 hours' notice so that they would be ready to undertake rescue operations in Egyptian towns affected by anti-foreign rioting. He hoped that, if it became necessary for British troops to intervene, they would be able to rescue not only British subjects but all white nationals of foreign countries resident in Egypt. He did not intend that there should be any intervention by British troops unless the situation made it evidently and urgently necessary.

The Meeting –

Agreed that the Commanders in Chief Middle East should be instructed to bring troops in the Canal Zone to 72 hours' notice and to report what operations they could undertake, if the eventuality arose, for the rescue of British subjects and white nationals of other foreign countries resident in Egypt.

3. EAST/WEST TRADE

The Foreign Secretary suggested that before Mr Stassen returned to the United States it would be desirable for the Prime Minister to see him and the United States Ambassador in London. Meetings between the President of the Board of Trade and Mr Stassen had been proceeding during the day and he hoped that some measure of agreement would be reached so that the British and Americans might present a united front to the Paris group.

The Prime Minister said that he would be glad to see Mr Stassen before he left.

Sir Winston S. Churchill to Anthony Eden
Prime Minister's Personal Minute M.63/54
(Premier papers, 11/701)

29 March 1954
Personal and Private

I was startled by the word 'insuperable' used in this account of your talk with Lord Hankey.[1] I understand the Chiefs of Staff have come round to the CIGS's view, provided the figure is 15,000 and not 10,000. I thought this matter still awaited the further consideration and final decision of the Cabinet. The confusion in Egypt makes the subject less urgent than all this Hydrogen

[1] Maurice Pascal Alers Hankey, 1877–1963. Secretary to Committee of Imperial Defence, 1912–38. Knighted, Feb. 1916. Secretary to War Cabinet, 1916–18; to Cabinet, 1919–38. Director, Suez Canal Co., 1938–9, 1945–63. Baron, 1939. Minister without Portfolio, Sep. 1939 to May 1940. Chancellor of the Duchy of Lancaster, 1940–1. Paymaster-General, 1941–2. Chairman, Scientific Advisory Committee, 1941–2; Technical Personnel Committee, 1941–52. Member, Advisory Council on Scientific Research and Technical Development to Minister of Supply, 1947–9.

business which has swooped down on us, and also, I think, than East–West trade. But in about a fortnight we must have another Cabinet upon it.

Sir Winston S. Churchill to President Dwight D. Eisenhower
Prime Minister's Personal Telegram T.51/54
(Premier papers, 11/1074)

29 March 1954
Top Secret

My dear Friend,

There is widespread anxiety here about the H-bomb and I am facing a barrage of Questions tomorrow about the March 1 explosion. Our instruments here record a second explosion in the series mentioned in our private talks at Bermuda on the 26th instant.

2. I am well aware of all your difficulties in view of the McMahon Act etc. and of the efforts you are making to obtain greater freedom to give us information and I shall do my utmost to safeguard our common interests as they are developing. It would be a great help to me if I could say that in return for the facilities we accorded to American aircraft at the Australian experiments the American authorities had agreed to our sending aircraft to collect samples of debris at very great heights.

3. I should also like to say that apart from this act of reciprocity we have no information as yet of the results of the experiment, but we hope it may be possible within the limits of existing US legislation to give us a report of what occurred.

4. I shall of course repulse all suggestions – and there are many – that we should protest against the continuance of your experiment. I have to speak at 3.30 p.m. GMT Tuesday, 30th. The Prof is also telegraphing to the Admiral.

President Dwight D. Eisenhower to Sir Winston S. Churchill
Prime Minister's Personal Telegram T.52/54
(Premier papers, 11/1074)

30 March 1954
Immediate
Dedip
Top Secret
No. 1256

Greatly appreciate your message. Admiral Strauss has just returned from the Pacific and I shall not see him until tomorrow. I understand, however, that he has been in touch with your Ambassador and that the first two points you raise have been covered to your satisfaction.

Sir Winston S. Churchill: speech
(Hansard)

30 March 1954   House of Commons

THE HYDROGEN BOMB

The development of the hydrogen bomb raises strategic and political issues which are so momentous and far-reaching that they cannot be adequately discussed within the limits of a statement at the end of questions. I do not propose to make any general statement on these issues. I will, however, deal briefly with some of the specific suggestions made in the particular questions which have been placed on the Order Paper, although the bulk of them would not have been reached in ordinary circumstances.

In the first place, I must make it clear that our knowledge of these American experiments is necessarily limited. The United States Government are prevented by their own legislation from divulging secret information about them. I can say, however, from our own scientific knowledge that there is no foundation for the suggestion that these explosions are 'incalculable', in the sense that those making the tests are unable to set limits to the explosive power of the bomb or to calculate in advance what the main effects will be. I greatly regret, as do our American friends, that any injury or damage should have been suffered by third parties as a result of the recent experiment; but I understand that the injuries suffered by persons outside the area which had been cleared for the purposes of the test – that is the 1st March test – are neither serious nor lasting.

It is being suggested that further tests should be the subject of international consultation or control. The restrictions imposed by the United States law, to which I have already referred, would make this impracticable. But, even if this were not so, I should not myself be ready to propose it, for reasons which I will now mention.

International rules have, of course, been prescribed to regulate the testing of conventional weapons; and these, appropriately amended to meet the greatly increased risks of experiment with atomic or hydrogen weapons, have, we believe, been carefully applied in all the experiments carried out by the United States authorities. I am sure that those responsible for conducting these tests will continue to take the most rigorous precautions to minimize the risks involved. The House will have noticed that, since the explosion of 1st March, they have taken the additional precaution of enlarging considerably the area which shipping and aircraft are warned to avoid on the occasion of further experiments of this nature.

It has now been announced in Washington by the Chairman of the Atomic Energy Commission that another experiment was carried out in the Pacific on 26th March, since that one which we had already heard on 1st March. Both the experiment and the extra precautions taken to warn shipping in the vicinity are stated to have been successful. The experiment is described as being one of a 'test series', which will continue during April. I hope it may be found possible within the limits of existing United States legislation to give us information about what occurs. Our own instruments, which are highly developed, of course recorded the explosion of Friday last as soon as sound waves or pressure waves reached us.

As is well known, the President is appealing to Congress for a greater latitude of communication on certain nuclear matters with us. In view of what we have learned by our own scientific researches, and also in view of the progress of the Soviets in this sphere, I am sure that consultation is to the advantage both of Great Britain and the United States. I trust nothing will be said here which will set back the many favourable tendencies in this direction which are now evident in the United States.

It is being suggested that I should endeavour to persuade the United States Government to abandon their series of experimental explosions of hydrogen bombs. We have no power to stop this. And I am sure that it would not be right or wise for us to ask that it should be stopped. When similar experiments were conducted by the Russians, I cannot remember that anyone suggested that such representations should be made to the Soviet Government. The experiments which the Americans are now conducting in the Pacific are an essential part of the defence policy of a friendly Power without whose massive strength and generous help Europe would be in mortal peril. We should indeed be doing a great disservice to the free world if we sought in any way to impede the progress of our American allies in building up their overwhelming strength in the weapon which provides the greatest possible deterrent against the outbreak of a Third World War.

Together with our friends in the Commonwealth and our Allies, we have laboured long to secure international agreement on disarmament and to limit the competition in armaments which is denying to the peoples of the world so many of the benefits which modern science could provide. But no satisfactory arrangements could be made to limit the use of atomic weapons except as part of an international agreement on disarmament as a whole. There could be no security in such an agreement unless it included provision for effective inspection and enforcement. We ourselves have repeatedly offered to accept such provision. But it would be idle to suppose that such an agreement could be concluded with any reasonable expectation of its observance until conditions of confidence between the nations have first been established. We, Sir, speaking for Her Majesty's Government, shall lose no opportunity of securing an easement of world tension, but at the same time we must persevere, with the other nations of the free world, in our policy of upholding, at the necessary level, our united military strength.

Cabinet: conclusions
(Cabinet papers, 128/27)

31 March 1954
Secret
11.30 a.m.
Cabinet Meeting No. 23 of 1954

1. On 29th March the Prime Minister had discussed with some of his Ministerial colleagues the terms of a statement which he was proposing to make in the House of Commons in reply to a number of Questions about the series of test explosions of hydrogen bombs which the United States authorities were conducting in the Pacific. These questions, which had been tabled by members of the Labour Opposition, implied that it was the duty of the Government to use their influence to persuade the United States authorities either to abandon this series of tests or at least to bring it under some form of international control. In his statement on 30th March the Prime Minister had made it clear that the Government were not prepared to make any such representations to the United States Government or to take any other action which might impede American progress to building up their overwhelming strength in nuclear weapons, which provided the greatest possible deterrent against the outbreak of a third world war.

The Prime Minister said that it was now clear that, in view of the public anxiety which these experiments had aroused, the House of Commons should be given an early opportunity for a full debate on this question. The Cabinet endorsed this view.

The Cabinet –
   (1) Invited the Chief Whip to seek the agreement of the Opposition that a debate should be held on 5th April on the questions arising from the current series of nuclear explosions in the Pacific.
   (2) Agreed that the Prime Minister and the Foreign Secretary should speak on the Government's behalf in this debate.

The Cabinet also considered what answer should be returned to a Question by Mr Hamilton, MP,[1] for answer that day by the Under-Secretary of

---

[1] Malcolm Avendale Douglas-Hamilton, 1909–64. Served in RAF, 1929–32, 1939–46. Worked in civil aviation, 1934–9. OBE, 1943. DFC, 1944. MP (Unionist) for Inverness, 1950–4. Died in an airplane crash in Cameroon.

State for Air, asking how many RAF aircraft had made flights in the vicinity of the recent test explosion in the Pacific and whether they had suffered any damage.

The Cabinet were informed that, by arrangement with the United States authorities, RAF aircraft were operating in the area for the purpose, without damage, after each of the explosions on 1st and 26th March. Two other aircraft which had been assigned to this duty had been lost in transit between Australia and the base in the Pacific from which the experimental flight was to have been made. One was believed to have fallen into the sea, and its crew had been posted missing: the second had made a forced landing on an island, without injury to the crew. It had been intended that these operations should remain secret; but President Eisenhower had now agreed that the Prime Minister might disclose some limited information about them if he thought this essential for the purpose of satisfying opinion in Parliament.

Alternative draft answers to the question were considered by the Cabinet. The first was to the effect that it would not be in the public interest to disclose in detail all the measures taken by British and American authorities to gain scientific information about the effects of nuclear explosions, wherever they occurred; but it would be added that no British Service personnel had suffered any radioactive effects of nuclear explosions in the Pacific on 1st and 26th March; and that no injury or damage had been suffered by this aircraft or its crew on either occasion. The answer would go on to disclose that two other aircraft assigned to this duty had been lost in transit between Australia and the base in the Pacific from which the experimental flight was to have been made.

The Prime Minister said that he greatly preferred the second of the alternative drafts. He thought it would be unwise to withhold from the House information about the loss of two of the aircraft assigned to this duty. The Cabinet accepted the Prime Minister's view.

The Cabinet –

(3) Agreed that the information contained in the longer of the two draft answers to this Question should be given to the House – by the Under-Secretary of State for Air, if the Question was reached that afternoon; or, if it was not reached and was subsequently withdrawn, by the Prime Minister in the course of his speech in the forthcoming debate on 5th April.

[. . .]

4. The Cabinet had before them a memorandum by the Chiefs of Staff (D(54)17) outlining a military plan for assisting Jordan in the event of major aggression by Israel.

The Minister of Defence said that at the meeting of the Anglo-Jordan Joint Defence Board in September, 1953, our representatives had been pressed to say what action we should take to honour our obligations under the Treaty in the event of a major attack on Jordan by Israel. The Board was due to meet again on 5th April and, if we failed to give any indication of our intentions, the Jordanians would suspect that we were not going to honour our obligations. The Chiefs of Staff had therefore prepared a plan for military action, which involved the invasion of Israel by British forces from the south. Was it politically acceptable that a plan of this kind should be disclosed at the meeting of the Board? Quite apart from that question he himself thought it would be wise that the armoured squadron now at Ma'an should be sent to Mafraq to train with the Arab Legion. That would be at once an assurance to Jordan and a warning to Israel that if an act of aggression were committed British forces would be involved.

The Chief of the Imperial General Staff said that the memorandum before the Cabinet had been prepared in the absence of the Chiefs of Staff themselves, who did not wish to support the recommendation that this particular plan should be disclosed at the meeting of the Anglo-Jordan Joint Defence Board. The plan itself was militarily sound, and it would be difficult to give effective support to Jordan if we were limited to helping the Jordanian forces to defend their own territory because it would take too long to move any substantial numbers of British forces into Jordan. The Chiefs of Staff had in any event hoped to build up the armoured squadron at Ma'an to the strength of an armoured regiment and to move it to Mafraq, but that could not be done in the immediate future. Our intentions in this respect might, however, be disclosed at the meeting of the Anglo-Jordan Joint Defence Board on 5th April, and this might be sufficient to convince the Jordanians that we had plans for carrying out our obligations under the Treaty.

The Prime Minister said that he was much relieved to hear that the Chiefs of Staff were not in favour of disclosing to the Jordanians a plan involving British invasion of Israel. Leakage of such a plan would have very grave consequences. Would it not be possible either to defer the meeting arranged for 5th April or, if it must be held, to avoid any disclosure of military plans?

The Foreign Secretary said that it was laid down in our Treaty with Jordan that when a threat of aggression existed immediate consultation would take place between the two Powers. On the other hand it was also laid down in the Treaty that it was their first duty to try to resolve problems by peaceful means. It could not be denied that a threat now existed and it would be valuable if the Prime Minister would send a message to the Prime Minister of Israel reminding him of our obligations under our Treaty with Jordan and urging him to avoid any provocative action.

The Foreign Secretary said that he would like to consider further the suggestion made by the Chief of the Imperial General Staff that the disclosure of plans at the meeting of the Anglo-Jordan Joint Defence Board on 5th April should be confined to our intentions to increase the armoured squadron to a regiment and to move it to Mafraq. He thought that something on these lines might meet the immediate necessity for giving some reassurance to Jordan.

The Cabinet –
(1) Agreed that the substance of the plan outlined in D(54)17 should not be divulged to Jordan at the meeting of the Anglo-Jordan Joint Defence Board on 5th April.
(2) Invited the Foreign Secretary to consider the instructions to be given to our representatives on the Anglo-Jordan Joint Defence Board in the light of the Cabinet's discussion.
(3) Took note that the Foreign Secretary would submit to the Prime Minister the terms of a message which he might send to the Prime Minister of Israel.

[. . .]

April 1954

Sir Winston S. Churchill to President Dwight D. Eisenhower
Prime Minister's Personal Telegram T.57/54
(Premier papers, 11/1074)

1 April 1954
Emergency
Top Secret, Personal and Private
No. 1293

My dear Friend,

I am grateful to you for permission to speak about the aircraft in reply to a Question. As we are going to have a full dress Debate on Monday the Question has been postponed. I send you herewith the Answer I was going to give[1] which I think meets most of Strauss's misgivings. I shall now weave it into my argument. Meanwhile any topical comments upon it will be welcome.

2. Another matter far more important presses upon me. The foundation of my argument is that the United States Government is bound by the McMahon Act and cannot disclose forbidden information even to their closest friends. You are appealing to Congress for more flexibility in view of our own knowledge independently acquired and the general diffusion of knowledge on this subject. Our Opposition, especially its anti-American Left Wing, are trying to put the blame for the present restriction of information on to me and this increases my difficulty in defending, as I have done and will do, your claim to keep your secrets as agreed with the late Socialist Government. I am also supporting, as you will have seen, your continued experiments.

3. In view of the attacks, however, I am sure you will agree that they only course open to me is to quote and publish the text of my agreement with FDR in 1943, which completely vindicates my own care of British interests. You will remember I showed it to you in Bernie's flat before you had assumed power, on my way to Jamaica in January, 1953. It will prove decisively that the Opposition, not I, are responsible for our present position, and how great is

---

[1] Reproduced immediately below.

April 1954   1511

the difference between the situation which I handed over when I was thrown out by the Election of 1945 from the new position which I inherited from the Socialists in 1951.

4. The fourth clause of this document about commercial possibilities contains a prediction by me that I was content to leave the future of commercial atomics to the President of the United States, 'as he considered to be fair and just and in harmony with the economic welfare of the world'. This has now been vindicated in a striking manner by your scheme announced in UNO on December 8, 1953.

I feel I have a right to disclose this document which I signed with your predecessor eleven years ago, and which has since been superseded by other Treaties agreed between Great Britain and the Truman Administration. I am nevertheless explaining my positon and intentions to you because of our personal friendship and our various talks about the document. It would be an encouragement to me to hear from you that you are content with the course I am taking.

5. Our talks with Stassen went off very well and will I am sure produce fruitful and harmless results.

Sir Winston S. Churchill to President Dwight D. Eisenhower
(Premier papers, 11/1074)

1 April 1954
Emergency
Top Secret
No. 1294

Following is text referred to in Paragraph 1.

The United States authorities agreed that we should have certain limited facilities for collecting scientific data bearing on the effects of the present series of nuclear experiments in the Pacific. This arrangement was made in return for similar facilities which we had granted to the Americans on the occasion of our own nuclear test in Australia. For this purpose an aircraft of the Royal Air Force made a flight in the vicinity of the explosion of March 1, some hours after it occurred; a similar flight was also made on March 27. No injury or damage was suffered by this aircraft or its crew, on either occasion.

I think, however, that the House should know that two Canberra aircraft which had been assigned to this duty were lost in transit between Australia and the base in the Pacific from which the experimental flights were to have been made. Of these, one is believed to have fallen into the sea and its crew of three have been posted missing. The second made a forced landing on an island with the loss of the aircraft but without injury to the crew. Her Majesty's Government greatly regret the loss of life and I feel sure that the House would wish me to express our sympathy with the relatives. The House will understand, however, that the loss of those two aircraft was in no way due to the risks of the special mission which they were to have undertaken.

John Colville to Sir Winston S. Churchill
(*Premier papers, 11/682*)

2 April 1954

This long and emotional letter[1] from the Queen of Greece is a plea that you personally should intervene in the Cyprus question. She says: 'All we want is an open door where discussions would be possible which might determine a gradual evolution of the Cyprus question to the satisfaction of our countries.'

She speaks a lot of the friendly help given to England by Greece during the war, but very little of the help which we gave to the Greeks. Cyprus has never been a Greek possession, at any rate never since the fall of the Byzantine Empire. After the Knights Templar had ruled it for 300 years it fell to Venice and then to the Turks. It came to us in 1878. The Queen of Greece has, I am told, recently taken to meddling in politics to a very undesirable extent. She bases everything on her friendship with General Smuts whose example she quotes copiously in this letter. I really hardly think it is necessary to ask the Foreign Office for a draft reply, though you will doubtless wish to send them a copy of this letter. I submit a draft for your consideration.

The Queen implies that it would be nice if she could see you personally. This is probably a reference to the disappointment which the King and Queen of Greece feel that they are not being invited for their State Visit to England this year. The Swedes are coming and also the Emperor of Abyssinia[2] so that the King and Queen of Greece will have to wait until 1955. I am sure you will not want to refer to this matter in your reply.

---

[1] Reproduced above (pp. 1497–9).
[2] Haile Selassie, 1892–1975. Acceded to Imperial Throne of Abyssinia, 1930. Exiled, 1936. Returned, 1941. Deposed, 1974.

April 1954

Sir Gerald Kelly[1] to Sir Winston S. Churchill
(*Churchill papers, 2/345*)

2 April 1954

My dear Winston,

When I came to Chartwell I saw amongst other things a very slightly indicated picture of the Cap d'Ail, of pines against the sea, which you said amused you because, you said, the pines seemed to be fighting. It looked very well in your studio and wonderfully complete considering how short a distance you had gone, but in the raking light of the Royal Academy it does not look so good and the Hanging Committee have asked me to write and beg you to send the other version which is more complete.

There was also another picture, of the approach to an island outside Venice which I thought extremely lovely and I was bitterly disappointed that you did not send it along. Will you help by instructing Mr Patrickson[2] to bring these two pictures to the Academy?

The Fountain in Shadow does not look very well: it is too dark and I know I begged you to send it, but I think I was wrong.

Otherwise the Exhibition[3] is gradually forming itself, and I promise you that too many of your pictures will not be hung. But I do beg you to allow me — and it is the last time I shall bother you so — to let us have the approach to the island and the other version of the Cap d'Ail.

This is the 'positively last time' I can bother you.

Lord Woolton to Sir Winston S. Churchill
(*Churchill papers, 6/4*)

2 April 1954

You asked for an appreciation of the most suitable month for a General Election.

<u>The Spring</u> is impossible because of the complications of Easter, Whitsuntide, the local elections, and the Budget.

<u>Summer.</u> June to September is complicated by holidays, and particularly by the Wakes weeks of Lancashire. Holidaymakers do not get the postal

---

[1] Gerald Festus Kelly, 1879–1972. Educated at Eton and Trinity Hall, Cambridge. Associate, Royal Academy, 1922; Academician, 1930. Member, Royal Fine Arts Commission, 1938–43. Painted State Portraits of the King and Queen, 1945. Knighted, 1945. Commander of Legion of Honour, 1950. Membre correspondant de la section de peinture de l'Académie des Beaux Arts de l'Institut de France, 1953. Academico Correspondiente de la Réal Academia de Bellas Artes de San Fernando, Madrid, 1953. Commander of Order of Oranje Nassau, 1953.

[2] Frank Patrickson, 1909–58. Owner, J. J. Patrickson and Sons, Ltd. Glazed, varnished and framed paintings for Churchill, 1940s and 1950s.

[3] The Royal Academy Summer Exhibition.

vote. Furthermore, they are the worst months for interesting the farming community.

Autumn. October is the best month of the year for elections. Open-air meetings are still possible, and door-to-door canvassing is not too great a strain.

Winter. The new register comes into force on the 16th March, but it must be in the Party's hands three or four weeks before polling day; after that the holidays and the Budget interference. January and February obviously are not good months, though the country was lucky in exceptionally fine weather in 1950 when polling was on the 23rd February.

Conclusion. I arrive at the conclusion that October is the best month, and the alternatives are late May or late February, but neither of these have much to commend them.

President Dwight D. Eisenhower to Sir Winston S. Churchill
(Premier papers, 11/1074)

2 April 1954
Secret

Dear Winston,

I have your letter[1] received today.

I give you quickly my reaction which on both counts is affirmative. The proposed text referred to in paragraph 1 is quite in order from our standpoint. With reference to the matters dealt with in your second third and fourth paragraphs I can only say that I am, to use your word 'content' with the course you plan. Of course some of this history is not fully known to me but I certainly would not feel disposed to interpose any objection. I am confident you have weighed this matter with the wisdom which you always bring to bear on these momentous matters.

Harold Stassen has just told me of his talks and I share your judgment of the outcome.

---

[1] Reproduced above (pp. 1511–12).

April 1954 1515

Sir Winston S. Churchill to President Dwight D. Eisenhower
Prime Minister's Personal Telegram T.65/54
(Premier papers, 11/1074)

5 April 1954
Emergency
Dedip
Top Secret
No. 1385

My dear Friend,
  Thank you so much for your most kind and considerate telegram. I hope you will be 'content' with the way I am dealing with the problem in my speech tomorrow.

President Dwight D. Eisenhower to Sir Winston S. Churchill
(Premier papers, 11/645)

5 April 1954
Top Secret

Dear Winston,
  I am sure that, like me, you are following with the deepest interest and anxiety the daily reports of the gallant fight being put up by the French at Dien Bien Phu. Today, the situation there does not seem hopeless.
  But regardless of the outcome of this particular battle, I fear that the French cannot alone see the thing through, this despite the very substantial assistance in money and material that we are giving them. It is no solution simply to urge the French to intensify their efforts, and if they do not see it through, and Indochina passes into the hands of the Communists, the ultimate effect on our and your global strategic position with the consequent shift in the power ratio throughout Asia and the Pacific could be disastrous and, I know, unacceptable to you and me. It is difficult to see how Thailand, Burma and Indonesia could be kept out of Communist hands. This we cannot afford. The threat to Malaya, Australia and New Zealand would be direct. The offshore island chain would be broken. The economic pressures on Japan which would be deprived of non-Communist markets and sources of food and raw materials would be such, over a period of time, that it is difficult to see how Japan could be prevented from reaching an accommodation with the Communist world which would combine the manpower and natural resources of Asia with the industrial potential of Japan. This has led us to the hard conclusion that the situation in Southeast Asia requires us urgently to take serious and far-reaching decisions.
  Geneva is less than four weeks away. There the possibility of the

Communists driving a wedge between us will, given the state of mind in France, be infinitely greater than at Berlin. I can understand the very natural desire of the French to seek an end to this war which has been bleeding them for eight years. But our painstaking search for a way out of the impasse has reluctantly forced us to the conclusion that there is no negotiated solution of the Indochina problem which in its essence would not be either a face-saving device to cover a French surrender or a face-saving device to cover a Communist retirement. The first alternative is too serious in its broad strategic implications for us and for you to be acceptable. Apart from its effects in Southeast Asia itself, where you and the Commonwealth have direct and vital interests, it would have the most serious repercussions in North Africa, in Europe and elsewhere. Here at home it would cause a widespread loss of confidence in the cooperative system. I think it is not too much to say that the future of France as a great power would be fatally affected. Perhaps France will never again be the great power it was, but a sudden vacuum wherever French power is, would be difficult for us to cope with.

Somehow we must contrive to bring about the second alternative. The preliminary lines of our thinking were sketched out by Foster in his speech last Monday night when he said that under the conditions of today the imposition on Southeast Asia of the political system of Communist Russia and its Chinese Communist ally, by whatever means, would be a grave threat to the whole free community, and that in our view this possibility should now be met by united action and not passively accepted. He has also talked intimately with Roger Makins.

I believe that the best way to put teeth in this concept and to bring greater moral and material resources to the support of the French effort is through the establishment of a new Ad Hoc grouping or coalition composed of nations which have a vital concern in the checking of Communist expansion in the area. I have in mind in addition to our two countries, France, the Associated States, Australia, New Zealand, Thailand and the Philippines. The United States Government would expect to play its full part in such a coalition. The coalition we have in mind would not be directed against Communist China. But if, contrary to our belief, our efforts to save Indochina and the British Commonwealth position to the south should in any way increase the jeopardy to Hong Kong, we would expect to be with you there. I suppose that the United Nations should somewhere be recognized, but I am not confident that, given the Soviet veto, it could act with needed speed and vigor.

I would contemplate no role for Formosa or the Republic of Korea in the political construction of this coalition. The important thing is that the coalition must be strong and it must be willing to join the fight if necessary. I do not envisage the need of any appreciable ground forces on your or our part. If the members of the alliance are sufficiently resolute it should be able to make clear to the Chinese Communists that the continuation of their material support to the Viet Minh will inevitably lead to the growing power of the forces arrayed against them.

My colleagues and I are deeply aware of the risks which this proposal may involve but in the situation which confronts us there is no course of action or inaction devoid of dangers and I know no one who has firmly grasped more nettles than you. If we grasp this one together I believe that we will enormously increase our chances of bringing the Chinese to believe that their interests lie in the direction of a discreet disengagement. In such a contingency we could approach the Geneva Conference with the position of the free world not only unimpaired but strengthened.

Today we face the hard situation of contemplating a disaster brought on by French weakness and the necessity of dealing with it before it develops. This means frank talk with French. In many ways the situation corresponds to that which you describe so brilliantly in the second chapter of 'Their Finest Hour', when history made clear the 1940 breakthrough should have been challenged before the blow fell.

I regret adding to your problems. But in fact it is not I, but our enemies who add to them. I have faith that by another act of fellowship in the face of peril we shall find a spiritual vigor which will prevent our slipping into the quagmire of distrust.

If I may refer again to history, we failed to halt Hirohito, Mussolini and Hitler by not acting in unity and in time. That marked the beginning of many years of stark tragedy and desperate peril. May it not be that our nations have learned something from that lesson?

So profoundly do I believe that the effectiveness of the coalition principle is at stake that I am prepared to send Foster or Bedell to visit you this week, at the earliest date convenient to you. Whoever comes would spend a day in Paris to avoid French pique; the cover would be preparation for Geneva.

Sir Winston S. Churchill: speech
(Hansard)

5 April 1954　　　　　　　　　　　　　　　　　　　　　　　　　House of Commons

THE HYDROGEN BOMB

We are, I think, all agreed in admiring the thoughtful and inspiring speech of the Leader of the Opposition, and we are agreed with almost everything that he said. My difficulty is that I do not feel that he has bridged the gulf between the awe-inspiring facts which he mentioned and the practical method of solving them by the Motion − moderate, and certainly well-intentioned − which he has placed upon the Paper.

There is a gap between the evils and perils which we can all see, which have often been stated, and not only stated this afternoon, and the practical steps which can, in the circumstances, be taken. It will be my duty this afternoon to inflict upon the House, instead of very agreeable sentiments, a number of unpleasant facts which lie around us and about us and with which we have to deal. I hope that I may have the indulgence of the House, because the questions are full of complications, and I only wish that they could be solved by eloquent and passionate appeals.

Nevertheless, I cannot feel that this is a day of tribulation. We are all naturally concerned with the prodigious experiments which are being carried out in the Pacific, but I do not think that there will be any difference between us that we would rather have them carried out there than in Siberia. We might, I think, reflect for one moment, at the beginning of this debate, on how we should feel in this House this afternoon if it were the Soviet Government instead of the United States Government which were carrying out this test series of hydrogen explosions and were circulating to the world films and photographs of what they look like. Indeed, before we come to anything else, let us all thank God for sparing us that. It would, indeed, be a dark day if the Soviet Government were able to confront the free world with this sort of demonstration and to tell us what they would like us to do about it, and about quite a lot of other things as well.

I in no way detract from the sombre picture which the right hon. Gentleman the Leader of the Opposition has painted, but our present position is certainly not as bad as it would be if circumstances were altered as I have suggested. In fact, I believe that what has happened, what is happening, and what is to happen in the near future in the Pacific Ocean increases the chances of world peace far more than the chances of world war. I also believe that we have time – though not too much time – to survey the problems which now confront us and the whole world and to talk them over in their new proportions, not only in public discussion but intimately and privately with our American friends and allies. That, of course, is what we shall do and what we have been doing.

When saying this, I must also repeat what I said last week – that I shall not ask the United States Government to stop their series of experiments, which will go on throughout April. After full consultation with our technical experts, I can repeat the assurance which I gave, 'that there is no foundation for the suggestion that these explosions are "incalculable", in the sense that those making the tests are unable to set limits . . .' – even if not exact limits – 'to the explosive power of the bomb, or to calculate in advance what the main effects will be' – (Official Report. 30th March, 1954; Vol. 525, c. 1846.). The biological aspect of experiments of this character also requires profound study. Hitherto the physical has been the main subject of discussion. If it were proved, for instance, that a very large number of hydrogen explosions could, in their cumulative effect, be detrimental to the health, or even the life, of the whole human race – without any need for a declaration of war upon itself – the effect would certainly afford a new common interest between all men, rising above military, political or even ideological differences. That aspect, the biological aspect, must certainly receive the constant study of scientists in every country. I am assured by our scientists, I may say, that the remainder of the series of experiments contemplated in the Pacific could not possibly affect appreciably such an issue, as some of these biologists have led us to suppose.

Mr Sydney Silverman (Nelson and Colne): Do they know what is happening?

Sir W. Churchill: We must not forget, moreover, that no one has more interest in being right in this particular matter than the people of the United States, who have the greatest need to take all precautions, since the Marshall Islands are much nearer to them than to us, or indeed to most other nations. My own impression is that this biological aspect tends to be greatly exaggerated.

I hope that the House will not expect me to answer all the questions that have been asked, or that have been raised in our minds, by recent events in the atomic or nuclear sphere. Such a task would far exceed the limits of mortal strength and Parliamentary time. I am not a technical authority. I remember Mr Asquith, as Prime Minister, saying, 'I am not a business man, but I have often been called upon to give business men advice when they were in a difficulty.'

I certainly cannot claim to be a technical expert. I can only deal selectively with some of the main points which occur to me. Besides, even since this debate was arranged an immense amount of information about the 1st March explosion has been published in the United States. Admiral Strauss, in his masterly speech of Wednesday last, which was reported verbatim in some of our newspapers, gave a tremendous account which everyone can read for themselves. I hope, however, that the public realise that all the photographs which are appearing in the newspapers, and the films which may soon be released, are related not to the explosion of 1st March, 1954, but to that at Eniwetok atoll of 2nd November, 1952.

All the facts about this were, until quite lately, kept secret under the McMahon Act. The secrecy imposed by the Act, which only Congress can alter, has indeed proved decisive. However, as a result of the action taken by the right hon. Gentleman the Leader of the Opposition in past years, we have made atomic bombs of our own. He has not replied, in contemplation of these difficulties by merely wringing his hands. He took practical, secret and effective action, and we stand, at any rate, on that basis today. Our technical knowledge has long been respected by the United States experts. We have, in fact, by our prolonged study and recent experiments in the atomic sphere, obtained an independent position. Canada has also from the beginning played an important part.

There is, I believe, a widespread desire among American executive authorities and scientists to interchange information with us and with the Canadians.

But, in spite of this, the fact remains that the first authoritative disclosure of the results of the explosion at Eniwetok atoll 18 months ago was made by Mr Sterling Cole, the very able successor to Senator McMahon, the Chairman of the Joint Congressional Atomic Energy Committee. It was made in his speech at Chicago on 17th February. This was printed and published, though very shortly, by many British newspapers.

Mr Cole said, for instance, that the thermo-nuclear test of 1952 tore a cavity in the floor of the ocean – a crater measuring a full mile in diameter and 175 feet in depth at its lowest point. Actually, I believe it was much more than 175 feet because the ocean floor was blown up so that it fell back into its place again and the pulverisation must have extended much deeper. Mr Cole said: '. . . if it occurred in a modem city the heat and blast generated in the 1952 hydrogen test would cause absolute destruction over an area extending three miles in all directions from the point where the hydrogen device exploded.' Finally, after describing the medium damage, 'the area of light damage would reach 10 miles from the point of detonation. In other words, an area covering 300 square miles would be blanketed by this hydrogen explosion.' Mr Cole also said that security prevented him from commenting on where the hydrogen weapons armament programme now stands – that is, the American programme – and from outlining the directions in which it is moving. 'But I can assure you' he said, 'that it is moving.' He added a remarkable comment with which I am in entire accord – namely, that 'it is more sinful to conceal the power of the atom than to reveal it'. This seemed to show some of the pressures that he was under, and his own courageous reaction to them.

He continued: 'Russia's capacity to deliver a crippling atomic or hydrogen weapon attack on the United States at present might be debatable; but beyond any question the Russians would be able to do so in one, two, or three years from now.' That, no doubt, is not only or even mainly because of the progress of Russia's science but because of the great distance which separates Russia from the United States – an advantage which we in this island certainly do not share. It is also affected by the character of bomber aeroplanes possessed by the different countries.

I was astonished at some of the facts which Mr Cole disclosed, and still more that his statement did not supersede all other matters of public interest here and in other countries. The fact that it seemed hardly to have been noted was the reason that I used very strong expressions in answering some questions in the House in the latter part of March. I hope, however, we shall not go too far in the opposite direction now, for nothing could be less helpful to us in our problems than panic or hysteria, especially when, as I have said, the actual physical results are of a favourable character to the free world. The House may rest assured that all the new facts that are being brought to our knowledge – and they are pouring in from public statements in all directions – are the subject of continuous study by Ministers and their technical advisers.

Speaking more generally, we must realise that the gulf between the conventional high explosive bomb in use at the end of the war with Germany on the one hand, and the atomic bomb as used against Japan on the other, is smaller than the gulf developing between that bomb and the hydrogen bomb. That is now in large-scale production, I believe, in the United States, and also, we believe, to a less degree, and possibly in a less potent form, it is in large-scale production in Soviet Russia. No words which I could use are needed to emphasise the deadly situation in which the whole world lies. These stupendous facts, although at present to our advantage, glare upon the human race. That is why I felt myself so much in agreement with what the right hon. Gentleman the Leader of the Opposition said.

With all its horrors, the atomic bomb did not seem unmanageable as an instrument of war, and the fact that the Americans have such an immense preponderance over Russia has given us a passage through eight anxious and troublous years. But the hydrogen bomb carries us into dimensions which have never confronted practical human thought and have been confined to the realms of fancy and imagination. The hydrogen bomb has been talked about in scientific circles almost as long as the atomic bomb, but nothing has emerged of a practical nature until the experiments at the atoll.

Admiral Strauss tells us that the Russians were the first to begin active and large-scale researches and work upon it. The United States conducted its first full-scale experiments at Eniwetok atoll 18 months ago. The first hydrogen explosion in Russia took place on 12th August, 1953, and its pressure waves were recorded and noted by instruments reporting both to the United States and Britain. According to the best intelligence that I have been able to acquire, the Soviets were well behind the United States even before the American explosion on 1st March of this year. But, on the other hand, they are much closer on the heels of the United States in the development of hydrogen bombs than they ever were in atomic bombs. We do not know what the Soviets are doing inside their vast ocean of land, and I shall make no predictions today.

It does not, however, follow that the hydrogen bomb is peculiarly favourable to the Soviets. Their enormous expanse of territory, which seemed to limit the atomic bomb to a very large number of military and quasi-military targets, is no longer able to give the same immunity to the far wider effect of the hydrogen bomb and the clouds of radioactive dust and vapour to which it may give rise. To us, in this overcrowded island, and to the densely populated regions of Europe, the new terror brings a certain element of equality in annihilation. Strange as it may seem – and I beg the House not to disdain it – it is to the universality of potential destruction that I feel we may look with hope and even with confidence.

Turning to our relations in these matters with the United States, the United

States Government are bound by their laws unless and until Congress alters them. We have no agreement with them which entitles us to claim any form of joint authority. They are acting entirely within their rights as agreed between them and the late Government. I am always ready to bear responsibility where I have power, but if there is no power there can, I think, be no real responsibility. Whether we like it or not, that is the position which we found when we came into office two and a half years ago.

I have no more wish than the right hon. Gentleman to deal with these awesome issues on party lines, and I acknowledge the public spirit which has animated the right hon. Gentleman and his principal colleagues. But that is not the mood of his official party Press or of many of his supporters. Attacks are being made on the Government, and particularly on me, from various quarters, which I ought not to ignore. Let me quote the words used by the hon. Member for Devonport (Mr Foot) on television last Friday. He said: 'I am attacking the British Prime Minister, the British Foreign Secretary, and the British Government because of their failure to demand from the Americans full information about this bomb.' But this is only one of the attacks made in the Press and on the public platform by Members of the party opposite. I must say that I do not see why blame of this kind should be put upon Her Majesty's Government.

Mr Harold Davies (Leek): For God's sake rise above it at this moment.

Sir W. Churchill: I have never seen much which the hon. Member was able to rise above. I do not really see why I should be blamed. When, after the Election in 1945, I quitted the office of Prime Minister which I had held during the war, our position was very different. I feel that it will be in the national interest, and can do nothing but good on both sides of the Atlantic, if I now make public for the first time the agreement which I made in 1943 with President Roosevelt, which was signed by both of us at Quebec. President Eisenhower has informed me that he is content that I should do so. The House will find this document in the Vote Office when I sit down. I thought it right to lay the facsimile before the House, but here are the salient facts. I wrote them out myself those many years ago. 'It is agreed between us' 'First, that we will never use this agency against each other.' That might even appear to have a jocular aspect, as we were all such close allies, fighting, but it was meant to show that the agreement extended far beyond the limits of the war – 'Secondly, that we will not use it against third parties without each other's consent.' 'Thirdly, that we will not either of us communicate any information about Tube Alloys' – They were called tube alloys; that was the code name – 'to third parties except by mutual consent.' 'Fourthly, that in view of the heavy burden of production falling upon the United States as a result of a wise division of war effort, the British Government recognise that any post-war advantages of an industrial or commercial character shall be dealt with as between the United States and Great Britain on terms to be specified by the President of the United States to the Prime Minister of Great Britain. The Prime Minister expressly disclaims any interest in these industrial and commercial aspects beyond what may be considered by the President of the United States to be fair and just and in harmony with the economic welfare of the world.' Then followed detailed arrangements to ensure full and effective collaboration between the United States and Britain and Canada, including the setting up of a committee in Washington to consider combined policy. The House will find all this set out in the document.

That was how things stood when the Socialist Government came into office. Any changes that have taken place from that position in the interval are their responsibility or their misfortune, and not mine. Her Majesty's Government are bound by them, nevertheless, and that was the position I had to put before the House last Tuesday. When we think of the importance which attaches to Clause 2 of the original agreement which I have read, namely, 'that we will not use it against third parties without each other's consent,' and also to the provisions for the constant interchange of information, it seems odd that the right hon. Member for Ebbw Vale (Mr Bevan), who rose and intervened the other day, and who was an important member of the Government which agreed to abandon these all-important provisions and precautions, should not have realised that he shares, also, a direct measure –

Mr Attlee: I do not understand the right hon. Gentleman saying that we abandoned any precautions. We did not abandon any of these agreements; we carried them on with the United States Government. Unfortunately, the Senate passed the McMahon Act, which prevented them carrying out those agreements.

Sir W. Churchill: I have to say, about the right hon. Gentleman to whom I alluded, that I hope he will be specially helpful now, in consequence of what happened. I do not say that there were not many reasons and facts operative at the end of the war which were different from those during its course, but considering that the abandonment of our claim to be consulted and informed as an equal was the act of the Socialist Administration –

Mr Attlee: I must ask the Prime Minister on what grounds he says we abandoned any claim. We did not abandon the claim; we made the claim, and I believe that the United States Administration were fully prepared to carry it out. They were prevented by the action of the Senate, which passed the McMahon Act, which prevented them giving the information. We did not abandon anything.

Hon. Members: Withdraw.

Sir W. Churchill: They abandoned the agreement, or took action which enabled the agreement to be destroyed. (*Interruption*) Hon. and right hon. Gentlemen opposite must not show so much uneasiness in the matter. I feel they have no ground for reproaching their successors with the consequences. (Hon. Members: 'Withdraw'.) I have nothing to withdraw.

Mr Ellis Smith (Stoke-on-Trent, South): On a point of order. There is doubt about statements that have been made with regard to the facts. My right hon. Friend the Leader of the Opposition has denied allegations that have been made. Before the Prime Minister proceeds, should he not accept that denial or otherwise?

Sir W. Churchill: I am coming to that aspect a little later, but I will transpose what I have to say to meet the wish of the House. I return to the Quebec Agreement as a whole – (Hon. Members: 'No'.). Why do not hon. Gentlemen opposite listen? Why do they say 'No', especially when they do not know what I am coming to? When I visited the United States two years ago, I showed this document that will soon be in the Vote Office to Senator McMahon, whom I had known for some time, and who was a man of the highest honour and outstanding patriotism to his own country. (An Hon. Member: 'So is McCarthy.') He said at once, 'If we had seen this agreement there would have been no McMahon Act.'

That was a remark made in a private conversation, and I should not have repeated it here if he had not a few weeks later said in public, on the occasion of our successful atomic experiment in Australia: 'The achievement of an atomic explosion by Great Britain, when an accomplished fact, will contribute to the keeping of the world peace because it will add to the free world's total deterring power. This event is likely to raise in still sharper focus the problem of atomic co-operation between ourselves and Great Britain. The British contributed heavily to our own war-time atomic project. But, due to a series of unfortunate circumstances, the nature of the agreements which made this contribution possible was not disclosed to me and my colleagues on the Senate Special Atomic Energy Committee at the time we framed the law in 1946. Now we may consider rethinking the entire situation with all the facts in front of us.' Alas, he died, and we and his fellow countrymen can mourn his loss.

Mr Attlee: I regret that the Prime Minister made an attack on me in this matter. I never reproached him with any of the terms of the Quebec Agreement with regard to the industrial side of it. The right hon. Gentleman said that we had abandoned it. He now tells me that Senator McMahon did not know of the Quebec Agreement. Surely, that is not a reproach on me. If it is a reproach on anybody it is on the United States Administration. The right hon. Gentleman will remember that I did not go by myself. I went with Lord Waverley to try to settle these matters. We had an agreement with the Administration, and we were informed they could not carry it out because of the Senatorial action in the McMahon Act. Surely it was not for me to send the McMahon Committee or Senator McMahon this information? If the right hon. Gentleman is making any attack, he is making it on the Truman Administration.

Sir W. Churchill: I did not intend – (Hon. Members: 'What? Did not intend what?') I did not intend — (*Interruption.*) I have no doubt whatever that before the McMahon Act was passed he ought to have confronted the people of the United States with the declaration. That is what I believe will be the view of history.

Mr E. Shinwell (Easington): Why did not the right hon. Gentleman?

Sir W. Churchill: I did. I made reference to it in a former Parliament. I hesitated to make a public disclosure as a private person, but I did communicate with Mr Truman on the subject, and he strongly appealed to me not to do so — (Hon. Members: 'Oh'.) — but I frequently urged the right hon. Gentleman to make this agreement public. This matter can be looked into and debated at length, but I am quite certain that if the agreement which I made had been made public, it is very unlikely we should have had facilities withdrawn from us.

Mr Herbert Morrison (Lewisham, South): It is important to get this clear. I understood that the right hon. Gentleman had made a private and secret agreement on this matter with President Roosevelt, which was not published. Of course, we were aware of it — those of us who were entitled to know — but at the time it was surely a secret, confidential agreement. Is the right hon. Gentleman suggesting that my right hon. Friend, notwithstanding that, should have published it over the heads of the United States Government? He does not know what action we took with a view to the non-passing of the McMahon Act, or to its modification later. Is he suggesting that, he having made a secret agreement, my right hon. Friend should have broken faith and published it?

Sir W. Churchill: I am of opinion that the agreement should have been circulated in confidential circles in the first instance to the American Government. (Hon. Members: 'Why?') The war was over, and there was no reason at all why this solemn agreement, signed by President Roosevelt and me, should not have been brought into proper consideration —

Mr S. Silverman: By whom?

Sir W. Churchill: — by the American Government.

Mr Attlee: What possible reason had I to suspect that the United States Government, with a Bill affecting an agreement like this with us, had not informed their own supporters and Senator McMahon? I did not know. They did not tell me. How could I know?

Sir W. Churchill: I think it would have been an obvious precaution to confront them with that agreement. (Hon. Members: 'Resign.') Anyhow, they were not confronted with it —

Hon. Members: By whom?

Mr Deputy-Speaker (Sir Charles MacAndrew): I hope we may have less noise.

Sir W. Churchill: I do not see what all this anger is due to if it is not through a feeling of considerable regret that other action was not taken at the time.

Mr James Callaghan (Cardiff, South-East): The right hon. Gentleman is dragging us down to the gutter.

Sir W. Churchill: The right hon. Gentleman said that I referred to the *quid pro quo* which was given in the new agreement – namely, giving up the right to commercial and industrial production. It can, of course, be said that in the fourth article of my agreement with President Roosevelt I abandoned all rights to the control of industrial and commercial nuclear power and left them entirely to the President of the United States. He was to act in accordance with what he considered was fair and just and in accordance with the welfare of the world; whereas the Socialist Government regained these rights in return for sacrifices in the share of the control of the military aspects.

I was, however, quite sure when I drafted this passage that it would never be in the interest of the United States to keep a monopoly of commercial atomic energy. The exchange which was made by the late Government lost us all right of control and even of information on the military aspect. As for the commercial, that has now, after 11 years, been offered to the whole world by President Eisenhower's proposals made in the address to UNO of 8th December last.

Mr Attlee: The right hon. Gentleman now says that we abandoned control over the military in exchange for advantages on the industrial side. We never had advantages on the industrial side. There was no bargain of that sort. I think it is a pity in this debate that all the time the right hon. Gentleman is attacking us for not developing atomic energy. I never mentioned the Quebec Agreement and giving away the industrial advantages. I was too loyal.

Hon. Members: Resign.

Sir W. Churchill: As for the commercial, that has now, after 11 years, been offered to the whole world by President Eisenhower's proposals made in the address to UNO on 8th December last.

Mr Julian Snow[1] (Lichfield and Tamworth): This is disgraceful.

Sir W. Churchill: In these proposals not only are knowledge and rights in the commercial sphere freely extended, but even what is thought to be an increasing proportion of the nuclear stockpile is to be transferred from war destruction to peace and plenty.

Mrs E. M. Braddock[2] (Liverpool, Exchange): No wonder we are in the mess we are in today. Why don't you get out? (*Interruption.*)

Mr Deputy-Speaker: There is so much noise going on that I cannot hear what the Prime Minister is saying. I ask hon. Members to contain themselves a little.

Sir W. Churchill: I therefore still feel that I was right in the choice which I made on the commercial aspect.

---

[1] Julian Snow, 1910–82. Served in RA, 1939–45. MP (Lab.) for Portsmouth Central, 1945–50; for Lichfield and Tamworth, 1950–70. Baron, 1970.

[2] Elizabeth Margaret Bamber, 1899–1970. Known as 'Bessie'. Married, 1922, John Braddock. Member, Liverpool City Council, 1930–61. President, Liverpool Trades and Labour Council, 1944. MP (Lab.) for Liverpool Exchange, 1945–70.

The question which has long confronted us is our relations on this subject with the Government and peoples of the United States. Intimate talks, of course, there have been both with President Truman and President Eisenhower. Private conversation is one thing; formal action is another. (An Hon. Member: 'It is the same thing with you.') In 1951, when I was a private person, I asked President Truman to agree to the publication of the Quebec Agreement, because I was cross-examining the right hon. Gentleman, then Prime Minister, in the House upon the subject at that time. He appealed to me not to make such a request in public and, being in a private station, I deferred.

President Eisenhower, like his predecessor, is equally bound by the McMahon Act and the determination evident up to the present, of Congress, to maintain it. British representatives are bound by what happened in the time of the late Government. We have no means but friendly persuasion of inducing the Americans either to desist from their series of experiments, even if we desired them to, or to supply us with secret information about them, and generally in the atomic sphere we have no means of compelling them, if their law forbids it.

The President is seeking from Congress more latitude in the application of the McMahon Act. I trust that nothing will be said in the House today which will arouse needless antagonism –

Hon. Members: You have said it.

Mrs Braddock: Look at the faces behind you.

Sir W. Churchill: – in Congress or throughout America. Nothing could be more disastrous to peace than a grave dispute – (An Hon. Member: 'You have started it.') – between Britain and the United States. I have not started it at all. I have obtained sanction to make public the solemn agreement made between President Roosevelt and myself.

Hon. Members: 'Oh'.

Mr Silverman: You have sacrificed the interests of humanity to make a cheap party point.

Sir W. Churchill: If there is nothing in the point, why is there so much excitement? Now let me say only –

Mrs Braddock: You have said too much.

Sir W. Churchill: Yesterday, the hon. Member for Coventry, East (Mr Crossman)[1] wrote in one of the Sunday papers: 'On Monday, when the H bomb will be debated, Sir Winston must tell Mr Eisenhower and Mr Dulles that they can either scrap their new H-bomb strategy and join with

---

[1] Richard Howard Stafford Crossman, 1907–74. Educated at Winchester School and New College, Oxford. Fellow and Tutor, New College, 1930–7. Leader, Labour Group, Oxford City Council, 1934–40. Married, 1937, Inezita Hilda Baker (div. 1952); 1954, Anne Patricia McDougall. Asst Editor, *New Statesman and Nation*, 1938–55; Editor, 1970–2. Deputy Director, Psychological Warfare, AFHQ Algiers, 1943; Asst Chief, SHAEF, 1944–5. OBE, 1945. MP (Lab.) for Coventry East, 1945–74. Member, Labour Party Executive Committee, 1952–67. PC, 1964. Minister of Housing and Local Government, 1964–6. Leader of the House and Lord President of the Council, 1966–8. Secretary of State for Social Services, 1968–70.

Britain in the plan for high-level talks or else face the prospect of "going it alone".'

Mr S. Silverman: That is right.

Sir W. Churchill: If this line of thought were adopted, it seems almost certain that 'the agonising re-appraisal' of which Mr Dulles spoke in another connection would follow. If the United States withdrew from Europe altogether – she might withdraw from Europe altogether – and with her three-quarter circle of hydrogen bases already spread around the globe, she would face Russia alone, as she certainly could.

I cannot doubt that war in these circumstances would be nearer than it is today when the anxiety of the United States, to their abiding honour, is so largely centred upon the safety and freedom of Western Europe and the British Isles.

It is a delusion to suppose that a declaration of our neutrality would make us immune from danger from Russia. The very inferiority of Russia in atomic and hydrogen weapons would make it necessary for them to use to the utmost their enormous preponderance in conventional warfare. A simultaneous counter-attack on Western Europe would be the only form of immediate reprisal and of securing territorial hostages, which the Soviet Government could take, so although we still have the Channel, the British Isles would be laid open to every conceivable form of air attack. These facts should surely be weighed by the House before light-hearted and lightheaded suggestions of challenging the United States 'to go it alone' are given the slightest countenance.

I can repeat that we have full confidence in the humanity and sense of fair play of the United States and of their desire to maintain the close and friendly relations with us which are the foundation of our alliance and of the security of the free world.

I now come to the Motion on the Order Paper. (Hon. Members: 'Sit down.') I do not have to sit down until I choose to or the rules of order require it. We do not dissent in principle from the Motion which the Opposition have placed upon the Paper, and I congratulate the right hon. Gentleman – (Hon. Members: 'Oh'.) – on having procured agreement to it. We shall not divide against this Motion provided that it is clearly understood that the word 'immediate' does not commit us to action at an unsuitable time or lead only to courting a polite deadlock or even providing a refusal.

That indeed would not be a help, but a disastrous hindrance to the hopes and desires which are widespread on both sides of the House, for an easier relationship between both sides of the world. Nothing would be simpler than for my right hon. Friend the Foreign Secretary to propose to the State Department in the United States and to the Soviet Foreign Minister that a meeting of Heads of States and Governments should be held forthwith; and if an unfavourable answer was received from either of them reporting the same to the House with appropriate expressions of regret. We must try for something better than that.

It seems to me moreover that, with the Geneva Conference impending at the end of this month, you could hardly pick a more ill-chosen moment to propose a meeting of the Heads of State and Governments. I had certainly thought that we must see what happens there before attempting to use what is, after all, a very unusual reserve procedure.

It must also be remembered that the position of a President of the United States is intrinsically different from that either of Mr Malenkov or me. We are only Heads of Governments. The President is the Head of the State, and he may well take a different view of his duties in time of peace to that which his predecessors took of their duties in time of war.

When in May last year I suggested a personal and to some extent informal meeting of this character, the situation was different from that which exists today. Stalin had just died, and Malenkov had newly assumed the leadership in Russia. I thought it would be a good thing if friendly, personal relations could be established between leaders and if we could form a clearer view of what was then called the 'New Look'. I am still in favour of that, but the topic has changed.

A far more precise and definite objective is now before us, and there is also perhaps – I say perhaps – a new vehicle of procedure. The President in his speech to the United Nations after the meeting at Bermuda, when he had shown it to me, though it was entirely on his initiative, had already proposed a new consultative and co-operative machinery, limited, it is true, to the industrial atomic sphere in which all those Powers directly concerned in atomic production, including of course Russia, are to take part. I think that it was a most important event.

It is quite true that the present objective is to develop the industrial possibilities and commercial possibilities of atomic energy and to wean the nations away from the destructive side, even at the expense of the military stockpile. This profoundly conceived American thought, to which the most powerful man in the world has given eloquent expression, seems to offer a chance to the United States, Russia, Britain and the British Commonwealth – I am speaking of the circle of atomic Powers – travelling farther together, perhaps even into the domains of hydrogen warfare.

For instance, if Russia, the British Commonwealth and the United States were gathered round the table talking about the commercial application of atomic energy, and the diversion of some of their uranium stockpile, it would not seem odd if the question of the hydrogen bomb, which might blow all these pretty plans sky-high, cropped up, and what I have hoped for, namely a talk on supreme issues between the Heads of States and Governments concerned, might not have proved so impossible as it has proved hitherto.

When President Eisenhower told me and my right hon. Friend the Foreign

Secretary at Bermuda what he was going to say to UNO, I at that moment felt the hope that this might lead to the kind of consultations which are now set forth in the Motion which the right hon. Gentleman has spontaneously proposed. But that is only one idea, and other more direct and quicker methods may be found. We shall not weary in the search for them.

Meanwhile, in accordance with the Agreement reached at Berlin, we have thought it right, together with the United States and French Governments, to propose the calling together of the Disarmament Commission of the United Nations, in order that comprehensive solutions of the problem of disarmament may be considered. Her Majesty's Government have been preparing the ground for this initiative for some weeks, and my right hon. Friend the Foreign Secretary will tell us more about it when he closes the debate tonight.

As we go forward on our difficult road, we shall always be guided by two main aims of policy. One is to lose no opportunity of convincing the Soviet leaders and, if we can reach them, the Russian people, that the democracies of the West have no aggressive designs on them. The other is to ensure that until that purpose has been achieved we have the strength necessary to deter any aggression by them and to ward it off if it should come. We shall continue at the same time to seek by every means open to us an easement in international tension and a sure foundation on which the peoples of the world can live their lives in security and peace. I thank the House for its most considerate attention.

Sir Winston S. Churchill to President Dwight D. Eisenhower
Prime Minister's Personal Telegram T.69/54
(Premier papers, 11/1074)

6 April 1954
Immediate
Top Secret
No. 1438

My Dear Friend,

I have received your most important message of April 5.[1] We are giving it earnest Cabinet consideration.

---

[1] Reproduced above (pp. 1515–17).

Sir Winston S. Churchill to Queen Frederica of Greece
(*Premier papers, 11/682*)

7 April 1954

Madam,

Lord Leicester[1] brought me Your Majesty's letter.[2] I shall show it to the Foreign Secretary, but while we fully share your feelings on the subject of Anglo-Greek friendship it would not be right for me to leave Your Majesty in doubt of our conviction that this is not the time, in the interests either of Greece, Great Britain, or wider still of NATO, for discussion about changes in the government of Cyprus.

The island is of vital importance to the defence of the Middle East and of the Mediterranean. While that remains the case, disturbance of the present regime could do nothing but harm to us all. I remember with emotion the friendly feelings shown by the Greek people in the war to the British armies who came to help defend them, first from Nazi invasion and later from Communist revolution. If a third world war should come it might well be that British blood would once again be shed to save Greece from invasion. I can assure Your Majesty that withdrawal from Cyprus would certainly not help to that end and might, indeed, fatally weaken the combination on which the safety of us all depends.

I beg you to convey my respectful good wishes to the King and remain
Your Majesty's obedient servant.

Cabinet: conclusions
(*Cabinet papers, 128/27*)

7 April 1954
Secret
Cabinet Meeting No. 26 of 1954

[. . .]

4. The Cabinet had before them a memorandum by the Foreign Secretary (C(54)134) reporting a proposal by the United States Government for the formation of a coalition of interested countries to resist Communist encroachment in South-East Asia and for the publication by them, before the Geneva Conference, of a declaration warning China against continuing to aid the Vietminh rebels in Indo-China.

---

[1] Thomas William Edward Coke, 1908–76. Educated at Eton College and Royal Military College, Sandhurst. Entered Scots Guards, 1928. Married, 1931, Elizabeth Yorke: three children. Equerry to Duke of York (later King George VI), 1934–7. Capt., 1938. Maj., 1945. Succeeded as 5th Earl of Leicester, 1949. Lt-Col., Home Guard, 1952–6. Hon. Col., 1st Cadet Battalion, Royal Norfolk Rgt.

[2] Reproduced above (pp. 1497–9).

The Prime Minister read to the Cabinet a letter[1] which he had received from President Eisenhower enlarging upon this proposal and suggesting that Mr Dulles, the United States Secretary of State, should come to London forthwith to discuss it.

The Foreign Secretary said that there would be some solid advantages in the formation of a coalition of the United States, United Kingdom, France, Australia, New Zealand, Siam, the Philippines and the Associated States of Indo-China. It would remove the anomaly of our exclusion from the ANZUS pact and would contribute directly to the security of Hong Kong and Malaya, and of the whole area of South-East Asia. He feared, however, that the United States Government were less interested in the creation of this coalition as a permanent security system than in the declaration which they wished the coalition to make before the Geneva Conference. This was to take the form of a warning to China that, if she continued to aid the Vietminh rebels, the coalition Powers would take naval and air action against the China coast in addition to direct intervention in Indo-China. He doubted whether such a threat would cause China to withdraw air from the Vietminh. It seemed much more likely to lead to China's withdrawal from the Geneva Conference, and that would be a serious shock to public opinion in the United Kingdom and France. Moreover, if China were not intimidated by the threat, the coalition would be compelled either to withdraw ignominiously or to embark on warlike action against China. This would give China every excuse for invoking the Sino-Soviet treaty, and might lead to a world war. He could not see that there was any military urgency for making a declaration of this kind. In three or four weeks' time the rains would start in Indo-China and there could then be no military activity for some months. The French certainly could not lose the war in Indo-China before the rains began. He therefore believed that the best course was to try to persuade the Americans to re-shape their plan so that it could be made to give security in South-East Asia in the future without endangering the Geneva Conference. He would like Mr Dulles to visit London early in the following week, and in the meantime he would work out an alternative plan of action which was not open to the objections applicable to Mr Dulles' present proposal.

In discussion the following points were made:

(a) Mr Dulles had already explained his proposals to the Australian and New Zealand Ambassadors[2] in Washington. The Australian

---

[1] Reproduced above (pp. 1515–17).

[2] Leslie Knox Munro, 1901–74. Born in Auckland, New Zealand. Educated at University of Auckland. Lecturer in Constitutional Law and Roman Law, University of Auckland, 1925–38; Dean of Faculty of Law, 1938. Married, 1927, Christine Mary Priestley: one child (d. 1929); 1931, Muriel Olga Sturt: one child. Associate Editor, *New Zealand Herald*, 1941; Editor, 1942–51. New Zealand Ambassador to US, 1952–8. New Zealand Representative to UN, 1952–8. KCMG, 1955. KCVO, 1957. Chairman, First Political Committee, UN, 1957. President of UN General Assembly, 1957–8. MP (New Zealand National Party) for Waipa, 1963–9; for Hamilton West, 1969–72.

Ambassador had drawn particular attention to Mr Dulles' insistence that the Americans would not be prepared to give direct military assistance in Indo-China unless the United Kingdom were also ready to make a contribution.

(b) Careful thought should be given to the form which any military assistance to Indo-China should take. The American Chiefs of Staff were thinking primarily in terms of supporting action by naval and air forces; but, as the New Zealand Prime Minister had pointed out, past experience (*e.g.* in Korea) suggested that limited action of this kind would be only a prelude to intervention by land forces. There was no indication whether the Americans had it in mind that air action in Indo-China, or against China itself, would include the use of atomic or hydrogen bombs. That was a point which Mr Dulles should be asked to clarify during his visit.

(c) President Eisenhower had suggested that the preparations for the Geneva Conference would afford a convenient pretext for Mr Dulles' visit to London. The British public would, however, connect it with the current American tests of the hydrogen bomb, and would expect it to lead to some further pronouncement on that question.

The Prime Minister said that he shared the Foreign Secretary's doubts about the wisdom of making the proposed declaration before the Geneva Conference. On the other hand, any proposition which led to closer co-operation between the United Kingdom and the United States deserved very careful consideration. The best course would be for him to tell the President that we should be glad to see Mr Dulles in London at the beginning of the following week, but that we could not offer any opinion on the merits of the American plan until it had been further clarified and studied. Meanwhile, we should tell the Governments of Australia, New Zealand and France of our invitation to Mr Dulles, and promise to keep them informed of the results of our conversations with him. The Australian Prime Minister had already sent a message putting forward very much the view taken by the Foreign Secretary, that we should use the period of the rains in Indo-China for working out a coalition on the lines proposed by the Americans.

The Cabinet –

(1) Took note that the Prime Minister would inform President Eisenhower that he would welcome a visit by Mr Dulles early in the following week, but did not wish to pronounce meanwhile on the merits of the American proposal outlines in C(54)134.

(2) Took note that the Foreign Secretary would work out means of adapting the United States plan so as to further the security of South-East Asia without endangering the prospects of a successful outcome from the Geneva Conference.

[. . .]

April 1954

Sir Winston S. Churchill: speech[1]

('Winston S. Churchill, His Complete Speeches', volume 8, pages 8559–60)

7 April 1954

AMERICA AND BRITAIN

Rochester was the home of my grandparents, and my mother was born in Brooklyn, so it is with both pride and emotion that I accept the degree of Doctor of Laws from the Board of Regents of the University of the State of New York. I take it as a remarkable honour that now, for the first time in one hundred and seventy years you confer a degree *in absentia*. I am only sorry for the *absentia*. Three thousand miles of sea keep us apart, but science, in one of its more beneficial manifestations, is able to record my thanks to you in person, and certainly no ocean divides me or indeed my countrymen, from you in thought and spirit tonight.

I am not a lawyer, but I have obeyed a lot of laws, and helped to make a few. Law, language, and literature unite the English-speaking world, and all sorts of other things are happening which fortify these mighty traditions with ever-growing practical considerations of safety and survival. The rule of law, calm, without prejudice, swayed neither to the right nor to the left however political tides or party currents may flow, is the foundation of freedom. The independence of the judiciary from the executive is the prime defence against the tyranny and retrogression of totalitarian government. Trial by jury, the right of every man to be judged by his equals, is among the most precious gifts that England has bequeathed to America.

Great have been our divergencies since 1776. But in respect of the law and the maintenance of the English common law, Great Britain and the United States have marched together. Indeed it is a fact that American law is more wedded to the older versions of English law than is the case in Britain, where in the first half of the nineteenth century a great deal of technical modernization was effected. Although I like old things better than new, I believe our revised version has many conveniences in procedure. Going back to 1776, you may have heard that as a lineal descendant on my mother's side from a Captain in Washington's armies,[2] I am a member of the Cincinnati. As I told them when admitted to the Society I must have been on both sides then. Certainly in judging that historic quarrel I am on both sides now. Sex was not born till protoplasm – or protozoa if you prefer – divided itself. But for this split the sexes would not have had all the fun of coming together again.

Naturally we have our differences. They are differences of method rather

---

[1] Accepting, in absentia, a Doctorate of Law from the University of the State of New York.

[2] Lebbeus Ball I, 1738–1806. Born in Springfield, Mass. Married, 1762, Thankful Stowe: three children. Capt., Massachusetts Rgt., 1775. Maj., 1781. Great-great-great-grandfather of Winston Churchill.

than of purpose. I am a great believer in democracy and free speech. Naturally when immense masses of people speak the same language and enjoy the fullest rights of free speech they often say some things that all the others do not agree to. If speech were always to be wise it could never be free, and even where it is most strictly regulated it is not always wise. But where British and American relations are concerned I remain an incurable optimist.

I remember when I first came over here in 1895 I was a guest of your great lawyer and orator, Mr Bourke Cockran.[1] I was only a young Cavalry subaltern but he poured out all his wealth of mind and eloquence to me. Some of his sentences are deeply rooted in my mind. 'The earth,' he said, 'is a generous mother. She will produce in plentiful abundance food for all her children if they will but cultivate her soil in justice and in peace.' I used to repeat it so frequently on British platforms that I had to give it a holiday. But now today it seems to come back with new pregnancy and force, for never was the choice between blessing and cursing more vehemently presented to the human race. There was another thing Bourke Cockran used to say to me. I cannot remember his actual words but they amounted to this: 'In a society where there is democratic tolerance and freedom under the law, many kinds of evils will crop up, but give them a little time and they usually breed their own cure.' I do not see any reason to doubt the truth of that.

There is no country in the world where the process of self-criticism and self-correction is more active than in the United States. You must not think I am talking politics. I make it a rule never to meddle in the internal or party politics of any friendly country. It is hard enough to understand the party politics of your own. I end where I began in my thanks to you for the compliment you pay me tonight. Your country and your population are far bigger than ours even when our sister Commonwealths are added, but whenever we are working together we seem to be more than twice as strong. It is my faith that if we work together there are no problems that we cannot solve, no dangers which we cannot ward off from ourselves, and no tangles through which we cannot guide the freedom-loving peoples of the world.

---

[1] William Bourke Cockran, 1854–1923. Known as 'Bourke Cockran'. Born in Carrowkeel, Ireland. Emigrated to US, 1871. Congressman (Dem.) from New York, 1887–9, 1891–3, 1893–5, 1904–9, 1921–3.

1536   APRIL 1954

Sir Winston S. Churchill to President Dwight D. Eisenhower
Prime Minister's Personal Telegram T.70/54
(Premier papers, 11/1074)

7 April 1954
Personal and Secret

My dear Friend,

We discussed your proposal about Indo-China in the Cabinet this morning and we are certainly giving it a great deal of thought. It is however a topic which raises many problems for us and I am sure you will not expect us to give a hurried decision. We shall be very glad to see Foster here and talk the matter over with him. If Monday next, April 12, were convenient to him it would suit us well to open the talks that day.

Evelyn Shuckburgh: diary
('Descent to Suez', page 161)

8 April 1954

Two terrible days, in which I have been completely exhausted and out of temper. The Eisenhower plan for the Far East worrying everybody and Dulles is to visit us next Monday. The questions is, can we 'go along' with him at all on his project? Certainly we are all thinking that an anti-Chinese 'declaration' immediately before Geneva would be regarded by Western opinion as a poor contribution to the success of the Conference. But maybe we can announce some line-up in support of the French, to strengthen our bargaining position at Geneva. The only trouble is, the Americans don't want to bargain and think any division of Indo-China would be disaster.

Ike has announced that he will not make bigger H-bombs than he needs!

Saw Winston in the House this afternoon, during speeches in aid of the Entente Cordiale, and thought he looked terribly old. AE says he thinks the poor old boy must be going to have another stroke quite soon – that he is ashen grey and taking nothing in. He said to AE wasn't it 'splendid news' that *Izvestia* has called for a cease-fire in Indo-China, to which AE says he replied: 'Don't you see it is a trap; there is no line there; it is a trap and they would overrun the whole place' – and the old boy was quite crestfallen.

[. . .]

Sir Winston S. Churchill to Clement Attlee
(Churchill papers, 2/28)

9 April 1954

In his personal statement yesterday Herbert Morrison said that the War Cabinet were never informed of the Quebec Agreement. You may have seen in the *Daily Telegraph* this morning a reference to a telegram of mine addressed to 'Deputy Prime Minister and War Cabinet' at the end of the Quebec Conference – which I published in Volume V of my book (pages 83–84). This opened: 'We have secured a settlement of a number of hitherto intractable questions, e.g. the South East Asia Command, Tube Alloys and French Committee recognition.' You will have noticed that this message was specifically addressed to you and the War Cabinet. It was my wish that they should be informed, and I should hardly have expressed such a wish if I had not known that members of the War Cabinet were aware of the significance of the code word 'tube alloys'. I have ascertained today that, after the advance copy of the telegram had been shown to you in this form, the words 'Tube Alloys' were omitted in the copies which were circulated to the War Cabinet. I certainly bear no responsibility for that omission. I imagine that the explanation is that this was among those specially secret matters which in those days were explained orally to the War Cabinet or Defence Committee but were not written down.

Herbert Morrison's statement of yesterday seems to have been designed to further the argument that my negotiations on this subject with President Roosevelt in 1943, and the Agreement which resulted from them, were personal, rather than official, in character. I think, therefore, that I ought to direct your attention to the letter which I sent to you on this subject on the 12th of February, 1951, and your reply of the 14th of February.[1] You will note the sentence in your letter: 'While the Quebec Agreement was made between Roosevelt and yourself, it was of course in your capacities as President and Prime Minister.'

I am not thinking of publishing this letter and certainly would not do so without your agreement.

---

[1] Both reproduced in *The Churchill Documents*, vol. 22, *Leader of the Opposition, August 1945 to October 1951*, pp. 2002 and 2004.

April 1954

Sir Winston S. Churchill: speech
('*Winston S. Churchill, His Complete Speeches*', volume 8, pages 8560–1)

13 April 1954 House of Commons

BASUTOLAND, BECHUANALAND AND SWAZILAND

There can be no question of Her Majesty's Government agreeing at the present time to the transfer of Basutoland, Bechuanaland and Swaziland to the Union of South Africa. We are pledged, since the South Africa Act of 1909, not to transfer these Territories until their inhabitants have been consulted and until the United Kingdom Parliament has had an opportunity of expressing its views. General Hertzog[1] himself, in 1925, said that his party was not prepared to incorporate in the Union any Territory unless its inhabitants wished it.

It is the interest, as it is also the desire, of this country and of South Africa, that the friendship which has developed so strongly between us over the years should remain unbreakable. I therefore sincerely hope that Dr Malan and his Government, with whom we have hitherto happily co-operated on so many problems we share in common, will not needlessly press an issue on which we could not fall in with their views without failing in our trust.

My noble Friend the Secretary of State for Commonwealth Relations is also making a statement on this subject in another place.

Defence Committee: minutes
(*Cabinet papers, 131/14*)

14 April 1954
Top Secret
12 p.m.
Defence Meeting No. 5 of 1954

[. . .]

3. REINFORCEMENTS FOR SHAPE IN THE FIRST SIX MONTHS OF WAR

The Committee had before them a memorandum by the Minister of Defence (D(54)21) reporting a request from the Supreme Allied Commander, Europe (General Gruenther) for information about any additional forces we could expect to put at his disposal in the first six months of war.

---

[1] James Barry Munnik Hertzog, 1866–1942. Born in Wellington, South Africa. Educated at Victoria College, South Africa, and University of Amsterdam. Married, 1894, Wilhelmina Neethling: three children. Gen., Boer Forces, during Boer War, 1899–1902. Signatory, Treaty of Vereeniging, 1902. Minister of Justice, Union of South Africa, 1910–12. Leader, Nationalist Party of South Africa, 1914–34. PM, 1924–39. Leader, United South African Party, 1934–9.

The Minister of Defence said that General Gruenther was at present engaged in trying to estimate the military situation in his Command in 1957, taking account of new weapons. In order to carry out this exercise effectively, he needed information from all the members of NATO about the additional forces they expected to be able to put at his disposal in the first six months of war. This request went a good deal further than the information now available to him, which was confined in the main to land forces available in the first thirty days and air forces immediately available at the outbreak of war. He and the Chiefs of Staff thought that the information should be given. It did, however, raise certain difficulties. We should in fact have very few forces available in the extended period and we might be faced with the suggestion that what additional forces we should have should now be committed to SACEUR. If that request were made, he did not think we could go beyond the two territorial army divisions already committed; we must leave ourselves free to decide what use to make of the others in the light of the situation at the time.

In discussion the following points were made:

(a) The ultimate plan was to raise up and equip eleven and two-thirds territorial divisions, but only the first four of these would have received modern equipment and war reserves by 1960. The rest would have training scales of equipment sufficient to fit them for home defence, but not for operations against a first-class enemy on the continent. In the present financial stringency, it was not possible to give these divisions modern equipment at any earlier date.

(b) If the Committee decided to give General Gruenther the information he required, the Canadians might be glad to know in advance that we were going to do so.

The Prime Minister said that General Gruenther was entitled to all the information he needed for working out his plan. The slow rate at which additional territorial army divisions became available would no doubt be a disappointment to him, but, even if they were all available within the first six months, it might be quite unrealistic to suppose that we should be able to send them to the continent in the early stages of a war of the type we had to expect.

The Committee:

(1) Authorised the Minister of Defence to accept SACEUR's proposals to send officers from his Staff to discuss the question of reinforcements for SHAPE in the first six months of war with the Ministry of Defence; and agreed that in the discussions the United Kingdom representative would follow the general line indicated in D(54)21.

(2) Invited the Commonwealth Secretary to let the Canadian Government know that we intended to give SACEUR the information for which he had asked.

[. . .]

April 1954

Cabinet: conclusions
(Cabinet papers, 128/27)

15 April 1954　　　　　　　　　　　　　　　　　　　　Prime Minister's Room
Secret　　　　　　　　　　　　　　　　　　　　　　　　House of Commons
11.30 a.m.
Cabinet Meeting No. 29 of 1954

1. The Foreign Secretary drew attention to the decision taken by the Defence Committee, at their meeting on the previous day, that after the end of the Geneva Conference the Hong Kong garrison should be reduced by gradual and unobtrusive stages to the level required for internal security purposes. If this decision became known to the United States authorities, it would prejudice the prospects of establishing a system of collective defence in South-East Asia and the Western Pacific. And if the Chinese got to know of it, negotiation at Geneva would be made even more difficult. He hoped, therefore, that nothing would be said to indicate to the Governor of Hong Kong, or to the military commanders in the Far East, that a decision had already been taken to reduce the garrison after the Geneva Conference.

The Prime Minister agreed that the decision taken by the Defence Committee must be kept most secret. For the time being the Governor of Hong Kong should be told that no action was being taken on the proposal to reduce the garrison and that the matter would be reviewed after the Geneva Conference. In the meantime, no hint of any kind should be given that a reduction of the garrison was contemplated.

The Cabinet –
Invited the Colonial Secretary to inform the Governor of Hong Kong that no immediate action would be taken to reduce the garrison, that the matter would be reviewed after the Geneva Conference, and that in the meantime no hint should be given that any reduction was contemplated.

2. The Cabinet had before them memoranda by the Chiefs of Staff (D(54)19) and the Foreign Secretary (C(54)148) on the military arrangements for safeguarding civilians in Egypt in an emergency.

The Foreign Secretary said that the Chiefs of Staff were now suggesting that we should be content with plans for (i) sending a strong flying column to bring out from Cairo such British subjects as could assemble within the Embassy precincts in an emergency, and (ii) sending warships into Alexandria. He could not think that these plans were adequate. Provisions ought also to be made for a more powerful follow-up operation, which would preserve British and foreign lives and property in Cairo and Alexandria by restoring order in these cities. If a situation arose which called for intervention by us, we might have an opportunity to set up an alternative Government and we should be ill-advised to miss such an opportunity. The Egyptians already knew that we had plans for occupying the Delta, and this knowledge was a powerful guarantee of their

April 1954

good behaviour. If we now restricted our plans in the way proposed by the Chiefs of Staff, we should be abandoning this useful negotiating card. He felt that, so long as we retained forces in the Canal Zone, we ought to be ready to intervene effectively in the Delta if the situation demanded it.

The Chief of the Imperial General Staff said that the object of the modified plan was to enable a start to be made with the redeployment of the fighting troops in the Canal Zone. So long as we accepted a firm commitment to occupy the Delta in an emergency, no reduction could be made in the garrison of the Canal Zone. Moreover, if we had to restore order in Cairo and Alexandria and support an alternative Government, it was likely that reinforcements would be needed from the United Kingdom.

In discussion the following points were made:
- (a) It was impossible to forecast the scope and nature of the operations which might be required if we had to intervene in the Delta. It would therefore be wise to have a number of alternative plans to meet the various contingencies that might arise. The choice of any particular plan could not be made in advance.
- (b) If plans had to be based on the assumption that all troops now in the Canal Zone would be available for these operations there could be no preliminary reductions and no contraction of the Base, since the reduction of forces and the contraction of the Base were complementary moves which had to proceed simultaneously.
- (c) On the other hand, it was suggested that plans for intervention in the Delta should be related to the troops available in the Canal Zone at any given time in accordance with the plans for contracting the Base.

The Prime Minister said that at all stages we must be ready to intervene in the Delta as effectively as we could with the forces available in the Canal Zone. This did not mean that plans for the contraction of the Base should not be made, although no forces should be withdrawn from the Canal Zone without further reference to the Cabinet. The Chiefs of Staff should prepare plans for intervention in the Delta on varying assumptions regarding the local situation and the forces available in the Canal Zone at the various stages of redeployment.

The Cabinet –
- (1) Instructed the Chiefs of Staff to prepare plans for intervention in the Delta with the forces at any time available in the Canal Zone, on the lines indicated by the Prime Minister.
- (2) Agreed that plans for the contraction of the Canal Zone Base and the reduction of forces should continue to be made, but should not be put into effect without further reference to the Cabinet.

The Prime Minister said that the readiness of the United States Government to join in an Anglo-American initiative for the establishment of a system of collective defence for South-East Asia and the Western Pacific had encouraged him to hope that they might now be ready to join with us in similar assurances about the security of the Middle East and the Suez Canal. If the Egyptians were confronted with a firm Anglo-American declaration on the requirements for security in that area, we should have a good prospect of reaching a satisfactory agreement which would enable us to reduce our forces without loss of prestige. We should not need to ask the Americans to provide either forces or money. An international agreement, in which the British and Americans took the lead, would be a sufficient guarantee of the security of the area and of the right of international passage through the Suez Canal, and no great show of force should be required. He thought that the moment was opportune for suggesting a scheme of this kind to the Americans.

The Foreign Secretary said that it was not easy to create a system of collective defence in the Middle East. In South-East Asia there were a number of large and small Powers directly involved by territorial and other interests. The countries of the Middle East were less willing to be drawn into a collective defence pact. Moreover, the Americans had so far taken the line that they would take no part in defence negotiations or arrangements with Egypt unless the Egyptians invited them to do so. He would, however, examine the possibility of devising some workable scheme which he might have an opportunity of discussing with the United States Secretary of State during the Geneva Conference.

The Cabinet –
(3) Took note that the Foreign Secretary would examine the possibility of putting forward practical proposals for a system of collective defence in the Middle East.

[. . .]

5. The Cabinet had before them a memorandum by the Home Secretary (C(54)121) summarising the arguments for and against the suggestion, made in the Cabinet's earlier discussions on 24th February and 17th March,[1] that legislation might be passed to restrict publication of the details of criminal prosecutions for homosexual offences.

The Home Secretary said that in his judgment the objections to such legislation outweighed any advantage it might have. He was specially impressed with the difficulty of drawing a distinction, as regards publication, between homosexual offences and other sexual offences – or, for that matter, crimes of violence, which were often associated with sexual irregularity or misconduct. There was also force in the argument that, if the Government supported this legislation and at the same time declined to hold an enquiry, they would be open to the criticism that they were trying to suppress the publication of evidence showing the need for an enquiry.

---

[1] See Cabinet: conclusions of Mar. 17, reproduced above (pp. 1482–4).

The Home Secretary said that in these circumstances he felt obliged to press his earlier proposal for the holding of an independent enquiry into the law relating to prostitution and homosexual offences. As, however, the Cabinet were reluctant to add to the number of Royal Commissions now sitting, he was ready to agree that this enquiry should be made by a Departmental Committee rather than a Royal Commission.

The Prime Minister said that if the Home Secretary was prepared to take the responsibility for appointing a Departmental Committee to enquire into these matters, the Cabinet need not raise objection to this modified proposal.

The Cabinet –
  (1) Agreed that a Departmental Committee should be appointed to enquire into the law relating to prostitution and homosexual offences.
  (2) Took note that the Home Secretary would consult with the Prime Minister on the membership of the proposed Committee.

6. The Cabinet had before them a memorandum by the Home Secretary and the Colonial Secretary (C(54)141) seeking guidance on the line they should take in forthcoming discussions with Dr Borg Olivier, the Prime Minister of Malta, about Malta's future status.

The Colonial Secretary said that the offer was still open that Malta should be brought under the authority of the Queen in Council, on the analogy of the Channel Islands and the Isle of Man, with the Home Secretary as the responsible Minister. It seemed likely, however, that the Maltese would be unwilling to accept this offer. The possible alternatives appeared to be:
  (i) to accede to Dr Borg Olivier's desire that Malta should be accorded a status comparable with that enjoyed by Southern Rhodesia before Central African federation;
  (ii) to develop a closer relation between Malta and the United Kingdom on the lines favoured by the Labour Party in Malta;
  (iii) to appoint a Royal Commission to examine the working of Malta's present constitution, her financial problems and the question of some change in her present status.

As regards (i), a request that responsibility for handling the affairs of Malta in London should be transferred to the Commonwealth Secretary had already been rejected. The idea of closer integration of Malta with the United Kingdom, implicit in (ii) above, must depend very largely on whether Parliamentary representation of Malta at Westminster could be seriously considered. He himself did not consider that it could and he understood that his view was shared by the Labour Opposition in the House of Commons. The Opposition were also doubtful about the wisdom of any arrangement which might make this country's social services available to the population of Malta, which the island's economy could not wholly support. There were risks in the appointment of a Royal Commission, which might submit recommendations which the Government could not accept. It seemed possible, however, that Ministers might find themselves in a position in which the appointment of a Commission was unavoidable.

In discussion there was general agreement that representation of Malta in the Parliament at Westminster could not be contemplated.

The Commonwealth Secretary said that further reflection had confirmed him in the view that the Cabinet had been right to reject the request that responsibility for handling Malta's affairs should be transferred to him. He was, however, apprehensive about the possible consequences of the appointment of a Royal Commission and he hoped that the two Secretaries of State would find it possible, in their discussions with Dr Borg Olivier, to explore the position and report further to the Cabinet before a decision was taken to appoint a Royal Commission.

The Prime Minister said that it did not seem necessary at this stage to rule out the possibility that it would eventually be necessary to adopt a negative attitude towards Malta's present attempts to obtain some change in her constitutional status.

The Colonial Secretary pointed out that Malta's claims tended to evoke special sympathy and support in this country on account of her unique position in having been awarded the George Cross.

The Cabinet –
(1) Took note of C(54)141 and of the views expressed in discussion.
(2) Authorised the Home Secretary and the Colonial Secretary to initiate discussions with the Prime Minister of Malta and invited them to refer the matter again to the Cabinet before bringing these discussions to a conclusion.

[. . .]

Evelyn Shuckburgh to John Colville
(Premier papers, 11/593)

15 April 1954
Top Secret

The attached minute from the Secretary of State to the Prime Minister was brought back by Mr Eden after a conversation with Sir Winston Churchill, and a minute written upon it, as you will see, at the bottom of the page.

Mr Eden has now asked me to explain to you the position as follows.

We have already once persuaded the Americans to agree to a postponement of the approach because of the Berlin Conference. We were able to use arguments there which would not be valid in connection with Geneva. If we now ask for a delay until after Geneva, we shall run into very great difficulty with the Americans. They, unlike us, have an effective fighting force in Austria and will be supplying any military equipment which the Austrians eventually require. They are, therefore, particularly interested in this approach to the Austrians and we understand that they are in fact about to go ahead with the Austrians on their own.

In these circumstances Mr Eden feels that there would be no advantage in our refusing to join in the discussions and that the best way of keeping the matter under some control is to join with the Americans and French in the approach to the Austrians. It should be mentioned that the discussions would be secret and oral and nothing would be committed to paper. Furthermore, they would be held with trusted Austrian Ministers who have successfully preserved the secrecy of previous talks on similar matters. We do not therefore think that there is a serious risk that the discussions might prejudice the success of the Geneva Conference.

Mr Eden hopes that the Prime Minister will agree.[1]

John Colville to Evelyn Shuckburgh
(Premier papers, 11/593)

16 April 1954
Top Secret

I showed the Prime Minister your Top Secret letter of April 15 about the use of Austrian manpower in the event of war.

The Prime Minister is not at all happy about the proposal. He still thinks it would be a great pity to have these discussions before Geneva. However discreet the Austrian Ministers may be, there is always a risk of a leakage in matters of this kind (perhaps in Washington or Paris?). Should the Russians get wind of what we were doing it could only have an ill effect on them if, by chance, they were contemplating any concessions or steps towards a détente. Are the advantages which we stand to gain of sufficient importance to warrant this risk? The Prime Minister feels that we ought not to be dragged into this against our better judgement just because the Americans want it. He would prefer us to go back to the Americans, to offer the strongest arguments against an untimely initiative such as they propose and to say that we should be strongly averse to any action of this kind until after the Geneva Conference. What great disadvantage could there be in a month's delay over such an issue?

I am sending a copy of this letter to Hanna[2] at the Ministry of Defence.

---

[1] Churchill wrote at the bottom of the page: 'No wonder the Russians want to keep control and not to make a Peace with Austria.'

[2] W. N. Hanna. Secretary to Minister of Defence, 1954–5.

1546   April 1954

Sir Winston S. Churchill to Colonel Christian de Castries[1]
(Premier papers, 11/645)

18 April 1954

We in Great Britain have watched with admiration the heroism and endurance with which your gallant troops have held Dien Bien Phu in the face of repeated bitter assaults by an enemy far superior in numbers. I salute you and your men whose exploits bring glory to France and are an example which inspires us all.

Evelyn Shuckburgh: diary
('Descent to Suez', page 167)

21 April 1954

[...]

Went over to see Jock Colville about a peerage for Oliver Harvey. He told me the PM is *not* now thinking of retiring at Whitsun (!) but 'might go to the end of the session *provided* he is not given any impression that he is being pushed'. In other words, no one is to say a hard word to him, or speak of his retirement in any way. Jock also said that the PM had been impressed with the way AE had faced a hostile House in defending him (WSC) over the Quebec agreement, and was more disposed on account of this to consider him fit to succeed. I expressed astonishment at this, and Jock added, 'Oh, but he has not been at all sure that the Government could hold together if he were to retire.' AE's comment on what I told him of this was that Whitsun is the last date his colleagues will stand. If the Old Man doesn't go then, the Government will break up – several of them will resign. We shall see.

[...]

Sir Winston S. Churchill to President Dwight D. Eisenhower
(Premier papers, 11/666)

22 April 1954
Top Secret, Private and Personal

My dear Friend,

I am told that you will be in Washington between May 20 and 24, before you receive the Emperor of Abyssinia. I should very much like to have some

---

[1] Christian Marie Ferdinand de la Croix de Castries, 1902–91. French Army officer. Educated at Saumur Cavalry School. Commissioned, 1926. POW, 1940–1. Served in North Africa, Italy, and France, 1941–6. Lt-Col., 1946. Brig.-Gen., 1953. Charged with defending Dien Bien Phu, 1953. POW, 1954.

talks with you. I would stay at the Embassy and probably a night or two with Bernie. We shall know more than we know now about several things – mostly tiresome. I should keep the plan secret till the last moment. Do you like the idea?

Sir Winston S. Churchill to Anthony Eden
Prime Minister's Personal Telegram T.77/54
(Premier papers, 11/670)

23 April 1954
Emergency
Secret and Personal
No. 901

Your telegram No. 241.

I wonder whether it is wise to deliver this broadside about NATO before (repeat before) the Geneva Conference opens on matters concerning the other side of the world. We shall of course have to decline the Soviet proposal to join NATO but it may well be asked why this could not be deferred till after the conference is over or has clearly broken down. The timing now will certainly require explanation. What were Bidault's objections mentioned in paragraph 3 of telegram under reference?

Anthony Eden to Sir Winston S. Churchill
Prime Minister's Personal Telegram T.78/54
(Premier papers, 11/670)

23 April 1954
Emergency
Secret
No. 256

Your telegram No. 901.

M Bidault's main concern was of an internal character. He has a very difficult meeting of his Cabinet on Saturday, at which he has to obtain their approval for the line he is to adopt at Geneva. They are much divided, and he himself has not yet determined his own attitude finally. He was, therefore, afraid that if he asked the Cabinet at the same time to approve the reply to the Soviet Union about European security it would gravely add to his task. Those who are defeatist about prospects of Geneva would accuse him of throwing into the pool something which was likely to reduce the prospects of success. He does not himself hold this view.

2. We were all agreed that if our reply is not delivered to the Russians

before Geneva begins, Molotov's first action on Monday could be to ask why this Note has not been answered. He will point to the meeting of the NATO Council in Paris this week, and ask their attitude to his proposal that the Soviet Union should join NATO. By this means he could force the question of European security on to the agenda of the Geneva Conference. We must avoid this if we are to have any prospect of getting down to business on the two Far Eastern issues for which the Conference has been called.

3. Moreover, this is a NATO matter. The meeting is now taking place and it is surely natural that the reply should emerge from the meeting.

Sir Winston S. Churchill to Anthony Eden
Prime Minister's Personal Telegram T.81/54
(Premier papers, 11/670)

24 April 1954
Immediate
Secret and Personal
No. 907

Your telegram No. 256.

1. You must decide how to play the hand.

2. Your paragraph 2, first sentence. Surely the answer could be that we did not want to darken the prospects of a Conference about quite different issues. I do not see how he could 'force the question of European security onto the agenda of the Geneva Conference' except as a means of preventing the very Far Eastern Conference for which he has pressed and for which they all have come.

3. Your paragraph 3. It will be thought odd that the reply has been delayed to hit off this particular moment.

4. I sympathise deeply with you in all your trials which are also ours. I have a feeling things have turned more sour. Sour is an understatement.

President Dwight D. Eisenhower to Sir Winston S. Churchill
(Premier papers, 11/1074)

24 April 1954
Top Secret

Dear Winston,

Of course you will be welcome. I agree with you that it is high time that we make certain of our common understanding of current and impending events that affect both our countries intimately. I am temporarily out of Washington but will be back there Monday at which time I shall cable you again as to exact dates.

APRIL 1954 1549

Sir John Martin[1] to Sir Winston S. Churchill
(Premier papers, 2/193)[2]

25 April 1954

Dear Prime Minister,

Thank you so much for my copy of *Triumph and Tragedy*.

I am proud and deeply grateful to have received the six volumes as your gift. How vividly they bring back those great years. The concluding pages recalled to me the memory of how, when at the height of the Blitz of 1940 I said that I should like to survive 'to see the end of the film', you answered that 'the scenario of history has no end'.

Long may you live to see the continuing story unroll.

Record of a conversation
(Premier papers, 11/645)

26 April 1954 Chequers
Top Secret

    Present: The Prime Minister
    Admiral Radford,[3] USN
    Captain George Anderson,[4] USN
    Mr J. R. Colville

Admiral Radford said that the fall of Dien Bien Phu, and failure by the United States and Great Britain to take appropriate action would be a great victory for the Communists and a turning point in history. The French Government would collapse and be replaced by a new Government with neutralist tendencies. EDC would not be ratified and NATO itself might well be destroyed. He had been present at a meeting of Congressional leaders at which

---

[1] John Miller Martin, 1904–91. Entered Dominions Office, 1927. Seconded to Malayan Civil Service, 1931–4. Secretary, Palestine Royal Commission, 1936–7. Private Secretary to PM (Churchill), 1940–1; Principal Private Secretary, 1941–5. Asst Under-Secretary of State, Colonial Office, 1945–56; Deputy Under-Secretary, 1956–65. Knighted, 1952. High Commissioner, Malta, 1965–7. His memoir, *Downing Street: The War Years*, was published shortly after his death in 1991.

[2] This letter was handwritten.

[3] Arthur William Radford, 1896–1973. Born in Chicago, Ill. Educated at US Naval Academy. Entered US Navy, 1914. Ensign, 1916. Lt, 1920. Lt-Cdr, 1927. Cdr, 1936. Married,1939, Miriam J. Ham Spencer. Head, Aviation Training Div., Washington DC, 1941–3. Capt., 1942. Cdr, Carrier Division Seven, 1943. DC of Naval Operations, 1944. Task Force Cdr, 1944–5. Deputy Chief of Naval Operations for Air, 1945. RAdm., 1947. VAdm., 1948. Vice-Chief of Naval Operations, 1948. Adm., 1949. High Commissioner of the Trust Territory of the Pacific Islands, 1949. Cdr, US Pacific Fleet, 1949–53. Chairman, JCS, 1953–7.

[4] George Whelan Anderson Jr, 1906–92. Born in New York City. Educated at US Naval Academy. Entered Navy, 1923. Ensign, 1927. Lt junior grade, 1930. Lt, 1932. Married, 1933, Muriel Buttling: two children (d. 1947); 1948, Mary Lee Sample. Lt Cdr, 1935. Cdr, 1937. Capt., 1940. RAdm., 1954. VAdm., 1957. Adm., 1961. Chief of Naval Operations, 1961–3. US Ambassador to Portugal, 1963–6. Chair of the President's Intelligence Advisory Board, 1970–6.

it was made clear that Congress would approve action to save Indo-China but only if England was willing to cooperate. He believed that if Indo-China fell and there was Communist infiltration elsewhere in SE Asia, not only would the food supplies of Japan and other Asiatic peoples in Siam and Burma be lost but Australia and New Zealand would be threatened. Japanese thoughts would turn towards Asiatic Communism with which they would believe the future to lie. The nationalists in Morocco would rise against the French, and would be harshly suppressed. This would spread disquiet and disorder into Africa and the Middle East. This was the critical moment at which to make a stand against China and he did not think that the Russians, who were frightened of war, would go openly to the aid of the Chinese. The situation would however be much worse in five years and indeed every day that passed meant a proportionate gain for the Communist powers at our expense. He said that if we cooperated over this the United States would be willing to help us in other spheres and that he thought that there would be no difficulty in revoking the present American policy of aloofness with regard to our difficulties in Egypt.

The Prime Minister said that he admitted the fall of Dien Bien Phu might be a critical moment in history. It reminded him of the situation at Warsaw in 1919 when the Russian revolutionary armies, under the command of a former Lieutenant, were sweeping westwards and were halted by Pilsudski[1] with the help and advice of General Weygand[2] and Lord d'Abernon.[3] The tide had been checked and rolled backwards. This was another such point in history, but how to roll back the tide in this instance was a very different problem. The British people would not be easily influenced by what happened in the distant jungles of SE Asia; but they did know that there was a powerful American base in East Anglia and that war with China, who would invoke the Sino-Russian Pact, might mean an assault by Hydrogen bombs on these islands. We could not commit ourselves at this moment, when all these matters were about to be discussed at Geneva, to a policy which might lead by slow stages to catastrophe.

[1] Józef Klemens Piłsudski, 1867–1935. Born in Zulow, Poland. Educated at Kharkov University. Joined Polish Socialist Party, 1893. Founder, editor, writer, *Robotnik*, 1894. Married, 1899, Maria Koplewska (d. 1921); 1921, Aleksandra Szczerbinska: two children. Banished to Siberia, 1887–92. Commandant, Bde I, Polish Legions, 1914–16. Chief of State, Republic of Poland, 1918–22. CGS, Polish Army, 1922–3. PM of Poland, 1926–8, 1930. General Inspector of the Armed Forces, 1926–35.

[2] Maxime Weygand, 1867–1965. Born in Brussels. Educated at École Spéciale Militaire de St-Cyr. On active service, WWI, 1914–18. Col., 1914. Brig.-Gen., 1916. Maj.-Gen., 1918. CoS, Allied Armies in France, 1918–20. Lt-Gen., 1920. Gen., 1923. C-in-C, Levant, 1923–4. Member, Supreme War Council, 1924–31. Director, Centre des Hautes Études Militaires, 1924–30. CoS, Army General Staff, 1930–1. Vice-President, Supreme War Council, 1931–5. Inspector-General of the Army, 1931–5. On active service, WWII, 1939–45. C-in-C, Allied Forces in France, 1940. Minister of National Defence, 1940. C-in-C of the Armed Forces, 1940. Minister of War, Vichy Government, 1940. Delegate-General of Vichy Government in French Africa, 1940–1. Governor-General of Algeria, 1941. German POW, 1942–5. French political prisoner, 1945–6.

[3] Edgar Vincent, 1857–1941. Knighted, 1887. MP (Cons.) for Exeter, 1899–1906. Baron D'Abernon, 1914. Ambassador to Berlin, 1920–6. Viscount, 1926.

The Prime Minister said he had learnt two significant facts in the last few days. One was that the Russians had ostentatiously flown over Moscow a large jet bomber of a type capable of reaching the United States. This had been seen by the American Air Attaché and was no doubt meant to be seen. What could this mean? Its interpretation seemed to him on the whole favourable because if the Russians were trying to impress us with their strength they were obviously not contemplating some secret blow. Secondly it had come to his knowledge that the Americans now possessed a hydrogen bomb which did not have to be filled with liquid hydrogen, which could be stored for years rather than hours and which could be carried much more easily to its target. It was possible, indeed probable, that the Russians had the same knowledge though they certainly had far smaller capacity for production. However this might be it was clear that given the present state of Russian aviation, the immediate Russian target was more likely to be East Anglia or London than the United States.

The Prime Minister went on to impress on Admiral Radford the danger of war on the fringes, where the Russians were strong and could mobilise the enthusiasm of nationalist and oppressed peoples. His policy was quite different: it was conversations at the centre. Such conversations should not lead either to appeasement or, he hoped, to an ultimatum; but they would be calculated to bring home to the Russians the full implications of Western strength and to impress upon them the folly of war. Conversations might or might not be fruitful but they would be understood by people in this country far better than fighting in SE Asia and were indeed already supported by a Resolution of the House of Commons. It might be true, as Admiral Radford had said, that we could not be sure the Russians would support the Chinese, but it was evident that in entanglements on the fringes of the Communist world the Soviet had everything to gain without the loss of a single Russian soldier.

The Prime Minister thought nothing more important than the close alliance of the English-speaking peoples and the continued effective cooperation of Great Britain and the United States. He had devoted a great part of his life and strength to this end. But we could not allow ourselves to be committed against our judgment to a policy which might lead us to destruction, the more so when we believed that the action which the Americans now proposed was almost certain to be ineffective. We could do nothing to save Dien Bien Phu and the French must realise that they had not the strength to hold down all Indo-China with the forces at their disposal. The loss of the fortress must be faced. The sensible policy for the French was to withdraw to such areas as they could securely hold and on that basis, after we had seen what came out of the Geneva Conference, the Cabinet would be willing to consider the situation in the closest consultation with their American allies.

Admiral Radford and Captain Anderson both said that they understood the British point of view, but they still felt that the risks were not as great as we supposed and that postponement of effective resistance could only bring upon us further misfortunes. The Admiral would be seeing President Eisenhower on the following day and would certainly report to him all that Sir Winston had told him. Cooperation with Great Britain was the keystone of his policy and he was certain that without it both the United States and the United Kingdom would drift to disaster.

Sir Winston S. Churchill: speech
('Winston S. Churchill, His Complete Speeches', volume 8, pages 8561–2)

27 April 1954 House of Commons

THE GENEVA CONFERENCE

Mr Attlee (by Private Notice) asked the Prime Minister whether he has any statement to make with regard to the meeting of the Foreign Ministers in Paris.

Sir W. Churchill: The meeting of the Foreign Ministers in Paris marked the fifth anniversary of the signing of the North Atlantic Treaty and reviewed in its military aspects the international situation. No doubt hon. Members will have read the communiqué issued after the meeting, which, for convenience, I am circulating in the Official Report.

While in Paris there were naturally conversations between the Foreign Ministers especially about the grave local situation in French Indo-China. No decisions were taken in advance of the Conference at Geneva. All the Powers concerned are now in session there. The preliminary stage of procedure which has so often absorbed much time and energy has been settled, with the full agreement of the Four Powers who initiated the Conference, with a smoothness and celerity which is at least a good augury for the spirit which should animate the proceedings. The House will, I am sure, be anxious that nothing should be said here today which would render more difficult the momentous discussions and vital contacts which are now in progress.

The episode of the siege of the French fortress of Dien Bien Phu, the fate of which now hangs in the balance, creates a violent tension in many minds and at a time when calm judgment is most needed. The timing of the climax of this assault with the opening of the Geneva Conference is not without significance but it must not be allowed to prejudice the sense of world proportion which should inspire the Conference and be a guide to those who are watching its progress.

Three of the Commonwealth countries are represented by high authorities at the Conference, and the closest intimacy and sense of unity prevails between them and us. My right hon. Friend the Foreign Secretary is also in constant touch with the other members of the Commonwealth. In order that his Cabinet colleagues and he should be in full agreement, he returned to this country last Saturday, and we had lengthy meetings on Sunday at which all the questions pending were considered, and we had the advantage of the professional advice of the Chiefs of Staff. As a result we have the fullest confidence in the wisdom of the course which we have agreed my right hon. Friend should follow in circumstances so largely governed by the unknown.

Her Majesty's Government are not prepared to give any undertakings about United Kingdom military action in Indo-China in advance of the results of Geneva. We have not entered into any new political or military commitments. My right hon. Friend has, of course, made it clear to his colleagues at Geneva that if settlements are reached there Her Majesty's Government will be ready to play their full part in supporting them in order to promote a stable peace in the Far East.

Sir Winston S. Churchill to Anthony Eden
Prime Minister's Personal Telegram T.83/54
(Premier papers, 11/645)

27 April 1954
Immediate
Secret
No. 37

M Massigli came to see me this morning with an urgent appeal from M Laniel that we should join with the Americans in the statement, for the purpose of influencing Congress, which has been in discussion. I told him that we had decided that we would not at this stage make any commitments in advance of the Agreement mentioned to Parliament by you before we separated. He brought an Officer with him, who has seen General Brownjohn at the Ministry of Defence, and Massigli assured me that he had given them a much more favourable review both of the conditions at Dien Bien Phu and of the proposed American air-strike, than our Chiefs of Staff had apparently obtained. I said I would of course examine the Report of our experts upon this but that I could not feel that it was likely to make any difference to the decision which you had already announced to M Bidault in your Paper.

2. I expressed my deep sympathy with the French in their agony but I said I thought it a great mistake to have left this large and important Force in so isolated a position.

President Dwight D. Eisenhower to Sir Winston S. Churchill
(*Premier papers, 11/666*)

27 April 1954
Top Secret

Dear Winston,
   Please let me refer again to your suggestion that we have a meeting to talk over things of great significance to our two countries.
   I am continually impressed by the drastic change in the world situation that each day seems to bring us in this obviously critical period. Likewise, I am deeply concerned by the seemingly wide differences in the conclusions developed in our respective governments, especially as these conclusions relate to such events as the war in Indochina and to the impending conference at Geneva.
   In order that our talks may have the maximum fruitfulness, I think it best to await the return of Foster to Washington before you and I try to work out firm details as to timing and subjects of our conversations. Foster will bring back to me valuable impressions and conclusions that I should study before you and I meet to explore why we seem to reach drastically differing answers to problems involving the same sets of basic facts. Certainly I agree with the thought, implicit in your suggestion, that we must reach a true meeting of minds so that we may work more in concert as we attack the critical questions of the day.
   I assure you that I am anxious, as I have always been, to reach a common understanding that will be squarely based upon existing fact and to which both governments can logically adhere to their mutual advantage.

Cabinet: conclusions
(*Cabinet papers, 128/27*)

28 April 1954
Secret
11.30 a.m.
Cabinet Meeting No. 30 of 1954

[...]
   3. The Prime Minister said that on Sunday, 25th April, he had held two emergency meetings with the Ministers immediately available to consider a proposal, put forward by the United States Government, for Anglo-American military intervention in Indo-China. A record of those meetings had been circulated as C(54)155. He had no doubt that the Foreign Secretary had been right in recommending that the United Kingdom should decline to associate themselves with any immediate declaration of intention to check the expansion of Communism in South-East Asia or to join in any precipitate

military intervention in Indo-China. He thought it possible that the United States authorities might eventually be brought to share our view on this matter.

The Prime Minister said that the French Ambassador in London had on the previous day brought him a further message from the French Prime Minister urging reconsideration of this decision. He had felt obliged to reject this further appeal. Since 25th April the Chiefs of Staff had also reviewed the position afresh in the light of representations made by a French military officer who had been sent over specially from Paris; but they adhered to their opinion that air intervention of the kind proposed would not be effective in saving the garrison at Dien Bien Phu.

The Commonwealth Secretary drew attention to a telegram from the Foreign Secretary (Geneva telegram No. 25) embodying the text of a message which he was proposing to send to the Prime Ministers of India, Pakistan and Ceylon. This emphasized the importance of securing the widest possible measure of support for any settlement on Indo-China which might be secured at the Geneva Conference. It disclosed our willingness to guarantee such a settlement, and enquired whether these Commonwealth countries could be associated with such a guarantee in any way. The three Prime Ministers were also to be asked whether there was any other action which they thought the Commonwealth countries might take, individually or collectively, to reinforce the settlement and to take advantage of the resulting relaxation of tension.

The Commonwealth Secretary said that he was in full agreement with the terms of the message which the Foreign Secretary was proposing to send.

The Cabinet –
(1) Took notice of the Prime Minister's statement.
(2) Invited the Commonwealth Secretary to arrange for a personal message from the Foreign Secretary on the lines of the draft embodied in Geneva telegram No. 25 to be despatched at once to the Prime Ministers of India, Pakistan and Ceylon.

[. . .]

Sir Winston S. Churchill: speech
('Winston S. Churchill, His Complete Speeches', volume 8, pages 8562–3)

28 April 1954   Royal Academy, London

ROYAL ACADEMY BANQUET

I am very much obliged to Sir Gerald Kelly for proposing the toast of Her Majesty's Ministers, and for the compliment which he has paid to me. I cannot help regretting that after what may well have been a prolonged meditation he has not been able to find anything to say about our politics good or bad, or indifferent, but has simply commended us to the natural kindness of this distinguished gathering. A more fertile theme would perhaps have been 'the difficulties of Her Majesty's Ministers', and he could have expatiated on these without giving any offence to the Leader of the Opposition whom we are so glad to see here tonight and who, I believe, has his difficulties too.

Sir Gerald has, however, decided to keep clear of politics and politicians as long as they do not send pictures to the Royal Academy, or otherwise trespass upon the domains of art. This prudent course imposes, however, disadvantages upon the politician who is called upon to reply. He is like a painter invited to produce a masterpiece but unprovided with any particular subject wherewith to fill his canvas. He has got to provide it all out of his own head or else embark upon a dreary vindication of conduct which has neither been impugned or even praised. Sir Gerald need not have restricted himself in this way. Her Majesty's Ministers are quite used to being criticized and even if they were paid a tribute I am sure Mr Attlee would not have been offended. He is quite used to putting up with things. Let me therefore confine myself to more agreeable topics than politics.

I was very glad when it was decided a few years ago to revive the Royal Academy Banquet after the war, and we are grateful to Sir Alfred Munnings[1] not only for his strong initiative but for the controversial element with which he enlivened the proceedings. It is with genuine regret that we face the fact tonight that this is the last Royal Academy dinner over which Sir Gerald Kelly will preside. The Presidents of the Royal Academy are esteemed figures in British life. None has been more tireless in his search for the welfare of the Academy and of British Art in general than Sir Gerald. During his Presidency we have had the Dutch Exhibition and the Flemish Exhibition. Seldom if ever have there been exhibitions at Burlington House which surpassed them either in the quality of the pictures or in the crowds they have attracted. For these remarkable selections we have Sir Gerald Kelly's personal labours and persistence to thank. His successors will take over the Presidency at a high level of popularity and acclaim.

Last year I spoke of conventional and unconventional Art, and of the controversies and compromises which exist between them. It was with a shock that a few months ago I heard that warfare was now being classified in 'conventional' and 'unconventional' forms and that these had become the official expressions on the continent of Europe. These hitherto harmless, inoffensive terms now strike a knell in all our hearts. Indeed we may ask ourselves whether we should go on with the routine, ceremonies, and festivities of our daily round when dangers are growing which might end the life of the human race. I have no doubt what the answer is to that question, namely, that the more the human mind is enriched and occupied and the conditions of our

---

[1] Alfred James Munnings, 1878–1959. Educated at Norwich School of Art, 1892–8. Associate, Royal Academy, 1919; Member, 1925; President, 1944–9. Associate, Royal Society of Painters in Water-Colours, 1921; Member, 1929. Knighted, 1944. KCVO, 1947.

life here are improved and our capacities enriched the greater is the chance that the unconventional weapons will lead not to general annihilation but to that outlawry of war which generation after generation has sought in vain.

In the course of a few bewildering years we have found ourselves the masters or indeed the servants of gigantic powers which confront us with problems never known before. It may be that our perils may prove our salvation. If so this will depend upon a new elevation of the mind of man which will render him worthy of the secrets he has wrested from nature. In this transfiguration the Arts have a noble and vital part to play. We therefore have no need to reproach ourselves for levity in coming here tonight.

Sir Winston S. Churchill: speech
('Winston S. Churchill, His Complete Speeches', volume 8, pages 8863–5)

30 April 1954   Albert Hall, London

GRAND HABITATION OF THE PRIMROSE LEAGUE

This is the third time in my third administration that I have presided as Grand Master at the annual meeting of the Primrose League. A year ago almost to a day I was able to speak of the steady growth of strength of Her Majesty's Government at home and abroad, and to point to the deep cleavages and personal rivalries which distract our Socialist opponents. All this is as true and even more obvious today than it was last time. We have pursued with steadfast perseverance our heavy task of undoing the harm which six years of Socialist rule has brought upon our country.

We are increasingly encouraged by our achievements. These would have been impossible without the devotion to national duty which the Conservative and National Liberal Members of Parliament have shown in the discharge of their public duty, and the efficiency of the management of Parliamentary business of our whips department in the House of Commons, and the ever-improving and widening strength of the party organization which Lord Woolton has built up throughout the country. The result is that in a world of so much disturbance and confusion this small island on which so many burdens have fallen presents to many distressed and distracted a spectacle of calm, reasonable, and methodical government, combining the workings of free and progressive democracy with the fame and traditions of the past. This fulfils in fact and spirit the message of Tory democracy which Lord Beaconsfield left behind him and which Lord Randolph Churchill revived and preserved by founding our Primrose League.

No member of the Government had to shoulder a harsher burden than Mr Butler. When he became Chancellor of the Exchequer we were sliding into bankruptcy and only his stubborn sense of duty and disdain of fleeting popularity has enabled us to regain that solid foundation of solvency without which not merely the well-being but the very survival of our immense population could not be maintained.

In spite of the programme of rearmament which we accepted from our predecessors with a salute – for in this respect they did their duty; in spite of the load of debt which we have incurred largely for the sake of helping other peoples and world causes; in spite of the faithful development of what is called the Welfare State, which was largely conceived in the war-time Coalition Government, which I had the honour to lead – in spite of all this our reserves have grown larger month by month and are now three hundred and fifty million pounds above the low level which they reached in early 1952 before we had arrested the Socialist landslide. The pound sterling has never since the war been stronger or more stable.

There is an American recession going beyond what happened in 1949, and which then struck so heavy a blow at our financial economy. But owing to Mr Butler's resolute, patient discharge of his duty, it has so far made no impression upon our production, our employment, or the buoyancy of our markets. Three weeks ago there was a hullabaloo about the Budget. Where is the howling now? Of course we all feel the weight of taxation, the highest in the free world, but only time filled by exertion, invention, and industry, and public and private thrift, can render relief possible.

It costs the Socialists nothing to clamour for large new additions to our expenditure. They should instead have acknowledged the intense effort we are making to sustain the progress of our social life. It seems indeed astonishing to me that not one of them has even mentioned the fact that Mr Butler has, in this year's Budget, alone amid all the strains and struggles, produced no less than sixty-five million pounds additional for social services. It was indeed a magnificent achievement to have combined this new extension of our housekeeping with the strengthening of our solvency and the growth of our reserves.

An even more crude and ridiculous example of Socialist ill-nature and irresponsibility is the attack upon our Minister of Education, Miss Florence Horsbrugh. She is denounced as a harsh, cruel Tory reactionary, stinting and maltreating our education system in every direction. She has in fact produced the largest and most generous education estimates for which Parliament has ever been asked to vote at any time by any Government of any party.

Today we have as our principal speaker Mr Harold Macmillan. You are right to give him a hearty cheer. You will be able now to judge him by his words; you can already judge him by his deeds. He had a predecessor; I never could understand why a man so personally ambitious as that predecessor did not try to make a name for himself – an honourable name, I mean – by a record building of houses for the British people who needed them so bitterly after the War. I should have thought it would have appealed equally to any public man whether he were a philanthropist, a statesman, or simply a careerist. However, the fact remains that he thought two hundred thousand houses a year was all he could do and devoted his energies to mocking at our pledge to build three hundred thousand or more. I would say more about this gentleman this afternoon but for the fact that I do not like hitting a man when he is down.

Now here you have before you on this platform the Minister whose name will for ever be associated with the most substantial forward step in building houses to meet an urgent need, and who is now working night and day – for that is what he does – not only to build new houses but to repair those that are falling into ruin and to resume in full activity the clearance of slums on which the Conservative Government was so fruitfully engaged before the War.

Before I sit down I must turn from our complicated but manageable situation at home to the sombre scene of foreign affairs which should rightly weigh upon all thinking minds. Although in this fearful twentieth century Britain has found a path of victory and has grown in national fame, we must face the fact that a vast world has grown and is growing up around us in which all the strength and loyalty of the Commonwealth and all the wisdom and experience of our race will be needed if we are to hold the rank and wield the influence which we have for so many generations commanded. How fortunate it is that at the conferences at Berlin and Geneva we have the reputation, skill and knowledge of Anthony Eden to assert our influence and plead with authority and patience the cause of peace through strength. It is right we should waft him a message of confidence and encouragement from this great meeting.

Our policy today is to preserve our friendship with France, and to convince the French people that their own safety as well as the freedom of Europe will not be achieved without bringing Germany back into the family of Europe and enabling her to play the worthy part she has accepted in the defence of Western Europe under the supreme authority of the United Nations. Secondly, we should establish relations with Russia which in spite of all distractions and perils will convince the Russian people and the Soviet Government that we wish them peace, happiness, and ever-increasing, ever-expanding prosperity and enrichment of life in their own mighty land and that we long to see them play a proud and splendid part in the guidance of the human race. And the foundation of all is our friendship and brotherhood with the United States of America, whose exertions and sacrifices since the War ended will long shine in history, and without whose unrivalled power chaos or subjugation might overwhelm us all.

May 1954

Cabinet: conclusions
(Cabinet papers, 128/27)

3 May 1954   Prime Minister's Room
Secret   House of Commons
5 p.m.
Cabinet Meeting No. 31 of 1954

1. The Minister of State drew the Cabinet's attention to a message from the Foreign Secretary (Geneva telegram No. 113) regarding the embarrassments arising at the Geneva Conference from the divergence of view between the United Kingdom and United States Governments on the question of any immediate military intervention in Indo-China. Despite these, the Foreign Secretary considered that, pending the outcome of the negotiations at Geneva, we must decline to be drawn into the war in Indo-China or even into promising moral support for measures of intervention of which the full scope was not yet known. We should, however, continue to assure the Americans of our readiness to work with them in establishing a system of collective defence, with the widest possible Asian support, to guarantee whatever settlement could be achieved in Indo-China and to assure the security of Southeast Asia generally. The Foreign Secretary had discussed this situation with the Ministers for External Affairs of Canada, Australia and New Zealand, and had assured himself that they were in full agreement with his views.

The Prime Minister said that he was sure that the Cabinet would endorse the policy which the Foreign Secretary was pursuing. At the same time it must be recognized that the fall of Dien Bien Phu, which now seemed inevitable, would afford great encouragement to Communists throughout the world. We must seek to counter its effects by pressing forward, as soon as the Geneva Conference was over, the efforts to establish an effective system of collective defence for Southeast Asia and the Western Pacific.

The Cabinet –
Took note with approval of the message from the Foreign Secretary embodied in Geneva telegram No. 113.

[. . .]

MAY 1954   1561

Lord Bracken to Sir Winston S. Churchill
(*Churchill papers, 2/212*)

3 May 1954

My dear Winston,
　Here is Hodge's review of your book.
　I ought to know something about your capacity for work as I have had plenty of opportunities of witnessing it since the far-off days when you were living at Hosey Rigg and rebuilding Chartwell. Having read the last volume of the six which you have had to write in the intervals of leading the Opposition and the Government, I can only say that there never was and never will be such an animal as WSC. I think I could pass an examination in all the volumes you have sent me from time to time: the last is the best.
　Your children and grandchildren have every reason to bless you for undertaking this Herculean labour for them. I grieve beyond all telling that no benefit from it can come to Clemmie and you.
　I had great fun at Chartwell – thank you very much.

Cabinet: conclusions
(*Cabinet papers, 128/27*)

5 May 1954
Secret
11.30 a.m.
Cabinet Meeting No. 32 of 1954

　[. . .]
　5. The Cabinet considered proposals by the Lord Privy Seal (C(54)157) for a provisional legislative programme for the 1954–55 session of Parliament.
　The Lord Privy Seal said that, by the end of the present session, the Government would be able to claim, broadly speaking, that they had carried through the legislation to which they had committed themselves and the Cabinet must, therefore, decide which of the alternative projects mentioned in paragraphs 3 and 4 of his memorandum should be adopted as the main element in the legislative programme for the next (and perhaps the last) session of the present Parliament. In making this choice the Cabinet must bear in mind that the session might prove to be shorter than earlier sessions of the present Parliament. Decisions on the main items of the programme should be taken soon in order that the necessary work of preparation and drafting might proceed.
　The Minister of Transport reminded the Cabinet that they had accepted a commitment to include a Road Traffic Bill in next session's programme. In The Queen's Speech at the opening of the present session it had been stated that Ministers were 'attentively examining the Road Traffic Acts with a view

to introducing further legislation to improve road safety and promote orderly use of the roads'.

Attention was also drawn to the probable need for legislation to effect some of the economies in public expenditure which were now in contemplation. This might make substantial demands on Parliamentary time.

The Cabinet's subsequent discussion was concerned with the proposals for (i) legislation on health, welfare and safety in nonindustrial employment and closing hours of shops, and (ii) legislation necessary to permit the final dismantling of emergency powers.

The Cabinet had before them a memorandum by the Home Secretary, the Secretary of State for Scotland, the Minister of Labour and the Minister of Agriculture (C(54)122), proposing that the provisional programme for the next session should include legislation on health, safety and welfare in non-industrial employment and closing hours of shops, and a memorandum by the Lord President (C(54)128) reporting the views of the Home Affairs Committee on this question.

The Home Secretary said that the reports of the Gowers[1] Committee on these matters had been made in 1947–9 and it was becoming increasingly difficult to resist pressure from interested organisations for legislation to give effect to the Committee's recommendations. There was undoubtedly practical justification for such legislation, and the Government should consider whether they could afford to delay much longer reforms which affected so large a proportion of the working population. On the other hand, this legislation would occupy much Parliamentary time and would involve employers generally in fresh obligations and expenditure.

The Minister of Labour said that responsible trade union leaders attached considerable importance to this matter as well as to the proposals for a National Occupational Health Service on which the Cabinet had on 28th April deferred a decision. There would be advantages in taking some action to satisfy them, but he recognized that these plans for further social progress must now be looked at afresh in conjunction with any proposals for securing economy in public expenditure.

The Minister of Transport said that in principle it was certainly difficult to justify the continued exclusion of railways from statutory requirements in respect of health, welfare and safety; but he believed that any fresh expenditure which the British Transport Commission might find it possible to incur in the immediate future ought to be devoted to increasing the wages of the more

---

[1] Ernest Arthur Gowers, 1880–1966. Educated at Rugby and Clare College, Cambridge. Principal Private Secretary to Lloyd George (at the Exchequer), 1911–12. Chief Inspector, National Health Insurance Commission, 1912–17. Secretary, Civil Service Arbitration Board, 1917–19. Director of Production, Coal Mines Dept, 1919–20. Permanent Under-Secretary for Mines, 1920–7. Knighted, 1926. Chairman, Board of Inland Revenue, 1927–30. Chairman, Coal Mines Reorganization Commission, 1930–5; Coal Commission, 1938–46. Chairman, Royal Commission on Capital Punishment, 1949–53.

highly-skilled men rather than to improving the conditions of employment of railway workers generally.

The Lord President said that opinion in the Home Affairs Committee on this matter had been very evenly divided but it had been recognized that, however justifiable this legislation might be in principle, it was not likely to be viewed with favour by a majority of Government supporters in Parliament or the country.

The President of the Board of Trade said that he would deprecate legislation which would have the effect of adding to the existing difficulties and handicaps of industrial employers.

The Prime Minister said that in his view priority in further social progress should be accorded to improvement of the position of old age and war-disability pensioners, but plans for legislation on the lines recommended by the Gowers Committee should in the meantime continue to be studied.

The Home Secretary said that in paragraph 4 of C(54)157 the possibility was mentioned that the whole structure of emergency powers might be abandoned before the end of the present Parliament. With the cooperation of his colleagues he had been able to bring about a considerable reduction of these powers, but there were strong arguments for making a special effort to complete the process during the lifetime of the present Government. First, it was the Government's declared intention to dispense with all emergency powers which were not needed and to embody the remainder in permanent legislation. Secondly, the revocation of these powers would put it beyond the power of a future Government to revive economic controls without fresh Parliamentary authority.

In discussion the view was expressed that, while this aim was desirable in principle and in accord with Conservative opinion, the legislation needed for its attainment would contain features which would be highly controversial and unpalatable to Government supporters.

The Prime Minister said that the project appeared to him, nevertheless, to be one deserving of further study. It would be in keeping with the Government's general theme and purpose, and it would involve no fresh expenditure of public money.

The Cabinet –
    (1) Invited the Home Secretary to arrange for his Committee on Emergency Legislation to investigate the possibility of dispensing altogether with emergency powers before the end of the present Parliament, and to report to the Cabinet.
    (2) Appointed a Committee consisting of:
    Lord Privy Seal
    Lord President
    Home Secretary
    Chancellor of the Exchequer

Secretary of State for Scotland
Minister of Housing
Chief Whip

to consider the provisional legislative programme for the next session in the light of the Cabinet's discussion and to make recommendations thereon to the Cabinet.

[. . .]

Sir Winston S. Churchill to Gwilym Lloyd George
Prime Minister's Personal Minute M.84/54
(Premier papers, 11/661)

10 May 1954

Would you please let me know to what extent the date of the Local Elections was taken into account when May 8 was fixed as the end of butter rationing. It has been suggested to me from several quarters that the consequent rises in price of butter in the coming week may work to the advantage of the Socialists, as did the reduction of the cheese ration just before the Local Elections two years ago.

President Dwight D. Eisenhower to Sir Winston S. Churchill
(Premier papers, 11/1074)

12 May 1954
Secret

Dear Winston,

In my message of April 26[1] I promised you a further reply after I had had an opportunity to talk with Foster concerning the timing of your visit to Washington. I have now had the opportunity to discuss it with him and we are agreed that some time in June would be best from our point of view. By then Geneva will have unfolded further and we will both better know where we stand in the matter of Indochina, where I think a greater show of unity is essential. In addition to this consideration, the present series of our tests will not have been evaluated until the early days of June and it would be useful for progress on that front if I had the results of those before me when we talked.

Let me know how your schedule looks for June and we can then agree on the most convenient date for both of us.

---

[1] Reproduced above, dated Apr. 27.

May 1954

Sir Winston S. Churchill to Anthony Eden
Prime Minister's Personal Telegram T.109/54
(Premier papers, 11/666)

12 May 1954
Immediate
Top Secret, Private and Personal
No. 399

I am sorry you cannot come over for I do not yet understand why Dulles departed and I should much have liked a talk. However I trust you still have hopes of some fruitful result. Perhaps you will send a letter to The Queen.

2. I have just had a visit from Winthrop Aldrich. He brought me the paper marked 'A' (contained in telegram No. 400) which you will see is nothing more than the communiqué proposed to be issued tomorrow and kindly communicated the day before to us. I expressed suitable acknowledgement and mentioned that I feared it was inaccurate as we understood that the final test was to be made tonight and while he was with me a message arrived from the Embassy further postponing his inaccurate information.

3. Later on during our talk the further message enclosed at 'B' (contained in telegram No. 401) reached him from the Embassy. As you know I have not sent any reply to the President's message of April 27.[1] If you look at the date in relation to my proposal of May 20 it looks as if Dulles' return must have been a surprise to the President.

4. I propose to send the following reply.
Begins.

My dear Friend,
    How would Friday June 18 suit you or will you be going away for the weekend? I could stay four or five days at your convenience at the Embassy. I am most anxious to survey with you the whole question of sharing information about the Bomb, etc. It will be most valuable to learn your evaluation of the latest series of tests. I should also welcome a talk with you about the Indo-China imbroglio. If you preferred weekdays I could start Sunday June 20.
    Kindest regards,
    Winston[2]

Ends.

---

[1] Reproduced above (p. 1554).
[2] This message was sent on May 13 as T.112/54.

May 1954

Sir Winston S. Churchill to Desmond Flower[1]
(Churchill papers, 4/24)

12 May 1954

My dear Desmond,

I received the letter from your Father[2] with great pleasure and now I thank you for yours.

Looking back it seems incredible that one could have got through all these six volumes and I suppose nearly two million words. Our relations have indeed been pleasant and memorable.

I shall look forward to seeing the cartoons but I should prefer to look at them before accepting the dedication. I hope they are not all complimentary!

With kind regards

Anthony Eden to Sir Winston S. Churchill
Prime Minister's Personal Telegram T.111/54
(Premier papers 11/666)

13 May 1954
Immediate
Top Secret, Private and Personal
No. 266

I do not think there is any mystery about Dulles' departure. He said as far back as Berlin that he could only stay here a few days.

2. I am very sorry I could not come this weekend. If the French Government falls today and the conference has to go into recess, it may still be possible. Otherwise I will do my best to come next weekend for a talk with you. I wonder whether the dates of a visit to Washington could be left open until we are able to discuss them together then.

3. I don't like Prince Consort as a title.[3] What about Prince of the Realm?

---

[1] Desmond John Newman Flower, 1907–97. Only son of Sir Newman Flower. Educated at Lancing and King's College, Cambridge. Entered Cassell & Co., 1930; Director, 1931; Literary Director, 1938; Acting Director, 1939–40. On active service, 1940–5 (despatches, MC, 1944). As Deputy Chairman of Cassell, 1952–8, and Chairman, 1958–71, he supervised the printing, publishing and sale of Churchill's *The Second World War* and *A History of the English Speaking Peoples*. In 1991 he published his memoirs, *Fellows in Foolscap*.

[2] Walter Newman Flower, 1879–1964. Educated at Whitgift School. Joined the publishing firm Cassell & Co., 1906; purchased the firm in 1927; subsequently its Chairman and President. Knighted, 1938.

[3] For Prince Philip.

President Dwight D. Eisenhower to Sir Winston S. Churchill
(Premier papers, 11/666)

15 May 1954
Top Secret

Dear Winston,

Friday, June 18th suits me very well. It will give us a good weekend for talks. I hope very much you are counting on bringing Anthony with you so that he may talk with Foster. The two of them could help us keep our talks related to the many delicate aspects of the world situation. Moreover, their presence should be helpful to them in implementing any ideas we might agree upon.

My thought is that we should see that social affairs are kept at a minimum or totally eliminated, so that we could have the maximum time for leisurely discussions. Do you agree with this or would you like to make some different suggestion?

The matter of announcements, so far as I am concerned, can be determined by Foster and Anthony, but if you have any particular thought on this point, I will be glad to have it.

Sir Winston S. Churchill to President Dwight D. Eisenhower
Prime Minister's Personal Telegram T.117/54
(Premier papers, 11/666)

15 May 1954
Top Secret
Private and Personal
No. 2202

My dear Friend,

So many thanks for your telegram of May 15. Of course I should like to bring Anthony with me. I agree that social affairs should be eliminated though probably I should be urged as on all previous occasions to lunch with the Washington Press Club where the proceedings have always been confidential.

I did not think any announcement was urgent. We might discuss this at the end of May when perhaps Geneva will be over.

Sir Winston S. Churchill to Anthony Eden
Prime Minister's Personal Telegram T.116/54
(Premier papers, 11/666)

15 May 1954
Immediate
Top Secret, Private and Personal
No. 470

1. Thank you for the text of the answer I am to give on Monday; it seems all right. I will study it over the weekend. You seem to have been making good progress and I think the Opposition will be in a better temper.

2. You will have received the reply enclosed from the President to my telegram to him of May 13 and I am sending him the answer also enclosed.

3. I like the President's idea that he and I shall have talks rather than formal meetings and that we should avoid social functions. I am especially glad there is no idea of bringing the French in.

4. I hope you will be able to come. Please let me know as soon as you can. My own card for June is rather full and no other date would suit me as well as the 18th. The weekend concession of the President is certainly convenient for just the kind of contact I want.

5. Let me know what are your prospects for coming over next Saturday 22nd and whether I can offer you any hospitality. Will you bring Bedell with you, I should like to see him.

PS. I invited Lester Pearson to Chequers but he could not come.

Sir Winston S. Churchill: speech
(Hansard)

17 May 1954   House of Commons

HER MAJESTY'S RETURN FROM HER COMMONWEALTH TOUR

I beg to move, that a humble Address be presented to Her Majesty, assuring Her Majesty, on the occasion of Her return from Her historic Commonwealth Tour, of the loyal and affectionate welcome of this House to Her Majesty and his Royal Highness the Duke of Edinburgh. Mr Speaker, there is no duty which the House of Commons could discharge with keener pleasure or deeper conviction than to approve the Motion it now falls to me to move.

When the background of this formidable century rises in our minds with all its struggles and achievements; with all its increases in power and peril, with all its anxieties and unsolved problems, the gleaming episode of the Queen's journey among her peoples, their joy in welcoming her and the impact of her personality upon their vast numbers constitutes an event which stands forth without an equal in our records, and casts a light – clear, calm, gay and benignant upon the whole human scene.

To the people of these islands, for whom we speak in this House, the Sovereign has rendered a service of lasting value – which could have sprung from no other source – a service involving not only tireless exertion but an element of danger – through air travel and other hazards – of which everyone concerned was conscious except herself. Sir, we thank God she is safe home again, and we in the Mother of Parliaments express our gratitude to her and to her husband the Duke of Edinburgh for the work that they have done together, which no one else could do.

Let us survey and salute the service to which our Address of welcome bears testimony. Although we have grown and progressed in many ways since the great Victorian age, a gigantic world has come into being and into contact around us in which, if judged by material tests alone, we have been surpassed. The Queen's journey of nearly six months has reminded all the nations of the message we have brought and of the causes for which we stand.

The Constitutional Monarchy surely founded in the hearts of its people; the Crown the servant not the master of the State; the harmonious reconciliation of the past with the present; the spirit of individual freedom, tolerance, fair play; the capacity at the same time to change and to endure: all these facts and themes have been presented as was never before possible, for all the world to see.

From beginning to end this Royal pilgrimage has reasserted human values, and given a new pre-eminence to the grace and dignity of life. This has not been confined to those who participated in the ceremonies or belong to our wide and varied association. All over the globe there has been a sense of kindly feeling and of generous admiration. Even Envy wore a friendly smile: 'How lucky they are to be able to personify the authority and symbolism of the State and combine tradition and modernity in so captivating a way.' Indeed, I believe that far beyond her Realms men and women have gained an accession of moral strength and good humour at a time when these virtues were never more needed to help mankind to use their hearts as well as their brains and so find their way through the problems and perils which baffle intellect alone.

Indeed, it may well be that the lively sense of universal brotherhood, and of the bright hopes of the future, may stir in all humanity these qualities which will enable it to control and survive the dread agencies which have fallen into its as yet untutored hands. I assign no limits to the reinforcement which this Royal journey may have brought to the health, the wisdom, the sanity and hopefulness of mankind. And we in the House of Commons welcome the opportunity of putting on record, in the most earnest and solemn manner open to us, our acknowledgment of the memorable benefits which we have received.

Sir Winston S. Churchill: speech
(Hansard)

17 May 1954   House of Commons

SOUTH EAST ASIA (DEFENCE)

I am obliged to the right hon. Gentleman and other hon. Members for postponing these Questions until now.

The Geneva Conference is now entering on its fourth week. The immediate object of the discussions about Indo-China is to bring the fighting to an end on terms acceptable to both sides. My right hon. Friend the Foreign Secretary is doing all in his power to help in finding an agreed basis for this, and I am sure the House would not wish that anything should be said which might make his task more difficult. Moreover, the situation is in constant flux. As those who have put these Questions on the Paper have no doubt seen for themselves, it has undergone changes even since last Thursday. I certainly feel sympathy with the desire of many Members of the House to discuss more fully than is possible at Question time the whole foreign situation in all its bearings, but I cannot yet fix a suitable occasion. It certainly would be a great advantage – I think we should all agree to this – if the Foreign Secretary himself were present to give his own account of the events which have taken place and set his own proportion upon them.

All I will therefore say today is that until the outcome of the Conference is known, final decisions cannot be taken regarding the establishment of a collective defence in South-East Asia and the Western Pacific. Meanwhile it will be clear from the statements already made that Her Majesty's Government have not embarked on any negotiation involving commitments.

These problems of future policy to which I have just referred are, of course, quite distinct from the question of the examinations undertaken without commitment by existing military agencies, to which my right hon. and learned Friend the Minister of State referred in reply to a Question on 10th of May. They are equally distinct from the conversations which, as reported in the Press, have been in progress during the past few days between the United States and French Governments about the situation in Indo-China.

In our consideration of all these matters, we are maintaining the closest touch with the Governments of India, Pakistan and Ceylon, and also with the Government of Burma. All these Governments are being kept fully informed from day to day of the development of events at the Geneva Conference, since we fully realise that they will be closely affected by its outcome and may feel willing to make a contribution towards it. There is, of course, also very intimate consultation with the Governments of Canada, Australia and New Zealand through their Delegations at Geneva as well as through the usual channels of Commonwealth consultation.

It should not, however, be thought that the terms of this statement cast any doubt upon our readiness to examine, when the outcome of the Geneva Conference is clearer, the possibility of establishing a system of collective security and defence in South-East Asia and the Western Pacific within the framework of the United Nations. We shall certainly do so. But our immediate task is to do everything we can to reach an agreed settlement at Geneva for the restoration of peace in Indo-China. Her Majesty's Government are resolved to do their utmost to achieve this aim and to exercise their influence to ensure that any acceptable settlement shall be backed by effective international guarantees.

Lord Ruffside[1] to Sir Winston S. Churchill
(*Premier papers, 11/680*)

21 May 1954

Dear Prime Minister,
In view of the reference by the Spanish Foreign Office, which I heard on the wireless at lunch today about a suggestion that you had offered to discuss Gibraltar at a secret session, would a letter as enclosed to the *Times* be helpful?
If so, by all means pass it on to them. I trust that by so doing I will not be breaking the law!

Sir,
A reference has been made to an alleged statement by the Prime Minister made during a secret session implying that he would be prepared to discuss giving Gibraltar to Spain.[2] As in my then position of Speaker, deputy Speaker or deputy Chairman of Ways and Means, I was in the Chair for a large portion of every secret session debate, and I certainly heard every one of the Prime Minister's speeches, so I can say with certainty that nothing of the kind alleged was ever said by him. Even, if I had missed it, there would have been considerable comment afterwards, and this I would have heard of, and I heard nothing of the kind.

---

[1] Douglas Clifton Brown, 1879–1958. Educated at Trinity College, Cambridge. MP (Cons.) for Hexham, 1918–51. Deputy Speaker of the House of Commons, 1938–43; Speaker, 1943–51. PC, 1941. Viscount Ruffside, 1951.

[2] The substance of the statement is reproduced in Churchill to Halifax, 26 June 1940, in *The Churchill Documents*, vol. 15, *Never Surrender, May 1940–December 1940*, p. 424. This statement was later explicitly repealed.

May 1954

Sir Winston S. Churchill to Lord Ruffside
(Premier papers, 11/680)

22 May 1954

My dear Ruffside,

Thank you for your letter about Gibraltar. I certainly think it would carry weight if you wrote to *The Times* as you propose and would dispose of the allegations that have been made. I therefore return the letter which you sent me to see so that you can send it to the Editor.

Sir Winston S. Churchill to Lady Churchill
(Baroness Spencer-Churchill papers)[1]

22 May 1954

My darling Clemmie,

I am so glad your journey[2] was so swift & smooth, & I await with eagerness your account of all the arrangements.

Here all is well but hard. I have no less than 3 speeches next week –

Payment of MP's on which I have got my way: (not without miaouings): the women's meeting at the Albert Hall & a debate on Friday about the atomic agreement which I published. That is indeed a packet.

Anthony has at last decided to come & all is in train.

Do let me know about your treatment & how it occupies & helps you.

Mrs Dean Acheson[3] has sent me one of her pictures, which she promised 3 years ago. Patrick says it is quite good. Oddly enough it is a scene in Antigua, which you have taken under your protection. I am just off to Chequers & will write to you tomorrow.

With all my love & prayers for your restoration to full health & strength.

Your ever loving husband
[Drawing of a pig]

Have you seen they have a new disease 'atrophia rhinitis'. I hope I shall escape it.

---

[1] This letter was handwritten.
[2] Lady Churchill had gone to Aix-les-Bains for treatment for neuritis.
[3] Alice Stanley, 1895–1996. Art major, Wellesley College, 1916. Married, 1917, Dean Acheson. Honourable mention, Society of Washington Artists, 1940.

Sir Winston S. Churchill to President Dwight D. Eisenhower
Prime Minister's Personal Telegram T.125/54
(Premier papers, 11/666)

24 May 1954
Immediate
Dedip
Top Secret and Personal
No. 2360

My dear Friend,

1. I am planning to leave for Washington on the 17th arriving 18th as outlined in our telegrams of May 13 and 15, and shall be at your convenience at the British Embassy for a few days thereafter. I think the announcement might be fitted in with Geneva as soon as possible, perhaps even this week. If you still like the idea, I will suggest the text of the communiqué.

2. The main and obvious topic is interchange of information about atomics, etc., and the progress of your great design to develop its harmless side. Apart from that we will talk over anything that crops up. For instance, I should like to reinforce Malaya; and Egypt is my first reserve. With your support a sound and dignified arrangement should be possible. I sincerely hope you will be able to postpone sending the Egyptians any aid until you and I have had our talks.

3. Anthony would like very much to come as you suggested, though perhaps he could not be there the whole time. I agree with you that it is essential to have him and Foster together and with us.

4. It seems to me that our meetings in the easy informal manner that we both desire may be a help in brushing away this chatter about an Anglo-American rift which can benefit no one but our common foes.

Cabinet: conclusions
(Cabinet papers, 128/27)

24 May 1954
Secret
10 a.m.
Cabinet Meeting No. 35 of 1954

1. The Cabinet had before them a memorandum by the Foreign Secretary, subsequently circulated as C(54)177, outlining the objectives which he was pursing in the discussions on Indo-China at the Geneva Conference.

The Foreign Secretary said that he believed there was a fair chance of securing agreement at Geneva on the terms for a cease-fire in Indo-China. He would continue to work for such a settlement; for he was gravely concerned about the dangers of the alternative courses of action which the United States

Government were likely to favour if a settlement were not now secured by negotiation. He therefore proposed to pursue the double objective of securing a cease-fire in Indo-China while at the same time keeping open the possibility of establishing at the appropriate moment an effective system of collective defence for South-East Asia as a whole. In this his main difficulty was to avoid lasting damage to Anglo-American relations. The Americans had not been wise in their handling of this situation. Though Mr Bedell Smith was personally most friendly and cooperative, he was acting under close directions from Washington, where opinion was divided. Some American authorities evidently thought that this was the moment to challenge the ambitions of Communist China, if necessary by force, and believed that this could be done without provoking Russian intervention. Some of them were probably influenced by the consideration that the risk of such intervention would be greater in a few years' time, when Russia had the power to deliver an atomic attack on North America. The American representatives at Geneva were therefore inclined to adopt an uncompromising attitude towards the Chinese. The Chinese, on the other hand, although they were not anxious for any fresh military adventure, were certainly not in a mood to be browbeaten. Mr Chou En-Lai, though courteous, was hard. He did not regard Korea as a failure and was not ready to accept dictation by the Western Powers. The Russians plainly wanted to secure a settlement: in the conduct of negotiations M Molotov had been skilful and constructive. But it was evident that the Chinese were not wholly under the control of the Russians. Nor, for that matter, were the Viet-minh representatives completely responsive to Chinese control. The French delegation were distracted and handicapped by the instability of their Government. There was no doubt that their interest lay in reaching a quick settlement on the best terms they could get, but it was hard for them to embrace such a policy and to risk its political consequences.

The Foreign Secretary said that he had little doubt that the proper course for him in this difficult situation was to persevere for a time in the attempt to secure a reasonable settlement. He was alive to the risk that the discussions might be unduly protracted, but it was only one week since holding of the first restricted session and he was sure that it would be right for him to devote at least another week to the search for an agreement. He recognised that, as things stood, the United Kingdom would be open to special criticism if the Communists improved their military position in Indo-China while discussions were proceeding at Geneva. But, short of military intervention in Indo-China, which the United Kingdom Government were not at present prepared to contemplate, there was no practical action which was being delayed by the continuance of the Conference at Geneva. We had already agreed that military plans should be discussed through the medium of the Five-Power Staff Agency. And, even if we had been willing to enter at once into international discussions of the proposal for collective defence arrangements for South-East

Asia, such discussions could not have had any immediate effect on the military situation in Indo-China.

In the Cabinet's discussion the following particular points were made:

(a) The Foreign Secretary said that there was evidently much talk in Washington about a rift in Anglo-American understanding. This was based partly on our refusal to support the American proposal for an air attack on the besiegers of Dien Bien Phu, and partly on our unwillingness to join in international discussions on a defence pact for South-East Asia before the end of the Geneva Conference. On the first point Anglo-American differences might not have become publicly known if the Americans had not disclosed them to the Press. On the second there should have been no room for misunderstanding. It was difficult to see why Mr Dulles should have thought that he could proceed at once to international discussion of the proposed defence pact, immediately after the end of the London talks, in spite of the fact that it had not then been decided which countries should be parties to the proposed pact. The prospects of concluding such a pact would in fact have been seriously jeopardized if Mr Dulles had proceeded with his proposal to discuss it in Washington with representatives of ten countries including no Asiatic countries save Siam and the Philippines.

(b) The Foreign Secretary said that, in this as in the particular problem of Indo-China, it was most important that the Western Powers should retain the goodwill of the leading countries of Asia. Precipitate actions for the establishment of a system of collective defence for Southeast Asia would certainly have alienated India; and, without India's goodwill, few of the other countries of Southeast Asia would have been willing to participate in it. Their participation was essential to its success; and, with time and patience, they might be brought to see its advantages. There was now some reason to believe that, if agreement were reached on a cease-fire in Indo-China, India would be ready to play a part, jointly with Norway, in supervising its observance.

(c) The Foreign Secretary said that the United States Government were likely to press their suggestion that Siam should invite the United Nations to send an Observation Commission to the frontiers of Siam and Indo-China. He doubted whether this would be a wise move. First, the appeal would have to be considered by a special meeting of the United Nations Assembly and the Assembly, once convened, could not be prevented from discussing other aspects of the problems now under negotiations at Geneva. Secondly, the Russians were likely to represent it as a manoeuvre devised by the Americans to justify their proposed intervention in Siam. Thirdly, it would seem inconsistent with the arguments developed by the Western Powers at Geneva for declining to negotiate a single settlement covering Laos and Cambodia as well as Viet Nam, namely, that military operations in the former were not on a scale comparable with those taking place in the latter. The Foreign Secretary said that on his return to Geneva he would put to the Americans the arguments against proceeding with this project at the present time and would do his utmost to dissuade them from going forward with it. But, if he failed to dissuade them by these arguments, he proposed that, with a view to avoiding further damage to Anglo-American friendship, he should assure them that they could rely on our support in the United Nations if such an appeal were made.

The Cabinet agreed that this plan of inducing Siam to make an appeal to the United Nations was ill-judged and ill-timed. The matter was not, however, of such importance that it need be added to the list of subjects on which we were publicly seen to be at variance with the United States. If, therefore, the Foreign Secretary failed to dissuade the Americans from proceeding with it, he should assure them that they could in the last resort rely on us to support them in the United Nations.

(d) The Foreign Secretary said that it was too early to say what line the Americans would take if all attempts to arrange a cease-fire in Indo-China were unsuccessful. This would depend on the outcome of the military talks now proceeding between the Americans and the French. It seemed unlikely that the French would accept the American conditions for sending land forces into Indo-China; but the Americans might be ready to give support with naval and air forces, and even this might lead to a state of general hostilities between the United States and China.

The Prime Minister said that it was clear from the Cabinet's discussion that the Foreign Secretary had the full support of his colleagues in his conduct of the negotiations at the Geneva Conference. It was also evident that he had won the support and goodwill of other Commonwealth Governments. It was right that he should persevere for a week or so longer in his efforts to secure a settlement on Indo-China. He would, however, continue to be aware of the risks of becoming involved in protracted negotiations which offered little prospect of a successful outcome.

The Cabinet –

Authorised the Foreign Secretary to pursue, in his negotiations at the Geneva Conference, the objectives set out in C(54)177.

2. The Prime Minister drew attention to a private Member's motion tabled by Sir Charles Taylor, MP,[1] for discussion in the House of Commons

---

[1] Charles Stuart Taylor, 1910–89. Educated at Trinity College, Cambridge. MP (Cons.) for Eastbourne, 1935–74. Married, 1936, Constance Ada Shotter: four children. Entered Royal Artillery,

on 28th May, inviting him to seek the agreement of the United States and Canadian Governments to the publication of a document setting out the history of Anglo-American cooperation in atomic energy development under agreements made during and since the war.

The Prime Minister recalled the exchanges which had taken place in the House of Commons since his disclosure on 5th April[1] of the agreement on these matters which he had reached with President Roosevelt at Quebec on 19th August, 1943 (Command 9123). Some Government supporters wished to press the political advantage which this disclosure appeared to have given them, and the present motion reflected the view that the Opposition would not object to the publication of further documents if they thought it was likely to further their cause. The Prime Minister said that he still considered that the publication of the Quebec Agreement had been fully justified for the purposes both of defending the Government against accusations of undue subservience to the United States and of inducing the United States to be more cooperative in sharing information on atomic energy development. Nevertheless, he did not consider that a debate on this private Member's motion would serve a useful purpose at this stage and, if his colleagues agreed, he proposed to take advantage of Sir Charles Taylor's willingness to withdraw his motion.

There was general support in the Cabinet for the view that further public controversy on this matter should, if possible, be avoided.

The Cabinet –

Took note that the Prime Minister would invite Sir Charles Taylor, MP, to withdraw his motion tabled for debate in the House of Commons on 28th May.

[. . .]

Sir Winston S. Churchill to Anthony Eden
Prime Minister's Personal Telegram T.126/54
(Premier papers, 11/666)

25 May 1954
Immediate
Top Secret and Personal
No. 684

Following is text of telegram received form the President today.

'Dear Winston,
    Many thanks for your letter to which I promptly reply. Please suggest

---

1937. Capt., 1939; Maj., 1941. Col., Staff College, 1941. Deputy Lieutenant of Sussex, 1948. Knighted, 1954.

[1] See speech of Apr. 5, reproduced above (pp. 1517–30).

announcement and timing as soon as convenient. I believe it should not name any topics. Am hopeful that you can stay with me at least for the weekend on your arrival and I can also put up an aide-de-camp at White House.
    Looking forward to good talks, I am
    As ever,
    Ike.'

2. We must defer to his wish about not mentioning topics beforehand. It would be better also to keep it all informal and private, and as a proof that differences of opinion can be argued at International Conferences between Allies like Britain and America, without any nonsense about rifts or breaches. It might suit you to come the night of the 20th, but let me know your wishes.

3. I hope the announcement can be made on Friday or Saturday. I will send you a draft which will mention April as the date when the project was first raised.

Anthony Eden to Sir Winston S. Churchill
Prime Minister's Personal Telegram T.127/54
(Premier papers, 11/666)

25 May 1954
Emergency
Top Secret and Strictly Personal
No. 445

    Your telegram No. 684.
    Many thanks for your message. You will wish me to be perfectly frank with you in this matter. I believe that it would be a grave mistake for the visit to be announced before the position here is clearer. Whatever the terms of the announcement, it would, if made now be assumed to be connected with Anglo-American differences about Indo-China. It would be thought that these differences had attained such serious proportions that you felt it necessary to visit the United States yourself in order to compose them.

2. This would put us into a most embarrassing position. And apart from personal considerations it might have a serious effect on the Conference itself and therefore increase those dangers which we discussed together during the weekend.

3. I look forward to seeing your draft of the terms of the announcement though I am less concerned about these than I am about the timing. I feel very strongly that the announcement should be delayed until we have achieved something here or until it is clear that nothing can be achieved. Ten days may decide that.

4. Having been away so much from England you will know how reluctant I am to set out again. But if I am to be with you, do not you think I should be with you all the time in Washington?

Sir Winston S. Churchill to Lady Churchill
(Baroness Spencer-Churchill papers)

25 May 1954

Darling,

The weekend at Chequers was a great success. Diana admirable. Jock in particular was enormously impressed with his long talk with her. Betty[1] came over and played Besique with me. I thought this was what she had played last time, but of course it was then Oklahoma, and she had not played Besique for years. However she had very good cards and held her own. Anthony and Clarissa enjoyed themselves, but poor Clarissa is, as you probably know, too ill to go back to Geneva. The Doctors have diagnosed duodenal trouble. I had very good talks with Anthony and we are in pretty close agreement on the Geneva issues, though of course I want to be very careful not to have a break with Americans. They are the only people who can defend the free world even though they bring in Dulles to do it. There are still hopes of a practical, minor result with an armistice or ceasefire for the local situation. Why are you angry with Bidault? He does not seem to have done anything wrong and is very friendly to us.

We all came up to London after dinner on Sunday and Monday was Payment of Members in the House.[2] It all worked out as I wished and had planned. The Tory Party are said to be very angry but they seem quite friendly in the Smoking Room and considering they were free to do whatever they liked and get paid a monkey for it, I think they will get over any moral sulkiness. I am trying to have the debate on Friday about the Quebec Agreement (about which there was that row in the House) withdrawn, as Attlee made a special and public appeal to me in the House to do so. It is really up his street and I am quite content to leave it there. This really is an intensely busy week. Today after all the excitement of Payment of Members, in which I avoided speaking, I have had Billy Graham[3] for half-an-hour, to see me.[4] He made a

[1] Lady Salisbury.
[2] Referring to the Members' Expenses debate of May 1954.
[3] William Franklin Graham Jr, 1918–2018. Born in Charlotte, NC. Educated at Bob Jones College, Florida Bible Institute and Wheaton College. Married, 1943, Ruth McCue Bell: five children. President, Northwestern Bible College, Minneapolis, 1948–52. Founder, Billy Graham Evangelistic Association, 1950.
[4] As Graham left the meeting, Churchill is reported to have said: 'I do not see much hope for the future unless it is the hope you are talking about, young man.' For an account of this meeting, see Billy Graham, *Just as I Am*, pp. 235–7, and David Aikman, *Billy Graham, His Life and Influence*, pp. 92–3.

very good impression and his latest triumph has been to convert the Archbishop of Canterbury.

I advised him not to allow mundane considerations to bulk too largely in his mission, to stick to the spiritual side. I think he finds anti-Communism a pretty good ally to salvation in the United States. After this quite agreeable meeting I had The Duke of Windsor to luncheon, who looked very well and made himself most agreeable. The American historians are bringing out some beastly documents in their eighth Volume,[1] but they will do no harm and I expect it is only put in to add some sensationalism to what would otherwise be a boring book. Talking of War historians, I have an overwhelming case against the Admiralty historian.[2] He belongs to the type of retired Naval Officers who think that politicians should only be in the Admiralty in time of War to take the blame for naval failures and provide the Naval Officers with rewards in the cases of their successes, if any.

Thursday, alas, I have to address the Women at the Albert Hall – Mrs Emmet[3] in the Chair.

This is a toil which lies ahead of me and I do not conceal from you that original composition is a greater burden than it used to be, while I dislike having my speeches made for me by others as much as I ever did.

Alas, I have had two bits of bad luck. The black swans have hatched out and there is only one alive and swimming about with its parents. One dead one has been retrieved. Vincent[4] has no idea what has happened to the other four. Perhaps they were stolen by somebody who was prowling around. The fox was certainly not guilty. However even one is very attractive riding on its Mama's back. The other piece of bad luck is more serious; Red Winter the Irish horse in whom I have a half share has a chill and is probably unfit to run in the £6,000 race which was one of our principal fixtures next Thursday. I suppose she got to hear that I had to go and address the Women and was offended.

As I have now got out of the debate on Friday on the Quebec Agreement I am able to go to Kempton and I have invited Randolph and June. From Kempton I go down to Chartwell. Maria has just arrived from Frinton where

---

[1] Of *Foreign Relations of the United States, 1940*, which dealt with the Duke of Windsor's contacts with German diplomats in Lisbon in 1940.

[2] The naval historian Capt. Stephen Roskill (1903–82), later a fellow of Churchill College, Cambridge, author of the multi-volume official history *The War at Sea*, in which he wrote, of the sinking of the *Prince of Wales* and *Repulse*: 'It is beyond doubt that Churchill initiated the idea of the two ships going East, and that the First Lord and the First Sea Lord, Mr Alexander and Admiral Pound, strongly opposed it at many meetings of the Defence Committee and Chiefs of Staff Committee. . . . In the end Alexander and Pound gave way' (Roskill, *The War at Sea*, vol. 1, pp. 553–9).

[3] Evelyn Violet Elizabeth Rodd, 1899–1980. Educated at Lady Margaret Hall, Oxford. Married, 1923, Thomas Addis Emmet: four children. Chairman, Conservative Women's National Advisory Committee, 1951–4; National Union of Conservatives, 1955–6. British Delegate to UN General Assembly, 1952, 1953. MP (Cons.) for East Grinstead Div. of East Sussex, 1955–64. Baroness, 1968.

[4] Victor Vincent, head gardener at Chartwell.

she has had very harsh weather but where the children enjoyed the beach and Jeremy wants to plunge into the sea. She and Christopher are dining tonight and everything is going most smoothly in the household.

I have used Miss Portal to put this down for me as I could not possibly have written it with my own hand during these exceptionally busy days. I enclose it in my letter as a bulletin.

Sir Winston S. Churchill to President Dwight D. Eisenhower
Prime Minister's Personal Telegram T.129/54
(Premier papers, 11/1074)

26 May 1954
Immediate
Dedip
Top Secret
No. 2405

My dear Friend,

I shall be delighted to come to you at the White House on June 18 for the weekend. I hope Anthony will come over at the same time.

2. I see no hurry for the announcement until things are clearer at Geneva. Anthony thinks that we should postpone it for perhaps ten days.

Sir Winston S. Churchill to Raymond Triboulet
(Premier papers, 11/671)

26 May 1954

My dear Monsieur Triboulet

I was much honoured by the invitation of the D-Day Commemoration Committee to attend the celebrations in Normandy on June 5 and 6. I am indeed sorry that the great pressure of my engagements prevents me from accepting. It would have given me so much pleasure to be present at the Tenth Anniversary of this historic occasion, and I should be obliged if you would convey my warm good wishes for the success of the ceremony to your Committee.

Sir Winston S. Churchill: speech
('Winston S. Churchill, His Complete Speeches', volume 8, pages 8569–73)

27 May 1954   Conservative Women's Meeting
Albert Hall, London

THE CONSERVATIVES' TASK

As the years go by the process of Government, I suppose in every modern country and certainly in our own, grows ever more complicated and elaborate. The burden thrown on all who take part in it becomes heavier to bear, and more difficult to discharge. So much is going on from day to day and from week to week that it is bewildering to keep track of all that the newspapers set before us, and still more keep a clear and correct proportion of the weight and value of facts and events. I have perhaps a longer experience than almost anyone, and I have never brooded over a situation which demanded more patience, composure, courage, and perseverance than that which now unfolds itself.

As I look at this great Hall, with its audience of serious and responsible women, on whom Her Majesty's Government rely for support, aid, and encouragement, I feel how important is the part you have to play in anxious times. We have lived through terrible wars with honour and success. But even in time of war, the complexity of the problems, mortal though they may be, is not so apparent. The choices open are not so numerous. Events govern and limit what can be done with hard rigidity. Failure closes many doors, and victory gives its own guidance to those on whom it shines.

But in time of peace – modern peace – especially peace after the ravages of war, there is such diversity of aim, such ceaseless clatter and minor turmoil, that efforts as strenuous as any of war and comradeship as loyal and true as we always found them are needed if calm and resolute progress is to be achieved. It is in that mood that I invite you to examine with me in the short time I shall address you this afternoon some of the outstanding facts that confront us and some of the tasks we must help each other to perform.

It is four years since I addressed this gathering with which each year you bring your Conference to a close. When I spoke to you in June, 1950, we were not responsible for the Government of the country. We had faced six years of war followed by five years of Socialist administration. Although the Socialist Government had stood up boldly in military matters, they had most improvidently overtaxed and squandered our already depleted resources. Blinded by partisanship and eager for popularity they had been led into some of the gravest economic and financial blunders by which a modern community can be afflicted. Nationalization has at a great cost been exposed even to its own supporters as the most complete of fallacies. The British people do not want Socialism. The less they have of it the more they will be pleased. The more they have of it the more they will be obstructed and annoyed, and the more their recovery will be delayed. It has been a very expensive lesson.

During the years of Socialist rule we had to live on our capital with our economic position getting worse and worse as the years passed by till finally, in 1951, we found ourselves on the very verge of collapse. Our trading balance was in heavy deficit. We were spending abroad at a rate far more than we were earning. Gold and dollar reserves were pouring out at an alarming rate; the cost of living here at home was soaring relentlessly and the purchasing power of the pound had fallen by nearly six shillings since the war had stopped.

This was the scene, not merely of confusion and extravagance but of wrong thinking and distorted design, which lay before us two years and seven months ago when the electors placed us in office and never, I say, in any period of history which I have studied, was a British Government called upon to face such a conglomeration of evils and errors with powers so impaired and a majority so small. Indeed our majority – only seventeen – was so slender that few there were who thought we could have maintained ourselves in our position, let alone face the vast problems by which we were surrounded. In those days I heard a story of a talk between two Socialist members. One said: 'We'll have them out in six months.' The other replied: 'We had much better let them stay three years and then we shall have some money to spend.'

And where do we stand today? The slender majority sustained by growing conviction and support in the country has shown to the world another form of British stability which has won their admiration and trust. And what of the tangles and confusions which we found? Has there not been a wonderful change, a combination on an immense scale of un-building folly and rebuilding natural health? Let me give some instances.

Take first of all finance. What do we see, and none can refute it? Bankruptcy banished by Butler. Soon after we became responsible the drain of our precious store of gold and dollars was stopped, and for two years we have been steadily rebuilding our reserves. Today they stand once more at over £1,000 million. The outside world, watching our efforts and seeing their results, has regained its confidence in our country. Sterling once again has become a currency which the world can trust. From the shadow of bankruptcy we have advanced to solvency. At home during the past years the cost of living has been very much steadier. Production has achieved new high records and the highest level of employment has been maintained. We salute Mr Butler, the Chancellor of the Exchequer, who has so faithfully and patiently followed the prudent though often unpopular courses which alone made this recovery possible.

There is another Minister you would wish to acclaim. You saw him yesterday. Major Gwilym Lloyd George (Food Minister), bearer of a famous name in our political history. You all know what he has been doing. We made it one of our first aims to get rid of the whole system of controls and restrictions as soon as possible. Major Lloyd George set about that task with a will, and from 4 July we shall all be finished with our ration books. One by one we have freed all the foods covered by the wartime rationing system which Socialists perpetuated in time of peace.

It seems a long time since our opponents used to cheer themselves up by jeering at Lord Woolton and his remarks about 'red meat'. They must look for something else. And what about that target of 300,000 houses which the Socialists said was absurd and impossible? We did even better than that last year and Mr Macmillan told you yesterday that we are going to do better still. At the same time we are building more factories and more schools. I will let you into a secret and I am sure Mr Macmillan won't mind. I will tell you how he got these results. He let the builders get on with the job.

Now we are going to tackle a no less urgent problem. We are going to demolish the slums and we are going to stop houses which are still sound, though old, degenerating into slums. One would have thought that the Socialists would have been able to rise above the envy they must feel at our success even in a field where their failure was so lamentable. I should have thought that there at least was an enterprise in which they could cooperate to help improve the living conditions of so many people. Instead they are making this the subject of a fresh campaign of misrepresentation against us. But time will vindicate our work and reputation.

There is another Socialist cry in the country which should not escape your attention. They say we are wielding a Tory axe to cut the social services. What are the facts? They are that we have improved all the social services and we are spending more this year on them than any Government at any time. That is true of education, health, housing, family allowances, and the whole field of the social services. I trust that you will make these facts widely known in the constituencies to counter the slanders of our opponents. To have made these improvements in spite of the many other heavy claims on our resources is a high tribute to the recovery the country has made under the present Government. Solvency, and yet the social services and education not only maintained but maintained at a higher level than ever before.

I could go on for much longer than I have a right to trespass on your patience. But how has it all been done? Just by hard, patient, steadfast work, without undue courting of popularity, and pursuing the theme which I think I coined some years ago, 'Set the people free.' And this only in little more than two and a half years. When we came in I pleaded that we should not be judged until we had three years' work to show.

I feel most strongly that the Conservative and National Liberal Party have not completed their task. I do not agree with the excitable newspapers who clamour for a premature election. The country ought to be governed by Parliament, and not be always seeking convulsion and change at elections. It is better even for a politician, let alone a statesman, if there are any to be found, to have his eyes on the stars rather than his ears on the ground. Very hard are the trials which lie before our crowded island, with its fifty millions, in the midst of this vast modern world. Only the exercise of its finest qualities, only the fame of its famous institutions, only the native genius of its people and their unfailing instinct will enable us to retrieve the great position which we had in the days of Queen Victoria and to command the comradeship, love, and admiration of the Commonwealth and Empire.

How strange it is to reflect that after two and a half years Britain has gained a reputation all over the world for being the faithful and the skilful friend of peace, and even I, who so often get scolded and abused, now wear a reputation as a seeker after peace which even in Russia would hardly be impugned. And now when I speak about our institution I come to a point where I ought to be rather careful. And here I am going to ask you a favour. I probably will not be asking you many more. It is not to change your opinion but only to consider mine in a friendly spirit. Of course you know what I am coming to. It is this payment of Members. I would like you just to hear what I have to say.

I am sure it is a very bad thing to have the tremendous affairs and responsibilities of the State discharged by men, a large number of whom are themselves seriously embarrassed. It is remarkable that six Conservatives and six Socialists on the Committee studied this question impartially and came to the same conclusion, namely, that there was real and widespread hardship. But I do not think myself we ought to regard this matter as one of compassion to individuals. I am thinking of the institution.

I have spoken to you of the pressures and strains we are under in the modern world. Great provinces have gone from us, stern rivals and competitors have sprung up on every side. But the institutions which this island, free for a thousand years from invasion, has developed within itself, win it a measure of respect and power which we cannot afford to cast away. There is the constitutional monarchy. There is the free system of law and justice and the ancient judicature which are honoured all over the world, particularly in the great republic of the United States without whom I warn you there is no path through our perils; and there is Parliament and the House of Commons.

When I think that our ancient and famous Parliament, which has so proudly confronted our foes for centuries, is now the most harassed and poorly sustained assembly of its kind among all the Parliaments of the civilized world, of which it has been the cradle and is still the model, I am convinced that a long-term and far-seeing view should be taken of these problems, and that Conservatives who are capable of doing so will be helping all or many of those causes that they cherish so dearly in their hearts. I have said I am not asking for your agreement but I do ask for your patient consideration of the facts which I venture to give to you and the course which I have not hesitated to advise.

There is also the question of the old-age pensioners. I have a right to speak of this for as Conservative Chancellor of the Exchequer it was I who reduced the pensionable age from seventy to sixty-five. I can assure you it is our deep desire that this infinitely vaster problem shall be solved in the present Parliament in a manner worthy of British humanity. If so it will be another example of wise and efficient service to the country by the Conservative Party in the true spirit of Tory Democracy.

Let me end on that cause of peace which is in all our hearts, and for which Mr Eden labours night and day. Two of our leading opponents had a bitter quarrel the other day, and one of them, Mr Morrison, said of the other, Mr Bevan, that he had lost the Socialists twenty or thirty seats when he denounced nearly half his fellow-countrymen as 'lower than vermin'. Mr Morrison may well be right about this but whatever advantage we gained from this insulting abuse was more than made up for by the campaign with which Mr Morrison was not unconnected of calling me a warmonger. There indeed a serious injury was done to our Party.

Our supreme policy is peace through strength, and it is our belief that if we pursue this course with steadfastness and courage, building up the strength of the free world while cultivating friendship with all its nations, seeking by every means and with tireless patience to abate tension and spread confidence and goodwill, we shall come safely through this anxious and also dangerous period, and that we may live to see – or you may – the awful secrets which science has wrung from nature serve mankind instead of destroying it and put an end to the wars they were called forth to wage.

Sir Winston S. Churchill to Lady Churchill
(Baroness Spencer-Churchill papers)

28 May 1954

My darling,

Your second letter arrived yesterday morning. I was deeply interested in the account you give of your treatment. It seems very severe. I am looking forward to your next report. Let me know whether Dr Forestier[1] is satisfied. Time passes away very quickly, and three weeks does not seem long for a cure. I hope and pray you are making progress. How is the Hambling[2] getting on? Is she having a stronger or a weaker dose than you?

The weekend party as I told you was most successful, and Diana was a great help. It was followed by a busy week. There is a real row in the Tory Party about the payment of Members, and there is no doubt it is very unpopular. Although it was quite certain that the so-called three Party resolution had a

---

[1] Jacques Forestier, 1890–1978. Born in Aix-les-Bains. On active service, WWI (Légion d'Honneur). Olympic Silver Medal, Men's Rugby, 1920. Married, 1922, Adrienne Japuis: seven children.

[2] Grace Hamblin, Lady Churchill's secretary, who had accompanied her to Aix-les-Bains and was being treated for rheumatic problems.

majority in the House, there is still much difference and confusion about the method, and Rab is much puzzled to know which way to steer.

The 17th is still my date for the aeroplane. Anthony will come too, and we are both invited to stay at the local palace (which will make things easier). I use those terms because one never can be sure what happens to letters in foreign countries in these highly civilized times. Anthony is doing very well at Geneva and seems to be entirely wrapped up in his task. Naturally he longs to have something to show at the end of it all. It will be very necessary to make sure that we do not have a rift. But I think it is going all right.

I began dictating this going down to Kempton where Prince Arthur was running. He was said to have a very good chance, and he certainly galloped ahead of all the others for three-quarters of the way. He then continued to go on at the same or even a faster pace, but the mass overtook him and he came in only fourth. He certainly looks beautiful and has a very long stride. It is thought now he may do better over two miles than over one and a half, and he will run that distance in a race at Ascot. Audrey Paydell Bouverie[1] turned up on the racecourse, having come over from Paris to see her horse run. She was very confident of it. It ran second and as I backed it both ways I was no loser. Randolph and June also came and I think enjoyed themselves.

L'Avengro is still reported to be galloping well. I am going to the Derby on Wednesday; if we are able to finish Cabinet at about 12.45 p.m., there seems to be a general desire on the party of my colleagues to go, and Rab is making a feature of it.

The police have now made a report on the death or disappearance of the cygnets. They say the criminals were carrion crows. The one survivor is said to be very well, and I hope to see him tonight riding on his Mamma's back. The big red fish in the garden pool are threatening to spawn, and I have got the Zoo expert coming over tomorrow to advise how best we ought to handle this very difficult problem. Max is coming to lunch tomorrow, and Violet is coming to stay the weekend. She as giving away prizes at a school about 20 miles from Chartwell, and was delighted to come. Mary and Christopher will, as you know, be staying in the house, and Sarah and her Husband are coming over to lunch on Sunday. We have lots of films and I hope some of them will be good.

I have only given one luncheon party, of eight. It was in honour of Odette,[2] whom Randolph located. He and June came, and so did Christopher and Mary, and I persuaded Betty to come for, I think, her first outing, apart from

---

[1] Audrey Evelyn James, 1902–68. English socialite. Married, 1922, Muir Dudley Coats: one child (d. 1927); 1930, Marshall Field III (div. 1934); 1938, Peter Pleydell-Bouverie (div. 1946).

[2] Odette Marie Céline Brailly, 1912–95. Married, 1931, Roy Sansom: three children (div. 1946); 1947, Peter Churchill (div. 1956); 1956, Geoffrey Hallowes. Allied Intelligence officer in Nazi-occupied France, 1942–5. Imprisoned, 1943; interrogated by the Gestapo 14 times and tortured. MBE, 1945. GC, 1946. Légion d'Honneur, 1950.

Chequers. She can get about on her crutches, though with much difficulty, and of course the lift was indispensable. The party was said to be very pleasant.

Otherwise I have dined & lunched with Christopher or Jock for company, and played a good deal of Bezique. Christopher has a lesson this morning & I shall soon see if he is a good pupil. I am writing in my bed at Chartwell after having a little sleep. I will write to you again Sunday & in the meanwhile send you all my fondest love.

Your ever loving husband
[Drawing of a pig]

PS. 15 stone exactly on your machine but rather battered & very sore eyes.

Sir Winston S. Churchill to Anthony Eden
Prime Minister's Personal Telegram T.131/54
(Premier papers, 11/666)

28 May 1954
Immediate
Dedip
Top Secret, Private and Personal
No. 756

I have received the following telegram from the president:
<u>Begins</u>

> Dear Winston:
>
> I shall be more than happy if Anthony also will be my guest at the White House during your stay there. This should provide maximum convenience for you both. Won't you please inform him as soon as possible that I should be pleased and complimented by his acceptance.
>
> I shall wait to hear from you with regard to the announcement. I agree that there is no hurry about it.
>
> With warm regard, as ever,
> Ike

<u>Ends.</u>

2. Unless I hear to the contrary during the day I shall accept this offer on your behalf. Ike's friendship is very important to Britain.

Francis Nolan¹ to Sir Winston S. Churchill
(Baroness Spencer-Churchill papers)

28 May 1954

Dear Sir,

I should be very grateful if, at the Light Brigade Dinner next Wednesday, you were to defend the honour and military integrity of my granduncle Captain L. E. Babbington Nolan,[2] ADC to General Airlie,[3] who carried the order for the charge. I am his last surviving grand-nephew. My father (an officer in the Durham and Gordon Highlanders) and six uncles and cousins were in the Crimean War. May I give you some information first hand from my father and my cousin, the late Col. J. G. Nolan,[4] RA and MP for Galway for about 45 years (Parnell's[5] staunch friend and defender).

They were both on the spot when Captain Nolan brought the order and heard Lord Cardigan,[6] in a very rude manner, demand to know the contents. My grand-uncle, who disliked Lord Cardigan on moral and other grounds refused his request and Cardigan then threatened him with a court martial if they both came out alive. My cousin saw Nolan, as the Charge started, point to the captured English guns, Cardigan pointed the other way. My grand-uncle was well read in military lore etc.; and both my father and cousin were dead sure that Cardigan was solely responsible for the ghastly tragedy. Please excuse my shaky writing but I am shortly entering my 80th year and a bit infirm from rheumatism.

PS. My mother was a great grand-niece of General Sir John Moore of Corunna[7] and her first cousin, Lady Butler,[8] painted the 'Charge'.

---

[1] Grand-nephew of L. E. Baggington Nolan, who delivered the charge order to the Light Brigade in 1854 during the Crimean War.

[2] Louis Edward Nolan, 1818–54. Born in York County, Canada. Entered British Army, 1839. ADC to Brig-Gen. Richard Airey, 1853–6.

[3] Richard Airey, 1803–81. Entered Army, 1821. Ensign, 34th Rgt of Foot, 1821. Capt., 1825. ADC to Commissioner, Ionian Islands, 1827–30. ADC to Governor, British North America, 1830–2. Lt-Col., 1838. Married, 1838, Harriet Mary Everard Talbot. Asst Adjutant-Gen., 1847–51. QMG, 1851–3. C-in-C of Gibraltar, 1867. Gen., 1871. Baron, 1876.

[4] John Philip Nolan, 1838–1912. MP (Home Rule) for Galway County, 1872, 1874–85; (Irish Parliamentary, Irish National League, Independent Nationalist) for Galway North, 1885–95, 1900–06. Lt-Col., British RA, 1857–81.

[5] Charles Stewart Parnell, 1846–91. MP (Home Rule League) for Meath, 1875–80; for Cork City, 1880–91. Chairman, Home Rule League, 1880–2. Leader, Irish Parliamentary Party, 1882–91.

[6] James Thomas Brudenell, 1797–1868. Educated at Christ Church, Oxford. MP for Marlborough, 1818–29; for Fowey, 1829–32; for Northamptonshire, 1832–7. Entered Army, 1824. Lt., 1825. Capt., 1826. Married, 1826, Elizabeth Johnstone. Maj., 1830. Lt-Col., 1830. Maj.-Gen., 1854. Lt-Gen., 1861. Inspector-General of Calvary, 1855. Succeeded as 7th Earl of Cardigan, 1837. KCB, 1855.

[7] John Moore, 1761–1809. Entered Army, 1776. MP for Lanark Burghs, 1784–90. Maj., 1787. Lt-Col., 1789. Maj.-Gen., 1798. Lt-Gen., 1804. Knighted, 1804. Commanded British forces during Peninsular War, 1807–14.

[8] Elizabeth Southerden Thompson, 1846–1933. One of the few female painters to achieve fame for historical and especially military battle paintings. Married, 1877, Lt-Gen. Sir William Butler.

Sir Winston S. Churchill to President Dwight D. Eisenhower
(Premier papers, 11/666)

29 May 1954
Top Secret, Private and Personal

My dear Friend,

Thank you so much for your message and invitation. We shall both be delighted to stay with you for the weekend.

Sir Winston S. Churchill to Francis Nolan
(Baroness Spencer-Churchill papers)

30 May 1954

My dear Sir,

Thank you very much for your most interesting letter[1] which I have read with great attention. I shall not venture at the 4th Hussars Dinner on Wednesday to trespass on the historical controversy which I have not studied in sufficient detail to attempt to pronounce. I never thought that Captain Nolan's honour or military integrity was in any way impugned. I dare say you have read a very interesting book called *The Reason Why* which has been lately published and has revived all those dramatic episodes. I am sure the Charge of the Light Brigade could never be considered as a 'ghastly tragedy' for its glory has long shone proudly upon the British Army.

Sir Winston S. Churchill to Lady Churchill
(Baroness Spencer-Churchill papers)

31 May 1954

My darling,

We had a jolly weekend. Mrs Landemare[2] distinguished herself as usual. Violet made herself most agreeable, and Mary made everything go well. Sarah came down for Luncheon and dinner yesterday and Antony for dinner. We had three films, of which one, with Danny Kaye,[3] was very lively and laughable, the second *Idiot*, a terrible Russian story, very effectively presented, and the third an American attempt at the same sort of thing, very

---

[1] Reproduced above (p. 1589).
[2] Georgina Landemare, 1882–1978. Cook for Clementine Churchill, 1930s–1953.
[3] David Daniel Kaminsky, 1911–87. Known as 'Danny Kaye'. Born in Brooklyn, New York. Married, 1940, Sylvia Fine: one child. Thirty-three acting credits, including starring roles in *The Secret Life of Walter Mitty* (1947), *The Inspector General* (1949), *White Christmas* (1954) and *The Court Jester* (1955).

grim and ghastly, as if there was nothing in life but infidelity, murder and suicide.

Things are not going too well at your place though there is still a hope of producing something. The Frogs are getting all they can for nothing, and we are getting nothing for all we can. I think my aeroplane journey may be very necessary. Meanwhile at home the MP's salaries or expenses, because the choice is still open, causes much concern, and I am motoring up now to see the executive of the 1922 Committee.

(It turned out all right. 2 hours)

I think we have made the best possible arrangements for the spawning. The Zoo man fully approved. Vincent has planted a lot of little flowering water weeds in the shingle amongst the stepping stones in the shallow part, offering the big fish attractive glades for their approaching honeymoon. During the Whitsun holiday I am going to take the little ones out of the spring pool and put them in the top one of all. I am sure the cold water has kept them back enormously compared to the others, which are really beautiful, and little more than two years old. The garden and the lawns are looking lovely, but the poor pink rhody was sold a pup by that unnatural spring in February which brought so many pink flowers now. Your wisteria trees on the other hand are magnificent. The real injury of the cold weather is to the gunnera. I doubt if it will be half the ordinary size.

There is no doubt that the weekend at Chartwell did me a lot of good. I feel much less tired than when I wrote to you last Friday,[1] although I have had to do a lot of paper work and read a lot of telegrams in the interval. The weather has been queer – 48 hours real heat between 70 and 80, then down to between 50 and 60, and cloudy; and now today, of course, when one is motoring up to London, brilliant sunshine though cool.

I am longing to get your next letter, and hope you will have some encouraging results to report.

I got back here (No. 10) at 6 p.m. after the '22' meaning to play Bezique. But very sensibly I went to sleep instead. Christopher is dining. Duncan flies to USA tonight.

All my love my dearest one. I think of you often amid the daily cares. Your ever loving husband.

[Drawing of a pig]

---

[1] Letter reproduced above (pp. 1586–8).

June 1954

Sir Winston S. Churchill to Sir David Maxwell Fyfe
Prime Minister's Personal Minute M.96/54
(Premier papers, 11/607)

1 June 1954

Where does the responsibility lie for organizing the demonstration of an atom bomb raid prepared for Coventry?[1] Who thought of the blood-stained old woman with the birdcage? I hope there is not going to be any more of this sort of thing at the Government expense. The Coventry City Council of course behaved as badly as they could. The newspapers made an absurd fuss. The one sensible feature is recorded in *The Times*, namely that only 100 adults and two or three hundred children were enticed to attend. This is creditable to the people of Coventry and puts things in their proper proportion.

Anthony Eden to Sir Winston S. Churchill
Prime Minister's Personal Telegram T.137/54
(Premier papers, 11/666)

1 June 1954
Immediate
Dedip
Personal and Top Secret
No. 540

I am becoming increasingly troubled at the international position which may develop about the time of our visit to the United States. The French seem convinced that about June 15 will be their danger period for Hanoi. There is

---

[1] The Experimental Mobile Column (a branch of the civil defence organisation) joined with 3,000 local civil defence units, including the Casualties Union, in Coventry on May 30 to demonstrate and simulate the immediate response to a nuclear strike. Fyfe replied to Churchill: 'The bloodstained old woman with the birdcage was supposed to represent one of the homeless persons attempting to rescue her belongings.'

also only too much evidence here that the main American concern is not now, if it ever has been, for the success of the conference, but with the preparations for intervention.

2. If we take these two things together the result may be that we would arrive in Washington just when the French were in grievous trouble and the American desire to intervene at its height. The call for us to take part in such an adventure would then be intensified and the strain on Anglo-American relations, when we had to decline, could be all the worse.

3. Moreover, there is the problem of the conference itself. I am doing everything in my power to push it along, even at the cost of some criticism from the Americans. But at the pace at which we move, I cannot feel any confidence that we shall have finished our work at the end of next week, even if things go well. We might be over the worst, but we are more likely to be in a dangerous phase. If I were then to leave this work and go with you to Washington wouldn't that seem all wrong?

4. I only put these thoughts to you because they are in my mind as part of the most troubled international scene I can ever recall.

Sir Winston S. Churchill to Anthony Eden
Prime Minister's Personal Telegram T.138/54
(Premier papers, 11/618)

1 June 1954
Immediate
Top Secret, Personal and Private
No. 850

Thank you for your personal telegram No. 614.

2. With reference to 587, below paragraph 5, is it not significant that the Socialist Congress should have accepted EDC at this juncture and that the MRP should have reaffirmed their faith? Do you think there might be any connection between this and no re-arrangement between France and the USA? I had always thought the Americans would stipulate for EDC in any deal.

3. When do you think you are likely to pay us another visit? We too have some worries.

4. Your 540 just received. Reading[1] is dining with me tonight.

---

[1] Gerald Rufus Isaacs, 1889–1960. Educated at Rugby School and Balliol College, Oxford. Married, 1914, Eva Violet Mon: three children. On active service with Royal Fusiliers, WWI. Lt-Col. Commanding Inns of Court OTC, 1923–5; Pioneer Corps Training Centre, 1939–41. Col., Staff, 1941–3. Brig., Director of Labour HQ, 21st Army Group, 1943–4. Hon. Col., Inns of Court Rgt, 1947–59. KStJ, 1948. Parliamentary Under-Secretary of State for Foreign Affairs, 1951–3. Minister of State for Foreign Affairs, 1953–7.

June 1954

Anthony Eden to Sir Winston S. Churchill
Prime Minister's Personal Telegram T.139/54
(Premier papers, 11/618)

2 June 1954
Immediate
Top Secret, Personal and Private
No. 550

Your telegram No. 850.

With reference to paragraph 2 of your telegram, I believe that the Socialist and MRP Congress results were only as expected. I do not think that we can attach particular significance to what happened.

2. As to paragraph 3, I plan to spend two or three days at home over the Whitsun weekend. I hope to see you then, and will send further particulars later.

Cabinet: conclusions
(Cabinet papers, 128/27)

5 June 1954
Secret
11 a.m.
Cabinet Meeting No. 39 of 1954.

[...]

3. The Prime Minister informed the Cabinet that he had suggested to President Eisenhower, towards the end of April, that he might pay a short visit to Washington early in the summer for informal talks on matters of current concern to the two Governments. The President, in assenting to this proposal, had suggested that the visit might be postponed until June, when he would expect to be fully informed of the results of the latest series of atomic tests in the Pacific. The President had also suggested that the Foreign Secretary should accompany the Prime Minister and take that opportunity of further conversations with Mr Dulles. In the result it had been arranged that the Prime Minister and the Foreign Secretary should arrive in Washington on Friday, 18th June, for a series of informal conversations over that week-end.

The Prime Minister said that he thought it important that this opportunity for personal discussion with the President should not be missed. He was specially concerned to take advantage of the President's willingness to discuss the problems created by the development of the hydrogen bomb, and for that purpose he proposed that Lord Cherwell should accompany him to Washington. The other matter which he was specially anxious to pursue with the

President was the possibility of securing some fresh American initiative which would enable us to reduce our military commitment in Egypt.

When these arrangements had been made it had seemed reasonable to assume that the Geneva Conference would be over by 18th June. This now seemed less likely; but it would be unfortunate if this opportunity for personal talks with the President had to be forgone because of the prolongation of the Geneva Conference.

The Foreign Secretary said that it would be difficult for him to go to Washington on 18th June if the negotiations at Geneva had not then been concluded. It would create a bad impression if he appeared to abandon the Conference for the sake of two or three days' discussions in Washington. He would, however, be reluctant to suggest that the Prime Minister should on this account postpone his proposed visit; for personal talks between the Prime Minister and the President at this junction might yield valuable results. On the other hand, he recognised that an embarrassing situation might arise if, while the Prime Minister was in Washington, the Geneva Conference broke down and strong political pressures developed in the United States in favour of military intervention in Indo-China.

In discussion several Ministers expressed the view that it would be unfortunate if the Foreign Secretary were prevented, by the continuance of the Geneva Conference, from accompanying the Prime Minister to Washington.

The Prime Minister said that he would be reluctant to postpone the proposed visit, as the President might be unable to find time for it at a later date. For the present therefore he would prefer to suggest no change in the existing arrangements, under which he and the Foreign Secretary were due to go to Washington on 18th June. Those arrangements could be reviewed in a week's time, in the light of progress made meanwhile at the Geneva Conference.

The Cabinet –

Agreed that a final decision on the proposed visit of the Prime Minister and the Foreign Secretary to Washington could be deferred until their next meeting on 15th June.

4. The Foreign Secretary said that, with the encouragement of the Government of Saudi Arabia, the United States oil company Aramco had sent a prospecting party over the Saudi Arabian border into territory where the Trucial Sheikhs claimed jurisdiction. There was good reason to believe that very substantial amounts of oil might be found in this area, and it was vital to British interests that the American company should not establish a claim to work it. They had no rights in the area, and it was known that their action in prospecting there would not be supported by the United States Government. He had therefore proposed that this prospecting party should be removed from the area, if necessary by force.

The Prime Minister said that, while he agreed that this party should be removed from the area, he had been reluctant to authorise the use of fire-arms

– especially as the British force immediately available seemed to be much smaller in numbers than the intruders. He would have preferred to wait until the prospecting party could be confronted with overwhelming forces, so that recourse to violence might be avoided.

The Foreign Secretary said that, so long as there was no delay in removing this party from the area, he would be quite ready to consider how his proposed instructions could be modified so as to reduce the risk of personal injury to United States citizens. It might be helpful if the Prime Minister could also send a personal message to President Eisenhower asking him to use his authority to recall this prospecting party.

The Cabinet –

Took note that the Foreign Secretary would arrange for the Minister of State to submit for the Prime Minister's approval (i) revised instructions for the removal of the prospecting party sent across the Saudi Arabian border by the American oil company Aramco, and (ii) the draft of a message on this subject which the Prime Minister might send to President Eisenhower.

[. . .]

Sir Winston S. Churchill to Lady Churchill
(Baroness Spencer-Churchill papers)

5 June 1954

My darling One,

I was delighted to get your telegram saying that you are coming home on the 12th. I trust it means that everything has gone as well as you expected. I hope to meet you at the Airport and drive you to Chequers. It is quite possible that Bedell Smith will pay me a visit for the weekend. If he does I will ask Diana and Duncan (if home) too.

Wednesday (2nd) was an active day. Cabinet till 12.30 p.m. Six or eight Ministers wanted to go to the Derby and I said that they were 'under starter's orders'. I went and lunched with the Derbys. It is wonderful how she has got over her terrible wounds. I could see no trace whatever on her neck of the bullet which so nearly severed her jugular vein.[1] I saw Sydney, who is very gay and valiant. Rab confided to me that he had bad news. I do not write it. In the evening we had a further two hours Cabinet about the MP's Pay, about which there is a tremendous petty row in the Tory Party. Rab takes a vehement view that we should conform to the Free Vote of the House, but the general feeling is overwhelming that there should be a compromise. The disadvantage of this is that the Opposition will get about three-quarters of what the House voted.

---

[1] Isabel, Countess of Derby, was sitting alone in the dining room at Knowsley one evening when a footman appeared with a gun and attempted to murder her. There appeared to be no motive; the footman was found guilty but insane.

This they will take and at the same time feel free to throw all the blame on us, saying, as they will be able to do with truth, that it was our scheme.

After that I presided as Colonel at the Fourth Hussars Balaclava centenary dinner. They were all very devoted. Ozier[1] and Tim Rogers[2] were both there.

Today also has been lively. Anthony returned and gave us a full account of the gloomy and confusing prospects at Geneva, where the French are paralysed and the Americans very difficult. The Communists are playing their winning hand with civility. A crisis may arise around Hanoi in the latter half of June. This causes complications with that other date I mentioned to you – the 17th. We shall know more in a week. It may well be that the Conference will end in time for Anthony to come with me. We had a two hours Cabinet on this sombre situation before going on to the more squalid but not less bewildering trouble of MPs' pay. Anthony lunched with me afterwards and we have a very perfect understanding, I think, about everything.

I then rushed off to Hurst Park where we had decided at the last moment to run PRINCE ARTHUR in the *Winston Churchill* Stakes. PREMONITION, who you will remember in the Leger, was 10 to 1 on, and the *Evening Standard* described PRINCE ARTHUR as 'only fit for a handicap'. However we hoped that he would do better over the longer distance of two miles than one-and-a half. He certainly did. PREMONITION is of course one of the best long-distance horses alive and we were 25 to 1. However PRINCE ARTHUR gave a performance which restored his reputation and value. For one thrilling second a hundred yards from home he took the first place; he was third, but even that paid his expenses for a good many months (£144.50). It was very exciting and I was very glad to have gone. An awful row arose between the 1st and 2nd, resulting from a Photo Finish between PREMONITION and her pace-maker which is in the stables same as the Queen used. The pace-maker looked like winning, whereas everything had been staked on the favourite, so the jockey of the pacemaker has been brought before the Stewards for having checked his horse to let the favourite win. One can make too much pace.

I am now on my way back to Chartwell. Christopher came up to see the race and has returned from Frinton. The weather has turned definitely warmer though it has been raining heavily most of the afternoon. (Today, Sunday, cloudy, rainy, windy, bloody). The children at Frinton have enjoyed themselves enormously and Maria consented to let Christopher come back and look after me. We have a film *Cyrano de Bergerac* tonight. I have forgotten the story but I believe it is good. (It was worth seeing). I stay at Chartwell till Tuesday when I come again to Hurst Part to see PIGEON VOLE run in a smallish race; he has a good chance of winning. Thereafter an Audience and

---

[1] John Ogier, 1921–77. Maj., 4th Queen's Own Hussars, 1944. ADC to Churchill, 1945.
[2] Anthony Dyke Darby Rogers, 1921–84. Known as 'Tim'. On active service with 10th Royal Hussars, and ADC to Churchill, WWII. Married, 1965, Sonia Pilkington. Founder of the Airlie Stud in Ireland and Churchill's principal adviser on bloodstock matters.

then an English-speaking Union Dinner with a nine minutes broadcast. I have to come up again for the Trooping of the Colour on the 10th.

Pamela L. came to luncheon on Friday before going to the Fourth of June at Eton to see Grandchildren and the fireworks. She sent you many messages. Her form of arthritis is in the left side and comes on in very sharp pain but only at intervals. She takes potent drugs. I am arranging for her to come to the Trooping of the Colour and bring a Grandchild. She came last year and asked if I could manage it. I am sure it can be arranged.

I have got a new weighing-machine. It stands next to yours in my bathroom. It says I am 14 stone and a half compared to the previous version of 15 stone on your machine and 15 stone & a ½ on the broken-down one at Chartwell. The two in London are to be tested on Tuesday next and if your machine is proved to be wrong you will have to review your conclusions and I hope abandon your regime. I have no grievance against a tomato, but I think one should eat other things as well.

<u>6 June, Sunday</u>

Darling, I rejoice you are coming home on Saturday for a Chequers weekend. Miss Marston[1] arranged with Mrs Hill[2] that the Chequers cook & kitchen maid shd come down here to Chartwell and cook all this week for me, so that I was able to give Mrs Landermere 9 days complete holiday. She was not vy well, and was delighted.

Diana, Celia & Edwina are coming to luncheon. Alas the weather! Also the father swan has got out of his pen and is now on the bottom lake. His wife & child are looking for him, & he tried hard to return. We were vy anxious lest he flies off too. I am going to get up and see what can be done. The anxieties are grievous.

Always your ever loving husband
[Drawing of a pig] 14½ stone (subject to confirmation)
All my love

---

[1] Lettice Marston, 1927–. One of Churchill's secretaries, 1946–53. Married Robert Shillingford.

[2] Rose Ethel Kathleen Hill, 1900–92. Secretary to Chief Commissioner of Girl Guides for All-India, 1930–2. Broadcast as a solo violinist, Calcutta, Bombay and Delhi, 1935–6. Returned to England, 1937. Churchill's first Residential Secretary, July 1937; lived at Chartwell from July 1937 to Sep. 1939. Churchill's Personal Private Secretary, 1939–46. MBE, 1941. Curator of Chequers, 1946–69.

Anthony Eden to Sir Winston S. Churchill
(Churchill papers, 6/4)[1]

7 June 1954

My dear Winston,

Thank you for listening so patiently to the problems of July. As it seems to me, a new administration must have the chance once formed to face Parliament for, I would suppose, at least two weeks before the recess begins.

If it cannot do this, it will not be able to prove itself or receive the vote of Parliament. Moreover if the new govt has not been endorsed by Parliament its authority to take decisions during the recess could be challenged with some justification.

I realize that this may be a more difficult time table for you. It occurs to me that someone like Norman Brook, who is familiar with such problems, might perhaps work out a programme under your direction, which we could then look at together. There is also the point that any new administration should have a fair chance of contact with its officials before the holidays.

Clarissa is better here, I think, but unhappily the duodenum cannot be expected to yield to treatment for some weeks yet. It is all very depressing for her, poor child, & worrying.

Sir Winston S. Churchill: speech
('Winston S. Churchill, His Complete Speeches', volume 8, pages 8573–4)

8 June 1954   English-Speaking Union Dinner

ANGLO-AMERICAN FRIENDSHIP

We are deeply indebted to the Duke of Edinburgh for presiding at this gathering of the English-Speaking Union and for expressing our welcome to General Gruenther in such just and powerful terms. This is a memorable and well-chosen occasion. Ten years ago last Sunday, the greatest expeditionary force that has ever sailed from any shores set out from our South Coast, for the Normandy beaches. A million men owing allegiance to the King were concentrated in a few weeks into the British bridgehead. They were matched by a million American citizens who had crossed the Atlantic like their fathers twenty-seven years before. They had come to help us liberate Europe, and as we hoped *all* Europe, from the grip of Hitler's tyranny and save the ancient civilization from which they themselves had sprung.

Today General Gruenther, standing where Eisenhower stood, commands forces not of two nations only but of fourteen. He also commands the respect

---

[1] This letter was handwritten.

and confidence of us all. He is a wise and skilful leader of a widespread military coalition which has been built up for the defence of law and freedom. We all earnestly pray that he will never be called upon to lead his armies into battle. It is the strength of the organized free world, personified at this great gathering by General Gruenther, with its measureless reserves and resources as yet unmobilized, which give us the right to hope that none will dare assail us.

The English-Speaking Union plays an active and vital part in the whole vast process of bringing the English-speaking nations of the world into unity and keeping them in effective harmony. We are entitled tonight to fix our thoughts on the might, and I think I may say majesty, of the unwritten alliance which binds the British Commonwealth and Empire to the great republic of the United States. It is an alliance far closer in fact than many which exist in writing. It is a treaty with more enduring elements than clauses and protocols. We have history, law, philosophy, and literature; we have sentiment and common interest; we have a language which even the Scottish Nationalists will not mind me referring to as English. We are often in agreement on current events and we stand on the same foundation of the supreme realities of the modern world.

When great and buoyant communities enjoy free speech in the same language, it is not surprising that they often say different things about the confused and tangled age in which we dwell. But nothing must divide us as we march together along the path of destiny. If the world is to be split in twain we know which side we are on and we believe that our unbreakable unity is the core to the safety and survival and to the freedom and peaceful progress of mankind. As I have several times said, our policy is 'Peace through Strength'. There is nothing contradictory in that. In fact I believe the two are inseparable.

When I spoke in the House of Commons on 11 May of last year,[1] Stalin had just died and new minds controlled the fortunes of Russia. I hoped that we should see from them a more realistic and less pedantic approach to world problems. But I added:

> This would be the most fatal moment for the free nations to relax their comradeship and preparedness. To fail to maintain our defence effort up to the limit of our strength would be to paralyse every beneficial tendency towards peace both in Europe and in Asia. For us to become divided among ourselves because of divergencies of opinion or local interests, or to slacken our combined efforts would be to end for ever such new hope as may have broken upon mankind and lead instead to their general ruin and enslavement. Unity, vigilance, and fidelity are the only foundations upon which hope can live.

---

[1] Speech reproduced above (pp. 998–1010).

Nothing that has happened in the past twelve months has made me alter my view that peace through strength must be our guiding star. It is the duty and also the interest of the Communist and free worlds that they should live in peace together and strive untiringly to remove or outlive their differences. Humanity stands today at its most fateful milestone. On the one hand science opens a chasm of self-destruction beyond limit. On the other hand she displays a vision of plenty and comfort of which the masses of no race have ever known or even dreamed. We in the West know which we would choose, but also that we can only reach it at the price of eternal vigilance. While preserving at great sacrifice and cost in building our military strength, we must never lose sight of the importance of a peaceful and friendly settlement of our differences with Russia.

What a vista would be open to all if the treasure and toil consumed on weapons of destruction could be devoted to simple and peaceful ends. It is not only the West who would benefit from it. The people of Russia have had to live a hard and tragic life and the twentieth century has been full of agony for them. They would dearly love the easement and the leisure, the comfort and the diversions, which could be theirs should those who rule them so decide. The English-speaking world, united in itself, and supported by its allies, is an unconquerable force. It asks nothing more than that it should be allowed in safety and freedom to use its wealth, its genius, and its power for the furtherance of peace, progress for all.

Sir Winston S. Churchill to President Dwight D. Eisenhower
Prime Minister's Personal Telegram T.155/54
(Premier papers, 11/666)

10 June 1954
Emergency
Dedip
Top Secret
No. 2680

My dear Friend,

I was very glad to hear through our Ambassador that your invitation to me and Anthony to spend a weekend with you might be postponed for one week, namely from the 18th to the 25th without causing you any inconvenience. This probably resolves the puzzle about whether Anthony could leave Geneva in time. He feels that it is his first duty to play the hand through at the Conference and not to incur reproach for breaking it up by his sudden departure.

2. Like you I feel that the sooner an announcement can be made without complicating Geneva the better and I will suggest a draft for your consideration in my next.

3. I look forward to those talks between you and me which we had always considered an essential part of the vital cooperation of the English-speaking world. I feel that we have reached a serious crisis in which the whole policy of peace through strength may be involved.

Sir Winston S. Churchill to President Dwight D. Eisenhower
Prime Minister's Personal Telegram T.160/54
(Premier papers, 11/1074)

11 June 1954
Immediate
Top Secret
Dedip
No. 2701

My dear Friend,

Anthony suggests that the following announcement which seems to me very suitable:

'Some weeks ago the President of the United States invited the Prime Minister and the Foreign Secretary to spend a weekend as his guests in Washington. The invitation was cordially accepted and it has been arranged for the visit to take place during the weekend beginning June 25.'

2. As to timing I should prefer to make the announcement to Parliament when it meets next Tuesday. This would be at 3.30 p.m. our time, i.e. 10.30 a.m. your time. This is quite agreeable to Anthony from the Geneva point of view.

3. I am so glad it is all arranged and I look forward keenly to seeing you again. Please give my regards to Foster.

President Dwight D. Eisenhower to Sir Winston S. Churchill
Prime Minister's Personal Telegram T.161/54
(Premier papers, 11/666)

11 June 1954
Immediate
Dedip
Top Secret and Personal

Dear Winston,

It is easy for me to make the change of one week and I am particularly glad that this will cause less inconvenience to Anthony. I shall be waiting for your suggested draft of the necessary announcement.

It will be like old times to have a weekend with you. I know that it will be interesting and enjoyable and I am certainly hopeful that it will be profitable for both our countries.

Sir Winston S. Churchill to Anthony Eden
(Churchill papers, 6/4)

11 June 1954

My dear Anthony,

I am not able to commit myself to what you suggest in your letter of June 7.[1] I am increasingly impressed by the crisis and tension which is developing in world affairs and I should be failing in my duty if I cast away my trust at such a juncture or failed to use the influence which I possess in the causes we both have at heart.

Before I can judge the issue I must see what emerges from our talks in Washington, and how they affect the various schemes I have in mind. I am sorry that this may entail a longer period than your letter contemplates. It will not I hope extend beyond the autumn which you mentioned to me as an alternative when we talked in the Cabinet Room last week.

I am most anxious to give you the best opportunity to prepare for an election at the end of 1955 and to establish the repute and efficiency of your Administration. I have however to offer wider reasons than this to history and indeed to the nation.

My personal regard and affection for you will ever weigh with me, and I am always ready to talk these matters over with you with all the frankness which our friendship makes possible between us.

Anthony Eden to Sir Winston S. Churchill
Prime Minister's Personal Telegram T.163/54
(Premier papers, 11/666)

12 June 1954
Immediate
Top Secret and Personal
No. 679

Dulles' charges made in his speech at Los Angeles, raise some important issues.[2] I saw Bedell Smith about them this morning when he told me that

---

[1] Reproduced above (p. 1599).

[2] In the course of this speech, made on 11 June 1954, Dulles had said: 'Last March, after the siege of Dien Bien Phu had begun, I renewed President Eisenhower's proposal that we seek conditions which would permit a united defense for the area. I went to Europe on this mission, and it seemed that there

Bidault had been much upset by the speech but that he had not realized that there was anything of importance left in the speech, dealing with Britain or with me. He had in fact telegraphed some amendments which he understood had been accepted. After some discussion with his staff, it seemed that today's *Times*' report might have been based on an earlier edition of the speech which was handed out separately in Washington. It seems that Dulles not only makes speeches daily but publishes several different texts of his speeches.

2. But these charges must be answered, and I shall have no difficulty in answering them. I am concerned, however, about the timing of my reply in relation to the announcement of our impending visit. I think that it will seem very strange if it is announced that we are going to Washington in the face of Dulles' unanswered charges. In fact, I do not see how personally I could do any such thing. But it does not look like being possible for me to return in time to make a statement in Parliament on Tuesday which is the day now proposed for the announcement. The only course that I can suggest is that the President should be asked to agree that the announcement should be deferred until I can be present in Parliament. It could be explained that this ought not to be later than about Thursday or Friday. It should not be necessary to offer the President any special explanation. I think he would consider it quite natural that I should wish to be in the House when the announcement is made.

3. I saw Molotov this morning and we had an almost wholly negative interview which is being telegraphed to you separately. All the same, this conference is proving difficult to wind up. The Communists clearly want to keep it going, and we have to be careful that the responsibility for the break is not ours. Molotov urged a plenary on Indo-China for Monday and restricted sessions afterwards. I told him I saw little of value in this while we were so divided. I have to go back and see him later tonight or tomorrow, but we cannot refuse a plenary for Monday if they ask for it. Bedell Smith and I are agreed to try to wind things up but we both understand the difficulty of doing this in the absence of a French Government when the French are the principals. Taking all in all, I have never known such a tangle.

4. I do not see how I can do better than try to work for a plenary on Indo-China on Monday, which might be the end of things. We have then still got to wind up Korea which I might leave Reading to do, but even then it would be physically pretty difficult to get to London in time for a statement on Tuesday. Yet I am sure I should make my statement at least on the day of the announcement of the visit, if not before.

5. I apologise for inflicting all this upon you, but what a birthday.

6. Casey has just arrived and is very apprehensive of the steps Americans may yet wish to take to intervene in Indo-China if this conference breaks down. I will telegraph his view later.

---

was agreement on our proposal. But when we moved to translate that proposal into reality, some of the parties held back because they had concluded that any steps to create a united defense should await the results of the Geneva Conference.'

Sir Winston S. Churchill to Anthony Eden
Prime Minister's Personal Telegram T.165/54
(Premier papers, 11/666)

13 June 1954
Immediate
Top Secret, Private and Personal
No. 1083

1. I telegraphed on June 11 to the President the exact proposals which you made to me for the terms and timing of the announcement and I have just received Makins' message that the President and Dulles accept both of these. In these circumstances very grave reasons would be needed to go back on our proposal.

2. I do not feel that what Dulles is reported to have said would justify such a step on my part. As you say he 'not only makes speeches daily but publishes several different texts of his speeches'. I have no doubt you have complete answers to the charges, some of which refer to events nearly a quarter of a century ago and none of which have attracted any attention over here. Indeed I think that the number of speeches and press interviews which are a feature of American public life greatly weaken the individual importance of their pronouncements.

3. I have been told that in diplomacy many difficulties are avoided by ignoring silly or ill-natured points made by other Governments. Even the Speaker (Cat) often says that he has not heard some disorderly or improper remarks and this process is well understood in the House of Commons. The matter might well be dealt with by a communication by Fife Clark to the newspapers or some of them.

4. Of course we should all be delighted if you could be over here on Thursday. I am sure however that the House will not want to hear from you a refutation of this chatter by Dulles and that they very earnestly desire the full statement which only you can make about the Geneva Conference even though it had not given its final croak. The Opposition including Attlee are asking me Questions on Tuesday on this subject and the Foreign Office are preparing a reply, no doubt in close touch with you and your staff. It would be much better if I could say instead that you yourself will be in your place on Thursday and will make a full statement. It might indeed be desirable to give the day to Foreign Affairs and this most important statement to which everyone would look forward. You might or might not think it worthwhile to refer to this particular floater in which Dulles has indulged but I hope you will consider very carefully whether a personal wrangle with your fellow Foreign Secretary in Washington would be a wise feature to introduce into a situation already as you say a tangle such as you have never known.

5. I therefore cannot agree to repudiate my proposal to the President which

was yours and which he has accepted. This would only be raking up a fresh dispute with our only power Ally at the moment when so many differences and divergences of a serious character are alive between our two countries.

6. It might indeed seriously diminish our influence over them on which perhaps maintenance of general peace depends. I therefore feel bound to adhere to your proposal that the announcement should be made in your words by me on Tuesday.

7. A far more serious aspect is that we shall be charged with having been sucked in by the Communists into breaking up the Conference so that they can ensure the doom of Hanoi etc. . . . The Military advice I get is that they are doomed anyway. I agree with Casey's view mentioned in your last paragraph that the breakdown of the Conference may lead to dangerous American decisions about intervention in Indo-China, that is why I am sure that a meeting between us and the President could not occur at a more opportune and even vital moment.

8. I am sorry that all this should be inflicted upon you on your birthday. I hope you got my message wishing you many more and happier ones.

Sir Winston S. Churchill to Anthony Eden
Prime Minister's Personal Telegram T.167/54
(Premier papers, 11/666)

13 June 1954
Immediate
Top Secret, Private and Personal
No. 1089

I am so glad about the Dulles Aunt Sally.[1] Few have noticed it and fewer still have bothered to try to understand it. It would be a very good plan for you to come over here on Thursday, and give the House an hour of the best. I am almost sure I can arrange a day for a Foreign Office Debate. I could pay my tribute later, before dinner, to your perseverance and influence for peace. It might be a good show, and we both I think stand rather well with the Opposition now. Even if you went back to Geneva the next day your visit here would be worth it from every point of view. Dulles, in British public opinion, stands nearly as low as McCarthy, but the latter is better found on TV. Let me know in a single word whether I shall try to book the Thursday. Why should not foreigners wait sometimes instead of only the English or, as the fashion goes, Britons. I am sure D will grovel when we meet him.

The rain never stops and never washes away our cares.

[1] 'Aunt Sally': something set up as a target for disagreement or attack.

Sir Winston S. Churchill to Anthony Eden
Prime Minister's Personal Telegram T.168/54
(Premier papers, 11/666)

14 June 1954
Immediate
Top Secret and Personal
No. 1090

Your telegram No. 689.

I accept and welcome your proposal. On Tuesday therefore I shall read the agreed announcement on the American visit and promise that you will make a statement on Geneva on the following Tuesday and that that day will be devoted to a Debate on Foreign affairs.

2. There is also this pay joke which we hope to settle on the allowance lines at Tuesday's Cabinet and then during the week I will bargain with the Opposition for fair play. Rab has developed a workable scheme which may well ease the Party strain. I understand that it is all being forwarded to you. If not let me know. I will now arrange that the pay scheme should be announced on Monday, June 21 so that Tuesday can be kept clear for you.

3. Please send me an OK.

President Dwight D. Eisenhower to Sir Winston S. Churchill
(Premier papers, 11/666)

15 June 1954
Secret

Dear Winston,

The announcement of your forthcoming visit in the terms you suggested is agreeable to us as well as your proposed time for its release.

Foster and I anticipate seeing you and Anthony with great pleasure.

Sir Winston S. Churchill to John Selwyn Lloyd
Prime Minister's Personal Minute M.106/54
(Premier papers, 11/702)

15 June 1954

What is the foundation for the report in the *Daily Express* about the renewal of talks in Cairo? The Cabinet have authorized no renewal of the talks and I understood from the Foreign Secretary that they were to await the conclusion of the Geneva Conference.

JUNE 1954

Sir Winston S. Churchill to Anthony Eden
Prime Minister's Personal Telegram T.175/54
(*Premier papers, 11/666*)

15 June 1954
Priority
Secret, Personal and Private
No. 1142

If you thought it worthwhile we could return on the *Queen Elizabeth* which leaves New York on Thursday, July 1 and gets to Southampton on the evening of Tuesday, July 6. That would give us a rest and we should miss only two Parliamentary days. We could arrange for a cypher staff on board to keep us in touch. We could keep open the option of returning by air if events made this necessary.

Sir Winston S. Churchill to Lord Beaverbrook
(*Beaverbrook papers*)

15 June 1954
Private and Confidential

My dear Max,

I think I ought to tell you about a point which may arise with the publication in the United States on June 20 of Volume VIII of *Documents on German Foreign Policy, 1918–1945*. The column deals with the period September, 1939, to March, 1940; and as you know, these documents from the archives of the German Foreign Ministry, while most interesting to historians, rarely claim much space in the news columns either in the United States or here.

I enclose three documents from the latest volume which make reference to the Duke of Windsor. As you will see, they are dispatches from the Minister in The Hague who reports that he 'might have the opportunity to establish certain lines leading to the Duke of Windsor' – then a member of the British Military Mission with the French Army Command and 'supposed to be most disgruntled' because he could not have a more active role. The documents are as vague in their references as they are dubious in their authority, which is simply that of a German diplomat trying to show his chief that he was exploring every avenue though unable to report any success along this particular line. Certainly these documents do not seem to me to be damaging to the Duke; but I am a little apprehensive that a few American newspapers who feel malice towards him may build up and distort these references, and cabled summaries may reach the British press.

Though I am inclined to think that the documents are too thin to carry any sort of news story, I thought you would like to be forewarned. I know that if such reports are cabled from the other side, the British press will weigh carefully their strength, including the reliability of their original sources; and as always I should be grateful for your help.

Sir Winston S. Churchill to Anthony Eden
Prime Minister's Personal Telegram T.179/54
(Premier papers, 11/666)

16 June 1954
Immediate
Top Secret, Private and Personal
No. 1147

Your telegram No. 731.

I emphasized your skill today in bringing in a bunch of Asian Powers, i.e. the Colombo lot on our side. This was generally cheered.

2. Camrose will only have a Memorial Service next week[1] so I shall be free on Friday to see you, which I shall look forward to doing.

3. Dulles evidently does not like our White House meeting. What he says counts for absolutely nothing here and the more he says it the more harmless does he become.

4. I should like to have met Molotov again and Chou En-lai for the first time. I have many prejudices to get over about the Chinese.

Sir Winston S. Churchill to Lady Camrose[2]
(Churchill papers, 2/213)[3]

16 June 1954

My dear Lady Camrose,

It is with great personal sorrow that I write to offer you my deepest sympathy in your irreparable loss. I know how you and Bill were devoted to one another, and depended upon each other in all the joys and griefs of human existence. His life and career do him honour achieved by few. His work remains as a living monument which will long endure for the good of our hard-pressed country. But the gap so unexpected must be a terrible agony to his nearest and dearest.

One comfort at least is its very suddenness; and to old people it must seem a blessing that the pain and worry of a lingering death was spared him.

Please accept my most fervent sympathy. I know your courage.

---

[1] Lord Camrose had died on June 15.

[2] Mary Agnes Corns, 1873–1962. Married, 1929, William Berry: eight children. Viscountess Camrose, 1941.

[3] This letter was handwritten.

Sir Winston S. Churchill to President Dwight D. Eisenhower
Prime Minister's Personal Telegram T.186/54
(Premier papers, 11/666)

17 June 1954
Immediate
Top Secret, Personal and Private
Dedip
No. 2800

My dear Friend,
Thank you so much for all the charming things you have said about our visit. The plan is greatly welcomed here. Its announcement may have healthy effects both on French and Chinese.

2. Would it suit your convenience if we stayed to dinner with you Sunday and slept the night at the Embassy? I thought I would stay at the Embassy day and night of the 28th and fly to Ottawa for 29th and 30th, then would stay two nights with Bernie, who has a reporter-proof country house an hour from New York. But these plans are of course flexible.

House of Commons: Oral Answers
(Premier papers, 11/675)

17 June 1954

GERMAN ARMY SURRENDER DOCUMENT (POSSESSION)

50. Mr G. M. Thomson[1] asked the Prime Minister if he will arrange for the original instrument of the surrender of the German Army at present in private possession to be recovered and placed in the national archives.

The Prime Minister: No, Sir, it seems to me that Field Marshal Montgomery set a valuable precedent by retaining in his own hands the original document of the battlefield surrender to him at Luneberg Heath of more than half-a-million well-trained enemy soldiers.

The fact that such trophies will hereafter be the personal property of the British Commander-in-Chief in the field should be an incentive to all young officers in the British Army to repeat the episode on the half-million scale whenever the public interest requires.

I do not think that any addition to the Queen's Regulations is necessary.

[1] George Morgan Thomson, 1921–2008. On active service, RAF, 1940–6. Married, 1948, Grace Jenkins: two children. Asst Editor, *Forward*, 1946; Editor, 1948–53. MP (Lab.) for Dundee East, 1952–72. Minister of State, FO, 1964–6. PC, 1966. Chancellor of the Duchy of Lancaster, 1966–7, 1969–70. Joint Minister of State, FO, 1967. Secretary of State for Commonwealth Affairs, 1967–8. Minister without Portfolio, 1968–9. European Commissioner for Regional Policy, 1973–7. Baron, 1977. Member, Social Democratic Party, 1981–8; Liberal Democratic Party, 1988–2008.

The practice may form part of the unwritten law. Its adoption would in any case be optional.

Mr Thomson: While everybody agrees in paying tribute to the brilliant military record of Field Marshal Viscount Montgomery, may I ask whether the Prime Minister is aware that there will be astonishment throughout the country that the right hon. Gentleman, above all people, with his high sense of constitutional propriety, should defend the purloining by a military leader of a document of surrender which belongs, above all, to all who contributed to the victory? Would not the right hon. Gentleman seriously reconsider the constitutional propriety of the course he is advocating?

The Prime Minister: I have considered the propriety, but I think the course that I recommend is far preferable to the use of the word 'purloining' by the hon. Gentleman which, in my opinion, is grossly unfair and ungrateful to a man to whose great achievements we all owe so much.

Brigadier Medlicott:[1] Is not it clear that the retention of this document by the distinguished officer in question is a small but very well-deserved tribute to one who made an imperishable contribution to our common victory?

The Prime Minister: I may say that had this document not been retained by the gallant Field Marshal it would have passed into American hands and been entirely out of the control of this country.

Mr Stokes: Does the Prime Minister realise the impossible position he is getting us into? Would he say, for example, that Sir Ivone Kirkpatrick would be entitled to keep the original document reporting his own interview with Rudolf Hess?[2]

The Prime Minister: I do not know what that has to do with it. I am sure that if the right hon. Gentleman were to be concerned in any way with procuring the surrender of 500,000 enemies of this country there would be no objection raised to his keeping the receipt for that transaction. But I can assure the House that there is no chance of anything like that happening.

Mr Stokes: No, but the Prime Minister has wilfully misunderstood me. I am not complaining that Field Marshal Lord Montgomery should have a record, but surely the original document should be the property of the nation. While he may be entitled to a copy surely that should be sufficient.

Several Hon. Members *rose* –

Mr Speaker: It is after half-past three and we cannot carry this further.

---

[1] Frank Medlicott, 1903–72. Entered Army, 1937. MP (Lib.) for Norfolk Eastern, 1939–50; for Norfolk Central, 1950–9. Maj., 1940. Col., 1941. Brig. 1943. CBE, 1945.

[2] Rudolf Hess, 1894–1987. Political Secretary to Hitler, 1920–31. Deputy Leader, Nazi Party, 1934–41. British POW, 1941–5.

President Dwight D. Eisenhower to Sir Winston S. Churchill
(Premier papers, 11/1074)

18 June 1954
Top Secret

Dear Winston,

Do you interpret the elevation of Mendes-France[1] and the pledges he has made as evidence of a readiness on his part to surrender completely in Southeast Asia: If this is so, can you give me some idea of your solution to the resulting problems? If you have formulated any thoughts of these delicate matters, I should like to have them so that I can give them some contemplation before we meet.

I understand that you and Anthony reach here about 10 a.m. on Friday. This will be splendid, as both Foster and I are looking forward eagerly to our talks.

Lord De L'Isle and Dudley to Sir Winston S. Churchill
(Premier papers, 11/586)

18 June 1954
Secret

1. You are aware of the generous and well meant suggestion from the Americans that they should provide us with some B.47 bombers by the end of next year. They suggested enough for two wings (i.e. 90 first line aircraft).

2. Having in mind the magnitude of this offer, both as a political gesture and for its military value, I have had it examined most carefully in all its aspects. The Chief of Staff has now reported the outcome. He represents that the disadvantages of accepting this offer greatly outweigh its apparent advantages and that in fact its acceptance has the gravest objections.

3. The reason for this conclusion requires explanation in detail, but I summarize some of the main points below:

(i) It would not be possible to find the aircrews of the requisite experience to man the B.47 squadrons by the end of next year in addition to manning the Valiant Squadrons due to be formed (the B.47 requires aircrews of considerable experience).

(ii) Apart from the aircrew difficulty the RAF has not the resources to form squadrons of B.47 bombers and at the same time proceed with its plan to form Valiant Squadrons. To cancel the Valiants, a

---

[1] Pierre Mendès-France, 1907–82. Left National Assembly to join French Air Force in 1939 at outbreak of war; served until France capitulated in May 1940. Fought with Free French Air Forces until joining de Gaulle's Government-in-Exile in 1941. Imprisoned by Vichy authorities, 1941. Escaped and rejoined Free French Air Force, 1942. French Minister of Economic Affairs, 1944. PM of France, 1954–5.

British aircraft of superior performance, would not be to our advantage. Neither would the rolling up of the Canberra Squadrons, just formed, assist, as these squadrons provide the lead in to the Valiant. There would be Ministry of Supply and political complications in cancelling Valiant and Canberra contracts.
(iii) All our experience leads to the conviction that it is not practicable to maintain complicated American aircraft, such as the B.47, serviceable under US aid arrangements. However generous the spirit of the initial gesture, practical difficulties would prevent our keeping the squadrons serviceable and this will lead to much criticism.
(iv) The B.47 needs longer and stronger runways than our own V bombers and we should have to extend our airfields. Apart from the cost the extension of runways to 10,000 feet creates special political and other problems.

4. I have discussed the American suggestion with the Minister of Defence and you will no doubt wish for further information. We shall have to consider most carefully how to explain to the Americans that this most generous suggestion would not in fact help us.[1]

President Dwight D. Eisenhower to Sir Winston S. Churchill
(Premier papers, 11/666)

18 June 1954
Top Secret

Dear Winston,

The arrangements you suggest are perfectly satisfactory. I would be delighted to have you stay with me Sunday night or at the Embassy whichever you prefer.

Harold Macmillan to Sir Winston S. Churchill
(Churchill papers, 6/4)

18 June 1954
Private and Confidential

Dear Prime Minister,

I have thought a great deal about the matter which you mentioned to me after the dinner on Wednesday. It was indeed kind of you to take me into your confidence. I appreciate this very much.

But I must tell you frankly that, in my view, if a new administration is to

---

[1] Churchill responded: 'Please see that the Minister of Supply has a copy of this at earliest and tell him that I hope to receive a minute from him sometime tomorrow, Sunday, or Monday morning' (M.109/54).

be formed during this year, it would be a very great advantage for Ministers to be installed in their new offices before and not after the summer holidays. Indeed, I think this is really essential. Otherwise, we shall really waste two or three very precious months.

Of course, there may be developments in the international sphere which would override these considerations. You and Anthony must judge these.

I need hardly say that I am not in the least concerned with my own position. But, if someone is to take on my job, the sooner he can start the better. And this applies all round.

Once more, I must tell you how much I appreciate serving you and the support and confidence which you have shown me.

Sir Winston S. Churchill to Duncan Sandys
Prime Minister's Personal Minute M.110/54
(Premier papers, 11/586)

19 June 1954

I have asked the Secretary of State for Air to send you a copy of a minute he wrote me on June 18.[1] Let me know when you receive it and try to give me your views by Sunday night or Monday morning. I also wish a statement for guidance about the bits and pieces promised on which no action was taken.

Sir Winston S. Churchill to Harold Macmillan
(Churchill papers, 6/4)[2]

20 June 1954

Dear Harold,

I received yr letter[3] yesterday morning.

I do not think it ought to have been written except in yr own hand.

I was well aware of your views.

---

[1] Reproduced above (pp. 1612–13).
[2] This letter was handwritten.
[3] Reproduced above (pp. 1613–14).

Sir Winston S. Churchill to President Dwight D. Eisenhower
Prime Minister's Personal Telegram T.197/54
(Premier papers, 11/649)

21 June 1954
Immediate
Top Secret, Private and Personal
Dedip
No. 2883

My dear Friend,

I have always thought that if the French meant to fight for their empire in Indo-China instead of clearing out as we did of our far greater inheritance in India they should at least have introduced two years' service which would have made it possible for them to use the military power of their nation. They did not do this but fought on for eight years with untrustworthy local troops, with French cadre elements important to the structure of their home army and with the Foreign Legion, a very large proportion of whom were Germans. The result has thus been inevitable and personally I think Mendes-France, whom I do not know, has made up his mind to clear out on the best terms available. If that is so, I think he is right.

2. I have thought continually about what we ought to do in the circumstances. Here it is. There is all the more need to discuss ways and means of establishing a firm front against Communism in the Pacific sphere. We should certainly have a SEATO corresponding to NATO in the Atlantic and European sphere. In this it is important to have the support of the Asian countries. This raises the question of timing in relation to Geneva.

3. In no foreseeable circumstances except possibly a local rescue could British troops be used in Indo-China and if we were asked our opinion we should advise against United States local intervention except for rescue.

4. The SEATO front should be considered as a whole and also in relation to our world front against Communist aggression. As the sectors of the SEATO front are so widely divided and different in conditions, it is better, so far as possible, to operate nationally. We garrison Hong Kong and the British Commonwealth contributes a division to Korea. But our main sector must be Malaya. Here we have twenty-three battalions formed into five brigades. You are no doubt aware of the operation contemplated in the event of a Communist invasion from Siam. I will bring the detailed plan with me. Alex, who I understand is coming over in July, will discuss it with your Generals. The question is whence are we to draw reinforcements. There are none at home; our last regular reserves are deployed. It would be a pity to take troops from Germany. On the other hand we have what are called 80,000 men in the Egyptian Canal Zone, which mean 40,000 well-mounted fighting troops. Here is the obvious reserve.

5. Now is the time the Middle East front should be considered together by the United States and Britain. I had hoped more than a year ago that the United States would act jointly with us in negotiating an agreement with the Egyptian military dictatorship in accordance with the terms already agreed between the British and American staffs. It was however felt at Washington that America could not go unless invited. The negotiations therefore broke down. Since then there has been a deadlock though the area of dispute is limited.

6. As time has passed the strategic aspect of the Canal Zone and Base has been continually and fundamentally altered by thermo-nuclear developments and by a Tito-Greeko-Turco front coming into being and giving its hand to Iraq and by America carrying NATO's finger-tips to Pakistan. I like all this improvement in which you and the power and resources of the United States have played so vital a part.

7. These events greatly diminish the strategic importance of the Canal Zone and Base, and what is left of it no longer justifies the expense and diversion of our troops, discharging since the war, not British but international purposes. As far as Egypt is concerned we shall not ask you for a dollar or a marine. I am greatly obliged by the way you have so far withheld arms and money from the Egyptian dictatorship.

8. The general theme of completing and perfecting in a coherent structure the world front against Communist aggression, which I suppose might in current practice be described as NATO, MEATO and SEATO, is of course one, but only one of the topics I am looking forward to talking over with you.

9. The other two have long been in my mind. One is the better sharing of information and also perhaps of resources in the thermo-nuclear sphere. I am sure you will not overlook the fact that by the Anglo-American base in East Anglia we have made ourselves for the next year or two the nearest and perhaps the only bull's eye of the target. And finally I seek as you know to convince Russia that there is a thoroughly friendly and easy way out for her in which all her hard-driven peoples may gain a broader, fuller and happier life.

10. You know my views, already publicly expressed in October 1953, about Germany. If EDC fails we ought to get her into NATO or a revised form of NATO under the best terms possible.

11. I would not have tried to put all this on paper but for your direct request.[1] So if there is anything it which you do not like, let it wait till we are together for our weekend meeting, to which I am so keenly looking forward.

---

[1] See Eisenhower to Churchill of June 18, reproduced above (p. 1612).

Anthony Eden to Sir Winston S. Churchill
(*Premier papers, 11/702*)

21 June 1954
PM/54/98

I have been thinking over your suggestion that we should ask the Americans to join us in negotiating a settlement with Egypt. I see the advantages which it might have politically. But I think I should warn you it may raise some serious difficulties.

First, it would make an agreement much more difficult for the Egyptians. The Americans are not more popular in the Middle East than we are – maybe less so. If Nasser were to accept an arrangement of this kind, he would be open to the charge of having allowed two Great Powers into the Canal Zone instead of one. Moreover, as I mentioned to you, I have some doubts whether admitting the Americans to a share in the supervision of our base installations would make the arrangement more popular at home.

Secondly, there is surely value in keeping control (as we should under the agreement which I propose) over the important staging facilities in the Canal Zone. The Americans will want to make use of these as they did recently in connexion with Indo-China. We should of course let them do so, but it would give us something to gain credit for.

Thirdly, I am apprehensive of the effect in other Middle East countries (especially Iraq and the Persian Gulf) if we appear unable to settle this business for ourselves and have to ask help from the Americans. You will have seen Dulles' recent disagreeable remarks (Washington telegram No. 1217). This makes me anxious that our approach to the Egyptians should not seem to be dictated by the Americans.

On the other hand, we do want support from the United States. I suggest that it should take three forms:
(i) Strong public approval of our new basis for agreement, possibly as an outcome of the Washington talks.
(ii) Some link to be made between American economic and financial aid to Egypt and the agreement reached by us.
(iii) A special public endorsement at the appropriate time of the passage relating to freedom of navigation through the Canal.

I really think that this is simpler than trying to bring the Americans into the negotiations. I cannot believe that the Egyptians would accept the other method and the result might be a setback to the prospect of reaching agreement.

Finally, I believe it is most important that we should give the Egyptians, before we leave for Washington, some indication that we hope shortly to renew negotiations and an outline of the plan we now have in mind. This would also help us to get American support agreed while in Washington and publicly expressed at the end of your talks there.[1]

[1] Churchill wrote here: 'For Cab. on Tuesday, 22nd'.

1618 June 1954

Duncan Sandys to Sir Winston S. Churchill
(*Premier papers, 11/586*)

21 June 1954

OFFER OF AMERICAN BOMBERS

1. In your minute of June 19th[1] you asked for my views about the American offer of B.47 bombers.

2. This proposal probably arises from the fact that the Americans are in danger of producing more aircraft than they will know what to do with.

3. The main arguments in favour of acceptance are as follows:
   (a) The monetary value of the planes offered to us is very substantial. They will cost the United States Government about $400 m.
   (b) The Americans naturally feel that their proposal is a generous one. If we decline it, our attitude may be misunderstood and criticised in the United States.
   (c) By accepting the American B.47's, we would have some medium bombers in service a few months earlier than if we waited for deliveries of our Valiants.

4. The following are the main arguments against acceptance:
   (a) Even if it were practicable, we should not be justified in expanding our bomber force beyond the size now planned. The B.47's would therefore have to be introduced into the RAF in place of, and not in addition to, British aircraft.
   (b) The performance of the American B.47 is inferior in important respects to the British Valiant, of which first deliveries are due later this year.
   (c) If the size of our medium bomber force is not to be increased, the acceptance of over 100 American planes would involve cancelling orders for a similar number of Valiants. We have placed firm orders for 128 Valiants at a cost of about 55 million. The manufacturers are tooled up to produce these over the next 2½ years and some 75 planes are already in the production pipe-line. Consequently the cancellation of all or a large part of the Valiant contract would entail exceedingly heavy nugatory payments and would have most serious effects on the Vickers–Armstrong aircraft works, which are making such an important contribution to our export trade.
   (d) It would not be possible to make room for the B.47's by reducing our force of Canberras, since experience in these light bombers is an indispensable step in the training of air crews for the medium bombers.

[1] M.110/54, reproduced above (p. 1614).

(e) We could not hope to produce sufficient medium bomber crews in time to match deliveries of both B.47's and Valiants. Aircraft would thus be grounded for lack of crews, and this would give rise to criticism both here and in America.

(f) Spares are not included with American aircraft or equipment supplied under the Mutual Aid Scheme, and have to be bought from the manufacturers. Unless, therefore a different arrangement were made for the B.47's, we should be involved in considerable dollar expenditure.

(g) By 1957, the B.47's will be obsolescent and will then probably be replaced in the United States Air Force by a more modern type. We should no doubt have to do the same. This would necessitate increasing our planned production of Vulcans or Victors. The additional expenditure would much more than offset any money saved by cancelling the Valiant.

(h) Moreover, if after only two years we were to scrap the American gift planes, which though obsolescent would still be in good condition, we would probably incur a good deal of criticism in the United States.

5. Taking all these factors into account, I have no doubt that we should decline the offer.

6. If so, we shall have to convince the Americans of the soundness of our reasons. Since this would involve detailed and technical discussion with the Americans, I suggest that it could best be handled through Service channels.

Cabinet: conclusions
(Cabinet papers, 128/27)

22 June 1954
Secret
11 a.m.
Cabinet Meeting No. 43 of 1954

1. The Cabinet considered memoranda by the Minister of State and the Minister of Defence (C(54)187 and 206) on the resumption of the defence negotiations with Egypt.

The Foreign Secretary said that the main points of the proposed new approach to the Egyptians were summarized in paragraph 8 of C(54)187. The essence of the plan was that we should reduce substantially the scope of our Base in the Canal Zone and should be content to have it maintained in peace by civil technicians. In return we could press for an agreement of longer duration: we might begin by asking for twenty years, and might accept twelve years or even ten. And, as we would now propose to remove much more equipment from the Base, we must stipulate that the withdrawal of British troops from the Canal Zone would be spread over two years instead of fifteen months. Draft Heads of an Agreement had been prepared in accordance with the proposals in C(54)187 and 206, and copies of these were circulated at the meeting.

The Minister of Defence said that the minimum military requirements in the Canal Zone were summarized in C(54)206. The Service authorities were now prepared to accept the disadvantages of having the Base maintained by civil technicians in peace. This meant, however, that a larger quantity of stores and equipment would have to be removed from the Base, and this process could not be completed in less than two years. Although there would be military advantage in securing an agreement of longer duration than seven years, it was more important that the evacuation period should not be reduced below two years.

In discussion the following particular points were made:

(a) Was it certain that civil technicians would be available to maintain the Base in peace? The Cabinet were informed that this problem had been discussed with some leading British contractors who were satisfied that they could accept a contract and provide the labour required – though they were not anxious to undertake the responsibility and considered that this method of maintaining the Base would be neither economical nor efficient.

(b) The Cabinet were reminded of the military advantages of transferring the Headquarters organization of the British forces in the Middle East from the Canal Zone to Cyprus. It was important that this move should be carried out as soon as it could be done without weakening our bargaining position in the defence negotiations with Egypt. There was some risk of premature disclosure of our intentions in the Press and the Foreign Office and Ministry of Defence might with advantage prepare an official announcement, to be held in readiness for immediate issue if need arose.

(c) The Chancellor of the Exchequer said that, as soon as the defence negotiations were resumed, he would wish to be free to remove the existing restriction limiting the right of the Egyptians to draw on their sterling balances within the limits of the Sterling Releases Agreement. He hoped that this restriction could be removed before the end of the summer.

(d) On 28th January the Cabinet had asked the Foreign Office and Ministry of Transport to keep under review the timing of further representations to the United States Government regarding the proposal that the maritime Powers should jointly seek from the Egyptian Government firmer guarantees regarding the freedom of navigation through the Suez Canal. The Minister of Transport was proposing to ask the Cabinet to consider this question again in relation to the proposed resumption of negotiations for a defence agreement with Egypt.

The Cabinet's main discussion turned on the manner in which the United States might be associated with the proposed defence agreement with Egypt and on the question whether, before the forthcoming discussions in Washington, any intimation should be given to the Egyptians of our readiness to resume the defence negotiations.

The Prime Minister said that, while he accepted the military argument for redeploying our forces in the Middle East, he continued to be impressed by the political disadvantages of abandoning the position which we had held in Egypt since 1882. This was bound to be deplored by certain sections of Conservative opinion, and the resulting political situation would not be made easier by the developments which were taking place in the Sudan. He believed that our withdrawal from Egypt could be made more palatable to public opinion in this country if it could be presented as a part of a comprehensive Anglo-American plan for building up a defensive front against Communist aggression throughout the world. He hoped that the forthcoming talks in Washington might result in a declaration foreshadowing the creation of a collective defence system in South-east Asia which would displace, or at least reduce the importance of, the ANZUS Pact, from which the United Kingdom had been excluded. Such a development would be welcomed by those sections of public opinion in this country which would be most disturbed by the surrender of our position in Egypt. A close Anglo-American association in the Middle East, parallel with that created in the Atlantic and proposed for South-East Asia, would help to mitigate the political effects of our proposed withdrawal from Egypt. Finally, he considered that our willingness to conclude a defence agreement with Egypt would be a useful bargaining counter in the forthcoming talks in Washington. He did not wish to be committed to resuming the negotiations before he had explored in those talks the extent to which the United States could be persuaded to support us in the negotiations, or even to be associated with us in them.

The Foreign Secretary said that he was doubtful whether the Americans would be willing to join us in the proposed negotiations with Egypt – or, for that matter, whether their direct association with the negotiations would make it easier to reach a satisfactory agreement. Their influence with the countries of the Middle East was not greater than ours: indeed, our own influence in the Middle East as a whole might be damaged if we seemed to be unable to settle our differences with Egypt without American help. The air staging facilities which we hoped to secure in the Canal Zone would certainly be of value to the Americans as well as to us; but there were political advantages in retaining sole rights to these and making them available to the Americans on request. For these reasons he would prefer that American support for our new approach to Egypt should take the form of: (i) strong public approval of our new proposals;

(ii) some link between our new defence agreement and their economic and financial aid to Egypt; and (iii) public endorsement at the appropriate stage of the clause in the agreement relating to freedom of navigation through the Suez Canal. In these circumstances he thought it would be wise if, before he left for Washington, he gave the Egyptians some reason to expect that the defence negotiations would be resumed after his return. He feared that, if he delayed this until after his return, it would be said that we had resumed the negotiations at the behest of the United States Government. This would weaken his bargaining position with the Egyptians and would also cause some political embarrassment in the House of Commons.

The Prime Minister said that, while he agreed that American support in the defence negotiations with Egypt might take the form suggested by the Foreign Secretary, he still believed that some tactical advantage would be lost in the forthcoming discussions in Washington if it were known at the outset that we were now ready to resume those negotiations. He would prefer to keep this issue open until the whole field of Anglo-American co-operation had been explored in the Washington talks.

The Foreign Secretary said that he would consider whether his purpose could be equally met by intimating to the Egyptian Government, before he left for Washington, that he had noted their efforts to maintain order in the Canal Zone and that he hoped that conditions there would continue to improve for as they had already been informed, the defence negotiations could not be resumed while conditions of disorder prevailed in the Zone.

In further discussion of the presentation of the proposed defence agreement with Egypt, the point was made that our strategic needs in the Middle East had been radically changed by the development of thermo-nuclear weapons. This development would of itself have led us to review the expedience of maintaining so large a concentration of stores, equipment and men within the narrow confines of the Canal Zone. Our withdrawal from Egypt could be presented as part of a redeployment of our forces in the Middle East based on a reassessment of our essential strategic needs in that area.

The Cabinet –

(1) Approved the proposal outlined in C(54)187 and 206 for a new approach to the conclusion of a defence agreement with Egypt.

(2) Took note that the Prime Minister and the Foreign Secretary would adopt the draft Heads of Agreement circulated at the meeting as a basis for their forthcoming discussions in Washington on the resumption of the defence negotiations with Egypt and that they would seek to enlist American support, on the lines which the Foreign Secretary had indicated, for the new approach which we proposed to make to the Egyptian Government.

(3) Took note that the Foreign Secretary would consider in the light of the Cabinet's discussion whether, before leaving for Washington, he

should make any communication to the Egyptian Government with reference to the defence negotiations, and would consult with the Prime Minister on the terms of such a communication.

[. . .]

President Dwight D. Eisenhower to Sir Winston S. Churchill
(Premier papers, 11/1074)

23 June 1954
Confidential

Dear Winston,

As you know, I had planned to keep social engagements to a minimum during your stay with me until Sunday night or Monday morning. I think we shall use luncheon and dinner periods for small business meetings, except for Friday evening when I thought a very few members of the Cabinet and their wives should come to meet you and Anthony. At Saturday's luncheon I shall hope to bring in a few of our top legislative people to meet with you for an hour or so. None of this will be formal, but it might be nice to have a black tie for the Friday evening affair. I understand that a group of associates will accompany you and Anthony to Washington. I would be pleased if you would select three or four of them as additional guests at dinner Friday night. I would appreciate your sending me their names.

Sir Winston S. Churchill to President Dwight D. Eisenhower
Prime Minister's Personal Telegram T.201/54
(Premier papers, 11/1074)

23 June 1954
Immediate
Top Secret, Private and Personal
No. 2927

My dear Friend,

I like all your plans very much indeed. I should be grateful if you would invite the following friends of mine to the dinner on Friday:
Lord Cherwell
Lord Moran
Sir Edwin Plowden
Sir Harold Caccia[1]

[1] Harold Anthony Caccia, 1905–90. Educated at Eton and Trinity College, Oxford. Entered Diplomatic Service, 1929. 3rd Secretary, Peking, 1932. Asst Private Secretary to Secretary of State for Foreign Affairs, 1936–9. On staff of Resident Minister in North Africa, Algiers, 1943. Vice-President,

2. I am a tardy riser so I think it would be better for me to leave the White House for the Embassy on Sunday night after dinner.

3. I have a feeling that this meeting to which I have so long looked forward is more timely now than at earlier dates. It may be that our all being together will make other people more careful.

Sir Winston S. Churchill to Sir Edward Bridges
Prime Minister's Personal Minute M.116/54
(Premier papers, 11/602)

24 June 1954

I enclose a minute which the Minister of Agriculture gave me after a discussion with me last night. I agree with his view that public disquiet about some of those censured in the Report[1] makes it desirable that they should not continue in their present duties and that they should be transferred to posts with different responsibilities. Please report to me after consultation with the Minister of Agriculture.

Sir Winston S. Churchill: speech
(Churchill papers, 5/54)

25 June 1954   Upon arrival at Washington National Airport

I have had a very comfortable journey from my Fatherland to my Mother's Land.

I have come with Anthony Eden to talk over a few family matters and try to make sure there are no misunderstandings.

The English Speaking family or Brotherhood is rather a large one and not entirely without a few things, and if we work together we may get along all right ourselves and do a lot to help our neighbours, some of whom – on both sides of the Iron Curtain – seem to face even greater problems than we do ourselves.

Allied Control Commission, 1943. Political Adviser to GOC British Land Forces, Greece, 1944. CMG, 1945. British Minister to Athens, 1945–9; to Vienna, 1950. Chief Clerk, FO, 1949. KCMG, 1950. Ambassador to Austria, 1951–4; to US, 1956–61. GCMG, 1959. GCVO, 1961. Permanent Under-Secretary of State, 1962. Head, Diplomatic Service, 1964–5. Baron, 1965. Provost of Eton, 1965–77.

[1] The Clark Report on the 'Crichel Down affair'. In 1938 the Air Ministry had used compulsory purchase laws to acquire much of the Crichel Down estate, owned by Lord Alington. In 1941 Churchill had promised in Parliament that after the war the land would be returned to its owners. Lord Alington having died on active service in 1940, the estate had passed in trust to his daughter, Mary, and her husband Cdr Marten. When the war ended, the Government failed to fulfil this promise. A public inquiry conducted by Sir Andrew Clark QC in 1954 ruled that the Ministry of Agriculture should resell the land to the Martens at a price they could afford.

John Colville: diary
('The Fringes of Power', page 692)

25 June 1954

On arrival at Washington we were met by Nixon, the Vice President, and Foster Dulles. Winston and Christopher are staying at the White House; I at the Embassy. I spent most of the day at the White House where, on arrival, W at once got down to talking to the President. The first and vast surprise was when the latter at once agreed to talks with the Russians – a possibility of which W had hoped to persuade the Americans after long talks on Indo-China, Europe, atoms; on all these the first impressions were surprisingly and immediately satisfactory while the world in general believes that there is at this moment greater Anglo-American friction than ever in history and that these talks are fraught with every possible complication and difficulty.

The White House is not attractive; it is too like a grand hotel inside. Moreover all the lights burn all the time which is extremely disagreeable at high noon – particularly as the sunshine is bright and the temperature in the 90°s.

This evening, after the official conversations – at which Eden and Dulles were present – the President gave a dinner for the PM to meet the American Cabinet. I was not bidden and went instead to dine with the Empsons,[1] in their garden, by the light of candles and fireflies. To bed, very tired, at 11 p.m.

John Colville: diary
('The Fringes of Power', pages 692–3)

26 June 1954

After a comfortable and delicious breakfast, to the White House for the morning. The PM was closeted with the President, again to his great satisfaction. Christopher and I made the acquaintance of his large staff and also swam in the indoor pool (water temperature 86 degrees). The PM met the leaders of Congress at lunch and (according to his own account) addressed them afterwards with impromptu but admirable eloquence! I lunched at the Embassy with the Makinses. They have delicious food provided by a French chef.

At the White House all the afternoon. Good progress, this time on Egypt. The PM elated by success and in a state of excited good humour. In the middle

---

[1] Charles Empson, 1898–1983. Educated at Harrow and Magdalene College, Cambridge. On active service, 1917–19. Joined Staff of Civil Commissioner, Baghdad, 1920. Consul, High Commissioner, Baghdad, 1924–32. Married, 1931, Monica Tomlin: two children. Commercial Secretary, High Commissioner, Baghdad, 1932–4. Commercial Agent for Palestine, 1934–8. Commercial Secretary, HM Embassy, Rome, 1938–9. Commercial Counsellor, HM Embassy, Cairo, 1939–46. Economic Minister, Special Commission in SE Asia, 1946–7. Commercial Minister, HM Embassy, Rome, 1947–50; HM Embassy, Washington DC, 1950–5. Ambassador to Chile, 1955–8.

of the afternoon meeting, while Christopher and I were sipping high-balls and reading telegrams in his sitting-room, he suddenly emerged and summoned us to go up to the 'Solarium' with him so as to look at a great storm which was raging. I can't imagine anybody else interrupting a meeting with the President of the United States, two Secretaries of State and two Ambassadors just for this purpose. The Russian visit project has now been expanded (by the President, so the PM says) to a meeting in London, together with the French and West Germans, at the opening of which Ike himself would be present.
[. . .]

Record of a meeting
(*Premier papers, 11/702*)

26 June 1954   The White House
Secret

EGYPT

Mr Eden began by giving a brief explanation of the new approach which HM Government proposed to make to the Egyptian Government in the immediate future. He said that HM Government had now decided to put forward a scheme whereby civil contract labour would be used in the base as opposed to military technicians. It had also been decided that we should drastically reduce the size of the base, but that we should still retain certain essential workshops and other facilities. This would mean that we should need longer to withdraw our military personnel and would want two years, rather than fifteen months, for the purpose. But at the end of the two years, under our scheme, there would be no British troops in the base either in or out of uniform.

This was a great concession to the Egyptians and HM Government considered that the agreement should consequently be for a longer period than the seven years previously proposed – for instance, ten or twelve years at least.

Mr Dulles agreed that, in logic, we had a good case for asking for a longer period of duration for the new scheme. So far as the Americans were concerned, their government would be glad if we could obtain the agreement of the Egyptian Government to fifty or even one hundred years. But he was not sure whether this was a case where logic would govern the Egyptian reaction. If the Egyptians did make trouble, he thought that we might overcome their objection in one of two ways. We might point out to them that since we were going to give up half the base in two years, we should be entitled to keep the other half of the base, not only for the seven years previously proposed but for an additional five years. This would make up for the unused bit of the seven-year period available from the half which, in fact, we were giving up in two years. This would give us a total of twelve years for the part of the base which we wished to retain.

Alternatively, would we consider an arrangement whereby the agreement for maintenance of the base was limited to a seven-year period but where the right to return would be of longer duration?

The President at this point enquired whether we had yet put our new scheme to the Egyptian Government.

Mr Eden explained that we had not done so but that HM Ambassador in Cairo had indicated that there were prospects of a move in the near future. Provided nothing untoward happened, it was our intention to act soon after the return of the Prime Minister to London. Meanwhile it was essential that there should be no leak.

Mr Dulles agreed with this and expressed the opinion that our proposal was a 'saleable proposition' and the President asked what HM Government would like the United States Government to do in order to help the negotiations forward.

The Prime Minister explained that his original thought had been that the best form which United States help might take would be for any agreement reached with the Egyptian Government to be between HMG and the US Government on one side and the Egyptian Government on the other. But he recognized that the United States Government had taken the stand that this was not possible unless the US Government were invited to participate by the Egyptian Government as well as by HM Government. There had then been a deadlock. He went on to say that a further idea had occurred to him. It was that if Field Marshal Alexander went out to sign an agreement with the Egyptian Government, General Bedell Smith might visit Egypt at the same time to give moral support. This would not entail any actual obligation for the US Government but it would be a signal means of emphasizing US interest and support.

Alternatively, if the US Government were willing to say publicly that they endorsed our approach, such other methods were not essential.

The President confirmed that the US Government could not actually sign any agreement unless they were asked to do so by the Egyptian Government as well as by HM Government. But they could say privately where they stood, and publicly when desirable.

Mr Byroade, in response to a question by Mr Dulles, said that it was the view of the State Department that agreement was more likely to come quickly if the US Government did not seek to be a party. That idea had already got into the press and the Egyptian Government had volunteered that they did not wish to see direct US participation. Mr Dulles said that, at the time of Lord Salisbury's visit last year, the question had arisen whether US aid to Egypt could be made conditional on a satisfactory United Kingdom agreement with Egypt about the base. He thought that this could not be done in quite that way. But it might be possible to try to maintain the two sets of negotiations in such a way that the final agreements would be made simultaneously. If this was to be done, we should have to keep in the closest touch in order to ensure that simultaneity could be achieved, since negotiations for American aid programmes usually took a certain amount of time to negotiate.

The President, summing up, repeated that the US Government would certainly give such support as they could. If we wished the US Government to say something privately to the Egyptian Government when we put forward our proposals, they would do so. If, later, there was to be a public announcement about the negotiations, the US Government would also be ready to make a public announcement of support. Further, if the negotiations prospered, the US Government would be ready to try to handle their economic (and military) aid negotiations so as to reach a simultaneous result.

Mr Dulles here suggested that the US Government's agreements with the Egyptian Government might point out that one of the reasons aid was being given was that the Egyptian Government, for their part, were providing military bases which would be of use to the West in case of an emergency.

The President endorsed this and said that, as things were, one of the conditions of giving aid was that the country concerned should be prepared to make bases available.

It was concluded that an agreed note should be initialled setting out the programme to be followed by both Governments in their negotiations with the Egyptian Government. This joint note is attached.

John Colville: diary
('The Fringes of Power', page 693)

27 June 1954

All day at the White House except for luncheon at the Embassy. At 10.30 a.m. the President, in his luxurious cinema, showed us *The White Heron*, a film of the Queen's tour.

The Russian project has shrunk again as Dulles has been getting at the President. W still determined to meet the Russians as he has now an assurance that the Americans won't object.

Invited to dinner with the President. Others there were, besides the PM and Eden, Dulles, Bedell Smith, Winthrop Aldrich, Roger Makins, Merchant,[1] Christopher Soames. Very gay dinner, during which the PM and the President spoke highly of the Germans and in favour of their being allowed to rearm. The President called the French 'a hopeless, helpless mass of protoplasm'.

---

[1] Livingston Tallmadge Merchant, 1903–76. Known as 'Livy'. US official and diplomat. Born in New York City. Asst Secretary of State for European Affairs, 1953–6, 1958–9. Ambassador to Canada, 1956–8, 1961–2. Under-Secretary of State for Political Affairs, 1959–61.

Eden took the other line, with some support from Dulles, and ended by saying he could not be a member of any Government which acted as Ike and Winston seemed to be recommending. After dinner we adjourned to the Red Room and worked collectively and ineffectively on the draft of a Declaration – a kind of second Atlantic Charter – which the PM and the President propose to publish. It seems to me a very messy affair.

The PM went to bed at 12.00 elated and cheerful. He has been buoyed up by the reception he has had here and has not as yet had one single afternoon sleep. His sole relaxation has been a few games of bezique with me. Roger Makins said he never remembered a more riotous evening.

Record of a conversation
(Premier papers, 11/618)

27 June 1954   The White House
Top Secret

At dinner at the White House on June 27 Mr Eden reverted to the question of EDC and German rearmament.

2. Mr Dulles repeated that the American military authorities were becoming restive and impatient. They felt that if a start was not soon made with German rearmament, the opportunity of doing it in a controlled and effective fashion might pass, and there were, of course, problems connected with the supply of equipment from American sources. The Pentagon had been given promises by the State Department first that the matter would be settled after the Berlin Conference and then after the Geneva Conference. There was some danger that if the prospect of taking action was put off indefinitely, the concept of peripheral defence would gain headway.

3. The President intervened to say that if the French did not proceed with EDC then they ought to be confronted with the choice of having Germany in the NATO. They should be asked to vote on one side or the other.

4. Mr Eden said that the trouble was that if EDC had been rejected the French would make equal difficulties about Germany's entry into NATO. Some of the French seemed to be under the illusion that Germany would enter NATO while accepting nearly all the restrictions they had been willing to accept in EDC. He was convinced that this was an illusion.

5. The President agreed. He himself had grave anxieties about German rearmament involving the recreation of a German national army and a German general staff. The NATO solution would have to permit both of these and he came back with renewed conviction to the conclusion that there was really no satisfactory alternative to the EDC.

6. General Bedell Smith also agreed. He too was greatly concerned at the prospect of the renewal of Germany military power on a national basis.

7. The President said that every effort must be made to strip the French of their illusions. If they did not come to a decision on the choice between NATO and the EDC in the near future he would regard them as 'a hopeless helpless mass of protoplasm'.

8. The Prime Minister said that if the French could not bring themselves to the point of a decision it would be necessary to proceed without them on the basis of the real elements of strength in the Western alliance. These lay in the United States, in Britain and in Germany.

Sir Winston S. Churchill: speech
(*Premier papers, 11/1015*)

28 June 1954   Press Club Luncheon, Washington DC

I am of the opinion that we ought to have a try for peaceful co-existence, a real good try for it, although anyone can see that it doesn't solve all the problems, but it may be that time, if it is accompanied by vigilance, will enable peaceful co-existence for a period of years, will create a very different situation to the one so full of peril, so doom-laden, as the present one under which we live.

I am most anxious that the real mood of the people of Russia should be known, and that every opportunity should be given for its expression.

The people of Russia have had a very rough time in the 20th century, the century of the common man.

The common man in no country has had a worse time than they have had in the 20th century, with all the bloody struggles in which they have had to engage, in the revolution and the disciplinary measures, internal stresses which have fallen upon them.

I have a sort of feeling – I may be quite wrong, I feel it with my fingertips, that is all I have got in the matter – I have a sort of feeling that there must be a very great wish in Russia to have a better time, among the masses of the people.

I think they would like to have some of the new wealth which science can give to all peoples in the world and to the masses of the people, to have more to eat and more various things to eat, and more and better houses and more knickknacks to put in the houses, and would like to have more cinemas with better programmes and, after all, democracy, once its material needs are met, deserves to have some fun.

So I would like to make quite sure that the Russian people would not feel that they might gain far more by a quarter of a century of peaceful development in their own country than they would by pressing matters to a point where we should all be led to a situation which baffles human imagination in its terror but which, I am quite sure, would leave us victorious, but victorious on a heap of ruins.

So I am very much in favour of patient, cool, friendly examination of what the Russian intentions are.

Now, they say you cannot ever believe what they say, but I do not think anyone wants to put one's foundation on words. A study of their real interests may give a key, a cue, to their intentions which one could trust. At any rate, I would like to make sure, and save the consciences of the democracies of the world, I would like to make sure that no step or stage has been neglected in endeavouring to test the reality and the imminence of our danger.

And, therefore, I am in favour of trying to find out where we are while, at the same time, exercising the strongest vigilance, and making it clear, as we are doing even here now in this building, the unbreakable unity of the English-speaking world of Britain and the United States in all these affairs.

You may some day hear that I have done something or other which looks as if I were going to become a Communist. Well, I assure you, that I have been all my life one of the really prominent people fighting this.

If I had been properly supported in 1919, I think we might have strangled Bolshevism in its cradle, but everybody turned up their hands and said, 'how shocking', and I even remember making a speech at Fulton six years ago, which didn't get a very warm welcome in the United States, because it was so anti-Russian and anti-Communist; but I am not anti-Russian; I am violently anti-Communist, but I do beg you to make sure that no stone is left unturned in this period to give them a chance to grasp the prospects of great material well-being, which will be offered to all those millions, and I am rather inclined to think, if I had to make a prediction, that they will not throw away such an opportunity; but, at any rate, as I say, the conscience of the Western World will be clear only if they are assured that every alternative but a directly hostile policy has been searchingly examined beforehand, and I am quite clear that the fact that we are working together and are known to be inseparable in our brotherhood is going to be one of the factors which will give the impression of strength, without which I am sure peace cannot be preserved.

John Colville: diary
('The Fringes of Power', page 694)

28 June 1954

Meeting in the President's office at 10.00 to discuss the Declaration (in which the PM had suddenly espied some Dulles-like anticolonial sentiments) and the draft minutes on Indo-China, EDC and Egypt. This was a much more orderly affair and was satisfactorily concluded.

At 12.30, having issued a separate and rather colourless communiqué on the subjects that have been discussed, we all set off for the Hotel Stattner[1] to

---
[1] Statler Hotel.

lunch with the Washington Press Club. A disgusting luncheon after which the PM answered written questions that had been handed in with his best verve and vigour. Everybody greatly impressed by the skill with which he turned some of the most awkward. Himself so pleased by his reception that when I leant over to collect his notes he shook me warmly by the hand under the impression that I was a Senator or pressman endeavouring to congratulate him.

After lunch the PM and Eden drove to the Embassy, whither they moved their headquarters this afternoon. I played bezique with a highly contented Winston (in spite of the fact that I won 26,600 in one solitary game), but at 6.00 he was still fresh enough to address, first, the Commonwealth ambassadors and after them the British press representatives. This was followed by a huge dinner at the Embassy, from which I mercifully escaped. I dined with Ed and Sarah Russel[1] at the Colony restaurant. Meanwhile at the Embassy the PM was holding forth about the Guatemala revolution (a current event) and, according to Tony Rumbold, making the Foreign Secretary look rather small in argument (the FS being all for caution and the PM being all for supporting the US in their encouragement of the rebels and their hostility to the Communist Guatemalan régime.) I talked to the PM as he went to bed and he said that Anthony Eden was sometimes very foolish: he would quarrel with the Americans over some petty Central American issue which did not affect Great Britain and could forget about the downtrodden millions in Poland.

John Colville: diary
('The Fringes of Power', pages 694–5)

29 June 1954

A hectic morning for me at the Embassy mainly concerned with arrangements for the publication of the Eisenhower–Churchill Declaration of principles, to which the Cabinet had suggested a few amendments. The PM went down to the White House at 11.30 to settle this and to take leave.

Luncheon party at the Embassy. The American guests were Dean Acheson, Eugene Meyer,[2] Senator Hickenlooper,[3] Mr Sterling Cole (Chairman of the

---

[1] Sarah Consuelo Spencer-Churchill, 1921–2000. Known as 'The Duchess'. Cousin of Winston S. Churchill; granddaughter of American heiress Consuelo Vanderbilt and Charles Spencer-Churchill, 9th Duke of Marlborough. Raised funds for charitable causes during WWII. Married, 1943, Edwin Fariman Russell: four children (div. 1966); 1966, Guy Burgos (div. 1967); 1967, Theodorus Roubanis (div. 1990).

[2] Eugene Isaac Meyer, 1875–1959. Educated at Yale University. Married, 1910, Agnes Elizabeth Ernst: five children. Stock investor and speculator, New York Stock Exchange. Co-founder, Allied Chemical Corp., 1920. Chairman, Federal Farm Loan Board, 1927; Federal Reserve, 1930–3. Purchased *Washington Post*, 1933. President, World Bank Group, 1946.

[3] Bourke Blakemore Hickenlooper, 1896–1971. Iowa State Representative, 1934–7. Lieutenant Governor of Iowa, 1939–42; Governor, 1943–4. US Sen., 1945–69. Co-Chairman, US Congress Joint Committee on Atomic Energy, 1947–9. Chairman, Republican Policy Committee, 1961–9.

Atomic Energy Commission), Mr Whitelaw Reid,[1] Ed Russel. I sat between the latter and Edwin Plowden. After lunch the PM became jocular. He said that if he were ever chased out of England and became an American citizen, he would hope to be elected to Congress. He would then propose two amendments to the American Constitution: (i) that at least half the members of the US Cabinet should have seats in Congress (ii) that the President, instead of signing himself Dwight D. Eisenhower a hundred time a day should be authorised to sign himself 'Ike'.

At 3.30 we left the airfield, seen off by the Vice President and Dulles, in a Canadian aircraft for Ottawa. Mike Pearson, Canadian Foreign Minister, travelled with us. I played bezique with the PM most of the way.

We reached Ottawa at 5.45 p.m. Guards of Honour of all three Services – the band in scarlet and bearskins – 'Rule Britannia' played as a special tribute to the PM, a short broadcast message (written by me), and a slow drive to the Chateau Laurier Hotel.

Dinner in the PM's suite: St Laurent, Howe (Minister of Defence), the Prof, Sir A. Nye[2] (High Commissioner), Christopher and self. Dinner excellent (caviare, etc.). Nye most interesting and agreeable, also Howe. St Laurent dumb and a little glum – possibly even a bit shocked. A most secret subject* discussed with apparent success. Left the party as soon as I could get away in order to record this and to draft a speech for the PM to broadcast tomorrow.

*The American threat to use the atomic bomb in Korea.

R. A. Butler to Sir Winston S. Churchill
Prime Minister's Personal Telegram T.211/54
(Premier papers, 11/667)

29 June 1954
Emergency
Top Secret
No. 3064

The Cabinet were most grateful for the opportunity to comment on the proposed declaration. They warmly congratulate you upon the success of your visit. Yesterday's statement has been well received over here.

We have only one point of substance on the proposed Declaration. We are seriously concerned about paragraph 3 and in particular about its first

[1] Whitelaw Reid, 1913–2009. Educated at Yale University. Married, 1948, Joan Brandon (div. 1959); 1959, Elizabeth Ann Brooks. In mechanical department, *Herald Tribune*, 1938; reporter, London bureau, 1940. Commissioned US Navy aviator, 1941. Returned to *Herald Tribune*, 1946; Editor and Vice-President, 1947; President, 1953; Chairman, 1955.
[2] Archibald Edward Nye, 1895–1967. On active service, 1914–18. Lt, 1916. Maj.-Gen., 1940. Director of Staff Duties, War Office, 1940. Lt-Gen., 1941. VCIGS, 1941–6. Knighted, 1944. Governor of Madras, 1946–8. UK High Commissioner in India, 1948–52; in Canada, 1952–6.

sentence. We assume that this paragraph is mainly aimed at the Satellites but it may also have grave repercussions for the British Empire. You will remember that the same trouble arose over the Atlantic Charter and that your speech in the House of Commons on September 9, 1941,[1] made it clear that even the more guarded words of the Charter did not apply to our Colonial Empire. We have consistently refused to acknowledge anything so vague as a 'right of self-determination'. This Wilsonian doctrine has caused enough trouble in its time and we would not have thought that a Republican Administration would insist upon it. Even President Wilson qualified it in his speech to Congress on February 11, 1918. Paragraph 3 of the Atlantic Charter was much more guarded and so was Article 1 (2) of the Charter of the United Nations. If this right is conceded will it not apply to any separatist movement anywhere? Will it not embarrass us in Cyprus? And what of the position which we have so strenuously maintained at the United Nations with regard to Colonial territories? Its effect in North Africa just at this moment would surely be serious? For all these reasons we think it most important that the Declaration should not contain the words 'uphold the right of self-determination'. We recognise that it may be difficult at this stage to propose a mere deletion. If so, the first sentence of this paragraph might be amended to read: 'we uphold the principles of self-Government and will earnestly strive by every peaceful means to secure the independence of all countries whose peoples desire and are capable of sustaining an independent existence'.

President Dwight D. Eisenhower and Sir Winston S. Churchill: declaration
(Premier papers, 11/667)

29 June 1954

As we terminate our conversations on subjects of mutual and world interest, we again declare that:
(1) In intimate comradeship, we will continue our united efforts to secure world peace based upon the principles of the Atlantic Charter, which we reaffirm.
(2) We, together and individually, continue to hold out the hand of friendship to any and all nations, which by solemn pledge and confirming deeds show themselves desirous of participating in a just and fair peace.
(3) We uphold the principle of self-government and will earnestly strive by every peaceful means to secure the independence of all countries whose peoples desire and are capable of sustaining an independent existence. We welcome the processes of development, where still

---

[1] Reproduced in *The Churchill Documents*, vol. 16, *The Ever-Widening War, 1941*, pp. 1185–96.

needed, that lead toward that goal. As regards formerly sovereign states now in bondage, we will not be a party to any arrangements or treaty which would confirm or prolong their unwilling subordination. In the case of nations now divided against their will, we shall continue to seek to achieve unity through free elections supervised by the United Nations to insure they are conducted fairly.

(4) We believe that that the cause of world peace would be advanced by general and drastic reduction under effective safeguards of world armaments of all classes and kinds. It will be our persevering resolve to promote conditions in which the prodigious nuclear forces now in human hands can be used to enrich and not to destroy mankind.

(5) We will continue our support of the United Nations and of existing international organizations that have been established in the spirit of the Charter for common protection and security. We urge the establishment and maintenance of such associations of appropriate nations as will best, in their respective regions, preserve the peace and independence of the peoples living there. When desired by the peoples of the affected countries we are ready to render appropriate and feasible assistance to such associations.

(6) We shall, with our friends, develop and maintain the spiritual, economic and military strength necessary to pursue these purposes effectively. In pursuit of this purpose we will seek every means of promoting the fuller and freer interchange among us of goods and services which will benefit all participants.

Sir Winston S. Churchill to Lady Churchill
(Churchill papers, 1/50)

29 June 1954

I think we have broken the backbone of our difficulties. I am very well. So glad Woodford was so successful. Off to Canada this afternoon. Hope cure is working. Fondest love.

JUNE 1954

Sir Frederick Hoyer Millar[1] to Sir Winston S. Churchill
Prime Minister's Personal Telegram T.216/54
(Premier papers, 11/678)

30 June 1954
Immediate
Confidential
No. 489

Federal Chancellor has asked me to convey following message to Prime Minister.

Begins.

On reading the Washington Communiqué of June 29, I hasten to express to you the deep satisfaction with which the Government of the German Federal Republic has welcomed the clear position which you and the President of the United States have taken up in regard to questions concerning Western Europe and the Federal Republic. This position is completely in accord with the views of the Federal Government. I thank you most particularly for the further confirmation that the German Federal Republic will take its place as an equal partner in the community of Western nations, where it can make it appropriate contribution to the defence, of the free world.

Ends.

2. Unless requested to the contrary, the Chancellor would propose to release the text of the message tomorrow evening for publication in morning papers of July 2.

John Colville: diary
('The Fringes of Power', pages 695–6)

30 June 1954

The PM and Anthony Eden went to a meeting of the Canadian Cabinet and at 12.00 noon the former addressed the press correspondents. He did not do it as well as in Washington, but it went down all right. Tony Rumbold and

---

[1] Frederick Robert Hoyer Millar, 1900–89. Educated at Wellington and New College, Oxford. Entered HM Diplomatic Service, 1923. 3rd Secretary, Berlin and Paris; 2nd Secretary, Cairo. Married, 1931, Jonkvrouw Anna Judith Elisabeth de Marees van Swinderen: four children. Asst Private Secretary to Secretary of State for Foreign Affairs, 1934–8. 1st Secretary, Washington DC, 1939. CMG, 1939. Counsellor, 1941–2. Secretary, British Civil Secretariat, Washington DC, 1943. Counsellor, FO, 1944. Asst Under-Secretary, 1947. Minister, British Embassy, Washington DC, 1948. KCMG, 1949. UK Deputy, NATO, 1950. UK Permanent Representative on NATO Council, 1952. UK High Commissioner in Germany, 1953–5. British Ambassador to West Germany, 1955–7. GCGM, 1956. Permanent Under-Secretary of State, FO, 1957–61. Baron Inchyra, 1962.

JUNE 1954 1637

I then lunched with Nicholas Monsarrat,[1] author of *The Cruel Sea*, and now Information Officer in the High Commissioner's Office. A gentle intelligent man, he prophesied that in South Africa it might well be that when Malan went, the extremists (Strydom[2] and Donges[3]) would get the upper hand. A republic would be declared, Natal would secede and out of the resulting civil war would come a great native uprising.

The PM would spend most of the afternoon reading the English newspapers so that he started his broadcast (to which I contributed a few sentences) very belatedly, recorded it after we were supposed to have left for the Country Club and in consequence made everything late throughout the whole evening. Our drive to the Country Club, in huge open Cadillacs, was impressive because of the affectionate cheering crowds. The dinner there, given by St Laurent, was also impressive, partly on account of two moving speeches made by the two Prime Ministers and partly because all the Canadian Ministers, etc., present were so delightful. I sat between Campney,[4] from Vancouver, who becomes Minister of Defence tomorrow, and Mr Beaudoin,[5] the Speaker. The latter, a French Canadian, was voluble, sentimental and rather a bore, the former interesting and redolent of that enthusiasm tempered by modesty which distinguishes the Canadians from their southern neighbours.

After dinner we had a tumultuous ovation at the airport and flew in a Canadian aircraft to New York, I playing bezique with a somewhat tired but very triumphant PM. Boarded the *Queen Elizabeth* at 1.00 a.m.

[1] Nicholas John Turney Monsarrat, 1910–79. Educated at Winchester and Trinity College, Cambridge. Married, 1939, Eileen Rowland: one child (div. 1952); 1952, Philippa Crosby: two children (div. 1961); 1961, Ann Griffiths. On active service in WWII. Joined RNVR, 1940. Lt, 1940. Lt-Cdr, 1943. Entered Diplomatic Service, 1946. Director, UK Information Office, Johannesburg, South Africa, 1946–53; in Ottawa, 1953–6. Author of *The Cruel Sea* (1951).

[2] Johannes Gerhardus Strijdom, 1893–1958. Known as 'Hans Strydom'. Born in Willowmore, South Africa. Educated at Universities of Stellenbosch and Pretoria. Farmer, 1912–14. Civil servant, 1914–17. Advocate, Supreme Court, 1918. Attorney, Nylstroom, 1918–34. President, Waterberg Agricultural Association, 1923–9. MP (National Party) for Waterberg, Transvaal, 1929–58. Married, 1931, Susanna Klerk: two children. Minister of Lands and of Irrigation, 1948–58. PM of South Africa and Leader of the National Party of South Africa, 1954–8.

[3] Theophilus Ebenhaezer Donges, 1898–68. Born in Klerksdorp, South Africa. Educated at University of Stellenbosch, South Africa University and London University. Called to Bar, Middle Temple, 1922. Co-Editor, *Die Burger*, 1924–7. Married, 1926, Billie Schoeman: two children. Cape Bar Legal Advisor, 1929–39. KC, 1939. MP (National Party) for Fauresmith, 1941–9; for Worcester, 1948–67. Minister of Interior, 1948–59. Minister of Finance, 1958–67. Leader, South Africa Delegation to UN, 1950, 1951. Cape Leader of National Party, 1954–66. Chancellor, University of Stellenbosch, 1959–68. State President Elect, South Africa, 1967. Author of *The Liability of Safe Carriage of Goods in Roman Dutch Law* (1925); *Municipal Law* (1940).

[4] Ralph Osborne Campney, 1894–1967. Born in Picton, Ontario. MP (Lib.) for Vancouver Centre, 1949–57. Parliamentary Assistant to Minister of National Defence, 1951–2. Solicitor-General of Canada, 1952–4. Minister of National Defence, 1954–7.

[5] Joseph Louis Fernand Rene Beaudoin, 1912–70. Born in Montreal, Canada. Educated at Séminaire de Ste Thérèse and University of Montreal. Called to the Bar, 1935. Married, 1939, Margaret Wespiser (div. 1958): four children; 1958, Alice Margaret Outram (div. 1964). MP (Lib.) for Vaudreuil-Soulanges, 1945–57. Canadian Delegate, UN General Assembly, 1947. Deputy Speaker, Canadian House of Commons, 1952; Speaker, 1953–7.

1638 JUNE 1954

Sir Winston S. Churchill: broadcast
(*Churchill papers, 5/54*)

30 June 1954

It is now fifty-three years since I first came to Canada on a lecture tour after the Boer War.

I was very kindly treated and I have been back several times since.

In those early days your population was a little over five millions.

When I come back to you now it is nearly fifteen millions.

What a tremendous expansion for a man to have witnessed in his life-time.

I knew all your famous Prime Ministers.

When I was an Under Secretary of State I met Sir Wilfrid Laurier and he had with him as an unknown Private Secretary one who became my cherished friend for so many years of peace and War – Mr Mackenzie King.

I had very close and agreeable personal talks with Sir Robert Borden[1] and Mr Bennett;[2] and now I am here at the invitation of Mr St Laurent who is so widely esteemed in his native land and has an influence for good throughout the world.

This morning with my friend Mr Eden and with Lord Cherwell I attended a meeting of the Canadian Cabinet.

This is the third time I have taken my place at that very large and stately table.

As I am a Canadian Privy Councillor, a rather rare bird, there was hardly any secret that your Ministers could not tell me, if there had been time.

But nowadays there is so much to talk about among people who can talk together in real confidence and friendship that I expect there were many things we could not cover in our session of an hour-and-three-quarters.

I also had the pleasure of meeting a strong body of your journalists.

I always get on with journalists.

I suppose it is because I am one myself and they feel we are in the same Trade Union.

I have had a lovely welcome from the people of Ottawa and it is a great comfort and stimulant to me to feel their warm, spontaneous spirit carrying with it approval of much that I have done in a very long life.

I have always enjoyed coming to Ottawa or it might be Quebec or Toronto and have often regretted that as on this occasion, time and pressure have prevented me going further afield throughout your vast domain.

---

[1] Robert Laird Borden, 1854–1937. Born in Grand Pré, Nova Scotia. MP (Cons.), 1896–1920. Leader, Canadian Conservative Party, 1901–20. PM of Canada, 1911–20. Chancellor of Queen's University, 1924–30.

[2] Richard Bedford Bennett, 1870–1947. Born in Hopewell Hill, New Brunswick. Educated at Dalhousie University. MP (Cons.) for Calgary East, 1911–21; for Calgary West, 1925–38. Minister of Justice, 1921. Minister of Finance, 1926. Leader, Canadian Conservative Party, 1927–38. PM of Canada, 1930–5. Viscount, 1941.

But I have been all over Canada in my time and I have most vivid pictures in my mind of many places from Halifax to Kicking Horse Valley and further on to Vancouver.

In fact, I think one of the only important places that I have never visited is Fort Churchill which was named after my ancestor John Churchill,[1] 1st Duke of Marlborough who succeeded the Duke of York, afterwards James II as Governor of the Hudson Bay Company.

All that part of the world is growing in importance, both commercial and strategic.

Nowadays, in fact, a wonderful thing about your country is that there is hardly any part of it where something new and very valuable may not spring to life either on the surface of the soil or underneath it.

It must be very inspiring to all of you and especially to those who have the responsibility of the Canadian Government upon their shoulders, to feel that you are the architects of a mighty structure whose future cannot be measured, but will certainly take its place in the first rank of Sovereign communities.

When all these hopes are fulfilled and all these glories come to you do not forget the Old Land; do not forget that little Island lost among the Northern mists which played so great a part in your early days and now regards you with such admiration and pride.

There is also France to which a strong and ancient element in the Canadian people look with the respect which children should show to their parents.

It must be a pleasure for French Canadians to feel that the bitter quarrels between France and Britain have passed into history and that we have shared our other perils and sufferings as friends and allies in this fearful twentieth century of strife.

I hope that those buoyant, modern pilgrims – I believe that there are nearly a million of them, who have gone forth from our Island shores since the end of the last War to find a new home among you have brought you some knowledge of the place which Canada holds in British hearts.

I can bring you good reports from the Old Country.

Honour and victory crowned our arms in the most terrible struggles the world has seen.

The cost has been heavy in the flower of our race, and in this you too have borne a grievous and splendid part.

It has also been heavy in material wealth and opportunities and very great continuing exertions will be needed from all classes in our country if we are to keep the high rank we still hold in the world.

---

[1] John Churchill, 1650–1722. Commissioned, Foot Guards, 1667. Served at Tangier, 1668–70. Sent with English troops to assist Louis XIV against the Dutch, 1672. Promoted Col. of English Rgt by Louis XIV, 1674. Married, *c.*1677, Sarah Jennings. Lt.-Gen., C-in-C and Peer of the Realm, 1685. Earl of Marlborough, 1688. Commander of English forces during Nine Years War, 1688–97. 1st Duke of Marlborough, 1702.

We are cheered by the comradeship of great and young democracies like the Commonwealths of Australia, New Zealand, and the Great Dominion (if that expression has not become obsolete) who gather around us in their strength and vitality.

We do not fear the future while we advance hand in hand together and in company with the United States.

We are resolved to do our duty whatever it may cost and we believe that we shall not fail.

Let us move forward bound together by those enduring ties of language, literature and law and by those principles of Parl. Government and the rights of the individual which are the characteristics of our civilization in every part of the world where it has been established.

We give thanks to Providence that we have come through so many trials and that in this period of perplexity and danger we have been granted the aid of the gleaming figure who is Queen of Canada and makes us in all lands of the Brit. Common. kinsmen because we are Her subjects and they command the envy and respect of the world.

Au revoir, mes amis Canadiens.

C'est toujours un plaisir pour moi de faire un séjour dans votre pays, que j'ose considerer presque comme le mien. Au revoir et dormez bien: c'est un avenir splendide qui vous attend demain.

Sir Winston S. Churchill to Mamie Eisenhower
(Churchill papers, 2/217)

30 June 1954　　　　　　　　　　　　　　　　　　　　　　　　　　　　　　Ottawa

Dear Mrs Eisenhower,

I am sincerely grateful to you both for the great hospitality you gave me at the White House and for the comfort and luxury which surrounded me. It made our talks so much easier for me and I know how much trouble you took to make my stay the highly agreeable occasion that it indeed was. Being in the bedroom which I know so well brought back many memories and certainly this last visit to the White House, so beautifully renewed inside by you, will remain among the pleasantest and most enjoyable.

July 1954

John Colville: diary
('The Fringes of Power', pages 696–7)

1 July 1954

A milling crowd came on board, Baruch, Giraudier[1] (a Cuban who keeps Winston supplied with cigars and brandy at home) to see the PM, Roger Makins, etc., to see Eden, Henry and Mimi Hyde to see me. Bags, newspapers, letters succeeded each other at confusing speed and all in a heat and humidity which seemed, if anything, to increase as we sailed away at noon, past Manhattan and down the Hudson River.

Lunched with the PM in the Verandah Grill. Oh, the changes that have taken place, in order to please the great dollar-producing clientele, since last we sailed on the *Queen Mary* in January 1953! The Verandah Grill food, which formerly equally or surpassed many famous French restaurants, has become Americanised and has sunk to a level of ordinariness, if not tastelessness, which bewilders and disappoints. The same applies in lesser degree to the service and the appearance of the ship's company.

We went on the bridge after lunch and then I played bezique with the PM till dinner-time. Dined in the Verandah Grill with Lord Moran and Tony Rumbold. Afterwards we saw a series of short films – all American. It is a pity, and rather a humiliating pity, that the Cunard line must go to these lengths to de-Anglicise themselves.

---

[1] Antonio Giraudier. Wealthy Cuban merchant, cigar maker and brewery owner. Met Churchill on the latter's 1946 visit to Cuba and sent him cigars every three months until Churchill's death in 1965, even after fleeing Cuba in 1961.

July 1954

R. A. Butler to Sir Winston S. Churchill
Prime Minister's Personal Telegram T.219/54
(Premier papers, 11/602)

1 July 1954
Immediate
Confidential
Personal
No. 5

CRICHEL DOWN

You will remember that the day you left you sent a minute to Bridges enclosing one from Dugdale suggesting that some of those censured in the Clark Report should be transferred to other posts.

2. We are in some difficulty, since such action would not be consistent with the Minister's announcement on June 15 (approved by the Cabinet) that 'no further action' was to be taken in relation to civil servants. If we decide on postings without some further procedure of a semi-judicial character, many will feel that the Government, having taken its decision in a judicial spirit, has reversed it in response to pressure.

3. The Cabinet have therefore agreed this morning that there should be an immediate enquiry by three individuals. This is not to review the Government's general decision or to go over the ground covered by the Clark Report, but to advise whether in order to maintain public confidence in the administration of the departments it would be reasonable in the public interest and with proper consideration for the position of the individuals affected, that any of these officers should be transferred from their existing duties to other posts.

4. We propose that the committee should consist of Sir Thomas Barnes,[1] the former Treasury Solicitor; Sir John Woods, former Permanent Secretary of the Board of Trade and now in business; and Sir Harry Pilkington,[2] Chairman of the FBI. We have complete confidence in the good sense and impartiality of these individuals, and if transfers are necessary their advice will enable this to be done while at the same time giving Ministers a basis on which they can revise their previous decision.

5. The Cabinet think it essential that we should be in a position to announce the results of this review in the debate. We are therefore obliged to go ahead immediately and I have authorised the committee on the Cabinet's behalf to start work forthwith.

[1] Thomas James Barnes, 1888–1964. Legal Adviser, Ministry of Shipping, 1918–20. Asst Solicitor, Board of Inland Revenue, 1919. Solicitor, Board of Trade, 1920–33. Knighted, 1927. Procurator-General and Treasury Solicitor, 1934–53.

[2] William Henry Pilkington, 1905–83. Known as 'Harry'. Educated at Magdalene College, Cambridge. Knighted, 1953. President, Federation of British Industries, 1953–5. President, Council of European Industrial Federations, 1954–7. Baron, 1968. President, Court of British Shippers' Council, 1971–4.

6. Because the Civil Service post mainly in question (Commissioner of Crown Lands) is a Crown appointment made on the Prime Minister's advice, the committee needs in form to be set up by you and not by the Minister of Agriculture. I trust that you will endorse this action which I have had to take on your behalf. The Cabinet are all satisfied that it is the only wise course.

7. The Committee will sit in private and their existence and findings will not be announced until the debate.

John Colville: diary
('The Fringes of Power', pages 697–8)

2 July 1954

Still very hot. Indeed today and yesterday are more oppressive than any day in Washington. The broken ice has moved further south than usual this year and we are taking the southern Gulf-Stream route.

The PM told me this morning he was decided on an expedition to Russia, where he would ask freedom for Austria as an earnest of better relations. Meanwhile Anthony Eden, who has only come back by sea because he wants to talk over future plans and to get a firm date for Winston to hand over to him, is feeling bashful about choosing the right moment and last night consulted me about this. I thought, and said, how strange it was that two men who knew each other so well should be hampered by shyness on this score. This morning the opportunity came and W tentatively fixed September 21st for the hand-over and early August for the Moscow visit. Returning to his cabin he then dictated to me a long telegram to Molotov proposing talks with the Soviet leaders in which the US would not, indeed, participate but could, W thought, be counted on to do their best with their own public opinion.

We all had a gay luncheon in the PM's dining-room, but after luncheon the fun began over the Molotov telegram. Eden went on deck to read; Winston retired to his sitting-room and had the telegram shortened and amended. He asked me to take it to Eden and to say he now intended to despatch it. Eden told me he disliked the whole thing anyway: he had been adding up the pros and cons and was sure the latter (danger of serious Anglo-American rift, effect on Adenauer and Western Europe, damage to the solid and uncompromising front we have built up against Russia, practical certainty that the high hopes of the public would be shattered by nothing coming of the meeting) far outweighed the pros. However, what he really disliked was Winston's intention of despatching the telegram without showing it to the Cabinet. Why couldn't he wait till we were home and let AE deliver the message to Molotov when he saw him at Geneva? Would I tell W that if he insisted, he must do as he wished but that it would be against his, Eden's, strong advice.

I imparted this to W, who said it was all nonsense: this was merely an unofficial enquiry of Molotov. If it were accepted, that was the time to consult the

Cabinet, before an official approach was made. I represented, as strongly as I could, that this was putting the Cabinet 'on the spot', because if the Russians answered affirmatively, as was probable, it would in practice be too late for the Cabinet to express a contrary opinion. W said he would make it a matter of confidence with the Cabinet: they would have to choose between him and his intentions. If they opposed the visit, it would give him a good occasion to go. I said this would split the country and the Conservative Party from top to bottom. Moreover if he went on this account, the new administration would start with a strong anti-Russian reputation. After a great deal of talk Eden was sent for and eventually agreed to a compromise which put *him* 'on the spot'. The PM agreed to send the telegram to the Cabinet provided he could say that Eden agreed with it in principle (which of course he does not). Eden weakly gave in. I am afraid the PM has been ruthless and unscrupulous in all this, because he must know that at this moment, for both internal and international reasons, Eden cannot resign – though he told me, while all this was going on and I was acting as intermediary, that he had thought of it.

Bezique with W till dinner, which Charles Moran, Tony Rumbold and I had downstairs. Then a film, followed by drinks with Gavin[1] and Irene Astor[2] who are travelling home on board.

Sir Winston S. Churchill to Konrad Adenauer
Prime Minister's Personal Telegram T.227/54
(Premier papers, 11/678)

2 July 1954
Immediate
No. 8

I was so glad to receive your telegram of June 30[3] and to know that the position which Her Majesty's Government and the United States Government have publicly adopted with regard to Germany has earned the approval of the Federal Government. The continued stability, prosperity and friendship of Western Germany are of the utmost importance to Great Britain and to the whole free world.

---

[1] Gavin Astor, 1918–84. Educated at Eton. On active service, WWII. Capt., Life Guards, 1940. Married, 1945, Irene Violet Freesia Janet Augusta Haig: five children. High Sheriff of Sussex, 1955. Deputy Lieutenant of Sussex, 1956; of Kent, 1966. Chairman, Times Publishing Co., 1959–66. President, Times Newspapers Ltd, 1967. Custos Rotulorum of Kent, 1972. Lord Lieutenant of Kent, 1972. 2nd Baron Astor, 1971.

[2] Irene Violet Freesia Janet Augusta Haig, 1919–2001. Married, 1945, Gavin Astor: five children. Lady Astor, 1971. CStJ.

[3] Reproduced above (p. 1636).

JULY 1954

Sir Winston S. Churchill to R. A. Butler
(Foreign Office papers, 800/762)

2 July 1954
Immediate
Top Secret
No. 11

I propose to send this personal and private telegram, with which Anthony agrees in principle, to Molotov. I hope you will like it. The matter is urgent.

Begins.
   Prime Minister to Molotov.
   Secret and Private.
   I wonder how my American expedition has reacted on what you feel about the wish I expressed on May 11, 1953[1] for a top level meeting of the Big Three, and upon the statements I have made from time to time in the House of Commons, that if this were impossible I would seek to make a contact myself with your Government if that were desired by them. It is clear to me that at the present time the United States would not participate, but you have no doubt read the very much more favourable statement made upon the subject by President Eisenhower in his Press Conference of June 30. [Her Majesty's Government do not of course have to obtain permission from anyone in such matters.][2] My feeling is that the United States would make it as good for me with their public opinion as they could.
   2. The question is: how would your Government feel about it? I should like to know before I ask the Cabinet to we make you an official proposal. Anthony Eden, with whom you have had so many friendly talks, would of course come with me. I have never had the pleasure of meeting Mr Malenkov or, as far as I can remember from the war time years, any other of your political colleagues.
   3. I should be very glad if you let me know if they like the idea of a friendly meeting, with no agenda and no object but to find a reasonable way of living side by side in growing confidence, easement and prosperity.
   4. Although our meeting, wherever held, would be simple and informal and last only a few days, it might be the prelude to a larger reunion where much might be settled. I have, however, no warrant to say this beyond my own hopes.
   5. With many thoughts of our war time comradeship, I ask you to let me know, as soon as you can, what you and your friends think.
   Ends.

---

[1] See speech of this date reproduced above (pp. 998–1010).
[2] Struck-through words in this and next para. were marked thus by Butler.

July 1954

Sir Winston S. Churchill to R. A. Butler
Prime Minister's Personal Telegram T.230/54
(Premier papers, 11/602)

3 July 1954
Immediate
Personal and Secret
No. 16

CRICHEL DOWN

I am concerned by your telegram.[1] I feel enquiries by three individuals would, if it became public, expose Her Majesty's Government, not without reason, to charge of being incapable of taking decisions which are their undoubted responsibility and ought to be well within their capacity. We have, of course, full liberty to seek advice and information on technical matters of law or service customary from any quarter, but we are supposed to decide for ourselves what is fair and right.

2. If as now appears, the Cabinet feel no further action, punitive or other, should be taken in relation to civil servants whose conduct is the cause of so much public wrath, we rest on the fact that the Minister has declared that he himself will bear the whole responsibility. This is a high and dignified line for him to take. It was in the hope of avoiding its implication that I wrote my minute to Bridges[2] which, you now tell me, produces no means of escape.

3. I should find it very difficult to sign a submission to the Crown for the appointment of the committee. Surely it must be kept informal and unofficial? We should welcome the benefit of their advice but have not need to invoke the shield of their authority.

John Colville: diary
('The Fringes of Power', pages 698–9)

3 July 1954

Cooler. Atlantic breezes instead of the Gulf Stream. Worked with W most of the morning and composed telegrams, descriptive of the Washington talks, to Menzies and Holland which the PM accepted. Drinks with the Astors before luncheon, which we had in the PM's dining-room with Charles Moran, Christopher and the Prof. The latter was in his best anecdotal form. I liked his apocryphal story of Victor Cazalet[3] and Lady Colefax having a race after an

[1] T.219/54, reproduced above (pp. 1642–3).
[2] M.116/54, reproduced above (p. 1624).
[3] Victor Alexander Cazalet, 1896–1943. Educated at Eton and Christ Church, Oxford. On active service, WWI, 1915–18 (MC). Member of Gen. Knox's staff in Siberia, 1918–19. MP (Cons.) for

electric lion. Victor won because Lady Colefax would keep on stopping to tell the public she had known the lion as a cub.

After lunch I succeeded in getting away with only one game of bezique and making Christopher take over. Saw Eden this morning. Got the impression he was aggrieved with W. which I don't find surprising. W, on the other hand, complains to me that he was trapped into sending the telegram to the Cabinet, had forgotten it was the weekend, and now he wouldn't get a reply till Monday. So he telegraphed to Rab saying that he assumed the telegram had already gone on to Moscow.

Dined in the Verandah Grill with the Astors and Tony Rumbold. Then joined the PM and Eden. The former was now quite reconciled to the Cabinet having been consulted about the Molotov telegram because Rab had telegraphed suggesting only one or two small amendments and had appeared generally satisfied with the main idea. So everybody went to bed happy and W and I played bezique, to my great financial advantage (six grands coups!) till nearly 2.00 a.m.

Sarah and Antony Beauchamp to Sir Winston S. Churchill
(Churchill papers, 1/50)

3 July 1954   RMS *Queen Elizabeth*

Bon voyage! It was a dazzling success with great impact on public opinion. All reactions indicate you were at peak form. Wish we could have been with you. Will be following shortly. All our love to you and chimp.[1]

R. A. Butler to Sir Winston S. Churchill
Prime Minister's Personal Telegram T.242/54
(Premier papers, 11/602)

4 July 1954
Immediate
Personal and Secret
No. 39

Your telegram No. 16. Crichel Down.[2]

I will send you a further message tomorrow Monday after comparing notes with those chiefly involved. I hope then to put the picture before you in better focus than I appear to have done hitherto.

Chippenham, 1924–43. Parliamentary Secretary, Board of Trade, 1924–6. Political Liaison Officer to Gen. Sikorski, 1940–3. Died in air crash.

[1] Churchill wrote underneath: 'Thank you so much darling! I wish we could have seen you.'

[2] T.230/54, reproduced above (p. 1646).

2. Meanwhile it may ease your mind to know that there is no question of your having to sign a submission to the Crown about this group of individuals which is advisory in capacity.

3. When you return, in addition to anything I send to the boat, I shall be able to tell you of some important aspects of this problem which have arisen since you left. The debate will not take place till the week after your return. Meanwhile I am satisfied we are steering the best course under the circumstances.

John Colville: diary
('The Fringes of Power', pages 699–700)

4 July 1954

The PM deep in Harold Nicolson's *Public Faces* and greatly impressed by the 1932 prophecy of atomic bombs. Went to church, which was packed. Then descended to the profane and played bezique till luncheon. The Astors, Christopher and I lunched with the PM who was in splendid form, describing the heart trouble he developed in consequence of dancing a *pas seul* after dinner at Blenheim some fifty years ago, elaborating the desirable results which would come from re-establishing the Heptarchy[1] in England (so as to ease the pressure on Parliament) and teaching Gavin, a non-smoker, to smoke cigars.

A Turkish bath this evening, followed by dinner with the Astors and Adrian Bailey[2] in the Verandah Grill, a cinema and a blood row between Winston and Anthony Eden. This arose in the following way. I went down about 11.30 to see how their dinner party (WSC, AE, the Prof, Moran, Christopher) was getting on. Everybody very jovial when suddenly Miss Gilliatt brought me a telegram from Roger Makins about the effects in America of a speech made by Senator Knowland,[3] who has evidently implied that we have been pressing the Americans to let Red China into UNO and has said that if this happens, the United States will leave the Organisation. Eden read the telegram first and said that he objected to HMG saying anything in reply to Knowland: it looked as if we minded. The PM then read it and wanted to issue a statement from this ship to the effect, first, that the matter had not been seriously discussed during the Washington talks and secondly that there was no question of our

[1] The seven kingdoms of Anglo-Saxon England (Northumbria, Mercia, East Anglia, Essex, Kent, Wessex and Sussex) before their union under a single monarch in the tenth century.

[2] John Adrian Bailey, 1930–?. Glass company director. Married, 1954, Mary Baillie-Hamilton (div. 1965): three children.

[3] William Fife Knowland, 1908–74. Educated at University of California, Berkeley. Married, 1926, Helen Davis Herrick (div. 1972): three children; 1972, Ann Dickson. Member (Rep.), California State Assembly, 1932; California State Senate, 1934–8. Chairman, Executive Committee, Rep. National Committee, 1940–2. 2nd Lt, 1942. Maj., 1945. Senator (Rep.) for California, 1945–59. Senate Majority Leader, 1953–5. Senate Minority Leader, 1955–9. Leader, California Republican Party, 1959–67. President, Editor and Publisher, *Oakland Tribune*, 1966–77.

recognising Red China while she was still in a state of war with the United Nations.

Eden said that if we made any such statement it would destroy all chance of success at Geneva: we ought to keep entry into UNO as a reward for China if she were good. The PM looked grave: he had not realised, he said, that what Knowland said was in fact the truth – Eden *did* contemplate the admission of China into UNO while a state of war still existed. Eden got red in the face with anger and there was a disagreeable scene. They both went to bed in a combination of sorrow and anger, the PM saying that Anthony was totally incapable of differentiating great points and small points (a criticism that has an element of truth in it).

Christopher and I then went to the Verandah Grill with Gavin and Rene, Tony Rumbold and two American girls. We danced and drank champagne till nearly 4.00 a.m.

John Colville: diary
('The Fringes of Power', page 700)

5 July 1954

The PM looked still grave and depressed this morning and dictated to me a minute about the Knowland question. Anthony Eden did not wake up till 12.00, but he seemed to have recovered his equanimity and was cheerful when I handed the minute to him. We lunched in the PM's dining-room (he staying in bed). In the afternoon I talked to Rene on deck, played bezique and at 6.30 there was a small cocktail party for fellow passengers given by the PM and Mr Eden.

We all dined in the PM's dining-room. It was a most amicable occasion, last night's differences resolved and the PM saying that provided AE always bore in mind the importance of not quarrelling violently with the Americans over Far Eastern questions (which affected them more than us) a way ought certainly to be found of bringing Red China into the United Nations on terms tolerable to the USA. This was followed by much quoting of Pope, Shakespeare and others on the PM's part and a dissertation on Persian and Arabic poets and writing by Eden (who apparently got a First in Oriental Languages at Oxford.) To bed at 2.00.

1650 JULY 1954

Sir Winston S. Churchill to President Dwight D. Eisenhower
Prime Minister's Personal Telegram T.246/54
(Premier papers, 11/1074)

7 July 1954
Emergency
Top Secret, Private and Personal
No. 3209

Dear Friend,

1. In the light of our talks and after careful thought I thought it right to send an exploratory message to Molotov to feel the ground about the possibility of a Two Power Meeting. This of course committed nobody except myself. The following is a summary of my message.

> (Begins) After referring to my speech of May 11, 1953 for a top level meeting of the Big Three, and to the statements I have made from time to time in the House of Commons, that if this were impossible I would seek to make a contact myself with the Soviet Government, I put the question, how would they feel about it. I should like to know this, I said, before we made any official proposal, or considered such questions as the time and place. I went on, 'I should be very glad if you would let me know if you would like the idea of a friendly meeting, with no agenda and no object but to find a reasonable way of living side by side in growing confidence, easement and prosperity. Although our meeting, wherever held, would be simple and informal and last only a few days, it might be the prelude to a wider reunion where much might be settled. I have, however, no warrant to say this beyond my own hopes. I ask you to let me know, as soon as you can, what you and your friends think.' (Ends)

2. This evening I received an answer from Molotov, which I send you textually. I should like to know how this strikes you.

> (Begins) I express my gratitude for your important message handed to me by Ambassador Hayter on the 4th of July.
>
> It is with interest that the Soviet Government got acquainted with this message, the importance of which is quite clear. You may be sure that your initiative will find here favourable attitude which it fully deserves especially in the present international situation in general.
>
> Your idea about a friendly meeting between you and Premier G. M. Malenkov as well as the considerations expressed by you regarding the aims of such a meeting, have met with sympathetic acknowledgement in Moscow. Mr A. Eden's participation in such a meeting who is closely connected with the development of the relations between our countries, is, of course, accepted as quite natural.

We feel that such a personal contact may serve to carrying out a broader meeting on the highest level, if it is accepted by all the parties who are interested in easing the international tension and in strengthening peace.

I deem it necessary to express to you the general opinion of the leading political statesmen in Moscow. They have often recalled about our friendly relations during the war and about the outstanding role which you personally played in all that.

Once again you have rightly reminded of this time. One may ask why during the years of war there existed between our countries the relations which had a positive significance not only for our peoples but for the destinies of the whole world, and why such relations cannot be developed in the same good direction now. As to us we are striving to this end and we are regarding your message from this point of view. (Ends)

3. We have many pleasant and enduring memories of our visit to the White House.

President Dwight D. Eisenhower to Sir Winston S. Churchill
Prime Minister's Personal Telegram T.248/54
(Premier papers, 11/1074)

7 July 1954
Emergency
Top Secret
No. 1406

Your telegram No. 3209.

You did not let any grass grow under your feet. When you left here I had thought, obviously erroneously, that you were in an undecided mood about this matter, and that when you had cleared your own mind I would receive some notice if you were to put your program into action. However, that is now past history and we must hope that the steps you have started will lead to a good result.

I shall, of course, have to make some statement of my own when your plan is publicly announced. I hope you can give me advance notice as to the date that you will make a public statement on the subject. In this way I will have time to prepare my own statement carefully.

I probably shall say something to the effect that while you were here the possibility of a Big Three meeting was discussed; that I could not see how it would serve a useful purpose at this time; that you then suggested an exploratory mission of your own; that I said this would be essentially your own responsibility and decision. Finally, I said that if you did undertake such a mission, your plan would carry our hopes for the best but would not engage our responsibility.

The fact that your message to Moscow was sent so promptly after you left here is likely to give an impression more powerful than your cautioning words that in some way your plan was agreed at our meeting. Of course, the dating of your message may not become public. This I think would be best because it will call for less explanation from me to the American public. In any event, I think you will agree that your program should be handled with the greatest delicacy to avoid giving either the misapprehension that we are in fact party to it, or the equally dangerous misapprehension that your action in this matter reflects a sharp disagreement between our two countries. I know that you will be aware of these twin dangers and I hope that by understanding and cooperation we can surmount this.

As to the content of Molotov's message as related in your cable, I can only observe that it must be almost exactly what you would have expected in the circumstances.

I am delighted that you enjoyed your visit here. I think that one of the major advantages we may have gained from it is what seems to me an obvious drawing together of Anthony and Foster in their thinking and relationships.

David Pitblado to Ronald Guppy[1]
(Premier papers, 11/585)

7 July 1954

Dear Guppy,
The Prime Minister has asked me to get a report from the Home Secretary on whether action cannot be taken on cruelty to animals grounds to prevent the deliberate spreading of myxomatosis.

I think I am right in addressing this to you but I am also sending a copy to Wilde[2] at the Ministry of Agriculture.

---

[1] Ronald James Guppy, 1916–77. Educated at St John's College, Cambridge. Entered Home Office, 1939. On active service, 1939–45. Married, 1943, Elsie Fuller: two children. Principal Private Secretary to Home Secretary, 1953–5; Asst Secretary, 1955. Asst Under-Secretary of State, Home Office, 1961–7, 1974. CB, 1967. In Dept of Education and Science, 1967–9. Secretary, Commission on the Constitution, 1969–73.

[2] G. L. Wilde. Lt, Royal Army Educational Corps, 1948. Secretary, Dept of Agriculture, Fisheries, and Food, ?–1955.

John Colville: recollection
('The Fringes of Power', page 701)

7 July 1954

The following day, July 7th, there was a Cabinet in the course of which WSC revealed his intention to meet the Russians and also another even more startling decision recently taken by the Defence Committee and communicated to St Laurent and Howe in Ottawa at dinner last Tuesday. In the evening I heard from Lord Swinton the reactions of the Cabinet, underlined even more forcibly by Harold Macmillan after dinner at No. 10 (an official dinner for Ismay in his capacity as Secretary General of the United Nations, during which I sat next to Sir W. Haley, editor of *The Times*). In consequence of all this Lord Salisbury said he must resign. I became much involved in the subsequent activities, being approached separately by Lord Swinton and the Lord Chancellor and asked by them to explain all the circumstances to Sir M. Adeane for the information and (as the Lord Chancellor thought) possible intervention of the Queen. Salisbury both dislikes the Russian project and objects to the PM's action in approaching Molotov without consulting and obtaining the agreement of the Cabinet. Lord Swinton has represented to him, first that this is the 'end of the voyage' with Winston and that a similar case is therefore unlikely to occur; secondly, that his resignation will do great harm to Anglo-American relations because it will be greatly played up by those who, like Senator Knowland, will cry out against the Russian talks and will be represented as a revolt by Lord Salisbury against an anti-American move on the part of Winston and Eden. Also, of course, it will be highly embarrassing to Eden.

Cabinet: conclusions
(Cabinet papers, 128/27)

7 July 1954
Secret
11.30 a.m.
Cabinet Meeting No. 47 of 1954

[...]

2. The Cabinet had before them a note by the Minister of State (C(54)220) covering a minute recording the agreement reached between the Prime Minister and the President of the United States regarding the resumption of defence negotiations with Egypt.

The Foreign Secretary said that the United States Government had come as far as to meet our requirements as we could reasonably expect. In particular, it should be most helpful to us that the provision of the United States economic aid to Egypt would be conditional on Egyptian fulfilment of any agreement relating to the Canal Zone base and that the United States would support publicly the principle of free transit through the Suez Canal. Conditions in the Canal Zone had improved considerably of late, and this made it easier to propose a resumption of negotiations. Our negotiators would be instructed to aim at an agreement to last for twenty years and to cover the case of aggression against Persia as well as Turkey, although it might not prove possible to obtain our full requirements on these points.

The Prime Minister said that the agreement reached with the United States Government in Washington was valuable both because it broadened the basis for the action which we now proposed to take, and because it would increase the chances that the Egyptian Government would abide by the terms of any agreement we might reach with them. In spite of his earlier doubts he was now satisfied that the withdrawal of British troops from Egypt could be fully justified on military grounds. Our requirements in the Canal Zone had been radically altered by the admission of Turkey to the North Atlantic Treaty Organisation and the extension of a defensive Middle Eastern front as far east as Pakistan. Furthermore, the advent of thermo-nuclear weapons had greatly increased the vulnerability of a concentrated base area and it would not be right to continue to retain in Egypt 80,000 troops who would be better placed elsewhere. It was also relevant that the conditions in the Canal Zone were damaging both to the morale of the Forces and to recruitment.

The Minister of Defence expressed his support for these views, and there was general agreement in the Cabinet that the defence negotiations with the Egyptian Government ought now to be resumed on the basis of the agreement reached with the United States Government in Washington.

The following further points were raised in discussion:

(a) The Secretary of State for Air recalled that it was intended to obtain from the Egyptian Government transit and servicing facilities for RAF aircraft at an Egyptian air force station on the lines of paragraph 10 of the draft Heads of an Agreement which had been before the Cabinet at their meeting on 22nd June. In seeking to obtain these facilities, it would be his aim that the Air Ministry should commit themselves to as little expenditure as possible on this object.

(b) The Minister of Transport said that British shipping interests would welcome the public support of the United States Government for a declaration affirming the rights of free transit through the Suez Canal.

(c) The military arguments in favour of a defence agreement on the lines proposed should, at an early stage, be explained in confidence to interested Government supporters, many of whom could probably be brought to support the proposed agreement if they could be satisfied that it was militarily sound. The most suitable forum for such explanations would probably be the Conservative Members' Foreign Affairs Committee, and an early meeting of this body might, therefore, be arranged at which the Foreign Secretary and the Secretary of State for War might speak.

The Foreign Secretary said that he would be ready to meet Conservative Members as suggested, but it did not seem necessary that action on the Government's proposals should be deferred in the meantime.

The Cabinet –
(1) Authorised the Foreign Secretary to arrange for the defence negotiations with the Egyptian Government to be resumed on the basis of the agreed minute annexed to C(54)220.
(2) Invited the Foreign Secretary, in consultation with the Secretary of State for War and the Chief Whip, to arrange for the military grounds for the proposed settlement with Egypt to be explained in confidence to interested Government supporters at an early date.

The Chancellor of the Exchequer said that as the defence negotiations were now to be resumed, he hoped that this opportunity could be taken to remove the restrictions on Egypt's withdrawals of her sterling balances in accordance with the Sterling Releases Agreement. In return for this the Egyptian Government were now prepared to facilitate increased trade with this country.

The Foreign Secretary said that he would prefer that this should not be handled as part of the defence negotiations. Indeed, there might be advantage in withdrawing the restriction before the defence negotiations were resumed.

The Cabinet –
(3) Authorised the Chancellor of the Exchequer to decide, in consultation with the Foreign Secretary, the appropriate moment for lifting the existing restriction limiting the exercise of Egypt's right to draw on her sterling balances in accordance with the provisions of the Sterling Releases Agreement.

[...]

5. The Prime Minister said that the Defence Policy Committee had approved, on 16th June, a proposal that our atomic weapons programme should be so adjusted as to allow for the production of hydrogen bombs in this country. His recent discussions in Washington and Ottawa had been conducted on the basis that we should produce hydrogen bombs. He therefore suggested that the Cabinet should now formally approve the proposal that hydrogen bombs should be produced in this country, and should endorse the preliminary action which had already been taken to this end.

The Prime Minister said that we could not expect to maintain our influence as a world Power unless we possessed the most up-to-date nuclear weapons. The primary aim of our policy was to prevent major war; and the possession of these weapons was now the main deterrent to a potential aggressor. He had no doubt that the best hope of preserving world peace was to make it clear to potential aggressors that they had no hope of shielding themselves from a crushing retaliatory use of atomic power. For this purpose the Western Powers must provide themselves, not only with a sufficient supply of up-to-date nuclear weapons, but also with a multiplicity of bases from which a retaliatory attack could be launched. They must put themselves in a position to ensure that no surprise attack, however large, could wholly destroy their power of effective retaliation. These considerations, in his view, made it essential that we should manufacture hydrogen bombs in the United Kingdom so as to be able to make our contribution to this deterrent influence.

The Lord President said that he accepted the strategic argument outlined by the Prime Minister. Plans were now in preparation for the production of hydrogen bombs in this country. If further scientists could be recruited, this additional production could be undertaken without serious disruption of the existing programme for the manufacture of atomic weapons. Some preliminary steps to this end had already been taken with the approval of the Defence Policy Committee.

The Lord Privy Seal said that the Cabinet had had no notice that this question was to be raised and he hoped they would not be asked to take a final decision on it until they had had more time to consider it.

The Cabinet –
Agreed to resume their discussion of this question at a later meeting.

Cabinet: Confidential Annex
(Cabinet papers, 128/40)

7 July 1954
Top Secret
11.30 a.m.
Cabinet Meeting No. 47, Minute 4, of 1954

The Prime Minister said that in the private conversations which he had held with President Eisenhower during his recent visit to Washington he had again canvassed the possibility of an informal meeting of Heads of Governments, on a three-Power or four-Power basis. The President had at first seemed ready to give this serious consideration and had discussed the possibility that, if such a meeting were held in London, he might attend the opening, and perhaps the concluding, stages – being represented in the interval by the Vice-President and the Secretary of State. Towards the end of the visit the President had been rather less forthcoming, possibly as a result of consultations with his Secretary of State, and had given the impression that it would be difficult for him to assent to such a meeting at the present time having regard to the state of opinion in the United States. Nevertheless, at his Press Conference on

30th June, he had said publicly that on this question he differed more in emphasis than in substance from the views which had been publicly expressed by the Prime Minister. He had recalled that he had always expressed his readiness to confer with anybody if the deeds of the other side convinced him that there was sincerity there. He had also said that the United States were sincere in their search for peace and that, if there were any proof that the other side would keep their agreements, he thought that 'all of us would be quite content to do almost anything to advance that cause'.

The Prime Minister said that, while these conversations with the President had related to the possibility of a meeting on a three-Power or four-Power basis, he had formed the impression while in Washington that the President would not be surprised if he sought an opportunity for a bilateral meeting with M Malenkov. When he had previously suggested this in May, 1953, the President had deprecated such a 'solitary pilgrimage'. But much had happened since then, and he believed that the President would not now seek to dissuade him from undertaking such a mission. On his journey home he had decided, after consultation with the Foreign Secretary, to send a personal message to M Molotov asking him how the Soviet Government would view the idea of a friendly meeting 'with no agenda and no object but to find a reasonable way of living side by side in growing confidence, easement and prosperity'. Such a meeting might be a prelude to a larger reunion, though he had no warrant to say this beyond his own hopes. The draft of his proposed message had been seen by the Chancellor of the Exchequer, who had suggested some valuable improvements; and the message had been despatched to Moscow on 4th July (Foreign Office Telegram to Moscow No. 873). On his return to London the previous evening he had received a friendly reply which included the statement that, in the view of the Soviet Government, such a personal contact might serve to pave the way for a broader meeting, if this were accepted by all the parties interested in easing international tension and in strengthening peace. Later in the evening he had discussed this exchange of messages with the Foreign Secretary, the Lord President, the Chancellor of the Exchequer and the Minister of Housing. With their agreement he had conveyed to President Eisenhower the substance of his message to M Molotov and the text of the latter's reply and had invited an expression of the President's view (Foreign Office Telegram to Washington No. 3209).

M Molotov's message had been delivered in person by the Soviet Ambassador in London. The Prime Minister had taken the opportunity of making it clear to the Ambassador that his was a personal message on which the Cabinet had not yet been consulted, and also that it had been sent without specific prior consultation with President Eisenhower.

It would be for the Cabinet to decide, when President Eisenhower's views were known, what further message should be sent to M Molotov. If a definite proposal for a meeting were to be made, place and timing would be important.

The meeting could hardly be held before the proceedings of the Geneva Conference had been brought to a head, and this might mean that it could not take place before the middle of August. He would be reluctant to go to Moscow, and he hoped that the Russians might agree to come to Stockholm or Vienna. As regards a larger meeting, it was evident that the Americans would not assent to this unless the Russians gave some practical proof of their sincerity. It was his hope that they might be persuaded to indicate for this purpose a firm intention to conclude a peace treaty for Austria.

The Foreign Secretary agreed that the Cabinet should now await the expression of the President's views. They should also take account of the probable reactions of this project upon public opinion in Europe. Such a meeting was likely to arouse particular apprehensions in Western Germany.

The Lord President said that he had had an opportunity for reflection since seeing these messages on the previous evening. He was glad that the Cabinet were not being asked to express a final opinion that day, for he would certainly wish to reserve his opinion until President Eisenhower's views were available. If the President were critical of this project, that would weigh heavily with him. For in present circumstances he thought it more than ever important to avoid anything which might seriously impair the partnership between this country and the United States.

At the end of the discussion the Prime Minister said that the texts of his exchange with M Molotov and of his message to President Eisenhower would be circulated to members of the Cabinet for their personal information. He would also arrange for his Private Secretary to make available to any member of the Cabinet who wished to see them the earlier messages which he had exchanged with President Eisenhower on this subject in 1953.

The Cabinet –

(1) Agreed to resume their discussion of this question as soon as the Prime Minister had received a reply to his message to President Eisenhower.

At the Prime Minister's request Lord Cherwell gave the Cabinet a summary report of the discussions which had been held in Washington and Ottawa on atomic questions.

The Americans had indicated their readiness to cooperate more fully with us in future over the whole field of atomic energy development. For the moment this full cooperation was precluded by the terms of their legislation, but most of these barriers would be removed by the amending legislation which, it was hoped, would be passed before Congress rose for the summer recess. Meanwhile, the Americans had undertaken to provide us with full information of the effects of their hydrogen bombs. They were also ready to give us details of the dimensions and characteristics of their bombs, so that RAF aircraft could be adapted to carry the United States type of bomb. They were anxious to collaborate with us in the interpretation of intelligence about atomic research and production in the Soviet Union. To the extent that this involved disclosure of their own atomic secrets, this had hitherto been precluded by the terms of their legislation; but it was now hoped that there could be closer collaboration in this when the amending legislation was passed.

The Americans were anxious to proceed with their plan for an international pool of uranium for the development of the civil use of atomic energy, despite the refusal of the Soviet Government to cooperate in this scheme. In view of the extent to which the Americans were now prepared to assist us in the development of our own atomic projects, it had been thought inexpedient to offer further opposition to the Atomic Bank Plan. We had therefore agreed that international discussions might go forward, but some time was likely to elapse before an effective international agreement was concluded.

The Canadian government had undertaken to explore the possibility of providing us with supplies of tritium, which would enable us to expedite the production of atomic weapons in this country.

The Cabinet –
(2) Took note of this statement by Lord Cherwell.

Cabinet: conclusions
(Cabinet papers, 128/27)

8 July 1954
Secret
11.30 a.m.
Cabinet Meeting No. 48 of 1954

[...]
2. The Cabinet resumed their discussion of the question whether our atomic weapons programme should be so adjusted as to allow for the production of thermo-nuclear bombs in this country.

The following were the main points raised in the discussion:
(a) What additional financial commitment would be involved?

The Cabinet were informed that the *net* additional cost of adjusting the programme so as to allow for the production of thermo-nuclear bombs would not be very substantial. The capital cost should not exceed £10 millions, and the thermo-nuclear bombs would be made in lieu of atomic bombs at a relatively small additional production cost. Much of the material needed for the production of the new type of bomb would have been required for the production of atomic bombs, and there would be a substantial degree of flexibility in the programme, since atomic bombs could be converted into thermo-nuclear bombs. In terms of explosive power the thermo-nuclear bomb would be more economical than the atomic bomb.

(b) Might we not wish to prevent the manufacture of thermo-nuclear bombs in Western Europe, particularly in Germany? Would it be easier for us to prevent this if we ourselves refrained from producing these weapons? Some of our other defence preparations were already based on the assumption that we should not engage in major war except as an ally of the United States: could we not continue to rely on the United States to match Russia in thermo-nuclear weapons?

In reply it was pointed out that the strength of these arguments was weakened by the fact that we had already embarked on the production of atomic weapons. There was no sharp distinction in kind between atomic and thermo-nuclear weapons; and, as we were already engaged in the manufacture of this kind of weapon, it was unreasonable that we should deny ourselves the advantage of possessing the most up-to-date types. The Foreign Secretary said that our power to control the production of thermo-nuclear weapons in Western Europe would not in his view be weakened by the fact that we ourselves were making these weapons.

(c) Was it morally right that we should manufacture weapons with this vast destructive power? There was no doubt that a decision to make hydrogen bombs would offend the conscience of substantial numbers of people in this country. Evidence of this was to be found in the resolutions recently passed by the Methodist Conference in London.

In reply the point was again made that there was no difference in kind between atomic and thermo-nuclear weapons; and that, in so far as any moral principle was involved, it had already been breached by the decision of the Labour Government to make the atomic bomb. It was also argued that the moral issue would arise, not so much on the production of these weapons, but on the decision to use them; and that the resolution of the Methodist Conference was directed mainly against the use of atomic weapons. The further point was made that, if we were ready to accept the protection offered by United States use of thermo-nuclear weapons, no greater moral wrong was involved in making them ourselves.

(d) No country could claim to be a leading military Power unless it possessed the most up-to-date weapons; and the fact must be faced that, unless we possessed thermo-nuclear weapons, we should lose our influence and standing in world affairs. Strength in thermo-nuclear weapons would henceforward provide the most powerful deterrent to a potential aggressor; and it was our duty to make our contribution towards the building up of this deterrent influence. It was at least possible that the development of the hydrogen bomb would have the effect of reducing the risk of major war. At present some people thought that the greatest risk was that the United States might plunge the world into war, either through a misjudged intervention in Asia or in order to forestall an attack by Russia. Our best chance of preventing this was to maintain our influence with the United States Government; and they would certainly feel more respect for our views if we continued to play an effective part in building up the strength necessary to deter aggression than if we left it entirely to them to match and counter Russia's strength in thermo-nuclear weapons.

(e) Doubt was expressed about the feasibility of keeping secret, for any length of time, a decision to manufacture thermo-nuclear weapons in this country. It was therefore suggested that thought should be given to the question how a decision to manufacture these weapons could best be justified to public opinion in this country and abroad.

It emerged from the discussion that there was general support in the Cabinet for the proposal that thermo-nuclear bombs should be manufactured in this country. Some Ministers asked, however, that there should be a further opportunity for reflection before a final decision was taken. Meanwhile, it was agreed that there should be no interruption of the preliminary planning which had already been put in hand.

The Cabinet –

Agreed to resume their decision of this question at a further meeting before the end of July.

3. The Cabinet continued their discussion of the possibility of an Anglo-Soviet Meeting.

The Cabinet's discussion on this question is recorded separately.[1]

4. The Cabinet were informed of the business to be taken in the House of Commons in the following week.

The Opposition had expressed the wish that foreign affairs should be debated, in Committee of Supply, on 14th July. It was now clear, however, that the Foreign Secretary would be obliged to return before then to the Geneva Conference. When they knew this the Opposition might suggest another subject for debate on the day. If, however, they still wished to hold a Foreign Affairs debate related mainly to the recent meeting in Washington, it might be convenient that the Prime Minister's statement on the Washington talks should be made in a speech opening that debate instead of after Questions on 12th July.

The Cabinet agreed that the proposed debate on the report of the Crichel Down Inquiry should be held in the week beginning 19th July.

The Lord Privy Seal said that, in his statement on business that day, he would say that the Government hoped to obtain the Second Reading of the Food and Drugs Bill before the House rose for the summer recess.

5. The Lord Privy Seal said that it was now quite clear that no Government time could be made available before the summer recess for Parliamentary proceedings on the Government's proposals for the reorganisation of the railways. It did not follow, however, that publication of the proposed White Paper

---

[1] See immediately following document.

on this subject need be deferred on this account. If, after the White Paper had been published, the Labour Opposition should wish to have it discussed before the recess, it could be indicated to them that the only means of arranging this would be by their making available one of their remaining Supply Days for this purpose.

The Minister of Transport said that the Railways Reorganisation Scheme represented an important result of the Transport Act of 1953 and he would deplore further delay in its publication, even though some time might elapse before the necessary steps could be taken to secure its approval by Parliament.

The Cabinet –

Authorised the Minister of Transport to publish without further delay the draft White Paper on the 'Railways Reorganisation Scheme' annexed to C(54)211.

[. . .]

Cabinet: Confidential Annex
(Cabinet papers, 128/40)

8 July 1954
Top Secret
11.30 a.m.
Cabinet Meeting No. 48, Minute 3, of 1954

The Prime Minister said that earlier that morning he had received President Eisenhower's reply to his message about the possibility of a bilateral meeting with M Malenkov. This was read to the Cabinet (Washington telegram No. 1406).[1] The Prime Minister said that he hoped that, if further explanations were given, a more favourable response might be elicited from the President; and he read to the Cabinet the text of a further message which he was proposing to send to him (Foreign Office telegram to Washington No. 3228). He suggested that the Cabinet should take no final decision until a further expression of the President's view was available. He made it clear, however, that he would not be disposed to accept an invitation to meet M Malenkov in Moscow.

The Foreign Secretary said that in the draft message to the President reference was made to the possibility of a meeting at Stockholm or Vienna. He hoped that the Prime Minister would also mention the possibility of a meeting at Berne. He himself believed that the meeting might have quite a different effect on opinion abroad if it were held at Berne immediately after the end of the Geneva Conference. This, in his view, would be more than a geographical difference. It would seem much more natural that he and M Molotov should

---

[1] Reproduced above (pp. 1651–2).

go from Geneva to Berne, at the end of the Conference, in order to confer there with the Prime Minister and M Molotov. The Prime Minister agreed to include, in his message to the President, a reference to the possibility of a meeting at Berne.

The Prime Minister said that some of his colleagues might think that the Cabinet should have been consulted before he had sent to M Molotov the personal and private message embodied in Foreign Office telegram to Moscow No. 873. It had been his practice as Prime Minister, both during the war and since the present Government took office, to exchange personal messages with Heads of Governments and more particularly with the President of the United States. Most of these messages had been seen before despatch by the Foreign Secretary, who could always suggest that reference should be made to the Cabinet if he thought this necessary. The Prime Minister hoped that he would continue to enjoy the confidence of his colleagues in continuing a practice which, in his opinion, had proved beneficial in the conduct of public affairs.

The Lord President said that he was glad that this opportunity had been given to discuss the constitutional aspects of this matter. He did not contest the right of a Prime Minister to determine policy. But, if a Prime Minister took a decision of policy which involved the collective responsibility of the whole Government without prior consultation with his Cabinet colleagues, any of his colleagues who dissented from the decision might thereby be forced to the remedy of resignation. The message which the Prime Minister had sent to M Molotov, though framed as a personal inquiry, was in his opinion an important act of foreign policy; and it would have been preferable that the Cabinet should have been given an opportunity to express their views on it before it was sent.

The Lord Privy Seal said that he also regarded this as an important act of policy, on which the Cabinet should have been consulted. For, although it was presented as a personal enquiry, it was bound to commit the Government to some extent to the view that this was an opportune moment for a meeting of the kind suggested. For his part, if his view had been sought, he would have been inclined to advise against making such an approach at the present time.

The Prime Minister suggested that a distinction could be drawn between an informal enquiry and a formal proposal for a meeting. The latter could clearly not have been made without the approval of the Cabinet. But he had not thought that the Cabinet would be in any way committed by a personal and preliminary enquiry; and he had understood that the Foreign Secretary, whom he had consulted, was of the same opinion.

The Foreign Secretary recalled that a draft of the message had been sent to the Chancellor of the Exchequer, and it had been in his mind at the time that the Chancellor would bring it to the notice of his Cabinet colleagues.

The Chancellor of the Exchequer said that the draft had reached him during the afternoon of Saturday, 3rd July, when he was in Norfolk. The telegram embodying it had been addressed to him personally, and copies had at that stage been shown only to senior officials in the Foreign Office and to the Prime Minister's Private Secretaries at 10 Downing Street. There was nothing in the telegram to suggest that the views of the Cabinet were being invited. Indeed, before he had been able to despatch his own comments, which he had formulated after discussion with senior Foreign Office officials, a further telegram had been received from the Prime Minister enquiring whether the message had been transmitted to Moscow. This had confirmed his view that he had not been expected to invite the views of other Cabinet colleagues – and it would in any event have been very difficult for him to do so when Ministers were dispersed at the weekend.

The Lord President said that the message had been despatched to Moscow on 4th July. The Prime Minister and the Foreign Secretary had arrived in London on 6th July and could then have held full consultation with their Cabinet colleagues. Was the message so urgent that its despatch could not have been delayed for three days?

The Prime Minister said that, in his anxiety to lose no opportunity of furthering the cause of world peace, he might have taken an exaggerated view of the urgency of the matter. There had seemed no reason to delay what he regarded as a personal and informal enquiry which could not commit his colleagues.

The Commonwealth Secretary said that in his view the constitutional position was clear. A Prime Minister was certainly free to conduct unofficial personal correspondence with Heads of other Governments. But, equally, in such correspondence a Prime Minister would take care to avoid committing the Cabinet to any act of policy without their prior approval. The practical question was whether any particular message sent in the course of such personal correspondence, had the effect of committing the Cabinet. Though it was clear that this had not been intended on the present occasion, had it produced this effect?

The Lord President said that in his opinion the Cabinet's freedom of action had to some extent been limited by the message which the Prime Minister had sent. When the Cabinet came to take a decision on the substance of the issue, they might wish to decide that it would be preferable not to go forward with this project for a meeting with M Molotov. But, if they so decided, and if the Russians then chose to give publicity to the messages exchanged between the Prime Minister and M Molotov, the public would be left with the impression that the Prime Minister had wished to arrange such a meeting but had been deterred from doing so by his Cabinet colleagues. That consideration might now influence the Cabinet's eventual decision.

The Colonial Secretary said that the constitutional position was as stated by the Commonwealth Secretary. The practical question was whether the collective responsibility of the Cabinet had in any way been involved by the informal approach which the Prime Minister had made to M Molotov. For himself he did not think it could be denied that it was now more difficult for the Cabinet to decide that this was not an appropriate moment for a bilateral meeting of the kind suggested in that message. Nevertheless, he thought it was still open to the Cabinet to decide not to proceed further with this project.

The Prime Minister agreed with this view. It might well be that, when President Eisenhower had replied to his further message, he would be convinced that it would be preferable not to proceed further with this project. In that event he would not feel obliged to give M Molotov any detailed reasons for his decision. It would suffice to thank him again for his cordial message and to say that we did not think it practicable to proceed further with this project at the present time. This, however, must be left for consideration in the light of a further expression of the President's views.

The Cabinet –

Agreed to resume their discussion of this question when President Eisenhower had replied to the further message which the Prime Minister now proposed to send him.

Sir Winston S. Churchill to President Dwight D. Eisenhower
Prime Minister's Personal Telegram T.249/54
(Premier papers, 11/1074)

8 July 1954
Immediate
Dedip
Top Secret, Private and Personal
No. 3228

Your telegram No. 1406.

I hope you are not vexed with me for not submitting to you the text of my telegram to Molotov. I felt that as it was a private and personal enquiry which I had not brought officially before the Cabinet I had better bear the burden myself and not involve you in any way. I have made it clear to Molotov that you were in no way committed. I thought this would be agreeable to you, and that we could then consider the question in the light of the answer I got.

2. Much grass has already grown under our feet since my telegram to you of May 4, 1953.[1] I should be grateful if you would glance again at our correspondence of that period. I have of course stated several times to Parliament my desire that a top level meeting should take place and that failing this I did not exclude a personal mission of my own. I have never varied, in the

---

[1] T.117A/53, reproduced above (p. 986).

14 months that have passed, from my conviction that the state of the world would not be worsened and might be helped by direct contact with the Russia which had succeeded the Stalin era. However as you say this is now past history.

3. I thought Molotov's reply was more cordial and forthcoming to what was after all only a personal and private enquiry than I had expected. It strengthens my view that the new Government in the Kremlin are both anxious about the thermo-nuclear future and secondly attracted by the idea of a peaceful period of domestic prosperity and external contacts. This is certainly my view of what is their self-interest. I was struck by the fact that they did not suggest a meeting in Moscow but respected my wish to leave the time and place entirely unsettled. Of course it would be much better to have even the Two Power meeting about which I enquired in Stockholm or Vienna or Berne and if the Cabinet decide to go forward with the project a margin of six or eight weeks would be open to us for fitting the timing into the movement of events both at Geneva and in Indo-China.

It is on all this that I most earnestly seek your advice, while being willing to bear the brunt of failure on my own shoulders.

4. I fear that grave military events impend in the Tonkin Delta and indeed throughout Indo-China. I have heard that General Ely[1] does not think that there is any hope of holding an effective bridgehead in the Delta. There is, I am told, no doubt which way the Viet Nam population would vote if they were freely consulted. I well understand the sense of disaster and defeat in Indo-China may produce a profound effect in the United States as well as far-reaching reactions in Siam and Malaya. It is my hope that an increasing detachment of Russia from Chinese ambitions may be a possibility and one we should not neglect.

5. Meanwhile we shall keep you most thoroughly informed and I shall not seek any decision to make an official approach until I hear from you again. All I have said to Molotov in thanking him for his telegram is that a few days will be needed before any reply can be sent. There can be no question of a public announcement before our two governments have consulted together about policy and also agreed on what it is best to say.

I have impressed on the Soviet Ambassador the importance of absolute secrecy.

---

[1] Paul Henri Romauld Ely, 1897–1975. Born in Salonika, Greece. Educated at Ecole Spéciale Militaire de St-Cyr, France. Lt, 1919. Capt., 1930. Lt-Col., 1942. Col., 1944. French Liaison Officer to SHAEF, 1944–5. Director of Infantry, Ministry of War, 1945. Maj.-Gen., 1946. Director, Military Cabinet, Ministry of the Army, 1945–7. Gen. Officer, 7th Military Region, 1947–9. CoS to Gen. de Lattre de Tassigny, 1948–9. French Representative on the Military Committee, Western Union, 1949–53. Head of French Military Mission to US, 1953. President of COS Committee and CoS of French Armed Forces, 1953–4, 1956–9. C-in-C, Indochina, 1954–5. Chief of National Defence, 1959–61.

President Dwight D. Eisenhower to Sir Winston S. Churchill
Prime Minister's Personal Telegram T.250/54
(Premier papers, 11/1074)

8 July 1954
Emergency
Top Secret
No. 1425

Your telegram No. 3228.

Thank you very much for your message just this minute received. Of course I am not vexed. Personal trust based upon more than a dozen years of close association and valued friendship may occasionally permit room for amazement but never for suspicion. Moreover, I cannot too strongly emphasize to you my prayerful hope that your mission, if you pursue it, may be crowned with complete success. My appreciation of the acute need for peace and understanding in the world certainly far transcends any personal pride in my judgments or convictions. No one could be happier than I to find that I have been wrong in my conclusion that the men in the Kremlin are not to be trusted, no matter how great the apparent solemnity and sincerity with which they might enter into an agreement or engagement.

Unfortunately, I find no reason for taking a brighter view of the Tonkin Delta situation than is expressed in your fourth paragraph. This, of course, is all the more exasperating to our people because they are well aware that ever since I came into office this Government has been suggesting and urging some internationalization of the Indo-China conflict so as to mark it clearly as another instance of Communist aggression against the independence of small countries. In this case I do not think it a harsh judgment to observe that the French have been wrong both from the viewpoint of world peace and of their own prestige. Again I suppose we must sadly observe that that is now history.

At this moment the international question that most engages the attention of our people is the possibility that some kind of armistice in Indo-China will be used as an excuse for raising the issue of Red China's entrance into the United Nations. You, of course, put the case very succinctly when you said to me that there can be no serious consideration of this proposition as long as the United Nations is at war with China over the Korean question. On this one matter I honestly believe that American opinion is so firmly fixed that, in the absence of a series of deeds that would evidence a complete reversal of Red China's attitude, the introduction of this question for debate in the United Nations would create real difficulty in this country. This is far less a matter of geography than of principle. I have heard it said that America makes a mistake in attempting to introduce moral codes into international relationships, and that morals and diplomacy have nothing in common. Be that as it may, the fact remains that the American people like to think that they are being just and fair in these matters and, therefore, they will not be browbeaten into accepting something that they consider completely unfair, unjust and immoral.

The bill of particulars against Red China includes, among many other things, its invasion of North Korea, where its armies still are stationed. Secondly, Red China, by its own admission, illegally holds a number of Americans as prisoners. This outrages our entire citizenry. Third, Communist China has been the principal source of the military strength used in the illicit and unjust aggression in Indo-China. Finally, Red China had been guilty of the most atrocious deportment in her dealings with the Western world. At Geneva it excoriated the United Nations and asked for the repudiation of decisions by that body. Red China has been worse than insulting in its communications to ourselves and others, while the public statements of its officials have been characterized by vilification and hatred.

Frankly, I have no worries whatsoever about the ability of your Government and this one to keep Anglo-American relationships on a sound friendly and cooperative basis as long as this one question which looms so importantly in the American mind does not rise up to plague us. I pray that you and our other friends may be able, as long as Red China persists in her inexcusable conduct, to help us keep this one matter from appearing on the agenda, either in the Security Council or in the General Assembly of the United Nations.

Cabinet: Confidential Annex
(Cabinet papers, 128/40)

9 July 1954
Top Secret
12.30 p.m.
Cabinet Meeting No. 49, Minute 1, of 1954

The Prime Minister read to the Cabinet the text of a further message from President Eisenhower (Washington telegram No. 1425) and a draft of the reply which he proposed to send (subsequently despatched as Foreign Office telegram to Washington No. 3256).[1] The greater part of the President's message was concerned with the situation in Indo-China and the representation of China in the United Nations. In his reply the Prime Minister proposed to press for a more definite expression of the President's views on some of the practical aspects of his proposal for a meeting with M Malenkov. He intended to make it clear that he would not accept an invitation to meet in Moscow and that, although a meeting in Stockholm or Vienna would be acceptable, the best plan would be to meet at Berne after the Geneva Conference. He also proposed to make more plain his intention to ask the Russians to give

---

[1] Reproduced below (pp. 1670–3).

some definite proof of their sincerity, as a preliminary to a wider meeting – e.g. an undertaking to ratify the Austrian Treaty and, perhaps, a promise to co-operate in the Atomic Bank Plan. He would urge the President to give him his views on these specific proposals before the Cabinet were asked to decide whether a formal proposal for a two-Power meeting should be submitted to the Soviet Government.

The Lord President said that he wished to make it clear that he was opposed in principle to the idea of holding a high-level meeting with the Russians without the participation of the United States. He had explained this to the Prime Minister in a private letter which he had sent to him after his speech in the House of Commons in 11th May, 1953, and nothing which had since occurred had changed his opinion on this point. The projected meeting, if it took place, would be an important act of foreign policy; and, if he remained in the Government, it would fall to him, as Leader of the House of Lords and spokesman for the Foreign Office in that House, to defend it publicly. This he would be unable to do. Therefore, as at present advised, he feared that he would have to resign from the Government if it were in the event decided that the Prime Minister should go forward with this project for a bilateral meeting with M Malenkov.

The Prime Minister said that, in their further discussions on this question, the Cabinet would wish to keep in mind the view which the Lord President had expressed. For the moment, however, he preferred to await a further expression of President Eisenhower's views; and he was not proposing to ask the Cabinet that day to take a final decision on the matter.

In further discussion Ministers recognised that they could not take a final decision on the expediency of proposing such a meeting until they knew the outcome of the negotiations on Indo-China which were now to be resumed at the Geneva Conference. If those negotiations resulted in an agreement from which the United States Government expressly dissociated themselves, it was arguable that a bilateral meeting between the Prime Minister and M Malenkov would at that moment give the impression that an even wider breach was being created between the United Kingdom and the United States. On the other hand it was arguable that in those circumstances – and, perhaps even more, if no agreement of any kind were reached at Geneva – it would be re-assuring to public opinion throughout the world that a further opportunity was being created for discussions with the Soviet Government which might yet avert the danger of world war. In either event it seemed clear that a final decision must await the outcome of the resumed negotiations at Geneva.

The Prime Minister suggested that the Foreign Secretary should take the opportunity, while at Geneva, to make it clear to M Molotov that this project could not proceed further until the outcome of the Geneva Conference was known. He might also put to him the advantages of Berne as a possible meeting-place.

The Foreign Secretary said that some thought should also be given to the questions which the Russians were likely to raise, if such a meeting were held. How would they react, for example, to the suggestion that they should give an undertaking to ratify the Austrian Treaty? Were they not likely to counter this by pressing the suggestion for a European security guarantee which they had put forward at the Berlin Meeting – a suggestion which, as Ministers would remember, was designed to prevent the establishment of a European Defence Community. As an alternative to the creation of that Community, they would probably suggest that a united Germany should be admitted to the North Atlantic Treaty Organisation, and that the Organisation should thereafter be widened to include the Soviet Union. As regards the project for a broader meeting, we must be prepared for them to press the suggestion that this should be on a five-Power basis, including Communist China. The Foreign Secretary suggested that further thought should be given to all these questions while he was in Geneva.

The Cabinet –

Agreed to resume their discussion of these matters at a later meeting.

Sir Winston S. Churchill to Mamie Eisenhower
(*Churchill papers, 2/217*)

9 July 1954

My dear Mrs Ike (pardon me),

I so much enjoyed my visit to the White House and send you both my warm thanks for the comfort and luxury with which you surrounded me. I have many pleasant, and I think I may say historic, associations with those rooms which I occupied last week, but none will remain more pleasant in my memory than those connected with my latest visit and I am indeed grateful to you both for your kindness and hospitality.

Sir Winston S. Churchill to President Dwight D. Eisenhower
(*Foreign Office papers, 800/762*)

9 July 1954
Immediate
Dedip
Top Secret, Personal and Private
No. 3256

Your telegram No. 1425.

I am very much relieved by your kind telegram which reassures me that no serious differences will arise between our two Governments on account of a

Russian excursion or 'solitary pilgrimage' by me. I feel sure that you will do your best for me in presenting it to the United States public. I accept the full responsibility as I cannot believe that my American kinsmen will be unanimous in believing I am either anti-American or pro-Communist.

2. I do not intend to go to Moscow. We can only meet as equals and though Stockholm, which you mentioned to me before you took office, or Vienna, are both acceptable, Anthony has proposed what I think is the best, namely, Berne. If Malenkov will come to Berne when Geneva is over, Molotov could meet him there and Anthony and I could have a few talks on the dead level.

3. My idea is to create conditions in which a Three-, or perhaps with the French a Four-Power Conference might be possible, perhaps, as I said to you, in London early in September. For this I feel, and I expect you will agree, that Russian deeds are necessary as well as words. I should ask them for a Gesture or as better expressed, 'an Act of Faith', after all Stalin's encroachments in Poland, Czecho, Korea, etc., which ruptured Anglo-American wartime comradeship with them, and created the world-wide union of the Free Nations, of which NATO is the first expression and METO and SEATO are coming along. The sort of Gesture I should seek at Berne would be, as I think I mentioned to you, an undertaking to ratify the Austrian Treaty on which all their conditions have been agreed, and to liberate Austria and Vienna from Russian military domination. Surely also it would be a help if they would accept your atomic theme which you told us about at Bermuda and afterwards proposed to United Nations.

4. But I am not asking any promise from you that even if the above Gesture were attained you would commit yourself to the Three- or Four-Power Conference in London, but naturally my hopes run in that direction.

5. Of course all this may be moonshine. The Soviets may refuse any meeting place but Moscow. In that case all would be off for the present. Or they will give nothing and merely seek, quite vainly, to split Anglo-American unity. I cherish hopes not illusions and after all I am 'an expendable' and very ready to be one in so great a cause.

6. I should like to know your reaction to what I have set out above before I formally ask the Cabinet to propose to the Soviets the Two-Power meeting as described.

PART II

7. Now let me come to the main subject of your telegram. Anthony and I were astonished on the voyage to read the Press extracts and other reports, etc., about the storm in the United States about the admission of Red China to United Nations against American wishes. Still more were we amazed (though not suspicious) that this seemed to be in some way or other linked with our visit as if we had come over for such a purpose. In fact it was hardly discussed. A brief reference was made to it on June 27 at the Foster–Anthony

talks in which Anthony is recorded by us as having said the following:

China

'Mr Eden said that he thought he knew something about the difficulties which the United States Government faced in relation to their policy towards China. But Her Majesty's Government also had their difficulties. In dealing with this problem, he wished to keep in step with the United States. But he could give no unequivocal guarantee that it would be possible to do so.'

8. There is also a very well-informed account in the Paris edition of the *New York Herald Tribune* of July 7. This states inter alia that Mr Eden 'according to information available here did not press his point but rather sought to reach a meeting of minds. In doing so he promised to give further thought to the question, to consult his Cabinet colleagues, and to enter into conversation with other Governments which perhaps were considering favourable action on the Red China view.'

9. The British position has in fact been defined in our absence but with our full agreement by the Foreign Office on July 5 (see *Herald Tribune* of July 7) as follows:

'The United Kingdom policy has been constant since 1951 when Mr Morrison, the then Foreign Secretary, stated that Her Majesty's Government believed that the Central People's Government should represent China in the United Nations. In view however of that Government's persistence in behaviour which was inconsistent with the purposes and principles of the Charter it appeared to Her Majesty's Government that consideration of this question should be postponed. That was the policy of the late Government and it has been the policy of the present Government. This policy was reaffirmed in July 1953 by the Chancellor of the Exchequer who stated that the only accretion or addition which he could make was the hope and trust that the day for settling this and other problems would have been brought nearer by the Korean armistice.'

10. I shall confirm this in the statement I am to make to the House of Commons on Monday next and also point out that since July 1953 there has been no settlement of the Korean question – the armies are still in presence – and the problem of Indo-China has assumed more serious proportions. I hope that will ease American minds. I am very sorry that this business which anyhow does not come up at United Nations till the third week in September should have been magnified by Knowland and others into a serious difference between the United States and Great Britain on which the Press on both sides of the Atlantic are having a good time. It has somewhat taken the bloom off the peach of our visit, especially as we have not yet been able to make clear

by deeds and policy the full measure of our agreement on what I think are far more urgent matters.

11. I need not say how deeply I feel the force of the arguments you use in the latter part of your last telegram. Although we do not think that any nation could never, repeat never, come in to United Nations we feel as strongly as you do that they should not come in as a result or at the time of successful and impenitent defiance of the Charter and while still persisting in this attitude. Meanwhile surely the easiest way is to postpone it? We have got enough difficulties in the world to face without it at present.

12. Meanwhile I cannot see why Anthony should not go on trying to persuade China to behave decently even if their conduct should make them more eligible ultimately for membership of the Club. I earnestly hope that all the talk and feeling that has been aroused about the issue will not spoil the prospects of a cease-fire leading to a settlement in Indo-China. Such a settlement would in no way weaken our resolve [. . .].

President Dwight D. Eisenhower to Sir Winston S. Churchill
(*Premier papers, 11/1074*)

11 July 1954

Dear Winston,

Thank you for your long cablegram. I shall study it over the weekend and send you a complete reply early next week.

Sir Winston S. Churchill: speech
(*Hansard*)

12 July 1954   House of Commons

A VISIT TO THE UNITED STATES AND CANADA

The Prime Minister (Sir Winston Churchill): Mr Speaker, I should first like to explain to the House how our visit to America arose. On 17th February of this year Mr Sterling Cole, the Chairman of the Joint Congressional Committee on Atomic Energy, made a speech which was reported at some length in the *Manchester Guardian*. I was astounded by all that he said about the hydrogen bomb and the results of experiments made more than a year before by the United States at Eniwetok Atoll.

Considering what immense differences the facts he disclosed made to our whole outlook for defence, and notably civil defence, depth of shelters, dispersion of population. anti-aircraft artillery and so forth – on which considerable expenditure was being incurred – I was deeply concerned at the lack of information we possessed, and in view of all the past history of this subject, into which I do not propose to go today, I thought I ought to have a personal meeting with President Eisenhower at the first convenient opportunity.

Very little notice was taken over here at first of Mr Sterling Cole's revelations, but when some Japanese fishermen were slightly affected by the radioactivity generated by the second explosion, at Bikini, an intense sensation was caused in this country, and the House will remember the hydrogen bomb Questions and statements of 23rd and 30th March, and the debate of 5th April.[1]

All this seemed to emphasise the need for me to see the President personally, therefore, having made inquiries about the President's engagements, proposed my coming to the British Embassy in Washington about 20th May and having some talks with him. This suggestion was at once cordially received by the President, and after some correspondence it was arranged that our two Foreign Secretaries would also be present. But as the Geneva meeting had in the meanwhile begun, and was protracted from week to week, a succession of postponements was inevitable and the final date was fixed for the weekend of 25th June, for which the President very kindly invited my right hon. Friend the Foreign Secretary and myself to be his guests at the White House.

Very full reports have been made public upon what followed. I had not in the first instance specified any particular topics for our private conversations, which would, as they so often have done on similar occasions, have ranged over the whole field of affairs. The thermo-nuclear problem was, of course, foremost in my mind, and it was evident that if we waited from May to June it would be possible to evaluate more exactly the results of the Bikini experiments which had been concluded.

In the meanwhile, many other questions had arisen connected with the Vietminh operations in Indo-China, which were being sustained by the Communist Government of China. There was also the state of affairs in Europe, including the failure of the French Chamber to ratify, or afford any prospects of ratifying, the Treaty of two years ago upon the European Defence Community, on which so much study, argument and negotiation had been previously consumed. It was evident that these matters would occupy a leading place in our talks.

On 23rd June, the day before our departure, my right hon. Friend the Foreign Secretary made two speeches in this House – one at the beginning and one at the end of the debate – which attracted great attention in the United States, and when we started by air on the night of the 24th it was reported that we should be facing a storm of hostile opinion on our arrival. The contrary proved to be true.

---

[1] See speech reproduced above (pp. 1517–30).

I have never had a more agreeable or fruitful visit than on this occasion, and I never had the feeling of general good will more strongly borne in upon me. I had many hours of conversation with the President alone, and also in company with my right hon. Friend and Mr Foster Dulles; and the two Foreign Ministers had prolonged and more detailed discussions at the State Department and at Mr Dulles's residence. Lord Cherwell, whom I had planned from the beginning to take with me, and Sir Edwin Plowden – Chairman of the Atomic Energy Authority – discussed at length with Admiral Strauss and other American authorities the technical matters connected with the current atomic and hydrogen problems.

In their discussions and in my talks with the President about the exchange of information and technical co-operation in this sphere we were, of course, governed by the conditions created by the United States legislation, by which the President himself and all his officials are equally bound. It would not be in the public interest for me to make any detailed statement upon what passed. I can only say that there was cordial agreement that both our countries would benefit from a wider latitude both in cooperation and in the exchange of knowledge. Far-reaching amendments to the McMahon Act had been proposed by the President some time ago, and as the result the Congressional Committee is preparing a Bill which, among other things, would enable the United States Government to impart more information to or exchange more information with, friendly and allied countries. As this Bill is now before Congress, I shall make no comment beyond wishing it a fair passage.

The United States experts are of course well aware of the very high level which has been reached independently by our own scientists on this whole subject, and we are also both aware of the formidable progress of the Russian Soviet Government. Close contact on this topic was kept by us with the Canadian Government, who have so long been a powerful factor in these affairs.

It would not be helpful for me at the present time to say more on this subject, except that I have every hope that more satisfactory conditions will prevail between our two countries in the future than has been the case since the war with Germany came to an end.

We spent four and a half days in Washington and we worked hard. We had no fixed agenda, but we had an exchange of views on all subjects of major current importance. We talked with perfect frankness and in full friendship to each other. We dispelled, I think, some misunderstandings – even some nightmares – from the minds of our American friends about the direction of our policies. I think we convinced them that we have changed none of our ultimate joint objectives, and that there is at any rate some wisdom in the means by which we are proposing to reach them.

The House has no doubt studied the two documents which were published in Washington on successive days about world affairs. The first was the communiqué or statement – which term the President prefers – usual on these occasions. And the second a reaffirmation of the Atlantic Charter together with further declarations relating to present circumstances.

In addition to our exchange of views on particular current problems, President Eisenhower and I decided to use this occasion to reaffirm the fundamentals on which the policies of our two Governments have been and will continue to be built. We did so in a declaration of six points. I would ask you, Mr Speaker, to bear in mind this declaration of our basic unity in days when the newspapers are so full of bickerings and disagreements; for these points of unity transcend all passing differences and give a framework within which the incidents of daily life can be amicably resolved and dealt with.

In that declaration we affirmed our comradeship with one another; we stretched out the hand of friendship to all who might seek it sincerely; we reasserted our sympathy for and loyalty to those still in bondage; we proclaimed our desire to reduce armaments and to turn nuclear power into peaceful channels: we confirmed our support of the United Nations and of subsidiary organisations designed to promote and preserve the peace of the world; and we proclaimed our determination to develop and maintain in unity the spiritual, economic and military strength necessary to pursue our purposes effectively. These are the principles which we share with our American friends.

No one, I think, should complain of these declarations, or still less mock at them, because of their necessarily general and sometimes vague character. When the representatives of two great countries, comprising hundreds of millions of people, are trying to set forth the principles which will be right and in the main acceptable to the immense number of men and women for whom they are responsible, it is not the occasion for the sharp and sprightly literary performances such as we so often have the pleasure of reading in our daily and weekly newspapers. Disagreement is much more easy to express, and often much more exciting to the reader, than agreement. The highest common factor of public opinion is not a fertile ground for lively epigrams and sharp antithesis. The expression of broad and simple principles likely to command the assent and not to excite the dissent of vast communities must necessarily be in guarded terms. I should not myself fear even the accusation of platitude in such a statement if it only sought the greatest good of the greatest number.

But for myself, on this occasion, I was thrilled by the wish of the President of the United States to bring our two countries so directly together in a new declaration or charter, and to revive and renew the comradeship and brotherhood which joined the English-speaking world together in the late war, and is now, if carried into effect, the strongest hope that all mankind may survive in freedom and justice. I can well understand that such a document may incur the criticism of mischief makers of all kinds in any country, but for myself I rejoice to have had the honour of adding my signature to it.

The Washington communiqué states that the President and the Prime Minister 'agreed that the German Federal Republic should take its place as an equal partner in the community of Western nations where it can make its proper contribution to the defence of the free world. We are determined to achieve this goal –' says the communiqué – 'convinced that the Bonn and Paris Treaties provide the best way.' Nobody can call that a platitude. It is a grave decision but not a new decision. It is a policy which has been steadfastly pursued by successive British Governments. The need for a German contribution to Western defence was recognised by all the members of NATO as long ago as December, 1950. There have, of course, been differences about how this contribution should be made. There has been no difference that it must be made.

It was the French Government which put forward this idea of a European Defence Community instead of an army based – as I had myself somewhat conceived – on the principles of a Grand Alliance. This French plan offered a means of associating Germany politically as well as militarily with the West, and of creating a partnership of nations in place of the rivalries and hatreds which have torn Europe for so many centuries.

After long negotiations the EDC Treaty was signed in May, 1952. It has been ratified by four of the six signatory States. Her Majesty's Government and the United States Government have given the most solemn and far-reaching pledges of their practical support and intimate partnership with the Defence Community. They have substantial armies now standing on what we must call the Eastern front, both of which, in the event of war, would serve in a single line of battle with the EDC under the supreme NATO commander. But although France was the author of the plan the French Chamber has so far been unable to ratify it. It is not easy to foresee, nor would it at this moment be wise to forecast, the consequences of this deadlock should it continue.

We have both in Britain and the United States to consider the position of Germany. Under the Bonn Treaty the Federal Government will not regain her sovereignty until the EDC Treaty comes into force. At present she remains in law a State under military occupation. The Federal Republic of Germany is willing and anxious to co-operate with the Western world, and it is right that she should do so on a footing of equality. Germany under Dr Adenauer has shown a very high degree of patience during the last two years when we have all been hoping, almost from month to month, that the French Chamber would ratify the Treaties signed by the representatives of France and supported by her Allies in the war.

It would indeed be a tragedy if this opportunity were lost of bringing Germany back into the European family while also at the same time preventing the recreation of a German national army. Dr Adenauer in his wisdom has made it clear that he much prefers an international army. To me, the bulk of whose public life has been spent in war or preparation for war with Germany, it seems little less than madness to leave that active and virile nation with no choice but to raise an independent national army – (Hon. Members: 'Oh!') – and to reject associations with her in the Western world.

Mr Bevan: On a point of order. I should like to ask your guidance, Mr Speaker, as to what we are to do about the statements to which we have just listened. (Hon. Members: 'Sit down.') Is it not a complete abuse of the proceedings of the House that it should have, not a statement which the House can study in preparation for the debate next Wednesday, not a statement of such urgency that it could not be withheld, but a series of opinions on policies – indeed, a speech which the right hon. Gentleman is now making? (Hon. Members: 'Why not?') Because it cannot be answered today. I respectfully submit to you, Mr Speaker, that this is a complete abuse of the proceedings.

Mr Speaker: I do not think there is any point of order in this for me. The Prime Minister is giving us an account of the subjects discussed at Washington – (Hon. Members: 'No'.) That is what I understood. Anything of an argumentative character can easily be discussed during the debate that we are to have next Wednesday. I think the Prime Minister ought to be allowed to finish his statement.

Several Hon. Members *rose* –

Mr Bellenger: May I raise at the end of the Prime Minister's statement –

Mr Speaker: I cannot have two right hon. Gentlemen standing at the same time. I understand that the right hon. Member for Bassetlaw (Mr Bellenger) is raising a point of order.

Mr Bellenger: At the end of the right hon. Gentleman's statement, will the House be permitted to put any question on these personal points, or are questions to be reserved for Wednesday when we properly discuss foreign affairs, as the right hon. Gentleman now seems to be doing?

Several Hon. Members *rose* –

Mr Speaker: Only one hon. Member can speak at a time. Naturally, I should have supposed that with the debate so imminent as Wednesday the House would desire to pass at once to the Orders of the Day.

Several Hon. Members *rose* –

Mr Speaker: The Prime Minister.

Mr Donnelly: On a point of order.

The Prime Minister *rose* –

Mr Speaker: Is the right hon. Gentleman speaking to the point of order?

The Prime Minister: Might I say, Mr Speaker, that I expressed through the usual channels my willingness to do whatever the House wished, to make the statement fully, as I am trying to do, today and then have the foreign affairs debate on Wednesday, or to make the statement on Wednesday at the beginning of the foreign affairs debate, or to have the foreign affairs debate this afternoon. However, the decisions which were reached, in agreement, were that I was to make the statement today, and I hope I may be allowed to do so, so that it may be studied and the whole subject debated on Wednesday.

Mr S. Silverman: On a point of order. Whatever may have been agreed between the usual channels would not, I feel sure, determine your judgment, Mr Speaker, on a point of order relating to the rights of the House. In so far as the right hon. Gentleman had given us or had intended to give us a factual account of what took place in Washington in preparation for the debate on Wednesday, that would have been one thing, but, as I understand it, my right hon. Friend the Member for Ebbw Vale (Mr Bevan) has put to you, as a point of order, that the Prime Minister is not doing that at all but is making an argumentative and very controversial speech about matters which are very much in dispute and which will be the subject of the debate on Wednesday. The point I am putting is that either the right hon. Gentleman should confine his statement to the facts of what took place or that his speech should be debatable today when he sits down.

Mr Speaker: I do not see how it is possible reasonably to give an account of conversations which were held embracing foreign affairs without some expression of views on the questions of policy which arose out of them. I cannot myself draw such a hard-and-fast line as the hon. Member invites me to draw. I have heard nothing in the Prime Minister's statement which is out of order. I do think it is the duty of the House to listen to him.

Mr Donnelly: Further to that point of order –

Hon. Members: Sit down.

Mr Speaker: What is the point of order? I have ruled on the first point of order.

Mr Donnelly: Might I respectfully make this submission to you, Mr Speaker? The system of making statements at the end of Questions has grown up in the last few years – (Hon. Members: 'No'.) – and it has been respected by the House because it is a convenient administrative arrangement for the House of Commons. What is extremely difficult for back-benchers is for a statement to be made which becomes a controversial speech and which is then not debated. The point which I am seeking to establish, and which my right hon. and hon. Friends have sought to establish, is that a tradition of this House has been violated and that the rights of hon. Members are to be prejudiced as a result. I respectfully put to you, as the Speaker of the House of Commons, that you should look into this matter and reconsider the Ruling which you have given.

Mr Speaker: There is nothing in this for me to look into. The practice of Ministers making statements upon policy is a very old one and by no means of recent origin. I honestly do not see how one can separate these matters of policy on which differences of opinion are held, from questions of fact as to what actually occurred. This arrangement has apparently been come to by some sort of common consent. It is rather an abuse of the system of points of order to interrupt this statement. Anything of a controversial character can be dealt with fully and freely on Wednesday, and that is the proper time to do it.

The Prime Minister: I think it is my duty, as far as I can, to avoid controversy, but it is necessary for me to do justice to the character of the conversation which we have had. I never have known, Mr Speaker, even before your Ruling today, that statements by Ministers were supposed to be confined only to subjects and issues on which everyone in the House was agreed. Even on domestic matters – very domestic matters – some differences of opinion have been felt about statements which it has been my duty to make quite recently. I assure the House that I have no wish to raise controversy. I thought it would be convenient for hon. Gentlemen to be able to consider the most scathing terms with which they could repel any point in my narrative on which they differ from me.

I was speaking on the question of bringing Germany into the system of European defence. The convictions of Her Majesty's Government upon this issue, as were those of our predecessors, are in full harmony with those of the United States. That is factual, anyhow.

We feel that we are bound to act in good faith towards Germany in accordance with the Treaties we have signed and ratified and also that those concerned in these decisions owe this to Dr Adenauer, who, during a score of long and weary months of delay and uncertainty, has never shrunk from facing unpopularity in his own country in order to keep his word and to range Germany definitely with what is called the Free World, including Britain and the United States. We welcome the statement of the new French Prime Minister, who has other anxieties on his hands, that France should now put an end to the present uncertainties, and that the French Chamber should take a decision before it separates for the Summer Recess.

The Treaty contains effective safeguards for the future peace of Europe – the EDC Treaty – and these safeguards the Federal Republic of Germany has freely accepted. Dr Adenauer has recently stated that the guarantees are a benefit for everyone concerned, the Germans not excepted. We earnestly hope that what Britain and the United States have said in unison at Washington may play its part in averting the measureless consequences which may follow from further delay by the French Chamber.

The Washington talks have helped to get Anglo-American discussion of the problems of South-East Asia back on to a realistic and constructive level. My right hon. Friend the Foreign Secretary has returned today to Geneva with the feeling that we have moved towards a common outlook on the problems now being discussed there. Further progress at the Geneva Conference depends largely on the results of the military negotiations now taking place between the French, the Associated States and the Vietminh. We and the United States share the hope that the parties will be able to reach an understanding which can be referred back to the Geneva Conference with some hope of success.

Our ideas about a guarantee of any settlement that may be reached at Geneva were explained to the Americans and are now better understood. It is hoped that, should an acceptable settlement be reached on the Indo-China problem, means may be found of getting the countries which participated at the Conference to underwrite it. We hope, too, that other countries with interests in the area might also subscribe to such an undertaking. This was the basis on which the idea was put to the Americans and it is one of the problems to be examined in Washington by the Anglo-United States Study Group set up as the result of our talks.

The other problem which this Group is studying is that of South-East Asia defence. We have to plan not only for the contingency of a negotiated settlement but for other eventualities less agreeable. The arrangements for collective defence in South-East Asia will proceed whether or not agreement is reached at Geneva, though their nature will depend on the results of the Conference. The concept of a collective defence system is not incompatible with the settlement we hope for at Geneva and, after all, the Communists have their own defensive arrangement in the form of the Sino-Soviet Treaty. There is no doubt that the Foreign Secretary's care and zeal in bringing the five Asian Colombo powers prominently into the situation is fully appreciated now by the United States Government. Their association would be and is regarded as important and welcome. All I say on the subject today is that there is no intention of presenting cut-and-dried formulas on a 'take it or leave it' basis to potential Asian members.

The Study Group is therefore examining methods of associating other countries with any settlement of the Indo-China problem that may be reached at Geneva. This involves a security arrangement for South-East Asia assuming an Indo-China agreement, or alternatively a security arrangement for South-East Asia assuming no agreement on Indo-China. The cases are different, quite different.

The joint statement issued in Washington on 28th June stated that if the French Government are confronted with demands which prevent an acceptable agreement regarding Indo-China, the international situation will be seriously aggravated. These words are not intended to be a threat; they are undoubtedly a blunt assertion of fact.

That is all I have to say today upon this complicated and dangerous subject. But I should not conceal from the House the deep anxiety which must naturally be felt lest the military events which are taking place become dominant, with a consequent serious increase of tension in every quarter. We meet under that direct and immediate anxiety.

I now come to a question which has suddenly received a degree of publicity out of all proportion, in my opinion, either to its importance or urgency when compared with the vital matters which I have been outlining. My right hon. Friend the Foreign Secretary and I were astonished on our homeward voyage to read the Press extracts and other reports which were sent us of the storm suddenly raised in the United States by Senator Knowland about the possibility of Communist China being admitted to UNO against American wishes, and still more that these reports seemed to be in some way or other linked with our visit as if we had come over for such a purpose. In fact, although it was mentioned, it played no notable part in our discussions, and was not an immediate issue. It cannot in any way be raised for some time and if it should be raised, which is by no means certain, we shall undoubtedly have a different situation to face than any which now exists.

The United Kingdom policy on the subject of the admission of Communist China to the United Nations has been unchanged since 1951 when the right hon. Gentleman the Member for Lewisham, South (Mr H. Morrison), then Foreign Secretary, stated that His Majesty's Government believed that the Central People's Government should represent China in the United Nations but that, in view of that Government's persistence in behaviour inconsistent with the purposes and principles of the Charter, it appeared to His Majesty's Government that consideration of the question should be postponed. That was the policy of the late Government and it has been the policy of the present Government, reaffirmed in July last by the Chancellor of the Exchequer.

Since then the Geneva Conference has discussed but failed to reach agreement on the reunification of Korea, and although the armistice remains in force the arrangements for its supervision have proved far from satisfactory. Although no actual fighting is taking place, the armies still remain in the presence of each other.

Moreover, as we can all see, the problem of Indo-China has assumed far more serious proportions. Indeed, as I have indicated, a military climax may well be approaching. No agreement has yet been reached at Geneva either about Indo-China or Korea. If such agreements were reached in either or both these theatres, the arrangements would still depend on good faith and co-operation, for which time would certainly be required. In these circumstances, although Her Majesty's Government still believe that the Central People's Government should represent China in the United Nations, they certainly do not consider that this is the moment for the matter to be reconsidered.

Before our return home, the Foreign Secretary and I paid a flying visit to Canada. We were received with glowing warmth of friendship and full understanding, and during our 30 vibrant hours in Ottawa we had very good talks with Mr St Laurent. We sat at the Canadian Cabinet table – I have the honour to be a Canadian Privy Councillor – and we carried away with us renewed conviction of the harmony in sentiment and policy of our two countries.

I have a final thought, which I do not think will raise disagreement, to present to the House, and I should be glad for it to travel as far as my words can reach. In the speech which my right hon. Friend the Foreign Secretary made in winding up the debate before our departure, in speaking about the relations of the Communist and free worlds, he used the remarkable phrase 'peaceful co-existence'. This fundamental and far-reaching conception certainly had its part in some of our conversations at Washington, and I was very glad when I read, after we had left, that President Eisenhower had said that the hope of the world lies in peaceful co-existence of the Communist and non-Communist Powers, adding also the warning, with which I entirely agree, that this doctrine must not lead to appeasement that compels any nation to submit to foreign domination.

The House must not under-rate the importance of this broad measure of concurrence of what in this case I may call the English-speaking world. What a vast ideological gulf there is between the idea of peaceful co-existence vigilantly safeguarded, and the mood of forcibly extirpating the Communist fallacy and heresy. It is, indeed, a gulf. This statement is a recognition of the appalling character which war has now assumed and that its fearful consequences go even beyond the difficulties and dangers of dwelling side by side with Communist States.

Indeed, I believe that the widespread acceptance of this policy may in the passage of years lead to the problems which divide the world being solved or solving themselves, as so many problems do, in a manner which will avert the mass destruction of the human race and give time, human nature and the mercy of God their chance to win salvation for us.

Cabinet: Confidential Annex
(Cabinet papers, 128/40)

13 July 1954
Top Secret
11.30 a.m.
Cabinet Meeting No. 50, Minute 2, of 1954

The Prime Minister read to the Cabinet President Eisenhower's reply to his latest message (Foreign Office telegram to Washington No. 3256)[1] regarding the proposed meeting with M Malenkov. The President had said that this project would not create any difference between the Governments of the United States and the United Kingdom or alter his confidence in the Prime Minister's dedication to the principles which had united the two countries in time of peril and now constituted the best guarantee of world peace. Though he feared the effect on public opinion in the United States, he would do his best to mitigate any immediate unfavourable reaction. On more specific points, the President had welcomed the Prime Minister's statement that he would not be willing to meet M Malenkov except on a basis of full equality. He had also been reassured by the Prime Minister's insistence that the Soviet Government should give proof of their sincerity by deeds as well as words; and he had agreed that it would help to re-establish public confidence if the

[1] Reproduced above (pp. 1670–3).

Russians would undertake to ratify the Austrian Treaty and to co-operate in the Atomic Bank Plan.

The Prime Minister said that he was gratified by the terms and the tone of the President's message.

The Cabinet were also informed of a conversation which the Foreign Secretary had held with M Malenkov in Geneva, in pursuance of the Cabinet's discussion on 10th July. This was reported in Geneva telegram No. 898. M Molotov had recognised that this project of a bilateral meeting could not proceed further until the outcome of the Geneva Conference was known. As regards the choice of meeting-place, the Foreign Secretary rejected a tentative suggestion by M Molotov that the meeting might take place within the Soviet Union, and had suggested London, or as an alternative, Berne. M Molotov had then said that his Government had not yet considered questions of time and place, but he would now communicate with them on this and would let the Foreign Secretary have their views in due course. The Foreign Secretary had deduced from this interview that, if it were finally decided to pursue this project, we need not exclude the possibility of persuading the Russians to accept London, or alternatively Berne, as the place for a meeting.

The Prime Minister said that he would not ask the Cabinet to reach decisions on this matter until after the Foreign Secretary had returned from the Geneva Conference.

President Dwight D. Eisenhower to Sir Winston S. Churchill
(Premier papers, 11/1074)

13 July 1954
Top Secret

Dear Winston,

I have given much thought to your meaty message of July 9.[1] You ask for my reactions to what you say about your proposed trip. You must, of course, know that never for one moment would this create any difference between two governments which are headed by you and me, or alter in the slightest my profound confidence in your dedication to the principles which have so often united our two nations in time of peril and which today constitute a most precious asset and the best guarantee of peace. I cannot, of course, undertake to deliver unto you what you refer to as the 'United States public'. I fear that it may reflect some doubts. But I pledge you that I will do my best to minimize whatever may be the immediate and unfavourable reaction. There will, I am confident, be general acceptance of the sincerity and lofty motivations of your

---

[1] Reproduced above (pp. 1670–3).

efforts. Probably the majority will consider it, as Hoover is supposed to have said of prohibition, 'a noble experiment'.

I am glad that you will not be willing to meet except on a basis of full equality, as indeed I had always assumed. Also, I am reassured that you share the view I have often expressed that Russian deeds are necessary as well as words. Certainly nothing but an evil purpose can prevent their liberation of Austria, where our Foreign Ministers at Berlin accepted all of the Soviet terms. The same applies to my atomic project which cannot possibly harm them and which could re-establish confidence if that be their desire.

Let me now turn to the other subject of your telegram, namely Red China. I too was amazed at the storm which was raised in the press about your presumed intentions. I cannot explain its origin. Foster's recollection is the same as Anthony's as to what he said and is as you put it in your message to me.

I have just been told of the statement on this matter which you have made today. The word came as I was writing this message to you. I am confident that what you have said will indeed ease American minds. Already I think, as a result of what Foster and I have said, there has been a subsiding of Congressional emotion and its action now contemplated does not bear the bellicose note which was originally threatened.

Neither Foster nor I have ever used the 'never, never' theme and we can only rejoice if ultimately the rulers of Red China behave as decent civilized persons. Even this, of course, would leave us the problem of loyalty to our friends on Formosa whom we cannot turn over to the untender mercies of their enemies. This, however, is a matter for the future.

Foster tells me that the talks here with reference to SEATO are going forward in good spirit and at good speed. I earnestly hope that we shall quickly create something to stop the onrush of Communism in Southeast Asia. The French position is crumbling alarmingly.

I am talking now with Foster about whether we should participate in the Geneva Conference. We have agreed that he should offer to meet with Anthony and Mendes-France in Paris tomorrow evening if they desire, with a view to seeing whether in fact we can create a 'united front'. Our great concern is to avoid getting into a position at Geneva where we should be forced to disassociate ourselves publicly and on the basis of principle from a settlement which the French feel they had to take. This would, I feel, do much more lasting harm to Western relations than if we did not appear at a high level at Geneva.

I am glad to see that you have resumed talks with the Egyptians. It would indeed be happy if this friction could be settled and your forces in the Suez made available as a more flexible reserve.

I feel confident that in these and other ways the value of our visit together will progressively manifest itself. The memories of it remain fresh and pleasant in my mind.

1686 JULY 1954

Sir Winston S. Churchill to President Dwight D. Eisenhower
Prime Minister's Personal Telegram T.256/54
(Premier papers, 11/1074)

13 July 1954
Immediate
Top Secret
No. 3352

Dear Friend,

I am deeply grateful for your most generous message. I will telegraph to you at length later.

Sir Winston S. Churchill: speech
(Hansard)

14 July 1954   House of Commons

REVIEW OF FOREIGN AFFAIRS

We have all listened with interest and attention to the calm speech which the right hon. Gentleman the Leader of the Opposition has delivered upon the subject of the statement which I was called upon to make last Monday and also on the general field of foreign affairs. I must say that when listening to the right hon. Gentleman, while paying every tribute to his moderation and desire to mention any fact which he thought fairness required, my general impression of his speech was that it was one long whine of criticism against the United States –

Mr George Craddock (Bradford, South):[1] Scandalous.

The Prime Minister: We are still allowed to debate and not merely to yelp from below the Gangway. It was one long criticism against the United States – (Hon. Members: 'Nonsense') – and, of course, of advancing the importance, if not the virtues, of Communist China. The right hon. Gentleman spoke of the entry of China into the United Nations organisation. I thought the statement I made on Monday covered that matter. (Hon. Members: 'No'.) Well, in principle one cannot conceive that China would be forever excluded from the United Nations, but, on the other hand, one really does not see why this particular moment would be well chosen for its admission when it is still technically at war with the United Nations – technically, I say – and when it is at this moment going to achieve a resounding triumph by the success of the stimulated war in Indo-China, in which it has played so great a part.

I am sure that to choose such a moment as this to try to force the entry of

---

[1] George Craddock, 1897–1974. MP (Lab.) for Bradford South, 1949–70.

Communist China into the United Nations would be to complicate altogether the very grave affairs we have to deal with in so many other questions and would be regarded as a most harsh and uncalled-for act of unfriendliness by the mighty people of the United States, to whom we all owe much and from whom no Government ever received more than the Government of the party opposite.

Mr Attlee: I do not think the right hon. Gentleman quite caught the import of my remarks. The point was that a large number of people say they will never have China in the United Nations and they will never do anything in regard to Formosa. My point was that unless we held out the prospect that when these things are settled that will happen, there will be no immediate settlement. I never suggested that at this very moment it could be done.

The Prime Minister: I am glad to hear that, because in any case it would be very difficult to deal with the matter at this very moment, there being no session of the United Nations – unless one were specially called – until the third week in September. Even then I do not think we could form our view clearly without a proper study of the circumstances as they existed at the time.

As I was listening to the speech of the right hon. Gentleman, I felt it was all for consideration for China and, very moderately expressed, but none the less very notable, criticisms of the United States. The right hon. Gentleman mentioned the word 'Korea'. I think I must ask him to look back a little on his own past – the good parts in it as well as the other parts. It is only a little while ago that he joined the United States in repelling Communist aggression in Korea. Although our country and the United States have made great sacrifices – our sacrifices have been such that many families in this country feel their pangs – there are 20 times as many casualties which fell on the Americans. And when a country has recently lost 20,000 killed and 80,000 or something like that – wounded, and poured out vast sums of money, it is natural that they feel certain emotions – I think that is the right word – certain emotional manifestations, about what happens in the country for which these sacrifices were made, and made with the full agreement and active support of the right hon. Gentleman.

It is surely not a moment, the present moment, when the situation is what it is in Indo-China; and when all these memories of Korea are still lively in the United States; and when no cessation of the technical war with UNO has been achieved, for us to raise such a matter in a strenuous fashion with the United States on a visit which was intended to clear up misunderstandings, and not to aggravate by sharp expression any of the necessary and natural differences which exist between great free communities working together.

The right hon. Gentleman spoke also about Chiang Kai-shek and Formosa. Chiang Kai-shek used to be very popular in this country. I remember his being thought to be the future leader of the new Asia. And, of course, his views about India and its connection with the British Crown caused no obstacles to the admiration with which he was regarded by the right hon. Gentleman and his friends on that side of the House. But I was rather astonished at the attempt which the right hon. Gentleman made to compare Chiang Kai-shek with General Burgoyne.[1] I must say, you could hardly pick two figures more different.

And also I thought it rather odd that, speaking of Guatemala, of what had happened in Guatemala, this should raise in his mind the memory and story of the life of John Wilkes.[2] These are very farfetched comparisons to bring together. Personally, I cannot see that if General Burgoyne had been established on Long Island, and had set up an independent State there, he would in any way have resembled what is the position of Chiang Kai-shek who, having for a very long time fought on our side, or on the American side, with American aid and support, was driven out of his country by a Communist revolution – which incidentally killed, I believe in cold blood, something which is estimated to be between two million and three million persons – and who took refuge upon Formosa, where he still remains. I certainly do not see anything in the conduct of China which has yet happened which should lead the American Government to deliver Formosa to Communist China.

Nor do I see any reason why at some subsequent date Formosa should not be treated in the manner which the right hon. Gentleman described, and placed in the custody of the United Nations. I know that the right hon. Gentleman does not want to harm our relations with the United States; but I can assure him that the speech he has made, although so temperately expressed, will undoubtedly make a bad impression – (Hon. Members: 'No'.) – and more difficult the settlement of the many awkward questions which we have to deal with in common with the United States. That is what I have to say about that.

We are not going to raise this question of the entry of Communist China into the United Nations at present. We think that September is the first time that it can be raised, and we believe that it might be better for all concerned, and for all the interests represented, that it should be postponed until a later period. I must point out to the Committee – before you start shouting with anger at me who has done you no harm – (Hon. Members: 'Oh'.) – we keep some of our indignation for the quarters to which it really belongs –

Miss Jennie Lee[3] (Cannock): Not today.

---

[1] John Burgoyne, 1722–92. Lt, 1st Royal Dragoons, 1745. Capt., 1747. Married, 1751, Charlotte Stanley Derby: one child. Served in Seven Years War, 1956–63. Lt-Col., 1758. MP for Midhurst, 1761–8; for Preston, 1768–92. Brig.-Gen., 1762. Governor of Fort William, 1769–79. Major-Gen., 1775. Surrendered to American forces at Saratoga, 1777. C-in-C, Ireland, 1782–4. Col., 4th Rgt of Foot, 1782–92.

[2] John Wilkes, 1727–97. Educated at University of Leiden, Dutch Republic. Married, 1747, Mary Meade: one child. MP (Radical) for Aylesbury, 1757–64; for Middlesex, 1768–9, 1774–90. Published *The North Briton*, 1762–3. Alderman of London, 1769; Sheriff, 1771; Lord Mayor, 1774; Chamberlain, 1779–97.

[3] Janet Lee, 1904–88. Known as 'Jennie'. Educated at Edinburgh University. MP (Lab.) for North Lanark, 1929–31; for Cannock, 1935–70. Married, 1934, Aneurin Bevan (d. 1960). Member, National

The Prime Minister: We follow the policy outlined by the former Secretary of State for Foreign Affairs which I described on Monday, and which, as far as I know, still continues to be the policy of the British Government, and which has commanded a very considerable measure of acceptance, if not of agreement, in the United States.

Mr Herbert Morrison (Lewisham, South): I quite agree that the timing and the moment for the raising of this is a matter for careful consideration; but the right hon. Gentleman ought to appreciate that the statement which I made, and to which I adhere, was made while hostilities were proceeding; and it should not be assumed from that that in the very different circumstances – though I wish they were still better – that now obtain, there is not such a change of circumstances as may well warrant a revision of the judgment then made in conditions of hostility.

The Prime Minister: I am quite sure that if at the present moment an agitation were set on foot to bring Communist China into the United Nations, the American feeling would be that they were succeeding in shooting their way in. Not only has there been no settlement in Korea, but there has been very grave aggravation of all our anxieties by what has happened, and is happening, in Indo-China. We all hope that better results may be achieved in Indo-China, and that more peaceful arrangements, bringing at any rate the fighting to an end, may be gained. If so, no one would deserve more praise for his extraordinary perseverance and skill than the Foreign Secretary, who, even at this moment, is tirelessly continuing his efforts with the utmost patience. I only hope that nothing that has been said, or will be said, in this debate will, by rousing American feeling, make his task and the prospect of success more difficult.

The right hon. Gentleman finished by saying something about the hydrogen bomb and about a possible meeting with Mr Malenkov. If today I have nothing to add to or subtract from anything which I have previously said upon this subject, and ask the Committee not to press me upon the matter, I can assure hon. Members that it is not because it does not hold a lively place in my mind. I certainly feel that it is extraordinary that the noble theme, as I called it, which President Eisenhower put forward to the United Nations has not received more acceptance from the Soviet, and it seems to me that it might well be a subject on which at a certain stage, and when the right time comes, there might be a meeting on the highest level; but all this must depend, as I said, not only upon the timing but also upon the course of events.

While I in no way diminish or recede from what I have said in the past, I could not refer to the topic without warning anyone who is sympathetic to the idea of the great risks which are run that not merely false hopes would be

Executive Committee, Labour Party, 1958–70; Chairman, 1967–8. Parliamentary Secretary, Ministry of Public Building and Works, 1964–5. Parliamentary Under-Secretary of State, Dept of Education and Science, 1965–7. PC, 1966. Minister of State, 1967–70. Baroness, 1970.

raised and broken but that the situation itself might be rendered more severe if such top-level meetings took place without any satisfactory effect.

I made a statement last Monday which was criticised in some quarters as having something in it of the nature of a speech. I certainly have no desire to detain the Committee for any length of time this afternoon. The right hon. Gentleman mentioned the question of Egypt and I was asked whether I would answer the Question of the right hon. and learned Member for Rowley Regis and Tipton (Mr A. Henderson) to the Foreign Secretary.

Mr H. Morrison: That was earlier.

Mr Arthur Henderson (Rowley Regis and Tipton): Before the Leader of the Opposition spoke.

The Prime Minister: I beg the right hon. and learned Gentleman's pardon. That is something to look forward to.

The right hon. and learned Gentleman asked whether we would make a further statement on the resumption of negotiations between Her Majesty's Government and the Egyptian Government over the Canal Zone. Discussions with the Egyptian Government have been resumed but no point has been reached at which any statement could be made at present.

Mr R. H. S. Crossman (Coventry, East): The right hon. Gentleman made one yesterday.

The Prime Minister: That is quite untrue. The hon. Member is never lucky in the coincidence of his facts with the truth. No question of the terms which are being discussed or may be discussed was involved; there was no question of stating them to a party committee. If ever they were stated at all, it would in the first instance be in the House of Commons, but I am very doubtful whether it would be a good thing to begin negotiations by a categorical statement of terms which would almost invest them with an air of an ultimatum, because one thing plays in with another and has to be balanced against another, and in these conversations it is a good thing to keep little things open at the same time and then probably find agreement among them. (Hon. Members: 'What about the 1922 Committee?')

The committee which I addressed last night was not the 1922 Committee. It was the military sub-committee of the Defence Committee, not the 1922 Committee, and it was in fact attended by practically the same Members. I hope that when I make inquiries about any of the very numerous similar committees and consultations which take place on the other side of the House, I shall be given an equally exact and suitable reply.

Mr E. Shinwell (Easington): *rose* –

The Prime Minister: This has nothing to do with the right hon. Gentleman. I am not prepared to give way. I raised the question of Egypt with the President when I was in Washington.

Mr Shinwell: The right hon. Gentleman is afraid to give way.

The Prime Minister: I am afraid that if I were to give way on such a point as this the right hon. Gentleman might think there was some truth in that allegation.

I raised the question of Egypt with the President. I have for some time been of the opinion that the United States have a strategic interest in Egypt as well as their interest in the international waterway of the Suez Canal and that the responsibility for both these matters should no longer be allowed to rest exclusively with Great Britain. Although, of course, the strategic importance of Egypt and the Canal has been enormously reduced by modern developments of war, it cannot be wholly excluded from American thoughts where the recent extension of NATO's southern flank to Turkey is concerned.

I have dealt with the suggestion which has been made in the papers that some announcement was made to Conservative Members of Parliament about the terms and negotiations with Egypt and I can give the Committee the assurance that nothing of that kind took place. We had discussions and arguments among ourselves, as I believe is not by any means confined to this party.

I have only a few points to add to the statement which I made on Monday. I am sometimes reproached with having led France to expect that Britain would be a full member of the European Defence Community. When in 1950 I proposed at Strasbourg the creation of a European army, I had in mind – and it is clear from my speech – the formation of a long-term grand alliance under which national armies would operate under a unified allied command. The policy of the alliance would, I assumed, be decided jointly by the Governments of the participating countries. My conception involved no supranational institutions and I saw no difficulty in Britain playing her full part in a scheme of that kind.

However, the French approached this question from a constitutional rather than a purely military point of view. The result was that when they and the other five Continental nations worked out a detailed scheme, it took the form of a complete merger of national forces under federal supranational control. The late Government, in a joint declaration made at Washington in 1951, gave their support to this EDC plan, but they made it clear that Britain, whilst ready to associate herself closely with the new organisation, would not be a full member. I agreed with this. That was the situation when we became responsible for the Government, and we have persevered in that policy ever since.

I still regret, looking back on the past, that the late Government did not accept the French invitation to take part in the framing of the plan of EDC. If they had, it might have been possible to obtain an agreement on a scheme of a less federalistic nature in which Britain could have played a fuller part. But regrets about the past and theoretical differences should not lead us to under-estimate the practical value in terms of defence which the EDC scheme offers, and for that reason I have no doubt whatsoever that the Government and the official Opposition are right in giving EDC their support and encouraging France to ratify the Treaty. But I do hope that disputes about the form of things will not be allowed to bulk too large.

A few months ago we agreed to dedicate a British division to the EDC, and this gave much satisfaction to our French friends. But, after all, what difference did it make in fact? The division was still composed of the same men; it wore the same uniform; it stood in the same place in the line of battle where it was intended by General Gruenther, the Supreme Commander, to place it. It could be moved about by him in peace or war. All that happened was that it was dedicated by us to the French conception of EDC, and this gave a good deal of pleasure.

But, after all, what counts in matters of defence are the physical facts. We must not lose our sense of proportion or allow theoretical differences to dim our vision of the outstanding realities on which our life and safety depend. What are these realities? By the combined working of the EDC scheme with NATO, the British, Canadian and United States forces would be brought into the Continental line of defence together with all their European comrades. All will stand together on the same front. All will be under a single commander, by whom all can be disposed and moved about in national homogeneous divisions. Surely, this giant fact should not be overlooked for the sake of complicated and almost metaphysical argument, however intricate or exciting it may be.

In the Washington statement to which I referred when I spoke on Monday, the President and I declared that we were 'agreed that the German Federal Republic should take its place as an equal partner in the community of Western nations where it can make its proper contribution to the defence of the free world. We are determined to achieve this goal, convinced that the Bonn and Paris treaties provide the best way.' We also said that we 'welcomed the recent statement by the French Prime Minister that an end must be put to the present uncertainties,' and expressed 'our conviction that further delay in the entry into force of the EDC and Bonn Treaties would damage the solidarity of the Atlantic nations'. Her Majesty's Government, like its predecessor, support wholeheartedly the policy of the European Defence Community. We are sure that this is the best and the safest way in which Germany can be rearmed and enabled to play its necessary and vital part in the scheme of European unity and reconciliation. There is a wider measure of agreement for EDC than for any other plan that has been conceived or proclaimed, and certainly the scheme for German participation in an international army with a force of 12 divisions cannot be regarded as excessive when we remember the strength of the Soviet armies.

These comprise an immediate strength in the forward areas of Europe of 30 active divisions, mostly armoured and mechanised, which could be increased to a total of considerably over 100 divisions at what is called in military parlance D plus 30. Moreover, NATO have already stated publicly that the Soviet world strength on the 30th day of mobilisation would, including the European satellite countries, amount to 400 divisions. I do not feel that the question of 12 German divisions ought to bulk out of all proportion when we consider the general situation.

We cannot tell, however, whether the French Assembly will ratify the EDC Treaty during their present session, which will probably end in August. This Treaty was signed by the French Government more than two years ago. If it does not come into force in the very near future, a most difficult situation will arise. The Bonn Conventions which bring the occupation of the German Federal Republic to an end cannot, as they at present stand, enter into force unless the EDC Treaty enters into force at the same time.

In this situation the German Federal Republic is still denied the political benefits of the Bonn Conventions signed by all the Governments concerned more than two years ago. Confronted by this problem, the British and United States Governments have come to the conclusion that in the unhappy event of the failure to ratify EDC, their aim could best be achieved by dissociating the Bonn Conventions in simultaneity from the passing of the EDC Treaty, and if possible this should be done by agreement between the four Powers which signed those Conventions. Any other course in the face of these long and indefinite delays would be contrary to the standards of good faith and fair play which we desire to maintain towards all nations, including those with whom we have been at war.

Mr Attlee: This is a very important statement. This would seem to give a great accession of sovereignty to Germany without the integration of German defence forces into a European Army. There is then a danger that Germany will rearm on her own. There may be provisions for control, but they become more and more difficult with each accession of sovereignty. I would ask, before this is definitely approved, that the House should be called together.

The Prime Minister: We have not gone away yet. We must consider all these matters when circumstances are before us.

I shall not attempt this afternoon to forecast what arrangements would be needed to secure the agreement of Germany to confine the use of her restored sovereign rights within standard limits of safety comparable to that which has been effected by EDC. It is clear, however, that discussions of these matters would entail the deferment of German rearmament for the time being, with the necessary provision of continued financial support for the Allied Forces in Germany during this period. I understand that some announcement in this sense is going to be made in the United States today.

Mr Aneurin Bevan (Ebbw Vale): I have been endeavouring to follow what the right hon. Gentleman said, especially in the last paragraph of his statement. I am sure the Committee would be obliged if he would repeat it, because he says that a similar statement is to be made by the United States, and we should like to know what it is.

The Prime Minister: The statement to which I have referred is this: It is clear that the discussion on what is to happen to Germany if EDC fails, and on what would happen in the course of restoring her liberties under the Bonn Conventions, would entail a deferment of German rearmament for the time being, with the necessary provision for the continued financial support for the Allied Forces in Germany, during this period.

The French Government have been informed of our intention to proceed along the lines I have indicated. Should the French Chamber fail to ratify the EDC Treaty, we still hope that we shall not be forced to separate the two Treaties and to make other arrangements to replace in some form or other the satisfactory plan of German rearmament set forth in EDC. If these difficulties are solved and if the EDC Treaty entered into force shortly, the problems to which I have referred would not confront us.

Mr William Warbey (Broxtowe):[1] This is an extremely important matter upon which the Committee desire elucidation. Can the Prime Minister say whether any time-limit has been set by Her Majesty's Government and the United States Government for the ratification of EDC by the French Parliament; and secondly, what would be the juridical position of the West German Government in relation to the creation of national armed forces in the event of the Bonn Conventions being brought into force?

The Prime Minister: No time-limit has been definitely fixed, yet at the same time we cannot go on keeping all this matter hanging in the air indefinitely. There must be a moment when, in justice and fair play to Germany, some relief similar to that which was signed in the Treaties of two years ago should be accorded. That would require other rearrangements in the military sphere. I should have thought there was very general agreement upon this being the way to proceed.

We are showing no impatience at all and are giving every opportunity to the French, but we recognise that we have to be fair with the Germans. If they were cut out of what they had been promised by all of us two years ago, it would be a very bad thing, and if we, so to speak, felt that we had been guilty of breaking faith with them or with Dr Adenauer.

I have had handed to me a communiqué issued in Paris at 4.30 p.m. today. Perhaps I might read it in conclusion to the Committee, as it is relevant to the matters which are in all our minds. It says that General Bedell Smith is going back to Geneva. The communiqué is as follows: 'We have had intimate and frank discussions. These have resulted in a clear understanding of our respective positions in relation to Indo-China. The United States Secretary of State,

---

[1] William Noble Warbey, 1903–80. Educated at King's College London and London School of Economics. Language teacher and interpreter, France and Germany, 1925–6. Master, Derby Municipal Secondary School, 1927–8. Secretary and Tutor, University Tutorial College, London, 1929–37. Married, 1931, Audrey Grace Wicks. Tutor-organiser, National Council of Labour Colleges, 1937–40. Chief English Press Officer to Norwegian Government in London, 1941–5. MP (Lab.) for Luton, 1945–50; for Broxtowe, 1953–5; for Ashfield, 1955–66.

Mr Foster Dulles, explained fully the attitude of his Government towards the Indo-China phase of the Geneva Conference and the limitations which that Government desired to observe as not itself having primary responsibility for the Indo-Chinese war.' 'The French Premier and Foreign Minister, Mr Mendes-France, expressed the view, with which Mr Eden, the Secretary of State for Foreign Affairs for the United Kingdom, associated himself, that it would nevertheless serve the interests of France and of the Associated States, and of the peace and freedom of the area, if the United States, without departing from the principles that Mr Dulles expressed, were once again to be represented at Geneva at the ministerial level.' 'Accordingly, President Eisenhower and Mr Dulles are requesting the United States Under-Secretary of State, General Bedell Smith, to return to Geneva at an early date.' This is as good a moment to sit down as I am likely to find.

Sir Winston S. Churchill to Sir David Maxwell Fyfe
Prime Minister's Personal Minute M.117/54
(Premier papers, 11/607)

15 July 1954

I certainly consider you should treat them[1] with the utmost censure which the law allows. What a mean and cowardly gesture for a City to refuse to give humanitarian aid to neighbouring towns in distress, at the same time expecting help themselves. I earnestly hope however you are eliminating the ridiculous aspects of the Civil Defence demonstration.

John Colville: diary
('The Fringes of Power', pages 701–2)

16 July 1954

Things came to a head today, at any rate within 10 Downing Street. Before luncheon Harold Macmillan came to see Lady Churchill and told her that the Cabinet was in danger of breaking up on this issue.[2] When he had gone she rang me up and asked me to come and see her. I in fact knew more about the situation than she did and since she proposed to 'open' the matter to Winston at luncheon, I suggested I should stay too.

She began by putting her foot into it in saying that the Cabinet were angry with W for mishandling the situation, instead of saying that they were trying to stop Salisbury going. He snapped back at her – which he seldom does – and

---

[1] Coventry City Council, which voted to abandon civil defence measures after the US Castle Bravo H-bomb test of March 1954.

[2] Regarding the details of a potential meeting with the Russians.

afterwards complained to me that she always put the worst complexion on everything in so far as it affected him. However, he did begin to see that Salisbury's resignation would be serious on this issue, whereas two days ago when I mentioned the possibility to him he said that he didn't 'give a damn'. On the other hand it became clear that he had taken the steps he had, without consulting the Cabinet, quite deliberately. He admitted to me that if he had waited to consult the Cabinet after the *Queen Elizabeth* returned, they would almost certainly have raised objections and caused delays. The stakes in this matter were so high and, as he sees it, the possible benefits so crucial to our survival, that he was prepared to adopt any methods to get a meeting with the Russians arranged.

Sir Winston S. Churchill to Anthony Eden
Prime Minister's Personal Telegram T.261/54
(Premier papers, 11/613)

17 July 1954
Immediate
Secret and Personal
No. 1471

1. I am sending you a letter I have received from Monty. I certainly do not think that we should press the Americans to give another two months' delay which presumably would alter the whole timetable of fulfilling the Bonn Convention as agreed by us with Ike at Washington. However we can talk this over when you return. You will have got my telegram which I sent you last night (the 16th) by now. Obviously we must wait until Geneva is decided. I am sorry to read in the newspapers that things are looking adverse on your front.

2. I am getting a good deal of abuse about Suez, etc. The fact that redeployment on every military ground is necessary, does not make it less unpleasant to carry out.

3. The feeling against Dugdale in the Party is serious and he may decide to tender his resignation and announce it in his opening speech. He has not done so yet.

4. We shall have to have Cabinet on Tuesday and Wednesday and I expect on Thursday. All good luck in the Geneva finish. No one can blame you whatever happens.

Sir Winston S. Churchill to Anthony Eden
(Premier papers, 11/613)

17 July 1954
Immediate
Secret
No. 1472

My immediately preceding telegram.
Following is text.

16 July 1954

My dear Winston

I had a long talk last night in Paris with General Koenig, who, as you know, is Minister of Defence in the Mendès-France Government. The conversation seems to me to be so important that I would like to let you know about it at once. It concerned two subjects, i.e. Indo-China and the EDC. I give below the main points of the conversation.

Indo-China

On this subject Koenig said that France had failed in the past to face up to practical realities and to enter into her responsibilities in a whole-hearted manner. She was now paying the price for that neglect and would have to swallow a bitter pill. But there was no alternative, and it was his opinion that if there was not some agreement reached, and the fighting was continued for much longer, France would suffer a military defeat.

It was, therefore, completely essential to get some acceptable solution to the problem, even if this involved partition of Viet Nam. It would then be essential for France to regain complete administrative control in that part of Viet Nam remaining to her. But I expect you know all about this, and you no doubt know the terms of the agreement that is likely to be reached. Koenig made the point that they have got to face up to practical realities and get the Indo-China problem disposed of in the best way possible: accepting the fact that it is entirely their own fault and due to mistakes made by previous French Governments.

EDC Treaty

The next fence to be taken will be EDC and Koenig is gravely disturbed about this fence. It is his definite opinion that as things stand today it will not be passed by the French Parliament; if it gets through the Assembly it will not get through the Senate.

Everyone is exhausted by the struggle to get a solution in Indo-China. The moment <u>that</u> has been achieved, American pressure demands that they go straight on to the EDC problem and get that through before Parliament rises for the Summer Recess. In other words, the two items have to be taken as 'one package'. If they bring the EDC up before Parliament and fail to get it through, which it seems may well happen, a very severe blow will be dealt at the possibility of ever getting it though at all. It might also result in the downfall of the Mendès-France Government and the loss of the only French Prime Minister who seems to be able to tackle these things in a realistic manner.

I have now lived in France for some time and I know a great many French people on varying levels, political and military. It is my definite view that the Western Allies are making a mistake in trying to rush the EDC through so soon after the Indo-China matter has been settled. I consider that Mendès-France needs a period of about two months after the solution of the Indo-China problem, and during those months he might be able to fix up things in such a way that there is a chance of getting the Treaty through his Parliament. It might happen that during these two months some small amendments could be made which would make the Treaty more acceptable to various political parties and which would not be objected to by the other five nations; but this of course I do not know. What I am quite certain about is that a delay of two months might save the whole thing from crashing.

I also believe that the only hope of getting such a delay of two months would be for the initiative in the matter to be taken by Her Majesty's Government. Certain nations, e.g. Germany, Belgium, America, have been very outspoken about the necessity of no further delay and I doubt if any approach would be successful other than one coming from the United Kingdom Government.

If, for instance, you could communicate with Ike and suggest that every chance be given to Mendès-France after the turmoil of Geneva is over, and that you reckon a delay of say two months would give him that chance, then I would suggest that such an approach would be well worthwhile.

What it really comes to is this: if Mendès-France goes into the EDC Battle in August, immediately after the Indo-China turmoil has subsided, he will crash almost for a certainty; if he can be given a period of about two months to sort things out, there is a possibility he may succeed.

That is how I see the matter.

Conclusion

I am sending this letter over to you by hand of an ADC and he has orders to take it direct to No. 10 Downing Street and ask that it be given to you at once.

I hope you will not mind me writing to you on this subject. But I do feel very strongly that this is one of those matters where a little time spent in preparing the ground may make a great difference to the peace of Europe. And after all, two months is not a very long time.

JULY 1954 1699

In war, time spent in reconnaissance and preparation is always justified. Is it not the same in this case?

I agree that there has been much time wasted in the past on these activities, but not by Mendès-France. If you give him a chance he may succeed. And it is worth waiting another two months, if it means success.

Yours always
Monty

Sir Winston S. Churchill to Sir Hartley Shawcross
(Churchill papers, 4/58)

17 July 1954

My dear Hartley Shawcross,

Thank you so much for your letter of July 6, and later your letter of the 13th. I think you were quite right to publish your rejoinder to Dorman Smith's outburst.

As to the publicity. I have long been used to lies being published in the Press and I have not often found it necessary to contradict them.

I think the whole thing is settled most satisfactorily. The great thing was to avoid the annoyance and expense of an action. This has been achieved by your patience and skill and personally I shall now put the matter from my mind.

PS. You promised me to send the account of your expenses through your Secretary.

Sir Winston S. Churchill to Anthony Eden
(Foreign Office papers, 800/762)

18 July 1954
Immediate
Dedip
Top Secret, Personal and Private
No. 1486

Your No. 957.

I agree with your para. 2[1] and think it should cover success or failure at Geneva. I hope, however, you will not say anything to dissuade Molotov from

---

[1] This para. read: 'If Molotov raises the topic with me, I will speak to him as you suggest. But if we succeed here, I may have to say something more before leaving. I suggest that it should be that you want to discuss the whole situation with me and the rest of the Cabinet on my return from Geneva.'

a future meeting. According to your No. 943 of July 16 he may not be very keen on it anyhow.

2. Thursday will be all right for discussing these issues at Cabinet and I should certainly like to have a talk with you beforehand when you get back on Wednesday. I shall judge the position in light of the then existing circumstances. At present my feeling is that failure at Geneva will make it all the more necessary that the meeting should take place and we at any rate should make 'officially' something like the suggestion I made 'personally' on the voyage and which you said you would support.

3. I hope that Salisbury will defer to your advice. I have heard nothing from him.

Anthony Eden to Sir Winston S. Churchill
Prime Minister's Personal Telegram T.263/54
(Premier papers, 11/650)

18 July 1954
Secret
No. 962

In my view we still have no more than a fifty–fifty chance of reaching an agreement here. The time limit which M Mendès-France has set himself expires next Tuesday, July 20.

2. I have been discussing with Bedell Smith since his return what we should do to enlist the fullest support of the Commonwealth and Asian countries either for any agreement which we may reach or for any action we may have to take in the serious situation that will arise should our efforts fail.

3. If an agreement is reached which the Americans can respect they will be ready to issue a statement making the points indicated in my second following telegram. There would be great advantage in persuading the Colombo Powers, as well as the Governments of Australia and New Zealand, to make similar statements on these lines.

4. If we get no agreement the Americans think it very important that the governments concerned should be ready to issue, with the least possible delay, some clear statement of their intention to press forward with the conclusion of a collective defence agreement for South East Asia and the South West Pacific. I think there is much of value in this idea. The important thing for us is that our Asian partners in the Commonwealth and the other Colombo Powers, as well as Australia and New Zealand, should be told what we have in mind and given an opportunity of joining in from the outset. They may not all agree to take part but their being consulted may make all the difference to the view they take of our later actions.

5. My third following telegram contains a draft, as agreed with Bedell Smith, of the declaration which all the participating Powers might be asked to make, either severally or individually. I recommend that Her Majesty's Government in the United Kingdom should in any event join with the United States Government and such other governments as are willing to take part in making individual statements on these lines.

6. I have agreed with Bedell Smith that subject to your views and those of any colleagues you may wish to consult I should send an urgent message to the Five Colombo Powers and also to Australia and New Zealand, giving them our views about the sort of action they might take in either eventuality and seeking their urgent comments. A message on these lines is contained in my immediately following telegram.

7. If you agree I hope that our High Commissioners at Canberra, Wellington,[1] New Delhi,[2] Karachi[3] and Colombo and Her Majesty's ambassadors at Rangoon and Djakarta[4] may be instructed immediately to deliver this message together with the accompanying drafts in my second and third following telegrams. I am repeating this telegram to them but they should of course not act until they receive final authority from London. I hope they may receive this in time to enable them to act tomorrow.

8. If you agree with my proposal the United States Government will make a similar communication to the Governments of the Philippines and Siam. Her Majesty's Ambassador at Washington should be instructed to inform the United States Government, and I shall tell Bedell Smith, as soon as you give your agreement.

9. I suggest that Her Majesty's Ambassador at Paris should also then inform the French Government of the action we are taking. I shall keep Mendès-France informed here.

10. Our High Commissioner at Ottawa should I think, also be authorised to keep the Canadian Government informed.

---

[1] Geoffrey Allen Percival Scoones, 1893–1975. Served in France during WWI, 1915–17 (despatches thrice, DSO, MC). GOC 19th Indian Infantry Div., 1941–2; IV Corps, 1942–4. KBE, 1944. GOC-in-C, Central Command, India, 1944–6. ADC to King George VI, 1947–9. High Commissioner to New Zealand, 1953–7.

[2] Peter Alexander Clutterbuck, 1897–1975. Served with Coldstream Guards during WWI, 1916–19 (despatches, MC). Deputy High Commissioner to South Africa, 1939–40. Asst Under-Secretary of State, Dominions Office, 1942–6. KCMG, 1946. High Commissioner to Canada, 1946–52; to India, 1952–5; to Republic of Ireland, 1955–9. GCMG, 1952.

[3] John Gilbert Laithwaite, 1894–1986. On active service in France, 1917–18 (wounded). Private Secretary to Viceroy of India Lord Linlithgow, 1936–43. Knighted, 1941. Under-Secretary (Civil), War Cabinet, 1944–5. Deputy Under-Secretary of State for India, 1944–5; for Burma, 1945–7. Ambassador to Dublin, 1950–1. High Commissioner to Pakistan, 1951–4.

[4] Oscar Charles Morland, 1904–80. Ambassador to Indonesia, 1953–6. Asst Under-Secretary of State, FO, 1956–9. KCMG, 1959. GBE, 1962.

Sir Winston S. Churchill to Anthony Eden
Prime Minister's Personal Telegram T.264/54
(Premier papers, 11/650)

19 July 1954
Immediate
Secret, Personal and Private
No. 1487

Your 962. At this hour, 1 a.m., I have not yet been able to consult any colleagues except Lord Swinton. We both approve your proposals and text. I will support them with my full authority. If you consider urgency requires it you are free to dispatch forthwith.

[. . .]

Sir Winston S. Churchill to Anthony Eden
Prime Minister's Personal Telegram T.268/54
(Premier papers, 11/650)

20 July 1954
Immediate
Top Secret and Personal
No. 1517

Your telegram No. 984.

I entirely agree. The supreme Geneva objective is Cease Fire and stopping the war in Indo-China, and no procedural differences with the United States should be allowed to prevent this. Moreover I think the arrangements proposed for SEATO are a necessary factor in the policy of Peace Through Strength. I hope we can be equally agreed upon the next step and I believe that this can also be balanced with the USA. I will bring your telegram to the notice of the Cabinet and urge them to reply as you wish. I cannot imagine there would be any difficulty but I will send you a confirmatory message before noon.

Cabinet: conclusions
(Cabinet papers, 128/27)

20 July 1954
Secret
11 a.m.
Cabinet Meeting No. 51 of 1954

1. The Prime Minister said that he had received a message from the Foreign Secretary (Geneva telegram No. 984) about the reluctance of the United States

Government to join in a multilateral declaration recognising any settlement on Indo-China which might be reached at the Geneva Conference. The United States representative at Geneva had made it plain that, even if the settlement was one which they could respect, they would be unwilling to do more than make a unilateral declaration taking note of the agreement and undertaking not to disturb it. The Foreign Secretary feared that this might give rise to procedural difficulties in the concluding stages of the Conference. He would do his best to overcome these without disclosing the differences between Western Powers. If, however, he found himself faced with the choice between losing an agreement because of the procedural difficulties and securing an agreement at the cost of some procedural difficulties between the United States and other Western Governments, he would feel obliged to choose the latter alternative.

In discussion there was general support for the view expressed by the Foreign Secretary.

The Cabinet –

Took note that the Prime Minister would at once inform the Foreign Secretary that he could count on the Cabinet's full support in pursuing the course indicated in paragraph 3 of Geneva telegram No. 984.

[. . .]

President Dwight D. Eisenhower to Sir Winston S. Churchill
(Churchill papers, 6/3B)[1]

22 July 1954　　　　　　　　　　　　　　　　　　　　　　　　The White House
Eyes Only
Top Secret

Dear Winston,

I have been thinking over some of the conversations we had during your recent visit, particularly those dealing with our joint pronouncement on the principles and purposes which will guide our international behaviour. I have in mind also your confidential statement that within a reasonable time you want to shift the responsibility of the Premiership to other shoulders – one reason being that you wish to give your successor a chance to establish himself politically before the next elections.

Considering these two matters together, I am certain that you must have a very deep and understandable desire to do something special and additional in your remaining period of active service that will be forever recognized as a mile-stone in the world's tortuous progress towards a just and lasting peace.

---

[1] President Eisenhower wrote in a covering letter: 'By this mail I am sending you a very long letter which I hope you will read when you have a bit of leisure time. I assure you that in writing it I am thinking only of our joint hope of welding among the nations of the free world bonds that will grow ever stronger and more durable.'

Nothing else could provide such a fitting climax to your long and brilliant service to your sovereign, your country and the world.

I am sure that some such thought of your conscious or sub-conscious mind must be responsible for your desire to meet Malenkov and to explore, so far as is possible, the purposes of his heart and the designs of his brain.

As you know, while I have not been able to bring myself to believe wholeheartedly in the venture, I most earnestly pray that you may develop something good out of what seems to me the bleakest of prospects. This I say not primarily because of my deep affection and respect for an old and valued friend and the satisfaction I would take in such a personal triumph of yours, but because the world so desperately needs to be strengthened in hope and faith and confidence that anyone who would not pray for the success of your venture would indeed be wicked.

Having said this, I must also say that because of my utter lack of confidence in the reliability and integrity of the men in the Kremlin and my feeling that you may be disappointed in your present hopes, my mind has been turning toward an exploration of other possibilities by which you would still give to the world something inspiring before you lay down your official responsibilities. It should be something that would so well serve the cause in which we believe that it would indeed be considered one of your finest contributions.

Another factor to be considered is that in far too many areas the Kremlin is pre-empting the right to speak for the small nations of the world. We are falsely pictured as the exploiters of people, the Soviets as their champion.

I suggest to you a thoughtful speech on the subject of the rights to self-government, so vigorously supported in our recent communiqué.

At first glance, this seems a thorny nettle to grasp. But I believe that by looking closely we can find that this is not necessarily so.

In our conversations, we agreed that in a number of areas people are not yet ready for self-rule and that any attempt to make them now responsible for their own governing would be to condemn them to lowered standards of life and probably to communistic domination. At the same time, we must never allow the world to believe that we are ready to abandon our stated purposes merely because of this obvious, negative truth.

Colonialism is on the way out as a relationship among peoples. The sole question is one of time and method. I think we should handle it so as to win adherents to Western aims.

We know that there is abroad in the world a fierce and growing spirit of nationalism. Should we try to dam it up completely, it would, like a mighty river, burst through the barriers and could create havoc. But again, like a river, if we are intelligent enough to make constructive use of this force, then the result, far from being disastrous, could redound greatly to our advantage, particularly in our struggle against the Kremlin's power.

To make use of the spirit of nationalism, we must show for it a genuine sympathy; we must prove that the obstacles that now prevent self-government in certain regions genuinely concern the free world and engage our earnest purpose to work for their elimination. This you and I stated in our joint communiqué. But to make it a real and vital thing in the lives of so many peoples throughout the world, we ought, I think, to make the whole matter a subject of more detailed explanation both as to objectives and as to methods for attaining them.

A speech on this matter – and no other could so well do it as you – should deal with the need for education and announce the cooperative purpose of great nations in the Western World to bring educational opportunities to all peoples we are able to reach.

The talk would not, of course, ignore the economic requirements of independent nations and would certainly dwell at length upon the advantages of voluntary agreements and associations in order to promote the freest and most fruitful kind of commerce. There would have to be discussed the burdensome responsibilities of self-rule; internal and external security; proper systems for the administration of justice; the promotion of health and the general welfare.

Finally, it seems to me that such a talk should announce a specific hope or aim in terms of the time limit for the attainment of our announced objectives. Possibly it might be said that our two nations plan to undertake every kind of applicable program to insure that within a space of twenty-five years (or by some other agreed upon, definite, date), all peoples will have achieved the necessary political, cultural and economic standards to permit the attainment of their goals.

If you could then say that twenty-five years from now, every last one of the colonies (excepting military bases) should have been <u>offered a right to self-government and determination</u>, you would electrify the world. More than this, you could be certain that not a single one of them would, when the time came, take advantage of the offer of independence. Each would cling more tightly to the mother country and be a more valuable part thereof.

Equally important with this particular announcement would be the outline of the program we propose jointly to undertake to help these nations achieve this level of progress.

The kind of talk that I am thinking of would seek to put this whole matter in such a light as to gain us friends – to be positive rather than negative. The attitude should be that we recognize great difficulties, some of which will take time to overcome, but that we know the job can be done.

Of course, in developing such a subject, one would want to contrast, if only by passing reference, this great purpose and development with the practice of the communists in Eastern Europe and wherever their evil power reaches. A good bit of cold war campaigning could be carried on in such a talk without ever making that particular objective an obvious one. For the same reason, reference could be made again to the plan for making nuclear science serve the peaceful interests of all nations, particularly in those areas where people are starved for adequate power.

I long to find a theme which is dynamic and gripping and which our two countries can espouse together. In this way, we can exercise the world leadership to which the communists aspire. Also by working together for concrete constructive goals, we can cement our relationship in a way which is only possible if there is fellowship in deeds. We found that fellowship in war, and we must equally try to find it in peace.

The theme I outline seems to me to be the one which best fills the need. It is, however, not a theme which the United States can develop alone without seeming to put the United States into opposition with Britain, which is the very result we do not want. Therefore, I bespeak your cooperation and indeed your initiative in opening what could be a great new chapter in history.

It seems to me that to say anything more in this letter would merely be repetitive or redundant. I am sending this through the mails rather than by cable because I want no other to see it except you and me.

Cabinet: Confidential Annex
(Cabinet papers, 128/40)

23 July 1954
Top Secret
11 a.m.
Cabinet Meeting No. 52 (Minute 3) of 1954

The Prime Minister said that, now that the Geneva Conference was over, the Cabinet must decide what further communication should be made to M Molotov in reply to his message of 5th July. After discussion with the Foreign Secretary he had prepared a draft telegram, which he read to the Cabinet. This suggested that it would be useful if, before an official proposal was made, agreement could be reached informally about the time and place for a meeting. It proposed that the meeting should not take place before the early part of September, and that it should be held in Berne, Stockholm or Vienna. It also threw out the suggestion that other Ministers, besides the Prime Minister and the Foreign Secretary, might attend.

The Prime Minister said that it might be convenient that he should carry this matter a stage further on a personal basis, and he asked whether the Cabinet would be content that he should send a personal and private message to M Molotov in the terms of his draft.

In the discussion which followed it was argued that such a communication, though expressed as a personal message from the Prime Minister, must now be regarded as engaging the collective responsibility of the Cabinet. Since the Prime Minister's return the Cabinet had been fully consulted on this matter

– indeed this was stated in the draft message – and any further communication must be taken as an expression of the Government's view.

This led to further discussion of the constitutional aspects of this matter which the Cabinet had considered at their meeting on 8th July.[1]

The Prime Minister said that when, in the course of the return voyage from his visit to Washington, he had reached the conclusion that the time was ripe for suggesting such a meeting, he had thought it better that he should himself take the responsibility for making the first informal approach to the Soviet Government. He had thought it would be preferable that the Cabinet should not be in any way committed at that stage, and that he should first explore the possibility on a purely personal basis. He had thought, and still thought, that it was perfectly proper for him to do this without prior consultation with the Cabinet. For the idea of such a meeting was not novel. It had been mentioned in his speech in the House of Commons on 11th May, 1953.[2] More recently, in the debate in the House of Commons on 5th April, 1954, the Government had accepted an Opposition motion welcoming 'an immediate initiative' by the Government to bring about a meeting between the Prime Minister and the Heads of the Administrations of the United States and the Soviet Union. The Prime Minister circulated a paper containing some extracts from speeches made in that debate, and drew particular attention to the Foreign Secretary's statement, in winding up the debate, that when the Government thought there was the least chance of such a meeting being fruitful they would not hesitate to go for it. In the light of this it had seemed natural that he should explore the possibility of proceeding with a project which, as his colleagues well knew, had been in his mind for some time past; and he was not prepared to admit that there was anything unconstitutional in the course which he had taken in making his preliminary approach to M Molotov on a purely personal basis. Before sending his message he had discussed the matter fully with the Foreign Secretary and had gained the impression that, while he would not himself have initiated the project, he did not disapprove it. If he had disapproved, he could have insisted that the matter should be referred to the Cabinet.

The Foreign Secretary said that it had been his view that the Cabinet should be consulted before the message was sent, and he had made this clear to the Prime Minister at the time.

The Chancellor of the Exchequer said that, when he had received the draft of the proposed message, he had understood that it had been sent to him for his personal comments only. It would have been possible, though very difficult, for him to have consulted the Cabinet at that stage, and he must accept personal responsibility for having decided not to do so. He had sent to the Prime Minister a full account of the circumstances in which he had received, and commented on, the draft message; this was on record and could be made

---

[1] See Cabinet: Confidential Annex of July 8, reproduced above (pp. 1662–5).
[2] Reproduced above (pp. 998–1010).

available to any of his colleagues who wished to pursue that aspect of the matter.

The Prime Minister said that he would not be prepared to abandon the practice, which he had followed for many years, of conducting personal correspondence with Heads of other Governments, and he could not accept the view that the despatch of his original message to M Molotov involved any constitutional impropriety. He was sure that there were many good precedents for actions such as this, in which preliminary enquiries or pourparlers had been carried out by a Prime Minister or a Foreign Secretary without prior consultation with all members of the Cabinet. Indeed, there must have been many occasions on which a Prime Minister or a Foreign Secretary had taken far more decisive action than this without the knowledge of all members of the Cabinet.

The Minister of Housing suggested that the Cabinet should now look to the future rather than the past. He himself shared the view originally expressed by the Lord President that the Prime Minister's message to M Molotov was an important act of foreign policy which engaged the collective responsibility of the Cabinet and that the Cabinet should have been consulted before it was sent. There seemed, however, to be little profit in prolonging discussion of the constitutional aspects of the matter. What the Cabinet had now to consider was how they could best deal with the situation which now confronted them. The Lord Privy Seal, the Commonwealth Secretary and the Colonial Secretary spoke in the same sense. There was general agreement that the Cabinet's discussion should now centre on the action to be taken in the situation which had now been reached.

The Lord President said that, though he had been the first to raise the constitutional aspects of this matter, his main concern now was with the international consequences of going forward with this project for a bi-lateral meeting between the United Kingdom and the Soviet Union. Some believed that the greatest threat to world peace came from the Russians. He himself believed that the greater risk was that the United States might decide to bring the East/West issue to a head while they still had overwhelming superiority in atomic weapons and were comparatively immune from atomic attack by Russia. He considered that during that period the supreme object of our policy should be to preserve the unity and coherence of the Western Alliance. Could we expect the Americans to respect the unity of that Alliance if, without their agreement, we embarked on bi-lateral discussions with the Russians? Was there not a great risk that they would thereby be encouraged to pursue independent policies and to take less account of our views on international affairs? The Soviet Government had that morning published a long statement on the results of the Geneva Conference. Though they welcomed this as proof that outstanding international difficulties could, with goodwill, be solved by peaceful means, they had gone out of their way to contrast the attitude of the

United States with that of other Western Powers and to suggest that American policy had an aggressive purpose. In view of this it would surely be most inopportune and most damaging to Anglo-American relations to embark, without consultation with the United States Government, on bi-lateral discussions with the Russians. It was his view that no further approach should be made to the Soviet Government without full consultation with the United States and other members of the Western Alliance.

The Prime Minister said that his message had not been sent without any consultation with the United States Administration. While he was in Washington he had held many informal talks with President Eisenhower about the prospects of arranging a three-Power or four-Power meeting at the highest level, and he had also mentioned to him and to Mr Dulles the possibility that he might propose a bi-lateral meeting with M Malenkov as a personal reconnaissance with a view to a later meeting on a broader basis. Though he had not said anything about the timing of such a bi-lateral meeting, they certainly had known that it was in his mind.

The Foreign Secretary said that his colleagues were entitled to a clear expression of his views on this question. He did not himself believe that any good would come from a bi-lateral meeting with the Russians at the present time. On all the main topics for discussion at such a meeting there was no prospect that any agreement could be reached. On European questions there was no sign that the Russians were ready to modify the uncompromising attitude which they had adopted at the Berlin Conference. On Germany, in particular, their attitude was unyielding. The proposals which they were likely to put forward at such a meeting were quite unacceptable to us, e.g. their plan for the abolition of atomic weapons, their own security plan for Europe and the demand that the Chinese People's Government should at once be recognised as the proper representatives of China in the United Nations. It was evident from the report of the latest conversation which the French Prime Minister had had with M Molotov (Foreign Office telegram No. 1781 to Paris) that on all these topics the Russians were still maintaining a wholly uncompromising attitude. On the other hand the Prime Minister was most anxious to make a personal attempt to discover, by conversation with the Russian leaders, whether a three-Power or four-Power meeting at the highest level would help to preserve world peace, and was convinced that some result might be achieved by this personal contact with the Russian leaders. As the Prime Minister, with all his long experience, felt so strongly that the attempt was worth making, the Foreign Secretary was ready to acquiesce – so long as the meeting was not held on Russian soil. For his part, therefore, he had not wished to raise objection to the despatch of a further message to M Molotov in the terms of the draft which the Prime Minister had read to the Cabinet. But he agreed that, before any such message was sent, it would be wise to study the announcement which the Soviet Government had issued that morning on the results of the Geneva

Conference. If the Russians were about to intensify their propaganda about the aggressive intentions of the United States, it might be more difficult to go forward with this project at the present time. It might be expedient that we should take the line that we could not attend a meeting with the Russians while they continued to use their propaganda machine for violent attacks on the policy of our American ally. For this reason he suggested that the Cabinet might defer their decision until he had had an opportunity to study more closely the announcement by the Soviet Government to which the Lord President had drawn attention.

There was general agreement in the Cabinet that there would be advantage in postponing a decision on this question until the following week, so that Ministers might have time to reflect further and to consider the significance of this statement by the Soviet Government.

In further discussion the following points were also raised:

(a) Reference had been made to the effect which a bi-lateral meeting with the Russians might have on Anglo-American relations. Account should also be taken to the effect of such a meeting on public opinion in Europe.

The Foreign Secretary said that, if it were decided to go forward with this project, the French and German Governments would have to be told in advance of the line we proposed to take and of the results we hoped to achieve. These preliminary explanations to the French and the Germans would need very careful handling. There was little doubt that the meeting would be a shock to public opinion in these and other countries of Western Europe.

It would be specially important that French opponents of the European Defence Community (EDC) should not be given the opportunity to use the meeting as a pretext for further delay in ratifying the EDC Treaty. If the project went forward, no announcement of the meeting should be made until after the French Parliament had completed their proceedings on the Treaty.

(b) In considering what further reply should be sent to the Soviet Government, account must be taken of the possibility that the Russians would at some future date disclose the fact that the approach had been made or even publish the correspondence. We might be put in an embarrassing position if it were disclosed that, having made this offer, we had then withdrawn it. This seemed to be an argument for making a further suggestion to the Russians on the lines of the draft prepared by the Prime Minister.

(c) It was at least possible that, if a further offer were made on these lines, the Russians would decline it or would insist that the meeting-place should be within the Soviet Union. That being so, it was for consideration whether the next message to the Russians should not be a

JULY 1954   1711

formal, rather than a personal, communication. For we might wish at some stage to disclose the reasons why this project had not come to fruition and we might feel precluded from publishing communications expressed as private and personal messages.

In this connection it was argued that the Government could not escape responsibility for these overtures on the basis that they had been made in personal correspondence between the Prime Minister and M Molotov. Any further message which was sent would be sent after full discussion by the Cabinet and would engage the full collective responsibility of Ministers. In any event the Government would certainly be held responsible by public opinion, whatever the form of the correspondence.

(d) There was reason to believe that, since Stalin's death, power in the Kremlin had been shared by a number of Russian leaders. If this were so, it might increase the reluctance of MM Malenkov and Molotov to attend a high-level meeting outside the Soviet Union. It was with this in mind that the Prime Minister was proposing to say in his message that he might wish to bring with him to a meeting one or two other Ministers in addition to the Foreign Secretary. The Russians might perhaps be more willing to attend a meeting on neutral ground if it could be attended by others of their leaders in addition to MM Malenkov and Molotov.

(e) Several Ministers said that, as this project had now been carried so far, the balance of advantage seemed to lie on the side of sending a further message to the Russians on the lines suggested by the Prime Minister. They agreed, however, that it was desirable that members of the Cabinet should have an opportunity to reflect further on the question over the week-end and should resume their discussion early in the following week.

The Cabinet –

Agreed to resume their discussion of this question at a further meeting on 26th July.

Cabinet: Confidential Annex
(Cabinet papers, 128/40)

26 July 1954
Top Secret
11.30 a.m.
Cabinet Meeting No. 53 (Minute 2) of 1954

The Prime Minister said that, since the Cabinet had last discussed on 23rd July his suggestion of a bi-lateral meeting with the Russians, the Soviet

Government had publicly proposed an early conference of all European Governments to consider the establishment of a system of collective security in Europe. This created a new situation, especially as it was clear from its terms that the Soviet Note had been drawn up after the end of the Geneva Conference. It was evident that the primary purpose of the Soviet Government, in making this public proposal at this time, was to influence the attitude of the French Parliament in their forthcoming discussion of the Treaty for the establishment of the European Defence Community. But he was satisfied that he could not proceed with his proposal for a bi-lateral meeting with the Russians while this suggestion of a much larger meeting of Foreign Ministers was being publicly canvassed. He had therefore prepared a revised draft of his message to M Molotov indicating that the larger meeting which the Soviet Government had now publicly proposed did not seem to accord with the plan for an informal bi-lateral meeting which he had previously had in mind, and asking whether this Soviet proposal was intended to supersede his plan. He proposed to include in this revised message a reference to the place and time which he had been intending to propose for a bi-lateral meeting: this would have the advantage of making it clear that he had not been prepared to attend a meeting in Moscow. The Foreign Secretary had independently prepared an alternative draft, which was similar in substance though somewhat different in wording. The Prime Minister read the two drafts to the Cabinet. He said that, if the Cabinet approved the substance of the proposed message, he could settle the wording in consultation with the Foreign Secretary.

In the course of a short discussion it was agreed that a new situation had been created by the publication of the Soviet Note of 24th July. Though it seemed unlikely that this Soviet proposal would be acceptable to the Governments of Western Europe, its recipients must be given time to consider it and the position must be reviewed again in the light of their response. Meanwhile, it was desirable that M Molotov should be given to understand that the Prime Minister's proposal for a bi-lateral meeting would be held in abeyance while the Soviet Note was under consideration.

The Cabinet –

Took note that the Prime Minister would send a personal message to M Molotov making it clear that his proposal for a bi-lateral meeting with M Malenkov must be regarded as held in abeyance pending the outcome of the Soviet proposal of 24th July for a conference of all European Governments on the creation of a system of collective security in Europe.

JULY 1954

Sir Winston S. Churchill to Vyacheslav Molotov
Prime Minister's Personal Telegram T.272/54
(Premier papers, 11/670)

26 July 1954
Immediate
Dedip
Top Secret, Private and Personal
No. 987

1. I am sorry not to have been able to reply before now to your prompt and agreeable message of July 5, but I am sure that from your talks with Mr Eden you will have realised that I had to wait until the end of the Geneva Conference. I am glad that an Agreement has been reached there and hope that it will not be disturbed.

2. After discussion with my colleagues I was about to send you a further message to suggest a meeting say at the end of August or in the first half of September at some half-way house such as Berne, Stockholm or Vienna. But in the meanwhile your Note of July 24 in reply to ours of May 7 has been published. This of course does not fit in with the plan I had in mind. My aim and hope was to bring about an informal Two-Power Talk between the Heads of our two Governments, but now after the Geneva Conference ended you have decided to propose a formal Conference of European States and of the United States to discuss again the proposals made some months ago by the Soviet Government on collective security in Europe, which I presume the Heads of Governments would not be expected to attend.

3. This has obviously superseded for the time being the small informal meeting I had suggested which might perhaps have been the prelude to a Three- or Four-Power Meeting at the top level.

House of Commons: Oral Answers
(Hansard)

29 July 1954

SUEZ CANAL ZONE BASE (ANGLO-EGYPTIAN AGREEMENT)

Captain Charles Waterhouse (Leicester, South-East):[1] It is never easy for a Member of this House to get up and take a view strongly opposed to that of a leader whom he highly respects and whom he has followed with loyalty

---

[1] Charles Waterhouse, 1893–1975. On active service, 1914–18 (MC). MP (Cons.) for Leicester South, 1924–45; for Leicester South East, 1950–7. Asst Postmaster-General, 1939–41. Parliamentary Secretary, Board of Trade, 1941–5. PC, 1944. Chairman, National Union of Conservative and Unionist Associations, 1952. Chairman, Tanganyika Concessions, 1957–66.

for so many years. It is never an easy task for any back bencher to follow the speeches made from the Front Bench, but when we have had two speeches such as we have had today, one of very high oratory, the other both of oratory and very close argument, it is more difficult still, and the House will, I hope, have sympathy with me.

Mr R. H. S. Crossman (Coventry, East): Which was which?

Captain Waterhouse: I always keep chronological order. The House will, perhaps, have sympathy with me when I am putting a view which is now, I know, definitely going to be disagreeable to my right hon. Friends on the Front Bench. I want to assure the House and my right hon. Friends, too, that there is not the smallest bitterness in anything I intend to say or that will be said by anybody from these benches so far as I know. We speak in sorrow. We speak, I am sure, with very real sincerity.

I should like with very great respect to make a passing reference to our late colleague, Sir Herbert Williams,[1] whose memorial service many of us attended this morning. Sir Herbert Williams took part in many hard fights in this House. He worked with us in this little party we have had in opposing what we believe to be a wrong policy. I believe it to be a cause of very deep regret in all parts of the House that he is not with us tonight.

There are not many aspects of this problem on which I can congratulate the Government, but I want to keep in as good odour with them as I can and, therefore, I shall start off by congratulating them on the manner in which this negotiation has been closed, although I certainly cannot congratulate them on the matter of its conclusion.

There is one very sound piece of advice which applies, I am told, both in matrimonial and in military matters, and that is, 'If you are going to run away run fast, run far, and run in good company.' Whether my right hon. Friends had that in mind or not I do not know, but they certainly decided that in this case we were going to run in good company when they sent the Secretary of State for War to do the deed. Nobody has had a better war record than he; nobody is more respected as a Minister than he. I wonder exactly what instructions he had. I have a very good idea of the sort of instructions he received – 'Get out there and sign an agreement. Don't bother too much about the terms. Get it signed.' I imagine the Patronage Secretary chipping in by saying, 'And mind it is signed by Tuesday, or you are likely to lose some of your holidays.' The Agreement was signed by Tuesday. Here it is, and in this piece of paper we have got all that is left of 80 years of British endeavour, thought and forethought.

[1] Herbert Geraint Williams, 1884–1954. Educated at University of Liverpool. Secretary, Machine Tool Trades Association, 1911–28. Secretary, Machine Tool Dept, Ministry of Munitions, 1917–18. MP (Cons.) for Reading, 1924–9; for South Croydon, 1932–45; for Croydon East, 1950–4. Parliamentary Secretary, Board of Trade, 1928–9. Knighted, 1939. Member, House of Commons Select Committee on Expenditure, 1939–44. Chairman, London Conservative Union, 1939–48; National Union of Conservative and Unionist Associations, 1948. Bt, 1953.

My right hon. Friend the Prime Minister at the start of his career wrote one of the finest books in the English language, *The River War*,[1] on this subject. It must be grave indeed for him now to have to take this decision. I am not saying that as a measure of blame; I have the very greatest sympathy, and I know how hard it must be for him to have so decided. I and my friends had feared that there would be a sell-out. This is not a sell-out. This is a give-away. Instead of having physical control of a great base, instead of having troops on the major waterway of the world, we have got this piece of paper in our hands. It is indeed a hard day for anybody on this side of the House to have to sit and support this Government which has, as we believe, not taken a wise decision on the Suez Canal.

My right hon. Friend the Secretary of State for War divided his speech into two portions; in one he discussed the terms, and in the other he discussed the reasons. I propose to follow him very closely in that. The terms are for the evacuation of all forces within 20 months. In other words, we have got to get out just as quick as our ships and our engineers can get us out. The stores, the equipment, installations, public utilities, communications, bridges, pipelines and wharves are to be handed over, and the Egyptian Government will assume responsibility for their security. We pay the bill.

Egyptian or British technicians will be sent in there under a contractor. That contractor will nominally be under the protection of the Egyptians. If any stuff is to be removed, we have got to discuss it with the Egyptians. If we want to do any building we have got to get their permission. We pay the bill for all this. We are actually to be allowed to use some of the airfields that we have built if we arrange when the flight is coming in and inform the Egyptians of the time of the flight, and if they give their consent.

What happens if these provisions are broken, as they may well be broken? We have got to be prepared for all that. Are we going to re-enter forcibly? Do hon. Members opposite welcome that? I doubt whether all hon. Members on this side would welcome that. Are we going back there by force, in the face of everything that we have said, in the face of a hostile Egypt? I do not believe that that is feasible at all. Really and truly, we have handed over £500 million worth of stores and buildings to the Egyptians, and if they like to use them against Palestine or against anybody else, who is going in to say, 'No, you will not?'

We have got the right of re-entry and a treaty for seven years. I do not mind whether this treaty is for seven years or 70 years. What do we mean by saying that we have gained a right of re-entry? If Egypt wants us in in some future emergency, as she wanted us in when she was threatened by the Italians, she will invite us in, treaty or no treaty. If she does not want us in when the time comes, this piece of paper is not going to get us in. We shall then have to fight

---

[1] Winston S. Churchill, *The River War* (London: Longmans, Green & Co, 1899).

our way in, with this treaty, just as we would have had to fight our way in without the treaty if Egypt at that time was not friendly to us.

In all such papers there is a little bit of light relief, and in this paper we find our light relief in Article 8 where we read that both parties express their 'determination . . . to uphold the 1888 Convention. . . .' That really is a pretty good one, considering that Egypt has consistently been breaking it for the past four years. It is for those reasons that I think this piece of paper is not worth anything at all to us, and it is because of that that I say we have not sold out but we have cleared out.

During the last Election my right hon. and hon. Friends spoke from the platforms and pointed out what we believed to be the errors of Abadan. We pointed to the right hon. Member for Lewisham, South (Mr H. Morrison) and told him that he had scuttled from Abadan. We pointed to my right hon. Friend the Foreign Secretary and said that, thank heaven, that policy would now be reversed. We said that the Canal would be re-opened and freed again. We said that we on this side of the House at least stood for a strong and definite principle. It is with very great regret that I say that if the electorate of this country had seen or foreseen this paper in 1951, we would not now be sitting on this side of the House.

What are the arguments that have been adduced to persuade us to this course? One good argument is sufficient to convince anyone of any honourable course, provided it is a good argument. If arguments are multiplied, doubts arise; but if arguments are changed, we have a right to have grave suspicions. When this proposal was started, when, as some hon. Members opposite suggested, we first thought of scuttling from Egypt under the preceding Government – and I do not hesitate to use the term – the main thing was nationality. It was wrong to fly in the face of Egyptian nationality.

I suggest that nationality is very like alcohol. It is extremely pleasant and it is definitely stimulating when it is taken in small quantities, and so is patriotism, but it is very dangerous and utterly besotting and misleading when it takes hold of a person, just as nationalism is bad when it takes hold of a nation. We have got to resist extreme nationalism because it is bad for the world and it is bad for the people who adumbrate it. It leads to murders. It leads to wars.

The second argument was that a friendly Egypt was necessary. That may be so, but the Egyptians have already said that there are two things necessary for Egypt; one is possession of the Canal. They have that. The other is a free hand in the Sudan, and the Leader of the Opposition mentioned that in his speech. Have we finished with the Sudan? Are we now saying to the Sudan, 'You have had your chance. You have not taken it. You can lump it'? If we are not doing that, then there is little chance immediately of a friendly Egypt. If we are doing that, then I say we are grossly betraying an almost sacred trust.

Then I come to the main argument, the strategic argument. Obviously, anything that I say will be considered against what my right hon. Friend has said. That is one of the troubles of this argument. Does my right hon. Friend come to the House as a very eminent, successful and fine soldier, a brigadier or a major-general? Does the Minister of Defence when he speaks in another place speak as the most respected soldier certainly in England and probably in the world? Or are they both speaking as representatives of the Cabinet putting over Cabinet policy? It is extremely difficult for us to decide, and in saying that, I am in no way attributing any dishonesty in motive or any dishonesty at all. But it is quite impossible to have at the head of a Department, in my view, a man who can take a Departmental view based on that of his advisers and completely exclude from his view the policy which he is in the Cabinet to sponsor.

[. . .]

Captain Waterhouse: [. . .] My last question: What is to be the position if this treaty is broken like the others? I believe it would be an advantage if it were made clear that if this treaty goes the way of the other three, we will no longer tolerate it and that this treaty, such as it is, is our last word. If that is not made clear, I feel strongly that in signing it we may have opened the grave of British greatness.

6.11 p.m.

Mr R. T. Paget (Northampton): I should be deeply interested to know what the right hon. and gallant Member for Leicester, South-East (Captain Waterhouse) means by 'our last word'. Does he mean war? Is it his view that if there be any breaches in the working out of the Agreement, the alternative is that we should invade Egypt? That is an alternative that we would all like to know about.

During the last Election, as the right hon. and gallant Member candidly and honourably pointed out, he and his colleagues on the benches opposite attacked people on this side of the House for scuttling from Abadan and pointed out that there would be a very different policy from the Prime Minister with regard to Egypt and the Canal. When we asked whether the alternative to that policy was war, the right hon. and gallant Member complained. What does this 'last word' mean?

[. . .]

We had an opportunity to get out on honourable and advantageous terms. General Neguib overthrew the wretched royal Government in Cairo and the people who had inflicted injuries upon us by their irresponsibility. I urged upon the right hon. Gentlemen at that time that we should have gone to Neguib then and said, 'We are delighted to see you. We want, as Ernest Bevin once said, to get out of the Canal Zone. You will, of course, realise that while the wretched King's Government was here we had nobody to whom we could hand over the base. Now, of course, a responsible strong man is in charge.

Now there is somebody to whom we can hand it over. All that there remains to do is to make our arrangements to leave.'

Neguib's whole prestige would have been built up on the fact not that he was going to get rid of the British but that he had done so. From that point onwards he would have gone into the negotiations for the arrangements committed to their success. He could not go back to his people and say, 'I have not got rid of the British after all.' He would have been committed to the fact that he had got rid of us, and we could have had any terms we liked for our withdrawal with the very best of good will from the new Egyptian Government. Under those circumstances, we would have come out not damaged, but with our prestige enhanced.

Instead of that, by delay we are having to withdraw on miserable terms, having carried a burden which has gravely injured our Army, which has weakened recruitment, and has weakened our defence position. Why has it happened? For one reason only. It was not because the Secretary of State for Foreign Affairs did not know what was the right thing to do. It was not because the Secretary of State for War did not know, but it was because of a back bench cabal in the Conservative Party encouraged under the table by the Prime Minister.

The Prime Minister (Sir Winston Churchill): That is an absolute untruth.

Mr Paget: Does the right hon. Gentleman say that he really was not obstructive in the Cabinet – and letting it be known to people behind him – to the wish of the Service Departments and of the Foreign Office to conclude an agreement to get out of Egypt?

Mr Ralph Assheton (Blackburn, West):[1] That is absolutely untrue.

The Prime Minister: I behaved with perfect correctness in my relations with my colleagues and with Members of the House. I have not in the slightest degree concealed in public speech how much I regretted the course of events in Egypt. But I had not held my mind closed to the tremendous changes that have taken place in the whole strategic position in the world which make the thoughts which were well-founded and well knit together a year ago utterly obsolete, and which have changed the opinions of every competent soldier that I have been able to meet.

I am not going to attempt, in interrupting the hon. and learned Gentleman, to lay this argument before the House, but I should be prepared to do so and to show how utterly out of all proportion to the Suez Canal and the position which we held in Egypt are the appalling developments and the appalling spectacle which imagination raises before us. Merely to try to imagine in outline the first few weeks of a war under conditions about which we did not

[1] Ralph Assheton, 1901–84. MP (Cons.) for Rushcliffe, Nottinghamshire, 1934–45; for City of London, 1945–50; for Blackburn West, 1950–5. Parliamentary Secretary, Ministry of Labour and Ministry of National Service, 1939–42; Ministry of Supply, 1942–3. Financial Secretary, Treasury, 1943–4. Chairman of Conservative Party Organization, 1944–6. Bt, 1945. Baron Clitheroe, 1955.

know when this Session commenced, and about which we had not been told – merely to portray that picture and submit it to the House would, I am sure, convince hon. Gentlemen of the obsolescence of the base and of the sense of proportion which is vitally needed at the present time, not only in military dispositions but in all our attempts to establish human relationships between nation and nation.

Vyacheslav Molotov to Sir Winston S. Churchill
(Foreign Office papers, 800/762)

31 July 1954
Priority
Dedip
Top Secret
Strictly Private and Personal
No. 1024

I have received your letter of the 27th of July.[1]

In your letter you write that our proposal, in the Note of July 24, to summon an all-European conference on the question of collective security in Europe has obviously replaced for some time the meeting of the Heads of our States proposed by you.

I must state, that we do not see the reasons for considering that the proposal for an unofficial meeting proposed in your letter of the 4th of July, a meeting furthermore without any kind of agenda, is necessarily dependent upon (has any bearing on) the question of the convocation of a conference concerned with the guaranteeing of security in Europe in the course of the ensuing months.

---

[1] Reproduced above, dated July 26 (p. 1713).

August 1954

Sir Winston S. Churchill to Members of the Cabinet
(Cabinet papers, 129/70)

3 August 1954
Top Secret
Cabinet Paper No. 263 of 1954

TWO-POWER MEETING WITH SOVIET GOVERNMENT

I should be glad if my colleagues would consider the enclosed general observations in connection with the telegrams to and from Mr Molotov already circulated.

1. The purpose of a Two-Power Top-Level meeting with the Soviet Government on neutral ground is to bring about a Top-Level Three or Four-Power meeting in London. For this latter a gesture of goodwill is required from the Soviet. This might either take the form of (1) an undertaking by the Russians to accept the Austrian Treaty on which all the Soviet terms have already been met, or (2) to participate in a cooperative spirit in President Eisenhower's attempt to deflect thermo-nuclear power to peaceful and productive aims instead of world destruction where it is now heading. Either or both of these symbols of goodwill must be forthcoming to give a chance of the United States being persuaded to accept the idea of the Head of their State and Government to participate in a Top-Level Conference at the present time (i.e., in the next few months).

2. I believe that the Russians would welcome the Top-Level meetings in the aforesaid order. Their reasons may well be:

First, that they are still far weaker in the thermo-nuclear sphere, including especially power of hostile delivery.

Secondly, that it is their interest and their wish to have an era of greatly increased material comfort and prosperity, even though it may be attended by a relaxation of Communist theory enforced by police control, and military discipline resting on normal patriotism.

The inter-play of the party and military forces is at present intricate. Combined as they would be in war or under threat of war, they of course give absolute domination throughout Russia and her satellites to the Kremlin Government. They are, however, fundamentally diverse, and even opposed, in character, tradition and mood. Given a prolonged period of peace, or at least of 'non-war confidence' and easement, one force might correct and modify the other. This process would not perhaps be harmful to the Free World.

3. These considerations have led me to believe that a (say) twenty years' period of 'peaceful coexistence' although not settling things precisely on paper, might well create a new era in human thought and temper favourable to the survival of individual liberty and the healthy evolution of human society. This hope should not be based on optimism about Communist or Russian good faith, but only on a correct estimate of Russian self-interest. All this of course has a constant and powerful ally in the widespread subconscious fear of destruction which Science will intensify.

4. Side by side with the above, and potentially and realistically more imminent is the argument which must be present in many American minds namely:

We alone have for the next two or perhaps three years sure and overwhelming superiority in attack, and a substantial measure of immunity in defence. Merely to dawdle means potential equality of ruin. Ought we not for the immediate safety of our own American people and the incidental rescue of the Free World to bring matters to a head by a 'show down' leading up to an ultimatum accompanied by an Alert?

5. This could be brought about by a war with China, even though unconventional weapons were not used in the first stage, or at any rate only the atom bomb. It is my opinion – for what it is worth – that the Kremlin would not in their present inferiority of thermo-nuclear power retaliate by opening the Third World War. They would give aid by ground and air forces to China, and in so doing would obtain a valuable hold on large Chinese territories which they have long coveted. At the same time, by boasting that they would not use their thermonuclear power (in reality weakness) they would command the moral and intellectual support of European and non-Communist Asian countries. This might so anger the United States that they would feel free to look after their own interests and use their own might in any way they thought fit.

6. If this happens the 'show down' leading up to an ultimatum would probably occur. Two alternatives are possible: first, the World War in which we and Western Europe might well be victims whatever we thought, said or did, but in which United States would at present time be victors; or secondly, that the Kremlin would give in, yielding the satellites and effective one-sided control of unconventional weapons and armaments generally. The risk of total War would however be extreme and of all the nations involved the United States would suffer the least.

I should be glad if my colleagues would ponder over these issues in priority to everything else.

7. It is on this background that the comparatively minor procedure that I have proposed should be measured, namely: the Two-Power Top-Level meeting at some halfway house, leading if possible to a Three or Four-Power Conference in London. It is clear that the Soviets would like this. While we must not be taken in or out-manoeuvred, it is a mistake to assume that the Soviet motives are necessarily in all cases vicious, or that what is their natural self-interest is necessarily antagonistic to ours. Their regime is both complex and rigid. The Note proposing the International Conference to explore further their Berlin suggestions, which the leading NATO allies rejected on the 7th of May, is in my opinion a piece of routine machine-made diplomacy. Having regard to the simple and cordial private telegrams I have interchanged with Mr Molotov, it is clumsy in its timing. I understand that the Foreign Offices of the three countries to whom it was addressed, Britain, the United States, and France, are now engaged in writing an argumentative diplomatic refusal which may well take three weeks or a month. This delay is not inconvenient to us as it meets M Mendes-France's desire for an unostentatious pause to enable him to see what he can do about EDC. French agreement to this would of course greatly aid Dr Adenauer's problems which are certainly becoming more acute. There is also the holiday season which must be treated with due respect.

8. However, I understand that we may count on the Soviet routine Note being rejected and out of the way by the end of August. We must then review the situation in the light of existing facts, and my last telegram to Mr Molotov (August the 1st) was intended to secure us the time and power to do so. These facts affect France and EDC, the United States and NATO, and also Adenauer and Dr John.[1] Unless a decisive and relevant change in the world situation arises from any of these, the Two-Power Top-Level meeting at a halfway house will stand as the only constructive proposal to an indefinite continuance of the cold war, relieved from time to time by diplomatic grimaces of the kind we have just received officially from Russia.

---

[1] Otto John, 1909–97. Born in Marburg. Involved in July 1944 plot to assassinate Hitler; escaped to England to avoid execution. Appeared as witness at Nuremberg War Crimes Trials. Married, 1949, Lucie Manén. President, West German Federal Office for the Protection of the Constitution, 1950. Secretly moved to East Germany, July 1954, and began to criticize Adenauer's policies; later claimed, after moving back to West Germany, that he had been forcibly taken to East Germany by the KGB.

AUGUST 1954 1723

Sir Winston S. Churchill to Lady Churchill[1]
(Churchill papers, 1/50)

3 August 1954

Delighted all well and attractive. Weather warm here. My cold better. Best love to you both from Winston and Chartwell Garrison.

Sir Winston S. Churchill to Vyacheslav Molotov
(Foreign Office papers, 800/762)

5 August 1954
Immediate
Dedip
Top Secret and Personal
No. 1026

Thank you for your letter of the 31st of July.[2] It was not my intention to convey that I had changed in any way from my original project. But your unexpected revival of your Berlin proposal created a new situation since it would not have been possible to have a large form international conference going on at the same time as the unofficial Two-Power top level meeting which I proposed and which I feel you think might do good.

The British, American and French Governments whom you addressed officially are now preparing their replies. Although Ministers in this and other countries are liable to be dispersed at this season of the year, I think it likely that an answer will be sent to your Diplomatic Note from the three Governments concerned in the course of this month. Let us therefore wait until we know what is going to happen about this and then re-examine my project in the light of events.

Sir Winston S. Churchill to Lord Simonds
Prime Minister's Personal Minute M.132/54
(Premier papers, 11/599)

7 August 1954

I shall be glad if you will look into this. Apparently the Foreign Secretary thinks they should be given permission to publish the short letter, marked 'A' in red by me, and its publication will of course lead to great curiosity about the

---

[1] Lady Churchill was taking a holiday on the Riviera with Sir Oswald Birley's widow, the artist Rhoda Lecky Pike (1900–81).
[2] Reproduced above (p. 1719).

long one.¹ The two must, I am sure, be considered together. I have not given such consideration to Ribbentrop's long letter. But surely Adenauer ought to be asked what he feels about it beforehand? Is it intended to improve relations and feeling towards the Germans? Will it help to revive the Nazis and make people think we are publishing it because we are softening towards them? As you know, I was always against the vindictive execution of the so-called war criminals at Nuremberg, and think they should have been put away for life on some solitary island. But the question we have to settle is, do we want this sort of publicity now? Surely another five or ten years should be allowed to pass.

It does not follow that only legal threats will deter the *Evening Standard*. If they are asked not to do it they will very likely defer to our wishes. Again, I repeat, the short letter can have no other purpose or consequence than to bring about the publication of the long one. Have they got the long one? There does not seem any particular hurry about this.

Sir Winston S. Churchill to President Dwight D. Eisenhower
(Premier papers, 11/1074)

8 August 1954
Private and Secret

My dear Friend,

I have been pondering over your very kind letter of July 22,² and I am most grateful to you for this further proof of our friendship. One has to do one's duty as one sees it from day to day and, as you know, the mortal peril which overhangs the human race is never absent from my thoughts. I am not looking about for the means of making a dramatic exit or of finding a suitable Curtain. It is better to take things as they come. I am however convinced that the present method of establishing the relations between the two sides of the world by means of endless discussions between Foreign Offices, will not produce any decisive result. The more the topics of discussion are widened, the more Powers concerned, and the greater the number of officials and authorities of all kinds involved, the less may well be the chance of gaining effective results in time or even of using time to the best advantage.

I have, as you know, since Stalin's death hoped that there could be a talk between you and me on the one hand, and the new Leaders of Russia, or as they might be, the Leaders of a new Russia, on the other. It will seem astonishing to future generations – such as they may be – that with all that is at stake no attempt was made by personal parley between the Heads of Governments to create a union of consenting minds on broad and simple issues. This should

---

¹ See letters from Ribbentrop reproduced in *The Churchill Documents*, vol. 21, *The Shadows of Victory, January–July 1945*, pp. 1776–82.
² Reproduced above (pp. 1703–6).

surely be the foundation on which the vast elaborate departmental machinery should come into action, instead of the other way round.

Fancy that you and Malenkov should never have met, or that he should never have been outside Russia, when all the time in both countries appalling preparations are being made for measureless mutual destruction. Even when the power of Britain is so much less than that of the United States, I feel, old age notwithstanding, a responsibility and resolve to use any remaining influence I may have to seek, if not for a solution at any rate for an easement. Even if nothing solid or decisive was gained no harm need be done. Even if realities presented themselves more plainly, that might bring about a renewed effort for Peace. After all, the interest of both sides is Survival and, as an additional attraction, measureless material prosperity of the masses. 'No' it is said, 'The Heads of Governments must not ever meet. Human affairs are too great for human beings. Only the Departments of State can cope with them, and meanwhile let us drift and have some more experiments and see how things feel in a year or two when they are so much nearer to us in annihilating power.'

Now, I believe, is the moment for parley at the summit. All the world desires it. In two or three years a different mood may rule either with those who have their hands upon the levers or upon the multitude whose votes they require.

Forgive me bothering you like this, but I am trying to explain to you my resolve to do my best to take any small practical step in my power to bring about a sensible and serious contact.

* * *

I read with great interest all that you have written me about what is called colonialism, namely: bringing forward backward races and opening up the jungles. I was brought up to feel proud of much that we had done. Certainly in India, with all its history, religion and ancient forms of despotic rule, Britain has a story to tell which will look quite well against the background of the coming hundred years.

As a matter of fact the sentiments and ideas which your letter expressed are in full accord with the policy now being pursued in all the Colonies of the British Empire. In this I must admit I am a laggard. I am a bit sceptical about universal suffrage for the Hottentots even if refined by proportional representation. The British and American Democracies were slowly and painfully forged and even they are not perfect yet. I shall certainly have to choose another topic for my swan song: I think I will stick to the old one 'The Unity of the English-speaking peoples'. With that all will work out well.

Enclosed with this private letter I send you the telegrams I have interchanged with Molotov since I sent you my last on the subject. I told the Bedell to tell you that I was 'an obstinate pig'. Alas, the best I can do.

Please believe me always your sincere friend,

August 1954

Sir Winston S. Churchill to Lady Churchill
(Churchill papers, 1/50)

8 August 1954

No news. Weather bad. Cold lingers. Cyprus silly. All well. We do hope you are having sunshine. Fondest love.

Sir Winston S. Churchill to Arabella Churchill
(Churchill papers, 1/51)

9 August 1954

Darling Arabella,

Thank you for your very kind letter.[1] I was very sorry I had to go away from Chequers without seeing you, and consequently I loved having your letter.

I hope you are very well. I am at Chartwell now. It is raining every day, but I have always been able to feed the fish and the black swans.

Your loving Grandpapa

Sir Winston S. Churchill to Lady Churchill
(Churchill papers, 1/50)

9 August 1954

Your lovely letter of the 5th just received. So glad you are having lovely weather. Here it hardly ever stops raining. My cold continues but all well. Best love. Writing. A good report from Nellie but she has not come here yet on account of treatment.

Sir Winston S. Churchill to Lady Churchill
(Baroness Spencer-Churchill papers)[2]

10 August 1954

My darling,

Last night your dear letter arrived. I was delighted to read the word 'heavenly' applied to the weather. I feel you have sunshine.[3] Here we have hardly had a gleam. Pouring rain, dull skies are not only abundant but unpleasant: But *you* have sunshine.

---

[1] Arabella had written to her grandfather: 'My dear Grandpa Thank you very much for having me to stay with you I had a lovely time at Chequers I did not see you to kiss you goodbye.'

[2] This letter was handwritten.

[3] Clementine Churchill was at Ste Maxime in the South of France.

I hope you find Rhoda a good companion. Fancy bathing in the open sea: Has she done any painting? Do you play cards?

Here I stay in bed most of the time and only go out to feed the fish. Gabriel[1] gets on very well with everyone except his yellow rival. He is very friendly to me & Rufus[2] and most attractive. My cold has now gone down on to my chest & turned into a cough, and Charles (who comes nearly every day) watches it vigilantly. I fear I have passed it on to Christopher, but I am giving him my remedies as well. I dined at the Farm last night & he and Mary came after here. I have had to avoid Charlotte Clementine[3] for more than a week, so as not to make her an untimely gift.

One gets no consolation at this moment from the animal world. All the Chartwell rabbits are dead & now the poor foxes have nothing to eat, so they attack the little pigs and of course have eaten the few pheasants. It is said they will perish & migrate & that then there will be no one to cope with the beetles and rats. Christopher paints a gloomy picture.

Christopher and I have jointly invested nearly £1000 in 8 Swedish 'Landrace' pigs: out of which he expects to make a fortune. They live at Bardogs and have remarkable figures

[Drawing of a pig]

Their hams are much admired – and there are only about 1200 of them in our Pig population of 5 millions. The Boar is said to be worth 5 or 6 hundred £s, & in two years we hope to make a fortune. As they can be kept on what is called 'a herd basis', they will not be income but a capital gain.

The Hamblin has just given me the latest reports about poor Nellion.[4] The hospital say they are satisfied with her progress under the rays. She can go out in the afternoons & is at her disposal. It is thought better that she stays at the hospital. The Hamblin will go see her tomorrow (Wed) and will find out what she would like to do about the weekend. I have sent her my love & flowers.

I do nothing, and enjoy it. It is nice having no plans except what one makes from day to day, & better still hour to hour. I see a few people at lunch and play a good deal of bezique with Christopher & Jack. I hold my own more or less.

Randolph has just rung up. He has returned & will come to lunch tomorrow or perhaps drive & sleep. Alexander Korda comes to lunch today, & Rab to dinner on Friday 13th (Blenheim day). I fear he has gotten anxieties, Jane P[5] keeps me informed.

My darling one I brood much about things, and all my moods are not equally gay. But it does cheer my heart to think of you in the sunlight and I pray that Peace & Happiness may rule your soul. My beloved darling come

[1] Clementine's Siamese cat.
[2] Churchill's poodle.
[3] Charlotte Clementine Soames, 1954– . Daughter of Christopher and Mary Soames; grand-daughter of Winston S. Churchill. Married, 1989, William Peel: one child.
[4] Clementine's sister, Nellie Romilly, was suffering from cancer.
[5] Jane Portal.

back soon refreshed & revived, & if possible bring the sun with you as wide as your lovely smile.

PS. I do not sign myself with my usual portrait, as I am not anxious to compete with the Landrace type.

Sir Winston S. Churchill to Lady Churchill
(Churchill papers, 1/50)

10 August 1954

Chestnut Mollflanders[1] in foal after all to Hyperion. Unexpected luck. Fondest love.

Anthony Eden to Sir Winston S. Churchill
(Churchill papers, 6/4)

10 August 1954

As to our home affairs, I admit that I am not happy. I don't think that you understand what a gap your departure must make. If there isn't sufficient time for the new Government to make its own name for itself in advance of the general election, then it will have no chance of survival. It will be hard enough anyway. But at least a year, beginning with a Party Conference, seems to me the minimum.

This is not, I am sure, a selfish view, nor a personal one, though I am convinced that it is correct and that there is no escape from it. As, however, we are both so much concerned, I hope you won't hesitate to talk to any of our colleagues about it while I am away. I know that this is what they would like.

---

[1] A Thoroughbred broodmare, acquired by Churchill in 1949.

August 1954　　　　　　　　　　1729

Vyacheslav Molotov to Sir Winston S. Churchill
(Foreign Office papers, 800/762)

11 August 1954

Priority
Dedip
Top Secret
No. 1070

I have received your message of August 6,[1] in which you say that you have not in any way changed your original plan and intend to return to this question.

As far as our proposal for an all-European Conference is concerned, and also as regards a conference of the Ministers of the Four Powers, this, as you know, is an answer to the corresponding Note of the Three Powers of May 7. Our reply was naturally postponed until the end of the Geneva Conference. For our part we consider that the positive results achieved at Geneva should contribute to the settlement of other questions as well.

In connexion with your comments on our Note of July 24, I consider it necessary to make this addition to my preceding letter.

John Colville to G. L. Wilde
(Premier papers, 11/585)

12 August 1954

Dear Wilde,
　　The Prime Minister feels that the cruelty to animals aspect of myxomatosis has not been receiving sufficient attention from the official point of view.[2] He would like to know what is the composition of the Ministry's Advisory Committee and what line they have taken about the deliberate spreading of the disease. The Prime Minister is at present considering whether or not to send a subscription to the RSPCA deliberately ear-marked for this purpose and to give full publicity to the fact that he has done so. He would be obliged for the Minister's comments on this.

---

　[1] Reproduced above (p. 1723), dated Aug. 5.
　[2] See Pitblado to Guppy, July 7, reproduced above (p. 1652). The practice of placing rabbits carrying myxomatosis in burrows to kill off wild rabbits began in 1953. It succeeded in killing 99% of wild rabbits in the UK before it was outlawed by the Pests Act of November 1954.

Field Marshal Lord Alexander to Sir Winston S. Churchill
(Premier papers, 11/706)

13 August 1954
Private and Personal

My dear Prime Minister,

On my return to the United Kingdom yesterday evening I find that during my absence on the North American Continent you had appointed a Committee called the Defence Review Committee of which Lord Swinton is acting as Chairman.

I understand that this Committee has already held a number of meetings. I shall send you my considered opinion of their findings when I have had the time and opportunity to study them fully. I would however point out that this Committee has been studying matters of Defence for which I am responsible and on which I have already expressed my views and recommendations to you. You will, I feel sure, appreciate that it will be very difficult for me to serve you if I don't enjoy your confidence.

Sir Winston S. Churchill to John Foster Dulles
Prime Minister's Personal Telegram T.282/54
(Premier papers, 11/618)

14 August 1954
Top Secret
Personal and Private

1. I have strongly supported your line in my messages to Mendes-France. I have indeed for a very long time, as you know, been wearied with this deeply injurious French procedure of delay. I hope however you will not fail to grip the NATO solution which I am sure can be arranged.

2. I am telegraphing to you because in Anthony's absence on holiday I have been promoted to the Foreign Office. I hope therefore you will treat me as kindly as you did when we talked about my Boston speech. I suppose you are watching the Attlee and Bevan excursion. How lucky you are in Washington never to have to worry about Party politics. Kindest regards.

Sir Winston S. Churchill to Field Marshal Lord Alexander
(Premier papers, 11/706)

15 August 1954
Secret

My dear Alex,

As you were away for a month the Cabinet felt you would wish the scrutiny of the Service Estimates not to be discontinued. Nigel Birch was at this small Committee on all occasions representing you and to make quite sure that everything was in order I took the Chair myself on the first occasion, thus making it a Cabinet Committee headed by the Prime Minister. I have been awaiting their report but so far nothing has arrived. I understand it is almost ready. Will you therefore take over from me from Monday on and make the report to me when you have approved it. The only reason why Duncan Sandys took part was because he had a lot of knowledge of the subject and is not ear-marked to any one particular Department. I shall look forward very much to hearing from you in the course of the next week or so what your final view is.

The French are running great risks both for themselves and NATO in their endless and I think disgraceful hindering of EDC. I fear that this, coupled with Chou En-lai's truculence and the Attlee–Bevan overtures, may lead to far-reaching United States developments.

It is ten months since I said publicly at Margate that we should go straight ahead on a NATO basis.[1] All this time has been deliberately wasted and Adenauer's position rendered daily more difficult.

R. A. Butler to Sir Winston S. Churchill
(Churchill papers, 6/4)[2]

16 August 1954

First, many thanks for a very pleasant evening. Second, thank you for letting me see a copy of your letter to Anthony. I think this puts your own decision against the background of world events in the best way possible. But of course it will come as a shock to him. I comment only because you asked me and not in order to approve or disapprove any action you think fit, or to interfere in your relations with Anthony.

I am glad that no reference is made to the Election. I could not bring myself to agree now to any idea of an early election. I cannot yet forecast my Budget. I have not got enough saving on 'Defence' & it is only now being realised what burdens we are carrying.

[1] Speech reproduced above (pp. 1237–46).
[2] This letter was handwritten.

Up till now you have always expressed yourself in favour of a long delay before an Election & have even mentioned early 1956. You have also warned me always of the snare & delusion of 'popular' budgets, quoting your own tea duty reaction!

I feel sure however that you do not mean to decide now on the Election or on the Leadership at the Election.

Sir Winston S. Churchill to Pierre Mendès-France
Prime Minister's Personal Telegram T.283/54
(Premier papers, 11/672)

17 August 1954
Immediate
Confidential
No. 1938

I have felt the strongest need and desire to meet you and nothing could be more convenient than if you would look in here on your way back by air from Brussels. Chartwell is only ten minutes from Biggin Hill Airfield. I hope you will include luncheon or dinner. Let me know who you will bring with you.

Sir Winston S. Churchill to R. A. Butler
(Churchill papers, 6/4)

17 August 1954

My dear Rab,

Please have a look at this version.[1] I hope it is the final edition and I wonder whether you think it worse or less bad than its precursor.

Sir Winston S. Churchill to Anthony Eden
Prime Minister's Personal Telegram T.284/54
(Premier papers, 11/672)

18 August 1954
Immediate
Top Secret, Personal and Private
No. 363

Kirkpatrick tells me that you have asked my advice whether to return or not. Mendès-France has proposed himself to come to see me at Chartwell

---

[1] Draft letter to Anthony Eden, finally sent 24 Aug. 1954, reproduced below (pp. 1751–2).

on the way back from Brussels. I do not think there is any difference between you and me on our attitude about EDC in which I am in full accord with the Foreign Office. I should welcome an opportunity of meeting MF and had proposed to receive him at Biggin Hill with a Guard of Honour of 615 Squadron which is conveniently stationed there. Whether he can come Saturday, Sunday or Monday is still, like much else, uncertain. I should of course exhort him to do his duty and thus avert what might be Dulles's reappraisal.[1] My position is exactly as I explained it at Margate ten months ago.[2] I do not think any international crisis will arise before the EDC debate in the Chamber, now again to be put off till August 28. I had not intended to call a Cabinet till Monday, 30th, unless something urgent cropped up. Should you decide to come home sooner other arrangements can easily be made.

I hope you are having a pleasant rest. I cannot plead the weather as any additional inducement.

Sir Winston S. Churchill to Members of the Cabinet
(Cabinet papers, 129/70)

18 August 1954
Top Secret
Cabinet Paper No. 271 of 1954

ANGLO-RUSSIAN RELATIONS

As my colleagues have been following so closely the discussions about a Top-Level Meeting with Russia, I circulate the following record of a conversation between Sir Frank Roberts and the First Secretary of the Soviet Embassy.

2. In my correspondence with the President I made it clear that my object was to make a Three or Four-Power Meeting in London possible and for this a gesture would be required from the Russians either on Austria, or on Eisenhower's Industrial Atomic proposal. Even then I made it clear that I could not commit the President to accepting the plan. The prospect to the Kremlin was certainly bleak. Their refusal, on the other hand, to come halfway to meet on neutral territory on the conditions I outlined on May 11, 1953 would have put us in a strong position in Parliament, and would have freed us from any complaint of not acting in harmony with the unanimous House of Commons' resolution of last Session. Certainly we should be better situated both at home and abroad either if they had refused, or if an announcement of a Conference had been made, than we are now. The Attlee–Bevan Moscow excursion and Malenkov contacts may not have done any serious international harm,

---

[1] The US Joint Chiefs were considering promoting German rearmament outside NATO, in the event of a French veto on it within NATO. Eden's diplomatic efforts forestalled such a veto.

[2] Speech reproduced above (pp. 1237–46).

but while avoiding all solid and serious issues it has given them a vague, sloppy initiative in the direction of peace, which may not be without its Electoral reactions.

3. We had however no choice in view of our loyalty to the European Defence Community (EDC). We must do our best to get this through. Speed and decision are far more important to us than changes in the form of the Treaty provided that they do not paralyse the whole project. Its real value is the fact that it brings a German Army in a strictly regulated form into the North Atlantic Treaty Organisation (NATO) front and under General Gruenther's command. EDC also commands the support of our official Opposition who would probably not commit themselves to other methods. But it was NATO not EDC that would ever have done any fighting.

4. I am very glad that M Mendes-France, whom I have been anxious to meet, has himself proposed to come to Chartwell on Monday on his way back from Brussels. I will keep my colleagues informed.

5. We are actively supporting the Americans on EDC. If it fails or evaporates in indefinite delays, a great effort must be made to achieve the same results through a recasting of NATO. The danger which I fear the most is Mr Dulles's 'agonised reappraisal'. Peripheral defence may well be doomladen. Its possibility is not receding.

R. A. Butler to Sir Winston S. Churchill
(*Churchill papers, 6/4*)

18 August 1954
Personal

Dear Prime Minister,

I value your confidence in asking me to look at your second epistle to Anthony. Since last Summer at the time of your severe illness we have all accepted that Anthony is to be your successor. I have therefore a loyalty to him which you realise that I must be careful not to abuse.

Up till my visit to you last Friday I thought you would hand over to your successor this Autumn leaving him time to mobilise his forces, his programme and public opinion.

You have now thought over the situation and have introduced a new argument, which you fortify with your experience, namely that you distrust the outlook for 'fag-end' successor Governments. This is an important argument; and no doubt in order to give it its full force, your second draft omits detailed description of the type of reconstituted Government which you envisage and leaves this as well as the detailed timetable of the changeover until you have talked to Anthony. I think this is right.

Now I come to your reference on page four to the Budget. First, I don't think that the handling of the Old Age Pensions depends on the Budget, and your sentence to this effect might be omitted. The Old Age Pension legislation will precede the Budget by several months. Second, I do not like making the election date and our future depend too much on the Budget as such. The historical precedents against doing this are as strong as the precedents you quote against 'fag-end' successor Governments. The Budget would, as in 1929, have to be reduced to the barest minimum in order to get the Finance Bill through in the short time which would lie between the Budget and the dissolution; and negotiations with the Opposition would be necessary, as we could not achieve even a minimum Finance Bill, without their cooperation, in the time.

Moreover, we are still far short of the savings I asked for on Defence. On the Home Front the Swinton Committee has already drastically reviewed the Civil Estimates. You tend to underestimate, in your references to my last Budget, the terrible burdens we are carrying. The Defence bill is twice what Cripps bore, and Social Services are up by £65 million. It is a wonder that we have produced the economic results we have. While I can still give you a good showing I can't exhibit magical results in the national accounts.

My instinct about the election is that the Party will do better if it appears normally to have gone on and done its job rather than that an abnormal summer date for an appeal should have been chosen. The summer is favourable to Labour outdoor speakers, as the Chairman of the Party must know, and historically less favourable to the Conservatives. So I am glad to see that you keep the election date open in your letter.

To sum up therefore I think the Party may suffer from an early election. This is my first reaction and I shall of course consider further. I realise that if no election is decided upon, the question of a successor Government will be more likely to remain open, but I think this issue will remain open in any case. You yourself leave open the detailed arrangements for the change-over. I quite accept that we might have a successor Government if the date for the election be postponed.

How we shall resolve all this I don't yet see, but you may be sure that I shall from now on expend a fund of understanding on your arguments and shall evaluate at its priceless worth the boon of your strength and experience in handling world events.

Sir Winston S. Churchill to Sir Ivone Kirkpatrick
(Premier papers, 11/618)*

18 August 1954

There is no alternative but a revised NATO 'peripheral' is ruin for Europe.

* Reference: Minute from Sir Ivone Kirkpatrick dated August 18, 1954 – PM/IK/54/139, about a recent conversation with General Bedell Smith.

Sir Winston S. Churchill to John Foster Dulles
(Premier papers, 11/618)

19 August 1954
Top Secret
Personal and Private

1. Thank you so much for your message. If EDC fails through the impotence of the French Chamber we surely ought to create some variant of NATO. I am having the problem studied here and may have some ideas to put before you and the President. I am distressed at Adenauer's position. I feel we owe him almost a debt of honour after all the risks he has run and patience he has shown. It ought to be possible to devise some safeguards for a NATO arrangement.

2. Mendes-France has proposed to visit me here at Chartwell on his way back from Brussels on Saturday, Sunday or Monday. I shall do all I can on the lines on which we are agreed.

Anthony Eden to Sir Winston S. Churchill
(Premier papers, 11/672)

19 August 1954   Vienna
Personal and Private
No. 202

Thank you. I am confident we agree about EDC.

2. Mendes France sent Quai d'Orsay official here yesterday with a message explaining his many difficulties. The messenger left for Brussels this morning with a non-committal reply of which Kirkpatrick knows tenor.

3. If agreement is not reached at Brussels, Chartwell meeting may assume more formidable proportions and take longer. I have asked the Foreign Office to keep me posted of Brussels progress and if required I can always fly back by RAF plane from here. Meanwhile I will await events.

4. Grateful for Cyprus correspondence. Before I left England I was asked about a visit and said my own judgment was against it this time.

5. I feel no enthusiasm for this Far Eastern journey.

Sir Winston S. Churchill to Lord Swinton
(Premier papers, 11/706)

19 August 1954
Personal and Private

My dear Philip,

I assumed that my correspondence with Alex[1] had been forwarded to you. I am sorry that in the pressure of these days that was not done. I hope however you have had agreeable contacts with him and that I shall receive your report agreed with him or with only minor differences. I am afraid he was vexed at Duncan's intervention. Please let me know how things are going and if there is anything you want me to do.

Sir Winston S. Churchill to Lady Churchill
(Baroness Spencer-Churchill papers)[2]

19 August 1954

Welcome Home, My Darling

I do hope you have got real good as well as pleasure out of your trip. We await you tonight with eagerness. All is well here except the weather.

I lunched yesterday with Mary & the children. They are a wonderful brood. Jeremy is a portent. I have not seen his like before. It is a lovely home circle and has lighted my evening years.

Gabriel is much more at home and I feed him personally twice a day. He is quite friendly with Rufus, but it is an armed neutrality which prevails with the yellow cat.

We bought another Indian pig for £300 on Tuesday at a sale where many of them were sold for £700 or more. A litter fetches £2000. Christopher is much excited about it all and may well be on a good thing.

Mr Cox who takes a sober view predicted that prices at the sale wd average about £80. Actually they averaged £290!

Mr Mendès-France (I have got a better pen) proposed himself to look in here on his way back from Brussels on Sunday or Monday. He will land at

---

[1] Reproduced above, (pp. 1730, 1731).
[2] This letter was handwritten.

Biggin Hill and I shall tell 615 Squadron to provide a Guard of Honour. I have been most anxious to meet him as he is a new face in France. I am so glad you will be here.

Osbert Peake came to dine & sleep last night and Christopher and I had 4 hours vy informative talk w him about OAP, which is the dominant feature of next year's Cons Programme. 7/6 a week addition wd be an event of first importance (most secret) and they say the people are quite content to lick a few more stamps (10d). This sort of approval wd enable us to restore all and more than the Six Years of Socialist misrule took in *real value* from the Old & Poor.

Peake hates Old people (as such) living too long and cast a critical eye on me. He told about his Father who was stone blind for 20 years and kept alive at great expense by 3 nurses till he died <u>reluctantly</u> at 91: and of course the Death Duties were ever so much more than they would have been if he had only been put out of the way earlier. I felt very guilty. But in rejoinder I took him in to my study and showed him the 4 packets of proofs of the History of the E S Peoples which bring 50,000 dollars a year into the island on my account alone. 'You don't keep me, I keep you'. He was rather taken aback. I think he will play a large part in this coming year. He has some very important ideas about Insurance. I think I may put him & his office in the Cabinet on account of the preeminence of the OAP in our decisive year. (Secret)

Bedell Smith has resigned at Washington now about policy but to gain Health & Wealth. I hope he will succeed. Longing to see you my Beloved.

Your devoted husband
[Drawing of a pig with caption 'New Style £750']

President Dwight D. Eisenhower to Sir Winston S. Churchill
(*Premier papers, 11/1074*)

20 August 1954
Top Secret and Personal

Dear Winston,

I have carefully studied your recent letter[1] and I think I fully understand your views and position.

Right now I am wondering how you will handle the Cypress situation. This, of course, is strictly one of your family problems and I am not mentioning it with any thought that my own opinions should have a bearing on such a matter. My indirect concern, though, arises out of resultant effects upon American opinion. You and I have devoted a lot of time and thought to keeping relationships between our two peoples both durable and cordial, and

---

[1] Of Aug. 8, reproduced above (pp. 1724–5).

I am anxious to be in a position to be as helpful as possible when there appears to be any chance of damage to those relationships.

If you should like to give me a little briefing on the matter, I might be in a position to do something. Incidentally, some of our people who have been travelling recently in Greece have come back and spread stories to the effect that Greece and Cypress are quite ready to be reasonable and conciliatory – of course I do not know how accurate are their observations and their reporting. But this kind of thing does serve to give you some idea of why I am interested in the other side of the story.

We had a recent jolt when we found that there had evidently been a most indiscreet, not to say reprehensible, passing of security information from one of our military officers to one of yours here in Washington. Secret parts of the atomic development were involved. While I am not aware that anything was passed which would go beyond limits permitted by the new law we are trying to get through the Congress, yet when we disclosed this incident to certain members of the Congress, it greatly endangered our bill. Frankly for a day or two I have been quite worried.

I am blaming no one, least of all the individual, whoever he was, of your Services. The fault must lie with our man. But you and I have enough problems to solve in getting our ducks set up in a row without having to overcome the difficulties occasioned by such gauche, unwarranted and illegal actions. If we find out who <u>our</u> man was, he will probably be handled roughly. It might not be a bad idea to let your Chiefs of Staff know that our mutual relationships are far too important and too much engage the attentions of heads of government to endanger them by some unwise attempt to get hold of individual but highly sensitive items. In this way they could possibly help our people from becoming indiscreet.

I am hopeful either tomorrow or the next day that I can move the Summer White House to Denver.[1] The season has been a wearing one and I am quite tired. Nevertheless, if you want to communicate with me, your letters or cablegrams will come through in their accustomed secrecy. I shall not be separated from adequate communications.

---

[1] To Lowery Field USAF base near Denver, which was established in the summer of 1954 for Eisenhower's golfing and fishing holidays in the Rockies.

Sir Winston S. Churchill to Anthony Eden
(Premier papers, 11/618)

20 August 1954
Top Secret

As it seems probable that the French Chamber will be incapable of reaching an effective decision on EDC, we must work out a good plan for bringing Germany into the NATO front. It must be ready soon: the study is urgent and you should get in touch at once with the Ministry of Defence. It may be that they have already made progress in contact with SHAPE and General Ismay.

Pray let me have whatever is available at earliest.

2. We should propose that Germany should join NATO. If France uses a veto we should make a new NATO which should coexist with the present arrangements if necessary without the French. Of course it would only be on paper. But so is the mass of verbiage called the EDC. We must try to get the new NATO into a form which we can put before the Americans. They ought to have seen that EDC was hopeless a year ago. However it does not follow they will refuse to consider a revised NATO now. They no doubt argued that to talk about the two alternatives at once would destroy whatever chance there was of EDC.

3. We are confronted by the question of what safeguards can be imposed upon a German army under NATO which would take the place of EDC. The idea of special treaties for a limited period, say 15 or 20 years, between Britain and Germany and between America and Germany, or better still, an Anglo-American treaty with Germany must be searchingly examined. By some such method Germany in consideration of guarantees of help against attack from any quarter (such as have already been given) will maintain an armed force of not more than an agreed size. I do not agree that absolute similarity and equality for Germany must be accepted as indispensable, though no doubt Germany will ask for it. Certainly they should not be worse off but perhaps a little better off than under the present EDC.

4. The immediate danger is Mr Dulles having an 'agonised reappraisal' out of which 'peripheral defence' would be produced. This would mean the complete destruction of all the arrangements which have at present been made in Europe. The United States would withdraw her armies from Germany and content herself with Spain while expecting us to accord her the base in Norfolk and thus make ourselves the bullseye of a future war. If we did not like this and asked them to go, they might tell us to defend ourselves. Unhappily we have nothing yet to do it with. But that is the line along which argument or thought they would move if EDC is not replaced or sustained by a revised NATO.

5. There is one even more horrible and deadly alternative namely that proposed by Mr Aneurin Bevan when he urged America to 'go it alone'. She is quite strong enough to do so. All that would happen is that we should have

no influence on her policy and no protection and that at present and for some years, the dangerous years, no means of defence. The impotence and intrigues of the French Chamber may destroy EDC spell the ruin of France and the subjugation of Western Europe through fear of Russia. Only a revised NATO to include Germany under safeguards can secure our freedom and the peace of the World.

Sir Winston S. Churchill to Gwilym Lloyd George
Prime Minister's Personal Minute M.140/54
(Premier papers, 11/662)

20 August 1954

1. Let me have urgently a brief statement of British consumption of foods in tons of staple foods, gallons of milk, and numbers of eggs, etc. How much did we eat in May, June and July? How does this compare (a) with pre-war, and (b) with the similar three months of 1947 and 1951?

2. Let me know the total money spent in the same three month periods on tobacco, wines and spirits.

3. Let me have the same figures making allowance for the increase of population.

4. This paper should aim at factual simplicity and it ought not to occupy more than one page. No percentage calculations are required, people don't eat percentages.

John Foster Dulles to Sir Winston S. Churchill
(Premier papers, 11/618)

21 August 1954
Secret

My dear Sir Winston,

Thanks for your message of August 19.[1] I certainly agree with you that we are under heavy obligation to Adenauer. It would be an incalculable disaster if there was a failure of his pro-Western policy to ally Germany with the West and to prevent the revival of German militarism.

2. I shall be greatly interested in knowing the outcome of your talks with Mendès-France. From here it seems that Mendès-France seems to think that only he has Parliamentary difficulties and that all of our other Parliaments will happily dance to the tune which his parliament sets.

3. So far as the US Congress is concerned, it is pretty well convinced that

---

[1] Reproduced above (p. 1736).

EDC is a test of the reliability of France and if by this test France seems dedicated to indecision and unreliability then that fact undermines the whole NATO concept because French soil is essential to an effective Continental defense system.

4. I cannot, therefore, be optimistic about a NATO substitute although we shall of course try to limit the scope of the disaster which will be caused if the French Government again proves undependable.

5. However, as I suggested in my reply to your earlier message, even if a NATO solution is acceptable in principle, I foresee a repetition of past indecision and procrastination in relation to the question of whether Germany will become a member on a discriminatory basis – which I doubt – or whether France will admit Germany on a basis of full equality – which I equally doubt. I imagine that even you might find it a bit difficult to get your Parliament to accept the latter view and I think that Adenauer will find it impossible to get his Parliament to accept discrimination.

6. I am, of course, keeping the President fully informed of our correspondence as 'Foreign Ministers'.

Field Marshal Lord Alexander to Sir Winston S. Churchill
(*Premier papers, 11/618*)

23 August 1954

ALTERNATIVES TO EDC

Your minute of 20th August addressed to the Foreign Office and Ministry of Defence.[1]

The Chiefs of Staff have given much thought to possible alternatives to EDC and have concluded that the only satisfactory alternative, which would provide reasonable safeguards over German rearmament, would be to bring Western Germany into NATO.

2. If France vetoed this and we went ahead with a new NATO without the French, the consequences would be very serious, for the use of French territory is essential to the defence of Western Europe. We must assume that, in those circumstances, France would be neutral and deny us the use of her territory. This would mean that:
    (a) we should cease to have the use of supply ports on the Channel and Atlantic coasts, and of transportation facilities in France. This would completely disrupt the American line of communication and our own plans for supporting our forces on the Continent in war. I do not think that it would be strategically acceptable to depend

---

[1] Reproduced above (pp. 1740–1).

in war on lines of communication through the North Sea ports, in view of their vulnerability to atomic and submarine attack; in any case, the cost of realigning the lines of communication would be immense.
(b) we should lose the use of airfields in France, which are vital to the defence of the Central Sector.
(c) we should have to replace at great cost the headquarters and signal communication system, which have been built up in France.
(d) we should also lose the use of naval ports and bases on the Mediterranean coast, including North Africa, which would seriously affect Allied ability to operate in the Mediterranean.

3. The French contribution to the armed forces of Saceur (14 1/3 divisions, about 500 aircraft, 4 major and about 40 minor naval units) would be withdrawn. It is true that, in time, we should obtain a German contribution of about equivalent size and almost certainly of greater operational value. But Saceur requires the German contribution in addition to the forces already at his disposal, to enable him to defend Western Europe. With our worldwide commitments, we could not possibly offer additional forces to replace the French forces withdrawn, and I am sure that the Americans would not be prepared to increase their forces in Europe.

4. For these reasons it is of the utmost importance to get France to agree either to Western Germany joining NATO or to an arrangement which would permit the rearming of Germany with safeguards, while France herself remains in NATO.

5. Your suggestion for a triangular alliance, superimposed on NATO, is attractive. Militarily, however, it is not an exact parallel to the Balkan Alliance; the main difficulty being that in Central Europe all the allied forces must be under one single Supreme Commander. This is not probably an insuperable difficulty; possibly the British or American Headquarters in Central Europe might provide the link between the German forces and the Supreme Allied Commander. It should also be possible to introduce into an alliance of this sort restrictions on Germany's rearmament under NATO. I am having the military implications of this alternative further examined.

6. I am sending a copy of this minute to the Foreign Secretary.

Sir Winston S. Churchill to John Foster Dulles
Prime Minister's Personal Telegram T.290/54
(Premier papers, 11/618)

23 August 1954
Emergency
Top Secret and Personal
No. 4229

Very many thanks for all your telegrams today. You and I have never been closer together on a live issue. I send you the telegram I sent on the nineteenth to Adenauer which had already been published. Here are the two messages I have just received from him and his circle. They look good.

2. Mendès-France arrives here noon tomorrow, and I shall urge him to stake his political fame on getting EDC through. I shall make plain the awful consequences which might follow from a flop. It is a choice between peace through strength and subjugation through weakness. Anthony returns in time for the meeting. We might all of us be in on a winner. We must keep in the closest touch. This is a time for vehement moral action. I suppose you could come over if need be.

3. Give this with all my respects to the President. The climate of opinion he is building makes the best results possible. Code name 'Bite', quite like old times.

Sir Winston S. Churchill to John Foster Dulles
(Premier papers, 11/618)

23 August 1954
Emergency
Top Secret
No. 4230

Following is text of personal message to Dr Adenauer of August 19:

I am thinking much of you and your difficulties. My belief is that all will come right in the end in one form or another and that your statesmanship will not be denied its reward.
  Winston Churchill

2. Literal translation of German Chancellor's reply is as follows:

Your message has done me much good in these so exceptionally difficult days. Your words have strengthened my confidence that it is still possible to achieve a good result. My judgement of the result of the Brussels conference has not made me pessimistic. I am convinced that it is still possible for Mendès-France to get the EDC through. The result of the conference gives him in my opinion the possibility of telling the Members of Parliament who are hesitating that he has achieved the utmost – more than his predecessors. My impression of his personality and cleverness is that he can bring it off. With hearty thanks.

John Foster Dulles to Sir Winston S. Churchill
Prime Minister's Personal Minute T.291/54
(Premier papers, 11/618)

23 August 1954
Top Secret

Am greatly cheered by your message. Let us 'bite' hard and I think we should get something not only digestible but invigorating. I eagerly await the results of your talk with Mendès-France. I agree that we must keep in closest touch and I could come over at your call, although I must be in Manila September 3, which is our September 2.

Give my best regards to Anthony and be sure to let me know what happens.

Sir Winston S. Churchill and Pierre Mendès-France: notes of a conversation
(Premier papers, 11/618)

23 August 1954   Chartwell
Top Secret

The Prime Minister began by describing the general world situation and warning M Mendès-France that there were four alternative policies for the West in Europe, which he developed in considerable detail:
(1) the EDC which was much the best;
(2) to bring Germany into NATO which was the next best;
(3) the empty chair policy under which all the other countries would be forced to go ahead without France with a reasonable German policy, leaving a chair for France to take when she was ready to do so; this would be regrettable but might become inevitable;
(4) peripheral defence with the withdrawal of United States and United Kingdom forces from the Continent of Europe; he was very much afraid that the United States might turn to such a policy, with all its grave dangers.

The Prime Minister made it very clear that French rejection of the EDC and refusal to find an acceptable alternative would leave France absolutely isolated. The position inside Germany and, indeed, the world position would not allow delay. We could none of us permit our policies to be frustrated further by the indecisions of the French Chamber, more especially as French parliamentary procedure apparently made it impossible for the Chamber to be dissolved and M Mendès-France to appeal to the country.

The Prime Minister mentioned his own earlier ideas for a European Grand Alliance but said that he had put his whole weight behind the EDC because that was preferred by France. He was sure that it was now much the best solution and drew attention to the far-reaching guarantees which the United Kingdom and the United States had given to France under the EDC arrangements. Those who rejected this would be undertaking a very heavy responsibility. He and the Foreign Secretary urged M Mendès-France to use his immense authority to get the EDC through the French Parliament and pointed out the very grave dangers France would be incurring if they rejected it. They made it clear that the United Kingdom were determined to work in close agreement with the United States and other European countries who had shown a more realistic appreciation of the needs of the European situation. The Prime Minister referred M Mendès-France to his Margate speech a year ago[1] with which the Foreign Secretary had been in full agreement. He gave him the following passage: 'I am sure that the decisions taken by the Socialist Government, which were supported by us at the time and are now being carried forward steadfastly and soberly by Her Majesty's Government, constitute the best chance – and indeed, I think it a good chance – of getting through this awful period of anxiety without a world catastrophe.' We at any rate are going to adhere faithfully to them, and do our utmost to promote the formation of the European Army, with a strong contingent of Germans in it. We, like the Americans, shall maintain our forces in Europe, thus restoring the French balance of equality with our new German associates. If European Defence Community should not be adopted by the French, we shall have no choice in prudence but to fall in with some new arrangement which will join the strength of Germany to the Western Allies through some rearrangement of what is called NATO.

M Mendès-France had previously referred himself to the Margate speech and said he was in entire agreement with it. He felt that if the French Chamber had then been confronted with the choice of either EDC or Germany in NATO, they would have chosen one or the other. He criticized the Bermuda Conference because it had left France with only one choice, i.e., EDC. But this was past history, and he must now consider what could best be done. His problem had been to attract the vote of the waverers on the Right in the French Parliament. He was convinced that the protocol he had presented at Brussels would have obtained a majority for the EDC. But he had received no help from the other Powers present in Brussels, and had returned empty

[1] Reproduced above (pp. 1237–46).

handed. The United Kingdom Ministers demurred at this description of the Brussels Meeting and M Mendès-France said that anyway he had returned with absolutely nothing for the purpose he had in mind. He himself doubted whether it was wise to put the issue to the vote next week as the result was certain to be rejection, and there was no agreed alternative. But he was alone in this view. Opponents and advocates of the EDC alike in France and everyone outside France wanted the issue decided. He would therefore see that this was done. But he could not make it a question of confidence without destroying his Cabinet.

The United Kingdom Ministers urged him nevertheless to put the issue as strongly as he could to the French Chamber and to point out in no uncertain terms that EDC was much the best solution for France.

Some discussion then took place on alternatives, accepting M Mendès-France's argument that the EDC would be rejected.

The Foreign Secretary told him that the Foreign Office had given much thought to this problem in recent months but had found no alternative free from very serious difficulties. We could not expect the Germans to give us anything like the same safeguards in 1954 as we had obtained in the Bonn and Paris Treaties. Nor could Dr Adenauer wait for another prolonged round of negotiations. M Mendès-France said that what was wanted was a very simple solution under ten main heads which could be put into operation within two months. He agreed that the German situation was dangerous and was most anxious to help Dr Adenauer. He was also against German neutralism and for German rearmament as he had made clear in the key passages of the Brussels Communiqué which he had himself drafted. He was also very ready to give Germany back her political sovereignty at once and to announce this to the Assembly.

The United Kingdom Ministers said that German entry into NATO would be the best alternative solution. The problem was, however, to obtain the necessary safeguards. Moreover, there were many other countries concerned and the problems were not such as could be rapidly decided and agreed among many countries under ten main headings.

There was no simple 10-point solution, and it was, they feared, unrealistic to think of reaching agreement on a solution alternative to the Bonn and Paris Treaties in two months.

M Mendès-France then mentioned very generally another idea of associating the United Kingdom with the six EDC Powers in some modified structure within NATO which would control something equivalent to the armaments pool restricted to the Six Powers. He did not, however, go into any detail beyond saying that what France wanted was something with which the United Kingdom was associated. He did not make it clear whether Germany was or was not to be a member of NATO as well.

In all this part of the discussion M Mendès-France was very definite that a

France which rejected the EDC would never dare to reject an alternative even that of German entry into NATO. He did not seem very much concerned with the problem of safeguards under such a solution. In reply to the Prime Minister he asserted that France would not deny the use of facilities, including expensive infrastructure, on French soil to her NATO allies. But he later said that he could not answer for a Popular Front Government, which might succeed his own. He insisted that he must be helped by the United Kingdom if he was to get the necessary results within the next few weeks. It would be most dangerous if France remained isolated as she had been in Brussels.

M Mendès-France was critical of the pressure brought to bear in Brussels by United States representatives there. He said that the other Ministers in Brussels had expected him to give way at the last session and had been very surprised and disappointed when he had not done so. They had explained their inability to meet him further by saying that they had been asked to make so many earlier concessions to France with the result that they could not do so again, more especially as they were not sure that even M Mendès-France could deliver the goods.

M Mendès-France spoke very strongly against the American proposal for a meeting of the four ratifying Powers plus the United States and the United Kingdom. This would do no good and might do much harm. He thought that the other EDC Powers would not be enamoured of it.

On the Chartwell communiqué, M Mendès-France had been very determined not to include anything which endorsed the Brussels communiqué, although he was very ready to bring in the idea of the necessity for early action. Before leaving M Mendès-France had shown keen interest in methods for bringing the Bonn Conventions into force and wanted to know more about this in order that he might put the matter in the proper perspective to the Assembly next week. He was given a general idea of the recommendations of the Anglo-American Study Group.

The impression given by M Mendès-France was that whilst being very firm and definite in explaining that EDC would not pass and in proclaiming his belief in Western unity, the necessity for German rearmament, his opposition to German neutralism, he had not faced up to the very real difficulties about producing an acceptable solution within the very short time limit he mentioned. The United Kingdom Ministers, like the five EDC Ministers at Brussels, were thus left in some uncertainty about M Mendès-France's real position and intentions.

ANNEX

Foreign Office Telegram to Washington No. 4241 of August 23, 1954

Please give the following to Mr Dulles:
Begins.
At our meeting with Mendès-France today the Prime Minister and I impressed upon him with all the force at our command the grave dangers

which France and the whole Western world would incur if the French Assembly refused to ratify the EDC Treaty. The Brussels Conference had shown that France was isolated from her European partners and she would be altogether isolated if the French Chamber continued to refuse a decision on the German defence contribution. We urged Mendès-France strongly to put all his authority behind the EDC Treaty with the Spaak interpretations as much the best solution for France. He said he would put this issue to the vote next week, but he was quite definite that it would be rejected and that his Cabinet would not agree to make the vote a question of confidence. He agreed, however, that the attempt must be made, although the strength of his advocacy is uncertain.

2. We urged Mendès-France to make it clear to the Assembly that, if they rejected the EDC, some other solution of the German problem must be found, with or without France, without delay. He did not dissent and was ready to consider German entry into NATO, with or without some smaller grouping within NATO. He said he was ready as a first step to give Germany her political sovereignty without any delay and to announce this in the debate. A simple solution to the problem of German rearmament must then be found within two months. We warned him of the difficulties of finding and bringing into force any such solution which Germany and everyone else concerned could accept in so short a time. We concluded on the note that he must try to persuade France to accept the EDC as much the best way out, but that if this were impossible the Germans must receive their political equality immediately and be included within some acceptable defence framework, preferably NATO, very shortly thereafter. We impressed upon him, in particular, that we intended to work in close agreement with the United States Government and that we had a debt of honour to Adenauer and those European countries who had ratified the EDC.

3. Mendès-France argued strongly against a meeting of United States, United Kingdom, Germany and Benelux. Though we did not tell Mendès-France so we also see difficulties about such a meeting and think that the other countries concerned must be expected to do so. In any event, nothing of the kind can take place until after the French vote next week. We are giving urgent thought to some alternative procedure which would meet your objective and I will telegraph to you again very soon.

4. Meanwhile a fuller account of today's proceedings is being given to United States Embassy here.

Ends.

Sir Winston S. Churchill to John Foster Dulles
Prime Minister's Personal Telegram T.292/54
(Premier papers, 11/618)

24 August 1954
Emergency
Top Secret, Private and Personal
No. 4245

The visit passed off as follows. The first thing Mendes France said, and we affirmed, was that he was absolutely sure that the Chamber would not, repeat not, agree to EDC but were also determined that the matter should be debated. The French Cabinet were resolved to have a free vote. They would certainly be beaten but not probably by enough to have an election. Mendès-France seemed much hurt that everybody should have voted against France at Brussels. We made the obvious reply.

2. I was surprised to find that Mendès-France was himself much keener about NATO. I suppose it is because of the deep feeling in France that in EDC they will be boxed up in civil and military affairs with the much more active and powerful Western Germany, whereas in the NATO system the United Kingdom and the United States counter-balance Germany to her proper proportions. He furnished no solution about how to persuade Germany to make some substitute for the EDC safeguards. We told him that France would never get so good a bargain with Germany as they had got in EDC. He did not contradict this but pleaded helplessness. I was very sorry for him but gave him no comfort and pointed out that we should not agree to be governed by the impotence of the French Chamber. I was pleased at his attitude towards Adenauer and Germany.

3. Anthony who was with me for the three out of our four-hour talk was in full agreement though we had no chance of talking things over beforehand. He said he would send you a fuller account from the Foreign Office.

4. Thank you very much for your message just received. I think that there is nothing that can be done before the impending Debate in the Chamber and there will be time enough for our discussions after that result is known and you have finished your Manila expedition. I am now handing back to Anthony and wishing you all luck.

Sir Winston S. Churchill to Anthony Eden
(Churchill papers, 6/4)[1]

24 August 1954

My dear Anthony,

I have been pondering over your letter of August 10[2] but thought it better to wait till you came back before replying.

I am sorry you are not happy about home affairs. We have both had a hard fifteen months. During the first part of them I was much grieved and troubled by your illness and the uncertainty as to whether and when you could return. Since these fears have happily passed away, I have been oppressed by a series of suggestions that I should retire in your favour. I have done my best to discharge the Commission I hold from Crown and Parliament, and I am glad to say that I have not missed a single day in control of affairs, in spite of a temporary loss of physical mobility a year ago. Now I have good reports from my doctors, and I do not feel unequal to my burden.

I have no intention of abandoning my post at the present crisis in the world. I feel sure that with my influence I can be of help to the cause of 'peace through strength', on the methods of sustaining which we are so notably agreed. I trust therefore I may count on your loyalty and friendship during this important period, although it will not, as I hoped in my letter to you of June 11,[3] be ended by the autumn.

At another level coming to Party affairs, I have reflected long and deeply on the domestic scene by which we are confronted. The dominant fact is that the changes in the rating valuations are said to make it overwhelmingly desirable to have the election before November, 1955. It does not seem to me that the brief spell which remains till then gives the best chance to the Party or offers a propitious outlook to my successor. Certainly he would court a very heavy responsibility which in fact rests on me. He would have to present in twelve or thirteen months the impression of something new and different which would spread the sense of improvement. But we must ask ourselves whether this is likely in the prevailing circumstances. It is certain that one half of the country, instead of judging the new Government fairly on its merits, will on the contrary make it their target for electioneering abuse and for unfavourable comparisons.

[1] The following paragraph, originally to be the first of the letter, was deleted from the version that was sent: 'It is certainly no easier to see ahead in world politics than when we last talked. The Attlee–Bevan meeting with Malenkov is a new event which must be weighed and measured as it deserves. We have yet to hear about their visit to China which I consider far more dangerous from the American point of view. Chou En-lai's threats last week about "determined Chinese action to liberate Formosa" may easily be deemed grave at Washington. I approved some strong telegrams, which Kirkpatrick had drafted, to Mendès-France not to dawdle or whittle away EDC, but I do not expect any result. It is a terrible example of the dominion of impotence' (*Churchill papers*, 6/4).

[2] Reproduced above (p. 1728).

[3] Reproduced above (p. 1603).

Woolton, whom as Party Chairman I have consulted, tells me that he has already expressed the opinion that such a procedure would be bad electoral tactics. Looking at the scene impartially, as I try to do when I am in a good humour, it seems to me that it might be wiser not to attempt, with the restricted resources available, to conquer the hearts of an audience the majority of whom are hostile Party men. Fag-end Administrations have not usually been triumphant. I can remember Rosebery after Gladstone and AJB[1] after Salisbury. Both were brushed aside in spite of their ability, experience and charm.

When our Cabinets resume regularly in September, we shall be concerned both with the severe pruning of the Estimates, on which the hopes of the Budget depend, and also with The Queen's Speech for what will be our final Session. There is not much margin of money, and the array of bills which have so far been paraded do not seem attractive. Departmental legislation occupies Parliamentary time, but rarely wins the mead of popular applause, most rarely from the Conservative Party.

Moreover, need we forget it – the present Government have not got a bad record, with Rab's and Harold's solid and memorable achievements and your own skill at the Foreign Office. Prosperity, Homes, Employment, Solvency, and 'Peace through Strength' is a theme both simple and majestic. This will, I trust, be made good by the 1955 Budget, saved up from last year, which we are trying so hard to sustain. Apart from this and earlier in the year the one obvious and outstanding task on which our domestic fortunes turn is the humane and large-scale handling of Old Age Pensions and kindred subjects. All this is a natural climax, and not a new venture.

As to the election, I ought to bear the responsibility for the past and leave to my successor a fair start and the hope of the future. We can discuss in detail the mechanism and timing by which such a transition could most effectively be achieved. I would in any case stand as a Conservative at the polls.

I fear a great many of our colleagues will be abroad on their holidays during September, and certainly the Cabinet before the new Session will be exacting. One thing stands forth. There must be a thorough reconstruction of the Government. This is itself will end the uncertainty which has arisen from your physical affliction and my own.[2]

---

[1] Arthur James Balfour.
[2] Churchill sent a copy of this letter to Harold Macmillan with the note: 'On this basis we can certainly plan the future and arrive at what you so aptly described as a prospectus and not a sample.'

Harold Macmillan: recollection
('Tides of Fortune', pages 539–41)

24 August 1954

On my return from a short holiday, I got a message inviting me to Chartwell. Churchill was in a relaxed and amiable mood. In the course of luncheon, which lasted until nearly 4 p.m., after a certain amount of desultory discussion about Soviet policy, EDC, NATO, Adenauer's position, the French confusion, and the like, we got to the real point. He had now made up his mind not to resign in September as had been the original plan. He reminded me that I had protested against this as being too late to allow for a successful Government to be formed before the end of the year. He therefore made it clear that he proposed to stay as long as he could. He produced in favour of this plan a number of arguments:

> First, he (and he alone in the world) might be able to steer through the complications of Foreign Policy and international problems. He had a unique position. He could talk to anybody, on either side of the Iron Curtain, either by personal message or face to face. Having now fully recovered his health, he could not abandon (his) commission. . . . Secondly, a 'fag end' government, formed at the end of a Parliament, could never succeed. Such brilliant figures as Lord Rosebery and Arthur Balfour had been swept away, in spite of their talents and their charm, when they had to succeed to Gladstone and Salisbury. It would be much better for Eden if he (Churchill) were to go on till the Election. Or, perhaps, it might be wise to let Eden become PM just *before* the election. That could be decided later. Thirdly, he was PM and nothing could drive him out of his office, so long as he could form and control a Government and have the confidence of the House. This continual chatter in the lobbies and the press about his resignation was intolerable. It arose, of course, from his illness last year. But he was now recovered. Naturally, like any man of nearly 80, who had had *two* strokes, he might die at any moment. But he could not undertake to die at any particular moment! Meanwhile, he did not propose to resign.

Naturally, all this did not pour out in a single flood of rhetoric. There were pauses, questions and silent broodings, and I had to make appropriate remarks at intervals in order to encourage him to tell the whole story. When he pressed me for my opinion, I thought it right to give it sincerely and truthfully. I said:

> That (i) there was no reason to suppose that the foreign problems were temporary or passing; (ii) that there were arguments the other way about the 'fag end' administration. We needed a new impetus and a new theme. Anthony Eden might give us these. It was impossible for him. (iii) Since he had repeatedly told everybody that he proposed to resign this autumn, it

was he who was responsible for this widespread (even general) assumption. He had said farewell to the Women's Party Conference at the Albert Hall this summer.[1] But much more important, he had many times in the last few months told Anthony that he was on the point of 'handing over'. First he had told him the Queen's return, that is May; then he had said, July; finally, in a letter, written on June 11th (which I had seen),[2] he had categorically told Eden that he would resign the Premiership in September. Anyway, what had he now said to Eden?

Churchill naturally did not much like this, but as always treated what I said calmly and courteously. I had once observed to him that I could speak to him more frankly than some of his colleagues. He had long treated Eden as an eldest son, and even if Eden were to break down in health, there were many senior to me. In the case of great estates, the eldest son can never speak to his father about the wisdom of handing over property; a younger son who had nothing to gain is the person who should undertake the task, however disagreeable. It was in such a spirit that I had always spoken to him, and he had accepted this as a fair point.

I now asked again – what had he said to Eden and what was this new plan? It proved to be that Eden should become Deputy Prime Minister, Leader of the House, and responsible for the 'home front'. He would speak in the country; he would take control of the party machine; he would 'plan' the programme for the next election. He would be, as it were, to use an analogy of commerce, the managing director, while Churchill remained as chairman. If only Eden would agree to this, all would be plain sailing. I replied frankly that I thought this decision would be a severe shock to Eden and that he would be much more likely to wish to stay at the Foreign Office. At any rate, I urged him not to let things drift but to bring them to a head. We really must settle, and within a few weeks, what was to be done and how we were to plan our work. To this Churchill agreed and undertook to send Eden a letter in these terms.

But it was not only the question of the Premiership which must be settled. The Government had ceased to function with full efficiency; many of the Ministers were unsuited to their posts; no one coordinated policy; Cabinets were becoming long and wearisome, as well as too frequent. The Parliamentary Party, already discontented, might soon break up into groups and cabals; the whole party machine was losing grip. All this was due to the continual uncertainty, discussed openly in the Press, as to Churchill's intentions.

---

[1] Speech reproduced above (pp. 1582–6).
[2] Reproduced above (p. 1603).

President Dwight D. Eisenhower to Sir Winston S. Churchill
(Premier papers, 11/618)

25 August 1954

Dear Winston,
I have read with keen interest the account of your conversation with Mendès-France.[1] I feel a deep sense of satisfaction that you and your government are in accord with Foster and me and this administration in our efforts. If we could only figure out some way to bring Mendès-France to see his historic opportunity or to put a little backbone into the French Assembly, there would be an immediate spiritual transformation throughout the whole region and there would be rapidly developed a defensive program and organization in which all of us could have confidence.

Sir Winston S. Churchill to Sir Ivone Kirkpatrick
Prime Minister's Personal Minute M.146/54
(Premier papers, 11/670)

25 August 1954

Your minute PM/IK/54/150.*
These were the two gestures I suggested as being perhaps the means of rendering a top level 3 or 4-Power conference in London possible which the President might attend himself. They are now to be wasted in fending off another meeting of the Berlin type which we and the Americans had already decided we did not want.

* Reply to Soviet Note.

Sir Winston S. Churchill to Lady Churchill
(Baroness Spencer-Churchill papers)[2]

25 August 1954   Chequers

My darling & beloved Clemmie,
Do forgive me for my lapse this morning. I was preoccupied with dictating a message to Ike. I only wanted the Portal not to go back to the office but wait in the next room while we had a talk. I was enraptured by your lovely smile of greeting, & longing to kiss you. And this I spoiled by clumsiness & gaucherie.

[1] Reproduced above (pp. 1745–9).
[2] This letter was handwritten.

I cherish your morning comings & I beseech you to be noble & generous as you always are to your thoroughly penitent & much ashamed, but loving & hopeful

PS. You have been so bright & splendid here and I have thanked God to see you much stronger. I will try to do better.

Sir Winston S. Churchill to Lady Churchill
(Churchill papers, 1/50)[1]

25 August 1954

My darling one,

I did not worry you with the enclosed yesterday.[2] Harold thought I ought to send it, it has gone. The responsibility is mine. But I hope you will give me your love.

Anthony Eden to Sir Winston S. Churchill
(Churchill papers, 6/4)

25 August 1954

My dear Winston,

Thank you for your letter of yesterday, and for telling me of your changed plans since our conversations and your letter of June 11.[3]

The problem was not a personal one for any of us, but how the government is to be carried on and the future of the party best assured.

In any event it is clearly urgent to reach a decision as to how these purposes can be realized, & I assume that you will wish to discuss with those of your colleagues with whom you talked over the whole problem some months ago.

---

[1] This letter was handwritten.
[2] Letter to Eden of Aug. 24, reproduced above (pp. 1751–2).
[3] Reproduced above (p. 1603).

August 1954

Sir Winston S. Churchill to Anthony Eden
(Churchill papers, 6/4)[1]

26 August 1954

My dear Anthony,

Of course we must try to make the best plans possible to win the Election and to save the world. They are not necessarily opposed. I shall be glad to have a talk with you tomorrow at noon at No. 10, if this would be convenient. Send me a telephone message tonight.

Anthony Eden: diary
(Robert Rhodes James, 'Anthony Eden, A Biography', pages 385–6)

27 August 1954

Rab & Harold asked to see me at 11.

Rab said that he had been much embarrassed, that he had a double loyalty to W & to me & had told W so. He was convinced that W was determined to stay. Neither pretended that this was nationally desirable. The issue was what to do. Rab clearly wanted me to consider whether I could take over Home front & leadership of the House. This he urged would make me PM in everything but name. Harold did not conceal his concern at attempting to carry on with W as he now is. Nor did I. The reshuffle was merely a device to enable him to carry on longer while doing even less. He would then do nothing except interfere with FO. This might have disastrous results. We all agreed that it was essential to have a meeting of a number of colleagues soon.

We were all pretty gloomy but friendly. A disagreeable feature of this whole business is that in the reshuffle I am sure we will find W actuated by animus against Bobbety, Harry Crookshank & perhaps Lord Chancellor.

After long talk with Harold & Rab walked across to see W.

Interview opened stiffly. He paid various compliments about FO documents since my return. I did not respond. Eventually we got to the point. He asked me what I thought of the position. I said 'I have your letter, you have mine, what more is there to say?'

He then launched out into a long rigmarole as to how he felt better (he didn't look it & his argument was often confused – for instance when later he discussed whether I should stay at FO or lead the House he gave the arguments for one in support for the other). He also argued that this was a bad time for him to go; not possible for the new administration to make its mark in the last year. This was Woolton's view too. Unfortunate I had been ill when he had

[1] This letter was handwritten.

his stroke last year. Now better wait until he fell ill again, or nearer the election when he would give me all the help he could.

I said I had explained what I thought many times. If I was not fit to stand on my own feet now & choose an administration now, I should probably be less so a year from now. The Gov't was not functioning well & this was putting a heavy strain on all his senior Ministers. These were able men but there was no coordination.

Of course he didn't like this & said he had never missed a day since his illness. I said that wasn't the point. There was no coordination on home front & Cabinets dragged on far too long. There was much argument about this which got us nowhere. I said that I would have been glad of the chance to take over a year ago, but it meant less to me now, & would mean less still next year if I were still there. I added that I envied Oliver (Lyttelton) & would like to do as he had done.[1] He replied that the Party would never forgive me if I did, that they were counting on me, etc. I was young. It would all be mine before sixty. Why was I in such a hurry? Anyway if I felt like it he would be ready for me to take over Leadership of House and home front. I showed no enthusiasm and felt none.

He said there was another alternative, that I might lead a rebellion of five or six Ministers. But that would be very grave. I said of course it would & he knew perfectly well that I was the last person to want to do this after our many years of work together.

Then there was some emotion, after which I said I would like to talk it all over with political colleagues together. He didn't like this much, but eventually agreed as long as it was a discussion of reconstruction and not of his resignation (it wasn't put like that, but that is what it amounted to).

Sir Winston S. Churchill to Anthony Eden
(Churchill papers, 6/4)

27 August 1954

My dear Anthony,

I was deeply touched this morning by your kindness to me.

---

[1] i.e. retire from politics altogether.

AUGUST 1954

Cabinet: conclusions
(*Cabinet papers, 128/27*)

27 August 1954
Secret
3.30 p.m.
Cabinet Meeting No. 57 of 1954

1. The Cabinet had before them a memorandum by the Foreign Secretary (C(54)276) about the course to be adopted if the European Defence Community (EDC) Treaty should be rejected by the French Assembly after their forthcoming debate.

The Foreign Secretary said that there was every likelihood that the Treaty would be rejected by the French Assembly within the next few days. It was vital that, until the critical vote had taken place, no encouragement should be given publicly to the idea of any alternative to the Treaty. He could, however, envisage no better than to bring Germany into the North Atlantic Treaty Organisation (NATO), in agreement with France and the United States and subject to the safeguards set out in the annex to C(54)276. The difficulties in the way of this alternative were undoubtedly formidable. Not only had the attitude adopted by M Mendès-France at and since the recent Brussels Conference seriously antagonised the other signatories of the EDC Treaty, but the Labour Party in this country were not committed to supporting any plan involving German rearmament other than EDC and might well take advantage of the opportunity of restoring Party unity on this issue by opposing the admission of Germany into NATO. If the Cabinet agreed with his view about the course which should be taken in the event of French rejection of the Treaty, he would at once inform the United States Government confidentially of what we had in mind: he expected them to agree to our taking the initiative. The first step would be to seek the views of Dr Adenauer, and this he would propose to do in the first instance through our High Commissioner in Bonn. It seemed unlikely that the German Federal Government would feel able to accept all the limitations outlined in the annex to his paper, but as many as possible of these must be secured. It was doubtful whether a majority would be obtainable in the present French Assembly for any proposals involving German rearmament, but M Mendès-France had expressed the view that on a second occasion the Assembly would find it harder to take an entirely negative decision.

The Prime Minister said that it had not been difficult to convince the United States Government that their plan for a postponement of the French Assembly debate and for the immediate summoning of an Eight-Power conference was unsound (Foreign Office telegram No. 4293 to Washington). The words which, in agreement with the Foreign Secretary, he had used in his speech to the Conservative Party Conference at Margate in October, 1953,[1] remained as true today as when he had spoken them:

> 'I am sure that the decisions taken by the Socialist Government, which were supported by us at the time and are now being carried forward steadfastly and soberly by Her Majesty's Government, constitute the best chance – and indeed, I think it a good chance – of getting through this awful period of anxiety without a world of catastrophe.
>
> We, at any rate, are going to adhere faithfully to them and do our utmost to promote the formation of the European Army with a strong contingent of Germans in it. We, like the Americans, shall maintain our forces in Europe, thus restoring the French balance of equality with our German associates.
>
> If EDC should not be adopted by the French, we shall have no choice in prudence but to fall in with some new arrangement which will join the strength of Germany to the Western allies through some rearrangement of the forces of NATO.'

French fears of German predominance in the comparatively restricted EDC might not have the same force in respect of the wider community of NATO, including, as it did, the United States and United Kingdom. The isolation in which France would find herself if she rejected EDC would, moreover, be likely to induce her to cooperate in seeking an alternative to it.

The Minister of Housing suggested that a NATO solution might be made more palatable both to French opinion and to the Labour Party in this country if, for this purpose, NATO could be made at least to appear to have been modified in the direction of the European idea. Was it possible, for example, for Germany formally to adhere to the Brussels Treaty which continued to subsist within the North Atlantic Treaty? He would send some suggestions on these lines to the Foreign Secretary.

The Commonwealth Secretary said that he would be opposed to any associating of the United Kingdom with continental countries closer than that envisaged in connection with the EDC, as it seemed likely that this would encourage tendencies in certain Commonwealth countries to turn towards the United States.

The Cabinet –

(1) Agreed in principle that, in the event of rejection of the EDC Treaty by the French Assembly, it would be necessary to work to bring Germany into NATO, subject to as many as possible of the safeguards set out in the annex to C(54)276.

(2) Authorised the Foreign Secretary to proceed on the general lines suggested in C(54)276 and in the course of discussion.

---

[1] Reproduced above (pp. 1237–46).

[. . .]

4. The Prime Minister said that he understood that the South African Minister of Defence,[1] during his forthcoming visit to this country, was likely to try to reopen discussion on the transfer of the Simonstown base to the South African Navy. This base had always been of first-rate strategic importance, but its value appeared to be even greater now in the light of the reduced importance of the Suez Canal and the greater uncertainty about the degree of cooperation in defence matters which was to be expected of the South African Government in the future. He had asked the Minister of Defence to report on the suitability of Durban as an alternative base to Simonstown, but it was not clear that Durban could be relied upon in all circumstances. He therefore felt doubtful whether in any circumstances we ought to consider abandoning our present legal right to perpetual use of the Simonstown base.

The Commonwealth Secretary said that the object of the forthcoming discussions with the South African Minister of Defence, Mr Erasmus, was to encourage the South African Government to take a broader view of their responsibilities in Commonwealth defence. There were grounds for believing that Mr Erasmus might prove to be reasonably forthcoming. In any event there was not at present any intention to modify the conditions for transfer of the Simonstown base which had been agreed upon in 1951.

The Minister of Defence said that, even from the point of view of our use of the Simonstown base, it was important to ensure the fullest possible cooperation of the South African Government in order to safeguard the continued supply of labour, water and electric power to the base.

The Prime Minister said that there was certainly no objection to seeing what, if anything, Mr Erasmus had to say on the subject of the Simonstown naval base. But, before any encouragement was given to him to think that the United Kingdom Government might be ready to reopen the question of transfer, the matter must be brought again before the Cabinet. World conditions had substantially changed even since 1951, and it was by no means certain that conditions for the transfer of the base which had been considered sufficient at that time would prove on examination to meet adequately the conditions of today.

The Cabinet –

Took note of these statements.

5. The Prime Minister said that it had been brought to his notice that the Argentine Ministry of Agriculture had approached the Bristol Aeroplane Company about buying Sycamore helicopters for crop-spraying. They wished

---

[1] François Christiaan Erasmus, 1896–1967. Born in Merweville, Cape Colony. Educated at University of Cape Town. Taught in Transvaal. Registrar to Judge-President of the Cape. Advocate, Cape Town, 1925–7. Deputy Attorney-General, South West Africa, 1927–8. Asst Organiser, National Party, Cape Province, 1928–30; Chief Secretary, 1930–48. MP (National Party) for Moorreesburg, 1933–61. Minister of Defence, 1948–59. Minister of Justice, 1959–61. Ambassador to Italy, 1961–5.

to buy 5 now, and might order up to 50 later. At the end of 1953 the Argentine Navy had wanted to buy helicopters from us, but we had been unwilling to agree, since they might have been used against us in the Antarctic. He did not himself feel sure that the helicopters the Argentines now wanted would not in fact be used to our detriment.

The Foreign Secretary said that, although there was no certain guarantee that the Argentines would not use these helicopters against us, they had already bought for their Navy American helicopters which were larger and more suitable for use in the Antarctic. On balance, he recommended allowing the sale of not more than 10 Sycamore or similar helicopters to Argentina, and that the matter should be re-examined if the Argentines wished to place a larger order.

The Secretary of State for Air said that orders for these helicopters would represent a valuable export, since they cost £40,000 each. He had no objection to the sale, provided the Argentines did not pre-empt helicopters needed by the Services.

The Cabinet –

Agreed that not more than 10 Sycamore or similar helicopters should be sold to the Argentine Ministry of Agriculture; and that, if the Argentines later wished to place a larger order, the matter should be considered again by the Cabinet.

6. The Minister of State for Colonial Affairs said that the announcement of the policy approved by the Cabinet on 26th July[1] had provoked a violent reaction in Greece, but there had been only minor and isolated incidents in Cyprus. Indeed, except for the extreme nationalists and the Communists, there was considerable apathy among the people of Cyprus. Archbishop Makarios[2] had preached three sermons of a political nature, but not in such terms as would warrant a prosecution for sedition. As regards the enforcement of the laws against sedition, it had been the intention that the Governor should issue a warning that the law would be enforced, but that this would be in general terms, whereas the publication of detailed prohibitions, some of which might not be applicable in present circumstances, had understandably aroused widespread criticism. The Colonial Secretary had since expressed the view to the Governor[3] that seditious behaviour which did not lead to violence

---

[1] That Britain would reaffirm its intention to retain sovereignty over Cyprus but also offer constitutional changes which would mark a further stage in the development of self-governing institutions in the island (Cabinet Meeting No. 53 of 1954, *Cabinet papers, 128/27*).

[2] Mikhail Khristodoulou Mouskos, 1913–77. Known as 'Makarios III'. Born in Panayia, Cyprus. Educated at the National and Kapodistrian University of Athens, Greece, and Boston University, US. Entered Kykkos Monastery, 1926. Bishop of Kition, Cyprus, 1948. Archbishop of Cyprus, 1950. President, Republic of Cyprus, 1960–74, 1974–7.

[3] Robert Perceval Armitage, 1906–90. Born in Nungambakkam, Madras. Educated at New College, Oxford. District Officer, Kenya Colony, 1929. Married, 1930, Gwladys Lyona Meyler: two children. Secretary to Member for Agriculture and Natural Resources, 1945; Administrative Secretary, 1947. Under-Secretary, Gold Coast, 1948; Financial Secretary, 1948; Minister for Finance, 1951–3. Governor and C-in-C, Cyprus, 1954–5. Governor of Nyasaland, 1956–61. KStJ, 1954.

AUGUST 1954   1763

might conveniently be overlooked. The Colonial Office were taking active measures to explain publicly the case for the Government's policy in Cyprus.

The Prime Minister said that the publication of repressive laws against sedition had been unwise and had led to unnecessary trouble. It would do no harm to allow demonstrations in Cyprus, provided they did not lead to violence, which did not appear likely.

The Foreign Secretary said that it was necessary to explain our policy, and the reasons for it, in as convincing a way as possible before the matter came up for discussion in the United Nations in September. The claim to Cyprus, which Greece was pressing, was a fabricated one and we should be ready to expose this. Many Greeks, particularly those with a liberal outlook, were not in sympathy with present Greek policy, but could not say so because there was no freedom of expression in Greece. We could point out that the Greek record of administration in the Dodecanese, since it had been restored to them, was deplorable compared with our own in Cyprus. We had a good case and it might be helpful if a small Committee of Ministers were set up to supervise its presentation.

In discussion the following further points were made:
(a) Pakistan had now indicated that she fully supported the United Kingdom on this issue. There had been criticism from the New Zealand Minister for External Affairs, but this might not reflect the general state of public opinion in New Zealand, and showed the need for a proper explanation of our policy.
(b) It was suggested that an examination should be made of the laws against sedition in Cyprus, with the object of putting into reserve such of them as need not be used unless a state of emergency were declared. It was pointed out that in Cyprus, as in other Colonial territories, seditious intent included the intention to change the sovereignty of the Colony, regardless of whether there was any incitement to violence.
(c) The Foreign Secretary expressed the view that, since it should be our aim to show that conditions were not abnormal in Cyprus, it would be unwise for the Colonial Secretary to visit the island at the present time, and that the Cabinet should be consulted before any decision was taken to pay such a visit.

The Cabinet –
(1) Took note of the statement by the Minister of State for Colonial Affairs.
(2) Invited the Prime Minister to arrange for a small Committee of Ministers to be set up to consider the presentation of the Government's policy towards Cyprus.

7. The Cabinet had before them a memorandum by the Prime Minister (C(54)272) covering a report by the Ministry of Labour about the rise of 3 points in the Retail Prices Index figure published for July; a note (C(54)277)

containing statistics of the consumption of food and expenditure on tobacco, beer, wines and spirits provided by the Ministry of Food at the Prime Minister's request; and a memorandum by the Minister of Food (C(54)274) about the level of meat prices since decontrol.

The Parliamentary Secretary, Ministry of Labour, said that, as the Index figure was calculated from the actual prices which people were prepared to pay on a particular day, it was not possible to make accurate forecasts of future changes in the Index figure. In so far as any estimates could be made, the Index figure for August might show a fall of 1 point; but a rising trend must be expected for the rest of the year, as there would be increases in rents and fares as well as in the cost of some foods and other items.

The following points were made in discussion:

(a) The increasing difficulty of making reliable forecasts was a result of freeing the economy and removing price controls.

(b) The increase in retail meat prices was due in part to the fact that consumers were prepared to pay a price which allowed butchers to take a somewhat higher rate of profit than they had been allowed while meat was controlled. In fact, the public were willingly paying for the better cuts of meat.

(c) When prices were controlled, it was the controlled price which was taken for the purpose of calculating the Index figure, although in some cases, for example meat, consumers might well, on occasion, have paid more than the controlled price.

(d) It was agreed that there was no general discontent about the cost of living, but it was pointed out that a rise of 3 points in the Index figure nevertheless provided a basis for claims for increased wages, and in some cases wages increased automatically with a rise in the Index.

The Prime Minister said that it was clear from the statistics of food consumption that the level of prices did not deter consumers, and the statistics of expenditure on tobacco, beer, wines, and spirits showed that the people generally were prosperous. It should not be difficult to find arguments to meet Opposition propaganda based on the rise in the Retail Prices Index figure for July.

The Cabinet –

Took note of C(54)272, C(54)277 and C(54)274.

[...]

10. The Foreign Secretary said that two subordinate employees in the British Embassy in Moscow had, when intoxicated, assaulted Russians, including a Russian policeman. One was employed as a wireless operator, but not in such a position that his predicament gave rise to anxiety on security grounds. The Ambassador wanted to send the employees concerned back to the United Kingdom, but the Russians were insisting on bringing them

to trial for hooliganism. A trial could be avoided if they were given refuge in the Embassy premises, but there were difficulties about such a course since the employees concerned had families, and in any case there was no doubt that they had committed an offence. We could, therefore, either stand on their claim to diplomatic immunity but without taking measures to prevent their arrest, or we could waive any claim to diplomatic immunity for them. If they were tried, they might well receive severe sentences.

He had asked the Soviet Ambassador to transmit a personal message to the Soviet Foreign Minister expressing the hope that the Russians would not insist on bringing these men to trial since that would lead to unnecessary friction. Subject to this, he had come to the view that we should waive diplomatic immunity in this case.

The Prime Minister said that he agreed with the course proposed by the Foreign Secretary. If the Russians inflicted vindictive sentences it would then be proper to take whatever measures were open to us; but this was not a case in which diplomatic immunity should be claimed.

The Cabinet –

Agreed that diplomatic immunity should be waived in this case.

Anthony Eden to Sir Winston S. Churchill
(Churchill papers, 6/4)[1]

28 August 1954

My dear Winston,

Thank you for your letter.[2] I would like to give further thought to alienation of FO & home front. Perhaps we could discuss this further & whenever our meeting takes place I would be glad to have views upon it. There are strong arguments both ways as to what it is best to do for the side.

Sir Winston S. Churchill to Anthony Eden
(Premier papers, 11/618)

29 August 1954
Private and Personal

My dear Anthony,

I suppose there has never been a more magnificent example of the power of impotence than what the French Chamber is providing us with. Washington has shown itself in this last stage more patient and tolerant than ever

---

[1] This letter was handwritten.
[2] Of Aug. 24, reproduced above.

before. I grieve for the much maltreated famous Benelux as well as for faithful Adenauer and I feel exactly as I did at our Party Conference ten months ago on the words which we agreed upon together. This policy is I am sure feasible provided the UK and the US are agreed upon it. I don't see why 'the empty chair' phase should not give the French Chamber six months to do their duty while they will be continually confronted by the formidable march of events and the awful consequences which they are bringing upon themselves through their selfishness and ingratitude towards their fellow-sufferers and rescuers alike.

2. About the suggested Eight Power Meeting. I should be glad if you would consider whether we should press the President to come himself and make it Top Level. This could certainly add to the impression it would make and to the latitude of its decision. This again might be followed, though it seems very improbable no, but a Big Four Top-Level with the Bear or Bears in London. It doesn't follow we should grovel to them.

I am less alarmed about a cold confrontation in the true facts, then I am about the sands running out in the American Year-glass. (Two-three years.)

3. About NATO – (see no. 645 from UK High Commissioner in Australia). I do not feel quite sure that the gap of your not going to Manila would be filled in world or American or Commonwealth eyes by Reading, though no doubt he would do the work well. I still think Philip[1] as Secretary of State for Commonwealth Relations would be very appropriate. You could instruct him about the point you had in mind.

However, it may be that an eight Power Meeting in Europe will prevent Dulles going himself and thus alter the balance from a new angle. How shabbily Nehru is behaving!

4. Today we have sunshine for the third day running and my buddleia may well have sixty Red Admiral, Peacocks and Tortoiseshells feeding on them. I planned them on purpose four years ago and till this weekend I had bewailed the decline of our butterfly population. Perhaps a crusade by the Almighty as some small amendment by the human-race for the filthy torture of rabbits.

Clemmie and I send our best love to Clissa.[2]

PS. Your letter has just arrived. I think you are right to weigh the alternatives. I will write again later today or tomorrow.

---

[1] Philip Cunliffe-Lister, Lord Swinton.
[2] Clarissa.

Christopher Soames to Sir Winston S. Churchill
(*Churchill papers, 6/4*)[1]

29 August 1954

I told Swinton of your intentions. He as much interested and said that events were moving so fast he thought you should stay. He added that you would need to reconstruct and that you should have someone to take a firmer grip on Home Affairs. He thought Macmillan should do it. I naturally said nothing of what was in your mind on this except that you were aware of the need for a strong Chairman of Home Affairs Committee. He said that in the reconstruction that you must make he hoped that he would not be moved to another job. He thought it necessary he should stay where he was.

He wants me to say that he thought your decision would be well received on the whole by your colleagues, though some most notably AE would be disappointed.

We had a good day's shooting yesterday, 105 brace.

Bill de Lisle is here and sends you his regards.

I long to know how your talk with Anthony went.

Yours very affectionately
Chimp

Sir Winston S. Churchill to Bernard Baruch
(*Churchill papers, 2/210*)

29 August 1954
Top Secret
Personal and Private

My dear Bernie,

The Kremlin did not turn out to be particularly keen on the visit and though the issue of the rendezvous being on neutral ground was never mentioned I have no reason to believe they liked the idea. I should certainly not go to Moscow. My hope, as you know, was to have talks which might lead to a larger Top Level meeting at a later date. That I have a very good British warrant in pursuing this matter you can judge from the resolution unanimously passed by the House of Commons last Session, a copy of which I enclose.

I am also on pretty strong ground about EDC, etc. It is not ten months since I addressed the Conservative Party Annual meeting and I cannot express our policy today better than in repeating what I said then.[2] The French Chamber

---

[1] This letter was handwritten.
[2] Speech reproduced above (pp. 1237–46).

with its extraordinary constitution has enabled an indefinite stalemate to be maintained, greatly to the injury of our vital interests in the attitude of Germany.

I was glad to hear again about Jimmy Byrnes.[1] I like what I saw of him personally very much as I remember with pleasure your and his visit to me when I was ailing at Miami. I cannot think he treated us very fairly over the Atomic Bomb by not letting the Congressional Committee see the text of my Agreement with FDR, – a memorable document of undoubted American constitutional validity. However we are now going on all right on our own after losing several years and spending a lot.

You will, I am sure, be glad to hear that I am not thinking of retirement at the present time. I feel earnestly I still have something to contribute to the cause of 'Peace through Strength'. I am sure that I shall always get a fair hearing in my Mother's Land. I have seemed to gather vigour as this year has progressed and can do a long and thorough day's work especially if I get a good sleep in the middle of the day. I am not however trying any of your equestrian or high-diving exercises at the present time though I am most envious. Still, we have never been rivals.

I doubt if I shall leave England except for a week or two before the end of the holidays, and after that the Party and the Parliament resume their sway.

My mind is continually oppressed by the thermo-nuclear problem, though I still believe it is more likely to bring War to an end than mankind.

Mind you let me know if there is any prospect of your coming over here.

Lord Bracken to Lord Beaverbrook
(Beaverbrook papers)

31 August 1954

Luce's consistent hostility to Britain and to Churchill puzzles me. In his last issue of *Time* his London correspondent declares that Churchill horned in on the delicate French political situation by inviting Mendès-France to visit him at Chartwell. This statement is altogether untrue. Mendès-France pressed Churchill to see him for a few hours at his 'country residence'.

---

[1] James Francis Byrnes, 1882–1972. Born in Charleston, SC. Representative (Dem.) for South Carolina's Third Congressional District, 1911–25. US Senator (Dem.) from South Carolina, 1931–41. Associate Justice, US Supreme Court, 1941–2. Head of Office of Economic Stabilization in Washington DC, 1942. Director of Office of War Mobilization, 1943. Secretary of State, 1945–7. *Time* magazine's Man of the Year, 1947. Governor of South Carolina, 1951–5.

August 1954

Duncan Sandys to Sir Winston S. Churchill
(Churchill papers, 6/4)[1]

31 August 1954
Private

My dear Winston,
　I was so glad to hear from you last night about your decision to carry on. This will, I am sure, be almost universally welcomed here and abroad.
　[. . .]

---

[1] This letter was handwritten.

September 1954

Sir Winston S. Churchill to John Foster Dulles
(*Premier papers, 11/657*)

1 September 1954
Secret
No. 4395

Many thanks for your message. I also much regret that we shall not be meeting in Manila, but I am sure you will agree that in view of the urgent and anxious situation in Europe my place is here.

2. I think that we are very close on the text of the treaty and Gerald Reading, who is representing us in Manila, will explain to you our views on the points you raise. We still feel strongly that the balance of advantage lies against having observers from the three Associate States.

3. This deplorable vote in Paris[1] will open a chapter of problems for the free world. Our work together will be more important than ever and I will do everything in my power to help.

Cabinet: conclusions
(*Cabinet papers, 128/27*)

1 September 1954
Secret
3 p.m.
Cabinet Meeting No. 54 of 1954

1. The Cabinet had before them a note by the Foreign Secretary (C(54)280) covering draft telegrams of instruction to our representatives at Bonn, Washington and Paris on the situation arising from the rejection of the European Defence Community (EDC) Treaty by the French Assembly.

[1] Refusal to ratify the EDC Treaty.

The Foreign Secretary said that action was required (i) to bring the Bonn Conventions into force apart from the EDC Treaty; and (ii) to devise an alternative means of obtaining an early German defence contribution within the framework of the North Atlantic Treaty Organisation (NATO).

The decision of the French Assembly had had a stunning effect upon our partners in the Western Alliance and only M Spaak had so far communicated his views to us officially: these were generally in line with our own thinking, although we could not share his suggestion that France should be given a further opportunity for considering the EDC plan. It was, in his view, essential that we should act promptly both to prevent a further deterioration of the position and to forestall proposals from other quarters which might not seem to us wise. He had therefore circulated the four draft telegrams annexed to C(54)280: these had since been amended in some respects, including, in particular, a redrafting of paragraph 5 of the longer draft telegram to the High Commissioner at Bonn. The first step was to seek the agreement of the United States Government to our approaching the Federal German Chancellor on the lines of the draft telegrams to Bonn. He would add to the draft telegram to Washington a paragraph emphasizing the need for prompt action and asking for early American agreement to our taking the proposed initiative. If this agreement were forthcoming, and if thereafter Dr Adenauer should prove receptive to our proposed approach to him, it should be our aim to convene within, say, two weeks a meeting of the six EDC Powers, together with the United Kingdom and the United States, if possible in London.

The Cabinet should be under no illusions about the difficulties which would confront such a meeting. Thus, the German Government might well see little attraction in the Bonn Conventions now that they were not to be counter-balanced by the admission of Germany to EDC. They might also be reluctant to enter into any form of agreement on a German defence contribution if this involved Germany's acceptance of restrictions and obligations not shared equally by her future partners. The French Government, on the other hand, might not feel able to bring the Bonn Conventions into force unless they continued to embody conditions which Germany would not find acceptable in present circumstances. On the question of Germany's defence contribution, it might be possible to devise means whereby the German Army would be restricted in practice to the twelve divisions for which the EDC Treaty provided, but there was likely to be difficulty over the questions of her Air Force and her participation in atomic and thermo-nuclear preparations, from which she was to have been altogether debarred under the arrangements hitherto contemplated.

If it should prove impossible to promote agreement between France and the remaining seven Powers, the choice would lie between proceeding without France or leaving Germany free to pursue an independent policy, involving possibly some arrangement with Soviet Russia. If the need arose to decide between these two alternatives, we should be bound, in his view, to choose the former.

The Prime Minister said that the decision of the French Assembly had put the German Government into a strong tactical position *vis-à-vis* Germany's Western Allies and had, in his view, presented them with a rare opportunity to restore Germany's moral standing and expose the failure of France to rise to the needs of the hour. If Dr Adenauer were to issue, promptly, spontaneously and without waiting for demands on Germany to be formulated, a generous public declaration to the effect that the German Government would not seek to derive advantage from the predicament now facing her partners in the Western Alliance, and that she continued to recognize that her contribution to Western defence must remain subject to limits acceptable to her partners, this would be likely greatly to further her cause, besides reassuring her neighbours. He had it in mind to address a personal message to Dr Adenauer immediately, urging him to consider making a declaration on these lines.

The Foreign Secretary said that he would welcome a message in this sense from the Prime Minister to Dr Adenauer but the suggested terms of such a public declaration should, in his view, be kept as general as possible.

Support was expressed for this view on the ground that, by issuing a detailed declaration of Germany's intentions, Dr Adenauer might prompt French comment to the effect that German declarations were not enough and that her undertakings must be formally embodied in any agreement which might be evolved.

The following were the main points made in subsequent discussion:

(a) The draft telegram to HM Ambassador at Paris instructed him to approach the French Government on the bringing into force of the Bonn Conventions but to make no reference to the contemplated approach to Dr Adenauer about alternative means of obtaining a German defence contribution. Was it right that the French should be left without any indication of our intentions on this second point?

The general view of the Cabinet was that, while it would be unwise to expose ourselves to the accusation of having misled the French government in this matter, there would be some advantage in adopting a course which would make it clear to them that their conduct in regard to the EDC Treaty had compelled us to enter into discussions with the German Government in which we did not yet desire French participation. At this stage, therefore, we should inform the French Government, and likewise the other EDC countries, but only in general terms, that, besides taking up the question of the bringing into force of the Bonn Conventions, we were taking steps to consult Dr Adenauer about the possible alternatives to the EDC as a means of obtaining a German defence contribution.

(b) The point was made that the French Assembly's rejection of the EDC Treaty had inflicted a grave wound on the concept of a European community which, although it might be staunched would not be likely to heal for a long time to come.

(c) It was suggested that the French rejection of EDC had been due more to reluctance to surrender national control of the French Army than to opposition to German rearmament in principle. A German defence contribution which did not involve such a surrender seemed likely, therefore, to prove more acceptable to French opinion, particularly if the alternative should prove to be the isolation of France.

The Cabinet –

(1) Took note that the Prime Minister would address an urgent personal message to Dr Adenauer on the general lines suggested by him in the discussion.

(2) Authorised the Foreign Secretary to issue instructions to our representatives at Bonn, Washington and Paris on the lines of the drafts attached to C(54)280, subject to necessary drafting amendments and to the additional modifications suggested in discussion.

2. The Minister of Defence said that, at the request of the South African Minister of Defence, he had arranged an informal meeting at which Mr Erasmus had raised the question of the Simonstown naval base and made it clear that his main aim was that the base should now be handed over to the Union of South Africa. It had been pointed out to him that, in view of the strategic importance of Simonstown to the whole Commonwealth, the Governments of Australia and New Zealand would have to be consulted about any arrangements in regard to it. Mr Erasmus had also been reminded that the negotiations in 1951 had broken down on the question of availability of the base, and that it was essential that it should be freely available to the Royal Navy in peace, and to the Royal Navy and our Allies in war. Furthermore, the base must be efficiently organized and maintained. Mr Erasmus had indicated that South Africa would be prepared to meet these requirements, but it had been impressed upon him that any South African proposal about the future of the base would have to be referred to the Cabinet. The Minister of Defence suggested that, at a further meeting which he and the Commonwealth Secretary expected to have with Mr Erasmus, they should, while avoiding any commitment, try to obtain a clear picture of what he had in mind about the future of the base; and he would then bring the matter again before the Cabinet.

The Prime Minister said that he was reluctant to contemplate any transaction which would be presented as yet another surrender of the rights and responsibilities of the United Kingdom. The political pressure engendered by the colour problem might lead South Africa at some time to sever her ties with the United Kingdom and the rest of the Commonwealth. Indeed, this consideration might underline the Union's desire to have the base handed over to her.

The Commonwealth Secretary said that although, under the existing agreement, the United Kingdom had a perpetual right to use the Simonstown naval base, the defences of the base were owned and manned by the South African Government. The base was of little value without their full cooperation, and in any case the repair facilities were very limited. In war we should always need in addition the facilities of Cape Town and Durban. An agreement with South Africa which safeguarded our requirements at Simonstown would be preferable to having no agreement and being unable to use Simonstown in practice because of South African hostility.

The Cabinet –

Authorised the Minister of Defence and the Commonwealth Secretary to ascertain what proposals Mr Erasmus might have in mind for the future of the Simonstown naval base, on the understanding that no commitment would be incurred in regard to the future of the base without further reference to the Cabinet.

Sir Winston S. Churchill to President Dwight D. Eisenhower
Prime Minister's Personal Telegram T.294/54
(Premier papers, 11/1074)

3 September 1954
Immediate
Top Secret, Private and Personal
No. 4447

I should like you to see the following message I sent to Dr Adenauer which I believe had a fairly good reception. I will write again soon in answer to your letter of August 20.[1] Kindest regards, Winston.

> Message begins. It seems to me that at this critical juncture a great opportunity has come to Germany to take her position among the leaders of free Europe. By a voluntary act of self-abnegation she could make it clear that in any new arrangement as a substitute for EDC she would not ask for a level of military strength beyond that proposed in the EDC plan or to be agreed with her partners in Western defence. This would invest the new Germany with a moral dignity and respect far more worth having than merely claiming the right to create as many divisions as she chose or as anybody else and plunging into an endless legalistic argument on the subject. This might well be expressed in terms in no way derogating

[1] Reproduced above (pp. 1738–9).

from the equal and honourable status of the German Federal Republic and would indeed open a new chapter by the very fact that the decision was taken on the initiative of Germany herself. I beg you to think this over as coming from one who after so many years of strife has few stronger wishes than to see the German nation take her true place in the world wide family of free nations. Ends.[1]

Sir Winston S. Churchill: note
(Churchill papers, 2/128)

4 September 1954

I do not consider that 'surprise' is an object to be aimed at in fixing a General Election. It is not conducive to the public interest that tactics of this kind should be pursued. Events may compel but a 'snap' Election for its own sake brings its own revenges with it.

Sir Winston S. Churchill to President Dwight D. Eisenhower
Prime Minister's Personal Telegram T.296/54
(Premier papers, 11/1074)

5 September 1954
Immediate
Top Secret, Private and Personal
No. 4482

I have now received the following answer to the message which I sent to Dr Adenauer.

Message Begins. Dear Sir Winston. I thank you for the personal message which you have sent me at this critical juncture. The thoughts and sentiments which you express in it have greatly moved me.

I can assure you that nothing is further from my mind than to waste time, which is becoming even more precious, in theoretical disputes, or to slip into extreme courses, now that difficulties have arisen in the way of the well-considered solution envisaged by the EDC treaty as regards the strength of the German defence contribution. The idea of a link with the allocation of forces in the EDC plan had already occurred to me as well. But above all I share your view that the solution must consist in a voluntary act of self-limitation, if it is to give Germany moral dignity and respect. I

[1] On Sep. 6, Eisenhower responded: 'I think your message to Dr Adenauer is perfect. I hope he responds favourably.'

therefore note with gratitude that you too consider that the solution should have a form which in no way prejudices the equal and honourable status of the German Federal Republic.

With great admiration for the historic task which you are accomplishing for Europe and the peace of the world. I am yours very sincerely, Adenauer. Message ends.

Cabinet: conclusions
(Cabinet papers, 128/27)

8 September 1954
Secret
3 p.m.
Cabinet Meeting No. 59 of 1954

1. The Foreign Secretary recalled that, in the situation arising from the rejection of the European Defence Community (EDC) Treaty by the French Assembly, we had made it our first concern to ascertain Dr Adenauer's views on possible alternative means of associating Germany more fully with the free world and obtaining an early German defence contribution. Telegram No. 705 from our High Commissioner in Bonn showed that Dr Adenauer did not share our desire for an early conference of the eight or nine Powers most closely concerned but favoured discussions with us on a bilateral basis leading to a plenary meeting of the Council of the North Atlantic Treaty Organisation (NATO). The Foreign Secretary said that in these circumstances he proposed himself to visit the Benelux capitals, Bonn and Paris, in that order, for exploratory discussions with the Governments of the countries concerned. On the military side he still thought there was no alternative to bringing Germany into NATO, subject to as many safeguards as Dr Adenauer could be brought to accept. It seemed to him possible, however, that general agreement to Germany's admission would not be obtainable without an undertaking on our part to retain on the continent of Europe, so long as the present emergency situation might persist, say three divisions, compared with the four and a half divisions we now had there in practice, and the single division which we had undertaken to commit to EDC. He recognised that such an undertaking would have to be made subject to a suitable proviso to safeguard our balance of payments. On the political side he regarded suggestions for a modified form of EDC as quite impracticable, but some new proposal whereby the concept of a European community could be kept alive within the NATO framework would in his view be welcomed alike by our Allies and by responsible opinion in this country. The plan which he now had in mind for this purpose was that Germany and Italy should be invited to adhere to the Brussels Treaty, which

would thereby be no longer directed against Germany but transformed into an instrument covering all Western Europe and providing for mutual assistance in the event of aggression either by one of the parties or by an outside Power. A suggestion on these lines might, apart from its other advantages, dispose Dr Adenauer more favourably towards the programme of future action which we considered more appropriate than that which he at present favoured.

In discussion there was support for the line of approach proposed by the Foreign Secretary. It was pointed out that, so long as the EDC plan – to which we had seen objections of principle from the outset – had held the field, we had felt under no obligation to propose constructive alternatives. But the position had now changed. Extension of the scope of the Brussels Treaty, which had the advantage of a duration of fifty years, would provide a focus for those in all countries, including Western Germany, who still clung to the conception of a united Europe. Germany and Italy would thereby be enabled to take their part in the cultural and kindred activities which were already being pursued under the Treaty's aegis. Some doubts were, however, expressed about the wisdom and the necessity, at least at this stage, of our undertaking any rigid commitment as to the size of the forces which we should retain on the Continent, and it was suggested that this matter would be better left for discussion in due course through the normal machinery of NATO.

The Prime Minister said that, while he did not question the wisdom of the proposal to extend the Brussels Treaty to cover Germany and Italy, he would welcome an opportunity to refresh his mind about the exact nature of the obligations which the Treaty imposed. He felt more serious doubts about the prudence of our entering into firm commitments as to the forces we should retain on the Continent in the absence of any corresponding commitment on the part of the United States Government. In any case ought not France to be left for a time in anxiety about her Allies' intentions, rather than rewarded for her recent actions by further promises of British support?

The Foreign Secretary said that in his forthcoming discussions he would be careful to avoid encouraging the belief that we should be prepared to enter into more definite commitments as to the forces which we would retain on the Continent. But, on his return, he might well find himself compelled to seek Cabinet approval to our entering into such commitments as the price of a settlement of the problems confronting us.

The Cabinet –

Authorised the Foreign Secretary, in his forthcoming discussions in the Benelux capitals, Bonn and Paris, to explore the possibilities of promoting a solution of the problems arising from the French rejection of the EDC Treaty through admitting Germany to the North Atlantic Treaty Organisation, subject to all possible safeguards, and enabling her to adhere concurrently to the Brussels Treaty.

[. . .]

September 1954

Sir Winston S. Churchill to President Dwight D. Eisenhower
Prime Minister's Personal Telegram T.297/54
(Premier papers, 11/1074)

9 September 1954
Immediate
Top Secret, Private and Personal
No. 4587

My dear Friend,

Thank you so much for your message of September 6. Adenauer's response was good and I think his attitude is easier.

2. We are all agreed that an 8-Power meeting of Allies, plus Canada, would be the right move now and prefer it to the 16 NATO Powers proposal, which might well follow it, and we should like very much to have it in London which is a big and well known place and has stood by the Thames for quite a long time without having a conference of this kind. Anthony, who knows all the Continental personalities involved from long experience, feels that he could smooth out difficulties, queries and objections, of which there are no lack, better by personal contacts than by the interminable interchange of coded messages and arguments. He is, therefore, at the desire of the Cabinet, proposing to start on a flying circuit of Brussels, Bonn, Rome and Paris to see what he can do. We shall keep you and Foster fully and punctually informed.

3. If he succeeds, it seems to me not improbable that we might reach a considerable measure of agreement and that the NATO meeting would follow as the second stage.

4. Of course it is always my hope that the prospects of an improvement in our affairs, arising out of a London conference might be so good, or the results in sight become so good, that you might be able to come yourself, at least for the finale, and make that State visit I mentioned to you at the White House. But that of course is not a matter which requires decision now.

5. I have read what has been disclosed to our people in Washington about the Pentagon's views on reappraisal. This, I am sure, would mean disaster if it actually came to pass. I hope, none the less, that if such ideas are shaping themselves in Washington, you will let the French know about them at an early stage. It might help them to do their duty.

Anthony Eden: diary
(Robert Rhodes James, 'Anthony Eden, A Biography', pages 387–8)

10 September 1954

W came to luncheon with Clemmie. He was in very poor shape & claimed of dizziness caused by reading in the car. They were very late & hadn't seen Makins, his only appointment of the day.

Had further talk with Patrick[1] & Harold.[2] They were gloomy at the prospect of the Party if W remained & a little inclined to complain, perhaps rightly, that I had made things too easy for him. I am quite clear that Ministry of Defence gambit is impossible & told them so. They were keen to press for departure on birthday. I don't think we can succeed, but no harm in trying.

Anthony Eden: diary
(Robert Rhodes James, 'Anthony Eden, A Biography', page 388)

11 September 1954

Woke up at seven, finished my box & wrote to W & Harold. W will not like the letter but I had to tell him that no scheme of reconstruction so far devised was any good if the Govt was to function & we were to have best chance of winning next election. Both Harold & Patrick were insistent that I should write this because W is now merely fiddling with names of juniors & all the old men in Cabinet are still to stay. But it isn't easy for an 80 year old to sack a 70 year old.

C[3] came to see me off. Also all six Ambassadors; quite a party.

Sir Winston S. Churchill to President Dwight D. Eisenhower
Prime Minister's Personal Telegram T.300/54
(Premier papers, 11/1074)

12 September 1954
Immediate
Deyou
Top Secret, Private and Personal
No. 4621

My dear Friend,
  I promised to keep you fully informed of Anthony's tour.
  2. He had a successful talk yesterday with Benelux Ministers, whom he found robust and realistic.

[1] Buchan-Hepburn.
[2] Macmillan.
[3] Clarissa.

3. They are disturbed at growth of nationalism in Germany and fear that the dangers which confront us all are not apprehended by Mendes-France or the French Chamber.

4. They are agreed on German entry into NATO with such safeguards as we can extract in present German atmosphere. They are also attracted by suggestion which Anthony laid before them of modifying the Brussels Treaty so as to admit Germany and Italy. We want of course to keep this idea secret until we can put it to the French.

5. As to procedure they considered that whilst NATO Council must be brought in, a preliminary Nine Power meeting should be held. They hope this would take place in London as soon as possible after Anthony's tour, and be followed by a NATO meeting.

6. Finally they consider that we must proceed rapidly on lines on which we are all agreed and do what we can to convince the French. But we must be ready to go ahead without France in the last resort (policy of the empty chair) making clear our intention in Paris in good time.

Sir Winston S. Churchill to President Dwight D. Eisenhower
Prime Minister's Personal Telegram T.306/54
(Premier papers, 11/1074)

14 September 1954
Immediate
Deyou
Top Secret, Private and Personal
No. 4643

My dear Friend,

You will have seen the message which Anthony sent Foster last night on his talks in Bonn.

Anthony found Adenauer in fairly good health and as quick as ever though aged since their last meeting. Adenauer much liked the Brussels Treaty idea which he described as a most happy thought and psychologically valuable as providing a focus for European policies and keeping alive German youth's faith in the European idea. It was also important, he thought, to devise means of saving Mendes-France's face.

We must now see how the talks in Paris go but on present form it looks as if there will be plenty to discuss with Foster, if, as we hope, he can pay us a visit.

Sir Winston S. Churchill to President Dwight D. Eisenhower
Prime Minister's Personal Telegram T.312/54
(Premier papers, 11/1074)

15 September 1954
Immediate
Deyou
Top Secret, Private and Personal
No. 4673

My dear Friend,
Anthony's talks in Rome went well. The Italians accepted unreservedly as a basis for discussion the ideas which had emerged from the talks in Brussels and Bonn. Piccioni[1] said that the consolidation of Europe with the association of the United Kingdom would weaken neutralist tendencies in Italy.

2. Anthony emphasised the part which the Italians could play in influencing the French. Piccioni said he could not guess the French reaction and expressed concern at what would happen in the event of French rejection. He enquired whether we would then be prepared to go ahead. Anthony replied that the mood of the Benelux Governments was to go ahead and leave the French to come along later, and this seemed also to be Adenauer's thought. He explained that the British Government had not yet taken a decision, but he certainly intended to make it clear in Paris that the French could not be allowed to frustrate our plans indefinitely. He added that it was unfortunate that the issues had never been explained to the French people by their public men and that the French had probably convinced themselves that American talk of reappraisal was bluff.

3. Piccioni agreed that the French could not be allowed to impede progress indefinitely and said he would try to influence the French in the right direction.

President Dwight D. Eisenhower to Sir Winston S. Churchill
(Premier papers, 11/1074)

15 September 1954

Dear Winston,
Your report on the progress of Anthony's tour is very helpful to me. It is encouraging to know that the Benelux people are thinking along constructive and realistic lines. We will look forward to the more detailed account of your proposals which Anthony has promised to send Foster at the end of his tour.

---

[1] Attilio Piccioni, 1892–1976. Born Poggio Bustone in Italy. Educated at Universities of Rome and Turin. Served in Italian Air Force, WWI. Secretary, Italian Christian Democracy Party, 1946–9. Minister of Justice, 1950–1. Foreign Minister, 1954–5, 1962–3. Head, Italian Delegation to UN, 1958. Senator (Christian Democrat) for Lombardy, 1958–1963.

In the meantime, we are trying to pull together some useful ideas to contribute with respect to both the plan for German membership in NATO and a course of action in the unhappy event that the French refuse to go along. I feel that you and we should agree on this latter point as soon as possible since I am not certain that anything less drastic will bring the French to their senses.

Sir Winston S. Churchill to Lord Leathers
(Premier papers, 11/615)

16 September 1954
Personal and Secret

When you left the Government you told me that I could always call upon your services in time of need. I am now taking you at your word.

2. We have been considering how we can cut down our vast defence expenditure, and how in the new world of hydrogen bombs we should reallocate what we can afford between the Services. One great source of economy would be the speeding up of our withdrawal from the Canal Zone. When the Anglo-Egyptian Agreement is signed we shall have twenty months in which to do this. The military Chiefs claim that the period cannot be reduced without substantial additional cost on account of shipping diversion. There are 400,000 tons of stores to be moved and 8,000 vehicles. In addition the Civil Contractors, who are to run the Base when the soldiers have left, must have time to take over.

3. It is my hope that we can shorten the period of withdrawal to one year. The Egyptians are much more friendly now and I feel sure we can count on their help in modifying this particular part of the Agreement.

4. Would you be willing to examine the problem from an independent point of view and tell me what you think could be done? There is nobody else who combines an expert knowledge of the machinery of Government as well as with my own unqualified personal confidence.

5. I do hope you can undertake this burden. Needless to say all official assistance would be put at your disposal. You could either fly back from Cape Town on the date you were proposing to leave by sea or, if you wished, I would arrange to have as much of the material as possible flown out by Confidential Bag to Cape Town so that you could study it on the return voyage.

SEPTEMBER 1954

President Dwight D. Eisenhower to Sir Winston S. Churchill
(*Premier papers, 11/1074*)

16 September 1954

Dear Winston,
Thank you very much for keeping me posted with reference to the European developments and the talks which Anthony is having. As you probably know by now, Foster is leaving today to have a quick trip where he will talk with Anthony and also with Adenauer. This will help us to make our own plans. Foster will carry to you our latest thinking on these matters.

Sir Winston S. Churchill to President Dwight D. Eisenhower
Prime Minister's Personal Telegram T.314/54
(*Premier papers, 11/1074*)

18 September 1954
Immediate
Dedip
Top Secret, Private and Personal
No. 4719

My dear Friend,
Thank you very much for your message of September 15.[1] I am glad I was a good reporter. I made my living as a journalist. I believe you have them in your country too.

2. Foster lunched with me and Anthony today and we had an agreeable and helpful talk. As you know, EDC was very different from the Grand Alliance theme I opened at Strasbourg in August, 1950.[2] I disliked on military grounds the Pleven European Army plan which began with mixing races in companies if not platoons. At that time when I saw you in Paris I was talking of it as 'sludgy amalgam'. However, when I came to power again I swallowed my prejudices because I was led to believe that it was the only way in which the French could be persuaded to accept the limited German army which was my desire. I do not blame the French for rejecting EDC but only for inventing it. Their harshness to Adenauer in wasting three years of his life and much of his power is a tragedy. Also I accepted the American wish to show all possible patience and not compromise the chances of EDC by running NATO as a confusing rival.

3. All this time I kept one aim above all others in view, namely a German contribution to the defence of an already uniting Europe. This, I felt, was your

---

[1] Reproduced above (pp. 1781–2).
[2] Speech of 11 Aug. 1950, reproduced in *The Churchill Documents*, vol. 22, *Leader of the Opposition, August 1945 to October 1951*, pp. 1827–32.

aim too, and I am sure we both liked the plan better when the intermingling was excluded from all units lower than a division. But it was to get a German army looking Eastward in the line with us that commanded my thought, and also I felt yours, with all its military authority. Although the French have rejected EDC, I do hope and pray that you and I still keep the German contribution as our No. 1 target and also to get them on our side instead of on the other.

4. When Anthony recently proposed taking the Brussels Treaty of 1948 turned upside down, as a model for preserving the cause of European unity, coupled with a variant of NATO to include Germany, I thought it was a first rate plan. I hope earnestly that it will commend itself to you. It may lead on as time passes to united Europe and also gain for us both what we have tried for so hard, namely, the German comradeship. Now Foster tells me that there is a widespread feeling in America that it has not got any, or at least enough, 'supra-national' characteristics. I hope this will not prevent you giving it all the help you can. European federation may grow but it cannot be built. It must be a volunteer not a conscript.

5. After all if the realities can be achieved and if Gruenther can form a front including French and German armies by whose side we and you stand, we need not worry too much about the particular theories which are favoured or rebuffed. Above all we should not lose more time when what we have worked so long and hard to win may now be within our grasp.

6. I have been distressed to hear talk (not from Foster) about the withdrawal of American forces from Europe and even that a German contingent might fill the gap. If the United States loses or seems to lose its interest in Europe there might well be a landslide into Communism or into a kow-towing to Soviet influence and infiltration which would reduce the continent to satellite status. I really do not see how we British could stay there by ourselves.

7. Forgive me burdening you with all this but I feel it a great comfort when I am sure our thoughts are marching along the same roads. You may imagine how pleased I was by your applying the word 'perfect' to my message to Adenauer.

Sir Winston S. Churchill to President Dwight D. Eisenhower
Prime Minister's Personal Telegram T.315/54
(Premier papers, 11/1074)

18 September 1954
Immediate
Top Secret, Personal and Private
No. 4736

My dear Friend,

I did not complicate my long telegram to you about Europe by referring to the isolated question of Cyprus about which you wrote to me on August 20.[1]

A factual note is being prepared which I will send by airmail, but I understand our Embassy in Washington has already supplied the State Department with information. A simple test is to compare the conditions prevailing in Cyprus with those in the Greek Islands and particularly in Rhodes since the Greeks took them over from the Italians. Cyprus has never known more rapid progress while in the others there is a grievous decline.

I feel it is my duty to tell you that the failure of the United States to support us at UNO would cause deep distress over here and add greatly to my difficulties in guiding public opinion into the right channels in much larger matters.

It cannot be disputed that our claim against the inscription of this question affecting our own external affairs is justified by the statutes and spirit of UNO. If any such item were discussed by the Assembly, we would of course walk out. Injury would be done to that institution of which the United States and Britain and her Commonwealth are the main pillars. Cyprus would acquire utterly disproportionate publicity and be magnified by the enemies of the English Speaking world on both sides of the ocean into marked difference between us. I do trust therefore that we shall not be confronted with American abstention.

Sir Winston S. Churchill to Sir Alexander Cadogan[2]
(Premier papers, 11/594)

24 September 1954

My dear Cadogan,

My attention has been drawn to the fact that on the evening of Saturday, September 18, the BBC in their 9 o'clock news bulletin quoted two Labour Party speakers in respect of the proceedings of the Council of Europe

---

[1] Reproduced above (pp. 1738–9).
[2] Alexander George Montagu Cadogan, 1884–1968. Educated at Eton and Balliol College, Oxford. British Minister to China, 1933–5; Ambassador, 1935–6. Knighted, 1934. Deputy Under-Secretary of State for Foreign Affairs, 1936–7; Permanent Under-Secretary, 1938–46. Permanent British Representative at the UN, 1946–50. Government Director, Suez Canal Co., 1951–7. Chairman, BBC, 1952–7.

Assembly at Strasbourg as compared with one Ministerial speaker, and that the total coverage for the Labour Party was twice the amount of time given to Mr Nutting, Under Secretary of State for Foreign Affairs.

I am also informed that in the 11 o'clock and mid-night news bulletins there was no mention of Mr Nutting's remarks, whereas prominence was given to the views of the Labour Party speakers.

In view of the national importance of this item I think it is most unfortunate that the BBC on this occasion did not maintain their normal standard of impartiality, and I hope that you will be able to give me your assurance that this inequitable reporting will not occur again.

Anthony Eden to Sir Winston S. Churchill
(Churchill papers, 6/4)[1]

26 September 1954

My dear Winston,

I think there was force in what you said to me about the difficulty of my leaving the FO now for some post entirely concerned with the home front. But I am glad that we do not have to decide this at the moment. I shall be ready to do so when this week of conference is over.

But I am sure that we must concentrate on whatever gives us the best chance of winning the next general election. From that angle I am concerned – as I have said – at the prospect of going on at the FO until within a few weeks of the general election.

If I am to lead the party there, this doesn't seem to me to give time or opportunity for any leadership or to develop any theme.

As for the reconstruction proposed it has occurred to me, & probably to you, that in order to make it thorough you might think fit to ask for the resignation of all your colleagues.

In any event I would like to submit some suggestions which I hope might be considered and which are designed to bring in younger men & new blood. I feel that our party's fortunes will be deeply influenced by these decisions.

---

[1] This letter was handwritten.

September 1954

Sir Winston S. Churchill to Anthony Eden
(Churchill papers, 6/4)[1]

28 September 1954

My dear Anthony,

I like yr thought of my calling for all Ministers' resignations. It looks more <u>thorough</u> and also avoids insidious exceptions which cause pain. I am looking for precedents if any there be. The Queen will not return to London before October 11.

Meanwhile we have the 9 Power Conference and the week after there is our Party Conference – with a <u>speech</u> for me!

I am glad you think you may be able to decide about the FO when your Conference is over, and perhaps after this week. That wd be a great simplification. Of course I shall welcome any advice you may give about the changes and I fully agree with what you say about their importance to the future fortunes of the Party.

I wish you all success in your gt task at Lancaster House. I have a feeling that the chances are improving.

There is quite a lot going on!

Sir Alexander Cadogan to Sir Winston S. Churchill
(Premier papers, 11/594)

29 September 1954

My dear Prime Minister,

Thank you for your letter of September 24th.[2]

The reports in our News bulletins of the proceedings of the Council of Europe Assembly, as of other events, are compiled on the best assessment we can make of each item according to its news value; not on the basis that, irrespective of news value, an equal number of lines should be allotted to the speakers of the two main British parties.

I think you must have been misinformed about the 9 p.m. news bulletin of September 18th. The speeches qualifying for mention on news value were reported there in chronological order, as follows:

M Spaak – 14 lines (including 2½ lines reporting a question interjected by Mr Robens, one of the British Labour delegates).

Mr Callaghan – 9 lines

Mr Nutting – 8 lines

So far from the total coverage for the Labour Party being twice the amount of time given to Mr Nutting, the reports of Mr Callaghan's and

---

[1] This letter was handwritten.
[2] Reproduced above (pp. 1785–6).

Mr Nutting's speeches were approximately of equal length. The 2½ lines given to Mr Robens' question to M Spaak had to be included in the report of M Spaak's speech, because the question and M Spaak's answer to it were concerned with the possibility of whether the United States would withdraw her troops from Europe if Western Germany were not rearmed – a point that had supplied the keynote of M Spaak's speech.

As to the 11 p.m. and midnight news summaries, Mr Nutting's speech was regrettably omitted from the very short report – 11 lines – of the debate that was given in these two summaries. This was the result of inadvertence and was a misjudgment of news value. It was an editorial mistake and, as such, we are dealing with it.[1]

---

[1] Churchill forwarded this letter to Eden.

October 1954

President Dwight D. Eisenhower to Sir Winston S. Churchill
(Premier papers, 11/1074)

1 October 1954
Top Secret

Dear Winston,
Foster has kept me informed on the progress of the talks now going forward in the Nine Power Conference. Both officially and personally I am most deeply appreciative of the contribution that Britain has offered to make to advance European unity. Of course I understand fully your reluctance to move without parallel commitment by us. However, our constitutional processes do not permit this, but I am certain that so long as Europe is moving toward unified action, you can always be sure of our effective cooperation on the continent. In this statement I know I speak for the tremendous majority of the citizens of our country.
In this often confused world, it is encouraging to witness the enlightened and courageous statesmanship exhibited by you and Anthony. In this instance, as in so many others, I have the greatest admiration for your judgments and actions.
Please give my warm regards to Anthony, and, as always, the best to yourself.

Sir Winston S. Churchill to Lord Salisbury
(Churchill papers, 6/4)

1 October 1954
Private and Personal

My dear Bobbety,
Thank you very much for your letter. I thought well of Anthony's suggestion of a general resignation of Ministers which would at the same time give the impression of the thoroughness of the reconstruction and avoid invidious particularising of individuals. It had in fact been moving in my own mind. On

the other hand one must see first how many are to go. I have told Anthony I should welcome any suggestions he should volunteer to make. At present I only see two cases of Cabinet rank which would be painful and I cannot get the Chief Whip to suggest more than a very few Junior Ministers who can be said to have not done their work well. He also points out that with a majority of seventeen even a few embittered men may endanger the life of the Government. When I have finally decided who are to be dropped I shall be better able to judge whether it is worthwhile calling for eighty-three resignations or whether the ordinary process would be wiser.

There is a lot of talk about the need for a younger, stronger personnel in the Cabinet and Government and also for bringing in new men of real distinction and exceptional quality and experience into its ranks. I ask repeatedly for names. On the other hand for one who is pleased to come in an equal number would be angered at being turned out and four or five times as many disappointed at not having been chosen. Always there confronts us the majority of seventeen and also the fact that the personal efficiency and character of the Government is high.

I have not mentioned any names in this letter in writing, but I shall be very glad to renew the conversation we had at luncheon the other day.

Konrad Adenauer to Sir Winston S. Churchill
(Premier papers, 11/676)

4 October 1954   Bonn

Dear Sir Winston,

On my return to Bonn, permit me to express to you my great satisfaction at the outcome of the Nine-Power Conference, which was assembled at your initiative. I consider that the most important result of this Conference is that it has removed the great uncertainty which had arisen within the community of the free peoples since the decision of the French National Assembly on the 30th August, and the abandonment of the Treaty of the European Defence Community. At the Nine-Power Conference in London, the unity of the Western World, so gravely menaced, has been restored.

For the Federal Republic this Conference means both a decisive step forward on the road to the re-establishment of her sovereignty and her admission to both the great treaty systems of the Western World, the Brussels Pact and the North Atlantic Organisation. With it, as soon as the treaties are ratified, the Federal Republic of Germany will take her place in the free world as a partner with equal duties and equal rights.

In this hour, when we may hope that European unity is now at last becoming a reality, permit me, dear Sir Winston, to thank you sincerely for the excellent and friendly counsel which you have given me in these weeks, and for the historic decision of the British Government to retain their troops on the continent. It was this that created the decisive conditions for this happy turn of events.

Cabinet: conclusions
(Cabinet papers, 128/27)

5 October 1954
Secret
11 a.m.
Cabinet Meeting No. 63 of 1954

The Prime Minister said that the Cabinet would wish to record their satisfaction that the Nine-Power Conference had reached so successful a conclusion and to convey to the Foreign Secretary their appreciation on the distinguished part which he had played in bringing this about. The influence of the United Kingdom in international affairs had been greatly strengthened by the settlement which had been reached, and would be still further enhanced by the agreement on Trieste which was due to be signed in London that day.

The Joint Parliamentary Under-Secretary of State for Foreign Affairs[1] said that, during his recent visits to countries in the Middle and Far East, he had been impressed by the widespread evidence of the prestige enjoyed by the United Kingdom. The criticism of the West which was voiced in Eastern countries was more often directed at the United States than at this country.

In discussion it was suggested that the British press were not showing enough recognition of the success with which the United Kingdom Government had assumed the lead in international affairs. The recent visit of leading members of the Opposition to Russia and the Far East had been reported with more attention than the solid progress of the Government in resolving intractable international problems. The Chancellor of the Exchequer said that, in the absence of the Commonwealth Secretary, he had it in mind to discuss with some of his colleagues what measures could be taken to further the presentation of the Government's achievements. A meeting between Ministers and the Lobby Correspondents might be arranged for this purpose.

The Joint Parliamentary Under-Secretary of State for Foreign Affairs said that substantial progress had been made in the negotiations which Mr Nutting was conducting with the Egyptian Government in Cairo. The Egyptians were, however, still reluctant to accept the inclusion in the Agreement of a clause prescribing that the Agreement, after it was signed, would be subject to ratification by Her Majesty's Government. They were concerned lest a provision to this effect would result in delaying final confirmation of the Agreement

[1] Dodds-Parker.

and so afford an opportunity for discontented elements in Egypt to undermine the position of the Egyptian Government by provoking incidents, which in turn might induce the United Kingdom Parliament to oppose ratification. Mr Nutting had accordingly sought authority to give the Egyptian Government an assurance that arrangements would be made to afford Parliament an opportunity of debating the new Agreement before the end of October. The Cabinet would recall that Lord Reading had given an undertaking in the House of Lords on 15th December, 1953, that provision would be made in the Anglo-Egyptian Agreement for its ratification and that, before ratification took place, full opportunity would be afforded for debate in Parliament.

The Lord Privy Seal suggested that the Government's obligation to provide facilities for a debate might be held to have been honoured already by the debate which had taken place on the Heads of Agreement. He doubted whether the Government need take the initiative in arranging a further debate in Parliament before ratification, though a debate would have to be arranged if there were a demand for it in Parliament.

The Prime Minister said that it was important that the new treaty with Egypt should, in accordance with normal custom, include a ratification clause. If a debate should prove to be necessary – and he expected that it would be – arrangements could no doubt be made without undue difficulty. If necessary, an indication could be given to the Egyptian Government that Her Majesty's Government expected that ratification would have been effected by the end of November and possibly by the end of October.

The Cabinet –

Invited the Joint Parliamentary Under-Secretary of State for Foreign Affairs to arrange guidance to be sent to Mr Nutting in Cairo accordingly.

[. . .]

Sir Winston S. Churchill: speech
('*Winston S. Churchill, His Complete Speeches*', volume 8, pages 8593–601)

9 October 1954   Conservative Party Conference
Blackpool

'PEACE THROUGH STRENGTH'

When we were returned to power three years ago I asked that we might be judged not by promises but by results. I ask the same today and I seek it with an assurance based not merely on hopes but on facts.

The facts cannot be challenged. They are obvious and convincing. Both the position and prospects of Britain are decidedly better than they were when we became responsible in October, 1951. In the vast, tumultuous world which towers up around us under the shadow of the nuclear age no single country can control its destiny alone. We have done our best. We have tried to govern with general consent and goodwill but we have not shrunk – and we shall not shrink – from doing unpopular things when convinced that they are in the public interest. Today I can assert that both our material well-being at home and our influence and credit of all kinds abroad, show a marked advance.

Indeed I must say that we have done better than I dared to hope. If I may quote my broadcast during the election – I said: 'Too much harm has been done in these last six years for it to be repaired in a few months. Too much money has been spent for us to be able to avoid another financial crisis. It will take all our national strength to stop the downhill slide and get us back on the level, and after that we shall have to work up.'[1] And a few weeks later when I had formed the Government I said: 'We shall require at least three years before anyone can judge fairly whether we have made things better or worse.' Well, Ladies and Gentlemen, the three years have ended, or nearly ended. We survey the scene without complacency but, I admit, with growing confidence. We feel entitled to ask for your approval and encouragement both in what has been done and in the important work this Parliament still has to do.

After all the excellent and outspoken speeches which have marked our Conference this year, I shall not attempt to describe in detail the series of obvious improvements in the British position and prospects. It would take too long. I can only pick out the salient points.

Thanks to a wise and resolute financial policy with a lot of saying 'No,' we have restored national sovereignty – solvency. (I think it is quite a natural mistake to make – the two go together very well.) We are rebuilding the precious reserves which three years ago were draining away at an alarming rate. We are paying our way again and re-paying the dollar loans our predecessors contracted. There is a new spirit of confident endeavour in the land. Indeed, I think you were right yesterday to acclaim the man to whom this solid and vital result is mainly due – Rab Butler, the Chancellor of the Exchequer. He has, of course, been greatly helped by the close understanding and association in which he has worked with Mr Thorneycroft, President of the Board of Trade, whose forceful and sprightly contribution to this Conference was so successful on Thursday.

In our administration we reversed or arrested the policy of the Socialist Government in many ways in order to give a freer rein to enterprise and effort. We let the traders trade and we let the builders build. Our aim has been freedom, not control. The ration book has gone down the drain with the identity card. Two-thirds of the wartime regulations we inherited have been scrapped – all have been carefully preserved for the Socialist system. Form-filling has ceased to be our national pastime. More people are at work than ever before.

[1] See broadcast of 8 Oct. 1951, reproduced in *The Churchill Documents*, vol. 22, *Leader of the Opposition, August 1945 to October 1951*, pp. 2177–82.

This year, as has been pithily said, I think by the Home Secretary – no – pithily said by him and by others, our countrymen and women ate more, earned more, spent more, saved more than has ever happened before in all our records. No one has put this better than Mr House-builder Macmillan – Mr Harold Macmillan – in his recent broadcast, and no band of friends and fellow-workers are more capable than this great audience of impressing the truth upon the electors by personal exertion, and may I add they will be greatly aided through the powerful political organization which under Lord Woolton is now at the service of Tory democracy. And all this has been done, let me remind you, with a House of Commons majority of sixteen, now eighteen. This achievement – incredible as it would have seemed before it happened – is due to the devotion of our Members of Parliament and also to the excellent arrangements of our Whips Office under the tireless vigilance of Patrick Buchan-Hepburn.

This afternoon, my Lords, Ladies and Gentlemen, it is my task to take a general view. The business of Government has become vastly more complicated since I first meddled in public affairs. In a free country everyone has the right to find fault with everything he thinks is wrong and to express himself to all who care to listen. Powerful organs of comment and criticism act upon us with ceaseless activity and spread opinion daily, and almost hourly. There are few mistakes or shortcomings which do not get the attention they deserve and this healthy process, while it increases the severity of the Ministerial ordeal, also brings about the constant correction on which the progress of human society depends.

I feel we may be sure that a respectful verdict will be granted to our Government by history. And even if we are not mentioned we may console ourselves with the reflection that history has been described by Gibbon as 'little more than a register of the crimes, follies, and misfortunes of mankind'. So perhaps our modest contribution will be overlooked. I must say that I had throughout a feeling that Britain, and also the quivering world, stand in need of a breathing space. This is not a time for violent ideological conventions. The productive forces which are now working have only to be allowed to unfold and grow in a calm and healthy atmosphere to create material well-being for all to a degree never before within practical reach. The process is cumulative. A cog-wheel is mounted this afternoon. It goes on turning for years, helping to make things for us, and there are lots of cog-wheels. Let the productive forces run in fullness and in freedom. Don't let it all be spoiled by class hatred or doctrinal pedantry.

We live in a land where party government has been a habit for centuries. As the Liberal Party has suffered misfortune from the general acceptance of so many of its ideals, the two-party system of Conservatives and Socialists looks likely to last some time. Naturally there is rivalry and partisanship. There are immense doctrinal differences between them. The opposition holds that free enterprise is unfair. Our view is that the Socialist economy is a gigantic fallacy. Passions are excited. Powerful organizations search for points of difference, work up controversies, and attack one another. But as each Party is supported by more than 12,000,000 voters they must have a great deal in common. British Conservatives and Socialists mingle together in daily life without, I think, the same degree of bitterness which so often afflicts the internal politics of other countries.

When necessary for the safety of our island we work together. This happens not only in wartime but as you saw a few years ago we supported all the necessary measures taken by the Socialist Government in foreign policy and defence, even though we thought their domestic policy disastrous. And here I will say that Mr Attlee and Mr Morrison and the majority of their followers – I believe it was a majority – strengthened by the leaders of the trade unions, have shown firmness and consistency on several important occasions in dealing with our foreign policy for the broad continuity of which they have unquestionable responsibility.

I am sorry that Mr Attlee did not have more success in his trip abroad, but even our football team came a cropper in Moscow and they never meant to go to China. They did not, of course, represent the full strength of Britain and that may apply to Mr Attlee's team also. Certainly the politicians said several things which were not helpful to our affairs, but we are all very glad they came back safely and we hope they will do better next time.

Foreign nations, friendly and not so friendly, should realize that there is a core of strength and union in our island people and throughout the British Commonwealth which can and must be counted upon in all the difficulties and anxieties of the present time.

It is in this setting that I will now proclaim the guiding aims and principles of the Conservative Party, which perhaps after fourteen years' service – of which you have so kindly reminded me – as your leader, I am supposed to be acquainted with.

We stand for the maintenance of freedom, national and individual, in accordance with the well-tried laws and customs of our island. We hold, as the Home Secretary said yesterday, that the people should own the state and not the state the people. As a foundation for this we seek to develop a property-owning democracy. We believe that more and more people should be owners as well as earners. We like to see families living in their own homes and, as Mr Macmillan told you yesterday, we are making it possible for ever larger numbers to do so.

We welcome the increasing tendency of large industrial firms to introduce profit-sharing and co-partnership schemes, thus enabling the workers to become owners of a share in their work and giving them an interest in its fortune.

Our desire is to stimulate thrift. We rejoice that the personal savings last year were nearly £900 million compared with £100 million in 1950. We believe that a continuing rise in the standard of living is in harmony with the way of life and is what the British people want, and we believe that that is the most practical answer to the mean-minded equalitarianism that grudges greater earnings to anyone but themselves.

We are resolved firmly to maintain those basic standards which are dictated by the humanities and below which no one must fall. We seek the means to raise them progressively as the years go by. This can only be done by exceptional diligence, exertion, enterprise, invention, and skill. The genius of our race in these latter qualities is today recognized all over the world. Incentive and opportunity must be our watchwords. There is an expression widely used in industry which aptly illustrates my thought. 'Differentials', the term I have in mind, provide recognition of extra skill, responsibility, or effort and are therefore one of the keys to progress. Our industrial eminence as a nation owes much to the famous craftsmanship of our workers. Rewards for extra skill and effort have had in the past, and still have, an important part to play in stimulating the increasing volume and quality of our output. It is on this increase that the continued process of raising our general standard and of the advance of the main body of our society alike depend.

I now come to something which we cannot feel happy about – on the contrary: the grievous injustice and hardship which is inflicted on the old-age pensioners and others in similar positions by the shrinkage in what money can buy during the reign of the Socialist Party from 1945 to 1951. We have only so far partially remedied this evil by the half-crown added by the Chancellor to pensions in 1952. We are going to complete our task as soon as we receive the report of the expert committee which has for some time been at work upon the problems of old age among what has become a longer living population. Here I may say a word about this longer living. It is not the people over seventy who are responsible. Some of them are rather hardy but I can assure you that they die off on the average at the former rate. It is the infants, the children, the people under fifty years whose lives have been prolonged by the discoveries of medical science and the improvement of hygiene. Excuse this diversion.

The old-age pensioners will be a principal feature of the next Session of Parliament. It seems to me extraordinary that the Socialist Party during the six years when they spent so much money and when they represented themselves as bringing about a collectivist Utopia – the dawn of a new world – should until a few months before the last General Election have looked on helplessly at a diminution of upwards of five shillings in the true value of the pensions of the old-age and other pensioners. Reckless inflation of the currency inflicted this loss of five shillings a week upon the very class one might have thought they – the then Ministers – would have found themselves bound above all to protect. But now they pose as their champions. Even this morning their party organ says 'Old-age pensioners are the most helpless section of the community.' But when they had the power they were guilty for six long years of careless and unfair neglect. They were so full of airy – perhaps windy is a better word – windy schemes for assailing wealth and its creative enterprise that they forgot about the plight of the aged. While the Socialists nearly reduced Britain to bankruptcy in the pursuit of visionary schemes of nationalization and other forms of ground nuts,[1] while their eyes were fixed upon distant mirages, they allowed this misfortune to develop at their feet.

It was not only a misfortune but an injustice. Under the system of national insurance old-age pensions, with the beginnings of which I was associated in my Liberal days and which as Conservative Chancellor of the Exchequer I made begin at sixty-five instead of seventy, under this system everybody contributes and a serious and prolonged fall in what they can buy in return for their contributions is morally a breach of faith to a system of compulsory thrift.

It's quite true that there is also the system of national assistance. This was first started by the Conservatives in 1934 and it has grown steadily under all Governments ever since. It is still indispensable as a measure of humanity to the weak, unfortunate, and poor. But the guiding purpose of national insurance – and I am speaking about what I know – has been throughout to substitute organized state aided and employer aided thrift for grants of assistance based inevitably upon a means test. A society built on and around national insurance and private thrift is sounder, healthier, and ranks, in my opinion, far higher than one based on public assistance and the means test, which should – must – be reserved for emergencies and exceptions. That at any rate is the new policy of this vast sphere of our force of Tory Democracy and Liberalism.

Since power came to us three years ago we have already sought, as I have said, to mitigate the evil by raising the pensions. Now the Chancellor of the Exchequer has sufficiently restored our solvency and prosperity to be able to remove the injustice inflicted upon old-age pensioners and others in the same category during the Socialist regime. That we are going to do.

I may say, Mr Chairman, I should not speak with such severity about our political opponents – after all, I am sure they did not mean to be callous – it was just muddleheadedness – were it not for the fact that their party machines are deliberately trying to pose as the guardians and saviours of the old-age pensioners, and throw the blame on us for what they did themselves.

Now you have heard the Minister of Pensions (Mr Osbert Peake) speaking in detail on this subject to the Conference on last Thursday afternoon. He is a master of this subject, to which he has most earnestly devoted himself. I have great confidence in his judgment and in his knowledge. He will handle in Parliament next Session the complicated legislation required.

---

[1] Possibly a reference to the British Labour government's failed Groundnut Scheme of 1946, which was cancelled in 1951 after £49 million was spent to grow peanuts in modern-day Tanzania.

Now, Mr Chairman, I must ask this great audience to look abroad and to survey with me some aspects of the world scene, in which we have a part to play and on which all our lives depend.

An attempt is being made by a large section of the Socialist Party, spurred on by Communist propaganda, to gain votes and popularity by reviving and inflaming the feelings of bitterness and anger which were aroused in all our minds by the frightful atrocities of which Hitler was the cause and moving spirit. They would never have taken place if he had not made himself Dictator of Germany. Peoples who let themselves fall into the grip of dictatorship and totalitarian tyranny cannot escape the consequences of their carelessness and folly and heavily have the Germans suffered for them. The foundation and prime purpose of the British and American constitutions – and, I believe, indeed of the French constitution – is to safeguard their countries against falling under the rule of dictators or oligarchies. That is no longer our British problem. We have others but at least we are secure against that form of danger.

But the misdeeds or mistakes of peoples stand apart on a totally different footing to the crimes committed in their name by dictators, the tyranny of whose personal will-power is obtained by violence and enforced by fear. It would be disastrous to the human race if in learning – as they have to learn – the hard lessons of experience, they were to let their minds and actions be dominated by feelings of hatred and revenge against whole nations or races because of the deeds of a tyrant by whom these nations had been misled, bullied, and subjugated. As the great Burke said, 'I do not know the method of drawing up an indictment against a whole people.' In mighty, highly organized communities, many millions of ordinary men and women are swept along by events and authority and by the feeling that they cannot desert their country, right or wrong. I believe myself that the mass of the people in all countries are kind, decent folk who wish to live their lives in neighbourly fashion with their fellow-men and women. Naught but ruin awaits the world if communities of scores of millions are taught and allow themselves to journey along dominated by feelings of hatred against other vast collections of bewildered mortals. Let the dictators whose wickedness wrought the fearful deeds – deeds which would never have happened without their despotic personal power – carry their awful record into history. Let Hitler take his shame to Hell. Let the peoples extend the hand of friendship and forgiveness to each other and walk forward together through the mysteries of life in freedom, justice, and peace.

But it is not only to Germany and Hitler that I apply these thoughts in this present momentous crisis in world fortunes and perhaps in the fate of mankind. Stalin was for many years Dictator of Russia and the more I have studied his career the more I am shocked by the terrible mistakes he made and the utter ruthlessness he showed to men and masses with whom he acted. Stalin was our ally against Hitler when Russia was invaded, but when Hitler had been destroyed Stalin made himself our principal object of dread. After our joint victory became certain his conduct divided the world again. He seemed to be carried away by the dream of world domination. He actually reduced a third of Europe to a Soviet satellite condition under compulsory Communism. These were heartbreaking events after all we had gone through. But a year and a half ago Stalin died – that is certain – and ever since that event I have cherished the hope that there is a new outlook in Russia, a new hope of peaceful co-existence with the Russian nation and that it is our duty, patiently and daringly, to make sure whether there is such a change or not. It is certainly the interest of the Russian people, who have experienced a terrible half-century of war, revolution, and famine, it is certainly in their interest – and interest is always a thing we should consider in estimating the conduct of foreign countries – it is certainly in their interest to have an easier and more prosperous generation with more food, more fun, and more friends.

While I have life and strength I shall persevere in this, though I feel with Mr Eden that the Soviet attitude about Germany and Austria is far from encouraging at the present time. But there is one risk that we must never run. Our policy is 'peace through strength'. We must never willingly or unwittingly run the risk of 'subjugation through weakness'. Our strength can only be founded on the unity, precautions, and vigilance of the free nations of the world. This community of states and peoples, comprising, as it does, the greater part of mankind, has as its vanguard the Nine Powers which met in London last week under the Presidency of our Chairman. For the policy of this country, the Cabinet, who were consulted at every stage, bear full responsibility. I think Lord Beaverbrook has been rather unfair in doing me out of my share of the blame. But there is no doubt that the initiative which led to the London Conference sprang from our Foreign Secretary who journeyed round Europe to make it possible. Without his energy and boldness the London Conference would not have taken place and without his knowledge, experience, tact, and skill, it could never have reached its favourable conclusion. I profoundly believe that this Agreement may well become a monument and a milestone in our march towards that peaceful co-existence which is our heart's desire and during which the lasting peace of the world may find its sure foundation. This, if it is fairly treated, will be indeed the most important of a series of successes which have distinguished the recent conduct of the Foreign Office.

The conventional military forces of which the NATO Powers dispose are, of course, much fewer than those of Russia and the Soviets have no need to fear their attack, if such an idea were possible among the free nations. In fact there is no doubt that Soviet Russia could overrun the whole of Europe and make the life of the British Isles impossible, but for the fact that the United States possesses today that superiority in nuclear weapons which, while it is maintained, will be, I believe – that is all I can do – a decisive deterrent against a Communist aggression.

I must remind you of what I said a year ago at our Conference at Margate[1] – there have often been other times in my political life when I have not been keen to read out what I said a year ago. This is what I did say at Margate:

> I am sure that the decisions taken by the Socialist Government, which were supported by us at the time, and are now being carried forward steadfastly and soberly by Her Majesty's Government, constitute the best chance – and indeed I think it a good chance – of getting through this awful period of anxiety without a world catastrophe.
>
> We, at any rate, are going to adhere faithfully to them and do our utmost to promote the formation of the European Army, with a strong contingent of Germans in it. We, like the Americans, shall maintain our forces in Europe, thus restoring the French balance of equality with our new German associates.
>
> If EDC should not be adopted by the French, we shall have no choice in prudence but to fall in with some new arrangement which will join the strength of Germany to the Western Allies · through some rearrangement of the forces in NATO.

Well, I am content with that.

That is in effect what we are doing now through the combination of the Brussels Treaty of 1948 with the machinery of NATO through which the United States bring their mighty and indeed overwhelming power to the aid and protection of Europe. Without this aid on the Continent, the advance of Soviet Communism, which has already swallowed the satellite nations, could continue irresistibly by infiltration and intrigue with force in the background until despair produced a landslide into submission among the civilized countries in Europe.

I have always thought that the growth of ever closer ties with the United States, to whom we and our sister Commonwealth are bound, by language, literature, and law, is one, is the supreme factor in our future and that together we of the English-speaking world may make the world safe for ourselves and everybody else. There is no other case of a nation arriving at the summit of world power, seeking no territorial gain, but earnestly resolved to use her strength and wealth in the cause of progress and freedom.

Had this conception been visible to the American Governments fifty years ago we all, themselves included, might have escaped the two fearful World Wars which have brought such misery upon our generation and have made the twentieth century on a far larger scale the most tragic period since the Fall of the Roman Empire, fifteen hundred years ago. For America to withdraw into isolation would condemn all Europe to Russian Communist subjugation and our famous and beloved island to death and ruin. And yet six months ago

---

[1] Speech reproduced above (pp. 1237–46).

a politician who has held office in a British Cabinet and who one day aspires to become the Leader of the Labour Party did not hesitate to tell the Americans to 'go it alone'.

One cannot imagine any more fatal disaster than that this evil counsellor should be taken at his word on the other side of the Atlantic. There is already in the United States no little talk of a return to isolation and the policy is described as 'Fortress America'. We may, however, be sure that all the strongest, wisest forces over there, irrespective of party, will not allow the great Republic to be turned from the path of right and duty and that they will disdain the taunts of impudence as effectively as they confront the burden of toil and danger. I have been for many years in close relation with leading figures in American life and government and I can assure you that true and friendly comprehension between our kindred nations has rarely reached a higher standard than at the London Conference, over which Mr Eden presided with so much influence and distinction.

The particular task upon which we have been engaged is not yet done and many difficulties and complications lie ahead. The London Agreement represents the widest possible measure of common agreement in present circumstances. Major concessions were made by all the governments concerned. I think I am entitled to refer specially to the contribution made by this country and also by Dr Adenauer. I see it has been suggested in Paris that the French Prime Minister should now be asked to reopen negotiations and seek further major concessions to meet this and that requirement. This in my view is quite out of the question.

I repeat what Mr Eden said on Thursday. He said then:

I am measuring my words when I say that if our agreement is not ratified I know of no other way of creating a system into which Germany can be fitted to the general benefit of all concerned.

I have therefore to end my speech upon a grave and serious note, although I still have unconquerable hope that we shall come through all right in the long run and play a great part in helping others. I have good hopes that, if the free nations persevere soberly and patiently together, we may yet rescue the future of mankind.

Sir Winston S. Churchill to President Dwight D. Eisenhower
(Premier papers, 11/1074)

10 October 1954
Personal and Private
NOT SENT

My dear Friend,

1. I have waited till now to thank you for your most kind and welcome message of October 1[1] which gave great pleasure to me and Anthony. We are both concerned about the French attitude and you will perhaps have seen what I said yesterday on Anthony's advice about refusing to reopen negotiations for further concessions. We both feel that we have no choice but to move towards 'the Empty Chair' policy unless there is some early relief from the rule of a self-paralysed Chamber. If the Chamber turns us down next week it will seem important that we should both impress our views on the French and let them know what they are running in to. My own hope is strong that they will in the end do their duty and that if there was an Empty Chair it would not remain vacant very long. I am conscious that an anxious period lies before us, though the Soviet reaction to the London Agreement has so far seemed milder than might have been expected.

2. I should be obliged if you would send over privately someone who could explain to me the technical details of what I was told was the Pentagon Plan of becoming independent of the French infrastructure for a spell and especially what the timetable of moves would be if unhappily we had to take action in this sense. I have of course the general picture in my mind and will call it in our correspondence 'The Crab'. It might well be that very polite and quiet technical discussions with the French experts about the different stages of bringing it in would be a healthy process when the time comes. They might feel the pinch.

---

[1] Reproduced above (p. 1789).

October 1954

Sir Winston S. Churchill to Anthony Eden
Prime Minister's Personal Minute M.189/54
(Premier papers)

10 October 1954
Private and Personal

I am in full agreement with the message you propose. It does not conflict in any way with my general view; namely, that the Americans have a duty of honour to prevent Formosa being overrun and the Chiang refugees put to the same fate as the alleged 2,000,000 liquidated by the Chinese Communists. If the Americans use their overwhelming naval and air power the loss of Quemoy really does not affect the defence of Formosa.[1] Vide, the Channel Islands in our war. At the same time, if they make Formosa immune from all attack they cannot escape responsibility for aggressive action by Chiang's people against China.

Sir Winston S. Churchill to Lady Churchill
(Churchill papers, 1/50)

10 October 1954

I have looked at your speech.[2] It seems to be full of vivid and lively thoughts. I have only scribbled a few queries. The word 'preventative' should certainly be 'preventive'.

Christopher has arranged with Macleod, the Minister of Health, that if you let him have your copy some time tomorrow morning, he will look it through personally and see if there are any points which should be corrected or modified. Perhaps your Secretary will communicate with his. You should use a special messenger from the Private Office to send it round to him.

Sir Winston S. Churchill to Anthony Eden
(Churchill papers, 6/5)

11 October 1954

1. I should like Selwyn Lloyd to come from the Foreign Office and to be considered for either Education or Supply. Is this agreeable to you?

---

[1] The British and Americans disagreed with each other over whether or not to defend militarily the Quemoy and Matsus Islands, which were being shelled by mainland China owing to Chiang's residence there. The British viewed the islands as insignificant strategically to the defence of Formosa (Taiwan); the Americans believed they must be defended. Dulles even threatened the use of nuclear weapons against China. Neither Britain nor America intervened militarily. The islands remain Republic of China territory today.

[2] To the Professional Nurses and Midwives Conference.

2. Do you want Nutting made Minister of State, observing that this would entail Privy Councillorship under existing law, or would you be content with his being leading Under Secretary?

3. Who would you desire for the vacancy?

4. Can you promise Hopkinson an Embassy by the close of the year? If so, Munster[1] could become Minister of State, Colonies (peripatetic), and Lord John Hope Under Secretary, Colonies.

5. I am available if you wish to talk to me.[2]

Winston S. Churchill to Anthony Eden
(*Churchill papers, 6/5*)

13 October 1954
Private and Personal

I have been thinking further about Dodds-Parker. In spite of what I said to you, I wonder if you would consider keeping him after all. The new junior appointments would then be, as at present envisaged by me:

Commonwealth	Deedes[3]
War	Ian Harvey[4]
Foreign Office	Lord John Hope
Housing	Maclean[5]
Education	Walker-Smith[6]
Board of Trade	Harmar Nicholls[7]

[1] Geoffrey William Richard Hugh FitzClarence, 1906–75. Educated at Charterhouse. Succeeded his uncle as 5th Earl of Munster, 1928. Paymaster-General, 1938–9. Parliamentary Under-Secretary of State for War, Feb.–Sep. 1939. ADC and Military Assistant to Lord Gort, 1939. GSO to Malta, 1942. Parliamentary Under-Secretary of State for India and for Burma, 1943–4; at Home Office, 1944–5; at Colonial Office, 1951–4. Minister without Portfolio, 1954–7. PC, 1954. KBE, 1957.

[2] Eden responded the same day: '1. Yes. 2. Yes. Minister of State. 3. I will put up some suggestions. 4. Please see my separate minute.'

[3] William Francis Deedes, 1913–2007. Educated at Harrow. Reporter, *Morning Post*, 1931–7; *Daily Telegraph*, 1937–9. On active service, RA, 1939–45. Married, 1942, Evelyn Hilary Branfoot: five children. MP (Cons.) for Ashford, 1950–74. Editor, *Daily Telegraph*, 1974–86; columnist, 1986–2007. Baron, 1986.

[4] Ian Douglas Harvey, 1914–87. Educated at Christ Church, Oxford. On active service, 1939–45. Member, Kensington Borough Council, 1947–52. Married, 1949, Clare Mayhew: two children. Representative for Kensington, London County Council, 1949–52. MP (Cons.) for Harrow East, 1950–9. Parliamentary Under-Secretary of State, FO, 1958.

[5] Fitzroy Hew Royle Maclean, 1911–96. Educated at Eton and King's College, Cambridge. Diplomat in Paris, 1934–7; in Moscow, 1937–9. MP (Cons.) for Lancaster, 1941–59; for Bute and North Ayrshire, 1959–74. Head of British Liaison Mission with Tito, Yugoslavia, 1943–5. CBE, 1944. Married, 1946, Veronica Nell Fraser-Phipps: two children. Maj.-Gen., 1947. Financial Secretary, War Office, 1954–7. Bt, 1957. KT, 1993. Author of *Escape to Adventure* (1950).

[6] Derek Colclough Walker-Smith, 1910–92. Educated at Christ Church, Oxford. Called to the Bar, 1934. MP (Cons.) for Hertford, 1945–55; for East Hertfordshire, 1955–83. Economic Secretary to the Treasury, 1956–7. Minister of Health, 1957–60. Baron, 1960.

[7] Harmar Harmar-Nicholls, 1912–2000. Married, 1940, Dorothy Elsie Edwards: two children.

I think this look rather good.
Pray let me know what you think.¹

Field Marshal Lord Alexander to Sir Winston S. Churchill
(Premier papers, 11/844)

14 October 1954

My dear Prime Minister,

The work on the Government joint White Paper on Defence and Civil Defence is held up because the Ministers concerned are divided in their views as to the way in which our new policy would best be presented to Parliament.

My own view is that the substance of the draft I sent you contains the right approach because it gives a frank and true picture of what we believe to be the facts and conditions to be faced in the event of war in this thermo-nuclear age.

A different point of view is held by some Ministers who think that for reasons of security and public morale it would be wiser to present the case in a less direct and more optimistic form.

In my opinion the whole object of the White Paper is to give Parliament a full appreciation of the situation as we see it, not only because it is our duty to present the true picture, but to give the public a background against which to understand the reasons for the changes we are proposing in our defence policy and the consequent re-organisation of our Fighting Forces, together with our plans for Civil Defence with which they are linked.

Before we can proceed further with the White Paper which should be tabled as soon as possible after Parliament meets, this divergence of opinion amongst Ministers must first be resolved.

Since your experience and wisdom in these matters can solve this problem, I would appreciate your advice and direction, at your earliest convenience.

Konrad Adenauer to Sir Winston S. Churchill
(Premier papers, 11/676)

15 October 1954
Translation

Dear Sir Winston,
I learnt with delight of the great speech which you made in Blackpool on

---

Called to the Bar, Middle Temple, 1941. Magistrate, Darlaston Urban District Council, 1946. MP (Cons.) for Peterborough, 1950–74. Parliamentary Private Secretary to Asst Postmaster-General, 1951–5. Parliamentary Secretary, Ministry of Agriculture, Fisheries and Food, 1955–7; Ministry of Works, 1957–60.

¹ Apart from the appointment of Lord John Hope as Joint Parliamentary Under-Secretary of State for Foreign Affairs, none of the recommended appointments was made.

Saturday afternoon. I am deeply moved by the good and conciliatory words with which you spoke of the German people and I thank you for them from my heart, just as I also thank you for your friendly reference to the contribution which I myself may have made to the success of the London Conference.

Sir Winston S. Churchill to Harold Macmillan
(Churchill papers, 6/6)

16 October 1954
Private

My dear Harold,

I write to confirm the result to our talks about the Ministry of Defence. It has given me much pleasure to submit your name to The Queen for appointment to this key post in the Government on the morrow of your record achievement in housing. In this case, however, economy and quality are at least as important as magnitude and numbers.

Sir Winston S. Churchill to Field Marshal Lord Alexander
(Churchill papers, 6/6)

17 October 1954
Private

My dear Alex,

Although this letter adds nothing to our agreeable talk, I feel that there should be a formal record of what has happened.

I am deeply indebted to you for your distinguished and most helpful services. During these years of transition and uncertainty the whole foundation of Defence as we understood it all our lives has been replaced by problems awful in their character and largely beyond human control, or even comprehension. Your commanding thought and that of the Chiefs of Staff, namely that Deterrents must largely replace defence, is the only means that I shall ever see in my lifetime which gives the hope of peace and safety to your country, and indeed to mankind.

I could not resist your wish to lay down for private reasons the great office which you accepted at my earnest desire.

With every good wish for a long and happy future for you and Margaret.[1]

---

[1] Margaret Diana Bingham, 1905–77. Married, 1931, Harold Alexander: four children. Viceregal Consort of Canada, 1946–52. GBE, 1952.

OCTOBER 1954

Sir Winston S. Churchill to Lady Churchill
(Baroness Spencer-Churchill papers)[1]

18 October 1954   Chartwell

My darling,

I hope you will find time & energy to look through the enclosed cuttings from the country Press. They give a more widely representative view of the national opinion than do the London papers. They are certainly encouraging. I send them up to you at once.

Sir Winston S. Churchill to Private Office
(Premier papers, 11/595)

19 October 1954

Let me have a factual statement of the facilities afforded to Archbishop Makarios. In what ways were the Colonial Office responsible for them? What enquiries were made by the BBC before deciding upon this? The Colonial Office official who was summoned to the Cabinet said that they were not consulted in any way before the arrangements were made and that Mr Hopkinson regretted them greatly. These attempts by the BBC to build up enemies of England are deplorable. At least they might ask and consider the opinion of responsible Ministers of the Crown in matters of foreign and Colonial policy. Let me have a textual report of the dialogue. According to my information it is quite untrue to say that the Archbishop got the worst of it. I was astonished that men like Sir Alexander Cadogan and Sir Ian Jacob should have approved the proposal of *The Observer* newspaper. I am told that they knew nothing about it. Who then makes these decisions? Certainly the responsible Members of the organization should give their personal opinion and decision on matters of this importance. When I rang up Sir Ian Jacob it was evident that he had never heard of it but by then it was imminent and too late to prevent it. The Foreign Secretary took a very serious view. I propose to write a formal letter to the BBC when I am supplied with all the available facts.

---

[1] This letter was handwritten.

Sir Winston S. Churchill to Sir Alexander Cadogan
(Premier papers, 11/595)

22 October 1954

My dear Cadogan,

I am disturbed by the action of the BBC last Friday, October 15, in broadcasting an interview with the Archbishop of Cyprus. The Foreign Secretary had not heard of the intention until a few hours before the broadcast was due and he was much distressed. I have now enquired into the circumstances.

It appears that the Archbishop was first televised by the BBC on his arrival at London Airport on October 13 and the film was subsequently broadcast. The following day, a Mr Bonarjee[1] of the BBC *Home and Abroad* programme telephoned to the Colonial Office to say that he had invited the Archbishop to broadcast again. He thought that the Colonial Office might wish to suggest questions for the interviewer. The Colonial Office were not asked whether they thought well of the idea. They were merely informed of what had been decided and were asked for their collaboration in drafting the questions.

When I left the Cabinet and rang up Sir Ian Jacob, it was clear that he did not know anything about the impending broadcast. The interview was apparently arranged by the organiser of the BBC *Home and Abroad* programme on his own initiative. We have since been told that it was the BBC's object to employ a skilful questioner who would expose the weakness of the Archbishop's case. On the contrary a study of the transcript makes it clear that the Archbishop gave carefully pre-arranged answers in written form, and seemed to be making a good and reasonable case against Great Britain from the Communist point of view. One of his statements was 'we look on Communism as a kind of Trades Union Movement for the improvement of the workers' lot'.

I do not consider that the BBC should be used for the publicising of people hostile to this country and the gratuitous advertisement of their case. It astonishes me that matters of such serious importance should not be mentioned to the Government beforehand and that they should not even receive any prior consideration from the responsible heads of the BBC.

I cannot believe that men with so distinguished a record of service to the State as yourself and Sir Ian Jacob could have been content to stand by and see the BBC used to exploit anti-Colonial prejudice for the satisfaction of those whose greatest wish is to destroy the British Commonwealth and Empire.

---

[1] Stephen Wilson Bonarjee, 1912–2003. Educated at St Andrews University. On staff, *Manchester Guardian*, 1938. On active service, WWII. Radio producer, BBC, 1945–72; radio editor, 1962–72.

OCTOBER 1954

Sir Winston S. Churchill to Konrad Adenauer
(*Premier papers, 11/676*)

24 October 1954

Dear Dr Adenauer,

You have recently sent me two charming letters[1] by which I was gratified. It is now my turn to congratulate you on the skill, patience and resolve which you have shown for so long and which seem at last to have reaped the reward which they merit. Allow me to say how much I admire your personal contribution to the future peace and prosperity of Germany and of Europe as a whole.

Sir Winston S. Churchill to Field Marshal Lord Alexander
(*Cabinet papers, 131/14*)

28 October 1954

1. I wish the Chiefs-of-Staff Committee without delay to meet and consider the functions of any Military Command that is to be created in Cyprus for the Middle East.

2. The Forces at their disposal are to consist of one Armoured Division (13,500 combatants) for which one Brigade is in Cyprus, one Brigade in Libya and two Detachments of 700 each in Jordan and Malta. For this there also exists or is about to be created a Divisional Staff and of course there exist the two Brigade Staffs.

3. It would appear that the Divisional Staff, located in Cyprus, would be sufficient to discharge the duties of Middle East Headquarters and to manipulate the four Detachments aforesaid, provided that some moderate additions were made for the purpose of Intelligence and transmission of signals including coding and decoding to a dispersed Divisional unit.

4. It is to be observed that all political issues are decided and guidance given upon them by the Cabinet and the Defence Committee of the Cabinet. Secondly that all strategic questions are in the sphere of the Minister of Defence, having at his disposal the Chiefs-of-Staff, themselves advised by the General Staff. None of these political or strategic duties need to be entrusted to the Cyprus Commander. He will of course be kept fully informed and invited to express an opinion like any other Officer commanding a detached Division.

---

[1] Reproduced above (pp. 1790, 1805–6).

November
1954

Sir Winston S. Churchill to Lady Violet Bonham Carter[1]
(Churchill papers, 2/423)

4 November 1954

My dear Violet,

I have been reading the book about me which Cassells are publishing on my birthday.[2] Of the many kind and far too flattering articles in it, there is one which means more to me than all the remainder and which indeed moves me deeply. It seems that after all these years you still believe me to be a glow-worm. That is a compliment which I find entirely acceptable.

Sir Winston S. Churchill to Lord Cecil[3]
(Chelwood papers)

4 November 1954

My dear Bob,

You have done me a great honour in contributing a chapter to the book which Cassells are publishing about me on my birthday. To be described as a 'Man of Peace' by you is high praise indeed. I esteem it the more because I

---

[1] Helen Violet Asquith, 1887–1969. Elder daughter of H. H. Asquith, Lib. PM 1908–16. Educated in Dresden and Paris. Married, 1915, Sir Maurice Bonham Carter (d. 1960). President, Women's Liberal Federation, 1923–5, 1939–45; Liberal Party Organization, 1945–7. A Governor of the BBC, 1941–6. Unsuccessful Parliamentary candidate (Lib.), 1945, 1951. Member of Royal Commission on the Press, 1947–9. DBE, 1953. Baroness, 1964. Wrote *Winston Churchill as I Knew Him*, 1965.

[2] *Winston Spencer-Churchill, Servant of Crown and Commonwealth*, edited by Sir James Merchant. Wrapped around the dustjacket was a birthday card, which readers could detach and post to the Prime Minister. Lady Violet's contribution was entitled 'Winston Churchill As I Know Him'. After his death, she would publish a book on their long friendship using that title in the past tense.

[3] Edgar Algernon Robert Cecil, 1864–1958. Known as 'Bob'. Third son of 3rd Marquess of Salisbury. Educated at Eton and University College, Oxford. MP (Cons.) for East Marylebone, 1906–10; for Hitchin, 1911–23. Under-Secretary of State for Foreign Affairs, 1915–18. Minister of Blockade, 1916–18. Asst Secretary of State for Foreign Affairs, 1918. Viscount Cecil of Chelwood, 1923. Lord Privy Seal, 1923–4. President of the League of Nations Union, 1923–45. Chancellor of the Duchy of Lancaster, 1924–7. Nobel Peace Prize, 1937.

remember one occasion, some 50 years ago at Birmingham, when you were prepared to be a 'man of war' in my defence. Nothing pleases me more than that you should be one of those who have helped to make this book so agreeable to me.

Sir Winston S. Churchill: speech
('The Unwritten Alliance', pages 192–5)

9 November 1954   The Lord Mayor's Banquet
The Guildhall

It is always a stately and agreeable event for Her Majesty's Ministers to be invited to the Guildhall on this important civic occasion. I am indebted to you for all the goodwill you have shown to my colleagues, and for the kindness and compliments which you have bestowed on me. Last year your predecessor appealed to the Government to get a move on – though he may have used a more ceremonious expression – to get a move on with repairing the ruin inflicted on the City in the war. The request did not go unanswered. In fact we had already begun to issue licences on a far greater scale than had been thought possible earlier, and this year we have issued over thirteen million pounds' worth, on which some progress has been made. We cannot beat this record, because tomorrow morning we are abolishing licences altogether and leaving you to a large extent to be the judges in your own affairs, subject only to the approval of the town and country planning authorities to whom you will, I have no doubt, have a lot to say. Personally I must confess that there was one quite old ruin which seemed to me to deserve at least as much attention as those which owed their destruction to Hitler. I am very glad that thanks to the generosity of Mr Bridgland[1] we rescued the Temple of Mithras from the progress of modern civilization, whether in its destructive or reconstructive form. I must congratulate you on having got a magnificent new roof over your heads and amid all the problems of housing for the people not to have left Gog and Magog out in the cold.

This is now the fourth Guildhall speech I have made in my present tenure of office and I am very glad that I can once again report to you a definite improvement in our own affairs, and it seems to me also in the moods of and the fortunes of the ever-growing and quivering world around us. We live in an age where the mood decides the fortunes rather than the fortunes decide the mood. If the human race wishes to have a prolonged and indefinite period of material prosperity, they have only got to behave in a peaceful and helpful way towards one another, and science will do for them all that they wish and more than they can dream. If of course their wish is to be quarrelsome and think

[1] Aynsley Vernon Bridgland, 1893–1966. Educated at Adelaide University. Chairman, Aynsley Trust Ltd.

it fun to bite one another, there is no doubt that every day they can kill each other in a quicker and more wholesale manner than ever before. The choice is theirs. Man is becoming increasingly master of his own fate and increasingly uncertain about it, and I think he is beginning to understand this fact better than he has ever done before.

In our own island we are conscious of having more influence over other countries than we used to have in this present century and certainly since the war, in which we did the best we could. We have tried to show ourselves well-informed, sedate, persevering, and resolute. We have not shrunk either at home or abroad from doing things which we believed were necessary, even though anyone could see they might be unpopular, and we have found a strong measure of responsibility among many of the Leaders of the Opposition and among the strongest – I did not say the loudest – elements in their rank and file. This, and the sober, stable view of the great trade unions, have aided Her Majesty's Government in the conduct of foreign affairs, and given the feeling that a government in this ancient kingdom has a stature and substance considerably above the ordinary ins and outs and ups and downs of party politics. In fact, although we no longer play so dominating a role in the modern world as we used to, we are nevertheless a people whose opinion is very widely respected. Encircled by our sister Commonwealths, we are felt to deserve attention from enlightened men and women of varied outlook in many lands.

In our active political life we have undoubtedly here at home a great measure of that bipartisanship, as it is called, which plays such a large part in the United States and is going to play a larger part there in the years that lie before us. This seeks to lift a lot of important things above ordinary electioneering, without in any way preventing free speech or a healthy measure of initiative. All this is to the good. We must also make sure that a most complete understanding prevails among all members of our Commonwealth, whose unity and majesty shine ever more brightly and are kept alive by intimate and timely consultation. I feel sure this great company gathered here tonight will welcome the plan we have made for another Commonwealth and Empire Conference. When the Prime Ministers of so many powerful communities assemble in London at the end of January, I have no doubt they will be impressed by the strength of our financial structure, the increasing confidence it commands over the land and sea, and the reserves it controls. For this we ought certainly to pay due tribute to the Chancellor of the Exchequer who is here with us tonight.

Several important negotiations have been successfully carried through in the past year. The Persian oil is flowing again. We are once more reaping the benefit of what British foresight and industry has created. In Europe the great city of Trieste, which has so long been a cause of friction between two of our friends and a cause of anxiety and expense to us, has been the subject of a friendly and reasonable agreement. In Africa, a settlement has been reached with Egypt which will relieve us of a heavy burden which it was no longer our military interest to bear. A revolution in the science of destruction has profoundly changed the factors and values by which men have hitherto been guided – or misguided. This is not primarily because particular localities or bases are more vulnerable than they were, though that is no doubt the case. It is because the entire character and timetable of any future war has undergone a cataclysmic change, the like of which has never been known to mortal man. It would be wrong not to notice a thing like that.

Finally, we can claim to have taken a leading part in finding a way through the maze of intricate and baffling negotiations which have so long delayed the reentry of Germany in the community of the West. After many heart-searchings and disappointments, ending in the collapse of EDC, we had an international conference in London – yes, fancy that, for once it was actually in London – at which nine Western powers agreed how Germany might contribute to the defence of Europe without becoming a threat to French security. The energy and initiative of our Foreign Secretary, Sir Anthony Eden, was throughout supported by the patience of Dr Adenauer, who has fought hard, long, and at last successfully, for a European solution of the problems confronting his country, and by the imaginative wisdom of the other statesmen who assembled here. When the agreements, which were later signed in Paris, have been ratified, it may be that the ancient antagonism of France and Germany will have passed from life into history and this itself may only be a better chapter in a new and brighter story than in our time we have had to tell.

I am one of those who believe that the powers of the West and of the East should try to live in a friendly and peaceful way with each other. It would certainly not be to anyone's disadvantage if they tried. We don't agree with Soviet Communism or with their system of one-party uniformity. We think there is a great deal to be said for nature and variety, and that governments are made for men, not men for governments. But if the Soviets really like being governed by officials in a sealed pattern, and so long as they do not endanger the safety or freedom of others, that is a matter for them to decide themselves for themselves. Nothing is final. Change is unceasing and it is likely that mankind has a lot more to learn before it comes to its journey's end.

One thing is certain: with the world divided as it is at present, the freedom of our vast international association of the free peoples can only be founded upon strength and strength can only be maintained by unity. The whole foundation of our existence stands on our alliance, friendship, and an increasing sense of brotherhood with the United States, and we are also developing increasingly intimate ties with France, Germany, Italy, and the Low Countries which are stronger and more practical than any that have yet been devised. From these solemn and important agreements we hope that we shall be able to create that peace through strength which will allow time to play its part and bring about an altogether easier relationship all over the world. We might even find ourselves in a few years moving along a smooth causeway of peace and plenty instead of roaming around on the rim of Hell. For myself I am an optimist – it does not seem to be much use being anything else – and I cannot believe that the human race will not find its way through the problems that confront it, although they are separated by a measureless gulf from any they have known before. I look forward to the time when, to use Sir Anthony Eden's words, having brought about a stability and a common purpose in the West, we shall have established the essential basis on which we can seek an understanding with the East. Thus we may by patience, courage, and in orderly progression reach the shelter of a calmer and kindlier age.

Sir Winston S. Churchill: speech
(Churchill papers, 2/336)

12 November 1954   Harrow School

Ladies and Gentlemen,

Thank you very much for this kind welcome. The Head Master[1] has asked me whether I would say a few words to you, reminding you that this is the fifteenth time running, without missing once, that I am here. The first time I came it certainly was a time rather like the last verse of 'The Silver Arrow'. It was a time of great anxiety and peril, and we seemed to be all alone in the world with mighty powers rising against us, and Allies falling away, and others, who we hoped would come in, still delaying on their path. We were all alone for a whole year. But I can assure you who are seated before me that there was no real doubt; that, if there was anxiety, it was not anxiety over what was going to happen to any of us. It was only whether we should succeed in carrying out our unconquerable purpose. We succeeded in doing so. We held our own. The island was inviolate. None was able to cross the water.

Every person, whatever his task, discharged it with spirit and zeal; and we found after a year had passed a vastly altered world. Many things that had looked hopeless had become self-evident, accomplished and achieved. The country had indeed a fine period in its history then. I daresay it may prove that it will be thought to be – what I ventured to say at the time – our finest hour. But what had rendered it possible had been prepared through generations, growing and developing in generations, and I am sure that the forces and influences in our life which gave us the strength to be worthy of our duty at that moment, that these causes and influences are still travelling on with us all. You are the heirs of fathers who have set as fine an example in the fighting

---

[1] Robert Leoline James, 1905–82. Educated at Jesus College, Oxford. Asst Master, St Paul's School, 1928. Married, 1939, Maud Eliot W. M. Gibbons: two children. Headmaster of Chigwell School, 1939–46. High Master of St Paul's School, 1946–53. Headmaster of Harrow, 1953–71. Chairman of Council, Heathfield School, 1960–79.

field and in the general struggle as any that our history shows, and we are sure that you, in your turn, will carry on the torch when older hands have let it fall and will enable our country, although only a small island in a vast world of power around us, to maintain its great influence and authority and to build upon its established honour not only a security for itself; it will act also as an example and, in a way, bring a lasting salvation maybe to men and weak people all over the world who are in danger and in suffering. I feel that the continuity must be very apparent in your minds. It is in mine.

I remember being a little boy here, not a very happy little boy I must admit. I was not much good at the games and even less good, I am sorry to say, at the lessons. But I got the feel of a common spirit that this was the building-place for the life of England and of Britain; and it has always been a great help to me when I have felt worried or anxious about things.

Now you have sung these songs. I have always asked you to sing them since 1940 and I pick some every time. I am rather sorry not to have asked for 'Euclid'. I always thought there was one good point about 'Euclid'. You were almost invited to argue back with people. I am sorry to see it has dropped out of your curriculum. But perhaps it may one of these days be sung. One ought to be able to stand up for one's own point of view and what one believes in, without in any way overlooking other people's points of view.

One of the great things about our country today is that, though we have our party differences and class distinctions, in the great things that matter, and in the most difficult things that most matter, there is a strong national spirit which stands uppermost. The ordinary groupings of politicians or people arguing about public affairs must not make us forget that.

I thank you very much for giving me such a warm welcome. As usual I have brought a number of friends with me. Some I know and run across. I see the Chief Whip there, and Sir Walter Monckton who prevents any trouble breaking out, at least I hope he will. And then there is my friend Leo. I have had several adventures with him. But I am glad to say that in the seventy or eighty years that have followed we have nearly always got along together – but not always. And that is very important. Make quite sure that you must not bring politics into private life. You must not let the ordinary flow and ebb of political affairs interfere with loyalty and friendship.

I almost seem to have been preaching a sermon. We have still some more excellent songs to sing, and although I have been here fifteen times, it is my intention to come a sixteenth time.

NOVEMBER 1954

Cabinet: minutes
(*Cabinet papers, 130/106*)

19 November 1954   Prime Minister's Room
Top Secret   House of Commons
11.30 a.m.
Gen. 476/1st Meeting

MEETING OF MINISTERS ON MIDDLE EAST DEFENCE
Middle East Joint Headquarters

The Meeting had before them a note by the Secretaries of Defence Committee (D(54)37) covering a minute addressed to the Prime Minister by the Minister of Defence and a memorandum by the Chiefs of Staff outlining the proposed functions of the Higher Command Organisation in the Middle East which was to be established in Cyprus.

The Prime Minister said that the principle of setting up a Joint Services Headquarters in Cyprus, following our withdrawal from Egypt, had been approved by the Cabinet. He had, however, been concerned to learn that, notwithstanding the great reduction which was taking place in the size of our forces in the Middle East, the plans of the Service Departments envisaged a total administrative strength of 7,000 in the new Middle East Command. It appeared that irrespective of the staff attached to combatant forces at the various Middle East stations, there would be nearly 2,500 administrative personnel in the new Joint Headquarters in Cyprus. The capital cost of the Headquarters was estimated at £30 millions, and the annual cost of the staff would be £2 millions a year. The advent of nuclear weapons had created a new strategic situation in the Middle East and the Government had rightly laid emphasis on the need for redeployment of our forces from Egypt. The same considerations should be applied to the structure of the new Command Headquarters to be formed in Cyprus. He accepted the necessity to provide a Joint Headquarters in the Middle East to carry out those essential functions which could not be undertaken by the divisional and brigade staffs. But all large issues of policy affecting defence plans for the Middle East would continue to be decided by the Cabinet or the Defence Committee, and he was not convinced that some at least of the planning functions which it was proposed to carry out in Cyprus could not be fulfilled equally well by Service staffs in London. The costly new Headquarters to be built on an undeveloped site in Cyprus would in modern conditions be hardly less remote than London from widely dispersed areas falling within the purview of the Middle East Command. Moreover, if war should come, reinforcement of our forces in the Middle East was unlikely to be possible, at any rate in the opening stages. The Middle East Headquarters should therefore be designed in the main for the functions which it must carry out in peace.

NOVEMBER 1954 1817

The Minister of Defence[1] said that the plans so far made by the Service Departments for the staffing of the Cyprus Headquarters were provisional. They could not be finally settled until decisions had been taken on the functions which the Headquarters would be called upon to perform. A broad definition of these functions had been put forward by the Chiefs of Staff in paragraph 5 of their memorandum (D(54)37) and, if this was acceptable, he would ascertain in consultation with the Service Ministers the minimum number of staff which would be required to carry out those functions. It was already evident that the numbers originally proposed were unnecessarily large.

The Foreign Secretary said that in the changed strategic situation there was clearly no need to maintain so elaborate a Headquarters Organisation in the Middle East as we had done in the past. This consideration applied to the Foreign Service staff (in the British Middle East Office) as well as in the military Headquarters. But, before the minimum number required in either case could be finally determined, it was necessary to agree upon their new role. He agreed with the general outline of their functions in D(54)37, and he would be willing to collaborate with the Minister of Defence in working out a more detailed directive. The reduction which was taking place in the military strength which we deployed in the Middle East made it all the more necessary to preserve the ability of the Middle East Headquarters to encourage and coordinate the contribution which Middle East countries could themselves make to the stability of the area.

In further discussion the following points were made:
   (a) In defining the tasks of the Joint Service Headquarters in the Middle East, account should be taken of the relations between our own defence planning for this area and that of NATO, and the probable extent of United States and Commonwealth assistance in the defence of the Middle East in war.
   (b) The status of the Command should be maintained at a level which would enable it to command the respect of Commonwealth countries, notably South Africa and Pakistan, whose assistance would be essential to the execution of our own plans for the defence of the area.
   (c) Some adjustments had already been made by the War Office and the Air Ministry in their provisional plans for the staffing of the Joint Services Headquarters. These would have the effect of reducing the number of Army officers at the Headquarters from 172 to 127, and the number of Air Force officers from 159 to 131. Further economies were being sought by the Service Departments, but a major reduction in the total provisional complement of over

[1] Harold Macmillan.

2,000 could not be achieved without a radical alteration in the functions of the Headquarters as outlined in D(54)37.

(d) The site of the new Headquarters in Cyprus had been selected on the advice of the Government of Cyprus.

The Committee –

Invited the Minister of Defence to draw up, in consultation with the Foreign Secretary, a more detailed statement of the functions of the Joint Service Headquarters in the Middle East and the related part of the British Middle East Office, and of the minimum organization required to discharge those functions.

Sir Winston S. Churchill: speech
('*Winston S. Churchill, His Complete Speeches*', volume 8, pages 8604–5)

23 November 1954   Woodford

THE UNITY OF THE FREE NATIONS

It is in foreign affairs, especially those affecting Europe, that the greatest measure of unity in the nation arises. On our side there is complete and natural agreement and the Socialists voted among themselves to support the London and Paris Agreements, in which Mr Anthony Eden, I should say Sir Anthony,[1] was the prime mover, by 124 to 72. The Socialists did not repeat that when it came to a vote in the House. That means that more than three-quarters of the people's representatives have definitely declared themselves for rearming Germany and including her in the ranks of the NATO Powers.

This might have been a very unpopular policy within ten years of our war with Hitler and the terrible things that were done then. Certainly if anyone when Germany surrendered unconditionally had predicted that we should be allied within ten years, very few people would have believed them here and still fewer over in America.

This vast reversal of British, American, and of European opinion was brought about only by the policy of Soviet Russia itself and above all by Stalin, the Dictator, who was carried away by the triumphs of victory and acted as if he thought he could secure for Russia and Communism the domination of the world.

I believe I was the first well-known person to publicly state the fact that we must have Germany on our side against Russian Communist aggression. Even before the war had ended and while the Germans were surrendering by hundreds of thousands, and our streets were crowded with cheering people, I telegraphed to Lord Montgomery directing him to be careful in collecting

---

[1] The Order of the Garter had been conferred on Eden by the Queen on Oct. 20.

the German arms, to stack them so that they could easily be issued again to the German soldiers whom we should have to work with if the Soviet advance continued.

When in 1950 I said in the House of Commons that there was no effective defence of Western Europe without a rearmed Germany, Mr Attlee said it was an irresponsible statement. A little more than a year later he accepted the policy himself in alliance with the United States, whose opinion had decisively altered. I do not mention this to criticize Mr Attlee. I think a statesman in responsible office shows courage rather than inconsistency in changing his mind if he is convinced that his country's safety and freedom are involved.

The world front that has been established and is being strengthened against Russian Communist aggression will, I believe, preserve mankind from another disaster infinitely more fearful than any we have ever known or even dreamed of in our wildest nightmares.

None of the free countries now banded together must flinch or waver and Britain, still one of the most powerful in the world, has undoubtedly played and will play a leading part. We at this moment are highly respected as a nation for our far-sighted vision and calm, indomitable resolve.

But meanwhile another great event has happened. Stalin died and new men sharing the power together are at the head of Russia. It was in May last year that I advocated that we with our allies should work towards a closer contact with Russia in order to make sure whether that great people had undergone an important change of mood and outlook under their new leadership. This is still my purpose. Our policy is Peace through Strength.

Nothing could be more foolish than for us to begin these closer contacts with Soviet Russia by a break-up with the unity among themselves of the free nations. That was what threatened us all when the French Chamber refused to ratify the EDC Agreements which they had themselves devised and shaped and on which so much precious time had been spent. The arrangements which have been made as the result of Sir Anthony Eden's exertions are, I believe, in many ways an improvement on EDC, and when they have been ratified the path will be clear for those contacts with Soviet Russia from which I still hope and indeed, increasingly hope, a peaceful and easier and ever more prosperous future for the whole world may spring and grow.

NOVEMBER 1954

Lady Churchill to Sir Winston S. Churchill
(Churchill papers, 2/423)[1]

23 November 1954

Winston,

Yesterday, when I opened the 'Churchill House' at Seven oaks, one of the old lady residents gave me this blotter for you. It seems that 500 old ladies live in the 47 Churchill Houses,[2] sprinkled up & down the country. Each of these residents contributed towards this gift.

Wow!

Your devoted old Clem Pussy Bird –

The 'waiting list', for a room in a Churchill house is over 7000!

Cabinet: conclusions
(Cabinet papers, 128/27)

24 November 1954
Secret
10 p.m.
Cabinet Meeting No. 79 of 1954

Prime Minister's Room
House of Commons

1. The Prime Minister said that he thought it would be right that he should make a general statement on defence during the forthcoming Debate on the Address. He had in mind a broad appreciation, which, without treating problems of defence in any detail, would present in symmetric form many points which had already been made separately. It would be necessary soon to announce certain changes which it had been decided to make in our defence programmes, such as those affecting Anti-Aircraft Command and the Auxiliary Air Force; and it was preferable that these changes should be made known in the context of a broad statement on defence policy. It would be convenient if arrangements could be made which would enable him to make his statement on 6th December, but he would be willing, if necessary, to make it somewhat earlier, possibly on 2nd December.

The Lord Privy Seal said that the Parliamentary time-table for the Debate on the Address could not be determined until the terms of any amendment tabled by the Opposition was known. He would sound the Opposition through the usual channels, but they would probably not be willing to come to any definite arrangements until they had had an opportunity of seeing the terms of The Queen's Speech. If it became necessary to concede another day for the

---

[1] This letter was handwritten.
[2] The 'Churchill Houses' were run by the Church Army Housing Association, whose first home for the homeless was established in 1890.

Debate on the Address, this might jeopardise the time-table for the passage of the Pensions Bill.

The Cabinet —

Invited the Lord Privy Seal to make informal inquiries with a view to arranging that a Government statement on defence should take place on Monday, 6th December, or failing this, on Thursday 2nd December.

[. . .]

Moshe Sharett[1] to Sir Winston S. Churchill
(Churchill papers, 6/6)

26 November 1954   Jerusalem

Israel unites today with Britain and the nations of the world in paying homage to your matchless record and statesmanship. In one of the bleakest crises in the history of civilisation, it was given to you, by supreme feat of personal determination and inspired national leadership, to save the cause of freedom, to give sublime expression to the faith and fervour of man in his resistance to tyranny, and to lead your own brave people and its allies from defeat to victory.

Your staunch advocacy of the Zionist idea, your belief in its justice and ultimate triumph, and your joy in its consummation with the rise of an independent Israel, have earned for you the everlasting gratitude of the Jewish people. They will never forget your steadfast support of the policy of the Balfour Declaration, your forceful interventions on its behalf, your long and unbroken friendship with Chaim Weizmann, and your resolute step in giving their sons the long-yearned-for chance of fighting the mortal enemy as a national unit under their own flag. Your continuing personal interest in the efforts and aspirations of Israel reverberates deeply in our people's hearts. May you long be spared to persevere in your noble endeavours for security, international understanding, and universal peace, and to continue to excite the admiration of the world by the brilliance of your mind and the tenacity of your spirit.

---

[1] Moshe Sharett, 1894–1965. Born in Kherson, Russian Empire. Educated at Istanbul University and London School of Economics. On active service, WWI. Married, 1922, Tzipora Meirov. Asst Editor, *Davar*, 1925–31. Secretary, Political Dept, Jewish Agency, 1931–3; Head, 1933–48. Foreign Minister, Provincial Government of Israel, 1948–9. Elected to Knesset, 1949. Minister of Foreign Affairs, 1949–56. PM, 1954–5.

NOVEMBER 1954

Sir Winston S. Churchill: speech[1]
('The Unwritten Alliance', pages 198–200)

26 November 1954   University of Bristol

I always enjoy coming to Bristol and performing my part in this ceremony, so dignified and so solemn, and yet so inspiring and reverent. It is almost three years since I last had the pleasure of presiding at a ceremony such as this. I do regret indeed that my wife could not come with me but she felt the need of a few days' rest in order to regather her strength and I shall take great pleasure in carrying to her personally the message sent to her by Sir Robert Sinclair,[2] my old friend, who has expressed it in such happy words, and also your enthusiastic endorsement of it.

I said I always enjoy coming here, and may I say I rather like wearing this. It was my father's robe as Chancellor of the Exchequer in 1886 and was most carefully preserved by my mother until I had the opportunity of wearing it as Chancellor myself, but also as Chancellor of this University. The alterations which had to be made are really not by any means fundamental.

Now in the interval of my first coming here, and in the interval even of the last three years, many things have happened and I am bound to say that I cannot look around this hall with its war scars upon it without remembering that occasion when I came during the war and when in a neighbouring building we went through with extreme exactness our ritual and formalities, and the dons came in in their robes, wearing them over their dripping wet and smoke-stained garments in which they had been fighting the fire which, while we were engaged in our ceremony, was still smouldering next door. That was an event which always sticks in my mind and I do not feel any great urge or hurry to have the inside of this building changed. It is at any rate an historical adornment which will keep it going until other measures have in due course been taken.

As I cast my mind back over the quarter of a century which I have been your Chancellor I go back to the summer of 1929. Prosperity was high. We were not perhaps quite back where we had been before the cataclysm of the First World War but peace seemed assured, we had forgotten our wrongs, we had forgiven our enemies, and it seemed that all we had to do was to march forward under the banner of the League of Nations to a still brighter horizon. How quickly the vision faded. That very autumn the American slump set in. It was followed by unemployment on a hideous scale, by the restriction of foreign markets and a decline in our own financial position so rapid and so

---

[1] The Chancellor's Address, given at the Conferment of Degrees ceremony.
[2] Robert John Sinclair, 1893–1979. On active service, WWI (wounded, despatches). Married, 1917, Mary Shearer Barclay. MBE, 1918. Asst Secretary, Imperial Tobacco Co., 1920–7; Secretary, 1927–33; Director, 1933–9; Deputy Chairman, 1939–47; Chairman, 1947–59; President, 1959. KBE, 1941. KCB, 1946. Pro-Chancellor, Bristol University, 1946–70. Baron, 1957.

unexpected that within two years many countries were on the brink of ruin and we not far from it.

You all know the familiar story of how the 1930s crept on, a story of hopes not merely deferred but destroyed and of growing dangers which none of the great parties in the state, to be quite frank, would face and in which most people even refused to believe. I have often said that the Second World War was the most unnecessary war in history. Today we are in point of time as nearly removed, as nearly as far removed, from the Second World War as we were from the Treaty of Versailles on the day I became your Chancellor. Once again the country has regained a large measure of its lost prosperity. Once again we are trying to establish a rule of law for the world under the auspices of most of the great nations. In this case we have the measureless advantage denied us in the days after the First World War, the measureless advantage that the United States is principal champion and servant and member of the United Nations Organization. Had that happened twenty years before we might indeed have had a very different story to tell.

Now that we have much stronger forces in the United Nations, and it is supposed to represent the common thought of all the world, the illusions of a calm passage lying before us are no longer in our minds. We have learnt by practical experience and bitter disappointments to believe that the path to the future is more likely than not to be a harsh and stony one and that terrible pitfalls await the nations, and indeed the world, if they allow themselves to advance incautiously and recognize the vanity of our past illusions it does not follow that we should despair of the issues before us or that we should cast aside generous hopes and aspirations.

The University is a treasure house of the country's future; now more than ever before the fate of the world will be shaped by the hands of the generation that is growing to maturity. Let us hope that the examples which we can provide will not be rejected as unworthy. If they are wise the young figures who leave this University will seek in the past, both near and distant, precepts which will help to guide them even through the nuclear age. It might well be said that a clear choice lies before mankind. One has no doubt what mankind would do, if they were able, by some power or other, through some institution or some measure of meeting or agreement, one has no doubt what they would do, which line they would take of the two alternatives. On the one hand science with all its marvels and humanity with its noble instincts could combine to open vistas of a splendour never seen before; on the other all will collapse in hatred, confusion, and it might well be obliteration.

Let us therefore close no doors. We might indeed be vigilant, we must indeed be firm in upholding the principles we believe to be just, but let us resolve with patience and with courage to work for the day when all the men in all the lands can be brought to cast aside the dark aspirations which some have inherited and others have created. Then at last together we shall be able to strive in freedom for the enjoyment of the blessings which it has pleased God to offer to the human race.

President Dwight D. Eisenhower to Sir Winston S. Churchill
(*Premier papers, 11/1074*)

28 November 1954   The White House

Dear Winston,

    I know I speak for my fellow countrymen, as I enthusiastically do for myself, in sending you warmest congratulations on reaching a new landmark in a life that is in itself a series of great landmarks.

    We Americans have known you and of you over the years – as roving war reporter, as adventurous solider, as administrator and parliamentarian and, increasingly with each passing year, as statesman and defender of freedom.

    We have seen the great Anglo-American partnership grow and flourish, with you as one of the staunch advocates. In the dark times of war, and the anxious ones of uncertain peace, this partnership has sustained us all and given us strength.

    Now, as you reach four score, we Americans salute you as world statesman, as unconquerable warrior in the cause of freedom, as our proven friend of many valiant years.[1]

Cabinet: conclusions
(*Cabinet papers, 128/27*)

29 November 1954
Secret
5.30 p.m.
Cabinet Meeting No. 80 of 1954

    1. The Prime Minister said that since the Cabinet's discussion on 24th November it had occurred to him that it would be convenient if Ministers could have some private talks with leading members of the Opposition on defence policy before any general statement was made on this subject in Parliament. He had had an opportunity during the weekend to mention this possibility informally to the Leader of the Opposition, whose first reaction had not been unfavourable. If, after consulting his colleagues, Mr Attlee was able to fall in with this suggestion, it might perhaps be publicly stated in the Debate on the Address that this course was to be followed.

---

[1] Churchill responded on Nov. 29: 'Thank you so much for your letter which I greatly value. I am writing.'

NOVEMBER 1954   1825

In discussion there was general agreement that Opposition leaders should be given the opportunity of confidential discussions on defence problems, if they were willing to accept it.

[. . .]

3. The Cabinet had before them a memorandum by the Chancellor of the Exchequer (C(54)344) recommending that means should be sought to restrict the growing scale of Government expenditure on subsidised houses for the double purpose of reducing Government expenditure and of furthering other forms of capital investment. They also had before them a memorandum by the Minister of Health (C(54)348) drawing attention to the need for the further development of hospital services.

The Chancellor of the Exchequer said that, while the general economic position gave no cause for anxiety, there were some signs of a tendency towards inflation. This must be held in check. One of the measures which the Government could take to this end was so to adjust their policy as to avoid a situation in which the building industry became overloaded with competing claims for capital investment. He was on this account anxious to reduce the amount of government expenditure on housing. There was every likelihood that the momentum which had been given to house-building by private enterprise would be maintained in 1955 and 1956. The time had therefore come to restrict the number of subsidised houses which local authorities were authorized to build; and he hoped that authorisations in 1955 could be limited to about 140,000 as against the present level of 180,000. This would leave room for further expansion of industrial investment and for meeting some of the other claims to capital investment, e.g., in roads, schools and hospitals.

The Minister of Housing said that he accepted the general objective proposed by the Chancellor of the Exchequer and was willing to adopt a total of 140,000 authorisations in 1955 as a target for his own guidance in determining the allocations to be made to local authorities for subsidised house building. No publicity should, however, be given to this figure; for any public announcement of so low a target would be regarded by local authorities as incompatible with the Government's intention to resume the campaign for slum clearance. Moreover, he would certainly have to make some concessions to meet representations from particular local authorities.

The Prime Minister said that he was glad that the Minister of Health had drawn the Cabinet's attention, in C(54)348, to the need for further capital expenditure on hospitals. He had been impressed by the extent to which this country was falling behind others in the provision of up-to-date hospitals, and by the urgent need to improve the hospital services in London and elsewhere. He considered that a great campaign should be undertaken to improve this part of our social services as soon as the Government's programme for pensions was completed.

The Cabinet –
Endorsed the proposals of the Chancellor of the Exchequer in C(54)348 for reducing the scale of future Government expenditure on housing.

Sir Winston S. Churchill: speech
('Winston S. Churchill, His Complete Speeches', volume 8, pages 8687–9)

30 November 1954   Westminster Hall

EIGHTIETH BIRTHDAY

This is to me the most memorable public occasion of my life. No one has ever received a similar mark of honour before. There has not been anything like it in British history, and indeed I doubt whether any of the modern democracies has shown such a degree of kindness and generosity to a party politician who has not yet retired and may at any time be involved in controversy. It is indeed the most striking example I have ever known of that characteristic British Parliamentary principle cherished in both Lords and Commons 'Don't bring politics into private life'. It is certainly a mark of the underlying unity of our national life which survives and even grows in spite of vehement party warfare and many grave differences of conviction and sentiment. This unity is, I believe, the child of freedom and fair play fostered in the cradle of our ancient island institutions, and nursed by tradition and custom.

I am most grateful to Mr Attlee for the agreeable words he has used about me this morning, and for the magnanimous appraisal he has given of my variegated career. I must confess, however, that this ceremony and all its charm and splendour may well be found to have seriously affected my controversial value as a party politician. However, perhaps with suitable assistance I shall get over this reaction and come round after a bit.

The Leader of the Opposition and I have been the only two Prime Ministers of this country in the last fourteen years. There are no other Prime Ministers alive. Mr Attlee was also Deputy Prime Minister with me in those decisive years of war. During our alternating tenure, tremendous events have happened abroad, and far-reaching changes have taken place at home. There have been three general elections on universal suffrage and the activity of our Parliamentary and party machinery has been absolutely free. Mr Attlee's and my monopoly of the most powerful and disputatious office under the Crown all this time is surely the fact which the world outside may recognize as a symbol of the inherent stability of our British way of life. It is not, however, intended to make it a permanent feature of the Constitution.

I am sure this is the finest greeting any Member of the House of Commons has yet received and I express my heartfelt thanks to the representatives of both Houses for the gifts which you have bestowed in their name. The portrait[1] is a remarkable example of modern art. It certainly combines force and candour. These are qualities which no active Member of either House can do without or should fear to meet. The book with which the Father of the House of Commons (Mr David Grenfell)[2] has presented me is a token of the goodwill and chivalrous regard of members of all parties. I have lived my life in the House of Commons, having served there for fifty-two of the fifty-four years of this tumultuous and convulsive century. I have indeed seen all the ups and downs of fate and fortune, but I have never ceased to love and honour the Mother of Parliaments, the model to the legislative assemblies of so many lands.

The care and thought which has been devoted to this beautiful volume and the fact that it bears the signatures of nearly all my fellow members deeply touches my heart. And may I say that I thoroughly understand the position of those who have felt it their duty to abstain. The value of such a tribute is that it should be free and spontaneous. I shall treasure it as long as I live and my family and descendants will regard it as a most precious possession. When I read the eulogy so gracefully and artistically inscribed on the title page, with its famous quotation from John Bunyan, I must confess to you that I was overpowered by two emotions – pride and humility. I have always hitherto regarded them as opposed and also corrective of one another; but on this occasion I am not able to tell you which is dominant in my mind. Indeed both seem to dwell together hand in hand. Who would not feel proud to have this happen to him and yet at the same time I never was more sure of how far it goes beyond what I deserve.

I was very glad that Mr Attlee described my speeches in the war as expressing the will not only of Parliament but of the whole nation. Their will was resolute and remorseless and, as it proved, unconquerable. It fell to me to express it, and if I found the right words you must remember that I have always earned my living by my pen and by my tongue. It was a nation and race dwelling all round the globe that had the lion heart. I had the luck to be called upon to give the roar. I also hope that I sometimes suggested to the lion the right places to use his claws. I am now nearing the end of my journey. I

---

[1] The portrait, by Graham Sutherland, caused Churchill great distress. 'It makes me look half-witted, which I ain't,' he told Clementine. Sympathetically, she promised him that it would never see the light of day. Around 1955–6, she removed it from storage at Chartwell and on her instructions her secretary Grace Hamblin and her brother burned it. See Lady Soames: recollection, reproduced below (pp. 1914–15).

[2] David Rhys Grenfell, 1881–1968. A coal miner (underground) from age 12 to age 35, Miners' agent, 1916. MP (Lab.) for Gower, 1922–59. Member, Forestry Commission, 1929–42. CBE, 1935. Secretary for Mines, 1940–2. Chairman, Welsh Tourist Board, 1948. PC, 1951. 'Father of the House', 1953–9 (Churchill had first been elected 22 years earlier, in 1900, but had been out of the Commons 1922–4).

hope I still have some services to render. However that may be and whatever may befall I am sure I shall never forget the emotions of this day or be able to express my gratitude to those colleagues and companions with whom I have lived my life for this superb honour they have done me.

President Dwight D. Eisenhower to Sir Winston S. Churchill
(*Premier papers, 11/1074*)

30 November 1954

You will be deluged, I know, with messages of felicitation on your eightieth birthday from all over the world. I have myself sent one through our State Department,[1] but I want to add to that deeply felt but somewhat official note, a sense of my appreciation of the privilege that has been mine to call you friend – in the truest sense of the word – for these many years. Mamie and I join in warmest affection and admiration for you.[2]

Sir Winston S. Churchill to Dorothy Richardson[3]
(*Churchill papers, 2/423*)

[30] November 1954

Dear Miss Richardson,

I received with great pleasure the beautiful silver blotter from the Tenants of all the Churchill Houses,[4] and I should like, through you, to express my very warm thanks for this most useful and acceptable gift. It will be constantly on my desk, and will be a reminder to me of the goodwill so kindly expressed in the message of greetings inscribed on it. Pray convey to all those concerned my appreciation of their thought of me.

---

[1] Letter of Nov. 28, reproduced above (p. 1824).

[2] Churchill responded on Dec. 1: 'I am most grateful for your personal message. I am writing when I can get my head above water.'

[3] Dorothy Emily Richardson. Secretary, Church Army Housing Association. One of the organizers of the Churchill Houses. MBE, 1963.

[4] See letter from Lady Churchill, reproduced above (p. 1820).

December 1954

House of Commons: Debate
(Hansard)

1 December 1954   House of Commons

DEBATE ON THE ADDRESS

Mr E. Shinwell (Easington): Although, Mr Speaker, you have indicated that the subject of defence may be debated in the course of the day, it is not my intention to deal in detail with that subject. It seems to me, however, that there is an unfortunate omission in the Gracious Speech. No reference is made to a possible reduction in defence expenditure although upon more than one occasion we have been promised a review of our military organisation, and suggestions have been made that that review would inevitably effect a substantial reduction in costs.

The Gracious Speech does contain a reference to the creation of a strategic reserve, but that appears to me to be somewhat strange, because, as we know, there has been a sharp decline in Regular recruitment. So far, the Government have not indicated their readiness to agree to the Opposition's proposal, made on more than one occasion, for an inquiry into the operation of the National Service Acts. No reference is made in the Gracious Speech to the Government's intentions about the Army Act, a subject which created considerable controversy in the House some time ago.

I wish to direct the attention of hon. Members to two items of major importance. One is a speech delivered by the right hon. Gentleman the Prime Minister in his constituency of Woodford on 23rd November.[1] The other is the speech delivered by the Foreign Secretary yesterday, in which he made some observations about confidence in the Government's economic and social policy. As I listened to him, I thought that the Foreign Secretary's incursion into the domestic sphere was somewhat unfortunate. I shall say something more about that before I sit down.

---

[1] Reproduced above (pp. 1818–19).

The speech delivered by the Prime Minister on 23rd November overshadows much that appears in the Gracious Speech. It is relevant to some items in the Speech; for example, there is a reference to the need for promoting peace with our neighbours, none of the neighbours being excepted. That, I take it, is the desire of every hon. Member of the House. Subject to any explanation which the right hon. Gentleman may offer in elucidation, or any attempt to illuminate and enlighten our minds as to his intentions in making that speech, and also upon the content of the signal alleged to have been sent to Field Marshal Montgomery towards the end of the last war, I would say that – putting it very mildly and without using strong language, however much one might be tempted – it was a most unfortunate and inopportune prelude to a four-Power conference.

The speech undoubtedly sharpened public interest; of that there can be no doubt. There has been considerable excitement, confusion and bewilderment in the public mind, and there are doubts whether the right hon. Gentleman actually intended to say what he did. However, we shall see. I am sorry to engage in controversy with the right hon. Gentleman immediately after his birthday celebrations.

The Prime Minister (Sir Winston Churchill): Quite right.

Mr Shinwell: The right hon. Gentleman forgives me. I am grateful to him.

The Prime Minister: Do your duty.

Mr Shinwell: The right hon. Gentleman has advised me to do my duty. That I shall do faithfully – by the right hon. Gentleman and by the British public.

Let us, first, get the facts right. That is very important. What was the statement which the right hon. Gentleman made, as reported in – and here I mention the newspaper – *The Times*, a reputable organ which usually supports the Government? The statement was that he had instructed Field Marshal Montgomery – I doubt whether he was a Field Marshal at the time, but there is no doubt who is meant – to collect and stack surrendered German arms so that they could easily be issued again to the German soldiers with whom we should have to work if the Soviet advance continued. (hon. Members: 'Hear, hear'.) I take note of the approval given to the Prime Minister's comments. I hope that hon. Members opposite will appreciate the implications of that approval.

The whole point is whether he sent such an order, if so, exactly what it contained, and whether, in fact – and this is perhaps more pointed – he contemplated rearming German troops in order to fight the Russians in certain eventualities. That is a fair question on the basis of the right hon. Gentleman's speech. An hon. Member on this side of the House, I think my hon. Friend the Member for Nelson and Colne (Mr S. Silverman) – he is still my hon. Friend, and we can handle these matters without any help from the other side of the House – did venture to address a Question to the Prime Minister on this subject.

The Prime Minister directed my hon. Friend's attention, in turn, to the last volume of his war memoirs, in which certain signals were published, which the Prime Minister, as I understand him, alleged were in complete agreement with the signal he was alleged to have sent to Field Marshal Montgomery. Now it so happened, quite fortuitously, that I was familiar with that volume. It so happened that, after its publication or immediately before actual publication, I was asked to review it for the *Daily Herald*, so I was more or less familiar with the telegrams and to my surprise, in view of what the right hon. Gentleman said in his speech, I could not recall any telegram giving specific instructions to Field-Marshal Montgomery or General Eisenhower or anybody else in control of the Allied Forces to that effect – none whatever.

If we are to get the facts right, there is no better testament than the right hon. Gentleman's own words, and for the purpose of our argument we had better accept that they are in the book. Let us, therefore, stand by the book. On 12th May, 1945, the Prime Minister sent the following message to President Truman:

> I am profoundly concerned about the European situation. I learn that half the American Air Force in Europe has already begun to move to the Pacific theatre. The newspapers are full of the great movements of the American armies out of Europe. Our armies also are, under previous arrangements, likely to undergo a marked reduction. The Canadian Army will certainly leave. The French are weak and difficult to deal with. Anyone can see that in a very short space of time our armed power on the Continent will have vanished, except for moderate forces to hold down Germany.

That message, and similar messages to General Eisenhower and the then Foreign Secretary, were obviously in line with the right hon. Gentleman's apprehensions of a Russian advance. Towards the end of the war, the Russians had taken advantage of the situation in the Balkan countries – Roumania, Bulgaria and Hungary – to inspire Communist uprisings. Moreover, it was apprehended, as, indeed, many of us knew at the time, and it was even better known to those in the Government, that the Russians did contemplate an advance to the north towards the Scandinavian theatre.

When discussing the merits or demerits the possibility of a sharp and substantial advance by the Soviet forces naturally created alarms and apprehensions in the mind of the Government and in the minds of the Western allies, because they did know what the Russians were likely to be up to. The Prime Minister, being so apprehensive in the message to which I have just referred, added this:

> Surely, it is vital now to come to an understanding with Russia, or see where we are with her, before we weaken our armies mortally or retire to the zones of occupation. This can only be done by a personal meeting. I should be most grateful for your opinion and advice. Of course, we may take the

view that Russia will behave impeccably, and no doubt that offers the most convenient solution. To sum up this issue of a settlement with Russia before our strength has gone seems to me to dwarf all others.

No one can take exception to those words. It was quite proper that we should try to reach an understanding with our allies. That is something quite different, however, from sending a message to Field Marshal Montgomery in which he was instructed to stack and collect surrendered German arms in order to contest the issue with Russia in certain eventualities, and, by so doing, continue the war.

The Prime Minister: Of course, if they went on.

Hon. Members: With German troops?

Mr Shinwell: All I say at the moment is that there is something quite different – (Hon. Members: 'No'.) If hon. Members do not appreciate the distinction between seeking an understanding with our former ally through a conference, and issuing instructions, almost at the same time, as I shall show, to Field Marshal Montgomery to prepare to use German Nazis, indoctrinated Nazis and unscreened Nazis, in order to fight a former ally – if they do not appreciate the distinction there, then there is something wrong either with their judgment or their intelligence, or both.

The Prime Minister sent that signal three days before, on 9th May, to General Eisenhower, and, by the way, it occurs to me that if any instructions of this sort should have been sent, and even if it was desirable to send such instructions at all, they should have been sent to General Eisenhower and not to Field Marshal Montgomery, because General Eisenhower was in control of the allied forces and not Field Marshal Montgomery.

What was the message to General Eisenhower? It was as follows:

> I have heard (said the Prime Minister) with some concern that the Germans are to destroy all their aircraft *in situ*. I hope that this policy will not be adopted in regard to weapons and other forms of equipment. We may have great need of these some day, and even now they might be of use, both to France and especially in Italy. I think we ought to keep everything worth keeping. The heavy cannon I preserved from the last war fired constantly from the heights of Dover in this war.
>
> There is great joy here.

That last remark referred to the fact that the Germans had surrendered.

It is, of course, perfectly true that many weapons and much equipment salvaged from the First World War – surrendered by the Germans or captured from them – were used in the Second World War because we were not well enough prepared. (Hon. Members: 'Hear, hear'.) Hon. Members opposite ought to be careful, because they gave precious little support to the right hon. Gentleman when he made speeches from below the Gangway. (Hon.

Members: 'Neither did you'.) Hon. Members opposite say that neither did we. But one expects it from the supporters of the right hon. Gentleman – from the same party – even if one does not expect it from the official Opposition. The less said by hon. Members opposite about their conduct in that matter, the better.

The following day the right hon. Gentleman sent a further message in which he said: 'If the Germans are destroying equipment it is in violation of the act of surrender and I shall be glad to have any particulars which will enable me to punish the offenders.' Then he sent a message to the Foreign Secretary, who was in San Francisco. All these messages were sent about the same time. In it, he said: 'Today there are announcements in the newspapers of the large withdrawals of American troops now to begin month by month. What are we to do?' Please note the interrogation. 'Great pressure will soon be put on us (at home) to demobilise partially. In a very short time our armies will have melted, but the Russians may remain with hundreds of divisions in possession of Europe from Lübeck to Trieste, and to the Greek frontier on the Adriatic,' and so on.

These were the messages sent to the appropriate authorities, to President Truman, the right hon. Gentleman's opposite number, to General Eisenhower who was in control of the allied forces, and to the Foreign Secretary. All very good. At the same time – I now revert to the right hon. Gentleman's speech at Woodford – the right hon. Gentleman apparently sent a signal to Field Marshal Montgomery which does not appear in the book. Why this omission from these memoirs? Why, at this late stage – nine years after – is that signal disclosed? What was the purpose of the disclosure – that remarkable revelation? What was the intention? Was the intention to seek an understanding with the Russians? Was this the overture or part of the symphony? The right hon. Gentleman, no doubt, will give us his version of the matter.

I wish to say to the right hon. Gentleman positively – if he will give me his attention, because it concerns him personally – that neither in the message to Truman nor to Eisenhower is there the slightest indication of the intention to use these weapons for rearming the surrendered Germans, and it is to that point that the right hon. Gentleman must reply. Indeed, I cannot find in the book any reference to the rearming of the surrendered Germans.

What was Field Marshal Montgomery's comment when he was asked about the Woodford speech? I have searched both the American Press and the British Press, and all I can find is that Field Marshal Montgomery said that he had received the telegram, but that he was not going to say anything about what happened – a remarkable exhibition of reticence upon his part. I know him well; I have had experience of him, and I have a very great regard for him, as everybody knows.

In view of Field Marshal Montgomery's remarkable reticence, I put these questions to the Prime Minister. I hope that he will take notice of them, because

I expect him to reply to them. Did he actually suggest to the Field Marshal that it might be necessary to rearm the German troops and to work with them against the Russians? Did he, before taking this remarkable step, consult Truman or Eisenhower, or, for that matter, any of his Cabinet colleagues? If not, why not? Why did he not refer to this suggestion in his message to Eisenhower on 9th May? Or has something been excised from the published text of that message which is contained in the book?

There is a further question. Was anything more heard of the suggestion when the right hon. Gentleman made it nine years ago? Was it made in a signal and then, having been made, abandoned – nothing more being heard about it until the Prime Minister appeared in Woodford and was inspired to make this remarkable disclosure?

I feel that in the interest of the House as a whole – indeed, in the interest of the Government – and in the interest of the promotion of world peace and of a better understanding with Soviet Russia, which, I understand, is the desire of the right hon. Gentleman, and in the interest of a satisfactory conclusion of a four-Power pact – as everybody appreciates, we are entering on a very difficult phase – we are entitled to have the actual text of the message to Field Marshal Montgomery, and also his answer to it. I think that we are also entitled to a full explanation of why the right hon. Gentleman took this remarkable step in this extraordinary way.

I hope that hon. Members will not be violent with me when I make the observation that perhaps no such message was ever sent.

The Prime Minister indicated assent.

Mr Shinwell: The Prime Minister nods. We shall soon find out, because, after all, the Prime Minister must have the signal, either in the archives of the Foreign Office or in the files of the War Cabinet. It must be somewhere. Even though the right hon. Gentleman brought it out of his head just like that, it must be based on something substantial, on something that happened, if, indeed, it did happen.

On the other hand, the Prime Minister's memory may have been confused. After all, the speech was made nine years after the event. He may have confused the message with some ideas on the subject, and may have thought that he had actually sent such a message. You know the sort of thing that happens, Mr Speaker. The right hon. Gentleman pays a visit to his constituency on the eve of his birthday celebrations. There is a jollification and a warm welcome – that is natural – and he is with people who do not like the Russians.

He does not like the Russians very much himself. He did not like them very much in 1918, and he does not care very much for them now. Therefore, he thought to himself, 'I will say something about these Russians which will surprise you.' So he did. He surprised us very much, and also alarmed us. That may have happened, and, as I say, the right hon. Gentleman may have got the messages all mixed up.

Finally, may I put this question to the right hon. Gentleman? Whether there was such a message or not, and even if he had got the messages mixed up, as *The Times* put it, what made him say it?

Did he intend to continue the war? Imagine the effect on the troops, on the gallant remnants of the Desert Rats who were fighting in Normandy at the end of the war, if they had been asked, having destroyed Rommel and his forces, to be associated with the Nazi German troops against our former allies.

Moreover, did the right hon. Gentleman consider the possible reaction on our own people? I can remember what happened during the war: the vast assemblies throughout the country praising our gallant Russian allies, the vast sums of money raised, and hon. Members on the other side of the House helping all they could to glorify Russia. Indeed, it is very doubtful whether we could have gained the victory without the help of our Russian allies.

Mr Rupert Speir[1] (Hexham) *rose* —

Mr Shinwell: Something remarkable has happened. One would have expected a sharp response to the speech of the right hon. Gentleman from official Soviet sources. It is true that something was said in *Pravda* about 'betrayal' as the result of this revelation, but there has been no official comment, so far as I can see. I wondered about that.

I venture to ask this question — I do not know what the answer is but I ask the question, nevertheless: could the Russians have known what the right hon. Gentleman was thinking about at the time, and what he was up to? They might have known, and if they knew that we were prepared to associate with the Nazi forces at that time and to avail ourselves of their support, the knowledge might have coloured their policy and outlook ever since.

Let us not forget that suspicion breeds suspicion and does not help to promote harmony in foreign relations. I must ask the Prime Minister to clear the matter up. Let him produce the telegram, if there is such a telegram. We are entitled to have it. If there is no such telegram, let him be quite frank and forthright with the House and say, 'There was no such thing', and that this was a mistake on his part because he was confused about the matter. That is quite acceptable, and we can let it go at that.

I must say to the Prime Minister, rather more in sorrow than in anger, that in view of this disclosure and if there is any substance in what he said, I doubt very much whether he is the right person to engage in negotiation with Soviet Russia. If I had to engage for business purposes somebody who I knew was working against me I should be very careful. Anyway, we shall see.

No doubt the right hon. Gentleman will illuminate our minds on the subject. Let us get the full facts from him. Nothing less will suffice. In this field of foreign relations the right hon. Gentleman, like Caesar's wife, must be above suspicion. (*Interruption.*) I assure hon. Members that any inference

---

[1] Rupert Malise Speir, 1910–98. MP (Cons.) for Hexham, 1951–66.

that I am suspecting the right hon. Gentleman of feminine qualities is quite wrong.

The Prime Minister: It was Caesar's wife, not Caesar.

Mr Shinwell: That is what I said. I do not require the right hon. Gentleman to correct me. I am familiar with Shakespeare's work; I learned it when I was in prison. Unless the Prime Minister can illuminate our minds on the subject I have dealt with, I am afraid that people abroad as well as at home will hardly feel that the right hon. Gentleman has done the right thing in making that speech.

I do not wish to detain the House for more than a few moments longer. (Hon. Members: 'Hear, hear'.) There is nothing to prevent hon. Members from leaving the Chamber if they wish. They have my permission. If I am disturbing them, I am sorry. I am entitled to put these questions to the Prime Minister.

I want to make a reference to the Foreign Secretary's speech yesterday and I will come to the point quickly, for the sake of brevity. He said that the present Government had undertaken salvage operations. The characteristic amiability of the right hon. Gentleman appears to have been somewhat marred by an unfortunate omission; he forgot about the salvage operations that we had to undertake in 1945, at the end of a devastating and costly war.

Consider the difficulty then. Practically all our resources had vanished. Many other difficulties presented themselves to the Labour Government at that time, and hon. Gentlemen opposite are well aware of them. If they are not they are more ignorant than I thought. The Foreign Secretary indulged in some boasting about the improved conditions of the people, but he ought not to have forgotten that many of the social Measures now acceptable in all quarters of the House were vigorously opposed by hon. Members opposite.

There is something more. The Chancellor of the Exchequer is not present, but I venture to put this point in his absence. He made a statement the other day in reply to a Question in the House. I am amused by the Chancellor of the Exchequer. He is always patting himself on the back, a kind of exercise that no doubt contributes to his excellent physical condition. On that occasion he told the country that there were 18 million people in this country whose wages and salaries were below £500 a year, and that of the 18 million 8 million actually had wages of less than £250 a year. What is the use of talking about confidence, social stability, security, of having solved problems or made a substantial contribution to social requirements, if we have 18 million people who have to live on wages and salaries of that kind in face of the high and increased cost of living?

In spite of what the Minister of Pensions and National Insurance has said this afternoon we propose, in the course of this debate on the Address to challenge the whole range of Government policy. We propose to do more than that. We propose to challenge the Tory Party conception of the organisation of society – of its conception of the right social order. That is our intention – let it face that challenge.

The right hon. Gentleman is very anxious – I can see him straining at the leash –

The Prime Minister: No, no.

Mr Shinwell – to pounce upon me, so I await his reply – it may be his onslaught – without anxiety but with eager expectancy and with interest.

The Prime Minister (Sir Winston Churchill): I must say that, considering that the right hon. Gentleman the Member for Easington (Mr Shinwell) was making a partisan speech in a controversial debate, I think that he has shown a great consideration for fairness. There is a lot more of that in him than many people would think from watching his ordinary conduct of events. But let me deal with the matter which occupied the main part of his speech, and let me say what I have to say directly to the House.

When I spoke at Woodford, I was under the rooted impression that not only had I sent this telegram to Field Marshal Montgomery, but also that I had published it a year ago in the sixth volume of my account of the Second World War. In fact, the telegram was not published in the book. I am also sorry that, in my speech at Woodford, I failed to observe the rule which I have so often inculcated in others, 'Always verify your quotations.' Otherwise, I should certainly not have made this particular point, which was in no way necessary to my argument at this time. I must also admit the truth of what the *Manchester Guardian* said, to the effect that historical events are best treated in their context. I hope that I shall remember that next time. Therefore, I express my regrets to the House for what I said last week.

The right hon. Gentleman has asked for the text of the message. Indeed, I should be very glad to give that to the House – when I find it. It may well be that I never used these precise words in a telegram to a general – not a field marshal; I beg pardon for that – to General Montgomery as he was at that time. Indeed, it may be, as the right hon. Gentleman has several times suggested, that it was never sent at all. (Hon. Members: 'Oh'.) I do not want to argue all the way through. At any rate, it has not been traced in the official records, though a search of the utmost extent has been made, and is still continuing. I have asked Field Marshal Montgomery, and he replied that he would be back on the 4th of this month and would, at my request, look through any private records that he may have.

There are, as the right hon. Gentleman said, various explanations of this. I do not exclude one, which he himself suggested, that the message might have been mixed up. He said that I might have been confused in my mind. 'You know the sort of thing that happens' – those, I think, were his words.

We all make factual mistakes from, time to time, and the hon. Member below the Gangway who asked me a Written Question, hit the wrong general altogether.

Mr Sydney Silverman (Nelson and Colne) *rose* –

The Prime Minister: I beg his pardon, but I am only indicating that mortals are fallible.

Mr Silverman: Perhaps the right hon. Gentleman might like to know that, although I did inadvertently omit the name of Field Marshal Montgomery from my Question, it was not a matter of putting down the name of the wrong general but of putting down the name of only one general instead of both. What I had in mind was what my right hon. Friend had in mind; that such a message, if sent, would normally be expected to go to the Commander-in-Chief, who was General Eisenhower.

The Prime Minister: I am obliged to the hon. Gentleman. I only introduced the point to show how error is human.

Here are some other reasons, however. It may be that the telegram to General Eisenhower, which has been published in my book, superseded my original intention of sending such a message to General Montgomery. In any case, all was happily overtaken in a few days by events. An entirely new situation presented itself. The immediate emergency did not mature.

No Cabinet assent was sought for this particular telegram. It was only of a precautionary character, and, if it were sent at all, it went only as one of scores of similar messages which were passing at the time about the German surrender. Anyhow, if there is any question of responsibility, and if there is any telegram and any question of responsibility for it, I accept it for myself.

When I come to the facts of what I did in 1945, of what I intended to do – certainly, it was in my mind; I am not making any concealment of that – of the motives animating them, I have no misgivings. In those days of victory, the thought which filled my mind was that all the efforts we had made to free Europe from a totalitarian regime of one kind might go for naught if we allowed so much of Europe to fall into the grip of another totalitarian regime from the East.

This is the theme of the sixth volume of my book. This was the tragedy which came on us in our hour of triumph. The realisation of it filled many of the messages which I sent at that time. I sent a great many at different levels. I may easily have been in error as to any particular one. The attitude of our Russian allies at that time gave ample grounds for this fear. We had taken up the sword in 1939 on behalf of the independence of Poland. What was happening to Poland in 1945? What has happened to it since?

I also had at this time the gravest anxieties about the fate of Denmark. The time of this is about the first fortnight in May, 1945. If the Soviet forces had overrun Denmark, they would have controlled the Baltic, with all that that involves. In such circumstances, the same kind of situation would have arisen as that which, four years later, compelled the Western world to create NATO, to contemplate the EDC arrangements, and now to sign the London and Paris Agreements.

The situation which we faced in May, 1945, was grave and threatening. I can find no better words to describe it than those which I used in my telegram of 12th May to President Truman, the telegram which I have called the 'Iron Curtain telegram' and which the right hon. Gentleman has done me the honour to quote. I do not think I did anything inconsistent with that, and, as it states absolutely my line of thought, I would ask the indulgence of the House, as it has been quoted, while I read it. This is to President Truman:

> I am profoundly concerned about the European situation. I learn that half the American Air Force in Europe has already begun to move to the Pacific theatre. The newspapers are full of the great movement of the American armies out of Europe. Our armies also are, under previous arrangements, likely to undergo a marked reduction. The Canadian Army will certainly leave. The French are weak and difficult to deal with. Anyone can see that in a very short space of time our armed power on the Continent will have vanished, except for moderate forces to hold down Germany.
>
> 2. Meanwhile, what is to happen about Russia? I have always worked for friendship with Russia but, like you, I feel deep anxiety because of their misinterpretation of the Yalta decisions, their attitude towards Poland, their overwhelming influence in the Balkans excepting Greece, the difficulties they make about Vienna, the combination of Russian power and the territories under their control or occupied, coupled with the Communist technique in so many other countries, and above all their power to maintain very large armies in the field for a long time. What will be the position in a year or two, when the British and American Armies have melted and the French has not yet been formed on any major scale, when we may have a handful of divisions, mostly French, and when Russia may choose to keep two or three hundred on active service?
>
> 3. An iron curtain is drawn down upon their front. We do not know what is going on behind. There seems little doubt that the whole of the regions East of the line Lübeck–Trieste–Corfu –

right from the north to the Mediterranean –

> will soon be completely in their hands. To this must be added a further enormous area conquered by the American Armies between Eisenach and the Elbe, which will, I suppose, in a few weeks, be occupied, when the Americans retreat, by the Russian power. All kinds of arrangements will have to be made by General Eisenhower to prevent another immense flight of the German population westward as this enormous Muscovite advance into the centre of Europe takes place. And then the curtain will descend again to a very large extent, if not entirely. Thus a broad band of many hundreds of miles of Russian-occupied territory will isolate us from Poland.
>
> 4. Meanwhile, the attention of our peoples will be occupied in inflicting

severities upon Germany, which is ruined and prostrate, and it would be open to the Russians in a short time to advance if they chose to the waters of the North Sea and the Atlantic.

I will read this following passage again, although it was quoted just now by the right hon. Gentleman, because it governed my thoughts:

> Surely it is vital now to come to an understanding with Russia, or to see where we are with her, before we weaken our armies mortally or retire to the zones of occupation. This can only be done by a personal meeting. I should be most grateful for your opinion and advice. Of course, we may take the view that Russia will behave impeccably, and no doubt that offers the most convenient solution. To sum up, this issue of a settlement with Russia before our strength has gone seems to me to dwarf all others.

I must apologise for having to dwell so much on these quotations. Having done so, I may say that I shall be very glad to place sufficient numbers of copies of my sixth volume in the Reading Room of the House of Commons in case they may serve the convenience of hon. Members in verifying these facts.

Even if the telegram does not exist, in general spirit it is not contrary to my thoughts. In addition to what would inevitably have come to pass had the Soviets continued their advance into the Low Countries and towards the sea, there was another set of considerations to be borne in mind. As we had in General Montgomery's theatre alone more than a million disarmed German prisoners of war who had surrendered to us – to us, I say – I felt we were responsible for taking measures for their protection, and if we were unable to carry out our terms of capitulation or to afford them that protection for which we were responsible, it might become a matter of honour as well as of policy to give them back their arms.

No trouble could, in any case, have arisen with the Soviets unless they had continued their advance to a point at which they forced the breaking out of a new war between Russia and her Western allies. To prevent such a disaster, it might have been a help to warn them that we should certainly in that case rearm the German prisoners in our hands, who altogether, including those in Italy, numbered 2½ million. It was never necessary to tell them, because they did not do what I felt we had to consider. In this event, the modest precaution I had in mind of stacking the arms might have been found convenient. However, all those matters are far above the level on which this particular routine business like arrangement was suggested.

I may say that I did not judge the German army of that time, whatever may have been their political label, by that label. I think the majority were ordinary people compelled into military service and fighting desperately in defence of their native land. I also suggest to the House that in modern times war should not be decided on questions of nationality or of the past conduct of any nation, but only on the new guilt of aggression. I am sure that resistance to aggression must be our dominating thought. That was where I stood at the moment of victory in the first part of May, 1945, and that is where I believe a large majority of the House stands today.

I am not unduly disheartened by any Russian reaction to what I said last week. *Pravda*, like the *Daily Worker*, can always be turned on or off at will. In my recent thoughts I have always tried to measure what are the true Russian interests at this present time in history. There lies the key. Personally, I believe their interest is in peace and plenty. *The Times* newspaper, to which the right hon. Gentleman referred, in the very full report that it gave of my speech, omitted altogether in any of the editions I have seen the references I made to Soviet Russia which were intended to balance the other statements so fully printed. I suppose they were preoccupied with their leading article.

There is, however, a very good report in the *Manchester Guardian* which I hope the House will forgive me quoting – hon. Members have been very indulgent when I have been quoting so much of myself – because I should like to give publicity to it. This is what I said at Woodford on 23rd November. It ought to be read with what *The Times* has already quoted:

> But meanwhile another great event has happened. Stalin died, and new men sharing the power together are at the head of Russia. It was in May last year that I advocated that we, with our allies, should work towards closer contact with Russia in order to make sure whether that great people had undergone any important change of mood and outlook under their new leadership. This is still my purpose.

In fact, that is the only explanation of my presence here today. It is still my purpose.

> Our policy is peace through strength. Nothing could be more foolish than for us to begin these closer contacts with Soviet Russia by a break-up of the unity among themselves of the free nations. That was what threatened us all when the French Chamber refused to ratify the EDC agreements, which they had themselves devised and shaped, and on which so much precious time had been spent.
>
> The new arrangements which have been made as a result of Sir Anthony Eden's exertions are, I believe, in many ways an improvement on EDC, and when they have been ratified the path will be clear for those contacts with Soviet Russia from which I still hope and, indeed, increasingly hope a peaceful and easier and even more prosperous future for the whole world may spring and grow.

That is all I have to say on the personal point that has been raised. I hope that the House will remember that I have done what I have very rarely done, formally expressed my regret for an observation which I made, not on the spur of the moment, in a speech in the country. I am very sorry that I have had to take up so much of the time of the House on what is and has been largely a personal explanation.

The larger issues raised in the speech of the right hon. Gentleman the Member for Easington about defence will be answered with other questions by my right hon. Friend the Minister of Defence when he speaks later in the debate. I will content myself with a few general observations.

The advance of the hydrogen bomb has fundamentally altered the entire problem of defence, and considerations founded even upon the atom bomb have become obsolescent, almost old-fashioned.

Mr Emrys Hughes (South Ayrshire): The whole lot.

The Prime Minister: Immense changes are taking place in military facts and in military thoughts. We have for some time past adopted the principle that safety and even survival must be sought in deterrents rather than defence – deterrents – and this, I believe, is the policy which also guides the United States. This does not mean that such precautions as are possible should not be taken. It certainly does not justify any part of the British community in failing in its duty to render all help to these precautions and in reciprocating the measures for ambulance and salvage aids which are being taken by their neighbours.

It is evident that the world as a whole is faced with problems which affect the existence of the human race. While we are trying to solve these, we must not cast away the conventional weapons in which the Soviet Government have a vast superiority. If we were to do so, we should lay it open to the Soviets to subjugate the whole of free Europe and advance to the sea and ocean in a Communist wave without meeting any effective, organised resistance.

Although I have spoken of the overwhelming superiority – I was going to say that I do not think that this should be taken alone, because the mere fact that they are at a disadvantage in the nuclear would make it necessary for them to stake out claims in Western Europe with their great military forces, also so as to have hostages for any negotiations, and also to improve the sites from which they could discharge their missiles of a very dangerous character which they have.

Although I have spoken of the overwhelming superiority in conventional weapons of the Soviets, I would mention that I do not believe that a surprise attack with conventional weapons would be made upon the Western front. There would certainly be discernible movements of troops which would raise both the alert and the alarm, and this would certainly bring the use of nuclear weapons into discussion of a decisive character by the heads of all the great States that are involved.

If the Soviets, as the weaker nuclear Power, resolved to make, which I do not believe they would, a treacherous surprise attack, it is inconceivable, to my mind, that they would begin with ground forces on the Western front and so compromise the advantage of a surprise attack by nuclear weapons. On the other hand, their weakness in nuclear weapons would make it all the more important, as I have said, for them to secure large areas of territory in Western Europe. This question of the nuclear weapons, therefore, remains the supreme issue.

In this interim period, when everything is in a state of transition, it is not possible to present a complete design of defence, allied or national. Certain important practical modifications are being made in our military arrangements, especially in regard to the use of anti-aircraft artillery. My right hon. Friend the Minister of Defence will deal with this in his speech. The fact that they afford financial relief is not their purpose, but only an incidental effect – a welcome, but an incidental effect. I must advise the House to take their time before discussing in detail the whole of our system of defence. Full opportunities will, of course, be open when the Estimates are considered in the New Year, and I should hope myself to be able to make a far more clear and concrete statement of the position in February than would be possible now. My right hon. Friend proposes this evening, in the main, to confine himself to the actual practical measures, partial though they may be, which will shortly come into operation and which should be made known to the House.

I have one more point to make. I cannot help recalling that the late Government, several times, very courteously invited some of our leaders when we were in Opposition to meet them in confidential discussion and consultation. So far, nothing of this kind has taken place in this Parliament. I believe that there would be many advantages in such a conference which, after all, deals with matters that affect all parties equally.

The subjects would not all be suitable, or suitable in all respects, for public debate and discussion at the present time. But an interchange of knowledge and views between leading members of both parties would, I believe, be a real advantage. As there are, as I have said, powerful and recent precedents for it, I hope it may not pass unnoticed. It is for the right hon. Gentleman the Leader of the Opposition to consider this matter and let us know at his convenience whether he would like this course to be adopted. If so, we should be perfectly willing to make the necessary arrangements. I thank the House for the great indulgence with which it has listened to my statement.

December 1954

Sir Winston S. Churchill to President Theodor Heuss[1]
(Churchill papers, 2/422)

1 December 1954

Dear President Heuss,

I received today from the hand of Herr Blankenhorn a letter bearing your good wishes for my Birthday, for which I am sincerely obliged to you. It contained also an expression of sentiments at once so friendly and so flattering that I could not fail to be moved by them and by the trouble which you have taken to express them so agreeably.

My feelings towards the great Nation at whose head you stand have always been admiring and, when circumstances did not dictate the contrary, friendly. I am certainly glad that I have lived to see the genius and high qualities of the German people turn once again to the exercise of their traditional skill in the arts of peace and that Germany has once again taken her place among the free Nations of Europe.

Sir Winston S. Churchill to Konrad Adenauer
(Churchill papers, 6/6)

1 December 1954

My dear Dr Adenauer,

I am delighted with the magnificent Birthday present which, in your generosity, you have given me and which Herr Blankenhorn so kindly brought here this afternoon. It is a striking example of modern German craftsmanship and one of which I am proud to be the possessor. Please accept my most sincere and heartfelt thanks.

The letter which accompanied your gift has moved me profoundly. As I hope you know, I am high on the list of your admirers as a statesman and as a patriot. It is therefore pleasant indeed to read such words from your pen and to be told by you that the German people hold me high in their esteem. For my part I trust that I shall live long enough to see Germany not only confirmed as the peaceful and stabilising influence in Europe, to which it is her true mission to be, but also, under your wise guidance, established at home in justice, prosperity and contentment.

Secret
PS. I did not send my congratulations on your Electoral victory, because I always try to keep out of other people's politics.

[1] Theodor Heuss, 1884–1963. Born in Brackenheim, Germany. Educated at Universities of Berlin and Munich. Married, 1908, Elly Heuss-Knapp: one child. Chairman, Democratic People's Party of Germany, American Zone, 1946–7. Founder, Democratic Party in Germany, 1947. Chairman, Free Democratic Party, 1948. President, Federal Republic of Germany, 1949–59.

December 1954   1845

Sir Winston S. Churchill to Lord Birkenhead[1]
(Churchill papers, 6/6)

2 December 1954

My dear Freddy,

I am sorry that you feel you have no alternative but to resign. I had hoped that you might perhaps be willing to remain in your present Office, with the administrative improvements which I have caused to be made. However, I see that your mind is made up and I therefore feel bound to accept your resignation. I thank you for the services which you have rendered to us over so many years and for the way in which you have presented important aspects of the Government's case in the House of Lords.

Sir Winston S. Churchill to Jacques Pol Roger[2]
(Churchill papers, 6/6)

2 December 1954

My dear Monsieur Pol-Roger,

I am much distressed that I was not aware of your presence in England at the time of my party on December 1. It would have given me great pleasure to receive you. I tried tonight to repair the error by intercepting you at the theatre but alas, I was not successful.

Sir Winston S. Churchill to Queen Elizabeth II
(Churchill papers, 2/475)[3]

3 December 1954

Madam,

I am deeply grateful for Your Majesty's gracious gift to me on my birthday wh is a source of intense pleasure and pride to me and my wife. We have already taken these beautiful coasters into daily use and they are greatly admired by all who have seen them. I was much honoured by the presence of so many members of Your Majesty's family and am writing to thank them for their participation and for their initials.

I am also much obliged to Your Majesty for letting me have the vacant

---

[1] Frederick Winston Furneaux Smith, 1907–75. Churchill's godson. Only son of 1st Earl of Birkenhead; succeeded as Earl, 1930. Joined 53rd Anti-Tank Rgt, 1938. Capt., 1940. Maj., 1942. Political Intelligence Dept, FO, 1942. British Military Mission to Yugoslav Partisans, 1944–5. Lord-in-Waiting to the Queen, 1952–5. Biographer of, among others, his father (1933), of Lord Halifax (1965) and of Churchill (completed by his son, the 3rd Earl).
[2] Jacques Pol Roger, 1905–64. Married, 1933, Odette Wallace.
[3] This letter was handwritten.

subscription to Aureole. I shall buy the most suitable mare I can find in the December sales and hope for the future.

Madam I am still overcome by the kindness – far beyond my deserts – wh I have received from the highest and the humblest in the land. From the latest accounts it looks as if this mood might soon change in certain quarters: but I have confidence that I shall enjoy Your Majesty's favour as long as I live. At least that is my cherished hope.

And with my humble duty,
I remain
Your Majesty's faithful and devoted servant

Sir Winston S. Churchill to Moshe Sharett
(Churchill papers, 6/6)

4 December 1954

I am deeply touched by the kind message of good wishes which you sent me for my birthday.[1] I am happy to be assured that I have the esteem of the people of Israel, whose courageous struggle for their national home I have watched with sympathy and admiration over so many years. What you say in your message has therefore given me very great pleasure.

Sir Winston S. Churchill to General Sir Bernard Paget[2]
(Churchill papers, 6/6)

4 December 1954

My dear General Paget,

Thank you for your invitation to the inspection of the In-Pensioners on May 28. I value the compliment you have paid me but think that I must decline since I try to spend the weekends away from London.

I am glad to hear that a decision has been reached to rebuild the Infirmary in the grounds of the Royal Hospital and that a start is being made in planning this work.

---

[1] Reproduced above (p. 1821).

[2] Bernard Charles Tolver Paget, 1887–1961. Entered Army, 1907. On active service, 1914–18 (wounded twice, despatches four times, DSO, MC). Maj.-Gen., 1937. As Cdr, 18th Div., in Norway in 1940, extracted two brigades from the Dombaas–Aandalsnes area during a seven-day action that won specific praise from Churchill in the House of Commons. CB, 1940. CGS, Home Forces, 1940–1. C-in-C, South-Eastern Command, 1941. C-in-C, Home Forces, 1941–3. Knighted, 1942. Gen., 1943. C-in-C, 21st Army Group, 1943. C-in-C, Middle East Force, 1944–5. Governor, Royal Hospital Chelsea, 1949–56.

Sir Winston S. Churchill to Sir William Rootes
(Churchill papers, 6/6)

4 December 1954

My dear Sir William,

How very kind of you and your colleagues to offer me one of your new Humber Estate cars as a birthday present. I am most touched by your thought and look forward to receiving it. I know it will be very useful to me at Chartwell.[1]

Sir Winston S. Churchill to William Morrison
(Churchill papers, 6/6)

6 December 1954

My dear Mr Speaker,

I am much complimented by your proposal to give a dinner party in my honour at which members of the war-time Coalition Government who are still Members of the House of Commons would be present. I understand that Wednesday, December 15, would be a suitable date from your point of view and it would certainly be very agreeable for me.

I am most grateful to you.

Sir Winston S. Churchill to President Dwight D. Eisenhower
(Premier papers, 11/1074)

7 December 1954
Top Secret, Personal and Private

My dear Friend,

I am so sorry that the pressure upon me of events both large and small has been so unceasing that I have not replied other than by telegrams to your last three most kind letters,[2] including the two about my birthday. I am so grateful to you for all that you wrote. Our comradeship and friendship were forged under hard conditions, and stood the test of war and aftermath. They always remain for me a possession of inestimable value. Thank you so much.

About the present and future. I think our two countries are working together even more closely than I can ever remember. They certainly need to do so. I greatly admired your speech on Thursday last about China in the teeth of

---

[1] The car was a 1956 Humber Hawk Mark VIA estate, which Churchill owned until around 1960. The Hawk was often sent to join Churchill on his holidays in the South of France, where it was used to transport his painting paraphernalia.

[2] Of Oct. 1, Nov. 28 and Nov. 30, reproduced above (pp. 1789, 1824 and 1828).

the brutal maltreatment of your airmen.[1] In my view China is not important enough to be a cause of major hazards. Many people over here exaggerate the power and importance of China as a military factor, and talk about six hundred million Chinese who, we are told, have all become Communists.

I am old-fashioned enough to look to steel as a rather decisive index of conventional military power, and of manufacturing and communication capacity. Crude steel output in 1953 of the non-Soviet world was 182.2 million tons, and that of the total Soviet bloc 51.7 million tons. Of this China contributed 1.7 million tons. I have had a number of other principal metals examined from this viewpoint and enclosed a list, (A).[2]

These figures seem to me to deserve taking into account when thinking about the power to conduct modern war of the six hundred million Chinese now said to exist. It may be a different picture in a decade. When I was young I used to hear much talk about 'The Yellow Peril'.

I am thinking of course only on a 'conventional' basis. But you have no reason to be worried about the nuclear balance. It is Soviet Russia that ought to dominate our minds. That is one of the reasons for my pleasure at your speech and the profound sense of proportion which it revealed.

I still hope we may reach a top level meeting with the new regime in Russia and that you and I may both be present. We can only contemplate this on the basis of the London Agreement and a united NATO. In spite of the tyrannical weakness of the French Chamber I still hope for ratification by all Powers in the first few months of the New Year. It is in the hope of helping forward such a meeting that I am remaining in harness longer than I wished or planned. I hope you will continue to look to it as a goal in seeking which we could not lose anything and might gain an easier and safer co-existence – which is a lot. When I had my last Audience with The Queen she spoke of the pleasure with which she would welcome a State visit by you to London. This might be combined in any way convenient with a top level meeting. Anyhow, please keep it high in your mind among your many cares and hopes.

Best wishes to Mrs Eisenhower.

Manganese Ore	–	China 82,000 tons
		Non-Soviet World 5,772,000 tons
Chrome Ore	–	China Nil
		Non-Soviet World 3,036,000 tons
Tungsten concentrates	–	China 21,000 tons
		Non-Soviet World 48,393 tons (This seems to be their only strong point)

---

[1] At a press conference on Dec. 2, Eisenhower had condemned China for continuing to imprison as spies 13 American airmen captured during the Korean War.
[2] Reproduced at the end of this letter.

Nickel	–	China Nil
		Non-Soviet World 160,697 tons
Aluminium	–	China 5,000 tons
(Primary)		Non-Soviet World 2,183,000 tons
Copper	–	China 7,000 tons
(Blister)		Non-Soviet World 2,552,000 tons

Sir Winston S. Churchill to Lord Quickswood
(*Churchill papers, 2/196*)

8 December 1954

My dear Linky,

Thank you so much for your charming letter which I greatly value. I wish indeed you could have been in Westminster Hall but you were absolutely right to husband your strength. I have had a very hard time this last three weeks. Kindness can be as exacting as nagging and I have had both harmony and discord rolling over each other inside my octogenarian nut. My prevailing mood is to have received kindness utterly beyond my deserts.

I am certainly not going to give all my money to charitable objects. The greater part of it has been sent by those who have expressed their wish that it should be for me to use personally. There is quite enough for both.

In November 1955 I shall begin publishing my *History of the English-Speaking Peoples*, a work I completed before the last War began. It will take four volumes. I lay one egg a year and will amuse myself with polishing and improving each in turn. It encourages me to see how good and tense your thought is although you are five years ahead of me, and I wonder whether it would amuse you to read the first volume which is practically in its final stage? I am therefore sending you down the first half-dozen chapters to read in your leisure. Please let me know whether you would like some more. The volume itself goes down to the Battle of Bosworth.

Sir Winston S. Churchill to Dr Anders Österling[1]
(*Churchill papers, 6/6*)

10 December 1954

Dear Doktor Österling,

It is my privilege, as a winner of the Nobel Prize for Literature, to recommend a candidate for next year's award. I should like to put before the Swedish

---

[1] Anders Österling, 1884–1981. Born in Helsingborg, Sweden. Educated at Lund University. Married, 1916, Greta Sjöberg: one child. Member, Nobel Committee, Swedish Academy, 1921–81. Permanent Secretary, Swedish Academy, 1941–64; Chairman, 1947–70.

Academy's Nobel Committee the name of Professor George Trevelyan,[1] OM, Master of Trinity College, Cambridge, who is certainly among the greatest living English historians. The Committee will be familiar with Professor Trevelyan's work which has ranged over many years, covering such varied fields as the Italian struggle for unity in the 19th Century, the War of the Spanish Succession and, in recent times, a most notable social history of England. Professor Trevelyan, connected both by blood and by literary tradition with Lord Macaulay, is a master of English prose whose writings will, in my opinion, attain an enduring fame not only in the Works of history but in the wider field of English literature.

Sir Winston S. Churchill to Members of the Cabinet
(Churchill papers, 2/217)

14 December 1954
Top Secret
Cabinet Paper No. 390 of 1954

NOTES ON TUBE ALLOYS, 1954

I circulate to my colleagues these few notes in case they may be a help to our representatives at the NATO Council. I should be glad to know the Cabinet's view upon them.

Part I

1. The only sane policy in the next few years is Defence through Deterrents. This we have already adopted and although we ourselves have no effective nuclear deterrents we are making progress. Meanwhile the United States has probably at least five times the nuclear power of Soviet Russia. Our moral and scientific support of the United States and presently British possession of nuclear weapons of the highest quality and on an appreciable scale, together with their means of delivery (though these are under serious reproach) should greatly reinforce the Deterrent power of the free world.

2. The danger of the next two or three years is that the United States, feeling itself being caught up by the Soviet Government, should make a forestalling nuclear attack on Russia, and might be provoked by some episode in China. We should assume that the United States would be restrained by their strong, moral and spiritual convictions from such an act. They might

---

[1] George Macaulay Trevelyan, 1876–1962. Educated at Harrow and Trinity College, Cambridge. Commandant, 1st British Ambulance Unit for Italy, 1915–18. Regius Prof. of Modern History, Cambridge University, 1927–40. OM, 1930. Master of Trinity College, Cambridge, 1940. Chancellor of Durham University, 1949–57. Author of *The Life of John Bright* (1913), *British History in the Nineteenth Century, 1782–1901* (1922), *England Under Queen Anne*, 3 vols (1930–4) and *English Social History, A Survey of Six Centuries, Chaucer to Queen Victoria* (1944).

even be prepared to make a Declaration, in which we should join, that they (and NATO) will never be the first to use nuclear weapons except in reply to a major act of aggression. That at any rate is the policy we should pursue and at the right moment proclaim.

3. A more grievous and less improbable peril is that Soviet Russia, fearing a nuclear attack before she has caught up the United States and created, either through equality or 'Saturation', deterrents of her own, should attempt to bridge the gulf by a surprise nuclear attack. American superiority in nuclear weapons, presently to be reinforced by the British, must be so organized as to make it clear that no surprise nuclear attack could prevent immediate retaliation on a far larger scale. This is an essential of the deterrent policy – our only hope.

4. For this purpose not only must the nuclear superiority of the NATO Powers be stimulated in every possible way but their means of delivery of bombs must be expanded, improved and varied. Smaller varieties should be designed capable of being carried by bombers from any large-scale airfield without the necessity of making the tell-tale prolongation of the take-off concrete track. Bases should be established in as many parts of the world as possible. Camouflage should be used to convey the impression of numbers as well as to disguise reality. It is probably, though we have not been told details, that a great deal of this has already been done by the United States. We should aid them in every possible way.

5. The Soviet Government should certainly be informed, though not in detail, of the policy that is being pursued and of our power to achieve it. Thus they should be convinced that a surprise attack could not exclude immediate retaliation. 'Although you might kill millions of our peoples and cause widespread havoc by a surprise attack, we certainly could within four hours of this outrage deliver five times the weight of nuclear material which you have used, and continue retaliation on that scale. We have already hundreds of bases for attack from all angles and have made an intricate study of suitable targets.' This would make the Deterrent effective except in the case of lunatics, or dictators or plotters in the kind of position of Hitler in his final phase.

6. The question of how and when this information should be imparted to the Soviets requires consideration. Perhaps they know already. Perhaps a talk, formal or informal, between some of our scientists, strictly limited as to detail, and some of theirs, might be a method. Such conversations might accompany a top level conference for peaceful co-existence, and for measures to sustain it.

7. It seems an unwise and useless procedure for NATO Governments to spread alarm through the free world without having definite practical measures in mind and in hand. Much has already become public, but the truth is happily mingled with fiction and exaggeration to so great an extent that panic has not occurred. The world goes on its daily journey in spite of a remote

doom-laden impression. It would be foolish to destroy this uncertainty by publishing precise facts and details which have not yet leaked without having some practical policy to declare at the same time.

8. I was informed by our nuclear experts early in August of the developments set forth in the Minister of Defence's paper of December 9. They are now embellished by the statements of the effects of 'fall out' and the intricate consequences of windborne radio-active matter on animals, on grass and vegetables, and the passing on of these contagions to human beings through food, thus confronting measureless numbers who have escaped all direct effects of the explosions with poisoning or starvation or both. Here again the only cure is successful Deterrents.

9. The broad effect of all the latest developments is to spread almost indefinitely and at least to a vast extent the area of mortal danger. This should certainly increase the deterrent upon Soviet Russia by putting her enormous spaces and scattered population on an equality or near-equality of vulnerability with our small densely-populated Island and with Western Europe. It is an ironic fact that we have reached a stage in this topic where safety may well be the child of terror, and existence the twin brother of annihilation. Here again all depends upon Deterrents, immune against surprise and well understood by all persons on both sides who have the power to control events.

Part II

1. It is on the foregoing general background that we should consider the practical problems of the Western front. The Soviets are between five and ten times as strong as the NATO forces. They could, if they so decided, advance across Germany and the Low Countries and through France to the sea and to the Atlantic. This would of course be a major war, with hundreds of thousands of allied troops killed or captured and all Western Europe north of the Pyrenees, with all its capitals, falling into Russian hands. No-one can believe that these events would occur, whether the Russians used nuclear weapons or not, without the whole nuclear power of the United States, and of Britain (when we have anything worth speaking of) being thrown in, with the consequent Soviet rejoinder. The reaction of this colossal and measureless event upon the Soviet military advance might be to bring it to a standstill in confusion. It is probable, however, that in the next two years the Soviet nuclear attack would be concentrated on Britain with measureless but certainly immense local destruction. That is at any rate a belief which the Russians would not be likely to discourage.

2. People say: 'What is the use of maintaining conventional forces at immense expense when the issue will only be settled in the atomic sphere'? This query overlooks the fact that unless NATO maintains a front which could only be broken by a major act of war, the Communist forces could peter forward gaining control of large indefinite areas and populations. There must

be a line drawn to break which will require a Russian military effort on a large scale. This will prevent the seepage above mentioned. It would also require discernible preliminary Soviet troop movements, which would give the immediate Alert, and this is of undoubted value to the stronger nuclear power. The conclusion which may be drawn here is that though our conventional forces are only a fraction of the Russian, they nevertheless play a vital part in our security. They must be strong enough to prevent surprise or infiltration.

3. On the other hand I cannot conceive that the Russians, if they were resolved on mortal war, would be so foolish as either to make a sudden attack only with their front-line conventional elements or reveal their intent by the preliminary reinforcing moves essential to their initial success. If they were resolved to stake all, as they would have to do, on a sudden assault, why should they throw away their only chance while they are the weaker nuclear power of surprise by Hydrogen bombs?

4. The picture sometimes presented to us of war beginning by a sudden conventional attack on the Western front with or without preparatory movements is wholly unreal. There is therefore no real need for our military Commanders to claim the authority to turn on nuclear weapons without the sanction of governments. It may well be that the fourteen governments concerned would be well advised to entrust this decision to two or three of their number, possibly the NATO Standing Group countries, or best of all to the United States and Britain, who alone possess the nuclear weapon (Britain as yet on a petty scale).

5. It may also be asked: 'If the Russians can gain nothing and only spoil their nuclear surprise on the Western front, why do they maintain these enormous and costly conventional forces'? The answer seems simple. The fact that Russia is far weaker in the nuclear sphere makes it all the more necessary for her to gain at the outset territorial hostages from the West. If, during and in spite of the confusion of the nuclear war, they were able to occupy Paris and Brussels and spread themselves out over the conquered lands, they would have an important counter for negotiation, and bases for the discharge at Britain of missiles very injurious and additional to their atomic stockpile. Moreover it is probable that even at this stage the Allies would be shy of dropping a Hydrogen bomb on the Bois de Boulogne, and thus destroying the population of Paris.

6. Therefore I conclude that the Soviets have a good reason for maintaining the means to make a conventional attack on Western Europe, and that the NATO powers would be most unwise not to present at any rate a delaying front till their nuclear superiority should manifest itself.

7. We must now look at the structure of the NATO defensive force. It already possesses nuclear artillery, and it is probable the Russians have also similarly equipped their forces. Some Americans argue that nuclear artillery, including field rockets, is only a modern expansion of artillery firing high explosives, and that no new principle is involved in firing more powerful shells

at a hostile army in the field. I have always contended that even though the use of nuclear weapons is confined to combatants and only incidentally strikes the civil population, yet the multiplication of explosive power is so gigantic that a wide gulf yawns between the two. Anyhow, the other side would be the judge of whether it paid him to treat the use of nuclear artillery against him as the beginning of wholesale nuclear war.

8. But the authority for which the NATO Commanders are asking is much wider than the use of nuclear artillery. There are three sections of nuclear warfare:

    First, nuclear artillery, including rocket missiles,

    Second, the use on a great scale of nuclear bombs by the Tactical Air Force, and

    Third, the Strategic Nuclear Air Force.

To give the right to decide on launching the nuclear attack by the Tactical Air Force to the NATO Commanders would undoubtedly give them the power to begin, without consulting their Governments, World Nuclear War. Hitherto there has been an impression that nuclear artillery firing at combatants might be accepted by both sides, but no one can possibly believe that the Tactical Air Force, which is planned to carry hundreds of Hydrogen bombs and double the number of Atomics, is in the same class as nuclear artillery. It is indeed indistinguishable from the main Strategic Nuclear Air Force, and it would be folly to use the one without the other.

9. It would surely be impossible at this stage to obtain agreement with the Soviets that nuclear artillery could be recognized on both sides as belonging to the field of conventional armaments. General Gruenther considers that it gives him his only chance of making an effective defence for a short time against the existing overwhelming conventional forces of his potential opponents. In fact, it is no good imagining that it could be separated in principle or practice from the rest of the atomic field. This could only be included in a much larger and deeper agreement on the problem as a whole.

10. To sum up this portion of the argument:

    (a) We should not agree to invest NATO Commanders with the right to use nuclear weapons, including nuclear artillery, without the sanction of the governments under whom they serve. They must plan for both alternatives. They may deploy for the full one.

    (b) To prevent delay by a large number of Powers who have nothing to contribute in this sphere, we should seek a devolution of authority upon two or three nations, preferably the only two who have any nuclear strength to offer.

    (c) We and the Americans should seek an opportunity of discussing the issue with the Soviets on the highest level at the earliest practicable date. Time should not be wasted as it is both short and deadly. They are certainly catching up, both in nuclear weapons and their delivery, with every month that passes, and although they may not overtake the United States, with British reinforcements approaching, they may easily reach a 'saturation' point where, although one Power is stronger than the other, both are capable of inflicting mortal injury. The grave mistake was in not coming to terms with Russia when the United States had the Atomics and they had none.

11. In attempting to forecast the conduct of the Soviet Government, who have absolute executive power, it is prudent to study what their real interest is. No one can doubt that they will have a far better chance of world domination if they wait until they have overtaken the United States in nuclear weapons or at least have achieved 'saturation'. It would indeed be folly for them not to wait for two or three years. We therefore need not take immediate alarm at Molotov's rough words, designed no doubt to play upon the French Chamber. The next two or three years may well be the safest the world will see for a long time.

We should remain calm and firm.

Dido Cairns[1] to Sir Winston S. Churchill
(Churchill papers, 2/423)

14 December 1954

Dear Sir Winston,

Your budgerigar 'Toby' should arrive on Friday. I do hope you will like him. I am sure he will not take long to get to know you, especially if you allow him to perch on the rim of your Brandy glass. He will enjoy doing this.[2]

He brings you my love and best Christmas wishes.[3]

---

[1] Diana Katherine Soames, 1917–97. Known as 'Dido'. Married, 1939, Hugh William Cairns: three children.

[2] Toby the budgerigar (parakeet) quickly insinuated himself into Churchill's affections and travelled everywhere with him. Toby was taught to drink and once had to be fished out of a brandy glass. He often perched on visitors' heads, sometimes leaving a token of esteem – 'hoping to be remembered', according to Churchill. One recipient of these tokens, Rab Butler, muttered as he wiped his bald pate: 'The things I do for England.' The bird often nibbled at books and manuscripts, Piers Brendon wrote, 'thus indicating, in his master's view, that he had read them'. A secretary who showed Churchill a set of nibbled page proofs was told: 'Oh! Yes, that's all right, give him the next chapter.' In 1960, to Churchill's great distress, Toby flew out of a Monte Carlo hotel window and was lost. A replacement could not match Toby's personality (Brendon, *Churchill's Bestiary*, p. 54.)

[3] Churchill replied on Dec. 17: 'We have received Toby in great state. Thank you so much. Merry Christmas.'

President Dwight D. Eisenhower to Sir Winston S. Churchill
(Premier papers, 11/1074)

15 December 1954
Top Secret

Dear Winston,

You have given a flawless exposition of Red China's relative weakness if we have under consideration only the possibility that she might launch aggressive war against either of our two countries. However, it is clear that our vital interests can be seriously damaged by operations that she is capable of carrying out against weaker areas lying along the boundaries of her territory. We saw what she tried to do in Korea and was foiled only by the intervention of strong allied forces, and we likewise saw what gains she made in the Indo-China region due to the political and military weakness of one of our allies. She can pay any price in manpower, with complete indifference to the amount. Consequently, she is a distinct threat to the peace of the world as long as she may be sufficiently irresponsible to launch an attack against peoples and areas of tremendous importance to us. This imposes on us the burden of supporting native forces in the region and of supplementing these with some of our own units.

Here I shall not outline the importance to the Western World of Japan and the island chain extending on to the Southward, as well as the bits of mainland on the Pacific that still remain in the possession of the free world. The moral, political and military consequences that could follow upon the loss of important parts of this great chain are obvious to both of us and to the staffs that work for us in the military, economic and diplomatic fields. So I think it dangerous to dismiss too complacently the risks that the bad faith, bad deportment and greed of Red China pose to our world. Some of our citizens are particularly sensitive to this threat and openly argue that it would be a mistake to allow this threat to endure and extend until the day comes when Red China may actually achieve the capacity to endanger us directly. I know that neither of us is blind to this possibility, even though we consider that such a development is somewhat doubtful and in any event its attainment would involve such a long time that world conditions and balances of power could well have been radically changed in the meantime. But, of course, I agree with you that our attention and watchfulness should be directed mainly to Moscow.

Incidentally, I was interested in your renewed suggestion of a top-level meeting with the regime in Russia. I have always felt, as you know, that it would be a mistake for you and me to participate in a meeting which was either essentially social or exploratory. A social meeting would merely give a false impression of accord which, in our free countries, would probably make it more difficult to get parliamentary support for needed defense appropriations. Within the captive world it would give the impression that we condone the present state of affairs. And if these are to be exploratory talks, should they not be carried out by our foreign ministers, so that heads of government would come in only if some really worthwhile agreement in is likely prospect?

The latter, I fear, is not an early possibility. There are still several months to go before we shall know where we are on the London and Paris accords and all the indications are that if they go through, the Russians will probably 'play tough', at least for some little time. Therefore, I do not see the likelihood of our foreign ministers usefully meeting for some considerable period. So, I am bound to say that, while I would like to be more optimistic, I cannot see that a top-level meeting is anything which I can inscribe on my schedule for any predictable date. I regret this the more because if a top-level meeting were to take place, and if it led to a personal visit to London, I would indeed be very happy.

I hope you will find some way of letting the Queen know how deeply I appreciate her gracious reference to the possibility of such a visit.

Foster and I have just had luncheon together and now he starts immediately for the NATO meeting. We discussed a number of matters, including a series of urgent requests that in our view practically amount to demands received from Mendes-France. He wants us to make public pronouncements supporting his statements affecting the Saar, Morocco and commitments of American troops to Europe. Important as French cooperation is to the great NATO plan, Mendes-France seems to forget that the safety, security and welfare of France are far more directly and intimately involved in the projects now under discussion than is the future of this country or of yours. One of the virtues of EDC was that it contained an acceptable solution of the Saar problem and it was French desertion of that plan that insured its defeat.

I see no good reason for this government to re-state its intentions about the stationing of American troops in Europe or take a position as to the Saar arrangement[1] at least until the French Parliament has by some positive action shown itself capable of making decisions in keeping with the responsibilities of a great European power. I have asked Foster to confer with Anthony on these matters. Likewise, I have asked him to avoid any rigid position of refusal in considering the seemingly unreasonable requests of Mendes-France, but I am determined that we shall begin to realize some dividends on the constant pledges and pronouncements that seem to be expected of us.

I like your phrase 'tyrannical weakness'. It sharply defines the situation.

As you know, I occasionally flatter myself by attempting to paint likenesses of friends. I would be tremendously intrigued by the effort to paint one of you. Would it be an intolerable burden on you to allow an artist friend of mind to

---

[1] The coal-rich Saarland, on the Franco-German border, was occupied and exploited by France from the 1919 Versailles Treaty until 1935, when it reverted to Germany. In 1946, France set up an economic union with the Saarland. After France rejected EDC in Aug. 1954, a new agreement resulted in a referendum, through which the Saarland became part of West Germany. At this time, too, the French Government was resisting independence for Morocco, which nevertheless came in 1956.

visit you long enough to take a few photographs and draw a few hasty color sketches that I would use in such an attempt? The final result would, of course, not be good, but also it might not be so bad as to be unendurable. If you feel this would not make an unjustified demand upon your time, I could send my artist friend over soon after the first of the year. I should think that something about thirty minutes to an hour would be sufficient for what I would need from him. This is just an idea and I shall not be at all offended by your inability to entertain it.

Lord Bracken to Lord Beaverbrook
(Beaverbrook papers)

15 December 1954

W is in tearing spirits though a bit tired after all the jubilations. He tells me they greatly pleased him but he doesn't want any more.

Sir Anthony Eden: diary
(Robert Rhodes James, 'Anthony Eden, A Biography', page 392)

21 December 1954

Felt far from well all day, & temperature in evening but determined to have my talk with W after dinner. Mentioned to Bobbety on telephone that I was going & he told me there was something I should know. He would come round & see me.

He did, and told me that Fred W(oolton) had told him in H of L that afternoon that W had asked him & James (Stuart) & Rab to stay behind after Cabinet. He had then raised & discussed with them possible Spring election (without a word to me). Fred had also said to Bobbety that of course no one would dream of wanting a March election except to get rid of W.

Rab had been against it. James had kept silent. Evidently a preparatory lobbying. Interesting, considering he (Churchill) has consistently refused a meeting with me present. He never mentioned this talk when I saw him later, nor admitted prior consultation except with Rab night before.

Set out for No. 10 at 9.30. Found Clemmie there with W. She was charming & worried at my colour. W said he supposed I had been living too well in Paris. Then when Clemmie had gone after a long pause he said 'What do you want to see me about'? in his most aggressive tone.

I said that he had had my letter and said he would be ready to discuss it. And slowly the argument began. At first he would have nothing. All was as well as possible. There was no hurry for an election or for him to hand over, the end of June or July would do very well. Laboriously I explained first that the new administration should have a chance to establish itself with the public. This gave us none. Second that it would place me in a much stronger position if I could take over in a month when an election was possible. Then, if my authority or mandate was challenged I would have the option either to fight it out in Parliament or to say very well let the country judge, & go to the country. This I could not do in July.

He wasn't much interested in this but when I had made it quite clear that I was not interested either in taking over at the end of June he eventually agreed to meeting at 3 p.m. with the people I chose. But it was all most grudging. There was much rather cruel '*divide et impera*'. For instance, he asked me how I got on with Harold. I said 'very well, why'? He replied 'Oh, he is very ambitious'. I laughed.*

* In 1965 Eden noted that 'This was the only occasion I recall when Winston warned me about a colleague.'

Sir Anthony Eden: diary
(Robert Rhodes James, 'Anthony Eden, A Biography', pages 392–3)

22 December 1954

Meeting of Ministers at 3 p.m. on lines I had asked for last night. Not a pleasant business. Rab had told me yesterday evening on telephone how unsatisfactory whole position was, that Cabinet I had missed had taken no decision etc., etc. All of which did not prevent him coming out with a mass of technical arguments against an election in March. Harold eventually debunked all this by saying that if there was an emergency he could presumably overcome these difficulties, to which Rab somewhat naively replied 'Yes'.

After a certain amount of further desultory conversation & explanation of value of an option to a new Govt, W rounded on me and said it was clear we wanted him out. Nobody contradicted him. Earlier he had said that I had made no difficulty about end of July last year. I replied that he had first said Queen's return if not sooner. End of July had been an afterthought.

At the end W said menacingly that he would think over what his colleagues had said & let them know his decision. Whatever it was he hoped it would not affect their present relationship with him. Nobody quailed. James (Stuart) said afterwards to me that it had been painful but absolutely necessary. He had to be told he could not pursue a course of 'such utter selfishness'.

Later Bobbety & Harold repaired to my room at FO. We gloomily surveyed the scene. It was clear to us that Rab would give no help. I said that I had said my say & they agreed that no more could be expected of me. Therefore they would try to hold a meeting without W or me of the remaining colleagues (still in London) before Christmas. Bobbety charged himself with this task &

later Rab assured him that he would attend and only wished to be helpful. What the result of all this may be I cannot tell except that the old man feels bitterly towards me, but this I cannot help. The colleagues are unanimous about drawling Cabinets, the failure to take decisions, the general atmosphere of *'apres moi le déluge'* & someone had to give a heave.

Sir Winston S. Churchill to Dido Cairns
(Churchill papers, 2/423)

23 December 1954

My dear Dido,

I am writing to let you know that Toby is settling in very happily and is giving me a lot of enjoyment. He has a blue cage and a green cage and has stayed the weekend at Chartwell and will come with me to Chequers tomorrow to spend Christmas. He is quite delightful and friendly and already sits on my glass and even my spectacles. I am so grateful to you for thinking of giving me such a charming token for my Birthday.

Please accept my best wishes for Christmas and the New Year.

Sir Winston S. Churchill to Lady Churchill
(Baroness Spencer-Churchill papers)

25 December 1954 Chequers

My Beloved Darling,

Buy yourself something you like out of this and keep the rest for a Christmas without a

[Drawing of a pig]
All my love,

Sir Winston S. Churchill to Lady Lytton
(Lytton papers)[1]

29 December 1954

Dearest Pamela,

We have had a family gathering of all our nine grandchildren & their parents which has been vy pleasant but also exacting. I have had many thoughts about you & have wondered how you spent yr Christmas, hoping that all was well & happy. I sent you a sample of volume one of my history

---

[1] This letter was handwritten.

of the ESP thinking that perhaps it might amuse you, if you had any time to spare. I trust it reached you safely. The French and the Railway crises[1] have filled any gaps in my own occupations.

With my best love and all fond wishes for 1955.

I remain,
Your always devoted

Sir Winston S. Churchill to Major-General Sir Edward Spears[2]
(Churchill papers, 2/199)

31 December 1954

Dear Louis,

I am very shy about giving away my pictures outside the family circle. They are like children to me, often very badly behaved but still regarded. All good wishes for the New Year.

---

[1] On 21 Dec. 1954, the National Union of Railwaymen announced that their members would go on strike from 9 Jan. 1955 unless awarded a 15% wage increase. They received a wage increase, and the strike was called off on the evening of Jan. 6.

[2] Edward Louis Spears, 1886–1974. Capt., 11th Hussars, 1914. Four times wounded, 1914–15 (MC). Liaison Officer with French 10th Army, 1915–16. Head of British Military Mission to Paris, 1917–20. MP (Nat. Lib.) for Loughborough, 1922–4; (Cons.) for Carlisle, 1931–45. Churchill's Personal Representative with the French PM, May–June 1940. Head of British Mission to de Gaulle, 1940. Head of Mission to Syria and the Lebanon, 1941. 1st Minister to Syria and the Lebanon, 1942–4. Knighted, 1942. Bt, 1953.

January 1955

Sir Winston S. Churchill to Randolph S. Churchill
(Churchill papers, 1/51)

2 January 1955

My dear Randolph,

I have read your article about 'Who Chooses the Tory Leader?', and was most interested to learn of these facts, of most of which I was unaware. I like the terse and cool method you adopt in your recent writings.

I have also read in the *Evening Standard* of yesterday your article about Yugoslav politics. This also was good and clear, and I am particularly grateful to you for telling me how to pronounce 'Geelas' and 'Ded-ee-ay'. I have not yet read the article about Anthony's successor.[1] It seems to have got mixed up with other papers, or did you take it away?

With all good wishes for the New Year,

Your loving Father

Sir Winston S. Churchill to Lord Birkenhead
(Churchill papers, 6/6)

2 January 1955
Private

My dear Freddie,

At the Other Club the other night I suggested to you deferring your resignation from the Government until my own departure. As, however, the date of this still remains 'buried in impenetrable obscurity' I do not feel I ought to press you on the point. I am therefore telling Lord Salisbury to proceed on the basis of my letter to you accepting your resignation of October 23. So much has happened since the Government was reconstructed in October that there could be no foundation for any critical comment. I am most sorry that

[1] As Foreign Secretary.

you want to go, but I thoroughly realize the good reasons you have. I hope, however, it will not mean that you give up politics, but that on the contrary you will take a more active part in the House of Lords than has hitherto been open to you.

With all good wishes to you and Sheila for the New Year.

Sir Winston S. Churchill to Lady Violet Bonham Carter
(Churchill papers, 6/6)

2 January 1955

My dear Violet,

I have taken an unconscionable time in answering your letter of December 13 about the appointment of a Royal Commission on Voting. I have also received a letter from the Secretary of the Committee, Mr Pollard,[1] in which he suggests that if I am too much pressed myself, one of my colleagues, who would naturally be the Home Secretary, should receive the Deputation. I think this would be much better. I shall not be responsible for leading the Conservative Party at the General Election, whenever it comes, and any effective decision would have to be taken by my successor. There is an overwhelming disapproval in the Conservative Party of any approach to PR[2] in any form. My own opinion has hardened against it, in view of the ruin it has brought to every Parliament to which it has been applied. Look at the French Chamber with all its groups.

I am therefore sending Mr Pollard's letter on to the Home Secretary. This one is personal to you, with all my good wishes for the New Year.

Sir Winston S. Churchill to Irene Ward[3]
(Churchill papers, 6/6)

2 January 1955

Dear Miss Ward,

You wrote to Christopher Soames on December 14 about the Answer which I gave to your Question on December 9 on problem families.

The circular you mention was issued by the Minister of Health after

[1] Robert Spence Watson Pollard, 1907–84. Born in York, England. Married, 1938, Beatrice Elise Pascall. Author of *The Problem of Divorce* (1958) and *Family Problems and the Law* (1959).

[2] Proportional representation: an electoral system in which divisions in an electorate are reflected proportionally in the elected body. Churchill opposed it, feeling it would lead to a plethora of political parties and unstable coalitions. Lady Violet, a lifelong Liberal, supported it as it stood to favour the Liberals, now a distant third of the main parties behind the Conservatives and Labour.

[3] Irene Mary Bewick Ward, 1895–1980. CBE, 1929. MP (Cons.) for Wallsend-on-Tyne, 1931–45; for Tynemouth, 1950–74. DBE, 1955. CH, 1973. Baroness, 1974.

consultation with the Home Secretary and the Ministers of Education and Housing and Local Government. All these Ministers are in agreement that the various local services which may help problem families should work in cooperation. My Answer to your Question stated that problem families cannot be dealt with in isolation from the rest of the community. It would be impracticable for one Department to be responsible, for instance, for rehousing a particular type of family, for providing local health services, for seeing that children attend school, for visiting in connection with National Assistance payments and for providing accommodation for children who need to be removed from the family. This example shows that the services must continue to be administered by the various Departments which are responsible for them in relation to the community as a whole.

I do not think that local authorities wish to shirk their responsibilities. I hope that by now they are well aware of the need for cooperation among their various services, but the central Departments concerned are in close touch on the matter and are keeping it under review.

With good wishes for the new year,

Sir Winston S. Churchill to Major T. C. Shillito[1]
(Churchill papers, 6/6)

5 January 1955

Dear Major Shillito,

Please accept my warm thanks, and convey them to the other members of your Association, for the very kind letter of good wishes which the surviving Defenders of Ladysmith sent me on my birthday. Long after we that are left have gone, the name of Ladysmith will be found in the select list of battles famous in the annals of the British Army. I was indeed proud to be saluted by its Garrison on my 80th birthday.

I shall always remember galloping in with the SALH in the first relief to get through, and dining with Sir George White.[2] I was disappointed that he gave us Bully Beef instead of the horseflesh on which you had all lived so long.

---

[1] T. C. Shillito. Served in Second Boer War, 1899–1900, including defence of Ladysmith, a siege which was relieved by a British force including Winston Churchill. Lt, 1916. Capt., 1917.

[2] George Stuart White, 1835–1912. Ensign, 27th Inniskilling Rgt, 1853. VC, 1881. C-in-C, India, 1893–8. Gen., 1899. Commanded troops at Ladysmith against Boer Army. Governor of Gibraltar, 1900–4. FM, 1903. OM, 1905. Governor, Royal Hospital Chelsea, 1905–12.

Sir Anthony Eden: diary
(Robert Rhodes James, 'Anthony Eden, a Biography', page 395)

6 January 1955

Motored up to Cabinet. Met at 11.30. Explained to us that we didn't yet know what Robertson proposed to say at meeting this afternoon. No certainty ether that NUR would even now accept. Considerable evidence of communist desire for row. RAB told me when he joined W and I at luncheon later of this evidence & that he would rather have row now than later.

W & I had rather a sharp altercation at Cabinet. He attacked me for having been bellicose from the start & added 'You'll get your strike alright'. I countered that he had chucked the reins on the horse's neck & said I agreed with *Times* and *M Guardian*'s[1] leaders this morning.

C[2] & I lunched with W and Clemmie. Argument continued more mildly there. He said I was a Tory, that my City experience had done me no good & had imbued me too much with rights of private property. I said I had been brought up to believe this was a liberal principle. Clemmie agreed. There was much talking at luncheon about the handing over, Clemmie talking to C about showing her kitchen etc. Rab told me in the late afternoon that he would like it to be Commonwealth Conference, but that Easter was more probable.

Sir Winston S. Churchill to the Reverend Dr Donald Soper[3]
(Churchill papers, 6/6)

6 January 1955

Dear Dr Soper,

In a letter of December 31, signed by yourself and others, you expressed the hope that I would take an immediate initiative in calling high level talks with Russia and America early in the new year, for the purpose of considering anew the problem of the reduction and control of armaments.

Her Majesty's Government have in fact invited the Governments of the United States, France, the Soviet Union and Canada to hold further meetings of the United Nations Disarmaments Sub-Committee on this important matter in London next month. As I said in the House of Commons on October 19, it would be improper to cut across these negotiations.

It was announced in the House of Commons on December 6 that Her Majesty's Government would be represented in the Disarmament Sub-Committee's

---

[1] *Manchester Guardian*'s.
[2] Clarissa Eden.
[3] Donald Oliver Soper, 1903–98. Prominent Methodist minister, socialist and pacifist. Born in London. Educated at St Catharine's College, Cambridge. Married, 1939, Marie Gertrude Dean: four children. Baron, 1965.

discussions by the Minister of State for Foreign Affairs, Mr Nutting. As regards the suggestion for high level talks on Disarmament, the Foreign Secretary said in the House of Commons on that occasion that if the result of these discussions is encouraging, we shall certainly be ready to contemplate a meeting at a higher level. He stressed, however, that the Government must be free to use whatever method and time they think best.

Sir Winston S. Churchill to President Dwight D. Eisenhower
Prime Minister's Personal Telegram T.3/54
(Premier papers, 11/1074)

11 January 1955
Priority
Secret
No. 130

Should be delighted to see your artist friend and am much honoured at the prospect.[1] Am writing at length about other matters.

Sir Winston S. Churchill to President Dwight D. Eisenhower
(Churchill papers, 2/217)

12 January 1955
Top Secret, Private and Personal

My dear Friend,

I waited to answer your letter of December 15[2] until the vote had been taken in the French Chamber[3] and after that our Governments were in such complete accord that I let the days slip by. There are still opportunities open to the French obstructers for making serious delays. Anthony and I are in full agreement with you that there can be no Four Power Conference of any kind until ratification is complete, and we feel of course that everything reasonable in our power should be done to press for a definite decision. I suppose they could, if they chose, spread the whole process out for four or five months. I am sure you will agree that this would be a most improvident way of wasting the ever-shortening interval of time before the Soviets have developed their nuclear strength, including delivery, though not to anything approaching equality with you, to what is called 'saturation point', namely

---

[1] See Eisenhower to Churchill of 15 Dec. 1954, reproduced above (pp. 1856–8).

[2] Reproduced above (pp. 1856–8).

[3] The French National Assembly ratified the Paris and London agreements on 28 Dec. 1954. Formal agreement was also required by the Council of the Republic. Thus Churchill's following letter to Mendès-France.

the power to inflict mortal injury upon the civilized structure of the free world.

Britain will, of course, be stronger in two or three years in nuclear weapons. I visited some of our secret establishments last week, and was struck by their progress and prospects, both in the atomic and in the hydrogen sphere ('sphere' is apposite in more senses than one). We are making atomic bombs on a steadily increasing scale, and we and our experts are confident that we have the secret, perhaps even with some improvements, of the hydrogen bomb. I am very glad that the difficulties about the 'fittings' which you promised me at Bermuda have been solved, and that your officers have been over here talking to ours. Thank you very much.[1]

Looking back and knowing your views throughout the story, I cannot but regret that you had not the power at the time the McMahon Act was under discussion. If the agreement signed between me and FDR had not been shelved, we should probably already have been able to add a substantial reinforcement to your vast and formidable deterrent power. We have, however, through Attlee's somewhat unconstitutional exertions in making vast sums available for nuclear development without disclosing the fact to Parliament, mastered the problems both of the atomic and the hydrogen weapons by our own science independently. The inevitable delay must, however, be regarded as a severe misfortune to our common cause from which your convictions would have saved it.

I enclose a paper which I wrote for my colleagues before the recent NATO Meeting in Paris. This secured a very large measure of agreement between them and in several cases the same opinion had been spontaneously reached. I feel pretty sure that you and I were thinking separately on the same or similar lines – as we have done before.

I cabled you on Monday about your artist friend. I need hardly say I shall be greatly honoured to be one of your subjects in an artistic sense. Although my experiences as a model have not been altogether agreeable lately I submit myself with great confidence to your well-balanced love of truth and mercy.

With every good wish

Believe me always; your dear friend

---

[1] The US had provided Britain with information on external fittings of nuclear bombs as part of its increased sharing of information on atomic matters.

Sir Winston S. Churchill to Pierre Mendès-France
(Churchill papers, 6/6)

12 January 1955
Private and Personal

My dear Monsieur Mendes-France,

Thank you very much for your letter. I renew my congratulations to you on your success in the Chamber. I feel that your difficulties in dealing with all the vehement and self-centred groups must be enormous. Your courage and vitality have given me an impression of French leadership which I had not sustained since the days of Clemenceau. Pray accept my earnest compliments.

I have for some time felt a strong desire to establish a direct personal contact with the new leaders of the Soviet Government such as might lead to a fruitful Four-Power Conference. But these thoughts of mine received a rude check when the Soviets requested a Four-Power meeting of the Foreign Secretaries, apparently with the object of stimulating opposition in the French Chamber to the Ratification of EDC.

After this came the London Conference and Sir Anthony Eden's initiative was there, and subsequently at Paris, crowned by the Agreements which you by your determination and skill managed, though by a very small majority, to pass through the Chamber. I am well aware that the Treaty has also to pass the Conseil de la Republique and of the many opportunities for uncertainty and delay which still remain.

I still hold most strongly to my conviction that a Top Level Meeting might be productive of real advantages if the time and circumstances were well chosen. This view was, as you know, expressed in an unanimous resolution by the House of Commons last year. I cannot feel however that at this juncture any negotiation with the Soviets about a Four-Power Meeting even though conditional on the Agreements having been previously ratified, would help our common cause. Weakness makes no appeal to the Soviets. To mix up the process of ratification with what might well follow soon afterwards would very likely dilute both Firmness and Conciliation. The sooner we can get our united ratification the sooner the Top-Level Four-Power Conference may come.

Although we have every sympathy with you in your difficulties and admiration for your exertions, the fact should be accepted that I and my colleagues are wholeheartedly resolved that there shall be no meeting or invitation in any circumstances which we can foresee between the Four Powers, either on the Foreign Secretaries level or on that of the Heads of Governments, until the London–Paris Agreements have been ratified by all the signatories. In this we are in the closest accord with the United States. I cannot believe there is the slightest chance of any change of attitude on this point in either of our two countries. Indeed I fear that an indefinite process of delay may well lead to the adoption of other solutions which are certainly being studied on both sides of the Atlantic.

I, myself, am very much opposed to the withdrawal of all American and British troops from the continent. You may count on me to oppose to the best of my ability the strategic conception known as 'peripheral'. On the other hand I should feel bound, whether as Prime Minister or as a Private Member, to support the policy known as 'The Empty Chair', although this would involve large changes in the infra-structure of NATO, both military and political. I feel that the United States with their immense superiority of nuclear weapons and acting in association with Great Britain, the British Commonwealth and the German Federal Republic, will be strong enough, at any rate during the next few years, to afford to the Benelux countries and our other Allies for whom we have a deep regard, and also the German Federal Republic to whom we are bound in honour, a definite and substantial security based on physical and moral deterrent power.

In this breathing space much may be achieved. But having ever since 1910 worked and fought with and for France, for whose people I have a deep affection, I should feel the utmost sorrow to see her isolated and losing her influence with the rest of the free world. I hope indeed that it will fall to you to save your country from this evil turn of fortune.

Please accept for yourself and Madame Mendes-France all my good wishes for the New Year and my earnest hopes that you may continue at the helm.

Cabinet: conclusions
(Cabinet papers, 128/28)

13 January 1955
Secret
11.30 a.m.
Cabinet Meeting No. 3 of 1955

1. The Cabinet had before them telegrams which the Colonial Secretary had exchanged with the Governor of Kenya on a proposal that a new offer should now be made that Mau Mau terrorists who surrendered voluntarily would not be prosecuted for any offence committed before the date of the offer (Kenya telegrams Nos. 21, 29 and 34 and Colonial Office telegrams to Kenya Nos 7, 8 and 9).[1]

The Colonial Secretary said that intensive military operations were now being launched against two of the main strongholds of the terrorists, and this was a favourable moment for an offer of new surrender terms. It was, however, the view of the War Council in Nairobi that such an offer should not be made unless it could be stated at the same time that no further proceedings would be taken against members of the Kikuyu Guard and other loyal supporters of the

---

[1] By 1954 Kenyan Government forces were rapidly overcoming the Mau Mau rebels. Military operations ended in late 1956, the Government instituted substantial land reforms, and the first elections for native Kenyans to the Legislative Council took place in 1957. Kenya became independent in 1963.

Government for misdemeanours committed in the course of their activities against the terrorists. The Colonial Secretary said that he shared this view: it would be impossible to satisfy public opinion in Kenya that it was right to offer clemency to terrorists and at the same time to continue investigations designed to uncover irregularities committed by those, whether European or African, who had sought to help the Government to restore order.

In a preliminary discussion questions were raised about the legal basis of the proposals put forward by the Governor of Kenya. Doubt was also expressed about the wisdom of linking a new surrender offer with a suspension of further investigations into misdemeanours by members of the Kikuyu Guard and other loyalists. This latter proposal though it might be welcomed in Kenya, might give rise to misgivings in this country.

The Cabinet –

Agreed to resume their discussion of these proposals at a further meeting later in the day.

The Prime Minister said that he had been surprised at the manner of the announcement of General Erskine's impending transfer from his appointment as Commander-in-Chief in Kenya. It seemed strange that this change of command should be announced at a moment when military operations in Kenya were being intensified. The change was certainly one on which he should have been consulted.

The Secretary of State for War said that General Erskine had been appointed to this post for a period of two years, which was due to expire in May; that his transfer, and the choice of his successor, had been settled in consultation with the Colonial Secretary; and that, as had been made clear in the announcement, his departure from Kenya would be delayed beyond May if the state of military operations then made this desirable. He greatly regretted that, by an oversight, the announcement had been made without prior consultations with the Prime Minister.

The Prime Minister asked that further steps should be taken to ensure that he was consulted in future on all military appointments which might affect other Departments or arouse public interest, so that he might have an opportunity of bringing them to the notice of the Cabinet.

[. . .]

Sir Winston S. Churchill to Lord Salisbury
(Churchill papers, 6/6)

14 January 1955

My dear Robert,

Your letter of the 12th: I saw Chesham[1] today amid the Cabinets. I formed a very favourable impression of him. I reminded him that I knew his Father in the 10th Hussars, this was apparently correct. He was delighted and what he called 'thrilled' to accept the Office.[2] I explained to him that I was most anxious to make the representation of Departments by Lords in Waiting a reality and that a room would be found and facilities given by the official spokesman in the House of Lords to familiarise and identify himself with the work of the Department. Anyhow he seemed very pleased with the idea. I think you will find a good aid in him. I must say I think he would do very well at the Admiralty, unless you have other plans I would suggest this to you. I did not of course mention it to him. If he were associated with the Admiralty, there would be heaps of work for him to do. Ships, dockyards, sailors' institutes etc. to get in touch with.

He has accepted and apparently has no Directorships. I have told him to write to you and I told him that I would be writing to you. Please advise me when I should make a Submission to The Queen.

Sir Winston S. Churchill to Lord Leathers
(Churchill papers, 2/422)

15 January 1955
Private and Confidential

My dear Fred,

It was a complete surprise to me though by no means an unwelcome one when Lord Moynihan[3] and Mr Martell[4] started the idea of making me a birthday present by popular subscription, and I am indeed proud that over three hundred and fifty thousand people should have responded. The great majority

---

[1] John Charles Compton Cavendish, 1916–89. Educated at Trinity College, Cambridge. Married, 1937, Mary Edmunds Marshall: four children. Capt., Royal Artillery, 1939–45. JP for Buckinghamshire, 1946. Joint Parliamentary Secretary to Minister of Transport, 1959–64. PC, 1964. 5th Baron Chesham, 1952. Lord-in-Waiting to Queen Elizabeth II, 1955–9.

[2] As Lord-in-Waiting.

[3] Patrick Berkeley Moynihan, 1906–65. Baron, 1936. Served in RA, 1939–45.

[4] Edward Drewett Martell, 1909–89. Educated at St George's School, Harpenden. Married, 1932, Ethel Maud Beverley. Served in RAC, 1939–45. Member (Lib.), London County Council, 1946–9. Unsuccessful Parliamentary candidate (Lib.) for Rotherhithe (by-election), 1946; for Hendon North, 1950; (Ind.) for East Ham, 1957; (Cons.) for Bristol South East (by-election), 1963. Formed People's League for the Defence of Freedom, 1956. Joined Conservative Party, 1962. Chairman, Hastings Conservative Association, 1963.

of these have, I understand, expressed their wish that their gift should be personal to me. Others would like them to be devoted to charitable purposes, to use the legal term, in which I take an interest. This also is very agreeable to me. I have long had an idea of building a small museum at Chartwell in which many things of personal interest could be displayed including numbers of my pictures and the trophies which have been given me. This building would also include sanitary accommodation and one or two resting-rooms needed by visitors to Chartwell who would also have access to the House when that has been handed over to the National Trust to whom it now belongs.

Apart from this I have long been associated with the Church Army enterprise which is called The Churchill Homes for Elderly People.

But if further Funds were at my disposal I should like to encourage the study and use of the English language in the Public Schools and other educational establishments. I have my own ideas based on my own experience for inculcating the writing of good and simple English and also for stimulating the learning of famous passages of English prose and poetry by heart. It is not possible for me to give thought and care to these plans at present, but it would be a great pleasure to develop them if sufficient resources were placed at the disposal of the Trust.

Sir Winston S. Churchill to Gresham Cooke[1]
(Churchill papers, 6/6)

15 January 1955

My dear Cooke,

I have no hesitation in commending you to the electors of the Twickenham Division. Your wide experience in industrial affairs, the value of the contribution you make to the export drive, and your special knowledge of road traffic problems are excellent qualifications for a member of Parliament at the present time.

This is a straight fight between a supporter of the Conservative Government and a supporter of one or other faction of the Socialist Opposition. The question for any doubting elector to ask himself or herself before deciding how to vote is therefore quite a simple one: 'Is the country – and am I and my neighbours – likely to be better off under the present Government than we should be if the Socialists were put in charge again?'

Unless the intending voter has a very short memory or has closed his mind

[1] (Roger) Gresham Cooke, 1907–70. Secretary, British Road Federation, 1935–8. Hon. Secretary, German Road Delegation, 1937. Grand Council, FBI, 1946–55. Chairman, Highways Committee, 1948–55. Board of Trade Exhibition Advisory Committee, 1947–55. MP (Cons.) for Twickenham, 1955–70. Parliamentary Private Secretary to Economic Secretary to the Treasury, 1957–8. Joint Secretary, Cons. Parliamentary Transport Committee, 1955–8. Member, Council of Europe, Western European Union Assembly, 1962–4.

to realities, he has only to look around him to find the right answer. Under its Socialist rulers, who even then were quarrelling among themselves (as they still are), the country had six years of short commons, recurring crises, and perpetual anxiety, culminating in near-disaster. Three years of Tory Democracy have transformed the whole scene. Freed from much needless muddling by Whitehall, the nation has leapt ahead to work out its own progress by its own native genius and with the overall guidance and help that it is a modern Government's business to give.

The hideous shadow of war has become more remote. There is scarcely a home in the land whose burdens have not been lightened. Even the less fortunate among us who depend on National Insurance pensions and benefits are assured of better times in the near future.

I ask the citizens of Twickenham to cast their votes in accordance with the facts known to them. And I hope that no Conservative will be so over-confident of your victory that he will leave it to others to make your majority secure. Every vote counts and every vote is needed. I wish you a large poll and a resounding majority.

The Right Reverend Neville Gorton[1] to Sir Winston S. Churchill
(*Churchill papers, 6/6*)

16 January 1955

Dear Prime Minister,

I venture to write to you on the matter of a broadcast by a Mrs Knight.[2] I could not object to people of real eminence giving their philosophic positions on the third programme or the other responsible broadcasts. Nor do I wish The Church to be thought to be asking for a closed shop for weak positions.

But I object to this particular Broadcast for this reason. It was addressed to parents in their homes on the care of their children.

It reached them with the authority of the BBC and the prestige of the microphone.

It was introduced by a series of cheap sneers at the Christian Faith, and ended by telling parents to tell their children not to believe in God.

I write to you as a bishop whose main job is the pastoral care of his people – their homes and their children.

---

[1] Neville Vincent Gorton, 1888–1955. Educated at Marlborough and Balliol College, Oxford. Deacon, 1914. Priest, 1916. Asst Chaplain, Sedbergh School, 1914–34. Married, 1926, Ethel Ingledew Daggett: three children. Headmaster, Blundell's School, Tiverton, 1934–43. Bishop of Coventry, 1943–55.

[2] Margaret Kennedy, 1903–83. Educated at Girton College, Cambridge. Married, 1936, Arthur Knight. Editor, *Journal of National Institute of Industrial Psychology*, 1926–36. Lecturer in Psychology, University of Aberdeen, 1936–70. Published *A Modern Introduction to Psychology* (1948), *William James: A Selection from His Writings* (1950) and *Morals Without Religion* (1955).

Some time back I was asked by the secretary of the association of probation and welfare officers of the whole of the Midlands to spend a day with them and to hold a service with them at their Conference on 'Young People in Trouble'.

I speak for every one of us, said the secretary – for we all know that the only answer to this mounting evil is the Christian Faith back in the homes of our people.

At a conference on juvenile Delinquency at the Police college the same thing was said.

I am in close touch with Homes for spastic children and probation schools – I find there deeply Christian masters finding for them in Christian faith recovery of mind and body.

Next the Nation in the Education Act thro' Parliament laid down the teaching of the Christian Faith as the basis of the system of national education. I speak not of Church schools but of numbers of local state schools where superb Christian men and women are devotedly building the life of their schools on a Christian instruction too often up against the indifference of parents.

But I also see in these huge new housing estates numbers of young parents, many with a precarious hold on the Christian Faith but many also fumbling their way back for the sake of their children. These young people have no critical defences. What faith they have was submitted in the Broadcast to an ignorant attack but a need to them with the apparent authority of a pseudo-science and its to them imposing jargon.

It is with these things in mind or rather these people and their children that I write to you. I apologise for the circumstantial length of this letter.

But to generalize about so urgent a matter might mean nothing in particular.

Lord Bracken to Lord Beaverbrook
(Beaverbrook papers)

17 January 1955

There is a lot of political news which cannot easily be put down in writing. Our friend, under no pressure from Clemmie, Eden or other ministers, intends to depart before July. Naturally this news is in our bond of secrecy.

He says, without any sign of regret, that it is time he gave up. His only wish now is to find a small villa in the South of France where he can spend the winter months in the years which remain to him.

I am certain that he will not change his mind. All his plans are made and when he leaves No. 10 Jock Colville will resign from the Civil Service to take a job in the City early in July.

I have no doubt that many foolish Tories will rejoice in the news. They may well be disillusioned by the result of the next General Election.

Sir Winston S. Churchill to Lord Halifax
(Churchill papers, 6/6)

20 January 1955

My dear Edward,

I shall be glad to see Dr Helen Keller[1] in my room at the House of Commons at 4 p.m. on Thursday, February 17. I hope this will be convenient.

Sir Winston S. Churchill to Clement Attlee
(Churchill papers, 6/6)

23 January 1955
Private

My dear Attlee,

We have been considering again the financial and administrative arrangements for Chequers and I think that you will like to know what has been decided. As you know, the resources of the Trust have for many years had to be supplemented. This has been done by the Ministry of Works taking responsibility for a large number of services, with the inevitable consequence of divided control. A further complication is that it was necessary last year to provide a grant-in-aid from the Treasury to meet the deficit on the Income and Expenditure Account of the Trust which had accumulated over a number of years.

We have come to the conclusion that we should replace the Ministry of Works services by an annual cash grant-in-aid to the Trust from the Treasury with the help of which the Trustees can control the whole Estate. This will be more convenient and we hope also more economical. Provision for such a grant-in-aid is being made in next year's Estimates. This provision will be higher next year than in recent years because we have decided to go ahead with the replacement of the present central heating system. You will remember that there have long been plans for the installation of an oil burning system which should reduce running costs, particularly in labour.

---

[1] Helen Adams Keller, 1880–1968. American author and political activist, famous for being the first deaf-blind person to earn a college degree. Educated at Radcliffe College, Harvard University.

Sir Winston S. Churchill to the Right Reverend Neville Gorton
(Churchill papers, 6/6)

24 January 1955
Private and Confidential

My dear Bishop,

Thank you so much for your letter[1] which arose no doubt out of the telephone message I asked Brendan to send you.

I have considered the whole subject in the interval and have decided not to plunge into this controversy in my present position. It may however amuse you to see, in confidence, the sort of comment I had felt provoked into making. Please let me have it back when you have read it. I think all the points you make are valid and weighty.

ENCLOSURE

Thank you for your letter referring to the recent broadcasts by Mrs Knight. I willingly express my personal view about them. I am all for free speech and free thought, and our Island is founded on and famous for these principles. Everyone has a right, subject to the well-known laws of the land, to express his own opinions to as many as care to listen. Full and keen discussion may at any time be opened between British subjects by argument, discourse, or literature of every kind. I have therefore no fault to find with Mrs Knight for expressing the convictions which she holds as often as she gets a chance. She might even feel that they were suitable to the doom-laden world of nuclear power in which we now dwell. It might seem logical to her that the spiritual side of human nature should keep pace with our physical discoveries so that universal obliteration should engulf all the bodies and all the souls together. The theme would at any rate wear a more up-to-date garb than the usual atheistic propaganda.

The misbehaviour, as such it may be termed, must be ascribed to those who gave Mrs Knight the opportunity of using an elaborate mechanical process perfected in recent years to plunge into millions of homes and pour out a selection of hackneyed assertions, which must have caused pain to many people of all ages.

The process of delivery should be scrutinised. 13,872,633 instruments to receive broadcasting messages have been purchased by British householders. These gather families and friends around them during convenient hours of the day or night. Many of those who come to listen have no notion of the sort of thing they are going to hear. Indeed, surprise is an asset to the performance. It is on this basis that advice is given to parents to bring up their children upon a denial of the Divinity of Christ. The apparatus

[1] Reproduced above (pp. 1873–4).

is so widespread that many millions of people who had not prepared their minds for the controversy were confronted with an assault upon beliefs which they have cherished all their lives. This is not a case of the individual being overborne by the mass. He is overborne by the machine with all its plugs, knobs and switches and the organisation which markets the stuff.

It is an anti-social act to use a modern invention to cause needless and purposeless mental distress in a wholesale manner on a vast scale. Firm faith will no doubt be stimulated. But it is inhumane to brush away even a crumb of comfort from young or old in their journey through this hard world, or quench a gleam of hope in an aching heart. The responsibility for a callous and indiscriminate use of these new, gigantic and ever more powerful scientific agencies rests, on this occasion, primarily on those who bestowed the opportunity on Mrs Knight. The blame for hurting lots of ordinary people by the clumsy misuse of robot machinery falls upon them.

President Dwight D. Eisenhower to Sir Winston S. Churchill
(*Churchill papers, 2/217*)

25 January 1955
Top Secret

Dear Winston,
Permit me to refer to paragraph eight, page two, of your top secret memorandum[1] on tube alloys. Our conclusions here on the particular subject of that paragraph do not fully conform to yours. We believe that consequences would not be so far reaching as you describe.

On the other hand, your paper seems to me to under-emphasize a point of such moment that it constitutes almost a new element in warfare. I refer to the extraordinary increase in the value of tactical or strategic surprise, brought about by the enormous destructive power of the new weapons and the probability that they could be delivered over targets with little or no warning. Surprise has always been one of the most important factors in achieving victory. And now, even as we contemplate the grim picture depicted in your memorandum, we gain only a glimmering of the paralysis that could be inflicted on an unready fighting force, or indeed upon a whole nation, by some sudden foray that would place a dozen or more of these terrible weapons accurately on target.

I personally believe that many of our old conceptions of the time that would be available to governments for making of decisions in the event of attack are no longer tenable. I think it possible that the very life of a nation,

---

[1] Of 14 Dec. 1954, reproduced above (pp. 1850–5).

perhaps even of Western civilization, could, for example, come to depend on instantaneous reaction to news of an approaching air fleet; victory or defeat could hang upon minutes and seconds used decisively at top speed or tragically wasted in indecision.

I completely agree with all that you say about deterrents. The principal weakness of this policy is that it offers, of itself, no defense against the losses that we incur through the enemy's political and military nibbling. So long as he abstains from doing anything that he believes would provoke the free world to an open declaration of major war, he need not fear the 'deterrent'. Since he knows that we, in our democracies, are honestly devoted to peace and by instinct and training abhor the thought of mass destruction and attacks that would necessarily involve helpless people, he knows that there is a great area of fruitful opportunity open to him lying between the excitation of a global war on the one hand and passive acceptance of the status quo on the other. At this moment, the Kremlin and Peiping are driving forward with their plans and purposes in this realm of relative safety. However, there can be local deterrents as well as global deterrents. The theory of the deterrent should, at the very least, logically be backed up by the most careful studies on our part to decide upon the conditions under which we would find it necessary to react explosively. A concomitant problem would be how we could inform the enemy of the first decision so that he would not, through miscalculation, push us to the point that global war would result.

I share your feelings of satisfaction in the progress of your country toward nuclear stockpile; I share your regret that through unfortunate circumstances of the past, that development is not further advanced.

In Europe we must now wait final action in the French and German Parliaments on our latest plans for military cooperation in that area, particularly between these two ancient enemies. Nothing must be done that could give a reason or excuse for delay in this work. Just as you deplore the delays that were experienced in your country in the initiation of your atomic project, so I bitterly regret that all of us did not put our shoulder to the wheel some three years ago when the prospects for the approval of EDC looked bright. All the free world could breathe easier today had that venture been a success.

Respecting the Far East – yesterday I sent a message to the Congress to clarify the intention of this nation in the region of the Formosa Straits. It would be a pity if the Communists misinterpreted our forbearance to mean indecision and precipitated a crisis that could bring on a nasty situation.

I note that in the memorandum accompanying your letter, your Government fears that during the next two or three years the United States may, through impulsiveness or lack of perspective, be drawn into a Chinese war.

I trust that my message to the Congress reassured you as to our basic attitudes and sober approach to critical problems.

It is probably difficult for you, in your geographical position, to understand how concerned this country is with the solidarity of the Island Barrier in the Western Pacific. Moreover, we are convinced that the psychological effect in the Far East of deserting our friends on Formosa would risk a collapse of Asiatic resistance to the Communists. Such possibilities cannot be lightly dismissed; in our view they are almost as important, in the long term, to you as they are to us.

I am certain there is nothing to be gained in that situation by meekness and weakness. God knows I have been working hard in the exploration of every avenue that seems to lead toward the preservation and strengthening of the peace. But I am positive that the free world is surely building trouble for itself unless it is united in basic purpose, is clear and emphatic in its declared determination to resist all forceful Communist advance, and keeps itself ready to act on a moment's notice, if necessary.

Thank you very much for your nice reply concerning my artist friend. Right now I have in some odd moments been attempting to copy a photograph I have of a portrait painted of you some years ago. It shows you sitting down, in semi-formal attire, with a cigar in your right hand. But I would far rather work on something that was not a mere slavish copy.[1]

I have earnestly instructed my artist friend to be as sparing of your time as possible. Incidentally he was born, raised and trained in Britain. He has been an American citizen for only three or four years. His name is Thomas E. Stephens.[2] I think it best that he makes contact with you through the American Embassy, and I am asking Winthrop to contact your secretary at the proper time. If present plans go through, Mr Stephens will be in Britain next week.

With my continuing warm regard, and with my sincere wishes for your health, strength and happiness.

The Right Reverend Neville Gorton to Sir Winston S. Churchill
(Churchill papers, 6/6)

27 January 1955

My dear Prime Minister,

Thank you for the great kindness of your personal letter[3] and for allowing me to read that superb statement. But what a loss of ammunition directed not to Mrs Knight but to so much that is needed in this country. But it is a great spiritual encouragement to a spiritually hard-pressed bishop.

I would dare to say this that when Brendan after a long gap began at the

---

[1] The portrait Eisenhower had copied was a reproduction of a famous 1942 painting by the Hungarian artist Arthur Pan.

[2] Thomas Edgar Stephens, 1884–1966. Welsh-American painter. Born in Cardiff. Educated at Art School of Cardiff University, Heatherly School, London, and Académie Julian, Paris.

[3] Reproduced above (pp. 1876–7).

worst point of the war to write to me several long personal letters which I felt brought to me something of your own faith and mind I did pray regularly for you. And I do continue that now. So many would want to tell you something like this.

God bless you in all you have carried and still carry for us all.

Sir Winston S. Churchill to Maria Julius Heusch[1]
(Churchill papers, 6/6)

28 January 1955

My dear Oberburgermeister,

I am deeply complimented by the honour which has been paid me by the City of Aachen in awarding me the International Charlemagne Prize for 1955, and by your most agreeable invitation to visit Aachen to receive this award. It will give me very great pleasure to come to Aachen for this purpose. It is difficult for me at this stage to be sure that the 19th of May will be a possible date and I will therefore take advantage of your kindness in leaving it open whether the ceremony might take place on some other day. I will write to you again about this as soon as I can see the position more clearly.

Sir Winston S. Churchill to Konrad Adenauer
(Churchill papers, 6/6)

28 January 1955

My dear Adenauer,

Thank you so much for your letter about the invitation from the City of Aachen. It is kind of you to write in such terms and I hope to be able to go to Aachen to receive the International Charlemagne Prize. It will indeed give me great pleasure if you yourself are able to be there. I am not yet sure that it will be possible for me to come on the 19th of May and I have taken advantage of the readiness of the City of Aachen to leave it open for the present whether the ceremony might take place at some other time.

---

[1] Maria Julius August Aloys Aegidius Hermann Heusch, 1906–81. Born in Aachen, Germany. Educated at Université de Lausanne. Head, Aachen Chamber of Commerce and Industry, 1945–81. Mayor of Aachen, 1952–73.

Sir Winston S. Churchill to Sir Anthony Eden
Prime Minister's Personal Minute M.21/55
(Premier papers, 11/867)

29 January 1955

1. I am in full agreement with you about doing our best for 'Oracle'.[1] There is no doubt that this policy is not only right but generally acceptable over here. We must wait and see what happens.

2. Chou En-lai's attitude, expressed in Peking telegram no. 104 of January 28 is not encouraging. The Chinese may not even come or only come to disagree.

3. If 'Oracle' fails it seems to me that it might be wise for the United States to take the following line:
   (a) To defend Formosa and the Pescadores at all costs and by all means, including counter-attack.
   (b) To announce their intention to evacuate all the Coastal Islands, including Quemoy, in the same way as they are clearing Chiang's troops out of the Tachens and to do this within three months.
   (c) To treat any proved attempt to hamper their withdrawal as the beginning of War between the United States and China.

4. The object of this is to free the Americans from having to look on while Chiang's 50,000 men on Quemoy and any other detachments elsewhere on the coastline, were scuppered while they did nothing. This, I am sure, would be intolerable to them. On the other hand, they had much better, in their own interests, get Chiang out of the Coastal Islands and draw a clear, clean line about Formosa, which is what they really want. If they could invest this process with a dictatorial air as an ultimatum concession and would evidently be doing what they themselves had decided and not what they had been compelled to do or badgered into doing, and if the Chinese submitted to the three months period of delay and strictly obeyed it, the American sense of humiliation would be greatly diminished and they would also be praised all over the free world.

5. I do not know whether there is any chance of the Americans accepting this sensible withdrawal under cover of their formidable threats and military precautions and also the whole thing being on their initiative and decision. They would say in effect: 'As negotiations have become impossible nothing is left to us but to decide the matter for ourselves; this is what we are going to do. Beware!'

6. Will you let me know whether you think there is anything in the above. We ought at any rate to be thinking of our next move if 'Oracle' fails.

---

[1] 'Oracle': a diplomatic initiative to get the UN Security Council to denounce the PRC's shelling of ROC-controlled islands in the Straits of Taiwan. The operation involved New Zealand, the UK and the US, and was ultimately a failure.

PS. I expect that Dulles has gone away because Ike has taken over the show. It is really in his hands after the Congress resolutions. He has gathered all the Staff people together and made it clear that he and he alone is to decide. I do not think it improbable that the sort of thing I put on paper might appeal to him and the American people would follow. The reports from Washington about the newspapers show a very varied panorama of opinion. I can always send him a telegram if we are agreed.

Cabinet: conclusions
(Cabinet papers, 128/28)

31 January 1955
Secret
11.30 a.m.
Cabinet Meeting No. 8 of 1955

[. . .]

2. The Foreign Secretary said that the Soviet Government had now asked for an immediate meeting of the Security Council to consider 'acts of aggression by the United States against the People's Republic of China in the area of Taiwan and other islands of China'. It need not be assumed that their motives were necessarily hostile: it was conceivable that their resolution had been framed with a view to making it possible for the Chinese Communist Government to send representatives to the discussions in the Security Council. As a result of consultations between the representatives in New York of the United Kingdom, United States, New Zealand and France, it was now proposed that this request by the Soviet Government should be placed on the agenda of the Security Council simultaneously with that previously put forward by the New Zealand Government – on the understanding that the New Zealand item would be discussed first and that any communication inviting the Chinese Communist Government to be represented at the ensuing discussions should be related to that request.

The Foreign Secretary said that, while the discussions in the Security Council were likely to last for several days, it was not too early to consider what line we should take if they produced no result. To assist the Cabinet in considering this he had put together some suggestions, in the form of a draft telegram to Her Majesty's Ambassador in Washington. Copies of this draft were handed round. If Ministers were in broad agreement with the general line there suggested, it might be adopted as a basis for discussion at the forthcoming Meeting of Commonwealth Prime Ministers. It was fortunate that we should have that opportunity for ascertaining the views of other Commonwealth Governments on this question.

JANUARY 1955 1883

In discussion of this draft the following points were made:
(a) Further consideration should be given to the terms of paragraph 11 of the draft. First, there might be some inconsistency between this and what was said in paragraph 7. Secondly, reference might be made to the human, as well as the juridical, arguments against accepting the Communists' claim to Formosa. In many countries public opinion would be impressed by the argument that the followers of Chiang Kai-shek now in Formosa should not be abandoned to the Communists. Thirdly, the analogy with Cyprus and Gibraltar might be put in more general terms.
(b) The Prime Minister said that he had made some suggestions to the Foreign Secretary about the advice which we might offer to the United States Government. It was important that the Administration should not get into a position from which they could not extricate themselves without the appearance of a diplomatic defeat. On the other hand, if they took a firm stand on a reasonable position, it seemed unlikely that the Chinese Communists would press their claims to a point at which they ran the risk of provoking general hostilities with the United States.
(c) It would be helpful if the Foreign Secretary would circulate, for the information of the Cabinet, a note on the juridical position in relation to Formosa.

The Cabinet –
(1) Took note that the Foreign Secretary, in the light of the points raised in the Cabinet's discussion and of the suggestions communicated to him by the Prime Minister, would recast the draft telegram to Her Majesty's Ambassador at Washington which he had circulated as a basis for the Cabinet's discussion.
(2) Took note that, during the forthcoming Meeting of Commonwealth Prime Ministers, the opportunity would be taken to ascertain the views of other Commonwealth Governments on the present situation in the Far East.
(3) Agreed to consider at a further meeting what advice might be given to the United States Government on this subject if no practical results emerged from the current discussion in the Security Council.

[...]

1884 JANUARY 1955

Commonwealth Prime Ministers' Conference: minutes
(Premier papers, 11/825)

31 January 1955
Meeting No. 1, Minute 1, of 1955

Sir Winston Churchill welcomed the other Commonwealth Prime Ministers, who had come great distances to take part in the family councils of the Commonwealth. In particular, he welcomed the Prime Minister of Ceylon, as a newcomer to the Meetings, and Mr Swart[1] who had come to represent the Prime Minister of South Africa.

He recalled that the last Meeting had been held at a time of general rejoicing at Her Majesty's Coronation. Now, after eighteen months had passed, the Prime Ministers were meeting with storm clouds from the Far East casting a grave and menacing shadow over the world. He hoped that their discussions would help them to see how the Commonwealth could use its underlying unity and strength to disperse those clouds.

Since the last Meeting a number of problems had been solved: the Persian oil dispute had ended; we had come to an understanding with Egypt about the Suez Canal base; Italy and Yugoslavia had reached agreement over Trieste; and in Indo-China fighting had been brought to an end. Moreover, the long argument over EDC had been ended and a basis had been found for bringing the German Federal Republic into a Western European Union. In each of these settlements the Foreign Secretary had played a leading part: he had reaped the reward of long months of patient and skilful negotiation. The Governments of the Commonwealth approached world problems from different angles, but they were united by the same high purposes and could discuss world issues with freedom and frankness. In the months ahead Commonwealth countries might well have to exert their combined influence and strength to prevent humanity from plunging to disaster.

Mr St Laurent expressed the deep appreciation of the Government and people of Canada for this opportunity of discussing international problems for the benefit of the Commonwealth and of the whole free world. He congratulated Sir Anthony Eden on the great part he had played in dealing with the many dangers to peace. The Paris Agreements had been the best solution, in the circumstances, of a most difficult problem: he regarded them as designed, not primarily to give Germany the right to rearm, but rather to restore her sovereignty and allow her to play her part in maintaining the peace of the world. Canada was concerned, as were other countries, with the situation in the Far

[1] Charles Robberts Swart, 1894–1982. Known as 'Blackie'. Born in Winburg, Orange Free State (OFS). Educated at University College of OFS, South Africa, and Columbia University, New York. MP (National Party) for Ladybrand, OFS, 1923–38; for Winburg, OFS, 1941–59. South African Minister of Justice, 1948–59. Minister of Education, Arts and Science, 1949–50. Deputy PM and Leader of the House, 1954–9. Acting PM, 1958. Governor-General of the Union of South Africa, 1960–1. President of South Africa, 1961–7.

East; and it was to be hoped that, on this occasion again, the deliberations at this Commonwealth meeting would serve to help, not only Commonwealth countries, but also the cause of freedom throughout the world.

Mr Menzies, in thanking Sir Winston Churchill for his welcome, said that the nature of these Commonwealth meetings was not always fully appreciated. At other international conferences delegates met as relative strangers and under the compulsion to make the conference a success, or an apparent success, or to admit failure. There was no need to do this when one was among friends: Commonwealth Prime Ministers met to extend the bounds of their knowledge and to talk frankly to one another. He associated himself with the congratulations offered to Sir Anthony Eden on his conduct of foreign policy during the past year.

Mr Holland said that the eyes of the world were on this Meeting, and he hoped that the countries of the Commonwealth would be able to give the world confidence in the prospects of peace. New Zealand rejoiced in the growing strength of Britain and felt that the Commonwealth was the greatest international force for good the world had ever known.

Mr Swart said that the Prime Minister of South Africa much regretted that he was not able to be present; but the Meeting coincided with his first Session of Parliament as Prime Minister, and it was out of the question for him to attend. The Government of South Africa had expressed the hope that Prime Ministers' Meetings should not in future be held during the period January–June, when the South African Parliament was in session.

Mr Swart emphasised that, contrary to the impressions which had arisen, the policy of the Government of South Africa was not one of isolation. One the contrary, South Africa realised the implications of her strategic position, and her Government stood for full cooperation with the free world.

Mr Nehru, in thanking Sir Winston Churchill for his welcome, said that the Meeting was especially opportune because of the situation in the Far East. Although it would be wrong to minimise the difficulties of that situation, it would be helpful to consider it from the different viewpoints of the countries of the Commonwealth.

In the course of his opening remarks, Mr Nehru made a statement on the outlook of the Chinese Government, which is recorded in Minute 3 below.

Mr Mohammed Ali also expressed his appreciation of the invitation to the Meeting. He said that the Commonwealth was unique as a free association of free nations and that, with growing understanding of the problems and points of view of other countries, this cooperation could be increased. To this end he hoped that Commonwealth meetings could be held at regular intervals, and he agreed with Mr Swart that it would be useful if they could be planned in advance to suit the convenience of all Prime Ministers. Pakistan had made it clear that she was definitely allied with the free world, and wished to make as effective a contribution as possible to the preservation of world peace.

Sir John Kotelawala said that he had recently visited a number of countries all over the world and was convinced that no one wanted war. In relation to the situation in the Far East, it should be remembered that Asia was now free and that Asian countries would like to handle their own affairs. China might therefore be ready to respect Asian opinion as regards the Formosa question. In this connection it was of interest that Choi-En-Lai had invited him to visit China, despite the fact that he was known to be anti-Communist and that Ceylon had no diplomatic relations with China. The three Prime Ministers from Asia who were present at this Conference would, he felt sure, be prepared to assist by talking to China, if it was felt that the situation could be improved by such an approach.

Sir John Kotelawala also referred to the need for economic aid to Asia. He said that at heart the under-developed countries of Asia wanted to remain democratic. But it was necessary for them to improve their standards of living; political ideologies and talk of freedom meant little to people if they were starving. Economic aid to the countries of Asia was therefore necessary if they were to play their proper part in international affairs.

Sir Godfrey Huggins also expressed his appreciation of the invitation to the conference. He felt that the true nature of these Meetings, as a means of consultation between Commonwealth countries, was now more fully understood.

February 1955

James de Rothschild to Sir Winston S. Churchill
(Churchill papers, 2/197)

1 February 1955

My dear Winston,

May I hope you will read these few lines? In asking you to do so, I am counting on the friendship you have always shown me.

Do you remember our stay in Jerusalem in 1921? You then laid the foundations of the Jewish State by separating Abdullah's Kingdom from the rest of Palestine. Without this much-opposed prophetic foresight, there would not have been an Israel today.

Now I see in *The Times* that at the Imperial Conference you are likely to discuss future admissions to the Commonwealth.

I have drawn up a short paper – which I enclose – on the reasons for including Israel among these, and the summary of this is annexed to this note.

I hope you may find time to glance at it in the welter of your tumultuous occupations. This is a matter to which I have given much anxious thought for many years and I think at last, it is right in the picture today.

It seems to me an exciting idea with large-scale possibilities and it needs a stout-hearted champion like you.[1]

PS. I have not sent a copy to Anthony and will only do so if I hear from you.

---

[1] In the margin, Churchill wrote a note to Eden: 'This is a big question. Israel is a force in the world & a link w the US.'

February 1955

Commonwealth Prime Ministers' Conference: minutes
(Premier papers, 11/867)

4 February 1955
Secret
Meeting No. 6, Minute 1, of 1955

1. FAR EAST
(Previous Reference: PMM (55) 2nd Meeting, Minute 1)

Sir Anthony Eden said that the answer which the Peking government had made to the invitation to send representatives to the United Nations made it clear that they were not prepared to come to the Security Council on any basis which was likely to be acceptable to the majority of members of the Council. Their refusal showed a considerably different attitude from the less extreme line taken by the Russians at the Security Council meeting. One thing was certain; the reaction in the United States would not be good. American opinion had been developing gradually in the direction of moderation, but the Chinese reply would weaken the position of those whose policy was to evacuate the Chinese Nationalist forces from the coastal islands and strengthen those who were working to bring matters to a head.

In this new situation we had to consider what was our objective. We could try to get the whole problem settled, for which purpose several methods might be available, such as an Assembly Resolution or a specially convened conference of the nations most directly concerned. But it was perhaps too much to hope that a general settlement could thus be reached. It would be preferable to concentrate on trying to secure the establishment of a neutral sheet of water between the mainland of China on the one hand and Formosa and the Pescadores on the other. This could not be achieved by agreement except at a meeting at which the Peking Government were represented. There was, however, the possibility of a third course – to obtain an American assurance that they would withdraw from all the coastal islands, coupled with an undertaking by the Peking Government that they would not interfere with the operation.

The immediate problem was to decide what was to be done in the Security Council. He was apprehensive about proceeding with a resolution in the Security Council. Inevitably, any resolution which would be acceptable to the Americans would be vetoed by the Soviet Union. The result, therefore, would only be to demonstrate a division of opinion in the Security Council and to bring China and Russia closer together. Moreover, the Americans might well then ask us what we proposed to do to support them. This would be extremely embarrassing, since public opinion in the United Kingdom would not favour giving even moral support to defending the retention of the coastal islands, still less support of a material kind. The only other possible course might be to have further private discussions with the Russians. The United Kingdom had not yet received an answer to the note which had been given to the Soviet Chargé d'Affaires in London two days earlier, and reports in the Soviet Press had been hostile. Nevertheless, it was possible that a fresh approach to the Russians would be worthwhile.

Mr Holland said that he thought that there would be great value in a period of delay, to give time for consideration and study. He read out to the meeting the terms of the draft resolution which it had been proposed that the New Zealand representative should table in the Security Council. Although he did not think that the resolution, in itself, would have led to trouble, especially if the Peking Government had come to the meeting, it was very likely that in present circumstances such a resolution would be vetoed, and would lead to further difficulties.

Mr Pearson said that if the question were simply dropped in the Security Council, it would be a clear demonstration that the Security Council was powerless to take any effective action which was not approved by the Peking Government. The terms of the Chinese reply suggested that this might be exactly what the Peking Government had wished to demonstrate. On the other hand, if we proceeded with a resolution, it was likely to be vetoed in the Security Council, and this would inflame United States public opinion. The United States Administration might then feel themselves compelled to take some further action, in the Security Council or elsewhere, which it might be difficult for the rest of the free world to support; and if we did not support the United States, it would be seen that the Western Powers were divided, which would be a victory for Peking. We should therefore try to avoid taking any action until we saw how public opinion in the United States was developing.

Mr Nehru said that he agreed that it would be desirable to wait over the weekend to see what the reactions to the uncompromising reply from Peking would be. Although the reply had been in harsher language than he had expected, a refusal had not been unexpected. It was clear that, if progress was to be made, the Peking Government had to be brought into consultation. Any decision by the Security Council in the absence of representatives from Peking (even if it were not vetoed by the Russians) would be regarded by the Chinese as an order which, clearly they would not be prepared to carry out. The Peking Government bore no allegiance to the United Nations; the United Nations did not recognise them and they could reasonably say that they did not recognise the United Nations.

Mr Menzies said that wisdom required that we should not be in a hurry to take action. Resolutions, even good ones, would get us nowhere and we should find the road to hell paved with them. The action which was likely to follow a resolution in the Security Council might well exacerbate the Americans, and force them to take up a position from which they would find it difficult to retreat. It might be that the best line would be for the Commonwealth to have private talks with the United States to see whether, even at some danger to their prestige, they could be persuaded to undertake the evacuation of the Nationalist forces from the coastal islands. If it were clear to the Peking Government that the United States was taking constructive action of this sort, they might well be prepared not to put any obstacles in the way of evacuation.

Sir Winston Churchill said that it was essential always to appreciate how this situation was regarded by Americans. Never before had such a great nation been threatened with war by so weak a power. It was only too likely that the attitude of the Peking Government would strengthen the hand of the militant elements in the United States who saw advantages in bringing matters to a head now, while the balance of power, especially in thermo-nuclear weapons, was so decisively in favour of the Americans. We must be careful not to give an opportunity to Americans of that way of thinking to say that their allies were of no use, and that the United States must therefore act alone, and at once. It was by no means certain that the Russians, who appreciated the preponderant power of the United States at the present time, would want to give the Chinese active support. If the Russians were to give active support, they would throw away all chance of surprise in the use of their own atomic weapons, since the whole military potential of the United States would be instantly alerted. It was contrary to the Russians interest to commit themselves to support of Peking at this stage; knowing this, the Americans might well feel that they could safely take action against China alone.

If President Eisenhower could succeed in determining a sound policy based on a position of strength, he could declare publicly that, since there was no purpose in trying to negotiate with the Peking Government, the United States Government had accordingly decided upon the action which, with their overwhelming power, they would take. This action would be to ensure the safe evacuation of all forces from the coastal islands, so that there would be a wide barrier of water between China, and Formosa and the Pescadores. This operation would be carried out in three months or less. If Peking should interfere with it, the United States would take such military measures as were necessary to remove that interference. It might well be that President Eisenhower would feel himself capable of valiant and daring actions of this kind for peace, and it would be wrong to do anything at this moment which might make it more difficult for him to bring that about. It did not seem that the Commonwealth would be involved in the actual process of withdrawal, since our obligations under the United Nations were limited to Formosa and the Pescadores.

In reply to a question from Mr Pearson,

Sir Anthony Eden said that he felt sure that Chiang Kai-shek was doing all he could to persuade the United States not to evacuate the Tachen Islands. He was not sure what numbers were involved, but the total was small. There were not more than a thousand civilians in Quemoy; presumably these would be given the opportunity to be evacuated if they wanted.

Sir Anthony Eden informed the Meeting that, in the light of the discussion

FEBRUARY 1955 1891

which had taken place, he proposed to send a telegram to the United Kingdom Ambassador in Washington, saying that the Commonwealth Prime Ministers had been anxiously watching developments in China, and were of the opinion that it would be wise to avoid any precipitate action in order to give time for reflection. The telegram might also say that the Prime Ministers had been much impressed by the calm and restrained way in which President Eisenhower was handling the situation.

Cabinet: conclusions
(*Cabinet papers, 128/28*)

4 February 1955
Secret
5 p.m.
Cabinet Meeting No. 9 of 1955

[...]
2. The Cabinet were informed that the Prime Minister of Pakistan had now put before the Meeting of Commonwealth Prime Ministers a definite programme of constitutional change by which Pakistan would become a republic in the course of 1955. He had assured the other Commonwealth Prime Ministers that it was the unalterable will of the Pakistan people to adopt a republican form of Constitution, but that it was equally their desire that Pakistan should remain a full member of the Commonwealth. He had made it clear that it was the policy of the Pakistan Government to maintain the closest association with the other members of the Commonwealth and to align themselves firmly with the Western Powers.

In the discussion at the Commonwealth Meeting the Prime Ministers of the United Kingdom, Australia and New Zealand had expressed their profound regret at Pakistan's decision to renounce her allegiance to the Crown. In the course of this discussion the suggestion had been made that the wishes of the Pakistan people might have been met by an arrangement by which the Governor-General would in future be elected instead of being appointed by the Crown; but it seemed clear that their nationalist aspirations would not be satisfied with anything less than the declaration of a republic. This being so, the other Commonwealth Prime Ministers had unanimously agreed to accept Pakistan's proposal that she should continue to be a full member of the Commonwealth after becoming a republic.

The Prime Minister said that, with very great regret, he had made the necessary submission to Her Majesty on behalf of all the Commonwealth Prime Ministers. The decision would be announced that evening, in the form of a declaration approved by all the representatives of Commonwealth Governments attending the Commonwealth Meeting.

In discussion there was general agreement with the Prime Ministers. The decision would be announced that evening, in the form of a declaration approved by all the representatives of Commonwealth Governments attending the Commonwealth Meeting.

In discussion there was general agreement with the Prime Minister's view that Pakistan's decision to adopt a republican form of Constitution was greatly to be regretted.

It was suggested that in recent years there had been too great a tendency to describe the advancement of dependent peoples in terms of 'independence' instead of 'self-government' and that these references to 'independence' had tended to encourage the view that full sovereignty was incompatible with continued allegiance to the Crown. The Colonial Secretary undertook to consider this point.

The Cabinet —

Took note that the representatives of all the Commonwealth Governments attending the Commonwealth Meeting had agreed that Pakistan should continue to be a full member of the Commonwealth even though she adopted a republican form of Constitution.

[. . .]

4. The Prime Minister said that other Commonwealth Prime Ministers had now been informed of the Government's decision to proceed with the development and production of thermo-nuclear weapons. The Government would be embarrassed if there were any premature disclosure of this decision, and he had thought it right that the Cabinet should have an opportunity of considering whether an official announcement should be made in advance of the publication of the Defence White Paper. He himself was satisfied that public reception of this decision would be less favourable if it were announced in isolation; and he would much prefer that it should be made public in the White Paper in the context of the Government's defence policy as a whole.

The Cabinet were reminded that a White Paper was also to be presented on the civil uses of atomic energy. It had been assumed hitherto that this would be published a few days before the Defence White Paper. There would be advantage in publishing the Government's programme for civil development of atomic energy before announcing their decision to produce thermo-nuclear weapons. This was an additional reason for announcing the latter decision in the Defence White Paper.

The Cabinet —

Agreed that the Government's decision to proceed with the development and production of thermo-nuclear weapons should be announced in the Defence White Paper, which was due to be presented to Parliament on 17th February.

[. . .]

FEBRUARY 1955 1893

Commonwealth Prime Ministers' Conference: minutes
(Premier papers, 11/867)

7 February 1955
Secret
Meeting No. 7, Minute 1, of 1955

1. FAR EAST
(Previous Reference: PMM (55) 6th Meeting, Minute 1)

Sir Anthony Eden said that on 2nd February he had asked the Soviet Government, through the Soviet Chargé d'Affaires in London, to urge the Peking Government to accept the invitation to attend the proposed discussion in the Security Council on the situation in the Far East. However, the Peking Government had now refused this invitation. On 4th February M Molotov had given the United Kingdom Ambassador in Moscow a statement of the views of the Soviet Government. The salient feature of this was a proposal that the problem should be considered at a special conference to which the United States, the Peking Government, the Soviet Union, the United Kingdom, France, India, Burma, Indonesia, Pakistan and Ceylon should be invited: it had been suggested that the United Kingdom, the United States and India might take the initiative in arranging such a conference. M Molotov had been asked by the United Kingdom Ambassador to continue to keep this proposal secret. It had been passed on to the United States Government on 5th February. It was unlikely that such a conference would be acceptable to the Americans, since it was not to include the Chinese Nationalists and it would take the matter out of the United Nations.

The United Kingdom Government had also given their general views on the situation to the United States Government. They had expressed the view that no good result would flow from further discussion on the substance of this issue in the Security Council, but that later on a conference might usefully be held, if possible under the aegis of the United Nations. The essential preliminary was to bring the fighting to an end and for this purpose it was necessary to know what the United States wished eventually to achieve. The United Kingdom Government believed that the United States aim was that Nationalist troops should be withdrawn to Formosa and the Pescadores, and that the coastal islands should be evacuated. If the United States held this view but were unable for political reasons to express it in public, it might be possible for the United Kingdom to take some initiative which would reduce the risk of an incident. Finally, the United Kingdom Government had indicated that, while they would not regard the Soviet proposal in its present form as acceptable, the door should not be closed on the possibility of a conference, even if it was held otherwise than under the aegis of the United Nations.

The United Kingdom Ambassador in Washington would shortly obtain the reaction of Mr Dulles to these views. It was the former's view that the United States would not be prepared to define her objectives in the Formosa Straits, even confidentially. While it was probably true that most of the Administration realised that Nationalist China must eventually withdraw from the coastal islands, they would not be prepared to admit this in public; and Mr Dulles' reply was likely to be that he could not clarify the United States position, beyond the statements which had already been made, until the evacuation of the Tachen Islands had been completed. The United Kingdom Ambassador had suggested that this reluctance to clarify their objectives was due, not so much to anxiety about the political repercussions in the United States, as to a desire to avoid making a major concession to the Peking Government and lowering the morale of Nationalist China. The Ambassador therefore doubted whether it was wise to press the United States Government to clarify their position publicly, and had suggested that it might not be essential that this should be done before approaches were made to the Peking Government.

Sir Anthony Eden said that there was also a report that Mr Chou En-lai had sent a telegram to the Secretary-General of the United Nations suggesting that direct discussions between the United States and the Peking Government might be possible.

Mr Nehru said that the Indian Ambassador at Peking had reported that the Peking Government broadly agreed with the Soviet proposal, but would also be ready to discuss the situation with the Secretary-General of the United Nations. They would also be prepared to enter into direct discussions with the United States Government, as the party principally concerned in the dispute over the Formosa Straits. They were not, however, prepared to accept any proposal which would have the effect of recognising, even inferentially, that there were two Chinas. The Ambassador had added that, so far as he could see, no warlike preparations were being made in China.

Mr Menzies said that, while it was true that uncertainty about the United States position was embarrassing, their policy was understandable. Formosa was of first-rate importance to the United States and, in view of the danger of undermining the morale of the Chinese Nationalists, they must feel that the possibility of evacuating Quemoy must be handled with delicacy. On the other hand, the United States were most unlikely to plunge into war over Quemoy. The best course seemed to be to allow time for passions to cool. Meanwhile, the evacuation of most of the coastal islands would probably have been completed.

Mr Holland suggested that in these circumstances there was little point in proceeding with a debate in the Security Council on the New Zealand resolution. A meeting might have to be held to consider the reply which had been received from the Peking Government, but this should be arranged in such a way as to avoid any substantive discussion of the New Zealand or Russian resolutions.

Mr Pearson suggested that appropriate steps should be taken to prevent the President of the Security Council from taking the initiative of calling an early meeting. But any member of the Council could call a meeting; and, if any did, the best course would be to handle it as a procedural discussion and to avoid discussion of either resolution. There was always a possibility that if a meeting took place the United States might wish to go ahead with a cease-fire resolution, even though the Peking Government were not represented, and this might lead to difficulties.

Sir Anthony Eden said that Formosa was recognised as belonging to Nationalist China by some members of the United Nations but not by others; it would therefore be very difficult to get a resolution through the Assembly on this question which would command general support. The immediate objective should be to discourage the Security Council from meeting.

There was general agreement with this view.

Mr Menzies said that the problem of the Formosa Straits should be kept so far as possible out of the arena of public debate. At the present stage this would tend to exacerbate the situation and was likely to have the result that countries would take up positions from which they would find it embarrassing to withdraw. It would be monstrous if these offshore islands became a casus belli. As regards Formosa and the Pescadores, on the other hand, while the juridical position was uncertain, it was strategically important for the United States to keep control of these islands. There would be great uneasiness in Australia if, through the surrender of Formosa, a break was made in the chain of islands which were of material importance to the defence of the South Pacific. Such a surrender would lead to Communist infiltration in to Indonesia and the Philippines. The best course would be to secure a neutralised sheet of water between the mainland of Communist China, with its offshore islands, and Formosa with the Pescadores. It might be possible, by means of private persuasion by all members of the Commonwealth where their pressure was most likely to be effective, to bring about such a solution.

Whether this was possible depended on what were the real aims of the Peking Government. If their immediate objective was simply to recover the coastal islands, they would be likely to connive at an evacuation; but if they wanted to destroy a substantial portion of Chiang Kai-shek's forces, the evacuation of the coastal islands might well be the occasion for hostilities. The Commonwealth included countries which were particularly well placed to sound and to influence China and the United States, and perhaps to help to bring them to the point at which they could hold direct talks.

Sir Winston Churchill said that the military dangers of an evacuation of Quemoy were great and such an operation might tempt the Chinese Communists to harass the garrison as it dwindled. The United States might therefore be justified in warning the Peking Government that any interference with the operation would be punished. But there was an essential difference between

Formosa and the coastal islands. The retention of Formosa by Nationalist China could be defended on the ground that it represented a sanctuary for an ally whom, in honour, the United States could not abandon. But the coastal islands were more in the nature of bridgeheads for an invasion of China. It was understandable that the occupation of these islands by the Chinese Nationalists angered the Peking Government. It would not be unreasonable for the Peking Government to ask for assurances that, if they agreed to the peaceful evacuation of the coastal islands, Chiang Kai-shek would not be allowed to use Formosa as a base for the invasion of China. The United States were naturally concerned to avoid lowering the morale of the Chinese Nationalist forces; but, even if plans for a return to China were dropped, these men would have an assurance of sanctuary and freedom for their lifetime. In twenty years' time, when it was no longer a sanctuary for men who were sheltering from Chinese Communist vengeance, it would be easier to settle the ultimate status of Formosa.

Commonwealth Prime Ministers' Conference: minutes
(Premier papers, 11/867)

8 February 1955
Secret
Meeting No. 8, Minute 1, of 1955

1. FAR EAST
(Previous Reference: PMM (55) 7th Meeting, Minute 1)

The Meeting were informed of the attitude of the United States Government to the situation in the Far East, as disclosed by Mr Dulles in talks which he had had on the previous day with the United Kingdom and New Zealand Ambassadors in Washington.

Sir Anthony Eden mentioned two further factors which also had to be considered. First, the Soviet proposal for a special conference, which had hitherto been kept secret, was now on the point of becoming public. Second, M Malenkov had that morning resigned from his position as Prime Minister of the Soviet Union. The ostensible reason for his resignation was the failure of his agricultural policy, but there had been earlier reports of rivalry between M Malenkov and M Krushchev, but it might be that the policy of collective leadership which had been followed since the death of Stalin had given way to the traditional Russian preference for individual leadership. M Krushchev, if he was to succeed, would no doubt owe his position to his control of the Communist party.

Sir Anthony Eden said that, in present circumstances, he remained opposed to the discussion of the New Zealand resolution in the Security Council. The

United States Government had given no indication of their attitude towards the Soviet suggestion for a special conference. They evidently needed more time for reflection; but an uncomfortable position would develop if weeks were allowed to pass without any clarification of their policy. As the Soviet proposal was now to become public, the United Kingdom Government would be pressed to state their reaction. It would be their aim to keep the diplomatic channel open by pointing out, in the reply to the Soviet Union, that certain alterations would have to be made in the proposal for a meeting if it was to lead to any useful result. For example, the Chinese Nationalist Government would have to be represented at the conference. It was clear that the United States Government were not prepared to negotiate, inside or outside the United Nations, about the present situation unless the Chinese Nationalist Government were represented.

Mr Menzies said that he was not sure, from these reports, that the United States Government were closing their minds to the possibility of eventual evacuation of Quemoy and Matsu. They clearly felt that evacuation at the present time would place too grave a strain on the morale of the Chinese Nationalists. But it might be that they would contemplate eventual evacuation at a time when this could be undertaken without such grave risk to the authority of the Nationalist Government. But the United States Government were possibly under-estimating their great ability to influence Nationalist morale.

The Meeting agreed to resume consideration of the international situation in the Far East later in the day.

Neither the United Kingdom nor Australia nor any other free country would want to become involved in a war over Quemoy. We should, therefore, be careful not to encourage the United States to become so involved. If the United States got into a war with China, that might well develop into a world war, and it would be too late for any of us then to say that we did not know the gun was loaded.

Would the Russians want to start a world war over Quemoy? He could not believe that they would, all the indications were that their internal advice will be against precipitating a war.

Would the Chinese Communists want a world war over Quemoy? In his view they would not. For, as a war over Quemoy could arise only by Communist China's aggression, Russia might well say: 'This is not within the terms of our bargain. If you are attacked, we stand with you under our treaty but if you go and buy a war unnecessarily that is your business.'

What, then, were the respective points of view of Communist China and Nationalist China? It seemed to him that what the Peking Government wanted was physical possession of the off-shore islands, with the loss of face which this would involve for Chiang Kai-shek. If they could see that these islands were to be evacuated and handed over, would they insist on military action to destroy the retreating troops? This, surely, was open to serious doubt. They were more likely to regard the evacuation itself as a sufficient blow to Nationalist China's morale. He therefore concluded that, if it could be made known to the Peking Government, not by public declaration but by ordinary diplomatic means, that the off-shore islands were to be ceded, there would be much wild talk but very little, if any, shooting.

The attitude of Chiang-Kai-shek was more doubtful. He alone among people outside the Communist curtain had a vested interest in a world war, because he would see in it his only prospect of reestablishment on the mainland of China. He might, therefore, set out to create incidents and thereby to precipitate a war. For control over him we must rely on President Eisenhower. Formosa's chance of survival depended on American aid; and the President could influence Chiang as nobody else could.

This reasoning reinforced his belief that this was not a time for public declarations which might, in some contingency, lead to war. To make threats without performing them would be to make the worst of all worlds. His conclusion, therefore, was this. Neither we nor the United States wanted war, least of all about the off-shore islands. Some 'face saving' manoeuvre might be needed, but in the long run it was better to have one's face damaged than to lose one's head. The sensible practical course was surely to persuade the United States Government, by private representations, to make it clear to Chiang Kai-shek that the off-shore islands were strategically important only for a Nationalist attack upon the mainland; that America would support no such project; and that the firm American protection of Formosa and its adjacent waters was worth far more to Nationalist China than any adventure in the off-shore islands which would enjoy little if any world support. Simultaneously, Mr Nehru might be able to exercise his influence in Peking by indicating to the Chinese Communist Government that, if they kept quiet, they would get the offshore islands and that a world war would have been avoided. The situation was one which called for quiet persistent and persuasive diplomacy.

From the point of view of Australia and, indeed, Malaya, it would be fatal to have an enemy installed in the island chain so that by a process of island-hopping Indonesia might be reached and Malaya and Australia to that extent exposed to serious damage either in the rear or on the flank. But the off-shore islands had nothing to do with the defence of Formosa. They were important only for Nationalist China's ambitions. We should discourage the United States Government from getting into a position in relation to the off-shore islands in which they would find themselves bound to enter upon operations of war.

To sum up, he was confident that neither the United States nor the United Kingdom nor the British Commonwealth nor the free world as a whole wished to make the off-shore islands an occasion of war. He was also confident that the influence of Moscow would be in the same direction; and that Communist China, while willing to pick up the bits if they could be picked up cheaply, would not seriously want to become involved in a major struggle with the United States. If all this was correct, the task of the Commonwealth Governments was to remove heat, to play for time, to avoid public debate, and to use their versatile diplomatic resources to exercise the maximum of influence both in Washington and Peking.

In further discussion there was general agreement with the views expressed by Mr Menzies.

Mr Mohammed Ali, while agreeing with Mr Menzies on the immediate issue, said that in his opinion the Peking Government intended eventually to play for bigger stakes than the coastal islands. Their ultimate aim was to liquidate the Nationalist forces and to end Chiang's pretensions that he could provide an alternative government of China. They were also concerned to secure for themselves the representation of China in the United Nations and to bring to an end the period of American influence over Formosa. It was clear that the Commonwealth countries could not at present contemplate the cession of Formosa to Communist China or the surrender of the refugees on Formosa to the mercies of the Chinese Communists. Peking's claims to Formosa must therefore be resisted for some time to come. Meanwhile, tension would be eased if some concession could be made. He wondered whether it would be possible, at the appropriate stage, to support the claim of the Peking Government to represent China in the United Nations, on the basis that the Government of Chiang-Kai-shek would be treated as nothing more than the Government of Formosa?

Mr Jooste[1] said that the South African Government had serious misgivings about the present policy of the United States Government in respect of the coastal islands. They feared that American action in support of the Nationalists in this area might provoke incidents which might lead on to general war.

Sir Winston Churchill said that, while he was in general agreement with Mr Menzies' conclusions, he could not altogether exclude the possibility that some incident might occur on Quemoy which would inflame public opinion in the United States to a point at which the Administration would be forced to take vigorous action. If the Nationalist forces were to be evacuated from Quemoy, they would have to be withdrawn in stages; and in that process there would come a point when those left on the island could easily be overcome by Communist forces. If the Communists seized that opportunity to butcher the remaining detachments of Nationalist troops on the island, a situation might well arise in which the United States Government would feel compelled, in honour, to take retaliatory action. If such a situation arose, he was not sure

---

[1] Gerhardus Petrus Jooste, 1904–90. Entered public service, Union of South Africa, 1924. Private Secretary to Minister of Finance, 1929–34; in Dept of External Affairs, 1934–7. Légation Secretary, 1937–40. Chargé d'Affaires ad interim, 1937–40; to Belgian Government-in-Exile, 1940–1. Head of Economic Div., Dept of External Affairs, 1941–6; Head of Political and Diplomatic Div., 1946–8. Ambassador to US, 1948–54. Permanent Delegate to UN, 1948–54. High Commissioner of Union of South Africa in London, 1954–6.

that the United States would be willing to limit themselves to the use of conventional weapons. It was this possibility which most disturbed him, and make him feel that there was a real risk that a series of incidents might be set in train which could lead on to widespread hostilities.

Mr St Laurent, in concluding the discussion, said that the pooling of information and exchange of views at this Meeting would be of great value to all Commonwealth Governments in their future consideration of this problem. Those of them which were in a position to exercise influence in Washington, Peking and Moscow would be better able to do so in the light of the discussions which had taken place at this Meeting.

Commonwealth Prime Ministers' Conference: minutes
(*Premier papers, 11/825*)

8 February 1955
Secret
Meeting No. 9, Minute 2, of 1955

2. CONCLUSION OF PROCEEDINGS

Mr St Laurent said that he would wish, on behalf of himself and of the other Commonwealth Ministers, to express gratitude for the initiative taken by the United Kingdom Government in convening this Meeting and for the hospitality which they had extended to visiting Delegations. He also wished to express, on behalf of all, their appreciation of the way in which Sir Winston Churchill had presided over the Meeting. Throughout their discussions they had benefited greatly by his guidance, based on an unrivalled experience, and to him personally they owed a great debt.

Mr Nehru said that Mr St Laurent had spoken for all other Commonwealth Ministers and there was nothing he need add. But he would like to say that all those who had attended the Meeting had benefited greatly by the discussions, which would be of great value in helping Commonwealth Governments to take their future decisions on the matters which had been considered at the Meeting.

Sir Winston Churchill said that, on behalf of the United Kingdom Government, he wished to express similar sentiments. The presence of other Commonwealth Ministers in London at this time had itself helped to increase the influence which Commonwealth Governments could exercise on world affairs; and it was fortunate that, by coincidence, this Meeting had been held at a time of such serious international tension. The discussions had shown what a large measure of agreement there was between Commonwealth Governments on all major questions and they had confirmed him in his view that the Commonwealth countries could make a great contribution towards the preservation of world peace. It had been a pride and an honour for him to receive the other Commonwealth Ministers and to preside over their discussions.

Meeting of Commonwealth Prime Ministers: communiqué
(Premier papers, 11/825)

9 February 1955

The Governments of the member nations of the Commonwealth are resolved to do their utmost to ease international strain. It is their aim, not only to bring any open hostilities to an end, but to promote conditions in which real peace can grow and thrive so that freedom and plenty may be enjoyed by all peoples.

Since the last Meeting of Commonwealth Prime Ministers in 1953, agreements have been reached in various parts of the world which have had the effect of removing differences and widening the area of understanding among Governments and peoples. The Prime Ministers welcomed the settlement of the Trieste dispute. They recorded their satisfaction that, in the Middle East, the United Kingdom's differences with Egypt and Iran had been resolved. They looked forward to closer collaboration between all the countries of that area so that its economic development and the welfare of its peoples could be advanced. They welcomed, in South-East Asia, the end of hostilities in Indo-China and stressed the need for strict adherence to the conditions of the Geneva Agreement and for increased welfare and stability in that area.

The Prime Ministers were informed that the Commonwealth countries associated with the North Atlantic Treaty were convinced that the early ratification of the Agreements reached in London and Paris and the acceptance of Federal Germany into the community of the Western nations would mark an important advance towards the security and cohesion of Western Europe.

The Prime Ministers met at a time of tension in the Far East. In view of developments which occurred during their Meeting, their discussion of this problem assumed a special significance. They were confident that the intimate and personal discussion which they had held at this Meeting would be a valuable foundation for future consultations, with one another and with other countries directly concerned, and for the development of their policies on this question.

The Prime Ministers noted the improvement in the outlook for world trade and prosperity which had taken place since the Commonwealth Finance Ministers met at Sydney in January, 1954. They recognised that Commonwealth countries had made a substantial contribution to this by maintaining the stability of their currencies, by continuing their development programmes, in which the Colombo Plan had played its part, and by expanding their production.

They had also continued their progressive approach towards the widest practicable system of trade and payments, which best serves the interest of the sterling area and Canada.

The Prime Ministers affirmed their determination to continue these policies of economic progress. They agreed, in particular, that all Commonwealth countries should strive to develop further their resources and their earning power. By these means they could best consolidate their strength and make an increased contribution to economic stability throughout the world.

The Prime Ministers gave anxious thought to the problems of nuclear energy. The latest discoveries confront humanity with a force which is almost beyond the capacity of man's brain to comprehend or measure. They present a choice and a challenge. Is this vast power to be developed for the benefit of man, or is it to be used to bring ruin upon that human race?

The Prime Ministers once again declare that their countries will never embark upon aggression. Indeed, it is their hope that, when the peoples of the world understand the magnitude of the disaster which world war would bring, all nations will shrink from violence and follow peaceful means of settling their differences. The annihilating power of the new weapons renders it imperative that sanity should prevail and that war should be prevented.

It is the aim of the Commonwealth countries to work for a disarmament agreement which includes forces and weapons of all kinds and is both comprehensive and effective. Commonwealth Governments have already devoted much time and thought to producing and furthering practical plans to achieve this purpose, and two of the Commonwealth countries are members of the Sub-Committee of the United Nations Disarmament Commission.

With international accord on disarmament, it would become possible to turn the vast resources of atomic energy increasingly into channels which benefit mankind. The Prime Ministers were informed of the progress made by the United Kingdom Government in the use of atomic energy for industrial and other peaceful purposes. They look forward to the prospects of continued close cooperation between the United Kingdom and other Commonwealth countries in the development of the civil uses of atomic energy.

In the course of this Meeting, the Prime Minister of Pakistan informed the other Prime Ministers that Pakistan was about to adopt a republican form of constitution but desired to remain a member of the Commonwealth. They were assured that the people of Pakistan were resolved to maintain, despite this constitutional change, their steadfast adherence to the Commonwealth and their recognition of the Crown as the symbol of the free association of its sovereign members. In a declaration issued on February 4 they signified their agreement that Pakistan should continue on this basis to be a full member of the Commonwealth after becoming a republic. All the Prime Ministers reaffirmed that their countries would remain united as free and equal members of the Commonwealth, freely cooperating in the pursuit of peace, liberty and progress.

The Commonwealth is a unique association. Its countries contain a fourth of the world's population, embracing people of many races and religions. Among its members are countries of importance in all quarters of the globe. Its strength and influence in the world today are derived from this and from a common outlook which, in spite of differences of geography, religion and race, evokes a broadly similar response to most international problems of the day.

The Commonwealth countries do not pursue any selfish purpose. They seek no aggrandisement and will always oppose aggression. In concert with all who share their ideals, they are resolved to do their utmost to further the cause of peace throughout the world.

President Dwight D. Eisenhower to Sir Winston S. Churchill
(Premier papers, 11/1074)

10 February 1955   The White House
Top Secret – Eyes Only

Dear Winston,

I have heard how earnestly you supported throughout the Conference of Prime Ministers the proposition that nothing must create a serious rift in British–American relationships. Not only do I applaud that sentiment, but I am most deeply grateful to you for your successful efforts.

I realize that it has been difficult, at times, for you to back us up in the Formosa question and, for this reason, I want to give you a very brief account of our general attitude toward the various factors that have dictated the course we have taken. You understand, of course, that we have certain groups that are violent in their efforts to get us to take a much stronger, even a truculent position. The number that would like to see us clear out of Formosa is negligible. I know that on your side of the water you have the exact opposite of this situation.

Because the Communists know these facts, there is no question in my mind that one of the principal reasons for their constant pressing on the Asian frontier is the hope of dividing our two countries. I am sure that we, on both sides of the water, can make quite clear that, no matter what may be our differences in approach or even sometimes our differences in important convictions, nothing is ever going to separate us or destroy our unity in opposing Communist aggression.

We believe that if international Communism should penetrate the island barrier in the Western Pacific and thus be in a position to threaten the Philippines and Indonesia immediately and directly, all of us, including the free countries of Europe, would soon be in far worse trouble that we are now. Certainly that whole region would soon go.

To defend Formosa, the United States has been engaged in a long and costly program of arming and sustaining the Nationalist troops on that island. Those troops, however, and Chiang himself, are not content now, to accept irrevocably and permanently the status of 'prisoners' on the island. They are held together by a conviction that someday they will go back to the mainland.

As a consequence, their attitude toward Quemoy and the Matsus, which they deem the stepping stones between the two hostile regions, is that the surrender of those islands would destroy the reason for the existence of the Nationalist forces on Formosa. This, then, would mean the almost immediate conversion of that asset into a deadly danger, because the Communists would immediately take it over.

The Formosa Resolution,[1] as passed by the Congress is our publicly stated position; the problem now is how to make it work. The morale of the Chinese Nationalists is important to us, so for the moment, and under existing conditions, we feel they must have certain assurances with respect to the offshore islands. But these must be less binding on us than the terms of the Chino-American Treaty, which was overwhelmingly passed yesterday by the Senate. We must remain ready, until some better solution can be found, to move promptly against any Communist force that is manifestly preparing to attack Formosa. And we must make a distinction – (this is a difficult one) – between an attack that has only as its objective the capture of an off-shore island and one that is primarily a preliminary movement to an all-out attack on Formosa.

Whatever now is to happen, I know that nothing could be worse than global war.

I do not believe that Russia wants war at this time – in fact, I do not believe that even if we became engaged in a serious fight along the coast of China, Russia would want to intervene with her own forces. She would, of course, pour supplies into China in an effort to exhaust us and certainly would exploit the opportunity to separate us from your country. But I am convinced that Russia does not want, at this moment, to experiment with means of defense against the bombing that we could conduct against her mainland. At the same time, I assume that Russia's treaty with Red China comprehends a true military alliance, which she would either have to repudiate or take the plunge. She would probably be in a considerable dilemma if we got into war with China. We believe our policy is the best that we can design for staying out of such a fight.

In any event, we have got to do what we believe to be right – if we can figure out the right – and we must show no lack of firmness in a world where our political enemies exploit every sign of weakness, and are constantly attempting to disrupt the solidarity of the free world's intentions to oppose their aggressive practices.

---

[1] A mutual security treaty between the US and Nationalist China was written in Dec. 1954 and ratified by the US Senate on 5 Feb. 1955.

Though thus sketchily presented, this has been the background of our thinking leading up to the present day. I devoutly hope that history's inflexible yardstick will show that we have done everything in our power, and everything that is right, to prevent the awful catastrophe of another major war.

I am sending you this note, not merely because of my realization that you, as our great and trusted ally, are entitled to have our thoughts on these vital matters, but because I so value, on the more personal side, the opportunity to learn of your own approach to these critical problems.

Again my thanks to you for giving Thomas Stephens so much of your valuable time, and my apologies that he appeared in London in what was, I know, a most difficult and exhausting week for you.

Cabinet: conclusions
(Cabinet papers, 128/28)

15 February 1955
Secret
11.30 a.m.
Cabinet Meeting No. 13 of 1955

1. The Foreign Secretary said that he was increasingly disturbed by the risk that the United States administration would commit themselves to support the continued occupation of Quemoy and the Matsu Islands by Chinese Nationalist Forces. The Administration were being led to believe, by reports from their representatives in Moscow and elsewhere, that the Russians were ready to support the Peking Government in an offensive policy; and this made them reluctant to make any move which might be interpreted as a gesture of appeasement. It was also known to be the view of some of the senior military advisers in Washington that the recent Government changes in Moscow had reduced the likelihood that the Soviet Government would risk a major war, and that the United States could therefore afford to take a very firm line in the Far East. Against this general background it was disturbing to learn, from Washington telegram No. 414, that the Administration were thinking of making a public declaration of their policy which would imply that, in present circumstances at any rate, some of the coastal islands were regarded by them as necessary for the defence of Formosa.

In discussion there was general agreement with the Foreign Secretary's view that the United States Government would not be able to command the support of large sections of world opinion if at this stage they publicly committed themselves to a policy which might involve them in giving active support to the Chinese Nationalists in Quemoy and the Matsus. The Prime Minister said that it suited the Communists' purpose to divide Western opinion on this question, and the United States Government would be falling into an obvious trap if they made a public declaration which had the effect of dividing that opinion still further. Peking's threats to seize Formosa by force were idle words: in fact it would be quite impossible for the Chinese Communists to mount an effective attack against Formosa in the face of United States opposition. It was, therefore, both unnecessary and unwise for the United States Government to make any public declaration implying that they paid serious attention to these threats.

The Foreign Secretary read to the Cabinet a draft of a message on this question which he was proposing to send to the United States Secretary of State. The Prime Minister informed the Cabinet of the substance of a personal message which he was proposing to send to President Eisenhower.

The Cabinet –

Took note of these statements and approved the terms of the messages which the Prime Minister and the Foreign Secretary were proposing to send to Washington on this question.

[. . .]

Sir Winston S. Churchill to President Dwight D. Eisenhower
Prime Minister's Personal Telegram T.6/55
(Premier papers, 11/879)

15 February 1955
Immediate
Dedip
Top Secret, Personal and Private
No. 697

My dear Friend,

We have all here been watching with the closest attention your decisions and moves in the Formosan crisis. For the last three weeks I have been wanting to write to you. Your most kind letter of February 10[1] has reached me and I find that much I had already put on paper still represents my steadily growing theme. Anthony and I, who have composed this message together, wish to do our utmost to sustain you and help you lead world opinion. There is wide recognition of the efforts you have made to keep out of war with China in spite of gross provocation. As you know, I feel strongly that it is a matter of honour for the United States not to allow Chiang Kai-shek and his adherents, with whom the United States have worked as Allies for so many years, to be liquidated and massacred by Communist China, who are alleged to have already executed in cold blood between two and three millions of their opponents in their civil war. Our feeling is that this is the prime and vital point. According

---

[1] Reproduced above (pp. 1431–2).

to our lights we feel that this could and should be disentangled from holding the offshore islands as bridgeheads for a Nationalist invasion of Communist China. Besides this we do not think that Formosa itself, while protected by the United States, ought to wage sporadic war against the mainland.

2. So the problem before us at this stage centres on what should be done about the offshore islands, which we here have to admit are legally part of China and which nobody here considers a just cause of war. You know how hard Anthony and I have tried to keep in step with you and how much we wish to continue to do so. But a war to keep the coastal islands for Chiang would not be defensible here.

3. I had understood that the United States Government had so far been resolved to resist Chiang's pressure to give assurances about these islands, even in return for Chinese Nationalist evacuation of the Tachens,[1] and had succeeded in doing so. I hope your last sentence on page 2[2] does not conflict with this.

4. I cannot see any decisive relationship between the offshore islands and an invasion of Formosa. It would surely be quite easy for the United States to drown any Chinese would-be invaders of Formosa whether they started from Quemoy or elsewhere. If ever there was an operation which may be deemed impossible it would be the passage of about a hundred miles of sea in the teeth of overwhelming naval and air superiority and without any tank and other special landing-craft. You and I have already studied and indeed lived through such a problem both ways.

5. Guessing at the other side's intentions is, as you say, often difficult. In this case of Quemoy, etc., the Communists have an obvious national and military purpose, namely, to get rid of a bridgehead admirably suited to the invasion of the mainland of China. This seems simple.

6. Diplomatically their motives are more fanciful. It may be, as your third paragraph suggests, that the absurd Chinese boastings about invading Formosa are inspired by the Soviet desire to cause division between the Allies in the far more important issues which confront us in Europe. It costs very little to say, as the Chinese are now reported to be doing, that 'the possession of the Tachens will help the liberation of Formosa'. It adds to the pretence of Communist China's might and is intended to provoke the United States into actions and declarations which would embarrass many of us, and add influence to Communist propaganda.

7. I have already expressed my convictions about your duty to Chiang

---

[1] The Tachen (Dachen) islands are made up of 29 islets and rocks with a total area of 5.6 square miles off the coast of Taizhou. In pursuance of the Formosa Resolution, passed by Congress on 29 Jan. 1955 and ratified by the Senate on 5 Feb. 1955, the US Navy evacuated 14,500 civilians and 14,000 servicemen and guerrilla fighters to Taiwan. The Tachens were subsequently occupied by the Chinese People's Liberation Army.

[2] Sentence reading: 'We must remain ready, until some better solution can be found, to move promptly against any Communist force that is manifestly preparing to attack Formosa.'

whom you rightly called your 'brave Ally'. But I do not think it would be right or wise for America to encourage him to keep alive the reconquest of the mainland in order to inspirit his faithful followers. He deserves the protection of your shield but not the use of your sword. ('Sword' in this case is a rather comprehensive term.) The hope of Chiang subduing Communist China surely died six years ago when Truman on Marshall's advice gave up the struggle on the mainland and helped Chiang into the shelter of Formosa.

8. We were of course glad to see your decision, now bloodlessly carried out, to evacuate the Tachen islands, but we still feel very anxious about what may happen at the Matsus and Quemoy. The operation of evacuating 50,000 Nationalist troops might present serious dangers, especially to the rearguard. On the other hand to linger on indefinitely in the present uncertainty, might well reach the same conclusion by a slower process.

9. Before I got your message I had been wondering whether the following threefold policy would be acceptable and I send it now for your consideration.
   (a) To defend Formosa and the Pescadores as a declared resolve.
   (b) To announce the United States intention to evacuate all the offshore islands including Quemoy in the same way as the Tachens, and to declare that they will do this at their convenience within (say) three months.
   (c) To intimate also by whatever channel or method is thought best that the United States will treat any proved major attempt to hamper this withdrawal as justification for using whatever conventional force is required.

This would avoid the unbearable situation of your overwhelming forces having to look on while Chiang's 50,000 men on Quemoy and any other detachment elsewhere on the offshore coastline were being scuppered. To me at this distance the plan seems to have the merit of being simple, clear, and above all resolute. It would I believe command a firm majority of support over here. It puts an end to a state of affairs where unforeseeable or unpreventable incidents and growing exasperation may bring about very grave consequences.

10. To sum up, we feel that the coastal islands must not be used as stepping stones either by the Communists towards the conquest of Formosa or the Nationalists towards the conquest of China. But they might all too easily become the occasion of an incident which would place the United States before the dilemma of either standing by while their allies were butchered or becoming embroiled in a war for no strategic or political purpose.

11. If this is so, the right course must be to make sure that the United States are not put in the position of having to make such a decision over the coastal islands. This can only be done by taking advantage of the present lull to remove the Nationalists from Quemoy and the Matsus – as they have already been removed from the Tachens – before they become the occasion

of further dangers. Opinion in this country, and so far as can be judged in the Commonwealth, would regard such a decision as right in law, in morals and in worldly wisdom.

12. Our long friendship made me wish to put these thoughts before you and now I have the generous invitation of your closing paragraph. Anthony and I deeply desire to do our utmost to help you and our strongest resolve is to keep our two countries bound together in their sacred brotherhood.

Lady Violet Bonham Carter to Sir Winston S. Churchill
(Churchill papers, 6/6)

15 February 1955
Private

Dearest Winston,

Thank you for your letter and its enclosure.

I am a little puzzled by its purpose – i.e. why you send me a letter you have written (and not sent), to the Bishop of Coventry[1] instead of sending it to him? (Nor do I understand why you are sending it to Sir Ian Jacob – whom it concerns more directly – instead of writing to him direct?).

As you know I have had no responsibility for the BBC since my Governorship expired in 1946. I should however have supported the policy statement issued by the Governors in 1947 on the broadcasting of 'affirmations of widely differing beliefs and unbeliefs . . . made constructively'.

And as you may, or may not, have noted, the British Council of Churches recommended (in 1949) 'That the experiments in controversial religious discussion should be continued and extended to cover a wider range of listeners'.

I did not hear the twelve talks broadcast in the Light Programme (in 1953) under the title 'Question Mark' – six by Christians and six by unbelievers – with the approval and advice of the Religious Advisory Committee.

But I did hear Bertrand Russell[2] argue for three quarters of an hour with Father Copplestone[3] – against the existence of God – (and Bertrand Russell carried and discharged far heavier guns than Mrs Knight)! So far as I know these precedents left you unmoved?

I do not happen to agree with Mrs Knight's views, but (like Voltaire) I

[1] The letter was in fact sent; it, and the Bishop's reply, are reproduced above (pp. 1876–7, 1879–80).
[2] Bertrand Arthur William Russell, 1872–1970. Educated at Trinity College, Cambridge, 1893; Fellow, 1895–1916, 1919–20, 1944–9. Founder, Beacon Hill School, 1927. 3rd Earl Russell, 1931. Lecturer, London School of Economics, 1937. OM, 1949. Nobel Prize in Literature, 1950.
[3] Frederick Charles Copleston, 1907–94. Educated at Marlborough and St John's College, Oxford. Entered Catholic Church, 1925; Society of Jesus, 1930. Ordained priest, 1937. Prof. of History of Philosophy, Heythrop College, Oxford, 1939–70; Gregorian University, Rome, 1952–68; University of London, 1972–4. Dean of Faculty of Theology, University of London, 1972–4. Visiting Prof., University of Santa Clara, Calif., 1974–5, 1977–82; University of Hawaii, 1976. Gifford Lecturer, University of Aberdeen, 1979–80.

believe that she has every right to express them. If Free Speech means anything it cannot be confined to certain prescribed media or subjects.

The air is now the most far-reaching medium of communication in existence and our religious belief, or unbeliefs, are certainly among the most important themes which concern the human mind.

Your indictment of 'a machine with all its plugs, knobs and switches' – 'robot machinery' etc., is an indictment of broadcasting itself.

You yourself have used its 'robot machinery' to good purpose on many occasions and it is at present being used to pour thousands of hours of Christian doctrine into millions of homes every day of every week.

To say that the machine becomes unholy when it transmits what we disagree with is the pure milk of Totalitarianism – as practised by every dictator to this day.

Our Christianity would not be worth much it if could not stand up to two mild and platitudinous twenty-minute talks.

In our long friendship we have often passionately agreed and sometimes differed – but now – for the first time – I feel that we are not talking the same language. I therefore enclose, to make my meaning clear (and for the edification of the Bishop of Coventry) a statement of the case for freedom, in far better language than I could attempt, by a master of the subject – John Stuart Mill.[1]

My love to you as always.

PS. I apologize for the length of the Mill quotation – but its quality makes it well worth reading.

Lieutenant-General Sir Ian Jacob to Sir Winston S. Churchill
(Churchill papers, 6/6)

16 February 1955

My dear Prime Minister,

Thank you very much for sending me a copy of the letter[2] you contemplated sending to the Bishop of Coventry. I very fully appreciate the view that you express in the letter. It is one of the hardest tasks imposed on the Governors and on myself who have to direct the output of the BBC, to exert our influence with a full sense of responsibility particularly as it is always a matter of opinion whether this course or that should be followed. The output is considerable and unceasing, and with the passage of time has come to embrace

---

[1] John Stuart Mill, 1806–73. Philosopher, economist and civil servant. Worked for East India Co., 1823–58. Married, 1851, Harriet Taylor. MP (Lib.) for Westminster, 1865–8. Published *System of Logic* (1843), *Principles of Political Economy* (1848), *On Liberty* (1859) and *The Subjection of Women* (1869).

[2] Reproduced above (pp. 1876–7).

an exceedingly wide range of human thought and activity. To hold the scales between free speech and the full expression of differing opinions on the one hand, and irresponsibility on the other is the main task, and it is inevitable that there will be occasions when in the opinion of some we do not altogether succeed.

I return the copy of your letter as requested.

Cabinet: conclusions
(Cabinet papers, 128/28)

17 February 1955
Secret
11.30 a.m.
Cabinet Meeting No. 15 of 1955

1. The Cabinet considered a memorandum by the Colonial Secretary on the problem presented by the growth of Indian communities in British Colonial territories.

The Colonial Secretary said that, although he sought no immediate decisions on this problem, he had thought it right to bring it to the notice of the Cabinet since it was one which Ministers should have constantly in their minds. There were substantial Indian communities in many of the Colonies, both in Africa and elsewhere, and their rate of natural increase was alarming. In some Colonies this was already giving rise to racial tension.

In discussion the following points were made:

(a) The attitude of the Indian Government towards these communities should be closely watched. It was at present their professed policy that Indians settled overseas should regard themselves as members of the community in which they lived. It was, however, stated in paragraph 10 of C(55)10 that, while professing this policy, the Indian Government lost no opportunity to foster links between India and these overseas communities.

(b) Close attention should be given to the activities of Indian Commissioners in Colonial territories. The Indian Government had recognized that these representatives should not intervene in the domestic politics of the countries where they were stationed; and it was open to us to press, as we had done successfully in the past, for the recall of any Indian Commissioner whose activities transgressed this principle.

The title 'Commissioner' gave these representatives a higher local status than that of the Trade Commissioners of other Commonwealth countries. It was for consideration whether those countries should not be asked to change the title of their representatives, so as

to deprive the Indian Commissioners of the superior status which they now enjoyed.
  (c) Colonial Governments could take steps to restrict further immigration of Indians. The Indian Government had not disputed the right of other Commonwealth countries to restrict Indian immigration into their territories.
  (d) In paragraph 16(e) of C(55)10 it was proposed that public action should be taken in the United Nations and elsewhere to counter tendentious speeches and actions by Indian representatives. It was suggested that on most occasions it would be preferable, and more effective, to proceed by way of private representations to the Indian Government.

The Prime Minister said that, while he recognized the gravity of this problem, he did not think the time was opportune for any drastic action in respect of it which might give offence to the Indian Government. India was in a position to exercise a moderating influence in Asia; and it was specially important at the present time that she should maintain the closest possible association with us in the handling of the major international problems of the day. It need not be assumed that in all Colonies Indian communities would prove an embarrassment to us: in some they might even be a balancing factor. Thus, although the problem should be carefully watched, precipitate action should be avoided.

The Lord President doubted whether action could be long delayed. He was specially impressed by the considerations summarized in paragraph 10 of C(55)10. He believed that in this matter the policy of the Indian Government was likely to be influenced by their desire to champion coloured peoples and to encourage opposition to Colonial rule.

The Cabinet –

Took note of C(55)10 and agreed to resume their consideration of this problem later in the year.

[. . .]

FEBRUARY 1955

Sir Winston S. Churchill to Spyros Skouras[1]
(Churchill papers, 6/6)

18 February 1955

My dear Mr Skouras,

I must tell you what a great success are the CinemaScope arrangements which have been made at Chartwell. We had our first performance last week, during which we saw *The Robe* and the film *Pageants and Pastimes* which you have been so kind as to give me. I am delighted with the new vista that now opens before me and shall henceforward find still greater enjoyment in my Chartwell cinema. I am much indebted to you for your generous gift and want to tell you how justified I see you were in the enthusiasm with which you advocated these new leisures.

Evelyn Shuckburgh: diary
('Descent to Suez', pages 250–1)

18 February 1955

We went to lunch with the Queen and Duke of Edinburgh, in honour of the Shah and his Queen. Queen Elizabeth, the Churchills, Edens, Tommy Lascelles, Nuttings,[2] Harold Nicolsons,[3] Peter Flemings,[4] Salisbury-Jones[5] and some Household. Really excellent lunch, far beyond the cooking of

---

[1] Spyros Panagiotis Skouras, 1893–1971. President of 20th Century Fox. Born in Skourohorion, Greece. Migrated to US, 1910. Married, 1920, Saroula Bruiglia: five children. Formed Skouras Brothers Co., 1924. Took over Fox West Coast Theater, 1932. Merged Fox with Twentieth Century Pictures to form 20th Century Fox, 1942. President, 20th Century Fox, 1942–62.

[2] Gillian Leonora Strutt, 1918–?. Married, 1941, Anthony Nutting (div. 1959): three children.

[3] Victoria Mary Sackville-West, 1892–1962. Known as 'Vita'. Daughter of 3rd Baron Sackville. Author. Married, 1913, Harold Nicolson. Wrote *Country Notes in Wartime* (1940). Columnist at *The Observer*, 1946–61. CH, 1948.

[4] Robert Peter Fleming, 1907–71. Known as 'Strix'. Educated at Eton and Christ Church, Oxford. Commissioned, Grenadier Guards, 1930. Married, 1935, Celia Johnson: three children. On active service, WWII, 1939–45. Commanded 4th Battalion, Oxford and Bucks Light Infantry (TA), 1951–4. High Sheriff of Oxfordshire, 1952. President, Oxfordshire Branch of Country Landowners' Association, 1960–71. Deputy Lieutenant, Oxfordshire, 1970. Published *One's Company, A Journey to China in 1933* (1934), *The Flying Visit* (1940) and *The Fate of Admiral Kolchak* (1963).
Celia Elizabeth Johnson, 1908–82. English actress. Nominated for Academy Award for Best Actress for *Brief Encounter* (1945). Six-time BAFTA Award nominee and and winner of BAFTA Award for Best Actress in a Supporting Role for *The Prime of Miss Jean Brodie* (1969).

[5] Arthur Guy Salisbury-Jones, 1896–1985. Commissioned, Coldstream Guards, 1915. Liaison Officer in Syria, 1924–6. Served in Jebel Druze campaign, 1925–6. Commanded 3rd Battalion Coldstream Guards, Palestine, 1938–9. Served in Syria, Italian Somaliland, Greece and Crete, 1939–44. Head, Military Mission to South Africa, 1941–4. Served at Supreme HQ Allied Expeditionary Force, 1944–5. Head, British Military Mission to France; Military Attaché, Paris, 1946–9. ADC to HM King George VI, 1948–9. HM Marshal, Diplomatic Corps, 1950–61. Chairman, Franco-British Society, 1963–7.
Hilda de Bunsen, 1900–95. Married, 1931, Arthur Salisbury-Jones: two children.

Government hospitality. After lunch the children and the two corgis came in and played around. They were quite unspoilt and natural, yet very well behaved, and their grandmother took them round to talk to people. The little princess[1] was fascinated by Winston, who sat slumped in his chair, looking just like the Sutherland portrait. I was drawn into some talk with him, and he said the FO was 'riddled with Bevinism' on Middle East questions, i.e. anti-Jewish. He had heard (from James de Rothschild) that the Israelis would like to join the British Commonwealth. 'Do not put that out of your mind. It would be a wonderful thing. So many people want to leave us; it might be the turning of the tide.' I congratulated him on the success of the Commonwealth Prime Ministers Conference. He said, 'I have worked very hard with Nehru. I told him he should be the light of Asia, to show all those millions how they can shine out, instead of accepting the darkness of Communism.' 'But you ought to let the Jews have Jerusalem; it is they who made it famous.' He also said that large numbers of the refugees ought to be settled in the Negev. I'm not sure whether he was aware that this is something the Israelis are resisting. I was surprised that the guests of honour were not given an opportunity to talk to any of the 'Persian experts' (Harold Nicolson, etc.) whom we had so carefully collected for them. They talked to the Queen and Duke exclusively before, during and after lunch.

Lady Soames: recollection
('Clementine Churchill', page 501)

[undated]

It was during the voyage to New York[2] that my mother told Christopher and me that the Graham Sutherland portrait of my father was no longer in existence. We were both flabbergasted. We knew the picture had been sent to Chartwell not long after the presentation, and had been stored away there. But the information Clementine now imparted to us was a total surprise. She told us that Winston's deep dislike of the picture, and the bitter resentment at the manner in which he had been portrayed, weighed more and more on his mind during the months that followed its presentation in November 1954, to such an extent that Clementine told us she had promised him that 'it would never see the light of day'. As far as I know, she consulted no one about her intention, and it was entirely on her own initiative that some time in 1955 or 1956 she gave instructions for the picture to be destroyed. I do not believe

---

[1] Anne Elizabeth Alice Louise, 1950–. Second child and only daughter of Queen Elizabeth II and Prince Philip, Duke of Edinburgh. Participated in 1976 Olympic Games as a member of the British equestrian team. Married, 1973, Capt. Mark Phillips (div. 1992); 1992, Cdr Tim Lawrence. Princess Royal, 1987–. Grand Master of the Royal Victorian Order, 2007.
[2] In February 1965.

Clementine ever specifically told Winston the steps she had taken: but her original pledge calmed him, and reassured him that the actual portrait which he so heartily loathed would not be seen by generations yet unborn. (But of course photographs had been taken of the picture.)

As time went by there were spasmodic, but persistent enquiries about the portrait, and requests for it to be exhibited on permanent loan or for specific exhibitions. These enquiries were at first easily parried, both Winston's and Clementine's dislike for the picture soon becoming a well-known fact. The very small number of people who came to know of its fate were all of the same mind – namely, that whatever the enquiries, or the speculation, the facts should not be revealed in Clementine's lifetime. It was therefore inevitable that from time to time a few of us were forced to be less than candid when questioned on the subject. Clementine herself simply refused to discuss the matter at all, except with those of us who knew the story. And even with us, it was not a topic frequently touched upon.

Sir Winston S. Churchill to Queen Elizabeth II
(Churchill papers, 6/6)

19 February 1955

Madam,

Your Majesty will remember the project that Auxiliary squadrons of the Royal Air Force should no longer form part of the RAF front line and should be deprived of their own operational aircraft. I understand that the Secretary of State for Air explained to Your Majesty the suggestion that each Auxiliary squadron should be linked for training purposes with a regular squadron in Fighter Command, although retaining its identity, its Honorary Air Commodore, its headquarters and a flight of Meteors or Vampires for training purposes.

After further consideration, it is felt that, while it will never be possible for the Auxiliary squadrons to be ready on the outbreak of war for service against the latest type of bomber, there will nevertheless be a useful part which they could play against older types of enemy aircraft and in support of operations against invasion by air or sea.

For these reasons it is now proposed to make no change in the organisation of the squadrons, apart from what may be necessary to give the pilots training in the new swept-wing aircraft. This will be explained in parliament during the debates on the Defence and Air Estimates, but I feel it my duty first to inform Your Majesty of this change of plan.

February 1955

President Dwight D. Eisenhower to Sir Winston S. Churchill
(Premier papers, 11/879)

19 February 1955
Top Secret

Dear Winston,

I greatly appreciate the message[1] from you and Anthony. I have studied it long and carefully, as has Foster. Quite naturally, it distresses us whenever we find ourselves in even partial disagreement with the conclusions that you two reach on any important subject. It is probably that these differences frequently reflect dissimilar psychological and political situations in our two countries more than they do differences in personal convictions based upon theoretical analysis. Nevertheless we clearly recognize the great importance to the security of the free world of our two governments achieving a step by step progress both in policy and in action.

Diplomatically it would indeed be a great relief to us if the line between the Nationalists and the Communists was actually the broad strait of Formosa instead of the narrow straits between Quemoy and Matsu and the mainland. However, there are about 55,000 of the Nationalist troops on these coastal islands and the problem created thereby cannot, I fear, be solved by us merely announcing a desire to transplant them to Formosa.

Foster and I have been working very hard over recent months, and he has been in close touch with Anthony, in the attempt to lay a basis for what we have hoped may prove a gradual but steady solution.

There are two important points that must be considered at every step of any analysis of this exceedingly difficult situation.

The first is that this country does not have decisive power in respect of the offshore islands. We believe that Chiang would even choose to stand alone and die if we should attempt now to coerce him into the abandonment of those islands. Possibly we may convince him in the future of the wisdom of this course, but to attempt to do more at this time would bring us to the second major point, which is: we must not lose Chiang's army and we must maintain its strength, efficiency and morale. Only a few months back we had both Chiang and a strong, well-equipped French army to support the free world's position in Southeast Asia. The French are gone – making it clearer than ever that we cannot afford the loss of Chiang unless all of us are to get completely out of that corner of the globe. This is unthinkable to us – I feel it must be to you.

In order to make an express or tacit cease-fire likely, we have, with difficulties perhaps greater than you realize, done, through our diplomacy, many things.

---

[1] T.6/55, reproduced above (pp. 1906–9).

1. We rounded out the far Pacific security chain by a treaty with the Nationalists which, however, only covered specifically Formosa and the Pescadores, thus making it clear to Chiang and to all the world that we were not prepared to defend the coastal positions as treaty territory.
2. We obtained from Chiang his agreement that he would not conduct any offensive operations against the mainland either from Formosa <u>or from his coastal positions</u>, except in agreement with us. Thus we are in a position to preclude what you refer to as the use of those offshore islands as 'bridgeheads for a Nationalist invasion of Communist China', or as a base for 'sporadic war against the mainland' or 'the invasion of the mainland of China'. Under present practice we do not give agreement to any such attacks unless they are retaliatory to related, prior, Communist attacks. In these respects we have done much more than seems generally realized.
3. Furthermore, we obtained an agreement from the Nationalists closely limiting their right to take away from Formosa military elements, material or human, to which we had contributed if this would weaken the defense of Formosa itself.
4. We made possible the voluntary evacuation of the Tachens and two other islands.
5. Finally, we secured the acquiescence of the Chinese Nationalists to the United Nations proceedings for a cease-fire, although the Chinese Nationalists were extremely suspicious of this move and felt that it could permanently blight their hopes.

All this was done, as I say, in consultation between Anthony and Foster and in the hope that this would provide a basis for a cease-fire.

However, what we have done has apparently been interpreted by the Chinese Communists merely as a sign of weakness. They have intensified their threats against Formosa and their expressions of determination to take it by force. Also, they continue to hold, in durance vile, our airmen who were captured by them in the Korean war and who should have been freed by the Korean armistice.

There comes a point where constantly giving in only encourages further belligerency. I think we must be careful not to pass that point in our dealings with Communist China. In such a case, further retreat becomes worse than a Munich because at Munich there were at least promises on the part of the aggressor to cease expansion and to keep the peace. In this case the Chinese Communists have promised nothing and have not contributed one iota toward peace in the Formosa area. Indeed, they treat the suggestion of peace there as an insult.

I am increasingly led to feel it would be dangerous to predicate our thinking and planning on the assumption that when the Chinese Communists talk about their resolve to take Formosa, this is just 'talk', and that they really would be satisfied with the coastal islands. I suspect that it is the other way around. What they are really interested in is Formosa – and later on Japan – and the coastal islands are marginal. They do not want to have another Chinese government in their neighborhood, particularly one which has military power and which poses a threat to their center if ever they attack on their flanks.

Therefore, I think that if the Chinese Nationalists got out of Quemoy and the Matsus, they would not be solving the real problem, which is far more basic. I repeat that it would more likely mean that this retreat, and the coercion we would have to exert to bring it about, would so undermine the morale and the loyalty of the non-Communist forces on Formosa that they could not be counted on. Some, at least, might defect to the Communists or provide such a weak element in the defense of Formosa that an amphibious operation could give the Communists a strong foothold on Formosa.

You speak about our capacity to 'drown' anybody who tried to cross the Formosa Straits. However, we do not and cannot maintain at that spot at all times sufficient force to cope with an attack which might come at any time both by sea and by air and which would presumably operate from several different points and be directed against several different points on what is a very considerable body of land. It took us two days to assemble the force necessary to insure the safety of the Chinese Nationalists evacuating from the Tachens. Now most of that force has returned to its normal bases which are the Philippines Japan, and Okinawa. The Chinese are past masters at the art of camouflage and, as bitter experience in Korea taught us, they can strike in force without detectable preparations. We must rely upon a loyal and dependable force of Nationalists on Formosa to deal with any who, for the reasons indicated, we might be unable to 'drown' before the attackers reached that island.

And if perchance there should be any serious defection on Formosa, that would be a situation which we could not possibly meet by landing Marines or the like to fight the Chinese Nationalist defectors on the island. Such a development would undermine the whole situation.

All of the non-Communist nations of the Western Pacific – particularly Korea, Japan, the Philippines, and, of course, Formosa itself, are watching nervously to see what we do next. I fear that, if we appear strong and coercive only toward our friends, and should attempt to compel Chiang to make further retreats, the conclusion of these Asian peoples will be that they had better plan to make the best terms they can with the Communists.

I know that your government's intelligence sources are very good. But this is a situation which we have worked with and lived with very intimately. We do have considerable knowledge, and the responsibility. Surely all that we have done not only here, but in Korea with Rhee, amply demonstrates that we are not careless in letting others get us into a major war. I devoutly hope that there may be enough trust and confidence develop between our two peoples so that when judgments of this kind have to be made, each could, in the last analysis, trust the other in the areas where they have special knowledge and the greatest responsibility.

It would surely not be popular in this country if we became involved in possible hostilities on account of Hong Kong or Malaya, which our people look upon as 'colonies' – which to us is a naughty word. Nevertheless, I do not doubt that, if the issue were ever framed in this way, we would be at your side.

We are doing everything possible to work this situation out in a way which, on the one hand, will avoid the risk of war, and, on the other hand, preserve the non-Communist position in the western Pacific, a position which, by the way, is vital to Australia and New Zealand. However, if the Chinese Communists are determined to have a war to gain Formosa, then there will be trouble.

I see I have made this as long, and perhaps as complicated, as a diplomatic note. For that I apologize!

Sir Winston S. Churchill to Sir Anthony Eden
(Premier papers, 11/879)

19 February 1955
Secret and Private

My dear Anthony,

Herewith I send you Ike's reply, which reached me too late for your departure. It is a much better letter than the one we answered and has, as he says, been concerted with Foster. It is a real and sincere attempt to make us understand the American point of view.

They do not mean to let Japan go red. I also feel they may easily get tired of being insulted by the Chinese Communists. In this connection I send you a paper I had prepared of the abuse which Chiang and Chou-en-lai etc., are hurling at each other. I should have thought it was rather a dangerous thing for Chou-en-lai to say that he will in certain conditions wipe the aggressors, meaning the Americans, off the face of the earth.

We must go forward with patience and with courage, being very thankful we can talk so intimately to the heads of the greatest power in the world.

The Soviets, it seems to me, are playing a dangerous game if they are stimulating Communist China to talk big about Formosa. They are quite right in thinking that this provokes the Americans into awkward and unhandy policy which loses them support in Britain and in Europe. They are quite wrong if they think the consequences will divide the free world, or be very agreeable to China should they go too far.

I will watch the situation as a cat does a tiger. I am seeing Rab on Monday on what you spoke to me about and Harold later in the day about the Defence Debate.

God speed you and Clissa on your journey.

Sir Winston S. Churchill to Sir Edwin Plowden
Prime Minister's Personal Minute M.39/55
(Premier papers, 11/1055)

19 February 1955
Secret

You have no doubt seen the latest Soviet bid for banning nuclear weapons. Please examine the following point for me.

When this matter was considered at various times after the late War, the possibilities of a concealed stockpile had not arisen, and it was agreed that inspection could observe the gigantic plants necessary to produce the uranium and also to extract the plutonium, etc., therefrom. But how could inspection ensure that, say, a cubic yard of plutonium, etc., had not been overlooked and hidden somewhere? Then after the United States and Britain had scrapped all their stockpile and plant it might be discovered and mentioned with many apologies by the Soviets. It is true that between this cubic yard and bomb equipment there is a large scale and complicated process. Would re-created plants for this have to be of a certainly detectable size, on the assumption that agreed United Nations inspectors are mooching about in all countries? Although re-creation of these plants, whether discoverable or not, would necessarily precede any atomic attack, the fact that the Soviets would be the only power in the world with the cubic yard stockpile would give them, I suppose, several years start of anybody else. They might then acquire a position of great advantage, in which they could say that nothing was further from their thoughts than to give an equipment outfit to their cubic yard, and they would not think of doing this as long as we allowed them to have their way bit by bit in the cold war. But possessing or controlling as they would no doubt overwhelming superiority in conventional weapons and in manpower, the Free World would have no power to prevent them equipping the cubic yard. This they could do at their leisure while holding off forcible conventional counter measures and enjoying a period of aggregable bargaining power.

Pray let me have your thoughts on this in Christian language and not more than three or four pages.

I am sending a copy of this minute to Prof.

FEBRUARY 1955

Sir Winston S. Churchill to Queen Elizabeth II
(Churchill papers, 6/6)

20 February 1955

Madam,

I enclose herewith the latest letter[1] I have received from President Eisenhower. It is a very sincere and intimate expression of American views and on some points of their intentions. It has evidently been a matter of joint consultation between him and Dulles and I expect other advisers, and must be regarded as a more finished product than his previous one. I like his reference to Hong Kong and Malaya. I do not think, and nor apparently does he, that the main Russian aim at this moment is war. Their hope is to divide Britain and the United States by words. They find 'Formosa' a very useful word. Nonetheless, the situation about the offshore islands is more than ever full of danger. It is a great anxiety, but nothing like what we should feel if there were no United States.

Sir Winston S. Churchill to Lady Violet Bonham Carter
(Churchill papers, 6/6)

20 February 1955

My dear Violet,

I sent my letter[2] to you because we argued the topic at Downing Street and I wanted to put it to you that the use of robot machinery raises other questions than those of free speech. I sent it to Ian Jacob because I thought he would be interested. I have had a very nice latter back from him. It is astonishing that the mechanical aspect does not command its due proportion of your thought. One can understand why John Stuart Mill did not deal with it in the quotation you sent me.

Sir Winston S. Churchill to Lieutenant-General Sir Ian Jacob
(Churchill papers, 6/6)

20 February 1955

My dear Jacob,

Thank you very much for your letter.[3] I realise how great your difficulties are. The responsibility for the use of the vast machinery of radio and TV is at once formidable, novel and perpetual. In this case I think there would have

[1] Reproduced above (pp. 1916–19).
[2] Reproduced above (pp. 1876–7).
[3] Reproduced above (pp. 1910–11).

been no trouble if the topic had been part of a rather high-grade programme like the Third Programme. What vexed me was the millions of humble homes affected.

I am very glad you are standing up against the idea of anticipating the Parliamentary Debate on the H bomb.

Sir Winston S. Churchill to Jawaharlal Nehru
(*Churchill papers, 6/6*)

21 February 1955

My dear Nehru,

I am so much obliged to you for sending me the fascinating book of paintings taken from the Ajanta Caves. The reproductions are beautifully executed and I am indeed happy to possess such a wonderful book. It also gives me great pleasure that it should have come from you, and that our personal relations, after all that has happened, are so agreeable. I hope you will think of the phrase 'The Light of Asia'. It seems to me that you might be able to do what no other human being could in giving India the lead, at least in the realm of thought, throughout Asia, with the freedom and dignity of the individual as the ideal rather than the Communist Party drill book.

I am so glad your Sister[1] is in so important a position over here.

House of Commons: Written Answers
(*Premier papers, 11/879*)

23 February 1955

CHINA (COASTAL ISLANDS)

48. Mr Hector Hughes[2] asked the Prime Minister if he will make a comprehensive statement up to date specifying the Government's present policy on the hostilities now taking place in the Far East relating to Formosa and the islands off the Chinese coast, which have been referred to the United Nations organisation.

The Prime Minister: A very full statement was made by my right hon. Friend the Foreign Secretary on the 14th of this month and I have only somewhat general observations to make upon this anxious subject today.

---

[1] Vijaya Lakshmi Nehru, 1900–90. Married Ranjit Sitaram Pandit, 1921. Indian Ambassador to Soviet Union, 1947–9; to US, 1949–52. President, UN General Assembly, 1953. High Commissioner of India to UK, 1954–61. Governor of Maharashtra, 1962–4. Representative to UN Human Rights Commission, 1979.

[2] Hector Hughes, 1887–1970. Educated at University College, Dublin. MP (Lab.) for Aberdeen North, 1945–70.

There is a great difference between the coastal islands of China and the island of Formosa. As there is no question of our being involved militarily or indeed or our being needed in the defence of the coastal islands, we should be careful of what advice we should offer our friends and Allies upon it.

The decision on whether or when these particular islands should be evacuated is not one the burden of which falls upon Her Majesty's Government and we must recognise the natural preoccupations of other Governments who are immediately affected by the threatened attack from Communist China. This is especially true at a time when the Chinese Communists keep stridently asserting that the islands are to be regarded as a stepping stone to the seizure of Formosa itself, with all that that must mean for the Chinese Nationalists under Generalissimo Chiang Kai-shek, who have been given shelter and protection there by the United States, and to whom the United States are bound by over 14 years' comradeship in war, both against the Chinese Communists and the Japanese invaders of China.

Government of Israel: press release
(Government of Israel Archives)

24 February 1955

The Ambassador of Israel, Mr Eliahu Elath, called this afternoon at 10 Downing Street to present to the Prime Minister, on behalf of the Prime Minister and Government of Israel, their eightieth-birthday gift.

This is an album of original woodcuts of Old Jerusalem by the Israel artist Jacob Steinhardt,[1] and the title page bears the following inscription:

'These woodcuts of Old Jerusalem are respectfully presented by the Government of Israel to one who, in a career of world-wide impact, has shown himself deeply alive to the appeal of this Land and to the fate of its people.'

Sir Winston has been known for many years past as a firm supporter of the Zionist movement and the cause of Israel, as well as a personal friend of the late President Weizmann. He himself said, as a Washington Press Conference last June:

'I am a Zionist. Let me make that clear. I was one of the original ones, after the Balfour Declaration, and I have worked faithfully for it.'

'I think it a most wonderful thing that this community should have established itself so effectively, turning the desert into fertile gardens and thriving townships, and should have afforded a refuge to millions of their co-religionists who had suffered so fearfully under the Hitler, and not only Hitler, persecution. I think it's a wonderful thing.'

The full accounts given by the Israel press of Sir Winston's eightieth

[1] Jacob Steinhardt, 1887–1968. German–Israeli artist. Served in German Imperial Army during WWI. Fled Germany to Palestine, 1933. Director, Bezalel Academy of Art and Design, 1954–7.

birthday celebrations in London were closely followed by his many friends and admirers in that country. The Album now presented is a small token of Israel's admiration and enduring gratitude for the man who saved the world from Nazi domination, thus securing for all its peoples – Israel among them – the renewed hope of peace, freedom and progress.

Sir Anthony Eden to Sir Winston S. Churchill
Prime Minister's Personal Telegram T.12/55
(Premier papers, 11/879)

25 February 1955
Emergency
Secret
No. 172

If you and colleagues see no objection, I should be glad if you would authorize action in Peking, Moscow, New Delhi and Ottawa as suggested in my telegrams to these posts.

2. You will realize my reluctance to offer to go to Hong Kong to meet Chou En-lai. But my conversation with Foster Dulles yesterday evening has convinced me that the situation is grave and urgent action is imperative and that I should at least offer to meet Chou En-lai half way if there is any prospect of finding a basis for negotiation.

Sir Winston S. Churchill to Sir Anthony Eden
Prime Minister's Personal Telegram T.13/66
(Premier papers, 11/879)

25 February 1955
Emergency
Secret
No. 237

I am sure your colleagues would wish you to act upon your own judgement about trying to arrange a personal meeting with Chou En-lai at Hong Kong or on its borders (repeat borders). I should deprecate stating explicitly at this stage that you are willing to go on to Chinese territory. I am accordingly authorizing Mr Trevelyan[1] to act as you propose but asking him to omit the words 'or even nearby on Chinese territory'.

[1] Humphrey Trevelyan, 1905–85. UK Counsellor in Baghdad, 1948. Economic and Financial Adviser, UK High Commission for Germany, 1951–3. Chargé d'Affaires, Peking, 1953–5. KCMG, 1955. Ambassador to Egypt, 1955–6; to Iraq, 1958–61; to Soviet Union, 1958–61. Baron, 1968. KG, 1974.

2. I have only so far consulted Rab as the decision only covers a reasonable approach of a tentative nature and in line with our general policy.

3. We are having quite an interesting time over here too. It is not going too badly.

March 1955

Sir Winston S. Churchill: speech
(Hansard)

1 March 1955   House of Commons

DEFENCE

I beg to move, 'That this House approves the Statement on Defence, 1955, Command Paper No. 9391'. This Motion stands in my name, and it is supported by my right hon. Friends the Foreign Secretary, the Chancellor of the Exchequer and the Minister of Defence.

We live in a period, happily unique in human history, when the whole world is divided intellectually and to a large extent geographically between the creeds of Communist discipline and individual freedom, and when, at the same time, this mental and psychological division is accompanied by the possession by both sides of the obliterating weapons of the nuclear age.

We have antagonisms now as deep as those of the Reformation and its reactions which led to the Thirty Years' War. But now they are spread over the whole world instead of only over a small part of Europe. We have, to some extent, the geographical division of the Mongol invasion in the thirteenth century, only more ruthless and more thorough. We have force and science, hitherto the servants of man, now threatening to become his master.

I am not pretending to have a solution for a permanent peace between the nations which could be unfolded this afternoon. We pray for it. Nor shall I try to discuss the cold war which we all detest, but have to endure. I shall only venture to offer to the House some observations mainly of a general character on which I have pondered long and which, I hope, may be tolerantly received, as they are intended by me. And here may I venture to make a personal digression? I do not pretend to be an expert or to have technical knowledge of this prodigious sphere: of science. But in my long friendship with Lord Cherwell I have tried to follow and even predict the evolution of events. I hope that the House will not reprove me for vanity or conceit if I repeat what I wrote a quarter of a century ago:

We know enough (I said) to be sure that the scientific achievements of the next 50 years will be far greater, more rapid and more surprising than those we have already experienced. . . . . High authorities tell us that new sources of power, vastly more important than any we yet know, will surely be discovered. Nuclear energy is incomparably greater than the molecular energy which we use today. The coal a man can get in a day can easily do 500 times as much work as the man himself. Nuclear energy is at least one million times more powerful still. If the hydrogen atoms in a pound of water could be prevailed upon to combine together and form helium, they would suffice to drive a 1,000 horse-power engine for a whole year. If the electrons – those tiny planets of the atomic systems – were induced to combine with the nuclei in the hydrogen, the horse-power liberated would be 120 times greater still. There is no question among scientists that this gigantic source of energy exists. What is lacking is the match to set the bonfire alight, or it may be the detonator to cause the dynamite to explode.

This is no doubt not quite an accurate description of what has been discovered, but as it was published in the *Strand* Magazine of December, 1931 – twenty-four years ago – I hope that my plea to have long taken an interest in the subject may be indulgently accepted by the House.

What is the present position? Only three countries possess, in varying degrees, the knowledge and the power to make nuclear weapons. Of these, the United States is overwhelmingly the chief. Owing to the breakdown in the exchange of information between us and the United States since 1946 we have had to start again independently on our own. Fortunately, executive action was taken promptly by the right hon. Gentleman the Leader of the Opposition to reduce as far as possible the delay in our nuclear development and production. By his initiative we have made our own atomic bombs.

Confronted with the hydrogen bomb, I have tried to live up to the right hon. Gentleman's standard. We have started to make that one, too. It is this grave decision which forms the core of the Defence Paper which we are discussing this afternoon. Although the Soviet stockpile of atomic bombs may be greater than that of Britain, British discoveries may well place us above them in fundamental science.

May I say that for the sake of simplicity and to avoid verbal confusion I use the expression 'atomic bombs' and also 'hydrogen bombs' instead of 'thermo-nuclear' and I keep 'nuclear' for the whole lot. There is an immense gulf between the atomic and the hydrogen bomb. The atomic bomb, with all its terrors, did not carry us outside the scope of human control or manageable events in thought or action, in peace or war. But when Mr Sterling Cole, the Chairman of the United States Congressional Committee, gave out a year ago – 17th February, 1954 – the first comprehensive review of the hydrogen bomb, the entire foundation of human affairs was revolutionised, and mankind placed in a situation both measureless and laden with doom.

It is now the fact that a quantity of plutonium, probably less than would fill this Box on the Table – it is quite a safe thing to store – would suffice to produce weapons which would give indisputable world domination to any great Power which was the only one to have it. There is no absolute defence against the hydrogen bomb, nor is any method in sight by which any nation, or any country, can be completely guaranteed against the devastating injury which even a score of them might inflict on wide regions.

What ought we to do? Which way shall we turn to save our lives and the future of the world? It does not matter so much to old people; they are going soon anyway, but I find it poignant to look at youth in all its activity and ardour and, most of all, to watch little children playing their merry games, and wonder what would lie before them if God wearied of mankind.

The best defence would of course be bona fide disarmament all round. This is in all our hearts. But sentiment must not cloud our vision. It is often said that 'Facts are stubborn things'. A renewed session of a sub-committee of the Disarmament Commission is now sitting in London and is rightly attempting to conduct its debates in private. We must not conceal from ourselves the gulf between the Soviet Government and the NATO Powers, which has hitherto, for so long, prevented an agreement. The long history and tradition of Russia makes it repugnant to the Soviet Government to accept any practical system of international inspection.

A second difficulty lies in the circumstance that, just as the United States, on the one hand, has, we believe, the overwhelming mastery in nuclear weapons, so the Soviets and their Communist satellites have immense superiority in what are called 'conventional' forces – the sort of arms and forces with which we fought the last war, but much improved. The problem is, therefore, to devise a balanced and phased system of disarmament which at no period enables any one of the participants to enjoy an advantage which might endanger the security of the others. A scheme on these lines was submitted last year by Her Majesty's Government and the French Government and was accepted by the late Mr Vyshinsky as a basis of discussion. It is now being examined in London.

If the Soviet Government have not at any time since the war shown much nervousness about the American possession of nuclear superiority, that is because they are quite sure that it will not be used against them aggressively, even in spite of many forms of provocation. On the other hand, the NATO Powers have been combined together by the continued aggression and advance of Communism in Asia and in Europe. That this should have eclipsed in a few years, and largely effaced, the fearful antagonism and memories that Hitlerism created for the German people is an event without parallel. But it has, to a large extent, happened. There is widespread belief throughout the free world that, but for American nuclear superiority, Europe would already have been reduced to satellite status and the Iron Curtain would have reached the Atlantic and the Channel.

Unless a trustworthy and universal agreement upon disarmament, conventional and nuclear alike, can be reached and an effective system of inspection is established and is actually working, there is only one sane policy for the free world in the next few years. That is what we call defence through deterrents. This we have already adopted and proclaimed. These deterrents may at any time become the parents of disarmament, provided that they deter. To make our contribution to the deterrent we must ourselves possess the most up-to-date nuclear weapons, and the means of delivering them.

That is the position which the Government occupy. We are to discuss this not only as a matter of principle; there are many practical reasons which should be given. Should war come, which God forbid, there are a large number of targets that we and the Americans must be able to strike at once. There are scores of airfields from which the Soviets could launch attacks with hydrogen bombs as soon as they have the bombers to carry them. It is essential to our deterrent policy and to our survival to have, with our American allies, the strength and numbers to be able to paralyse these potential Communist assaults in the first few hours of the war, should it come.

The House will perhaps note that I avoid using the word 'Russia' as much as possible in this discussion. I have a strong admiration for the Russian people – for their bravery, their many gifts, and their kindly nature. It is the Communist dictatorship and the declared ambition of the Communist Party and their proselytising activities that we are bound to resist, and that is what makes this great world cleavage which I mentioned when I opened my remarks.

There are also big administrative and industrial targets behind the Iron Curtain, and any effective deterrent policy must have the power to paralyse them all at the outset, or shortly after. There are also the Soviet submarine bases and other naval targets which will need early attention. Unless we make a contribution of our own – that is the point which I am pressing – we cannot be sure that in an emergency the resources of other Powers would be planned exactly as we would wish, or that the targets which would threaten us most would be given what we consider the necessary priority, or the deserved priority, in the first few hours.

These targets might be of such cardinal importance that it would really be a matter of life and death for us. All this, I think, must be borne in mind in deciding our policy about the conventional forces, to which I will come later, the existing Services.

Meanwhile, the United States has many times the nuclear power of Soviet Russia – I avoid any attempt to give exact figures – and they have, of course, far more effective means of delivering. Our moral and military support of the United States and our possession of nuclear weapons of the highest quality and on an appreciable scale, together with their means of delivery, will greatly reinforce the deterrent power of the free world, and will strengthen our influence within the free world. That, at any rate, is the policy we have decided to pursue. That is what we are now doing, and I am thankful that it is endorsed by a mass of responsible opinion on both sides of the House, and, I believe, by the great majority of the nation.

A vast quantity of information, some true, some exaggerated much out of proportion, has been published about the hydrogen bomb. The truth has inevitably been mingled with fiction, and I am glad to say that panic has not occurred. Panic would not necessarily make for peace. That is one reason why I have been most anxious that responsible discussions on this matter should not take place on the BBC or upon the television, and I thought that I was justified in submitting that view of Her Majesty's Government to the authorities, which they at once accepted – very willingly accepted.

Panic would not necessarily make for peace even in this country. There are many countries where a certain wave of opinion may arise and swing so furiously into action that decisive steps may be taken from which there is no recall. As it is, the world population goes on its daily journey despite its sombre impression and earnest longing for relief. That is the way we are going on now.

I shall content myself with saying about the power of this weapon, the hydrogen bomb, that apart from all the statements about blast and heat effects over increasingly wide areas there are now to be considered the consequences of 'fall out', as it is called, of wind-borne radio-active particles. There is both an immediate direct effect on human beings who are in the path of such a cloud and an indirect effect through animals, grass and vegetables, which pass on these contagions to human beings through food.

This would confront many who escaped the direct effects of the explosion with poisoning, or starvation, or both. Imagination stands appalled. There are, of course, the palliatives and precautions of a courageous Civil Defence, and about that the Home Secretary will be speaking later on tonight. But our best protection lies, as I am sure the House will be convinced, in successful deterrents operating from a foundation of sober, calm and tireless vigilance.

Moreover, a curious paradox has emerged. Let me put it simply. After a certain point has been passed it may be said, 'The worse things get the better.'

The broad effect of the latest developments is to spread almost indefinitely and at least to a vast extent the area of mortal danger. This should certainly increase the deterrent upon Soviet Russia by putting her enormous spaces and scattered population on an equality or near-equality of vulnerability with our small densely-populated island and with Western Europe.

I cannot regard this development as adding to our dangers. We have reached the maximum already. On the contrary, to this form of attack continents are vulnerable as well as islands. Hitherto, crowded countries, as I have said, like the United Kingdom and Western Europe, have had this outstanding vulnerability to carry. But the hydrogen bomb, with its vast range of destruction and the even wider area of contamination, would be effective also against nations whose population hitherto has been so widely dispersed over large land areas as to make them feel that they were not in any danger at all.

They, too, become highly vulnerable; not yet equally perhaps, but, still, highly and increasingly vulnerable. Here again we see the value of deterrents, immune against surprise and well understood by all persons on both sides – I repeat 'on both sides' – who have the power to control events. That is why I have hoped for a long time for a top level conference where these matters could be put plainly and bluntly from one friendly visitor to the conference to another.

Then it may well be that we shall by a process of sublime irony have reached a stage in this story where safety will be the sturdy child of terror, and survival the twin brother of annihilation. Although the Americans have developed weapons capable of producing all the effects I have mentioned, we believe that the Soviets so far have tested by explosion only a type of bomb of intermediate power.

There is no reason why, however, they should not develop some time within the next four, three or even two years more advanced weapons and full means to deliver them on North American targets. Indeed, there is every reason to believe that within that period they will. In trying to look ahead like this we must be careful ourselves to avoid the error of comparing the present state of our preparations with the stage which the Soviets may reach in three or four years' time. It is a major error of thought to contrast the Soviet position three or four years hence with our own position today. It is a mistake to do this, either in the comparatively precise details of aircraft development or in the measureless sphere of nuclear weapons.

The threat of hydrogen attack on these islands lies in the future. It is not with us now. According to the information that I have been able to obtain – I have taken every opportunity to consult all the highest authorities at our disposal – the only country which is able to deliver today a full-scale nuclear attack with hydrogen bombs at a few hours' notice is the United States. That surely is an important fact, and from some points of view and to some of us it is not entirely without comfort.

It is conceivable that Soviet Russia, fearing a nuclear attack before she has caught up with the United States and created deterrents of her own, as she might argue that they are, might attempt to bridge the gulf by a surprise attack with such nuclear weapons as she has already. American superiority in nuclear weapons, reinforced by Britain, must, therefore, be so organised as to make it clear that no such surprise attack would prevent immediate retaliation on a far larger scale. This is an essential of the deterrent policy.

For this purpose, not only must the nuclear superiority of the Western Powers be stimulated in every possible way, but their means of delivery of bombs must be expanded, improved, and varied. It is even probable, though we have not been told about it outside the NATO sphere, that a great deal of this has been already done by the United States. We should aid them in every possible way. I will not attempt to go into details, but it is known that bases have been and are being established in as many parts of the world as possible and that over all rest the United States Strategic Air Force, which is in itself a deterrent of the highest order and is in ceaseless readiness.

The Soviet Government probably knows, in general terms, of the policy that is being pursued, and of the present United States strength and our own growing addition to it. Thus, they should be convinced that a surprise attack could not exclude immediate retaliation. As one might say to them, 'Although you might kill millions of our peoples, and cause widespread havoc by a surprise attack, we could, within a few hours of this outrage, certainly deliver several indeed many times the weight of nuclear material which you have used, and continue retaliation on that same scale.' 'We have', we could say, 'already hundreds of bases for attack from all angles and have made an intricate study of suitable targets.' Thus, it seems to me with some experience of wartime talks, you might go to dinner and have a friendly evening. I should not be afraid to talk things over as far as they can be. This, and the hard facts, would make the deterrent effective.

I must make one admission, and any admission is formidable. The deterrent does not cover the case of lunatics or dictators in the mood of Hitler when he found himself in his final dug-out. That is a blank. Happily, we may find methods of protecting ourselves, if we were all agreed, against that.

All these considerations lead me to believe that, on a broad view, the Soviets would be ill-advised to embark on major aggression within the next three or four years. One must always consider the interests of other people when you are facing a particular situation. Their interests may be the only guide that is available. We may calculate, therefore, that world war will not break out within that time. If, at the end of that time, there should be a supreme conflict, the weapons which I have described this afternoon would be available to both sides, and it would be folly to suppose that they would not be used. Our precautionary dispositions and preparations must, therefore, be based on the assumption that, if war should come, these weapons would be used.

I repeat, therefore, that during the next three or four years the free world should, and will, retain an overwhelming superiority in hydrogen weapons. During that period it is most unlikely that the Russians would deliberately embark on major war or attempt a surprise attack, either of which would bring down upon them at once a crushing weight of nuclear retaliation. In three or four years' time, it may be even less, the scene will be changed. The Soviets will probably stand possessed of hydrogen bombs and the means of delivering them not only on the United Kingdom but also on North American targets. They may then have reached a stage, not indeed of parity with the United States and Britain but of what is called 'saturation'.

I must explain this term of art. 'Saturation' in this connection means the point where, although one Power is stronger than the other, perhaps much stronger, both are capable of inflicting crippling or quasi-mortal injury on the other with what they have got. It does not follow, however, that the risk of war will then be greater. Indeed, it is arguable that it will be less, for both sides will then realise that global war would result in mutual annihilation.

Major war of the future will differ, therefore, from anything we have known in the past in this one significant respect, that each side, at the outset, will suffer what it dreads the most, the loss of everything that it has ever known of. The deterrents will grow continually in value. In the past, an aggressor has been tempted by the hope of snatching an early advantage. In future, he may be deterred by the knowledge that the other side has the certain power to inflict swift, inescapable and crushing retaliation.

Of course, we should all agree that a worldwide international agreement on disarmament is the goal at which we should aim. The Western democracies disarmed themselves at the end of the war. The Soviet Government did not disarm, and the Western nations were forced to rearm, though only partially, after the Soviets and Communists had dominated all China and half Europe. That is the present position. It is easy, of course, for the Communists to say now, 'Let us ban all nuclear weapons.' Communist ascendancy in conventional weapons would then become overwhelming. That might bring peace, but only peace in the form of the subjugation of the Free World to the Communist system.

I shall not detain the House very much longer, and I am sorry to be so long. The topic is very intricate. I am anxious to repeat and to emphasise the one word which is the theme of my remarks, namely, 'Deterrent'. That is the main theme.

The hydrogen bomb has made an astounding incursion into the structure of our lives and thoughts. Its impact is prodigious and profound, but I do not agree with those who say, 'Let us sweep away forthwith all our existing defence services and concentrate our energy and resources on nuclear weapons and their immediate ancillaries.' The policy of the deterrent cannot rest on nuclear weapons alone. We must, together with our NATO allies, maintain the defensive shield in Western Europe.

Unless the NATO Powers had effective forces there on the ground and could make a front, there would be nothing to prevent piecemeal advance and encroachment by the Communists in this time of so-called peace. By successive infiltrations, the Communists could progressively undermine the security of Europe. Unless we were prepared to unleash a full-scale nuclear war as soon as some local incident occurs in some distant country, we must have conventional forces in readiness to deal with such situations as they arise.

We must, therefore, honour our undertaking to maintain our contribution to the NATO forces in Europe in time of peace. In war, this defensive shield would be of vital importance, for we must do our utmost to hold the Soviet and satellite forces at arm's length in order to prevent short-range air and rocket attack on these islands. Thus, substantial strength in conventional forces has still a vital part to play in the policy of the deterrent. It is perhaps of even greater importance in the cold war.

Though world war may be prevented by the deterrent power of nuclear weapons, the Communists may well resort to military action in furtherance of their policy of infiltration and encroachment in many parts of the world. There may well be limited wars on the Korean model, with limited objectives. We must be able to play our part in these, if called upon by the United Nations organisation. In the conditions of today, this is also an aspect of our Commonwealth responsibility. We shall need substantial strength in conventional forces to fulfil our world-wide obligations in these days of uneasy peace and extreme bad temper.

To sum up this part of the argument, of course, the development of nuclear weapons will affect the shape and organisation of the Armed Forces and also of Civil Defence. We have entered a period of transition in which the past and the future will overlap. But it is an error to suppose that, because of these changes, our traditional forces can be cast away or superseded. The tasks of the Army, Navy and Air Force in this transition period are set forth with clarity in the Defence White Paper. The means by which these duties will be met are explained in more detail in the Departmental Papers which have been laid before the House by the three Service Ministers.

No doubt, nothing is perfect; certainly, nothing is complete, but, considering that these arrangements have been made in the first year after the apparition of the hydrogen bomb, the far-seeing and progressive adaptability which is being displayed by all three Services is remarkable. (Hon. Members: 'Oh'.) I understand that there is to be a motion of censure. Well, certainly, nothing could be more worthy of censure than to try to use the inevitable administrative difficulties of the transitional stage as a utensil of party politics and would-be electioneering. I am not saying that anyone is doing it; we shall see when it comes to the vote.

The future shape of Civil Defence is also indicated in broad outline in the Defence White Paper. This outline will be filled in as the preparation of the new plans proceeds, but the need for an effective system of Civil Defence is surely beyond dispute. It presents itself today in its noblest aspect, namely, the Christian duty of helping fellow mortals in distress. Rescue, salvage and ambulance work have always been the core of Civil Defence, and no city, no family nor any honourable man or woman can repudiate this duty and accept from others help which they are not prepared to fit themselves to render in return. If war comes, great numbers may be relieved of their duty by death, but none must deny it as long as they live. If they do, they might perhaps be put in what is called 'Coventry'. (*Laughter.*) I am speaking of the tradition, and not of any particular locality.

The argument which I have been endeavouring to unfold and consolidate gives us in this island an interlude. Let us not waste it. Let us hope we shall use it to augment or at least to prolong our security and that of mankind. But how? There are those who believe, or at any rate say,

> If we have the protection of the overwhelmingly powerful United States, we need not make the hydrogen bomb for ourselves or build a fleet of bombers for its delivery. We can leave that to our friends across the ocean. Our contribution should be criticism of any unwise policy into which they may drift or plunge. We should throw our hearts and consciences into that.

Personally, I cannot feel that we should have much influence over their policy or actions, wise or unwise, while we are largely dependent, as we are today, upon their protection. We, too, must possess substantial deterrent power of our own. We must also never allow, above all, I hold, the growing sense of unity and brotherhood between the United Kingdom and the United States and throughout the English-speaking world to be injured or retarded. Its maintenance, its stimulation and its fortifying is one of the first duties of every person who wishes to see peace in the world and wishes to see the survival of this country.

To conclude, mercifully, there is time and hope if we combine patience and courage. All deterrents will improve and gain authority during the next ten years. By that time, the deterrent may well reach its acme and reap its final reward. The day may dawn when fair play, love for one's fellow men, respect for justice and freedom, will enable tormented generations to march forth serene and triumphant from the hideous epoch in which we have to dwell. Meanwhile, never flinch, never weary, never despair.

Sir Anthony Eden to Sir Winston S. Churchill
Prime Minister's Personal Telegram T.15/55
(Premier papers, 11/879)

2 March 1955
Immediate
Secret
No. 241

The following are my preliminary thoughts on what we should do about the Chinese reply[1] which is uncompromising and does not yet offer much prospect of reaching a settlement by discussion.

2. We might conclude that no useful purpose was to be obtained by continuing this exchange. It would then be for consideration whether we should decide on what line and on what conditions we were prepared to stand and

---

[1] In reply to Eden's suggestion that he and Zhou Enlai meet in Hong Kong, Zhou proposed Peking.

make this clear first to the United States Government and perhaps later in public. I assume that we should exclude the coastal islands and continue to encourage the United States to withdraw the Nationalists from them. With this in view we might express readiness to join with the United States and others in preventing any attempt by the Chinese Communists to seize Formosa and the Pescadores by force before a proper attempt had been made to settle their future by way of peaceful negotiations. We may be driven later to something like this but I would myself be against such action at this stage and would prefer to continue for the time being to show patience.

3. I have accordingly drafted a reply to the Chinese, text of which is in my immediately following telegram and I would like to discuss this on my return to London with you and the colleagues. (?Meanwhile) I think it is still possible for some method to be devised for bringing hostilities to an end and for persuading the Americans to remove the Nationalists form the coastal islands.

4. The Burmese Prime Minister[1] whom I have just seen in Rangoon suggested that there should be a meeting in Delhi between ourselves, the Indians, the Russians and the Chinese to discuss without agenda or commitment how a peaceful settlement could be achieved. His view was the Chinese were so suspicious that no progress could be made without personal contact and he was by no means sure that the Russians could be relied upon to give them sensible advice in private.

5. I told U Nu that I did not think it was possible for us to participate in such a meeting with one of the principals involved (China) without any representation from the other side. He seemed to see the point. I will make this clear to him in a considered reply from Delhi.

6. No doubt Nehru will have further ideas.

7. A further object of my continuing exchanges with Chou En-lai is that I do not wish to accede as yet to United States pressure for further discussion in the Security Council. Dulles will, I know, be anxious to go ahead in New York when he gets back to Washington and I can see no profit and some danger in this.

8. I hope that you will be broadly in agreement with my present thinking.

---

[1] Nu, 1907–95. Known as 'U Nu'. Born in Wakema, British Burma. Educated at Rangoon University. Married, 1935, Mya Yi: five children. Foreign Minister, 1943–4. Minister of Information, 1944–5. First PM of Burma, 1948–56, 1957–8, 1960–2.

Sir Winston S. Churchill to Sir Anthony Eden
Prime Minister's Personal Telegram T.16/55
(Premier papers, 11/879)

3 March 1955
Immediate
Secret and Personal
No. 423

Your Nos. 241 and 242.

1. I have consulted the Cabinet this morning. There is as usual general agreement between us on the policy. As to timing Chou-en-lai's suggestion that you should come to Peking seemed a pretty impudent response to your friendly offer to meet him in Hongkong. It might do him no harm to wait a few days as you propose in paragraph 3 of 242. I have called a Cabinet for 4 o'clock Monday afternoon.

2. We had a great success on Defence last night. We repulsed the Vote of Censure by a 107 majority and there was a thorough split between Bevan and Attlee of whom the latter behaved very well.

3. Rab's strong measures about Finance are generally recognised as wise and courageous. Altogether we shall have a good report to make to you.

All good wishes for your return journey. Give my love to Clarissa.

President Dwight D. Eisenhower to Sir Winston S. Churchill
(Premier papers, 11/1074)

4 March 1955

Dear Winston,

I send you this purely personal note to thank you once again for your courtesy in seeing Mr Thomas E. Stephens. Because of the pressure we have been under here – and lately it has seemed heavier than usual – I have not yet had a chance to see Mr Stephens' sketches, but I look forward eagerly to seeing how his artist's eye has captured your spirit and personality. I am certain no artist can ever do it to my complete satisfaction.

Please give my affectionate regard to Clementine, and, as always, the very best to yourself.

March 1955

Sir Winston S. Churchill to President Dwight D. Eisenhower
Prime Minister's Personal Telegram T.18/55
(Premier papers, 11/879)

4 March 1955
Immediate
Dedip
Top Secret, Private and Personal
No. 939

My dear Friend,

I have been as you may have noticed from the newspapers rather hunted lately by politics[1] and have not found the time or the strength to answer your deeply interesting letter of February 19.[2] I was very glad to see from reports of your interviews with the Press that we are in such good agreement about the H Bomb and all that.[3] All went very well in the House of Commons. Considering we only have a majority of sixteen, the fact that the Opposition Vote of Censure was rejected by 107 votes was a remarkable event and entitles me to say that our policy of 'Defence through Deterrents' commands the support of the nation. I will be writing to you again soon in more detail.

Lady Churchill to Sir Winston S. Churchill
(Churchill papers, 1/55)

4 March 1955

My darling Winston,

By my present Will I have bequeathed to Moorfields Westminster and Central Eye Hospital, of City Road, London EC1, my eyes, in order that they may, if possible, be used for therapeutic purposes. To carry this into effect it is essential that the nearest eye hospital should be notified immediately upon my death. The necessary steps must be taken by the Hospital authorities within a few hours of my death and it is therefore most important that they should be notified quickly.

I have told Doctor Barnett, my two Executors, Leslie Rowan[4] and Peregrine Churchill,[5] and Miss Hamblin.

---

[1] On Mar. 2, Churchill took part in a debate on the Defence White Paper, which proposed the development of a British H-bomb.

[2] Reproduced above (pp. 1916–19).

[3] On Mar. 2, in a press conference, Eisenhower enunciated a policy of nuclear deterrence.

[4] Thomas Leslie Rowan, 1908–72. Married, 1943, Catherine Patricia Love: two children. Private Secretary to PM, 1941. Principal Private Secretary to PM, 1945. KCB, 1949. Economic Minister, British Embassy, Washington DC, 1949–51. Head of Treasury Overseas Finance Div., 1951–8. Chair, British Council, 1971–2.

[5] Henry Winston Spencer-Churchill, 1913–2002. Known as 'Peregrine'. Jack Churchill's younger son, brother to John and Clarissa (Eden). Educated at Harrow and Cambridge. An inventor and company director.

March 1955

Sir Winston S. Churchill to Clement Davis
(Churchill papers, 6/6)

6 March 1955

My dear Davies,
The next Session of the Consultative Assembly of the Council of Europe will open in Strasbourg in mid-May. We propose that the United Kingdom delegation should, as previously, consist of nine members of the Conservative Party, eight of the Labour Party, with a convenient number of substitutes.

I should be obliged if you would let me have the name of a representative and a substitute from the Liberal Party. I will then write to them in accordance with the usual practice and invite them to serve as representatives of the United Kingdom Parliament.

The same delegation would also represent the United Kingdom at the Assembly of Western European Union, when that body is constituted.

Sir Roger Makins to Sir Anthony Eden
(Foreign Office papers, 800/844)

10 March 1955 Washington DC
Immediate
Top Secret
No. 539

Mr Dulles sent for me this afternoon and said he had an idea about which he wished to conspire with us. It was that the President should send a letter to President Coty to the following effect.

2. The two countries[1] are now moving into the final stages of the ratification of the Paris Agreements and President Eisenhower had been considering how best to solemnise this great step towards the strengthening of the Atlantic community. He noted that all fifteen nations concerned in one way or another with the restoration of sovereignty to Western Germany and its admission to Western European Union and the North Atlantic Treaty Organisation would have completed their parliamentary processes by the tenth anniversary of the surrender of Hitler's Germany, and no doubt President Coty would also have reached the same conclusion as President Eisenhower that 'for political reasons May 8, the tenth anniversary of V-E Day, marks the date beyond which it will not be possible to continue the occupation of Germany'. He therefore wished to suggest that France should play host to a meeting or series of meetings in early part of May which would dramatise for the Western countries what has been achieved in the last decade. This would also give an opportunity to lay plans for a meeting with the Soviets in a sustained effort to ease tensions and

---
[1] The US and France.

to reduce the risk of war. President Eisenhower would be glad to come to Paris in response to an invitation for such a purpose, and his thought would be that Sir Winston Churchill, Dr Adenauer and himself might be invited to meet with President Coty to exchange the instruments of ratification of the treaties now before the respective legislatures. In advance of such a ceremony the four Foreign Ministers might meet with a view to preparing, for the consideration of the Heads of Governments, proposals in regard to unification of Germany, the conclusion of the State Treaty for Austria, and the general security of Europe as a whole, on the basis of which the Soviet Union might then be invited to meet in an earnest effort to solve these problems. At some point during these proceedings, it would be desirable to convoke an extraordinary meeting of the Council of NATO. In conclusion the President might say that it seemed to him appropriate to meet in France to mark not only the return of Germany as a sovereign member of the family of nations, but also the new era in Franco-German relations which would be opened with Germany's entry into WEU and NATO. It would be an occasion which would also demonstrate to the world the role that France is playing in the achievement of that resolution, strength and unity in Europe which is now in prospect.

3. This is the rough outline of the proposed letter and a final draft has not been prepared.

4. Mr Dulles asked my view of this proposal and I said I thought it might do the trick. As put to me the proposal only involved a formal meeting of the North Atlantic Treaty Council when the four heads of Government were present in Paris, I suggested that this should be made more flexible in order that the NATO Council if necessary be called together in connexion with the meeting of the four Foreign Ministers. Mr Dulles agreed with this.

5. I then said that I must of course obtain your views. Mr Dulles asked me to do so, emphasising that this was at the moment a proposal of the highest secrecy which had been worked out by the President and himself. He begged you to treat it in the most confidential manner possible.

6. I hope you may be able to send me your observations, for transmission to Mr Dulles, before the weekend.

President Dwight D. Eisenhower to Sir Winston S. Churchill
(Premier papers, 11/845)

10 March 1955   The White House

My dear Mr Prime Minister,

At the time when there was under consideration the treaty to establish a European Defense Community, I made a public announcement of certain principles which would guide United States policies and actions with respect to Western Europe in the event that treaty should be ratified. Now, in substitution for that community, a plan has been evolved for a Western European Union. Obviously that union and related arrangements signed at Paris on October 23, 1954, when brought into force, will serve the vital interests not only of the members of the union, but of the peoples of the free world, including the United States. The United States has twice been drawn into wars which originated in Europe and today it maintains forces there to help minimize the possibility of another war. It is in the interest of the United States to help reduce such dangers.

To this end the United States committed itself to the North Atlantic Treaty. This treaty is in accordance with the basic security interests of the United States, and the obligations which the United States has assumed under the Treaty will be honoured.

The member nations are seeking to make the Atlantic Alliance an enduring association of free peoples within which all members can concert their efforts toward peace, prosperity and freedom. The success of that association will be determined in large measure by the degree of practical cooperation realized among the European nations themselves. The Western European Union and the related arrangements agreed upon in Paris are designed to ensure this cooperation and thereby to provide a durable basis for consolidating the Atlantic relationship as a whole.

It is my belief that the proposed arrangements when effective:

Will promote progress toward unity in Western Europe and draw together those whose past differences have led to recurrent war and gravely depleted Europe's human, material and moral strength;

Will restore sovereignty to the Federal Republic of Germany, a sovereignty which has now been withheld for ten years, during which time the Government and people of that republic have demonstrated that they are capable of worthily discharging their responsibilities as a self governing member of the free and peaceful world community;

Will, by controlling armament levels through an appropriate agency of the Western European Union, assure against militarism;

Will provide a core of unity at the heart of the North Atlantic Treaty organization, thus permitting adoption of practical defensive measures which offer good hope that any enemy attack could be stopped at the threshold;

Will enable the Federal Republic of Germany to make its appropriately measured contribution to international peace and security, in keeping with the spirit of the North Atlantic Treaty organization;

Will, through action of the North Atlantic Treaty Council, assure a closer integration of the armed forces in Europe of the member countries, thereby giving assurances that these forces cannot be used for nationalistic aggression or otherwise than for the security purposes envisaged by the North Atlantic Treaty.

At London on September 29, 1954, the United States Secretary of State, in

order to facilitate efforts to produce an effective collective defense of Western Europe, indicated the conditions under which the United States might be prepared to make a policy declaration similar to that which was announced when the earlier European Defense Community plan was under consideration. I am glad to affirm that when the Paris Agreements have been ratified and have come into force, it will be the policy of the United States:
- (1) To continue active in the various organic arrangements established under the North Atlantic Treaty Organization and to consult with other members of NATO on questions of mutual concern, including the level of forces from the respective NATO countries to be placed at the disposal of the Supreme Allied Commander Europe;
- (2) To consult, if so desired, with the agency for the control of armaments of the Western European Union with a view to assisting in the achievement of its objective of controlling armaments and preventing unjustified military preparations within the members of the Union;
- (3) To continue to maintain in Europe, including Germany, such units of its armed forces as may be necessary and appropriate to contribute its fair share of the forces needed for the joint defense of the North Atlantic area while a threat to that area exists, and will continue to deploy such forces in accordance with agreed North Atlantic strategy for the defense of this area;
- (4) To cooperate in developing the closest possible integration among the forces assigned to NATO in Western Europe, including those contributed by the German Federal Republic, in accordance with approved plans developed by the Military Agencies and the Supreme Commanders of the North Atlantic Treaty Organization in accordance with the resolution adopted by the North Atlantic Council on October 22, 1954;
- (5) To continue to cooperate toward Atlantic security by sharing information authorized by Congress with respect to the military utilization of new weapons and techniques for the improvement of the collective defense;
- (6) In consonance with its policy of encouraging maximum cooperation among the free nations of Europe and in recognition of the contribution which the Brussels Treaty, as amended, will make to peace and stability in Europe, to regard any action from whatever quarter which threatens the integrity or unity of the Western European Union as a threat to the security of the parties to the North Atlantic Treaty calling for consultation in accordance with Article IV of that treaty.

In accordance with the basic interest of the United States in the North Atlantic Treaty, as expressed at the time of ratification, the treaty was regarded as of indefinite duration rather than for any definite number of years. The United States calls attention to the fact that for it to cease to be a party to the North Atlantic Treaty would appear quite contrary to our security interests when there is established on the continent of Europe the solid core of unity which the Paris Agreements will provide.[1]

Sir Winston S. Churchill to Sir Beverley Baxter[2]
(Churchill papers, 6/6)

11 March 1955

I was interested to hear that you are thinking of writing a life of Neville Chamberlain.

You asked whether you would be allowed for this purpose to consult the Cabinet records of the period. I fear that, unless an entirely new practice is instituted, this would not be possible. No decision has yet been taken on the question whether, and if so after what lapse of time, Cabinet records should be made available to historians. This is an interesting, and in many ways difficult, question. A Committee on Departmental Records (Cmd. 9163) recently recommended that Cabinet papers should be opened to inspection after 50 years: but this proposal has not yet been carried into effect and, even if it were, it would mean that the Cabinet records of Chamberlain's Government would not be available to historians until the 1980's. This might be a little late for your purpose.

When you refer to a rule that Cabinet papers may be quoted only by permission of the Prime Minister of the day, you are thinking, I believe, of the practice by which a former Minister may see again Cabinet papers which he saw while in office but may not publish any extract from them without the permission of the Sovereign, which is normally sought through the Prime Minister of the day. That procedure is designed to permit disclosures by Privy Councillors which would otherwise be contrary to their Oath. But it applies only to disclosures of Cabinet proceedings by people who themselves shared in those proceedings: it has no application to biographies written by others.

---

[1] Aldrich wrote to Churchill the same day: 'The White House will release the text of the assurances to the press at three o'clock this afternoon, Washington time.'

[2] Arthur Beverley Baxter, 1891–1964. Served in Canadian Engineers, 1918. Joined London *Daily Express*, 1920; Managing Editor, 1924; Editor-in-Chief and Director, 1929–33. Managing Editor, Sunday Express, 1922. Editor-in-Chief, Inveresk Publications, 1929. Public Relations Counsel, Gaumont British Picture Corp. Ltd, 1933–5. Editorial Adviser, Allied Newspapers, 1938. MP (Cons.) for Wood Green, 1939–50; for Southgate, 1950–64. Fellow, Royal Society of Literature. Knighted, 1954. Published *The Parts Men Play* (1920), *The Blower of Bubbles* (1920), *Strange Street* (1935), *First Nights – and Noises Off* (1949) and *First Nights and Footlights* (1955).

Sir Winston S. Churchill to Sir Anthony Eden
(Churchill papers, 6/4)

12 March 1955

1. Makins' tel. no. 539[1] is of prime importance. It is the first time President Eisenhower has responded to my appeals beginning on May 11, 1953[2] and has shown willingness to visit Europe in person and after securing ratification of the London and Paris Agreements, to 'Lay plans for a meeting with the Soviets in a sustained effort to reduce tensions and the risk of War'. This proposal of a meeting of Heads of Governments which he would attend himself must be regarded as creating a new situation which will affect our personal plans and time-tables.

2. It also complicates the question of a May Election to which I gather you are inclining. Your proposed last sentence of your paragraph 7 might be dangerous as it seems to suggest that the Party politics of a snap-Election to take advantage of Socialist disunity would be allowed to weigh against a meeting of the Heads of Governments which would give a chance to the world of warding off its mortal peril. The British national reaction to this would not be favourable.

3. It would I think be wrong to assume that the French Senators or the French people would be disdainful of a procedure which would accord to France the leading position in Europe. Certainly it seems unwise to adopt personal estimates of when they would regard honourable treatment as flattery or factual appraisal of consequences as threats. Anyhow we should not allow such estimates to be the main factor in our decisions upon the tremendous issues which have now been opened by the President and Dulles.

4. The magnitude of the Washington advance towards a Top Level Meeting is the dominant fact now before us and our reply must not underrate it or fail to encourage its development.

5. I shall be most interested to see the actual draft of what you propose to say. I presume you are circulating Makins' tel. no. 539 to the Cabinet who must be consulted. Meanwhile a cordial interim message should be sent for Makins to deliver. It may well be this is what you have in mind.

---

[1] Reproduced above (pp. 1939–40).
[2] See speech of this date, reproduced above (pp. 998–1010).

March 1955

Sir Anthony Eden to Sir Winston S. Churchill
(Churchill papers, 6/4)

12 March 1955

1. I have your message of today.
2. I was not aware that anything I had done in my public life would justify the suggestion that I was putting Party before country or self before either.
3. I am circulating the telegram to our colleagues as you suggest. I must ask that we discuss it at an early Cabinet; at latest Monday morning.
4. I will send no reply to Dulles' message meanwhile.

Sir Winston S. Churchill to Sir Anthony Eden
(Churchill papers, 6/4)

12 March 1955

Your paragraph 2. Nothing in my minute suggested or was intended to suggest that you were putting Party before country or self before either. What I meant, and mean, is that the last sentence of paragraph 7 of your minute PM/55/21 would be taken to imply a snap Election in May. This would in any case rouse a Party struggle of intense bitterness. That our treatment of the Eisenhower–Dulles proposal was in any way associated with our electoral schemes, and this became known, as it well might, would certainly be made the grounds for a Socialist charge that we had discouraged a Top Level approach to the international problem for reasons connected with our Party tactics. That is why I deemed the sentence dangerous in this context.

I am distressed that you should have read a personal implication, which I utterly repudiate, into a discussion of policy. There are enough difficulties already without misunderstanding between you and me after all these years.

Cabinet: conclusions
(Cabinet papers, 128/28)

14 March 1955
Secret
12 p.m.
Cabinet Meeting No. 23 of 1955

The Cabinet had before them a telegram from Her Majesty's Ambassador at Washington (Washington telegram No. 539)[1] outlining a plan, evolved by President Eisenhower and his Secretary of State, for holding in Paris early

---

[1] Reproduced above (pp. 1939–40).

in May a series of international meetings designed to demonstrate the progress towards European unity, which had been made in the ten years since the defeat of Hitler's Germany. This plan was based on the assumption that all the countries concerned with the restoration of sovereignty to Western Germany and its admission to Western European Union and the North Atlantic Alliance would have completed their ratification of those Treaties by the tenth anniversary of VE-Day. It was proposed that President Eisenhower should come to Paris in order to exchange the instruments of ratification with the Heads of Governments of the United Kingdom, France and Germany. This, it was suggested, would also give an opportunity to make plans for a Meeting with the Soviet Government, in pursuance of the policy of the Western Powers to ease international tension and to reduce the risk of war. Therefore, in advance of the ceremony for exchanging the instruments of ratification, the four Foreign Ministers might meet to prepare, for the consideration of Heads of Governments, proposals on the unification of Germany, the Austrian State Treaty and the general security of Europe as a whole, on the basis of which the Soviet Government might be invited to attend a Meeting for the discussion of those problems. In the course of these proceedings, an extraordinary meeting of the North Atlantic Council might also be held. Mr Dulles had invited the views of the United Kingdom Government on this plan.

The Foreign Secretary said that Mr Dulles had previously suggested that, if the French delayed unduly their ratification of the Paris Agreements, other means would have to be found of emphasising the independence of Western Germany. It seemed likely, therefore, that the primary purpose of this new plan was to ensure French ratification of the Paris Agreements. It should not be assumed that it was certain to have this effect on the French; and it might be doubtful whether the Germans would appreciate the choice of the tenth anniversary of VE-Day as the most suitable date for a ceremonial exchange of ratifications of the Paris Agreements. A more important consideration, however, was the effect which the announcement of this plan might have on the Soviet Government. If it were announced before the French Senate debated the Agreements, the Russians were likely to counter it by a public declaration that, if the French ratified the Agreements, they would decline the proposed invitation to a Four-Power Meeting. A Russian declaration on those lines would probably cause some French Senators to revert to the earlier idea that a Four-Power Meeting should be held before the Agreements were ratified.

The Foreign Secretary said that, if it were the primary purpose of this plan to prepare the way for a Four-Power Meeting, he would wish to give it his support. But, if that were its object, it would be more likely to produce results if both the announcement and the invitation were withheld for some time after the ratification of the Paris Agreements. He would like also to know what kind of Four-Power Meeting was envisaged by the Americans. There was nothing in this telegram to suggest that they had in mind a Meeting of Heads of Governments. Indeed, the subjects suggested for preliminary discussion by the four Foreign Ministers implied that what the Americans had in mind was a continuation of the Berlin Conference – though, for the resumption of those discussions no further preparation by the Western Powers was necessary. The main question for the Cabinet to consider was whether an early announcement of the plan outlined by Mr Dulles was likely to further our primary purpose of securing a fruitful Four-Power Meeting with the Russians. He himself doubted whether it would improve the prospects of securing such a Meeting.

The Prime Minister said that he attached primary importance to the President's willingness to come to Europe for the purpose of making plans for a Four-Power Meeting with the Russians. This was a new and significant initiative, and we should welcome it. We should certainly say nothing to discourage it. Many people, both in this country and elsewhere in Western Europe, would have high hopes that such a visit would make a significant contribution towards the preservation of world peace. Even though it might be true that the primary purpose of the plan was to ensure French ratification of the Paris Agreements, it would give us an opportunity to discuss with the President means of securing a fruitful Meeting with the Russians. We should therefore be ill-advised to brush it aside or deny ourselves the chance of turning it to good account.

The following were the main points made in the Cabinet's discussion:

(a) It was open to some doubt whether the plan outlined by Mr Dulles would have the desired effect of ensuring French ratification of the Paris Agreements. Earlier American attempts to influence the outcome of Parliamentary proceedings, in France and in Italy, had not been successful. This move might even have the effect of stiffening some sections of French opinion against ratification – especially if it provoked a sharp reaction from the Soviet Government. This was, however, a point which might be left to the judgment of the French Government.

(b) Similarly, it was for the German Government to raise objection, if they wished, to the emphasis which the plan would lay on the tenth anniversary of VE-Day. To many Germans that was the anniversary, not of Germany's defeat, but of Hitler's downfall.

(c) Whatever its effect on the French or the Germans, the plan would do nothing to make it more likely that the Russians would accept an invitation to a Four-Power Meeting. They had consistently opposed the Paris Agreements; and, although they would probably accept them in the end as facts of the international situation, they could hardly be expected to accept an invitation to a Four-Power Meeting which was issued soon after, and linked with, the ratifications. The plan outlined by Mr Dulles did not seem to take sufficient account of the problems of timing: neither the timing proposed for the original announcement, nor the timing of the proposed invitation to the Four-Power Meeting, seemed likely to appeal to the Soviet Government.

(d) There was nothing in the telegram to suggest that President Eisenhower would himself be willing to take part in the Conferences proposed, either at the original meetings in Paris or at a subsequent Four-Power Meeting with the Russians. The plan contemplated that the preparatory work in Paris would be undertaken by Foreign Ministers and that the President would attend only for the formal ceremony of exchanging instruments of ratification. It could not therefore be assumed that the President would be willing to attend a Four-Power Meeting of Heads of Governments.

The conclusion which emerged from the Cabinet's discussion was that precipitate action on the lines proposed by Mr Dulles, though it might help to ensure French ratification of the Paris Agreements, was not likely to improve the prospects for a Four-Power Meeting with the Russians which might produce fruitful results. Indeed, it was more likely than not that the Russians would decline an invitation issued in the circumstances envisaged in this plan. On the other hand, much good might come from a visit to Europe by President Eisenhower; and we should certainly do nothing to discourage the initiative which he had shown in suggesting it. Many of the difficulties which had been mentioned in the Cabinet's discussion could be avoided if any immediate announcement of his plans could be confined to a statement that he was willing to come to Europe later in the summer – perhaps in June. Though this announcement could be made before the French debate on the Paris Agreements, it need not be linked specifically with the ratification of those Agreements and could refer more generally to the easing of international relations in Europe and the possibility of a Four-Power Meeting with the Russians. The issue of a specific invitation to the Soviet Government to attend such a Meeting could then be deferred until the President was in Europe. The promise of a visit by the President later in the year, together with the prospect that a Four-Power Meeting might be held later, would be more valuable in reducing international strain than an earlier visit by the President on the basis proposed in Mr Dulles' plan coupled, as seemed inevitable, by an immediate Soviet rejection of the accompanying proposal for a Four-Power Meeting.

The Cabinet –

Invited the Foreign Secretary, in the light of their discussion, to prepare a draft reply to the proposal outlined in Washington telegram No. 539, and agreed to resume their discussion when this draft was available.

Sir Winston S. Churchill: speech
(Hansard)

14 March 1955   House of Commons

[. . .] The Leader of the Opposition has moved a Motion of censure on the Government. The terms may be admired for their earnest attempt to present a collection of words and ideas which may be acceptable to the bulk of his followers. I hope sincerely that the word 'followers' is the right word. The Amendment which we have put on the Order Paper in answer to the right hon. Gentleman's Motion represents, I believe the bulk of responsible opinion on both sides of the House, has the merit of being practical in character and is aimed at producing the largest measure of unity not only of a party but of the country as a whole at an important moment in our foreign affairs.

If I may, I should like to comment a little on the Motion. I notice that the Leader of the Opposition calls for a Three-Power conference. It is quite true that the Resolution of the House of 5th April, 1954, mentioned only three Powers, but a busy year has passed since then in this clattering world. Is it the up-to-date conclusion of the Opposition that only those Powers who possess the secret of the hydrogen bomb should meet in an attempt to decide the future of the world? That would be, I am sure, a very unwise declaration. Clearly, it would encourage any ambitious State to qualify, which would be the very opposite of the right hon. Gentleman's argument. I am sure he does not wish for a number of other States, large and small, responsible and irresponsible, to embark upon an elaborate series of experiments of the kind the effects of which would cause such justifiable concern.

Moreover, we cannot agree that France and Germany at this time should be dissociated from the task of resolving the fears and disputes which beset Europe and the world today. Indeed, to mention only three Powers would give serious offence when, I am sure, none was intended, and would give that offence at a time when France is taking, or about to take, decisions important to her welfare and also to the policy which both parties in the House have supported. It certainly affords an additional reason for the House to prefer the words of the Amendment to the Motion of censure.

I am also unfavourably struck by the word 'immediately' in the Motion. I agree that there should be no question of indefinite delays. But the French Council of the Republic is meeting on the 21st of this month, so I am told, to decide this issue, and we shall know one way or another then. In view of that going on at the present time, I should have thought that it was not possible to conceive a worse time than the immediate present for us to propose a resolution for immediate efforts to be made to promote a Three-Power conference.

With the debates on the ratification of the London and Paris Agreements approaching their decisive point, the Soviets would certainly not agree to such a meeting except on a basis of further postponement of ratification. This we could in no circumstances consider, and I do not believe that the Leader of the Opposition would wish us to. In an interview which the right hon. Gentleman gave to the *News Chronicle* on 16th February he is reported as saying: 'I believe that ratification should go ahead with all possible speed and that Four-Power negotiations should take place when it has been completed.' Her Majesty's Government endorses that view, and that, indeed, is the burden of the Amendment which we are moving in reply to the right hon. Gentleman's Motion of censure.

I do not wish to deal with this matter in a controversial mood – more than is really necessary in receiving a Motion of censure. I must now ask the House to allow me to survey the past, because it all comes into the present – the present is only the heir of the past – and I give my assurance that I will summarise this as concisely as I can.

I was greatly disappointed when, now nearly two years ago, I was prevented by illness from going to meet President Eisenhower at Bermuda. I was most anxious to set before him personally the argument which I had used in my speech of 11th May, 1953,[1] shortly after Marshal Stalin's death, in favour of a top-level meeting with his successor, the new leader of the Soviet Government, Mr Malenkov. It is not true to suggest, however, that the whole proposal was allowed to drop on account of my falling out. On the contrary, a conference was held at Washington, instead of Bermuda, in the middle of July, 1953, at which Lord Salisbury – who took my place and that of my right hon. Friend the Foreign Secretary who was also struck down, who was also ill – raised all the arguments which I would have used in favour of a meeting of the heads of Governments.

The idea of a top-level, Four-Power meeting – it was Four-Power even then – with a fluid or flexible agenda, was presented forcefully to the Americans and to the French. They could only be brought to agree to an invitation to the Russians for a meeting of the four Foreign Ministers to discuss specifically free elections in Germany, German reunification, and the conclusion of the Austrian Treaty. This was duly conveyed to the Soviet Government. It was the utmost we could get.

From 15th July, 1953, we entered upon a period of tripartite Notes and Soviet rejoinders and counter-rejoinders after agreement with the three allied Powers, France, America and ourselves – quite a lengthy and elaborate process. From 15th July we entered upon this period and it did not end until November. At the beginning of December, 1953, we were able to arrange the long delayed conference of the heads of the British, American and French Governments at Bermuda, and here a reply to the Russians was agreed.

The reply was to propose that a Four-Power meeting on the Foreign Ministers' level should take place in January, 1954, in Berlin. This meeting lasted for

---

[1] Reproduced above (pp. 998–1010).

three weeks and covered a wide field of differences between the Soviets and the Western Powers. The discussion was certainly valuable and the contacts were undoubtedly useful. I believe, from accounts that have been given me, personal contacts were also agreeable. They were certainly forthright. They did not, however, lead to any agreement on the grave points at issue.

The most fruitful result of the Berlin Conference was the birth of the Geneva Conference, which began in April, 1954 – we are getting on in the story – and eventually arrived at the arrangements for an armistice and settlement of the Indo-China problem. On this we are living unrestfully now, but living – I mean there is no killing going on, no war going on. However, the hope of a peaceful and lasting solution has by no means vanished in this theatre, so that we cannot say that the Geneva Conference, to which my right hon. Friend devoted such enormous care and energy, has not produced results.

While all this was going on, in June, 1954, I visited Washington and my right hon Friend detached himself for the time being from Geneva and came with me. We passed a very busy week at the White House in the most friendly and intimate conversations with the President. Anglo-American relations had been disturbed by events at Geneva and my right hon. Friend and I were very glad that we were able to reach agreements upon many points. These agreements did not, however, include the top-level meeting with the Soviet Government for which I continued to work. There was, on the other hand, certainly no slamming of the door, no slamming down of the idea, of the plan. I felt it was one which we should all consider.

This brings me to our latest effort, which I must describe in rather more detail as I mentioned it the other day. I gave a brief outline of this to the House during our defence debate. I made an intervention in the speech of the right hon. Gentleman the Member for Ebbw Vale (Mr Bevan), whose absence, and particularly whose illness, we all regret. I made this intervention which, though unstudied, was not incorrect and, I hope, not unhelpful. If the House would permit me, I should like to tell the story more fully this afternoon so as to make sure that it can be judged in its perspective and proportion.

On our homeward voyage from the United States in the first week of July last, I sent a personal and private telegram to Mr Molotov,[1] of which I, of course, informed the President.[2] After referring to my speech of 11th May, 1953, for a top-level meeting of the Big Three, and to the statements I had made from time to time in the House of Commons that, if this were impossible, I would seek to make a contact myself with the Soviet Government, I asked Mr Molotov how they would feel about it. I should like, I said, to know this before we made any official proposal or considered such questions as those of time and place. I said that I should be very glad if he would tell me whether

---

[1] See Churchill to Butler, 2 July 1954, reproduced above (p. 1645).
[2] See T.246/54, reproduced above (pp. 1650–1).

he would like the idea of a friendly meeting with no agenda and no objective but of living side by side in growing confidence, easement and prosperity.

Although our meeting, wherever held, would be simple and informal and last only a few days, it might be, I suggested, the prelude to a wider reunion where much might be settled. I said, however, that I had no warrant to say this beyond my own hopes. I ended by referring to our war comradeship. I saw quite a lot of him in the war; he was sometimes very cordial and human.

On 5th July I received a very friendly and encouraging reply from Mr Molotov,[1] for which I thanked him. We had, in any case, to wait until after the Geneva Conference, to which the Foreign Secretary had to return, was concluded. It was not until 26th July that I was able to address Mr Molotov again.[2] I said that after discussion with my colleagues I was about to send him a further message to suggest a meeting, say, at the end of August or in the first half of September at some halfway house such as Berne, Stockholm or Vienna.

In the meanwhile, however, the Soviet Note of 24th July, 1944 – (Hon Members: 'July, 1954.') – Yes, 1954 – things were much easier in 1944 – had been published, proposing a formal conference of European States and of the United States to discuss again the proposals made some months before by the Soviet Government at Berlin on collective security in Europe. This seemed to have obviously superseded for the time being the small informal meeting that I had suggested which might perhaps have been the prelude to a Four-Power meeting at the top level. I have always attached great importance to that.

No, I had no right or authority to propose a Three-Power meeting any more than we have today. I was proposing a Two-Power meeting, an informal meeting between me and my right hon. Friend on the one hand and Mr Malenkov and Mr Molotov, on the other hand, or anyone else they chose to bring, at some neutral place where we could talk over things.

I do not mind telling the House that I had in mind to tell the Soviet that if they wanted to bring the United States along they would have to make some change in their general attitude, and I would have suggested that the signature of the Treaty with Austria and also their joining the proposal which was made about this time by the President of the United States for the civil use of atomic power – which they have done since – would be very good topics which might make it possible to make it a three-Power conference and evidently it would soon become a four-Power, and, very likely, a five-Power, conference. However, it never came off, because I never had the opportunity. I am glad to say that there is an understanding between America and Russia about the use of civil atomic energy. That is being developed.

To this, Mr Molotov replied that he did not see the reasons for considering that my proposal for an informal meeting had any bearing – I am paraphrasing

---

[1] See T.246.54, reproduced above (pp. 1650–1).
[2] T.272/54, reproduced above (p. 1713).

this – on the question of the convocation of a conference concerned with the guaranteeing of security in Europe.[1]

I answered that I had not changed in any way from my original project, but that the unexpected revival of his Berlin proposal at this juncture created a new situation, since it would not have been possible to have a large formal international conference going on at the same time as the unofficial Two-Power top-level meeting which I had suggested.[2] The British, American and French Governments, who had been addressed officially by the Soviets, were already preparing their replies for the formal conference. It was, therefore, necessary to wait until we knew what was going to happen about the Four-Power conference before re-examining my project in the light of events.

Mr Molotov apparently saw no reason why the two conferences should not go on together. This was a fair matter of opinion. I am not complaining at all. We thought this impossible, as the one would certainly confuse or paralyse the other. That was our view. There the matter rested.

Meanwhile, the Soviet proposal for a Four-Power Foreign Secretaries' conference had the effect for which I could not help feeling it was designed, namely, to dissuade the French from ratifying the EDC treaties. I had always assumed that it was to be taken for granted.

As I have been deeply interested in the cause of United Europe for a good many years, I must remind the House of the sequence of events – I apologise for these digressions – since the Russian-Communist menace became apparent. I have consistently endeavoured, in opposition or in Government, to promote an alliance of the free world against it. I was, I think, the first to point out that this involved that Germany must rejoin the European family, and I hoped France would lead her back, and, also, I was the first, I think, in this House to state that there was no possibility of effective defence against Soviet Russia without a German Army. However, years have passed since then, and great new developments have occurred.

I had always thought that the forces of the West should be grouped on the principles of a grand alliance, but the French preferred to aim at a cosmopolitan Army, thus avoiding the creation of a German Army, and they presently elaborated their plan of the European Defence Community. As this seemed to be the only way of reconciling France to the inclusion of Germany, the advocates of Western Defence had no choice but to defer to French ideas.

Three years of lamentable delay followed before the French were able to perfect the highly complicated arrangements which they had in mind. Right hon. Gentlemen opposite had experience of some of those three years of indecision. In the end, an arrangement was agreed upon by all the Powers concerned on which a cosmopolitan Army for the West could be founded. This agreement collapsed because of the French refusal to ratify it, as we

---

[1] See Molotov to Churchill, 31 July 1954, reproduced above (p. 1719).
[2] See Churchill to Molotov, 5 Aug. 1954, reproduced above (p. 1723).

all remember. Meanwhile, under the NATO provisions an elaborate military infrastructure had been created in France. To prevent the French from ratifying EDC was, therefore, an obvious and quite reasonable Soviet objective.

The strain of these three years upon Dr Adenauer has been most grievous, and no one but that valiant patriot and idealist, for he is both, could have endured it. It is not a question of the NATO forces gaining an addition of 12 divisions that moves me personally. Even with them, the Western front could not be a guarantee against the overpowering Russian strength in conventional weapons. Twelve German divisions are, to me, a symbol rather than a physical factor. They may, indeed, be used as a peaceful guard against uncontrolled or unlimited German rearmament and thus would be consistent at once with European unity and German self respect.

What is of major consequence to the causes we serve is the ranging of the mighty German race and nation with the free world – not on the wrong side – instead of allowing it by infiltration, or territorial bribery, or by actual force, or by our own tragic memories to be amalgamated with the satellite States to carry the doctrine and control of Moscow into world supremacy.

Earnestly as I desire to get a peaceful arrangement for co-existence brought about with Russia, I should regard it as an act of insanity to drive the German people into the hands of the Kremlin and thus tilt into Communist tyranny the destiny of mankind. Moreover, the only safe policy for us to pursue is, as we have often stated, peace through strength. Without unity there can be no strength. For the Western Powers to abandon EDC and have nothing to put in its place in Europe would have presented us divided and in vacuity before the mighty Communist oligarchy and dictatorship and its satellites.

Weakness makes no appeal to Moscow. To mix up the process of ratification with what might well follow soon afterwards would very likely dilute both firmness and conciliation. The sooner we can get our united ratification settled, the sooner the top-level Four-Power conference may come, it may be Five-Power. On the other hand, it might well be that one retreat would lead to another and, far from assuaging differences, would stimulate further aggression from the East and slowly arouse the reluctant anger of the West.

We went through all this in the years before the war, which I remember only too well. Therefore, we felt that we must on no account allow our earnest desire to bring about a top-level conference of great Powers to expose us to the charge of having thrown doubt and disarray into the ranks of NATO. We were, therefore, convinced that Her Majesty's Government had no choice but to suspend for the time being the proposal I had made to Mr Molotov.

I am sure that the more this matter is considered by the House and studied in detail, the more it will be seen that our efforts to act in accordance with the unanimous Resolution of the House of 5th April, 1954, have been sincere and untiring and that we have in no way been disloyal to the resolution, or lukewarm, or dithering – a word that was used the other day – in pursuing our purpose across one obstacle after another. Our policy throughout has been simple, earnest, straightforward and we shall faithfully persevere in it.

I must, however, point out that several important changes have occurred in the situation since May, 1953, and also since August last when, I think, there was a visit paid to Moscow by some of the right hon. Gentlemen opposite. The Malenkov regime has gone. New forces rule. The 'New Look' which I wished to explore in May, 1953, has been succeeded by another 'New Look'. Some hon. Members opposite may no doubt contend that this change might have been averted if a meeting had taken place. I doubt very much whether this assertion has any foundation at all.

In a Press interview on 1st January this year Mr Malenkov was asked whether he would welcome diplomatic talks leading to a Four-Power conference. He refused to give an affirmative reply and said with emphasis that the efforts of the Western Powers to settle the German problem were not compatible with the proposal to hold a Four-Power conference. We have yet to ascertain the feelings and policy of his successor.

So far, the new 'New Look' has not raised any extravagant hopes of improvement. But anyhow, it is so easy to assume, as is done in some influential quarters, that all would have been well if only Mr Malenkov had had due encouragement from us and of course from the United States. This is all pure guesswork. I would go into this subject a little more if we had the right hon. Member for Ebbw Vale in his place, because he has dealt with it both in and outside the House and I should very much relish the opportunity of replying to some of the points he made. However, I will not attempt to do so in his absence.

But it was on the basis of the convictions and reasoning that I have described, that I replied on 12th January[1] to a letter from Mr Mendes France. Extracts from this letter were imparted to the French Senate Commission on Foreign Affairs last Thursday by M Pinay, the Foreign Secretary. They have been referred to in various garbled forms in the Press all over the world.

I am to be asked at Question Time tomorrow whether I will publish the text of this letter. I should be very glad to do so, as it places M Pinay's quite friendly quotation in its proper context. It expresses views I strongly hold and which are very correctly represented by the Amendment I have moved to the Motion of censure. It was, however, a private and personal letter, and although I certainly feel that the House may expect to be informed of a communication of which part has already been quoted in the Parliament of another country I must first seek Mr Mendes France's views. If it is agreeable to him – which I should think would not be unlikely – I will in due course take steps to lay the full text as a White Paper. I hope that that can be done before the end of the month.

---

[1] Letter reproduced above (pp. 1868–9).

I have now given the House a factual account of what the Government have done to bring about top-level two, three, four, or a Five-Power conference. None excludes the others and, of course, it might be hoped that a smaller meeting would lead to a larger one. I think it is a well founded and reasonable suggestion that a Three-Power conference may get a Four-Power meeting, or a Five-Power meeting and then there is the basis for solid agreement.

I was not cross. I voted for the unanimous Resolution which mentioned a Three-Power conference, but I do not think that now is a good opportunity to stress that point when these critical discussions are going on in France. I carefully stated, if I remember rightly, that I was sure no offence was meant – but it would be tactless to do it now, and that is one of the reasons why I prefer our Amendment to the Motion of censure. That is what I am arguing about.

I have now given the House a factual account of what we have done. I have tried very hard to set in motion this process of a conference at the top level and to bring about actual results. Although I do not pretend to measure what the recent changes in the Soviet oligarchy imply, I do not feel that they should in any way discourage us from further endeavours.

I must here, however, say very seriously to the House that it is a mistake to suppose that to bring about such a meeting of any of these classes is an end in itself. It is only a means to an end. It is by no means certain that the end will be agreeable. To have a conference at an ill-chosen moment, or in unfavourable circumstances, would only raise false hopes and probably finish by leaving things worse than before.

If this happened those concerned would have to bear the responsibility not only for a futile procedure but for using up in a wasteful manner what might be at the right moment an important shield against rash or violent action and have thus weakened the resources, both moral and practical, of peace-seeking peoples. It would be wrong and foolish, in timing our procedure, to run the risk of dividing the allies of the Free World. That would only make the danger greater and the potential defence, whether mental or physical, weaker.

I think I have trespassed too much on the great kindness and indulgence of the House to allow me to go so far back over the past. I think that if I were to try to explain the motives which animated me every time I have been called upon to address a public meeting in this country, I should be going really too far and would lose at once the patience of the House and that general attitude of indulgence which I have received from it.

I have now finished speaking about the European situation, but before I sit down I must look across the Atlantic. One thing stands out in my mind above all others; that is the increase of our friendship and understanding with our ally the United States. I circulated last Friday to the House, with what I believe is almost a record for speed, the White Paper, which I have already mentioned, containing the letter which the President has written to me and other Prime Ministers of the Western European Union.[1]

The President's statement renews the pledges which the United States gave to the EDC. When the Paris Agreements are ratified – may I just summarise them to the House – the United States undertakes to maintain its fair share of forces in Europe so long as a threat to the North Atlantic Treaty area exists. The United States will work closely with the Western European Union and will regard any action, from whatever quarter, which threatens its integrity or unity, as a threat to the security of the members of NATO, including the United States itself.

Finally, the United States will continue to play its full part in NATO, and if, in the President's words a solid core of unity is established in Europe the interests of the United States will require its continued membership of the North Atlantic Treaty for a period of indefinite duration. These assurances are of the highest value not only for Western European Union but for NATO and for the free world as a whole. They are of particular importance for the United Kingdom which has undertaken great obligations and risks, very serious when undertaken alone, but assuming an altogether different character when supported and sustained by undertakings of this kind from the United States.

The pledge which we gave last September in the conference which my right hon. Friend, by his extraordinary vigour and enterprise, brought about in London – that pledge made the Paris Agreements possible and is an integral part of those Agreements. Our commitment is most powerfully reinforced and our peril most importantly reduced by the President's new statement.

My feeling is – when the right hon. Gentleman spoke he said that he thought that there were some changes of opinion in the United States – that the wish of the United States for peace grows stronger at the same pace as their capacity for war. They give great consideration to our views. They show marked respect for our experience of the European scene. But this very attention which they pay to what we advise is accompanied by serious irritation of their public opinion at anything they take to be unfair criticism.

For instance, when criticisms are made that the President has not come over here – or come over yet to our international conferences – it must always be remembered that the President of the United States is not only the head of a State, and that he has powers of action in emergencies far beyond those granted to any other individual in the modern world. At the same time, he is morally and legally bound to other institutions of equal status in the long-established structure of the American Constitution. He cannot move about as freely as the ordinary heads of Governments. Both his immediate predecessors have created recent precedents for journeys of the President beyond the territories of the United States; and there are many earlier ones.

[1] Reproduced above (pp. 1940–3).

No President of the United States has ever had the knowledge and experience of Europe and of the very group of problems now confronting us as is possessed by President Eisenhower, and I do hope that nothing will be said on this side of the Atlantic, and particularly in this House, which will raise new inhibitions in American minds against the freedom of his personal movements. I still believe that, vast and fearsome as the human scene has become, personal contacts of the right people in the right place, at the right time may yet have a potent and valuable part to play in the cause of peace which is in our hearts.

Cabinet: conclusions
(Cabinet papers, 128/28)

15 March 1955
Secret
11 a.m.
Cabinet Meeting No. 24 of 1955

1. The Cabinet considered a draft message to the United States Secretary of State, which the Foreign Secretary had prepared in the light of their discussion on the previous day, commenting on the American plan for holding in Paris early in May a series of international meetings designed to demonstrate the progress made towards European unity. This set out some of the main difficulties which the Cabinet had seen in the specific plan outlined by Mr Dulles, and suggested that these might be avoided if the President were to announce, before the French debates on the ratification of the Paris Agreements, his willingness to visit Europe some time later in the summer, perhaps in June. It also suggested that the announcement of such a visit need not be linked specifically with the ratification of the Paris Agreements: it could refer more generally to the easing of international relations in Europe and the possibility of a top level Four-Power Meeting with the Russians.

Discussion showed that the Cabinet were in general agreement with the terms of the draft telegram. The Prime Minister said that he attached particular importance to the reference to a top level meeting with the Russians. This should ensure that the United States Government would make it plain whether they envisaged a meeting of Heads of Governments of the Four Powers or further meetings of Foreign Ministers in continuation of the Berlin Conference.

The Cabinet –

Authorised the Foreign Secretary to send a message to the United States Secretary of State in the terms of the draft submitted to the Cabinet (subsequently despatched as Foreign Office telegram to Washington No. 1057).
[. . .]

March 1955

Sir Winston S. Churchill to Lady Churchill
(Baroness Spencer-Churchill papers)

15 March 1955
Most Secret
Burn or lock up

My darling Clemmie,

The Cabinet met for the purpose of approving the answer to be sent to the long Makins telegram I showed you.[1] However, Anthony had been unable to compose a draft and we had a wandering talk over the whole field, at the end of which he asked whether this made any difference in the planned dates on which we had agreed. I pointed out that it was unprecedented to discuss such matters at Cabinet, and most of the Ministers seemed very embarrassed. I made it clear that I should be guided by what I believed was my duty and nothing else, and that any Minister who disagreed could always send in his resignation. The poor Cabinet, most of whom knew nothing about the inner story, seemed puzzled and worried. Of course, as you know, only one thing has influenced me, and that is the possibility of arranging with Ike for a top level meeting in the near future with the Soviets. Otherwise I am very ready to hand over responsibility. I thought this Makins message offered a new chance, and that is why I am testing it. Thus the Cabinet ended, and I had to concentrate on my speech. Later in the day Winthrop Aldrich brought a message to the Foreign Office from Washington to the effect that Ike was not willing himself to participate in a meeting with Russia. Whether this referred to a top level meeting at a later date or not is still uncertain. It may only apply to the immediate meeting of the Four Powers referred to in the Makins note, but this I understand is to be, like all the other failures, upon the Foreign Office level. We are now going to meet again today to settle the answer to America. Of course, if it is clear that Ike will not in any circumstances take part in the near future in a top level meeting, that relieves me of my duty to continue and enables me to feed the hungry. This will soon settle itself.

I had a nice talk with Bobbety after the Cabinet, and I told him that the 9th in any case was on, but the date of return would have to be settled later.[2] He quite understood. I think it probable, however, that Ike will be negative and obstinate, in which case I should be free. We must see how things go on today, but it may be there will be further delays. Anyhow we are working on the basis of the 9th as planned.

There is a very good report of my speech in *The Times* which perhaps you may find time to read. The Opposition was in a pitiable plight. A majority of 30, when one only has 16, on a Vote of Censure is remarkable.

I do hope the rest is doing you good,[3] and will keep you informed.

[1] Reproduced above (pp. 1939–40).
[2] It had been arranged that Lord Salisbury would go to Washington on Apr. 9 to put the case for a top-level meeting to the Americans.
[3] Lady Churchill was at Chequers, having suffered a return of her neuritis.

March 1955

Sir Winston S. Churchill to President Dwight D. Eisenhower
Prime Minister's Personal Telegram T.21/55
(Premier papers, 11/845)

18 March 1955
Immediate
Deyou
Top Secret, Private and Personal
No. 1125

My Dear Friend,

I am so glad you disclaimed responsibility for the issue of the Yalta papers. Personally I do not at all mind their publication though I feel a strong line should be drawn by Governments between formal and plenary sessions on the one hand and after dinner conversations on the other. Also I think people should know whether they are being reported by Interpreter Bohlen[1] or not. Otherwise so far as I am concerned I am very content with the tale. What worries me is whether its publication at this moment may not endanger the French ratification of the London and Paris agreements.

2. I thought your letter to me and the other NATO Prime Ministers was a splendid declaration which doubles our strength and halves our risks.[2] I am sorry we shall never meet in a Top Level confrontation of our would-be friends, but I hope indeed this applies to political occasions only.

3. With my sincere good wishes.

PS. How are you getting on with the portrait? I hope you will show it to me when it is finished and I warn you I shall claim full rights of retaliation.

Konrad Adenauer to Sir Winston S. Churchill
(Premier papers, 11/845)

18 March 1955   Bonn

Dear Sir Winston,

I was greatly moved by your statement on the German defence contribution in your speech in the House of Commons on the 14th of this month,[3] as well as by the friendly remarks you then made about myself. I am delighted to be able to inform you today that the Bundesrat has dealt with the Paris

[1] Charles Eustis Bohlen, 1904–74. Known as 'Chip'. US diplomat, 1929–69. Served in State Dept during WWII. Roosevelt's interpreter at the Teheran (1943) and Yalta (1945) Conferences. Key adviser to Harry Truman, 1947. US Ambassador to Soviet Union, 1953–7; to the Philippines, 1957–9; to France, 1962–8.
[2] On Mar. 10, Eisenhower wrote to the premiers of France, West Germany, Great Britain, Italy and the Benelux countries to urge unity of purpose and defence.
[3] Reproduced above (pp. 1949–58).

Treaties, including the agreement on the Saar, thus bringing to a close the negotiations on ratification in the Bundestag and Bundesrat.

I take this opportunity to express once again my deep gratitude for the decisive contribution made by the British Government to overcome the crisis last August which endangered our efforts to construct an effective system of European defence. The speedy initiative which you seized immediately after August 30, 1954, established the foundations which enable us today to look forward with confident hope to the moment when a German defence force will join with the forces of the other free nations of Europe to ensure the maintenance of freedom and peace in Europe.

With my sincerest thanks and best wishes

President Dwight D. Eisenhower to Sir Winston S. Churchill
(Churchill papers, 2/217)

22 March 1955   The White House
Top Secret

Dear Winston,

The last sentence of your letter,[1] with its implication that you are soon to withdraw from active political life, started, in my memories, a parade of critical incidents and great days that you and I experienced together, beginning at the moment we first met in Washington, December, 1941. Since reading it I have been suffering from an acute case of nostalgia.

First I recall those late days of 1941, when this country was still shuddering from the shock of Pearl Harbor. I think of those occasions during the succeeding months when I was fortunate enough to talk over with you some of the problems of the war, and I especially think of that Washington visit of yours in June of '42, when we had to face the bitter reality of the Tobruk disaster.

Somewhere along about that time must have marked the low point in Allied war fortunes. Yet I still remember with great admiration the fact that never once did you quail at the grim prospect ahead of us; never did I hear you utter a discouraged word nor a doubt as to the final and certain outcome.

Later, of course, we were often together as we planned the 'Torch' Operation,[2] the Sicilian venture, the move into Italy, and the campaign through Normandy. Then, in these later years, starting with my return to Europe in January of '51, I have valued beyond calculation my opportunities to meet with you, especially when those meetings were concerned with the military and diplomatic problems of the free world and our struggle against the evil conspiracy centering in the Kremlin. Because I do so highly value this long association and friendship with you, I echo your hope that

[1] T.21/55, reproduced above (p. 1960).
[2] 'Torch': Allied invasion of North Africa, Nov. 1942.

the impending divergence of our lives will apply to political occasions only. Indeed, I entertain the further hope that with greater leisure, you will more often find it possible to visit us in this country – after all, we do have a fifty percent share in your blood lines, if not in your political allegiance.

Of course both Foster and I have been unhappy about the affair of the Yalta papers. Actually we had hoped that we had made adequate arrangement for an indefinite postponement of the appearance of the documents; an unexplained leak finally put the State Department in the position that it had either to release the papers publicly or to allow one lone periodical a complete scoop in the matter.

As for myself, you know how earnestly I have argued that no matter what else might happen, really good international friends cannot ever afford to be guilty of bad faith, one toward the other. I pray that you do not consider that any such thing was intended in this case.

Ever since 1945, I have argued for the declassification of war records in order that our countries could profit from past mistakes. But I have also insisted that where documents touch upon our combined alliances and arrangements of the late war, published accounts should be limited to a recitation of fact and decision – they should not include mere conversation or gossip.

I think the entire subject is one to which we should give some attention because I am certain that future political battles will create, in some instances, irresistible demands for the publication of particular papers. At least I suspect that this will be true in this country and consequently I think we should prepare as intelligently as possible for this eventuality.

Foster has just returned from Canada where he had a series of very fine visits with the members of the Canadian Government. While there, he had an opportunity to explain the reasons for our attitude in the Formosa matter.

As you know, I am dedicated to the idea that unless the free world can stand firmly together in important problems, our strength will be wasted and we shall in the long run be ineffective in our struggle to advance freedom in the world and to stop the spread of Communism. I believe it to be especially important that we seek to understand each other's viewpoints in Southeast Asia, because in that region we have a very delicate – sometimes dangerously weak – situation and one to which the future welfare and fortunes of the free world are definitely related. If we can achieve the kind of common understanding and thinking that we should, then I feel that there will never be any doubts as to this country's readiness to stand firmly by the side of any other free nation opposing aggression in that region. We have no possessions in that immediate area. Consequently, we cannot be accused of any support of colonialism or of imperialistic designs. We recognize situations that have been properly and legally established and we certainly want to halt Communism dead in its tracks.

To do this, one of the essentials is a strong and continuous land defense of Formosa. This can be done – certainly under present conditions – only by Chiang Kai-shek and his troops. This in turn means that their morale and their vigor, their training and equipment, must all be adequately assured. Until the time comes that they themselves feel that their morale can be sustained, even though their forces are withdrawn from all of their outlying positions, we must be exceedingly careful of the pressures we attempt to apply to Chiang to bring about such a result.

Except for this one feature, I agree entirely with the thoughts you have expressed in your former letters on this touchy subject, and I hope also that you have no difficulty of seeing the importance of this morale feature in Formosa.

As to the 'portrait': since Mr Stephens has come back, I have had no opportunity to meet with him to go over the work he did on my behalf. However, in the meantime I discovered a small black and white print of a portrait of you that was painted some years ago. In order to obtain some practice in the task I had set for myself, I have painted a small canvas, using this photograph as a guide. I do not know the name of the original artist, but it is a picture of you sitting in a straight-backed chair, in a panelled study, and holding a cigar in your right hand. Considering my lack of qualification in this field, it did not turn out badly and I have had a color photograph made of it, which I am forwarding with this letter.

Actually, I have not had time to complete every detail of this particular canvas because I must say that it is difficult for me to give a fairly realistic impression of the stripes in a statesman's trousers. I could wish that, at least for the day you sat for that portrait, you could have worn your wartime 'zipper suit'.

With my affectionate regard and my most prayerful wishes for your continued good health and happiness

Sir Winston S. Churchill to Edgar Faure[1]
(Premier papers, 11/845)

23 March 1955
No. 390

I warmly welcome your decision to insist upon ratification of the Paris Agreements without any amendment or suspensory clause. I share your hope that the completion of ratification will enable us to enter into discussions with the Soviet Government at the earliest suitable opportunity thereafter. I agree

[1] Edgar Faure, 1908–88. French lawyer and politician. Member, National Assembly, 1946–58. Secretary of State for Finances, 1949–50. Minister of Budget, 1950–1. Minister of Justice, 1951–2. PM, 1952, 1955–6. Minister of Finance and Economic Affairs, 1958. Minister of Agriculture, 1966–8. Minister of Education, 1968–9. Minister of State, Ministry of Social Affairs, 1972–3. President, National Assembly, 1973–8. Member of European Parliament, 1979–81. Wrote detective novels under the pseudonym Edgar Sanday.

with you that we should ourselves take the initiative and I am willing that officials should shortly start consideration of the joint policies to be pursued by the Allies at a meeting with the Russians. Good luck to you.

Cabinet: conclusions
(Cabinet papers, 128/28)

23 March 1955
Secret
11.30 a.m.
Cabinet Meeting No. 26 of 1955

1. The Cabinet were informed of the business to be taken in the House of Commons in the following week.

The Prime Minister said that ten years had now passed since the death of Earl Lloyd George;[1] and he proposed to invite the House of Commons on 28th March to present an Address to The Queen praying that a monument to his memory be erected in the Palace of Westminster. The Cabinet endorsed the Prime Minister's proposal.

[. . .]

Lady Churchill to Sir Winston S. Churchill
(Churchill papers, 1/50)

25 March 1955   Chequers

This weekend will be the last that we shall spend and sleep at Chequers. We shall want to say Goodbye to everybody here and I am sure you will like to say something to them.

Next weekend we had planned to spend in London because of the Birthday party you are giving for me on Friday April the 1st, and because the Queen is coming to dinner on the Monday, and of course I should want to be all that day in London trying to make the arrangements as perfect as possible. I wonder if you would like to come down to Chequers to lunch on Sunday the 3rd, after which we could make our farewells, and then go back to Downing Street? If you liked we could ask a few people to dinner there on Saturday the 2nd and again on Sunday the 3rd. I am sending you this minute so that you have time to consider it before we meet here tomorrow evening.

---

[1] David Lloyd George, 1863–1945. Educated at a Welsh Church school. Solicitor, 1884. MP for Caernarvon, (Lib.) 1890–1931, (Ind. Lib.) 1931–45. President of the Board of Trade, 1905–8. PC, 1905. Chancellor of the Exchequer, 1908–15. An original member of the Other Club, 1911. Minister of Munitions, May 1915 to July 1916. Secretary of State for War, July–Dec. 1916. PM, Dec. 1916 to Oct. 1922. OM, 1919. Earl, 1945.

March 1955

Sir Winston S. Churchill to Lord Moran
(Churchill papers, 1/81)

28 March 1955
Private

My dear Charles,

As I mentioned to you the other day it would in my opinion be a mistake for me to inflict upon you the burden of coming out with me to Sicily. At this particular time it would give the appearance that I had resigned through ill-health, which is not true. At the same time there is no doubt that I need a rest and sunshine, so I hope you will sign the very simple paper which the Bank of England requires for an addition to the normal currency. As you may not be familiar with this, I send you the new form which is of course entirely private.

Perhaps you will let me know how many of the minors[1] I ought to take. I thought about two a week. I think it very likely I shall be back during the first week of May and anyhow I am sure you would come to my aid if anything goes wrong; but I feel quite well thanks to your attention and all I need at present is agreeable occupation and an occasional sight of the sun.

Sir Winston S. Churchill: speech
(Hansard)

28 March 1955   House of Commons

I beg to move, that this House will, tomorrow, resolve itself into a Committee to consider an humble Address to Her Majesty praying that Her Majesty will give directions that a Monument be erected at the public charge to the memory of the late Right Honourable the Earl Lloyd-George of Dwyfor, with an inscription expressive of the high sense entertained by this House of the eminent services rendered by him to the Country and to the Commonwealth and Empire in Parliament, and in great Offices of State. There is, I believe, general agreement that the House made a wise rule when it prohibited the introduction of a Motion of this character for ten years after the death of the statesman concerned. This rule is comparatively new, and has been used only once, in 1938, in the case of that honoured figure Lord Oxford and Asquith.

Ten years is long enough to allow partisan passions, whether of hatred or of enthusiasm, to cool, and not too long to quench the testimony of contemporary witnesses. We combine by this method the memories and feelings of men who knew David Lloyd George long and well with that sense of sober

---

[1] Medication to improve circulation of the blood.

proportion and perspective which ever changing time alone can give and keep on giving.

I had originally drafted this Motion to include the phrase, within the precincts of the Palace of Westminster, but because of the views which were expressed to me by the Leaders of the Labour and Liberal Parties – and, may I say, I much regret the absence and the cause of the absence of the Leader of the Liberal Party – I shall not ask the House to prejudge this matter. Some may prefer Parliament Square to the precincts of the Palace of Westminster. At any rate, it is better to leave the question open for much longer consideration than would be possible this afternoon.

I will not, however, conceal my personal opinion. David Lloyd George was a House of Commons man. He sat here for one constituency for fifty-five years. He gave sparkle to our debates. He guided the House through some of its most critical years, and without the fame and authority of the Mother of Parliaments he could never have rendered his services to the nation.

The Committee which this Motion will set up will no doubt wish those who were nearest him to express their opinion as to where he would have chosen his monument to be. He might have liked it to be as near this Chamber as possible.

The duty that falls to me this afternoon strikes a curious coincidence. It is exactly ten years ago to the day, 28th March, since I stood at this box, in my present office, and, at the first opportunity after Lloyd George's death, addressed the House on his career.[1] The discussion that followed is well worth re-reading. There will be seen the unanimity and the fervour of the testimony given to his work from all parts of the House.

I was perplexed, I admit, when I was thinking of how to commend this Motion to you, Mr Speaker, to find, on looking back, that I had already said much that I now wish to say. My friendship for this remarkable man covered more than forty years of House of Commons life, including long periods during which I served with and under him as his Cabinet colleague. Whether in or out of office, our intimate and agreeable companionship was never darkened, so far as I can recall, by any serious spell of even political hostility.

As a first-hand witness, as I may claim to be, I wish to reaffirm the tribute I paid to his memory on his death. I feel that what was said then has only grown and strengthened and mellowed in the intervening decade. There were two great spheres of his activity and achievements. He launched the Liberal and Radical forces of this country effectively into the broad stream of social betterment and social security along which all modern parties now steer.

His warm heart was stirred by the many perils which beset the cottage homes, the health of the bread winner, the fate of his widow, the nourishment and upbringing of his children, the meagre and haphazard provision

---

[1] Speech reproduced in *The Churchill Documents*, vol. 21, *The Shadows of Victory, January–July 1945*, pp. 780–3.

of medical treatment and sanatoria, and the lack of any organized accessible medical service from which the mass of the wage earners and the poor in those days suffered so severely. All this excited his wrath. Pity and compassion lent their powerful wings.

He knew the terror with which old age threatened the toiler – that after a life of exertion he could be no more than a burden at the fireside and in the family of a struggling son.

When I first became Lloyd George's friend and active associate, more than fifty years ago, this deep love of the people, the profound knowledge of their lives and of the undue and needless pressures under which they lived, impressed themselves indelibly upon my mind. Most people are unconscious today of how much of their lives have been shaped by the laws for which Lloyd George was responsible. Health insurance, and old-age pensions, were the first large-scale State-conscious efforts to fasten a lid over the abyss without pulling down the structures of civilised society.

Now we move forward confidently into larger and more far-reaching applications of these ideas. I was his lieutenant in those bygone days, and shared, in a minor way, in the work. He was indeed a champion of the weak and the poor and I am sure that as time passes his name will not only live but shine on account of the grand, laborious, constructive work he did for the social and domestic life of our country.

But the second phase of his life's work, upon which his fame will rest with equal and even greater firmness, is his guidance of the nation in the First World War. Here I will venture to quote directly what I said ten years ago: 'Although unacquainted with the military arts, although by public repute a pugnacious pacifist, when the life of our country was in peril he rallied to the war effort and cast aside all other thoughts or aims. He was the first to discern the fearful shortages of ammunition and artillery and all the other appliances of war which would so soon affect, and in the case of Imperial Russia mortally affect, the warring nations on both sides. He saw it before anyone. He presented the facts to the Cabinet even before he went to the Ministry of Munitions. Here he hurled himself into the mobilisation of British industry. In 1915, he was building great war factories that could not come into operation for two years. There was the usual talk about the war being over in a few months, but he did not hesitate to plan on a vast scale for two years ahead. It was my fortune to inherit the enormous overflowing output of those factories. When he became the head of the Government in the political convulsions of 1916, he imparted immediately a new surge of strength, of impulse, far stronger than anything that had been known up to that time, and extending over the whole field of war-time Government . . . All this was illustrated by the successful development of the war; by the adoption of the convoy system, which he enforced upon the Admiralty and by which the U-boats were defeated; by the unified command on the Western Front which gave Marshal Foch the power to lead us all to victory. . . . In these and in many other matters which form a part of the story of those sombre and tremendous years we can observe and measure the depth we owe him. As a man of action, resource and creative energy he stood, when at his zenith, without a rival.' – There is one further episode which I will mention. It fell to the lot of most of us who are here today to have to face a second world war. Lloyd George had been long out of office. Nearly a generation had passed since he ceased to be Prime Minister, but upon 3rd September, in the solemn debate which marked our entry into the new struggle, he spoke words which gave confidence to many and comfort to all. I will read them to the House: 'I have been through this before, and there is only one word I want to say about that. We had very bad moments, moments when brave men were rather quailing and doubting, but the nation was firm right through, from beginning to end. One thing that struck me then was that it was in moments of disaster, and in some of the worst disasters with which we were confronted in the war, that I found the greatest union among all classes, the greatest disappearance of discontent and disaffection, and of the grabbing for right and privileges. The nation closed its ranks then. By that means we went through right to the end, and after 4½ years, terrible years, we won a victory for right. We will do it again.' – That is what he said of this occasion, and I am glad to read it to the House again.

In supporting the motion which is on the Order Paper the House will, I believe, be acting in harmony with its traditions, and it will also strengthen the national faith in the wisdom and propriety of its judgment and the guidance which it gives. When the history of Britain for the first quarter of the twentieth century is written it will be seen how great a part of our fortunes in peace and in war was shaped by this one man.

President Dwight D. Eisenhower to Sir Winston S. Churchill
(*Churchill papers, 2/217*)

29 March 1955   The White House
Eyes Only – Top Secret

Dear Winston,

I have no doubt that you and your Cabinet find it necessary, just as we do, to ponder daily on the world situation and to calculate as carefully as you can every move to be made as you strive to straighten out some specific portion of the tangled mess that we call international relations.

Of one thing I have always been completely confident – that you are as fully dedicated as I am to promoting between our two governments and our two peoples clear unity of purpose and common understanding of the obstacles we face so as to double our strength as we push forward in the search for an honorable peace.

It is because of this confidence in our common intent — indeed, I hope I may say our indestructible personal friendship — that I venture to bring up an apparent difference between our two governments that puzzles us sorely and constantly. Although we seem always to see eye to eye with you when we contemplate any European problem, our respective attitudes toward similar problems in the Orient are frequently so dissimilar as to be almost mutually antagonistic. I know that you could make the same observation regarding us; possibly this fact troubles you and your associates just as much as it does us.

I beg of you <u>not</u> to think of this letter as a complaint, or as any effort to prove that we are right and you are wrong. In writing to you in this vein I am interested in one thing and one thing only — how can we and our two governments come closer together in our thinking so as to achieve a better result in matters that are serious and fateful for both our nations? I know that frankness on my part will not be interpreted as accusation or recrimination.

I assume that the existence of the differences I mention is so clearly, even sadly, recognized on both sides of the water as to require no elaboration. The words Formosa, Quemoy and Matsu typify them today, as Manchuria in 1931.

The conclusion seems inescapable that these differences come about because we do not agree on the probable extent and the importance of further Communist expansion in Asia. In our contacts with New Zealand and Australia, we have the feeling that we encounter a concern no less acute than ours; but your own government seems to regard Communist aggression in Asia as of little significance to the free world future.

As I once explained to you, we are not interested in Quemoy and Matsu as such. But because of the conviction that the loss of Formosa would doom the Philippines and eventually the remainder of the region, we are determined that it shall not fall into the hands of the Communists, either through all-out attacks or, as would appear to be far more likely, through harassing air attacks, threats and subversion.

The only way in which pressure of the latter type can be successfully resisted is to sustain a high morale among Chiang's forces. The danger of internal subversion and consequent collapse in Formosa is always present; Chiang feels this keenly and we believe it necessary to help him combat it.

In fact, we feel this is vitally important to the interests of the entire Western world.

Of course I would personally be very happy, both as a political leader and as an ex-soldier who may have a bit of competence in the strategic field, to see Chiang, <u>voluntarily</u> and in accordance with what he believed to be his own best interests, withdraw from Quemoy and the Matsus.

But I am just as unwilling to put so much pressure on him that he might give up the entire struggle in utter discouragement. It's at this point that you and ourselves seem to part company. But we cannot understand how the free world can hold Formosa except as Chiang provides the necessary ground forces.

Another apparent difference between us that added to our bewilderment occurred in connection with Foster's recent visit to the Far East. He urged the Government of Laos, while it still has the ability to do so, to clean out the areas in that country where Communist elements are establishing themselves in some strength. The Laos Government is fully justified in taking such action under the terms of the Geneva agreements. When Laotian officials expressed to Foster some concern lest such action on their part provoke attack from the Viet Minh and the Chinese Communists, he assured them that aggression from without would bring into play the Manila Pact. This would mean assistance from the other signatories of the Pact to preserve the territorial integrity of Laos.

Some time after this conversation, we heard that both the British and the French Ambassadors in Laos informed that Government that under no circumstances could Laos expect any help against outside aggression, under the terms of the Manila Pact, if such aggression should result from their own efforts to rule their internal affairs.

As a result, we have a situation in which the Communists, in the affected areas of Laos, grow stronger and stronger, and we face a possibility of ultimately losing that entire territory to the Communists, just as we lost North Vietnam.

Another point bothers us. This country believes that the existence of the Chi Nat[1] Government confers upon all of us one advantage that is not often publicly noted. Throughout the Far East there are great numbers of 'émigré' Chinese. These people, in most cases, possess sort of a dual citizenship – one pertaining to the country in which they reside; the other to China. Up to date, millions of these people have preserved their allegiance to Chiang and have not become Communist cells menacing the countries where they are now residents. This affects the Philippines, Indonesia and, of course, other areas much as Malaya and Hong Kong.

This is another fact that points to the very great desirability of sustaining Chiang's prestige and the morale of his followers. If the Chinese National Government should disappear, these émigré Chinese will certainly deem themselves subjects of the Chinese Communist Government and they will quickly add to the difficulties of their adopted countries. Indeed, where their numbers are quite strong, I believe that their influence might become decisive and that no outside aid that any of us could bring to bear could prevent these regions from going completely Communist. Do not such possibilities concern you?

As we consider such developments and possibilities, it seems to me we cannot fail to conclude that the time to stop any advance of Communism in Asia is here, now.

---

[1] Chinese Nationalist.

We have come to the point where every additional backward step must be deemed a defeat for the Western world. In fact, it is a triple defeat. First, we lose a potential ally. Next, we give to an implacable enemy another recruit. Beyond this, every such retreat creates in the minds of neutrals the fear that we do not mean what we say when we pledge our support to people who want to remain free. We show ourselves fearful of the Communistic brigands and create the impression that we are slinking along in the shadows, hoping that the beast will finally be satiated and cease his predatory tactics before he finally devours us. So the third result is that the morale of our friends crumbles.

Of course it is easy to say that this is a gross overstatement of the case. Because the ChiComs[1] have no great fleet and cannot now attack across the seas, it is natural to underestimate their potential strength and the fearful eventual results of the crumbling process. So I believe it critically important that we make a sober estimate of what we are up against.

Two decades ago we had the fatuous hope that Hitler, Mussolini and the Japanese war lords would decide, before we might become personally involved, that they had enough and would let the world live in peace. We saw the result.

Yet the Communist sweep over the world since World War II has been much faster and much more relentless than the 1930s sweep of the dictators. I do believe that all of us must begin to look some of these unpleasant facts squarely in the face and meet them exactly as our Grand Alliance of the 40's met our enemies and vanquished them.

You and I have been through many things where our judgments have not always been as one, but, on my part at least, my admiration and affection for you were never lessened. In this long experience, my hope is rooted that the two of us achieve a personal concord that could, in turn, help our two governments act more effectively against Communists everywhere.

My warm greetings to Clemmie, and, of course, my very kind regard to yourself.

Lord Moran to Sir Winston S. Churchill
(Churchill papers, 1/89)

29 March 1955

My dear Prime Minister,

Your decision has worried me a great deal – I do not think I am being alarmed without good reason.[2]

Dunhill,[3] whose judgment I trust, said when I told him about the bleeding:

---

[1] Chinese Communists.
[2] See Churchill to Moran of Mar. 28, reproduced above (p. 1965).
[3] Thomas Peel Dunhill, 1876–1957. Educated at Clinical School, Melbourne Hospital, 1903. Married, 1914, Edith Florence Affleck McKellar (d. 1942). On active service in WWI. CVO, 1919.

'It is imperative that the Prime Minister should be investigated to establish the cause of the bleeding, or alternatively that he takes you with him in case there is a severe haemorrhage.'

But apart from this, and in my judgment far more important, is the question of the circulation, on which after all everything turns. It seems that after nursing the circulation for months we are, overnight as it were, to leave it to its own devices. Surely to break off the minors, to take none for a month, is just to invite trouble. I am thinking of the effect on the circulation of the withdrawal of the minors, discarding a proved ally at what may well be the height of the battle. For it does mean giving them up; no doctor who knew his job would countenance you taking minors when not under observation. Indeed taking minors without skilled supervision would be the most hazardous of all.

The point at issue is whether my going with you gives the appearance you are not in good health. The same point, you may remember, was raised before you went off to sign the Atlantic Charter. It was then decided at the last moment that if I went it might suggest you were not in good health. I thought at the time there was nothing in this, and subsequently when I went regularly no one ever thought it was because you weren't fit. Incidentally, if the decision taken before the Atlantic Charter had not been reversed when you went to America in December, 1941, I should not have gone with you, and an American doctor would have been called in when you had the heart attack after opening a window in the White House. It would then have got about everywhere that you had had a heart attack.

When Dunhill told me what in his view were the two alternatives, I said that I thought you would not take me because you had got it into your head that if I went people would think you were not in good health. He was very much surprised, saying people had come to take my going for granted, as part in fact of routine arrangements. And that when you went to Bermuda and to America fairly recently no one talked about the Prime Minister being unfit.

I travel a good deal about England in connection with Awards, and I know pretty well what people think about my going on these journeys. It is taken as a precautionary measure, an insurance, common enough in history, as the records of the College of Physicians prove; a measure which became a routine during the war, and a fairly frequent happening since the war. It has never suggested to anyone that you were in poor health. On the other hand my not going will certainly not be taken as a sign that you are in good health. Those who notice my absence will say that you may be going abroad for some time and that probably your doctor could not get away for so long. I do not hope to persuade you that this is a mistaken policy, but I cannot help telling you how profoundly I am concerned with the course you are taking.

CMG, 1919. Asst to Dr George Gask, St Vincent's Hospital, London, 1920. Surgeon to the Royal Household, 1928. Hon. Surgeon to George VI, 1930. KCVO, 1933. Hon. Fellow, Royal College of Surgeons, 1939.

MARCH 1955

Sir Winston S. Churchill to Konrad Adenauer
(Premier papers, 11/845)

30 March 1955

Dear Dr Adenauer,

I am indeed obliged to you for the kind things which you said in your letter of March 18.[1]

My remarks about you in my speech in the House of Commons[2] were most sincerely meant. Your contribution to the cause of Western Europe has been a noble one and the creation of the new system which is now emerging is due to a large extent to your statesmanship at the London and Paris Conferences. I much admire your success in steering the Paris Agreements through to ratification despite all the difficulties which beset them.

Please accept my sincere congratulations and good wishes.

Sir Michael Adeane to Sir Winston S. Churchill
(Churchill papers, 6/4)[3]

31 March 1955   Buckingham Palace
Secret

Dear Prime Minister,

The Queen was having her portrait painted this evening but I was able to deliver your message just before luncheon.

Her Majesty said at once that she was most grateful to you telling her privately of your intention and that I was to emphasize in replying to you that she fully understood why it was that when she received you last Tuesday there still seemed to be some uncertainty about the future.

She added that I must tell you that, though she recognized your wisdom in taking the decision which you had, she felt the greatest personal regrets and that she will especially miss the weekly audiences which she has found so instructive and, if one can say so of State matters, so entertaining.

The Queen told me to say that she was particularly sorry to hear that Lady Churchill's neuritis was still giving trouble and that I was to ask you to give her best wishes to Lady Churchill for her birthday tomorrow with her hopes that it may be free from pain.

I enclose a copy of the Court Circular of 26 October 1951 for which you asked me. On that occasion both important announcements formed part of one circular, but on this our plans will be for two announcements on two consecutive days.

[1] Reproduced above (pp. 1960–1).
[2] Reproduced above (pp. 1949–58).
[3] This letter was handwritten.

March 1955

Sir Winston S. Churchill to Lord Moran
(Churchill papers, 1/89)

31 March 1955

My dear Charles,

Thank you so much for your letter.[1] It is generous to you to wish to sacrifice yourself in this way especially as Dr MacKenna tells me that you are still suffering a good deal of pain. I really cannot feel it would be a good thing for me to advertise my departure as if it were on grounds of health. It is one thing for you to accompany me on an official journey and quite another when I am a private person. In this case all the publicity of a public journey would be involved without my having any official status. Health therefore would be the only reason.

As to the latter, I have not seen Dunhill for a year-and-a-half so he cannot know much about me. Though my eye is troublesome at the moment I feel very well and I am quite sure there is nothing wrong. Come and look me up tomorrow if you feel well enough.

---

[1] Reproduced above (pp. 1971–2).

April
1955

Sir Winston S. Churchill to Sir Anthony Eden
Prime Minister's Personal Minute M.60/55
(Premier papers, 11/879)

1 April 1955
Secret

I have received the enclosed[1] from the President. It seems to me a serious statement of his position. We can talk about it when you come to see me at 7 o'clock tomorrow.

Sir Winston S. Churchill to President Dwight D. Eisenhower
(Churchill papers, 2/217)

April 1955
NOT SENT

My dear Friend,
I have to thank you for your two memorable letters of March 22 and 29.[2] By the time you get this very inadequate reply I shall have resigned my Office as Prime Minister and relinquished my direction of British policy. Anthony Eden and I have long been friends and lately even related by marriage; but quite apart from personal ties I feel it is my duty, as Leader of the Conservative Party, to make sure that my successor has a fair chance of leading the Conservatives to victory at the next Election, which, under the Quinquennial Act, falls at the end of October 1956. The choice of the date is indeed one of the extraordinary complication, into which Luck and Hazard enter on a remarkable scale. I feel that the decision should be taken by the man whose fortunes are governed by the result. It will in many ways be a disaster to most of the causes with which we are both concerned if the Socialist Party in its present

---

[1] Reproduced above (pp. 1968–71).
[2] Reproduced above (pp. 1961–3, 1968–71).

feebleness and disarray should again obtain what might be a long lease of power in Britain. I do not feel sure that our national vitality and wisdom would survive the event and the impression it would make on the world. At any rate I did not feel that I ought to overhang the situation unless I were prepared to lead the Party in the Election myself. This at my age I could not undertake to do. Hence I have felt it my duty to resign.

To resign is not to retire, and I am by no means sure that other opportunities may not come upon me to serve and influence those causes for which we have both of us worked so long. Of these the first is Anglo-American brotherhood, and the second is the arrest of the Communist menace. They are, I believe, identical.

Lord Moran to Sir Winston S. Churchill
(Churchill papers, 1/89)

2 April 1955

My dear Prime Minister,

I have given a good deal of thought to one point: how can the considerable risks inherent in the course you are taking be minimized? And I have decided that taking minors for the next ten days is after all not indicated. On the contrary it is better to drop them now. It is unlikely that there will be any immediate reaction, because you have, I think, gone as long before without them, without mishap. But if there were, I should be available to deal with the situation.

For a long time I have been following a long term plan, the purpose of which was to brace and maintain the circulation at any rate at its present level, and as part of this plan I'd given particular attention to the time immediately following your resignation and to a possible reaction then. It is difficult not to feel discouraged when I see these carefully worked out plans go sky high. Particularly as I have not the consolation of believing that real and substantial advantages on the medical side have been set aside for some solid and tangible and not imaginary gain. Now the political world and the country have been told that you had a stroke they will not think of you as in good health whatever is done or said.

However I must now put aside the feeling of disappointment that my plans as your doctor have gone awry, and not lose heart, but do what can be done in the circumstances.

I shall be available at any time any day till Wednesday at midnight, when I go to Cornwall to see if a change of scene will bring some sleep which I rather badly need.

APRIL 1955

Sir Winston S. Churchill to Sir Anthony Eden
(Churchill papers, 6/4)

2 April 1955

The following are my ideas about our changing guard.

Cabinet, Tuesday at noon – Parliamentary business and Foreign Affairs, after which I will say what I am going to do. We might then go upstairs to the pillared room and have a photograph taken. There is supposed to be one, Norman Brook says, of every Cabinet. I shall not attend the House on Tuesday. I am expecting to arrange 4.30 as the time of my Audience. I understand that my Successor will be summoned to the Palace probably about noon on Wednesday, when he will become responsible. On Wednesday afternoon at 4 p.m. I am having a Staff party for the typists and messengers and some others from No. 10, and a party from Chequers. I shall leave for Chartwell before 6 p.m. Clemmie has various household things to settle, and would be proposing to join me Thursday evening. I am arranging that the Cabinet Room and offices shall be at my Successor's disposal (I hope yours) if you want a Cabinet, from Thursday onwards. As far as the residential quarters are concerned, it will take about a week to have all our stuff cleared out, and as Easter intervenes, it would seem convenient that Miss Hamblin, my Wife's Secretary, should have till, say, the 20th to do this. Thereafter the whole building will be at your disposal, but I expect you will be a few days getting the house in order before you can move in. I am going now to Sicily on the 12th. I understand you have been planning a meeting at Chequers for the weekend after this; we have a good deal of stuff of our own to remove from there, but this can be done thereafter. I hope there will be no hurry about the fish, as I have to arrange for their removal, care and reception, which is all a complicated business.

Sir Winston S. Churchill to Lord Moran
(Churchill papers, 1/89)

3 April 1955

My dear Charles,

I shall need to take a couple of minors on Monday and Tuesday, and perhaps another on Wednesday. After that I do not think there will be any need, unless you advise it, for me to take any when I am abroad. I shall only be living an ordinary life, and hope to get a sleep every day.

It occurred to me that it might be well for you to enquire privately about a doctor in Syracuse or Taormina whom I could see from time to time and who could report to you. You did this before with great advantage at Cap d'Ail.

April 1955

Sir Winston S. Churchill: speech
(Churchill papers, 5/57)

4 April 1955   No. 10 Downing Street

Your Royal Highness,
Your Graces,
My Lords, Ladies and Gentlemen.

I have the honour of proposing a Toast which I used to enjoy drinking during the years when I was a Cavalry Subaltern in the Reign of Your Majesty's Great-great-Grandmother, Queen Victoria.

Having served in office or in Parliament under the four Sovereigns who have reigned since those days, I felt, with these credentials, that in asking Your Majesty's gracious permission, I should not be leading to the creation of a precedent which would often cause inconvenience.

Madam, I should like to express the deep and lively sense of gratitude which we and all your peoples feel to you and to His Royal Highness the Duke of Edinburgh for all the help and inspiration we receive in our daily lives and which spreads with ever-growing strength throughout the British Realm and the Commonwealth and Empire. Never have we needed it more than in the anxious and darkling age through which we are passing and which we hope to help the world to pass.

Never have the august duties which fall upon the British Monarchy been discharged with more devotion than in the brilliant opening of Your Majesty's reign.

We thank God for the gift he has bestowed upon us and vow ourselves anew to the sacred causes and wise and kindly way of life of wh Your Majesty is the young, gleaming champion.

The Queen.

John Colville: recollection[1]
(Randolph Churchill papers)

4 April 1955

On 4 April 1955, the Prime Minister gave a farewell dinner at 10 Downing Street for the Queen and the Duke of Edinburgh. This had been greatly altered in appearance. The idea had been suggested that there should be a small dinner of twelve persons, none of whom would be common members of the Cabinet but would be great grandees, such as the Dukes of Norfolk and Northumberland. However it became clearer as the arrangements were made that more and more people would be offended if they were not asked, and

---

[1] Recorded by Randolph Churchill, 1965.

indeed they were. The dinner was expanded to some fifty persons although very few members of the Cabinet were asked. Among the original grandees among whom I had been invited to advise were Lord and Lady Home.[1] Lord Home was at that time Under-Secretary of State for Scotland, and it had occurred to me that he was a suitable Scottish grandee; he was left in the list and the Secretary for State for Scotland, Mr James Stuart was left out.

The great day arrived and I was asked by Lady Churchill to arrange the guests in exact order of precedence by referring to the table of precedence in *Burke's Peerage*. This I duly did and since all the grandees were there apart from other commoner types the order was remarkable. Also it was quite clear that since the Queen and Prince Philip could not be expected to walk around and shake hands with all present it was so arranged that they stood in the pillared room at 10 Downing Street and the guests would marshal in strict order of precedence next door and would march past. Now the first in order of precedence were the Lord Chancellor followed by the Dukes. The Secretary of State for Foreign Affairs and Lady Eden came very low down on the list, in fact after the younger sons of earls. However this did not suit the book of the Secretary of State for Foreign Affairs and Lady Eden, who jumped the queue immediately before the Duchess of Westminster[2] and after the Duke and Duchess of Norfolk.[3] The poor Duchess of Westminster, not realizing that this was going to happen, strode forward and put her foot right through Lady Eden's train which was torn from her shoulders. This was observed by the Duke of Edinburgh, who was heard to say in a loud voice: 'That's torn it, in every sense.'

However, in spite of this original and immediate misunderstanding and misfortune, the dinner went ahead very well and the placement was excellent. I found myself sitting next to the Chief Whip who attacked me venomously on the subject of Lord and Lady Home having been invited and not the Secretary of State for Scotland. The Chief Whip was Mr Patrick Buchan-Hepburn. He said that he was very glad that I was leaving the Foreign Office as I had really got too jumped up for my position and that a new regime was coming

---

[1] Alexander Frederick Douglas-Home, 1903–95. MP (Cons.) for South Lanark, 1931–45; for Lanark, 1950–1. Married, 1936, Elizabeth Hester (1908–90): four children. Parliamentary Private Secretary to Neville Chamberlain, 1937–40. Succeeded as 14th Earl Home, 1951. Minister of State, Scottish Office, 1951–5. Secretary of State for Commonwealth Relations, 1955–60; for Foreign Affairs, 1960–3. Disclaimed peerage, 1963. PM, 1963–4. Leader of the Opposition, 1964–5. Secretary of State for Foreign and Commonwealth Affairs, 1970–4. Baron, 1975.

[2] Viola Maud Lyttelton, 1912–87. Married, 1946, Robert Grosvenor, 5th Duke of Westminster: three children. Flying Officer, WAAF, 1942–5. Lord Lieutenant of Fermanagh, 1979–87.

[3] Miles Francis Stapleton Fitzalan-Howard, 1915–2002. Eldest son of 3rd Baron of Howard of Glossop. On active service in France, North Africa, Sicily and Italy during WWII (MC). Married, 1949, Anne Mary Teresa Constable-Maxwell: five children. CB, 1960. Retired from military service with rank of Maj.-Gen., 1965. CBE, 1966. Director of Service Intelligence, 1966–7. Succeeded his second cousin as 17th Duke of Norfolk and Earl of Arundel, 1975. KG, 1983. GCVO, 1986.

Anne Mary Teresa Constable-Maxwell, 1927–2013. Married, 1949, Miles Francis Stapleton Fitzalan-Howard: five children. CBE, 1992.

in which would stand no nonsense of this kind. I became very violent and said how dare he say such a thing about Sir Winston Churchill to whom he owed everything. We had a fiendish row at dinner and he turned his back on me in fury and turned to his neighbour on the other side, who turned out to be Lady Bridges,[1] which upset him very much because he had nothing to say to her.

After dinner everything went very well, except for the extraordinary behaviour of Mr Randolph Churchill who more or less in the manner of Groucho Marks[2] pursued Lady Eden all around the room with a draft poem for *Punch* which he had written, which caused her ladyship untold trouble. There was also a little bit of difficulty about Lady Morrison of Lambeth,[3] recently married, who insisted on sitting next to the Queen and regaling her with conversation.

However in due course all the great departed and nobody was left except Sir Winston Churchill in his last night at 10 Downing Street. I went up with him to his bedroom and he sat down on his bed resplendent in his Garter, his Order of Merit, his knee breeches, and he stared at the window and said nothing and I also said nothing because I felt that he was thinking that this was his last night after so many years at 10 Downing Street, and perhaps pondering all that had happened in that room. However his mind was in fact on something else, because after about a minute, he suddenly fixed me with a stern glare and said: 'I don't think that Anthony can do it'.

Cabinet: conclusions
(Cabinet papers, 128/28)

5 April 1955
Secret
12 p.m.
Cabinet Meeting No. 28 of 1955

[. . .]

6. The Prime Minister said that he intended to submit his resignation to Her Majesty at an audience that afternoon. His resignation would carry with it the resignation of the whole Administration. Other Ministers need not tender their resignations to The Queen, but they should regard their offices as at the disposal of his successor. Meanwhile they should carry on the necessary administration of their Departments until a new Government was formed. Ministers of Cabinet rank who were not members of the Cabinet would be so informed at a meeting which he was holding later in the day. Junior Ministers would be similarly informed by letter.

---

[1] Katharine Dianthe Farrer, 1896–1986. Born in Abinger, Surrey. Married, 1922, Edward Ettingdean Bridges: four children.
[2] Marx.
[3] Edith Meadowcroft, 1908–? Businesswoman. Married, 1955, Herbert Stanley Morrison.

April 1955

The Prime Minister said that it remained for him to wish his colleagues all good fortune in the difficult, but hopeful, situation which they had to face. He trusted that they would be enabled to further the progress already made in rebuilding the domestic stability and economic strength of the United Kingdom and in weaving still more closely the threads which bound together the countries of the Commonwealth or, as he still preferred to call it, the Empire.

The Foreign Secretary said that his Cabinet colleagues had asked him to speak on this occasion on behalf of them all. It therefore fell to him to express their sense of abiding affection and esteem for the Prime Minister and their pride in the privilege of having served as his colleagues. He himself had enjoyed this privilege for sixteen years, others for varying shorter periods; but all, whatever the length of their service, had the same strong feelings of affection for him. If in a succeeding Government they met with success, this would be largely due to the example which he had shown them: if they did less well, it would be because they had failed to learn from his experience and skill as a statesman. They would remember him always – for his magnanimity, for his courage at all times and for his unfailing humour, founded in his unrivalled mastery of the English language. They would always be grateful for his leadership, and for his friendship, over the years that had passed; and they would hope to enjoy in future his continuing interest and support in their endeavours.

Sir Winston S. Churchill: note
(Churchill papers, 2/197)

[5] April 1955

I tendered my resignation to The Queen, which Her Majesty accepted. She asked me whether I would recommend a successor and I said I preferred to leave it to Her. She said the case was not a difficult one and that She would summon Sir Anthony Eden.

After some further conversation Her Majesty said She believed that I wished to continue in the Commons but that otherwise She would offer me a Dukedom. I said that I would like to go on in the Commons while I felt physically fit but that if I felt the work was too hard I would be very proud if She chose to reconsider Her proposal.

I expressed my deep gratitude to Her Majesty for Her kindness.

April 1955

John Colville: recollection[1]
(Randolph Churchill papers)

5 April 1955

Another matter[. . .] was the question of Sir Winston's dukedom. I must take the credit for this personally because I suggested to Sir Michael Adeane, who succeeded Sir Alan Lascelles as Principal Private Secretary to the Sovereign, that when the Prime Minister resigned, since he was quite different from any other Prime Minister, it would be quite appropriate if he were offered a dukedom. To which the reply was that no more dukedoms would ever be given except to Royal personages. However it did seem appropriate. Could I give the undertaking that the Prime Minister would refuse it? I said I would take some soundings. So on the next possible occasion I asked Sir Winston what would happen if when he resigned the Queen were to offer him a dukedom? To which he said nothing would induce him to accept it. First of all what could he be Duke of? Secondly even if he were Duke of Westerham, what would Randolph be? He could only be Marquis of Puddleduck Lane which was the only other possession he had apart from Chartwell. And thirdly, and quite seriously, he wished to die in the House of Commons as Winston Churchill. He therefore told me that even if this unlikely event came to pass he would certainly decline it. I rushed to the telephone and rang up Sir Michael Adeane and said that he could safely tell the Queen that the dukedom could be offered.

Accordingly when Sir Winston went to Buckingham Palace on 5 April 1955, to resign, the dukedom was duly offered. I was greatly disturbed because as I saw the Prime Minister going off in his frock coat and his top hat and knowing as I did that he was madly in love with the Queen – and this was clear from the fact that his audiences had been dragged out longer and longer as the months went by and very often took an hour and a half, at which I may say racing was not the only topic discussed, – I was rather alarmed that sentimental feelings might indeed make him accept at the last moment. In which case I knew that both the Queen and Sir Michael would be very angry with me for having given this pledge.

When he returned from his audience the first thing I said to him as we sat in the Cabinet room was 'How did it go?' With tears in his eyes he said 'Do you know, the most remarkable thing – she offered to make me a Duke.' With trepidation I asked what he had said. 'Well you know, I very nearly accepted, I was so moved by her beauty and her charm and the kindness with which she made this offer, that for a moment I thought of accepting. But finally I remembered that I must die as I have always been – Winston Churchill. And so I asked her to forgive my not accepting it. And do you know, it's an odd thing, but she seemed almost relieved.'

[1] Recorded by Randolph Churchill, 1965.

April 1955

Sir Winston S. Churchill to Sir Robert Howe
(Churchill papers, 6/6)

5 April 1955
Private

My dear Howe,

You sent me a long and interesting account of the state of the Sudan at the close of your Governor Generalship. I am indeed obliged to you for the trouble which you have taken to keep me informed and, now that your stewardship is ended, let me congratulate you on the skill and patience with which you have presided over the government of the Sudan. You have done this in circumstances which must often have been exasperating and cannot have been anything but distressing to you as an Englishman.

Queen Elizabeth II to Lady Churchill
(Baroness Spencer-Churchill papers)[1]

5 April 1955
Buckingham Palace

Dear Lady Churchill,

This is just a line to try and express our thanks for such a delightful evening at No. 10 last night.

It was a most interesting and friendly party and we enjoyed it all greatly. I only hope we did not stay too late and tire you all out completely!

Though I don't think it was intentional that your kind invitation to dinner should be a farewell occasion, in fact I could not have been more perfectly amazed, coming just before Today's resignation.

I hope you will both now have time for rest and relaxation in the sun in Sicily.

With renewed Thanks,
Yours Sincerely, Elizabeth R.

---

[1] This letter was handwritten.

April 1955

Prince Philip to Lady Churchill
(Baroness Spencer-Churchill papers)[1]

6 April 1955   Buckingham Palace

Dear Lady Churchill,
    This is a most inadequate note of thanks for the perfectly delightful dinner on Monday.
    It was such a friendly and happy occasion that I find it hard to realize that it must have been rather a sad moment for you.
    I do hope that your holiday in Sicily will do you good and that when you come back your arm will be fully recovered.
    Again many thanks for a charming evening.

Yours sincerely,
Philip

Anthony Montague Browne to Sir Winston S. Churchill
(Churchill papers, 6/4)

6 April 1955

You wished to know the economies of staff achieved in the Cyprus Headquarters under the present proposals. They are as follows:

	Present Proposals	October 1954 Proposals	Saving
Army	447 (177 Officers and 270 Other Ranks)	485 (172 Officers and 313 Other Ranks)	55 Officers and 43 Other Ranks
Air Force	316 (94 Officers and 222 Other Ranks)	473 (162 Officers and 311 Other Ranks)	68 Officers and 89 Other Ranks

For the moment the Army are seeking a 'temporary increase' on their final figure, bringing the total up to 450 (138 Officers and 312 Other Ranks). This is intended they say, to deal with the stockpiling of equipment moved from the Canal Zone and a 'building programme covering Jordan, Libya, and Cyprus'.
    The Naval figures are not yet available, but I understand that they are much smaller than the other two Services since the Navy's main requirements are met from the Malta Headquarters.

---

[1] This letter was handwritten.

April 1955

Harry S Truman to Sir Winston S. Churchill
('Defending the West, The Truman–Churchill Correspondence', page 215)

6 April 1955

I feel as I know the whole free world feels – that something has gone and will be most difficult to replace.

We all know that we cannot go on forever. I wish that you could have gone on indefinitely.

My association with you was one of the highlights of my life.

Your contributions to the salvation of the free world from the totalitarians and the tyrants have never been equalled in history.

May your retirement be no retirement but a happy relief from responsibility and a continued contribution to the safety and welfare of this old world.

Lord Camrose[1] to Sir Winston S. Churchill
(Churchill papers, 2/481)[2]

7 April 1955

Dear Sir Winston,

I write, as my brother[3] has also done, to say how distressing it has been that the *Daily Telegraph* has not been able to pay the immense tribute to yourself which we should have liked to have done.[4]

My father would have been very sad.

Sir Anthony Eden to Sir Winston S. Churchill
(Churchill papers, 2/216)

8 April 1955

My dear Winston,

I promised you a few reflections on this problem of the Election.

There is no doubt that other things being equal the autumn would suit us better. The 26th of May is uncomfortably near the Whitsun holiday. But unfortunately other things are not equal. It seems that we are now about 70% convertible, though I confess that I was not clear at the time that we had

---

[1] John Seymour Berry, 1909–95. Educated at Eton and Christ Church, Oxford. MP (Cons.) for Hitchin, 1941–5. Served in WWII as Major, City of London Yeomanry, RA, 1939–45. Deputy Chairman, *Daily Telegraph*, 1939–87. Vice-Chairman, Amalgamated Press, 1942–59. Baron, 1954.

[2] This letter was handwritten.

[3] William Michael Berry, 1911–2001. Married, 1936, Pamela Smith: four children. Chairman and Editor-in-Chief, *Daily Telegraph*, 1954–87. Baron Hartwell, 1968. 3rd Viscount Camrose, 1995.

[4] Strike action by maintenance workers in Fleet Street was at this time preventing publication of all British national newspapers except the *Guardian*, which was produced and printed in Manchester.

moved so far. However having done so it seems that the best course is probably to go completely convertible. If we are to do this there must be confidence in our country's political future. We cannot be sure that there will be such confidence in the fourth year of the Parliament with the advent of a Socialist Government as a possibility.

Therefore as it seems to me the financial remedy which we have to use, should our exchange position deteriorate further, would probably be effective after a General Election but might not be so before. This as I see it is the disagreeable reality which pushes us towards a May Election. As you know I have been tempted to try to show that we can be a good Administration for at least six months before appealing to the Country but I am increasingly compelled to take account of these distasteful economic factors.

Over and above all this we are finding increasing difficulty in selecting any date early next year. These wretched valuations, though they do not come into force until April, are likely to become known as early as December, or in any event in January. This seems to rule out a month by which you and I had both been much attracted.

I should be grateful if you would treat this letter as between ourselves alone because I am not showing a copy of it to anybody.

I fear that the decision cannot be taken on Tuesday but we are fixing a code word with you.

Clarissa joins me in love to you and Clemmie. We were so touched by your telegram.

Sir Anthony Eden to Sir Winston S. Churchill
(Churchill papers, 2/216)[1]

11 April 1955   Chequers

My dear Winston,

This is just to send the warmest love from us both to you & to Clemmie with every good wish for the journey and for sunshine and a happy holiday in Sicily.

Pitblado will tell you the latest development on the election front. There is no change of significance, but the strike outlook continues to cause some worry. It is not very possible to estimate how this will work out.

He will keep you posted, meanwhile – bon voyage.

---

[1] This letter was handwritten.

Sir Winston S. Churchill to Bernard Baruch
(Churchill papers, 2/210)

14 April 1955   Sicily

My dear Bernie,
A fortnight has passed since you wrote me your very kind letter of March 30. You will have seen that in the meanwhile my position has become one of greater freedom and less responsibility. I am glad to be freed from responsibility which was not in every case accompanied by power, and have not yet made any plans concerning the new freedom. It is very nice to reach a milestone in the journey on which I may sit and rest.

Of course all our plans are affected by the uncertainty about the Election, which I expect to go home to fight in the Woodford constituency in the first week of May, when I imagine the dissolution will be announced, but all is still unsettled, as it ought to be in any well-constructed human society. Thank you so much for your good wishes to Clemmie and 'all of the families' and pray accept the same from me.

PS. I am afraid I shall not be much use to Mary Martin.[1]

Sir Winston S. Churchill to Harold Macmillan
(Churchill papers, 2/191)

15 April 1955   Sicily
Secret

My dear Harold,
Some time ago I made enquiries about General Bor Komorowski,[2] who I had heard was in financial difficulties. I was told by the Foreign Office that in addition to his small earnings as a silversmith, he receives a pension of £40 a month from 'C'. I now learn that he gives part of this to other indigent Poles. Moreover although, until recently, he also received £20 a month from a fund at General Anders'[3] disposal, this income has now ceased. I therefore hope

---

[1] Mary Martin, 1913–90. American actress and Broadway star. Known for her role as Peter Pan in the 1954 Broadway production.

[2] Tadeusz Komorowski, 1895–1966. Known as 'Bór-Komorowski' from his codename, 'Bór'. Joined Army of Polish Republic, 1918. On active service, 9th Cavalry, Russo-Polish War, 1919. Commandant, Central Cavalry School, Grudziądz, 1938–9. Deputy C-in-C, Polish Home Army, 1939–43. C-in-C, Polish Home Army, 1943–4. Ordered Home Army to rebel against the Nazi occupiers and attempt to capture Warsaw before the advancing Red Army, 1 Aug. 1944. POW, 1944–5. PM, Polish Government-in-Exile, 1947–9. Lived in the UK during his retirement.

[3] Władysław Anders, 1892–1970. CoS to Inspector-General of Cavalry, 1925–6. CO, Cavalry Bde Samodzielnej, 1926–37; Cavalry Bde Nowogrodzkiej, 1937–9. GOC Operational Cavalry Group, 1939. POW, Soviet Union, 1939–41. GOC Forces in Soviet Union, 1941–2; 5th Div., 1941–2; Army of the East, 1942–3; II Corps (Italy), 1943–6. Inspector-General of Polish Forces in the West, 1945–54.

you may think of increasing the pension from secret sources. He is a very gallant man whose only reward has been exile and penury.

I meant to do this before leaving office, but it has followed me here.

Sir Winston S. Churchill to Lord Camrose
(Churchill papers, 2/481)

24 April 1955   Sicily

My dear Seymour,

Thank you so much for your letter.[1] I am so sorry the *Daily Telegraph* tribute was never published. It would I am sure have gone far beyond what I deserve. But that might have been expected by the oldest correspondent of the *Daily Telegraph* still alive. I hope to see you ere long at the Other Club. I have so many memories of your dear Father, who was so kind to me for so many years.

Sir Winston S. Churchill to Lady Churchill
(Churchill papers, 1/55)

24 April 1955

Schopenhauer[2] has said 'We look upon the present as something to be put up with while it lasts, and as a means of helping us towards our goal. Most people when they get to the end of their life find they have lived throughout ad interim.' Such is the view of the pessimistic philosopher.

When we get home on Tuesday night we shall soon find ourselves in the General Election. I shall ask Miss Sturdee and Mrs Shillingford[3] to help till the end of May. (Mrs Shillingford anyhow does the work of the Constituency.) If an additional shorthand writer is required to typewrite speeches many good ones are available. It is necessary to wait till the result of the Election is known before making plans. If we win, I shall hope for a long spell abroad. If, on the contrary, we are beaten, a new and more difficult situation will arise.

We really must wait and see what happens. Meanwhile Miss Hamblin will, I hope, continue to do exactly what she is doing now. I was hoping Miss Wood[4] could give me half her time.

After the present deluge of correspondence has been disposed of, and time does a lot, I must look out upon a prospect of a vast reduction in letters which

---

[1] Reproduced above (p. 1985).

[2] Arthur Schopenhauer, 1788–1860. Philosopher. Born in Danzig. Educated at Universities of Gottingen and Berlin. Lecturer, University of Berlin, 1820. Published *The Fourfold Root of the Principle of Sufficient Reason* (1813), *On Vision and Colors* (1816), *Theory of Colors* (1830) and *The World as Will and Representation* (1944).

[3] Formerly Lettice Marston.

[4] Heather Wood, 1936–. Secretary to Lady Churchill, 1953–5.

have to be answered and a continuing decline in quantity. The *English-Speaking Peoples*, which is to be my main work, does not require new composition but is almost entirely revision and done by hand.

I am quite agreeable to a junior being engaged.

Sir Winston S. Churchill to Lord Rothermere
(Churchill papers, 2/197)

27 April 1955
Private

My dear Esmond,

Thank you so much for your very kind letter of three weeks ago. I am so glad that the National Press has resumed its strong and active life.[1] I missed it very much, but I feel sure you were right in the course you took. I am sure that the spectacle of four Socialists, at the head of seven hundred unskilled, highly paid men, being able to inflict this vast and far-reaching injury upon the nation with its cruel hardships on many sides, cannot be reconciled with any process of democracy. I believe it has made a deep impression upon the nation, and I hope the new Parliament will consider basically the new problems which have come to us as the examples of the malignant activities of Communism.

We are having beautiful weather in Sicily on the day of our departure. Otherwise the gleams of sunshine have been few and far between. The Sicilians regarded our disappointment with characteristic shrewdness, 'We are very glad to see him here, but what a pity he should have thought it necessary to bring his English weather with him.' Now I expect they will say, 'Thank God he has taken it away.'

Sir Winston S. Churchill to Lord De La Warr
(Churchill papers, 2/184)

27 April 1955

My dear Buck,

Thank you very much for your letter on my resignation. I did not want to go but I thought it was my duty, and I fervently hope the results to the party at the Election will show that this view was right.

My main purpose is, however, to thank you for the three and a half years excellent work which you did in the difficult office which I asked you to fill for a period marked by such complex problems, about which there were bound

---

[1] The national newspaper strike had ended on Apr. 21.

to be different sets of opinion and through which you steered your way with so much success. Being an old and old-fashioned animal, I am no enthusiast for the TV age, in which I fear mass thought and actions will be taken too much charge of by machinery, both destructive and distracting. I have greatly admired the way in which you have managed these difficult problems.

Sir Winston S. Churchill to Duchess of Kent
(*Churchill papers, 2/197*)

27 April 1955

Madam,

I am most grateful to you for writing to me on my departure from power. The red lilies which you sent me when I was ill in 1942 have brought a healthy and buoyant posterity. This year was, I think, the best crop we have yet had. They always remind me of Your Royal Highness's kindness.

In thanking Your Royal Highness for writing, I cherish the hope that we shall meet in future days.

Sir Winston S. Churchill to R. A. Butler
(*Churchill papers, 2/481*)

28 April 1955

My dear Rab,

It was very nice of you to write to me in all the hurry of the budget days and give me such a good account. In the main I am sure the Budget will be a help and Gaitskell's attitude will receive the contempt it deserves. The only point I should have differed on was the half-measure about the purchase tax easements in the cotton trade. Now that you cannot think of a quota any more because of India's favourable reactions to its disciplinary menace, would it not be possible to go the whole hog – or perhaps it would be better to say the 'whole little pig' – about the purchase tax? This is my only suggestion.

I hope we shall meet soon. I am not coming to the House during this Parliament.

Everybody feels you have been a pillar of strength to my Administration. I should like to record once again my warmest thanks to you for your services.

April 1955

John Colville to Sir Winston S. Churchill
(Churchill papers, 1/66)[1]

29 April 1955

My Dear Winston,

Since you bid me address you like this, I take you at your word.

First let me thank you for your kindness in taking me to Sicily, at no cost to myself. Though it is not an island for which I have developed any notable affection, I certainly have a very highly developed one for those I went with and my memories are not of the grey skies but of Lady Churchill and you, with whom the North Pole or Katmandu would be enjoyable.

But what I really want to say, and that is much more difficult, is that my official association with you, which began fifteen years ago, has meant more to me in every way than anything else ever has or can in my future career. To have been at Downing Street in the summer and autumn of 1940 is something on its own, and yet no month or year since then, whether during the war or in your second administration, has ever seemed an anticlimax to those great days; and I suspect I shall become a famous bore on the subject to my descendants as the years go by, because it will always seem to me that the years I spent with you were the really important years of my life.

I am coming up to London for the night on Tuesday, and will call upon you either that afternoon or on Wednesday morning to pay my respects and to be of any service.

With my love to Lady Churchill and many regards, both grateful & affectionate

[1] This letter was handwritten.

May 1955

Sir Winston S. Churchill to Major-General Sir Hugh Tudor[1]
(Churchill papers, 2/201)

May 1955

My dear Hugh,

Thank you so much for your letter of April 6. I did not wish to continue to bear my burdens any longer. This was not because I felt unequal to them, but one has to think of one's successor, and make sure that he has a fair chance – both for his own sake and for that of the party.

I have read your correspondence with the First Commoner in England.[2] He was deeply interested in it all, and I am so glad that the contacts you had with him at Loos and thereafter were so well maintained.

Please keep in touch with me.

Sir Winston S. Churchill to Lord Rothermere
(Churchill papers, 2/137)

4 May 1955

My dear Esmond,

Thank you so much for your letter. I knew you would be offended by the *Tribune*'s allegations. It is an odious rag.

I have for a long time been much impressed with the Leading Articles in the *Daily Mail*, which I am told are written by Mr Murray.[3] I wondered whether he

---

[1] Henry Hugh Tudor, 1871–1965. On active service, South Africa, 1899–1902. Brig.-Gen. commanding the artillery of 9th (Scottish) Div., 1916–18. Maj.-Gen. commanding 9th Div., 1918; commanding Irregular Forces in Ireland (the 'Black and Tans'), 1920–1. GOC special gendarmerie in Palestine (known as 'Tudor's lambs'), with rank of AVM, 1922. Lt, 1923. Published *The Fog of War* (1959).

[2] Prince Philip, Duke of Edinburgh.

[3] George McIntosh Murray, 1900–70. Educated at Archbishop Tenison's School. On staff of *Farnham Herald*, 1923; *Dudley Herald*, 1925; *Hampshire Herald*, 1925. Married, 1927, Irene Bill (d. 1953): two children; 1967, Loris Taylor. Joined *Southern Daily Echo*, 1930; *Sunday Dispatch*, 1931; *Daily Mail*, 1933. Chief Leader Writer, *Daily Mail*, 1939–70. Member, Press Council, 1953; Vice-Chairman, 1957; Chairman, 1959–63. Director, Associated Newspapers Ltd, 1955. Published *The Life of King George V* (1935), *His Majesty King Edward VIII* (1936), *King George VI and the Coronation* (1937) and *The Impatient Horse* (1952).

would care to give me privately a little help in one or two of the speeches I have to make; for instance, I can speak at Bedford on the 17th and at Walthamstow on the 19th. I have a good many speeches to make, and my difficulty is that they may well be reported. A little reinforcement would be most welcome. If he liked the idea we might arrange a meeting. I should not take up much of his time, and should anyhow like to make his acquaintance.

Oscar Nemon[1] to Sir Winston S. Churchill
(Churchill papers, 2/195)[2]

5 May 1955

Dear Sir Winston,

The photographs which you will find with this letter represent the sculpture you did a year ago. I beg you not to underrate the artistic value of this work which would be considered by any expert as outstanding for a first attempt.

The clay model still shows the imprints of your fingers which bear witness to the fact that the sculpture is the same as you left it. I shall make a bronze patina on the plaster and leave it at your house at Hyde Park Gate.

I cannot let this opportunity pass without once more expressing my really very deep appreciation of the interest you have shown in my work and of the precious moments of your Time, it has been my great privilege to spend with you.

I wish your endless interests may keep you forever young and active in the arts.

Sir Winston S. Churchill to Lord Beaverbrook
(Beaverbrook papers)

12 May 1955   Chartwell

My dear Max,

My Election Address is to be issued on Saturday for the Sunday papers. I thought you would like to see one earlier, even though it is too late to make any changes.

I think things are going very well.

I am so glad about the Big Four talks.[3]

---

[1] Oscar Nemon, 1906–85. Born in Osijek, Croatia. Trained as a sculptor at the Académie des Beaux Arts, Brussels, 1925. Gained renown after sculpting Sigmund Freud. Created his first bust of Churchill in 1951. Produced the famous sculpture of Churchill that stands in the House of Commons, 1969. Other notable sitters include Queen Elizabeth II, Gen. Eisenhower and Lady Thatcher.

[2] This letter was handwritten.

[3] The Big Four talks, involving the British, French, Soviet and US foreign ministers, were held in Geneva in July and August 1955.

May 1955

Sir Winston S. Churchill: speech
('Winston S. Churchill, His Complete Speeches', volume 8, pages 8646–50)

16 May 1955   Woodford

ELECTION ADDRESS

We have come to the end of what I believe will prove to be regarded as a creditable and even memorable Parliament. I am deeply interested in the result of this General Election for outstanding reasons. First, we ask for a vote of goodwill and approval for the work which the Conservative and Unionist Government I had the honour to lead have done for the country in three and a half years of power. More important, however, than approval of the past is to arm us with a substantial majority to carry forward the good work we have done into new fields of well-being, hope and opportunity.

I felt it my duty to resign my office as Prime Minister at a time under conditions which would give whoever the Queen summoned to be my successor a fair chance of seeking a mandate from the country. This alone would give him the authority to confront and master the many difficult and anxious problems of our small and crowded island which is capable of exerting so great an influence for peace and progress upon the mighty modern world. In my successor, Sir Anthony Eden, we have a statesman long versed in Parliamentary and Cabinet Government, both in peace and war, and respected for his record in many lands, but in none more than his own. It is with full confidence founded on comradeship and cooperation through nearly twenty fateful years that I have passed the torch to him, and I call upon the electors of Britain as a whole to give him generous and effective support. In this I can assure him the electors of Woodford are determined to set an example. It is generally recognized that we have a good account to give. Our record shines in any comparisons which may be made between what we took over and what we now present.

Under the Conservative Government the nation has made an undoubted and remarkable recovery. From the brink of national bankruptcy we advanced to a greater prosperity than we have known before. More people than ever before in time of peace have been kept in steady and profitable employment. Earnings have outstripped prices, instead of lagging behind as they did under our predecessors. The nation has achieved a higher standard of living than ever before, eating more, enjoying more goods of every kind, and saving more. At the same time important advances and improvements in the social services have been made. We have more than restored to the old-age pensioners and other pensioners the damage Socialist finance did to the purchasing power of their weekly benefits. Family allowances have been increased. We did even better than our undertaking – so much derided – to build those 300,000 houses a year, and at the same time we built more schools than ever and have launched a programme for new hospitals.

None of all this was achieved by accident. It was done by 'setting the people free'. We ended rationing, drastically reduced controls and State trading, and made reductions in taxation, to restore incentives and encouragement to those British qualities and energies upon which our high position in the world was built, and upon which it alone can be maintained. I cannot believe that the electorate will wantonly or lightly reverse those policies and change the course which has thus far brought such beneficial results, in order to return to the discredited and discarded theory and practice of Socialism, with its paraphernalia of restrictions and regulations, its penal taxation and its recurring economic crises and doses of austerity.

The renewed threat of nationalization will disrupt and disorganize industries upon whose smooth working we rely for the export trade on which we live. We must never forget how precarious and artificial are the means by which a nation like ours keeps itself alive and prosperous, how easy it would be for us to lose the means of our support in a vast, swiftly developing, and highly competitive world. Nothing would be easier than to cast all we have regained away. Of all countries in the world, Britain is the least suitable for the Socialist experiment. Of all times, now would be the worst time for us to try it.

I have had a leaflet printed, which I have had carefully checked, and which I am circulating throughout the constituency, giving the facts and figures of the improvements we have brought about or welcomed during our solid tenure of office, and which affect every part of the country and every class of its people. It is indeed a wonderful tale of recovery and revival during a Parliament in which we started with a majority of only sixteen. That in itself is a proof of the unity and loyalty of the Conservative Party, and the spontaneous faithfulness with which its members discharge their duties.

It was indeed a time of effort and exertion, from which sprang the recovery and revival of Britain. After six years of war followed by six years of Socialism, we found ourselves on the verge of bankruptcy. Many of the hardships and restrictions of war were gleefully maintained by the Socialists, and of course a large part of the authority which in time of war must be exerted by the State for the safety of the nation is an essential part of the Socialist conception of the rule of the State over the individual.

The Socialist Party who claim to guide us all are themselves in rather an uncomfortable plight. Mr Attlee, who was my war-time Deputy Prime Minister, is certainly tough or he would not have kept the lead of his Party for so long. I have no doubt he wished to do the right thing. He has bluntly and boldly declared himself in favour of our making the hydrogen bomb. He could hardly do otherwise, considering that he made the atomic bomb secretly for four years without even telling Parliament. He has also been in favour of maintaining the unity of the Western Powers and the solidarity of NATO. But all the time he has to keep 'on side' with his Party.

His real struggle is less with the Tories than with his own Left Wing followers.

His choice is therefore a hard one. The best he can do is to be a piebald. I will give you some examples. He has had to declare himself in favour of renationalizing steel. This would be one of the most harmful things to British industry, British exports, and the prosperity of our country that a harassed politician could pick out to do. Amidst intense and growing competition the British steel industry has achieved new records of expansion and prosperity and displayed amazing quality and vigour. We should all rejoice that the Conservative Government took over in time to rescue it from the half-witted treatment which the Socialists had in store for it.

Now besides steel he has to add the chemical industry to the nationalizer's execution list. Did you, I wonder, observe the interesting fact that on the very morning that the Socialist manifesto announced the decision to nationalize chemicals, the biggest firm in the industry, well-known as the ICI, declared the results of their profit-sharing scheme? They are crediting their 75,000 employees with a bonus equal to a shilling in the pound on their wages, a total of over two and a half million pounds, which will be used to buy for the wage-earners shares in the company. This is a fine example to industry as a whole.

By developing and spreading voluntary systems of co-partnership and profit-sharing the wage earners in any undertaking can increasingly feel their own interest in the industry on which they and their families depend. There is a real Tory democratic flavour about these ideas. I hope they will flourish and prosper. It seems to me a much better plan than to hand these intensely complicated industries, vital to our welfare, over to a horde of officials in Whitehall. However well-meaning they may be, they are bound to stick to rigid rules and to play for safety at a time when flexibility, ingenuity, contrivance, and daring, are qualities absolutely needed in this fiercely competitive world.

So much for the harassed Mr Attlee and the nationalization flop. His next proposal is to make a strong election point of cutting the call-up. When he said this extremely foolish thing Sir Anthony Eden knocked him out by his prompt and strong reply. 'It would be criminal folly,' said the Prime Minister, 'to weaken ourselves before the negotiations begin. It is only our present strength and unity with our Allies that has made this negotiation possible. I would rather lose every vote at this election than take a step which might imperil its success.'

Fancy, at this time, when all hopes are centred on the forthcoming conference with Russia, when we know that the strength of Britain is that she seeks peace for its own sake and not merely to avoid the burdens or dangers for which the duty calls; fancy, when the meeting of the Big Four at the summit holds the first place in all our thoughts and hearts, the Leader of the Socialist Party feeling himself compelled to try to gain popularity in his Party and votes in the election by saying something which might give the impression to the Communist world that Britain is on the run.

This is no time for the freedom and peace-seeking democracies to show weakness or disunion. In fact it might be fatal. Everyone knows that a reduction of armaments fair and square all round including the call-up period is what we all want. That is one of the main objects and hopes of a friendly meeting with the Russians, and nothing would be more likely to make that meeting fail than for Britain to go to such a conference whining that she cannot bear the expense or burden.

Now let me come to Mr Bevan. (I always pronounce the name 'Bevan' very carefully, as I have a high regard for the memory of Ernest Bevin, a great trade unionist and a true patriot.) He is the politician who causes most anxiety to every friend and ally of Britain all over the world. Undoubtedly his influence in the Socialist Party is great and growing. This is the man, this voluble careerist, who has called at least half his fellow countrymen all sort of names which have been helpful on our Party platform.

His latest taunt is that the Tories cannot be Christians. I will give you his own words: 'Toryism and Christianity are inconsistent with each other. For a long time people suffered pain, hardship, anxiety, and grief, not because we did not possess the knowledge necessary to relieve them, but because they were too poor to buy their knowledge.' What is the ground on which this accusation that half his fellow-countrymen are not worthy to be called Christians is founded? It is an obvious and palpable untruth. The whole creation of the national Health Service and indeed a great part of the modern welfare state was planned and prepared by the National Coalition Government of which with its great Conservative majority I was the head, and which I never invited Mr Bevan to join. Now I leave the two rivals for the leadership of the Socialist Party to present themselves in their own way to the electors.

I turn to wider and more inspiring subjects. I turn to the international scene. When I made my speech on 11 May 1953[1] – two years ago almost to the day – I was acting Foreign Secretary as well as Prime Minister. I felt that the death of Stalin was a milestone in Russian history. When Mr Malenkov took over I sustained the impression that there might be a 'New Look' in the Soviet policy, and that anyhow we ought to make sure. I therefore suggested to President Eisenhower that there should be a meeting of what is called the Big Three.

He felt, however, that it was better that any talks that might occur should be conducted on the Foreign Secretary level. His position as Head of a State as well as head of a Government was, of course, an important distinction, though it had not restricted the action of his predecessors. I am very glad that he has now expressed his willingness to attend a meeting at the summit with the Heads of Government of Britain, France, and Russia. The arrangements which are proposed for the Foreign Secretaries to be there at the same time and for their separate meeting seem also to me practical and sensible.

---

[1] Reproduced above (pp. 998–1010).

What I had proposed was that the Heads of Government should meet together and talk things over in a broad way as only the Heads of Government can. To have consenting minds at the top is far the best beginning for all the work which has to be done at other levels to give effect to their wishes. This is a much surer way of getting good results than beginning with the Foreign Secretaries who, however skilful and sincere, are definitely responsible for presenting all the difficulties, and it is still better than establishing 'working parties' to make sure none of the difficulties are overlooked. However, as I could not persuade my great American friend, we had to make the best of the second alternative, and many lengthy but valuable fruitful discussions have taken place without, however, securing any major result in the fundamental relations of the great Powers concerned.

Meanwhile, two years have passed and much has happened. Two years is a long time nowadays. We have a new scene. New men are masters in the Kremlin. It is by no means certain that there is not another 'New Look' on other faces with more powerful forces behind them which may still be most beneficial to the overwhelming masses of people all over the world who wish to dwell in peace with one another and have a fuller share of life with all the benefits which the benignant forms of science are capable of bestowing upon them to an almost limitless extent.

I rejoice that this is so, and I congratulate Sir Anthony Eden and Her Majesty's Government upon the good fortune which has attended their effort to bring about, though under different conditions, the policy for which I have faithfully striven. Moreover, the Heads of Government of Britain, the United States and France go to this meeting strong and united, seeking the peace of the world, the welfare of all mankind, and that period of relaxed tension, disarmament, and all-round prosperity which is within our reach and may soon be within our grasp. I have been a lifelong opponent of Communism which I am convinced is a fallacious philosophy, fatal to individual and democratic liberty and imposing itself by the tyrannical rule, either of dictators or oligarchies working through a numerous hierarchy of officials or would-be officials. But this is an internal issue for the Russian people to settle for themselves.

At this juncture, the British electors have the great opportunity of casting their votes in favour of the sincere effort for a friendly way of living between States great and small which has now to be made and nations all over the world are waiting on tenterhooks to see if Britain will rise to the occasion. In this terrible twentieth century, our country has played an honourable and famous part. Britain is regarded as fearless and unconquerable. Let us make sure we do not cast away by casual or careless behaviour the reputation upon which both our influence in the world and our safety depend.

Sir Winston S. Churchill: speech
('Winston S. Churchill, His Complete Speeches', volume 8, pages 8650–4)

17 May 1955   Bedford

ELECTION ADDRESS

Captain Soames won this constituency for the Conservatives in 1950. During the last few years he has been my Parliamentary Private Secretary. He has therefore a deep knowledge of events as they are seen from the top. He has shown the greatest discretion, and although he has been prevented by his confidential knowledge from making as many speeches as he would have liked, he has built himself up a very solid reputation in the House of Commons. I am delighted to come down here tonight and urge you to return him by an even larger majority than before. I am also quite glad to see my daughter on the platform. She is a very keen politician too, and it is lucky that she and her husband are in complete agreement on the political questions of the day.

The consequences of this election could be grave for us all. No doubt except for the Communists and their fellow-travellers, we live together in a neighbourly way without the political factions and hatreds which convulse many other countries. There is no fierce internal conflict between us, such as I have seen in many other elections. Nevertheless, we could make a mistake which would cost us dear. A tremendous world now towers up around our fifty million people in this small island. They will only be able to keep themselves alive by their skill and diligence in up to date production and by maintaining the tolerant and liberal way for life which we have slowly evolved throughout the century.

At a General Election it is the duty of the Head of the Government and Leader of the Party to unfold the policy for the new Parliament, to which he is personally pledged. I did not feel that at my age I should incur such new and indefinite responsibilities, and I thought that it would be right and proper to leave my successor free to choose for himself both the moment and the programme for the election.

It is a source of great satisfaction to me that it has fallen to my friend, Sir Anthony Eden, to take my place as Prime Minister and Leader of the Conservative and Unionist Party. We have worked together in one way and another for nearly twenty years, in peace and war, in office and out of it, and I know that our Party and our nation have in him a capable and experienced leader who deserves their confidence and a policy which claims their support.

In my broadcast after the last General Election[1] I said: 'We do not seek to be judged by promises but by results. After six years of Socialism we have a right to have a fair try. . . . We require at least three years before anyone can

---

[1] Reproduced above (pp. 145–9).

judge fairly whether we have made things better or worse'. Well, we have had three years, indeed three years and a half, and we are ready to be judged fairly. It is for our countrymen to say whether we have made things better or worse. I have no doubt what they are going to say, and all the free democratic world will rejoice when they have said it.

Both the Socialists and the Liberals have paid tribute to the achievements of the Conservative Government. The *Socialist Commentary*, a serious monthly publication catering for the more responsible sections of that Party, has written: 'On the whole the country is – and feels – more prosperous.'

The Liberal Party Manifesto says: 'It would be ungenerous not to admit that since the last General Election we have gone some way to arrest the decay which set in with the second post-war Labour Government. . . .'

And Lord Samuel has said: 'I should feel the greatest anxiety for the economic stability of our country if this election should give an absolute control in the House of Commons to the Labour Party.'

Step by step we ended rationing, drastically reduced the controls and state trading, and by solid and substantial reductions in taxation restored incentive and opportunity to those forces of ingenuity, enterprise, good management, and thrift upon which our high position in the world was built, and upon which it can alone be maintained.

The result of these policies, steadfastly pursued in the face of misrepresentation and abuse from our opponents, has been that more people than ever before in time of peace have been kept in steady and profitable employment. I saw a newspaper headline the other day dealing with one of the Gallup Polls on the election. It said there are 'Fewer Don't Knows'. That does not surprise me. If the British people know one thing, it is that they are better off in every way than they were four years ago, and that the election is being fought on that record, with the promise of a continuance of the successful policy which has given us all a booming, buoyant Britain. In that respect the British people are not a 'Don't Know' nation. They are a 'Do Know' nation.

Nor did this Government, which I had the duty to form and head, neglect the social services which the genius of our race, under various parties, has built up over the years. We more than restored to the old-age pensioners and others the damage Socialist finance did to the purchasing power of their weekly benefits. We increased the family allowances. We did even better than our undertaking to build those 300,000 houses a year, and at the same time we built more schools than ever, and have launched a programme for new hospitals.

With this fine record of achievement to its credit the new Conservative Government is asking for a mandate to continue the good work for a further term, and its aim is a clear period of five years in which it can plan ahead for further advances in national well-being. I can conceive no greater folly at this time than for the electorate to turn head over heels – or heels over head – into discredited Socialism and nationalization, with all its paraphernalia of restrictions and regulations, its penal taxations and its recurring economic crises and doses of austerity.

It is of the utmost importance that no Conservative should let himself be lulled into complacency or slackness in his political duty by the brilliant results of the borough elections. There are many marginal House of Commons seats. Margins count more than averages in elections. So they do on the turf. The Gallup Polls, which I always like to read when they go the way I want, are founded on averages. By all means let us have good averages, but to win a race every horse must have a good gallop too.

We must be on our guard against some new version of the 'war monger' lie, which the Socialists, in their desperate greed for office, which is their only bond of unity must be prepared to let off at the last moment.

I was very glad to read in the *Daily Mirror* today the following declaration solemnly printed in the largest type:

> We supported the Tory Government's decision to make the British H-Bomb. And we still support that decision.
>
> The Labour Party takes the same view and has officially said so.
>
> The *Mirror* does not believe that the H-Bomb should be allowed to become a scare issue in the General Election.

Lady Megan Lloyd George[1] is a convert to Socialism. This is big jump for anyone, especially for her father's daughter, to take. I must repeat to you what I said in 1908 when I was working with that famous man:

> Liberalism has its own history and its own tradition. Socialism has its own formulas and aims. Socialism seeks to pull down wealth; Liberalism seeks to raise up poverty. Socialism would destroy private interests; Liberalism would preserve private interests in the only way in which they can safely and justly be preserved, namely, by reconciling them with public right. Socialism would kill enterprise; Liberalism would rescue enterprise from the trammels of privilege and preference. Socialism assails the preeminence of the individual; Liberalism seeks, and shall seek more in the future, to build up a minimum standard for the mass. Socialism exalts the rule; Liberalism exalts the man. Socialism attacks capital; Liberalism attacks monopoly.

Looking out upon a wider scene, I am very glad to learn that the prospects of a meeting at the Summit of what are called the Big Three or Four have lately so markedly improved. I worked very hard for this, but I was also resolved that it should not be a substitute for the unity of the Free World as represented

---

[1] Megan Lloyd George, 1902–66. Younger daughter of David Lloyd George. MP (Lib.) for Anglesey, 1929–51; for Carmarthenshire, 1957–66. President, Women's Liberal Federation, 1936, 1945. Chairman, Welsh Parliamentary Party, 1944–5. Deputy Leader of the Liberal Party, 1949–51. Joined Labour Party, 1957. CH, 1966.

by the North Atlantic Treaty Organization, to which I rejoice Germany has been added. My policy has always been peace through strength, and above all through the friendship and united action of the English-speaking peoples. No one can say for certain that the results of a top-level meeting will fulfil our hopes, but the stronger and more united are the nations of the Free World, the better are the chances of a good outcome. It ought to be possible to reach a position where there is a general sense of easement throughout the world, and where the cost and burden of armaments can be fairly reduced all around.

The Socialist Party claim to govern the nation. One would expect they would have some coherent thought or principle on the dread subject of the H-bomb, which torments the minds of all serious people. The contrary is the truth. On no subject is the Socialist poverty of thought and imagination, their contradictions and differences, and their unfitness to solve the problems that confront us more lamentably exposed than in the jumble of discordant declarations about the hydrogen bomb. Their official statement of policy says (I am quoting the words):

> Until world disarmament can be achieved, weapons of mass destruction in the hands of Britain and her Allies in NATO form the most effective deterrent against aggression by a potential disturber of the peace. . . .

That is at any rate a perfectly clear and plain statement. But Mr Bevan's paper, *The Tribune*, said on the 13th of this month, that is, only four days ago, that Mr Attlee had said: 'The idea of the H-bomb as a deterrent is a profound delusion.' Is this true, or is it merely Bevanism? Mr Attlee should tell us without further delay.

Then again, some Socialists believe the H-bomb should be made and tested. Others want it made but not tested. Surely that is the climax of silliness. Fancy making a deadly thing like this, and not knowing what it really was. Some of the Socialists say that it should be made and tested, but not used until we have first been attacked by this kind of weapon. That would be like a man saying: 'I carry a pistol in self-defence but you can trust me not to use it until I am shot dead.' Others again believe that nuclear weapons should be banned, but that orthodox weapons should continue to be manufactured; and still others want to ban all nuclear and orthodox weapons alike.

In all this welter of mental disunity and moral confusion into which the Socialist Party are plunged Mr Bevan holds the winning place. At one time he favours the manufacture of the bomb. At another time he opposes it. He was a Minister in the Socialist Government that gave orders without consulting Parliament for the manufacture of the atomic bomb. He shared the responsibility for that. In a Debate in the House of Commons last March he said: 'I myself cannot see there is any logical difference between the H-bomb and the atom bomb.' But a few weeks later he said: 'I am profoundly opposed to the manufacture of the bomb.' The nation would be most unwise to trust their safety and it might be their survival, to these chaotic and muddle-headed jabberings.

This is no time for panic. It is indeed the moment for calm, prudent, clear-headed, resolute behaviour. Above all, this is the time for talking things out in a fair and friendly manner with other people who have the same, or indeed far greater dangers to face than we have. I am for a top-level conference at the Summit. I have worked for it for two years. Let us do our best for our fellow-men, and let us put our trust in God. All will come right.

Robert Armstrong[1] to Sir Winston S. Churchill
(Churchill papers, 2/135)

17 May 1955

Between 1946 and 1951 the industrial production rose by about 34%. Between 1951 and the first quarter of 1955 it has risen by about 13%. Thus Mr Attlee's claim that production rose considerably faster under the previous Government is statistically true.

The apparently slower rate of increase of production since 1951 is due almost entirely to the setback of 1952. Between 1951 and 1952 industrial production fell by about 3%. This was due partly to the steel shortage, but mainly to the worldwide fall in demand for textiles, clothing and other consumer goods which occurred in 1951/1952. Since 1952 production has been kept rising at 6.5% per annum, which is quite as good as 1946–1951 record.

The answer to Mr Attlee might, therefore, apply in two parts. The period of the Labour Government's term of office, and particularly the earlier years of it, covered the period of demobilization and restrictions, when there was a large return of manpower into industry, and switch from defence to civil production. It would therefore have been not merely surprising but disgraceful if there had not been a considerable increase in production in those years.

The second part of the answer to Mr Attlee might be that production fell in 1952; the causes of this fall were inherent in the economic crisis which the present Government found when it came into office. By the end of 1952 inflation had been checked, the balance of payments strengthened, and production brought back on its upward trend. Since then production has been rising by 6.5% a year, which is just as good as what was achieved by the Labour Government.

---

[1] Robert Temple Armstrong, 1927–. Asst Principal, Treasury, 1950–5. Private Secretary to Reginald Maudling (Economic Secretary to Treasury), 1953–4; to R. A. Butler (Chancellor of the Exchequer), 1954–5. Principal, Treasury, 1955–7, 1959–64. Principal Private Secretary to PM, 1970–5. Deputy Under-Secretary of State, Home Office, 1975–7. CVO, 1975. Permanent Under-Secretary of State, 1977–9. KCB, 1978. GCB, 1973. Baron, 1988.

Christopher Soames to Sir Winston S. Churchill
(*Churchill papers, 2/137*)

18 May 1955

Thank you so much for coming to our meeting. Everyone is rejoicing at its success and you gave new life to our workers and supporters. Much love.

Sir Winston S. Churchill: speech
(*'The Unwritten Alliance', pages 262–5*)

19 May 1955   Walthamstow and Chigwell

ELECTION ADDRESS

Nearly 40,000 electors recorded their votes at the last election. The Socialist candidate[1] won by only 1,020, and he won because a Liberal candidate split the vote by taking 2,815, for which he forfeited his deposit. Now we have a new Liberal candidate. For what is he asking your support? He will certainly poll fewer votes than his predecessor. He will certainly forfeit his deposit. But he offers to the Socialists their only chance of winning the seat. The main ideas of Liberalism have been adopted or penetrated all over the world. It is strange that this triumph of a noble theme should have carried with it the decline of the Liberal Party. Its main ideas are not disputed in civilized States. I have no doubt that it is beneath the fame and dignity of Liberalism as a theme to seek to prove its existence as a Party, not by returning Liberals, but by so disturbing the electoral system as to procure the return of Socialists on a minority vote. That is the only danger here in East Walthamstow. I am sure that it would be deeply injurious to the reputation of the Liberal Party if this were to happen. The behaviour of Lady Megan Lloyd George has not been well received in the Liberal Party, and the attempt to use her to procure the return of minority Socialists in various parts of the country is one which has evoked general condemnation, or perhaps ridicule.

I see that Mr Philip Fothergill,[2] a Liberal, made a thoughtful contribution to this controversy. He said that the Labour Party was drifting farther away from Liberalism than ever, and no Liberal revival would ever take place under the direction of anybody yet within sight of Transport House. But I can quote you higher authority. There is Lord Samuel, a man greatly respected and older even than me: 'I should feel the greatest anxiety for the economic stability

---

[1] Harry Wright Wallace, 1885–1973. MP (Lab.) for Walthamstow East, 1929–31, 1945–55.
[2] Philip Charles Fothergill, 1906–59. Educated at Wheelwright School, Dewsbury, and Bootham School, York. Worked in the textile industry for most of his life. Chairman and Managing Director of C. P. Fothergill & Co. Ltd, Dewsbury. Chairman, Liberal Party, 1946–9; President, 1949–52; Joint Treasurer, 1954–9.

of our country if this election should give an absolute control in the House of Commons to the Labour Party'. Now I appeal to all to all Liberals in this constituency to satisfy their consciences that whatever they do they do not sacrifice the fundamental principles of Liberalism in upholding the rights of the individual against the State by so using their vote as to send a Socialist candidate to Parliament.

We declare ourselves inveterately opposed to any further nationalization of industry. We have repealed the nationalization of steel. We have repealed the nationalization of transport. Steel is a tremendous success and is bounding ahead as a great key feature in our prosperity. The liberation of transport has been more difficult. It is always easier to do harm than to undo it, but I have no doubt that unless it is interrupted the liberation of transport will be as beneficial to the country as its nationalization to the country was injurious. Further we come to those large bodies of practical domestic reform set forth in our manifesto 'United Peace and Progress' and from a very slightly different angle in Liberal election literature. No doubt there are points upon which Liberals and Conservatives do not agree, but how petty they are, how small they are in scale and importance compared to the great body of fundamental principles and practical schemes of application on which both the anti-Socialist parties are in full accord.

Let me mention to you some of the great issues on which Conservatives and Liberals are agreed and which constitute the elements of the common cause vital to our national welfare. First, we proclaim that the State is the servant and not the master of the people. We reject altogether the Socialist conception of a division of society between officials and the common man. We repudiate their policy of levelling down to a minimum uniformity above which only politicians and their agents may rise. We stand for the increasingly higher expression of individual independence. We hold most strongly to the Declaration of Human Rights as set forth by the United Nations at Geneva in 1948.

Co-partnership and profit sharing form a prominent part of the Liberal Party's policy for industry. I would therefore draw the attention of the Liberals to the situation in the chemical industry. There, one of the largest firms, ICI, recently announced the result of their profit-sharing scheme. Its seventy-five thousand employees have been given a bonus equal to a shilling in the pound on their wages. Between them they will get two and a half million pounds, which will be used to buy them shares in the company. On the same day that this was announced the Socialists brought out their plan to nationalize the industry. Nationalization of course would kill profit-sharing stone dead. Is that what Liberals really want? Judging from what has happened on the railways and in the mines, it will be a matter of losses, not profits, and no one would dislike nationalization more than the wage-earners in the industry when they got it. It is the duty of every man and woman who agrees upon the main principles and practical steps which will benefit the nation to make sure that these are not overwhelmed by the ignorant and absolute doctrine of Socialism against which the British nation stands today in marked recoil.

I am astonished that Mr Attlee would allow his name and authority in the country and in his Party to be used in Bevanite propaganda against the H-bomb. Last week's *Tribune* quoted him prominently on the front page as saying that the idea of the H-bomb as a deterrent was a profound delusion. When I spoke at Bedford on Tuesday, the 17th,[1] I challenged Mr Attlee on the subject. Yesterday (Wednesday), he referred to this speech, but he did not clear the matter up. On the contrary, he only confused and clouded the issue. I invite him to declare publicly whether or not he stands by the plain declaration he made in the House of Commons on March 2: 'We are driven to rely on deterrents. That is simply the knowledge on the part of any would-be aggressor, or breaker of the peace, that retaliation would be devastating and certain.' This declaration is, of course, completely in line with the official statement of policy recently issued by the Labour Party, which said: 'Until world disarmament can be achieved, weapons of mass destruction in the hands of Britain and her allies in NATO form the most effective deterrent against aggression by a potential disturber of the peace.' If, in a desire to catch votes, or to keep on terms with the Bevanites, Mr Attlee undermines confidence in the sincerity of these declarations, he is doing his country no service.

That was certainly the view of Sir Hartley Shawcross at Bolton last month when he said: 'The most deplorable internal dissensions we have had in the Labour Party have done great harm to the country. Abroad people have been gravely confused and misled as to what would be the foreign policy of a Labour Government.' Let Mr Attlee give a plain answer to my question. Mr Attlee now slides off the main point into the evil effects which tests and experiments in nuclear weapons may have upon the population and upon the children. I was assured, as Prime Minister, by the highest scientific opinion, that nothing that had happened so far had produced any dangerous or injurious effects. But it does not follow, if this process continues indefinitely over the years, that the increased radio-activity of the atmosphere would not be harmful. That is what we want to prevent. That is one of the first things we should have to talk about with the Soviets. What do they think we want this top-level conference for if it is not to try to deal with all these dangers that impend upon the world, and to try to see if a friendly and sensible agreement may be reached which would give the human race the blessings of science without its curses? The electors must be careful when they give their vote.

I have another point on which I wish to challenge Mr Attlee directly. I was much astonished to read a statement attributed to him, as follows: 'Labour will strive to increase the nation's wealth through increasing production. Under the

---

[1] Speech reproduced above (pp. 1999–2003).

Tories the rise in output has fallen by half.' I found that my Socialist opponent in Woodford,[1] basing himself no doubt upon the authority of his leader, has repeated the statement that under the Tory Government 'the annual increase in industrial production is only half of what it was under Labour'. Now this is a grossly misleading picture of the course of events – and a grotesque distortion of the present situation. What is the truth? We all know that there was a setback in 1952 – a crisis we inherited from the Socialists. But since then production has been surging ahead as fast as ever and certainly faster than in the last two years of Socialist government. What is more, our gross national production last year was over one thousand million pounds higher than in 1951 – and that is allowing for price changes. In addition to the blunt, indisputable, and brutal fact that last year's industrial production far exceeded anything produced by the Socialists in their period of power.

It must be remembered that our increase in production was achieved on top of all the increases which naturally took place after the end of the war, when people went back from war service and war production to industry. It is much harder to jump seven feet than six feet. We have established a record for annual industrial production far higher than the Socialists, and judging by the outturn of the first quarter in this year, 1955, the production this year should be higher still, if it is not spoiled by the financial convulsions and restrictions which would follow the return of the Socialists.

Sir Winston S. Churchill: speech
('Winston S. Churchill, His Complete Speeches', volume 8, pages 8657–8)

23 May 1955   Woodford

[. . .] Mr Bevan is already looking for excuses for defeat. He accuses us of altering the constituency boundaries in our favour. The accusation is as false as it is unworthy.

The whole method of changing constituency boundaries to meet shifts of the population was decided by an all-party agreement during the war, when Mr Herbert Morrison was Home Secretary, and the present Act under which the official and impartial Boundary Commission work was passed after the war by the Socialist Government. They laid down the rules. The Conservative Government which I led accepted in full and without alteration the findings of these impartial commissions and gave effect to them.

Our conduct in these matters has been distinguished by the highest impartiality and is in strict accordance with procedure for which the Socialists were themselves responsible. We have fairly and impartially carried out the law as the Socialists shaped it and as the non-party commissions recommended it.

---

[1] Arnold Keith M. Milner.

We have made no changes in the boundaries of constituencies not recommended by the commission.

I have never seen a general election more calm than this one. Yet the decision which has to be made on Thursday might affect the well-being and destiny of our people in their daily lives at home and in their influence at an anxious moment upon the nations of the whole free world.

Do not be lulled into a false sense of security by the broad sense of agreement which we feel exists among our fellow-countrymen, or think in terms of mass effects, averages, and Gallup Polls. Every man or woman who has a vote is responsible for recording it according to what he really believes is for the nation's good. Apathy, complacency, idleness, chatter, or indifference may often be faults. On Thursday they will be crimes.

Sir Winston S. Churchill to Alan Hodge
(Churchill papers, 4/27)

26 May 1955

My dear Hodge,

I send you Chapter II,[1] in which I have made a good many amendments, and ask various questions. Please look at it over the weekend, and make sure it is with the printers as soon as possible. We can discuss the outstanding points later on.

I should be glad of any comments in the meantime.

Sir Winston S. Churchill to Alan Hodge
(Churchill papers, 4/27)

26 May 1955

Page 6 and its neighbours seem to me worthy of expansion. Is it to be suggested that William[2] knew what he was doing and planned a balanced society, or did it all simply happen as the result of his actions? Was he a man capable of comprehending these issues, or did he simply try to build up his own power? Was there an aim? Was there a design? Or did it simply work out that way?

I should like to talk it over with you, and perhaps you will let me know if there is any interesting literature upon the subject. I do not remember who

---

[1] Of vol. 1 of *The English-Speaking Peoples*. Vols 1–4 would be published between 1956 and 1958.
[2] William I, c.1028–87. Known as 'William the Conqueror'. Born in Falaise, Normandy. Eldest child of Robert I of Normandy. Married, 1052/3, Matilda, daughter of Baldwin V of Flanders. Invaded England at the Battle of Hastings, 1066. Crowned King of England in Westminster Abbey on Christmas Day 1066.

helped me on this period sixteen years ago. Perhaps Bill Deakin will remember. I should write to him if you thought that would help.

Sir Winston S. Churchill to Bernard Baruch
(Churchill papers, 2/210)

26 May 1955

My dear Bernie,

I was very glad indeed to get your letter of May 19, and to read the kind things you say in it.

I am looking forward to the end of the Election. Although I have not taken a full part in it, I have found the work quite sufficient. The result will be known within twenty-four hours, and will, of course, affect my future plans. If, as I hope, the Conservative party gain a majority of fifty or more, I propose to take a good long rest at Chartwell, and then perhaps in the autumn I shall try some painting somewhere in the South of France.

I am most grateful to you for suggesting that I should come and stay with you on Long Island. I do not feel, however, that I shall be able to cross the Atlantic this year, as I have declined several important engagements over there. I have at the moment a great desire to stay put and do nothing.

Lord Beaverbrook to Sir Winston S. Churchill
(Churchill papers, 2/137)[1]

27 May 1955

My dear Winston,

This big vote[2] must be gratifying to you for the result is due to your wise & far seeing foreign policy & your sound administration at home.

---

[1] This letter was handwritten.

[2] In the poll on May 26, the Conservatives won 345 seats with 49.7% of the popular vote; Labour won 277 (46.4%); and the Liberals won 6 (2.7%). The Conservatives had an overall majority of 60 in the House of Commons.

May 1955

Sir Norman Brook to Sir Winston S. Churchill
(Churchill papers, 2/181)[1]

27 May 1955

Dear Sir Winston,

You have been much in my thoughts during this Election, and should like to send you my sincere congratulations on its result. For it is a most remarkable testimony to the record and achievement of your Government over the past 3½ years. The real issue was whether the people was content with the Government they had had. And it is very evident that they were. The drop in the Labour vote is surely significant. I am sure you must be gratified by the way things have gone.

I have not forgotten my promise is keep you informed of what goes on. During the Election nothing much has happened in Cabinet circles: but, now that Government is about to be resumed, I shall have things to tell you.

Meanwhile, my best congratulation and all good wishes.

Sir Winston S. Churchill to Sir Norman Brook
(Churchill papers, 2/181)

29 May 1955

My dear Norman,

Thank you so much for your letter of May 27. I think everything has gone off in a very satisfactory manner, and I feel that the Prime Minister is well established in the goodwill and confidence of the country. The stability of Britain plays a great part in the stability of the world.

Let us have a talk together when you are less busy.

Sir Anthony Eden to Sir Winston S. Churchill
(Churchill papers, 2/216)

30 May 1955

My dear Winston,

I am getting a little sunshine at Chequers today. Until now I have had to devote all my time to the railway dispute.

First let me thank you again for all that you did in the Election. I think that the result has fully justified the decision to hold it now. I have not forgotten that you were in favour of that decision.

The strike situation both in the docks and on the railways is very disturbing.

---

[1] This letter was handwritten.

We shall have to try to find some ways of preventing these inter-union squabbles being carried to these lengths. At the same time we must try to carry the Trade Union movement with us. This should be possible since the TUC are very properly extremely worried themselves. Unhappily their authority is limited.

We are taking the necessary emergency measures and a State of Emergency will be proclaimed and the necessary Regulations made tomorrow. These Regulations have to be laid before Parliament and approved within seven days, and for this reason and also because Parliament will want to discuss the situation if the strike goes on, I fear we shall have to bring forward the formal Opening of Parliament and The Queen's Speech to Friday, June 10. We shall be discussing this with the Opposition Leaders tomorrow. This unfortunately gives us less time to prepare The Queen's Speech and we are at work upon it this week.

I am not thinking of reconstructing the Government at all for the present. For one thing I haven't time, and it might be better to make changes just before the Summer Recess so as to have the new team well in the saddle when Parliament resumes in the Autumn.

Our exchanges about the Four-Power Conference are continuing. The President has suggested that the top-level meeting should be held either around July 20 or towards the end of August. The latter date would give more time for preparation and make it more easy to have a rather longer meeting but we do not want to appear to be holding back. The French seem to prefer August to July.

I have of course been very happy to include in my Birthday Honours recommendations the names which you sent me from Sicily. The only exception is the Prof. You know how much I like him and that I value all the help which he has given us but I am not making many recommendations for peerages and none for any award higher than a barony. You gave the Prof a CH only two years ago and he is till helping us in the atomic world and indeed in other ways. I will be prepared to consider him again for a Viscountcy a little later.

I should have been happy to recommend Miss Davies[1] for a DBE, but she herself has asked that this recommendation should not be made, since she feels herself amply rewarded by the CBE, with which her predecessor, Miss Watson,[2] retired at the end of the war. It is of course a source of deep and continuing pleasure to her to know that you wished her to be recommended for this signal honour.

Clarissa and I send our love to you both and hope that you will come and have a night with us when you are next in London.

---

[1] Gwen Davies. Worked for Sir Horace Wilson, 1939. Secretary to PM, 1942–5. Replaced Edith Margaret Watson as Private Secretary to PM, 1945.

[2] Edith Margaret Watson (?–1953). Private Secretary to Andrew Bonar Law, 1916–23. CBE, 1919. Private Secretary to PM, 1922–45. CVO, 1937.

May 1955

Sir Winston S. Churchill to Sir Anthony Eden
(Churchill papers, 2/216)

31 May 1955

My dear Anthony,

Thank you very much for your letter in these busy and anxious days. Firmness in the strike is vital. It can only be based on patience at the outset. The national response may be overwhelming. You are indeed wise to try to get the TUC with you. A few days more or less should be borne. The timing of the strike by its leaders so as to hit the holiday makers will be judged very cruel. Personally, I have always had a great liking for engine drivers, and am astonished at their behaviour. Perhaps they are pained themselves. Increased tension may be a necessary phase.

I did not like the idea of a Christmas strike, but now the weather is less severe and it should be faced. I am sure you will be supported. Of course, there are great numbers of potential volunteers and it is not so very hard to drive an engine with safety and three quarters efficiency. This, however, would raise grave issues with the TUC. I shall come to the House for the formal opening, and having tried a good many, I shall try to get the corner seat below the gangway.

I think you are very wise not to reconstruct the Government in a hurry or a crisis.

I do not see much difference between August and July. I was sorry I could not persuade Ike to test the Malenkov 'New Look' in 1953. Krushev has the Army in a way that Malenkov did not, so that if there is a 'New Look' it may be more fruitful. I do not think the Russian Army wants war. There is no such thing as military glory now. Soldiers would be safer than civilians, though not so comfortable as in time of peace. Surveying the scene from my detached position, I feel the corner will be gradually turned, and that the human race may be subjected to the tests of extreme prosperity.

I am sorry about the Prof. It would, of course, have been attributed to me. I could, I believe, have had a resignation list of my own, had I tried. The matter, however, is not one to which I attach much importance, and the Prof certainly much less.

I congratulate you on the manner you fought the election. You did not seem to me to put a foot wrong, and one is a centipede on such occasions. Now, however, may be the appointed hour. All good luck.

I have put my thoughts on paper as I am sure you would like me to do.

June 1955

Field Marshal Lord Montgomery to Sir Winston S. Churchill
(Churchill papers, 2/143)

4 June 1955   Hampshire

My Dear Winston,

When I was in Copenhagen the other day I went to see the bust of yourself[1] which has been erected there. I thought it was an extraordinary fine piece of work. I was photographed looking up at you and I send you a copy of that photo. It seems right from every point of view that you should be up on a pedestal and that I should be below and looking up at you.

I shall hope to see you at the Rehearsal at St James's Palace on the 8th of June and also at the Garter service at Windsor on Monday the 13th of June.

I am going tomorrow to Normandy for the weekend to attend the unveiling of the war memorial at Bayeux on Sunday and some anniversary celebrations near Caen on 6th of June: the anniversary of D-Day.

My love to you and Clemmie.

Sir Norman Brook to Sir Winston S. Churchill
(Churchill papers, 2/181)

9 June 1955

Dear Sir Winston,

I am sorry that I have not sent an earlier reply to your letter of May 25 about the operation against the German dams in May, 1943.

This operation was considered several times by the Chiefs of Staff Committee, who appointed a special Sub-Committee to supervise its preparation. Until about March, 1943, the main emphasis was on the development of a spinning bomb, given the code name 'Highball', to be used against battleships. The development of this technique was pressed forward with great urgency.

[1] By Oscar Nemon.

The weapon which was used against the dams was a variation of it, called 'Upkeep'. Operational use of both types of weapon was to be dependent upon trials in April and early May, 1943. On May 13, when you and the Chiefs of Staff were in Washington, the Vice-Chiefs were informed in London that the 'Upkeep' trials had proved successful. They were asked to agree that this weapon should be used at once for operations against the dams, on the ground that it would be a long time before conditions were again as favourable for attack upon them. A telegram recommending this course was sent to the Chiefs in Washington. They were warned that an attack against the dams might prejudice the later use of the other weapon, 'Highball', against battleships, but it was thought that this risk should be accepted. From the subsequent telegrams and minutes it is clear that the Chiefs of Staff immediately agreed to the operation and that you were informed in writing that they had done so. The operation took place on the night of May 16.

The success of the operation was reported to you, in Washington, and you at once sent a telegram of congratulation to the squadron in the following terms:

> 'Please convey to the crews of the Lancasters of No. 617 Squadron who attacked the Mohne, Eder and Sorpe Dams my admiration and my congratulations on this outstanding and very gallant action. They have struck a blow which will have far reaching effects.'

This, however, is the only written comment of yours which I can find about the operation. I imagine that you had discussed it with Portal, but there is no trace in the records of any minutes or directions by you about it.

Sir Winston S. Churchill to Alan Hodge and Denis Kelly
(*Churchill papers, 4/27*)

12 June 1955

CHAPTER VII, PAGE 9

No explanation has been given about who and what the Hotentots[1] were. The text has remained unaltered about them. Is the Frederick mentioned a Holy Roman Emperor?

Also page 9. We are talking very freely about Henry III's son Edmund.[2] Something more should surely be inserted about the new King Henry III.[3]

---

[1] 'Hottentots': antiquated term for the Khoikhoi, a nomadic group of non-Bantu tribesmen from south-west Africa.

[2] Edmund Crouchback, 1245–96. Lord Warden of the Cinque Ports, 1264. Lord High Steward, 1265–96.

[3] Henry of Winchester, 1207–72. King Henry III of England, 1216–72.

He succeeded as a minor at 9. I do not notice any reference to his definitely succeeding to the throne. He is planning an expedition in 1229 to take an army to France and quarrelling with Hubert de Burgh.[1] We are now on page 9 learning of his son Edmund for the first time. At least a paragraph must record his early years on the throne and his development as a ruler. How old was Edmund in October 1255? He had already been on the throne 39 years. Do not delay reprinting, but please meditate upon strengthening the structure of the fact that he is King.

I have also sent John[2] to the printer, but there are only passing illusions to losing the crown jewels in the Wash and the surfeit of lamphreys of which he died.

Harold Macmillan to Sir Winston S. Churchill
(*Churchill papers, 2/131*)

15 June 1955
Confidential

Dear Winston,

I hear that you feel unable to keep your engagement with U Nu, the Prime Minister of Burma, which had been arranged for next Tuesday, June 21. I know, of course, that the reasons for your decision are very good ones. But I think you would want me to let you know why the effect on the Burmese is likely to be bad.

When U Nu was asked what he would like to do during his visit to this country, one of his first requests was that he could be given an opportunity 'to pay his respects' to you. I have no doubt that in making this request U Nu had in mind your former attitude to the leaders of the Burmese independence movement, of which he of course was one, and that he himself would regard his call on you as in some sense an act of final reconciliation. Now that his intention of calling on you has been made public, I am sure that your inability to see him, however good the reason, could not fail to be interpreted by the Burmese as a sign that you did not wish for such a reconciliation, and would be bound to cause resentment and offence, as well as great disappointment.

I am afraid that things have not gone as well as might have been hoped in the arrangements for this visit. The Prime Minister will be at the Guildhall when the Burmese had hoped that he would be able to accept a luncheon invitation from them. I myself shall be out of the country and able to take no part in the programme. If now this key engagement with you has to be cancelled,

---

[1] Hubert de Burgh, 1170–1243. 1st Earl of Kent and Justiciar of England and Ireland. One of the most influential men in England during the reigns of King John and King Henry III.

[2] John Lackland, 1166–1216. King John of England, 1199–1216. It was in fact Henry I who died of a surfeit of lampreys.

I am very much afraid that most of the value of a visit designed to generate goodwill will be destroyed.

If you could possibly see your way to change your mind, we should of course be happy to explain to U Nu that there are special reasons why he must keep his visit very short. I know he would not mind this. But I am afraid that he might mind very much being deprived of the opportunity to make a gesture on which he seems to have set his heart.

Sir John Rothenstein[1] to Sir Winston S. Churchill
(Churchill papers, 1/25)

15 June 1955

Dear Sir Winston,

At the last meeting of our Board of Trustees it was agreed that they would welcome the inclusion in the collection of an example of your work as a painter, and I was authorized to make their views known to you.

I don't believe I need tell you what pleasure the decision of the Trustees gave me and how glad I should be of an opportunity of discussing this most interesting possibility with you.

Anthony Montague Browne to Sir Winston S. Churchill
(Churchill papers, 2/131)

20 June 1955

Here with brief notes on U Nu prepared by the FO for your talk this afternoon.

VISIT OF U NU, PRIME MINISTER OF BURMA
NOTE FOR SIR WINSTON CHURCHILL

U Nu the Prime Minister of the Union of Burma is in the United Kingdom for a week's goodwill visit. A personality report is attached. He will be calling on Sir Winston Churchill at 5 p.m. on Tuesday, June 21.

U Nu will visit the US officially after his visit here. He has just ended official visits to Israel and Yugoslavia. He intends to discuss the Formosa situation with President Eisenhower and to try to contribute towards an agreement between China and the United States on the solution of this problem

Sir Winston Churchill may like to say that although, to our regret, Burma chose to leave the Commonwealth on attaining her independence, many of the old ties of respect and indeed affection remain between us, and he hopes

---

[1] John Knewstub Maurice Rothenstein, 1901–92. Museum curator and art historian. Director, Tate Gallery, London, 1938–64. CBE, 1948. Knighted, 1952.

that our past association has helped her leaders to overcome the many problems confronting a new state making its way in a troubled area of the world.

We for our part have responsibilities and a contribution to make in Asia. If we withdraw our influence, the results would be unpredictable but uncomfortable for all. Our interests and Burma's coincide. Burma, with uneasy neighbours, may rely on us to do all we can to see that the independence we gave her is preserved from destruction by others.

Biographical Notes

U Nu

Prime Minister of the Union of Burma
Born in 1907.
Educated at Rangoon University.

He was President of the Rangoon Students Union in 1935 and was a leader of the Students' strike that year, which is regarded as a landmark in the history of Burma's progress toward independence. He joined the Nationalist Thakin Party and after the war emerged as one of the leading figures of the Anti-Fascist People's Freedom League. Following the assassination of Aung San[1] in the summer of 1947 he succeeded him as Deputy Chairman of the Executive Council and, when Burma obtained her independence on January 4, 1948, became Prime Minister. He has continued in office ever since.

U Nu is an Independent in politics but his Government is formed predominantly by the Burma Socialist Party. He is a devout practising Buddhist.

U Nu's Government follows a policy of neutrality and has felt unable to join the South East Asia Collective Defence Treaty. Internally the Burmese Government is strongly anti-Communist and has to deal with two insurgent outlawed Communist parties. In foreign affairs, however, it is Burma's policy to promote friendship with Communist China and to work for East–West understanding.

Mrs Nu (otherwise Daw Mya Yi)[2]

Mrs Nu takes a leading part in activities connected with Buddhism and in social and welfare work. She speaks no English. U and Mrs Nu have four children.

---

[1] Aung San, 1915–47. Educated at Rangoon University. Led students' strike, 1936. Secretary General, 'Dobama Asiayone' nationalist organization, 1939–40. Founder and Secretary-General, Communist Party of Burma, 1939. Fled Burma to China to avoid British arrest warrant for his attempt at organizing revolts. Aided Japan in return for promises of Burmese independence. Organized revolts against Japan after doubting sincerity of promises. Deputy Chairman, Executive Council, Burma, 1946. Signed agreement with British PM Clement Attlee for Burma's independence, 1947. Assassinated, 19 July 1947.

[2] Daw Mya Yi, 1910–93. Married, 1935, U Nu: five children.

U Nu is accompanied by his Private Secretaries U Thant[1] and U Hla,[2] and by his ADC Captain Pye Soe.

Sir Winston S. Churchill: speech
('The Unwritten Alliance', pages 266–8)

21 June 1955   Guildhall

I regard it as a very high honour that the City of London should decide to set up a statue of me in this famous Guildhall, which I have so often visited and spoken in during the last half century. I must admit that I think that the House of Commons has made a good rule in not erecting monuments to people in their lifetime. But I entirely agree that every rule should have an exception. The fact that you have done so in my case will both prove the rule, and emphasize the compliment.

I greatly admire the art of Mr Oscar Nemon whose prowess in the ancient realm of sculpture has won such remarkable modern appreciation. I also admire this particular example, which you, my Lord Mayor,[3] have just unveiled, because it seems to be such a very good likeness. But on this point, as indeed in any other part of this ceremony, I cannot claim to be either impersonal or impartial. I am indeed an interested and biased party. However, the responsibility belongs to the Corporation of the City of London. I feel that I can safely leave it on their broad shoulders, and that, so far as I am concerned, I am fully entitled to enjoy their kindness to my heart's content.

My only regret to-day is that my dear wife, without whom I should certainly not have deserved this reward, has been prevented from coming by the painful accident[4] from which her many well-wishers and friends will be glad to learn she is making a steady recovery. I should especially have liked her to have been present at the speech of the Lord Mayor which of course she will have heard and seen through the scientific agencies which now play so large a part in our daily lives, and cast their fierce light upon us with amicable intent.

---

[1] Thant, 1909–74. Known as 'U Thant'. Teacher, National High School, Pantanaw, 1928–31; Headmaster, 1931–42, 1943–7. Secretary, Educational Reorganizing Committee, Burma, 1942–3. Press Director, 1947. Director of Broadcasting, 1948. Secretary, Ministry of Information, 1949. Private Secretary to PM, 1951–7. Burmese delegate to the UN, 1952–3; Permanent Representative, 1957–61. Vice-President, UN General Assembly, 1959; Acting Secretary-General, UN, 1961–2; Secretary-General, 1962–71.

[2] U Hla Maung, 1911–92. Born in Meiktila, Burma. Educated at University of Yangon. President, Rangoon University Students' Union, 1939. Joined Diplomatic Service, 1948. Secretary of Ministry of National Planning. Burmese Ambassador to China, 1951–9; to UK, 1961–8; to US, 1968–70.

[3] Cuthbert Lowell Ackroyd, 1892–1973. Educated at University of London. On active service, WWI; Capt., RA. Married, 1927, Joyce Wallace Whyte: two children. Member, Corporation of London, 1940–70. Chairman, Guildhall Library Committee and Art Gallery, 1945. Sheriff, City of London, 1945–50. Lord Mayor of London, 1955–6. Underwriting Member of Lloyd's. Chairman, Licensing Sessions, City of London, 1957–62.

[4] Early in June Lady Churchill had fallen and broken her left wrist.

I am most grateful to you, my Lord Mayor, for the great kindness with which you have spoken about my work and character, and I shall not hesitate to include it among my testimonials if ever I should be looking for another job. If I were not already ruddy in complexion I should certainly have blushed in a noticeable manner. My hope is that your successors will not find it their duty in my lifetime at any rate, to make any 'agonizing re-appraisal', to quote a famous and up-to-date diplomatic expression, of the verdict you have pronounced with so much eloquence and generosity.

It has been my lot to live as a grown-up person through more than half of the most violent century in human record. I remember well the scene which spread before us at the close of the Victorian era. The vast majority of the nation looked with confidence upon our island as the centre of a vast empire spreading all over the world, as its leader in commerce, manufacture, and invention, as the model of orthodox finance and fiscal policy, as the author of Parliamentary government and all guarded by the unchallengeable power of a navy which only cost about £20 millions a year. Little did we realize how mighty was the world which was growing up around us, or how terrible and gigantic were the struggles into which all its people were to be plunged. Now we look out upon a different prospect. All the values and proportions are changed. We have emerged on the victorious side from two world wars in which scores of millions have perished. They were wars which in their scope and scale seemed far to surpass our resources, and at times to threaten us with doom.

To-day we see our small island, with its dense population and delicate, complex, elastic but still precarious means of existence, no longer enjoying the ascendance and power of bygone days, but yet preserving in no small measure the respect and goodwill of large portions of mankind, and exercising in the new and far larger organization into which we have come, and which we have helped to found, a worthy and, I believe, growing share of influence. If this is so, it is because in the fearful ordeals of peace and war through which we have passed we have done our duty, and have faithfully sought the maintenance of peace from motives superior to the fear of death or destruction. We may all be proud to have lived through such a period, and I do not feel that our generation has any need to be abashed before our ancestors, or the famous ages of our history of which this hall so vividly reminds us.

But now I leave the past, and I leave the present. It is to the future that we must turn our gaze. I confess that, like Disraeli, I am on the side of the optimists. I do not believe that humanity is going to destroy itself. I have for some time thought it would be a good thing if the leaders of the great nations talked freely to one another without too much of the formality of diplomacy. I am very glad that this is now going to happen. We must not count upon complete and immediate success. Whatever is the outcome, we must persevere in the maintenance of peace through strength. A period of relaxation of tension may well be all that is now within our grasp. But such a phase would not be sterile. On the contrary it would give the time for science to show the magnitude of her blessings rather than of her terrors; and this again may lead us into a more genial climate of opinion and resolve. Let us go boldly forward and play our part in all this.

Sir Winston S. Churchill to General George C. Marshall
(Churchill papers, 2/144)

25 June 1955

My dear Marshall,

I am so sorry that I have not found an opportunity to answer the letter with which you honoured me last month. To the 'avalanche of congratulations' succeeded the tumult of the General Election, and much other difficult personal business connected with my departure from office. This has most adversely affected the very letters I put away meaning to answer myself.

I deeply value all that you say. Our wartime comradeship is one of my most cherished memories of those tremendous days.

My wife joins with me in sending you and Mrs Marshall[1] our best wishes.

Sir Winston S. Churchill to Harold Macmillan
(Churchill papers, 2/131)

30 June 1955

My dear Harold,

Thank you so much for your letter. I was glad to see U Nu, and much admired his celestial baby's face (?)

The query is confidential.

AMB[2] is a great help to me in my official & semi-official aftermath.

---

[1] Katherine Boyce Tupper, 1882–1978. Educated at American Academy of Dramatic Arts and later Comédie-Française. Married, 1911, Clifton Stevenson Brown (d. 1928): three children; 1930, George C. Marshall. Published *Annals of an Army Wife* (1946).

[2] Anthony Montague Browne.

Sir Winston S. Churchill to Lady Lytton
(Churchill papers, 1/56)[1]

30 June 1955   Chartwell

My dearest Pamela,

I was sweet of you to write me yr letter about the Guildhall, but I am indeed sorry for the cause wh prevented you from coming. I do pray that you are better & free from pain. I have just heard that you are back at Knebworth so I hope for the best.

I put yr letter aside when I got it, as I do my most important or cherished communications, and, as alas often happens, one trifle after another put me off from day to day, with renewed resolve & continued deferment. Do forgive me for I have wanted to write to you every single day and I am ashamed at myself.

I wish you could have been at the show. It is the last engagement I have, and I am vy chary of adding to them. I have a protracted desire to avoid the public kindness. But this Guildhall statue was certainly worth the worry these things take me now. I am getting much older now the stimulus of responsibility & power has fallen from me, and I totter along in the shades of retirement.

They now tell me you are 'a little better today'. I do trust indeed that this is a real gain.

Clemmie & I wd love to come to The Manor House one day. Alas she is suffering a great deal of pain from her neuritis, & for the last three weeks has been a complete invalid with her broken wrist and the shock of her fall. I spend my days between Chartwell & 28, with the Book as my main task.

This tardy letter is meant to carry you my love and every good wish. Please send me a line to say how you are and that you forgive my stupid delay.

                                                                                             Your ever loving
                                                                                               and devoted
                                                                                                     W

Excuse the scrawl. It is due to age!

[1] This letter was handwritten.

June 1955

Sir Winston S. Churchill to Harry S Truman
('Defending the West, The Truman–Churchill Correspondence', page 216)

30 June 1955
Paraphrase[1]

My dear Harry,

Of all the letters I received on my resignation none has given me more pleasure than yours.[2]

You wrote of my contribution to history, but it was your decision at the outset of the Korean War and before that with the establishment of NATO which are responsible for the degree of calm we now have, and that together must ensure your reputation and the gratitude of the free world.

---

[1] Header reproduced from *Defending the West*.
[2] Reproduced above (p. 1985).

July 1955

Sir Winston S. Churchill to Lord Woolton
(Churchill papers, 2/202)

4 July 1955

My dear Fred,

I expected the announcement which appeared in all the papers last week of your retirement from the Chairmanship of the Conservative Central Office, and I think you are quite right in choosing this time for so important a change.

There is no doubt that when you took over in 1945 the Socialists and many others believed that their ascendancy in the State and the perpetuation of their fallacious doctrine would endure. This might well have happened, but for your influence, authority and exertion. I shall always be very proud to have taken this all-important decision, not so much for the Tory party, but for our precarious and at the same time powerful island community. Your country has every reason to be grateful to you.

For myself, you have been an immense support, and I rejoice that after our two hard fought elections you were able to remain in charge. I know no one better, the efforts and personal sacrifices which you made to keep the flag flying. It is indeed a fitting conclusion to our joint work that after nearly four years of steadfast administration we should have seen the Party restored to full strength and the nation steadily advancing in efficiency and prosperity.

Pray accept my warmest gratitude, and convey my sentiments to your wife,[1] without whom you could never have survived victorious.

---

[1] Maud Matthews.

July 1955

President Dwight D. Eisenhower to Sir Winston S. Churchill
(Churchill papers, 2/217)

15 July 1955   The White House

Dear Winston,

Soon Anthony and I will be meeting with the French and the Russians at Geneva. As you know, I feel sure that the Western nations could not, with self-respect, have earlier consented to a Four Power Summit meeting. Yet I cannot escape a feeling of sadness that the delay brought about by the persistently hostile Soviet attitude toward NATO has operated to prevent your personal attendance at the meeting.

Foster and I know – as does the world – that your courage and vision will be missed at the meeting. But your long quest for peace daily inspires much that we do. I hope that in your wisdom you will consider that we there do well; certainly we shall do the best of which we are capable in the opportunities we may encounter in Geneva.

Personally I do not expect, and I hope the people of this country and of the world do not expect, a miracle. But if we can inch a little closer to the dream that has been yours for these many years, if together at the meeting table we can create a new spirit of tolerance and perhaps, in concert, come to the realization that force and the threat of force are no longer acceptable in dealings among nations, we shall gain much that will help us in the long and complicated processes that must come after the Summit meeting.

As I leave Washington, my thoughts are with you, as indeed they are on many, many days. I hope you are enjoying to some degree the greater leisure that is yours.

Please give my affectionate regard to Clemmie, and, as always, the best to yourself.

Your old friend,

John Colville to Sir Winston S. Churchill
(Churchill papers, 1/66)

17 July 1955

My dear Winston,

I treasure the silver V-sign, commemorating your Second Administration, and am placing it on my watch-chain as an object to be very especially prized.

I hope that during the last week of July or any time in August you will let me know if you feel the need of either companionship or Bezique, and I will be at your disposal.

Sir Winston S. Churchill to President Dwight D. Eisenhower
(Churchill papers, 2/217)

18 July 1955

My dear Friend,

I am deeply grateful to you for your letter[1] and the thought that prompted you. I was touched by what you said when I resigned, and I had two of your letters with me at the time which I had not answered. What often happens is that one puts on one side the most important features in one's correspondence in order to do justice to them in the reply, and then keeps putting them off from day to day for less important things. I can only beg you to forgive, as I am sure you will, my neglect.

It is a strange and formidable experience laying down responsibility and letting the trappings of power fall in a heap to the ground. A sense not only of psychological but of physical relaxation steals over one to leave a feeling both of relief and denudation. I did not know how tired I was until I stopped working.

I cannot help, however, feeling satisfied with the way things have turned out. I am fortunate to have a successor whose mind I know and whose abilities are of the highest order. I had to consider the interests of the Party I have led for 14 years and I was convinced that this was the time to ask the verdict of the nation on what we had done in 3 years of office. Moreover, I have for a long time felt that at my age I should not be justified myself in leading in the election when I could not feel any assurance that I could carry out in an effective manner any new programme to which I pledged myself. I was very pleased with the result, and, indeed, on the whole I feel that we Changed Guard at Buckingham Palace at the right time and in the right way.

I am very glad that the meeting 'at the summit' is now taking place, and I will gladly do anything in my power from a distance and a private station to help it to a good result. I have never indulged in extravagant hopes of a vast, dramatic transformation of human affairs, but my belief is that, so long as we do not relax our unity or our vigilance, the Soviets and the Russian people will be increasingly convinced that it is in their interests to live peaceably with us. There is a strong reaction from the post-war mood of Stalin. Abundance for hundreds of millions is in sight and even in reach. These processes of growth require time, and one improvement can easily lead to another.

I do not relish the idea of 'saturation' in the nuclear sphere. If, however, that is accompanied by the undoubted fact that a full scale nuclear war means not the mastery of one side or the other but the extinction of the human species, it may well be that a new set of deterrents will dominate the soul of man.

I will convey your very kind message to Clemmie, and thank you once

---

[1] Reproduced above (p. 2024).

again for thinking of me at this busy and momentous time. I hope indeed that you will find it possible to visit our island before you return home. I should look forward so much to a talk.

Sir Anthony Eden to Sir Winston S. Churchill
(Churchill papers, 2/216)

19 July 1955
Secret

Dear Winston,

Our proceedings[1] have opened on rather a quiet note like the general election. It is too early to tell what the week may bring. The Russians are polite in private talk, so far as we have had any, and moderate in tone in public. However, most of what they said today was the mixture as before. We have all the bears to dinner tomorrow.

The President, with whom I had a useful talk alone yesterday, said he had written to you. He seems to be in good heart and not too unhappy to find himself here.

Sir Anthony Eden to Sir Winston S. Churchill
Prime Minister's Personal Telegram T.96/55
(Premier papers, 11/981)

20 July 1955
Immediate
Dedip
Top Secret
No. 50

So far the Russians are showing little sign of movement in our discussions. The Foreign Secretaries are to try tomorrow to work out the instructions which might be given to them on the subjects of German reunification and European security. However, our private discussions have been more hopeful and it seems clear that both the Russians and the Americans want to get some positive result from the Conference. The Russians talked freely when they dined last night, which was encouraging as they had said nothing but civilities when dining with the United States and French. Bulganin told me that he could not go back to Moscow having agreed to the immediate unification of Germany. Neither the army nor the people would understand it. It would be said that it was something Stalin would never have agreed to. This was no doubt true.

---

[1] At the Four-Power Summit in Geneva.

JULY 1955 2027

I do not think that the Russians are now trying to divide us from the United States, but are rather looking to us as a possible bridge. I have discussed the Far Eastern situation both with the President and with the Russians. There is no lack of understanding on either side of the dangers over Quemoy and Matsus, but the United States are as reluctant as ever to take any firm decision about the islands.

Randolph S. Churchill to Sir Winston S. Churchill
(*Churchill papers, 1/56*)

22 July 1955

My dearest Papa,
 You will remember that some months ago you asked me to open on your behalf the new Churchill Hall of the Riverside Conservative Club in Cardiff. I gladly agreed to do so but owing to a series of accidents the plan has miscarried.
 I flew back specially from Geneva this morning in order to carry out this engagement. Unfortunately, partly owing to the mistake of a new secretary and partly to the inefficiency of British Railways, I was put into the wrong train, a thing that has never happened to me before. I got out at Reading where I very nearly succeeded in having the train I should have been on flagged. I just failed by seconds. I then tried to charter a plane and drove to Blackbushe Air Field. This plan too miscarried and in the end I was forced to abandon the enterprise.
 I am deeply sorry to have let you down in this matter and I am of course writing to the Club expressing my deepest regret and offering, if they wish, to visit them on some other occasion.

Sir Anthony Eden to Sir Winston S. Churchill
(*Churchill papers, 2/216*)

25 July 1955

My dear Winston,
 I do not think that there is much to add to the instructions to the Foreign Secretaries which were finally agreed and to the speeches in the closing session of the Conference. Bulganin then restated the whole Soviet position without real modification, although in reasonably amiable terms. The treatment of the Conference by *Pravda* bears out the impression that this was primarily for the record. But we have a very long way to go before we get a solution over Germany.
 I had two further good private talks with Bulganin, Krushchev and Molotov,

in one of which they showed greater interest in our security ideas than they had in open session.

There is one further development of importance which I hope to announce on Wednesday and which Pitblado will tell you about.

I am off to Winchester, where I have my Audience.

Sir Winston S. Churchill to Elizabeth Gilliatt
(Churchill papers, 1/66)

28 July 1955

My dear Miss Gilliatt,

I am indeed sorry that you wish to leave my service. It never occurred to me that such a small drop of only 18 inches could cause such a grave injury. I am afraid you have suffered a great deal of pain.

I hope you will come to see me, for I shall be in England all of August, and there is plenty of time to talk over our troubles and decide what is best to do.

I am deeply grieved by what you tell me.

August 1955

Lady Churchill to Sir Winston S. Churchill
(Churchill papers, 1/55)[1]

5 August 1955

My Darling,

It was very sweet of you to come with me to the Airport. It sent me off happy in my laborious effort to regain my health.[2]

The flight was magnificent. The last hour there were heavy clouds right & left of the plane; but we flew in perfect sunshine.

When we touched down at Zürich however, the air-field was water-logged & we had just missed a short but horrid thunderstorm.

Zürich is a beautiful town & it was more than half an hour's drive through it to the railway station.

I tucked up comfortably in the Station hotel for 2 hours & then began the rather tedious 5 hour journey (with a change) to St Moritz. Dinner on the train was delicious & we were made most welcome in this very comfortable hotel. The pain is considerable but supportable; I have given myself an injection,[3] but hope soon to do without. Tomorrow I'm seeing the spa doctor to see if he can soothe the neuritis away with some magic peat or pine baths.

All my love Darling,
Your devoted Clemmie

PS: I'm spending today in my room so as to get use to the altitude.

---

[1] This letter was handwritten.
[2] Lady Churchill was travelling to St Moritz to take a recommended cure for persistent neuritis.
[3] Pethidine injections, self-administered on doctor's recommendation to alleviate the pain.

Sir Winston S. Churchill to Lady Churchill
(Baroness Spencer-Churchill papers)[1]

5 August 1955   Chartwell

Darling,

Monty came to lunch today. He was vy amusing & made most thorough inquiries about you. I told him all there was to tell. We all went down to the Pool with Jeremy[2] who was a gt success.

I am eagerly awaiting news of you & hope to receive some on Monday. It may well be that you will have a set back for a few days and that then the attacks of pain will lessen. Several people have told me that they have had <u>arthritis</u> and after a bit it has worn off & so why shd not <u>neuritis</u> do the same? Anyhow do not Despair. I beg you not to do that. I am <u>sure</u> you will find a remedy. I know it may be hard, but you have valiant blood. This is the third letter I have tried to write to you and always failed. I love you so much and am determined to persevere.

It will be easier when I have one of your own dear letters to begin on.

                                                      Always your loving husband.

Sir Winston S. Churchill to Lady Churchill
(Baroness Spencer-Churchill papers)[3]

8 August 1955   Chartwell

My darling,

I was so glad to get your letter & to learn the details of yr journey. I had been waiting eagerly for it. Now it has come I take up my pen to answer aided by Toby[4] who is sitting on the sheet of note paper insisting on lapping the ink from my pen in order to send you a personal message. He has come down here greatly improved and there is no doubt that he knows I am writing to you and that he wishes to join in. He is a wonderful little bird. He pecked and scribbled with his beak and what I have written so far is as much his work as mine. He has gone back to his cage now (by my bedside) so perhaps I may write better. (I have also had my pen refilled.)

Monty evidently enjoyed himself and has given me a letter to send you. He has asked to come Sunday 11th September. You may well be here & <u>high time too</u>. You will find a lot of changes which I hope you will like. (Toby is back again on my hand.) This is really a joint message so I make him sign it.

I have had Hodge down for a couple of days & in a quarter of an hour

---

[1] This letter was handwritten.
[2] Jeremy Soames.
[3] This letter was handwritten.
[4] Budgerigar.

expect Bill Deakin. I must bring him along if I can. I am directing him with Hans[1] who comes at about 4.

I can't harden my heart to get rid of the old van. & am going to keep it for a bit, so as to let the secretaries & Miss Hamblin do some of their short trips for a while. (Toby is back.) But you can settle when you come home.

My dearest one you have all my love. Do write to me & don't give up hope.

Your ever devoted husband.

Joel Hurstfield[2] to Sir Winston S. Churchill
(Churchill papers, 4/27)

10 August 1955

Dear Sir Winston,

I write to thank you for your kind letter of 5th August and to add that I shall be happy to give any further assistance in connection with the Tudor section[3] that you might require.

I shall be out of London for two short periods from August 13th–21st, and from September 2nd–12th, but apart from these, I should be very ready to come and discuss with you any aspect of this material upon which you have been working.

Sir Winston S. Churchill to Lady Churchill
(Baroness Spencer-Churchill papers)[4]

10 August 1955   Chartwell

Darling,

Your letter of the 8th has reached me this morning. I am enchanted that you feel better. This is really good news after only three days. Let me know what the local doctor says after his blood tests, and also what he prescribes. I am sure it is a good thing to take all opinions which are authoritative on a question like this – but whether you act upon them is another. Still the remedies proposed <u>may</u> be harmless & fit in with the regime of the Spa. And there is always the chance of hitting the bull's eye. There are so many cures or alleviations.

---

[1] Hans Heinrich von Halban, 1908–64. Educated at University of Zurich. Physicist. Worked on nuclear fission at the College of France, Paris, 1937–40. Invited to work on the Manhattan Project after fleeing France. Helped establish the British Atomic Energy Research Establishment under the direction of Lord Cherwell.

[2] Joel Hurstfield, 1911–80. British historian. Prof., University of London, 1962–79. Author of several books on Elizabethan politics.

[3] Of *History of the English-Speaking Peoples*.

[4] This letter was handwritten.

You must be popping up and down a lot to drop down 5000 feet to lunch with Mildred Gosford.[1] I have a distinct recollection of her – tho I do not suppose I shd recognise her. It must have been a wonderful drive, and how amusing to meet the friends of girlhood!

I have been working at my book & Christopher and Mary have made all sorts of plans to fill in the 11 days (wh begin tomorrow) which I am bound to say seems attractive. Violet is coming here for Saturday. Today we have the Ismays. He tells me that his sinus is much better since he had his teeth pulled out & that perhaps he will not have to have another operation. But about this I will write in my next.

Anthony & Cleopatra[2] have chosen the 10th September for their visit and Christopher will be available. They only stay one day. I do hope you will be back flourishing, Monty lunches on the 11th September & I am trying to persuade them not to go till after lunch.

Tender love my dearest Clemmie
Your devoted husband

Toby has signed.

Sir Winston S. Churchill to Lady Churchill
(*Baroness Spencer-Churchill papers*)[3]

11 August 1955   Chartwell

My darling,

I am indeed glad that you have had such a favourable accommodation. Do let me know how things go on. Your letter (No. 8) has just arrived. I sent mine by Christopher's Mama on the night of the 5th, so it ought to have got there in good time. This is my fourth & I hope to keep a steady flow.

Mary & Ch have started on their journey by motor car & will be motoring all day to Braithwaites where they are going to stay till they go to the Swintons, I dined with them last night, vy pleasant.

Christopher has made some good arrangements for me in their absence. Violet is coming this week and I am expecting the Delawares[4] to luncheon on Sunday. I have also asked for the next Sunday (27th)[5] Juliet Duff[6] & she has

---

[1] Mildred Carter, 1889–1965. Known as 'Millie'. Childhood friend of Clementine Churchill. Married, 1910, Archibald Charles Montagu Brabazon Acheson, 5th Earl of Gosford (div. 1927): five children.
[2] Anthony and Clarissa Eden.
[3] This letter was handwritten.
[4] Earl and Countess De La Warr.
[5] Actually Aug. 28.
[6] Juliet Lowther, 1881–1965. Only child of 4th Earl of Lonsdale. Married, 1903, Robert Duff (killed in action, 1914); 1919, Keith Trevor, MC (div. 1926).

telegraphed saying she can. I am so sorry that Mrs Jack has died. You will indeed be grieved. She was a vy good friend of yours. Miss Hamblin told me. She is writing you about it.

I have taken charge of the children and have just watched them bathe & all went well. They are dear little things. They leave us on Thursday next for the sea side. Mary returns the day after and will stay with me till she leaves for you. I hope that she will give you good reports of all our goings on at Chartwell.

Darling you have my dearest love
Your devoted husband

Sir Winston S. Churchill to Lady Churchill
(Baroness Spencer-Churchill papers)[1]

13 August 1955　　　　　　　　　　　　　　　　　　　　　　　　　　　　Chartwell
Blenheim Day

My darling,

I am getting quite festive, Violet is staying with me today & tomorrow: I have asked Pamela, who proposed herself, to come on Thursday 18th & Juliet for the weekend of the 27th, when Lord & Lady De la War are coming to lunch. This is a record.

Violet made herself vy agreeable last night and argued a great deal about her Papa, the Liberal Party & all that. Mr Hodge who has now gone to retrieve his family was thrilled, I am to have a string of painters (to whom I shall give a fleeting glimpse) next week & Mr Laughlin who comes over from Ireland to talk 'Book'. There are others filling in the intervals.

My plans were deranged by Meg & Jock. Jock was smitten by appendicitis & had to have an operation on the 11th. He has come through all right, but it was vy sudden & unwarned.

Now I want to hear your news. I am expecting a letter with a full account of yr progress. What a wonderful thing it will be if you have had <u>less</u> neuritis and <u>fewer</u> injections! It is a week & 2 days since you left. In the meantime I can do no more than hope.

With all my love
Your devoted husband

---

[1] This letter was handwritten.

Sir Winston S. Churchill to Lady Churchill
(Baroness Spencer-Churchill papers)

17 August 1955   Chartwell

My darling,

I am still awaiting your reply to my telegram before sending any further chapters. If, as I suppose, you have the first revise with you up to the end of 'The Saxon Dusk', it will be easy to send some of the early chapters of William the Conqueror, etc. from a later revise, and then Mary can bring the rest when she comes. I expect to hear from you today. But I should like you to read it in sequence, and to have the latest edition.

I am so glad you like it, and what you say about it is a great encouragement to me. I have read Volume 1, which includes Books I, II, and III, three times now, and have, I think, a good deal improved it. I am delighted at what you say about helping a lot of people to read history, and that it will have results which may be compared with 'Painting as a Pastime'.

I am still waiting anxiously for further reports on the new treatment. It sounds very hopeful. Do not hesitate to prolong your stay for another week if the doctor thinks it will do good.

I will write you again later in the day. Mr Laughlin, the Canadian publisher, who is a very nice man, is coming to lunch.

With all my love
Your devoted

PS. Montague-Brown is just off & we have to post in London to catch the Air Mail.

Sir Winston S. Churchill to Lady Churchill
(Baroness Spencer-Churchill papers)[1]

20 August 1955   Chartwell

My darling,

Mary comes home today & stays with me. She leaves on Monday & will bring you all the news. Pamela cd not come for the weekend, but Randolph is coming with little Winston; but June is abroad.

Your letter dated 18 has just reached me. It tells me what I wanted. There has been a definite improvement during the fortnight. This is anyhow to the good, and I feel you are right to postpone yr return. I have only one engagement – the 7th (the Cinque Ports) which I wd not recommend you to attempt & have duly prepared them. So that if you feel you want a day or two more

---

[1] This letter was handwritten.

you cd take them. On the other hand it wd be vy nice to have you here from the 5th onwards.

Anthony & Clarissa are coming on the 10th – sleep the night and remain till after luncheon on 11th, when Monty lunches. They leave in the afternoon. I shd be a bit stiff with Einstein.[1] We <u>saved</u> Greece from being inside the Iron Curtain by our personal exertions. Cyprus has never had any pledge from us that she wd be handed over to the Greeks who have never had her. Although I do not say that this is a decisive argument, we have embarked upon a clearance plan for Egypt which is based upon our base in Cyprus, & we are not likely to choose this moment (above all others) to compromise it. The Greek revilings leave me quite cold – or indeed hot me up. I will see if I can put something more down for Mary to bring.

Tender love my dearest one. I am struggling along with my book – much bucked up by yr approval –

All my love & many kisses
Your devoted & loving husband
[Drawing of a pig]

PS. I go out harvesting every day in the new Land Rover.

Randolph S. Churchill to Sir Winston S. Churchill
(Churchill papers, 1/56)[2]

21 August 1955 Chartwell

PENSÉES MATINALES ET FILIALES (PRESQUE LAPIDAIRES)

Power must pass and vanish. Glory, which is achieved through a just exercise of power – which itself is accumulated by genius, toil, courage and self-sacrifice – alone remains. Your glory is enshrined for ever on the imperishable plinth of your achievement; and can never be destroyed or tarnished. It will flow with the centuries.

So please try to be as happy as you have a right and (if it is not presumptuous for a son to say it) a duty to be. And, by being happy, make those who love you happy too.

All on one sheet of paper!

With devoted love,

---

[1] Lewis David Einstein, 1877–1967. American diplomat and historian befriended by Clementine Churchill on her travels. Born in New York City. Educated at Columbia University. Married, 1904, Helen Ralli. 3rd Secretary, US Embassy, Constantinople, 1903, 1915; Chargé d'Affaires, 1908. US Ambassador to Costa Rica, 1911; to Czechoslovakia, 1921–30. Published *Inside Constantinople: A Diplomatist's Diary during the Dardanelles Expedition* (1918), *Roosevelt: His Mind in Action* (1930), *Divided Loyalties* (1933) and *A Diplomat Looks Back* (1968).

[2] This letter was handwritten.

Lady Churchill to Sir Winston S. Churchill
(Churchill papers, 1/55)[1]

21 August 1955

My darling,

Yesterday three more chapters of your book arrived, & I have devoured them eagerly. I am more & more interested. I'm rather sad that you have left out the bit about 'Edith the Swan-neck'. Wasn't she Harold's wife? And I thought it was she who begged William for her Husband's body? But now I see it was his Mother.

I'm longing for Mary's arrival. Do send Heather Wood a message of thanks. She has been charming capable & companionable.

Your loving

Lady Churchill to Sir Winston S. Churchill
(Churchill papers, 1/55)[2]

24 August 1955

My Darling,

It is a great joy having Mary with me.

Yesterday we went for a drive with Mr Einstein. We both set upon him about Cyprus, (with the help of your letter) after which he became quite amenable.

I have just been speaking to you on the telephone.

Today Mary went out climbing with Barbie & Herbert Agar.[3] I followed in a pony chaise as far as I could & then awaited their return on the sunny terrace of a small hotel.

We all lunched in the most beautiful high valley, with a glacier in the far distance & a waterfall in the middle distance & rushing [. . .] streams all round. We were about 8000 feet up.

I'm getting on with the cure & feel stronger, but can't walk more than ½ a mile which is mortifying.

I'm just going to start out in the new chapters you have sent me. I love your book. Darling Winston take care of yourself.

Your loving & devoted
[Drawing of a cat]

---

[1] This letter was handwritten.

[2] This letter was handwritten.

[3] Barbara Lutyens, 1898–1981. Long-standing friend of Pamela Digby, Randolph Churchill's first wife. Married, 1920, David Euan Wallace (d. 1941): three children; 1945, Herbert Sebastian Agar.

Herbert Sebastian Agar, 1897–1980. Educated at Princeton University. Chief Quartermaster, USNR, 1917–18. Pulitzer Prize for History, 1934. Special Assistant to US Ambassador in London, 1942–6. Married, 1945, Barbara Lutyens Wallace. Director, Rupert Hart-Davis Publishers, 1953–63.

The 25th

Mary has just been having a lawn-tennis lesson from a very good professional. She really has a lovely style & looks charming in her short tennis dress. The Agars (Alas) have just gone away, motoring home via Bâle & Nancy.

God bless you my darling and us both,

Sir Winston S. Churchill to Major-General Sir Hugh Tudor
(Churchill papers, 2/201)

25 August 1955

My dear Hugh,

I was, like you, much distressed to hear that Will Y. Darling[1] was taken ill in the House of Commons. His wife has written to me in a tone which gives me every hope that he will take his place in the new session.

I am indeed enjoying the period of comparative leisure, and it is a real relief for me to be freed from the burdens of Prime Minister. The worst thing about it is that when you let all these responsibilities drop you feel your power falls with the thing it held.

Sir Winston S. Churchill to Lady Churchill
(Baroness Spencer-Churchill papers)[2]

26 August 1955   Chartwell

My darling,

Mary arrived last night & Randolph & Winston. We had a vy pleasant dinner (after a bathe, wh I witnessed), and saw a vy good film. She will tell you all about it. I asked her to give you a good account of me, & she said she would.

I am looking forward to seeing you on the 5th or 6th September. If you cannot come then a later date will do, but the 7th I shall be at the Cinque Ports & will not be back till after 6. I can of course send cars. The 8th wd set mine free, as well as yours. But all can be arranged.

---

[1] William Young Darling, 1885–1962. Educated at Edinburgh University. Trained for business in Edinburgh and London. Enlisted in Black Watch, 1914. Served in WWI, 1915–18, and in Ireland, 1920–2. Member, Edinburgh Town Council, 1933; City Treasurer, 1937–40. Nat. Government candidate, West Lothian, 1937. Chief ARW, 1938–9. District Commissioner, South Eastern Scotland, 1939–41. Lord Provost of Edinburgh, 1941–4. Chairman, Scottish Council on Industry, 1942–6. Director, Royal Bank of Scotland, 1942–57. MP (Cons.) for South Edinburgh, 1945–57.

[2] This letter was handwritten.

Randolph is vy pleasant and likes his house, in which he is now established vy much.[1]

It will be delightful having you back. There is much for you to see. All my love,

Your devoted husband

I can write better than this – but writing in bed enables me to make it a joint performance.

Mary Soames to Sir Winston S. Churchill
(Churchill papers, 1/56)[2]

27 August 1955

My Darling Papa,

I am enjoying myself so much here with Mama. I do think she is improved but not quite better yet. I think the Cure Baths etc. have an accumulating and beneficial effect. But I think she becomes very easily exhausted, I am sure that when she returns home she must go <u>her own pace</u>.

We are both devouring and enjoying enormously yr. *Eng. Spking Peoples*. It is a thrilling & moving panorama of events. I had already read a few chapters, but it is very satisfying to be able to read a whole section off at a time. And the chapters do lead most skilfully one into the other. I think people will be thrilled when it is published, & full of additional admiration and amazement at its author.

I fly home next Tuesday 30th – arriving at 7.10 p.m. I wonder if your car could meet me? And might I dine with you? If this is convenient, please don't wait dinner for me, as I might be late, but perhaps I could join in when I arrive? I will make all possible haste at the airport end.

I will sleep in my own 'bunny'[3] at the farm, as the next day the children return – & I must kiss them – pack & set off in the evening (of the 31st) to join my dear Chimp.

Darling Papa, my thoughts are so often with you. I do look forward to our holiday in France all together.

With dearest love,
Your loving & devoted daughter,

---

[1] In the summer of 1955, the Churchill family trust financed Randolph's purchase of Stour, a pink brick house in the rambling village of East Bergholt, Suffolk. The rear garden overlooked the Stour valley with views of Dedham Church. A storeroom built just outside the house was the first home of the Churchill Papers. Randolph was devoted to Stour and lived there until his death in 1968.

[2] This letter was handwritten.

[3] Her bed.

Sir Winston S. Churchill to Lady Churchill
(Baroness Spencer-Churchill papers)

28 August 1955

My darling,

I am so glad that my letter was of some use in dealing with Mr Einstein. He is not the great Einstein, who died earlier in the year. This I should have known.

Christopher leaves this afternoon. His visit has been very pleasant. We went to Windsor races yesterday, and won a good victory. The race is worth £1,000, but of course the second gets £200, the third £100 and the jockey and trainer each ten per cent. But still, the value of the horse has probably been raised from very little to a couple of thousand, and we hope she will win another race this autumn. Although we have not sold anything this year, there is every prospect of balancing the racing account.

I am so glad that you will come with me on the 15th to Max's villa. It is all arranged, and we shall, I am sure, be very happy with Mary and Christopher. I am also glad that you are going to go through with your cure, and will expect you to dinner on the 5th.

I sent you two more chapters yesterday. I am so glad you like the book. I am much encouraged by it. You now have the whole of Book II, ending with 'The Black Death', which reduced the population of the world by at least a third at the time when it was certainly not over-crowded. Let me know how you get on, for there is a third Book included in the volume, which is, I think, a good one.

Poor Mrs Shillingford has lost her baby, which is a great blow to her, but renders all the changes unnecessary as she would like to continue the constituency work. Let me repeat yr ending. God bless you my darling and us both.

Sir Winston S. Churchill to Richard Nixon
(Churchill papers, 2/131)

29 August 1955

My dear Mr Vice-President,

I have before me the Resolution[1] which the United States Senate adopted on July 28. The Senate's action does me the highest honour, and I would be indeed obliged if you would convey to the Members of the Senate my most sincere thanks. I am moved by your gesture, which recalls to me the occasions when I had the great privilege of addressing Congress.

---

[1] Commending Churchill, in the wake of his retirement from the premiership, for 'his contributions on behalf of freedom and world peace' and expressing the Senate's 'profound hope that Sir Winston Churchill may be spared for many more years of useful and honorable service'.

The compliment which you have paid me has few precedents, and I value most highly this mark of friendship from your famous and powerful assembly.

With renewed thanks to the United States Senate and to you personally, Mr Vice-President.

Sir Winston S. Churchill to George A. Smathers[1]
(Churchill papers, 2/131)

29 August 1955

My dear Senator,

I have written formally to the Vice-President of the United States asking him to convey my thanks to the Senate for the Resolution which they did me the great honour of passing on July 28. I would now like to express my warm thanks to you, and through you to your fellow sponsors of the Resolution personally for the leading part you played in the matter. The compliment and the felicitous terms in which the Resolution was couched meant much to me.

---

[1] George Armistead Smathers, 1913–2007. US Representative (Dem.) for Florida's 4th District, 1947–51. US Senator, 1951–69. Secretary, Senate Democratic Conference, 1960–7. Chair, Senate Aging Committee, 1963–7; Senate Small Business Committee, 1967–9.

September 1955

Sir Winston S. Churchill: speech
('The Unwritten Alliance', page 270)

7 September 1955   Hastings

THE CINQUE PORTS

Mr Speaker, Your Worships, Jurats, Aldermen, Freeman, Councillors and Combarons, I am greatly honoured today to be bidden to this Court, and by the kindness with which I have been treated. The portrait by Mr Bernard Hailstone[1] which you have presented to me, Mr Speaker, is one which, as you have rightly said, reminds us of those grim struggles of the past. I direct that it should be hung in the Maison Dieu Hall at Dover, side by side with the portraits of other Lords Warden of the Cinque Ports. Mr Hailstone has certainly portrayed in a worthy manner the individual who was, and is still your Lord Warden, and if that be your wish, I am more than content that he should take his place in the long line of those who have endeavoured to serve you well.

I take a great pride in holding the office of Lord Warden of the Cinque Ports. When you approach the end of a long life there is a comfort in looking back on the past, and belonging to an institution of such age and dignity. I am deeply grateful to you, and above all to the Speaker, whom I now address for the first time, for allowing me, and even inviting me to attend the Court of Brotherhood and Guestling, and to see for myself how much business you have to deal with, and, if I may say so, how admirably you discharge it. I am most grateful, Mr Speaker, for your many compliments.

It is quite true that I was called upon to play a part in the War, and, oddly enough, that this entailed many visits to the Cinque Ports. In fact I paid as many visits before October, 1941, when I received from King George VI this

---

[1] Bernard Hailstone, 1910–87. English painter, known for his portraits of the Royal Family and civilian workers in WWII. Educated at Sir Andrew Judd's School, Tonbridge. Trained at Goldsmiths' College and Royal Academy School. Married, 1934, Joan Mercia Kenet Hastings: one child. National Fire Service, London (Fireman Artist), 1939–42. Official War Artist to Ministry of Transport, 1942–4. Official War Artist to SEAC, 1944–5.

cherishable appointment, as I did in later years. Although we had many difficult and dangerous situations to contend with, the worst was over in the autumn of 1941. We were no longer alone. Russia, who could not believe it in spite of our warnings, was substituted by Hitler's Germany as the target for the 1941 offensive, and after that Japan came in – and all that.

We now have to look forward, and not back. We now have to think of the perils of the future, and not those of bygone years. And here we find the United States drawn to us ever more closely as the years go by, and, with the British Commonwealth of Nations, making fair play for all a realizable hope.

Sir Anthony Eden to Sir Winston S. Churchill
(*Churchill papers, 2/216*)[1]

12 September 1955   Chequers

My dear Winston,

I don't know how to thank you for your princely present. As you know I have a weakness for a good cigar, and I shudder to think how many of yours I have smoked in these years.

But I do regard this particular brand the best I have ever enjoyed, and I am proportionally delighted.

Clarissa and I so much enjoyed our visit and I my talks with you about our problems. Whatever else happens they will always be there in some form.

We both send our best wishes for your stay in France. With this autumn nip in the air, you have chosen the right moment for the change of climate.

Love and gratitude from us both.

Sir Winston S. Churchill to Lord Beaverbrook
(*Beaverbrook papers*)

18 September 1955

My dear Max,

We are all spreading out beautifully.[2] The Soames are in your jolly little house, which has everything they can want. I wish they were going to stop longer. I have begun painting that other daub half way down the wall and I shall still have another try at it. Everything is going as well as it can, and I look forward to a delightful rest. Clemmie has taken another good turning, and I hope she may get a real break.

[1] This letter was handwritten.
[2] At La Capponcina, Max Beaverbrook's house at Cap d'Ail in the South of France.

There are so far as I can see no lizards, but there are two cats with whom we have made friends, or sort of friends. The violet heather looks lovely. Thank you so much for lending me this beautiful place.

When exactly are you thinking of going to Canada?

Sir Winston S. Churchill to Lord Moran
(Churchill papers, 1/54)

26 September 1955

My dear Charles,

I have been very well, and lived an idle life except at the Book and painting. I have taken one minor so far since arriving, in two parts. Memory lags and tickles tease. I eat, drink and sleep well.

I am sorry about Ike.[1] He will be a great loss.

Kindest regards to you and your wife.

Sir Winston S. Churchill to John Raeburn Green[2]
(Westminster College papers)

29 September 1955

Dear Mr Green,

I am grateful to you for the invitation which you have extended to me to be present at the inauguration of Dr Robert L. D. Davidson[3] as fifteenth President of Westminster College. I am only sorry that, much as I should like to be present in person at the Convocation, this will not be possible.

It was within your hospitable walls, more than nine years ago, that I had the honour of speaking about the perils and opportunities of the world as I then saw them. Since then we have experienced many of the dangers about which I spoke, and even now the benefits of lasting peace and freedom from tyranny are still denied to millions of people. There have been many changes in the world in the last nine years, but although in recent months some of the

---

[1] President Eisenhower suffered a coronary thrombosis on Sep. 25. It appeared that he would not run for office again, but in February 1956 he announced that he would.

[2] John Raeburn Green, 1894–1973. Educated at Westminster College, Fulton, Mo., and Harvard Law School. Married, 1917, Elisabeth Haskell Cox. Member, Legal Section, Secretariat of the League of Nations, 1920–1. Democratic nominee for Congress, 1928. President, Board of Trustees, Westminster College, 1953.

[3] Robert Laurenson Dashiell Davidson, 1907–98. Known as 'Larry'. Educated at Dickenson College and Temple University. Served US Navy, 1941–5. Associate Dean and Associate Prof. of Social Science, Westminster College, 1945–55; President, 1955–73. As President, oversaw the building of the Churchill Memorial and Library. President Emeritus of Westminster College, 1973–98.

clouds seem to have rolled away, we still require that constancy of mind and persistency of purpose which I described when I spoke to you.

The years which have passed since then have also seen continued co-operation between our two great English-speaking peoples. This close and fraternal relationship which I suggested was necessary for our mutual strength and security will, I know, be continued in the future.

It is not only for itself that I value the invitation which you have sent me, but as a symbol of this relationship. I know that Westminster College, under its new President, will continue in its generous attitude of friendship towards all those who share the ideals which have led our countries in the past and lead them still.

Sir Winston S. Churchill to Alan Hodge and Denis Kelly
(Churchill papers, 4/27)

30 September 1955

I have made a preliminary attempt at the Preface. Print it at once, and see they get to work at it first thing on Monday morning. I do not consider that this is its final form.

It would be very nice if one or both of you could come out about the 10th of October as my guests. There is an excellent hotel in Cap d'Ail.

October
1955

Lord Moran to Sir Winston S. Churchill
(Churchill papers, 1/54)

3 October 1955

My dear Winston,

I was delighted to hear from you,[1] and to get such an excellent report. It is most encouraging.

I was hoping that Ike was nearly out of the wood. Probably today's bulletin means only a temporary set-back. There is only one danger in coronary thrombosis, the liability of a second attack. In the first fortnight this is not at all a remote possibility, but after that time the chances are much better, though the danger is always present. I don't remember how many years it is since Cunningham,[2] the sailor, had a coronary thrombosis, I think after cutting down a tree. The man to whom the Ministry of Health most often turns for advice had a bad coronary thrombosis nine years ago, and has led an active life since. He often helps Dorothy in the garden. If I were in Ike's shoes I should count it no more than a provisional notice to quit.

I rashly undertook to review the book about Group-Captain Cheshire[3] for the *Sunday Times*. He reminds me of Wingate,[4] and there is the same

[1] See letter of Sep. 26, reproduced above (p. 2043).
[2] John Henry Dacres Cunningham, 1885–1962. Entered RN as a Cadet, 1900. Served as Navigator on HMS *Renown*, 1917, and HMS *Lion*, 1918. Asst CNS (Air), 1937; 5th Sea Lord and Chief of Naval Air Services, 1938. Commanded 1st Cruiser Sqn, 1938–41. Took part in the Norwegian campaign (evacuation of Namsos), May 1940. Naval Cdr, Dakar expedition, Sep. 1940. 4th Sea Lord and Chief of Supplies and Transport, 1940–2. Knighted, 1941. C-in-C, Levant, 1943. C-in-C, Mediterranean, and Allied Naval Cdr, 1943–5 (including Anzio and South of France landings). 1st Sea Lord, 1946–8.
[3] Geoffrey Leonard Cheshire, 1917–92. Educated at Stowe School and Merton College, Oxford. Served in RAF, reaching rank of Gp Capt., 1937–46. Official British observer at dropping of atomic bomb on Nagasaki, Aug. 1945. Founded Leonard Cheshire Disability, 1948. Baron, 1991.
[4] Orde Charles Wingate, 1903–44. Born in India. Educated at Charterhouse. 2nd Lt, RA, 1923; Capt., 1936. Attached to Sudan Defence Force, 1928–33. On special appointment (Intelligence) in Palestine and Transjordan, 1936–9 (wounded, despatches, DSO). On active service, 1939–44 (despatches, two bars to DSO), first in Abyssinia, and then as Cdr, Special Force, India Command in Burma. Killed in an aeroplane crash during a tropical storm, while on a visit to one of his units, 24 Mar. 1944.

instability. I am half-way through the book, and unless he becomes more attractive I think I shall get out of the review.

Sir Winston S. Churchill to Lord Beaverbrook
(Beaverbrook papers)

6 October 1955   La Capponcina

My dear Max,

We have had a very pleasant three weeks here, and Clemmie is better. The Chef is excellent, and the garden lovely. I have painted another picture, and so far I have not spoiled it, which is something.

We dined with the Prefet des Alpes Maritimes[1] the other night, and I was glad to feel myself sincerely in the mood to congratulate France on clearing out of the United Nations <u>pro tem</u> and also on not going to Russia <u>now</u>. I am getting a bit tired of this Nehruism, and I gather you are too. The Americans must have learned a lot.

Mr Billmeir[2] of Lloyds has lent us a very convenient 200-ton yacht which awaits our beck and call. Clemmie is delighted with it, and I went to San Remo yesterday. But really I very rarely leave the garden which I like so much.

I think of you in your <u>cold, bleak, winter-ridden country</u> with wonder and admiration that you have made this sacrifice for me. But perhaps you like to do it. That would only make it better.

Clemmie sends her love.

Sir Winston S. Churchill to Lord Beaverbrook
(Churchill papers, 2/211)

10 October 1955   La Capponcina

My dear Max,

Life at your Villa is so pleasant and peaceful that I wonder whether you could keep me longer than the 31st October. I could then fly over for my engagements in England in November and December, and return to this sunshine world. I hope, however, that if this were possible you would allow me to engage my own cook and pay for the housekeeping, because I do not want to be a burden on you. When you said to me that you were not returning yourself till the 1st March I wondered whether something like this might be possible.

---

[1] Pierre-Jean Moatti, 1912–84. French lawyer and civil servant. Born in Constantine, Algeria. Educated at College of Law of Algiers. Married, 1940, Isabella Béatrice Carmélite Shomorowsky. Prefect of Oise, 1951–4; of Alpes-Maritimes, 1954–67.

[2] Jack A. Billmeir, 1900–63. Founded Stanhope SS Co., 1934. Member of Shipowners' Advisory Panel of Lighthouse Commencement, 1946–57. Prime Warden, Shipwrights' Co., 1962–3.

It may be, however, that you have already made other arrangements, in which case my goodwill and gratitude to you continue unabated.

Alan Hodge to Sir Winston S. Churchill
(Churchill papers, 4/26)

10 October 1955

Dear Sir Winston,

I am greatly looking forward to seeing you on Saturday next.

With the help of Mr Deakin, I have been reading through the page proofs of the first book of your Volume. Nothing arises with which we should trouble you. As neither of us felt expert on this period, we thought it worthwhile to ask a member of the British Museum staff to scrutinise dates and names and facts. He has done so – his name is Mr R. A. G. Carson.[1] He has fished patiently, but not caught more than five or six sprats, the biggest of which is that Constantius, on page 29, was not born at York but died there. It is reassuring to know that he has found so little to question. I would suggest that he deserves payment in excess of his findings. Would you agree to pay him 25 gns.?

Sir Winston S. Churchill to Lady Churchill
(Baroness Spencer-Churchill papers)

20 October 1955   La Capponcina

My darling,

Today it is raining, and the prophets predict at least two days of similar weather. There is no doubt you were well advised to leave when you did.

I have been working at the book. I hope that Miss Pugh gave you the ninth and tenth sections. You must not judge by the end. It is incomplete, and I have not looked at it (except 'The Great Republic') for fifteen years. There is, however, plenty of time, as it is not required till October 1958.

I have bidden Hodge and Kelly to lunch each day, and dined alone with Anthony. We have been to the Casino on two occasions, and so far I am £90 to the good, (never having staked a fiver). I think, however, I shall probably go again as no mention of it has appeared.

I am perplexed at Max not answering. Ten days have passed. If by the end of the week no reply by letter or telegram is received, I shall return to England on the 31st. There is no doubt I am in better health.

---

[1] Robert Andrew Glendinning Carson, 1918–2006. Educated at Kirkcudbright Academy and Glasgow Caledonian University. Capt., RA, 1940–6. Asst Keeper, Dept of Coins and Medals, British Museum,1947; Deputy Keeper, 1965–78; Keeper, 1978–83. Wrote *Late Roman Bronze Coinage* (1960) and *Coins of the Roman Empire* (1990).

I will keep you informed by telegrams. The posts often take three or four days. You seem to be having stormy weather.

Tell me what yr doctor said. Are you not making slow but sure progress? I think so much of you and all your kindness to your poor [drawing of a pig]. I am looking forward to a letter from you when the post comes tomorrow. You have been gone 5 days. But I expect you will say 'where is yours'. The common difficulty is that there is little to tell.

All my love & many kisses,
Your ever loving husband

Christopher Soames to Sir Winston S. Churchill
(Churchill papers, 1/56)

23 October 1955

My dear Sir Winston,

I am afraid Pinnacle[1] didn't run very well. I was not very pleased with Nightingall,[2] as it was obvious during the race that she was not at her best and, as I pointed out to him afterwards, it should not be necessary to take a horse to the racecourses to find that out.

The Stud is going according to plan, and Carey Foster[3] is spending a lot of time there getting it organised in the way he wants. The foals are not looking so well as they did when they were at Chartwell, and I am a little worried about them: but they are always bound to go back a bit after they have been weaned, and I hope that soon they will begin to pick up again. Carey Foster agrees that they do not look as well as they should, but hopes for better things before long.

The Farm Accounts look very well, and I think that you will be pleased with the results following on the wonderful harvest that we had this year. I believe Cox[4] is writing to you to give you details.

The Conference was not very exciting, though your telegram was well received. Anthony got a good cheer, but there is a widespread feeling that the Government hasn't got a firm enough grip of affairs – there is too much drift and not enough evidence of decision on many outstanding problems. I am sending you under separate cover a copy of *The Recorder* of this week and last week which reflects the opinion of many.

As you know, the House meets again on Tuesday; and I will write to you during next week to let you know what I hear.

[1] Thoroughbred acquired by Churchill in 1953. Won only one race, in 1955.

[2] Walter Nightingall, 1895–1968. Racehorse trainer. Trained to be a jockey, but retired at age 14 after fracturing his skull at Windsor racecourse. Trained horses for Churchill, including (as well as Pinnacle) Welsh Abbott, Tudor Monarch and Colonist.

[3] Arnold Carey Foster. Veterinarian. Churchill's Stud Master, 1955.

[4] Percy Walter Cox, 1888–1975. Estate Manager at Chartwell.

Lady Churchill and Sarah are coming down to Chartwell for the weekend and are mealing with us. We have not yet seen them since they got back. Mary and the children are all well and send you much love. We all hope that you will come home soon. It was lovely being with you at the Villa, and we both enjoyed it so much: it was sweet of you to give us such a lovely holiday. I quite understand your not being in any hurry to come back, but for purely selfish reasons we do hope that you will do so soon.

Sir Winston S. Churchill to Lady Churchill
(*Baroness Spencer-Churchill papers*)

26 October 1955   La Capponcina

My darling,
The weather is very pleasant – bright and calm. The only change is that it has become a little cooler. I am very glad that Sarah is coming out again on Friday. She will have your room. Anthony M. B. is going home for a week Sunday next, and it will be very nice to have Sarah with me. I am going to invite Bill Deakin to spend a prolonged weekend also. He has been working a great deal at the book. I am reading the volume to be delivered in the first fortnight in November through again. This will be my final. I think it is all right, and will in three or four days turn to the re-read of Volume II.

As regards my correspondence with Max, which I forwarded to you on Monday, he showed himself most kind and obliging, and if on reflection you are still for it I will accept for January and February. I think the fortnight's voyage will do you good, though I will not commit myself finally at this stage whether or not to save time by flying. It is only twenty-two hours, and I am not a good sailor. How many tons is the *Caronia*? However, we can talk this over when I get back on the 15th November. I will, however, write and accept Max's invitation for Pancake House.[1]

I am bidden tomorrow to lunch with Reves and Madame R[2] at the St Pol Restaurant, which I believe is where you went the other day, and I will look at the Matisse Chapel after lunch.

Darling your doctor's account is very vague. Perhaps Sarah will bring me details. I send this letter by Hodge & Kelly who are returning home today, so it will reach you tonight, i.e., quicker than a telegram. I am certainly better & am sure I shall be able to do the speeches all right – within the limits. I have a fine set of notes from Christ. The dinner shd be easy.

[1] Nickname for Beaverbrook's home in Nassau.
[2] Wyn-Nelle Russell, 1916–2007. Known as 'Wendy'. Born in Marshall, Texas. Married, 1933, Al Schroeder (div. 1938): one child; 1940, Paul Baron (div. 1946); 1964, Emery Reves (d. 1981). Began her magazine modelling career in New York, 1939. Responsible for revitalizing Villa La Pausa after Emery purchased the French estate from Coco Chanel, 1953. Benefactor, Dallas Museum of Art, 1985; Wendy and Emery Reves Center for International Studies, William & Mary College, 1989.

I hear from Christopher that you are going to spend the weekend at Chartwell & that they are 'meeting' you. This seems a good idea. The time passes fairly quickly here. I have been every night to the Casino! & not a word in the Press, & am still playing on my winnings. When they stop I shall stop too.

Darling one I think of you so much & of how we are to lead a happy life. I was quite content with Nov. 15 as my date for going home. It will be interesting to get in touch with political affairs again.

I am so glad you like the Nassau plan.

Sarah will bring me news of Diana. I have some now. She is vy dear to me.

I am afraid this is a vy discursive letter, but I know you will receive it with kindness & I hope pleasure.

Always my tender love my dear one & many many kisses.

Your devoted husband

[Drawing of a pig]

Christopher Soames to Sir Winston S. Churchill
(Churchill papers, 1/56)[1]

27 October 1955

My dear Sir Winston,

The party did not like the budget – too many bitter memories of how we used to attack the Socialists when they increased the purchase tax to combat inflation. Now we do the same thing. Broadly speaking they felt it wd have been better to have removed the subsidies on bread and milk and increased the National Assistance level so as not to hurt the poorest. Also they feel that Rab's excuses for not doing more to prune Government expenditures were very lame. You will have seen that Rab has put purchase tax onto essential homeland goods like cooking utensils – this will bring him in £15 million in a full year. Why, people ask, annoy people to this extent for so small a return? Rab seems <u>very</u> tired, mentally as well as physically.

Anthony took me on one side in the lobby. He was full of charm, very agreeable and waxed confidential. He told me, for <u>no one's ears but your own</u>, that the reason that he had postponed the reshuffle was because he had decided to move Rab to Harry Crookshank's job. He therefore had to wait until this budget and its aftermath of the Finance Bill was out of the way, otherwise it wd have meant a double shuffle. Anthony couldn't have been nicer. He said it was on his conscience that he owed you an explanation as to why he had postponed the changes, but that he had been so overwhelmed of late that he had not had time to write to you as he would have wished. He added that he felt he also owed me an explanation which I thought was indicative and hopeful.

---

[1] This letter was handwritten.

Lady Churchill kindly invited me to stay here this week. On Tuesday the Barlow-Wheelers[1] came to lunch. Apparently all is fine at Woodford and they are much looking forward to your visit on the 18th. Lady Churchill has a slight cold and is deeply worried about Diana; she is coming to Chartwell this weekend and will meal with us like last weekend. I hope we will be able to comfort her a little.[2]

Maria is here tonight and goes back to Chartwell tomorrow. She asked me to send you much, much love. We all long for your return.

PS. A number of back-benchers turned up to me yesterday and asked me to take over the Chairmanship of the 1922 Committee!

Sir Winston S. Churchill to Lady Churchill
(Baroness Spencer-Churchill papers)

30 October 1955   La Capponcina

My darling,

I think it would be a very good idea for me to stay the 15th, 16th and 17th at No. 28, and motor to the Hawkey Hall for the Monkhams Dinner on the Friday, 18th. We could motor back to Chartwell thereafter thro the Blackwall Tunnel. I should like to stay at Chartwell the weekend and possibly longer. I have given the Headmaster of Harrow the choice of Wednesday 23rd and Thursday 24th November for my visit to Harrow to hear the Harrow songs. Perhaps the cook problem will be solved by then.

I have had a full letter from Christopher, and I think it is working out very satisfactorily. He will probably represent the War Office in the House of Commons instead of the Admiralty when the reconstruction of the Services takes place.

Sarah is back and great fun. You will probably see AMB early next week. I am relying on him to convey these letters. They reach their destination faster than a telegram.

I will today write to Max accepting Pancake House for January and February.

The Billmeirs came to lunch yesterday. I thought very well of them both. I do not think that the epithet 'cocky' at all applies to him. He struck me as being a very simple, active, and competent man. After lunch they took us to see a villa here which has been empty for twenty years, in a vast forest exactly above Monte Carlo, which would have much to recommend it if I were twenty years younger and everything else was the same. You need not have any anxiety that I shall commit you to anything.

---

[1] William Hubert Barlow-Wheeler, 1909–81. Known as 'Hugh'. Churchill's political agent in Woodford.

[2] Diana frequently suffered from depression.

I must include my weather report. The morning hitherto is overcast, but the sun is now coming through and I think we are going to have a fine afternoon.

Darling I am indeed sorry for yr cold: but I think yr bed-sitting room is a good place for a cure. I send you all my love, & hope we may make good plans for the New Year. You have my most tender thoughts. It is quite cleared-up now & I wish indeed you were with us.

Your ever loving & devoted husband
[Drawing of a pig]

November 1955

Sir Winston S. Churchill to Sir Gerald Kelly
(Churchill papers, 2/124)

2 November 1955

My dear Sir Gerald,
   Thank you for your kind suggestion,[1] but I do not contemplate such a display in my lifetime.

Sir Winston S. Churchill to Lady Churchill
(Baroness Spencer-Churchill papers)

9 November 1955   La Capponcina

My Darling,
   I am looking forward to returning on Monday and seeing you all again. I think you will find me better, and I have no doubt about getting through all right on Friday at Hawkey Hall.
   I have studied carefully the results of your consultation with Barlow Wheeler, and I will do what you advise in making good the arrears of £50 per annum and in writing to him a note of appreciation.
   We have engaged ourselves in reconnoitring houses, but without any result. Do not be alarmed therefore by anything you read in the *Nice-Matin*.
   Will you give us dinner on Monday night. It would be nice to ask Anthony M. B. and his wife, and of course I should like to see Randolph and June, and Mary and Christopher if they are free.
   I am leaving my speech till I return. The Government seem to be getting through all their Parliamentary difficulties all right, but it is difficult to judge from out here.

---

[1] Kelly had asked if the Royal Academy could mount an exhibition of Churchill's paintings, which were held at Chartwell.

Darling one I think so much of you & hope & trust you are making progress. I love you vy much my dearest Clemmie & feel sure you reciprocate these sentiments wh spring from my heart.

> Your devoted husband
> [Drawing of a pig]

Sir Winston S. Churchill to Field Marshal Lord Montgomery
(Churchill papers, 2/143)

9 November 1955

My dear Monty,

I had hoped to give you a budgerigar for your birthday, but Commander Fogg Elliot,[1] who rears and trains them, has told me that he was unable to get one ready for you in time. Accordingly I propose to give you the bird for Christmas. I hope you will like this.

Sir Winston S. Churchill to Lord Beaverbrook
(Churchill papers, 2/211)

9 November 1955 La Capponcina

My dear Max,

I am approaching the end of a delightful visit here. We leave on Monday. I have Diana and Sarah with me, and Montague Browne, who used to be my Private Secretary and is a great friend. Diana seems very well, though she is still undergoing hospital treatment. It has all been a very pleasant break, and I now return rested, and I think invigorated, to England for a few weeks before I again become your guest at Pancake House. You have been very kind to me, and I am most grateful to you for it.

---

[1] Oliver Fogg-Elliot, 1902–78. Retired RN Cdr known for breeding excellent budgerigars, including one named Toby that Dido Cairns gifted to Churchill. See letter of 14 Dec. 1954, of reproduced above (p. 1855).

NOVEMBER 1955

Sir Winston S. Churchill to Alan Hodge
(Churchill papers, 4/27)

10 November 1955   La Capponcina

My dear Hodge,

I send you 'A', which is a note by Wood[1] on copyright. It seems to me very stupid that the works of celebrities like Caesar and Tacitus should be unquotable except with their translators' names. Surely anyone has a right to translate Caesar himself, and the numbers of words are very small. I have written to Cassells on the subject, and forwarded to you a copy of my letter to them.

Reves has given me back the amended text which I proposed of the Preface. He has had lengthy telephonings with French, German, Italian and Scandinavian publishers, showing what they want for their editions. I am quite willing to cut out 'of the English-speaking peoples' at the bottom of the first page in the foreign editions. I think that the words I have deleted in red at the bottom of page 3 and beginning of page 4 are not important and can be omitted from all editions, including the English. I am a little more doubtful about the closing sentence. Perhaps you will let me know when I arrive next week.

Mr Literary Wood made me feel that a vortex might break out in the detailed final correction of the First Volume which could be avoided if he were out here. The posts are very tardy. As a matter of fact it will be better to settle things in England, which we will do next week. I have told him to go back on Saturday. I think Cassells should have told me about turning over to Clowes.[2] However, we will settle everything in the weekend following my return.

I have a speech of modest dimensions which a little overhangs me till Friday, 18th, but I will see you on Tuesday morning and you could tell me how things are going.

Sir Winston S. Churchill to Alan Hodge
(Churchill papers, 4/27)

12 November 1955

I send you by Mr Wood four more signatures. I have worked on those into which Mr Wood has put the corrections which have reached him from the various quarters. You are responsible for sending them to the printer.

The only point of importance is on page 127 – 'seven hundred vessels'

---

[1] Charles Carlyle Wood, 1875–1959. Editor and proof-reader for Churchill, first in the 1930s, working on *Marlborough*, and again from 1948 on *The Second World War* and *A History of the English-Speaking Peoples*. Referred to by Churchill as 'Mr Literary Wood' to distinguish him from the financial consultant 'Mr Accountant Wood'.

[2] William Clowes & Sons, printers.

carrying only seven thousand men is absurd. I expect myself that the seven thousand men were warriors in character and substance, and that they had eight or ten thousand more armed dependants. However, this cannot be proved, and modern historians are trying to cut down the numbers in all the battles. Let me know what your solution is. Later on, in the Battle of Towton, another instance occurs, where the Lancastrian fugitives, although now put at a very small number, are able to dam the stream and make bridges with their bodies. I should think myself there were fifty thousand men at Towton.

I have one more of Wood's corrected proofs which I have not yet seen. Six more have arrived this morning.

Sir Winston S. Churchill to Alan Hodge and Denis Kelly
(Churchill papers, 4/27)

November 1955[1]

Although these two chapters, the Saxon Dusk and The Norman Invasion, are in different books, they are very closely related, and in fact overlap. From the time Godwin dies in 1053 (see page 10, volume I, chapter VIII) Harold 'was virtual ruler of England for the next thirteen years'. During this period all his adventures and contacts with William of Normandy took place. The contacts between Normandy and England were very close during the last twenty years of the reign of Edward the Confessor. Westerham Church is built with stone from Ouisterham, where we landed in 1944 in Normandy, and the name of Westerham as well as the stone may have come from there. The relationship of these two chapters must be reconsidered.

Coming to chapter IX: pages 2, 3 and 4 have a good many repetitions, and require simplifying. It is of no use introducing, as on page 3, an epitome of the history of Normandy, which had already been playing a great part in our affairs, and was itself nearly a hundred years old. It might well be that a good deal of the first part of chapter IX should be included in chapter VIII. IX would then begin with a summary of England at the death of Edward the Confessor, and next a summary of Normandy, already interwoven in volume VIII until the death of Edward the Confessor, with any comparison that may be convenient. The narrative beginning on page 4 reads well to pages 5, 6, 7 and 8, and of course the Battle of Hastings is a good tale.

---

[1] The day is not specified on the original document.

Sir Anthony Eden to Sir Winston S. Churchill
(Churchill papers, 2/216)

13 November 1955

My dear Winston,

Welcome home. I hope that you have had plenty of sunshine.

We have had our troubles, economic and otherwise, but are battling through.

Geneva was not good. The Bear would only move backwards. The question is what we should do next. I am inclined to think that there should be no further meeting of Foreign Secretaries until we have had a go at Bulganin and Khrushchev as our guests here in April.

Ike is recovering but I am afraid it will be a little time yet before he can do serious business again. Adenauer is also better but I fear not too stalwart. You can imagine how we have missed them both.

Do let us know when you will be in London and come and have a quiet meal with us.

Clarissa and I send all love to you both.

Sir Winston S. Churchill to Sir Anthony Eden
(Churchill papers, 2/216)

15 November 1955

My dear Anthony,

Thank you so much for your kind letter of welcome.

I have watched with attention your battle, and it seems to me that you are getting along pretty well. I have got a speech in my Constituency to deliver on Friday, and this hangs over my head in a disproportionate manner.

Do you think you and Clarissa would come to luncheon or dinner on Tuesday or dinner on Wednesday next?

Randolph S. Churchill to Sir Winston S. Churchill
(Churchill papers, 2/127)

15 November 1955

The two dominant events in world affairs since I spoke to you last have been the breakdown in the Geneva talks and the grave deterioration of our affairs in the Eastern Mediterranean and the Middle East. No one could have tried harder or acted in better faith to procure understanding with the Russians than did President Eisenhower and Sir Anthony Eden; and their efforts have been admirably sustained by Mr Foster Dulles and Mr Macmillan. I myself shared the hope that the new Soviet regime which came to power after the death of Stalin might be prepared to discuss in a genuine mood of conciliation methods by which East and West could live together, but it now seems plain that Soviet Russia is determined to persevere with the cold war.

The interval between the two Geneva meetings has been used by Russia to make as much mischief as possible in the Middle East. The Russian tactics have taken the cynical form of irresponsibility placing arms in the hands of the Egyptians, who have ever since 1949 shown that they wished to destroy the State of Israel which was brought into being by the actions of the United Nations.

The situation is one of great delicacy. It may be taken for granted that neither Britain nor the United States would stand idly by and allow the Egyptians and their allies to pitch the Jews into the sea. It would not, however, be a satisfactory answer to the problem simply to give more arms to the Jews as the Egyptians are armed by the Communists. Such a policy pursued by the great powers could only end in war, and what we wish to achieve is peace. It seems to me that urgent and unwearying thought must be concentrated on finding a means whereby either the United Nations or the great powers of the West can provide effective safeguards to restore the balance of power and the balance of arms in the Eastern Mediterranean. Britain, France and the United States are already committed up to the hilt to defend Egypt against Israeli aggression, and Israel against Egyptian aggression. What we need to do now is to make effective plans to discourage any such aggression, and to make sure that if aggression comes it will be the aggressor who will be defeated. A solution of this problem should surely not be beyond the wit or the strength of the Western Powers.

Sir Winston S. Churchill: speech
('The Unwritten Alliance', pages 273–4)

18 November 1955　　　　　　　　　　Monkhams Ward Dinner and Dance

CONSTITUENCY SPEECH

I will not conceal from you the pleasure that I felt at the result of the General Election. Not for ninety years had a Government improved its position at a subsequent election, and it was naturally a source of considerable satisfaction that we managed to increase our majority to so significant an extent last May. This result was due to the fact that the people had seen the Conservative Party in power for three years in difficult circumstances with a minute majority in the House and had liked what they had seen. It was also due to the hard work of thousands of keen party workers up and down the country who had not spared themselves in their efforts to support the Government and to keep the

Conservative cause and Conservative ideals before the eyes of the people. We seek a free and varied society where there is room for many kinds of men and women to lead honourable, useful, and happy lives. We are fundamentally opposed to all systems of rigid uniformity in our national life, and we have grown great as a nation by indulging tolerance rather than logic across the centuries.

It is very nice to be back in Woodford again. It is quite a time since we were last together. One way and another I have been rather busy these last few years, and when Parliament rose for the summer recess I thought it would be a good idea to take a holiday abroad and get some rest and sun. It was very enjoyable, but there is nothing like coming home again. My wife and I have spent a few days in our home in London, and here we are in our political home of Woodford.

I am not going to make a long speech tonight, because the purpose of this gathering is to dine and to dance. I have, however, put a few notes on paper, because I have always been a bit shy of the really extemporary speech ever since I heard it said that an extemporary speech was not worth the paper it was written on.

A lot of things have been happening in the political world recently, and there is certainly plenty to think and talk about. We had an autumn Budget. The Socialists have pounced on this with glee, for as they have no policy themselves to put before the nation they grasp every opportunity to pour scorn on the efforts of the Government to steer the country through its difficulties. Of course, the Socialists are in great difficulties themselves. They appreciate that the electorate has at last realized that the whole theme of Socialism has been based upon the fallacy of nationalization. They realize that if they continue with their long-proclaimed policy to nationalize all the means of production, distribution, and exchange, they have no chance of gaining the support of the majority of the electorate. Yet if they remove nationalization from their policy, there is very little left of Socialism. They now say that they are going to spend three years thinking up a new policy. And so for the next three years the country is fated to suffer the Opposition party in the House of Commons without an alternative policy, indulging in nothing more useful than vituperation and destructive criticism. This is not a very helpful contribution to the process of Parliamentary government.

I much look forward to the Young Conservative Rally on 5 December when I will unfold my thoughts about the political situation and the problems that assail us. But tonight I only want to say how truly delighted Lady Churchill and I are to be back with our friends in Woodford. I hope you will all have a most agreeable and successful evening, and that you will enjoy the dance. I am afraid my days of dancing are over, but I would like to watch you doing it, and I look forward to being back again with you in a fortnight's time.

Sir Winston S. Churchill: speech
(Churchill papers, 2/336)

24 November 1955   Harrow School

I thank you all very much for your kindness and the welcome you have given me. But I thank you all the more for the songs which you have sung and the beautiful way in which you have sung them.

I was a three-yearer and even a four-yearer – I achieved that when I was here. But what about the sixteen-yearer? Because I have been coming for sixteen years if I calculate it rightly – this is my sixteenth visit here since the beginning of the Great War and every time you have cheered my heart and have given us a very jolly hour.

Now we have had alas a sad loss since last year. Mr Leo Amery has gone. He used to come down with me. Half a dozen times we came from London together and went back together and I know how great was his interest in Harrow and how great was his love of Harrow. I am sure that you will think it right of me to mention in passing his name.

We have, I rejoice to see, Lord Alexander, my comrade and officer in the great war, who is looking as fresh and as fit as ever and could, I have no doubt, if circumstances required it walk off and lead an army in any direction we wished. Also I see some of my colleagues here who have come down. They have an all-night sitting, I believe, to go back to. But I am going to take advantage of the Chief Whip's courtesy to go to bed. But all the same I think that it is a very agreeable gathering that we have here and I hope that it may long continue. I will certainly come as long as I am here available on duty.

Sir Winston S. Churchill to Lord Beaverbrook
(Churchill papers, 2/211)

26 November 1955

My dear Max,

[. . .]

I am very sorry to abandon my visit to Nassau, and worried by the fear that I have caused you inconvenience. I had, however, become increasingly attracted to the Riviera, which is so handy to get at and avoids long journeys. You have been so kind to me, and the nine weeks I spent as your guest were so pleasant and peaceful that, as perhaps you have seen, I have been looking about for a dwelling of my own where we could be neighbours. I am now exploring two retreats. The late French Premier, or was he President, Tardieu,[1] found a place

---

[1] André Pierre Gabriel Amédée Tardieu, 1876–1945. Educated at Lycée Condorcet. Sat in French Chamber of Deputies for Seine-et-Oise, 1914–24; for Territoire de Belfort, 1926–36. Minister of Liberated Regions, 1919–20. Minister of Transportation, 1926–8. Minister of the Interior, 1928–30.

in the mountains behind Mentone about ten miles inland, which they would sell furnished, I believe, for 27 million francs, which is approximately £27,000. Tardieu built this place. He guillotined the mountain to make a flat space and built upon the summit a rather jumbled house, which I think a little alteration might make acceptable to me.

Another place which seems suitable is in the Eze curve, called Chateau St Laurent. The proprietor came to see me yesterday. He has already got a villa on the peninsula Saint Jean Cap Ferrat, and is quite willing to rent St Laurent to me for, say, a couple of years, with the option to buy it at the end. This would in any case give me the opportunity of looking around.

Of course neither of these is as nice as yours. But I do not want to take advantage of your kindness and generosity, or abuse the hospitality you have so abundantly given me.

Clemmie is now definitely better, and she was very grateful to you for offering your 'big and beautiful' garden. I do hope we have not upset your plans by our not being able to come to Nassau.

What date do you contemplate publishing your new book? I think you said to me March. If so, it will be all right, because I do not come out in volume form in England or America till 23rd April.

President Dwight D. Eisenhower to Sir Winston S. Churchill
(Churchill papers, 2/217)

26 November 1955

Dear Winston,

This medallion, struck to commemorate your eighty-first birthday, is a timely recognition both of your lifelong friendship toward the United States and of the incalculable debt owed you by all mankind for your unfaltering defense of peace with justice, and the freedom of men.

The English-speaking peoples – and the entire world – are the better for the wisdom of your counsel, for the inspiration of your unflagging optimism and for the heartening example of your shining courage. You have been a towering leader in the quest for peace, as you were in the battle for freedom through the dark days of war.

In that light, the medallion is a token of America's enduring gratitude. But more than that, it sharpens in our minds today the eternal faith that the forces of evil cannot triumph over men whose courage is many times fortified by dedication to human freedom, to human rights, to the God-guided destiny of free men.

Warm sentiment is mingled with gratitude as I send this medallion, provided

---

PM, 1929–30, 1930, 1932. Minister of Agriculture, 1931. Minister of War, 1932. Minister of Foreign Affairs, 1932. Minister of State (without portfolio), 1934.

by American friends of yours, to commemorate your birthday. Millions of my countrymen join me in tribute to you on this anniversary and in best wishes for long and happy years ahead.

Sir Winston S. Churchill to Sir Anthony Eden
(Churchill papers, 1/56)[1]

27 November 1955
Chartwell

My dear Anthony,

I had a long talk with RAB yesterday, and I advised him to accept yr offer of leadership of the HofC, without connecting himself with any Departmental office.

It is true that in war time a seat in the War Cabinet gains by such an addition, but in Peace it is only a burden. He seemed convinced.

I think you will have to review your invitation to the Russians in the light of Khrushchev's Indian exhibition;[2] but April is still a long way off.

Sir Anthony Eden to Sir Winston S. Churchill
(Churchill papers, 2/216)[3]

29 November 1955

My dear Winston,

Thank you so much for your letter and for telling me of your talk with RAB. I am most grateful.

The bears are certainly behaving ill; perhaps it would do the British public no harm to see them do so. But, as you say, we don't fortunately have to decide on that yet.

Every good wish for tomorrow.

Sir Winston S. Churchill to President Dwight D. Eisenhower
(Churchill papers, 2/217)

30 November 1955

My dear Friend,

I am deeply grateful for the honour you have done me in presenting me with the beautiful medallion, and for associating with it the friends I am proud to have in the United States.

[1] This letter was handwritten.
[2] Khrushchev was in India, where he was vigorously denouncing capitalism and the West.
[3] This letter was handwritten.

Your letter has moved me more than I can tell you. As you know, it is my deepest conviction that it is on the friendship between our two nations that the happiness and security of the free peoples rests – and indeed that of the whole world. Your eloquent words have once more given me proof, if it were needed, that you share my own feelings and reciprocate my personal affection.

White House: press release
(*Churchill papers, 2/217*)

30 November 1955

The President has sent a special medallion to Sir Winston Churchill for presentation on the occasion of Sir Winston's 81st birthday, November 30. The presentation was made in England on behalf of the President by Ambassador Winthrop W. Aldrich.

The citation on the medal reads:

'Presented to Sir Winston Churchill by President Dwight D. Eisenhower on behalf of his millions of admiring friends in the United States for courageous leadership and in recognition of his signal services to the defense of freedom in which cause his country and the United States have been associated in both peace and war.'

The medallion, three inches in diameter, is of gold. The artist was Mr Gilroy Roberts,[1] head sculptor and engraver of the United States Mint. The face of the medallion bears a representation of Sir Winston's head and shoulders, as taken from the President's portrait of him. The citation is inscribed on the reverse, together with a design of clasped hands flanked by the British and United States shields.

---

[1] Gilroy Roberts, 1905–92. Born in Philadelphia. Asst Engraver and Sculptor, US Mint, 1936–7. Staff Member, Washington DC Bureau of Engraving and Printing, 1937–44. Head Assistant to Chief Engraver, 1944–8. 9th Chief Engraver and Sculptor, US Mint, 1948–64. Best known for designing the John F. Kennedy Half Dollar following President Kennedy's assassination in 1963.

December 1955

Sir Winston S. Churchill: speech
('The Unwritten Alliance', pages 275–9)

5 December 1955   Woodford

YOUNG CONSERVATIVES

The ten eventful years since the war have seen a remarkable resurgence of the Conservative Party on the foundation of universal suffrage. In this nothing has been so important, or so encouraging for the future, as the great accession of strength we have received from the growth and expansion of the Young Conservative movement. For many years our opponents claimed to be the party of youth and the future. It is only too true that earlier generations of young people were misled by the chimera of Socialism, and mistakenly believed that it offered the best prospects for their country and the world. Since the war we have seen Socialism in practice. The practice was a lot less attractive than the theory.

As the fallacies of Socialist theory became apparent more and more young people turned with growing hope and conviction to the Conservative Party. The Young Conservative movement has grown at a remarkable pace, and today its membership of 150,000 makes it the largest movement of its kind in the free world. This splendid body of eager and alert youth played a worthy part in removing the Socialist Government from office, and in securing a Conservative victory at the polls in two successive elections. It is good to learn, too, that your movement is showing no signs of resting on its laurels after these solid achievements. Since the election last May more than fifty new branches have been formed. That is a most hopeful sign.

Our opponents may well envy us this growing and sustained support from the rising generation. In the House of Commons we have nearly three times as many Members under forty as sit on the Opposition benches, and in the party organizations up and down the country they suffer from the same lack of younger workers. At their last annual conference at Margate the Socialists spent a good deal of time in bemoaning the absence of young blood in their movement. The absence is so marked that they have even decided to wind up the Labour League of Youth. Let us then rejoice at the evidence that the principles of Tory democracy appeal to youth with ever-growing power. They appeal because they strike a chord in the breast of every man and woman who puts country first. Our strength springs from the fact that we are a party which serves no class or section. We put the nation first.

There are many reasons why the Socialists have failed to attract youth. Today after more than four years in opposition they still have no policy, no message to give to the country, on any of the big issues of the day. Nationalization of all the means of production, distribution, and exchange was long proclaimed by the Socialist Party as the foundation of their movement. It is certainly the sole practical way in which they could put Socialism into force. But now they are not sure of a single important industry which they would nationalize if they had the power. They hope they will be able to settle their differences, and work out a policy during the next three or four years, in time for the next election. Meantime, they occupy themselves in petty fault-finding about day-to-day affairs in the hope of finding something that will give them a good war-cry. But there will not be an election for three or four years and no one can tell what we shall be talking about then.

'We must go back to the classroom', one of their leaders, Mr James Griffiths, has stated. Well, I don't suppose you want to go back to the classroom with them. Some of you haven't long left it, and now you want to venture out into an expanding future. You have had the advantage of seeing the two rival theories at work in recent years. We had six years of Socialist control, with its shortages, and queues, rationing and austerity, and three major financial and economic crises. Abroad we saw a weakening of our position in the world, and a sad decline from the heights to which, thanks to the valour and determination of our people, we had climbed in 1945.

Since our Conservative policy of national growth was given a chance to work four years ago, there has been a marked improvement in our affairs and prospects. Production has risen, and our general living standards have improved. Shortages have largely disappeared and rationing is not only abolished but forgotten. Nor have any of the fears our opponents professed to entertain been realized. Employment has reached new peaks this year and unemployment has been the lowest ever recorded in peacetime. No savage axe has been wielded against the social services: on the contrary they have been expanded and improved. Wages have risen faster than prices. We are undoubtedly as a nation better fed, better housed, and better off in most material ways than we have ever been.

Who can doubt that the country has chosen wisely between the two roads presented to it? Along one road lay the Socialist State, with all-powerful officials deciding increasingly how everybody shall live, and spending more of what everybody earns. As the State counts for more, the individual man and woman counts for less. On the other road, the Conservative road, the goal is a free life in which there is growing opportunity for the able, and growing protection for the weak and unfortunate. We seek a life in which everybody is encouraged to earn more – and keep more of what is earned: a life in which living standards rise as production rises: and in which more of us can take pride in ownership, and in our working lives enjoy a pride in partnership.

Nobody should be in any doubt that progress can be sustained only by continuing exertions and by every use of ingenuity and adventurous enterprise. The world outside does not owe us a living. We have to earn it, and earn it in a fiercely competitive world. There never has been a nation like ours, densely populated, unable to feed itself from its own resources, but keeping alive by trade and industry and winning for itself a standard of living such as few other countries enjoy. In no other great country in the world would the penalty of failure to earn that livelihood be as heavy or far-reaching.

I am firmly convinced that the one hope of success lies in the quality and native genius of our island race. We must give full scope to the spirit of adventure, adaptability, enterprise, hard work, and contrivance which brought us to a commanding position in the world, and which alone can retain it for us. We have had some reminders this year of the precarious foundations of our existence. Once again our imports have tended to outstrip our exports, there has been a drain on our resources, and measures have been necessary to reduce and limit our home demand on materials and manpower. These measures have not been popular. It will be an ill day when a Conservative Government shrinks from doing right out of any consideration of electoral popularity or favour. Gallup Polls no doubt have their proper place in our modern life, but popularity or unpopularity are poor guides to conduct. From time to time restraint is needed. We must certainly never allow our hard-won prosperity to force up our prices and costs so that our goods cannot compete with those of other countries in world markets. That would be fatal to every hope we cherish for the future. To realize those hopes the Conservative Party puts its faith in expansion, not restriction. If our country faces problems it also has great opportunities. We live in a rapidly expanding age of new discovery, exciting days when the power of science is opening up new vistas of infinite possibility. To seize these chances, to lead the world in the new industrial revolution as we did in the earlier one, is a task for youth.

I have no doubt you have all been following the exhibition which the heads of the Russian State have been making of their tour through India and Burma. It has certainly been a surprising spectacle, and one which Her Majesty's Government will no doubt study carefully before they allow it, with suitable variants, to be repeated here. But the behaviour of their leaders must not lead us to suppose that Russian power and capacity is not growing in many other directions. I will take only one example tonight – technological education. This is an all-important subject in which Great Britain has allowed herself to fall behind. We are already surpassed by Russia on a scale which is most alarming. In the last ten years Soviet higher technical education for mechanical engineering has been developed both in numbers and in quality to an extent which far exceeds anything we have achieved. This is a matter which needs the immediate attention of Her Majesty's Government. It is very fitting that I should talk to the young men and girls I see before me upon it. The Ministry of Education have hitherto relied upon the universities and they have no doubt done their best, but large technical schools should immediately be founded and brought into full and active life if we are – not to keep abreast but even to maintain – our proportionate place in the world. We live in an age of mechanization. Not only do mechanics relieve the body of its labours, but they relieve the mind. Machines can be got which will add up and multiply at a rate and on a scale we could not have been taught at school. I am all for your using machines, but do not let them use you.

We had a debate in Parliament last week about television and whether it should be prevented from anticipating debates impending in the House of Commons. The House of Commons thought not, and I think they were right. But, it is asked, what about free speech? I am all for free speech. I am all for a state of affairs where every man and woman should form his own opinion and express the same to as many as care to listen. But that is quite a different thing to a man getting hold of an instrument and talking, as he could do in this country, to fifteen million people on the particular topics which the House of Commons has indicated that it is going to discuss. Who is going to give this man access to the instrument of such superhuman power? Surely that is a matter which wants looking into before we accord to anyone such an extraordinary multiplication of human power. The House of Commons has been fully justified in taking its time over this, and not allowing its authority to be weakened. Part, perhaps the largest part, of the secret of our country's enduring greatness has been our gift of ensuring the continuity of our island life, of changing with the age while still remaining true to the spirit of the ages. Let our aim continue to be to preserve the inheritance our fathers bequeathed to us, and upon the firm and strong foundations of the past to build for the years to come. High tasks await you. History and geography alike have laid upon us special responsibilities and have given us a place still unique in the world. We have close ties and associations with the British Empire and Commonwealth, with the Atlantic community and the English-speaking world, and with the continent of Europe. To rise to the full opportunity this gives us, we must be solvent and economically strong, faithfully and resolutely earning our own living by the sweat of our brow, and the exertion of our minds. We must make our full contribution to the united strength of the free nations upon which peace depends, and we must develop the resources, and raise the living standards of the Commonwealth and Empire. You will, I am confident, be equal to your opportunity.

DECEMBER 1955

Sir Winston S. Churchill: speech
(*'Winston S. Churchill, His Complete Speeches'*, volume 8, pages 8667–8)

7 December 1955   Drapers' Hall, London

THE WILLIAMSBURG AWARD

I am honoured by the Award which the Williamsburg Trustees have made to me, and I am glad indeed to be the first to receive it.[1] I saw myself nine years ago the wonderful memorial which Mr Rockefeller's father[2] has raised to the history of the United States, and the link which he has provided with the past. No more fascinating gleam exists of a vanished world, embodying as it does the grace, the ease, and the charm of bygone colonial days.

I am also profoundly touched by the personal kindness which has led so many Americans, when I was unable to go to them, to come over here and give this truly remarkable dinner in the Drapers' Hall in London. This memorable event is a proof – if proof were needed – of the unity of thought and sentiment which has come into being between us during this tragic century, and which, I venture to say, is the most important thing in the world. The horizons of life are dark and confused, but I think that most of us here have the sort of feeling that we shall not go far wrong if we keep together. I am very glad to learn that Sir Anthony Eden and the Foreign Secretary, Mr Harold Macmillan, whom we are all so glad to see here tonight, are going over in the New Year for another talk about all those tiresome and difficult matters in which our common interests are involved. They will talk about them on foundations strong, and ever growing stronger, and which will never be broken by force or the threat of force.

Colonial Williamsburg has added a new element to our strength and unity. The Award, and the conception which Mr Rockefeller's father embraced, transcends the bounds of race, creed, and geography, and brings the whole free world within its sphere. The choice is world wide. This, in my view, constitutes the strength of its appeal, and the fact that you should give your first Award to one who is a British subject establishes an even higher and wider level than those bounded by nationality.

I am, however, by blood half American and on my mother's side I have the right to enjoy the early memories of Colonial Williamsburg as much as anyone here. I delight in my American ancestry which gave me in five generations a claim to membership of several celebrated historical institutions across the

---

[1] The Williamsburg Award 'is given to those who have helped preserve and perpetuate the values exemplified by 18th century Williamsburg – liberty, courage, devotion to the dignity of the individual, and responsible citizenship'.

[2] John Davison Rockefeller Jr, 1874–1960. US financier and philanthropist. Educated at Brown University. Best known for financing and directing the construction of the Rockefeller Center in New York City, which employed over 40,000 people during the Great Depression. Helped launch the restoration of Colonial Williamsburg in 1927.

Atlantic. Jerome Park in New York shows that my grandfather took an interest in horse-racing.

It gave me extreme pleasure to hear you read the message which President Eisenhower has sent on this occasion. He is a great friend of mine. For the last fourteen years we have worked together, and it is but a week ago that I had the honour to receive from him the Medallion which bore the imprint of a picture painted with his own hands. His message tonight comes from Gettysburg, and there we have one of those famous names which teach us to forget and forgive as well as to remember.

The Trustees of Colonial Williamsburg have come in a body and have brought with them distinguished guests. Mr Baruch, Mr Harriman, General Bedell Smith were prevented at the last moment from joining our company tonight. I am very glad, however, that we have Admiral 'Betty' Stark[1] and Lew Douglas, who works so tirelessly for Anglo-American unity, and General Gruenther, the NATO Supreme Allied Commander in Europe. My own British friends, comrades, and colleagues are too numerous for me to attempt to mention, and I can only express my gratitude that they should be here tonight. It has been to me an occasion I shall never forget.

Mr Winthrop Rockefeller[2], you have presented to me a Town Crier's Bell as it was made at Colonial Williamsburg in the days of our forefathers. The words you have inscribed on it are inspiring. Its silver tone is gentle. I shall ring it whenever I feel there is duty to be done.

Harold Macmillan to Sir Winston S. Churchill
(Churchill papers, 2/210)

13 December 1955
Confidential

Dear Winston,

You wrote to me from Cap d'Ail on October 10 enclosing a letter from Bernard Baruch Junior, in which he suggested that a British honour should be conferred upon his father.

I have now had time to go into this matter carefully (I am sorry it has taken so long) and have consulted the appropriate authorities. I fear that for the following reason it would be very difficult to fall in with Mr Baruch's suggestion.

We made it a rule during the war – and the rule was reaffirmed after

---

[1] Harold Rainsford Stark, 1880–1972. Known as 'Betty'. Ensign, US Navy, 1905. Capt., USS *West Virginia*, 1933–4, Adm., 1939. Chief of Naval Operations, US Naval Forces in Europe, 1942–5. Present at the Atlantic Conference. Relieved of command following controversy regarding withheld information over Japanese movements leading up to the attack on Pearl Harbor.

[2] Winthrop Rockefeller, 1912–73. Educated at Yale. Served in WWII. Governor of Arkansas, 1967–71.

the war – not to offer awards to any civilian officials or employees of the United States Government in respect of wartime services. This was because under the American Constitution such persons cannot accept foreign awards without the consent of Congress; and we held it to be inconsistent with the dignity of the Crown that an honour conferred by the Sovereign should be subject to the approval of a foreign legislature. We felt obliged to apply this rule not only to salaried officials but also to those who, like Mr Baruch, served the Government for a nominal remuneration (the so-called 'dollar-a-year' men), since they were equally affected by the Constitutional embargo. I understand that for that reason proposals to honour amongst others Wendell Willkie[1] and Harry Hopkins[2] were turned down. Indeed, so far as I know, no British honours have been given to any United States civilians who worked with the United States Government in connexion with the war effort, whether their services were official or unofficial.

Nor do I see how Bernard Baruch could be given an honour in connexion with his work as Chairman of the United Nations Atomic Energy Commission. His undoubtedly great services in that field were rendered in the main to an international body and were not of the kind which we normally recognize by a British award.

I am told that, when Prime Minister, you did actually consider Bernard Baruch for a high honour, in 1954, but that owing to these difficulties you decided to drop the idea. I need hardly say that nothing would give me greater pleasure than to have been able to further a recommendation in which you had taken personal interest. I know that I can count on your friendly understanding of my difficulty.

I return herewith the letter from Mr Bernard Baruch Junior.

Sir Winston S. Churchill: speech
('Winston S. Churchill, His Complete Speeches', volume 8, pages 8668–9)

16 December 1955   Mansion House, London

It is a great pleasure to me to become a Freeman of Belfast and Londonderry. It is all the greater because of the distinguished company who have come over here to give it to me. I thank the Lord Mayor of London for making it possible for us to meet here in this well-known room. I feel embarrassed by

---

[1] Wendell Lewis Willkie, 1892–1944. Born in Indiana. A lawyer and initially a Democrat. Became a Republican in opposition to Roosevelt's New Deal. Republican Party nominee for the Presidency, 1940. Roosevelt's personal emissary to Britain, Soviet Union and China, 1940–1.

[2] Harry Hopkins, 1890–1946. Director of the (New Deal) Works Progress Administration, 1935–8. Secretary of Commerce, 1938–40. Administrator of Lend-Lease, 1941–5. President Roosevelt's closest aide; lived at the White House when he was not on wartime missions to London or Moscow, or in hospital (in 1937 he underwent surgery for cancer of the stomach). Travelled to Moscow on a mission for President Truman, May 1945.

the trouble I have caused. It arises from need and desire to allow a period of rest and quiet to intervene between my laying down the office of Prime Minister and the resumption of civic duties, however attractive or honourable they may be. I can only ask your pardon and that of the people of Belfast and Londonderry for any shortcomings on my part. I am encouraged by your generosity to hope for a favourable response.

I can look back over nearly sixty years of Irish politics in which I have been often actively involved. If my memory serves me rightly, we did not always find ourselves in close and intimate agreement. But for the last thirty-five years of shock and change we have acted together, and when thirty years ago I spoke in the Ulster Hail you accepted with enthusiasm the statement which I made. Let me quote it to you today:

> I can really say that I have tried to do my duty according to my lights, not only in sustaining and supporting the Ulster Government in these difficult years, but also in treating with fair play and consideration the developing Irish Free State, and I am sure the prosperity and peace and well-being of the Irish Free State ranks in your minds only second to that of your own and is intimately connected with your own interests.

I said also:

> I have a very strong feeling that the worst of Ulster's trials and anxieties are over, I may cherish the hope that some day all Ireland will be loyal because it is free, will be united because it is loyal, and will be united within itself and united with the British Empire.

That is thirty years ago, and although names and former relationships have been changed, there is a growing measure of goodwill between the Irish Republic and Northern Ireland which it will not be within the power of a small minority to alter.

I was very glad to see that the Irish Republic has become a member of the United Nations, for I believe the passage of years and a general broadening of thought will show many points on which we shall be in agreement. On none more shall we find ourselves in agreement than in combating the movement towards Communism which has already ceased to make progress in the minds of men and is only sustained by strong governmental systems in countries where other expressions of human thought are not allowed. Both the Lord Mayor of Belfast[1] and the Mayor of Londonderry[2] have in their speeches reminded us of what we went through in the Second Great War, and have

---

[1] Robert John Rolston Harcourt, 1902–69. High Sheriff of Belfast, 1949. Member of Northern Ireland Parliament for Belfast, 1950–5. Lord Mayor of Belfast and *ex officio* member of the Senate, 1955–7. JP for Belfast. Knighted, 1957.

[2] Samuel Sydney Dowds. Married, 1930, Isobel MaCloskie. Optician in Londonderry. Mayor of Londonderry, 1954–7. Chair, Northern Ireland Tourist Board, 1958.

spoken all too kindly of my part in those events. I am glad you think I did my duty, and that both these famous and ancient cities should wish to inscribe my name on their list of Freemen is a distinction which I am proud to enjoy. They are indeed both lists of fame and honour. It is indeed remarkable that the three field marshals whom we have with us today, the most celebrated soldiers we had in the War, 'Brookey', 'Alex', and 'Monty', should all be Irish. They certainly adorn the record which Belfast and Londonderry have made of famous men across the centuries.

Belfast and Londonderry had a great share in the War. To them we owe our routes across the Atlantic Ocean which alone enabled us to dispense with Cork and Kinsale. It was for that reason that the victorious powers did not hesitate to appoint the place of surrender of the enemy's submarine fleet in your harbour. That was a signal honour.

The great exertions made in shipbuilding in both these historic seaports during the War led to a considerable disturbance of the balance of local industry. This has resulted in a proportion of unemployment in Northern Ireland – over six percent – which, translated into terms of the United Kingdom, would mean over a million and a quarter unemployed over here. I am very glad that Lord Chandos, who is with us today, has become Chairman of the Northern Ireland Development Council, whose main business is to bring new industries into Ulster. He tells me that the plant he is establishing at Larne at a cost of eight million pounds has already made its impression upon the unemployed labour, that they are adaptable and easily trained and that the facilities on a general scale to industrialists attracted to establish themselves there by Lord Brookborough's Government are producing good results. All this is satisfactory, and will we hope continue.

Let me thank you in conclusion once again for all your kindness to me, and above all for recognizing the help and inspiration which my wife has been to me during so many years of toil and adventure.

1956

Sir Winston S. Churchill to Lord Beaverbrook
(*Churchill papers, 2/211*)

6 January 1956

Thank you so much for your generous invitation. I realised your difficulties and have made other arrangements to stay with Emery Reves at the Chanel Villa[1] during the latter part of January and all February. Meanwhile I shall be searching for a habitation and will keep you well informed. You are always so good to me.[2]

Sir Winston S. Churchill to John Selwyn Lloyd
(*Churchill papers, 2/128*)

8 January 1956
Private

My dear Selwyn Lloyd,

I am indeed obliged to you for your courtesy in letting me continue to see some of the Foreign Office telegrams. It is of considerable interest to me, and enables me, as a Privy Councillor, to keep in touch with what is going on.

I trust that you will have no objection to Montague Browne continuing to assist me and spending some time with me as conditions allow. As you know, I have a considerable 'aftermath' of foreign and other correspondence arising from my term in office, and it is a help to me to have some official point of liaison.

---

[1] La Pausa, in Roquebrune, Cap Martin, built by Coco Chanel in the early 1930s and purchased by Emery Reves in 1953.

[2] Churchill followed this telegram with one on Jan. 8: 'I have some unfinished daubs which I hope I may go to Capponcina to complete while staying with Reves' and another to Reves on the same date: 'Looking forward much to my visit.'

Field Marshal Lord Montgomery to Sir Winston S. Churchill
(Churchill papers, 2/143)[1]

14 January 1956

My dear Winston,

You will like to have news of the budgerigar. He is doing splendidly and is quite at home at Isington Mill. When I am away, over here or travelling, he lives with my servants and my Corporal batman is teaching him to talk. I hope to be able to report progress on this later on. He has been taught to have a bath in a saucer – and enjoys it.

I do hope you are well and enjoying your rest in the sun.

Sir Winston S. Churchill to Lady Churchill
(Baroness Spencer-Churchill papers)[2]

15 January 1956   La Pausa

My dear One,

I have been worried by your sore throat & temperature; but Drs Barnett & Rosenheim[3] have reassured me, & I now learn they are taking a normal course. If not I will return. I also rang up Maria whose promised morning telegram I await.

We have had so far nothing but clouds & rain. So I have not left this luxurious house & have passed the time mainly in bed revising the Book. They predict a gleam of sunshine this afternoon.

RAB came to dinner with the Birkenheads, but the occasion gave little opportunity for serious talk. Randolph has arrived and is staying with the Onassis[4] on the monster yacht. He had a dangerous voyage, but seems vy well. I do hope you will get back to 28 soon. Toby awaits you there expectantly & Rufus shd be in Vincent's care. The presence of one & the absence of the other shd make the house perfect for what I hope will form a short rest-cure.

Reves told me last night he intended to marry Wendy soon – but privately. She is a charming hostess and asked me to carry my respects to you. All is vy quiet here.

You have all my love, my Darling & I pray for your early cure. Wendy's mother had arthritis and was cured after 4 years of woe.

Your loving husband.

---

[1] This letter was handwritten.

[2] This letter was handwritten.

[3] Max Leonard Rosenheim, 1908–72. RAMC, 1941–6. Physician, South-East Asia Command, 1945–6. Physician, University College Hospital, 1946–50. CBE, 1955. Member, Medical Research Council, 1961–5. President, Royal College of Physicians, 1966–72. KBE, 1967. Baron, 1970.

[4] Aristotle Socrates Onassis, 1906–75. Known as 'Ari' or 'Aristo'. Greek shipping magnate who came to own the largest privately owned shipping fleet in the world. Born in Smyrna, Turkey. Married, 1946, Athina Mary Livanos (div. 1960): two children; 1968, Jacqueline Kennedy.

Sir Winston S. Churchill to Lady Churchill
(Baroness Spencer-Churchill papers)[1]

17 January 1956   La Pausa

My Darling,

All the children go home today by one route or another. Arabella & Celia were both vy sweet to me. Diana will give you accounts. She seems vy well & mistress of herself. Randolph brought Onassis (the man with the big yacht) to dinner last night. He made a good impression upon me. He is a vy able and masterful man & told me a lot about whales. He kissed my hand!

I have passed another morning in bed at the Book. I had a peep outside yesterday, but today the sun has definitely begun to shine & I shall take a walk in the garden after luncheon. We dine with Rab on Wednesday next.

I am so grieved & worried by the news that your throat has not cleared up entirely and that you had a temperature. Dr Rosenheim is a regular informant & he gives me full accounts twice a day. He says the arthritis is better & that his new treatment of it is answering.

My dear One I would so much like to kiss you now. I send you my love by this. You see I have written it by my own paw & no one has seen it. The children will take it home.

Sir Winston S. Churchill to Lady Churchill
(Baroness Spencer-Churchill papers)[2]

17 January 1956   La Pausa

My darling,

I have had so much pleasure & relief at hearing good news of you. Things sound so bad and to be at a distance is vy trying. But this morning when I was awakened at half past nine to hear from Doctor Rosenheim that your temperature was normal I was filled with joy.

I have passed the time since I arrived three quarters in bed & come down to meals. Reves & Wendy are most obliging. They ask the guests I like and none I don't. A few people have written & so we had last night Daisy Fellowes[3] & her young man Hamish Edgar.[4] Daisy was vy sprightly. I remember meeting her in 1918 when she was the Princess de Broglie in Paris. She is wonderfully well

---

[1] This letter was handwritten.
[2] This letter was handwritten.
[3] Marguérite Séverine Philippine, 1890–1962. Known as 'Daisy' and 'the Imbroglio'. Married, 1910, Prince Jean de Broglie (killed in action, 1918), hence her nickname; 1919, Reginald Ailwyn Fellowes, son of Lady Rosamond Spencer-Churchill, sister of Churchill's father. Her villa in the South of France was named Les Zoraïdes.
[4] 'Edgar': error for James Alexander Wedderburn St Clair-Erskine, 1909–73. Known as 'Hamish'. Companion to French society figure Daisy Fellowes. Educated at Eton and Oxford University. Served with Coldstream Guards, WWII.

maintained & kept us all agog. Her young man is coming to play bezique with me this afternoon at 4.

Arthur Soames has also written and he & his wife[1] are to dine tonight. On Wednesday we all go to lunch or dinner with RAB as the weather (which is unbroken clouds) permits. Thursday we are going to paint still-life & garden according as the sun shines.

My darling one I send you all my love. We have devised a means of getting the airplanes to carry the letters by making them into packages. I hope therefore this will reach you today.

With all my heart.
Your loving husband

Sir Winston S. Churchill to Lady Churchill
(Baroness Spencer-Churchill papers)[2]

19 January 1956   La Pausa

My darling One,

I have just heard from Dr Rosenheim that yr improvement continues and that in a few days he expects to return you to 28 & Toby. I am greatly relieved. He says you got up yesterday, & were the better for it. The hospitals have dangers of their own and I long to think of you in your own bunny. He has written me a long letter in wh. he says that arthritis and neuritis have troubled you much less. I do hope this is a proof that the new treatment is making headway.

We went out yesterday for the first time in the week that has slipped by since my arrival. We lunched with RAB who is coming to paint here tomorrow. He is a bit anxious. I reassured him. I shall have to get my paints out. I have not touched them yet.

This is the first day we have had blue sky in small patches, but it is only noon.

I have been working in bed at the Book & have almost finished Volume II. I don't think there will be any difficulty about my retirement, so that anything more I do can be stored in yr hands – if indeed I last so long.

I thought well of Onassis & perhaps I will go and inspect his yacht, wh he wants me to do vy much.

(A gleam of sunshine) Perhaps it portends the Spring. But I am not dependent on the weather except for painting. The days pass by quickly. My cough continues. I always hate having to get up.

My darling I loved your telegram. I do think you are out of the wood. We can then make plans at leisure.

Always your loving husband.

---

[1] Audrey Alma Humphreys. Married, 1949, Arthur Soames.
[2] This letter was handwritten.

PS. It is quite audible talking on the telephone when you feel fit for it. I shd love to hear your dear voice.

Sir Winston S. Churchill to Lady Churchill
(Baroness Spencer-Churchill papers)[1]

21 January 1956   La Pausa

My darling,

It is raining again! We have not had a sunshine day since I arrived – only a few faithful gleams. All the same the time has passed pleasantly. I don't get up till one thirty and have a two hours nap in the afternoon. I shd think I averaged 10 hours sleep a day, & the Book occupies my leisure. The final chapter of Vol II goes off today. I am content with it.

I was so much relieved at your increasing good news, & I hope you will soon be home again. Anthony[2] goes back tomorrow (Sunday) & wd like vy much to come to see you to give you a full account. I am vy much inclined to take him on. From what Norman Brook said I am sure I can deduct his salary from the literary expenses, & also that he can be 'seconded' so as not to leave the service or lose pension rights for two or three years. He is vy companionable & means eventually to choose another career. He is out flying now in Onassis' airplane. It will be his first flight in his own hands for <u>seven</u> years. However there is a pilot & (I hope) dual control.

We are going after luncheon to look at a house wh can be let furnished & in good order for several months at a time, & is said to have many attractions. I shall not commit you to anything permanent. I feel however that I am a burden here as they both mean to stay on – Nothing could exceed Wendy's kindness & they repulse with vigour all suggestions that they want me to go – even after February. Wendy will look after the housekeeping and she is a marvel at this. Do not have any worries. Everything will be temporary & I shall not be committed beyond a couple of months.

I am inviting Diana to come out here during AMB's absence. She said she would like to come & I think the scene & setting will do her good.

My darling one I love you dearly

Your devoted husband

PS. Anthony's air trip was a 'fiasco' (his own expression). The plane wd not get off the ground. So there was no accident. He is back & the motor car will take this letter. It shd reach you tonight.

---

[1] This letter was handwritten.
[2] Anthony Montague Browne.

Sir Winston S. Churchill to Lady Churchill
(Baroness Spencer-Churchill papers)[1]

22 January 1956   La Pausa

Darling,

Anthony leaves this morning and bears this. I am going to make him head of my private office. He will be 'seconded'. He will preserve his pension rights & can go back to the FO at any time. I can with Treasury sanction include his salary in my expenses. I am sure this is a good arrangement.

We went to look at a house yesterday – beautifully situated but in disrepair. I have been made so comfortable here and Wendy is so kind & charming that I am not hurrying renting another house. She persists in begging me to stay, saying in her husband's presence that I have done everything for him & that they never can repay etc. At any rate I shall stay till March. They are keeping a lovely room for you & are most eager you shd try it. Anyhow think it over during your rest cure at 28.

I am telegraphing to Diana to come out for ten days. She will be able to give you a full report.

My dear one I am planning to talk on the telephone to you as I want to hear your voice & to tell you how much I love you.

                                                         Your loving husband

PS. Weather still warm & sultry.

Sir Michael Adeane to Sir Winston S. Churchill
(Churchill papers, 2/532)[2]

24 January 1956   Buckingham Palace

Dear Sir Winston,

As you know the Queen is starting for Nigeria in a few days time and will be there for three weeks. Knowing what an interest you have taken, and take, in her travels she thinks you may like to see the programme which she is going to follow and of which I enclose a copy.

Her Majesty and The Duke of Edinburgh hope that you are finding some sun – there is not much here – and desire me to send you their best wishes. May I please send you my own?

---

[1] This letter was handwritten.
[2] This letter was handwritten.

Sir Winston S. Churchill to Field Marshal Lord Montgomery
(Churchill papers, 2/143)

25 January 1956   La Pausa

My dear Monty,

Thank you very much for your letter with news of the budgerigar.[1] I am so glad he is doing well, and to hear of the good arrangements you have made.

We have not had one day of sunshine since arriving here, but I am very comfortable and idle.

Sir Anthony Eden to Sir Winston S. Churchill
(Churchill papers, 2/216)

26 January 1956
Confidential

On setting out on this journey[2] we have made so often together I want to tell you how much I am thinking of our past experiences.

I was so glad to hear about you from Rab. Every possible good wish.[3]

Sir Winston S. Churchill to Lady Churchill
(Baroness Spencer-Churchill papers)[4]

26 January 1956   La Pausa

My darling,

Here is a vy nice message[5] from the Queen & my reply.[6] I pray she may come safely home. She works hard!

I hope you are settling down in 28, & you are right to plan from day to day. Wendy's mother had vy bad arthritis & was completely cured in a few months ten years ago by an American doctor & he thrust needles into the nerves affected so as to kill them. He is still the family physician. The truth is that there are many varieties & many cures, & it is hard to fit them together. They want to bring the doctor over here.

The weather has at last improved & yesterday we lunched in blazing sunshine at the Cafe de Madoil wh is on a peak overlooking St Jean Cap Ferrat. All the servants here bunched together & made a collective demand for a walk on their own. We are to stay here today.

[1] Reproduced above (p. 2074).
[2] Eden's first visit to the US as PM.
[3] Churchill replied: 'Thank you so much.'
[4] This letter was handwritten.
[5] See Adeane to Churchill, reproduced above (p. 2078).
[6] Reproduced immediately below.

Diana seems greatly better in every way. She gave me a gloomy account of the University College hospital, & said you got a touch of 'pneumonia' there. Between morning & night the doctor decided not to telegraph for me because you or they had shaken it off. These are disconcerting things to hear. I am sure it is much better to be ill at home & not get all the local illnesses wh the hospitals exist to cure.

Darling one take care of yourself. Do no work that does not amuse you. Make no plans for the present. I thought Diana's visit might – if all goes well – give you time to look round. If not I will come home & see you, & fly out again. They are vy nice people here & Wendy is charming.

Always yr loving & devoted

Sir Winston S. Churchill to Queen Elizabeth II
(Churchill papers, 2/532)[1]

26 January 1956   La Pausa

Madam,

It is very kind of Your Majesty to think of me at this hour of departure and to send me such interesting information about the journey to Nigeria. I had thought a great deal about it myself and all the exertions and sacrifices Your Majesty makes for the public interest. I have not troubled Your Majesty with a letter amid so much business, and that this gracious message should reach me from Yourself and the Duke gives me the keenest pleasure. May God protect Your Majesty and bring You both back safely to our shores.

I am looking forward to sending the first copy of the *History of the English-Speaking Peoples*, which will come out in April and occupies my time meanwhile, to Your Majesty.

---

[1] This letter was handwritten.

Sir Winston S. Churchill to Sir Michael Adeane
(Churchill papers, 2/532)

26 January 1956   La Pausa

My dear Adeane,

Thank you so much for sending me Her Majesty's gracious message and programme of her journey.[1]

I have found some sun here, though after ten days of surly weather.

I was deeply touched by The Queen's kindness in thinking of me at this juncture when so much is going on. Let me also thank you for your kind message.

Sir Winston S. Churchill to Bill Deakin
(Churchill papers, 4/27)

30 January 1956

My dear Bill,

Thank you so much for your letter and for the help you are giving me.

I am working hard at the third volume, and hope to make the Marlborough part more interesting.

---

[1] See Adeane to Churchill, reproduced above (p. 2078).

Sir Winston S. Churchill to Lady Churchill
(Baroness Spencer-Churchill papers)[1]

30 January 1956   La Pausa

My Darling,

    Assuming you have made up your mind to start with Sylvia[2] on the 17th, I shall come home on the 10th to see you off and return here about the 20th – probably with Montague Browne.

    I had hoped to persuade you to come and convalesce out here and that you would meet Wendy who is a vy charming person. But I feel that with Sylvia & the Ceylon sun your plan is a good one, and the weather here in February is vy half & half. (Today & yesterday unfit for human consumption) and once you have got through the Bay of Biscay you will have a good convalescent cruise. Be vy careful about Ceylon & do not treat it like England.

    Give me warning of any change because my plans depend on yours my dearest One. I spend the days mostly in bed, & get up for lunch and dinner. I am being taken through a course of Monet,[3] Manet,[4] Cezanne[5] & Co by my hosts who are both versed in modern painting and practise in the studio – now partly an office with Miss Maturin.[6] Also they have a wonderful form of gramophone wh plays continuously Mozart[7] and other composers of merit and anything else you like on 10-fold discs. I am in fact having an artistic education with vy agreeable tutors.

    Darling unless I hear to the contrary we meet on the 10th at 28.

                                                              All my love
                                               Your devoted husband
                                                 [Drawing of a pig]

---

[1] This letter was handwritten.

[2] Sylvia Laura Stanley, 1882–1980. Daughter of Edward Lyulph Stanley, 4th Baron Sheffield; cousin to Clementine Churchill. Married, 1906, Brig.-Gen. Anthony Morton Henley: four children. OBE, 1962.

[3] Oscar-Claude Monet, 1840–1926. French artist. Educated at Le Havre Secondary School of the Arts. Founder of Impressionist painting movement.

[4] Édouard Manet, 1832–83. French artist. Noted for his role in the transition from Realism to Impressionism.

[5] Paul Cézanne, 1839–1906. French artist. Post-Impressionist; chief linking figure between Impressionism and Cubism.

[6] (Verity) Gillian Maturin, 1931–85. Private Secretary to Sir Winston Churchill.

[7] Wolfgang Amadeus Mozart, 1756–91. Austrian musician and composer. Born in Salzburg. Married, 1782, Maria Constanze Cäcilia Josepha Johanna Aloysia Weber: two children. Composed a vast body of work in his short life, beginning at a precociously early age.

1956

Sir Winston S. Churchill to Lady Churchill
(Baroness Spencer-Churchill papers)[1]

3 February 1956　　　　　　　　　　　　　　　　　　　　　　　La Pausa

My darling,

Here I am, with Diana & Anthony, in gt comfort but nursing a sore throat with the aid of Dr Roberts[2] who is I think a good man. (I had him last time you will remember). Meanwhile you shd have reached Colombo & I hope are already safely ensconced. I await a letter. They tell me the posts take 3 or 4 days, which is pretty good – but it leaves me in an hour.

I had an interesting time in London, & saw a lot of Christopher & Maria & also of the PM. He is having a hard time & the horizon is dark whichever way one looks. The Defence debate was an awful flop. 12 millions to be evacuated according to Walter Monckton and what they do when the wind changes[3] (as it is sure to do in 3 weeks): the conditions of the air force: the state of the Navy: all vy disturbing. WM was not good at this difficult task – to which he is completely new; and Nigel Birch was deservedly shouted down.

Christopher goes into action next Monday & will I trust establish himself. He has a gt chance.

I give you my impressions gained in my corner seat,[4] which is most respectfully kept open for me by Hinchingbrooke, and wh I fill at the critical moment.

I have brought Toby out here! He can go home whenever I choose. There is no restraint in England now, so I took him along. He is a bit subdued, but I think it is only the change of scene. (He had a peck at this, but it did not come off.)

Pamela L has had to go into the University College Hospital for an operation on Monday. She has written me but the letter is still in the French post. Mary is finding out and will telephone to me. Operations unexpected are anxious at eighty.

I must close this letter now my dearest Clemmie.

　　　　　　　　　　　　　　　　　　　　　　Your ever loving husband.
　　　　　　　　　　　　　　　　　　　　　　　　　[Drawing of a pig]

---

[1] This letter was handwritten.

[2] John Roberts. Having been invalided out of RAF with a 90% disability pension, he practised medicine in Monte Carlo, with the permission of the French authorities, on the condition that he treated only British patients. Unlike Lord Moran, he kept no diary.

[3] The reference seems to be to the evacuation protocol for the planned response to a nuclear attack, and the danger of radioactive material being carried by wind many miles from the blast site.

[4] As a gesture of respect, the Conservatives always kept available for Churchill in the Commons Chamber the first corner seat below the gangway, which his father had formerly occupied. This was a place of honour, for above the gangway was the Government front bench.

Sir Winston S. Churchill to Lady Churchill
(Baroness Spencer-Churchill papers)[1]

4 February 1956   La Pausa

My darling,

    I have not been out for a week & for the last 3 days have not even been on the verandah. This is not because the weather is bad. The last three days have been cold (comparatively) but you would call them bright and sunny. The truth is that I stay a gt deal in bed and have taken (when I get up) to painting Cezanne. I will bring you 2 or 3 home with ease.

    My hosts are vy artistic, they paint & they collect. More than that they delight in the famous painters of Europe & I am having an education in art wh is beneficial. Also they play Mozart & others on these multiplied gramophones. I am responsible for the few guests who come. Wendy is vy hard working as well as gay. She organises the household & they seem to be devoted to her. I take them out every few days to give the servants a rest. Wendy has undertaken the outfitting & repairs of any house I may want. But I have decided to do what they wish and stay here through March. So there is no hurry. In fact, except for the Book, I am idle & lazy.

    My hope is that in April you will change ships at Suez & look in here for the Easter holidays. You wd like it & yr room awaits you.

    Darling One I send you all my love & many kisses.

                                               Your ever loving husband
                                               [Drawing of a pig]
                                                Torpid & recumbent

PS. I was enchanted by your voice & miaouw on the telephone. You gave me the impression of having got round the corner. I look forward so much to seeing you on the 10th.

Sir Winston S. Churchill to Lady Churchill
(Baroness Spencer-Churchill papers)[2]

8 February 1956   La Pausa

My darling,

    Your delightful letter reached me vy punctually, and I have just received that of the 6th with the tale about Rufus. I am glad he likes his new environment so much. I shall have a hard job to recall him to his duty! Toby will be a problem when we are both away.

    The day after tomorrow I shall be with you. I look forward to it so much, dearest one.

---

[1] This letter was handwritten.
[2] This letter was handwritten.

Wendy was enchanted by yr letter. They have devoted themselves to my comfort in every conceivable way & the month has passed vy smoothly. I have learned a lot I did not know about modern painters & musicians, & at their sincere request I shall come back here & not take a living place for March.

We dined with the Onassis' on their yacht two nights ago. He is an extraordinary man. He wanted to lend us the yacht to go to Ceylon! It is the most beautiful structure I have seen afloat. I did not accept.

My darling I shall see you soon. The sun is shining & the wind has dropped. We are going to luncheon at a café on a pinnacle.

All my love
Your devoted husband,
[Drawing of a pig]

Sir Winston S. Churchill to Lord Beaverbrook
(Churchill papers, 2/211)

13 February 1956

Thank you so much for your generous offer.[1] I am set on the Riviera and shall be staying with Reves the bulk of March and April pending finding a permanent residence. We shall be neighbours.

All good wishes.

Sir Winston S. Churchill to Lady Churchill
(Churchill papers, 1/55)

19 February 1956

Hope voyage has been peaceful and that Sylvia is recovered. All quiet at Chartwell. Am probably not going back this week as La Pausa is still frozen. Fondest love.

Lord Bracken to Lord Beaverbrook
(Beaverbrook papers)

20 February 1956

I spent the weekend with Winston who was in high spirits – he sees some advantages in being freed from the financial and economic woes which are crowding upon his successor.

---

[1] Asking Churchill to come as his guest to the Bahamas.

Lady Churchill to Sir Winston S. Churchill
(Churchill papers, 1/55)

23 February 1956

Lovely voyage but still very cold. We have just been inoculated against typhoid, cholera, etc. Thinking of you. Love.

Sir Winston S. Churchill to Lady Churchill
(Churchill papers, 1/55)

24 February 1956

Have postponed return Roquebrune till weather there improves. Hope now go next week. Love.

Sir Winston S. Churchill to Lady Churchill
(Churchill papers, 1/55)

26 February 1956

Hope your voyage prospers. Am returning Roquebrune Thursday. Cannot catch you with letters before Colombo.

Sir Winston S. Churchill to Lady Churchill
(Baroness Spencer-Churchill papers)[1]

27 February 1956

My darling one,

It is hard to catch you with a letter with your different ports of call, so I have telegraphed. I do hope you are <u>both</u> feeling better and that the Indian Ocean has been warm. As you voyage southwards you carry my thoughts with you. I got yr second letter this morning and this reply shd reach you at Colombo according to the Post Office.

I love you so much and envy yr three weeks in Ceylon. I hope the High Commissioner will make things go smoothly.

I spent the long weekend at Chartwell mostly alone. It was not fit for more than one peep out. I walked however round the ponds – 3 inches of ice, and down to the Farm. Mary & Christopher had the Fords[2] staying with them &

---

[1] This letter was handwritten.

[2] Edward William Spencer Ford, 1910–2006. Asst Private Secretary to the Queen, 1952–67. Knighted, 1957.

Virginia Brand, 1918–95. Married Edward Ford: two sons.

they all came to dine & see the film on Saturday. It was a vy good one, *The Four Feathers*, with lots of good pictures of the battle of Omdurman. These stirred my memory, though accuracy was not achieved.

I had made all arrangements for going back to Roquebrune on Monday, March 5, but Reves telephoned to say that the weather was now beautiful & the temperature 70 (here it is 35°). I therefore altered my plans which are now to set out on March 1 from London Airport with Diana & AMB to La Pausa. If no fresh snowfall recurs I shall start accordingly. I thirst for warmth, and Chartwell even with Mary & Christopher & Dido[1] does not make up for the sunny landscape my window reveals. The thaw however seems to have begun here too, & will I trust continue.

I came back this morning to attend the Debate on foreign affairs which are in a fog. Tomorrow & Wednesday Defence is the subject. I shall vote with the Government. Chandos is dining with me & I hope for a little Bezique.

You are quite right to go first of all to the Galle Face Hotel, they tell me in the House, and push out to the Lavinia afterwards.

I will write about your landing at Marseilles & bringing Sylvia with you to stay for a few days at La Pausa. I do hope she liked Vol. I. She is I am sure a good judge.

Tender love my darling Clemmie from yr old & battered [Drawing of a pig]

Sir Winston S. Churchill to Selwyn Lloyd
(*Churchill papers, 2/194*)

March 1956[2]

My dear Selwyn Lloyd,

It has been reported in the Press that the Queen is to be represented at the Prince of Monaco's[3] wedding by our Consul-General at Nice.[4] This has aroused a good deal of interest locally, and it has been represented to me that the decision is likely to give considerable offence in Monaco.

Of course, I do not know what scale of representation other countries are contemplating, nor if there are major difficulties in the way of our taking a

---

[1] Dido Cairns, Christopher Soames's sister.

[2] Original does not specify day within March.

[3] Rainier Louis Henri Maxence Bertrand Grimaldi, 1923–2005. Also known as 'Rainier III'. Prince of Monaco. Born in Monte Carlo, Monaco. Educated at Institut Le Rosey, Switzerland, University of Montpellier and Paris Institute of Political Studies. Served in French Army, 1944–7, attaining rank of Chevalier. Prince of Monaco, 1949–2005. Married, 1956, Grace Patricia Kelly (d. 1982): three children.

[4] Wolstan Beaumont Charles Weld-Forester, 1899–1961. Educated at Royal Naval Colleges, Osborne and Dartmouth. On active service, RN, 1914–18. Entered Foreign Service, 1927. Vice-Consul, Teheran, 1927. Acting Consul-General, Munich, 1939. Consul, Basra, 1940–2; Suez, 1943–4; Damascus, 1944–6. 1st Secretary, British Legation, Addis Ababa, 1947–9. Consul-General, Salonika, 1949–52; Oporto, 1952–5; Nice, 1955–7. CBE, 1957.

different course. I thought, however, that I should inform you of what I have heard because, although a small matter, it looks as though it may impair the very considerable goodwill the British enjoy down here.

I am receiving a selection of Foreign Office telegrams through the Consul-General at Nice, and I am so much obliged to you for your courtesy in making this arrangement. It is of considerable help and interest to me.

PS. Of course, the local comment does not reflect in any way on the Consul-General personally. It is only a question of the status of representation.

Anthony Montague Browne to Sir Winston S. Churchill
(Churchill papers, 2/341)

4 March 1956

There would be no political objection to your subscribing to this fund if you wished.[1]

(We are not very happy that the Israel Parliament should have set itself up in Jerusalem, which is supposed to be an international city, but this is rather a fine point.)

Anthony Montague Browne to Alan Hodge
(Churchill papers, 4/26)

4 March 1956   Roquebrune Cap Martin

Thank you so much for sending me the Bullock[2] notes and other documents on the late 19th century.

Sir Winston is now beginning to think that he might well write 1870 onwards himself, as he has such a close acquaintance with the period, both from his own early life and from the work he did for *Lord Randolph*. He is ruminating on getting me to delve further into 1763–1815, but quite on what lines I do not yet know. So for the moment I am marking time.

We are all much looking forward to seeing you.

---

[1] Churchill was asked by the FO to inscribe an ornamental candelabrum to be set up outside the Israeli Parliament building in Jerusalem as a gift from Britain.

[2] Alan Louis Charles Bullock, 1914–2004. Historian. Educated at Bradford Grammar School and Oxford University. First approached by Churchill as researcher on *History of the English-Speaking Peoples*, 1939. Married, 1940, Hilda Yates Handy: five children. Talks Editor for BBC European Service, 1940–5. Fellow in Modern History, New College, Oxford, from 1945. Head of St Catherine's Society, 1952; founding head of St Catherine's College, 1962. Fellow, British Academy, 1967. Published works included biographies of Hitler, Stalin and Bevin.

Sir Winston S. Churchill to Harry S Truman
('Defending the West, The Truman–Churchill Correspondence', page 218)

6 March 1956
Paraphrase[1]

My dear Harry,
Now that your trip to England is set, I am writing to ask if you will dine with me on the occasion of your visit.

Sir Winston S. Churchill to Bernard Baruch
(Churchill papers, 2/210)

6 March 1956

My dear Bernie,
Thank you so much for your letter. I must get hold of a copy of the speeches and listen to it myself, since you say they produce an effect on you.

You will be very welcome when you come over in the summer to come to Chartwell, and I hope that June or July will be the date.

You thrill me by what you say of riding on horseback and on foot to shoot quail. I am sure I could ride, but I have not done so for five years.

I do not like the look of things in general. I am not so sure that a suitable opportunity will be accorded to me in the next few years of righting the world, as you suggest. However, if an emergency arises during the time I am hanging about the guardroom, I hope you will consider that I have not failed. Personally, I think that the Soviets will exploit their peaceable policy another five or six years during which the United States is on duty. But we have made sufficient progress, though greatly hampered by the McMahon Act, to be able at the end of that time to send them back, whatever they choose to send us. It is on this that I rely for the safety of the world and the impossibility of war.

We will talk these things over when you come to Chartwell.

Every good wish to you and Elizabeth.

---

[1] Header reproduced from *Defending the West*.

Anthony Montague Browne to Captain Thomas Tilbrook[1]
(Churchill papers, 2/295)

6 March 1956

Dear Captain Tilbrook,

Thank you for your letter of February 27.[2] The answers to your questions are as follows:

1. Any good Havana Cigar.
2. I cannot guide you much, as Sir Winston is catholic in his tastes. He eats on the whole an English breakfast, and enjoys good food at other meals.
3. He usually breakfasts about 9.0, lunches at about 1.15 and dines at about 8.30, but here again he has no set rule.
4. He likes white wines, usually drinking hock for luncheon and champagne for dinner. He has no special favourite as regards to port and brandy.
5. He is usually called when he wakes up and rings for his servant.
6. We will bring the Cinque Ports standard for Sir Winston's car and for the flag pole. The size is approximately 4′ x 4′ for the flag pole.
7. Sir Winston will bring his own valet with him, Kirkwood.[3] It would be desirable for Kirkwood to sleep near Sir Winston and have a bell which rings in his room if this is conveniently possible.

Sir Anthony Eden to Sir Winston S. Churchill
(Churchill papers, 4/67)

11 March 1956

My dear Winston,

I have now received the first volume of *A History of the English Speaking Peoples* which you have so kindly inscribed for me. This is another milestone, and I am very pleased that you have marked it by sending me this present.

It is tough going here, but we are surviving.

Clarissa sends her love.

---

[1] Thomas William Tilbrook. Married Jacqueline Mackillican. British Military Adviser in Ottawa. Brig., Queen's Royal Irish Hussars.

[2] Regarding arrangements to be made for Churchill's visit to West Germany in May.

[3] James Kirkwood.

Sir Winston S. Churchill to Lady Churchill
(Baroness Spencer-Churchill papers)[1]

11 March 1956   La Pausa

My Darling,

I was so glad to get you letter of the 5th & to realize that we are only 5 or 6 days apart.

Pamela L had a kidney taken out, which is a shock at 79 and I was astonished to hear that the doctors said that she would be able to go home in 12 days; I hope she will not have a relapse.

Now the weather has clouded over again here & I have hardly been out of doors since I arrived. Perhaps it is saving up for your landing on April 5 at Marseilles. The Reves will be delighted to put you & Sylvia up. I must get back by the 12th as I have to preside at the Albert Hall Primrose League on the 13th. It is very comfortable here & Wendy makes herself most agreeable. I work in bed at the book every morning & Kelly is at the hotel & Alan Hodge relieves him on the 15th. This is the way to get the job finished I am sure.

I brought Toby out here with me and I have arranged for him to have 2 female companions. He did not take much interest in them & seems to prefer me. He is sitting at my side & my conscience feels easier. Diana is staying now till the 13th and Christopher & Mary are planning to come out on the 27th. And we can make arrangements all to go home together after the Easter Recess. However if this does not attract you I shall have done my best.

I am very glad that the 'Zoo' is so attractive, but I think it would be better not, repeat NOT, to bring more than three 30 inch elephants to Chartwell!

I enclose a cutting from the MG. It happened the day after I left. It was a silly thing to say.[2]

[Drawing of a pig] I have had a cough & sore throat but am recovered thanks to Dr Foster & Penicillin.

---

[1] This letter was handwritten.
[2] Gerard Fay, London correspondent for the *Manchester Guardian* and a close friend of Randolph Churchill, had written an article in the *Guardian* referring to recent articles by Randolph in the *Evening Standard* arguing that Eden should be replaced as PM because of his failings in the Middle East. Fay wrote: 'There have been some ironical musings on the question of whether Mr Churchill's chances of selection for a safe party seat are rather worse than before or whether, in some circumstances they might not be rather better. It is also asked, of course, whether or not as a political journalist he writes with any special knowledge of what his father might be thinking at the moment. Whichever is the case he has certainly stirred up plenty of gossip in his latest article' (*Manchester Guardian*, 7 Mar. 1956).

Lady Churchill to Sir Winston S. Churchill
(Churchill papers, 1/55)[1]

16 March 1956   The Mount Lavinia Hotel
Ceylon

My Darling,

Your letter has come suggesting that Sylvia & I should get off at Marseilles & join you & Mr Reves & Wendy at La Pausa.

Fundamentally I'm better, but I have had 2 set backs, the second one a threatening of my old enemy cystitis. This is being coped with efficiently by a very good doctor. But I do feel I need an uninterrupted voyage home. Our boat has been delayed in Australia, so we can't reach Tillner before the 12th so I shall await you with much longing either at Hyde Park Gate or Chartwell. I shall have much to tell you about this island. The rich are now being heavily taxed but the condition of the poor peasant is pitiable.

The Election is being conducted with barefaced self interest – We have taken refuge here 7 miles from Colombo but only for 3 days.

I bathed at 6.30 this morning at dawn. It was lovely. Later in the day it would be too hot.

We are being treated with the most lavish hospitality by the Prime Minister, Sir John Kotelawala. We have a loving Civil Servant attached to us who is our 'Shadow'.

The crows here & everywhere are quite menacing. They almost hop on to your breakfast tray & dispute with you your slice of pineapple.

                                         Your loving Clemmie [Drawing of a cat]

Sir Winston S. Churchill to Lady Churchill
(Baroness Spencer-Churchill papers)

17 March 1956   La Pausa

My darling one,

No news from Ceylon by letter or telegram! I do hope this is because you and Sylvia are enjoying yourselves.

Here all is peaceful & the weather 'mezzo tint' – I spend most of my time in bed. Tonight Pug Ismay & his wife with M de Staercke are coming for dinner. Both Kelly & Alan H are at their hotel working hard. I see them every morning. K goes home today with Book VIII, in a finished condition. I am still house-hunting on the basis of renting not buying; and I bear in mind that you must not be burdened with more housekeeping. I hope to have some proposals to put before you when we meet. When!

---

[1] This letter was handwritten.

Christopher & Mary come out on the 27th; & Nonie[1] on the 19th (for 5 days).

This is the last letter that will reach you before you sail for home.

Toby is flourishing. He sends you his best love. I have got him 2 females – blue for company who are ensconced in a large separate cage. Nothing has or will occur. He is very cool about them. (He made this blot and has been lapping the ink from my pen). How he knows I am writing to you I cannot tell.

Darling my fondest love

PS. I enclose a paper to show what I am considering now. It was written by AMB who is a wonderful addition.

Sir Winston S. Churchill to Alan Hodge
(Churchill papers, 4/27)

20 March 1956

My dear Hodge,

It will be necessary in Volume I, *Richard III*, to deal with all this modern argument that Crookback[2] did not murder the Princes, rules wisely and efficiently during his short reign, and has been slandered by the Tudors. Sir Alan Lascelles lent me a book about this some time ago. The argument is growing in strength. You should advise me of one or two really good authorities who would separately give their opinion on all the new facts for a reasonable fee. Please let me know. At any rate the pros and cons must be balanced.

Sir Winston S. Churchill to Lady Churchill
(Churchill papers, 1/55)

21 March 1956   La Pausa

Your March 16 letter[3] received this morning. Am much disappointed. Shall be home 11th. Writing Aden. Bon Voyage. Love

---

[1] Evelyn Noel Arnold-Wallinger, 1925–2016. Known as 'Nonie'. Married, 1950, Anthony Montague Browne (div. 1970): one child; 1973, Michael T. Pelloe (div. 1981); 1981, Henry Sargant.

[2] Richard of York, 1452–85. Took the throne after the death of his brother, Edward IV, as King Richard III of England, 1483. Killed at Battle of Bosworth, the final engagement of the Wars of the Roses.

[3] Reproduced above (p. 2092).

Sir Winston S. Churchill to Lady Churchill
(Baroness Spencer-Churchill papers)[1]

23 March 1956   La Pausa

My Darling,

    It is comforting to think of your ship paddling Home, & that we plan to dine together on the 12th of April at 28. Your buoyant telegram gave me joy. I am so glad you had a successful visit to Ceylon. I fear you are not yet clear of pain. Also, we must continue our search for a cure.

    I lunched with W. Somerset Maugham on Wednesday & he told me he was going to a watering place just north of Venice in May where the ancients took mixed baths & often shook off the different varieties of neuritis in bygone days. I will bring home the details. The cure takes 12 days & it might be worth trying. All say it is very pleasant to undergo, & return to Venice afterwards.

    Give my love to Sylvia. I hope she has benefitted by the voyage.

    Longing to see you my dearest one, with all my love.

Sir Winston S. Churchill to Lady Churchill
(Churchill papers, 1/55)

24 March 1956   La Pausa

    Hope you are having a pleasant voyage. It never leaves off raining here. Have written Aden. Love

---

[1] This letter was handwritten.

1956

Sir Winston S. Churchill to Edward Heath[1]
(*Churchill papers, 2/129*)

24 March 1956

My dear Heath,

Will you arrange for me not to be paired in favour of the Malta decision on Monday.[2] I am convinced this is a wrong and mistaken thing to do, and it will inflict lasting injury upon the character of the House of Commons.

Harry S Truman to Sir Winston S. Churchill
(*'Defending the West, The Truman–Churchill Correspondence', page 218*)

24 March 1956

Dear Sir Winston.

I certainly did appreciate your invitation of March 8th,[3] and, of course, I want to accept your invitation.

Definite arrangements have only been set for three affairs –
one for the Degree on Wednesday, June 20th,
one for the Pilgrims dinner on Thursday, June 21st,*
and one for the luncheon with the Lord Mayor on Friday, June 22nd.

You can be sure your invitation is a definite engagement and is most highly appreciated.[4]

* In his Pilgrims dinner address, Truman reaffirmed the importance of the English language and of the democratic way of life as the ties that bind 'our two countries'.

---

[1] Edward Richard George Heath, 1916–2005. Known as 'Ted'. On active service, RA, 1940–6. MP (Cons.) for Bexley, 1950–74; for Bexley Sidcup, 1974–83; for Old Bexley and Sidcup, 1983–2001. Master Gunner, Tower of London, 1951–4. Deputy Government Chief Whip, 1953–5. Parliamentary Secretary to the Treasury and Government Chief Whip, Dec. 1955 to 1959. Minister of Labour, 1959–60. Lord Privy Seal with FO responsibilities, 1960–3. Secretary of State for Industry, Trade and Regional Development, and President of the Board of Trade, 1963–4. Leader of the Opposition, 1965–70, 1974–5. PM, 1970–4. KG, 1992. Father of the House, 1992–2001.

[2] The Malta Round-Table Conference had recommended the admission of Maltese Members of Parliament to Westminster in order to appease the demand from within Malta for greater powers and eventual independence. On 26 Mar. 1956 the Secretary of State for the Colonies, Alan Lennox-Boyd, stated that he 'could not recommend to the House that they should increase the powers of the Maltese Government and Parliament' unless he could be 'sure of safeguarding the United Kingdom's own interests and imperial responsibilities in Malta'. Malta became independent in Sep. 1964.

[3] Reproduced above, dated Mar. 6 (p. 2089).

[4] Churchill responded on Apr. 4: 'Thank you for your March 24th letter. Mrs Churchill and I would be delighted to have you and Mrs Truman dine with us at our home, if this is agreeable, on Sunday, June 24th.'

Sir Winston S. Churchill to Lady Churchill
(Baroness Spencer-Churchill papers)[1]

26 March 1956 La Pausa

My darling,
'Many Happy Returns of the Day'.
I write this to reach you at Port Said on April 1.
I hope you have had a pleasant voyage, & that Sylvia has shared your progress. The weather here has been detestable; but the company is very quiet & friendly. I am sorry you will not join us, but I cannot promise anything like the shining blue skies of the Riviera. We have had a bout of rain, & I fear great distress will fall upon all engaged not only in flower growing but also in large scale agriculture.
Once more my best wishes for your Birthday. May you long enjoy life & hope.

Your ever loving husband

Alan Hodge to Sir Winston S. Churchill
(Churchill papers, 2/189)[2]

27 March 1956

Dear Sir Winston,
I greatly enjoyed being with you at Roquebrune. The hospitality of La Pausa is a thing I shall always remember with delight.
One of the best pieces of reconstruction you have done on your History was this time accomplished. Book Nine is taking splendid shape, and the alteration of interest between England, America and France is most impressively planned. The chapters you gave me to bring back have gone to press. The new printers are quick at their work; it is encouraging to have the fresh Revise coming in daily. Shortly I hope to submit to you a piece on Wellington and the Peninsular War.
I had a very agreeable flight back in Mrs Montague-Browne's company. Please give my regards to all at the Villa.

---

[1] This letter was handwritten.
[2] This letter was handwritten.

President Dwight D. Eisenhower to Sir Winston S. Churchill
(Churchill papers, 2/217)

29 March 1956   The White House

Dear Winston,

    Although from almost every British visitor to this city, I gain some news of you and of your welfare, it has been far too long since I have had the great privilege of hearing from you directly. A few minutes ago our old friend, Bernie Baruch, dropped in for a chat and, upon his departure, I determined to wait no longer before I started a letter to tell you that I still missed the occasional letters and far too infrequent personal conversations that we had up until the date of your retirement.

    The Soviets have gone through a bewildering series of turn-abouts and somersaults ranging all the way from the sweet kindness they tried to exude at Geneva to their latest and curious effort to deny that Stalin ever was a true Communist.

    It is amazing that so many people continue to believe, wholly or in part, the propaganda with which the Soviets cover the world. It seems to make no difference in many regions how often the Soviets reverse themselves or how often they are guilty of self-contradiction. On the other hand, the free world, continuing in its basic effort to raise the living standards of all and to increase the opportunity for less developed countries to earn their own independence and to improve their economies, is accused of a desire to dominate less fortunate peoples.

    The unity we have, on our side, is that which is dictated by the obvious self interest of each nation. Opposed to the unity of force, which is the pattern behind the Iron Curtain, our own methods leave each of us too often too much alone. These methods can, of course, be improved.

    We know that some lack of unity in any organization of 'equals' is inevitable. It is one of the prices each of us pays for independence and for the great privilege of self-government. Yet sometimes we are more than careless and therefore pay more than a greater price than necessary. By this I mean that the enlightened self-interest of each of us is much more nearly identical with that of our friends than sometimes appears obvious; a little more honest soul searching on the part of each of us would prove, I am convinced, that we could vastly improve our coordination, and therefore our security, without any additional cost of a material kind.

    The free nations know, for example, that the prosperity and welfare of the entire Western world is inescapably dependent upon Mid East oil and free access thereto. This is particularly true of all Western Europe, and the safety and soundness of that region is indispensable to all the rest of us.

    These facts should provide such a clear guide post for all our policies, actions, efforts and propaganda in the region that we would allow nothing to weaken the solidarity of our unified approach to our common problems. In the two countries where this truth is best recognized, yours and ours, I know that men of goodwill on both sides have earnestly struggled for years to concert our plans and thinking with respect to our common interests. Between the two of us, we have done better than most; even so, the different political climates in the two countries, the need that politicians feel to have themselves reelected even at the cost of demagoging against a friend, and differing national policies that go back sometimes a long ways into history, all combine to make very difficult the kind of cooperation of which I speak and which I believe is, in the long run, a vital necessity.

Of course the Mid East is merely the most important and bothersome of the problems that currently confront our nations. Moreover, the welfare of each of the fourteen NATO countries, as well as the fate of those many other nations that still live in freedom because of our strength, will eventually be determined by our success in making the processes of voluntary cooperation more effective than is a Gestapo in a dictatorship.

When we consider all of these difficulties against a back drop of scientific development that has brought to man the power of destroying an entire enemy nation – possibly at the cost of suicide – it is no exaggeration to say that each of us should pray earnestly for a bit more wisdom, a bit more understanding, a bit more capacity for dealing with these problems of limitless scope.

In spite of all this, I am by nature so optimistic that at times I am forced to laugh at myself in the thought that I am as inconsistent as is the most blatant of Soviet propaganda. Though the world is torn and threatened by the conflicting prejudices and ambitions of little men and of big, of great nations and small, yet somehow or other I think that through the ages the good qualities of men have, on the average, exerted more influence that have his baser ones. I believe this will continue and so I keep struggling to better myself, in a small way, to grapple with the questions that daily come before me for some kind of answer.

I derive a certain satisfaction in saying these things to you because I know that in your long life in positions of heavy responsibility, you must have often sensed similar feelings.

Yet when I started this letter, I had no other intention than to tell you how earnestly I pray that your health continues to be good, that Clemmie is well, and that you are both finding time to enjoy your own company and that of your family.

With deep and abiding affection from your old friend

Sir Winston S. Churchill to Lady Churchill
(Churchill papers, 1/55)

31 March 1956   La Pausa

Many happy returns of the day. Do think over whether you will not come on here from Marseilles. We can go home together by air on 10th or 11th. Love

Sir Winston S. Churchill to Lady Churchill
(Churchill papers, 1/55)

6 April 1956   La Pausa

Welcome darling.[1] I will talk to you on the telephone at 10 a.m.

Lady Churchill to Sir Winston S. Churchill
(Churchill papers, 1/55)

7 April 1956

So sorry darling but cannot sort and repack crumpled and inadequate clothes so am making straight for home. All my love.

Sir Winston S. Churchill to Alfred Rowse[2]
(Churchill papers, 4/28)

12 April 1956

My dear Rowse,

I am indeed obliged to you for your letter of April 7 and for all the trouble you have taken. Your comments are most valuable, and it is very good of you to have devoted so much time to my affairs.

Thank you also so much for sending me a copy of your review of Volume I. I am much complimented by what you say.

---

[1] Lady Churchill had just reached Marseilles. In their phone conversation, Churchill invited her to join him at La Pausa for four days.

[2] Alfred Leslie Rowse, 1903–97. British author and historian. Fellow of the Royal Society of Literature; President of the English Association, 1952. President, Shakespeare Club, Stratford-upon-Avon, 1970–1. Author of approximately 100 books including *Mr Keynes and the Labour Movement* (1936), *William Shakespeare, a Biography* (1963) and *Discovering Shakespeare* (1989).

Sir Winston S. Churchill to Lady Churchill
(Baroness Spencer-Churchill papers)[1]

13 April 1956

My Darling,
 'Welcome Home'.
 I long to see you & kiss you. You will find me putting the finishing touches on my speech. I hope you will approve of Miss Hamblin's plan for a long weekend at Chartwell.

Your ever loving husband,

Sir Winston S. Churchill: speech
('Winston S. Churchill, His Complete Speeches', volume 8, pages 8671–3)

13 April 1956

Primrose League Meeting,
Albert Hall, London

The Primrose League has endured the battle of life for seventy-three years and is now stronger and more active than ever. I am greatly complimented to be its Grand Master. Lord Randolph's League Number was Number 1, and I was very glad when you consented to my continuing to hold office after my resignation as Prime Minister a year ago. We have this year a great annual meeting, and we are very glad to welcome as our principal speaker the Colonial Secretary. In Mr Alan Lennox-Boyd we have a man who has for many years made our colonial relations his main political interest, and who since he took up office eighteen months ago has shown a tireless zeal and energy in the discharge of his difficult and variegated duties.

It is not, however, only in the colonial sphere that we are having a tough time. Our country faces baffling problems and grave difficulties, both in our domestic life here at home and in this turbulent and troubled world in which we live. We must not be in any way dismayed by the magnitude or the complexity of the tasks which face us; but it is right that we should squarely face them and take the measure of them. There is, I think, a general awareness of the underlying economic facts of our existence. They transcend our party differences, which, after all, are mainly the differences of the methods we should apply. There lies a very wide measure of common agreement about the nature of our problems.

The first problem is how we are to maintain the high standard of living to which we have become accustomed. We tend to take it as a right. But we must not forget that we are a people which is largely dependent upon imported food for its homes and imported raw materials for its factories. Can we sell enough

---

[1] This letter was handwritten.

overseas to pay for the imports which alone keep us going? Can we sell enough of the right quality, at the right price, and deliver it at the right time? These are the questions which affect every one of us here today, and I don't wonder that when we see how great and various are the movements of trade many people view our margin as precarious.

There have been disquieting signs of late that we have been falling down on some of the tests we have to apply. Our foreign competitors have been gaining on us. Our costs have risen with rising prices at home. All of you here will, I know, sustain and support our Conservative Government in the hard and unpopular measures they have deemed it their duty to take to remedy these defects in our economy. But that is not the end. We await Mr Macmillan's Budget on Tuesday. He has a very difficult task. But we can have confidence in him for, after all, he is the man who built the houses when all the wiseacres said it could not be done.

Of one thing I am sure. If we are to win this economic battle it will be by our very considerable store of skill and enterprise. The task is one for daring individuals, not for State planners and theorists. Nationalization has been proved to be a delusion to the dissatisfaction of many of its keenest advocates. The Socialist dogmas of state ownership and control are no remedy in the affairs of Britain. We are soon to have some visitors from Russia. They have a right to be treated with courtesy and goodwill, as guests in Britain are. I hope they will enjoy their time in this country, and that easier and more fruitful relations will emerge as a result of their visit. Peaceful coexistence is, after all, the first thing we are seeking, and to this easier personal relations between their national leaders and ours and a clearer comprehension of the way we live can make a valuable contribution.

And what of the United States? I do not share the views of those who think that they have failed in their duty, or will fail in their duty if the moment comes. They are a wise and experienced people. They learn from history. They know well that both the great wars which have darkened our lives and dishevelled the world could have been prevented if the United States had acted before they began to prevent them. Now a somewhat similar case has arisen, though on a much smaller scale. Egypt and Israel are face to face, and we and our American brothers have with France made a declaration in 1950 to the effect that we will not allow them to fight. The Secretary General of the United Nations and General Burns[1] are also doing their utmost to avert bloodshed, and they have our full support in their delicate, thankless, and humane task.

I think we can be perfectly sure that the United States as well as the United Kingdom will both intervene to prevent aggression by one side or the other. The need for this will probably never come; but it may come, and come at

---

[1] Eedson Louis Millard Burns, 1897–1985. Known as 'Tommy'. Cdr, 5th Canadian Armoured Div. and I Canadian Corps, Italy, WWII. Cdr, UN Emergency Force, Middle East, 1954–9. Chief Advisor to Canadian Government on Disarmament, 1960–9.

any moment, and if Israel is to be dissuaded from using the life of their race to ward off the Egyptians until the Egyptians have learnt to use the Russian weapons with which they have been supplied, and the Egyptians then attack, it will become not only a matter of prudence but a measure of honour to make sure that they are not the losers by waiting. For my part, I put my trust in President Eisenhower, that he will make the willpower of America felt clearly and strongly and felt in time. A firm faith that a continued drawing together, of the British Commonwealth and Empire on the one hand, while preserving all their personal identities, affords the surest guarantee of the safety of the whole world from the now measureless horrors of war. That is the road upon which our two countries should march.

Eliahu Elath to Sir Winston S. Churchill
(Government of Israel Archives)

13 April 1956

Dear Sir Winston,
I should like you to know with what deep gratification my Government and the people of Israel will receive your friendly references to our country in your speech to the Primrose League today. Our own heartfelt appreciation will, I know, be shared by all friends of Israel everywhere. We shall all hope and pray that these words, coming from you, will have their effect on those, in London and in Washington, in whose hands now lie the crucial decisions on the matters to which you referred, including that of the supply to Israel of adequate arms for her self-defence.

Sir Winston S. Churchill to Bernard Baruch
(Churchill papers, 2/210)

15 April 1956

My dear Bernie,
Thank you very much for your letter of April 9. I hope you will read my first volume in the original, as *Life* picks and chooses a good deal. Their pictures are very good.

I note your quotations from Woodrow Wilson. I did not think he was a very good President, but certainly he seems to have said some pithy things.

I see from your holograph note that you have been reading the tales they tell of Monte Carlo. I had no win, but came out quits after three days' play, which was not bad. Most of the reporters put in fairy-tales about Onassis. He is a friendly kind of man, but I did not depend on his invitation to go there.

I dare say you will have noticed that I spoke about the United States and

Ike at the Primrose League yesterday. I had a very nice letter from the President[1] after your visit to him.

I look forward to your visit at the end of June. Let me know the date of your arrival.

PS. Many thanks for your telegram just received.

Sir Winston S. Churchill to President Dwight D. Eisenhower
(Premier papers, 11/1690)

16 April 1956

Dear Ike,

How awfully kind of you to write me such a charming letter.[2] I read it with the greatest interest and pleasure. Our friendship has lasted through many anxious years, when we were concerned with matters that have passed, on the whole safely, into history.

But the fact that you should write to me so fully on the still grave situation which continues to afflict the world is not only a proof of your friendship, but a compliment of the highest order.

Our Russian guests are expected this week, and we shall soon see whether anything material results. We have only forty or fifty thousand professional communists in this country, but I suppose the people as a whole will treat them on the Malenkov lines. They have made an extraordinary volte-face about Stalin. I am sure it is a great blunder which will markedly hamper the Communist Movement. It would have been easy to 'play him down' gradually without causing so great a shock to the faithful. Stalin always kept his word with me. I remember particularly saying to him when I visited Moscow in 1940, 'You keep Rumania and Bulgaria in your sphere of influence, but let me have Greece.' To this bargain he scrupulously adhered during months of fighting with the Greek communists. I wish I could say the same about the Greeks, whose memories are very short.

I am so glad that you recognise so plainly the importance of oil from the Middle East. When I was at the Admiralty in 1913 I acquired control of the Anglo-Persian Company for something like £3,000,000, and turned the large fleet I was then building to that method of propulsion. That was a good bargain if ever there was one.

I am not unhappy about the present relations between our two countries. Eden stands very close to you. The forces which are at work will continue to draw us together, and I am sure that if we act together we shall stave off an actual war between Israel and Egypt. I am, of course, a Zionist, and have been

[1] Reproduced above (pp. 2097–8).
[2] Reproduced above (pp. 2097–8).

ever since the Balfour Declaration. I think it is a wonderful thing that this tiny colony of Jews should have become a refuge to their compatriots in all the lands where they were persecuted so cruelly, and at the same time established themselves as the most effective fighting force in the area. I am sure America would not stand by and see them overwhelmed by Russian weapons, especially if we had persuaded them to hold their hand while their chance remained.

We have always been in agreement about the information on the Atomic and Hydrogen Bombs being shared by both our countries. That is past now so far as the main secret is concerned, but we have lost two or three years in having to work it out for ourselves. I do not think, however, that a world war is likely to develop in the next decade. Till then we are, of course, defenceless against a Russian attack. After that we shall be able to say to the Russians, 'If you kill twenty or thirty million Englishmen, we have made unbreakable arrangements to kill double that number of Russians in the next few days.' The creation of such a situation would certainly be the end of nuclear war, except, of course, for accidents, which all nations have an equal interest in preventing.

I venture to send you a copy of my forthcoming book *A History of the English-Speaking Peoples*. The whole thing is finished now. I am afraid the Americans do not come into this volume, because it was only

> 'In fourteen hundred and ninety-two
> Columbus over the ocean flew.'

I am so glad to be able to tell you that Clemmie has returned from Ceylon far better than when she went. The monotony of the voyage, although cold and stormy, had good effects.

Let me finish by saying how relieved I am to hear of your recovery, and my admiration for the courage and stamina which enable you to face the ordeal of another term.

Lord Attlee to Sir Winston S. Churchill
(*Churchill papers, 4/67*)

21 April 1956

My dear Winston,

Thank you so much for sending me your most interesting *Birth of Britain*. I read it with much enjoyment. I am glad that you did full justice to the Wessex kings. What they did is often underrated. All good wishes.

Sir Anthony Eden to Sir Winston S. Churchill
(Churchill papers, 2/216)

21 April 1956

My dear Winston,

Thank you so much for letting me see your recent correspondence with Ike.[1] I have shown it to Norman Brook but to no one else.

I have now been able to study Ike's letter more carefully. I confess that I find it rather puzzling. I am not at all sure what the middle part of it is intended to convey. His intention may, however, have been to explain why it is that, although they are willing to work closely with us in discussing common policies for the Middle East, it is difficult for them to admit publicly that they are doing so – especially in an election year. There has been an unhappy revival of that phrase 'no ganging up' and we have strongly protested against it. Their unwillingness to let it be known that we are at one on this important issue diminishes the influence which each of us could exercise in the area. It also puts a considerable strain on our relations. We shall, however, survive this. I am resolved that we shall not be divided from our American friends over this crucial issue, however much we may be provoked by the outbursts of American columnists in support of Nasser.

Your answer to Ike was very good. I am, as always, most grateful to you for your help.

Dr John Plumb[2] to Sir Winston S. Churchill
(Churchill papers, 4/28)[3]

22 April 1956

Dear Sir Winston,

I was deeply touched by your kind and generous gesture of sending me a copy of your great work which I shall treasure as long as I should live. After the little that I had done to help, I did not expect so noble a gift. From what I have read so far, it is clear that this book possesses the greatest qualities which we have come to expect from your heart and mind – this same grandeur in the writing of history as in the making of it. Thank you very much.

I am sending you a copy of the first volume of the life of one of your illustrious predecessors, Sir Robert Walpole – which I am writing in the hope that

---

[1] Reproduced above, (pp. 2097–8, 2104–5).

[2] John Harold Plumb, 1911–2001. Known as 'Jack'. British historian. Ehrman Research Fellow, King's College, Cambridge, 1939–46. Fellow, Christ's College, Cambridge, 1946–78; Master, 1978–82. Prof. of Modern English History, Cambridge University, 1966–74. Knighted, 1982. Author of over 30 books, including *The First Four Georges* (1956), *Churchill Revised* (1969) and *The Commercialisation of Leisure* (1974).

[3] This letter was handwritten.

you may have a moment of leisure in the years ahead when you might care to glance at it.

With respect and admiration.

Duchess of Marlborough to Sir Winston S. Churchill
(Churchill papers, 4/67)[1]

23 April 1956

My dear Winston,

Thank you so very much for sending me your new book. I am delighted to have it. I started reading it last night in bed and I suddenly looked at the clock and saw it was 2.15 a.m.

I do hope I shall see you and Clemmie in the near future.

Lots of love dear Winston to you both.

George Trevelyan to Sir Winston S. Churchill
(Churchill papers, 4/67)[2]

23 April 1956   Cambridge

Dear Churchill,

It was a very kind thing of you to send me your book. It gives me the greatest delight to have it from you, and I have also had great delight in reading it. The Preface is a noble piece and will I have no doubt be read by people on both sides of the Atlantic for generations to come. The time will come when they will stop reading us professional historians but not you.

At the other end of the book I think your treatment of Richard III exactly right. There has been so much nonsense written about him on both sides, and you steer an even course. All through the book I like the way you keep your eye on personalities and on well known stories – it is the way to write popular history, though you put them all in their right place in scientific generalizations.

---

[1] This letter was handwritten.
[2] This letter was handwritten.

Sir Desmond Morton to Sir Winston S. Churchill
(Churchill papers, 4/67)[1]

23 April 1956

My dear Winston,

I am deeply touched at your continued kind remembrance of me by sending me a copy of the first volume of your *History of the English-Speaking Peoples*. May you live boldly and rejoice in seeing the remaining volumes given to the world – and long after that too.

Well do I remember the beginnings of the book at Chartwell before the last war, which seems as yesterday though too much has happened in between. I remember too talks then and even later, during the war itself, when, in your own forceful and uninhibited way, you professed with deep sincerity your conviction that the forging of a closer link between the peoples of the British Empire and the United States was an end to be sought above all others in this world, if progress and decent living were to be won for the human race.

You at least have done your utmost to guide our destinies toward that end and you have not failed.

Jo Sturdee to Sir Winston S. Churchill
(Churchill papers, 4/67)[2]

24 April 1956

Dear Sir Winston,

I was thrilled to receive from you yesterday a copy of your *Birth of Britain*, and have already devoured its first few chapters. How I wish our school history books had been as vivid and absorbing. I can hardly wait to read the rest of your story.

It really is most kind of you to remember me like this. I shall not only always treasure your gift, but will I know read it over and over again. Thank you so very much for your kindness and for this wonderful and enlightening story.

---

[1] This letter was handwritten.
[2] This letter was handwritten.

George Young[1] to Sir Winston S. Churchill
(Churchill papers, 4/67)[2]

25 April 1956

Dear Sir Winston,

Many thanks for the book. I have read it with equal admiration and enjoyment, and I look forward to its successor.

I now have your earliest and your latest work – Charles Dilke's[3] copy of the *Malakand Field Force* and *The Birth*. And what a world of experience and reflexion lies in between!

Lord Hankey to Sir Winston S. Churchill
(Churchill papers, 4/67)[4]

27 April 1956

Dear Winston,

I am both deeply touched and flattered by the receipt of the first volume of your *History of the English Speaking Peoples* and the good wishes you express to accompany it.

I greatly admire your amazing industry and courage in taking up again a task, begun before the war, which even a whole-time historian might approach with hesitation. But it is not your first labour of Hercules!

I have entered my 80th year on April Fool's Day (also Easter Day) and am still very active with weekly visits to Paris for the Suez Canal job (which you gave me after the war). I believe we shall be able to hold on to the Canal until the concession ends in 1968 and maybe beyond if we show courage – but that is a long story.

With very best wishes

---

[1] George Malcolm Young, 1882–1959. Member, British Mission to Petrograd, 1916–17. CB, 1917. Fellow of All Souls College, Oxford, 1905. Trustee, National Portrait Gallery, 1937–59. Member, Standing Commission on Museums and Galleries, 1938–59. Author of *Portrait of an Age* (1936) and *Stanley Baldwin* (1952).

[2] This letter was handwritten.

[3] Charles Wentworth Dilke, 1843–1911. Radical politician. MP (Lib.) for Chelsea, 1868–86; for Forest of Dean, 1892–1911. Baron, 1869. Parliamentary Under-Secretary for Foreign Affairs, 1880–2. PC, 1882. President, Local Government Board, 1882–5.

[4] This letter was handwritten.

President Dwight D. Eisenhower to Sir Winston S. Churchill
(Churchill papers, 2/217)

27 April 1956 The White House

Dear Winston,

The most enjoyable event in my week just past was the receipt of your fine letter.[1] I am especially grateful to you for the advance copy of your *History of the English Speaking Peoples*. I immediately plunged into its reading. I am anxious to see whether you make of Richard III a terrible villain as does Sir Laurence Olivier in his interpretation of Shakespeare's tragedy. Since your account of that period does not come until the end of the book, it will be some time before I can make the comparison – because my reading time is indeed limited.

Concerning my recovery from the coronary attack, I am largely dependent upon the doctors for an opinion. According to them, the clinical reports are excellent and show what they call 'as complete a recovery as can be expected in any case of extensive heart damage.' For myself, I sense no difference whatsoever in my feeling of health and strength as compared to my condition prior to the attack. The possible exception is that I do not always seem to have the same amount of zeal in tackling a new problem that I used to experience. When I mentioned this to one of my doctors, he merely grinned and said, 'Of course you are a bit older, too.'

In any event, at long last I have adopted your advice of former years to me to take a mid-day rest. Strangely enough, my doctors insist that this rest should be taken prior to lunch and so nowadays I have a very late luncheon – something on the order of two o'clock. The only difficulty about this is that I can no longer use the luncheon period for meetings at which much business can be done under comfortable and pleasant surroundings.

In my former letter, I did not mean to imply that I was disturbed about the relationships between our two countries. I merely meant to point out that even in the case of our two countries these relationships are not perfect. As you know I have long been a friend and admirer of Anthony; on top of this both Foster and I think that Anthony and Selwyn Lloyd make a splendid team. Of course we were initially disappointed when Macmillan left the Foreign Office because we felt we were getting on such a splendid basis of understanding and cooperation with him.

I regret, as you do, the two or three years wasted in your atomic development. Unquestionably you not only lost time, but also a considerable amount of money because the true circumstances were not understood by some fairly small characters <u>before</u> the Congress passed a law that tied the hands of the Executive Department. But I am delighted that you have gone so far in catching up and, of course, nowadays the law is not only less restrictive than it once

---

[1] Reproduced above (pp. 2103–4).

was, but I would not be astonished to see it still further liberalized within a year or so.

I do not fully share your conclusion that an end to nuclear war will come about because of realization on both sides that by using this weapon an unconscionable degree of death and destruction would result. I do think it might tend to reduce very materially the possibility of any new war; but I think it would be unsafe to predict that, if the West and the East should ever become locked up in a life and death struggle, both sides would still have sense enough not to use this horrible instrument. You will remember that in 1945 there was no possible excuse, once we had reached the Rhine in late '44, for Hitler to continue the war, yet his insane determination to rule or ruin brought additional and completely unnecessary destruction to his country; brought about its division between East and West and his own ignominious death.

I assure you that Mrs Eisenhower and I were delighted to have a good report on Clemmie's health. Please convey to her our warm greetings, and to yourself our best wishes for continued health and happiness.

Sir Winston S. Churchill to Wendy and Emery Reves
(Churchill papers, 2/532)

30 April 1956

My dear Wendy and Emery,

Let me thank you once more for your kindness and hospitality to me during my ten weeks with you. You certainly made up for the weather. Indeed I passed a peaceful and happy time under the shelter of your palatial roof.

With regard to your further attractive invitation, Lady Churchill is going to stay with a friend in Paris for a week beginning 24 May, and would like very much to come to stay with you for a few days after that. I will myself come over on Monday 28 or Tuesday 29 May, if that will suit you, and should like to stay until about the middle of the month, if you will keep me so long, when I must go home to take part in the Garter celebrations and racing engagements. Let me know if this is all right.

Lord Bracken to Sir Winston S. Churchill
(Churchill papers, 4/67)

1 May 1956

My dear Winston,

Thank you very much for sending me your book. It is very attractively produced and I look forward to reading it during my long flight to South Africa.

What a history your history has had! I remember my unavailing efforts to soothe the savage breast of the elder Flower when he was unreasonably demanding delivery at what he called the 'due date'. A better negotiator, dear Bill Camrose, suppressed his caterwaulings. Then came Korda and afterwards the resurrection of the faded old proofs. And now happily the book is launched and the back broken of most of the work required to produce three more volumes. I have never known a book to get a better press.

You are a marvellous animal.

Sir Winston S. Churchill: speech
('The Unwritten Alliance', page 288)

3 May 1956   St Paul's Cathedral

LORD CAMROSE MEMORIAL

The honour falls to me to pay a tribute to the late Lord Camrose by unveiling the modest yet impressive memorial which Sir Albert Richardson[1] has conceived. A large part of Lord Camrose's working life was spent within sight of St Paul's Cathedral. It is especially fitting that he should be commemorated here, not far from Fleet Street, in the splendid building of Sir Christopher Wren.[2]

When I heard of Lord Camrose's death in 1954 I said of him that: 'Patriotism and an earnest desire for a stable yet progressive society were his unswerving guides.' In dark and uncertain times, no man could be more steady and persevering. During the war his unfaltering confidence helped to sustain all those who knew him. It happened that Lord Camrose chose journalism as his profession and was always faithful to his choice. He sustained and built up a famous newspaper enterprise. He was a man who, it seemed to those who knew him, would have made his mark in any field of affairs. Wisdom, foresight, and pertinacity showed in all his thoughts and actions.

This country owes much to his staunchness of spirit. Nothing ever shook Lord Camrose and worry was a word that found no place in his vocabulary. To his friends and to the causes in which he believed he was steadfastly loyal. Throughout his life Lord Camrose was, in the words of John Bunyan, 'Valiant-for-Truth'.

---

[1] Albert Richardson, 1880–1964. English architect. Known for restoration of churches and his academic work on Georgian-era architecture. Prof,, University College London, 1919–46. Royal Gold Medal for Architecture, 1947. President, Royal Academy, 1954–6. Knighted, 1956.

[2] Christopher Wren, 1632–1723. English scientist and architect. Designed at least 51 churches, most notably St Paul's Cathedral, as well as many secular buildings, including the Royal Observatory, Greenwich; Trinity College Library, Cambridge; and the façade of Hampton Court Palace. Prof. of Astronomy, Gresham College, 1657–61. Founding member, Royal Society, 1662; President, 1680–2.

Aristotle Onassis to Sir Winston S. Churchill
(Churchill papers, 4/67)

9 May 1956 Monte Carlo

I was very touched to receive the first volume of your *History of the English Speaking Peoples*, the reading of which will, I am sure, be no less enjoyable than instructive. I am looking forward to spending a few quiet evenings with this, the latest of your literary-historical achievements.

On glancing at it, however, I was sad to notice an omission, which, knowing full well the pleasure you derive from free comment, I should like to take the liberty to point out to you here. There is no mention in the opening chapters of your book of the great old neighbour and compatriot of mine – Phyleas the Massaliot,[1] the historian and explorer who discovered Britain long before Caesar landed there.

I am afraid, too, that the Hellenic (in its wider sense) contribution to the fundamentals of British civilisation and culture is either ignored altogether or submerged in the ostentatious grandeur (not glory) of Rome.

With grateful thanks for your kind thought in sending me your book, I remain

Sir Winston S. Churchill: speech
('Winston S. Churchill, His Complete Speeches', volume 8, pages 8674–6)

10 May 1956 Aachen, West Germany

GRAND ALLIANCE OF EUROPEAN POWERS

It is for me a high honour to receive today the Charlemagne Prize in this famous German and European city of Aachen which some call Aix-la-Chapelle.

I am proud too that my name should be added to the distinguished list of the recipients of the prize who have all contributed so notably to the inspiring theme of European unity and brotherhood. I find it particularly pleasing that my immediate predecessor should be the Federal Chancellor himself. No individual has consciously done more than Dr Adenauer to bring Germany back into the circle of free nations who look out hopefully upon the future. I recall my first meeting with him at The Hague eight years ago, and I have followed with attention the great work which he has done for this country, and rejoiced in his success.

---

[1] Pytheas of Massalia, c.350–285 bc. Greek explorer and scientist, known for having circumnavigated Great Britain. Although records of his journeys have not survived, it is believed he may have travelled as far as Iceland and the Baltic Sea, making several scientific discoveries along the way.

It was indeed a remarkable conception of Dr Pfeiffer[1] and his fellow-citizens of Aachen to have created this prize and to have shaped the terms of its award. The name of Charlemagne[2] would occur naturally to you. Here is where Charles the Great was laid to rest. Before his sway, for hundreds of years after the Roman Empire had been broken into fragments, a far-reaching substratum of Europe's population had refused to accept as normal a world consisting of warring tribes, whose quarrels dominated their lives. Just as there was a universal church, people were then dimly aware that there should be some accepted authority to keep order within and prevent incursions from without. Thus the resuscitation of the Roman Empire under Charles the Great on that Christmas Day at the turn of the eighth century was welcomed by almost all with a sigh of relief, in the hope that it heralded a return to the peace and prosperity and to the larger unity which had once existed.

The idea was too good to be true. Unity was preserved for less than fifty years. Wars rent Europe for more than a thousand years. Indeed it was exactly eleven hundred years after Charlemagne's death, that in 1914 a war fiercer and more devastating than any which had gone before broke out between the states whose frontiers lie so close to this city. I do not need to trace the succeeding quarter century of fitful peace and flickering hopes which came to an end in 1939. Nor is it necessary today further to lament the six years which followed. You in this city know them well – but not in such a way, I am glad to think, as to prevent you from receiving me as you have done.

I have not been in Germany since I came to attend the meeting at Potsdam eleven years ago. I had to leave before it was concluded because of a General Election at home, and I did not return. Much has happened in those eleven years. In fact, in the first two years Russia pursued a policy which divided her from her allies. We have now been told on high authority that it was 'the Stalin policy' and Stalin, who was then all-powerful, is now dead. But meanwhile events moved. There followed very speedily during the Stalin policy a reconciliation between the British Commonwealth and the United States on the one hand, and the great mass of Western Germany on the other. This was indeed an historical event. It led to the formation of NATO which now includes no less than fifteen countries, from Canada and the United States to Turkey, and from Iceland to Italy and Portugal. This Treaty in which Germany is a partner is a solemn affirmation of the Unity of Europe, and of the resolve of the United States to come back across the

---

[1] Kurt Christian Theobald Pfeiffer, 1893–1987. Educated at University of Bonn. Ran family textile business, 1923–44. Mayor of Aachen under American Military Government, 1944–5. Founder and Chairman, Charlemagne Prize Committee, 1949–68. CBE, 1961.

[2] Charles the Great, 742–814. Known as 'Charlemagne'. Founded an expanded Frankish state known as the Carolingian Empire. King of the Franks, 768–814. King of the Lombards, 774–814. Holy Roman Emperor, 800–14.

Atlantic Ocean and take what cannot be less than the leading part in maintaining it.

In these considerations France and the valiant French people must be much in our thoughts. I have always felt – and I said at Zurich in 1946[1] – that one of the supreme duties and privileges of France after 1945 was to bury all bitterness and lead Germany by the hand back into the European family. The French contribution to European unity is very large, and the German reception has been invaluable. The conceptions of a former Charlemagne Prize winner, M Monnet, have played no small part therein. Now France is faced in North Africa with the gravest difficulties,[2] and her allies should give her their full support in her efforts to reach a just settlement.

NATO is a striking product and expression of a world wearied of war determined to build its own organization in such strength and power that there will be peace henceforward. The principle of the Treaty is simple and majestic. We all join hands together and are sworn to fight the aggressor, whoever he may be. A new question has been raised by the recent Russian repudiation of Stalin. If it is sincere we have a new Russia to deal with, and I do not see myself, why, if this be so, the new Russia should not join in the spirit of this solemn agreement. We must realize how deep and sincere are Russian anxieties about the safety of her homeland from foreign invasion. In a true Unity of Europe Russia must have her part. I was glad to see that Poland was already not unaffected by the changes in Russian outlook that have recently come to pass. It may be that other changes will follow. Czechoslovakia will recover her freedom. Above all, Germany will be reunited.

We should be rash and blameworthy were we to attempt to solve the problem of European unity, of which German reunification is a vital part, by any violent stroke. We must avoid violence. The only unity there might be then might be a unity of ashes and death.

Equally, it would be fatal for NATO now to relax and let apathy overtake what has been achieved by the planning and financial sacrifices made in the last eight years. I have spoken much of NATO and I do not wish to leave the impression that I regard it as the sole and exclusive effective expression of the moves towards European unity. No one can doubt the usefulness of the Western European Union, the Economic Committee, the Coal and Steel Community and the Council of Europe at Strasbourg, with all of which many of you here have been so closely concerned. But I believe that our main theme of salvation should be the Grand Alliance of the European powers, linked with Canada and the United States. I repeat that the spirit of this arrangement should not exclude Russia and the Eastern European states. It may well be that the great issues which perplex us, of which one of the gravest is the

---

[1] Speech reproduced in *The Churchill Documents*, vol. 22, *Leader of the Opposition, August 1945 to October 1951*, pp. 458–61.

[2] Between 1954 and 1962 France was engaged in hostilities with the Algerian National Liberation Front; the war ended with Algerian independence in 1962.

reunification of Germany, could then be solved more easily than they can by rival blocks confronting each other with suspicion and hostility. That is for the future. Let us go forward to it by reinforcing patiently and surely the arrangements which we have so far achieved. I thank you for your welcome.

Sir Winston S. Churchill to President Dwight D. Eisenhower
(Churchill papers, 2/217)

May 1956[1]   Chartwell
NOT SENT

I put off answering your letter of April 27[2] until I had got through my German visit. The speech was a serious pre-occupation and took me a lot of time to prepare. There were so many things not to say. As I know, I think very highly of Adenauer, and some years ago paid him the compliment of saying he was the greatest German Chancellor since Bismarck. I read a book about Bismarck lately by an Oxford don, which does not show him in a broad disinterested light. I asked Adenauer whether he had taken it as a compliment or a criticism. He was by no means reassuring on the matter.

The Germans received me very kindly. I had to make six other speeches, but as they were impromptu they caused no worry. The Fourth Hussars are quartered within forty miles of the Russian Zone, and I was much interested to see the modern composition of the Regiment. Fifty officers sat down to mess, and even that was insufficient for the tanks they had to manage. An American armoured division had just arrived for firing exercises, and hundreds of them came to welcome me. Altogether the visit leaves a pleasant memory in mind, and I was glad to see that in spite of the march of time I can still do four days continuous toil.

Sir Winston S. Churchill to Bernard Baruch
(Churchill papers, 2/210)

June 1956[3]
Private and Confidential

My dear Baruch,

Thank you for your letter of May 29. Alas, I have been unable to achieve what you know I would wish. The following, for your personal information, is an extract from the Foreign Secretary's reply[4] to my letter on the subject.

---

[1] Day not specified in original.
[2] Reproduced above (pp. 2109–10).
[3] Day not specified in original.
[4] See Macmillan to Churchill, 13 Dec. 1955, reproduced above (pp. 2069–70).

'We made it a rule during the war – and the rule was reaffirmed after the war – not to offer awards to any civilian officials or employees of the United States Government in respect of wartime services. This was because under the American Constitution such persons cannot accept foreign awards without the consent of Congress; and we held it to be inconsistent with the dignity of the Crown that an honour conferred by the Sovereign should be the subject to the approval of a foreign legislature. We felt obliged to apply this rule not only to salaried officials but also to those who, like Mr Baruch, served the Government for a nominal remuneration (the so-called "dollar a year" men), since they were equally affected by the Constitutional embargo. I understand that for that reason proposals to honour amongst others Wendell Willkie and Harry Hopkins were turned down. Indeed, so far as I know, no British honours have been given to any United States civilians who worked with the United States Government in connexion with the war effort, whether their services were official or unofficial.'

With much regret I feel that I must bow to this view.

Colonel George Wigg to Sir Winston S. Churchill
(Churchill papers, 2/131)

18 June 1956

Dear Sir Winston Churchill,

I have placed on the Order Paper, a copy of which I attach, a Motion to secure the erection of a monument to the memory of the late Lord Haldane,[1] the centenary of whose birth occurs on July 30th, 1956, and I wondered whether you would be good enough to add your name. As an inscription I have suggested the words written by Field Marshal Earl Haig[2] in the copy of his Dispatches which he handed to Lord Haldane at the end of the Victory Ride through London in 1919 (Lord Haldane describes the incident on page 288 of his Autobiography), and I am sure you will agree they are very appropriate.

I have long thought that Lord Haldane's work as an Army reformer is worthy of study in relation to current service problems, and his genius in this field has certainly not received the appreciation it merits. My motion,

---

[1] Richard Burdon Haldane, 1856–1928. MP (Lib.) for Haddingtonshire, 1885–1911. Secretary of State for War, 1905–12. Viscount, 1911. Lord Chancellor under Asquith (1912–15) and Ramsay MacDonald (1924).

[2] Douglas Haig, 1861–1928. Graduated from Royal Military College, Sandhurst, 1885. Commissioned into 7th Queen's Own Hussars, 1885. CB, 1901. ADC to King Edward VII, 1902–4. Inspector-General of Cavalry, India, 1903–6. Maj.-Gen., 1904. KCVO, 1909. CoS, India, 1909–12. Lt-Gen., 1910. KCIE, 1911. KCB, 1913. ADC to King George V, 1914. Gen., 1914. C-in-C, British Armies in France, 1915–19. GCB, 1915. GCVO, 1916. FM, 1917. KT, 1917. OM, 1919. Earl, 1919. C-in-C of Forces in Great Britain, 1919–20.

therefore, seeks to recognise the memory and work of a great man in the hope that present and future generations will profit thereby. I very much hope you will give it your support.

Sir Winston S. Churchill to Colonel George Wigg
(*Churchill papers, 2/131*)

21 June 1956
Private

My dear Colonel Wigg,

Thank you for your letter of June 18. I had and have a high opinion of Haldane, but even so I do not feel that I could add my name to your Motion. There are, I think, far too many statues in London – not all of them very good – and the trend has been to add to them increasingly in recent years.

This does not mean of course that I oppose your suggestion in any way, but I do not think that I can actively support it. Pray nevertheless accept my thanks for thinking of me in this connection.

Harry S Truman: recollection
('*Defending the West, The Truman–Churchill Correspondence*', *pages 218–19*)

24 June 1956

Sir Winston and Lady Churchill met us at the door.[1] We stopped for pictures. Many of the neighbor people were at the gate. They gave a wave and a cheer as Mrs Truman & I entered.

Sir Winston and I had a most pleasant conversation about Potsdam, on agreements and Russian perfidy. I walked around the place with him, feeding the goldfish in two ponds and sitting in the garden watching his three grandchildren play. It was a scene long to be remembered and an experience never to be forgotten.

Mr Churchill is as keen mentally as ever. He still has the ability to meet quip with quip and to turn a phrase in his own inimitable manner. But his physical condition shows his 82 years. He walks more slowly and he does not hear well.

He told me that he could do whatever had to be done as he always did but that he'd rather not do it. He walked around and up and down steps with no more effort than would be expected of a man his age. He remarked that it would be a great thing for the world if I should become President of the United States again. I told him there is no chance of that.

Lord Beaverbrook impressed me very much. I had quite a conversation

---

[1] At Chartwell. This proved to be their last meeting.

with him. He is a great admirer of Sir Winston. He also told me that on this European trip, he thought I'd made the greatest ambassador of goodwill USA had ever had here. Quite a statement from that source. He also said that Margaret had done a wonderful piece of work along the same line. He may have been pulling my leg, but I don't think so.

It was all over too soon and we had to return to London.

John Wilson[1] to Sir Winston S. Churchill
(Churchill papers, 1/54)[2]

11 July 1956

Dear Sir Winston,

I have just learned from Lloyd's Bank that you recently renewed the deed under which you have been giving us an annuity.

Shirley and I have been exceedingly grateful for the help you have given us in the past seven years and we never for one moment imagined that the annuity would continue after this year. It is extraordinarily generous of you to continue to give it to us and we don't really know how to thank you. The money has been a tremendous help to us in setting up with our family and if anything should happen to my father it would help to enable us to make sure that my mother was provided for.

We can only say how very grateful we are to you for your great generosity. We both thank you very much indeed.

---

[1] Richard John McMoran Wilson, 1924–2014. Ordinary Seaman, HMS *Belfast*, 1943; HMS *Oribi*, 1944–6. Married, 1948, Shirley Rowntree Harris: three children. 3rd Secretary, Ankara, 1948; Tel Aviv, 1950. 2nd Secretary, Rio de Janeiro, 1953. 1st Secretary, FO, 1956; Washington DC, 1959; FO, 1961. Counsellor, British Embassy in South Africa, 1965. Head, West African Dept, 1968–73. British Ambassador to Chad, 1970–3; to Hungary, 1973–6; to Portugal, 1976–81. CMG, 1970. Succeeded his father as 2nd Baron Moran, 1977. British High Commissioner to Canada, 1981–4. KCMG, 1981. Elected to House of Lords, 1999.

[2] This letter was handwritten.

Lord Moran to Sir Winston S. Churchill
(*Churchill papers, 1/54*)[1]

13 July 1956

My dear Winston,

I hardly trust myself when I see you to tell you what I feel about your wonderful generosity in extending the covenant. It means a great deal to both my boys at this particular time. John is just back in the FO in Whitehall after 8 years abroad, and has to set up house with a young family without the allowances they got when abroad. Geoffrey[2] is just starting in English Electrics, and it is even more of a Godsend to him than to John. Besides apart from this they both feel the thrill of being helped by you. I am sending this because when talking to you I can never put into words what I so very deeply feel. Thank you very much.

Sir Winston S. Churchill to Lady Churchill
(*Baroness Spencer-Churchill papers*)

30 July 1956

My darling One,

Christopher was quite right in his judgement about flying. He rang up the proper authorities and was told that the clouds, which were 6,000 feet in England, were 3,000 feet in the neighbourhood of Dusseldorf. We started amid gusts, which the plane encountered with a few bumps, and reached our destination in one hour and fifty minutes. Immediately after our departure a really frantic hurricane of rain and wind broke on Chartwell and the neighbourhood. This stripped many branches off trees, and there is quite a mess for the gardeners to clear up. One of the front gates was blown down.

We were received with the utmost courtesy in Dusseldorf, and were all invited to luncheon with the Stewards at the hotel. I cannot imagine why Nightingall thought we could win this race, only on German interested assurances we would have a walk-over. The French horses were quite good. The paddock was invaded by the mob, who pressed around our horse, causing him to stream with sweat long before he even got to the course. We had a ten minutes hail and rain storm before the race, which made the ground even more boggy than it was after the heavy rain. As you know, Le Pretendant's[3] form largely depends on hard ground, but here he was slipping all over the

---

[1] This letter was handwritten.

[2] Geoffrey Hazlitt Wilson, 1929–. Educated at Eton and King's College, Cambridge. Fellow, Institute of Chartered Accountants, 1955; Chartered Institute of Management, 1959. Director, Blue Circle Industries, 1980–97. Chairman, Delta PLC, 1982–94. CVO, 1989.

[3] Thoroughbred owned by Churchill; half-brother to Colonist II. Won Churchill Stakes in Indiana, among other races, 1953–7, before being retired to stud.

place. The Irish horse ridden by Lester Piggott[1] was just behind us at the tail.

It all passed off very pleasantly, however. The Germans paid the expenses, and the Ambassador met us and accompanied us all the time. His wife is in Scotland. He asked after you. I must confess I thought you would be all right in the big aeroplane, though I was a little worried about the prospects of our flight in a six-seater. But I fear you had a very bumpy journey – perhaps even worse than we had.

I am on my way to the Royal luncheon, and afterwards am going to the House. Eden says he wants to see me, as he has much to tell. Personally, I think that France and England ought to act together with vigour, and if necessary with arms, while America watches Russia vigilantly.[2] I do not think the Russians have any intention of being involved in a major war. We could secure our rights in the Arab world, and France has every reason to resent Nasser's attitude and action in Algeria.

I do hope you will take a good rest and acquire height usage, and will recover from the bumpy journey and the long and very tiring motor drive.

Lady Churchill to Sir Winston S. Churchill
(Churchill papers, 1/55)[3]

1 August 1956   Palace Hotel, St Moritz

My darling,

Your letter has just come full of interesting information – (And my *Times* tells me that an old gentleman who lives close to us Dunton Green Sir Richard Lloyd-Roberts[4] was killed by the fall of an old walnut tree). Your flight to Dusseldorf was a gallant adventure and I grieve that you were not rewarded by good fortune. Was Lester Piggott pulling his horse too hard or was he really trying?!

I fear that AE will wait for America who for the 3rd time will arrive on the scene very late. I hope you may be able to influence him.

The weather here is lovely though crisp and I wish you were here to enjoy it. The sun is hot and high between 9 and 3. After that chill descends on this high world.

I am still very tired, but I'm sure in a few days, I shall recover. Yesterday I

---

[1] Lester Piggott, 1935–. Leading jockey. Winner of the Epsom Derby, 1954, 1957, 1960, 1968, 1970, 1972, 1976, 1977, 1983; 2,000 Guineas, 1957, 1968, 1970, 1985, 1992; 1,000 Guineas, 1970, 1981; Prix de l'Arc de Triomphe, 1973. Champion Jockey, 1960, 1964–71, 1981, 1982. Rode over 4,000 winners in Britain. Trainer, 1985–7.

[2] President Nasser of Egypt had nationalized the Suez Canal on July 26. He then closed the canal to Israeli shipping and blockaded the Gulf of Aqaba.

[3] This letter was handwritten.

[4] Richard Lloyd-Roberts, 1885–1956. Civil servant, Post Office and Labour Exchanges, 1903–16. Labour Officer, Brunner, Mond & Co. Ltd, 1916–27. Civil servant, Ministry of Labour, 1948–51. Member, Industrial Disputes Tribunal, 1952–6.

went for a short drive with my old crony, Mr Einstein, but we were both of us too exhausted to enjoy it!

I think Monsieur Mollet is being rather brave. What do you think of digging a second canal? Is Lord Birdwood[1] who writes in the *Times* old 'Birdie'[2] or his son.

With my dear love
[Drawing of a cat]

Sir Winston S. Churchill to Lady Churchill
(Baroness Spencer-Churchill papers)

3 August 1956   Chartwell

My darling One,

Your letter of the 1st arrived the morning of the 3rd, which is pretty good. Tomorrow is the 4th of August, a date which used to be very memorable in our minds.[3] I was away from Chartwell when Sir Richards Lloyd-Roberts was killed by the fall of the old walnut a few miles away. There are dangers everywhere, even in the safest places. Lester Piggott, was, I think, in the same position as we were, completely messed up by the boggy ground. I do not feel that Le Pretendant has lost his place, but it will take him a month to recover.

Give my regards to Mr Einstein. I am very glad he has turned up to give you company. August, from which we had hoped so much, has so far lived up to the reputation it inherited from July. I wish indeed I could spend a day or two with you. This is not meant to be ungrateful for the two hours of sunshine I have had tonight. I do hope you will continue to gain strength and to eat up your bruises. I will inquire about Lord Birdwood. The original must be very old, if he is still alive.

I am pleased with the policy being pursued about Suez. We are going to do our utmost. Anthony told me everything, and I even contemplated making a speech, but all went so well in the Thursday debate that this would have been an unnecessary hazard. As I am well informed, I cannot in an unprotected letter tell any secrets, but I feel you may rest assured that there will be no ground of complaints on what we try to do. The French are very sporting, and it is nice to feel they are working with us, and that we and the Americans are both agreed. We have taken a line which will put the canal effectively on its

---

[1] Christopher Birdwood, 1899–1962. Educated at Royal Military College, Sandhurst. Married, 1931, Elizabeth Vere Drummond Ogilvie (div. 1954): two children; 1954, Joan Pollack Graham. Entered Indian Army, 1917. ADC to GOC Australian Corps, 1918–19. British Officer in Charge of King's Indian Orderly Officers, 1932, 1939. Baron, 1951.

[2] William Riddell Birdwood, 1865–1951. Lt, Royal Scots Fusiliers, 1883. GOC Australian and New Zealand Army Corps (ANZAC), 1914–18. Knighted, 1914. FM, 1925. C-in-C, India, 1922–30. Master of Peterhouse, Cambridge, 1931–8. Baron, 1938.

[3] On 4 Aug. 1914, Britain declared war on Germany.

international basis, and will also make it secure until long after 1968. Anthony has told my Anthony to keep himself fully informed from Downing Street, and I am actually reading large bundles of telegrams from day to day.

Violet is coming to spend the night of Bank Holiday with me, and thereafter I have Juliet on Friday the 11th.[1] I propose to ask Pamela for the following week. It is Bernie Baruch's 87th Birthday on Sunday the 19th. Randolph has gone off to America after giving me a dreadful beating up about supporting such a Government as this. I took the brunt of it off myself by a film, and he was astonished the next morning (Wednesday) when he saw the newspapers which I could not reveal to him until they were published. There is only one opinion in the House of Commons, and this fully covers the use of force as and when it may be necessary.

My dearest Clemmie do persevere in getting back yr strength and we can make some plans together with all my love.

Your devoted husband.
[Drawing of a pig]

Sir Winston S. Churchill: note
(Churchill papers, 2/130)

6 August 1956

Questions relating to method of control. EM[2] not adapted military. The Prime Minister is always in fact Minister of Defence. It might be well for him to assume it in fact, though probably without making it a formal change. Harold Macmillan, who has recent experience, could take on the job with which he is fully acquainted, giving WM sick leave. Again, however, the Prime Minister's authority and constant supervision would be required.

In the war I knew the three Chiefs of Staff better than we know them now. The airman[3] is very little known. According to my ideas there would be nothing incongruous in your[4] asking one or both ministers to be present.

The military operation seems very serious. We have a long delay when our intentions are known. The newspapers and foreign correspondents are free to publish what they choose. A censorship should be imposed. In a month it should be possible for at least 1,000 Russian & similar volunteers to take over the cream of the Egyptian aircraft and tanks. This might expose us to much more severe resistance. I was not used readily to accept from the Air

---

[1] Aug. 11 was actually a Saturday in 1956.
[2] Error for WM, i.e. Walter Monckton, Minister of Defence.
[3] Dermot Alexander Boyle, 1904–93. Air ADC to the King, 1943. CBE, 1945. CB, 1946. AVM, 1949. KCVO, 1953. KBE, 1953. AOC-in-C, Fighter Command, 1953–5. Air Mshl, 1954. CAS, 1956–9. Air Chf Mshl, 1956. GCB, 1957. Mshl of the RAF, 1958.
[4] i.e. Eden's.

Force numbers of aircraft which could be used by us from various stations. For instance, it seems to me unreasonable not to use at least 100 Canberras in Cyprus alone, and generally to follow the principle of 'more than enough.'

The more one thinks about taking over the Canal, the less one likes it. The long causeway could be easily obstructed by a succession of mines. We should get much of the blame of stopping work, if it is to be up to the moment of our attack a smooth-running show. Cairo is Nasser's centre of power. I was very glad to hear that there would be no weakening about Libya on account of the Prime Minister etc., but that both the armoured divisions, properly supported by air, with any additional forces that may be needed, would be used.

On the other side a volte face should certainly free our hands about Israel. We should want them to menace and hold the Egyptians and not be drawn off against Jordan.

Lady Churchill to Sir Winston S. Churchill
(Churchill papers, 1/55)[1]

9 August 1956
Palace Hotel, St Moritz

My darling,

I have been reassuring myself and comforting myself by reading again your letter of August the 3rd. Because to me, the Suez situation seems perplexing and deteriorating. I too thought of August the 4th 1914 but when I said to Mr Einstein, 'This is a memorable day for us,' he didn't know of what I was thinking, but of course the Americans did not wake up till years later. I pray that this time they will help sooner.

Do explain to me why Israel has not been bidden to the Conference. I listened to Anthony last night. It was hard to hear but I'm afraid I was disappointed by what I did hear. There was no inspiration.

The weather here since two days is lovely, really hot sun and a light cool breeze.

The leg and foot are static but any day now I hope for improvement. I have a balcony to my bedroom which is pleasant.

Your devoted and loving
[Drawing of a cat]

---

[1] This letter was handwritten.

Sir Winston S. Churchill to Lady Churchill
(Baroness Spencer-Churchill papers)

11 August 1956   Chartwell

My darling One,

The weather is awful. We had one lovely day, not a cloud from dawn to dusk, and I hoped it marked a decided turn. Since then we have not had a gleam, and lots of rain.

Like you, I am anxious about the situation in the Middle East. I suppose the reason why they did not bring Israel in was that they were afraid she would become uncontrollable. But she is there in the background, and I have no doubt that if it comes to war she will join in. One can never be quite sure whether a number of 'volunteers' will not be mixed up with the Egyptians, who manage the Russian aeroplanes and tanks. There is no doubt that this would involve hard fighting, but I think we will have enough troops on the move. Naturally I am worried about this pow-wow, which was to have finished by the end of August at the latest. I do not see myself how it is to be closured and wound up, and I am not sure that Selwyn Lloyd is the man. However, there is nothing for it but to go on with the programme. The President is quite right in saying that if he stays out America will balance Russia. The unity of Islam is remarkable. There is no doubt that Libya, whom we have paid £5,000,000 a year, like Jordania, to whom we paid £10,000,000 or more, are whole-heartedly manifesting hostility. You will be home before anything serious happens.

I shall go up to London next Wednesday to see my Optician about my left eye, which is very bloodshot, and I will take occasion to make some contacts then. I have not worried Anthony since I saw him.

Christopher has been to Paris, but comes back today. I rather gather that Maria follows a little later.

I am so glad you are having sunshine. It is indeed dreary gazing out through rain-spotted windows on the grey mists that wrap the weald of Kent. I have been reading about Disraeli and Gladstone to come after the American Civil War Book.

I hope to have good news for you about MGM (Metro-Goldwyn-Meyer). It appears that I retained the television and film rights[1] and that they are just my ordinary property. This makes a great difference. I will explain it all to you when we meet.

Juliet[2] is coming to luncheon today and will stay till Monday. If I remember right she plays Bezique.

---

[1] Relating to *My Early Life* (*A Roving Commission* in the US).
[2] Juliet Duff.

4 p.m.

Juliet is here, and she had brought the new book with her and sends you lots of love. We are sitting in yr rose garden wh is really <u>hot.</u>

All my love,
Yr Devoted Husband,
[Drawing of a pig]

Sir Winston S. Churchill to Lady Churchill
(Baroness Spencer-Churchill papers)

14 August 1956   Chartwell

My darling One,

I enclose you a cutting which I tore from today's *Mirror*. It is a pretty odious piece of money-grubbing. Nevertheless I expect it represents at least a large minority of the country. I think it may be a reflection of Harold Macmillan's views. He expressed them fairly and frankly to me last week. They point to the futility of taking the Canal and having a hundred thousand troops to find to guard it, instead of what he favours if need be going for Cairo and the Egyptian state.

The Russians have come over with a delegation of fifty – the numbers being picked, according to AMB, to proselytize the rest of the Conference. I really don't see how they (HMG) will be able to cope with the clatter of voices and get the thing wound up by the end of August. You will be home in plenty of time for the <u>fun</u>, if any.

Today it is partly cloudy, but bright, and I am sitting on a seat in the garden dictating a letter to Miss Maturin, who sends you her regards.

I had Miss Thorson[1] of the MGM down here yesterday. She is a really clever woman. The negotiations are settled in principle on the basis of seventy thousand down, and God knows how many millions in the future as a result of fifty per cent of the profit. The extraordinary thing is that it is practically certain that this fifty-year-old story is my own property and not taxable.

I have to make arrangements for reading four or five minutes from the text. Miss T worked up a good extract, which I considered and polished this morning, and which I will deliver on Saturday next in my study. I think it is all very good, and will unfold it to you at better length when you arrive.

---

[1] Marjorie Thorson, 1912–99. Born Minneapolis, Minnesota. Educated at University of Southern California and the University of California at Berkeley. Married, 1938, Arthur William Bernal (div.); 1957, Henry McIlvaine Parsons. Joined MGM, Story Dept, 1935. Executive Story Editor, MGM, *c.*1965. Office of War Information, 1941–5.

Mary says she had a long and lovely letter from you. She has come back to look after her brood, and is dining with me tonight. Christopher is wrapped up in his office duties, as you can imagine.

All my love
[Drawing of a pig]

Sir Winston S. Churchill to Lady Churchill
(Baroness Spencer-Churchill papers)

15 August 1956

My darling One,

I came up to London today and had a lunch to which I invited Christopher, Nigel Birch, and Antony Head. We talked over all our affairs. I think it would be very difficult to arrive at a good result. After lunch I received the Lions deputation who gave me 'Rusty'.[1] They are an interesting body of charitable intentions. They gave me a beautiful plaque which I will have put on the cage. I send you a letter which will explain them.

What I have to tell you about is the downfall of my hopes about the film. Apparently, I sold it in 1941 to the Warner Brothers for £7,500! They have done nothing about it all the time, and when we asked Nicholl Manisty[2] if there was any record of any truck with them, they said 'No.' However, yesterday afternoon they wrote a letter saying they had found a document which coupled with the American records make it quite clear that I had no possession. It was very careless of Nicholl Manisty not to give an answer, and of course Moir[3] and all my people were misled. This seemed such a good thing and so simple that I am sorry that it falls to the ground. It was after all only an additional resource, but none the less it is a disappointment.

I brought Rufus up today and sent him to Miss Lobban[4] who has shaved him beautifully. He looks as good as ever. There is no doubt the doctor made a great cure of him. He put a 2½" needle in his broken left jawbone, which now seems to work perfectly, though of course he has no teeth. He eats good meals, and I think I may look forward to a reasonable prolongation of his life. They begin the conference tomorrow, and I imagine that very considerable difficulties still encroach upon them. The Grenadier Guards are leaving today! What a tangle. However this is settled, I expect we must look to Israel for the next move.

[1] A lion.
[2] A firm of solicitors.
[3] Anthony Forbes Moir, 1903–67. Solicitor and legal adviser to Winston Churchill. Married, 1939, Bettine Ethel Read Hardy. Senior Partner, Fladgate & Co., solicitors, c.1957; Stephenson Harwood & Tatham, solicitors, 1958–67.
[4] Bella Lobban. Ran a London kennel that cared for Churchill's poodle, Rufus, in his absence.

My dearest I have been absorbed all day with difficult points ranging from War to my financial affairs. I long to see you and am so glad it will be a week tomorrow.

Your loving and devoted husband,
[Drawing of a pig]

Sir Winston S. Churchill to Wendy Reves
(Churchill papers, 2/532)

16 August 1956   Chartwell

My dear Wendy,

I was very sorry you could not visit this country with Emery. It would have been very jolly to see you again. Emery will have told you about my present plans which remain to visit you about the middle of September. I hope that the Egyptian situation will not develop in a way to delay or prevent it. I don't see why it should. I look forward to coming back to Pausaland again, and will do the same thing about the motorcar and Mario[1] if that can be arranged.

I have been toiling at the book, but have not made the progress I expected. I hope, however, that it will all be finished by the end of January. Five months.

I am sorry that the Princess[2] did not reply to your flowers. Did you make it clear that they came from you and not from me? She wrote a very nice letter in answer to mine. She may be tripping over the irregularity. It makes it difficult for people in formal surroundings.

Clemmie has gone to St Moritz. She had a painful fall before leaving. She thought it was only bruises, but knee and ankle have been afflicted by a torn muscle, and she is unable at present to walk. She is coming back here on Thursday next.

The weather is disappointing. When June failed, I hoped for July. When July disgraced itself, my thoughts turned to August. We have had the most curious changes of weather. Sometimes the most beautiful day without a cloud in the sky, but nearly always succeeded by periods of rain and gales. I wonder what sort of weather you are having and whether the lavender has fulfilled your courageous hopes?

Christopher's official work takes him up to London a great deal, and Mary has her brood but I can live a solitary life without great discomfort.

---

[1] Emery Reves's chauffeur.

[2] Grace Patricia Kelly, 1929–82. Born in Philadelphia. Appeared in roughly a dozen movies and two dozen television shows in the late 1940s and early 1950s. Winner of Golden Globe Award for Best Supporting Actress, 1953; Academy Award for Best Actress, 1954; Golden Globe Award for Best Actress, 1954. Married, 1956, Rainier Louis Henri Maxence Bertrand Grimaldi: three children. Princess Consort of Monaco, 1956–82.

Sir Anthony Eden to Sir Winston S. Churchill
(*Churchill papers, 2/216*)

17 August 1956
Top Secret and Personal

My dear Winston,

Thank you so much for your letter about the documents and your good wishes for the Conference.

We are only at the beginning but there are some encouraging elements. Most important of all, the Americans seem very firmly lined up with us on internationalisation. Secondly, there are signs that the Middle Eastern States who are also oil producers, e.g. Iraq, Persia, and Saudi Arabia, are in varying degrees opposed to Nasser's plans. In other Arab States demagogy howls in support of Nasser.

Preparations about which I spoke to you are going forward with some modifications, which should lead to simplification of our plan should the need arise. I am sure that you will think this all to the good.

It is difficult to judge about public opinion. The left-wing intellectuals and some liberals are all out against us. The BBC is exasperating me by leaning over backwards to be what they call neutral and to present both sides of the case, by which I suppose they mean our country's and the Dancing Major's.[1] I am, however, seeing Jacob[2] this afternoon. He and nearly all the seniors have been away on leave. I hope we can improve on past performances.

Bob Menzies has been very helpful and it would help me if you would tell him so when you see him. I will keep you posted.

I was sorry to be away on Monday, but I needed a few hours off. I am very fit now.

Clarissa joins me in love.

Sir Winston S. Churchill to Lady Churchill
(*Baroness Spencer-Churchill papers*)

23 August 1956   Chartwell

Welcome my darling – I am so glad you are safely home. Maria brings this with all my love.

---

[1] Salah Salem, 1920–62. Egyptian military officer and politician. Commanded artillery units in Egyptian Revolution, 1952. Served with Nasser on Egyptian Revolutionary Command Council. Earned the nickname 'Dancing Major' after being photographed dancing with Sudanese in local garb.

[2] Sir Ian Jacob, BBC Director-General.

Sir Winston S. Churchill to Wendy Reves
(Churchill papers, 2/53)

4 September 1956

My dear Wendy,

Thank you so much for your delightful letter. It gives me keen pleasure to reflect that I can make my plans a fortnight from today. On Monday, therefore, the 17th of September, I will revisit Pausaland. I hope I may bring Montague Browne with me, and I shall indeed look forward to finding you and Emery safely ensconced in the villa.

The only thing that might alter my plans will be WAR. In that case I should have to attend Parliament, and whatever sittings may be necessary.

Sir Winston S. Churchill to Lady Churchill
(Baroness Spencer-Churchill papers)

12 September 1956

My darling One,

Some flowers to salute our 48th anniversary!

All my love

Sir Winston S. Churchill to Lady Churchill
(Baroness Spencer-Churchill papers)

19 September 1956 La Pausa

My darling,

It is all very bright and peaceful here. The air is cool yet the temperature is warm, and in the sun of course it is very hot. Since the beginning of the month they have not had a rainy day. So far I have not moved from the house and the verandah, but we are going to the Chateau de Madrid for luncheon today. They are asking the Prof out here, and I hope he will come. I have not done a stroke of work, but have read about three-quarters of *Tono Bungay*.[1] Yesterday the Kemsleys[2] came to luncheon. I found him very friendly and agreeable.

Dr Roberts has examined me and finds me in very good health. I have started resolutely on the Baruch hearing aid, and am getting very used to wearing it. I can even hear the bird talk when I am alone.

[1] Novel by H. G. Wells, published 1908.

[2] James Gomer Berry, 1883–1968. Newspaper proprietor; brother of Lord Camrose. Married, 1907, Mary Lilian Holmers: seven children (d. 1928); 1931, Edith Merandon Du Plessis (d. 1976). Bt, 1928. Baron Kemsley, 1936. Chairman, Kemsley Newspapers Ltd, 1937–59. Editor-in-Chief, *Sunday Times*, 1937–59. Trustee, Reuters, 1941; Chairman, 1951–9. Viscount, 1945. One of his six sons was killed in action in Italy in 1944.

I do hope your improvement has been continuous. The recovery seemed almost miraculous, and it was a joy to me to see you getting better every day.

My dear One all my love

[Drawing of a pig]

Sir Winston S. Churchill to Lord Cherwell
(Churchill papers, 2/214)

19 September 1956   La Pausa

My dear Prof,

I enclose you a very pleasant and attractive invitation. The weather is beautiful – sunny yet cool. The sooner you come the better. Accept my introduction to Wendy, and send a telegram.

Sir Anthony Eden to Sir Winston S. Churchill
(Churchill papers, 2/216)

21 September 1956

My dear Winston,

Thank you so much for the present of cigars. This was really generous of you.

I am not very happy at the way things are developing here, but we are struggling hard to keep a firm and united front in these critical weeks, firm is even more important than united.

Foster assures us that US is as determined to deal with Nasser as we are – but I fear he has a mental caveat about November 6. We cannot accept that.[1]

Jawaharlal Nehru to Sir Winston S. Churchill
(Churchill papers, 4/67)

22 September 1956   New Delhi

My dear Sir Winston,

This is a belated acknowledgement of your book which you were so kind as to send me. This is the first volume of *The History of the English Speaking Peoples*. It is a delight to read this book and I am very grateful to you for sending it.

I trust you are keeping well.

---

[1] Eden had proposed the setting up of a Canal Users' Association, which would enforce free passage of the Suez Canal from 6 Nov. 1956. This deadline was rejected by the US.

Sir Winston S. Churchill to Lady Churchill
(Baroness Spencer-Churchill papers)

24 September 1956   La Pausa

My dearest,

Your letter has just arrived. You seem to have changed your plan. Does this mean that you will go on early with the improvements to Chartwell? How is Maria provided for?

Here all is peaceful and I am glad to say that the whole book team is hard at work.

Thank you so much for dealing with poor Ivor's[1] funeral.

I am wearing Bernie's hearing-aid every day when in company and I find it a great relief. It is complete and in perfect order and I think I shall get used to the habit of using it. I quite agree that it is a necessity.

I have not tried any painting yet, although there has been plenty of sunlight. The Prefect[2] and his wife are coming to dine on Thursday next. So far we have had no strangers as company.

I had a letter from Anthony thanking me for the cigars, and incidentally showing a robust spirit. I am so glad they are going to the Security Council immediately. I see he is to be in Paris tomorrow or the next day. I must say I am very glad the burden does not rest on me.

I stay in bed all the morning, and am very pleased with the way the book is getting on, and I think you will be both pleased and surprised at the way the work is going.

My darling One,[3]

It is such a pleasure to receive your letters – the handwriting is so strong and you can dash them off with a vigour which shows that your tumbles and their consequences are now steadfastly relegated to the background.

I must say I am attracted by this neighbourhood & am cherishing the idea of La Dagoniere when I have ended my visit here, in the opening days of November. If all my plans work out and I can return in January – (I shall know next week) we shall have a large canvas to paint and we must try to fit ourselves into the design with the utmost pleasure & company.

                                                          My tender love
                                                     Your devoted husband
                                                     [Drawing of a pig]

Toby sends his salutations which I enclose [. . .]

---

[1] Churchill's cousin, Lord Ivor Churchill.
[2] Pierre-Jean Moatti.
[3] Churchill continued from this point in his own hand.

Sir Winston S. Churchill to Maurice Shock[1]
(Churchill papers, 4/28)

25 September 1956   La Pausa

It would be very nice if you could spend the weekend with Alan at his hotel as my guest. I should like to meet you very much. I can get you a seat in the plane Friday or Saturday.

Sir Winston S. Churchill to Gheorghe Gheorghiu-Dej[2]
(Churchill papers, 2/184)

October 1956[3]

Dear Secretary-General,

I am writing to you at the instance of Mr Frederick William Deakin of St Antony's College, Oxford, who has been associated with me in my literary work for many years. He is the son-in-law of Mr Liviu Popescu-Nasta,[4] who, I understand, was sentenced in Bucharest to twenty years' imprisonment in 1950. According to reliable information, Mr Nasta is now dangerously ill and paralysed in a prison hospital. His wife and son, who live in Bucharest, would in no way be in a position to look after him even if he were released on medical grounds and Mr Deakin hopes that the Roumanian government would consider allowing the family as a whole to join him and his wife in England so that he could assume full care and responsibility.

I consider that, on humanitarian grounds alone, this an entirely correct request, and earnestly hope that you will feel able to give it every due consideration.

---

[1] Maurice Shock, 1926–2018. Served in Intelligence Corps, 1945–8. Lecturer in Politics, Christ Church and Trinity College, Oxford, 1955–6. Fellow in Politics, University College, Oxford, 1956–77; Estates Bursar, 1959–74. Vice-Chancellor, Leicester University, 1977–87. Rector, Lincoln College, Oxford, 1987–94. Author of *The Liberal Tradition, From Fox to Keynes* (1967).

[2] Gheorghe Gheorghiu-Dej, 1901–65. Born in Bârlad, Romania. Joined Communist Party of Romania, 1930. General Secretary, Romanian Communist Party, 1944–54, 1955–65. President, State Council, 1961–5.

[3] Day not specified in original.

[4] Liviu Popescu-Nasta, 1891–1956. Born in Brasov, Romania. Correspondent for *New York Times* in Bucharest, 1944–56. Sentenced in 1950 to 20 years' hard labour by the Communist-controlled Romanian Government. Fell ill and died six years later.

Sir Winston S. Churchill to Lady Churchill
(Baroness Spencer-Churchill papers)

2 October 1956   La Pausa

My Darling,

I just cannot think what I meant by 'princely gift'. Perhaps when I get to Chartwell I may find something in the early letters of the monument room which will reveal it.

It continues to be lovely here. We have had, since the electric storms reduced the tension, four lovely days and have no reason not to hope for more.

You do not say anything in your letters to me about how your health is faring. Has the pain gone completely away from the leg, and does it come back to the shoulder? I will telephone again in a day or two.

Here all goes very quietly. The Chateau de Madrid is closed for two months' holiday and we have the chef to cook for us. The food is therefore excellent, though as you know I do not eat so much as I used to. I have done a great deal of work at the book and not painted yet. Mr Shock, who brings this letter this afternoon, has done me a very good note on the first Gladstone and Disraeli chapter, and I look forward to receiving another fertile wodge in a fortnight. He is a very nice young man, and I am glad to have had him at the hotel for the weekend. There are only three more chapters in the last book to be composed after which there will only be bits and pieces and final revise. I am keeping the printers and my whole outfit very busy.

The Prof arrived last night. It was nice of him to face this journey. He is having a dreadful fight with Duncan, and the papers, particularly the *Spectator*, are making it as bad as they can. I cannot see what right D has to use his powers to stir up all this trouble.

I also enclosed a very nice letter I have had from poor Ivor's widow.[1] I have answered it myself, but perhaps you will keep it for me till I return.

I never heard a word from anyone about Collusion running last Saturday, though I see now that he was not placed.

With all my love
Your devoted husband

---

[1] Elizabeth Cunningham, 1914–2010. Known as 'Betty'. Married, 1947, Ivor Charles Spencer-Churchill (d. 1956), a first cousin once removed of Winston Churchill.

Sir Norman Brook to Sir Winston S. Churchill
(Churchill papers, 2/181)

4 October 1956
Top Secret and Personal

Dear Sir Winston,

I understood that a bag was going to you from the Foreign Office today, and I thought you might like to have from me a brief note on developments in the Suez situation.

The PM had rather a difficult time with the French, during his visit to Paris, though he managed to bring matters to a successful conclusion on the second day. The French Ministers showed a good deal of impatience and irritation at the delays in reaching a settlement. They have never seen the same need to go to the Security Council – for the old reason, I suppose, that it is easier for a Socialist Government to be tough than it is for a Conservative Government facing Socialist Opposition. And they continue to be anxious to bring this issue to a head before they have to meet their own Parliament later in the month. They would still prefer therefore an early recourse to force. They also feel very strongly that we should lose no time in bringing Nasser down. For they believe that, if he is not checked, the consequences for Europe as a whole will be very serious. It is not, in their view, a matter only of oil supplies. They fear that, if Nasser succeeds, the existing Governments in other Arab States will be overthrown and that the whole of the Middle East will pass under the influence, not so much of Egypt, as of Russia – and that, if that happens, Europe will be ripe for the picking. For all these reasons they are extremely reluctant to accept the American view that it is better 'to play this long'.

The Americans have certainly not been helpful. It is clear now that we should have been in a much better position here, and should have had a much less divided public opinion, if we had gone to the Security Council at the time when Parliament met. This, as you know, is what we ourselves would have preferred to do. But we were restrained by the Americans who urged us most strongly to hold our hands and give room for the trial of their plan of 'the users' association'. At that stage they presented this plan as a practical means of bringing the issue to a head. But the Second London Conference, at which this plan was discussed, was much less successful than the first – and by the end of it most of the 'teeth' had been removed from that plan. Now, at his latest Press Conference, Dulles has gone so far as to say that it never had any teeth at all. His other statements about colonialism and about our differences 'on fundamental issues' must surely have the effect of encouraging Nasser – and perhaps the Russians too.

Our best hope of bringing Nasser to his senses was to preserve a firm front among the Western Powers – and particularly between the United States, France and ourselves. I fear that, during the last week or so, the Western position has been seriously weakened by public statements made in the United States. This at any rate is the PM's view – and I am sure that it will be held even more strongly by the French.

You may like to know that the PM was deeply impressed by the youth and vigour of M Mollet's Government. He says that they are by far the best French Government he has seen since the war. Over Suez they are tough and uncompromising. He believes that we may be at the beginning of something like a renaissance of strength in France.

We have had no indications yet what course the discussions in the Security Council are likely to take. It seems inevitable, however, that we should be pressed to accept negotiation in some form or other. We do not think it will be possible to reject out of hand all suggestions for negotiation. Possibly the most acceptable form for us would be direct negotiation between ourselves, the French and the Egyptians. It is too early to say how these discussions will go. We feel here, however, that the next ten days will be difficult. And it may well be that by the 15th or 16th October we shall face a critical choice – unless there has emerged from the Security Council some proposal for a method of negotiation which we can accept.

We are at last having some reasonable weather here. This encourages me to hope that you are doing even better on the Mediterranean.

With all good wishes.

Sir Winston S. Churchill to Lady Churchill
(Baroness Spencer-Churchill papers)

5 October 1956 La Pausa

My dear One,

Delighted to get your letter. I am sorry about Rose, but I think she should be operated on. Let me have a telegram if anything goes wrong. I certainly have never felt a twinge since I was treated.

I had a very long and full letter from Christopher last night which had taken four days to travel here in the official bag. The very secret matters with which it dealt – horse racing – required these precautions. I am not quite sure whether I will come home for the 12th or not. It would be more natural to salute the Parliament on the 23rd. Christopher writes with great confidence about the horse. If I come I shall come on the 12th and leave again on the morning of the 14th. Where will you be – London or Chartwell? I will come to either place. I will give you at least three days' notice if I do not come.

The weather is still bright and warm and clear, the breeze cool. Since this morning a mistral has broken upon us. I am very foolish in not getting up to take advantage of it.

Do let me know when you write how you are progressing.

I agree with you about Suez and Dulles and Nasser. I think Gaitskell with his determined speech on August 2 is responsible to a large extent for the Government committing themselves by large troop movements. It would be very hard to use force now.

Progress on the book continues. There are only two or three chapters to do. My darling I send my best love

Your devoted husband
[Two drawings of pigs]
[...]

Maurice Shock to Sir Winston S. Churchill
(Churchill papers, 4/28)[1]

5 October 1956   Oxford

Dear Sir Winston,

Thank you so much for making my visit to Monte Carlo possible; it was a delightful experience. Not only did I see something of the Riviera – in itself a considerable thing which I had not done before – I met you and was fortunate enough to have the opportunity of talking about a great many things. In every way I spent a most enjoyable few days, and not a little of their pleasure was due to your kindness and consideration.

My next chapter is progressing. I will send it to you as soon as it is fit to be seen.

Lady Churchill to Sir Winston S. Churchill
(Churchill papers, 1/55)[2]

9 October 1956

My darling,

'Prof' rang me up to say how much he had enjoyed visiting you & that during his five days at La Pausa the weather had been lovely. I am so very glad.

I feel ashamed & mortified by Randolph's libel action.[3] I fear he will lose, which will be expensive; if he wins I expect the damages will be one ¼. 'Prof' said, however, that you were not using your hearing-aid 6h. I do hope you will. Mary & I are going to Kempton Park with Christopher to see your Horse win. Tender Love my Darling

[Drawing of a cat]

---

[1] This letter was handwritten.

[2] This letter was handwritten.

[3] Against the *People* newspaper for having described him as 'a paid hack'. The jury awarded him £5,000 in damages and legal expenses.

1956

Sir Winston S. Churchill to Lady Churchill
(Baroness Spencer-Churchill papers)

12 October 1956   La Pausa

My dearest One,

I am so glad you and Mary are going to see the horse run on Saturday. I hope it will not rain and that Le Pretendant will fulfil our hopes. You might tell Christopher to send me a telegram, or better still ring me on the telephone, whatever happens.

The weather is very good. Yesterday was one of the finest days I have seen out here. I invited hosts and guests to lunch with me at the Vistaero, which is really a most beautiful villa perched on a peak from which you can look down a thousand feet or more. We came home and I went for my usual daily walk in the garden. Wendy was taken ill, having, it is presumed, eaten something, but today she has recovered.

I plan to come home on the 22nd, and am looking forward so much to seeing you. Toby sends his love, but has not given me any overt sign which I can enclose.

I admit I was astonished that Randolph won his action, and at the damages. It is quite true that he is not a 'paid hack', but I did not think that a jury would draw so firmly the very refined distinction between his vocabulary and the *People*'s. He seems to have acquitted himself well in the box. I have written him a letter of congratulation.

I was so glad to hear from your own lips that you have made a recovery from the many evils which haunted you. I do hope it will last.

With my fondest love
I remain
Your devoted husband
[Drawing of a pig] (more like a mouse than a pig)

Jane Hodge[1] to Sir Winston S. Churchill
(Churchill papers, 2/189)

13 October 1956

Dear Sir Winston

I did not dare, yesterday, try to tell you just how much our holiday had meant to me, because I was afraid, if I did, I should disgrace myself by weeping. Afterwards, in the plane, I wished I had had the courage to make my farewells properly by kissing you gratefully on both cheeks.

---

[1] Jane Aiken, 1917–2009. American-born British author. Married Angus Smart (div.); 1948, Alan Hodge: two children. Author of several books including *Only a Novel*, *The Double Life of Jane Austen* (1972), *One Way to Venice* (1974) and *A Death in Two Parts* (2000).

After my fourteen perfect days, it is almost too good to be true to find it splendidly fine here. I am just off to fetch my daughters. When they ask me where I have been, I shall tell them I have been visiting the world's kindest great man.

Alan says you will forgive me for typing this because my handwriting is so particularly tiresome.

Sir Winston S. Churchill to Lady Churchill
(Baroness Spencer-Churchill papers)[1]

15 October 1956   La Pausa

My darling,

The time has passed very quickly & I am now within a week of coming home – five weeks to a day it will be. It has been a very pleasant spell, quiet and peaceful, I wish you had come for a week or so, I have not decided anything about a permanent residence or indeed anything except read the papers.

I have begun painting one picture – a large long one of the view to the Eastward; and have progressed so well that after three days it is still an attraction to me. Today it rains, but there is hope of clearing in the afternoon.

Sarah is coming on Thursday & the prospects give great pleasure all round. I am going to speak to her on the telephone in an hour or so. Do you know the Baroness Jean de Rothschild,[2] she is a great friend of Wendy's, and I think an agreeable woman. <u>She plays Bezique</u>. Her husband[3] – a Vienna Rothschild – is 72 and she about thirty years younger. She leaves on Wednesday when Sarah arrives.

I hope the Queen was not too vexed at being beaten. It was just as well I wasn't there as there would have been embarrassing cheers & counter-cheers. I agreed to let the colt go to the USA yesterday on Christopher's advice.

The book is going to be finished in time; but I have not heard so far from the Revenue. The man who dealt with my affairs says that there is a good deal of holiday making just now.

I am so glad to have your good reports confirmed by Sarah who says you are very well. I look forward so much to seeing for myself. My dearest

With all my love
Your devoted husband
[Drawing of a pig] resting

Anthony E made a good speech at the conference.

---

[1] This letter was handwritten.

[2] Ivy Sweet, 1908–2003. Known by her stage name 'Jeanne Stuart' and as 'Jeanne de Rothschild'. British stage and film actress. Married, 1933, Bernard Docker (div. 1935); 1952, Eugène Daniel von Rothschild (d. 1976). Acted in over a dozen films in the 1930s and 1940s.

[3] Eugène Daniel von Rothschild, 1884–1976. Member of the Vienna branch of the Rothschild family. Served in Austrian Army, WWI. Married, 1925, Catherine 'Kitty' Wolf (d. 1946); 1952, Ivy 'Jeanne' Sweet.

Anthony Montague Browne: note[1]
(Baroness Spencer-Churchill papers)

[Undated]

The villa is situated on a promontory above Monte Carlo Beach about 100 ft. above the sea. The property comprises practically the whole of the point except the Western seaboard which belongs to the Monte Carlo Beach Hotel. It is isolated, but within a few minutes of the centre of Monte Carlo, and is undoubtedly one of the best positions one could find on the coast. The villa is in very bad condition and war-damaged, and the garden is overgrown.

The Société des Bains de Mer, the company which controls the Casino, the Hotel de Paris, the Beach Hotel, etc., own the villa. They have for some time been proposing to reconstruct it as a luxury annex to the Beach Hotel or something similar. Mr Onassis, who is the largest single shareholder in the company, has made the following proposal:

The Company must in its own interest reconstruct the villa or else raze it and build something new on the site. They would like to erect the new building to the specifications of Sir Winston, and let it to him furnished for his lifetime at a rent to be agreed – probably £1500 a year. (Various figures were mentioned, but £1500 a year seemed the most likely.) The reconstruction would probably cost the Company in the neighbourhood of £40,000–£50,000. Their preliminary proposal is that it should be rebuilt as a one-storey 'colonial' type house with five–seven bedrooms. When Sir Winston no longer required the property it could be modified without much difficulty to meet the Company's requirements as a Hotel. Staff and if necessary cooking could be provided from the Beach Hotel which is a few minutes away.

At first sight there do not seem to be many snags. But the possible ones are:
1. The point is exposed and in rough weather extremely windswept.
2. The railway passes behind the point (but further away than is the case at La Capponcina.)
3. The point is somewhat overlooked by houses on the hill behind, though from a distance.
4. In high summer one might be disturbed by noise from the Beach Hotel swimming pool which is below the house on the West side.
5. It would take ten to twelve months to reconstruct the house or build a new one.

---

[1] Relaying a suggestion by Aristotle Onassis for a permanent residence or villa for Churchill in the South of France.

Anthony Montague Browne to Sir Winston S. Churchill
(Churchill papers, 2/130)[1]

17 October 1956
Secret

My dear Sir Winston,

I went to No. 10 today and had a talk with Bishop, the Prime Minister's principal private secretary.[2] He has put most of his news in the attached letter to me, which he gave me at the time. It speaks for itself. Bishop's only addition orally was to say that military action was 'by <u>no</u> means ruled out'.

There is little else on the official side. The Colonial Office tell me that Harding is confident that, given enough troops, he could break the back of the terrorism in Cyprus in a few months. There are thought to be only about 70 'hard-core' terrorists organised in gangs in the mountains, plus a few individual gun-men in the towns. The morale of our people is good, but the Greek Cypriot police are in rather a bad way, being under almost unbearable pressure on themselves and their families.

Norman Brook sends you his love, but has no particular news. He seemed a little depressed.

The news in the rest of the letter is on a separate sheet, not confidential.

I enclose the CRO notes for your Smuts speech. They are rather disappointing, I think, and not the draft they had proposed. I am endeavouring to put something together myself.

I was detained rather long at No. 10, and on arrival at the FO, where I am writing this, found that they had already put your telegrams in the Bag. They will therefore be rather numerous.

Nonie and I are deeply grateful to you for so generously bringing her out. She so much enjoyed her stay and your kindness and attentions – and the painting and the cigars! – touched us both deeply.

Lady Churchill and Sarah both seem well and in very good spirits. Sarah will of course be giving you all family news.

I have been engaged in a frantic attempt to get our flat ready by November 1. So far, so good.

Au revoir. Thank you again so much for your many kindnesses.

With our congratulations on Prétendant's triumph.

---

[1] This letter was handwritten.
[2] Frederick Arthur Bishop, 1915–2005. Served in RAF and Air Transport Auxiliary, 1942–6. Asst Secretary, Cabinet Office, 1953–5. Principal Private Secretary to PM, 1956–9. Deputy Secretary of the Cabinet, 1959–61. Ministry of Agriculture, Fisheries and Food, 1961–4. Permanent Secretary, Ministry of Land and Natural Resources, 1964–5.

Frederick Bishop to Anthony Montague Browne
(Churchill papers, 2/130)

17 October 1956
Secret

My dear Anthony,

This is by way of bringing you up to date with the latest developments on Suez, in case it may be of help in your communications with Sir Winston Churchill.

On the whole the Prime Minister was satisfied with the outcome of the debate in the Security Council. Of course, it was not easy to decide what form of resolution was best, to be consistent with the line which the Prime Minister wished to take in his speech after the Party Conference at Llandudno, and it was even harder to carry the French with us in formulating such a resolution, particularly as Mr Dulles and the Secretary-General had also to be considered. As it came out, with considerable emphasis on the 18 Power proposals, it was about right. The fact that the Russians vetoed it was a help rather than a disadvantage from the political point of view.

We have tried to make it clear that we regarded the Security Council as having taken the matter only a very little way forward towards a settlement. The fact that Mr Dulles and President Eisenhower welcomed the resolution 'with a prayer of thanksgiving in their hearts' does not seem to have misled people here, at any rate, into undue optimism.

Immediately the Foreign Secretary returned, the Prime Minister and he decided to accept an invitation from the French Prime Minister to go over to Paris to talk about the next steps. The Prime Minister is only just back, but there seems no doubt that, broadly speaking we and the French still see eye to eye about how to carry the matter forward. Probably our diplomatic attitude will be to repeat that it is up to the Egyptians to put forward practical proposals to seek a settlement in accordance with the principles agreed at the Security Council; until they do, we stand by the 18 Power proposals as the best basis.

But this straightforward diplomatic picture is now overlaid with the complicated situation between Iraq, Jordan and Israel. Seemingly the Jordanians are unwilling to take the risk that the Israeli assertion that the entry of Iraqi troops into Jordan would be regarded by them as an aggression may be more than a bluff, and the Iraqi troops are held near the frontier. It may be that, because of our part in all this and our assurances to Jordan, Britain will now be seen to be of more value to the Arab States than Egypt. On the other hand, if the result of these movements has been to make Western help more suspect in Arab eyes, the position of the Government of Jordan may be endangered, and even Nuri may be affected. But the latter seems safe enough at present.

On the whole, the events of the last few days seem to have made the cracks in Arab solidarity a little more evident.

I think that that is all, to date. Needless to say, the precautionary measures are being fully maintained. The Prime Minister's repetition that no responsible Government could undertake in the present circumstances that force will never be used, is becoming more widely appreciated, as the limitations of the United Nations are demonstrated, for example by Russia's use of the veto last Saturday.

Dr John Roberts to Lord Moran
(Churchill papers, 1/54)

25 October 1956

Dear Lord Moran,

As you will know from my telephone conversation with you, Sir Winston has had an attack of cerebral spasm. During the attack he lost the use of right leg, right arm, left side of face, and Broca's area. After an injection of 3 cc's of coramine the signs of spasticity passed off. I put him on a fat-diminished diet, vitamin pp papaverine and aminophyline.

He has made very good progress, and has even been out in the garden.

Today I have taken blood tests for cholesterol, urea and coagulation time, and I shall forward the results of these tests to you with Sir Winston on his return.

Lord Moran to Sir Winston S. Churchill
(Churchill papers, 1/54)

29 October 1956

My dear Winston,

I was a little worried last night because Dr Roberts in his letter of October 25 to me said you were on (1) a vitamin, (2) a fat diminished diet and (3) aminophyline.

Aminophyline is a depressant of the circulation and directly contraindicated. However, from what I can gather you are not taking aminophyline now. The diet, the vitamins and the papaverine are all right: anyway they will do no harm, though I doubt if they will do any good. But I didn't want any depressant of the circulation used. Brain[1] agrees about <u>not</u> using aminophyline. I shall be back Wednesday evening and could see you 9 p.m. with Brain. This will suit Brain. If you would rather see him alone, he will I'm sure fit in.

---

[1] Walter Russell Brain, 1895–1966. Neurologist and physician to Winston Churchill. Educated at Mill Hill School and New College, Oxford. Friends Ambulance Unit, 1914–18. Fellow, Royal College of Physicians, 1931; President, 1950–6. Knighted, 1952. Baron, 1952.

There has never been any question of[1] the anticoagulants are dangerous so the regulation time does not arise. Cholesterol is a long time consideration. There are the blood tests he suggested. I shall not wake you.

Sir Winston S. Churchill to Donald Forbes[2]
(Churchill papers, 3/14)

3 November 1956

My dear Alderman Forbes,

I think that my Constituents may wish to have a brief statement of the reasons that lead me to support the Government on the Egyptian issue. The British connection with the Middle East is a long and honourable one. Many of the States there owe their origin and independence directly to us. In peace we have assisted them in many ways, financially, technically, and with our advisors in every sphere. In war we have defended them, at great cost. Above all, we have endeavoured to confer on them the benefits of justice and freedom from internecine war. In the last few years the United States, France and we ourselves have been principally concerned with keeping the peace between Israel and her neighbours.

In spite of all our endeavours, the frontiers of Israel have flickered with murder and armed raids. Egypt, the principal instigator of these incidents, had openly rejected and derided the Tripartite Declaration by which we, the French and the Americans sought to impose restraint. The last few days have brought events to a head. Israel, under the gravest provocation, erupted against Egypt. In this country we had the choice of taking decisive action or admitting once and for all our inability to put an end to the strife. Unfortunately, recent months have shown us that at present it is not possible to hope in this area for American cooperation on the scale and with the promptness necessary to control events. Her Majesty's Government and the Government of France have reacted with speed. I regret profoundly that the Egyptian reaction has forced the present course on us. But I do not doubt that we can shortly lead our course to a just and victorious conclusion.

We intend to restore peace and order to the Middle East, and I am convinced that we shall achieve our aim. The American alliance remains the keystone of our policy. I am confident that our American friends will come to realize that, not for the first time, we have acted independently for the common good. World peace, the Middle East, and our national interest will surely benefit in the long run from the Government's resolute action. They deserve our support.

---

[1] that.
[2] Donald Logan Forbes, 1908–94. Chairman, Woodford Constituency Party. FCA. JP. CBE, 1987.

Sir Anthony Eden to Sir Winston S. Churchill
(*Churchill papers, 2/216*)[1]

5 November 1956

My dear Winston,

I cannot thank you enough for your wonderful message.[2] It has had an enormous effect, and I am sure that in the US it will have maybe an even deeper influence.

These are tough days – but the alternative was a slow bleeding to death.[3]

Sir Winston S. Churchill to President Dwight D. Eisenhower
(*Churchill papers, 2/217*)

23 November 1956
Private and Personal

My dear Ike,

There is not much left for me to do in this world, and I have neither the wish nor the strength to involve myself in the present political stress and turmoil. But I do believe, with unfaltering conviction, that the theme of Anglo-American alliance is more important today than at any time since the war. You and I had some part in raising it to the plane on which it has stood. Now, whatever the arguments adduced here and in the United States for or against Anthony's action in Egypt, to let events in the Middle East become a gulf between us, would be an act of folly, on which our whole civilisation may founder.

There seems to be a growing misunderstanding and frustration on both sides of the Atlantic. If they be allowed to develop, the skies will darken indeed and it is the Soviet Union that will ride the storm. We should leave it to the historians to argue the rights and wrongs of all that has happened during the past years. What we must face is that at present these events have left a situation in the Middle East in which spite, envy and malice prevail on the one hand and our friends are beset by bewilderment and uncertainty for the future. The Soviet Union is attempting to move into this dangerous vacuum, for you must have no doubt that a triumph for Nasser is an even greater triumph for them.

The very survival of all we believe may depend on our setting our minds to forestalling them. If we do not take immediate action in harmony, it is no exaggeration to say that we must expect to see the Middle East and the North African coastline under Soviet control and Western Europe placed at the mercy of the Russians. If at this juncture we fail in our responsibility to act

---

[1] This letter was handwritten.
[2] Statement supporting the Government published in the *Manchester Guardian* on 5 Nov. 1956. See *Winston S. Churchill*, vol. 8, *Never Despair*, pp. 1220–1.
[3] Churchill responded: 'Thank you for your kind words. I am so glad it was a help.'

positively and fearlessly we shall no longer be worthy of the leadership with which we are entrusted.

I write this letter because I know where your heart lies. You are now the only one who can so influence events both in UNO and the free world as to ensure that the great essentials are not lost in bickerings and pettiness among the nations. Yours is indeed a heavy responsibility and there is no greater believer in your capacity to bear it or true wellwisher in your task than your old friend.

Sir Desmond Morton to Sir Winston S. Churchill
(Churchill papers, 4/67)[1]

22 November 1956

Dear Winston,

How charming and kind of you still to keep me in mind and to send me a copy of Volume II of your great *History of the English Speaking Peoples*. From your first volume I have frequently quoted in lecturing at various Universities and with great effect. As I only got it yesterday, I have not yet had time to read Vol. II, but already note with gratitude and admiration your most fair, and unhappily prophetic, dealing with the Faith, which that very great man, Thomas More[2] and my negligible self have professed. In your words, '. . . that the break with Rome carried with it the threat of a despotism freed from every fetter', at the top of page 52, the mind immediately turns to the antithesis of everything which 'Rome' has stood for, namely atheistic Communism.

Would to Heaven that you were twenty years younger and could now lead our country into a just peace and out of the morass into which we seem to have staggered – doubtless with the best intentions! Above all that you could ensure the healing of the rift between us and the great English-speaking Republic, whose intentions are doubtless equally good, but whose grave lack of knowledge, understanding, and dexterity fills me with alarm.

Ten days ago I had to lunch two influential Democrats on their way from New York to Persia, on business. Their sympathies were wholly with us and the French. One of them, who was with me in the Middle East in 1950 and knows a great deal about that part of the world, expressed vehemently his horror at the complete lack of understanding he had experienced in the State Department. He criticized us too for our 'bad propaganda' in the USA, which, he claimed, could only be understood by the handful, like himself, who had stayed in and understood the Middle East situation; claiming that we should have started by considering, rightly, that no Americans even knew where the Middle East lay on the map. He was also very critical of the British

[1] This letter was handwritten.
[2] Thomas More, 1478–1535. English statesman known for his opposition to King Henry's VIII separation of the English Church from the Roman Catholic Church.

Government's political handling of the Suez affair, asking why Anthony had not told the whole story of the Anglo-French intervention in the first speech he made in the House, instead of apparently 'making up his excuses for it as the affair developed'. He said that the fate of the Russian armies and bases, if brought out at the beginning, would have moved the whole American people, even if not immediately Dulles & the State Department.

Anyway, this letter is to wish you very well and more than that, it is to wish you happiness and content in a much-troubled world.

President Dwight D. Eisenhower to Sir Winston S. Churchill
('Finest Hour', No. 114, Spring 2002, page 36)

27 November 1956
Top Secret

Dear Winston,

I agree fully with the implication of your letter[1] that Nasser is a tool, possibly unwitting, of the Soviets, and at the back of the difficulties that the free world is now experiencing lies one principal fact that none of us can afford to forget. The Soviets are the real enemy of the Western World, implacably hostile and seeking our destruction.

When Nasser took his high handed action with respect to the Canal, I tried earnestly to keep Anthony informed of public opinion in this country and of the course that we would feel compelled to follow if there was any attempt to solve by force the problem presented to the free world through Nasser's action. I told him that we were committed to the United Nations and I particularly urged him, in a letter of July thirty-first, to avoid the use of force, at least until it had been proved to the world that the United Nations was incapable of handling the problem.

Sometime in the early part of October, all communication between ourselves on the one hand and the British and the French on the other suddenly ceased. Our intelligence showed the gradual buildup of Israeli military strength, finally reaching such a state of completion that I felt compelled on two successive days to warn that country that the United States would honor its part in the Tri-Partite Declaration of May, 1950. In short, that we would oppose clear aggression by any power in the Mid-East. But so far as Britain and France were concerned, we felt that they had deliberately excluded us from their thinking; we had no choice but to do our best to be prepared for whatever might happen. . . .

The first news we had of the attack and of British–French plans was gained from the newspapers and we had no recourse except to assert our readiness to

---

[1] Reproduced above (pp. 2144–5).

support the United Nations, before which body, incidentally, the British Government had itself placed the whole Suez controversy.

Nothing would please this country more nor, in fact, could help us more, than to see British prestige and strength renewed and rejuvenated in the Mid-East. . . . All we have asked in order to come out openly has been a British statement that it would conform to the resolutions of the United Nations. The United Nations troops do not, in our opinion, have to be as strong as those of an invading force because any attack upon them will be an attack upon the whole United Nations and if such an act of folly were committed, I think that we could quickly settle the whole affair.

This message does not purport to say that we have set up our judgment against that of our friends in England. I am merely trying to show that in this country there is a very strong public opinion upon these matters that has, I believe, paralleled my own thinking. I continue to believe that the safety of the western world depends in the final analysis upon the closest possible ties between Western Europe, the American hemisphere, and as many allies as we can induce to stand with us. If this incident has proved nothing else, it must have forcefully brought this truth home to us again. A chief factor in the union of the free world must be indestructible ties between the British Commonwealth and ourselves. . . .

So I hope that this one may be washed off the slate as soon as possible and that we can then together adopt other means of achieving our legitimate objectives in the Mid-East. Nothing saddens me more than the thought that I and my old friends of years have met a problem concerning which we do not see eye to eye. I shall never be happy until our old time closeness has been restored. With warm regard and best wishes for your continued health,

Sir Harold Nicolson: diary
('The Later Years', page 321)

28 November 1956

I broadcast for Mau Mau. The BBC are very fussy about not making any controversial remarks about Suez. I go on to Enid Jones'[1] house in Hyde Park Gate where there is to be a presentation to Alan Moorehead[2] of the Duff Cooper prize for his *Gallipoli*. We are greeted by Diana (Cooper) looking too beautiful, and I find all Duff's special friends there – all somewhat aged in appearance. Then Winston comes in with Clemmie. He is very tottery and is helped to a chair. I say a few introductory words, and then Winston reads

---

[1] Enid Bagnold, 1889–1981. Author and playwright. Married, 1920, Sir Roderick Jones (d. 1962), chairman of Reuters. Great-grandmother to Samantha Sheffield, wife of former PM David Cameron.

[2] Alan McCrae Moorehead, 1910–83. Educated at Scotch College, Melbourne, and Melbourne University. *Daily Express* War Correspondent, Mediterranean and North African fronts, 1939–43.

from a piece of paper his bit about Duff. He hands the prize to Moorehead, who replies in excellent terms. Meanwhile Winston has drunk his glass of champagne and says to me, 'I think I should like to say a little more.' So up he gets and adds a few charming and impromptu words. It is a moving occasion.

Sir Winston S. Churchill: speech
(Churchill papers, 5/60)

28 November 1956   29 Hyde Park Gate

THE PRESENTATION OF THE FIRST DUFF COOPER MEMORIAL PRIZE
TO ALAN MOOREHEAD

No one could help feeling honoured at being the first recipient of this prize which is founded to commemorate a man who made a distinguished place for himself in the field of letters, and whose qualities of mind and heart, of courage and integrity, earned him a unique place in the affections of his hundreds of friends.

It must be a further matter of pride to Mr Moorehead that this literary prize should come to him at the unanimous choice of three such eminent writers and scholars as Sir Maurice Bowra,[1] Sir Harold Nicolson, and Lord David Cecil.[2]

I, too, am proud and happy that Diana should have wished me to make the presentation on behalf of the Trustees. It is nearly two years since Duff died, but his memory is cherished in our hearts, and it is agreeable to reflect that when all of us in this room are ourselves no more, the annual bestowal of this prize will keep his memory bright in the field of literature which he did so much to adorn.

George Trevelyan to Sir Winston S. Churchill
(Churchill papers, 4/67)[3]

29 November 1956

Dear Winston,

Will you allow me to congratulate you on your 82nd birthday, and thank you very sincerely for sending me the 2nd volume of your great history. I like

---

[1] Cecil Maurice Bowra, 1898–1971. Classical scholar and academic. On active service, Royal Field Artillery, 1917–18. Educated at New College, Oxford. Fellow, Wadham College, 1922–38. Vice-Chancellor, Oxford University, 1951–4. Knighted, 1951.

[2] David George Brownlow Cecil, 1905–81. Styled Lord Burghley. Educated at Cambridge University. Olympic hurdler, 1924; Gold Medal, 1928; Silver Medal, 1932. MP (Cons.) for Peterborough, 1931–43. Governor of Bermuda, 1943–5. Chairman, Organising Committee, 1948 London Olympics. Succeeded his father as 6th Marquess of Exeter, 1956.

[3] This letter was handwritten.

it even better than the first. For one thing it is ground with which your mind is more familiar than the Middle Ages, and in the second place the story of this new volume has an artistic unity culminating in 1688, which no one could have made of the Middle Ages culminating at Bosworth Field. I heartily congratulate you.

Sir John Colville: recollection
('The Fringes of Power', pages 721–2)

29 November 1956

On Thursday, November 29th, Winston had told me in reply to a direct question that he thought the whole operation[1] the most ill-conceived and ill-executed imaginable. It was at luncheon at 28 Hyde Park Gate. I had begun by asking him if he would have acted as Eden had if he had still been Prime Minister. He replied, 'I would never have dared; and if I had dared, I would certainly never have dared stop.' He also said that if Eden resigned he thought Harold Macmillan would be a better successor than R. A. Butler.

Field Marshal Lord Montgomery to Sir Winston S. Churchill
(Churchill papers, 2/143)[2]

6 December 1956   Versailles

My dear Winston,

I am flying to London on the 13th to attend the dinner of the Other Club: since you are to be in the chair.

In all my military experience I have never known anything to have been so 'bungled' as the Suez affair. You would not have handled it that way. Nor would you have gone off to Jamaica.[3] Under such conditions the captain of the ship does not go sea bathing – he dies on the bridge.

---

[1] The Suez intervention. Eden had ordered a ceasefire on 6 Nov. 1956 without previously notifying France or Israel, England's co-combatants. English and French troops completed withdrawal by the end of Dec. 1956; the Israelis remained until Mar. 1957.

[2] This letter was handwritten.

[3] Eden suffered from cholangitis, an abdominal infection that was probably the result of his 1953 gallstone surgery, during which a bile duct was lacerated. He was prescribed amphetamines (Benzedrine), which may have exacerbated his symptoms. He went to Jamaica in an attempt to convalesce in the warm climate.

President Dwight D. Eisenhower to Sir Winston S. Churchill
(Churchill papers, 4/67)

6 December 1956   Augusta, Georgia

Dear Winston,

Because I so greatly enjoyed the first volume of your magnificent and exciting *History of the English-Speaking Peoples*, I have hopefully and quite without shame looked forward to receiving the second one. *The New World* is, of course, destined to interest me tremendously. I am more than grateful to you for sending me a copy, personally inscribed, and particularly glad that it reached me here in Augusta where I find I have a little more time than usual for reading.

With deep gratitude for your thought of me, and warm personal regard.

Alan Hodge to Anthony Montague Browne
(Churchill papers, 4/28)

19 December 1956

My Dear Anthony,

There are two matters of payment which Sir Winston might like to consider. One concerns Maurice Shock. Sir Winston felt that he should be paid £200 for the drafting he has done. So far he has been given £100 and perhaps the balance should now be made up.

The other point concerns India. Dr A. P. Thornton,[1] Department of History, King's College, Old Aberdeen, has read the chapter on the Indian Empire in Book Eight, and also the passage on the Indian Mutiny in Book Ten. He made a number of useful suggestions, which have been adopted and passed by Sir Winston. I think that some sum such as £20 or £25 might be sufficient reward for his labours.[2]

---

[1] Archibald Paton Thornton, 1921–2004. Served in East Riding Imperial Yorkshire Yeomanry during WWII, 1939–45; Capt. Lecturer in History, Trinity College, Oxford, 1948–50; University of Aberdeen, 1950–7. Prof., Chairman of History and Dean of Arts, University College of West Indies, 1957–60. Dept of History, University of Toronto, 1960–7; Chairman, 1967–72. Retired, 1987. Author of several books including *West-India Policy under the Restoration* (1956), *The Imperial Idea and its Enemies* (1959) and *Imperialism in the 20th Century* (1978).

[2] Churchill wrote on the original letter 'Yes' for £25 to Thornton and 'Yes' to make the balance up to Shock.

1957

Sir Anthony Eden to Sir Winston S. Churchill
(Churchill papers, 2/216)[1]

9 January 1957

My dear Winston,

I have heavy news about health. The benefit of Jamaica is not significant. More troubling is that over Christmas & the New Year I have had a return of internal pain, which, apart from its fatiguing effect, worries the doctors in relation to my past operation.

In short they say firmly (and I have refused to accept one opinion & this is outcome of 3 apart from my own doctor) that I am endangering my life – & shortening it – by going on. This in itself, as you will know, would not influence me. What is troublesome is that the immediate result is a gradually increasing fatigue. In short I shall be less & less able physically to do my job as weeks go by.

This seems to me an impossible position. The more so since they give me little hope that I can continue as I am doing without collapse until Easter, & virtually no hope, if I attempt to go on, until the end of summer.

Bobbety & Norman Brook both agree that it will be of no use for me to drag on for such a short period of time. I am very sad, but I did not want you to know by any hand but mine.

PS. I expect this to be announced by 6.30 p.m.[2]

---

[1] This letter was handwritten.
[2] On this date the Queen accepted Eden's resignation as PM. She then sent for Harold Macmillan.

Sir Winston S. Churchill to Lady Churchill
(Churchill papers, 2/216)

9 January 1957   Chartwell

Darling,

Poor Anthony has just sent me this. You will have the secret for about an hour.

Keep the letter to give me. Let no one see it again.

Your own ever loving,

Sir Anthony Eden to Sir Winston S. Churchill
(Churchill papers, 2/216)

17 January 1957   Chequers
Personal

My dear Winston,

Thank you so much for your letter and also for the very kind message you sent me. We have carefully weighed the advantages and disadvantages of this journey, but the doctors seem convinced that it is best to get away to entirely different surroundings. We hope to have a real rest at the other end in a lovely house near Auckland by the sea which Holland[1] has found for us, and then perhaps on to the Barrier Reef before we finally come home. I so look forward to seeing you then.

I am naturally very sad that this had to be at this time, but with the doctors all lining up one behind the other I am quite sure that there was no choice.

Nor have I felt in the last days that the decision was wrong, odious as it was.

Love from us both.

Sir Winston S. Churchill to Lady Churchill
(Baroness Spencer-Churchill papers)

18 January 1957   La Pausa

My darling One,

I have been worrying about Christopher. There is no doubt that the naval appointment will be promotion, which gives him the spokesmanship in the House of Commons and all that flows from that. I am afraid the Navy is to be shockingly cut, and it may be trouble will arise over that.

We arrived here very smoothly, and I have done nothing ever since. Today is lovely sunshine, the air chilly, but the sun warms everything. I aimed at

---

[1] Sidney Holland, PM of New Zealand.

getting up before lunch, and am now sitting dressed on the terrace enjoying the sunshine in an overcoat.

Wendy was delighted to have Sarah, and addressed her on the telephone in a decisive manner. She is coming, I think, either tomorrow or the next day. Wendy would also like to have Mary at the same time as AMB & Sarah, and I think she will arrange this for the beginning of February. I gave her your lovely present, which was a touching scene. She put a powder puff inside, and is using it regularly now. She will have written to you herself on this.

I had a telephone message from Brendan to say that Bernie was seriously ill, so I have both telegraphed and written. He has never lost his interest in life, a kind of long latent joie de vivre, which I have not been able to acquire.

I have started to read *Brave New World*. My 'boys' arrive today, and dine tonight. I have no doubt I shall succeed in finishing the job by the end of the month.

I think you are absolutely right to try and see the effect of freeing yourself from drugs, but I am most anxious to know how things proceed. Do let me know how you get on.

PS. I have got an aurist coming with Dr Roberts tomorrow & am going to have a good try to work a cure.

Joan Ronald to Sir Winston S. Churchill
(*Churchill papers, 4/28*)

20 January 1957

Dear Sir Winston,

I am reading and enjoying Volume Two of your *History of the English-Speaking Peoples*. Might I be so bold as to bring to your notice a slip which you may wish to correct in future editions?

On page 50 you mention that Jane Seymour[1] was 'about twenty-five' (i.e. in 1533) while on page 56 you say 'and when she died, still aged only twenty-two. . . .' (i.e. in 1537). My husband and I feel that she must have had (like yourself!) the secret of perennial youth![2]

---

[1] Jane Seymour, 1508–37. Queen of England, 1536–7. Married, 1536, as his third wife, King Henry VIII: one child (King Edward VI). Died from complications arising from childbirth.

[2] Gillian Maturin, Churchill's secretary, wrote to Mrs Ronald on Jan. 28: 'Sir Winston Churchill has asked me to thank you for your letter of January 20 in which you point out a discrepancy in the Second Volume of his *History of the English-Speaking Peoples*. This is being attended to.'

Sir Winston S. Churchill to Lady Churchill
(Baroness Spencer-Churchill papers)

22 January 1957   La Pausa

My darling Clemmie,

Thank you so much for your delightful and informative letter which reached me yesterday, Monday. The Aurist took two large pieces of wax out of my ears, and I certainly hear more clearly since then. He is awaiting the technical report that the people who examined me in England must have made. I am sure that French medicine is much ahead of English. I had a sore throat which was cured immediately by a box of tablets that Dr Roberts produced out of his bag, and I cannot find any minor ailment that the French have not got a ready cure for. Another cure which meets all needs is a small pill taken after lunch to provoke sleep. A quarter of it sends me to sleep for two hours in the afternoon, whereas the English version failed completely. It is said to be perfectly harmless & widely used. They have adopted all the modern dodges and in a moment produce them from their wallet. There must be at least half a dozen common afflictions which are driven off in this easy way.

I agree with you about the American Ambassadress.[1] She gave us the little pill box we use on the dining room table every day. I return you herewith Clarissa's letter. I agree with you in the choice of epithet. We hope that Sarah will come tomorrow. They are very fond of her here, and look forward much to seeing her. I am doing a good deal of work, and I think I shall have the Book finished in time. If not, there is at least one extra week to spare in February.

Sarah gave me the news about yourself last night, but do let me know about it too. I am so glad you will come. I cannot describe to you the joy which your present gave. By now you will have received Wendy's letter which she showed me.

The skies are clouded today & it may be the week's perfect weather is about to pass. But it will soon return & bring you with it – <u>I hope</u>.

Sir Winston S. Churchill to Lady Churchill
(Baroness Spencer-Churchill papers)[2]

24 January 1957   Alpes Maritimes

My darling,

I send you herewith the notification from Lloyds' that they have bought me £29,900 odd of shares from duty at my death. I hereby give it to you as I promised & hope you will long live to enjoy it.

---

[1] Ann Clare Boothe Luce. Although she had resigned her post in Italy on 27 Dec. 1956, her replacement did not officially take up his post until 6 Feb. 1957.

[2] This letter was handwritten.

I have asked Lloyds' to let you know that I wish to make the transfer to you; and you consult Moir upon any steps you shd take to bring it under your effective control as soon as possible.

I am vy glad to be able through my own exertions & be able to testify in this way my love & gratitude to you.

Your ever-devoted husband

Sir Winston S. Churchill to Lord Moran
(Churchill papers, 1/54)

26 January 1957 Alpes Maritimes

My dear Charles,

Thank you so much for sending me the ear chart and report. I will let you know developments.

The French seem to have an outfit of very good effective remedies, all made up as popular medicines. For instance, I enclose you a specimen of a white lozenge which Dr Roberts gave me at once and urged me to use with freedom in order to provoke sleep after luncheon. One (a quarter) is certainly effective. It gave about two hours' sleep. Roberts said these lozenges were widely used, and there was no sort of complaint about them locally. He advised me to try a half at night instead of the reds. I cross-examined him as well as I could about the effect on lowering the blood pressure. This he said is much less than the red, though he recognised the evil. I certainly had a good night without red or yellow. My blood pressure is 80/140 this morning, and the pulse 67.

I was interested to have your account of events at home. Here we are getting quite a lot of sunshine, and my Book is rapidly nearing completion.

Sir Winston S. Churchill to Lady Churchill
(Baroness Spencer-Churchill papers)

3 February 1957   Alpes Maritimes

My darling One,

    I have been so hunted with winding up these proofs of the Book and other things before the date when I retire, and I have not been able to write to you as I should wish.

    All is well here. Sarah is a great pleasure. I was very glad to hear your news of Jeremy. I sent him a telegram which I hope he got. In ten days I shall be with you, the 13th. They both hope you will come out with me when I return on the 16th.

    It is foggy today, but I hope it will clear. I have had vy good weather till the last 2 days. With all my love, my dearest one.

                                                                 [Drawing of a pig]

PS. Moir has arrived & is staying till Wednesday next.

Lady Churchill to Sir Winston S. Churchill
(Churchill papers, 1/55)[1]

4 February 1957

My darling,

    Miss Maturin tells me she is joining 'the Troop' tomorrow; so I hasten to send you a line bringing you my love.

    I think I should love to go with you when you return to La Pausa on the 16th. I'm writing to Wendy to ask her if she can have me.

    I forgot to tell you that I had a letter from Lord Kemsley asking me to write some recollections for the *Sunday Times*. I thanked him but said that for the moment I didn't feel like putting pen to paper.

    The red camellia opposite the dining-room window is just coming into bloom & in a fortnight there will be at least 50 camellias. The almond tree is also about to explode into blossom. 'Prof' is coming to luncheon next Thursday & I have invited Leslie Rowan & will write to meet him.

                                                                      Your loving
                                                                [Drawing of a cat]

---

[1] This letter was handwritten.

1957

Lord Moran to Sir Winston S. Churchill
(Churchill papers, 1/54)

4 February 1957

My dear Winston,

The 'reds' that you have taken for a long time contain one and a half grains of seconal and nothing else. The white lozenge, which you have sent me, is precisely the same, namely one and a half grains of seconal and nothing else. The lozenge is therefore exactly the same as a 'red' only the red coating was not added.

To confirm this I took the lozenge to the head dispenser at St Mary's. He knew these lozenges and was familiar with the fact that in France seconal is not always coated red. He confirmed that the lozenges were 'reds' in everything but colour.

To be quite sure we rang up Rousel, the manufacturers of these white lozenges, and they confirmed that the whites are identical with the reds.

I can only suppose that Roberts does not know what is in them as he suggested using them 'instead of the reds at night', and also said that the effect in lowering the blood pressure was 'much less than the red'. I imagine if Roberts knew he was really using a 'red' after luncheon he would hesitate to use a drug depressant to the circulation, in a dose of one and a half grains, twice in twenty-four hours.

The delay in answering your letter was due to the fact that I wanted to be quite sure of the facts and when I telephoned Rousel on Saturday I found that they were not open on Saturdays.

On Tuesday Collins, the publishers, are giving a party at the Dorchester to launch Alanbrooke's book.[1] Arthur Bryant[2] and Alanbrooke are speaking and Portal is to be in the Chair. Black Rod at the House of Lords is Horrocks,[3] who commanded the XIIIth Corps in the desert, and he told me he was appearing on television with Alanbrooke.

Delighted to hear of the sunshine and that the book is nearly completed.

In case Roberts might get a stroke, perhaps it might be wise not to show him this letter.

---

[1] *The Turn of the Tide, 1939–1943*, edited by Arthur Bryant.
[2] Arthur Wynne Morgan Bryant, 1899–1985. Succeeded G. K. Chesterton as writer of 'Our Note Book', *Illustrated London News*, 1936–85. Chairman, St John and Red Cross Library Dept, 1945–74; Ashridge Council, 1946–9; Society of Authors, 1949–53. Author of dozens of books including *The Spirit of Conservatism* (1929), *The American Ideal* (1936) and *The Medieval Foundation of England* (1965).
[3] Brian Gwyne Horrocks, 1895–1985. Known as 'Jorrocks'. Instructor at Staff College, Camberley, 1938–40. CO, 2nd Battalion Middlesex Rgt, France, 1940; 9th Infantry Bde, 1940–1. GOC 44th Infantry Div., 1941–2; 9th Armoured Div.; XIII Corps, North Africa, 1942; X Corps, Dec. 1942 to Apr. 1943; IX Corps, North Africa, 1943 (wounded); XXX Corps, North-West Europe, 1944–5. GOC-in-C, Western Command, 1946–7. GOC British Army of the Rhine, 1948–9. Retired, 1949. Gentleman Usher of the Black Rod, 1949–63.

Sir Winston S. Churchill to Lady Churchill
(Baroness Spencer-Churchill papers)[1]

6 February 1957   Alpes Maritimes

My dearest One,

For three days only a short shaft of sunshine. However we are still gay, for it will give a better chance later on for Moir has been unlucky.

How sweet of you to say you will come out with when I come. I am looking forward to finishing up the book – it is nearly ended. I hope you like what you have read of it. Today week I start for home. I think Duncan seems to have done well in US & the relations are good again.

With tender love & many kisses your dearest pig.

Sarah Beauchamp to Sir Winston S. Churchill
(Churchill papers, 1/56)[2]

12 February 1957

Darling Papa,

You have worked so hard and done so well – <u>Do</u> take today as easily possible – you have 'The Journey' <u>tomorrow</u> – Lunch with Macmillan and the other club the <u>next</u> day and Mr Moir on Friday morning and then the journey <u>back</u> on Saturday – Wow – you are so well at the moment – it would be silly to spoil – <u>Please</u> rest this afternoon and try not to read too much today so as to rest the pore eye!

Love – Love – Love – <u>don't</u> bite me.

[Drawing of a mule]

Sir Winston S. Churchill to Lady Churchill
(Baroness Spencer-Churchill papers)[3]

11 March 1957   Alpes Maritimes

Darling,

I have tried to make the best arrangements possible to convey this letter to you today. It is Sunday, and the Prefet & Madame le Prefet[4] are coming for luncheon. I have made up my mind to give him the picture of the swans, & I shall tell him that you chose it for him. We have quite fallen in love with it.

---

[1] This letter was handwritten.
[2] This letter was handwritten.
[3] This letter was handwritten.
[4] Isabella Béatrice Carmélite Shomorowsky, 1909–2004. Born in Leipzig, Germany. Married, 1940, Pierre-Jean Moatti.

Alas such is generosity; we must do our duty. But really it is vy beautiful, & I hate parting with it, I never thought anything of it while it hung for years in my bedroom & 28. Now it is a wreath. But I think he will like it & show it to lots of people. I hope so anyhow Voila!

Yesterday we were given lunch by Onassis at the Chateau de Madrid, & we ate a whole large tin of caviar, which must have cost him a fortune. (He has one at present.) As his wife was held up at St Moritz by snow she could not reach us till after the meal. So his sister came as a hostess. She looked vy nice. Her teeth were much admired. The conversation centred on politics & oil. I reminded him that I had bought the Anglo-Persian for the Admiralty forty or fifty years ago and made a good profit for the British Government about 3 or 4 hundred millions! He said he knew all about it. All this reminded me of poor Hopkins – but I think we did it together, I enjoy the credit.

Darling One all passes peaceably & quietly here. Toby has just flown on to the page I have written, and thrown it on the floor.

What a lovely letter you sent me by Anthony! It was a duck. I feel all over of a purr when I read it through. I send you in return my most tender love my dearest Clemmie.

Your devoted and ever loving husband
[Drawing of a pig]

PS. Next week – tomorrow – I am going to look at a House. But none shall be bought without your approval.

Sir Winston S. Churchill to Lord Alanbrooke
(Churchill papers, 2/179)

12 March 1957　　　　　　　　　　　　　　　　　　　　　Alpes Maritimes

My dear Brookie,

Thank you for sending me a copy of your book. On the whole I think that I am against publishing day to day diaries written under the stress of events so soon afterwards. However, I read it with great interest, and I am very much obliged to you for what you say in your inscription.[1]

---

[1] The inscription reads: 'To Winston from Brookie with unbounded admiration, profound respect, and deep affection built up in our 5 years close association during the war. Some of the extracts from my diaries in this book may contain criticisms, and references to differences between us. I hope you will remember that these were written at the end of long and exhausting days, often in the small hours of the morning, and refer to momentary daily impressions. These casual day to day impressions bear no relation to the true feelings of deeprooted friendship and admiration which bound me so closely to you throughout the war. I look upon the privilege of having served you in war as the greatest honour destiny has bestowed on me.'

Sir Winston S. Churchill to Lady Churchill
(Baroness Spencer-Churchill papers)

15 March 1957   Alpes Maritimes

My Darling,

I have been giving a good deal of thought to finding a suitable dwelling out here, and I think I have hit upon one. It is one of three detached in a cul-de-sac of four at the base of Cap Martin. It comprises an acre of ground, and is on the sea facing west. I was very much struck with the convenience of the house. I could live on the ground floor and no lift would be necessary. The layout is really well considered. There are five master bedrooms and four, perhaps five servants'. It was a surprise to find anything so close to Pausaland. The house is unpretentious but most compactly planned. I asked Wendy and Emery to go and see it the next day. There is no doubt they are very much impressed with it, and so was Sarah. The price put on it is 30,000,000 francs, or £30,000, but I have every reason to believe it could be had much cheaper. My own feeling is that an offer of, say, £16,000 cash down might certainly lead to purchase at, say £20,000.

We have looked at a great many houses, and Anthony has gone this afternoon for a preliminary exploration of Cannes and Mougins possibilities. All these seem to be much dearer. This also applies to others of the many I have looked at Cap Ferrat and in the Nice region. We will go on with our explorations, and bring you home a comprehensive report.

The weather is vy cloudy and windy, & rather cold. What a contrast to what you are having in England! Pug Ismay & his wife are coming to dine tonight – they are staying with Daisy, but they have full liberty & so Wendy does not have to worry about asking them.

                                              Always your loving and devoted
                                                         [Drawing of a pig]
                                                 Meant to be lying down.

Sir Winston S. Churchill to Lady Churchill
(Baroness Spencer-Churchill papers)[1]

17 March 1957   Alpes Maritimes

Darling – Here is a damnable thing – the House I wrote to you about was offered by the agents at thirty million francs but now that my name is mentioned to the owner – a swindling, Italian prince, he has put it up to forty-seven million, of course I will not touch it on these terms. So we are all at sea again.

---

[1] This letter was handwritten.

Anthony is off today to look at 2 Houses at Cannes. There is one at 25 million and one all on one floor. But I do not like the idea of Cannes vy much.

It is vy nice to think I shall be home again in 60 hours, Darling one I look forward to being with you so much.

[Drawing of a pig]
A vy small one but black and smudged

Sir Winston S. Churchill to Lady Churchill
(Baroness Spencer-Churchill papers)

[March] 1957   Alpes Maritimes

My darling One,

Here I have found another swift & trustworthy Aide-de-camp – Mr Desmond Flower, the head of Cassells – who came to dine last night, & will be in London tomorrow. He will take this letter to you tomorrow, & assumes full responsibility for its delivery. I trust him with the mission. He leaves his hotel to go to the Paris plane at 10.30. It is now 10.7, & the car is waiting. There is therefore just time for me to write and tell you that I love you dearly, & that I am looking forward to the 22nd when I trust I shall have dinner & tell you all the news. I have been reading the short stories of W. Somerset Maugham. They are quite good, & have so far interested me that I am nearly late for lunch & dinner every day. I have no other news except that I visited 2 houses yesterday & am sure they wd not commend themselves to your eye. I am going to persevere & will make an extensive report.

The sun is shining, the air & sky are clear & warm. You have my fondest love, my darling, your ever devoted husband.

[Drawing of a pig]

Sir Winston S. Churchill: speech
('Winston S. Churchill, His Complete Speeches', volume 8, pages 8677–9)

3 May 1957   Albert Hall, London

THE PRIMROSE LEAGUE

It is a year since I last presided at your annual meeting in this hall.[1] That year has been a testing time both for our country and our party. This crowded gathering this afternoon is a potent reminder of the massive, solid, and unshakeable support which our Tory party has behind it, and which it will

---

[1] See speech reproduced above (pp. 2100–2).

always enjoy so long as it continues to serve the enduring interests of our country.

We all deplore the illness which struck down Sir Anthony Eden a few months ago. We rejoice to read the better accounts of his progress and we all wish him a speedy restoration to full health and strength. Our party, as indeed our country, owes him its gratitude for a lifetime of work upon the causes we all serve. Indeed, those who at home and abroad attacked the resolute action which, in company with our French allies, he took last autumn, may now perhaps have reason to reconsider their opinions. I do not think that the attitude then adopted by the United Nations has been helpful either to the free world or to the cause of peace and prosperity in the Middle East.

However, events have moved on since those days, and we must not be discouraged from continuing to take our full share of leadership in world affairs. Now the burden has fallen upon Mr Harold Macmillan. Mr Macmillan has been proved and tested in most of the high offices of State. He can count upon the unswerving support which our party always accords to its Leader. Mr Macmillan will devote himself wholeheartedly and with imaginative vigour to the well-being of our country and to upholding the true traditions of Tory democracy. You of the Primrose League need no reminder from me of what those traditions are. High among them at home is what Disraeli called the improvement of the condition of the people.

It is nearly six years now since the Socialist Government were removed from office, and I was entrusted with the formation of a Conservative administration. Those six years have witnessed a remarkable improvement in the condition of all the people. All the people. The Tory Party is not and will never become the vehicle or instrument of any one class or section.

Look back to 1951, and look around today. We are better fed. There is more to buy in the shops, and the nation is earning more with which to buy it. The burden of taxation, though still heavy, has begun to be relieved. We are better housed. To have built 1½ million new houses in our first five years is a striking vindication of the programme we placed before the electors. And just as the new houses are going up, those blots on our great cities – the slums – are coming down.

But we Tories and Conservatives will never delude the country into believing that there are easy short cuts to prosperity, that all we have to do is help ourselves to bigger and better benefits. The standard of living we enjoy, the social services we provide come out of what we earn by selling our products in an increasingly competitive world. It was for that reason that I was so glad to see that our Chancellor of the Exchequer, Mr Peter Thorneycroft, resisted the temptation to win easy votes in his Budget last month.

Cheap popularity can prove itself very dearly bought. The Chancellor distributed his reliefs not where they would evoke the loudest cheers, but where they would do most good in expanding production and improving our competitive power in world markets. He was right to do that and he can count upon the full backing and support of all true Conservatives.

Back in 1945, when our arms had achieved victory and we were thinking again of the tasks and problems of peace, I ventured to give the newly formed Socialist Government a word of advice on the opening day of the new Parliament. 'What we desire is freedom,' I said. 'What we need is abundance. Freedom and abundance – these must be our aims.' That was nearly twelve years ago.

My advice – as has sometimes been the case before in the course of my public life – was little heeded at the time; but I have been spared to see the policy adopted and some of its advantages reaped.

As a party we can count ourselves fortunate in the number of young men always at hand to fill the gaps time causes in our ranks. One of them is your speaker this afternoon, Lord Hailsham.[1] He is a man of independent mind, and outspoken and not always orthodox views. We don't mind that in the Primrose League. Indeed, looking back over the years I am not sure whether I have invariably succeeded in being notably orthodox myself.

At about the time my father was bringing the Primrose League into being, Lord Hailsham's grandfather was founding the Polytechnic. Education is in his blood. It is a task of prime importance with which he has been entrusted, for in the keen international race before us the prizes will go to the nation which has the highest skill of brain and hand. Where we are behind we must catch up; where we lead we must stay ahead. But man does not live by bread alone. Our aim must be men and women not only skilled and diligent in earning a living, but having access to those deep wells in which lie the secrets of the future.

The world around us is changing fast. For good or ill new and disturbing powers are falling into the hands of mankind. They may bring an unsurpassed blessing or a senseless and meaningless wholesale destruction. We must hope that man's wisdom will match his widening knowledge. In fostering that growth in wisdom, I am certain that our party, with its deep roots in the past, has a noble part to play.

---

[1] Quintin Hogg, 1907–2001. MP (Cons.) for Oxford, 1938–50; for St Marylebone, 1963–70. On active service, 1939–45. Succeeded his father as 2nd Viscount Hailsham, 1950. 1st Lord of the Admiralty, 1956–7. Minister of Science and Technology, 1959–64. Disclaimed his peerage for life, 1963. Secretary of State for Education and Science, 1964. Lord Chancellor, 1970–4, 1979–87. Baron, 1970.

Sir Anthony Eden to Sir Winston S. Churchill
(Churchill papers, 2/216)

5 May 1957

Thank you so much for your speech which has I am sure exactly hit the mood of second thoughts which now prevail here. It has had of course an excellent reception here.[1] I am still making good progress and we look forward to our journey to Canada on Monday. Love to you and Clemmie from us both.

Sir Winston S. Churchill to Winston Churchill
(Churchill papers, 1/56)

11 May 1957

My dear Winston,

I believe that next year you are hoping to go to Christ Church. I am glad about this, because it is one of the finest colleges in Oxford.

I have been making inquiries, and I hear that the competition is keen and the examination stiff. It will therefore mean sustained work if you are to be successful. I do hope you will be, my dear Winston.

Winston Churchill to Sir Winston S. Churchill
(Churchill papers, 1/56)

14 May 1957   Eton College, Windsor

Dear Grandpapa,

Thank you so much for your letter, which I have just received.

I was hoping to go to Christ Church in October of next year, but because there are lots of boys who will not be doing National Service and who will want to go to a University next year, I do not think I will be able to go until October 1959.

When I had dinner with you at Chartwell the other evening the Prof told me that I would have to work very hard to get into Oxford.

I am enjoying your third volume of the *English-Speaking Peoples*, it is so much easier reading than the History books we read at school and your vivid description brings it all to life. I am in the middle of the chapter on the French Revolution – just before Trafalgar when Villeneuve[2] evades Nelson,[3] to escape

---

[1] In the US.

[2] Pierre-Charles-Jean-Baptiste-Silvestre de Villeneuve, 1763–1806. Commander of French and Spanish fleets defeated at Battle of Trafalgar, 1805.

[3] Horatio Nelson, 1758–1805. C-in-C, Mediterranean Fleet, 1803–5. Led RN to victory against Napoleon's navy in Battle of Trafalgar, during the course of which he was killed.

to its West Indies. I will finish the book by the end of this week and send it back to you.

I went sailing yesterday on the Thames at Bourne End, which is eleven miles from Eton and is meant to be the best river-sailing in England. We went there by bicycle and we had a wonderful afternoon; the sun shone all the time and there was such a strong wind that we nearly capsized. Sailing on a river of course is not as much fun as on the sea. Father is thinking of getting a small sailing-boat in Suffolk, as we are only twelve miles from the sea, and a good sailing place called West Mersea.

It is most amusing the way Toby likes pecking at the letter. Please give my love to Grandmama.

Your loving grandson,

Winston Churchill to Sir Winston S. Churchill
(Churchill papers, 1/56)

16 May 1957   Eton College, Windsor

Dear Grandpapa,

I return herewith the 3rd volume of the *English-Speaking Peoples*, which you so kindly lent me. I enjoyed it very much indeed and I am sure I will do better in the History paper of School certificate as a result of reading it.

Please forgive the messy way in which I have packed the book, as I did not have a box of the right size. Please give my love to Grandmama.

Your loving grandson,

Sir Winston S. Churchill to Winston Churchill
(Churchill papers, 1/56)

18 May 1957

My dear Winston,

Thank you so much for your letters and for returning Volume III. I am glad you enjoyed reading it.

I am off to Roquebrune tomorrow morning. Toby is already there.

Yr loving grandfather

Sir Winston S. Churchill to Lady Churchill
(Baroness Spencer-Churchill papers)

21 May 1957   La Pausa

Darling,

We arrived and all is well. Today the skies are without a cloud and the temperature is warm. Toby as you can see sends his love and salute. I am going to get up and paint in half-an-hour. Yesterday was not quite so good, but still pleasant. Great progress has been made in and with the garden, and the lavender covers almost all. Sarah & AMB are very happy & will write you for themselves. The cold & clouds of England are left behind.

Wendy was obviously disappointed to learn that you wd not come, but could see you at Capponcina in September. I was exhausted yesterday and slumbered well.

Your visit to me the night before I left was very precious. Do not let the idea that I am 'mean' to you tear your mind. As a matter of fact I take every lawful opportunity of passing money to you in a way which will avoid the 67% toll which the State will almost certainly take at my death & will continue to do so as long as I am able. Your life of devotion & kindness to me has made my own one both happy & successful. (Toby is busy and attentive.) I am weary of a task wh is done & I hope I shall not shrink when the aftermath ends.

My only wish is to live peacefully out the remaining years – if years they be. But you, dearest one, have the twilight of a glorious spell upon you in all probability. So be happy & and do not let misconceptions of me darken & distort your mind.

                                             With all my love and many kisses xxx
                                                                            I remain
                                                                Your loving husband

Sir Winston S. Churchill to Lady Churchill
(Baroness Spencer-Churchill papers)

21 May 1957   La Pausa

My Darling,

Your delightful letter has just arrived.

Alas rain & clouds kept us all indoors yesterday, but Welsh Abbot's victory by six lengths brightened the afternoon. Wendy has had a cold but is now recovering and is most kind and agreeable. She & Sarah paint flowers all day in the hall & I have (two days ago) begun a large indoor picture which I think you may like when it is finished, I am occupied with *I Claudius*[1] which is quite readable. The days pass smoothly & pleasantly.

How vy interesting is your account of the lunches at the French Embassy & at home to the Rowans! I shd have enjoyed being there! But I envy you your forthcoming visit to Hatfield with the meeting with Adlai Stevenson.[2] He is vy well thought of in English political circles & I hope he will run again for the Presidency; but that is a long time yet.

I am sending this letter to Hatfield. Give my love to Betty & tell her I am playing a gt deal of Besique. Emery has learned to play it vy well. We have had a gt number of vy small games for vy small stakes (1/-) in which Anthony joins. I do not know whether skill predominates yet.

Darling one do write again and tell me about Hatfield and Adlai. I shall be home again in three weeks (14 June). I hope Christopher will come as planned. The weather must improve by then.

With all my love
I remain
Your loving and devoted husband

The whole party here send you their salutations.

Sir Winston S. Churchill to Lady Churchill
(Baroness Spencer-Churchill papers)[3]

28 May 1957 La Pausa

My darling,

I expect & hope that you had an interesting Sunday & that you will tell me all about it & Adlai Stevenson when you have time. I am vy glad the Frogs are trying to form a solid government in France & that Guy Mollet will be the head of it.

It has been sullenly cloudy with winds & rain for four days running & I am waiting to finish my picture of the verandah through the Olive trees impatiently. I see the Doctor every few days, but not with any definite cause. Dr Roberts is a vy nice fellow and he looks me over with a reassuring air which has a beneficial effect.

---

[1] An historical novel by Robert Graves in the form of an autobiography of the Roman Emperor Claudius. Originally published in 1934, in the 1970s it was turned into a successful television series.

[2] Adlai Ewing Stevenson II, 1900–65. Born in Los Angeles. Educated at Princeton University, Harvard University and Northwestern University School of Law. Chief Attorney, Federal Alcohol Control Administration, 1933–5. Principal Attorney and Special Assistant to Secretary of Navy, 1940–4. Governor of Illinois, 1949–53. Presidential Candidate (Dem.), 1952, 1956. US Ambassador to UN, 1961–5.

[3] This letter was handwritten.

I send you a cheque for £400 wh I beg you to cash & keep. It is a part of my policy to send you money from time to time for reasonable sums which can be considered insurance from the death duties of 67 per cent.

Randolph's birthday! I sent him a message, and will send him a present if you will look around & let me have it when I come home on the 14th. Christopher is coming out here on the 7th, having I hope witnessed the victory of Holiday Time[1] which runs on the 6th, and of which he has hopes.

With love & kisses xxx
From your devoted husband,

PS. I hope you will enjoy your visit to Ireland. I wd like to go there. I believe they wd be nice to me.

John Colville to Sir Winston S. Churchill
(Churchill papers, 1/108)

30 May 1957

My Dear Winston,

You will remember that Rothschilds agreed, early in 1956, to let you have 10,000 shares in the British Newfoundland Corporation Ltd. (BRINCO) at a price of $3 a share. I am glad to say that these shares have recently been changing hands at $6 to $6.50, which means that you have doubled your capital. It would be difficult to sell your whole holding, because the market is a very limited one and I think it would be unwise to do so because they may well increase still further in value. However, I have spoken to Rothschilds who think that they could, without depressing the price very much, sell 5,000 shares for you. If this were done you would, at $6 be recouping your whole capital and be left with 5,000 shares at a book cost of nothing. Would you let me know if you would like this to be done? I so very much look forward to seeing you when you get back in June.

Sir Winston S. Churchill to Lady Churchill
(Baroness Spencer-Churchill papers)[2]

1 June 1957 La Pausa

My darling,

I am vy glad to hear about yr visit to Hatfield & the conversation with Adlai. His succession to Ike wd no doubt be popular in England. But it is the Americans who have to choose!

[1] One of Churchill's racehorses.
[2] This letter was handwritten.

Now I write to you on another glorious 1st of June. The weather is a little better & I painted for 2½ hours yesterday. Today I give a luncheon to the company & the Billmeirs who start tonight in their yacht for Corsica.

Wendy seemed unhappy at our going to the Capponcina in September, but cheered up when I said it was only for a month & I wd come back afterwards.

You will have gone to Ireland before I write again in all probability. I hope you will enjoy yr stay there, let me know about the Irish people, I am worried about them, they come to England in large numbers instead of building up their own country.

The weather improves every minute and we lunch at the Chateau de Madrid & will deliver suitable messages to our guests from you.

Thank you for going to see Pamela at Knebworth. It is a picturesque estate. What fun it was winning two races in one day! Quire an event for a beginner. Christopher is vy clever about horses & the stud has become numerous & valuable: & pays for itself so far.

Always your loving husband
[Drawing of a pig]

Sir Winston S. Churchill to Lady Churchill
(Baroness Spencer-Churchill papers)[1]

5 June 1957   La Pausa

Darling,

Your fourth letter has just arrived. I telegraphed to Randolph on his Birthday & was vy glad when hr thanked me for the garden chairs along with you. He recognised they were a joint present. But I can claim no credit for it.

I am absorbed in *Wuthering Heights*. There is no doubt it deserves its fame. One can see it is a good book, I am ¾ the way through.

Here we have mainly clouds & I spend my mornings in bed. But in the occasional gleams I have painted 2 landscapes which are worth bringing home to show you.

Christopher comes the day after tomorrow (Friday) & I am looking forward to seeing him and hearing his news. We are going to lunch in Italy today at the Restaurant across the frontier. Did you go there – I forget. I would rather stay at home. The Prefect is coming, His wife is still in Paris. They are both coming by Sunday next when Christopher will have joined us.

I read what you say about Clarissa & Anthony and I agree with it. They bear their lot with courage.

Here is a letter from the Governor of the West Indies[2] which I think you will like to read. He has had a rough time. But I do not think we shd make it

---

[1] This letter was handwritten.
[2] Lord Hailes.

worse. Poor Patrick! They will get along all right. But it was a chilling episode.

The French are dawdling & dithering over their new Government & their large deficit. Algeria is a shocking situation. I think 15 days has lasted long enough. The politicians must be enjoying their 'Crisis'. I hope they will pull through & beat the Algerian terrorists.

I envy you your heat wave. The world has become as muddled as its people about the weather, and it is a relief to find the shelter of Victorian Literature, when the alternative wd be to stare out at really bloody prospects from the windows.

I hope you have had *rain* or will have it as the ground is reported shockingly hard & stiff – good for my horses on the whole.

My dearest one, I love you from a gloomy background I fear. The only thing that cheers me this morning is the new bath of wh you write. I shall look forward to wallowing in it.

Tender love my darling. Your devoted husband.

PS Anthony has returned from his cruise with the Billmeirs. He flew back from Corsica (of which he gives good account) in a plane lent him by Onassis, & piloted by him.

[Drawing of a pig]
xxxxxxxxx for you
Toby chose it unprompted

Winston Churchill to Sir Winston S. Churchill
(Churchill papers, 1/56)[1]

19 June 1957   Eton College, Windsor

Dear Grandpapa,

I am sorry I did not come and watch you at the Garter ceremony on Monday; it must have been awfully hot in all your robes.

I go riding every Tuesday and Thursday at the Life Guards barracks in Windsor; it is great fun, about fifteen of us go. We ride inside a large riding school and we are instructed by a large army officer, with a large moustache and a large whip. The horse which I chose was a huge black charger called 'Colonist'! He jumped very well and I just managed to hold on and keep him between my legs.

I was very sorry to read in the newspapers that you auctioned your herd yesterday and that Bardog's will be going too, soon.

I hope you and Grandmama are well; please give her my love.

Your loving grandson,

[1] This letter was handwritten.

Sir Winston S. Churchill to Winston Churchill
(Churchill papers, 1/56)

23 June 1957

My dear Winston,

Thank you so much for your letter. I am glad to hear that you are getting some riding, and enjoying it. I went to Ascot yesterday to see Le Pretendant run, but he did not do quite as well as I hoped.

We miss the Jersey herd, but we still have the Belted Galloways. I am not parting with them.

Yr loving grandfather,

Sir Anthony Eden to Sir Winston S. Churchill
(Churchill papers, 2/216)[1]

23 June 1957

My dear Winston,

I am so sorry that Horace Evans & my US surgeon[2] are firm that I must stay quiet here this summer. I should have loved to come to London to see you or to Chartwell but I fear that these journeys are beyond my strength at present.

It is lovely weather here, and we spend much of our time in the garden. We also do a little leisurely house-hunting; Clarissa with rather more energy. We hope to find something a little larger than this.

The Canadian elections were interesting. Diefenbaker[3] is a good man, I think. He did much better than anyone expected & he held the initiative. He was rigorously critical of St Laurent over Suez, and he drew the bigger crowds, throughout the campaign. St Laurent made the mistake of trying to imitate Ike and be a God above the battle. That did not work in Canada.

I am also much encouraged by increasing American understanding of our Suez action. *New York Times* so much better than our own which seems to have returned to the Dawson[4] appeasement days. In view of this Canadian & US attitude it seems to me important that we should not renege on what we have done, or we should lose the respect we are still gaining. I have told Harold that this is my view and that Socialists have more cause to wish to forget their Suez conduct than we.

[1] This letter was handwritten.
[2] Richard Cattell.
[3] John George Diefenbaker, 1895–1979. MP (Cons.) for Lake Centre, 1940–53; for Prince Albert, 1953–79. Leader of Official Opposition, 1957. PM of Canada, 1957–63.
[4] George Geoffrey Robinson, 1874–1944. Educated at Eton and Magdalen College, Oxford. Fellow of All Souls, 1896. Private Secretary to Milner, British High Commissioner in South Africa, 1901–5. Editor, *Johannesburg Star*, 1905–10; *The Times*, 1912–19, 1923–41. Took the surname Dawson, 1917.

But enough of politics. I find it pleasant to read again – books not newspapers. When we have a little more room for documents and papers, I may feel disposed to try my hand at some account of the Thirties. You have always told me what a good companion the writing of a book can be.

Clarissa sends her love. She rang you up when she was in London but, alas, you were away.

Jo Sturdee to Sir Winston S. Churchill
(Churchill papers, 1/144)

25 June 1957

Dear Sir Winston,

I write to let you know that I shall shortly be giving up my office here and going to work for Lord Ismay while he is writing his book. This means that I shall no longer be able to deal with the mail which you receive from the General Public. I am very sorry about this, because I have enjoyed doing this meagre task for you, and I like to think that, because of their letters to you, some good has been done for some of the less fortunate people who write to you for help. The letters are up to date and the files could be handed over tomorrow. But I expect you will need a little time to make alternative arrangements about this part of your many interests and worries.

You receive approximately eight letters a week from the General Public, with many more of course on the occasion of your birthday and at Christmas-time. I do not know if you will need anyone else to do this work, under your own personal staff, perhaps on a part-time basis, but if you do I can thoroughly recommend Miss Delia Morton,[1] who has been working here for more than a year and who knows how to deal most of the mail. She is 22, very intelligent and a very nice person.

I do want to thank you very much for allowing me to do this work for you up till now. I am sorry in many ways to be giving it up, and I hope you really will let me know if there is anything I can do to help over this or anything else.

Sir Winston S. Churchill to Anthony Eden
(Churchill papers, 2/216)

26 June 1957

My dear Anthony,

I was very pleased to receive your substantial letter.[2] I met Horace Evans at Ascot, and was glad to hear all he said about you. You should nurse your strength.

---

[1] Churchill did indeed hire Delia Morton to work as a secretary.
[2] Reproduced above (pp. 2171–2).

The Canadian elections were certainly a great surprise to me, and I shall look forward to meeting Diefenbaker next week. I am bidden by Macmillan to the Dinner on Tuesday. I quite agree with you about the *Times*.

I was so sorry not to get Clarissa's message. Clemmie joins me in sending both of you our best love, with every good wish for a full recovery. Do let me know if there is any way in which you think I can be of help.

I am getting older with every day that passes, but I still hope to see us get the better of Nasser. I am sure it would be a very good thing for you to write a book about the 30s, and you will find plenty of material. But there is no reason why this should be the end of the story which you have to tell, and I am sure it will be good all through.

Sir Winston S. Churchill to Alan Lennox-Boyd
(Churchill paper, 2/214)

3 July 1957

My dear Alan,

How very kind of you to write to me. I shall greatly miss him,[1] even though I have no duties to perform. He was a great companion during my eleven years of Office and before the war. I do not think we ever disagreed on general matters.

Thank you so much for your kindness in thinking of me.

Sir Winston S. Churchill: speech
('Winston S. Churchill, His Complete Speeches', volume 8, pages 8679–81)

6 July 1957 Constituency Fete
Royal Wanstead School

ONE NATION

My wife and I are so pleased to be with you this afternoon at your Fete in this very lovely setting. I want first of all to thank Mr Charles French,[2] the Governors of the Royal Wanstead School, and the Headmaster[3] for their kindness in again allowing us to use their beautiful grounds, and for the great help they have given us.

A Fete is an admirable method of getting people together in pleasant circumstances, and of raising much needed funds for the Association; but it requires a great deal of organization and work, and we are very grateful to the Committee and everyone in all the Branches who have worked so hard

---

[1] Lord Cherwell, who died on July 3.
[2] Charles S. French, President of the Board of Governors, Royal Wanstead School.
[3] John F. Lavender, 1916–2002.

to ensure success. I hope that you are all having an enjoyable afternoon and spending as much as you can.

At your last Fete here in 1954 I was unfortunately unable to be present, as I was in the United States conferring with the President, but I spoke to you here in 1951.[1] What changes have come about since then! It is all too easy to see the imperfections of present affairs, and to forget the miseries of Socialism in action, the rationing of everything, and the controls so necessary in the war but preserved after it to bolster up an unsuccessful doctrine. The costly failures which we have endured between 1945 and 1951 have not cured the Socialists of their views.

Mr Gaitskell has hinted at the punitive measures that would be taken against shareholders if the Socialists were returned to power. Therein, of course, he is attacking the whole concept of private property, for the shareholders are after all nothing more than the owners of the industries in which they have invested. I certainly do not see how the country's economy could get on without them. Perhaps the trade unions will have something to say about Mr Gaitskell's latest departure, for I understand that they themselves are substantial shareholders in many enterprises, and have done rather well out of it. And this is only a small part of what a renewal of Socialist Government would bring us. Another five years of mis-rule would do mortal harm to our slowly revived hopes of well-being.

There is one domestic matter above all others which occupies our thoughts and the thoughts of the Government – the cost of living. We have not yet halted the rise, but we have slowed it down considerably. Under the Socialists the index rose by over forty per cent. Since we came in it has risen by only a little over twenty per cent. We must persevere and improve still more. There must be no rise at all.

Remember, too, that whereas under Socialism taxation rose every year with monotonous regularity, under Conservatism almost every Budget has brought concessions which have helped all classes of society. We should all like to see still more concessions, particularly for the aged, and for those on fixed incomes. I am sure they will come.

In the field of international affairs our achievement in developing unassisted the hydrogen weapon is a hopeful contribution. We have all followed the technical controversy on the effects of nuclear tests. Some protagonists have been less honest than others, and I have no doubt that our possession of this perfected means of large-scale destruction is most welcome in many quarters. I myself believe that the weight of evidence lies on the side of those who believe the effects of tests on the present scale to be negligible from the point of view of the health of the human race. But even if this were not so, what are these effects compared with the misery and annihilation of another

---

[1] Speech reproduced in *The Churchill Documents*, vol. 22, *Leader of the Opposition, August 1945 to October 1951*, (pp. 2116–20).

war? Every addition to the free world's armoury increases the chances of permanent peace. I do not suggest that Soviet Russia desires war, but how much more careful will the leaders of the Communist world be to refrain from steps that might lead to it when they realize that their own total destruction would inevitably ensue. I have for long referred to nuclear weapons as 'deterrents'. As far as Britain and America are concerned, that is their purpose, and it will always remain so.

I am happy to see that our relations with our American partner are being restored to their normal warm temperature. Make no mistake. It is in the closest association with our friends in the Commonwealth, America, and NATO that our hopes of peace and happiness lie. Neither we nor they can afford estrangements. The concept of the United Nations was a remarkable one, but in its present form it has shown itself impotent in a time of crisis and effective only against those who are prepared to respect its opinion. To rely solely on the United Nations Organization would be disastrous for the future.

However, the horizon is by no means black, and certainly our position in the world is the better for improvements in our own country. Six years of Conservative Government have changed a good deal. But these things take time. Industry and good sense are only starting to bear fruit. As time goes on the improvements will become more apparent, and all, I repeat all, may share in the prosperity to come. The Conservative Party strives for the good of the whole nation, irrespective of class. We do not seek to bribe a section of the electorate at the expense of the rest. We are one nation, and we all share the results of the nation's effort, the nation's industry, and the nation's glory.

None of you here, I am quite confident, share the gloomy views being expressed in some quarters about the prospects before our party. Some of the experts, or at least those who would like to be taken for experts, read a lot into the figures of by-election voting and the fluctuations of the Gallup Polls. Well, I have been in this game for quite a few years now, and I have always found that in politics you want to take a long view and not be too much influenced by what is going on at the moment. It is not the ripples the wind may cause on the surface of the water that really count in navigation, but the deeper and stronger tides and currents that flow underneath and may not be detected by the casual observer. The British people, I am firmly convinced, are fundamentally and instinctively opposed to the whole alien conception of State Socialism, with all that it implies in the loss of individual freedom and the stifling of individual ambition and effort.

The years since 1951, when our Conservative Government took over in the nick of time, have seen a remarkable transformation in the affairs of our nation. Too many people have forgotten the shortages, the restrictions, the rationing and the queues: they take all the improvements for granted. Some of them grumble that there have not been even more of them. But the policy of the Government has been, first to make sure we do not lose what has been gained so painfully, and then go on to make further progress. Many of the steps taken in the past year or two have of necessity been unpopular, and therefore easy for our opponents to misrepresent. But the next year or two will show their wisdom in the beneficial results they produce.

But while we can be confident, we must not be either complacent or lazy. We would be very foolish to sit back in the comfortable belief that time is on our side. That is as easy a mistake, and as fatal a mistake, to make in politics as it is in war. Time is on no man's side, and no party's side. Time is neutral; but it can be made the ally of those who will seize it, and use it to the full. So I hope that all of you who believe in our party, and who know how much depends upon its success, will be diligent over the coming months in your work on its behalf, and in boldly and actively stating our case, and refuting and repelling the attacks which are made upon us. And you can all start this afternoon by helping to provide the funds which are the sinews of our political campaign.

Anthony Montague Browne to Sir Winston S. Churchill
(<i>Churchill papers, 2/131</i>)</center>

8 July 1957

BRITAIN IN EUROPE

When you welcome those at the meeting on Tuesday, July 9, you said you would speak two or three sentences impromptu. I nevertheless submit a few very banal lines. The main theme of the meeting is expected to be the question of our association with the European Common Market.

The list of those present is attached below.

Draft

I am complimented that it falls to me to welcome here the distinguished personalities who are to speak today on the theme 'Britain in Europe'. The European Movement has played a leading part in preparing the climate of opinion in which the concrete developments of European Unity in the past ten years have become possible to Governments, and acceptable to their peoples. It is well that the ground should thus slowly be prepared, particularly in this country where the difficulties to be overcome are perhaps greater than among the Continental countries. At this time we contemplate the problem of our association with the European Common Market and its compatibility with our obligations and links within the Commonwealth and Empire. The advantages of a successful outcome are very great to all sides – it may be greater than any of the previous measures in this field. ~~I urge our Continental friends to reflect on what is at stake and to do all in~~

~~their power to ease our decision~~. Politically and economically the fates of Britain and Continental Europe are intertwined, yet to sacrifice the Commonwealth association would be most damaging to both you and ourselves. Both advantages must be preserved for either to flourish.

Sir Winston S. Churchill: speech
('Winston S. Churchill, His Complete Speeches', volume 8, pages 8681–2)

9 July 1957

United Europe Meeting
Central Hall, Westminster

EUROPE – UNITE!

My message to Europe today is still the same as it was ten years ago – unite. Europe's security and prosperity lie in unity. Much has already been achieved and we are on the verge of further big decisions. We all welcome the formation of a common market by the six nations, provided that it is a step towards the creation of a free trade area, to which the whole of free Europe will have access. If, on the other hand, the European trade community were to be permanently restricted to the six nations, the results might be worse than if nothing were done at all – worse for them as well as for us. It would tend not to unite Europe but to divide it – and not only in the economic field.

We, in Britain, have our special relationship with our fellow-members of the British Commonwealth, and nothing will make us sever the bonds which link us together. But there is no necessary inconsistency between our position in the Commonwealth and our participation in a European free trade area. We genuinely wish to join a European free trade area, and if our continental friends wish to reach agreement, I am quite sure that a way can be found and that reasonable adjustments can be made to meet the essential interests of all.

It is a pleasure to me to take part again in a gathering to promote the cause of a united Europe, which has for so many years been near to my heart. I wish you all continued success in this great enterprise. Let us therefore go forward together with courage and patience.

John Colville to Sir Winston S. Churchill
(Churchill papers, 2/182)[1]

9 July 1957

My Dear Winston,

I got back yesterday from a business trip to Portugal, too late, alas, to go to the Prof's funeral. I feel that much as we all miss him, there is one person above all to whom his death will be a shattering blow, and since we cannot feel sorrow for the dead we can only express it with the living. Without you, the Prof might have been a great scientist, but he could never have been what he was or achieved what he did. In a sense, indeed, you created him and the result gave his friends untold satisfaction and his country immeasurable service.

Meg and I had arranged to take him to a play next week, and I can scarcely bear to think I shall see him no more. But our loss is as nothing to yours, and it is for that reason I feel I must write to you.

Do not, I beg, think of replying.

Yours ever

Sir Winston S. Churchill to Lord Beaverbrook
(Beaverbrook papers)

13 July 1957   Chartwell

My dear Max,

I must thank you most warmly for your welcome and for the beautiful salver that you have given me. It will always remind me of the year 1940, when the Club of which you are President played a decisive part in our getting through the year when we were all alone. I accept with alacrity the title of Master Member of the 1940 Club which you wish to confer upon me.

Thank you so much for all your personal kindness and friendship.

---

[1] This letter was handwritten.

Sir Winston S. Churchill to Lady Olivier[1]
(Churchill papers, 2/195)

18 July 1957

My dear Vivien,

I hope you will succeed in your defence of the St James's Theatre, though as a parliamentarian I cannot approve of your 'disorderly' method. If a fund is needed, as seems to be possible, I shall be very glad to subscribe £500 to it. I fear it is all that I can promise to do at present, but I shall be definitely committed to the cause.

I thought your *Titus Andronicus* was a great presentation. I was too far away to hear, but I very much enjoyed the evening, and especially seeing you again.

Sir Anthony Eden to Sir Winston S. Churchill
(Churchill papers, 2/216)[2]

25 July 1957

My dear Winston,

It was very kind of you and Clemmie to come to see us yesterday. Your visit gave us so much pleasure; I enjoyed every moment of it. I can only hope that you were both not too exhausted when you got back to London.

I am sorry that I forgot the volume of *Lee's Lieutenants* when you left. However, I will have it wrapped up and dispatched when my secretary comes down next week. I am sure that you will enjoy it for Freeman always writes well. I should be grateful if you could let me have it back some time because I have not read it yet myself. There is no hurry about this at all. Although it is a second volume of a series I am sure that it will read well by itself, for each deals with a distinct period. The cavalry's part in this period, Jeb Stuart,[3] a young Pelham[4] & the use of new tactics, make more sympathetic study than the latest activities of N. Cousins.[5] Clarissa sends her love to you and Clemmie.

---

[1] Vivian Mary Hartley, 1913–67. Known by her stage name, 'Vivien Leigh'. Educated at Royal Academy of Dramatic Art, London. Acted in films including *Gone With the Wind* (1939), *Waterloo Bridge* (1940), *That Hamilton Woman* (1941), which was Churchill's favourite, and *A Streetcar Named Desire* (1951). Married, 1940, Laurence Olivier (div. 1960).

[2] This letter was handwritten.

[3] James Ewell Brown Stuart, 1833–64. Known as 'Jeb'. Confederate cavalry commander during American Civil War. Died from wounds received in battle.

[4] John Pelham, 1838–63. A brilliant young artillery commander who served with J. E. B. Stuart's cavalry during American Civil War. Died from wounds received in battle.

[5] Norman Cousins, 1915–90. American political journalist and author. Educational Editor, *New York Evening Post*, 1935–6. Managing Editor, *Current History* magazine, 1936–9. Editor, *Saturday Review*, 1940–71, 1973–8. Author of several works including *Talks with Nehru* (1951), *The Improbable Triumvirate* (1972) and *The Pathology of Power* (1987).

Sir Winston S. Churchill to Robert Davidson
(Churchill papers, 2/566)

26 July 1957

My dear Mr Davidson,

I am indeed obliged to you for your letter of July 12 telling me of the opening of your 'Churchill Room' and inviting me to be present. It is with much regret that I must decline, as my arrangements will not allow of my coming to the United States in the foreseeable future.

I am glad to hear that Westminster College has invited the Queen to open the 'Churchill Room', but I fear that I could not properly seek to influence Her Majesty's decision.

I remember well my most agreeable visit to Westminster College, and with warm personal good wishes.

Sir Winston S. Churchill: speech[1]
('Winston S. Churchill, His Complete Speeches', volume 8, pages 8682–4)

31 July 1957   The Guildhall

LIBERTY AND THE LAW

I am very glad that it has fallen to me to propose the toast of the Legal Profession and at the same time to welcome the many illustrious American guests who have come from within and outside the ranks of the profession. Several thousand members of the American Bar Association have come to our island for part of their Annual Convention. That is a remarkable fact, and a compliment of which we are all deeply sensible.

It illuminates a great truth. In the main, Law and Equity stand in the forefront of the moral forces which our two countries have in common, and rank with our common language in that store of bonds of unity on which I firmly believe our life and destiny depend. You are 160 millions and we, with our Dominions gathered round us, are 70 or 80 millions, and if we work together there is no doubt that we shall together represent a factor in the development of the whole world which no one will have cause to regret. The alliances of former days were framed on physical strength, but the English-speaking unity can find its lasting coherence above all in those higher ties of intellect and spirit of which the law and language are a supreme expression.

Last week you visited Runnymede. There was the foundation, on which you have placed a monument. It has often been pointed out that the 5th and 14th Amendments of the American Constitution are an echo of the Magna

---

[1] Delivered to the Law Society Dinner for the American Bar Association.

Carta. No person shall under the 5th Amendment be deprived of life, liberty, or property without due process of law, and the 14th Amendment says that no State shall deprive any person of life, liberty, or property without due process of law, nor deny any person within its jurisdiction equal protection of the laws. National governments may indeed obtain sweeping emergency powers for the sake of protecting the community in times of war or other perils. These will temporarily curtail or suspend the freedom of ordinary men and women, but special powers must be granted by the elected representatives of those same people by Congress or by Parliament, as the case may be.

They do not belong to the State or Government as a right. Their exercise needs vigilant scrutiny, and their grant may be swiftly withdrawn. This terrible twentieth century has exposed both our communities to grim experiences, and both have emerged restored and guarded. They have come back to us safe and sure. I speak, of course, as a layman on legal topics, but I believe that our differences are more apparent than real, and are the result of geographical and other physical conditions rather than any true division of principle. An omnipotent Parliament and a small legal profession, tightly bound by precedent, are all very well in an island which has not been invaded for nearly 2,000 years. Forty-nine states, each with fundamental rights and a different situation, is a different proposition.

Between Magna Carta and the formulation of the American Constitution we in Britain can claim the authorship of the whole growth of the English Common law. Our pioneers took it with them when they crossed the Atlantic. For many centuries in the Middle Ages English lawyers would not admit that the law could be changed, even by Parliament. It was something sacrosanct, inviolable, above human tampering, like right and wrong. And this seems to have been the view of the English Chief Justice, Coke,[1] as late as the early sixteen hundreds. His dream of a Supreme Court above the legislature for Great Britain vanished in the Civil War. The Supreme Court survived and flourished in the United States. England was too compact and too uniform a community to have need of it. But the Supreme Court in America has often been the guardian and upholder of American liberty. Long may it continue to thrive.

There are wider aspects to these considerations. Justice knows no frontiers. Within our considerable communities we have sought to regulate our affairs with equity. We have now reached the point where nations must contrive a system and practice to resolve their disputes and settle them peacefully. We have not succeeded so far in this. Some have tried at one swoop in the hour of victory to draw up an all-comprehending scheme such as the Charter of the United Nations to meet most international possibilities. In a recent speech that most distinguished Australian statesman, Mr Menzies, said that justice

---

[1] Edward Coke, 1552–1634. Leading English lawyer, legal scholar and politician during the reigns of Elizabeth I and James I.

was not being achieved there. A serious charge, but it is true. I do not throw in my lot with those who say that Britain should leave the United Nations. But it is certain that if the Assembly continues to take its decisions on grounds of enmity, opportunism, or merely jealousy and petulance, the whole structure may be brought to nothing.

The shape of the United Nations has changed greatly from its original form and from the intention of its architects. The differences between the Great Powers have thrown responsibility increasingly on the Assembly. This has been vastly swollen by the addition of new nations. We wish these new nations well. Indeed, we created many of them, and have done our best since to ensure their integrity and prosperity. But it is anomalous that the vote or prejudice of any small country should affect events involving populations many times its own numbers and affect them as momentary self-advantage may direct. This should be changed. There are many cases where the United Nations have failed. Hungary is in my mind. Justice cannot be a hit-or-miss system. We cannot be content with an arrangement where our new system of international laws applies only to those who are willing to keep them.

I do not want tonight to suggest an elaborate new charter for the United Nations, but I think we can all agree that its present conception is imperfect, and must be improved.

The mere creation, however, of international organizations does not relieve us of our individual responsibility – at least not until the international systems are truly reliable and effective. It falls to the righteous man individually to do what he can and to form with his friends alliances that are manifestly crowned with justice and honour. Such are the North Atlantic Treaty and the other combinations of the Free World. Such, I trust and believe, is the union of the English-speaking peoples. The Legal Profession.

Sir Anthony Eden to Sir Winston S. Churchill
(*Churchill papers, 2/216*)[1]

1 August 1957

My dear Winston,

Herewith the Freeman.[2] I do not want it back. I will arrange to get another from USA in due course.

What an excellent speech you made to the American lawyers. Bob Menzies will be pleased and he deserves that support. I know that he feels that he has lately been carrying the burden of this argument, somewhat unsupported among other Empire Statesmen. He did not tell me so, but he so remarked to Cilcennin a while ago. Your views of course count for more with him than anything all other contemporaries could say.

---

[1] This letter is handwritten.
[2] See Eden to Churchill, July 25, reproduced above (p. 2179).

We are enjoying this return of sunshine and warmth, and go to Max's Somerset home this afternoon where Nicholas[1] joins us. Very exciting.

Clarissa sends her love.

Sir Winston S. Churchill to Sir Anthony Eden
(Churchill papers, 2/216)

8 August 1957

My dear Anthony,

Thank you so much for your letter, and for sending me the Freeman, which I have begun to read and am enjoying.

I am very glad to hear that you liked what I said about the United Nations. Certainly Bob is one of our greatest assets, and he deserves all the support we can give him.

Clemmie and I both look forward to seeing you and Clarissa again soon.

Desmond Flower to Sir Winston S. Churchill
(Churchill papers, 4/26)

30 August 1957

Dear Sir Winston,

I have very great pleasure in sending you herewith the first copy to come from the printers of Vol. III of *A History of the English-Speaking Peoples*. I hope that you will like it. The red morocco copy for your set will follow as soon as the binders have finished it.

May I ask for your views regarding the title for the fourth and last volume. I know that you have up to the present called it *The Nineteenth Century*. But we feel that this has not quite got the majestic rightness of the titles which you have given to the previous volumes. May we suggest for your consideration *The Great Democracies*. I need hardly point out that after *The Age of Revolution*, the period covered by the fourth volume saw the emergence of the United States not only as a power but also as the growing ally of this country – apart from the Daughters of the Revolution who still live happily in the distant past – and that period witnessed the start of an alliance of the two great democracies which was to resist and rebut within the lifetime of us all the next challenge from the Age of Dictatorship.

We do feel that the title which we offer for your consideration is apposite, a good selling point title, and one which is in accord with your own views and

---

[1] Nicholas Eden, 1930–85. Served in KRRC, 1949–51. ADC to Governor-General of Canada, 1952–3. Lt-Col., Royal Green Jackets, 1967–70. Earl of Avon, 1977. Lord in Waiting, 1980–3. Parliamentary Under-Secretary of State, Dept of Energy, 1983–4. Under-Secretary of State for the Environment, 1984–5.

public expression over many years. We should feel very happy if this suggestion appealed to you enough for it to be adopted.

For the jacket of the last volume we have been fortunate enough to get for the front the lovely Winterhalter[1] of Victoria and the Prince Consort beside her and her children about her knees, which is in the collection of Her Majesty; and for the back a remarkably interesting painting of Abraham Lincoln in conference in the Admiral's cabin of a Federal warship. I feel sure that they will make a jacket which will please you.

I understand that you are going to the South of France on Sunday: may I express the hope that the weather will be lovely and that you will have all the pleasures for which you could ever wish.

Sir Winston S. Churchill to Desmond Flower
(Churchill papers, 4/26)

31 August 1957

My dear Desmond,

Thank you very much for your letter, and for the delightful book which accompanied it. I think the jacket is brilliant.

It is not for me, who has retired, to decide upon the question of the title of Volume IV, but I think the change you propose is a great improvement.

I am most interested to hear of the beautiful paintings which you have secured for the jacket of Vol. IV.

Sir Winston S. Churchill: speech
('Winston S. Churchill, His Complete Speeches', volume 8, page 8684)

3 September 1957   Geneva

PARLIAMENT – SPOKESMAN OF THE PEOPLE

Since the Inter-Parliamentary Conference last met in London, twenty-seven years ago, free Parliamentary institutions have confronted, and have triumphantly overcome, the heaviest assault ever made upon them.

I rejoice that at this meeting the Inter-Parliamentary Union is stronger than ever before, and particularly that it now contains representatives of the Parliaments of many nations which have recently achieved independence, as well as newcomers from older Assemblies which have decided to join the Union.

Our Parliament has survived because it made itself the spokesman not of government but of the people. In the fiercest clash of debates we have

---

[1] Franz Xaver Winterhalter, 1805–73. German artist, known for his portraits of European royalty.

jealously guarded the right of every Member freely to speak for his constituents and for himself. If your Conference will follow this tradition, it can make a significant contribution to toleration between ideologies and understanding between nations. Thus alone can freedom endure and mankind live in peace.

Sir Winston S. Churchill to Lord Beaverbrook
(Churchill papers, 2/211)

11 September 1957   Alpes Maritimes

My dear Max,

Clemmie and I are so much enjoying your hospitality here. The weather has been excellent on the whole, and I have managed to do a little painting. Clemmie seems to be benefiting much from the change, and finds your Housekeeper and your staff most pleasant and helpful.

The chair is a great success, and I use it daily both up and down. It was ready for me the day after we arrived, and makes a considerable difference to the ease of living.

We have gone out very little since being here, except to luncheon with the Reves at Roquebrune, and a few visits to the Casino, with indifferent fortune. A number of friends have lunched and dined with us here, including Mrs Anna Rosenberg,[1] whom I expect you know.

I do not care for the look of things in the Middle East. By their action on Suez the Americans have put an end to the chance of using anything but words and money, and they are not always enough. The stock markets drift from bad to worse, especially the Canadian oil and gas companies. I wonder if they have reached their lowest point?

I trust all goes well with you, and that you are enjoying the Canadian autumn.

With so many thanks again for all your kindness.

---

[1] Anna Marie Lederer, 1902–83. American public official and consultant. Married, 1919, Julius Rosenberg (div. 1962); 1962, Paul G. Hoffman. Secretary to President Roosevelt's Labor Victory Board, 1942–5. Member, US National Commission for UNESCO, 1946–50. Member, Advisory Commission of the President on Universal Military Training, 1946–7. Asst Secretary of Defense, 1950–3.

Anthony Montague Browne to J. A. Billmeir
(Churchill papers, 2/180)

21 September 1957

Sir Winston will be writing to thank you for your letter of September 17. Both he and Lady Churchill were so touched by your renewed thought of them. Unfortunately, there has been a continuous flow of engagements that have kept us all at La Capponcina, and we have not been able to take advantage of your hospitality. It is a great pity.

All is well out here, and the weather excellent. Sir Winston paints and visits the Casino, and my Wife and I potter about with Lady Churchill and swim. In between tides swarms of people descend on us or we on them.

The forest fires here have been very serious, and Roquebrune village was threatened. The fire reached the outlying houses and burnt some of them before it was put out. 'Onskaboet' seemed to be quite intact when I drove past it, and there has been no damage in that neighbourhood.

I follow with anxiety the freight rates. It can be no consolation to you to see the stock markets all falling the downward trend, particularly our Canadian gas and oil companies.

We move to Roquebrune on October 1, and will be back in England by the middle of the month.

Sir Winston S. Churchill to Lady Churchill
(Baroness Spencer-Churchill papers)[1]

7 October 1957

My darling,

Your two lovely letters have just arrived. Everything you are doing about the pictures seems well calculated. The frames ought to be wooden. I shall look forward to seeing the results. I certainly think the Lawrence Farm pictures shd be considered.

Yesterday (Sunday) we went over to Mortola &, after an excellent luncheon, we were inspired to visit your favourite house. The owners were most agreeable. The poor lady was charming – crippled though she be. She had <u>not</u> known of your visits though this would have delighted her. She knows you from of old. You did not tell me she had offered to lend you her house & grounds in 1945 – but we were about to start for Marakesh. I felt vy sorry for her. She was absolutely charmed to see me.

I clambered up to the square terrace, & we all sat and talked. She had sent her conveyance. It was Queen Victoria's special Chair, in which I was wheeled

---

[1] This letter was handwritten.

about from the top to the bottom (the sea) & the bottom to the top, & saw everything, accompanied by the whole family – husband, son, son's wife and my own party. (The Reves had to go back from the house because Wendy had terribly high heels but they enjoyed themselves vy much and all they saw) It is indeed a wonderful spot.

I am sorry to say that Anthony MB has to return on the 11th as his mother is to be seriously examined for heart trouble. Monty arrives on the same day for a weekend,

With tender love
My dearest one
Your ever loving husband
[Drawing of a pig]
[...]

Sir Winston S. Churchill to Harold Macmillan
(Churchill papers, 2/210)

10 October 1957   La Pausa
Private

My dear Harold,

You may remember that when you were at the Foreign Office in October 1955 I wrote to you about an Honour for Bernie Baruch. You explained to me in a letter dated December 13, 1955[1] why you did not feel able to accept this suggestion.

I would now like once more to put the idea before you. Bernie is approaching the end of his life, and there is no doubt that he has been a staunch friend of our country. I do not think that an Honour in his case could be interpreted by the Foreign Office as a bad precedent which would get them into difficulties elsewhere. The occasion of the Queen's visit would be a particularly happy one, and I really do not see that it could do anything but good in America. Will you let me know what you think?

---

[1] Reproduced above (pp. 2069–70).

Sir Winston S. Churchill to Randolph S. Churchill
(Churchill papers, 1/56)

11 October 1957

My dear Randolph,

Thank you very much for sending me your pamphlet about Bevan and Cousins.[1] I had seen your article on the same subject in the *Express*.

We have had an agreeable and sunny stay down here, and I have been able to do some painting. I return to England on October 21.

Yr lovg father,

Sir Winston S. Churchill to Lady Churchill
(Baroness Spencer-Churchill papers)[2]

11 October 1957

Darling,

Your letter has just arrived. I send the answer back by Anthony. It will reach you today. Queen V's chair was pushed by the entire Mortola family & the 3 gardeners.

The satellite[3] itself etc. does not distress me. The disconcerting thing is the proof of the forwardness of Soviet Science compared to Americans. The Prof was as usual vigilant and active. Plenty of warnings were given but we have fallen hopelessly behind in technical education, & the tiny bit we have tends to disperse & scatter about America & the Dominions. This is the mechanized age, & where are we? <u>Quality and of the Front rank</u> indeed we still possess. But numbers are lacking. The necessary breeding ground has failed. We must struggle on; & looking to the Union with America.

After inviting Christopher & Mary to come out in Anthony's place Wendy has asked Diana, who seemed quite pleased to come. We are going to luncheon in the Onassis Yacht today.

I have painted two (2) pictures, one is rather good.

Tender love & many kisses xx
From your devoted husband
[Drawing of a pig]

---

[1] Frank Cousins, 1904–86. Born in Bulwell, Nottinghamshire. Married, 1930, Annie Judd: four children. Joined Transport and General Workers' Union, 1933. National Secretary, Road Transport Group, 1948. Asst General Secretary, TGWU, 1955–6; General Secretary, 1956–69. President, International Transport Workers' Federation, 1958–60, 1962–4. Minister of Technology, 1964–6. MP (Lab.) for Nuneaton, 1965–6.

[2] This letter was handwritten.

[3] On 4 Oct. 1957, the Soviet Union had successfully launched into orbit the first satellite, Sputnik 1.

Randolph S. Churchill to Sir Winston S. Churchill
(Churchill papers, 1/56)

14 October 1957

My dearest Papa,

I was so glad to get your letter and to hear that you have been having some sunshine. I look forward to seeing you very much when you get back.

The Tory Conference was a triumph and I greatly enjoyed it. Lord Woolton asked specially to be remembered to you as he would like you to know that 'you are often in his thoughts'.

Michael Foot has written a remarkable book about Swift. For a polemical pamphleteer it is strangely objective. It is called *The Pen and the Sword* and is concerned with the intrigues that led up to the Treaty of Utrecht. He is very fair about Marlborough and in his list of sources says of your life, 'No other book on the subject deserves to be mentioned in the same breath.' I am sure you will find it interesting. I am sending you a copy by air mail under separate cover.

Sir Winston S. Churchill to Lady Churchill
(Baroness Spencer-Churchill papers)[1]

18 October 1957   La Pausa

Darling,

We had a slip-up in organization wh arose from the strike of Electric & Gas workers on the 16th & the Communist Demonstrations of the 17th. The first caused some inconvenience; the second was a flop. Otherwise all has run smoothly, and my vy pleasant visit will end on Monday.

I took Mrs Lees Milne[2] & my hosts out to lunch yesterday at the Vistaero (on the spike of the hills) and I think it went all right. Mrs LM is quite interesting and revives memories of my old friend Tom.[3]

Wendy had an alarm of Flu yesterday but temperature has dropped to normal this morning after American medicine. I hope I am not going to plunge into an epidemic myself on return. I am going to paint this morning after ending *Black Arrow*[4] wh I have entirely forgotten.

Looking forward to seeing you on Monday, ever your loving husband.

[Drawing of a pig]

---

[1] This letter was handwritten.
[2] Alvilde Bridges Milne, 1909–94. British gardening and landscape expert. Married, 1933, Anthony Freskin Charles Hamby Chaplin (div. 1950): one child; 1951, George James Henry Lees-Milne.
[3] George Tom Molesworth Bridges, 1871–1939. Mrs Lees-Milne's father. Served in British Army, 1892–1922. KCMG, 1919. Governor of South Africa, 1922–7. KCB, 1925.
[4] *The Black Arrow: A Tale of the Two Roses*, a novel by Robert Louis Stevenson (1888).

Sir Winston S. Churchill to Winston Churchill
(*Churchill papers, 1/56*)

18 October 1957

My dear Winston,

Thank you so much for your letter. I was very sorry to hear you had influenza, and do hope you are quite well again now.

We have had many days of beautiful sunshine both here and at Capponcina, and the time has passed very pleasantly. I have done some painting in the garden, and also completed two flower studies in my room.

I return to England on October 21, and look forward to seeing you again.

Yr loving grandfather

Sir Winston S. Churchill to Nicholas Soames
(*Churchill papers, 1/56*)

24 October 1957

My dear Nicholas,

I was very pleased to get your letter of October 13. That was indeed an interesting visit on which you were taken by your Father and Mother. It is always a good thing to meet when young the leading men of the nation.

I think your handwriting is very good, and above all plain.

Your ever-loving grandfather,

Sir Winston S. Churchill: speech
(*Churchill papers, 2/336*)

25 October 1957   Harrow School

I should just like to thank you from the bottom of my heart for your kindness in receiving me and for singing me these beautiful songs. They have roused in my heart many a memory and I think that you will all find that you have in your Harrow Songs a companion with whom you can walk through life and it may well be that you will find that they are as good a companion as any and a means of retaining memories of the School and youth which cannot be equalled. I thank you most sincerely for your kindness and I pay you every compliment for the excellence of your singing.

Anthony Montague Browne to Frederick Bishop
(Churchill papers, 2/211)

31 October 1957
Personal and Confidential

In a recent letter to Sir Winston Lord Beaverbrook referred to 'the British Government giving a dirty deal to the Canadians. They made a public proposal of Free Trade without giving warning to the Dominion Government.'

From Foreign Office Intel No. 162 of September 30 it appears that the Canadians were in fact informed in advance. There might be advantage in putting Lord Beaverbrook right on the point, and Sir Winston would be prepared to write to him confidentially giving the information in the Intel. Would you let me know if the Prime Minister would like him to do this?

Sir Winston S. Churchill to Lord Beaverbrook
(Churchill papers, 2/211)

November 1957[1]

My dear Max,

In your interesting letter of October 5 you referred to the British Government giving 'a dirty deal to the Canadians. They made a public proposal of Free Trade without warning to the Dominion Government.' I have learnt that this was not the case. For your confidential information, this is what happened. When Mr Diefenbaker stated his objective of a 15% diversion of Canadian trade from the United States to the United Kingdom, we considered various possible means by which this could be attained. The most promising method would be a free trade area under which tariffs and other impediments to trade would be progressively reduced over a long period in accordance with the GATT and other international obligations. The Minister of Agriculture was accordingly authorised to put this proposal informally to Canadian Ministers during his visit to Ottawa on September 9 and 10. The leak to the Press of September 27 gave rise to damaging rumours, and Thorneycroft therefore told the Press on September 29 that an Anglo-Canadian Free Trade area was indeed one of the proposals which we had put forward for the expansion of Anglo-Canadian trade. So, whatever the merits or demerits of the proposal, I do not think that the Government were guilty of your particular charge.

I am now back in London, and contemplating our usual autumn weather. Clemmie has had an operation on her foot. It was successful, but she is laid up for the time being.

I told you about my pictures being exhibited in the United States. I thought

[1] Day not specified in original.

of sending them on to Canada. What do you think of the idea, and at what centres do you think they should be exhibited?

Sir Anthony Eden to Sir Winston S. Churchill
(Churchill papers, 2/216)[1]

4 November 1957

My dear Winston,

Thank you very much for the Third Volume of the History. I am already embarked, and enjoying the opening chapters of the voyage; it is grand writing & proud reading.

I suppose that our American friends now regret that the numerous attempts you and I made to break down the barriers of the McMahon Act, or find a way round them, all failed.

As late as January 1956 I made a further attempt with Eisenhower. Much was promised, but scarcely anything performed. Repeated reminders met with excuses, Congress, the impending elections, etc, etc.

And now we are, the Russians know, how many laps behind.

We were rather disappointed with the result of the blood tests in London. Everything else was showing improvement. I am to have another in a week or two & see whether the improvement we have been hoping for is at last beginning to show itself.

Clarissa sends her love.

Sir Michael Adeane to Sir Winston S. Churchill
(Churchill papers, 2/127)

7 November 1957   Buckingham Palace
Personal and Confidential

My dear Sir Winston,

The Queen sees in the instructions for the Ceremony at the Cenotaph on Sunday next that your name is on the list of those attending.

Her Majesty has commanded me to write you this note to express her concern that you should be thinking of standing for some time in the cold or damp and hopes that you will not consider doing so unless the weather is exceptionally fine or warm.

The Queen desires me to tell you that she gladly excuses you from any obligation that you may feel to be present. Indeed Her Majesty hopes that you will not take the smallest risk to your health by prolonged exposure to November weather which this Ceremony entails.

---

[1] This letter was handwritten.

Sir Winston S. Churchill to Sir Anthony Eden
(Churchill papers, 2/216)

9 November 1957

My dear Anthony,

Thank you for your letter of November 4.[1] I am so glad you are enjoying the book.

I am indeed disappointed to hear that you are not satisfied with the result of your blood test, and I anxiously await your news of a further one. But still, it is very good to know that you are feeling better.

Clemmie is recovering from an operation on her foot, which was successful. She sends you both her love.

I am so glad to learn from Brendan that you have found a new house in Cornwall.

Richard Nixon to Sir Winston S. Churchill
(Churchill papers, 4/67)

3 December 1957

My dear Sir Winston,

I wish to thank you for your continued thoughtfulness in sending me Volume III of *A History of the English-Speaking Peoples*.

Judging from the first two volumes of your great work, I know that rewarding hours of reading await me. Naturally, I shall be particularly interested in that portion of *The Age of Revolution* which deals with the birth of our infant Republic, and I know that your magnificent style of writing will bring to life this and other revolutionary events of the one hundred and twenty-five years covered in this volume.

I want you to know that your completed work will always be a prized possession in my personal library, and I would like to again thank you for making it available to me and to extend my very best wishes.

Sir Winston S. Churchill to Lord Beaverbrook
(Churchill papers, 2/211)

4 December 1957

My dear Max,

Thank you so much for your most kind invitation and the offer of the Capponcina. I am, however, engaged to go in January and February to La Pausa, and I fear that I should upset the Reves if I changed. I do not

---

[1] Reproduced above (p. 2192).

expect to visit America until after the middle of April.

Let me know when you are coming over to England. There are lots of things I want to talk to you about.

Sir Winston S. Churchill to Sarah Beauchamp
(Churchill papers, 1/55)

12 December 1957

I enclose an extract from a letter of Dr Barnett's about your Mother's health. As he says, she is in a state of nervous tension and fatigue and we want to avoid anything that adds to the strain. I think it will be best if we keep Christmas as quiet as possible and, although we both much look forward to seeing you, if you defer coming over until you join me at Pausaland, and visit London on our return. I am sorry about Christmas and we shall all miss you then, but Pausaland will be in mid-January and I gather that this might also suit you professionally.

Sir Winston S. Churchill to President Dwight D. Eisenhower
(Churchill papers, 2/217)

16 December 1957
Personal

My dear Ike,

Welcome to Europe. I am so glad that your health has unquestionably permitted the adventure. It would have given me great pleasure if you had been able to include this little island in your tour, and we should not have been behindhand in showing you what we think and feel about you.

I have gone through all the business of looking out thirty-five pictures, which I have now placed in the competent hands of Mr Hall.[1] I do hope they will be considered worthy of the honour you have done them, and I hope myself to come to Washington in the closing half of April.

---

[1] Joyce Clyde Hall, 1891–1982. American businessman and founder of Hallmark Cards, Inc. Born in David City, Nebraska. Married, 1922, Elizabeth Ann Didlay: three children. Founded Norfolk Post Card Co., 1908; Hall Brothers Co., 1928 (renamed Hallmark Cards, 1954). Instrumental in organizing the exhibition of Churchill's paintings in the US and Canada in 1958, and also produced two sets of Christmas greetings cards bearing Churchill's works. Retired, 1966.

Sir Winston S. Churchill to Lord Beaverbrook
(Beaverbrook papers)

16 December 1957

My dear Max,

I am sending thirty-five pictures to be exhibited in the United States. The President has pressed me repeatedly to do this, and he himself will write a foreword to the catalogue. The pictures will, of course, go to Canada as well. I fancy they will be shown in Montreal, Toronto and Vancouver, and stop a week or ten days at each place. It occurs to me that you might like to show them in your gallery at the University. If so, let me have a telegram, and I will put you in touch with Mr Hall of Kansas City who is responsible for arranging the whole show. It may well be that you will not care to have them. You have only to say the word, which I shall quite understand, and not be in any way offended. I felt, however, in view of all your kindness to me, that this was a thing I ought to do.

I am going out to La Pausa on the 15th of January, and shall stay there for at least a month. When are you coming back to England? Let me know your plans.

1958

Sir Anthony Eden to Sir Winston S. Churchill
(Churchill papers, 2/216)[1]

2 January 1958

My dear Winston,

A wonderful Christmas present has arrived from you & Clemmie – Hock of that superb 1921 vintage. We look forward to a festive enjoyment of it. Thank you so much.

We are comfortably settled in here and I hope soon to begin work on the book. All I have done so far is to read one or two critics; e.g. Kennedy.[2] His book is a most unimpressive performance – some of it very naïve. However, it should be useful as a stimulus to deal with his criticism which is in particular aimed at the first Greek campaign. Our point does not seem to have occurred to him – or others. We could not have waged the second Greek campaign – Christmas 1944 – if we had not waged the first one, 1941. The Greeks would be behind the iron curtain today but for both. It's true they would have been able to squawk less there.

Meanwhile I do not like the present day news. Why in the world do we have to join with Dulles to send arms to Tunisia; this seems an abrupt denial of our Suez policy. As I see it, the French are fighting for life, for all our lives in Algeria. The oil is there & if the French have it & can control it, the dependence on the Canal will be less and we can be firm at last with Nasser.

I liked your message to the Primrose League so much. Unless NATO powers will support each other in other continents, the organisation will hardly survive. I feel very sorry for the Dutch. The Americans couldn't even vote for them against the Indonesian claim to New Guinea at UNO; miserable.

[1] This letter was handwritten.
[2] John Noble Kennedy, 1893–1970. Entered RN, 1911; RA, 1915. On active service, 1915–18 (mentioned in despatches, MC); South Russian campaign, 1919 (mentioned in despatches). Deputy Director of Military Operations, War Office, 1938; Director of Plans, 1939. Cdr, RA, 52nd Div., France, 1940. Director of Military Operations, War Office, 1940–3. ACIGS (Operations and Intelligence), 1943–5. Knighted, 1945. Governor of Southern Rhodesia, 1946–54. Chairman, National Convention of Southern Rhodesia, 1960. Wrote *The Business of War* (1957).

Health is tiresome a real unnecessary fever pulled me down rather. However we are hopeful that with the New Year all will now mend.

Love, & gratitude to you and Clementine for the present. Every good wish for 1958.

Sir Winston S. Churchill to Sir Anthony Eden
(*Churchill papers, 2/216*)

4 January 1958

My dear Anthony,

We are so glad you liked the 1921 Hock.

I agree with you about Kennedy being unimpressive. I suppose that he was kept at home till the War was over. I have not read his book, but only looked at the parts that concern me.

I share your opinions about the blunder that was made in sending arms to Tunisia. Why we could not keep out of that I cannot imagine. I told Harold this when I lunched with him last.

Elizabeth Nel[1] to Sir Winston S. Churchill
(*Churchill papers, 1/143*)

11 January 1958   Port Elizabeth, South Africa

Dear Sir Winston,

When I last wrote to you I did not intend intruding upon you again. Now however I feel I should do so, even though perhaps by this time you have almost forgotten me. I want to tell you about the following before it reaches your ear from outside. For ease of reading I will type this letter.

I have written a book about my war experiences. It is not the same as the one you objected to in 1947. I don't like that one either, and have scrapped it entirely. My book is to appear in condensed form in the *Ladies' Home Journal* in April of this year, and subsequently is to be printed as a book.

Please believe me, I have read again and again through the manuscript, and am quite, quite sure there is nothing in its harmless pages which could give you cause for grievance. I have said nothing, in substance, that has not already appeared in print, as far as concerns you, my revered employer. I will of course send you a copy as soon as it is possible to do so.

I want to tell you why I have done this, after all these years, and you must

---

[1] Elizabeth Layton, 1917–2007. One of Churchill's two personal secretaries, 1941–5. Accompanied Churchill on most of his overseas journeys, including to Washington DC (1943), Cairo (1943), Moscow (1944), Athens (1944) and Yalta (1945). After the war, married Lt Frans Nel, a South African Army officer who had been a POW in Germany from 1942 to 1945. Author of *Mr Churchill's Secretary* (1958).

pardon me if this letter is rather a long one. I do most particularly want you to understand.

First of all, it must be admitted, I want to help Frans, my husband. We now have three children, two daughters and a son. We have both put up a good battle to give them the home they need, but they have talents we cannot at present afford to develop. Frans is a man of many abilities, both practical and artistic. But he is one of a family of twelve, and has had to work hard for every single thing he has. I can see great possibilities in our children; we both want to give them every chance. Whatever may accrue to us from my writings will be used for their benefit.

But there are other reasons. I find it difficult to resign myself entirely to a life of domestic interests, after working for you. I have kept quiet for a long time, but I cannot forget those years. I have a great urge to write something, and a great urge to tell people about you; and writing my book, my one big chance, has given me a new lease of life. If it is a success I shall try to write something else, perhaps about South Africa.

Further, I feel that someone ought to write about you from the secretarial angle. Someone ought to put on record the dictating of your speeches, which I found so thrilling, and those evenings when you worked late in the Cabinet Room and the course of history was moulded. It is something people want to know about, and I do not think there is anything wrong in their knowing. Those days will never be repeated.

That's all. I hope all is well with you and Lady Churchill and that you are enjoying your lives, and I send remembrances and good wishes to you both.

Lord Stuart: recollection
(*'Within the Fringe', pages 116–17*)

17 January 1958

I referred earlier to our occasional friendly bickerings about the rival merits of the Stuarts and the Hanoverians. When Winston had more or less completed *The English-Speaking Peoples* he asked me to read what he had written about Prince Charles Edward Stuart[1] and the 1745 rising, and to let him have my comments.

I read it with interest and wrote to him from my family's house in Moray. I said that I was writing from a room looking out towards a road, less than a mile and a half away, along which the Prince's army had marched from

---

[1] Charles Edward Louis John Casimir Sylvester Severino Maria Stuart, 1720–88. Known as 'Bonnie Prince Charlie'. Eldest son of James Stuart, whose father, King James II, was deposed in 1688 during the Glorious Revolution, and thus Stuart heir to the throne of Great Britain. Born in Rome. Married, 1772, Louise Maximilienne Caroline Emmanuele of Stolberg-Gedern.

Kinloss to Nairn, and then on to Culloden the following day, where they were faced with the Duke of Cumberland[1] and his army a day later. I explained frankly that my family had not participated, believing it to be a lost cause without French troops and money.

I added that I was glad to note that he too disliked Cromwell, but that his dislike could not be greater than mine because my family had been fined 3,000 guineas on account of their Stuart sympathies. I concluded by expressing relief that, according to our records, we had not paid much more than half of the fine before the Restoration relieved us.

The Churchillian reply, which gave me great pleasure, was typical:

My dear James,
I have just reached here and your letter catches me up. Here for the moment we have delicious sunshine, which I value greatly. Heath[2] told me I could go away, which was very kind of him. Do your wayward steps ever lead you to the Riviera? If so, let me know.

Your reminiscences of the '45 are very interesting. I am sure you would have had your head cut off.

Sir Winston S. Churchill to Lady Churchill
(Baroness Spencer-Churchill papers)

18 January 1958 La Pausa

My darling,
The muff is a great success here. I use it at all meals, and on the whole it achieves its purpose. It is vy cold.

We had Onassis to dinner on Thursday night, and I in no way committed myself or you to a voyage. It all went off very pleasantly. I have spent the greater part of my days in bed, but sit for a couple of hours in the sunshine from 2:30 till 4:30. It is very pleasant & bright.

I agree with you that Sarah got out of it as well as she could.[3] I sent her the following telegram, of which I hope you will approve: 'Let me know your plans. Congratulations and love from Papa.' I will keep you informed of any correspondence with her. Personally I hope she will find it possible to come here as soon as she has finished her local engagements.

---

[1] William Augustus, 1721–65. Third and youngest son of King George II of Great Britain and Ireland. Best known for his role in the suppression of the Jacobite Rising of 1745–6. Born in London. Rose to the rank of Lt-Gen. and was a capable military commander.

[2] Edward Heath, Government Chief Whip.

[3] In Jan. 1958 Sarah had been arrested for drunkenness in Los Angeles. According to the *Daily Mail* of Jan. 14, 'She was held for nearly eight hours in the county jail before being released on £9 bail.' On Jan. 16 she pleaded guilty to being drunk in public and was fined $50.

I think the Edens would like to come, and therefore we must fit things in in good time, as space is limited and I think the Reveses would like to make plans for the latter part of February.

We had another lovely day today – the third running, and for the moment the prospects are good. I hope you will find it possible to come, if only for a few days. Wendy is very well, and has put on weight without impairing her figure in any way. She has written to you.

I have been reading a Russian novel, which has made a great impression in America as it is critical of the Russian world and yet the author has apparently been permitted by the Russian government to publish it and print an edition of thirty thousand copies for Russian use. This is a step in the right direction, and we should watch it with attention.

The Dynevors[1] are coming to dinner tomorrow. I have not heard anything about Christopher's father,[2] who, as you know, has been far from well. I will pick my way through these complications.

I shall send this letter off tomorrow, Sunday, and am told it ought to reach you on Monday.

The enclosed has just arrived from Sarah. She has arranged to come in the first week of February.

With all my love my dearest darling

Sir Winston S. Churchill to General George C. Marshall
(Churchill papers, 2/144)

18 January 1958

My dear Marshall,

It was a great pleasure to hear from you. I am so glad you have found pleasure and interest in the books that I have written.

We have a difficult position here, but if we hold firmly to NATO I think it will be clear after a few years of anxiety.

With all good wishes to Mrs Marshall and to you.

---

[1] Charles Arthur Uryan Rhys, 1899–1962. Served in Grenadier Guards, attaining rank of Capt., 1918–20, 1939–45. MP (Cons.) for Romford, 1923–9; for Guildford, 1931–5. Parliamentary Private Secretary to PM, 1927–9. Married, 1934, Hope Mary Woodbine Soames: one child. Chairman, Cities of London and Westminster Conservative Association, 1948–60. 8th Baron Dynevor, 1956. President, University College of South Wales and Monmouthshire, 1950–62.

[2] Arthur Granville Soames, 1886–1962. 2nd Lt, Coldstream Guards, 1905; Lt, 1907. Married, 1913, Hope Mary Woodbine Parish (div. 1934): three children, including Christopher (married Mary Churchill, 1947); 1934, Annette Constance Jardine, née Fraser (div.); 1948, Audrey Alma Humphreys. Sheriff of Buckinghamshire, 1926–7.

Sir Winston S. Churchill to Lady Churchill
(Baroness Spencer-Churchill papers)[1]

22 January 1958　　　　　　　　　　　　　　　　　　　　　　　　　La Pausa

My darling Clemmie,
　No word from Sarah yet; but I assume she adheres to the 3rd or 4th as the date of her arrival here. The sun shines every day and I hope to begin painting *indoors* fairly soon. At present I am dawdling in bed till lunch, but I agree with what you write in yr letter to Wendy that the mornings are best. Today we are going to lunch at the Chateau de Madrid, wh shd be good both for food and sunlight.
　I get a bad report of the weather at home, tho I shd like to be in Parlt for the Thorneycroft debate, and I nearly came home for it. Laziness however decided my conduct.
　Toby is brisk and kind and sends you messages. He flits into Wendy & is much encouraged. He spends the bulk of his mornings on my bed table.
　I send you my best love, and hope you will come out soon.
　　　　　　　　　　　　　　　　　　　With my deepest affection always
　　　　　　　　　　　　　　　　　　　　　　　　Your loving husband

Sir Winston S. Churchill to Lady Churchill
(Baroness Spencer-Churchill papers)[2]

23 January 1958　　　　　　　　　　　　　　　　　　　　　　　　　La Pausa

My darling Clemmie,
　I have started painting again: <u>indoors</u> for the snow is on the hills all round. Flowers arranged by Wendy is the subject & she has painted for three days herself just from memory. It is much better to have a model. The sun shines brightly & today I got up before luncheon and sat in the porch.
　Not a word from Sarah! She really ought not to neglect her trusted friends. They do not know when to expect her, & the house only holds three! I am sending her a telegram which I trust will be effective. Randolph sent me a nice one but telling nothing about her movements.
　My darling – I love you so much. You are a sweet 'Clemmie Cat'. I would like so much to give you my loving kisses. My heart goes with this scrawl.
　　　　　　　　　　　　　　　　　　　　　　　　Your affectionate husband.

---

[1] This letter was handwritten.
[2] This letter was handwritten.

Anthony Montague Browne to Sergeant Edmund Murray
(Churchill papers, 1/143)

24 January 1958
Private

Lady Churchill is rather worried by the amount that gets into the Press when Sir Winston is at La Pausa – false rumours about his health today, and in the past details of his day-to-day life. You know the sort of thing I mean. Can you throw any light on where this comes from? Do you think it is any of the staff there, or the police at the gate?

I should be grateful if you could drop me a line about it, as Lady Churchill is most distressed, and has asked me to do what I can to stop it.

Anthony Montague Browne: recollection
('Long Sunset', page 226)

[January 1958]

The serious press, both French and international, was a fact of life and generally acceptable, but the local paparazzi and stringers were a bore, always managing to turn up and buzz about like unzappable armoured bluebottles wherever WSC was going. Clearly someone was tipping them off and presumably being remunerated for doing so. I therefore told the suspect, and him alone, that the following day we were going up high into the mountains to a remote village for lunch. The next day was very hot. I waited until noon, when the French police guard came to find out our plans, and told them that we were lunching at the villa. They later regaled me, rocking with laughter, with stories of the fury of the paparazzi, who had toiled up the remote and narrow mountain roads on motor scooters in the boiling sun. I think the mole must have had a thin time in the bar that evening.

Lady Churchill to Sir Winston S. Churchill
(Churchill papers, 1/55)

25 January 1958

My Darling,

I have just telegraphed to Wendy to ask if I may come stay at La Pausa on February the 18th.

I have seen in the *Daily Mail* that 1,221 persons visited your Exhibition[1] in one day at Kansas City and that this is a record. I am so happy about this. I

---

[1] Arranged by Joyce Hall of Hallmark Cards.

know you will have been disappointed that the Exhibition was not opened by an American, but I hope this will be put right in the other great Cities. It was most unlucky about the blizzard.

I was disquieted by the report (in the *News Chronicle*) that you were indisposed & very tired, but so relieved that it was baseless: I wonder who starts these rumours.

Poor Charles Moran has come rather a bad toss over his speech to the Doctors & Dentists. He said the Medical Profession was a ladder where at the top were the Specialists & those who 'fell off' had to become General Practitioners.

People are quite angry about it & there has been a stream of angry letters, mostly to the *Manchester Guardian*. One woman wrote she presumed that some of these who reached the top of the ladder were made Peers & that the Noble Lord was talking through his Coronet! I lunched with Pamela Churchill the other day to say goodbye to young Winston before he went back to Eton. He is now beginning to grow & he has a man's voice, low & rather attractive.

I took Edwina & a party of her friends to the Theatre another night & we all came back to dinner here. It was great fun & we all enjoyed it. She knows some very agreeable & intelligent young men.

Tonight I am taking Diana out to a play. I so much want to see you Darling.

Your loving Clemmie
[Drawing of a cat]

Sir Winston S. Churchill to Lady Churchill
(Baroness Spencer-Churchill papers)[1]

27 January 1958   La Pausa

My dearest One,

This is the new paper wh the Reves have at last invented. You will recognize the gate wh is of an attractive design.

What an interesting letter you have written me, wh I have just got. I thought Moran was making a mistake when I read what he wrote, & I do not wonder he has had a bad reaction. The doctors are not a happy tribe just now.

I was delighted you had fixed a date for your visit to La Pausa. It is still a long way off! But I will wait with patience. Wendy was vy pleased too. She looks forward so much to seeing you.

The pictures seem to have got off all right at Fulton, though the hurricane made it difficult for those interested to get there. I don't think it will do any harm either to me or them.

I shall be interested to see the result of repainting my study, & I think you

---

[1] This letter was handwritten.

are quite right to close Chartwell till I come back – bringing I hope summer with me.

Your loving and devoted husband,

This might reach you tomorrow, let me know the date, Toby is sitting on the paper.

Sir Winston S. Churchill to Lady Churchill
(Churchill papers, 1/55)

31 January 1958

I send you the letters I have exchanged with the President of which I talked to you on the telephone. I did not see what else I could do. It will be a very short visit to America, only a week, of which three and a half days will be spent at the White House and the rest with Bernie, either in New York or at his country place. I do hope you will be able to come with me, but I shall quite understand if you feel that a double flight across the Atlantic is more than the experience will be worth. I hope and trust, however, that you will come.

I am sitting here in the garden under the balcony. We have only had one cloudy day, and all the rest have been lovely and sunny and really not cold. I expect March will be very warm out here, and I am keeping it unplanned.

Sir Winston S. Churchill to Albert McCleery[1]
(Churchill papers, 1/56)

8 February 1958   La Pausa
Personal

Dear Mr McCleery,

My daughter, Sarah, has told me how kind and staunch you have been, and what this has meant to her both professionally and personally. I hope you will accept my most warm thanks for what you have done. It is very helpful to me to know that Sarah has such good friends in America.

---

[1] Albert K. McCleery, 1911–72. American television producer (NBC). Married, 1930, Sanny Sue Bailey. Served during WWII, attaining the rank of Lt.-Col.

Sir Anthony Eden to Sir Winston S. Churchill
(Churchill papers, 2/216)

11 February 1958
Personal

My dear Winston,

I am so sorry that we could not accept Mr Reves's kind invitation to go out to the South of France early next month. I am now embedded in documents and beginning to put thoughts down on paper, and I must keep at it for as long as we have Daisy's lovely house, i.e., the end of March.

The world news seems to me to get steadily darker. Perhaps that is how retired politicians often view events.

I am very sad for the French about Algiers. It is being a terrible ordeal for them. Tunis was a tragedy and I suppose that someone blundered in the choice of target. However, I noticed also in today's *Times* that some civilians in Aden were shot up as a result of trouble with tribesmen set on from the Yemen. Nobody, however, would mind about that for anything that Nasser or his satellites do is sacrosanct.

I came across the enclosed remarkable article as an advertisement in *The New York Times* a few days ago. I send it to you on the chance that you may not have seen it because it expresses my sentiments clearly and vigorously.

Clarissa is well and I think that I am steadily gaining strength at last.

We both send our love.

Yours always

Sir Winston S. Churchill to Sir Anthony Eden
(Churchill papers, 2/216)

14 February 1958   La Pausa

My dear Anthony,

Thank you so much for your letter. It was such good news to know that your health is really improving, and that the book is going well.

I can only agree with you that the world picture seems to grow progressively blacker. I was interested to see that advertisement you sent taken from the *New York Times*. I suppose the company in question are losing their plantations in Indonesia.

Clemmie joins me here next Tuesday, and Sarah is now staying. I plan to go home for a week or ten days towards the end of the month.

Let me know when you can come out here.

Anthony Montague Browne to Sir Winston S. Churchill
(*Churchill papers, 1/60*)

21 February 1958

I have spoken to Major Charteris[1] at Buckingham Palace, who tells me that the Queen is being kept closely informed of your news, but that the Palace much like to hear from here direct. I therefore gave our present news,[2] and will continue to do so.

Major Charteris told me that there would be no objection to telling the press that the Queen was inquiring after you. He added that there was no need to[3] you to reply to Her Majesty. However, I submit a short draft:

> 'My Wife and I are deeply grateful to Your Majesty for your most kind inquiries.
> – Winston Churchill'[4]

Gillian Maturin to Sir Winston S. Churchill
(*Churchill papers, 1/60*)

22 February 1958

The little post office at Roquebrune has been very busy with the large number of telegrams which are being received here. I went down to see them this afternoon and thanked them on your behalf. They were all very concerned about you, and asked me to give you their very good wishes for your recovery.

There are only five people running the post office, and they have been working very hard for you (though with the greatest pleasure). Would you care, perhaps at the end of your stay here, to give a signed photograph to be hung in the Post Office?[5]

---

[1] Martin Michael Charles Charteris, 1913–99. Educated at Eton and Royal Military College, Sandhurst. Private Secretary to Princess Elizabeth, 1950–2. Asst. Private Secretary to the Queen, 1952–72. Private Secretary to the Queen and Keeper of HM's Archives, 1972–7. Permanent Lord-in-Waiting to the Queen, 1978–99. Provost of Eton, 1978–91.

[2] On Feb. 18 Churchill had succumbed to a chest cold which rapidly turned into pneumonia. Lord Moran flew out to France to treat him, and bulletins were issued on the patient's condition.

[3] for.

[4] Churchill wrote 'Yes'.

[5] Churchill wrote in the margin: 'Yes'.

1958

Richard Nixon to Sir Winston S. Churchill
(Churchill papers, 1/60)

24 February 1958

My dear Sir Winston,

Along with your countless admirers throughout the world, I was pleased to learn that you are recovering so nicely from your recent illness. That is the kind of encouraging good news all of your friends want to hear!

In a recent letter from Mr Joyce Hall, he told me about the enthusiastic reception your exhibit received at the Nelson Gallery in Kansas City. The fact that all previous one-day attendance records were broken on the opening day is, I am sure, indicative of the way your work will be received everywhere in the United States. It was a great disappointment for me not to be among those present on the first day of the showing.

Both Mrs Nixon[1] and I hope to have an opportunity to see your canvases before they leave our country, and we look forward with pleasure to welcoming you to Washington again soon.

Our kind regards to you and Lady Churchill,[2]

Harold Macmillan and Hugh Gaitskell to Sir Winston S. Churchill
(Churchill papers, 1/60)

27 February 1958

At Question Time today whole House asked that a message of congratulation should be sent to you on your recovery, conveying the warm good wishes of us all.[3]

Lord Bracken to Sir Winston S. Churchill
(Churchill papers, 1/60)

27 February 1958

My dear Winston,

I am pleased and relieved beyond all telling by the news of your rapid recovery.

---

[1] Thelma Catherine Ryan, 1912–93. Known as 'Pat'. Born in Ely, Nevada. Educated at Fullerton Junior College and University of Southern California. Married, 1940, Richard Milhous Nixon: two children. Second Lady of the United States, 1953–61; First Lady of the United States, 1969–74.

[2] Churchill responded on Mar. 4: 'I am touched that with your many burdens you should have taken the time to write me such an agreeable letter. Thank you so much. I too am much looking forward to our meeting.'

[3] Churchill responded on Feb. 28: 'I am deeply honoured that the House of Commons should send me a message as you have done. I hope soon to be once more in my seat. Meanwhile please accept my grateful thanks.'

If you were to write a book on *Health Without Rules* it would outsell all your other books and would soar above the fantastic sales of Mary Baker Eddy's[1] *Science and Health With Key to the Scriptures*. It is claimed by Christian Scientists that this book has already sold 50 million copies, but as Madam Baker Eddy only attained the trifling age of 62, your book would be a much more authoritative guide to the best means of attaining long life!

As the Inland Revenue would take away any profits you would derive from such a masterpiece, this must remain one of the great unwritten books of our age.

PS. Could you take the chair at the Other Club on March 27th?

Sir Winston S. Churchill to Lady Lytton
(Churchill papers, 1/60)

12 March 1958   La Pausa

It gave me so much pleasure to receive your letter this morning. I purred. I am afraid you are having awful weather in England, and I am really looking with one eye at the weather at home and another at snow and sunshine out here.

My illness came on all of a sudden, but the doctors were quite ready to grapple with it. I hope the weather in England will permit my return next Tuesday, for that I propose to do if nothing goes wrong.

Sir Winston S. Churchill to Odette Pol Roger[2]
(Churchill papers, 1/60)

15 March 1958   La Pausa

My dear Odette,

How charming of you to send me the case of delicious champagne. It is making my recovery most cheerful and pleasant. Thank you so much.

I am much better now, and shall be returning to England soon.

---

[1] Mary Baker Eddy, 1821–1910. Founder, Church of Christ, Scientist. Founded Massachusetts Metaphysical College, 1881; *Christian Science Journal*, 1883; Christian Science Publishing Society, 1898; *Christian Science Monitor*, 1908. Author of several books including *Science and Health with Key to the Scriptures* (1875) and *The Manual of The Mother Church* (1895).

[2] Odette Wallace, 1911–2000. Married Jacques Pol-Roger (d. 1956).

Lady Churchill to Mary Soames
('Clementine Churchill', page 465)

15 March 1958

Papa, for the first time shews hesitation about going to America – I think Alas – he feels definitely weaker since his illness – He certainly made a marvellous recovery, but without the mass use of antibiotics he would have sunk and faded away. . . . If Papa does go to America . . . would you go with him in my place? I don't feel strong enough, I am ashamed to say; but I think a member of his family should go. . . . Of course – I hope he won't go – If he does not make one or two speeches & television appearances, the visit will be a flop as regards the American People – who . . . want to see and hear him. Then if he lets himself be persuaded to make public appearances it will half kill him. Monty, the dear creature has just arrived & thinks Papa is crazy to contemplate this idea. . . .

Clarissa Eden to Sir Winston S. Churchill
(Churchill papers, 1/60)[1]

18 March 1958

Dearest Uncle Winston,

Anthony was going to write to you himself but unfortunately he had one of his attacks a day or two ago & isn't able to. I expect he will be all right shortly. We were so relieved to hear that you had made such a quick recovery and will be back with us soon – when we hope we can meet.

I hope you weren't all deafened by Prince Albert's guns.[2]

We send you our fondest love, & Aunt Clemmie too.

Please take care of yourself.

Sir Winston S. Churchill to President Dwight D. Eisenhower
(Churchill papers, 2/277)

March 1958[3]   La Pausa

My dear Ike,

It is with the greatest regret that I have to tell you that I was compelled to put off my visit to you. I had been making good progress, but I have had a setback, which will mean that I have to take things quietly for a time.

You can imagine what a disappointment this is. I had been so much looking

---

[1] This letter was handwritten.
[2] The reference is to the salute fired to mark Prince Albert's birthday, Mar. 14.
[3] Day not specified in original.

forward to seeing you, and I do trust that your arrangements will not be too disturbed.

When the exhibition of my pictures reaches Washington, I hope that you will have time to look at them and choose one for yourself.

I hope that it will be possible to make a rendez-vous later in the year. Meanwhile, Clemmie joins me in sending you both our warmest good wishes.

Harold Macmillan to Sir Winston S. Churchill
(Churchill papers, 2/220)

22 March 1958

Dear Winston,

I have been told that you have postponed your return to this country for a few days. I am sure this is wise and will give you a much better chance of coming back really fit. The weather here has been very cold. I need hardly say that I greatly look forward to seeing you some time after you come back for a talk. You will have read that I am going to see Ike in June.

It was good of you to let me know about Churchill College, and I read what you said about it with great interest. It is an exciting development. I am told that the University Grants Committee[1] are to consider the question of the grant to be given round about the end of the month, and I have asked to be kept informed.

Harold Macmillan to Sir Winston S. Churchill
(Churchill papers, 2/220)

25 March 1958
Confidential

Dear Winston,

The Americans have asked us to agree to the downgrading and subsequent publication in *Foreign Relations of the United States 1943, Volume II Europe* of the enclosed five messages which you sent to President Roosevelt in 1943.

I am prepared to agree but, before telling them so, I should be glad to know whether you have any objection.

Although the text of your message No. 325 of June 23, 1943[2] has not yet been published the gist of it appears on pages 157–159 of Volume V of your Memoirs.

---

[1] From 1918 to 1989, this body advised the British Government on the distribution of grant funding among British universities.

[2] Reproduced in *The Churchill Documents*, vol. 18, *One Continent Redeemed, January–August 1943*, pp. 1697–8.

The Russians have already published your message to President Roosevelt No. 326 of June 23, 1943.

I should be grateful if you would return the documents with your reply.

Sir Winston S. Churchill to Clarissa Eden
(Churchill papers, 1/60)

25 March 1958

Thank you so much for your letter.[1] I am indeed sorry to hear that Anthony has been ill again. Do let me know how he progresses.

I myself have had a slight setback, but I hope soon to be about again and back in England.

Sir Winston S. Churchill to Harold Macmillan
(Churchill papers, 2/220)

27 March 1958
Private and Confidential

My dear Harold,

Many thanks for your letter.

I got your message about the Torrington by-election. I think that on the whole I would rather not mix myself up in this particular election on personal grounds, though of course I hope you will win it.

I have had a slight setback, but I shall soon be about again. I look forward to seeing you on my return.

Sir Winston S. Churchill to Harold Macmillan
(Churchill papers, 2/220)

27 March 1958
Confidential

My dear Harold,

Thank you for your letter of March 25.[2] I do not claim any right of veto on the publication of these telegrams. On the other hand, I think that the timing is important, even today. It seems to me unhelpful to draw attention to our suspicions of de Gaulle at a time when he may still have services to render to France. Could it not be deferred for rather longer.

[1] Reproduced above (p. 2209).
[2] Reproduced above (pp. 2210–11).

Sir Anthony Eden to Sir Winston S. Churchill
(Churchill papers, 2/216)

2 April 1958

My dear Winston,

Welcome home. I am so glad that you have so completely routed the whole army of germs, virus and other foes. The weather does not seem to have been too kind to you and it has been quite odious here. We like this house and I have been concentrating on this book,[1] particularly the Suez period. Hardly exhilarating fare, and I have learnt much to add to the gloom. If the Canadians had been as good as the Australians and the Americans as quiet as the Russians in the first four days we should have been home with a margin to spare, and there would be no Nasser in Cairo now, at least not on his throne. But enough of these sad records, & would-have beens.

We go to the cottage for a few days at Easter to make a break for both of us.

We both send our love to you & Clemmie. Happy Easter.

Lord Beaverbrook to Lord Bracken
(Beaverbrook papers)

6 April 1958

I have just been to Rome for Easter Sunday. Mass was said to 300,000. It was an immense scene.

I saw Winston for fifteen minutes or more. He was certainly clear in mind and I do hope that by this time he is strong in body.

Sir Winston S. Churchill to Lord Beaverbrook
(Beaverbrook papers)

11 April 1958   Chartwell

My dear Max,

Thank you so much for your letter and your most kind and hospitable offer. Clemmie and I are touched by your thought of us, and we should very much like to take advantage of it at some time. May I let you know?

As you will have seen in the newspapers, I have put off my visit to America. It is a disappointment, but it seems best.

I much enjoyed seeing you at the airport, and I hope we shall meet again soon.

<u>I have another attack with temperature and am under full medical treatment. How bloody!</u>

---

[1] *The Memoirs of Sir Anthony Eden, Full Circle* (London: Cassell, 1960).

1958

Lord Beaverbrook to Lord Bracken
(Beaverbrook papers)

13 April 1958

I saw Churchill at the airfield and talked with him for a while. He was clear in his head though not firm on his feet. He said he was going to America and I offered to make the sea journey with him. I have had a telegram today said 'I am laid up again. Writing.'

I am sure he is wise to cancel the journey. He would find Eisenhower in a very gloomy mood America is terribly depressed.

Sir Winston S. Churchill to Sir Anthony Eden
(Churchill papers, 2/216)

15 April 1958

My dear Anthony,

Thank you so much for your letter.[1] I was very glad to have news of you and to know that the book is making progress. I look forward with the greatest interest to reading it. A great deal has been written on Suez, but you will give the 'authorised' version.

I have been laid up afresh, and am only just beginning to improve. As I expect you know, I have had to put off my visit to America, at any rate for the time being.

I much look forward to seeing you. We must meet soon.

Clemmie joins me in sending you both affectionate good wishes.

Richard Nixon to Sir Winston S. Churchill
(Churchill papers, 4/67)

21 April 1958

My dear Sir Winston,

I want you to know of my deep appreciation for your continued thoughtfulness in seeing to it that I received a copy of the fourth and final volume of your great work – *A History of the English-Speaking Peoples*.

As you perhaps know, I am soon to depart on an official trip to South America and, because of the many attendant preparations, I do not anticipate any leisure time before then. However, I can assure you that *The Great Democracies* will be first on my reading list when I return.

I was very pleased to read the good news this morning that you are on the road to recovery and, although your planned visit to Washington has been

---

[1] Reproduced above (p. 2212).

cancelled, I hope that it can take place in the near future.

Mrs Nixon joins me in sending our warm regards to you and Lady Churchill.

Lord Bracken to Lord Beaverbrook
(*Beaverbrook papers*)

21 April 1958

Alas, Winston is not very well. Moran has been at Chartwell for four or five days and his normal imperturbability seems rather dinted. He told me he would like to come up and have a talk with me on Monday and I, of course, am at his service.

Our friend Winston is, of course, a medical marvel. He has disregarded all the normal life-threatening rules and has witnessed, doubtless with regret, but with some complacence, the burial of most of his doctors, save Charles. But the sun is Churchill's great life-maintainer and the lack of it has probably played some part in creating his present condition. After I meet Moran, I will give you a summary of our talk.

Anthony Montague Browne to Sir Winston S. Churchill
(*Churchill papers, 2/368*)

22 April 1958

Mr Christ has submitted a draft message[1] that you may wish to send the Primrose League on Friday. It seems a good one.[2]

Winston S. Churchill to the Primrose League
(*Churchill papers, 2/368*)

25 April 1958

I am sorry that I cannot be with you to do honour to my old friend, Harold Macmillan, on this the first occasion on which he is addressing the Primrose League as Prime Minister and Leader of the Conservative and Unionist Party. He faces heavy tasks and responsibilities both at home and abroad, but I know that he can rely on the enthusiastic, whole-hearted and active support of every member of your audience. We can all take pride in the part our country has

---

[1] Reproduced immediately below.
[2] Montague Browne wrote to Christ on Apr. 24: 'Sir Winston has asked me to thank you so much for your thought in drafting a message for the Primrose League. He considered it very good, and has sent it on with no amendments. Sir Winston asks me to send you his very good wishes.'

played over the centuries in preserving the freedom of the world. None of us need doubt that if we remain true to the faith and the principles which have guided and inspired us in the past, we have it in our power to make still greater contributions to the well-being of mankind. It was to uphold that faith and those principles that my father helped to found your League, and there was never more need of your united endeavours than there is today.

Anthony Montague Browne to Sir Winston S. Churchill
(Churchill papers, 2/571)

28 April 1958

When the Trustees of the technological College lunch with you on May 6[1] you may wish to consider making the following point to them:

Among the Trustees are representatives of our great industries and of science. There is no representative of organized labour, and at some time in the future this might militate against the total success of the scheme. Should not a carefully chosen and responsible trade union leader be in some way associated – perhaps as a Trustee?

When Jock saw Mr Gaitskell to tell him of the plan the latter gave it his warm approval, but made this point to Jock. Jock feels he cannot himself put it forward to the Trustees.

Sir Anthony Eden to Sir Winston S. Churchill
(Churchill papers, 2/216)

29 April 1958

My dear Winston,

Thank you so much for your letter. We are both looking forward to coming to see you the weekend of May 17th.

I was so sorry to hear about your complaint, for it is a brute, I think. You have done magnificently to throw it off so well.

I look forward to a talk about events. I observe that the Americans are now offering to release some of his money to Nasser. I suppose this is intended to make him feel good towards the West when he flies to Moscow. I am sure that it will have just the opposite effect and make him more attractive to Moscow. Also, the more the Americans cosset Nasser the more difficult it will be for those who are standing out against him like Chamoun[2] in Syria, the king in

---

[1] Churchill wrote here: 'Yes. BF [before] May 5'.

[2] Camille Nimr Chamoun, 1900–87. Member, Lebanese Parliament, 1934–52, 1960–4, 1968–87. Ambassador to UK, 1944–6. President of Lebanon, 1952–8. President, National Liberal Party, 1958–85. Deputy PM, 1984–7.

Libya[1] and Nuri. I feel very sorry for the French over Algeria. I think it likely that but for the help the insurgents get from Egypt the whole thing would have been over long since.

The fourth volume of *A History of the English-Speaking Peoples*, *The Great Democracies*, has just arrived. Thank you so much for it. I look forward to the happiest hours in its company. I have already dipped, out of order, into the American Civil War, superbly told.

This weather is glorious and more than recompense for politics.

We both send our love to you and Clemmie.

Lord Bracken to Lord Beaverbrook
(Beaverbrook papers)

29 April 1958

Moran had lunch with me today and was more gloomy than usual about our friend.

Winston Churchill to Sir Winston S. Churchill
(Churchill papers, 1/56)[2]

29 April 1958

Dearest Grandpapa,

I trust your illness has gone and that you are now in good health. And I hope you can now go out and do some painting. Here it's been wonderfully warm for the last three days. It seems that spring is here at last.

I have just finished my exams but do not go home until Wednesday. The fourth volume of *The English-Speaking Peoples* has been given a very prominent display in the local bookshop. I have so far read the first five chapters and find it easy-reading. It has very great clarity and forthrightness, and is much more interesting to read than other books which I have read covering such a large period.

It does not seem that the libel action is going to be brought against father, does it? I am spending the first half of next holidays with him at Stour.

Please give my love to grandmama.

Your loving grandson

---

[1] Muhammad Idris bin Muhammad al-Mahdi as-Senussi, 1889–1983. Chief of the Senussi order, 1916. Emir of Cyrenaica, 1920; of Tripolitania, 1922. Went into exile, 1922. King of Libya, 1951–69. Deposed in 1969 by *coup d'état* led by Muammar Gaddafi.

[2] This letter was handwritten.

Admiral of the Fleet Lord Louis Mountbatten to Sir Winston S. Churchill
(Churchill papers, 2/194)

22 May 1958

My Dear Sir Winston,

How very kind of you to have inscribed the set of your *History of the English-Speaking Peoples* to my grandson Norton.[1] He will be a proud boy and indeed even prouder when he is grown up.

I am sure he will be delighted too that your budgerigar has taken a small bite out of volume II, as it will add to its historic significance.

Sir Winston S. Churchill to Lady Churchill
(Churchill papers, 1/55)

1 August 1958
La Capponcina

Very hot and very fine. Have done nothing at all except order some thin clothes. The Onasses are dining tonight. Otherwise all tranquil. Max has passed the day on his boat I have remained ashore. Pamela lunched with us looking admirable and leaves for Venice tonight. Take my love to Maria & Christopher and the rest of the family and accept my fondest thoughts from a completely idle

Harold Macmillan to Sir Winston S. Churchill
(Churchill papers, 2/220)

7 August 1958

Dear Winston,

I hope you are having better weather than we are. We have had very poor days since you left.

I called to see Brendan last week. He is certainly very gallant and talked as well and gaily as ever.

We are rather disappointed that the summit meeting did not come off. It seems as if Khrushchev was much more impulsive than Stalin and, if possible, even more crooked. However, since I cannot go in one direction, I have decided to go in another.

---

[1] Norton Louis Philip Knatchbull, 1947–. Married, 1979, Penelope Eastwood: three children. 3rd Earl Mountbatten of Burma, 2017.

Sir Winston S. Churchill to Lady Churchill
(Baroness Spencer-Churchill papers)[1]

8 August 1958   La Capponcina

Darling,

The days pass monotonously but pleasantly & quickly. More than a week has gone since I arrived. I have done nothing but play bezique with Anthony – seven games a day! – and have won thirty shillings.

Max & Dalmeny[2] go out in their boat, which is a flat bottomed contrivance and enables them to face rough weather. I have not accompanied them. They go along the coast, 5 or 6 hours a day, and seem to enjoy it – I think it is a bit risky – although the sea is calm & the sun shines bright. You will have to try it when you arrive.

I brought Daisy Fellowes to the Villa & we lunched together. She is very well preserved. Lady Derby[3] is also here & they are trying to get her from dinner again at this moment. She is very nice and seems to have recovered from the stormy episodes of which you know.

It is very hot & beautiful, & time passes swiftly. I <u>long</u> to have you here & I am sure you would find it agreeable, 'Toby' is on my bed at the moment & I have had a large cage constructed which serves as an exercise ground for him.

We have been deeply moved by Brendan's death[4] – but I am sure it was best for him. His will about no memorials for him made us resist a return journey tomorrow which we had contemplated.

Darling one I am eagerly looking forward to seeing you. I rejoice that the doctors give a good report, & that progress continues steady to the eye.

This is an awful scrawl, but I write in bed & have almost lost the art of legibility.

Always your loving & devoted husband

Lady Churchill to Sir Winston S. Churchill
(Churchill papers, 1/55)[5]

9 August 1958   Chartwell

My Darling,

You are much in my thoughts.

You will miss Brendan so much and so will Max. Please give him a message of sympathy.

---

[1] This letter was handwritten.

[2] Neil Archibald Primrose, 1929–. Married, 1955, Alison Mary Deirdre Reid: five children. 7th Earl of Rosebery, 1974.

[3] Isabel Milles-Lade, 1920–90. Married, 1948, Edward John Stanley, 18th Earl of Derby.

[4] Lord Bracken died on Aug. 8 as a result of cancer of the throat.

[5] This letter was handwritten.

I am sorry there is to be no Memorial Service for him. So many would have liked by their presence to pay a tribute of affection and respect.

I'm packing up & leaving Chartwell & till I leave Tuesday (at Cock-crow!) I shall be at Hyde Park Gate. Diana is coming up from the Isle of Wight to spend Monday with me. It is very sweet of her.

I liked Beverley Baxter's article on Brendan in the *Express* this morning. I will write to you from Tangier. Meanwhile I am your poor devoted

John Colville to Sir Winston S. Churchill
(Churchill papers, 2/212)[1]

11 August 1958

My dear Winston,

I know how much you loved Brendan and what this breach with the happier past will mean to you. You, of course, were everything to him and whenever I have seen him in this last few weeks he has scarcely spoken of anybody else. I, who have known him so much less long and intimately, am broken hearted by his going, and this gives me some glimmering of what you must feel.

This news was broken to me by Mr Baruch, whom I met at Saratoga Races last Friday. He asked me to send you his love and to say that he was thinking of you.

Meg and I look forward to seeing you on Sept 5th when, DV,[2] we shall arrive at La Capponcina in bezique-playing mood.

Mary Soames to Sir Winston S. Churchill
(Churchill papers, 1/55)[3]

12 August 1958

Darling Papa,

I think often of you enjoying blue skies and golden sunshine – we are happy, but alternately drenched by showers and dried by gusts of wind!

I have thought much of you also since Brendan died. You and Max must indeed grieve for such a friend as he was.

We had Mama to stay for a few days – it was lovely for us all, and the children revelled in having her here. I think she enjoyed the slight hurly-burly of Hamsell holiday life – which is quite hectic! I am so glad her eye improved enough for her to leave today for Tangier. I'm sure she'll enjoy staying with the Nairns.[4]

---

[1] This letter was handwritten.
[2] *Deo volente*: 'God willing'.
[3] This letter was handwritten.
[4] Bryce James Miller Nairn, 1903–78. Born in Marrakech, Morocco. British Consul at Marrakech,

Chimp has been able to spend several consecutive days at home, which is lovely for us all. The days fly by, we are busily occupied with our riding, which covers a variety of activities from catching the ponies (quite vital, and not in the least a foregone conclusion!) and brushing, dressing to finally (somewhat exhausted by all these previous operations) actually going for a ride! But we all love it – and the bigger children are really getting quite efficient in all departments.

Next week we go to Yorkshire and Scotland. Great preparations and plans are afoot. Chimp and I, Nicholas and Emma and one large black dog and sundry sporting equipment, have all somehow, got to be put in – or on top of one car!

We all send our dearest love.

Always your loving

Sir Winston S. Churchill to Harold Macmillan
(Churchill papers, 2/220)

23 August 1958
Personal

My dear Harold,

Only two days ago I received your letter of August 7.[1] Meanwhile, the end had come. He was one of my best friends and a man whose sterling qualities we all admired. They talk of starting a memorial for him, but I do not think that a scholarship for some university would meet the case. Have you any ideas?

I have followed as well as I can the tangled negotiations with Kruschev. I am very glad you are giving your mind the job, and let me congratulate you on the remarkable response that the whole nation now gives to your conduct of power. How silly the resignation of the Finance Minister[2] looks now.

1944; at Bordeaux, 1944; at Madeira, 1949. Consul-General, Tangier, 1950. CBE, 1960. Wrote *Portuguese East Africa, Mozambique, Economic and Commercial Conditions in Portuguese East Africa* (1955).

Margaret Nairn, 1903–90. Skilled painter. Guest, along with Churchill, at the Château de Bordaberry in the Basque region of France, July 1945. During this holiday, she persuaded Churchill to paint his first post-WWII picture

[1] Reproduced above (p. 2217).
[2] Peter Thorneycroft.

Sir Winston S. Churchill to Lord Beaverbrook
(*Churchill papers, 2/211*)

5 September 1958   La Capponcina

This very night your white cat killed a rat which he brought to my feet at dinner. Am writing full particulars. May I restore fish ration?

Sir Winston S. Churchill to Lord Beaverbrook
(*Churchill papers, 2/211*)

5 September 1958   Alpes Maritimes

My dear Max,

I have greatly enjoyed my stay at the Capponcina and all your kindness in making me so welcome. If we may, we should like to remain here until about the 23rd when we have been invited to go on a cruise with Onassis. After that, we shall go directly home, probably from Spain.

I must tell you the remarkable story about the white cat. I gave him supper last night, and the next thing I knew half an hour later was that he had brought a beautiful rat he had killed, and laid it at <u>my</u> feet. The incident was so remarkable and personal that it should be recorded.

I am very glad that you liked my companionship. It has now become very feeble, though none the less warm. It was a great pleasure to me to get your letter, and to realise that the ties we formed so many years ago and strengthened in the days of war have lasted out our lifetime. Thank you for what you so eloquently say.

I hope you enjoy the United States and New Brunswick and do not stay away too long.

Clemmie joins me in renewed thanks to you for all your kindness.

Anthony Montague Browne to Randolph S. Churchill
(*Churchill papers, 1/57*)

6 September 1958

We are under increasing pressure from the Press here who want to photograph Sir Winston and Lady Churchill on their Golden Wedding, and also are asking us for details of what is planned for the day and who is going to be here. On their instructions, I am saying that there will be no photographs taken at the villa, that the occasion is a private family one with only members of the family and close friends present, and that in general no details will be given. Copies of a photograph of Sir Winston and Lady Churchill taken earlier this year are being made available to the Press both here and in London.

This course is no doubt very unsatisfactory from the newspapers' point of view, but it is the specific wish of Sir Winston and Lady Churchill, and I see no difficulty in pursuing it.

I thought that it might be helpful to you to know about what is happening. Would you pass the information on to Diana or anyone else you think should know?

Anthony Montague Browne: note
(<i>Churchill papers, 1/57</i>)</div>

[September 1958]

Randolph Churchill and his three sisters are marking the anniversary of their parents' Golden Wedding on September 12 by giving them an avenue of golden roses at Chartwell. This, of course, cannot be planted until late in October and cannot flower until next year. So they have decided to present their parents on the day with a large, illuminated vellum book in which there will be a dedication, a list of the 28 roses to be planted and a plan of the proposed avenue.

Someone has suggested that it would be nice if this book were to be further enriched and embellished with individual pictures of the 28 roses. The idea is that they should be painted in watercolour by 28 of the leading English flower painters.

I enclose a list of some of the painters joined in this enterprise. If you would like to take part in this tribute, would you let me know as soon as possible? So that all the pictures may be of the same size I will send you paper of the appropriate size and quality – also some specimens of the rose.

It is not intended that total conformity be sought. Some may choose to paint a bud and some a flower in bloom. Some may favour a strictly botanical exposition; some may prefer something more imaginative.

While conforming to the integral conception of the book a wide variety of expression would be desirable.

Sir Winston S. Churchill to Lord Beaverbrook
(<i>Churchill papers, 2/211</i>)</div>

10 October 1958

My dear Max,

Thank you so much for your letter. I should of course be honoured if you spoke about the Cambridge College and myself.

We had a most successful cruise with Onassis,[1] concluding at Gibraltar,

---

[1] From Sep. 22 to Oct. 10, Churchill cruised the Mediterranean on the first of eight voyages as the guest of Aristotle Onassis on board his yacht *Christina*.

where we were very well received by everybody, including the apes! I am only staying here until the 12th when I go to Roquebrune until Parliament reassembles at the end of the month.

Clemmie and I are so grateful to you for your renewed offer of La Capponcina. I should very much like to take advantage of it and will communicate with you again.

I hope by now your worries over your Picture Gallery are decreasing.

I look forward to your news.

Sir Winston S. Churchill to Lady Churchill
(Baroness Spencer-Churchill papers)[1]

14 October 1958

My darling One,

Yesterday, Monday, was a perfect day. Today begins not quite so good – it is cloudy, but I think it will improve. We shall see. All is peace & quiet here. It is six months – so they calculate – since I was last here. They all send appropriate messages. I am passing the morning in bed – reading a book about ancient Greece which is rather good. Tomorrow I shall try to paint, and Murray is getting the outfit ready. But I am doubtful, inert & lazy.

I wonder what you will be doing & when you will set off for Chartwell. Would you give some food to the fish? They are very appreciative. And the black swans. I never visited them this time. It was too wet for the car, & I do not care about walking – much.

You have all my fondest love my dearest. The closing days or years of life are grey and dull, but I am lucky to have you at my side. I send you my best love & many kisses.

Always your devoted

PS. We had Onassis to dinner last night. He was very lively.

Sir Winston S. Churchill to Lady Churchill
(Baroness Spencer-Churchill papers)

22 October 1958
Personal

My darling,

The days pass quickly and peacefully here. We see a few old friends at meals. The papers seem to hold no news. The most interesting thing we have

---

[1] This letter was handwritten.

is Dr Galleazzi-Liza[1] who Emery tells me came to see him two years ago when the Pope[2] was in excellent health and proposed to sell him for an enormous sum of money the aftermath of his illness.[3] Emery scornfully refused him, but was not all surprised at what has occurred. He, Emery, had intended to expose the man, but it has all come out without his being called upon to intervene. I think he will be made an example of.

We are going to lunch with the Onasses tomorrow at their yacht, and I will deliver your beautifully framed photograph to Mrs O,[4] and give her suitable messages from you.

We are examining the possibility of going to lunch next Sunday upon the *Randolph*, an American aircraft carrier. They have the idea that they can pick us up in one of their special helicopters and drop us on the ship itself. We have invited the captain and his wife[5] to lunch on Friday to look into the possibilities. I have never been in a helicopter, and would like to make a voyage which would certainly save a great deal of toil.

I shall look forward to reading Monty's book when you have done with it. He seems to have stirred the waters up a little bit. I am personally keeping myself from reading a copy, and have not indulged in the *Sunday Times* serials.

Darling, I have found very little to say, but I am enjoying myself very much, and my health is pronounced by Doctor Roberts[6] to be much better than it was two years ago.

Always your loving husband

PS. I am delighted that you will come to Paris. Shall I make arrangements through the Embassy for you to stay there the night before, (November 5)? It may be that Anthony will already have worked this out for you. I have not been in Paris for five years.

---

[1] Riccardo Galeazzi-Lisi, 1891–1968. Personal physician to Pope Pius XII, 1939–58. Hon. member, Pontifical Academy of Sciences.

[2] Eugenio Maria Giuseppe Giovanni Pacelli, 1876–1958. Ordained priest, 1899. Appointed to Papal Secretariat of State, 1901. Secretary, Congregation for Extraordinary Affairs, 1914. Pope Pius XII, 1939. In 1949, issued a decree condemning Soviet totalitarianism while excommunicating any and all Catholics who collaborated with the Communists.

[3] In other words, to sell Reves literary rights to details of the Pope's death.

[4] Athina Mary Livanos, 1929–74. Known as 'Tina'. Daughter of shipping magnate Stavros Livanos. Married, 1948, Aristotle Onassis (div. 1960); 1961, John Spencer-Churchill (div. 1971); 1971, Stavros Niarchos.

[5] Bernard Max Strean, 1910–2002. Educated at US Naval Academy, Annapolis, 1933. Married, 1936, Janet Lockey (d. 1987); 1988, Susan (surname unknown). Naval aviator during WWII. Credited with a direct bomb hit on a Japanese aircraft carrier during Battle of the Philippine Sea, June 1944.

[6] Dafydd Myrddin Roberts, 1906–77. Educated at Medical School, Cardiff and London Hospital. Married, 1936, Eileen Vera Roberts (div. 1954): two children. Worked at Cardiff Royal Infirmary, 1934–5. Commissioned Flying Officer Medical Branch, RAF, 1938; Flight Lt, 1942. District Medical Officer, Poulton-le-Fylde, 1944–9. Started practicing in Cap d'Ail, Monte Carlo, 1953.

John Colville to Sir Winston S. Churchill
(Churchill papers, 2/212)

29 October 1958

My dear Winston,

I enclose a letter to you, asking for a subscription to a memorial to Brendan, which is identical with what I have sent to all his personal friends. I have sent out the appeal on a list supplied by Brendan's Secretary and vetted by Oliver,[1] Lord Radcliffe,[2] etc. In many cases they are writing covering letters. We hope we may raise about £25,000 so as to build a worthy memorial. I have sent off most of the letters and will let you know how good the response is.

I hope you have been having a lovely time at Roquebrune and that the helicopter was fun!

John Colville to Sir Winston S. Churchill
(Churchill papers, 2/212)

27 October 1958

My dear Winston,

Some of Brendan Bracken's friends believe that there are many of those who knew and loved him who would wish to join them in raising some memorial that will fittingly commemorate his great personal qualities and his distinguished public service.

In considering how best to pay tribute to his memory, they have had especially in mind his devoted interest in architecture and education. They also feel it is appropriate that his name should be permanently associated with that of Winston Churchill.

For these reasons they hope to collect a sum of money to build, within the confines of Churchill College, Cambridge, an individual room or feature (for instance a Reading Room, Hall or Lecture Room) which would be separately identified by the name of Brendan Bracken. This suggestion has the strong support of Sir Winston Churchill and of the other Trustees of the College.

No public appeal will be made and we are seeking subscriptions from Brendan's friends by means of a personal approach. An alphabetical list of the subscribers will be prepared, not for publication but for retention at Churchill College.

[1] Oliver Lyttelton, Lord Chandos.
[2] Cyril John Radcliffe, 1899–1977. Served in Labour Corps during WWI. Educated at New College, Oxford, 1921. Called to the Bar, 1924. Director-General, Ministry of Information, 1941–5. KBE, 1944. GBE, 1948. PC, 1949. Baron, 1949. Lord of Appeal in Ordinary, 1949–64. Chairman, Royal Commission on Taxation of Profits and Income, 1951–5; Constitutional Commission for Cyprus, 1956; Radcliffe Committee, 1957–9; Committee on Security Procedures and Practices in the Public Service, 1961. Trustee, British Museum, 1957; Chairman of Trustees, 1963–8. Viscount, 1962.

If you wish to send any amount, large or small, would you be kind enough to forward your subscription to me, c/o Philip Hill, Higginson & Co., Limited, at the above address. Cheques should be made out to the Bracken Memorial Fund.[1]

Sir Winston S. Churchill: speech
('Winston S. Churchill, His Complete Speeches', volume 8, page 8687)

6 November 1958   Paris

I am going to speak English today. I have often made speeches in French, but that was wartime, and I do not wish to subject you to the ordeals of my darker days.

I am particularly happy that it should be my old friend and comrade, General de Gaulle, who should be paying me this honour.[2] He will always be remembered as the symbol of the soul of France and of the unbreakable integrity of her spirit in adversity. I remember, when I saw him in the sombre days of 1940, I said, 'Here is the Constable of France'. How well he lived up to that title!

Now he is back again in a position of the greatest and gravest responsibility for his country. The problems which confront us are no less important than our struggle for survival eighteen years ago. Indeed, in some ways they may be more complicated for there is no clear-cut objective of victory in our sight. It is harder to summon, even among friends and allies, the vital unity of purpose amidst the perplexities of a world situation which is neither peace nor war.

I trust that I may be permitted these observations of a very general character. I think that I can claim always to have been a friend of France. Certainly your great country and your valiant people have held a high place in my thoughts and affection in all the endeavours and great events with which we have been associated in the last half-century. Some of these events have been terrible: they have brought great suffering on the world and on our peoples. The future is uncertain, but we can be sure that if Britain and France, who for so long have been the vanguard of the Western civilization, stand together, with our Empires, our American friends, and our other allies and associates, then we have grounds for sober confidence and high hope.

I thank you all for the honour you have done me.

Vive la France!

---

[1] Churchill wrote to Colville on Nov. 12: 'I send you herewith the cheque for £1,000 which I promised as a contribution to Brendan's memorial.'

[2] The Croix de la Libération, the highest award given to those who served with the Free French forces. On this day, Churchill became the 1,054th and last recipient of the order, founded by de Gaulle on 16 Nov. 1940 to recognize distinguished services by French or foreign citizens who aided in the liberation of France. The order had been discontinued in 1946; de Gaulle reactivated it to present the final one to Churchill.

1958

Sir Winston S. Churchill to Lord Beaverbrook
(*Churchill papers, 2/211*)

14 November 1958

My dear Max,

I am ashamed not to have answered your letter of September 20 before, and not to have thanked you for offering to lend me your house at Capponcina until April. I know you will forgive me.

I am afraid I shall not be able to take advantage of your kindness. We are going to Marrakesh, and after six weeks there from January 7 on, for another cruise in Onassis' yacht.

I have now come home to London and Chartwell after a very nice visit to Paris. Is there any chance of your coming home at the end of the year?

The Government seems to be well established here, and the Opposition do not seem formidable to me. I have become a regular attendant on the three inside days of the week, and am wondering whether I can screw myself up to make a speech. I am going to have a preliminary in my Constituency which is very quiet.

All my best good wishes

Sir Winston S. Churchill: speech
(*Churchill papers, 2/336*)

27 November 1958   Harrow School

Ladies and Gentlemen,

It gives me great pleasure to come here once again for the eighteenth time, the eighteenth time, and listen to these tunes and words which touch my heart and have inspired my actions and my life. I must say that I think the Harrow Songs are an invaluable part of the life of Harrow and I earnestly trust you will always devote to them the attention which I see you have given to them tonight and will enable on a future occasion an equally charming performance to be given me.

Sir Winston S. Churchill to Lady Cecil[1]
(Chelwood papers, 47/76)

29 November 1958

Dear Lady Cecil,

 I must express my sorrow at your Husband's death after a long and famous life. I remember the first time I met him. Linky and I were going to make a speech against Mr Chamberlain's policy in the Town Hall of Birmingham, and there were rumours that the meeting would be broken up by riotous Tories. However, when we arrived at the London Railway Station we found a large carriage full of young men who announced that they were going down with us to see that we were not interrupted. This was the first time I met your late Husband, with whom afterwards I had so many pleasant connections.

 You have my deepest sympathy.

---

[1] Eleanor Lambton, 1868–1959. Daughter of George Lambton, 2nd Earl of Durham. Married, 1889, Edgar Algernon Robert Gascoyne-Cecil, 1st Viscount Cecil of Chelwood.

1959

Sir Winston S. Churchill: speech
('Winston S. Churchill, His Complete Speeches', volume 8, pages 8689–91)

6 January 1959　　　　　　　Woodford Conservative Association Meeting
　　　　　　　　　　　　　　　　　Kensington Palace Hotel, London

A VOTE OF CONFIDENCE

I am very glad to have this opportunity of meeting the full Executive Council of our Division, and will start by wishing you good fortune in the New Year.

The last two years have had their difficult moments, and we therefore owe a debt of gratitude to those of you who have borne the heaviest burden, who have rallied our workers when spirits have been low, and spurred them on to renewed efforts as the tide has turned again in our favour.

I am very grateful to you all. You have just completed a magnificent job in the recruiting drive, Roll Call for Victory. I was told in September last that we hoped to make a thousand new members. Now Colonel Barlow-Wheeler tells me that the figure is in fact over 1,800. This is splendid, and I congratulate you all. I know that it is personal leadership and drive that have produced success. We must not relax now. Now we have to organize ourselves for the General Election some time this year or next. We must be ready to help our neighbours in marginal seats as before, and still produce a solid Conservative majority in our old Tory stronghold of Woodford. The Conservative Party has very good hopes throughout the country, and the Conservative Party in Woodford will play its part.

Seven years ago, when the Conservative Party became responsible for our national affairs, you may remember we were targets for a good deal of abuse. Almost before we had had time to sit down at our desks our opponents were shouting: 'Where is the red meat Lord Woolton promised us?' 'When are you going to build those three hundred thousand houses?' 'When are you going to set the people free?' 'Where is the freedom and where is the abundance?' At about that time I made a broadcast. I said that when a train was running on the wrong line downhill you could not try to stop it by building a brick wall across the track. You had to slow it down, stop it, and go into reverse back to the junction to change over the points and get on to the right line. This process, I warned the country, would take three years, at the end of which time we should be quite prepared to be judged by results. Well, you know all that happened. Before the three years were up we had brought all food rationing to an end. We were building those three hundred thousand houses a year and more. We had begun the process, which has since continued, of reducing taxation, of limiting the powers of the State, and of restoring freedom to the individual citizen, the trader, and the farmer.

The recent action taken by the Government in freeing the pound sterling from some of the controls imposed on it is clear evidence of our improved position. The freer the pound the easier it is for the City of London to maintain its position as a great money market, with all the benefits which accrue to the whole country from this position. I notice that Mr Gaitskell has taken exception to what has been done. But so far, at least, the pound does not seem to have suffered from being set free – indeed to the contrary, I myself think that this is a great step forward. I look forward to the time when the pound is as freely and universally circulated as was the gold sovereign, and is as much sought after by foreign countries.

From our policy of freedom, abundance has flowed. The past seven years have seen an improvement in the general standard of living of our people more marked that in any similar period of time that I can recall in the whole of my long life. I rejoice to see it and my hope is that it will continue unabated and unchecked. But here I must recall something else which I said in that same broadcast of seven years ago, for it is just as true and just as important as when I said it. We have no assurance, I said, that anyone else is going to keep the British lion as a pet. We have to stand firmly on our own feet and pay our way in the world. It is because we have done that in these past seven years that our affairs have prospered.

A country like ours, so dependent on its overseas trade for its very existence, must inevitably face difficulties from time to time. Even when the train is on the right line it still faces steep gradients and dangerous curves. When these difficulties or dangers arrive – as they did just over a year ago – it is imperative that those in charge should take prompt action. The stakes are too high for any hesitation or vacillation, or any nice weighing of popularity or electoral advantage.

In the autumn of last year the Government, under Mr Harold Macmillan, did not hesitate to apply a number of stern remedies to master the economic difficulties which threatened us. Our party paid the price at the time in votes lost at by-elections, but the country benefited by the restoration of world confidence in our currency. And today the country is showing its appreciation in the growing support it is giving to our Government and party, and the increasing confidence it is displaying in them. Over the years I have found that in the long run the politician and the party that wins the most support is the one that sets out to do what it believes to be right, not what it fancies will be immediately popular.

There is another and rather harder lesson that I have learned. That is that the British people are reluctant to give any party a vote of gratitude for what has been done. The transformation of our affairs since 1951 has been marked and wholly beneficial; but do not, I beg you, believe that the electors will give you their votes solely on that account. It is a vote of confidence, rather than a vote of thanks that we seek; the future, not the past that we look to; and we can point to the past seven years as evidence that we have both the resolve and the ability to carry those plans and policies through.

I have seen with special satisfaction that among those plans a high priority is given to developing education and especially technical education. Three years ago in a speech I made in Woodford to a gathering of Young Conservatives I attempted to direct the attention of the country as a whole to the dangerous lead the Russians were gaining in this all-important field of legitimate competition. I am glad to feel that what I had to say was heeded. The Government have launched a new programme to develop technical education at all levels, and it is making good progress. Let none of us underestimate the importance of all of this. There is no task which should take greater pride of place in our national effort.

In 1958 the world has undergone many changes. In the Middle East, we mourn the death of the King of Iraq,[1] his uncle,[2] and Nuri Pasha. These three men were most loyal servants of their country and true friends of their allies. They were swept away in the convulsion of the Arab peoples that is still going on. I trust that counsels of peace and moderation will prevail, and that the Arab peoples and Israel will get the long period of prosperity and peaceful development they need.

Our own record there is a fine one. Our reputation rests on the great traditions of justice, fair government, and peace to which our administrators, soldiers, and ambassadors have been faithful. The British monument in the Middle East is to be found in harbours, dams, roads, and hospitals that we caused to be built, in the great oil industry that we created and developed, in the law and education which we brought, and in the graves of our dead, who died in preserving those countries from foreign invasion.

Here in Europe, I am very glad to see my old friend and wartime colleague,

---

[1] Al-Malik Faysal Ath-thani, 1935–58. Known as 'Faisal II'. Last King of Iraq, 1939–58. Killed during Baghdad uprising, 14 June 1958. Author of *How to Defend Yourself* (1951).

[2] Abd al-Ilāh, 1913–58. Known as 'Abdullah'. Son of King Ali ibn Hussein of Hejaz. Regent of Iraq, 1939–53; Crown Prince, 1943–58. In March 1941, the pro-German Rashi Ali al-Gaylani, a former PM of Iraq, seized power in Baghdad, forcing Emir Abdullah to flee; he returned with British aid in May. Killed during the Baghdad uprising, 14 June 1958.

General de Gaulle, now presiding over the destinies of his great country. We all fervently wish for the success of France in restoring her economy, which is potentially so prosperous. In General de Gaulle and Dr Adenauer in Germany we are fortunate to have two wise and forceful leaders of their countries who are also proved friends of Great Britain. Twelve years ago, in 1946, I expressed the hope that France would lead Germany by the hand back into the European community. I am happy to see each new development of Franco-German friendship, and I trust that Britain and the United States, bound increasingly together, will continue always to lend them support and help.

John Colville to Sir Winston S. Churchill
(Churchill papers, 1/91)[1]

26 January 1959

My dear Winston,

Meg and I loved our stay at Marrakech, every minute of it, and are more than grateful to you for including us in such an agreeable party. We left with sorrow and are still pining for that delectable view of the Atlas, for our nightly games of poker and for the pleasures of your company. The whole excursion was entirely delightful.

We had a very successful Press Conference about Churchill College yesterday. The press turned up in force, sending leading representatives (for instance Colin Coote[2] himself came to represent the DT) and Lord Weeks[3] handled them admirably. As far as I can see, only the *Times* – which has all along been captious and tiresome – published a disquieting article. Having seen the long-haired and insalubrious reporter whom they sent, I was certainly not surprised. Great stress was laid by Lord W on your anxiety to get the college operating before it was completed and on the plans for doing this.

With again so many thanks from us both,

---

[1] This letter was handwritten.
[2] Colin Reith Coote, 1893–1979. On active service during WWI (DSO). Member of Gloucestershire Rgt, 1914–17. Married, 1916, Marguerite Doris Wellstead: two children (div. 1925). MP (Lib.) for Wisbech, 1917–18; for Isle of Ely, 1918–22. Correspondent, *The Times*, Rome, 1922–6. Writer for *The Daily Telegraph* from 1942; Deputy Editor, 1945–50; Editor, 1950–64. Knighted, 1962.
[3] Ronald Morce Weeks, 1890–1960. Joined Pilkington Brothers, 1912. On active service, 1914–18 (despatches thrice, DSO, MC and bar). Retired from Army, 1919. Director, Pilkington Brothers, 1926; Chairman, 1939. Rejoined Army, 1939. CoS, Territorial Div., 1939. Brig., General Staff, Home Forces, 1940. Maj.-Gen., Director of Army Equipment, 1941. Lt-Gen., Deputy CIGS, 1942–5. Knighted, 1943. Deputy Military Governor and CoS, British Zone, Control Commission of Germany, 1945. Retired from Army, 1945. Chairman, British Scientific Instrument Research Association, 1946–51. National Advisory Council on Education for Industry and Commerce, 1948–56. Baron, 1956. British Government Representative on Board of British Petroleum, 1956–60.

Harry S Truman to Sir Winston S. Churchill
('Defending the West, The Truman–Churchill Correspondence', page 224)

2 February 1959

Dear Sir Winston,

I was very sorry indeed that you could not make the visit to the University of Missouri.[1]

I had hoped you might have another 'Iron Curtain' speech in your system and would like to have a place to release it, but, of course, if you can't come that is all there is to it. Maybe a future date can be arranged for the same purpose.

I am always most happy to hear from you and I sincerely hope that you had a wonderful rest and vacation in Marrakech.

Please give my very kindest regards and best wishes to Lady Churchill and Mrs Truman joins me in that request.

Sir Winston S. Churchill to Lady Violet Bonham Carter
(Churchill papers, 2/520)

5 March 1959

Thank you so much for your letter, which I was happy to receive on my return from London. We had a very successful time, first in Marrakech and then cruising on the Onassis' yacht to the Canary Islands and the Moroccan coast. The weather was on the whole kind, and I painted one or two pictures.

We were only at Gibraltar for a few hours and I did not see Archie.[2] I did not know he was there.

Tomorrow I leave for Roquebrune, but will be back in London about April 10. I think that I will be making a speech in my constituency on April 20, and thereafter I plan to go to Washington to stay with the President on May 4, and spend a few days in New York with Bernie before coming back to London.

I shall look forward to reading Mark's[3] speech. It is kind of you to think of sending it to me. I hope you enjoy your trip to Berlin, and I shall much look forward to seeing you again when we are both back.

---

[1] On 20 Dec. 1958, Truman had extended an invitation to Churchill to visit the University of Missouri to receive its Distinguished Service Award in Journalism. On 4 Jan.1959, Churchill sent his regrets, saying his visit to the US in May would be too brief to allow it.

[2] Archibald Sinclair, Lord Thurso.

[3] Mark Raymond Bonham Carter, 1922–94. Son of Sir Maurice Bonham Carter and Helen Violet Asquith (Lady Bonham Carter); grandson of H. H. Asquith; uncle to actress Helena Bonham Carter. On active service, Grenadier Guards, 1941–5. Captured by the Germans in Tunisia, 17 Mar. 1943; escaped from a prison camp in Italy, returning to England Oct. 1943. Married, 1955, Leslie Nast. Member, UK delegation to Council of Europe, 1958–9. MP (Lib.) for Torrington, 1958–9. Director, Royal Opera House, Covent Garden, 1958–82. Governor, Royal Ballet, 1960–85. Vice-Chairman and Governor, BBC, 1975–81. Baron, 1986.

Sir Winston S. Churchill to Lady Churchill
(Baroness Spencer-Churchill papers)

8 March 1959   La Pausa

Clemmie, Beloved One,

I arrived in due course and was met by the Préfet and Emery Reves. I found Nice and Roquebrune and all between wrapped in fog and shrouded impenetrably by clouds. Rain poured on my unfortunate meeters who had to wait three quarters of an hour while the delayed landing took place. However, they all seemed pleased to see me, and Emery drove me on here as quick as he could.

We had a second day of rain yesterday, but today, Sunday, all is bright, although more storms are predicted passing along the coast in our direction. I have not been out so far, but unless a shower intervenes I shall do so before lunch.

Wendy, who came to meet me, was delighted to get your letter, and she will no doubt answer it herself. She has presented me with a gold clip which holds attached to my coat a white napkin. I think you will like this when you see it, as it prevents food from dropping on my clothes. In fact it is the very thing which you would have suggested yourself.

Today they are all voting all over France and I presume, though I do not know, that de Gaulle will triumph.

I sent for Dr Roberts and he is dealing with all my ticklings which have come back in a very tiresome fashion.

My darling, I think a great deal about you & our troubles. I hope for a letter soon to tell me about Sarah. I think they treated her vy roughly at Liverpool & roused her fiery spirit.[1] I hope she will convince you that her affliction is a part of the period difficulties which are common to women at the change of life, & above all that she will persevere at her profession.

I am so sorry for the burden this rests on you & hope that staying with Mary & Christopher will relieve your troubles. Dearest my thoughts are with you. It all falls on you: 'Poor lamb!'. With all my love I remain a wreck (but with its flag still flying) & send you my best love and many kisses. I await your letter.

I found Toby safely here & he just got on my elbow to remind me that I must mention him in writing to you, or he wd be offended.

                                                                                Your loving husband

---

[1] 'After an evening on stage, she [Sarah] had tried to find her way back to her hotel. [. . .] Those who found her – 'slightly distracted', as she recalled – instead of calling for a taxi, called for the police. She was taken to court, fined £2, and dismissed. The case was blown up mightily by the Press' (Gilbert, *Winston S. Churchill*, vol. 8, *Never Despair*, p. 1286).

Sir Winston S. Churchill to Anthony Moir
(Churchill papers, 2/517)

10 March 1959 La Pausa

My dear Moir,

During some twenty years I have exchanged a great number of minutes and letters with Sir Anthony Eden which he thinks it would be opportune to publish in the near future. He is now collecting his minutes to me, and says that my communications to him exist in printed form among my papers.

I would very much like to look through these minutes, and wonder whether you could find them and have them sent here. I would be interested to have all my communications to Sir Anthony in whatever form they may exist.

Doreen Pugh to Sir Winston S. Churchill
(Churchill papers, 1/149)

12 March 1959

Prince Rainier and Princess Grace ask if you would lunch with them at the Palace on Monday next, March 16. It will be a small party of eight or ten only, consisting of the Prince and Princess, the Queen of Spain,[1] yourself if you can come, and a few officials of the Palace. They would like to invite Mr and Mrs Reves too.

(The Queen of Spain is staying at the Palace for the first birthday of Prince Albert[2] who is her godchild.)[3]

Sir Winston S. Churchill to Lady Churchill
(Baroness Spencer-Churchill papers)

13 March 1959 La Pausa

My darling,

I have been thinking about the Sarah incident and I have come to the conclusion that it went off as well as it could be expected. I am very glad that Sarah is to do another three weeks in the provinces, and I hope she will realise how much it means to her if she can clear her reputation by good behaviour in the future.

---

[1] Victoria Eugenie Julia Ena, 1887–1969. Born at Balmoral Castle, Scotland. Married, 1906, Alfonso XIII of Spain (d. 1941): seven children. Queen Consort of Spain, 1906–31.

[2] Albert Alexandre Louis Pierre Grimaldi, Albert II, Prince of Monaco, 1958–. Son of Prince Rainier III and Grace Kelly. Married, 2011, Charlene Wittstock (b. 1978). Five times Olympic bobsled finalist.

[3] Churchill wrote on this note: 'Yes'.

I hope your dinner with the Cholmondeleys[1] went off as expected and that you were victorious in bezique.

We have been invited to go to the Palace for luncheon on Monday and all three have accepted. Tomorrow, Saturday, we lunch with the Préfet. The day after we shall go on board the yacht, and on Friday we lunch with Daisy Fellowes.

It is fine today though misty. I have spent long hours in bed. Toby has just bitten off the flicks of blue which he sends you with his love, and mine dearest.

Your loving husband

Sir Winston S. Churchill to Lady Churchill
(Baroness Spencer-Churchill papers)

16 March 1959　　　　　　　　　　　　　　　　　　　　　　　　　　La Pausa

Dearest Clemmie,

Your two letters of the 13th and 14th have both arrived, and I am delighted by their contents. Also a very nice letter from Juliet with an extravagant tribute from Gerald Kelly who I did not think was in a good temper. I enclose you this letter.

Wendy has started a new cure for my habit of dropping food upon my coat front. She presented me with a gold snap locket which fastens securely the table napkin in position on my coat for all danger to be averted. She gave it to me on my arrival, and I am using it regularly with good results.

We are off this morning at 12.30 for lunch with the Prince at the Palace. The Queen of Spain is to be there.

We have had two days of brilliant weather, and I walked each day in the garden. Yesterday Paul Maze[2] and his wife came to lunch. He talked a good deal about painting, and will come and paint with me. I found it too cold to go on painting yesterday morning, but I will try again tomorrow. It is not quite so bright today.

I think it will be best to put the celebration of your Birthday off until Sunday, April 12, at Chartwell. I choose Sunday because then Sarah will be able to

---

[1] George Horatio Charles Cholmondeley, Earl of Rocksavage, 1883–1968. On active service in South Africa, 1901–2. Married, 1913, Sybil, sister of Sir Philip Sassoon. On active service in France and Flanders, 1914–18. Maj., RAF, 1920. Succeeded his father, 1923, as 5th Marquess of Cholmondeley. Joint Hereditary Lord Great Chamberlain; bore the Royal Standard at the coronation of King George VI.

Sybil Rachel Betty Cecile Sassoon, 1894–1989. Married, 1913, George Horatio Charles Cholmondeley: three children. Styled Marchioness of Cholmondeley, 1923. Superintendent, WRNS, 1939–46. CBE, 1946.

[2] Paul Lucien Maze, 1887–1979. Anglo-French painter. Naturalized British subject, 1920. Married, 1921, Margaret Nelson. Personal Staff Officer to Arthur 'Bomber' Harris, WWII.

come. Also it will give me more time to make the necessary arrangements after I return on Monday the 6th. Let me know if this will be convenient.

Tender love my darling
Your affectionate loving

Sir Winston S. Churchill: speech

(*'Winston S. Churchill, His Complete Speeches', volume 8, pages 8691–5*)

20 March 1959   Hawkey Hall, Woodford

It is a long time since I have made a speech in public, and I am justified in looking back some way into the past. I was astonished at the result of the 1945 election. I thought it would be much more beneficial to the country to allow the Government that won the war to win the peace. I have never felt more sure of this than I do now. Then we had only fancy to go on, but now we have the record of seven years' solid work done by the Conservative Government on the one hand to set against the Socialist performance. The Socialists have, I think, accomplished the hard task of convincing the people of this country that their rule does not mean prosperity. Now let us look into this.

In August, 1945, when the War was won and the country had chosen to entrust the task of Government to the Socialist Party, I ventured as Leader of the Opposition to address a few words to this New House of Commons. I urged the new Government to set the nation free as soon as possible.

'What we desire,' I said, 'is freedom; what we need is abundance. Freedom and abundance – these must be our aims.' Not for the first time in my life I had the experience of finding that my words were not heeded. It took more than six years, and considerable exertions by those who support the Conservative cause, before the country could be persuaded to reject the fallacies of Socialist doctrines, and to try instead the method of setting the people free. Now we can judge the results. They have been undoubtedly beneficial. They are here for all of us to see. Perhaps we take them all for granted.

I do not propose to worry you with a long catalogue of the many improvements that have been brought about since 1951. I will content myself with this simple, but very telling comparison.

For every pound saved under the Socialists £6 has been saved under the Conservatives. For every house built under the Socialists two have been built under the Conservatives. For every school place provided under Socialism, two have been built under the Conservatives. For every pound spent on major road schemes under the Socialists £4 is being spent by the Conservatives. For every pound on the wrong side in our overseas trading accounts under the Socialists, £1 15s. has been earned on the right side under the Conservatives. For every family with a car in 1951, there are two under the Conservatives. For each home with a television set under the Socialists in 1951, eight homes have a set under the Conservatives.

On top of that there have been other benefits. Taxation bears less heavily than it did, notably on parents with children to educate and on the elderly who have to live on pensions or the savings of a lifetime's work. All of you, I know, would wish to congratulate Mr Heathcoat Amory,[1] the Chancellor of the Exchequer, on his latest instalment of this healthy Tory process of lightening the burden of taxation – letting the money fructify in the pockets of the people, as they used to say in my young days. That always seemed to me a very sensible thing to do.

The Socialists have spared no expense in producing a policy for the next election. There is a great deal in it that is sound sense, as well as a lot more that is all sound and all nonsense. But while our opponents have been talking, we Conservatives have been getting on with the job. While they have been talking about more schools, we have been building them. While they are talking about the need for more teachers, we are training them. Against all their words, we can set deeds. No propaganda, however slick or skilful, can demolish the houses we have built, or re-erect the slums we have cleared.

I find it difficult to believe that when the time comes for the country to make its choice at the next General Election it will lightly or wantonly cast away all the advantages it has so laboriously gained.

We live by trade. To buy the food and the raw materials we need to keep our large population fed, clothed, and at work, we must export one-third of what we produce. During the whole of the war I had no greater anxiety than watching the weekly figures of our shipping losses. The mine and the submarine threatened to cut the lifeline by which our country breathes. But now that this danger has passed away, failure to sell our goods in the markets of the world would cut our lifeline just as surely. The effects might be slower, but they would be no less sure.

I was glad to read that Mr Harold Macmillan reminded the country of these facts just after his return from Moscow. 'If we can lessen the tension and resolve our difficulties, what we shall have achieved is competitive co-existence. And the accent will be, and is now, on competition,' said the Prime Minister. 'We must show the free world,' he went on, 'that we can produce the goods.'

For myself I am quite certain that Socialist planning has no constructive part to play in these tasks. Socialist controls, regulations, and directions can be made to apply to every citizen here at home, but not beyond our shores. You cannot direct the foreigner to buy British goods. You cannot order him to hold sterling if he has lost confidence in it.

Socialism could not help us in our task; but it could and would hinder. It

---

[1] Derick Heathcoat Amory, 1899–1981. Served in WWII (wounded). Retired as hon. Lt-Col., 1948. MP (Cons.) for Tiverton, 1945–60. Minister of Pensions, 1951–3. Chancellor of the Exchequer, 1958–60. Viscount, 1960.

would impose the most severe handicaps upon every British industry. There would be the handicap of the vastly increased taxation necessitated by their costly programme for increased expenditure in state services. There would be the handicap of doubt and uncertainty engendered by their threats of further nationalization throughout a wide but unspecified area of industry. There would be the handicap of renewed controls to sap confidence and interfere with the initiative and risk-taking which are the essentials of all sound business enterprise. Their unsound financial projects would inevitably mean a revival of the inflation of which the Conservative Government has at last rid itself. The return of inflation would be a national – indeed international – tragedy, the first victims of which would be those least able to help themselves – the old, the young, and the sick.

Any failure to pay our way in the world, or any loss of confidence overseas in our currency, would inevitably lead to unemployment on a scale we have not, mercifully, known since the war. Ten years ago we were given some timely reminders of that by some leading Socialist Ministers. Good specimens are speeches by Herbert Morrison and Aneurin Bevan. They told us at that time that there would have been one and a half million or more unemployed if it had not been for Marshall Aid. We must all rejoice that at that time our American allies so generously helped us to meet our difficulties. Nor need we feel any sense of shame because we accepted it. If the war left us poor, it was an honourable poverty.

Today the scene has changed. We do not ask for or expect external aid. Our pride is to stand squarely on our own feet. The whole aim of Conservative policy has been to maintain employment at the highest possible level by keeping our industrial costs competitive and by maintaining world confidence in our currency. Fourteen years have passed since we victoriously concluded the war, and since then the governments of this country, both Socialist and Conservative, have had to struggle with tough problems. Most of these are certainly not of our own making.

However, I see that Mr Khrushchev in his recent speech at Leipzig referred to me as the author of the Cold War. I am certainly responsible for pointing out to the free world in 1946, at Fulton in America, the perils in complacently accepting the advance of Communist imperialism.[1] But apart from this, my conscience is clear. It was not Britain who in 1939 so cynically compounded with Hitler, and later so greedily devoured the half of helpless and hapless Poland, while the Nazis took what was left. It is not Britain who has advanced her frontiers, absorbing many sovereign peoples who had made great contributions to civilized history. On the contrary, I suppose we are the only nation who fought throughout the war against Germany, and who, far from receiving any reward, have greatly diminished in our tenure on the surface of the globe.

---

[1] Speech reproduced in *The Churchill Documents*, vol. 22, *Leader of the Opposition, August 1945 to October 1951*, pp. 227–35.

But we are very willing to forget old scores. I seek, and have always sought, nothing but peace with the Russians, just as after the War I did my utmost to bring Germany back into the circle of the European family. Both Russia and England have all to gain and nothing to lose from peace. The Soviets hope that the doctrines of Karl Marx[1] may eventually prevail. We on our side trust and believe that as the mild and ameliorating influence of prosperity begins at last to uplift the Communist World, so they will be more inclined to live at ease with their neighbours. This is our hope. We must not be rigid in our expression of it; we must make allowances for justifiable Russian fears; we must be patient and firm.

We have all followed with admiration and hope the tireless efforts of Mr Macmillan, so ably seconded by the Foreign Secretary, in his journeys to Moscow and to the capitals of our principal allies. It is, of course, too early to be sure of the final achievement, but already the date of 27 May, when the Russians said that they would hand over their Berlin responsibilities to the East Germans, has lost something of its threatening character. I think that we have moved both from the position in which we either had to sacrifice our rights and the position of the free world in Berlin, or face the possibility of military action. It is unnecessary for the Soviet leaders to assure us that the use of armed force in Berlin would inevitably unleash a general conflict. We are well aware of this. We are well aware, too, that there is no chance of the world being spared the use of nuclear weapons if the war came.

The German problem under consideration is, in itself, a comparatively simple one. We hope, if possible, to see a reunited Germany. The terms of unification should be such that the true will of the German people is expressed and that the country does not fall under the domination of the Soviets. We in the West know that our intentions to Russia and the satellites are peaceful. We would never seek to make use of Germany as an offensive base against them. But with the background of the last war Russian fears of a resurgent Germany are reasonable, even if they are not justified. We must take account of them. The Soviets on their side must realize that we cannot contemplate a further increase in the number of countries and peoples they so tyrannically control. West Germany is our ally in NATO. We cannot abandon her. Berlin recently showed with an overwhelming vote where her sympathies lie. We cannot abandon the Berlin people either.

On basic issues we are at one. But I will say that I should like to see the Western allies show more sympathy for each other's problems. Clearly, to achieve our purposes in our talks with the Soviets we must be united and strong. With these few remarks I shall leave the subject. We all know that the

---

[1] Karl Heinrich Marx, 1818–83. Educated at Universities of Bonn and Berlin, 1835–6. Philosopher, sociologist and economist. Author of *The Communist Manifesto* and *Das Kapital*.

General Election is approaching. On that you know your duty. On past record and on character, on promise and on personalities, the Conservative Government deserves your support to bring continued and growing prosperity at home and to ensure lasting peace in the world. For my part I shall be ready to offer myself once again as a candidate in your constituency which I have had the honour of representing for nearly thirty-five years.

Denis Kelly to Sir Winston S. Churchill
(Churchill papers, 2/517)

25 March 1959

1. Here are your war-time minutes to Sir Anthony Eden for the years 1940–1944.[1] I will send you the 1945 minutes and your telegrams for the whole war in a few days.

Time prevented me flagging all your minutes, but the position of the remainder is indicated on the front of each of the monthly prints and also marked by a marginal cross in red ink on the relevant page.

At a rough guess, you sent Sir Anthony about one thousand minutes during the recent war. Adding in the enclosures, the total is nearly 1,500 pages of text.

2. His replies are approximately the same length. He told me he has copies of these (minus enclosures) except for the years 1941 and 1942. A Civil Servant has been tracking down these missing years. It has taken three months spare time research and amounts to about five hundred pages. These are being photographed at Government rates and work out at one shilling per page for one copy.

3. Your pre-war communications with Sir Anthony are among the archives of the Chartwell Literary Trust. They are not catalogued in detail. I reckon they would take a fortnight's full-time work to trace and extract and collate, plus perhaps another month to have them copied and/or photographed.

4. Your post-war interchanges are:
   a) Among your papers at Chartwell, which are un-catalogued. These cover the period when you were out of office.
   b) Either at No. 10 or in the archives of the Cabinet Office, when you were Prime Minister for the second time.

I am very vaguely acquainted with (a) and totally ignorant of (b).

Digging this lot out would entail perhaps another two months whole-time work. This is rather difficult for me to undertake at present without neglecting the Bar. But I would very much like to do it if you feel the cost is justifiable. It

---

[1] See Churchill to Moir of Mar. 10, reproduced above (p. 2235).

would, if properly edited, make a good book. May I know your wishes before embarking on the work outlined in paragraphs 3 and 4?

5. Please give my love to Wendy and Emery. I have not yet seen your Royal Academy Exhibition, but, flu permitting, hope to do so in two or three days' time.

Anthony Montague Browne to Sir Winston S. Churchill
(Churchill papers, 2/517)

27 March 1959

I see that Denis Kelly speaks of a total of between two and three months whole-time work necessary to collate your Minutes to Sir Anthony Eden. Before you undertook the expenses that this would involve, you might wish to consider what profit you could derive from publication.

(a) The Minutes you wrote to Sir Anthony Eden up to 1946 belong to the Chartwell Trust, to whom, as you will remember, you handed over your archives. I understand no profit could derive to you personally from the publication of these Minutes, though it would to the Trust.

(b) From 1946 to 1951, when you returned to the Prime Ministership, your Minutes belong to you personally, and the publication of them would presumably profit you directly. You would, of course, have to safeguard most closely the benefit you derived from your literary retirement, and I do not know if publication would be thought to jeopardise this.

(c) From 1951 until your resignation in 1955 your Minutes to Sir Anthony Eden I think are Crown Copyright. Of course, you would always be allowed <u>access</u> to them, just as you were to write the War History, and presumably if they were published as part of a book you were writing, just as many of your Minutes were published in your War Memoirs, there would be no difficulty. If on the other hand the Minutes of your Second Premiership were published without any supporting text you might have difficulty over the Crown Copyright. (I think the legal argument might be that as these Minutes were produced during your period of paid Office under the Crown they could not be the <u>sole</u> contents of a work from which you derived personal profit.)

All these points need clearing up, and I would suggest that the best thing to do would be to have a talk with Mr Moir and Sir Norman Brook after your return to England.

1959

Sir Winston S. Churchill to Lady Churchill
(Baroness Spencer-Churchill papers)[1]

29 March 1959   La Pausa

Clemmie darling,

I am getting better slowly from a curious illness which has lasted a whole week mostly spent in bed. Anthony brought me news & relief & will tell you about it. I come home in a week and will occupy myself with your Birthday celebrations which are fixed for the 12th.

The entertainment here of the Prince & Princess was a great success, and we had yesterday Ari & Tina.[2]

With all my love,
Your loving husband,

Sir Winston S. Churchill to Wendy Reves
(Reves papers)

April 1959

My dear Wendy,

I have been so far from well since I returned that I have had the greatest difficulty in getting through my various functions. The one in the Constituency was certainly the most severe, but I managed it all right after all. I am now better, and am going to America to stay with the President on the 4th of May.

It was so nice of you to have me out there and I shall propose myself again some to you and Emery.

With all good wishes my dear Wendy & best of love.

Your own devoted

Denis Kelly to Anthony Montague Browne
(Churchill papers, 2/517)[3]

8 April 1959

Dear Anthony,

I have been thinking about the Churchill–Eden correspondence.

1. <u>Crown copyright</u> could be got over if the documents were linked by a commentary as was done with Sir Winston's War Memoirs.

---

[1] This letter was handwritten.

[2] Christina Onassis, 1950–88. Daughter of Aristotle Onassis and heiress to his fortune. Born in New York City. Educated at Queen's College, London. Married, 1971, Joseph Bolker (div. 1972); 1975, Alexandros Andreadis (div. 1977); 1978, Sergei Kauzov (div. 1980); 1984, Thierry Roussel (div. 1987): one daughter. Took control of the Onassis shipping empire when her father died in 1975.

[3] This letter was handwritten.

2. This commentary ought, I feel, to be written by an outsider – not necessarily by me, though of course I would very much like to do it. An outsider would get a more critical & detached approach. Naturally, he would consult both the statesmen involved.

3. <u>Finance</u>: Their respective Trusts could commission this outside editor i.e. pay him a fee, & then share the proceeds of the sales of the book.

Anthony Moir to Anthony Montague Browne
(Churchill papers, 2/517)

13 April 1959

Dear Anthony,

Thank you for the letter of the 9th April enclosing one which you have received from Denis Kelly, which I return.

With regard to the points which Denis makes:

1. This is a point which I think only Sir Norman Brook can advise upon. I should have thought, however, that if all of the Minutes passing between Sir Winston and Sir Anthony were to be published in one volume, even though a commentary was included, the Crown would probably not agree to such a publication.
2. Whoever was commissioned to write the commentary could of course consult fully with Sir Anthony, but, once again, it would be impossible for Sir Winston to take any part which could possibly be construed as a literary activity.
3. If Denis' suggestions as to finance were adopted, it would mean that the Trustees' respective shares of the proceeds would be taxable. It would be infinitely better, if practicable, to get someone such as a publishing house to buy the right of access to the documents and then commission someone to write the book.

Sir Winston S. Churchill to Bernard Baruch
(Churchill papers, 2/298)

23 April 1959

My dear Bernie,

I have delayed answering your letter until I was sure about my arrangements. My plans are now these: I shall arrive in Washington on May 4, come to New York after luncheon on May 8, and leave for London on the night of May 10. If you could have me from May 8 until May 10, it would be most agreeable.

Clemmie is still not well, and will not be accompanying me. My entire party will therefore be Anthony Montague Browne, Sheppard, my valet,[1] and Sgt. Murray of Scotland Yard. If you could accommodate me and Sheppard I would be most grateful. Montague Browne has been invited to stay with Dixon who I think lives in the same building as you.

We shall be coming by air from Washington on the 8th, either in the President's aircraft or the Ambassador's. I will let you know the exact time later.

As regards the arrangements for entertaining which you so kindly suggest, I think that small numbers to luncheon or dinner would be preferable to a large party, if this meets with your approval. I would leave it to you to decide who they should be. I would like, if I may, to propose on one occasion Mr Giraudier, who is the Cuban who for many years has corresponded with me and provided me with cigars. He is an agreeable man. I expect you know of him.

I am much looking forward to seeing you.

Anthony Montague Browne to Bernard Baruch
(Churchill papers, 2/298)

23 April 1959
Private and Confidential

You will have had by the same post Sir Winston's letter about the visit. I should tell you for your strictly private information that Sir Winston has not been very well, and we were in doubt as to whether he should go. However, he is determined to visit America again, so that is that! I know that you will safeguard him from fatigue as much as possible.

If it can be arranged for him to have a bell that rings in Sheppard's room, this is the best arrangement, as he needs him at quite frequent intervals.

I much look forward to seeing you again.

---

[1] Sheppard, a trained nurse, succeeded James Kirkwood as Churchill's valet.

Anthony Montague Browne to Lord Nicholas Gordon-Lennox[1]
(Churchill papers, 2/298)

23 April 1959
Private

I think that the Ambassador should know that Sir Winston has not been well lately, and we have all hoped that he would cancel his visit. However, he is resolutely determined not to do this, so we are making the best of it and endeavouring to minimize fatigue.

As you know, he is declining all invitations outside the programme you have so kindly arranged for him. He is not making any speeches, and although I have no doubt that he can cope with the remarks on arrival at either New York or Washington, we would like to keep them to a minimum. In particular, it would be best for him not to be over-run with the Press at both places on arrival. Washington, the terminal point, would seem to be the logical place for him to be greeted and say a few words.

We hope that it will be possible for there to be no speeches at the luncheons or dinners. Of course, Sir Winston is almost certain to get up at the end of the meal and say a few sentences of thanks to his hosts.

We should like, if possible, to minimize the amount of walking he has to do, and in particular the climbing of stairs. Sheppard, his valet, is a trained nurse, and looks after him very well. Perhaps it could be arranged for a bell to ring from Sir Winston's bedroom to Sheppard's?

I do not know if diet hints are any help to you? If they are, Sir Winston has no particular dislikes and enjoys good cooking! He likes on the whole to drink a still white wine at luncheon, and champagne at dinner.

I leave it to you to pass on as much of all this as you see fit to the White House, and I hope it does not sound too imperious to our hosts.

One small final point. Could you let me know what bits of the programme I feature in, so that I can make outside arrangements if I am not on deck?

---

[1] Nicholas Charles Gordon-Lennox, 1931–2004. Second son of Frederick Charles Gordon-Lennox, 9th Duke of Richmond and 4th Duke of Gordon. Private Secretary to HM Ambassador to US, 1957–61; at HM Embassy, Santiago, 1961–3; to Permanent Under-Secretary, 1963–6. Head of Chancery, HM Embassy, Madrid, 1966–71. Seconded to Cabinet Office, 1971–3. Head of News Dept, FCO, 1973–4; of North America Dept, 1974–5. Counsellor and Head of Chancery, Paris, 1975–9. Asst Under-Secretary of State, FCO, 1979–84. Ambassador to Spain, 1984–9. KCMG, 1986. KCVO 1989.

Lord Moran to Sir Winston S. Churchill
(*Churchill papers, 1/54*)

2 May 1959

My dear Winston,

I was rather sad when you said this morning that you wished that you were not going on this trip. I expect you feel that this visit is only worthwhile if you can do it really well. But I believe that this is still possible.

Any doubts I have had are not concerned with any vascular accident or emergency; after all it is good odds against anything of that kind happening. I only wonder if you will be in such good form that people in the States will say: 'I'd like to remember him like that'.

I am sure it is possible to tune your circulation so that you will be in such form. I say this because your circulation still responds to 'Minors' if used at the right time, and when it is safe to use them judging from the pulse tension – perhaps using more 'Minors' than we have done hitherto. So far we have used the 'Minors' only before speeches etc. But I had it in mind to use them to keep you in top form throughout your visit (which is short enough to make that possible).

I was pretty certain that 'Minors' so used would make the difference between your visit being an outstanding success and merely one where your form might be compared sadly with what they remembered in former times.

That is why I was very sorry when you decided not to take me. I have learnt so much about your circulation in the last nineteen years and what can be done to tone it up that I believe I could have made up the difference. I wanted you so much to bring off this trip so that people would talk of it as a wonderful thing in itself and not just talk of your former visits. I wanted them to say how marvellous it was that in your eighty-fifth year you were so much 'on the spot' and plainly in a state when you could give Ike the advice he so obviously needs.

I want you to know that if there is any change in your plans I am ready at this end.

Sir Winston S. Churchill to Lady Churchill
(*Baroness Spencer-Churchill papers*)[1]

5 May 1959   The White House

My dearest Clemmie,

Here I am. All goes well & the President is a real friend. We had a most pleasant dinner last night, & caught up my arrears of sleep in eleven hours. I

---

[1] This letter was handwritten.

am invited to stay in bed all the morning & am going to see Mr Dulles after luncheon. Anthony will send you more news. I send my fondest love darling.

Sir Winston S. Churchill: speech
(Churchill papers, 2/298)

5 May 1959   The White House

Mr President and Gentlemen,

I am grateful to you for allowing me to have the honour to be associated with the Toast of the Queen.

It is remarkable how much you have contributed to using this new link of the Crown to bring together these vast populations which are on either side of the Atlantic to awake development of the world. It is a most remarkable and most encouraging thing.

I am very much complimented that our host, the President should have invited here tonight so remarkable a gathering of many of the most distinguished figures of the United States of America. It is a great honour to meet you all, I can assure you that I deeply feel it as such. To come across the Atlantic and to see so many friends and so many elements in the union of our peoples has been a great and memorable joy to me.

Here at this table, to look around, sit those whose decision can perhaps influence the destiny of mankind more deeply than any other group of men you could find.

We are all of us here today faced with complex and difficult problems. They are perhaps harder to resolve than those which confronted us in the last war, in the days of our closest comradeship. And yet, in a way, you did not run the risk of making mistakes, of slipping here or there in minor matters, such as we sometimes experience nowadays in time of peace.

I would suggest to you that the solution today is the same as it was then. I feel most strongly that our whole effort should be to work together. It resounds in my mind, a precious and hopeful thought. That anyone should be cast aside as 'only another country' is ridiculous. We have got to work together. I think that it is in close and increasing fellowship, the brotherhood of English-speaking peoples, that we must work.

It is that I look at, first and foremost, and I was very pleased indeed to have the opportunity of coming over here and telling you, late in the day, what I have always lived up to, namely: the union of the English-speaking peoples. I am sure that it is in a close and increasing fellowship with you, our American friends and brothers, that our brilliant future rests.

Consider, broadly speaking, there's a very large mass of people – we are small, but we are eighty millions, with Canada, Australia and New Zealand brought in. You are 175 millions – well, how does that add up? It seems to me, adding it up, it's more or less 300 millions, pretty near. Anyhow, a few more years of your tenure of office will easily see that raised three million a year and building up, and there you will be.

And let us be united. Let us be united, and let our hopes lie in our unity. Because we understand each other. We understand when things go wrong, or things are said, or anything like that, we really can afford to pass them by.

We understand each other, and we hope that the realization of this truth will continue to increase on both sides of the Atlantic, to the lasting benefit of the free world – and above all, the people of Britain and America.

I earnestly hope that an effort will be made, a fresh further effort forward, to link us together. Because it is really of the utmost importance that we, who think so much alike, as well as speaking, who think so much alike, should see clearly before us the plain road onwards through the future.

Now, Mr President, I have detained you some time, but I must ask this distinguished company to join me in a drinking the health of the President of the United States, which I now propose.

Anthony Montague Browne to Sir Harold Caccia
(*Churchill papers, 2/298*)

21 May 1959
Private and Confidential

I said that I would send you an account of Sir Winston's stay in the White House covering the part of his visit when you were not with him. I fear that it will not contain anything that is either new to you or particularly interesting, but here it is.

Sir Winston had his principal talks with the President at luncheon on May 5 and May 6. The conversation, which was of a very general nature, ranged much over personalities, with the President returning more than once to how wounded he had been by Field Marshal Montgomery's television interview.[1] He said that he was willing to believe that the Field Marshal had been seduced by Ed Murrow,[2] whom he described as 'a snake,' but that it was really too much that Lord Montgomery, who had repeatedly invited himself to stay at the White House, should make a personal attack of this nature. He added that when he had been appointed Supreme Commander of Overlord, Sir Winston had told him that he could sack any British officer who proved difficult, but

---

[1] *Montgomery Speaks His Mind*: filmed in Hampshire; released in the US 28 Apr. 1959.

[2] Edward R. Murrow, 1908–65. Born Egbert Roscoe Murrow. Known as 'Ed'. American broadcast journalist. Asst Director, Institute of International Education, New York, 1932–5. Director of Talks and Education, Columbia Broadcasting System (CBS), 1935–7; Director of European Operations (London), 1937–46. Known for his opening phrase 'This is London' and his closing phrase 'Goodnight, and good luck'. Flew on 25 Allied combat missions in Europe, on which he reported. Had a romantic affair with Pamela Churchill, 1944–5. Vice-President of CBS, 1945.

that he had not exercised this right in the case of Field Marshal Montgomery! Sir Winston succeeded to a great extent, I think, in smoothing the ruffled feathers, but it was surprisingly evident how affected the President is by personal criticism levelled at him from abroad. He also referred with asperity to attacks on him in the British Press, and for someone in his position seemed surprisingly thin-skinned.

The President spoke warmly of the Prime Minister. He said, 'That's a man you can really do business with. And he's quick, too.' He went on to speak unfavourably of the French in general, and General de Gaulle in particular. He clearly has a paternal feeling for the NATO military machinery, dating no doubt from his tenure at SHAPE, and he thought that the French might well wreck it. He spoke of Algeria and General de Gaulle's illogical position in maintaining that it was an internal French affair, and at the same time seeking NATO endorsement of the French position and policy there. From there the President launched into a disquisition on the position of colonial countries in Africa. This was on the classical American line of 'give it to them before they take it' and seemed greatly to over-simplify the problems.

Sir Winston raised with the President the question of discrimination against British contractors and the trend towards protection to the detriment of our exports, as mentioned in the Foreign Office brief. The President appeared sympathetic, but said that he had a difficult time in selling the desirability of a liberal American policy in this direction. He added that he had heard that the President of the Board of Trade was going to offer the Russians a five-year credit scheme, and that this would break the NATO front on the subject. If we did this the Dutch or probably the West Germans would want to follow suit. He was then working on a message to us about it. This has of course resolved itself since.

During the three days we were in the White House the President showed an affection care and consideration for Sir Winston and spent a great deal of time with him. He looked well and seemed alert. He said that he is troubled by deafness, but this was not apparent. His working day seems to be from about half-past nine in the morning until luncheon. In the afternoon, when he was not with Sir Winston, he seemed either to be resting or taking light exercise.

The President spoke with what seemed relief of the approach of the end of his tenure. I do not think that this was assumed. In general he seemed rather less than optimistic, but perhaps this was caused by Mr Dulles' decline, which was much in his mind. At one point he concluded his remarks about the future of NATO with approximately these words: 'The big question is, will the West have the endurance and the tenacity and the courage to keep up the struggle long enough?' (Mr McElroy[1] spoke in rather similar terms to Sir Winston and hinted to him that Great Britain was not pulling its weight in defence matters.

---

[1] Neil Hosler McElroy, 1904–72. Educated at Harvard University, 1925. President, Proctor & Gamble, 1948–57. US Secretary of Defense, 1957–9. Medal of Freedom, 1959.

I did not hear this conversation, but Sir Winston said that the sense of it was quite clear.)

To sum up, the President seemed relaxed, healthy and following a regime that was light enough to keep him so. His outlook seemed on the melancholy side, and it did not appear that his mind was receptive to ideas differing from these he already held.

I apologise for writing at such length, particularly as this will add very little to what you know.

President Dwight D. Eisenhower to Sir Winston S. Churchill
(*Churchill papers, 2/217*)

26 May 1959 																																		The White House

Dear Winston,

Thank you so much for inscribing for me one of the photographs taken on our memorable trip to Gettysburg earlier this month. I can't tell you how delighted I am to have it.

Stories are still appearing in some of our magazines about your visit to this country. America of course claims at least half of you as her very own, and just to have you here once again did us all good. I most sincerely trust that you have completely recovered from the exhaustion that the journey must have provoked.

Just as I was dictating this note, your telegram about Foster came to my desk.[1] I am grateful for your sympathy. At the same time, may I mention how touched I was by the statement you issued Sunday? His death, inevitable though it had seemingly been for some time, nonetheless came as a blow both personally and officially.

Incidentally, for the time being I have put the *Valley of the Ourika and Atlas Mountains*[2] in my office, so that I may display it proudly to each and every visitor there.

---

[1] Dulles, who had been suffering from cancer for some time, died on May 24 at Walter Reed Army Medical Center.

[2] A 1948 painting by Churchill, which he gave to Eisenhower in 1959 after visiting the President's farm.

President Dwight D. Eisenhower to Sir Winston S. Churchill
(Churchill papers, 2/217)

26 May 1959 The White House

Dear Winston,

I take the liberty of quoting to you a paragraph from an editorial appearing in the *Montreal Gazette* from April 30, 1959. I do not send this to you in any attempt toward self-glorification; I simply want to assure you that in one particular, at least, one editor commended both you and me for avoiding the pitfall of unjustified criticism of colleagues.

'Sir Winston Churchill, in his memoirs of the Second World War, deliberately omitted complaints about France, which his subordinates later printed. In the same way, Eisenhower's memoirs of the conflict were carefully edited; for the sake of Western unity, they contained no bitterness'.

'Like Churchill, Eisenhower's greatness grows as his critics multiply. Politically, this may be twilight for him. But, in twilight, his shadow lengthens every day'.

Please give my warm greetings to your Lady and, of course, all the best to yourself.

Harry S Truman to Sir Winston S. Churchill
('Defending the West, The Truman–Churchill Correspondence', page 225)

27 May 1959

Dear Sir Winston,

I have not received a letter in a long, long time that pleased me so much as yours of the twenty-first.[1] I was very anxious for you to understand the situation and to know that I had no intention of appearing discourteous to you. Circumstances developed which left me no other course of action.

Sometime I hope that you and I can discuss the attitudes that prevail here. They are fantastic.

Please say to Lady Churchill that Mrs Truman was highly pleased to receive the message signed by you both.

If you have need of a second-class campaign orator for your re-election and are certain that I would not cost you any votes, I will be glad to come over to make my contribution.

---

[1] Churchill had written to Truman wishing Mrs Truman, who had recently been ill, a speedy recovery and regretting that he and Truman had missed each other in Washington.

1959

Anthony Montague Browne to Sir Winston S. Churchill
(Churchill papers, 2/194)

1 June 1959

This letter is rather hard to decipher, but it would appear from the note at the end that Munuswamy[1] collapsed and died while he was dictating it.

Do you wish to send his Widow a message and a final present?[2]

Sir Winston S. Churchill to President Dwight D. Eisenhower
(Churchill papers, 2/217)

13 June 1959

Thank you so much for your two letters, and for sending me the extract from the *Montreal Gazette*. I was glad to see that the Editor put our names together in this matter! I agree with you that nothing is ever lost by restraint in these things. It was good of you to write to me about it.

I have most agreeable memories of my visit to you. It was a great source of pleasure to me to meet your wife again and stay with you, and to see the faces of so many of my old friends. You made this, my most recent visit – I hope that it is not my last visit – a most memorable one. I hope that all goes well with you, and that we may one day see you over here.

Sir Anthony Eden to Sir Winston S. Churchill
(Churchill papers, 2/517)

17 June 1959
Private and Personal

My dear Winston,

We are both so disappointed not to be able to come up to luncheon tomorrow. There is a small broken bone in Clarissa's foot which is mending well but I fear she will be immobile for a week or two at least. It is really very bad luck for the cruise was such an enjoyable success.

I have been at work on the book and I have virtually decided to publish first, as a separate volume, the years 1951–57. The chief reason for this is that I wrote these first as being fresh in my memory. If I had gone back to the early 1930s I fear that I would have forgotten a great deal of the 1950s by the time I reached them. Also, I have been influenced by the importance of getting our own story out for those years before others do so.

I look forward to showing you the complete story when I have got it into

---

[1] P. Munuswamy, c.1879–1959. Churchill's butler during his military service in Bangalore, 1896.
[2] Churchill wrote: 'Yes, £5'. Churchill had sent £5 a year to Munuswamy since 1945.

shape. Meanwhile, there are one or two chapters which concern us both, particularly that which deals with the changing of the guard between us. I have asked Alan Hodge to show you this. I hope you will think that it treats the subject fairly and I should be grateful for any comments you may have, either as to substance or as to wording.

Clarissa and I both send love to you and Clemmie.

Sir Winston S. Churchill to Sir Anthony Eden
(*Churchill papers, 2/517*)

19 June 1959

My dear Anthony,

Thank you so much for your letter and for sending me the Chapter about the changeover in 1955. I have read it with great interest and I do not think that I have any particular comment to offer. I look forward to seeing the rest as they come along.

We were so sorry not to see you, and I do trust that Clarissa's foot will soon be completely mended. I look forward to seeing you soon.

Sir Winston S. Churchill to Sir Anthony Eden
(*Churchill papers, 2/517*)

16 August 1959

My dear Anthony,

I wonder if you could let me know in greater detail what you had in mind about the possible publication of the Minutes we have exchanged over the years? I first heard of the idea last March from Reves. At that time I caused inquiries to be made into the possibilities, and there seemed to be difficulties.[1] It might be useful to you, for your strictly private information, to know how my Archives stand.

1. My papers prior to 1946 are the property of Chartwell Trust. The Trust, of course, gives full weight to any wishes which I express, but nevertheless these papers are not my personal property.
2. My papers between 1946 and 1951 are mine without any complications.
3. My papers which issued between 1951 and 1955 are, of course, subject to Crown Copyright. You are well aware of the arrangements by which the Crown allow one access to one's Minutes, but if documents which are Crown copyright constitute the sole text of

---

[1] See correspondence reproduced above (pp. 2235, 2241–2, 2242, 2244).

a book and are not merely illustrations or appendices of the text, there could be copyright difficulties.

What, of course, complicates the position for me is that I have retired[1] as an author, and I cannot therefore write anything myself, or, indeed, perform any services with regard to the publication of the Minutes.

It was so nice seeing you both before we came away, and I do hope that your health will show real improvement.

Sir Winston S. Churchill to Lady Churchill
(Baroness Spencer-Churchill papers)

22 August 1959   Alpes Maritimes

Darling One,

We have been overwhelmed by weather and I expect you have had a dose of the same. Immediately after breakfast, from a grey sky, rain began to drip – and pour and everything became sopping, and all who showed a nose out of doors were sopped. I remained in bed and watched the patter from my verandah ledge. I certainly saw more rain in those few hours than we have seen since we sallied forth from London. This letter is at present confined to weather conditions, for these are the only ones which constitute my outlook.

Max and I dined together alone last night, and were entertained – or I was – by the lizards on the wall, who each got their fly before they went to bed.

The white cat has just put head and shoulders in the room where I am at present dictating my letter to you. I think you will find it will reach you before you go to the hospital. I send you all my fondest love and trust indeed that things may go well with you in a graver ordeal than I am likely to encounter inside any limits I can foresee.

Best of all good fortune in the operation,[2] & tender love forever.

---

[1] Churchill was using the word 'retired' here in the legal rather than the conventional sense. His accountants found it useful from a tax standpoint to declare him 'retired' as an author when he was not involved in book projects.

[2] Lady Churchill was about to undergo surgery to correct a drooping eyelid, the result of a prolonged attack of shingles. The operation, carried out by Sir Benjamin Rycroft, was a complete success.

1959

Sir Anthony Eden to Sir Winston S. Churchill
(Churchill papers, 2/517)

22 August 1959
Personal

My dear Winston,

Thank you for your letter telling me the position in respect of your archives. I think that the idea about the minutes was originally Reves', but it seemed to me to have a good deal to commend it.

Over the years you and I must have exchanged many thousand minutes. The majority of these may have been upon matters of only ephemeral interest. On the other hand, others among them may deal with matters of permanent concern to history. You have used some of your minutes to me in the books you have already published. I am proposing to use a very few of my minutes to you in my book.

I think it likely that a diligent study of all these minutes through the years, from 1939–1955, would reveal sufficient worthwhile material to form a book. To judge of this it would be necessary to read through all the minutes, yours and mine, which would be quite a task. I should be ready to undertake this, once the book is out of the way. Meanwhile, I could this autumn look through one or two of the years, which would help me to judge whether the operation was justified supposing you were prepared to consider it further.

If we decide on this, it would be necessary to have an editor. Indeed, this would be indispensable to judge from paragraph 3 on page 2 of your letter. I think that, once we had determined our preliminary opinion about the operation, it would be necessary to approach the authorities about the Crown Copyright. I do not imagine that the choice of an editor will present any difficulties. His task would be limited to a brief summary of the international or domestic events which formed the background of our exchanges.

I am sorry not to have been able to send out my proofs of Book III, Suez, before now, but I have been wretchedly held up by the printers' strike and have still not received them myself. We have had to work so far on some rather grubby efforts which *The Times* discreetly put together.

On the other hand, I have had a visit from the editor and manager of the paper (McCall's)[1] which is to serialise the book in the United States. To my pleasure, and somewhat to my surprise, he expressed himself in warmest terms about the book. It is true that he subsequently admitted that he had always been a supporter of our Suez action, but it is a relief to me to know that the text seemed to him a clear and fair account of all we had been through, which he judged would deeply impress the American people.

[1] Herbert R. Mayes, 1900–87. Managing Editor of *The American Druggist*, 1927–34. Editor of *Pictorial Review*, 1934–7. Managing Editor, *Good Housekeeping*, 1937; Editor, 1937–58. Editor of *McCall's Magazine*, 1958–62. President and CEO, McCall Corp., 1962–5. Retired, 1965.

I confess to being unhappy at the present state of Anglo-French relations, and on some other international topics as well. I cannot see why the International Bank has to go offering Nasser money for the Canal at this time when he is refusing transit not only to Israeli ships but to Israeli trade. This seems to me the worst form of appeasement.

I hope that you enjoyed your cruise. We have had such wonderful weather here that the garden & farm have been very rewarding.

Clarissa & I send our love to you & most cordial greetings to Max.

Anthony Montague Browne to Captain Peter Aurand[1]
(Churchill papers, 2/217)

22 August 1959   La Pausa

I have now discussed with Sir Winston the possibility of his returning to see the President during his stay in London. As Sir Winston is well installed here, and Lady Churchill will be in hospital in England at the time, it seems best for him to stay and not return for so short a time. Sir Winston will be writing to the President, saying how sorry he is that he will be unable to see him.[2] I regret too the chance of seeing more of you, but I hope there will be another opportunity.

Sir Winston S. Churchill to Emery Reves
(Churchill papers, 2/532)

September 1959[3]

My dear Emery,

You and Wendy are much in my thoughts, and I do hope that you are continuing to make good progress.[4]

Here the Election is approaching its climax and I am gradually drawn into it more and more. I think however, on the whole, that our chances are still good, though not so good as they ought to be. However, in another week we shall know for certain. Indeed you may not get this letter before the results come in. I have had two charming letters from Wendy and hope the rest she has taken amid her anxieties will do her lasting good.

It was a great disappointment to me not to come out again to Pausaland.

---

[1] Evan Peter Aurand, 1917–89. US Naval Academy, 1938. Married, 1941, Patricia Lucille Riley (d. 1988). Naval aviator in WWII; Navy Cross. Naval aide to the President, 1957–61. Retired as VAdm., 1972.

[2] In fact a meeting did take place.

[3] Day not specified in original.

[4] Emery Reves had suffered a coronary thrombosis.

We have, however, had enchanting weather here and not a day on which the sun has not shone brightly.

With all good wishes for your complete recovery, believe me,

Rear-Admiral Christopher Bonham-Carter[1] to Anthony Montague Browne
(Churchill papers, 2/571)

2 September 1959   Buckingham Palace

Dear Montague Browne,

Thank you for your letter of the 20th August.

I have had a further discussion with His Royal Highness The Duke of Edinburgh and he has asked me to say that he will be pleased to accept the Visitorship of Churchill College, Cambridge.

Sir Winston S. Churchill to Wendy Reves
(Reves papers)

4 September 1959   Chartwell

My dear Wendy,

I am so grieved at the bad news about Emery, but I hope that six or eight weeks will enable him to recover. It is a lucky thing your Mother is with you. She ought to be a comfort to you in these difficult days.

Here we have beautiful weather every day and we might almost be at Pausaland. Clemmie is home from the hospital. We both read your letters with deep interest, and feel a great deal for you in all your anxiety and care.

It was always great fun and pleasure coming to Pausaland, and taking my daily walks with you.

I hope we shall have some more,

---

[1] Christopher Douglas Bonham-Carter, 1907–75. Served during WWII, 1939–45. Commanded Second Frigate Flotilla, 1949–51. Naval Attaché, Rome, 1951–3. Commanded HMS *Glasgow*, 1955–6. Rear-Adm. 1957. Chief of Staff, Mediterranean, 1957–9. Treasurer to Duke of Edinburgh, 1959–70; Treasurer and Private Secretary, 1970.

Sir Winston S. Churchill to David Ben-Gurion[1]
(Churchill papers, 2/128)

11 September 1959
Private

My dear Prime Minister,

I was very sorry to miss you in the South of France, but I quite understood how you were placed, and I am very much obliged to you for writing to me such a long and interesting letter.

I will reflect carefully on what you say. For myself, I believe that your view may perhaps be on the melancholy side. However, there is no doubt that we should be well advised to bear in mind the possibilities you discussed.[2]

I often think of your Country, and I view with admiration the way in which you are undertaking your great tasks. I trust that we shall have another opportunity of meeting before long, and with all good wishes, I remain,

Sir Winston S. Churchill to Prince Philip, Duke of Edinburgh
(Churchill papers, 2/571)

15 September 1959

Sir,

I have learned that Your Royal Highness has consented to become the Visitor of Churchill College at Cambridge. I write in the name of my fellow Trustees to express to you our gratitude. Your decision will give the greatest pleasure to all those associated with the College, and Your Royal Highness' well known interest in scientific development in this country makes the honour which you have done us even more welcome.

---

[1] David Ben-Gurion, 1886–1973. Recognized as founder of the State of Israel. Attended University of Warsaw, 1905. Studied Law, Istanbul University, 1912. General Secretary, Zionist Labour Federation in Palestine, 1921–35. Declared establishment of State of Israel, 14 May 1948. Leader of Israel in Arab–Israeli War, 1948. First Israeli PM and Minister of Defence, 1949–63.

[2] Ben-Gurion wrote of the likelihood, in his opinion, that any gesture of goodwill made by the Soviet Union towards non-Communist countries, such as the Khruschchev–Eisenhower talks, the Foreign Ministers' conference or a summit conference, was meant solely 'to lull the free world to sleep and weaken its consciousness of the imperative need for unity'.

Harold Macmillan to Sir Winston S. Churchill
(Churchill papers, 2/128)

28 September 1959
Private and Confidential

Dear Winston,

Thank you so much for sending me the letter from Ben Gurion (which I am returning as requested). I was very interested to see this and to learn the way his own thoughts are moving.

I hope you are well. Everyone up here is in good heart and in spite of what the newspapers say we have not yet given up hope! Indeed, we are calmly confident.

Sir Winston S. Churchill: speech
('Winston S. Churchill, His Complete Speeches', volume 8, pages 8697–700)

29 September 1959   Hawkey Hall, Woodford

ADOPTION MEETING

I am much touched by your action, Ladies and Gentlemen, in doing me the honour of adopting me as your candidate for the ninth time. We have had eight victories running, and I am sure that if everyone plays his part as you have always done we shall increase our score on 8 October.

Thirty-five years have now passed since you first adopted me, and it is a source of great satisfaction and pleasure to my wife, the President of your Association, and to me that we have been sustained over this long period by your unfailing confidence and goodwill. The Conservative campaign has opened in this election on a wave of optimism for a Conservative victory. I find a most solid basis of national prosperity on which we can build, and every class of society in this country has benefitted demonstrably from eight years of Conservative rule. But do not let us allow ourselves to be lulled into a false sense of security.

You will, I am confident, spare some of your time and energy in neighbouring seats where the forces of Socialism are stronger and our own may be hard pressed. It is not merely that we require to gain a decided victory on our own ground. We seek with determination to participate in a general success.

And here let me point out that there was a time when public opinion polls registered the unpopularity which the Government were incurring through the stern but necessary measures they were taking. As a party we never allowed that to depress or disturb us. Today when the public opinion polls tell a very different story we must not allow them to elate us unduly, or let them lead us into the pitfalls of over-confidence. Moreover, we must not forget the large number of candidates which the Liberal Party have seen fit to put forward, many of them in marginal constituencies. We have no Liberal opponent here, but they constitute a considerable factor in the country as a whole.

Mr Grimond, the leader of the Liberals, has discussed the suggestion that to vote for his party is to waste a vote. He maintains that a Liberal vote enforces good behaviour on the Socialists and Conservatives. How absurd! The Socialists, I have no doubt, will pursue their destructive trend blandly indifferent to any mild and ameliorating Liberal wind. If they return to power the policies they have outlined will undo what has been laboriously achieved in the last eight years. So I say, in spite of Mr Grimond, do not vote Liberal; do not let the Socialists in.

The country next month will be deciding two very important questions. The first, which concerns affairs at home, is this: Does the country wish to travel further along our Conservative road of freedom and opportunity; or does it wish to turn back and go down the Socialist road of controls and state interference of every kind?

Fortunately nowadays people can make their choice on the basis of fact, not just simple theory. They had six long years of the Socialist method. It brought us one crisis after another. It never succeeded in ending shortages, whether of houses, food, or fuel. In those days taxation was kept at penal levels. Rationing, often even harder than what was necessary during the war, was rigorously maintained. Prices rose remorselessly to the detriment especially of those living on fixed incomes, and those relying on pensions and other social service benefits.

Since then we have had eight years of the Conservative policy of freedom and incentive. The transformation has been remarkable. The houses have been built. Rationing has long since ended. The shortages have disappeared. Taxes have come down. Prices have been steady for the past year and more. Pension rates have been improved and the social services have been extended.

Mr Macmillan is giving the country a good account of his stewardship. I was always confident that he would be able to do that. But could anybody seriously imagine that this happy state of affairs would continue under a Socialist administration? The past provides the best pointer to the future. Look, for instance, at the record of the three last Socialist Chancellors of the Exchequer. In each case taxes went up, and the value of money went down. And, of course, the same thing would happen again. The only difference next time would be that taxes would go up even higher and the value of money fall even lower. That would be the inevitable result of Socialist extravagance, combined with another round of experiments in nationalization, municipalization, public accountability, or whatever they choose to call it.

Their whole policy would inevitably undermine the very foundations of that considerable degree of prosperity which it has taken eight years of exertion to build up. To build may have to be the slow and laborious task of years. To destroy can be the thoughtless act of a single day. Let us pray that 8 October is not such a day.

All that we have gained and all the further gains which we look to the Conservative Government to make in the years ahead rest upon the foundation of the country's economic strength. Under Conservative Governments our economy is sound and buoyant, the pound is strong, we are paying our way in the world. Weaken those foundations – as Socialist policies inevitably would – and the whole edifice would be imperilled.

There is another foundation too, which we must never forget. Without peace abroad there can be no prosperity at home. The second point on which the electorate must decide is, as the Prime Minister has said, who is to represent us in the negotiations that will undoubtedly take place in the next months between the West and the Soviets. I am not speaking of a 'Summit' meeting, because there is no certainty that it will take place in the immediate future. For myself, I hold that such a meeting is desirable, and whether or not concrete agreements spring from it, the chances of peace can only be increased by meetings between leaders. The very fact of there being a further peace conference to look forward to, with renewed chances of reaching understanding, means that there is less danger of one side or the other being driven to extreme steps in the meanwhile. For the leaders of the nations of the world to meet each other as they are doing now must be a good thing.

The world faced a dangerous situation last November when what amounted to a six months' ultimatum was served on the West about the future of Berlin. It was vital that more should be learned about the mood and intentions of the Soviet leaders. The Macmillan mission revealed some willingness on the Russian side to negotiate. There followed the conference of Foreign Ministers in Geneva, and now we are having the visit between Mr Khrushchev and President Eisenhower, which has opened even wider paths.

Here let me say that it gave me very great pleasure to meet the American President once again when he was in London the other week. He is a true friend of this country and a champion of the whole free world. We are fortunate to have men of his experience and calibre on the international stage at this time. For we face a period of protracted and complicated negotiations. In this period two things are vital. Firmness of purpose can be accompanied by flexibility of method; but we must avoid all temptation to buy a temporary peace at the price of a surrender of vital interests.

Mr Khrushchev has now made a most striking proposal for disarmament. So far, we know very little about it, except for his brief though most important reference to a plan for total disarmament which occurred in a speech which also covered other matters. We must know more. How is this disarmament to be controlled? For it is on this point that so many past discussions have foundered.

Our own position is clear. We aim at the cessation of nuclear tests as one of the first steps in a balanced programme of disarmament, covering both nuclear and conventional weapons. But there must be effective international control. One-sidedly to deprive ourselves of our arms, and in particular of the nuclear deterrent, will be suicidal.

The years in which I have been concerned in these matters have not caused me to revise my opinion that you are more likely to obtain a hearing for your views if you have some substantial stake in the balance of world power. And these stakes, for good or ill, are still much measured in military language. To strip ourselves of our nuclear weapons without any clearly safeguarded agreement would be greatly to weaken the West, and to deprive us of a voice in the settling of our destinies. By all means let us go forward to disarmament, but let us all go forward together.

Do not think from these words that I mean in any way to diminish from the importance and scope of what Mr Khrushchev has suggested. The goal he envisages is one for which all countries and their leaders must yearn.

To represent us in the talks that may lead us to the fulfilment of our hopes I put my trust in Mr Macmillan. He has behind him at the highest level a most solid background of experience and service to the country in foreign affairs. He and Mr Selwyn Lloyd, who has so ably seconded him, can be accorded great credit for their tenacity of purpose and their patience. These qualities will be needed again and again in the coming months, and if a Conservative Government is returned we could view our representation with sober confidence and high hope.

Whether that would be equally true of another Government, divided among itself on policy, forced time after time to compromise to appease its own extremists, is the question which the country will have to decide on 8 October.

Sir Winston S. Churchill to Emery Reves
(Churchill papers, 2/532)

29 September 1959

My dear Emery,

I was so glad to see your handwriting again. Thank you very much for your letter which we have all read with the greatest interest and sympathy. We are thankful that at any rate you have been spared too much pain, but the immobility must be very hard to bear. I am glad you intend to emulate the President.

Here we are much engaged with the Election. I am making some speeches in my Constituency. I am conducting my campaign from Chartwell where we are still having the most beautiful weather.

With very good wishes to you. I hope that your progress, though it must be slow, will be steady.

Anthony Montague Browne to Sir Winston S. Churchill
(Churchill papers, 2/571)

29 September 1959

When you go to plant the oak tree (and thereby 'lay the foundation stone') of your College at Cambridge on October 17, how do you wish to travel?

By road from Chartwell, it would take you 3¼ hours.

By air from Biggin Hill it would take you approximately half an hour. The charge for chartering an aircraft for this distance, however, would be £60. This would be a Dove similar to the aircraft in which you went to the races at Düsseldorf and Newmarket.[1]

Sir Winston S. Churchill to Lord Beaverbrook
(Beaverbrook papers)

4 October 1959   Chartwell

My dear Max,

It was so kind of you to suggest that I should come to the Capponcina when you are there. If opportunity offers, I would certainly much like to pay you a visit and to add to the many happy days I have spent there in your company.

I have looked again at the reproductions of your pictures in *Time* Magazine. They are very fine and you are much to be congratulated on making this remarkable display available in Canada. It covers a great range, and will give pleasure for many years to come.

I have now drunk the excellent bottle of 1928 champagne which you so kindly brought for me. I enjoyed it much and it does not seem to have lost any of its sparkle, in spite of its great age. Thank you so much for it, and also for your splendid gift of the 1934 and 1947 vintages, which I look forward to drinking.

Sir Winston S. Churchill to Emery Reves
(Churchill papers, 2/532)

14 October 1959

My dear Emery,

It gave me pleasure to receive a letter from you and to know that you are making satisfactory progress. You must certainly take every care not to do too much too quickly. You are very wise to take all precautions.

---

[1] Churchill chose to fly.

Thank you also for sending me the cheque. I trust the recordings will be a success.

The Election has gone very well and I think we can look forward to a period of stability at home.[1]

I look forward to seeing you again.

Sir Winston S. Churchill to Wendy Reves
(Churchill papers, 2/532)

14 October 1959

My dear Wendy,

I was so glad to have good news of Emery, but I was distressed to know that you are still weak and not yourself. I do trust that this will clear up soon.

The Election has given us a majority of a size that is surprising,[2] and which will I think enable us to run our affairs in a stable way for some time to come. I myself am back in the House once more.

Anthony Montague Browne to Sir Winston S. Churchill
(Churchill papers, 2/571)

15 October 1959

I attach below the programme for Cambridge.

Below that is a list of the guests at the luncheon at King's College. You will be sitting on the right of the Provost of King's, Mr Noel Annan,[3] who is one of the most active Trustees. On your other side will be Sir John Cockcroft, the Master of the College.

Lady Churchill will be on the Provost's left, and beyond her Lord Tedder, the Chancellor of the University and another of your Trustees.

You will notice that Mr Frank Cousins and his wife have been asked to the luncheon and ceremony. Mr Cousins is head of the Transport and General Workers Union (Mr Bevin's Union), who gave £50,000 to the College as a memorial to Mr Bevin – you refer to it in your speech. Mr Cousins, as you know, is Chairman of the Trades Union Council and has been on the Left

---

[1] In the British general election of Oct. 8, the Conservative Party was returned to power with 365 seats (49.4% of the vote); Labour won 258 seats (43.8%), the Liberals 6 (5.9%).

[2] The Conservative Government under Harold Macmillan had a majority of 101 over the Liberal and Labour parliamentary parties combined. For details see immediately preceding footnote.

[3] Noël Gilroy Annan, 1916–2000. Commissioned, Intelligence Corps, 1941; Served during WWII. Fellow of King's College, Cambridge, 1944–56; Lecturer in Politics, 1948–66. Provost of King's College, 1956–66; of University College London, 1966–78. Trustee of Churchill College, Cambridge, 1958–76. Baron, 1965.

~~wing of it~~. However, he has been most helpful over the College, as this gift shows.

You will no doubt remember that Mr William Carron[1] of the Amalgamated Engineering Union is one of your Trustees. He will not be present at the luncheon.

Sir Winston S. Churchill: speech
('Winston S. Churchill, His Complete Speeches', volume 8, pages 8704–6)

17 October 1959   Cambridge

CHURCHILL COLLEGE CEREMONY

This is for me a most happy occasion. It is certainly an unusual honour and distinction that a college bearing my name should be added to the ancient and renowned foundations which together form the University of Cambridge. It is seldom easy to graft a new branch on a well-grown tree, and the thanks of my fellow Trustees and myself are much due to the University for the gracious and hospitable reception which they have accorded to this endeavour.

As you are well aware, the outlay for the building and endowment of so large a College must be on a generous scale. It has been matched by the generosity of the contributors. The success of our Appeal bears witness to the farsightedness of those who recognize what the significance of Churchill College could be in the new and challenging era which lies before us. All kinds of people have subscribed. British industry has contributed on a massive scale, and we have been assisted by individuals and small firms as well as by the giants of industry, finance, and commerce. From other quarters too, we have received heartening support. I am able to announce today that the Ford Foundation in America have granted the College a million dollars. It is a princely gift. It is a mark of confidence in what Churchill College can grow to be, and I am sure this confidence will not be misplaced. We are deeply grateful.

Here in Britain, we may also announce today that the Transport and General Workers Union have given fifty thousand pounds in memory of that statesman and patriot, the late Mr Ernest Bevin. Bevin was a man of courage and of vision, with whom I worked in pleasant accord during five arduous years. He never failed his colleagues or his country. I rejoice that, on the initiative of the great trades union he led with so much devotion, his name should be commemorated here. With this generous gift the Library will be built.

---

[1] William John Carron, 1902–69. President, Amalgamated Engineering Union, 1956–67. Director, London Board, Co-operative Printing Society, 1956–68. Director, British Productivity Council, 1957–68. Director, Bank of England, 1963–9. Director, Fairfield Shipbuilding and Engineering Co., Glasgow, 1966–8.

A great deal has already been done. The plans have, I trust, been well and truly laid, and even though still more be needed to complete and endow, we have sufficient to begin our labours with the highest hope and enthusiasm.

The College is fortunate to secure as its first Master that distinguished physicist, Sir John Cockcroft, whose name is known and respected far beyond our own shores.

We are honoured that the Duke of Edinburgh is to be the College Visitor. It is singularly appropriate that His Royal Highness should occupy this position. He has amply shown his interest in the progress of scientific knowledge and the development of technology in this country and the Commonwealth. I hope that he will see our aspirations for Churchill College worthily fulfilled.

The College recalls to me the names of two of my dearest friends: Brendan Bracken, to whom education was of unceasing interest and who bequeathed many of his personal possessions to the College. To his memory the Reading Room is fittingly dedicated. And Lord Cherwell – the Professor – who strove so earnestly and so well to awaken our country to the shortages we faced in the sphere of technology. His name is recorded elsewhere, but his inspiration remains and his memory should be held bright among the scientists of tomorrow.

Perhaps what we seek to achieve here is only a beginning, but I hope that it may also be seen as an example. At any rate throughout the land the wind is blowing in the right direction. The appointment of a Minister of Science (Lord Hailsham) is something that we can all welcome. It is not a party or political matter. More than any other country in the world, Britain must rely on the enterprise and trained ingenuity of her people. The emphasis should be on the word 'trained'. Here I know, of course, that I am preaching to the converted, but this aspect of our affairs cannot be overstated. Since we have neither the massive population, nor the raw materials, nor yet adequate agricultural land to enable us to make our way in the world with ease, we must depend for survival on our brains, on skilled minds that are at least proportionately equal to those in the United States and Soviet Russia.

This is far from being achieved, and even when it is, we shall only have reached a quantitative target. In quality, we should endeavour to outstrip our friends and our rivals as we have done in the past. Let no one believe that the lunar rockets, of which we read in the Press, are merely ingenious bids for prestige. They are manifestations of a formidable advance in technology. As with many vehicles of pure research, their immediate uses may not be apparent. But I do not doubt that they will ultimately reap a rich harvest for those who have the imagination and power to develop them, and to probe ever more deeply into the mysteries of the universe in which we live.

I trust and believe that this College, this seed that we have sown, will grow to shelter and nurture generations who may add most notably to the strength and happiness of our people, and to the knowledge and peaceful progress of the world. 'The mighty oak from an acorn towers; A tiny seed can fill a field with flowers.'

Sir John Cockcroft to Sir Winston S. Churchill
(Churchill papers, 2/571)[1]

18 October 1959

Dear Sir Winston,

I send my personal thanks for the very fine start you gave yesterday to the building of Churchill College. Your speech at the tree planting was very much appreciated and I will have a recording placed in the Bevin Library as the first of its treasures.

Press release
(Churchill papers, 2/571)

18 October 1959

Churchill College, Cambridge, was formally inaugurated on Saturday afternoon when Sir Winston Churchill planted an Oak tree (*Quercus robur*) and a Black Mulberry tree (*Morus nigra*) on the site. Sir Winston travelled to Cambridge in a chartered aircraft from Biggin Hill, accompanied by Lady Churchill. The Chancellor of Cambridge University, Lord Tedder, most of the Trustees of the new College, including the Master, Sir John Cockcroft, and leading representatives of the University and of Industry attended the ceremony (list attached). Sir Winston used a stainless steel spade kindly presented by the Architects, Messrs Richard Sheppard, Robson and Partners. The Provost and Fellows of King's College entertained Sir Winston and Lady Churchill and about 150 other guests to luncheon at King's College before the ceremony.

Two new outstanding donations have just been received, and were announced at the ceremony. As a contribution to an institution devoted to the advancement of science in the name of Sir Winston Churchill, the Ford Foundation has presented the sum of one million dollars to help start the College during the first few years.

The Transport and General Workers Union has decided to give £50,000 to Churchill College to be used in the construction of the College Library in memory of Mr Ernest Bevin after whom it will be named.

[1] This letter was handwritten.

Sir Winston Churchill and the Trustees have accepted both these gifts with the deepest gratification.

Other donations so far subscribed and promised, including a recent generous contribution from the Amalgamated Engineering Union, amount to £3,055,000. Although this sum allows the Trustees to proceed with the building of the College, yet another £1 million is required for the final equipment and for adequate endowment.

The recently formed United States Churchill Foundation propose shortly to launch an appeal with three principal objectives:
1) 'to provide scholarships and fellowships both for American citizens and others at Churchill College;
2) to enable members of Churchill College to attend courses at Universities and Technological institutions in the United States;
3) to help towards the final appeal target.'

The Duke of Edinburgh will be the first Visitor of Churchill College. The Trustees will shortly submit a petition to the Queen in Council for the granting of a Royal Charter.

The preparation of the site will begin this autumn and tenders for the first buildings were invited this week. These will be the flats for married members of the College; they should be completed in less than twelve months. They will be used initially to house Graduate students so that the College will be operating on a small scale at the beginning of the next academic year. The building of the main part of the College will not start till next year. The first Undergraduates are to join the College in October 1961, and the numbers and activities of the College will grow with the completion of each successive stage of construction.

The Architects, Messrs Richard Sheppard, Robson and Partners, are at present engaged in modifying their competition designs for the central block of buildings in order to take account of the new Bevin Library and other benefactions which affect the layout of the College.

Sir Winston S. Churchill to Noël Annan
(Churchill papers, 2/571)

21 October 1959

My dear Annan,

Please accept my very warm thanks for the hospitality which King's College so kindly accorded to us on Saturday. It was a most agreeable occasion which I shall remember with much pleasure. The way in which the University has welcomed the new College is most heartening, and I know how much you have done personally.

Sir Anthony Eden to Sir Winston S. Churchill
(*Churchill papers, 2/571*)

31 October 1959
Personal

My dear Winston,

Thank you so much for your letter. I am so glad that you found the proofs interesting. I hope that the volume as a whole will present the public with a consecutive theme and show that we were faced, and are still, with the same problems as in the 'thirties: dictators in whose word little faith can be placed. I certainly number Nasser among these and I am troubled about the future of Israel, where the Arab boycott seems to be meeting with some success.

This volume is now finished, except for the final reading of proofs, which is due to begin next week. It will be serialised towards the end of January in *The Times* and published at the end of February.

Health has been rather tiresome and I had a second high fever within three weeks, with higher temperatures than at any time since the operation. I contrived to touch 105°. However, I am better again now and we are just hoping they will not return for a while.

We plan to leave for the West Indies in December and hope to be in London next month. We will get into touch and propose ourselves to see you.

Clarissa and I send love to you and Clemmie. We are so glad that the eye operation[1] was completely successful.

Sir Winston S. Churchill: speech
('*Winston S. Churchill, His Complete Speeches*', volume 8, pages 8706–7)

31 October 1959   Woodford

THE WOODFORD STATUE

I am deeply obliged to my old friend, Field Marshal Montgomery, for the very kind things he has said of me and for the graceful way in which he has expressed them. When I consider the war years of his own brilliant achievements and his long career of devoted service to our country, I reflect that of him it may well be said, 'I have built a monument more lasting than bronze.'

It is not easy to speak of a work of art portraying oneself. I should like, nevertheless, to congratulate the Trustees on their choice of such a distinguished young sculptor, and to offer Mr McFall[2] my sincere compliments on his work.

---

[1] On Lady Churchill. See p. 2255 n.2 above.

[2] David Bernard McFall, 1919–88. Educated at Royal College of Art. Master of Sculpture, City and Guilds of London Art School, Lambeth, 1956–75. Created by commission the bronze figure of Sir Winston Churchill located at Woodford Green.

The theme of what I have to say to you is brief. It is one of gratitude to the people of Wanstead and Woodford for the signal honour which you now pay me, and for the way in which you have sustained and supported me during the thirty-five years in which I have had the privilege of representing you in Parliament. I am heartily thankful to you all. This ceremony seems to sum up the many expressions of kindness which my wife and I have received from you over the years.

Thirty-five years. That is more than half my adult life. It is certainly a period of history in which much has been built up and much torn down in this troubled world.

The question we may ask ourselves is how the balance lies between progress and ruin. When we contemplate the squalid and brutal destruction of the last war, man's ingenuity in perfecting the means of his own annihilation, and the jealousy, anxiety, and hatred that consume a large part of the globe, it is easy to give a melancholy answer. Certainly it is far from reassuring to consider the position of much of Asia and Africa. The Middle East flickers with barely repressed violence and enmity. In East Asia vast and ever expanding populations are reaching a critical stage in their development. They are on the move, and none knows whither. In many undeveloped areas of the world former systems of government are being thrown aside, and new nations are rising. We wish them well. We may watch them anxiously and take a justifiable pride in true progress there.

Many of these countries owe their very existence to Great Britain. In war we have defended them at great cost. In peace we have assisted them financially, technically, and with our advisers in every sphere. Above all, we have endeavoured to confer on them the benefits of justice and freedom which we have so long enjoyed ourselves in these islands. Yet amidst this sombre and perplexing scene there is much that is bright.

With all our political differences we in this country are, I think, more united than we have ever been in time of peace. Certainly we may disagree, but I see no hatred. The way ahead is a broad and clear one.

In Western Europe many of the age-old enmities are at last dispersing and the outlook for a closer unity of those who share the common fruit of Western civilization, both here and overseas, is full of promise. There is no reason why these developments should conflict with our ever closer association with the countries of the Commonwealth and the United States. Nor, I believe, should the problems that confront the West in their relations with Soviet Russia and her allies be unsuperable. Some progress has already been made, and the tensions that caused us anxiety have been slackened by meetings between the leaders. I trust that this initiative will be vigorously maintained.

It is not only in the realm of war that science is advancing with giant strides. In the formidable manifestations of the new technology, both in the East and the West, the prospect of man's adventure into the mysteries of the universe in which he lives stirs the imagination.

In all this we in Britain have a great part to play, a leading part. By our courage, our endurance, and our brains we have made our way in the world to the lasting benefit of mankind. Let us not lose heart. Our future is one of high hope. I thank you all for the reception you have accorded me.

Sir Winston S. Churchill to Wendy Reves
(Reves papers)

9 November 1959   Chartwell

My dear Wendy,

You are often in my thoughts. I do trust that Emery is continuing to make good progress, and that you yourself are feeling much better and stronger again now. Such anxiety as you have endured is indeed wearing. I hope that the outlook at Pausaland is becoming daily brighter.

Here, all is well. The new Parliament has taken up its duties, and I go to the House a good deal. We are at Chartwell at the weekends, of course. It has been a wonderful autumn, and the trees here are beautiful.

Sarah is touring in a new play called *The Night Life of a Virile Potato*. It seems to be meeting with considerable success, and we hope very much that it will get to London.

Sir Winston S. Churchill: speech
(Churchill papers, 2/336)

12 November 1959   Harrow School

Thank you very much for your wonderful welcome this evening. We have had a grand performance which lives again like the Songs that we have spoken of in the past. We have had indeed a memorable occasion, and everyone who has been present and taken part in it – and I have thought that there are not many who have not taken some part or other in it – will feel that they have perpetuated a glorious memory which will long continue to give strength to those who have it.

Anthony Montague Browne to Sir Winston S. Churchill
(Churchill papers, 2/179)

16 November 1959

DR ADENAUER'S VISIT

Dr Adenauer arrives on Tuesday and leaves on Thursday. He is not accompanied by any of his Family. The purpose of his visit is to have confidential talks with the Prime Minister and the Foreign Secretary.

The Foreign Office tell me that one of our main hopes is to disperse the suspicion which they think Dr Adenauer entertains towards Mr Macmillan personally. Apparently Dr Adenauer thinks that Mr Macmillan leans towards 'disengagement', i.e. leaving a vacuum in Europe between the West and the Soviets. He also feels that Mr Macmillan is too soft in his dealings with the Russians and too keen to compromise.

The Foreign Office also say that Dr Adenauer is apt too much to discount Britain as a whole and to feel that in the Western Alliance only the opinion of Washington and Paris is of importance.

The Foreign Office hope that you may be able to express yourself in general terms towards convincing Dr Adenauer (a) that Mr Macmillan is entirely robust in his attitude towards the Russians, but seeks only step by step arrangements to lessen tension, and (b) that he does not favour disengagement as such.

The Foreign Office also hope that you will urge on Dr Adenauer the continuing importance of Great Britain on the Continent of Europe and the danger that the Continentals would run in feeling that they could form any lasting separate arrangements without us.

Jawaharlal Nehru to Sir Winston S. Churchill
(Churchill papers, 2/444)

17 November 1959　　　　　　　　　　　　　　　　　　　　　　　New Delhi

On the occasion of Sir Winston Churchill's 85th birthday, I should like to send my greetings and good wishes to him and my tribute to one of the great men of our age. Sir Winston and I were opposed to each other on the political plane for long years, and we did not agree with each other about some matters which were of vital importance to us in India. But, since the question of India's independence was settled by agreement and to the mutual advantage of both India and the United Kingdom, those old differences have not come in the way of our coming closer to one another. I consider it a privilege to have his friendship over which the shadow of the past does not fall.

Wendy Reves to Sir Winston S. Churchill
(Churchill papers, 2/532)

19 November 1959

Dear, dear Sir Winston,

Wow . . . !!! I am very long, indeed, in writing to you but things have been very bad for me and you must forgive me <u>this</u> time for my <u>badness</u> in neglecting to write! You surely know, by now and after all of these faithful years, that whether I write or not – you are never out of my thoughts – so there!!

We read, with anxiety that you were indisposed and as you know – we telephoned yesterday to find out the facts from Anthony. I felt elated to hear that you had just received Adenauer and that you were better. . . . I worry much. Silly me!! I should know, by now, that you are stronger than all . . . an exception to every rule and it is a joyful thought . . . if only I would think clearly more often! (Ha!)

I have read of all of the bad weather in England but I must tell you that here it has been perhaps, even worse.

(Here I was stopped in mid air by mommie's accident to her legs.)

Floris Chocolates Ltd to Lady Churchill
(Churchill papers, 2/444)

23 November 1959

Dear Lady Churchill,

I thank you for your telephone message and understand that the cake has to be delivered on Monday 30th November between 9 and 10 a.m.

The cake is 22 inches in diameter and the Album is the size of a telephone directory.

The Album contains some 120 letters of good wishes from all over the world, signed by Presidents of States, Prime Ministers, Governor Generals, Administrators Ambassadors etc. Among the many beautiful letters addressed to Sir Winston, I wish to mention just ten names, sent to us, to be lodged in the Album.

Each Country has contributed one ounce of material which is baked into the Cake. I enclosed a list of the Countries, Nations and Territories from where contributions of material were received.

The stamps from letters and parcels were made into little flags and now these adorn the Cake.

There is quite a lot of material left, as the contributions, in many cases, were much more than one ounce. We have undertaken to make the surplus material into Christmas Cakes and to send these to a Children's Hospital.

The elaborate work to create this Global Cake started back in July and it is regretted indeed that this wonderful display of the rare materials, sent with so much enthusiasm from every part of the world, as a tribute to Sir Winston, will not be enjoyed and not even seen by him.

The envelopes from exotic places with the stamps on them is in itself a rare sight.

I would be pleased if these would be at least inspected by someone and to take all of it or part of it away, as bottles of spirit etc. and many other such ingredients are not suitable for children's Christmas Cakes. Perhaps this may be done after the Birthday.

Sir Winston S. Churchill to President Charles de Gaulle
(Churchill papers, 2/523)

26 November 1959
Private and Personal

My dear President,

I am indeed obliged to you for your thought in sending me a specially printed copy of *Le Salut*. I look forward with great interest to reading it and to renewing my memories of our association in the War.

I follow with close attention your work in the great task you have undertaken. There is much to cheer us in the international scene, and notably I send you my fervent good wishes for the success of your initiative in Algeria.

In Europe I trust that our two countries may not diverge after all we have been through together. It would be a tragedy if the minor differences which have arisen on matters of trade were to lead to real divisions of opinion on larger matters. I am convinced that you share my anxiety over the dangers that would arise from any feeling that Britain could be set aside, and I was very glad to know that the recent conversations between our Foreign Secretaries have gone well.

With renewed thanks for your thought of me, and all good wishes for the future, I remain,

Yours very sincerely

Konrad Adenauer to Sir Winston S. Churchill
(Churchill papers, 2/443)

27 November 1959
Unofficial Translation

My dear Sir Winston,

On the occasion of your 85th birthday I should like to send you my most cordial congratulations. May you be able to assist your people, Europe and the Free World as a whole with your wisdom and experience for many years to come. I recall with vivid emotion our first meeting in The Hague and the words with which you then addressed my countrymen. After all, you were the first after this terrible war had ended who threw out the challenge for European community and for the unification of our old continent. In very difficult years you have thus rendered unforgettable services not only to your country but to all free countries through your personal achievements and your never-failing courage.

During my last visit to London I was very pleased to be able to talk to you and to learn your opinion on the problems which are of our common concern.

I hope that you will enjoy the enclosed engraving which depicts the siege of Bonn by your great ancestor, the Duke of Marlborough.

I wish you from all my heart many happy returns. May I ask you to remember me to Lady Churchill?

With most cordial regards

Wendy Reves to Sir Winston S. Churchill
(Churchill papers, 2/532)[1]

29 November 1959

My dear –,

I am enclosing a letter that I began two days ago. I was already very late then in writing and now I am so late that it is time to say Merry Christmas almost!! As I was writing to you two days ago – mommie was working in the garden and had a terrible accident and I was stopped in mid-air and mid-letter. A tremendous rock fell on her left leg, which was outstretched at that moment (all of the walls have been falling from the heavy rains that we have had!) we had a terrible time in getting her well enough to walk and to sail home and I fear that I once again neglected you – alas!

However, with treatment of massage and hot air pressure, she was able to sail on schedule, which was Thursday. I am feeling very lonely without her!

The weather has been beastly and except for a very few shining days we have had torrents of rain and the garden is flooded and I am most discouraged – poor lamb!

Emery is well on his way to recovery – it is, however, a slow and tedious process and we can only hope that we may be able to travel to a sunnie spot before too long. We cannot know until another series of tests are given with good results – we dangle in the air at the moment! Would it not be fun if you and Lady Churchill could come with us to a glamorous and sunny place for

[1] This letter was handwritten.

a three weeks holiday and then back to good ole 'Pausalaud' for one more of our happy times together????

Tomorrow is your birthday, dear, and I know it will be a joyous one – I cannot believe that you will be eighty-five – so young in heart you are to me. I dare to send you a hundred kisses for this occasion and to tell you that your real present awaits you here. I hope to lure you back with that! (Ha!)

Such love I send you, dear Sir Winston, you must reuse in every line of this letter and also much love to Lady Churchill and the 'family'.

Your Devoted

House of Commons: Oral Answers
(Hansard)

30 November 1959

Mr Hugh Gaitskell (Leeds, South). I hope that it will be in order, Mr Speaker, if I offer to the right hon. Gentleman the Member for Woodford (Sir W. Churchill) our warm congratulations and best wishes and affectionate greetings on his eighty-fifth birthday.

The Secretary of State for the Home Department (Mr R. A. Butler). May I support the Leader of the Opposition, Sir, and, on behalf of the whole House, including the right hon. Gentleman and his hon. Friends, offer our most heartfelt good wishes to my right hon. Friend?

Sir Winston Churchill (Woodford). May I say that I most gratefully and eagerly accept both forms of compliment.

Sir Winston S. Churchill to Konrad Adenauer
(Churchill papers, 2/443)

5 December 1959

My dear Chancellor,

I am most grateful to you for your delightful gift. It was indeed interesting to see this print of the siege of Bonn by my ancestor. I trust the citizens do not bear me any inherited illwill!

I was greatly touched by your letter[1] in which you so eloquently expressed such very complimentary and agreeable thoughts. I, too, very much enjoyed your visit to London, and I hope that we shall have another opportunity soon for a discussion.

---

[1] Reproduced above (pp. 2275–6).

Sir Winston S. Churchill to Lord Beaverbrook
(Beaverbrook papers)

5 December 1959

My dear Max,

How very kind of you to give me such a splendid gift of champagne. Wine of that year is getting rarer and rarer, and I was touched by your thought of me.

I much enjoyed our luncheon on Monday.

Sir Winston S. Churchill to Jawaharlal Nehru
(Churchill papers, 2/444)

21 December 1959

My dear Prime Minister,

It was most kind of you to address to me such an agreeable message on my Birthday,[1] and of India to send a contribution to the remarkable cake which I was given on that occasion.[2]

I warmly reciprocate your good wishes, and my thoughts are with you in your many burdens and responsibilities.

---

[1] Reproduced above (p. 2273).
[2] See letter from Floris Chocolates Ltd, reproduced above (pp. 2274–5).

1960

Anthony Montague Browne to Sir Winston S. Churchill
(Churchill papers, 2/343)

10 January 1960

Please see Jock's letter. He has since spoken to me on the telephone, and we wondered if you would like to ask the Prime Minister, in confidence, his feelings about Lord Lambton?[1] Not to have Lord Lambton is perhaps a rebuff to Lord Beaverbrook, one of the oldest members of the Club, who put him forward?[2]

Anthony Montague Browne to John Colville
(Churchill papers, 2/343)

10 January 1960
Private

I showed your letter of January 9 to Sir Winston and also put to him a brief note suggesting that he should write to the Prime Minister to seek his feelings about Lambton, because, to my mind, it might be rather a rebuff to Lord Beaverbrook to turn him down out of hand.

Sir Winston has said that he wants Alan Hodge and that he does not want either John Wyndham[3] or Lambton. He was not disposed to hear any

---

[1] Antony Claud Frederick Lambton, 1922–2006. MP (Cons.) for Berwick upon Tweed, 1951–73. Parliamentary Under-Secretary of State, MoD, 1970–3. Personal Private Secretary to Foreign Secretary, 1955–7. Author of several books including *Snow and Other Stories* (1983), *Elizabeth and Alexandra* (1985) and *Pig and Other Stories* (1990).

[2] As a new member of the Other Club.

[3] John Edward Reginald Wyndham, 1920–72. Private Secretary to Minister Resident, Algiers, 1941–5. Married, 1947, his second cousin once removed Pamela Wyndham-Quin. Private Secretary to the PM (Harold Macmillan), 1957–63. Baron Egremont, 1963. Succeeded his father as 6th Baron Leconfield, 1967.

arguments either about the embarrassing position of Lord Winterton[1] or the rebuff to Lord Beaverbrook. So there we are.

Anthony Montague Browne to Sir Norman Brook
(Churchill papers, 2/531)

16 January 1960
Private and Confidential

Sir Winston has asked me to thank you so much for all the trouble you took in writing to him from Lagos. He was very interested to read what you had to say.

The Press in London have been very much stirred up by what they believe to be Sir Winston's imminent death, and in consequence Monte Carlo is full of journalists. However, I am glad to be able to tell you that on the whole Sir Winston seems much better. He had a day or two in bed with a mild recurrence of the infection he suffered in London (liver or gall bladder), but is now about again and, apart from melancholy and boredom, is more alert than I have seen him for a long time. Of course, one may be proved wrong tomorrow, but it does not look like it at the moment.

The weather has been deplorable for the last week, and there are not sufficient entertaining people down here to provide the little visits that Sir Winston welcomes more out here than in England. Lord Beaverbrook has left, but Onassis is very attentive, and Sir Winston is fond of him and amused by him. Incidentally, the Press reports that Sir Winston is Onassis' guest are incorrect. Sir Winston pays his way.

Lady Churchill is in excellent spirits and health, and the 'penthouse' in which we live on the top of the Hotel de Paris is very agreeable in spite or because of its featureless luxury.

I will speak on the telephone or telegraph to Stephen on February 2, so that he can telegraph you a report. There is no date yet set for our return to England, but I think that Sir Winston may possibly move up to stay with the Reves at Roquebrune in February which will release me.

I do hope all goes well with you.

---

[1] Edward Turnour, 1883–1962. Educated at Eton and New College, Oxford. MP (Cons.) for Horsham, 1904–51. Succeeded his father as 6th Earl Winterton, 1907; as an Irish peer, continued to sit in the House of Commons. Served at Gallipoli, in Palestine and in Arabia, 1915–18. Under-Secretary of State for India, 1922–4, 1924–9. Chancellor of the Duchy of Lancaster, 1937–9. Paymaster-General, 1939. Chairman, Inter-Governmental Committee for Refugees, 1938–45. Father of the House of Commons, 1945–51.

Note: books for Sir Winston on cruise
(Churchill papers, 1/153)

March 1960

The Bell of Rye	P. Lindsay
Konigsmark	A. E. W Mason
Call of the Wild	J. London
The Man Who Went Back	Warwick Deeping
Uther & Igraine	" "
The Pursuer	Louis Golding
No Price for Freedom	Philip Gibbs
Brothers Karamazov	Dostoievsky
Sard Harker	John Masefield
Conquer	" "
Judas	Eric Linklater
Secret Battle	A. P. Herbert
The King's Mirror	Anthony Hope
Mansfield Park	Jane Austen
Action at Aquila	Hervey Allen
The Borgia Testament	Nigel Balchin
Arrow of Gold	Joseph Conrad
Master of Ballantrae	R. L. Stevenson
A Gun for Sale	Graham Greene
National Velvet	Enid Bagnold
In the Wilderness	Sigrid Undset
Dalliance and Strife	F. Bancroft
Beatrix	Balzac

John Stow[1] to Sir Winston S. Churchill
(Churchill papers, 1/153)

22 March 1960   Barbados

Dear Sir Winston,

    I write on behalf of the Government and people of the loyal and ancient Island of Barbados to let you know how honoured this Island has been to have you and Lady Churchill and your party within our shores during the past two days.

    Your visit to Bridgetown and your drive through the streets has given

---

[1] John Montague Stow, 1911–79. Commissioner of Saint Lucia, 1947–53. CMG, 1950. Chief Secretary, Jamaica, 1955–9. KCMG, 1959. Governor and C-in-C, Barbados, 1959–66. GCMG, 1966. KCVO, 1966. Governor-General, Barbados, 1966–7.

intense joy and satisfaction to thousands of people here and will long be remembered especially by the school children.

The people of Barbados (known as Little England) are intensely loyal to the Throne and the spontaneous enthusiasm which was shown today reflects their admiration of you, Sir, as the embodiment of the fighting spirit of Britain.

May I wish you and Lady Churchill a safe voyage to England and may I respectfully ask you to accept the warm good wishes of us all.

Sir Winston S. Churchill to Lord Beaverbrook
(Beaverbrook papers)

20 April 1960   Chartwell

My dear Max,

Thank you so much for your letter of the 18th, and for your promise to give me the photograph from the *Daily Express* which I should very much like to see.

I cannot accept your offer of the house. I am tied up here and my plans are still vague. Owing to winning a £6,000 race yesterday I have moved into the Derby sphere, which I cannot desert, so I cannot take your most attractive proposal. Good fortune ties me by the legs, but I shall look forward to seeing you at the end of this month and I hope you will find a day or two for lunch or dinner. I am so glad you have conquered the return of asthma.

Clemmie was very pleased to get your message.

Harold Macmillan to Randolph S. Churchill
(Churchill papers, 2/619)

22 April 1960

Dear Randolph,

I have just read your *Life of Lord Derby*. I feel I must write to tell you how admirably you have handled the whole period. Your book constitutes in my opinion an absolutely first class account of the politics of some thirty or forty years. You have used very skilfully the figure of Lord Derby on which to hang this admirably written and very well documented work. I congratulate you most sincerely.

PS. I dined with your father two nights ago and thought him pretty well. I told him my view about your book which pleased him very much.[1]

---

[1] It was Randolph's *Life of Lord Derby* that persuaded Churchill to allow Randolph to write his official biography. See letter of May 23, reproduced below (p. 2285).

Anthony Montague Browne to Major-General John Hamilton[1]
(Churchill papers, 2/541)

5 May 1960
Private

Thank you for your letter of May 4.[2] It now seems rather unlikely that Sir Winston will be in London on July 13, but I will let you know definitely as soon as possible.

I discussed the bust question with Sir Winston and Lady Churchill. They both agree that one of Nemon's works would be best. I think that Sir Winston himself likes the one that the Queen has at Windsor, and Lady Churchill feels that the one at Sedbergh is the best. No doubt, if it is decided to have one of Nemon's works, the best thing would be to go to his Studio and examine the many studies he made of Sir Winston.

The suggestion about Graham Sutherland was <u>not</u> smiled on at all. Neither Sir Winston nor Lady Churchill ever liked it. Speaking for myself, it seems to me to fall down completely as a portrait, whatever its merits may be as a work of art. In addition to this, it is a singularly disagreeable sepia colour, and I would not call it an ornament to any wall.

I am afraid that there is no question of Sir Winston selling any of his pictures, and at the moment he is inclined to keep as many as possible around him. However, I think that if it is intimated to him that his fellow Trustees would much like one of his pictures, this might be arranged, and something more might possibly be forthcoming later.

First editions of Sir Winston's books are extremely hard to come by. He himself has not got a complete collection of them, I do not think. The only way to obtain them is to put an order in the hands of someone of repute in the book trade, perhaps Mr Wilson of Bumpus,[3] and ask him to cast the net. This usually produces the desired results in the long run.

If it were not first editions you seek, I have little doubt that Sir Winston would himself be able to help.

I am putting all this on paper in case we do not meet when you are in London.

---

[1] John Robert Crosse Hamilton, 1906–85. Educated at Royal Military Academy and Caius College, Cambridge. 2nd Lt, RE, 1925. On active service, WWII, 1939–45. Acting Brig., 1947. Lt-Col., 1948. Col., 1950. Maj.-Gen., 1956. CoS, HQ Malaya Command, 1955–6. Director of Military Operations, War Office, 1956–9. Retired, 1959. Bursar, Churchill College, Cambridge, 1959–72.

[2] Hamilton's letter contained four points: a notice of the 13 July 1960 meeting of the Churchill College trustees; a request for Sir Winston's opinion of which bust and portrait of him the College should display; a request for Sir Winston to donate or purchase one or two of his paintings to the College; and a request for a complete set of Sir Winston's works, preferably first editions.

[3] John Gideon Wilson, 1876–1963. Well-known London bookseller. Managing Director of J. & E. Bumpus Ltd, Oxford St, London, 1941–59. Vice-President of the Council, Royal Society for the Encouragement of Arts, Manufactures and Commerce, 1945–55. Member, Library Society, 1947–63. CBE, 1948. Author of *The Business of Bookselling* (1930).

Anthony Montague Browne to Stanley Martin[1]
(*Churchill papers, 2/511*)

10 May 1960

Many thanks for the note on President Ayub Khan[2] which I now return to you.

The President, accompanied by his military secretary, called on Sir Winston yesterday and stayed for 35 minutes. The conversation was of a general nature about the world political situation.

The President said that in his view Russia and China might ultimately fall out, but it would not be until China's industrial development was on a par with Russia's, and this could not happen for forty years or so. Meanwhile, he thought that Chinese expansionism would lie southwards, perhaps even as far as Australia. He thought there was a strong case for arming Germany and Japan to the greatest extent possible so that they could act in some sense as guardians of the no-man's-land (sic) that lay on either side of the Communist bloc.

Turning to India, the President said that Mr Nehru had taken the view that China was India's unalterable friend and that Pakistan was a perpetual foe. This had now been proved wrong, but Mr Nehru did not seem to be really ready to settle differences with Pakistan, so that their two armies could 'look outward instead of inward'.

The President said that he had hoped for some small conciliatory gesture from South Africa. He fully realised that the situation there could not be changed rapidly, but he much regretted that Mr Louw[3] should be proving so rigid.

I am sending a copy of this letter to Samuel[4] in the Foreign Office.

---

[1] Stanley William Frederick Martin, 1934–. Asst Private Secretary to Foreign Secretary, 1959–62. 1st Secretary, Canberra, 1962–4; Kuala Lumpur, 1964–7. Associate Head of Protocol Dept, FCO, 1986–92. Author of *The Order of Merit, One Hundred Years of Matchless Honour* (2006) and *Honouring Commonwealth Citizens* (2007).

[2] Mohammad Ayub Khan, 1907–74. Educated at Aligarh Muslim University and British Royal Military College, Sandhurst. 2nd Lt,14th Punjab Rgt, 1928. C-in-C, Pakistan Army, 1951–8. President of Pakistan, 1958–69. Minister of Defence, 1958–66. Minister of Interior, 1965.

[3] Eric Hendrik Louw, 1890–1968. South African MP for Beaufort West, 1924, 1938. Trade Commissioner in US and Canada, 1925–9. High Commissioner in London, 1929–30. Minister of Economic Affairs, 1948–55. Minister of Finance, 1955–7. Minister of Foreign Affairs, 1957–63.

[4] Adrian Christopher Ian Samuel, 1915–2010. Known as 'Ian'. Served in RAF during WWII. HM Foreign Service: 1st Secretary, 1947; Counsellor, 1956. CMG, 1959. Principal Private Secretary to Secretary of State, 1959–63. CVO, 1963. Minister, HM Embassy, Madrid, 1963–5.

Sir Winston S. Churchill to Randolph S. Churchill
(Churchill papers, 2/619)

23 May 1960
Private and Confidential

My dear Randolph,

I have reflected carefully on what you said. I think that your biography of Derby is a remarkable work, and I should be happy that you should write my official biography when the time comes. But I must ask you to defer this until after my death.

I would not like to release my papers piece-meal, and I think that you should wait for the time being and then get all your material from my own Archives and from the Trust. In any case I do not want anything to be published until at least five years after my death.

Randolph S. Churchill to Sir Winston S. Churchill
(Churchill papers, 2/619)

24 May 1960

Dearest Papa,

Your letter has made me proud and happy. Since I first read your life of your father, thirty-five years ago when I was a boy of fourteen at Eton, it has always been my greatest ambition to write your life. And each year that has passed since this ambition first started in my mind, has nurtured it as your heroic career has burgeoned.

When the time comes, you may be sure that I shall lay all else aside and devote my declining years exclusively, to what will be a pious task, fascinating and I suppose, a remunerative task.

Thank you again from the bottom of my heart for a decision which, apart from what I have already said, adds a good deal to my self-esteem and will, I trust, enable me to do honour in filial fashion, to your extraordinarily noble and wonderful life.

Your loving son,
Randolph

PS. Last time I was at Chartwell, you said you would like to see the letter[1] which Harold wrote me about my Derby book. I enclose a copy.

---

[1] Reproduced above (p. 2282).

Anthony Montague Browne to Ian Samuel
(*Churchill papers, 2/508*)

9 July 1960
Confidential

I do not think that cocktail party diplomatic conversation is usually worth repeating, but the following may be of interest.

I met recently a member of the Soviet Embassy one Ivan Glasgov (?). He apparently knew me by name and told me that he had seen in the Press that Sir Winston Churchill had been considering visiting Leningrad but had cancelled it. Was this true? I said it was. Mr Glasgov said what a pity, because the Russians would have given Sir Winston 'a wonderful welcome'. I said that after the breakdown of the Summit and notably the way in which Sir Winston's friend President Eisenhower and our ally America had been subjected to gross abuse, it was rather difficult for Sir Winston to pay a friendly visit. Mr Glasgov said that the Russians were simple people and reacted violently. How would we like it if the Russians flew aeroplanes over us and then said that they were going to go on doing so? I made the conventional rejoinders about not breaking up the Summit, the President's undertaking that there would be no more flights, and so forth. Mr Glasgov expressed the hope that Sir Winston would come to Russia another time, and we parted.

I am sending a copy of this letter to Philip de Zulueta.[1]

Michael Creswell to John Selwyn Lloyd
(*Churchill papers, 1/152*)

16 July 1960 British Embassy
Confidential Belgrade
No. 77

Sir,

I have the honour to report that on July 14 Sir Winston and Lady Churchill, travelling on board Mr Onassis' yacht, *Christina*,[2] called at the port of Split in order to pay a visit to President Tito and Madame Broz.[3]

2. Owing to the coincidence of Sir Winston's cruise with the state visit to Yugoslavia of the Sudanese President,[4] it proved a little difficult to dovetail the

---

[1] Philip de Zulueta, 1925– 89. Private Secretary to Ambassador Sir David Kelly, 1950–2; to PM Sir Anthony Eden, 1955–7; to PM Harold Macmillan, 1957–63; to PM Sir Alec Douglas-Home, 1963–4.

[2] The fifth *Christina* cruise, to the Adriatic and Eastern Mediterranean, took place between July 14 and Aug. 3.

[3] Jovanka Budisavljević, 1924–2013. Married, 1952, Josip Broz Tito. First Lady of Yugoslavia, 1953–80.

[4] El Ferik Ibrahim Abboud, 1990–83. Commissioned in Egyptian Army, 1918–25; Sudan Defence

arrangements. At one time it had been hoped that President Tito would be able to receive him and Lady Churchill on the island of Brioni, but this proved impossible owing to the timing. A rendezvous at Split was, however, arranged on the day on which President Tito would be there at the end of the visit of General Abboud, and Sir Winston and Lady Churchill were received in the President's villa on the coast outside the town, off which the *Christina* anchored at 12 noon.

3. The party was greeted by a representative of the President's personal staff, by Her Majesty's Consul and by myself, and later by the Secretary-General of the President's household and by the Deputy Chief of the Yugoslav Naval staff, who accompanied them in the launch of their visit to the villa. After a tea party ashore, Sir Winston and Lady Churchill, accompanied by myself and my wife and by Mr and Mrs Montague Browne, returned to the yacht where they and Mr Onassis shortly afterwards received President Tito and Madame Broz and various members of his staff for a cocktail party. The President was then taken round the ship, in which he showed great interest.

4. President Tito's reception of Sir Winston was cordial in the extreme and he was obviously extremely touched to be able again to meet Sir Winston, whom he had not seen since his own state visit to London in 1953. Their conversation was concerned principally with war-time memories; and current topics were only touched upon lightly. In answer to a question from Sir Winston, Tito said that he was on the whole an optimist as regards the world situation, as he was convinced that none of the Great Powers would take it upon themselves to cause the world cataclysm which would result from a war with modern weapons. He said that the Yugoslav Army was powerful and well-equipped, but added, somewhat regretfully I thought, that they had no nuclear weapons. As regards the situation in the Congo, Tito quoted a remark by President Abboud on the situation there to the effect that order must be restored in the Congo at once, a sentiment with which he appeared to agree. It is encouraging to note that both the Sudanese President and Tito seem to be unaffected by current Soviet propaganda on this subject.

5. I am quite sure that Sir Winston's visit, coming at this time, was an excellent opportunity – of which he made full use – for President Tito to show his sympathy and friendship for Great Britain. It came in the middle of a long series of state visits from Yugoslavia's uncommitted friends, and the President has already received the Heads of State of Indonesia,[1] the UAR and

---

Force, 1925–64. Served with British Army in North Africa during WWII. Cdr, Sudan Defence Force, 1949; C-in-C, 1956. After overthrowing civilian government, Abboud led the new military government as President, 1958–64. Dissolved his government in 1964.

[1] Kusno Sosrodihardjo, 1901–70. Also known as Sukarno. Imprisoned in a Dutch jail in Bandung for opposing colonialism, 1929–31. Exiled to Flores and Sumatra, 1933–42. Led Indonesian forces under Japanese rule, 1942. Declared Indonesia's independence and served as its first President, 1945–67.

the Sudan, and expects later this year the Kings of Nepal[1] and Afghanistan.[2] Although for obvious reasons he concentrates the emphasis of his publicity upon these visits, he is no less anxious, I think, to show that he has not forgotten his old friends.

Sir Winston S. Churchill to John Colville
(*Churchill papers, 2/343*)

11 August 1960

My dear Jock,

Thank you for your letter about the Other Club. I would like to consider further the financial difficulties of the Club before I give you my views. Anthony has put forward the following suggestion, but I have not adopted it. I should however be glad of your views on it: 'A circular should be sent to all the Members of the Club telling them its financial difficulties. All Members should be asked to contribute whatever they see fit. The richer Members would no doubt contribute more, but the list of contributions would not be published and no-one would therefore be embarrassed.'

I have considered the list of new members. I should be quite willing to support a somewhat shorter list, and if you think it would be desirable, consult the Prime Minister on it.

 Duke of Devonshire[3]
 Mr Peter Thorneycroft
 Mr John Profumo
 Lord Rothschild[4]
 Duke of Northumberland[5]

---

[1] Mahendra Bir Bikram Shah Dev, 1920–72. Born in Kathmandu, Nepal. King of Nepal, 1956–72. Staged a coup in 1960, dissolving the parliament and suspending the constitution. Promulgated new constitution in 1962.

[2] Mohammed Zahir Shah, 1914–2007. Married, 1931, Humaira Begum: eight children. Assumed throne after father's assassination. Last King of Afghanistan, 1933–73. Renounced his rule when his cousin Mohammed Daoud Khan staged a coup and established a republican government, 1973. Lived in exile in Italy, 1973–2002.

[3] Andrew Robert Buxton Cavendish, 1920–2004. Commissioned, Coldstream Guards, 1940. Served in Italy during WWII (MC, 1944). Married, 1941, Deborah Mitford. Maj., 1945. Succeeded as 11th Duke of Devonshire, 1950. Under-Secretary of State for Commonwealth Relations, 1960–2. Minister of State for Commonwealth Relations, 1962–4.

[4] Nathaniel Mayer Victor Rothschild, 1910–90. Married, 1933, Barbara Judith Hutchinson (div. 1945); 1946, Teresa Georgina Mayor. 3rd Baron Rothschild, 1937. Served in military intelligence during WWII, 1939–45. American Legion of Merit and Bronze Star, 1948. Director, BOAC, 1946–58. Research Vice-Chairman, Shell, 1961–3; Chairman, 1963–70.

[5] Hugh Algernon Percy, 1914–88. Educated at Eton College and Christ Church, Oxford. 10th Duke of Northumberland, 1940. Lord-in-Waiting to the King, May–July 1945. Married, 1946, Elizabeth Scott. KStJ, 1957. 9th Lord Percy, 1957. KG, 1959. Chancellor, Northumberland University, 1964–88. Lord Steward of the Household, 1973–88.

Mr Ted Heath
Sir John Wheeler Bennett[1]
Sir Humphrey De Trafford

I agree that November 3 would be a good date and that the Prime Minister should be asked to be in the Chair.

I look forward to seeing you here next week.

Sir Winston S. Churchill to Wendy Reves
(Churchill papers, 2/532)

15 August 1960

Would you and Emery like me to come and stay with you on Tuesday September the 6th for about ten days. Much want to see you both.

Emery Reves to Sir Winston S. Churchill
(Churchill papers, 2/532)

21 August 1960

My dear Sir Winston,

Your telegram suggesting to come to Pausaland on the 6th September was a great surprise for us. Since last winter when you declined our repeated and even persistent invitation and went to the Hotel de Paris, we have been convinced that you had decided not to come back to us. We could understand that cruises had a greater attraction to you than our villa, but we could not interpret your decision to stay at a hotel rather than at Pausaland in any other way than that we had done something, or behaved in a manner which prevented you from returning to us.

This was a sad conclusion we had to draw, but no matter how painful, 'facts are better than dreams'. . . . Our, perhaps foolish, dream was that during the years 1956, 1957, and 1958, when you spent a third of each year at Pausaland, we had become friends. Both Wendy and I are devoted and dedicated to the ideal of friendship which is for us the only real joy in life.

You cannot imagine how shocked we were when two years ago we suddenly

---

[1] John Wheeler-Bennett, 1902–75. Asst Publicity Secretary, League of Nations Union, 1923–4. Director of Information Service on International Affairs, Royal Institute of International Affairs, London, 1924–30. Head of NY Office of British Political Warfare Mission in the US, 1942–4. Attached to British Prosecuting Team at War Criminal Trials, Nuremberg, 1946. OBE, 1946. Lecturer in International Politics, New College, Oxford, 1946–50. Fellow of St Antony's College, Oxford, 1950–7. CMG, 1953. Governor, Radley College, 1955–67. Fellow of the Royal Society of Literature, 1958. FBA, 1972. Published 18 books including *The Nemesis of Power* (1953), *King George VI, His Life and Reign* (1958) and *The History Makers, Leaders and Statesmen of The 20th Century* (1973).

remarked that all kinds of intrigues started destroying this friendship and a few months later we realized that these forces had succeeded in destroying what was a happy and lovely companionship.

It is not possible for me to describe the humiliations and sufferings we had to endure which left deep marks both in Wendy and in me. During the past two years Wendy has suffered deeply and dangerously with mental depressions. There is a certain way of disregarding other people's feelings which drive sensitive human beings to the border of insanity. I am fully aware that all of this was not intended, and that you were a victim, perhaps even more than we were.

During my long life I developed the capacity to end a big cry in laughter and today I can only smile at the past two years. How childish and unnecessary all those intrigues were, how easy it would have been to maintain our beautiful relationship and to add to it anything that might have attracted you! But Wendy is not yet capable to master a deep emotional stress and her wounds are still open. She is a different woman, disillusioned and unbelieving. The doctors warned me most seriously to let her live a quiet life and to protect her from any possible emotional stress.

You must believe me that all this makes me heartbroken and terribly unhappy. I pray that the 'Pausaland atmosphere' will return, that all this nightmare will one day be forgotten and that you will enjoy again, together with us, the peace and privacy of Pausaland. But this can only return gradually, and I am very much afraid that if we precipitate matters, you may be disappointed. I want you to find here, when you return, the old and happy atmosphere and not a strained and unhappy one.

I sincerely hope that this will be possible. Should we not be able to defeat the intrigues that so unnecessarily separated us, then I am anxious to preserve the memories of our association during the years 1955–58. After all, what does one keep in life as time passes? A certain number of memories. . . . I do not know what memories you have of those years, but mine are unforgettable. It was a tremendous happiness for me to be able to put at your disposal a home, a garden, a piece of sunny sky, a fireplace, Wendy's devotion – which contributed so much to your recovery after your illness and retirement. And for all this you repaid me bountifully with your incomparable company. This memory I cherish more than anything and I shall not permit anyone to destroy it.

Please forgive me for pouring out my heart to you. Probably it is a mistake. But only sincerity and frankness may dissipate all the clouds of misunderstanding and bring back the pleasures of our old friendship.

Wendy must undergo medical examinations in Paris between the 4th and 12th September. This date was fixed last June. We may have to stay longer there but, if all goes well, we shall return to Roquebrune the middle of the month. In October we are planning to go to New York. So this year, unfortunately, I cannot invite you, but I hope that if you will spend the months of

September–October at Capponcina, or some other place on the Riviera, you will come to Pausaland as frequently as possible. And . . . And I do hope that after this we shall be able to arrange a new reunion at Pausaland during the winter.

I am longing to see you and trust that we shall soon meet on the Cote d'Azur. Should you not come down in September, I would come to London, if you will allow me to pay you a visit.[1]

General Lord Ismay to Sir Winston S. Churchill
(Churchill papers, 2/526)

20 September 1960

My dear Sir Winston,

It is wonderful news to hear that you have accepted the invitation of the *Daily Telegraph* and Heinemann to the dinner in honour of my memoirs on Monday, the 26th September. You cannot imagine what immense pleasure this will give to everyone, and particularly to the author.

I would like to have asked if I might do ADC and accompany you to the dinner, in the same way as I do to the Other Club, but perhaps I ought to be there at least a quarter of an hour ahead of the appointed time, in order to receive the guests. I imagine that we will be about twenty strong.

I hope you will allow me to send you a specially bound copy of the book as soon as it is ready. It isn't worth reading, so it may as well look nice.

Kathleen[2] joins me in much love to Clemmie.

PS. I have just been in hospital for a week, but am now much better.

Sir Winston S. Churchill to Harry S Truman
(Churchill papers, 2/536)[3]

21 September 1960

My dear Harry,

My thanks for sending me a copy of your post-retirement memoirs for my library.[4]

Your thoughts on affairs in retirement are most interesting.

---

[1] The Reveses had been deeply wounded by their omission, on Lady Churchill's insistence, from the guest list for the Churchills' first and subsequent cruises on *Christina* as guests of Aristotle Onassis. Anthony Montague Browne provides an account of the episode in *Long Sunset*, pp. 242–3.

[2] Laura Kathleen Clegg, 1897–1978. Married, 1921, Hastings Ismay.

[3] This was the final letter that passed between the two men.

[4] *Mr Citizen* (1960), Truman's memoirs of his years in retirement and reflections on his Presidency.

Lady Churchill to Emery and Wendy Reves
(Churchill papers, 2/532)

23 September 1960   Monaco

I write to let you know that Winston and I and Anthony will be coming to stay at the Hotel de Paris next Wednesday for two or three weeks.

Winston showed me Emery's letter, which had grieved him. He was surprised and sorry that you should feel the way you do. I do not think that any good purpose would be served by debating what Emery said, but I do want you to know that as far as we are concerned there are no intrigues; and we are all deeply grateful for the hospitality we have enjoyed with you.

We hope that you will come to luncheon with us one day at the Hotel de Paris.

Sir Winston S. Churchill to Lord Beaverbrook
(Beaverbrook papers)

6 October 1960   Monaco

My dear Max,

It is so kind of you and Lady Dunn[1] to lend us the magnificent motor car. It is a great help to us and Clemmie goes up to Mont Agel in it as often as the weather allows. I have also been enjoying La Capponcina: I have painted there on two days and sat in the sun in your beautiful garden on a third. But our stay is punctuated by heavy storms which are doing much damage and costing lives all over Southern Europe.

As I told you in my telegram I greatly admired your book,[2] and I am glad that the critics have shown a just appreciation of it in their reviews.

I hope that you are enjoying the Canadian autumn, and that we shall meet again soon.

---

[1] Marcia Anastasia Christoforides, 1909–94. Known as 'Christofor'. Born in Sutton, England. Married, 1942, James Hamet Dunn, 1st Bt (d. 1956); 1963, Lord Beaverbrook (d. 1964). Chancellor of Dalhousie University in Halifax, Canada, 1968–90. In 1971, The Angry Brigade, a British terrorist group, attempted to assassinate Lady Beaverbrook.

[2] Max Aitken Beaverbrook, *Friends: Sixty Years of Intimate Personal Relations with Richard Bedford Bennett* (1959).

Anthony Montague Browne to Peter Baker[1]
(Churchill papers, 1/146)

6 October 1960   Monaco
Private and Personal

Dear Peter,

I am not sure if you are the right person to bother with this but may I use you as an intermediary if you are not? At one time and another the *Express* and the *Evening Standard* have said that Sir Winston is staying here as Onassis' guest. This is not in fact the case, as we are staying at the Hotel de Paris under our own arrangements. Now Onassis has been a kind and generous host to us often and he is a great friend, so any denial on our side would seem ungracious and rude. If you could contrive to slip something in straightening it out it might be a good thing, but don't do so if this causes any difficulty, and don't take the matter up officially as this is a private note to set the record straight.

I might also point out that you (meaning the *Express* newspapers) have said that Sir Winston is painting at Mont Agel, and that Sarah, who is here, is his eldest daughter: Sir Winston is in fact painting at La Capponcina some 2,500 feet below and many miles away from Mont Agel, and Sarah is his third child and second daughter! But this does not of course matter.

It is far too long since we have met and I hope that when I am back in London at the end of this month we shall be able to do so.

Sir Winston S. Churchill to Wendy Reves
(Reves papers)

9 October 1960   Monte Carlo

My dear Wendy,

I am so sorry to hear that you were vexed with me, and I cannot allow you to leave for America without telling you that the months I spent at your charming house were among the brightest in my life, and I shall always think of them as such.

I hope that you will carry with you to the New World my sincere and warmest thanks and affection.

---

[1] Peter G. Baker. Editor, *Films and Filming*, 1955–66. Deputy Editor, *Daily Express*, c.1964. Producer of *The David Frost Show*, 1969–72; *The Frost Programme*, 1973; *Scene*, 1976.

Anthony Montague Browne to John Colville
(Churchill papers, 2/343)

13 October 1960   Monte Carlo

Sir Winston has asked me to thank you for your letter of October 11. He thinks it would be best to put the names of the candidates[1] up on November 3 and invite them to the following dinner if they are elected.

The weather here has been patchy but Sir Winston has managed to get some painting and has begun three pictures. He also goes daily to the Casino!

We are returning I hope on October 25, and should much like to see you some time thereafter. Most of the things I wanted to talk to you about have died a natural death, but there are still one or two.

Lady Churchill sends her love.

Anthony Montague Browne to Ian Samuel
(Churchill papers, 2/523)

26 October 1960
Confidential

When he was in Monte Carlo Sir Winston heard of President de Gaulle's intended visit to the South of France, and expressed a wish to call on him at the Prefecture at Nice to return the courtesy that the President had paid him while in London.

This was arranged, and Sir Winston, Lady Churchill and I went to the Prefecture on October 22 at 7 p.m. and spent half-an-hour with the President and Madame de Gaulle.

The conversation was of a general nature but three points which may be of interest to you emerged:

1. The President asked Sir Winston whether, had he been Prime Minister, he would have gone to the General Assembly. From the way the question was phrased he obviously expected and hoped for the answer 'No'. Sir Winston replied that he had not considered the question in light of conditions then existing, but that he did not believe that Mr Kruschev and the anti-Whites should be allowed to have it all their own way without being answered, and he entirely supported the Prime Minister.
2. In the course of a discussion on the forthcoming American Election, President de Gaulle stated firmly that he supported Nixon, hoped very much that he would get in, but feared that Kennedy was in the lead.

---

[1] For membership of the Other Club; see Churchill to Colville of Aug. 11, reproduced above (pp. 2288–9).

3. On Algeria the President reiterated the theme of his recent public speeches. He did so, however, in a somewhat tired and discouraged tone of voice, particularly when referring to his difficulties at home. This may simply have been due to the fatigue of his programme which seemed very heavy.

In general the President seemed very weary but relaxed and calm. His manner throughout the visit was charming and affectionate to Sir Winston.

I enclose a second copy of this letter in case you should wish to send it to our Embassy in Paris, and I am also copying it to Philip de Zulueta.

Anthony Montague Browne to Sir Winston S. Churchill
(Churchill papers, 2/336)

9 November 1960

The younger brother[1] of King Hussein of Jordan[2] is at Harrow. In view of your friendship with his grandfather, King Abdullah, and King Hussein's present courageous stand against Egypt and Syria, Jock has suggested that when you go for Songs tomorrow you might ask for the boy to be introduced to you?

I think that this would undoubtedly do good and be a mark of your memory of King Abdullah, our friend.

Sir Winston S. Churchill: speech
(Churchill papers, 2/336)

10 November 1960   Harrow School

I am always very glad when the day comes round for me to turn up here, and to have the opportunity of hearing these old Songs and bringing back to my mind the notes which they always recall. And I shall always welcome the opportunity of coming. Thank you very much indeed for the entertainment you have given me and I hope I shall be fit and able to come on the day when I shall have accomplished my twenty-first year!

Thank you very much indeed for inviting me down here and singing these old songs to me.

---

[1] Hassan bin Talal, 1947–. Prince of Jordan. Educated at Harrow School and Christ Church, Oxford. Crown Prince, 1965–99. Founded Royal Scientific Society, 1970. Chairman, UN Advisory Board on Water and Sanitation, 2013–. Replaced as Crown Prince with his nephew Abdullah by King Hussein, Jan. 1999.

[2] Hussein bin Talal bin Abdullah bin Hussein, 1935–99. Educated at Victoria College in Alexandria, Egypt; Harrow School and Royal Military Academy, Sandhurst. Crowned King of Jordan following his father's abdication; reigned 1952–99. In 1994, signed a peace treaty with Israel.

Press release
(Churchill papers, 1/61)

16 November 1960

Sir Winston has fallen and broken a small bone in his back. He was seen today by Lord Moran and Mr Seddon,[1] and will have to remain in bed for a little time.

Duchess of Kent to Lady Churchill
(Baroness Spencer-Churchill papers)[2]

17 November 1960

Dear Clemmie,

I was so very sorry to read about Winston's accident. I want to send you these few lines just to say I am thinking of you & realize what an anxious time this is for you. I do pray he is not suffering & that he will soon be much better.

With all kind remembrances to you both.

President Dwight D. Eisenhower to Sir Winston S. Churchill
(Churchill papers, 1/61)

17 November 1960   Augusta, Georgia

Dear Winston,

All the people in America are distressed to learn of your accident. None more so than I. I do trust that the whole business is not too painful, and while I know you will not enjoy the enforced period in bed I hope you will do exactly what the doctors say. Do take care of yourself. Mamie joins me in affectionate regard to Clemmie and yourself.

---

[1] Herbert John Seddon, 1903–77. Instructor in Surgery, University of Michigan, 1930–1. Resident Surgeon, Royal National Orthopedic Hospital, Stanmore, 1931–40. Nuffield Professor of Orthopedic Surgery, Oxford, 1940–8; Director of Studies, Institute of Orthopedics, 1948–65. CMG, 1951. President, British Orthopedic Association, 1960–1. Chair of Orthopedic Surgery, National Fund for Research into Crippling Diseases, 1965–7.

[2] This letter was handwritten.

Press release
(Churchill papers, 1/61)

18 November 1960

Sir Winston has had a rather disturbed night, but his spinal injury is progressing satisfactorily and is giving no anxiety.

Private addition for the Press themselves
Lady Churchill expresses her appreciation to the Press for their consideration in not telephoning the house.

Press release
(Churchill papers, 1/61)

19 November 1960

Sir Winston did not have a very good night but the pain of his injury is less.

Sir Winston S. Churchill to Lord Beaverbrook
(Beaverbrook papers)

3 December 1960

My dear Max,
The beautiful clock which you and Lady Dunn brought me sits by my bed side. I so much admire it. Thank you most heartily for this remarkable gift. And thank you also dear Max for coming to see me. I did enjoy it.

Sir Winston S. Churchill to Harold Macmillan
(Churchill papers, 5/521)

22 December 1960
Private and Confidential

My dear Harold,
The arrangements for Churchill College at Cambridge have gone forward rapidly, and there are now already Advanced Students working there. Within a year we shall have undergraduates, and the competition for entry seems to be keen. The buildings are now being erected, and though I myself do not admire the architecture there is no doubt that it will meet the needs of the College well. Cockcroft, whose name you suggested to the Trustees as the Master, is working most energetically and I think that all are delighted that he should have accepted the positon.

All this brings to my mind the part that Jock Colville has played. It was he, together with the Prof, who first brought this concept to me, and it is he who throughout has been the leading spirit in hastening the work and guiding the Appeal, which has now realized over three million pounds in Britain, with a hoped-for five million dollars to come from America. I should like there to be a record of all he has done so that if, at a later date, his name should be scrutinized by the Honours Committee his services in this respect should not be forgotten. I hope and believe that the College will contribute worthily to the advance of technology in Britain, and Colville has played a major part in the foundation.

1961

Sir Winston S. Churchill to Lord Beaverbrook
(Beaverbrook papers)

1 March 1961
Private

My dear Max,

I know that you allow your cartoonists a free hand, but I was unpleasantly struck by the enclosure to this letter perpetrated by Vicky[1] in the *Evening Standard*. I am sorry that something so contrary to your own way of thinking – and to mine – should appear in one of your papers.

We had an agreeable dinner at the Other Club last night, and we missed you. We elected as new members Wyndham, Lambton and Alan Hodge.

Clemmie has gone into St Mary's Hospital, Paddington. There is nothing organically wrong but she is to be given a complete rest, which I hope will restore her before long.

I sail from Gibraltar on the *Christina* on March 9 and will be in the West Indies about March 22.

I do trust that your health is now completely restored. Please let me know.

Sir Winston S. Churchill to Lady Churchill
(Baroness Spencer-Churchill papers)

March 1961 *Christina*

Smooth sea and weather beautiful hope soon for news of you.[2] Tender love
With all my love
Your loving husband,

---

[1] Victor Weisz, 1913–66. Known as 'Vicky'. Cartoonist for German anti-Hitler journal *12 Uhr Blatt*, 1928–33. Migrated to England as a refugee, 1935. Cartoonist for *News Chronicle*, 1941–54; *Daily Mirror*, 1954–8; *Evening Standard*, 1958–66.

[2] The sixth *Christina* cruise, from Mar. 9 to Apr. 12, sailed from Gibraltar to the Caribbean and ended in New York City. Churchill then flew home.

Sir Winston S. Churchill to Lady Churchill
(Baroness Spencer-Churchill papers)[1]

20 March 1961 *Christina*

My darling Clemmie,

Here is a line to keep us posted in my own handwriting – <u>all done myself!</u> And to tell you how much I love you: We have travelled ceaselessly over endless seas – <u>quite smoothly</u> for weeks on end and now here we are – within a few days of meeting <u>Ari</u> and his family. This is the moment for me, to show you that I still possess the gift of writing & continue to use it. But I will not press it too far.

Ever your devoted

Sir Winston S. Churchill to Lady Churchill
(Baroness Spencer-Churchill papers)

25 March 1961 *Christina*

Leaving today for Becquia to see Anthony and Clarissa. We have had pleasant meetings with Patrick and Diana Hailes[2] and I see Harold this afternoon. The weather is hot and my cold has now gone. I do trust you are feeling better and hope for good news of you. Tender love

Sir Winston S. Churchill to Lady Churchill
(Baroness Spencer-Churchill papers)

31 March 1961 *Christina*

Have had agreeable voyage in Grenadines and Anthony and Clarissa lunched on board. We are now bound for Jamaica and Haiti. If convenient for you I propose to fly home on April 13. We will travel via New York which is shortest air route.[3]

---

[1] This letter was handwritten.
[2] Diana Mary Lambton, 1914–80. Married, 1936, W. Hedworth Williamson (d. 1942): one child; 1945, Patrick Buchan-Hepburn. Styled Lady Hailes, 1957, when her husband was raised to the peerage.
[3] This would be Churchill's final visit to the US.

Anthony Montague Browne: recollection
('Long Sunset', pages 289–90)

10–12 April 1961 New York City

The greeting the City gave WSC was great, with fire-boats escorting *Christina* with their hoses playing vertically, and helicopters overhead. The following night, braving the elements, some of WSC's friends came onboard from police boats: Bernie Baruch, bolt upright and aquiline as ever, and Marietta Tree[1] accompanied by Adlai Stevenson. Marietta was an enchanting American, the wife of Ronnie Tree, an heir to the Marshall Field fortune and a former British MP. [. . .]

Towards the end of dinner I was called to take an urgent message on the telephone. The message was cryptic: 'Call Operator 17 in Washington.' This I did, and to my no small surprise found myself addressing President Kennedy.[2] He was markedly friendly. Either he had the famous Royal memory for small-fry or else he had been exceedingly well briefed, for he spoke of our meeting in Monte Carlo. He then asked if WSC would come and spend a day or two in Washington with him. He would send the Presidential aircraft to New York to pick him up and would alter his own schedule to accommodate him.

Here was a dilemma. I had to decide at once, and I knew that if I asked WSC, he would accept immediately. It was just possible that WSC could achieve one of his tours de force and summon up the energy to carry off the occasion. But it was highly unlikely, and he had not kept sufficiently up-to-date with world events to sustain a serious high-level conversation. The thought of America, and indeed the world, seeing him at his worst was not endurable. So I took it on myself to decline the invitation without further reference. I explained the reasons briefly to the President. His charm was legendary and it was very evident in what he said. 'I understand your reasons, and I feared that this would be the case. Please give him my warmest and most admiring good wishes. And I think your decision does you credit.' I was moved. I only told WSC of the good wishes at that time, but later, with great trepidation, I gave him the gist of the whole conversation. To my surprise he took it totally calmly, and sent a cable to the President thanking him for his thought.

At the end of dinner, Adlai Stevenson proposed WSC's health with the words: 'To the man who was the world's conscience and the saviour of our freedom.'

---

[1] Marietta Endicott Peabody, 1917–91. Married, 1939, Desmond FitzGerald (div. 1945): one child; 1947, Ronnie Tree: one child.

[2] John Fitzgerald Kennedy, 1917–63. Educated at Harvard University, 1940. Lt, US Navy, 1941–5. Navy and Marine Corps Medal and Purple Heart, 1944. US Representative (Dem.) for Massachusetts 11th District, 1947–53. Married, 1953, Jacqueline Lee Bouvier. US Senator for Massachusetts, 1953–60. US President, 1961–3. Signed proclamation declaring Churchill an honorary citizen of the US, Apr. 1963 (see speech reproduced below, pp. 2342–3). Assassinated in Dallas, Texas by Lee Harvey Oswald, 22 Nov. 1963. Kennedy and Churchill exchanged messages but never met.

Lord Hailes to Sir Winston S. Churchill
(Churchill papers, 1/55)

21 April 1961   Trinidad

Dear Sir Winston,

I feel I must write a few lines now that you are home again, to say what immense pleasure it gave Diana and me, and those thousands who greeted you, to see you in Port of Spain.

I have never seen such crowds and such enthusiasm in Port of Spain, and it was very moving to see Negro, Indian, and Chinese alike with the same expression on their faces – sheer delight and above all, <u>gratitude</u>. In fact, I found it so moving that I had to think of other things to avoid shedding tears.

We just missed you by one day in Jamaica, where I had to go to open a Caribbean Trade Fair. However I met Harold and Dorothy again and saw them off to Washington.

Diana and I are both suffering a little from lack of temperate climate, and we want very much to come back to England this Summer/Autumn if we can. We shall hope to see you again then, if we may.

Thank you once more for visiting us and Trinidad. It did us all a lot of good. Diana sends her love.

Sir Anthony Eden to Anthony Montague Browne
(Churchill papers, 2/517)

9 May 1961
Personal

My dear Anthony,

With some reluctance I trouble you with another matter.

The first time that I heard Sir Winston speak was at Sunderland on or about January 8th, 1920. I have a vivid and, I hope, correct recollection of the speech when, referring to Soviet ambitions, he said 'The ghost of the bear comes padding across the snows.' I would like to put this into my book, but the account of the speech in *The Times*, which is brief, does not give this sentence. I wonder whether there are any records which will confirm that my memory is right. If so, I shall be most grateful. If not, I will take the risk.

Sir Anthony Eden to Anthony Montague Browne
(*Churchill papers, 2/517*)

15 May 1961
Personal

Dear Anthony,

I write to tell you that research has produced the quotation from Sir Winston's speech in Sunderland and I apologise for having bothered you about it. I had it about right.

There is, however, one other point about which I would crave help. On August 7th, 1936, Sir Winston wrote me a letter about the Spanish situation, a part of which he put in *The Gathering Storm*.

Unhappily, I have not a copy of my reply because I wrote it by hand while I was away on holiday. It may be, in view of our relations at the time, that it did contain some serious discussion of the Spanish policy, or, of course, it may be that it was only a brief acknowledgement. If it does not make a lot of work, do you think it possible to look it up.

Forgive me for causing so much trouble. I hope all is well at No. 28 & Lady Churchill better.

PS. Paris was most interesting. De Gaulle sour and pessimistic upon world scene. There is uneasiness in France that all the internal trouble may not yet be over.

Anthony Montague Browne to Sir Anthony Eden
(*Churchill papers, 2/517*)

16 May 1961

Many thanks for your letter of May 15. Our researches into the Sunderland speech had not been as successful as yours. We were about to fall back on the British Museum files!

We will certainly look for your letter acknowledging Sir Winston's of August 7, 1936 and let you know as soon as possible.

I must apologise for the slowness of our research. Sir Winston no longer has an archivist, and as you can imagine his papers are extremely extensive. Moreover all papers prior to 1946 belong to the Chartwell Literary Trust and not to Sir Winston personally, and a lot of them are housed in Lloyds Bank and at the Cabinet Office!

Sir Winston was most interested in your Paris news. I am glad to say that he is in good health and spirits, and that Lady Churchill on the whole is a good deal better.

Anthony Montague Browne to M. J. Wilmshurst[1]
(*Churchill papers, 2/506*)

2 June 1961
Confidential

Many thanks for your note about Mr Ben-Gurion which Sir Winston found helpful.

Their conversation lasted about twenty minutes and the only points of interest that arose were these: Mr Ben-Gurion said that in his view Iraq would 'survive' and be strong enough to contain her own Communists. He was more doubtful about the survival of Jordan which hung on the life of one brave man, to wit, the King. He said that Egypt was slowly preparing for war, that they had twenty and possibly more MIG 19 fighters which were better than anything the Israelis had, and about 200 Russian Army and Airforce instructors. He said that he had asked the Prime Minister to make available suitable weapons to deal with the air side.

Sir Winston S. Churchill to David Ben-Gurion
(*Churchill papers, 2/506*)

2 June 1961
Private

My dear Prime Minister,

It gave me great pleasure to see you here.

I now send you a copy of my book, *Thoughts and Adventures* which contains the essay on Moses. I have re-read it, however, and I would not particularly wish it to be remembered as one of my literary works. But as I promised to send it to you, here it is.

I hope that we shall have another opportunity of meeting again, and meanwhile I send you my earnest good wishes for the great tasks in which you are engaged.

---

[1] Michael Joseph Wilmshurst, 1934–2006. Served in Foreign Service from 1953 until retiring in 1989. Asst Private Secretary to Foreign Secretary, 1960–2.

Anthony Montague Browne to Arthur Lourie[1]
(Churchill papers, 2/506)

4 June 1961

I enclose a copy of Sir Winston's book, *Thoughts and Adventures*, with a covering letter from Sir Winston to Mr Ben-Gurion. As you will see from the letter, Sir Winston does not think very much of the essay himself!

Arthur Lourie to Anthony Montague Browne
(Churchill papers, 2/506)

9 June 1961

Dear Mr Montague Browne,

I am most grateful to you for your letter of 4 June, 1961, and for arranging for Mr Ben-Gurion to receive a copy of Sir Winston's book. I know that he will deeply value the book and the covering letter.

Permit me, too, to thank you for making possible the interview last week. It was a moving occasion also for those of us who accompanied Mr Ben-Gurion to the talk.

Sir Winston S. Churchill to Lady Churchill
(Baroness Spencer-Churchill papers)[2]

[June 1961]   Hotel de Paris, Monte Carlo

My darling,

We seem to have only just arrived after our dashing start, but the weather is lovely and even better than we left behind us. The Prefect[3] met us and was all over us with good will. We sailed off through to Monte Carlo & arrived in time for an excellent dinner. Since then we have had the best weather by night & day. Each day better than the last.

I send you my best love & wish I could have persuaded you to join us.

With many kisses
Yours devotedly,

---

[1] Arthur Lourie, 1903–78. Political Secretary, Jewish Agency Office in London, 1933–48. Director, American Zionist Emergency Council, 1940–5. Member, Jewish Agency delegation to San Francisco Conference, 1945. Director, Jewish Agency UN Office, 1946–8. Israeli Consul-General in New York, 1948–52. Ambassador to Canada, 1957–9; to UK, 1960–5. Deputy Director-General, Ministry of Foreign Affairs, 1965–72.

[2] This letter was handwritten.

[3] Pierre-Jean Moatti.

Sir Winston S. Churchill to Lady Churchill
(Baroness Spencer-Churchill papers)[1]

[June 1961]   Hotel de Paris, Monte Carlo

My darling One,

I write, as I promised to salute you with love and kisses. You will recognise the handwriting, for it is my own. It is a feat.

We got here all right, and I am sitting up in bed looking at the view, which you know so well. The sun is shining brightly and perhaps it will continue to shine. I hope so.

I am going out for a drive this afternoon in the mountains and look forward to it.

I send you this letter with all my love and hope you will like to get it.

Sir Winston S. Churchill to Lady Churchill
(Baroness Spencer-Churchill papers)[2]

[June 1961]   Hotel de Paris, Monte Carlo

My dearest Clemmie,

Here is a letter in my own paw. All is vy pleasant and the days slip by. We are steadily wiping off old friendship's debts with lunches & dinners. I find it vy hard to write a good letter and wonder at the rate with which my friends accomplish their daily tasks. It is amazing they can succeed so well.

But now here I have written what is at least the expression of my love Darling. When I was young I wrote fairly well, but now at last I am played out. You have my fondest love.

Your devoted

PS. I am daily astonished by the development I see in my namesake. He is a wonderful boy. I am so glad I have got to know him.

Sir Winston S. Churchill to Lady Churchill
(Baroness Spencer-Churchill papers)[3]

[June 1961]   Hotel de Paris, Monte Carlo

My darling,

I am writing you a letter with my own paw, from lovely sunshine. We are all

---

[1] This letter was handwritten.
[2] This letter was handwritten.
[3] This letter was handwritten.

going to bask in it from the balcony. I hasten to send you this assurance of my devotion. How I wish you were here.

Tender love

Sir Winston S. Churchill to Lady Churchill
(Baroness Spencer-Churchill papers)[1]

25 June 1961   Hotel de Paris, Monte Carlo

My darling Clemmie,

I am looking forward a great deal to coming home. We have had wonderful weather here, but you seem to have had a fine show too. There is nothing like England when it chooses to be good. I am most eager to get back & to sit in the sunlight.

Here we have had a jolly time. Every day we have ranged the country & climbed some new fortress. There is no lack of these, & the French are proud of their defences in this much fought over land.

I have not, so far, visited the Casino. But I think I will go before I go.

Tender love my darling. I am longing to kiss you.
You are a sweet duck.

Anthony Montague Browne to Major-General John Hamilton
(Churchill papers, 2/571)

5 July 1961
Private

Many thanks for your letter of June 30.

Sir Winston's preference would be for the smaller luncheon if this fits in with the views of his fellow Trustees, the Master and yourself.

I think October 14 would be all right, but you will perhaps understand if subsequent events make it impossible for Sir Winston to attend. Moreover, I fear that he would not be able to make a speech – but you probably did not expect one.

Sir Winston was interested to hear news of the College and asked me to thank you and to send you his good wishes. I do hope that nothing will prevent his attending.

---

[1] This letter was handwritten.

Anthony Montague Browne to Delmar McCormack Smyth[1]
(*Churchill papers, 2/576*)

6 July 1961
Private

Dear Mr Smyth,

I am sorry to have been so long in answering your letter of June 7: Sir Winston has only recently returned to this country, and I myself have been abroad.

I very much regret that it does not look as though Sir Winston will be able to fit in a meeting before you go down. For your strictly private information, his health is somewhat uncertain, and we have to be very careful not to make too many engagements for him, as they tire him much, particularly if it involves meeting a large number of people.

I am so sorry to have to send you a disappointing answer, but I have no doubt that you and your colleagues will understand.

Sir Winston S. Churchill to Lord Beaverbrook
(*Beaverbrook papers*)

20 July 1961

My dear Max,

Thank you so much for sending me a copy of *The Donkeys*, which I am reading with interest.

Clemmie and I greatly enjoyed seeing you and Lady Dunn last Sunday, and I do hope that we shall meet again before long.

Alan Hodge to Sir Winston S. Churchill
(*Churchill papers, 2/526*)

22 August 1961

My dear Sir Winston,

Jane and I were delighted to see you on Sunday at Chartwell, and my daughters were entranced by the opportunity of meeting you. They will be telling their grandchildren about the occasion many years hence.

My older girl[2] felt she had had such an exciting day that she went to bed as

---

[1] Delmar McCormack Smyth, 1922–2011. President of McCormack Smyth Ltd, 1947. Attended Churchill College as the first Fellow Commoner, a fellowship established in honour of Churchill's life and work, 1960–2. Dean of York's Atkinson College, 1963–9. Founding member and first Chairman of The Churchill Society for the Advancement of Parliamentary Democracy, 1984.

[2] Jessica Mary Hodge, 1949–. Married Simon Orebi Gann: two daughters.

soon as we got home, in order to recollect her impressions in tranquillity. The younger one,[1] with the red head, stayed up and played a hand of bezique with me. It seemed very appropriate.

Sir Winston S. Churchill to Doris Moss[2]
(Anthony Montague Browne, 'Long Sunset', pages 273–4)

August 1961

My dear Mrs Moss,

The problem of British and Commonwealth relations with the European Economic Community occupies a position of major importance and interest. I feel that it may be useful to you if I send you my general thoughts on the matter.

For many years, I have believed that measures to promote European unity were ultimately essential to the well-being of the West. In a speech at Zurich in 1946,[3] I urged the creation of the European Family, and I am sometimes given credit for stimulating the ideals of European unity which led to the formation of the economic and the other two communities.

In the aftermath of the second world war, the key to these endeavours lay in partnership between France and Germany. At that time this happy outcome seemed a fantasy, but it is now accomplished, and France and West Germany are more intimately linked than they have ever been before in their history. They, together with Italy, Belgium, Holland and Luxembourg, are welding themselves into an organic whole, stronger and more dynamic than the sum of its parts. We might well play a great part in these developments to the profit not only of ourselves, but of our European friends also.

But we have another role which we cannot abdicate: that of leader of the British Commonwealth. In my conception of a unified Europe, I never contemplated the diminution of the Commonwealth. It is most important to consider correctly the initiative taken by the Government in applying formally for accession to the Treaty of Rome, the statute that set up the European Economic Community. This application for membership is the sole way in which, so to speak, a reconnaissance can be carried out to find out for certain whether terms for British membership of the Community could be agreed which would meet our special needs as well as those of the Commonwealth and of our partners in the European Free Trade Association.

---

[1] Joanna Marrack Hodge, 1953–. Educated at Somerville College and Wolfson College, Oxford; PhD, 1983. Hanseatic Scholar, Stiftung FvS, 1978–81. Junior Research Fellow, Wolfson College, 1981–5. Senior Lecturer in Philosophy, Manchester Metropolitan University, 1991–6; Reader, 1996–2000; Prof. from 2000. Published *Heidegger and Ethics* (1995) and *Derrida on Time* (2007).

[2] Chair of Churchill's Woodford constituency.

[3] Reproduced in *The Churchill Documents*, vol. 22, *Leader of the Opposition, August 1945 to October 1951*, pp. 458–61.

In the negotiations that we expect will take place in the coming months, the Six Countries should recognise that the Commonwealth is one of the most valuable assets that we could bring, for them as well as for ourselves, and should be ready to work out arrangements to prevent any damage to Commonwealth interests. There are other considerations. We have obligations to the other European countries who are members of the European Free Trade Association. The Government have emphasised that satisfactory arrangements for them are a pre-condition for our entry into the Economic Community, or Common Market as it is called. The position of our farmers is also of major significance.

To sum up my views, I would say this: I think that the Government are right to apply to join the European Economic Community, not because I am yet convinced that we shall be able to join, but because there appears to be no other way by which we can find out exactly whether the conditions of membership are acceptable.

Sir Winston S. Churchill to Emery and Wendy Reves
(Churchill papers, 1/149)

2 September 1961   Alpes Maritimes

Dear Emery and Wendy,

Many thanks for your telegram Alas I cannot lunch or dine before my departure as you so kindly suggest. All good wishes.

Sir Winston S. Churchill to Aristotle Onassis
(Churchill papers, 1/148)

8 September 1961

My dear Ari,

I was sorry not to see you again before I left Monte Carlo. I had a most agreeable stay, and I would like to tell you again how grateful I am to you for all the arrangements you have made and which the Société des Bains de Mer so effectively carry out, to make my stays at the top of the Hotel de Paris so easy and pleasant.

My grandson, Winston, came out for some time and much enjoyed himself.

I look forward to seeing you before long, and hope that you will come and see me when you are in England.

Anthony Montague Browne to Lord Beaverbrook
(Churchill papers, 2/519)

23 September 1961

The Sunday before we left Monte Carlo, Sir Winston wanted at short notice to visit La Capponcina. Madame Franco was out for a few hours, and so Sgt Murray climbed over your wall and let the car in! I hope that you will excuse this breaking and entering of your property?

Sir Winston is very well, and more alert intellectually than for some time. He asks me to put to you this question: Is the French Canadian population of Canada going to outnumber the British Canadian, and if so, when, and what are the results going to be?

I do hope all goes well with you. The weather here is mild and pleasant, and Berlin seems to be simmering down just for the moment. I am very much struck by the idea of moving the United Nations there as a final freeze on the German situation without re-unification.

Anthony Montague Browne to Sir Winston S. Churchill
(Churchill papers, 2/506)

23 September 1961

Sir Winston

It is Ben-Gurion's 75th birthday on September 27. Do you wish to send him a message? You have not done so in previous years.[1]

Anthony Montague Browne to Major-General John Hamilton
(Churchill papers, 2/571)

25 September 1961

I am sorry to have been so long in letting you know Sir Winston's decision, but now, in the light of all the circumstances, he feels that it might be best if Lord Tedder would lay the Foundation Stone,[2] and he himself will not come. The journey, even if we lay on an aircraft, is quite a long and tiring one, and although Sir Winston is much better than he was some months ago, I do not think he feels quite up to this public occasion when, whatever the arrangements, he would think himself bound to make a brief speech.

I am indeed sorry, particularly as you have been so considerate and painstaking with the arrangements.

I myself hope to come with my Wife, although I feel that we are getting in under false pretences now!

[1] Churchill wrote on this note: 'Yes'.
[2] At Churchill College, Cambridge.

David Ben-Gurion to Sir Winston S. Churchill
(Churchill papers, 2/506)

2 October 1961

My dear Sir Winston,

I was deeply moved to receive your greeting on the occasion of my birthday, and rejoiced to see that you still remember such trifles. It recalled to my mind the few unforgettable moments I spent with you at the beginning of June, and I cherish as a precious possession your book of essays, which includes that on Moses.

I hold you in esteem and affection, not only – not even mainly – because of your unfailing friendship to our people and your profound sympathy with its resurgents in our ancient homeland. Your greatness transcends all national boundaries.

I happened to be in London, from the beginning of May till September 1940, and I heard the historic speeches in which you gave utterance to the iron determination of your people and yourself to fight to the end against the Nazi foe. I saw you then not only as the symbol of your people and its greatness, but as the voice of the invincible and uncompromising conscience of the human race at a time of danger to the dignity of man, created in the image of God. It was not only the liberties and the honour of your own people that you saved. If your advice had been taken in the last year of the war, the grave crisis over the question of Berlin, which has aroused the apprehensions of the civilized world, would never have arisen, and some of the East European countries would have remained within the bounds of Western Europe.

Your words and your deeds are indelibly engraved in the annals of humanity. Happy the people that has produced such a son.

In profound admiration and esteem,

Sir Winston S. Churchill to Lord Tedder
(Churchill papers, 2/571)

9 October 1961

My dear Teddy,

I enclose a message for the ceremony at Churchill College on October 14, which I should be much obliged if you would read out. I am so sorry that I cannot be there, and it is good of you to undertake the laying of the foundation stone.

Sir Winston S. Churchill to Dr Francis Crick[1]
(*Churchill papers, 2/571*)

9 October 1961
Private

Dear Dr Crick,
   I was sorry to learn that you have resigned from Churchill College, and I am puzzled at your reason. The money for the Chapel was provided specifically for that purpose by Mr Beaumont[2] and not taken from the general College funds.
   A chapel, whatever one's views on religion, is an amenity which many of those who will live in the College may enjoy, and none need enter it unless they wish.

Dr Francis Crick to Sir Winston S. Churchill
(*Churchill papers, 2/571*)

12 October 1961

Dear Sir Winston,
   It was kind of you to write. I am sorry you do not understand why I resigned.
   To make my position a little clearer I enclose a cheque for ten guineas to open the Churchill College Hetairae fund. My hope is that eventually it will be possible to build permanent accommodation within the College, to house a carefully chosen selection of young ladies in the charge of a suitable Madam who, once the institution has become traditional, will doubtless be provided, without offence, with dining rights at the high table.
   Such a building will, I feel confident, be an amenity which many who live in the college will enjoy very much, and yet the instruction need not be compulsory and none need enter it unless they wish. Moreover it would be open (conscience permitting) not merely to members of the Church of England, but also to Catholics, Non-Conformists, Jews, Moslems, Hindus, Zen Buddhists and even to atheists and agnostics such as myself.
   And yet I cannot help feeling that when you pass on my offer to the other Trustees – as I hope you will – they may not share my enthusiasms for such

---

[1] Francis Harry Compton Crick, 1916–2004. Worked in British Admiralty Research Laboratory, 1940–7. After the war, moved to Cambridge, where he worked at the Strangeways and Cavendish Laboratories. Proposed double-helix structure for DNA, 1953. Nobel Prize in Medicine, 1962. Non-resident Fellow, Salk Institute for Biological Studies, San Diego, 1962–73. Ferkhauf Foundation Visiting Prof., Salk Institute, 1976–7.

[2] Timothy Wentworth Beaumont, 1928–2008. Asst Chaplain, St John's Cathedral, Hong Kong, 1955–7. Vicar, Christ Church Kowloon Tong, Hong Kong, 1957–9. Honourable Curate, St Stephen's Rochester Tow, London, 1960–3. Representative of Diocese of London in Church Assembly, 1960–5. Baron, 1967. Liberal Party Chairman, 1967–8; President, 1969–70. Vicar, St Philip and All Saints with St Luke, Kew, 1986–91.

a truly educational project. They may feel, being men of the world, that to house such an Establishment, however great the need and however correctly conducted, within the actual College would not command universal respect. They may even feel my offer of ten guineas to be a joke in rather poor taste.

But that is exactly my view of the proposal of the Trustees to build a chapel, after the middle of the 20th century, in a new College and in particular in one with a special emphasis on science. Naturally some members of the College will be Christian at least for the next decade or so, but I do not see why the College should tacitly endorse their beliefs by providing them with special facilities. The churches in the town, it has been said, are half empty. Let them go there. It will be no further than they have to go to their lectures.

Even a joke in poor taste can be enjoyed, but I regret that my enjoyment of it has entailed my resignation from the College which bears your illustrious name.

Understandably I shall not be present on Saturday. I hope it all goes off well.

Sir Winston S. Churchill: statement
(Churchill papers, 2/571)

14 October 1961

A few days ago the first undergraduates of Churchill College joined the Foundation. I welcome them most warmly, together with the second intake of post-graduates. It is a source of great satisfaction that the culmination point of our enterprise should now be reached, and I am truly sorry that I cannot be present. The College has now begun to fulfil the purposes for which it was created, and all those who have contributed to it through funds or through work can be well pleased. I trust that every effort will be made to complete the buildings on or before the promised date so that there may be no delay in bringing the College up to its full strength as quickly as possible.

Two years ago I planted an oak on the site of the College. Since then the manifestations of the formidable advance in technology of America and Russia, to which I referred, have multiplied. Britain must not be left behind. It is inconceivable that our country, with its traditions of pioneering and discovery in every field and its magnificent resources of men and intellectual power should be constrained by our own inactivity to wait for other countries to impart to us the knowledge they have gained. Whether in the fields of pure research or applied technology, whether in the adventure into space or in the minute investigation of the substance of our globe, we must as always before be with the leaders. It is to further this high aim that Churchill College was founded.

Sir Winston S. Churchill to David Ben-Gurion
(Churchill papers, 2/506)

16 October 1961
Private

My dear Prime Minister,

I am indeed obliged to you for your graceful and charming letter.[1] It gave me great pleasure to read what you said, and I would like to assure you again of my very warm good wishes both for the State of Israel and for you personally.

Lord Tedder to Sir Winston S. Churchill
(Churchill papers, 2/571)

16 October 1961

Dear Sir Winston,

This is to report that the laying of the Foundation Stone of Churchill College went through without a hitch. I hope I did justice to your grand message – it was certainly loudly applauded and was, I know, deeply appreciated by our other Trustees and by the College. I have taken the liberty of arranging to send the silver trowel, which was used for the laying ceremony, on to you as soon as it has been suitably inscribed.

As you will have heard, the current stage is almost two months behind schedule but they hope to be able to make up the lost time.

You may like to know that both the Oak and the Mulberry tree are flourishing.

With every good wish,

Sir Winston S. Churchill to Harold Macmillan
(Churchill papers, 2/508)

19 October 1961
Private and Confidential

My dear Harold,

Anthony Eden dined with me last night, and we talked of Ghana. I find that he shares the increasing perturbation with which I view the Queen's forthcoming visit there.

I have the impression that there is widespread uneasiness both over the physical safety of the Queen and, perhaps more, because her visit would seem

---

[1] Reproduced above (p. 2312).

to endorse a regime which has imprisoned hundreds of Opposition members without trial and which is thoroughly authoritarian in tendency.

I have little doubt that Nkrumah[1] would use the Queen's visit to bolster up his own position.

No doubt Nkrumah would be much affronted if the visit were now cancelled and Ghana might leave the Commonwealth. I am not sure that that would be a great loss. Nkrumah's vilification of this country and his increasing association with our enemies does not encourage one to think that his country could ever be more than an opportunist member of the Commonwealth family.

Is it too late for the Queen's plans to be changed?

Harold Macmillan to Sir Winston S. Churchill
(Churchill papers, 2/508)

19 October 1961
Private and Confidential

Dear Winston,

Many thanks for your letter of October 19. The Ghana problem is indeed a difficult one.

It is a great tragedy that this visit did not take place when it was originally planned over a year ago, for then things were calm. Unfortunately, it had to be postponed owing to the Queen's baby.[2] Now there is this dilemma to which you refer. If the visit were cancelled and The Queen continued Her tour of Sierra Leone and Gambia, that would be tantamount to dismissing Ghana from the Commonwealth. Whether or not we ought to face this is what worries me continually. We hope that the New Commonwealth with all its weaknesses will be a kind of League of Nations owing some allegiance to British ideals and the Throne is the symbol of this. We get very angry with some Commonwealth countries because of their follies but after all we have committed considerable follies here in our own history, including cutting off the head of our King. The people of Ghana have got to learn. Can we help them best by throwing them out of the body corporate or by trying to keep them in the community?

I am informed on very good authority by men whom I trust, like Jackson,[3]

---

[1] Kwame Nkrumah, 1909–72. Organized 5th Pan-African Congress, 1945. Founder, Convention People's Party, 1949. Leader of Government Business for the Gold Coast, 1951–2. PM, 1952–7. PM of Ghana, 1957–60. President, 1960–6. Third Chairperson of Organization of African Unity, 1965–6. Overthrown in military coup, 1966.

[2] Andrew Albert Christian Edward, 1960–. Second son of Queen Elizabeth II and Prince Philip, Duke of Edinburgh. Served in Royal Navy, 1978–2001. CVO, 1979. Fought in Falklands War, 1982. Cdr, 1999. Married, 1986, Sarah Ferguson (div. 1996): two children. 1st Duke of York, 1986. KG, 2006.

[3] Robert 'Jacko' Jackson, 1911–91. Served in Royal Australian Navy, 1929–41. OBE, 1941.

who has been there for several years, that Nkrumah has not yet wholly sold out to the Russians. If Ghana is thrown out of the Commonwealth Russia will move in. In the Congo they were in a difficulty, because the United Nations held the only port and the rest of the country is unapproachable except by very long-range aircraft and not easily supplied. That was the reason why we defeated their efforts eighteen months ago. But West Africa, with the advantage of a sea position, is very different. Indeed, all the reasons which made West Africa attractive first to the Danes and then to ourselves make it equally feasible for Russian occupation. All these things I have to ponder.

Against this there is the terrible burden of deciding about the Queen's personal security. I need hardly say that her wish is to go. That is natural with so courageous a personality. But I am having further discussions about the security position and if it deteriorates we shall have to cancel the visit. I am bound to tell you that I would not like it cancelled on political grounds, for the arguments are much in favour of holding on to the British connection with Ghana and hoping for better times. And there are very many people in Ghana to whom the Crown still has real meaning. But The Queen's personal safety is the real argument in my view which would finally weigh in favour of cancellation. We are still, therefore taking the line that the visit should continue but I can tell you privately that we may have to cancel it at the last moment. If we did so, it would be on security grounds and we would try to get Dr Nkrumah to say that he did not wish to subject the Queen to any risk.[1]

Sir Winston S. Churchill to Lord Tedder
(*Churchill papers, 2/571*)

20 October 1961

My dear Tedder,

Thank you so much for telling me of the Laying of the Foundation Stone.[2] I am very sorry that I could not be there, and it was good of you to deputise for me.

I should be very glad to have the silver trowel but, as you laid the Stone, I think that it would be appropriate for you to retain it yourself.

Director-General, Anglo-American Middle East Supply Centre, 1942–4. CMG, 1944. Senior Deputy Director-General, UNRRA, 1945–7; Asst Secretary-General for Coordination, 1948. Secretary, Australian Dept of National Development, 1950, 1951. Chairman of Independent Ghana's Commission for Development, 1957–62. KCVO, 1962. Assisted in reformation of UN's Development System, 1968–9. Under Secretary-General of UN, 1972–87.

[1] Churchill responded: 'My dear Harold, thank you so much for answering my letter about Ghana so fully. I will reflect with every care on what you say' (*Churchill papers, 2/508*).

[2] Letter reproduced above (p. 2315).

Anthony Montague Browne to Lord Beaverbrook
(Churchill papers, 2/519)

16 November 1961

I thought that you would like to know that Sir Winston is contemplating a descent on the Hotel de Paris from about December 4 for a fortnight. It will be his fifth this year. (Personally, I have all the disadvantages of being Monegasque while still paying income tax!)

Sir Winston is well, but rather bored with events and disturbed by the international scene and notably by the Queen going to Ghana and thus endorsing Nkrumah's corrupt and tyrannical regime.

I do hope that you yourself have recovered from the disagreeable Menier's disease. I much look forward to seeing you at Sir Winston's birthday dinner.

PS. Within twenty-four hours of Sir Winston reaching his decision to go to Monte Carlo, the *Daily Express* telephoned asking if I could confirm that he was doing so! I was/much impressed and said that I would give them detailed and accurate descriptions of our plans if they would tell me where they got their news from. They did not feel inclined to accept my offer!

Anthony Montague Browne to Ian Samuel
(Churchill papers, 1/155)

21 November 1961
Private and Confidential

Sir Winston is proposing to go on a cruise with Mr Onassis some time during the next two months. This time, instead of going to the West Indies as before, Mr Onassis is contemplating going down through the Suez Canal and spending some time in the Red Sea and possibly at Aden.

I should be grateful if you could let me know if you foresee any difficulties or objections to what is proposed. We should probably touch at some Saudi port and probably at Port Sudan, as well as Aden, and of course would be in Egyptian territory while going through the Canal.

Knowing Sir Winston's feelings about the Egyptians I do not think he would be willing to meet any of their dignitaries, even if they on their side proposed to send any aboard. Moreover, it is widely known in the Arab world that Sir Winston has always been pro-Zionist. On the other hand he had agreeable relations with the Saudis because of his connection with the late Ibn Saud, and also with the Sudanese through his friendship with The Mahdi. So perhaps it would all balance out.

I am sending a copy of this letter to Philip de Zulueta.

Sir Winston S. Churchill to Lady Churchill
(Baroness Spencer-Churchill papers)

[December 1961]   Monte Carlo

My darling,

Here I am with a pen in my hand & a full sheet of paper before me. I believe I could write a whole letter jobbed in a strong hand together without difficulty; and I think I will take this business up again.

We are now half way through our journey & are already counting the days when the red bricks of Chartwell will shine before us. I am a shocking scribbler & the more I try to write a letter the worse it looks.

I love you vy much indeed my darling Clemmie but I think I have lost the art of writing & when the page is finished I am quite ashamed of all my remaining efficiency as an author, but I am sure you will like to receive this.

                                                                                 Many kisses

Sir Winston S. Churchill to Lord Beaverbrook
(Beaverbrook papers)

2 December 1961

My dear Max,

Thank you so much for sending me the most interesting and beautifully bound book on the Wines of France. I am indeed glad to have this in my possession and I admire the way in which it is put together and the fine illustrations. But more than this, it pleased me to have your letter and your company at dinner on my Birthday. I think you know how much your friendship has meant to me over the years.

Yours ever,

1962

John Cockcroft to Anthony Montague Browne
(Churchill papers, 2/571)

2 January 1962　　　　　　　　　　　　　　　　　　　　　　　Churchill College
　　　　　　　　　　　　　　　　　　　　　　　　　　　　　　　　　　Cambridge

Dear Montague Browne,

　The College has decided to have a few drawings made, first of all of its Senior Fellows, paying for these from monies which I receive from time to time for lectures and broadcasts.

　We have been considering whether we should have drawings made of our Trustees, particularly non-Cambridge Trustees.

　We are having the drawings made by a young artist, Robert Tollast,[1] who has recently painted a very good portrait of R. A. Butler.

　Do you think it is at all possible that Sir Winston would be willing to sit for a drawing? About one hour would suffice. Needless to say we should very much like to have an original drawing of him, since it does not appear to be possible to obtain a portrait.

Anthony Montague Browne to Lord Beaverbrook
(Churchill papers, 2/519)

8 January 1962
Private

　Sir Winston noticed in the Londoners' Diary of January 1 the paragraph about Neville Chamberlain which indicated that Sir Winston had demanded Chamberlain's final resignation and that the latter was deeply hurt.

　Sir Winston's own remembrance was that they had parted on good terms, and I have checked through the unpublished correspondence between them at the time, which seems to bear this out. The formal letter of resignation and

---

[1] Robert Tollast, 1915–2008. English portrait painter liked by Churchill. Educated at Westminster School of Art. Diplomatic Service, 1940–8. Professional portrait painter, 1948–2008.

its acceptance were naturally couched in warm terms, but there is no hint of any pressure being put on Chamberlain in the private correspondence, nor is there any indication of this being done orally.

Sir Winston wondered if you remembered something about the incident that he does not? If the passage did not emanate from you personally, perhaps the writer has been mis-informed, and in this case Sir Winston thought that it might be a good thing to put it right, if you could?

I have been daily at Chartwell, and find Sir Winston physically well enough, but in low spirits and without energy or interest. I think that this is partly because he has not been outside the house for a long time owing to the severe weather. However, he does not show any inclination to go abroad at the moment. Lady Churchill has had a bad cold, but otherwise is all right.

I am much looking forward to reading your new books.[1]

Anthony Montague Browne to John Cockcroft
(Churchill papers, 2/571)

8 January 1962
Private and Confidential

Dear Master,

Thank you for your letter of January 2. I have discussed this with Sir Winston and more fully with Lady Churchill. They neither of them like the idea very much. I think Lady Churchill feels that Sir Winston is now too old to pose and that in any case it might be better for the College to have a picture that represented him more as he was in his great days.

Lady Churchill has an extremely good and little known portrait of Sir Winston painted after the war by the late Sir Oswald Birley.[2] I wonder if you would feel that a copy of this or a sketch drawn from it might meet with your approval? If it did, Lady Churchill would be very glad to lend the picture for the purpose.

On another topic: Sir Winston wrote to Lord Hailsham about the idea of getting young scientists to sign some form of contract to work in Britain or for British firms for a specified time. I enclose a copy of Lord Hailsham's answer (with his permission of course), which Sir Winston thought you would like to see. I do not think that Sir Winston himself is entirely convinced by this answer.

---

[1] Beaverbrook published two books in 1962, *My Early Life* and *The Divine Propogandist*.
[2] Oswald Hornby Joseph Birley, 1880–1952. Born in New Zealand. Educated at Harrow and Trinity College, Cambridge. On active service, Royal Fusiliers, 1914–16; Intelligence Corps, 1916–18. MC, 1919. Maj., Sussex Home Guard, 1940–3. Knighted, 1949. Known for his portraits of Winston Churchill, King George V, Queen Mary, King George VI, Queen Elizabeth the Queen Mother and Queen Elizabeth II.

Anthony Montague Browne to General Lord Ismay
(*Churchill papers, 2/526*)

16 January 1962

Sir Winston asks me to say that if you are going to the Other Club on the 25th, he hopes you will pick him up at Hyde Park Gate on your way.

I hope all is well with you: Nonie and I went to church in Tewkesbury Abbey on Christmas morning and thought we might see you, but in view of the extreme cold I suppose that you were not able to go out of doors.

I have little news. Sir Winston has been rather low and depressed for some time, and taking very little interest in affairs. But in the last two days he seems brighter. He has been continuously here,[1] and I am rather weary of commuting!

I do hope to see you at the Other Club.

Sir Winston S. Churchill to Lord Beaverbrook
(*Beaverbrook papers*)

24 January 1962

My dear Max,

Anthony has shown me your correspondence about Chamberlain's final resignation. Thank you for what you say about not carrying passengers. I like this compliment, and you yourself were certainly never a passenger!

When Chamberlain's health deteriorated, he offered me his resignation without any prompting from my side. We parted on friendly terms and as far as I knew he never bore me the slightest animosity. That was why I caused Anthony to write to you.

I do hope all goes well with you. I am contemplating coming out to the South a little later in the Parliamentary Session, and of course your being out there is the greatest inducement to me to come.

Sir Winston S. Churchill to Queen Elizabeth II
(*Churchill papers, 2/532*)

5 February 1962

Madam,

At the conclusion of the first decade of your Reign, I would like to express to Your Majesty my fervent hopes and wishes for many happy years to come.

---

[1] Chartwell.

It is with pride that I recall that I was your Prime Minister at the inception of these ten years of devoted service to our country.

With my humble duty,
I remain,
Your Majesty's faithful
Subject and servant,

Anthony Montague Browne to Philip de Zulueta
(Churchill papers, 1/155)

23 February 1962
Private and Confidential

It now seems likely that Sir Winston will go on a cruise starting on approximately April 5 from Monte Carlo and visiting Libya and the Lebanon, before returning via Greece.[1] This presents no problem as of course both Libya and the Lebanon are reasonably friendly and uncommitted.

I fear much, however, that Sir Winston will insist on visiting Israel. I had thought that our host, Mr Onassis, would have been debarred from going there because of his oil interests and his relations with the Arab countries, but I find that this is not so. I will do what I can to persuade Sir Winston not to go to Israel, but I cannot guarantee it in view of his long association with Israel and his outspoken feelings as a Zionist.

I will let you know how things develop, and possibly as a last resort the Prime Minister might consider writing to Sir Winston if it is thought that it would be really harmful for Sir Winston to stop in Israel.

I am copying this letter to Ian Samuel in the Foreign Office.

Anthony Montague Browne to Lord Beaverbrook
(Churchill papers, 2/519)

14 March 1962

Many thanks for your letter of March 12. As I think I told you, Sir Winston has been meditating on a cruise, and now the plans look something like this: Leave Monte Carlo on April 6 on the *Christina* and go to Libya (this was Sir Winston's own idea; he wants to see the Greco-Roman remains at the Leptis Magna and Cyrene). Then we shall probably go to the Lebanon, and home by April 30 via either Monte Carlo, Venice, or Athens.

Besides the usual entourage, Bill Deakin and his wife will probably be

---

[1] Churchill's seventh cruise aboard *Christina*, Apr. 6–28, toured the Mediterranean.

accompanying us. I think you know him? He is Master of St Antony's at Oxford, was Fitzroy Maclean's predecessor in Yugoslavia during the war, and worked for Sir Winston in the 1930s.

All this is not fully settled yet, so it is for your ear alone.

Sir Winston has ups and downs, but on the whole is pretty well, though his hearing has deteriorated further in the last six months.

Anthony Montague Browne to Sir Ponsonby Moore Crosthwaite[1]
(Churchill papers, 1/155)

22 March 1962
Private and Confidential

This is to let you know that Sir Winston is in all probability going on a cruise in Onassis's yacht the *Christina* which may possibly take him to Beirut, during the month of April. On present plans we are sailing from Monte Carlo on April 6 and going to Libya, and thence to Beirut. As always on these cruises there is no fixed itinerary and plans are of the vaguest, but I thought that you would wish to have warning.

As you know, Sir Winston is now eighty-seven and his vigour and hearing have very much deteriorated. He would not expect any unusual facilities or attentions, and any official ceremonies would be undesirable. What has happened in the past on our cruises, of which there have been about eight, is that on arrival at a capital city we have continued to live on board the yacht, and Sir Winston pays brief visits to the shore usually lasting not more than an hour or two each. He usually dines and lunches on the yacht, and he and our host would, I know, be very pleased if you would come and dine and perhaps bring one or two suitable local dignitaries if you saw fit. However, we could arrange all this nearer the time.

According to present arrangements our party will consist of Sir Winston; our host Ari Onassis; Theodore Garofalides and his wife[2] (he is Onassis's brother-in-law and a distinguished surgeon with a hospital in Athens); Bill Deakin and his wife (you no doubt know Bill, but in case not he is Master of St Antony's College in Oxford, was Fitzroy Maclean's predecessor in Yugoslavia, and is an old friend of Sir Winston's); our host's two children, Alexander,[3] aged fourteen, and Christina, aged eleven; and my wife, eight-year-old daughter,

---

[1] Ponsonby Moore Crosthwaite, 1907–89. British Diplomatic Service, 1932–52. Deputy UK Representative to UN, 1952–8. Ambassador to Lebanon, 1958–63; to Sweden, 1963–6.

[2] Theodore Garofalides, 1900–?. Brother-in-law of Aristotle Socrates Onassis.
Artemis Onassis, 1902–81. Sister of Greek shipping tycoon Aristotle Socrates Onassis.

[3] Alexander Onassis, 1948–73. Son of shipping tycoon Aristotle Onassis. President of Olympic Aviation, 1971–3. Died in an airplane crash at the age of 24.

and self. Sir Winston will also bring a nurse and his Scotland Yard detective Sergeant Murray.

I will let you know anything further as soon as it is settled, but it may not be until shortly before we arrive owing to the snipe-like nature of our movements. I leave it to you to decide when to tell the Lebanese authorities, but perhaps you would leave this as late as possible.

When we are at sea, telegrams can reach the yacht if addressed 'Yacht *Christina*, ELLU', and it is also possible to talk on the radio telephone.

There is of course no need for any special Embassy arrangements and if, for instance, you were going to be away when we came there would be absolutely no necessity for you to change your plans, though we should be sorry to miss you.

The Foreign Office and No. 10 know about our plans.

Lord Moran to Theodore Garofalides
(Churchill papers, 1/155)

4 April 1962

My dear Theodore,

I wonder if it might help you if I said a word about Sir Winston in case he has any trouble while on the yacht.

He has had several attacks of Cholangitis with some pain over the gall bladder and fever. In one of these attacks he had jaundice. I think that the attacks are shortened if he is put on an antibiotic when he gets the symptoms and the fever. We have used aureomycin and terramycin in the ordinary doses.

From time to time he has symptoms due to sluggishness of the cerebral circulation. But these generally clear up pretty quickly, and I am doubtful whether any treatment has much influence on the length and severity of these attacks.

At present, Sir Winston is in pretty good form. I trust you may have good weather and a very pleasant cruise.

Note: books for Sir Winston on cruise
(Churchill papers, 1/155)

4 April 1962

Outrageous Fortune	Murray
Enormous Shadow	Harling
War in the Desert	Glubb
The Governor	Thomas

Persuasion	Austen
Arm Me Audacity	Pape
Bless This House	Lofts
The Mary Deare	Innes
The Day They Robbed the Bank of England	Brophy
The Way to the Lantern	Lindop
Captain of Marine	White
The Brave White Flag	Ford
Bernard Baruch: The Public Years	
The Hussar	Rezzori
Claudius the God	Graves
Disputed Barricade	Maclean
The Bull from the Sea	Renault
The Loser	Ustinov
Count Belisarius	Graves
Devil's Brood	Duggan
Northanger Abbey	Austen
Revolution & Roses	Newby
Pilgrim?	Philby

Total 23

Anthony Montague Browne to Lord Beaverbrook
(Churchill papers, 2/519)

25 April 1962

I am so sorry not to have replied before to your letter of April 7, which followed me in our snipe-like wanderings round the Mediterranean and has only just caught up.

Sir Winston was much interested to see the cutting about Churchilliana in the Beaverbrook Art Gallery and has asked me to thank you for sending it to him.

I should much like to see the Jagger picture:[1] while some of Sutherland's studies that I saw at the time seemed admirable the final result was a most disagreeable khaki-coloured caricature.

We had a successful cruise with excellent weather and no rough seas, but I fear that for Sir Winston it is in many ways a diminishing return as he is increasingly disinclined to go ashore at the points we visit. I expect that he will be here for some time and very likely go to the South of France in a month or so.

---

[1] David Jagger, 1891–1958. Painted a portrait of Churchill in 1939.

1962

Randolph S. Churchill to Sir Winston S. Churchill
(*Churchill papers, 1/136*)

28 May 1962

Dearest Papa,

Immersed as I am in the study of your wonderful and fascinating life, I fell to speculating this morning while walking round my garden on my fifty-first birthday of what you had accomplished by the time you had reached my present age. It is extraordinary to realise that you had been Chancellor of the Exchequer for about a year: that you had already lived several lives: that you had served in six wars and campaigns; that you had written nine successful books and were, on your fifty-first birthday, while Chancellor of the Exchequer, working on Volume 3 of *The World Crisis*. You had been Under-Secretary of State for the Colonies, President of the Board of Trade, Home Secretary, First Lord of the Admiralty, Minister of Munitions, Secretary of State for War and Air and Secretary of State for the Colonies.

It is a sobering thought for me, but an encouraging one, that on your fifty-first birthday very much less than half of your life's work was accomplished. From this I 'take heart of grace' (from one of your favourite operettas, *The Pirates of Penzance*) and derive many encouraging thoughts for the future of my son Winston who is only twenty-one and who flew over today from Oxford for my birthday luncheon.

We both salute you, the author of our being.

Your loving son

Sir Shane Leslie to Lady Churchill
(*Churchill papers, 2/571*)

6 June 1962

My dear Clemmy,

Last weekend I paid a visit to Churchill College, Cambridge – and was entertained by the Master Sir J. Cockcroft. I am the first relative of the Founder-Nominee to visit them. It is all a building but they will soon have a Hall and their great desire is a central portrait of Winston. Of course as a scientific college they most want Graham Sutherland's strange portrait. If Winston does not like it it might be a good opportunity to lay it aside where it will descend the ages in a more or less public position.

In any case they are enthusiastic at the idea of any portrait which can be spared.

There is no hurry but I thought you might mention the idea to Winston sometime. We shall be here till August but I would return from Ireland in October when next term commences if the project succeeds.

They would be delighted if I accompanied you to Cambridge for you to make the presentation!

Lady Churchill to Sir Shane Leslie
(Churchill papers, 2/571)

8 June 1962

Thank you for your letter. I was interested to hear of your visit to Churchill College.

I must tell you that I hope that Graham Sutherland's insulting portrait of Winston will never be shown anywhere in my lifetime. It caused such pain to him & to those who love him to see him so odiously depicted that it spoilt his 80th birthday.

I think that Sir John Cockcroft may have forgotten that he has been in correspondence with us earlier this year, and he had arranged for an artist called Robert Tollast to copy the Oswald Birley sketch which I have here.

I am so sorry that you had all this trouble in vain. Winston is well.

Press release
(Churchill papers, 1/62)

28 June 1962

Sir Winston had a fall early this morning and suffered a fracture of the neck of the femur. He is in Monaco Hospital and it is not yet certain whether he will remain there or be flown back to England. The Press are requested not to telephone either the hospital or Sir Winston's medical advisers but to await bulletins.

Harold Macmillan to Sir Winston S. Churchill
(Churchill papers, 1/63)[1]

29 June 1962

Dear Winston,

I am so sorry about your accident; but very glad to hear that you have got home all right. I hope you will soon be well enough for your friends to come & see you.

With deep affection

---

[1] This letter was handwritten.

Diana Sandys to Sir Winston S. Churchill
(*Churchill papers, 1/63*)[1]

29 June 1962

Darling Papa,

I am so sorry about your beastly accident & I do hope you are not having too much pain. Let me know when you would like a visit. I'm so anxious about you.

Love & blessing
Diana

Queen Elizabeth II to Sir Winston S. Churchill
(*Churchill papers, 1/63*)

[June] 1962

I am so distressed to learn of your accident. My husband and I send you our best wishes for your speedy recovery.

Anthony Montague Browne to General Lord Ismay
(*Churchill papers, 1/63*)

2 July 1962

Thank you very much for your letter. I told both Sir Winston and Lady Churchill that you had written and they have asked me to let you know how much they value your sympathy.

I am glad to say that the Boss is getting on pretty well and has been up two or three times in a chair. This, as of course you know, is to avoid pneumonia. So far all is well, but the next two or three days are a little anxious. On the whole things have gone much better than we expected.

Arabella Churchill to Sir Winston S. Churchill
(*Churchill papers, 1/63*)[2]

2 July 1962

Darling Grandpapa,

I am so sorry to hear about your accident, I wish I could come and see you in hospital, when I come up from school. I do hope your leg does not hurt terribly, and not keep you awake at night. Here is some Foie Gras for you to eat

---

[1] This letter was handwritten.

[2] This letter was handwritten.

in bed, and here is a photograph of me. Please give my love to Grandmama, I have not seen either of you for so long, and I would love to.

Do get better soon

Lots of love,

Anthony Montague Browne to Lord Moran
(Churchill papers, 1/62)

4 July 1962
Private

I am taking off six days next week in the High Alps from Monday, July 9, until Sunday, the 15th. I will, of course, leave a telephone number, and can be back within about eight hours if needed. I thought I would go then after discussion with Lady Churchill, as it seems better for me to be away while Sir Winston is in hospital rather than when he comes out.

I understand that the date of his departure cannot definitely be fixed, but I believe from what your colleagues have said that it is likely to be between July 17 and 24.

Lady Churchill presumes that it would be best for Sir Winston to go straight to Chartwell rather than to come here.[1] But you may have other views. I am sure that Lady Churchill will fall in with whatever you consider best. Here in London the problem of getting Sir Winston up and down stairs arises, but we have in the past met this with a carrying chair.

Meanwhile, Lady Churchill has raised with me two other points,
1. Should Sir Winston have a special bed or would his ordinary bed here or at Chartwell suffice?
2. When Sir Winston leaves hospital, is he likely to be confined to his room, or if he wishes can he, for instance, go to the cinema at Chartwell? If this were so, I suppose we would have to arrange for him to be carried up and down stairs in a carrying chair.

I wonder if it would be possible for us to have a preliminary talk about these points before I leave next Monday. I will be at your disposal, perhaps here on the telephone if you think that that is sufficient.

---

[1] Hyde Park Gate. Alterations were made to the house to eliminate the need for Churchill to use stairs.

1962

Field Marshal Lord Montgomery to Lady Churchill
(Churchill papers, 1/63)[1]

5 July 1962

My dearest Clemmie,

I was so glad to hear your voice on the telephone this morning. I will be in London on Wednesday next week – the 11th July. Can I go and see Winston then? I only want to look into his eyes, shake his hand, wish him good luck – and go out. Two minutes, that is all.

I am so very fond of him.

President John F. Kennedy to Sir Winston S. Churchill
(Churchill papers, 1/63)

6 July 1962

Dear Sir Winston,

We have been encouraged by the reports of the progress you have made and heartened again by your display of indomitable courage in the face of adversity. The wishes of all our peoples as well as those of Mrs Kennedy[2] and I go to you.

Randolph S. Churchill: diary
(Randolph Churchill papers)

11 July 1962

Went to London this morning. Lunched with CSC at Hyde Park Gate; then to Christies to look at furniture in sale tomorrow; thence driving 3.30 to Middlesex Hospital to see WSC.

He was, considering everything, looking well; he was sweetly affectionate, absent-minded and bloody minded. His great grievance was a metal tent over his left foot (to keep the sheet and counterpane from pressing on his left leg.) He asked for the nurse, whom I got, and said to her: 'Couldn't you take this damn thing away?' She said 'No' and withdrew. A little later he said with great pathos to me 'Wouldn't even you take it away?' I did, and then regretted it and went out and called the nurse who came back and replaced it rather violently, hurting one of his toes in doing so. All nurses are madly in love with doctors and obey their orders unthinkingly. WSC's hope of living

---

[1] This letter was handwritten.
[2] Jacqueline Lee Bouvier, 1929–94. Educated at Vassar College and George Washington University, 1951. Married, 1953, John Fitzgerald Kennedy (d. 1963); 1968, Aristotle Onassis (d. 1975). First Lady of the US, 1961–3.

is in his will power and not in the skill of doctors however experienced and devoted.

If he continues to be frustrated in small matters he will blow up and die.

A little later, Sergeant Murray, the detective, poked his nose round the door and WSC said 'Won't you take this thing away?' 'No Sir Winston' said that disciplined man 'the nurses say you must keep it there.'

I was with him for forty minutes and as I have been told that it was a good thing for him to wiggle his toes and move his left ankle, I tickled his toes through the counterpane. He wriggled them with great effect and when the counterpane was removed I looked at his toes. They were still as beautifully shaped as ever and the nails were exquisitely manicured.

He did not seem to want me to leave. When I said 'Would you like me to come and see you again?' He reacted more brightly and coherently than at any time during our talk: He said 'Next time you come to see me I hope I will receive you in the House of Commons.'

Lady Soames: letter to the Editor
('Finest Hour', No. 117, Winter 2002–2003, page 9)

11 July 1962

Your last issue reported an article in the *Daily Mail* quoting Field Marshal Montgomery, who stated in 1962[1] that he had found my father 'protesting against Britain's proposed entry into the Common Market'. I wish to record that Montgomery's statement not only took advantage of a private conversation with an old man who had only recently sustained a bad accident and had flown home for an operation; it also misrepresented my father's views. What I remember clearly is that not only my father, but all of us – particularly my mother – were outraged by Monty's behaviour, and he was roundly rebuked.

Anthony Montague Browne: recollection
('Long Sunset', page 274)

11 July 1962

Field Marshal Montgomery emerged [from Middlesex Hospital] to tell the waiting press, quite truthfully, that 'the patient was in excellent form'.

[1] Montgomery's remarks to the press were made one week after publication of his article, 'I Saw We Must Not Join Europe', *Sunday Express*, 3 July 1962, in which he wrote: 'The intention behind the Rome Treaty is something more than the Common Market; there would be little point in the Treaty if that was to be all; the "something more"; is political unity, a Federation on the model of the USA. We could not possibly take part in that; it might well mean that we would have our laws made for us by Europeans and not by our Parliament.'

Unfortunately he went on to declare that WSC was totally and fundamentally opposed to Britain joining the EEC. This was not an invention, but a serious misinterpretation of an old and sick man's views by a totally black-or-white-and-no-middle-ground interpreter. I heard it on my car's radio as I drove home from the Middlesex, where I had left Monty. Consulting nobody, I immediately released to the press a statement of WSC's views on the subject that he had embodied in a private and unpublished letter to his Constituency Chairman, Mrs Moss, in August 1961.[1] [. . .]

It might have been better to keep total silence, but this would have implied a negative stance, particularly in view of Monty's indiscreet intervention. So, after agonising, I had cobbled together as best I could what I, feeling that I knew WSC's thoughts better than any one else at that time, considered could do the least harm.

However, when Monty gave his account of WSC's views, I received a telephone call from Philip de Zulueta at Number Ten. 'The Prime Minister has asked me to find out "What the hell that boy Browne is doing,"' he said mildly. I bristled and suggested that he wait and see what WSC's formal views were when the Constituency letter was published that evening. This was not good enough, and a messenger arrived from Number Ten for a copy. The milk-and-water contents did not get anyone anywhere, but it took the heat off and pacified both Macmillan and the Euro-antis.

Anthony Montague Browne to Lord Moran
(Churchill papers, 1/62)

16 August 1962

When Sir Winston leaves hospital, we must consider how to thank the many people who have been helpful to him. I wonder if you could give me any thoughts you have on the matter?

With the help of our nurses, we are compiling a list of nurses, porters, etc., at the hospital, but this leaves unmentioned the more eminent figures of Brigadier Hardy-Roberts,[2] the Matron[3] and Assistant Matron,[4] and of course the surgeons and doctors. I presume that those who have attended Sir Winston will be sending in their accounts sooner or later, and I was thinking in terms of framed signed photographs for those less directly concerned,

---

[1] Reproduced above (pp. 2309–10).
[2] Geoffrey Hardy-Roberts, 1907–97. Served in British Army, 1926–37, 1939–45. Sat on London County Council, 1938–46. CBE, 1944. CB, 1945. Secretary-Superintendent of Middlesex Hospital, 1946–67. High Sheriff, Sussex, 1965. Master of Her Majesty's Household, 1967–73. Extra Equerry to the Queen, 1967–97. KCVO, 1972.
[3] Marjorie Jane Marriott, 1903–82. Matron and Superintendent of Nurses at Middlesex Hospital, 1946–65. President, General Nursing Council of England and Wales, 1958–60, 1962–3. OBE, 1959.
[4] Gillian 'Sunny' Keefe Morton, 1939–. Nurse at Middlesex Hospital.

and for Professor Seddon and Mr Newman[1] possibly an inscribed silver cigarette box. What do you think?

Sir Winston S. Churchill to F. A. Richardson[2]
(Churchill papers, 1/62)

22 August 1962

Dear Mr Richardson,

Would you please convey to the Ambulance driver and his assistants my warm thanks for the skill and care with which they brought me home from the Middlesex Hospital yesterday?

Doreen Pugh to Emery Reves
(Churchill papers, 4/26)

4 September 1962

Dear Mr Reves,

So sorry to bother you, but can you tell us if Professor Enéas Camargo of Brazil translated the *History of the English-Speaking Peoples* vol. 2 from English into Portuguese? He says he did and asks for an autograph, and if he really did we think he probably deserves it. But we thought we should check with you first.

I do hope you and Wendy are well.

Sir Winston is doing tremendously well, and has even walked, with assistance, down the steps into the garden here. He is delighted with his new bedroom [. . .].

Sir Winston S. Churchill to Marjorie Marriott
(Churchill papers, 1/62)

17 September 1962

My dear Miss Marriott,

Now that I have so much recovered, I should like to express to you my gratitude for the remarkable skill, care and devotion with which you and all your staff looked after me in the Middlesex Hospital. I have written to many who were associated with me individually, but everything I encountered at the

---

[1] Philip Harker Newman, 1911–94. Conjoint diploma from Middlesex Hospital Medical School, London University, 1934. Served in British Army, 1939–45. DSO, 1940. MC, 1942. Consultant Orthopedic Surgeon at Middlesex Hospital, 1945–76; at Royal National Orthopedic Hospital, 1946–76. President, British Orthopedic Association, 1976. CBE, 1976.

[2] Superintendent of Ambulance Services, Middlesex Hospital.

Middlesex Hospital made a strong impression on me, and I hope that you will accept my very warm thanks and good wishes, together with a copy of my *History of the English-Speaking Peoples*, which I have signed for you.

Sir Winston S. Churchill to Lady Churchill
(Baroness Spencer-Churchill papers)[1]

[October 1962]

Darling,

I hope you are going on well & that we may come together again tomorrow. I have found it quite lonely & will rejoice to see us joined together in gaeity and love. Dearest one I place myself at your disposal & intend to take a walk in the park hand in hand. With many Kisses.

Sir Winston S. Churchill to Lady Churchill
(Baroness Spencer-Churchill papers)[2]

[1962]

Darling,

Please let me know how you are. I do hope you are getting on & will soon be thriving again.

Yours ever
Pig

Anthony Montague Browne to Lord Beaverbrook
(Churchill papers, 2/519)

15 October 1962

I have not written to you, as there has not been a great deal of news lately. Sir Winston's health seems stationary: he is in fairly good spirits and is in many ways intellectually better than before his accident, but his mobility is not increasing and he is very bored. He was pleased and complimented by your photographs and letter about his bust. Do you think it would be appropriate for him to write to Lady Dunn?

I think that it is just possible that Sir Winston will be able to go to Monte Carlo after Christmas, if General de Gaulle has not done a Goa[3] by then.

---

[1] This letter was handwritten.
[2] This letter was handwritten.
[3] Comparing the possibility of de Gaulle rejecting the March 1962 Evian Agreements, which granted Algeria independence, to the Indian invasion in Dec. 1951 of Goa, a Portuguese territory on the Indian subcontinent.

I think everyone is a bit alarmed about the India–China conflict. I hope that we shall not be foolish enough to get involved. I should give India just as much assistance as she gave us at Suez.

My only real news is that Sir Winston is putting Lord Moran's name forward for the Other Club!

I do trust that your own health is improving.

Randolph Churchill: diary
(Randolph Churchill papers)

17 October 1962

WSC confirmed to Winston at luncheon the anecdote about coffee and Lady Astor.[1]

Pamela Lady Lytton was present at luncheon. CSC said to Winston before she arrived 'She is an old flame of your grandfather's. She knew him before I did and after we were married she tried to take him away from me; but I did not allow this.'

Sir Winston S. Churchill: statement
(Churchill papers)

22 November 1962

I am honoured that Westminster College should wish to commemorate the speech I made at Fulton on March 5, 1946.[2] The removal of a ruined Christopher Wren church, largely destroyed by enemy action in London in 1941, and its reconstruction and re-dedication at Fulton, is an imaginative concept. It may symbolise in the eyes of the English-speaking peoples the ideals of Anglo-American association on which rest, now as before, so many of our hopes for peace and the future of mankind.

---

[1] Nancy Witcher Langhorne, 1879–1964. Born in Virginia. Married, 1897, Robert Gould Shaw (div. 1903); 1906, 2nd Viscount Astor. MP (Cons.) for Plymouth Sutton, 1919–45 (the first woman to take her seat in the Westminster Parliament). CH, 1937. According to this anecdote, Lady Astor said to Churchill, 'If I were your wife, I'd give you poison in your coffee' – to which he replied: 'If you were my wife, I'd drink it.'

[2] Reproduced in *The Churchill Documents*, vol. 22, *Leader of the Opposition, August 1945 to October 1951*, pp. 227–35.

Randolph Churchill: notes of a conversation
(*Randolph Churchill papers*)

1 December 1962

TALK WITH MRS MURIEL WARDE[1]

RSC called on Mrs Muriel Warde at Cannon Hall, Cannon Place, London, NW3.

RSC was ushered in through a number of rooms, including the dining room, to a sitting room overlooking the one acre garden, where Mrs Warde sat with her feet in a foot cosy. Early in our talk she said: 'Would you like to have half a glass of port? I have got some rather good port – I opened a bottle the other day.' I said: 'Yes, I would', it then being 11.45 a.m.

The butler came and Mrs Warde ordered a glass of port and 'the usual' for her. He returned in two minutes with a glass of port for RSC and a glass of white wine. She said: 'I usually have that at this time of day.'

At an early stage RSC asked her about the letters (see correspondence attached from Lady Listowel) from WSC.

> MW: 'Oh! I have sent all the letters – they are not love letters – to the bank, sealed, and with a note saying 'Not to be opened till after my death.'
>
> RSC: 'Could you not give them instructions to send them to me: I would have them copied and return them to the bank in another sealed envelope.'
>
> MW: 'Well, I will have to think about that.'

WSC first met MW at a party at Hindlip when they were both eighteen. She was very shy, but quickly made friends with Winston, who said that he 'hated parties'. This remark put her at her ease and they soon became close friends. Winston stayed quite often at Tranby Croft.

She repeated what she had already written to RSC about WSC walking up and down the drive at Tranby Croft greatly bored trying to improve the enunciation of his S's:

'The Spanish ships I cannot see, for they are not in sight.'

> RSC: 'Do you remember where these lines came from?'
>
> MW: 'No!'
>
> RSC: 'We will find out.'
>
> MW: 'All the young guardsmen whom Winston was apt to meet in his early manhood hated him. They thought him "too clever", and used to ask me what on earth I saw in him. He found them very boring.'
>
> RSC: 'How well had you known my father and was it true that he had proposed to you?'
>
> MW: 'Oh, he proposed repeatedly, but it was merely good manners on

[1] Muriel Thetis Wilson, 1875–1964. Youngest daughter of Arthur Wilson of Tranby Croft. Married, 1919, Richard Edward Warde, 1884–1932.

his part.' She went on: 'You see, there were three of them – all cousins – Freddy Guest,[1] Winston, and there was another one who became a duke – who was it – yes, Sunny Marlborough. They all travelled around together: I saw a lot of them.'

RSC: 'What about Ivor Wimborne[2] – the old dog?'

MW: 'No, I never thought much of him.'

RSC: 'Why didn't you accept my father?'

MW: 'I liked both the other cousins better.'

RSC: 'Well, they married very well. Freddie married Amy Phipps[3] and Sunny married Consuelo Vanderbilt.'

MW: 'Well, you see I was not nearly an heiress. I only had £4,000 a year. My father said to me: "All you'll have is £4,000 a year – perhaps £8,000 a year but not a penny more.'

RSC complimented MW on her fine garden, which she said was of about an acre. She pronounced it 'arker'. She had bought it sixteen years before when she found she could not live in her house in the South of France, Marylands, because the Treasury would not allow her more than £2,000 p.a. across the exchange. She had bought the house from a man who had been Private Secretary to Sir Ernest Cassell[4] and she was shocked at how run down the house was. She said that she had no direct heirs but had asked one of her nephews whether he would like to live in the house. He had replied: 'Not on your life,' so, she continued, 'I suppose it will be sold on my death and the proceeds divided among my family.'

RSC noticed on the wall a charcoal drawing of MW by Sargent.[5] He expressed his admiration for it. It was dated 1907.

RSC: 'Could I borrow that and have it photographed to put in either the first or the second volume?'

---

[1] Frederick Edward Guest, 1875–1937. Third son of 1st Baron Wimborne. Churchill's cousin. Served in South African War as Capt., Life Guards, 1899–1902. Private Secretary to Churchill, 1906. An original member of the Other Club, 1911. Treasurer, HM Household, 1912–15. ADC to Sir John French, 1914–16. On active service in East Africa, 1916–17. Patronage Secretary, Treasury (Chief Whip), May 1917 to Apr. 1921. PC, 1920. Secretary of State for Air, Apr. 1921 to Oct. 1922. MP (Lib.) for Stroud Div. of Gloucester, 1923–4; for Bristol North, 1924–9. Joined Conservative Party, 1930. MP (Unionist) for Plymouth, 1931–7.

[2] Ivor Churchill Guest, 1873–1939. Served in Imperial Yeomanry, 1896–1902. MP (Cons., Lib.) for Plymouth, 1900–6 (following Churchill to the Liberals in 1904); for Cardiff, 1906–10. Baron Ashby St Ledgers, 1910. Paymaster General, 1910–12. Lord-in-Waiting, 1913–15. 2nd Baron Wimborne, 1914. Lord Lieutenant of Ireland, 1915–18. 1st Viscount Wimborne, 1918.

[3] Amy Phipps, 1873–1959. Prominent women's suffragist, philanthropist and aviation enthusiast. Daughter of American industrialist Henry Phipps. Married, 1905, Frederick Guest: three children.

[4] Ernest Joseph Cassel, 1852–1921. Merchant banker and philanthropist: attained net worth of over £7 million. Royal Order of Vasa, 1900. PC, 1902. Order of Osmanieh, 1903. Commander of the Légion d'Honneur, 1906. GCB, 1909. Order of the Rising Sun, first class, 1911. Order of the Red Eagle, first class with brilliants, 1913.

[5] John Singer Sargent, 1856–1925. Born in Italy of American parents. Renowned landscape artist and portraitist of society figures.

MW: 'Oh, I don't think so. You see, Sargent did just what I wanted. I said to him, draw me with a long neck, and you see' – she said triumphantly – 'he did what I told him.'

RSC: 'I am going to publish a drawing by Violet, Duchess of Rutland,[1] of Pamela Lytton in the first volume, and it would be a serious blemish on the book if we did not have a picture of you.'

MW: 'How soon can you send it back?'

RSC: 'Within a week.'

And RSC was allowed to take it off the wall and take it away.

RSC: 'Did you know Pamela Lytton very well?'

MW: 'Yes, I knew her very well – well, perhaps not very well. She didn't like me: but she was very pretty.'

Earlier in the conversation MW had said that she had an old friend, who was a neighbour – a Colonel Pitt, who usually looked in on Saturdays, and I hoped that I could persuade him (who sounded like the 'homme d'affaires') to get the letters from the bank. But when half an hour had passed and I was not offered another half glass of port I began to excuse myself.

She escorted me through the dining room and showed me the Laszlo[2] oil painting of herself, which she said was far inferior to the Sargent, and a picture of her mother in later life, who looked like a glorious grande dame.

Colonel Pitt never showed up, and I went off with the Sargent drawing and got into my motor car, telling the butler on the way (whom I forgot to tip) that Mrs Warde had authorised me to take the picture away, but that I would return it after being photographed within a week.

RSC had tried in the morning to buy some photographic albums in which to put his photographs of his garden to present to WSC and CSC. Hatchards had discontinued the business and the firm recommended by Natalie in Jermyn Street were closed on Saturdays. On the way back from Hampstead RSC thought of Wallace Heaton,[3] and the driver said the head office was in Bond Street whither we went. As RSC was getting out of the car he thought that Wallace Heaton might well photograph the Sargent drawing – so he left it there, with the instruction to return the original to Mrs Warde on Wednesday and to send three copies to RSC.

[. . .]

---

[1] Marion Margaret Violet Manners, 1856–1937. Artist. Marchioness of Granby, 1888–1906. Duchess of Rutland, 1906–37.

[2] Philip Alexius de Laszlo, 1869–1937. Born in Hungary. Settled in London, 1907. Successful portrait painter of royal and aristocratic clients.

[3] Wallace Evans Heaton, 1877–1957. Purchased Watsons of High Street photographic business in Sheffield, 1902. Founding member, Photographic Dealers Association, 1914; President, 1920. Opened photography shop in London as Wallace Heaton Ltd, 1919. Awarded Royal Warrant by King George VI, 1938.

1963

Sir Winston S. Churchill to Paul-Henri Spaak
(Anthony Montague Browne, 'Long Sunset', page 273)

31 January 1963
Not Sent

My Dear Spaak,

I was moved by your eloquent remarks.[1] It is to me further proof, if this were needed, of your statesmanship and far-sighted approach to the problems that confront us. The future of Europe if Britain were to be excluded is black indeed. [. . .]

Anthony Montague Browne to Sir Frank Roberts
(Churchill papers, 2/533)

13 February 1963
Private and Confidential

I do not know if this letter will catch you or not before you leave, but I wanted to explain my silence on the matter we discussed at Patsy Jellicoe's[2] party.

---

[1] On Jan. 14, France vetoed British membership in the EEC. On Jan. 29, Spaak, addressing the 17th ministerial meeting between the EEC Member States and the UK, stated: 'The movement to unite Europe and give it back its place in the world has, like every great movement, days of victory and days of defeat. Today is incontestably a day of defeat. Great Britain has been excluded without valid reason in the opinion of five of the delegations of the Common Market, from the negotiations over its entry. [. . .] As soon as one member of a Community seeks to force all the others into decisions of capital importance for its life, the Community spirit ceases to exist. It will be extremely difficult, I am convinced, to continue to develop economic Europe. As for the political Europe of which we had dreamed as a necessary consequence of economic organisation, I do not know when it will be possible to speak of this again, since there is no doubt that confidence has been destroyed.'

[2] George Patrick John Rushworth Jellicoe, 1918–2007. Known as 'Patsy'. Son of John Jellicoe, who served as Admiral of the Grand Fleet during Churchill's tenure as 1st Lord of the Admiralty. 2nd Earl, 1935. Educated at Trinity College, Cambridge. On active service in WWII with Coldstream Guards and SAS (DSO, despatches thrice, MC, wounded), serving alongside Randolph Churchill. 8 Commando, 1940–1. 3rd Battalion, Coldstream Guards, 1941–2. 1st SAS Rgt, 1942–3. SBS, 1943–4. Negotiated with the Italians at Rhodes and Leros during Dodecanese campaign.

The fact is that since we spoke, Sir Winston, though physically well, has been somewhat lethargic and indifferent to events. In the circumstances, I did not feel that a meeting would produce anything useful of the kind we had in mind, so I let it slide.

I did, however, talk to Sir Winston and Lady Churchill about your departure to Bonn. They both send you their warmest good wishes, and Lady Churchill sends her remembrances of your very agreeable meeting in Moscow in 1945.

Anthony Montague Browne to Lord Beaverbrook
(Churchill papers, 2/519)

21 February 1963

I was so glad to hear that your health had sufficiently recovered for you to go to the South of France. This is indeed good news, and I hope that the warmer climate will restore you fully and rapidly.

I have little news, but I think that it is possible that Sir Winston will go down briefly to the Hotel de Paris before the Spring. He speaks of it from time to time, but never reaches a conclusion as to whether he really wishes to or not. He attended the meeting of the Other Club and much enjoyed it, though he finds it extremely difficult to hear, and his hearing-aid only increases the confusion of many people speaking.

I was very glad to see that your initiative in the *Evening Standard* has stirred up interest in the 'intellectual hemorrhage'. I enclose a cutting from today's *Daily Mail* on the Royal Society's Report. You may note that they have even stolen your headline!

You will have seen that Randolph is suing *Private Eye*.[1] Undoubtedly Sir Winston himself was libelled, but I am not so sure about Randolph. Clearly Sir Winston can ride over these matters and should not sue, quite apart from the physical difficulties of possibly having to appear in the witness-box, and so on.

Would you please give my affectionate regards to Lady Dunn?

POW, 1943; escaped shortly afterwards. Combined Operations, 1944–5. Married, 1944, Patricia Christine O'Kane: four children (div. 1966); 1966, Philippa Ann Dunne: three children. Minister of State, Home Office, 1962–3. PC, 1963. 1st Lord of the Admiralty, 1963–4. Lord Privy Seal, 1970–3. Leader of the House of Lords, 1970–3. KBE, 1986. Baron, 1999.

[1] This was the first libel case against *Private Eye*, which had published a cartoon of Randolph Churchill ('Rudolph Rednose') at home surrounded by 'hacks' and 'hirelings' helping him to write the biography of his father. *Private Eye* eventually paid £3,000 in damages and printed a full-page apology in the London *Evening Standard*.

Sir Winston S. Churchill to Lord Beaverbrook
(Beaverbrook papers)

5 March 1963

My dear Max,

I am fascinated by your account of Lloyd George.[1] It is a most remarkable work and will long be read and remembered for the entertainment it offers, quite apart from its enormous value to the historian. I am so glad to see that the reviewers do it justice.

Sir Winston S. Churchill to Lady Churchill
(Baroness Spencer-Churchill papers)[2]

8 April 1963

My darling one,

This is only to give you my fondest love and kisses <u>a hundred times repeated</u>. I am a pretty dull & paltry scribbler; but my stick as I write carries my heart along with it.

Yours ever & always

President John F. Kennedy: speech
(American Rhetoric Online Speech Bank)

9 April 1963   The White House

Members of the Congress, Members of the Cabinet, His Excellency the British Ambassador, Ambassadors of the Commonwealth, old friends of Sir Winston led by Mr Baruch, ladies and gentlemen:

We gather today at a moment unique in the history of the United States.

This is the first time that the United States Congress has solemnly resolved that the President of the United States shall proclaim an honorary citizenship for the citizen of another country. And in joining me to perform this happy duty, the Congress gives Sir Winston Churchill a distinction shared only with the Marquis de Lafayette.[3]

In proclaiming him an honorary citizen, I only propose a formal recognition of the place he has long since won in the history of freedom and in the affections of my – and now his – fellow countrymen.

Whenever and wherever tyranny threatened, he has always championed

---

[1] Lord Beaverbrook, *The Decline and Fall of Lloyd George* (1963).

[2] This letter was handwritten.

[3] Marie Joseph Paul Yves Roche Gilbert du Motier, 1757–1834. Marquis de Lafayette. Officer, Musketeers, 1771. Capt., Dragoons, 1775. Maj.-Gen., US Army, American War of Independence.

liberty. Facing firmly toward the future, he has never forgotten the past. Serving six monarchs of his native Great Britain, he has served all men's freedom and dignity.

In the dark days and darker nights when England stood alone – and most men, save Englishmen, despaired of England's life – he mobilized the English language and sent it into battle. The incandescent quality of his words illuminated the courage of his countrymen.

Indifferent himself to danger, he wept over the sorrows of others. A child of the House of Commons, he became its father. Accustomed to the hardships of battle, he has no distaste for pleasure.

Now his stately ship of life, having weathered the severest storms of a troubled century, is anchored in tranquil waters – proof that courage and faith and zest for freedom are truly indestructible. The record of his triumphant passage will inspire free hearts all over the globe.

By adding his name to our rolls, we mean to honor him; but his acceptance honors us much more. For no statement or proclamation can enrich its name now – the name Sir Winston Churchill is already legend.

Sir Winston S. Churchill: statement[1]
('Winston S. Churchill, His Complete Speeches', volume 8, pages 8709–10)

9 April 1963   The White House

HONORARY UNITED STATES CITIZENSHIP

Mr President, I have been informed by Mr David Bruce[2] that it is your intention to sign a Bill conferring upon me Honorary Citizenship of the United States.

I have received many kindnesses from the United States of America, but the honour which you now accord me is without parallel. I accept it with deep gratitude and affection.

I am also most sensible of the warm-hearted action of the individual States who accorded me the great compliment of their own honorary citizenships as a prelude to this Act of Congress.

It is a remarkable comment on our affairs that the former Prime Minister of a great sovereign state should thus be received as an honorary citizen of another. I say 'great sovereign state' with design and emphasis, for I reject the view that Britain and the Commonwealth should now be relegated to a tame and minor role in the world. Our past is the key to our future, which I firmly

---

[1] Read by Randolph Churchill at the White House.
[2] David Kirkpatrick Este Bruce, 1898–1977. Maryland House of Delegates, 1924–6, 1939–42. Head, OSS, 1943–5. US Ambassador to France, 1948–52; to West Germany, 1957–9; to UK, 1961–9; to NATO, 1974–6. Chief, US Liaison Office to People's Republic of China, 1973–4.

trust and believe will be no less fertile and glorious. Let no man underrate our energies, our potentialities and our abiding power for good.

I am, as you know, half American by blood, and the story of my association with that mighty and benevolent nation goes back nearly ninety years to the day of my Father's marriage. In this century of storm and tragedy I contemplate with high satisfaction the constant factor of the interwoven and upward progress of our peoples. Our comradeship and our brotherhood in war were unexampled. We stood together, and because of that fact the free world now stands. Nor has our partnership any exclusive nature: the Atlantic community is a dream that can well be fulfilled to the detriment of none and to the enduring benefit and honour of the great democracies.

Mr President, your action illuminates the theme of unity of the English-speaking peoples, to which I have devoted a large part of my life. I would ask you to accept yourself, and to convey to both Houses of Congress, and through them to the American people, my solemn and heartfelt thanks for this unique distinction, which will always be proudly remembered by my descendants.

Jacqueline Kennedy Onassis: recollection
('Finest Hour', No. 79, Spring 1993, page 10)

9 April 1963

We met in [Jack's] office. Randolph was ashen, his voice a whisper. Someone said he had been up most of the night. 'All that this ceremony means to the two principals,' I thought, 'is the gift they wish it to be to Randolph's father – and they are both so nervous it will be a disaster.'

The French windows opened and they went outside. Jack spoke first but I couldn't listen – every second was ticking closer to Randolph. Then the presentation. Randolph stepped forward to respond: 'Mr President'. His voice was strong. He spoke on, with almost the voice of Winston Churchill, but while others could imitate Sir Winston, Randolph's voice was finer.

He sent his words across the afternoon, that most brilliant, loving son. His head was the head of his son beside him – Randolph and Winston – those two names that would for ever succeed each other as long as Churchills had sons. And Randolph speaking for his father. Always for his father.

But that afternoon, the world stopped and looked at Randolph. And many saw what they had missed. After, in the Green Room – the happy relief – Randolph surrounded, with his loving friends – we so proud of him and for him – he knowing he had failed no one, and had moved so many. I will for ever remember that as Randolph's day.

Harold Macmillan to Sir Winston S. Churchill
(*Churchill papers, 2/539*)

10 April 1963

Dear Winston,

I gave a dinner last night for General Lemnitzer.[1] He used to be American Deputy to Field Marshal Alexander in the Mediterranean Campaign and is now the Supreme Allied Commander in Europe. Field Marshals Alexander and Harding, Lord Mountbatten and General Strong[2] all came. We and others present unanimously agreed to send you a message recalling the days when we worked together under your leadership. We wished also to express our delight at your versatility which allows you to combine being a loyal British subject with being a good United States citizen.

Sir Winston S. Churchill to Lady Churchill
(*Baroness Spencer-Churchill papers*)

19 April 1963   Monte Carlo

My darling one,

Nonie will carry this letter.

We have passed the afternoons for the most part in long drives, and have found them most agreeable.

I must say it would be a great pity to blot these apartments out from our use. They are both comfortable and sleek. We have had markedly fine weather. The sun has shone repeatedly every day, and has backed up our many repetitions of plunges.

I wish I had you with me, and I do hope you will not write it off as a gone concern. There is no doubt that these rooms are very pleasant.

I think on the whole that with your wedding episodes which may play their role, I would come home on the 25th. Thank you so much for your telegram received today. All the same, I am looking forward to getting home and seeing you again.

---

[1] Lyman Lemnitzer, 1899–1988. Instructor at West Point, 1926–30, 1934–5; at Coast Artillery School, 1936–9. Brig.-Gen., 1942. Maj.-Gen., 1944. Gen. and Cdr of US Army in the Far East, 1955. Cdr, Far East Command and United National Command, 1955–7. CoS, US Army, 1957–60. Chairman, JCS, 1960–2. SACEUR, 1963–9.

[2] Kenneth William Dobson Strong, 1900–82. Chief of Intelligence, AFHQ Mediterranean, 1943–4; SHAEF, 1944–5. Director-General of Political Intelligence Dept, FO, 1945–7. First Director of Joint Intelligence Bureau, MoD, 1948–64; of Intelligence, MoD, 1964–6.

2346 1963

Lady Churchill to Sir Winston S. Churchill
(Baroness Spencer-Churchill papers)[1]

19 April 1963

My Darling Winston,
    Thank you so much for your loving letter.
    I am so glad you are having a pleasant interlude; but I look forward much to your return on the 25th. I hope Darling you are thinking carefully about the letter Christopher wrote to you. He read it to me before he despatched it & I agree with all he says.
    I don't see how you can stand next year without campaigning & fighting for your seat. And it would be kind to let your Executive Council know now, before they become too restive.

                                                   All my love Darling

Lady Churchill to Christopher Soames
(Mary Soames, 'Clementine Churchill', page 484)

1 May 1963

    ... In tomorrow's newspapers you will see Winston's letter to his Chairman telling her that he will not stand again at the next General Election.
    I feel your excellently reasoned letter was a contributory cause to it being written *at last*!
    I am much relieved as the situation at Woodford was becoming increasingly uneasy...

Harold Macmillan to Sir Winston S. Churchill
(Churchill papers)

14 May 1963

Dear Winston,
    I think you must have been pleased with your reception in the House of Commons today. It was a great occasion for us all. If you could find the poem about the ducks[2] I would be very glad to have it. I hope you enjoyed the set-to I had with the Leader of the Opposition. It was quite in the good old-fashioned style of knockabout.

---

[1] This letter was handwritten.
[2] A poem about the ducks in St James's Park, published in *Punch*, which Churchill had committed to memory. It contained the following lines:
Besoide the worter in Sin Jimes's Pork,
I've stritched meself ter snooze hunder this ole tree –
But cawn't, fur all the keckle, screech, an' squork,
From these yere ducks an' swans, an' sim'lar poultry!

1963

Sir Winston S. Churchill to Harold Macmillan
(*Churchill papers*)

18 May 1963

My dear Harold,

Thank you so much for your agreeable letter. I much enjoyed seeing you at luncheon too. But, alas, no one can find the poem about the ducks: it does not seem ever to have been put on paper. Though I think that it appeared in *Punch* at about the turn of the century. I am so sorry.

Anthony Montague Browne: recollection
(*'Long Sunset'*, pages 298-300)

June 1963

I was surprised when in 1963 WSC accepted Ari's invitation and left on 8 June on the last and the least fortunate cruise.¹ The guest list was partly ours and partly our host's. I had suggested Jock and Meg Colville, both because WSC enjoyed their company and because Jock had long hoped to be invited. Young Winston came, and finally, after a tussle, WSC was persuaded to include Randolph. The latter had after all introduced Ari to WSC and had maintained a dignified silence over the successive failures to take him. [. . .]

Randolph had hitherto behaved well, treating his father with respect and affection, and I was congratulating myself on having pushed for his inclusion. Alas, it was premature. 'Mai sans nuages, et Juin – poignardé.' Suddenly at dinner he erupted like Stromboli. For no apparent reason his rage was directed at his father, but then he began to particularise with violent reproaches relating to his wartime marriage. What he said was unseemly in any circumstances, but in front of comparative strangers it was ghastly. Nonie intervened with great courage, but Randolph, who was fond of her and normally treated her with regard, swept her aside as 'a gabby doll' – the mildest of his remarks that evening. I was equally unsuccessful in trying to divert his abuse from his father. Short of hitting him on the head with a bottle, nothing could have stopped him. Ari did his best, but was ignored. It was one of the most painful scenes I have ever witnessed. I had previously discounted the tales I had heard of Randolph. Now I believed them all.

WSC made no reply at all, but stared at his son with an expression of brooding rage. Then he went to his cabin. I followed him and found him shaking all over. I feared that he would suffer another stroke, and sat drinking whisky and soda with him until he was calmer. I will not record what he said, but it was plain that means must be found to remove Randolph from the ship.

---

¹ Churchill's eighth and final cruise aboard the Onassis yacht *Christina*, during which it toured the Mediterranean and Aegean, ended on July 4.

I sought out Ari, who was quite extraordinarily upset. 'But how could we have prevented it?' he said repeatedly. He had already reached the same conclusion as me, and was a jump ahead. Randolph was writing for, I think, the *News of the World*. Ari telephoned the King of Greece's Royal Chamberlain and arranged for either the King or Queen Frederika, who was a controversial figure in Britain at the time, to give Randolph an exclusive interview at their palace on the eastern Greek mainland. The next morning a cable of invitation was received. Randolph was pleased and flattered, but how was he to get there in time? Ari said that we would put into Corfu that evening and an Olympic Airways aircraft would fly Randolph to Athens. After a harmonious but rather silent dinner Randolph departed, humming 'Get me to the Church on time'. I accompanied him in the launch to the harbour. After a while he fell silent, and I saw that he was weeping.

'Anthony,' he said, 'you didn't think that I was taken in by that plan of Ari's and yours, do you? I do so very much love that man [WSC], but something always goes wrong between us.' I could only hope that there would be enough time left for Randolph to demonstrate his love, and WSC his.

Lady Churchill to Sergeant Edmund Murray
(Churchill papers, 1/143)

6 July 1963
Private

It was most unfortunate that you should have said to Sir Winston that you were sure that his Constituents would like him to stand again. This is not the case. They all honour and respect Sir Winston, but they realise that he could not fight an Election, and the Executive Council, numbering ninety persons representing the whole Association, were relieved to receive Sir Winston's letter saying he did not intend to stand at the next General Election.

What you said upset Sir Winston, which is sad. Although I do not believe that you wished to distress him, your uninformed comment was in fact most unhelpful. Naturally, his decision was made after consultation in a number of quarters, and the matter is settled and a prospective candidate has been adopted.[1] Would you therefore be so kind as not to say anything like this to him again?

You may like to know that the new candidate is coming to make Sir Winston's acquaintance on Saturday, July 13, when I am giving a Garden Party for the Executive Council.

---

[1] Charles Patrick Fleeming Jenkin, 1926–2016. Married, 1952, Alison Monica Graham. MP (Cons.) for Wanstead and Woodford, 1964–87. Secretary of State for the Environment, 1983–5. Baron, 1987.

1963

Anthony Montague Browne to Lord Beaverbrook
(Churchill papers, 2/519)

23 August 1963
Private

Many thanks for your letter. Nonie and I are touched and delighted by your invitation. We should love to take it up and come and see you, but assuming Sir Winston to be well enough, we are committed to a family holiday in Elba with Jane[1] starting on September 4, and until then I think that I must stay here. I wonder how long you are going to be at the Capponcina, because when Jane has gone back to school we should so much like to come if you would have us.

You say nothing of your own health, so I hope it is good.

The photograph of you and Sir Winston which I have had framed for Christofor is now ready, but it would probably get broken if sent through the post, so I will keep it for the present, unless someone is going out to you soon.

Sir Winston's state is stationary, which is a little worrying. He showed early signs of improvement, but they have not been maintained, and he cannot get up very much as when his foot is lowered to the ground it becomes discoloured, indicating that the impediment in the circulation is still there. Lady Churchill is very depressed, but, as you know, she is resilient and I have no doubt will recover her spirits.

Sir Winston is mentally much better than he was, and it is a great pity that his physical condition does not march with it.

May I say how delighted I am to see the Express newspapers defending our South African friends. I enclose a copy of a sad letter from a South African clergyman which may interest you. I am trying to get some sort of constructive answer for him, but I fear that one cannot urge Sir Winston to engage on this crusade himself, although I know where his sympathies most strongly lie.

Lady Soames: recollection
('Clementine Churchill', pages 479–80)

1 September 1963

It was school holiday time, and I was away with my family in France. But I received worrying accounts from Chartwell from both Grace Hamblin and from Monty, who had been to stay with my parents and who gave me a detailed report on them both. Winston was evidently improving physically, and his circulation was restored. 'But, as you know,' Monty wrote on 1st September 1963,

---

[1] Jane Montague Browne, 1953–. Married, 1978, Piers Hoare-Temple.

He can't now read a book or paper; he just lies all day in bed doing nothing.*
This has been a great strain on Clemmie, and she finally collapsed under it all and took to her bed the day after you and the children looked in on your way to France. She really is worn out. Winston dislikes being left alone all day with his nurses, and dislikes having meals alone; Clemmie found it a strain having to talk loudly to make him hear.

Since I have been here I have been with him all day, trying to interest him in things and showing him photographs of us two in the war. He is now definitely on the mend. He will recover. My view is that Clemmie is now the problem; she is worn out and needs rest. . . .

*It must be remembered that Winston's state varied very much, and this was a particularly bad period following on the specific circulatory trouble in his foot; he was by no means continuously bedridden.

Anthony Montague Browne to Lord Beaverbrook
(Churchill papers, 2/519)

3 September 1963

I thought that you would like to know that Sir Winston is making good, though slow, progress, and he is now getting up every day and seeing a film after dinner. Mentally, he continues a great deal better than during the summer.

Lady Churchill is feeling very depressed and unwell, and thinks that she is seriously ill, though the doctors say there is nothing organically wrong at all. In fact, therefore, she is having a prolonged rest in bed.

I do hope that all goes well with you and Christofor, and I much look forward to seeing you.

Lady Churchill to Sir Winston S. Churchill
(Churchill papers, 1/135)[1]

12 September 1963   Chartwell

My darling Winston,
   Today we have been married 55 years
   September the 12th 1908
   September the 12th 1963

                                                              Your loving
                                                                Clemmie

[1] This letter was handwritten.

Anthony Montague Browne to Field Marshal Lord Montgomery
(Churchill papers, 2/529)

26 September 1963

Many thanks for your letter. I have been intending to telephone you and give you the news, which is on the whole good.

Lady Churchill is resting at Mary's house, and every medical test has proved negative. However, she is still feeling rather low.

Sir Winston has improved considerably, not so much physically as in hearing and morale. When the Prime Minister visited him yesterday, he was in particularly good form and talked more than he has for a long time. I have arranged a series of visitors for dinner: Norman Brook, Jock Colville, Leslie Rowan and Alan Hodge, etc., and Sir Winston has films on the odd evening when he is by himself. So I think I can give you a good report.

I entirely agree with what you say about moving up to London. Mary feels the same thing and is urging it on Lady Churchill, so I hope we shall soon be back here. From my own point of view, it would be a great release!

I will keep you posted on any new developments.

May I say in conclusion how touched everyone around Sir Winston is by your devotion and care of him.

Anthony Montague Browne to Field Marshal Lord Montgomery
(Churchill papers, 2/529)

8 October 1963

I thought that you would like a progress report. Sir Winston is physically much the same, with perhaps a slight improvement. He is depressed by Lady Churchill's absence, but he is mentally clear and alert.

Lady Churchill is now in the Westminster Hospital, and there is no change in her condition. She has had sedation, and I have not been to see her, but have written to her saying that I will wait until I get a message asking me to do so.

A number of Sir Winston's friends and family have visited him, and we have not had many blank days. However, we are going up to London, I hope, today week, where, as you have pointed out, it will be much easier for people to come and see him, and where he himself can call on Lady Churchill.

Lady Soames: recollection
('Clementine Churchill', page 481)

19 October 1963

Diana had a great gift for friendship, and there were in particular three or four people to whom she could, and did, normally turn, in moments of depression or worry. In the family, her closest relationship was with Sarah. Together they had faced much, and each would always rush to the other's rescue in moments of crisis. As ill-chance would have it, at the time she took her life her main 'props-and-stays' were all away from London, and Celia also was staying in the country over that weekend. Edwina had seen her mother on the afternoon of Saturday, 19th October, and had found her in good spirits. Diana was due to lunch with her mother at the hospital the following day, and to dine with her father on that same Sunday evening. And so the dreadful news, when it broke upon us all, was not only totally unexpected, but seemingly inexplicable.

Both Winston and Clementine, although through different causes, were spared the sensations of extreme shock and grief that such a sudden and tragic event must normally bring. The lethargy of extreme old age dulls many sensibilities, and my father only took in slowly what I had to tell him: but he then withdrew into a great and distant silence. Despite her illness, it was absolutely necessary for my mother to know about Diana without delay, for she always listened to the news on the radio, and usually read the newspapers. Owing to the nature of her illness, she was under fairly heavy sedation, and so what I had to break to her was mercifully filtered and softened. I went to see her every day, and little by little she took it all in. But it was a merciful dispensation that they were both spared the necessary, but chill formalities and details of the inquest.

Clementine was enough recovered to return home the day before Diana's funeral, but neither of her parents was well enough to go to the service. However, both were present at the crowded and moving Memorial Service which was held the following week in St Stephen's, Walbrook, the church in the City of London the crypt of which houses the headquarters of the Samaritans. Diana's ashes lie near her parents' grave at Bladon.

Lord Beaverbrook to Lady Churchill
(Mary Soames, 'Clementine Churchill', pages 486–7)

30 November 1963

My dear Clemmie, What a burden you have borne over so many years – and with what charm & dignity. How much the Nation & the World owes to you for all your labours. And on this *89th birthday* I send you this message.

Many many intimates sending Winston messages of love & devotion will think of you. Max.

John Colville to Anthony Montague Browne
(Churchill papers, 2/514)

9 December 1963

My Dear Anthony,

I enclose copies of some correspondence I have had with the Prime Minister about my suggestion for making Sir Winston a Life Member of the House of Commons.

I think that the decision is unimaginative of the powers that be, and apart from giving great pleasure to Sir Winston, it would give great pleasure to the country.

Anthony Montague Browne to John Colville
(Churchill papers, 2/514)

11 December 1963
Private

Thank you so much for your letter of December 9 about Sir Winston's Life Membership. If I may say so, the mixture of eloquence and conciseness with which you write on major topics makes your letters a pleasure to read as well as extremely persuasive.

I am not altogether surprised by the answer from the Prime Minister. I have been led to believe that he himself would not be averse from the proposal, but that others are strongly opposed to it. It is perhaps appropriate that those responsible for our own 'very rapidly closing twilight' should not wish to honour the setting sun. So I suppose we must await a Socialist Government who may treat him more honourably than his 'friends'. It would not be the first time.

Funnily enough, at the French Embassy last night Anthony Wedgwood Benn[1] raised the matter with me and spoke of a Bill which would 'allow Sir Winston to sit in the House'. Whether this is the same as Life Membership, I do not know. In any case, we can only wait on events. I think you have done nobly in trying to promote the idea.

---

[1] Anthony Neil Wedgwood Benn, 1925–2014. MP (Lab.) for Bristol South East, 1950–60, 1963–83; for Chesterfield, 1984–2001. Succeeded as 2nd Viscount Stansgate, 1960; renounced peerage, 1963. Postmaster-General, 1964–6. Minister of Technology, 1966–70. Chairman of the Labour Party, 1971–2. Secretary of State for Industry, 1974–5; for Energy, 1975–9. President, Stop the War Coalition, 2001–14.

1964

Anthony Montague Browne to Lord Beaverbrook
(Churchill papers, 2/519)

17 January 1964
Private

Thank you very much for your letter of January 15. I have noted the date for the 1940 Club, I know that, as always, Sir Winston will greatly enjoy it.

I have been meaning to write to you for some time to give you such news as there is. Sir Winston has basically been on decline, but in the last two or three days he has suddenly staged one of the astonishing come-backs with which he has so often surprised us. Last night, for instance, he talked to me clearly and connectedly about the Prime Minister's speech in the House, to which he has listened. So one simply cannot tell, but I do rather wish that he would not go to the House, so that people will remember him from his great days.

In this connection, I told you privately of the proposal that he should be made an Honorary Member of the House by a special Act. I now learn that the Government have no intention of doing this, though I gather that the Prime Minister personally would like it. The Socialists, on the other hand, may conceivably go ahead if they win the Election! Or at least so Anthony Wedgwood Benn, who owes Sir Winston a debt of gratitude over his support on the Peerage issue, told me a few weeks ago.

Lady Churchill I think is better, but subdued. Randolph is delighted at the reception of his paper-back.[1] Sarah is still in the United States. Mary is making preparations for the eventual writing of her Mother's biography. And that concludes my family news.

I was delighted at the sane and helpful attitude the Express Newspapers are taking over the road problem. It is absurd to try and shuffle off the lamentable state of our roads and concentrate on the criminal drunken driver. I am rather glad that few people remember that it was Sir Winston, as Chancellor of the Exchequer, who first raided motor taxation for general finance purposes!

---

[1] *The Fight for the Tory Leadership: A Contemporary Chronicle* (1964).

It is always satisfactory when people are consistent. Macleod is certainly that: as you once said, 'the dirk in the stocking'.

Nonie and I are most grateful to you for your invitation, and would love to take it up.

With affectionate good wishes from us both to you and Christofor,

Anthony Montague Browne to Lord Beaverbrook
(Churchill papers, 2/519)

11 March 1964
Private

Thank you very much for your letter. [. . .]

I had had news of you from Max, and I gather that you are coming back soon. I rejoice that the treatment you had is proving efficacious.

Sir Winston is well, but a little down and apathetic. Lady Churchill is greatly cheered by the good news of Randolph: we had all feared that it would be cancer, but it was only, I understand, scar tissue and chronic pneumonia which made it desirable to remove a lobe of the left lung, and he should make a complete recovery. I had a long talk with him the night before the operation, and found him, as one would expect, very calm, courageous and dignified.

With love to Christofor, and looking forward to seeing you soon.

Lady Churchill to Sir Winston S. Churchill
(Churchill papers, 2/514)

18 April 1964

Winston,

The Government and the Members of the Opposition have been thinking what would be the best way of marking the end of your time in Parliament. They propose that you should be given a Vote of Thanks. This would be passed unanimously by the House, and then a special Committee consisting of the Prime Minister, the Leader of the Opposition and the Leader of the Liberal Party would wait upon you here at Hyde Park Gate to hand you a copy of the Resolution.

Would you be agreeable to this?

Lady Churchill to Anthony Montague Browne
(Churchill papers, 2/514)

19 April 1964
Private

Yesterday afternoon I gave Winston this little note. At first he seemed to pretend not to understand it, but later on he said he thought it would be very suitable. You will notice that I have carefully left out any suggestion that he could possibly be in the House when the Vote of Thanks is proposed. I did not show him the wording of the Resolution.

Later on in the afternoon he seemed very sad and depressed.

Sir Robert Menzies to Sir Winston S. Churchill
(Churchill papers, 1/59)

1 June 1964
Canberra

My dear Winston,

I understand that the pair of black swans which the Australian Government sent over to you some years ago are no longer breeding, and that as a consequence your flock is rather diminished.

I should therefore be very pleased if you would accept from the Australian Government a new pair of swans, which we hope will quickly establish themselves at Chartwell. Sir Edward Hallstrom,[1] of the Taronga Park Zoo in Sydney, assures me that the birds we are sending are breeding, and he expects them to continue to do so.

I have asked our High Commissioner, Sir Eric Harrison,[2] to make arrangements to present the swans to you. We expect that they will be despatched from Sydney in the next few weeks.

With all best wishes for your continued good health.

---

[1] Edward John Lees Hallstrom, 1886–1970. Australian Manufacturer and philanthropist. Trustee, Taronga Zoological Park Trust, 1941–67; Vice-Chairman, 1945–51; President, 1951–9; Honorary Director, 1959–67. Received awards from Société Royale Zoologique de Belgique (1964) and Zoological Society of San Diego (1966).

[2] Eric John Harrison, 1892–1974. Served in Australian Imperial Force, 1916–19. Member (United Australian Party, Lib.) of Australian House of Representatives, 1931–56. Postmaster-General and Minister of Repatriation, 1939–40. Deputy Leader, United Australia Party, 1944–5; Liberal Party, 1945–56. Minister of Postwar Reconstruction, 1949–50. Resident Australian Minister in London, 1950–1. Minister for Defence Production and Vice-President of the Executive Council, 1951–6. KCVO, 1954. Minister for the Army and Navy, 1955–6. Australian High Commissioner in London, 1956–64. KCMG, 1961.

Doreen Pugh to Sir Winston S. Churchill
(Churchill papers, 2/513)

5 June 1964

Sir Winston

You will remember that Mr Harold Wilson, the Leader of the Opposition, spoke to you in the House yesterday.

He had just returned from Russia, and he brought with him good wishes to you from all the Soviet leaders, and particularly Mr Mikoyan.

Sir Winston S. Churchill to Harold Wilson
(Churchill papers, 2/513)

6 June 1964

My dear Wilson,

I am so much obliged to you for bringing me the agreeable messages from the Russians. What you said reminded me of my own visits there in days gone by. Thank you very much.

Sir Winston S. Churchill to Sir Robert Menzies
(Churchill papers, 1/59)

7 June 1964

My dear Bob,

I was delighted to receive your letter. Clemmie and I would be very pleased to have a new pair of swans. The old flock suffered from the depredations of foxes during the severe winter of 1962–1963, and the present surviving trio show no signs of breeding. They are very much a part of Chartwell, and it makes me happy to think that you should seek to help us in preserving them.

I often reflect on our long comradeship, and I hope that I shall see you when you are over here.

Anthony Montague Browne to Lady Violet Bonham Carter
(Churchill papers, 2/520)

15 June 1964
Private and Confidential

This letter is typed to save you my handwriting (recently described as the only unbreakable cypher).

First, let me say that I feel you have every right to criticise such matters in any way you see fit, and I am naturally not at all offended that you should do so.

Some time ago, after discussions with Lady Churchill, and to some extent with Sir Winston himself, it was decided that he would not send any further message except on banal topics. An exception to this will have to be made at the General Election as he could hardly fail to send his successor candidate a message of goodwill, and this is bound to be to some extent controversial since we hope that he will win the seat. But Sir Winston was deeply and obviously moved at Lord Beaverbrook's death,[1] and in the last years no one had been closer to him. He had spent weeks staying with Lord Beaverbrook, and their mutual visits were as regular as their health allowed. Lady Churchill and I both felt that it would be a most marked omission if Sir Winston did not send a message on this occasion.

In one sentence it is very difficult to sum up a friendship. But Lord Beaverbrook was his oldest (male) friend: he met him six years before he met Bernie, and saw far more of him. In recent years Lord Beaverbrook was one of the very few whose visits consistently caused Sir Winston to light up, and certainly in my time with him now going back twelve years, he confided in him as much as anyone both on personal and political matters. Sir Winston told me several times that if Britain had been invaded in 1940 and we had had to fall back north of the Thames, he would have ruled Britain with a triumvirate of himself, Beaverbrook and Ernest Bevin; (this is of course strictly private). Once it was decided to send a message, it would have been impossible to hedge and qualify the deep and undoubted affection which Sir Winston felt for Lord Beaverbrook.

In conclusion may I say how much I welcome your letters on any topic and at any time, and I am honoured that you should confide in me in this way.

Anthony Montague Browne to Sir William Hayter
(*Churchill papers, 2/525*)

22 June 1964
Private

Many thanks for your letter of June 20. Alas, in his 90th year, Sir Winston's vigour and interest has greatly declined, and now he sees no one except his family and a few very old friends. I am so sorry, but, quite frankly, I think it would do more harm than good if his homonym came to see him. If he does get a First in PPE, I will ask Sir Winston to send him a message of congratulation which I hope will achieve something.

It was so nice to hear from you, and we do hope to see you and Iris[2] again

---

[1] Lord Beaverbrook died on 9 June 1964.
[2] Iris Marie Grey, 1911–2004. Married, 1938, William Hayter.

soon. Perhaps we may look in on you when we drive through Oxford to Herefordshire sometime in the summer, if you are there.

Nonie sends her love.

Sir Alec Douglas-Home: speech
(Hansard)

28 June 1964

I beg to move, That this House desires to take this opportunity of marking the forthcoming retirement of the right honourable Gentleman the Member for Woodford by putting on record its unbounded admiration and gratitude for his services to Parliament, to the nation and to the world; remembers, above all, his inspiration of the British people when they stood alone, and his leadership until victory was won; and offers its grateful thanks to the right honourable Gentleman for these outstanding services to this House and to the nation. I move this Motion in the full confidence that it will be supported by every right hon. and hon. Member of the House, and in the knowledge that all who have ever served here with the right hon. Gentleman the Member for Woodford will feel that they share at once in the sadness and in the grandeur of this essentially parliamentary occasion, sadness because the right hon. Gentleman's long membership of the House is coming to an end, and grandeur because of the honour and the lustre which the parliamentary career of the right hon. Gentleman has brought to the House of Commons. Not least of the honours of which we are sensible is that it has so evidently remained a pleasure to the right hon. Gentleman in recent days to attend our sittings.

Hon. Members may imagine how difficult it was to decide how adequately to record our thanks for this lifetime of service, but those of all parties who met to consult together were soon agreed that whatever was to be done must be something in keeping with the history of the House and in keeping with its character as the representative forum of the nation and as the House of Commons. We have chosen, by common consent, a method of trying to convey our thanks adopted by the House on 1st July, 1814, in respect of the Duke of Wellington. I feel that this precedent in itself will give the right hon. Gentleman pleasure, appealing to his vivid sense of the sweep of history.

Today is not the occasion to review the services of the right hon. Gentleman, those which he has given both to the House and to the nation. For anyone at any time that would be a daunting task. If I were to begin to undertake the tale of when the right hon. Gentleman was first elected to the House I should be intimidated, for it is from the year 1900, with only but a short interval, that he has been a Member of the House throughout the progress of this century. I myself first remember his speeches from his place in the corner seat below the Gangway in the 1930s when he was seeking to catch the ear of Parliament and the country and to give urgency to the preparations for the war which he himself had long foreseen was due to come. Then we knew him as the Prime Minister in war, exercising the unparalleled authority with which he commanded the House at that time through all the adversities and through the triumphs of the battle until victory was ours and his. At all times we remember him, whether as backbencher, as Minister, or as Prime Minister, for the inimitable style with which he has always adorned our debates and our proceedings, with that extraordinary gift of words, compelling in their simplicity, which made an appeal to the hearts of millions and gave them leadership which was inspired.

In this place the right hon. Gentleman went through and took us through the whole range of the emotions. He has loved the parliamentary fight and I think that his opponents would concede that he has won most of them. I never remember an occasion, though, however dramatic and alarming – as was sometimes the case – the parliamentary storm might be, when the magnanimity and humanity of the right hon. Gentleman has not taken charge. Time and again I have seen that ferocious frown turn to the smile with which he has acknowledged the quality of a worthy opponent, and time and again it was like the sun coming out from behind the thunder cloud, with all its healing power.

The right hon. Gentleman is a man of the strongest principles and holds very strong ideas, but he is essentially broad minded, and everybody has felt and known that he has felt the people with his heart. He said on one occasion: 'My views represent a continual process of adjustment to changing events.' It may be that the right hon. Gentleman has found the ultimate wisdom which so often eludes lesser men.

But today it is enough and it suffices to unite in saluting one of the most famous personalities that this House has ever known and one of its most faithful servants. Therefore, when a few of us are selected by the House to go and convey the respect and the gratitude of every right hon. and hon. Member in it, I hope that we may say that everybody in the House today will always be filled with pride that we have had the right to call the right hon. Gentleman the Member for Woodford our colleague and our friend.

Anthony Montague Browne to Lord Kilmuir
(*Churchill papers, 2/512*)

1 July 1964
Private and Confidential

Thank you very much for your letter of June 30, which I have discussed at length with Lady Churchill. If Sir Winston were in health and intellectual vigour he would certainly wish to assist the Speaker.[1] But it is now widely known that Sir Winston is no longer capable of formulating considered opinions on difficult matters, nor of marshalling the arguments to support them: it might therefore be felt that words were being put into his mouth. We want to avoid any risk of this, and Lady Churchill hope that you will understand if Sir Winston does not comply with what you suggest in the circumstances.

There is a subsidiary point: at the end of this Session Sir Winston is to receive an All-Party Resolution of Thanks for his services, and it would be in any case a little embarrassing for him to be involved in a political controversy near that time.

Anthony Montague Browne to Sir Winston S. Churchill and Lady Churchill
(Churchill papers, 2/514)

22 July 1964

The Resolution of Thanks from the House of Commons to Sir Winston will come before the House on Tuesday afternoon, July 28, after Questions. As soon as it has been debated, the following will come to Hyde Park Gate to present it to Sir Winston, who will hand them his reply:

The Prime Minister
The Leader of the Opposition
The Leader of the Liberal Party
The Leader of the House (Mr Selwyn Lloyd)
The Deputy Father of the House, Sir Thomas Moore[2] (if he is well enough)
Mr Shinwell
The Clerk Assistant (Mr Lidderdale)[3]

Sir Winston will receive them in the dining room at Hyde Park Gate, and after the exchange of the Resolution and Sir Winston's thanks, they will be given champagne.

Two photographers* from the National Press Association rota will be allowed to take photographs.

* Mr Priest, AP and Mr Joseph D. Mail.

---

[1] Kilmuir had requested Churchill's endorsement of Speaker of the House Sir Harry Hylton-Foster, a Conservative MP who was opposed by both Liberal and Labour parties.
[2] Thomas Cecil Russell Moore, 1886–1971. Entered Army, 1908. On active service in France, 1914–15. GHQ, Ireland, 1916–18. On active service in Russia, 1918–20; Ireland, 1920–3 (OBE, 1918, CBE, 1919, despatches twice). Retired with rank of Lt-Col., 1925. MP (Cons.) for Ayr Burgh, 1925–50; for Ayr, 1950–64. Knighted, 1937. Bt, 1956.
[3] David William Shuckburgh Lidderdale, 1910–88. House of Commons Clerk, 1934. Commissioned, Rifle Bde, 1939. Served in Tunisian and Italian campaigns. CB, 1963. Clerk of the House, 1974–6. KCB, 1975. Published *The Parliament of France* (1951) and (with Gilbert Francis Montriou Campion) *European Parliamentary Procedure* (1952).

2362   1964

Anthony Montague Browne to Lady Violet Bonham Carter
(Churchill papers, 2/520)

25 September 1964
Strictly Private

After some thought, I told Lady Churchill of our conversation. I have myself reflected further on the matter and there have been further talks; it literally gave me a sleepless night, which does not happen often.

The outcome is that Sir Winston is going to send two short messages, one to his successor candidate and the other to the Prime Minister: they have both been cut to the bone.

I am strengthened in my feeling that this is the right course by an incident yesterday. Sir Winston, who, as you know, fluctuates very much in his awareness of events, was particularly good at luncheon. He was asked, 'You have been asked to send messages supporting the Conservative party in the General Election to your successor candidate and the Prime Minister. Do you wish to do so or not?' He replied very clearly, 'Yes, I will do it.' With this, I am content that brief messages of general support of the Conservative government are right.

I only write to tell you this, as I know what a devoted friend you are, and how strongly you feel.

PS.[1]
I really do not think you should have used the word 'forgery' to me. Sir Winston has had things drafted for him for many years, even when he was Prime Minister. If they represent his views, and he signs them, they are not 'forgeries'. These messages, of the briefest and most general support for the Conservatives, fulfil this condition: Sir Winston undoubtedly supports the Conservatives.

In case you should think personal feelings come into it, I myself believe the Conservatives are slightly the lesser of two evils! But this is irrelevant.

Anthony Montague Browne to Sir Henry d'Avigdor-Goldsmid[2]
(Churchill papers, 2/609)

23 November 1964
Private

Dear d'Avigdor-Goldsmid,
Thank you for your letter of November 20. The only message Sir Winston

[1] This postscript was handwritten.
[2] Henry Joseph D'Avigdor-Goldsmid, 1909–76. Maj.-Gen., Royal West Kent Rgt, 1939–45 (DSO, MC, 1945). Married, 1940, Rosemary Margaret Horlick. 2nd Bt, 1940. MP (Cons.) for Walsall, 1955–74.

is putting out on his birthday is one of thanks for messages received. I enclosed the proposed text, but it should not, of course, be made public until December 1.

In addition, Sir Winston will be sending specific 'thank-yous', but the scale of his birthday post is so vast that these will have to be restricted to a very small number. To give you an example, on his 80th birthday, he received more than thirty thousand messages, and the indications are already that this time there will be more.

Lady Soames: recollection
('Clementine Churchill', page 488)

30 November 1964

Winston's ninetieth birthday brought an avalanche of good wishes. The Queen sent him flowers, and many people gathered in the street outside No. 28 on the eve of his birthday and on the day before, when, carefully dressed and looking benevolent, Winston appeared at the open window of the drawing-room so that the Press could take some happy birthday photographs. The little crowd of well-wishers cheered and clapped and sang 'Happy Birthday to You'. Before luncheon on the actual day Clementine arranged for all his secretarial, nursing and domestic staff to gather in his bedroom to drink his health in champagne. She took this opportunity to thank them all for their loyal and devoted care. Clementine's present to him was a small golden heart enclosing the engraved figures '90'. It was to hang on his watch chain, and joined the golden heart with its central ruby 'drop of blood' which had been her engagement present to him fifty-seven years before. During the afternoon the Prime Minister called to bring Winston and Minnie, and Arabella, Julian Sandys, Edwina and Piers Dixon, Celia Kennedy (Sandys); and Cousin Sylvia. The only guests not members of the family were Jock and Meg Colville, and Anthony and Nonie Montague Browne. Monty had been invited but was himself ill in hospital. The house glowed with candlelight and flowers, and we were united yet one more time in drinking first Winston's health and then Clementine's. But this birthday evening had for us all a poignant quality – he was so fragile now, and often so remote. And although he beamed at us as we all gathered round him, and one felt he was glad to have us there – in our hearts we knew the end could not be far off.

1965

Lady Soames: recollection
(Mary Soames, 'A Churchill Family Album', pages 112–16)

January 1965

Although in these last years Winston was slowly declining – yet his health was remarkable when one considered all he had been through and his mounting tally of years. [. . .] When he left the House for the last time in July 1964, he had been a Member of Parliament almost continuously for over half a century, and he had represented the same constituency for forty years. [. . .] And now, in these last two years, the pace of life for Winston was very slow: it was like a broad, weary river, gently meandering on. Sometimes he seemed quite content: even though he might not say very much, one knew he was glad one was there. But sometimes he withdrew a great distance from us – and who knows what thoughts or images moved across the screen of his consciousness from the long saga of his life, so crowded with events and people? And, even now, Chartwell did not fail him: in the summer days he loved to sit out in his chair on the lawn, and gaze away across the valley and the lakes to the green and misty blue distances of the Weald. One felt he was at peace with himself and with the world:

'I warmed both hands before the fire of life; It sinks, and I am ready to depart.' (Walter Savage Landor)[1]

Sir Winston Churchill died at his home at 28 Hyde Park Gate, London, at 8 a.m. on Sunday 24 January 1965. It was seventy years to the day since his father had died.

---

[1] Walter Savage Landor, 1775–1864. English poet who composed a significant number of his works in Latin. Best known for his series *Imaginary Conversations* (1824–9).

Walter Hallstein[1] to Harold Wilson
(Premier papers, 13/205)

24 January 1965

On behalf of the Commission of the European Economic Community I would ask you to convey to Her Majesty's Government the British Parliament and people our deep distress at the passing of Sir Winston Churchill. We share your sense of loss and wish to be associated in your tributes to a great statesman and great European.

Lester Pearson to Harold Wilson
(Premier papers, 13/205)

24 January 1965   Ottawa

I was deeply distressed and saddened to learn of the death of Sir Winston Churchill.

On behalf of the Canadian people, in whose hearts Sir Winston has long had a special place, I wish to extend sincerest sympathy to the British people to whom the passing of such a great citizen and outstanding leader must bring deep sorrow. His death, after so many years of great achievement and of devoted service to the people of his country, marks an irreplaceable loss, not only to Britain but to the Commonwealth and to the world.

We, in Canada, share that loss with the people of Britain. We rejoiced with you in his triumphs, and we lament with you his death.

Alexei Kosygin[2] to Harold Wilson
(Premier papers, 13/206)

24 January 1965

Dear Prime Minister,

Please accept the sincere condolences of the Soviet Government and of myself personally on the occasion of the passing of the outstanding British

[1] Walter Hallstein, 1901–82. Lecturer, University of Rostock, 1928–39. Prof., University of Frankfurt, 1939–42. Drafted into German armed forces, 1942. POW, 1944–5. Vice-Chancellor, University of Frankfurt, 1945–8. Head of German delegation to Schuman Conference, 1950. State Secretary, Federal German Foreign Office, 1951–8. President, Commission of the European Economic Community, 1958–67. President, European Movement, 1968–74. Member (Christian Democratic Union) of the Bundestag, 1969–72.

[2] Alexei Kosygin, 1904–80. Volunteer in Red Army, 1919–21. Deputy Chairman, Council of People's Commissars, 1940–3; Chairman, 1943–6. Member, Politburo, 1948–52, 1960–80. Minister of Finance, 1948. Minister for Light Industry, 1948–53. Deputy Chairman, Council of Ministers, 1953–6, 1960–4. Chairman, State Planning Committee, 1959–60. Chairman, Council of Ministers, 1964–80.

statesman Sir Winston Churchill. The tireless activity of Sir Winston Churchill in the years of the war against Hitlerite Germany is remembered and the grief of the British people over this loss is shared in the Soviet Union.[1]

Józef Cyrankiewicz[2] to Harold Wilson
(Premier papers, 13/206)

24 January 1965

On the passing away of Sir Winston Churchill please accept, Mr Prime Minister, expressions of profound and sincere sympathy which I convey to you on behalf of the government of the Polish People's Republic. And on my own, Sir Winston Churchill's name has been indelibly inscribed in history among the most outstanding statesmen of Great Britain. The Polish people will keep him in memory as one of the great and unflinching leaders of the anti-Nazi coalition in the Second World War, when our two nations fought together for a complete victory over the forces of brutal oppression, destruction and genocide. Sir Winston Churchill will go down in history as one of the founders of that victory.

Mohammad Ayub Khan to Harold Wilson
(Premier papers, 13/206)

24 January 1965

Deeply grieved to learn of the death of Sir Winston Churchill. With his passing away the world has lost one of the greatest statesmen of the century, the Commonwealth one of its ablest and dedicated leaders, and England one of her most illustrious sons. On my own behalf and on behalf of the government and the people of Pakistan I extend to you and to the people of your country our sincerest condolences.

---

[1] Wilson replied on Jan. 27: 'My colleagues and I thank you and the Soviet Government most warmly for your kind message of sympathy on the death of Sir Winston Churchill. We have greatly welcomed this expression of sympathy from our wartime allies' (*Premier papers, 13/206*).

[2] Józef Cyrankiewicz, 1911–89. Educated at Jagiellonian University, Kraków. Captured by Germans and interned at Auschwitz, 1941–5. Secretary-General, Polish Socialist Party, Central Executive Committee, 1945. Polish PM, 1947–52, 1954–70. Chairman, Polish Peace Committee, 1973–86.

President Charles de Gaulle to Lady Churchill
(*Premier papers, 13/205*)

24 January 1965

Chère Madame,

Du fond du coeur, nous prenons part, ma femme et moi, à la peine profonde qui vous atteint et qui atteint les vôtres, en meme temps que l'Angleterre et tous les hommes de coeur du monde entier. En France, la mort de Sir Winston Churchill est réssentié partout avec beaucoup de chagrin.

Pour moi, je vois disparaitre en la personne de ce très grand homme, mon compagnon de guerre et mon ami.

Veuillez agréer, chère Madame, mes hommages très respectueux.[1]

Ludwig Erhard[2] to Harold Wilson
(*Premier papers, 13/205*)

24 January 1965

In namen der Bundesregierung spreche ich Ihnen zum Tode von Sir Winston Churchill tiefempfundene Anteilnahme aus. Das Vereinigte Koenigreich hat mit ihm einen der grossen Staatsmaenner seiner Geschichte, die Welt einen hervorragenden Kaempfer fuer die freiheitliche demokratische Ordnung verloren. Seine Verdienste um das freie Europea, fuer dessen Einheit er unermuedlich eingetreten ist, sein Muehen, die Entfaltung des europaeischen Erbes auch fuer die Zukunft zu sichern, werden unvergessen bleiben.[3]

---

[1] 'Dear Madam,

'From the bottom of our hearts, we take part, my wife and I, in the deep pain that afflicts you and yours, and at the same time all of England and all men around the world. In France, the death of Sir Winston Churchill is felt everywhere with much sorrow.

'For me, this marks the disappearance of the spirit of this very great man, my war comrade and my friend.

'Please accept, dear Madam, my very respectful regards and homage.'

[2] Ludwig Wilhelm Erhard, 1897–1977. Economics Minister for Bavaria, 1945–6. Director, Advisory Committee for Money and Credit, 1947–8; Economic Council for Joint Anglo-US Occupation Zone, 1948–9. Economics Minister, Federal Republic of Germany, 1949–63. Chancellor, 1963–6.

[3] 'In the name of the Federal Government I express to you heartfelt condolences on the death of Sir Winston Churchill. In him the United Kingdom has lost one of the great statesmen in her history, and the world an exemplary fighter for the liberal democratic order. His merits for the free Europe whose unity he has tirelessly advocated, as well as his toiling to preserve the development of the European legacy, even for the future, shall never be forgotten.'

2368   1965

Lal Bahadur Shastri[1] to Harold Wilson
(*Premier papers, 13/205*)

24 January 1965

The world will remember Sir Winston Churchill for long as a leader of unparalleled courage and tenacity of purpose. He was a forceful writer and a great parliamentarian of his time. On behalf of the Government and the people of India I offer our heartfelt condolences on the passing away of Sir Winston Churchill.

Amir Abbas Hoveyda[2] to Harold Wilson
(*Premier papers, 13/205*)

24 January 1965

It has been with a sense of profound sorrow that my colleagues and I have learnt news of the death of Sir Winston Churchill. His demise has deprived the world of the irreplaceable wisdom political insight and the exemplary valour of a man who shall live in history as one of the most illustrious figures of our time. In this hour of your great national loss I hasten to extend to you Mr Prime Minister and to the British government and nation expression of my deepest condolences.

Levi Eschkol[3] to Harold Wilson
(*Premier papers, 13/205*)

24 January 1965

May I ask you to deliver to the government and people of Great Britain the sentiments of deep mourning which have swept Israel at the news of the death of Sir Winston Churchill. The British people and free men everywhere have lost a leader of unique stature, a statesman of supreme ability and courage, and architect of history, the providential leader of an embattled Britain and

---

[1] Lal Bahadur Shastri, 1904–66. Member, United Provinces Legislature Assembly, 1937–40. Imprisoned, 1940–1, 1942–6. State Parliamentary Secretary, Uttar Pradesh, 1947. Indian Minister of Police and Transport, 1947–50; of Railways, 1952–6; of Home Affairs, 1961–3; of External Affairs, 1964. PM, 1964–6.

[2] Amir Abbas Hoveyda, 1919–79. Iranian Foreign Office, 1945–57. Board member, National Iranian Oil Company, 1958–64. Finance Minister, 1964–5. PM, 1965–77. Sentenced to death and executed by Islamic Revolutionary Court, 1979.

[3] Levi Eschkol (originally named Levi Shkolnik), 1895–1969. Volunteered with Jewish Legion, 1918–20. Secretary-General, Workers' Party of the Land of Israel, 1942–4; Tel Aviv Workers' Council, 1944–8. Director-General of Israeli Ministry of Defence, 1948–9. Member (Lab.) of the Knesset, 1951–69. Minister of Agriculture, 1951–2. Finance Minister, 1952–63. PM, 1963–9. Founder of Israeli Labour Party, 1968.

of the imperilled world. It was his indomitable championing of human liberties and of fundamental human decencies that in the end rid mankind of the dreadful plague of Nazism. It will be hard to find his equal again.

We in Israel are profoundly aware of all that he accomplished for the reestablishment of our statehood. For that staunch and unswerving friendship, this and all coming generations of our people will ever treasure his memory in abiding gratitude and regard.

Private Office to Harold Wilson
(Premier papers, 13/205)

25 January 1965

There are, as you can imagine, masses of telegrams from foreign and Commonwealth statesmen on the death of Sir Winston Churchill.

In the case of the most distinguished of our allies, e.g., the United States, the Soviet Union, etc., I will draft replies from you for delivery through our Ambassador/High Commissioner in the capital concerned. For the rest, it will, I consider, be sufficient for HM Ambassador/High Commissioner in the capital concerned merely to go round and formally thank the Government to which he is accredited for their message of sympathy.

All the messages will, of course, be kept in the archives.

Jean Duvieusart[1] to Harold Wilson
(Premier papers, 13/205)

25 January 1965

Please accept on behalf of the Bureau and Members of European Parliament and myself the expression of our deepest sympathy for the irreparable loss which your country has suffered in the passing of one of its great sons. Not only do we mourn with the people of Britain the death of a dauntless guardian of democracy but also that of a great European and a man of vision to whom this nascent commonwealth of European nations owes so much. The great contribution he made to the creation of a free and united Europe will indeed remain as a permanent memorial to his wisdom.

---

[1] Jean Pierre Duvieusart, 1900–77. Member (Christian Social Party), Belgian Chamber of Representatives, 1944–9. Minister of Economic Affairs, 1947–50, 1952–4. PM, 1950. President of the European Parliament, 1964–5. Founding member of Walloon Rally Party, 1968.

Willi Stoph[1] to Harold Wilson
(Premier papers, 13/205)

25 January 1965

Exzellenz, gestatten Sie mir, aus Anlass des Ablebens von Sir Winston Churchill, der eine bedeutsame Rolle bei der Niederschlagung des deutschen Faschismus gespielt hat, mein aufrichtiges Mitgefuehl zu uebermitteln.[2]

Sir Alexander Bishop[3] to Commonwealth Relations Office
(Premier papers, 13/205)

25 January 1965   Nicosia
Immediate
Confidential
No. 95

Following are texts of messages received from Vice President[4] addressed to Lady Churchill and Prime Minister.

'Lady Winston Churchill,
Is it possible that a man who has brought a new lease of life of the Free World and who has enriched history to such an extent should pass away? This is the feeling of the Turks in Cyprus in conveying their condolences to you over the death of the mortal Sir Winston'

and

'The Right Honourable Harold Wilson, Prime Minister.
House of Commons.
Mankind has sustained a heavy loss with the passing away of Sir Winston and it is with profound grief that the Turks of Cyprus have received the sad news. In paying tribute to him at this sad moment words are too inadequate to describe the man who has brought new meaning and new heights to human greatness and who added new dimensions to eternity. Please accept the condolences of the Turkish people of Cyprus.'

---

[1] Willi Stoph, 1914–99. Interior Minister of East Germany, 1952–5. Defence Minister, 1956–60. First Deputy Prime Minister, 1960–4. Chairman of the Council of Ministers (Socialist Unity Party), 1964–73, 1976–89. Chairman of the State Council, 1973–6.

[2] 'Excellence, allow me to convey my sincere sympathy on the occasion of the passing of Sir Winston Churchill, who played a momentous role in the abolition of German fascism.'

[3] (William Henry) Alexander Bishop, 1897–1984. Served with Dorset Rgt in Mesopotamia and Palestine, 1914–19; in India, 1919–25. War Office, 1933–5. Colonial Office, 1937–9. Served during WWII, 1939–44. Director of Quartering, War Office, 1944–5. Regional Commissioner for North Rhine Westphalia, 1948–50. Director of Information Services and Cultural Relations, Commonwealth Relations Office, 1962–4. British High Commissioner in Cyprus, 1964–5.

[4] Fazıl Küçük, 1906–84. Known as an advocate for Turkish Cypriot rights and an opponent of British colonial rule in Cyprus. Co-founder of Association of the Turkish Minority of the Island of Cyprus, 1943. First Vice-President, Republic of Cyprus, 1959–73.

1965

Friedrich Wahlen[1] to Harold Wilson
(*Premier papers, 13/205*)

25 January 1965

In my own name and in that of my colleagues on the Committee of Ministers of the Council of Europe I send to you and to your countrymen deepest condolences on the death of Sir Winston Churchill. His action in defence of freedom has won him a lasting place among those few who have decisively influenced the course of mankind at one of the greatest hours of your nation's history. His subsequent contribution to peace and to European unity will ever be remembered and honoured by us especially in this Council of Europe which he did so much to form. Please convey the expression of our profound sympathy to Lady Churchill.

House of Lords: tributes
(*Hansard*)

25 January 1965

DEATH OF SIR WINSTON CHURCHILL

The Lord Privy Seal (The Earl of Longford):
My Lords, I have it in command to deliver to your Lordships a Message from Her Majesty The Queen.
Then Her Majesty's message was presented and read to the House by the Lord Chancellor as follows:

> I know that it will be the wish of all my people that the loss which we have all sustained by the death of the Right Honourable Sir Winston Churchill, Knight of the Garter, should be met in the most fitting manner and that they should have an opportunity of expressing their sorrow at the loss and their veneration of the memory of that outstanding man who, in war and peace, served his country unfailingly for more than fifty years and in the hours of our greatest danger was the inspiring leader who strengthened and supported us all. Confident in the support of Parliament for the due acknowledgement of our debt of gratitude and in thanksgiving for the life and example of a national hero, I have directed that Sir Winston's body shall lie in State in Westminster Hall and that thereafter the funeral service shall be held in the Cathedral Church of St Paul. Elizabeth Regina.

---

[1] Friedrich Traugott Wahlen, 1899–1985. Swiss agronomist and politician. Deputy Director-General, UN Food and Agriculture Organization, 1958–9. Member (Party of Farmers, Traders and Independents), Swiss Federal Council, 1958–65. Head, Dept of Justice and Police, 1959; Dept of Economic Affairs, 1960; Political Dept, 1961, 1962–5; Dept of Economic Affairs, 1961. Member of the Committee of Ministers, Council of Europe, from 1962.

The Earl of Longford: My Lords, I beg to move that the Message from Her Majesty the Queen be taken into consideration forthwith.

Moved accordingly, and, on Question, Motion agreed to.

[. . .]

Earl Attlee: My Lords, as an old opponent and colleague, but always a friend, of Sir Winston Churchill, I should like to say a few words in addition to what has already been so eloquently said. My mind goes back to many years ago. I recall Sir Winston as a rising hope of the Conservative Party at the end of the 19th century. I looked upon him and Lord Cecil as the two rising hopes of the Conservative Party. Then, with courage, he crossed the House – not easy for any man. You might say of Winston Churchill that to whatever Party he belonged he did not really change his ideas: he was always Winston.

The first time I saw him he was at the siege of Sidney Street,[1] when he took over command of the troops there, and I happened to be a local resident. I did not meet him again until he came into the House of Commons in 1924. The extraordinary thing, when one thinks of it, is that by that time he had done more than the average Member of Parliament, and more than the average Minister, in the way of a Parliamentary career. We thought at that time that he was finished. Not a bit! He started again another career, and then, after some years, it seemed again that he had faded. He became a lone wolf, outside any Party; and, yet, somehow or other, the time was coming which would be for him his supreme moment. It seems as if everything led up to the that time in 1940, when he became Prime Minister of this country at the time of its greatest peril.

Throughout all that period he might make opponents, he might make friends; but no one could ever disregard him. Here was a man of genius, a man of action, a man who could also speak superbly and write superbly. I recall through all those years many occasions when his characteristics stood out most forcibly. I do not think everybody always recognised how tender-hearted he was. I can recall him with the tears rolling down his cheeks, talking of the horrible things perpetrated by the Nazis in Germany. I can recall, too, during the war his emotion on seeing a simple little English home wrecked by a bomb. Yes, my Lords, sympathy – and more than that: he went back, and immediately devised the War Damage Act. How characteristic! Sympathy did not stop with emotion; it turned into action.

Then I recall the long days through the war – the long days and long nights – in which his spirit never failed; and how often he lightened our labours by that vivid humour, those wonderful remarks he would make which absolutely dissolved us all in laughter, however tired we were. I recall the eternal friendship for France and for America; and I recall, too, as the most reverend

---

[1] An incident in London in 1911, when gunfire was exchanged between a force of military and police officers and two Latvian revolutionaries. Churchill was Home Secretary at the time.

Primate[1] has said already, that when once the enemy were beaten he had full sympathy for them. He showed that after the Boer War, and he showed it again after the First World War. He had sympathy, an incredibly wide sympathy, for ordinary people all over the world.

I think of him also as supremely conscious of history. His mind went back not only to his great ancestor Marlborough but through the years of English history. He saw himself and he saw our nation at that time playing a part not unworthy of our ancestors, not unworthy of the men who defeated the Armada and not unworthy of the men who defeated Napoleon. He saw himself there as an instrument. As an instrument for what? For freedom, for human life against tyranny. None of us can ever forget how, through all those long years, he now and again spoke exactly the phrase that crystallised the feelings of the nation.

My Lords, we have lost the greatest Englishman of our time – I think the greatest citizen of the world of our time. In the course of a long, long life, he has played many parts. We may all be proud to have lived with him and, above all, to have worked with him; and we shall send to his widow and family our sympathy in their great loss.

[. . .]

The Earl of Avon: My Lords, this is a day not only of national mourning but of mourning throughout the Free World. For Sir Winston's service was to mankind, and for this his place will always be among the few immortals. Many of your Lordships knew Sir Winston well, and worked with him closely at one or other period of his career. But this afternoon, as has been apparent from almost every speech, our minds go back more especially to that period of the Second World War which he himself called our 'finest hour', and which was certainly his.

It seems to me in every sense appropriate that this sad occasion should be so exceptionally signalised as in this Royal Message – and not only because of Sir Winston's qualities of true greatness in leadership above all. These in themselves would be cause enough for the Message which we have received. But there is also another reason: that Churchill epitomised, at the same time as he led, the nation, at a time of brave and (why should it not be said?) splendid resistance against odds which might have seemed overwhelming. So, my Lords, as we mourn and honour Sir Winston, we reverence also all those who fell to bring victory to a cause for which he had dedicated himself and us. They are now together.

My Lords, what follows is a suggestion to which I expect, of course, no immediate reply or comment, and which I make with some temerity, but from messages I have received I believe that it is not only my thought. It seems to me that the nation would feel glad if there could be a 'Churchill day'.

---

[1] Michael Ramsay, 1904–88. Ordained priest, 1929. Bishop of Durham, 1952–6. Archbishop of York, 1956–61. 100th Archbishop of Canterbury, 1961–74. Baron, 1974.

This could be most appropriately connected, perhaps, with some date in that summer of 1940, when both Churchill's leadership and this country's will to resist, whatever the cost, expressed themselves so gloriously. They could then be enshrined together for as long as our calendar endures.

I should like also to associate myself with the messages to Lady Churchill. No tribute, however penned or phrased, could out-measure what is deserved.

My Lords, courage is never easy to define. Sometimes it is shown in the heat of battle; and that we all respect. But there is that rarer courage which can sustain repeated disappointment, unexpected failure, and even shattering defeat. Churchill had that too; and he had need of it, as the noble Earl, Lord Attlee, will remember, not only for days but sometimes for weeks and for months. Looking back now at the war, victory may seem to have been certain. But it was not always certain; and when news is bad, it is very lonely at the top.

Like one or two of those who are with us in this House this afternoon, I saw much of Sir Winston then – often many times a day, not only at official meetings but in such periods of comparative relaxation as there were, at meals and, as was his wont, late into the night. I grew to respect and love him, even though the argument might sometimes be sharp.

My Lords, there is the granite type which feels little. Sir Winston was nothing of that at all. He felt deeply every blow of fortune and every gleam of hope. Alert, eager and questioning as his temper was, he could hold on through all tides and tempests; and he had that gift, rare and difficult to discharge in statesmanship, of knowing when to reject 'No' as an answer, recognising that the arguments against any positive action could always be trusted to marshal themselves. During those war years his mind was always projected to the next move, and in this he was aided by an energy which was something much more than zest for life. With that constitution, Sir Winston would have survived any strain in any age, but he loved best the present one in which he lived. I have heard it said in criticism that his opinions were of his own generation. Certainly they were. And that was his strength, because he was at the same time open-minded and comprehending as are very few men in this century. He saw clearly and further than most, and he spoke fearlessly and without favour of what he saw. He sensed the danger for his country with the instinct of the artist and the knowledge of the historian.

As we cast our minds back this afternoon and pay tribute to his memory, there is, of course, nothing for which we in this Assembly shall remember him more than as a Parliamentarian. He called himself a 'child of the House of Commons'. But he was, of course much more than that. He had been brought up in a great Parliamentary age. I remember how he used to tell me how in those days speeches, even of Under-Secretaries, were fully reported in the Press. With awe, almost, he spoke of those days. And the great figures that dominated that period gave him an intimate sense of the power of Parliament which he never lost, just as he never forgot that Parliament put him where he was in 1940. It was a memory with him always.

So, my Lords, as we say farewell to him now, we thank this, the greatest of all Parliamentarians whom we shall know; and we can best enshrine his work by devoting ourselves to the same thing, to those cherished thoughts, traditions and beliefs to which he held, through life, till death.

[. . .]

Baroness Asquith of Yarnbury: My Lords, I must ask your indulgence as a newcomer among you and as one who speaks, as we all speak today, under the stress of deep personal grief. I think it is hard to realise that that indomitable heart, to which we all owe our freedom and our very existence, has fought its long, last battle and is still. I count myself infinitely blessed in having known Winston Churchill as a close and dear and life-long friend. But, from the day of our first meeting in my early youth, I saw him always in a dual perspective. Through and beyond my friend, well known and dearly loved, I saw one of the greatest figures of all time upon the stage of history.

Few shared my view in those days; nor, indeed in thirty years' time. But, despite frustrations and setbacks and disappointments, I was always conscious that his ultimate confidence in himself remained unshaken. He had no doubts about his star. Even in those early days he felt he was walking with Destiny and that he had been preserved through many perils in order to fulfil its purpose. I think he might have said with Keats:[1] There is an awful warmth about my heart, like a load of Immortality. And he was right. For in his own life he has taken his place among the immortals.

My Lords, for me it would be vain to attempt to assess the elements that have gone to the making of this epic character – statesman, orator, artist in action, fighter from first to last – and withal the most human of human beings. Many of his great qualities have been extolled in the eloquent and moving speeches we have listened to this afternoon, and I would associate myself with the noble Viscount, Lord Dilhorne[2] (and I think the noble Earl, Lord Avon, mentioned it), in putting courage first: his courage, the courage that accepts and hurls back every challenge; courage which he himself esteemed as the highest of human virtues, because, as he once said to me, 'It guarantees all the rest'.

Then, greatness of heart. From all small things he had a grand immunity. He never wished to trample on a fallen foe, whether a political opponent or a defeated nation. For though he believed and said that the only answer to defeat is victory, his enmity could not survive once victory was won. My hate had died with their surrender he wrote about the ruins of Berlin. He never hated nations – or men – as such. He hated only their ideas. 'You knock a

---

[1] John Keats, 1795–1821. English Romantic poet. Published *Poems* (1817), *Endymion* (1818) and *Lamia, Isabella, The Eve of St Agnes, and Other Poems* (1820). The quotation is from a letter of Sep. 1818 to John Hamilton Reynolds.

[2] Reginald Edward Manningham-Buller, 1905–80. MP (Cons.) for Daventry Div. of Northamptonshire, 1943–50; for South Northamptonshire, 1950–62. Member, Parliamentary Delegation to USSR, 1945. Solicitor-General, 1951–4. Attorney-General, 1954–62. 1st Viscount Dilhorne, 1962. Lord High Chancellor of Great Britain, 1962–4.

man down in order to pick him up in a better frame of mind – and you may pick him up in a better frame of mind', he once said. And then there was his vitality, a flame which all the waters of the world were powerless to quench. He seemed to have been endowed by Fortune with a double charge of life and with a double dose of human nature.

But, transcending all, was his warm and wide humanity. His character spanned the whole gamut of human possibilities – its frailties, foibles, grandeur and nobility'. He could be Puck[1] or prophet, sage or wit, above the battle, in the scrum, an epic poet or a tease. What other Leader of the Opposition has ever kissed his hand to an infuriated Government Front Bench? That is what I once saw him do. And how he brought not only fortitude but gaiety to our grimmest hours! We are expecting the coming invasion. So are the fishes! Thus he broadcast to the French people from a basement during the crashes of an air raid. Hearing his chuckle, we ignored the bombs and laughed with him.

He shared our tears. When he saw gallant Londoners sticking up little, pathetic Union Jacks among the ruins of their homes, he was totally unmanned and wept. An old woman said: 'You see, he really cares; he is crying.' They recognised a human being, vulnerable to their own simplest emotion; one who shared their common clay and had invested it with a new glory. At last he was not only understood but loved, as few Prime Ministers have ever been.

I think that few men's lives have touched such heights and depths of triumph and disaster, and it was sometimes in his darkest days that I thought him greatest. I am thinking of the thirties (to which the noble Earl, Lord Attlee, has referred), when he was in the shadows, at odds with his own Party and with all the powers that be. He saw so clearly the danger, the deadly peril which encompassed us, and he saw the choice which we must make. To him it was a stark, simple, moral choice: it was a choice between tyranny and freedom, good and evil, life and death. He dedicated all his powers of vision, passion, and expression to awakening the sleeping conscience of the nation, both to its peril and to its honour. And he failed. The awakening came from the fulfilment of the doom he prophesied and did his utmost to avert.

I have heard him called 'erratic', 'unreliable', 'not a safe man'. Not safe enough to fill the armchair of a humdrum office in safe days, but when all was at stake, when our own survival and the fate of civilisation were rushing towards the rapids, then we saw him, in the lightning flash of danger, as the one man strong enough to save.

How did he save us? The answer is, by being himself. When all was desperate, he wildly hurled himself into the scale and saved the world. He threw in the nation, too. He created in each one of us his own heroic image of ourselves, so that we were transmuted by his faith into the people he believed

---

[1] Also known as Robin Goodfellow. A mischievous fairy, sprite, or demon in English folklore. Portrayed as a 'shrewd and knavish sprite' in Shakespeare's *A Midsummer Night's Dream*.

in. We were that people, but we did not know it until he had revealed us to ourselves.

And now – there can be no leave-taking between him and the people that he served and saved. I think that many of us today may be feeling that by his going the scale of things has dwindled, our stature is diminished, that the glory has departed from us, that there is nothing left remarkable beneath the visiting moon. When yesterday I looked for the last time on his face from which all age and all infirmity had dropped away – young, calm and resolute in death – I thought: 'Is there anything, or is there nothing left that we can do for him?' Then I remembered the words of his Victory broadcast – when he urged us not to fall back into the rut of inertia, confusion and 'the craven fear of being great'. And I knew that the resolve to keep unbroken that pattern of greatness which he impressed upon the spirit of the nation is the tribute he would ask from us today.

On question, Motion agreed to, nemine dissentiente: ordered, that the said Address be presented to Her Majesty by the Lords with White Staves.

NATO: record of a meeting
(Premier papers, 13/205)

26 January 1965   Paris
11.00 a.m.

TRIBUTE TO SIR WINSTON CHURCHILL

1. The Council stood to observe one minute's silence in honour of the passing of Sir Winston Churchill.

2. The Chairman[1] then spoke as follows:

'We have met today to honour the memory of Winston Churchill and to pay our tribute of sorrow at his passing. To his family, and above all to Lady Churchill, who for fifty-six devoted years shared his triumphs and supported him in his adversities, we offer our deep sympathy. Today, a whole nation will be in mourning. To the British people also, we say "your grief is ours".

For Winston Churchill will not be mourned in Britain alone. To countless multitudes all over the world, his name has become the symbol of resistance to tyranny of every kind; of refusal to surrender to the aggressor and the bully; of refusal to admit that brute force and naked materialism are the dominant factors in human affairs. To him more than any one man, we owe it that our lives and liberties remain to us, and that our children may grow up and prosper as free men and women. Of him in the years

---

[1] Charles Paul de Cumont, 1902–90. Chairman, Belgian JCS, 1959–63. Chairman, NATO Military Committee, 1962–3, 1964–8.

of war it may in truth be said that "his shoulders held the sky suspended". What he did then, the world will for ever remember.

But Churchill's services to mankind did not end with the Second World War. "Last time" – he said at Fulton in 1946 – "I saw it all coming, and cried aloud to my fellow-countrymen and to the world, but no one paid any attention." Once again, in the years that followed, he was the first to warn us of the renewed perils we were facing, and the first to point out the way to meet them. At Fulton, in 1946, he warned us that:

"From Stettin on the Baltic to Trieste on the Adriatic, an iron curtain has descended across the Continent."

At Zurich in 1946, he called for that partnership between France and Germany which has since become the corner stone of the policies of both countries, and urged Europe to build up her political unity and her common defence in terms which foreshadowed both the European Economic Community and the Atlantic Alliance.

In the years between the wars, he had been a voice crying in the wilderness. This time, his appeal was heard. It is fitting that in this Council of all places, we should recall how he who did more than any other single individual to win the war, pointed out the way to preserve peace.

The greatest Englishman of his time – warrior, statesmen, man of letters – has gone to his rest. You will remember the words in which, in his Memoirs, he described how in May 1940 he received the Seal of Office from his King.

"I felt as if I were walking with destiny, and that all of my past life had been but a preparation for this hour and this trial."

How that hour was met, how that trial was surmounted, has passed into history.

No words of mine can add to his fame.

Stat magni nominis umbra.

No words of mine can convey the vivid sense of personal grief and loss which we all feel, whether, as I was privileged to do in my days in London, we knew and worked with him personally, or whether he was to us only a voice on the radio, a light in the darkness, an embodiment of the valiant people he led. "Never" – he said nearly a quarter of a century ago – "Never in the field of human conflict was so much owed by so many to so few." Never has humanity owed so much to the inspiration, the driving force, and the indomitable will of one man. Let us see to it that we are worthy of the heritage he has left us.'

[. . .]

4. The United Kingdom Representative[1] spoke as follows:

---

[1] Evelyn Shuckburgh.

'Mr Secretary General[1] and my dear colleagues: I thank you for the moving words spoken in your name by the Secretary General and the Doyen.[2] I shall certainly convey to Lady Churchill and to my Government the warm messages of condolence and sympathy which the Council has expressed.

I think we all feel, as our Doyen has said, that Winston Churchill belonged in a real sense to all of us. At the time of the highest crisis in our lives, when we all most needed the encouragement and strength of true leadership, he provided it, and he called up out of the depths of our consciousness noble and generous instincts rooted in the past of our peoples. His voice rose with the true note of liberty. He was the sort of man in whom everybody can recognize some part of his own ambitions and ideals.

Therefore, while I proudly accept in the name of Her Majesty's Government the generous tributes which have been paid to Winston Churchill as an Englishman and as my country's greatest statesman, I also join you in paying tribute to him as a European, a profound believer in the Atlantic partnership and a prime example of Democratic Man.'

Private Office to Harold Wilson
(Premier papers, 13/174)

28 January 1965

SIR WINSTON CHURCHILL'S FUNERAL: COMMONWEALTH BUSINESS

It is gradually becoming clearer who will be attending the funeral and what the items of business should be.

On the Commonwealth front there are clearly two major items of business and one of less importance:

(i) Southern Rhodesia. It is not yet certain whether Mr Smith[3] will be coming; but if he does clearly this will be the most important piece of business of all.[4]

---

[1] Manlio Brosio.
[2] The Chairman, de Cumont.
[3] Ian Douglas Smith, 1919–2007. Served in RAF, 1939–45. Member (Lib.), Southern Rhodesia Legislative Assembly, 1948–53. MP (United Front), Federation of Rhodesia and Nyasaland, 1953–61. Founding member and Vice-President of Republican Front, 1962; President, 1964–87. Deputy PM and Minister of the Treasury of Southern Rhodesia, 1962–4. PM of Rhodesia, 1964–79. Leader of the Opposition, Zimbabwe, 1980–7.
[4] In 1964 and 1965, negotiations took place between Harold Wilson and Ian Smith, PM of Rhodesia, over the conditions under which England would come to terms with the Rhodesian independence movement.

(ii) Confrontation.[1] Both Sir Robert Menzies and Mr Holyoake[2] will be present; this therefore seems an excellent moment to have a proper talk about confrontation, to discuss both the Australian and New Zealand military effort and perhaps also President Johnson's[3] letter.

(iii) Problems of Anglo-Canadian Trade. Mr Lester Pearson will be coming and obviously you should take advantage of his visit to leave him in no doubt what we think about things.

Other Commonwealth representatives appear to be of lower status and in any case there is no particular business to discuss with them.

I have asked the PUS at the CRO to produce a plan and suggested that thereafter the Commonwealth Secretary might come and discuss it with you.

My own view is that, depending on who is present, you might aim to give a Commonwealth Lunch on Friday, January 29. This will be a fairly muted social occasion.

Then it would seem desirable perhaps to have a working meal with Sir Robert Menzies and Mr Holyoake present to go over the problems of confrontation.

I will do a separate note about 'foreign' visitors, when we know who is coming. So far only Chancellor Erhard has specifically asked to see you and I have told the German Ambassador that you will of course be very glad to see him. Possibly Saturday afternoon, and in any case after you have seen the President/Vice-President, whoever comes.

Harold Wilson: recollection
('The Labour Government, 1964–1970', pages 70–1)

29 January 1965

It was my duty the following afternoon to appear at the bar of the House bearing a message from the Queen, informing Parliament of her royal wish that the body of Sir Winston should lie in state in Westminster Hall. I had given instructions that the seat he occupied for so many years after his retirement from office, below the gangway immediately next to the Government front bench, should be left empty throughout the afternoon. One unthinking back-bencher sought to claim it and was sharply hustled on to another bench.

[1] The reference is to the violent confrontation between Indonesia and Malaysia, also known as the Borneo Confrontation. The Commonwealth PMs had met in 1964 and expressed concern about any members of the Commonwealth becoming involved in the confrontation.

[2] Keith Jacka Holyoake, 1904–83. MP (Reform, National) of New Zealand Parliament for Motueka, 1932–8; for Pahiatua, 1943–77. Deputy PM, 1954–7. Deputy Leader of the Opposition, 1947. Deputy PM and Minister of Agriculture, 1949–57. PM, 1957, 1960–72. Governor-General of New Zealand, 1977–80.

[3] Lyndon Baines Johnson, 1908–73. Born in Stonewall, Texas. Served in US Navy, 1940–2. US Representative (Dem.) from Texas' 10th District, 1937–49. US Senator from Texas, 1949–61. Senate Majority Whip, 1951–3. Senate Minority Leader, 1953–5. Senate Majority Leader, 1955–61. Vice-President, 1961–3. 36th US President, 1963–9.

I ended my tribute with these words:

> We are conscious only that the tempestuous years are over; the years of appraisal are yet to come. It is a moment for the heartfelt tribute that this House, of all places, desires to pay in an atmosphere of quiet. For now the noise of hooves thundering across the veldt; the clamour of the hustings in a score of contests; the shots in Sidney Street, the angry guns of Gallipoli, Flanders, Coronel and the Falkland Islands; the sullen feet of marching men in Tonypandy; the urgent warnings of the Nazi threat; the whine of the sirens and the dawn bombardment of the Normandy beaches – all these now are silent. There is a stillness. And in that stillness, echoes and memories. To each whose life has been touched by Winston Churchill, to each his memory. And as those memories are told and retold, as the world pours in its tributes, as world leaders announce their intention, in this jet age, of coming to join in this vast assembly to pay honour and respect to his memory, we in this House treasure one thought, and it was a thought some of us felt it right to express in the parliamentary tributes on his retirement. Each one of us recalls some little incident – many of us, as in my own case, a kind action, graced with the courtesy of a past generation and going far beyond the normal calls of parliamentary comradeship. Each of us has his own memory, for in the tumultuous diapason of a world's tributes, all of us here at least know the epitaph he would have chosen for himself: 'He was a good House of Commons man.'

Early on the Saturday morning, the last of the three hundred thousand who had filed past the bier in Westminster Hall came through. I had arranged, as a parliamentary tribute to Sir Winston, that in place of the rota of soldiers who mounted guard in Westminster Hall, three party leaders – Prime Minister, leader of the Opposition and leader of the Liberal Party – together with Mr Speaker, should mount guard for a short period. This we did late on the Friday evening. The four of us, in full morning dress, took up our positions at the corners of the catafalque.

It was only for a few minutes. It was for an age.

The next day there was the great procession from Westminster Hall to St Paul's – the service of tribute, attended by presidents, prime ministers and war leaders from all over the world. Then the solemn progress following the coffin down to the river, where it was taken by launch to Waterloo and then to the train – and so to Sir Winston's last resting place at Bladon.

Lady Soames: recollection
(Mary Soames, 'A Churchill Family Album', pages 112–16)

30 January 1965

For three days Winston Churchill lay in state in Westminster Hall, and 320,000 people waited for hours (by day and by night) in bitter weather to file through the great Hall to take their leave of one who had become a legend in his own lifetime.[1] On Saturday 30 January, the funeral procession wound its long, magnificent way to St Paul's Cathedral, through streets lined by immense crowds of solemn, silent people. Below, the coffin is borne by Grenadier guardsmen into St Paul's, where a vast congregation was headed by the Queen who – waiving all custom and precedence – awaited the arrival of her greatest subject. Following behind the coffin are Clementine with Randolph, and other members of the close family.

Richard Crossman: diary
('The Diaries of a Cabinet Minister', pages 141–3)

30 January 1965

Winston's funeral. All through the week London had been working itself up for the great day. The lying-in-state in Westminster Hall had taken place on Wednesday, Thursday, and Friday. I went on all three evenings, taking Molly and our doorman, Arthur, on one night, Anne[2] and Tommy Balogh[3] the second night, and then on the third night Mr Large who cuts my hair. Each time one saw, even at one o'clock in the morning, the stream of people pouring down the steps of Westminster Hall towards the catafalque. Outside the column wound through the garden at Millbank, then stretched over Lambeth Bridge, right round the corner to St Thomas's Hospital. As one walked through the streets one felt the hush and one noticed the cars stopping suddenly and the people stepping out into the quietness and walking across to Westminster Hall. We as Members of Parliament could just step into the Hall through our side door.

I really hadn't wanted to go to the funeral. But it was obvious that I couldn't

---

[1] On 24 Jan. 1965, the day Churchill died, Queen Elizabeth II declared that his body was to lie in State at Westminster Abbey. On 15 Sep. 1965, the 25th anniversary of the Battle of Britain, at the request of the Queen and Parliament, a memorial stone was placed at the entrance to Westminster Abbey in memory of Sir Winston Churchill.

[2] Anne Patricia McDougall, 1920–2008. Married, 1954, Richard Crossman: two children. Published Richard Crossman's diaries after legal battle with the Cabinet Office, 1974.

[3] Thomas Balogh, 1905–85. Economic staff, League of Nations, 1931. National Institute of Economic Research, 1938–42. Lecturer at Balliol College, Oxford, 1938; Fellow, 1945. Oxford University Institute of Statistics, 1940–55. Fellow and Reader in Economics,1945–73. Member, Economic and Financial Committee of the Labour Party, 1943–64. Baron, 1968. Chairman, Fabian Society, 1969–70. Minister of State, Dept of Energy, 1974–5.

be known to have stayed away and I was a bit surprised, but also relieved, when Anne finally rang up and said she would like to go too and would come up on Friday. We spent the evening with Mark Childs,[1] who for some years has been, I suppose, the number three American political columnist. He had come over to cover the funeral. We discussed old times, particularly his visit during the Suez crisis when he had been, on request, first to see Anthony Eden, who told him nothing, and then to hear Harold Macmillan give him a hair-raising interview in which he was requested to send a personal message to the American Secretary of the Treasury begging him to go easy on the pound. He told us how next day, when he was seeing Anthony Eden, Macmillan had come into the room and said to him, 'Have you sent that telegram yet?' He then began to ask me about Gordon Walker, who had been built up by the American press as a strong, courageous man, almost a statesman. I am afraid that I said that he is really a pretty poor politician who got into Herbert Morrison's good books as a result of his attitude in the Oxford by-election at the time of Munich. Having got into the Attlee Cabinet as a Morrison man and risen to be Commonwealth Secretary, he was a solid Gaitskellite until Hugh died; and then during the contest for the leadership switched from George Brown to Harold Wilson at the critical moment.

We had a pleasant evening dining at Overtons. Then Anne and I went back to bed, or rather to find Kathleen[2] and Tam[3] sitting quietly by our fire and we chatted before going to sleep to prepare for the great day.

On Saturday Molly called for us at 9 a.m. in the morning, because instructions were that we had to get past Aldwych by 9:40. We were through Trafalgar Square by 9:20 and then we joined the stream of establishment cars wending their way, down the Strand, down Fleet Street, to St Paul's. We got there about 9:55 and were decanted suddenly and unexpectedly. We crept past various kinds of guards and found ourselves with places right forward under the dome. Anne was sitting next to Ray Gunter,[4] our Minister of Labour, and I next to Field Marshal Harding, who I had last seen in Cyprus when I was lunching with him, and his wife had turned to me and said, 'You're a very wicked man, Mr Crossman, last time you were here in Nicosia you were the cause of murder and destruction.' Harding is a little

---

[1] Marquis W. Childs, 1903–90. Worked for United Press, 1923–5, 1944–53; for *Saint Louis Post-Dispatch*, 1926–44, 1954–74; Chief Washington Correspondent, 1962–8. Pulitzer Prize for Commentary, 1970.

[2] Kathleen Mary Agnes Wheatley, 1937–. Married, 1963, Tam Dalyell: two children. National Trust for Scotland Administrator at The Binns, 1972. Chairman, Royal Commission on Ancient and Historical Monuments of Scotland, 2000–5.

[3] Tam Dalyell, 1932–2017. Born in Edinburgh. Educated at Eton College. Married, 1963, Kathleen Mary Agnes Wheatley. On active service, Royal Scots Greys, 1950–2. MP (Lab.) for West Lothian, 1962–83; for Linlithgow, 1983–2005. Personal Secretary to Richard Crossman, 1964–70. Member, European Parliament, 1975–9. Father of the House of Commons, 2001–5.

[4] Raymond Jones Gunter, 1909–77. Enlisted in Royal Engineers, 1941; Staff Capt., 1944–5. MP (Lab.) for South East Essex, 1945–50; for Doncaster, 1950–1; for Southwark, 1959–72. Chair, Labour Party National Executive Committee, 1964–5. Minister of Labour, 1964–8. Minister of Power, 1968.

man who is always falling over his sword every time he gets down on his knees to pray. However, he relieved my boredom by conducting a conversation with me throughout the whole service in a fairly high-pitched, audible whisper. I had brought with me Conrad's *Youth* to fill the intervals but I didn't read anything because the whole period before the service started was taken up by arrivals – arrivals by the lord mayor; the arrival of the procession of foreign ambassadors; then the foreign kings; they came at ten- or twenty-minute intervals and filled up the stage. Meanwhile there was also St Paul's to look at. Thanks to TV and the lighting, one could see the mosaics which one had never seen before and the whole decoration of the chancel. The mosaics were not very good but the general appearance under the lighting was magnificent. As for the service itself, it was fairly straightforward and very badly conducted by the Dean.[1] My chief memory is of the pall-bearers, in particular poor Anthony Eden, literally ashen grey, looking as old as Clement Attlee. And then of the coffin being carried up the steps by those poor perspiring privates of the Guards, sweat streaming down their faces, each clutching the next in order to sustain the sheer weight. As they came past us they staggered and they weren't properly recovered when they had to bring the coffin down the steps again to put it on the gun carriage to be taken to Tower Bridge. My other chief memory was the superb way the trumpets sounded the Last Post and the Reveille. The trumpeters were right up in the Whispering Gallery, round the inside of the dome, and for the first time a trumpet had room to sound in a dimension, a hemisphere of its own. But, oh, what a faded, declining establishment surrounded me. Aged marshals, grey, dreary ladies, decadent Marlboroughs and Churchills. It was a dying congregation gathered there and I am afraid the Labour Cabinet didn't look too distinguished either. It felt like the end of an epoch, possibly even the end of a nation.

When it was all over and we got out and stood on the steps at the west end, I feared the worst, and the worst came. The procession had of course been magnificently organized to the last split second so that the coffin arrived at the Tower of London, was got on to the boat and off the boat at Waterloo perfectly on time. But once the procession was over the Earl Marshal couldn't have cared less about those who had taken part. There we were, a couple of thousand people, waiting on the steps of St Paul's for cars which came one by one inconceivably slowly. We stood there for thirty minutes in a bitter wind and then Anne and I walked for five minutes to the underground at Blackfriars and I left her to go back to Vincent Square and on from there by car to the country, while I went to the Garrick for lunch with my publisher,

---

[1] Walter Matthews, 1881–1973. Ordained priest, 1907. Vicar of Christ Church, 1916–18. Dean of King's College, London, 1918–32; of Exeter, 1931–4; of St Paul's, 1934–67; of the British Empire, 1957–67.

Jamie Hamilton.[1] The Ministry was shut so I slipped into a cinema after lunch and saw a slick, novelettish little Terence Rattigan[2] show called *The Yellow Rolls Royce* which amused me a great deal. Then I walked home to do an hour and a half's reading and preparing papers before I went back to the House of Commons to the southern region of the Labour Party's annual dinner, which was being held in the Members' dining-room. I was only there because Harold Wilson had to look after the foreign guests at the funeral and gave instructions that I should take his place. I don't think he could have been conscious that the chairman would be Sydney Irving[3] in whose constituency I had given Span permission to build the model village of Hartley!

Afterwards I walked home and found Tam and Kathleen sitting watching for the second time the film of Churchill's funeral. I could see the things I hadn't seen – the scene at the Tower and the boat on the river and the landing-stage. I must say it was impressive. There was a stature, an ashen magnificence about the whole thing which made me think of Tennyson's 'Passing of Arthur'. But chiefly I reflected on the mood of the regional dinner I had just been addressing. And I asked myself, are we going to be driven out of office? Because if there were an election now there would be a landslide against us. I believe we shall get through this awkward period mainly because the Conservatives are still disunited and unable to strike. So if we keep our heads and do our job, there is no earthly reason why we shouldn't fight on into the summer, losing a lot of the local elections on the way I daresay, but still surviving. And once we get through to the summer and things pick up again we can settle down to go on for a year or two.

Dwight D. Eisenhower: broadcast[4]
(BBC Sound Archives)

30 January 1965

Upon the mighty Thames, a great avenue of history, move at this moment to their final resting place the mortal remains of Sir Winston Churchill. He was a great maker of history, but his work done, the record closed, we can almost hear him, with the poet say:

---

[1] James Hamish Hamilton, 1900–88. Born in Indianapolis, Indiana. Educated at Caius College, Cambridge. Married, 1929, Jean-Forbes Robertson (div. 1933); 1940, Yvonne Vicino Pallavicino: one child. Established publishing firm of Hamish Hamilton Ltd, 1931.

[2] Terence Rattigan, 1911–77. Educated at Trinity College, Oxford. Author of 27 plays and numerous screenplays.

[3] Sydney Irving, 1918–89. MP (Lab. and Co-op) for Dartford, 1955–70, 1974–9. Opposition Whip, 1959–64. Deputy Chief Whip and Treasurer of the Household, 1964–6. Deputy Speaker, 1966–70. Baron (Life Peer), 1979.

[4] This statement was broadcast as Churchill's casket was carried up the Thames to travel by rail to Bladon churchyard.

> Sunset and evening star,
> And one clear call for me!
> Twilight and evening bell,
> And after that the dark!
> And may there be no sadness of farewell
> When I embark.[1]

As I, like all other free men, pause to pay a personal tribute to the giant who now passes from among us, I have no charter to speak for my countrymen – only for myself. But, if in the memory, we journey back two decades, to the time when America and Britain stood shoulder to shoulder in global conflict against tyranny, then I can presume – with propriety, I think – to act as spokesman for the millions of Americans who served with me and their British comrades during three years of war in this sector of the earth.

To those men Winston Churchill was Britain – he was the embodiment of British defiance to threat, her courage in adversity, her calmness in danger, her moderation in success. Among the Allies, his name was spoken with respect, admiration and affection. Although they loved to chuckle at his foibles, they knew he was a staunch friend. They felt his inspirational leadership. They counted him a fighter in their ranks.

The loyalty that the fighting forces of many nations here serving gave to him during that war was no less strong, no less freely given, than he had, in such full measure, from his own countrymen.

An American, I was one of those Allies. During those dramatic months, I was privileged to meet, to talk, to plan and to work with him for common goals.

Out of that association an abiding – and to me precious – friendship was forged; it withstood the trials and frictions inescapable among men of strong convictions, living in an atmosphere of war.

The war ended, our friendship flowered in the later and more subtle tests imposed by international politics. Then, each of us, holding high official posts in his own nation, strove together so to concert the strength of our two peoples that liberty might be preserved among men and the security of the free world wholly sustained.

Through a career during which personal victories alternated with defeats, glittering praise with bitter criticism, intense public activity with periods of semi-retirement, Winston Churchill lived out his fourscore and ten years.

With no thought of the length of the time he might be permitted on earth, he was concerned only with the quality of the service he could render to his nation and to humanity. Though he had no fear of death, he coveted always the opportunity to continue that service.

---

[1] From 'Crossing the Bar' by Alfred Lord Tennyson (1889).

At this moment, as our hearts stand at attention, we say our final affectionate though sad good-bye to the leader whom the entire body of free men owes so much.

In the coming years, many in countless words will strive to interpret the motives, describe the accomplishments and extol the virtues of Winston Churchill – soldier, statesman, and citizen that two great countries were proud to claim as their own. Among all things so written or spoken, there will ring out through the centuries one incontestable refrain: Here was a champion of freedom.

May God grant that we – and the generations who will remember him – heed the lessons he taught us: in his deeds; in his words; in his life.

May we carry on his work until no nation lies in captivity, no man is denied opportunity for fulfilment.

And now to you, Sir Winston, my old friend – farewell.

Lady Churchill to Harold Wilson
(Premier papers, 13/170)

9 February 1965
Private and Confidential

My dear Prime Minister,

It is so very kind of you to say that Anthony Montague Browne may stay on to help me with the many matters arising from Winston's death. The immediate clearing up can be quite quickly accomplished, but there are some long-term matters with which he is intimately acquainted and where I should welcome his assistance and advice.

He is in touch with the Foreign Office over his future. After thirteen years away from the Foreign Office, of which only three were at Downing Street, he thinks that it may be difficult for him to go back. However, nothing has been settled yet, and certainly the stories in the newspaper of his taking employment with Mr Onassis are entirely untrue.

May I express to you my true and heartfelt thanks for the wonderful and sustaining way in which many Government Departments have helped me in recent days? I am thinking not only of the State Funeral, but of many other matters. I know that much of this is due to your personal sympathy.

Appendices

Appendix A: Ministerial Appointments, 1 November 1951 to 5 April 1955

THE CABINET

Prime Minister and First Lord of the Treasury
  Winston S. Churchill
Lord Chancellor
  Lord Simonds (to 18 Oct. 1954)
  Lord Kilmuir (from 18 Oct. 1954)
Lord President of the Council
  Lord Woolton (to 24 Nov. 1952)
  Lord Salisbury (from 24 Nov. 1952)
Lord Privy Seal
  Marquess of Salisbury (to 7 May 1952)
Leader of the House of Lords
  Marquess of Salisbury
Lord Privy Seal and Leader of the House of Commons
  Harry Crookshank (from 7 May 1952)
Chancellor of the Exchequer
  R. A. Butler
Secretary of State for Foreign Affairs
  Anthony Eden
Secretary of State for the Home Department and Welsh Affairs
  Sir David Maxwell Fyfe (to 18 Oct. 1954)
  Gwilym Lloyd George (from 18 Oct. 1954)
Chancellor of the Duchy of Lancaster
  Lord Woolton (from 24 Nov. 1952)
Minister of Agriculture and Fisheries
  Sir Thomas Dugdale (to 28 July 1954; in Cabinet from 3 Sep. 1953)
  Derick Heathcoat-Amory (from 28 July 1954)

Minister for the Co-ordination of Transport, Fuel and Power
   Lord Leathers (to 3 Sep. 1953, when office abolished)
Minister of Defence
   Winston S. Churchill (to 1 Mar. 1952)
   Lord Alexander (to 18 Oct. 1954)
   Harold Macmillan (from 18 Oct. 1954)
Minister of Education
   Florence Horsbrugh (to 18 Oct. 1954; seat in Cabinet from 3 Sep. 1953)
   Sir David Eccles (from 18 Oct. 1954)
Minister of Food
   Gwilym Lloyd George (to 18 Oct. 1954)
   Derick Heathcoat-Amory (from 18 Oct. 1954)
Minister of Health
   Harry Crookshank (to 7 May 1952)
Minister for Housing and Local Government
   Harold Macmillan (to 18 Oct. 1954)
   Duncan Sandys (from 18 Oct. 1954)
Minister of Labour and National Service
   Sir Walter Monckton
Minister of Materials
   Lord Woolton (from 1 Sep. 1953)
Minister of Pensions
   Osbert Peake (seat in Cabinet from 18 Oct. 1954)
Paymaster-General
   Lord Cherwell (to 11 Nov. 1953)
President of the Board of Trade
   Peter Thorneycroft
Secretary of State for the Colonies
   Oliver Lyttelton (to 28 July 1954)
   Alan Lennox-Boyd (from 28 July 1954)
Secretary of State for Commonwealth Relations
   Lord Ismay (to 12 Mar. 1952)
   Lord Salisbury (to 24 Nov. 1952)
   Lord Swinton (from 24 Nov. 1952)
Secretary of State for Scotland
   James Stuart

LAW OFFICERS

Attorney-General
   Sir Lionel Heald (to 18 Oct. 1954)
   Sir Reginald Manningham-Buller (from 18 Oct. 1954)

Lord Advocate
   James Clyde (to 30 Dec. 1954)
   William Rankine Milligan (from 30 Dec. 1954)
Solicitor-General
   Sir Reginald Manningham-Buller (to 18 Oct. 1954)
   Sir Harry Hylton-Foster (from 18 Oct. 1954)
Solicitor-General for Scotland
   William Rankine Milligan (from 2 Nov. 1951)

OTHER MINISTERIAL APPOINTMENTS

Chancellor of the Duchy of Lancaster and Minister of Materials
   Lord Swinton (to 24 Nov. 1952)
First Lord of the Admiralty
   James Thomas
Minister for Economic Affairs (office abolished 24 Nov. 1952)
   Sir James Salter
Minister of Fuel and Power
   Geoffrey Lloyd
Minister of Health
   Iain Macleod (from 7 May 1952)
Minister of Materials
   Lord Swinton (to 24 Nov. 1952)
   Sir James Salter (from 24 Nov. 1952)
Minister of National Insurance (combined with Ministry of Pensions Sep. 1953)
   Osbert Peake
Minister of Pensions
   Derick Heathcoat-Amory (to 3 Sep. 1953)
   Osbert Peake (from Sep. 1953, with seat in Cabinet from 18 Oct. 1954)
Minister of Supply
   Duncan Sandys (to 18 Oct. 1954)
   John Selwyn Lloyd (from 18 Oct. 1954)
Minister of Transport
   John Maclay (to 7 May 1952)
   Alan Lennox-Boyd (to 28 July 1954)
   John Boyd-Carpenter (from 28 July 1954)
Minister of Works
   Sir David Eccles to 18 Oct. 1954)
   Nigel Birch (from 18 Oct. 1954)
Paymaster-General
   Lord Selkirk (from 11 Nov. 1953)

Postmaster-General
    Lord De La Warr (from 5 Nov. 1951)
Secretary of State for Air
    Lord De L'Isle and Dudley
Secretary of State for War
    Antony Head

Appendix B: Abbreviations

AA: anti-aircraft
AB: atomic bomb
ACIGS: Assistant Chief of the Imperial General Staff
ADC: aide-de-camp
Adm.: Admiral
AE: Anthony Eden
AFC: Air Force Cross
AFHQ: Allied Force Headquarters
AIOC: Anglo-Iranian Oil Company
Air Chf Mshl: Air Chief Marshal
Air Mshl: Air Marshal
AMB: Anthony Montague Browne
ANZAM, Anzam: Australia, New Zealand and Malaya
ANZUS, Anzus: Pacific Security Treaty between the United States, Australia, and New Zealand
AOC: Air Officer Commanding
AOC-in-C: Air Officer Commanding-in-Chief
ARW: Air Raid Warden
A/S: anti-submarine
Asdic: anti-submarine sonar detection device
Asst: Assistant
ATS: Auxiliary Territorial Service
Aus.: Australia
AVM: Air Vice-Marshal

BAOR: British Army of Occupation on the Rhine
BBBC: British Board of Boxing Control
BBC: British Broadcasting Corporation
Bde: Brigade
BEF: British Expeditionary Force
BMA: British Medical Association

BOAC: British Overseas Airways Corporation
Brig.: Brigadier
Brig.-Gen.: Brigadier-General
Bt: Baronet

C: Chief of the Secret Intelligence Service
Capt.: Captain
CAS: Chief of the Air Staff
CB: Companion of the Order of the Bath
CBE: Commander of the Order of the British Empire
CBS: Columbia Broadcasting System
CCS: Combined Chiefs of Staff
Cdr: Commander
CDS: Chief of the Defence Staff
CEO: Chief Executive Officer
CGS: Chief of the General Staff
CH: Companion of Honour
CIA: Central Intelligence Agency
CIE: Companion of the Order of the Indian Empire
CIGS: Chief of the Imperial General Staff
C-in-C: Commander-in-Chief
CIO: Congress of Industrial Organizations (US)
CMG: Companion of the Order of St Michael and St George
CNAS: Chief of Naval Air Services
CNS: Chief of the Naval Staff
CO: Commanding Officer
Co.: Company
COCOM: Co-ordinating Committee
Col.: Colonel
COMNAVNORTH: Commander, Allied Naval Forces in the North Sea
Cons.: Conservative [Party]
Co-op.: Co-operative [Movement]
Corp.: Corporation
CoS: Chief of Staff
COS: Chiefs of Staff
CPC: Combined Policy Committee
Cpl.: Corporal
CRO: Commonwealth Relations Office
CSO: Chief Staff Officer
CStJ: Commander of the Order of St John
CVO: Commander of the Royal Victorian Order

d.: died
DBE: Dame Commander of the Order of the British Empire
DC: District of Columbia
DCAS: Deputy Chief of the Air Staff
DCI: Director of Central Intelligence
DCIGS: Deputy Chief of the Imperial General Staff
DCM: Distinguished Conduct Medal
DCNS: Deputy Chief of the Naval Staff
DCVO: Dame Commander of the Royal Victorian Order
Dem.: Democrat (US)
Dept: Department
DFC: Distinguished Flying Cross
diss.: [marriage, company] dissolved
div.: divorced
Div.: Division
DL: Doctor of Laws
DRP: Defence Research Policy
DSC: Distinguished Service Cross
DSIR: Department of Scientific and Industrial Research
DSM: Distinguished Service Medal
DSO: Distinguished Service Order
DT: *Daily Telegraph*

EASTLANT: East Atlantic
E-boat: German *Schnellboot* ('fast boat')
EDC: European Defence Community
EEC: European Economic Community
EQ: Enlisted Quarters

FBA: Fellow of the British Academy
FBI: Federation of British Industries (UK); Federal Bureau of Investigation (US)
FCO: Foreign and Commonwealth Office
FDR: Franklin Delano Roosevelt
Flt Lt: Flight Lieutenant
FM: Field Marshal
FO: Foreign Office
FRCP: Fellow of the Royal College of Physicians
FRS: Fellow of the Royal Society
FRSA: Fellow of the Royal Society of Arts

GATT: General Agreement on Tariffs and Trade
GB: Great Britain

GBE: Knight Grand Cross of the Order of the British Empire
GC: George Cross
GCB: Knight Grand Cross of the Order of the Bath
GCIE: Knight Grand Cross of the Order of the Indian Empire
GCMG: Knight Grand Cross of the Order of St Michael and St George
GCSI: Knight Grand Commander of the Order of the Star of India
GCVO: Knight Grand Cross of the Royal Victorian Order
Gen.: General
GHQ: General Headquarters
GOC: General Officer Commanding
GOC-in-C: General Officer Commanding-in-Chief
GP: General [Medical] Practitioner
Gp Capt.: Group Captain
GSO: General Staff Officer (I, II)

HHC: Headquarters and Headquarters Company
HM: His/Her Majesty's
HMG: His/Her Majesty's Government
HMS: His/Her Majesty's Ship
Hon., hon.: honorary, honourable
HQ: headquarters
HRH: His/Her Royal Highness

IAEA: International Atomic Energy Agency
Iberlant: Iberian Atlantic Area
IBRD: International Bank for Reconstruction and Development
Inc.: Incorporated
Ind.: Independent
IFF: Identification Friend or Foe
IMF: International Monetary Fund
IRA: Irish Republican Army

JCS: Joint Chiefs of Staff
JP: Justice of the Peace
Jr: Junior
JSM: (British) Joint Staff Mission in Washington DC

KAR: King's African Rifles
KBE: Knight Commander of the Order of the British Empire
KC: King's Counsel
KCB: Knight Commander of the Order of the Bath
KCIE: Knight Commander of the Order of the Indian Empire

KCMG: Knight Commander of the Order of St Michael and St George
KCVO: Knight Commander of the Royal Victorian Order
KG: Knight of the Garter
KRRC: King's Royal Rifle Corps
KStJ: Knight of Grace in the Venerable Order of St John
KT: Knight of the Thistle

Lab.: Labour [Party]
Lib.: Liberal [Party]
LL.D: Doctor of Laws
LOM: Legion of Merit
LPC: Lord President of the Council
Lt: Lieutenant
Lt-Cdr: Lieutenant-Commander
Lt-Col.: Lieutenant-Colonel
Ltd: Limited [Company]
Lt-Gen.: Lieutenant-General

Maj.: Major
Maj.-Gen.: Major-General
MBE: Member of the Order of the British Empire
MC: Military Cross
M-Day: mobilisation day
ME: Middle East
MEDO: Middle East Defence Organisation
MELF: Middle East Land Forces
MoD: Ministry of Defence
MP: Member of Parliament
MRP: Mouvement Républicain Populaire (France)
Mshl of the RAF: Marshal of the Royal Air Force
MVD: Soviet Ministry of Internal Affairs

Nat.: National
Nat. Gov.: National Government
NATO: North Atlantic Treaty Organization
NCO: non-commissioned officer
NFU: National Farmers Union
NHS: National Health Service
NKVD: Narodnyy Komissariat Vnutrennikh Del, the Soviet People's Commissariat for Internal Affairs (security service)
NUP: National Unionist Party (Sudan)
NUR: National Union of Railwaymen
NZEF: New Zealand Expeditionary Force

OAP: old age pension(s)
OBE: Office of the Order of the British Empire
OC: Officer Commanding
OEEC: Organization for European Economic Co-operation
OM: Order of Merit
OStJ: Officer of the Order of St John
OSS: Office of Strategic Services
OTC: Officer Training Corps

PAYE: Pay As You Earn (income taxation)
PC: Privy Councillor
pdr: pounder
PhD: Doctor of Philosophy
PM: Prime Minister
POW: prisoner of war
PPE: Philosophy, Politics and Economics
PQ: Parliamentary Question
PR: proportional representation
PRC: People's Republic of China
Prof.: Professor
PUS: Permanent Under-Secretary
PWE: Political Warfare Executive

QC: Queen's Counsel
QM: HMS *Queen Mary*
QMG: Quartermaster-General

RA: Royal Artillery
RAAF: Royal Auxiliary Air Force
RAB, Rab: R. A. Butler
RAC: Royal Armoured Corps
RAdm.: Rear-Admiral
RAF: Royal Air Force
RAFVR: Royal Air Force Volunteer Reserve
RAMC: Royal Army Medical Corps
RASC: Royal Army Service Corps
RE: Royal Engineers
Rep.: Republican (US)
RFC: Royal Flying Corps
Rgt: Regiment
RN: Royal Navy
RNAS: Royal Naval Air Service
RNVR: Royal Naval Volunteer Reserve

ROC: Republic of China
ROK: Republic of Korea
RPF: Rassemblement du Peuple Français

SAC: Supreme Allied Commander
SACEUR, Saceur: Supreme Allied Commander, Europe
SACLANT: Supreme Allied Commander Atlantic
SACMED: Supreme Allied Commander, Mediterranean Command (NATO)
SACSEA: Supreme Allied Commander, South East Asia
SALH: South African Light Horse
SAS: Special Air Service
SBS: Special Boat Service
SE: South-east
SEAC: South East Asia Command
SEATO: Southeast Asia Treaty Organization
SED: Sozialistiche Einheitspartei Deutschlands (East German Communist Party)
Sgt: Sergeant
SHAEF: Supreme Headquarters, Allied Expeditionary Force
SHAPE: Supreme Headquarters, Allied Powers Europe
SIS: Secret Intelligence Service
SOE: Special Operations Executive
S of S: Secretary of State
SPD: Sozialdemokratische Partei Deutschlands
Sqn: Squadron
Sqn Ldr: Squadron Leader
SRP: Socialist Republican Party (Sudan)
SS: Schutzstaffel

TA: Territorial Army; Tube Alloys
TCC: Temporary Council Committee (NATO)
TGWU: Transport and General Workers Union
TUC: Trades Union Congress

UAR: United Arab Republic
UJ: Uncle Joe, i.e. Stalin
UK: United Kingdom
UKAEA: United Kingdom Atomic Energy Agency
UKHC: United Kingdom High Commission(er)
UNESCO: United Nations Educational, Scientific and Cultural Organization
Union.: Unionist
UN(O): United Nations (Organisation)
UNRRA: United Nations Relief and Rehabilitation Administration

UNRWA: United Nations Relief and Works Agency for Palestine Refugees in the Near East
US, USA: United States of America
USAF: United States Air Force
USN: United States Navy
USNR: United States Naval Reserve
USS: United States Ship
USSR: Union of Soviet Socialist Republics

VAdm.: Vice-Admiral
VC: Victoria Cross
VCAS: Vice-Chief of the Air Staff
VCIGS: Vice-Chief of the Imperial General Staff
VCS: Vice-Chief of Staff
VE: Victory in Europe
VT: variable time

WAAF: Women's Auxiliary Air Force
Wg Cdr: Wing Commander
WRNS: Women's Royal Naval Service
WVS: Women's Voluntary Service
WWI: First World War
WWII: Second World War

YWCA: Young Women's Christian Association

Appendix C: Churchill's Travels, December 1951 to 1963

Date	Destination	Description
1951		
17 Dec.	Paris	Diplomatic visit accompanied by Eden. Returned to London Dec. 19.
30 Dec.	New York	Embarked at Southampton on RMS *Queen Mary*, arriving New York 4 Jan. 1952.
1952		
5 Jan.	Washington DC	Flew in President Truman's plane to Washington for White House talks on NATO.
9 Jan.	New York	Guest of Bernard Baruch.
11 Jan.	Ottawa	Became honorary member of Canadian press corps. Speech at banquet given by Canadian Government in his honour.
15 Jan.	Washington DC	Became member of Society of Cincinnati. Address to Congress.
19 Jan.	New York	Guest of Bernard Baruch.
22 Jan.	Southampton	Embarked at New York on RMS *Queen Mary*, arriving Southampton Jan. 28 and travelling on to London.
9 Sep.	La Capponcina, Côte d'Azur	Holiday to Southern France with Clementine. Elected honorary Mayor of Cap d'Ail. Returned to London Sep. 25.
1 Oct.	Balmoral, Scotland	Guest of the Queen. Returned to London Oct. 4.
9 Oct.	Scarborough	Conservative Party Conference. Returned to London Oct. 14.
30 Dec.	New York	Embarked at Southampton on RMS *Queen Mary* with Clementine, Mary, and Jock Colville, arriving New York 5 Jan. 1953.

1953

5–8 Jan.	New York	Meeting with President-Elect Eisenhower at Bernard Baruch's apartment. Meetings with John Foster Dulles, Winthrop Aldrich, Governor Dewey, and again with Eisenhower.
8 Jan.	Washington DC	Flew in President-Elect's aircraft. Stayed at British Embassy. Meeting with outgoing President Truman at White House.
9 Jan.	Ocho Rios, Jamaica	Holiday. Worked on war memoirs. Flew back to London, arriving Jan. 29.
17 Apr.	Glasgow	Speech to Scottish Unionist Association Annual Meeting at Green's Playhouse. Returned to London Apr. 20.
17 Sep.	La Capponcina	Holiday at Lord Beaverbrook's villa with Christopher and Mary Soames and Miss Portal. Painted and worked on war memoirs. Returned to London Sep. 30.
10 Oct.	Margate	Speech to Conservative Party Conference.
1 Dec.	Bermuda	Flew out for tripartite talks with the United States, including President Eisenhower, and France. Stayed at Mid Ocean Golf Club. Returned to London Dec. 11.

1954

24 June	Washington DC	Flew out with Eden on diplomatic visit to United States and Canada.
25 June	Washington DC	Visited President Eisenhower, Vice-President Nixon, John Foster Dulles and others at the White House.
29 June	Ottawa	Meetings with Canadian Prime Minister and Cabinet. Returned to New York June 30.
1 July	London	Embarked at New York on RMS *Queen Elizabeth*, arriving Southampton July 6 and travelling on to London.
8 Oct.	Blackpool	Speech to Conservative Party Conference. Returned to London Oct. 9.
26 Nov.	Bristol	Delivered Chancellor's Address at Bristol University's degree conferment ceremony.

1955

12 Apr.	Sicily	Holiday with Clementine after resigning as Prime Minister on April 5. Stayed at the Villa Politi at Syracuse, where he was joined by Lord Cherwell and Jock Colville. Painted. Returned to London Apr. 27.
17 May	Bedford	Election address on behalf of Christopher Soames.
7 Sep.	Hastings	Received portrait as Lord Warden of Cinque Ports, painted by Bernard Hailstone, at the Court of Brotherhood and Guestling of the Cinque Ports.
15 Sep.	La Capponcina	Holiday at Lord Beaverbrook's villa. Joined by Clementine and Mary and Christopher Soames. Painted and worked on his *History of the English-Speaking Peoples*. Returned to London Nov. 13.

1956

11 Jan.	La Pausa, Cap Martin	Holiday at Emery Reves' villa. Painted.
18 Jan.	Monte Carlo	Holiday continued. Lunch with R. A. Butler.
19 Jan.	La Pausa	Holiday continued with R. A. Butler. Dined with Aristotle Onassis on his yacht, *Christina*. Returned to London Feb. 10.
27 Feb.	La Pausa	Holiday. Returned to London Apr. 11.
10 May	Aachen (Aix-la-Chapelle), West Germany	Received Charlemagne Prize.
31 May	La Pausa	Holiday. Returned to London June 14.
30 July	Düsseldorf	Brief horse-racing excursion.
19 Sep.	La Pausa	Holiday. Returned to London end October.

APPENDICES 2403

1957

18 Jan.	La Pausa	Holiday. Returned to London Feb. 20.
16 Feb.	La Pausa	Returned to London Mar. 22.
3 Sep.	Geneva	Speech to Inter-Parliamentary Union Conference.
11 Sep.	La Pausa	Holiday. Returned to London Oct. 21.

1958

13 Jan.	La Pausa	Holiday. Painted. Visited *Christina*. Contracted bronchial pneumonia and fevers, which prolonged his stay. Returned to London Apr. 1.
31 July	La Capponcina	Holiday with Lord Beaverbrook.
22 Sep.	South of France	Embarked on *Christina* for Mediterranean cruise, concluding at Gibraltar Oct 10. Returned to London.
	Worthing	Saw Sarah in Terence Rattigan's play *Variations on a Theme*.
12 Oct.	La Pausa	Holiday.
6 Nov.	Paris	Received the Croix de la Liberation from General de Gaulle. Returned to London Nov. 14.

1959

7 Jan.	Marrakech	Holiday with Clementine.
18 Feb.	Marrakech	Embarked on *Christina* for cruise of Canary Islands and Moroccan coast. Returned to London Mar. 2.
6 Mar.	La Pausa	Painting holiday. Returned to London Apr. 6.
4 May	Washington DC	Visit to the White House. US visit concluded May 10.

22 July	Mediterranean	Embarked on *Christina* for cruise of Greek and Turkish waters, concluding Monte Carlo Aug. 13.
22 Aug.	La Capponcina	Holiday continued. Returned to London Sep. 4.
17 Oct.	Cambridge	Naming and tree-planting ceremony at Churchill College, University of Cambridge.

1960

2 Jan.	Monte Carlo	Holiday. Returned to London Feb. 10.
8 Mar.	Gibraltar	Embarked on *Christina* for cruise of Caribbean.
21 Mar.	Barbados	Cruise continued.
22 Mar.	Trinidad and Tobago	Cruise continued.
25 Mar.	St Lucia	Cruise continued.
26 Mar.	Antigua	Cruise continued.
28 Mar.	Martinique	Cruise continued.
31 Mar.	St Thomas	Cruise continued.
1 Apr.	Puerto Rico	Cruise ended. Returned to London Apr. 3.
10 July	Venice	Embarked on *Christina* for Mediterranean cruise.
14 July	Split (Adriatic port)	Cruise continued. Visited President Tito.
19 July	Athens	Cruise continued.
22 July	Rhodes	Cruise continued.
28 July	Athens	Cruise ended. Returned to London Aug. 4.
28 Sep.	Hôtel de Paris, Monte Carlo	Holiday with Clementine and Anthony Montague Browne. Visited La Capponcina. Returned to London Nov. 3.

APPENDICES 2405

1961

9 Mar.	Gibraltar	Embarked on *Christina* for cruise via Caribbean to New York. Accompanied by Anthony and Nonie Montague Browne with their daughter Jane.
22 Mar.	Port of Spain, Trinidad	Cruise continued.
10 Apr.	New York	Cruise ended. Returned to London, Apr. 14.
June	Hôtel de Paris	Holiday.
21 Aug.	Hôtel de Paris	Holiday accompanied by grandson Winston. Visit to La Capponcina. Returned to London Sep. 8.
Early Dec.	Hôtel de Paris	Holiday. Returned to London Dec. 13.

1962

6 Apr.	Monte Carlo	Embarked on *Christina* for cruise of western Mediterranean with various other guests.
14 Apr.	Libya	Aboard, informed that he will receive Grand Sash of the High Order of Sayyid Mohammed bin Ali al-Sanusi. Returned to London Apr. 28.
27 June	Monte Carlo	Holiday. Visited La Capponcina. Fell and fractured his pelvis. Returned to London June 29.

1963

11 Apr.	Monte Carlo	Holiday. Visited La Capponcina. Returned to London Apr. 25.
21 June	Monte Carlo	Embarked on *Christina* for Mediterranean and Aegean cruise, calling at Athens. Returned to London July 4.

Appendix D: Two Additional Documents

This speech excerpt is included here for two reasons. First, it did not find its way into volume 12 of The Churchill Documents, *which covers the period 1929 to 1935. Second, it contains sage advice to all who endeavour to learn from the lessons of the past and from the examples of its greatest characters.*

Winston S. Churchill: speech
('Winston S. Churchill, His Complete Speeches', volume 5, pages 4674–5)

14 December 1929   Bristol University

ADVICE TO STUDENTS

[. . .] I never myself had the advantage of a university education. I was not thought clever enough to profit by it to the full. I was put to be trained in technical matters of a military college, and almost immediately afterwards things opened out very quickly into action and adventure. In those days England had a lot of jolly little wars against barbarous peoples that we were endeavouring to help forward to higher things, and I found myself scurrying about the world from one exciting scene to another. During years appropriate to study and the accumulation of knowledge, I was a pack-horse that had to nibble and browse such grass as grew by the roadside in the brief halts of long and wearying marches. But see how very lucky you all are. You are a most fortunate crowd of quadrupeds, to use a neutral term. (*Laughter.*) You are admitted to a spacious paddock with the very best herbage growing in profusion. You are pressed to eat your fill. I hope you are going to take advantage of that. . . . The most important thing about education is appetite. Education does not begin with the university, and it certainly ought not to end there. I have seen a lot of people who got cleverer until about 21 or 22 years of age, then seemed to shut down altogether and never made any further progress. [. . .] Take full advantage of these years when the wisdom of the world is placed at your disposal, but do not spend too much time in buckling on your armour in the tent. The battle is going on in every walk and sphere of life.

Similarly, this humorous doctor's note is not included in volume 12 of The Churchill Documents, *and it would be a shame to publish the final document volume without it.*

Dr Otto Pickhardt: prescription for Winston S. Churchill
(Churchill papers, 1/400)

26 January 1932

This is to certify that the post-accident convalescence of the Hon. Winston S. Churchill necessitates the use of alcoholic spirits especially at meal times. The quantity is naturally indefinite but the minimum requirements would be 250 cubic centimeters.[1]

---

[1] Churchill wrote on this prescription: 'Keep on hand'.

Appendix E: Orders, Decorations, Medals and Honours Conferred on Winston Churchill, 1951 to 1965

This appendix reproduces adapted excerpts from Douglas S. Russell's book *The Orders, Decorations and Medals of Sir Winston Churchill* (1990). The editor is grateful to Douglas Russell for his permission to use elements of his book in this final volume of *The Churchill Documents*.

QUEEN ELIZABETH II'S CORONATION MEDAL, 2 JUNE 1953

Queen Elizabeth II was crowned on 2 June 1953, and soon afterwards a coronation medal struck by the Royal Mint was issued as her personal souvenir of the event to no fewer than 129,051 notables in the Government, the Commonwealth, the military and society. Not the least notable was the PM, the Right Honourable Sir Winston Churchill, KG, OM, CH, TD, MP, appointed to be and soon to be installed as Knight of the Garter.

Following the Coronation ceremony, hundreds of thousands of spectators lined the route of the grand Coronation procession between Westminster Abbey and Buckingham Palace. Churchill rode in a closed carriage with Mrs Churchill and was one of the most popular persons present; only Queen Elizabeth II and Queen Salote of Tonga received louder cheers and applause.

Queen Elizabeth II's Coronation Medal is similar in design to that of King George VI. The medal is struck in silver and is 31.25 mm in diameter. The obverse shows the bust of the Queen wearing a royal crown and robe, facing to the right. There is no inscription on the obverse and, as on the Queen Victoria Jubilee Medals, the Queen's figure appears alone without that of her consort. The reverse of the medal features the royal cipher E II R in block letters in the centre beneath a royal crown. Surrounding the cipher is the inscription Queen Elizabeth. II. 2ND JUNE 1953 in block letters. The medal has knob and ring suspension identical to those of King George V's Jubilee Medal and King George VI's Coronation Medal. The ribbon is of red silk 31.25 mm wide, with two narrow blue stripes in the centre and a narrow white strip on each edge.

NOBEL PRIZE FOR LITERATURE, 11 DECEMBER 1953

Churchill learned on 16 October 1953 that he had been awarded the Nobel Prize for Literature. The award came with a £12,100 tax-free cash prize, about which Churchill wrote to his wife, 'Not so bad!' By October 1953, Churchill had written and published thirty-five books, nineteen of which were collections of his speeches. Many of these were multi-volume works, such as *The River War, Lord Randolph Churchill, The World Crisis, Marlborough: His Life and Times* and *The Second World War.* After 1953, he would go on to write and publish his four-volume *A History of the English-Speaking Peoples.*

Churchill intended to accept the award in person, but the December 4–8 Bermuda Conference between the heads of state of the United Kingdom, the United States and France required that Clementine and Mary travel to Stockholm to accept the prize in Churchill's absence. Of the Bermuda Conference and the Nobel Prize, official biographer Martin Gilbert writes, 'There were those who thought that Churchill should have been awarded the Nobel Prize for Peace. Ironically, the prize for literature came on the day of his greatest disappointment since the war, to build at Bermuda a path to the Summit which, as he had envisaged it, would also have been a path to peace.'[1]

KNIGHT COMPANION OF THE MOST NOBLE ORDER OF THE GARTER, APPOINTED 24 APRIL 1953, INSTALLED 14 JUNE 1954

The Most Noble Order of the Garter was founded in 1348 by Edward III and is the senior British order in precedence of honour and in history. The selection for the Order is now made personally by the Sovereign and is given in only one class, knight. Membership is limited to the Sovereign and twenty-five knights. A limited number of royal heads of state may be admitted as honorary members. It is one of the most prestigious orders in the world and the highest honour for military and civil service a Briton may receive.

Following his election defeat on 26 July 1945, Churchill went to Buckingham Palace and offered his resignation. At their meeting King George VI offered Churchill the Order of the Garter. Few commoners have been given this high distinction since the Order was created. But Churchill was one of the few ever to decline the Garter. The official statement from Buckingham Palace on 30 July was, 'After Mr Churchill had tendered his resignation to the King last Thursday his Majesty asked him to accept the Order of the Garter in recognition of his great services throughout the war. Mr Churchill, however, begged his Majesty that, in present circumstances, he might be allowed to decline the offer.'[2] Churchill explained his reason for declining the Garter a few days later to Sir Alan Lascelles: 'For me, I felt the times were too sad for honours or rewards. After all, my great reward is the kindness and intimacy with which the King has treated me during these hard and perilous years which we have endured and enjoyed in common.'[3]

In 1952, now Elizabeth II's principal private secretary, Sir Alan Lascelles

---

[1] *Winston S. Churchill*, vol. 8, *Never Despair, 1945–1965*, p. 938.
[2] *The Times*, 31 July 1945, p. 4.
[3] Reproduced in *The Churchill Documents*, vol. 22, *Leader of the Opposition, August 1945 to October 1951*, pp. 4–5.

made a discreet inquiry of Churchill's principal private secretary, John Colville, and learned that if it were offered again, Churchill would accept the Order of the Garter.[1] Churchill did not make the decision quickly or easily. In the words of Sir Norman Brook, Secretary of the Cabinet from 1947 to 1962, Churchill

> would have preferred to keep unchanged the name by which he had always been known and to remain plain 'Mr Churchill'. Though he had always been avid for medals, he was not interested in titles. This was why he was reluctant for so long to accept the offer of the Garter. He would have liked, characteristically, to have it both ways, to accept the Garter but retain the 'Mr'. During the long period when he was struggling with this dilemma, he once said to me: 'I don't see why I should not have the Garter but continue to be known as Mr Churchill. After all, my father was known as Lord Randolph Churchill, but he was not a Lord. That was only a courtesy title. Why should not I continue to be called Mr Churchill as a discourtesy title?'[2]

At a dinner at Windsor Castle on 24 April 1953 the Queen offered, Churchill accepted, and he was duly invested as a Knight Companion of the Most Noble Order of the Garter. He was now entitled to add KG to his name and was ever after referred to as Sir Winston. The installation ceremony was held on 14 June 1954, at St George's Chapel at Windsor Castle.

The rules of the Order require that the insignia of the Order be returned to the sovereign upon the death of a knight. Churchill's insignia were returned to Queen Elizabeth by Randolph Churchill in a private ceremony at Windsor Castle on 5 April 1965. Later, his badge of the Order was re-loaned for exhibit at Chartwell by special permission of Her Majesty the Queen. The collar of the Order displayed at Chartwell is not Sir Winston's but another collar kindly loaned by the Central Chancery of the Orders of Knighthood.

ORDER OF LIBERATION, FRANCE, AWARDED 6 NOVEMBER 1958

In November 1958, Churchill was in Paris at the invitation of President Charles de Gaulle to receive the Order of Liberation (Ordre de la Libération), sometimes referred to as the Cross of the Liberation. It was de Gaulle's plan to express his appreciation to Great Britain and Churchill as soon as he returned to office in 1958. He made good his intention by announcing the award of the Order of Liberation on 18 June 1958, as one of his first acts upon assuming power that month.

The Order of Liberation was founded on 16 November 1940 by de Gaulle to recognize distinguished or exceptional services by French citizens

---

[1] Martin Gilbert, *Winston S. Churchill*, vol. 8, *Never Despair, 1945–1965*, pp. 822–3.
[2] Memoirs of Lord Normanbrook, quoted in Sir John Wheeler-Bennett, ed., *Action This Day* (New York: St Martin's Press, 1969), p. 45.

or foreigners who aided in the liberation of France in the Second World War. It was awarded to veterans of the Resistance, to members of the Free French Forces and to various distinguished and high-ranking foreigners. The order was given in only one class, the members of which were called Companions of the Liberation. One thousand and fifty-three awards were made before the award was discontinued by decree in January 1946. It is likely that Churchill was the last recipient of the order.

The award ceremony took place on 6 November 1958, in the garden of the Hôtel Matignon in Paris, de Gaulle's headquarters. Present were Madame de Gaulle and Lady Churchill, officials of the French government and a number of British diplomats. Following the review of a military honour guard and playing of the national anthems, the General pinned the cross of the Order on Churchill's chest. In his remarks at the ceremony, de Gaulle stated that the award was a reminder that France knew what it owed Churchill and that de Gaulle admired him more than ever. He ended, characteristically, with 'Long live Churchill, long live Britain, long live France!'

The citation for the award of the Order of Liberation to Churchill stated, in part, 'Trusted in France when it was most difficult, lending her the moral and material aid of Britain, her ally. Thus contributed directly to the liberation and the victory. Will remain in history illustrious of the highest.'

MOST REFULGENT ORDER OF THE STAR OF NEPAL, FIRST CLASS, NEPAL, 29 JUNE 1961

The Most Refulgent Order of the Star of Nepal (Nepal Tārā) was created by King Tribhuban Bir Bikram Shah Deva in 1918 to reward meritorious service to the Kingdom or to the cause of international peace. It may be awarded to foreigners for the latter reason. It is the sixth-ranking of Nepalese orders and the highest order which may be granted to foreigners. It is awarded in five classes, of which Churchill received the first or highest class (supra deepta Mānyavara Nepal Tārā). The order was bestowed upon Churchill by the Nepalese ambassador in London on 29 June 1961.

The badge of the Order is circular, with a white enamel field at the centre surrounded by a thin band of gold, a wider band of red enamel and a thin band of gold on the edge. The badge is worn suspended from an elaborate collar of gold gilt. The collar consists of twenty crosses and a like number of six-pointed stars connected by gold chain links. The badge may also be worn suspended from a sash riband, with a band of dark red on the left fading into pink and then into a white centre band, which fades into yellow and finally orange on the right side. The star of the Order is one of the most unusual and most beautiful of all breast stars. It consists of a sixteen-pointed star, between the rays of which are red enamel rays symbolic of flame. The central medallion consists of a miniature badge of the Order in gold and enamel placed upon a multi-coloured enamelled scene of the Himalaya mountains. The entire medallion is surrounded by a band of gold.

GRAND SASH OF THE HIGH ORDER OF SAYYID MOHAMMED BIN ALI AL-SANUSI, LIBYA, AWARDED 14 APRIL 1962

The last of the foreign orders Churchill received was conferred upon him by King Idris I of Libya on 14 April 1962. The award was made during a visit to Libya as part of Churchill's seventh and final Mediterranean cruise on Aristotle Onassis' yacht. Churchill was then eighty-seven years old, in declining health and not much inclined to public ceremony. The brevet for the Order which was forwarded to Churchill via the British Embassy at Tripoli and the Foreign Office in London stated in part: 'In the Name of God Almighty Merciful. From Idris I, King of the United Kingdom of Libya, under the kind protection of Almighty God, To His Excellency the Right Honourable Sir Winston Churchill. In recognition of your high and noble qualities, and in appreciation of the bonds of friendship, we have conferred on you the Grand Sash of the High Order of Sayyid Mohammed bin Ali al-Sanusi. . . . Written at the Royal Palace of Dar al-Salam in Tobruk . . .'

The Grand Sash of the High Order of Sayyid Mohammed bin Ali al Sanusi was created in 1951 by King Idris I to recognize exceptional merit in either the civil or military service. It is awarded in four classes, of which the Grand Sash is the highest. The order is now considered obsolete, because Libya created new orders following the revolution which ended the monarchy in 1969.

HONORARY CITIZENSHIP, UNITED STATES, 9 APRIL 1963

On 9 April 1963, Sir Winston S. Churchill became the second foreigner up to that point to be made an honorary citizen of the United States of America, the first being the Marquis de Lafayette. However, Churchill was the first to be made an honorary citizen because of a US Congressional resolution. Randolph and his son Winston travelled to the ceremony, held in the White House Rose Garden. Averell Harriman, Dean Acheson, three sons of Franklin Roosevelt and the 92-year-old Bernard Baruch were also in attendance. Both President Kennedy's and Winston Churchill's remarks, which were read by Randolph to those in attendance, are reproduced in this volume.

Index

CSC = Clementine Spencer-Churchill
RSC = Randolph S. Churchill
WSC = Winston S. Churchill

Abboud, El Ferik Ibrahim, 2286–7, 2286 n.4
Abd al-Ilāh (Abdullah), 2231, 2231 n.2
Abdel Rahman Ali Taha, Faisal, 961, 961 n.4
d'Abernon, Lord (Edgar Vincent), 1550, 1550 n.3
Abdullah I bin al-Hussein (King of Jordan), 1007, 1007 n.1
d'Avigdor-Goldsmid, Henry Joseph, 2362–3, 2362 n.2
Acheson, Alice Stanley, 1572, 1572 n.3
Acheson, Dean Gooderham
  biographical information, 5 n.2
  defence: Atlantic Command proposals, 212–13, 221–2; Atomic Security discussions, 175; European Defence Community, 162, 189, 803; German rearmament, 42, 50, 318–20; US disarmament proposals, 5
  Far East and South-East Asia: British trade with China, 165–6, 166–8; defence issues, 162; exclusion of UK from Pacific Tripartite Treaty, 650–1; Korea, 85–6, 183–4, 318; US–UK policy towards China, 184–5, 272–3, 354–5
  Middle East: Anglo-Iranian Oil Company, 93, 182–3, 608, 627 n.1, 658–9; Middle East Command, 163, 181; Persian nationalisation law, 603; US–UK policy towards Egypt, 182, 803
  NATO: command structure, 143; reform proposals, 171–2, 190; Secretary-General candidates, 300–1, 320–1, 322–4
  Russia, 161–3
  WSC visits US (1953), 802, 807, 809–10, 811
Ackroyd, Cuthbert Lowell, 2018–19, 2018 n.3
Acland, Richard Thomas Dyke, 473, 473 n.2
Adams, Philip, 1458–9, 1459 n.1
Adeane, Michael Edward, 813, 813 n.1, 1973, 2078, 2081, 2192

Adenauer, Konrad
  biographical information, 64 n.2
  Adenauer visits England (1959), 2273
  Anglo-German relations, 1790–1, 1805–6, 1809, 1844, 1961, 1973
  Four Power Conference proposals, 1141, 1186, 1193, 1344–5
  meets with Eisenhower, 936, 945
  Nine Power Conference, 1790–1
  Paris discussions, 64–5
  publication of letters from von Ribbentropp, 1723–4
  war criminals release and sentencing proposals, 139, 502–3, 629–30
  and WSC: New Year's greetings exchanged with, 151, 157; WSC accepts Charlemagne Prize from City of Aachen, 1880; WSC praises Adenauer, 1456, 2112, 2232; WSC praises French/German reconciliation, 725, 1003; WSC's eighty-fifth birthday, 2275–6, 2277; WSC's opinion of Adenauer, 945, 2115
  see also European Defence Community (EDC); Foreign Ministers Washington conference (1953); Germany; NATO (North Atlantic Treaty Organisation)
Africa: *see* Egypt; Kenya; South Africa; Sudan
Agar, Barbara Lutyens, 2036, 2036 n.3
Agar, Herbert Sebastian, 2036, 2036 n.3
agriculture: *see* food
Airey, Richard, 1589, 1589 n.3
air force: *see* Royal Air Force (RAF)
Air Ministry, 136–8, 235–6, 1468
Aitken, William Maxwell: *see* Beaverbrook, Lord ('Max')
Akers, Wallace, 939–42, 942 n.2
Akihito, Emperor of Japan, 1131, 1131 n.3
Alanbrooke, Lord (Alan Francis Brooke)
  biographical information, 12 n.3
  England (April 1953 WSC speech), 965
  farewell dinner for Eisenhower (1952), 440
  The Hinge of Fate, 1026–7, 1028–9
  memoir, 2157, 2157 n.1, 2159, 2159 n.1

2414　INDEX

Alanbrooke, Lord (Alan Francis Brooke) *(continued)*
　Ministry of Defence organisation and functions, 12–13
　NATO infrastructure accounting for WSC, 13
Albert II, Prince of Monaco, 2209, 2209 n.2, 2235, 2235 n.2
Albert, Prince (Francis Albert Augustus Charles Emmanuel), 299, 299 n.3
Aldrich, Winthrop Williams
　biographical information, 798 n.1
　Egypt, 886–7, 927–8, 994
　Three Power (Bermuda) Conference (1953), 1042, 1081–2, 1114–15, 1119–20
　WSC invites Eisenhower to England (1953), 1181, 1182, 1187
　WSC meets with (1953), 798, 927, 927–8
　WSC meets with Gromyko, 950–1
Alexander, Sir Harold Rupert Leofric George
　biographical information, 135 n.4
　Colville's opinion of, 363
　domestic affairs: Food Stocks Index, 396; protected accommodation for Government staffs, 338; Service officers' pensions, 1306–8; tax-free educational allowances for Armed Forces officers, 603–4
　Europe: Alexander dines with Massigli and Juin, 423–4; European Defence Community, 1731; European Defence Community alternatives, 1742–3; European Movement Economic Conference, 135; farewell dinner for Eisenhower (1952), 440; French military system assessment (1953), 1025–6, 1038–9; Italy, 1383; reinforcements for SHAPE in the first six months of war, 1538–9; structure of defence command, 864–5
　Germany: authorisation to make atomic weapons (proposed), 431, 431 n.1; joint military planning with German authorities, 857–8; NATO membership (proposed), 1742–3; rearmament, 326
　Kenya, 649, 915
　Middle East: Anglo-Jordan Joint Defence Board, 1507–9; British military Headquarters relocated to Smyrna (proposed), 1314; British troop quarters in, 343–4; move of British Middle East Headquarters to Cyprus (proposed), 744, 1809; redeployment of British troops in, 1211–12, 1211 n.3, 1312, 1314–15; Russian threat against, 378–9
　Royal Navy: fuel oil reserves, 324, 376–7, 377 n.1, 399; Naval Cadet training, 1302–3; Royal Naval Base at Simonstown, 335, 1761, 1773–4

Russia: East/West trade, 1398–400; location and strength of Soviet forces (1954), 1427, 1429–30, 1469, 1471–2, 1485
South-East Asia: Burmese Government Defence Agreement, 1204–5; Five Power military planning conference (1953), 1015–16; Indo-China war, 984–5, 988, 1076
WSC praises, 662, 719
see also defence; Egypt; Korea
Alexander, Lady Margaret Diana Bingham, 1806, 1806 n.1
Alexander, Ulick, 1217, 1217 n.2
Algeria, 2114, 2114 n.2, 2170, 2196, 2205, 2216, 2250, 2295, 2335 n.3
Allan, Rupert, 921–2, 921 n.2
Allen, Carleton Kemp, 835–6, 835 n.2
Allen, George Rolland Gordon ('Peter'), 497, 497 n.3
Allen, William Denis, 1317, 1317 n.1, 1328
Amery, (Harold) Julian, 131, 385, 385 n.3, 392, 465, 1117
Amery, John, 461, 461 n.3
Amery, Leopold Charles Maurice Stennett ('Leo')
　biographical information, 134 n.1
　Eastern European Conference, 134–5, 152–3
　Harrow School (November 1952 WSC speech), 719
　Harrow School (November 1955 WSC speech), 2060
　peerage suggested for, 461, 465
　United Europe, 135–6
Amory, Derick Heathcoat, 2238, 2238 n.1
Amr Pasha (Abdelfattah Amr), 413–14, 413 n.1
Anderson, George Whelan, Jr, 1549–52, 1549 n.4
Anderson, Sir John (Lord Waverly), 814–15, 814 n.1, 939–42
Anders, Władysław, 1987, 1987 n.3
André, Gérard, 423, 423 n.2
Andrew, Prince (Andrew Albert Christian Edward), 2316, 2316 n.2
Anglo-American relations
　admission of British officers to US National War College, 226
　British requests for monetary and/or material aid from the US, 119
　Cherwell's opinion of, 496
　China, 634, 634 n.1, 1100–1, 1667–8
　Dulles and Stassen visit London, 823–4, 837–8
　Eisenhower discusses importance of Anglo-American unity regarding Soviets, 2097–8, 2103–4
　Eisenhower's opinion of Eden, 2109

INDEX 2415

Eisenhower urges WSC to offer self-government to all colonies, 1703–6, 1703 n.1, 1725
Finnish tanker SS *Wiima*, 962, 962 n.3, 964, 970–1, 973, 975–6, 979–81
Green invites WSC to Westminster College Convocation, 2043–4
Holland meets with Eisenhower and Nixon, 1067
Indo-China war, 1575
joint commitment to thwart Communist expansion in Asia, 1968–71, 1975, 1975–6
Pilgrims' Dinner societies, 669, 669 n.1
Three Power (Bermuda) Conference (1953), 1361
Trieste frontier dispute, 1287
Truman reiterates importance of unity to WSC, 603
US repudiation of secret wartime agreements, 852–3, 854–5, 863–4
and WSC: WSC describes irrevocable nature of, 422; WSC meets with Eisenhower (1953), 797; WSC's eighty-first birthday commemorative medallion, 2061–2, 2062–3, 2063; WSC stresses importance of unity, 667–8, 669–71, 930–1, 1800–1, 2101–2, 2175; WSC warns Mountbatten against anti-American attitude, 157, 157 n.1
WSC speeches: Address to the United States Congress (January 1952), 212, 213–20, 242, 289–91; America and Britain (April 1954), 1534–5; Anglo-American friendship (June 1954), 1599–601; upon arrival at Washington National Airport (June 1954), 1624; A Visit to the United States and Canada (July 1954), 1673–83; White House visit (1959), 2248–9
see also US–UK Washington discussions (1952); US–UK Washington discussions (1954)
Anglo-Iranian Oil Company: *see* Persia
Annan, Noël Gilroy, 2265, 2265 n.3, 2269
Anne, Princess Royal (Anne Elizabeth Alice Louise), 1914, 1914 n.1
Anstruther-Gray, William John St Clair, 702, 702 n.1
'Ardent', 659, 659 n.1, 726–7, 727 n.1
Argentina, 651, 1761–2
Armitage, Robert Perceval, 1762–3, 1762 n.3
Armstrong, Robert Temple, 2003, 2003 n.1
army: *see* British Army
Ashley-Cooper, Anthony (Lord Shaftesbury), 780, 780 n.1
Asquith, Emma Alice Margaret Tennant ('Margot'), 516–17, 516 n.2

Asquith, Helen (Lady Violet Bonham Carter)
biographical information, 1810 n.1
at Chartwell, 2033, 2122
Mrs Knight's BBC broadcast, 1909–10, 1921
Royal Commission on Voting, 1863
WSC's death, 2375–7
WSC's declining health (1964), 2357–8, 2362
WSC thanks for 'glow-worm' compliment, 1810, 1810 n.2
WSC thanks for letter, 2233
Asquith, Herbert Henry, 261, 261 n.3, 516, 1519
Asquith, Raymond Herbert, 516, 516 n.3
Assheton, Ralph, 1718, 1718 n.1
Astor, Gavin, 1644, 1644 n.1
Astor, Irene Violet Freesia Janet Augusta Haig, 1644, 1644 n.2
Astor, John Jacob, V, 515–16, 515 n.1, 537, 538
Astor, Lady (Nancy Witcher Langhorne), 2336, 2336 n.1
Athlone, Lord (Alexander Augustus Frederick William Alfred George), 918, 918 n.3
Atlantic Charter, 1634, 1634 n.1
atom bomb and atomic energy
Anglo-American information exchange, 160, 223–4, 798, 945, 1299, 1492–3, 1576–7, 1594, 1616, 1658–9, 1675, 1739, 1867, 1867 n.1, 2104, 2109–10
atom bomb: Anglo-American White Paper on, 1334, 1358, 1364; atomic weapons security, 174–6, 196, 358; Attlee suggests HofC control of atom bomb, 1269; British atom bomb tests, 266, 284–5; British evacuation plans, 2083, 2083 n.3; British hydrogen bomb production, 1689, 1927, 1938, 1938 n.1, 2001, 2006, 2174; British production capability, 106, 196; as defence against war, 424; Eisenhower promotes deterrence policies, 1938; Eisenhower's thoughts on potential use of, 903, 1633; Eniwetok tests, 805; Experimental Mobile Column nuclear strike demonstration, 1592, 1592 n.1; hydrogen bomb tests (1954), 1500, 1503, 1503–4, 1506–7, 1510–11, 1511–12, 1514, 1515, 1519, 1521; NATO report on Soviet and NATO strengths, 434–5; New Mexican desert tests, 808, 813, 813–15, 814–15; personnel security procedures, 554; potential effects of, 479–80, 482, 519–20, 1470–1, 1520, 1673–4, 1927, 1930; Russian production capability, 1520, 1521; *The Times* article hydrogen bomb tests (1954), 1500; US airbase in East Anglia, 98–100, 284
atomic energy: Atomic Energy Commission discussions, 186; Atomic Energy

atom bomb and atomic energy *(continued)*
    atomic energy *(continued)*
        Corporation, 1392–3; Atomic Energy Tests in Australia (Oral Answers), 282–3; British programme (1952), 770–2; Eisenhower's 'Atoms for Peace' speech, 1357, 1357 n.1, 1358, 1365, 1374, 1374 n.2, 1376, 1487–8, 1529–30; international Atomic Energy Administration (proposed), 1334, 1374, 1374 n.2, 1376; Ministerial organisation of British programme, 268, 329, 332, 347, 358, 363, 390–1, 939–42
    disarmament: arms control talks (1955), 1865, 1866–7, 1928–9; Soviet proposal for nuclear weapons ban, 1920; US proposals, 5–6
    McMahon Act, 173–4, 175–6, 186–7, 284–5, 798, 1510, 1519, 1523–7, 1527, 1867, 2192
    Quebec Agreement of 1943, 173, 186, 1510–11, 1522–7, 1537, 1577, 1768, 1867
    and WSC: WSC discusses potential use of with Eisenhower, 1470–1, 1487–8; WSC promotes deterrence policies, 94–5, 219–20, 1850–5, 1877–8, 1929–35, 1938, 2002, 2110; WSC and Truman discuss justification for use of on Japan, 805, 806–7
    WSC speeches: Atom Bomb Test, Australia (October 1952), 682–5; Debate on the Address (November 1953), 1276–7; The Hydrogen Bomb (March 1954), 1504–6; The Hydrogen Bomb (April 1954), 1517–30, 1526, 1527; Debate on the Address (November 1954), 1842–3
    see also Cold War
Attila, 1353, 1353 n.3
Attlee, Clement Richard
    biographical information, 19 n.1
    defence: Adoption of a New Army Rifle (February 1954 WSC speech), 1416; American airbase in East Anglia, 99; Atlantic Command proposals, 213; Defence White Paper (March 1952), 316; Longley-Cook's Naval Intelligence paper, 144–5; National Service periods, 868–9, 1297
    domestic affairs: Chequers Trust arrangements, 1875; Coronation, 693–4, 694 n.1; General Election (1955), 1995–6, 2006–7; Stone of Scone, 267–8
    economics: post-war industrial production rates, 2003, 2006–7; sterling balances and UK indebtedness, 26; UK economic position (1952), 708

    foreign affairs: ANZUS and ANZAM, 775–6; China, UN admission (proposed), 1686–7; Egypt, 1000, 1269; Europe, 385–7, 392, 394, 440; Germany, 1003, 1244–5, 1693, 1819; Guatemala, 1688; Russia, 1689, 1730, 1733–4, 1795
    and WSC: Mr Clement Attlee (November 1953 WSC speech), 1305–6; WSC congratulates on Order of Merit, 19; WSC criticises Attlee, 1241; WSC's death, 2372–3, 2372 n.1; WSC sends *Birth of Britain* to, 2104; WSC thanks for eightieth birthday wishes, 1826
    see also atom bomb and atomic energy; Labour Party
Auchinleck, Sir Claude John Eyre ('The Auk'), 1027, 1027 n.2
Aung San, 2017, 2017 n.1
Aurand, Evan Peter, 2257, 2257 n.1
Australia
    ANZUS and ANZAM, 769, 775–7, 799
    atom bomb: Atom Bomb Test, Australia (October 1952 WSC speech), 682–5; Atom Bomb Test, Press Correspondents (Oral Answers), 392; Atomic Energy Tests in Australia (Oral Answers), 282–3; British atom bomb tests, 266, 284
    British COS Defence Policy and Global Strategy report, 624
    exclusion of UK from Pacific Tripartite Treaty, 650–1
    Governor-General of Australia appointment for Queen Mother (proposed), 410
    Indo-China war, 1532–3, 1570–1, 1700–1
    Korea: armistice talks, 86; British Deputy Chief of Staff (proposed), 506, 518, 548; US proposals for total embargo and severing of diplomatic relations with China and North Korea, 633
    Middle East, 314–15
    postponement of Slim's appointment as Governor-General to, 855, 855
    Royal Visit: costs of, 110–11, 111; postponement of, 269
    South-East Asia, 1015–16
Austria, 746–7, 1499, 1544–5, 1545, 1545 n.1
Avon, Earl of: *see* Eden, (Robert) Anthony

Bailey, John Adrian, 1648, 1648 n.2
Baker, Peter G., 2293, 2293 n.1
Baldwin, Robert Maurice, 720, 720 n.1
Baldwin, Stanley, 261, 261 n.4, 507, 856
Balfour, Arthur James, 261, 261 n.2, 1752
Ball, Lebbeus, I, 1534, 1534 n.2
Balogh, Thomas, 2382, 2382 n.3
Bao Dai (Nguyen Vinh Thuy), 1340, 1340 n.1
Barber, Anthony Perrinott Lysberg, 19–20, 19 n.3

Index

Baring, Evelyn, 1437–8, 1437 n.1
Baring, George Rowland Stanley, 1247, 1247 n.3
Barlow-Wheeler, William Hubert ('Hugh'), 2051, 2051 n.1, 2229
Barnes, Thomas James, 1642, 1642 n.1
Baruch, Bernard Mannes
  biographical information, 227 n.3
  British honour for (proposed), 2069–70, 2115–16, 2187
  foreign affairs: Europe, 797, 1767–8; Israeli-Egyptian relations (1956), 2102–3; Three Power (Bermuda) Conference (1953), 1309, 1311; US policy towards Korea (1953), 800; WSC discusses Soviet actions with, 2089; WSC proposes meeting with Malenkov (1954), 1767
  illness, 2153
  WSC's friendship with, 266–7, 553, 2089
  WSC's political career, 1768, 1987, 2009
  WSC visits US, 227, 796–7, 1610, 2244–5, 2245, 2301
Baruch, Bernard M., Jr, 797, 797 n.1, 2069–70
Bathurst, Charles (Lord Bledisloe), 1385, 1385 n.1, 1387, 1394–5
Battle, Lucius Durham, 331, 331 n.1
Batt, William Loren, 127–8, 127 n.2
Baxter, Arthur Beverley, 1943, 1943 n.2
Beaconsfield, Lord (Benjamin Disraeli), 919, 919 n.4
Beamish, Tufton Victor Hamilton, 387, 387 n.2, 1117
Beards, Paul Francis Richmond, 239, 239 n.2
Beauchamp, Antony
  biographical information, 118 n.2
  marriage to Sarah Churchill, 416–17, 499, 541, 1255, 2166
  Stereo Realist camera for WSC, 118, 118 n.4
  television broadcasts of WSC (proposed), 533–4
Beauchamp, Sarah: *see* Churchill, Sarah Millicent Hermione Spencer (WSC's daughter)
Beaudoin, Joseph Louis Fernand Rene, 1637, 1637 n.5
Beaumont, Timothy Wentworth, 2313, 2313 n.2
Beaverbrook, Lord ('Max')
  biographical information, 584 n.1
  Big Four (Geneva) Summit (1955), 1993
  Bracken complains about anti-WSC Press coverage, 1768
  British trade deal with Canada (1957), 2191
  Chamberlain's resignation as PM, 2320–1, 2322
  Chartwell renovations, 907–8
  at Chequers, 1180

  Churchilliana in Beaverbrook Art Gallery, 2326
  death of, 2358, 2358 n.1
  Duke of Windsor, 1107–8, 1189, 1608–9
  General Election (1955), 1993, 2009
  German Army, 1220
  likelihood of domestic strikes in 1954, 1380
  opinion of Eden, 808
  opinion of Salisbury, 1180
  sends eighty-ninth birthday greetings to CSC, 2352–3
  Truman's opinion of, 2117–18
  and WSC: *Daily Mirror* campaign against, 1405; friendship with, 907, 2049, 2054, 2060–1, 2073, 2085, 2195, 2264, 2278, 2282, 2297, 2308, 2319, 2342, 2358; in Jamaica with, 808; La Capponcina visits, 627, 627 n.2, 1220, 1221, 2042–3, 2046, 2046–7, 2054, 2185, 2217, 2218, 2221, 2221, 2223, 2227, 2255; Master Member of 1940 Club honour for, 2178; Press coverage of WSC's Monte Carlo visits, 2318; US exhibit of WSC's paintings, 2195; WSC asks about French Canadian/British Canadian populations, 2311; WSC comments on political cartoons, 1170, 1180, 2299; WSC comments on recent events (1953), 908, 908 n.1, 908 n.2, 908 n.3; WSC declines US invitation, 2193–4; WSC discusses politics with, 2185, 2227; WSC meets with at No. 10 Downing Street, 584–5; WSC plans to step down as PM (1955), 1874–5; WSC praises Beaverbrook's memoirs, 2292, 2292 n.2; WSC's eightieth birthday, 1858; WSC's health, 1189, 2212, 2212, 2213, 2216, 2335–6, 2341, 2349, 2350, 2354–5, 2355; WSC's spirits after stepping down as PM (1956), 2085
Beddington-Behrens, Edward, 134, 134 n.2
Bedell Smith, Walter ('Beetle')
  biographical information, 174 n.1
  completion of Volume 6 of *The Second World War*, 943, 944, 1141, 1141–2, 1142 n.1, 1167, 1167 n.2, 1171, 1172, 1178, 1198, 1313
  Finnish tanker SS *Wiima*, 973
  Indo-China war, 1574, 1603–4, 1694–5, 1700–1
  Korea, 1040–1, 1048–9
  Middle East: Arab-Israeli peace prospects, 898; British defence negotiations with Egypt (1954), 1627; Saudi claims on Trucial Sheikdoms, 884–5; US aid to Persia, 884; US–UK defence negotiations with Egypt (proposed),

Bedell Smith, Walter ('Beetle') *(continued)*
  Middle East *(continued)*
    886–7, 892–4, 896–7, 897–8, 902, 903–4, 904
  resigns from Washington post, 1738
  Washington meeting (1954), 1628, 1629
  Windsor Papers, 1159
  WSC visits US (1953), 802
Bedri, Ali, 961, 961 n.5
Belgium, 1159
Bellenger, Frederick John, 579, 579 n.1, 1438–9, 1678
Bell, Ronald McMillan, 1117, 1117 n.4
Benelux, 162–3, 189, 581
Ben-Gurion, David, 2259, 2259 n.1, 2259 n.2, 2260, 2304, 2305, 2311, 2311 n.1, 2312, 2315
Benn, Anthony Neil Wedgwood, 2353, 2353 n.1, 2354
Bennett, Richard Bedford, 1638, 1638 n.2
Beria, Lavrentiy Pavlovich
  biographical information, 911 n.1
  execution of, 1161, 1161 n.3, 1176, 1183, 1225
  purges in Georgia, 969, 970
  Tito's opinion of, 911
  WSC offers to meet with Molotov in Moscow (proposed), 990–1
Bermuda Conference: *see* Three Power (Bermuda) Conference (1953)
Bermuda parliamentary system, 1349
Bernal, John Desmond, 344, 344 n.3
Berry, James Gomer (Baron Kemsley), 2129, 2129 n.2, 2156
Berry, John Seymour (Lord Camrose), 1985, 1985 n.1
Berry, Mary Agnes Corns (Lady Camrose), 1609, 1609 n.2
Berry, William Ewert: *see* Camrose, Lord (William Ewart Berry)
Berry, William Michael, 1985, 1985 n.3
Beswick, Frank, 684–5, 684 n.1, 756, 758
Bevan, Aneurin ('Nye')
  biographical information, 102 n.1
  Attlee and Bevan visit Moscow (1954), 1730, 1733–4
  BBC debates between Junior Members of government, 589, 594
  defence: European Defence Community, 1693–4, 1740–1; The Hydrogen Bomb (April 1954 WSC speech), 1523; rearmament programme, 102–3, 739; UK defence production programme, 576, 577
  Eisenhower's opinion of, 1159
  HofC: budget debates (1953), 957; Foreign Affairs debates, 302, 1359; interruptions to WSC's speeches, 968; Motion of Censure (December 1952 WSC speech), 753, 759, 762; A Visit to the United States and Canada (July 1954 WSC speech), 1678–9
  Labour Party: nationalisation of rented land (proposed), 1050–2; political friction between Attlee and Bevan, 588; WSC mocks Labour criticism of Conservative housing policies, 663
  Marshall Plan, 2239
  Morrison criticises, 1586
  RSC sends WSC pamphlet on Bevan and Cousins, 2188
  WSC's opinion of, 109, 753, 1997, 2002–3
Bevin, Ernest
  biographical information, 29 n.1
  WSC praises, 29, 94, 286, 667, 1003, 1997, 2266
  WSC's opinion of, 109, 963
Bidault, Georges-Augustin
  biographical information, 1083 n.2
  Europe: French support for EDC, 1162–4, 1166, 1168, 1329, 1335–7, 1345–6, 1361–2, 1448; Germany, 1154–5, 1162–3
  Five Power (Geneva) Conference proposals, 1342, 1433–4, 1448
  Four Power Conference Proposals (1953), 1162–4, 1166, 1166–7, 1168, 1185–6, 1342–5
  Indo-China war, 1339–42, 1553, 1603–4, 1603 n.2
  Russia, 1162, 1182, 1185–6, 1547, 1547–8, 1548
  Suez Canal, 1338–9
  Three Power (Bermuda) Conference (1953): European Defence Community, 1335–7, 1349; planning, 1083, 1279, 1281, 1282, 1288, 1289; Plenary Meeting #1, 1317–18; postponement, 1122; Soviet Government policies, 1319–21
Biesterfeld, Bernhard Graf von, 701, 701 n.1
Big Four (Geneva) Summit (1955)
  Eden reports on to WSC, 2026, 2026–7, 2027–8, 2057
  Eisenhower mentions that he will miss WSC's presence at, 2024, 2025–6
  planning, 1993
  RSC discusses with WSC, 2057–8
Billmeir, Jack A., 2046, 2046 n.2, 2051, 2186
Birch, Evelyn Nigel Chetwode, 481–2, 481 n.3, 1731
Birdwood, Christopher, 2121, 2121 n.1
Birdwood, William Riddell, 2121, 2121 n.2
Birkenhead, Lord (Frederick Winston Furneaux Smith), 1845, 1845 n.1, 1862–3

Index

Birley, Oswald Hornby Joseph, 2321, 2321 n.2
Birtchnell, Cyril Augustine, 365–7, 365 n.3
Bishop, Frederick Arthur, 2140 n.2, 2141–2, 2191
Bishop, (William Henry) Alexander, 2370, 2370 n.3
Bismarck, Otto von, 251, 251 n.2
Blackett, Patrick Maynard Stuart, 504–5, 504 n.3
Blandford, Lord (John George Vanderbilt Henry Spencer-Churchill, later 11th Duke of Marlborough), 191, 191 n.3, 412–13, 413 n.3
Blankenhorn, Herbert, 1164, 1164 n.1
Bledisloe, Lord (Charles Bathurst), 1385, 1385 n.1, 1387, 1394–5
BOAC (British Overseas Airways Corporation), 1481–2
Boer War, 1864
Bogra, Sahibzada Mohammad Ali
  biographical information, 1062 n.1
  Commonwealth PMs meeting (1953): Middle East discussion, 1086–7; Soviet foreign policy and Western Europe discussion, 1062–3
  Commonwealth PMs meeting (1955), 1885, 1899
  Pakistan adopts republican form of Constitution, 1891–2, 1902
  Three Powers meeting (proposed), 1062–3
Bohlen, Charles Eustis ('Chip'), 1960, 1960 n.1
Bonaparte, Charles-Louis Napoléon (Napoléon III), 919, 919 n.1
Bonaparte, Napoléon, 444, 939, 965, 965 n.5, 1452–3
Bonarjee, Stephen Wilson, 1808, 1808 n.1
Bonham-Carter, Christopher Douglas, 2258, 2258 n.1
Bonham Carter, Mark Raymond, 2233, 2233 n.3
Boothby, Robert John Graham
  biographical information, 45 n.2
  The Economic Position (July 1952 WSC speech), 582
  Europe: Council of Europe, 386, 392, 403, 1117; United Europe, 45, 131, 133; Western Union (European Army), 83–4
  Fife-Clark's opinion of, 595
  Russia, 949–50, 950 n.1
  thanks WSC for Chartwell visit, 779
Borden, Robert Laird, 1638, 1638 n.1
Borneo Confrontation, 2380, 2380 n.1
Boswell, James, 495, 495 n.3
Botha, Louis, 62, 62 n.2
Bouchier, Cecil Arthur
  biographical information, 300 n.1
  Korea: military situation in, 300, 300 n.2;

replacement of Bouchier as UK COS representative, 547–8, 566; return of POWs to Communist China, 397–8, 397 n.3, 400, 400 n.1
Bowen, Edward Ernest, 112, 112 n.2
Bowie, Robert Richardson, 1328, 1328 n.1
Bowles, Francis George, 1440, 1440 n.1
Bowra, Cecil Maurice, 2148, 2148 n.1
Boyce, Harold Leslie, 31, 31 n.1, 32
Boyd-Carpenter, John Archibald, 546, 546 n.2
Boyle, Dermot Alexander, 2122, 2122 n.3
Bracken, Brendan
  biographical information, 410 n.4
  Bracken Reading Room at Churchill College, 2267
  Daily Mirror campaign against WSC, 1405
  death of, 2218, 2218–19, 2218 n.4, 2219, 2220
  Eden's opinion of Soames, 410
  likelihood of domestic strikes in 1954, 1380
  Macmillan meets with, 2217
  memorial proposals, 2225, 2225–6, 2226 n.1
  pessimism regarding Conservative Government, 445
  and WSC: anti-WSC Press coverage, 1768; Crisp seeks to sell private letters from WSC, 1177–8; Hodge's review of Volume 6 of *The Second World War*, 1561; sends well wishes to, 2207–8; thanks WSC for copy of *Birth of Britain*, 2110–11; WSC plans to step down as PM (1955), 1874–5; WSC's eightieth birthday, 1858; WSC's health, 2212, 2213, 2214, 2216; WSC's spirits after stepping down as PM (1956), 2085
Braddock, Elizabeth Margaret Bamber ('Bessie'), 1526, 1526 n.2, 1527
Bradley, Omar Nelson
  biographical information, 174 n.3
  China, 243–4, 287
  defence: Atlantic Command proposals, 213; atomic weapons, 174; European Defence Community, 190; Middle East Command reorganisation proposals, 181–2
  Korea: armistice talks, 183, 729; military situation in, 300; napalm bombing in, 605, 627–8, 628–9; US–UK policy towards, 243–4
  WSC visits US (1953), 802
Brailly, Odette Marie Céline, 1587, 1587 n.2
Brain, Walter Russell, 2142–3, 2142 n.1
Brentano di Tremezzo, Heinrich von, 135, 135 n.2
Bridges, Sir Edward
  biographical information, 8 n.2
  CSC lunches with, 191

2420　INDEX

Bridges, Sir Edward *(continued)*
  defence: British Armed Forces Service Estimates revisions, 155; manpower, 8, 239, 261; Ministerial organisation of British atomic energy programme, 268, 329, 332, 347, 939–42; Ministry of Defence contracting procedures, 303 n.1, 330, 330 n.3
  domestic affairs: Committees, Sub-Committees and Working Parties list, 37; communications, 373–4, 378, 499, 510–11; Crichel Down, 1624, 1624 n.1, 1646; Financial Committees interim report, 114
Bridges, George Tom Molesworth, 2189, 2189 n.3
Bridges, Katharine Dianthe Farrer, 1980, 1980 n.1
Bridges, Thomas, 768, 768 n.2
Bridgland, Aynsley Vernon, 1811, 1811 n.1
Brind, Eric James Patrick, 37, 37 n.2, 624, 701
British Armed Forces
  amnesty for deserters (proposed), 567–8, 782–4
  call-up of reservists, 100–1
  Greek memorial to UK soldiers, 248, 345–6
  Home Guard re-establishment, 100, 874
  Korea Military Situation (May 1952 WSC speech), 468–70
  Loss of Rifles file, 46
  manpower allocations, 95–6, 100–1, 149–50, 476–7
  military service deferments for jockeys, 1049–50, 1054
  Ministry of Defence staff, structure and responsibilities, 7
  National Service periods, 23, 96, 868–73, 1462
  NCOs and substantive rank, 303–4
  new armed forces security procedure, 554, 561
  service estimates (1952–1953), 142
  see also British Army; Royal Air Force (RAF); Royal Navy
British Army
  3rd Infantry Division, 306
  6th Armoured Division, 91, 149, 306
  Adoption of a New Army Rifle (February 1954 WSC speech), 1410–19, 1431
  American vehicles for, 127–8
  4th Hussars Light Brigade Dinner (1954), 1589, 1590, 1597
  manpower: allocations, 149–50; call-up of reservists, 100–1; Class Z reserve, 477, 477 n.1; estimates, 126–8, 579–80; NCOs and substantive rank, 303–4, 327, 346

  Royal Welsh Fusiliers, 1047, 1118, 1233, 1290, 1352, 1352 n.1, 1352 n.2
British Broadcasting Corporation (BBC)
  BBC debates between Junior Members of government, 537, 589, 594–6
  broadcasting White Paper, 426–7
  coverage of Egyptian closure of Suez Canal, 2128
  Forum discussion on cliques, 45
  interview with Archbishop Makarios, 1807, 1808
  Ministerial broadcasts for Government actions, 538
  Mrs Knight's BBC broadcast, 1873–4, 1876–7, 1879–80, 1909–10, 1910–11, 1921, 1921–2
  'Opposite Numbers' debate proposal, 537, 594–6, 601
  WSC complains to Cadogan about inequitable BBC political reporting, 1785–6, 1787–8
British Commonwealth
  Accession Proclamation, 255–6
  Canada broadcast (June 1954 WSC speech), 1640
  Commonwealth Advisory Committee on Defence Science, 332–3
  Commonwealth Economic Conference: Eden departs for, 647; meeting planning, 571–2; proposed, 513–14, 558–9, 560, 561; WSC praises results of, 708
  Commonwealth Finance Ministers meeting, 211
  Commonwealth PMs meeting (1953): agenda, 1060; Commonwealth PMs and Cabinet meeting (1952), 745–53; concluding speeches, 1097; Europe, 1095, 1096–7; Far East and South-East Asia discussion, 1069–78; Korea, 1069–71, 1072–6, 1084, 1094; Middle East discussion, 1084–91, 1094; planning, 464–5; Press relations and communiqués, 1061, 1069, 1078, 1091, 1093–4, 1095, 1096–7; South-East Asia, 1076–7; Soviet foreign policy and Western Europe discussion, 1061–9; Three Powers meeting (proposed), 1093–4; WSC looks forward to, 709–10; WSC's opening statement, 1060
  Commonwealth PMs meeting (1955): British development and production of hydrogen bombs, 1892; communiqué, 1901–3; conclusion of proceedings, 1900–1; Far East discussions, 1888–91, 1893–6, 1896–900; Pakistan adopts republican form of Constitution, 1891–2, 1902; welcome and preliminary remarks, 1884–6

INDEX

Coronation Naval Review, 635
costs of Royal Visit to Australia and New Zealand, 110–11
Dominion PMs receive copies of COS Defence Policy and Global Strategy report, 550–1
economics, 438–9, 2309–10
Egypt, 991–2
European affiliation with (proposals), 135–6
Indian communities in British Colonial territories, 1911–12
Indo-China, 355
Ismay appointed Secretary-General of NATO, 334
Korea, 86, 336, 1393–4
UK defence plans, 314
US disarmament proposals, 5–6
WSC praises abiding power of, 214, 422
WSC's goal for unity and consolidation of, 82–3, 148, 220
British Guiana, 1229–30, 1233–4, 1237, 1246–7
British Overseas Airways Corporation (BOAC), 1481–2
Brockway, Archibald Fenner, 699, 699 n.1, 713
Bromley-Davenport, Walter Henry, 392, 392 n.1
Brook, Norman Craven
biographical information, 7 n.1
Cabinet: access by former Ministers to Cabinet and other official papers, 298, 298 n.2, 1446–7, 1447; Brook keeps WSC informed of activities of, 2010; food budget discussions, 430; liaison for Departmental communications with Cabinet, 116; Scampton airfield extension (proposed), 1468, 1469
communications: Eden's war-time minutes to WSC, 2244; use of 'Top Secret' rather than 'Most Secret', 370, 377–8, 378 n.1
Conservative Government: Committees, Sub-Committees and Working Parties list, 37, 46, 55–6, 56 n.1; Defence Committee formation, 60; General Election (1955), 2010; Government Information Services Committee, 84–5, 85 n.1; Ministry of Defence, 7–8, 303 n.1, 330, 330 n.3; Service Department memoranda circulation protocols, 70; Service Ministers' meetings on non-operational matters, 116, 116–17; WSC considers stepping down as PM (1953), 1188; WSC plans to step down as PM (1954), 1599; WSC steps down as PM (1955), 1977
defence: atom bomb and atomic energy, 329, 332, 599, 808; COS Defence Policy and Global Strategy report, 494,

498; Economic Debate on defence programme, 550; inter-Allied machinery for concerted Western defence, 132; move of British Middle East Headquarters to Cyprus (proposed), 744; production programme, 533, 541–2; reduction of Military Mission staff in Washington, 261
domestic affairs: Coronation, 687–8, 687 n.1; Diplomatic Immunities Bill, 772; Eden steps down as PM, 2151; RAF aircraft production programme, 70, 79; Television Bill, 1368–9, 1373; UK economic position (1952), 507; 'Valiant' aircraft prototype crash, 211
foreign affairs: Egypt, 1427, 2134–5; Harriman meets with WSC in Paris (1951), 141–2; NATO, 232, 232 n.1, 920–1; Sudan, 713–14; Three Power (Bermuda) Conference (1953), 1053, 1081–2, 1318; US–UK Washington discussions, 39, 40–1
opinion of Soames, 507
and WSC: WSC asks about 'Highball' and 'Upkeep', 2013–14; WSC completes *The Second World War*, 647, 1171, 1172–3, 1176; WSC's health (1960), 2280
Brooke, Alan Francis: *see* Alanbrooke, Lord (Alan Francis Brooke)
Brooke, Basil Stanlake, 1238, 1238 n.1
Brosio, Manlio Giovanni, 352, 352 n.4, 2379
Brown, Douglas Clifton (Lord Ruffside), 1571, 1571 n.1, 1571 n.2, 1572
Browne, Anthony Arthur Duncan Montague
biographical information, 1057 n.1
Adenauer visits England (1959), 2273
British trade deal with Canada (1957), 2191
Chamberlain's resignation as PM, 2320–1, 2322
Churchill College: foundation stone ceremony, 2311; inauguration ceremony, 2264, 2264–5; portraits of Fellows, 2320, 2321; trustees luncheon, 2307
Eden's war-time minutes to WSC, 2242, 2243–4, 2244
Eden writes memoirs, 2302, 2303
employment after WSC's death, 2387
feeds false story to paparazzi about WSC's plans, 2202
foreign affairs update for WSC, 2140
head of WSC's private office, 2077, 2078
A History of the English-Speaking Peoples, 2088, 2150
Israel, 2088, 2088 n.1, 2304, 2305
letter from Munuswamy, 2253, 2253 n.2
Montgomery's remarks on European Economic Community, 2332–3

Browne, Anthony Arthur Duncan Montague *(continued)*
  move of British Middle East Headquarters to Cyprus (proposed), 1984
  notes for WSC's visit with U Nu, 2016–18, 2020
  The Other Club, 2279, 2279–80, 2322
  Suez Canal closure and Gulf of Aqaba blockade (1956), 2141–2
  and WSC: Coronation, 1057–8; Golden Wedding anniversary (WSC and CSC), 2221–2, 2222; HofC Life Member status (proposed), 2353; HofC Resolution of Thanks (1964), 2356, 2361; at La Capponcina, 2311; at La Pausa/Cap Martin, 2077, 2078, 2257; Mediterranean cruises with Onassis, 2318, 2323, 2324–5, 2326, 2347–8, 2347 n.1; meets with de Gaulle, 2294–5; message to Primrose League, 2214, 2214–15, 2214 n.2; in Monte Carlo, 2318; ninetieth birthday, 2362–3, 2363; Press coverage of WSC's friendship with Onassis, 2293; residence for in South of France, 2139; technological college Trustees luncheon, 2215; visits West Germany (1956), 2090; visits US (1959), 2245, 2246, 2249–51; WSC visits US (1961), 2301; WSC writes messages of support for Macmillan and Jenkin (1964), 2362
  see also health (WSC)
Browne, Evelyn Noel Arnold-Wallinger ('Nonie'), 2093, 2093 n.1, 2322, 2349
Brownjohn, Nevil Charles Dowell, 741, 741 n.1, 1024, 1024–5, 1101, 1553
Brownlow, Lord (Peregrine Francis Adelbert Cust), 808, 808 n.1, 809
Bruce, David Kirkpatrick Este, 2343, 2343 n.2
Brudenell, James Thomas (Lord Cardigan), 1589, 1589 n.6
Brundrett, Frederick, 939–42, 940 n.4
Bryant, Arthur Wynne Morgan, 2157, 2157 n.2
Buchan, Alastair Francis, 1330, 1330 n.1, 1349
Buchan-Hepburn, Patrick George Thomas
  biographical information, 48 n.1
  Cabinet discussion items, 66
  defence White Paper, 252
  meat ration and supply projections (1951–1952), 48–9
  radio broadcast, 588
  regulars retention and call-up of reservists for Korean War (proposed), 252
  WSC postpones stepping down as PM (1954), 1779
  WSC steps down as PM (1955), 1979–80
  WSC visits with, 2300, 2302
  WSC wishes to avoid political broadcasts and electioneering atmosphere, 66
Buchan, Priscilla Jean Fortescue (Lady Tweedsmuir), 386, 386 n.5
Bulganin, Nikolai Alexandrovich, 990–1, 990 n.3
Bullock, Alan Louis Charles, 2088, 2088 n.2
Bulwer-Lytton, Edward Antony James, 985, 985 n.2
Bulwer-Lytton, Victor Alexander George Robert, 985, 985 n.1
Bundock, George, 926, 926 n.2
Burgoyne, John, 1688, 1688 n.1
Burke, Edmund, 205, 205 n.1
Burma, 1077, 1570–1
Burmese Government Defence Agreement, 1204–5
Burns, Eedson Louis Millard ('Tommy'), 2101, 2101 n.1
Butler, Lady (Elizabeth Southerden Thompson), 1589, 1589 n.8
Butler, Richard Austen
  biographical information, 1 n.1
  Colville's opinion of, 1170
  Commonwealth Finance Ministers meeting, 195, 211
  Commonwealth PMs meeting (1953), 1060, 1095
  Coronation, 398, 922
  domestic affairs: Cabinet Committees, 46; calculation of electricity charges, 44; civil aviation, 280–1, 280 n.1; electoral reform proposals, 833–4; housing subsidy, 2; provision of married quarters for US Armed Forces in the UK, 737–8; Savoy Hotel case, 1420–1; tax-free educational allowances for Armed Forces officers, 604; transfer of funds to Duke of Windsor, 732, 733
  Egypt: American nun murdered in, 232; Canal Zone negotiations, 376, 992; Sterling Releases Agreement, 790–1, 839, 1203–4, 1210, 1378–9, 1620, 1655; US arms for, 989–90
  foreign affairs: British trade with Japan, 904; Germany, 43, 425–6; Israeli oil supply financing request, 401–2, 424, 424 n.5; Persia, 996, 1197; Press coverage of UK leadership in, 1791; Russia, 1183–4, 1186–7, 1188, 1645, 1645 n.2, 1647, 1662–5, 1707–8; Three Powers meeting (proposed), 1036; UN admission for China (proposed), 1672, 1682; Washington meeting (1954), 1633–4, 1634 n.1
  and WSC: at Chartwell, 1169–70; with WSC at La Pausa/Cap Martin, 2074,

2076; WSC praises Butler, 491, 642, 1557–8, 1583, 1793; WSC's eighty-fifth birthday (Oral Answers), 2277; WSC sends condolences after death of Butler's father, 727; WSC suffers stroke (1953), 1130, 1139, 1147; WSC thanks after stepping down as PM, 1990; WSC wishes to meet with Menzies, 381
see also Conservative Government; defence; domestic affairs; economics
Butler, Sydney Courtauld, 1328, 1328 n.4, 1596
Byrnes, James Francis, 1768, 1768 n.1
Byroade, Henry Alfred, 927–8, 927 n.1, 1627–8

'C' (John Alexander Sinclair), 538–9, 538 n.2
Cabinet
 atom bomb: British production of hydrogen bombs, 1655–6, 1659–61, 1892; Defence White Paper (1955), 1892; history of Anglo-American cooperation in atomic energy development, 1576–7; hydrogen bomb tests (1954), 1501, 1506–7; information exchange among UK, US and Canada, 1658–9; Ministerial organisation of British programme, 390–1, 939–42, 1299; New Mexican desert tests, 808, 814–15; US consultation with UK prior to use of, 1492–3; WSC promotes deterrence policies in 'Notes on Tube Alloys, 1954', 1850–5
 China: British trading practices with, 866–8, 1046; 'Oracle' and Formosa, 1882–3; Quemoy and Matsus Islands, 1905–6, 1937; UN admission (proposed), 1205–6, 1668, 1671–3
 communications: access by former Ministers to Cabinet and other official papers, 296–7, 298, 298 n.2; Cabinet Papers Access (Oral Answers), 1438–40; circulation of telegrams to Ministers, 1384, 1384 n.1; Ministerial co-ordination with Cabinet on public announcement of executive decisions, 253–4; papers for Neville Chamberlain biography, 1943; political broadcast planning (December 1951), 129; timing of announcements for curbing expenditures, 118–19
 Coronation: amnesty for British Armed Forces deserters (proposed), 783–4; Committee, 398; Coronation Oath, 850–1, 850 n.1; date, 265–6, 269, 281, 398; Latin version of Royal Title, 834–5; Naval Review, 635, 644, 658, 922; preparations, 682; televising of (proposed), 682, 687–8, 687 n.1, 688–9, 690–1, 693–4; uniforms, 488; Westminster Abbey seating allocations, 691–2, 743
 economics: association between Western Europe and Commonwealth countries (proposed), 438–9; British requests for monetary and/or material aid from the US, 119; Civil Service retirement age, 253–4; Local Loans Fund procedures, 671–2; timing of education cuts announcements, 114–15, 116; UK economic position (1951), 1–4, 16–17; UK economic position (1952), 459–60; US tariffs on British goods, 400; Washington discussions (1953), 863
 Elizabeth II: costs of Royal Visit to Australia and New Zealand, 110–11; Family name for children and descendants, 274, 274 n.2, 281, 377; Her Majesty visits the Temple of Tooth in Ceylon, 1438; Parliamentary Address to Her Majesty on the occasion of her departure for Australia and New Zealand, 1299–300; Western Australia visit, 1479–81
 English politics: Cabinet appointments, 735, 736, 1188; Cabinet Ministers speaking in by-elections, 680; electoral reform proposals, 833–4; House of Lords reform proposals, 834; Welsh affairs debate planning, 73; WSC seeks Welsh Under-Secretary assistant for Fyfe, 10
 Europe: British role in future of European movement, 348–9; European Defence Community, 1166, 1759–60, 1770–3, 1776–7; Nine Power Conference (1954), 1791; Western Union (European Army), 119–20, 140; WSC views and policy on United Europe, 81–3
 foreign affairs: Anglo-American relations, 1594–5, 1633–4; Anglo-Norwegian fisheries case, 568–9, 784; British Guiana political situation (1953), 1229–30, 1229 n.2, 1233–4, 1246–7; British trade with Japan, 904; Burmese Government Defence Agreement, 1204–5; Central Africa federation proposals debate planning, 73; Ceylon riots, 1195; Commonwealth PMs and Cabinet meeting (1952), 745–53; Five Power Conference on Trieste (proposed), 1300; Germany, 138–9, 425–6, 858–9, 1759–60; Indian communities in British Colonial territories, 1911–12; Malaya, 30, 840, 859–60; Pakistan, 1381–2, 1891–2; Press coverage of UK leadership in, 1791; South Africa, 52–4, 73–4; Three Power (Bermuda) Conference planning, 1284, 1288; Three

Cabinet *(continued)*
  foreign affairs *(continued)*
    Power meeting (proposed), 1035–6, 1047; UK fisheries dispute with Iceland, 784–5
    Foreign Ministers conference in Washington (July 1953): Adenauer's policies, 1152–3; Anglo-American differences in policy towards Soviet Union, 1149–50; European uncertainties, 1153–4; purpose, 1148–9; Soviet policies towards Germany, 1150–1; Western policies towards Germany, 1151–2, 1154–5; Western policy towards Soviet Union, 1149
    Four Power (Berlin) Conference (1954): conclusion of, 1444; Eden reports on to Cabinet, 1447–9; expansion of trade with Soviet bloc (proposed), 1395; Five Power (Geneva) Conference proposals (1954), 1401–2, 1403; planning, 1389–90; US military aid to Pakistan (proposed), 1381–2
  George VI, King, 254–5, 255–6
  Indo-China war: Geneva negotiations (1954), 1702, 1702–3; UK refuses to send transport aircraft to the French, 988; US aid to France, 789; Western coalition of aid for France (proposed), 1530, 1531–3, 1554–5, 1560
  Kenya: British troop reinforcements despatched to (1953), 915; clemency for General China (proposed), 1437–8, 1445, 1459; detention of Mau Mau supporters, 1445–6; Griffiths' Court Martial, 1350–1; Mau Mau society, 649–50, 1035, 1869–70, 1869 n.1
  Korea: armistice talks, 505–6, 929, 1029–30, 1046; bombing of power stations on Yalu River, 512, 514–15; British Deputy Chief of Staff (proposed), 505–6, 518–19, 551, 555; British policy towards, 294; British troops' availability for deployment to, 1126; napalm bombing in, 628–9, 628 n.1; Parliamentary statements on Korea Mission, 512, 518–19; Political Conference, 1205–6; US proposals for total embargo and severing of diplomatic relations with China and North Korea, 616
  Middle East: Anglo-Jordan Joint Defence Board, 1507–9; Anglo-Jordan Treaty of 1948, 1300–2, 1303–5; Arab League meeting, 1390; Command reorganisation proposals, 30–1; Cyprus and Anglo-Greek relations, 1762–3, 1762 n.1; Joint Services Headquarters staffing and costs, 1816–18; move of British Middle East Headquarters to Cyprus (proposed), 1620, 1809; Persia, 601, 650, 656, 1196–7, 1197; redeployment of British troops in, 1312; Saudi claims on Trucial Sheikdoms, 787–8, 790, 1595–6
  Ministerial appointments, 1 November 1951–5 April 1955, 2389–90
  Parliament: Cabinet meeting times, 36; final dismantling of emergency powers, 1563–4; Food and Drugs Bill, 1661; Foreign Affairs debate, 1661; HofC Standing Committee meetings, 1401; legislation on health, welfare and safety in nonindustrial employment, 1562–3; Members' Expenses, 1607; Parliamentary Delegation visit to Canada, 567; Parliamentary Private Secretary procedures, 301–2; provisional legislative program (1954–1955), 1561–4; Railways Reorganisation White Paper, 1661–2; Road Traffic Bill, 1561–2; University franchise and representation in the HofC, 10–11, 15–16
  Sudan: Anglo-Egyptian agreement regarding, 826–8, 829–31, 841–3, 952; Egyptian propaganda regarding Sudanese elections, 1046–7; postponement of opening of Sudanese Parliament, 1458–9; Sudanese PM's anti-British speech (1954), 1444; Sudan's right to self-government, 10
  Windsor Papers, 1188, 1189, 1199
  WSC rests at Chartwell (1953), 1139
  WSC steps down as PM (1955), 1977, 1980–1
  see also Conservative Government; defence; domestic affairs; Egypt; food; Russia

Caccia, Harold Anthony, 1623, 1623 n.1, 2249–51
Cadogan, Alexander George Montagu, 1785–6, 1785 n.2, 1787–8, 1808
Caffery, Jefferson, 849–50, 849 n.1, 862, 897–8, 903–4, 904
Cairns, Diana Katherine Soames ('Dido'), 1855, 1855 n.1, 1860, 2087
Callaghan, (Leonard) James, 706, 706 n.2, 1418, 1419, 1526
Campbell, Alan Hugh, 43, 43 n.2, 43 n.4
Campney, Ralph Osborne, 1637, 1637 n.4
Camrose, Lady (Mary Agnes Corns Berry), 1609, 1609 n.2
Camrose, Lord (John Seymour Berry), 1985, 1985 n.1, 1988
Camrose, Lord (William Ewart Berry)
  biographical information, 250 n.2
  completion of Volume 6 of *The Second World War*, 250, 1171, 1176

INDEX 2425

Crisp seeks to sell private letters from WSC, 1175–6
death of, 1609
Lord Camrose Memorial (May 1956 WSC speech), 2111
WSC recalls fond memories of, 1988
Canada
British trade with, 381, 389, 2191, 2380
defence: atom bomb information exchange among UK, US and Canada, 1299, 1658–9; British COS Defence Policy and Global Strategy report, 622, 623; Canadian F86 fighters for NATO, 314; Canadian Navy programme, 201; reinforcements for SHAPE in the first six months of war, 1539; UK declines to provide immediate assistance to French at Dien Bien Phu, 1570–1
East/West trade with Russia, 1400
Eighty-fifth Anniversary of Confederation (1952), 206–7
Korea, 86, 506, 518, 548
Parliamentary Delegation visit, 567
WSC visits (1954), 1636–7, 1638–40, 1682
see also UK–Canada joint Cabinet meeting (1952)
Canal Zone
Anglo-Egyptian Agreement, 1715, 1716, 1718, 1791–2, 1812
British Government's intention to 'safeguard the international highway', 10, 28
British military intervention in (proposed), 36, 36 n.2, 47, 47 n.1, 56–7, 111–12, 233, 233 n.2, 237–8, 273–4, 273 n.1, 839
British troops in (1953), 799, 861, 916, 974, 978
British troops' readiness in case of attacks (1953), 812, 827–8, 830–1, 849, 856–7, 860–1, 861 n.1, 991–2, 997, 998
British troops' readiness for evacuation of, 1198
British withdrawal from, 325–6, 1427, 1782
Canal Zone Base, 1485, 1486, 1486–7, 1487, 1502–3
English and French withdrawal from (1956), 2149, 2149 n.1
Four Power proposal for Middle East defence, 107, 217–18, 218, 275–6, 325–6, 327–9, 724
garrison costs and stores, 381–2, 394, 394 n.1, 891–2
international importance of Suez Canal, 1337–8
maritime Powers seek guarantees of freedom of navigation through Suez Canal, 1407–8, 1620–1, 1654

Montgomery criticises Eden's handling of Suez affair, 2149, 2149 n.3
situation report, 1017–20, 1018
Suez Canal closure and Gulf of Aqaba blockade (1956), 2120, 2120 n.2, 2121–2, 2122–3, 2123, 2124, 2128, 2130, 2130 n.1, 2131, 2134–5, 2136, 2141–2, 2143, 2144, 2144–5, 2144 n.2, 2145–6, 2146–7, 2171, 2383
UK defence negotiations, 269–70, 274–6, 277–9, 369–70, 375–6, 379–80, 382, 384, 387–8, 413, 600, 600 n.1, 695–7, 748, 770, 789–90, 790, 844–7, 847–8, 849–50, 852, 853, 853 n.1, 855, 860–1, 861 n.1, 1616, 1627, 1691
US–UK combined defence negotiations (proposed), 182, 220, 695–7, 799, 846–7, 847–8, 849–50, 852, 855, 860–3, 878, 879, 883, 885, 886–7, 889–90, 890, 891, 892–4, 894, 895, 896, 896–7, 897–8, 898, 899–901, 902, 903–4, 904–5, 908–9, 910–11, 911–12, 922, 927–8, 930–2, 932–3, 933, 946, 948–9, 963, 1002
US–UK defence negotiations (1953), 1020–1, 1021–2, 1021 n.1, 1084–91, 1087–8, 1102–4, 1106–7, 1108–10, 1116–17, 1118, 1140, 1158, 1158, 1201–4, 1203, 1209–11, 1210, 1210, 1213, 1249–52, 1300, 1308–9, 1314, 1337–9, 1348–9, 1355–7, 1366, 1377–8, 1379–80
US–UK defence negotiations (1954), 1405–7, 1420, 1422–3, 1430–1, 1436, 1475–9, 1490–2, 1502–3, 1617, 1617 n.1, 1619–23, 1626–8, 1653–5
Canterbury, Archbishop of (Geoffrey Francis Fisher), 283, 283 n.1, 682, 688–9
Cardigan, Lord (James Thomas Brudenell), 1589, 1589 n.6
Cariappa, Kodandera Madappa ('Kipper'), 1112, 1112 n.1
Carney, Robert Bostwick, 181–2, 181 n.1
Carr, Leonard Robert, 411, 411 n.2
Carron, William John, 2266, 2266 n.1
Carson, Robert Andrew Glendinning, 2047, 2047 n.1
Casey, Richard Gardiner, 65 n.1, 67–8, 1604, 1606
Cashmore, John, 409, 409 n.1
Cassel, Ernest Joseph, 2338, 2338 n.4
Cassels, Archibald James Halkett, 1075, 1075 n.1
Castle, Barbara, 291, 291 n.1, 472, 1100
Castries, Christian Marie Ferdinand de la Croix de, 1546, 1546 n.1
Cattell, Richard Barley Channing, 1036–7, 1036 n.3, 2171

Cavendish, Edward William Spencer (Duke of Devonshire), 2288, 2288 n.3
Cavendish, Elizabeth Vere ('Betty'), 588, 588 n.4
Cavendish, John Charles Compton (Baron Chesham), 1871, 1871 n.1
Cazalet, Victor Alexander, 1646–7, 1646 n.3
Cecil, David George Brownlow, 2148, 2148 n.2
Cecil, Edgar Algernon Robert ('Bob'), 1810–11, 1810 n.3, 2228
Cecil, Lady (Eleanor Lambton Gascoyne-Cecil), 2228, 2228 n.1
Ceylon
  Ceylon riots, 1195
  CSC visits (1956), 2082, 2086, 2092, 2093, 2104
  economic situation, 898–9
  Her Majesty visits the Temple of Tooth, 1438
  UK declines to provide immediate assistance to French at Dien Bien Phu, 1570–1
Cézanne, Paul, 2082, 2082 n.5
Chamberlain, (Arthur) Neville, 283, 283 n.2, 507, 1943, 2320–1, 2322
Chamberlain, Joseph, 507, 507 n.1, 508
Chamberlain, (Joseph) Austen, 507, 507 n.2
Chamoun, Camille Nimr, 2215, 2215 n.2
Chancellor of the Duchy of Lancaster: *see* Swinton, Lord (Philip Cunliffe-Lister); Woolton, Lord (Frederick James Marquis)
Chancellor of the Exchequer: *see* Butler, Richard Austen
Channon, Henry ('Chips')
  biographical information, 9 n.1
  WSC takes oath as PM (1951), 9
  WSC privately lauded in 1922 Committee meeting (1952), 387
  WSC publicly criticised in HofC, 387, 968
  WSC returns to HofC (1953), 1256
  Debate on the Address (1953), 1277–8
Channon, Henry Paul Guinness, 1256, 1256 n.1
Charles the Great (Charlemagne), 2113, 2113 n.2
Charles, Prince of Wales (Charles Philip Arthur George), 293, 293 n.1, 294
Charteris, Martin Michael Charles, 2206, 2206 n.1
Chartwell
  black swans at, 1580, 1587, 1598, 2223, 2356, 2357
  butterflies at, 1766
  CinemaScope installed at, 1913
  CSC at, 191
  CSC suggests invitation for Menzies, 425
  Eden visits, 2032, 2035, 2057

  film nights, 347, 410, 507, 2037, 2087
  fish pond and fish tanks, 507, 588, 1591, 1727
  Mary and Christopher Soames decline to live permanently at, 91–2
  Mary Soames at, 2034, 2037, 2126
  pigs at, 1727, 1737
  renovations at, 584–5, 907–8
  RSC at, 91–2, 588, 1727, 2037–8, 2122
  Trumans dine with WSC and CSC at, 2117–18, 2117 n.1
  WSC describes to CSC, 553, 588, 1591, 1727, 1737, 2086
  WSC invites Baruch to, 2089
  WSC rests at after stroke, 1139, 1147
Chartwell Literary Trust, 2241, 2242, 2243–4, 2254–5, 2303
Chequers, 191, 1875
Cherwell, Lord (Frederick Lindemann, 'the Prof')
  biographical information, 12 n.2
  at Chartwell, 588
  death and funeral of, 2173, 2178
  Food Stocks Index, 388–9, 396
  NATO report on Soviet and NATO economic and military strengths, 296
  RAF, 77, 77 n.1, 463–4, 466
  Three Power (Bermuda) Conference (1953), 1125, 1290, 1291, 1314
  US–UK Washington discussions, 39, 164, 170
  Volume 6 of *The Second World War*, 497
  Washington meeting (1954), 1646–7
  WSC invites to La Pausa, 2130, 2133, 2136
  WSC praises, 2267
  WSC's drinking habits, 207
  see also atom bomb and atomic energy; defence; domestic affairs; economics
Chesham, Baron (John Charles Compton Cavendish), 1871, 1871 n.1
Cheshire, Geoffrey Leonard, 2045–6, 2045 n.3
Chetwynd, George Roland, 758, 758 n.1
Chiang Kai-shek
  biographical information, 184
  British relations with, 801, 983–4, 1064
  Formosa, 1898, 1904, 1904 n.1
  Quemoy and Matsus Islands, 1905–6, 1906–9, 1916–19, 1919–20, 1922–3, 1962–3, 1969–70
  A Review of Foreign Affairs (July 1954 WSC speech), 1687–8
  US relations with, 983–4
  US–UK policy towards Far East and South-East Asia, 184–5, 243–4
Chichester, Edward Arthur Donald St George Hamilton (Lord Donegall), 410, 410 n.2
Chichester, Gladys Jean Combe (Lady Donegall), 410, 410 n.3

INDEX

Chick, Alfred Louis, 1028, 1028 n.2
Chief of the Air Staff: *see* Dickson, William; Slessor, John Cotesworth
Chief of the Imperial General Staff (CIGS): *see* Harding, Allan Francis John; Slim, William Joseph ("Bill")
Chiefs of Staff (British)
  China, 272–3
  European Defence Community alternatives, 1742–3
  Falkland Islands, 299
  food, 337
  Germany, 42, 50, 857–8, 1742–3
  Indo-China war, 355–7, 1553, 1554–5
  Italy, 1383
  Korea: British Deputy Chief of Staff (proposed), 505–6, 506, 518–19, 525–6, 529, 547–8, 548, 551, 552, 555; COS Committee meeting minutes on armistice talks, 85–8; napalm bombing in, 627–8; provision of Commonwealth occupation forces in, 336; WSC asks for COS opinion on military situation in, 68–9, 77–8, 80
  Middle East: Anglo-Jordan Joint Defence Board, 1507–9; Israeli role in defence of, 993–4; Joint Services Headquarters staffing and costs, 1816–18; move of British Middle East Headquarters to Cyprus (proposed), 744, 1809; redeployment of British troops in, 1211–12, 1211 n.3
  South-East Asia: ANZUS and ANZAM, 769; British policy towards Chinese aggression in, 354–5; Five Power military planning conference (1953), 1015–16; Malaya defence planning, 839–40
  see also defence; Defence Committee; Egypt
Chiefs of Staff (US)
  admission of British officers to US National War College, 225–6
  China: British policy towards Chinese aggression in South-East Asia, 354–5; US–UK policy towards, 272–3
  defence: British COS Defence Policy and Global Strategy report, 623, 624, 652–5; Naval Command agreements with US and France, 740–1; US disarmament proposals, 5; US–UK defence negotiations with Egypt (proposed), 886–7
Childs, Marquis W., 2383, 2383 n.1
China
  British bombing of Manchuria, 86
  British policy towards, 286–92
  British recognition of Communist China, 198, 244, 524, 983–4, 1066

British trade with, 165–8, 166–8, 866–8, 884, 898–9, 1046
Chinese Nationalist troops in Burma, 1077
Chinese production of steel and other metal ores (1953), 1848–9, 1856
Eisenhower assesses potential danger of, 1856
Eisenhower relieves Seventh Fleet of China defence responsibilities, 732–3, 836, 844
Finnish trade with, 964, 970–1
Formosa, 198, 1878–9, 1881–2, 1882, 1888–91, 1890–1, 1893–6, 1896–900
Formosa Resolution, 1903–5, 1904 n.1
Indo-China war, 1532, 1536
Korea: armistice talks, 241–2; continuing imprisonment of US airmen captured during Korean War, 1847–8, 1848 n.1; potential air threat to UN forces in, 87–8; truce negotiations, 1069–71; WSC asks McLean for COS opinion on military situation in, 68–9
'Oracle', 1881, 1881 n.1, 1882–3
Quemoy and Matsus Islands, 1803, 1803 n.1, 1905–6, 1906–9, 1916–19, 1919–20, 1921, 1922–3, 1962–3, 1969–70
Russia, 975, 1320, 1448
Tachen (Dachen) Islands, 1907, 1907 n.1
UN admission (proposed), 1066, 1069, 1074, 1100, 1205–6, 1452, 1648–9, 1649, 1667–8, 1671–3, 1681–2, 1685, 1686, 1688–9
US policy towards (1953), 945
US–UK policy towards, 40, 162–3, 185, 216, 272–3, 289
WSC's opinion of Communist China as adversary, 615–16
see also Chiang Kai-shek; Zhou Enlai
Cholmondeley, George Horatio Charles (Earl of Rocksavage), 2236, 2236 n.1
Cholmondeley, Sybil Rachel Betty Cecile Sassoon (Marchioness of Rocksavage), 2236, 2236 n.1
Christ, George Elgie, 70, 70 n.2
Christoforides, Marcia Anastasia ('Christofor', Lady Dunn), 2292, 2292 n.1, 2297, 2308, 2349
Chuikov, Vasily Ivanovich, 924, 924 n.1
Churchill, Charles Richard John Spencer, 972–3, 972 n.4
Churchill, Clementine Hozier (CSC; later Baroness Spencer-Churchill)
  biographical information, 13 n.2
  attends theatre performance with Montgomery, 1053
  bequeaths her eyes to Moorfields Westminster and Central Eye Hospital, 1938
  at Chartwell, 191, 594
  at Chequers, 191, 1959, 1959 n.3, 1964

2428 INDEX

Churchill, Clementine Hozier (CSC; later Baroness Spencer-Churchill) *(continued)*
Christmas greetings exchanged with the de Gaulles, 785, 789
daughter Diana, 1328, 2352
dines with Queen Elizabeth, 1964
eighty-ninth birthday greetings from Beaverbrook, 2352–3
friendship with Jock Colville, 13–14
health: broken left wrist, 2018, 2021; eyelid surgery, 2255, 2255 n.2, 2270; foot operation, 2191, 2193; medications, 2153; nervous tension and fatigue, 2194, 2350, 2351, 2354; neuritis, 2029, 2029 n.2, 2029 n.3, 2030, 2031, 2033, 2034, 2036, 2038, 2039, 2048, 2049, 2074, 2075, 2076, 2133; St Mary's Hospital stay, 2299
No. 10 Downing Street, 13–14, 585
politics: CSC advises against appointing Duncan as Secretary of State for War, 156; discusses with WSC, 1695–6; Eden steps down as PM, 2152; Eisenhower promotes association of free nations for salvation of liberty, 1442; Three Powers meeting (proposed), 1037–8, 1042; WSC and CSC host farewell dinner for Eisenhower (1952), 440–1, 460–1; WSC decides to not stand for re-election (1963), 2346, 2348; WSC postpones stepping down as PM (1954), 1756, 1807; WSC steps down as PM (1955), 1977, 1979–80, 1983, 1984, 1988–9
son Randolph, 1215, 1218
speech at Professional Nurses and Midwives Conference, 1803
suggests Chartwell invitation for Menzies, 425
travel: Barbados visit (1960), 2281–2; Bermuda trip planning (1953), 1121, 1125, 1141; Cap d'Ail holiday (1955), 2042–3, 2046; Ceylon trip (1956), 2082, 2086, 2092, 2093, 2104; Ireland visit, 2168, 2169; Italy trip (1952), 539, 540, 541, 544, 545, 553; Jamaica trip (1953), 797; Sicily trip (1955), 1983, 1984, 1986, 1989; Tangier visit, 2219; with WSC in Alpes Maritimes, 2185, 2186
and WSC: abdication of Edward VIII (Duke of Windsor), 1107–8; 'Churchill Houses', 1820, 1820 n.2; CSC suggests monetary legacy for Miss Hamblin, 816; Fiftieth Wedding anniversary (WSC and CSC), 2221–2, 2222; Fifty-Fifth Wedding anniversary (WSC and CSC), 2350; HofC Resolution of Thanks (1964), 2355, 2356, 2361; Nemon bust of WSC, 2283; Nobel Prize for Literature, 1247–8, 1253, 1353–4; poor relations with RSC, 677; portrait of WSC for Churchill College, 2321; sails for US on *Queen Mary* with WSC, 791; Soviet launch of Sputnik satellite, 2188; Sutherland portrait of, 1827 n.1, 1914–15, 2327, 2328; US exhibit of WSC's paintings, 2202–3; War Memorial inauguration, 678–9, 679 n.2; WSC apologises for rudeness to CSC, 1755–6; WSC hopes to see CSC (1962), 2335; WSC's death, 2367, 2367 n.1, 2370, 2374, 2387; WSC's eighty-fifth birthday cake, 2274–5; WSC sends birthday greetings to, 2096; WSC sends flowers for 48th anniversary, 2129; WSC's friendship with Beaverbrook, 2358; WSC's ninetieth birthday, 2363; WSC transfers money to CSC, 2154–5, 2166, 2168; WSC visits US (1958), 2204; WSC visits US (1959), 2247–8
see also correspondence (CSC and WSC); health (WSC)
Churchill College
chapel, 2313, 2313–14
Churchill College Ceremony (October 1959 WSC speech), 2266–8
Churchill College and University Grants Committee, 2210, 2210 n.1
Churchill College Visitorship, 2258, 2259, 2267, 2269
Crick resigns from, 2313, 2313–14
foundation stone ceremony, 2311, 2314, 2315, 2317
inauguration ceremony, 2264, 2264–5
inauguration press release, 2268–9
portraits of Fellows, 2320, 2321, 2327–8, 2328
trustees luncheon, 2307
WSC plans to honour Colville for efforts in creation of, 2297–8
Churchill, Diana: *see* Sandys, Diana Churchill
Churchill Family Trust, 34–5
Churchill, John (1st Duke of Marlborough), 1639, 1639 n.1
Churchill, Mary: *see* Soames, Lady (Mary Churchill)
Churchill, Pamela (Pamela Digby), 1196, 1196 n.2
Churchill, Randolph Frederick Edward Spencer (RSC)
biographical information, 29 n.2
at Chartwell, 91–2, 588, 1727, 2037–8, 2122
conversation notes from talk with Mrs Muriel Warde (1962), 2337–9
Eastern European Conference, 134
films of, 499

INDEX 2429

Foyle's literary luncheon speech, 1215, 1215 n.2, 1218
health, 2355
libel suit against *People* newspaper, 2136, 2136 n.3, 2137
libel suit against *Private Eye* newspaper, 2341, 2341 n.1
opinion of Eden as PM, 2091, 2091 n.2
Sarah Churchill corresponds with, 417
serves as Gold Staff Officer at Coronation, 832
Stour house, 2038, 2038 n.1, 2216
and WSC: birthday present for RSC, 2168, 2169; Churchill Family Trust arrangements, 154–5; Derby biography, 1386, 1387, 2282, 2282 n.1, 2285; Golden Wedding anniversary (WSC and CSC), 2221–2, 2222; Honorary United States Citizenship (April 1963, read by RSC on behalf of WSC), 2343–4, 2344, 2412; Lord Randolph biography, 932; Mediterranean cruise, 2347–8; opening of Churchill Hall at Riverside Conservative Club, 2027; Privilege Case, 1386, 1386 n.3; RSC cancels attendance at Conservative Annual Conference, 660, 674, 674–6; RSC congratulates WSC on formation of Government, 29; RSC expresses grief over poor relations with, 674–7, 778 n.1; RSC reflects on WSC's career and achievements, 2327; RSC reports on Tory Conference, 2189; RSC's Blenheim essay, 1385; RSC sends well wishes, 1218, 1221; RSC thanks WSC for Christmas present, 786, 786 n.2; RSC wishes WSC good luck in upcoming Washington discussions, 154; title for book of WSC's speeches, 778, 778 n.2, 779; WSC chooses RSC to write his official biography, 2285; WSC falls and fractures femur (1962), 2331–2; WSC's Address to US Congress, 220, 220 n.1; WSC steps down as PM (1955), 1980, 2035; WSC thanks for copies of RSC's articles, 1862; WSC thanks RSC for pamphlet on Bevan and Cousins, 2188; WSC voices concern for RSC's health, 674

Churchill, Lord Randolph Henry Spencer, 932, 932 n.1

Churchill, Sarah Millicent Hermione Spencer (WSC's daughter)
biographical information, 79 n.3
acting career, 231, 2234, 2234 n.1, 2235, 2272
Allan's Coronation articles for *Look* magazine, 921–2
attends WSC's speech to US Congress, 210
CSC's nervous tension and fatigue, 2194
death of Queen Mary, 921
describes Brooklyn plaque dedication to WSC, 416
friendship with Margaret Truman Daniel, 227
Los Angeles arrest for drunkenness, 2199, 2199 n.3
marriage to Antony Beauchamp, 416–17, 499, 921, 1255, 2166
sends birthday greetings to WSC, 79–80
sends holiday greetings to WSC, 645
sends well wishes to WSC, 1254–5, 1647
television series, 416, 416 n.2
with CSC in Italy, 499, 541, 544, 553, 589
with WSC in Alpes Maritimes, 2153, 2154, 2156, 2158
WSC suffers stroke (1953), 1160–1, 1161 n.1

Churchill, Winston Spencer (WSC)
death of, 2364
funeral, 2379–80, 2381, 2382, 2382–5, 2385–7, 2387
honours and awards: Charlemagne Prize, 1880, 2112–13; Churchill Room at Westminster College, 864, 2180; Croix de la Libération (November 1958), 2226, 2410–11; Grand Sash of the High Order of Sayyid Mohammed bin Ali al Sanusi, 2412; honorary US citizenship (1963), 2342–3, 2343–4, 2344, 2412; Master Member of 1940 Club, 2178; Most Refulgent Order of the Star of Nepal, 2411–12; Nobel Prize for literature, 1247–8, 1253, 1254, 2408–9; Order of the Garter, 972–3, 973 n.1, 2409–10; Queen Elizabeth II's Coronation Medal, 2408
personal life: bathing, 813; drinking habits, 207, 302, 1184, 1278, 1318, 2090, 2208, 2246, 2264, 2278, 2407, 2407 n.1; eightieth birthday, 1824, 1824 n.1, 1826–8, 1828, 1844, 1845–6, 1847, 1858, 1864, 1871–2, 1923–4; eighty-first birthday, 2061–2, 2062–3, 2063, 2069; eighty-second birthday, 2148; eighty-fifth birthday, 2273, 2274–5, 2275–6, 2277; ninetieth birthday, 2362–3, 2363; pride in American ancestry, 210, 2068–9, 2344; quarrel with Lord Moran, 51; smoking habits, 302, 2090
race horses, 493, 493 n.2, 1597, 1728, 2039, 2048, 2119–20, 2133, 2135, 2136, 2137, 2138, 2168, 2169
reading lists, 2281, 2325–6
'retirement' as an author, 2255, 2255 n.1
Rufus II (family dog), 2126

Churchill, Winston Spencer (WSC) *(continued)*
  signed photograph for Roquebrune post office, 2206
  Sutherland portrait of, 1827, 1827 n.1, 1914, 1914–15
  television and film rights to *My Early Life*, 2124, 2125, 2126
  Toby the budgerigar (pet parakeet), 1855, 1855 n.2, 1855 n.3, 1860, 2030, 2074, 2076, 2084, 2091, 2093, 2131, 2137, 2159, 2165, 2166, 2201, 2217, 2218, 2234
  travels, December 1951–1963, 2400–5
  tributes to, 2365, 2365–6, 2366, 2367, 2368, 2368–9, 2369, 2370, 2371, 2371–7, 2377–9, 2380–1, 2382 n.1, 2385–7, 2385 n.4
  see also Chartwell; correspondence (CSC and WSC); health (WSC); painting (WSC)
civil aviation, 280, 280–1, 281 n.1, 728–9, 1481–2
Clarke, Henry Ashley, 721–2, 721 n.1
Clark, Mark Wayne
  biographical information, 470 n.1
  Korea: Alexander visits battlefront, 470–2; armistice talks, 729; British Deputy Chief of Staff (proposed), 505–6, 525–6, 526, 529, 551, 552; British troops' availability for deployment to, 1125–6; Korea Truce Talks (June 1953 WSC speech), 1099
Clark, Thomas Fife, 508–9, 508 n.3, 537, 594–6, 601
Clausewitz, Carl von, 424, 424 n.2
Claxton, Brian Brooke, 197, 197 n.1
Clementis, Vladimír, 746, 746 n.1
Clutterbuck, Peter Alexander, 1701, 1701 n.2
coal industry
  coal imports, 2–3, 17–19, 27
  coal production, 141
  Conservative Party policies, 1242
Cochrane, Ralph Alexander, 540, 540 n.1
Cockcroft, John Douglas, 939–42, 941 n.1, 2265, 2267, 2268, 2320, 2321, 2327, 2328
Cockran, William Bourke, 1535, 1535 n.1
Cocks, Frederick Seymour, 473, 473 n.3
Coke, Edward, 2181, 2181 n.1
Coke, Thomas William Edward, 1531, 1531 n.1
Cold War
  American airbase in East Anglia, 98–100, 284
  Anglo-American unity, 667–8, 669–71, 930–1, 958, 2097–8, 2103–4
  British use of Austrian manpower in the event of war, 1499, 1544–5, 1545, 1545 n.1
  Conservative Party 'peace through strength' policy, 1456, 1529–30, 1586, 1600, 1819, 1841–2, 2002

COS Defence Policy and Global Strategy report, 494, 498, 542–3, 544, 550–1, 623, 624, 652–5
COS memorandums on likelihood of war with Soviet Union through 1955, 841, 1248–9
Eisenhower: emphasises importance of avoiding global war, 1904–5; promotes association of free nations for salvation of liberty, 1431–2, 1442, 1457, 1467, 1468, 1469–71; relieves Seventh Fleet of China defence responsibilities, 732–3
inter-Allied machinery for concerted Western defence, 132, 142–4
'Jujitsu', 228, 228 n.1
propaganda: Communist accusations of US germ warfare, 648, 648–9, 659, 678; Communist propaganda regarding South-East Asia, 198; Eisenhower complains about Soviet propaganda to WSC, 1431
risk of parachute attack on the UK, 882–3
Russia: alert procedures in case of imminent Russian attack on Western Europe, 445–6, 446 n.1; Ben-Gurion's opinion of Soviet goodwill gestures, 2259, 2259 n.2, 2260; British acquisition of MiG 15 aircraft, 881; COS memoranda on likelihood of war with Soviet Union through 1955, 816–22, 841, 1223–7, 1248–9; Eden promotes idea of 'peaceful co-existence' with Communists, 1682–3; Eisenhower's 'Atoms for Peace' speech, 938–9, 943, 944, 945, 945 n.1, 949, 949 n.3, 1357, 1357 n.1; germ warfare propaganda, 648, 678; Khrushchev criticises WSC, 2239; location and strength of Soviet forces (1954), 1408, 1426, 1441–2, 1464–6, 1465, 1466, 1469, 1471–2, 1485, 1490; Malik attends Chequers luncheon with WSC, 1373–6; Russian MiG shoots down British bomber in Hamburg–Berlin air corridor (1953), 908, 908 n.3, 910, 912–13; Soviet attitudes towards Europe, 1447–8; Soviet disarmament proposals, 6, 2262–3; Soviet launch of Sputnik satellite, 2188, 2188 n.3; Soviet proposal for nuclear weapons ban, 1920; US bomber attack on Soviet U-boat bases, 539–40, 540; Western Summit meeting (1960), 2286; WSC discusses likelihood of war, 67–8, 201, 434–5, 625, 722, 1276–7, 1852–5; WSC discusses Soviet actions with Baruch, 2089; WSC hopes for Anglo-American approach to Stalin, 611; WSC hopes for peace with, 2240;

WSC's concerns regarding after German surrender (1945), 1838–41
Three Powers meeting (proposed), 1032–3, 1033, 1033–4, 1035–6, 1037–8, 1042, 1043–4, 1047, 1052, 1053, 1062–4, 1065, 1066
UK defence production programme, 574–5, 869
and WSC: WSC discusses prevention of third world war, 204–5, 315–16; WSC downplays likelihood of third world war, 95, 148, 217; WSC promotes deterrence policies, 94–5, 219–20, 306, 1799, 1842–3, 2006, 2174–5; WSC seeks abatement of through negotiations, 28–9; WSC's forecast of Third World War opening phases (1953–1954), 793–6
WSC speeches: The Sinews of Peace (Iron Curtain speech, March 1946), 68, 214, 285–6, 805, 2043–4, 2233, 2239, 2336, 2378; The Path of Duty (November 1951), 33; Defence (March 1953), 869; The Government's Record (April 1953), 958; Foreign Affairs (November 1953), 1285–8; The Berlin Conference (February 1954), 1449–57; Defence (March 1955), 1926–35; Press Club Luncheon (June 1954), 1630–1
Colefax, Sibyl Halsey, 45, 45 n.4, 1646–7
Coleman, Cyril Frederick Charles, 1124, 1124 n.1
Cole, William Sterling, 1470–1, 1470 n.1, 1520, 1632–3, 1673–4, 1927
Collick, Percy Henry, 1455, 1455 n.3
Collins, Lawton, 225–6, 225 n.1
Colville, (Elizabeth) Harriet, 1054, 1054 n.3
Colville, Helen Cynthia Milnes, 191, 191 n.2
Colville, John Rupert ('Jock')
biographical information, 13 n.4
Bracken's death and memorial proposals, 2219, 2225, 2225–6, 2226 n.1
Chartwell film nights, 347, 410
at Chequers, 363, 443–4, 1180–1, 1183–5, 1186–7, 1188, 1189–90
Cherwell's funeral, 2178
Conservative Government: Conservative Party Conference (1953), 1235; public standing of (1952), 475; relations between WSC and Eden, 823, 1176; WSC orders reduction of British staff in Washington, 194; WSC plans to step down as PM (1954), 1546, 1643
domestic affairs: Churchill College, 2232; Civil Servant status for WSC's Private Secretaries, 55, 66–7; Coronation, 722, 1054–5, 1107–8; Craig's sentence, 730; Diplomatic Immunities Bill, 772; No. 10 Downing Street renovations, 585; The Other Club, 2279, 2279–80, 2288–9, 2294; penal servitude laws, 730–1; Queen's Plates for racing in Ireland, 1216–17, 1217, 1230–1; road haulage denationalisation, 384; Transport Bill, 443, 446; UK economic position (1952), 475, 495–6, 507; WSC asks about deliberate spreading of myxomatosis among wild rabbits, 1729, 1729 n.2; WSC muses on need for coalition government, 441; WSC plans to honour Colville for efforts in creation of Churchill College, 2297–8
foreign affairs: Adenauer's policies and proposals, 1165 n.1; ANZUS and ANZAM, 800; British use of Austrian manpower in the event of war, 1544–5, 1545, 1545 n.1; Cyprus and Anglo-Greek relations, 1512; employment of British and Soviet citizens in their respective Embassies in Moscow and London, 500, 529–30, 538–9; Indo-China war, 1549–52; Mansergh's appointment, 773–4; Persian oil negotiations, 611; US repudiation of secret wartime agreements, 863–4; WSC and Casey discuss likelihood of war with Russia, 67–8; WSC dines with Massigli and Juin, 423–4; WSC meets with Aldrich, 927; WSC meets with Eisenhower and Dulles (1953), 812; WSC meets with Gromyko, 950–1; WSC proposes meeting with Malenkov (1954), 1653, 1695–6, 1695 n.2; WSC speaks to US Congress, 208–9; WSC suggests Azores meeting with Eisenhower, 1235
opinions: of Dewey, 801; of Dulles, 802, 1348; of Eden, 384; of Eisenhower, 802; of Mountbatten, 156; of White House, 1625
personal life: appendicitis, 2033; Clarke offers Chancery job to, 721–2; friendship with CSC, 13–14; marriage to Margaret Egerton, 14, 347; Private Secretary to Princess Elizabeth, 14
Three Power (Bermuda) Conference (1953): arrivals, 1316; Communism in the East and West, 1326–7; Eisenhower voices anti-Russian views, 1317; Plenary Meeting #1, 1317–18; Press coverage, 1318, 1324; WSC meets privately with Eisenhower, 1317; WSC relaxes on the beach, 1317
US trip with WSC (1953): Eisenhower hosts dinner parties, 800–2, 802–3; New York

Colville, John Rupert ('Jock') *(continued)*
  US trip with WSC (1953) *(continued)*
    Press conference preparation, 796; *Queen Mary* voyage, 791, 791–2, 793; WSC dines with Eisenhower and Baruch, 796–7
  Washington meeting (1954): arrivals, 1625; dinner parties, 1628–9; return to England on RMS *Queen Elizabeth*, 1641, 1643–4, 1646–7, 1648–9; White House swimming pool, 1625; WSC interrupts talks to view thunderstorm, 1625–6
  and WSC: BRINCO stock shares, 2168; Colville notes depressed mood of, 441, 495, 496; Colville suggests Life Member of HofC status for, 2353; Colville thanks after WSC steps down as PM, 1991; Colville thanks for silver V-sign for watch-chain, 2024; D-Day Commemoration at Arromanches, 383–4; in Jamaica, 808, 809; in Morocco, 2232; Queen Elizabeth offers Dukedom to, 1982; speechwriting duties for WSC, 463; WSC asks about 'Cincleastlant', 'Cincaireastlant' and 'Comsubeastlant', 611; WSC complains about Eden, 823; WSC suffers stroke (1953), 1130, 1169–70, 1174; WSC considers stepping down as PM, 1189–90; WSC plans to step down as PM (1955), 1874–5; WSC steps down as PM (1955), 1978–80, 1991; WSC's advancing age, 463, 594, 721; WSC's ninetieth birthday, 2363; WSC's private reaction to Eisenhower's election as President, 721
Colville, Margaret Egerton ('Meg'), 14, 14 n.2, 363, 1054–5
Combe, Gladys Jean (Lady Donegall), 410, 410 n.3
Commonwealth: *see* British Commonwealth
communications
  broadcasting: BBC debates between Junior Members of government, 594; explanatory Ministerial broadcasts for Conservative Government actions, 515–16, 537, 538; White Paper, 426–7; WSC inquires about teleprompter for television screen tests, 1397, 1397 n.2; WSC suggests Ministerial Statement from Woolton, 66
  Cabinet: access by former Ministers to Cabinet and other official papers, 296–7, 298, 298 n.2; Cabinet Papers Access (Oral Answers), 1438–40; circulation of telegrams to Ministers, 1384, 1384 n.1; Ministerial co-ordination on public announcement of executive decisions, 253–4; papers for Neville Chamberlain biography, 1943; political broadcast planning (December 1951), 129; timing of announcements for curbing expenditures, 118–19
  dates format in official correspondence, 499, 510–11
  description of 'parka' for WSC, 239
  Eden's war-time minutes to WSC, 2244
  length of telegrams, 535–6, 942, 1190, 1190–1
  letters to WSC from the general public, 2172
  publication of war-time messages from WSC to FDR, 2210–11, 2211
  Service Department memoranda circulation protocols, 70
  use of 'Top Secret' rather than 'Most Secret', 373–4, 378
  WSC corrects Ross on Swift quotation, 765, 768, 768 n.3
  WSC deals with correspondence after stepping down as PM (1955), 1988–9
  WSC directs Erskine to minimise Press communiqués and interviews, 153
  WSC offers to buy family papers from Leslie, 1473
  see also British Broadcasting Corporation (BBC)
Communism
  Korea: armistice talks, 59; British POWs returning from, 978–9; COS Committee meeting minutes on armistice talks, 85–8; increase of Communist forces in during armistice talks, 78; potential air threat to UN forces in, 87–8
  non-admission of foreigners to events in England organised by Soviet propaganda groups, 344
  reports of Communists among Rhodes Scholars, 835–6
  reports of individuals with Communist associations on Board of Trade statutory bodies, 503–5
  US–UK policy towards Far East and South-East Asia, 184–5
  WSC predicts freeing of Eastern Europe from, 793
  WSC states anti-Communist, pro-Russian stance, 1631
  see also Cold War
Conservative Government
  Bracken's pessimism regarding, 445
  Cabinet: appointments, 735, 736, 2050, 2062; appointments (proposed), 1803–4, 1804–5, 1804 n.2, 1805 n.1; Committees, 46; Ministerial appointments, 1 November 1951–5 April 1955, 2389–90

Index

communications: announcement of upcoming Bills (1952), 639–44; failure to announce key decisions (1952), 594; Ministerial broadcasts for Conservative Government actions, 515–16; political broadcast planning (December 1951), 129

defence programme: The Government's Record (April 1953 WSC speech), 957–8; March 1952 proposals, 305–16; 'peace through strength' policy, 958; planning, 24

domestic affairs: agriculture policies, 1274–5; budget planning (1956), 2101; High Court Judges' remuneration, 913–15, 916–17; housing, 421–2, 663; London repair and rebuilding efforts, 1285; Ministerial salaries, 16, 21

economics: economic policies (1959), 2238–9; European Economic Community, 2309–10; taxation policies, 421, 956, 957, 2238; UK economic position, 205–6, 553, 1583; WSC requests Cabinet paper on state of nation's affairs at start date of Conservative Government, 72; WSC requests records on state of nation's affairs as of start date of Conservative Government, 95

Eden: Eden appoints Butler as HofC leader, 2062; Eden expects to form new Government (1953), 1170, 1176; Eden forms new Government (1955), 1977, 2011; Eden steps down as PM (1957), 2151, 2151 n.2, 2152, 2162; Eden visits US (1956), 2079, 2079 n.3; Queen Elizabeth's support for Eden as PM, 813; relations between WSC and Eden, 823, 1180, 1182, 1212, 1228–9, 1235–6, 1236–7, 1285, 1643–4, 1647, 1648–9, 1649, 1728, 1751–2, 1754, 1756, 1757–8, 1758, 1765, 1767, 1779, 1858–9, 1859–60, 1865, 1945, 2144 n.3, 2254

foreign affairs policies, 667–8, 2143, 2144, 2144 n.2

General Election (1959), 2265 n.2

industry: Cotton Import Committee, 421; denationalisation policies, 421, 443, 475; relations with TUC, 953–4; timber trade policies, 421; Transport Commission and Road Haulage permits, 365–7

law officers, 2390–1

Macmillan becomes PM (1957), 2151 n.2, 2162

Macmillan's political ambitions, 1859

Ministerial appointments, 2391–2

Party concern with conduct of, 410–11

Press conjecture on new Government formation, 1199

support for Butler as PM, 813

timing of general election, 1513–14, 1734–5, 1751–2, 1757–8

timing of new Government formation (1955), 1858–9, 1859–60, 1865, 1944, 1945, 1985–6, 1986

and WSC: Attlee's criticisms of formation of, 24–5; RSC congratulates WSC on formation of, 29; 'Working Men Tories' letter from Jack Binns to WSC on 'Labour lies', 494, 494 n.1; WSC appeals for Labour Party cooperation with, 638; WSC considers stepping down as PM (1952–1953), 742, 767, 812, 1174, 1181, 1188, 1189–90, 1212–13, 1216, 1235; WSC plans to step down as PM (1954), 1472, 1546, 1599, 1603, 1613–14, 1614, 1643, 1728, 1731–2; WSC postpones stepping down as PM (1954), 1575, 1731–2, 1732, 1734–5, 1751–2, 1751 n.1, 1752 n.2, 1753–4, 1756, 1757, 1757–8, 1765, 1767, 1768, 1769, 1779, 1786, 1787; WSC steps down as PM (1955), 1973, 1975–6, 1977, 1979, 1980, 1981, 1992, 2037, 2039–40, 2039 n.1, 2040; WSC wishes to avoid electioneering atmosphere, 66, 113, 145–6, 215, 420–1, 1238–9, 1270–1, 1456

see also Cabinet

Conservative Party

policies: economics, 1243; education, 2231; 'peace through strength', 1456, 1529–30, 1586, 1600, 1819, 1841–2, 2002; proportional representation, 1863, 1863 n.2; railways, 1242; social services, 1584

Torrington by-election, 2211

UK financial situation (1952), 508–9

Woolton: appointed Chancellor of the Duchy of Lancaster, 735; ineffectiveness as Chair of, 410; steps down as Chair of Conservative Central Office, 2023; WSC plans to replace Woolton with Lyle as Chair, 410

and WSC: reaction to WSC's praise of Shinwell, 110; WSC decides to not stand for re-election (1963), 2346, 2348; WSC disapproves of advertisements of his books with Party literature, 271; WSC provides messages of support for Macmillan and Jenkin (1964), 2362

WSC speeches: The State of the Nation (December 1951), 145–9; Grand Habitation of the Primrose League (April 1952), 407–9; The Conservatives'

Conservative Party *(continued)*
  WSC speeches *(continued)*
    First Six Months (May 1952), 418–22;
      The First Year (October 1952),
      660–9; Press Association Luncheon
      (June 1952), 489–91; Lord Mayor's
      Banquet (November 1952), 722–6;
      The Government's Record (April
      1953), 952–8; Conservative Party
      Conference (October 1953), 1235,
      1237–46, 1254; Grand Habitation
      of the Primrose League (April 1954),
      1557–9; The Conservatives' Task
      (May 1954), 1582–6; 'Peace Through
      Strength' (October 1954), 1792–801,
      1795–7; Bedford Election Address
      (May 1955), 1999–2003; Constituency
      Speech (November 1955), 2058–9;
      Young Conservatives (December 1955),
      2064–7; Primrose League Meeting (April
      1956), 2100–2; The Primrose League
      (May 1957), 2161–3, 2164; Primrose
      League address (April 1958), 2214–15;
      A Vote of Confidence (January 1959),
      2229–32; Woodford constituency (March
      1959), 2237–41; Woodford constituency
      Adoption Meeting (September 1959),
      2260–3
  see also English politics
Cooke, (Roger) Gresham, 1872–3, 1872 n.1
Cooper, Alfred Duff ('Duff'), 128, 128 n.1, 1387,
  1409, 1409 n.2
Cooper, Anne Frances May Clifford, 588, 588
  n.8
Cooper, John Julius, 588, 588 n.7
Cooper, Lady Diana (Diana Olivia Winifred
  Maud Manners), 588, 588 n.6, 2147, 2148
Coote, Colin Reith, 2232, 2232 n.2
Copleston, Frederick Charles, 1909, 1909 n.3
correspondence (CSC and WSC)
  Aix-les-Bains (1954), 1572, 1579–81, 1586–8,
    1590–1, 1596–8, 1635
  Alpes Maritimes (1957), 2156, 2158, 2158–9,
    2160, 2160–1, 2161
  Bermuda (1953), 1328–9, 1351
  Cap d'Ail (1953), 1213, 1214–15, 1215 n.2,
    1216, 1217–18, 1219, 1221
  Cap d'Ail (1955), 2047–8, 2049–50, 2051–2,
    2053–4
  Cap d'Ail/La Capponcina (1958), 2217,
    2218, 2218–19
  Cap d'Ail/La Capponcina (1959), 2255
  Christina cruise (1961), 2299, 2299 n.2, 2300
  Christmas letters and gifts, 1377, 1860
  Italy (1952), 539, 540–1, 544–5, 553, 584–5,
    585, 586, 587, 587–9
  La Pausa/Cap Martin (1956), 2074, 2075,
    2075–6, 2076–7, 2077, 2078, 2079–80,
    2082, 2083, 2084, 2084–5, 2085, 2086,
    2086–7, 2091, 2092, 2092–3, 2093,
    2094, 2096, 2099, 2099 n.1, 2100,
    2129–30, 2131, 2133, 2135–6, 2136,
    2137, 2138
  La Pausa/Cap Martin (1957), 2152–3, 2154,
    2166, 2166–7, 2167–8, 2168–9, 2169–70,
    2186, 2188, 2189
  La Pausa/Cap Martin (1958), 2199–200,
    2201, 2202–3, 2203–4, 2204, 2223,
    2223–4
  La Pausa/Cap Martin (1959), 2234, 2234 n.1,
    2235–6, 2236–7, 2243
  Monte Carlo (1961), 2305, 2306, 2306–7,
    2307, 2319
  Monte Carlo (1963), 2342, 2345, 2346
  Riviera (1954), 1723, 1723 n.1, 1726, 1726–8,
    1728, 1737–8
  St Moritz (1955), 2029, 2030, 2030–1, 2031–2,
    2032–3, 2033, 2034, 2034–5, 2036,
    2037–8, 2039
  St Moritz (1956), 2119–20, 2120–1, 2121–2,
    2123, 2124–5, 2125–6, 2126–7, 2128
  Washington (1952), 190–1, 227, 231, 233
Cortines, Adolfo Tomás Ruiz, 1232, 1232 n.1
Coty, Jules Gustave René, 1377, 1377 n.1,
  1939–40
Council of Europe
  association between Western Europe and
    Commonwealth countries (proposed),
    438–9
  Boothby suggested as replacement for Spaak,
    392, 403
  British proposals regarding future of, 359
  British role in future of European movement,
    348–9
  UK delegations, 385–7, 392, 1117, 1939
  United Europe discussions, 133, 133 n.2
  see also United Europe; Western Union
    (European Army)
Cousins, Frank, 2188, 2188 n.1, 2265–6
Cousins, Norman, 2179, 2179 n.5
Coventry, Bishop of (Neville Vincent Gorton),
  1873–4, 1873 n.1, 1876–7, 1879–80,
  1909–10, 1910–11
Cox, John William, 1316, 1316 n.1, 1349, 1737
Cox, Percy Walter, 2048, 2048 n.4
Craddock, George, 1686, 1686 n.1
Craig, Christopher, 730, 730 n.1
Cranborne, Lord: *see* Salisbury, Lord (Robert
  Gascoyne-Cecil, 'Bobbety')
Creswell, Michael Justin, 968, 968 n.2, 969, 997,
  2286–7
Crick, Francis Harry Compton, 2313–14, 2313
  n.1
Cripps, Richard Stafford, 403–5, 403 n.2

Crisp, Charles Birch, 1175–6, 1175 n.1, 1177–8
Cromwell, Oliver, 1044, 1044 n.2, 2199
Crookshank, Harry Frederick Comfort, 9–10, 9 n.3, 191, 252, 532, 1468, 1469
Crossman, Anne Patricia McDougall, 2382–3, 2382 n.2, 2384
Crossman, Richard Howard Stafford, 1527–8, 1527 n.1, 1690, 1714, 2382–5
Crosthwaite, Ponsonby Moore, 2324–5, 2324 n.1
Crowther, Geoffrey, 545–6, 545 n.2
Crowther, James Gerald, 344, 344 n.4
Cumberland, Duke of (William Augustus), 2199, 2199 n.1
Cummings, Arthur Stuart Michael, 1170, 1170 n.2
Cumont, Charles Paul de, 2377–8, 2377 n.1
Cunliff-Lister, Philip: *see* Swinton, Lord (Philip Cunliffe-Lister)
Cunningham, Sir Andrew Browne, 965, 965 n.2
Cunningham, John Henry Dacres, 2045, 2045 n.2
Currie, James, 362, 362 n.3
Cust, Caroline Elizabeth Maud, 809, 809 n.1
Cust, Edward John Peregrine, 809, 809 n.2
Cust, Peregrine Francis Adelbert (Lord Brownlow), 808, 808 n.1, 809
Cyprus
  BBC interview with Archbishop Makarios, 1807, 1808
  British military presence in, 2140
  British troops withdrawal (proposed), 696–7
  Cyprus and Anglo-Greek relations, 1497–9, 1512, 1531, 1738–9, 1762–3, 1785
  Cyprus Convention of 1878, 1497 n.2
  move of British Middle East Headquarters to (proposed), 696–7, 744, 748, 1620, 2035, 2036
  New Zealand troops in, 751
  RAF base in (proposed), 338
  WSC's death, 2370
Cyrankiewicz, Józef, 2366, 2366 n.2
Czechoslovakia, 745–6

Dalton, Edward Hugh John Neale, 457, 457 n.2
Dalyell, Kathleen Mary Agnes Wheatley, 2383, 2383 n.2
Dalyell, Tam, 2383, 2383 n.3
Danckwerts, Harold Otto, 371, 371 n.1, 442
Daniel, Margaret Truman, 210, 210 n.2, 227, 806, 806–7
Darling, William Young, 2037, 2037 n.1
Davidson, Robert Laurenson Dashiell ('Larry'), 2043, 2043 n.3, 2180
Davies, Clement, 385–7, 385 n.1, 392, 473, 1939
Davies, Gwen, 2011, 2011 n.1
Davies, Harold, 473 n.1, 577, 875, 1522
Daw Mya Yi (Mrs Nu), 2017, 2017 n.2
Dawson, George Geoffrey Robinson, 2171, 2171 n.4
Deakin, Arthur, 429, 429 n.1, 491–2
Deakin, Frederick William Dampier ('Bill')
  biographical information, 495 n.1
  at Chartwell, 495
  cruise with WSC, 2323–4
  A History of the English-Speaking Peoples, 2009, 2030–1, 2047, 2049, 2081
  Popescu-Nasta family, 2132
  Volume 6 of *The Second World War*, 497, 497 n.5, 647, 686
Deakin, Livia Stela Nasta ('Pussy'), 686, 686 n.1
Dean, Gordon Evans, 223–4, 223 n.2
de Burgh, Hubert, 2015, 2015 n.1
Deedes, William Francis, 1804, 1804 n.3
defence
  civil defence: air-raid warning system, 253; Coventry civil defence demonstration, 1695, 1695 n.1; Defence and Civil Defence White Paper, 1805; Director-General of Civil Defence Operations position (proposed), 493; Home Fleet review, 596, 596 n.1; Home Guard, 10, 307, 1264–5; Home Guard future planning, 1264–5; Home Guard for Northern Ireland, 340; planning, 407, 435–8, 436–7, 437, 546–7, 1934
  CSC advises WSC against appointing Sandys as Secretary of State for War, 156
  Defence Review Committee, 1730, 1731, 1735, 1737
  handling of defence matters during Alexander's absence, 481–2
  'Jujitsu', 228, 228 n.1
  Macmillan appointed Minister of Defence, 1806
  'Mainbrace' military exercise, 616, 616 n.1, 624
  manpower: British forces and European Defence Community, 434; call-up of reservists, 307–8, 873; estimates, 234–5, 562, 567; French Army manpower estimates, 117; Hong Kong garrison reduction, 1540; Militia battalions disbandment, 780; National Service Act, 1292–4; National Service periods, 305, 308–10, 565, 566, 580–2; NCOs and substantive rank, 327, 346; reduction of Military Mission staff in Washington, 261; regulars retention and call-up of reservists for Korean War, 235–6; regulars retention and call-up of reservists for Korean War (proposed), 235–6, 252; staff reductions, 90, 295, 295; training, 307

INDEX

defence *(continued)*
planning: British Defence Programme Annual Review, 717; civil defence, 407, 435–8, 436–7, 437, 546–7; Commonwealth Advisory Committee on Defence Science, 332–3, 333, 349, 349–50; Conservative Government planning (March 1952), 305–16; COS Defence Policy and Global Strategy Report, 476–7, 494, 498, 542–3, 544, 550–1, 623, 624, 652–5; general war reserves, 337–8; move of British Middle East Headquarters to Cyprus (proposed), 696–7; North Atlantic Treaty associations, 466, 466 n.1; Paris discussions with Adenauer, 64–5; Statement on Defence (1954), 1428–9; state of war plans and preparations (1953), 1016; TCC report, 172, 232, 232 n.1, 305–6; US–UK Washington discussions, 40–1, 144; WSC acknowledges previous Labour Government policy efforts, 94–5, 146; WSC questions need for defence White Paper, 252; WSC thanks Sandys for Middle East defence planning paper, 339
production programme: ammunition, 509, 530–1, 534; budget reduction effects, 652–5, 710–12; Debate planning, 73, 532–3, 550, 1820–1, 1824–5, 1920; Defence Programme budget (1953–1954), 710–12, 714–18; Defence Programme loan precedents, 669, 673–4, 674 n.1; Loss of Rifles file, 46; previous Labour Government programme, 23, 305, 316; programme estimate reductions (proposals), 136–8; rearmament, 101–5, 102, 117, 117 n.1, 117 n.2, 117 n.3, 117 n.4, 170, 214–15, 306, 509, 556–8, 572–80, 576–7, 662, 739, 875–7; reduction of Army steel requirements, 260; rifle production programme, 103–5; rifle standardisation, 177–8; rifle stocks and dispersement accounting, 12; Service estimates, 541–2; strategic stockpiling suspension (proposed), 2, 4; tank production programme, 150–1, 152, 153, 228, 303, 303 n.1, 308, 330, 342
WSC asks for review of Defence speech, 91
WSC meets with Menzies to discuss, 484
WSC's Address to US Congress, 220
WSC speeches: Defence (December 1951), 94–108; Defence White Paper (March 1952), 304–16; Defence (March 1953), 868–78; Adoption of a New Army Rifle (February 1954), 1410–19; Defence, German Rearmament (March 1954), 1460–7; Defence (March 1955), 1926–35
see also atom bomb and atomic energy; British Army; Cold War; Defence Committee; Europe; Ministry of Defence; NATO (North Atlantic Treaty Organisation); Royal Air Force (RAF); Royal Navy; U-boats
Defence Committee
atom bomb tests, 808, 814–15
Atomic Energy Programme, 769, 770–2
British COS Defence Policy and Global Strategy report, 652–5
Chequers Defence Committee staff conference conclusions, 973–4
Coronation Naval Review, 1016–17
Defence Programme: Admiralty production programme, 123–6; aircraft production programme, 120–3; Army estimates, 126–8; budget reduction effects, 652–5, 710–12; DRP Committee Progress Reports, 208, 253; Progress Report meeting minutes, 120–3, 123–6, 126–8; state of war plans and preparations (1953), 1016; war reserves, 336–7, 337, 337–8
Egypt: British defence negotiations with, 770; British military base in, 338; British troops' readiness in case of attacks (1953), 991–2; Canal Zone reinforcements, 974, 976–7; Canal Zone situation report, 838–9, 1017–20; 'Rodeo', 974, 977; US–UK defence negotiations (1953), 1021–2, 1355–7
Europe, 864–5, 1538–9
formation, 60
Hong Kong garrison reduction, 1540
Indo-China war, 988
Israeli role in Middle East defence, 993–4
Kenya, 881–2
Korea: British Deputy Chief of Staff (proposed), 547–8; provision of Commonwealth forces in, 336; reduction of Commonwealth forces in, 1393–4; treatment of British POWs returning from, 978–9; US–UK policy towards, 840–1
Pakistan, 880–1
protected accommodation for Government staffs, 338
Russia: British acquisition of MiG 15 aircraft, 881; location of Soviet forces (1954), 1429–30; submarine strength, 357
Service Ministers' meetings on non-operational matters, 116–17, 158
South-East Asia: ANZUS and ANZAM, 769, 775–7; British action in the event

of French withdrawal from Indo-China, 355–7; British policy towards Chinese aggression in, 354–5; Five Power military planning conference (1953), 1015–16; Malaya defence planning, 839–40
Statement on Defence (1954), 1428–9
Sudan, 977–8
de Freitas, Geoffrey, 439–40, 439 n.1
de Gasperi, Alcide, 417, 417 n.2, 1125, 1130, 1137, 1137 n.1, 1147
de Havilland, Geoffrey, 549, 549 n.4
de la Bère, Rupert, 1284–5, 1285 n.1
De La Warr, Lord (Herbrand Edward Dundonald Brassey Sackville, 'Buck'), 339–40, 339 n.1, 1989–90
De L'Isle and Dudley, Lord (William Philip Sydney)
biographical information, 57 n.1
Australasia tour costs, 462
Civil Service staff reductions, 90
Coronation, 947
Egypt, 1654
Gatwick Airport development, 728–9
Middle East, 534, 729
Pakistan, 880–1
provision of married quarters for US Armed Forces in the UK, 737–8
RAF: aircraft production programme, 57–8, 118, 120, 229; 'Ardent' air-defence training exercise, 659, 659 n.1, 726–7, 727 n.1; jet aircraft pilot casualties, 552, 592; rocket propulsion for jet fighters, 363; 'Valiant' aircraft prototype crash, 211
Russian MiG shoots down British bomber in Hamburg–Berlin air corridor (1953), 912–13
sale of Sycamore helicopters to Argentina, 1761–2
US offers B-47 bombers to England, 1612–13, 1613 n.1
Dempsey, Miles Christopher, 1264, 1264 n.1
Dening, Esler Maber, 525–6, 525 n.1
Denny, Michael Maynard, 123–4, 123 n.2
Derby, Isabel (Countess of Derby), 1596, 1596 n.1
Derby, Lady (Isabel Milles-Lade Stanley), 2218, 2218 n.3
Derby, Lord (Edward George Villiers Stanley), 1386, 1386 n.2, 1387
de Rothschild, James Armand Edmond, 727, 727 n.2, 1887, 1914
Deshmukh, Chintaman Dwarakanath, 745, 751–2, 751 n.2
de Trafford, Humphrey Edmund, 1054, 1054 n.2, 1179, 2289

Devonshire, Duchess of (Evelyn Emily Mary Petty-FitzMaurice), 444, 444 n.1
Devonshire, Duke of (Edward William Spencer Cavendish), 2288, 2288 n.3
Dewey, Thomas Edmund, 801, 801 n.3, 804
Dibdin, Thomas John, 112, 112 n.1
Dickson, William, 816–22, 822 n.2, 880–1, 881, 1223–7
Diefenbaker, John George, 2171, 2171 n.3, 2172, 2191
Digby, Edward Henry Kenelm, 433, 433 n.5
Digby, Pamela (Pamela Churchill), 1196, 1196 n.2
Dilhorne, Lord (Reginald Edward Manningham-Buller), 2375, 2375 n.2
Dilke, Charles Wentworth, 2108, 2108 n.3
Dillon, Clarence Douglas, 1044, 1044 n.1, 1082
Dimitrov, Georgi Mihov ('Gemeto'), 134, 134 n.4
Diplock, William John Kenneth, 1483, 1483 n.1
Disraeli, Benjamin (Lord Beaconsfield), 919, 919 n.4
Dixon, Pierson John ('Bob'), 1190, 1190–1, 1190 n.3
Dodds-Parker, Arthur Douglas, 19–20, 19 n.2, 1791
domestic affairs
broadcasting White Paper, 427
Civil Servant status for WSC's Private Secretaries, 55, 66–7
Civil Service staff reductions, 90
corporal punishment, 685–6, 686, 733–4
Crichel Down, 1624, 1624 n.1, 1642–3, 1646, 1647–8
Criminal Statistics for England and Wales (1951), 589–91, 591, 591 n.1
dispersal of funds of disbanded Militia battalions, 780, 780 n.2, 788, 1419–20, 1420 n.1
electricity charges, 44, 48
employment of coloured people in public service sector, 1423–4
felling of elms in Kensington Gardens, 1473, 1474, 1474 n.1
hospital services development, 1825
International Women's Day conference in England, 344
Leeds Police tribunal inquiry (proposed), 1483–4
National Assistance Board and Ministry of National Insurance amalgamation (proposed), 391
national newspapers maintenance workers' strike, 1985, 1985 n.4, 1989
non-admission of foreigners to events in England organised by Soviet propaganda groups, 344–5, 345

domestic affairs *(continued)*
  old age pensions, 1585–6, 1735, 1796–7
  postal services curtailment (proposed), 339–40
  Prison Officers Association, 478, 480–1, 482
  prison warden reductions, 444, 445, 445 n.1, 445 n.2
  'problem families' and child welfare, 1863–4
  prostitution and homosexuality laws, 1482–3, 1542–3
  provision of married quarters for US Armed Forces in the UK, 737–8
  Rent Restriction Acts amendments (proposed), 657–8
  reports of Communists among Rhodes Scholars, 835–6
  Royal Commission on certification and detention of mental patients, 1256–7
  Royal Commission on Voting, 1863
  Savoy Hotel case, 1420–1, 1425, 1428, 1428 n.2, 1440–1
  Service officers' pensions, 1306–8, 1308
  Straffen's life sentence and potential release, 637, 645
  Television Bill, 1368–9
  WSC asks about deliberate spreading of myxomatosis among wild rabbits, 1652, 1729, 1729 n.2
  WSC speeches: House of Commons speech (November 1951), 19–29; The State of the Nation (December 1951), 145–9; King George VI (February 1952), 257–9; Transport, Government Policy (May 1952), 447–55; Press Association Luncheon (June 1952), 489–91; The Economic Position (July 1952), 570–83, 586; The Government's Tasks (September 1952), 638–44; Debate on the Address (November 1952), 701–10; Westminster Abbey Appeal (January 1953), 824–6; England (April 1953), 964–7; Commonwealth Parliamentary Association (May 1953), 1044–5; Debate on the Address (November 1953), 1268–77, 1277–8, 1280; National Service (November 1953), 1294–9; Royal Academy Banquet (April 1954), 1555–7; University of Bristol Chancellor's Address (November 1954), 1822–4; Parliament–Spokesman of the People (September 1957), 2184–5; Churchill College Ceremony (October 1959), 2266–8; Churchill College foundation stone ceremony (October 1961), 2314
  see also economics; education; food; House of Commons (HofC); housing; industry; railways; transport

Dominion Governments: *see* British Commonwealth
Don, Alan Campbell (Dean of Westminster), 267–8, 267 n.1, 682
Donegall, Lady (Gladys Jean Combe), 410, 410 n.3
Donegall, Lord (Edward Arthur Donald St George Hamilton Chichester), 410, 410 n.2
Donges, Theophilus Ebenhaezer, 1637, 1637 n.3
Donnelly, Desmond Louis, 1100–1, 1100 n.1, 1678–9
Dorman-Smith, Eric Edward, 1026–7, 1026 n.1, 1028–9, 1030–1
Doud, Elivera Mathilda Carlson, 1052, 1052 n.1, 1053, 1125
Douglas-Hamilton, Malcolm Avendale, 1506–7, 1506 n.1
Douglas-Home, Alexander Frederick, 1979, 1979 n.1, 2359–60
Douglas, Lewis Williams, 544, 544 n.2, 736, 2069
Dowds, Samuel Sydney, 2071–2, 2071 n.2
Drayson, George Burnaby, 412, 412 n.1
Drew, George Alexander, 203–4, 203 n.3
Driberg, Thomas Edward Neil, 344, 344 n.1, 471
Duff, Juliet Lowther, 2032–3, 2032 n.6, 2124–5
Dugdale, Thomas Lionel
  biographical information, 357 n.1
  agriculture policies, 1274–5
  Crichel Down, 1624, 1624 n.1
  farm economy and cost of home-raised food, 1385, 1387, 1388–9, 1394–5
  felling of trees, 1473
  food budget discussions, 430
  fruit and sugar supplies, 483
  marketing of home-produced meat and bacon after end of meat rationing, 1258–62, 1265–7
  Milk Marketing Board resumes operations (1954), 1265–7, 1266 n.1
  pork production levels, 357
  potato acreage projections (1952), 357–8
Duke, Neville Frederick, 229, 229 n.1
Dulles, John Foster
  biographical information, 152 n.1
  China: Formosa, 1882, 1893–6, 1896–900; Quemoy and Matsus Islands, 1803, 1803 n.1, 1916–19, 1919–20, 1921, 1936, 1962; UN admission (proposed), 1205–6, 1685; US complaints about British shipping and trading practices with, 866–8, 884
  death of, 2251, 2251 n.1
  Europe: European Defence Community, 837, 883–4, 884 n.1, 1163–4, 1345–6,

1362, 1367, 1367 n.1, 1368, 1377, 1426, 1629–30, 1730, 1736, 1741–2, 1744, 1745, 1748–9, 1750, 1770; NATO meetings in, 823–4; Nine Power Conference, 1789; US–UK policy towards, 883–4
  foreign affairs: ANZUS and ANZAM, 804; atom bomb, 1492–3, 1528; Five Power (Geneva) Conference proposals (1954), 1403, 1433–4, 1448; Four Power Conference proposals (1953), 1344; Korea, 152, 804, 1118, 1118 n.2; publication of Yalta papers, 1962; South-East Asia, 775, 1575, 1970; US suggests Four Power meeting as part of NATO Council (1955), 1939–40, 1944, 1945, 1945–8, 1958
  Germany: NATO membership (proposed), 1742, 1744, 1748–9, 1750, 1778, 1780, 1783–4; rearmament, 1629–30, 1733, 1733 n.1, 1734, 1736, 1740; Western policy towards, 1154–5
  Middle East: Arab–Israeli peace prospects, 887; Persia, 798, 804, 836–7, 878–9, 884, 888–9
  Russia: Anglo-American differences in policy towards, 1149–50; Eisenhower considers meeting with Soviets, 906, 907; strains of Cold War on economy, 1068–9; US–UK policy towards, 1159; Western policy towards, 1162, 1183, 1185–6, 1188; WSC offers to meet with Molotov in Moscow (proposed), 986–7, 995
  WSC meets with (1953), 798, 798–800, 801
  WSC's opinion of, 801, 802
  WSC suggests Azores meeting, 1232
  see also Anglo-American relations; Egypt; Foreign Ministers Washington Conference (1953); Indo-China war; Three Power (Bermuda) Conference (1953)
Duncan, James Alexander Lawson, 381, 381 n.1, 389
Dunhill, Thomas Peel, 1971, 1971 n.3, 1974
Dunn, James Clement, 1473, 1473 n.1
Dunn, Lady (Marcia Anastasia Christoforides, 'Christofor'), 2292, 2292 n.1, 2297, 2308, 2349
Duvieusart, Jean Pierre, 2369, 2369 n.1
Dynevor, Baron (Charles Arthur Uryan Rhys), 2200, 2200 n.1

Eade, Charles Stanley, 353, 353 n.1, 362, 428–9
Eccles, David McAdam
  biographical information, 361 n.2
  Coronation: procession route seating, 692; safety of bridge between Westminster Abbey and Parliament, 1027, 1034, 1034 n.2; Westminster Abbey seating allocations, 692, 743
  domestic affairs: civil defence planning, 436–7; felling of elms in Kensington Gardens, 1473, 1474, 1474 n.1; housing programme, 641, 663, 1240; industry double-shift work proposals, 361–2; structural steel safety and supplies, 389–90, 634
economics
  currency: 'commodity sterling dollar' concept, 495, 495 n.2; Exchange Control policies, 393, 406, 406 n.3; Pound Sterling controls, 2230; sterling balances and UK indebtedness, 2, 4, 26, 147–8, 359–61, 361 n.1
  domestic affairs: Bracken's criticisms of Butler's financial policies, 445; budget planning and general election timing, 1734–5, 1752; Civil Service estimates, 234–5; Civil Service retirement age, 253–4; Civil Service staff reductions, 88–9, 89 n.1; county court judges' and judicial officers' salaries, 11, 30; expenditures and remuneration of medical specialists, 370–1, 371 n.2, 441–3, 443 n.1; Financial Committees interim report, 114; Government expenditure reductions, 3, 4, 17; High Court Judges' remuneration, 680–2, 913–15; housing investment programme (1953), 564; land taxation policies, 706–7; Local Loans Fund procedures, 671–2; Members' Expenses debate, 1596–7, 1607; MPs' remuneration, 988–9; old age pensions, 347; purchase taxes, 249, 260, 1990, 2050; remuneration of general practitioners and medical specialists, 441–3; salaries and cost of living, 1836; Scottish Judges' tax concessions and remuneration, 681–2; Supplementary Estimates, 767, 780–1; unemployment in textile and clothing industries, 368–9, 372, 372 n.1; War Office estimates, 234; 'Working Men Tories' letter from Jack Binns to WSC on 'Labour lies', 494, 494 n.1; WSC praises Butler's proposed budget (1952), 408
  trade: British arms exports, 578, 875–6; British imports of Canadian cheese, 381, 389; British rubber exports to Russia, 347, 362; British rubber exports to Russia and China, 353, 362, 428–9; cotton importing and marketing, 1105, 1111; East/West trade with Russia, 1399, 1454; Paris Group, 1390,

economics *(continued)*
  trade (continued)
    1390 n.1; trade control and embargoed goods 'short list', 1390–2; UK exports of aluminium to US, 202; UK raw material exports to US, 187–8; US tariffs on British goods, 400, 405
  UK economic position: 1951, 1–4, 20–1, 26–7, 26, 33–4; 1952, 214, 239, 419–20, 459–60, 460, 495–6, 508–9, 553, 570–1, 572, 577, 587, 641–2, 661–2, 708–9, 709; 1953, 955–7, 1239, 1273; 1954, 1792–3, 1793; 1959, 2230–1
  US assistance to England, 21, 213
  Washington discussions (1953), 801, 804, 836, 863
Eddy, Mary Baker, 2208, 2208 n.1
Eden, Beatrice Helen Beckett, 227, 227 n.2
Eden, Clarissa Churchill
  biographical information, 594 n.4
  at Chartwell, 2032, 2035, 2057
  Eden's surgery complications, 1036–7, 1161–2
  health issues, 1579, 1599
  marriage to Anthony Eden, 594, 596, 596 n.3, 1579, 2171–2, 2172, 2179, 2183, 2205
  sends well wishes to WSC, 2209, 2211
  WSC's opinion of, 594
  WSC steps down as PM (1955), 1979, 1980
Eden, Nicholas, 2183, 2183 n.1
Eden, (Robert) Anthony
  biographical information, 5 n.1
  domestic affairs: access by former Ministers to Cabinet and other official papers, 296–7; Anglo-Norwegian fisheries case, 568–9, 784; Conservative Party economic and social policies, 1829, 1836–7; death of George VI, 254–5, 254 n.1; dock and railway strikes, 2010–11; London municipal elections, 350; memorial for Lord Camrose, 1609; non-admission of foreigners to events in England organised by Soviet propaganda groups, 344; sale of Sycamore helicopters to Argentina, 1761–2; Trades Union Congress, 2012, 2100
  economics: Civil Service estimates, 234–5; Commonwealth Economic Conference, 647; International Economic Conference in Moscow, 412; US tariffs on British goods, 400, 405; Washington discussions (1953), 836, 844, 863
  foreign affairs: arms at British Embassy in Teheran, 592; Austria, 1499, 1544–5, 1545 n.1; Cold War, 1467, 1499, 1682–3; Commonwealth PMs praise Eden, 750; Conservative Government policies, 667–8; Cyprus, 1762–3, 1807, 1808; Cyprus and Anglo-Greek relations, 1531; dines with Massigli and Juin, 423–4; diplomatic immunity privileges for international organisations, 584; Eight Power Meeting proposals, 1766; Falkland Islands, 299; HofC debate (December 1953), 1355; Hong Kong garrison reduction, 1540; Iceland, 784–5; Italy, 1300, 1383, 1386; Japan, 898–9, 904; Kenya, 915, 926; Leather's unauthorised statements about WSC, 679; Malaya, 65, 72, 859–60; Menzies criticises UN, 2182, 2183; Pakistan, 1381–2; Turkey, 700, 700 n.2, 748; United States Government, 119, 731, 1232; UN meeting in New York (1952), 702; US–UK cooperation regarding, 750; US–UK policy towards Far East and South-East Asia, 163; WSC considers departure from Foreign Office for Eden, 507; WSC praises Eden's conduct as Foreign Secretary, 408, 425, 731, 731 n.1, 929, 1243, 1285, 1559, 1799, 1813; WSC sends well wishes to Eden during US visit (1953), 895
  Israel: Arab–Israeli peace prospects, 879–80; British jet aircraft for, 680, 693; de Rothschild recommends admitting Israel to British Commonwealth, 1887, 1887 n.1; oil supply financing request, 424, 424 n.5
  NATO: Secretary-General candidates, 320, 320–1, 322–4; Soviets wish to join, 1547, 1547–8, 1548; US suggests Four Power meeting as part of NATO Council (1955), 1939–40, 1944, 1945–8, 1958
  Persia: nationalisation law, 603; oil negotiations, 182–3, 199–200, 608, 620, 621, 622, 626, 627 n.1, 646, 650, 656, 749; US aid to, 884, 885, 888–9, 889 n.1; US–UK policy towards, 878–9
  personal life: Beaverbrook's opinion of Eden, 808; Eden writes memoirs, 2212, 2212 n.1, 2213, 2235, 2241–2, 2242, 2253–4, 2254, 2254–5, 2256, 2270, 2302, 2303; Eisenhower sends well wishes, 997; gall-bladder surgery, 932, 939, 944, 944 n.1, 963, 971; health issues, 553, 588, 1180, 1182, 2149 n.3, 2150, 2164, 2171–2, 2172, 2192, 2193, 2197, 2205, 2209, 2211, 2270; marriage to Clarissa Churchill, 594, 596, 596 n.3; opinion of Soames, 410; Order of the Garter honour for, 1818, 1818 n.1; surgery complications, 998, 998 n.1, 1036–7, 1047–8, 1161

INDEX   2441

Sudan: Anglo-Egyptian agreement regarding, 826–8, 829–31, 841–3, 922; elections and self-government planning, 35, 35 n.1, 38–9, 43, 43 n.4, 713–14, 747, 1355; postponement of opening of Sudanese Parliament, 1458–9
Three Power (Bermuda) Conference (1953): planning, 1279, 1281, 1283, 1290; Plenary Meeting #1, 1317–18; Press communiqués, 1337, 1337 n.1; WSC meets privately with Eisenhower, 1317
and WSC: Chartwell visits, 2032, 2035, 2057; Eden declines visit to La Pausa, 2205; Eden discusses politics with (1958–1959), 2196, 2197, 2205, 2212, 2215–16, 2257; Eden sends New Year's greeting to (1958), 2196–7; Eden sends well wishes, 2212, 2213; Eden's war-time minutes to, 2235, 2241–2, 2242, 2243–4, 2244, 2254–5, 2256; Eden thanks for gift of cigars, 2042, 2130; Eden thanks for volumes of *A History of the English-Speaking Peoples*, 2090, 2192, 2193, 2216; *New York Times* article on WSC's US visit (1953), 809–10, 811; proof copies of Cabinet Papers, 1384; WSC and CSC visit Eden, 2179; WSC's death, 2373–5
see also Anglo-American relations; Big Four (Geneva) Summit (1955); China; Conservative Government; defence; Egypt; Europe; Four Power (Berlin) Conference (1954); Germany; Indo-China war; Korea; Middle East; Russia
Edinburgh, Duke of (Philip Mountbatten) biographical information, 206 n.1
Churchill College Visitorship, 2258, 2259, 2267, 2269
Coronation, 687–8, 1054–5
in Peers' Gallery during HofC debates, 299
position for at opening of Parliament, 672–3, 673 n.1
Western Australia visit, 1479–81
WSC steps down as PM (1955), 1978–80, 1984
WSC visits Balmoral, 611
Edmund Crouchback, 2014–15, 2014 n.2
education
Advice to Students (December 1929 WSC speech), 2406
Conservative Party policies, 2231
educational expenditures in Germany, 251–2
labour representation for technological college Trustees, 2215
school leaving age alteration proposals, 140–1, 150, 249, 249 n.2, 421, 500, 500 n.1
tax-free educational allowances for Armed Forces officers, 603–4

Teachers' Superannuation Bill, 1459–60
technological education, 2066–7
timing of education cuts announcements, 114–15, 115, 116
see also Churchill College
Edward, King (Edward the Confessor), 824–5, 825 n.1
Edward VII, King, 262, 262 n.1
Edward VIII, King: *see* Windsor, Duke of
Egerton, Margaret: *see* Colville, Margaret Egerton
Egypt
abdication of King Farouk, 566, 566 n.2
American nun murdered in, 232
British defence negotiations with, 695–7, 770, 861–2
British Embassy in Cairo, 592
British jet aircraft for, 680, 693, 693 n.1, 876
British occupation of Delta to safeguard civilians (proposed), 1540–1
British policy towards, 71, 199, 625, 724, 1235
British rearmament of Egyptian forces (proposed), 591, 593
civil affairs planning, 1019
Daily Express article on renewal of talks in Cairo, 1607
Defence Committee situation report, 838–9
economic situation in, 698, 698 n.1
Egyptian Government: anti-British speeches, 968, 969; Foreign Affairs (May 1953 WSC speech), 1000–3; General Election (1952), 364, 397; Naguib Government, 623; Naguib's attitude towards England, 569, 593; political corruption in, 947; Wafd (Hizb al-Wafd) political party, 325, 325 n.1; WSC questions possibility of ongoing relations with, 247
Egyptian propaganda, 937–8, 938, 946–7, 951, 961–2
exile of Mohammed Ali Tewfik, 637, 637 n.3
fellaheen, 600, 600 n.2, 623
General Election planning (1952), 364–5, 369–70, 397, 397 n.2
Maher Pasha, 593, 593 n.2
Middle East: British manpower estimates, 1207, 1207 n.1; defence planning, 861–2, 1541–2; Egyptian armed forces in the Sinai, 1018; Egyptian blockade of Israel, 1395–6; Iraqi proposal for Gaza Strip, 63–4; move of British Middle East Headquarters to Cyprus (proposed), 744; withdrawal of British troops from Cyprus (proposed), 696–7
Nahas Pasha, 325–6, 325 n.2, 364–5, 382
New York Times article on WSC's US visit (1953), 810

Egypt *(continued)*
  oil supplies for civilian population, 9
  Operation Redeployment, 1354–5, 1366
  potential for strikes and riots in (1954), 1501–2
  'Rodeo', 233, 233 n.1, 237–8, 273, 974, 977, 991–2, 1017–18, 1022, 1023, 1024, 1024–5
  Sterling Releases Agreement, 790–1, 839, 1203–4, 1210, 1378–9, 1620, 1655
  US arms for, 989–90, 991, 994, 995, 996–7
  US economic aid to, 1367–8, 1369–71, 1372, 1376, 1378
  US policy towards (1953), 803
  US training of military officers, 112
  WSC cruises the Mediterranean with Onassis, 2318
  WSC directs Howe to not travel through Cairo, 982
  WSC proposes to deal with all Egypt matters while Eden attends Four Power Conference, 1396
  WSC recommends that British Community should evacuate from, 1010
  WSC's opinion of Eden's policy efforts, 347
  see also Canal Zone; Sudan
Einstein, Lewis David, 2035, 2035 n.1, 2036, 2039, 2121, 2123
Eisenhower, Dwight David ('Ike')
  biographical information, 30 n.1
  Europe: British contribution to air defence of, 58; Council of Europe, 359; European Defence Community, 800, 933, 945, 1120, 1121, 1121 n.2, 1122, 1158–9, 1164, 1368, 1371, 1372–3, 1629–30, 1692–3, 1755, 1774–5, 1775–6, 1775 n.1, 1778; Nine Power Conference, 1789; Supreme Commander of NATO forces in, 30–1, 82, 97; US support for Western European Union (Paris Agreements), 1940–3, 1943 n.1, 1956–8; Western Union (European Army), 83–4, 84, 108–9, 140, 154, 158, 200
  foreign affairs: Arab–Israeli peace prospects, 879–80, 887, 898; Big Four (Geneva) Summit (1955), 2024, 2025–6; Cyprus and Anglo-Greek relations, 1738–9, 1785; describes difference between 'command' and 'leadership' to Eden, 909; Eisenhower's World Peace declaration, 958, 959–61, 963, 971–2; Five Power Conference proposals (1953), 1279, 1279 n.1; Four Power Conference proposals (1953), 110–11, 1168, 1169, 1171, 1276; France, 1628, 1630; Israeli–Jewish relations, 799–800; Japan, 898–9; meets with Eden, 731; South-East Asia, 775–7, 799, 1515, 1970; Turkish relations with Russia, 1079; US–UK cooperation regarding, 750; Washington discussions (1953), 836, 844; Yugoslavia, 911, 912
  Germany: Adenauer meets with Eisenhower, 936, 945; NATO membership (proposed), 1779–80, 1781, 1781–2, 1783, 1783–4, 1802; Paris Agreements (1955), 1866, 1866 n.3, 1878; rearmament, 1629–30, 1831–3, 1838; response to French refusal to ratify EDC, 1774–5, 1775 n.1
  Korea: armistice talks, 729, 939, 939 n.2, 959–60, 963–4, 971–2, 1040–1, 1046, 1048–9, 1053; British troops' availability for deployment to, 1125–6, 1130–1; Korea Truce Talks (June 1953 WSC speech), 1098; Rhee's release of 25,000 POWs, 1118, 1118 n.2, 1119–20; transport of Indian troops to, 1112, 1112 n.1; US policy towards (1953), 800, 903, 945; US–UK policy towards, 749–50; WSC suggests ouster of Rhee, 1120, 1123
  NATO: command structure, 219, 725; infrastructure planning, 271–2; Mediterranean Command proposals, 272; reorganisation proposals, 272; US suggests Four Power meeting as part of NATO Council (1955), 1939–40, 1944, 1945–8, 1958, 1960
  Persia: Anglo-Iranian Oil Company, 749; US aid to, 884, 885, 888–9; US–UK policy towards, 798, 799, 799 n.1, 804, 878–9, 996
  personal life: health, 1045, 2043, 2043 n.1, 2057, 2109; Montgomery's criticism, 2249–50, 2252, 2253; sends well wishes to Eden, 932
  Presidency: inauguration speech, 803–4; Press relations, 729; summer White House in Colorado, 1739, 1739 n.1; US Presidential election (1952), 416, 440–1, 495, 540, 544, 643, 668, 713, 714, 723
  Truman subpoenaed by House Un-American Affairs Activities Committee, 1290, 1290 n.1
  and WSC: Atlas Mountains painting, 2251, 2251 n.2; commemorative medallion for WSC's eighty-first birthday, 2061–2, 2062–3, 2063, 2069; completion of Volume 6 of *The Second World War*, 936–7, 943, 944, 1141, 1167–8, 1171, 1172, 1178, 1313; Eisenhower hosts dinner parties for (1953), 800–2, 802–3; Eisenhower meets with in

INDEX 2443

England (1959), 2257, 2257 n.2, 2262;
Eisenhower paints portrait of, 1857–8,
1866, 1867, 1879, 1879 n.1, 1937,
1960, 1963; Eisenhower sends birthday
wishes, 739, 1824, 1824 n.1, 1828,
1828 n.2, 1847; friendship with, 1960,
1961–2, 2098, 2103, 2109, 2150, 2204,
2209–10; Order of the Garter honour
for WSC, 972, 972 n.1; US exhibit of
WSC's paintings, 2194, 2195, 2210;
Windsor Papers, 1141, 1159; WSC
congratulates on Presidential election
(1952), 713, 714, 723; WSC and
CSC host farewell dinner for (1952),
440–1, 460–1; WSC declines to invite
Eisenhower to address Parliament, 274;
WSC invites to England (1953), 1181,
1181–2, 1182, 1187; WSC's funeral,
2385–7, 2385 n.4; WSC's health,
1137, 1140, 1158, 2296; WSC's Nobel
Prize for literature, 1253; WSC's
opinion of Eisenhower, 809; WSC's
private reaction to Eisenhower's
election as President, 721, 1174; WSC
suggests Azores meeting, 1231, 1232,
1234–5, 1235; WSC visits US (1953),
796–7, 799–800, 1257, 1257 n.1; WSC
visits US (1959), 2233, 2247–8, 2248–9,
2249–51, 2251, 2253; Yalta papers,
1960, 1962
see also Anglo-American relations; atom bomb
and atomic energy; China; Cold War;
Egypt; Indo-China war; Russia; Three
Power (Bermuda) Conference (1953)
Eisenhower, Mamie Geneva Doud
biographical information, 739 n.1
Bermuda trip planning (1953), 1052, 1053,
1125, 1141
birthday good wishes for WSC, 739
WSC and CSC host farewell dinner for
(1952), 460–1
WSC thanks for hospitality, 1640, 1670
Elath, Eliahu, 624–5, 624 n.2, 1923–4, 2102
El Glaoui, Thami, 935, 935 n.2, 1058, 1112–13
Elizabeth II, Queen
biographical information, 14 n.1
Accession Declaration, 689–90, 690 n.1
Accession Proclamation, 255–6
Auxiliary RAF squadrons, 1915
China, 1921
Commonwealth Parliamentary Association
(May 1953 WSC speech), 1044–5
Commonwealth tour (1953–1954):
Her Majesty's Return From Her
Commonwealth Tour (May 1954 WSC
speech), 1568–9; Her Majesty visits the
Temple of Tooth in Ceylon, 1438; HofC

notes imminence of, 1269; Parliamentary
Address to Her Majesty on the occasion
of her departure, 1299–300; Western
Australia visit, 1479–81
corgis, 1914
Coronation: Allan's Coronation articles
for *Look* magazine, 921–2; amnesty
for British Armed Forces deserters
(proposed), 783–4; authorisation of
proposed changes to Coronation Oath,
850–1, 850 n.1; The Coronation of
Queen Elizabeth II, An Introduction
to a Royal Broadcast (June 1953 WSC
speech), 1057; Coronation uniforms,
488; date, 265–6, 269, 281, 398; Duke
of Windsor does not attend, 732, 736–7,
766; gift of crown from El Glaoui, 1058,
1112–13; Latin version of Royal Title,
834–5; Naval Review, 635, 644, 658,
838, 838 n.1, 853–4, 854 n.1, 854 n.2,
922, 1016–17, 1104, 1104 n.1; Nehru
attends, 1055; parties and celebrations,
1054–5; procession route seating, 692;
safety of bridge between Westminster
Abbey and Parliament, 1027, 1034,
1034 n.2; Stone of Scone, 265–6, 267–8;
televising of (proposed), 682, 687–8, 687
n.1, 688–9, 690–1, 693–4; Thanksgiving
Service, 1092–3; Westminster Abbey
seating allocations, 691–2, 743; WSC
attends, 1057–8; WSC's grandson
Winston serves as page for Portal at, 832;
Zhou Enlai sends greetings to Queen
Elizabeth, 1073
David Lloyd George memorial proposal,
1964, 1965–8
death of George VI, 254, 259, 262–5
dines with CSC, 1964
Eden steps down as PM, 2151 n.2
Family name for children and descendants,
274, 274 n.2, 281, 377
Ghana visit security, 2315–16, 2316–17, 2318
Nigeria visit, 2078, 2079, 2080, 2081
position for Duke of Edinburgh at opening of
Parliament, 672–3, 673 n.1
postponement of Royal Visit to Australia and
New Zealand, 269
proper description of Prince Charles in
Church of England and Church of
Scotland Prayers, 293, 294
Queen's Plates for racing in Ireland, 1216–17,
1217, 1221–2, 1229, 1230–1
race horses, 2138
returns to England from Kenya, 256
Salisbury appointed Secretary of State for
Commonwealth Relations, 334
sends well wishes to CSC, 1973

Elizabeth II, Queen *(continued)*
  Trooping the Colour, 489
  and WSC: completion of *The Second World War*, 923, 926–7, 1172–3; excuses WSC from attending Cenotaph Ceremony, 2192; offers Dukedom to WSC, 1981, 1982; Order of the Garter, 972–3, 973 n.1, 2409–10; Queen Elizabeth II's Coronation Medal, 2408; sends well wishes to WSC after his stroke, 1138, 1138 n.2; WSC congratulates on first decade of Reign, 2322–3; WSC considers stepping down as PM, 1181; WSC falls and fractures femur (1962), 2329; WSC invites Eisenhower to England (1953), 1181–2, 1187; WSC's death, 2371–2, 2380; WSC's eightieth birthday, 1845–6; WSC's ninetieth birthday, 2363; WSC steps down as PM (1955), 1973, 1978, 1978–80, 1980, 1981, 1983; WSC thanks Her Majesty for concern about his health, 2206, 2206 n.2; WSC visits Balmoral, 611, 1200–1, 1201 n.1; WSC voices faith in, 267
Elizabeth, Queen Mother, 254, 254 n.2, 259, 262, 264, 410, 588
Elliot, William
  biographical information, 209 n.2
  admission of British officers to US National War College, 225–6
  Atlantic Command proposals, 213
  Korea, 472–3, 605, 627–8
  NATO, 271–2
  US bomber attack on Soviet U-boat bases, 540
  WSC speaks to US Congress, 209
  WSC visits US (1953), 802
Ely, Paul Henri Romauld, 1666, 1666 n.1
Embry, Basil Edward, 865, 865 n.1
Emmet, Evelyn Violet Elizabeth Rodd, 1580, 1580 n.3
Empson, Charles, 1625, 1625 n.1
English politics
  Cabinet appointments, 735, 736, 1188
  Cabinet Ministers speaking in by-elections, 680
  Conservative Party disapproval for proportional representation, 1863, 1863 n.2
  Daily Mirror campaign against WSC, 1405
  electoral reform proposals, 833–4
  General Election (1955): Bedford Election Address (May 1955), 1999–2003; Conservative Party victory, 2009, 2009 n.2, 2010, 2058–9; constituency boundaries, 2007–8; timing, 1985–6, 1986, 1987, 2010, 2012; Walthamstow and Chigwell Election Address (May 1955), 2004–7; Woodford Election Addresses (May 1955), 1994–8, 2007–8; WSC discusses with Baruch, 2009; WSC praises Eden, 1994, 1999
  General Election (1959), 2257, 2263, 2265, 2265 n.1, 2265 n.2
  General Election timing and 'snap' Elections, 1775
  Government member participation in London municipal election speeches, 350
  House of Lords reform proposals, 834
  Quinquennial Act, 1270
  Torrington by-election, 2211
  Welsh affairs debate planning, 73
  WSC recalls success of National Coalition Government, 1306
  WSC seeks Welsh Under-Secretary assistant for Fyfe, 10
  WSC writes letter of political support for Cooke, 1872–3
Erasmus, François Christiaan, 1761, 1761 n.1, 1773–4
Erhard, Ludwig Wilhelm, 2367, 2367 n.2, 2367 n.3, 2380
Erskine, George Watkin Eben James ('Bobby'), 153, 153 n.1, 233, 1350–1, 1870
Eschkol, Levi, 2368–9, 2368 n.3
Europe
  Atlantic Command designations, 617, 617 n.2
  Austria, 746–7, 1499, 1544–5, 1545, 1545 n.1
  Belgium, 1159
  Benelux, 162–3, 189, 581
  Brind's Command of Allied Forces in Northern Europe, 701
  British role in future of European movement, 348–9, 349 n.1
  Central and Eastern European Commission, 128
  C-in-C, Allied Forces, Northern Europe, 701
  Commonwealth PMs meeting (1953): Soviet foreign policy and Western Europe discussion, 1061–9, 1095, 1096–7
  Czechoslovakia, 745–6
  defence of Western Europe, 245, 246, 287–8, 306, 1933–4
  Eastern European Conference, 134–6, 136 n.1, 152–3, 154, 155, 155 n.4
  European Economic Community, 2309–10, 2332, 2332–3, 2332 n.1, 2340, 2340 n.1
  Four Power Conference proposals (1953), 1344–5
  German armaments industry controls (contractual negotiations and security safeguards), 318–20
  Gibraltar, 1571, 1571 n.2, 1572
  Grand Alliance of European Powers (May 1956 WSC speech), 2113–15
  Holland, 837, 1159

INDEX 2445

New York Times article on WSC's US visit (1953), 809–10
Nine Power Conference (1954), 1789, 1790–1, 1791, 1799
Ridgway relieved of SHAPE duties, 1184
structure of defence command, 865
US–UK policy towards, 162–3, 883–4
see also Council of Europe; European Defence Community (EDC); France; Germany; Turkey; United Europe; Western Union (European Army); Yugoslavia
European Defence Community (EDC)
  Adenauer's policies, 1152–3, 1361
  alternatives to, 1742–3
  British support for, 1120, 1121, 1121 n.2, 1122, 1156–7, 1160, 1166, 1244–5, 1278–9, 1281, 1372–3, 1734
  Foreign Affairs (May 1953 WSC speech), 1004–6, 1117
  French refusal to ratify, 1745–9, 1750, 1755, 1759–60, 1765–6, 1767–8, 1770, 1770–3, 1772–3, 1774–5, 1775–6, 1775 n.1, 1776–7, 1778, 1953–4
  French support for, 1162–4, 1166, 1168, 1329, 1332, 1335–7, 1344, 1345–6, 1361–2, 1377, 1448, 1456, 1629–30, 1691–4, 1697–9, 1710, 1722, 1732–3, 1736, 1740–1, 1741–2, 1744, 1744–5, 1745
  joint military planning with German authorities, 857–8
  Pleven Plan, 133, 140
  Soviet attitudes towards Europe, 1447–8
  treaty ratification (1952), 746
  treaty ratification, 746, 837, 925, 1744–5
  US support for, 800, 1158–9, 1163–4, 1325, 1367, 1367 n.1, 1368, 1371, 1593, 1594
  Western policies towards Germany, 1151–2, 1636, 1644, 1677, 1813
  WSC discusses with Acheson, 803
  WSC stresses importance of, 1117, 1122, 1160
  see also Foreign Ministers Washington Conference (1953)
Evans, Horace, 1036–7, 1036 n.2, 1479–81, 2171, 2172
Evans, Lincoln, 532, 532 n.1
Evans, Stanley Norman, 1455, 1455 n.1
Evatt, Herbert Vere, 650–1, 650 n.1
Everest, Elizabeth Anne ('Woom'), 1221–2, 1221 n.4
Ewbank, Robert Withers, 299, 299 n.1

Fadden, Arthur William, 211, 211 n.3
Faisal I, King of Syria (Faisal bin Abdulaziz Al Saud), 884, 884 n.3
Faisal II, King of Iraq (Al-Malik Faysal Aththani), 2231, 2231 n.1

Falkenburg, Bob, 1330, 1330 n.4
Falkenburg, Eugenia Lincoln ('Jinx'), 1330–1, 1330 n.3
Falkenhorst, Nikolaus von, 139 n.4, 631
Falkland Islands, 299
Far East
  British policy towards, 750
  Dodds-Parker notes anti-US sentiment in, 1791
  exclusion of UK from Pacific Tripartite Treaty, 650–1
  Hong Kong, 840, 867
  Pacific Treaty proposal, 804
  Siam, 1071, 1076
  US–UK policy towards, 184–5
  US–UK Washington discussions planning, 40
  see also China; Japan; Korea
Farouk (King of Egypt)
  biographical information, 182 n.1
  abdication of, 566, 566 n.2, 594, 1001
  British military intervention in Canal Zone, 237–8
  Egyptian General Election (1952), 364–5
  Sudan, 270–1
  US–UK policy towards Egypt, 182, 199
  see also Egypt
Faure, Edgar, 1963–4, 1963 n.1
Fay, Gerard, 2091, 2091 n.2
Fechteler, William Morrow, 165–6, 165 n.2, 179, 213, 226, 540
Fellowes, Marguérite Sévérine Philippine ('Daisy'), 2075–6, 2075 n.3, 2218
Felton, Monica, 978, 978 n.1
Ferdinand, Archduke (Franz Ferdinand Carl Ludwig Joseph Maria), 1360, 1360 n.1
Finnish tanker SS *Wiima*, 962, 962 n.3, 964, 970–1, 973, 975–6, 979–81, 980
Fisher, Geoffrey Francis (Archbishop of Canterbury), 283, 283 n.1, 682, 688–9
Fitzalan-Howard, Bernard Marmaduke (Earl Marshal), 682, 682 n.1, 687–8, 688–9, 690–1, 691–2, 737, 766
Fitzalan-Howard, Miles Francis Stapleton (Duke of Norfolk), 1979, 1979 n.3
Fitzclarence, Geoffrey William Richard Hugh (Earl Munster), 1804, 1804 n.1
Five Power (Geneva) Conference (1954)
  Eden reluctant to leave for Washington meeting with WSC, Dulles and Eisenhower, 1592–3
  Eden reports on to Cabinet, 1597
  Indo-China war: cease-fire proposals, 1573–6; Molotov proposes plenary and restricted sessions on, 1604; UK declines to provide immediate assistance to French at Dien Bien Phu, 1560, 1570–1, 1606
  proposals (1954), 1401–2, 1403, 1403–4, 1427, 1433–4, 1452

Fleischmann, Manly, 187–8, 187 n.1
Fleming, Celia Elizabeth Johnson, 1913, 1913 n.4
Fleming, Robert Peter ('Strix'), 1913, 1913 n.4
Flower, Desmond John Newman, 1566, 1566 n.1, 2161, 2183, 2183–4, 2184
Flower, Walter Newman, 1566, 1566 n.2
Fogg-Elliot, Oliver, 2054, 2054 n.1
food
  agriculture policies, 1274–5
  bananas, 508
  British imports of Canadian cheese, 381, 389
  British wheat stocks (1952), 337
  Conservative Conference agriculture debate, 1241
  costs: farm economy and cost of home-raised food, 1385, 1387, 1388–9, 1394–5; food budget discussions, 430; price increases for bacon, butter, margarine, sugar and cheese (1952), 636–7; Retail Prices Index, 1763–4
  Food Stocks Index, 364, 388–9, 396, 417
  meat: Argentine meat exports to Britain, 651; British meat ration and supply projections (1951–1952), 27, 48–9; British population and meat consumption rates, 423, 427–8; marketing of home-produced meat and bacon after end of meat rationing, 1258–62, 1261–2, 1265–7; meat consumption (1953), 1240–1, 1241; pork production levels, 357; weekly meat ration levels, 729
  Milk Marketing Board resumes operations (1954), 1265–7, 1266 n.1
  potato acreage projections (1952), 357–8
  pre- and post-war staple foods consumption rates, 1741
  rationing: bread subsidy, 482–3, 483 n.1; butter and margarine rations, 535, 1056, 1056 n.1, 1564; Christmas bonus reductions (1951), 66, 74–5; end of food rationing (1954), 1583–4; fruit and sugar supplies, 483; post-war rationing (1951), 147; sugar ration, 1108; unrationed food import reductions, 3, 4
Foot, Michael Mackintosh, 595, 595 n.1, 1522, 2189
Forbes, Donald Logan, 2143, 2143 n.2
Ford, Edward William Spencer, 2086–7, 2086 n.2
Ford, Virginia Brand, 2086–7, 2086 n.2
foreign affairs
  Anglo-American Conversations (January 1952), 239–47
  ANZUS and ANZAM, 775–7
  Council of Europe proceedings debate (proposed), 439–40
  Foreign Ministers London conference (1953), 1235, 1235 n.1, 1257
  HofC: China, Coastal Islands (Written Answers), 1922–3; Debate on the Address (December 1954), 1829–43; Foreign Affairs debate, 302; Foreign Affairs Debate planning, 24, 27; German Army Surrender Document (Oral Answers), 1610–11; Israel Loan Request (Oral Answers), 456–7; World Peace, President Eisenhower's Declaration (Oral Answers), 959–61, 963
  Three Power meeting (proposed), 1033
  WSC promotes 'fraternal association' of English-speaking world, 83, 148
  WSC reflects on gulf between Russia and the West, 215–16
  WSC speeches: Canadian Government banquet (January 1952), 203–7; Vote of Censure (February 1952), 283–92, 283 n.3; NATO (October 1952), 669–71; Debate on the Address (November 1952), 702; Lord Mayor's Banquet (November 1952), 722–6; Foreign Affairs (May 1953), 998–1010, 1012, 1117, 1182–3, 1236–7, 1245, 1276; Conservative Party Conference (October 1953), 1243–6; Debate on the Address (November 1953), 1275–6; Foreign Affairs (November 1953), 1284–8; Foreign Affairs (December 1953), 1359–65; The Berlin Conference (February 1954), 1449–57; Basutoland, Bechuanaland and Swaziland (April 1954), 1538; The Geneva Conference (April 1954), 1552–3; Her Majesty's Return From Her Commonwealth Tour (May 1954), 1568–9; South East Asia Defence (May 1954), 1570–1; Canada broadcast (June 1954), 1638–40; A Review of Foreign Affairs (July 1954), 1686–95; Lord Mayor's Banquet (November 1954), 1811–14; The Unity of the Free Nations (November 1954), 1818–19, 1829–30, 1833, 1837–8, 1841–2; Motion of Censure (March 1955), 1949–58; Grand Alliance of European Powers (May 1956), 2112–15; One Nation (July 1957), 2173–6; Europe–Unite! (July 1957), 2177; Liberty and the Law (July 1957), 2180–2
  see also Big Four (Geneva) Summit (1955); Canal Zone; Cold War; Egypt; Five Power (Geneva) Conference (1954); Foreign Ministers Washington

INDEX 2447

Conference (1953); Four Power (Berlin) Conference (1954); France; Germany; Indo-China war; Korea; Russia; Three Power (Bermuda) Conference (1953)
Foreign Ministers Washington conference (1953)
  European Defence Community, 1162–4, 1166, 1168
  European uncertainties, 1153–4
  Four Power Conference proposals (1953), 1162–4, 1166, 1166–7, 1168, 1169, 1171, 1173–4
  Germany: Adenauer's policies and proposals, 1152–3, 1165, 1165 n.1, 1167; reunification of, 1162–3; Soviet policy towards, 1150–1, 1166
  purpose, 1148–9
  Russia: Anglo-American differences in policy towards, 1149–50; Soviet policies towards Germany, 1150–1; Western policy towards, 1149, 1162, 1166
  Salisbury reports on to Foreign Office, 1162–4
Foreign Office
  Germany, 1165, 1165 n.1
  germ warfare propaganda report, 678
  Korea: British policy towards, 294; COS Committee meeting minutes on armistice talks, 85–8; return of POWs to Communist China, 461, 465, 484–5, 486, 527–8
  length of Foreign Office telegrams, 535–6
  Middle East: Anglo-Iranian Oil Company, 620, 622; Egypt, 36, 36 n.2, 63–4, 698, 698 n.1, 904; Iraqi proposal for Gaza Strip, 63–4; Israel, 731, 731–2, 971; redeployment of British troops in, 1211–12, 1211 n.3
  Russia: Big Three meeting (proposed), 1031; Diplomatic Immunities Bill, 772; employment of British and Soviet citizens in their respective Embassies in Moscow and London, 538–9, 612; Western policy towards, 1180–1, 1183–5, 1185–6, 1186–7, 1188, 1199, 1235–6
  Sudan, 1011
  Three Power (Bermuda) Conference planning, 1033–4
  Western Union (European Army), 83–4
  see also foreign affairs
Foreign Secretary: *see* Eden, (Robert) Anthony
Forestier, Jacques, 1586, 1586 n.1
Formosa
  'Oracle' and Formosa, 1881–2, 1882–3, 1888–91, 1893–6
  A Review of Foreign Affairs (July 1954 WSC speech), 1687–8
  treaty with Japan, 198, 216
  US protection of, 1898, 1904, 1904 n.1

US–UK policy towards, 291, 1878–9
see also China
Forster, Edward Morgan, 411, 411 n.1
Foster, Arnold Carey, 2048, 2048 n.3
Fothergill, Philip Charles, 2004, 2004 n.2
4th Hussars Light Brigade Dinner (1954), 1589, 1590, 1597
Four Power (Berlin) Conference (1954)
  Austrian independence discussions, 1453
  The Berlin Conference (February 1954 WSC speech), 1449–57
  conclusion of, 1443, 1443 n.1
  European Defence Community, 1447, 1448–9
  Five Power (Geneva) Conference proposals, 1401–2, 1433–4
  German rearmament, 1454–6
  Molotov's role as elder statesman of Kremlin, 1421–2
  Molotov's speech at, 1404
  opening meetings at, 1397, 1398
  planning, 1388, 1388 n.1
  WSC proposes to deal with all Egypt matters in HofC while Eden attends, 1396
  WSC recalls during HofC debate, 1950–1
  WSC updates Eden on Cabinet affairs during, 1696
France
  Algeria, 2114, 2114 n.2, 2170, 2196, 2205, 2216, 2250, 2295, 2335 n.3
  British relations with, 1288
  defence: European Defence Community, 837, 933, 1677; French Army manpower estimates, 117; National Service periods, 581; Naval Command agreements with US and France, 740–1; St Cyr Special Military School, 1025, 1025 n.1, 1038; US disarmament proposals, 5–6; WSC requests assessment of French military system (1953), 1025–6, 1038–9
  Eisenhower's opinion of the French, 1628, 1630
  Europe: European Economic Community, 2340, 2340 n.1; Grand Alliance of European Powers (May 1956 WSC speech), 2114; Western Union (European Army), 82, 83–4, 108–9, 119–20, 140
  Five Power (Geneva) Conference proposals, 1342
  Foreign Affairs (May 1953 WSC speech), 1004–6
  Germany: relations with, 164; unification proposals, 352; WSC encourages French/German reconciliation, 81, 82, 149, 725, 1288
  Russia, 975, 1320
  Saarland, 1857, 1857 n.1

France *(continued)*
  Suez Canal closure and Gulf of Aqaba blockade (1956), 2134–5, 2141, 2145–6, 2146–7
  Three Power (Bermuda) Conference (1953): planning, 1032–3, 1033, 1033–4, 1035–6, 1037–8, 1042, 1043–4, 1047, 1052, 1053, 1062–4, 1065, 1066, 1081–2, 1083, 1092, 1110, 1110–11, 1114–15, 1279; postponement, 1118, 1119–20, 1122, 1122–3
  see also European Defence Community (EDC); Foreign Ministers Washington conference (1953); Indo-China war; Western Union (European Army)
Franckenstein, Georg Freiherr von und zu, 1453, 1453 n.1
Franks, Oliver Sherwell
  biographical information, 194 n.1
  admission of British officers to US National War College, 225–6
  Atlantic Command proposals, 212–13
  Korea, 318
  NATO, 322, 331, 334 n.1
  Persia, 602, 618, 658–9
  WSC addresses British staff in Washington, 194
Fraser, Richard Michael, 509, 509 n.1, 1050–2
Fraser, William Jocelyn Ian, 240, 240 n.1, 367, 408, 682–4
Frederica of Hanover, 1497–9, 1497 n.1, 1512, 1531
French, Charles S., 2173, 2173 n.2
Fuchs, Emil Julius Klaus, 176, 176 n.1, 358
fuel and energy
  calculation of electricity charges, 44, 48
  coal imports, 2–3, 27
  coal industry, 1242
  coal production, 141
  see also Persia
Fyfe, David Patrick Maxwell
  biographical information, 10 n.1
  defence: air-raid warning system, 253; atom bomb, 479–80, 482, 1592, 1592 n.1; British refusal to participate in Western Union (European Army), 83; civil defence planning, 407, 435–8, 546–7; Coventry civil defence demonstration, 1695, 1695 n.1; Director-General of Civil Defence Operations position (proposed), 493; Home Guard future planning, 1264–5; Statement on Defence (1954), 1428–9
  domestic affairs: Accession Proclamation, 254–5; amnesty for British Armed Forces deserters (proposed), 783–4; broadcasting White Paper, 427; Coronation Oath, 851; corporal punishment, 686, 733–4; Criminal Statistics for England and Wales (1951), 589–91, 591, 591 n.1; employment of coloured people in public service sector, 1423–4; Leeds Police tribunal inquiry (proposed), 1483–4; non-admission of foreigners to events in England organised by Soviet propaganda groups, 344–5, 345; prison warden reductions, 444, 445, 445 n.1, 445 n.2; prostitution and homosexuality laws, 1482–3, 1542–3; Straffen's life sentence and potential release, 637, 645; WSC asks about deliberate spreading of myxomatosis, 1652
  WSC appoints Llewellyn as Under-Secretary assistant for, 10, 25–6
  WSC praises, 409

Gafencu, Grigore, 134, 134 n.3
Gairdner, Charles Henry, 1480, 1480 n.1
Gaitskell, Hugh Todd Naylor
  biographical information, 406 n.2
  Defence (March 1953 WSC speech), 874
  The Economic Position (July 1952 WSC speech), 571, 572, 582
  Exchange Control policies, 406
  The Government's Record (April 1953 WSC speech), 955
  labour representation for technological college Trustees, 2215
  One Nation (July 1957 WSC speech), 2174
  Pound Sterling controls, 2230
  WSC's eighty-fifth birthday (Oral Answers), 2277
Galeazzi-Lisi, Riccardo, 224 n.3, 2224, 2224 n.1
Gann, Jessica Mary Hodge, 2308–9, 2308 n.2
Garbett, Cyril Forster (Archbishop of York), 474, 474 n.2
Garner, Joseph John Saville, 536, 536 n.3
Garner, Robert L., 93–4, 93 n.2
Garofalides, Artemis Onassis, 2324, 2324 n.2, 2325
Garofalides, Theodore, 2324, 2324 n.2
Gascoyne-Cecil, Eleanor Lambton (Lady Cecil), 2228, 2228 n.1
Gascoyne-Cecil, Hugh, ('Linky'): *see* Quickswood, Lord (Hugh Gascoyne-Cecil, 'Linky')
Gascoyne-Cecil, Robert Arthur James: *see* Salisbury, Lord (Robert Gascoyne-Cecil, 'Bobbety')
Gascoyne-Cecil, Robert Arthur Talbot, 1286, 1286 n.1

Index

Gaulle, Charles de
 biographical information, 785 n.1
 Eden meets with, 2303
 publication of war-time messages from WSC to FDR, 2211
 sends Christmas greetings to WSC, 785, 789
 WSC meets with, 2294–5
 WSC praises, 2231–2, 2234
 WSC receives Croix de la Libération, 2226, 2410–11
 WSC's death, 2367, 2367 n.1
 WSC thanks for letter and copy of *Le Salut*, 2275
Gaulle, Yvonne Charlotte Anne Marie Vendroux de, 789, 789 n.3
Gault, James Frederick, 461, 461 n.1
Geoffrey-Lloyd, Geoffrey William, 17–19, 17 n.1, 44
George III, King, 919, 919 n.6
George IV, King, 919, 919 n.5
George V, King, 262–3, 262 n.2, 918
George VI, King
 biographical information, 142 n.2
 British Armed Forces service estimates (1952–1953), 142
 Cabinet reviews draft of King's Speech on the Opening of Parliament, 10–11, 15–16
 death of, 254–5, 254 n.1, 261–5, 267
 King George VI (February 1952 WSC speech), 257–9
 South Africa visit planning, 61–2
 WSC praises in Ottawa speech, 206
 WSC serves as Lord Warden of the Cinque Ports, 2041
Germany
 Berlin: Berlin airlift, 95; Russian MiG shoots down British bomber in Hamburg–Berlin air corridor (1953), 908, 908 n.3, 910, 912–13; Soviet interruption of free circulation within, 1115, 1116, 1116 n.1, 1124, 1126–7, 1127, 1128–9, 1129–30
 British Overseas Information Services work in, 85
 British policy towards, 251–2
 British relations with, 745, 1288
 defence: Beaverbrook's opposition to German Army, 1220; cost of British forces stationed in, 425–6; German participation in defence of Western Europe, 81, 84, 1692–3; joint military planning with German authorities, 857–8; Western Defence contribution and security controls, 40, 41–3
 educational expenditures in, 251–2
 elections in, 1110, 1114, 1118, 1126–7, 1165, 1167, 1193–4, 1389–90, 1451–2
 foreign affairs: Adenauer meets with Eisenhower, 936, 945; French/German reconciliation, 81, 82, 149, 725, 1288; Paris discussions with Chancellor Adenauer, 64–5; response to French refusal to ratify EDC, 1774–5, 1775 n.1; Soviet claims about Potsdam Conference conclusions, 464, 467–8
 fox hunting in, 412–13, 413 n.3
 German Army Surrender Document (Oral Answers), 1610–11
 partition of, 949
 publication of letters from von Ribbentropp, 1723–4, 1724 n.1
 rearmament of, 41–3, 50, 318–20, 326, 1455, 1629–30, 1733, 1733 n.1, 1736, 1741–2, 1742–3, 1744, 1747, 1818–19, 1830–5, 1831–3, 1837–8, 1838
 reunification of, 352, 352 n.3, 1126–7, 1128–9, 1129–30, 1141, 1143–6, 1156–7, 1163, 1165, 1165 n.1, 1330, 2114–15, 2240
 Saar Government, 359, 745, 1960–1
 Saarland, 1857, 1857 n.1
 war criminals: arrest of Naumann, 858–9; Eden discusses release of German Military Commanders with WSC, 502–3, 629; Eden recommends release of Mackensen, 631; release of Kesselring, 630–1; release of, 630–1; release and sentencing proposals, 138–9, 502–3, 629–30; sentencing proposals, 139, 629; sick leave release for von Manstein, 631; WSC proposes release of German Generals from prison, 85
 WSC disagrees with anti-German propaganda, 1798
 WSC's death, 2367, 2367 n.3, 2370, 2370 n.2
 WSC speeches: Defence, German Rearmament (March 1954), 1460–7; Foreign Affairs (May 1953), 1003; Grand Alliance of European Powers (May 1956), 2112–15
 WSC visits (1956), 2115
 see also European Defence Community (EDC); Foreign Ministers Washington conference (1953); NATO (North Atlantic Treaty Organisation); Western Union (European Army)
Geyer, Albertus Lourens, 61–2, 61 n.3
Gheorghiu-Dej, Gheorghe, 2132, 2132 n.2
Gibraltar, 1571, 1571 n.2, 1572
Gifford, Walter Sherman, 119, 119 n.1, 301, 320–1, 322–4, 626, 631, 802
Gilbert, Bernard William, 939–42, 940 n.1

Gilliatt, Elizabeth, 55, 55 n.2, 66–7, 67, 1648, 2028
Giraudier, Antonio, 1641, 1641 n.1, 2245
Gladstone, William Ewart, 473, 694, 919, 919 n.3
Gloucester, Duke of (Henry William Frederick Albert), 918, 918 n.1
Glubb, John Bagot ('Glubb Pasha'), 1087, 1087 n.1
Goethe, Johann Wolfgang von, 1286, 1286 n.3
Goettling, Willy, 1115, 1115 n.4
Gog and Magog, 32–3, 32 n.1, 1285
Gopalan, Kunnathu Puthiyaveettil Rayarothu, 1079–80, 1079 n.1
Gordon-Lennox, Nicholas Charles, 2246, 2246 n.1
Gore-Booth, Paul Henry, 1082, 1082 n.2
Gorton, Neville Vincent (Bishop of Coventry), 1873–4, 1873 n.1, 1876–7, 1879–80, 1909–10, 1910–11
Goschen, John Alexander, 1117, 1117 n.3
Gosford, Lady (Mildred Carter Acheson), 2032, 2032 n.1
Gothic, SS, 110–11
Gould, Ronald, 1459–60, 1460 n.1
Gowers, Ernest Arthur, 1562–3, 1562 n.1
Graham, William Franklin, Jr, 1579–80, 1579 n.3, 1579 n.4
Greece
  Anglo-Greek relations, 1498–9
  Eden recalls British war-time campaigns in, 2196
  Foreign Affairs (May 1953 WSC speech), 1006
  Greek memorial to UK soldiers, 248, 345–6
  NATO command structure, 40
  NATO membership (1952), 725
  Truman doctrine, 68
Green, John Raeburn, 2043–4, 2043 n.2
Grenfell, David Rhys, 1827, 1827 n.2
Grey, Paul Francis, 934–5, 935 n.1
Griffiths, Gerald Selby Lewis, 1350–1, 1350 n.1
Griffiths, James, 755, 755 n.2, 2065
Gromyko, Andrei Andreyevich, 950–1, 950 n.2, 962
Gruenther, Alfred Maximilian
  biographical information, 774 n.1
  European Defence Community, 1692, 1734, 1784
  location and strength of Soviet forces (1954), 1408, 1426, 1441–2, 1465, 1466, 1469, 1471–2, 1485, 1490
  reinforcements for SHAPE, 1538–9
  WSC praises, 1599–600
Guest, Amy Phipps, 2338, 2338 n.3
Guest, Frederick Edward, 2338, 2338 n.1
Guest, Ivor Churchill, 2338, 2338 n.2

Gunter, Raymond Jones, 2383, 2383 n.4
Guppy, Ronald James, 1652, 1652 n.1
Gustaf VI Adolf (King of Sweden), 1253, 1253 n.1

Hägglöf, Bo Gunnar Rickardsson, 1247–8, 1247 n.4
Haig, Douglas, 2116, 2116 n.2
Hailes, Lady (Diana Mary Lambton), 2300, 2300 n.2, 2302
Hailes, Lord: *see* Buchan-Hepburn, Patrick George Thomas
Hailsham, Lord (Quintin Hogg), 2163, 2163 n.1, 2321
Hailstone, Bernard, 2041, 2041 n.1
Halban, Hans Heinrich von, 2031, 2031 n.1
Haldane, Richard Burdon, 2116–17, 2116 n.1
Hale, Charles Leslie, 699, 699 n.2, 713
Haley, William John, 1500, 1500 n.1
Halifax, Lord (Edward Frederick Lindley Wood), 345–6, 345 n.2, 669, 1875
Halle, Katherine Murphy, 180, 180 n.1, 207
Hall, Joyce Clyde, 2194, 2194 n.1, 2195, 2207
Hall-Patch, Edmund Leo, 802, 802 n.4
Hallstein, Walter, 2365, 2365 n.1
Hallstrom, Edward John Lees, 2356, 2356 n.1
Hall, William Glenvil, 84, 84 n.1, 131
Hall, William Webster, 864, 864 n.1
Hamblin, Grace Ellen, 816, 816 n.2, 1586, 1727, 1827, 1938, 1977, 1988
Hamilton, James Hamish, 2385, 2385 n.1
Hamilton, John Robert Crosse, 2283, 2283 n.1, 2283 n.2, 2307, 2311
Hampden, John, 1364, 1364 n.1
Hankey, Maurice Pascal Alers, 1502–3, 1502 n.1, 2108
Hanna, W. N., 1545, 1545 n.2
Harcourt, Robert John Rolston, 2071–2, 2071 n.1
Harding, Allan Francis John
  biographical information, 822 n.1
  Anglo-Jordan Joint Defence Board, 1507–9
  Canal Zone Base, 1485, 1486, 1486–7, 1487, 1502–3
  COS memorandums on likelihood of war with Soviet Union through 1955, 816–22, 1223–7
  WSC's funeral, 2383–4
Hardy-Roberts, Geoffrey, 2333, 2333 n.2
Harmar-Nicholls, Harmar, 1804, 1804 n.7
Harmsworth, Esmond Cecil (Lord Rothermere), 1190, 1190 n.1, 1215, 1989, 1992–3
Harriman, William Averell
  biographical information, 141 n.1
  admission of British officers to US National War College, 225–6

Index

attends Eisenhower's dinner party for WSC (1953), 802
defence: NATO reform proposals, 171; TCC report, 172, 232, 232 n.1; UK aircraft for US NATO use, 331; UK production programme, 190
meets with WSC in Paris (1951), 141–2
US–UK policy towards Russia, 164
Harrison, Eric John, 2356, 2356 n.2
Harrison, William Kelly, Jr, 527–8, 527 n.2, 1076, 1099
Harrod, Henry Roy Forbes, 359–61, 359 n.1
Harrow School speeches (WSC)
December 1951, 112–13
November 1952, 719–20, 719 n.1, 721
November 1953, 1310–11, 1310 n.1, 1814–15
November 1955, 2060
October 1957, 2190
November 1958, 2227
October 1959, 2272
November 1960, 2295
Hartley, Vivien Mary (Vivien Leigh), 2179, 2179 n.1
Harvey, Arthur Vere, 351–2, 351 n.1
Harvey, Ian Douglas, 1804, 1804 n.4
Harvey, Oliver Charles, 191, 191 n.5, 383–4, 1122–3, 1127
Hassan bin Talal, Prince of Jordan, 2295, 2295 n.1
Havenga, Nicolaas Christiaan, 745, 751, 751 n.1
Hayter, Iris Marie Grey, 2358–9, 2358 n.2
Hayter, William Goodenough, 1291, 1291 n.1, 2358–9
Head, Antony Henry
biographical information, 10 n.2
at Chequers, 444
defence: Adoption of a New Army Rifle (February 1954 WSC speech), 1415, 1416; Army estimates (1951–1952), 126–8; Army manpower estimates, 587, 766–7; British troop quarters in Libya, 343; Burmese Government Defence Agreement, 1204–5; Home Guard, 10, 1264–5; Loss of Rifles file, 46; National Service periods, 565, 566; NCOs and substantive rank, 303–4, 327, 346; Royal Navy manpower estimates, 766; tank production programme, 152, 153
domestic affairs: Civil Service staff reductions, 90; Coronation uniforms, 488; dispersal of funds of disbanded Militia battalions, 780, 780 n.2, 788, 1419–20, 1420 n.1; Dunkirk memorial, 266; tax-free educational allowances for Armed Forces officers, 603–4
Indo-China war, 984–5

Kenya, 1349–50, 1350–1
see also Egypt
Head, Dorothea Ashley-Cooper, 444, 444 n.2
Heald, Lionel Frederick, 365–7, 365 n.1
health (WSC)
alcohol prescription, 2407, 2407 n.1
circulatory health and travel plans, 777, 788
colds, 231, 233, 267, 1727
CSC worries about Press reports regarding, 2202, 2203
deafness, 594, 1113, 1219, 2077, 2117, 2129, 2131, 2136, 2153, 2154, 2155, 2179, 2324, 2341
decline of, 1536, 1779, 2117, 2147, 2186–7, 2192, 2245, 2246, 2280, 2301, 2308, 2335–6, 2340–1, 2341, 2349, 2349, 2349–50, 2349–50, 2350, 2351, 2354–5, 2355, 2357, 2358, 2358–9, 2360–1, 2361 n.1, 2362
fall and fractured femur (1962), 2328, 2329, 2329, 2330, 2331, 2331, 2331–2, 2333–4, 2334, 2334–5
fall and fractured spine (1960), 2296, 2296, 2297
Juler examines and treats WSC's eyes, 788
medications, 1280, 1965, 1965 n.1, 1972, 1976, 1977, 2154, 2155, 2157, 2247, 2325
Moran wishes to accompany WSC on Sicily trip, 1965, 1971–2, 1974, 1976
Nicolson notes unhealthy appearance of, 302
pneumonia, 2206, 2206 n.2, 2207, 2208, 2209, 2209–10, 2211, 2212, 2213, 2214
Shuckburgh notes WSC's bad cold, 411
stroke (1953): Bedell Smith sends well wishes, 1167 n.2; daughter Mary reacts to, 1138; daughter Sarah sends well wishes, 1160–1, 1161 n.1; Eden sends well wishes, 1161; Eisenhower sends well wishes, 1158, 1170–1; Marshall sends well wishes, 1143, 1160; Queen Elizabeth sends well wishes, 1138, 1138 n.2; recovery from, 1138, 1138 n.2, 1146–8, 1168–9, 1169–70, 1174, 1177, 1184, 1189, 1200–1, 1201, 1201 n.1, 1212–13, 1213, 1215–16, 1217–18, 1218, 1219, 1220, 1221, 1235, 1255, 1255 n.2; suffered during dinner for de Gasperi, 1125, 1130, 1137, 1137 n.1, 1138, 1147, 1200–1, 1201, 1201 n.1; WSC describes to Eisenhower, 1140
stroke (1956), 2142, 2142–3
weight, 1588, 1598
Heath, Edward Richard George ('Ted'), 2095, 2095 n.1, 2199, 2289
Heaton, Wallace Evans, 2339, 2339 n.3
Helm, Alexander Knox, 1382, 1382 n.1

2452 INDEX

Helmore, James Reginald Carroll, 940, 940 n.5
Henderson, Arthur, Jr, 314, 314 n.1, 472, 1099, 1690
Henderson, Arthur, Sr, 314, 314 n.2
Henderson, John Scott, 481, 481 n.2
Henderson, Loy Wesley, 608–9, 608 n.1, 620, 836–7, 878–9
Henley, Sylvia Laura Stanley, 2082, 2082 n.2
Henriques, Robert David Quixano, 1388–9, 1388 n.3
Henry of Winchester (King Henry III of England), 2014–15, 2014 n.3
Hertzog, James Barry Munnik, 1538, 1538 n.1
Hess, Rudolf, 1611, 1611 n.2
Heusch, Maria Julius August Aloys Aegidius Hermann, 1880, 1880 n.1
Heuss, Theodor, 1844, 1844 n.1
Hickenlooper, Bourke Blakemore, 1632, 1632 n.3
el-Hilaly, Ahmed Naguib, 364, 364 n.1
Hill, Austin Bradford, 442, 442 n.1
Hill, Rose Ethel Kathleen, 1598, 1598 n.2
Hinchingbrooke, Lord (Alexander Victor Edward Paulet Montagu, 'Hinch'), 352, 352 n.2
A History of the English-Speaking Peoples (Churchill)
  Browne assists WSC with, 2088, 2150
  Butler muses that WSC should focus on, 1212
  corrections, 2153, 2153 n.2
  CSC reads draft chapters, 2034, 2036, 2038, 2039
  Deakin assists WSC with, 2009, 2030–1, 2047, 2049, 2081
  Hodge assists WSC with, 1208, 2008, 2008–9, 2014–15, 2030–1, 2044, 2047, 2055, 2055–6, 2056, 2088, 2092, 2093, 2096, 2150
  Kelly assists WSC with, 2044, 2056, 2092
  Mary Soames reads draft chapters, 2038
  Rowse provides comments and review of, 2099
  Stuart comments on Bonnie Prince Charlie section, 2198–9
  Volume 1, WSC sends to friends and acquaintances, 2090, 2104, 2105–6, 2106, 2107, 2108, 2110–11, 2112, 2130
  Volume 2: Portuguese translation of, 2334; WSC sends to Eisenhower, 2150; WSC sends to Morton, 2145; WSC sends to Trevelyan, 2148–9
  Volume 3: Flower sends first bound copy to WSC, 2183; Nixon thanks WSC for copy of, 2193; WSC sends to Eden, 2192
  Volume 4: Nixon thanks WSC for copy of, 2213–14; suggested titles for, 2183–4, 2184; WSC sends to Eden, 2216
  WSC revives work on, 1220, 1312–13, 1849

  WSC works on after stepping down as PM, 1989, 2030–1, 2031, 2032, 2033
  WSC works on at Alpes Maritimes, 2156, 2158
  WSC works on at Cap d'Ail, 2043, 2044, 2047, 2049, 2055, 2055–6, 2056
  WSC works on at Chartwell, 2127
  WSC works on at La Pausa/Cap Martin, 2074, 2075, 2076, 2077, 2080, 2081, 2084, 2088, 2092, 2093, 2096, 2099, 2133, 2136, 2138, 2154
Hitler, Adolf, 33, 444
Hoare-Temple, Jane Montague Brown, 2349, 2349 n.1
Ho Chi Minh (Nguyen Sinh Cung), 1341, 1341 n.1
Hodge, Alan
  biographical information, 1208 n.1
  at Chartwell, 2308–9
  Eden writes memoirs, 2254
  A History of the English-Speaking Peoples, 1208, 2008, 2008–9, 2014–15, 2030–1, 2044, 2047, 2055, 2055–6, 2056, 2088, 2092, 2093, 2096, 2150
Hodge, Jane Aiken, 2137–8, 2137 n.1, 2308–9
Hodge, Joanna Marrack, 2309, 2309 n.1
Hogg, Quintin (Lord Hailsham), 2163, 2163 n.1, 2321
Holland, 837, 1159
Holland, Sidney George
  biographical information, 211 n.2
  ANZUS and ANZAM, 769, 775–7, 799
  Commonwealth Economic Conference (proposed), 560
  Commonwealth Finance Ministers meeting, 211
  Commonwealth PMs meeting (1953): Commonwealth PMs and Cabinet meeting (1952), 745, 750, 751; Far East and South-East Asia discussion, 1075–6; McCarthyism, 1067; Middle East discussion, 1088; Soviet foreign policy and Western Europe discussion, 1066–7, 1068; Three Power meeting (proposed), 1066–7
  Commonwealth PMs meeting (1955), 1885, 1889, 1894
  Eden visits New Zealand, 2152
  Egypt, 1088
  praises Eden, 750
Hollis, Maurice Christopher, 472, 472 n.1
Holmes, Stephen, 1480, 1480 n.2
Holyoake, Keith Jacka, 2380, 2380 n.2
Home Guard, 10, 307
Home Secretary: *see* Fyfe, David Patrick Maxwell
Hong Kong, 840, 867

Index

honours and awards
  Attlee receives Order of Merit, 19
  British honour for Baruch (proposed), 2069–70, 2115–16, 2187
  KCMG honour for Gault, 461
  Order of the Garter for Eden, 1818, 1818 n.1
  WSC: Becoming a Member of the Society of Cincinnati, 209–10; Charlemagne Prize, 1880, 1880, 2112–13; Churchill Room at Westminster College, 864, 2180; The Cinque Ports (September 1955), 2041–2; Croix de la Libération (November 1958), 2226, 2410–11; Freeman of Belfast and Londonderry (December 1955), 2070–2; Grand Sash of the High Order of Sayyid Mohammed bin Ali al Sanusi, 2412; honorary US citizenship (1963), 2342–3, 2343–4, 2344, 2412; Master Member of 1940 Club, 2178; Most Refulgent Order of the Star of Nepal, 2411–12; Nobel Prize for literature, 1247–8, 1253, 1353–4, 2408–9; Order of the Garter, 972–3, 973 n.1, 2409–10; Queen Elizabeth II's Coronation Medal, 2408

Hood, Alexander, 1042, 1042 n.2, 1349
Hope, John Adrian, 386, 386 n.3, 1117
Hopkins, Harry, 2070, 2070 n.2
Hopkinson, Henry Lennox D'Aubigne, 129–31, 129 n.1
Hopwood, Joseph Stanley, 481, 481
Horowitz, David, 401–2, 401 n.1, 430
Horrocks, Brian Gwyne ('Jorrocks'), 2157, 2157 n.3
Horsbrugh, Florence Gertrude, 115, 115 n.1, 116, 500, 500 n.1, 968
Horton, Edith Cook Snyder ('Drucie'), 544, 544 n.4
Hottentots, 2014, 2014 n.1
House of Commons (HofC)
  atom bomb: Atom Bomb Test, Official Report, 458–9; Atom Bomb Test, Press Correspondents (Oral Answers), 392; Atomic Energy (Oral Answers), 367–8; Atomic Energy Tests in Australia (Oral Answers), 282–3; The Hydrogen Bomb (April 1954 WSC speech), 1517–30; The Hydrogen Bomb (March 1954 WSC speech), 1504–6; hydrogen bomb tests (1954), 1501, 1506–7; US consultation with UK prior to use of, 1492–3
  defence: Adoption of a New Army Rifle (February 1954 WSC speech), 1410–19; defence debates (1956), 2083; Defence, German Rearmament (March 1954 WSC speech), 1460–7; Defence (March 1955 WSC speech), 1926–35; Statement on Defence (1954), 1428–9
  domestic affairs: budget debates (1953), 955–7; Cabinet Papers Access (Oral Answers), 1438–40; Coronation Oath, 850–1, 850 n.1; Debate on the Address (November 1952 WSC speech), 701–10; Debate on the Address (November 1953 WSC speech), 1268–77, 1277–8, 1280; Duke of Edinburgh in Peers' Gallery during HofC debates, 299; George VI, King, 254–5, 261–5; Her Majesty's Return From Her Commonwealth Tour (May 1954 WSC speech), 1568–9; High Court Judges' remuneration, 913–15, 916–17; Maltese MPs, 2095, 2095 n.2; Members' Expenses debate, 1579, 1586–7, 1596–7, 1607; Ministerial salaries, 21; Motion of Censure (December 1952), 753–64, 753 n.1; MPs' remuneration, 988–9; Nationalised Industries Select Committee report, 1392–3; National Service Act, 1292–4; Private Members' days and Ten Minutes Rule, 702, 1268–9; Soames reports on Budget debate to WSC, 2050; Sir Stafford Cripps (April 1952), 403–5; Television Bill, 1368–9, 1373; television coverage of upcoming Debates, 2067; Transport, Government Policy (May 1952), 447–55; University franchise and representation in HofC, 10–11, 15–16, 22
  Egypt: British defence negotiations with (1954), 1690–1; Suez Canal Zone Base, Anglo-Egyptian Agreement (Oral Answers), 1713–19; US–UK defence negotiations (1953), 1308–9, 1355–7, 1359–60
  foreign affairs: Anglo-American Conversations (January 1952), 239–47; The Berlin Conference (February 1954 WSC speech), 1449–57; China, Coastal Islands (Written Answers), 1922–3; Council of Europe proceedings debate (proposed), 439–40; Debate on the Address (December 1954), 1829–43; Foreign Affairs debate, 302; Foreign Affairs Debate planning, 24, 27; Foreign Affairs (December 1953 WSC speech), 1359–65; The Geneva Conference (April 1954 WSC speech), 1552–3; German Army Surrender Document (Oral Answers), 1610–11; Indo-China war, 1694–5; Israel Loan Request (Oral Answers), 456–7; Motion of Censure (March 1955 WSC speech), 1949–58;

House of Commons (HofC) *(continued)*
  foreign affairs *(continued)*
    A Review of Foreign Affairs (July 1954 WSC speech), 1686–95; South East Asia Defence (May 1954 WSC speech), 1570–1; Three Power meeting (proposed), 1033; World Peace, President Eisenhower's Declaration (Oral Answers), 959–61, 963
  Korea: armistice talks, 929; Korea Military Situation (May 1952), 468–74; The Korean War (July 1952), 520–5, 525
  and WSC: HofC sends well wishes to WSC (1958), 2207, 2207 n.3; interruptions to WSC's speeches, 21, 23, 99, 309, 311, 316, 571, 582–3, 586, 706, 755–7, 758, 968, 1272, 1523, 1524–5, 1678–9; Life Member of HofC status for WSC (proposed), 2353, 2354; luncheon for (1963), 2346, 2346 n.1, 2347; MacAndrew instructs Members to resume seats when WSC does not give way, 103, 582; Resolution of Thanks (1964), 2355, 2356, 2359–60, 2361; WSC criticises jaded nature of (1952), 638; WSC publicly criticised in HofC, 387, 968; WSC returns to HofC (1953), 1256; WSC's corner seat, 2083, 2083 n.4, 2380; WSC's death, 2380–1; WSC's eighty-fifth birthday (Oral Answers), 2277; WSC takes oath as PM (1951), 9
House of Lords, 16, 25, 834, 2371–7
housing
  building program reduction proposals, 1–2
  'Churchill Houses', 1820, 1820 n.2, 1828, 1872
  Conservative Government policies, 663, 1795
  construction programme, 422, 641, 663, 1240
  housing subsidy, 2
  investment programme (1953), 563–5
  Rent Restriction Acts amendments (proposed), 657–8
  subsidised housing expenditures, 1825, 1826
  WSC praises Ministry of Housing, 641, 663, 1240
  WSC speeches: The Government's Tasks (September 1952), 641; The Government's Record (April 1953), 954–5; Conservative Party Conference (October 1953), 1240; Debate on the Address (November 1953), 1272–4; The Conservatives' Task (May 1954), 1584
Hoveyda, Amir Abbas, 2368, 2368 n.2
Howe, Clarence Decatur, 196, 196 n.1, 1633
Howe, Robert George
  biographical information, 39 n.1
  Egypt: Egyptian propaganda, 937–8, 938, 946–7, 951, 961–2; US–UK defence negotiations (1953), 1020–1, 1021 n.1; WSC directs Howe to not travel through Cairo, 982; WSC proposes to deal with all Egypt matters while Eden attends Four Power Conference, 1396
  Sudan: Anglo-Egyptian agreement regarding, 937–8, 938, 946–7, 951, 952, 1011, 1020; elections in, 1355; elections and self-government planning, 35 n.1, 39; Lloyd suggests Howe not return to, 1081; postponement of elections in, 952; Umma Party, 961–2; WSC praises Howe's service as Governor General of, 1983
Howson, Edmund Whytehead, 112, 112 n.3
Huggins, Godfrey Martin, 465, 465 n.1, 745, 1068, 1886
Hughes, Emrys
  biographical information, 282 n.5
  atom bomb tests, 282–3, 458–9, 684
  defence, 308, 312, 871, 1842
  Korea, 474, 1100
Hughes, Hector, 1922–3, 1922 n.2
Hull, Cordell, 1237, 1237 n.1
Hull, John Edwin
  biographical information, 879 n.1
  Egypt: US–UK defence negotiations (1953), 1108–10; US–UK defence negotiations (proposed), 879, 883, 886–7, 891, 892–4, 896–7, 897–8, 899–901, 903–4, 931, 933
Humphrey, George Magoffin, 996, 996 n.1
Humphreys-Davies, George Peter, 939–42, 940 n.3
Hunt, David Wathen Stather, 43, 43 n.1, 43 n.4, 249, 249 n.2, 331
Hurcomb, Cyril William, 365–7, 365 n.4
Hurstfield, Joel, 2031, 2031 n.2
Hussein, King of Jordan (Hussein bin Talal bin Abdullah bin Hussein), 2295, 2295 n.2
Hyde, Hartford Montgomery, 386, 386 n.2
Hyde, Henry, 796
Hyde, Marie Emily de la Grange ('Mimi'), 796, 796 n.1
Hynd, John Burns, 755, 755 n.1, 1417

Ibn Saud (Abdul Aziz ibn Abdurrahman el Feisel Al Saud), 749, 749 n.1, 787–8, 884–5, 2318
India
  aircraft for, 341
  British arms supplied to, 340–1
  Commonwealth Advisory Committee on Defence Science, 332–3, 349, 349–50
  Indian communities in British Colonial territories, 1911–12
  India/Pakistan situation, 60–1, 2284
  Korea, 750, 1084

INDEX 2455

UK declines to provide immediate assistance to French at Dien Bien Phu, 1570–1
Indo-China war
  Anglo-American differences regarding, 1578
  British action in the event of French withdrawal from, 355–7, 749, 751, 839–40
  British air transport resources for, 974
  British and Western policy towards, 1615, 1666
  cease-fire proposals, 1573–6
  Dien Bien Phu, 1546, 1560, 1566, 1568, 1570–1, 1603–4, 1603 n.2, 1609
  Dulles' speech on Western defence of, 1603–4, 1603 n.2, 1605, 1606, 1606 n.1
  effect of on French Army, 185, 244, 752
  French position in (1953), 983, 984, 1025–6, 1038–9, 1070–1, 1339–42
  French position in (1954), 1696, 1697, 1698
  Geneva negotiations (1954), 1700–1, 1702, 1702–3
  Molotov proposes plenary and restricted sessions on at Five Power Conference, 1604
  potential for French surrender in, 1612
  Tonkin Delta, 1666, 1667
  UK refuses to send transport aircraft to the French, 984, 984–5, 988
  US aid to France, 749, 751, 752, 789
  US role in, 984–5, 1604, 1606, 1694–5
  US warns China against further aggression, 197–8
  US–UK policy towards China, 272–3
  Western coalition of aid for France (proposed), 1515–17, 1530, 1531–3, 1536, 1549–52, 1552, 1552–3, 1553, 1554–5, 1603–4
  WSC asks for clarification on Saigon situation, 982–3, 984
  WSC speeches: Foreign Affairs (May 1953), 1000, 1004, 1117; South East Asia Defence (May 1954), 1570–1
Indonesia, 2380, 2380 n.1
industry
  Conservative Party policies, 1242–3, 2005–6, 2101
  cotton importing and marketing, 1105, 1105–6, 1105 n.1, 1111
  double-shift work proposals, 361–2, 362 n.1, 393
  Electrical Trades Union strike, 1206
  engineering industry wages, 636
  Nationalised Industries Select Committee report, 1392–3
  post-war industrial production rates, 2003
  Trades Union Congress, 4, 638–9, 663, 665, 666–7, 953–4, 1242–3

unemployment figures (1953), 953
unemployment in textile and clothing industries, 368–9, 487–9
WSC criticises Labour Party nationalisation policies, 1241–2, 1996, 2101
WSC praises British trade unionism and trade union leaders, 638–9, 663, 666–7, 1242–3
see also coal industry; steel industry; transport
'influence mines', 319, 319 n.1
Iraq, 63–4, 748, 748 n.1, 2141–2
Ireland, 1222
iron: *see* steel industry
Irvine, Arthur James, 961, 961 n.1
Irving, Sydney, 2385, 2385 n.3
Isaacs, Gerald Rufus (Marquess of Reading), 1593, 1593 n.1
Ismay, Sir Hastings Lionel ('Pug')
  biographical information, 7 n.2
  Accession Proclamation, 254–5
  defence: Commonwealth Advisory Committee on Defence Science, 333; inter-Allied machinery for concerted Western defence, 132; Ministry of Defence staff, structure and responsibilities, 7–8
  England (April 1953 WSC speech), 965
  Europe: European Defence Community, 1408, 1426; location and strength of Soviet forces (1954), 1408, 1426, 1441–2, 1469, 1471–2, 1485, 1486, 1490
  foreign affairs: South Africa, 52–4; Three Power (Bermuda) Conference (1953), 1125, 1292, 1325; US–UK Washington discussions, 39
  NATO: defence Annual Reviews, 920–1; infrastructure, 271–2; Mediterranean Command proposals, 272; reorganisation proposals, 272; Secretary-General appointment, 333, 334, 339, 724
  opinion of Mountbatten, 156
  writes memoirs, 2291
  and WSC: *The Hinge of Fate* (Churchill), 1029; thanks WSC for copy of Volume 6, 1408; WSC falls and fractures femur (1962), 2329; WSC praises, 670; WSC requests reduction in length of telegrams, 942; WSC requests ride to Other Club meeting, 2322
Ismay, Laura Kathleen Clegg, 2291, 2291 n.2
Israel
  defence: Anglo-Jordan Joint Defence Board, 1507–9; Anglo-Jordan Treaty of 1948, 1300–2, 1303–5; British jet aircraft for, 680, 693, 876; Iraqi proposal for Gaza Strip, 63–4; Middle East defence role, 993–4; US support for, 803

Israel *(continued)*
  foreign affairs: Arab–Israeli relations, 879–80, 1087; British relations with, 624–5; de Rothschild recommends admitting Israel to British Commonwealth, 1887, 1914; draft aide memoire to, 963; Egyptian blockade, 1395–6; Foreign Affairs (May 1953 WSC speech), 1006–7; Israeli-Egyptian relations (1956), 2101–2, 2103–4, 2124; relations with Jordan and Iraq, 2141–2
  Israeli Parliament building in Jerusalem, 2088, 2088 n.1
  Negeb region, 731–2
  oil supply financing request, 401–2, 402 n.1, 424, 424 n.5, 430, 456–7
  Sarah Churchill attends 4th birthday celebration of, 416
  and WSC: eightieth birthday gift for WSC, 1923–4; WSC hopes to visit (1961), 2323; WSC meets with Ben-Gurion, 2304, 2305; WSC praises establishment of, 217; WSC's death, 2368–9; WSC's support for, 1821, 1846

Italy
  anti-British and anti-US demonstrations in, 1287
  Five Power Conference on Trieste (proposed), 1300
  German reunification proposals, 352
  Yugoslavia: Italian relations with, 1287, 1363; Western Powers' relations with, 747

Itote, Waruhiu ('General China'), 1437–8, 1437 n.2, 1445, 1459

Jackson, Robert ('Jacko'), 2316–17, 2316 n.3
Jacob, Edward Ian Claud
  biographical information, 132 n.1
  BBC: coverage of Egyptian closure of Suez Canal, 2128; interview with Archbishop Makarios, 1808; Mrs Knight's broadcast, 1910, 1921, 1921–2
  defence: COS Defence Policy and Global Strategy report, 494, 545; Economic Debate on defence programme, 550; handling of defence matters during Alexander's absence, 481–2; inter-Allied machinery for concerted Western defence, 132, 142–4; manpower estimates, 562; manpower recruiting projections, 563, 563 n.1; National Service periods, 597; production programme, 562
  The Hinge of Fate (Churchill), 1029
  'Rodeo' Operations names, 597
Jagan, Cheddi, 1246–7, 1246 n.1
Jagger, David, 2326, 2326 n.1

Jamaica, 797, 808, 809, 908, 908 n.2
James, Henry, 594, 594 n.1
James II, King, 1312, 1312 n.2
James, Robert Leoline, 1814, 1814 n.1
Japan
  British relations with, 749
  British trade with, 904
  economic situation, 898–9
  New Mexican atom bomb tests, 815
  release of British sailors sentenced to hard labour, 613, 613 n.1, 614
  US–UK policy towards, 40, 184–5, 217
Jebb, Hubert Miles Gladwyn, 797, 797 n.3, 906, 983–4
Jeffrey, George Johnstone, 293, 293 n.3
Jellicoe, George Patrick John Rushworth ('Patsy'), 2340, 2340 n.2
Jenkin, Charles Patrick Fleeming, 2348, 2348 n.1, 2362
Jenkins, Thomas Gilmour, 365–7, 365 n.2
Jenks, Bertha Wells, 194, 250–1, 250 n.2
Jerome, Leonard Walter, 1473, 1473 n.2
John 'Lackland', King, 2015, 2015 n.2
John, Otto, 1722, 1722 n.1
Johnson, Hewlett, 648, 648 n.1
Johnson, Lyndon Baines, 2380, 2380 n.3
Johnston, Thomas, 1272–3, 1273 n.1
Joliot-Curie, Frederic, 344, 344 n.2
Jones, Alfred Lewis, 508, 508 n.1
Jones, Enid Bagnold, 2147, 2147 n.1
Jones, John Henry ('Jack'), 756, 756 n.1
Jones, William Alton, 598, 598 n.2, 602, 836–7, 879, 884, 888–9
Jooste, Gerhardus Petrus, 1899, 1899 n.1
Jordan
  Anglo-Jordan Joint Defence Board, 1507–9
  Anglo-Jordan Treaty of 1948, 1300–2, 1303–5
  British relations with, 748
  British troops stationed in, 845–6
  Hassan bin Talal, Prince of Jordan, 2295, 2295 n.1
  Hussein, King of Jordan (Hussein bin Talal bin Abdullah bin Hussein), 2295, 2295 n.2
  relations with Iraq and Israel, 2141–2
Joy, Michael Gerard Laurie, 982–3, 982 n.1, 984
Juin, Alphonse Pierre, 244, 244 n.1, 423–4
'Jujitsu', 228, 228 n.1
Juler, Frank Anderson, 788, 788 n.2
Junor, John Donald Brown, 1180, 1180 n.1

Kāšāni, Sayyed Abu'l-Qāsem, 749, 749 n.2
Kaye, Danny (David Daniel Kaminsky), 1590, 1590 n.3
Keats, John, 2375, 2375 n.1

Kekkonen, Urho, 1078, 1078 n.1
Keller, Helen Adams, 1875, 1875 n.1
Kelly, Gerald Festus, 1513, 1513 n.1, 1555–6, 2053, 2053 n.1
Kelly, Grace Patricia, 2127, 2127 n.2, 2235, 2236
Kelly, Richard Denis Lucien
  biographical information, 497 n.4
  Eden's war-time minutes to WSC, 2241–2, 2243–4, 2244
  A History of the English-Speaking Peoples, 2044, 2056, 2092
  The Second World War, 497, 1028–9
Kemsley, Baron (James Gomer Berry), 2129, 2129 n.2, 2156
Kennedy, Jacqueline Lee Bouvier, 2331, 2331 n.2, 2344
Kennedy, John Fitzgerald, 2196, 2197, 2301, 2301 n.2, 2331, 2342–3
Kennedy, John Noble, 2196, 2196 n.2
Kent, Duchess of (Princess Marina), 632, 632 n.1, 1990, 2296
Kent, Duke of (George Edward Alexander Edmund), 259, 259 n.1
Kenya
  British troop reinforcements despatched to (1953), 915, 926
  clemency for General China (proposed), 1445, 1459
  detention of Mau Mau supporters, 1445–6
  Erskine departs from Kenya post, 1870
  Griffiths' Court Martial, 1350–1
  Labour MPs visit, 698, 699, 713
  Mau Mau revolt, 649–50, 754–5, 754 n.1, 757–9, 1035, 1869–70
Kerr, Hamilton William, 386, 386 n.1
Kesselring, Albert, 139, 139 n.2, 502–3, 629, 630–1
Khalil, Sayed Abdallah, 947, 947 n.1
Khama, Seretse, 52–4, 52 n.2, 73–4
Khama, Tshekedi, 52–4, 52 n.1, 73–4
Khan, Genghis, 1353, 1353 n.4
Khan, Mohammad Ayub, 2284, 2284 n.2, 2366
Khrushchev, Nikita Sergeyevich
  biographical information, 1319 n.1
  criticises WSC, 2239
  in India, 2062, 2066
  Macmillan's opinion of, 2217, 2220
  Soviet Government policies, 1319–20
  Western Summit meeting with (1959), 2262–3
King, William Mackenzie, 203, 203 n.2, 1638
Kipling, (Joseph) Rudyard, 825, 825 n.2, 825 n.3
Kirkpatrick, Ivone Augustine
  biographical information, 319 n.3
  circulation of telegrams to Ministers, 1384, 1384 n.1
  civilian injuries and deaths and Soviet interruption of free circulation within Berlin, 1116
  European Governments conference proposal, 1755
  German rearmament, 319, 1736
  NATO Secretary-General candidates, 321, 323
  Russian MiG shoots down British bomber in Hamburg–Berlin air corridor (1953), 924
  WSC proposes to deal with all Egypt matters while Eden attends Four Power Conference, 1396
Kirkwood, James, 2090, 2090 n.3
Knatchbull, Norton Louis Philip, 2217, 2217 n.1
Knight, Margaret Kennedy, 1873–4, 1873 n.2, 1876–7, 1879–80, 1909–10, 1910–11, 1921, 1921–2
Knollys, Edward George William Tyrwhitt, 209, 209 n.1
Knowland, William Fife, 1648–9, 1648 n.3, 1649, 1653, 1672–3, 1681–2
Knox, Robert Uchtred Eyre, 693–4, 693 n.2
Koenig, Marie Joseph Pierre François, 424, 424 n.1, 1696, 1697–9
Koirala, Matrika Prasad, 282, 282 n.1, 282 n.2
Komorowski, Tadeusz ('Bór-Komorowski'), 1987–8, 1987 n.2
Köprülü, Mehmet Fuat, 747, 747 n.1
Korda, Alexander, 549, 549 n.3, 550
Korea
  armistice: negotiations, 46–7, 59, 59 n.2, 85–8, 107, 132, 152, 183–4, 185, 197, 199, 241–2, 521–2, 729, 750, 751–2, 929, 939, 939 n.2, 959–60, 963–4, 971–2, 1040–1, 1046, 1048–9, 1053, 1177; public warning statement on signed Armistice, 331, 332; truce negotiations, 1064–5, 1069–71, 1073–4, 1084, 1094
  bombing: napalm bombing, 605, 612, 627–8, 628–9, 628 n.1; power stations on Yalu River, 512, 514–15, 523
  British presence: Alexander visits, 470–2, 501, 501 n.3; British casualties, 522; British contribution to Korean war efforts, 209; British Deputy Chief of Staff (proposed), 505–6, 518–19, 525–6, 529, 547–8, 551, 552, 555; British ships in Japanese waters (1952), 718, 720; British troop establishments and fighting strengths, 1101; British troops' availability for deployment to, 1125–6, 1130–1; Commonwealth forces in, 336, 751, 1393–4; description of 'parka' for WSC, 239; Parliamentary statements on Korea Mission, 512, 518–19; regulars retention

Korea *(continued)*
  British presence *(continued)*
    and call-up of reservists for Korean War (proposed), 252; replacement of Bouchier as UK COS representative, 547–8, 566; UK policy towards, 286–92, 317–18, 318, 326; WSC asks for COS opinion on military situation in, 68–9, 77–8, 80
  Indian troops in, 1112
  New Zealand forces in, 751
  Prisoners of War (POWs): Alexander visits, 501; continuing imprisonment of US airmen captured during Korean War, 1847–8, 1848 n.1; release of captured British diplomats, 923–4, 923 n.1, 924–6, 934; return of POWs to Communist China, 369, 371–2, 397–8, 397 n.3, 400, 400 n.1, 402, 411, 461, 465, 484–5, 486, 511–12, 511 n.2, 523–4, 527–8, 528, 536, 735, 736, 750, 934–5, 999–1000, 1389–90; Rhee's release of 25,000 POWs, 1118, 1118 n.2, 1119–20; treatment of British POWs returning from Korea, 978–9
  UN forces in, 87–8
  US embargo proposal, 609–10, 615–16, 616, 633–4, 634 n.1
  US military in: casualties, 161, 216, 522; forces and expenditures, 164, 216–17, 1000; military situation reports, 300, 300 n.2, 300 n.3; US proposal to use atomic bomb on, 1329, 1331
  US–UK policy towards, 40, 46–7, 86, 289, 749–50, 840–1
  WSC speeches: Korea Military Situation (May 1952), 468–74; The Korean War (July 1952), 520–5, 525; Lord Mayor's Banquet (November 1952), 723; Foreign Affairs (May 1953), 999–1000; Korea Truce Talks (June 1953), 1098–101; Debate on the Address (November 1953), 1275; A Review of Foreign Affairs (July 1954), 1687
Kosygin, Alexei, 2365–6, 2365 n.2, 2366 n.1
Kotelawala, John Lionel, 1438, 1438 n.2, 1886, 2092
Kramer, Erich Maria (Erich Maria Remarque), 1214, 1214 n.3
Krock, Arthur Bernard, 251, 251 n.1
Küçük, Fazil, 2370, 2370 n.4

Labouchere, Henry, 495, 495 n.4
Labour Government
  remuneration of general practitioners and medical specialists, 441–3
  'Working Men Tories' letter from Jack Binns to WSC, 494, 494 n.1
  WSC acknowledges previous Government's defence policy efforts, 94–5, 146
  WSC criticises previous Government: non-participation in Schuman Plan and Western Union discussions, 200; policies, 288–92, 294, 296, 302, 407–8, 418–19, 443, 448–53, 454–5, 641–2, 661–3, 757–8, 1582–3, 2237–8; rearmament programme, 572–4, 575
Labour Party
  Attlee's Opposition leadership, 204, 408, 420–1, 701–2, 1268–70, 1272, 1274, 1295, 1364, 1449, 1460–1, 1517–18, 1824–5, 1949–50
  Egypt, 931
  High Court Judges' remuneration, 913–15
  House of Lords reform proposals, 834
  Morrison criticises Bevan, 1586
  MPs' remuneration, 988–9
  nationalisation of rented land (proposed), 1043, 1050–2
  National Service Act, 1292–4
  political friction between Attlee and Bevan, 588, 1244
  Service officers' pensions, 1306–8
  World Peace, President Eisenhower's Declaration (Oral Answers), 959–60
  WSC appeals for cooperation, 20–1, 23, 638, 1794–5
  WSC criticises, 953–4, 1558, 1995–6, 2174
  WSC praises, 1812
  WSC speaks to US Congress, 209
  WSC speeches: Conservative Party Conference (October 1953), 1240; Constituency Speech (November 1955), 2059; Defence, German Rearmament (March 1954), 1463–5; interruptions to WSC's HofC speeches, 968; Motion of Censure (December 1952), 753–64, 753 n.1; Motion of Censure (March 1955), 1949–50; National Service (November 1953), 1294–9; Vote of Censure (February 1952), 285–92; Young Conservatives (December 1955), 2065–6
Lafayette, Marquis de (Marie Joseph Paul Yves Roche Gilbert du Motier), 2342, 2342 n.3
Laithwaite, John Gilbert, 1701, 1701 n.3
Lambton, Antony Claud Frederick, 2279, 2279–80, 2279 n.1
Lambton, Katherine de Vere Beauclerk, 1215, 1215 n.3
Landemare, Georgina, 1590, 1590 n.2, 1598
Landor, Walter Savage, 2364, 2364 n.1
Langhorne, Nancy Witcher (Lady Astor), 2336, 2336 n.1
Lang, John Gerald, 123, 123 n.1
Laniel, Joseph, 1231, 1231 n.1
  Three Power (Bermuda) Conference (1953):

European Defence Community, 1346, 1361–2; Laniel becomes ill during, 1327, 1352; planning, 1043–4, 1279, 1281, 1282, 1283–4, 1288, 1289
Western coalition of aid for France in Indo-China (proposed), 1553
WSC suggests Azores meeting with Eisenhower, 1231, 1232
Lascelles, Sir Alan Frederick ('Tommy')
biographical information, 61 n.1
completion of *The Second World War*, 923, 926–7
Duke of Windsor does not attend Coronation, 732
George VI plans South Africa visit, 61–2
Princess Margaret's engagement to Peter Townsend, 1107
transfer of funds to Duke of Windsor, 733
Laszlo, Philip Alexius de, 2339, 2339 n.2
Laughlin, Henry Alexander, 1196, 1196 n.1, 2033, 2034
Laurier, Henri Charles Wilfrid, 203, 203 n.1, 1638
Lavender, John F., 2173, 2173 n.3
Law, Andrew Bonar, 1220, 1220 n.3
League of Nations, 263
Leather, Edwin Hartley Cameron, 679, 679 n.4
Leathers, Lord (Frederick James)
biographical information, 2 n.2
Anglo-Norwegian fisheries case, 568–9
British trade with China, 1046
coal imports, 2–3
Egypt, 1203, 1209–11, 1782
electricity charges, 44, 48
Maclay's illness and Ministerial duties, 415
Persian oil negotiations, 622
Royal Navy fuel oil reserves, 324
transport: direct coach licenses, 382–3, 382 n.1; Ministry of Transport duties, 431–2, 431 n.2; nationalised railways and road transport planning, 431–2, 475–6; road and rail fares public committee proposal, 478; Transport Bill, 383, 401, 545–6; Transport Commission and Road Haulage permits, 365–7
UK defence production programme, 1782
WSC suggests using birthday gift subscriptions for Chartwell museum or studies of the English language, 1871–2
LeBaron, Robert F., 186, 186 n.2
Lee, Janet ('Jennie'), 1688, 1688 n.3
Lee Meng ('Lee Ten Tai'), 859–60, 859 n.2
Legge-Bourke, Edward Alexander Henry, 457, 457 n.1
Leigh, Vivien (Vivien Mary Hartley), 2179, 2179 n.1

LeMay, Curtis Emerson, 539–40, 539 n.3
Lemnitzer, Lyman, 2345, 2345 n.1
Lennox-Boyd, Alan Tindal
biographical information, 317 n.1
Anglo-Norwegian fisheries case, 568–9
Cyprus and Anglo-Greek relations, 1762–3, 1762 n.1
death of Lord Cherwell, 2173
Gatwick Airport development, 728–9
Indo-China war, 355
sale of Hermes aircraft by BOAC, 1481–2
transfer from Colonial Office to Ministry of Transport, 462–3
transport: bus and railway fare increases, 317, 351–2; nationalised railways and road transport planning, 475–6; Railways Reorganisation White Paper, 1661–2; Road Traffic Bill provisional legislative program (1954–1955), 1561–2; Transport Bill, 486, 543, 545–6; Transport Commission and Road Haulage permits, 365–7
WSC praises, 2100
Leopold III (King of Belgium), 736, 736 n.1, 766
Le Rougetel, John Helier, 335, 335 n.1
Leslie, John Randolph Shane, 544, 544 n.1, 1473, 2327–8, 2328
Liberal Party, 833–4, 2261
Lidderdale, David William Shuckburgh, 2361, 2361 n.3
Lindemann, Frederick: *see* Cherwell, Lord (Frederick Lindemann, 'the Prof')
Lindgren, George Samuel, 706, 706 n.3
Lippmann, Walter, 1256, 1256 n.2
Lipton, Marcus, 458, 458 n.1, 579, 687–8, 687 n.1
Llewellyn, David Treharne, 25–6, 25 n.2
Lloyd George, David, 1964, 1964 n.1, 1965–8, 2342
Lloyd George, Gwilym
biographical information, 3 n.2
food: bananas, 508; bread subsidy, 482–3, 483 n.1; British imports of Canadian cheese, 381; British population and meat consumption rates, 423, 427–8; butter and margarine rations, 535, 1056, 1056 n.1, 1564; end of food rationing (1954), 1583–4; farm economy and cost of home-raised food, 1385, 1387, 1388, 1394–5; Food Stocks Index, 364, 388–9, 396, 417; fruit and sugar supplies, 483; marketing of home-produced meat and bacon after end of meat rationing, 1258–62, 1265–7; meat consumption (1953), 1241; meat ration and supply projections (1951–1952), 27; Milk Marketing Board resumes

Lloyd George, Gwilym *(continued)*
food *(continued)*
operations (1954), 1265–7; pre- and post-war staple foods consumption rates, 1741; Retail Prices Index, 1763–4; sugar ration, 1108; unrationed food import reductions, 3, 4; weekly meat ration levels, 729; WSC asks for justification of Christmas bonus reductions, 66, 74–5
Lloyd George, Megan, 2001, 2001 n.1, 2004
Lloyd, John Selwyn Brooke
biographical information, 503 n.1
Argentine meat exports to Britain, 651
China, 1046, 1077
defence: 'Mainbrace' military exercise, 616, 616 n.1; Montgomery advises against sending British troops to Denmark, 1041, 1041 n.1; Statement on Defence (1954), 1428–9
Finnish tanker SS *Wiima*, 962, 962 n.3, 975–6, 979–81
Five Power (Geneva) Conference proposals (1954), 1433–4
France, 1036
Germany, 503, 629–30
Japan, 613, 613 n.1, 614
Korea, 512, 518–19, 609–10, 615–16, 1069–71, 1072–3
Middle East: British military base in Gaza (proposed), 614; British troop quarters in Libya, 343; Israel, 963; Persian oil negotiations, 622, 650; US aid to Persia, 601
Prince of Monaco's wedding, 2087–8
Russia, 949–50, 950 n.1, 989, 1078, 1083
Siam, 1071
South-East Asia, 1077
WSC meets with Tito (1960), 2226–8
WSC praises, 2263
WSC thanks for continuing access to Foreign Office telegrams, 2073
see also Egypt; Indo-China war; Sudan
Lloyd-Roberts, Richard, 2120, 2120 n.4, 2121
Lobban, Bella, 2126, 2126 n.4
Longden, Gilbert James Morley, 1117, 1117 n.2
Longley-Cook, Eric William, 144–5, 144 n.1, 145 n.1, 786, 786 n.3
Lord Chancellor: *see* Simonds, Gavin Turnbull
Lord President of the Council: *see* Salisbury, Lord (Robert Gascoyne-Cecil, 'Bobbety'); Woolton, Lord (Frederick James Marquis)
Lord Privy Seal: *see* Salisbury, Lord (Robert Gascoyne-Cecil, 'Bobbety')
Lord Randolph Churchill (Churchill), 271
Louise (Queen of Sweden), 1253, 1253 n.2
Louis XIV, King of France, 1313, 1313 n.1

Lourie, Arthur, 2305, 2305 n.1
Louw, Eric Hendrik, 2284, 2284 n.3
Lovett, Robert Abercrombie
biographical information, 5 n.3
defence: Atlantic Command proposals, 178, 212–13, 220–1; atomic weapons, 173, 174–6; NATO reform proposals, 171; rifle standardisation, 177; USAF aircraft production levels, 806; US disarmament proposals, 5; US expenditures, 163–4
WSC and Truman discuss justification for use of atom bomb on Japan, 807
Luce, Ann Clare Boothe, 800–1, 800 n.1, 2154, 2154 n.1
Luce, Henry Robinson, 1312–13, 1312 n.1, 1313–14
Luce, William Henry Tucker, 1081, 1081 n.1
Lyle, Charles Ernest Leonard ('Mr Cube'), 410, 410 n.1
Lyon King of Arms, Lord (Thomas Innes of Learney), 293, 293 n.2
Lyttelton, Oliver
biographical information, 2 n.1
banana trade, 508
Bracken memorial proposals, 2225
British Guiana political situation (1953), 1229–30, 1233–4, 1246–7
Conservative Party expresses confidence in, 1237
Coronation, 1049
Eden envies retirement of, 1758, 1758 n.1
Indian communities in British Colonial territories, 1911–12
Kenya: clemency for General China (proposed), 1445, 1459; detention of Mau Mau supporters, 1445–6; Labour MPs visit to, 698, 699, 713; Mau Mau society, 649–50, 1035, 1869–70
Malaya: British military commitments in, 30, 1071–2; defence planning, 840; Lee Meng's death penalty sentence, 859–60; Lyttelton visits Far East region (proposed), 65, 72
NATO Secretary-General candidates, 323
Sudan, 1028
UK economic position, 2, 4, 459–60
WSC approves Singapore visit, 15
Lyttelton, Viola Maud (Duchess of Westminster), 1979, 1979 n.2
Lytton, Lady (Pamela Frances Audrey Plowden), 432, 432 n.1
CSC refers to as WSC's old flame, 2336
kidney removal operation, 2091
Order of the Garter honour for WSC, 985
unveiling of WSC statue at London Guildhall, 2021
WSC lunches with, 1598

Index

WSC mentions 'German Democratic Report' to, 432
WSC sends Christmas greetings to, 1860–1
WSC thanks for well wishes, 2208

MacAndrew, Charles Glen, 94, 94 n.1, 103, 582, 754, 755–7, 758, 1525, 1526, 1678–80
MacArthur, Douglas, 544, 544 n.3
MacArthur II, Douglas, 1082 n.1, 1325
　Three Power (Bermuda) Conference (1953): planning, 1081–2
Macaulay, Thomas Babington, 824, 824 n.1
MacDonald, Malcolm John, 322, 322 n.1, 525, 526, 982–3, 984
MacKenna, Robert Merttins Bird, 1280, 1280 n.1
Mackensen, Friedrich August Eberhard von, 139, 139 n.3, 629, 631
Mackeson, Harry Ripley, 1190, 1190 n.2
Mack, William Henry Bradshaw, 651, 651 n.1
Maclay, John Scott
　biographical information, 280 n.1
　civil aviation: arriving passengers service charge, 280, 280–1, 281 n.1
　direct coach licenses, 382–3, 382 n.1
　illness and Ministerial duties, 415, 415 n.2, 423
Maclean, Donald Duart, 176, 176 n.3
Maclean, Fitzroy Hew Royle, 1804, 1804 n.5
Maclean, Melinda Marling, 1215, 1215 n.5
Macleod, Iain Norman
　biographical information, 386 n.6
　Council of Europe, 386
　expenditures and remuneration of medical specialists, 441–3, 443 n.1
　Prison Officers Association, 478, 480–1, 482
Macmillan, Dorothy Evelyn Cavendish, 191, 191 n.1
Macmillan, (Maurice) Harold
　biographical information, 1 n.2
　Bracken's death, 2220
　British honour for Baruch (proposed), 2069–70, 2115–16, 2187
　CSC lunches with, 191
　defence, 1806, 1920
　domestic affairs: Churchill College and University Grants Committee, 2210, 2210 n.1; Gatwick Airport development, 728–9; Lambton's proposed membership in The Other Club, 2279, 2279–80; praises RSC's *Life of Lord Derby*, 2282; Torrington by-election, 2211
　economics, 671–2, 2230–1
　foreign affairs: Adenauer visits England (1959), 2273; Council of Europe, 348–9, 349 n.1, 352; Five Power (Geneva) Conference proposals (1954), 1433–4; Germany, 352, 352 n.3, 2240, 2240; Middle East, 1809, 1816–18; Montgomery's remarks on European Economic Community, 2333; Russia, 1653, 1695, 1695 n.2, 1708, 2217, 2220, 2260, 2262–3
　Her Majesty's security during Ghana visit, 2315–16, 2316–17, 2317 n.1, 2317
　HofC: Colville suggests Life Member of HofC status for WSC, 2353, 2354; luncheon for WSC (1963), 2346, 2346 n.1, 2347; Resolution of Thanks for WSC (1964), 2355, 2361; sends well wishes to WSC (1958), 2207, 2207 n.3
　and WSC: publication of war-time messages from WSC to FDR, 2210–11, 2211; sends well wishes to, 2210; WSC meets with U Nu, 2015–16, 2020; WSC plans to honour Colville for efforts in creation of Churchill College, 2297–8; WSC praises MacMillan, 1558–9, 1794, 2162, 2220, 2261–3; WSC's health, 1146–8, 2328; WSC's honorary US citizenship, 2345
　see also Conservative Government; housing
Maffey, John Loader (Lord Rugby), 1217, 1217 n.3
al-Mahdi, Abd al-Rahman, 1039, 1039 n.2, 1080, 1355, 2318
Mahendra Bir Bikram Shah Dev (King of Nepal), 2288, 2288 n.1
Maher Pasha, Aly, 593, 593 n.2
'Mainbrace' military exercise, 616, 616 n.1, 624
Makarios III (Mikhail Khristodoulou Mouskos), 1762–3, 1762 n.2, 1807, 1808
Makins, Alice Brooks Davis, 792, 792 n.1
Makins, Roger
　biographical information, 174 n.2
　Anglo-American relations, 1605
　atomic weapons, 174
　dines with WSC on the *Queen Mary*, 792
　Eden's surgery complications, 1047–8
　Egypt, 902, 903–4, 904, 908–9
　European Defence Community, 1122
　Korea, 1048, 1048–9, 1123
　Russia, 985, 986, 986–7, 1022–3, 1031
　Three Power (Bermuda) Conference planning, 1033–4, 1039, 1081–2, 1125
　Three Power (Bermuda) Conference postponement, 1119–20, 1122
　US suggests Four Power meeting as part of NATO Council (1955), 1939–40, 1944, 1958, 1959
　Washington meeting (1954), 1628–9, 1648
　WSC visits US (1953), 805–6, 809–10, 811
Malan, Daniel Francois
　biographical information, 61 n.2

Malan, Daniel Francois *(continued)*
  Basutoland, Bechuanaland and Swaziland (April 1954 WSC speech), 1538
  Commonwealth Economic Conference (proposed), 558
  Commonwealth PMs meeting (1953): Middle East discussion, 1090; Soviet foreign policy and Western Europe discussion, 1062, 1065–6, 1068; Three Power meeting (proposed), 1066
  Egypt, 1090
  George VI plans South Africa visit, 61–2
  Korea, 1066
Malaya
  ANZUS and ANZAM, 769, 775–7
  Borneo Confrontation, 2380, 2380 n.1
  British action in the event of French withdrawal from Indo-China, 355–7, 749
  British military commitments in, 30, 106–7, 1071–2
  British policy towards Chinese presence in, 615
  British tin mines and rubber plantations in, 107
  defence planning, 840, 974
  Lee Meng's death penalty sentence, 859–60
  Lyttelton visits Far East region, 65, 72
Malenkov, Georgy Maksimilianovich
  biographical information, 905 n.1
  Attlee and Bevan visit Moscow (1954), 1730, 1733–4
  Eden tries to discern Molotov's relations with, 1421–2
  resigns as Russian PM, 1896
  Russia: Big Three meeting (proposed), 1031; British policy towards, 1182–3; Eisenhower considers meeting with Soviets, 905; purges in Georgia, 969, 970; Soviet economic policies, 1224; US–UK policy towards, 930; WSC offers to meet with Molotov in Moscow (proposed), 990–1
  Tito's opinion of, 911
  WSC comments on weak political position of, 1183
  WSC proposes meeting with, 1484, 1500, 1529, 1650–1, 1656–8, 1662–5, 1668–70, 1670–1, 1683–4, 1684–5, 1689, 1706–11, 1711–12, 1713, 1719, 1720–2, 1723, 1767, 1951–3
Malik, Yakov Alexandrovich, 950–1, 951 n.1, 1031, 1373–6
Malta, 429, 491–2, 599, 1543–4
Manchuria, 86, 87–8
Manet, Édouard, 2082, 2082 n.4
Manners, Diana Olivia Winifred Maud (Lady Diana Cooper), 588, 588 n.6, 2147, 2148

Manners, Marion Margaret Violet (Duchess of Rutland), 2339, 2339 n.1
Manningham-Buller, Reginald Edward (Lord Dilhorne), 2375, 2375 n.2
Mansergh, Maurice James, 773, 773–4, 773 n.2, 774
Manstein, Erich von, 139, 139 n.1, 502–3, 629, 631
Manuel, Archibald Clark, 309, 309 n.1, 758
Margaret, Princess (Countess of Snowdon), 588, 588 n.5, 1107
Margerie, Roland Jacquin de, 1349, 1349 n.1
Marie, André, 1110–11, 1110 n.2, 1114–15, 1118
Marina, Princess (Duchess of Kent), 632, 632 n.1, 1990, 2296
Marlborough, Duchess of (Alexandra Mary Cadogan Spencer-Churchill), 617, 617 n.3, 2106
Marples, Alfred Ernest, 641, 641 n.1, 663, 1240
Marquis, Frederick James: *see* Woolton, Lord (Frederick James Marquis)
Marriott, Marjorie Jane, 2333, 2333 n.3, 2334–5
Marshal, Earl (Bernard Marmaduke Fitzalan-Howard), 682, 682 n.1, 687–8, 688–9, 690–1, 691–2, 737, 766
Marshall, George Catlett
  biographical information, 194 n.2
  Anglo-Greek relations, 1498
  attends Coronation, 1055
  attends Eisenhower's dinner party for WSC (1953), 802
  meets with Bertha Jenks, 194–5, 250
  New Mexican atom bomb tests, 814–15
  thanks WSC for holiday greetings, 194
  Volume 6 of *The Second World War*, 647
  WSC sends painting of Atlas Mountains to, 1101
  WSC suffers stroke (1953), 1143, 1160
  WSC thanks for letters, 2020, 2200
Marshall, Katherine Boyce Tupper, 2020, 2020 n.1
Marsh, Edward Howard, 811, 811 n.1
Marston, Lettice, 1598, 1598 n.1, 1988
Martell, Edward Drewett, 1871, 1871 n.4
Martinaud-Déplat, Léon, 1219, 1219 n.2
Martin, Basil Kingsley, 45, 45 n.3
Martin, John Miller, 1549, 1549 n.1
Martin, Mary, 1987, 1987 n.1
Martin, Stanley William Frederick, 2284, 2284 n.1
Marx, Karl Heinrich, 2240, 2240 n.1
Mary, Princess Royal and Countess of Harewood (Victoria Alexandra Alice Mary), 918, 918 n.2
Mary, Queen (Mary of Teck), 917–18, 917 n.1, 919–20, 921

INDEX 2463

Massigli, Odette Isabelle Boissier, 423, 423 n.3
Massigli, René, 423–4, 423 n.1, 1500, 1553
Matsumoto, Shunichi, 1131, 1131 n.1
Matthews, Harrison Freeman ('Doc'), 176, 176 n.4, 802
Matthews, Walter, 2384, 2384 n.1
Maturin, (Verity) Gillian, 2082, 2082 n.6, 2153, 2156, 2206
Maudling, Reginald, 735, 735 n.6
Maugham, William Somerset, 1214, 1214 n.2, 2093, 2161
Maurice, Frederick Barton, 504, 504 n.2
Mawby, Raymond Llewellyn, 666, 666 n.1
Mayer, René Joël Simon, 1032–3, 1032 n.1, 1033, 1033–4, 1035–6, 1037–8, 1043–4, 1127
Mayes, Herbert R., 2256, 2256 n.1
May, Henry Farnum, 541, 541 n.1
Mayhew, Christopher Paget, 287, 287 n.1
Maze, Paul Lucien, 2236, 2236 n.2
McCarthy, Joseph Raymond, 1065, 1067, 1067 n.2, 1606
McCleery, Albert K., 2204, 2204 n.1
McCloy, John Jay, 321, 321 n.1
McCormick, Lynde Dupuy, 241, 241 n.3, 539–40
McCrary, Eugenia Lincoln Falkenburg ('Jinx'), 1330–1, 1330 n.3
McElroy, Neil Hosler, 2250, 2250 n.1
McFall, David Bernard, 2270, 2270 n.2
McGovern, John, 1455, 1455 n.2
McGrigor, Rhoderick Robert, 69, 69 n.1, 212, 511, 816–22, 1223–7
McLean, Kenneth Graeme
  biographical information, 37 n.1
  Admiralty management of British coastal waters, 37–8
  Atlantic Naval Command arrangements, 49–50, 49 n.1
  British Army manpower allocations, 149–50
  comparison of US and British Fleet tonnages and personnel in the Atlantic, 77
  Defence Committee formation, 60
  Egypt, 71
  Korea, 68–9, 77–8, 80
  RAF detection of U-boats, 77, 77 n.1
McLeavy, Frank, 447, 447 n.1
McMahon, Brien, 186–7, 186 n.1, 284, 798, 1520, 1523–7
McNeil, Hector, 300–1, 300 n.4
Médecin, Jean, 1220, 1220 n.2
Medlicott, Frank, 1611, 1611 n.1
Mellish, Robert Joseph, 282, 282 n.4, 458
Menderes, Adnan, 725, 725 n.1
Mendès-France, Pierre
  biographical information, 1612 n.1
  European Defence Community, 1697–9, 1722, 1741–2

Indo-China war: French position in (1954), 1697, 1698; Geneva negotiations (1954), 1700–1; potential for French surrender in, 1612; US role in and policy towards, 1694–5
  Paris Agreements (1955), 1868–9, 1955
  WSC invites to Chartwell, 1732, 1732–3, 1737–8
Menthon, François de, 134, 134 n.7
Menzies, Robert Gordon
  biographical information, 314 n.3
  ANZUS and ANZAM, 769, 775–7, 799
  black swans for Chartwell, 2356, 2357
  Borneo Confrontation, 2380
  British Atomic Energy Programme, 770–2
  Commonwealth PMs meeting (1953): agendas and procedures, 1060; Commonwealth PMs and Cabinet meeting (1952), 745, 750, 753; Europe discussion, 1095, 1096–7; Korea truce negotiations, 1074, 1076; Three Power meeting (proposed), 1065; US Government and McCarthyism, 1065
  Commonwealth PMs meeting (1955): Far East discussions, 1889–90, 1894, 1895, 1897–9; praise for Eden's foreign affairs achievements, 1885
  criticises UN, 2181–2, 2182, 2183
  CSC suggests Chartwell invitation for, 425
  Middle East: Commonwealth PMs meeting (1953) discussion, 1088–9; Egypt, 1088–9; Royal Australian Air Force fighter wing stationed in, 314–15; US–UK defence negotiations with Egypt (proposed), 846–7, 847–8, 861, 901
  nationalised railways and road transport planning, 475–6
  postponement of Slim's appointment as Governor-General to Australia, 855
  praises Eden, 750
  WSC discusses defence issues with, 484
  WSC wishes to meet with, 381, 384, 395, 396
Merchant, Livingston Tallmadge ('Livy'), 1628, 1628 n.1
Meyer, Eugene Isaac, 1632, 1632 n.2
Middle East
  British military in: Commonwealth PMs meeting (1953) discussion, 1084–91; Gaza base (proposed), 338; Headquarters relocated to Cyprus (proposed), 1809; Headquarters relocated to Smyrna (proposed), 1314; Joint Services Headquarters staffing and costs, 1816–18; troop quarters in Libya, 343, 343
  British troop quarters in Libya, 343–4
  defence: British contribution to air defence of, 58; British COS Defence Policy and

2464　INDEX

Middle East *(continued)*
　defence *(continued)*
　　Global Strategy report, 653; Command reorganisation proposals, 30–1, 181, 181–2; Defence Organisation proposals, 542, 844–5, 886, 887; Four Power proposal, 246–7; Royal Australian Air Force fighter wing stationed in, 314–15; Western defence planning, 748
　　Dodds-Parker notes anti-US sentiment in, 1791
　　Iraq, 63–4, 748, 748 n.1, 2141–2
　　New York Times article on WSC's US visit (1953), 809–10
　　Russian actions in, 2057–8
　　Saudi claims on Trucial Sheikdoms, 749, 787–8, 790, 884–5, 1595–6
　　Syria, 748
　　US–UK policy towards, 161, 162, 163, 799, 2098, 2101–2, 2103, 2105, 2144–5, 2145–6, 2146–7
　　US–UK Washington discussions planning, 40
　　see also Canal Zone; Egypt; Israel; Jordan; Persia; Sudan
Middleton, George Humphrey, 620, 620 n.2
Mikoyan, Anastas Ivanovich, 1319–20, 1319 n.2, 2357
Millar, Frederick Robert Hoyer, 1636, 1636 n.1
Mill, John Stuart, 1910, 1910 n.1, 1921
Mills, Percy Herbert, 505, 505 n.1
Milmo, Helenus Padraic Seosamh, 1030–1, 1030 n.1
Milne, Alvilde Bridges, 2189, 2189 n.2
Minister of Agriculture: *see* Dugdale, Thomas Lionel
Minister of Defence: *see* Alexander, Sir Harold Rupert Leofric George; Macmillan, (Maurice) Harold
Minister of Education, 25
Minister of Food: *see* Lloyd George, Gwilym
Minister of Fuel and Power: *see* Geoffrey-Lloyd, Geoffrey William
Minister of Health: *see* Crookshank, Harry Frederick Comfort; Macleod, Iain Norman
Minister of Housing and Local Government: *see* Macmillan, (Maurice) Harold
Minister of Labour: *see* Monckton, Walter Turner
Minister of Materials: *see* Salter, James Arthur; Swinton, Lord (Philip Cunliffe-Lister)
Minister of State: *see* Lloyd, John Selwyn Brooke
Minister of State for Colonial Affairs: *see* Lennox-Boyd, Alan Tindal
Minister of Supply: *see* Sandys, Duncan Edwin
Minister of Transport: *see* Lennox-Boyd, Alan Tindal
Minister of Works: *see* Eccles, David McAdam

Ministry of Defence
　Alanbrooke's note on organisation and functions of, 12–13
　contracting procedures, 303 n.1, 330, 330 n.3, 341–3
　germ warfare propaganda report, 647, 648–9, 659, 678
　Headquarters reductions (proposed), 49
　Ministerial organisation of British atomic energy programme, 268, 329, 329, 332, 358
　NATO TCC report, 232
　propaganda Directorate, 622–3
　Service Department interactions, 70, 158
　Service Department memoranda circulation protocols, 70
　staff reductions (proposed), 239
　staff, structure and responsibilities, 7–8
　WSC serves as Minister of while PM, 24–5
　see also defence
Ministry of Supply, 303 n.1, 330, 330 n.3, 358, 509
Ministry of Transport, 384, 853–4
Moatti, Isabella Béatrice Carmélite Shomorowsky, 2131, 2158, 2158 n.4
Moatti, Pierre-Jean, 2046, 2046 n.1, 2131, 2158, 2305
Mohammed Zahir Shah (King of Afghanistan), 2288, 2288 n.2
Moir, Anthony Forbes, 2126, 2126 n.3, 2155, 2156, 2158, 2235, 2244
Mollet, Guy, 134, 134 n.8, 2120
Molotov (Vyacheslav Mikhailovich)
　biographical information, 905 n.2
　Eden offers to discuss foreign relations with, 934
　Eisenhower considers meeting with Soviets, 905
　European Governments conference proposal, 1711–12, 1713, 1719, 1722, 1723, 1729
　Five Power Peace Pact proposals, 975
　Four Power (Berlin) Conference (1954), 1404, 1443, 1443 n.1
　Indo-China war, 1574, 1604
　Korea: armistice talks, 1047, 1048–9, 1053, 1059; release of captured British diplomats, 923–4, 934; WSC suggests Eden meet with Molotov, 924, 924–5
　sends well wishes to Eden, 1059
　Soviets wish to join NATO, 1547–8
　Three Power (Bermuda) Conference, 1059, 1289, 1291
　Tito's opinion of, 911
　WSC offers to meet with in Moscow (proposed), 985, 986, 986–7, 989, 990–1, 995

Index

WSC proposes meeting with Malenkov
 (1954), 1643–4, 1645, 1645 n.2, 1647,
 1650–1, 1651–2, 1653, 1656–8, 1662–5,
 1665–6, 1699–700, 1699 n.1, 1706–11,
 1711–12, 1713, 1719, 1720–2, 1723,
 1728, 1951–3
WSC sends copy of The Government's
 Record speech to, 962, 962 n.1
Monaco, Prince of (Rainier Louis Henri
 Maxence Bertrand Grimaldi, Rainier III),
 2087, 2087 n.3, 2235, 2236
Monckton, Walter Turner
 biographical information, 230 n.1
 aircraft production programme, 230
 Conservative Government relations with
  TUC, 953–4
 cotton importing and marketing, 1105
 military service deferments for jockeys, 1054,
  1179
 sale of Hermes aircraft by BOAC, 1481–2
 Service Departments and Central Workers
  Union of Malta negotiations breakdown,
  429
 unemployment in textile and clothing
  industries, 368–9
 Windsor Papers, 1199
 WSC praises, 667, 1815
Monet, Oscar-Claude, 2082, 2082 n.3
Monnet, Jean, 82, 82 n.2
Monsarrat, Nicholas John Turney, 1637,
 1637 n.1
Montagu, Alexander Victor Edward Paulet
 (Lord Hinchingbrooke, 'Hinch'), 352,
 352 n.2
Montgomery, Sir Bernard Law
 biographical information, 119 n.2
 at Chartwell, 587, 597–8, 2030, 2032
 at Chequers, 363, 444, 1184
 Colville's opinion of, 444, 597–8
 defence: manpower estimates, 562, 565, 567;
  Montgomery advises against sending
  British troops to Denmark, 1041, 1041
  n.1; production programme, 562
 England (April 1953 WSC speech), 965–6
 Europe: Brind's Command of Allied Forces in
  Northern Europe, 701, 773; European
  Defence Community, 1697–9; European
  Economic Community, 2332, 2332–3,
  2332 n.1; Germany, 1143–6, 1610–11,
  1818–19, 1830–5, 1837–8; location and
  strength of Soviet forces (1954), 1472,
  1485; Mansergh's Northern Europe
  appointment, 773, 773–4, 774; NATO
  status memoranda, 1131–6, 1143–6;
  Western Union (European Army),
  composition of, 119–20, 159, 159 n.1
 Indo-China war, 1696

Middle East, 1314, 2149, 2149 n.3
 opinion of Roberts, 1184
 television interview criticising Eisenhower
  (1959), 2249
 and WSC: discussion of US military mistakes
  during World War Two, 1184; fall and
  fractured femur (1962), 2331; invites
  WSC to theatre performance, 1053,
  1056; Montgomery invited to speak at
  1900 Club, 1424, 1425; pneumonia,
  2209; sends well wishes after WSC
  suffers stroke, 1139; The Woodford
  Statue (October 1959 WSC speech),
  2270; WSC gives budgerigar to
  Montgomery, 2054, 2074, 2079; WSC's
  health (1963), 2349–50, 2351
Moorehead, Alan McCrae, 2147–8, 2147 n.2,
 2148
Moore, John, 1589, 1589 n.7
Moore, Thomas Cecil Russell, 2361, 2361 n.2
Moran, Lady (Dorothy Dufton Wilson), 51,
 51 n.2
Moran, Lord (formerly Sir Charles Wilson)
 biographical information, 51 n.4
 criticises General Practitioners, 2203
 Eden's surgery complications, 1036–7
 Eisenhower's health, 2045
 expenditures and remuneration of medical
  specialists, 370–1, 371 n.2, 441–3, 443
  n.1
 Lady Moran apologises to WSC on behalf
  of, 51
 The Other Club, 2336
 WSC's annuity for Moran's sons, 2118, 2119
 WSC's health: circulatory health and travel
  plans, 777, 788, 2247; colds, 1727;
  medications, 1280, 1965, 1965 n.1,
  1972, 1976, 1977, 2043, 2155, 2157,
  2247, 2325; Moran wishes to accompany
  WSC on Sicily trip, 1965, 1971–2,
  1974, 1976; pneumonia, 2214, 2216;
  WSC suffers stroke (1953), 1137 n.1,
  1138, 1138 n.2, 1146, 1184, 1255, 1255
  n.2, 1329; WSC suffers stroke (1956),
  2142–3; WSC visits US (1959), 2247; fall
  and fractured spine (1960), 2296; fall and
  fractured femur (1962), 2330, 2333–4
More, Thomas, 2145, 2145 n.2
Morgan, Frederick Edgworth, 939–42, 940 n.6
Morland, Oscar Charles, 1701, 1701 n.4
Morrison, Edith Meadowcraft, 1980, 1980 n.3
Morrison, Herbert Stanley
 biographical information, 22 n.1
 domestic affairs: access by former Ministers to
  Cabinet and other official papers, 296,
  1438–9; Coronation, 693–4; criticism of
  Bevan, 1586; Defence White Paper

Morrison, Herbert Stanley (continued)
  domestic affairs (continued)
    (March 1952), 309, 310; General Election (1955), 2007–8; railway shareholders compensation, 705–6; Steel Nationalisation Act, 704; Transport, Government Policy (May 1952 WSC speech), 447–8, 454–5; University franchise and representation in the HofC, 22
  foreign affairs: atom bomb, 1525, 1537; China UN admission (proposed), 1672, 1682, 1689; Egypt, 28, 1690, 1716; German rearmament, 1455; HofC Foreign Affairs debate, 302; Marshall Plan, 2239; Vote of Censure (February 1952 WSC speech), 283–4, 287; World Peace, President Eisenhower's Declaration (Oral Answers), 959–60
Morrison, John Granville, 1268, 1268 n.1
Morrison, William Shepherd ('Shakes'), 9, 9 n.2
Morton, Delia, 2172, 2172 n.1
Morton, Desmond John Falkiner, 646, 646 n.1, 2107, 2145
Morton, Gillian 'Sunny' Keefe, 2333, 2333 n.4
Mossadeq, Mohammed
  biographical information, 93 n.1
  Kāšāni's opposition to, 749
  meets with Jones, 598, 602
  overthrow of Mossadeq's Government, 1196–7
  WSC suggests joint US–UK appeal to, 606, 607–8, 611, 614–15
  see also Persia
Moss, Doris, 2309–10, 2309 n.2
Mott-Radclyffe, Charles Edward, 386, 386 n.4
Mountbatten, Lord Louis ('Dickie')
  biographical information, 156 n.2
  Colville's opinion of, 156
  Family name for children and descendants, 274 n.2
  thanks WSC for sending *A History of the English-Speaking Peoples* to his grandson Norton, 2217
  WSC's deafness, 1113
  WSC warns against anti-American attitude, 157, 157 n.1
Mountbatten, Philip: see Edinburgh, Duke of (Philip Mountbatten)
Moynihan, Patrick Berkeley, 1871, 1871 n.3
Mozart, Wolfgang Amadeus, 2082, 2082 n.7
Munnings, Alfred James, 1556, 1556 n.1
Munro, Leslie Knox, 1532–3, 1532 n.2
Munster, Earl (Geoffrey William Richard Hugh FitzClarence), 1804, 1804 n.1
Munuswamy, P., 2253, 2253 n.1
Murphy, Robert, 525 n.2, 526

Murray, Edmund, 118, 118 n.3, 2202, 2245, 2311, 2325, 2332, 2348
Murray, George McIntosh, 1992–3, 1992 n.3
Murrow, Edward R., 2249, 2249 n.2
Mussolini, Benito Amilcare Andrea, 1086, 1086 n.1, 1287

Naguib Yousef Qotp Elkashlan, Mohamed
  biographical information, 569 n.1
  attitude towards England, 569, 593
  Canal Zone: British troop reinforcements despatched to (1953), 916; Defence Committee situation report, 838–9; negotiations, 600, 748; Suez Canal Zone Base, Anglo-Egyptian Agreement (Oral Answers), 1717–18
  Egyptian propaganda, 937, 961–2
  Foreign Affairs (May 1953 WSC speech), 1000–3
  Sterling Releases Agreement, 790–1
  WSC directs Howe to not travel through Cairo, 982
  WSC voices optimism regarding Naguib Government, 623, 625, 680, 724
  see also Egypt; Sudan
Nahas Pasha, Mostafa, 325–6, 325 n.2, 364–5, 382
Nairn, Bryce James Miller, 2219, 2219 n.4
Nairn, Margaret, 2219, 2219 n.4
Nasr, Salah ed Din, 947, 947 n.2
Nasser, Gamal Abdul
  biographical information, 1422 n.1
  Egypt: Suez Canal closure and Gulf of Aqaba blockade (1956), 2120, 2120 n.2, 2121–2, 2122–3, 2130, 2130 n.1, 2134–5, 2136, 2146–7; US aid to, 2215; US–UK defence negotiations (1954), 1422–3, 1617
  WSC's opinion of, 2173
NATO (North Atlantic Treaty Organisation)
  command structure: Atlantic Command proposals, 221–2, 240–1; Greece and Turkey, 40; Ismay appointed Secretary-General of, 333, 334, 339; Mediterranean Command proposals, 272; Middle East Command reorganisation proposals, 30–1; Secretary-General candidates, 300–1, 320, 320–1, 322–4
  defence: alert procedures in case of imminent Russian attack on Western Europe, 445–6, 446 n.1; British contributions to tactical bomber force for, 120–1; Canadian F86 fighters for, 314; COS Defence Policy and Global Strategy report, 542–3; Naval Command agreements with US, France and UK,

INDEX

740–1; UK aircraft for US NATO use, 331; UK defence production programme, 557–8, 567, 572, 578, 715, 717–18; WSC's preferred organisation of military forces for, 97

Eisenhower's opinion of future of, 2250

Europe: British role in future of European movement, 348; defence of Western Europe, 1933–4; European Defence Community, 746, 1005, 1156–7; European unity, 219; Grand Alliance of European Powers (May 1956 WSC speech), 2113–15

Germany: authorisation to make atomic weapons (proposed), 431, 431 n.1; German membership in NATO (proposed), 1616, 1629–30, 1740–1, 1742–3, 1744, 1745–9, 1750, 1759–60, 1770–3, 1776–7, 1778, 1779–80, 1781, 1781–2, 1783, 1783–4, 1790–1, 1800–1, 1802, 1813, 1818–19; German participation in defence of Western Europe, 81, 1692–3; Paris Agreements (1955), 1866, 1866 n.3, 1868–9, 1878, 1884–5, 1940–3, 1943 n.1, 1954, 1955, 1956–8, 1963–4, 1973; rearmament of, 1734, 1736; Western Defence contribution and security controls, 41–3

Greece and Turkey become members of (1952), 725

Lisbon Conference (1952), 315

military status memorandum, 1131–6

NATO Council (1955), 1857, 1939–40, 1944, 1945, 1945–8, 1958, 1959

planning: Annual Reviews, 920–1; British COS Defence Policy and Global Strategy report, 652–5; British Defence Programme Annual Reviews, 712, 717–18, 920–1; infrastructure accounting and planning, 13, 271–2; military status memorandum, 1131–6; National Service periods, 581; NATO report on Soviet and NATO strengths, 296, 434–5; political status memorandum, 1143–6; reform proposals, 170–2, 190; reorganisation proposals, 141, 143, 272; TCC report, 232, 232 n.1

Russia: location and strength of Soviet forces (1954), 1408, 1426, 1441–2, 1465, 1466; report on Soviet and NATO strengths, 296, 434–5; Soviets wish to join NATO, 1547–8; Western policy towards, 196, 1245–6; WSC promotes deterrence policies in 'Notes on Tube Alloys, 1954', 1850–5

WSC praises, 94, 205, 218–19, 724–5

WSC's death (Tribute to Sir Winston Churchill), 2377–9

WSC stresses importance of Anglo-American unity for Cold War defence, 669–71

Naumann, Werner, 858–9, 858 n.2

Navarre, Henri Eugène, 1339, 1339 n.1

Navarro, Elizabeth, 797, 797 n.2

navy: *see* Royal Navy

Nazimuddin, Khawaja, 745, 752, 752 n.1

Needham, Noel Joseph Terence Montgomery, 678, 678 n.2

Nehru, Jawaharlal
biographical information, 536 n.2
attends Coronation, 1055
British relations with Chiang Kai-shek, 1064
Commonwealth Economic Conference (proposed), 536–7, 543, 558
Commonwealth PMs meeting (1953): Europe discussion, 1095, 1096–7; Korea, 1072–3, 1074, 1094; Middle East discussion, 1089–90, 1094; South-East Asia, 1076–7; Soviet foreign policy and Western Europe discussion, 1063–4, 1068–9
Commonwealth PMs meeting (1955): conclusion of proceedings, 1900; Far East discussions, 1885, 1889, 1894, 1914
Egypt, 1089–90
Four Power Conference proposals (1953), 1063–4
Indian relations with Pakistan, 2284
Korea, 1064–5, 1094, 1112
Soviet Government after death of Stalin, 1079–80
thanks WSC for copy of *Birth of Britain*, 2130
WSC encourages Nehru to lead anti-Communists efforts in Asia, 1922
WSC's eighty-fifth birthday, 2273, 2278
WSC thanks for book of Ajanta Caves paintings, 1922

Nehru, Vijaya Lakshmi, 1922, 1922 n.1

Nel, Elizabeth Layton, 2197–8, 2197 n.1

Nelson, Horatio, 2164, 2164 n.3

Nemon, Oscar, 1993, 1993 n.1, 2013, 2018, 2283

Newman, Philip Harker, 2334, 2334 n.1

New York Times article on WSC's US visit (1953), 809–10, 811

New Zealand
ANZUS and ANZAM, 769, 775–7, 799
British COS Defence Policy and Global Strategy report, 624
costs of Royal Visit to, 110–11, 111
exclusion of UK from Pacific Tripartite Treaty, 650–1
Five Power military planning conference (1953), 1015–16

New Zealand *(continued)*
  Indo-China war, 1532–3, 1570–1, 1700–1
  Korea, 86, 518, 548, 751
  postponement of Elizabeth II's Royal Visit to, 269
Nguyen Sinh Cung (Ho Chi Minh), 1341, 1341 n.1
Nguyen Vinh Thuy (Bao Dai), 1340 n.1, 1340
Nicholls, John Walter, 1012, 1012 n.1
Nicholson, Cameron Gordon Graham, 1024, 1024 n.2
Nicholson, Godfrey, 474, 474 n.1, 1100
Nicolson, Harold George, 45, 45 n.1, 302, 1189, 2147–8, 2148
Nicolson, Nigel, 302, 302 n.1
Nicolson, Victoria Mary Sackville-West ('Vita'), 1913, 1913 n.3
Nightingall, Walter, 2048, 2048 n.2
Nikonov, Aleksandr, 1012–14, 1013 n.1
Nixon, Richard Milhous
  biographical information, 1067 n.1
  Holland meets with, 1067
  sends well wishes to WSC, 2207, 2207 n.2
  thanks WSC for volumes of *A History of the English-Speaking Peoples*, 2193, 2213–14
  Washington meeting (1954), 1625
  WSC thanks for US Senate Resolution, 2039–40, 2039 n.1, 2040
Nixon, Thelma Catherine Ryan ('Pat'), 2207, 2207 n.1, 2214
Nkrumah, Kwame, 2316, 2316 n.1, 2317
Nobel, Alfred Bernhard, 1353, 1353 n.2
Noble, Andrew Napier, 980, 980 n.1
Noel-Baker, Philip John, 520–1, 520 n.1, 525, 1101
Nolan, Francis, 1589, 1589 n.1, 1590
Nolan, John Philip, 1589, 1589 n.4
Nolan, L. E. Babbington, 1589, 1589 n.2, 1590
Noon, Firoz Khan, 60–1, 60 n.1
Norfolk, Duke of (Miles Francis Stapleton Fitzalan-Howard), 1979, 1979 n.3
North Atlantic Treaty Organisation: *see* NATO (North Atlantic Treaty Organisation)
Northern Ireland, 487–8, 1238, 2070–2
Northumberland, Duke of (Hugh Algernon Percy), 2288, 2288 n.5
Norway, Anglo-Norwegian fisheries case, 568–9
Nutting, Gillian Leonora Strutt, 1913, 1913 n.2
Nutting, Harold Anthony, 385–7, 385 n.2, 1117, 1160, 1791–2, 1913
Nu ('U Nu'), 1936, 1936 n.1, 2015–16, 2016–18, 2020
Nye, Archibald Edward, 1633, 1633 n.2

Oates, Peter Geoffrey, 678–9, 678 n.3
O'Brien, Thomas, 954, 954 n.1
Odlum, Victor Wentworth, 700, 700 n.1, 700 n.2

Ogier, John, 1597, 1597 n.1
oil: *see* Persia
Olivier, Giorgio Borg, 1049, 1049 n.2, 1543–4
Onassis, Alexander, 2324, 2324 n.3
Onassis, Aristotle Socrates ('Ari')
  biographical information, 2074 n.4
  Press coverage of WSC's friendship with, 2293
  residence for WSC in South of France, 2139, 2139 n.1
  RSC's friendship with, 2074, 2075
  thanks WSC for copy of *Birth of Britain*, 2112
  WSC cruises the Mediterranean with, 2222–3, 2222 n.1, 2227, 2236, 2281, 2286–7, 2291 n.1, 2318, 2323, 2323–4, 2324–5, 2347–8, 2347 n.1
  WSC dines with, 2085, 2102, 2159, 2188, 2199, 2217, 2223, 2224
  WSC thanks for hospitality, 2310
Onassis, Athina Mary Livanos ('Tina'), 2224, 2224 n.4
Onassis, Christina, 2243, 2243 n.2, 2324
Österling, Anders, 1849–50, 1849 n.1
Osuský, Štefan, 134, 134 n.5
The Other Club, 1409, 2279, 2279–80, 2288–9, 2294, 2299, 2322, 2336, 2341

Pace, Frank, Jr, 177–8, 177 n.1
Pacelli, Eugenio Maria Giuseppe Giovanni (Pope Pius XII), 224 n.3, 2224, 2224 n.2
Padmore, Thomas, 939–42, 940 n.2
Paget, Bernard Charles Tolver, 1846, 1846 n.2
Paget, Reginald Thomas, 309, 309 n.2, 754, 1419, 1717–18
Pahlavi, Mohammed Reza (Shah of Iran), 878–9, 878 n.2
painting (WSC)
  in Bermuda, 1282
  at Cap d'Ail, 1213, 1216, 1513, 2042, 2043, 2046
  at La Pausa/Cap Martin, 2073 n.2, 2076, 2084, 2138, 2166, 2167, 2169, 2188, 2201, 2236
  in the Mediterranean, 2233
  Painting as a Pastime (Churchill), 250, 2034
  Royal Academy Banquet (April 1954 WSC speech), 1555–7
  Royal Academy exhibition of WSC paintings (proposed), 2053, 2053 n.1
  for Royal Academy Summer Exhibition, 1513
  Sarah Churchill sends holiday greetings to WSC, 645
  in southern France, 2009, 2185, 2186, 2190, 2293, 2294
  US exhibit of WSC's paintings, 2191–2, 2194, 2195, 2202–3, 2207, 2210
  WSC gives Atlas Mountains painting to Eisenhower, 2251, 2251 n.2

INDEX

WSC gives swans painting to Moatti, 2158–9
WSC lends painting box to Duchess of Kent, 632
WSC painting displayed at Tate Gallery, London, 2016
WSC sends painting of Atlas Mountains to Marshall, 1101
WSC sends painting to Spears, 1861
Pakenham, Francis Aungier, 144, 144 n.2, 786
Pakistan
  adopts republican form of Constitution (1955), 1891–2, 1902
  aircraft for, 341
  British arms supplied to, 340–1
  Commonwealth Advisory Committee on Defence Science, 333
  Indian relations with, 2284
  India/Pakistan situation, 60–1
  loan of British destroyer to (proposed), 880–1
  military collaboration with Turkey (proposed), 1381–2
  UK declines to provide immediate assistance to French at Dien Bien Phu, 1570–1
  US military aid to (proposed), 1381–2
  WSC meets with Khan, 2284
Palmerston, Viscount (Henry John Temple), 919, 919 n.2
Papagos, Alexandros, 1498–9, 1499 n.1
Parker, Harold
  biographical information, 12 n.1
  defence: DRP Committee Progress Reports, 253; French Army manpower estimates, 117; rearmament programme, 117, 117 n.1, 117 n.2, 117 n.3, 117 n.4; rifle stocks and dispersement accounting, 12; WSC asks for review of Defence speech, 91
  Royal Navy: Admiralty defence programme progress report, 75–6, 79; notes on reservists, demobilisation, civilian staff and new construction, 70–1, 75–6; WSC questions focus of naval ship-building programme, 69
Parliament
  Accession Declaration, 689–90, 690 n.1
  authorisation of proposed changes to Coronation Oath, 850–1, 850 n.1
  British Guiana political situation (1953), 1237, 1247
  corporal punishment debate in House of Lords, 685–6
  draft of King's Speech on the Opening of Parliament, 10–11, 15–16
  House of Lords reform proposals, 16, 834
  Hunt recalls WSC's praise of Shinwell, 109–10
  Motion of Censure (December 1952), 753–64, 753 n.1

Parliamentary Address to Her Majesty on the occasion of her departure, 1299–300
Parliamentary Private Secretary procedures, 301–2
position for Duke of Edinburgh at opening of, 672–3, 673 n.1
University franchise and representation in the HofC, 10–11
Unveiling of a Commemorative Panel (October 1952 WSC speech), 694
War Memorial inauguration, 678–9
WSC criticises jaded nature of (1952), 638
WSC declines to invite Eisenhower to address Parliament, 274
WSC reflects on new Parliament and hopes for cooperation with Opposition, 20–1, 23, 33–4
see also House of Commons (HofC)
Parnell, Charles Stewart, 1589, 1589 n.5
Parodi, Alexandre, 1083, 1083 n.1, 1122, 1349
Paton, John, 242, 242 n.1
Patrickson, Frank, 1513, 1513 n.2
Paul (King of Greece), 856, 856 n.1
Paymaster-General: *see* Cherwell, Lord (Frederick Lindemann, 'the Prof')
Peake, Osbert, 1308, 1308 n.1, 1738, 1797
Pearson, Lester Bowles ('Mike')
  biographical information, 198 n.1
  Anglo-Canadian Trade issues, 2380
  Commonwealth Economic Conference, 647
  Commonwealth PMs meeting (1955), 1889, 1890, 1895
  Communist propaganda regarding South-East Asia, 198
  Korea, 750
  NATO Secretary-General candidates, 322
  WSC's death, 2365
Peel, Charlotte Clementine Soames, 1727, 1727 n.3
Pelham, John, 2179, 2179 n.4
Penney, William George, 683, 683 n.1, 684–5, 939–42
Perak, Sultan of (Yussuf Izzuddin Shah Ibni Almarhum Sultan Abdul Jalil Karamatullah Nasiruddin Mukhataram Shah Radziallah), 859, 859 n.3
Percy, Hugh Algernon (Duke of Northumberland), 2288, 2288 n.5
Persia
  Anglo-Iranian Oil Company: joint US–UK negotiations, 182–3, 199–200, 602, 602 n.2, 606, 606–7, 607–8, 611, 614–15, 618–19, 619–20, 619 n.1, 620–1, 621, 622, 626, 626–7, 627 n.1, 631, 643, 650, 655–6, 656; Mossadeq responds separately to joint US–UK message, 650, 655–6, 658–9; settlement terms, 646; WSC bemoans loss of, 642–3

Persia *(continued)*
  British relations with, 749, 1363
  Jones meets with Mossadeq, 598, 602
  nationalisation law, 603
  New York Times article on WSC's US visit (1953), 810
  US aid to, 601, 607, 615, 619, 749, 836–7, 884, 888–9
  US negotiations with Mossadeq, 93–4, 598, 602, 608–9, 620, 658–9, 878–9, 879
  US–UK policy towards, 798, 804, 878–9, 996
  Zahedi Government, 1197
Peter II (King of Yugoslavia), 736, 736 n.3, 766
Petter, Ernest Willoughby, 507, 507 n.3
Petty-FitzMaurice, Evelyn Emily Mary (Duchess of Devonshire), 444, 444 n.1
Pfeiffer, Kurt Christian Theobald, 2113, 2113 n.1
Phillips, Morgan Walter, 761, 761 n.1
Phoulivong, Sisavang, 982–3, 982 n.2, 984
Piccioni, Attilio, 1781, 1781 n.1
Pierssené, Stephen Herbert, 1043, 1043 n.1, 1050–2
Piggott, Lester, 2120, 2120 n.1, 2121
Pilgrims' Dinner societies, 669, 669 n.1
Pilkington, William Henry ('Harry'), 1642, 1642 n.2
Pilsudski, Józef Klemens, 1550, 1550 n.1
Pinay, Antoine, 424, 424 n.3, 746, 1955
Pitblado, David Bruce
  biographical information, 155 n.3
  Coronation Thanksgiving Service, 1092–3
  description of 'parka' for WSC, 239
  Eastern European Conference, 155
  nationalisation of rented land (proposed), 1050–2
  Three Power (Bermuda) Conference (1953), 1325
  Transport Commission and Road Haulage permits, 365–7
  US arms for Egypt, 989–90
  WSC asks about deliberate spreading of myxomatosis, 1652
Pitt, Edith Maud, 1268, 1268 n.2
Pitt, William (the Elder), 210, 1170, 1170 n.1
Pitt, William (the Younger), 207
Pius XII, Pope (Eugenio Maria Giuseppe Giovanni Pacelli), 224 n.3, 2224, 2224 n.2
Plastíras, Nikólaos, 248, 248 n.1, 345–6
Pleven, René, 82, 82 n.1, 133, 140
  WSC meets with (1951), 130
Pleydell-Bouverie, Audrey Evelyn James, 1587, 1587 n.1
Plowden, Edwin Noel Auguste, 323, 323 n.2, 1675, 1920

Plowden, Pamela Frances Audrey: *see* Lytton, Lady (Pamela Frances Audrey Plowden)
Plumb, John Harold ('Jack'), 2105–6, 2105 n.2
Plym, HMS, 683–4
Pollard, Robert Spence Watson, 1863, 1863 n.1
Pollitt, Harry, 666, 666 n.2
Pol Roger, Jacques, 1845, 1845 n.2
Pol Roger, Odette Wallace, 2208, 2208 n.2
Pontecorvo, Bruno, 176, 358
  biographical information, 176 n.2
Popescu-Nasta, Liviu, 2132, 2132 n.4
Portal, Sir Charles Frederick Algernon ('Peter'), 323, 323 n.3, 440, 832, 965
Portal, Jane Gillian, 55, 55 n.3, 66–7, 67, 1581, 1727
Porter, George, 457, 457 n.3
Pound, Alfred Dudley Pickman Rogers, 965, 965 n.3
Powell, (John) Enoch, 299, 299 n.2
Powell, Richard Royle, 654, 654 n.1, 939–42
Pownall, Henry Royds, 497, 497 n.2, 1029
President of the Board of Trade: *see* Thorneycroft, Peter
Price, Henry Alfred, 702, 702 n.2
Price, Morgan Philips, 368, 368 n.1
Priestman, John David, 1352, 1352 n.3
Primrose, Archibald Philip (Lord Rosebery), 495, 495 n.5, 1049–50, 1054
Primrose, Neil Archibald, 2218, 2218 n.2
Princess Victoria sinking, 908, 908 n.1
Profumo, John ('Jack'), 735, 735 n.8, 2288
propaganda
  Astor recommends explanatory Ministerial broadcasts for Conservative Government actions, 515–16
  Communist accusations of US germ warfare, 648, 648–9, 659, 678
  Communist propaganda regarding South-East Asia, 198
  Egyptian, 937–8, 946–7, 951, 961–2
  Eisenhower complains about Soviet propaganda to WSC, 1431
Pugh, Doreen, 1217, 1217 n.1, 2334, 2357
Pym, John, 1364, 1364 n.2
Pytheas of Massalia, 2112, 2112 n.1

Quemoy and Matsus Islands, 1905–6, 1906–9, 1916–19, 1919–20, 1922–3, 1962–3, 1969–70
Quickswood, Lord (Hugh Gascoyne-Cecil, 'Linky')
  biographical information, 461 n.2
  describes his health and happiness to WSC, 461–2, 465
  Korean return of POWs to Communist China, 461, 465, 484–5, 486, 511–12, 511 n.2

Index

suggests peerage for L. S. Amery, 461, 465
WSC works on *History of the English-Speaking Peoples,* 1849

Radcliffe, Cyril John, 2225, 2225 n.2
Radford, Arthur William, 1549–52, 1549 n.3
railways
  Conservative Party policies, 1242
  nationalised railways and road transport planning, 431–2, 475–6
  Railways Reorganisation White Paper, 1661–2
  Robertson appointed head of British Railways, 1271–2
  shareholders compensation, 705–6, 706 n.1
  Transport, Government Policy (May 1952 WSC speech), 453–4
  National Union of Railwaymen threaten strikes (1955), 1861, 1861 n.1, 1865
Ramadier, Paul, 134, 134 n.6
Ramsay, Michael, 2372–3, 2373 n.1
Rana, Shanker Shamsher Jang Bahadur, 282, 282 n.3
Rapp, Thomas Cecil, 1024, 1024 n.4
Rattigan, Terence, 2385, 2385 n.2
Reading, Marquess of (Gerald Rufus Isaacs), 1593, 1593 n.1
Reid, Helen Miles Rogers, 801, 801 n.1
Reid, Whitelaw, 1633, 1633 n.1
Remarque, Erich Maria (Erich Maria Kramer), 1214, 1214 n.3
Remer, Otto Ernst, 994, 994 n.1
Renton, David Lockhart-Mure, 387, 387 n.1
Reston, James Barrett, 809–10, 809 n.4, 811
Reuter, Ernst Rudolf Johannes, 135, 135 n.3
Reves, Emery
  biographical information, 250 n.1
  estrangement from WSC, 2289–91, 2291 n.1, 2292, 2310
  A History of the English-Speaking Peoples: assists WSC with, 2055; Portuguese translation of Volume 2, 2334
  recovery from coronary thrombosis, 2257–8, 2257 n.4, 2258, 2263, 2264–5, 2272, 2276
  The Second World War completion, 250
  WSC plans May visit (1956), 2110
  WSC plans January visit (1958), 2193–4
  WSC stays at La Pausa Villa, 2073, 2073 n.1, 2073 n.2, 2074, 2110, 2187, 2224, 2234
Reves, Wyn-Nelle Russell ('Wendy')
  biographical information, 2049 n.2
  CSC writes to, 2292
  estrangement from WSC, 2289 n.1, 2291 n.1, 2292, 2293, 2310
  husband Emery's recovery from coronary thrombosis, 2258, 2272, 2276

sends well wishes to WSC, 2274, 2276–7
WSC plans September visit (1956), 2127, 2129
WSC asks about visiting La Pausa (1960), 2289
WSC stays at La Pausa Villa, 2049, 2074, 2075, 2077, 2078, 2082, 2084, 2110, 2153, 2166, 2169, 2187, 2200, 2201, 2234, 2236
WSC thanks for hospitality, 2243
Reynaud, Paul, 83–4, 83 n.1, 114, 130, 133, 134, 1047, 1053
Reynolds, Frank Umhlali, 62, 62 n.1
Rhee, Syngman
  biographical information, 501 n.2
  Alexander meets with, 501
  Korea: Korea Truce Talks (June 1953 WSC speech), 1099; Rhee's release of 25,000 POWs, 1118, 1118 n.2, 1119–20; truce negotiations, 1029–30, 1040, 1064–5, 1073, 1074, 1075, 1076, 1084; WSC suggests ouster of Rhee, 1120, 1123
Rhodes Scholars, 835–6, 835 n.1
Rhys, Charles Arthur Uryan (Baron Dynevor), 2200, 2200 n.1
Richard III, King, 2093, 2093 n.2, 2106, 2109
Richardson, Albert, 2111, 2111 n.1
Richardson, Dorothy Emily, 1828, 1828 n.3
Richardson, F. A., 2334, 2334 n.2
Riches, Derek Martin Hurry, 1028, 1028 n.3
Rickett, Denis Hubert Fletcher, 802, 802 n.5
Ridgway, Matthew Bunker
  biographical information, 540 n.3
  Brind's Command of Allied Forces in Northern Europe, 701
  European Defence Community, 857–8
  Mansergh's appointment, 773, 773–4
  Middle East defence planning, 861–2
  NATO command structure, 725, 1005
  Naval Command agreements with US and France, 740
  relieved of SHAPE duties, 1184
  US bomber attack on Soviet U-boat bases, 540
  WSC praises, 670, 671
Robens, Alfred, 579–80, 579 n.2, 761, 953, 1244
Roberts, Dafydd Myrddin, 2224, 2224 n.6
Roberts, Frank Kenyon, 1182–3, 1182 n.2, 1184, 1317, 1330, 1331
  WSC's health (1963), 2340–1
Roberts, Gilroy, 2063, 2063 n.1
Roberts, John, 2083, 2083 n.2, 2129, 2142, 2153, 2154, 2155, 2157, 2167
Robertson, Brian Hubert
  biographical information, 830 n.1
  Egypt: British troops' readiness in case of attacks (1953), 830–1; US-UK defence

Robertson, Brian Hubert *(continued)*
   Egypt *(continued)*
      negotiations (1953), 1021–2, 1106–7, 1109–10, 1116–17, 1140, 1201–4, 1209–11, 1355–7; US–UK defence negotiations (proposed), 946, 948–9, 1002, 1018
   National Union of Railwaymen threaten strikes (1955), 1865
   Robertson appointed head of British Railways, 1271–2
Robinson, Joan Violet Maurice, 504, 504 n.1
Rockefeller, John Davison, Jr, 2068, 2068 n.2
Rockefeller, Winthrop, 2069, 2069 n.2
Rocksavage, Earl of (George Horatio Charles Cholmondeley), 2236, 2236 n.1
Rocksavage, Marchioness of Sybil Rachel Betty Cecile Sassoon Cholmondeley, 2236, 2236 n.1
'Rodeo', 233, 233 n.1, 237, 273, 597, 974, 977, 991–2, 1017–18, 1024
Rodionov, Georgiy Mikhailovich, 1373, 1373 n.2
Rogers, Anthony Dyke Darby ('Tim'), 1597, 1597 n.2
Romilly, Edmund Humphrey Samuel, 588, 588 n.2
Romilly, Giles Samuel Bertram, 588, 588 n.1
Romilly, Nellie Hozier, 587, 587 n.1, 588, 1215, 1727
Roosevelt, Franklin Delano (FDR), 251, 647, 793, 863, 983, 1522, 1525, 1526, 2210–11
Rootes, William Edward, 234, 234 n.1, 1847, 1847 n.1
Roper, Harold, 391, 391 n.1
Rosebery, Lord (Archibald Philip Primrose), 495, 495 n.5, 1049–50, 1054
Rosenberg, Anna Marie Lederer, 2185, 2185 n.1
Rosenheim, Max Leonard, 2074, 2074 n.3, 2075
Roskill, Stephen, 1580, 1580 n.2
Ross, William, 765, 765 n.1, 768, 768 n.3
Rothenstein, John Knewstub Maurice, 2016, 2016 n.1
Rothermere, Lord (Esmond Cecil Harmsworth), 1190, 1190 n.1, 1215, 1989, 1992–3
Rothschild, Eugène Daniel von, 2138, 2138 n.3
Rothschild, Jeanne de (Ivy Sweet), 2138, 2138 n.2
Rothschild, Nathaniel Mayer Victor, 2288, 2288 n.4
'Rotor', 121, 121 n.1, 230
Rowan, Thomas Leslie, 1938, 1938 n.4
Rowse, Alfred Leslie, 2099, 2099 n.2
Royal Air Force (RAF)
   aircraft production programme, 57–8, 70, 79, 96, 102, 117, 117 n.4, 118, 120–3, 136–8, 229, 230, 230–1, 578–9
   aircraft sound barrier issues, 549, 550
   Air Defence Committee blackout policy, 418
   'Ardent' air-defence training exercise, 659, 659 n.1, 726–7, 727 n.1
   jet aircraft pilot casualties, 617
   'Jujitsu', 228, 228 n.1
   manpower: call-up of reservists, 101; estimates, 207, 228, 234, 312–14, 463–4, 466, 873; regulars retention and call-up of reservists for Korean War, 235–6; training, 314
   rocket propulsion for jet fighters, 363
   Russian MiG shoots down British bomber in Hamburg–Berlin air corridor (1953), 908, 908 n.3, 910
   Scampton airfield extension (proposed), 1468, 1469
   US offers B-47 bombers to England, 1612–13, 1613 n.1, 1614, 1618–19
   'Valiant' aircraft prototype crash, 211
Royal Navy
   Admiralty defence programme progress report, 75–6
   Admiralty management of British coastal waters, 37–8, 105–6, 241
   Atlantic Command proposals, 179, 212–13, 221–2, 240
   Atlantic Naval Command arrangements, 49–50, 49 n.1, 740–1, 742
   British ships in Japanese waters (1952), 718, 720
   comparison of US and British Fleet tonnages and personnel in the Atlantic, 77
   Coronation Naval Review, 635, 644, 658, 838, 838 n.1, 853–4, 854 n.1, 854 n.2, 922, 1016–17, 1104, 1104 n.1
   Defence Programme: Admiralty production programme, 123–6, 124; expenditure reduction proposals, 126, 136–8; loan precedents, 669; Navy Estimates (1951), 96; Navy Estimates (1952), 310–12; progress report, 75–6, 79
   fuel oil reserves, 324, 336–7, 337, 376–7, 377 n.1
   German rearmament, 319
   'influence mines', 319, 319 n.1
   Longley-Cook Report, 144–5, 145 n.1, 786
   manpower: call-up of reservists, 101; civilian staff numbers, 125–6; demobilization, 70; estimates, 579, 766; Naval Cadet training, 1043, 1258, 1262–3, 1302; notes on reservists, demobilisation, civilian staff and new construction, 70–1, 75–6; recall of Naval Fleet Reservists, 742, 764–5, 764 n.2, 772–3, 782, 792

Index

Mediterranean Fleet visit to Sea of Marmora, 1174–5
Royal Naval Base at Simonstown, 335
territorial waters measurement, 569
visit to Soviet Black Sea ports (proposed), 1198, 1199
WSC questions focus of naval ship-building programme, 69
Royal Welsh Fusiliers, 1047, 1118, 1233, 1290, 1352, 1352 n.1, 1352 n.2
Ruffside, Lord (Douglas Clifton Brown), 1571, 1571 n.1, 1571 n.2, 1572
Rugby, Lord (John Loader Maffey), 1217, 1217 n.3
Rumbold, Horace Anthony Claude ('Tony'), 1236, 1236 n.1, 1632, 1636
Rundstedt, Karl Rudolf Gerd von, 502, 502 n.1
Russell, Bertrand Arthur William, 1909, 1909 n.2
Russia
Anglo-Russian relations, 1404, 1733–4, 1798–800
British Ambassador's quarterly report on (1953), 934–5
British Embassy employees assault Russians, 1764–5
Diplomatic Immunities Bill, 792
East/West trade, 1390–2, 1395, 1398, 1398–400, 1448–9, 1454, 1488–9, 1494, 1494–6, 1496, 1500, 1502, 1514, 1616
European Governments conference proposal, 1711–12, 1713, 1722
foreign affairs: Big Three meeting (proposed), 1031, 1645, 1997–8; Boothby meets with Zhivotovski, 949–50, 950 n.1; Eden meets with Molotov (proposed), 924, 924–5, 934; Eisenhower considers meeting with Soviets, 905, 906, 907, 971–2, 986–7; Eisenhower considers meeting with Stalin, 803; Five Power (Geneva) Conference proposals (1953), 1279, 1279 n.1, 1342; Five Power Peace Pact proposals, 6, 975; Foreign Affairs (May 1953 WSC speech), 1007–9, 1012; Four Power Conference proposals, 1063, 1162–4, 1166, 1166–7, 1168, 1169, 1171, 1173–4, 1180–1, 1185–6, 1284, 1362, 1959; Malik attends Chequers luncheon with WSC, 1373–6; Molotov's role as elder statesman of Kremlin, 1421–2; *Pravda* article on Soviet foreign policy, 1012–14; proposed summit meeting (1958), 2217, 2220; proposed summit meeting (1959), 2262–3; Soviet foreign policies, 925, 1061–9, 1320–1; WSC meets with Gromyko, 950–1, 962; WSC proposes meeting with Malenkov (1954), 1643–4, 1645, 1645 n.2, 1647, 1650–1, 1651–2, 1653, 1656–8, 1661, 1662–5, 1665–6, 1667, 1668–70, 1670–1, 1673, 1683–4, 1684–5, 1686, 1689, 1695–6, 1695 n.2, 1699–700, 1699 n.1, 1704, 1706–11, 1708, 1711–12, 1713, 1720–2, 1724–5, 1733–4, 1856–7; WSC proposes meeting with Molotov, 985, 986, 986–7, 989, 990–1, 995, 1022–3, 1643–4
Formosa, 1893–4, 1896–900
International Economic Conference in Moscow, 412
Mediterranean Fleet visit to Sea of Marmora, 1174–5
Middle East, 2057–8
potential air threat to UN forces in Korea, 87–8
purges in Georgia, 969, 970, 1078
Russian Air Force, 313
Soviet aircraft production levels, 806
Soviet claims about Potsdam Conference conclusions, 464, 467–8
Soviet economic policies, 1224, 1319–20
Soviet Government after death of Stalin, 934–5, 938–9, 958, 987, 987 n.2, 1007–9, 1061–2, 1064, 1066, 1078, 1079–80, 1083, 1149, 1224–7, 1236, 1275–6, 1711
Stalin's 'doctor's plot', 934, 934 n.1, 939, 1078
UK policy towards, 930, 1010, 1180–1, 1182–3, 1374
US policy towards, 1181
US–UK policy towards, 161–4, 197, 222–3, 930, 936, 1009, 1141, 1159
Western policy towards, 40, 745, 1008–9, 1182–3, 1183, 1183–4, 1186–7, 1188, 1193–5, 1199, 1235–6, 1245–6
and WSC: Mikoyan sends good wishes to, 2357; WSC's death, 2365–6, 2366 n.1
see also Cold War; Foreign Ministers Washington conference (1953)
Rutland, Duchess of (Marion Margaret Violet Manners), 2339, 2339 n.1

Sackville, Herbrand Edward Dundonald Brassey (Lord De La Warr, 'Buck'), 339–40, 339 n.1, 1989–90
es Said, Nuri Pasha, 63–4, 63 n.1, 2141–2, 2231
Salem, Salah, 2128, 2128 n.1
Salisbury-Jones, Arthur Guy, 1913, 1913 n.5
Salisbury-Jones, Hilda de Bunsen, 1913, 1913 n.5
Salisbury, Lord (Robert Gascoyne-Cecil, 'Bobbety')
biographical information, 16 n.1, 302 n.3
defence: atom bomb and atomic energy,

Salisbury, Lord (Robert Gascoyne-Cecil, 'Bobbety') *(continued)*
  defence *(continued)*
    1299, 1655–6; British arms supplied to India and Pakistan, 340–1; Debate planning, 1820–1; Royal Naval Base at Simonstown, 334–5
  domestic affairs: Checham accepts Lord-in-Waiting position, 1871; Conservative Government, 1858–9, 1859–60, 2151; Conservative Party, 1243, 1789–90; High Court Judges' remuneration, 916–17; House of Lords reform proposals, 16; MPs' remuneration, 988–9; Parliamentary provisional legislative program (1954–1955), 1561–4; Railways Reorganisation White Paper, 1661–2; Salisbury appointed Lord President of the Council, 735
  Europe: Council of Europe, 386, 438–9; European Defence Community, 1156–7, 1158–9, 1162–4
  foreign affairs: China, 355, 1199; Egypt, 1140, 1158, 1191–3, 1197–8, 1209–11, 1227–8; exclusion of UK from Pacific Tripartite Treaty, 650–1; Four Power Conference proposals (1955), 1959; Germany, 251–2; HofC Foreign Affairs debate, 302; Korea, 336, 548, 552, 1393–4; Persia, 1196–7; Sudan, 713–14; Three Power meeting (proposed), 1036
  Russia: refusal to attend Austrian Treaty Conference, 1200; Royal Navy visit to Soviet Black Sea ports (proposed), 1174–5, 1198; Western policy towards, 1183, 1183–5, 1185–6, 1186–7, 1188, 1193–5, 1199, 1236–7; WSC proposes meeting with Malenkov (1954), 1653, 1662–5, 1668–70, 1695–6, 1700, 1708–9
  Secretary of State for Commonwealth Relations, 333, 334
  and WSC: WSC describes strained relations with to CSC, 553, 585; WSC rests at Chartwell after stroke, 1147
  see also Foreign Ministers Washington conference (1953)
Salter, James Arthur, 735, 735 n.5, 1105, 1190
Samuel, Adrian Christopher Ian ('Ian'), 2284, 2284 n.4, 2286, 2318
Sanders, Arthur Penrose Martyn, 1024, 1024 n.1
Sanders, Edgar, 860, 860 n.1
Sandys, Celia Mary, 44–5, 44 n.5
Sandys, Diana Churchill
  biographical information, 44 n.1
  death of, 2352
  depression suffered by, 2051, 2051 n.2
  insulin treatments, 1328
  thanks WSC and CSC for Family Trust arrangements, 44–5
  WSC falls and fractures femur (1962), 2329
  with WSC at La Pausa/Cap Martin, 2080, 2083, 2091
Sandys, Duncan Edwin
  biographical information, 17 n.2
  defence: aircraft production programme, 57–8, 121–2, 230, 230–1; ammunition production, 509, 530–1, 534; Army estimates (1951–1952), 127; Atomic Energy Programme (1952), 770–2; contracting procedures, 342; CSC advises WSC against appointing Sandys as Secretary of State for War, 156; Defence Programme budget (1953–1954), 716; Defence Review Committee, 1731, 1737; Economic Debate on defence programme, 550; Ministerial organisation of British atomic energy programme, 347, 358, 390–1, 1299; Ministry of Defence contracting procedures, 303 n.1, 330, 330 n.3; new armed forces security procedure, 554; production programme, 532, 558; programme estimate reductions (proposals), 136–8; reduction of Army steel requirements, 260; *Sunday Express* article on atom bomb testing, 599; tank production programme, 150–1, 152, 303, 303 n.1, 342; US offers B-47 bombers to England, 1612–13, 1613 n.1, 1614, 1618–19; WSC thanks Sandys for Middle East defence planning paper, 339
  domestic affairs: Churchill Family Trust arrangements, 44–5; Civil Service staff reductions, 90; coal imports and British steel production, 17–19; Sandys's political career, 588; Steel Nationalisation Act, 643, 666; structural steel safety and supplies, 369, 389–90, 634; unemployment in textile and clothing industries, 488, 781; WSC postpones stepping down as PM (1954), 1769
  economics: British export of cars to US (proposed), 260; East/West trade with Russia, 1398–400; Supplementary Estimates, 767, 780–1; UK economic position (1952), 460
  Europe: Eastern European Conference, 136, 136 n.1, 152–3; Western Union (European Army), 130
Sandys, Edwina, 44–5, 44 n.4
Sandys, Julian Winston, 44–5, 44 n.3

Index

Sargent, John Singer, 2338–9, 2338 n.5
Sarnoff, David, 624–5, 624 n.3
Saudi claims on Trucial Sheikdoms, 749, 787–8, 790, 884–5
Savage, Alfred William Lungley, 1233–4, 1233 n.1
Savoy Hotel case, 1420–1, 1425, 1428, 1428 n.2, 1440–1
Schmidt, Carlo, 135, 135 n.1
Schopenhauer, Arthur, 1988, 1988 n.2
Schuman, Jean-Baptiste Nicolas Robert
   biographical information, 41 n.1
   Germany: Coal and Steel Plan and reconciliation of France and Germany, 82; rearmament of, 41–2, 50, 318–20; Saar Government, 359, 745; WSC praises French/German reconciliation, 725
   Western Union (European Army), 130–1, 158
Schurmer, Percy Lionel Edward, 21, 21 n.1
Schuyler, Cortlandt Van Rensselaer, 1485, 1485 n.2
Scoones, Geoffrey Allen Percival, 1701, 1701 n.1
Scoones, Reginald Laurence, 1028, 1028 n.1
Scotland, 488, 568–9, 681–2, 952–8
Scott, Vreda Esther Mary Lascelles (Mollie), 968, 968 n.1
Second World War
   Battle of the Atlantic, 204
   D-Day Commemorations, 353, 383–4, 1227, 1581, 2013
   Dunkirk memorial, 266
   Eisenhower recalls memories of in letter to WSC, 1961
   'Highball' and 'Upkeep', 2013–14
   Montgomery criticises Eisenhower (1959), 2249–50
   Montgomery and WSC discuss US mistakes made during, 1184
   'Terminal' (Potsdam Conference), 464, 467–8, 815, 1003, 1151
   'Torch', 1961, 1961 n.2
   WSC describes as most unnecessary war in history, 1823
   WSC muses about possible prevention of, 33
   WSC recalls Pacific theatre actions, 204
   Yalta Agreement, 854–5, 863–4
The Second World War (Churchill)
   completion of publication of, 250
   Morton thanks WSC for copy of *Closing the Ring*, 646
   Quebec Agreement of 1943, 1537
   Volume 4 (*The Hinge of Fate*), 1026–7, 1028–9, 1030–1
   Volume 6 completion, 497, 647, 686, 793, 923, 936–7, 943, 944, 1313
   Volume 6 praised by Luce, 1313–14

Secretary of State for Air: *see* De L'Isle and Dudley, Lord (William Philip Sydney)
Secretary of State for the Colonies: *see* Lyttelton, Oliver
Secretary of State for Commonwealth Relations: *see* Ismay, Sir Hastings Lionel ('Pug'); Salisbury, Lord (Robert Gascoyne-Cecil, 'Bobbety'); Swinton, Lord (Philip Cunliffe-Lister)
Secretary of State for the Co-ordination of Transport, Fuel, and Power: *see* Leathers, Lord (Frederick James)
Secretary of State for Scotland: *see* Stuart, James Gray
Secretary of State for War: *see* Head, Antony Henry
Seddon, Herbert John, 2296, 2296 n.1, 2334
Selassie, Haile, 1512, 1512 n.2
Senanayake, Dudley, 745, 1067–8, 1091
Senanayake, Stephen, 1438, 1438 n.1
as-Senussi, Muhammad Idris bin Muhammad al-, 2215–16, 2216 n.1
Seydoux Fornier de Clausonne, Roger, 1328, 1328 n.2
Seymour, Horatia, 611, 611 n.1
Seymour, Jane (Queen of England), 2153, 2153 n.1
Shaftesbury, Lord (Anthony Ashley-Cooper), 780, 780 n.1
Shakespeare, William, 825, 825 n.4
Sharett, Moshe, 1821, 1821 n.1, 1846
Shastri, Lal Bahadur, 2368, 2368 n.1
Shawcross, Hartley William, 859, 859 n.1, 1699, 2006
Shaw, George Bernard, 965, 965 n.4
Shigeru, Yoshida, 197, 197 n.2
Shillingford, Lettice Marston, 1598, 1598 n.1, 1988
Shillito, T. C., 1864, 1864 n.1
Shinwell, Emanuel
   biographical information, 101 n.1
   Cabinet Papers access, 1439–40, 1446–7
   Conservative Party economic and social policies, 703, 704, 1836–7
   defence: Admiralty management of British coastal waters, 241; Adoption of a New Army Rifle (February 1954 WSC speech), 1412–13, 1414, 1415–16; Atom Bomb Test, Australia (October 1952 WSC speech), 684; call-up of reservists, 101; Defence, German Rearmament (March 1954 WSC speech), 1462; Defence White Paper (March 1952), 316; National Service periods, 310, 565, 566, 580–2, 597, 871–2, 1295; rifle production programme, 104–5
   foreign affairs: British defence negotiations

Shinwell, Emanuel *(continued)*
  foreign affairs *(continued)*
    with Egypt (1954), 1690–1; Foreign Affairs (December 1953 WSC speech), 1359; German rearmament, 1830–5; Israel Loan Request (Oral Answers), 456; Korea Military Situation (May 1952 WSC speech), 471
  WSC praises statesmanlike speech and patriotism of, 108, 109–10
Shock, Maurice, 2132, 2132 n.1, 2133, 2136, 2150
Shoosmith, Stephen Newton, 566, 566 n.1, 729
Shuckburgh, (Charles Arthur) Evelyn
  biographical information, 155 n.2
  Conservative Government: Eden's health, 1036–7, 1182; Party concern with conduct of, 410–11; Queen Elizabeth's support for Eden as PM, 813; relations between WSC and Eden, 823; Windsor Papers, 1199; WSC considers stepping down as PM, 742, 767; WSC plans to step down as PM (1954), 1472, 1546
  Europe: British use of Austrian manpower in the event of war, 1544, 1545, 1545 n.1; Eastern European Conference, 155; Germany, 1165 n.1
  foreign affairs: employment of British and Soviet citizens in their respective Embassies in Moscow and London, 500, 529–30; Four Power Conference proposals (1953), 1173–4; hydrogen bomb tests (1954), 1500; Three Power (Bermuda) Conference (1953), 1317; US–UK defence negotiations with Egypt (1953), 1183; Western coalition of aid for France in Indo-China (proposed), 1536; Western policy towards Russia, 1182–3, 1199
  impressions of the US, Truman and the White House, 160–1
  WSC lunches with Queen Elizabeth and Shah of Iran, 1913–14
  WSC meets with Eisenhower and Dulles (1953), 812
  WSC meets with Gromyko, 950–1
  WSC's death, 2378–9
  WSC's declining health, 1536
Shurmer, Percy Lionel Edward, 578, 578 n.1
Siam, 1071, 1076
Sillitoe, Percy Joseph, 539, 539 n.1
Silverman, Samuel Sydney
  biographical information, 99 n.1
  American airbase in East Anglia, 99–100
  Far East and South-East Asia, 243–4
  Defence White Paper (March 1952), 310, 311, 313
  Atom Bomb Test, Australia (October 1952), 685
  Motion of Censure (December 1952), 755, 756, 759
  The Hydrogen Bomb (April 1954), 1519, 1525, 1527, 1528
  Debate on the Address (December 1954), 1830
Simmons, John F., 160, 160 n.1
Simonds, Gavin Turnbull
  biographical information, 11 n.1
  Accession Proclamation, 254–5
  authorisation of proposed changes to Coronation Oath, 850–1, 850 n.1
  corporal punishment, 685–6
  county court judges' and judicial officers' salaries, 11, 30
  diplomatic immunity privileges for international organisations, 583–4
  High Court Judges' remuneration, 680–2
  Maclay's illness and Ministerial duties, 415, 415 n.2
  publication of letters from von Ribbentropp, 1723–4, 1724 n.1
Simon, Lord John Allsebrook, 834, 834 n.1, 859
Sinclair, Archibald Henry Macdonald (Lord Thurso), 1409, 1409 n.1
Sinclair, John Alexander ('C'), 538–9, 538 n.2
Sinclair, Robert John, 1822, 1822 n.2
Skouras, Spyros Panagiotis, 1913, 1913 n.1
Slánský, Rudolf, 746, 746 n.2
Slessor, John Cotesworth
  biographical information, 120 n.1
  NATO: infrastructure planning, 271–2; Mediterranean Command proposals, 272; reorganisation proposals, 272
  Naval Command agreements with US and France, 740–1
  RAF aircraft production programme, 120–1, 229
  RAF jet aviation fuel reserves, 337
  US bomber attack on Soviet U-boat bases, 539–40
Slim, William Joseph ("Bill")
  biographical information, 127 n.1
  defence: Army estimates (1951–1952), 127; Army manpower estimates, 587; British wheat stocks (1952), 337; rifle standardisation, 178; tank production programme, 152, 153
  Egypt: British Defence Agreement proposals (1953), 1227–8; British military base in, 338; 'Rodeo', 976–7; US–UK defence negotiations (1954), 1435; US–UK defence negotiations (proposed), 695–7, 846–7, 847–8, 849–50, 855, 860–1, 861, 862, 883, 889–90, 890, 891, 892–4,

896–7, 897–8, 899–901, 904, 910–11, 931, 933, 946, 1002
foreign affairs: British policy towards Chinese aggression in South-East Asia, 354–5; British troops in Kenya, 881–2; Korea, 336, 506; location of Soviet forces (1954), 1429–30; postponement of Slim's appointment as Governor-General to Australia, 855
Middle East: Anglo-Jordan Treaty of 1948, 1303–5; British troop reinforcements despatched to Sudan (1953), 978; Command reorganisation proposals, 181–2; redeployment of British troops in, 1314–15
Smathers, George Armistead, 2040, 2040 n.1
Smith, Ellis, 522, 522 n.1, 1524
Smithers, Waldron, 473, 473 n.4
Smith, Frederick Winston Furneaux (Lord Birkenhead), 1845, 1845 n.1, 1862–3
Smith, Ian Douglas, 2379, 2379 n.3
Smuts, Jan Christian, 53, 53 n.1, 1497, 1512
Smyth, Delmar McCormack, 2308, 2308 n.1
Snowdon, Countess of (Princess Margaret), 588, 588 n.5, 1107
Snow, Julian, 1526, 1526 n.1
Snyder, John Wesley, 163, 163 n.1, 164, 170, 802
Soames, Arthur Christopher John
biographical information, 34 n.3
Chartwell: Mary and Christopher decline to live permanently at Chartwell, 91–2; pigs at, 1727, 1737; visits Chartwell, 2039, 2051
domestic affairs: family life, 2220; taxation relief proposals, 697–8; unemployment in textile and clothing industries, 372, 372 n.1
Montgomery's remarks on European Economic Community, 2332, 2332 n.1
political career, 1999, 2004, 2050, 2051, 2083, 2126, 2127, 2152
Russian outreach regarding meeting between WSC and Malenkov, 1484
Three Power (Bermuda) Conference (1953), 1316, 1317
Washington meeting (1954), 1625–6, 1628
and WSC: attends Eisenhower's dinner parties for WSC (1953), 801–2, 802; in Cap d'Ail with WSC, 1215–16, 2049; Colville warns Soames against too-close relations with WSC, 410; in Jamaica with WSC, 809; at La Pausa/Cap Martin with WSC, 2093; Mary thanks WSC and CSC for Family Trust arrangements, 34–5; race horses, 2135, 2136, 2137, 2168, 2169; return flight from Germany (1956), 2119–20; sails for US on *Queen Mary* with WSC, 791; WSC postpones stepping down as PM (1954), 1767; WSC's funeral, 2382; WSC decides to not stand for re-election (1963), 2346
Soames, Arthur Granville, 2076, 2200, 2200 n.2
Soames, Arthur Nicholas Winston, 433, 433 n.1, 2190
Soames, Audrey Alma Humphreys, 2076, 2076 n.1
Soames, Charlotte Clementine, 1727, 1727 n.3
Soames, Jeremy Bernard, 598, 598 n.1, 2030
Soames, Lady (Mary Churchill)
biographical information, 13 n.1
at Chartwell, 91–2, 2034, 2037, 2126
CSC's return to 10 Downing Street (1951), 13–14
CSC's Tangier visit, 2219
death of sister Diana, 2352
family life, 2219–20
political career, 1999, 2004
in St Moritz with CSC, 2036–7, 2038
and WSC: in Cap d'Ail with WSC, 2049; in Jamaica with, 797, 809; at La Pausa/Cap Martin with, 2093; sails for US on *Queen Mary* with WSC, 791; thanks WSC and CSC for Family Trust arrangements, 34–5; WSC's health, 1138, 1201, 1215–16, 2209, 2349–50, 2364; WSC's ninetieth birthday (1964), 2363
Soper, Donald Oliver, 1865, 1865 n.3
Sosrodihardjo, Kusno (Sukarno), 2287, 2287 n.1
The Sound Barrier (film), 549, 550
South Africa
Bamangwato affairs, 52–4, 73–4
Basutoland, Bechuanaland and Swaziland (April 1954 WSC speech), 1538
British COS Defence Policy and Global Strategy report, 624
Commonwealth PMs and Cabinet meeting (1952), 745, 751
Korea, 518, 548, 634
political future of, 1637
Royal Naval Base at Simonstown, 334–5, 1761, 1773–4
South-East Asia
ANZUS and ANZAM, 769, 775–7, 799, 1621
Borneo Confrontation, 2380, 2380 n.1
British policy towards Chinese aggression in, 354–5
Communist propaganda regarding, 198
Five Power military planning conference (1953), 1015–16
Indonesia, 2380, 2380 n.1
US–UK policy towards, 184–5
see also Indo-China war; Malaya

Southern Rhodesia, 561, 2379, 2379 n.4
Soviets: *see* Russia
Spaak, Paul-Henri Charles
  biographical information, 130 n.1
  Council of Europe, 133, 392
  Eastern European Conference, 134
  European Defence Community, 1214, 1771
  European Economic Community, 2340, 2340 n.1
  Western Union (European Army), 130–1
  WSC declines invitation to Hague Congress, 1213–14
Spears, Edward Louis, 1861, 1861 n.2
speeches (WSC)
  Anglo-American relations: Address to the United States Congress (January 1952), 212, 213–20, 242, 289–91; America and Britain (April 1954), 1534–5; Anglo-American Conversations (January 1952), 239–47; Anglo-American friendship (June 1954), 1599–601; upon arrival at Washington National Airport (June 1954), 1624; A Visit to the United States and Canada (July 1954), 1673–83; White House visit (1959), 2248–9
  atom bomb and atomic energy: Atom Bomb Test, Australia (October 1952), 682–5; Debate on the Address (November 1953), 1276–7; The Hydrogen Bomb (March 1954), 1504–6; The Hydrogen Bomb (April 1954), 1517–30, 1526, 1527; Debate on the Address (November 1954), 1842–3
  Cold War: The Sinews of Peace (Iron Curtain speech, March 1946), 68, 214, 285–6, 805, 2043–4, 2233, 2239, 2336, 2378; The Path of Duty (November 1951), 33; Defence (March 1953), 869; The Government's Record (April 1953), 958; Foreign Affairs (November 1953), 1285–8; The Berlin Conference (February 1954), 1449–57; Defence (March 1955), 1926–35; Press Club Luncheon (June 1954), 1630–1
  Conservative Party: The State of the Nation (December 1951), 145–9; Grand Habitation of the Primrose League (April 1952), 407–9; The Conservatives' First Six Months (May 1952), 418–22; The First Year (October 1952), 660–9; Press Association Luncheon (June 1952), 489–91; Lord Mayor's Banquet (November 1952), 722–6; The Government's Record (April 1953), 952–8; Conservative Party Conference (October 1953), 1235, 1237–46, 1254; Grand Habitation of the Primrose League (April 1954), 1557–9; The Conservatives' Task (May 1954), 1582–6; 'Peace Through Strength' (October 1954), 1792–801, 1795–7; Bedford Election Address (May 1955), 1999–2003; Constituency Speech (November 1955), 2058–9; Young Conservatives (December 1955), 2064–7; Primrose League Meeting (April 1956), 2100–2; The Primrose League (May 1957), 2161–3, 2164; Primrose League address (April 1958), 2214–15; A Vote of Confidence (January 1959), 2229–32; Woodford constituency (March 1959), 2237–41; Woodford constituency Adoption Meeting (September 1959), 2260–3
  defence: Defence (December 1951), 94–108; Defence White Paper (March 1952), 304–16; Defence (March 1953), 868–78; Adoption of a New Army Rifle (February 1954), 1410–19; Defence, German Rearmament (March 1954), 1460–7; Defence (March 1955), 1926–35
  domestic affairs: Advice to Students (December 1929), 2406; House of Commons speech (November 1951), 19–29; The State of the Nation (December 1951), 145–9; King George VI (February 1952), 257–9; Transport, Government Policy (May 1952), 447–55; Press Association Luncheon (June 1952), 489–91; The Economic Position (July 1952), 570–83, 586; The Government's Tasks (September 1952), 638–44; Debate on the Address (November 1952), 701–10; Westminster Abbey Appeal (January 1953), 824–6; England (April 1953), 964–7; Commonwealth Parliamentary Association (May 1953), 1044–5; Debate on the Address (November 1953), 1268–77, 1277–8, 1280; National Service (November 1953), 1294–9; Royal Academy Banquet (April 1954), 1555–7; University of Bristol Chancellor's Address (November 1954), 1822–4; Parliament–Spokesman of the People (September 1957), 2184–5; Churchill College Ceremony (October 1959), 2266–8; Churchill College foundation stone ceremony (October 1961), 2314
  foreign affairs: Canadian Government banquet (January 1952), 203–7; Vote of Censure (February 1952), 283–92, 283 n.3; NATO (October 1952), 669–71; Debate on the Address

(November 1952), 702; Lord Mayor's Banquet (November 1952), 722–6; Foreign Affairs (May 1953), 998–1010, 1012, 1117, 1182–3, 1236–7, 1245, 1276; Conservative Party Conference (October 1953), 1243–6; Debate on the Address (November 1953), 1275–6; Foreign Affairs (November 1953), 1284–8; Foreign Affairs (December 1953), 1359–65; The Berlin Conference (February 1954), 1449–57; Basutoland, Bechuanaland and Swaziland (April 1954), 1538; The Geneva Conference (April 1954), 1552–3; Her Majesty's Return From Her Commonwealth Tour (May 1954), 1568–9; South East Asia Defence (May 1954), 1570–1; Canada broadcast (June 1954), 1638–40; A Review of Foreign Affairs (July 1954), 1686–95; Lord Mayor's Banquet (November 1954), 1811–14; The Unity of the Free Nations (November 1954), 1818–19, 1829–30, 1833, 1837–8, 1841–2; Motion of Censure (March 1955), 1949–58; Grand Alliance of European Powers (May 1956), 2112–15; One Nation (July 1957), 2173–6; Europe–Unite! (July 1957), 2177; Liberty and the Law (July 1957), 2180–2
General Election (1955): Bedford Election Address (May 1955), 1999–2003; Walthamstow and Chigwell Election Address (May 1955), 2004–7; Woodford Election Addresses (May 1955), 1994–8, 2007–8
Harrow School: December 1951, 112–13; November 1952, 719–20, 719 n.1, 721; November 1953, 1310–11, 1310 n.1, 1814–15; November 1955, 2060; October 1957, 2190; November 1958, 2227; October 1959, 2272; November 1960, 2295
honours and awards: Becoming a Member of the Society of Cincinnati, 209–10; The Cinque Ports (September 1955), 2041–2; Freeman of Belfast and Londonderry (December 1955), 2070–2; Honorary United States Citizenship (April 1963, read by RSC on behalf of WSC), 2343–4, 2412; The Nobel Prize for Literature (December 1953), 1353–4; WSC receives Croix de la Libération (November 1958), 2226
Korea: Korea Military Situation (May 1952), 468–74; The Korean War (July 1952), 520–5, 525; Lord Mayor's Banquet (November 1952), 723; Foreign Affairs (May 1953), 999–1000; Korea Truce Talks (June 1953), 1098–101; Debate on the Address (November 1953), 1275; A Review of Foreign Affairs (July 1954), 1687
tributes: Sir Stafford Cripps (April 1952), 403–5; King George VI (February 1952), 257–9; Unveiling of a Commemorative Panel (October 1952), 694; The Death of Queen Mary (March 1953), 917–18, 919–20; The Coronation of Queen Elizabeth II, An Introduction to a Royal Broadcast (June 1953), 1057; Mr Clement Attlee (November 1953), 1305–6; Eightieth Birthday (November 1954), 1826–8; David Lloyd George memorial proposal (March 1955), 1965–8; WSC toasts Queen Elizabeth (April 1955), 1978; Unveiling of WSC statue at London Guildhall (June 1955), 2018–20, 2021; The Williamsburg Award (December 1955), 2068–9, 2068 n.1; Lord Camrose Memorial (May 1956), 2111; The Presentation of the First Duff Cooper Memorial Prize to Alan Moorehead (November 1956), 2148; The Woodford Statue (October 1959), 2270–2
WSC book collection of, 778, 778 n.2, 779
WSC draft speech notes from Browne (July 1957), 2176–7
WSC inquires about meeting Murray for help with speeches, 1992–3
Speir, Rupert Malise, 1835, 1835 n.1
Spencer-Churchill, Alexandra Mary Cadogan (Duchess of Marlborough), 617, 617 n.3, 2106
Spencer-Churchill, Arabella, 154–5, 154 n.2, 588, 1726, 2329–30
Spencer-Churchill, Elizabeth Cunningham ('Betty'), 2133, 2133 n.1
Spencer-Churchill, Henry Winston ('Peregrine'), 1938, 1938 n.5
Spencer-Churchill, Ivor Charles, 972–3, 972 n.2, 973 n.1, 2131, 2133
Spencer-Churchill, John George Vanderbilt Henry (Lord Blandford, later 11th Duke of Marlborough), 191, 191 n.3, 412–13, 413 n.3
Spencer-Churchill, Sarah Consuelo ('The Duchess'), 1632, 1632 n.1
Spencer-Churchill, Susan Mary Hornby, 191, 191 n.4
Spencer-Churchill, Winston (WSC's grandson) biographical information, 92 n.1
at Chartwell, 432–3, 433, 2037
at Chequers, 154–5

Spencer-Churchill, Winston (WSC's grandson) *(continued)*
  hopes to attend Oxford, 2164
  Mary and Christopher Soames decline to live permanently at Chartwell, 92
  reads *A History of the English-Speaking Peoples,* 2164–5, 2165, 2216
  sends WSC birthday greetings, 743
  serves as page for Portal at Coronation, 832
  writes to WSC about horse riding, 2170, 2171
  writes to WSC about school activities, 433, 679, 743, 743 n.3, 1444
  with WSC in Monte Carlo, 2310
  WSC sends stamps to, 493, 498, 764, 767, 1111–12, 1443, 1444
  WSC's love for, 2306
  WSC writes to from La Pausa, 2190
Spender, Percy Claude, 633, 633 n.1
Spens, William, 441–3, 441 n.1
Staercke, André de, 1408, 1408 n.1
Stafford, Lord (Basil Francis Nicholas Fitzherbert), 1049–50, 1049 n.3, 1054
Stalin, Josef Vissarionovich Djugashvili
  biographical information, 14 n.3
  death of, 883, 883 n.2, 934
  Pravda article on Soviet foreign policy, 1013
  Soviet Government after death of, 934–5, 938–9, 958, 987, 987 n.2, 1007–9, 1061–2, 1064, 1066, 1078, 1079–80, 1083, 1149, 1224–7, 1236, 1275–6
  Truman recalls Potsdam meetings with, 802–3
  and WSC: exchange of greetings (1951), 14, 14 n.4; WSC cites Stalin as reason for Western alliance, 1450, 2113; WSC hopes for Anglo-American approach to, 611; WSC recalls April 1945 communications with, 1008–9; WSC seeks abatement of Cold War through negotiations, 28–9, 625
  see also Russia
Stanley, Edward George Villiers (Lord Derby), 1386, 1386 n.2, 1387
Stanley, Isabel Milles-Lade (Lady Derby), 2218, 2218 n.3
Stanley, Oliver Frederick George, 404, 404 n.1
Stark, Harold Raynsford ('Betty'), 2069, 2069 n.1
Stassen, Harold
  biographical information, 823 n.1
  Anglo-American relations, 823–4, 837–8
  East/West trade with Russia, 1391–2, 1496, 1500, 1502, 1511, 1514
  European Defence Community, 1164
  NATO meetings in Europe, 823–4
St Clair-Erskine, James Alexander Wedderburn ('Hamish'), 2075–6, 2075 n.4

Steel, Christopher Eden ('Kit'), 802, 802 n.3
Steele, Mildred Helen Shay, 1330, 1330 n.2
steel industry
  artillery ammunition, 509
  British armaments exports, 577–8
  Iron and Steel Bill, 532, 643–4, 663–4, 665–6, 703–4, 754, 755, 757–9, 1242
  nationalisation repeal, 9–10, 22–3
  Nationalised Industries Select Committee report, 1392–3
  rearmament programme, 509, 576–7
  Royal Navy annual requirements, 124–5
  steel production, 709
  structural steel safety and supplies, 389–90, 634
  UK steel imports from US, 142, 188
Steinhardt, Jacob, 1923, 1923 n.1
Stephens, Thomas Edgar, 1879, 1879 n.2, 1937, 1963
Stettinius, Edward Reilly, Jr, 854–5, 854 n.4
Stevens, John Felgate, 1229–30, 1230 n.1
Stevenson, Adlai Ewing, II, 2167, 2167 n.2, 2168, 2301
Stevenson, Sir Ralph Clarmont Skrine
  biographical information, 36 n.1
  Egypt: abdication of King Farouk, 566, 566 n.2; British defence negotiations with, 274–6, 849–50; British troops' readiness in case of attacks (1953), 998; exile of Mohammed Ali Tewfik, 637 n.3; possible British military intervention in, 36, 36 n.2, 47, 47 n.1, 56–7, 273–4, 273 n.1; US–UK defence negotiations (proposed), 887, 904, 933; WSC proposes to deal with all Egypt matters while Eden attends Four Power Conference, 1396; WSC recommends that British Community should evacuate from, 1010
Stikker, Dirk U., 323, 323 n.1, 466, 466 n.1
Stimson, Henry Lewis, 815, 815 n.2
St Laurent, Louis Stephen
  biographical information, 195 n.2
  Canada–UK joint Cabinet meeting (1952), 195–6, 197, 199, 202, 203, 206
  Commonwealth PMs meeting (1953):
    Commonwealth PMs and Cabinet meeting (1952), 745, 750–1; concluding speeches, 1097; Korea truce negotiations, 1073; Middle East discussion, 1090–1, 1094; Soviet foreign policy and Western Europe discussion, 1063
  Commonwealth PMs meeting (1955):
    conclusion of proceedings, 1900; Far East discussions, 1900; Paris Agreements, 1884–5
  foreign affairs: COS Defence Policy and Global Strategy report, 623; Egypt,

INDEX

1090–1, 2171; Four Power Conference proposals (1953), 1063; Korea, 750–1; WSC praises formation of NATO, 205
WSC meets with (1954), 1633, 1637, 1638, 1682
Stoddart-Scott, Malcolm, 274, 274 n.1
Stokes, Graham Henry, 1024, 1024 n.3
Stokes, Richard Rapier, 1051, 1051 n.1, 1611
Stone of Scone, 265–6, 267–8, 267 n.2
Stopford, Frederick William, 1184, 1184 n.1
Stoph, Willi, 2370, 2370 n.1
Stow, John Montague, 2281–2, 2281 n.1
Strachey, John, 960, 960 n.2, 1415, 1417, 1462–3
Straffen, John Thomas, 480–1, 480 n.1, 637, 645
Strang, William
  biographical information, 38 n.1
  Anglo-American relations, 962, 962 n.3, 964, 970–1, 979–81
  Chequers Defence Committee staff conference conclusions, 973–4
  domestic affairs: length of Foreign Office telegrams, 535–6; relations between WSC and Eden, 823
  foreign affairs: Egypt, 63–4, 889–90, 890, 969, 989–90; European Defence Community, 1156–7; Germany, 64, 64–5, 1116, 1116 n.1; Indo-China war, 983, 984; Israel, 731–2, 963; Korea, 526, 527–8, 536, 538, 545, 1101; Sudan, 38–9, 43, 1039; US reaction to WSC's Washington visit (1952), 863–4
  Russia: Mediterranean Fleet visit to Sea of Marmora, 1174–5; purges in Georgia, 969, 970; Soviet claims about Potsdam Conference conclusions, 464, 467–8; Soviet reaction to WSC's Foreign Affairs speech (May 1953), 1012; Western policy towards, 1183–5, 1186–7; WSC offers to meet with Molotov in Moscow (proposed), 989
Strauss, George Russell, 367–8, 367 n.1, 704
Strauss, Jacobus Gideon Nel, 53, 53 n.2
Strauss, Lewis Lichtenstein
  biographical information, 1291 n.4
  atom bomb: Anglo-American White Paper on, 1334, 1358; hydrogen bomb tests (1954), 1503–4, 1510, 1519, 1521
  Three Power (Bermuda) Conference (1953), 1291, 1334
Strean, Bernard Max, 2224, 2224 n.5
Strijdom, Johannes Gerhardus (Hans Strydom), 1637, 1637 n.2
Strong, Kenneth William Dobson, 2345, 2345 n.2

Stuart, Charles Edward ('Bonnie Prince Charlie'), 2198–9, 2198 n.1
Stuart, James Ewell Brown ('Jeb'), 2179, 2179 n.3
Stuart, James Gray
  biographical information, 265 n.1
  amnesty for British Armed Forces deserters (proposed), 783–4
  comments on Stuart section of *A History of the English-Speaking Peoples*, 2198–9
  corporal punishment, 733–4
  Home Guard future planning, 1264–5
  marketing of home-produced meat and bacon after end of meat rationing, 1261–2
  Scottish Judges' tax concessions and remuneration, 681–2
  Stone of Scone, 265–6
  timing of new Government formation (1955), 1858–9, 1859–60
Sturdee, Nina Edith ('Jo'), 55, 55 n.1, 66–7, 67, 1988, 2107, 2172
submarines: *see* U-boats
Sudan
  Anglo-Egyptian agreement regarding, 922, 937–8, 938, 946–7, 951, 952, 978, 1011, 1020, 1475–9
  British policy regarding Egyptian claims, 270–1, 275
  British troop reinforcements despatched to (1953), 974, 977–8
  Egyptian propaganda regarding Sudanese elections, 1046–7, 1080
  elections in, 952, 1355
  Farouk and US–UK policy towards Egypt, 182
  Lloyd suggests Howe not return to, 1080 n.1, 1081
  Naguib's attitude towards England, 569, 593
  National Unionist Party, 1011
  self-government: claims, 10, 275, 413–14; draft Statute, 713–14; Egyptian recognition of, 387–8; planning, 35, 35 n.1, 38–9, 43, 43 n.4, 747
  Sudan claims, 275, 413–14
  Sudanese Parliament opening postponement, 1458–9
  Umma Party, 961–2
  WSC praises Howe's service as Governor General of, 1983
  WSC suggests al-Mahdi travel to England without stopping in Cairo, 1039
Suez Canal: *see* Canal Zone
Sutherland, Graham, 1827 n.1, 1914–15, 2283, 2327–8, 2328
Swart, Charles Robberts ('Blackie'), 1884, 1884 n.1, 1885

Sweet, Ivy (Jeanne de Rothschild), 2138, 2138 n.2
Swinton, Lord (Philip Cunliffe-Lister)
  biographical information, 71 n.1
  defence: aircraft production programme, 230; defence programme planning, 295, 295 n.1; Defence Review Committee, 1730, 1735, 1737; loan of British destroyer to Pakistan (proposed), 880–1; Ministry of Defence contracting procedures, 303 n.1, 330, 330 n.3; RAF manpower estimates, 207; Royal Naval Base at Simonstown, 1761; Royal Navy new construction figures, 71; service estimates, 207
  domestic affairs: authorisation of proposed changes to Coronation Oath, 851; BBC debates between Junior Members of government, 537, 589, 594–6; employment of coloured people in public service sector, 1423–4; House of Lords reform proposals, 834; housing programme, 641, 663; 'Opposite Numbers' debate proposal, 594–6, 601; price increases for bacon, butter, margarine, sugar and cheese (1952), 636–7; Savoy Hotel case, 1425, 1428; Swinton appointed Secretary of State for Commonwealth Relations, 735; WSC postpones stepping down as PM (1954), 1767
  economics: Conservative Party publication on UK financial situation (1952), 508–9; cotton importing and marketing, 1105; 'Working Men Tories' letter from Jack Binns to WSC on 'Labour lies', 494, 494 n.1
  foreign affairs, 1400; Ceylon riots, 1195; Egypt, 889–90, 890, 989–90, 991–2, 1210; France, 1036; Indo-China war, 1554–5; Kenya, 881–2; Malta's status and relations with UK, 1543–4; Russia, 1079–80, 1653, 1664–5
Swope, Herbert Bayard, 801, 801 n.2
Sydney, William Philip: *see* De L'Isle and Dudley, Lord (William Philip Sydney)
Syers, Cecil George Lewis, 1195, 1195 n.1
Syria, 748

Taft, Robert Alphonso, Sr, 416, 416 n.3, 544, 1049
Tardieu, André Pierre Gabriel Amédée, 2060–1, 2060 n.1
Taylor, Charles Stuart, 1576–7, 1576 n.1
Tedder, Arthur William, 440, 440 n.1, 2265, 2268, 2311, 2312, 2315, 2317
Temple, Henry John (Viscount Palmerston), 919, 919 n.2

Templer, Gerald Walter Robert, 1072, 1072 n.1
Tennyson, Alfred, 2386, 2386 n.1
'Terminal' (Potsdam Conference), 464, 467–8, 815, 1003, 1151
Tewfik, Mohammed Ali, 637, 637 n.2, 637 n.3
Tewson, Vincent, 140–1, 140 n.1, 150, 249, 599
Thomas, Ivor Owen, 757, 757 n.1, 758, 760
Thomas, James Purdon Lewes
  biographical information, 8 n.1
  Anglo-Norwegian fisheries case, 568–9
  Atlantic Command designations, 617, 617 n.2
  British ships in Japanese waters (1952), 718, 720
  Coronation Naval Review, 635, 644, 658, 838, 838 n.1, 853–4, 854 n.1, 854 n.2, 922, 1016–17, 1104, 1104 n.1
  costs of Royal Visit to Australia and New Zealand, 111
  German rearmament, 319, 326
  Home Fleet review, 596, 596 n.1
  loan of British destroyer to Pakistan (proposed), 880–1
  Longley-Cook Report, 144–5, 145 n.1, 786, 786 n.4
  Maltese employment conditions, 599
  manpower: Civil Service staff reductions, 90; defence staff reductions, 295; legislation regarding regulars retention and call-up of reservists for Korean War (proposed), 235–6, 252; Naval Cadet training, 1043, 1258, 1262–3, 1302; recall of Naval Fleet Reservists, 742, 764–5, 764 n.2, 772–3, 782, 792
  Ministry of Defence staff, structure and responsibilities, 8
  Paul (King of Greece) visits Portsmouth, 856
  Royal Navy: Admiralty expenditure reduction proposals, 126; Admiralty management of British coastal waters, 37–8, 105–6; fuel oil reserves, 337, 376–7, 377 n.1; Naval Command agreements with US and France, 740–1; Royal Naval Base at Simonstown, 335; WSC questions focus of naval ship-building programme, 69
  Service Ministers' meetings on non-operational matters, 113–14, 158
  US bomber attack on Soviet U-boat bases, 539–40
Thomas, Thomas George, 25, 25 n.1
Thomson, George Morgan, 1610–11, 1610 n.1
Thorneycroft, Peter
  biographical information, 330 n.1
  defence: Defence Programme budget (1953–1954), 716; Ministry of Defence contracting procedures, 303 n.1, 330, 330 n.3
  economics: housing investment programme

Index

(1953), 564; UK economic position (1952), 460; UK economic position (1954), 1793; unemployment in textile and clothing industries, 368–9, 372, 372 n.1
individuals with Communist associations on Board of Trade statutory bodies, 503–5
proposed membership in The Other Club, 2288
Savoy Hotel case, 1420–1, 1425, 1428, 1428 n.2, 1440–1
trade: British imports of Canadian cheese, 381, 389; British rubber exports to Russia, 347, 362; cotton importing and marketing, 1105, 1111; East/West trade with Russia, 1399, 1454; trade control and embargoed goods 'short list', 1390–2; US tariffs on British goods, 400, 405
WSC criticises, 2220
WSC praises, 2162–3
Thornton, Archibald Paton, 2150, 2150 n.1
Thorson, Marjorie, 2125, 2125 n.1
Three Power (Bermuda) Conference (1953)
arrivals, 1316
atom bomb: Anglo-American White Paper on, 1334, 1358; Eisenhower's attitude toward use of, 1329–30; Eisenhower's draft 'Atoms for Peace' speech, 1319, 1325, 1329–30, 1333, 1333 n.2, 1333 n.3, 1334; international Atomic Energy Administration (proposed), 1334; storage of US bombs in England, 1332
bilateral US–UK discussion topics, 1333, 1333 n.1
China: Communism in the East and West, 1326–7; WSC's remarks on meeting with versus recognition of, 1324–5
conclusion of, 1346, 1349, 1351, 1352
dinner party at, 1325
Egypt and the Middle East, 1337–9, 1348–9, 1359
European Defence Community, 1335–7; British support for, 1329, 1331, 1331–2, 1335–7; French support for, 1335–7, 1344, 1345–6, 1349, 1361–2; German role in, 1330; US support for, 1325, 1329, 1331, 1331–2, 1335–7, 1362
Far East, 1326–7, 1348, 1363
Four Power Conference proposals, 1342–5, 1347–8, 1362
French presence at, 1348
German reunification, 1330
Indo-China, 1339–42, 1348
Korea, 1325, 1329, 1331, 1348
Laniel unable to attend, 1327
meeting minutes, 1319–24, 1327–8, 1335–7, 1337–9, 1339–45, 1345–8

NATO, 1347
planning, 1032–3, 1033, 1033–4, 1035–6, 1037–8, 1039, 1042, 1043–4, 1047, 1052, 1053, 1081–2, 1083, 1091, 1092, 1110, 1110–11, 1114–15, 1118, 1119–20, 1120–1, 1122, 1122–3, 1125, 1137, 1279, 1280–1, 1281, 1282, 1283, 1283–4, 1284, 1289, 1290, 1291, 1292, 1309, 1311
Plenary Meeting #1, 1317
postponement, 1118, 1119–20, 1122
Press communiqués, 1324, 1328, 1337, 1337 n.1, 1346–8
Press coverage, 1318, 1324, 1327, 1349, 1360, 1365
procedures, 1319, 1327–8
Royal Welsh Fusiliers at, 1047, 1118, 1290, 1352, 1352 n.1, 1352 n.2
Russia: Eisenhower voices anti-Russian views, 1317; Soviet Government policies, 1319–24; trade policy towards, 1318–19, 1322–3; WSC note on satellite problem, 1318; WSC promotes twofold 'double dealing' policy towards, 1317, 1322
WSC meets privately with Eisenhower, 1317, 1360
WSC reflects on results of, 1451
WSC reports on to HofC, 1360–5
Thurso, Lord (Archibald Henry Macdonald Sinclair), 1409, 1409 n.1
Tilbrook, Thomas William, 2090, 2090 n.1
The Times article on hydrogen bomb tests (1954), 1500
Tito, Josip Broz, 417, 417 n.1, 911, 2286–8
Tito, Jovanka Budisavljević, 2286–7, 2286 n.3
Tizard, Henry Thomas, 208, 208 n.1, 253
Todd, Garfield, 561, 561 n.1
Tollast, Robert, 2320, 2320 n.1, 2328
Townsend, Peter Wooldridge, 1107, 1107 n.1
Trades Union Congress (TUC), 4, 638–9, 663, 665, 666–7, 953–4, 1242–3
transport
Australian nationalised railways and road transport planning, 475–6
bus and railway fare increases, 317, 351–2
civil aviation, 280, 280–1, 281 n.1
Colville disagrees with denationalisation proposals, 446
direct coach licenses, 382–3, 382 n.1
railway statutes, 640
Road Haulage Association, 448
road haulage denationalisation proposals, 384, 640–1, 663–5, 705
Road Haulage permits, 365–7
road and rail fares public committee proposal, 478

transport *(continued)*
  Road Traffic Bill provisional legislative program (1954–1955), 1561–2
  Transport Commission and Road Haulage permits, 365–7
Transport Bill
  'C' licenses, 640, 665
  Conservative Party Conference (October 1953 WSC speech), 1242
  Debate on the Address (November 1952 WSC speech), 703, 705–6
  The Government's Tasks (September 1952 WSC speech), 640–1, 644
  Press comments on, 545–6
  proposals, 383, 401
  WSC dictates speech notes for, 443
Tree, Arthur Ronald Lambert Field, 13, 13 n.3
Tree, Marietta Endicott Peabody, 2301, 2301 n.1
Trench-Gascoigne, Alvary Douglas Frederick
  biographical information, 923 n.2
  Korean release of captured British diplomats, 923–4, 924–5, 934
  Russia: British policy towards, 930, 1010; Eden offers to discuss foreign relations with Molotov, 934; *Pravda* article on Soviet foreign policy, 1012–14; purges in Georgia, 970; quarterly reports on (1953), 934–5
Trevelyan, George Macaulay, 1849–50, 1850 n.1, 2106, 2148–9
Trevelyan, Humphrey, 1924, 1924 n.1
Triboulet, Raymond, 353, 353 n.2, 383–4, 1227, 1581
tributes
  Bracken memorial proposals, 2225
  Dunkirk memorial, 266
  Lord Haldane monument proposal, 2116–17, 2117
  War Memorial for MPs, 678–9
  to WSC: Death of Sir Winston Churchill (House of Lords), 2371–7; Nicolson records television obituary of WSC (1953), 1189
  WSC speeches: Sir Stafford Cripps (April 1952), 403–5; King George VI (February 1952), 257–9; Unveiling of a Commemorative Panel (October 1952), 694; The Death of Queen Mary (March 1953), 917–18, 919–20; The Coronation of Queen Elizabeth II, An Introduction to a Royal Broadcast (June 1953), 1057; Mr Clement Attlee (November 1953), 1305–6; Eightieth Birthday (November 1954), 1826–8; David Lloyd George memorial proposal (March 1955), 1965–8; WSC toasts Queen Elizabeth (April 1955), 1978; Unveiling of WSC statue at London Guildhall (June 1955), 2018–20, 2021; The Williamsburg Award (December 1955), 2068–9, 2068 n.1; Lord Camrose Memorial (May 1956), 2111; The Presentation of the First Duff Cooper Memorial Prize to Alan Moorehead (November 1956), 2148; The Woodford Statue (October 1959), 2270–2
Truman, Elizabeth Virginia Wallace ('Bess'), 2252, 2252 n.1
Truman, Harry S
  biographical information, 68 n.1
  atom bomb, 173–6, 223, 1524–5, 1527
  atomic energy, 223–4
  British trade with China, 165–6, 166–8
  defence: Atlantic Command proposals, 179, 212–13, 221–2, 240; Middle East Command reorganisation proposals, 182; NATO reform proposals, 172; naval Command arrangements in the Atlantic, 49–50, 49 n.1; rifle standardisation, 177–8, 1413; TCC report, 172; UK aircraft for US NATO use, 331; UK defence budget, 331; US disarmament proposals, 5
  House Un-American Affairs Activities Committee subpoena, 1290, 1290 n.1
  Persia: Anglo-Iranian Oil Company, 602, 602 n.2, 606–7, 608–9, 618–19, 619–20, 619 n.1, 620–1, 622, 626, 626–7, 627 n.1, 631, 643, 650, 655–6, 656, 658–9; Jones meets with Mossadeq, 598, 602; nationalisation law, 603; WSC suggests joint appeal to Mossadeq, 606, 607–8, 611, 614–15
  Russia, 222–3, 1839–40
  US Presidential election (1952), 416
  and WSC: completion of *The Second World War*, 928, 1031–2; Truman plans England visit (1956), 2089, 2095, 2095 n.4; Truman reiterates importance of Anglo-American unity to WSC, 603; Trumans dine with WSC and CSC at Chartwell, 2117–18, 2117 n.1; WSC's opinion of Truman, 68, 793, 807; WSC steps down as PM (1955), 1985, 2022; WSC thanks for copy of memoirs, 2291, 2291 n.4; WSC visits US (1953), 720–1, 721, 802–3, 805–6; WSC visits US (1959), 2233, 2233 n.1, 2252, 2252 n.1
  see also US–UK Washington discussions (1952)
Tryon, Charles George Vivian, 1216–17, 1216 n.1, 1221–2, 1229, 1230–1
TUC (Trades Union Congress), 4, 638–9, 663, 665, 666–7, 953–4, 1242–3

INDEX 2485

Tudor, Henry Hugh, 1992, 1992 n.1, 2037
Tunisia, 2196, 2197, 2205
Turkey
  British relations with, 747
  desire for inclusion with NATO forces in Europe, 30–1
  Foreign Affairs (May 1953 WSC speech), 1006
  Mediterranean Fleet visit to Sea of Marmora, 1174–5
  Middle East: Command reorganisation proposals, 30–1; redeployment of British troops in, 1211–12, 1211 n.3
  NATO command structure, 40
  NATO membership (1952), 725, 748
  Turkish fears of Soviet attack on, 700, 700 n.2
Turnour, Edward (Lord Winterton), 2279–80, 2280 n.1
Tweedsmuir, Lady (Priscilla Jean Fortescue Buchan), 386, 386 n.5

U-boats
  Admiralty management of British coastal waters, 105
  Admiralty production programme, 123–4
  anti-U-boat measures, 311–12
  'Asdic', 319, 319 n.2
  Atlantic Command proposals, 178–9, 200–1
  Battle of the Atlantic, 204
  in the Black Sea, 511
  British defences against, 125
  RAF detection of, 77, 77 n.1
  Russian submarine strength, 357
  US bomber attack on Soviet U-boat bases, 539–40
  WSC questions focus of naval ship-building programme, 69
U Hla Maung, 2018, 2018 n.2
UK–Canada joint Cabinet meeting (1952)
  Atlantic Command proposals, 200–1
  atomic weapons, 196
  economics: Canadian–UK trade imbalances, 202–3; UK economic position, 202; UK exports of aluminium to US, 202; UK rearmament programme, 202
  Far East, 197–9
  Middle East, 199, 199–200
  Soviet Union, 196–7
  St Laurent's welcoming remarks, 195–6
  Western Union (European Army) composition, 200
Umberto II (King of Belgium), 736, 736 n.2
Unionist Party, 952–8
United Europe
  Baruch hopes for, 797
  Council of Europe discussions, 45, 131, 133, 133 n.2
  European affiliation with British Commonwealth (proposed), 135–6
  European Army, 81–2
  European Federation proposals, 81
  German participation in defence of Western Europe, 81
  WSC discusses with Massigli and Juin, 423–4
  WSC encourages French/German reconciliation, 81, 82, 149, 218
  WSC promotes 'fraternal association' of English-speaking world, 83
  WSC promotes safety and revival of, 422
  WSC views and policy on (remarks to Cabinet), 81–3
United Nations (UN)
  atom bomb: disarmament proposals, 6, 197; Eisenhower's 'Atoms for Peace' speech, 1357, 1357 n.1, 1358, 1365; US disarmament proposals, 5–6
  China: Chinese Nationalist troops in Burma, 1071, 1077; Eisenhower relieves Seventh Fleet of China defence responsibilities, 732–3; UN admission (proposed), 1066, 1069, 1074, 1100, 1205–6, 1452, 1648–9, 1649, 1667–8, 1671–3, 1681–2, 1685, 1686, 1688–9
  Egypt: General Election planning (1952), 397; Suez Canal closure and Gulf of Aqaba blockade (1956), 2131, 2134–5, 2141–2, 2144–5, 2146–7
  General Assembly meetings: Paris (1951), 24, 98; New York (1952), 702
  Indo-China, 1575–6
  Korea: Alexander reports on Korea visit to WSC, 501; armistice talks, 59, 183–4, 241–2, 505–6, 723, 750, 1046; bombing of power stations on Yalu River, 512, 514–15; British Deputy Chief of Staff (proposed), 506, 518–19, 529, 547–8; Korea Military Situation (May 1952 WSC speech), 471–3; Korea Truce Talks (June 1953 WSC speech), 1098–101; napalm bombing in, 605, 612, 628–9; potential air threat to UN forces in, 87–8; provision of Commonwealth occupation forces in, 336; public warning statement on signed Armistice, 331; return of POWs to Communist China, 402, 484–5, 511–12, 511 n.2, 523–4, 527–8, 723; truce negotiations, 1069–71, 1072–6, 1084; US proposals for total embargo and severing of diplomatic relations with China and North Korea, 609–10, 615–16
  'Mainbrace' military exercise, 616, 616 n.1, 624
  Menzies criticises, 2181–2, 2182, 2183

United Nations (UN) *(continued)*
  WSC discusses prevention of third world war, 204–5
  WSC reflects on formation of, 1823
United States Air Force (USAF), 806
United States Government
  Anglo-American relations: British requests for monetary and/or material aid from the US, 119; Finnish tanker SS *Wiima*, 962, 962 n.3, 964, 970–1; use of 'Top Secret' rather than 'Most Secret', 373–4, 377–8
  Congressional limits on Presidential powers, 902–3
  Eden meets with Eisenhower, 731
  Eight Power Meeting proposals, 1766
  exclusion of UK from Pacific Tripartite Treaty, 650–1
  Formosa, 1893–4, 1896–900
  Germany, 42, 425–6
  House Un-American Affairs Activities Committee, 1290, 1290 n.1
  Indo-China war, 749, 751, 752, 1531–3, 1549–52, 1700–1, 1702–3
  Korea: armistice talks, 1029–30, 1046, 1047, 1047–8; British criticism of US policy towards, 523–4; Korea Military Situation (May 1952 WSC speech), 474; Korea Truce Talks (June 1953 WSC speech), 1098–101; return of POWs to Communist China, 400, 400 n.1, 402, 411, 736; truce negotiations, 1073–6, 1084; US proposals for total embargo and severing of diplomatic relations with China and North Korea, 609–10, 615–16, 633–4
  McCarthyism, 1065
  Middle East, 1595–6
  Russia: Five Power Peace Pact proposals, 975; trade control and embargoed goods 'short list', 1390–2; Western policy towards, 1185–6, 1186–7, 1188, 1193–5; WSC offers to meet with Molotov in Moscow (proposed), 1022–3; WSC proposes Russia visit (1954), 1708–10
  South-East Asia, 775–7, 1015–16
  US Presidential election (1952), 416, 440–1, 495, 540, 544, 643, 668, 713, 714, 722–3
  and WSC: Address to the United States Congress (January 1952), 213–20; WSC thanks Nixon for US Senate Resolution, 2039–40, 2039 n.1, 2040
  Yugoslavia, 747
  see also atom bomb and atomic energy; Egypt; US–UK Washington discussions (1952); US–UK Washington discussions (1954)
U Nu, 1936, 1936 n.1, 2015–16, 2016–18, 2020

US–UK Washington discussions (1952)
  Anglo-American Conversations (January 1952 WSC speech), 239–47
  British arrivals, 160
  China, 162–3, 165–8
  defence: Atlantic Command proposals, 178–9, 221–2, 240–1; atomic energy, 223–4; atomic weapons, 173–6, 186–7, 223; European Defence Community, 188–9; NATO reform proposals, 170–2, 190; rifle standardisation, 177–8; TCC report, 162, 162 n.1, 172; UK production programme, 168–70, 190; US spending on, 163–4
  discussion planning, 39, 40–1, 144
  economics: prevention of economic crises, 163, 164, 170; raw materials, 169–70, 187–8, 223; UK economic position, 164, 168–70
  Europe: German military production, 162; Western Union (European Army), 162
  Far East and South-East Asia, 184–5, 243–6
  Korea: armistice talks, 183–4, 241–2, 245–6; US casualties, 161, 241; US–UK policy towards, 242–6
  Middle East: Egypt, 182, 220, 224; Middle East Command, 180–2; Persia, 182–3; US–UK policy towards, 161, 162
  Russia, 161–4, 222–3
  Shuckburgh's impressions of the US, Truman and the White House, 160–1
  summary communiqué, 191–3
  Truman cuts off WSC's remarks at, 160
  Truman makes concluding remarks, 224
  WSC makes witty remarks during, 180
  see also Cold War; US–UK Washington discussions (1954)
US–UK Washington discussions (1954)
  arrivals, 1625
  departures, 1633, 1641
  dinner parties, 1628–9, 1632, 1632–3
  Egypt, 1625, 1626–8
  European Defence Community, 1629–30, 1677, 1680, 1692–3
  German rearmament, 1628, 1629–30, 1636, 1677, 1680
  joint Declaration of Principles, 1631, 1632, 1633–4, 1634–5, 1675–6
  planning, 1546–7, 1548, 1554, 1564, 1565, 1566, 1567, 1568, 1573, 1577–8, 1578–9, 1581, 1587, 1588, 1590, 1592–3, 1594–5, 1601–2, 1602, 1602–3, 1604, 1605–6, 1607, 1608, 1609, 1610, 1612, 1613, 1623, 1623–4, 1624
  Press Club Luncheon, 1630–1, 1632
  Russian talks (proposed London meeting), 1625, 1626, 1628

Index

South East Asia, 1680–1, 1682
A Visit to the United States and Canada (July 1954 WSC speech), 1673–83
see also Cold War; US–UK Washington discussions (1952)
U Thant, 2018, 2018 n.1
Uthwatt, Augustus Andrewes, 707, 707 n.1

Valdés Armada, Félix Juan, 444, 444 n.3
Valdés y Ozores, María, 444, 444 n.4
'Valiant' aircraft prototype crash, 211
Vandenberg, Arthur Hendrick, 215, 215 n.1, 223
Vandenberg, Arthur Hendrick, Jr, 223, 223 n.1, 225–6, 806
Vanderbilt, Consuelo Balsan, 516–17, 516 n.1, 2338
Van Fleet, James Alward, 501, 501 n.1
van Starkenborgh Stachouwer, Jonkheer Alidius Warmoldus Lambertus Tjarda, 1408, 1408 n.2
van Zeeland, Paul, 130, 130 n.2
Victoria Eugenie Julia Ena (Queen of Spain), 2235, 2235 n.1, 2236
Victoria, Queen (Alexandrina Victoria), 261, 261 n.1, 262, 2184
Villeneuve, Pierre-Charles-Jean-Baptiste-Silvestre de, 2164, 2164 n.2
Vincent, Edgar (Lord d'Abernon), 1550, 1550 n.3
Vincent, Victor, 1580, 1580 n.4, 1591
Vyshinsky, Andrei Yanuarevich, 6, 6 n.1, 183–4, 185, 197

Wafd (Hizb al-Wafd) political party, 325, 325 n.1
Wahlen, Friedrich Traugott, 2371, 2371 n.1
Walker, Patrick Gordon, 131, 131 n.1
Walker-Smith, Derek Colclough, 1804, 1804 n.6
Wallace, Harry Wright, 2004, 2004 n.1
Wallinger, Geoffrey Arnold, 1499, 1499 n.2
Warbey, William Noble, 1694, 1694 n.1
Warde, Muriel Thetis Wilson, 2337–9, 2337 n.1
Ward, George Reginald, 549, 549 n.1, 550, 617
Ward, Irene Mary Bewick, 1863–4, 1863 n.3
Ward, John Guthrie ('Jack'), 1115, 1115 n.1, 1124, 1127, 1128–9, 1129–30
Warfield, Wallis (Duchess of Windsor), 541, 541 n.2, 800–1, 1107–8
Waterhouse, Charles, 1713–17, 1713 n.1
Watkinson, Harold Arthur, 1206, 1206 n.1
Watson, Edith Margaret, 2011, 2011 n.2
Waverly, Lord (Sir John Anderson), 814–15, 814 n.1, 939–42
Webster, Daniel, 1286, 1286 n.2
Weeks, Ronald Morce, 2232, 2232 n.3
Weisz, Victor ('Vicky'), 2299, 2299 n.1

Weizmann, Chaim
biographical information, 51 n.1
Israeli oil supply financing request, 401–2, 402 n.1, 424, 424 n.5, 430, 456–7
WSC pays tribute to, 724, 727, 1006
WSC's friendship with, 1923
WSC thanks for gift of oranges and grapefruits, 362
WSC thanks for letter and sends good wishes, 51
Weld-Forester, Wolstan Beaumont Charles, 2087, 2087 n.4
Welensky, Roy, 462–3, 462 n.1
Wellesley, Gerald (Duke of Wellington), 679, 679 n.1
Western Union (European Army)
composition of, 97–8, 119–20, 129–31, 140, 159, 159 n.1
Conservative Delegation letter to Consultative Assembly regarding, 131
Council of Europe discussions regarding, 129–31
French participation in, 82
German participation in, 96–7, 218
UK non-participation in, 83–4, 98, 108–9, 114, 129–31, 154, 188–9, 200, 205, 218–19
US–UK discussions (1952), 188–90
WSC's views on necessity of German and French participation in, 81–2
Westminster, Dean of (Alan Campbell Don), 267–8, 267 n.1, 682
Westminster, Duchess of (Viola Maud Lyttelton), 1979, 1979 n.2
Weygand, Maxime, 1550, 1550 n.2
Wheeler-Bennett, John, 2289, 2289 n.1
Whistler, Reginald Hector, 809, 809 n.3
White, George Stuart, 1864, 1864 n.2
Whiteley, John Francis Martin, 1416, 1416 n.1
White, Thomas Walter, 395, 395 n.2
Wigg, George Edward Cecil, 1418, 1418 n.1, 2116–17, 2117
Wilde, G. L., 1652, 1652 n.2, 1729
Wiley, Alexander, 1141, 1141 n.1
Wilhelm (Emperor of Germany), 251, 251 n.3
Wilkes, John, 1688, 1688 n.2
William Augustus (Duke of Cumberland), 2199, 2199 n.1
William I, King (William the Conqueror), 2008, 2008 n.2
Williams, Herbert Geraint, 1714, 1714 n.1
Willkie, Wendell Lewis, 2070, 2070 n.1
Wilmshurst, Michael Joseph, 2304, 2304 n.1
Wilson, Charles Edward, 142, 142 n.1
Wilson, Charles McMoran: *see* Moran, Lord (formerly Sir Charles Wilson)

Wilson, C. P., 292, 292 n.1
Wilson, Geoffrey Hazlitt, 2119, 2119 n.2
Wilson, Harold, 2357, 2365, 2365–6, 2366, 2366 n.1, 2367, 2367 n.3, 2368, 2368–9, 2369, 2370, 2370 n.1, 2371, 2387
Wilson, Sir Henry Maitland ('Jumbo'), 440, 440 n.2, 814
Wilson, John Gideon, 2283, 2283 n.3
Wilson, Richard John McMoran, 2118, 2118 n.1, 2119
Wilson, Thomas Woodrow, 263, 263 n.1, 1634
Windsor, Duchess of (Wallis Warfield), 541, 541 n.2, 800–1, 1107–8
Windsor, Duke of
  biographical information, 263 n.2
  abdication of, 263, 1107–8
  attends Eisenhower's dinner party for WSC (1953), 800–1
  CSC mentions in letter to WSC, 541
  death of Queen Mary, 918
  does not attend Elizabeth's Coronation, 732, 736–7, 766
  references to in *Documents on German Foreign Policy* publication, 1608–9
  transfer of funds to, 732, 733
  Windsor Papers, 1141, 1159, 1188, 1189
  WSC meets with, 1580, 1580 n.1
Wingate, Orde Charles, 2045–6, 2045 n.4
Winterhalter, Franz Xaver, 2184, 2184 n.1
Winterton, Lord (Edward Turnour), 2279–80, 2280 n.1
Winterton, Thomas John Willoughby, 1287, 1287 n.1, 1383, 1386
women, International Women's Day conference in England, 344
Wood, Charles Carlyle, 2055, 2055–6, 2055 n.1
Wood, Edward Frederick Lindley (Lord Halifax), 345–6, 345 n.2, 669, 1875
Wood, Heather, 1988, 1988 n.4, 2036
Woodcock, George, 491–2, 491 n.1
Woods, John Harold Edmund, 939–42, 942 n.1, 1642
Woolton, Lord (Frederick James Marquis)
  biographical information, 3 n.1
  broadcasting: BBC debates between Junior Members of government, 594; White Paper, 426–7; WSC inquires about teleprompter for television screen tests, 1397, 1397 n.2; WSC suggests Ministerial Statement from Woolton, 66
  Conservative Government: Cabinet Committees, 46; general election timing, 1513–14, 1751–2, 1757–8; timing of new Government formation (1955), 1858–9, 1859–60; Transport Commission and Road Haulage permits, 365–7
  Conservative Party: Woolton appointed Chancellor of the Duchy of Lancaster, 735; Woolton's ineffectiveness as Chair of, 410; Woolton steps down as Chair of Conservative Central Office, 2023; WSC disapproves of advertisements of his books with Party literature, 271; WSC plans to replace Woolton with Lyle as Chair, 410
  description of Prince Charles in Church of England and Church of Scotland Prayers, 293, 294
  food: Argentine meat exports to Britain, 651; food budget discussions, 430; meat ration and supply projections (1951–1952), 27; unrationed food import reductions, 3, 4
  sends regards to WSC, 2189
  WSC praises, 1238, 1557
World Federation of Scientific Workers, 344
World War II: *see* Second World War
Wren, Christopher, 2111, 2111 n.2, 2336
Wyatt, Woodrow Lyle, 104, 104 n.1, 105, 456–7, 1410, 1412, 1414–15, 1465
Wyndham, John Edward Reginald, 2279, 2279 n.3

Yalta Agreement, 854–5, 863–4
York, Archbishop of (Cyril Forster Garbett), 474, 474 n.2
Yoshida, Shigeru, 1131, 1131 n.2
Younger, Kenneth Gilmour, 960, 960 n.1
Young, George Malcolm, 2108, 2108 n.1
Yugoslavia
  Five Power Conference on Trieste (proposed), 1300
  Foreign Affairs (May 1953 WSC speech), 1006
  Italian relations with, 1287, 1363
  Western Powers' relations with, 747
  WSC meets with Tito (1960), 2226–8

Zahedi, Fazlollah, 1197, 1197 n.1
Zhivotovski, Georgi Mikhailovich, 949–50, 949 n.4
Zhou Enlai
  biographical information, 934 n.2
  Coronation greetings to Queen Elizabeth, 1073
  Eden offers to meet with, 1924, 1924–5, 1935–6, 1937
  Formosa, 1894
  Indo-China war cease-fire proposals, 1574
  repatriation of Korean POWs, 934–5
  WSC's opinion of, 1609
Zulueta, Philip de, 2286, 2286 n.1, 2323, 2333